Contents

All of the papers used in this book are recyclable and made from wood grown in managed, sustainable forests. They are manufactured at mills certified to ISO 14001 and/or EMAS.

About the Good Beer Guide

Your guide to the best pubs & beer in the UK

If you want to know where to find a great pub serving great beer, then let this guide be your constant companion. But it's far more than just a pub guide – it will also direct you to breweries and their beers as well as keeping you up-to-date on the pub and beer scene.

A guide of different parts

Pubs are the central core of the Guide, the essential outlets for real ale. But the *Good Beer Guide* has always played a number of roles. Its Breweries section complements the pub listings by detailing all the producers of cask beer and their regular ales. And as well as listing some 4,500 of the finest outlets for real ale, over 1,750 breweries and 7,500 beers, the Guide also contains lively and informative consumer features on beer, pubs, beer festivals and brewing. In the introduction to this edition on pages 6–9 we look at CAMRA's campaigns to cut the tax burden on pubs and oppose the anti-alcohol lobby. On pages 10–13 we celebrate the work done by publicans, community groups, women brewers and pub pioneers.

Comprehensive breweries listing

Uniquely, the *Good Beer Guide* includes a complete listing of British breweries and their core beers, along with CAMRA tasting notes. Breweries are monitored on a regular basis and each brewery is visited by CAMRA members, who speak to the brewer and check on the beers being produced before reporting to the Guide. When a new brewery comes on stream, a liaison officer will be appointed to ensure the Breweries section of the Guide is accurate and up to date.

Swannay brewery, Orkney (p943)

Democratically selected entries

The way in which pubs are chosen is equally meticulous. Much of CAMRA's 190,000 membership is involved and those members who cannot be active or attend regular meetings are invited to recommend pubs via email or branch websites.

Branch areas are broken down into local sections so pubs can be monitored regularly. The quality of beer in each pub is assessed using a national beer scoring system. Special branch meetings are convened once a year where short-lists are presented and then members vote on the final selection for the Guide.

National Beer Scoring System

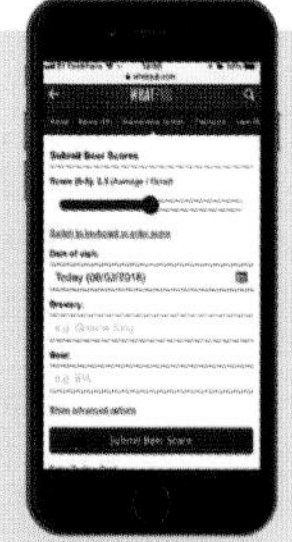

In selecting pubs for the Guide, CAMRA branches use beer scores submitted by members through a National Beer Scoring System (NBSS) to help them identify places that serve consistently good beer. NBSS uses a simple 0–5 scale and scores are submitted online. Any CAMRA member can submit a beer score for a pub anywhere in the country by going to CAMRA's online pub guide **www.whatpub.com**, logging in as a member and selecting 'Submit Beer Scores'.

Regular inspections

The entries in most pub guides are chosen either by small editorial teams or by members of the public, whose recommendations are not necessarily checked. However, every pub that appears in this Guide has been visited regularly, by CAMRA members. We offer full entries, with no unchecked 'lucky dip' sections of pubs sent in at random. Readers' recommendations are passed to local CAMRA branches, who take this feedback into account during their survey work.

It's not only about quality beer

The key driving force of the Guide – beer quality – has not changed in over four decades. However, the Guide also takes account of the history and architecture of pubs and such important aspects as food, family and disabled facilities, gardens, special events such as mini-beer festivals, and even the standard of the toilets. CAMRA volunteers are called on to be minor

CAMRA's GOOD BEER GUIDE 2019

Project Manager Emma Haines

Contributing Editor Tim Hampson
Editors Ione Brown, Simon Tuite
Project Assistance Joe Baxter, Katie Button, Julie Hudson
Sales & Marketing Toby Langdon

Head of Publishing Simon Hall

Vale Inn, Bollington, Cheshire, p7 (Photo: The Vale Inn)

Special thanks to 190,000 CAMRA members who carried out research for the pub entries; the Campaign's Regional Directors and Area Organisers, who co-ordinated the pub entries; the Campaign's Brewery Liaison Co-ordinators and Brewery Liaison Officers, who carried out research for the brewery entries; Rick Pickup for assistance co-ordinating the brewery entries; Alex Presland for technical support; Iain Barker and Christine Beatty at AMA Dataset; Michael Slaughter for advising on heritage pubs; all CAMRA's staff and CAMRA's National Executive for their help and support.

Thanks also to the publicans, breweries and others who have kindly contributed their photographs.

Photo credits: [Key: t = top; b = bottom; c=centre; l = left; r = right] Cover: (l&C) Cath Harries, (r) Plunkett Foundation; p9 Michael Slaughter; p17 Neal Revell/Clear-Capture Photography (www.clear-capture.com); p18 (l) Nick Alexander, (r) Phil Dickson-Earle; p19 (l) Neal Revell/Clear-Capture Photography (www.clear-capture.com), (r) Louise Hanzlik @ Beer_Talk.

Design: Colour pages design: Keith Holmes, Thames Street Studio; cover design: Dale Tomlinson. *Typeset in Guardian Sans and Dax.*

Maps & illustrations: Pubs section maps: David and Morag Perrot, PerroCarto; illustrations Keith Holmes.

Production: Database, typesetting of listings and indexes: AMA Dataset Ltd, Preston.

Printing: Printed and bound in the UK by CPI William Clowes, Beccles, Suffolk.

Published by the Campaign for Real Ale Ltd, 230 Hatfield Road, St Albans, Herts, AL1 4LW. www.camra.org.uk

ISBN 978-1-85249-354-7

Crown Inn, Pantygelli, Gwent (p599)

essayists, describing all aspects of the pubs they choose. We know, from the feedback we receive, that users of the Guide want to read detailed information about pubs before deciding whether to embark on a journey to visit them.

Town & country pubs

In addition to detailed descriptions, users want a good spread of pubs. Unlike some guides that concentrate on rural pubs, we recognise that most people live in towns and cities and expect a good selection of pubs in those areas. But we don't neglect suburban and country pubs: on the contrary, CAMRA campaigns for the survival of rural pubs that are often hubs of their communities.

We strive hard to ensure that all areas of the country are covered. Each county or region has an allocation of pubs based on a calculation of factors such as its population, number of licensed premises and levels of tourism. As a result, the *Good Beer Guide's* reach is unparalleled.

Proudly independent

Unlike with many of our competitors, all entries in our guide are free. CAMRA is a proudly independent organisation and there are no hidden costs of appearing in the *Good Beer Guide*. Guides that charge for entries restrict consumer choice as not all publicans want to pay the fees demanded.

CAMRA is a broad church and the Guide reflects that by choosing pubs across a wide spectrum that will appeal to people from all walks of life, regardless of income and background.

Keeping up to date

The Campaign has more than 200 branches. Each branch surveys the pubs in its area and monitors not only the quality of the cask beer in each one but also changes of ownership or management that could affect the ale on offer and the overall standard of the pub. In addition, branch officers liaise frequently with breweries in their areas and keep a close eye on the local brewing scene.

Both CAMRA's national website and its monthly newspaper *What's Brewing* publish regular information about, and updates to the Guide, including pubs that have closed or where beer quality has declined. These changes are also reflected in the Good Beer Guide mobile app that, alongside an e-book and sat-nav POI file, give readers access to the Guide in many different formats (see page 1046).

Such rigorously updated information provides CAMRA and the *Good Beer Guide* with an unrivalled overview of Britain's beer scene.

The improved Good Beer Guide app is a great partner to the printed edition (p1045)

More pub-finding resources

There are limits to the size of the *Good Beer Guide*. We believe – thanks to our members' efforts and the recommendations sent in by readers – that we offer a choice of the very best pubs throughout the country. But the Guide is complemented by other resources, including local pub guides produced by CAMRA branches which are available at beer festivals and local outlets, and the online **www.whatpub.com** – CAMRA's highly-visited official guide to all known real ale outlets in the country.

CAMRA also produces a constantly changing range of other books on the subjects of beer, pubs and brewing. Some of the latest are shown on pages 1043–1044. For the full list visit **www.camra.org.uk/books**.

Updates & reader feedback

You can keep your copy of the Guide up to date by visiting the *Good Beer Guide* area of the CAMRA website: **www.camra.org.uk/gbg**. Click on 'Updates to GBG 2019' where you will find information about changes to pubs and breweries.

The Guide is keen to hear from readers. If you wish to recommend a pub or feel that one you have visited fell below your expectations, then we would like to know. Please use the Readers' recommendations form at the back of the book or contact the editor at **gbgeditor@camra.org.uk**.

Introduction

Pubs and beer matter

Despite the many pressures on people's time and wallets, the pub is still the most popular place to go out to. And when people visit a pub, it's highly likely they will drink at least one beer, which has been brewed in the United Kingdom, using ingredients grown here too. This 46th edition of the *Good Beer Guide* will guide you to the best pubs *and* beer. Each edition is similar in that it includes the very best pubs in the country, all of which have been carefully selected by CAMRA members. But each is unique in that it provides an annual snapshot on the state of the pub and brewing industry for the year of publication.

The current UK brewing scene is incredibly vibrant and diverse. In 46 years of publishing the *Good Beer Guide*, CAMRA has seen the number of breweries rise from 105 to more than 1,750. Today, every UK Parliamentary constituency has at least one brewery within its boundary, and many of these breweries were established during the last 10 years. They can be found in city centres and remote rural locations. Some are run as lifestyle businesses, whilst others have far more ambitious plans. Most are run by people who care deeply about their carbon footprint, sustainability and the environment.

Collectively, this wealth of diverse companies are big employers of people, too. Importantly, they are often a source of employment for younger adults. Many of the people working in UK breweries are under the age of 25. And what an astonishing assortment of beers they make. More than 40 years ago most brewers only made a mild and perhaps two bitters. Some might have made a winter warmer or a Christmas ale. How times have changed. Today, customers going to a pub can expect to find milds, bitters, golden ales, wheat beers, rye beers and even sour beers. There are stouts and imperial stouts, IPAs and double IPAs.

Forty-six years ago, most beers were made with malt, hops, water and yeast. This quartet of natural ingredient are still the principle components of beer. But today, it is not unusual to find brewers who have added other ingredients to their repertoire – these could include vanilla, lemongrass or fresh summer fruits. The only limitation is the imagination of the brewer. Who would have thought people would be drinking peanut butter milk stout?

Cask ale has a taken on a modern hue. It's become a drink for aspirant millennials. And the idea that beers is only sold by the pint to men finishing a shift at a factory now seems old-fashioned and from a long-gone era. Many pubs now offer beer by the third of a pint. The smaller-sized glasses offer drinkers the opportunity to try a wider range of beers and experience more of the fantastic aromas, flavours and colours today's brewers are creating.

Taxing times for pubs & consumers

Pubs and brewing are a great British success story. For locals and tourists, Britain's pubs are a beacon. They offer something uniquely British and are often identified as a major attraction by some 13 million foreign visitors every year.

But this success cannot be taken for granted. Despite the vibrancy of the pubs sector, with new breweries and pubs opening every week,

Andrew Birkby, Jaega Wise, William Harris and James Birkby of London's Wild Card brewery. Established in 2013, the brewery and tap room now employs 16 people in the local area

18 pubs are also being forced to close each week. Changing consumer tastes, legislation, taxation and planning laws can all affect the viability of a pub or brewery.

Pubs are being hit hard by a triple whammy of one of the highest rates of beer duty across Europe, rapidly rising business rates, and VAT. A third of the cost of a pub pint is now made up of various taxes. Typically, when a consumer spends £4 on a pint in a pub more than £1.40 will go to the taxman. Did you know that the UK pays nearly 40% of all beer duty in the EU but only consumes around 12% of the beer?

Tax breakdown on a £4 beer

15p is business rates

49p is beer tax

67p is VAT

15p is other taxes

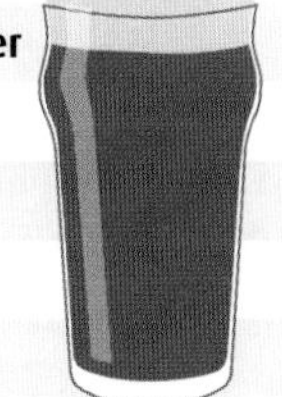

In the last Budget, the Chancellor gave the beer drinker and pubgoer some relief, but in the cold light of day the drinker's glass seems half empty rather than half full. While temporary business rate relief in England and a beer duty freeze have been welcomed, CAMRA is calling on the Government to implement a fundamental review of the tax system. Britain's impending departure from the EU provides potential new opportunities to support pubs, such as lower rates of tax for draught beer sold in pubs.

Strengthening the Pubs Code

CAMRA campaigned long and hard for the introduction of the Pubs Code and Adjudicator (PCA). It was with good reason. Some pub-owning businesses had established a monopoly over the supply and cost of products to their tenants and were enforcing increasingly high rents. The result was that viable businesses became unsustainable and communities were at risk of losing their pubs.

The first 18 months of the operation of the Code were plagued by delays, and the PCA was too slow to respond to emerging issues. There was evidence the PCA had struggled with a significantly under-resourced office and deficiencies in the Code. This lead to a backlog of issues and uncertainty among some tenants over the future of their contracts. Uncertainty leads to doubt, which has in some case been followed by the closure of potentially viable pubs.

CAMRA says the Government should undertake an urgent review and public consultation of the Pubs Code to identify the necessary improvements required to deliver the core principles of the Code. Two years into its operation, the national pub companies are continuing to exploit gaps in the legislation and operation of the Pubs Code and are not abiding by the spirit of the Code.

A CAMRA fact-finding exercise uncovered reports of obstructive tactics deployed by pub companies when tenants were attempting to break free of tie. Now, urgent changes are needed to the Pubs Code Regulations to allow the original aims of the legislation to be achieved.

A review must be carried out as soon as is practicably possible and include a full public consultation to allow for the collection of evidence of the workings of the Code so far from tied pub tenants and other key stakeholders, including groups representing tenants and other industry experts.

Providing a voice of moderation

Drinkers' Voice is an initiative which CAMRA has been involved in which seeks to bring the public back into the debate on alcohol and health. For too long the alcohol and health debate has been dominated by the anti-alcohol lobby, which has sought to de-normalise drinking and restrict people's access to alcohol.

Drinkers' Voice claims the anti-alcohol lobby has influenced people's attitude towards drinking alcohol and has led to the government issuing some of the lowest alcohol consumption guidelines in Europe.

The new guidelines, issued in 2016, replaced the former suggested limits of 21 units of alcohol a week for men and 14 for women with a new limit of 14 units for both sexes. These new guidelines have been widely criticised and rejected – indeed, a Drinkers' Voice poll revealed that 70% of drinkers don't pay attention to them.

Drinkers' Voice chairman Bryan Davies said: 'We believe it is important that people understand the benefits of drinking alcohol as part of a healthy lifestyle. We want people to talk about how enjoying a drink with friends enhances their wellbeing, and how scientific evidence shows that moderate drinking can help heart and cognitive health.

'The freedom to enjoy drink in moderation, without fear of being criticised by anti-alcohol campaigners is, I believe, a fundamental right of all responsible citizens.'

You can find out more information about Drinkers' Voice by visiting their website: **www.drinkersvoice.org.uk**.

The on-going fight to save pubs

Campaigners in Kent have been celebrating after winning CAMRA's prestigious Pub Saving Award, which recognises communities that save their beloved local pub from closure.

The campaigners were recognised for their work in saving the Harrow in Stockbury, a 200-year-old village pub which faced closure after it was put up for sale in 2016. Now the pub is a thriving community hub with social lunches for vulnerable people, book swaps and an internet cafe.

The campaigners secured the £380,000 needed to buy the pub through a network of 140 shareholders, money from the Plunkett Foundation, which helps rural communities, and community pub support programme More Than A Pub. The pub re-opened last year and is now described as a 'buzzing and thriving' part of Stockbury.

The campaigners raised awareness of the pub's plight in the local community by engaging with local papers and hosting various events such as quiz nights and BBQs in the village centre.

Harrow Community Benefit Society (CBS) Group chair Chris Porter said: 'It is a fantastic achievement to have saved this pub from closure thanks to the help of hundreds of people – stakeholders, villagers, councillors, press, MPs and groups like Pub is the Hub and Plunkett.

'Through these efforts our little community is better connected than ever before. It is an absolute delight to receive this award from CAMRA and to be able to show other communities that it is possible to save their local from disappearing forever.'

Praising the winner, Paul Ainsworth, who organises CAMRA's Pub Saving Award said: 'The Harrow CBS group used every tool available to save their beloved pub from closure, and it is an absolute delight to celebrate this with our Pub Saving Award. Once a pub is closed, it is too often lost for ever and their success should be a great inspiration to other communities faced with losing their local – pubs really can be saved.'

Staff at the Craufurd Arms celebrate their recognition by CAMRA's Pub Saving Awards

The runner-up in the competition was the Craufurd Arms Community Group, which attracted the attention of judges after saving the **Craufurd Arms** (see page 46), the last pub in North Maidenhead, Berkshire, using the combined efforts of everyone from residents all the way up to the Prime Minister. Support also came from Sir Robert and Lady Georgina Craufurd, after whose family the pub is named.

When the pub was threatened by closure the local community sprung to action to raise the required funds to purchase the pub, with a guide price of £325,000. They secured the support of the local community through residents' surveys, public meetings and social media engagement.

Craufurd Arms Society chairman Mark Newcombe said: 'With the help of our members and supporters the Craufurd Arms – our pint-sized community pub – has been able to thrive and prosper as a vital social and community hub and a profitable business.

'The fact that we managed to raise the funds in such a short period of time is a testament to the incredible efforts of the committee, investors, supporters and CAMRA members.'

ENCOURAGING COMMUNITY PUB OWNERSHIP

One way of breathing life into threatened pubs is to make it easier for communities to buy their pubs. Now, more help is at hand thanks to the Plunkett Foundation with the support of CAMRA and pub trade organisations.

A network of community pub leaders is being created. The network will offer informed advice on how to set up, run and ensure the sustainability of a community-owned venture. Much more than just a place to drink, pubs are the soul of many communities, too many of which have been stricken by the loss of other local services.

CAMRA's vision is to have quality real ale and thriving pubs in every community. With a properly working Pubs Code and better advice for communities who want to buy their local, there is every chance it could happen.

Saving post war pubs

Not all pubs have a long and glorious history going back hundreds of years – pubs built in the post-war period are also important and valuable community and cultural assets. CAMRA is seeking protection and recognition of pubs built post-war which have remained at the heart of their communities for more than 50 years and play a unique role in Britain's history and culture.

The Campaign has highlighted three of the very best intact surviving pubs which were recently turned down for listing due to restrictive criteria being applied including: the White Admiral in Harlow, built in 1953, the Palomino in Newmarket, built in 1963, and the Punch Bowl in Worcester, built in 1958.

Each of these pubs are central to their surrounding living environment, but modern pressures for change make them some of the most threatened and vulnerable buildings in the country. Many other pubs designed in this period have fallen by the wayside simply because their architecture reflects austerity and functionality, rather than grandeur and theatrics. This means that some fantastic survivals from this period risk being lost forever, along with a whole cultural era that is now seriously under-represented in the national heritage listings.

Giving a pub Grade-II Listing marks it as nationally important to our historic heritage and provides it with extra legal protection within the planning system.

The 1960s interior of the Palomino, Newmarket

Mind the gender gap

Research conducted by CAMRA a few years back showed more than half of all women now visit the pub regularly and that many were willing to give real ale a try.

However, a report commissioned by Dea Latis, a group set up to inform and educate women about beer, has found the UK has the lowest percentage of female beer drinkers in the world, despite the 'craft' beer boom.

The Gender Pint Gap report also concluded that outdated sexist marketing, misunderstanding about the calorie content of beer and negative perceptions about flavours in beer all contributed to British women avoiding drinking beer.

The research is the first carried out about female attitudes to beer in almost a decade. Dea Latis wanted to discover if the UK's brewing boom has inspired more women to drink beer.

The report concludes with a 'Beer Drinking Women's Manifesto' which urges women who drink beer to become advocates; encouraging sampling, asking for different volumes and glassware and dispelling myths about calories and acceptability.

Discriminatory marketing

CAMRA has also condemned sexist and other discriminatory marketing in the brewing industry and will not be promoting brands that use it or stocking their beers at festivals. The recent Manchester Beer Festival trialled a policy that prevented beers with discriminator imagery or names being invited to supply. Volunteers also enforced CAMRA's Code of Conduct and Volunteers' Charter, designed to ensure volunteers and members of the public do not experience discrimination of any kind at CAMRA festivals or events.

Constant values

Despite the changing fortunes of pubs and the brewing industry, there is one constant – real ale is central to CAMRA's aims and activities.

CAMRA wants more people to discover the joy of drinking good cask conditioned beer in a well-run, caring and atmospheric pub or club, which reaches out to all people.

The pub as an institution is a great survivor, and its epitaph has been written many times – from the passing of the Defence of the Realm Act in World War One, through to the introduction of a second TV channel in the 1950s, people have forecast the demise of the pub. As we spend more on our homes and gardens, the pressure on consumers' disposable income increases. But the resilience of pubs is in how they have responded to consumer lifestyle changes and pressure.

For the pub to retain its position as the most popular place for people to go out, we need to support them with our time and our custom, and discover some of the wonderful drinking places within these pages.

The great British pub

Pubs come in all shapes and sizes

The British pubs is a unique institution – a place where people from all walks of life can come together to meet, drink, talk, eat, listen to music, support a sports team and to socialise. In a competitive market, pubs are increasingly playing to their strengths and choosing to specialise, but whatever form a pub comes in, the best are still places where everyone can find welcome.

Micropub movement grows bigger

The rise of the micropub is one of the pub phenomena of recent years. Some see them as one of the drivers which could help revive the beleaguered British High Street, many of which are struggling as retail shops close.

The first British micropub was opened in east Kent in 2005, by Martyn Hillier, after a licensing law change which made it easier for new pubs to open in buildings which had previously been used for something else. Since then, micropubs have popped up in antique shops, sweet shops and even an undertaker's, and they now number more than 330. Typically they are small, trade from high street and town centre units, have a strong cask beer focus and a very loyal, local following.

The growing micropub scene is bringing real ale to places where a traditional pub would not be appropriate, filling gaps on high streets and improving choice for drinkers.

Micropub pioneer Hillier, who is also co-founder of the Micropub & Microbrewery Association, believes the conventional pub model has let customers and licensees down. His pub the **Butchers Arms in Herne**, Kent (see page 227) is based in what used to be his wife's florists shop. The building had a been a butchers in a previous incarnation. Hillier wanted to create a pub where cask and conversation were equal, successful partners, so he created a design that took away the physical barrier between the licensee and the customers. The Butchers has no bar, the beer is served from casks racked in the back of the shop, and the seating is around the edges, meaning all the customers are facing into the room. The pub seats 18 comfortably – 'any more and people have their backs to each other' – and Hillier says his business is 50% about the cask beer on offer, and 50% about the conversation.

Micropub pioneer Martyn Hillier opened the Butchers Arms in his wife's old florists shop

Hillier says: 'For CAMRA, micropubs are the last piece of the jigsaw,' in terms of supporting both cask ale and local pubs. 'I think the market can support at least 500. Every village should have one.'

Hillier, who was named CAMRA's Campaigner of the Year in 2015 for his pioneering work, believes the number of micropubs will continue to grow. He cites the fact that the **Weavers Real Ale House in Kidderminster** (see page 521), a relatively new one-room micropub was named in the final four of CAMRA's pub of the year competition as sign of the growing success of the micropub concept.

The Weavers is deceptively spacious inside, with bench seating along the sides, plenty of tables and a conversational atmosphere. Light and airy, the walls display pictures of old Kidderminster and beer memorabilia. It serves eight beers, four ciders and a perry on handpump.

Weavers Real Ale House owner Dean Cartwright said: 'We took over the running of the pub just two years ago and are over the moon to be in the final four. While we've slightly modernised it and extended the beer range, we've also retained the quirky front-room feel to the pub.

'We have a small team of incredibly enthusiastic and friendly staff who love to talk about real ale in a welcoming and conversational atmosphere. It's just amazing to be this far in the competition out of thousands of pubs across the country – it means a lot to know how much some people care about the pub.'

CAMRA Regional Director Garry Timmins is an enthusiast for micropubs, believing they are a catalyst for a real ale revival. He said: 'The Weavers Real Ale House was the first micropub to

Weavers Real Ale House, Kidderminster

Tiny Rebel's new Brewery Bar, Rogerstone

open in Kidderminster and has helped spur a real ale revival in pubs across the town.

'The friendly welcome, convivial atmosphere for a chat and consistently excellent quality wide range of ales and ciders quickly developed a following and made it into a must-visit venue for visitors to the town. Above all, the greatest credit is due to the bar team whose friendliness, knowledge and enthusiasm shine through whenever anybody enters, and help to make it into an outstanding pub.'

Cornwall's first micropub is the **Pilchard Press Alehouse in St Ives** (see page 87). Situated in a cellar, down a side alley off the harbourside, it serves six-real ales, three of which come from Cornwall. There is a wooden bar and a few stools and two tables and chairs. It has space for about 25 people.

The **Little Ale House in Bromsgrove**, Worcestershire (see page 519) serves up to seven ales straight from the cask. The house beer, Half Cut, is brewed by Woodcote Manor. A range of ciders and perries are stocked. Take out containers are available, as are fresh rolls and Scotch eggs.

Tapping in to new markets

As an antidote to the national trend of pub closures, many breweries are opening their own thriving tap rooms. About a third of small breweries now run a tap bar, says the Society of Independent Brewers (SIBA).

SIBA chief executive Mike Benner said: 'A high percentage of our members now have tap rooms and they are becoming as important to local communities as pubs are. They have always existed but are making a comeback because today consumers are very much into the idea of independence and local beer.'

In July 2017, when Tiny Rebel opened a brand new £2.6m brewery in Rogerstone on the outskirts of Newport, South Wales it also includes a **Brewery Bar** (see page 599), with restaurant and conference venue for private functions. The directors believe this offers something unique to the UK, where everything is done on site from start to finish. Their brewery bar has also created an important hub for the local community.

Tiny Rebel director and co-founder Brad Cummings said: 'In just five years we have gone from home-brewing in a garage to a purpose-built and world-class facility.

'What was most important to us was to create a space for people to enjoy what Tiny Rebel represents. But we'll also be able to increase the breadth of what we can produce and support continued growth from our new home.

'When it comes to the location of the site, Newport is our home and where Tiny Rebel all began – so it is only right that we invest in the city as we grow our business.'

The Hop Studio brewery has created its own tap room, by converting an empty shop building in Pocklington, East Yorkshire. The development has created ten new jobs. The bar, called the Market Tap, will have the town's biggest beer range, with 18 beers on the bar at a time, as well as a large selection of bottled beers and ciders, a broad wine range and bar food. Nine of the beers on the bar will be Hop Studio's, and the other nine lines will be used to showcase beers from other leading Yorkshire breweries.

Hop Studio owner Dave Shaw said: 'Pocklington is a great town and it has new shops, and lots of new housing going up, but there are no other bars like this here and I think there are a lot of people whose beer tastes are not yet being met in the town. We will have an excellent wine selection as well. There has been a lot of excitement as people have seen it coming together.

'Accessing the market can be difficult for smaller breweries. The big brewers can be more aggressive on price and big pub companies do not give us a lot of access. More and more breweries are opening their own tap rooms, and it is a good way for us to have a direct route to the market.'

Gastropubs offer a warm welcome

Cambridge Professor Christel Lane says that the development of the gastropub has made pubs more welcoming to women and wider society.

In her academic book *From Taverns to Gastropubs* Professor Lane, a Fellow of St John's College, argues that while some pubs have switched to becoming food first, they have not entirely changed their identity, and some have become more popular local venues as a result of the move.

She says gastropubs have often been unfairly accused of helping to kill off the classic British alehouse. But according to her study, the rise of the gourmet pub has been unfairly maligned. Rather than tearing the soul out of British pubs, she argues that so-called 'gastrification' is a natural evolution, which has preserved some of their most cherished features, while also meeting changing social expectations.

She said: 'The character of the pub has always changed over the centuries and the gastropub is part of that.'

She found that, while gastropubs have shifted the emphasis away from drinking and towards eating, they have not completely distorted the identity of an English pub. Many have become social hubs for their local communities. They are also among the most patriotic champions of classic British cooking, from pies and roasts, to bread and butter pudding.

Although they are sometimes portrayed as posh eateries, her study found that gastropubs promote and value casual drinking, because of the relaxed environment that this creates for diners and drinkers alike. 'The future is casual dining,' one publican explained, 'and the pub is the perfect melting pot for that'.

Like traditional pubs, many gastropubs have become important centres for their community. Alongside quiz nights and Rotary meetings, her research threw up examples of gastropubs that host book groups, pensioners' clubs, choir meetings, cookery schools, mums and babies groups, environmental awareness meetings, and even a pitch for petanque.

The **Clarence in Bury**, Greater Manchester (see page 326) is just one example of a pub where fine dining and real ale go hand in hand. The pub even has its own brewery, Silver Street, which stared life in the pub's basement but last year moved to premises in the nearby Britannia Mill. The brewery's staff delight in offering beer and food matching suggestions.

The **Punchbowl Inn in Crosthwaite,** Cumbria (see page 94) marries the charm of a Lake District pub with good food. A beer can be enjoyed after a long country walk, and if you feel hungry, just order something from the award winning menu.

'Ultimately, much of the criticism of gastropubs seems to have less to do with what they actually offer, and more with the fact that people miss a past society which is no longer there.'

She argues that the development of food in pubs has made them more welcoming to wider sectors of society, particularly women, improving the gender balance and has generally made pubs less threatening than they might once have been.

Lane said: 'The rise of the gastropub does not just mean a culture has been lost; something has been gained. Women were once almost completely excluded from pubs; now they are a target market.'

Villagers solve their lack of a pub

The villagers of Grafham, Cambridgeshire have a community shop, a community bus and finally they are going to build their own pub. Campaigners have been given planning permission by Huntingdonshire District Council to build a pub on wasteland owned by the parish council.

For the last seven years residents who wanted a beer either had to drink at home or at a beer festival run by campaigners. Now, work has begun on building a log cabin which will be used as a pub.

The Pub at Grafham director Kevin Sharp said the community interest company now had planning permission granted to build a wooden log cabin for use as a community pub. He said the pub would cost £50,000 to build and make operational.

Sharp said: 'With all of the funds now secured from selling shares around the village we are excited to announce that the builders are due to start work on the building of the facility at the end of July with an expected completion date of the end of September.

'Over the last couple of years, a group of people have been working at bringing a permanent pub to our village. The pub, like the beer festival, will act as a free house, and will only sell local beers from our many local microbreweries. Working with the community and local councils we hope is to keep our overheads low so that we can pass savings on to our customers, whilst not compromising on quality beer. We have engaged the village through open meetings and information events and we even ran a competition to name the pub – which will be the Grafham Trout.

'When so many good pubs are closing, we think the model we have used would be of value to other villages who have no pub within walking distance and is a great example of the community coming together to build a pub for not half as much money as you would imagine.'

CAMRA celebrates women in brewing

CAMRA's 2018 Kidderminster Beer & Cider Festival decided to mark the centenary of women's suffrage by celebrating women working in brewing. The festival sourced half of its beers from breweries that employ female brewers (brewsters), including two local to Kidderminster: Hop Shed and Pershore.

Festival Organiser Nick Yarwood said: 'We have seen a huge resurgence of female brewers at both large and small breweries in recent decades. Women were the primary brewers for thousands of years, and brewsters have pioneered some really innovative and exciting ways of making beer more recently. Their contribution to the industry should be celebrated and promoted.'

Pershore brewery brewster Elizabeth Barnett said educating beer drinkers about microbrewing is incredibly important. 'Nothing is automated at our brewery – everything is done by traditional, manual process and I am involved in every step of the process.

'You can usually find me emptying out the mash tun, and most people are frankly astonished to see me getting stuck in and not just sitting behind a desk.

'We need to do more to show people that women are actually capable of making beer and can produce some really exciting ones – pushing boundaries and adding new ingredients.'

She welcomes the collaborative atmosphere across the industry, which she says has been incredibly helpful having learnt on the job without formal training.

Sarah Saleh, brewer and co-founder of Hop Shed, also spoke at the festival. Saleh began brewing in a garage at home and quickly got the bug for it, before taking part in some formal training at Brewlab in Sunderland.

Saleh said: 'Being based on a hop farm I only use British hops in the beers I brew. I enjoy developing recipes for new varieties of hops and showing you don't need American hops to produce really flavoursome beers.'

Hop Shed brewer Sarah Saleh

More needs to be done to attract the female beer drinker

Despite the strides forward being made by women in brewing, female drinkers are being left behind.

Beer Sommelier and women's beer group Dea Latis director Annabel Smith said: 'We know that the beer category has seen massive progress in the last decade – you only need to look at the wide variety of styles and flavours which weren't available widely in the UK ten years ago.

'Yet it appears the female consumer either hasn't come on the same journey, or the beer industry just isn't addressing their female audience adequately. Overtly masculine advertising and promotion of beer has been largely absent from media channels for a number of years but there is a lot of history to unravel. Women still perceive beer branding is targeted at men.'

Dea Latis' Annabel Smith

Fellow Dea Latis member Lisa Harlow said: 'Our research has shown many misconceptions which women still hold about beer, such as calorific content, self-image and pre-conceptions about taste. It was disheartening in our supposedly enlightened times that so many of our female respondents cited "being judged by others" as a reason for not drinking beer. Perhaps we need some high-profile celebrity advocates to show women that it is acceptable to drink beer?'

Beer writer, sommelier and certified Cicerone, Melissa Cole said the beer industry has managed to disenfranchise women from their once-loved drink over the last 70 years or so.

'It highlights everything from societal pressures to inappropriate serves to ingrained misogyny and more as just some of the issues and challenges the brewing industry to do something about it.

'But it's not just criticism, it's got rational advice on how the new, and old, guard of brewing can make beer relevant to 51 per cent of the population again; but it's also only just the start and I hope more long-overdue funding is provided to help address this issue.'

Award winning pubs & clubs

Pub of the Year

A Merseyside pub was named CAMRA's National Pub of the Year in 2018 just five years after it was boarded up for closure.

When owners Andy and Denise Evans took over the running of the **Cricketers Arms in St Helens** (see page 350) in 2013, it was boarded up and hadn't served cask ale since the 1980s. It is now a well-established local community pub with an excellent selection of 13 locally-sourced cask ales, including five session pale ales and two bitters, as well as IPAs, porters, stouts and lagers. Ten ciders are available year-round, with 20 in the summer.

Alongside this impressive ale and cider range, the pub installed a microbrewery in summer 2018, and plans to task its customers with naming the pub's beers. Visitors can also take part in a number of social nights including regular beer festivals, dominoes, jam nights, pub quizzes, karaoke and pool teams, as well as enjoy a new whiskey and gin bar.

The Cricketers Arms regularly wins local CAMRA awards, but this is the first time it has won a national title. Paul Ainsworth, CAMRA's National Pub of the Year coordinator said: 'After winning the regional award in both 2015 and 2016, it's a well deserved third time lucky for the Cricketers to be named CAMRA's national Pub of the Year.

'In less than five years, Andy and Denise have converted a boarded up pub on the brink of closure into a true destination pub for beer lovers across the country. What impressed me the most is that the Cricketers is a genuine community pub where people from all walks of life come together to socialise. It is a shining example of how a pub, which seems destined for closure, can have its fortunes turned around when in the right hands.'

The Cricketers Arms in St Helens has gone from a borded up boozer to an award-winning local

Owner Andy Evans said: 'We are over the moon to be named the top pub in the country after just a few short years of renovations. We've done everything we can to make this a welcoming community pub and still have exciting developments ahead of us. As well as expanding the beers available, we created a beer garden and put greens in the ground, and have big plans to install a microbrewery this year. We are very proud to be part of the cask ale scene and look forward to celebrating with our locals!'

Pubs entered for the Pub of the Year Award are judged by CAMRA on atmosphere, level of service, value for money and community focus, but extra weighting is, of course, given to the quality of the real ale, cider and perry.

Denise and Andy Evans celebrate the Cricketers Arms being awarded National Pub of the Year

The three other finalists in the Pub of the Year competition were:

Wigan Central, Wigan,
Greater Manchester (see page 342)

Located in a pair of 19th century railway arches, just yards away from Wigan's two railway stations, this two-roomed pub has a railway-themed interior, including screens with a with a live feed of arrival and departure times from both stations. The pub is the brainchild of Patsy and John Slevin, owners of the nearby Prospect Brewery, and it serves a range of their beers, alongside real ales from all over the country, four real ciders and continental bottled beers. The pub is a venue for regular music nights, as well as meet-the-brewer events and beer and food matching.

CAMRA's National Pub of the Year competition considers all the criteria that make for a good pub. The competition is judged by the Campaign's 190,000-plus members. Each branch selects its top pub. The branch winners are entered into 16 regional competitions, with the regional winners battling it out to reach the final stages of the competition. Look out for the 🏆 symbol against pub entries in the Guide and see 'Award-winning pubs' on pages 1037-1039 for the winning branch pubs.

Stanford Arms, Lowestoft, Suffolk (see page 445)

A Pub of the Year finalist two years running, the Stanford Arms has been run for the last six years by husband a wife team David and Samantha Burd. Up to 12 real ales, with a focus on East Anglian breweries, are available from the open-plan L-shaped bar, and up to six ciders are served on gravity. They stock a range of craft cans and bottles, and always have a sour ale available. The bar has been beautifully refurbished with pews salvaged from a local church, and there is a woodburner, courtyard garden, aviary and a wood-fired pizza oven. The pub holds a themed food evening on Wednesdays, pizza night on Fridays and there is live music on Sunday afternoon.

Weavers Real Ale House, Kidderminster, Worcestershire (see page 521)

This one-room micropub, a short walk from the railway station, is deceptively spacious inside, with plenty of bench seating and tables. It serves eight ales on handpump, including the house beer Unbeweavable from Pig Iron Brewery, which pub owner Dean Cartwright runs in nearby Rowley Regis. Four ciders and a perry are also available, plus six craft beers. The Weavers doesn't serve cooked food, but cobs are always available, and customers are welcome to bring their own food from the nearby takeaways.

Club of the Year

The **Flixton Conservative Club in Manchester** (see page 340) won the prestigious CAMRA Club of the Year award in 2018 after a recent transformation saw a wider range of real ales and ciders brought in.

Keith Spencer, Chairman of CAMRA's Clubs Working Group says: 'The Flixton Conservative Club has transformed itself over the last five years under new stewardship by expanding the real ale offering from just two to six at a time. The club is reaping the benefits and has become a thriving hub to the local community and a worthy winner of this year's award.'

The well maintained club runs a number of social events for the local community including brewery nights, quiz events and sports teams including snooker. There is even a walking group and a popular chess club that meets once a week in the club's function room. Regular entertainment takes place over the weekend with music, bingo and competitions. The club previously won the local CAMRA Club of the Year award but this is the first time it has made it through to the national round.

The Flixton Conservative Club in Manchester serves a wide range of real ales and ciders

Nigel Porter at Flixton Conservative Club says: 'This really is a total team effort. The Club is very fortunate in having a very supportive committee, really friendly and knowledgeable bar staff and a great bunch of members who just show so much enthusiasm for everything we do. The quality of our real ale has been paramount to the success of the Club and a great deal of the credit for that needs to go to all of the terrific brewers who supply us and support us in so many ways.'

Club Mirror's Head of Judges Caroline Scoular said: 'The four super regional winners were truly impressive clubs. The range and quality of ales was surpassed only by the quality of their welcome. Congratulations to them all for making the final four, and very well done to Flixton, a very worthy winner.'

The other finalists in the Club of the Year competition were:

Appleton Thorn Village Hall, Appleton Thorn, Cheshire (see page 71)

This ex-school, turned village hall was named CAMRA National Club of the Year in 2008 and has been a finalist in 2010, 2015 and 2017. A central bar serves a large function room and a smaller lounge. A changing range of beer is on offer, with paddles of thirds available. Five real ciders are also stocked. An annual beer festival is held in October. Quizzes and occasional live music nights also feature. Non-members pay a minimal fee for admission.

The Club of the Year competition is run by CAMRA in conjunction with the journal Club Mirror to find the best real ale clubs in the country. One of the criteria for entry into the competition is that clubs must admit CAMRA members, both men and women. A number of the best real ale clubs feature in the *Good Beer Guide* alongside recommended pubs. As well as admitting CAMRA members, many will also admit non-members carrying a copy of this book. See individual entries for more information.

Albatross Club (RAFA), Bexhill on Sea, East Sussex (see page 459)

Winner of the National Club of the year award in 2016, and a finalist in 2017, the Albatross Club is a welcoming, popular and friendly RAFA club. Local beers feature strongly here, from such as Three Legs, Gun and Rother Valley; other beers are nationally sourced. There are regular folk, jazz and quiz nights and meat raffles; additionally, the club stages very popular public beer festivals. CAMRA members are always welcome to sample the range of quality ales on offer.

Real Ale Farm (RAF), Gilfach Fargoed, Glamorgan (see page 587)

Housed in the former Gilfach Fargoed Fawr Farm– built in the 17th century and the the oldest surviving building in Bargoed – the Real Ale Farm offers the best range and quality of beer for miles, with up to five guest ales and two ciders or perries. Felinfoel Double Dragon is always available and there is usually one other from the Felinfoel range, alongside other beers from breweries both local and further afield, selected for flavour and interest. Numerous charity events and the occasional beer festival are hosted. Visitors are welcome but must be signed in. The short walk from Gilfach Fargoed station presents a modest but energetic climb.

Pub Design Awards

When the Campaign for Real Ale announced the very best pub designs across Britain, the winners included the "longest bar in Britain", a 1930s neo-Georgian roadhouse, a former Victorian coffeehouse, and a tastefully modern new-build pub.

The **Fitzroy Tavern in London's Fitzrovia**, which has been skillfully restored to its former Victorian-era glory won the Refurbishment award after Samuel Smiths returned the pub to its 1897 guise, installing new partitions and wrought-iron pub signs. The surviving tiling has been sensitively restored and the new wallpaper and repo carpets have been well-chosen.

The **Greenwood Hotel in Northolt**, London – an historic high street landmark – won the Conservation award. Still as much of a hub for the local community as it was in 1939, the fine, sympathetic conservation work executed at this pub shows how subtlety and respect can often achieve more than big-budget transformation.

Greenwood Hotel in Northolt, London

The **Sail Loft in Greenwich**, London has taken home the rarely-given New build award for its tasteful display of modern design, setting a wonderful example of "how to do it well" with floor-to-ceiling glazing, finishes of decent quality, a well-crafted island servery and very pleasant seating.

The only winner outside of London, the **Bowland Beer Hall in Clitheroe**, Lancashire (see page 244) took home the Conversion to Pub Use award after it was splendidly converted from a former textile mill by local architect Charles Stanton. It now boasts the longest bar in Britain and is the centrepiece of a larger regeneration scheme, which already includes an impressive food hall showcasing regional produce and plans for a future gym and hotel.

Bowland Beer Hall in Clitheroe, Lancashire

Sean Murphy, CAMRA's Pub Design Awards coordinator says: 'Our 2017 winners celebrate an enormously wide variety of building styles and contexts – from a modern new build to a historic high street landmark, from a textile mill conversion to a Victorian restoration. The sheer diversity of these winners, and their evident commercial success, shows just how vibrant a pub can be – and what an agent of regeneration it can provide – if treated with respect and sensitivity for both building and clientele.'

CAMRA's Pub Design Awards aim to find the most stunningly designed pubs in the UK. The awards, held in association with Historic England, recognise high standards of architecture in the refurbishment and the conservation of existing pubs. See **www.camra.org.uk/pub-design-awards**.

CAMRA beer festivals

A showcase for breweries old and new

With the astonishing range and variety of beers available today, even the best-stocked pub is limited by the number of its handpumps and the size of its cellars. For a true showcase for some of the best emerging brewing talent in the UK today, pay a visit to a CAMRA beer festival, and try some of the hundreds of different beers, ciders and perries on sale.

There are around 200 CAMRA festivals – local, regional and national – held throughout the country. They are joined in the beer drinkers' calendar by festivals run by other organisations: the Campaign welcomes all events that attract beer lovers but it feels its festivals have something special to offer.

CAMRA beer festivals play a key role in spreading the message about good beer in Britain. They have also played an important role in the campaign to roll back the power of giant breweries and offer a wider choice of beer. In the early days of CAMRA, when outlets for real ale were diminishing, festivals proved that good beer was still alive and available.

Many beer events just offer pale and golden ales. But Britain has a rich beer heritage and CAMRA festivals stress that heritage by also featuring such styles as dark mild, porter, stout and barley wine. Darker beers come into their own in the colder parts of the year and many festivals feature autumn and winter events, culminating in the Great British Beer Festival – Winter, currently held in Norwich in February.

CAMRA's festivals also feature innovative new styles of beer, including those aged in wood or made with the addition of fruit, herbs and spices. A number of festivals also make available beers suitable for vegans and vegetarians as well as beers that are gluten-free. And just about every festival will also feature cider and perry, drinks growing fast in popularity and which CAMRA has supported for many years.

There's no hard sell at CAMRA festivals. The atmosphere is relaxed and many events will offer small tasters of beer so visitors can sample before buying. Prices for both entry and beer are kept as low as possible. Wherever possible, there will be ample seating provided along with family rooms for visitors with children. There can be talks and tastings while live entertainment ranges from jazz, folk and blues to light classical.

Food is a key element of most festivals, often including 'street food' and food made by local artisans who share the ideals of craft brewers.

It's food – and beer – for thought. On the following pages you will find a festival near you. Come and raise a glass to the best of British.

CAMRA festival volunteers are happy to offer samples and recommend beers and ciders

CAMRA festivals offer a range of attractions, alongside the beer choice. Here are just a few festivals that offer slightly more.

- **Live music:** Nottingham – There is live entertainment throughout the festival, with a varied selection of music styles.
- **Food:** Manchester – A wide range of food stalls provide everything from snacks and sweets to tacos, burgers and hearty meals.
- **Winter ales:** GBBF Winter, Norwich – CAMRA's premier festival for winter beers. The Champion Winter Beer of Britain is judged at the festival.
- **Family-friendly:** Canterbury – An outdoor festival that welcomes families, with children's entertainers on the Saturday.
- **Cider & perry:** Reading – With over 150 real ciders and perrys available. CAMRA's National Cider & Perry Championship is judged here.
- **Beers by the sea**: Eastbourne – Held on Eastbourne seafront, you can enjoy your beer at outside tables with fine sea views.
- **Vintage transport:** Woodcote – A vintage transport rally, featuring over 600 vehicles, including vintage cars and motorbikes.

CAMRA beer festivals through the year

Beer festivals come in all shapes and sizes but offer a wide choice for discerning drinkers. Some festivals feature beers for such seasons as harvest time and winter but all offer a warm welcome with good food and, in many cases, live entertainment and family facilities. The listing below shows all the planned CAMRA beer festivals for 2019, although please note that some festivals, dates and details are to be confirmed. For more information visit **www.camra.org.uk/events**.

January
Colchester – Winter
Ely – Winter
Exeter – Winter
Manchester
Salisbury – Winter

February
Norwich – Great British (Winter)
Atherton – Bent & Bongs Beer Bash
Bishop's Stortford
Bradford
Chappel – Winter
Chelmsford – Winter
Chesterfield
Darlington – Spring
Dorchester
Dover – White Cliffs Winter
Fleetwood
Gosport – Winter
Hucknall
Jersey – Winter
Liverpool
Pendle
Redditch
Stevenage
Stockton – Ale & Arty
Tewkesbury – Winter

March
Brighton – Sussex
Bristol
Burton upon Trent
Chester – Cheshire
Coventry
Horsham – Equinox
Leicester
Loughborough
Rugby
Seascale
St Neots – Booze on the Ouse
Walsall
Wantage
Wigan
Winchester

April
Bolton
Bury St Edmunds – East Anglian
Chippenham
Doncaster
Farnham
Gloucester
Hull
Isle of Man
Larbert – Falkirk
Maldon
New Mills
Newcastle upon Tyne
Oldham
Paisley
Skipton
Thanet

May
Banbury
Barnsley
Bexley
Cambridge
Colchester
Eastbourne – Beer & Cider by the Sea
Glenrothes – Kingdom of Fife
Kidderminster
Kingston
Lincoln
Macclesfield
Newark
Newport – Tredegar House Folk Festival
Reading
Stourbridge
Wrexham – North Wales
Yapton
Yaxley

June
Braintree
Bromsgrove
Glasgow
Hitchin
Leeds
Lewes – South Downs
Nuneaton & Bedworth
Old Harlow – Gibberd Garden
Salisbury
Southampton
Stockport
Stratford-Upon-Avon
Tenterden – Kent & East Sussex Railway
Thurrock
Wolverhampton

Left: Reading Beer and Cider Festival. Right: Hitchin Beer and Cider Festival

Left: Repertoire Dogs playing at the Chelmsford Beer Festival. Right: Cambridge Beer Festival

July
Bromley
Canterbury – Kent
Chelmsford – Summer
Chorlton
Derby
Devizes
Ealing
Edinburgh – Scottish
Epping – Ongar Railway
Hereford – Beer on the Wye
Maidenhead
Market Bosworth – Rail Ale
Shrewsbury
Southampton
Stafford
Stowmarket – Summer
Winchcombe – Cotswold
Woodcote – Veteran Transport Rally
Wyke Regis – Wykefest

August
London – Great British
Clacton-on-Sea
Darlington
Durham
Grantham
Peterborough
Swansea
Ulverston
Worcester

September
Barnsley
Belper – Amber Valley
Bridgnorth – Severn Valley
Burnley
Calderdale
Cannock
Cardiff – Great Welsh
Chappel
Crewe – Rail Ale
East Malling (Kent)
Faversham – Hop
Harbury
Jersey
Melton Mowbray
Moreton-in Marsh – North Cotswolds
Nottingham
Plymouth
St Albans
St Helens
Scunthorpe
Tamworth
York

October
Alloa
Ascot
Basingstoke – OctoberFest
Bedford
Birmingham
Carmarthen
Chesterfield – Market
Egremont (Cumbria)
Falmouth
Gainsborough
Kendal – Westmorland
Louth
Matlock
Milton Keynes – Concrete Pint
Norwich
Oxford
Poole
Richmond (North Yorkshire)
Sheffield – Steel City
Solihull
South Woodham Ferrers
Southport
Spa Valley Railway (West Kent)
St Ives (Cambs) – Booze on the Ouse
Stoke-on-Trent – Potteries
Sunderland
Swindon
Troon – Ayrshire
Twickenham
Wakefield
Weymouth
Worthing

November
Bath
Belfast
Cambridge – Winter
Carlisle
Dudley
Grimsby
Harwich & Parkeston
Normanton
Redhill
Rochdale
Rochford
Shifnal
Uttoxeter
Watford
Woking

December
London – Pig's Ear

Cask Marque

Championing beer quality

Cask Marque are delighted to again sponsor the CAMRA Good Beer Guide in what is our 20th anniversary year for this not for profit organisation.

We now have over 10,000 pubs with the Cask Marque award for beer quality. These pubs undergo two unannounced visits a year from one of our 50 assessors who check the cask beers for temperature, appearance, aroma and taste. Fail on one beer and you fail the inspection. Any consumer complaints trigger a further mystery drinker visit. Over a period of a year they make 22,000 pub visit and inspect in excess of 70,000 pints.

Back in 1998 40% of pubs were failing their Cask Marque inspections. Today this figure is down to 8.5%. However, last year we undertook a mystery drinker exercise on **non** Cask Marque pubs and 49% failed, so quality is still an issue for the industry and the consumer.

Today our plaque is recognised by 77% of cask ale drinkers. Customers should be reassured when they see this and Cask Marque pubs listed in the Good Beer Guide are highlighted with a symbol.

Scores on the cellar doors

For a pub to join Cask Marque they must undertake a cellar inspection and we then give the cellar a star rating.

This has proved a popular addition to Cask Marque, as best practice in the cellar increases both yields (7%+) and beer quality.

The number of new pubs in the scheme is increasing, as a further 2,000 pubs have volunteered to have this assessment. We have therefore decided to trade mark the logo. Do look out for the window stickers.

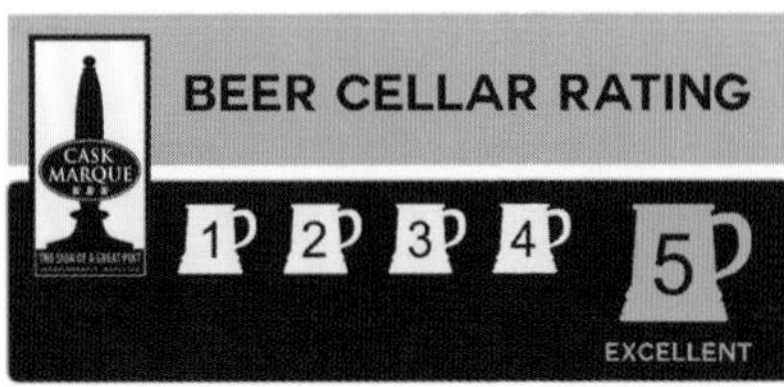

Our ratings scheme assesses cellarmanship

Cask Marque and Cyclops Beer

Cask Marque are proud to announce ownership of the Cyclops Beer Scheme, which has become the industry standard for educating, engaging and enthusing both drinkers and bar staff alike.

Cyclops Beer is a scheme which was launched by the industry to de-mystify and simplify some of the flavour profiles of cask ale, for both consumers and publicans. Using easy to understand language and symbols, it describes the colour, aroma and taste of over 10,000 beers in the UK, boasting tasting notes from more than 444 breweries. Cyclops notes are increasingly found on pump clips, bottle labels, websites and phone apps to navigate the sometimes bewildering array of beers available. Cyclops Beer notes can also be printed off and used on cask containers at beer festivals.

Cask Marque assessors make 22,000 pub visits a year

Have some fun!

The CaskFinder app, free to download from either the App Store or Play Store, is used 60,000 times a month to find Cask Marque pubs. It is also the home of the World's Biggest Ale Trail covering all of the 10,000 Cask Marque pubs. Just scan the QR code on the Cask Marque certificate in the pub and win prizes.

The app has now been upgraded to add two important features:

- Scan the pump clip with the app and it will give you the Cyclops description of the beer and information on the brewery.
- More Ale Trails have been added to make it easier to win prizes. For example, there is a Tetley Ale Trail around Leeds, and also ones for seven National Trails, such as Hadrian's Wall and the South West Coastal Path.

Download the app now at **www.cask-marque.co.uk/app**.

Stayinapub.co.uk

This is a sister company to Cask Marque and lists 1,700 pubs with accommodation that you can book online.

Pubs have challenged restaurants with their great food offer and now are investing heavily in accommodation to develop a third income stream after food and drink. This is particularly important for the survival of the country pub and accommodation is frequently as good, if not better, than many hotel offers.

Enjoy a pint with the locals, have great food and a comfortable bed for the night, all under one roof. What could be better!

Take a look at the website and see some of the fabulous pubs in this sector and sign up for the monthly newsletter – **www.stayinapub.co.uk**

National Walking trails

Cask Marque and Stay In A Pub have teamed up with Visit England to create ale trails along the Seven National Trails. Each ale trail on the CaskFinder app is sponsored by a brewery and the brewery issues prizes based on the number of pubs you visit. This is all part of a £1.4m project to encourage inbound tourists to visit our shores. Visit England say that one of the top 3 attractions for tourists is to visit a British pub.

This is endorsed by the fact that 16% of enquires received on the Stay In A Pub website come from abroad. You can easily find pub accommodation on these walks by visiting the Stay In A Pub website. **www.stayinapub.co.uk**.

A FINAL WORD

To find out more about Cask Marque, please do visit our website at **www.cask-marque.co.uk** and we hope you will join with us in championing beer quality in the glass to make sure you get served the perfect pint every time.

All about beer

A history of brewing innovation

The brewing of beer on these islands dates back thousands of years. From the start of history, it seems, we've known about beer. From its simple begvinnings as a mix of grains and water to the sophisticated, vibrant industry we have today, civilisation and beer have been partners on the same road.

Little remains of what brewers in the UK were doing more than 4,000 years ago. However, traces can be found of more recent activity. Brewing began on the Three Tuns site in Bishop's Castle, Shropshire in the 16th century and its brewing licence was granted in 1642. A small tower brewery from the 19th century, which still has some remnants from 16th century, survives. The Three Tuns was also one of only four pub breweries running when CAMRA was founded in the 1970s. Today there are hundreds.

Shepherd Neame, Faversham, Kent – which is also home to a fabulous museum and visitor centre – also has a claim to be the country's oldest brewery. The company traces brewing on its site to 1698, making it the oldest continuous brewery site in the country, though brewing on the site probably began even earlier.

One of the best examples of a Victorian tower brewery still in operation is the glorious Hook Norton, in the village of the same name in Oxfordshire. Its one of the oldest independent breweries in the country. Hook Norton, now in the hands of the fifth generation of the family who founded it, began brewing in 1849. The current premises were built in 1900 and much of the original equipment, including a 25 horsepower steam engine can be seen by people on a brewing tour.

Arkell's in Swindon, Wiltshire is another venerable survivor. The brewery was established in 1843 by John Arkell and the family still brew beer in the original Victorian brewhouse.

The oldest breweries incorporated as limited companies date back to 1880. Marston's in Burton upon Trent, and Wadworth in Devizes were both registered that year.

Brewing also has another claim in the history of industrial Britain. The first trademark registered in the UK was the Bass Red Triangle, in 1876.

The rise of new breweries

The past decade has seen a resurgence of independent brewers as younger people get a taste for beer. These new companies are quick and nimble, and able to respond rapidly to consumer calls for more information on ingredients and niche products. The growing consumer demand for gluten free and vegan beers has also been a boon for the new wave of brewers who have identified these gaps in the offerings of more conventional brewers.

A feature of many of the new wave of brewers is the shunning of words like 'traditional', and images of handpumps. Beer is modern, relevant and hip and promoted using bright and breezy imagery and names for beer. Indeed, the trend has become so popular that imitation has become the sincerest form of flattery as national and international brewers have released their own craft style branding.

The craft beer revolution has seen the number of UK breweries rise to more than 2,500 – the highest since the 1930s. The rise in the number of breweries opening is remarkable. In 1970 according to the British Beer and Pub Association there were 191 and the industry seemed in decline. However, recent years have seen boon times for openings, and between 2000 and 2016 the number of breweries in the UK increased by 1,750.

Beers from Tap Social Movement, which provides training for people serving prison sentences

Brewers with a social conscience

'Local' and 'community' are important words for many of the new wave of brewers. According to the Society of Independent Brewers (SIBA), 84% of independent breweries support charities, with 21% supporting more than five charities.

Many of the new wave of brewers make social purpose the core of their business. The Tap Social Movement, a 1,000-litre brewery in Oxford, was founded in 2016 to provide training and opportunities for effective rehabilitation for people serving prison sentences. The three co-founders, Amy Taylor, Paul Humpherson and Tess Taylor, all have a background in the criminal justice system.

Similarly, the Hophurst brewery in Hindley, Wigan was started in 2014 by Stuart Hurst. His passion for producing craft ales has been combined with 20 years of supporting businesses and re-skilling unemployed people to create a social enterprise brewery that employs people over the age of 50 and guides them through a training programme.

Breweries are also supporting people with learning difficulties. Ignition in Sydenham, south London employs and trains people with learning disabilities to brew beer, whilst the Norton brewery in Runcorn, Cheshire was created as a social enterprise by Halton Borough Council to provide employment opportunities for people with learning disabilities, autism and other disabilities. It opened in 2011 with a 2.5-barrel plant.

Braxx Porter is a full-flavoured alcohol free beer

The environment

Environmental awareness is part of the ethos of many small brewers. Sue Jefferson set up the Keswick brewery in Cumbria in 2006. The 10-barrel brewery is designed to be environmentally friendly. It uses sheep wool to insulate its brewing vessels, which reduces its environmental impact.

The family-run Otter brewery is set high up in the Blackdown Hills. Environmental responsibility lies at the heart of its operations. The brewery's eco cellar has been built underground and is naturally chilled. The beers are made using water from the brewery's own springs and locally-sourced ingredients.

The Stratford Upon Avon brewery in Warwickshire was the first brewery in the town since the Flowers brewery shut in the 1960s. It was set up by Richard Williams in 2014 on his family farm, which lies on the River Avon. The brewery has been developed with an environmentally-friendly approach, using the farm's own small solar farm, wind turbine and bore hole. All the spent hops and malts from the brewing process are sent to the pigs on the farm, meaning zero waste. From the field to the glass, and back again. Brewing is a virtuous task.

Going low

Full-flavoured, traditionally brewed low alcohol beers could soon become regulars feature in many pubs, and at CAMRA beer festivals for those who aren't drinking but still want to enjoy the event.

In 2018 CAMRA's Great British Beer Festival in London offered an alcohol-free beer range from the Dutch-based Braxzz brewery. It was the first time a non-alcoholic beer range was available at the 41-year-old festival.

Festival organiser Catherine Tonry said: 'Alcohol-free beer has become increasingly important in recent years and brewers have been keeping pace with consumer demands – there are now some fantastic innovations in the sector and a much wider range of styles and flavours than ever before. We are thrilled to provide an alcohol-free alternative to festival-goers who cannot or choose not to drink.'

In 2016 Rob Fink founded Big Drop Brewing in 2016. He believed there was a lack of choice in low/no alcohol beers so decided to start brewing his own. The brewery is dedicated solely to producing full-flavoured 0.5% beer and launched its first beer – a stout – two years ago.

Fink said: 'When new duty rates were introduced in 2011 for low strength beers below 2.8%, brewers rushed out new beers, wanting to take advantage of tax breaks whilst searching for the holy grail of brewing; a full flavoured, well-rounded reduced alcohol beer that tasted of, well, beer.

'There was talk of the sector making up 10% of the overall beer category but the optimism was ill-placed, and it never happened. Marketing budgets were reallocated and just a few, better established beers remained.'

However, since then Fink says, inspired by the craft beer revolution, experimentation with different brewing techniques and influences from around the world, people are getting the taste for low alcohol.

Fink said: 'A huge part of that evolution has been a new wave of no and low alcohol beers and we wait with bated breath to see if things will be different this time, can they take a sizeable share of sales and will they last the course?' There's certainly momentum that suggests they will.

How beer is brewed

Barley is beer's building block. Other grain can be used and many brewers blend in small amounts of wheat or oats and even rye, but barley is the preferred grain because it works in perfect harmony with hops and yeast.

British barley enjoys a world-wide reputation: the finest varieties are known as 'maritime barley' as they grow close to the coast. Norfolk, with its rich alluvial soil, grows some of the best barley, such as Maris Otter, suitable for brewing. Scotland also enjoys a good reputation for its barley, where the Golden Promise variety is prized.

But barley has to be turned into malt before brewing can begin. Once it's harvested, the grain is taken to a maltings where it's steeped in water to absorb moisture before being spread on heated floors or inside rotating drums where it starts to germinate. Once germination is under way, the grain is transferred to an oven known as a kiln. Heat dries the grain and, depending on the temperature, produces pale or darker malts.

All beer, regardless of colour, is made mainly from pale malt as it has the highest level of enzymes – natural chemical catalysts – that can convert starch within the grain into fermentable sugars crucial to the brewing process. Higher malting temperatures produce brown, black and chocolate malts, which are used for colour and flavour in darker beers.

Roasted barley, which is not malted, is often featured in stouts while a method similar to toffee-making produces specialist crystal malts used for colour and flavour. Depending on the mix of malts the brewer chooses, the grain will contribute aromas and flavours similar to Horlicks, Ovaltine, oatmeal biscuits, Ryvita, almonds and other nuts, as well as notes of honey, butterscotch, caramel, tobacco and vanilla.

The annual harvest also produces beer's other key ingredient: hops. In common with grain, hops need good soil, in this case loamy or sandy soil that retains a good supply of water. Kent, Herefordshire and Worcestershire are the main hop-growing counties of England.

Hops grow at great speed in the spring and summer and once harvested they are dried by warm air in special sheds or oast houses. Hops contain acids, oils and resins that deliver bitterness to beer along with fragrant aromas of spice, pepper, grass, cedar wood and citrus fruit. The oils and tannins in the plant help stabilise beer and prevent infection. English hops are prized for their spice and pepper notes. Fuggles and Goldings are the best known traditional varieties but new hops have been introduced in recent years, including First Gold, Boadicea, Endeavour and Jester: the last two have been bred to give the aromas and flavours of grapefruit, mango and tropical fruits demanded by many modern brewers.

The brewing process

When malt reaches the brewery, it's ground in a mill into a powder called grist ①. Grist and hot water (called 'liquor') flow into the mash tun,

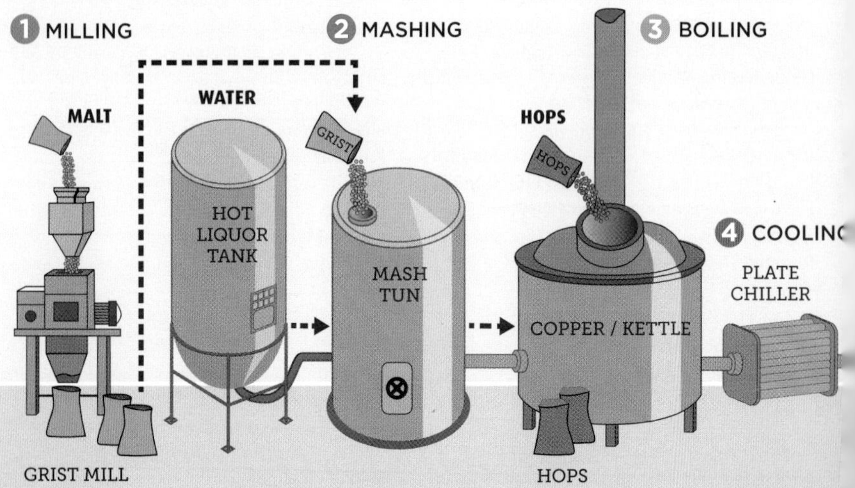

where the porridge-like mixture of grain and water starts the brewing process ❷.

Brewing water can come from springs, bore holes or from the public supply. It will be filtered and brewers often add such sulphates as gypsum and magnesium to enhance the flavours of malt and hops.

The mixture is left to stand in the mash tun for some two hours and during that time enzymes in the malt convert the remaining starch into fermentable sugar. When starch conversion is complete, the brewer and his team will run the sweet extract, called wort, to a second vessel, the copper, where it's vigorously boiled with hops ❸.

The copper boil lasts between 1½ and 2 hours. The hopped wort is passed through a cooler to lower the temperature ❹ and is then pumped to fermenting vessels. These can be open or closed, upright or horizontal, but it's here that the liquid starts the conversion of malt sugars to alcohol with the aid of yeast ❺.

Yeast is a fungus that feeds on sugary liquids. Every brewery will have its own yeast culture that's carefully guarded and stored, as it gives its own important 'house character' to the beer.

Ale fermentation is rapid and lasts for a week – it's a method known as 'warm fermentation' to distinguish it from the cold fermentation method used to make genuine lager. Yeast converts malt sugar into alcohol and carbon dioxide and creates a dense, rocky blanket on top of the liquid. It also produces natural chemical compounds called esters that give off aromas reminiscent of apples, oranges, pear drops, banana, liquorice, molasses and, in especially strong beers, fresh leather. These add to the complexity of the finished beer.

Eventually the yeast will be overcome by the alcohol it has created and the yeast blanket is skimmed from the vessel. The beer will rest for several days in conditioning tanks to mature and to purge unwanted rough alcohols and esters ❻.

Then comes the major divide in the world of brewing. One route leads to brewery-conditioned beer that is filtered, pasteurised and carbonated. The other creates Britain's great contribution to the world of beer: cask-conditioned ale.

Cask ale is unique as it's not finished in the brewery but in the pub cellar. From conditioning tanks, it's racked into casks ❼. Finings may be added to clear the beer and additional hops may be placed in the casks for extra aroma and flavour. Brewing sugar can be added to encourage a strong secondary fermentation.
The beer that reaches the pub cellar is said to be 'still working' as remaining yeast turns the final sugars into alcohol and CO_2.

Casks have to be vented to allow some of the natural gas to escape. A cask has two openings: a bung at the flat end where a tap is inserted to serve the beer; and a shive hole on top. A soft porous peg of wood, known as a spile or peg, is knocked into the shive, enabling some of the CO_2 to escape. As fermentation dies down, the soft spile is replaced after 24 hours by a hard one that leaves some gas in the cask: this gives the beer its natural sparkle, known as 'condition'.

Inside the cask, finings sink to the floor, attracting yeast in suspension. When the publican is satisfied that the beer has 'dropped bright', plastic tubes or 'lines' are attached to the tap and the beer is drawn by a suction pump activated by a handpump on the bar.

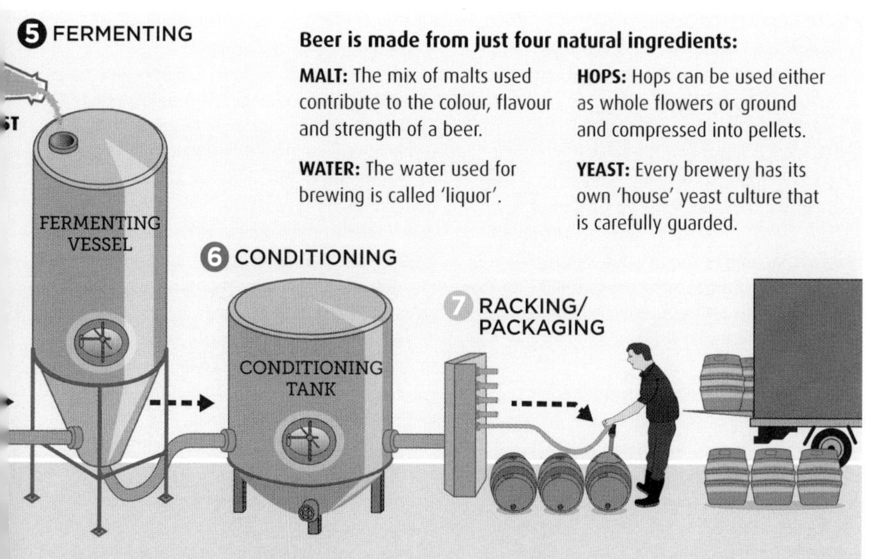

Beer is made from just four natural ingredients:

MALT: The mix of malts used contribute to the colour, flavour and strength of a beer.

WATER: The water used for brewing is called 'liquor'.

HOPS: Hops can be used either as whole flowers or ground and compressed into pellets.

YEAST: Every brewery has its own 'house' yeast culture that is carefully guarded.

Beer appreciation

The best way to enjoy a beer is in good company in a pub, club or a brewery tap. The sipping of a well-served ale can inspire discussion, and beer can be the key to unlocking memorable conversations. It's much more than an alcoholic liquid in a glass, beer is a liquid art form, and one which, with a little more knowledge, can be enjoyed even more.

Liquid art

We can increase our appreciation of beer and savour its qualities by sampling and tasting. Gently swirl the liquid in the glass to release the aroma or the 'nose' and discover the malt, hop and fruit notes that emerge. Allow the beer to trickle over the tongue, which picks up bitterness, sweetness and salt, and enjoy the palate or 'mouthfeel' as the beer coats the cheeks. Finally, the beer passes down the back of the throat in what is known as the 'finish'.

A beer's aroma gives you clues about its taste and character

Tasting

All the senses are involved when enjoying a beer:

Sight – We drink with our eyes, our visual sense whets the appetite and anticipation sets the taste buds tingling. What colour is the beer: light, dark, cloudy or crystal clear? Are there lots of bubbles and does it have a big foaming collar of foam on top, or is it tight, discrete and somewhat more restrained? And are there bubbles of carbon dioxide rising up the beer?

The answers to these questions are an indicator to the style of the beer and can be an indicator of its condition.

Touch – What temperature is the glass? Each beer has an optimal serving temperature. The ideal temperature for most ales is between 11 and 13°C. But stronger ales can be served warmer: the higher temperature releases soaring fruity aromas and esters, enhancing the beer flavour. Likewise, a cool crisp golden ale can be served slightly cooler.

Aroma – Our noses can detect more than 1,000 aromas. Can you discern some notes of citrus fruit? If it is a rich, dark stout is there a hint of coffee? In a barley wine you might detect some swirling winey almost sherry-like aromas. In a German style wheat beer, expect a flourish of bubblegum flavours.

The malts used will give a beer a rich biscuit or Ovaltine-like character. Hops will add their own distinctive note. English hops deliver a restrained spicy, peppery, earthy, wood and resinous note. American hops are renowned for their profound citrus notes, with grapefruit to the fore. Traditional European hops are called 'noble', and varieties offer cedar wood, mint, pine kernels and lemon zest. New Zealand hops have a vinous fruit character. One popular variety, Nelson Sauvin, is so called as a result of flavours similar to Sauvignon wine. There is currently a trend in brewing to use aroma hop varieties with wonderful strong flavours, which are sourced from all over the world. Some of the hops with the most intense aromas are grown in the New World, just like with wine. North America, New Zealand and even Eastern Europe are producing hops with distinct citrus, floral and fruit-like aromas.

British hops are unique due to the latitude of the UK, the climate, the soil, the terroir, the hours of sunshine and the breeding history. It is this unique and sustainable terroir that gives British hops a lower level of myrcene than hops grown elsewhere in the world producing hop aromas which are much more delicate and complex than other world hops.

Taste – Anticipate the first sip and then enjoy it. Let it caress your tongue. Our mouths have a battery of taste buds, which can detect salt, sweet, bitter, sour and umami.

A common misconception is that certain parts of the tongue can only detect certain taste. Not so, though certain areas may more susceptible to certain sensation than others. Some beer can play tricks: a hoppy aroma, may not always follow through on the taste. Is the beer fruity? Can you detect dark fruit flavours or even a hint of malted biscuits? The mouth feel of the beer is important too, does it feel good on your tongue? Is there a satisfying level of bitterness?

And don't forget to swallow. Ideally there should be a slow warming feeling as the beer is swallowed, which should linger, but not for too long, on the back of the throat.

Temperature

To enjoy the aromas and flavours of a beer, cask beer should be served at the correct temperature. Too warm and unwanted aromas will be released.

Too cold and the clean, fresh vibrancy of the beer could be lost. A very low temperature could make the beer cloudy – a chill haze.

The ideal serving temperature for most cask beers is between 11 and 13°C. Cask Marque audits to a required range of 10–14°C allowing a little leeway. Some cask ales are meant to be dispensed at lower temperatures, particularly summer beers. These have been specially brewed in order that no chill haze occurs at temperatures where other cask ales might be affected.

Other draught beers – lagers and keg are usually served between 5 and 8°C. Some draught beers are served even colder using glycol cooling systems and flash coolers Such beers are normally poured between 0 and 5°C.

Most bottled real ales should be served at between 8 and 12°C, other bottled beers are served colder.

The dimple glass

Many pubs serve beer in a dimple or tankard glass, although some people see them as old-fashioned. However, on the warmest days, beer served in a tankard rather than a standard nonic pint glass stays at the best drinking temperature for longer. Research by Brewlab – a provider of training services to the brewing industry – showed the drinkability of beer and ale is vastly improved when consumed from a tankard.

My beer is cloudy

For many years, many beer drinkers believed the perfect pint should be crystal clear. But times are changing and some perfectly good beers are being served cloudy. In some beer bars, cloud is the new normal and quite acceptable. So, before you send a cloudy beer back check with the bar staff. If they are on top of their game they will know if the murk is good or bad.

Serving beer in a dimple glass can ensure it remains at the best drinking temperature

German-style Weiss beers have traditionally been served cloudy, but today some of the country's best brewers, including Kernel, Fuller's and Moor, are serving some of their beers unfined and unfiltered. The recent haze craze comes from America, where many beers such as New England IPAs can look as turbid as a Massachusetts sea fog.

Supporters of the hazy brews say they are packed with tropical fruit and protein flavours which filtering takes out.

Historically, cloudy real ale was a sign that the beer had not been conditioned properly, and that can still be true. But bright people can still enjoy hazy beer. A good rule of thumb is, if it doesn't smell right it is probably off.

And for those who despair of hazy beers, beware the latest US trend for milkshake IPAs, some made with flour for added murk or others with added fruit puree. As ever, judge a beer with all of your senses: it beer might look more like a smoothie that a crystal clear pint, but if it tastes great, it is.

Insist on quality beer

Real ale, when it's conditioned with care, should be bright, sparkling, with a lively head and served cool and refreshing (though some beers, such as wheat beers, may be intentionally cloudy). As a consumer, forking out a high price for beer, don't be afraid to take your pint back to the bar if it is not in good condition. Bar staff should replace it and might not be aware of an issue unless you tell them.

Take your pint back to the bar if:

- Your beer is served either too warm or too cold. Real ale should be served cool – around 11–12°C. It's a myth that it should be served at room temperature. Warm beer tastes bad. But bear in mind that some Golden Ales are meant to be served cooler than other styles.
- Your beer smells of acetone, vinegar or stale bread.
- The pint has no head, is totally flat and out of condition.
- It's not only flat but hazy and has yeast particles or protein floating in the liquid.

British beer styles

Britain may be embarking on a new relationship with the rest of Europe but it will not be immune to beer styles from the continent. Many brewers in the UK are now producing their interpretations of such styles as Belgian lambic and saison, along with German wheat beers.

But our own distinctive beer styles are far from ignored or forgotten. Bitter remains the most popular style and Mild ale still enjoys support, particularly in the West Midlands, South Wales and Merseyside. Golden Ale has become enormously popular and most breweries now have at least one version in their portfolios. Brewers are also becoming more adventurous and are adding to beer's pleasure with versions that are aged in wood or which use such ingredients as herbs, spices, coffee, chocolate and fruit.

Brewers are also digging deep in to the rich treasure trove of older styles. Porters and stouts from the 18th century are now widely available. But undoubtedly the most dramatic revival comes in the shape of India Pale Ale or IPA, a great style of the 19th century that almost disappeared in the 20th but has now been restored to its place of honour in the ale pantheon.

A number of brewers are producing 'sour beers' based on the traditional Belgian style known as lambic. Such beers do not use conventional brewers' yeast but allow wild yeasts in the atmosphere to turn malt sugars into alcohol. These beers have a tart and acidic character and offer a fascinating glimpse of what the earliest beers tasted like many centuries ago.

PORTER & STOUT

Porter was a London beer that created the first commercial brewing industry in the world in the early 18th century. Its name came from its popularity with London porters who needed calories to help sustain them in their hard manual labour. The origins of the beer are disputed but the most recent research suggests Porter, first called 'Entire', was blended in the brewery from pale, mild and aged or 'stale' beer. The strongest version of Porter was called Stout Porter, later shortened to just Stout.

Porter and Stout were exported from London to the rest of the British Isles and, as a result, Arthur Guinness built his own Porter brewery in Dublin. During World War One, when the British government restricted the use of malt, heavily roasted versions in particular, in order to divert grain and energy to bread making and the arms industry, Guinness and other Irish brewers came to dominate the market. In recent years, Porter and Stout have returned to popularity in Britain, the United States and Australasia, with brewers digging into old recipes books to create genuine versions of the style.

Look for a jet-black colour and expect a dark and roasted grain character with burnt fruit, espresso or cappuccino coffee, liquorice and molasses. The beer should have a deep bitterness to balance the richness of malt and fruit. Milk Stout, made by a few brewers, uses lactose or 'milk sugar' to give a creamy character to the beer.

MILD

Mild developed in the 18th and 19th centuries as drinkers started to demand a slightly sweeter and less aggressively hopped beer than Porter. Mild Ale was drunk primarily by industrial and agricultural workers who needed to refresh themselves after long hours of arduous labour. Early Milds were much stronger than modern versions, which tend to fall into the 3% to 3.5% category though a number of brewers are bringing strength back to the style. Mild is usually dark brown in colour, due to the use of well-roasted malts or roasted barley, though there are paler versions such as Banks's Mild and Timothy Taylor's Golden Best. Look for a rich malty aroma and flavour, with hints of dark fruit, chocolate, coffee and caramel, with a gentle underpinning of hop bitterness.

OLD ALE

Old Ale is another style from the 18th century, stored for many months or even years in wooden vessels where the beer picked up some lactic sourness from wild yeasts and tannins in the wood. As a result of the sour taste, it was dubbed 'stale' by drinkers and the beer was one of the components of the early Porters. In recent years, Old Ale has made a return to popularity, due primarily to the success of such beers as Theakston's Old Peculier and Gales' Prize Old Ale. Contrary to expectations, Old Ales do not have to be especially strong and can be no more than 4% alcohol. Neither do they have to be dark: Old Ale can be pale and bursting with lush malt, tart fruit and spicy hops. Darker versions will have a more profound malt character, with powerful hints of roasted grain, dark fruit, polished leather and fresh tobacco. The hallmark of the style is a lengthy period of maturation, often in bottle rather than cask.

BARLEY WINE

Barley Wine dates from the 18th and 19th centuries when England was often at war with France and it was the duty of patriots, usually from the upper classes, to drink ale rather than French claret. Barley Wine had to be strong – often between 10% and 12% – and was stored for as long as 18 months or two years. Fuller's Vintage Ale (8.5%) is a bottle-conditioned version of its Golden Pride and is brewed with four different varieties of malts and hops every year. Expect massive sweet malt and ripe fruit of the pear drop, mandarin orange and lemon type, with chocolate and coffee if darker malts are used. Hop rates are generous and produce bitterness and peppery, grassy and floral notes.

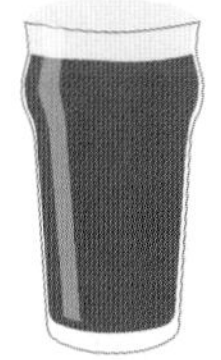

BITTER

At the turn of the 19th and 20th centuries, brewers built large estate of 'tied' pubs and they moved away from beers stored for months or years and developed 'running beers' that could be served after a few days of conditioning in pub cellars. Bitter was a new type of running beer: it developed from Pale Ale but was usually copper coloured or deep bronze due to the use of slightly darker malts, such as crystal, that gave the beer fullness of palate. Best is a stronger version of Bitter but there is considerable crossover. Bitter falls into the 3.4% to 3.9% band while Best Bitter is 4% upwards, though a number of brewers call their ordinary Bitter 'best'. A further development of the style comes in the shape of Strong Bitter of 5% or more: Fuller's ESB and Greene King Abbot are well-known examples. With ordinary Bitter, look for spicy, peppery and grassy hop character, a powerful bitterness, tangy fruit and juicy/nutty malt. With best and strong Bitters, malt and fruit character will tend to dominate but hop aroma and bitterness are still crucial to the style, often achieved by 'late hopping' during the copper boil or by adding additional hops to casks as they leave the brewery.

BURTON ALE

As the name suggests, the origins of Burton Ale lie in Burton upon Trent, but the style became so popular in the 18th and 19th centuries that most brewers had 'a Burton' in their portfolio and the expression 'gone for a Burton' entered the English language. Bass in Burton at one time had six different versions of the beer, ranging from 6% to 11.5%: the strongest versions were exported to Russia and the Baltic States. In the 20th century, Burton was overtaken in popularity by Pale Ale and Bitter but it was revived with great success in the late 1970s with the launch of Ind Coope Draught Burton Ale. When Allied Breweries broke up, the beer was owned by Carlsberg, who stopped production in 2015. But the style has been recreated by Burton Bridge Brewery in its home town. Other versions of the style exist under different names: Young's Winter Warmer was originally called Burton. Bass No 1, brewed occasionally, is called a barley wine but is in fact the last remaining version of a Bass Burton Ale. Look for a bright amber colour, a rich malt and fruit character underscored by a solid resinous and cedar wood hop note.

PALE ALE

According to a legend in the 19th century, when a sailing ship bound for India with a cargo of IPA foundered off the coast at Liverpool, the casks were brought ashore and news of both the colour and taste of Pale Ale spread throughout the country. IPAs were brewed for the domestic market as a result but the Burton brewers were keen to produce versions with lower alcohol and hop rates that didn't require months to mature. The spread of the railway system allowed brewers in Burton to move beer around the country at speed and Pale Ale was dubbed 'the beer of the railway age' as a result. The clamour for Pale Ale was so great that brewers from London, Liverpool and Manchester opened second breweries in Burton to make use of the mineral-rich water to make their own versions of the style. From the early 20th century, Bitter began to overtake Pale Ale in popularity and a result Pale Ale became mainly a bottled product. A true pale ale should be different to Bitter, similar in colour and style to IPA and brewed without the addition of coloured malts. It should have a spicy/resinous aroma and palate with biscuit malt and tart fruit from the hops. Many beers called Bitter today should properly be labelled Pale Ale.

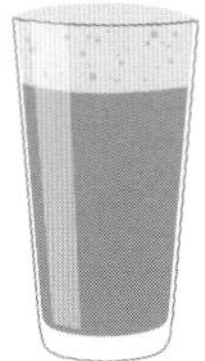

IPA

India Pale Ale changed the face of brewing in the 19th century. The new technologies of the Industrial Revolution enabled brewers to use pale malts to design beers that were pale bronze in colour. The first 'India Ales' were brewed in London and were probably based on October Beers that were matured for many months and were ideally suited to a long sea journey to India. But London was soon eclipsed by Burton-on-Trent with its spring waters rich in minerals that brought out the fullest flavours of malt and hops. 19th century IPAs were high in both alcohol and hops to keep them in good condition during the journey to the colonies. Its life span was brief, driven out of Africa and India by German lager beer. But the style has made a big comeback in recent years and is now made in abundance throughout the world. Look for a big peppery hop aroma and palate balanced by juicy malt and tart citrus fruit.

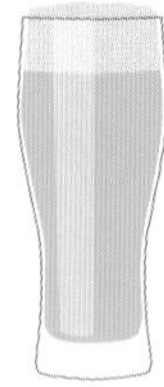

GOLDEN ALE

Golden Ales have become so popular with both drinkers and brewers that the style now has its own category in the annual Champion Beer of Britain competition. Exmoor Gold, Hop Back Summer Lightning and Rooster's Yankee started the trend in the early 1980s and other brewers quickly followed in a rush to wean younger drinkers from mass-produced lager to the pleasures of cask ale. The style is different to Pale Ale in two critical ways: Golden Ale is paler, often brewed with lager malt or specially produced low colour ale malt and, as a result, hops are allowed to give full expression, balancing sappy malt with luscious fruit, floral, herbal, spicy and resinous notes. While brewers of Pale Ale tend to use such traditional English hop varieties as Fuggles and Goldings, imported hops from North America, the Czech Republic, Germany, Slovenia and New Zealand give radically different notes to Golden Ale. As a result these beers offer a new and exciting drinking experience. They are often served colder than draught Bitter and some brewers, such as Fuller's, have installed special cooling devices to ensure the beer reaches the glass at an acceptably refreshing temperature.

SCOTTISH BEERS

Historically, Scottish beers tend to be darker and maltier than beers south of the border, the reflection of a colder climate where beer needs to be nourishing. It's an urban myth, though, that Scottish beers are less heavily hopped than English ones. The classic traditional styles are Light, Heavy and Export, which are not dissimilar to Mild, Bitter and IPA. They are also known as 60, 70 and 80 Shilling ales from a 19th century system of invoicing beers according to strength. A 'Wee Heavy' or 90 Shilling Ale, now rare, is the Scottish equivalent of barley wine. Many of the newer brewers in Scotland are producing beers lighter in colour and with pronounced hop character.

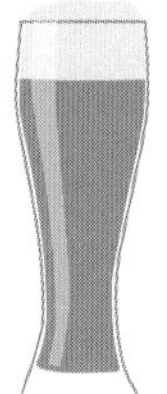

WHEAT BEER

Wheat beer is a style closely associated with Bavaria and Belgium and its popularity in Britain has encouraged many brewers to add wheat beers to their portfolios. The title is something of a misnomer as all 'wheat beers' are a blend of malted barley as well as wheat, as the latter grain is difficult to brew with and needs the addition of barley, which acts as a natural filter during the mashing stage. But wheat, if used with special yeast cultures developed for brewing the style, gives distinctive aromas and flavours, such as clove, banana and bubblegum, that make it a complex and refreshing beer. The Belgian version of wheat beer often has the addition of herbs and spices, such as milled coriander seeds and orange peel – a habit that dates back to medieval times.

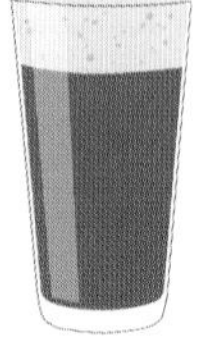

FRUIT/SPECIALITY BEERS

Brewers endlessly search for new flavours to reach out to a wider audience for their beers. The popularity in Britain of Belgian fruit beers has not gone unnoticed and now many domestic brewers are using fruit in their beer. Others have gone the extra mile and add honey, herbs, heather, spice and even spirits – brandy and rum feature in a number of speciality beers, while beers matured in Bourbon, whisky and Cognac casks have become a major development in both this country and the US. It's important to dispel the belief that fruit and honey beers are sweet: the ingredients add new dimensions to the brewing process and are highly fermentable, with the result that beers that use the likes of cherries or raspberries are dry and quenching rather than cloying.

SOUR BEER

Also known simply as 'Sours', this is a style brewed in both the UK and US by brewers fascinated by Belgian lambic beer, made by 'wild' or spontaneous fermentation. Instead of carefully cultivated brewer's yeast, lambic is left open to the atmosphere to allow wild yeasts to attack the sugars in the extract known as wort and begin the fermentation process. Elgood's brewery in Wisbech, Cambridgeshire, makes a fine example of lambic as it has the 'cool ships' or open cooling trays that enable the wort to be attacked by passing yeasts. Following the first fermentation, true lambics are stored in wooden casks for a year or more. The main wild yeast, *Brettanomyces*, is used by modern brewers to inoculate their worts and gain the required sour or acidic character. Other good examples of British sours come from Wild Beer, Kernel and Burning Sky.

SAISON

Saison is another Belgian beer style now finding favour in Britain and other countries. It originates in Wallonia, the French-speaking region of Belgium, and was a seasonal beer brewed by farmers to refresh their labourers during the busy harvest period. Such leading Saison brewers as Dupont, based on a farm, now brew their beers on a full-time basis. In sharp contrast to lambic, Saison should have a rich malty/fruity palate balanced by earthy, spicy and peppery hops. Some Saisons are made with the addition of 'botanicals' such as ginger, black pepper and aniseed. British interpretations come from Adnams, Brew By Numbers, Partizan and Poppyland.

Ten of the best

Tim Hampson selects some of the best interpretations of British beer styles

10 OF THE BEST

MILD: Rudgate Ruby Mild

A rich ruby colour, this 4.4% mild is a smooth, complex beer. The aroma begins with a hint of summer strawberries before giving way to a swirl of nutty smokiness. The taste is soft and luxuriant without much bitterness.

BITTER: Church End Goat's Milk

Named Champion Beer of Britain by CAMRA in 2017, this easy drinking 3.8% beer is pale in colour. The heart of the beer comes from pale barley, crystal malt and oats. Two aromatic US hops, Chinook and Cascade give it a beguiling citrus nose.

BEST BITTER: Tiny Rebel Cwtch

A well balanced, easy drinking beer, at 4.6%. It was named the CAMRA Champion Beer of Britain in 2015. A blend of six malts provide a solid, smooth biscuit base. A blend of three aromatic US citrus hops make this a very special Welsh red ale.

GOLDEN ALE: Blue Monkey Infinity

A pale golden colour, this 4.6% American-inspired beer shines like the sun on a summer's morning. It's made with lashings of Citra hops which gives it swathes of fruity aromatics including lime, grapefruit, mango, lychee, and gooseberry. It's an alcoholic fruit salad in a glass.

STRONG BITTER: Fuller's ESB

Pale and crystal malts add malted biscuit and luscious toffee notes to this mahogany-hued 5.5% brew. A multi-award winning CAMRA champion beer, a flourish of English hops adds notes of citrus and pepper to this sublime brew.

PORTER & STOUT: Siren Craft Broken Dream Breakfast Stout

Deep black in colour, at 6.5%, this silky smooth stout has notes of coffee, dark fruit, roasted malts overlain with a patina of sweet chocolate. An initial burst of bitterness gives way to a long dry finish.

IPA: Burning Sky Devil's Rest IPA

Full in flavour, this is an English IPA influenced by the rock and roll of American craft brewing. A big, bold 7% beer, with lashings of Simcoe and Centennial hops added in at the boil and then dry-hopped after fermentation, giving it a big aroma of orange marmalade.

BARLEY WINE: Chiltern Bodger's Barley Wine

Class in a glass, this 8.5% beer really does stand out as a heavenly, sipping beer. Golden to the eye it exudes juicy fruit, almost vinous notes. A solid Marris Otter malt base is overlain by the spiciness of classic English Fuggles and Goldings hops

SPECIALITY: Magic Rock Common Grounds

Full bodied, this 5.4% coffee porter is brewed with seven malts and seven different coffees. Made in collaboration with Yorkshire coffee roaster Dark Woods, it is full of rich fruit flavours and swirls of chocolate, vanilla and coffee. The finish is sweet and nutty.

FRUIT BEER: Hawkshead Damson Stout

On its own, this malty, warming stout is something special, but steep whole damsons grown in the Lyth Valley, Cumbria in the beer, and this 4.5% brew takes on a fruity hue. It's a harmonious marriage of fruit and chocolate, with the damsons adding a satisfying tartness.

CAMRA's Beers of the Year

The beers listed below are CAMRA's Beers of the Year. They were short-listed for the 2018 Champion Beer of Britain competition, held at the Great British Beer Festival in August, or the Champion Winter Beer of Britain competition, held in February that year. Each beer was found by a panel of trained CAMRA judges to be consistently outstanding in its category and they all receive a 🍺 against their entry in the Breweries section. In the Champion Beer of Britain finals, the best beers from each category in both competitions are judged together to decide the overall national winner. For the full results visit **www.camra.org.uk/cbob**.

GOLDEN ALES
Abbeydale, Moonshine
Allendale, Golden Plover
Baker's Dozen, Electric Landlady
Bishop Nick, Heresy
Blue Monkey, BG Sips
Driftwood, Lou's Brew
Flowerpots, Perridge Pale
Fyne, Avalanche
Grey Trees, Diggers Gold
Hawkshead, Cumbrian Five Hop
Kelburn, Jaguar
Marble, Pint
Moor, Nor'Hop
Oakham, JHB
Purple Moose, Cwrw Eryri/Snowdonia Ale
Salopian, Hop Twister
Salopian, Oracle
Windsor & Eton, Knight of the Garter

BITTERS
Acorn, Barnsley Bitter
Backyard, The Hoard
Bank Top, Flat Cap
Barngates, Cat Nap
Black Iris, Snake Eyes
Brewster's, Hophead
Church End, Goat's Milk
Grey Trees, Caradogs
Humpty Dumpty, Swallowtail
Loch Lomond, Southern Summit
Mighty Oak, Captain Bob
Old Dairy, Red Top
Orkney, Red MacGregor
Purple Moose, Cwrw Madog/Madog's Ale
Reunion, Opening Gambit
St Austell, Trelawny
Teignworthy, Reel Ale
Timothy Taylor, Boltmaker

MILDS
Castle Rock, Black Gold
East London, Orchid Vanilla Mild
Greene King, XX Mild
Holden's, Black Country Mild
Penzance, Mild
Rhymney, Dark
Strathaven, Craigmill Mild
Timothy Taylor, Golden Best

BEST BITTERS
Ashover, Littlemoor Citra
Bath, Gem
Bishop Nick, 1555
Eden River, Gold
Elland, Nettlethrasher
Hawkshead, Red
Hook Norton, Old Hooky
Kelburn, Red Smiddy
Mantle, MOHO
Milton, Sparta
Mordue, Workie Ticket
Old Dairy, Copper Top
Purity, Mad Goose
St Austell, Tribute
Salopian, Darwins Origin
Swannay, Scapa Special
Tiny Rebel, Cwtch
Welbeck Abbey, Harley

PORTERS
Ayr, Rabbie's Porter
Dunham Massey, Dunham Porter
Elland, 1872 Porter
Fownes, King Korvak's Saga
Grain, Slate
Lincoln Green, Tuck
Red Cat, Mr M's Porter
Roam, Porter
VOG, Dark Matter

STRONG BITTERS
Bays, Devon Dumpling
Black Sheep, Riggwelter
Blue Monkey, Ape Ale
Dark Star, Revelation
Grey Trees, Afghan Pale
Hooded Ram, Mosaic Single Hop Pale Ale
Kinver, Half Centurion
Papworth, Robin Goodfellow
Swannay, Orkney IPA

STRONG MILDS & OLD ALES
Derby, Quintessential
Jennings, Sneck Lifter
Milton, Medusa
Old Dairy, Snow Top
Orkney, Dark Island
Peakstones Rock, Submission
Theakston, Old Peculier
Tintagel, Excalibur
Untapped, Ember

STOUTS
BAD, Dark Necessities
Barngates, Goodhew's Dry Stout
Boss, Black
Bristol Beer Factory, Milk Stout
Cairngorm, Black Gold
Fixed Wheel, Blackheath Stout
Milton, Nero
Siren Craft, Broken Dream Breakfast Stout
Thornbridge, Saint Petersburg Imperial Russian Stout

BARLEY WINES & STRONG OLD ALES
Black Isle, Hibernator
Boot, Beast
Burton Bridge, Thomas Sykes
Coniston, No. 9 Barley Wine
Exmoor, Beast
Green Jack, Ripper Tripel
Kissingate, Six Crows
Monty's, Magnitude
Vocation, Life & Death

SPECIALITY BEERS
Bank Top, Port O Call
Colchester, Brazilian Coffee & Vanilla Porter
Cromarty, Red Rocker
Derventio, Cleopatra
Hanlons, Port Stout
Purple Moose, Cwrw Ysgawen/Elderflower
Salopian, Lemon Dream
Saltaire, Triple Chocoholic
Weird Beard, Black Perle

CHAMPION WINTER BEER OF BRITAIN
Green Jack, Ripper Tripel

CHAMPION BEER OF BRITAIN 2018
Siren Craft, Broken Dream Breakfast Stout

The Pubs

Smith's Tavern, Ashbourne, Derbyshire, p102 (Photo: Dave Etheridge)

NORTHERN ISLES
SHETLAND
HIGHLANDS & WESTERN ISLES
ABERDEEN & GRAMPIAN
TAYSIDE
LOCH LOMOND, STIRLING & THE TROSSACHS
FIFE
ARGYLL & THE ISLES
EDINBURGH & LOTHIANS
GREATER GLASGOW & CLYDE
BORDERS
AYRSHIRE & ARRAN
DUMFRIES & GALLOWAY
NORTHUMBERLAND
TYNE & WEAR
NORTHERN IRELAND
CUMBRIA
DURHAM
NORTH YORKSHIRE
ISLE OF MAN
LANCASHIRE
WEST YORKS
EAST YORKS
GREATER MANCHESTER
SOUTH YORKS
MERSEYSIDE
CHESHIRE
DERBYSHIRE
NOTTINGHAM-SHIRE
LINCOLNSHIRE
NW WALES
NE WALES
STAFFORD-SHIRE
SHROPSHIRE
LEICESTERSHIRE
RUTLAND
NORFOLK
WEST MIDLANDS
CAMBRIDGE-SHIRE
MID WALES
WORCESTER-SHIRE
WARWICK-SHIRE
NORTHAMPTON-SHIRE
SUFFOLK
HEREFORD-SHIRE
BEDFORD-SHIRE
BUCKINGHAM-SHIRE
WEST WALES
OXFORD-SHIRE
HERTFORD-SHIRE
ESSEX
GWENT
GLOUCS & BRISTOL
GLAMORGAN
GREATER LONDON
BERKSHIRE
WILTSHIRE
KENT
SURREY
SOMERSET
HAMPSHIRE
CHANNEL ISLANDS
WEST SUSSEX
EAST SUSSEX
DEVON
DORSET
ISLE OF WIGHT
CORNWALL

England

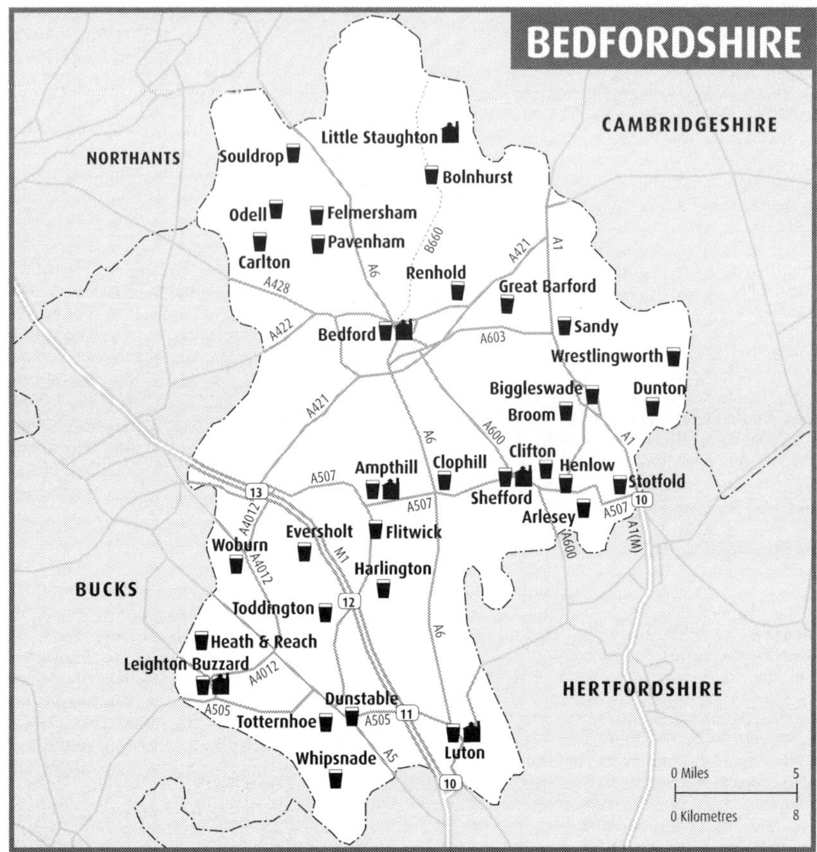

Ampthill

Albion 🄻

36 Dunstable Street, MK45 2JT

✪ 11.30-11 (midnight Fri & Sat); 12-10.30 Sun
☎ (01525) 634857

B&T Shefford Bitter, Golden Fox, Dragon Slayer; Everards Tiger; 8 changing beers 🄷

An award-winning, proper, narrow-fronted Victorian pub with one large bar and 12 handpumps serving a range of the local B&T beers as well as Everards Tiger and eight constantly changing ales mainly from microbreweries. Two regular real ciders and a guest are also served. Beer and cider festivals are held at least annually. There are a meeting room and a secluded patio garden towards the rear. English music nights feature once a month on a Wednesday. Twice Bedfordshire CAMRA Pub of the Year. 🛏❀♣🍎🚌🐾

Arlesey

Vicar's Inn 🄻

68 Church Lane, SG15 6UX

✪ 5-midnight; 12-4, 7-midnight Sat; 12-4, 7-11 Sun
☎ (01462) 731215

Eagle IPA; 1 changing beer (sourced nationally) 🄷

Opposite St Peter's Church, handy for the train station and popular with the local community, the pub opened in the 1860s as part of the Charles Wells estate and became a free house in 2001. There are two bars – a large lounge and a smaller public bar in which the local cribbage and dominoes teams can regularly be found. Historical local pictures feature together with beer jugs and other memorabilia. Complimentary cheese and biscuits are often available.
Q🛏❀⛺⇌♣P🚌(72,96)

Bedford

Bear

92 High Street, MK40 1NN

✪ 12-11 (2am Fri & Sat); 1-11.30 Sun ☎ (01234) 630235

4 changing beers (sourced nationally) 🄷

Traditional town-centre pub now restored to its original name. There is one long bar running back from the small street frontage, giving access to the rear garden. A small, separate room without a bar caters for diners. A wide choice of real ales and Westons Old Rosie cider are available. Thursday is quiz night and there is occasional entertainment on Saturday. Local CAMRA Young Members Pub of the Year 2018. 🛏❀☾⇌🍎🚌🐾📶

Castle 🄻

17 Newnham Street, MK40 3JR

✪ 12-11 (midnight Thu); 11.30-midnight Fri; 11-midnight Sat
☎ (01234) 353295 🌐 castlebedford.co.uk

Courage Directors; Eagle IPA; Young's Bitter, Special; 3 changing beers (sourced nationally) 🄷

Lively two-bar town pub with a pleasant walled patio garden, five minutes from the town centre and convenient for the Bedford Blues rugby ground. Lunches are served daily and evening meals on weekdays only. Current guest beers with tasting notes are listed on the website. A guesthouse behind the pub provides five en-suite bedrooms. Local CAMRA Pub of the Year 2016.

Devonshire Arms

32 Dudley Street, MK40 3TB (1 mile E of town centre S of A4280)

5-11; 4-midnight Fri; 12-midnight Sat; 12-10.30 Sun

(01234) 301170 devonshirearmsbedford.co.uk

Bombardier; Courage Directors; Young's London Gold; 3 changing beers (sourced regionally) Ⓗ

Pleasant Victorian pub in a residential area. Guest and seasonal ales are mainly from Eagle Brewery, the two ciders and perry are from Westons. Beer and cider festivals are held each year. The front bar has bare floorboards and an open fire, while there is a separate rear bar. The garden has a gazebo for smokers and a no-smoking paved area. A range of wines is sold by the glass or bottle. Local CAMRA Cider Pub of the Year 2018. Q (4)

King's Arms

24 St Mary's Street, MK42 0AS

11-11; 12-midnight Fri & Sat; 2-9 Sun (01234) 354494

thekingsarmsbedford.co.uk

Greene King IPA; Morland Old Speckled Hen; 3 changing beers (sourced nationally) Ⓗ

This busy former coaching inn has several interconnecting rooms, and a conservatory providing a quiet area. There is a quiz on Monday evening, free pool on Tuesday, a ukulele band on Wednesday, TV poker on Thursday and live performances by top local bands every Saturday evening. A selection of bottle-conditioned beer is available. No food at weekends.

(St Johns) P

Pilgrim's Progress

42 Midland Road, MK40 1QB

10-midnight (01234) 363751

Greene King Abbot; Ruddles Best Bitter; 8 changing beers (sourced nationally) Ⓗ

The Pilgrim's became a Wetherspoon hotel in 2016, and offers a choice of five internal areas and two outdoor seating spaces, one of them no-smoking. The bar is popular with all ages but not usually overcrowded, even on weekend evenings. There are views into the kitchen, and the varied food menu includes dietary information and low-calorie options. The normal Wetherspoon Club offers are available. Convenient for public transport, the location provides a good view of the town centre. Q

Three Cups

45 Newnham Street, MK40 3JR (200yds S of A4280 near rugby ground)

12-11; 11-11.30 Fri & Sat; 12-10.30 Sun

(01234) 352153 threecupsbedford.co.uk

Greene King IPA; Morland Old Speckled Hen; 5 changing beers (sourced nationally; often White Park) Ⓗ

Comfortable inn dating from the 1770s, now a Greene King Local Hero pub offering local microbrewery beers, including at least two from White Park Brewery, which holds the lease. Tasting thirds are available for all beers. Locally sourced home-cooked meals are served. Old wood panelling helps retain some of the pub's original character. Five minutes from the town centre and close to Bedford Blues rugby ground. Local CAMRA Pub of the Year 2017 and Town Pub of the Year 2018. P

Wellington Arms

40-42 Wellington Street, MK40 2JX (off A6 N of town centre)

12-11; 12-10.30 Sun (01234) 308033

Adnams Southwold Bitter; B&T Shefford Bitter; Draught Bass; 9 changing beers (often B&T) Ⓗ

A traditional street-corner pub and a key part of the Bedford real ale scene for 20 years. There is always an interesting selection of 12 ales and two real ciders on handpumps. Draught continental beers and a range of bottled Belgian beers are also available. There is a courtyard for drinkers and smokers. A friendly pub with a mixed clientele, it can get busy on Friday and Saturday evenings. Winner of a local CAMRA special real ale award in 2017.

White Horse

84 Newnham Avenue, MK41 9PX

12 (4 Mon)-11; 12-midnight Fri & Sat; 12.30-10.30 Sun

(01234) 409306 thewhitehorsebedford.co.uk

Courage Directors; Eagle IPA; Young's London Gold; 2 changing beers (sourced regionally) Ⓗ

Three seating areas, each with their own style, are served from a single bar. The smartphone quiz on Sunday and traditional quiz on Tuesday are popular, as is the Monday evening jazz. Other musical events are advertised on Facebook. Food is freshly cooked to order with a choice of roasts on Sunday (booking advised), and afternoon tea can be ordered for groups. The beer and wine selection is complemented by a wide choice of gins.

P (4)

Biggleswade

Golden Pheasant

71 High Street, SG18 0JH

12-midnight (1am Fri & Sat); 12-11.30 Sun

(01767) 313653 goldenpheasantpub.co.uk

Eagle IPA; 5 changing beers (sourced nationally) Ⓗ

A double-fronted Charles Wells Speciality Beer House located in the heart of Biggleswade, featuring six ales on handpump and four changing real ciders. The single bar has traditional pub seating which can be moved around to accommodate the local darts team as well as other local groups who hold meetings here. The pub has a strong community focus and regularly holds charity fundraising events with live music, taking advantage of the spacious patio area when the weather permits. Q

REAL ALE BREWERIES

B&T Shefford
Brewhouse & Kitchen Bedford
Crown Little Staughton (NEW)
Eagle Bedford
Kelchner Ampthill (NEW)
Leighton Buzzard Leighton Buzzard
Rockhopper Luton
White Park Bedford

Bolnhurst

Plough

Kimbolton Road, MK44 2EX (on W side of B660 S of turning to Thurleigh) TL088587
closed Mon; 12-3, 6.30-11; 12-3 Sun ☎ (01234) 376274
bolnhurst.com
Adnams Southwold Bitter; 2 changing beers (sourced regionally) H
Award-winning pub restaurant dating in part from the Tudor period, serving excellent food and beer. The main bar has a wood-burning stove and a second room is used for dining and functions. There is a large garden with decking beside a small pond. The pub has no prominent signage, just a modest sign hanging on a post by the road entrance. Closed from Christmas until the second week of January each year. **Q P**

Broom

Cock ★

23 High Street, SG18 9NA
12-11; 12-10 Sun ☎ (01767) 314411
thecockatbroom.co.uk
Greene King Abbot; 3 changing beers (sourced nationally; often Butcombe, Caledonian, Tring) G
Spacious pub with many areas in which to imbibe including a games room decorated with old enamel signs, a snug with a bottle collection, a relaxing room with a fish tank, a restaurant serving home-prepared meals and an attractive garden with tables and benches. Beer is served at the top of the cellar steps in another hop-bedecked area with tables and chairs. Quizzes, skittles, a Sunday meat raffle and an annual music festival also feature. The cider is typically from Apple Cottage. **Q P**

Carlton

Fox

High Street, MK43 7LA (off Turvey Rd S of village centre)
12-11 (10 Mon & Tue); 12-9.30 Sun ☎ (01234) 720235
thefoxatcarlton.pub
Eagle IPA; Fuller's London Pride; 2 changing beers (sourced regionally) H
A charming thatched community pub with a warm welcome and an attractive garden popular with families. Guest beers are often from local microbreweries. Good-value home-cooked lunches are served (daily except Mon) and evening meals Wednesday to Saturday. There is a regular quiz on Thursday evening, occasional themed food evenings and spring and summer bank holiday festivals, using an outbuilding in the garden as an additional bar. Local CAMRA Country Pub of the Year 2016 and 2017. **Q P** (25)

Clifton

Admiral

1 Broad Street, SG17 5RJ
3-11; 11-1am Fri & Sat; 11-11 Sun ☎ (01462) 811069
5 changing beers (sourced nationally; often B&T, Harvey's, Robinsons) H
Friendly, knowledgeable staff help customers choose from five real ales, usually including something dark, while Westons Old Rosie cider is also on pump. The original beer house maintains its nautical theme with maritime pictures and model ships. There are darts, board games, monthly live music, a monthly quiz and an annual beer festival. Food includes dripping-fried fish & chips Fridays, weekend breakfasts, Sunday roasts and Monday steak night, plus stone-baked pizzas on some summer weekends. Local CAMRA Most Improved Pub in 2018. (71)

Clophill

Stone Jug

10 Back Street, MK45 4BY (500yds off A6 at N end of village) TL083381
12-3 (not Mon), 6-11; 12-midnight Fri & Sat; 12-10.30 Sun
☎ (01525) 860526 stonejug.co.uk
Otter Amber; St Austell Trelawny; 3 changing beers (sourced nationally; often B&T) H
Originally three 16th-century cottages, this popular village local has an L-shaped bar serving two drinking areas and a family/function room. Excellent home-made lunches are available Tuesday to Saturday. The guest beers are often from local microbreweries, the cider is Westons Old Rosie. Picnic benches at the front and a rear patio garden offer outdoor drinking space in fine weather. Parking can be difficult at busy times. A good pit stop for the Greensand Ridge Walk and a former CAMRA Pub of the Year.
Q P (44,81)

Dunstable

Gary Cooper

Grove Park, Court Drive, LU5 4GP
8am-midnight (1am Fri & Sat) ☎ (01582) 471452
Greene King Abbot; Ruddles Best Bitter; Sharp's Doom Bar; 7 changing beers H
Large, airy, modern Wetherspoon bar serving a selection of up to seven guest ales, often local. The usual range of JDW craft beer is also stocked. Situated in Grove Park leisure area, its patio overlooks the Grove House gardens, with many bus routes stopping outside. The pub is named after the famous Hollywood star, who attended the local grammar school between 1910 and 1913. Busy on Friday and Saturday nights.

Globe

43 Winfield Street, LU6 1LS
12-11 (midnight Fri & Sat); 12-10.30 Sun
☎ (01582) 512300
B&T Shefford Bitter, Edwin Taylor's Extra Stout; Everards Tiger; 7 changing beers H
Popular beer destination and community local where 13 handpumps boast a good range of regular B&T beers, five ever-changing microbrewery beers, a real cider and a perry. More than 20 Belgian beers are also available. Bare boards, bar stools, breweriana and a famous plank at the end of the bar create a traditional town pub atmosphere buzzing with conversation. Acoustic music night is Tuesday. Regular beer festivals are held. A former Bedfordshire and local CAMRA Pub of the Year. **Q** (70)

Pheasant Inn

208 West Street, LU6 1NX
11-11 (11.30 Fri & Sat); 12-11 Sun ☎ (01582) 662706
the-pheasant-inn-dunstable.co.uk
Mad Squirrel Hopfest; Sharp's Doom Bar; 4 changing beers (sourced nationally) H
A just-out-of-town-centre pub and B&B on a bus route, with a large main bar and function room

selling six real ales. Beers are also available to take away, often from local breweries. All major sports are screened and traditional pub games can be played. Outside are a covered and heated front smoking area, rear garden, large umbrellas and a car park. Free curry is served on Friday when you buy a pint. An annual beer festival features and live music on occasion. P

Victoria

69 West Street, LU6 1ST

11-11.30 (midnight Fri & Sat); 12-midnight Sun

(01582) 662682

House beer (by Tring); 3 changing beers

The Victoria is a popular town-centre pub near the police station on West Street. It usually offers three varying ales from microbreweries plus a house beer from the local Tring Brewery. Darts, dominoes and crib are popular as well as televised sports in the bar. There is a separate function room available next to the rear courtyard.

Dunton

March Hare

34 High Street, SG18 8RN

6-11 (midnight Thu); 3-midnight Fri & Sat; 12-10.30 Sun

(01767) 600258 themarchharedunton.co.uk

6 changing beers (sourced nationally; often Digfield, Eagle, Otter)

Community-spirited CAMRA hosts ensure the pub always has beers of varying styles and gravities. The L-shaped, brick-faced bar contains remnants of oak beams and the counter extends through a dividing wall with beer engines on both sides. Newspapers and games both traditional and modern are available. Two beer festivals, wassailing in early New Year, occasional live musicians, plus a welcoming fire and sun-soaked garden in the appropriate seasons add to the pub's appeal. Opens at noon on summer Saturdays.
Q (188)

Eversholt

Green Man

Church End, MK17 9DU

closed Mon; 12-3, 6-11; 12-11 Sat; 12-6 Sun

(01525) 288111 greenmaneversholt.com

Sharp's Doom Bar; Tring Side Pocket for a Toad; 1 changing beer (sourced nationally)

A genuine free house in Church End, one of the many 'Ends' that make up the village of Eversholt. It features flagstone floors, exposed brick fireplaces and has a large patio garden. Freshly prepared, good-quality food is served in the bar and the separate restaurant (not Sun eve). Conveniently placed for the nearby and popular tourist attractions of Woburn. P

Felmersham

Sun

Grange Road, MK43 7EU

4-11 (10 Mon); 3.30-11 Fri; 12-11 Sat; 12-10 Sun

(01234) 781355

Eagle IPA; 2 changing beers (sourced regionally)

Pretty thatched community pub owned by a local family. The guest beer range changes weekly and often includes ales from local microbreweries. Home-made pie-on-a-plate snacks are available at most times. The pub has a family-friendly rear garden and is convenient for visits to the historic parish church and a nature reserve just across the river. There is a quiz on the first Wednesday of the month and occasional beer festivals are held. A former local CAMRA Pub of the Year.
P (50)

Flitwick

Crown

Station Road, MK45 1LA

11.30-3, 5.30-11; 11.30-midnight Fri & Sat; 12-11 Sun

(01525) 713737 crownflitwick.co.uk

Sharp's Doom Bar; 3 changing beers (sourced nationally)

This large, tidy and thriving estate pub was successfully rescued by the current tenants who are keen on their real ales – interesting guest beers are common. Varying craft keg beers are also available. There is a games room with TV, jukebox and pool table. Saturday music nights are popular. Outside is a large garden with patio and children's play area. A good range of traditional pub food is served (not Sun eve).
P (42,C2)

Great Barford

Anchor Inn

High Street, MK44 3LF (by river 1 mile S of village centre) TL134517

12-3, 6.30 (5 Fri)-11; 12-11 Sat; 12-10.30 Sun

(01234) 870364 anchorinngreatbarford.co.uk

Eagle IPA; Young's Bitter; 4 changing beers (sourced nationally)

Busy inn next to the church, overlooking a medieval bridge across the River Great Ouse. At least two guest beers are usually available from an extensive range offered by the pub company. Good home-cooked food is served in the bar and restaurant, as well as a fine selection of wines. The pub is popular with river users in the summer. Occasional themed food nights are held, mainly during the winter months. Q P (27)

Harlington

Carpenters Arms

Sundon Road, LU5 6LS

12-3, 6-11.30; 12-midnight Fri & Sat; 12-11 Sun

(01525) 872384 thecarpentersarmsharlington.com

Greene King IPA; Wainwright; Woodforde's Wherry; 1 changing beer (sourced nationally; often Purity)

Situated in the heart of Harlington, this traditional low-beamed watch-your-head village pub was first licensed in 1790 and has listings of landlords from then until the present day. Three regular and one changing guest ales are available. Food is reasonably priced with good helpings – Monday is burger night. The railway station and bus service along with a range of country walks make this a popular stop-off. Q P (42)

Heath & Reach

Axe & Compass

Leighton Road, LU7 0AA

12-midnight (01525) 237394

theaxeandcompass.pub

3 changing beers

This village community pub has been a free house since 2014. The older front bar, with its low beams, is a lounge and dining area while the rear public bar has gaming machines, pool table and a TV screen. The large garden includes a children's play area. Regularly appearing guest beers often come from local breweries such as Hornes, Tring and Leighton Buzzard. Accommodation is available in a separate lodge. (150)

Henlow

Engineers Arms

68 High Street, SG16 6AA

12-midnight (1am Fri & Sat); 12-10.30 Sun

(01462) 812284 engineersarms.co.uk

10 changing beers (sourced nationally; often Leighton Buzzard, Tring) H

Local CAMRA Pub of the Year 2018, this popular free house offers 10 rotating ales and six ciders from across the UK. The cosy front bar has a fireplace, books, local history pictures and brewery memorabilia. The rear section features photographs of sporting heroes and two large TV screens showing a myriad of live sporting events. It has monthly disco evenings and regular live music. The back patio hosts legendary beer and cider festivals, plus comedy nights and barbecues.

Old Transporter Ale House

300 Hitchin Road, SG16 6DP

closed Mon; 3-10.30; 12-11 Fri & Sat; 12-9 Sun

(01462) 817410 theoldtransporter.co.uk

6 changing beers (sourced nationally; often Potbelly, Tring) G

Located near RAF Henlow, this cosy single-room beer house offers up to six ales direct from the cask, mainly from local and regional breweries. Real ciders are available, mostly from Lilley's, plus a range of snacks. There is a regular darts team and a large-screen TV for live rugby matches. Occasional events include live music evenings, quiz nights, raffles and mini beer festivals often featuring dark beers. The pub opens at noon on weekdays during the summer months.
(71,188)

Leighton Buzzard

Bald Buzzard Alehouse

6 Hockliffe Street, LU7 1HJ

4-9; 12-10 Fri & Sat; closed Sun & Mon 07581 146491

baldbuzzard.co.uk

7 changing beers (sourced locally; often Blackened Sun, Chiltern, Dark Star) G

This award-winning micropub opened its doors in July 2015. A small but perfectly formed premises, it has a clever bespoke chiller room with sliding glass doors behind the bar containing 12 casks on stillage and three or four ciders. There is also a selection of bottled beers, weiss beer, wines and more. The generous pork pies are popular.
Q (70,150)

Black Lion

20 High Street, LU7 1EA

12-11 (midnight Fri & Sat); 12-10.30 Sun

(01525) 853725 blacklionlb.com

Draught Bass; Oakham Bishops Farewell; house beer (by Nethergate); 5 changing beers (sourced nationally) H

With 17th-century origins, this traditional alehouse features exposed beams, wooden floors and an open fire. Eight handpumps dispense beers from the likes of Hook Norton, North Cotswold, Hornes, Phipps and XT. Eight changing real ciders are available and an impressive bottled beer menu lists over 100 continental and British beers. There is a large paved garden. Bar snacks are served and bring-your-own cold lunches are welcome. Local CAMRA Pub of the Year 2015 to 2018.
Q (70,150)

Leighton Buzzard Brewing Company Brewery Tap

Unit 31, Harmill Industrial Estate, Grovebury Road, LU7 4FF (2nd left from Grovebury Rd)

12-5 Wed & Thu; 12-8 Fri; 10-8 Sat; closed Sun-Tue

07538 903753 leightonbuzzardbrewing.co.uk

Leighton Buzzard Cuckoo, Narrow Gauge, Restoration Ale, Black Buzzard; 2 changing beers (sourced locally; often Leighton Buzzard) G

The brewery tap for the Leighton Buzzard Brewing Company, a core range of its beers plus some varying ales are sold at the bar. There is also a good range of bottled and canned artisan beers from other like-minded breweries as well as real cider. Beers are available to drink on the premises and to take home. Open days take place on one Saturday per month in the spring and summer (check the website for dates), with various local food offerings and occasional live music. P

Red Lion

1 North Street, LU7 1EF

10-11 (midnight Fri & Sat); 11-11 Sun (01525) 374350

Greene King Abbot; 2 changing beers (sourced nationally) H

Dating back to the 17th century, this is a town centre institution. An old-fashioned pub with old-fashioned values, the manager of over 20 years offers a warm welcome. The public bar has all the traditional pub games and the main bar resembles a living room with comfy chairs, a large fish tank, TV and the pub's dog wandering around. As well as the well-kept ales there is a choice of 21 Irish and Scottish single malt whiskies. (70,150)

Swan Hotel

50 High Street, LU7 1EA

6 (7 Mon)-midnight; 7-midnight Sat; 7-11.30 Sun

(01525) 380170

Greene King Abbot; Rebellion IPA; Ruddles Best Bitter; Sharp's Doom Bar; 6 changing beers (sourced nationally) H

A former coaching inn dating from the 17th century and renovated by Wetherspoon. With good-value food and 39 guest rooms, the Swan is busy and bustling for much of the week. A single long bar serves two rooms, a conservatory and a courtyard. Guest beers may come from local microbreweries such as Chiltern, Mad Squirrel, Tring and Vale, and real cider is available in the summer months. Friendly service is assured and families are welcome until 11pm. Events include biannual beer festivals. Q (70,150)

Luton

Black Horse

23 Hastings Street, LU1 5BE

3 (1 Sat & Sun)-11 (01582) 965290

the-black-horse-luton.com

3 changing beers (sourced nationally; often Leighton Buzzard, Oakham, Tring) H

Back-street pub near Luton town centre usually serving three ever-changing ales, often from local breweries. Entertainment includes a popular jukebox, sports TV, dartboard, pool table and a stage for live music events. There is a covered outdoor seating area for smokers. Food includes a good-value 'Get what you're given' Sunday roast. ♘◐⇌♣P🚌🐾

Bricklayers Arms

High Town Road, LU2 0DD

🕒 12-11 (midnight Fri & Sat); 12-10.30 Sun
☎ (01582) 611017 🌐 bricklayersarmsluton.co.uk

Batemans XB; 5 changing beers (sourced nationally; often Oakham) Ⓗ

Quirky High Town pub run by the same landlady for over 30 years. Popular with Hatters fans on match days, it has TVs in both bars and a quiz night every Monday. The six handpumps serve a variety of guest beers from breweries all over the nation, with a choice of light, amber and often a mild brew. Draft Belgian beers and two real ciders are also available. ❀⇌♣●🐾 ᯤ

Great Northern

63 Bute Street, LU1 2EY

🕒 11-11 (midnight Fri & Sun); 11-10.30 Sun
☎ (01582) 729311

Sharp's Doom Bar; St Austell Tribute Ⓗ

This may be the smallest pub in Luton. Its name was changed in the 1860s when the Great Northern Railway was built right on its doorstep. It still retains Victorian green wall tiles as well as a table featuring quirky brass pint glass holders at each corner. Sports are shown on TV. There is a smoking area at the rear. ⇌♣●

White House 🄻 ✔

1 Bridge Street, LU1 2NB

🕒 8am-midnight (1am Fri & Sat) ☎ (01582) 454608

Greene King Abbot; Ruddles Best Bitter; Sharp's Doom Bar; 6 changing beers (sourced nationally) Ⓗ

The White House is a large town-centre Wetherspoon pub offering the chain's usual range of keenly priced food and drinks. Following refurbishment in 2017 it now serves six different guest ales across the two bars, often including local ales from the Vale or Tring breweries. This is a bright and clean pub in the Galaxy Centre, conveniently located for several bus routes. Q♘❀◐◑♿⇌●🚌

Odell

Bell

81 High Street, MK43 7AS

🕒 11.30-11; 12-10.30 Sun ☎ (01234) 910850
🌐 thebellinodell.co.uk

Greene King IPA, Abbot; 4 changing beers (sourced nationally) Ⓗ

Handsome thatched village pub with a large garden near the River Great Ouse. With the Harrold-Odell Country Park just down the lane, this is a popular stop for walkers. Sympathetic refurbishment and a series of linked but distinct seating areas help retain a traditional pub atmosphere. Good-value quality food includes a Sunday roast, steak and chips night Monday and pie and chips night Tuesday. Local CAMRA Most Improved Pub 2016. Q♘❀◐◑P🚌(25,26)🐾 ᯤ

Pavenham

Cock 🄻

High Street, MK43 7NJ

🕒 closed Mon; 12-2.30 (not Tue & Wed), 5-11; 12-11 Sat; 12-10 Sun ☎ (01234) 822834

Fuller's London Pride; Greene King IPA; 2 changing beers (sourced regionally; often Grainstore, Tring, White Park) Ⓗ

A friendly village pub with a warm welcome and an interesting choice of ales. Food includes fish and chips on Friday evening, roast lunch on Sunday and a breakfast club on the first Saturday of the month. Sunday roasts may be replaced by a garden barbecue from June to September. Occasional beer festivals are held in the garden, which opens directly on to the Ouse Valley Way footpath. Local CAMRA Most Improved Pub 2018.
❀◐◑♣P🚌(25,29)

Renhold

Polhill Arms 🍷 ✔

25 Wilden Road, MK41 0JP (at Salph End)

🕒 12 (4.30 Mon)-11; 12-10.30 Sun ☎ (01234) 771398
🌐 polhillarms.co.uk

Hardys & Hansons Bitter; 5 changing beers (sourced nationally; often Greene King) Ⓗ

Family-friendly village local with a welcoming atmosphere and a large garden, play area and restaurant. An interesting collection of pub and brewery artefacts and airship memorabilia is displayed. Traditional pub food is served including fish and chips (not Sun or Mon eves). There are regular quiz nights, live music and busy darts and skittles matches. Two real ciders are available in the winter months, four in the summer. Local CAMRA Pub of the Year 2018.
♘❀◐◑♣●P🚌(27)🐾 ᯤ

Sandy

Sir William Peel ✔

39 High Street, SG19 1AG

🕒 12-11 (10.30 Sun) ☎ (01767) 680607
🌐 sirwilliampeel.webs.com

Batemans XB; 3 changing beers (sourced nationally; often Oakham) Ⓗ

Converted from two cottages in 1838 and now open plan, a U-shaped bar faces the entrance with, on the right, a digital jukebox and library. The area to the left – where a free Sunday cheeseboard is served – leads to the rear patio and disused stables, both of which host the April beer and July cider festivals. A disco and karaoke feature on the last Saturday of each month. Three or four real ciders are served, often from Westons. There is seating outside at the front to catch the sun.
♘❀⇌♣●P🚌(73,188)🐾 ᯤ

Shefford

Brewery Tap 🄻

14 North Bridge Street, SG17 5DH

🕒 11.30-11; 12-10.30 Sun ☎ (01462) 628448

B&T Shefford Bitter, Golden Fox, Dragon Slayer; Everards Tiger; 2 changing beers (sourced nationally) Ⓗ

The Tap is primarily a drinkers' pub, offering four regular beers and two, usually stronger, guest ales. Breweriana adorn an open-plan interior divided into two distinct areas, plus a family room at the rear. Lunchtime rolls are available. Darts, dominoes and cribbage teams are supported, as is a golf society. The rear patio garden is heated on cool evenings. Car park access is through an archway beside the pub. P (71,72)

Souldrop

Bedford Arms

High Street, MK44 1EY (½ mile W of A6)
closed Mon; 12-3, 5-11; 12-midnight Fri & Sat; 12-10 Sun
(01234) 781384
Black Sheep Best Bitter; Greene King IPA; Sharp's Doom Bar; 2 changing beers (sourced nationally; often Phipps) H
Large village pub created partly from a 17th-century hop and ale house. Guest beers are often from local microbreweries. The restaurant has a central open fireplace and offers traditional, hearty pub favourites with daily specials and a roast on Sunday. A games room with skittles runs off the main bar. The spacious garden with pétanque is popular with families in summer. A former local CAMRA Country Pub of the Year.
P (26)

Stotfold

Crown

39 The Green, SG5 4AL
12-11.30 (1.30am Fri & Sat); 12-11 Sun (01462) 731061
Greene King IPA H, Abbot G; 1 changing beer (sourced regionally; often Greene King) H
Recently refurbished to a high standard, this busy open-plan pub features window shutters and a picket fence. The main bar area has several large-screen TVs for live sports and a roaring open fire in winter months. The games area has pool, dominoes and darts. Monthly live music, karaoke and DJ nights are held. Sandwiches are served and functions can be catered for. A third stronger beer is served direct from the cellar, usually Abbot Ale, plus two real ciders from Westons.
P (97)

Toddington

Cuckoo

Market Square, LU5 6QJ
5-11; closed Sun (01525) 877780
thecuckootoddington.co.uk
4 changing beers (sourced nationally) H
A larger than usual micropub located in the old town hall, this 15th-century Grade II-listed building has a small bar, separate games room with pool and darts and an upstairs function room. At least four mainly local beers are on offer, often from Leighton Buzzard and Tring, plus one changing cider. No TV, music or food, just good beer, conversation and a quiz on alternate Thursdays.
Q (42,E)

Totternhoe

Old Farm Inn

16 Church Road, LU6 1RE
5-midnight Mon; 12-3, 5-11 Tue-Thu; 12-midnight Fri & Sat; 12-11 Sun (01582) 674053 oldfarminndunstable.co.uk
Fuller's London Pride, ESB; 2 changing beers H
Located in the conservation area of Church End, this charming village pub boasts two inglenooks. The public bar with its low boarded ceiling is where you will find good conversation and where traditional pub games are played. Dogs are welcome in the front bar and there is a child-friendly garden. Monday is folk music night, Thursday is quiz night. Tasty home-cooked food is served including popular Sunday roasts (no food Mon or Sun eves). Beer festivals are held in May and August.
Q P (61)

Whipsnade

Old Hunters Lodge

The Crossroads, LU6 2LN
11.30-2.30, 6-11; 11.30-11 Fri & Sat; 12-10 Sun
(01582) 872228 oldhunterslodge.co.uk
Greene King Abbot; 2 changing beers H
A beautiful 15th-century thatched inn set on the outskirts of Whipsnade village close to the world-renowned Whipsnade Zoo. The cosy main bar, with soft seating as well as traditional dining tables, is warmed by a log fire. The side bar includes many old features such as the inglenook fireplace. Separate restaurant areas may be used as function rooms. The picturesque front garden makes a lovely area for summer dining and drinking. The six guest rooms include a bridal suite.
Q P (35)

Woburn

Woburn Ale House

11 Market Place, MK17 9PZ
3 (5 Mon)-11; 12-11 Sat & Sun (01525) 290142
woburnalehouse.com
Hornes Triple Goat Porter; Leighton Buzzard Restoration Ale; 4 changing beers (sourced locally; often Hornes, Tring) H
Charming bar in a former flower shop with six handpumps for cask ales and two for varying ciders and perries. Local beers feature heavily, often from Hornes Brewery and Leighton Buzzard Brewing Company. There is also a wide variety of up to 40 different and interesting artisan keg, canned and bottled beers. With a relaxed atmosphere, comfortable seating and no TVs or music, there is nothing to distract from pleasant conversation.
Q (49)

Wrestlingworth

Chequers

43 High Street, SG19 2EP
5-10.30 Mon; 12-3, 5-11 Tue-Thu; 12-midnight Fri & Sat; 12-10.30 Sun (01767) 631818 chequersfreehouse.co.uk
Adnams Southwold Bitter; Black Sheep Best Bitter; Young's Bitter; 3 changing beers (sourced nationally; often Woodforde's) H
This venerable Grade II-listed pub's 17th- and 18th-century origins can still be seen in the shape of the bowed wood beams and ceiling. To the left are tables with pew benches where home-made meals are served (not Mon) and on the right is more seating and a CD jukebox. A separate room opposite the entrance has darts and a projector screen for sport. A popular local for several groups and teams, in summer Westons cider is available and there is an outdoor beer festival.
P (188)

Public transport information

Leave the car behind and travel to the pub by bus, train, tram or even ferry...

Using public transport is an excellent way to get to the pub, but many people use it irregularly, and systems can be slightly different from place to place. So, below are some useful websites and phone numbers where you can find all the information you might need.

Combined travel information

The national **Traveline** system gives information on all rail and local bus services throughout England, Scotland and Wales. Calls are put through to a local call centre and if necessary your call will be switched through to a more relevant one. There are also services for mobiles, including a next-bus text service and smart-phone app. The website offers other services including timetables and a journey planner with mapping:

- 0871 200 22 33
  www.traveline.info

LONDON

In London use Traveline or **Transport for London (TfL)** travel services. TfL provides information and route planning for all of London's transport networks, including London Underground and Overground, Docklands Light Railway, National Rail, buses, River Buses, Tramlink, Barclays Cycles and cycle routes. Detailed ticketing information helps you find the most cost-effective ways to travel in London. There are also live departure boards, service and traffic updates; mobile services and more:

- 020 7222 1234
  www.tfl.gov.uk

Train travel

National Rail Enquiries covers the whole of Great Britain's rail network and provides service information, ticketing, online journey planning and other information.

- 08457 48 49 50
  www.nationalrail.co.uk

Coach travel

The two main UK coach companies are **National Express** and **Scottish Citylink**. Between them, they serve everywhere from Cornwall to the Highlands. Their websites offer timetables, journey planning, ticketing, route mapping, and other useful information. CAMRA members can benefit from 20% off travel with National Express*. See **www.camra.org.uk/benefits**.

- National Express: 08717 81 81 81
  www.nationalexpress.com
- Scottish Citylink: 08705 50 50 50
  www.citylink.co.uk

Scottish ferries

Caledonian MacBrayne (CalMac) operate throughout Scotland's Hebridean and Clyde islands, stretching from Arran in the south to Lewis in the north. They run 475 sailings per day in summer and around 350 per day in winter.

- 0800 066 5000
  www.calmac.co.uk

Northern Ireland & islands

For travel outside mainland Britain but within the area of this Guide, information is available from the following companies:

NORTHERN IRELAND

- Translink: 028 9066 6630
  www.translink.co.uk

ISLE OF MAN

- Isle of Man Transport: 01624 662 525
  www.iombusandrail.info

JERSEY

- Liberty Bus: 01534 828 555
  www.libertybus.je

GUERNSEY

- Island Coachways: 01481 720 210
  www.buses.gg

Public transport symbols in the Guide

Pub entries in the Guide include helpful symbols to show if there are stations and/ or bus routes close to a pub. There are symbols for railway stations (⇌); tram or light rail stations (🚊); London Underground, Overground or DLR stations (⊖); and bus routes (🚌). See the 'Key to symbols' on the inside front cover for more details.

**Membership benefits are subject to change.*

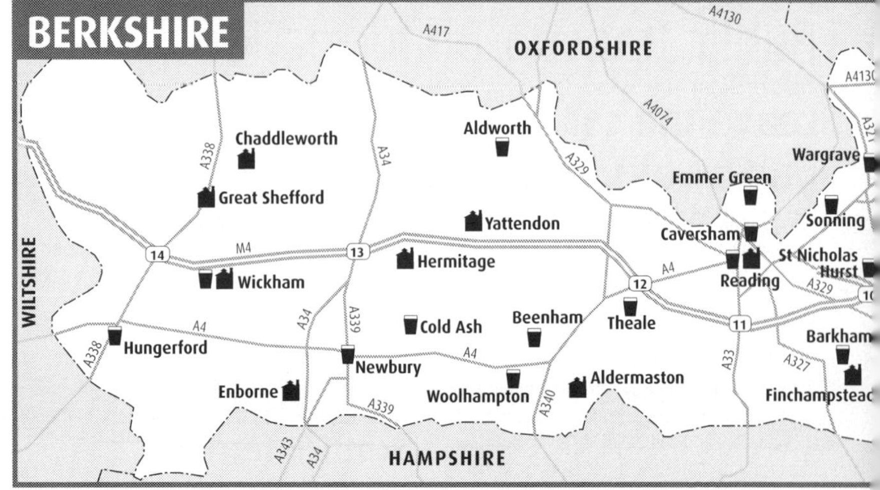

Aldworth

Bell Inn ★ 🄻

Bell Lane, RG8 9SE (250yds off B4009)

✪ closed Mon; 11-3, 6-11; 12-3, 7-10.30 Sun

☎ (01635) 578272

Arkell's 3B; West Berkshire Maggs' Magnificent Mild; house beer (by West Berkshire); 2 changing beers (sourced locally; often Loose Cannon, Rebellion, West Berkshire) ⊞

This traditional village inn dates back to 1340 and has been owned by the same family for nearly 130 years. Providing a welcome break for ramblers enjoying the nearby Ridgeway and Downs, it is famed for a range of hot filled rolls, delicious desserts, fine beers and a historic interior. Local ciders are from Tutts Clump plus Lilley's from Somerset. The delightful garden is well used all year round, providing extra space on busy days. It is a former national, regional and local CAMRA Pub of the Year. **Q☙❀◐♣●P🐾**

Barkham

Bull 🄻

Barkham Road, RG41 4TL (on B3349 jct with Barkham St)

✪ 12-11 (7 Sun) ☎ (0118) 976 2816 🌐 thebullbarkham.com

Gale's HSB; Rebellion Smuggler; Sharp's Doom Bar; Timothy Taylor Landlord; 2 changing beers (sourced locally; often Rebellion) ⊞

Grade II-listed pub and restaurant at the heart of its community, featuring etched glass windows and a working inglenook fire. Formerly a smithy, the old forge can still be seen. Up to six real ales are served, including some from local breweries. Authentic Thai dishes are a speciality, with food freshly prepared from ingredients mostly sourced locally (no food Sun eves). The pleasant garden hosts three beer festivals and other events every year. Dogs are welcome in the bar only. **Q❀◐◑P🚌**(3)**🐾**

Beenham

Six Bells 🄻

The Green, RG7 5NX (at Bucklebury end of main road through village)

✪ 12-2.30 (not Mon), 6-11; 12-2.30, 6.30-11 Sat; 12-3 Sun

☎ (0118) 971 3368 🌐 thesixbells.co.uk

West Berkshire Good Old Boy; 2 changing beers (sourced locally; often Loddon, Vale, West Berkshire) ⊞

This cosy two-bar local has a separate back room for functions and community meetings, and four letting rooms. One of the bars extends to a comfortable conservatory. A LocAle pub, it serves West Berks Brewery's Good Old Boy along with two guest ales. All food is home cooked. Wednesday is the popular pie and pudding night. A welcoming pub in all seasons – in winter there are open fires and in summer enjoy the flower-filled patio. Ideally located as a base for walkers. **Q❀🛏◐◑●P🚌📶**

Binfield

Binfield Club

Forest Road, RG42 4HP (at mini roundabout jct with Terrace Rd South)

✪ 11-11 (11.30 Fri & Sat); 12-10.30 Sun ☎ (01344) 420690

🌐 binfieldclub.com

Courage Best Bitter; Sharp's Doom Bar; Shepherd Neame Spitfire; 1 changing beer (sourced nationally; often Wadworth) ⊞

A CAMRA-friendly club offering first-class facilities, it has been branch Club of the Year for the last two years. It is home to a myriad of local groups, both community and charitable, attracting all ages and bringing a lively atmosphere which fosters a genuine spirit of inclusiveness. The club is truly at the heart of the community, with free parking available for visitors. Regular charity events are held. CAMRA members are welcome on production of a membership card. **Q☙◐◑♿♣P🚌**(150,151)**📶**

Bracknell

Cannie Man 🄻 ✔

Bywood, Hanworth, RG12 7RF

✪ 12-11 (11.30 Fri & Sat); 12-10.30 Sun ☎ (01344) 307620

🌐 cannieman.co.uk

House beer (by Ringwood); 4 changing beers (sourced nationally; often Brains, Hogs Back, Rebellion) ⊞

Community pub appealing to the largest section of the local area. Up to four changing real ales are

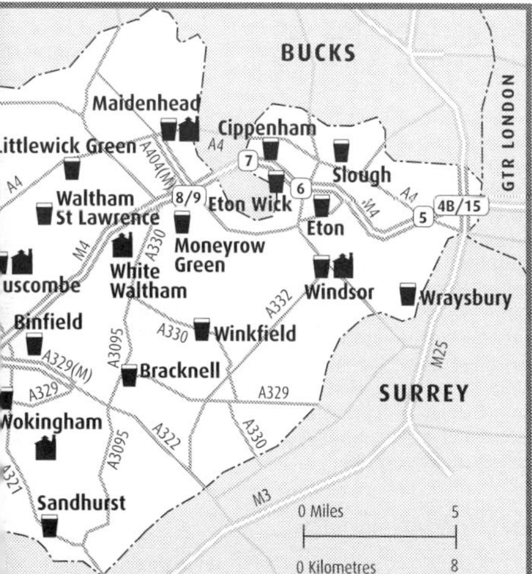

served including the house beer, Seven Zero Hero, from Ringwood. The pub has proudly raised thousands of pounds for local charitable causes and also sponsors a local football team. Pool and darts teams play here and there are two sports TVs. Outside seating with wooden benches is accessed via a side entrance. Children are welcome until early evening. Entertainment features on Friday and Saturday nights. ❀♣P🚌ᯤ

Old Manor 🏆 L ✓

Grenville Place, RG12 1BP (at College roundabout jct with Church Rd)

⏲ 8am-midnight (1am Fri & Sat) ☎ (01344) 304490

Greene King Abbot; Ruddles Best Bitter; Sharp's Doom Bar; 6 changing beers (sourced nationally; often Binghams, Loddon) H

Celebrating 20 consecutive years in this Guide and retaining elements of its Tudor origins – the Monks Room in particular – this Wetherspoon pub is one of the oldest buildings in Bracknell. Three regular real ales are available and up to six changing guests, split between two bars, accompanied by Old Rosie and Black Dragon ciders. It attracts a mixed clientele and gets busy on Friday and Saturday evenings. There are three outdoor seating areas to enjoy, weather permitting. Children are welcome. Local CAMRA Pub of the Year.

Q❀◑♿≠●P🚌(53)🐾ᯤ

Caversham

Fox & Hounds L

51 Gosbrook Road, RG4 8BN

⏲ 12-midnight (11 Sun) ☎ 07540 816293

8 changing beers (often Oakham, Siren, Wild Weather Ales) H

With two wins and a runner-up in the last three local CAMRA Pub of the Year awards, the Fox is a popular and lively community hub. It now proudly displays a blue plaque commemorating that in 1960 John Lennon and Paul McCartney worked behind the bar and performed as the Nerk Twins. Up to eight regularly changing beers and six or more ciders and perries are available. Serves excellent pizzas and Sunday roasts.

❀◑♣●P🚌🐾ᯤ

Griffin L ✓

10-12 Church Road, RG4 7AD

⏲ 11-11; 11-midnight Fri; 11-10.30 Sun ☎ (0118) 947 5018

Brains Rev James; Greene King IPA; 4 changing beers (often Loddon) H

There has been a pub on this site since the 1800s (when eels were fished in the nearby River Thames and brought to be sold in the pub). The current pub was built in 1916 and offers good food and ale with numerous specials on chalkboards and regular themed produce weeks. The spacious pub with a heated rear patio garden offers plenty of opportunity for a quiet drink or a big family meal. There is usually a LocAle at the bar.

❀◑♿●P🚌🐾ᯤ

Cippenham

Barleycorn L

151 Lower Cippenham Lane, SL1 5DS

⏲ 12-midnight (12.30am Fri & Sat); 12-11.30 Sun

☎ (01628) 603115

7 changing beers (sourced nationally) H

A traditional single-bar pub, recently refurbished, with seating on one side and a pool table on the other. It caters well for a strong local following. Around the walls is a large number of bottles and jugs. Of the six guest ales there is always one from Rebellion and a strong ale. The remaining four guests come from around the country. There are a couple of sports TVs and occasional live music. The nearby public car park is free. Q❀♣●P🚌(5)🐾ᯤ

Cold Ash

Castle Inn L ✓

Cold Ash Hill, RG18 9PS

⏲ 11.30-11.30 (midnight Fri & Sat); 12-11 Sun

☎ (01635) 863232 🌐 thecastleatcoldash.co.uk

Courage Best Bitter; Fuller's London Pride; Sharp's Atlantic; West Berkshire Good Old Boy; 2 changing beers (sourced nationally; often Exmoor, Otter, Ringwood) H

This popular, traditional pub is over 170 years old and has been run by same family for the last 25 years. The staff are friendly and welcoming. It serves four regular cask ales, two rotating guest beers and real cider. Reasonably priced food is available every day lunchtimes and evenings, except Monday which is quiz night. Occasional live music features and darts and other pub games are played. There is a meat raffle on Friday. In winter there is an open fire. ❀◑♣●P🚌(41)🐾ᯤ

REAL ALE BREWERIES

Binghams Ruscombe
Bond Brews Wokingham
Butts Great Shefford
Double-Barrelled Reading (NEW)
Elusive Finchampstead
Hermitage Hermitage
Indigenous Chaddleworth
INNformal 🛢 Wickham
New Wharf Maidenhead
Siren Craft Finchampstead
Stardust White Waltham
Two Cocks Enborne
West Berkshire Yattendon
Wild Weather Aldermaston
Windsor & Eton Windsor
Zerodegrees 🛢 Reading

Emmer Green

Black Horse

16 Kidmore End Road, RG4 8SE

12-11 ☎ (0118) 947 4111

Courage Best Bitter; Sharp's Doom Bar H

The Black Horse moved to its present site before 1870, allegedly to remove temptation from the adjacent chapelgoers at its original location in old Peppard Road. In Victorian times, the pub yard doubled as the local fire station. Nowadays, this well-kept two-bar local has pool and sports TV in its public bar, while the quieter lounge bar has a real fire. You can sit outside at the front or on the enclosed rear patio. Q

Eton

George Inn

77 High Street, SL4 6AF

8am-11 (10 Sun) ☎ (01753) 861797

georgeinn-eton.co.uk

Windsor & Eton ParkLife, Windsor Knot, Guardsman, Conqueror; 2 changing beers (sourced locally) H

Windsor & Eton Brewery's first pub, opposite Eton bridge. The recent refurbishment is now complete, including a new bar with six ales all from the brewery. Breakfast is served daily 8-10am. The wooden floors, carriage lamps and candles help to create a warm atmosphere. Please note the range of Windsor & Eton beers can change depending on the number of specials/seasonals available. Real cider is sold in summer. The Hop House is available for private parties. Q (10)

Eton Wick

Greyhound

The Walk, 16 Common Road, SL4 6JE

12-11; 11.30-midnight Fri & Sat; 11.30-10 Sun

☎ (01753) 868633 greyhoundetonwick.co.uk

Fuller's London Pride; Rebellion IPA; Windsor & Eton Knight of the Garter H

A proper, friendly locals' pub with a clean, contemporary air. A free house, it serves only local real ales. Food is available Monday to Friday lunchtimes. Unusually for this part of the country, it has a skittle alley, which is available to hire. Live music is a regular attraction. Karaoke is held on the second Saturday of every month.

P (10)

Hungerford

Hungerford Arms

113 High Street, RG17 0NB

12-11 (11.45 Fri & Sat); 12-10 Sun ☎ (01488) 682154

hungerfordarmspub.co.uk

Morland Old Speckled Hen; 1 changing beer (sourced nationally; often Timothy Taylor) H

This welcoming high-street pub is divided into two areas with an island bar, with drinking on one side and dining on the other. There are TV screens showing horse racing and other sports in the bar area. At least three ales including a house beer are available. The pub offers a traditional menu and serves snacks all day. Events include race festival previews, quiz nights and live music. The courtyard and large garden offer comfortable seating.

Hungerford Club

3 The Croft, RG17 0HY (on foot via Church Lane, by road via Church St and Croft Rd)

12-3, 7-11; 12-5 Sun ☎ (01488) 682357

hungerford-club.co.uk

Fuller's London Pride; 1 changing beer (sourced nationally) H

Visitors are welcomed at this friendly sports and social venue that is home to tennis and bowls club members. Snooker, billiards and other indoor games are also played. There is a comfortable lounge where you can sit and enjoy your beer and engage in conversation with the members. A changing guest ale is often available. It hosts outdoor events, including a beer festival every August bank holiday. Show this Guide or CAMRA membership card to gain entry.

Q P

Littlewick Green

Cricketers

Coronation Road, SL6 3RA

12-11 ☎ (01628) 822888 cricketers-berkshire.co.uk

Hall & Woodhouse Badger Best Bitter; 1 changing beer (sourced regionally) H

The Cricketers is in a quintessentially British pub location by the village green and cricket pitch, which featured in Midsomer Murders. A refurbished terrace area at the front overlooks this idyllic setting. Hall & Woodhouse seasonal beers are available at times. In winter, wood-burning stoves keep the pub cosy. A limited bus service is available along the Bath Road.

Q (4,127)

Maidenhead

Craufurd Arms

15 Gringer Hill, SL6 7LY

12-midnight (1am Fri & Sat) ☎ (01628) 675410

craufurdarms.com

Rebellion IPA; West Berkshire Good Old Boy; Windsor & Eton Knight of the Garter; 2 changing beers (sourced locally; often Stardust, Windsor & Eton) H

The pub was registered as an Asset of Community Value and is now owned by the community. The building dates back to the late 1800s and was close to Craufurd College, a private school for boys, hence the unusual spelling. A cosy single bar hosts a multitude of activities – crib on Monday, ladies' darts Tuesday, gents' darts Wednesday and Thursday quiz night. Two large screens show Sky and BT sports. Live music features on occasion.

(Furze Platt)P (5,8)

Grenfell Arms

22 Oldfield Road, SL6 1TW

12-11.30 (1am Fri & Sat); 12-10.30 Sun ☎ (01628) 620705

grenfellarmsmaidenhead.co.uk

Greene King IPA, IPA Gold; 6 changing beers H

A welcoming wood-panelled two-room pub situated a short walk from the town centre and the Thames, offering eight recently refurbished bedrooms. There are eight handpumps on the bar, four for Greene King beers, including a seasonal, and four for rotating guests from local micros. Two real ciders are offered, normally Orchard Pig and Hogan's. Breakfast is served from 10am followed by traditional pub food lunchtimes and evenings. The recent garden makeover adds to the attraction in summer. Q P (53,4)

Maidenhead Conservative Club

32 York Road, SL6 1SF

11-11 (midnight Fri & Sat); 11-7 Sun ☎ (01628) 620579
maidenheadconclub.co.uk

Fuller's London Pride; 4 changing beers H

A friendly real ale outlet close to the station and local CAMRA branch Club of the Year 2017. The four guests ales come from mainly local independent breweries, and a selection of bottle-conditioned beers is available. Crib nights are held during the week and a quiz night on the last Wednesday of the month. The TV lounge has been refurbished. Your CAMRA membership card allows entry for a minimal fee. Public parking is nearby. P (4)

Moneyrow Green

White Hart

SL6 2ND

12-11 (10 Mon; 11.30 Fri); 12-9 Sun ☎ (01628) 621460
thewhitehartholyport.co.uk

Greene King IPA; 3 changing beers H

A welcoming, traditional pub half-a-mile south of the village. The guest beers include one LocAle and two non-Greene King ales. The wood-panelled lounge features leather sofas and log fires in winter. The larger public bar has wooden flooring, a TV and traditional pub games including bar billiards. There is a regular quiz night on a Monday and open mic on the second Tuesday of the month. Outside is a large, fenced beer garden with a pétanque pitch and children's play area. P (53)

Newbury

Catherine Wheel

35 Cheap Street, RG14 5DB

12-11 (1am Thu; 2am Fri & Sat) ☎ (01635) 569897
thecatherinewheel.com

West Berkshire Good Old Boy; 4 changing beers (often Binghams, Longdog, Wild Weather Ales) H

Refurbished in 2014, this increasingly popular town-centre pub serves a changing selection of beers from six handpumps on the main bar. Additionally, over 100 UK and international beers are available in chilled bottles. A gin bar is housed in the covered courtyard. Winner of the CAMRA branch's 2017 Cider Pub of the Year award, it also offers 18 boxed ciders and local bottled ciders. The landlord arranges beer festivals, Meet the Brewer events and trips. The food menu, based around Pieminister pies, satisfies customers' appetites. Local CAMRA Pub of the Year.

Cow & Cask

1 Inches Yard, Market Street, RG14 5DP

12-2 (not Tue & Wed), 5-9; 12-2, 4.30-10 Fri; 12-9 Sat; closed Sun & Mon ☎ 07517 658071 cowandcask.co.uk

3 changing beers (sourced regionally; often Indigenous, Longdog, Ramsbury) G

Housed in a former shop near the bus and train stations, Berkshire's first micropub has dispensed around 500 different beers since it opened in November 2014. The bar serves up to four ales, most – but not all – locally sourced, and at least two ciders. Gin, wine, non-alcoholic drinks, pork pies and snacks are also available. Friendly conversation is the order of the day. A monthly quiz night, occasional raffles and traditional pub games such as crib are popular. Q

Hatchet Inn

12 Market Place, RG14 5BD

7am-midnight (1am Fri & Sat) ☎ (01635) 277560

Greene King Abbot; Ruddles Best Bitter; Sharp's Doom Bar; 5 changing beers (sourced nationally; often Loddon, Ramsbury, Two Cocks) H

Set back from the Corn Exchange in the Market Place, both front entrances to Newbury's Wetherspoon hotel are flanked by outdoor tables that face any afternoon sunshine. Different areas within the large interior space offer various seating styles, including sofas near the fireplace. Two sets of handpumps are positioned at each end of the divided bar, with several beers from local breweries. Real ciders are poured from refrigerated boxes. Breakfast is served until noon and main meals until 11pm. Q P

King Charles Tavern

54 Cheap Street, RG14 5BX

11.30-midnight (1am Thu-Sat); 12-midnight Sun
☎ (01635) 36695 kctavern.com

West Berkshire Good Old Boy; house beer (by Greene King); 6 changing beers (sourced nationally; often Butts, Oakham, St Austell) H

Close to the bus and rail stations, the King Charles has a central bar surrounded by three drinking areas, two with open fireplaces. Up to eight ales are on offer, with guests often from local breweries such as West Berkshire, Loose Cannon, XT and Loddon. Locally sourced, freshly prepared food is a speciality. Note the old map of Newbury on the ceiling in the right hand bar.

Reading

Alehouse

2 Broad Street, RG1 2BH

11-11 (midnight Fri); 12-10.30 Sun ☎ (0118) 950 8119

9 changing beers (often West Berkshire) H

One of Reading's quirkiest pubs, The Alehouse always leaves an impression on visitors. As a champion of microbreweries, both local and from further afield, there are frequently rare and unusual ales to be found on the pumps. Often busy around the bar area, those wishing for a more peaceful drink can take advantage of the secluded cubbyholes at the back of the pub.

Castle Tap

120 Castle Street, RG1 7RJ

11-11.30 (midnight Fri & Sat); 12-10.30 Sun
☎ (0118) 958 0473 thecastletap.co.uk

4 changing beers H

Alongside its ever-changing selection of real ales and ciders, The Castle Tap boasts an excellent range of bottled and canned beers. While offering a warm welcome to visiting real ale aficionados and craft beer fans, it maintains a friendly local atmosphere. The frequent live music and other events are well worth checking out. And for those feeling peckish, cheeseboards are available. The back room can be booked for functions. P

Eldon Arms

19 Eldon Terrace, RG1 4DX

5-11 (11.30 Fri & Sat); 5-10.30 Sun ☎ (0118) 958 6048
eldonarmsreading.co.uk

Loddon Hullabaloo; 6 changing beers (often Binghams, Salopian) H

Unexpectedly reopened as a free house in 2017 after being sold by Wadworth, this back-street local is just 10 minutes' walk from the centre of Reading. It offers a range of beers from Berkshire and further afield, as well as ciders. A traditional pub, it caters for all the family including canine visitors. A small courtyard garden is at the back for those warmer summer evenings, and on colder days you can relax in the bar and enjoy the atmosphere and the open fires.

Fisherman's Cottage

224 Kennet Side, RG1 3DW

closed Mon; 12-11.30 (midnight Fri & Sat); 12-10 Sun
(0118) 956 0432 thefishermanscottagereading.co.uk

4 changing beers (often Siren, Wild Weather Ales)

A thriving, traditional free house on the towpath of the River Kennet. Four ales on handpump are complemented by changing beers on six keg taps and a large selection of bottled and canned beers. The menu is based around tapas and paella, cooked by the I Love Paella company, including a good selection of vegetarian and vegan dishes. The garden is a summer delight, including beach hut-style seating booths. P

Foresters Arms

79-81 Brunswick Street, RG1 6NY

4-11; 12-midnight Fri & Sat; 12-11 Sun 07860 863387

2 changing beers (often Timothy Taylor)

Traditional back-street local with two bars linked by a side corridor, and recognised by CAMRA as having a historic interior of some regional importance. The front bar is a home-from-home, with a proper fire, carpet and sports TV. The rear room hosts a pool table and darts, leading to a recently renovated garden, ideal for a sunny evening pint. The licensees and staff are enthusiastic about cask-conditioned ales and encourage the locals to help choose the beers. No hot food is served, but an impressive array of snacks is available.

Greyfriar

53 Greyfriars Road, RG1 1PA

11.30-11 (midnight Thu-Sat); 12.30-7 Sun
(0118) 958 0560 thegreyfriarreading.co.uk

Hogs Back HBB; 7 changing beers (often Elusive, Siren, Wild Weather Ales)

A local success story, coming back from a long period of closure a few years ago and on the shortlist for the CAMRA branch's Pub of the Year in 2017. A refit in late 2017 saw the beer range extend to eight handpumps and 14 keg lines, all offering ales from independent breweries. Occasional tap takeovers feature. Convenient for the railway station and popular with the after-work crowd.

Hop Leaf

163-165 Southampton Street, RG1 2QZ

2-midnight; 1-1am Fri & Sat; 12-midnight Sun
(0118) 931 4700

Downton New Forest Ale; Hop Back Citra, Crop Circle, Taiphoon, Summer Lightning; 1 changing beer

The licensees recently celebrated their 10th anniversary at this traditional local. A good selection of pub games are on offer, which includes bar billiards, crib and backgammon, as well as a pinball machine. The pub stocks six Hop Back Brewery beers plus a selection of ciders and perries. Fans of classic rock will enjoy the landlord's choice in music. A variety of pub snacks is available and a good range of daily newspapers is provided. There is a buy-12-get-one-free loyalty card on pints.

Nag's Head

5 Russell Street, RG1 7XD

12-11 (midnight Fri); 11-midnight Sat 07765 880137
thenagsheadreading.co.uk

12 changing beers

With a wide range of real ales, real cider and perry always on offer, visitors can be sure to find something to their taste here. Dedication to quality has made the pub a multiple winner of local CAMRA Pub and Cider Pub of the Year awards, and it was regional winner of both in 2017. There is also a craft beer wall with vessel and dispense type clearly indicated on the adjacent blackboard. A selection of board games is kept for those wanting to while away a few sociable hours.
P

Park House (University of Reading)

Whiteknights Campus, RG6 6UR

12-11; closed Sat & Sun (0118) 378 5097 https://reading.ac.uk/catering

5 changing beers (often Rebellion, Siren, Titanic)

The university's old Senior Common Room is now open to the public. Five ales, mostly LocAle, are usually available in an array of styles. It is a popular venue for the mature university community and can get busy in the early evening. Open from midday during university term time and from 4pm during the Christmas and Easter holidays – if in doubt, please ring in advance. Almost uniquely, the bar is cashless. Non-accredited vehicles are not allowed on campus until after 5pm but a regular bus service drops off inside the campus.
Q (21,21A)

Retreat

8 St John's Street, RG1 4EH

4.30-11; 12-11.30 Fri & Sat; 12-11 Sun
(0118) 9376 9159 theretreatpub.co.uk

6 changing beers (often Butcombe, Harvey's, Sharp's)

A well-loved back-street boozer with a traditional layout and feel. A good range of real ales is squeezed onto the small bar. The landlord tends to concentrate on well-known regional brands; however, there is a selection of more eclectic choices available in bottles, as well as a number of ciders. The pub is locally renowned for regular live music and hosting community events. A quiz night is held every second Wednesday of the month.
Q

Ruscombe

Royal Oak

Ruscombe Lane, RG10 9JN (on B3024 E out of Twyford)

12-3 Mon; 12-3, 6-11; 12-4 Sun (0118) 934 5190
burattas.co.uk

Fuller's London Pride; 2 changing beers (often Binghams)

Across the road from Binghams Brewery, the pub's open-plan area is divided between cosy seating areas and a dining space. Through the restaurant is a bright conservatory overlooking the beautifully kept garden, excellent for families in summer. The interior is comfortably furnished and decorated with quirky objects and antiques – many are for sale. Also known as Buratta's, the pub is noted for its food, but welcomes drinkers with up to three real ales including one from Binghams, and a fine range of wines. Q (127)

St Nicholas Hurst

Wheelwrights Arms

Davis Way, RG10 0TR (off B3030 opp entrance to Dinton Pastures)

12-11 (10.30 Sun) (0118) 934 4100

thewheelwrightsarms.co.uk

Wadworth IPA, Horizon, 6X, Swordfish; 2 changing beers (sourced nationally; often Wadworth) H

Refurbished family-run community pub serving up to six Wadworth real ales including two changing guests. One or two real ciders, including Old Rosie, are also available. The pub is a handy stop-off for cyclists, walkers and their dogs visiting nearby Dinton Pastures, and is also popular with local diners and drinkers. The rear garden is ideal for families in the summer. Two fires inside make for a cosy drinking and dining experience in the colder months. Q P (128)

Sandhurst

Rose & Crown

108 High Street, GU47 8HA (on A321, 20yds W of jct with New Rd)

12-11 (midnight Fri & Sat); 12-10 Sun (01252) 878938

roseandcrownsandhurst.info

Otter Bitter; 6 changing beers (sourced nationally; often Bond Brews, Hammerpot) H

Friendly community local offering one permanent and up to six changing real ales. At least one of these will be locally sourced, and real ciders alternate on one of the handpumps. Beer festivals are held at Easter and Halloween when the pub is elaborately decorated by the licensees, who also dress up for the occasion. Good-quality food is served throughout (no food Mon lunch). Booking is strongly advised for Sunday lunches. Live music plays most Monday and Saturday evenings. P (194)

Slough

Moon & Spoon

86 High Street, SL1 1EL

9am-midnight; 8am-midnight Fri & Sat; 8am-11 Sun

(01753) 531650

Greene King Abbot; Ruddles Best Bitter; Sharp's Doom Bar; 4 changing beers H

This Wetherspoon establishment has 12 handpumps offering three regulars beers accompanied by up to four constantly changing guest ales, always including one from a local brewery. A couple of ciders are also usually available, often Old Rosie and Black Dragon. At the entrance is an eye-catching sculpture made of 1,148 spoons. The usual Wetherspoon extensive all-day food menu is available. Soft lighting gives the pub a cosy feel, especially at quieter times. (8,2)

Sonning

Bull Inn

High Street, RG4 6UP (next to St Andrew's Church)

10-11 (11.30 Fri & Sat); 10-10.30 Sun (0118) 969 3901

bullinnsonning.co.uk

Fuller's London Pride; Gale's HSB; 3 changing beers (sourced nationally; often Butcombe, Fuller's) H

This delightful, characterful 16th-century pub is leased to Fuller's by the adjacent church. Most of the pub is set for dining but the Village Bar is for drinkers. It serves an excellent range of quality food, from sandwiches to fine dining. The pub is a great base for a Thames-side walk – and features in the novel Three Men and a Boat. Boutique accommodation is available. Q P

Theale

Fox & Hounds

Station Road, Sheffield Bottom, RG7 4BE (20 mins' walk from village, 15 mins from station)

11-3, 5-11; 11-11 Fri & Sat; 11-10.30 Sun

(0118) 930 2295 foxandhoundstheale.co.uk

Wadworth IPA, 6X, Bishops Tipple; 2 changing beers (often Wadworth) H

Well worth the walk from the village, station or canal. Formerly known as The Drum & Monkey when it was used by local farmers, it is now an efficiently run and comfortable Wadworth's house (with some of the brewery's old signs adorning the walls), catering for a wide range of customers. There is an emphasis on food, although you are welcome to come in just for a beer. Garden and patio areas to the front and side are ideal for a comfortable summer's pint. P

Waltham St Lawrence

Bell

The Street, RG10 0JJ

12-3, 5-11; 12-11 Sat; 12-10.30 Sun (0118) 934 1788

thebellwalthamstlawrence.co.uk

Loddon Hoppit; 4 changing beers (often Binghams, Butts, Stardust) H

A relaxed and unfussy 14th-century pub, bequeathed to the village in 1608, which continues to function as the village local. The same licensees have managed the pub since 2004 and are proud to promote real ales and ciders from small independent brewers. The food menu offers bar snacks as well as restaurant meals, using locally sourced ingredients where possible. You will also find log fires in the winter and a good-sized beer garden for sunny summer days. Q (4A)

Wargrave

Wargrave & District Snooker Club

Woodclyffe Hostel, Church Street, RG10 8EP

7-11; closed Sat & Sun 07739 785552

wargravesnooker.co.uk

2 changing beers H

The club opens weekday evenings and shares the building with the local library. The regularly changing beers reflect members' recommendations, with two on in the winter months and one in the summer. The TV's default is off, though the Six Nations and Rugby World Cup are an exception. Visitors may show this Guide or CAMRA membership card for entry (£3 fee to use the snooker tables). Winner of CAMRA branch Club of the Year for several years. (850)

Wickham

Five Bells

Baydon Road, RG20 8HH (N side of B4000 in Wickham)
12-3, 5-10 (11 Fri); 12-11 Sat; 12-10 Sun
(01488) 657300 fivebellswickham.co.uk
INNformal INNHouse Bitter; 7 changing beers (sourced regionally; often INNformal, Mad Squirrel, Wild Weather Ales)
A 17th-century pub with a thatched roof, wooden floorboards and low exposed beams. The large single-room interior has an open fire and a central bar with nine changing real ales and four real ciders. Another four bag-in-box real ciders are kept in the fridge. Three of the changing real ales come from the INNformal Brewery which is located on-site. There is also one Belgian beer on draught and many more in bottles. The seasonal food menu changes regularly – look for the daily specials board. Q

Windsor

Acre

Donnelly House, Victoria Street, SL4 1EN
11-11 (midnight Fri & Sat); 12-10.30 Sun
(01753) 841083 theacrewindsor.com
Windsor & Eton Guardsman; 2 changing beers
Formerly the Liberal Club, now a free house open to all. The name refers to the adjacent Bachelors Acre. Three ales are on offer, with Windsor & Eton's Guardsman a permanent feature and two regularly changing guests, often from local breweries. Freshly made rolls, pies and pasties are available daily. Live music is hosted every Saturday night. Two screens show live sporting events and there are excellent facilities for darts. Now with a new cellar bar. (2)

Carpenters Arms

4 Market Street, SL4 1PB
11-11 (midnight Fri & Sat) (01753) 863739
Fuller's London Pride; St Austell Nicholson's Pale Ale; Sharp's Doom Bar; 5 changing beers (sourced nationally)
Situated on a narrow cobbled street close to the castle, this excellent, recently refurbished Nicholson's pub has been voted local CAMRA Pub of the Year several times. The elegantly decorated interior is on three levels, the lowest of which is reputed to house a passageway to the castle. On the floor by the entrance are Ashby's Brewery tiles, harking back to the pub's former owners. The three regular beers are supplemented by five interesting guests, usually including something dark. (71,702)

Corner House

22 Sheet Street, SL4 1BG
11-11 (midnight Thu; 1am Fri & Sat); 12-11 Sun
(01753) 862031 thecornerhousepub.co.uk
Big Smoke Solaris Session Pale Ale; 9 changing beers
This Grade II-listed building was completely refurbished in a traditional style by new owners in 2017 and designated as an ale and cider house. Fifteen handpumps serve 10 regularly changing real ales, five ciders and 10 keg lines. A good selection of traditional pub food is available. Upstairs is a function room. Unusually, there is a small, partly covered roof terrace, to cater for smokers and those wishing to savour the air. Pub quiz night is Monday.

Queen Charlotte

6 Church Lane, SL4 1PA
12-11 (midnight Fri & Sat); 12-10.30 Sun
(01753) 859268 queencharlottewindsor.co.uk
6 changing beers
The pub takes its name from the nearby Queen Charlotte Street which is listed as the shortest street in Britain. Situated in Windsor's historic centre, there are good views of Windsor Castle's Henry VIII Gate from the outside seating area. The local community is well represented among the clientele and the vicar from the nearby parish church can sometimes be seen working behind the bar. An extensive drinks menu includes six constantly changing cask beers, with several from local breweries. Q

Winkfield

White Hart

Church Road, SL4 4SE (opp St Mary's Church)
12-11 (7 Sun) (01344) 882415
thewhitehartwinkfield.co.uk
Rebellion IPA; Sharp's Doom Bar; 1 changing beer (sourced locally; often Rebellion)
Former 16th-century inn, now a quiet village pub with an open fire and separate dining area. Three handpumps serve the two regular ales and one local guest. The kitchen is 5-star rated and known for its home-cooked food. Meals are served every lunchtime and most evenings (not Sun or Mon), and the dining area is available to hire. The large well-maintained garden has a sunny aspect to enjoy in warmer times. Dogs are allowed in the bar area only. Q (162)

Wokingham

Broad Street Tavern

29 Broad Street, RG40 1AU
12-11 (midnight Fri & Sat); 12-10.30 Sun
(0118) 977 3706 broadstreettavern.co.uk
Wadworth IPA, Horizon, 6X, Bishops Tipple, Swordfish; 1 changing beer (sourced nationally; often Bath Ales, St Austell)
Popular town-centre pub serving five Wadworth beers alongside a changing guest and Westons Old Rosie cider. The entrance corridor is flanked by two cosy wood-panelled rooms, one with a real fire, leading to the bar and further upholstered seating. The large courtyard garden at the rear with patio heating makes for a pleasant summer visit. Children are welcome every day until 6pm. A pub quiz is on Tuesday and live music on Friday. (4)

Crispin

45 Denmark Street, RG40 2AY (opp Denmark St car park)
12-11 (midnight Fri & Sat); 12-10.30 Sun
(0118) 978 0309 crispinpub.co.uk
Hogs Back HBB; 4 changing beers (sourced regionally; often Rebellion, Siren, West Berkshire)
One of the oldest pubs in Wokingham, named after St Crispin, the patron saint of cobblers (hence the pub's sign). A 15th-century town-centre free house, up to five real ales and five real ciders are available. No food is served but you can bring your own food as long as you purchase a drink from the bar. Beer and cider festivals are held seasonally and there is a garden with a gazebo and seating for warmer months. (4,4X)

Hope & Anchor

Station Road, RG40 2AD (jct with Shute End)

12-11 (midnight Fri); 12-1am Sat ☎ (0118) 978 0918
hopeanchor.co.uk

Brakspear Bitter; Wychwood Hobgoblin; 3 changing beers (sourced nationally; often Bond Brews, Hogs Back, Marston's) H

Seventeenth-century coaching house with an old-fashioned feel. It gets its maritime name due to its construction from former ships' timbers. Welcoming staff dispense ales from the Marston's range, plus one from a local brewery. A substantial range of gins is also available. The delightful secluded garden features a barbecue and heated smoking area. Live bands play on Saturday evening and a board game night is held on the second Wednesday of the month. Three en-suite bedrooms are available. ♣ (4)

Queen's Head

23 The Terrace, RG40 1BP

12-11 (12.30am Fri & Sat); 12-10.30 Sun
☎ (0118) 978 1221 queensheadwokingham.co.uk

Greene King Abbot; Morland Original Bitter; house beer (by Hardys & Hansons); 3 changing beers (sourced locally; often Binghams, Hogs Back, Loddon) H

A 15th-century timber cruck-framed building, this is a Greene King Local Heroes pub that serves three local ales alongside three of its own. Third-pint paddles are available to try a selection of beers, as well as treats for four-legged friends. The pub has a strong community following, with darts played beside a cosy real fire and an Aunt Sally pitch in the secluded, landscaped rear garden. Local CAMRA Pub of the Year 2015-2017, and Country Pub of the Year 2015-2016. ♣ (4)

Woolhampton

Rowbarge

Station Road, RG7 5SH

11-11 (10.30 Sun) ☎ (0118) 971 2213

House beer (by Phoenix); 5 changing beers (sourced regionally; often Indigenous, Vale, Wild Weather Ales) H

Eighteenth-century Brunning & Price pub alongside the towpath of the Kennet & Avon Canal, with the station of Midgham a short walk away. Its idyllic location attracts the walking and cycling community, with ample routes around the pub. With five handpumps offering a changing ale selection, regular Meet the Brewer events and an established summer beer festival, the Rowbarge is a beer lovers' destination. A varied menu, outdoor barbecues and real fires in the winter add to the attractions. ♣P

Wraysbury

Perseverance

2 High Street, TW19 5DB

12-11 (8 Sun) ☎ (01784) 482375 thepercy.co.uk

Otter Ale; 3 changing beers (sourced nationally) H

Comfortable pub with several seating areas. The larger front room has soft sofas, a piano and a large inglenook fireplace with a real log fire. Another seating area, again with an open fire, leads through to the rear dining area, which has well-stocked bookshelves. Outside, the garden is delightful. Three guest ales are always varied and sourced from some of the more interesting breweries around the country. Regular beer festivals are held. Quiz night is Thursday and live music plays on Sunday afternoon.
Q ♣P (10,305)

Bell Inn, Aldworth

Askett

Stable Bar at The Three Crowns 🄻

HP27 9LT (150yds W of A4010)

⏲ closed Mon & Tue; 3-10 Wed-Fri; 12-10 Sat; 12-6 Sun

☎ (01844) 347166 🌐 thethreecrownsaskett.co.uk

Shepherd Neame Spitfire; 1 changing beer (sourced locally) 🄷

The Stable Bar is a new and welcome extension to the more food-oriented Three Crowns, converted from the pub's outbuildings. Aimed at drinkers and arguably the area's first micropub, one of its handpumps always serves a locally sourced ale. The cosy and welcoming pub is easily accessible by public transport despite its location in a chocolate box village in deepest Midsomer Murders country.

Q🛏❀◑♿⇌P🚌(300)📶

Aylesbury

Hop Pole Inn 🄻

83 Bicester Road, HP19 9AZ (near Gatehouse Industrial Area)

⏲ 4.30-10.30 Mon; 12-2.30, 4.30-11 Tue-Thu; 12-midnight Fri & Sat; 12-10.30 Sun ☎ (01296) 482129

🌐 aylesburybrewhouse.co.uk/thehoppoleaylesbury

Vale Best IPA, Gravitas; 7 changing beers 🄷

Well worth a short stroll out of the town centre, this is Vale Brewery's flagship pub complete with its own brewhouse. It regularly offers nine cask ales including three or four guests among the Vale and brewhouse beers. There is also a good range of mostly Belgian beers available. It hosts a long-running quiz on Tuesday nights and a ukulele night on the second and fourth Wednesdays of each month. Occasional live music features at the weekend. Meals can be enjoyed in its dining area, prepared with fresh, locally-sourced ingredients.

King's Head

Market Square, HP20 2RW

11-11; 12-10.30 Sun ☎ (01296) 718812

farmersbar.co.uk

Chiltern Pale Ale, Beechwood Bitter; 2 changing beers

Dating from circa 1455, this is the oldest courtyard inn in England and was donated by the Rothschild family in 1924. When Chiltern Brewery took over the running of the Farmers Bar for the National Trust it became the first bar in the country to be no-smoking and free from piped music. Small brewers' beers often appear alongside the Chiltern ales. Lunches here feature ingredients freshly sourced from local suppliers, with cheese and chutney made using the brewery's beers.

Q

Old Millwrights Arms

83 Walton Road, HP21 7SN

12-11 (midnight Fri); 12-1am Sat ☎ (01296) 488161

oldmillwrightsarms.com

Greene King IPA; 8 changing beers

Vibrant community pub with much on offer to interest all including an open mic night, comedy night, Dungeons & Dragons night and board games night. The Thursday quiz is well attended. Allied with up to nine real ales, this is a popular venue. Food is served daily with pizzas a speciality.

P

Bourne End

KEG Craft Beer Tasting Bar

12 Oakfield Road, SL8 5QN (next to the Co-op)

11-9 (10 Fri); 11-11 Sat; 12-6 Sun ☎ (01628) 529369

kegcraftbeer.co.uk

2 changing beers (sourced locally)

Opened in November 2016, this is a small, comfortable micropub with a warm welcome for all. The bar offers two regularly changing cask ales, six craft keg beers and four or five real ciders. Beers may be sourced locally or from around the world. The music is from the owner's vast collection of vinyl records. Parking is available either in front of the shops or in a nearby car park. (36)

Cheddington

Old Swan

58 High Street, LU7 0RQ

12-11 (midnight Fri & Sat) ☎ (01296) 662171

theoldswancheddington.co.uk

Fuller's London Pride; 3 changing beers (sourced locally; often XT)

A charming 16th-century Grade II-listed thatched free house, sympathetically refurbished in 2015, which offers a warm welcome to walkers and their dogs, drinkers and diners alike. An open fire and low beams contribute to a comfortable, cosy atmosphere in the bar. Lunchtime, main and children's menus featuring locally sourced ingredients are available daily (not Sun eve). Cheddington station is one mile away, the Grand Union Canal and Ridgeway Path are nearby walkers' routes. QP(164)

Chesham

Gamekeepers Lodge

Bellingdon Road, HP5 2NN

12-11.30 (1am Fri & Sat) ☎ (01494) 793491

gamekeeperslodgechesham.co.uk

Rebellion IPA; 2 changing beers (sourced nationally)

A welcoming local on the outskirts of Chesham. The Poachers' Bar is popular with regulars and has a large screen, pool table and dartboard. The relaxed Museum Bar deserves its name for the fascinating displays that crowd the walls – you can see historical photographs of Chesham, military memorabilia and the occasional stag's head. Good-value, traditional English food is served in the Museum Bar and a restaurant area at the back of the pub. Live music often features at weekends.

P

Dagnall

Red Lion

21 Main Road North, HP4 1QZ

12-11 (10.30 Sun) ☎ (01442) 843020

theredliondagnall.co.uk

Sharp's Doom Bar; 1 changing beer (sourced regionally)

A warm welcome awaits at this professionally run 1740s free house, offering well-kept beers and home-made food using fresh ingredients. An open fire, wood-burning stove and a rear dining room with watercolour paintings by a local artist all add to the homely atmosphere. A quiz night every second Monday and Tuesday curry night (booking advised) are popular. Children are welcome and dogs in the bar. Whipsnade Zoo is three miles to the north-east. P

Downley

De Spencer Arms

The Common, HP13 5YQ (across common from village on flint track beyond the end of Plomer Green Lane)

12-11 (midnight Fri & Sat); 11.30-10 Sun

☎ (01494) 535317 ledespencersarms.co.uk

Fuller's London Pride, ESB; 2 changing beers (sourced nationally)

REAL ALE BREWERIES

Abington Buckingham
Aylesbury Aylesbury
Blackened Sun Milton Keynes: Stacey Bushes
Blackpit Stowe
Bootlegger High Wycombe
Brewhouse & Kitchen Milton Keynes (NEW)
Bucks Star Milton Keynes: Stonebridge
Chiltern Terrick
Concrete Cow Bradwell Abbey
Fisher's High Wycombe
Haresfoot Chesham
Hillfire Aylesbury
Hope Springs Wendover (brewing suspended)
Hornes Bow Brickhill
Malt Prestwood
moogBREW Taplow
Old Luxters Hambleden
Rebellion Marlow Bottom
Vale Brill
Willy's Brew Stone (NEW)
XT Long Crendon

The pub, named after the notorious 15th Baron le Despencer, whose family still own the surrounding estate, is a busy, traditional village inn offering four real ales, good wines and home-cooked food. It is popular with walkers (dogs welcome too) and cyclists, and just a quarter of a mile by road or across the common from the village hall bus stop. Quiz nights, music nights, beer and food events add to the attraction of this cosy flint pub on Downley Common.

Emberton

Bell & Bear

12 High Street, MK46 5DH

5-10 Mon; 12-2.30, 5-11; 12-11 Fri & Sat; 12-8 Sun

(01234) 711565 bellandbear.net

4 changing beers (sourced regionally; often Banks's, Leighton Buzzard, Marston's) H

A stone-built pub with a slate roof serving a variety of interesting beers and real ciders. There is always at least one local beer, and local cider from Virtual Orchard. The old building houses a long narrow bar with a Northamptonshire skittles table in the far corner. There is a separate restaurant for fine dining (closed Sunday evening, Monday all day, and Tuesday lunchtime.) The restaurant is popular and booking in advance is recommended. Parking is on the street outside. **Q** **P** (21)

Farnham Common

Stag & Hounds

18 The Broadway, SL2 3QQ

12-midnight (1am Fri & Sat) (01753) 647716

stagnhounds.co.uk

10 changing beers H

Cosy one-room pub with an interesting selection of seating such as comfy sofas and beer casks as stools. The cellar can be viewed through a window near the side entrance. Ten changing beers are generally available, five from local and national microbreweries and five from the Greene King stable, alongside a good selection of ciders and bottled beers from around the world. A beer bat serves three third-pint glasses, allowing a good number of ales to be tasted. Major sporting events are screened on TV. Outside there is a small front patio, a pleasant garden area at the rear and a covered, heated smoking area to the side.

Q **P** (X74)

Fenny Stratford

Chequers

48 Watling Street, MK2 2BY

closed Mon; 12-3 (not Tue & Wed), 5-11; 12-11 Sat; 12-8 Sun (01908) 374527

Vale Best IPA, Gravitas H**; 4 changing beers (sourced regionally)** H/G

Recent extensive refurbishment has made much better use of the available space. The bar offers two regular beers from Vale and four other changing ales, two on gravity dispense. There is also an interesting selection of craft keg beers, some from local breweries, and an extensive choice of bottled beer, mostly Belgian. The food includes burgers, steak, chicken and vegetarian options. There is a small courtyard garden at the rear furnished with wooden tables and benches. Local CAMRA Pub of the Year 2018.

Q **P** (18,X31)

Red Lion

11 Lock View Lane, Simpson Road, MK1 1BY

12-11 (midnight Fri & Sat); 12-10.30 Sun

(01908) 372317

3 changing beers (sourced nationally; often Camerons, Gale's, Woodforde's) H

A popular lockside pub on the Grand Union Canal with a real ale enthusiast landlord and three changing real ales, contrasting in style and strength. Up to five real ciders include Old Rosie, Rosie's Pig, Thatchers Cheddar Valley and Heritage. There is a room with a large-screen TV as you enter and beyond is the main bar with TV and pool table. Through the bar a corridor leads to the canalside garden. Local CAMRA Cider Pub of the Year 2018.

P (18)

Great Kimble

Swan

Lower Icknield Way, HP17 9TR

12-3, 5-10 (11 Thu-Sat); 12-7 Sun (01844) 275288

kimbleswan.co.uk

Tring Moongazing; 2 changing beers (sourced locally; often Hillfire, Tring) H

Situated in a village at the foot of the Chiltern Hills in excellent hiking, horse riding and cycling country, the Swan is a genuine, family-owned free house with a warm welcome. The building dates back to the 18th century and is reputedly haunted by a former landlady. Many rotating ales from local breweries such as Hillfire are championed by the pub. Late evening opening hours can vary, especially in the winter.

P (300)

Haddenham

Rising Sun

9 Thame Road, HP17 8EN

12-2.30, 5-11; 12-midnight Fri & Sat; 12-10.30 Sun

(01844) 291744

XT Four; 5 changing beers (sourced locally) H

This bustling village pub boasts six real ales on handpump, with favourites from XT Brewing as well as unusual new Animal Brewing Company creations, plus an ever-changing selection of guest ales, craft beers and ciders. With a newly landscaped garden and treats on tap for canine companions, this family and pooch-friendly pub blends the best of old and new seamlessly.

Q (280)

Hanslope

Club

28 High Street, MK19 7LQ

12-2.30 (not Tue-Thu), 6-11; 5-11 Fri; 12-11 Sat & Sun

(01908) 510337

Adnams Ghost Ship; 2 changing beers H

The name has been changed from Hanslope Working Men's Club to The Club at Hanslope. It has two rooms designated the Bar and the Lounge, and serves Adnams Ghost Ship as its regular beer alongside two guest ales. It offers darts, skittles, pool, cards, quizzes and monthly bingo on a Friday. A beer festival is held over the Easter weekend. Non-members are welcome at all times for a 50p entry fee. Local CAMRA Club of the Year 2016 and 2017. **P**

Cock Inn

35 High Street, MK19 7LQ
4-11; 12-11 Sat & Sun ☎ (01908) 510553
Great Oakley Wagtail; Greene King IPA; 1 changing beer (sourced regionally; often Great Oakley, Magpie) H
A pub with one large L-shaped room, with a pool table, dartboard and a large-screen TV at one end and a real fire at the other. The bar is directly in front of you as you enter and serves Greene King IPA, Great Oakley Wagtail and a guest ale. There is BT Sport on the TV and live music is staged once a month. ❀♿♣P🚌🐾📶

Hedgerley

White Horse L

Village Lane, SL2 3UY (in old village, near church)
11-2.30, 5-11; 11-11 Sat; 12-10.30 Sun ☎ (01753) 643225
thewhitehorsehedgerley.co.uk
Rebellion IPA; 7 changing beers (often Mallinsons, Mighty Oak, Oakham) G
Local CAMRA Pub of the Year on numerous occasions including 2017, this village pub offers an impressive range of real ales. New breweries often feature, as well as favourites from Oakham, Mallinsons and Mighty Oak. A draft Belgian beer and three real ciders are also available. This classic pub has a well-tended garden and a heated, covered patio area. Regular beer festivals are held, the largest of which is over the Whitsun weekend and is a must for real ale enthusiasts.
Q❀◖♣●P🐾📶

High Wycombe

Belle Vue ✔

45 Gordon Road, HP13 6EQ
4.30-11; 3.30-midnight Fri; 12-1am Sat; 12-10.30 Sun
☎ (01494) 524728 thebv.pub
Adnams Ghost Ship, Broadside; 4 changing beers H
A Guide regular with a community atmosphere, this friendly pub has an open fire in winter, five real ciders from Westons and hosts regular music events. It is situated next to the railway line (take the north exit from the station). The name is a mystery as the only view from the pub is the brick wall enclosing the railway. It was once the corner building of a terrace of workers' houses but they have now all gone. ❀⇌♣●🚌🐾📶

Bootlegger L

Amersham Hill, HP13 6NQ
12-midnight (1am Fri & Sat); 12-11 Sun
☎ (01494) 525457 thebootleggerpub.co.uk
10 changing beers (sourced locally; often Chiltern, Rebellion, Vale) H
Formerly the Flint Cottage situated opposite the railway station, this is a spacious bar with an outside drinking area. Twelve real ales are available on handpump, as well as bottled beers, some or which are real ale. Beers come from smaller, as well as local, breweries. No food is served but you are welcome to bring your own or have your takeaway delivered. Plenty of seating is available although it does get busy when sport is on and when Wycombe Wanderers are playing at home. ❀♿⇌●🚌🐾📶

Mad Squirrel Brewery Shop Emporium

4-5 Church Street, HP11 2DE
11-9.30 (10 Fri & Sat); 11-9 Sun ☎ (01494) 395980
redsquirrelbrewery.co.uk
Mad Squirrel Mister Squirrel H, London Porter H/A; 4 changing beers (sourced nationally) P
The tasting bar and bottle shop opened in 2016 and has a downstairs bar with seating as well as more seating upstairs. At least two cask ales are available alongside a range of craft keg beers, plus plenty of choice to take away. There is a walk-in chiller offering a range of real ale in a bottle plus cans, some of which are real ale in a can. You can enjoy a pizza with your favourite beer.
◖◗♿⇌●P🚌📶

Ivinghoe

Rose & Crown L ✔

Vicarage Lane, LU7 9EQ
12-11 (10.30 Sun) ☎ (01296) 668472
roseandcrownivinghoe.co.uk
Sharp's Doom Bar; Tring Side Pocket for a Toad; 2 changing beers (sourced locally) H
Hidden away but clearly signposted, this 300-year-old free house has an open fire and slate floors throughout. It offers a varied choice of guest beers and is popular with locals, cyclists, walkers and visitors from the campsite nearby. There is a quiet restaurant to the rear leading to a courtyard. Reasonably priced traditional British food is served Tuesday to Sunday lunchtime. Recommended parking is in Ladysmith Road, Wellcroft Road and beside the village green. ❀◖◗▲♣🚌(61)🐾📶

Lacey Green

Black Horse ✔

Main Road, HP27 0QU
12-3 (not Mon), 5-11; 12-11 Thu (midnight Fri & Sat); 12-11 Sun ☎ (01844) 345195 blackhorselaceygreen.co.uk
Brakspear Bitter; 3 changing beers (sourced nationally) H
Noted for its friendly atmosphere, this village pub in the heart of the Chilterns offers one regular and three regularly changing ales and one changing real cider. Walkers, cyclists and children are welcome and there is a play area in the enclosed garden to the rear which features Aunt Sally. Excellent, freshly prepared, home-cooked food is available, including traditional Sunday lunch (under sixes eat for free) and full English breakfast 9-11am Tuesday to Saturday. Q❀◖◗♿♣●P🚌(300)🐾📶

Whip Inn L

Pink Road, HP27 0PG
11-11; 12-11 Sun ☎ (01844) 344060 thewhipinn.co.uk
6 changing beers (sourced nationally) H
With six cask ales from local, micro and national breweries, the Whip is a perennially popular village inn, high in the Chilterns. The pub is now under the same management as the Bootlegger in High Wycombe and has maintained its high standards and warm welcome throughout a tasteful refurbishment in 2017. Sitting right on the Chiltern Way, it is popular with walkers and cyclists. The attractive, enclosed garden overlooks the Lacey Green windmill. ❀◖◗♣P🚌(300)🐾📶

Little Missenden

Crown Inn

HP7 0RD (off A413, between Amersham and Gt Missenden)

11-2.30, 6-11; 12-3 Sun ☎ (01494) 862571
thecrownlittlemissenden.co.uk
St Austell Tribute; 3 changing beers (sourced nationally; often Oakham, Otter, Timothy Taylor) H
This lovely old village pub is a Guide regular and was local CAMRA Pub of the Year 2016. It has been in the same family for almost 100 years. A friendly locals' pub, popular with walkers, it has a large garden to the rear. A warming log fire awaits you on cold wintry days and good pub grub at lunchtimes. Four real ales and four real ciders are on offer. Three double en-suite rooms are available. Q

Littleworth Common

Blackwood Arms

Common Lane, SL1 8PP SU937863
closed Mon; 12-11; 12-10 Sun ☎ (01753) 645672
theblackwoodarms.net
Brakspear Bitter, Oxford Gold; Wychwood Hobgoblin; 3 changing beers (sourced locally) H
A delightful Victorian country pub brought back to life by an enthusiastic couple after a long period of closure. Close to Burnham Beeches and popular with walkers and diners, an attractive garden with plenty of seating is well used in summer, while in winter there is a roaring fire. Three guest ales are offered, one from the Marston's group plus two free of tie. Dog- and horse-friendly, hay can be provided. Cider is available in the summer only. Q

Jolly Woodman L

Littleworth Road, SL1 8PF
closed Mon; 11-3, 6-10 Tue; 11-10.30 Wed & Thu; 11-11 Fri & Sat; 12-6 Sun ☎ (01753) 644350 thejollywoodman.com
3 changing beers H
Attractive country pub close to the northern edge of Burnham Beeches. A rotating Rebellion ale is always available. The spacious garden is popular in good weather and has plenty of seating. Once a month, on a Monday evening, the pub opens for a jazz session (a cover charge is made for non-diners) – check the website for dates. There is a charity quiz evening every Thursday. Q P

Long Crendon

Eight Bells L

51 High Street, HP18 9AL
12-11; 12-10 Sun ☎ (01844) 208244 8bellspub.com
Ringwood Fortyniner; XT Four; 2 changing beers H
Charming and characterful village pub with a glorious beer garden. It is renowned for slaking the thirst of ale aficionados and for serving Long Crendon cider while diners can devour local produce. XT Four, from less than a mile away, and Ringwood Bitter are permanent fixtures on two of the four handpumps, joined by guest ales from across the country. Beer festivals are held over the Easter weekend and August bank holiday. Q P (110)

Loudwater

Derehams Inn

5 Derehams Lane, HP10 9RH
11.30-3.30, 5.30-11; 11-midnight Fri & Sat; 12-11 Sun ☎ (01494) 530965 derehamsinn.co.uk
5 changing beers H
A friendly local located up a lane off the London Road, with a car park at the rear. Outside is a covered smoking area with a pool table and a garden space. An annual beer festival is held at the beginning of July. This is a traditional pub where families and dogs are welcome. Formerly known as the Bricklayers Arms, it has been run by Graham and Margaret for almost 20 years. Q P

General Havelock

114 Kingsmead Road, HP11 1HZ
12-3, 5-11.30; 12-11.30 Fri-Sun ☎ (01494) 520391
generalhavelock.co.uk
Fuller's London Pride, ESB; Gale's Seafarers Ale; 3 changing beers H
The General Haverlock was purchased by Fuller's in 1986 and has been run by the same family since then. It was originally farm buildings before conversion to a pub. The decor is a strange mix of antiques and bric-a-brac. Six ales are available at all times, mostly from Fuller's, plus guest ales. TVs are brought out for England football matches and some other events. There is an open fire in the winter and the garden is a peaceful haven in the summer. P (35)

Loughton

Talbot

33 London Road, MK5 8AB
11.30-11; 10-11 Sat; 10-10.30 Sun ☎ (01908) 827296
Fuller's London Pride; Purity Pure UBU; house beer (by Black Sheep); 7 changing beers H
A large pub with a single bar, the room is divided into several seating areas. The bar area with its 12 handpulls is for adults only. Under-18s are welcome if dining. Food is served all day every day, including brunch at the weekend. On Monday all real ales are £2.49 per pint. Wednesday is quiz night. P (24,25)

Lye Green

Black Cat

Lycrome Road, HP5 3LF (off A416)
11-2.30, 5-11 (7 Mon); 11-11 Sat; 12-10.30 Sun ☎ (01494) 773966 blackcatchesham.co.uk
Timothy Taylor Landlord; Young's Bitter; 1 changing beer (sourced nationally) H
A lovely, warm and welcoming community pub with a log fire. A regular Guide entry, it serves well-kept beers and has been awarded Timothy Taylor's Champion Club status. Great home-cooked food is on the menu at good-value prices, including breakfast 9am-noon Monday to Saturday. The pub holds a weekly quiz night and hosts darts, cribbage and dominoes matches. There is an attractive fenced garden with children's games. Dogs are welcome on a lead outside mealtimes. P (730)

Marlow

Royal British Legion L

Station Approach, SL7 1NT (by train station)
7-11 (midnight Fri & Sat); 11-4 Sun ☎ (01628) 486659
rblmarlow.co.uk
Jennings Bitter; 5 changing beers H
The Royal British Legion club, situated next to Marlow railway station, is a friendly venue holding two beer festivals a year. A wide range of cask ales is available. Although a private members' club,

guests are welcome – show a copy of this Guide or a CAMRA membership card for entry. Various events are held including jazz and music nights. This popular club has been a local CAMRA Club of the Year and regional Club of the Year for the past four years. ❀♿⇌♣●P🚌📶

Marlow Bottom

Three Horseshoes L ✔

Burroughs Grove Hill, SL7 3RA

⏲ 11.30-11; 12-6 Sun ☎ 0800 612 5564

Rebellion IPA, Mutiny, Roasted Nuts; 1 changing beer Ⓗ

Recently refurbished, this large open-plan pub is a short bus ride from both High Wycombe and Marlow. Popular with diners, the pub has an extensive specials board, open fires and a pleasant garden. Drinkers are welcome too, as are well-behaved children and dogs, and the close proximity of the Rebellion Beer Company means the six Rebellion ales on offer are always in great condition. Q❀◐P🚌(800,850)🐾

Marsworth

Red Lion L ✔

90 Vicarage Road, HP23 4LU (opp church)

⏲ 11-3, 5-11; 11-11 Sat; 12-10.30 Sun ☎ (01296) 668366

🌐 redlionmarsworth.co.uk

Fuller's London Pride; 5 changing beers (sourced regionally) Ⓗ

Genuine 17th-century village pub close to the Grand Union Canal. A central bar serves three areas: an upstairs bar with comfortable sofas, a small snug, and a public bar with an open coal-burning fire. A separate games area hosts bar billiards, darts and shove-ha'penny. Five or more well-kept beers, some from local breweries, are on handpump and the kitchen serves generous portions of home-cooked food. There is a beautiful garden to the rear. Q🐴❀◐♣●P🚌(164)🐾📶

Milton Keynes: Central

Moon under Water ✔

Xscape, Avebury Boulevard, MK9 3NN

⏲ 8am-midnight (1am Fri & Sat) ☎ (01908) 528854

Greene King Abbot; Ruddles Best Bitter; 8 changing beers Ⓗ

A popular large single-room Wetherspoon pub in the busy Xscape leisure complex. The front of the pub is fully glazed and overlooks the outdoor seating area and car park beyond. Inside, there is a long serpentine bar with 10 handpumps. The room extends beyond the bar on two levels to the entrance inside Xscape. The traditional Wetherspoon food menu is served and the pub participates in the chain's beer and cider festivals. ❀◐♿●P📶

Wetherspoon's L

201 Midsummer Boulevard, MK9 1EA

⏲ 7am-midnight (1am Fri & Sat) ☎ (01908) 606074

Greene King Abbot; Ruddles Best Bitter; Sharp's Doom Bar; 9 changing beers Ⓗ

A popular meeting place for local CAMRA members, this bar is unbeatable for price and beer range, with 12 handpumps, several dispensing local beers. A beer shop was introduced in 2016 and a wide range of canned and bottled craft beers is available for off-sales. The usual Wetherspoon food menu is served from early morning until late evening. Local CAMRA Pub of the Year 2017. ❀◐♿⇌P🚌📶

Naphill

Wheel ✔

100 Main Road, HP14 4QA

⏲ 12 (4.30 Mon)-11; 12-10.30 Sun ☎ (01494) 562210

🌐 thewheelnaphill.com

Greene King IPA Reserve; Ruddles Best Bitter; 2 changing beers Ⓗ

Popular with locals and visitors alike, this traditional village local has a cosy atmosphere, with two bar areas – one small and another that leads to the dining area. There is a large garden which is ideal on summer days. A warm welcome is extended to all – including ramblers in muddy boots enjoying the nearby walks. This pub has been in the Guide for a number of years and prides itself on serving good cask ale. Q❀🛏◐♣P🚌🐾📶

Newport Pagnell

Cannon

50 High Street, MK16 8AQ

⏲ 11-11 (midnight Fri & Sat) ☎ (01908) 211495

Banks's Amber Ale; Marston's Pedigree; 2 changing beers (often Ringwood, Wychwood) Ⓗ

A family-run town-centre free house with one bar and four handpumps. There is a heated external smoking area and a large car park to the rear. The car park is accessed from Union Street which runs behind the pub and the High Street. There is a room in an outbuilding used for regular events such as open mic nights and is available to hire. ❀P🚌

Oving

Black Boy L ✔

Church Lane, HP22 4HN

⏲ 12-11; 12-6 Sun ☎ (01296) 641258

🌐 theblackboyoving.co.uk

3 changing beers (sourced locally; often Chiltern, Leighton Buzzard, XT) Ⓗ

Delightful 17th-century inn with a roaring fire in winter. Summer visits are also a treat, with wonderful views across the local countryside from the huge beer garden. The restaurant opposite the bar is separated from the drinking area by a wooden mesh around the archway. The drinking areas offer flagstone floors and wooden beams. With good food, friendly staff and a great atmosphere, this is a cosy pub and a pleasure to visit. 🐴❀◐●P🐾📶

Penn Street

Squirrel L ✔

HP7 0PX

⏲ 12 (4 Mon)-11; 12-1am Fri; 12-10.30 Sun ☎ (01494) 711291 🌐 thesquirrelpub.co.uk

5 changing beers (sourced locally; often Rebellion, Tring, Vale) Ⓗ

A delightful pub by the village green where the local cricket team plays. Three to five real ales are available plus a cider. Good food is on offer and families are welcome, with a fenced garden and play equipment outside. There is also an outdoor decked heated area with comfy chairs. Inside, logburners warm the bar and comfortable seating spaces. Themed quiz nights with food are held monthly on a Monday, and live music on Friday evening. P (1)

Quainton

George & Dragon

32 The Green, HP22 4AR

closed Mon; 12-2.30, 5-11; 12-11.30 Sat; 12-3, 6-10.30 Sun (01296) 655436 georgeanddragonquainton.co.uk

6 changing beers (sourced locally)

Free house with an adjoining coffee shop, always offering four LocAles plus two guests. It has a friendly public bar with darts, a jukebox and a TV, and a saloon bar dedicated to dining, although home-cooked food is served throughout. Parts of this well-maintained and delightful pub date back to the 1700s, with traditional English features such as inglenook fireplaces, beams and a quarry-tiled floor. Regular beer festivals overlooking the green feature in summer. P (16)

Radnage

Crown

City Road, HP14 4DW

11-3, 5-midnight Mon & Tue; 11-midnight Wed-Sun (01494) 482301 crownradnage.co.uk

Rebellion IPA; 2 changing beers

Nestled in a picturesque Chiltern village, this place is just a five-minute drive from junction 5 of the M40. It is a family-friendly pub with a large garden and modern accommodation. The pleasant one-room bar offers a warm welcome, with good home-cooked food and an open fire in the winter months. Real local ales and real local cider are dispensed on gravity. P

Stoke Goldington

Lamb

Main Street, MK16 8NR

12 (5 Mon)-11; 12-7 Sun (01908) 551233 thelambatstokegoldington.co.uk

Tring Brock Bitter, Death or Glory; 2 changing beers (sourced regionally)

This village is a few miles from Milton Keynes and Northampton on the B526. The bar area has a dartboard and a Northamptonshire skittles table. The pub serves home-cooked food using local seasonal produce (no food Mon). Cider is typically Old Rosie. The garden has a stage for music events. There is ample parking and walking groups are encouraged to park early and order food before their walk to enjoy on their return. Q P

Stoke Hammond

Three Locks

Leighton Road, MK17 9DD

12-11 (01525) 270214 thethreelocksstokehammond.com

5 changing beers (sourced regionally; often Hornes, Tring, XT)

Popular canalside hostelry that supports breweries in the area, with three or four changing beers, usually local. The cider can come from nearby producer Virtual Orchard, or may be from traditional producers around the country. A beer festival is held over the late May bank holiday. The pub is particularly popular in summer, with customers arriving by road and narrowboat. Inland Waterways Association members receive a 10 per cent discount on food. There is plenty of outdoor seating alongside the locks. P (70)

Stone

Rose & Crown

2 Oxford Road, HP17 8PB (at jct with Upper Hartwell)

12-11; 11-9.30 Sun (01296) 749160 roseandcrownstone.co.uk

2 changing beers (sourced locally)

A recent refurbishment has given the pub a stylish feel. The Willy's Brew microbrewery has been installed at the rear and provides all the ales on offer. Food includes home-made traditional pub classics alongside Jamaican dishes made to the landlady's family recipes. The Sunday carvery and seniors' menu on weekday lunchtimes are popular. There is a lovely beer garden area to the rear. P (280,110)

Taplow

Oak & Saw

Rectory Road, SL6 0ET

4.30-10 Mon; 12-11 (midnight Fri) (01628) 604074 oakandsaw.co.uk

Brakspear Bitter; Sharp's Doom Bar; 1 changing beer (sourced locally)

Situated opposite the village green and church in an idyllic setting, this pub offers good pub food and three real ales, including the Rebellion monthly. The food is home made and features local produce. The meat, including venison, comes from a farm and butchery just 20 miles away. There is a covered smoking area to the rear and a large decked patio which is popular in the summer. Dogs are allowed in non-dining areas. Q P

Twyford

Crown Inn

The Square, MK18 4EG

4-11; 12-midnight Fri-Sun (01296) 730216 thecrowntwyford.co.uk

1 changing beer

This freehold inn is central to the life of the village. The present landlady, Joan, has seen the other local pubs decline and close. The Crown is a deceptively large brick building opposite the village hall. A spacious bar area leads through to an even larger lounge/function area on the left. Serving one frequently changing beer from the barrel, it is usual to have seven different beers on during the week. P (16)

Wendover

King & Queen

17 South Street, HP22 6EF

11 (3 Mon)-11; 11-midnight Fri & Sat; 12-11 Sun (01296) 696872 thekingandqueen.squarespace.com

Young's Special; 2 changing beers

The pub is situated just off the High Street within easy reach of the station. It has three rooms, one a restaurant serving good food. It has been refurbished without losing its ambience and has an impressive wall map of the local countryside in one room. A wood fire helps to provide a warm winter welcome for walkers returning from the nearby Chiltern Hills. Q P

Whaddon

New Lowndes Arms

4 High Street, MK17 0NA

closed Mon; 5-10 Tue; 12-midnight (10 Wed; 10.30 Thu); 12-6 Sun ☎ (01908) 508373 thenewlowndesarms.co.uk

Fuller's London Pride; Sharp's Doom Bar; 1 changing beer (sourced locally) H

Reopened under new ownership in March 2017 following closure for over a year, this village pub has a single-room bar divided into two areas with additional restaurant seating. There is a large garden to the rear with views over the surrounding countryside. Accommodation is available in a separate building. The pub is popular with walkers at weekends. Q

Wheeler End

Chequers ✔

Bullocks Farm Lane, HP14 3NH (turn left down single track road about 400yds past West Wycombe heading towards Stokenchurch; pub is on left about 2 miles down) OS806926

12-11 (midnight Fri & Sat); 12-8.30 Sun ☎ (01494) 883070 chequersinnwheelerend.co.uk

Fuller's London Pride, ESB; Gale's Seafarers Ale H

A 300-year-old English country pub set in a beautiful part of the Chilterns with spectacular views of the surrounding area. The tastefully decorated L-shaped room has a low wooden-beamed ceiling, and a wood-burning stove set back in a large fireplace gives it a warm welcome in winter months. A separate dining area gives access to the beer garden. A Fuller's pub with a Master Cellarman certificate awarded to the tenant, The Chequers is highly regarded by locals.

Willen

Ship Ashore ✔

Granville Square, MK15 9JL

11.30-11 (midnight Fri & Sat) ☎ (01908) 694360

House beer (by Black Sheep); 4 changing beers H

A smart, modern pub on a residential estate not far from Willen Lake and its recreational facilities. The pub comprises one large bar but pillars and half walls break up the area to give a more intimate feel. There is a constantly changing selection of real ales plus the house beer, Ember Pale Ale, brewed by Black Sheep. On Monday all real ales are £2.49 per pint. Food is served all day. There is a small garden outside. (2)

Wooburn Common

Royal Standard

Wooburn Common Lane, HP10 0JS (follow signs to Odds Farm)

12-11 (10.30 Sun) ☎ (01628) 521121

theroyalstandard.biz

Hop Back Summer Lightning H**; St Austell Tribute** G**; 7 changing beers** H

A regular in the Guide, this is a traditional rural pub, convenient for Odds Farm Park. Its changing guest ales include one dark beer of a higher ABV. Up to eight real ciders are also usually available. Dogs and families are welcome and it is a popular stopping-off point for walkers. There is ample parking in the car park at the side of the pub. Well worth seeking out. Q

Woolstone

Cross Keys

34 Newport Road, MK15 0AA

11-11 ☎ (01908) 528145 crosskeysmiltonkeynes.co.uk

Courage Directors; Young's Bitter; 2 changing beers H

Set in a period building with a thatched roof, the pub's bar and restaurant were refurbished in early 2018. The food is home made using fresh local produce. The patio and garden to the rear are popular in summer. Situated close to the Grand Union Canal and local parkland, walkers are made welcome. Beer festivals are held during the summer and there is a quiz every Tuesday. Q (18)

Black Cat, Lye Green (Photo: Bob Steel)

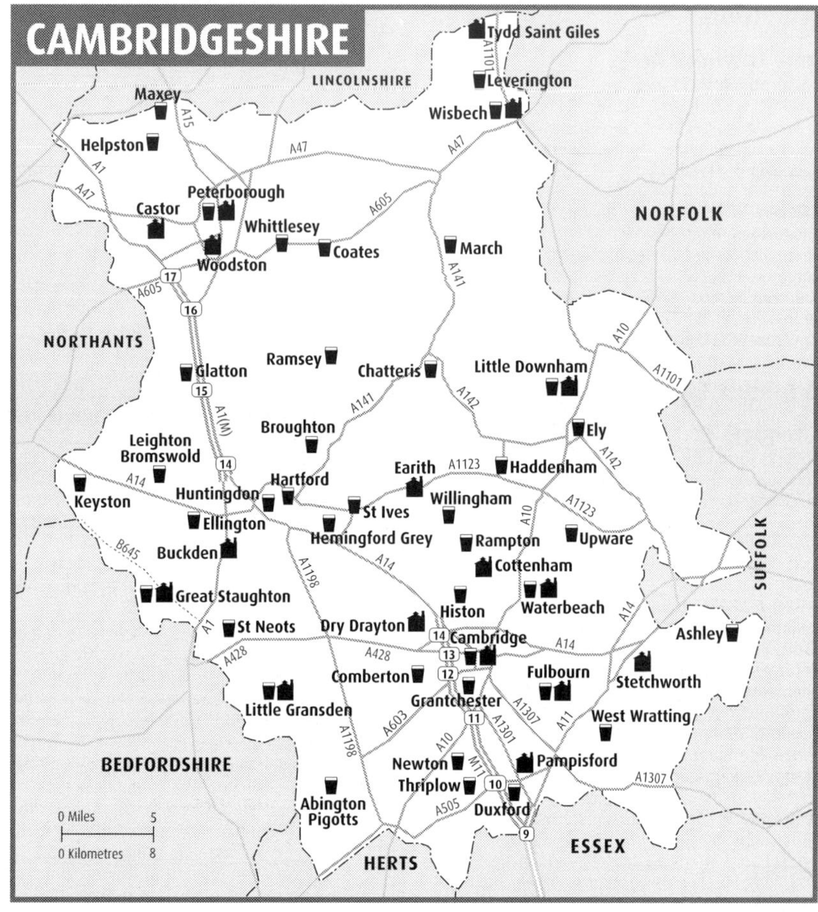

Abington Pigotts

Pig & Abbot

High Street, SG8 0SD (off A505 through Litlington)
12-3, 6-11; 12-11 Sat; 12-10.30 Sun ☎ (01763) 853515
pigandabbot.co.uk
Adnams Southwold Bitter; Fuller's London Pride; 2 changing beers (often Humpty Dumpty, Mighty Oak, Woodforde's) Ⓗ
Located in a surprisingly remote part of the south Cambridgeshire countryside, this Queen Anne-period pub offers a warm welcome. The interior has exposed oak beams and two fires, including a large inglenook featuring a wood-burning stove. A comfortable restaurant offers home-made traditional pub food, specialising in fresh fish and chips, steak and kidney puddings and pies. Two guest beers are stocked, often from Burton Bridge, Humpty Dumpty, Mighty Oak, Timothy Taylor or Woodforde's. A former local CAMRA Pub of the Year. **Q❀◐♿♣P**

Ashley

Crown Inn

24 Newmarket Road, CB8 9DR
3-11 (9 Mon); 12-11 Sat; 12-10 Sun ☎ (01638) 730117
thecrowninnashley.co.uk
Mighty Oak Captain Bob; 3 changing beers Ⓗ

This family-friendly community hub was first recorded as a pub in 1712, though parts of the building predate this. Formerly owned by Greene King, The Crown became free of tie in January

REAL ALE BREWERIES

Angles Peterborough
Bexar County Peterborough
Calverley's Cambridge
Cambridge Cambridge
Castor Castor
Crafty Beers Stetchworth
Downham Isle Little Downham (NEW)
Draycott Buckden
Elgood's Wisbech
Fellows Cottenham
Lord Conrad's Dry Drayton
Mile Tree Wisbech
Milton Waterbeach
Moonshine Fulbourn
Oakham Peterborough
Papworth Earith
Rocket Great Staughton
Son of Sid Little Gransden
Three Blind Mice Little Downham
Turpin's Pampisford
Tydd Steam Tydd Saint Giles
Xtreme Peterborough: Woodston

2014. Mighty Oak Captain Bob features regularly alongside up to three guest ales. Real ciders, direct from the box, are also available. Pub games include darts, pool and, in the enclosed rear garden, pétanque. Local CAMRA Pub of the Year 2016. 🐎❀◐◑♣●P🚌🐾📶

Broughton

Crown Inn

Bridge Road, PE28 3AY
11.30-3, 6.30-11; 11.30-6 Sun ☎ (01487) 824428
thecrowninnrestaurant.co.uk
Mauldons Moletrap Bitter; 2 changing beers (sourced locally) [H]
The Crown Inn is an idyllic early 19th-century Grade II-listed building next to the village church, set in picturesque grounds in a conservation area. A free of tie, family-run venue, it can seat up to 40 diners, with a bar and à la carte menu, but retains a sociable drinking area. There is a separate space suitable for private use. The decor is modern yet comfortable, with scrubbed pine tables and a stone floor. Q❀◐◑●P🐾📶

Cambridge

Blue Moon

2 Norfolk Street, CB1 2LF (off East Road)
5-12.45am (2.45am Fri & Sat); 5-10.30 Sun
☎ (01223) 500238 cambridge.pub/blue-moon
Adnams Mosaic; 3 changing beers (often Dark Star) [H]
A 1960s pub originally called The Man on the Moon. Since 2013 it has been a sister pub to the Cambridge Blue, hence the name change. It offers changing real ciders and real ales alongside 10 craft keg beers, with tap takeovers once a month. The front bar contains old pictures of Cambridge pubs and hand-drawn portraits of the staff. The larger back bar has a pool table and arcade machines. Local CAMRA Young Members Pub of the Year 2017. 🐎◑♿♣●P🚌🐾📶

Calverley's Brewery Tap [L]

23A Hooper Street, CB1 2NZ
6-10.30 Thu & Fri; 11-10.30 Sat; closed Sun-Wed
☎ (01223) 312370 calverleys.com
2 changing beers (often Calverley's)
Close to Mill Road, the brewery was established in a former garage in 2013. Due to its popularity, Calverley's is now open for on-sales on Thursday and Friday evenings and all day Saturday. It offers two of its beers direct from the cask. The bar is in the same room as the brewing equipment, with tables in a side room and others outside. Additional seating can be found in one of the outbuildings. Various gourmet food vans provide snacks.
Q🐎❀◑🚌

Cambridge Blue

85-87 Gwydir Street, CB1 2LG
12-11 (10.30 Sun) ☎ (01223) 471680 cambridge.pub/the-blue
Dark Star Hophead, American Pale Ale; Woodforde's Wherry [H]; 14 changing beers [H]/[G]
Ever-popular side-street pub close to Mill Road. A large rear extension leads to its garden which frequently has a marquee. Breweriana and pumpclips provide much of the decoration. Up to 14 ales from microbreweries nationwide are dispensed by handpump or gravity from the taproom. Up to seven real ciders and perries and a large selection of international bottled beers are also kept. The main beer festival is held in the summer. Cambridge University Real Ale Society Pub of the Year 2017. 🐎❀♿♣●🚌🐾📶

Castle Inn

38 Castle Street, CB3 0AJ
11.30-11 ☎ (01223) 353194
thecastleinncambridge.com
Adnams Lighthouse, Southwold Bitter, Ghost Ship, Broadside; 5 changing beers (often Adnams) [H]
This 1740s pub was acquired by Adnams in 1994 and respectfully renovated. Family run, it offers a great selection of the brewery's own beers and two or more changing guest ales. Originally two buildings, they have been combined to create a number of separate drinking areas over two floors, including a downstairs snug. To the rear is a suntrap garden next to the mound of the long-gone castle. Excellent food is served every session including a wide selection of specials.
Q🐎❀◐◑🚌(B)🐾📶

Elm Tree

16A Orchard Street, CB1 1JT
11-11; 12-10.30 Sun ☎ (01223) 502632
theelmtreecambridge.co.uk
8 changing beers (sourced nationally; often B&T, Eagle) [H]
Back-street pub close to Parker's Piece, decorated with breweriana, quirky bric-a-brac, photos and Belgian flags. The short bar is near the entrance with seating around and beyond. Jointly owned by B&T and Eagle, they have three handpumps each. Six other pumps offer changing guest ales alongside real cider or perry. Complementing these is a menu of around 100 bottled Belgian beers – the landlord has written a book on the subject and is happy to advise. Regular live music features.
🐎♿♣●🚌(PR3,X5)🐾

Flying Pig [L]

106 Hills Road, CB2 1LQ
12-11 (midnight Fri); 7-11 Sat & Sun ☎ (01223) 354623
theflyingpigpub.wordpress.com
Crouch Vale Brewers Gold; Dark Star Hophead; Rudgate Ruby Mild; 3 changing beers [H]
Much-loved, cosy and friendly pub with a local feel that defies its main road location. A beer and music venue, its walls and ceiling are adorned with an eclectic collection of old posters and pig paraphernalia. In the evening the intimate lighting is enhanced by candles. Ales often come from local breweries and craft keg beers are also available. Basic pub grub is served weekday lunchtimes only. Live music plays on Tuesday, Thursday, Saturday and some Fridays. The pub hosts an annual Pigfest charity music festival. ❀◐⇌●🚌📶

Free Press

7 Prospect Row, CB1 1DU
12-11 (midnight Fri & Sat) ☎ (01223) 368337
freepresskitchen.co.uk
Greene King XX Mild, IPA, Abbot; 4 changing beers (often Greene King) [H]
Close to Parker's Piece, this intimate, friendly pub serves high-quality food and great beer. Greene King-tied, the elusive XX Mild is a regular, alongside three guest ales. A pub for over 120 years, it just avoided the 1970s Kite area redevelopment, and is identified by CAMRA as having a regionally important historic pub interior. Only the tiny snug is original – the rest a loving

reconstruction. There is a walled garden at the rear. Named after a Temperance movement newspaper that lasted for just one edition. Q

Geldart

1 Ainsworth Street, CB1 2PF (off Mill Rd)

closed Mon; 5-11.30 (1am Fri); 12-1am Sat; 12-midnight Sun (01223) 314264 the-geldart.co.uk

Adnams Ghost Ship; Caledonian Deuchars IPA; Oakham Citra; St Austell Tribute; 4 changing beers (sourced nationally) [H]

Large two-bar back-street corner pub with an enclosed patio garden behind. It is decorated throughout with film and music memorabilia. The pub has a good reputation for its home-made food and its beers, with a restaurant area to the right of the entrance and a bar area to the left. Eight ales and a wide selection of malt whiskies and rums are available. The changing guest beers always include a dark one. The food includes 'hot rocks' available in both bars. Frequent live music is hosted.

Haymakers

54 High Street, CB4 1NG

12-11 (midnight Fri & Sat); 12-10.30 Sun (01223) 311077

Milton Pegasus; 7 changing beers (often Milton) [H]

Milton Brewery's second of three Cambridge pubs, popular with locals and employees from the nearby science park. There are drinking areas either side of the door and a snug with its own bar access. Dark wood and warm colours abound. A good-sized beer garden is to the rear. The car park contains the largest pub cycle park in Cambridge, leaving few spaces for cars. Eight real ales, including three guests, are on offer plus four real ciders or perries. P

Hopbine

11-12 Fair Street, CB1 1HA

11-11 (12.30am Thu-Sat) (01223) 367204 thehopbine.co.uk

6 changing beers [H]/[G]

Large pub close to Midsummer Common. It was sold in 2011 by Admiral Taverns and is now leased by the tenants of the Portland Arms. Free of tie, it offers up to six different real ales, often from East Anglian microbreweries including local ones. Real ales are £3 a pint on Thirsty Thursday evenings. Continental bottled beers are also offered. The food ranges from pub classics to hot rock grills. Local CAMRA LocAle City Pub of the Year 2018.

Kingston Arms

33 Kingston Street, CB1 2NU

12-3 (not Tue & Wed), 5-11; 12-midnight Fri; 11-midnight Sat; 12-11 Sun (01223) 319414 kingston-arms.co.uk

Crouch Vale Brewers Gold; Hop Back Summer Lightning; Mighty Oak Oscar Wilde; Oakham JHB; Thornbridge Jaipur IPA; Woodforde's Wherry; 4 changing beers [H]

A classic, cosy, side-street pub that is popular with drinkers and diners. Windows and mirrors keep the interior light and welcoming. Its rear walled garden has canopies and heaters, making it popular all year round. Twelve handpumps offer regular and changing beers, usually two dark ales, as well as two changing ciders or perries. A selection of Belgian and other bottled beers is stocked. Home-cooked food is available at all sessions including Saturday breakfast. Q

Live & Let Live

40 Mawson Road, CB1 2EA

11.30-2.30 (not Wed & Thu), 5.30-11; 11.30-2.30, 6-11 Sat; 12-2.30, 7-11 Sun (01223) 460261

Nethergate Umbel Ale; Oakham Citra; 3 changing beers [H]

A discreet corner local, just off Mill Road, with roadside cycle parking. It has a single bar and a small snug to the rear, furnished with simple tables and chairs plus stools at the bar. Wood panelling and railway and beer memorabilia add to a yesteryear atmosphere. It is a pub for contemplation and conversation. Its five ales cover a range of styles and strengths, alongside three changing ciders or perries. Rum festivals are held twice a year. Q

Maypole

20A Portugal Place, CB5 8AF

11.30-midnight (1am Fri & Sat); 12-11.30 Sun (01223) 352999 maypolefreehouse.co.uk

16 changing beers [H]

The Maypole has been in the capable hands of the Castiglione family since 1982, initially as tenants, latterly as owners. Showcasing quality beers won the landlord the CAMRA branch's first Real Ale Champion award. Up to 16 ever-changing ales are kept, including LocAles, more during festivals, mostly from micros. It has a busy front bar and quieter back bar downstairs plus a function room upstairs. There is a large patio to one side. Food focuses on home-cooked Italian dishes and English pub classics. Local CAMRA Pub of the Year 2018.

Mill

14 Mill Lane, CB2 1RX

11-11 (midnight Thu-Sat) (01223) 311829 themillpubcambridge.co.uk

7 changing beers (sourced locally; often Cambridge Brew House) [H]

Set in a honeypot riverside location across from Laundress Green, the building has been refurbished – improvements include an attractive wood-panelled side room. A vintage radiogram plays vinyl records. The curved wooden bar has eight handpumps, including one for cider. The beer range shows a strong commitment to local ales, including those brewed at sister pub the Cambridge Brew House. Tasty food is made with locally sourced ingredients. Local CAMRA LocAle (City) Pub of the Year 2017 and Young Members Pub of the Year 2018.

Chatteris

Ship

34 Bridge Street, PE16 6RN

5 (3 Fri)-11; 12-11 Sat & Sun 07880 326263

Sharp's Doom Bar; Timothy Taylor Landlord; 2 changing beers (often Deeside, Tydd Steam) [H]

A community free house dating from the 1850s. Originally known as The Ship, then called Walk the Dog, it is now The Ship again after reopening in 2012. The single L-shaped room is adorned with much maritime memorabilia. Games include scrabble, chess, darts, dominoes and crib, with a pool table in the small back room. A quiz is held once a month. The pub supports two charities, Macmillan and the Stroke Association, and a local cricket team. A winner of a CAMRA Merit Award. Q P (33)

Coates

Vine

4 South Green, PE7 2BJ
4-11; 2-midnight Fri; 9am-midnight Sat; 12-10.30 Sun
(01733) 840343
Grainstore Ten Fifty; 2 changing beers H
Overlooking the village green, this free house has two rooms – a lively bar/lounge and separate restaurant with bar. Meals are served lunchtimes and evenings, plus breakfast on Saturday. The varying beer list includes a LocAle. The large outdoor area has pétanque terrains and a children's play area. Entertainment includes live bands. Local buses pass in front of the pub. Opening times may vary. P (33)

Comberton

Three Horseshoes

22 South Street, CB23 7DZ
closed Mon; 12-2.30, 5.30-11 (midnight Fri); 12-midnight Sat; 12-11 Sun (01223) 262252
Adnams Lighthouse; Greene King IPA; 3 changing beers H
Hanging baskets adorn the front of this red tile roofed village pub. The long, low-ceilinged main bar has a cosy alcove at one end and a small raised area at the other. The brick-fronted bar takes up much of the central section. A separate games room lies off to the left. On the walls are historic photos of the village and its sports players. The large garden has play equipment for children. The pub is popular with local clubs and societies and sponsors the village football and cricket teams. P (18)

Duxford

Plough

57 St Peter's Street, CB22 4RP
11-11 (01223) 833170 theduxfordplough.co.uk
Adnams Southwold Bitter; Everards Tiger; 3 changing beers H
Thatched building first recorded as a pub in the 1820s. A single bar is divided into two distinct areas, one side for diners, the other for drinkers. Food is prepared on-site and is available every day. A range of regular and changing ales is kept, more than 500 in recent years, often including local beers, plus four changing ciders and perries. The nearest pub to Duxford Airfield and the Imperial War Museum, the pub is home to Duxford United football club, local badminton players and three darts teams. Cambridge & District CAMRA Cider Pub of the Year 2017. P (7)

Ellington

Mermaid

High Street, PE28 0AB
closed Mon; 12-3, 5.30-11; 12-11 Sat; 12-10.30 Sun
(01480) 891106 themermaidellington.co.uk
3 changing beers (sourced locally; often Digfield, Nobby's, Oakham) H
Quintessential English village pub, parts of which date from around the 13th century, with the main range dating from the early 17th century. The oak-beamed bar has a welcoming atmosphere, with a fire for the winter months. There is a separate upper snug with a wood-burning stove. In warmer weather, the garden offers an idyllic setting near the village church and includes a pétanque pitch. Quality bar food is available, with a choice of eight hand-made dishes, alongside a full à la carte menu. Q

Ely

Prince Albert

62 Silver Street, CB7 4JF (opp cathedral car park)
11-11.30; 12-10.30 Sun (01353) 663494
Greene King XX Mild, IPA, Abbot; 5 changing beers (sourced nationally; often Milton, Purity, Timothy Taylor) H
A pub with two distinct characters – the front is a music-free drinkers' bar with a friendly atmosphere and a mixture of bench seating, stools and regulars (who are almost part of the furniture). The rear area is a recently renovated restaurant serving meals and snacks (booking advisable on Sundays). Outside is a secluded garden perfect for summer days. The pub is not far from Ely's cathedral and less than a mile from the railway station.
Q

Townhouse Pub

60-64 Market Street, CB7 4LS (nr Ely Museum)
11-11 (1.30am Fri & Sat); 12-11 Sun (01353) 664338
thetownhousepub.co.uk
4 changing beers (often Grainstore, Nethergate, Three Blind Mice) H
A Grade II-listed former Georgian townhouse, this is now a popular modern bar with a spacious conservatory and enclosed garden. The five handpumps serve a range of changing guest ales from local breweries, including Three Blind Mice. A popular annual beer festival is held in July. A DJ plays music from 9pm on Friday and Saturday and live music is hosted on Sunday afternoon.

Fulbourn

Six Bells

9 High Street, CB21 5DH
11.30-2.30, 5-midnight; 11.30-2am Fri; 12-2am Sat; 12-11 Sun (01223) 880244 thesixbellsfulbourn.co.uk
Adnams Southwold Bitter, Broadside; Greene King IPA; Woodforde's Wherry; 2 changing beers H
Traditional thatched village pub and former coaching inn. The main bar has low ceilings, a real fire and many cosy corners. The second bar is smaller. Beyond the rear car park is one of the largest beer gardens in the area. Regular ales are mostly from regional brewers, guest ales from across the country. Home-cooked, locally sourced food is served in the bar and separate dining room. The function room hosts a twice-monthly trad jazz club. A regular in this Guide. P

Glatton

Addison Arms

Sawtry Road, PE28 5RZ
12-3, 6-11 Mon; 12-11 (01487) 830410
addison-arms.co.uk
House beer (by Digfield) H**; 3 changing beers (sourced regionally; often Angles Ales, Digfield, Nene Valley)** H/G
Grade II-listed pub built at the start of the 18th century and named after the playwright and politician Joseph Addison (co-founder of The Spectator), who was a relative of the first landlord.

The pub offers at least three real ales and a real cider, with a focus on local producers. Food prepared from fresh locally sourced supplies is always popular. There is a thriving Sunday night quiz. The house beer, Addison Ale, is Digfield Shacklebush. Q🛏❀◑♿♣P🚌(46A)🐾📶

Grantchester

Green Man L ✔

59 High Street, CB3 9NF (in village centre)
11-11; 12-10.30 Sun ☎ (01223) 844669
thegreenmangrantchester.co.uk
Adnams Southwold Bitter; Oakham Citra; 3 changing beers H
A 17th-, possibly 16th-century building, the Green Man was first recorded as a pub in 1847. Complete with low ceilings and oak beams, it has an L-shaped bar and a separate restaurant area off to the right. To the left and back are more seating areas. Outside is sheltered seating and a long narrow garden reaching down to Grantchester Meadows, making the pub accessible from Cambridge by punt. Q🛏❀◑🍎P🚌(18)🐾

Great Staughton

White Hart

56 The Highway, PE19 5DA (on B645)
12-2 (not Mon & Tue), 4-11; 12-2, 4-midnight Fri; 12-midnight Sat; 12-11 Sun ☎ (01480) 861131
whitehartgreatstaughton.co.uk
Batemans XB, XXXB; 1 changing beer H
Passing through the narrow entrance to this fine small former coaching inn takes you back to the days of horse-drawn coaches. The Grade II-listed building dates back to 1630 but has been extended and altered. It has a main bar, a small pool room at the front and a restaurant at the rear. Traditional pub food is served lunchtimes and evenings Thursday to Saturday and noon-3pm Sunday.
Q🛏❀◑P🚌🐾📶

Haddenham

Three Kings L ✔

1 Station Road, CB6 3XD
11-11; 11.30-10 Sun ☎ (01353) 749080
threekingsely.co.uk
Greene King IPA; 2 changing beers (sourced nationally) H
This 17th-century building has been updated over time but retains its rustic framework and charm with plenty of exposed old beams, cosy areas and an inglenook fireplace. While this village pub focuses on fine food, it is also keen to promote high-quality ales and cider and is well supported by local drinkers. At the rear is a relaxing courtyard drinking area and a large car park.
Q🛏❀◑♿🍎P🚌🐾📶

Hartford

King of the Belgians L

27 Main Street, PE29 1XU (on old village high street parallel to B1514)
11-11 (midnight Fri & Sat); 12-10.30 Sun
☎ (01480) 52030 kingofthebelgians.com
4 changing beers (sourced locally; often Digfield, Elgood's, Nene Valley)
A 16th-century inn in a picturesque setting. This true village pub in the heart of the community actively supports local charities. It hosts a beer festival in May and another in late August. An ever-changing selection of four real ales and ciders is available alongside good-value food. Oak beams and a copper-topped bar characterise the public bar, and there is a separate peaceful dining area. Entertainment includes regular quizzes, games nights and open mic nights on the first and third Mondays of the month. Q🛏❀◑♣🍎P🚌🐾📶

Helpston

Bluebell L

10 Woodgate, PE6 7ED
11-3, 5-11; 11-11 Sat; 12-10.30 Sun ☎ (01733) 252394
bluebellhelpston.co.uk
Castor 12th Man; Fuller's London Pride; 1 changing beer (often Adnams) H
Quiet 17th-century stone village pub with the main entrance to the side. There are two wood-panelled bars, a number of dining areas, and a snug named after local poet John Clare who worked in the pub as a pot boy and lived next door. Beers come from Adnams and Castor plus two rotating guests from breweries around the country. Good-value food is served lunchtimes and evenings. There are plans to have guest rooms. Q🛏❀◑♿🍎P🚌🐾📶

Hemingford Grey

Cock L

47 High Street, PE28 9BJ (off A14, SE of Huntingdon)
11.30-3, 6 (5 Fri)-11; 11.30-11 Sat; 12-10.30 Sun
☎ (01480) 463609 cambscuisine.com
Brewsters Hophead; Elgood's Cambridge Bitter; Great Oakley Wagtail; 1 changing beer H
This village inn and restaurant has won local, regional and national awards. The cosy pub has recently been refurbished to provide more comfortable facilities and is popular with locals who enjoy the well-kept locally sourced beers and real Cromwell cider produced in the village. The separate restaurant features an extensive fish board, meat, game and excellent home-made sausages (booking essential at all times). During the summer, occasional beer festivals are held in the beer garden. Q❀◑♿⛺🍎P🚌(5)🐾📶

Histon

Red Lion ✔

27 High Street, CB24 9JD
10.30-11 (midnight Fri); 12-11 Sun ☎ (01223) 564437
theredlionhiston.co.uk
Adnams Ghost Ship; Tring Side Pocket for a Toad; 6 changing beers (often Batemans, Lacons) H
The two bars of this free house are adorned with a wonderful collection of breweriana and historical photos. The left-hand bar features the TV, while the nine handpumps are in the right-hand bar which is quieter and child free. Guest beers always include a mild. There are also Belgian and German beers on draught, a range of continental bottled beers, two ciders and a perry. Two beer festivals are held each year – the Easter aperitif and the main event in September. Local CAMRA Pub of the Year 2017 and Dark Ale Pub of the Year 2018.
❀⇆◑♿♣🍎P🚌📶

Huntingdon

Falcon 🄻

Market Hill, PE29 3NR
10-midnight (1am Fri & Sat); 11-11 Sun
☎ (01480) 457416 falconhuntingdon.co.uk
J Church Gold Testament; Olde England Ales Charles I; Potbelly Best; Wychwood Hobgoblin Gold, Hobgoblin; 14 changing beers (often Ringwood, Thwaites) Ⓗ
An established venue steeped in local history. This former coaching inn used to be Oliver Cromwell's recruiting station and the gates from the market square were once the entrance to Huntingdon Prison. The ever-changing selection of beers includes the landlord's very own J Church and many more from Northamptonshire breweries. Choose from up to 18 handpumps, alongside a range of real ciders. Good-value food is served every day. CAMRA branch Mild and Dark Ales Pub of the Year 2017. Q

Old Bridge Hotel 🄻 ✔

1 High Street, PE29 3TQ (at S end of High St on ring road)
11-11 (10.30 Sun) ☎ (01480) 424300 huntsbridge.com
3 changing beers (sourced locally; often Hart Family Brewers, Nene Valley) Ⓗ
A handsome ivy-clad hotel in an 18th-century former private bank at the southern end of the High Street. It has a prominent position on the banks of the River Great Ouse close to the riverside footpaths. Imaginative and high-quality food is served in the terrace restaurant, the covered patio and the garden area. Drinkers can also relax in the bar or lounge. The award-winning Old Bridge Wine Shop offers wine tasting as a diversion and there is an emphasis on local and regional beers. The bus station is a short walk away.
QP

Keyston

Pheasant 🄻

Loop Road, PE28 0RE (on B663, 1 mile S of A14, E of Thrapston)
closed Mon; 12-3, 6-11 Tue-Thu; 12-11 Fri & Sat; 12-5 Sun
☎ (01832) 710241 thepheasant-keyston.co.uk
Adnams Southwold Bitter; 2 changing beers Ⓗ
The village is named after Ketil's Stone, probably an Anglo-Saxon boundary marker. Created from a row of thatched cottages in an idyllic setting, the pub offers high-quality food, fine wines and well-kept cask ales. There is a splendid lounge bar and three dining areas. Regularly changing guest beers are offered, usually from Nene Valley or Digfield. Food is served 12-2pm, 6.30-9.30pm daily, 12-3.30pm Sunday. The pub appeared in the first edition of the Guide in 1974. QP

Leighton Bromswold

Green Man 🄻

39 The Avenue, PE28 5AW (1 mile N of A14, W of Huntingdon)
closed Mon; 12-2.30, 4.30-11; 12-5 Sun
☎ (01480) 890238 greenmanleightonbromswold.co.uk
4 changing beers (often Digfield, Nethergate, Young's) Ⓗ
A delightful local in a charming village on a ridge near the Northamptonshire border. The pub provides a congenial focus for the small village community and attracts visitors from a wide area. The regularly changing range of four real ales often includes beers from Nethergate, Young's, Digfield, Oakham and Buntingford. Good food is served 12-1.45pm, 7-9pm daily, 12-3pm Sunday. Hood skittles is popular and there is a pétanque court. A real fire adds atmosphere in winter. P

Leverington

Rising Sun Inn 🄻

Dowgate Road, PE13 5DH
12-2 (not Mon), 6-11; 12-11 Fri; 12-4 Sun
☎ (01945) 583754
Elgood's Cambridge Bitter; 2 changing beers (often Elgood's) Ⓗ
Comfortably furnished inn with an enclosed garden. It dates back to at least 1872 and was refurbished a few years ago but the bar retains the feel of a true village local. Cambridge Bitter is served alongside two changing beers including Elgood's seasonals and guests. Well known for good-value quality food, Wednesday is steak night and the restaurant hosts regular themed nights. Dogs and children are welcome. Closing time may be earlier if there is no trade. A CAMRA branch Gold Award winner in 2016. P

Little Downham

Plough

106 Main Street, CB6 2SX (W end of village)
12-3 (not Mon), 6-11; 12-midnight Fri & Sat; 12-3, 6-10.30 Sun ☎ (01353) 698297
2 changing beers (sourced regionally) Ⓗ
An early Victorian Grade II-listed pub, well preserved in character and charm. At least two changing regional cask ales are usually on offer. An annual beer festival is held in early September. Excellent Thai cuisine is available to eat in or take away. The pub has a good community spirit and supports traditional pub games and local customs. Children are welcome until 9pm. P (125)

Little Gransden

Chequers 🏆 🄻

71 Main Road, SG19 3DW
12-2, 7-11; 12-11 Fri & Sat; 12-5, 7-10.30 Sun
☎ (01767) 677348 chequersgransden.co.uk
4 changing beers (sourced locally) Ⓗ
Village pub owned and run by the same family for over 60 years and in this Guide for 24. The unspoilt middle bar, with its wooden benches, roaring fire and a collection of decoy birds that seem to be gathering on the beam over the bar, is a favourite spot to catch up on the local gossip. The pub's Son of Sid brewhouse supplies the pub and local beer festivals. Fish & chips are a highlight on Friday night (booking essential). Winner of numerous CAMRA awards. QP

March

Rose & Crown 🄻 ✔

41 St Peters Road, PE15 9NA
12-11 (midnight Fri & Sat) ☎ (01354) 652077
St Austell Cornish Best Bitter; 6 changing beers (often Oakham, Tydd Steam) Ⓗ
Traditional community pub, over 150 years old, with two carpeted rooms and low beamed ceilings. There is a real fire in the main bar and a pool table in the smaller bar. Six real ales are usually on offer, mainly from microbreweries, including one from

Oakham, and up to seven traditional ciders. A mini beer festival is held at Easter. Good-quality food is served lunchtimes and evenings. Quiz night is Thursday. Q P (33,46)

Ship Inn

1 Nene Parade, PE15 8TD

12-11 Mon & Tue; 9am-midnight Wed & Thu (12.30am Fri & Sat); 9am-10.30 Sun ☎ (01354) 607878

Woodforde's Wherry; 4 changing beers (often Church End, Tydd Steam) H

Thatched Grade II-listed riverside pub built in 1680 with extensive riverside moorings. The unusual carved beams are said to have 'fallen off a barge' during the building of Ely Cathedral. A quaint wobbly floor and wall lead to the toilets and a small games room. Reopened in 2010 as a free house, following a major refit, the pub has a friendly and welcoming atmosphere. A large collection of pumpclips is on display. Monthly live music showcases local bands. An annual beer festival is held in September.
Q (33,46)

Maxey

Blue Bell

39 High Street, PE6 9EE

1.30-11 (11.30 Sat); 12-6 Sun ☎ (01778) 348182

Abbeydale Absolution; Fuller's London Pride, ESB; Oakham Bishops Farewell; 5 changing beers (sourced regionally; often Grainstore, Oakham, Woodforde's) H

Originally a limestone barn, the building was converted many years ago and reflects the rural setting in which it is found. Paraphernalia of country life adorn the stone walls and shelves of the two-roomed interior. Nine handpumps dispense a range of quality ales from large and small breweries far and wide. It is a popular meeting place for groups including birdwatchers and golfers. A former local CAMRA Pub of the Year.
Q P (22,413)

Newton

Queen's Head

CB22 7PG

11.30-2.30, 6-11; 12-2.30, 7-10.30 Sun ☎ (01223) 870436

Adnams Southwold Bitter, Broadside; 2 changing beers G

This village local is one of a handful of pubs to have appeared in every edition of this Guide. The list of landlords since 1729, displayed on the wall in the simply furnished public bar, has just 18 entries. The cosy lounge has a welcoming fire in the colder months. Guest beers are often Adnams seasonals. Simple but excellent food centres on soup and sandwiches. The King and Kaiser are reputed to have stopped here for a pint in the early 1900s.
Q P (31)

Peterborough

Bumble Inn

46 Westgate, PE1 1RE

12-10 (8 Mon); 12-11 Fri & Sat; 12-6 Sun

thebimbleinn.wordpress.com

5 changing beers (often Axholme, North Riding, Tyne Bank) H

Local CAMRA Pub of the Year for 2018, this micropub opened in 2016 in what was a chemist's shop. Minimalist in style, it has five handpumps dispensing quality ales from far and wide – expect the unusual. Order a taster paddle of three third-pints if you want to try a selection. Rare bottled and canned beers are also stocked plus two craft keg beers and Korev Cornish keg lager. Regular tap takeovers and food nights add to the attraction. Tea, coffee, soft drinks, home-made pasties, pies and Scotch eggs are available.

Charters

Town Bridge, PE1 1FP (down steps at Town Bridge)

12-11 (midnight Fri & Sat); 12-10.30 Sun

☎ (01733) 315700 charters-bar.co.uk

Oakham JHB, Inferno, Citra, Bishops Farewell; 2 changing beers (often Exit 33) H/G

The converted Dutch grain barge from circa 1907 sits on the River Nene near the city centre. An oriental restaurant is on the upper deck and food is also served in the bar. Up to 12 beers are on offer plus cider. The large garden with a marquee, bar and landing stage for boats is popular in summer. Live music plays some weekends and in summer outside the pub. It gets busy on football match days. Close to the Nene Valley Railway.
P

Draper's Arms

29-31 Cowgate, PE1 1LZ

8am-midnight (1am Fri & Sat) ☎ (01733) 847570

Brewsters Hophead; Grainstore Ten Fifty; Greene King IPA, Abbot; Sharp's Doom Bar; 5 changing beers (often Oakham, Xtreme Ales) H

A converted former draper's shop, built circa 1899, this is one of two Wetherspoon pubs in the city. The interior is broken up with wood-panelled intimate spaces and dividers. The beer range, with many from local microbreweries, is dispensed through 10 handpumps. Food is served all day and regular beer and wine festivals are held throughout the year. Quiz night is Wednesday. A regular top 10-listed real ale pub within the company's chain. Close to bus and rail stations. Q

Frothblowers

78 Storrington Way, Werrington, PE4 6QP

3-9; 12-10 Sat; 12-6 Sun ☎ 07434 686336

5 changing beers (often Froth Blowers, Hopshackle, Mile Tree) H

A new micropub in a former tanning parlour, set in a row of small shops on a housing estate in the north of the city but easily accessed by bus. It offers five handpumps, six real ciders and a selection of bottled beers. The landlords have introduced various activities and events including neighbour nights with board games, a quiz, live acoustic music, a wine festival and a cider festival. It can get crowded on Friday and Saturday evenings.
Q P (1)

Hand & Heart ★

12 Highbury Street, PE1 3BE

3-11.30 (midnight Fri); 12-midnight Sat; 12-11.30 Sun

☎ (01733) 564653 thehandandheart.com

5 changing beers (sourced regionally; often Brewsters, Rockingham, Tydd Steam) H

This 1930s back-street pub is on CAMRA's National Inventory of Historic Pub Interiors. The separate bar and quiet back room are connected by a drinking corridor. Beers are from five handpumps and the cellar, often including some hard-to-find ales. Live music plays on the second Thursday of the month and a cheese club is held on the last Thursday.

Home-made Scotch eggs and rolls are usually available. The large garden has an outside bar and stage used for beer festivals and music events. A former local CAMRA Pub of the Year, it became free of tie in 2016. Q❀♣🍎🚌(1)🐾📶

Ostrich Inn 🄻

17 North Street, PE1 2RA

🕐 12-11; 11-1am Fri & Sat ☎ (01733) 746370

Oakham JHB; house beer (by King's Cliffe); 3 changing beers (sourced locally; often Tydd Steam) 🄷

Refurbished in 2009, this side-street single-room pub reopened with its original name restored. The U-shaped bar features many pictures and posters of bygone breweries and famous acts who appeared in the city. Up to five regularly changing beers are on offer, many from local breweries, alongside a few craft keg lines. A large gin selection is also stocked. Live music plays most weekends. The small enclosed patio is a suntrap.
🐴❀♿⇌♣🍎🚌🐾

Palmerston Arms 🄻

82 Oundle Road, PE2 9PA

🕐 3-11.30; 2-midnight Fri; 12-midnight Sat; 12-11.30 Sun ☎ (01733) 565865

Batemans Gold, XXXB 🄶**; Castle Rock Harvest Pale; Oakham Citra** 🄷/🄶**; 10 changing beers (sourced regionally; often Ossett, Robinsons)** 🄶

Popular 400-year-old listed stone-built locals' pub. Owned by Batemans Brewery, three of its beers are rotated alongside nine or more different ales, including some from Oakham Ales. Traditional cider, perry and an extensive range of malt whiskies are also available. Most beers are served straight from the cellar, which can be seen through a large glass panel behind the bar. Rolls and a variety of snacks tempt customers. Live music features most weekends and occasional philosophy nights. Busy on football match days.
❀♣🍎🚌(1,24)🐾📶

Ploughman 🄻

1 Staniland Way, Werrington, PE4 6NA

🕐 4-11; 2-11.30 Fri; 12-11.30 Sat & Sun ☎ (01733) 327696

10 changing beers (sourced regionally; often Castor, Tiny Rebel) 🄷

A rejuvenated two-roomed community pub brought to the forefront of the city's real ale outlets by the enthusiastic licensee. Ten handpumps serve beers both from local breweries and from afar. An annual beer festival features early in July. Many activities are held including charity events and poker nights and live music plays at weekends. A two-times local CAMRA Pub of the Year.
❀♣🍎P🚌(1,22)

Woolpack ✔

29 North Street, Stanground, PE2 8HR (in old part of Stanground village by River Nene)

🕐 12-11 (11.15 Fri & Sat); 12-10.45 Sun ☎ (01733) 753544

Black Sheep Best Bitter; Timothy Taylor Landlord; 2 changing beers (sourced regionally; often Tydd Steam) 🄷

Originally constructed in 1711, a medieval wall remains in the garden and the old barn used to be the village mortuary (last used in the 1850s and said to be haunted). The beer garden leads to the old River Nene, with boat moorings available. The L-shaped bar has TV and a dartboard, and is adorned with old photos and prints. Quiz night is Sunday and occasional live music plays. Two guest beers are usually available. The pub is on the city Green Wheel route and welcomes children and dogs. Local CAMRA Pub of the Year in 2016.
Q🐴❀◐◑♣🍎🐾📶

Yard of Ale

72 Oundle Road, PE2 9PA

🕐 12-11 (midnight Fri & Sat) ☎ (01733) 348000

Digfield Fools Nook; Oakham Bishops Farewell; Sharp's Doom Bar; Tydd Steam Barn Ale; 2 changing beers (often Hop Back, Lacons, Rooster's) 🄷

Built on land that was part of the Palmerston Arms stable yard and originally called the New Inn, this 120-year-old pub was fully refurbished in 1993, becoming a free house. It was taken on by the team from the nearby Swiss Cottage in 2017. The large open-plan single room is divided into four distinct areas and tastefully decorated in shades of grey, with a warm wood bar and surround. Entertainment includes live sport on screen, a pool table and live music at the weekend. Outside is a patio area and beer garden. 🐴❀🚌(1)📶

Rampton

Black Horse

6 High Street, CB24 8QE

🕐 closed Mon; 12-3 (not Tue & Wed), 5-11; 12-11 Sat; 12-6 Sun ☎ (01954) 251867

3 changing beers (sourced regionally) 🄶

This two-bar former Greene King pub has been a free house for several years. The left bar is mainly for diners, the right bar is for drinkers. Outside there is parking on both sides of the building and a large beer garden to the rear. Up to five ever-changing real ales are served on gravity from a stillage behind the bar. Traditional British pub food is served. 🐴❀◐◑♿♣🍎P🐾📶

Ramsey

Angel

76 High Street, PE26 1BS

🕐 12-11 (midnight Fri & Sat); 12-10.30 Sun ☎ (01487) 711968

Adnams Ghost Ship; 3 changing beers (often Grainstore, Lacons) 🄷

Reopened in 2016 after extensive refurbishment by the new owners, the pub has a bar area with fixed seating and country-style restaurant. It retains a serving hatch and the original stained-glass windows. Four real ales are available. Food includes popular Sunday lunches and occasional themed evenings. A pool table and dartboard provide entertainment. Friendly staff and locals create a great atmosphere for real ale drinkers.
Q🐴❀◐◑♿♣🍎P🚌(31)🐾📶

St Ives

Oliver Cromwell 🄻

13 Wellington Street, PE27 5AZ

🕐 11-11 (11.30 Thu; 12.30am Fri & Sat); 12-11 Sun ☎ (01480) 465601 🌐 theolivercromwell.co.uk

Adnams Southwold Bitter; Oakham JHB; 4 changing beers (often Lacons, Nene Valley, Nethergate) 🄷

Popular pub near the town quay and old town bridge. A true free house, it offers two regular and four rotating beers, often from regional microbreweries. A selection of Belgian bottled beers complements the cask beers. Local Cromwell cider is always available alongside two changing ciders. Lunchtime meals are freshly prepared and use local ingredients. Live music plays every Thursday evening. The rear patio is a suntrap in the summer. Beer festivals are held in June and November.

Royal Oak

13 Crown Street, PE27 5EB

11-11 (2am Fri & Sat); 12-midnight Sun (01480) 462586

Oakham Inferno; 5 changing beers (often Nobby's, Oakham, Tydd Steam)

Busy town-centre pub, one of a number of historic listed pubs in St Ives, whose most famous inhabitant was Oliver Cromwell. Despite the 1502 date over the door, most of the building is 18th century. The room layout and character were happily preserved in a sensitive renovation in the 1990s. A changing choice of five beers is usually from local SIBA breweries. The house beer is brewed by Greene King. Traditional cider is available. Live music plays on Saturday evenings.

St Neots

Ale Taster

25 Russell Street, PE19 1BA

4-10.30 (11 Fri); 12-11 Sat; 12-6 Sun (01480) 581368

3 changing beers (sourced regionally)

A traditional small back-street pub run in the style of a micropub. It features up to three changing beers served from stillage behind the bar. Up to five real ciders and perry are also sold. Beer and cider are from local producers as much as possible. Five large fridges display a wide selection of bottled beers from around the world. The pub encourages conversation, with quiet background music and no electronic machines.
Q P (X5)

Olde Sun

11 Huntingdon Street, PE19 1BL

12-11 (01480) 216863 yeoldesun.moonfruit.com

Woodforde's Wherry; 5 changing beers (often Adnams, Elgood's, Woodforde's)

Low-beamed and cosy traditional town-centre pub with two large inglenook fireplaces, three bar areas and a secluded patio. The jukebox is zoned allowing quiet areas for conversation. Shove-ha'penny and bar billiards are played. Five constantly changing guest beers come from various regional breweries including Adnams, Elgood's, Marston's, Thwaites and Woodforde's. A mild and other dark beers are usually among the range. A former local CAMRA winner of Mild/Dark Ales Pub of the Year. (X5)

Pig 'n' Falcon

9 New Street, PE19 1AE (behind Barretts department store)

6-midnight Mon; 11.30-midnight Tue & Wed; 11-midnight Thu & Sun; 11-2.30am Fri & Sat 07951 785678

pignfalcon.co.uk

Greene King IPA, Abbot; Potbelly Best; 5 changing beers (sourced locally; often Potbelly, Three Blind Mice)

This busy town-centre free house has up to six real ales and five real ciders, focusing on beers from microbreweries and unusual beers including milds, porters and stouts. A good range of bottled ciders, UK and foreign bottled beers includes Trappist ales. Four beer festivals are held each year. Live blues and rock nights are hosted Wednesday through to Sunday. Outside is a large, imaginatively created, covered and heated beer garden. Three Blind Mice beers are real ale served in KeyKegs.
(X5)

Thriplow

Green Man

2 Lower Street, SG8 7RJ

closed Mon; 11-11; 12-7 Sun (01763) 208855

thegreenmanthriplow.co.uk

4 changing beers (sourced regionally)

Purchased by villagers in 2013, the inn's cosy interior is divided in two. To the left is an area with a village-pub feel, complete with open fire, and to the right a larger area mostly used for dining. The pub has a reputation for good food and beer – the ales tend to come from smaller regional breweries. There is outside seating both on the green in front and in the pleasant garden.
Q P (31)

Upware

Five Miles Inn

Old School Lane, CB7 5ZR

11-11 (midnight Fri & Sat) (01353) 721654

fivemilesinn.com

Morland Old Speckled Hen; 3 changing beers (sourced nationally)

Located off the beaten track, next to the River Cam and overlooking part of the Fens, the pub's full name is the Five Miles From Anywhere No Hurry Inn. Four ales are on handpump with an occasional fifth beer from the cask during the summer, along with one real cider. A selection of food is available in the bar and separate restaurant. Visitor moorings and services are provided for narrowboats/motor cruisers, and there is a large car park for those arriving by land. P

Waterbeach

Sun Inn

Chapel Street, CB25 9HR

5-11; 12-midnight Fri-Sun (01223) 861254

Woodforde's Wherry; 3 changing beers

The small, cosy lounge is dominated by a huge fireplace, while the simply appointed public bar, with its woodblock floor, is always lively. There is a small meeting room and a function room upstairs where regular gigs are held. An annual beer and music festival features over the early May bank holiday weekend. There is no food on Monday or on Sunday evening. The pub hosts the local CJ's café from 9am Friday and Saturday.
(9)

West Wratting

Chestnut Tree

1 Mill Road, CB21 5LT

12-3 (not Mon), 5.30-11.30; 12-midnight Fri & Sat; 12-10.30 Sun (01223) 290384 chestnuttreepub.co.uk

Greene King IPA; 3 changing beers

Impressive two-bar Victorian-style pub with modern extensions creating a roomy, comfortable interior. On the left is a nicely furnished public bar with a pool table and on the right is a lounge bar mainly for dining. The pub hosts darts, pool and pétanque teams, and a small lending library. Originally a Greene King house, it has been free of tie since the present owners bought it in 2012.

Greene King IPA is regularly available, with three guest beers mainly from micros, sometimes local. Q P (19)

Whittlesey

Boat Inn L

2 Ramsey Road, PE7 1DR

4-midnight; 11-midnight Fri-Sun ☎ (01733) 202488
quinnboatinn.wordpress.com

Grainstore Ten Fifty H; 3 changing beers (sourced regionally; often Grainstore) H/G

This corner pub has two rooms – a public bar with sports TV and a lounge with an unusual boat-shape bar. Up to seven traditional ciders and perries supplement the real ales, some of which are served direct from the cask. It hosts a whisky club on the second Friday of the month. Open mic music nights feature on some Tuesdays and Fridays. Outside is a pétanque terrain. Closing times are flexible. P (31)

George Hotel

10 Market Place, PE7 1AB

7am-midnight (1am Fri & Sat) ☎ (01733) 359970

Adnams Ghost Ship; Greene King Abbot; Oakham Bishops Farewell; Ruddles Best Bitter; Sharp's Doom Bar; 5 changing beers H

Built in the late 1700s, the building was significantly altered in the mid-19th century before getting a Grade II listing in 1974. Once a popular locals' haunt with a basic bar and comfortable lounge, it was then closed down until it was refurbished and reopened by JD Wetherspoon in 2010. Now once again a local favourite, it offers a large selection of up to 10 real ales and five ciders alongside Wetherspoon's good-value food menu. P

Letter B L

53-57 Church Street, PE7 1DE

5-11; 3.30-midnight Fri; 12-midnight Sat; 12-11 Sun
☎ (01733) 206975 theletterb.co.uk

Sharp's Doom Bar; 4 changing beers (often Tydd Steam) H

Winner of numerous CAMRA awards over the years including County Pub of the Year and County Cider Pub of the Year. The pub is over 200 years old, with two bars, a small side room and a rear patio area. A beer festival is held in January during the Straw Bear festival weekend, which is popular with locals and visitors. In recent years the cider range has expanded rapidly to complement the five real ales on handpump. Popular charity events are hosted. Q (31,33)

Willingham

Bank Micropub

High Street, CB24 5ES

closed Sun & Mon; 6-10 Tue; 5.30-10 Wed (11 Thu-Sat)
☎ (01954) 200045 thebankmicropub.co.uk

6 changing beers G

Formerly a village bank, this micropub opened in late 2012. The single room has a short bar rescued from a closed Cambridge pub. The walls are decorated with photos of local interest. Up to six real ales are available direct from the cask, with regional and local beers featuring strongly. A large range of craft ales includes three served from keg. The Bank offers a warm welcome and the casual visitor is certain to be included in local conversation. Q

Wisbech

Red Lion L

32 North Brink, PE13 1JR

11.30-3, 6 (5 Fri)-11; 11.30-3, 7-midnight Sat; 12-11 Sun
☎ (01945) 582022

Elgood's Cambridge Bitter, Golden Newt; 1 changing beer H

This is the nearest Elgood's pub to the brewery and is very comfortable, with a pleasant, relaxed atmosphere. Drinkers and diners are well catered for with quality ales and excellent food served every day. There is always a specials board alongside the menu. The main access is via a side passage which links the North Brink road to the rear car park and patio. Baby changing facilities have been added. Q P (X1)

Queen's Head, Newton (Photo: Katie Button)

CHESHIRE

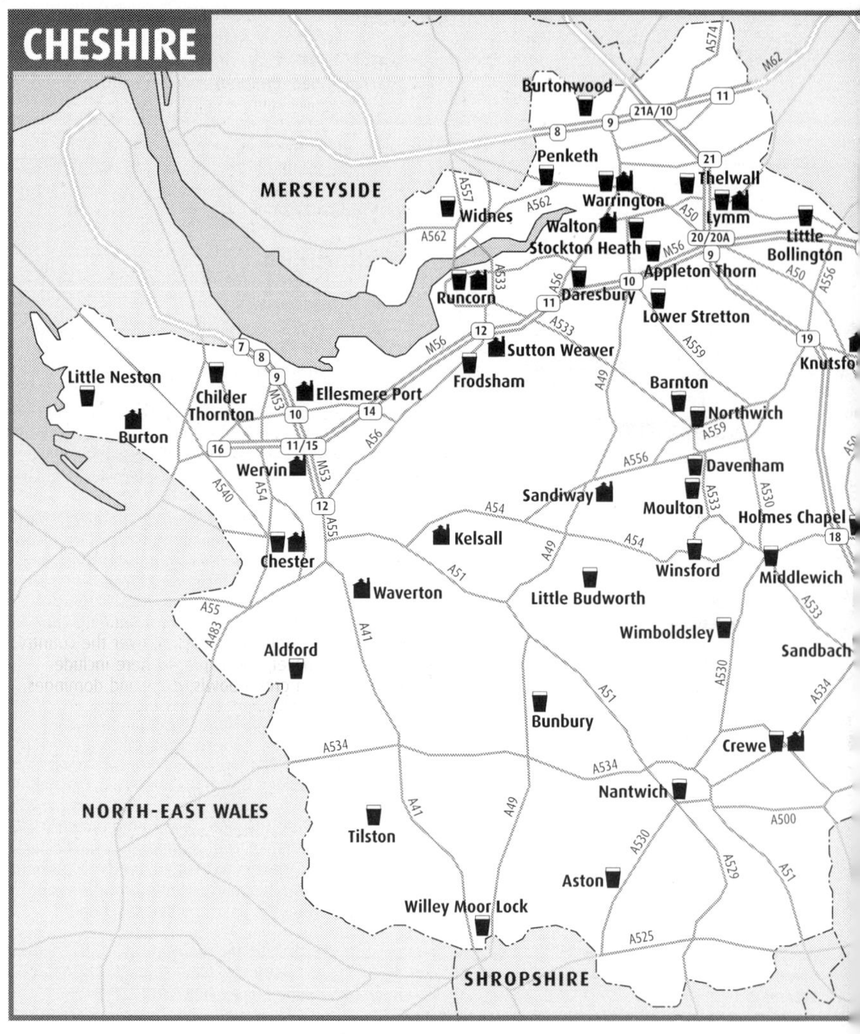

Aldford

Grosvenor Arms

Chester Road, CH3 6HJ (on B5130)
12-11 (10.30 Sun) (01244) 620228
grosvenorarms-aldford.co.uk
Timothy Taylor Landlord; Weetwood Eastgate; house beer (by Phoenix); 4 changing beers (sourced nationally)
Fine Victorian building with a stylish, upmarket interior. There are several rooms, all with an open aspect to the central bar. A garden room at the rear leads to a lawn and terrace with plenty of seating for the heady days of summer. Four changing guest beers, always including a mild, complement the three regular beers from Phoenix, Timothy Taylor and Weetwood. High-quality food is available.
Q P (C56)

Allgreave

Rose & Crown

Buxton Road, SK11 0BJ (on A54 between Bosley and Buxton)
closed Mon; 11-3, 5.30-11; 11-11 Sat; 11-10 Sun
(01260) 227232 roseandcrownallgreave.co.uk
5 changing beers (sourced regionally)
An historic old coaching inn and former toll house and smithy, nestling against the hillside in the beautiful Peak District overlooking Shutlingsloe – the Cheshire Matterhorn. It serves up to five often local cask ales complemented by a highly regarded food menu. Accommodation makes this a destination pub and a great base for walking in the area. This cosy inn with roaring logburners is a real gem and worth seeking out. P

Alsager

Lodge

88 Crewe Road, ST7 2JA (jct Crewe Rd and Station Rd, opp Church Rd)
4-11 (midnight Fri); 2-midnight Sat; 2-11 Sun
(01270) 873669
House beer (by Marston's); 7 changing beers (sourced nationally; often Dark Star, Oakham)
The ever-welcoming hosts offer varied, rapidly changing ales from seldom-seen breweries, both

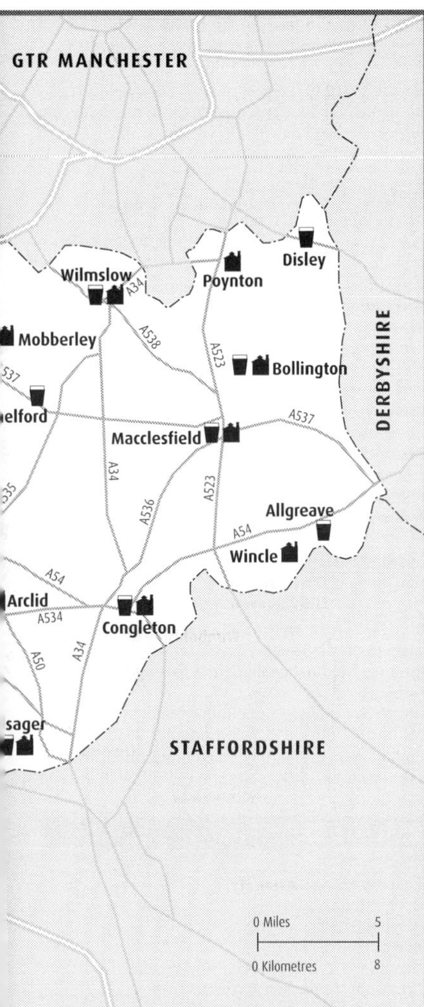

local and national. A good range of European beers is also available and up to three real ciders. With an inviting open fire in the winter months, it is always well worth a visit, especially after a seasonal walk on the snowdrop and bluebell trails at nearby Rode Hall. **QP**

Appleton Thorn

Appleton Thorn Village Hall

Stretton Road, WA4 4RT

closed Mon-Wed; 7.30-11.30 Thu-Sat; 1-4, 7.30-10.30 Sun

(01925) 261187 appletonthornvillagehall.co.uk

8 changing beers (sourced nationally; often Castle Rock, Facer's, Mallinsons) H

A former CAMRA National Club of the Year and finalist in 2018. A central bar serves a large function room and a smaller lounge. A changing range of beer is on offer, with paddles of thirds available. Five real ciders are also stocked. An annual beer festival is held in October. Quizzes and occasional live music nights also feature. Non-members pay a minimal fee for admission. **QP** (8,8E)

Aston

Bhurtpore

Wrenbury Road, CW5 8DQ (just off A530)

12-11.30 (midnight Fri & Sat); 12-11 Sun

(01270) 780917 bhurtpore.co.uk

11 changing beers (sourced nationally) H

A friendly community pub featuring in the Guide for the 26th consecutive year. It boasts an excellent range of 11 changing ales from a mixture of local breweries and some further afield, as well as real ciders including the local Wrenbury. A wide selection of bottled beers is also available. There are two other rooms, one with a pool table and TV. The restaurant serves locally sourced food, with curries a speciality. **QP** (72)

Barnton

Barnton Cricket Club

Broomsedge, Townfield Lane, CW8 4QL (200yds from A533, down a narrow drive to the left of Barnton Community Primary School)

6-11.30 (midnight Fri); 4-midnight Sat; 12-11 Sun

(01606) 77702 barntoncc.co.uk

Sharp's Doom Bar; 3 changing beers (sourced nationally) H

A former CAMRA National Club of the Year, this popular, friendly and multi award-winning club sells real ales from breweries all over the country. As well as cricket, sports played here include squash, crown green bowls, darts and dominoes. Monday is poker night. Food is available Wednesday to Saturday evening and Sunday lunchtime, with curry night Wednesday and steak nights Thursday and Friday. Open from 1.30pm Saturday during the cricket season mid-April to mid-September. Show your CAMRA membership card for admission. **P** (4,46)

Bollington

Poachers Inn

95 Ingersley Road, SK10 5RE

12-2 (not Mon), 5.30-11; 12-midnight Fri & Sat; 12-11 Sun

(01625) 572086 thepoachers.org

Storm Beauforts Ale; Weetwood Old Dog; 3 changing beers (sourced locally) H

Family-run, community free house generating a friendly atmosphere with a lovely suntrap garden for summer and a coal fire in winter, near Gritstone Trail and Peak District National Park. The pub enthusiastically supports local breweries. Real cider and bottled beers are also available. Popular with ramblers, cyclists and dog walkers, good-value, home-prepared locally sourced food is served. Events include Wednesday pie night, monthly quizzes and golf days. **P** (10,392)

Vale Inn

29-31 Adlington Road, SK10 5JT

12-2.30, 5-11; 12-11 Fri & Sat; 12-10.30 Sun

(01625) 575147 valeinn.co.uk

Bollington Long Hop, Bollington Best; 6 changing beers (sourced nationally; often Bollington) H

Close to the Macclesfield Canal and Middlewood Way, this mid-stone terraced single-room pub is the tap for the nearby Bollington Brewing Co. It features up to six of its own beers with an occasional guest and two ciders. Keg lines have also been recently installed. The renovated beer garden (separate from the pub) overlooking the recreation ground is ideal for a lazy summer evening watching the cricket. Good home-cooked food is served – booking recommended at busy times. (10,392)

Bunbury

Dysart Arms

Bowe's Gate Road, CW6 9PH (jct of Bowe's Gate Rd, College Lane and Wyche Lane)
11.30-11; 12-10.30 Sun (01829) 260183
dysartarms-bunbury.co.uk
House beer (by Brunning & Price); 5 changing beers (sourced regionally; often Salopian, Storm, Weetwood)
Situated opposite the imposing St Boniface Church, the pub takes its name from the Tollemache family who were the Earls of Dysart and local landowners. The original building was a farmhouse dating from the mid 18th century, with a tasteful modern extension added in 1996. The interior is a careful mix of wooden beams, extensive bookcases and tiled floors, conveying a pleasant and homely atmosphere. An excellent and extensive fresh food menu is available, with many ingredients sourced locally.

Burtonwood

Fiddle i'th Bag

Alder Lane, WA5 4BJ
12-3, 5.45-11; 12-11 Sat & Sun (01925) 225442
3 changing beers (sourced nationally)
Is this really a pub? Comparisons have been made with a museum, or even a junk shop. Heaps of memorabilia occupy most of the seats and bar area. The friendly and enthusiastic staff offer tasters of the frequently changing beers from three handpumps behind a pile of teddies, empty tobacco tins, busts of film stars and hordes of WWII relics. The mixture of locals and visitors seem to enjoy the ambience, the well-kept beers and the wholesome food. (329)

Chelford

Egerton Arms

Knutsford Road, SK11 9BB
12-11 (12.30am Fri & Sat); 12-10.30 Sun
(01625) 861366 chelfordegertonarms.co.uk
5 changing beers (sourced locally; often RedWillow, Tatton)
Originally a 15th-century stables, this is now a large single room with rural decor, real fires and an intimate atmosphere. The pub offers excellent food and a good range of up to seven beers, usually including one from the local Tatton and RedWillow breweries, two from other local breweries and more from regional/national breweries. Real cider is available in summer. Regular beer and food events take place, including food matching with local brewers' beers. Live music plays occasionally and quiz night is the last Thursday of the month.

Chester

Bear & Billet

94 Lower Bridge Street, CH1 1RU
11.30-11 (midnight Fri); 11-midnight Sat; 10-11 Sun
(01244) 311886
Okell's Bitter; 4 changing beers (sourced nationally; often Salopian, Okell's)
Grade I-listed, 17th-century, timber-framed building close to the river on three floors. TV screens show sport on all floors. There is a small outside space to the rear. A quiz and live folk music are hosted on Sunday evening. Up to five beers are available, usually including two from Okell's, together with a real cider.

Cellar

19-21 City Road, CH1 3AE
3-12.30am; 12-1.30am Fri & Sat; 12-12.30am Sun
(01244) 318950 thecellarchester.co.uk
Marble Pint; 5 changing beers (sourced nationally; often Burning Sky, Hammerton, Hawkshead)
Friendly, modern bar at street level with a cellar also available for functions. It is renowned for its excellent selection of ales, three real ciders, five craft keg beers and an extensive bottled beer range. Sport features on TV, particularly at weekends. Bar snacks are available, free bacon sandwiches on Sunday and free food during major sporting events. Dogs are welcome except Friday and Saturday nights when the bar can be busy.

Cornerhouse

4-8 City Road, CH1 3AE
12 (3 winter)-midnight; 12-1.30am Fri & Sat; 12-11.30 Sun
(01244) 347518 cornerhousechester.com
Salopian Oracle; Timothy Taylor Landlord; 2 changing beers (sourced nationally; often Hawkshead, Marble)
Attractive candlelit mock-Tudor building featuring lots of bare brick and wood flooring. It offers two regular beers and two changing ales, one of which is usually dark, plus a selection of bottled beers and

REAL ALE BREWERIES

4Ts Warrington
Beartown Congleton
Beer Refinery Wervin
Blueball Runcorn
Bollington Bollington
Borough Crewe (brewing suspended)
Brewhouse & Kitchen Chester
Brewhouse & Kitchen Wilmslow
Britman Burton
Buccaneer Sutton Weaver
Chapter Sutton Weaver
Cheshire Brewhouse Congleton
Coach House Warrington
Front Row Congleton
Goodall's Alsager
Happy Valley Macclesfield
Lymm Lymm
Macclesfield Macclesfield
Manning Congleton
Merlin Arclid
Mobberley Mobberley
Norton Runcorn
Oaks Ellesmere Port
Pied Bull Chester
Poynton Poynton
RedWillow Macclesfield
Sandiway Sandiway
Spitting Feathers Waverton
Stag Walton
Storm Macclesfield
Tatton Knutsford
Tipsy Angel Warrington
Weetwood Kelsall
Wincle Wincle

an extensive wine list. Live music is hosted Thursday to Saturday and a quiz on Sunday. There is a free-to-hire function room upstairs. Outdoor seating is at the front of the pub. Food is of the platter variety (meats and cheeses) plus snacks. Opening and closing times may vary Monday to Thursday in winter.

Cross Keys

2 Duke Street, CH1 1RP

closed Mon & Tue; 12-11; 12-10.30 Sun (01244) 344460

Joule's Blonde, Pale Ale, Slumbering Monk; 3 changing beers (sourced nationally; often Joule's)

Attractive red-brick building with a stylish interior featuring oak floors, wood panelling and stained glass windows depicting other Joule's hostelries. Three regular Joule's beers and a seasonal Joule's are complemented by two changing guests and up to four real ciders. A large upstairs room is available for hire. The small terrace beer garden catches the afternoon sunshine. A choice of pies is always available and a traditional roast on Sunday. The pub hosts a popular quiz each Thursday and live Irish music on the second and fourth Wednesdays of the month.

Deva Tap

121 Brook Street, CH1 3DU (at city end of Hoole Bridge close to railway station)

4-11 (9 Mon; 10 Tue); 3-midnight Fri; 12-midnight Sat; 2-10 Sun (01244) 314440

5 changing beers (sourced regionally)

The interior here is fairly open plan but still has the feel of three separate rooms – a small area by the door, a larger seating area in the middle and the bar at the far end. The exterior has an unusual but stunning roof line and there is a small courtyard with picnic tables. The bar has five handpumps.

Goat & Munch

52 Garden Lane, CH1 4EW

closed Mon; 2-10 (10.30 Fri & Sat); 2-7 Sun

07807 198267 goatandmunch.com

4 changing beers (sourced regionally; often Peerless, Salopian)

Chester's first micropub occupies a former electrical appliance repair shop in the Garden Quarter – an area heavily populated by students. The front room features a bar front made from old pallets, and furniture includes Swedish high tables and chairs plus some bench seating. There is also a brighter side room with additional seating. The four real ales tend to be from independent breweries such as Oakham or Salopian. Discounted beers are available on Tuesday.

Lodge Bar

8-10 Hoole Road, Hoole, CH2 3NH (on A56 ½ mile from railway station and ring road)

11-11 (midnight Fri & Sat) (01244) 324971

lodgebar.co.uk

3 changing beers (sourced nationally; often Abbeydale, Rudgate, Salopian)

Lounge-style bar, part of the Bawn Lodge hotel. To the right of the bar is intimate alcove seating and a large side lounge. Three handpumps serve a changing range of beers at competitive prices and there is good-value food available all day. A large beer garden is at the front, popular in summer, with heating for the winter months.

P

Old Harkers Arms

1 Russell Street, CH3 5AL (down steps off City Rd to canal towpath)

10.30-11; 12-10.30 Sun (01244) 344525

harkersarms-chester.co.uk

Weetwood Cheshire Cat, Eastgate; house beer (by Phoenix); 6 changing beers (sourced nationally; often Derby, Hawkshead)

Upmarket pub converted from the ground floor of a former Victorian canalside warehouse. Timber flooring, traditional wooden furniture and cast-iron pillars provide an insight to its history. Blackboards list the real ales with tasting notes – usually six guests including a selection of bitters, stouts, milds or porters. Many are from local breweries. Ciders and perries are listed separately and served from the cellar. Food is available all day (booking advised for busy weekend periods). Outside seating offers views of the canal.

Q

Olde Cottage Inn

34-36 Brook Street, CH1 3DZ

4-11 (midnight Fri); 2-midnight Sat; 2-11 Sun

(01244) 324065 oldecottagechester.co.uk

4 changing beers (sourced nationally; often Otter, Sharp's)

Welcoming traditional community hostelry on a popular eating and drinking street between the bus interchange and the railway station. To the left of the central bar is the games room with pool, darts and a bagatelle table (a game rarely seen outside Chester). The main bar has another dartboard, small TV and a real fire for colder weather. Beers are competitively priced and include one free of tie. Various loyalty and discount schemes are available. CAMRA Champion Pub of Cheshire 2016.

Telford's Warehouse

Canal Basin, Tower Wharf, CH1 4EZ (just off the city walls)

12-1am (11 Mon & Tue; 12.30am Wed & Thu)

(01244) 390090 telfordswarehousechester.com

Salopian Oracle; Weetwood Cheshire Cat; Young's Bitter; 3 changing beers (sourced nationally; often Hawkshead, Tatton, Three Tuns)

Popular former Georgian warehouse adjacent to the Shropshire Union Canal. Industrial artefacts adorn the interior and a large glass frontage overlooks the canal basin. During the day a relaxed atmosphere prevails, while evenings are livelier, with events such as salsa dance classes and live concerts, when an admission charge may apply. The regular beers are supplemented by guest ales which are often from local micros. Children are welcome in the upstairs restaurant. The annual beer festival is usually held in October.

P (1A)

Childer Thornton

Halfway House

New Chester Road, CH66 1QN (on A41 close to M53 jct 5)

3-11.30; 12-midnight Sat; 12-11 Sun (0151) 339 2202

4 changing beers (sourced nationally; often First Chop, Ringwood, Weetwood)

Friendly, traditional former coaching inn dating from the 1770s, based at the midpoint between Chester and New Ferry. It retains much of the original character, with several drinking areas offering smart, comfortable seating. The community feel is evident, with darts and dominoes teams plus a golf society. The pub can be busy when sporting events are on TV. Quiz night is Thursday.

Congleton

Barley Hops

2 Swan Bank, CW12 1AH
closed Mon; 3-8 (10 Fri); 12-8 Sat; 1-6 Sun
(01260) 270164 barleyhops.co.uk
3 changing beers (sourced locally)
In an impressive street corner location, this well-stocked bottled beer specialist is also a micropub. Three handpumps dispense predominantly local ales, with local cider in bottles. The bottled beer selection focuses on British beers but there are well-chosen foreign beers as well. Occasional Meet the Brewer events and other specialist spirit events are hosted. Closing times may vary according to demand. Q (38,42)

Prince of Wales

4-6 Lawton Street, CW12 1RP
4 (12 Thu)-11; 12-midnight Fri & Sat; 12-10.30 Sun
(01260) 280714
Joule's Blonde, Pale Ale, Slumbering Monk; 3 changing beers (sourced regionally; often Joule's)
Reopened in 2015, this pub is now owned by Joules Brewery. The interior has been divided into three areas, creating snug corners, warmed by a real fire. The interesting decor features green-tiled walls and enamel signs, adorned with lots of artefacts. At least one of the three guest beers here are often local. Food is served Sunday only. There is a good-sized outdoor drinking area behind the pub.

Young Pretender

30-34 Lawton Street, CW12 1RS
4-11; 12-1am Fri & Sat; 12-11 Sun (01260) 273277
thebeerparlours.co.uk
5 changing beers (sourced nationally)
Modern town-centre bar set within a part Grade II-listed building, with a strong community base. Bonnie Prince Charlie allegedly slept here, hence the name. The single large room is divided into smaller areas. It offers a varied range of five real ales plus one real cider. The real ales always come from the Manchester and east Cheshire area. A popular meeting point for local groups, regular Meet the Brewer evenings, Sunday quizzes, film nights and pub games all feature.
P

Crewe

Borough Arms

33 Earle Street, CW1 2BG (on Earle St railway bridge, with entrance up steps in adjoining Thomas St)
5-11; 12-midnight Fri & Sat; 12-11 Sun
10 changing beers (sourced nationally; often Fyne Ales, Oakham, Salopian)
Ten handpumps serve constantly changing real ales, with one or two more dispensing real ciders, alongside a large selection of continental draught and bottled beers. The L-shaped bar has three distinct seating areas on split levels. Another seating area downstairs accesses a secluded walled beer garden and smoking area. The West Coast Main Line runs within 6ft of the beer garden and the pub is a short distance from Crewe Heritage Centre, where the Rail Ale Festival is held each September. Q P

Hops

Prince Albert Street, CW1 2DF (opp Lifestyle Centre at S end of Prince Albert St)
11 (5 Mon)-11.30; 12-11.30 Sun (01270) 211100
6 changing beers (sourced nationally)
Originally a railway foreman's house built around 1844, Hops is now one of the foremost real ale pubs in south Cheshire, with six beers of varying strengths and types always on handpump. Interesting craft keg beers are also available and up to six real ciders and perries. It is also a haven for Belgian bottled beer. With a European-style sun terrace out front, it is a must-visit establishment if you are in the area. Q

Daresbury

Ring o' Bells

Chester Road, WA4 4AJ (just off A56 in centre of the village)
12-11 (10.30 Sun) (01925) 740256
Greene King IPA; 4 changing beers (sourced locally; often Weetwood)
Once the village courthouse, this 19th-century pub still retains many original features, including a listed horse trough. Although food oriented, this Chef & Brewer hostelry has five handpumps serving beers from local breweries. Outside the pub is Daresbury parish church which was once officiated over by The Rev Charles Dodgson, better known by his pen name Lewis Carroll – many of the author's sayings and characters are dotted around the pub. P (X30)

Davenham

Davenham Cricket Club

Butchers' Stile, Hartford Road, CW9 8JG (left down a narrow driveway after Mount Pleasant Rd)
closed Mon; 4.30-8.30; 4-11 Fri & Sat (01606) 48922
davenham.play-cricket.com
4 changing beers (sourced locally; often Beartown, Brimstage, Mobberley)
This family-oriented club is a community facility in an idyllic village setting. Extensive seating in front of the pavilion makes it the perfect place to enjoy beer, cricket and the summer warmth. The local football club is made welcome and sporting events are shown on TV. There is a refurbished main lounge. Four handpumps serve real ale mainly from local breweries. During the cricket season the opening hours are extended. Show your CAMRA membership card for admission. P

Disley

Malt Disley

22 Market Street, SK12 2AA (on A6 in village centre)
4-11; 12-11 Fri & Sat; 12-10 Sun (01663) 308020
maltdisley.co.uk
5 changing beers (sourced locally)
Converted from a shop, this spacious micropub has more seating downstairs and is a well-run and comfortable addition to the local micro scene. Five changing cask beers are available, often from local micro breweries, as well as a cask cider. Live music events feature on the last Sunday of each month.
Q (199)

White Lion

135 Buxton Road, SK12 2HA (on A6 towards E end of village)
12 (6.30 Mon)-11; 12-12.30am Fri & Sat
(01663) 762800
9 changing beers (often Adnams, Ossett, Purity)
Originally the 'red house', which gave the name to the adjacent road, this multi award-winning pub is now painted white. Nine different real ales are on offer, many from micros and all selected from SIBA member breweries. The contemporary interior is open plan apart from a separate dog room. A short walk from Peak Forest Canal (bridge 26).
P (199)

Frodsham

Helter Skelter

31 Church Street, WA6 6PN
11-11 (11.30 Fri & Sat); 12-11 Sun (01928) 733361
thehelterskelter.net
Oakham Bishops Farewell; Salopian Oracle; Weetwood Bitter; 7 changing beers (sourced nationally; often Ossett, Thornbridge)
A local CAMRA award winner offering three regular cask ales plus a further seven constantly changing guest beers from local and national micros. Two rotating guest ciders and a variety of imported bottled beers are also available. The single-room bar has a friendly, relaxed atmosphere attracting both locals and travellers. Excellent food is served in the bar and upstairs restaurant. Dogs are welcome and there are water bowls aplenty.
(21,48)

Kash 22 Brew & Chew

22 Church Street, WA6 6QW
4 (12 Thu)-11; 12-midnight Fri & Sat; 12-10.30 Sun
(01928) 733116
4 changing beers (sourced locally; often Blueball)
A friendly bar near the town centre and railway station, with knowledgeable staff. Four cask lines serve changing guest beers, often including two from local breweries. A popular and varied hot food menu using locally sourced ingredients is available every day. There is a large beer garden to the rear. Live music at least four nights a week creates a jovial vibe for a mixture of ages, and the bar is generally busy on these nights.
(21,48)

Holmes Chapel

Bottle Bank

24-26 London Road, CW4 7AL
12-10.30 (11.30 Thu-Sat); 2-10.30 Sun (01477) 534380
4 changing beers (sourced locally)
New bar and off-licence in the former NatWest bank building (hence the name). There are two rooms behind the front bar, one of which is the former strong room, which can be reserved for functions. Four changing cask pumps are supplemented by eight draught beers. Third-pints are available and the knowledgeable bar staff discuss beer styles with authority. A large range of British and foreign bottled beers is also stocked to drink or take away. Bar snacks are available.
(42,316)

Little Bollington

Swan with Two Nicks

Park Lane, WA14 4TJ (signposted off A56)
12-11 (10.30 Sun) (0161) 928 2914
swanwithtwonicks.co.uk
Timothy Taylor Landlord; Black Sheep Best Bitter; Dunham Massey Big Tree Bitter; house beer (by Coach House); 2 changing beers (sourced locally)
Spacious, traditionally styled country pub. To the front is the drinking area warmed by two large fires in chilly weather. In the middle is the bar and beyond that the restaurant. The house beer is typically accompanied by at least two local beers, often from Dunham Massey, and two nationally sourced ales. There is a varied food offering including gluten-free dishes. P

Little Budworth

Egerton Arms

Pinfold Lane, CW6 9BS
closed Mon; 3-11 Tue-Thu; 12-midnight Fri & Sat; 12-11 Sun
(01829) 760424 egerton-arms.co.uk
6 changing beers (sourced locally; often Blackjack, Heavy Industry, Tatton)
Situated on the edge of the village, this traditional, unspoilt and friendly pub offers a range of continental lagers and bottled world beers in addition to cask ales. Food includes a range of home-made burgers, specials and, on Thursday, pizza. A woodburner creates a warm, cosy atmosphere in winter. The beer garden is a sunny place to watch cricket in summer. The pub hosts a summer beer festival and winter Oktoberfest. Regular live music and themed events also feature.
P

Little Neston

Harp

19 Quayside, CH64 0TB (turn left at bottom of Marshlands Rd, pub is 300yds on left)
12-midnight (12.30am Fri & Sat); 12-11 Sun
(0151) 336 6980
Joseph Holt Bitter; Peerless Triple Blonde; Timothy Taylor Landlord; 2 changing beers (sourced nationally)
Former coal miners' inn with a basic lounge and a public bar warmed by a real fire in winter. Evening food is only available on a Tuesday for the popular curry night. In a glorious location on the Deeside to Neston stretch of the National Cycle Network, the pub overlooks the Dee Marshes and North Wales. It has a recently enlarged garden and a drinking area abutting the edge of the marshes.
QP (22,487)

Lower Stretton

Ring o' Bells

Northwich Road, WA4 4NZ (200yds from M56 jct 10)
5.30-11 (midnight Fri); 4.30-10.30 Sun 07791 572555
Lees Brewer's Dark; Merlin Dark Magic; Wood Shropshire Lad; 3 changing beers (sourced locally; often Merlin)
A small village local with no music or games machines. The main room, served by a single bar, leads to two smaller rooms for quieter drinking. Three regular and up to three rotating guest beers are available, including a mild, often from local microbreweries. A quiz night is held on the second

and fourth Tuesdays of the month, and a folk session on the first Tuesday of most months.
Q P (45,46)

Lymm

Brewery Tap

18 Bridgewater Street, WA13 0AB
12-11 (midnight Thu; 11.30 Fri & Sat) (01925) 755451
lymmbrewing.co.uk
Dunham Massey Dark; Lymm Bitter, Bridgewater Blonde; 4 changing beers (sourced locally; often Dunham Massey, Lymm)
Modern venue in the red-brick former post office, a stone's throw from the Bridgewater Canal. The well-lit bar is complemented by a tastefully decorated front room with subdued lighting, comfy armchairs and a wood-fired stove. Four guest ales are either from the microbrewery under the pub or nearby Dunham Massey. One rotating real cider is also available. An open mic night is held twice a month.

Bull's Head

32 The Cross, WA13 0HU (in village centre)
12-midnight (1am Fri & Sat) (01925) 753614
Hydes Original, Lowry; 3 changing beers (sourced regionally)
Situated next to the Bridgewater Canal humpback bridge leading out of the village, this unspoilt and inviting pub with its thriving local trade is well worth a visit. No food is served and conversation is the norm. A comfortable lounge with real fire is at the front of the pub, while the public bar is at the rear. Beers include two regulars from Hydes alongside three changing ales from the Hydes seasonal and Beer Studio ranges and the guest list.

Macclesfield

Park Tavern

158 Park Lane, SK11 6UB
4-11; 12-midnight Fri & Sat; 12-11 Sun (01625) 667846
park-tavern.co.uk
Bollington Long Hop, Best; 4 changing beers (sourced locally; often Bollington)
Dating from around 1825, this popular community local showcases the range of local Bollington Brewery beers plus occasional guest ales and two real ciders. Regular events include film nights in a mini cinema and function room upstairs. Quizzes and science talks are also held regularly. Food is available Thursday to Saturday. The train station is a 15-minute walk or there is a bus stop outside.

RedWillow

32A Park Green, SK11 7NA
closed Mon; 4-11 (midnight Thu); 3-midnight Fri; 12-midnight Sat; 12-10.30 Sun (01625) 503253
redwillowbar.com
RedWillow Headless; 4 changing beers (sourced regionally)
Stylish tap for the local RedWillow Brewery, offering a changing range of RedWillow and other guest beers and a real cider on five handpumps. A large screen above the bar displays an additional range of craft keg beers. Food is served every day, mainly pizza and charcuterie. The large open-plan bar can be noisy at busy times. A front terrace is popular for outdoor drinking.

Treacle Tap

43 Sunderland Street, SK11 6JL
4-11; 12-midnight Fri & Sat; 12-11 Sun (01625) 615938
thetreacletap.co.uk
3 changing beers (sourced locally)
A former saddlery shop, this small single-room bar opened in 2010 and is now well established as one of the towns' most reliable real ale outlets. Three handpumps rotate beers from smaller regional brewers and a range of craft keg and bottled beers is also on offer. Food is available every day, mainly pies with changing fillings. Plenty of community activities keep the pub busy with local trade.
Q

Waters Green Tavern

96 Waters Green, SK11 6LH
12-3, 5-11; 12-11 Sat; 12-10.30 Sun (01625) 422653
7 changing beers (sourced regionally; often Abbeydale, Acorn, Elland)
A mainstay in the Guide for over 20 years, this gem of a traditional free house benefits from the vast experience of the long-serving landlord and his son. Seven changing handpulled beers plus a real cider and good value home-cooked food can be enjoyed in the open-plan interior, with two seating areas, one with a real fire, and a separate pool room. Ideally located for the town centre and both rail and bus stations.

Wharf

107 Brook Street, SK11 7AW
12-2.30, 4-11 (11.30 Tue-Thu); 12-midnight Fri; 3-midnight Sat; 3-11.30 Sun (01625) 261879 thewharfmacc.co.uk
Butcombe Original; 4 changing beers (sourced locally; often Oakham)
A former Cheshire CAMRA Pub of the Year, this one-room free house has a central bar with a cosy lounge area with real fire on one side and a pool table on the other. It offers a superb range of regular and changing cask beers, plus real cider. This traditional wet-led pub is well worth the short walk up the hill from the town, especially when it is hosting one of its regular music nights.
(58)

Middlewich

King's Lock

1 Booth Lane, CW10 0JJ
closed Mon; 12-11 (01606) 836894
kingslockinn.com
3 changing beers (sourced regionally)
Traditional lockside public house with a friendly atmosphere on the outskirts of Middlewich on the junction of the Middlewich and Trent & Mersey canals. It offers three revolving real ales and one real cider, with an emphasis on local ales. A varied daily food menu is available. The comfortable barged beam bar has a tiled floor and welcoming fire. Monthly acoustic nights feature and the pub participates in the annual summer boat music and arts festival. An attractive beer garden is adjacent to the lock.
P

White Bear Hotel

Wheelock Street, CW10 9AG (on lower end of Wheelock St, just off St Michael's Way)
11-11 (midnight Fri & Sat); 12-10.30 Sun
(01606) 837666 thewhitebearmiddlewich.co.uk
4 changing beers (sourced locally)

Free house dating from 1625 with a rotating range of four real ales and a traditional cider on handpull. The licensee supports the LocAle scheme and sources unusual micro beers. Close to the church and near the canal, there are four distinct drinking areas here, all comfortably furnished. Excellent good-value food is served in the restaurant. Monday from 5pm is real ale discount night.
P (37,42)

Moulton

Lion Hotel

74 Main Road, CW9 8PB
5-11; 4-midnight Fri; 2-midnight Sat; 2-10.30 Sun
(01606) 606049
Wychwood Hobgoblin; 4 changing beers (sourced locally; often Cheshire Brewhouse, RedWillow, Tatton)
Located in the centre of the village, this is a welcoming community-focused pub and former local CAMRA Pub of the Year. Six handpumps dispense quality ales and ciders, mainly from local breweries. Quiz nights and themed music events are always popular. A complimentary cheeseboard is offered on Friday evening. A beer garden to the side and decking to the front enable customers to take advantage of the warm summer months.
P

Nantwich

Black Lion

29 Welsh Row, CW5 5ED (opp Cheshire Cat)
12-3 (not Mon), 5-11; 12-11 Sat; 12-10.30 Sun
(01270) 628711 blacklion-nantwich.co.uk
Weetwood Bitter, Cheshire Cat, Eastgate, Old Dog; 3 changing beers (sourced regionally)
A traditional black & white-fronted inn dating from the 17th century, standing among the historic buildings of Welsh Row. Its beautiful plaster and wood-beamed interior retains the expected bowed walls and creaking floorboards. An open fire welcomes you into an open-plan area. The small Hop Room features hop bines on the ceiling and a pot-bellied stove for heating. There is a restaurant upstairs and a covered beer garden to the side.
Q (84)

Crown

High Street, CW5 5AS (between NatWest and Caffè Nero)
11-11.30 (midnight Fri & Sat); 11-11 Sun
(01270) 625283 crownhotelnantwich.com
Salopian Shropshire Gold; 3 changing beers (sourced regionally)
Recently refurbished, this three-storey building was burned down in the Fire of Nantwich in 1583 and quickly rebuilt using timbers from Delamere Forest. Now Grade I listed, it features an abundance of old beams, wattle and daub walls, roaring fires and the strangest uneven bespoke flooring to be found in Cheshire. The bar offers a selection of four real ales including one from the Salopian Brewery plus three rotating guest ales. Live music plays on Thursday nights.
P (84)

Vine Inn

42 Hospital Street, CW5 5RP (near St Mary's Church)
12-midnight; 11.30-midnight Sat (01270) 619055
vineinnnantwich.co.uk
Hydes Original; 3 changing beers (sourced regionally)
A 17th-century two-storey building with its floor below street level and an open-plan interior with distinct levels. Beers are from the full Hydes range, often including two from the Beer Studio. Guests are sourced from Hydes craft ale range. Good-value food is served at lunchtime. On Monday there is a 50p discount on a pint of real ale.

Northwich

Salty Dog

21-23 High Street, CW9 5BY
11-11; 12-10.30 Sun salty-dog.co.uk
Tatton Gold; 3 changing beers (sourced locally; often Bollington, Merlin, RedWillow)
Opened in spring 2017, this former shop retains its picturesque black & white exterior. The pub's landlord and co-owner played drums in punk band The Business. Comedy nights are hosted as well as live music, with some events chargeable. A room at the rear has a jukebox, table football, retro arcade and a quiz machine. An extensive range of bottled British and European beers is available. The staff are particularly knowledgeable about all the beers.

Penketh

Ferry Tavern

Station Road, WA5 2UJ
5.30-9.30 Mon; 12-11 (midnight Fri & Sat); 12-10.30 Sun
(01925) 791117 theferrytavern.com
Exmoor Gold; Salopian Oracle; 6 changing beers (sourced nationally)
Access involves crossing a railway line and a canal before reaching this popular pub nestling alongside the River Mersey. Eight handpumps dispense the two regular beers plus six national ales, with brewery tap takeover evenings showcasing favourite breweries. Food includes the famous fish and chips plus locally made pies at the weekend. The large beer garden is thronged in the summer, often with walkers and cyclists.
P (32)

Runcorn

Ferry Boat

10 Church Street, WA7 1LR
8am-midnight (1am Fri & Sat) (01928) 583380
Greene King Abbot; Ruddles Best Bitter; Sharp's Doom Bar; 2 changing beers
Large, busy Wetherspoon pub opposite Runcorn old town bus station. The pub name derives from the river crossing that used to operate between the towns of Runcorn and Widnes (on the opposite bank of the River Mersey) before the building of the Manchester Ship Canal in the 1890s. The Brindley Theatre is 200 yards away. A welcome real ale pub in a mainly keg desert.
P

Norton Arms

125-127 Main Street, WA7 2AD
12-11 (midnight Fri & Sat); 12-10 Sun (01928) 567642
thenortonarms.co.uk
Greene King IPA; 3 changing beers (sourced nationally)

Another year in the Guide for this Grade II-listed, two-roomed, oak-beamed pub in the centre of Halton Village. Although sports TV dominates, with three screens, this pub is still a nice find and can get busy at weekends. Beers are on four handpumps, with third-pint taster glasses available. Due to the age of the pub, access is tricky – the door is up a flight of stone steps. Quiz nights, live music and open mic nights all feature.

Prospect

70 Weston Road, WA7 4LD
12-11 (10.30 Sun) (01928) 561280
Adnams Broadside; Timothy Taylor Landlord; 2 changing beers H
This traditional pub has ale on three handpumps and cider on one. The lounge is decorated with local memorabilia and has a real fire. The pub prides itself on sourcing local produce for its food and commits to local businesses whenever possible. Situated high above the Rivers Mersey and Weaver, it has views reaching from Liverpool to North Wales. Q P

Sandbach

Beer Emporium

8 Welles Street, CW11 1GT (off Hightown roundabout, down one-way street)
12-8 (10 Thu-Sat) (01270) 760113
thebeeremporium.com
5 changing beers H
This friendly and welcoming bar and bottle shop is a conversion of a former butcher's premises, retaining much of the original features including the façade and interior tiling. Five constantly changing cask ales are available and one keg line (sometimes KeyKeg). There is an esoteric selection of cans and bottles of beer (including bottle-conditioned), plus cider and perry from the UK and further afield. On the first Thursday of the month the pub hosts Brewers Anonymous for keen home brewers. Q (37,38)

Stockton Heath

Costello's Bar

23 Walton Road, WA4 6NJ
12-11 (midnight Thu; 11.30 Fri & Sat) (01925) 600910
costellosbar.co.uk
Dunham Massey Big Tree Bitter; Lymm Bridgewater Blonde; 5 changing beers (sourced locally; often Dunham Massey, Lymm) H
Welcoming and friendly modern real ale bar owned and run by Dunham Massey Brewing. There are seven handpumps, with five cask ales on rotation and two mainstays, always including at least one dark beer, one mild and one strong ale. Real cider is also sold. All cask ale is provided by Dunham Massey and Lymm Brewing. Free newspapers are on offer. Live music features every Sunday. Local CAMRA Pub of the Year 2018.

Thelwall

Little Manor

Bell Lane, WA4 2SX
10.30-11 (10.30 Sun) (01925) 212070
littlemanor-thelwall.co.uk
Coach House Cromwells Best Bitter; house beer (by Phoenix); 6 changing beers (sourced locally) H
A large upmarket food-based pub with a changing range of mainly local cask ales. The pub is tastefully furnished and has attractive garden areas for dining alfresco in the summer. A regularly changing food menu suits all tastes and is available throughout the day. First built for the Percivals as a family house in the 1600s, their crest has been adopted for the pub sign. Details of country walks around the pub are available from the website or bar.
Q P (5,6)

Tilston

Carden Arms

Mount View, Church Road, SY14 7HB
closed Mon; 12-11 (01829) 250900
cardenarms.co.uk
Coach House Gunpowder Mild; Salopian Shropshire Gold; Weetwood Eastgate; 2 changing beers (sourced locally; often Peerless, Spitting Feathers, Wincle) H
Stylishly renovated free house with wood and tiled floors, rugs, two real fires, traditional furniture and attractive framed pictures on the plain white walls. In addition to the three regular beers are two guests, often from local microbreweries. There is a separate dining room and the adjoining old stable is available for groups of up to eight people. The pub is on Sustrans Route 70 and popular with cyclists. For warmer weather there is outside seating to both the front and rear.
Q P (41)

Warrington

Bear & Bottle

90-92 Mersey Street, WA1 2BP
2-11; closed Wed; 12-1am Fri & Sat; 12-9 Sun
(01925) 635893 bearandbottle.co.uk
4 changing beers (sourced nationally; often Exmoor, Oakham, Salopian) H
A long-established pub renamed and given a modern feel in late 2016, owned and managed by well-known and highly regarded local operators. There is a jukebox and sports TV plus darts and dominoes, but the pub is generally fairly quiet during the week. However, it gets extremely busy on Saturday night when a live band usually plays. In addition to the cask ales there is an international selection of canned and bottled beers.
P

Looking Glass

41-43 Buttermarket Street, WA1 2LY
8am-midnight (1am Fri & Sat) (01925) 405030
Greene King Abbot; Ruddles Best Bitter; Sharp's Doom Bar; Theakston Old Peculier; house beer (by Coach House); 5 changing beers (sourced nationally; often Kelham Island, Peerless, Thornbridge) H
This Wetherspoon is on two levels with a small bar upstairs. Jabberwocky is produced for the pub by local brewery Coach House. The patio area in front opens out onto the pedestrianised town centre. Guest ales often include high ABV beers sourced nationally. Q

Lower Angel

27 Buttermarket Street, WA1 2LY (in pedestrianised town centre)
11-11 (midnight Sat); 12-10 Sun (01925) 653326

Weetwood Bitter; 6 changing beers (sourced nationally) Ⓗ
Enjoy a step back in time here, with a traditional vault and lounge layout and sheltered beer garden. Memorabilia from the former Walker's Brewery and stained-glass windows remain. The summer room to the rear is adorned with hundreds of pumpclips. The pub supports local charities and a visit at Halloween or Christmas is a must to see the decorations. The six changing beers are mainly from independent breweries.

Tavern

25 Church Street, WA1 2SS
12 (4 Mon & Tue; 3 Wed & Thu)-midnight
07747 668817
8 changing beers (sourced nationally; often Fyne Ales, Mallinsons, Oakham) Ⓗ
A regular Guide entry, this single-room pub has eight ever-changing beers – two from local 4Ts, one bitter, one dark, one session and three pale choices providing a good range for the discerning drinker. There is a board by the bar which is religiously updated to show beer name, price, style and strength. Multiple TVs allow different sporting events to be shown simultaneously. The large covered smoking area at the rear offers seating and TV.

Widnes

Premier

93-99 Albert Road, WA8 6JS
8am-midnight (12.30am Fri & Sat) (0151) 422 4920
Greene King Abbot; Ruddles Best Bitter; 3 changing beers Ⓗ
The Premier cinema and later the Carpenters bottling plant is now a Wetherspoon pub, on the edge of the shopping centre. It has a pleasant atmosphere and a changing clientele depending on the time of day. Sgt Thomas Mottershead VC, who died in 1917 while serving on the Western Front with the Royal Flying Corps, used to visit the Premier cinema and his statue appeal was launched at the pub.

Willey Moor Lock

Willey Moor Lock Tavern

Tarporley Road, SY13 4HF (400yds off A49, around 1½ miles N of Whitchurch)
12-2.30, 6-10.30; 12-3, 6-11 Sat; 12-3, 6-10.30 Sun
(01948) 663274 willeymoorlock.co.uk
6 changing beers (sourced nationally) Ⓗ
This family-run free house is a former lock-keeper's cottage, accessed from the car park via a footbridge over the Llangollen Canal. The pub is popular with boaters and walkers on the Sandstone Trail, especially in summer. Outside seating is available by the canal and in the attractive beer garden. Good-value meals are served lunchtimes and evenings. Three changing beers, many from local brewers, increase to six in summer. There is a campsite close by. QP

Wilmslow

Brewhouse & Kitchen

6-12 Swan Street, SK9 1HE
11-11 (midnight Fri & Sat); 12-11 Sun (01625) 441850
brewhouseandkitchen.com/wilmslow
Brewhouse & Kitchen Secret Genius, Fustian Cut, Bollin Ruby, Lucky Sam; 2 changing beers (sourced locally; often Brewhouse & Kitchen) Ⓗ
Opened in 2016, this brewery diner is a new concept to the area. The decor is unsurprisingly beer related, with lamps made from beer glasses and bottles. Brewed on the premises, the six cask ales have locally themed names. Food focuses on steaks and burgers but there is also a selection of vegetarian and vegan dishes. The menu has suggested beer pairings for most dishes. See the website for the current beer selection.
(130,88)

Old Dancer

16 Grove Street, SK9 1DR
12-midnight (1am Fri & Sat) (01625) 530775
theolddancer.co.uk
5 changing beers (sourced nationally) Ⓗ
Lively café-bar on the main pedestrian shopping street. It is furnished mainly with simple wooden tables set on boarded floors, the walls decorated with striking hand-painted murals on a dance theme. Six handpumps serve an interesting range of beers including local ales and a cask cider. Tea, coffee and food are available noon-10pm, including cakes and a selection of award-winning pies. The bar hosts live music on Saturday, film and quiz nights, science nights, a writers' group and a book club. (130,88)

Wimboldsley

Verdin Arms

Nantwich Road, CW10 0LW (on A530 adjacent to railway bridge over West Coast Main Line)
closed Mon; 5-10.30 (01270) 522275
3 changing beers (sourced regionally) Ⓗ
Originally the Plough Inn, the pub was renamed the Verdin Arms in the 1890s in honour of Sir Joseph Verdin, a local philanthropist who founded a school and hospital in nearby Middlewich. Bought in 2016 from Robinsons, it is now a genuine free house with three changing real ales and a real cider on handpump. There are three distinct and comfortable drinking areas and a pool room. Well worth a visit. QP

Winsford

Queen's Arms

Dene Drive, CW7 1AT (opp Winsford Cross shopping centre)
8am-midnight (1am Fri & Sat) (01606) 595350
Greene King Abbot; Ruddles Best Bitter; Sharp's Doom Bar; Wychwood Hobgoblin Gold; 4 changing beers (sourced regionally) Ⓗ
Modern open-plan Wetherspoon pub close to the shops and town centre. Large windows front a bright, comfortable interior, with two unobtrusive TV screens for sport. Good attention is paid to the beers on offer, and a loyal following of regular real ale drinkers help to choose the guest ales – stronger brews are among their favourites. Frequent Meet the Brewer sessions are held. The patio area with decking at the front provides a sunny outdoor spot. QP

CORNWALL

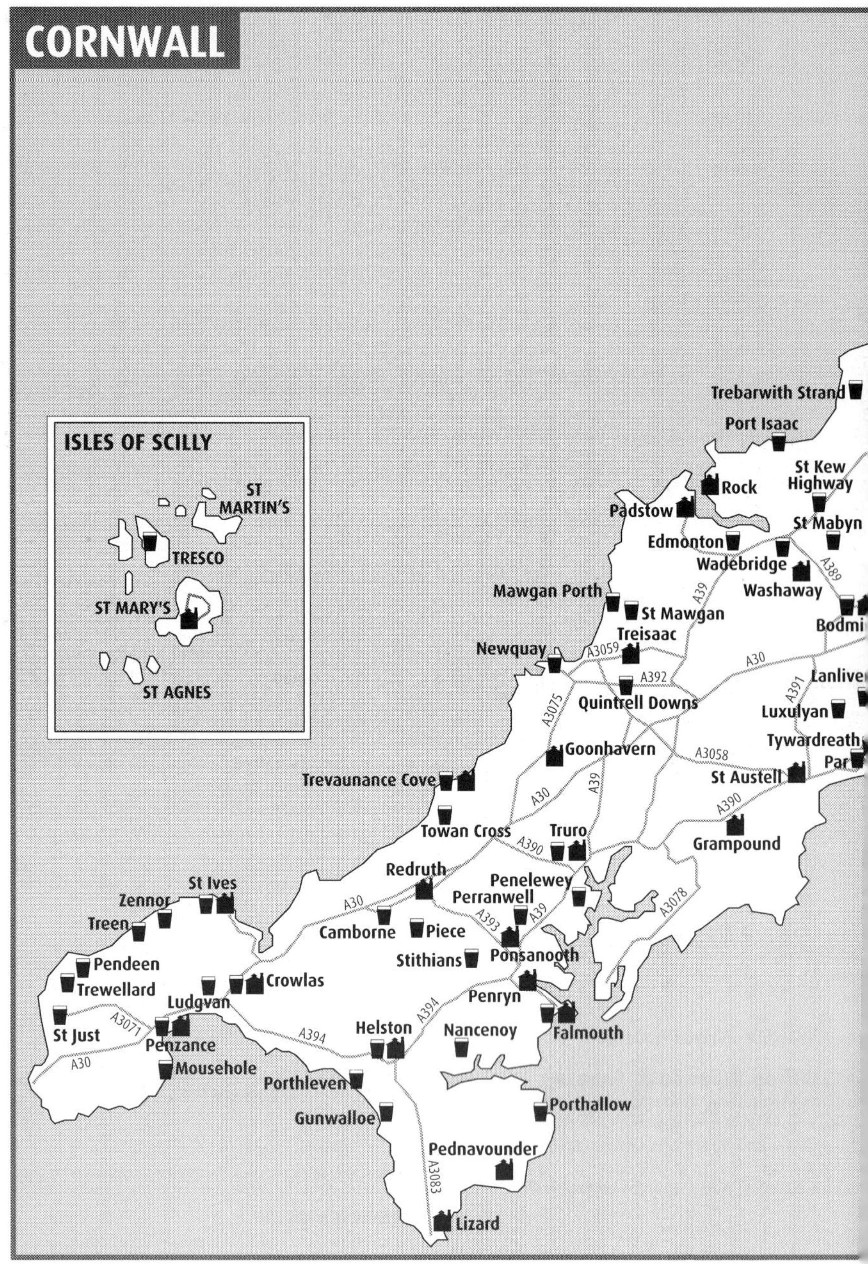

Altarnun

Rising Sun

PL15 7SN (off A30, NW of Five Lanes village) SX215825

12-2.30, 5.30-11; 12-11 Sat; 12-10.30 Sun

(01566) 86636 therisingsuninn.co.uk

Skinner's Lushingtons; 3 changing beers (sourced nationally; often Altarnun)

A thriving 150-year-old community pub and tap for nearby Altarnun Brewery on the outskirts of town. The interior of this characterful building is cosy and warm, with beamed ceilings and an open fireplace, and antique guns and various pictures on the walls. Deceptively spacious, the pub offers ample seating in the bar, two small annexes for pool and drinkers, and a separate restaurant. Outside, there is a large patio and grassed area for games. Food always uses locally sourced ingredients.

Q P

Bodmin

Chapel an Gansblydhen

Fore Street, PL31 2HR (near top of main street)

9am-midnight (10.30 Sun) (01208) 261730

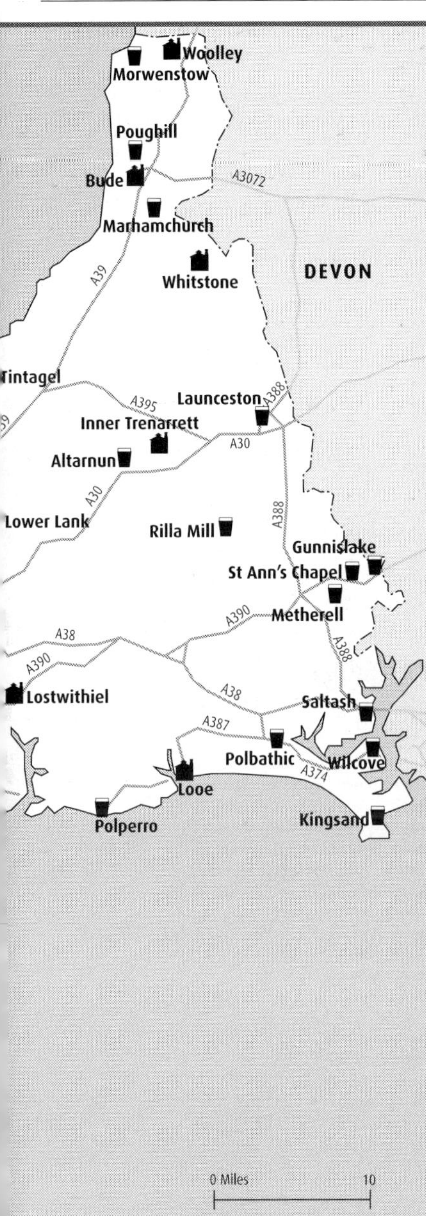

Greene King Abbot; Ruddles Best Bitter; Sharp's Doom Bar; 4 changing beers (often Cornish Crown, Harbour, Tintagel) 🄷
This busy town-centre pub has been converted from a former Methodist chapel, with many original features restored or retained. Seven ales are on offer, several from Cornish microbreweries, with two draught ciders as well. The pub supports the popular CAMRA pub guide which covers the Bodmin district, and outings to local breweries are run from time to time. Two beer festivals and a real cider festival are held annually, and a popular quiz night each Sunday. Q❀♣

Hole in the Wall 🄻 ✔
16 Crockwell Street, PL31 2DS (entrance from town car park)
12-11 (8 Sun) ☎ (01208) 72397
Butcombe Original; Sharp's Doom Bar, Sea Fury; 3 changing beers (sourced nationally; often Adnams, Dartmoor, Sharp's) 🄷
Popular locals' pub built in the 18th century as a debtors' prison. The building can be accessed direct from the public car park or through a secluded, leafy garden containing its own hop bine and stream, and presided over by a rather bleached stuffed lion. The single bar, which is subdivided by archways, contains a large and eclectic collection of antiques and military memorabilia. Upstairs is a separate function room. The pub has twice won local CAMRA Pub of the Year. Q❀♿♣

Camborne

John Francis Basset ✔
21 Commercial Street, TR14 8JZ
9am-midnight (1am Fri & Sat) ☎ (01209) 721720
Greene King Abbot; Ruddles Best Bitter; Sharp's Doom Bar; 5 changing beers 🄷
Wetherspoon pub in the town centre, in the former market house built by architect William Bond in 1866. Previous uses of the building have included a cinema, night club and a pub called the Corn Exchange. Named after a prominent former local mine owner, it is a large, airy, open-plan venue with high ceilings, tall windows and a single long bar offering an impressive selection of varying beers. A wide variety of meals is served all day 7am-11pm. Q❀♿

Crowlas

Star Inn 🄻
TR20 8DX (on A30, 3 miles E of Penzance)
11.30-11; 12-10.30 Sun ☎ (01736) 740375
Penzance Mild, Crowlas Bitter, Potion No 9; 4 changing beers (sourced nationally; often Coastal) 🄷
Roadside free house and former Cornwall CAMRA Pub of the Year, home to the Penzance Brewery. The long U-shaped bar dispenses real ales from the pub's own brewhouse and two or three from other microbreweries. There is a pool table to the right, a comfy raised seating area, a cosy lounge area with leather sofas and chairs, and an adjacent meeting room. This is essentially a beer-drinkers' local where conversation is the main entertainment, with no noisy machines to distract. ❀♣P

Edmonton

Quarryman Inn 🄻
PL27 7JA (just off A39 near Royal Cornwall showground)
12-11 (11.30 Sun) ☎ (01208) 816444
thequarryman.co.uk
Otter Bitter; Skinner's Lushingtons; 2 changing beers (sourced regionally; often Padstow) 🄷
Near the county showground, this highly popular traditional free house is well worth seeking out. Its quiet, comfortable interior features a slate-floored public bar and carpeted lounge, both with dining areas. The light, airy and eclectic decor includes sporting memorabilia and local art. The ever-changing beer menu offers up to four quality ales, generally local. Local produce is used for the food menu. The atmosphere is convivial and family-

friendly, and conversation flourishes – but mobile phone usage is prohibited. Q(11A,95)

Falmouth

'Front

Custom House Quay, TR11 3JT

11-11 (midnight Fri & Sat); 11-10.30 Sun 07977 813494

Sharp's Sea Fury; 9 changing beers (sourced regionally; often Atlantic, Skinner's, Tintagel) H

A warm welcome awaits at this quayside cellar-style bar. Friendly, knowledgeable staff are on hand to serve from 14 handpumps arranged along the bar, 12 dedicated to real ales and two to ciders. Cornish breweries are well represented, and there are regular brewery showcase sessions which can be local or regional. There is a popular Sunday quiz and other evening entertainment. No food is available, but you may bring your own. The pub offers a 10 per cent discount on real ales and ciders before 6pm. Q

Beerwolf Books

3-4 Bells Court, TR11 3AZ (up side alley off main shopping street)

10-midnight; 12-11 Sun (01326) 618474

beerwolfbooks.com

7 changing beers (sourced nationally; often Marble, Penzance, Shiny) H

Pub or bookshop? Actually, it's both! Popular with all ages, this former maritime storage loft and pleasant outside courtyard is tucked away off Market Street. It is accessed via a steep flight of stairs, at the top of which is the bookshop, while to the right is the bar with its seven handpumps dispensing an adventurous selection of constantly changing beers. Four further handpumps ensure that cider lovers are not forgotten. No food, but you may bring your own. Q

Oddfellows Arms

Quay Hill, TR11 3HA

12-11 (10.30 Sun) (01326) 218611

House beer (by Sharp's) H**; 1 changing beer (sourced locally; often Skinner's)** H/G

This small, unpretentious and traditional single-bar community pub is tucked up a hilly side street off the town centre and is popular with locals and visitors alike. Decorated with old photographs, it has a convivial atmosphere in which to enjoy the three beers normally on offer, with sometimes a fourth racked up at the back of the bar. A small room to the rear hosts the dartboard, pool table and real fire. The pub organises various festivals throughout the year, often involving food made by the locals. Q

Seven Stars ★

The Moor, TR11 3QA

11-11; 12-10.30 Sun (01326) 312111

Draught Bass; Sharp's Atlantic, Sea Fury; 2 changing beers (sourced locally) G

This timeless and unspoilt town-centre local has been in the same family for 165 years. Its originality is rightly recognised by CAMRA's National Inventory of Historic Pub Interiors. It has a lively, narrow taproom and two quiet snugs at the back. The old bottle-and-jug hatch still remains for outdoor drinkers. Beers are served on gravity from a unique, eccentrically designed stillage. Bass is ever-present, as are beers from Sharp's Brewery. The planked bar ceiling is festooned with a collection of key fobs, while the ancient bar top shows distinct signs of warping, and is often covered in an eclectic selection of bar towels. No food is served, but you may eat your own on the benches outside. A real gem that should not be missed. Q

Gunnislake

Rising Sun Inn

Calstock Road, PL18 9BX (off A390) SX432711

12-11 (midnight Fri & Sat) (01822) 832201

rising-sun-inn.co.uk

Brains Rev James; Dartmoor Legend, Jail Ale; Otter Bitter; 2 changing beers (sourced regionally) H

Friendly, oak-beamed country inn dating from the 17th century, lying in a conservation area in a rural setting off the beaten track. It has much charm and character, and serves a good choice of up to six ever-changing real ales, normally from Cornish or other West Country breweries. Exposed stone walls and wooden beams display an extensive collection of chinaware. Outside, the beautiful terraced garden affords views of the Tamar Valley. Food is available daily except Monday and Tuesday in winter. Q(79)

Gunwalloe

Halzephron Inn

TR12 7QB (off A3083 Helston-Lizard road) SW657224

11-11; 12-10.30 Sun (01326) 240406

halzephron-inn.co.uk

Sharp's Doom Bar; Skinner's Porthleven; 3 changing beers (sourced nationally) H

REAL ALE BREWERIES

Ales of Scilly St Mary's: Isles of Scilly
Altarnun Inner Trenarrett
Atlantic Treisaac
Black Flag Goonhavern
Black Rock Falmouth
Blue Anchor Helston
Bude Bude
Castle Lostwithiel
Coastal Redruth
Cornish Chough Lizard
Cornish Crown Penzance
Dowr Kammel Lower Lank
Driftwood Trevaunance Cove
Dynamite Valley Ponsanooth
Fish Key Looe
Forge Woolley
Fowey Lostwithiel
Granite Rock Penryn
Harbour Bodmin
Keltek Redruth
Leafy Hollow Washaway
Lizard Pednavounder
Longhill Whitstone
Padstow Padstow
Penzance Crowlas
Rebel Penryn
Sharp's Rock
Skinner's Truro
St Austell St Austell
St Ives St Ives
Tintagel Tintagel
Treen's Ponsanooth
Tremethick Grampound
Woodman's Ponsanooth

This quiet, welcoming 500-year-old inn was once the haunt of smugglers, who used a shaft from the pub to a still existing underground tunnel. The two traditional bars remain – the lounge doubling as a restaurant with an adjacent snug. Another restaurant area is in an extension to the rear. Accommodation is in two en-suite rooms. The pub name derives from the old Cornish 'als yffrin' meaning 'cliffs of hell' – timbers from many nearby shipwrecks were incorporated into the pub's structure. Q P

Helston

Blue Anchor

50 Coinagehall Street, TR13 8EL

10-midnight (1am Fri & Sat) ☎ (01326) 562821

spingoales.com

Blue Anchor Jubilee IPA, Middle [H], Special [H]/[G]; 1 changing beer (sourced locally; often Blue Anchor) [H]

A former monks' rest, this 15th-century brewpub is one of the oldest in Britain, changing little over the years and retaining much of its original character. Two separate small bars are found to the right of the central passageway, one with an open fire, and two sitting rooms to the left, all with slate floors. To the rear are a skittle alley and partly covered garden area with its own bar and barbecue. An anchor is visible on the thatched roof.
Q

Coinage Hall ✔

9-11 Coinagehall Street, TR13 8ER

8am-midnight (1am Fri & Sat) ☎ (01326) 565344

Ruddles Best Bitter; Sharp's Doom Bar; 4 changing beers (sourced locally; often Cornish Chough, Skinner's) [H]

This pub in a former furniture store takes its name from when locally mined tin was assayed in the coinage hall. Surprisingly large and deep inside, it spans four separate levels, with steps between them and a number of distinct drinking or dining spaces all the way through. The single long bar usually offers up to four changing local microbrewery beers. The lowest level at the rear leads out to a patio for alfresco drinking. There is also a roof terrace. Q

Kingsand

Rising Sun

The Green, PL10 1NH

closed Mon; 12-11 (10.30 Sun) ☎ (01752) 822840

Dartmoor Legend; Sharp's Atlantic; 1 changing beer (sourced locally; often Dartmoor) [H]

Once the Customs and Excise house in this village of narrow streets, and close to the coastal footpath, this is now a welcoming inn, at once both popular and quiet. Its single, spacious bar room is carpeted throughout and has partly wood-panelled walls. Prints and photos depicting old Kingsand and other nautical themes abound, and an interesting collection of toby jugs is displayed. The beer from Sharp's Brewery may occasionally vary. Vehicle access is difficult, especially in the summer months. P

Lanlivery

Crown Inn

PL30 5BT (off A390, in village centre)

12-11; 12-10.30 Sun ☎ (01208) 872707

thecrowninncornwall.co.uk

Sharp's Doom Bar; 2 changing beers (sourced locally; often Skinner's) [H]

Picturesque 12th-century listed building in a long farmhouse style, with the main bar and snug at one end. The rest of the interior comprises a comfortable lounge with an inglenook fireplace, containing a huge wood-burning stove, and the restaurant. An old well in the conservatory can be viewed through its glass cover. Food is available daily, with most of the ingredients sourced locally. Snacks are served all day in summer. Accommodation is in the former piggery, and wheelchair-accessible. Q P

Launceston

Bell Inn

1 Tower Street, PL15 8BQ

12-11 (10.30 Sun) ☎ (01566) 779970

House beer (by Holsworthy Ales); 5 changing beers (sourced regionally) [H]

Cosy 14th-century town hostelry originally built to house stonemasons erecting the nearby church. Conversation rules in this locals' pub, with a changing range of mostly local beers and two ciders, although the selection may be reduced out of season. A separate family room, available for local groups to use, has some ancient frescoes uncovered when previous owners stripped away decades of modernisation. Chess and other board games are played. Food is limited to a pasty or pork pie. Q

Ludgvan

White Hart

Churchtown, TR20 8EY (on B3309)

11.30-2.30, 5.30-10.30; 11.30-10.30 Wed & Thu (11 Fri & Sat); 11.30-10 Sun ☎ (01736) 740574

whitehartludgvan.co.uk

Fuller's London Pride; Sharp's Doom Bar; Skinner's Betty Stogs; 2 changing beers [H]

A recently refurbished 14th-century inn by the village church. Bare floorboards reflect the pub's age, and two large wood-burning stoves, wooden partitions, interesting furniture and photographs lend the alcoves and corners an authentic atmosphere. It has a separate restaurant, front dining room and a tiny snug under the stairs. Patios at the front and back and a large, quiet garden with wooden benches at the rear allow for alfresco drinking. All the real ales are handpumped, despite what it says on the board on the wall outside.
P (16)

Luxulyan

King's Arms ✔

Bridges, PL30 5EF SX048580

11-11 ☎ (01726) 850202 kingsarmsluxulyan.org

St Austell Trelawny, Tribute, Proper Job, HSD; 1 changing beer (sourced locally; often St Austell) [H]

Archetypal Cornish granite pub known locally as Bridges, with a welcome for locals and visitors alike. The large L-shaped bar caters for both drinkers and diners – a varied food menu is served daily along with Sunday roasts. Unusually, the pub has a defibrillator on site. The Kings can be accessed via the beautiful Luxulyan Valley, a World Heritage Site whose industrial past is still visible.

The pub is on the local rail ale trail and hosts a beer festival every June.
(101)

Marhamchurch

Buller's Arms Hotel

Helebridge Road, EX23 0HB (off A39 S of Bude)
12 (4 Mon-Fri winter)-11 (01288) 361277
thebullersarmshotel.com
Greene King Abbot; St Austell Cornish Best Bitter; Sharp's Atlantic; Tintagel Arthur's Ale; house beer (by Tintagel); 1 changing beer (sourced locally; often Longhill)
Large, community-oriented village pub/hotel with a spacious beamed and slate-flagged bar room. Decorative bric-a-brac includes buffalo horns, a stuffed fox and a badger at one end of the room, while the other end hosts a dartboard, pool table and an upright piano. The beers may vary occasionally but are generally from local breweries. The pub holds quiz nights and monthly live weekend entertainment. An under-fives soft play area is available most afternoons, and birthday party hosting on Saturday.
Q (218)

Mawgan Porth

Merrymoor

TR8 4BA (beside B3276 coast road, overlooking beach)
10-midnight (11 Sun) (01637) 860258
merrymoorinn.com
St Austell Tribute; Sharp's Doom Bar, Original; 1 changing beer (sourced locally; often Bath Ales)
Originally a café whose owner served in the North African campaign, hence the name. Now an atmospheric pub run by the same family since 1961, it is very much at the heart of the local community and raises huge sums for charity every year. Large picture windows overlook the sandy beach just 50 yards away. It is naturally busy in the season, and has a large beer garden, a spacious main bar and a separate family room.
P (A5,171)

Metherell

Carpenter's Arms

Lower Metherell, PL17 8BJ SX408695
2-11; 12-midnight Fri & Sat; 12-10.30 Sun
(01579) 351148
Sharp's Doom Bar; 2 changing beers (sourced locally)
Hard to find down a network of country lanes, this timeless, friendly 15th-century pub is full of character and atmosphere. The public bar is flagged with slate, while heavy black beams are held in place by massive exposed stone walls, in contrast to the larger lounge, which also functions as a dining area. All food is freshly cooked on-site. The guest ales change constantly. Outdoor seating is on the suntrap terrace and the pub hosts a monthly local produce market. Q P (79)

Morwenstow

Bush Inn

Crosstown, EX23 9SR (off A39 N of Kilkhampton) SS208150
12-midnight (11 Sun) (01288) 331242
thebushinnmorwenstow.com
St Austell Tribute, HSD; 1 changing beer (sourced locally; often Forge, Tintagel)
Unassuming from the outside, this little gem is an ancient former chapel, dating in parts back to 950AD. Inside, it is simply furnished, with slate floors, granite walls and exposed beams in two small bar rooms, one of which is subdivided into separate drinking areas. Conversation is the main entertainment, although there is occasional live music. A large garden offers outstanding views over the Tidna Valley and out to sea. Four en-suite rooms and a two-person holiday cottage are available. Q P (217,219)

Mousehole

Old Coastguard Hotel

The Parade, TR19 6PR
10.30-11.30 (01736) 731222
oldcoastguardhotel.co.uk
3 changing beers (sourced locally)
Built on the sloping cliff at the village edge, this attractive hotel was formerly the coastguard station. Its wooden-floored single-bar interior has several stepped levels accommodating numerous drinking and dining areas, tastefully furnished throughout. An ever-changing beer menu generally features locally brewed ales. An interesting food menu is available daily. The large terraced tropical-style garden down the cliff affords stunning views of St Clement's Isle and Mounts Bay. Parking is in the adjoining public car park.
Q (6)

Nancenoy

Trengilly Wartha Inn

TR11 5RP (off B3291 near Constantine) SW732283
11 (12 Sun)-3.15, 6-11 (01326) 340332
trengilly.co.uk
Penzance Potion No 9; Sharp's Original; 2 changing beers (sourced locally)
This versatile inn lies in extensive grounds including a lake, in an isolated, steeply wooded valley – the pub's name means 'settlement above the trees'. Originally a farmhouse, it has a variety of rooms and furnishings, the wood-beamed bar displaying pictures by local artists. A conservatory extension doubles as a family room. The real ales are mainly from local microbreweries, while a wide-ranging and imaginative food menu uses fresh local produce from named suppliers. Accommodation includes garden rooms and safari tents. Q P

Newquay

Red Lion

North Quay Hill, TR7 1HE (NW of town centre overlooking harbour)
12-midnight (01637) 872195 redlionnewquay.co.uk
Sharp's Doom Bar, Atlantic, Sea Fury; Skinner's Betty Stogs, Cornish Knocker, Porthleven; 2 changing beers (sourced nationally; often Thornbridge, Timothy Taylor)
Deceptively spacious open-plan pub with a flagstoned bar, overlooking the north quay of Newquay's historic harbour. It offers eight real ales and six real ciders, and was CAMRA Cornish Cider Pub of the Year in 2016. With a diverse food menu and live bands on Friday and Saturday nights, it attracts both locals and tourists. Warmed by a log

fire in winter, the pub is within easy walking distance of the town centre and is dog-friendly. P

Par

Royal Inn

66 Eastcliff Road, PL24 2AJ (outside railway station)
11-11 (midnight Fri & Sat) ☎ (01726) 815601
royal-inn.co.uk
Sharp's Doom Bar, Original; 2 changing beers (sourced regionally) Ⓗ
Large one-bar establishment, a family pub serving bar food and full meals in the separate raised dining room, and popular for eating out. In warmer weather, the large patio allows alfresco eating and drinking. The pub acquired its 'Royal' tag when the then Prince of Wales' train broke down nearby in the late 19th century. Quiz night is Wednesday, live performances are on Saturday evenings. Accommodation comprises 15 en-suite rooms. P (24,25)

Pendeen

North Inn ✔

TR19 7DN (on B3306)
12-midnight ☎ (01736) 788417
thenorthinnpendeen.co.uk
St Austell Cornish Best Bitter, Tribute, Proper Job Ⓗ
Welcoming locals' pub in an old mining village, close to the famous Geevor and Levant tin mines. The single large room has beamed ceilings and is carpeted throughout; the decor includes mining and other local pictures, and a tank of tropical fish. The food menu features a comprehensive range of curries. The inn is close to the coastal path and offers accommodation in two double rooms as well as a campsite. The small upstairs restaurant affords outstanding seaward views. Q P

Penelewey

Punchbowl & Ladle ✔

TR3 6QY (1 mile off A39 near Playing Place)
10.30-11 (midnight Fri & Sat); 12-11 Sun
☎ (01872) 862237 punchbowlandladle.com
St Austell Cornish Best Bitter, Tribute, Proper Job, HSD Ⓗ
Rambling 15th-century two-bar thatched country pub on split levels, with many cosy nooks and snugs, and a separate restaurant area. The main bar area attracts a lively mix of drinkers and diners; the smaller bar at the rear is mainly used by locals enjoying a quieter beer and a chat. The decor includes plenty of bric-a-brac – brasses, mugs and a large collection of bottle openers – and pictures of sailing ships mixed in with old local scenes, complemented by a large model of a ship.
Q P (493)

Penzance

Crown 🄻

Victoria Square, TR18 2EP
12-11 (midnight Fri & Sat); 12-10.30 Sun
☎ (01736) 351070 thecrownpenzance.co.uk
4 changing beers (sourced locally; often Cornish Crown) Ⓗ
Close to the railway and bus stations, and brewery tap for Cornish Crown, this small, traditional community local is tucked away behind the main shopping street. Offering a relaxed, friendly atmosphere, it has a tidily furnished bar with upholstered window seats and a huge mirror covering one wall, and a cosy two-table snug at the rear. The real ales are usually from Crown, although an occasional guest brew appears. You may bring your own food, with plates provided.
Q

Dock Inn

17 Quay Street, TR18 4BD
11-11 (midnight Fri & Sat); 11-10.30 Sun
☎ (01736) 362833
Blue Anchor Middle; Sharp's Doom Bar; 1 changing beer (sourced locally; often Penzance) Ⓗ
Old and traditional one-time fishermen's pub near the dockside, close to the Scilly ferry pier. The pub extends through two old cottages, with the bar in the upper level, and a comfortable lounge next door also serving as a dining area. The decor includes a large picture mirror, nautical and mining pictures and bric-a-brac including a stuffed bird in a cage. A ship's figurehead oversees proceedings in the bar. The guest beer is often from Penzance Brewery. P

Perranwell

Royal Oak 🄻

TR3 7PX
11.30-3, 6-midnight; 11.30-midnight Fri & Sat; 12-11.30 Sun ☎ (01872) 863175
theroyaloakperranwellstation.co.uk
Sharp's Doom Bar; 3 changing beers (sourced locally; often Harbour, Skinner's) Ⓗ
Small, sociable 18th-century cottage-style village community pub with an emphasis on good food – most of the tables are set for meals, but drinkers are equally welcome, as the many locals at the bar will testify. Booking for meals is advisable however, especially evenings. The beers vary frequently and are often from local breweries. The pub holds monthly quiz nights and fundraising events for local charities.
Q P (36,46)

Piece

Countryman Inn

TR16 6SG (on Four Lanes-Pool road) SW679398
11-11 (midnight Sat); 12-11 Sun ☎ (01209) 215960
Courage Best Bitter, Directors; St Austell Tribute; Skinner's Betty Stogs, 7 Hop; Theakston Old Peculier; 1 changing beer (sourced nationally) Ⓗ
Once a grocery shop for the miners, this is now a lively community pub set high among old copper mines near the distinctive landmark of Carn Brea. The larger of the two bars is overlooked by a granite fireplace and a massive cast-iron, coal-fired cooking range, while the smaller room is more of a public bar in style and welcomes families. The pub hosts entertainment most nights, and a raffle in support of local charities on Sunday lunchtime.
P (442)

Polbathic

Halfway House 🄻

PL11 3EY (on A387 between Trerulefoot and Torpoint)
12-11 (midnight Fri & Sat) ☎ (01503) 232986
halfwayhousepolbathic.co.uk

Dartmoor Jail Ale; St Austell Tribute; 1 changing beer (sourced regionally; often Exeter) Ⓗ
Sixteenth-century former coaching inn, village local and community library. It is surprisingly large inside, with separate public and lounge bars, and further rooms beyond that used for dining. The smallish public bar is the focus of the pub's daily life, hosting the pool table and dartboard, and features an unusual stone fireplace with an old wagon wheel above. A large beer garden at the rear is on a steep hillside and reached via flights of steps. ♨❀⇌◑♿♣●P🚌(72)🐾

Polperro

Blue Peter Inn 𝕃 ✔

Quay Road, PL13 2QZ (far end of W side of harbour)
⏲ 8.30am-11 (10.30 Sun) ☎ (01503) 272743
🌐 thebluepeterinn.yolasite.com
St Austell Tribute; Sharp's Original; 4 changing beers (sourced regionally; often Bays, Cornish Crown, Harbour) Ⓗ
Named after the naval flag, this friendly inn is reached up a flight of steps near the quay, and is the only pub with a sea view in the village. In summer the pub offers up to five ales from Cornwall and Devon, and a varied menu of home-cooked dishes available all day. Featuring low beams, wooden floors, unusual souvenirs and work by local artists, the pub is popular with locals, fishermen and visitors – and their dogs.
♨◑Å♣🐾📶

Crumplehorn Inn 𝕃

The Old Mill, Crumplehorn, PL13 2RJ (on A387, top of town near coach park)
⏲ 10-11; 11-11 Sun ☎ (01503) 272348
🌐 thecrumplehorninn.co.uk
Rebel Bal Maiden, Penryn Pale Ale; St Austell Trelawny, Tribute; Tintagel Castle Gold, Harbour Special; 1 changing beer Ⓗ
Once a mill and mentioned in the Domesday Book, this 14th-century inn at the entrance to the village still has a working waterwheel outside. The split-level bar has three comfortable areas with low ceilings and flagstone floors, and a spacious outside patio by the millstream offers large umbrellas as sunshades. A varied menu includes locally sourced food. Accommodation is B&B or self-catering. In summer, catch the milk float tram down to the harbour from the nearby public car park. Q♨❀⇌◑Å♣P🚌🐾📶

Port Isaac

Golden Lion ✔

13 Fore Street, PL29 3RB
⏲ 12-11 (midnight Sat; 10.30 Sun) ☎ (01208) 880336
🌐 thegoldenlionportisaac.co.uk
St Austell Tribute, Proper Job, HSD; 1 changing beer (sourced locally; often St Austell) Ⓗ
This fine old 18th-century pub in the heart of Port Isaac has several drinking areas and a small balcony overlooking the harbour. Beware the slightly uneven bare-boarded floors, which together with Victorian cast-iron fireplaces earn it recognition on CAMRA's inventory of historic pub interiors. The games room downstairs was originally the Bloody Bones locals' bar, and boasts a smugglers' tunnel down to a causeway on the beach. A small flagstoned courtyard at the rear offers alfresco drinking. ♨❀◑♣🚌(96)🐾📶

Porthallow

Five Pilchards

TR12 6PP (down narrow lanes, NNE of St Keverne) SW797232
⏲ 12-11 summer; 12-3 (not Mon), 6-11; 12-11 Sun winter
☎ (01326) 280256 🌐 thefivepilchards.co.uk
4 changing beers (sourced regionally; often Bays, Cornish Chough) Ⓗ
In an isolated beachside location, this popular community local is well worth finding. Its open-plan layout has distinct drinking and dining areas, furnished with wooden settles, tables and chairs. The bar area with its wood-planked floor and beamed ceiling is festooned with nautical odds and ends of all kinds, overlooked by enormous scale models of local harbour tugs and a lifeboat. There are up to four real ales offered, frequently changing but usually including a Bays brew, and a locally made cider. Q♨❀⇌◑♣●P🐾

Porthleven

Ship Inn

Mount Pleasant Road, TR13 9JS
⏲ 11-midnight ☎ (01326) 564204
🌐 theshipinnporthleven.co.uk
Sharp's Cornish Coaster, Doom Bar; Skinner's Porthleven; Tintagel Harbour Special; 1 changing beer (sourced locally; often Black Rock) Ⓗ
Seventeeth-century fishermen's inn perched on the south-west corner of the harbour, accessed up a steep flight of steps. It enjoys a commanding view over the harbour; here you can sit comfortably and watch the rough seas on stormy days. The open, if rambling, split-level interior has wooden and slated floors, and beams decorated with an eclectic mix of coins, banknotes, beermats and brass artefacts, and sketches of local characters. A large log fire warms the pub in winter. ♨❀◑🚌(U4)🐾

Poughill

Preston Gate Inn

Poughill Road, EX23 9ET (just outside Bude, on Sandymouth Bay road) SS224077
⏲ 11-11 ☎ (01288) 354017 🌐 prestongateinn.co.uk
Dartmoor Jail Ale; Skinner's Lushingtons; 2 changing beers (sourced locally; often Holsworthy Ales, Tintagel) Ⓗ
Cosy 16th-century building, originally two cottages, opening as a village pub in 1983. The spacious U-shaped room hosts a dartboard at one end of the bar; the other, roomier, end has more seating and a roaring log fire in winter. Conversation rules here, and the pub is home to darts and quiz teams. Meals include monthly theme nights (booking advised). The beer range may reduce in winter and the cider varies. The name Preston comes from the Cornish word for priest.
Q♨❀◑Å♣●P🚌(128)🐾📶

Quintrell Downs

Two Clomes

East Road, TR8 4PD (on A392)
⏲ 11.30-11 ☎ (01637) 879737
Sharp's Doom Bar; 2 changing beers (sourced locally; often Harbour, Padstow) Ⓗ
Named after the two ovens situated either side of the open fireplace – which is now fitted with a

wood-burning stove – this 18th-century free house is popular for dining out. Various extensions to the original building have added a large restaurant (booking is advisable, even in winter). The pub, on the Atlantic Coast Line Rail Ale Trail, is conveniently situated on a main route into Newquay, and close to campsites. ❀◑◗♿Ⓐ⇌♣P🚌(21,92)🐾

Rilla Mill

Manor House Inn

PL17 7NT (NE of Liskeard off B3254)
🕓 12-3, 5-11; 12-11 Sat & Sun ☎ (01579) 362354
🌐 manorhouserilla.co.uk
Draught Bass; Sharp's Original; 1 changing beer (sourced locally) Ⓗ
This is a comfortable, traditional 17th-century inn and restaurant in the upper Lynher Valley, on the edge of Bodmin Moor, allegedly haunted by three ghosts. It has three main rooms, one of which has a slated and carpeted floor, the other two comprising the restaurant areas. The changing beer is frequently varied but generally sourced from a local brewery, and meals also use local produce. The pub is situated near the Sterts open air theatre and a dairy that makes Cornish cheeses.
Q❀◑◗♣P🚌(236)🐾

St Ann's Chapel

Rifle Volunteer Inn

PL18 9HL (on A390)
🕓 11.30-11 ☎ (01822) 833038 🌐 theriflevolunteer.co.uk
St Austell Tribute; 2 changing beers (sourced regionally; often Keltek) Ⓗ
A former mine captain's house, converted to a coaching inn during the mid-19th century. The main bar has been extended to accommodate a conservatory, popular with diners for its view over the garden. Meals are made using locally sourced ingredients. A separate public bar caters for more dedicated drinkers and hosts a pool table and dartboard. The changing beer, usually from a local brewery, varies regularly. The pub offers panoramic views across the Tamar Valley and is in good walking country. Q❀◑◗♿♣●P🚌(79)🐾

St Ives

Pilchard Press Alehouse ✔

Wharf Road, TR26 1LF
🕓 closed Mon & Tue; 4-11; 12-11 Sun ☎ (01736) 791665
6 changing beers (sourced locally) Ⓗ/Ⓖ
Cornwall's first micropub, the Pilchard Press opened in 2016, with space for around 20-25 people. Easy to miss, it is situated up an alley off the harbour front. This friendly pub has up to six real ales in casks racked up on an interesting wooden stillage. Real cider is sometimes available. The wood-topped bar has a few bar stools to sit on and there are two tables with chairs and a smaller chessboard table. Note that the pub may close early if the beer runs out. QⒶ⇌●🚌🐾

St Just

Star Inn ✔

1 Fore Street, TR19 7LL
🕓 11.30-midnight (11.30 Sun) ☎ (01736) 788767
🌐 thestarinn-stjust.co.uk
St Austell Cornish Best Bitter, Tribute, Proper Job; 2 changing beers (sourced regionally; often Bath Ales, St Austell) Ⓗ
Banter is guaranteed at this simple 18th-century granite inn, where good ale and conversation rule. The pub has changed little over time, its atmospheric interior, with wooden furnishings and an open fire, generating a traditional ambience. Celtic flags adorn the beamed ceiling, and artefacts of former mining and maritime activities are displayed on the walls. An adjacent snug is used for various activities, and there is a walled beer garden. Up to five ales are offered, but no food is available. Q❀♿Ⓐ♣🚌🐾

St Kew Highway

Red Lion Inn Ⓛ

PL30 3DN (just off A39)
🕓 12-3 (not Mon-Fri), 5.30-11; 12-11 (4 winter) Sun
☎ (01208) 841271 🌐 redlionstkew.com
3 changing beers (sourced regionally; often Padstow) Ⓗ
Fully community-oriented, this picturesque and friendly family-run 17th-century pub is central to village activities. Its L-shaped single bar interior divides distinctly in two – the front area mainly for drinking, though it includes an elevated dining space, and the rear a restaurant for more leisurely dining. Comfortably furnished throughout, open fires add to the pub's cosy, relaxed ambience. Up to three ales are offered, two in winter, all from local breweries. Interesting freshly cooked meals feature local produce. Well worth a visit.
Q❀◑◗ⒶP🚌(95)🐾

St Mabyn

St Mabyn Inn

Churchtown, PL30 3BA
🕓 12-midnight (11 Sun) ☎ (01208) 841266
🌐 stmabyninn.com
Sharp's Doom Bar, Sea Fury; Tintagel Cornwall's Pride; 1 changing beer (sourced locally) Ⓗ
Near the church stands this popular, attractive, 17th-century free house, a village local where conversation thrives. It features a single bar with adjoining snug, games room and stylish well-appointed restaurant, and an attractive beer garden outside. Open fires and wood furnishings including settles, stained-glass partitions and windows add character, complemented by an interesting collection of toby jugs, horse brasses and vintage advertising. With four quality ales and an ever-changing menu specialising in local produce, this pub is one to seek.
Q❀◑◗♿Ⓐ♣●P🚌(55)🐾

St Mawgan

Falcon Inn Ⓛ

TR8 4EP (near Newquay airport)
🕓 11-11 (midnight Fri & Sat); 12-11 Sun summer; 11-3, 5.30-11; 11-midnight Fri & Sat; 12-11 Sun winter
☎ (01637) 860225 🌐 thefalconinnstmawgan.co.uk
Dartmoor Legend; 2 changing beers (sourced locally; often Harbour, Padstow) Ⓗ
Attractive community pub at the centre of this village in the idyllic setting of the Lanherne Valley. The single bar exudes a warm, welcoming atmosphere, with the decor reflecting country life. The pub is popular for meals, served in a separate

dining room. There is also a games room and a large garden. The pub's history dates back to 1758 and its name comes from the coat of arms of the owners of the estate. P (A5)

Saltash

Union Inn

Tamar Street, PL12 4EL (on waterfront beneath bridges)
11-11; 12-10.30 Sun (01752) 844770
Dartmoor Legend, Jail Ale; Sharp's Doom Bar [H]; 2 changing beers (sourced regionally; often Bays) [G]
The frontage of this riverside local, overlooked by the Tamar bridges, is strikingly painted as a union flag. The single bar offers a selection of real ales and a varying guest beer, usually on gravity in the cellar. The draught cider is Sam's Devon Dry. Outside drinking is at tables overlooking the river. Live music features on Tuesday or weekend evenings. Tamar Street, the pub's location, used to be known as Pickle Cock Alley, as shellfish were sold through open windows. Q P

Stithians

Seven Stars Inn

Church Road, TR3 7DH
12-11 (midnight Fri & Sat) (01209) 860003
sevenstarsstithians.net
St Austell Trelawny, Tribute; 1 changing beer (sourced nationally; often Bath Ales) [H]
Lively cottage-style village local, used by a broad cross-section of the community and supportive of local events and sports teams. The pub was originally purpose-built as a farmhouse extension to serve the drinking needs of tin miners at the end of the 19th century. The original bar and lounge (note the adjacent twin front doors) are now merged into one L-shaped drinking/dining area, with a later extension added towards the rear housing the pool table.
Q (36,442)

Towan Cross

Victory Inn

TR4 8BN
12-11 (01209) 890359
St Austell Tribute; Skinner's Betty Stogs, Lushingtons; 1 changing beer (sourced locally) [H]
Built originally to serve local miners, this 16th-century inn is now a convivial family-run free house sitting atop the cliffs above Porthtowan. The open-plan interior separates into drinking and dining areas with an adjoining conservatory. A large beer garden and a capacious car park adjoin the pub. Comfortably furnished throughout, its atmosphere is quiet and relaxing. Various sporting souvenirs decorate the bar area. An interesting, good-quality menu is offered daily. An additional local ale is usually available in the summer.
Q P (304,315)

Trebarwith Strand

Mill House Inn

PL34 0HD (off B3263, near Tintagel) SX058865
11-11; 12-10.30 Sun (01840) 770200
themillhouseinn.co.uk
Tintagel Castle Gold, Cornwall's Pride [H]; house beer (by Tintagel) [G]
Converted 16th-century corn mill and waterwheel set beside a stream in a deep wooded valley. This friendly inn has a stone-flagged bar area accessible up a flight of steps by the adjacent drinking terrace, with a dartboard and pool table. The restaurant is in an extension, offering an imaginative, daily changing food menu. While the Mill House is primarily a food and accommodation establishment, drinkers are nevertheless welcome in the bar, with a mix of local beers from nearby Tintagel Brewery. Q P

Treen

Gurnard's Head Hotel

TR26 3DE (on B3306, Lands End-St Ives coast road)
10-11 (11.30 Sun) (01736) 796928
gurnardshead.co.uk
St Austell Tribute; 3 changing beers (sourced locally) [H]
Named after the nearby headland, this strikingly coloured inn stands near the coastal path. Its wood-floored interior comprises a large bar, cosy snug and stylish restaurant. Wooden furnishings, comfy sofas and open fires create a relaxed atmosphere, with local art adorning the walls. The ever-changing beer range features mainly Cornish microbreweries. Daily variations to the food menu reflect availability of local produce. Community-oriented, the pub holds weekly Cornish cultural evenings, and other events are staged in the large lawned gardens.
Q P (7,16A)

Tresco (Isles of Scilly)

New Inn

Townshill, TR24 0QG
11-11 summer; closed Mon & Wed; 11-3 (not Tue), 6-11; 11-10.30 Sun winter (01720) 423006
Sharp's Doom Bar; 3 changing beers (sourced locally; often Ales of Scilly, St Austell, Skinner's) [H]
Excellent old pub near New Grimsby harbour, a haven between demanding coastal walks and the boat to St Mary's. Extensions to the garden and a covered pavilion have added to the attractions of this popular real ale outlet. The varying beers are mostly from Cornish breweries, often Skinner's and St Austell, and local brewer Ales of Scilly is frequently represented. Beer festivals are held over the spring and late summer bank holidays.
Q

Trevaunance Cove

Driftwood Spars

Quay Road, TR5 0RT
8am-11 (1am Fri & Sat); 11-11 Sun (01872) 552428
driftwoodspars.com
Sharp's Doom Bar; 5 changing beers (sourced locally; often Atlantic, Driftwood, Harbour) [H]
This friendly brewpub has it all! A former 17th-century sail loft and mine warehouse, it features three wood-beamed bars, lead-light windows and cosy open granite fireplaces. The decor is mainly smuggling and shipwreck-themed. Upstairs, the restaurant affords panoramic views across the bay, while over the road the beer garden adjoins the Driftwood Brewery, whose beers are always on the bar alongside favourite regional guests.
Q P (57,87)

ENGLAND

Trewellard

Trewellard Arms

Trewellard Road, TR19 7TA (on B3318/B3306 jct)
12-11 (midnight Sat); 12-10.30 Sun ☎ (01736) 788634
6 changing beers (sourced regionally; often Bays, Tintagel) Ⓗ
Formerly the nearby Geevor mine owner's residence, this is now a thriving family-run free house, where a warm welcome is assured. Its cosy interior accommodates a spacious open-beamed single bar and pleasant restaurant with secluded dining space. Open fires enhance the homely atmosphere. A varying beer menu offers up to six ales and two ciders, and good-value home-cooked food is available. The frontage includes a paved patio area and an extensive car park. A beer festival is held each May. **Q**♣**P**

Truro

Old Ale House

7 Quay Street, TR1 2HD (near the bus station)
11-11 (11.30 Mon & Fri; midnight Sat); 12-10.30 Sun
☎ (01872) 271122 old-ale-house.co.uk
Skinner's Betty Stogs, Hops 'n' Honey, Lushingtons, Cornish Knocker, Porthleven Ⓗ**; 3 changing beers (sourced regionally; often Skinner's)** Ⓗ/Ⓖ
This relaxed, friendly and lively city-centre pub is Skinner's brewery tap. The main bar is atmospheric, with subtle lighting, wooden floors, beamed ceiling, scattered artefacts and a barrel of free monkey nuts. Seating is plentiful, while upstairs is a quieter drinking area and function room. Up to 13 real ales and six real ciders are on offer, as well as an impressive range of up to 40 craft keg and foreign beers. Customers may bring in their own food. **Q**♣

Rising Sun

Mitchell Hill, TR1 1ED
11.30-midnight; 12-midnight Sun; closed Mon winter
☎ (01872) 240003 risingsuntruro.co.uk
Fuller's London Pride; Skinner's Betty Stogs; 2 changing beers (sourced locally; often Skinner's) Ⓖ
Near the city centre up a steep hill, this award-winning pub is worth seeking out. Its narrow frontage belies a spacious interior accommodating a small public bar with adjacent dining area, a lounge bar and a raised restaurant area. Comfortably furnished throughout, the decor includes old Truro scenes. Up to four ales from a wide beer range are dispensed straight from casks. The locally sourced food menu is popular – booking is advised. Outside is a sheltered patio where periodic beer festivals are held.
Q♣**P**

Tywardreath

New Inn

Fore Street, PL24 2QP
12-11 ☎ (01726) 813901
Draught Bass Ⓖ**; St Austell Trelawny, Tribute, Proper Job; 1 changing beer** Ⓗ
Built in the mid-18th century by mine owners, this classic village pub is a perfect example of a community local and the hub of village life. Groups meet here regularly, and fêtes are held in the extensive gardens. Although tied to a brewery, the landlord serves a guest beer and Draught Bass, which the pub is covenanted to sell in perpetuity. Pub games, good conversation and regular live music provide the entertainment. There is a separate restaurant area to the rear.
Q♣**P**(24)

Wadebridge

Ship Inn

Gonvena Hill, PL27 6DF (across bridge from town centre)
12-2, 5-11; 12-10 (5 winter) Sun ☎ (01208) 813845
shipinnwadebridge.co.uk
Sharp's Doom Bar, Sea Fury; 1 changing beer (sourced locally) Ⓗ
Across the river from the town centre, this award-winning pub is a popular local venue. Its extensive, stylish interior accommodates a single lounge bar adjoining a split-level and well-appointed restaurant, in turn leading to a courtyard and suntrap patio decking. Open fires and a tasteful, nautical-style decor contribute to a relaxing atmosphere. Beamed ceilings, leaded windows and wooden and upholstered furnishings all add character. The additional guest ale is often chosen by customer ballot. Local produce features in the ever-changing food menu.
Q♣**P**

Wilcove

Wilcove Inn

PL11 2PG (off A374, 1 mile from Torpoint ferry)
SX430564
5.30-11; 12-midnight Fri & Sat; 12-10.30 Sun
☎ (01752) 812381 thewilcoveinn.co.uk
St Austell Tribute; Sharp's Doom Bar; 1 changing beer (sourced locally; often Roam) Ⓗ
Traditional country village pub, tucked away beside a secluded creek off the River Tamar. Food is an important part of its trade, but it is community-focused, welcoming children and dogs on leads, and holding quiz nights and an annual beer festival in aid of charity. The changing beer is usually from a microbrewery. On fine days, enjoy the palm trees in the garden and views across the river. Beware, though, that spring tides can often flood the road and car park. **Q**♣**P**

Zennor

Tinners Arms

TR26 3BY (off B3306 St Ives-St Just coast road)
11.30-11; 12-10.30 Sun ☎ (01736) 796927
tinnersarms.com
House beer (by St Austell); 2 changing beers (sourced locally; often Skinner's) Ⓗ
Popular with cliff walkers and tourists drawn by a local mermaid legend (explained in the nearby museum), this ancient village free house is near the Penwith north coast. The atmospheric interior accommodates a single bar and adjacent restaurant, the cosy ambience enhanced by exposed granite walls and wood beams, open fires, wall panels and rustic furnishings. An attractive food menu features local produce. Outside are a sheltered beer garden, adjacent car park and cottage accommodation. Folk music features on Thursday evening.
Q♣**P**

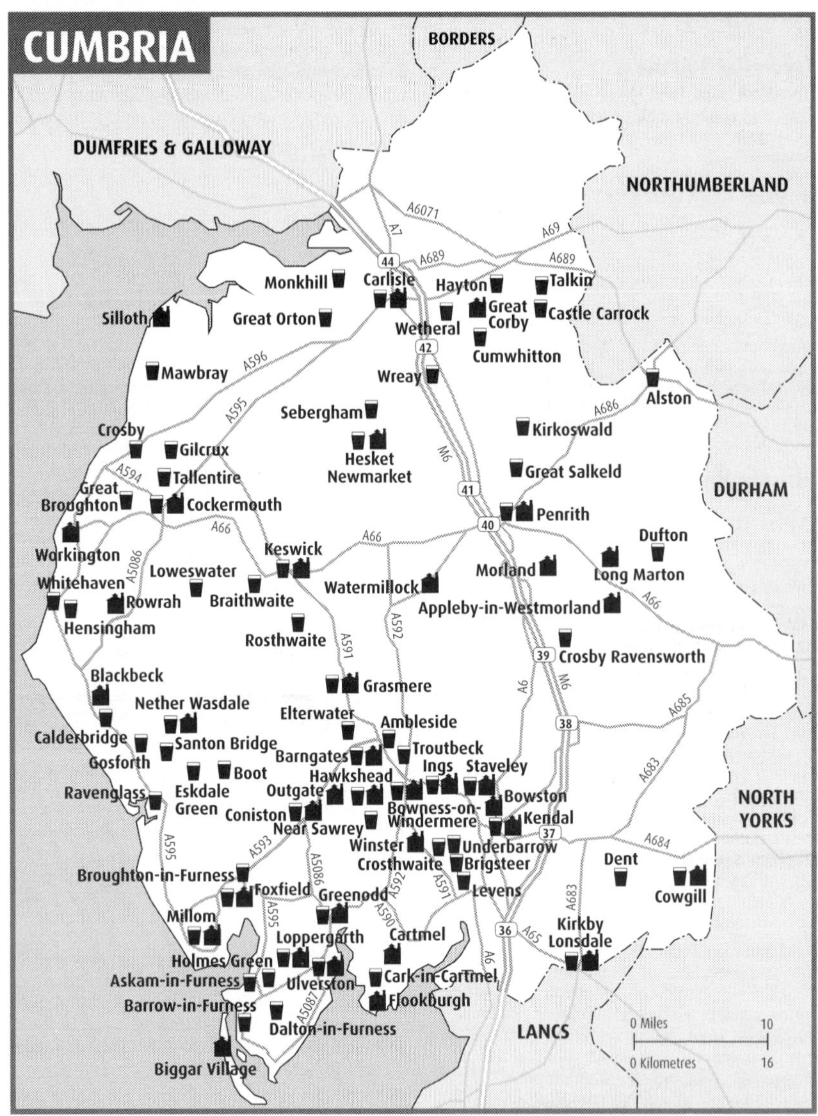

Alston

Cumberland Inn 🄻

Townfoot, CA9 3HX

12-11 ☎ (01434) 381875 alstoncumberlandhotel.co.uk

4 changing beers Ⓗ

A family-run 19th-century inn set in an Area of Outstanding Natural Beauty overlooking the South Tyne River. Close to the Coast-to-Coast cycle route and Pennine Way, it is an ideal base to explore the highest market town in England. Guest beers have come from Hesket Newmarket, Consett Ale Works, Allendale, High House Farm and Mordue as well as breweries further afield. Old Rosie is a regular real cider, with two or three other changing ciders and perries. Q❀⇌◑●P🚌🐾

Turks Head

Market Place, CA9 3HS

3-1am; 12-1am Sat & Sun ☎ (01434) 381148

Caledonian Deuchars IPA; 1 changing beer Ⓗ

Overlooking the market cross and cobbled square, the Turks Head dates from 1646 and was the first public house in the town. Now a traditional drinkers' venue, it has a cosy real fire in winter and is home to darts teams as well as dominoes players. The pub is a popular stop-off for walkers in the area. Hours of opening are flexible so please check before travelling. ❀♣P🚌🐾

Ambleside

Lily Bar

12-14 Lake Road, LA22 0AD

12-11 (midnight Fri & Sat) ☎ (015394) 33175

thelilybar.co.uk

Cumbrian Legendary Ales Loweswater Gold; 3 changing beers (sourced locally) Ⓗ

A former wine bar with a large main bar catering for locals and visitors alike, and especially popular with the local student population. Live music is often featured, with an open mic night on the first Sunday of the month. There is a good selection of bottled beers and an extensive range of cocktails. Occasional comedy nights are also a feature.

Askam-in-Furness

Railway Inn

24 Ireleth Road, LA16 7DJ
7-midnight; 3-1am Fri; 12-1am Sat; 12-midnight Sun
(01229) 467366
Cumbrian Legendary Ales Loweswater Gold; 2 changing beers (sourced nationally) H
A welcoming refurbished pub a short walk from Askam-in-Furness station. It has two separate rooms, with a public bar containing the dartboard and TVs for Sky and BT Sports, plus a lounge bar which has some comfortable seating and a pool table. Main sporting events are also shown in the lounge on a large screen. Three real ales are served of which two are from local breweries.
Q (7)

Barngates

Drunken Duck Inn

LA22 0NG (signed off B5286)
11.30-11; 12-10.30 Sun (015394) 36347
drunkenduckinn.co.uk
Barngates Cat Nap, Cracker, Tag Lag; 3 changing beers (sourced locally) H
Standing high above Ambleside, this is a traditional Lakeland dwelling, reflecting the simplicity, beauty and longevity of its natural environment. Water is drawn from the fells for the beers brewed at the on-site Barngates Brewery. The bar has six handpumps and serves all the Barngates beers on rotation. The outside seating area at the front offers commanding dramatic views of the fells to the north-east. Q P

Barrow-in-Furness

Duke of Edinburgh

Abbey Road, LA14 5QR
11-midnight (01229) 821039
dukeofedinburghhotel.co.uk
Lancaster Amber, Blonde, Red; Wainwright; 4 changing beers (sourced nationally) H
On the edge of the town centre near the station, the Duke does not get as noisy as similar bars in the town. The place has an airy feel with modern, comfortable furniture and a fine open fire. Paintings by local artists are displayed. Good-quality, reasonably priced bar meals are served. There is a separate restaurant and large function room. Beers are mainly from Lancaster (owned by the same company), with guest ales too.
P

King's Arms

Quarry Brow, Hawcoat, LA14 4HY
5.30-11; 4-midnight Fri; 12.30-midnight Sat; 1-midnight Sun (01229) 828137
Bowness Bay Swan Blonde; Cumbrian Legendary Ales Loweswater Gold; Kirkby Lonsdale Monumental Blonde; 6 changing beers (sourced locally) H
Popular local inn selling mainly from local micros, including Barngates, Bowness Bay, Cross Bay, Cumberland, Cumbrian Legendary Ales and Kirkby Lonsdale. A beer menu on a chalkboard lists forthcoming attractions. The pub, which has been here since the 1860s, has been extensively extended and renovated, and features an open bar with adjacent separate rooms. Friendly staff give a warm welcome. Well-behaved dogs are allowed in one of the rooms. Q

Boot

Brook House Inn

CA19 1TG (200yds from Dalegarth Station)
9am-11 (019467) 23288 brookhouseinn.co.uk
Cumbrian Legendary Ales Langdale; 6 changing beers H
In the heart of the western Lake District in the beautiful Eskdale valley and close to the terminus of the Ravenglass and Eskdale Railway, this popular family-run tourist pub is renowned for its wide range of cask ales, ciders and good food. Together with other pubs in the Eskdale valley, it provides the focal point for an annual beer festival held in June. Q P

Hardknott Bar & Café at the Woolpack Inn

CA19 1TH (¾ mile E of Boot village on approach to Hardknott Pass)
8am-11 (019467) 2328 woolpack.co.uk

REAL ALE BREWERIES

Appleby Morland
Barngates Barngates
Beckstones Millom
Biggar Biggar Village
Blackbeck Blackbeck
Bowness Bay Kendal
Brack'N'Brew Watermillock
Brewshine Kendal
Carlisle Carlisle
Coniston Coniston
Cumbrian Legendary Hawkshead
Dent Cowgill
Derwent Silloth
Eden River Penrith
Ennerdale Rowrah
Fell Flookburgh
Foxfield Foxfield
Grasmere Grasmere (NEW)
Great Corby Great Corby
Greenodd Greenodd
Handsome Bowston
Hawkshead Staveley
Healey's Loppergarth
Helm Bar Appleby-in-Westmorland
Hesket Newmarket Hesket Newmarket
Jennings Cockermouth
Kendal Kendal (brewing suspended)
Keswick Keswick
Kirkby Lonsdale Kirkby Lonsdale
South Lakes Ulverston
Strands Nether Wasdale
Tarn Hows Outgate
Tirril Long Marton
Tractor Shed Workington
Ulverston Ulverston
Unsworth's Yard Cartmel
Watermill Ings
Westmorland Kendal
Wild Boar Bowness-on-Windermere
Winster Valley Winster (brewing suspended)

Barngates Goodhew's Dry Stout; Bowness Bay Amazon Amber; 10 changing beers Ⓗ
This iconic inn on Hardknott Pass has an approach that is surrounded by the stunning scenery of the Eskdale valley and is a popular tourist pub, serving food, cask ales and draught ciders. It has 10 handpumps. The lounge and Walker's bar offer an attractive mix of traditional and modern styles. It participates in the annual Boot beer festival in June, holds a cider festival in April, and hosts live music and quiz nights. Local CAMRA Cider Pub of the Year 2017.

Bowness-on-Windermere

Boathouse

Windermere Marina Village, LA23 3JQ
11-11; 9am-11 Sat & Sun ☎ (015394) 22785
theboathouse-windermere.co.uk
Bowness Bay Swan Blonde; Coniston Bluebird Bitter; 2 changing beers (sourced regionally) Ⓗ
Overlooking the enclosed Windermere marina and adjacent to the Hawkshead ferry, this modern bar complex is a calm haven in the tourist maelstrom. Enjoy quality beers and a tasty plate on the sheltered suntrap terrace with great views of the yachts, the lake and the hills beyond that are reminiscent of the Italian lakes or the south of France. A wall of windows provides protection from the elements if the weather is more Lake District-style. The disabled facilities are excellent.
(Windermere)P

Braithwaite

Middle Ruddings Country Inn

CA12 5RY (W end of village)
10.30-11; 12.30-10.30 Sun ☎ (017687) 78436
middle-ruddings.co.uk
3 changing beers Ⓗ
Comfortable family-run country inn where they are passionate about food and real ale – usually brewed in Cumbria. The bar comprises two rooms and a lounge, and a separate conservatory restaurant serves home-made food using locally sourced produce. Well-behaved dogs are allowed in the bar areas. It also serves real ciders and an increasing range of bottle-conditioned ales. It hosts an annual beer lovers' dinner and is a winner of a number of CAMRA awards.
QP(X5)

Brigsteer

Wheatsheaf Inn

LA8 8AN
10-11; 10-10.30 Sun ☎ (015395) 68938
thewheatsheafbrigsteer.co.uk
Bowness Bay Swan Blonde; Hawkshead Bitter; 2 changing beers (sourced nationally) Ⓗ
Village pub offering great real ale, delicious food and superior accommodation, including a comfortable bunkhouse. Parts of this historic inn date back to 1762 and it has been an alehouse since early 1800. A member of the Individual Inns group, the Wheatsheaf has been delightfully refurbished with a great deal of attention and care. It has a series of rooms and cosy corners, log fires and an inviting bar area serving an excellent selection of local ales. QP

Broughton-in-Furness

Manor Arms

The Square, LA20 6HY
12-11.30 (midnight Fri & Sat); 12-11 Sun
☎ (01229) 716286 manorarmsthesquare.co.uk
Cumberland Corby Blonde; Hawkshead Windermere Pale; 6 changing beers Ⓗ
An outstanding free house owned by the Varty family for more than 28 years. Set in an attractive Georgian square, it has been the recipient of many CAMRA awards and is the local CAMRA Pub of the Year 2018. Real ale dominates, and the choice usually includes a dark beer along with traditional cider and perry. A mini beer festival is held every day. Two fires keep the pub warm and the bar staff are always friendly. Q

Calderbridge

Stanley Arms Hotel

CA20 1DN (on the A595)
12-11.30 ☎ (01946) 841235 stanleyarmshotel.com
Titanic Plum Porter; 4 changing beers Ⓗ
This late-Georgian hostelry is on the A595 at the southern edge of this small village. Standing next to a bend in the River Calder, it has an extensive beer garden and fishing rights, and is at the gateway to Ennerdale. Locally sourced produce features in the meals served in the two-room bar and restaurant. In addition to the Cumbrian ales offered, Titanic Plum Porter is a regular beer.
QP

Cark-in-Cartmel

Engine Inn

LA11 7NZ
12-11; 12-10.30 Sun ☎ (015395) 58341
theengineinncartmel.co.uk
Lancaster Blonde; Timothy Taylor Landlord; 3 changing beers (sourced nationally) Ⓗ
A 17th-century inn, refurbished in 2010, a short walk from the station and an excellent end to the walk from Grange described in CAMRA's Lake District Pub Walks book. There is an open bar area with a cosy fire, separate rooms away from the bar and a riverside beer garden. Five en-suite rooms are available. The pub has its own loyalty card scheme. Regular live music is a feature on Saturday evenings. P

Carlisle

301 Miles From London

Carlisle Citadel Station, Court Square, CA1 1QZ
8am-8 (9 Fri & Sat); 11-6.30 Sun ☎ (01228) 593301
6 changing beers Ⓗ
Within Carlisle railway station on Platform 4 and well placed for the Settle to Carlisle terminus. It was the station buffet in the 1950s and features much of the fabric of the old building and other railway heritage, including the original stone fireplaces. Named 301 Miles From London because Carlisle folklore claims that is the distance from the capital, although it is actually thought to be 299 miles.

Beehive

Warwick Road, CA1 1LH (on A69)
11.30-11 (midnight Fri & Sat); 12-11 Sun
☎ (01228) 549731

Morland Old Golden Hen; 3 changing beers (often Greene King, Marston's)
Large, popular pub opposite Carlisle football and rugby grounds on the A69 leading into town (home fans only for some games). There are lots of TV screens for Sky, showing multiple channels at the same time when necessary. Food is served all day. It has a regular quiz on Thursday night, a large covered outdoor smoking area, and live music most Friday evenings. Completely refurbished following devastating flooding in December 2015. P

Fat Gadgie

5 Devonshire Street, CA3 8LG
2 (3 Mon)-midnight; 12-midnight Sat & Sun
(01228) 812880 thefatgadgie.co.uk
4 changing beers
Opened in May 2017 after the closure of a specialist ale bar in the same premises, the new owner has refurbished the space to provide a pleasant, quiet drinking environment without the distraction of television or gaming machines. This city-centre bar serves a range of cask ales from far and wide, changing the range frequently and targeting the discerning drinker. The Fat Gadgie adds to a series of unusual bar names in this area of the city. Q

King's Head Inn

Fisher Street, CA3 8RF
10-11; 11-midnight Sat; 12-11 Sun
kingsheadcarlisle.co.uk
4 changing beers
An excellent-city centre pub, winner of many CAMRA awards, serving a range of ales from four handpumps. Pictures of old Carlisle adorn the internal walls and outside is an explanation of why the city is not in the Domesday Book. Good-value meals are served at lunchtime. Children and dogs are not allowed. The spacious covered courtyard has a large-screen TV and regularly hosts live music.

Spinners Arms

Cummersdale, CA2 6BD
6-midnight; 5-midnight Fri; 12-midnight Sat & Sun
(01228) 532928 thespinnersarms.org.uk
Carlisle Spun Gold, Flaxen, Magic Number
Cosy family-friendly hostelry, an original Redfern pub with unique and original features. It is less than half a mile from Carlisle's south-western boundary, close to the Cumbrian Way and National Cycle Route 7, which run alongside the picturesque river Caldew. There is regular live music, with Irish music sessions every first and third Wednesday. Children are welcome until 9pm and well-behaved dogs are permitted. The pub is the brewery tap for Carlisle Brewing Co, showcasing its beers on five pumps. P (75)

Woodrow Wilson

48 Botchergate, CA1 1QS
8am-midnight (1am Fri & Sat) (01228) 819942
Cumberland Corby Ale, Corby Blonde; Greene King Abbot; Marston's Old Empire; Ruddles Best Bitter; Sharp's Doom Bar; 6 changing beers (sourced nationally)
One of two almost adjacent Wetherspoons, this pub is in a refurbished Co-op building named after the former US president, whose mother was born in Carlisle. Up to 12 handpumps offer the largest range of real ales to be found in Carlisle. Food is available all day till 10pm. At the rear there is a spacious outdoor seating area, heated patio and smokers' area. Children are welcome in some areas until 8pm. P

Castle Carrock

Duke of Cumberland

CA8 9LU (near Brampton)
closed Mon & Tue; 12-midnight (01228) 670341
the-dukeofcumberland.co.uk
2 changing beers (often Derwent, Hesket Newmarket)
At the heart of this charming village, the Duke reopened in 2009 and is now successfully re-established. A local following also sees it as the centre for the annual Marr Folk Festival in July. At the foot of the northern Pennines, it is ideally located for outdoor activity enthusiasts, who can enjoy real ale and sample the home-made food, which has a growing reputation. The layout separates the games/TV area from the dining area. Dogs are not allowed inside the pub. P

Cockermouth

Castle Bar

14 Market Place, CA13 9NQ
11-11 (midnight Fri & Sat); 12-10.30 Sun
(01900) 829904 cockermouth.org.uk/castlebar
Cumbrian Legendary Ales Loweswater Gold; Jennings Cumberland Ale, Bitter; Titanic Plum Porter; 2 changing beers
A foodie pub in the town's Market Place with a refurbished interior that retains many historic features, lending character to this fine medieval building. There are three floors, with the main bar on the ground floor, restaurant on the first floor and a relaxing room with comfortable leather sofas on the second. Outside is a terraced beer garden. Booking for meals is advisable at weekends. Available for private functions.

New Cock & Bull

7 South Street, CA13 9RT (opp Sainsbury's)
3-11; 11-midnight Fri & Sat; 12-11 Sun (01900) 827999
thenewcockandbull.co.uk
Coniston Bluebird Bitter; Cumberland Corby Fox, Corby Blonde; 5 changing beers
This popular town-centre community pub charges competitive prices and offers a consistently good range of cask beers. The venue is on three levels and is sensitively modernised, offering quieter, more comfortable surroundings if required. It has occasional live music. No meals are served but it does have interesting bar snacks. It promotes Fizz Fridays, and has five real ales on offer including some from Cumbrian breweries.

Swan Inn

52-56 Kirkgate, CA13 9PH
5.30-11.30 (midnight Fri); 12-midnight Sat; 12-11 Sun
(01900) 822425 swaninncockermouth.com
Fyne Ales Jarl; Jennings Bitter, Cumberland Ale, Cocker Hoop; 1 changing beer
A true community pub well supported by locals. This 17th-century hostelry has flagged floors, exposed beams and a real fire. There are quiet nooks and crannies providing space for two quiz teams. It hosts a monthly whisky club and folk music sessions, and has six handpumps with three

of the beers from the local Jennings Brewery. There is a large-screen TV at the back of the pub used for showing sports.

Coniston

Black Bull Inn & Hotel

LA21 8DU

8.30am-11 (10.30 winter) (015394) 41335
blackbullconiston.co.uk

Coniston Bluebird Bitter, Bluebird Premium XB, No.9 Barley Wine, Old Man Ale, Oliver's Light Ale, Special Oatmeal Stout; 3 changing beers (sourced locally)

A 16th-century coaching inn, the tap house for the on-site Coniston Brewing Company, serving good food in traditional, comfortable surroundings. Six regular beers, available from 11am, are supplemented by other beers from the brewery on rotation. The spacious bar and lounge are well frequented by tourists in this hugely popular area. The outside seating space is perfect for the summer months, in a spectacular location near Coniston Old Man. Dogs are not allowed in the restaurant. P (X12,505)

Sun

LA21 8HQ

11-11 (015394) 41248 thesunconiston.com

Barngates Red Bull Terrier; Coniston Bluebird Premium XB; Cumbrian Legendary Ales Loweswater Gold; 4 changing beers (sourced locally)

Take the Walna Scar road up from Coniston village, or down from Coniston Old Man, to visit this 16th-century pub and hotel. The deliberately unmodernised dual-level bar has atmosphere and character, with slate flooring, exposed beams and stone walls, heated by a large open range. The slate-topped bar offers up to eight cask ales, mostly from local brewers. The conservatory and terrace complete the picture, with delightful views over the garden. Dogs are not allowed in the conservatory. Winter opening hours vary. QP

Cowgill

Sportsman's Inn

LA10 5RG

closed Mon; 12-3, 7-11; 12-11 Sat & Sun
(015396) 25282 thesportsmansinn.com

Pennine Natural Gold; 2 changing beers (sourced locally)

Set in an Area of Outstanding Natural Beauty, this 17th-century inn has fabulous views of Dentdale. The Grade II-listed building has been in the same family for 30 years. Natural Gold from Pennine is the permanent beer of choice, with two additional changing local ales. The pub sits on the Dalesway route and is close to Dent station on the Settle-Carlisle line, making it an ideal base for touring the Yorkshire Dales. QP

Crosby

Stag Inn

CA15 6SH

11 (3 Tue)-11; 12-10.30 Sun (01900) 812549
staginncrosby.com

3 changing beers

Welcoming pub that is popular with locals and visitors, set in a great location with views over the Solway Firth to Scotland. It has a large bar with two serving points and quiet corners, and a dining area with an extensive menu to suit all tastes, including vegetarian and vegan options. Beers are from the Marston's range and usually also include one from the local Jennings Brewery. P

Crosby Ravensworth

Butchers Arms

CA10 3JP

closed Mon & Tue; 5-11 Wed; 12-11 Thu; 12-midnight Fri & Sat; 12-11 Sun (01931) 715202
thebutcherscrosby.co.uk

3 changing beers (sourced regionally)

Successful community-owned village pub, reopened by former PM David Cameron in 2011. It has friendly welcoming staff and is co-run by the daughter of the Appleby Brewery owner, whose real ale is always on handpump. It has a games room with interesting traditional challenges, and a separate eating area for fine dining. Various pub events throughout the year include music, food-themed nights and quizzes. A dedicated smoking shelter is in the attractive rear garden. Occasionally snow-bound in winter. QP

Crosthwaite

Punch Bowl Inn

Lyth Valley, LA8 8HR

11-11 (015395) 68237 the-punchbowl.co.uk

Barngates Tag Lag; Bowness Bay Swan Blonde; 2 changing beers (sourced regionally)

Outstanding dining venue ranked in the top 50 gastropubs in the UK. Its old-fashioned pub atmosphere, complete with log fires, blends with contemporary dining in a stunning rural location overlooking the Lyth Valley. It boasts a traditional bar, informal lounge/dining areas and a formal restaurant. A selection of regional beers is on offer as well as a changing local ale. There is an outside terrace – a perfect place for summertime eating and drinking. QP

Cumwhitton

Pheasant Inn

CA8 9EX

5.30-11; 12.30-midnight Sat; 12-9 Sun (01228) 560102
pheasantinncumwhitton.co.uk

Cumberland Corby Blonde; 1 changing beer

Originally a farm cottage, a pub was added in around 1810. The building, once known as the Red Lion, has had various extensions and internal alterations to arrive at the popular hostelry it is today. The bar and games room have stone-flagged floors and a roaring fire in winter, while the dining room offers a comfortable environment to enjoy the excellent food on offer. Quiz nights are the first and third Thursdays in the month. QP

Dalton-in-Furness

Brown Cow

10 Goose Green, LA15 8AQ

10-midnight; 11.30-midnight Sun (01229) 462553

Black Sheep Best Bitter; 5 changing beers (sourced nationally)

A warm and friendly atmosphere awaits visitors to this 400-year-old coaching house, which has retained plenty of original features including beams, brasses, local prints and an open fire. A winner of many awards for its six real ales, the pub also serves excellent food from a full and varied menu. Meals can be enjoyed in the 100-seater restaurant or, on warmer days, in an outside area with seating for 80. P (6,X6)

Dent

Sun Inn

Main Street, LA10 5QL

11-11; 12-10.30 Sun (015396) 25208

sunınndent.co.uk

Kirkby Lonsdale Monumental Blonde, Tiffin Gold; 2 changing beers (sourced nationally)

A lovely local pub in the heart of Dent village, this 300-year-old inn sits on the cobbled street near St Andrew's Church. It has wooden floors together with traditional bench seating, wooden stools and armchairs. In the winter, coal fires are welcoming for weary walkers. There is a beautiful peaceful garden to the rear – perfect for the summer. It serves two ales from Kirkby Lonsdale and up to two national beers. Q P

Dufton

Stag Inn

CA16 6DB

6 (4 Thu & Fri; 12 Sat)-11; 12-10.30 Sun

(017683) 51608 thestagdufton.co.uk

3 changing beers (sourced regionally)

Lovely old pub on the green in this tranquil fellside village. An old black range in the bar and a stove in the snug greet locals, cyclists and walkers from the Pennine Way which passes the door. Well-kept interesting ales are complemented by a varied menu using locally sourced produce. The dining room and garden have spectacular views over the Pennines. An annual beer festival is held in August. Q P

Elterwater

Britannia Inn

LA22 9HP

10.30-11 (015394) 37210 britinn.co.uk

Coniston Bluebird Bitter; Jennings Sneck Lifter; 5 changing beers (sourced locally)

In the heart of glorious Langdale, this cosy pub has five rooms and real fires. Food and beers are locally sourced and the varied menu offers home-made pies. Britannia Ale is sold, brewed by Coniston in the style of Timothy Taylor Landlord. Pictures from the surrounding area taken by a former employee adorn the walls and are for sale. Dogs, children, muddy boots and dripping waterproofs are always welcome here. A true Lakeland experience. P (516)

Eskdale Green

Bower House Inn

CA19 1TD (short walk from Irton Road Station)

12-midnight (019467) 23244 bowerhouseinn.com

Cumbrian Legendary Ales Loweswater Gold; Hawkshead Bitter; Timothy Taylor Landlord; 3 changing beers

An eclectic mix of quaint, elegant buildings and secluded arbours in beautifully tended gardens, close to Irton Road station on the Ravenglass and Eskdale narrow gauge railway. The dining room offers oak-panelled seating and beamed ceilings, and there is a real fire in the bar. It is a community focal point, with a local cricket team, darts, charity quizzes and themed food evenings. Q P

Foxfield

Prince of Wales

LA20 6BX

closed Mon & Tue; 2.45-11 Wed & Thu; 11.45-11 Fri & Sat; 12-10.30 Sun (01229) 716238

princeofwalesfoxfield.co.uk

6 changing beers (sourced nationally)

This pub is testament to what is achievable through passion and hard work – numerous awards have been presented over the years. Guest ales come from house breweries Foxfield and Tigertops, plus others from carefully selected nationwide breweries, always including a mild. Check the website for various events throughout the year. B&B accommodation is excellent. Food is available at times. Payment is by cash only. The railway stops outside. Q P

Gilcrux

Barn Bistro

CA7 2QX NY114380

closed Mon; 12 (5 Tue)-11 (016973) 23289

barnbistro.co.uk

Jennings Bitter; 2 changing beers

This converted barn, with exposed beams and an open fire, has four handpumps offering Jennings Bitter plus beers usually brewed in Cumbria. It also has an excellent whisky selection and hosts a whisky club. There is a separate area for dining. The pub is situated in the centre of the village and has both front and rear beer gardens. It holds an annual beer festival. Well-behaved dogs are welcome until 6pm. Opens on Mondays in August and bank holidays. Q P

Gosforth

Gosforth Hall Inn

Wasdale Road, CA20 1AZ (next to St Mary's Church)

12-midnight (019467) 25322 gosforthhall.co.uk

3 changing beers

A Grade II-listed inn, once a 17th-century farmhouse, featuring an original sandstone fireplace with a 1673 shield above and a priest hole behind it. The recently renovated patio with its boules pitch provides an extra bar for alfresco dining in summer. Four varying real ales are generally Cumbrian, and there is an annual beer festival. Bar food and Rod's pies satisfy the heartiest of appetites. Local CAMRA Pub of the Year 2017. Q P

Grasmere

Tweedies Bar (Dale Lodge Hotel)

Red Bank Road, LA22 9SW

12-11 (midnight Fri & Sat) (015394) 35300

dalelodgehotel.co.uk

Coniston Old Man Ale; Cumbrian Legendary Ales Loweswater Gold; Hawkshead Windermere Pale; 8 changing beers (sourced nationally)

In the heart of Grasmere, this amazing pub continues to gain notoriety in the real ale world with 10 handpumps on the go plus real cider – from

Nottinghamshire! The walls are adorned with pumpclips from beers past and present, through familiar breweries to unusual ones. The famous Grasmere Guzzler festival is held on the first weekend in September. You need to head on down here! ⛀❀⇌◑●P⊟(555,599)🐾ᯤ

Great Broughton

Punch Bowl Inn 🏆

19 Main Street, CA13 0YJ

✪ closed Mon-Wed; 8-11 Thu; 5-11 Fri & Sat; 12-3, 6-11 Sun
☎ (01900) 267070

2 changing beers Ⓗ

A community pub run by a committee of local volunteers, saved from closure in 2012. Although it has limited opening hours, this is more than compensated for by the quality and variation of the Cumbrian real ale it serves. It always has two locally sourced beers, which constantly change. Originally a 17th-century coaching inn, this is very much a community and locals' pub. The decor is adorned with rugby memorabilia and water jugs. Q⛀♣P🐾ᯤ

Great Orton

Wellington Inn

CA5 6LZ

✪ closed Mon & Tue; 12-2, 6-11; 12-3, 6-10.30 Sun
☎ (01228) 710775

3 changing beers (sourced locally; often Derwent, Keswick) Ⓗ

Set in a quiet village, this is an attractive country inn, serving good-value meals using ingredients sourced locally, including meat from the renowned local butcher. Two handpumps serve ales from the Robinsons' range as well as seasonal beers. Live music is being reintroduced here with open mic nights on an occasional basis. There is space for 10 touring caravans on the adjacent campsite. Q⛀❀◑♿♣P

Great Salkeld

Highland Drove 𝕃

CA11 9NA

✪ 12-2.30 (not Mon), 6-11; 12-midnight Sat
☎ (01768) 898349

Theakston Black Bull Bitter; house beer (by Eden); 1 changing beer Ⓗ

Just off the main road through this attractive village, everything here is of a high standard. On entering the exceptionally well-stocked bar you will see a lounge and games room either side with the award-winning Kyloes restaurant upstairs, all with well-chosen decor featuring exposed timber and brickwork embellished with Highland-style soft furnishings, brass and copper ornaments. Excellent food is available every day except Monday lunchtime, and themed nights have recently been introduced. Watch out for the Highland cows! ⛀❀⇌◑♿⛺♣🐾ᯤ

Greenodd

Ship 𝕃

Main Street, LA12 7QZ

✪ closed Mon; 5-11 (midnight Fri); 2-midnight Sat; 12-10.30 Sun ☎ (01229) 861553 🌐 theshipinngreenodd.co.uk

Greenodd Citra, Coal Wharf, Kiln, Roundabout; 1 changing beer (sourced locally) Ⓗ

A traditional village inn attracting a good mix of locals and visitors. Five handpumps serve beers selected from a range of over 20 brewed by the on-site Greenodd Brewery. The pub has recently been refurbished and its open plan interior features slate floors, stone walls, exposed beams and open fires, with a separate quiet room to the rear. Locally produced food is served. Not all X6 buses stop at Greenodd. ⛀♣P⊟(X6)🐾ᯤ

Hawkshead

King's Arms Hotel 𝕃 ✔

The Square, LA22 0NZ

✪ 11-midnight ☎ (015394) 36372
🌐 kingsarmshawkshead.co.uk

Hawkshead Bitter; Cumbrian Legendary Ales Loweswater Gold; 2 changing beers (sourced locally) Ⓗ

Characterful 500-year-old village inn on the square of this historic settlement. The traditional interior features beamed ceilings, an open fire and a hand-carved king in the bar supporting the floor above. Good food is available in the bar and dining area. The patio is south-facing on the edge of the square. Frequent live music and twice-yearly beer festivals take place. It is family friendly and dogs are welcome in the bar area. There is plenty of parking in the village. Winter hours vary. Q❀⇌◑♣⊟(505)🐾

Hayton

Stone Inn

CA8 9HR

✪ 12-2, 5.30-11 (midnight Fri); 11-midnight Sat; 12-10.30 Sun ☎ (01228) 670896 🌐 stoneinnhayton.co.uk

Thwaites Original; 2 changing beers (often Hadrian Border) Ⓗ

A traditional family-run venue in the village of Hayton. A community pub, it is home to the local leek club. There is an upstairs dining room which can be hired for small gatherings. A fine pair of 1904 Christ Church Boat Club oars adorn one wall, and ask to see the CAMRA mirror. There are two changing ales, often from a local brewery, as well as the regular Thwaites Original bitter. ⛀◗♣P🐾ᯤ

Hensingham

Globe Inn

95 Main Street, CA28 8QX

✪ closed Mon; 2-1am Tue-Thu; 2-midnight Fri; 12-midnight Sat; 12-11 Sun ☎ (01946) 590772
🌐 theglobehensingham.co.uk

2 changing beers Ⓗ

An open-plan L-shaped inn that is family run, friendly and sociable – very much a locals' pub. It has TVs throughout as well as a jukebox, and provides an area with sofas specifically for drinkers. It usually serves Cumbrian beers on the two handpumps. The pub motto is 'Strangers leave as friends'. Food is served in the evening, except Sunday when it is lunchtime only. There is an upstairs function/dining room. ⛀❀◑⊟ᯤ

Hesket Newmarket

Old Crown 𝕃 ✔

CA7 8JG

⏲ 5.30-11; 12-2.30, 5-11 Fri; 12-11 Sat & Sun
☎ (016974) 78288 🌐 theoldcrownpub.co.uk
Hesket Newmarket Haystacks, Black Sail, Helvellyn Gold, High Pike, Doris' 90th Birthday Ale, Brim Fell; 4 changing beers (sourced locally; often Hesket Newmarket) Ⓗ
Sitting in the heart of this lovely fellside village, the Old Crown is a showcase for the Hesket Newmarket brewery, which is immediately behind the pub. It is well known as the first co-operatively owned pub in the country and is popular with locals and visitors alike; Prince Charles and Sir Chris Bonington are among its supporters. Closed Monday to Thursday afternoons in winter, with no meals anytime on winter Mondays.
Q❀◐♣🐾

Holmes Green

Black Dog Inn Ⓛ

Broughton Road, LA15 8JP (from Dalton-in-Furness 1 mile past South Lakes Safari Zoo) SD233761
⏲ closed Mon; 4-midnight Tue-Thu; 3-midnight Fri & Sat; 2-9 Sun ☎ (01229) 462975
Cumbrian Legendary Ales Esthwaite Bitter, Loweswater Gold; 3 changing beers (sourced nationally) Ⓗ
With five real ales on offer, including some from local microbreweries, a warm welcome awaits from the landlord and locals alike. This recently refurbished former coaching inn with two real fires, quarry-tiled floor and rustic beams retains plenty of character. Live music is hosted monthly (usually the last Saturday), as well as open mic nights plus beer and music festivals. It has an outdoor decked seating area. Quality home-made burgers are served on Friday evenings. Q❀◑P🐾

Ings

Watermill Inn Ⓛ

LA8 9PY
⏲ 11-11; 11-10.30 Sun ☎ (01539) 821309
🌐 watermillinn.co.uk
Watermill Collie Wobbles, Wruff Night; 9 changing beers (sourced locally) Ⓗ
A multi award-winning family-owned pub and brewery (recently renamed Windermere Brewing Company). It has 11 handpulls dispensing mainly its own beers. Two bars are served by central counters, one with windows opening on to the brewery. It hosts the longest-running single-site storytelling club in the country (on the first Tuesday of the month) and serves good bar meals. Dogs are allowed in the River Bar and provided with biscuits and water. Q❀◐♿♣P (555)🐾

Kendal

Factory Tap Ⓛ

5 Aynam Road, LA9 7DE
⏲ closed Mon; 4-10 Tue-Thu; 3-11 Fri & Sat; 3-9 Sun
☎ (015394) 82541 🌐 thefactorytap.co.uk
Bowness Bay Swan Blonde; 7 changing beers (sourced regionally) Ⓗ
With a deserved reputation as one of the finest real ale pubs in Cumbria, there is an impressive range of nine handpulled beers here, many regional. Sited in converted cottages in Kendal's creative quarter, it has been sympathetically restored, retaining original features complemented by industrial chic furniture; upstairs there are generous lounges blending old and new. Outside there is a terrace area and walled beer garden. Alongside regular street food weekends, beer festivals are held in October and May.
Q❀♿⇌P🐾

Masons Yard 24

22 Stramongate, LA9 4BN
⏲ 11-11 ☎ (01539) 727979 🌐 masonsyard24.co.uk
Bowness Bay Swan Blonde; Cumbrian Legendary Ales Loweswater Gold; Hawkshead Bitter; 3 changing beers (sourced regionally) Ⓗ
Brought back to full potential by quality craftsmanship over two years, this free house, established in 1826, has six handpumps dispensing different regional beers. An extensive brasserie menu is served at most times. The rear garden includes a new toilet block, two large covered areas (one can be heated) and ample seating. The pub has its own certified well water and a 1.25-barrel nanobrewery. Local CAMRA Pub of the Year 2018. Q❀◐♿⇌🐾

Ring o' Bells Ⓛ

37-39 Kirkland, LA9 5AF
⏲ 12 (6 Thu)-11; 12-midnight Fri & Sat ☎ (01539) 720326
🌐 ringobellskendal.webs.com
Coniston Bluebird Bitter; Thwaites Nutty Black; 1 changing beer (sourced locally) Ⓗ
Community is the watchword in this pub and a helping hand is extended to all – together with a warm welcome from the family owners and the customers alike. The skilfully run original cellar ensures quality local ales that change regularly by popular request from a wide-ranging selection. A roaring fire warms the taproom throughout the winter; sunny tables tempt you outside in the summer. Adjacent to the parish church, it has a river nearby, and serves tasty home-made food. A true local on every level. Q❀◐♣P🐾

Romney's Ⓛ

72 Milnthorpe Road, LA9 5HG
⏲ 11-11.45 ☎ (01539) 720956 🌐 romneyskendal.co.uk
Bowness Bay Swan Blonde; 4 changing beers (sourced regionally) Ⓗ
Kendal's most popular pub has the town's largest volume of real ale sales, all at competitive prices. The A6 location is a bonus, with a large car park before entering the one-way system into the town centre. The interesting range of beers is always a temptation. It is a welcoming hostelry for weary travellers and locals alike, with a wide choice of food including carvery and beer tapas. Self-catering modern apartments are available. It has an excellent children's adventure area and a summer suntrap garden. ❀◐♿P🐾

Keswick

Pheasant Inn ✔

Crosthwaite Road, CA12 5PP
⏲ 12-11 ☎ (017687) 72219
🌐 thepheasantinnkeswick.co.uk
Jennings Bitter, Cocker Hoop, Cumberland Ale; 1 changing beer Ⓗ
Comfortable and popular with diners, this edge-of-town pub serving a good selection of Jennings beers is well worth seeking out. It has two areas – one primarily for dining, the other, in front of the bar, suitable for drinking, with bar meals available. It has low beams and a flagged floor and offers a welcoming open fire for the cooler months. A

number of original Wilks (John Wilkinson) artworks adorn the walls. The Ladyside Pike Alpine Club meets here. **Q**

Kirkby Lonsdale

Orange Tree

9 Fairbank, LA6 2BD (turn left past churchyard, hotel is on your right)

11-11 (midnight Fri & Sat) (015242) 71716

theorangetreehotel.co.uk

5 changing beers (sourced locally) H

Situated close to the church in this lovely old market town, the welcoming front bar of this family-run hotel and free house presents a varying selection of Kirkby Lonsdale ales with local guest beers and good wholesome meals. Cosy dining areas are to the rear. The bar has a rugby theme and proves popular with local teams. A small beer festival is staged on the first weekend in December. A sister pub to the Royal Barn. (567)

Royal Barn

New Road, LA6 2AB

10-9.30 (11 Thu-Sat); 11-10 Sun (015242) 71918

kirkbylonsdalebrewery.com

Kirkby Lonsdale Jubilee Stout, Monumental Blonde, Ruskins Bitter, Singletrack, Stanley's Pale Ale, Tiffin Gold; 6 changing beers (sourced locally) H

Impressive taphouse for the Kirkby Lonsdale Brewery, with weekly on-site brewing taking place. It has 12 handpumps and eight keg taps plus real cider and a large selection of international craft beers. Opened in 2016 and busy from the outset, the venue is known locally as the Barn. Snacks, cakes and bottles to take away are all available. It can be hired for private functions. Live music and other events are listed on social media. **P**

Kirkoswald

Crown Inn

CA10 1DQ

12-4 (not Mon-Thu), 6-11.45 (01768) 870410

Jennings Bitter; 2 changing beers H

Friendly village pub in the main street, well supported by its locals. A pool table is to be found upstairs, and a traditional coal fire helps create a good atmosphere on cold winter nights. Visitors travel from some distance for the excellent food (booking advisable) which has a leaning to Italian styles and is freshly prepared to order. Usually there are two guest real ales along with Jennings bitter as the regular.

Levens

Hare & Hounds Inn

LA8 8PN

12-11; 12-10.30 Sun (015395) 60004

hareandhoundslevens.co.uk

Bowness Bay Swan Blonde; 4 changing beers (sourced regionally) H

A proper village pub, full of character and offering an impressive menu of local cask ales and craft beers. Originally a 16th-century coaching inn, it is a free house serving up to five real ales, showcasing the best in Cumbria. This thriving pub is everything a village hostelry should be, with the main bar serving four comfortable areas and a welcoming dining room with stunning views across the Lyth Valley. The fare is quality comfort food; the pizzas are a must. **Q** **P**

Loppergarth

Wellington Inn

Main Street, LA12 0JL (1 mile from A590 between Lindal and Pennington)

closed Sun & Mon; 6-11 (midnight Fri & Sat)

(01229) 582388

Healey's Blonde, Dark Mild, Give it Some, Golden; 1 changing beer (sourced locally) H

Superb village local with its own microbrewery (Healey's), a custom-made stainless steel plant which is viewable from the snug. Four handpumps, occasionally five, primarily dispense Healey's beers. These include an award-winning blonde, a golden bitter, a traditional darker best bitter, a superb mild, and occasional specials. Wood-burning stoves make this a cosy pub with games, books and good conversation. There is a quiz on alternate Saturdays. Well-behaved dogs on leads are welcome.

Loweswater

Kirkstile Inn

CA13 0RU (off B5289, 7 miles S of Cockermouth) NY140210

11-11; 12-10.30 Sun (01900) 85219 kirkstile.com

Cumbrian Legendary Ales Esthwaite Bitter, Grasmoor Dark Ale, Langdale, Loweswater Gold; 2 changing beers H

This 16th-century inn lies a short walk from both Loweswater and Crummock and is surrounded by stunning countryside. It is the brewery tap for Cumbrian Legendary Ales and has six handpumps, one of which dispenses Loweswater Gold – a previous Champion Golden Ale of Britain. There are four seating areas plus a separate dining room. It can be busy at mealtimes as it is popular with tourists and locals alike. An annual beer festival is held in April. **Q** **P**

Mawbray

Lowther

CA15 6QT

6-11 Mon & Thu; closed Tue & Wed; 5-midnight Fri & Sat; 12-11 Sun (01900) 881750 mawbraypub.co.uk

Derwent Parsons Pledge; 2 changing beers H

Traditional 19th-century pub with a contemporary feel set in a village close to the Solway coast. It has two rooms plus a conservatory and attracts customers from the wider local area. It is a supporter of village events and holds a quiz night on a Monday. Food is available in the evening and Sunday lunchtime, beers come from the local brewery in nearby Silloth. Winter opening hours vary. **Q** **P**

Millom

Punch Bowl

The Green, LA18 5HJ

closed Mon; 5.30-11 (midnight Sat); 5.30-10.30 Sun

(01229) 774457 the-punch-bowl.co.uk

6 changing beers (sourced nationally) H

A vibrant locals' pub enthusiastically run by landlord Nick. CAMRA award-winning Beckstones beers brewed in the village are sold, along with one or two from further afield. It has wood and slate floors, plus a woodburner to keep the pub cosy and warm. Good food is served on Wednesday, Friday and Saturday evenings till 8pm. It is well worth the walk of just over a mile if you are taking the train. Q P

Monkhill

Drovers Rest

CA5 6DB

12-2, 5-11 Mon-Wed; 12-11 (01228) 576141

4 changing beers H

A traditional country pub close to the popular Hadrian's Wall path with strong community focus. Although opened up, the interior still has the feel of three distinct rooms. The bar area is cosy and welcoming, with a roaring fire in winter. Some interesting historical State Management Scheme documents adorn the walls. The Drovers is an oasis for lots of different and sometimes obscure (for the area) real ales. Winner of the CAMRA super regional Pub of the Year award.
P (93)

Near Sawrey

Tower Bank Arms

LA22 0LF (on B5285 2 miles S of Hawkshead)

12-11; 12-10.30 Sun (015394) 36334

towerbankarms.co.uk

Barngates Tag Lag; Cumbrian Legendary Ales Loweswater Gold; Hawkshead Bitter; 2 changing beers (sourced locally) H

A 17th-century Lakeland inn with slate floors, oak beams and a cast-iron range with open fire, next to the National Trust Hill Top (Beatrix Potter's home). It delivers great local flavours in food, beer and atmosphere. Five handpumps serve local beer, and cider and perry are available too. Families and dogs are welcomed. There is a seasonal bus service connecting to the Windermere ferry and Hawkshead. Phone to check winter hours.
Q P

Nether Wasdale

Strands Inn

CA20 1ET

12-11; 12-10.30 Sun (019467) 26237

thestrandsinn.com

Strands Brown Bitter, Errmmm..., Green Bullet, Irresponsibly, Pied Piper, T'errmmm-inator; 6 changing beers H

Along winding, wooded and gently hilly lanes, this picturesque village is a delightful surprise with its view of the highest mountains in England just a few miles away. Strands has its own brewery, with any six of around 30 beers on the bar and more in bottles – try them all in May at the festival of beers. There is no mobile phone reception in the valley but the pub has free Wi-Fi. Local CAMRA Pub of the Year in 2016. Q P

Penrith

Dockray Hall

Great Dockray, CA11 7DE

11-11; 12-10.30 Sun (01768) 210676

dockrayhall.com

Cumbrian Legendary Ales Loweswater Pale Ale, Grasmoor Dark Ale, Loweswater Gold, American Invasion H

Grade I-listed 16th-century inn with many original features including three large fireplaces. King Richard III is known to have stayed here during his exploits in the area and there used to be a tunnel between the hall and nearby Penrith Castle. Fully refurbished in 2016, it sells a range of beers from Cumbrian Legendary Ales. Good food using local produce is available all week. Sister pub of the Kirkstile Inn, Loweswater. P

Fell Bar

52 King Street, CA11 7AY

4-midnight; 1-midnight Sat & Sun (01768) 866860

6 changing beers H

A small and intimate venue in the centre of Penrith with three floors, only becoming a pub in 2012. It is the tap for Fell Brewery but offers a range of other cask ales and craft beers as detailed on the blackboard near the bar. The Fell holds regular quiz nights and also hosts a beer club.

Ravenglass

Inn at Ravenglass

Main Street, CA18 1SQ (N end, overlooking Irish Sea)

12-11; 11-11 Sun (01229) 717230

theinnatravenglass.co.uk

Bowness Bay Swan Blonde; Hawkshead Bitter; 3 changing beers H

This pub offers excellent views of the estuary of three rivers, with some stunning sunsets. Set in a small coastal village, the 17th-century inn is full of character and offers a good choice of Cumbrian real ales. It is close to Ravenglass station for mainline connections to Carlisle and Barrow and for access to the narrow gauge Ravenglass and Eskdale Valley Railway. From here it is easy to get to the Western Lakes valleys. P (6)

Rosthwaite

Scafell Hotel

Borrowdale, CA12 5XB (on B5289)

12-11; 12-10.30 Sun (017687) 77208 scafell.co.uk

Jennings Bitter; 4 changing beers H

Located on the main road through picturesque Borrowdale, the Riverside Bar is open to non-residents. Popular with walkers, it is the home of the classic annual Borrowdale fell race. Set among the fells, it has a river view from the bar. Food served in the bar is of good value and quality. It has a good selection of malt whiskies, and a large open fire for the cooler times. There is plenty of comfortable seating in the main bar area.
P (78)

Santon Bridge

Bridge Inn

CA19 1UX (on road from Gosforth to Eskdale)

11-11 (019467) 26221 santonbridgeinn.com

Jennings Cumberland Ale; 6 changing beers H

The Bridge Inn, with low beams, creaking floors and cosy log fire, once a modest mail coach halt, is now a fine, comfortable country inn well located at a junction of roads into Wasdale and Eskdale. Seven beers are from local, regional and national breweries. It is home to the World's Biggest Liar competition, held every November. Good food is sourced locally. The clientele is a mix of guests, tourists and locals. Q P

Sebergham

Sour Nook Inn

Sour Nook, CA5 7DY

closed Mon & Wed; 5-11 Tue; 11.30-11 Thu; 11.30-midnight Fri & Sat; 12-11 Sun ☎ (016974) 76242

sournookinn.co.uk

2 changing beers (often Hesket Newmarket)

On the B5305 on the southern edge of the village, this pub has a Tack Room bar, a pool/darts room, function room and restaurant. Meals are locally sourced and reasonably priced (no food Wed). The area tractor group meets here on a regular basis, and the local fells pensioner group meets fortnightly for lunch. It usually serves at least one guest ale from the local Hesket Newmarket brewery in addition to Sour Nook (Tetley Bitter). P

Staveley

Beer Hall

Mill Yard, LA8 9LR

12-7 (11 Fri & Sat); 12-8 Sun ☎ (01539) 825260

hawksheadbrewery.co.uk

Hawkshead Bitter, Brodie's Prime, Cumbrian Five Hop, Lakeland Gold, Red, Windermere Pale; 16 changing beers (sourced locally)

At the heart of the vibrant Mill Yard complex of local and artisan businesses, this unusually modern two-storey tap bar serves a variety of local tapas and larger meals. Very much a centre of excellence and a showcase for the adjoining brewery's ales, it also has a selection of new KeyKeg beers and bottled varieties. Large and popular beer festivals take place in March and July. There are lots of walking and cycle routes nearby. Q P (555)

Eagle & Child Hotel

Kendal Road, LA8 9LP

11-11; 12-10.30 Sun ☎ (01539) 821320

eaglechildinn.co.uk

5 changing beers (sourced locally)

With an astonishing selection of artefacts and pictures, a varied menu with an extensive list of daily specials, and open fires, this eclectic hostelry really is a must-visit. The 555 bus stops right outside and the pub is in a bustling village with much to offer including the nearby Lakesline railway station. The wide range of interesting beers is predominantly Cumbrian. There is a busy quiz night weekly. It has a lovely quiet orchard behind and a popular front garden overlooking the River Kent. Q P (555)

Talkin

Blacksmiths Arms

CA8 1LE

12-midnight ☎ (016977) 3452 blacksmithstalkin.co.uk

Black Sheep Ale; 2 changing beers

Since taking over in 1997, the present owners have made this probably the most popular pub in the vicinity. The winning formula includes four real ales, a superbly stocked bar, friendly efficient staff, no television and meticulous attention to detail. With a golf course and country park within two miles and plenty of other outdoor activities locally, it attracts visitors from far outside north Cumbria to this Area of Outstanding Natural Beauty. Q P

Tallentire

Bush Inn

CA13 0PT

closed Mon; 6 (6.30 Thu; 5 Fri)-midnight; 12-2, 7-11 Sun ☎ (01900) 823707

3 changing beers

An old-fashioned pub that usually serves at least one ale from a Cumbrian brewery. This hub of the community and home of the cricket team hosts a traditional music session on the last Wednesday of the month. The Grade II-listed building has exposed beams, stone floors and a wood-burning stove. Well-behaved dogs are welcome. Food is served in the bar and separate dining room, Thursday to Saturday, March to December. Q P

Troutbeck

Mortal Man

LA23 1PL

10.30-midnight ☎ (015394) 33193

themortalman.co.uk

Coniston Bluebird Bitter; Cumbrian Legendary Ales Loweswater Gold; Hawkshead Bitter; 1 changing beer (sourced locally)

Scenically located pub that is a particular favourite of walkers enjoying the many varied routes and spectacular views of Windermere and the Troutbeck Valley. A main bar with side rooms serves food throughout the day, and it also has an excellent function room suitable for meetings. The garden seating is among the best in the area. Regular quizzes and folk nights take place, with a popular beer festival in the summer. Westmorland Cider Pub of the Year, with usually at least six ciders available. Q P

Ulverston

Devonshire Arms

Braddyll Terrace, Victoria Road, LA12 0DH

4-10.30; 12-midnight Fri & Sat; 12-10.30 Sun ☎ (01229) 582537

Abbeydale Moonshine, Deception, Absolution; Bank Top Flat Cap; Saltaire Blonde; 1 changing beer (sourced nationally)

Conveniently situated between the bus and train station, the Dev is a real ale paradise with a warm, friendly atmosphere. Four TVs provide comprehensive sports coverage; two dartboards and a pool table are also available. Five constantly changing cask ales and a real cider are dispensed, all from handpump, and the pub has received numerous awards from CAMRA over the years. The outside seating area is popular in summer. A Sunday meat raffle is drawn at 6pm. P

Mill

Mill Street, LA12 7EB

11-11 (midnight Fri & Sat); 11-10.30 Sun ☎ (01229) 581384 mill-at-ulverston.co.uk

Lancaster Amber, Black, Blonde, Red; 6 changing beers (sourced nationally)

Town-centre converted flour mill with an interesting layout. The original waterwheel is central to the ground floor, fed from the stream channelled alongside the first-floor outdoor terrace. Food is served in both the bar and, on weekends, in the upstairs restaurant (booking recommended). Tuesday is quiz night and open mic night is Wednesday. A recently opened loft bar/function suite serves wine and cocktails on Friday and Saturday evenings. Dogs are welcome in the bar area.

Old Friends

49 Soutergate, LA12 7ES

4 (2 Thu)-11; 2-midnight Fri; 12-midnight Sat; 12-10.30 Sun (01229) 208195 oldfriendsulverston.co.uk

6 changing beers (sourced locally) H

Welcoming old-fashioned locals' pub about 200 yards uphill from the town centre. There is a cosy snug in front of the bar with an open fire; another seating area with TV is separated by a passageway with a hatch to the bar. Beers are mostly from local brewers plus two brewed by the Old Friends. A popular quiz night is held every Tuesday and there is a wonderful beer garden at the back with heating in the winter.

Stan Laurel Inn

31 The Ellers, LA12 0AB

7-11 Mon; 12-2.30, 6-11 (midnight Fri & Sat); 12-11.30 Sun (01229) 582814 thestanlaurel.co.uk

Ulverston Flying Elephants, Lonesome Pine; 5 changing beers (sourced locally) H

Just off the centre of Stan Laurel's home town, the Stan offers a warm welcome to locals and visitors alike. Six handpulls serve a variety of mainly locally brewed beers, always featuring Ulverston Brewing Co. Excellent-value quality food is available (no food Mon). Adjacent to the bar is a large room with pool and darts and a smaller room primarily used by diners. In winter a log-burning stove adds to the comfortable ambience. Well-behaved dogs are welcome in the bar.

Q P (6,6A)

Sun Inn

6-14 Market Street, LA12 7AY

10-1am (3am Fri & Sat) (01229) 585044 thesuninnulverston.co.uk

6 changing beers (sourced regionally) H

Tastefully refurbished Grade II-listed coaching inn in the heart of Ulverston town centre. The bar carries a selection of six guest beers, ranging from small local breweries to the larger more well-known brands. Along with a warm welcome, you can expect a number of screens for watching sports, a large heated beer garden, en-suite hotel rooms and delicious food served daily.

P (6,X6)

Swan Inn

Swan Street, LA12 7JX

3.30-11; 2-midnight Fri; 12-midnight Sat; 12-11 Sun (01229) 582519

9 changing beers (sourced nationally) H

The pub has an open-plan feel yet there are three distinct areas for darts, TV watching or just good conversation by the fire. Live music features occasionally, while a jukebox allows all genres of music to be played. All Premier League football and major BT sports events are screened, and a Sunday night quiz rounds off the entertainment. A large beer garden behind the pub is popular in summer.

(6,X6)

Underbarrow

Black Labrador

LA8 8HQ

12-3, 6-11; closed Tue; 12-11 Sat & Sun (015395) 68234 theblacklabrador.co.uk

Hawkshead Bitter; 2 changing beers (sourced locally) H

A 16th-century inn on a scenic route between Kendal and Windermere. The flagstone-floored main bar includes large sofas and an inglenook fireplace, and there are separate dining and function rooms. The pub is popular with locals, walkers and those who love good beer and good food. A new extension includes a large lounge (with sliding glass doors, creating a semi-outside space in summer) and accessible toilets.

Q P

Wetheral

Wheatsheaf Inn

CA4 8HD

12-11 (midnight Fri & Sat); 12-11.30 Sun (01228) 560686 wheatsheafwetheral.co.uk

Cumberland Corby Ale; 2 changing beers H

An early 19th-century village pub, just a few minutes' walk from the village green and railway station, deservedly popular with locals and visitors. Along with Corby Ale from Cumberland Brewery there are two ales from other local breweries. Good-value bar meals are served Wednesday to Sunday (booking advisable at weekends). The regular Tuesday night quiz is well supported.

P (75)

Whitehaven

Vagabond

9 Marlborough Street, CA28 7LL

5-11; 4-midnight Fri; 12-midnight Sat; 12-9 Sun (01946) 66653 thevagabondpub.co.uk

4 changing beers H

The Vagabond is situated just off the historic harbourside of this Georgian town. The name commemorates naval commander John Paul Jones who raided Whitehaven in 1778. The traditional two-storied, wooden-floored pub offers a welcoming atmosphere. It has a reputation for good beer and quality food – especially its stone-baked pizzas. Beers are constantly changing, with choices and styles from Cumbrian, Scottish and national micros. Q

Wreay

Plough Inn

CA4 0RL

7-11 Mon; closed Tue; 12-3, 5.30-11 (016974) 75770 theploughwreay.co.uk

Hawkshead Lakeland Gold; 2 changing beers (sourced locally) H

Dating back to 1786, this historic pub is set in the heart of a picturesque village. Now tastefully modernised, the bar was built using bricks rescued from an old Cumbrian mill race. Locally sourced, excellent food is served in the split-level bar and dining area, with two cask ales from Cumbrian breweries usually available. The village guardians, whose display of clay pipes can be seen inside, continue to use it as their meeting place. Quiz night is Monday. Q P

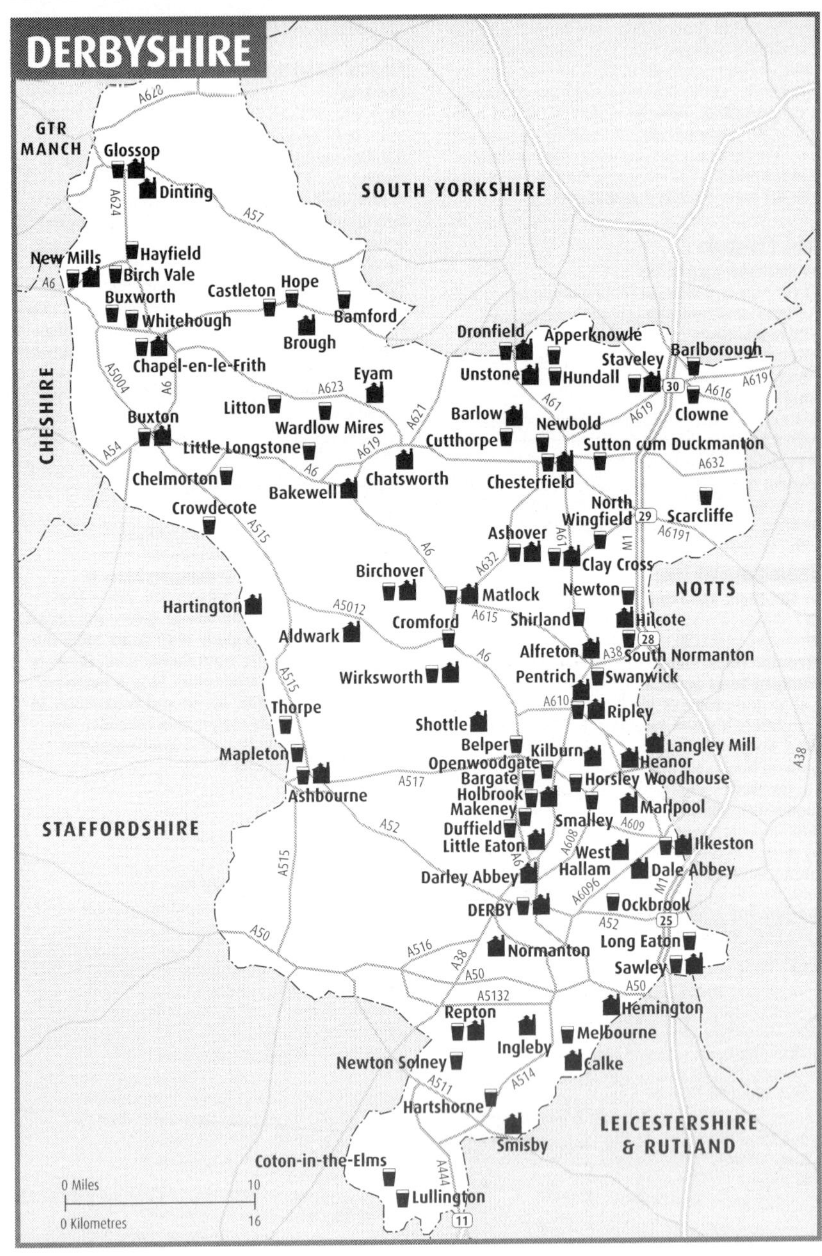

Apperknowle

Traveller's Rest 𝕃

High Street, S18 4BD SK384782

⏲ 12-11 ☎ (01246) 460169

Neepsend Blonde; Timothy Taylor Landlord Ⓗ**; 3 changing beers (sourced nationally; often Church End, Coastal, Welbeck Abbey)** Ⓗ/Ⓖ

A regular winner of CAMRA branch awards, this is a traditional country pub at the edge of the village, serving a good range of beers, ciders and perries. The outdoor drinking area provides splendid sweeping views over the Drone Valley. Good-quality food is available much of the time, with the cheeseboards and pork pie platters being particularly popular. Live music features strongly.

Q⛴❀◑⛺♣●P🚌🐾ᯤ

Ashbourne

Smith's Tavern ✔

36 St John Street, DE6 1GH

⏲ 12-11 (midnight Fri & Sat) ☎ (01335) 300809

Banks's Sunbeam; Brakspear Bitter; Marston's Pedigree; Ringwood Fortyniner; 3 changing beers (sourced regionally) Ⓗ

Small, highly traditional town-centre pub, with as many as seven real ales on. Beers come from the

Marston's portfolio, from which the landlord makes the widest possible selection; he is also allowed one free choice guest ale, served at weekends, always from a local brewery. The pub is a frequent winner of local CAMRA branch awards. Q

Ashover

Old Poets' Corner

Butts Road, S45 0EW (downhill from church)
12-11 (01246) 590888 oldpoets.co.uk
Ashover Littlemoor Citra, Poets Tipple, Font; 10 changing beers
Home of the award-winning Ashover Brewery, this large Brewers' Tudor pub is a frequent CAMRA award winner. The staff welcome walkers and dogs and provide excellent food and beer. Choose from up to 10 beers, including seasonal ones from Ashover, with a range of guest ales, traditional ciders, bottled Belgian beers and country wines. The pub hosts three beer festivals a year, weekly quizzes and regular live music.
QP(63,64)

Bamford

Anglers Rest

Taggs Knoll, S33 0DY
11-11; 12-11 Sun (01433) 659317 anglers.rest
Acorn Barnsley Bitter; Black Sheep Best Bitter; 3 changing beers (sourced locally; often Abbeydale, Bradfield, Kelham Island)
At the heart of Bamford and not far from Ladybower Reservoir, this is a community hub in every sense, where the locals have been running the pub (and associated post office and café) since 2013. The main bar is the focal point and is extremely popular with families, walkers and particularly cyclists, who have access to dedicated cycle parking and a DIY repair shop. There is also a quieter snug. Good-value, rustic bar food is served Wednesday to Sunday.
QP(273,274)

Bargate

White Hart

Sandbed Lane, DE56 0JA
5-11; 3-11 Fri; 12-11 Sat & Sun (01773) 827397
Fuller's London Pride; Hardys & Hansons Bitter; 4 changing beers (sourced nationally; often Oakham)
Local CAMRA Pub of the Year 2017 and 2018, the White Hart is a cosy two-roomed pub in the heart of Bargate above the town of Belper. With a reputation for friendly staff, good beer and a welcoming atmosphere, it is popular with locals and has an excellent selection of changing cask ales. A large beer garden is situated to the rear and walkers are welcome anytime. Bar snacks are usually available. P(7.1)

Barlborough

Pebley Inn

Rotherham Road, S43 4TH (on A618)
3-11; 12-11 Fri & Sat; 12-10.30 Sun (01246) 810327
thepebleyinn.co.uk
3 changing beers (often Abbeydale, Dukeries, Fuggle Bunny)
An old coaching inn built around 1770, standing on the old Sheffield to Newark turnpike, recently refurbished inside and out. This is a country pub with an urban feel, in the middle of nowhere but worth searching out. It has two rooms, one for meals, the other for drinkers, and occasionally holds beer festivals in its large garden overlooking Pebley Lane. P

ENGLAND

REAL ALE BREWERIES

Abstract Jungle Langley Mill
Aldwark Artisan Aldwark (NEW)
Amber Ripley
Ashover Ashover/Clay Cross
Aurora Ilkeston
Barlow Barlow
Birch Cottage Sawley (NEW)
Birchover Birchover
Black Hole Little Eaton
Boot Repton
Bottle Brook Kilburn
Brampton Chesterfield
Brunswick Derby
Buxton Buxton
Chapel-en-le-Frith Chapel-en-le-Frith
Collyfobble Barlow (NEW)
Dancing Duck Derby
Derby Derby
Derventio Darley Abbey
Draycott Dale Abbey
Drone Valley Unstone
Eyam Eyam (NEW)
Falstaff Derby: Normanton
Gaol Wirksworth
Globe Glossop
Grasshopper Langley Mill
Hairy Brewers Holbrook
Hartshorns Derby
Haywood Bad Ram Ashbourne
Hemlock Hemington (NEW)
High Peak Chapel-en-le-Frith
Hopjacker Dronfield
Howard Town Glossop
Instant Karma Clay Cross
Intrepid Brough
John Thompson Ingleby
Landlocked Alfreton
Leadmill Heanor
Leatherbritches Smisby
Littleover Derby
Marlpool Marlpool
Matlock Wolds Farm Matlock
Middle Earth Derby (brewing suspended)
Moody Fox Hilcote
Mouselow Farm Dinting
Mr Grundy's Derby
Muirhouse Ilkeston
Nutbrook West Hallam
Old Sawley Sawley
Peak Chatsworth
Pentrich Pentrich
Raw Staveley
Rock Mill New Mills
Rowditch Derby
Shiny Little Eaton
Shottle Farm Shottle
Thorley & Sons Ilkeston
Thornbridge Bakewell
Tollgate Calke
Torrside New Mills
Townes Staveley
Urban Chicken Ilkeston
Whim Hartington

Belper

Angels Micro Pub
Market Place, DE56 1FZ
✪ closed Mon-Wed; 12-10
Oakham Citra; Thornbridge Jaipur IPA; Titanic Plum Porter; 5 changing beers (sourced nationally) Ⓖ
A small, friendly bar offering real ales, an excellent choice of real ciders, wines, gins and juices, more like a mini beer festival than a pub. A full selection (up to eight ales and eight ciders at times) from Thursday gradually decreases as Sunday approaches and the beer is drunk. Locally sourced pork pies and cheeses are served. Live artists perform most Sunday afternoons. A quirky and popular micropub. ≈●🚌🐾

Arkwright's Real Ale Bar 𝕃
5 Campbell Street, DE56 1AP
✪ 4-11; 12-11 Sat & Sun ☎ (01773) 823117
🌐 arkwrightsbar.com
Marston's Pedigree Ⓖ**; 6 changing beers (sourced nationally)** Ⓗ
Situated below the Strutt Club in the town centre, this is a modern, friendly one-roomed bar regularly serving six real ales, ciders and perry. Named after Sir Richard Arkwright, an important 18th-century mill owner, it is a popular pub. Bar snacks are always available. Live acoustic music is a regular feature. The TV is only in use for major sporting events and, when coupled with a no under-14s rule, a quiet and relaxing environment for adults to enjoy a drink is ensured. Q❀≈♣●🚌🐾📶

Birch Vale

Printers Arms
Thornsett Road, SK22 1AZ (in village of Thornsett)
✪ 4.30-11.30 (midnight Fri & Sat); 12-9 Sun
☎ (01663) 744650
Storm Silk of Amnesia; 3 changing beers (sourced regionally; often Joseph Holt, Storm) Ⓗ
Small but perfectly formed, this modernised friendly village local, with accommodation and a well-maintained children's play area, overlooks the Sett Valley. A changing range of three (sometimes four) ales alongside the regular Storm beer are offered at competitive pricing for the area. It is well known for the excellent-value early evening meals – meal plus a pint – Wednesday to Friday. The pub is very much the centre of the local community, with a well-used pool table and dartboard.
❀🛏◗♣P🚌🐾📶

Birchover

Druid Inn 𝕃
Main Street, DE4 2BL
✪ closed Mon & Tue; 12-11; 12-10.30 Sun
☎ (01629) 653836 🌐 druidinnbirchover.co.uk
5 changing beers (sourced regionally; often Abbeydale, Acorn, Oakham) Ⓗ
Nestling under Rowtor Rocks in historic Birchover, this traditional rural free house has a main bar area featuring open fires at both ends. Both landlord and landlady are passionate about beer, with the pub offering regular real ales from breweries including Abbeydale, Acorn and Oakham and, occasionally, Sarah Hughes and Church End. There is a mixed clientele comprising locals and tourists visiting the Peak District National Park. Excellent home-cooked food is served in both the bar and separate restaurant. Q❀◖◗♿▲P🚌(172)🐾📶

Buxton

Ale Stop
Chapel Street, SK17 6HX
✪ 11 (12 Mon)-10; 12-9 Sun ☎ 07403 528605
3 changing beers (sourced nationally) Ⓗ
The first micropub in the High Peak, its two rooms converted from a former wine shop off Buxton Market Square. Beer is the thing here, with three changing beers from microbreweries up and down the country, as well as two real ciders from Sandford Orchards. The objective is to bring to Buxton beers that are rarely, if ever, seen in the town. The knowledgeable owner and staff ensure a warm and friendly welcome. An eclectic choice of background music on vinyl is played.
♿♣●🚌🐾📶

Cheshire Cheese
37-39 High Street, SK17 6HA
✪ 12-11 (midnight Fri & Sat) ☎ (01298) 212453
Everards Tiger; Titanic Steerage, Iceberg, White Star, Plum Porter, Captain Smith's Strong Ale; 4 changing beers Ⓗ
A double-fronted building of considerable age, reopened after refurbishment under the management of Titanic in 2013. The pub is open plan but split into several distinct areas; low ceilings with original beams add to the cosy atmosphere. There is a quiet area at one end which features an open fire. The bar boasts an impressive array of 10 handpulls serving a range of Titanic beers and guests. Thursday is pie night and there is a quiz on Sunday. Q❀◖◗♿▲♣●P🚌🐾📶

Buxworth

Navigation Inn
Brookside, SK23 7NE (off B6062)
✪ 11-midnight (10 Mon & Tue); 11-11 Sun
☎ (01663) 732072 🌐 navigationinn.co.uk
Timothy Taylor Landlord; Wainwright; 3 changing beers Ⓗ
Multi-roomed 18th-century pub in attractive countryside. It caters for all tastes, families and walkers and dogs are welcome, and there is a pleasant outdoor drinking area. Good-value food and real fires complement a warm and welcoming atmosphere. The guest beers tend to be from micros. The pub stands alongside the magnificent renovated Peak Forest Canal Basin, once the terminus of the limestone-carrying Peak Forest Tramway from the quarries high up at Dove Holes.
❀🛏◖◗♣P🐾

Castleton

Olde Nag's Head 𝕃 ✔
Cross Street, S33 8WH
✪ 12-11 (midnight Fri & Sat) ☎ (01433) 620248
🌐 yeoldenagshead.co.uk
Black Sheep Best Bitter; Bradfield Farmers Blonde; 5 changing beers (sourced locally; often Abbeydale, Bradfield, Intrepid) Ⓗ
The bar area of this busy family-run 17th-century coaching inn has a feature fireplace, exposed stone walls and carved wooden chairs, and is adjacent to the stylish restaurant. The impressive array of handpumps dispenses what is possibly the largest range of cask beers in the Hope Valley, mainly from local breweries. There is a quiz on Friday night and live music every Saturday night.
❀🛏◖◗▲●P🚌(173,272)🐾

Chapel en le Frith

Old Cell Ale Bar

10-12 Market Place, SK23 0EN

4 (5 Wed)-11; closed Tue; 12-11 Sat & Sun

07709 163316

3 changing beers (sourced locally) H

The Old Cell is a micropub on the historic marketplace, where all visitors are warmly welcomed. The original purpose of the building was the local lock-up. The bar area is well furnished with benches, tables and chairs. A range of three changing beers, often featuring local micros, is available, as well as gins. A selection of bottled beers is also stocked, often from the local brewery in the town. QP(199)

Chelmorton

Church Inn

Main Street, SK17 9SL

12-3, 6-11; 12-11 Fri-Sun (01298) 85319

thechurchinn.co.uk

Adnams Southwold Bitter; Marston's 61 Deep, Pedigree; 2 changing beers (sourced locally; often Abbeydale, Thornbridge) H

In beautiful surroundings opposite the local church (look for the unusual weathervane), this traditional village pub caters both for locals and walkers. The main room is laid out for dining, with good home-cooked food on offer; however, a cosy pub atmosphere is maintained, with a low ceiling and real fire. Guest beers are usually from local micros. There is an excellent patio area outside, and you can park on the road in front of the pub. Monday is quiz night. Q

Chesterfield

Beer Parlour

1 King Street North, Whittington Moor, S41 9BA

4-11; 12-midnight Sat; 1-10 Sun 07870 693411

the-beer-parlour.co.uk

8 changing beers (often Double Top, Thornbridge, Timothy Taylor) H

This former bottle beer shop with a few handpumps moved into its current larger premises and is now a rustic one-roomed bar with a warm, friendly feel, its comfy seating making it seem like a real micropub. It has a choice of eight real ales, ciders and perries, a range of bottled beers and Belgian and other continental beers. It is a local CAMRA award winner where you can opt to take a beer home too. Close to Chesterfield FC Proact Stadium. Q

Chesterfield Alehouse

37 West Bars, S40 1AG

12-10 chesterfieldalehouse.co.uk

6 changing beers H

Chesterfield's first micropub is a short walk from the historic marketplace. The split-level building has a small seating area leading up a few steps to the serving area, where you will find six regularly changing beers, always with a stout or a porter present, not to mention a range of bottled world beers, six KeyKeg beers, ciders and wines. Traditional pub snacks are available, and there is a popular free cheese night every Tuesday. Free-to-air sports are often shown in the upstairs room. Q

Neptune Beer Emporium

46 St Helen's Street, S41 7QD

4-9 Mon; 4-11 Tue-Thu; 4-midnight Fri; 12-midnight Sat; 3-11 Sun (01246) 220146

8 changing beers (sourced locally) H

Now a free house and a self-styled beer emporium, this is a compact back-street local serving an excellent range of beers in two drinking areas either side of a central bar. The changing list of real ales showcases many local breweries, complemented by an extensive selection of continental and craft keg beers on draught and in bottles, all displayed on a descriptive chalkboard. Regular live music takes place.

Real Ale Corner

415 Chatsworth Road, Brampton, S40 3AD

closed Mon; 1 (3 Tue)-7; 11-10 Fri & Sat; 1-5 Sun

(01246) 202111

2 changing beers H

There is a warm, friendly atmosphere in this bottle shop which maintains a pub feel, helped by having extended the seating area to the outside. Two real ales can be enjoyed while browsing the 150 bottles of beer; it specialises in beers that you cannot buy from the supermarket, as well as nine ciders and wines. It has a CAMRA-friendly home delivery service within five miles, and gift vouchers and gift packs are available. Q

Rose & Crown

104 Old Road, Brampton, S40 2QT

12 (3 Mon & Tue)-11; 12-midnight Fri & Sat

(01246) 563750 roseandcrownbrampton.co.uk

Brampton Golden Bud, Best; Everards Tiger; 6 changing beers (often Brampton) H

Everards' Project William renovation enabled the Brampton Brewery to open its first tied house. A compact snug provides room for group meetings, while the main room has plenty of quiet corners, and there are outdoor drinking areas to the front and rear. Memorabilia from the original Brampton Brewery festoon the walls. Quiz night is Tuesday, and Sunday lunches are served. An annual beer festival is held to mark St George's Day. Four Brampton beers are always available, including a dark ale. Local CAMRA Pub of the Year 2018. P(170)

Clay Cross

Rykneld Turnpyke

4 John Street, S45 9NQ

2-11.30 (midnight Fri); 12-midnight Sat; 12-11.30 Sun

(01246) 250366

12 changing beers H

It is a welcome return to the Guide for this establishment after being refurbished following a devastating fire. Formerly the Egstow Working Men's Club, the Rykneld Turnpyke (named after Rykneld Street, the old road between Chesterfield and Derby) has one large room divided into different areas, with comfortable seating. There is an excellent choice of up to 12 reasonably priced beers from brewers who are mostly local, including the on-site Instant Karma Brewery which can be seen through a viewing panel at the rear. Cribbage and dominoes are always available.

(51,54)

Clowne

Centre

Recreation Close, S43 4PL

7-11; 5-11 Sat & Sun ☎ (01246) 819546

4 changing beers (often Timothy Taylor)

A council-run community centre widely used by the locals for functions. The Rock and Blues Club has live bands every Sunday and there is a popular quiz night on Tuesday with free food. The venue is well cared for, with a relaxed and friendly atmosphere, and hosts a beer festival in May. The Timothy Taylor beer is always changing, and there are guest beers. Ample car parking is available. P

Coton-in-the-Elms

Black Horse

17 Burton Road, DE12 8HJ (centre of village)

4-11 (midnight Fri); 1-midnight Sat; 12-10.30 Sun
☎ (01283) 762947 theblackhorsederbyshire.co.uk

Draught Bass; Joule's Pale Ale; Marston's Pedigree; 1 changing beer (sourced regionally)

Lively and popular free house, owned by the licensee, with a bright and airy main room divided into bar and lounge areas by glass-topped wood partitions. A small snug, served through a hatch, features a bar billiards table. The guest beer is often from a local microbrewery, and over 25 ciders/perries are stocked (sources vary). A free cheeseboard is offered weekday evenings and weekend lunchtimes. Quiz night is Tuesday and live music is played monthly on a Sunday. Accommodation is a two-person self-catering holiday flat. Q P (22)

Cromford

Boat Inn

Scarthin, DE4 3QF (small road behind shops from Greyhound car park)

12-midnight; 12-11.30 Sun ☎ (01629) 258083
the-boat-inn.co.uk

4 changing beers (sourced locally; often Abbeydale, Dancing Duck, Whim)

Built in 1772, the beamed ceilings, exposed stone walls and open fire give the main bar a cosy atmosphere. A small snug area, dining room and cellar bar with Sky and BT Sports cater for most, if not all, needs. Home-cooked meals are served every day 12-9pm. Live music takes place every Friday and Saturday night. The beer garden overlooks the large mill pond.

Crowdecote

Pack Horse Inn

SK17 0DB (nr Buxton)

closed Mon & Tue; 12-3, 6-11; 12-3, 6-10.30 Sun
☎ (01298) 83618 thepack-horseinn.co.uk

4 changing beers

Friendly and welcoming pub on the side of the hill in the Upper Dove Valley just yards from the Staffordshire border, remote and rural but well worth the effort to visit. The knowledgeable landlord has a passion for quality real ales. Separate drinking areas in the main bar create a cosy feel and there is a dining room and pool room on the lower level. It is open bank holiday Mondays but may close early weekday evenings.

Cutthorpe

Gate Inn

Overgreen, S42 7BA

11.30-11; 12-11 Sun ☎ (01246) 276923

Black Sheep Best Bitter; Fuller's London Pride; 4 changing beers

This pub is set in a beautiful scenic rural location with views overlooking two counties. Two beers from local breweries are usually on the bar including Peak, Bradfield and Thornbridge. Meals are served all day until 9pm in the large dining areas to the left and rear of the main bar area. Although remote, it is only a 10-minute walk from the nearest bus stop at Linacre Reservoir.
Q P

Derby

Alexandra Hotel

203 Siddals Road, DE1 2QE

12-11 (midnight Fri); 11-midnight Sat ☎ (01332) 293993
alexandrahotelderby.co.uk

Castle Rock Harvest Pale; 5 changing beers (sourced nationally)

A Castle Rock pub serving four of its beers and up to five guests, including a mild and a stout or porter. There are also more than 50 UK and continental bottled beers of varying styles. Themed food nights are held approximately monthly. The lounge is adorned with breweriana and the bar with railway memorabilia. A Class 37 locomotive cab resides in the car park. This venue was the birthplace of Derby CAMRA in 1974.
Q P

Babington Arms

11-13 Babington Lane, DE1 1TA

8am-midnight ☎ (01332) 383647

Draught Bass; Greene King Abbot; Marston's Pedigree; Ruddles Best Bitter; Small World Thunderbridge Stout, Twin Falls; 11 changing beers (sourced nationally)

This Wetherspoon pub is a converted furniture showroom close to the city centre. It boasts a huge range of real ales, many from local microbreweries, and typically has six ciders on handpump or gravity dispense. The back end of the large bar has some half-partitioned banquette seating and caters for family eating. At the front of the pub there is a small fenced-off area where outdoor drinkers can smoke.

Brunswick Inn

1 Railway Terrace, DE1 2RU

11-11 (11.30 Fri & Sat); 12-10.30 Sun ☎ (01332) 290677
brunswickderby.co.uk

Brunswick White Feather, Triple Hop, The Usual; Everards Beacon Hill, Tiger; Timothy Taylor Landlord; 10 changing beers (sourced nationally)

Originally part of the railway village, this multi-roomed pub was restored and opened as Derby's first multiple choice real ale house in 1987. A purpose-built brewery was added in 1991 and it has since become one of the best-known free houses in the country. Owned by Everards, the range of up to 16 real ales includes at least six from Brunswick, the in-house brewery. It gets busy on Derby County match days. Local CAMRA Pub of the Year 2016 and 2017 and Cider Pub of the Year 2018. Q P

Exeter Arms

13 Exeter Place, DE1 2EU

12-11 (11.30 Wed & Thu; midnight Fri & Sat); 12-10.30 Sun (01332) 605323 exeterarms.co.uk

Dancing Duck Ay Up, Dark Drake; Marston's Pedigree; 4 changing beers H

A joint venture between Dancing Duck Brewery and a local food and drink entrepreneur has resulted in a fine range of beers and an excellent dining experience, all put together in a pub with old-world charm. The small bar has an open fire and leads to several other rooms, including a wooden-settled snug with an old-fashioned range. The adjoining atmospheric cottage dating from about 1815 has now been incorporated into the pub. It has a popular and quirky quiz on Monday evenings.

Falstaff

74 Silverhill Road, DE23 6UJ

12-11 (midnight Fri & Sat) (01332) 342902 falstaffbrewery.co.uk

Falstaff Fist Full of Hops, Phoenix, Smiling Assassin; 1 changing beer H

A 20-minute walk from the city centre rewards you with this atmospheric and reputedly haunted free house. Originally a coaching inn before the neighbourhood was built up, it is now the Falstaff Brewery tap and has long been the best real ale house in the Normanton area of Derby. The rear lounge is a shrine to Offilers' Brewery, with a display of memorabilia. Other collectables can be viewed throughout the games room and second bar room. Q

Five Lamps

25 Duffield Road, DE1 3BH

12-11 (midnight Fri & Sat) (01332) 348730 fivelampsderby.co.uk

Draught Bass; Everards Tiger; Peak Ales Chatsworth Gold; St Austell Proper Job; Thornbridge Jaipur IPA; house beer (by Derby); 8 changing beers (sourced regionally) H

Since it reopened in 2010, the pub has gone from strength to strength thanks to the dedication of the licensees and staff. Fourteen handpumps showcase many local ales from breweries such as Derby, Peak and Whim. The Lamps is essentially open plan, but has many little nooks and crannies giving it a homely feel. It has been tastefully refurbished with wood panelling and leather seating in a traditional style. P

Flowerpot

23-25 King Street, DE1 3DZ

12-11 (11.30 Wed & Thu; 12.30am Fri & Sat) (01332) 204955 theflowerpotderby.co.uk

Marston's Pedigree; Oakham Bishops Farewell; Sharp's Doom Bar H**; Whim Hartington IPA** H/G**, Flower Power** H**; 9 changing beers (sourced nationally)** H/G

Dating from around 1800 but much expanded from its original premises, this vibrant pub reaches back from the roadside frontage and divides into several interlinking rooms. One room provides the stage for regular live bands; another has a glass cellar wall revealing rows of stillaged firkins, which can be seen from the bar and from the road outside. Up to 14 real ales and two ciders are offered. Good en-suite accommodation is available.

Furnace Inn

Duke Street, DE1 3BX

2-11; 11-midnight Fri & Sat; 11-11 Sun (01332) 385981 shinybrewing.com/the-furnace-inn

8 changing beers (sourced nationally) H

Since it reopened in 2012 the pub has transformed into a real ale mecca. A former Hardys and Hansons pub, it is now the tap for Furnace Brewery. Up to eight real ales and three ciders/perries are served, plus guest beers from all over. There are two distinct open-plan rooms with a central bar. Poker and cheese nights feature weekly, with regular beer festivals held throughout the year.

P

Golden Eagle

55 Agard Street, DE1 1DZ

12-11.30; 12-11 Sun

Morland Old Golden Hen; Titanic Plum Porter; 3 changing beers (sourced nationally) H

Completely refurbished by the Titan Brewery, it is now the brewery tap. The pub's original name has also been restored after many changes. A mural on the outside pays homage to Derby history. Inside, the single room has a wooden floor throughout. It is comfortable and welcoming, with a table next to the bar for newspapers and local interest books. The upstairs function room hosts a poker night on Sunday and there is live acoustic music every Thursday evening. P

Last Post

1 Uttoxeter Old Road, DE1 1GA

11-11 (8 Mon-Wed) (01332) 296737

4 changing beers (sourced nationally) H

This former post office was Derby's second micropub and consists of a large single room with the bar towards the rear. The four changing beers vary continuously and one is usually dark. There is an interesting variety of whiskies on offer as well. Live acoustic music can be heard every evening from Thursday to Sunday. The small rear yard is a dedicated smoking area. Beer festivals coincide with those of the local CAMRA branch.

(8)

Little Chester Ale House

4a Chester Green Road, DE1 3SF

3-10.30; 12-11 Fri & Sat; 12-10.30 Sun

Hartshorns Ignite; 3 changing beers (sourced nationally) H

Derby's first micropub, on the edge of a tree-lined conservation area and in the historic Little Chester part of the city, the site of Roman Derventio, near where two ancient wells can still been seen. This former shop has one small main room with a narrower passageway containing the bar. It has four changing beers, including three from local Hartshorns brewery, the pub's owner.

Q

Old Bell Hotel

51 Sadler Gate, DE1 3NQ

12-11 (1am Fri & Sat) (01332) 723090 bellhotelderby.co.uk

Dancing Duck Dark Drake; Draught Bass; 6 changing beers (sourced locally) H

One of Derby's best-loved pubs continues to be restored to its former magnificence. The front Tavern Bar features a range of real ale and craft kegs, but discerning drinkers should seek out the Tudor Bar to the rear, which only ceased being a men-only bar in 1975. This 18th-century coaching inn is a welcome oasis in Sadler Gate, a premier shopping street in the Cathedral Quarter. The exterior Tudor-style half-timbering was only added in 1929.

Olde Dolphin Inne ★

5a Queen Street, DE1 3DL (close to cathedral)
11.30-11 (midnight Fri & Sat); 12-11 Sun
(01332) 267711 yeoldedolphin.co.uk
Draught Bass; Greene King Abbot; Sharp's Doom Bar, Atlantic; 4 changing beers (sourced nationally) H
Claimed to be Derby's oldest pub, it certainly looks the part, with a number of small rooms including a traditional snug which has a real fire in winter and conversation all year round. There is regular live music on the large outdoor patio. Food is provided in the bar areas, as well as in the upstairs steak restaurant open Thursday to Saturday evenings. A music quiz is held on Tuesday evenings and a general knowledge quiz on Sunday evenings.
QP

Peacock Inn

87 Nottingham Road, DE1 3QS
11 (3 Mon)-11; 11-midnight Fri & Sat; 12-10.30 Sun
(01332) 583308
Draught Bass; Marston's Pedigree; Whim Arbor Light, Hartington IPA; house beer (by Leatherbritches); 4 changing beers (sourced nationally) H
This attractive 18th-century stone-built roadside pub used to be a staging post on the main coach road out of Derby, which ran alongside the old Derby Canal. Two rooms on different levels are divided by a central bar, with wooden floors, stove burners, photos of old Derby and Derby County memorabilia. Up to nine real ales and two ciders and/or perries feature. Beer festivals are held in the large covered garden area to the rear.
Q

Rowditch Inn

246 Uttoxeter New Road, DE22 3LL
7-11; 12-2, 7-11 Sat & Sun (01332) 343123
Marston's Pedigree; Rowditch St Stephens, St Andrews; 1 changing beer H
This welcoming roadside hostelry has an unexpectedly deep interior which divides into two bar areas and a small snug. There is a display cabinet of pub memorabilia, and the pumpclips adorning the walls testify to the myriad of guest ales. Downstairs, at the rear, the garden is a peaceful haven. The output of the pub's brewery is almost exclusively consumed on the premises. Well worth the walk or the five-minute bus ride from the city centre. Q

Silk Mill Ale & Cider House

19 Full Street, DE1 3AF
12-11 (midnight Fri & Sat); 12-10.30 Sun
(01332) 349160 thesilkmillderby.co.uk
Dancing Duck Ay Up; Draught Bass; 5 changing beers H
Handsome stone-faced building named after the historic silk mill nearby, which marks the start of the Derwent Valley World Heritage Trail. To the right of the entrance is the Offilers' Lounge with a cosy real fire, ideal for drinkers. There is a dedicated dining area to the rear of the pub – booking is recommended at peak times. The central bar has nine handpumps shared between real ales and ciders. Quirky decorative ornaments and fittings are used throughout. P

Smithfield

Meadow Road, DE1 2BH
12-10.30; 12-midnight Fri-Sun (01332) 986601
smithfieldderby.co.uk
Draught Bass; 7 changing beers (sourced nationally) H
The Smithfield rests near the town centre on the banks of the River Derwent opposite Bass's Rec. The large main bar boasts an eclectic range of new interesting beers supported by Draught Bass. A separate quiet room with a real fire overlooks the patio, itself against the river. The pub has regular live music and many beer-related activities. Local CAMRA Pub of the Year 2018. P

Standing Order

28-32 Iron Gate, DE1 3GL
7am-12.30am (2am Fri & Sat); 7am-midnight Sun
(01332) 207591
Draught Bass; Greene King Abbot; Kelham Island Pale Rider; Marston's Pedigree; Ruddles Best Bitter; Sharp's Doom Bar; 12 changing beers H
Named after the building's former role as a bank, it became the first, grandest and certainly the tallest of the three Wetherspoon outlets in Derby. It features full-size reproductions of paintings of Derby worthies from the time of the Industrial Revolution. There are a few quieter corners, but generally this has the feeling of a busy city-centre pub. A good changing selection of guest ales is available. Alcohol is served from 9am.
Q

Dronfield

Coach & Horses

Sheffield Road, S18 2GD
4-10.30 Mon; 12-11 (midnight Fri & Sat); 12-10.30 Sun
(01246) 413269 mycoachandhorses.co.uk
Thornbridge Brother Rabbit, Lord Marples; 1 changing beer (sourced nationally; often Thornbridge, Drone Valley, Mallinsons) H
The pub is next to Sheffield FC's ground on the northern edge of Dronfield. It is operated by Thornbridge Brewery and showcases a good range of the regular and seasonal beers, plus guest ales, across a wide range of beer styles on six handpulls. The large outdoor drinking area is particularly popular. Good-value meals are served daily. Quiz night is Sunday, open mic acoustic night Monday.
QP(43)

Dronfield Arms

Chesterfield Road, S18 2XE
4-11; 3-midnight Fri; 12-midnight Sat; 12-10.30 Sun
(01246) 414413 dronfield-arms.co.uk
Abbeydale Moonshine; Hopjacker The Mark, Pyrites, The Grifter; 3 changing beers (sourced nationally; often Drone Valley, Magic Rock, RedWillow) H
This became Dronfield's first brewpub when the Hopjacker Brewery was opened in 2015. The brewery is downstairs in the former restaurant and is on display to customers through a glass panel in the floor of the main bar. Seven handpulls offer Hopjacker and a guest range. Quiz night is Tuesday at 8.30pm. P(44)

Duffield

Town Street Tap

17 Town Street, DE56 4EH

closed Mon; 4-10 Tue-Thu; 12-10.30 Fri & Sat; 12-5 Sun ☎ 07925 461706 thetownstreettap.co.uk
6 changing beers (sourced nationally) G
On the main road through Duffield, this micropub for Tollgate Brewery has been converted into a modern, uncluttered drinking space with table service. Of the six changing real ales, two are from the Tollgate range and at least one is dark. In addition, four ciders are available and takeouts come in containers or from the Bottle Shop. Walkers with boots are welcome, and there is free tea and coffee for drivers, pork pies and Scotch eggs for the hungry. Local CAMRA Country Pub of the Year 2018. **QP**

Glossop

Crown Inn ★
142 Victoria Street, SK13 8JF (on Hayfield Road out of town centre)
5-11; 12-11 Fri & Sat; 12-10.30 Sun ☎ (01457) 862824
Samuel Smith Old Brewery Bitter H
Stone-built end-of-terrace locals' pub, a few minutes from the town centre and railway station, built in 1846 and acquired by the brewery in 1977, and on CAMRA's National Inventory of Historic Pub Interiors. A curved bar serves two snugs, each with real fires in winter, and a pool/games room. Pictures of bygone Glossop add to the traditional character. An enclosed outdoor drinking area is provided in the rear yard. **Q** (390)

Queen's Arms
1 Shepley Street, SK13 7RZ
10.30-midnight ☎ (01457) 853005
queens-arms-hotel-old-glossop.co.uk
Joseph Holt Bitter; Morland Old Speckled Hen; Thornbridge Jaipur IPA; Wainwright; 3 changing beers (sourced locally) H
Situated in the Old Glossop part of town, below the Bleaklow hills, a pleasant 15-minute walk from the town centre through Manor Park. Popular with locals, visitors and hikers, it now serves breakfasts from 10.30am and the licence also covers the sale of alcohol from this time. A standard pub menu is offered downstairs; the Queen Spice Indian restaurant is on the first floor. Live entertainment takes place on Tuesdays and Saturdays while Thursday is quiz night. Local CAMRA Derbyshire Pub of the Year in 2017. (390)

Star Inn
2 Howard Street, SK13 7DD (next to railway station)
2-11 (midnight Fri); 12-midnight Sat; 12-10.30 Sun ☎ (01457) 853072
4 changing beers (sourced regionally; often Abbeydale, Howard Town, Pictish) H
A popular town-centre pub, run by a dedicated CAMRA member. A large comfortable main room, where conversation predominates, features wood panelling. A smaller room is to the rear. Guest beers are mainly from local microbreweries and real draught cider is served. Regular beer and cider festivals are held throughout the year. Close to the railway station, the pub is an ideal starting/finishing point for walking within the Dark Peak area. **QP**

Hartshorne

Admiral Rodney Inn
65 Main Street, DE11 7ES (on A514.)
5-11; 11-11 Sat; 12-11 Sun ☎ (01283) 227771
Exmoor Gold; 5 changing beers (sourced nationally) H
A traditional friendly village pub dating back to the early 19th century, but rebuilt and extended in the late 20th century to provide an open-plan L-shaped drinking area while retaining the original oak beams in the former snug. There is also a secluded raised area tucked away behind the bar. Additional guest beers often feature at weekends. There is cheese tasting on the first Monday of the month, a quiz night on Sunday, and occasional live music. The grounds include a cricket pitch, home of Hartshorne Cricket Club. **P** (2)

Hayfield

George Hotel
14 Church Street, SK22 2JE
11.45-11 (11.30 Fri & Sat); 12-11 Sun ☎ (01663) 743691
georgehotelhayfield.co.uk
Banks's Amber Ale; Ringwood Boondoggle; 2 changing beers (sourced nationally) H
Rambling stone-built 16th-century pub in the centre of the village. Originally a mail house, the Derby Militia was formed here in 1808. In addition to the handpulled ales, Thatchers Heritage cider is served. Two comfortable lounges, a cosy bar area, and a separate dining room await the visitor. The interior includes stained-glass mullioned windows and a magnificent cast-iron range fireplace incorporating a real fire in winter. Hikers and cyclists are welcome. Close to Hayfield bus station. **P**

Royal Hotel
Market Street, SK22 2EP
11-11 ☎ (01663) 742721 theroyalhayfield.co.uk
5 changing beers (sourced locally) H
An imposing stone pub, built as a coaching inn in the 18th century, close to the church, cricket ground and River Sett. The interior boasts oak panels and pews, creating a relaxing atmosphere; real fires blaze in winter. Guest beers from local micros are always available. A restaurant and function room complete the facilities (food is served all day in summer). The village is the base for many leisure activities in the Dark Peak and was the birthplace of actor Arthur Lowe. **QP**

Holbrook

Spotted Cow
12 Town Street, DE56 0TA
12-11 (midnight Fri & Sat) ☎ (01332) 880798
thespottedcowholbrook.co.uk
Marston's Pedigree; 5 changing beers (sourced locally) H
A community-owned pub with a range of local beers from nearby microbreweries. It has been restored to its former status as an historic ale house, has a good selection of wines and spirits, and serves locally sourced food. Traditional roast only is served on Sundays. The Spotted Calf, a next-door coffee bar/café, shares the facilities and is run by the Holbrook Community Society. **P**

Hope

Cheshire Cheese Inn

Edale Road, S33 6ZF

closed Mon; 12-3, 6-11; 12-11 Sat; 12-9 Sun
(01433) 620381 thecheshirecheeseinn.co.uk

Bradfield Farmers Blonde; 3 changing beers (sourced locally; often Bradfield, Peak Ales)

A cosy country inn dating from 1578, with an open-plan bar area and a smaller room at a lower level that was probably originally used to house animals, but now is mainly used as a dining area. Home-cooked meals using local produce are served lunchtimes and evenings. The pub is in good walking country but the parking is limited as the road outside is narrow. Q P

Horsley Woodhouse

Old Oak Inn

176 Main Street, DE7 6AW

4 (3 Thu & Fri; 12 Sat)-11; 12-10.30 Sun (01332) 881299

Changing beers (sourced nationally; often Bottle Brook, Leadmill)

As the taphouse for the Leadmill Brewery, the Old Oak features an extensive variety of Leadmill beers, plus a couple of guests. This is a traditional pub boasting four rooms of differing character, some having open fires, and is homely and welcoming. At weekends drinkers can enjoy the RuRAD bar – effectively a mini beer festival offering ales dispensed on gravity from craft brewers near and far alongside the more local Leadmill and Bottle Brook beers. Local CAMRA Pub of the Year 2016. Q P

Hundall

Miners Arms

Hundall Lane, S18 4BP

12-midnight (01246) 414505

Drone Valley Dronny Bottom Bitter; Pictish Alchemists Ale; 3 changing beers (sourced nationally; often Church End, Drone Valley, Welbeck Abbey)

On the high ridge above Unstone, this is a traditional village local which has thrived since its change of ownership in 2015. The beer garden to the rear provides an excellent space in which to enjoy the wide range of beers and ciders always available. The Miners operates a Monday Club, when real ale and cider are £2.30 a pint for all customers. Local CAMRA Pub of the Year 2016-2018. Q P

Ilkeston

Burnt Pig

53 Market Street, DE7 5RB

closed Mon-Wed; 11-11 07538 723722

5 changing beers

This micropub is now well established as a busy and popular local, which extends over three rooms with a collection of historical pub memorabilia. Hosted and run by its welcoming and enthusiastic owner Simon, it dispenses five varying beers and a good selection of real ciders and continental bottled beers. Also on offer are tasty cheeses to take away, and it still supplies its famous pork scratchings. This is a pub not to be missed. Q

Dewdrop

24 Station Road, DE7 5TE

4 (3 Fri; 12 Sat)-11; 12-10.30 Sun (0115) 932 9684

Oakham Bishops Farewell; house beer (by Oakham); changing beers (often Acorn, Blue Monkey, Castle Rock)

A heritage Victorian pub next to the new Ilkeston railway station on the outskirts of town, ideal as a first port of call to the real ale scene in Ilkeston or a relaxed visit before returning to the train. The layout is unchanged, with three rooms. The bar and lounge are separated by the serving area. A small room is offset from the entrance and provides a quiet area to sit. Eight beers plus three ciders are available, and there is pub food. Q (27)

Observatory

14A Market Place, DE7 5QA (E side of Market Place)

8am-midnight (0115) 932 8040

Greene King Abbot; Ruddles Best Bitter; Sharp's Doom Bar; 4 changing beers (often Exmoor)

A Wetherspoon that honours John Flamsteed, first Astronomer Royal, who was born locally, and which used to be a bank. The large bar, with a glass frontage, dispenses seven cask beers. This pub has ground-floor toilets. Upstairs is a smaller eating and drinking area and an outside terrace. It is a short walk to Wharncliffe Road for all bus routes. Q

Prince of Wales

69 South Street, DE7 5QQ

4-11; 12-11 Fri-Sun (0115) 932 5452

3 changing beers

A two-roomed ex-Shipstone's pub and a welcome new entry to the Guide, with a smaller lounge to the left and a popular bar to the right. The serving area is central to both. Throughout the year the pub offers brewery takeovers, increasing the number of beers available. Three handpumps dispense well-kept ales and support local breweries such as Falstaff and Blue Monkey.

Little Longstone

Packhorse Inn

Main Street, DE45 1NN

12-3, 5-11; 12-11 Sat & Sun (01629) 640471
packhorselongstone.co.uk

Black Sheep Best Bitter; Thornbridge Wild Swan, Lord Marples, Jaipur IPA; 2 changing beers (often Thornbridge)

A small pub that began life as two miners' cottages, but has been welcoming drinkers since 1787. Just a short walk from stunning views of Monsal Head, dogs and walkers are welcome. Fresh local produce is a passion, an ethos also extended to the beers, which always include a choice from the nearby Thornbridge Brewery. There is a pleasant beer garden. Food is available all day at weekends. (173)

Litton

Red Lion

Church Lane, SK17 8QU

12-11 (midnight Fri & Sat); 12-10.30 Sun
(01298) 871458 theredlionlitton.co.uk

Abbeydale Absolution; Peak Ales Bakewell Best Bitter; 2 changing beers (sourced locally; often Abbeydale, Peak Ales)

Nestling on the green and the only pub in the village, the Red Lion is a welcome refuge for locals and visitors alike. There is a large fireplace warming several rooms off a central passageway. Not to be missed, the annual wakes week is at the end of June with events including a well dressing on the village green, during which the pub holds a beer festival. Fresh food is served all day, every day. (65,173)

Long Eaton

Hole in the Wall

Regent Street, NG10 1JX

4-11.30; 11-12.30am Fri & Sat; 12-11.30 Sun

(0115) 973 4920

Draught Bass; Nottingham Extra Pale Ale; Oakham Citra, Bishops Farewell; 1 changing beer H

This regular Guide entry has retained its charm and is an unchanged two-roomed local. The walls of both rooms in the bar are covered with pub memorabilia collected by the landlord, who has had 30-plus years at the helm. It is a well-established local which has maintained its high standard of beer quality over the years. The pub offers a choice of four regular beers and one guest ale. Wheelchair access is via the rear entrance. Q

York Chambers

40 Market Place, NG10 1LT

1 (4 Mon)-10; 11-11 Fri & Sat; 12-10 Sun

(0115) 946 0999

6 changing beers (sourced nationally) H

This micropub, formerly a bank before becoming a café, has a little-changed interior, with high ceilings and an impressive wood-panelled fireplace. It serves six changing real ales straight from the cask; the temperature-controlled cellar is in full view of the bar. A range of ciders and quality wines is also available. It is a popular and friendly establishment and is close to a number of bus routes. Local CAMRA Pub of the Year 2018. Q

Lullington

Colvile Arms

Main Street, DE12 8EG (centre of village)

6-11 (10 Mon); 5-11.30 Fri; 12-11.30 Sat & Sun

07510 870980 thecolvilearms.com

Draught Bass; Marston's Pedigree; 2 changing beers (sourced regionally) H

Leased from the Lullington Estate, the seat of the Colvile family until the early 1900s, this popular 18th-century free house is at the heart of an attractive hamlet. The public bar comprises an adjoining hallway and snug, each featuring high-backed settles with wood panelling. The bar and a comfortable lounge are on opposite sides of a central serving area. A second lounge/function room overlooks the beer garden and lawn. QP

Makeney

Holly Bush ★

Holly Bush Lane, DE56 0RX

12-11; 12-10.30 Sun (01332) 841729

hollybushinnmakeney.co.uk

Fuller's London Pride; Greene King Abbot; Marston's Pedigree; Timothy Taylor Landlord; 4 changing beers (sourced nationally) H

The Holly Bush is a late 17th-century Grade II-listed pub with great character. Once a farmhouse and brewery on the Strutt Estate, the pub stood on the main Derby turnpike before the new road (now the A6) opened in 1818. Dick Turpin reputedly drank here and the pub, recognised by CAMRA as having a nationally important historic interior, has various stone-flagged hideaways, and there are often welcoming fires in winter. The home-cooked lunchtime menu and bar snacks are available daily. Regular beer festivals take place, and walkers, families and dogs are welcome. QP

Mapleton

Okeover Arms

DE6 2AB (5 mins drive from Ashbourne; take road at side of George & Dragon in market square)

11-11 (01335) 350305 theokeover.co.uk

Peak Ales Swift Nick; 2 changing beers (sourced locally) H

A large pub set in a small village in good walking country that welcomes walkers, muddy boots and dogs. It is a free house with at least two, and sometimes three, ales on, plus a decent cider or perry. The modern bar area has a flagstoned floor and low ceiling. The dining room at the other end serves good food. Roasts are served on Sundays until they run out, after that it is back to the regular menu. P

Matlock

MoCa Bar

77 Dale Road, DE4 3LT

11-11 (1am Fri & Sat) (01629) 583973

7 changing beers (sourced locally; often Abbeydale, Blue Monkey, Thornbridge) H

This modern single-room bar has a sophisticated café feel, with wooden floors and chunky pine furniture. Comfortable seating is available in a large window area and on a decked terrace at the rear. Open plan, with music memorabilia adorning the walls, the MoCa Bar has seven handpulls featuring ales from dedicated breweries Abbeydale, Blue Monkey, Totally Brewed, Dancing Duck, Pentrich, Oakham and Thornbridge. There is a reduction in the price of real ales (except premium ales) Monday to Wednesday.

Thorn Tree Inn

48 Jackson Road, DE4 3JQ (up Bank Rd, left into Smedley St, 2nd right up Smith Rd, 1st left)

12-2 (not Mon), 5-11; 12-midnight Fri & Sat; 12-11 Sun

(01629) 580295

Draught Bass; Nottingham Extra Pale Ale; Timothy Taylor Landlord; 4 changing beers (sourced nationally) H

Perched high above Matlock town, this compact two-roomed traditional pub enjoys beautiful views from the heated patio area. Children and dogs are welcome. A haunted wall clock hangs in the lounge where regulars, ramblers and real ale enthusiasts convene to enjoy the atmosphere. Three permanent real ales are complemented by four different guests. Home-made food is served Tuesday to Friday lunchtimes, pie night is Wednesday 6-8pm, and Sunday lunch is served till 5pm. Bar snacks are available all day. Local CAMRA Pub of the Year 2018. Q

Twenty Ten

16 Dale Road, DE4 3LT

closed Mon; 12-10 (midnight Fri & Sat); 12-9 Sun
07710 427442 twentytenmatlock.co.uk

4 changing beers (sourced locally; often Matlock Wolds Farm) H

A stone's throw from the railway station, Twenty Ten nestles among the antique shops on Matlock's historic Dale Road. Bare floorboards and French chic furnishing lend the place a style not often encountered elsewhere. Focusing on LocAle, the establishment is an outlet for Matlock Wolds Farm ales. Children and dogs are welcome, and food is served throughout the day. Often quiet early doors, things liven up considerably on Friday and Saturday evenings with live music laid on.

Melbourne

Chip & Pin

8-10 High Street, DE73 8GN

closed Mon; 4.30-9.30; 12-9.30 Fri & Sat; 12-2.30 Sun
07957 806454 chipandpinpub.com

4 changing beers (sourced regionally) G

A micropub centrally located in Melbourne's old Midland Bank premises. It is owned by a group of local real ale enthusiasts who serve you at your table. The building has been sympathetically restored and comprises two rooms, a main drinking area and a meeting room for local groups. Real ales are available in third of a pint taster racks. Real cider, wine, soft drinks and snacks are also on sale. Sunday opening hours apply on bank holidays.
Q (2)

New Mills

Beer Shed

47B Market Street, SK22 4AA

closed Mon & Tue; 2 (4 Wed & Thu)-10.30
(01663) 742005

4 changing beers (sourced locally; often Rock Mill, Torrside) H

The Beer Shed is this town's first micropub, handily situated in the town centre close to New Mills Central railway station and bus station. The layout is rather unusual, with a small frontage and long narrow bar, but it serves its purpose well. There is a small downstairs room also. The three changing beers support local micros. The cheerful, intimate atmosphere makes for a pleasant drinking experience. Q

Newbold

Nag's Head Inn

37 Newbold Village, S41 8RJ

4-11; 12-midnight Sat; 12-11 Sun (01246) 297446

Sharp's Doom Bar; 5 changing beers (often Brampton) H

A pub built in 1760 and Grade II-listed, retaining its central bar layout, surrounded by four separate rooms, one of them with an open fire. Another historic building directly behind, the medieval Eyre Chapel, is accessed through the pub car park and is Grade II*-listed. Adjoining this is the Newbold Observatory which has public open evenings. On Tuesdays there is a discount on cask ales. Traditional cider is available in the summer months. P

Newton

New Inn

80 Main Street, DE55 5TE

closed Mon; 4-midnight (1am Fri); 12-1am Sat; 12-midnight Sun (01773) 873944

Dukeries IPA, Farmers Branch; 1 changing beer (sourced locally) H

Two Dukeries beers, a guest ale and a cider or perry adorn the bar in this welcoming village pub. Traditional Sunday lunch is served 12-4pm, Thursday is steak night, followed by quiz and bingo. Karaoke is every other Friday, while live music is a feature most Saturdays. Third-pint taster batons are available. The L-shaped bar has comfortable seating with a real fire. The outdoor area has had an impressive makeover and is popular in the summer months.
Q P

Newton Solney

Brickmakers Arms

9-11 Main Street, DE15 0SJ (on B5008, opp jct with Trent Lane)

5 (4 Fri; 1 Sat)-11; 12-11 Sun 07525 220103
brickmakersarms.pub

Burton Bridge Sovereign Gold, Bitter, Burton Porter, Stairway to Heaven; 1 changing beer (sourced regionally) H

A cosy local at the end of an 18th-century terrace of cottages; it was converted into a pub in the early 19th century for workers at a nearby brickworks. Internally, it features a narrow central bar leading at one end to a room served through a hatch, and at the other end to an impressive oak-panelled room. The street entrance hallway houses a small bring & take library, beyond which is a function/meeting room. Quiz night is Monday, bingo Tuesday and poker Thursday.
Q P (V3)

North Wingfield

Shinnon

99 Station Rd, S42 5JJ

4-11; 2-midnight Fri; 12-midnight Sat & Sun
07983 503932

2 changing beers (sourced regionally) H

Traditional two-room village community local with a friendly welcome. Formerly the Midland Hotel, the pub now takes its name from an early 20th-century landlady who wore her hair in a 'chignon'. Two handpumps serve regularly changing beers from local and regional breweries, usually a lighter beer and darker option. The pub is family friendly and dogs are allowed in the taproom only. Wednesday is quiz night. P

Ockbrook

Cross Keys

Green Lane, DE72 3SE

12-midnight; 12-11.30 Sun (01332) 662308
crosskeys-ockbrook.co.uk

Marston's Pedigree; Sharp's Doom Bar; Tetley Mild; 2 changing beers H

A traditional village pub with a quirky character and a selection of five real ales and one real cider. The bar has a low-beamed ceiling, a darts playing area, several screens for sports TV and a woodburner for the winter months. Events include karaoke, quizzes

and theme nights. Home-made food features stone-baked pizza. Outside there is a small terrace with seating at the front and a small enclosed garden and play area to the side.
P (9,9A)

Royal Oak

55 Green Lane, DE72 3SE
11.30-3, 5-11; 11.30-11.30 Fri & Sat; 12-11.30 Sun
(01332) 662378 royaloakockbrook.com
Draught Bass; 4 changing beers H
Attractive 18th-century pub with a number of small rooms. Run by the Wilson family since 1953, they have brought about many improvements while retaining the original character and features. Excellent home-cooked food is served Monday to Saturday lunchtimes and early evenings, with two sittings for Sunday lunch. A large function room allows the pub to host many community and public events including live music and open mic nights. Outside there are two pleasant gardens, one with an enclosed play area for children. Local CAMRA Country Pub of the Year 2016 and 2017.
QP (9,9A)

Openwoodgate

Black Bull's Head

2 Kilburn Lane, DE56 0SF
12-11; 12-10.30 Sun 07860 757741
blackbullshead.com
Draught Bass; Greene King Abbot; Oakham Bishops Farewell; 6 changing beers (sourced nationally; often Blue Monkey, Castle Rock, Dancing Duck) H
A two-roomed former Greene King pub, now a free house, offering a warm welcome in comfortable surroundings with real fires in the winter. Walls are adorned with historic photographs and newspaper clippings of local and national interest, with one wall dedicated to the RAF. The pub serves many real ales and ciders, and there are more available in the separate rustic Bedlam Bar, open Friday to Sunday. QP (6.4,6.x)

Repton

Boot

12 Boot Hill, DE65 6FT (from Repton Cross head down Brook End; pub is on right as road is joined by Boot Hill)
11-11.45 (01283) 346047 thebootatrepton.co.uk
Boot Repton Cross, Clod Hopper, Bitter, IPA; 3 changing beers (sourced regionally) H
Close to the Repton Cross at the centre of the village, this pub has been brought back to life by the local Bespoke pub company with a refurbishment and the addition of an on-site microbrewery supplying up to six of the real ales on the bar. There are two main rooms, one more devoted to dining. Accommodation is available.
P (V3)

Ripley

Talbot

1 Butterley Hill, DE5 3LT
2-10.30; 12-11.30 Fri & Sat; 12-10.30 Sun
(01773) 742382
8 changing beers (sourced nationally) H
A traditional Victorian flat iron-shaped pub, the Talbot is blissfully free of music, instead preferring the sounds of conversation, laughter and traditional games. It has a real fire in winter and an excellent selection of real ales pulled from casks stored on an original stone stillage. Bar snacks are usually available. Locally turned pump handles in various designs add to the enjoyment of this welcoming and friendly popular pub. Local CAMRA Cider Pub of the Year 2018. QP

Thorn Tree

Market Place, DE5 3HA
10-midnight (01773) 744479
6 changing beers (sourced nationally) H
A Pub People Company-owned pub, the Thorn Tree is busy, popular and welcoming. An excellent selection of well-kept real ales and ciders is available; the ales are from local microbreweries as well as breweries nationwide. The large bar room is separated into several distinct areas. Food is served during the day, live music often takes place on Sunday evenings, and there is a weekly general knowledge quiz on Tuesday.

Sawley

White Lion

Tamworth Road, NG10 3AT
12-11.30 (0115) 946 3061 oldsawley.com
Old Sawley Jobber, Little Jack, Tollbridge Porter; 3 changing beers H
Well established as the Old Sawley Brewery tap house, this pub normally offers four of its own beers and two to three guest ales. The building dates back to the 18th century and is close to the River Trent and Sawley Marina. It is a two-roomed premises, with both rooms warmed by real fires in the colder months. It has a large beer garden which often stages live music during the summer months. The expanding microbrewery is at the rear.
QP

Scarcliffe

Horse & Groom

Mansfield Road, S44 6SU
12-11 (01246) 823152
Black Sheep Best Bitter; Greene King Abbot; Morland Old Golden Hen; 3 changing beers (often Abbeydale, Brains, Welbeck Abbey) H
Up to seven beers along with a cider are served at this charming 500-year-old two-room rural pub, which has been owned and run by the same family for the last 19 years. The main bar is mobile phone-free. Its locally made pork pies are a must. Young families and dogs are welcome in the large conservatory, and accommodation is available on-site in a couple of cottages. The bus stop is outside the pub, and there is a large car park to the front.
QP (53)

Shirland

Shoulder of Mutton

Hallfieldgate Lane, DE55 6AA (on B6013, Wessington-Shirland crossroads)
5-11; closed Tue; 12-11 Fri & Sat; 12-10.30 Sun
(01773) 834992
3 changing beers H
Eclectic, 16th-century traditional drinking den, nestling on the edge of Amber Valley. The beer garden offers spectacular views and sunsets. It is a true free house where real people enjoy real ale from small breweries; there is no beer list on the wall because the ales change daily. The regular

customers are drawn from far and wide, fuelling the unique, easy atmosphere created by the irrepressible landlord and landlady. Dogs and hikers are welcome. Check out the teacups. Q❀⛺♣P🐾📶

Smalley

Bell 𝕃

35 Main Road, DE7 6EF (on A608)
12-2.30, 5-11; 11.30-11 Fri-Sun ☎ (01332) 880635
thebellsmalley.co.uk
Abbeydale Moonshine; Marston's Pedigree; Sharp's Doom Bar; 3 changing beers Ⓗ
Near Shipley Country Park, this mid 19th-century inn has three rooms in which brewing and other memorabilia adorn the walls. A drinkers' pub, it serves three regular beers plus guests, but is also renowned for food with a good and varied menu including daily home-made specials (no food Sun eves). Accommodation is in three self-catering apartments in converted stables, and there is a large attractive garden. Weekday opening hours may be extended in the summer. Quiz night is Wednesday. Q❀P (H1,Y1)📶

South Normanton

Devonshire Arms 🏆

137 Market Street, DE55 2AA (at M1 jct 28 take B6019; at first mini-roundabout turn right into Market St)
12-midnight ☎ (01773) 810748
Moody Fox Pale Tale; Sarah Hughes Dark Ruby Mild; 3 changing beers (often Acorn, Derventio, Thornbridge) Ⓗ
A genuine free house offering up to five real ales and three real ciders or perries. Sarah Hughes Dark Ruby and Moody Fox Hilcote Brew House are the regular beers. Home-cooked food is served until 9pm every day except Sunday, when a popular carvery is offered. Vegetarians, vegans and coeliacs are all catered for. Sky Sports is shown on three screens. It is the winner of many CAMRA awards including local Pub of the Year for an impressive 11 years running from 2008 to 2018.
♿♣P (9.1)🐾📶

Staveley

Speedwell Inn 𝕃

Lowgates, S43 3TT
5-11; 12-11 Sat; 12-10.30 Sun ☎ (01246) 472252
Townes Speedwell Bitter, Staveley Cross, Pynot Porter; 1 changing beer Ⓗ
The brewery tap for Townes beers, which have been brewed on the premises since 1997. Following the retirement of the original brewer in 2013, new owners Lawrie and Nicoleta are enhancing the traditional pub atmosphere and brewing ethos, while introducing a fresh vitality to the place. Open plan but with several distinct seating areas, the bar is the focal point for conversation. The pub is handy for walks on the Chesterfield Canal, and is a meeting place for all sorts of organisations. ♣ (70 77)🐾📶

Sutton cum Duckmanton

Arkwright Arms 𝕃

Chesterfield Road, S44 5JG (on A632 between Chesterfield and Bolsover)
11-11 (midnight Fri & Sat); 11-10.30 Sun
☎ (01246) 232053 arkwrightarms.co.uk
Greene King Abbot; Whim Arbor Light; 12 changing beers Ⓗ
A Brewers' Tudor-fronted free house where a varied range of 10 guest ales, many from local micros, is complemented by 12 ciders and four perries. Beer festivals are held at Easter and bank holidays, with mini events throughout the year. Quality food is served until 8pm Monday to Saturday, and until 3pm Sunday. The spacious beer garden has play equipment for children. A winner of numerous CAMRA awards, including East Midlands Cider Pub of the Year and local CAMRA Pub of the Year. ❀⛺♣P🐾

Swanwick

Steampacket Inn

Derby Road, DE55 1AB
2-11; 12-midnight Sat & Sun ☎ (01773) 607771
House beer (by Nottingham); 5 changing beers (sourced nationally; often Blue Monkey, Derby, Nottingham) Ⓗ
A friendly and welcoming Pub People Company hostelry in the centre of Swanwick, the Steampacket boasts an excellent and constantly changing range of well-kept real ales and ciders, many of them from local microbreweries. It regularly serves Nottingham Packet Pale, which is brewed specially for the Steampacket. It is a popular, lively pub at the weekends with regular live music and a beer festival in winter and summer. Tuesday is quiz night. A welcoming fire blazes in winter, and and it has outdoor tables for summer. Q♣P🐾📶

Thorpe

Old Dog

Spend Lane, DE6 2AT
11.30-11; 11.30-10.30 Sun ☎ (01335) 350990
theolddog.co.uk
4 changing beers (sourced locally; often Dancing Duck, Derby, Titanic) Ⓗ
Brilliantly revived pub that rose again in 2014 after a lengthy closure. Four real ales are always on, usually from local breweries, always including a dark ale. Excellent food is served at most times. Set alone outside the village, it is within easy walking distance of the Tissington Trail and Dovedale, and welcoming to all walkers and dogs. Local CAMRA Pub of the Year 2016. ❀♿P🐾

Wardlow Mires

Three Stags' Heads ★ 𝕃

Mires Lane, SK17 8RW (jct A623/B6465)
closed Mon-Thu; 7-11 Fri; 11-11 Sat; 12-10.30 Sun
☎ (01298) 872268
Abbeydale Deception, Absolution; house beer (by Abbeydale); 1 changing beer (sourced regionally) Ⓗ
A quaint 300-year-old pub with two small rooms, stone-flagged floors and low ceilings. Unspoilt, it is one of the few pubs in the area identified by CAMRA as having a nationally important historic pub interior. An ancient range warms the bar and the house dogs, one of which gave the name to the house beer – Black Lurcher. Traditional cider is only available in summer. Q❀⛺P (173)🐾📶

Whitehough

Old Hall Inn L

Chinley, SK23 6EJ (in village, 750yds off B6062)
12-11 ☎ (01663) 750529 🌐 old-hall-inn.co.uk
Marston's Saddle Tank; changing beers H
The 14th-century Whitehough Hall forms part of this quintessential country inn which has won the Great British Pub award for best cask pub in the region for several years and is a regular entry within this Guide. Eight ales, including seven changing guests from quality local micros, complement those available at the adjacent Paper Mill Inn (under the same ownership). A popular menu features dishes using local produce. A well-attended beer festival runs in September.
P (189,190)

Wirksworth

Feather Star L

15 St Johns Street, DE4 4DR
12-10.30 (11 Fri & Sat); 4-10 Sun ☎ 07931 424117
🌐 thefeatherstar.co.uk
4 changing beers (sourced locally) H
Opened November 2016 in a former antiques shop, this small, cosy micropub is full of character. The well-furnished main room has a logburner and wooden beams. There is further seating up the tight stairs, where the toilet is also to be found. There are four cask beers on handpump and a cider. A Feather Star is the name for a crinoid fossil found locally in the limestone around Wirksworth.
Q

Red Lion, Litton (Photo: Bob Steel)

Appledore

Champ 𝕃

Meeting Street, EX39 1RJ (just off quay)
closed Mon; 5-midnight ☎ (01237) 421662
champappledore.co.uk
Clearwater Expedition Ale; 3 changing beers (sourced locally) H
The brewery tap for nearby Clearwater Brewery, this is a cosy, quaint and quirky evening pub by the sea in the charming coastal village of Appledore, renowned for its history of shipbuilding. It keeps real ale on four handpumps, sometimes joined by a guest. Real cider is also available, together with a selection of Belgian and craft beers. Soul food is served 5-9pm Tuesday to Saturday. The Champ is renowned for its live music, which features regularly on Fridays and Saturdays, as well as popular evening open mic sessions every Tuesday, Wednesday and Thursday. It has an interesting and eclectic decor.

Ashburton

Exeter Inn 𝕃

26 West Street, TQ13 7DU (on main road through centre of Ashburton opp church)
11-2.30, 5-11 (midnight Fri & Sat); 12-3, 7-10.30 Sun
☎ (01364) 652013
Dartmoor IPA, Legend H
Built in 1131, with additions in the 17th century, this friendly local's original purpose was to house the workers building the nearby church. It is the oldest pub in Ashburton, with seated drinking areas either side of the entrance which leads to a wood-panelled, L-shaped canopy-covered bar to the right. There is also a rear bar with a seating area and small serving counter. It is reputed that Sir Francis Drake was a regular drinker at the inn on his journeys to London, as was Sir Walter Raleigh. There is a lovely secluded walled garden at the back. Local Thompstone's cider is sold.
Q

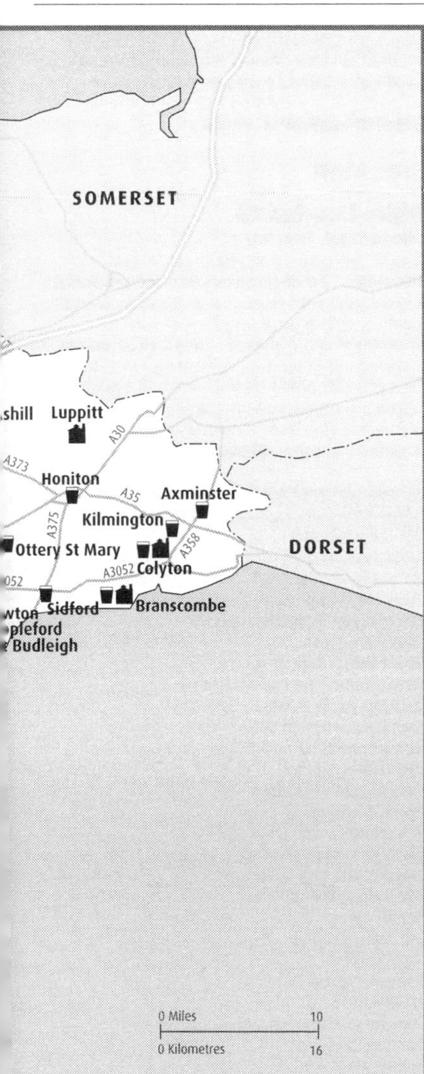

Ashill

Ashill Inn

EX15 3NL ST086113

12-2.30 (not Mon), 5.30-11; 12-4, 6.30-10.30 Sun
(01884) 840506

3 changing beers (sourced regionally)

A Grade II-listed pub, built in 1835, located in the Culm Valley. It is a charming small venue with a cosy bar and a recently extended restaurant area, with large windows which look out on to the garden. Local South-West brewery ales are served, and Orchard Pig Navel Gazer real cider. Good-value food is available, with produce mainly from local farms. Live music and special events are often featured. Q P

Axminster

Axminster Inn

Silver Street, EX13 5AH

10.30-midnight Mon-Wed; 10-12.30am Thu; 10.30-1am Fri & Sat; 11-midnight Sun (01297) 34947
axminsterinn.pub

Palmers Copper Ale, IPA, Dorset Gold, 200; 1 changing beer (sourced locally)

A friendly traditional pub, lying just off the town centre, with a real log fire for the winter months and a lovely enclosed beer garden to enjoy in the warmer weather. It is a Palmers house, offering a good range of the brewery's real ales. Good-value home-cooked food, often locally sourced, is served (contact pub for food times). Live music is featured. Free Wi-Fi is available, and there is a skittle alley and dartboard. P

Beaford

Globe Inn

Exeter Road, EX19 8LR (on main Exeter Rd in centre of village)

closed Mon; 5-11; 12-11.30 Fri-Sun (01805) 603920
globeinnpub.co.uk

GT Ales Thirst of Many; Sharp's Doom Bar; 1 changing beer (sourced nationally)

This 19th-century coaching inn recently reopened following renovation and has a warm, cosy atmosphere, attracting regulars and visitors. It offers a range of 40-plus bottled beers and ciders to complement a seasonal menu that uses the best ingredients from local producers. The drinks menu includes ales and gins from neighbouring breweries and distilleries, unique craft beers and ciders, and legendary bottled beer from around the globe.

Bere Ferrers

Olde Plough Inn

Fore Street, PL20 7JG (close to church and river)

11-3, 6-11; 11-11 Sun (01822) 840358
theoldeploughinn.co.uk

Sharp's Doom Bar; 3 changing beers (sourced locally; often Noss Beer Works, Roam, Summerskills)

A 16th-century village inn that has outstanding views over the River Tavy from the beer garden and is only a 15-minute walk from the station on the picturesque Tamar Valley line. Guest beers come from both local and popular national breweries. Inside, there are flagstone floors, exposed stonework walls, beamed ceilings, real fires and a welcoming atmosphere. Live music, acoustic nights and jam sessions feature, along with themed food nights.
Q (87)

Bideford

Appledore Inn

Chingswell Street, EX39 2NF

11-11; 12-10.30 Sun (01237) 476956
appledoreinnbideford.co.uk

Jollyboat Grenville's Renown; Sharp's Doom Bar, Original; 1 changing beer (sourced regionally)

Dating from the 15th century and one of the oldest inns in Bideford, this friendly family-run pub lies close to Bideford football ground. There is a single bar, with a restaurant area to the side and a paved beer garden at the rear. Four real ales are generally on tap, sometimes joined by a fifth served from the cask. The pub is renowned for the high-quality authentic Thai food served daily from 12 noon to 9pm. Q

Bittaford

Horse & Groom

Exeter Road, PL21 0EL

12-11 (midnight Fri & Sat) (01752) 892358

Dartmoor Jail Ale; house beer (by Hunters); 4 changing beers (sourced locally; often Roam, South Hams, Summerskills)

A family-owned pub with Oliver, a keen real ale enthusiast, serving good home-cooked food and with six pumps, two dedicated to real cider. The other pumps are predominantly ales from local breweries in south Devon and Cornwall. It has a long bar and separate dining area, with pictures of the former Moorhaven Hospital on the wall. A monthly quiz night is held, as well as a beer festival, and a cider and sausage festival, supporting local charities.

P (X38,Gold)

Bovey Tracey

Cromwell Arms

Fore Street, TQ13 9AE

11-11 (11.30 Fri & Sat); 12-11 Sun (01626) 833473

thecromwellarms.co.uk

St Austell Tribute; house beer (by St Austell); 3 changing beers (sourced nationally)

A 17th-century pub in the main square, with 14 letting rooms. One central bar is surrounded by other drinking areas which include a separate restaurant, with pictures of old Bovey on display. Up to five real ales from St Austell are in constant rotation, including seasonals and some guests. To the rear is an elongated garden with a pagoda and a wisteria-covered smokers' area adjoining the car park. An excellent bus service runs to Newton Abbot, with the stops being only yards away.

Q P

Bradninch

Olde White Lion

26 High Street, EX5 4QL

4-midnight; 12-midnight Fri; 12-1am Sat; 12-midnight Sun

(01392) 881263

Butcombe Original; Dartmoor Jail Ale; Otter Ale

A friendly, family-run locals' pub that caters for everyone, offering three real ales plus one real cider. Food consists of fish and chips on Friday evening, breakfast noon-4pm on Saturday, and a roast on Sunday (to order). There are many dark-oak beams plus a wood-burning stove. Music nights feature regularly, including a folk club on the first Tuesday of the month. The pub is involved with the annual music festival in June.

Q P

Branscombe

Fountain Head Inn

EX12 3BG (in main street 1 mile S of A3052)

11-3, 6-11; 12-10.30 Sun (01297) 680359

fountainheadinn.com

Branscombe Vale Branoc, Golden Fiddle, Summa That; 1 changing beer (sourced locally)

Popular with walkers, this beautiful 500-year-old pub is at the west end of this long straggly village in a beautiful coastal valley. It retains wood-panelled walls and flagstone floors with an inglenook fireplace. A beer festival is held on the nearest weekend to the longest day. The guest beer is from Branscombe Vale or another local brewery, and the cider is Branscombe Vale Pip. Good-value home-cooked food is served. Dogs are welcome, as are children (but not in the bar).

Q P (899)

Braunton

White Lion Inn

1 North Street, EX33 1AJ

12-11 (midnight Fri & Sat) (01271) 813085

Otter Amber; 2 changing beers (sourced nationally)

A locals' pub with three real ales usually available, together with a good selection of bottle-conditioned and craft beers. Good-value pub food is served, often with an interesting twist. Outside, there is an attractive beer garden and a good-sized function room upstairs. The White Lion has a nearby bus stop and is also close to the main Braunton campsite. Q P

REAL ALE BREWERIES

Art Brew Sutcombe
Bale Liddaton
Barum Barnstaple
Bays Paignton
Beer Engine Newton St Cyres
Bere Bere Alston
Black Tor Christow
Branscombe Vale Branscombe
Bridgetown Totnes
Buckland Bideford (NEW)
Checkstone Exmouth
Clearwater Bideford
Country Life Abbotsham
Crossed Anchors Exmouth
Darkplace Colyton (NEW)
Dartmoor Princetown
Devon Earth Buckfastleigh
Exe Valley Silverton
Exeter Exeter
Fat Belly Lynton
Fat Pig Exeter
Grampus Lee Bay
GT Braunton
Hanlons Half Moon Village
Holsworthy Clawton
Hunters Ipplepen
Isca Holcombe
Jollyboat Bideford
Madrigal Lynmouth
Moonchild Petrockstow
Morwell Morwellham (NEW)
New Lion Totnes
Noss Beer Works Lee Mill
Otter Luppitt
Platform 5 Newton Abbot
Powderkeg Woodbury Salterton
Red Rock Bishopsteignton
Riviera Stoke Gabriel
Roam Plymouth
Salcombe Ledstone
South Hams Stokenham
Sprey Point Teignmouth (NEW)
Stannary Tavistock
Summerskills Billacombe
Tally Ho! Hatherleigh
Teignworthy Newton Abbot
Totnes Totnes
Two Tone Shebbear (NEW)
Wizard Ilfracombe (NEW)
Yelland Manor Yelland

Brendon

Staghunters Inn 🄻

EX35 6PS SS767481

✪ 12-11 ☎ (01598) 741222 🌐 staghunters.com

Otter Bright; Exmoor Ale, Gold, Stag; 2 changing beers (sourced regionally) 🄶

Set deep in the Lyn Valley within Exmoor National Park, this family owned and run inn provides an ideal base for those exploring the local area. It has 14 well-appointed rooms, and dogs can stay overnight for a nominal charge. Up to four real ales are served on gravity, with the regular Exmoor and St Austell ales often joined by guests from other local breweries. Good locally sourced food can be enjoyed in the attractive restaurant.
Q❀◑◗⛺♣●P🐾📶

Bridford

Bridford Inn 🏆 🄻 ✔

EX6 7HT

✪ 12-11 (midnight Fri & Sat) ☎ (01647) 252250

🌐 bridfordinn.co.uk

Dartmoor Jail Ale; 3 changing beers (sourced regionally; often Brains, Inveralmond, Morland) 🄷

A 17th-century Devon longhouse on Dartmoor National Park converted to a pub in 1968 and now housing a village shop. The pub has a spacious open-plan interior for drinkers and diners, with old oak beams and an inglenook fireplace complete with an old bread oven and a woodburner. Fresh home-cooked quality food is served to order and outside there is a beer garden with picnic tables and the most stunning views. Highly regarded traditional ciders from Devon and Somerset producers are always stocked.
❀◑◗♿♣●P🚌 (360) 🐾📶

Brixham

Queen's Arms 🄻 ✔

31 Station Hill, TQ5 8BN (from Brixham library go up Church Hill East, then Station Hill)

✪ 4-11; 2-midnight Fri; 12-midnight Sat; 12-11 Sun

☎ (01803) 852074 🌐 thequeensarmsbrixham.co.uk

House beer (by Teignworthy); 5 changing beers (sourced nationally; often Oakham) 🄷

At the top of a short hill close to the town, the single-bar end-of-terrace pub has gained a well-deserved reputation for the quality of its six changing beers. The venue has a strong community ethos, a friendly atmosphere and, on cold winter nights, wood-burning fires. Live music at weekends and good-value Sunday lunches and Monday suppers are additional features. Local CAMRA Pub of the Year in 2016. ❀◑◗♣●P🚌

Brixton

Foxhound Inn 🄻

Kingsbridge Road, PL8 2AH

✪ 11-11 (midnight Fri & Sat); 12-11 Sun ☎ (01752) 880271

🌐 foxhoundinn.co.uk

Courage Directors; house beer (by Summerskills); 3 changing beers (sourced nationally; often Caledonian, Courage, Summerskills) 🄷

This 18th-century former coaching house is in a rural village just east of Plymouth, where it is well served by a frequent daytime bus service. The pub has two separate bars and a small restaurant. Traditional English meals are offered daily, using locally sourced ingredients. Look out for Red Coat, an ale crafted by the landlord, among four guest ales. A monthly charity quiz night is held. Local CAMRA branch Country Pub of the Year runner-up 2018. Q❀◑◗⛺♣●P🚌🐾

Broadclyst

New Inn 🄻

Whimple Road, EX5 3BX (½ mile E of village)

✪ 11-11 ☎ (01392) 461312 🌐 newinn-exeter.co.uk

Dartmoor Jail Ale; Hanlons Brewers Blend; Otter Bitter; Sharp's Doom Bar 🄷

Large, traditional 17th-century inn, with a recently extended car park to the rear, and a two-acre beer garden and play area. The spacious grounds host the village Year Seven football club. Freshly cooked food is served lunchtimes and evenings. There are three secluded rooms and the skittle alley can double as a function room. Regular events are held, plus an annual bonfire night.
Q❀◑◗♣●P📶

Buckland Monachorum

Drake Manor Inn 🄻 ✔

The Village, PL20 7NA

✪ 11-2.30, 6-11; 11.30-11.30 Fri & Sat; 12-11 Sun

☎ (01822) 853892 🌐 drakemanorinn.co.uk

Dartmoor Jail Ale; Sharp's Atlantic; 1 changing beer (sourced regionally; often Otter) 🄷

This cosy and friendly conversation-led inn was built in the 12th century to house the workers constructing the village church. It is divided into three areas but always retains a rustic and atmospheric feel. There is a wonderfully colourful suntrap garden to enjoy in the warmer months. Fine accommodation is to be found here and people come from far afield for the food. There is regular live music and food promotions. The cider is usually Thatchers Heritage.
Q❀◑◗♣●🚌 (55) 🐾📶

Butterleigh

Butterleigh Inn 🄻

The Green, EX15 1PN (opp church) SS9746108212

✪ 12-2.30 (not Mon), 6-11; 12-2.30, 6-midnight Fri & Sat; 12-3 Sun ☎ (01884) 855433 🌐 butterleighinn.co.uk

Cotleigh Tawny Owl; Dartmoor Jail Ale; Otter Ale; 1 changing beer 🄷

Situated in this small, quaint village, the Butterleigh is an excellent country pub with a mixed clientele creating a great atmosphere with diverse conversation. It has a main bar, lounge and a modern dining room. Good-value home-cooked food is served lunchtimes and evenings Tuesday to Saturday, with a carvery Sunday lunchtime. There is always a choice of four real ales, one a LocAle, plus Sandford Orchards Devon Scrumpy, Winkleigh Sam's Medium and a rotating guest cider.
Q❀◑◗♿♣●P🐾📶

Chagford

Ring o' Bells 🄻

44 The Square, TQ13 8AH

✪ 10-midnight ☎ (01647) 432466

🌐 ringobellschagford.co.uk

Dartmoor IPA, Jail Ale; Teignworthy Reel Ale; 1 changing beer (sourced locally) 🄷

A 16th-century inn in the centre of the town, although archives reveal there has been an inn on this site since well before this time. The bar has a large open fireplace and is comfortably furnished with bench and booth seating. At the rear of the bar there is a separate dining room, again with an open fireplace. From there a passageway leads to a pretty walled garden with plenty of seating and a smokers' shelter. (173,178)

Chillington

Bear & Blacksmith

TQ7 2LD

12-3 (not Mon), 6-11; 12-3, 5-11 Fri; 12-4 Sun
(01548) 581171 thebearandblacksmith.com

South Hams Wild Blonde; 2 changing beers (sourced regionally; often Sharp's) H

The pub reopened in April 2016 with a change of name after a complete refurbishment, including a brand new kitchen. Its name relates to a time when the last dancing bear was kept in the village – when it died its paws were put on show in the local blacksmith's forge. Awarded Silver by Taste of the West 2017/18. P (3)

Chittlehampton

Bell Inn

The Square, EX37 9QL (opp St Hieritha's parish church) SS636254

11-3, 6-midnight; 11-midnight Fri & Sat; 12-11 Sun
(01769) 540368 thebellatchittlehampton.co.uk

Exmoor Ale; Otter Ale; 5 changing beers (sourced regionally) H

Owned and run by the same family for more than 30 years, The Bell celebrated 20 continuous years of Guide inclusion in 2016. There is always a good selection of real ales, with four on handpump and up to four more regularly available on gravity. The bar area is notable for its sporting memorabilia, and good-value home-cooked food is served both here and in the adjoining restaurant. Well-behaved children and dogs are welcome.
P (658,859)

Chudleigh

Bishop Lacy Inn

Fore Street, TQ13 0HY

12-midnight (1am Fri & Sat) (01626) 854585

3 changing beers (sourced regionally; often Bays, Black Tor, South Hams) H

A Grade II-listed building dominated by an effervescent landlady; the witch dolls suspended from the bar belie her true personality. It is opposite the church and named after the Bishop of Exeter (1420-1455) who was reputedly responsible for the original town's water supply. The left-hand bar is dominated by an incredible fireplace which was once twice the size and was used to cure ham. A strong following of Exeter Chiefs rugby supporters are to be found here on match days. Beers are often local from Black Tor, Hanlons or Hunters. Q P

Chulmleigh

Old Court House

South Molton Street, EX18 7BW

11-11 (01769) 580045 oldcourthouseinn.co.uk

Butcombe Original; Dartmoor IPA; Exmoor Ale; 1 changing beer (sourced nationally) H

A traditional thatched country inn dating from 1633. Charles I stayed here in 1634 on his first tour of the West Country and a bedroom still contains an original Royal House of Stuart coat of arms. A replica hangs above the fireplace in the main bar. The three regular real ales are often joined by a guest beer in summer. Good home-cooked food can be taken in the bar area, the separate dining room, or the pretty cobbled courtyard garden.
(377)

Clyst St Mary

Half Moon Inn

Frog Lane, EX5 1BR

11-2.30, 5-10.30; 11-midnight Fri & Sat; 12-10.30 Sun
(01392) 873515 half-moon-inn.co.uk

Bombardier; Otter Bitter, Ale; 1 changing beer H

Friendly village pub with a great atmosphere. Locally sourced food at reasonable prices is served lunchtime and evenings (Sunday lunchtime only). There are always four real ales on offer and a wide range of wines. Quiz and bingo nights take place, and the pub is within walking distance of Exeter Chiefs and Westpoint Exhibition Centre. It has three en-suite B&B rooms. Q P

Cockwood

Ship Inn

Church Road, EX6 8NU (just off A379, outside Starcross, close to Cockwood harbour)

11-11; 12-10.30 Sun (01626) 890373
shipinncockwood.co.uk

Dartmoor Jail Ale; Exeter 'fraid Not; St Austell Tribute; 1 changing beer H

A busy family-run pub, close to the picturesque harbour at Cockwood, with a large beer garden with views of the estuary, and a log fire in winter. Popular with drinkers and diners alike, it offers a choice of four regular ales and usually one rotating guest, and has an excellent food menu. Meals are prepared with local produce where possible including a varied choice of locally caught fish. The bus stops 100 yards across the bridge.
Q P (2)

Colyton

Gerrard Arms

St Andrew's Square, EX24 6JN

12-3, 5.30-11 (midnight Fri); 12-3, 6-midnight Sat; 12-3, 7-10.30 Sun (01297) 552588 thegerrardarms.co.uk

Draught Bass; Otter Ale; St Austell Tribute; 1 changing beer H

Busy one-bar pub dating back to 1506 and next to the church, in this delightful little town with lots of lovely old cottages and tangled narrow streets and alleyways. There is a safe courtyard at the back, now with wheelchair access. The home-made food is good value but only served on Friday and Saturday, with a traditional roast lunch available on Sunday. In summer the lunchtime session may run on. Colyton station on the Seaton Tramway is a level walk. Q

Crediton

Crediton Inn

28A Mill Street, EX17 1EZ

⌚ 12-11; 12-4, 7-10.30 Sun ☎ (01363) 772882
🌐 crediton-inn.co.uk
5 changing beers Ⓗ
The framed deeds date this inn to 1878, with windows etched with the ancient town seal. It is a genuine free house, well supported by the locals. The handpumps have increased to 10, served by local breweries, with an ale festival in November. The skittle alley doubles as a function room. Good home-cooked food is available at weekends, with snacks and renowned Scotch eggs at other times. The welcoming owner is the longest-serving landlady in Crediton. ❀◐⇌♣●P🚌(5)🐾📶

Mitre
9 High Street, EX17 3AE (on A377 in town centre opp Co-op)
⌚ 1-1am; 12-1am Sat & Sun ☎ (01363) 772508
4 changing beers (sourced regionally) Ⓗ
A Grade II-listed free house, fondly known by older locals as Number Nine, located on the High Street. It has interesting pub decor, with beer-originated curios and other knick-knacks, and is well supported by local rugby, football and darts teams. It has live music every Saturday evening. The terraced garden, which is south-facing, is great for warmer months, and serves as the smoking area in all weathers. You can always depend on well-kept ales and good conversation. 🐎❀♿♣🚌🐾📶

Cullompton

Pony & Trap 🄻 ✔
10 Exeter Hill, EX15 1DJ (on B3181 S of town)
⌚ 12-3, 5-11; 12-4.30, 7.30-11 Sun ☎ (01884) 34182
Branscombe Vale Golden Fiddle; Dartmoor Jail Ale; Draught Bass; Exmoor Ale; Plain Sheep Dip; 3 changing beers Ⓗ
A traditional local with a good atmosphere and a mixed clientele. It has a smart interior featuring a logburner, making it cosy in winter; flowers and ornaments add a homely feel. Up to eight real ales could be on offer, plus four real ciders. Home-cooked food is served Saturday and Sunday lunchtimes only. There is a garden and seating area. Live music features once a month and pub games are played. Q❀◖♣●🚌(1)🐾

Dartmouth

Cherub Inn ✔
13 Higher Street, TQ6 9RB
⌚ 11-11; 12-10.30 Sun ☎ (01803) 832571
🌐 the-cherub.co.uk
Exeter Ferryman; St Austell Proper Job; South Hams Devon Pride; house beer (by St Austell); 1 changing beer (sourced locally) Ⓗ
The nautical town of Dartmouth is famous for its Tudor buildings, and the Cherub is one of the best. Grade II-listed, it is the oldest house in town and in the 14th century was a merchant's home. The bar is small and cosy, with many original features including old ships' timbers as beams. A lovely old staircase leads to the next two floors which house the restaurant. Q🐎◐Ă⇌P🚌🐾

Dawlish

Marine Tavern
2 Marine Parade, EX7 9DJ
⌚ 11-11.30 ☎ (01626) 865245 🌐 marinetaverndawlish.com
Dartmoor Best; Otter Ale; Sharp's Doom Bar; 1 changing beer (sourced nationally) Ⓗ
Traditional seaside pub with a suntrap patio at the front, and a sea view balcony which also provides a great look-out post for passing steam train specials. Good-value food is served all day in the peak summer season, and lunch and evenings at other times. Accommodation consists of four rooms, and children are welcome in an area away from the bar. Dogs are also welcome. Occasional live music is hosted, and there are interesting local photos to admire. 🐎❀🛏◐⇌🚌(2)🐾📶

Doddiscombsleigh

Nobody Inn ✔
EX6 7PS
⌚ 11-11; 12-10.30 Sun ☎ (01647) 252394
🌐 nobodyinn.co.uk
House beer (by St Austell); 2 changing beers (sourced locally) Ⓗ
A venerable village inn, mainly 15th century with some later additions, full of old beams and antique furniture. Part of the bar is used for meals, and a separate small restaurant is open Tuesday to Saturday evenings. Whisky is a speciality, with about 240 different malts stocked behind the bar. Five comfortable bedrooms are available and high-quality food is served every lunchtime and evening. Doddiscombsleigh is best approached from the A38 at the top of Haldon Hill.
Q❀🛏◐P🚌🐾📶

Dousland

Burrator Inn 🄻 ✔
PL20 6NP
⌚ 12-11 (12.30am Sat); 12-10.30 Sun ☎ (01822) 853121
🌐 theburratorinn.com
Dartmoor Jail Ale; Otter Amber; St Austell Tribute; Sharp's Doom Bar Ⓗ
This substantial pub is on the road between Yelverton, Burrator Reservoir and Princetown. Inside, there is a large bar area, with space for a pool table and two dartboards, along with various other rooms including a separate dining room. Food is served all day. Outside, there is ample parking and a garden incorporating a children's play area. The pub is frequented by locals, and visited by those living in the surrounding towns and city. A September beer festival is held.
Q🐎❀🛏◐♿♣P🚌🐾📶

Drewsteignton

Drewe Arms ★
EX6 6QN
⌚ 12-3, 5-11 (midnight Fri); 12-6 Sun ☎ (01647) 281409
🌐 thedrewearmsinn.co.uk
St Austell Tribute; 4 changing beers (sourced nationally) Ⓖ
A thatched, white-walled village pub in front of the parish church in a picturesque village square. It is an unmistakably English drinking hostelry with a historic interior and rustic charm. The venue is most famous for Aunt Mabel, who held the record as the longest-serving landlady, running the place for 75 years before retiring at 99. The pub serves excellent food using locally sourced ingredients and prides itself on maintaining the ales from cask to glass just as Mabel did. Guest beers are added in summer. Q🐎❀🛏◐♿Ă♣●P🚌(173)🐾📶

East Budleigh

Sir Walter Raleigh Inn

22 High Street, EX9 7ED (off B3178 opp Hayes Lane)
12-3, 6-11; 12-3, 7-10.30 Sun (01395) 442510
4 changing beers (sourced regionally) H
Set in the middle of a delightful village, the birthplace of Sir Walter Raleigh, this free house is a truly welcoming 16th-century country inn. Good-quality local pub food is served lunchtimes and evenings in addition to four varying real ales, and up to six real ciders. Originally two cottages, the buildings were converted into a Jacobean-style pub, retaining the original wooden beams throughout. This gem is well worth a visit for good-quality real ale, cider, pub food and friendly service. Q (157)

East Prawle

Pig's Nose Inn

TQ7 2BY
12-3, 6-11 (01548) 511209 pigsnoseinn.co.uk
Otter Bitter G**; South Hams Devon Pride** H/G**, Eddystone; 1 changing beer** G
Highly regarded 500-year-old smugglers' inn on the village green attracting birdwatchers and coastal walkers, boasting a cluttered and quirky maritime-themed interior. Gravity beers are racked behind the bar, and home-cooked locally sourced food is served. Children and dogs are welcome and have their own menus! Occasional live music events are held in a hall adjoining the pub. Children's games are available, as is knitting for adults. Closed Sunday evenings in winter.
Q

Exbourne

Red Lion

High Street, EX20 3RY (200yds N of jct with A3072)
SS602018
4-11; 12-11 Sat & Sun (01837) 851551
Exmoor Fox; Sharp's Original; 1 changing beer (sourced regionally) G
Traditional village local which dates back to the 16th century with no handpumps or taps of any description, as the landlord refuses to serve draught lager – casks are set on stillage at the end of the L-shaped bar. Beer festivals with live music are held twice per year. A repeat winner of local CAMRA Pub of the Year, most recently in 2017.
Q P

Exeter

Fat Pig

2 John Street, EX1 1BL (behind Fore St)
5-11; 12-11 Sat; 12-5 Sun (01392) 437217
fatpig-exeter.co.uk
3 changing beers (sourced locally) H
Formerly The Coachmakers Arms, this Victorian corner local was brought back to life in 2008 as a traditional pub, featuring a range of locally sourced food, including brewery-fed pork and sausages from a herd of rare-breed pigs. There are malt whisky evenings, a Monday quiz, and homebrew competitions. It has two sister bars nearby, one home to the Fat Pig brewery, tap bar and distillery, producing a cider, a wide range of ales and numerous whiskies.

George's Meeting House

38 South Street, EX1 1ED (nr bottom of South St)
8am-midnight (1am Fri & Sat) (01392) 454250
Dartmoor Jail Ale; Greene King Abbot; Ruddles Best Bitter; Sharp's Doom Bar; 6 changing beers (sourced nationally) H
This Wetherspoon opened in January 2005 having been sympathetically converted from a Unitarian chapel dating from 1760. Many of the original features remain unaltered; these include two upstairs galleries, a pulpit and stained-glass windows. A range of national, regional and local real ales and five real ciders are served. Food is available throughout the day until 10pm. A newer extension, which is at the rear of the main building, leads to more seating outdoors.
Q

Thatched House Inn

Exwick Road, EX4 2BQ
12-11 (11.30 Fri & Sat); 12-10 Sun (01392) 272920
thatchedhouse.net
Greene King Abbot; 8 changing beers (sourced locally; often Dartmoor, Hanlons, Salcombe) H
This thatched building dates from the 1600s and is a community pub next to the Exwick playing fields, opposite the Exeter College sports hub. It is close to the river, convenient for dog walkers, cyclists and sightseers. Seven real ales and one real cider are usually on sale, with great-value home-cooked food sourced from local ingredients and producers. On-street parking is available nearby, and the pub is on the Stagecoach F1 and F2 bus route.
Q

White Hart Hotel

66 South Street, EX1 1EE
12-11 (midnight Fri & Sat); 12-10.30 Sun
(01392) 279897 whitehartpubexeter.co.uk
Ringwood Razorback; house beer (by Ringwood); 2 changing beers (sourced nationally) H
One of Exeter's most ancient inns in a central position within the old city wall. Non-residents who wish to use the car park need to pay at the meter and redeem their ticket against food or drinks purchased in the bar. An extensive selection of freshly-cooked meals is available, complemented by a fine selection of real ales from the Marston's range. There are two conference rooms. B&B accommodation is in 55 en-suite bedrooms, including a full English.
Q P

Exmouth

Bicton Inn

5 Bicton Street, EX8 2RU
11-midnight (01395) 272589 bictoninn.co.uk
Dartmoor Jail Ale; Hanlons Port Stout; 6 changing beers H
A friendly and popular back-street local, offering good beer and chat. A community hub, traditional games are played here such as darts, pool and euchre, and regular live music events are featured (see website for details). Up to eight real ales and one real cider are normally on offer, usually including several LocAles. The snug is available for small gatherings and meetings. There is a logburner in the main bar. Two beer festivals are held during the year.

First & Last Inn L

10 Church Street, EX8 1PE (off B3178 Rolle St)
11-11 (11.30 Sat); 12-10.30 Sun ☎ (01395) 263275
Courage Directors; Otter Ale; Teignworthy Neap Tide H; 2 changing beers (sourced locally; often Checkstone) G
Victorian pub near the town centre with a public car park opposite. A genuine free house, it has three distinct areas and a courtyard patio with heated awnings. The Checkstone Brewery started here in 2016 and supplies the pub with changing ales from an increasing range. Games include pool and darts, and there is a skittle alley. Televised sport is prominent and there is regular live music. Up to nine ciders are on sale including Westons Old Rosie and Thatchers Traditional.
(57)

Grapevine

2 Victoria Road, EX8 1DL
12-11 (midnight Fri & Sat) ☎ (01395) 222208
thegrapevineexmouth.com
Crossed Anchors American Pale Ale; 4 changing beers H
The Grapevine brewhouse is a stylish Victorian free house in the centre of town. It is home to Crossed Anchors Brewing and Ruby Diner burger specialists. As well as serving up to four Crossed Anchors beers there is always a wide selection of guest ales, craft beers from the UK and around the world, and Green Valley Cyder. You will find a pub quiz on Mondays, live music at the weekends and a good selection of board games.
(57)

George Nympton

Castle Inn L

EX36 4JE (1 mile S of South Molton on the Chulmleigh road)
12-3 (not Mon & Tue), 5-11; 12-3, 6-11 Sat; 12-7 Sun
☎ (01769) 574945
Exmoor Ale; 1 changing beer (sourced regionally) H
A traditional Devon country pub. The main bar has a pleasant eating area offset, while the lounge bar can at times be used as a family room. Two real ales are kept, together with a local cider. The pub has gained a good local reputation for the quality and value of its food. Accommodation in three attractive and well-appointed rooms is also now available. QP

Heavitree

Pig & Pickle Taphouse

38A Fore Sreet, EX1 2QL
closed Mon; 5-11; 3-11 Fri; 12-11 Sat; 1-10 Sun
3 changing beers (sourced locally) H
Micropub in the Fat Pig mini estate. It has been converted from the old post office, with the original signs and old counter. It is a friendly and welcoming venue, with a quiz every Tuesday evening. Food is restricted to platters of ham and various pickles. Also featured is the Fat Pig range of whiskies, gins and bourbons. The three changing beers are all from Fat Pig. Old-style dimpled mugs are used.

Hemerdon

Miners Arms L

PL7 5BU
11-11 ☎ (01752) 336040 theminersarmspub.co.uk
Dartmoor Jail Ale; Draught Bass; house beer (by Dartmoor) H; 2 changing beers (sourced locally; often Dartmoor, St Austell) H/G
Dating from 1783, this pub is rich in history with its association with the close-by Drakelands mine. The three regular beers are supplemented by at least one other local ale. The friendly atmosphere and delightful location make it popular. The spacious children's play area enables alfresco meals to be eaten while enjoying a summer's day. There is also a conservatory with dining area and patio. Regular beer and cider festivals are held, as are quiz nights and other events. QP(59)

High Bickington

Golden Lion L

North Road, EX37 9BB (on B3217) SS600205
12 (4.30 Mon & Tue)-11; 12-10.30 Sun ☎ (01769) 561006
Forge Litehouse; 1 changing beer (sourced regionally) H
On the main road through the village and dating from the 19th century, this traditional Devon village pub is a genuine hub of the community. The single bar has an adjacent skittle alley which converts into a pleasant dining area. Good-value home-cooked food is served throughout most opening hours. Two competitively priced local real ales are usually available, together with a good choice of real ciders. Well-behaved children and dogs are welcome. QP(325)

Honiton

Holt L

178 High Street, EX14 1LA
11-3, 5.30-11; closed Sun & Mon ☎ (01404) 47707
theholt-honiton.com
Otter Bitter, Amber, Bright, Ale, Head H
The Holt has a cosy bar at street level and a fine-dining restaurant upstairs, both smartly decorated and with plenty of exposed wood. The kitchen is in full view of the clientele. A lunch menu of tapas and home-smoked food is served in the bar. Independently owned by two sons of the Otter brewing family, the Holt has won the Taste of the West best gastropub award. The head chef also runs popular bread-making and cookery courses.
Q

Horsebridge

Royal Inn

PL19 8PJ (off A384 Tavistock-Launceston road) SX401748
12-3, 6.30-11; 12-3, 6.30-10.30 Sun ☎ (01822) 870214
royalinn.co.uk
Otter Ale; St Austell Proper Job; Tintagel Castle Gold H; 3 changing beers (sourced regionally; often Draught Bass, Skinner's) G
Originally built as a nunnery in 1437 by French Benedictine monks and reported to have been visited by Charles I, the pub overlooks an old bridge on the River Tamar, connecting Devon to Cornwall. It features half-panelling, stone floors, log fires and traditional styling in the bar and lounge, with another larger room off the lounge. There is a terraced garden with sheltered seating and free Wi-Fi. Guest beers are usually served on gravity; the locally sourced food is recommended.
QP(115)

Iddesleigh

Duke of York

EX19 8BG (off B3217 next to church) SS570083
11-11; 12-10.30 Sun ☎ (01837) 810253
dukeofyorkdevon.co.uk
Adnams Broadside; Bays Topsail; 1 changing beer (sourced regionally) G
This iconic, traditional village inn is popular with locals and visitors alike. The thatched 15th-century cob building has an open fire in the bar, where the ales are dispensed on gravity. There are seven en-suite rooms and the pub also offers a courtesy bus to and from the pub for those living in surrounding villages. A beer festival is held every August bank holiday weekend. Please note that food times may vary in winter. Q🐴❀🛏◑♿⛺♣🍎🚌🐾📶

Ide

Poachers Inn L

55 High Street, EX2 9RW (3 miles from M5 jct 31, via A30)
12-midnight (1am Fri & Sat) ☎ (01392) 273847
poachersinn.co.uk
Branscombe Vale Branoc; Exeter Lighterman; 4 changing beers (sourced regionally; often Exeter, Palmers, Sharp's) H
Busy village pub with a friendly atmosphere, serving a varied menu of home-made locally sourced produce, including excellent-value fish and chips to eat in or take away on Wednesday evenings. Dogs are welcome in the comfortably furnished bar, with old sofas, chairs and a log fire in winter. There is also a large beer garden overlooking the Devon countryside. Usually five or six ales are on tap, with various guest beers from the West Country. Q🐴❀🛏◑⛺P🚌(360)🐾📶

Ilfracombe

Admiral Collingwood ✔

Wilder Road, EX34 9AP
8am-midnight (1am Fri & Sat); 8am-11 Sun
☎ (01271) 862373
Greene King Abbot; Ruddles Best Bitter; Sharp's Doom Bar; 3 changing beers (sourced nationally) H
On the site of the old Collingwood Hotel, this purpose-built Wetherspoon pub was awarded the best new-build award at the National Pub Design Awards in 2015. Situated on Ilfracombe's seafront, there are stunning views from the roof terrace, which is open from March to October. Since opening its doors it has earned a well-deserved reputation for its range of well-kept ales, many of which are from local breweries.
🐴❀◑♿🍎P🚌(21A)📶

Hip & Pistol L

8 St James Place, EX34 9BH
11-11 (11.30 Fri & Sat); 12-10.30 Sun ☎ (01271) 549651
GT Ales Blonde Ambition, Thirst of Many; Exmoor Stag; 2 changing beers (sourced nationally) H
Opened late 2017, it was converted from an old Georgian house. The building has been extensively modernised to provide a timber-fronted bar with a nautical theme. The flooring is a special feature, showing the bay around Ilfracombe in pictorial form, with local landmarks and shipwrecks from the past together with an impressive pub logo shown in an image of a compass. A minimum of four real ales and six ciders will always be on.
🐴❀◑♿⛺🍎🚆🚌(21)📶

Wellington Arms ✔

66-67 High Street, EX34 9QE
11-midnight; 10-midnight Sun ☎ (01271) 864720
St Austell Tribute; Sharp's Doom Bar; 3 changing beers (sourced locally) H
Originally two pubs and now a listed building, this friendly town local was refurbished in February 2018. There is a separate public bar, lounge bar and games room. The cosy lounge retains its original beams and large real open fire. TVs and music sound systems enable different channels to be shown in each area. The beer terrace has been completely overhauled, with new seating areas and two huge wide-screen TVs. Live music, quiz nights, rock and roll bingo and barbecues take place in summer. 🐴❀⛺♣P🚌🐾📶

Kilmington

New Inn L ✔

The Hill, EX13 7SF (in village, S of A35)
12-3 (not Mon), 6-11; 12-8 Sun ☎ (01297) 33376
newinnkilmington.com
Palmers Copper Ale, 200 H
Thatched Devon longhouse that became a pub in the early 1800s. It was rebuilt after a major fire in 2004, retaining a welcoming atmosphere and gaining excellent toilets with wheelchair access. There is a large, safe garden, and a well-used skittle alley. A quiz night is held monthly on the first Sunday, with other events that maintain the pub's position as an important part of village life. A meat draw is held on Fridays.
Q❀◑♿♣🍎P🚌🐾📶

Kings Nympton

Grove Inn L

EX37 9ST (in centre of village) SS683194
closed Mon; 12-3, 6-11; 12-4, 7-10 Sun ☎ (01769) 580406
Exmoor Ale G**; 3 changing beers (sourced regionally)** H
Attractive to locals and visitors alike, this 17th-century thatched village inn has flagstone floors and log fires, together with a pretty enclosed terrace to enjoy in summer. Four real ales are normally on tap, alongside a good range of local ciders. Award-winning food is served in the dining area, which is adjacent to the bar. Local CAMRA Pub of the Year 2016 and Cider Pub of the Year 2017.
Q🐴❀🛏◑♣🍎P🐾📶

Kingsbridge

Hermitage Inn

8 Mill Street, TQ7 1ED
2-11 (midnight Fri); 12-midnight Sat; 12-11 Sun
☎ (01548) 853234
2 changing beers (sourced regionally; often Dartmoor, Teignworthy) H
A friendly local pub with log fires and a charming enclosed beer garden. Here you will find good value with a warm welcome in the heart of Kingsbridge. A couple of real ales are normally available from mainly local breweries. There are home-made bar snacks on offer and basket meals on Friday nights and lunchtimes during the summer. Live music events are held throughout the year. Check the Facebook page for details.
Q🐴❀♿🍎🚌🐾📶

Kingskerswell

Lord Nelson

47 Fore Street, TQ12 5JB

3-11 (midnight Fri & Sat); 12-11 Sun (01803) 875628
lordnelsonkingerswell.co.uk

3 changing beers (sourced nationally; often Fuller's, St Austell) H

Known locally as The Nellie, this is a cosy two-bar pub in the centre of the village. The lounge bar has upholstered high-back bench seating, tables and a fireplace, as well as a snug, the Admiral's Cabin. The other bar has two open stone fireplaces and alcove seating, together with stools at the bar and at a high table. The bar's walls are adorned with Trafalgar memorabilia, horse brasses and 1960s-era photographs of the village. Regular guest beers are served. For Sunday lunches booking is advised.

Kingston

Dolphin Inn

TQ7 4QE (next to church)

12-3, 6-11; 12-11 Fri & Sat; 12-10.30 Sun
(01548) 810314 dolphininnkingston.co.uk

Butcombe Original; Dartmoor Jail Ale; 2 changing beers (sourced regionally) H

This Asset of Community Value is at the heart of village life. The main building of the pub was originally three 16th-century cottages before being joined together and converted. The cosy interior features exposed stonework and pleasant low lighting. Home-cooked food from locally sourced ingredients is served; there are themed food nights and special menus to accompany events such as the regular quiz. The current owners took over in 2016 and breathed new life into the venture. Open all day in summer. P (875)

Lapford

Old Malt Scoop Inn L

EX17 6PZ

12-midnight (2am Fri & Sat); 12-11.30 Sun
(01363) 83330 oldmaltscoopinn.com

St Austell Tribute; house beer (by Beer Engine); 3 changing beers (often Dartmoor, Exeter, Hanlons) H

In the village centre, this is an old coaching inn dating back to the 16th century. Its transition from run-down tied pub in 2015 to the comfortable free house it is today has been excellent for all. There are now four handpumps at the bar, three usually dispensing LocAle beers. The pub serves good-quality home-cooked food lunchtimes and evenings, including a traditional Sunday roast. Occasional live music events take place. The pub is family and dog friendly. P (5C)

Lewdown

Blue Lion Inn L

EX20 4DL

5 (6 Tue & Thu)-11; 12-midnight Sat; 12-3.30 Sun
(01566) 783238

Dartmoor Jail Ale; Otter Amber; Sharp's Doom Bar; 1 changing beer (sourced regionally) H

This family owned and run pub has grown around a 17th-century farmhouse and is an interesting building with beautiful views of the surrounding countryside. Extended and developed in the early 20th century as part of the Lewtrenchard estate, it is home to numerous local groups and supports several pub teams. Predominantly wet sales-oriented, it is also dog-friendly. An annual beer and music festival is held in late July/early August. P

Littlehempston

Tally Ho L

TQ9 6LY SX813627

closed Mon; 11-3, 5.30-11; 12-10.30 Sun
(01803) 862316 tallyhoinn.co.uk

Dartmoor Legend; 1 changing beer (sourced locally; often Teignworthy) H

Charming 14th-century stone-built pub saved by the local community from closure in 2014. The single-roomed bar with timber beams is furnished with pews and wooden settles and has a cosy feel that is complemented by two woodburners. The pub hosts numerous events including an annual beer festival, occasional local live music and a regular Sunday night quiz. Guest beers are from local breweries including Hunters and New Lion. The enclosed beer garden is to the rear of the pub. Q P (X64,177)

Lydford

Castle Inn

School Road, EX20 4BH

11-11 (01822) 820242 castleinnlydford.com

St Austell Trelawny, Tribute, Proper Job; 2 changing beers (sourced locally) H

Comfortable and welcoming 16th-century pub, which is open from 8am for breakfast. The 12th-century Lydford Castle is adjacent, and St Petroc's church and Lydford Gorge (National Trust) are close by. The pub is situated on the NCN27 Devon Coast-Coast, Dartmoor Way and West Devon Way cycle/walking routes. Up to three St Austell beers are served, supplemented by two changing guest beers, usually from Devon. A quiz night is held every Wednesday evening in aid of the local school. P (46)

Lympstone

Redwing Bar & Dining

Church Road, EX8 5JT

11.30-3, 5.30-11; 11.30-11 Fri-Sun (01395) 222156
redwingbar-dining.co.uk

Branscombe Vale Branoc; St Austell Proper Job; 1 changing beer (sourced locally) H

Formerly the Redwing, this delightful pub is set in a charming riverside village. The tastefully decorated premises include a long bar with some soft furnishings and a conservatory. There is also an upstairs function room. There is a large garden at the back and parking at the side. Excellent fresh food is served lunchtimes and evenings with a separate lunch menu Monday to Friday. Dogs are welcome in the bar. Q P

Lynton

Beggars Roost Inn L

Barbrook, EX35 6LD

12-11; 12-10.30 Sun (01598) 753645
exmoormanor.co.uk

Exmoor Stag; Otter Amber; Tetley Bitter; 1 changing beer (sourced nationally) H

Refurbished in early 2018, this is a pleasant country pub with a warm welcoming atmosphere and an attractive food menu. In lovely countryside close to Lynton, it is both family and dog friendly. Lunch and evening meals are available every day, and regular themed food nights are a feature all year round. A recent addition of a skittle alley upstairs has greatly improved both local and visitor enjoyment. Q

Sandrock Hotel

Longmead, EX35 6DH

11-11 (midnight Fri & Sat); 12-11 Sun ☎ (01598) 752000
sandrockhotel.co.uk

Exmoor Silver Stallion; Fuller's London Pride; Marston's Pedigree; Wychwood Hobgoblin Gold; 1 changing beer (sourced nationally) H

An Edwardian hotel and pub nestled between the wildly rugged Valley of the Rocks and the picturesque village of Lynton. Many of the original features have been retained and the large wood-burning stove adds to the cosy and welcoming atmosphere in the bar. There is also a pleasant beer garden to enjoy in summer and three recently refurbished rooms for accommodation. Four real ales are usually available and good-quality, reasonably priced food is served.
Q

Manaton

Kestor Inn

TQ13 9UF (on main road through village)

closed Mon & Tue; 11-11; 11-6 Sun ☎ (01647) 221626
kestorinn.com

Dartmoor Legend H**; Otter Bitter** H/G**; 1 changing beer (sourced locally)** H

This pub, within the Dartmoor National Park, is a spacious village inn with a warm welcome and a friendly atmosphere. It has a large open-plan L-shaped bar with plenty of seating together with a long, separate dining room, which can also be used for functions. It sells a selection of local real ales. The lobby area of the pub has become a small shop selling basic items, and a book exchange scheme is in operation. Sam's Medium Cider is sold.
P (271,671)

Meavy

Royal Oak Inn

PL20 6PJ (on village green)

11-11; 11-10.30 Sun ☎ (01822) 852944
royaloakinn.org.uk

Dartmoor Jail Ale; St Austell Proper Job; house beer (by Dartmoor); 1 changing beer (sourced regionally; often Otter) H

People come from miles around to enjoy the food and drink at this tucked-away, civilised but unpretentious 16th-century pub. In the summer, sit at one of the outside benches by the legendary tree and watch children play on the village green. In winter, sit in the public bar and enjoy the conversation, dogs and roaring fire. There is an interesting range of cider, with a festival in August and occasional live music. Local CAMRA branch Country Pub of the Year 2018.
Q (56)

Newton Abbot

Taphouse & Bottle Shop

Tuckers Maltings, Teign Road, TQ12 4AA (500yds from Newton Abbot railway station)

closed Mon-Wed; 5 (4 Fri; 12 Sat)-11; 4-10 Sun
☎ (01626) 334734 themaltingstaphouse.co.uk

Edwin Tuckers Devonshire Prize Ale; 2 changing beers (sourced nationally; often New Lion) H

A micropub based in the historic Tuckers Maltings which also houses the Teignworthy Brewery. The interior reflects the Maltings heritage; the furniture, made with recycled wood from the old barley storage bins, still exudes the aroma of its original function. The walls are draped with images reflecting the history of the Maltings, railway and town. A vast range of bottled beers and several craft beers are also available. No jukebox, TV or fruit machines here – beer and conversation prevail. Q P (12)

Teign Cellars

67 East Street, TQ12 2JR

11-11; 10.30-midnight Fri & Sat ☎ (01626) 332991
teigncellars.com

4 changing beers (sourced nationally) H/G

Originally an annexe of the workhouse that stood opposite from 1836, this is now a highly enterprising establishment. Divided into three areas with a bar of high stools, to the rear it has a shop selling 170 different bottled beers while to the front there is a comfortable area for diners. The food is excellent, which explains why it might become crowded at weekends. The real ales are often unusual for the area and there is a good range of cider. Q P

Newton Poppleford

Cannon Inn

High Street, EX10 0DW

11-2.30, 5.30-11 (midnight Thu & Fri); 11-midnight Sat; 12-11 Sun ☎ (01395) 568266 pubindevon.com

Exmoor Gold; 1 changing beer (sourced nationally) G

Cheery, welcoming, two-bar pub with tables for dining in the lounge bar and restaurant area. Real ales are served by gravity from stillage behind the bar. This is a friendly locals' pub with busy passing trade. Good-value home-cooked food, served lunchtimes and evenings, covers most traditional pub favourites and, locals say, is of a tasty standard. Well-behaved dogs are allowed. There are two large gardens, and a skittle alley. The only pub in the village, and a community hub.
Q P (52,157)

Newton St Cyres

Beer Engine

EX5 5AX (beside railway station N of A377)

11-11; 12-9 Sun ☎ (01392) 851282
thebeerengine.co.uk

Beer Engine Rail Ale, Piston Bitter, Sleeper Heavy; 2 changing beers H

A Victorian pub, built in 1850, on the Exeter to Barnstaple Tarka Line, half a mile north of the A377. Popular with drinkers and diners alike, it is well-frequented by locals, visitors and its own cricket team. The dining area adjoining the bar serves its own bread made with beer yeast as well as home-cooked food available lunchtimes and evenings using locally sourced produce. The pub brews its own ales, including four regulars and a

seasonal ale which, like the village pictures and old pub signs, reflect a railway theme.
Q🐎❀◑◐♿⇌P🐾

North Tawton

Railway Inn 𝕃

Whiddon Down Road, EX20 2BE (1 mile S of town, just off A3124 and next to old North Tawton railway station, closed in 1971) SS666000
⏲ 6-11 Mon-Thu; 12-3, 6-11 Fri & Sat; 12-3, 7-10.30 Sun
☎ (01837) 82789 🌐 therailwaynorthtawton.co.uk
Teignworthy Reel Ale; 1 changing beer (sourced regionally) Ⓗ
Family-run local where there is always a warm welcome and good value to be found. The Railway has now deservedly achieved no fewer than 21 consecutive appearances in the Guide. Reel Ale from Teignworthy is normally joined by a guest ale from one of the other West Country breweries, together with a real cider in summer. The dining room is popular in the evening (no food Thu), with light meals served at lunchtime. Guide dogs only.
Q🐎❀◑◐♣🍎P🚌📶

Noss Mayo

Ship Inn 𝕃

PL8 1EW
⏲ 11-11 ☎ (01752) 872387 🌐 nossmayo.com
Dartmoor Jail Ale; Noss Beer Works Mew Stone; St Austell Tribute; 1 changing beer (sourced locally; often Noss Beer Works) Ⓗ
Popular with ramblers and seafarers alike, this fine split-level pub is on an inlet of the Yealm estuary. Four ales and excellent food are available daily. A former local CAMRA Pub of the Year, it is an ideal start/finish point for a walk to sample the breathtaking river and sea views along the route of Lord Revelstoke's Drive. If sailing, ring ahead to ascertain the tide times and mooring availability. There is no bus service in the evening or on Sunday. Q🐎❀◑◐♿⛺♣P🚌(3)🐾

Ottery St Mary

London Inn

4 Gold Street, EX11 1DG
⏲ 12 (4 Mon)-11; 12-midnight Fri & Sat; 12-10 Sun
☎ (01404) 812045 🌐 londoninn.net
6 changing beers Ⓗ
A 17th-century coaching inn close to the historic 14th-century parish church. Good-value home-cooked food, using local ingredients where possible, is served lunchtimes and evenings, plus a traditional roast on Sunday. It is a typical locals' pub, offering one regional real ale and up to five guests. Four B&B rooms are available. Dogs are allowed in the bottom bar.
Q🐎❀🛏◑◐♿♣🍎P🚌(4)🐾📶

Volunteer Inn

Broad Street, EX11 1BZ
⏲ 12-midnight; 12-11 Sun ☎ (01404) 814060
🌐 volunteerinnottery.co.uk
Otter Bitter; 3 changing beers (sourced regionally) Ⓖ
The pub has been part of Ottery St Mary's history since 1810, when it opened as a dwelling, hostelry and recruitment centre for the Napoleonic War. In the centre of the town, it is popular. The front bar has been kept traditional and the rear bar is more modern. All real ales, mainly from local breweries, are delivered by gravity. Food is served seven days a week, including a traditional Sunday roast, in the recently refurbished restaurant.
🐎❀◑◐♿♣🍎🚌(4)🐾📶

Paignton

Henry's Bar 𝕃 ✔

53 Torbay Road, TQ4 6AJ
⏲ 11-11 (midnight Fri & Sat) ☎ (01803) 551190
🌐 henrysbarpaignton.co.uk
Sharp's Doom Bar; 3 changing beers (sourced nationally; often Exmoor) Ⓗ
Splendid traditional-style pub with a long bar and covered seating at the front, located on the main street running from the bus/railway stations to the beach. The venue is warm and welcoming, and the beers reasonably priced. On handpump there are three regular beers, one guest beer and Sam's traditional cider, plus various bottles and polyboxes. Home-cooked wholesome fairly priced food is served all day until 9pm, and there is a highly regarded roast on Sunday. Families are welcome until 10pm, there is free Wi-Fi, and it is dog friendly. 🐎❀◑◐⇌🍎P🚌🐾📶

Isaac Merritt 𝕃 ✔

54-58 Torquay Road, TQ3 3AA
⏲ 8am-midnight ☎ (01803) 556066
Dartmoor Jail Ale; Greene King Abbot; Ruddles Best Bitter; Sharp's Doom Bar; changing beers (sourced nationally; often Hanlons, Hunters, Teignworthy) Ⓗ
A Wetherspoon pub just five minutes' walk from both the bus/railway stations, popular with locals and visitors alike, being community oriented. The pub boasts a well-deserved reputation for the quality and extensive range of handpumped real ales, plus various ciders both bottled and polyboxed. The decor is themed around Isaac Merritt Singer, the inventor of the Singer sewing machine; there are seated alcoves, separate family dining, a covered/heated smokers' area, and wheelchair access for both pub and toilets.
Q🐎❀◑◐♿⇌🍎P🚌🐾📶

Plymouth

Artillery Arms 𝕃

6 Pound Street, Stonehouse, PL1 3RH (behind Stonehouse Barracks and Millbay Docks)
⏲ 12 (4 Mon & Tue)-11 ☎ (01752) 262515
Draught Bass; 2 changing beers (sourced locally; often Black Tor, Dartmoor, Summerskills) Ⓗ
Cracking back-street local tucked away in the old quarter of Stonehouse, close to the magnificent Grade I-listed Royal William Yard, and maintaining the area's military connections. Two South-West guest beers and Thatchers Heritage cider are normally available. An out-of-season beach party takes place on the last weekend of February and charity monkey racing also features. Also popular with local hockey teams, this place is a real find.
❀🍎🚌(34,34A)🐾📶

Bread & Roses 𝕃

62 Ebrington Street, PL4 9AF
⏲ 4-1am; 12-1am Sat; 12-11 Sun ☎ (01752) 659861
🌐 breadandrosesplymouth.co.uk
Exeter Avocet; 3 changing beers (sourced regionally; often Altarnun, Bude, Red Rock) Ⓗ
This friendly, sympathetically restored late Victorian pub is popular with university staff, but

also has a mixed clientele. Up to four different real ales are sold, which are organic/Fairtrade wherever possible, just like the snacks. The beers are selected from local and regional breweries, including small-batch and speciality beers unusual for the area. The Real Junk Food Project is supported on the first Sunday each month, from 1pm. (23,24)

Britannia Inn

2 Wolesely Road, Milehouse, PL2 3BH

8am-midnight (1am Fri & Sat) (01752) 607596

Dartmoor Jail Ale; Greene King Abbot; Ruddles Best Bitter; Sharp's Doom Bar; changing beers (sourced nationally; often Bays, Fuller's, Summerskills) [H]

An Edwardian pub, built in the 1830s and opposite the Plymouth city bus depot, Central Park and the Life Centre, and a short walk from Home Park, Plymouth Argyle FC. The pub itself was built by the grandfather of Captain Scott (of the Antarctic fame). Ten handpumps dispense at least one real cider, with Westons and other local ciders appearing regularly. Since becoming a JD Wetherspoon in 1999, the pub has established a well-earned reputation for its beer.

Dolphin Hotel

14 The Barbican, PL1 2LS

10-11 (midnight Thu-Sat); 11-11 Sun (01752) 660876

Dartmoor Jail Ale; Draught Bass; Otter Ale; St Austell Tribute; Sharp's Doom Bar; Skinner's Betty Stogs; 2 changing beers (sourced regionally; often St Austell, Sharp's) [G]

A Plymouth institution, this unpretentious hostelry is steeped in history. Up to eight ales are all dispensed by gravity from the cask. The character of this establishment is charming, with tiled floors, well-used wooden benches and a traditional open fire, all creating the perfect ambience. The walls are adorned with paintings by local artist, the late Beryl Cook, who painted many of the characters she encountered in The Dolphin. Local CAMRA City Pub of the Year runner-up 2018. (25)

Fawn Private Members Club

39 Prospect Street, Greenbank, PL4 8NY

3 (2 Fri)-11; 12-11 Sat & Sun (01752) 226385

Bays Topsail; 4 changing beers (sourced regionally; often St Austell, Sharp's, Teignworthy) [H]

This mid 19th-century establishment was originally the Fawn Inn/Hotel, prior to converting to a club. CAMRA members are welcome with a valid membership card; regular visitors will be required to join. Four guest ales from the local area are generally on the bar, as well as a rotating range of local cider from Countryman. The club is popular for rugby and other televised sports, and supports multiple darts and euchre teams. Local CAMRA branch Club of the Year 2018, and former regional Club of the Year runner-up.

Ferry House Inn

888 Wolseley Road, Saltash Passage, PL5 1LA

12-11.30 (01752) 361063 ferryhouseinn.com

Dartmoor Jail Ale; Sharp's Doom Bar, Atlantic; 1 changing beer (sourced regionally) [H]

A picturesque pub on the River Tamar with a warm welcome. Decking on the edge of the river gives splendid views both of Brunel's 1859 rail bridge and the later 1952 road bridges. Three regular West Country ales are served, as well as good home-cooked food. Both bars display photos dating back to the turn of the 20th century of Brunel's bridge and the Saltash foot ferry. Water bowls for dogs are provided in the public bar.

(St Budeaux Victoria Road) (13)

Fisherman's Arms

31 Lambhay Street, Barbican, PL1 2NN

11-midnight (1am Fri & Sat) (01752) 268243

fishermansarms.co.uk

Dartmoor Jail Ale; house beer (by Summerskills); 1 changing beer (often Otter) [H]

Owner Donna, her partner Lee, and his family have turned this former St Austell Brewery pub back into a traditional free house. The interior is welcoming, with several distinctly decorated areas. The dartboard has returned and a variety of games and puzzles is available. Ale and cider festivals are held twice a year. Traditional pub grub at affordable prices is supplemented by specials. On Sunday only the famous roast is available. Close to the Royal Citadel and the Barbican. Dogs are welcome.

(25)

Fortescue Hotel

37 Mutley Plain, PL4 6JQ

11-midnight; 12-11 Sun (01752) 660673

Bays Devon Dumpling; St Austell Proper Job; Skinner's Betty Stogs; 6 changing beers (sourced nationally; often Cornish Crown, Hunters, South Hams) [H]

This multi award-winning and lively local is frequented by a broad section of the community, and conversation flourishes. Nine real ales are usually on the bar, and up to six real ciders. A perfect Sunday can be spent here – a good-value home-cooked roast paired with a pint of Spingo Special, followed by a brain-teasing quiz in the evening. The patio beer garden draws crowds in the summer and is heated in winter. Note the interesting cricket memorabilia adorning the walls.

Minerva Inn

31 Looe Street, Barbican, PL4 0EA

11.30-11.30 (midnight Wed; 12.30am Thu & Fri); 12-12.30am Sat; 1-10.30 Sun (01752) 223047

minervainn.co.uk

St Austell Trelawny, Tribute; 2 changing beers (sourced locally; often Dartmoor, Roam, Summerskills) [H]

Plymouth's oldest pub, dating from circa 1540, within easy walking distance of the city centre and the historic Barbican. The pub has a long and narrow bar, leading through to a cosy seating area at the rear. Two guest beers are added to during spring and autumn beer festivals, where beer could, and does, come from all over the country. Live music takes place Thursday to Sunday evenings and Sunday lunchtime. The pub benefits from a varied clientele.

Nowhere Inn

21 Gilwell Street, PL4 8BU

6-1am (3am Fri & Sat); closed Sun (01752) 670592

4 changing beers (sourced locally; often Bridgetown, Roam, Summerskills) [H]

Old-fashioned back-street pub tucked away in the middle of the student campus. It is close to the city centre and easily accessible by public transport, and is frequented by an eclectic variety of patrons, from students to elderly locals. Quiz nights are held on Mondays, and live music on Thursdays. A changing selection of locally sourced ale draws in visitors hoping to catch a glimpse both of favourite brews and hard-to-find ones. A black beer is usually on the bar. ≥♣🚌🐾📶

Prince Maurice 🄻 ✔

3 Church Hill, Eggbuckland, PL6 5RJ

🕘 11-3, 6-11; 11-11 Fri & Sat; 12-10.30 Sun
☎ (01752) 771515

Dartmoor Jail Ale; Hanlons Stormstay; St Austell Tribute, Proper Job; Sharp's Doom Bar; Summerskills Whistle Belly Vengeance; 2 changing beers (sourced locally; often Hunters, Roam, St Austell) 🄷

There is very much a village feel to this four-times local CAMRA Pub of the Year, which sits between the church and village green. The seven regular ales are supplemented by a changing guest ale. It is named after the Royalist general, the King's nephew, who had his headquarters nearby during the siege of Plymouth in the Civil War. The two log fires keep you warm in winter, adding to the ambience. Food is not available at weekends. ♣P🚌(28A)🐾

Pub on the Hoe 🄻 ✔

159 Citadel Road, The Hoe, PL1 2HU

🕘 8am-midnight ☎ (01752) 202405
🌐 thepubonthehoe.co.uk/index

House beer (by Hunters); 6 changing beers (sourced locally; often Bays, Noss Beer Works, Roam) 🄷

This is a busy street-corner pub serving a mixed clientele and near Plymouth Hoe, where Sir Francis Drake famously played bowls. Up to six varying real ales supplement the house beer, Drunken Hoe, and two local real ciders. Good home-cooked food is served all day. The wood-panelled raised and lower deck seating areas add to the nautical theme. It is located just a short walk from the historic Barbican and is well worth a visit. Live sport is shown on the large screen TV. ♣🚌(25)🐾📶

Waterloo Inn 🄻

30 Waterloo Street, Stoke, PL1 5RS

🕘 10-midnight; 11.30-11 Sun ☎ (01752) 550090

Sharp's Atlantic; 1 changing beer (sourced regionally; often Hunters, St Austell, Summerskills) 🄷

Situated in the western part of the city, it lies between Stoke Village and Plymouth Albion's Brickfields rugby ground. Built around 1890, this is a welcoming back-street pub. There are two main seating areas within this open-plan hostelry, which also has a large airy conservatory and a partially covered beer garden. Many games teams support the pub. Sharp's Atlantic is usually found as well as one continuously changing regional beer. Full wheelchair access is via the garden; please ring ahead. ♿≥♣🚌(32,32A)🐾📶

Plympton

Union Inn 🄻

17 Underwood Road, PL7 1SY

🕘 4-11 (11.30 Fri); 2-midnight Sat; 12-11 Sun
☎ (01752) 336756 🌐 unioninnplympton.com

4 changing beers (sourced regionally; often Exeter, Summerskills, Tintagel) 🄷

The landlord is a beer hunter, sourcing changing brews to charm his customers' palates, and to create a year-round beer festival. The four beers on offer are sourced regionally, but could be from almost anywhere. It is the same with the cider selection, but Old Rosie appears regularly in this former local CAMRA runner-up Cider Pub of the Year. This traditional, cosy, early 19th-century inn is a family-run community venue with a warm welcome for all who enter. Q♣P🚌🐾📶

Portsmouth Arms

Portsmouth Arms

Burrington, EX37 9ND (on A377 approximately 4 miles S of Umberleigh)

🕘 4-11; 12-11 Fri-Sun ☎ (01769) 561117
🌐 the-portsmouth-arms-hotel.co.uk

Otter Bitter 🄷**; 1 changing beer (sourced regionally)** 🄶

Set in the heart of the Taw Valley, this traditional coaching inn is an ideal base for walkers, fishermen and those exploring the local area. There is a comfortable lounge bar with wood-burning stove, a restaurant serving hearty home-cooked food, a public bar with pool table and an attractive patio garden at the rear with views across the river. The regular Otter Bitter is joined by a rotating guest ale, which is invariably served directly from the cask. Q≥♣P🐾📶

Postbridge

Warren House Inn 🄻

PL20 6TA (on B3212 between Postbridge and Bennett's Cross)

🕘 11-10 (3 Mon & Tue); 12-10.30 Sun ☎ (01822) 880208
🌐 warrenhouseinn.co.uk

Otter Ale; 3 changing beers (sourced regionally; often Black Tor, Butcombe, Summerskills) 🄷

Isolated and exposed at 1,425 feet above sea level, this is one of England's highest pubs. Countryman cider features regularly, with up to three varying guest beers mainly from the West Country. The characterful main bar boasts two log fires – one never goes out! Excellent home-made food includes the famous rabbit pie, local lamb and delicious puddings with clotted cream. There is a large family room, and tables outside give breathtaking views over the moors. Open all day in summer. Q⛺P🐾

Ringmore

Journey's End Inn 🄻

TQ7 4HL

🕘 closed Mon; 11-3, 6-11.30; 12-11 Sat; 12-10.30 Sun
☎ (01548) 810205 🌐 journeysendinn.co.uk

House beer (by Red Rock); 3 changing beers (sourced locally; often Exeter, South Hams, Teignworthy) 🄶

The 13th-century inn takes its name from the famous WW1 play by RC Sherriff, which he started writing while staying here. Up to four Devon beers on gravity behind the bar are sold in summer, and three in winter. Real cider is also stocked in summer. The dining room is now the games room. The car park is 200 yards away opposite All Hallows church. Beer festivals are held in March and September. Q♣P🚌(875)🐾

St Giles on the Heath

Pint & Post

PL15 9SA (just off main road through village)

🕘 12-3 (not Mon), 6-11; 12-3, 6-midnight Fri & Sat; 12-6 Sun
☎ (01566) 779933

Holsworthy Ales Muck 'n' Straw; 1 changing beer (sourced regionally) 🄷

Close to the Devon and Cornwall county border, this was once the village post office; it then became a pub containing the post office, thereby acquiring its name. Today, although no longer housing the post office, this friendly family-run pub remains at the heart of the community, with skittles and darts teams and a fortnightly local charity quiz night. The regular Muck 'n' Straw from Holsworthy is usually joined by another local guest ale. Q P

Shaldon

Shaldon Conservative Club

Dagmar Street, TQ14 0DU
12-3, 5-11; 12-11 Sat & Sun ☎ (01626) 873667
Teignworthy Reel Ale; 2 changing beers (sourced nationally) [H]
On a side street in the heart of the village, this spacious open-plan clubhouse has a friendly welcome for card-carrying CAMRA members and temporary members. Providing live entertainment, televised sport of local and national interest, a weekly meat draw, snooker, bingo and card games, this comfortable and modern venue serves three real ales and a cider. A beer festival is usually held in August. (22)

Sidford

Rising Sun

School Street, EX10 9PF (on main A3052 by traffc lights in Sidford)
12-3, 5-midnight; 12-midnight Fri-Sun ☎ (01395) 516616
Branscombe Vale Branoc; Otter Ale; Sharp's Doom Bar; 1 changing beer (sourced locally) [H]
A proper local community hostelry, this spacious street-corner pub offers a warm and friendly welcome both to locals and newcomers. Traditional pub food is served lunchtimes all week and evenings Monday to Saturday. The garden is popular in summer. While having no car park of its own, it is only 200 yards from a public car park behind the local shops. Q P

Silverton

Lamb Inn ✔

Fore Street, EX5 4HZ
12-2.30, 6-11; 12-11 Sat & Sun ☎ (01392) 860272
thelambinnsilverton.co.uk
Otter Ale; 2 changing beers (sourced regionally) [G]
Popular family-run village pub with stone floors, stripped timber, old pine furniture and a large open real fire. A fine display of old pumpclips is a reminder of the long list of previous guest beers. Three ales are served by gravity from a temperature-controlled stillage behind the bar, at competitive prices. There is a function room and skittle alley. Good-value home-cooked food is served lunchtimes and evenings, plus a popular Sunday roast. Q (55B)

Slapton

Queen's Arms

TQ7 2PN
12-3, 5.30-11; 12-3, 6-10.30 Sun ☎ (01548) 580800
queensarmsslapton.co.uk
Dartmoor Jail Ale; Otter Ale; South Hams Wild Blonde; 1 changing beer (sourced regionally; often Salcombe) [H]
Splendid 14th-century village pub deep in the South Hams countryside only half a mile from Slapton beach, boasting a flower-filled garden in summer with patios at the rear and an open fire in the winter. WWII evacuation photographs adorn the walls depicting local life and history. An extensive menu is served, with daily specials – the chef is known for his home-made pies in winter – and popular Sunday roasts (booking advisable). A takeaway food service is available. Children and dogs are also welcome. Q P

South Molton

Town Arms Hotel ✔

124 East Street, EX36 3BU (100yds E of town square)
11-midnight (1am Fri) ☎ (01769) 572531
Exmoor Ale; Sharp's Doom Bar; 1 changing beer (sourced regionally) [H]
Main-street local near the centre of this small, historic market town which is ideally situated for exploring Exmoor. Popular with locals and particularly busy on market day (Thursday), there is a strong commitment to real ale. Although no cooked food is served, good-value filled rolls are usually available. The single main bar has an open fire and pool table, while there is also a quieter back room and accommodation in four rooms. P (X7,155)

South Zeal

Oxenham Arms

EX20 2JT (on main road through village at lower end)
11-11; 11-10.30 Sun ☎ (01837) 840244
theoxenhamarms.com
4 changing beers (sourced regionally) [H]
Originally built as a 12th-century monastery, the Oxenham was later an imposing manor house. It now has the unspoilt atmosphere of an old country inn, with low beams, flagstone floors and open fires. Two guest beers, usually from local breweries, join the regular Oxy Ale and Merry Monk house beers. Good food can be enjoyed either in the bar or in the separate AA-starred restaurant. During January and February the pub closes 3-6pm. Q P (178)

Spreyton

Tom Cobley Tavern

EX17 5AL (off A3124 in village) SX6986096761
6.30-10.30 Mon; 12-3, 6-11; 12-4, 7-10.30 Sun
☎ (01647) 231314 tomcobleytavern.co.uk
Changing beers (sourced locally) [H]/[G]
A choice of up to 14 West Country real ales plus 18-30 real ciders and perries is on offer here. It also serves a wide range of bar snacks plus an extensive full menu. There is an eye-catching display of CAMRA certificates from National Pub of the Year 2006 onwards covering local, regional and national awards. A true village community pub, it has darts, quizzes and social events. Dogs and children are welcome. There is a delightful garden and five en-suite guest rooms. Q P

Sticklepath

Devonshire Inn

EX20 2NW (in centre of village)
12-3 (not Tue), 6-11; 12-11 Fri & Sat; 12-3 Sun
☎ (01837) 840626

Dartmoor IPA; Holsworthy Ales Sunshine, Muck 'n' Straw; 1 changing beer (sourced regionally) G
An atmospheric step back in time, this unspoilt thatched local, with low ceilings and an open fire, was originally at the end of a terrace of Elizabethan cottages in this Dartmoor village. There is a leat running past the rear wall of the pub which helps cool the three real ales on stillage, as well as powering the waterwheel of the Finch Foundry Museum (NT) next door. QP

Teignmouth

Blue Anchor Inn

Teign Street, TQ14 8EG
12-midnight (01626) 772741
6 changing beers (sourced regionally; often Exeter, Summerskills, Teignworthy) H
A single-room pub that is a real ale destination, with eight handpumps serving beer and cider. Situated on the edge of the town, the outdoor areas are a riot of floral colour in spring and summer and a winter wonderland of seasonal joy at Christmas. Beer festivals are held every Easter and August bank holiday and the pub is a great supporter of local charities and events. Live music, a pool table, a jukebox and televised sport are all popular attractions.

Brass Monkey

Hollands Road, TQ14 8SR
11-midnight; 12-11 Sun 07708 910144
St Austell Tribute H
A warming, simple and straightforward pub with one bar, pool table and two TV screens, very much in contrast to other establishments nearby. Halfway between the railway station and town-centre bus bays, it is capable of being either quiet and relaxing for reading the newspaper, or more lively at the weekends when the enjoyable karaoke takes place, with everyone welcome. In addition there is a Tuesday quiz and bingo on Wednesday. Q

Thorverton

Exeter Inn

Bullen Street, EX5 5NG
12-2.30, 5-11 (midnight Fri & Sat); 12-11 Sun
(01392) 860206
St Austell Tribute; Sharp's Doom Bar; 1 changing beer (sourced regionally) H
A small, traditional, village-centre pub, full of character, run by the same family for over 60 years. The walls and ceilings are covered by a collection of weapons, armour, military equipment, artisan items and brasses. There is also a deep glass-covered well. An open log fire plus a wood-burning stove help give the interior a warm, welcoming atmosphere. The village car park can be found 200 yards to the west. (55B)

Tiverton

Courtenay's

10 Newport Street, EX16 6NH
closed Mon; 1.30-11 Tue; 3-11 Wed & Thu; 12.30-midnight Fri & Sat; 1-4 Sun
4 changing beers (sourced regionally) G
A micropub that opened in 2012 in a former street-corner pet shop and is named after the family who lived in the nearby Tiverton castle. The old curved windows now contain some fine etched glass. There are four cask ales from South-West regional breweries, plus six real ciders, set up behind the compact wooden bar. Local suppliers are preferred. A small carpeted seating area is off to one side of the bar. Toilet facilities are limited. Q

Topsham

Bridge Inn ★

Bridge Hill, EX3 0QQ
12-2, 6-10.30 (11 Fri & Sat); 12-2, 7-10.30 Sun
(01392) 873862 cheffers.co.uk/bridge.html
Branscombe Vale Branoc; changing beers G
This historic, cosy, 16th-century inn is beautifully positioned overlooking the River Clyst and meadows. Run by six generations of the same family (they celebrated 121 years in 2018), this hostelry is a delight to fans of real ale and was even visited by the Queen in 1998. A varying range of seven to nine ales sourced locally and from further afield is dispensed by gravity directly from the cellar. Traditional pub lunches such as ploughman's and sandwiches are offered.
QP(57,T)

Exeter Inn

68 High Street, EX3 0DY
4-11; 12-midnight Fri & Sat; 12-10.30 Sun
(01392) 873131
Teignworthy Beachcomber; 4 changing beers (sourced regionally) H
A pub since at least 1860, some of this partially thatched building dates from the 17th century when it was part of a farm. The Exeter is a friendly local serving up to five real ales and two ciders, plus occasional snacks such as rolls. Three TVs show various sports, while the front area is devoted to pool and darts. There is a small sheltered garden and smoking area at the side. Dogs are welcome.
(57)

Torquay

Crown & Sceptre

2 Petitor Road, St Marychurch, TQ1 4QA
12 (1 Mon & Tue)-4, 6-11; 12-11 Sat; 12-4, 7-11 Sun
(01803) 328290
Butcombe Gold; Courage Best Bitter, Directors; Dartmoor Jail Ale; Hanlons Yellow Hammer; Otter Ale; 2 changing beers (sourced nationally; often Harveys, Yeovil) H
Close to St Marychurch shopping precinct is this lovely old-fashioned local. It has two bars, the lounge with bare stone walls, open fire and bench and stool seating, and the bar with stall-type table and bench seating, lots of chamber pots and interesting stuff hanging from the ceiling. There are two garden areas and a small car park. Live music features at least three nights a week. Everyone is welcome including families and dogs. Run by the same family for over 40 years.
P

Hole in the Wall

6 Park Lane, TQ1 2AU
12-midnight (01803) 200755
holeinthewalltorquay.co.uk
Butcombe Blond; Dartmoor Jail Ale; Otter Bitter; Sharp's Doom Bar; 4 changing beers (sourced regionally; often Butcombe, Otter, St Austell) H

An atmospheric pub in a hidden location close to the marina, popular with tourists and locals. The low-beamed quirky interior boasts a large restaurant serving a variety of foods for all tastes. The narrow passageway with seating and adorned with flowers provides a perfect spot for alfresco drinking. Reputed to be Torquay's oldest pub, from around 1540, it is a real haven for real ale drinkers.

Kents

1 Ilsham Road, TQ1 2JG

11-11 (midnight Fri) ☎ (01803) 292522

thekentstorquay.co.uk

Otter Ale; St Austell Tribute; Sharp's Doom Bar; 1 changing beer (sourced regionally; often Exmoor) H

A traditional pub on a corner site with a large ornate bar and a separate restaurant. Family friendly, it is in Wellswood, a leafy suburb about one mile from the centre of Torquay and a third of a mile from the world-famous Kents Cavern. Kents has a first-class restaurant serving food throughout lunchtimes and evenings. Four regional real ales plus one guest are always on the bar and, additionally, over 30 gins are permanently stocked. Four regular beers are offered in the holiday season. Q P

Totnes

Albert Inn

32 Bridgetown, TQ9 5AD

12-11 (midnight Fri & Sat) ☎ (01803) 863214

albertinntotnes.com

Bridgetown Albert Ale, Bitter, Shark Island Stout; 1 changing beer (sourced locally) H

Named after the famous scientist Albert Einstein, the pub is 100 yards over the bridge over the River Dart in Bridgetown, and is an excellent example of an old-school community local. Pub teams, live music, quiz, culinary and theme nights all feature in this friendly hostelry. Three or more beer/cider festivals are held each year and it is also home to the Bridgetown Brewery. At the rear is a cosy beer garden with views of the River Dart. It is well worth making a visit to this welcoming pub.
Q P

Bay Horse Inn

8 Cistern Street, TQ9 5SP

12-11.30 ☎ (01803) 862088 bayhorsetotnes.com

New Lion Mane Event, Totnes Stout, Pandit IPA; 3 changing beers (sourced regionally; often Otter, Teignworthy) H

Traditional without being old-fashioned, this inn is at the top of Totnes' main shopping street. A community minded, friendly pub, it hosts live music including jazz and open mic, and quiz nights. Beer festivals are held twice yearly at Easter and over the August bank holiday. It has a superb beer garden in which many events are held. The pub is also the tap for New Lion Brewery and gives a warm welcome to all.
Q P (X64,164)

Royal Seven Stars Hotel

The Plains, TQ9 5DD

8am-11 (11.30 Fri & Sat) ☎ (01803) 862125

royalsevenstars.co.uk

Dartmoor Jail Ale; Sharp's Doom Bar; 2 changing beers (sourced locally; often Bays, New Lion) H

Prominently situated at the bottom of the main shopping street in Totnes, in the centre of the town, this former coaching house is dog and family friendly. It has 21 rooms, an excellent à la carte restaurant, and is a wedding venue with two function rooms. The hotel hosts live music every Friday night and has plenty of seating outside the front of the hotel, where events are also held in the warmer months. Q P

Totnes Brewing Company

59A High Street, TQ9 5PB (at top of High Street by market square)

5-midnight; 12-midnight Fri & Sat; 12-11.30 Sun

thetotnesbrewingco.co.uk

8 changing beers (sourced nationally; often Totnes) H/P

Popular and quirky brewpub serving an eclectic range of beers, with staff who are enthusiastic and knowledgeable about beer. The beer range, which is constantly changing, generally includes at least one ale brewed on the premises on handpump, among a range of guest ales on up to seven pumps. There is also a good range of KeyKeg ales. Takeaway food may be ordered in.
Q

Turnchapel

Boringdon Arms

13 Boringdon Terrace, PL9 9TQ

12-11 (midnight Fri & Sat); 12-10.30 Sun

☎ (01752) 402053

Dartmoor Jail Ale; Fuller's London Pride; Sharp's Atlantic, Sea Fury H

The Bori is a traditional former Regional CAMRA Pub of the Year, with six letting rooms – dogs welcome. It sits in the waterside village of Turnchapel, which is on the South-West Coastal Footpath, and benefits from a regular bus service from Plymouth, or via water taxi from the Barbican. The four regular ales are added to during four beer festivals each year. Good-value home-cooked food is served daily. There are two secluded gardens to the rear. Q (2,2A)

Weare Giffard

Cyder Presse

EX39 4QR

5-11 Mon & Tue; 11-midnight ☎ (01237) 425517

Timothy Taylor Landlord; 4 changing beers (sourced nationally) H

Welcoming village local with cosy bar and restaurant areas, two en-suite twin rooms and a beer garden. Up to four real ales are regularly stocked, alongside a minimum of nine real ciders and an interesting choice of gins and rums. Home-cooked food made from local produce is served Wednesday to Saturday and Sunday lunchtime. The pub is both dog and family friendly. Tuesday is live folk music night and new musicians are always welcome. Q P (7A)

Wembury

Odd Wheel

Knighton Road, PL9 0JD

12-3, 5-midnight; 12-midnight Sat & Sun

☎ (01752) 863052 theoddwheel.co.uk

Dartmoor Jail Ale; St Austell Tribute; Sharp's Doom Bar; 3 changing beers (sourced regionally) H

Friendly country pub tastefully refurbished several years ago, and at the northern end of this

picturesque village. The three regular beers are supplemented by up to three guest beers, mainly from Devon and Cornwall. Regular beer festivals are held. It is only a short distance from many walking routes, including the South-West Coast Path. Food is served daily, with ingredients from local suppliers. Outside, there is a terraced garden and play area for children. Dogs welcome.
P (48)

Whiddon Down

Post Inn

EX20 2QT (just off main A30 at crossroads of B3219 and A382)

12-11 (01647) 231242 thepostinnwhiddon.co.uk

Dartmoor Legend; Otter Amber; Teignworthy Reel Ale; 1 changing beer (sourced regionally) H

This welcoming, cosy yet spacious roadside inn on the northern edge of Dartmoor has a long history dating back to its origins as a post house. All four beers are from the West Country and there is usually a choice of two ciders from Sampford Orchards. Food, which is available daily, is sourced locally wherever possible. The beer garden is particularly attractive and has panoramic views.
Q P

Widecombe-in-the-Moor

Rugglestone Inn

TQ13 7TF (¼ mile from centre of village)

11.30-3, 6-11.30; 11.30-3, 5-midnight Fri; 11.30-midnight Sat; 12-11 Sun (01364) 621327 rugglestoneinn.co.uk

Dartmoor Legend; house beer (by Teignworthy); 1 changing beer (sourced regionally) G

The pub is a Grade II-listed unspoilt Dartmoor building converted to an inn in 1832. The name comes from a local logan stone. There is a cosy bar with a woodburner and two further rooms, one with an open fire. Beer is also served through a hatch in the passageway. A wide selection of home-cooked food is available. Across the stream is a large grassed seating area with the car park just down the road. Local farm Ashridge cider is sold. Q P (271,672)

Yarde Down

Poltimore Arms

EX36 3HA (2 miles E of Brayford on jct with unclassified road from South Molton to Simonsbath) SS725356

11-11 (01598) 710381

Exmoor Ale; Otter Bitter; 1 changing beer (sourced regionally) G

Dating from the 13th century, this old coaching inn lies in a remote area of glorious Exmoor countryside. The ivy-clad, beamed hostelry is so remote it generates its own electricity, and water is from a spring. It is an atmospheric and welcoming locals' pub, which retains many interesting and original features including, it is said, a friendly ghost. Q P

Ferry House Inn, Plymouth

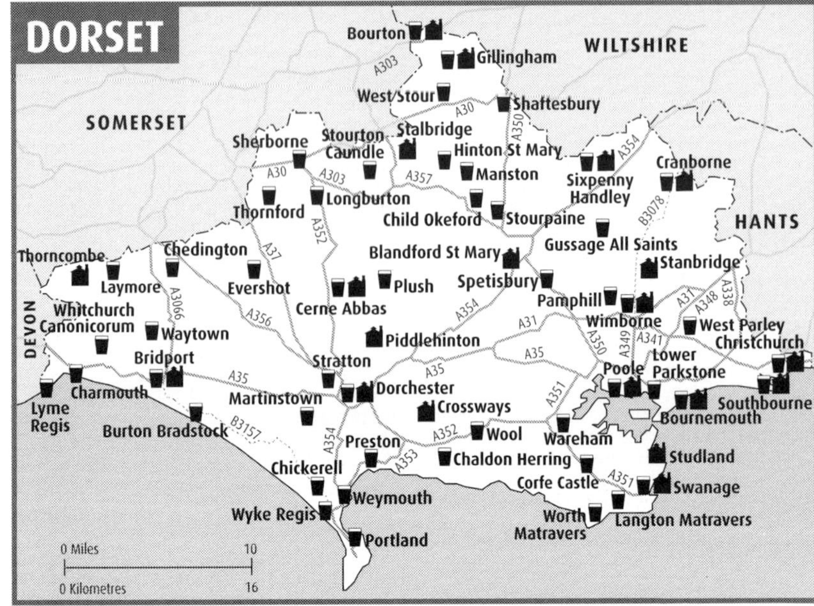

Bournemouth

All Hail Ale

10 Queens Road, Westbourne, BH2 6BE
12 (5 Mon)-10.30 ☎ 07786 045996
5 changing beers (sourced nationally) H
A vibrant micropub and bottle shop, this former restaurant has been skilfully converted, with wooden flooring and a polished wood bar and tables. Five handpumps serve a varying range of ales both from local and national breweries, alongside 10 keg lines with a varied and well-chosen selection on offer. A range of real ciders is also stocked. Beer-related slogans adorn the walls and a large blackboard lists the beers available.
Q

Cricketers ✔

41 Windham Road, Springbourne, BH1 4RN
11-11; 12-10.30 Sun ☎ (01202) 551589
Fuller's London Pride; 2 changing beers (sourced nationally) H
Bournemouth's oldest public house, dating from 1847, has two bar areas rich in mahogany and stained-glass windows. The vaulted upper section of the main bar was converted from the gym where world champion boxer Freddie Mills once trained. This friendly community pub offers two varying guest beers and Westons cider, and hosts an annual beer festival in October. Lunches are served at weekends, including excellent Sunday roasts. Away fans are welcome when AFC Bournemouth are playing at home.
P (2)

Firkin Shed

279 Holdenhurst Road, Springbourne, BH8 8BZ
closed Mon; 4 (3 Thu)-11; 12-midnight Fri & Sat; 3-11 Sun
☎ (01202) 302340
6 changing beers (sourced nationally; often Cerne Abbas, Siren, Vibrant Forest) G
The Shed is a quirky, award-winning, friendly, family-run micropub. Tables and benches hug the walls, which are decorated with flags, musical instruments, puppets and skulls. A shed is used as the bar, offering six constantly changing cask ales and 20-plus ciders from around the country. Beers are served straight from the cellar, viewable through the window in the rear corridor. Quality bar snacks are available. There is occasional live music. The pub is a mobile-free zone with fines payable to charity. (2)

Micro Moose 🏆

326 Wimborne Road, Winton, BH9 2HH
4-11; 12-11 Fri & Sat; 3-8 Sun ☎ (01202) 538542
micromoose.co.uk
4 changing beers (sourced nationally) H/G
Established when the Canadian owner decided to convert her coffee shop into a micropub advertising Great British Ales with Canadian Hospitality. This friendly and cosy bar offers a selection of local and regional ales served either on handpump or gravity. The bottled beer selection is Canadian-themed, as is the decor, complete with fluffy moose head. In common with other micropubs, sharing tables is encouraged. Local cider is also available and a good selection of bar snacks.
Q

Silverback Alehouse

518 Wimborne Road, Winton, BH9 2EX
12-10 (11 Thu-Sat) ☎ 07999 586730
silverbackalehouse.co.uk
4 changing beers (sourced nationally; often Blue Monkey, Cerne Abbas, Yeovil) G
Set on Winton's bustling high street, this micropub offers a welcome respite from the weekly shop. Four carefully chosen real ales from regional breweries are served on gravity alongside ales from the Nottinghamshire area. Four ciders are also on offer from small independent cider makers. Benches and tables set around the sides of the pub are served by friendly staff. Light snacks are available and you are welcome to bring in your takeaway. With a relaxed and friendly atmosphere, the bar is popular with locals and visitors alike.
Q

Bourton

White Lion

High Street, SP8 5AT

12-11; 12-10.30 Sun ☎ (01747) 840866

whitelionbourton.co.uk

Otter Amber; 1 changing beer H

The White Lion is a traditional inn dating from 1763. Originally separate rooms, the cosy bar with stone-flagged floor has been opened out but there is always a quiet corner to be found. It has a cosy, intimate restaurant and a large beer garden. The pub is set back from the B3081 with parking opposite as well as in the car park. Thatchers Original or Rich's Cider is served on handpump. Q P (X4)

Bridport

Pursuit of Hoppiness

15 West Street, DT6 3QJ

12-11 (midnight Fri & Sat); 12-10 Sun ☎ (01308) 427111

hoppiness.co.uk

6 changing beers (sourced nationally; often Eight Arch, Tapstone) H

Popular town-centre single-room micropub with room for around 25 people. There are six handpumps serving beers of all styles, changing regularly every few days – over 500 different beers from all over the UK were served in the first 15 months the pub was open. Six ciders are normally available including regulars Dorset Nectar and West Milton. Outdoor seating is available at the front. Q

Ropemakers Arms L ✔

36 West Street, DT6 3QP

10-11 (12.30am Fri & Sat); 12-4 Sun ☎ (01308) 421255

theropemakers.com

Palmers Copper Ale, IPA, Dorset Gold, 200, Tally Ho!; 1 changing beer H

Deceptively large pub situated in the centre of town serving the full Palmers range of beers. The interior is divided into lots of separate themed areas decorated with memorabilia and local history. There is a large partially covered courtyard at the rear and disabled access via the back door. Quality home-cooked food is from local suppliers. Music features on Friday and Saturday evenings. The pub closes around 4pm on Sundays in the winter (later on bank holiday weekends or if there is live music).

Tiger Inn ✔

14-16 Barrack Street, DT6 3LY

12-11 (midnight Fri & Sat) ☎ (01308) 427543

tigerinnbridport.co.uk

Sharp's Doom Bar, Atlantic; 4 changing beers (sourced regionally; often Gyle 59, Hop Back, Sharp's) H

A busy and popular Victorian pub tucked away near the town centre. The Tiger offers six changing real ales including occasional beers brewed on-site by the Stripey Cat Craft Brewery. The single bar has two distinct areas, with TV for major sporting events and pub games including darts and cribbage. There are two outdoor seating areas. Look for the rare Groves Brewery etched window and collection of old fishing rods on the ceilings. B&B is offered in seven en-suite rooms.

Burton Bradstock

Three Horseshoes L ✔

Mill Street, DT6 4QZ

12-3, 5-11; 12-11 Sat; 12-10.30 Sun ☎ (01308) 897259

threehorseshoesburtonbradstock.co.uk

Palmers Copper Ale, IPA, Dorset Gold, 200, Tally Ho!; 1 changing beer H

Three-hundred-year-old thatched pub and restaurant with suntrap seating at the front and in the beer garden. It serves good home-cooked food and is popular with families using the beach. The full Palmers range is available plus a Palmers seasonal beer or Dorset Orchards First Press cider. Open all day and serving food throughout April to September, Easter and summer school holidays and bank holidays. Dogs are welcome in the bar area. P (C1,X53)

Cerne Abbas

Royal Oak Inn L

23 Long Street, DT2 7JG

12-3, 5-11; 12-midnight Fri & Sat; 12-11 Sun

☎ (01300) 341797 theroyaloakcerneabbas.co.uk

3 changing beers (sourced regionally; often Cerne Abbas, Dartmoor, Lyme Regis) H

Set in the heart of the village, this traditional pub, built in 1540 of stone from the local abbey, is your quintessential pub with flagstone floors, beamed ceilings and an open fire. The beers are mainly from the south west, with a Cerne Abbas Brewery ale always available. The food is well served and plentiful and the ambience fantastic. Dogs and walkers are welcome. Open all day in summer, closed Tuesdays in winter. Q (X11)

Chaldon Herring

Sailor's Return L

DT2 8DN

closed Mon; 12-2.30, 6-11; 12-11 Sat; 12-10.30 Sun

☎ (01305) 854441 sailorsreturnpub.com

REAL ALE BREWERIES

Barefaced Bournemouth (NEW)
Brew Shack Sixpenny Handley
Brewers Folly Stanbridge (NEW)
Brewhouse & Kitchen Bournemouth
Brewhouse & Kitchen Dorchester
Brewhouse & Kitchen Poole
Brewhouse & Kitchen Southbourne
Cerne Abbas Cerne Abbas
Dorset (DBC) Crossways
Drop the Anchor Christchurch
Eight Arch Wimborne
Gyle 59 Thorncombe
Hall & Woodhouse (Badger) Blandford St Mary
Hattie Brown's Swanage
Isle of Purbeck Studland
King Alfred Bourton
Palmers Bridport
Piddle Piddlehinton
Sandbanks Poole
Sixpenny Cranborne
Small Paul's Gillingham
Southbourne Bournemouth
Stripey Cat Bridport
Way Outback Southbourne
Wriggle Valley Stalbridge

Otter Ale; Palmers Copper Ale; 1 changing beer (sourced regionally; often Cerne Abbas, Flack Manor, Otter) Ⓗ
Historic thatched inn situated on the fringe of a small, tranquil village, a few miles from the Jurassic Coast. The pub dates from the 1860s but the building is much older. There are a number of distinct dining and drinking areas of different shapes and sizes, with flagstoned floors throughout. Food comes mainly from local suppliers with many seasonal variations. Wednesday is pie night. The restaurant tends to be popular so booking is highly advisable. Q♘❀◑🍏P🐾📶

Charmouth

Royal Oak Inn Ⓛ ✔

The Street, DT6 6PE
10.30-11 (11.30 Fri & Sat); 10.30-9.30 Sun
☎ (01297) 560277 🌐 royaloakcharmouth.co.uk
Palmers Copper Ale, IPA, Dorset Gold, 200; 1 changing beer Ⓗ
The Royal Oak is a traditional family-run village pub situated on the Jurassic Coast. The friendly staff are welcoming of locals and visitors alike. It serves locally brewed Palmers beers and a local real cider. Food is freshly cooked using locally sourced produce. Dogs are allowed in the lower bar area. ♘❀◑⛺♣🍏🚌(X51,X53)🐾📶

Chedington

Winyards Gap Inn Ⓛ

DT8 3HY
11.30-3, 6-11; 11.30-11 Sat & Sun ☎ (01935) 891244
🌐 winyardsgap.com
Exmoor Ale; Otter Ale; 1 changing beer (often Branscombe Vale, Dorset, St Austell) Ⓗ
Split-level two-bar pub with flagstone floors and stunning views of the countryside. It is popular with diners and has outdoor seating and a large car park. Two real ales are available in winter and three or four in summer, with guest beers from Branscombe Vale, Dorset or St Austell breweries. The pub is only accessible via steps. Closed on Mondays in winter. Q♘❀🛏◑♣🍏P🚌(B1)🐾📶

Chickerell

Turk's Head Inn

6 East Street, DT3 4DS
11-11; 12-10.30 Sun ☎ (01305) 778565
🌐 theturksheaddorset.com
Dartmoor Jail Ale; Sharp's Doom Bar; 1 changing beer (sourced locally; often Dorset, Piddle) Ⓗ
Large food-oriented family-friendly pub serving up to three local guest ales in addition to the regulars, depending on the season. It has a separate restaurant but food is served throughout all day, including a popular carvery and the famous home-made steak and Jail Ale pie, with takeaways available. The outdoor children's play area has pigs, chickens and rabbits. Popular with locals and holidaymakers from the nearby camp and caravan sites. Q♘❀◑♿⛺♣🍏P🚌(8)🐾📶

Child Okeford

Saxon Inn

Gold Hill, DT11 8HD
12-3 (not Tue), 6-11 ☎ (01258) 860310 🌐 saxoninn.co.uk
Butcombe Original; Otter Bitter; 1 changing beer (sourced regionally; often Palmers) Ⓗ
This 300-year-old inn retains rustic charm despite significant extension following conversion from cottages in the 1950s. The bar area is cosy, with tables and chairs around the log fire. There are two distinct dining areas and a garden for alfresco meals. A varied menu of quality home-cooked food is available. A beer festival is held in September in the garden. The pub also offers B&B and is an ideal base for exploring rural Dorset. Q♘❀🛏◑♿♣P🐾📶

Christchurch

Saxon Bar Ale House

5 The Saxon Centre, Fountain Way, BH23 1QN
closed Mon; 4-10 Tue & Wed; 12-10 (11 Fri & Sat); 12-10.30 Sun ☎ (01202) 488931
4 changing beers (sourced locally) Ⓖ
This friendly, single-room micropub has perimeter seating and high tables. It offers a variety of well-chosen – often local – ales directly from the cask, as well as real ciders, all served directly to your table. The cellar can be seen from the pub and the walls are adorned with musical instruments, maps and other interesting curios. Hops and bottles hang from the ceiling. Specialty bar snacks and local spirits are also available. Look out for the Carlsbog urinal, not to be missed! Q⇌🍏🚌🐾

Thomas Tripp ✔

10 Wick Lane, BH23 1HX
11-11.30 (midnight Fri & Sat); 12-11.30 Sun
☎ (01202) 490498 🌐 thomastripp.co.uk
Ringwood Razorback, Fortyniner; 2 changing beers (sourced nationally; often Vibrant Forest) Ⓗ
Named after a legendary local smuggler, this vibrant, historic inn is situated just off the high street in the old town area. Good bar food is available lunchtimes and evenings, with speciality fish dishes served in the adjoining shack. There is a large paved patio area with sheltered alcoves. A wood-burning stove keeps the bar cosy in the winter. Live music plays several nights a week and the enthusiastic bar manager maintains an interesting choice of guest ales. Razorback is Ringwood Best. ♘❀◑♿🚌🐾📶

Corfe Castle

Corfe Castle Club

70 East Street, BH20 5EQ (off A351)
12-2.30, 6-11; 12-11 Sat & Sun ☎ (01929) 480591
Ringwood Razorback; Timothy Taylor Landlord; 1 changing beer (sourced nationally) Ⓗ
Friendly club in the village centre, formerly a school and built in Purbeck stone. The main bar has upholstered bench seating, TV for major sporting events and darts and shove ha'penny. An upstairs room has a pool table and can be hired for meetings. Filled rolls are available all day. The spectacular garden boasts a boules court and views over the Purbeck Hills. Convenient for the castle or steam railway, visitors are welcome with a CAMRA membership card or copy of the Guide. ❀⇌♣P🚌(40)📶

Cranborne

Sixpenny Tap

Holwell Farm, Holwell, BH21 5QP (1 mile from village centre on B3078)
4-7.30; 11.30-7.30 Fri; 11.30-4 Sat & Sun
(01725) 762006 sixpennybrewery.co.uk
Sixpenny Best Bitter, Gold, IPA; 1 changing beer H
Housed in a converted Victorian stables and packed full of quirky miscellaneous items, the Tap has quickly established itself as the heart of the local community. Conversation rules in the popular dog- and muddy boot-friendly bar. Sixpenny Brewery is next door and its range of beers is served with pride and enthusiasm. Many community events are held within the extensive courtyard. Ideally located for country walks, or as a stopping point for cyclists and horse riders – a hearty welcome awaits all.
QP

Dorchester

Blue Raddle

9 Church Street, DT1 1JN
12-3 (not Mon), 6.30-11; 12-11 Sat; 12-10.30 Sun
(01305) 267762 blueraddle.co.uk
Dartmoor Jail Ale; Otter Bitter; St Austell Tribute; 2 changing beers (sourced nationally; often Adnams, Cerne Abbas) H
Town-centre pub with a comfortable and cosy ambience and a friendly and enthusiastic landlord and staff, popular with a wide age range. Well-kept beers and a good selection of guest ales are complemented by a range of ciders. Locally sourced food is cooked and served to order lunchtimes Wednesday to Saturday and evenings Thursday to Saturday. The walls are covered in interesting and quirky pictures including Private Eye covers in the Gents. Folk music sessions feature regularly. No children are allowed but dogs are welcome. Q

Convivial Rabbit

Trinity House, Trinity Street, DT1 1TT (down alley next to Pennywise)
closed Mon & Tue; 12-10 (11 Fri & Sat); 3-10.30 Sun
convivialrabbit.co.uk
6 changing beers (sourced nationally)
Popular pop-up micropub with an ever-changing choice of around six real ales, of varying styles, on gravity from micro and independent British breweries. Local ciders, wines and spirits are also available. Folk music sessions are hosted on Sunday evening. Q

Royal Oak

20 High West Street, DT1 1UW
8am-midnight (1am Fri & Sat); 8am-11 Sun
(01305) 755910
Greene King Abbot; Ruddles Best Bitter; 6 changing beers (sourced nationally; often Butcombe, Dorset, Otter) H
A busy town-centre Wetherspoon pub offering a wide selection of frequently changing local and national ales on handpump, with regular beer festivals adding to the range. The pub offers a full food menu and is open for breakfast daily, welcoming children and families. To the rear is a sunny patio area with wheelchair access to the main internal area. Q

Evershot

Acorn Inn Hotel

28 Fore Street, DT2 0JW
11-11; 12-10.30 Sun (01935) 83228 acorn-inn.co.uk
3 changing beers (sourced regionally; often Dorset, St Austell) H
Small, attractive 16th-century inn mentioned in Thomas Hardy's Tess of the d'Urbervilles as the Sow & Acorn. The large flagstoned village bar at the back has a wood-burning stove. A smaller bar and restaurant are at the front. Two ales are always available, usually from Dorset Brewing Company or St Austell brewery. A third ale is added in the summer from breweries such as Dartmoor or Exmoor. The skittle alley can be hired for functions.
QP(B4)

Gillingham

Phoenix

High Street, SP8 4AY
10-11; 11-midnight Sat; 11-11 Sun (01747) 823277
Brains Rev James Gold; Sharp's Doom Bar; 1 changing beer (sourced regionally; often Bath Ales, St Austell) H
Originally built in the 15th century as a coaching inn when it had its own brewery and stables, it was rebuilt in the 17th century following a fire and renamed The Phoenix. It has an open-plan layout with a dining area to one side. There are two public car parks within walking distance and a small one to the rear. Good-value pub grub includes specials and traditional Sunday lunch. P(X2,X4)

Gussage All Saints

Drovers Inn

Bowerswain Hollow, BH21 5ET
closed Mon; 11-11 (9 Sun) (01258) 840550
droversinngussage.co.uk
5 changing beers (sourced locally) H
Located in a picturesque village in the heart of rural Dorset, this thriving, award-winning, community-owned pub is very much at the centre of local life. Friendly and cosy, The Drovers entices you in to sample its changing range of real ale and good-quality food. A popular book club and supper club meet here and there are quizzes, music nights and festivals throughout the year to keep you entertained. A British sign language service is available. Please check seasonal opening times.
QP

Hinton St Mary

White Horse

6 White Horse Lane, DT10 1NA
closed Mon; 12-2.30, 6-11; 12-5 Sun (01258) 472723
thewhitehorsehinton.co.uk
3 changing beers (sourced regionally; often Otter, Wriggle Valley) H
This 16th-century Grade II-listed stone building is a genuine old-fashioned public house at the heart of the community. With wooden beams throughout, the public bar features stone flooring and an open fire, while the lounge is used for dining. Three beers are usually available including one from the pub's own White Horse Craft Brewery. A new wood-fired pizza oven has been installed and parties and weddings can be catered for.
QP(309)

Langton Matravers

King's Arms

27 High Street, BH19 3HA

12-11 ☎ (01929) 422979

Ringwood Razorback; 3 changing beers (sourced nationally) Ⓗ

Dating back to 1743, this Purbeck stone-built pub, with original flagstone floors, has many quirky little rooms off a central bar area, and a suntrap rear garden. The seaside town of Swanage with its steam railway is close by, as are many fine walks where you can explore the Purbecks and the South-West Coast Path. A dog- and family-friendly pub serving fine pub food and well-chosen ales, this is a magnet both for locals and visitors. Q❀◑▲♣●🚌(40)🐾📶

Laymore

Squirrel Inn

TA20 4NT

5-10.30; 12-midnight Fri-Sun ☎ (01460) 30298

Sharp's Doom Bar; 1 changing beer (sourced nationally; often Fuller's) Ⓗ

Modernised country pub with a spacious single bar area and a separate function room with a double skittle alley and pool table. Two real ales, two draught ciders and a large selection of bottled cider are available. Camping can be arranged in the large outdoor area, and the barbecue hut, which sleeps four, can be hired. Families are welcome. ❀◑♿▲♣●P🚌(96)🐾📶

Longburton

Rose & Crown

DT9 5PD

12-3 (not Mon), 6-11; 12-4 Sun ☎ (01963) 210202

roseandcrownlongburton.com

5 changing beers (sourced regionally) Ⓗ

This lovely thatched 17th-century former coaching inn is a fascinating blend of traditional beams, stone flags and open fireplaces, set off by a contemporary decor. A free house, it offers one beer from Sharp's and four constantly rotating regional and local beers. Real cider is available in summer. Traditional pub food is served in the bar and restaurant. There is a large beer garden plus two B&B rooms in a separate building. Open all day on bank holidays.

Q❀◑♿♣●P🚌(X11)🐾📶

Lower Parkstone

Bermuda Triangle

10 Parr Street, BH14 0JY

12-3, 5-11; 12-midnight Fri & Sat; 12-11 Sun

☎ (01202) 748047 bermudatrianglepub.com

4 changing beers (sourced nationally; often Dark Star, Goddards, Sharp's) Ⓗ

This busy pub is decorated to reflect the Bermuda Triangle story. The single-room bar is on three levels – look out for the hidden stairway leading to the snug upstairs which is open at weekends. The walls and ceiling display a range of artefacts including maps, newspaper cuttings and ship and aircraft fittings. The bar has four handpumps offering a changing range of ales sourced locally and from throughout the UK. There is a covered patio area, occasionally used for barbecues and street seating. ❀⇌●P🚌(M1,3)🐾

Poole Ex-Servicemen's Club

66 North Road, BH14 0LY

12-3 (not Mon & Tue), 6-11; 12-11 Fri-Sun

☎ (01202) 744515

4 changing beers (sourced nationally) Ⓗ

A regular local CAMRA Club of the Year winner, this friendly social club is affiliated to the RBL and offers four ever-changing well-chosen ales and two real ciders. The club has a large main room, meeting rooms, pool table and beer garden. Numerous dartboards, an upstairs snooker room and a varied jukebox add to the bustle of this popular venue. Three beer festivals are held throughout the year. Visitors are welcome with a CAMRA membership card or copy of this Guide.

❀◑♿⇌♣●P🚌(M2,1)📶

Lyme Regis

Lyme Regis Brewery Tap

Mill Lane, DT7 3PU

10-5 ☎ (01297) 444354 lymeregisbrewery.com

3 changing beers (sourced locally; often Lyme Regis) Ⓗ/Ⓖ

The compact brewery tap and shop sells three Lyme Regis beers on handpump and occasionally a fourth on gravity. Bottled beers and ciders are also available. There is limited seating inside, with more available in an outside courtyard in the Town Mill complex. Formerly home of the Lyme Regis Brewery, increased demand has now led to beers being brewed off-site. Winter opening times are 11-3pm, but it is worth checking ahead as closing times can vary. Q❀🚌🐾📶

Royal Standard

25 Marine Parade, DT7 3JF

10-11 ☎ (01297) 442637

theroyalstandardlymeregis.co.uk

Palmers Copper Ale, IPA, Dorset Gold, 200 Ⓗ

Popular 400-year-old pub with a restaurant and beachside terrace. Interior stained glass, originally from the Three Cups Hotel, depicts the Duke of Monmouth landing on the nearby beach in the 1685 rebellion. Palmers seasonable beers are occasionally served and Tally Ho! is available in the winter, in addition to the four regular ales. Home-cooked meals feature local produce and freshly caught fish, with several vegetarian dishes on the menu. Ideal for families, the pub can be busy in the summer, and usually stays open late at weekends.

Q❀◑♿▲♣🚌(71)🐾📶

Manston

Plough Inn

Shaftesbury Road, DT10 1HB (on B3091 2 miles NE of Sturminster Newton) ST81351611

11.30-2.30, 6-11; 12-6 Sun ☎ (01258) 472484

ploughmanston.co.uk

Fuller's London Pride; Palmers Copper Ale; Sharp's Doom Bar; Timothy Taylor Landlord; 1 changing beer Ⓗ

This 450-year-old stone-built country inn has a single large bar with oak beams and unique plaster decorations on the ceiling and bar front, thought to be harvest fertility symbols. There is a large conservatory dining area, a covered patio, a large garden complete with pétanque rink and a campsite. Live music plays every Saturday night. An annual beer festival is hosted in May.

❀◑▲♣P🚌(309)🐾

Martinstown

Brewers Arms

DT2 9LB

closed Mon; 12-3, 6 (5 Fri)-11; 12-4 Sun
(01305) 889361 thebrewersarms.com

Palmers Copper Ale; 2 changing beers (sourced locally; often Cerne Abbas, Isle of Purbeck) G

Friendly, spacious village-centre pub with a light and airy decor. It is popular with walkers and cyclists visiting the nearby Ridgeway paths and Maiden Castle hill fort. Accommodation is offered in two en-suite rooms. Dogs are welcome in the bar area. The restaurant area can be busy, serving good traditional, home-made pub food, with curry night on a Tuesday. There is a quiz every Wednesday night. P (X51)

Pamphill

Vine Inn ★

Vine Hill, BH21 4EE (off B3082)

11-3, 7-10.30 (11 Thu-Sat); 12-3, 7-10.30 Sun
(01202) 882259

2 changing beers (sourced regionally) H/G

A former bakery, now owned by the National Trust and run by the same family for 117 years – the current landlady has been here over 30 years. The pub has two small bars plus an upstairs room; outside there is a large suntrap patio and garden. Two changing beers are served from local or regional breweries. At lunchtime there is a choice of ploughman's or toasties. This rural gem, popular with walkers and cyclists, has won many local CAMRA awards and is listed in the National Inventory of Historic Pub Interiors.
QP

Plush

Brace of Pheasants

DT2 7RQ

12-3, 6.30-11; 12-11 Sat (01300) 348357

Flack Manor Flack's Double Drop; Ringwood Razorback G

Originally a row of 16th-century cottages, this cosy village pub offers a friendly welcome for all. The main bar, with a real fire in winter, serves ales direct from the cask, with an occasional third beer added in summer. Superb food is on offer in the bar and restaurant areas – booking is a must. A large sloping cottage garden to the rear has tables and a covered area for smokers. Eight comfortable and stylish designer bedrooms are available. Closed Monday and Sunday evening in winter.
QP

Poole

Brewhouse

68 High Street, BH15 1DA

11-11; 11.30-11 Sun (01202) 685288

Milk Street Same Again, Beer; 2 changing beers (sourced nationally; often Dark Star, Milk Street, Oakham) H

This multi award-winning pub is a long-established feature of Poole High Street. It is a reliable source of interesting ales from Milk Street Brewery and well-chosen nationally sourced ales from microbreweries. Entering from the High Street you will find tables in the window, and past the busy bar area there is a space for pool and darts. Dogs are welcome in this no-frills traditional community pub, which offers a warm welcome to locals and visitors alike.

Poole Arms

19 The Quay, BH15 1HJ

11-11; 12-11 Sun (01202) 673450 poolearms.co.uk

Flack Manor Flack's Double Drop; Ringwood Fortyniner; St Austell Proper Job; 1 changing beer (sourced locally; often Dorset) H

A small and friendly waterfront pub on Poole Quay, steeped in history and famous for its green-tiled frontage. The building originates from 1635 and the locally produced tiles were added in the early 1900s. Not only is the beer excellent but seafood fans will love the menu (available noon-9pm). The single-roomed pub is adorned with historical pictures of the people, buildings and industries of Poole. Q

Portland

George Inn

133 Reforne, Easton, DT5 2AP

12 (3 Mon & Tue)-11; 12-10 Sun (01305) 820011
thegeorgeinn.org

Greene King Abbot; 3 changing beers (sourced nationally; often Black Sheep, Otter, Skinner's) H

A friendly, family-oriented local dating from the mid-18th century. It has four separate bar and dining areas and a large enclosed beer garden. Food is available daily Thursday-Sunday. The substantial Sunday roasts are popular, as is the Thursday evening curry and quiz. There are usually three constantly rotated guest ales on offer, as well as real ciders. Live music plays most Sunday afternoons and some Saturday evenings. A popular beer festival is held annually around St George's Day. (1,701)

Royal Portland Arms

Fortuneswell, DT5 1LZ (on main A354)

11-11.30 (1.30am Fri & Sat); 12-11 Sun (01305) 862255

2 changing beers (sourced regionally; often Cerne Abbas, Cotleigh, Yeovil) H/G

Dating back 200 years, this Portland-stone pub stands on the main road, with a public car park nearby. A basic one-bar pub, it offers a choice of regional ales and cider plus bar snacks. Live music plays on Friday and Sunday afternoon, and foodie events are popular such as the cheese club every Wednesday. George III is reputed to have stopped here for a drink and some Portland mutton on a visit to the island. Q (1,701)

Preston

Bridge Inn

Bridge Inn Lane, DT3 6BD

12-midnight (01305) 833380

Dartmoor Jail Ale; Ringwood Razorback; Sharp's Doom Bar H

Traditional family-run village pub built in the 18th century alongside the River Jordan, in a quiet valley just off the A353 and surrounded by stone cottages. The entrance leads to the single-bar lounge, to the left one step down is a snug with a dartboard, while to the right is a pool table. The separate restaurant serves traditional pub fare. Outside, the extensive beer garden features a children's play area. QP

Shaftesbury

Ship Inn ✓

24 Bleke Street, SP7 8JZ
⏲ 1-midnight (1am Fri); 12-1am Sat; 12-midnight Sun
☎ (01747) 853219
Butcombe Original; 3 changing beers Ⓗ
Stone-built town pub at the top of the steep Tout Hill. The single bar serves four different areas – the main bar, a games room with pool, darts, fruit machine and jukebox, a snug with an open fire, and a newly refurbished lounge bar. Outside there is a sunny patio and covered smoking area. No cooked food is available but you can order from local takeaways or bring your own. ❀🍎🚌🐾📶

Sherborne

Digby Tap ✓

Cooks Lane, DT9 3NS
⏲ 11-11; 12-11 Sun ☎ (01935) 813148 🌐 digbytap.co.uk
4 changing beers (sourced regionally; often Cerne Abbas, Otter, Teignworthy) Ⓗ
An institution in west Dorset, hidden away between the railway station and beautiful abbey church, and well worth seeking out. The owners of over 20 years have retained the old character and atmosphere, with four separate drinking areas, pine panelling, flagstone floors, old beams, settles and three fireplaces. Four beers, mostly from the West Country, offer superb value, as does the excellent lunchtime pub food. Q❀◐♿⇌♣🎯🚌🐾

Sixpenny Handley

Penny Tap

The Sports Pavilion, SP5 5NJ
⏲ 4.30-7 Wed & Thu; 4-7.30 Fri; 2-6 Sat; closed Sun-Tue
🌐 thepennytap.co.uk
4 changing beers (often Brew Shack, Sixpenny, Wriggle Valley) Ⓗ/Ⓖ
When the Sixpenny Brewery moved out of the village to larger premises elsewhere, the brewery tap also closed. A group of locals worked hard to establish a suitable outlet to fill the void and opted for the sports pavilion, creating a bar and cellar. It provides a focus for village sports and social events. A wide range of beer from local microbreweries is on offer. Opening times may be extended during local events including cricket. ⛺🍎P

Southbourne

Wight Bear Ale House

65 Southbourne Grove, BH6 3QU
⏲ 4-10 Mon; 12-11 (midnight Fri & Sat); 12-10.30 Sun
☎ (01202) 433733 🌐 thewightbear.co.uk
8 changing beers (sourced nationally) Ⓖ
This popular high-street micropub opened in 2015. There is no bar but knowledgeable Bear beer handlers will serve you at the high benches and tables surrounding the open-plan room. Convivial conversation rules and board games can be played in a mobile-free zone. Eight ever-changing ales from across the country are dispensed straight from the cask, alongside ciders and perries visible in the windowed cellar. Traditional bar snacks and bites are available and an excellent range of bottled and canned ales. Q🍎🚌🐾

Spetisbury

Woodpecker 𝕃

High Street, DT11 9DJ (on A350)
⏲ closed Mon; 12-3, 6-11; 12-11 Fri & Sat; 12-10 Sun
☎ (01258) 452658 🌐 woodpeckerspetisbury.co.uk
4 changing beers (sourced regionally; often Flack Manor, Palmers) Ⓗ
An imposing, comfortable, open-plan pub with feature fireplace situated on the edge of a picturesque Dorset village. The award-winning free house offers four changing ales plus real cider and perry. Excellent, reasonably priced home-cooked food is available including vegetarian options. The spacious garden hosts a cider festival in May and a beer festival in the autumn. St George's Day is celebrated with a popular vinyl and pie night. A perfect place in the countryside for whiling away an afternoon. Q🐴❀◐⛺🍎P🚌(X8)🐾

Stourpaine

White Horse Inn ✓

Shaston Road, DT11 8TA
⏲ 12-11 (midnight Fri); 10.30-midnight Sat
☎ (01258) 453535 🌐 whitehorse-stourpaine.co.uk
Fuller's London Pride; Sharp's Doom Bar; house beer (by Flack Manor); 2 changing beers (sourced regionally; often Piddle, Sixpenny) Ⓗ
Dating back to the early 18th century, this attractive, vibrant and popular pub is at the heart of its community, even containing the local shop and post office. Quality is the main emphasis, whether it is the real ales, food or service – the landlord and landlady take great care to welcome allcomers. It hosts many community events such as quizzes, theatre and folk music, and is close to the Bath to Bournemouth trailway. Recently becoming a free house, this pub is an atmospheric country gem.
🐴❀◐♣🍎P🚌(X3)🐾📶

Stourton Caundle

Trooper

Golden Hill, DT10 2JW (1½ miles E of A357) ST71491495
⏲ closed Mon; 12-2 (2.30 Sat), 7-11; 12-3.30, 7-11 Sun
☎ (01963) 362405 🌐 thetrooperinn.co.uk
3 changing beers Ⓗ
Stone-built, single-room community pub with a separate function room/skittle alley. There is an attached camping and caravan site and children's play area next to the beer garden. Good food is available lunchtimes and early evenings including a popular Friday fish and chips night. There are two guest ales and a farmhouse cider. The on-site microbrewery occasionally supplies one of the three ales. An annual beer festival is held in the spring. Dogs and walkers are welcome. A former CAMRA Regional Pub of the Year. Q❀◐⛺♣🍎P🐾

Stratton

Saxon Arms

20 The Square, DT2 9WG
⏲ 11-2.30, 5.30-11; 11-midnight Fri & Sat; 12-midnight Sun
☎ (01305) 260020 🌐 thesaxon-stratton.co.uk
Butcombe Original; Timothy Taylor Landlord; 2 changing beers (sourced nationally; often Otter, St Austell) Ⓗ
A thatched inn built of stone and flint in 2001. Set in the village square, with the church and village hall nearby, it is the hub of the community and

offers a warm, friendly welcome. Four ales are available plus cider and a decent wine list. There is locally sourced food and a real fire in winter. Dogs are welcome, but not in the restaurant area. Local CAMRA Pub of the Year 2017. Q🍺❀◑♣●P🐾📶

Swanage

Red Lion 𝕃

63 High Street, BH19 2LY

⏲ 11-11 ☎ (01929) 423533 🌐 redlionswanage.co.uk

Hop Back GFB; Otter Bitter; Sharp's Doom Bar; Timothy Taylor Landlord; 2 changing beers (often Palmers, Skinner's) Ⓖ

Popular 17th-century traditional inn in the heart of Swanage, serving up to six ales straight from the cask in the ground-floor cellar behind the public bar. The four regular beers are complemented by one or two well-chosen guests, depending on the season. There is also an excellent cider range – look for details on the blackboards. The lounge bar has a restaurant area where quality food is served, with curry and steak nights. The large, partly covered garden is extremely popular for whiling away a sunny afternoon. Q🍺❀🛏◑⇌●P🚌🐾📶

Thornford

King's Arms

Pound Road, DT9 6QD

⏲ closed Mon; 12-2.30, 6-11; 12-4 Sun ☎ (01935) 872294

🌐 kings-arms-thornford.com

Sharp's Doom Bar; 3 changing beers (sourced nationally; often Cerne Abbas) Ⓗ

Reverting to its previous name after a short period as The Lime Tree, this family-run pub is at the heart of the village, next to the unusual red-brick Victorian clock tower erected to commemorate Queen Victoria's Diamond Jubilee. It features a traditional cosy bar with separate contemporary restaurant. Open on bank holiday Mondays. Q🍺❀◑♣●P🐾📶

Wareham

Horse & Groom

St Johns Hill, BH20 4LZ

⏲ 10 (11 Mon)-midnight; 10-11 Sun ☎ (01929) 552995

Palmers 200; 3 changing beers (sourced regionally; often Dorset, St Austell) Ⓗ

An enthusiastic father and son partnership rescued this struggling pub, completely refurbishing it and now offering customers a range of beers and real ciders, regionally sourced, with an affinity to Palmers' ales. A light, airy, open-plan pub with a real fire, it has a jukebox and TV but they do not intrude or dominate conversation. Simple pub food is served and a pleasant garden area can be found tucked away at the rear. Live music plays occasionally, making this a pub for all. 🍺❀◑●🚌(40,X54)🐾📶

King's Arms ✔

41 North Street, BH20 4AD

⏲ 12-11 (10.30 Sun) ☎ (01929) 552503

🌐 kingsarmswareham.co.uk

5 changing beers (sourced regionally; often Exmoor, Otter, Skinner's) Ⓗ

Award-winning traditional thatched inn that has its roots in the 1500s and survived the great fire of 1762. This multi-roomed establishment has a flagstone-floored public bar, real fire, a drinking corridor and one room exclusively for dining, with an excellent range of home-cooked food on offer. To the rear is a large garden with a covered area for smokers. The five ever-changing guest beers are usually sourced from the West Country. Occasional live music features at weekends. Q🍺❀◑⇌●P🚌(40,X54)🐾📶

Waytown

Hare & Hounds 𝕃

Slape Hill, DT6 5LQ (2 miles S of Netherbury)

⏲ 12-3, 6 (7 Sun)-11 ☎ (01308) 488203

🌐 hareandhoundswaytown.co.uk

Palmers Copper Ale, IPA; 1 changing beer Ⓗ

Traditional village pub set in the breathtakingly beautiful Dorset countryside, with friendly staff and locals, real fires and three small rooms welcoming families, muddy boots and dogs. Palmers Dorset Gold, Tally Ho! or seasonal beers are available alongside the regulars. The menu and daily changing specials board include pub classics made with local ingredients, plus vegetarian and gluten-free options. With barbecues in summer and bar games in winter, this is a pub for all seasons. Q🍺❀◑♿♣●P🐾📶

West Parley

Owls Nest 𝕃

196 Christchuch Road, BH22 8SS

⏲ 11.30-2.30 (not Mon), 5-11; 11.30-2.30, 6-midnight Sat; 12-3, 6-10 Sun ☎ (01202) 572793

🌐 theowlsnest-westparley.com

4 changing beers (sourced regionally; often Eight Arch, Flack Manor, Yeovil) Ⓗ

Charming and welcoming, this Tudor-style building with beamed ceilings and a woodburner provides a comfortable ambience. Decorated with numerous adornments, owls feature heavily among miniatures, jugs and plates. Four handpumps dispense well-chosen local and regional ales. A beer and home-made pie festival has become an early-in-the-year favourite. There is occasional live music with an Irish session on the first Thursday of the month. Popular for its excellent home-made food, booking is recommended for diners. 🍺◑♿P🚌🐾📶

West Stour

Ship Inn

A30, SP8 5RP

⏲ 12-3, 6-11; 12-midnight Sat; 12-10.30 Sun

☎ (01747) 838640 🌐 shipinn-dorset.com

3 changing beers Ⓗ

Once a coaching inn, this popular roadside pub has views across the Blackmore Vale. The public bar features a flagstone floor and the separate light and airy restaurant area has stripped oak floorboards. There is a patio and large garden at the rear. This friendly pub is renowned for superb home-cooked food (no meals Sun eve) and comfortable accommodation. Six local ciders are usually available alongside three ales. Dogs are welcome in the bar. An annual beer festival is held in July. Q❀🛏◑♣●P🐾

Weymouth

Duke of Cornwall

1 St Edmund Street, DT4 8AS

closed Mon; 12 (5 Tue)-1am; 12-2am Fri & Sat
(01305) 776594 bestduke.com
Dartmoor Jail Ale; Skinner's Betty Stogs; 1 changing beer (sourced regionally; often Skinner's) H
Situated close to the picturesque Weymouth harbour, the Duke of Cornwall is an historic small pub serving Skinner's ales and Dartmoor Jail Ale plus over 100 different gins. The town centre is close by and the pub is easily accessed from the nearby railway station and via local bus routes. There is regular live music and the staff are welcoming, knowledgeable and always helpful.

Globe Inn
24 East Street, DT4 8BN
11-1am (01305) 786061
Dartmoor Jail Ale; St Austell Cornish Best Bitter, Proper Job; Sharp's Doom Bar; 2 changing beers (sourced regionally; often Cerne Abbas, Milk Street, Palmers) H
Free house with a friendly welcome, tucked away on a street corner, just 30 yards from the iconic harbourside. The Globe is only a short distance from the town centre, the beach and the esplanade, and offers a distinct change from the packed waterside. There is a jukebox and a separate games room with pool table, darts and pub games. A fun quiz is held on Sunday afternoon. Guest ales are not always available in the low season. The cider is Thatchers Cheddar Valley.

Whitchurch Canonicorum

Five Bells Inn
DT6 6RH
closed Mon; 12-2, 6.30-11 (01297) 489262
thefivebellsinn.co.uk
Palmers Copper Ale, IPA, 200; 1 changing beer H
A hidden gem nestled in the stunning Marshwood Vale. The pub serves traditional food prepared using locally sourced produce and is family-friendly, with a large beer garden and a seven-acre campsite with shower and toilet block. A seasonal beer from Palmers is served alongside the regulars. The winter opening times are listed above, but the pub opens all day every day in the summer. However, times can vary so please call ahead. QP

Wimborne

Green Man
1 Victoria Road, BH21 1EN
10 (11 Mon)-11; 10-midnight Fri & Sat (01202) 881021
greenmanwimborne.com
Wadworth IPA, 6X, Swordfish; 1 changing beer (often Wadworth) H
An 18th-century one-bar inn with open-plan drinking areas, a cosy woodburner and a separate restaurant, ideally located two mintues' walk from the centre of Wimborne. Excellent food, including breakfast, is served until 4pm, with a roast on Sunday. The garden has a marvellous floral display in summer, guarded by the green man in his red telephone box. A partially covered patio leads to the barn where pool and pub games are played. Please step over the green man when entering the pub. P

Taphouse
11 West Borough, BH21 1LT
11-11.30 (01202) 911200
thetaphousewimborne.co.uk
Sharp's Doom Bar; 6 changing beers (sourced nationally; often Brew Shack, Eight Arch, Sixpenny) G
Close to the historic town centre, the centrepiece of this narrow wood-panelled pub is the long hardwood bar, with beers displayed on a stillage behind. The pub offers seven ales from local and national microbreweries as well as some popular favourites. Always a bustling community pub full of atmosphere, conversation rules in the cosy window seating area and the suntrap patio outside. There is live acoustic music on Sunday. Q

Wool

Black Bear Inn
High Street, BH20 6BP
10.30-11 (midnight Fri & Sat); 10.30-10.30 Sun
(01929) 405541 blackbear.website
House beer (by Flack Manor); 3 changing beers (sourced nationally) H
This friendly community pub, located in the heart of Wool village and close to the many attractions of the Purbecks, offers so much more than the four cask ales. Hearty home-cooked food is available in the front bar and in the dedicated restaurant area to the rear. Curry nights, quizzes, pub walks and a breakfast club all contribute to this pub being at the heart of the village. The outside seating area is perfect for relaxing and enjoying the summer sun. QP(X54)

Worth Matravers

Square & Compass ★
Weston Road, BH19 3LF (off B3069)
12-11 (01929) 439229 squareandcompasspub.co.uk
5 changing beers (sourced regionally; often Hattie Brown's) G
A real gem, this multi award-winning pub is in CAMRA's National Inventory of Historic Pub Interiors and has appeared in every edition of the Guide. It has been in the same family since 1907, and two rooms either side of a serving hatch convey the impression that little has changed. Pasties are available along with home-made cider. Beer and cider festivals are held in October and November respectively. The sea-facing garden offers fantastic views across the Purbecks and fossils are displayed in a small adjacent museum. Closes 3-6pm in winter. Q(44)

Wyke Regis

Wyke Smugglers
76 Portland Road, DT4 9AB
11-11 (midnight Thu-Sat); 12-11 Sun (01305) 760010
thewykesmugglers.com
St Austell Proper Job; 3 changing beers (sourced nationally) H
A large, lively local hosting many community events. Regional guest beers often come from the SIBA south-west region. Good food is served every day except Monday. In winter, the dining area is set around the woodburner. There are racks for bicycles at the front and the skittle alley doubles as a function room. Dogs are welcome. There is live music at weekends and a beer and cider festival in the summer. P

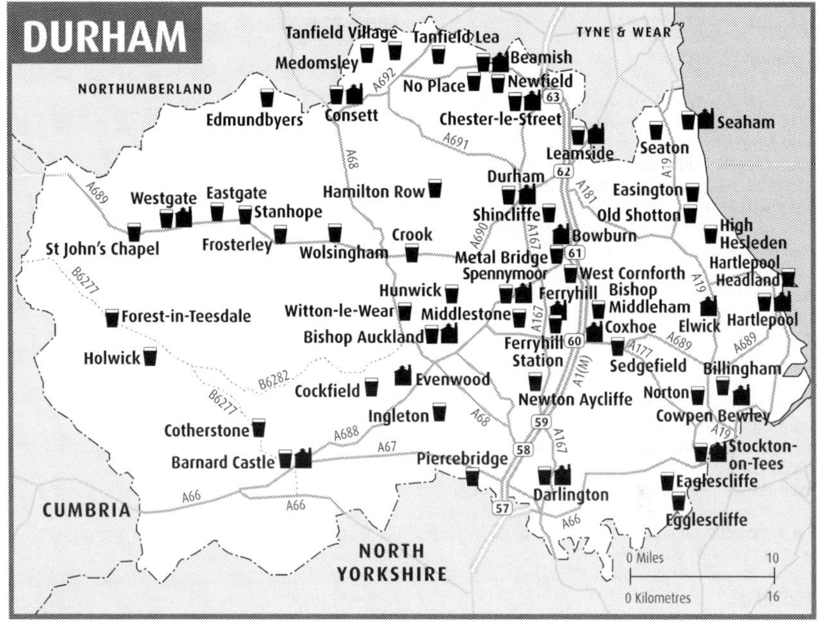

Co Durham incorporates part of the former county of Cleveland

Barnard Castle

Firkin Alley

2 Bakery Mews, DL12 8LZ (down alleyway next to YMCA charity shop, behind 20 Horsemarket)
⏲ closed Mon & Tue; 5-9.30 (10 Fri); 12-10 Sat; 3-8 Sun
☎ 07878 361111
5 changing beers Ⓗ
A new micropub established in 2016 housed in an ex-bakery storeroom, difficult to find down an alley off the main street. It has a bar downstairs and a spacious and comfortable room upstairs, tastefully fitted with warm wood surrounds. It offers a good and ever-changing ale selection, mainly from the region, plus a changing choice of cider. Well worth a visit, with hospitable licensees and a friendly, regular and local clientele. **Q**❀🍎🚌(75,76)🐾

Old Well Inn Ⓛ ✔

21 The Bank, DL12 8PH
⏲ 12-11 ☎ (01833) 690130 🌐 theoldwellinn.co.uk
Timothy Taylor Landlord; 5 changing beers Ⓗ
The boundary of this 17th-century town-centre inn incorporates part of the medieval castle wall. The pub has a cosy front bar and a comfortable lounge, a separate restaurant and an airy conservatory, plus an enclosed beer garden. At least five well-kept beers are available including four guests from local micros, usually including Mithril. Excellent food is served daily, and there is accommodation in 10 rooms. Two five-day beer festivals are held at Easter and October. The Castle Players meet here. CAMRA members get 30p off a pint.
Q❀🛏◐♿🚌(75,76)🐾📶

Beamish

Stables Bar & Restaurant Ⓛ

Beamish Hall Country House Hotel, DH9 0YB
⏲ 11-11 (midnight Fri & Sat); 11-10.30 Sun
☎ (01207) 288750 🌐 beamish-hall.co.uk/stables-restaurant-brewery
Stables Beamish Burn, Beamish Hall Best Bitter, Bell Tower, Bobby Dazzler, Old Miner Tommy, Silver Buckles; 1 changing beer Ⓗ
Attached to Beamish Hall Country House Hotel, with its own microbrewery. Stone floors, old beams and crackling log fires in winter help to create a relaxing environment. An extensive menu of locally produced food is served. Outside is a courtyard seating area and a play area, and Beamish Wild high ropes course is just yards away. An annual beer festival is hosted in January. A popular live music venue. **Q**❀🛏◐♿🍎**P**

Billingham

Greenholme Catholic Club Ⓛ

37 Wolviston Road, TS23 2RU (on E side of old A19, just S of Roseberry Rd roundabout, next to bus stop)
⏲ 7-midnight (12.30am Fri); 12.30-1am Sat; 12-midnight Sun
☎ (01642) 901143 🌐 billinghamcatholicclub.webs.com
3 changing beers Ⓗ
This Victorian mansion and former school is a friendly members' club, renowned for its vibrant R&B/rock scene, where a genuine welcome awaits CAMRA members. Dedicated and enthusiastic volunteers ensure that the club's reputation for serving 150 different beers annually continues. Three beers, two ciders and a perry are normally available, with up to eight ales during bank holiday weekend beer/music festivals. Regular quiz and open mic nights are also held. Local CAMRA 2018 Club of the Year. ❀♿♣🍎**P**🚉🚌(35,36)🐾

Bishop Auckland

Bay Horse

38-40 Fore Bondgate, DL14 7PE (50yds N of bus station)

11-11 (1am Fri & Sat); 12-11 Sun (01388) 609765
bayhorse-pub.co.uk
3 changing beers H
There has been a pub on this site since 1530, and this lively, open-plan L-shaped bar is a quiet relief from shopping during the week. With live music on Friday and karaoke on Saturday, it becomes joyfully boisterous at the weekend, and is popular for televised sport and the Sunday quiz. It retains its roots as a long-established, proper pub, with various pub games teams, and an eclectic choice of ales.

Green Tree
Cockton Hill Road, DL14 6EN (close to Station Bridge)
4-midnight (1am Thu); 12-1am Fri & Sat; 12-midnight Sun
(01388) 663249
2 changing beers H
A large pub at the south end of the shopping street. It has a bar with pool table area, a spacious lounge, and a big garden patio with a covered smoking area to the rear. Popular for TV sport and the Tuesday quiz, it hosts occasional live music. Interesting football and music memorabilia adorn the walls alongside paintings of the town by local artist Gaz Miller.

Pollards
104 Etherley Lane, DL14 6TU (400yds W of railway station)
12-2, 5.30-11; 12-3, 6-11 Sun (01388) 603539
5 changing beers H
This comfortable and busy establishment is a great combination of traditional pub and pleasant diner, 10-minutes' stroll from the town centre. Two of the four original areas, including the bar, boast open fires or logburners, while there is a spacious restaurant to the rear where the famous Sunday carvery can be enjoyed. A popular quiz on Sunday evening, good conversation and five well-kept ales top things off. **QP**

Bishop Middleham

Cross Keys L
9 High Street, DL17 9AR (1 mile from A177)
12 (2.30 Mon)-11 (01740) 651231 crosskeysbm.com
2 changing beers H
A busy family-run village inn with a good reputation for its food. It has a bar with a real fire, a lounge and a large restaurant at the back. The pub is opposite the remains of Forsters Brewery which closed in 1913 and it may well have been the tap house. The village has a series of walks through beautiful countryside. **Q**

Chester-le-Street

Butchers Arms
Middle Chare, DH3 3QD (off Front St)
11-11 (midnight Fri & Sat) (0191) 388 3605
butchersarms.org.uk
Jennings Cumberland Ale; Marston's Pedigree; 5 changing beers H
A cosy pub acknowledged for the quality of its beers, selling seven cask ales from the Marston's range. The pub is also noted for its food, with home-cooking a speciality; Sunday lunches are popular and good value. Teas and coffees are also served. Dogs are welcome and it is convenient for the railway station and all buses through the town. Quiz night is Tuesday. **Q** (21)

Lambton Worm L
North Road, DH3 4AJ
11.30-11 (midnight Fri & Sat); 12-10.30 Sun
(0191) 387 1162 thelambton.com
Sonnet 43 Abolition, Impressment, Seraphim, The Aurora, The Raven; 1 changing beer H
A bar at the front and gastro restaurant at the back offering traditional English food. Relaxed surroundings, friendly staff, a spacious bar area and plenty of tucked-away seating areas add to the ambience. Experimental and limited edition Sonnet 43 beers are often available alongside the core range. There is a patio drinking area to the rear, a weekly quiz on Tuesday, buskers' night on Wednesday and live music on Friday. Accommodation is in 14 boutique B&B rooms.
P (21)

Smiths Arms L
Forge Lane, Castle Dene, DH3 4HE NZ299507
12-11 (10.30 Sun) (0191) 385 7559
12 changing beers H
Somewhat off the beaten track, this traditional pub has a small cosy bar with an open fire, a room for pool and darts, and a larger lounge also with an open fire. The beers are sourced by the landlord, including up to 12 real ales, always including LocAle. Beer festivals are held in May and December. The pub is reputed to be haunted. Voted local CAMRA branch Country Pub of the Year 2017. **P** (71,78)

Wicket Gate L
193 Front Street, DH3 3AX
8am-midnight (2.30am Fri & Sat) (0191) 387 2960
Greene King Abbot; Ruddles Best Bitter; 5 changing beers H
This modern Wetherspoon Lloyds No.1 bar's name acknowledges the strong connection the town has with cricket. Situated close to the town club and the county club ground at the Riverside, various items of cricket memorabilia decorate the walls. It is roomy inside, with a central oval-shaped bar with service on both sides. (21)

REAL ALE BREWERIES
Barnard Castle Barnard Castle (NEW)
Black Paw Bishop Auckland (brewing suspended)
Blackhill Chester-le-Street
Camerons Hartlepool
Castle Eden Seaham
Consett Ale Works Consett
Crafty Monkey Elwick (NEW)
Crafty Pint Darlington
Durham Bowburn
George Samuel Spennymoor
Hill Island Durham
Hopburst Darlington
Mad Scientist Darlington
McColl's Evenwood
Roundhill Cowpen Bewley
Schoolhouse Darlington
Sonnet 43 Coxhoe
Stables Beamish
Stockton Stockton on Tees
Three Brothers Stockton on Tees
Village Brewer: Brew 22 Darlington
Weard'ALE Westgate
Working Hand Leamside
Yard of Ale Ferryhill

Cockfield

Queen's Head

106 Front Street, DL13 5AA
5-11; 11-11 Sat; 12-11 Sun ☎ (01388) 710981
2 changing beers H
Cosy, welcoming and popular pub opposite the church, serving two constantly changing beers from the Marston's range. It is open plan, but with distinct seating areas, as well as tables to the front. Bar staff will happily ask your opinion of the beers, and chat about which ones have proved popular. A proper community local, close to the historic Cockfield Fell and associated industrial archaeology. Q❀♣P (6,8)

Consett

Company Row

Victoria Road, DH8 5BQ
8am-midnight ☎ (01207) 585600
Greene King Abbot; Ruddles Best Bitter; 5 changing beers H
Modern pub named after the rows of houses built by the Derwent Iron Company for its workers, which were mostly demolished in the mid-1920s. The spacious and well-decorated Wetherspoon establishment is a real asset to Consett town centre. An excellent beer selection and good food make this social pub popular with a wide clientele of all ages. ❀♣

Grey Horse

115 Sherburn Terrace, DH8 6NE
12-11 (11.30 Wed & Thu; midnight Fri & Sat)
☎ (01207) 502585 greyhorseconsett.co.uk
Consett Red Dust, Steel Town Bitter, White Hot; 4 changing beers H
Traditional pub dating back to 1848. The interior comprises a lounge and L-shaped bar, with a wood-beamed ceiling. Consett Ale Works Brewery is located at the rear. Beer festivals are held twice a year, live entertainment is hosted on Thursday and a quiz on Wednesday. The coast-to-coast cycle route is close by. There is some bench seating outside at the front of the pub. ❀

Cotherstone

Red Lion

Main Street, DL12 9QE
6-10.30 Mon, Wed & Fri; closed Tue & Thu; 2-10.30 Sat & Sun ☎ (01833) 650236 theredlionhotel.blogspot.com
3 changing beers H
An 18th-century Grade II-listed coaching inn, built in stone and set in an idyllic village. Simply furnished, this homely local with two open fires has changed little since the '60s. There is no TV, jukebox or one-armed bandit, just good beer and conversation. Children and dogs are welcome. The house beer is Rowantree by Yorkshire Dales, and guest beers regularly come from Mithril. Up to six real ciders are kept. Local CAMRA Community Pub of the Year, the venue is used by various local clubs, and the small garden is a suntrap.
❀♣ (95)

Crook

Horse Shoe

4 Church Street, DL15 9BG
8am-midnight (1am Fri & Sat) ☎ (01388) 744980
Greene King Abbot; Maxim Double Maxim; Ruddles Best Bitter; 6 changing beers H
This busy and tasteful refurbishment has four interlinked drinking areas making up the main part of the pub, with a pleasant sheltered patio to the side. There is the usual Wetherspoon acknowledgement of previous use, in this case a butcher's, in the metal bar top. Local history is reflected in the decor, with a surprise at the top of the stairs in the shape of old mining equipment.
❀ (X1,X46)

Darlington

Britannia

1 Archer Street, DL3 6LR (next to ring road W of town centre)
12-11 (9 Sun) ☎ (01325) 463787
Camerons Strongarm; Draught Bass; John Smith's Bitter; 3 changing beers H
Warm, friendly, popular local CAMRA award-winning inn – a bastion of cask beer since 1859. The comfortable, traditional pub retains much of the appearance and layout of the private house it once was – a modestly enlarged bar and small parlour sit either side of a central corridor. Listed for its historic associations, it was the birthplace of teetotal 19th-century publisher JM Dent. Three guest ales complement the three regular ales.
♣P

Darlington Snooker Club

1 Corporation Road, DL3 6AE (corner of Northgate)
12-11; 11-1am Sat; 11-11 Sun ☎ (01325) 241388
4 changing beers H
First-floor, family-run and family-oriented private snooker club which in 2015 celebrated its centenary. A cosy, comfortable TV lounge is available for those not playing on one of the 10 top-quality snooker tables. Twice yearly, the club hosts a professional celebrity. Four guest beers from micros countrywide are stocked and two beer festivals are held annually. Frequently voted CAMRA Regional Club of the Year, it welcomes CAMRA members on production of a membership card or copy of this Guide.

Half Moon

130 Northgate, DL1 1QS
12 (5 Wed)-11 ☎ (01325) 469965 thecraftypint.co.uk
7 changing beers H
Across the ring road from the town centre, this relaxed and welcoming local reopened in 2013 as a real ale pub following a long period of closure. Seven guest beers include brews from micros unusual for the area as well as from the on-site Crafty Pint Nano Brewery. You have a choice of two ciders. ❀♣

Hole in the Wall

14-15 Horsemarket, DL1 5PT
11-11.30 (midnight Fri & Sat); 12-11 Sun
☎ (01325) 466720
7 changing beers H
Recently refurbished pub with a fine Edwardian frontage, smart wooden interior and large windows overlooking the town's Market Place. A wide range of ales is stocked alongside a variety of spirits. There is a full menu of traditional pub food, with a big emphasis on pies. The seating outside is pleasant for relaxing with a drink in the summer.

Number Twenty 2

22 Coniscliffe Road, DL3 7RG

12-11 (9 Mon); closed Sun ☎ (01325) 354590

Village Bull, Old Raby, White Boar; 7 changing beers H

Town-centre ale house with a passion for cask beer and a winner of many CAMRA awards. Ales are dispensed from up to 16 handpumps, including two real ciders and a stout or porter, along with 10 draught European beers. Huge curved windows, stained-glass panels and a high ceiling give the interior an airy, spacious feel. To the rear is the in-house nano distillery and microbrewery producing gin, vodka and ale. Sandwiches and snacks are available at lunchtime. Home of Village Brewer beers, commissioned from Hambleton by the licensee. Q

Old Yard Tapas Bar

98 Bondgate, DL3 7JY

11-11; 12-10.30 Sun ☎ (01325) 467385 tapasbar.co.uk

John Smith's Bitter; 5 changing beers H

Interesting mixture of a bar and Mediterranean taverna offering real ales alongside a fascinating blend of international wines and spirits in a friendly setting. Five guest beers from local micros and countrywide are stocked, with an extra two sometimes available in a further room. Although this is a thriving restaurant you are more than welcome to pop in for a pint and tapas. The pavement café is popular in good weather. TV is for sport only. Food is served lunchtimes and evenings Sunday to Friday and all day Saturday. Q

ORB Micropub

28 Coniscliffe Road, DL3 7RG

closed Mon & Tue; 5-10 Wed & Thu; 3-10.30 Fri; 12-10.30 Sat; 3-8 Sun ☎ 07903 237246

6 changing beers H

Traditional micropub in a former beauty salon with no TV or loud music, the first of its kind in Darlington. It provides local real ales, craft beers and a large range of single malt whiskies in relaxed surroundings with friendly, knowledgeable staff. An on-site microbrewery is planned (ORB stands for Orchard Road Brewery). Q

Quakerhouse

2 Mechanics Yard, DL3 7QF (off High Row)

11-11 (midnight Fri & Sat) ☎ (01325) 245052

quakerhouse.co.uk

9 changing beers H

Sixteen times local CAMRA Town Pub of the Year, and North-East Pub of the Year in 2015, this gem of a pub is located in one of the town's historic Yards. The lively bar offers nine handpulled guest beers from local and regional breweries and three changing real ciders. Friendly and welcoming, the pub is a popular music venue, with live music every Wednesday, as well as other nights, catering for all tastes from acoustic to rock, with free entry. P

Tanners Hall

63-64 Skinnergate, DL3 7LL

8am-midnight (1am Sat) ☎ (01325) 369939

Greene King Abbot; Ruddles Best Bitter; 7 changing beers H

A popular Wetherspoon town pub named after the local 18th-century leather trade that dominated the town. Its 12 handpumps provide a good selection of real ales including up to nine guests, often from local micros. The spacious interior makes it an ideal venue for holding its own beer festivals and Meet The Brewer nights as well as the chain's national events. Reasonably priced food is served until 11pm. Q

Durham

Colpitts Hotel

Colpitts Terrace, DH1 4EG

11-11; 12-10.30 Sun ☎ (0191) 386 9913

Samuel Smith Old Brewery Bitter H

This late-Victorian pub has changed little since it was first built. The unusual A-shaped building comprises a cosy snug, a pool room and the main bar area partially divided by a fireplace. As with all Samuel Smith's pubs, the noise comes from the chatter of conversation rather than from music or TV. A quiz is hosted on Tuesday evening. If you want to take a step back in time, this is the pub for you. Q

Court Inn

Court Lane, DH1 3AW

11-11 (midnight Fri & Sat) ☎ (0191) 384 7350

courtinn.co.uk

Timothy Taylor Landlord; 5 changing beers H

A busy venue with decor that reflects the location near the city's Crown Courts. Up to six real ales are on offer at any one time as well as two real ciders. A wide selection of food is served until 10.15pm daily. The pub is popular with students and prison staff, and offers a warm welcome to all visitors. (6)

Dun Cow

37 Old Elvet, DH1 3HN

11.30-10.30 (11 Wed & Thu); 11-11 Fri & Sat; 12-9.45 Sun ☎ (0191) 386 9219 duncowdurham.com

Black Sheep Best Bitter; Castle Eden Ale; Moorhouse's White Witch H

A Grade II-listed pub, parts of which date back to the 15th century. In 995AD, Lindisfarne monks searching for a resting place for the body of St Cuthbert came across a milkmaid looking for her lost cow. She directed them to Dun Holm (Durham), and the pub is named after the historic animal. There is a friendly front snug with a larger lounge to the rear. Three real ales are on offer. Q (58,59)

Half Moon Inn

86 New Elvet, DH1 3AQ

11-11 (midnight Fri & Sat); 12-11 Sun ☎ (0191) 374 1918

thehalfmooninndurham.co.uk

Draught Bass; Durham White Gold; Sharp's Doom Bar; Timothy Taylor Landlord H

Popular city-centre pub, reputedly named after the crescent-shaped bar that runs from the front room through to the lounge area. It has traditional decor throughout, with photos of the pub at the beginning of the 20th century, including many from the Miners' Gala. The large beer garden overlooks the river. A friendly venue with a relaxed atmosphere, it offers a good selection of ales to locals and visitors to the city. (6)

Head of Steam

Reform Place, DH1 4RZ (through archway from North Rd)

12-11 (midnight Fri & Sat) ☎ (0191) 383 2173

5 changing beers H

A popular pub with a continental feel, attracting beer lovers of all ages. As well as the four changing real ales, it offers an extensive choice of bottled beers from around the world and a range of real ciders. Tasting events are often held featuring a wide choice of ales and ciders. Excellent, good-value food is available and families are welcome during the day.

Market Tavern

27 Market Place, DH1 3NJ

11-midnight (12.30am Sat); 11-11 Sun ☎ (0191) 386 2069

Greene King IPA; 4 changing beers H

Located in Durham's historic marketplace, this pub offers a good selection of five local and national cask ales and one real cider. Despite refurbishments, the pub has managed to keep its traditional wooden alehouse appearance, and images of miners' banners take pride of place. Locals and visitors to the city are given a warm welcome, and good food based on pub classics is served until 9.30pm. Quiz night is Thursday.

Old Elm Tree

12 Crossgate, DH1 4PS

11.30-11 (midnight Fri & Sat) ☎ (0191) 386 4621

6 changing beers H

One of Durham's oldest inns, dating back to at least 1600. The interior comprises an L-shaped bar and a top room linked by stairs, with a friendly atmosphere attracting a good mix of locals, students and visitors to the city. A good range of ales and home-cooked food is available. The pub hosts a Wednesday quiz (arrive early), and a folk group on Monday and Tuesday.

P

Station House

North Road, DH1 4SE

closed Mon; 4-10.30 Tue-Thu; 12-11 Fri & Sat; 2-10.30 Sun

stationhousedurham.co.uk

4 changing beers G

Durham's first micropub offers a varying selection of local and national real ales and ciders straight from the cask. Customers are served through a hatch directly from the cold room, and there is a back-to-basics approach with an emphasis on conversation. This is a quirky, friendly and welcoming pub, and the two rocking chairs in the window are highly sought after. Beer festivals are held in March and October. Local CAMRA Town Cider Pub of the Year 2017-18 and North-East Regional Cider Pub of the Year 2017.

Q

Tap & Spile

Front Street, Framwellgate Moor, DH1 5EE

6 (5 Fri)-11; 12-3, 6-11 Sat; 12-3, 7-10.30 Sun

☎ (0191) 386 5451

8 changing beers (sourced nationally) H

This popular pub for real ale drinkers offers an excellent range of eight constantly changing real ales. There are two bars at one side while the other side can be partitioned into two – families are welcome in the side room until 9pm. Folk music night is Thursday and quiz night is Wednesday. The atmosphere is relaxed and locals and visitors from further afield are given a warm welcome.

P (21)

Victoria Inn ★

86 Hallgarth Street, DH1 3AS

11.45-11; 12-10.30 Sun ☎ (0191) 386 5269

victoriainn-durhamcity.co.uk

Big Lamp Bitter; Wylam Gold Tankard; 3 changing beers H

This family-run Grade II-listed Victorian pub has remained almost unchanged since it was built in 1899, and the quaint decor, coal fires, cosy snug and genuine Victorian cash drawer help create the old-world feel. Ales are mainly from local breweries, with a wide selection of single malt whiskies and whiskeys also on offer. No meals are served but toasties are available. Voted local CAMRA Town Pub of the Year for the 10th time in 2018, the Victoria is popular with locals, students and visitors to the city. Q (6,PR2)

Woodman Inn

23 Gilesgate, DH1 1QW

4-11; 12-12.30am Fri & Sat; 12-10 Sun ☎ (0191) 386 5515

woodmaninn.co.uk

Maxim Double Maxim; 2 changing beers H

Serving three real ales and a good selection of lagers, this traditional-style pub also offers a wide selection of spirits including gin and malt whisky. There is a pool table, dartboard and various other games, and popular karaoke on Saturday evening. Bar food is available throughout the day. Summer afternoon opening is often earlier to take advantage of the attractive beer garden with plenty of seating to the rear. The annual beer festival is popular.

Eaglescliffe

Cleveland Bay

718 Yarm Road, TS16 0JE (jct of A67 and A135, N of Tees bridge)

11-1am ☎ (01642) 780275 clevelandbay.co.uk

Camerons Strongarm; Timothy Taylor Landlord; Wainwright; 1 changing beer H

Popular locals' pub under the stewardship of an enthusiastic licensee with an enviable reputation for serving a selection of fine premium bitters. Third-pint glasses and tasting notes are available. The main bar, with four handpumps, has two sports TVs. There is also a lounge and a function room, where live bands play on Friday evening. A free finger buffet is served on Saturday afternoon, and a free lunch on Sunday. A former CAMRA branch Community Pub of the Year.

Q P (7,17)

Easington

Half Moon

The Green, SR8 3AZ (at top of village green)

11-3, 5-11; 11-11 Fri & Sat; 11.30-11 Sun

☎ (0191) 527 0203 halfmoonuk.com

Sharp's Doom Bar; 1 changing beer H

A welcoming, good-sized former Vaux Brewery hostelry which has undergone a recent interior refurbishment, in a prominent position at the head of the pleasant village green. Meals can be enjoyed in the bar or the restaurant lounge, with all the meats locally sourced. Two well-kept beers are always on offer. The pub's history can be traced back to the early 19th century when it was an inn owned by the church until 1866.

P (208)

Eastgate

Cross Keys

A689, DL13 2HW

5 (12 Sat & Sun)-midnight; closed Mon winter
(01388) 517234 crosskeyseastgate.co.uk
Allendale Wagtail Best Bitter; 1 changing beer H
A proper family-run Weardale pub, popular with holidaymakers and locals. The ancient 17th-century building has a pleasant interior with a lively, welcoming bar and a restaurant providing relaxed dining. The ceiling is adorned with tankards. A second Allendale beer is usually on offer. There is a beer garden to the rear. Comfortable B&B accommodation is available.
QP(101)

Edmundbyers

Baa

Low House Haven, DH8 9NL
4.30-10; 12-midnight Fri & Sat; 12-10 Sun
(01207) 255651 lowhousehaven.co.uk
2 changing beers H
Former Youth Hostel Association, and now independent, hostel dating back to 1600 when it began life as an inn. The cycle sheds have been converted into a welcoming stone-floored micropub-style bar, offering two well-kept ales, invariably from local breweries. Opening hours may vary, especially out of season, so check before travelling to avoid disappointment. Q

Egglescliffe

Pot & Glass

Church Road, TS16 9DQ (300yds E of A167, opp parish church)
12-2.30 (not Mon), 6-11; 12-2.30, 5.30-midnight Fri; 12-midnight Sat; 12-11 Sun (01642) 651009
Caledonian Deuchars IPA; Greene King IPA, Abbot; Jennings Cumberland Ale; Wychwood Hobgoblin; 2 changing beers H
A local CAMRA branch multi-award winner, this is a classic, cosy and old-fashioned place. Ever-popular, this multi-roomed 17th-century village local is in a quiet cul-de-sac. It has had the same licensee for approaching 20 years. A former licensee and cabinet maker, Charlie Abbey, whose resting place overlooks the pub, fashioned the ornate bar fronts from old country furniture. Tasting notes are available for the seven handpumps. Themed food evenings complement the good-value home-cooked food. Outside is a large, sometimes sunny, south-facing garden. QP(7,17)

Ferryhill Station

Surtees Arms

Chilton Lane, DL17 0DH
closed Mon; 4-11; 12-midnight Sat; 12-11 Sun
(01740) 655724 thesurteesarms.co.uk
Yard of Ale One Foot in the Yard; 4 changing beers H
Traditional pub serving locally and nationally sourced ales and ciders as well as beers from the on-site Yard of Ale Brewery (est 2008). Annual beer festivals are held in the summer and at Halloween. Live music and charity nights are regular events. Lunches are served on Sunday only. A large function room is available. A former regional CAMRA Pub of the Year and local branch Country Pub of the Year 2015. Q

Forest-in-Teesdale

High Force Hotel

High Force, DL12 0XH
11-11 (01833) 622306 thehighforcehotel.co.uk
4 changing beers H
Historic coaching inn located in beautiful Upper Teesdale and the North Pennines Area of Outstanding Natural Beauty. It is situated next to England's biggest waterfall in a spectacular setting amid magnificent scenery and superb attractions. If you are looking for a great place to stay while walking the Pennine Way, taking photographs, bird watching, sketching, cycling, stargazing, biking or kayaking, this is a little gem. With stripped floorboards, stone bars and an open fire, it offers a great selection of food and up to four ales, usually from Allendale and Mithril. QP

Langdon Beck Hotel

DL12 0XP (on B6277, 8 miles NW of Middleton in Teesdale)
11-10.30; 12-10.30 Sun; closed Mon winter
(01833) 622267 langdonbeckhotel.com
Great North Eastern Rivet Catcher; Wainwright H
Known as the Sportsman's Rest in the early 1800s, this pub is situated in the North Pennines, three miles from the spectacular High Force and Cauldron Snout waterfalls and close to the Pennine Way. The welcoming inn has long been a destination for walkers, fishermen and those seeking hospitality in scenic and peaceful surroundings, whether staying overnight or just long enough to enjoy the excellent food and drink. A beer festival is held over the late May bank holiday weekend.
QP

Frosterley

Black Bull

Bridge End, DL13 2SL
closed Mon-Wed; 11-11 Thu-Sat; 11-5 Sun
(01388) 527784 blackbullfrosterley.com
4 changing beers H
A truly unique, family-run pub next to the Weardale Railway and river, with four ales usually from local brewers, and up to four ciders and perries. Bare boards, stone flags featuring Frosterley marble, all manner of artefacts and antique furniture create a wonderful ambience. It offers high-quality, locally sourced food, and music, plays and story-telling. The outbuilding houses a peal of bells, visited by enthusiasts from across the country. Local CAMRA Country Cider Pub of the Year runner-up 2015-17.
Q(Weardale)P(101)

Hamilton Row

Black Horse

DH7 9AU
2-11.30; 12-midnight Sat; 12-11.30 Sun
(0191) 373 4576
3 changing beers H
A friendly local with an open fire at one end and a glass-fronted fire at the other helping to create a warm, cosy atmosphere. Three well-kept real ales always include one from a local brewery. Good-value Sunday lunches are served. There is a pool table. An excellent pub for walkers, it is handily situated adjacent to the Deerness Valley Way.
QP(52,725)

Hartlepool

Brewery Tap

Stockton Street, TS24 7QY (on A689, in front of Camerons Brewery)
11-4 (7 Fri); 12-5 Sat; closed Sun ☎ (01429) 868686
cameronsbrewery.com
Camerons Strongarm; 2 changing beers
When Camerons discovered that it owned a derelict pub, the former Stranton's future was secured – it was converted into the brewery tap, now in its 15th successful year. A strengthened marketing department has resulted in there now being 16 'monthly' specials, one of which is always available, together with Strongarm and another of the regular beers – IPA or Gold Bullion. Brewery tours start from here. Meetings and conferences, evening opening and social events, as well as superb buffets, can all be arranged.
P(1,36)

Causeway

Vicarage Gardens, Stranton, TS24 7QT (between Stranton Church and Camerons Brewery)
12-11 (midnight Thu & Fri); 11-midnight Sat
☎ (01429) 263000
Camerons Strongarm; Mansfield Cask Ale; 3 changing beers
Marvellous multi-roomed, red-brick Victorian building, dating from 1862, and Camerons' unofficial brewery tap for more than a century. The Causeway is now owned by Marston's, though the sales of Camerons Strongarm remain huge. Guest beers are sourced from Marston's. Good-value bar snacks are available. The licensees host an eclectic mix of live music most evenings and on Sunday afternoon, while the local Arts Association meets here on Tuesday evening. A previous local CAMRA multi award-winner. (1,36)

Rat Race Ale House

Station Approach, Hartlepool Railway Station, TS24 7ED (on Platform 1)
12.02-2.15, 4.02-8.15; 12.02-9 Sat; closed Sun & Mon
☎ 07903 479378 ratracealehouse.co.uk
4 changing beers
Formerly the station's newsagent, this is a drinker's paradise, with over 200 beers served annually, together with cider and perry and several bottled Belgian beers. Opening/closing times coincide with the arrival/departure of the coastal trains. No fizzy lager or beer, no spirits or alcopops, no TV or jukebox, no one-arm bandit, no bar! Over the last 10 years, more than 1,500 different beers, sourced from over 500 different breweries, have been served direct to the table by the landlord himself. A local CAMRA branch multi award-winner.
Q

Hartlepool Headland

Fisherman's Arms

Southgate, TS24 0JJ (on headland close to Fish Quay)
closed Mon; 2 (7 Wed)-11; 2-midnight Fri & Sat; 2-11 Sun
☎ 07847 208599
Maxim Double Maxim; 3 changing beers
The Fish, a local CAMRA multi award-winner, is a typically friendly, one-room locals' pub. Now free of tie, up to four beers are available, while a cider is served during the summer months. The pub's theme is Keeping Music Alive – it hosts well-supported open mic nights together with live music on Saturday. A popular quiz is held on Sunday. No jukebox, no TV, no one-armed-bandit. Two beer festivals, also with live music, are held annually. Winter opening hours may vary. Q(7)

Globe

26 Northgate, TS24 0LJ (on Headland, towards the Fish Quay in Old Hartlepool)
11.30-11; 11-11 Sun ☎ (01429) 860097
Camerons Strongarm
Opposite the port that was once bustling with shipbuilding, fishing boats, coal staithes and pit props, this recently refurbished local is under the stewardship of a friendly and experienced licensee with over 25 years of service to the trade. The price of Strongarm (ask for a Hartlepool Head) still represents remarkable value, reflecting the pub's freehold status, with savings negotiated with Camerons passed on to customers. A recent local CAMRA branch Community Pub of the Year.
Q(7)

High Hesleden

Ship Inn

Mickle Hill Road, TS27 4QD (signed from B1281, between A19 and Blackhall)
closed Mon; 6-11; 12-3, 6-11 Sat; 12-8 Sun
☎ (01429) 836453 theshipinn.net
7 changing beers
Now in its 18th year of family ownership, complete satisfaction is guaranteed at this rural gem. The landlord serves seven beers, some locally sourced, as well as real cider. His wife runs the superb restaurant offering top-quality food at reasonable prices, including mid-week early-doors two-course specials. There are stupendous coastal views from the well-kept gardens. Six motel-style chalets provide good-value accommodation. The pub closes during the owners' annual holidays, so check before making a long journey. A recent CAMRA Regional Pub of the Year.
QP(206)

Holwick

Strathmore Arms

DL12 0NJ (just outside Middleton-in-Teesdale)
12-midnight; closed Tue ☎ (01833) 640362
strathmoregold.co.uk
Mithril A66; Wainwright; 3 changing beers
Three miles off the B6277 at Middleton-in-Teesdale, this 17th-century stone and buttressed roadside pub has a welcoming bar with a stone flag floor, beams and real fire, and a separate lounge with a tiled floor and pool table. It offers a house beer from Mithril, Strathmore Gold, four guest ales (six in summer) and up to 20 ciders. A beer festival is held at the end of July. Food is served during all sessions. Regular live music plays on Fridays. Outside is a beer garden and four en-suite letting rooms are available. CAMRA Country Cider Pub 2016-18. P

Hunwick

Joiners Arms

13 South View, DL15 0JW
5-11 Mon & Fri; closed Tue; 6-11 Wed & Thu; 12-11 Sat; 11.30-11 Sun ☎ (01388) 605131
thejoinersarms.webnode.com
Timothy Taylor Boltmaker, Landlord

Family-run village local with a welcoming bar, restaurant, tiny snug and covered yard/pool room. This is a pub for proper conversation in the bar, along with the opportunity to enjoy its excellent well-kept beers. Quality locally sourced food is served Wednesday to Saturday evenings, and Sunday lunchtime in the restaurant. On Monday evening the bar hosts a cheese night.
❀◑♣P🚌(108,109)📶

Ingleton

Black Horse 🄻

Front Street, DL2 3HS
⏲ 5-11; 12-11 Sat & Sun ☎ (01325) 730374
🌐 blackhorseingleton.co.uk
Camerons Strongarm; 3 changing beers 🄷
Free house and restaurant set back from the road with a large car park, situated in a picturesque village. The friendly bar runs into the dining area. This is a popular community hostelry with a relaxed atmosphere serving excellent locally sourced food. Three guest ales come from local micros within a 30-mile radius of the pub. The restaurant menu is served Wednesday to Sunday. Local darts teams are supported. The weekly quiz night is on a Sunday. Q🧸❀◑♿♣P🚌(84)🐾📶

Leamside

Three Horseshoes 🏆 🄻

Pit House Lane, DH4 6QQ (½ mile N of A690, just outside West Rainton)
⏲ 11-11 ☎ (0191) 584 2394
🌐 threehorseshoesleamside.co.uk
Timothy Taylor Landlord; 5 changing beers 🄷
A country pub with an excellent restaurant, the Back Room (booking advisable). The traditional bar has open fires in winter and a large TV for sport. The attached Working Hand Brewery provides up to four real ales with names all linked to characters from the pub with a story to tell. Timothy Taylor Landlord is always available. The pub is home to a local cycle club and hosts a quiz on Sunday evening. Voted local CAMRA branch Country Pub of the Year 2018. Q🧸❀◑♿🍎P🐾📶

Medomsley

Royal Oak 🄻

7 Manor Road, DH8 6QN
⏲ 11.30-3, 5.30-11; 11-11 Sat; 12-11 Sun ☎ (01207) 560336
Hadrian Border Tyneside Blonde; 2 changing beers 🄷
The Royal Oak is a traditional country-style pub with a warm, welcoming country feel. It has a large bar with a selection of seating including soft sofas and leather chairs, and plenty of dining space. Outside, there is a large, attractive garden at the back and ample parking to the front. An excellent, friendly local, it offers a rotation of quality beers as well as good food. Quiz night is Sunday.
Q🧸❀◑♿P🚌🐾📶

Metal Bridge

Old Mill 🄻

Thinford Road, DH6 5NX
⏲ 12-11 (10.30 Sun) ☎ (01740) 652928
🌐 oldmilldurham.co.uk
4 changing beers 🄷
Originally a paper mill in 1813, the pub offers good-quality food and well-kept ales – four handpumps serve a diverse range, with local breweries supplying at least one of the beers. The food menu is extensive, with daily specials written on a board above the bar. Larger groups are welcome in the conservatory. Accommodation is of a high standard, with all rooms en-suite.
Q🧸🛏◑P

Middlestone

Ship Inn 🄻

Low Road, DL14 8AB (between Coundon and Kirk Merrington)
⏲ 4-11.30; 12-11.30 Fri-Sun ☎ (01388) 810904
🌐 theshipinnmiddlestonevillage.co.uk
6 changing beers 🄷
Regular drinkers come from far and wide to the Ship. It has a bar divided into three distinct areas with an open fire, and a large function room upstairs which is the location for occasional beer festivals. The rooftop patio has spectacular views, and there is always an event either taking place or imminent. Various pieces of Vaux memorabilia are on display – one of the many subjects of conversation. Sunday lunches are popular. A former Durham CAMRA Country Pub winner.
Q🧸❀◑♿♣🍎P🚌(56,99)🐾

Newfield

Newfield Inn 🄻

Front Street, DH2 2SP
⏲ 6-11.30; 12-11.30 Sat & Sun ☎ (0191) 370 0565
Maxim Ward's Best Bitter; 2 changing beers 🄷
A friendly two-roomed pub in the centre of the village, known locally simply as The Inn. It is owned by Maxim Brewery from nearby Houghton-le-Spring, with two of its beers and a guest on the bar. The pub offers accommodation, monthly live music, a regular Tuesday night quiz and football on TV. Families are welcome and there is a pleasant beer garden. Occasional beer festivals are held.
🧸🛏♿P🚌(78)

Newton Aycliffe

Turbinia 🄻

Parsons Centre, Sid Chaplin Drive, DL5 7PA
⏲ 12.30-midnight (1am Fri & Sat) ☎ (01325) 313034
🌐 turbiniapub.co.uk
4 changing beers 🄷
Named after the famous Tyneside ship, this friendly free house comprises a large lounge and function room, with traditional pub decor featuring a pictorial history of the Turbinia ship throughout. This local favourite serves an ever-changing variety of light and dark beers sourced locally and nationally, as well as a changing real cider. It hosts a beer and cider festival twice yearly. Darts, dominoes and pool can be found in the main bar during the week and live music at the weekend.
🧸♿♣🍎P🚌(7)📶

No Place

Beamish Mary Inn 🄻

DH9 0QH (follow signs to No Place off A693 from Chester-le-Street to Stanley)
⏲ 12-11 (10.30 Sun) ☎ (0191) 370 0237
🌐 beamishmaryinn.com
Big Lamp Sunny Daze, Lamplight Bitter; Consett White Hot, Red Dust; 5 changing beers 🄷

Full of character, this pub is well respected for its warm welcome, generously portioned pub grub and ample selection of well-kept real ale. The location is handy for visitors to the nearby world-renowned Beamish Open Air Museum. Consett Ale Works and Big Lamp beers are usually included among the range of LocAles on offer. Accommodation is available including twin, double and family rooms. Q

Norton

George & Dragon

109 High Street, TS20 1AA (80yds S of duck pond)
3-11; 12-midnight Fri & Sat; 12-11 Sun (01642) 554150
3 changing beers H
Traditional, ornate and unobtrusive, this three-roomed locals' pub has been described as 'how pubs used to be and how pubs ought to be'. It comprises a bar (where locals sit on leather benches and muse over wise quotations and photographs of yesteryear), two lounges, a pool room and sheltered outdoor drinking and smoking area. The three beers are always stronger premium bitters and include a darker brew, all chosen by the regulars themselves. On Monday, Stockton Folk Club meets in the back lounge. (35,37)

Hyde's Bar

Rowan Yard, Billingham Road, TS20 2RZ (at S end of High St)
1-11.30 (midnight Wed); 12-midnight Fri & Sat; 12-11 Sun
(01642) 550662
4 changing beers H
Comfortable, contemporary, friendly bar, located in the former workshop of John Hyde, a family-run joiner and builder's merchant for more than 50 years. The workshop was refurbished in 2016, making use of items recovered during the work, with its former use still readily apparent. Photographs from its heyday adorn the walls. Large patio doors open onto a south-facing courtyard area. Four guest beers and four ciders are served. Regular music nights feature throughout the week. Q (X10,35)

Old Shotton

Royal George L

The Village, SR8 2ND
11-11 (midnight Fri & Sat); 11-10.30 Sun
(0191) 586 6500 royalgeorgeoldshotton.co.uk
Timothy Taylor Landlord; 3 changing beers H
Pub and restaurant situated on the old village green, reopened after a major refurbishment of a virtually derelict establishment in 2014. The bar has been reinstated as well as a larger lounge and restaurant area. Owned by Working Hand Brewery, its beers are among the changing range of ales. Handpulled cider is always on offer. Traditional pub grub and bar snacks are available. Dogs are welcome with treats on the bar. QP

Piercebridge

Fox Hole L

Carlbury, DL2 3SJ (on B6275)
11-11; 12-10.30 Sun (01325) 374286
the-foxhole.co.uk
3 changing beers H
Set in a village with Roman origins, this venue sits almost centrally between the towns of Darlington, Barnard Castle, Bishop Auckland and Richmond. From the welcoming Wellie Bar through to the relaxed yet elegant dining room and alfresco dining terrace, the emphasis is on high-quality, carefully locally sourced food and drink combined with traditional pub values. A warm welcome and friendly service, along with three beers from local micros including Mithril three miles away, make this pub a must-visit. P (75,76)

St John's Chapel

Blue Bell Inn L

Hood Street, DL13 1QJ
5-1am; 12-1am Sat & Sun (01388) 537256
2 changing beers H
Originally a pair of terraced cottages, the Blue Bell is a friendly and cosy pub with a bar across the front of the building leading to a small pool room, and garden to the rear. Situated on the A689, it serves the local community and those who holiday in Upper Weardale. Popular for pub games, it also doubles as a library. Q (101)

Seaham

Hat & Feathers L

57-59 Church Street, SR7 7HF
8am-midnight (1am Fri & Sat); 8am-11 Sun
(0191) 513 3040
Greene King Abbot; Sharp's Doom Bar; 3 changing beers H
This Wetherspoon pub gets its name from the Doggarts store that occupied the site from the 1920s to the 1980s and had a department selling hats and feathers. Upstairs are old photographs depicting the headgear of the best dressed ladies of the time. Other interesting pictures show the past history of Seaham. The furnishings are a mix of modern and traditional styles, including comfortable settees. Outside is a plaque displaying a history of the building.

Seaton

Dun Cow L

The Village, SR7 0NA
4 (5 winter)-midnight; 12-midnight Fri-Sun
(0191) 513 1133
4 changing beers H
Excellent, friendly, unspoilt inn on the village green with public bar and lounge areas. A pub for good conversation or a game of darts, the TV is only turned on for special events. No meals are served but toasties are always available. The guest beer selection changes but usually comprises two light and two dark beers to satisfy all tastes. Regular busker and acoustic music nights are hosted. CAMRA branch Country Pub of the Year 2016.
P (238)

Sedgefield

Dun Cow L

43 Front Street, TS21 3AT
11-3, 6-11; 11-11 Sat; 12-10.30 Sun (01740) 620894
duncowinn.co.uk
Black Sheep Best Bitter; Theakston Best Bitter; 2 changing beers H
Run by the same landlord for over 40 years, this large and comfortable 18th-century inn has an excellent county-wide reputation for good food

using locally sourced produce as much as possible. It was the scene of a historic George Bush and Tony Blair lunch in 2003. There are three bars including a farmers' bar-cum-snug and restaurant. Four real ales are always available including at least one local beer. Q P

Shincliffe

Rose Tree

Low Road West, DH1 2NU (on A177 into Durham)
12-10.30 (11 Sat) (0191) 386 8512 rosetreeinn.co.uk
Black Sheep Best Bitter; Timothy Taylor Landlord; 1 changing beer H

The Rose Tree is a family-run pub and restaurant with an extensive beer garden, located in a picturesque village on the banks of the River Wear. Good food is offered, made with the best local produce wherever possible. There are two separate rooms and families and walkers are made welcome, as are well-behaved dogs in the bar. A selection of three handpulled ales is available. Q P

Spennymoor

Frog & Ferret

Coulson Street, DL16 7RS
11-11 (midnight Thu & Fri); 9am-midnight Sat; 12-8 Sun
(01388) 815840 thefrogandferretspennymoor.co.uk
5 changing beers H

Friendly, traditional family-run free house offering five constantly changing real ales, sourced from far and wide, with local and northern microbreweries well represented. The comfortably furnished lounge has a three-sided bar with brick, stone and wood cladding and a solid fuel burner. Sports TV is featured and well-behaved children are welcome until 9pm. Live music is hosted on a Saturday night. (6,21)

Grand Electric Hall

Cheapside, DL16 6DJ
8am-midnight (1am Fri & Sat) (01388) 825470
Greene King Abbot; Ruddles Best Bitter; Sharp's Doom Bar; 5 changing beers H

Formerly a cinema and bingo hall, this is a bright and airy Wetherspoon conversion, with film-themed decor and fittings. The main area is spacious with a high ceiling, and there is a smaller room on a lower level. Set in the centre of town, it boasts a large patio drinking area to the front which can be quite a suntrap in the summer months. (6,21)

Stanhope

Grey Bull

17 West Terrace, DL13 2PB
12-midnight; 11.45-midnight Sat (01388) 529428
3 changing beers H

At the foot of Crawleyside Bank at the west end of town, the pub has a busy bar area across the front and a lounge to the rear, served by a central bar. A community-focused hostelry with a warm welcome, it is convenient for the coast-to-coast cycle route. The tables to the front are popular in good weather. Q (101)

Stockton-on-Tees

Golden Smog

1 Hambletonian Yard, TS18 1DS (in a ginnel between High Street and West Row)
2-10 (01642) 385022
4 changing beers H

The town's first micropub is named after the environmental conditions that recently prevailed on Teesside. Four real beers and two real ciders are served alongside an impressive range of Belgian beers, some familiar, most not so familiar, but all served in matching glasses in the continental fashion. Third-pint glasses and bespoke tasting tables are also available. Local CAMRA Pub of the Year in 2018. Q

Hope & Union

9-10 Silver Court, TS18 1SL (E of High St, through a ginnel off Silver St)
11-11 (12.30am Sat); 12-11 Sun (01642) 385022
3 changing beers H

Tucked away in a square in the town's cultural quarter, the pub is named after a steam engine and a coach operated by the world's first steam passenger railway, the Stockton & Darlington, in 1825. This bright modern pub serves three interesting beers, a cider and a large selection of gins and whiskies. The cellar is on open display, as is the kitchen. Locally sourced and freshly cooked tapas-style dishes are served all day, every day.

Thomas Sheraton

4 Bridge Road, TS18 3BW (at S end of High St)
8am-midnight (11 Sun) (01642) 606134
7 changing beers H

This recently refurbished Wetherspoon pub is a fine conversion of the Grade II-listed Victorian law courts and named after one of the country's great Georgian cabinet makers, born in the town in 1751. The large, airy interior comprises several separate drinking and dining areas, together with a pleasant balcony and an outdoor terrace. The chain's nationally contracted beers are complemented by several regionally sourced guests, together with four ciders. Local CAMRA branch Cider Pub of the Year 2018. Q

Wasp's Nest

Wasp's Nest Yard, 1 Calvert's Square, TS18 1TB (E of High St, through a ginnel off Silver St)
11-11 (midnight Fri & Sat); 12-11 Sun 07789 277364
3 changing beers H

Tucked away in a square in the town's cultural quarter, between the Grade II-listed Georgian Theatre and the River Tees, the Wasps is now firmly established as an addition to the town's social life. This modern, contemporary and lively pub serves a selection of locally sourced beers, cider and perry. Third-pint bats are available. The pub's claim to fame is that it has the town's only outdoor courtyard patio drinking area. Q

Tanfield Lea

Tanfield Lea Working Men's Club

West Street, DH9 9NA
2-4, 7-11; 12-11.30 Fri & Sat; 12-2, 7-11 Sun
(01207) 238783
2 changing beers H

The village has no pub, reflecting its strong Methodist history, but guests are most welcome in this CIU-affiliated club, which has become something of a flagship for real ale in the area after a diet of keg beer for many years. TV sport is shown in the bar and there is a comfortable quiet lounge. Traditional club activities such as bingo take place and there is usually a live act on Sunday when nibbles are provided on the bar. Local CAMRA Club of the Year 2016-2018. ♣P (V7,V8)

Tanfield Village

Peacock

Front Street, DH9 9PX

4.30-10.30 Mon; 3-11; 12-midnight Sat & Sun
☎ (01207) 232720

Black Sheep Best Bitter; 1 changing beer H

A warm welcome is guaranteed in this friendly, traditional, two-bar pub in a pretty village, popular with locals and visitors alike – including bell-ringers from the church opposite. Lovely home-cooked meals are served Wednesday to Saturday evenings and Sunday lunchtime – the portions are generous and great value for money. There is a small beer garden and ample parking. Black Sheep is always available plus a changing guest beer.
Q♣P (V8)

West Cornforth

Square & Compass

7 The Green, DL17 9JQ (off Coxhoe-W Cornforth road)

5-11; 4-11 Fri; 12-11 Sat & Sun ☎ (01740) 653050

3 changing beers H

A proper drinking pub and friendly local on the village green in the old part of Doggy (the village's local nickname). It has sold real ale for 40 years and usually offers at least one local beer among its three guests. It is home to darts and dominoes clubs and hosts a well-attended Thursday night quiz. The pub has good views over to Wear Valley and Durham City. Q♣P (56)

Westgate

Hare & Hounds

24 Front Street, DL13 1RX

closed Mon; 6.30-11 Tue-Thu; 5.30-11 Fri; 3-11 Sat; 12-3, 6.30-9.30 Sun ☎ (01388) 517212
hareandhoundswestgate.blogspot.co.uk

Weard'ALE Chilled Nights, Dark Nights, Gold, Pilsner H

On the banks of the Wear, on the A689. The spacious stone-flagged bar is partially fitted out with items salvaged from the former village chapel, and is a great place to catch up on local news. The restaurant has a patio overlooking the river, while the beer is brewed beneath your feet. Food, including the famous Sunday carvery, is locally sourced. Local CAMRA Country Pub of the Year runner-up in 2015. Q♣P (101)

Witton-le-Wear

Dun Cow

19 High Street, DL14 0AY

6-11; 1-11 Sat; 12-11 Sun ☎ (01388) 488294

3 changing beers H

A welcoming local set back from the road through the village, with a single L-shaped room warmed by open fires at both ends. Dating from 1799, the bar is guarded by a sleeping fox who always seems to have just closed his eyes. There are benches to the left of the bar, and seating outside offering pleasant views over the Wear Valley. The decor includes some interesting football memorabilia.
Q♣P

Wolsingham

Black Lion

21 Meadhope Street, DL13 3EN (50yds N of marketplace)

6.30-11; 6-11 Fri; 12-11 Sat; 12-10.30 Sun
☎ (01388) 527772

5 changing beers H

Nationally recognised for its commitment to real cider, hidden away a minute from the marketplace, this welcoming, comfortable gem is a great place to relax. An open fire features in the single open-plan room, with a pool table to the rear and TV sport to the front. Local charities benefit from the efforts of the pub. Six or more ciders can be on offer. A former CAMRA North-East Region Cider Pub of the Year and local branch Country Cider Pub of the Year 2013-2018. Q♣ (101)

Rat Race Ale House, Hartlepool (Photo: Tom Stainer)

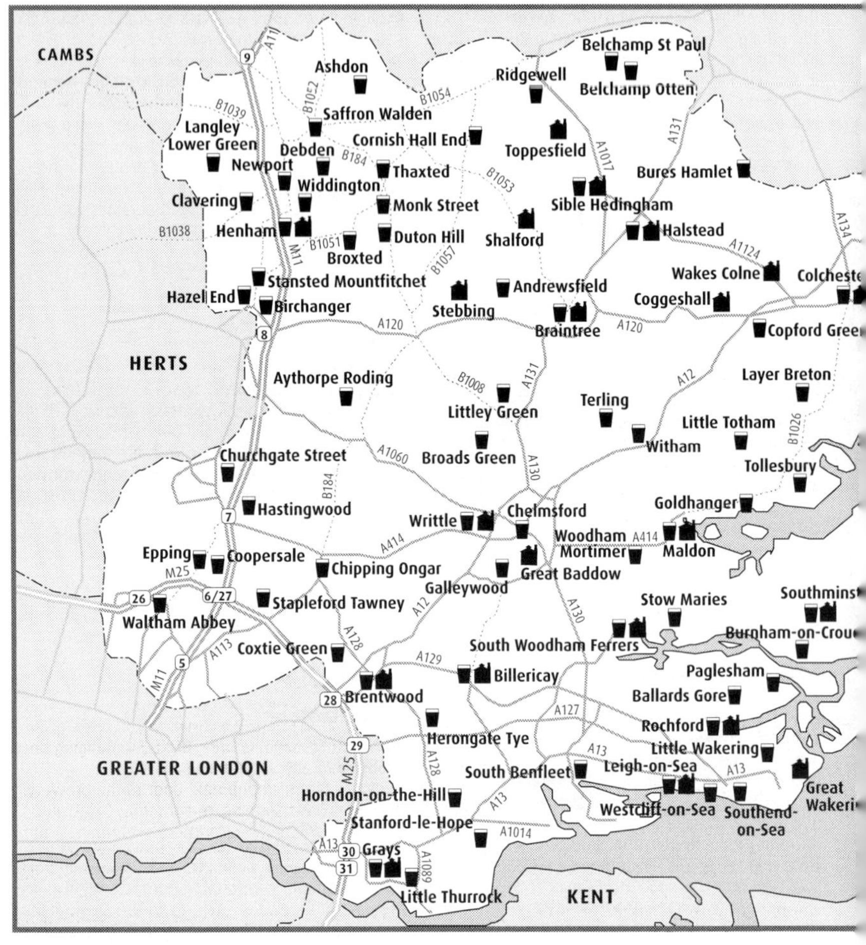

Andrewsfield

Millibar 𝕃

Stebbing Airfield, New Pasture Lane, CM6 3TH
(accessed by track beside runway, near Stebbing Green)
TL689248

11-9 ☎ (01371) 856744 🌐 andrewsfield.com/andrewsfield-millibar

Bishop Nick Ridley's Rite Ⓗ

Local training airfield which is a small grass strip, dominated by single-engine Cessna aircraft, a Mustang III and B17 Meteor IIIs. It is a local flying school, offering trial lessons up to a commercial pilot's licence. The bar manager is keen on local supply and has installed Ridley's Rite from Bishop Nick Brewery as his sole ale. There is also a range of bottled beers from Bishop Nick Brewery. The public are welcomed here and the bar stays open until 11pm if there are customers. **Q ◐P**

Ashdon

Rose & Crown

Crown Hill, CB10 2HA

closed Mon; 12-2.30, 5.30 (5 Fri)-11; 12-11 Sat; 12-7 Sun
☎ (01799) 584337

Woodforde's Wherry; 4 changing beers (sourced nationally) Ⓗ

The last remaining pub in this village which once had five more. The pub has an unusual layout and a room named after Oliver Cromwell where he is reputed to have kept prisoners, who illustrated the walls with their feelings at the time! Guest beers often include Nethergate and Essex-brewed beers. This pub is the focus of village social activities.
◐P

Aythorpe Roding

Axe & Compasses 𝕃

Dunmow Road, CM6 1PP (on B184 5 miles SW of Dunmow) TL594154

9am-11 (midnight Fri & Sat) ☎ (01279) 876648
🌐 theaxeandcompasses.co.uk

Adnams Ghost Ship; Bishop Nick Heresy; Fuller's London Pride; 1 changing beer (sourced regionally) Ⓗ

An 18th-century building, recently extensively refurbished. Drinkers are welcome, including a mixed clientele of walkers, locals and farming folk. The award-winning food consists of pub classics with a modern twist, all locally sourced, and the service is efficient and friendly. The pub hosts quiz and themed nights. On a sunny day the garden is a pleasant place to view the beautiful countryside and the nearby windmill. **Q◐ P** (17,18)

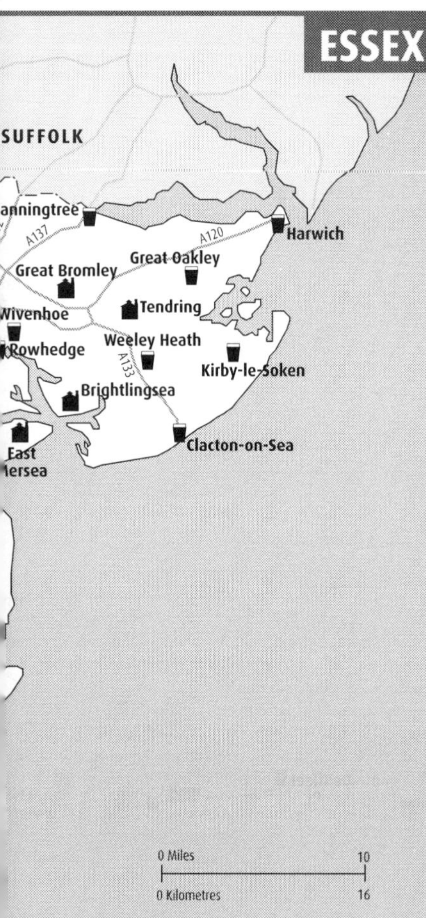

Ballards Gore

Shepherd & Dog

Gore Road, SS4 2DA (between Rochford and Paglesham)
12-11; 12-10.30 Sun ☎ (01702) 258658
shepherdanddog.co.uk
6 changing beers (sourced locally; often George's) H
A traditional country pub with beams throughout and a real fire, and a regular winner of local CAMRA awards. It is L-shaped, with the bar at the front offering six changing real ales including at least two from local breweries, plus a range of real ciders. Towards the back is the restaurant serving home-cooked food using local produce. It has seating outside at the front and in a beer garden to the rear, with an outside bar. Regular music events are popular. P (60)

Belchamp Otten

Red Lion L

Fowes Lane, CO10 7BQ (on very small single track lane, signed by duck pond) TL799415
12-3, 5.30-11; closed Tue; 12-6 Sun ☎ (01787) 278301
Adnams Southwold Bitter; 2 changing beers (sourced nationally) H
Lovely local pub, hidden away in the smallest of the Belchamps. The owner provides a warm welcome, with an open fire in winter. The pub has darts and a pool table, and runs occasional events. There are excellent views, good walks and cycle rides from here. The pub is not currently serving food but has delivery arrangements with local takeaway restaurants. A friendly Labrador greets you when you arrive. P

Belchamp St Paul

Half Moon

Cole Green, CO10 7DP TL792423
12-3, 6-midnight (11 Mon); 12-midnight Sat & Sun
☎ (01787) 277402 halfmoonbelchamp.co.uk
Greene King IPA; 2 changing beers (sourced nationally) H
Beautiful warm and friendly thatched rural inn dating from about 1685, opposite the village green. Three beers are available and guests change regularly. The pub is popular with locals and has an excellent choice of bar and restaurant meals (no food Sun eve or Mon). In the past the pub provided one of the locations for the first Lovejoy TV series. Original wooden beams and low ceilings remain in places. Q P

Billericay

Billericay Brewing Co Shop & Micropub

52 Chapel Street, CM12 9LS
10-6 Mon-Wed; 9am-9 Thu-Sat; 11-5 Sun
☎ (01277) 500121 billericaybrewing.co.uk
Billericay Zeppelin, Blonde, Dickie; 4 changing beers (sourced locally; often Billericay) G
Brewery tap micropub next door to the brewery. It serves at least six ales, mostly from Billericay, including gold, amber, dark and strong ales on gravity, plus bottled and craft beers. The micropub is also a beer shop where bottles can be bought

REAL ALE BREWERIES

Billericay Billericay
Bishop Nick Braintree
Brentwood Brentwood
Chelmsford Great Baddow (NEW)
Colchester Wakes Colne
Crouch Vale South Woodham Ferrers
Fallen Angel Writtle
Famous Railway Tavern Brightlingsea
Fox Meadow Braintree (NEW)
George's Great Wakering
Hart of Stebbing Stebbing
Keppels Rochford (NEW)
Leigh on Sea Leigh-on-Sea (NEW)
Maldon Maldon
Mersea Island East Mersea
Mighty Oak Maldon
Moody Goose Braintree
Mr Majolica Grays
Other Monkey Colchester (NEW)
Pumphouse Toppesfield
Red Fox Coggeshall
Saeburh Tendring (NEW)
Saffron Henham
Shalford Shalford
Silks Sible Hedingham
Sticklegs Great Bromley
Watson's Colchester
White Hart Halstead
Wibblers Southminster

from Billericay, other Essex and London breweries, foreign and craft breweries. Four beer festivals are held each year in March, June, September and December. The decor includes beer bottle lights, and seating on high stools, next to solid wooden tables. Q (100,222)

Coach & Horses

36 Chapel Street, CM12 9LU

11-11; 12-10 Sun (01277) 622873

thecoachandhorses.org

Adnams Broadside; Mighty Oak Captain Bob; Oakham Citra; Wibblers Dengie IPA; 2 changing beers (sourced nationally) H

Close to the high street, this welcoming one-bar pub with an inviting atmosphere has appeared in this Guide for over 20 years. Six ales are served, with one always from Oakham. Good-quality, home-made food is available lunchtimes and evenings, with curry night on Wednesdays (including Thai and Goan). The bar and food service is efficient and friendly. The walls are adorned with prints and decorative plates, and a collection of jugs and tankards hangs from the ceiling. Q P (100)

Railway

1 High Street, CM12 9BE

12-11 (10 Mon, midnight Fri & Sat) (01277) 652173

Dark Star Hophead; Wibblers Dengie IPA; 3 changing beers (sourced nationally) H

Friendly pub with a welcoming atmosphere which earns the tag line 'No.1 in the High Street'. It has served over 600 different real ales and won several local CAMRA awards. Guest beers are updated on social media. Regular events include a quiz and live music, and charity days. This community-oriented pub has three darts teams, and sponsors a local rugby team. Traditional bar games include shove-ha'penny with real ha'pennies. There is a beer garden outside, and an open fire indoors during winter. P

Birchanger

Birchanger Sports & Social Club

229 Birchanger Lane, CM23 5QJ

7-11 Mon, Tue & Thu; 12-2.30, 6-11 Wed; 12-11 Fri & Sat; 12-10.30 Sun (01279) 813441 birchangerclub.com

Greene King IPA; 3 changing beers (sourced nationally) H

A friendly, busy local social club where it is possible for CAMRA members to drink as guests. Many matches and events happen here, so the club can get busy. Beers change frequently as the turnover is high. The club has football, cricket, bowls, darts, crib and snooker teams, and regular quizzes plus bingo and bottle draws. It has won local CAMRA Club of the Year on several occasions. P (7,7A)

Braintree

King William IV

114 London Road, CM77 7PU

3-11; 12-midnight Fri-Sun (01376) 567755

kingwilliamiv.co.uk

4 changing beers (sourced nationally) G

Friendly free house, serving a changing range of real ales, usually featuring Essex microbreweries and at least one from the Moody Goose Brewery, located in the grounds of the pub. It also serves an interesting selection of ciders. There is a main bar and a small back bar with a dartboard. A large patio area with picnic tables and extensive gardens are used to host beer festivals and other events. This is a traditional drinking pub that does not offer cooked meals. Q P

Picture Palace

Fairfield Road, CM7 3HA

8-11.30 (1am Fri & Sat) (01376) 550255

Adnams Ghost Ship, Broadside; Greene King IPA, Abbot; Sharp's Doom Bar; 5 changing beers (sourced nationally) H

Originally a cinema, the Picture Palace, built in 1912, was replaced by the Embassy in 1930. This spacious pub retains the character of a picture house, with the floor sloping down to the long curved bar at the front, where the stage used to be. It has a large TV screen above it, and some eyecatching Art Deco installations. Additional TVs give a choice of channels. Trading as a Lloyds No.1 (Wetherspoon) bar, it is close to the bus and train stations.

Brentwood

Rising Sun

144 Ongar Road, CM15 9DJ (on A128, at Western Rd jct)

3-11.30 (midnight Fri); 12-midnight Sat; 12-10.30 Sun

07828 738549 rising-sun-brentwood.co.uk

Fuller's London Pride; Sharp's Cornish Coaster; Timothy Taylor Landlord; 2 changing beers (sourced nationally) H

Superb community local with five real ales. A charity quiz is held on Monday evenings, there are frequent darts matches in the public bar, and occasional chess evenings. Five handpumps in the saloon bar dispense three regular ales plus two guests, one of which is usually from Brentwood Brewery while the other is from anywhere. Framed prints of the local area decorate the walls. Outside there is a covered heated smokers' area and a patio. P (21,71,72)

Victoria Arms

50 Ongar Road, CM15 9AX (on A128)

11-11 (midnight Fri & Sat); 12-10.30 Sun

(01277) 223371

Adnams Ghost Ship; Harvey's IPA, Sussex Best Bitter; 3 changing beers (sourced nationally) H

Pleasant and comfortable Gray & Sons pub with a friendly atmosphere. Unusually for the area, there are normally two Harvey's beers available, as well as Ghost Ship and three changing beers. There are several TV screens, mostly showing sport, and an outside smoking area. Cribbage and other card games are available. Local CAMRA Pub of the Year 2018. P (498,21)

Broads Green

Walnut Tree

CM3 1DT

12-11 (01245) 360222

Adnams Southwold Bitter; Timothy Taylor Landlord; 1 changing beer (sourced nationally) G

Handsome Victorian pub overlooking the green. The front door opens into what was the bottle and jug, but is now a small snug. To the left is the wood-panelled public bar, little-changed since it was built in 1888. To the right is the slightly more modern saloon bar. Outside there is seating in front of the pub, a children's play area and a large garden. There is no food, the landlord preferring to concentrate on his beers and maintaining a traditional atmosphere. Q

Broxted

Prince of Wales

Brick End, CM6 2BJ

closed Mon; 11.30-11 Tue-Thu (midnight Fri & Sat); 12-11 Sun (01279) 850256 princeofwalesbroxted.co.uk

Greene King IPA; 5 changing beers (sourced nationally) H

Former Charrington's pub transformed into a welcoming community venue after the current landlords took over in late 2011. It has a comfortable split-level bar, an adjoining room with two woodburners, and a conservatory seating up to 50. Generously portioned pub grub, mostly locally sourced, will satisfy the most demanding appetite. There is a small garden to the rear. Up to five guest beers are served, with LocAle from Bishop Nick. P (6)

Bures Hamlet

Eight Bells

6 Colchester Road, CO8 5AE

12-3, 5-11.30; 12-11 Sat & Sun (01787) 227354

Greene King IPA, Abbot; 4 changing beers (sourced nationally) H

This hostelry has up to six real ales from Greene King and local guests such as Bishop Nick, Colchester and Nethergate. It is a traditional village pub with a landlord in his 37th year at the helm. Three separate drinking and dining areas are served by a large bar, and traditional pub food is available daily including specials and Sunday roasts. It hosts a monthly open mic night, a steel quoits team and has a separate function area. Walkers and cyclists are welcome. Q P

Burnham-on-Crouch

Queen's Head

26 Providence, CM0 8JU

2 (4 Mon)-11; 12-11 Fri-Sun (01621) 784825

Dark Star Hophead; Wibblers Dengie IPA; 2 changing beers (sourced nationally; often Oakham, Thornbridge, Tiny Rebel) H

Tucked down a quiet little lane off Burnham-on-Crouch's high street, this is a busy, welcoming locals' pub. An interesting choice of beer is offered, plus a selection of ciders. There are no carpets here, just a basic, comfortable pub interior with a wood-fired stove and pool table. Dogs are welcome. The sheltered patio-style garden is a delightful place to spend time on a summer's day. Burnham-on-Crouch railway station is 15 minutes' walk away. (31X)

Chelmsford

Ale House

24-26 Viaduct Road, CM1 1TS

11-11 (midnight Fri & Sat); 12-10.30 Sun (01245) 260535 the-ale-house-chelmsford.co.uk

12 changing beers (sourced nationally) H

A unique bar in Chelmsford, under the arches at the railway station, with one of the widest ranges of continuously changing beers in Essex, always including dark and stronger beers, plus four craft keg beers and 12 real ciders. There are also imported German beers on tap and a wide range of bottled beers from around the world. No food is served, but customers are welcome to bring their own. Quizzes are held on the last Sunday of each month and there are quarterly beer festivals.

Endeavour

351 Springfield Road, CM2 6AW

11-11; 12-11 Sun (01245) 257717

Adnams Ghost Ship; Harvey's Sussex Best Bitter; Mighty Oak Maldon Gold; Wibblers Dengie IPA; 1 changing beer (sourced nationally) H

Busy and friendly pub comprising three rooms. Cooked meals are served at lunchtimes and evenings, and sandwiches are available all day (Mon-Sat). Please book for the roast dinner on Sundays. All food is good value, locally sourced and home cooked. This is a true community pub, with darts and crib teams and regular charity events. The pub also shows BT Sports. There is a new attractive courtyard garden.

Hop Beer Shop

173 Moulsham Street, CM2 0LD

closed Sun & Mon; 12-9 (01245) 353570 thehopbeershop.co.uk

4 changing beers (sourced nationally) G

Essex's first micropub. Four beers are served by gravity, with local breweries always represented, as well as interesting beers from around the country, with usually a stout or porter and a golden beer. There are also craft keg beers, around 100 bottled beers from local and international breweries, and bottled cider, which may be drunk here or purchased to take home. The atmosphere is one of a traditional pub where people can meet and talk. Local CAMRA Pub of the Year 2016 and 2017, and Cider Pub of the Year 2018. Q

Ivory Peg

7 New London Road, CM2 0NA

8am-midnight (1am Fri & Sat) (01245) 253130

Adnams Broadside; Greene King Abbot; Ruddles Best Bitter; Sharp's Doom Bar; Wychwood Hobgoblin; 5 changing beers (sourced nationally) H

Town-centre pub with a single open-plan area at ground level, featuring large windows on to the street and a good collection of old photographs on the walls of the staircase to the toilets. Excavations prior to its building produced an ivory tuning peg from a medieval musical instrument (now in Chelmsford museum). Food is served all day. As with other Wetherspoon pubs, beer festivals are held twice a year with a cider festival in the summer. An accessible toilet is on the ground floor. Q

Oddfellows Arms

195 Springfield Road, CM2 6JP

12-11 (midnight Thu-Sat) (01245) 490514 theoddfellowsarms.com

Adnams Ghost Ship; Bishop Nick 1555; Dark Star Hophead; Wibblers Dengie IPA; 1 changing beer (sourced nationally) H

A pub with a modern wood interior, but maintaining the feel of a local. There is a large U-shaped bar area, with a back room containing a pool table leading out to the attractive decked garden/smoking area. Extensive home-made food is served weekday lunchtimes and evenings, and all day at weekends. It has a new barbecue real-wood smoker serving brisket, ribs and pulled pork. There are poker nights twice a week, quiz nights, karaoke, monthly live music and an annual beer festival. ❀◑♣P🚌📶

Orange Tree 🄻

6 Lower Anchor Street, CM2 0AS

⏲ 12-11 (midnight Fri; 11.30 Sat) ☎ (01245) 262664

🌐 the-ot.com

Dark Star Hophead; Mighty Oak Oscar Wilde; Plain Sheep Dip; 5 changing beers (sourced nationally) 🄷

The Orange Tree is one of the best real ale pubs in Chelmsford and has been local CAMRA Pub of the Year in recent years. It is a place for conversation and meeting friends, with separate public and saloon bars. A great range of real ales is on tap, always including something dark, plus craft keg beers. Food is served at lunchtimes, including a roast on Sunday, with a steak and curry night on Thursday evening. Quiz night is Tuesday.

Q♘❀◐♿♣●P🚌🐾📶

Queen's Head 🄻

30 Lower Anchor Street, CM2 0AS

⏲ 12-11 (11.30 Fri & Sat) ☎ (01245) 265181

Crouch Vale Essex Boys Best Bitter, Brewers Gold; 5 changing beers (sourced nationally) 🄷

Crouch Vale Brewery's first pub, this venue sells three of its beers permanently, with four guests which may include a Crouch Vale seasonal and always include a dark beer. The Victorian L-shaped pub has bare-board flooring and comfortable bench seating. Two fires make it cosy in winter. This popular local can be busy when there is a match at the nearby county cricket ground. The Essex Beard Club meets here once a year in February.

Q❀♣P🚌🐾📶

Railway Tavern 🏆 🄻

63 Duke Street, CM1 1LW

⏲ 10-11 (11.30 Fri & Sat); 12-8 Sun ☎ (01245) 280679

Greene King Abbot; Red Fox IPA; Sharp's Sea Fury; 5 changing beers (sourced nationally) 🄷

A Tardis-like corner pub, right outside Chelmsford station. Not surprisingly, a railway theme dominates. A Gray's house, it is long and narrow, with banks of handpumps at opposite ends of the central bar counter and seating towards the rear. There is a small enclosed garden where you can marvel at the ever-changing mural. There are craft beers and over 50 gins. It may stay open later on Sundays in summer. Dogs welcome after 2pm. Local CAMRA Pub of the Year 2018.

Q❀◐≹♣●🚌🐾📶

Woolpack ✔

23 Mildmay Road, CM2 0DN

⏲ 4-11; 12-midnight Fri & Sat; 12-11 Sun ☎ (01245) 259295

🌐 thewoolpack.wix.com/woolpackchelmsford

Greene King XX Mild; Hardys & Hansons Bitter; 7 changing beers (sourced nationally) 🄷

It is an easy walk from the town centre to this award-winning, friendly Victorian local. There are three rooms and a lounge area overlooking the large garden. Darts and a pool table are in a smaller room. Pub grub is served, specialising in different-flavoured sausages, with light snacks available until 11pm. Beer festivals are held at Easter and the first weekend in September, with up to 80 beers, ciders and perries. Smaller festivals take place at Halloween and in December.

♘❀◑♣●P🚌

Chipping Ongar

Cock Tavern 🄻

218 High Street, CM5 9AB (on A128)

⏲ 11-11 (midnight Fri & Sat) ☎ (01277) 365261

🌐 thecocktavern.com

Harvey's IPA; 3 changing beers (sourced regionally) 🄷

The Cock is a traditional, welcoming old pub in the centre of the attractive town of Ongar. It serves mostly local ales on handpumps and has a good selection of traditional pub food and a Sunday roast. Parking is available in the public car park by the library and it is close to the heritage Epping and Ongar Railway. Live music is played fortnightly.

♘❀◑≹♣●🚌🐾📶

Churchgate Street

Queen's Head

26 Churchgate Street, Old Harlow, CM17 0JT

⏲ 12-11 (10 Mon); 12-9 Sun ☎ (01279) 427266

🌐 tqhchurchgatest.co.uk

Adnams Southwold Bitter, Ghost Ship; Lacons Encore; Woodforde's Wherry, Once Bittern 🄷; 2 changing beers 🄷/🄶

Originally a Tudor building, with wooden beams spanning a spacious interior, The Queen's Head is believed to have been a pub since 1750. It is situated in a pleasant village street on the outskirts of Harlow. The smaller side bar has a fire in winter and there is a beach bar and barbecue in the summer. The home-made food is known for its fresh ingredients. There are regular quizzes, special events and a Friday burger and beer night.

Q❀◑♣P🚌(HSB1,HSB2)🐾📶

Clacton-on-Sea

Moon & Starfish

1 Marine Parade East, CO15 1PT

⏲ 8am-11.30 (1am Fri & Sat) ☎ (01255) 222998

Greene King Abbot; Ruddles Best Bitter; Sharp's Doom Bar; 6 changing beers (sourced nationally) 🄷

A regular in the Guide since 2014, this pub is opposite Clacton's historic pier and Pavilion Fun Park. The outside area to the front offers excellent views of the Clacton Air Show and the Clacton Carnival street procession during August. It holds two beer festivals and one cider festival each year, in common with other Wetherspoon pubs. Food is available daily. Q♘❀◑♿≹●🚌📶

Old Lifeboat House

39 Marine Parade East, CO15 6AD

⏲ 12-10 ☎ (01255) 476799

5 changing beers (sourced nationally; often Colchester, Greene King, St Austell) 🄷

This pub is frequented by locals and visitors alike and generally has five ales on the bar. It has been a regular in this Guide since 2011. Food is available on Wednesdays, when real ales are discounted by 50p. The pub hosts four darts teams: two that play on Mondays and two on Thursdays. The outdoor patio is a pleasant place to enjoy a summer pint.

❀◑≹♣●P▯🚌🐾📶

Clavering

Fox & Hounds ✔

High Street, CB11 4QR

4-11 (midnight Fri); 12-midnight Sat; 12-11 Sun
(01799) 550321 foxandhoundsclavering.co.uk
Adnams Ghost Ship; Marston's For Fox Sake; 1 changing beer (sourced nationally) H
A local drinkers' pub, the oldest remaining licensed premises in Clavering. It has a large car park and is a good place to start walks from in the middle of this village close to the River Stort. The pub runs events supporting the local school and charities, with a regular quiz on the second and fourth Tuesdays of the month. Excellent home-cooked and locally sourced pub meals are served including a Sunday Roast.

Colchester

Ale House

82 Butt Road, CO3 3DA
3-11; 12-midnight Fri; 12-11 Sat; 12-9.30 Sun
(01206) 573464 thealehousecolchester.co.uk
10 changing beers (sourced nationally) H
Free house with a large secluded walled garden at the rear. This award-winning pub has a wide range of ales, served both from handpump and on gravity, including at least one dark beer. Quiz nights are held every third Wednesday, with folk music sessions on the fourth Tuesday of the month. Darts, bar billiards and BT Sports are available. The nearest public car park is in Roman Circus Walk (CO3 3DG). It has a friendly landlady and staff. (Town) (64)

British Grenadier

67 Military Road, CO1 2AP
5-11.45; 2-midnight Fri; 12-midnight Sat; 12-3, 7-11.45 Sun 07832 215118
4 changing beers (sourced nationally) H
Welcoming local hostelry with a knowledgeable publican which has featured in the Guide for over 10 years. It is a Victorian two-bar inn with a pool table in the small rear bar and a dartboard in the main bar, which is heated by an open fire in the winter months. This former Adnams-tied pub is LocAle and serves real cider, offering a changing range of local, regional and nationally sourced beers and ciders via handpumps.
(Town)

Live & Let Live

12 Millers Lane, Stanway, CO3 0PS (in a small lane, less than 100yds from London Rd)
12-11 (midnight Fri & Sat) (01206) 574071
5 changing beers (sourced nationally) H
The Live's reputation continues to grow thanks to the publicans' great pride in the condition of their real ales and their regular beer, sausage and pie festivals. It is welcoming to families and dogs, appealing to a broad demographic, with a quiet homely saloon bar and a public bar offering sports TV, darts, pool, a comprehensive jukebox, plus a beer garden. Beers are competitively priced, as is the traditional home-cooked food, served lunchtimes daily and evenings Friday and Saturday. Highly commended local CAMRA Pub of the Year 2018. P

New Inn

36 Chapel Street South, CO2 7AX
12-11 (midnight Fri & Sat) (01206) 575277
theoldnewinnpub.co.uk
Bishop Nick Ridley's Rite; 7 changing beers (sourced nationally) H
Local CAMRA Pub of the Year 2017/2018 and Essex Pub of the Year 2017, offering up to eight real ales on handpump, plus four real ciders. It is a community hub with a garden. The saloon bar focuses on comfort and relaxation, while the public bar has music, TV sports and friendly conversation. Traditional pub food is served Tuesday to Saturday lunchtimes and evenings and Sunday roasts 12-5pm. Events such as tap takeovers and dark beer weekends are held. A plethora of pub games is on offer. Q (Town) P (64)

Odd One Out

28 Mersea Road, CO2 7ET
4.30-11; 12-11 Fri & Sat; 12-10.30 Sun (01206) 615102
7 changing beers (sourced nationally) H
The Oddie is a classic beer and cider house with saloon, lounge and side bars plus a function room for local community meetings, looking out on to the garden. There is always at least one beer from Colchester Brewery and up to six more changing guest ales and real ciders. To the rear is a secluded garden that allows for a quiet pint away from the busy road. It is a short walk from Colchester Town railway station and the historic town.
Q (Town)

Purple Dog

42 Eld Lane, CO1 1LS
11-11 (1am Thu); 10-1am Fri & Sat; 11.30-11 Sun
(01206) 564995 thepurpledogpub.co.uk
Adnams Ghost Ship; Sharp's Doom Bar; 4 changing beers (sourced nationally) H
One of the oldest inns in Colchester, dating back to 1647, this is a corner building in the town centre with an outdoor drinking area and wooden beams. Six handpumps provide mainly regional beers alongside the usual town-centre pub offerings, with seasonal beer festivals. An extensive menu, complemented by changing special dishes, is available daily. The pub hosts regular music events and a monthly quiz night. (Town)

Queen St Brew House

7 Queen Street, CO1 2PG
4 (3 Thu)-11; 3-12.30am Fri; 12-12.30am Sat; 12-10.30 Sun
07931 120806
2 changing beers (sourced nationally) H
Located close to Colchester Castle and the local Natural History Museum, this wooden-beamed building has been in commercial use for 600 years. It offers two handpumps alongside an extensive selection of bottled beer. A range of up to eight real ciders is also served. Beers are from all over Europe, though cask beers are usually sourced locally. The pub hosts regular live music and events, and a vinyl record player is available for music. (Town)

Three Wise Monkeys

60 High Street, CO1 1DN
11-midnight (1am Fri & Sat); 11-10.30 Sun
(01206) 543014 threewisemonkeyscolchester.com
6 changing beers (sourced nationally) H
Centrally located multi-level brew bar. The ground floor houses a spacious taproom, serving a range of local and national beers. The venue is host to regular beer, cider and brewery takeovers. Meals are served daily with a focus on American-style food and burgers. Live music and club nights take place on the top floor. There is also a basement gin bar with a boiler room/speakeasy vibe.
(Town)

Victoria Inn 𝕃
10 North Station Road, CO1 1RB
✪ 12-11 (midnight Fri & Sat); 2-11 Sun ☎ (01206) 514510
🌐 victoriainncolchester.co.uk
5 changing beers (sourced nationally) Ⓗ
A proper pub, serving two house beers and three changing guests. Nine real ciders and a selection of bottled and canned artisan ales are also available. Live music on Sunday afternoons, which in summer may be in the pleasant courtyard garden, is usually accompanied by roast potatoes and Yorkshire puddings. It holds a monthly cheese club, wine club and coffee mornings. Two annual themed beer festivals are staged. A previous local, county and regional CAMRA Pub of the Year, and local CAMRA Cider Pub of the Year 2018.
❀⇌(North)♣●🚌🐾📶

Coopersale

Theydon Oak 𝕃
9 Coopersale Street, CM16 7QJ
✪ 11-11; 12-8.30 Sun ☎ (01992) 572618
🌐 thetheydonoak.co.uk
Adnams Ghost Ship; Fuller's London Pride; St Austell Tribute; Woodforde's Wherry Ⓗ
An ancient pub with logburners and comfortable seating, lots of exposed beams, horse brasses and antiques; parts of the pub date back 400 years. A wide assortment of home-cooked food is served, for which the pub has a good reputation. It is in beautiful countryside, not far from Epping, and there is a footpath from Epping underground station. A beer festival is held in May and there are events throughout the year.
Q🐴❀◑◗●P🚌(381)📶

Copford Green

Alma 𝕃 ✔
School Road, CO6 1BZ (signposted from London Rd, Copford)
✪ 12-3, 5-11 (midnight Fri); 12-midnight Sat; 12-11 Sun ☎ (01206) 210607 🌐 thealma.org.uk
Greene King IPA, Abbot; Red Fox Hunter's Gold; 3 changing beers (sourced nationally) Ⓗ
Attractive 16th-century village pub, offering Greene King and guest beers, with a comfortable bar with various seating areas and garden. It was voted in the top three rural community pubs in north-east Essex. It holds a late Spring bank holiday beer festival with over 20 beers on offer. Quiz night is every first Thursday. Home-cooked food is served every lunchtime, and evenings from Wednesday to Saturday. The Sunday roast is popular. The pub also features an open fire, free Wi-Fi, sports TV, darts and pool.
Q🐴❀◑◗♿♣P🐾📶

Cornish Hall End

Horse & Groom 𝕃
B1057, CM7 4HF TL683366
✪ closed Mon; 12-11 ☎ (01799) 586306
🌐 thehorseandgroom.org
Greene King IPA; 4 changing beers (sourced nationally) Ⓗ
A pleasantly refurbished and redecorated village pub opposite the parish church, with a restaurant and garden. It runs beer festivals and events and is a warm and friendly place, with beers that change frequently. The pub is the social centre of this village, supporting many charities. It offers good food, and special lunches, carveries and fish and chips nights are regularly held. These can be popular, so they may need booking ahead.
Q🐴❀◑◗P🐾📶

Coxtie Green

White Horse 𝕃
173 Coxtie Green Road, CM14 5PX TQ564959
✪ 11.30-11 (midnight Fri & Sat); 12-11 Sun
☎ (01277) 372410 🌐 whitehorsebrentwood.co.uk
Fuller's London Pride; Greene King Abbot, IPA Reserve; 6 changing beers (sourced nationally) Ⓗ
Pleasant country free house with an extended comfortable saloon bar. The 10 handpumps normally dispense four regular beers and six guests, of which three are usually from Brentwood Brewery and the rest from anywhere. The pub is badged as the Brentwood Brewery Tap. Beer festivals are held in the large garden at the end of May and in October. There is a large children's play area in the garden to keep them happy. The local bus service is limited but reliable.
🐴❀◑♿♣●P🚌(71,72)🐾📶

Debden

Plough 🏆 𝕃
High Street, CB11 3LE
✪ closed Mon; 12-3 (not Tue), 5-11; 12-midnight Fri & Sat; 12-10 Sun ☎ (01799) 541899
Greene King IPA; 3 changing beers (sourced nationally) Ⓗ
The sole remaining village inn, with a restaurant and garden, now revitalised by a young, energetic couple. This warm and welcoming pub offers an extensive menu and runs beer festivals, events and other local celebrations. It offers an interesting and varied range of local beers. The pub is now an important social centre for the village and surrounding area, and a good base for walkers and cyclists. A monthly quiz night is normally held on the third Wednesday. Local CAMRA Pub of the Year 2018. Q🐴❀◑◗P🚌(6,313)

Duton Hill

Three Horseshoes 𝕃
CM6 2DX (1 mile W of B184) TL606268
✪ 6-11; 12-2.30, 6-11 Fri; 12-3, 6-11 Sat; 12-3, 7-10.30 Sun
☎ (01371) 870681
Mighty Oak Maldon Gold; 2 changing beers (sourced nationally) Ⓗ
Outstanding village local with a garden, wildlife pond and terrace overlooking the Chelmer Valley and farmland. The landlord often hosts a weekend of open-air theatre in July. A millennium beacon in the garden, breweriana and a remarkable collection of Butlin's memorabilia are pub features. A beer festival is held on the late spring bank holiday in the Duton Hill Den. Look for the pub sign depicting a famous painting – Our Blacksmith – by a former local resident, Sir George Clausen. Local and parish newspapers available. 🐴❀♿♣P🚌(313)🐾

Epping

Forest Gate Inn
111 Bell Common, CM16 4DZ
✪ 10-3, 5-11; 10-11 Fri & Sat; 12-8 Sun ☎ (01992) 572312

Adnams Southwold Bitter, Broadside; Bishop Nick Ridley's Rite [H]; 1 changing beer [H]/[G]
On the edge of Epping Forest, the pub is in a 17th-century building, with low ceilings and flag floors, run by the same family for 50 years. It is popular with locals, walkers and their dogs. Hot pub meals and soups are available in the bar, as well as in Haywards Restaurant next door, with a B&B. There is a large grassed seating area.
Q P

Galleywood

Eagle

Stock Road, CM2 8PS (on B1007)
12-11 (8 Mon; midnight Fri & Sat); 12-8 Sun
(01245) 269361
2 changing beers (sourced nationally) [H]
A Grade II-listed building, recently refurbished, with the cellar and kitchen also updated. The L-shaped bar has a mainly wooden floor with seating at the bar, at tables and in alcoves. There is a separate pool room. Freshly prepared home-cooked food is served, with a seniors' lunch club on Thursday. The Sunday roast is free for children. Quiz evenings are every Thursday, with karaoke on Friday and singers/groups on Saturday. Voted most improved pub 2017 by the local CAMRA branch.
Q P

Goldhanger

Chequers

Church Street, CM9 8AS
11-11; 12-10.30 Sun (01621) 788203
thechequersgoldhanger.co.uk
Adnams Ghost Ship; St Austell Proper Job; Sharp's Atlantic; Woodforde's Wherry; 2 changing beers (sourced nationally) [H]
Historic and characterful village inn with several timbered rooms, including a snug and games room with bar billiards. Up to six real ciders are served. There is an extensive menu, offering good quality food which is sourced locally. The rear courtyard is a suntrap in summer and fires in two of the bars provide warmth in winter. A beer festival is held annually in September. Excellent walks along the River Blackwater are close by.
Q P (95)

Grays

Theobald Arms

141 Argent Street, RM17 6HR
12-11 (midnight Fri & Sat) (01375) 372253
theosarms.co.uk
4 changing beers (sourced nationally) [H]
Genuine, traditional pub with a public bar that has an unusual hexagonal pool table. The changing selection of four guest beers features local independent breweries, and a range of British bottled beers is also stocked. Regular St George's weekend and summer beer festivals are held in the old stables and on the rear enclosed patio. Lunchtime meals are served Monday to Friday, and darts and cards are played. Local CAMRA Pub of the Year 2016. P

White Hart

Kings Walk, RM17 6HR
12-11.30 (midnight Fri & Sat); 12-11 Sun
(01375) 373319 whitehartgrays.co.uk

Crouch Vale Brewers Gold; Theakston XB; 3 changing beers [H]
Traditional local just outside the town centre, rejuvenated since it was taken over in 2006. The regular beers are supplemented by three guests (one usually dark) and a selection of over 30 bottled Belgian beers. Good-value meals are offered weekday lunchtimes. There is a meeting/function room and a large, secluded beer garden. Live music features on Saturdays. The pub supports pool and darts teams, and sport is screened on the TVs. Local CAMRA Pub of the Year 2017.
P

Great Oakley

Maybush Inn

Farm Road, CO12 5AL (nr B1414)
12-11 (1am Fri & Sat); 12-10.30 Sun (01255) 880123
maybushinn.co.uk
3 changing beers (sourced nationally) [H]
Since the Maybush's first appearance in the Guide last year, after being saved and opening as a community co-operative pub in February 2016, local owners have now purchased the building next door to provide a pub garden, restaurant and flats to rent to locals. Work on this is ongoing. The two-roomed pub is staffed entirely by volunteers who aim to ensure a warm welcome for all.
Q

Halstead

Dog Inn

37 Hedingham Road, CO9 2DB (on A1124)
4-11.30; 12-midnight Sat; 12-11.30 Sun
(01787) 477774 doginnhalstead.co.uk
4 changing beers (sourced nationally) [H]
Traditional, welcoming two-bar inn (one with a TV), close to the small market-town centre. Up to four different ales are on handpump, and there is a large beer garden to the rear, with fine views overlooking the valley. Live music takes place two Saturdays a month, plus folk music on the first Sunday afternoon of the month. B&B accommodation is also available.
Q (88)

White Hart Inn

15 High Street, CO9 2AA
11-11; 12-11 Sat; 12-10 Sun (01787) 475657
whitehartinnhalstead.co.uk
White Hart Golden Hart, Halstead Bitter; 2 changing beers (sourced nationally) [H]
The White Hart has its own brewery and gin distillery, located in the old stables at the rear of the inn. It started brewing in 2017 and is currently the only outlet for its own ales, apart from local CAMRA festivals. Originally a medieval hall building, believed to have been built in the 15th century, it comprises a traditional drinking area with comfy seating, beams, a fire, plus a dining area. Two permanent beers with its own mild or stout rotate alongside a guest.
P (88)

Harwich

Alma Inn

25 Kings Head Street, CO12 3EE
12-11 (midnight Fri & Sat) (01255) 318681
almaharwich.co.uk

Adnams Southwold Bitter, Broadside; 4 changing beers (sourced regionally) Ⓗ
This 16th-century building has been trading as an inn since 1859. Food is served daily. Two Adnams ales are always available, with four changing guest ales sourced from around East Anglia. The two real ciders, whenever possible, are from Herefordshire as they remind the landlord, Nick, of home. Local CAMRA Pub of the Year 2016.

Hanover Inn

65 Church Street, CO12 3DR
12-10.30 (11 Thu-Sat); 11.30-10.30 Sun
(01255) 502927 hanoverinn.co.uk
Green Jack Trawlerboys Best Bitter Ⓗ**; 3 changing beers (sourced nationally)** Ⓗ/Ⓖ
Since the current owners moved in during 2016 gradual yet sympathetic improvements have taken place. The cosy front bar remains a welcoming place of conversation, while the revamped and enlarged area to the rear is ideal for dining, with hearty, traditional food available lunchtimes and evenings. The function room upstairs can be hired for events. This buzzing community pub can be found in the heart of Old Harwich next to the church.

New Bell Inn

Outpart Eastward, CO12 3EN
11-3, 7-midnight; 11-midnight Fri & Sat; 12-midnight Sun
(01255) 503545 thenewbell.co.uk
Greene King IPA; Mighty Oak Oscar Wilde; 2 changing beers (sourced regionally) Ⓗ
A real ale destination both before and after changing hands in 2015, this pub continues to appeal. Lunchtime food is available (except Mon); in the evening, menus, cutlery and crockery are provided for those wishing to order from local takeaways. There are two real ciders normally on tap, often chosen by one of the pub's cider-drinking regulars – be warned though that they tend to be on the strong side.
Q

Hastingwood

Rainbow & Dove

Hastingwood Road, CM17 9JX
11.30-3 Mon; 11.30-3, 6-11 Tue-Fri; 12.30-3, 6-11 Sat; 12-6 Sun (01279) 415419
4 changing beers (sourced locally; often Adnams, Bishop Nick, Mauldons) Ⓗ
Originally a 16th-century farmhouse, Grade II listed with many original beams and a real fire in winter. It consists of small rooms, set up for dining, with limited seating for drinkers. The extensive garden has a large barn with seating, which is home to the beer festival. The pub is close to junction 7 of the M11. Dogs are permitted indoors, though not evenings and Sundays. Breakfast is served at the weekend. QP

Hazel End

Three Horseshoes

CM23 1HB
12-3, 6-11; 12-3 Sun (01279) 813429
threehorseshoeshazelend.co.uk
Adnams Southwold Bitter; Sharp's Doom Bar; 1 changing beer (sourced nationally) Ⓗ
A clean and friendly pub opposite the cricket green at Hazel End. It has been completely renovated and serves an impressive fish menu. A large extension, added after the renovation, has created more space to both eat and drink here comfortably. This is a good example of a once run-down premises being transformed into a thriving successful pub. It has low ceilings, black wooden beams and two wood-burning stoves. ΛP

Henham

Cock Inn

Church Street, CM22 6AL (1 mile off B1051) TL545286
12-3, 5-11; 12-midnight Fri & Sat; 12-10 Sun
(01279) 850347 thecockinnhenham.co.uk
Greene King IPA; Sharp's Doom Bar; 2 changing beers (sourced locally) Ⓗ
Traditional village pub opposite the church, with outdoor seating at the front and a garden at the rear. The snug has a large TV where major sporting events are screened, and a large separate dining room is next to the bar. The Saffron Brewery is 100 yards away and one of its beers is normally available here. There is a quiz night on the first Monday of the month. A special dish of the day is served on weekday lunchtimes (no food Sun eves).
QP(7,7a)

Herongate Tye

Olde Dog Inn

129 Billericay Road, CM13 3SD (¾ mile E of A128) TQ641909
11.30-11; 12-11 Sat; 12-9 Sun (01277) 810337
theoldedoginn.co.uk
Crouch Vale Brewers Gold; Greene King Abbot Ⓗ**; 3 changing beers** Ⓖ
This 17th-century weatherboarded inn is a family owned and run free house with traditional decor. It offers a variety of real ales including three regularly changing guests from countrywide microbreweries, along with more established national brands and its own locally brewed Olde Dog IPA. Two traditional ciders are also available. Food is served at the bar or in the separate restaurant area lunchtimes and evenings. Fish and chips is available to take away. Dogs are welcome in the area at the end of the bar known as the Dog House.
P

Horndon-on-the-Hill

Bell Inn

High Road, SS17 8LD
11-11; 12-10.30 Sun (01375) 642463 bell-inn.co.uk
Crouch Vale Brewers Gold; Greene King IPA; Sharp's Doom Bar; 2 changing beers (sourced nationally) Ⓗ
Popular 15th-century coaching inn, where beamed bars feature wood panelling and carvings, run by the same family since 1938. Note the hot cross bun collection; a bun has been added every Good Friday for more than 100 years. Three regular beers are on tap plus two guests, including ales from Essex breweries. The award-winning restaurant is open daily, lunchtimes and evenings. Booking is advisable. Gourmet nights are held – see website for details. Accommodation is available in 27 bedrooms. QP(11)

Kirby-le-Soken

Ship

35 Walton Road, CO13 0DT

11-11 ☎ (01255) 679149 theshipkirbylesoken.co.uk

Adnams Ghost Ship, Southwold Bitter; 3 changing beers (sourced nationally) H

Returning to the Guide for the first time since 1983, thanks to the hard work of the current owners, the Ship is now a free house with a restaurant area, a large beer garden containing a marquee, and an outside seating area to the front. Local CAMRA Cider Pub of the Year in 2017 and 2018, trays of three thirds of cider are available. It has a wide selection of menus. Well-behaved dogs are welcome. P (8)

Langley Lower Green

Bull

Park Lane, CB11 4SB TL437345

5-11; 12-2, 4-11 Fri; 12-11 Sat & Sun ☎ (01279) 777307

thebullpub.co.uk

Adnams Mosaic; Greene King IPA; 2 changing beers (sourced regionally) H

Classic Victorian village local with original cast-iron lattice windows, located in a tiny isolated hamlet, close to both Hertfordshire and Cambridgeshire. There is an aquarium in the lounge bar. The pub has a band of local regulars and hosts an open mic night on the last Tuesday of the month as well as occasional quiz nights. An annual beer festival takes place in September. If you plan in advance, a party can pre-book food at times it is normally unavailable. P

Layer Breton

Hare & Hounds

Crayes Green, CO2 0PN

9am-midnight (1am Fri & Sat) ☎ (01206) 330459

thehareandhound.co.uk

Bishop Nick Ridley's Rite; Greene King Abbot; Sharp's Doom Bar; 2 changing beers (sourced nationally) H

Attractive award-winning country pub with a single bar and a separate room for dining and functions, with cosy logburners. It has a garden with a pergola for outdoor eating and drinking. Three beer festivals a year are held, including the popular St George's Day festival. It has a community shop selling newspapers and a post office on Tuesday mornings and Thursday afternoons. A good-quality food menu is offered. Quiz night is the first Wednesday of the month and Thursday is steak night. Accommodation is available. P (92)

Leigh-on-Sea

Crooked Billet ✔

51 High Street, Old Leigh, SS9 2EP

12-11 (11.30 Fri); 11-10.30 Sun ☎ (01702) 480289

Adnams Southwold Bitter; St Austell Nicholson's Pale Ale; Sharp's Doom Bar; 3 changing beers (sourced regionally) H

Situated in Old Leigh fishing village, overlooking the Thames Estuary, this 16th-century pub has two small bars with bare floorboards and beamed ceilings. The walls are decorated with local village and fishing pictures. It has a small garden to one side and a larger seating area to the front, which is shared with a seafood merchant. It offers up to six real ales, with three regulars and three guests from the Nicholson's list. A short walk from Leigh-on-Sea station. P (21,26)

Mayflower

5-6 High Street, Old Leigh, SS9 2EN

11-11 (midnight Fri & Sat); 12-11 Sun ☎ (01702) 478535

mayfloweroldleigh.com

Crouch Vale Brewers Gold; George's Cockleboats; St Austell Proper Job; 2 changing beers (sourced regionally) H

Pleasant pub situated at the rear of a fish and chip restaurant at the far end of Old Leigh. LocAle is available from both George's and Crouch Vale, and usually a dark beer as well. Food is mainly fish dishes from the attached restaurant. There is an outdoor terrace with views across the Thames Estuary. One wall depicts the Pilgrim Fathers passenger manifest of those who sailed on the Mayflower. A former local CAMRA Pub of the Year. P (26)

Little Thurrock

Traitors' Gate L

40-42 Broadway, RM17 6EW (on A126)

12-midnight ☎ (01375) 372628

traitorsgatepub.wordpress.com

Greene King Abbot; 5 changing beers (sourced locally) H

Since it was taken over in autumn 2013, this pub has become a popular beer and live music venue. Six handpumps offer a rotating selection of beers, with an emphasis on Essex breweries. Look for the chalkboards above the bar listing current and forthcoming ales. Open mic night is Thursday, live bands play most Fridays. (22A,66)

Little Totham

Swan

School Road, CM9 8LB

12-11; 12-10.30 Sun ☎ (01621) 331713

Crouch Vale Brewers Gold; Mighty Oak Oscar Wilde; Timothy Taylor Landlord; 3 changing beers (sourced nationally) G

Grade II-listed three-roomed cottage-style pub, which includes a public bar and restaurant. There is a superb range of beers, mostly sourced locally, served direct from the cask from a chilled cellar, and a dozen or so ciders including Westons Rosie's Pig and Abrahalls Cracklin' Rosie perry. The walled front garden provides a safe play area and there is a large field to the rear for outdoor activities and events. The pub hosts an annual two-week beer festival in June. Q P

Little Wakering

Castle ✔

181 Little Wakering Road, SS3 0JW

12-11 (1am Fri & Sat); 12-10.30 Sun ☎ (01702) 216521

castleinnpub.co.uk

Fuller's London Pride; Sharp's Doom Bar; Timothy Taylor Landlord; 1 changing beer (sourced nationally) H

One of the oldest pubs in the area, dating back to 1620, where it started life as a wooden structure. It is believed that the cellar still has tunnels running to the church that was once used by smugglers. It is known locally for its home-cooked food, available every day. Sit by the cosy open fire in the

separate large two-bar area to enjoy one of the four ales. A family-friendly village pub that is also dog friendly, with a menu especially for dogs.
P

Littley Green

Compasses

CM3 1BU

12-3, 5.30-11.30 Mon-Wed; 12-11.30 (01245) 362308
compasseslittleygreen.co.uk

Bishop Nick Ridley's Rite; Crouch Vale Essex Boys Best Bitter; 3 changing beers (sourced nationally) G

Formerly Ridley's Brewery tap, this is a picturesque Victorian country pub in a quiet hamlet. A wood-panelled bar has benches around the walls and a tiled floor. Beers are drawn directly from casks in the half-cellar. It has an interesting range of three ciders and a perry. Renowned filled huffers (giant baps) are available lunchtimes and evenings, plus other traditional dishes. There are seats and tables outside and in the large gardens. Regular beer festivals are held. Accommodation comprises five high-quality rooms. Q P

Maldon

Carpenters Arms

33 Gate Street, CM9 5QF

11-11 (01621) 859896 carpentersarmsmaldon.com

Adnams Southwold Bitter; 5 changing beers (sourced nationally) H

This friendly back-street community Gray & Sons pub, with its ancient beams, is the local CAMRA Pub of the Year and Cider Pub of the Year for 2018. There is an outside seating area at the front of the pub as well as a rear patio area. A superb selection of over 20 ciders from around the UK and Normandy is served. A beer and cider festival is held annually in the summer. The pub actively supports darts, dominoes and cribbage teams.

Farmers Yard

140 High Street, CM9 5BX

12 (5 Mon)-9; 12-9.30 Fri & Sat (01621) 854202
maldonmicropub.co.uk

4 changing beers (sourced locally; often Maldon) G

Maldon Brewing Company's micropub and bottle shop is housed in a charming 400-year-old building on the High Street, which is Grade II listed. The small, timbered public room provides seating around the wall for a dozen people and has a similar number of standing places. The layout encourages locals and strangers to mingle and converse freely. The complete range of Maldon Brewing Company's bottled ales, two draught Belgian ales and three real ciders are also available. Children and dogs are welcome.
Q

Manningtree

Red Lion

42 South Street, CO11 1BG

12-11 (midnight Fri & Sat) (01206) 391880
redlionmanningtree.co.uk

Adnams Southwold Bitter; 2 changing beers (sourced nationally; often Colchester, Maldon, Nethergate) H

Friendly staff and well-kept ales have helped the oldest pub in Manningtree appear in the Guide for several years. A recent refurbishment added the Pump Room, which can be used for small functions; an older large function room upstairs is often a venue for live music and other events. Food is not available, but menus, crockery and cutlery are provided for ordering in takeaways.

Monk Street

Farmhouse Inn

Thaxted, CM6 2NR (off B184, 2 miles S of Thaxted) TL614288

11-11 (10 Mon; midnight Fri & Sat); 11-10 Sun
(01371) 830864 farmhouseinn.org

Greene King IPA; 2 changing beers (sourced locally) H

Built in the 16th century, this former Dunmow Brewery pub has been enlarged to incorporate a restaurant and accommodation; the bar is in the original part of the building. The quiet hamlet of Monk Street overlooks the Chelmer Valley, two miles from historic Thaxted. A disused well in the garden supplied the hamlet with water during World War II. The pub has a rear patio, front garden and a top field. Draught cider from Westons is usually sold. P(313)

Newport

White Horse Inn

Belmont Hill, CB11 3RF (on B1383)

12-11.30 (1am Fri & Sat) (01799) 540002
whitehorsenewport.co.uk

3 changing beers (sourced nationally) H

On the main road in the middle of Newport, this is a friendly drinkers' local, serving three different ales. It is an ex-Greene King house transformed into a pub focused on the community, having been purchased by a local business. Extensive repair work has been done to the building, and the change of ownership with a new licensee has raised its popularity as a beer drinkers' pub. Meals are on Tuesday and Thursday evenings only.
(301)

Paglesham

Plough & Sail

East End, SS4 2EQ (5 miles E of Rochford) TQ943923

12-3, 6-11; 12-10.30 Sat & Sun (01702) 258242
theploughandsail.co.uk

George's Wallasea Wench; Mighty Oak Maldon Gold; 1 changing beer H

A traditional pub a short walk from the River Roach, with an aviary in the garden, real fires, fine Essex ales and a warm welcome. It has a history dating back over 300 years. In 1890 over 30 oyster smacks were based in Paglesham, and the pub became a meeting place for the hardworking crews; it is still a community hub. The home-cooked food is popular so the restaurant is often busy. P

Ridgewell

White Horse Inn

Mill Road, CO9 4SG (on A1017) TL735408

5-11 Mon; 12-2, 5-11 Tue; 12-11 Wed-Sun
(01440) 785532 ridgewellwhitehorse.com

3 changing beers (sourced nationally) G

Set in a pretty village, which was home to the American 381st Heavy Bomb Group during WWII. A dark beer is often available here. Annual beer festivals are held in summer on the patio behind the pub. As well as a choice of excellent real ale and food, this pub offers 4-star accommodation in nine en-suite rooms at the rear of the pub and an interesting selection of good-quality wines to suit a variety of tastes.

Rochford

Golden Lion

35 North Street, SS4 1AB

11-midnight (1am Fri & Sat) (01702) 545487

goldenlionrochford.co.uk

Adnams Southwold Bitter; Greene King Abbot; Mighty Oak Maldon Gold; 4 changing beers (sourced nationally)

A longstanding Guide entry, this Grade II-listed weatherboarded free house has won many local CAMRA awards. As well as the three regular ales, there is usually one from Cotleigh along with three from interesting breweries. It holds two beer festivals a year, making use of the attractive patio-style garden, normally in May and October. Live football matches are occasionally shown on the large-screen TV. The wood-burning stove complements the decor perfectly.

Miley

1 Union Lane, SS4 1AP

12-midnight (1am Fri & Sat) (01702) 544229

4 changing beers (sourced nationally)

Friendly community local, which has been in the same family since opening 25 years ago. Four changing ales are sold, often from local microbreweries or large nationals such as Greene King. It is sports oriented, with two dartboards and a number of large-screen TVs. Live bands play most weekends (outside in summer) and there are monthly quiz and karaoke nights. Beers are £2.50 a pint on Monday and 12-4pm Tuesday-Thursday.

Rose & Crown

45 North Road, SS4 1AD

11-midnight; closed Fri & Sat (01702) 530112

Sharp's Sea Fury; 3 changing beers (sourced nationally)

This attractive corner pub in the Rochford conservation area is a good example of 1920s roadhouse style. A single bar serves two distinct areas – a lively public area with a pool table, and a quieter saloon with a dartboard. The large patio garden has an outbuilding serving real cider and cocktails and, in summer, seafood. Regular quizzes are held and there are often live bands at the weekend.

Rowhedge

Olde Albion

High Street, CO5 7ES

5-11 Mon; 12-3, 5-11 Tue & Wed; 12-11; 12-10.30 Sun

(01206) 728972

4 changing beers (sourced nationally)

Pleasant, welcoming community pub on the waterfront with a nautical theme, with a range of well-kept ales and ciders; over 500 different ales were available over the last year. A logburner in winter keeps customers warm, while in warmer weather there are tables and chairs on the greensward overlooking the River Colne. Beer festivals are held for St George's Day, Rowhedge Regatta, and one in autumn, plus the annual Carols on the Quay. (66)

Saffron Walden

King's Arms

10 Market Hill, CB10 1HQ

12-midnight (11 Mon; 12.30am Fri & Sat); 12-11 Sun

(01799) 522768 thekingsarmssaffronwalden.co.uk

Adnams Southwold Bitter; Oakham JHB; Woodforde's Wherry; 2 changing beers (sourced nationally)

Venerable, wooden-beamed multi-roomed pub, just off the market square. A mild or dark beer is often served in winter. There is live music at weekends, acoustic music on Thursdays and a monthly quiz. Welcoming log fires in the winter and a pleasant patio for alfresco eating and drinking are particular features. Food is served here at lunchtimes. QP

Old English Gentleman

11 Gold Street, CB10 1EJ (E of B184/B1052 jct)

11-midnight (11 Mon; 1am Fri & Sat); 11-11 Sun

(01799) 523595 oldenglishgentleman.com

Adnams Southwold Bitter; Woodforde's Wherry; 2 changing beers (sourced regionally)

An 18th-century town-centre pub with log fires and a welcoming atmosphere. It serves a selection of guest ales and an extensive menu of bar food and sandwiches. Traditional roasts and chef's specials are available on Sunday in the bar or dining area, where a variety of works of art is displayed. There is a heated patio at the rear.

Sible Hedingham

White Lion

6 Church Street, CO9 3NS

11-midnight; 12-midnight Sun (01787) 462534

3 changing beers (sourced nationally)

The last remaining pub in Sible Hedingham, serving as a local with occasional events and live music. Football is shown on TV frequently and there is a pool table. New tenants are making a success of this pub, which is friendly and hospitable. There is a function room with a small stage, available for hire. P

South Benfleet

South Benfleet Social Club

8 Vicarage Hill, SS7 1PB

12-11 (midnight Fri & Sat) (01268) 206159

5 changing beers

CAMRA East Anglia Regional Club 2018 and five times local branch Club of the Year, this family-oriented club gives a warm welcome to all; show a CAMRA membership card or a copy of this Guide for entry. Three handpumps are complemented by two more beers on gravity dispense. Regular beer festivals and LocAle also feature. TV sports, darts, pool, quiz nights and live music are part of the social scene. P

South Woodham Ferrers

Tap Room 19

19 Haltwhistle Road, CM3 5ZA

closed Mon; 4-9 (11 Fri); 2-11 Sat; 2-5 Sun

(01245) 322744

Crouch Vale Blackwater Mild, Essex Boys Best Bitter, Brewers Gold, Yakima Gold, Amarillo; 2 changing beers (sourced locally; often Crouch Vale) G
A friendly taproom, adjacent to the Crouch Vale brewery, with outdoor seating on a wooden veranda at the front. The bar staff are knowledgeable about the excellent range of beers they serve, straight from the casks in the climate-controlled cellar, which can be viewed through a window from the bar. There is a constantly changing selection of ciders. Brewery tours are available by appointment.
Q🛋❀♿⇌♣●P▯🚌(36)🐾📶

Southend-on-Sea

Mawson's Micro Pub 🏆 L

781 Southchurch Road, SS1 2PP
⏲ 4-11 (12.30am Fri); 12-12.30am Sat; 12-10 Sun
☎ (01702) 601781 🌐 mawsonsmicro.com
George's Wallasea Wench, Cockleboats; 4 changing beers (sourced nationally) H
Southend's first micropub opened in December 2015 and became an immediate success. Up to six ales are served on handpump with at least two from the local brewery, George's, and four guests which could include more from George's or Hopmonster. Foreign bottled beers, plus up to six draught and bottled ciders, complement the range. Local CAMRA Pub of the Year and Cider Pub of the Year 2017 and 2018. 🛋♿⇌(East)●🚌🐾📶

Railway Hotel L ✔

32 Clifftown Road, SS1 1AJ
⏲ 5-11 Mon; 12-11 Tue-Thu; 12-midnight Fri; 12-1am Sat; 12-10 Sun ☎ (01702) 343194 🌐 railwayhotelsouthend.co.uk
Adnams Southwold Bitter, Mosaic, Ghost Ship, Broadside; Crouch Vale Brewers Gold; house beer (by Marston's) H
Large Victorian hotel which has been recognised by CAMRA as having a historic interior of some regional importance. This community pub has a unique atmosphere and is music oriented; live music features most days and it has an excellent collection of vinyl records, played from a pulpit. It is one of the top 10 vegan pubs in the country, serving vegan food along with pizzas. Up to seven cask ales are available. 🛋❀◑♿⇌(Central)🚌📶

Southminster

Station Arms

39 Station Road, CM0 7EW
⏲ 12-2.30, 6 (5.30 Fri)-11; 2-11 Sat; 12-10.30 Sun
☎ (01621) 772225 🌐 thestationarms.co.uk
Adnams Southwold Bitter; 4 changing beers (sourced regionally; often Dark Star, George's, Mighty Oak) H
Multi award-winning traditional community pub, which attracts custom from far and wide. It has a weatherboarded exterior and a basic bareboarded interior with a real fire. A delightful courtyard garden with enclosed barn is to the rear, which hosts beer festivals and other events. The pub holds an annual conker championship, a harvest festival auction, Sunday meat raffles and monthly blues sessions. Free tasters of the beers are not available. Q❀⇌♣●🚌

Wibblers Brewery Taproom & Kitchen

Goldsands Road, CM0 7JW
⏲ closed Mon-Wed; 2-8 Thu; 2-10 Fri; 12-10 Sat; 12-6 Sun
☎ (01621) 772044 🌐 wibblers.co.uk/taproomkitchen
Wibblers Dengie IPA H**; 5 changing beers (sourced locally; often Wibblers)** H/G
Adjacent to the restored medieval tithe barn housing the Wibblers Brewery, this small taproom stocks a good range of beers produced next door. Furnished with high tables, stools and benches, it has further seating to the front of the building for those who enjoy their drinks alfresco in warmer weather. Meals use locally sourced ingredients wherever possible. The brewery hosts open days and various other events throughout the year. Southminster railway station is only a few minutes' walk away. Q🛋❀◑♿⇌●P🚌(31X)🐾📶

Stanford-le-Hope

Rising Sun L

Church Hill, SS17 0EU (opp church and near A1014)
⏲ 3-10.30 Mon; 12-midnight (10.30 Tue; 11 Wed; 11.30 Thu); 11-10.30 Sun ☎ (01375) 671097
5 changing beers H
Much-improved, two-bar, traditional town pub in the shadow of the church. The five guest beers are mainly from independent breweries, including LocAle beers, and up to three ciders or perries are stocked. Regular monthly live music is a feature. Beer festivals are held three times a year (spring, summer and winter) with the summer festival staged in the pub's large rear garden. A back bar is available for private functions. ❀⇌♣●P🚌🐾📶

Stansted Mountfitchet

Rose & Crown L

31 Bentfield Green, CM24 8HX (1 mile W of B1383)
TL505256
⏲ closed Mon; 12-3 (not Tue), 6-11; 12-midnight Fri & Sat; 12-9 Sun ☎ (01279) 812107 🌐 roseandcrownstansted.co.uk
Bishop Nick 1555; 2 changing beers (sourced regionally) H
Family-run Victorian pub near a duck pond on the edge of a small hamlet. This free house has been modernised to provide one large bar, but retains the welcoming atmosphere of an active village local. Food is home cooked and made from locally sourced produce. A large variety of gins is available. There is an old seven-inch singles jukebox and you are welcome to bring your own records to play. The pub has been extended to include a large snug. 🛋❀◑♣P🚌(7,7a)🐾📶

Stapleford Tawney

Moletrap

Tawney Common, CM16 7PU (3 miles E of Epping)
TL500013
⏲ 11.30-2.30 Mon; 11.30-2.30, 6-11; 12-4 Sun
☎ (01992) 522394 🌐 themoletrap.co.uk
Fuller's London Pride; 3 changing beers (sourced regionally) H
A 200-year-old pub in beautiful countryside, it offers a good selection of guest ales, normally including one dark one. Good-value home-cooked food is served (no food Sun and Mon eves). There is a cosy bar with a real fire in winter, and well-behaved children and dogs are allowed at the landlord's discretion. There is extensive outdoor seating with amazing views. In the middle of nowhere, it is difficult to locate without a sat nav, but is well worth it! Q🛋❀◑P🐾📶

Stow Maries

Prince of Wales

Woodham Road, CM3 6SA
11-11 (midnight Fri & Sat); 12-10.30 Sun
(01621) 828971 prince-stowmaries.net
Titanic Plum Porter; 6 changing beers (sourced nationally; often Crouch Vale, Dark Star, Titanic) H
Popular 17th-century weatherboarded pub with three cosy drinking areas, all with real fires. Interesting breweriana adorns the walls. The excellent food is prepared and cooked in-house. There is an extensive garden, and good accommodation is available. Many special events are held including Burns Night, a legendary firework display on the last Saturday in October, live music, summer barbecues and winter pizza nights on Thursdays using the Victorian wood-fired baker's oven. A major comedy event (with stars from the Edinburgh Fringe) is held in July.
Q P (593)

Terling

Monkey

1 Owls Hill, CM3 2PW
12-11; 12-10.30 Sun (01245) 233113
themonkeyterling.com
Adnams Southwold Bitter; St Austell Tribute H**; 1 changing beer (sourced nationally)** G
Built in 1840, this traditional English pub is probably the most prominent building in this small village and cannot be missed. Its name reflects the Lord Rayleigh coat of arms above the door. Having been closed for nearly four years, it has been extensively renovated in a modern way, while keeping its original style. There is a large bar area where clean dogs are welcome, a separate restaurant and a lounge at the back, the restaurant serving good-quality English dishes.
Q P

Thaxted

Maypole

Orange Street, CM6 2LT
12-11 (midnight Fri & Sat); 12-10.30 Sun
(01371) 831152
Greene King IPA; 2 changing beers (sourced nationally) H
A renamed ex-Ridley's pub all in one room, with a games/TV area, sofas, chairs and an area with tables. There is a garden and a car park at the rear. Up to four guest ales are served. The pub holds musical events and runs beer festivals, and is a beer drinkers' hospitable local. It has a pleasant patio at the rear. P (6,312)

Tollesbury

King's Head

1 High Street, CM9 8RG
12-11 (midnight Fri & Sat); 12-10.30 Sun
(01621) 869203
Bishop Nick Ridley's Rite; house beer (by Colchester); 3 changing beers (sourced nationally) H
Friendly village-centre pub with a long-serving landlord. Always good value. Tollesbury's maritime history is reflected in the main bar's many photographs of old racing yachts and the pub plays host to the annual East Coast Gaffers v Tollesbury Small Craft event. Walkers and birdwatchers are always welcome. Popular home-cooked food is served only on Friday lunchtimes. Pies and sandwiches are available from the bakery opposite. The public bar contains a pool table and dartboard.
Q P

Waltham Abbey

Woodbine Inn

Honey Lane, EN9 3QT
11.30-11 (1am Fri & Sat); 11.30-10.30 Sun
(01992) 713050 thewoodbine.co.uk
Adnams Ghost Ship H**; Bishop Nick Divine** H/G**; Mighty Oak Oscar Wilde** G**, Captain Bob** H**; 3 changing beers (sourced locally)** H/G
Essex CAMRA Pub of the Year 2018 and national finalist Cider Pub of the Year 2017, in Epping Forest and close to junction 26 of the M25. The pub has a separate restaurant, but concentrates on real ales and over 40 small-producer ciders, including London Glider which it makes itself. Food is home made, with local sausages, ham and steak as specialities. Dogs are welcome in the main bar, where there is bar billiards. The Ale Sampling Society and Comedy Club meet here monthly.
P (66,66A)

Weeley Heath

White Hart

Clacton Road, CO16 9ED (on B1441) TM153208
12-2.30, 4-11 (10 Mon); 12-11 Fri & Sat; 12-7 Sun
(01255) 830384
2 changing beers (sourced nationally; often Greene King, Mauldons, Woodforde's) H
After taking over the White Hart in 1996, it took Mark and Sally until 2002 for their first Guide appearance, but they have been in every Guide since. A large conservatory serves as a venue for various meetings. It was local CAMRA Pub of the Year 2017 and 2018 and Cider Pub of the Year 2016. There is a garden with a covered patio for smokers. Different sporting events are shown on various TV screens, and it has a real ale club, darts, pool and football teams. P

Westcliff-on-Sea

Cricketers

228 London Road, SS0 7JG (on A13 London Rd)
12-midnight Mon; 12-11 Tue & Wed; 12-midnight Thu; 12-1am Fri & Sat; 12-10.30 Sun (01702) 345053
Dark Star Hophead; Greene King Abbot; Mighty Oak Oscar Wilde, Maldon Gold; Sharp's Doom Bar H
A family-run, large street-corner Gray & Sons hostelry close to Southend. The pub has been split into a restaurant area and a bar area, with home-made food served until 9.30pm and roast dinners available on Sundays. Jazz nights are in the pub every second Wednesday of the month featuring Digby Fairweather, and quiz nights Mondays. The Venue adjoins the premises, so this popular pub can get busy on music nights. There is a discount for football fans on Southend United match days.

West Road Tap

2 West Road, SS0 9DA
closed Mon; 12-9 (10.30 Fri & Sat); 12-7 Sun
(01702) 330647 westroadtap.com
3 changing beers (sourced nationally)

Found near the Palace Theatre in Westcliff, this is a micropub and bottle shop serving up to three cask ales on gravity. The cask ale range is sourced nationally. Beer is also served from four KeyKeg dispensers, and an extensive fridge selection of craft beer in bottles and cans is available to drink on the premises or to take home. There are two real ciders from Dengie in Essex. Children are welcome until 7pm. **Q** ❀ ≋ 🍎 🚌 (1,27) 🐾

Widdington

Fleur de Lys

High Street, CB11 3SG TL538316
12-3 (not Mon & Tue), 6-11; 12-11.30 Fri & Sat; 12-10 Sun
☎ (01799) 543280 🌐 thefleurdelys.co.uk
Adnams Southwold Bitter, Broadside; Woodforde's Wherry; 2 changing beers (sourced nationally) H
Rumours of a ghost abound at this welcoming 400-year-old village local, which boasts a large open fireplace and beams. This was the first pub to be saved from closure by the North West Essex Branch of CAMRA after the branch's formation. Quality meals are offered with fresh local ingredients. The source of the River Cam and Prior's Hall Barn, an English heritage site, are both nearby. A bridge club is held here. ❀ ◐ ♿ ♣ 🍎 **P** 🚌 (301) 🐾

Witham

Battesford Court L ✔

100-102 Newland Street, CM8 1AH
8am-midnight (1am Fri & Sat); 8am-11 Sun
☎ (01376) 504080
Greene King Abbot; Ruddles Best Bitter; Sharp's Doom Bar; 5 changing beers (sourced nationally) H
A large Wetherspoon conversion of a former hotel of the same name. The 16th-century building was previously the courthouse of the manor of Battesford. It has distinct areas with wood panelling and oak beams, including a family area. Up to five regional beers are served, including something local, usually from Bishop Nick or Wibblers, plus up to two ciders and perries, usually from Westons and Gwynt y Ddraig. The standard Wetherspoon food offering is available.
Q ❀ ◐ ♿ 🍎 🚌 📶

Wivenhoe

Black Buoy ✔

Black Buoy Hill, CO7 9BS
11-11; 12-10.30 Sun ☎ (01206) 822425
🌐 blackbuoy.co.uk/index.html
Adnams Southwold Bitter; 5 changing beers (sourced nationally) H
Popular and welcoming community owned pub, now four times local CAMRA Rural Pub of the Year, serving an ever-changing range of beers. There is an area mainly for drinking, and other spaces for drinking and eating. A popular range of good-value home-cooked food is served. A pleasant outdoor area hosts beer festivals over the late May and August bank holidays. Open mic and quiz nights feature regularly as well as live music.
❀ 🛏 ◐ ♿ ≋ **P** 🚌 🐾 📶

Horse & Groom ✔

55 The Cross, CO7 9QL
10.30-3, 5.30-11 (11.30 Fri); 6-11 Sat; 12-4.30, 7-11 Sun
☎ (01206) 824928
Adnams Broadside, Ghost Ship, Southwold Bitter; 1 changing beer (sourced nationally) H
A real locals' pub, at the top end of Wivenhoe, comprising both public and lounge bars, with a range of ales from Adnams as well as locally sourced guests. Pub games include dominoes and darts. Children and dogs are welcome throughout and there is a small play area in the beer garden. It has a home-cooked menu including a roast lunch on Thursday and a regular curry club (no food Sun). There are excellent bus links from Colchester to the pub. **Q** ❀ ◐ ♣ **P** 🚌 🐾

Station Hotel ✔

27 Station Road, CO7 9DH
2-11; 12-11 Sat; 12-10.30 Sun ☎ (01206) 822991
Woodforde's Wherry; 2 changing beers (sourced nationally) H
This family-run, community pub, right next to the station, is particularly busy most evenings both with commuters and locals. It serves up to four ales on handpump and offers a warm welcome to all visitors; dogs have water and biscuits provided. The pub car park houses the local community chickens. Regular pop-up food and well-attended music events are advertised on the Facebook page and rugby will always be on the big-screen TV when there is a televised match.
❀ ≋ ♣ **P** 🚌 (61,62A) 🐾 📶

Woodham Mortimer

Hurdlemakers Arms

Post Office Road, CM9 6ST
12-11; 12-9 Sun ☎ (01245) 225169
🌐 hurdlemakersarms.co.uk
5 changing beers (sourced locally; often Maldon, Mighty Oak, Wibblers) H
It is worth making the short detour from the A414 to this lovely 17th-century Gray's pub, set in attractive grounds with a large beer garden, children's play area and ample parking. On offer is a good range of locally brewed beers and at least six ciders. Excellent locally sourced food is served daily. A beer festival and barbecue is held on the last weekend in June in the pub's barn and marquee. There is a monthly quiz night.
Q ❀ ◐ ♿ ♣ 🍎 **P** 🚌 🐾 📶

Writtle

Wheatsheaf L

70 The Green, CM1 3DU
11-11.30 (midnight Fri & Sat); 12-11 Sun
☎ (01245) 420672 🌐 thewheatsheafwrittle.co.uk
Adnams Southwold Bitter, Broadside; Maldon Drop of Nelson's Blood H**; Mighty Oak Oscar Wilde** G**, Maldon Gold; Wibblers Dengie IPA** H**; 2 changing beers (sourced nationally)** G
Traditional village pub built in 1813, with a small public bar, an equally compact lounge, and a covered patio by the road. It is a long-time favourite of the local CAMRA branch. The atmosphere is generally quiet, with the TV switched on only for occasional sporting events. Traditional pub food is served Tuesday to Saturday lunchtimes. Note the old Gray's sign in the public bar. **Q** ◐ ♣ **P** 🚌

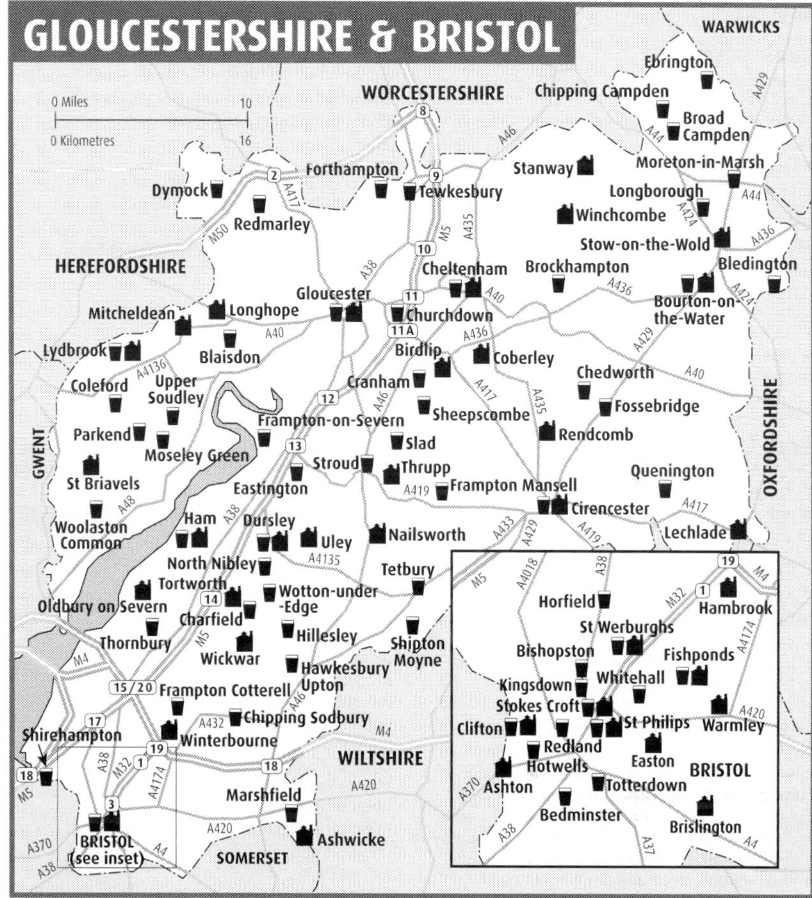

Blaisdon

Red Hart

GL17 0AH (centre of village; signed from A4136 E of Longhope or N of A48)

12-3, 6-11; 12-3, 7-11 Sun (01452) 830477

redhartinn.co.uk

4 changing beers (sourced nationally; often Bespoke, Kingstone, Wye Valley) H

This lovely award-winning old pub has worn flagstones in the bar, a welcoming fireplace and a veritable plethora of memorabilia as decoration. Guest ales are usually LocAle, alongside a local cider or perry from Severn Cider. The fabulous restaurant is popular and it can get busy, so be prepared to mix it with a rack of lamb, not to mention free-range children, if meals encroach into the bar area. Families are welcome to use the well-tended garden. P

Bledington

King's Head

The Green, OX7 6XQ (off B4450 on village green)

11-11 (01608) 658365 kingsheadinn.net

Flying Monk Elmers; Hook Norton Hooky; 3 changing beers (sourced regionally; often Wye Valley) H

Delightful 16th-century stone-built inn overlooking the village green. The pub has original beams, an open inglenook log fire and high-back settles. This free house, with 12 comfortable letting rooms, is renowned for its wide range of ales and food. Bledington is about four miles from Stow-on-the-Wold, and has good local walks to nearby villages, with Kingham station close by. The two guest beers are selected from local brewers in Gloucestershire and Oxfordshire. CAMRA award winner and finalist in the 2017 Pub of the Year. Q P

Bourton-on-the-Water

Mousetrap Inn

Lansdowne, GL54 2AR (300yds W of village centre)

11.30-11; 12-11 Sun (01451) 820579

themousetrapinn.co.uk

4 changing beers (sourced locally; often Battledown, North Cotswold, Prescott) H

Recently refurbished, this traditional Cotswold stone free house in the Lansdowne area of Bourton, close to the centre, offers three changing local beers. Service is friendly, with a warm welcome for locals, tourists, children and dogs. Meals include breakfast. A patio area in front of the pub with tables and hanging baskets provides a suntrap in the summer. CAMRA North Cotswold Seasonal Pub of the Year for winter 2107.
Q P (801,855)

Bristol

Bank Tavern

8 John Street, BS1 2HR (take lane next to arcade on All Saints St)
12-midnight (1am Thu-Sat) (0117) 930 4691
banktavern.com
4 changing beers
Popular compact one-bar pub, hidden away near the old city wall. The four beers are often from microbrewers from the South-West or further afield, and can be of any style. Two real ciders change constantly. Quirky humour and many varied events define the pub, and it is a great alternative to the more predictable establishments all around. It has a quiz on Tuesday and live music on Thursday. Quality food is served 12-4pm (booking is advisable for the award-winning Sunday lunch).

Beer Emporium

13-15 King Street, BS1 4EF
12-2am; 1-midnight Sun (0117) 379 0333
thebeeremporium.net
12 changing beers
On historic King Street, this cellar bar is set in three tunnels – one containing the bar, seating and a modern stained-glass window skylight, one for seating only, and a third housing the kitchens. A lift makes it accessible to all. Up to 12 changing cask ales are served and a wide range of world bottled beers. There is also a bottle shop just inside the entrance. The food is authentic Italian pizza and pasta, with vegetarian and vegan options.

Bridge Inn

16 Passage Street, BS2 0JF
12-11 (1am Fri & Sat); 1.30-11 Sun (0117) 929 0942
Dark Star Hophead; 4 changing beers
A short waterside stroll from Temple Meads station, this small, friendly pub is a good place to start your visit to Bristol as it is close to the shopping centre and other good pubs. An adventurous choice of ales is available including seasonal favourites. Weekday lunches are served 12-3pm and free cheese 'n' cracker feasts on Sundays at 6pm. Music memorabilia adorn the walls and board games are available to play. Thirty malt whiskies and selected vodkas, gins and rums are also on offer, together with Belgian bottled beers. Outside tables increase capacity during good weather.

Christmas Steps

2 Christmas Steps, BS1 5BS
11-midnight (1am Fri & Sat); 12-11 Sun
(0117) 925 3077 thechristmassteps.com
5 changing beers
Just off the city centre, this fascinating pub has welcomed drinkers since the 17th century and is one of Bristol's heritage treasures. The compact, cosy drinking areas reveal many original features and the top level includes a dining area. The food and drink are sourced locally where possible. Five real ales in a variety of styles are served including Crack ales brewed locally for the pub, as well as two real ciders.

Commercial Rooms

43-45 Corn Street, BS1 1HT
8am-midnight (1am Fri & Sat) (0117) 927 9681
Greene King Abbot; Ruddles Best Bitter; 10 changing beers (often Bath Ales, Butcombe, Great Western)
This centrally located, Grade II-listed building dating from 1810 was Bristol's first Wetherspoon pub. It offers up to 10 guest beers, and food is served from 8am until 11pm. There is a quieter galleried room at the rear, but the main bar does get busy at peak times. The interior features Greek revival-style decor, a stunning ceiling with dome, portraits and memorabilia from its days as a businessmen's club. Wheelchair access is via the side entrance in Small Street. Q

Cornubia

142 Temple Street, BS1 6EN
12-11; 12-6 Sun (0117) 925 4415 thecornubia.co.uk
8 changing beers
A cosy small pub with two linked rooms adorned with much patriotic memorabilia as well as countless pumpclips. Eight real ales are served, plus changing ciders in spring and summer. Pork pies and pasties are usually available. You can also

REAL ALE BREWERIES

Arbor Bristol
Bath Bristol: Warmley
Battledown Cheltenham
Beer Bores Ashwicke (brewing suspended)
Bespoke Mitcheldean
Brewhouse & Kitchen Bristol: Clifton
Brewhouse & Kitchen Cheltenham
Brewhouse & Kitchen Gloucester
Bristol Beer Factory Bristol: Ashton
Brythonic St Briavels
Ciren Cirencester
Clavell & Hind Birdlip (NEW)
Cocksure Oldbury-on-Severn
Corinium Cirencester
Cosmic Bristol: Fishponds (NEW)
Cotswold Bourton-on-the-Water
Cotswold Lion Coberley
Croft Bristol: Stokes Croft (NEW)
Dawkins Bristol: Easton
DEYA Cheltenham
Donnington Stow-on-the-Wold
Fierce & Noble Bristol (NEW)
Force Cirencester
Gloucester Gloucester
Goff's Winchcombe
Good Chemistry Bristol: St Philips
Great Western Bristol: Hambrook
Hal's Dursley (NEW)
Halfpenny Lechlade (brewing suspended)
Hillside Longhope
Incredible Bristol: Brislington
Keep Nailsworth
King Street Bristol
Left Handed Giant Bristol: St Philip's
Lydbrook Valley Lydbrook (NEW)
Moor Bristol
New Bristol Bristol
Prescott Cheltenham
Severn Tortworth (NEW)
Stanway Stanway
Stroud Thrupp
TAP Rendcomb
Three Engineers Winterbourne (NEW)
Tiley's Ham
Uley Uley
Wickwar Wickwar
Wiper and True Bristol: St Werburghs
Zerodegrees Bristol

enjoy a wide range of board games and books here. Live blues takes place on Thursday evenings, when anyone can come along and jam, and live bands some Saturdays. The outside area has seating and a boules piste.

Famous Royal Navy Volunteer

17-18 King Street, BS1 4EF
12-midnight (1am Fri & Sat) ☎ (0117) 316 9237
navyvolunteer.co.uk
8 changing beers H
The Volley, on historic King Street, is a much-loved part of Bristol's heritage. This listed 17th-century building has four bar areas, one of which is for dining. Its beers are available in third, half, two-third and pint measures from unmarked pumps. The wooden boards to the right of the bar show the current selection, but be aware that only the eight ales shown at the far right of the boards are served from the cask. Wheelchair access is via the rear entrance.

Gryphon

41 Colston Street, BS1 5AP
4-11.30 (1am Fri); 1-1am Sat; 6-11 Sun ☎ 07894 239567
6 changing beers H
A shrine to dark beer and great rock/heavy metal music. Posters, guitars and many pumpclips adorn the walls. Triangular in shape due to its corner plot, and just a few yards uphill from the Colston Hall, it has six handpumps dispensing rapidly changing brews, many dark and often strong. Live bands sometimes play upstairs and beer festivals are in March and September. Food is served evenings Wednesday to Saturday. It may open earlier on Sundays. Children and dogs are admitted at the licensee's discretion.

Lime Kiln

17 St Georges Road, BS1 5UU (behind City Hall – formerly Council House)
12-11; 12-10.30 Sun ☎ 07903 068256
6 changing beers H
Cosy city-centre free house just off College Green. The six handpumps dispense changing beers in a variety of styles. Many of the breweries featured are seldom seen in Bristol, but beers from local breweries are often stocked. There is also at least one traditional cider. You are welcome to bring your own food. A St Georges Road beer festival is usually held twice a year in conjunction with the nearby Three Tuns and Bag of Nails pubs. Runner-up local CAMRA Pub of the Year 2017.
P

No.1 Harbourside L

1 Canons Road, BS1 5UH
11-midnight (1am Fri & Sat); 12-10 Sun
☎ (0117) 929 1100 no1harbourside.co.uk
5 changing beers (often Arbor, Bristol Beer Factory, New Bristol) H
Modern pub/diner on the covered walkway on the quayside of the floating harbour and handy for city-centre buses. With early opening it is ideal for morning coffee, snacking or a cheeky early beer. Five handpumps usually feature two Bristol Beer Factory beers and three guests, often from Arbor, supplemented by a good selection of bottled beers and changing ciders. There are some tables outside from where you can watch the ferry boats arriving and departing. Live music features late evenings Wednesday to Saturday.

Seven Stars

1 Thomas Lane, BS1 6JG (just off Victoria St)
12-11; 12-10.30 Sun ☎ (0117) 927 2845 7stars.co.uk
8 changing beers H
Many who live miles away call this small free house their local. It has a pool table, a rock-oriented jukebox and outdoor seating. Eight pumps dispense a full range of styles and strengths from near and far plus ciders and perries. Quality acoustic acts play on weekend afternoons. Beeriodicals are held on the first Monday to Thursday of every month, with up to 20 beers from a different county each time. Anti-slavery campaigner Thomas Clarkson used this pub as a base during his research into the trade.

Three Tuns

78 St George's Road, BS1 5UR (300yds from Bristol Cathedral towards Hotwells)
12-11 (midnight Thu-Sat); 12-10.30 Sun
☎ (0117) 329 4310 the3tuns.com
7 changing beers (often Arbor) H
This independent pub has seven handpumps dispensing the full range of beer styles, with at least one from Arbor Ales and the rest from top-rated British brewers, as well as many unusual bottled beers and several ciders. The L-shaped interior has scrubbed wooden tables and mixed seating, plus a covered heated rear patio featuring an impressive mural by artist Silent Hobo. A small range of quality bar food is served. Quizzes take place, in addition to magic shows, live Irish music, movies and more.

Volunteer Tavern

9 New Street, BS2 9DX (very close to main Cabot Circus car park across carriageway from shops)
4 (12 Thu)-11; 12-midnight Fri & Sat; 1-10 Sun
☎ (0117) 955 8498 volunteertavern.co.uk
6 changing beers H
Tucked away in a side street but close to Cabot Circus shops and convenient for Old Market and its bus interchange, this pub dates from 1670 and is listed. There are always six changing beers including at least one dark one, plus two changing ciders. Live music features every Sunday evening. The large, fully enclosed, paved and heated garden is enjoyed all year round. Food is served every day with regular pop-up kitchens from local chefs and theme nights. Sunday roasts are hugely popular and booking ahead is advised. Local CAMRA Pub of the Year 2016.

Bristol: Bedminster

Bristol Beer Factory Tap Room

291 North Street, BS3 1JU
12-7 (9 Thu & Fri); 10-9 Sat; closed Sun ☎ (0117) 902 6317
Bristol Beer Factory Nova, Fortitude; 2 changing beers (often Bristol Beer Factory) H
Comfortable brewery taproom showcasing four rotating real ales from Bristol Beer Factory. Visitors are welcome to bring in food from local North Street bakeries/shops and the Tap Room provides both on and off sales. Regular beer events, both for the Bristol Beer Club and the general public, are held. The venue is open on a Sunday if Bristol City FC or Bristol RFC are at home at Ashton Gate, a short walk away. (24)

Hare

51 North Street, BS3 1EN

4-11 (midnight Fri); 2-midnight Sat; 2-11 Sun

(0117) 966 5740 theharepub.co.uk

Twisted Oak Leveret; 2 changing beers H

Narrow and homely pub up five steep steps from street level, serving two ever-changing guest beers as well as Twisted Oak Leveret (brewed especially for The Hare). The bar area and open back room are compact, with a steep flight of stairs leading to a partially covered rear garden patio area behind the pub which is used for barbecues in the summer. Pork pies and sausage rolls are available on the bar, but they are popular and often run out.

(24)

Spotted Cow

139 North Street, BS3 1EZ

12-midnight (11 Mon); 12-1am Fri & Sat; 12-11 Sun

(0117) 963 4433 thespottedcowbristol.com

Butcombe Gold; 4 changing beers (often Bristol Beer Factory, Milk Street, Tiny Rebel) H

An original Georges and Co Ltd sign is still prominent over the entrance to this single-bar pub that was for a while called 139 Degrees North. Guest beers usually come from independent breweries. A pleasant refurbishment has created a chilled atmosphere, with subdued lighting and mood music played at a non-intrusive volume. Quality food is sourced mainly from local suppliers, served lunchtimes (not Mon) and evenings. The pub has a sizeable garden which is busy and popular in the summertime.

(24)

Victoria Park

66 Raymend Road, BS3 4QW (250yds off St Johns Lane)

12-11 (11.30 Fri & Sat); 12-10.30 Sun (0117) 330 6043

thevictoriapark.co.uk

3 changing beers (often Bristol Beer Factory, Ringwood) H

A thriving red-brick pub in a residential area, but with the feel of a cosy country pub inside. There is a large, south-facing garden/patio area to the rear which features a wood-fired pizza oven and stunning views towards Dundry Hill. Three pumps serve quality beers, sometimes including a dark offering, and there is a large selection of bottled ales. Food is available all day and the seasonal award-winning menu is displayed on a chalkboard. Events take place throughout the week including films, a book club and a quiz.

(90,91)

Bristol: Bishopston

Annexe

Seymour Road, BS7 9EQ (directly behind Sportsman pub)

11.30-3, 5-11.30; 11.30-11.30 Sat; 12-11 Sun

(0117) 949 3931 the-annexe.co.uk

Fuller's London Pride; Otter Amber; Sharp's Doom Bar; Skinner's Betty Stogs; Timothy Taylor Landlord; Wye Valley HPA; 2 changing beers H

Community pub near Gloucestershire county cricket ground and not far from the Memorial Stadium, which means it can be busy on match days. The spacious interior also has a large conservatory/ family room to one side. Several TVs show live sport, including one on the partially covered patio outside. One or two of the guest beers can be fairly adventurous. Good-value wholesome food is served lunchtimes, with pizzas in the evening until 10.45pm (10.15pm Sun). No dogs allowed, even on the patio.

Bristol: Clifton

Eldon House

6 Lower Clifton Hill, BS8 1BT (off top of Jacobs Wells Rd)

12-11 (midnight Fri & Sat) (0117) 922 1271

theeldonhouse.com

Bath Ales Gem; 4 changing beers (often Bristol Beer Factory) H

Cosy end-of-terrace pub close to the busy Clifton Triangle area. Get off a bus near the top of Park Street and head a short way down Jacobs Wells Road. Four or five real ales are sold, including guests from well-chosen independent brewers, often local but occasionally from further afield. Good food including pizza is served daily and Sunday roasts are popular. Many events are hosted, including a Monday quiz and live music every Sunday and occasional Saturdays. The pub sometimes stays open later than advertised at weekends.

Lansdown

8 Clifton Road, BS8 1AF

4-11; 12-midnight Fri & Sat; 12-10.30 Sun

(0117) 973 4949 thelansdown.com

House beer (by Otter); 5 changing beers (sourced regionally; often Cheddar Ales, Great Western, St Austell) H

Traditional pub with a strong real ale offering, mainly from South-West breweries. Beers change every few months, but examples from Great Western and Cheddar Ales are frequently among the five or six on the bar, and there is usually a good mix of styles. An upstairs lounge/dining room is available for functions. Good food is served weekend lunchtimes and every evening. The courtyard garden, which is heated and covered in winter, shows rugby (Freeview) on a big screen and is the venue for occasional beer festivals.

(8,9)

Victoria

2 Southleigh Road, BS8 2BH (off St Pauls Rd)

4-11; 1-11 Sat; 12-10.30 Sun (0117) 974 5675

Dawkins Bristol Blonde, Bristol Best, Easton IPA; 3 changing beers (often Dawkins, Tiny Rebel) H

Cosy 19th-century Grade II-listed Dawkins tavern, tucked away just off the bottom of Whiteladies Road next door to the Clifton Lido. Seven handpumps offer beers from the Dawkins Brewery as well as some from independent breweries. A changing Tiny Rebel beer is often available as well as a dark beer and two real ciders. Two beer festivals are held each year. Parking close by can be difficult.

Bristol: Fishponds

Snuffy Jack's

800 Fishponds Road, BS16 3TE

5-10; 12-11 Sat; 12-4.30 Sun (0117) 965 5158

8 changing beers G

Bristol's third micropub, opened in 2017, is already popular despite a high number of other pubs and bars nearby. The name relates to a former head miller at the nearby Snuff Mills. Between four and eight real ales are served on gravity from a chilled cabinet, plus two or more changing real ciders. Local beers feature plus some from further afield, with all beer styles offered. Food is limited to bar snacks. Located conveniently close to multiple bus routes with direct links to many areas. Q

Bristol: Horfield

Drapers Arms

447 Gloucester Road, BS7 8TZ

5-9.30; 4-9.30 Fri; 12-9.30 Sat thedrapersarms.co.uk

5 changing beers G

Bristol's first micropub, opened in 2015, close to the Memorial Stadium and county cricket ground. It prides itself on an interesting and changing beer selection from in and around Bristol, with up to eight real ales served by gravity, frequently including a dark ale, and three real ciders. Wine and bar snacks are also available. There is no music or TV, but there is a warm welcome and a convivial, cosy atmosphere, with a focus on conversation. Local CAMRA Pub of the Year 2017. Q

Bristol: Hotwells

Bag of Nails

141 St Georges Road, BS1 5UW (5 mins walk from cathedral towards Hotwells)

12-11; 12-10.30 Sun

9 changing beers H

Close to the floating harbour, this small terraced free house dates from the 1860s and serves up to 10 changing cask ales, mainly from microbreweries, as well as a real cider. An eccentric list of pub policies includes no children or idiot pub crawls. The interior features terracotta colours, portholes in the floor, many pub cats roaming free, and eclectic music from a proper record player. Board games for the customers and toys for the cats make the pub a fun way to spend an evening. A quiz takes place every Thursday.

Grain Barge

Mardyke Wharf, Hotwell Road, BS8 4RU (moored on opp bank to SS Great Britain)

12-11 (11.30 Thu-Sat) (0117) 929 9347

grainbarge.co.uk

Bristol Beer Factory Nova, Fortitude; 3 changing beers (often Arbor, Bristol Beer Factory, New Bristol) H

Easily accessed on foot, by bus or ferry, this moored boat was built in 1936 and converted into a floating pub by Bristol Beer Factory in 2007. It boasts great views of the SS Great Britain, the floating harbour and passing boats from the top deck. Guest beers usually come from local breweries. Food nights include Wednesday pie and a pint, Thursday steak club and Sunday roasts. Other activities include a Monday night quiz, a Tuesday open mic night and live music on Thursdays in the downstairs Hold Bar.

Merchants Arms

5 Merchants Road, BS8 4PZ

4-11; 12-11 Fri-Sun (0117) 907 3047

4 changing beers H

Free-of-tie traditional pub close to the Cumberland Basin selling mainly South-West cask-conditioned ales. This hostelry is famous for home-made Scotch eggs, hand-finished pork pies and real Cornish pasties. Both of its rooms are furnished with dark-wood seating and there is a real log fire in the front room. Some sport is shown on the TV and there is a range of board games available. Regular poetry nights take place. There is a small free car park 50 yards behind the pub. Q P

Bristol: Kingsdown

Hare on the Hill

41 Thomas Street North, BS2 8LX

closed Mon; 5-11 (1am Fri); 3-1am Sat; 12-8 Sun

07480 624212 thehareonthehill.com

Moor Beer Nor'Hop; 4 changing beers (often Bristol Beer Factory, Butcombe, Good Chemistry) H

Small street-corner local with a traditional green-tile frontage. Five handpumps offer a range of locally brewed beers including one or two from the landlord's own Croft Ales. Food is provided by changing pop-up kitchens during the week, with roasts on Sunday. The pub is simply furnished with a light, airy feel throughout the stripped-back wood interior. Three TVs show big sporting events and there is occasional live music including Wednesday open mic and a pub quiz on Thursday.

Robin Hood

56 St Michael's Hill, BS2 8DX

4-11; 12-1am Fri & Sat; 12-10 Sun (0117) 929 9719

robinhoodbristol.co.uk

6 changing beers (sourced regionally; often Bristol Beer Factory, Cheddar Ales, Moor Beer) H

Originally a grocer's but a licensed premises since 1841, this Grade II-listed pub has a lovely arched-window frontage. Inside there are light magnolia walls, wooden flooring and furniture, and a pull-down screen at the back showing sports events. There are six handpumps serving brews from local breweries as well as from further afield, plus a traditional cider. Weekly events include a Wednesday quiz and live music on Thursday. Sunday roasts are served and pop-up kitchens provide food in the evening.

(9,72)

Bristol: Redland

Chums

22 Chandos Road, BS6 6PF

4-10.30; 12-11 Fri & Sat; 12-10 Sun (0117) 973 1498

chumsmicropub.co.uk

6 changing beers (often Butcombe, Cheddar Ales, Plain) H

Bristol's second micropub opened in 2016 in converted shop premises. Conversation rules here, with no TV, gaming machines or Wi-Fi; electronic communication devices should be used with discretion. Real ales are dispensed from six handpumps – two from changing breweries – always including a dark ale. Six traditional ciders are also served as well as a selection of wines and spirits. Simple bar snacks include filled rolls and cockles. Last orders are called half an hour before closing time. Local CAMRA Pub of the Year 2018. Q

Bristol: St Philips

Barley Mow

39 Barton Road, BS2 0LF (400yds from rear exit of Temple Meads station over footbridge)

12-11 (11.30 Fri & Sat); 12-10 Sun (0117) 930 4709

barleymowbristol.com

Bristol Beer Factory Nova, Fortitude; 6 changing beers (often Bristol Beer Factory) Ⓗ
Bristol Beer Factory's flagship pub is less than 10 minutes' walk from the rear exit of Temple Meads station. Eight handpumps offer three beers from the brewery plus five changing guests of varying styles from all over the UK. There is also an extensive bottled beer selection from around the world. Occasional beer-related events are held, along with a regular Monday night quiz. A small menu of quality food changes frequently and includes vegan dishes. Dogs are welcome in the rear beer garden. Runner-up local CAMRA Pub of the Year 2018. (506)

Bristol: St Werburghs

Duke of York

2 Jubilee Road, BS2 9RS (S side of Mina Rd park)
5-11; 4-midnight Fri; 3-midnight Sat; 3-11 Sun
☎ (0117) 941 3677
4 changing beers (sourced locally; often Arbor, Electric Bear, Moor Beer) Ⓗ
This well-hidden free house serves an eclectic clientele. Visit at night to experience the warm glow of the grotto-like interior. The decor comprises fairy lights, odd memorabilia, wooden floors, a refurbished skittle alley, local art and more. There are two rooms, with an extra bar upstairs offering a quite different feel. The exterior side wall features a Dali-esque '70s album cover mural depicting the Grand Old Duke of York nursery rhyme. Four handpumps serve unusual beers from local microbreweries plus others from the South-West. (5)

Bristol: Shirehampton

Lamplighters

Station Road, BS11 9XA
11-11 ☎ (0117) 279 3754 thelamplighters.co.uk
Bath Ales Gem; 3 changing beers (sourced regionally) Ⓗ
The friends of the Lamplighters worked hard to reopen this historic pub, which had been closed for several years. Built by a Mr Toy, a contractor for lighting half the parishes in Bristol, as his country residence, it became a hotel in 1810. Spacious and comfortable, this multi-levelled pub is able to accommodate sizeable groups and can hold functions. There is a pleasant garden overlooking the river. Good food is served every day and real cider from April to September, when it replaces one of the three guest ales.
P

Bristol: Stokes Croft

Canteen

80 Stokes Croft, BS1 3QY
11-midnight (1am Fri & Sat); 11-11 Sun
☎ (0117) 923 2017 canteenbristol.co.uk
5 changing beers Ⓗ
Situated inside a converted 1970s office block (which is now a cultural community centre), this café-style bar offers a wide range of drink, food and music. Basic furniture of plywood tables and steel-tube chairs sits in an open-plan area with a stage at the far end which hosts live music every evening. A long bar runs along the back wall serving five real ales, usually local ones, of varying strengths and styles, and up to three real ciders. An open kitchen provides a range of good value, locally sourced food. Outside a large patio overlooks the main road, with ample cycle parking.

Crofters Rights

117-119 Stokes Croft, BS1 3RW
5-midnight (1am Thu; 2am Fri); 2-2am Sat; 2-midnight Sun
☎ (0117) 231 0079
5 changing beers Ⓖ
This lively L-shaped and high-ceilinged pub, with stripped-back decor and a mixture of seating areas, offers up to five cask ales, sourced locally and from across the country. The cask ales come in a range of strengths and styles, and the real ciders are distinguished by the wooden tap handles. Pizzas are available from the side kitchen, which also has hanging cycle parking. A separate back room hosts a wide variety of events, live music, DJs, open mic and film nights.

Bristol: Totterdown

Oxford

120-122 Oxford Street, BS3 4RL
4-11; 3-midnight Fri; 2-midnight Sat; 12-11 Sun
☎ (0117) 907 5845
St Austell Tribute; 4 changing beers (often Arbor, Tapstone, Tiny Rebel) Ⓗ
Small single-bar urban and residents' pub. To one side of the central bar is an area with a stage and TV. The guest beers are often adventurous, usually from local breweries, but a large range of pumpclips on the walls shows a wide variety of guest beers from small to medium-sized breweries in the Bristol area and slightly further afield. Regular live music includes open mic, bands and jam sessions.

Bristol: Whitehall

Red Lion

206 Whitehall Road, BS5 9BP
4 (12 Thu)-12.30am; 12-3am Fri & Sat; 12-midnight Sun
☎ (0117) 329 1316
4 changing beers Ⓗ
Built at the beginning of the 20th century, this basic pub, which has a very late licence, has two rooms, one of which can be booked for private events. There is a pool table, dartboard, a table tennis table put up upon request, plus a real fire and a beer garden. The real ales change constantly, with least three during the week and a fourth at weekends – mostly unusual ones from microbreweries, normally including at least one dark beer, plus two real ciders. Live music features regularly. (6,7)

Broad Campden

Bakers Arms L

GL55 6UR (signed off B4081, at NW end of village)
12-3, 6-11; 12-11 Sat & Sun ☎ (01386) 840515
bakersarmscampden.com
North Cotswold Windrush Ale; Stanway Stanney Bitter; Wickwar BOB; Wye Valley HPA; 2 changing beers (sourced locally) Ⓗ
Fine old village local and genuine free house, first licensed as a public house in 1724. A photograph of the building in 1905 shows it as the village bakery and grain store. It boasts Cotswold stone walls, exposed beams and a fine inglenook. Excellent

food is available in the bar and dining room extension and there is a large garden and children's play area. Local guest beers alongside regular ales are served from its handsome oak bar. Local CAMRA Pub of the Year 2017.
Q

Brockhampton

Craven Arms

Kingsbury Street, GL54 5XQ (off A436 in centre of village in a cul-de-sac)
closed Mon; 12-3, 6-11; 12-11 Sat; 12-5 Sun
(01242) 820410 thecravenarms.co.uk
Otter Bitter; 3 changing beers (sourced regionally; often Butcombe, XT) H
A 17th-century family-run free house set in an attractive hillside village with outstanding views and walks. It has a cosy bar area with an open fire and a dining room separated by church-style stone windows. Four carefully selected beers are well looked after by the owner-chef. It is a regular Guide pub and a well-managed gem, run by a friendly family who organise functions for locals each month and a summer beer festival. Local CAMRA Pub of the Year runner-up 2018.
Q P

Charfield

Pear Tree Micropub

6 Wotton Road, GL12 8TP (on B4058 1½ miles from jct14 on M5)
2 (5 Mon & Tue)-9.30; 2-10.30 Sat; 12-9.30 Sun
(01454) 260663
Great Western Maiden Voyage; 3 changing beers (sourced regionally; often Abbey, Cheddar Ales, St Austell) G
This small one-roomed pub is popular with locals and visitors. The restored tiled flooring, the small wooden bar, the way the beers are dispensed through wooden casks mounted in an old fireplace, and the humorous murals covering most of the walls make it a most attractive location for drinkers. It offers up to four beers at busy times, usually from local and regional breweries. There is a large fenced seating area at the front.
Q P

Chedworth

Seven Tuns

Queen Street, GL54 4AE (NE of village near church)
12-3, 6-11; 12-11 Sat & Sun (01285) 720630
seventuns.co.uk
Hook Norton Hooky; Otter Amber; TAP Old Dairy Gold; 2 changing beers (sourced locally; often Box Steam, TAP) H
Attractive 17th-century stone-built village pub, recently reopened as a free house, with an excellent range of home-made food and local ales. There are two bars. It has an old, restored water wheel in the garden, where a stream flows noisily. The pub is within walking distance of the Roman villa and is thus on the path of many walkers and ramblers. Q P

Cheltenham

Charlton Kings Club

21 Church Street, Charlton Kings, GL53 8AP (opp church)
12-3, 6-11; 11.30-3, 6-midnight Fri; 12-midnight Sat; 12-11 Sun (01242) 525511
4 changing beers (often Butcombe) H
Popular village club in the heart of Charlton Kings, with a large lounge, separate sports bar and a skittle alley on the ground floor, plus a large function room and snooker room upstairs. Regular live music is played upstairs (Vonnies Blues Club) and also in the main lounge. Four regularly changing beers are sold, generally at least one from Butcombe, with guests sourced nationally. A beer festival is held annually in November. A small fee is charged for entry but card-carrying CAMRA members are welcome for free for an occasional visit. Bar snacks are available. P

Cheltenham Motor Club

Upper Park Street, GL52 6SA (first right off Hales Rd from London Rd lights, 100yds on right; pedestrian access from A40 via Crown Passage opp Sandford Mill Rd jct)
6-midnight; 12-midnight Sat; 12-3, 7-midnight Sun
(01242) 522590 cheltmc.com
Stroud Tom Long; 5 changing beers (often Moor Beer) H
Visitors are welcome at this friendly club just off London Road. It was National Club of the Year in 2013 and has won more than 17 other awards. Five regularly changing ales from across the country are served plus regular local Stroud Tom Long, at least one KeyKeg, and three real ciders, plus a range of bottled Belgian beers. A beer festival is held annually plus Meet the Brewer/takeover evenings. Home to local darts and pool teams.
Q P (B,51)

Jolly Brewmaster

39 Painswick Road, GL50 2EZ (off A40 Suffolk Rd, between Suffolks and Tivoli, 200yds S along Painswick Rd)
2.30-11; 12-11 Sat; 12-10.30 Sun (01242) 772261
7 changing beers (often Arbor, Bespoke, Moor Beer) H
Frequent and current local CAMRA Pub of the Year. Thirteen handpumps dispense a changing range of seven ales sourced nationally and six ciders. This busy and friendly community hub features original etched windows, a horseshoe bar and open fire. It is a traditional drinking pub with no food menu, but bar snacks such as pasties are generally available. The attractive courtyard garden is popular in the summer, with regular Friday barbecues. Quiz nights are Mondays and most Wednesdays.
Q (10,94U)

Kemble Brewery Inn

27 Fairview Street, GL52 2JF (off Northern ring road, jct of Fairview Rd/St Johns Avenue, turn left into Fairview St beside Machine Mart; pub is 100yds on right)
11-11 (midnight Fri & Sat); 12-11 Sun (01242) 701053
Wye Valley HPA, Butty Bach; 4 changing beers H
Small, popular, back-street local, hard to find but well worth the effort, fully refurbished in 2016. Originally a butcher's shop in 1845, it became a pub in 1847 and was soon producing ciders (hence the name), but not in recent times. Six ales are generally available from near and far, plus a cider. There is a small attractive walled garden to the rear. Guest chef night is Monday 7-9pm for charity.
Q

Moon Under Water

16-28 Bath Road, GL53 7HA (from the Strand, E end of High St, take Bath Rd; pub is 100yds on left)

8am-midnight (1am Fri & Sat) (01242) 583945
Greene King Abbot; Ruddles Best Bitter; Sharp's Doom Bar; 5 changing beers
An open-plan Lloyds No.1 just off the end of the pedestrianised high street. A decked area at the back overlooks the River Chelt and Sandford Park. Some five changing guest ales from breweries local to countrywide supplement the regular beers, plus Gwynt y Ddraig Black Dragon and Old Rosie ciders. The dance floor is only used Friday and Saturday from 8pm, with a generally quiet atmosphere at other times. Food is served 8am-11pm. Quiz night is Monday.

Sandford Park Alehouse

20 High Street, GL50 1DZ (E end of High St, past Strand on right)
12-midnight (11 Mon); 12-11 Sun (01242) 574517
spalehouse.co.uk
Oakham Citra; Purity Mad Goose; Wye Valley Butty Bach; 6 changing beers
Local CAMRA Pub of the Year 2016 and National Pub of the Year 2015, this smart contemporary alehouse has a U-shaped main bar area complete with bar billiards, a cosy front snug with a wood-burning stove and a large south-facing patio/garden. A function room/lounge showing TV sports is on the first floor. Ten handpumps feature constantly changing ales from microbreweries sourced nationally and locally, plus a cider and 16 speciality lagers and craft beers. Internal screens plus a website keep you informed.
Q

Strand

40-42 High Street, GL50 1EE (at E end of High St just past pedestrian area)
12-11 (midnight Fri & Sat); 12-10.30 Sun
(01242) 511848 strandpub.co.uk
5 changing beers (often Bespoke, Otter, Stroud)
Modern wine bar-style pub, offering five beers mainly from the region and generally featuring a brewery of the month, with one ale at £3 a pint, plus a cider. Good-value food is served daily, with gourmet burger night on a Wednesday from 6pm. An upstairs function room is available for hire, along with a cellar bar, home to live comedy and music nights. The large south-facing patio/garden provides a pleasant outdoor drinking area for those summer days.

Whittle Taps

1-3A Regent Street, GL50 1HE (near Everyman Theatre)
10-11 (midnight Fri & Sat) (01242) 222989
whittletaps.co.uk
4 changing beers (sourced nationally; often Purity, St Austell, Titanic)
This modern open-plan free house close to the Everyman Theatre (formerly the Slug & Lettuce) has recently undergone a major refurbishment in a rustic style. It now offers an extended range of up to four real ales plus six craft keg and three ciders. The new menu features an impressive range of pizzas, tapas and burgers as well as many other choices. It has good wheelchair access (one small step). Handy for pre-, post- or interval theatre drinks. It may stay open later Friday and Saturday if busy.

Chipping Campden

Eight Bells

Church Street, GL55 6JG
12-11; 12-10.30 Sun (01386) 840371
eightbellsinn.co.uk
Hook Norton Hooky; North Cotswold Best; Purity Pure UBU; Wye Valley HPA
The Eight Bells was originally built in the 14th century to house the stonemasons working on St James' Church, and was later used to store the peal of eight bells that were hung in the church tower. The inn was rebuilt using most of the original stone and timbers during the 17th century. What exists today is an outstanding example of a traditional Cotswolds inn, with a cobbled courtyard and an underground priest passage. Local CAMRA branch Pub of the Year runner-up 2018.
Q (21)

Chipping Sodbury

Horseshoe

2 High Street, BS37 6AH
10-11 (midnight Fri & Sat) (01454) 325658
horseshoechippingsodbury.co.uk
7 changing beers (sourced nationally)
One of the oldest buildings in the town and with a real cellar, this former stationery shop, then briefly a wine bar, was converted into a pub at the start of 2014. It serves seven beers, often unusual and mostly from the West Country, including dark and strong choices. The pub has three linked rooms with assorted furniture, a jukebox and TV, and a pleasant rear garden. A selection of freshly made rolls is available at lunchtimes.

Churchdown

Old Elm

Church Road, GL3 2ER
12-11 (midnight Thu & Fri); 10-midnight Sat; 10-10.30 Sun
(01452) 530961 theoldelminn.co.uk
Sharp's Atlantic; 4 changing beers (sourced locally; often Gloucester, Hillside, Stroud)
Set in the heart of the village, the Old Elm was fully refurbished before reopening in 2015, and is gaining a deserved reputation for its food (the menu features good vegetarian options). Serving five quality beers, including LocAles and some cider, it hosts lively quiz and music nights, and important rugby matches are shown in the sports bar. Families are welcome and the garden hosts a children's play area. There are five letting rooms.
P

Cirencester

Corinium Hotel

12 Gloucester Street, GL7 2DG (off A435 to N of town centre)
11-11; 11-10.30 Sun (01285) 659711
coriniumhotel.co.uk
3 changing beers (often Greene King, Wickwar)
An agreeable 2-star hotel with a discreet frontage entered via an attractive, narrow courtyard which leads into a slightly idiosyncratic interior, with a comfortable lounge area complete with woodburner. The varying thickness and layout of the walls hint at its heritage as an Elizabethan wool merchant's house. Guest ales include one LocAle. A modern vestibule leads into a smart dining room and the popular, pleasant suntrap of a garden at the rear of the premises. P

Drillmans Arms

34 Gloucester Road, GL7 2JY (on old A417, 200yds from A435 jct)
11-2.30, 5.30-11; 11-midnight Sat; 12-4, 7-10.30 Sun
(01285) 653892
Sharp's Doom Bar; 3 changing beers (sourced nationally) H
A lively Georgian inn, perched beside a busy thoroughfare, featuring a convivial lounge with woodburner, a pub games-dominated public bar and a popular skittle alley. Graced by the same landlady for over 25 years, this cracking free house features low-beamed ceilings, horse brasses, fresh flowers and brewery pictures, alongside well-priced pub lunches. An annual beer festival swamps the small front car park on August bank holiday weekends. It may close early some Sunday evenings. P

Marlborough Arms

1 Sheep Street, GL7 1QW
5-midnight; 12-midnight Fri-Sun
Box Steam Piston Broke; North Cotswold Windrush Ale; 6 changing beers (sourced nationally; often Corinium) H
This lively pub opposite the old GWR station is a real ale haven, offering eight beers from regional and microbreweries. Local CAMRA Cider Pub of the Year once again, it offers a plethora of interesting boxed ciders and perries. Brewery memorabilia adorn the walls, with pews and a deep-set fireplace adding character. The ceiling is disappearing behind the encroaching pumpclip collection. The rear patio is used for barbecues during its beer and cider festivals.

Coleford

Dog House Micropub

13-15 St John Street, GL16 8AP
5-10; 12-10 Sat; 12-3 Sun 07442 787015
thedoghousemicropub.co.uk
6 changing beers (sourced locally) H/G
Local CAMRA Pub of the Year, this friendly micropub is in an attractively fronted former chemist's shop, offering two changing ales on handpump, plus up to four more from the barrel, a couple of them usually LocAle. A cider fridge holds eight varying selections, plus a few Belgian beers. The pub's Facebook page highlights special events and music nights, which are invariably wonderful social occasions; with limited seating, arriving early is recommended. Q

Cranham

Black Horse Inn

GL4 8HP (off A46 or B4070)
12-3, 6-11.30 (10 Mon); 12-11.30 Fri & Sat; 12-9.30 Sun
(01452) 812217
4 changing beers (sourced regionally; often Wye Valley) H
A 17th-century stone-built free house almost hidden up a side lane in the village. It is a quiet idyll with no jukebox, TV or fruit machines, warmed by a proper fire. The lack of a reliable mobile phone signal in the village means that patrons here indulge in the traditional pursuit of conversation with friends, strangers and walkers taking a break after exploring the myriad woodland paths nearby. It welcomes dogs with well-behaved owners.
Q P

Dursley

New Inn

82-84 Woodmancote, GL11 4AJ (on A4135 Tetbury Road)
closed Mon-Wed; 2.30 (5 Thu)-11 (01453) 519288
newinnwoodmancote.co.uk
4 changing beers (sourced regionally; often Wye Valley) H
Known as a dog-friendly establishment, where the pub Labrador often helps provide the greeting, this welcoming, comfortable hostelry features a large L-shaped public bar with tiled floor and a smaller lounge. It serves an eclectic selection of regularly changing guest beers, usually from smaller local breweries, and often requested by regulars. There is a spacious suntrap of a garden at the rear which is popular on sunny days. Food is limited to the occasional freshly made roll. P

Old Spot Inn

2 Hill Road, GL11 4JQ (by bus station and free car park)
12-11 (01453) 542870 oldspotinn.co.uk
Uley Old Ric; 7 changing beers (sourced nationally) H
Excellent free house dating from 1776, serving great ales, ciders and perries. Named after the Gloucestershire Old Spot pig, a porcine theme blends with the extensive brewery memorabilia, low ceilings, wood-burning stoves and welcoming staff to create a convivial atmosphere. There is an attractive garden and a heated covered area. Freshly prepared food is served 12-3pm (4pm Sun). On the Cotswold Way, it is popular with walkers, and hosts regular events in the evenings.
Q

Dymock

Beauchamp Arms

GL18 2AQ (on B4216)
7-11 Mon; 11-2.30, 6-11; 12-3, 7-11 Sun
(01531) 890266 beauchamparmsdymock.co.uk
2 changing beers (often Wye Valley) H
On the Gloucestershire/Herefordshire border, this inn is one of the few parish-owned pubs in the country. It is one of the focal points of the parish and is a genuine village pub that warmly welcomes families and the visitors who come to enjoy the good food, fine beers and friendly company. It has three rooms and a log fire.
Q P

Eastington

Old Badger Inn

Alkerton Road, GL10 3AT (on Spring Hill)
12-11; 12-10.30 Sun (01453) 822892
oldbadgerinn.co.uk
Stroud Budding; Uley Bitter; Wye Valley Butty Bach; 4 changing beers (sourced regionally) H
Formerly The Victoria – closed by Punch in 2010 – the pub was reopened as a free house after being sympathetically renovated, modernised and extended. It was acquired by Wickwar in 2018. The large single bar features a wood-burning stove, with smaller rooms on either side plus a restaurant area – the pub has a formidable reputation for food. The walls are covered with brewery and other memorabilia. Outside there is a covered and heated patio and a large garden.
Q P (61,401)

Ebrington

Ebrington Arms 🄻

GL55 6NH (off B4035 in centre of village by green)
12-11 ☎ (01386) 593223 theebringtonarms.co.uk
North Cotswold Moreton Mild; 3 changing beers (sourced regionally) 🄷
A 17th-century Cotswold stone-built inn in a beautiful village with excellent walks. It has a cosy bar with a lovely open fireplace and six handpumps, three dispensing the pub's own Yubby ales. An excellent range of food is served from local suppliers, available seven days a week. It has five en-suite rooms, one with a four-poster bed. The Ebrington is a regular Guide entry and a sister pub to the Killingworth Castle in Wotton, Oxfordshire. It is a class-leading family-run pub with enthusiastic staff. P

Forthampton

Lower Lode Inn 🄻

GL19 4RE (follow sign to Forthampton from A438 Tewkesbury to Ledbury road) SO8788231809
12-midnight (2am Fri & Sat) ☎ (01684) 293224
lowerlodeinn.co.uk
Sharp's Doom Bar; 4 changing beers (often Bespoke, Brains, Malvern Hills) 🄷
Blessed with views across the River Severn to Tewkesbury Abbey, this attractive 15th-century brick-built establishment, with its three acres of lawns, is a popular stopover for boats and a Camping and Caravan Club site. Food advertised as simple and wholesome is excellent quality and value for money. It holds a beer festival in September. A small ferry operates from the Tewkesbury side from Easter to mid-September. Day fishing is available, plus en-suite accommodation. Opening times are reduced in winter so check the website.
QP

Fossebridge

Inn at Fossebridge

GL54 3JS (on A429)
12-11 ☎ (01285) 720721 fossebridgeinn.co.uk
Butcombe Original; North Cotswold Windrush Ale; Wadworth 6X; 2 changing beers (sourced locally) 🄷
In this pretty hamlet the Fosse Way drops into the Cotswolds valley of the River Coln, an Area of Outstanding Natural Beauty. This attractive one-bar inn boasts old timbers, a fine flagstone floor and open fires. It also benefits from an outstanding four-acre garden with a lake and river. A selection of regional ales and guests from local breweries can be enjoyed in cosy surroundings. Local CAMRA Pub of the Year 2018. QP

Frampton Cotterell

Rising Sun

43 Ryecroft Road, BS36 2HN
11.30-11.30; 12-11 Sun ☎ (01454) 772330
gwbrewery.co.uk/rising-sun
Draught Bass; Great Western Maiden Voyage, Classic Gold, Moose River; 2 changing beers 🄷
A longstanding Guide entry, this village local has a cosy log-burning stove. A single bar, with slate pillars and flagstone floors, attracts locals, and there is a refurbished restaurant in the warm conservatory. An extensive menu offers lunchtime snacks and more substantial evening meals. The pub is the brewery tap for the Great Western Brewing Company, and the guest beers are usually from small independent brewers. The skittle alley can also be used for private functions.
QP(46,82)

Frampton Mansell

Crown Inn

GL6 8JG (off A419 Cirencester to Stroud road opp Jolly Nice café & farm shop)
12-11 ☎ (01285) 760601 thecrowninn-cotswolds.co.uk
Uley Old Ric; Wickwar Cotswold Way; 2 changing beers (often Sharp's) 🄷
This thriving village local dates back to 1633 when it was a cider house with a slaughterhouse next door. The three rooms feature exposed stone walls and wooden beams, with an open fire in each. In summer lighted candles replace the fires. The suntrap front garden offers fine views over the Golden Valley. Families are welcome and there are children's books available. Good food is served. Attached is a modern 12-bedroom hotel annexe with ample car parking. P

Frampton-on-Severn

Three Horseshoes 🄻

The Green, GL2 7DY (off B4071)
11.30-2, 5.30-11 (1am Fri); 11.30-1am Sat; 11.30-10 Sun
☎ (01452) 742100 threehorseshoespub.co.uk
Sharp's Doom Bar; Timothy Taylor Landlord; Uley Bitter 🄷
Atmospheric 19th-century two-bar pub originally built by a farrier at the south end of England's longest village green. The food at this rural community venue is home-cooked, especially their unique 3-Shu pie, which is freshly baked to order. Both bars have coal fires, and dogs are welcome in the flagstoned public bar. Evening jamming sessions are popular (largely biased towards folk music), as are pasty baking competitions, conker contests and veggie Olympics. A double boules court hosts annual championships.
Q

Gloucester

Brewhouse & Kitchen

Unit R1, St Anne Walk, Gloucester Quay, GL1 5SH
11-11 (midnight Fri & Sat); 11-10.30 Sun
☎ (01452) 222965 brewhouseandkitchen.com/venue/gloucester-quays
Brewhouse & Kitchen Stevedore, Shed Head; 2 changing beers (often Brewhouse & Kitchen Gloucester) 🄷
Based in the bustling Gloucester Quays development, this smart bar and restaurant is part of the growing Brewhouse & Kitchen chain, brewing its own range of ales on-site. Customers can sit in comfort and enjoy a quality beer (with or without a meal), while watching the brewing process. On a fine day you can relax outside in the seating area by the side of the Gloucester-Sharpness Canal.

Fountain Inn 🄻

53 Westgate Street, GL1 2NW
11-11; 12-11 Sun ☎ (01452) 522562
thefountaininngloucester.com

Bristol Beer Factory Independence; Dartmoor Jail Ale; St Austell Tribute; 4 changing beers (often Butcombe) Ⓗ
An interesting 17th-century inn on the site of an alehouse, known to have existed in 1216. A passage leads from Westgate Street into a courtyard that is ablaze with flowers in the summer. The Cathedral Bar has a panelled ceiling and carved stone fireplace. The Orange Room serves as an overflow area or as a room for private functions. There is usually a LocAle beer or two, and the food menu is popular, especially on match days. ❀◑♿♣🐾📶

King Edward VII ✔

47 Old Cheltenham Road, Longlevens, GL2 0AN
🕒 11.30-11 (midnight Thu-Sat); 10-11 Sun
☎ (01452) 381273
Bath Ales Gem; Ember Pale Ale; Wadworth 6X; 2 changing beers (sourced nationally) Ⓗ
Red-brick pub built in 1907 by Mitchells & Butlers and renamed after Edward VII's visit to Gloucester in 1909. This large, popular community asset was given a total refit in 2001, featuring some practical modern styling and a large central bar layout, while keeping a real fire. The menu choices go down well with the locals, and the regularly changing guest ales are from the Ember Inns cask list. An attractive garden graces the front. ❀◑♿P🚌(94)🐾📶

Pelican Inn Ⓛ ✔

4 St Mary's Street, GL1 2QR (WNW of cathedral)
🕒 11-11.30 ☎ (01452) 387877
Wye Valley Bitter, HPA, Golden Ale, Butty Bach Ⓗ, **Wholesome Stout** Ⓗ/Ⓖ; **4 changing beers (sourced regionally; often Wye Valley)** Ⓗ
Local CAMRA Pub of the Year again, it was licensed as an alehouse in the 17th century. People believe that some of its beams are from Drake's Golden Hind, which began life as the Pelican. Rescued and refurbished by Wye Valley Brewery in 2012, its popularity has grown steadily, with the single bar dominated by conversation; there is a smaller room to the side and an attractive outdoor drinking area. The growing range of cider and perry increases during the summer. Q❀♿⇌♣🍎🚌🐾

Tank ✔

12-14 Llanthony Road, GL1 2EH
🕒 12-11 ☎ (01452) 690541 🌐 tankgloucester.com
Gloucester Cascade, Dockside Dark, American Pale; 4 changing beers (sourced nationally) Ⓗ
This brewery tap is a welcoming, urban warehouse-style bar with a contemporary feel, located in the heart of the Gloucester Docks redevelopment that opened in May 2015. The decor utilises the building's strengths, and is well worth a look. Though primarily selling Gloucester beers, there is a wide range of guest, craft and bottled beers and ciders. Food is available in the shape of local meats and cheeses served on platters, along with a selection of hand-made pizzas. ◑♿🍎🚌(10)📶

Ham

Salutation Inn Ⓛ

Ham Green, GL13 9QH (from Berkeley take road signposted to Jenner Museum)
🕒 5-11; 12-2.30, 5-11 Fri; 12-11 Sat; 12-10.30 Sun
☎ (01453) 810284 🌐 the-sally-at-ham.com
Butcombe Original Ⓗ
Multi award-winning rural free house, offering up to seven real ales and nine real ciders and perries, plus a bottled beer menu. The on-site microbreweries (Tiley's and Mills) produce hop-forward pale ales, traditional bitters and lambic beers. There are three bars (two cosy ones share a central woodburner) and a skittles alley/function room. Food is served at lunchtimes and on occasional evenings only; there are also folk nights and singalongs. Q❀◐♿♣🍎P🐾📶

Hawkesbury Upton

Beaufort Arms Ⓛ

High Street, GL9 1AU (off A46, 6 miles N of M4 jct 18)
🕒 12-11; 12-10.30 Sun ☎ (01454) 238217
🌐 beaufortarms.com
Bristol Beer Factory Independence; Butcombe Original; 3 changing beers (sourced regionally) Ⓗ
A wonderful Grade II-listed Cotswold stone free house, built in 1602, close to the historic Somerset Monument. It features separate public and lounge bars, a dining room, and a skittle alley/function room, which are all required to house a veritable plethora of ancient brewery and local memorabilia. It serves up to five ales and a traditional cider on handpump. It has an attractive garden with a barbecue used for local community activities. A great bunch of regulars assures a warm welcome. Q❀◑♿♣🍎P🚌🐾📶

Hillesley

Fleece Inn 🏆 Ⓛ

Chapel Lane, GL12 7RD (between Wotton-under-Edge and Hawkesbury Upton)
🕒 4.30-10 Mon-Wed; 12-11 Thu (11.30 Fri & Sat); 12-10 Sun
☎ (01453) 520003 🌐 thefleeceinnhillesley.com
Sharp's Atlantic; Wye Valley Butty Bach; 4 changing beers (often Arbor, Oakham, Tiny Rebel) Ⓗ
An attractive 17th-century village pub set in the heart of Hillesley. It has a single bar with a wood-burning stove, a separate lounge/dining room, and a snug area. The pub has up to six real ales and also features guest craft keg and draught cider. Food is served at lunchtime and in the evening up to 9pm. There is a large attractive lawned garden and private car park. Children and dogs are welcome and the garden has a safe play area. Q❀◑🍎P🚌🐾📶

Longborough

Coach & Horses

GL56 0QU (off A424 in village centre)
🕒 11-2.30, 5.30-11; 11-11 Fri-Sun ☎ (01451) 830325
🌐 coachnhorseslongborough.co.uk
Donnington BB, Gold, SBA Ⓗ
Dating from the 18th century, this village inn of Cotswold stone is perched on a bank overlooking a small green and war memorial. Located only one mile from the renowned Donnington brewery, this friendly, family-run, one-bar pub is the focal point of community activity in the village. Flagstone floors and an open fire greet locals and visitors alike, with the full range of good-value Donnington ales served along with home-cooked food. Q❀◑♣🐾📶

Lydbrook

Royal Spring Inn

Vention Lane, GL17 9RL (off B4228 to W of village)
☼ 12-3, 7-11 ☎ (01594) 860492
Brains Rev James; Fuller's London Pride; 1 changing beer (sourced regionally; often Wye Valley) Ⓗ
Traditional whitewashed community free house, in a lovely position up a narrow lane above the Wye. The carpeted floors in the attractive wooden bar areas do vary in depth, but help separate the pub games from diners enjoying their well-appreciated home-cooked food. A stream flows through a sloping, fenced rear garden that houses a menagerie, which is open as a playground and drinking area with some fantastic views. The adjacent cottage is available to rent.
♘❀◐♿⛺♣P

Marshfield

Catherine Wheel

39 High Street, SN14 8LR (if using postcode in sat nav check it is not showing Colerne)
☼ 12-11 ☎ (01225) 892220 ⊕ thecatherinewheel.co.uk
Butcombe Original; Fuller's London Pride; 1 changing beer (sourced locally; often Bath Ales) Ⓗ
An impressive building in a historic conservation area, much of it dating back to the 17th century, that feels like a traditional and cosy country pub. Well-sited for Bath and the Cotswolds, its simple, sympathetic decor complements the exposed stone walls and large open fireplaces. With a large bar area and adjoining rooms, overnight accommodation and wholesome freshly prepared food using local produce, this is a real ale pub that is well worth a visit. Q♘❀🛏◐♣P🚌🐾📶

Moreton-in-Marsh

Bell Inn Ⓛ ✔

High Street, GL56 0AF (on A429)
☼ 11-11 ☎ (01608) 651688 ⊕ thebellinnmoreton.co.uk
Prescott Hill Climb; Purity Pure UBU; Timothy Taylor Landlord; 2 changing beers (sourced locally; often Hook Norton, North Cotswold) Ⓗ
This old High Street coaching inn dating from the 18th century has been pleasantly refurbished. The interior consists of a mainly open-plan area which has been sympathetically divided into more intimate snug sections, with a real fire and good food. A large courtyard area is found through the old arched entrance, with an enclosed garden at the rear. It is famed for links with JRR Tolkien, the Lord of the Rings author, with a map of Middle Earth adorning the walls. Local and national ales are on tap. Q♘❀🛏◐♿⛺⇌P🚌🐾📶

Moseley Green

Rising Sun Ⓛ

GL15 4HN (off A48 at Blakeney toward Parkend and first left)
☼ 12-11 (midnight Fri & Sat) ☎ (01594) 562008
Wickwar BOB; 3 changing beers (sourced nationally) Ⓗ
Enjoying panoramic views from its isolated position amid defunct coal mines, this extended pub was built for miners in the early 1800s. Popular with cyclists, hikers, cavers and families, there are several patios, large gardens and a pond. It is hard to believe that trams and trains ran only yards from the pub doors. There is a bar on both floors (when busy), a games room and a special kids' menu in the dining areas. A local music ensemble rehearses here. ♘❀🛏◐♣●P🥤

North Nibley

Black Horse Inn Ⓛ ✔

1 Barrs Lane, GL11 6DT (on B4060)
☼ 12-11 (midnight Sat); 12-10.30 Sun ☎ (01453) 543777
⊕ blackhorse-northnibley.co.uk
Wickwar BOB; 3 changing beers (often Bath Ales, Bristol Beer Factory) Ⓗ
This comfortable local dates from the 16th century and is at the crossroads in the centre of village, sitting beneath the Tyndale Monument. There are usually four ales on tap, including guests, normally from local or regional breweries. Excellent locally sourced food is served at lunchtime and in the evening. It is a popular pub with the local community and with walkers on the nearby Cotswold Way. There are occasional live music events. Q❀🛏◐♣●P🚌🐾📶

Parkend

Fountain Inn & Lodge

Fountain Way, GL15 4JD (off B4234)
☼ 12-3, 6-11 ☎ (01594) 562189
⊕ thefountaininnandlodge.com
Brains Rev James; Sharp's Doom Bar Ⓗ
One-bar 200-year-old village pub in the heart of the forest, near the Dean Forest Railway terminus, with steam train trips from Lydney. The walls and ceilings in this large and popular venue are crammed with interesting artefacts and tools, many of which relate to the local area and are worthy museum pieces. It is frequented by tourists and locals alike, and has a welcoming atmosphere, a good standard of accommodation (some rooms accessible by wheelchair) and good food. Specialising in curries, it also boasts an award-winning children's menu. A bunkhouse, sleeping 32, caters for ramblers, in addition to the eight en-suite guest rooms. Quoits is played.
Q♘❀🛏◐♿⛺♣●P

Quenington

Keeper's Arms

Church Road, GL7 5BL (from Fairford turn right at village green)
☼ 12-3 (not Mon & Tue), 6-11; 12-3, 5.30-11 Fri; 12-3, 6-11 Sat; 12-3, 7-11 Sun ☎ (01285) 750349
⊕ thekeepersarms.co.uk
4 changing beers (sourced nationally; often Butcombe, Otter, St Austell) Ⓗ
Local CAMRA Pub of the Year, this wonderful community venue has been transformed into an attractive modern hostelry by the delightfully enthusiastic owner. Dogs, children, cricketers, cyclists, art lovers and ramblers are welcome in both the refurbished oak bar and the petite front garden. The unpretentious menus help fill both dining areas (no food Mon or Tue), with regular theme nights and quizzes proving popular. Two fireplaces give a pleasant glow in winter. Good accommodation is available in four swish en-suite rooms. ♘❀🛏◐P🐾📶

Redmarley

Rose & Crown

Playley Green, GL19 3NB (on A417)
12-3, 5.30-11 (01531) 650234
roseandcrownatredmarley.co.uk/pub-dining
St Austell Tribute; Wye Valley Butty Bach; 2 changing beers H
Well-appointed roadside inn with a family garden. The pub has undergone a major refurbishment since 2016 and prides itself on good food but, more importantly, on keeping a good pint. Accommodation is available in five rooms. This location, along with a large level car park and step-free entrance, makes it a great destination pub or a base from which to explore the lovely countryside and tourist attractions around Gloucestershire, Worcestershire and Herefordshire.
Q P

Sheepscombe

Butchers Arms

GL6 7RH (signed off A46 N of Painswick and B4070 N of Slad) SO8911610434
11.30-3, 6.30 (6 Fri)-11; 11.30-11 Sat; 12-10.30 Sun
(01452) 812113 butchers-arms.co.uk
Prescott Hill Climb; 2 changing beers (sourced regionally; often Butcombe, Derby, Mobberley) H
Handsome 17th-century Cotswold-stone pub overlooking a wooded valley. Its inn sign, a painted three-dimensional carving of a butcher quaffing ale while tethered to a pig, is world famous. An adventurous choice of ale from across the country is on the guest pump. In 2014 the lean-to outdoor toilets metamorphosed into a new bar, seamlessly executed in reclaimed stone and Welsh oak. This complements a quality inter-war refurbishment that added the generous bay windows and porch. The forecourt tables and sloping side garden are suntraps in summer. Q P

Shipton Moyne

Cat & Custard Pot

The Street, GL8 8PN (centre of village on Tetbury Rd)
11-3, 6-11 Mon; 11-11 (01666) 880249
Flying Monk Elmers; Hook Norton Hooky; Wickwar BOB; 1 changing beer (sourced nationally) H
Locally owned, this vibrant village inn has a unique sign (see the plaque inside). An equestrian haunt, as reflected by the memorabilia on the walls, this lovely pub has been recently updated with wheelchair accessible toilets and extended dining areas (the food is certainly popular). While the quieter snug is a favourite with families, the busy main bar and attractive front garden can, at times, appear to be the hub of the local dog walking society. Five letting rooms are available.
Q P

Slad

Woolpack

GL6 7QA (on B4070)
12-midnight (01452) 813429 thewoolpackslad.com
Stroud Budding; Uley Bitter, Old Spot Prize Strong Ale, Pig's Ear Strong Beer; 1 changing beer (sourced regionally; often Gloucester) H
Popular 17th-century inn clinging to the side of the Slad Valley with superb views. The Woolpack achieved fame through Cider With Rosie – author Laurie Lee was a regular and instrumental in saving the pub from closure. It has been thoughtfully restored, with built-in dark wooden settles in the end rooms. Outside there is a decked patio area down steps to the side. Monday is pizza night, prepared on the hob in the revolutionary oven designed by the pub's owner. Q

Stroud

Ale House

9 John Street, GL5 2HA (opp Cornhill farmers' market)
12-3, 5-11; 12-midnight Fri; 11-midnight Sat; 12-11 Sun
(01453) 755447
Burning Sky Plateau; Tiley's Special Pale; 6 changing beers (sourced nationally; often Salopian, Siren, Vibrant Forest) H
Built in 1837 for the Poor Law Guardians, this Grade-II listed building is a mecca for ale lovers. The bar occupies the former boardroom, where an all-year-round beer festival showcases ales from Siren, Electric Bear and many others, plus a cider and perry. Opposite is a blazing log fire and adjoining are two smaller rooms. Live music plays on Friday or Saturday, jazz once a month on a Thursday. A fiendishly difficult Sunday quiz is set by the landlord – who also prepares the specialty home-made curries, chillis and other dishes. Local CAMRA Pub of the Year. Q

Crown & Sceptre

98 Horns Road, GL5 1EG
3-11; 12-11 Fri & Sat; 12-10.30 Sun (01453) 762588
crownandsceptrestroud.com
Stroud Budding; Uley Bitter, Pig's Ear Strong Beer; 1 changing beer (sourced regionally; often Brains) H
Lively back-street local that is at the heart of its community. The walls display an eclectic mix of framed prints, posters and clocks. Local groups meet round a large oak table in a side room, including Knit and Natter on Tuesday. The pub also has its own motorcycle society. It is famed for its Up The Workers good-value set meal on Wednesday and Sunday roasts. Sport is screened in the back bar. A terrace to the rear offers panoramic views across the valley to Rodborough Common.
P (8,227)

Little George

21 George Street, GL5 3DP
closed Mon & Tue; 4-11 Wed-Fri; 12-11 Sat; 12-8 Sun
(01453) 750300 stroudmicropub.co.uk
Clearwater Mariners; Stroud Budding; changing beers (often Gloucester) H
The first micropub to open in Stroud, serving a wide range of ales and ciders from a gravity stillage, plus bottled and canned beers including a number from Belgium. A converted shop in the centre of the town, it has two simply furnished rooms, with space for around 40 people. Food consists of local pies, charcuterie, cheeses and cakes. Alternatively you can bring your own food or order a takeaway. Local CAMRA Cider Pub of the Year. Q

Prince Albert

Rodborough Hill, GL5 3SS (corner of Walkley Hill)
4-11.30 (12.30am Fri); 12-12.30am Sat; 12-10.30 Sun
(01453) 755600 theprincealbertstroud.co.uk
Otter Bitter; Stroud Budding; Timothy Taylor Landlord; 3 changing beers (sourced nationally; often Bristol Beer Factory, Gloucester , Sharp?s) H
Lively, cosmopolitan, Cotswold-stone pub below Rodborough Common that is simultaneously

bohemian, homely and welcoming, with a big reputation for live music. The L-shaped bar boasts an eclectic mix of furniture, fittings and memorabilia – the walls covered with film and music posters – and a log fire. The pub hosts a May beer festival, exhibitions and open mic nights. Some events are ticketed (phone or check website). Jamaica Inn Caribbean food is served Friday 5-9pm and Sunday 1-4pm. Alternatively bring your own food or phone for a takeaway.

Tetbury

Royal Oak

1 Cirencester Road, GL8 8EY (on B4067)
11-11 (11.30 Fri & Sat); 12-11 Sun (01666) 500021
theroyaloaktetbury.co.uk
Butcombe Haka; Moor Beer So'Hop; Stroud Tom Long; 2 changing beers (sourced regionally)
This wonderful award-winning pub utilises clever design to marry a traditional feel to a modern layout. The swathe of wooden surfaces provides a welcoming ambience, with a small fireplace adding warmth. Six handpumps include Severn Cider and a vegan ale from Moor – chosen to match the vegan menu dish. The one-pot option is popular, especially on quiz nights. Upstairs dining rooms and six letting rooms are further attractions, as are the lively music and beer festivals. P

Tewkesbury

Berkeley Arms

8 Church Street, GL20 5PA (between Tewkesbury Cross and abbey on old A38)
10-11 (01684) 290555
berkeleyarmstewkesbury.co.uk
Wadworth IPA, 6X, Swordfish; 2 changing beers (often Titanic, Wadworth)
A 15th-century half-timbered Grade II pub, just off Tewkesbury Cross. At the rear, a barn, which is believed to be the oldest non-ecclesiastical building in this historic town, is used for dining and also serves as a meeting room year round. Good-value home-cooked food is served daily in this two-bar establishment, and of particular note are the landlord's home-baked pies. Live music is performed on Friday and Saturday evenings. Q (41)

Nottingham Arms

129 High Street, GL20 5JU (on A38)
11-11 (midnight Thu-Sat); 12-11 Sun (01684) 276346
St Austell Tribute; Sharp's Doom Bar; Wye Valley HPA, Butty Bach
A 14th-century town-centre hostelry with two welcoming rooms, a public bar at the front and the restaurant behind. Framed photographs of old Tewkesbury adorn the walls. The pub is getting noticed for the excellent, well-priced food, served lunchtimes and evenings. Knowledgeable staff will happily tell you about the resident ghosts. Live music is performed on most Sunday evenings and Thursday is quiz night.

Royal British Legion Club

50 Church Street, GL20 5SN
8-11 (closed Tue); 7-11.30 Fri; 12-3, 7.30-11.30 Sat; 12-3, 7.30-11 Sun (01684) 293798
branches.britishlegion.org.uk/branches/tewkesbury
2 changing beers (often Exmoor, Froth Blowers, Ludlow)
Services club near the abbey located in a timber-framed building that used to be two pubs. The main lounge area is open to non-members. The venue has a great community feel; several clubs hold their meetings here and it has a team in the local crib league. There is live music every Saturday night. Local CAMRA branch Club of the Year 2016-18. Q (41)

Royal Hop Pole Hotel

94 Church Street, GL20 5RS (centre of town between abbey and cross)
7am-11 (01684) 278670
Great Western Old Higby; Greene King IPA; Hook Norton Old Hooky; Ruddles County; 4 changing beers (sourced locally; often Battledown, Exmoor, Prescott)
This well-known landmark is an amalgamation of historic buildings from the 15th and 18th centuries. It has been known as the Royal Hop Pole since being visited in September 1891 by Princess Mary of Teck (Queen Mary, Royal Consort of George V). The pub is mentioned in the Pickwick Papers. Purchased by JD Wetherspoon, it reopened in 2008. There is wood panelling on almost every wall of this spacious, multi-roomed drinking establishment, and it has a large patio and garden area at the rear. Q P

White Bear

Bredon Road, GL20 5BU (off N end of High St)
10-midnight (01684) 296614
famouswhitebear.co.uk
Salopian Oracle; Uley Old Spot Prize Strong Ale; 7 changing beers (sourced nationally; often Bristol Beer Factory, Sadler's, Uley)
Located on the north-western edge of the town, this good-value, friendly pub attracts ale and cider drinkers from far and wide. The open-plan L-shaped bar offers room to play pool and darts; there is also a skittle alley. Live music features every Sunday afternoon. The seven ales change frequently and include offerings from local and national award-winning breweries. At least five traditional perries and ciders are always stocked. P

Thornbury

Anchor Inn

Gloucester Road, BS35 1JY
11-11 (01454) 281375 theanchorthornbury.co.uk
Draught Bass; 5 changing beers
Licensed since 1695 and the second-oldest pub in Thornbury, this friendly, traditional inn has one regular beer and five changing guests, plus a real cider. Good home-cooked food is available daily. There are two large rooms, one of which has been split to provide a function/meeting area and is used by local artists as well. The pub also has its own darts, cribbage, dominoes and cricket teams and angling syndicate. The garden includes a boules piste and children's play area. P

Upper Soudley

White Horse Inn

Church Road, GL14 2UA (on B4227)

⏲ 7-11 (midnight Fri); 3-midnight Sat; 12-6 Sun
☎ (01594) 825968

2 changing beers (sourced nationally) Ⓗ

Built as a railway hotel next to the now defunct Soudley Halt, this hostelry has great views across the valley from the garden. It is an interesting venue for geologists and walkers, with the Blue Rock Trail and Soudley ponds. Run by an enthusiastic couple, this lovely old pub has a small main bar with a welcoming fireplace and two regularly changing guest ales. The old dining room down the passageway is used for functions, and leads through to a much-loved skittle alley.
♨❀♿♣●P🚌(717)🐾

Woolaston Common

Rising Sun

The Common, GL15 6NU (1 mile off A48 at Woolaston)
SO5901500924

⏲ 12-2.30, 6.30-11; 12-3, 6.30-midnight Sat; 12-3, 6.30-11 Sun ☎ (01594) 529282

Butcombe Adam Henson's Rare Breed; Wye Valley Bitter; 1 changing beer (sourced regionally) Ⓗ

Off the beaten track, this comfortable 350-year-old stone-built inn enjoys gorgeous views over the Forest of Dean. There is a welcoming main bar with an open fire and a small snug, both of which display part of the landlord's large collection of framed banknotes. Featured in the Circular Pub Walks of the Forest, the pub's varied menu of good home-cooked food is popular with ramblers (no food Mon & Tue lunchtimes). Some great locals help make for a convivial atmosphere. Q❀◑◗♣P

Wotton-under-Edge

Royal Oak Inn 🄻

3-5 Haw Street, GL12 7AG (on B4060 at top end of town)

⏲ 12-midnight ☎ (01453) 844366
🌐 theroyaloakwotton.com

Butcombe Original; Fuller's London Pride; Sharp's Doom Bar; 1 changing beer (sourced regionally; often Exmoor, Prescott, Wye Valley) Ⓗ

A large coaching inn with a friendly atmosphere. It has two comfortable bars, both with open fires, plus a large dining room with wooden beams. There is a full-size snooker table upstairs which is popular. This lively establishment supports the local community and welcomes walkers using the Cotswold Way. At the rear is a car park and enclosed garden containing a well-equipped children's play area. Q♨❀◑◗P🚌🐾📶

Berkeley Arms, Tewkesbury (Photo: Emma Haines)

Many entries in the Guide refer to pubs' support for CAMRA's LocAle scheme. The 𝕃 symbol is used where a pub has LocAle accreditation. The aim of the scheme is to get publicans to stock at least one cask beer that comes from a local brewery, usually no more than 30 miles away.

The aim is a simple one: to cut down on 'beer miles'. Research by CAMRA shows that food and drink transport accounts for 25 per cent of all HGV vehicle miles in Britain. Taking into account the miles that ingredients have travelled on top of distribution journeys, an imported lager produced by a multi-national brewery could have notched up more than 24,000 'beer miles' by the time it reaches a pub.

Supporters of LocAle point out that £10 spent on locally-supplied goods generates £25 for the local economy. Keeping trade local helps enterprises, creates more economic activity and jobs, and makes other services more viable. The scheme also generates consumer support for local breweries.

Support for LocAle has grown at a rapid pace since it was created in 2007. It's been embraced by pubs and CAMRA branches throughout England and has now crossed the borders into Scotland and Wales.

For more information, see the CAMRA website www.camra.org.uk and type 'locale' into the search window.

What is CAMRA LocAle?

- An initiative that promotes pubs which sell locally-brewed real ale
- The scheme builds on a growing consumer demand for quality local produce and an increased awareness of 'green' issues.

Everyone benefits from local pubs stocking locally brewed real ale...

- Public houses, as stocking local real ales can increase pub visits
- Consumers, who enjoy greater beer choice and locally brewed beer
- Local brewers, who gain from increased sales and get better feedback from consumers
- The local economy, because more money is spent and retained in the local economy
- The environment, due to fewer 'beer miles' resulting in less road congestion and pollution
- Tourism, due to an increased sense of local identity and pride – let's celebrate what makes our locality different.

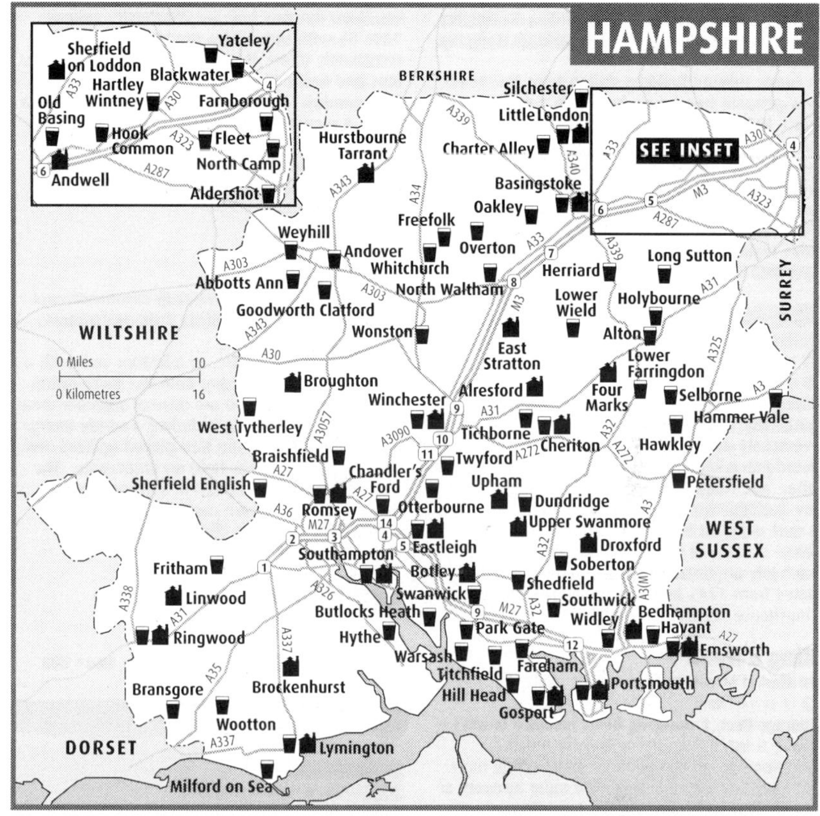

Please note: Ringwood Brewery renamed Best Bitter to Razorback but it is still available in some outlets as Best Bitter

Abbotts Ann

Eagle Inn

Duck Street, SP11 7BG

11.30-11; 12-10.30 Sun ☎ (01264) 710339

theeagleinn.wordpress.com

Bowman Wallops Wood; 3 changing beers (sourced locally)

In a picturesque village two miles south-west of Andover, this pub is at the heart of the community and friendly conversation rules. The regular Wallops Wood is supplemented by three changing beers, often from local breweries. A real cider made in the village is also served. A beer and cider festival is held over the second weekend of June. The public bar has pool and there is a skittle alley at the rear. Locally sourced food features (no evening meals Sun and Tue). P (87)

Aldershot

Garden Gate

2 Church Lane East, GU11 3BT

5-11 (midnight Thu; 1am Fri); 12-1am Sat; 12-10.30 Sun ☎ (01252) 219717

Black Sheep Bitter; Marston's Saddle Tank; St Austell Tribute; Surrey Hills Ranmore; Wainwright; 1 changing beer (sourced nationally)

A focal point of the local community, conversation and low-level background music reign here, with occasional live music. The bar is two rooms knocked into one; there is also a back room and a covered patio. Thursday night quizzes are well attended, and a monthly music quiz is held on a Sunday. The pub is as popular with dogs as it is with humans, and is close to the bus and train stations. Ranmore Ale is usually available, plus three more beers. P

White Lion

20 Lower Farnham Road, GU12 4EA

1-10.30 Mon; 1-11 Tue & Wed; 1-11.30 Thu; 1-midnight Fri; 12-midnight Sat; 12-10.30 Sun ☎ (01252) 323832

Triple fff Alton's Pride, Moondance; 2 changing beers (sourced nationally; often Triple fff)

Into its second decade of continuous entries in the Guide, the White Lion is well worth the trip out of the town centre. It began life in around 1857 as a beer house. A traditional two-room establishment, the back room is usually the quieter. A quiz and music bingo run on alternate Thursdays. It is one of the few Triple fff Brewery-run pubs, hence their LocAle beers are to the fore, often with a guest. Pub dog Millie welcomes others canines.

Alton

Eight Bells

33 Church Street, GU34 2DA (opp St Lawrence Church)

11.30-11; 12-10.30 Sun ☎ (01420) 82417

Bowman Swift One; Sharp's Doom Bar; 3 changing beers (sourced nationally; often Cotleigh, Longdog, Red Cat) Ⓗ
A Grade II-listed building dating from the 1640s, this genuine free house has been a pub since at least 1848. Guest beers come from far and wide but usually include at least one local brew and turnover can be rapid. One-third pint measures are available. The main bar is a haven for good beer and conversation while the rear drinking area has a TV for major sporting events. Nigel's not-so-secret beer festival follows the late summer holiday.
Q❀⇌🚌(13)🐾📶

George ✔
Butts Road, GU34 1LH
⏲ 11-11 (midnight Thu-Sat); 11-10.30 Sun ☎ (01420) 82331
🌐 thegeorgealton.co.uk
Sharp's Sea Fury; 4 changing beers (sourced nationally; often Longdog) Ⓗ
Previously named the Duke's Head, this Grade II-listed pub is friendly and well run, with five ales on offer, and frequently featuring a dark beer. Meals are available from a varied seasonal menu. There is a quiz night on the first Tuesday of the month, while occasional live music and the beer festival each July are detailed on the website. The building dates from 1745 and was previously the town's courthouse. 🛏❀◐◑P🚌(64)🐾📶

King's Head Ⓛ
28 Market Street, GU34 1HA (opp market square)
⏲ 12.30-1am ☎ (01420) 82313
Courage Best; 2 changing beers (sourced locally) Ⓗ
Grade II-listed, two-bar pub, very much a traditional local, combining a consistently high standard in beer quality with a rapid turnover of guest ales, which are usually local Hampshire brews. Happy Hour with 50p off a pint is 4.30-7pm Monday to Friday. The terraced garden at the rear backs on to the community centre car park which is sometimes the venue for live music on summer Sundays, but which otherwise gives a peaceful contrast to a bustling town-centre pub. 🛏❀🚌

Railway Arms Ⓛ
26 Anstey Road, GU34 2RB (opp Station Rd)
⏲ 12-11; 11-midnight Fri & Sat ☎ (01420) 82218
🌐 fffrailwayarms.com
Triple fff Alton's Pride, Pressed Rat & Warthog, Moondance; 3 changing beers (sourced nationally; often Brewsters, Red Cat, Triple fff) Ⓗ
Friendly pub close to the Watercress Line and mainline station, with a striking sculpture of a steam locomotive emerging from the front outside. Owned by Triple fff Brewery, its beers are supplemented by guests from a host of microbreweries. Real cider is from Mr Whitehead's and continental bottled beers are stocked. A rear function room is available for hire. The patio area out back, designed with a traditional railway theme, incorporates a covered smoking area.
❀⇌♣🍎🚌🐾📶

Andover

Angel Inn ✔
95 High Street, SP10 1ND
⏲ 9am-11 (midnight Fri & Sat); 11-7 Sun ☎ (01264) 351646
Morland Old Speckled Hen; 2 changing beers (sourced nationally) Ⓗ
The oldest building in Andover, saved when the town centre was redeveloped, this timber-framed courtyard inn was built by Winchester College 1445-55 with some later modifications but is remarkably intact. It is one of Hampshire's oldest inns and Grade II*-listed – look for the coaching light window. The upper bar was once used as a court. A pleasant small patio is at the rear and there is a sheltered courtyard at the front. Live music and karaoke feature as well as pool and darts. Breakfasts are good value. ❀◐🚌🐾

Town Mills ✔
20 Bridge Street, SP10 1BL
⏲ 11-12.30am ☎ (01264) 332540 🌐 thetownmills.co.uk
Wadworth IPA, 6X, Swordfish; 2 changing beers (sourced regionally) Ⓗ
Just off the town centre, in a historic mill with a working water wheel and with the River Anton passing through. There are several separate areas for dining and drinking including a comfy lounge upstairs. Pub games are also played upstairs and a well-supported quiz is held on Wednesday. The riverside garden is popular in summer. Usually three to four beers are available from the Wadworth's guest list. 🛏❀◐◑♿♣P🚌🐾📶

Basingstoke

Angel Ⓛ ✔
Unit R6, Lower Ground, Festival Place, RG21 7BB

REAL ALE BREWERIES
Alfred's Winchester
Andwells Andwell
Betteridge's Hurstbourne Tarrant
Botley Botley
Bowman Droxford
Brewhouse & Kitchen 🛢 Portsmouth
Brewhouse & Kitchen 🛢 Southampton
Brockenhurst 🛢 Brockenhurst (NEW)
Broken Bridge Upper Swanmore
CrackleRock Botley
Dancing Cows Lymington
Dancing Man Southampton
Emsworth Brewery Emsworth
Emsworth Brewhouse Bedhampton
Fallen Acorn Gosport
Flack Manor Romsey
Flowerpots 🛢 Cheriton
Irving Portsmouth
Itchen Valley Alresford
Little London Little London
London Road Brew House 🛢 Southampton
Longdog Basingstoke
Mash East Stratton
Newtown Gosport
Queen Inn 🛢 Winchester
Red Cat Winchester
Red Shoot 🛢 Linwood
Ringwood Ringwood
Sherfield Village Sherfield on Loddon
Southsea Portsmouth
Staggeringly Good Portsmouth
Steam Town 🛢 Eastleigh (NEW)
Tap It Southampton
Test Broughton (NEW)
Triple fff Four Marks
Unity Southampton
Upham Upham
Urban Island Portsmouth
Vibrant Forest Lymington

8am-12.30am (2am Fri & Sat); 8am-midnight Sun
(01256) 854800
Greene King IPA, Abbot; Sharp's Doom Bar; 7 changing beers (often Longdog, Vibrant Forest, Wild Weather Ales) H
Formerly a Lloyds No.1 Bar, this modern, spacious one-bar pub is at the edge of the restaurant quarter in the town's Festival Place shopping centre, handy for the nearby bus station and five minutes' walk from the rail station. Popular with younger people, it can get busy and often noisy in the evenings, especially at weekends. Lunchtimes attract a wider age range and tend to be quieter. The walls are adorned with TVs, all in silent mode.

Basingstoke Sports & Social Club

Fairfields Road, RG21 3DR (S end of town)
11-3, 5-11; 11-11 Fri & Sat; 12-10.30 Sun
(01256) 473646 basingstoke-sports-club.co.uk
Fuller's London Pride; Gale's Seafarers Ale; 3 changing beers (sourced nationally; often Andwells, Little London, Longdog) H
While technically a club, the public are welcome here. Founded in 1865 by local brewery owner and entrepreneur Colonel John May, this fine venue is home to cricket, rugby, football, racketball and squash. The wide-screen TV in the bar is dedicated to sports events. It has a full programme of social activities throughout the year and is currently home to the annual Hampshire OktoberFest. Opening hours and meal times vary.
P

Bounty Inn

Bounty Road, RG21 3BZ
12-11 (11.30 Fri & Sat); 12-10.30 Sun (01256) 320071
thebountyinnbasingstoke.co.uk
3 changing beers (sourced nationally; often Brains, Dartmoor, Red Cat) H
This 1830s pub is now one of Basingstoke's few remaining historic hostelries. The name acknowledges a gift of land, which includes the adjacent cricket ground, to the people of Basingstoke by local brewer John May in 1880. Three bars cater for a wide-ranging clientele including diners enjoying high-quality food. There is a pleasant south-facing rear garden. Hardy males might appreciate the last remaining outside Gents' toilet in the town. Three ales are usually served.
P

Maidenhead Inn

17 Winchester Street, RG21 7ED (top of town)
8am-midnight (1am Fri & Sat) (01256) 316030
Greene King Abbot; Ruddles Best Bitter; Sharp's Doom Bar; 4 changing beers (sourced nationally; often Loddon, Longdog, Wild Weather Ales) H
Formerly home to a building society and on the site of an inn of the same name, this JD Wetherspoon pub is in the sometimes lively Top of Town area, with five pumps dispensing local and guest ales. Beers from local breweries such as Andwell's, Longdog, Wild Weather and Loddon regularly feature. A dining area at the front leads to the compact bar, with further seating to the rear over two levels, complemented by a courtyard beer garden to the rear. P

Queen's Arms

Bunnian Place, RG21 7JE (100yds E of railway station)
11-11 (midnight Fri & Sat) (01256) 465488
thequeensarmspub.co.uk
Courage Best Bitter; Sharp's Doom Bar; 4 changing beers (sourced nationally) H
Just outside the main shopping area, this cosy pub is handy for all transport links. It attracts a wide-ranging clientele of all ages from all walks of life, and is a regular port of call for rail commuters. The choice of up to four guest beers is imaginative and the turnaround can be swift. Good-value home-cooked food is served lunchtimes and evenings. During warmer weather the shady courtyard garden at the rear is a popular attraction.
Q P

Blackwater

Mr Bumble

19 London Road, GU17 9AP
12-11 (midnight Fri); 11-midnight Sat; 12-10.30 Sun
(01276) 32691
Fuller's London Pride; 3 changing beers (sourced regionally; often Ascot Brewing Company, Binghams, Dark Star) H
A busy pub in the centre of Blackwater, near the station, a bus route and local shops. London Pride is the regular beer, with up to three other real ales, including LocAles, on tap; stout and porter are popular in the winter months. There is a large bar for drinking and conversation, while a smaller bar leads to the pool room, with three tables, which in turn leads out to the patio and smoking area. You can enjoy live music on Thursdays and Saturdays.
P (3)

Braishfield

Wheatsheaf

Braishfield Road, SO51 0QE
11.30-11; 12-10.30 Sun (01794) 368652
thewheatsheafbraishfield.co.uk
Flack Manor Flack's Double Drop; St Austell Tribute; Sharp's Doom Bar; 1 changing beer (sourced nationally) H
The Wheatsheaf is a handsome cream-painted country pub in southern Braishfield. A single bar serves several linked spaces including a restaurant area and a small games annexe. A homely feel is created by exposed brickwork and beams plus mismatched furniture. The garden gives views over farmland and wooded hills. The restaurant menu is good. Hillier arboretum with its visitor centre is nearby (reachable by footpath). Live music plays on Thursdays. P (35)

Bransgore

Three Tuns

Ringwood Road, BH23 8JH
11 (11.30 Sat)-11; 12-10.30 Sun (01425) 672232
threetunsinn.com
Otter Amber; Ringwood Razorback, Fortyniner; 2 changing beers (sourced nationally) H
This immaculate Grade II-listed building, white-painted and thatched, was originally an 18th-century farmhouse, and converted into a pub around 1900. There are two bars: a long comfortable lounge leading to a dining room, and a cosy snug. The pub has a good reputation for its food, often hosting wedding receptions in the barn or marquee. You can even get married here. Friendly knowledgeable staff, beer description boards and newspapers make this a great place just for a drink too. Q P (125)

Butlocks Heath

Roll Call ✔

Woolston Road, SO31 5FJ
12 (3 Mon & Tue)-11 ☎ (023) 8045 2358
therollcall.co.uk
Courage Best Bitter; Flowerpots Bitter; Upham Punter Ⓗ**; 1 changing beer (sourced locally)** Ⓖ
A two-bar pub with contemporary decor, pub signs on the walls and tankards hanging from the ceiling. A logburner is situated between the bars. In addition to the three handpumped core beers, the pub serves a guest local beer straight from the cask from Thursday to Sunday. Food, also served Thursday to Sunday, consists of home-made traditional pub meals plus a varied range of authentic curries. Outside is a patio and garden with a small children's assault course.
P (6,X15)

Chandler's Ford

Steel Tank Alehouse

1 The Central Precinct, Winchester Road, SO53 2GA
closed Mon & Tue; 3-10; 12-6 Sun ☎ 07379 553025
6 changing beers (sourced regionally) Ⓗ
Steel Tank is rhyming slang for bank, which this newly converted, thriving and popular micropub once was. The well-furnished interior and smart substantial seating arrangements make for a lively and sociable, conversational drinking atmosphere. The management team is passionate about supporting the local community and working with talented people and businesses on their doorstep. There is always a great variety of local beers and ciders – a dramatic increase in the area's real ale availability! Q P

Charter Alley

White Hart

White Hart Lane, RG26 5QA (1 mile W of A340)
closed Mon; 7-10 Tue; 12-2.30, 7-10 Wed; 12-2.30, 5.30-10 Thu; 12-2.30, 5.30-11 Fri; 12-2.30, 7-11 Sat; 12-3 Sun
☎ (01256) 850048 whitehartcharteralley.com
6 changing beers (sourced locally; often Hop Back, Langham, Loddon) Ⓗ
A cosy inn, built in 1819, the epicentre of this rural village, where allcomers are assured a friendly greeting. Welcoming features include log fires, oak beams and a capacious dining area, serving a variety of quality food and home-made pies. A stalwart Guide entry for the past 27 years, the breweriana-decorated main bar dispenses an array of ales that changes frequently, including a diverse range from its own small-scale Secret Brewing Company. The website shows beers that are on and coming soon. Q P

Cheriton

Flowerpots Inn

Brandy Mount, SO24 0QQ (½ mile N of A272 Cheriton/Beauworth crossroads) SU581283
12-2.30, 6-11; 12-3, 7-10.30 Sun ☎ (01962) 771318
flowerpotscheriton.co.uk
Flowerpots Perridge Pale, Bitter, Goodens Gold; 1 changing beer Ⓖ
An early 19th-century pub whose outbuildings are also home to the eponymous 10-barrel brewery. Its beers – three regulars plus seasonal and special brews – are served in the pub's two bars straight from the cask. Several real ciders, usually Westons, are stocked. Good home-cooked food is provided daily (no food Mon and Sun eves); on Wednesday evenings a Punjabi chef runs a curry night. The four-acre garden has many benches and a large marquee for rainy days. Q P (67)

Dundridge

Hampshire Bowman

Dundridge Lane, SO32 1GD (1½ miles E of B3035) SU578184
12-11 (midnight Fri); 12-10.30 Sun ☎ (01489) 892940
hampshirebowman.com
Bowman Swift One; West Berkshire Good Old Boy; 3 changing beers (sourced regionally; often Andwells, Flack Manor, Longdog) Ⓖ
Remote, traditional country pub with many interesting features. It typically serves five mostly local beers direct from the cask and up to 10 ciders. A wide variety of freshly prepared locally sourced food is available, including ever-changing specials. Outside is a large garden with patio and children's play area, which is popular during summer weekends. The pub welcomes walkers and their dogs, but keep your mobile hidden unless you want to add to the charity bottle!
Q P

Eastleigh

Steam Town Brew Co

1 Bishopstoke Road, SO50 6AD (on B3037)
11-11 ☎ (023) 8235 9139 steamtownbrewco.co.uk
4 changing beers (sourced nationally; often Steam Town) Ⓗ
Opened in late 2017, this is Eastleigh's first micropub and first brewery. The pub trades on the town's somewhat alien manufacturing past within an agricultural county, with decor extravagantly into the industrial shabby-chic mould. The in-house brewed beers are complemented by a changing selection from other small brewers. Live music including folk and jazz features several days per week. Unusually for a micropub, food is available daily in a dining area furnished with first-class train seating.

Emsworth

Blue Bell ✔

29 South Street, PO10 7EG
10-11 (midnight Fri & Sat); 12-11 Sun ☎ (01243) 373394
bluebellinnemsworth.co.uk
Sharp's Doom Bar; 2 changing beers (sourced nationally; often Dark Star, Emsworth Brewhouse, Irving) Ⓗ
A relatively recent addition to the town, the pub was built in 1960, replacing a much older premises with its own brewery further along the street. The move was made by a local businessman to improve access to properties behind the original pub. The brewery, however, was closed. Although modern, internally it has the look and feel of a much older pub. Being close to the harbour it is not surprising that the decor has a nautical feel.
(700)

Coal Exchange ✔

21 South Street, PO10 7EG
10.30-3, 5.30-11; 10.30-midnight Fri & Sat; 12-11 Sun
☎ (01243) 375866 thecoalexchange.co.uk

Fuller's London Pride; Gale's HSB, Seafarers Ale; 3 changing beers (sourced nationally; often Butcombe, Castle Rock, Fuller's) H
Located a short walk from Emsworth harbour, the pub's name derives from its use as trading place between local farmers and merchants delivering coal by sea. Formerly a Gale's pub, it has a somewhat unusual green-tiled frontage for one of their estate. Themed food evenings are held Monday to Thursday in addition to the award-winning lunchtime meals. A charity music and beer festival is held over one weekend in summer. (700)

Fareham

Delme Arms

1 Cams Hill, PO16 8QY
12-11 (midnight Fri); 11-midnight Sat; 12-10 Sun
(01329) 232638 delmearms.co.uk
Sharp's Doom Bar; 4 changing beers (sourced regionally) G
Situated on the eastern outskirts of Fareham, the premises were refurbished in 2014. There is a large main bar area, and a quiet upper bar which doubles as a restaurant and function room. There are two guest beers during the week, rising to four at weekends, and a local beer is normally available. Up to seven real ciders are also sold. A beer and cider festival takes place over the late May bank holiday weekend.
P (3,X4)

Lord Arthur Lee

100-108 West Street, PO16 0EP
8am-11 (midnight Fri & Sat) (01329) 280447
Greene King Abbot; Ruddles Best Bitter; Sharp's Doom Bar; 4 changing beers (often Ringwood) H
Spacious single-bar Wetherspoon pub with the walls hung with facts about historic locals including Lord Arthur Lee. The usual Wetherspoon food and beers feature, as well as its national beer festivals. The town's bus and train stations are in easy reach. There is a small garden area to the rear. The family area can get busy at lunchtime and early evening. Normally three guest beers are available weekdays and four at weekends.

Farnborough

Prince of Wales

184 Rectory Road, GU14 8AL
11.30-2.30, 5.30-11; 11.30-11 Fri & Sat; 12-10.30 Sun
(01252) 545578 theprinceinfarnborough.co.uk
Dark Star Hophead; Fuller's London Pride; Hogs Back TEA; Hop Back Summer Lightning; Ringwood Fortyniner; 5 changing beers (sourced nationally) H
After over 30 years in the Guide and many awards, this traditional local remains a haven for real ale drinkers. Five regular beers are served along with five guests, normally including a dark beer, and two real ciders. Evening meals are only available on Monday (curry night) and Friday (fish and chips). Quiz night is the first Sunday of each month and there is occasional live entertainment. A beer festival is held every October.
(North) P (41)

Swan

91 Farnborough Road, GU14 6TL (on A325)
11-11 (midnight Fri & Sat); 11.30-10.30 Sun
(01252) 510920 swanfarnborough.com
4 changing beers (sourced regionally; often Andwells, Hogs Back, Triple fff) H
A large, imposing building near Farnborough Airport, looking out directly over the runway. An ideal spot to book a garden table in Air Show week! Inside it is one large space, but with distinct drinking and dining areas, separated by partitions. It caters equally for diners and drinkers, with excellent food and a changing selection of four ales which are frequently LocAle. There are monthly live music and quiz nights and quarterly open mic nights. P (1,42)

Tilly Shilling

Unit 2-5, Victoria Road, GU14 7PG
8am-midnight (1am Fri & Sat) (01252) 893560
Greene King Abbot; Ruddles Best Bitter; Sharp's Doom Bar; 5 changing beers (sourced nationally; often Ascot Brewing Company, Binghams, Hogs Back) H
Modern town-centre Wetherspoon pub named after a celebrated engineer at the nearby Royal Aircraft Establishment. Its aviation theme includes a row of airline seats and various Spitfire memorabilia. The large rectangular open-plan lounge features a glass frontage that opens in good weather, extending the pub on to the pavement. Ten handpumps serve regular and changing guest beers. Real cider is dispensed from polypins at the end of the bar. Alcohol is on sale from 9am.

Fleet

Prince Arthur

238 Fleet Road, GU51 4BX
8am-midnight (1am Fri & Sat) (01252) 622660
Greene King Abbot; Ruddles Best Bitter; Sharp's Doom Bar; 4 changing beers (sourced nationally; often Twickenham, West Berkshire, Windsor & Eton) H
A traditionally designed pub in a building over 100 years old, with alcoves, wood surrounds and a rustic feel, named by Wetherspoon after Prince Arthur, son of Queen Victoria, who lived in Fleet in the 1890s while he was a British Army Commander at Aldershot. In July 2018 it celebrated 20 years since opening. Seven different casks ales are served including local ales from 12 breweries in Hampshire, Berkshire and Surrey. The leader of the Monster Raving Loony Party is a regular customer.
Q (7,10)

Freefolk

Watership Down Inn

Freefolk Priors, RG28 7NJ (just off B3400)
12-3, 6-11; 12-11.30 Fri & Sat; 12-9.30 Sun
(01256) 892254 watershipdowninn.com
5 changing beers (sourced locally) H
Built in 1840, in the Upper Test Valley, and still affectionately known locally as the Jerry, the pub has been named in honour of local author Richard Adams' book Watership Down, set in the downland to the north of the pub. Outside there is an extensive garden, patio and family area. The pub is popular with walkers and cyclists in the Test Valley. Each May a beer festival is held and occasional live music evenings arranged. It is close to the Laverstoke gin distillery. All beers are from local breweries. Q P (76)

Fritham

Royal Oak 🅛 ✔

SO43 7HJ (W end of village)

⏲ 11-3, 6-11; 11-11 Sat; 12-10.30 Sun ☎ (023) 8081 2606

Flack Manor Flack's Double Drop; house beer (by Ringwood); 4 changing beers (sourced locally; often Keystone, Stonehenge, Three Daggers) Ⓖ

A tiny thatched pub towards the end of a narrow no through road, over 40 years in this Guide. Seven beers are served, mostly local, straight from the cask, together with simple high-quality lunches using much local produce. Winter log fires and vast garden vistas in the summer make this a must-visit New Forest pub at all seasons. Accommodation is available in luxury shepherd's bothies. A large marquee often showerproofs the garden.
Q🐎❀🛏◐♿🐾

Goodworth Clatford

Clatford Arms ✔

Village Street, SP11 7RN

⏲ 11.30-10.30 (11.30 Thu; midnight Fri & Sat)
☎ (01264) 363298

Flack Manor Flack's Double Drop; 3 changing beers (sourced locally; often Longdog, Stonehenge) Ⓗ

A popular local in this pretty village. There is a dining room at one end where good-value home-cooked food is served. At the other end is the sports area, with a pool table, darts and TV. Four beers are served, mostly from local breweries, alongside traditional favourites. There is a large garden to the rear with a boules pitch.
Q🐎❀◐◑♿♣P🚌(15)🐾📶

Gosport

Junction Tavern

1 Leesland Road, Camden Town, PO12 3ND

⏲ 11-12.30am (11.30 Tue & Wed); 12-10.30 Sun
☎ (023) 9258 5140

3 changing beers (sourced regionally; often Broken Bridge, Langham) Ⓗ

The pub is on the site of Brockhurst Junction on the former Fareham to Gosport railway line which closed in 1953 and is now a cycle track and footpath. The three real ales are normally from independents and small breweries, and the pub is a mecca for cider drinkers, normally featuring four ciders and a perry from various suppliers. A beer festival takes place over the Easter weekend.
❀♣🍐🚌(E1)🐾📶

Queen's Hotel 🅛

143 Queens Road, Forton, PO12 1LG

⏲ 4.30-11.30 Mon-Thu; 11.30-2.30, 4.30-11.30 Fri; 11.30-11.30 Sat; 11.30-3, 7-11 Sun ☎ 07974 031671

🌐 queenshotelgosport.co.uk

Fallen Acorn Expedition IPA; Ringwood Fortyniner; Young's Bitter; 2 changing beers (sourced nationally) Ⓗ

No trip to Gosport is complete without a visit to this free house, which attracts visitors from all over the country. The guest ales change frequently and normally include a dark beer. Ales from the nearby Newtown Brewery appear occasionally, and real cider from Westons features quite often. A beer festival takes place in October. Snacks are available on Friday lunchtimes. **❀♣🍐🚌**

Hammer Vale

Prince of Wales

Hammer Lane, GU27 1QH

⏲ 11-11; 12-11 Sun ☎ (01428) 652600

🌐 princeofwaleshaslemere.co.uk

Fuller's London Pride; Gale's HSB; 2 changing beers (sourced nationally; often Fuller's) Ⓗ

Benefitting from a recent refurbishment, which revealed previously unknown doorways dating from the 1924 construction, this place is well worth a visit. It has a large outside seating area and car park and is well sited for walkers and campers. Mine hosts Nick and Heidi do excellent meals and bar snacks (no food Mon). Stories abound as to how such a large roadhouse was sited away from the main road. There are interesting stained-glass windows, one from Amey's of Petersfield.
Q🐎❀◐◑♿⛺♣P🐾📶

Hartley Wintney

Waggon & Horses

High Street, RG27 8NY

⏲ 11-11 (midnight Fri & Sat); 12-11 Sun ☎ (01252) 842119

Courage Best Bitter; Gale's HSB; 3 changing beers (sourced locally) Ⓗ

Current landlord Kasey served several years behind the bar of this award-winning local before taking over. HSB and Courage Best are regularly served alongside changing guest beers, often from microbreweries. The pub's lively public bar contrasts with a quieter lounge. Tables outside on the pavement enable guests to enjoy the atmosphere of the village, renowned for its unique shops. At the rear is a pleasant courtyard garden and a smokers' area. Food is served lunchtimes only, Monday to Saturday. **Q❀◐🍐🚌(7)🐾📶**

Havant

Old House at Home

2 South Street, PO9 1DA

⏲ 11-11; 12-10.30 Sun ☎ (023) 9248 3464

🌐 oldhouseathomehavant.co.uk

Fuller's London Pride; Gale's HSB, Seafarers Ale; 1 changing beer Ⓗ

This is one of the oldest buildings in Havant, although the 1339 date on the outside is about 200 years too early. It was originally five cottages and then a bakery (the remains of the oven can still be seen in the lounge) and one of only a few buildings to survive the fire of 1760. Beams recovered from the Spanish Armada were used in its construction and the last dancing bear in England reputedly performed in the pub. **🐎❀◐◑⇌♣🚌🐾📶**

Wheelwright's Arms 🅛 ✔

27 Emsworth Road, PO9 2SN

⏲ 11 (9 Sat)-11; 12-10 Sun ☎ (023) 9247 6502

🌐 wheelwrightshavant.co.uk

Upham Punter; 4 changing beers (sourced locally; often Fallen Acorn, Irving, Langham) Ⓗ

This imposing Edwardian pub on the edge of town has gained a good reputation for its quality food and drink. Up to five cask beers come from local micro and regional brewers, with a handpulled cider also offered. A range of bottled beers from the UK and abroad can also be found. The south-facing front terrace and secluded courtyard garden are popular in warm weather. Private hire space is available. The TV shows Rugby Union internationals. **Q🐎❀◐◑♿⇌♣🍐P🚌(27,700)🐾📶**

Hawkley

Hawkley Inn ✓

Pocks Lane, GU33 6NE

12-3, 5.30-11; 12-11 Sat; 12-9 Sun ☎ (01730) 827205
hawkleyinn.co.uk

Dark Star Hophead; Palmers Copper Ale; 5 changing beers (sourced regionally; often Flowerpots, Red Cat, Triple fff) H

Many country pubs now specialise in food but lose their way with beer. This free house has not, offering award-winning food paired with an excellent range of seven well-kept beers. Outside is a lovely, large, family-friendly garden and a sunny veranda. Accommodation is available in six refurbished rooms. The pub is welcoming to all, including walkers (the Hangers Way is nearby) and dogs. It holds a June beer festival and is a stopping point on the Alton Bus Rally in July.

Herriard

Fur & Feathers L

Back Lane, RG25 2PN (on old Basingstoke to Alton road)

closed Mon; 12-10; 11.30-11 Fri & Sat; 12-6 Sun
☎ (01256) 510510 thefurandfeathers.co.uk

Hogs Back TEA; Sharp's Doom Bar; 2 changing beers (sourced locally; often Flack Manor, Longdog, Red Cat) H

Family owned and run free house built in 1880 to service farm workers, now open plan with a central bar area and serving beers from an extensive list of Hampshire breweries. Two dining areas provide a pleasant atmosphere to enjoy the mouthwatering locally sourced daily changing menu. Reservations are recommended but a quiet pint can be enjoyed at any time. The well-appointed, secluded garden features paved and grassed areas. It was Hampshire Life Food and Drink Pub of the Year 2016. Please note that winter hours vary, so phone to confirm. Q P (13X)

Hill Head

Crofton ✓

48 Crofton Lane, PO14 3QF

11-11; 12-10.30 Sun ☎ (01329) 314222
thecrofton.co.uk

St Austell Proper Job; Sharp's Doom Bar; 4 changing beers (sourced nationally) H

A successful Punch Taverns outlet in a quiet residential area not far from the Solent. The guest beer range consists of ales from the Punch portfolio plus additional beers from SIBA. The premises consist of a main bar area plus a large dining area, and a function room with a skittle alley which gets booked up regularly. A beer festival takes place early in November. Home-cooked food is served all day. P (21,21A)

Holybourne

Queen's Head L

20 London Road, GU34 4EG

12 (4 Mon)-11.30; 12-11 Sun ☎ (01420) 768213
queensheadalton.co.uk

Hardys & Hansons Olde Trip; 2 changing beers (sourced nationally; often Greene King, Palmers, Triple fff) H

A friendly, unpretentious pub run by the same tenants for many years and a frequent entry in this Guide. A Greene King pub, it always has two guests, usually including one from local brewery Triple fff. The pub is in local darts and pool leagues and has a separate games room. There are occasional music nights. Outside there is a heated smoking refuge and an extensive family-friendly garden for use in the warmer months. Happy hour is 4.30-6pm Monday to Friday.
Q P (65)

Hook Common

Crooked Billet ✓

London Road, RG27 9EH

11.30-3, 6-11; 11.30-midnight Sat; 12-10 Sun
☎ (01256) 762118 thecrookedbilletpub.co.uk

Courage Best Bitter; Sharp's Doom Bar; 2 changing beers (sourced nationally) H

Just outside Hook, this has been a free house under the ownership of Richard and Sally for 32 years. In summer you can enjoy the pleasant riverside garden or air-conditioned bars, restaurant or snug. In winter, warm up around one of the traditional log fires. A fine selection of good food and real ales is always available. An annual beer and music festival is held over the August bank holiday weekend. Food is served until 8pm Sunday and quiz night is the first Monday of the month.
Q P

Hythe

Ebenezers L

18A Pylewell Road, SO45 6AR

11.30-2.40, 5.50-11; 11.30-11 Fri & Sat; 12-10.30 Sun
☎ (023) 8020 7799

Flack Manor Flack's Double Drop; Greene King Abbot; 2 changing beers (sourced locally; often Bowman, Flowerpots, Red Cat) H

Ebbs, as it is locally known, was built in 1845 as a chapel. It then became a school, a flour store and a furniture store before becoming a pub in 1998. The curved, open-plan bar serves four real ales. Home-cooked food plus Thai curries are available (no food Sun lunchtime). Lack of TV or pub games is an added attraction; just a nice atmosphere with conversation. Close by is the world's oldest working pier railway, serving the Southampton to Hythe ferry.

Little London

Plough Inn

Silchester Road, RG26 5EP

12-3, 5.30-11; 12-3, 6-11 Sat; 12-3, 7-10.30 Sun
☎ (01256) 850628

Otter Amber; Ringwood Razorback G**; 2 changing beers (sourced regionally; often Branscombe Vale, Church End, Little London)** H

Excellent traditional village pub and recent CAMRA Regional Pub of the Year. Enjoy beer gravity fed from casks behind the bar and sit in front of a log fire or in the peaceful garden. A good range of baguettes is available. It is popular with locals and also visitors to Pamper Forest and the nearby Roman remains in Silchester. Q P (14)

Long Sutton

Four Horseshoes

The Street, RG29 1TA (signed from B3349) SU748470

12-3 (not Mon), 6.30-11; 12-3 Sun ☎ (01256) 862488
fourhorseshoes.com
2 changing beers (sourced regionally; often Andwells, Palmers, Slater's) H
A truly rural pub, to the east of Long Sutton in a popular walking area. Formerly a Gale's tied house, it is now a free house normally offering up to two low-strength beers. There are twice-monthly quiz and jazz nights in the spacious but cosy bar which has two real fires. The pub serves simple English dishes with a popular roast on Sundays. It may not open at lunchtime so it is important to check in advance. **QP**

Lower Farringdon

Golden Pheasant

Gosport Road, GU34 3DJ (Farringdon crossroads on A32)
12-11; 12-10.30 Sun ☎ (01420) 588255
Courage Best Bitter; Dark Star Hophead; Sharp's Doom Bar, Atlantic; 3 changing beers (sourced nationally; often Andwells, Bowman, Cotleigh) H
The owners have run pubs in the area for over 10 years, and seven years ago brought their expertise to this delightful privately owned free house. The beers are well kept, with seven handpumps serving three fixed and four guest beers. The food is freshly cooked (with vegetarian options) – the fish and chips warrants special mention due to the secret recipe batter used. Easily accessible down the A32 four miles from Alton, this is a pub not to be missed. **QP**

Lower Wield

Yew Tree

Alresford, SO24 9RX SU636398
closed Mon; 12-3, 6-11; 12-10.30 Sun ☎ (01256) 389224
the-yewtree.org.uk
House beer (by Bowman); 1 changing beer (sourced locally; often Itchen Valley, Stonehenge, Triple fff) H
Out-of-the-way rural local set in picturesque rolling Hampshire countryside, with an old yew tree growing outside (hence the name), on a quiet lane opposite the local cricket pitch. The house beer is Bowman Meon Bitter and the guest normally comes from a local brewery. All real ales are sold at a reasonable price. The pub has a separate dining area where locally renowned and attractively priced food is served. Cyclists, ramblers and dog walkers are welcome. **QP**

Lymington

Monkey House

167 Southampton Road, SO41 9HA (on A337)
11-11; 12-10.30 Sun ☎ (01590) 676754
themonkeyhouse.co.uk
Brockenhurst Smokin Deer; Dancing Cows Pony; Flack Manor Flack's Double Drop; 1 changing beer (sourced locally; often Bowman, Brockenhurst, Piddle) H
Starting life as The Crown, the pub became known as The Monkey House as the landlord at the time kept monkeys. It later changed to The Tollhouse, after the nearby turnpike tollbooth. The real ales are all local and include an unfined beer from a new microbrewery in Brockenhurst. The lounge/dining room has a low, beamed ceiling and an open fire. The elegant bar (which is open to the roof) is wood-panelled, and has a fine fireplace and comfortable seating.
QP (6)

Milford on Sea

Wash House

27 High Street, SO41 0QF
11.30-11; 12-11 Sun ☎ (01590) 644665
thewashhousebar.co.uk
4 changing beers (sourced locally) H
Opened in mid-2017, this former launderette is now a smart, well-refurbished micropub with decor themed from its previous use. It serves four different real ales and four real ciders, plus a selection of wines and spirits and fresh coffee. The single room is nicely furnished with a selection of different seating. Although no meals are served, patrons can order gourmet burgers, via the bar staff, from the nearby La Perle café (owned and run by a former MasterChef finalist).
Q (X1)

North Camp

Farnborough Royal British Legion Club

51 Cambridge Road East, GU14 6QB
11.30-11 (midnight Fri & Sat); 12-11 Sun
☎ (01252) 543306
Palmers Dorset Gold; 2 changing beers (sourced regionally; often Flack Manor, Hammerpot, Hop Back) H
Show your CAMRA membership card or a copy of this Guide to enter this friendly social club. Set in a quiet, residential area, the venue comprises one large open-plan space with a central bar and a separate function room. It has a snooker table, pool table and dartboard. Social events include bingo, a meat raffle and occasional live music. Food is available lunchtimes and Thursday to Sunday evenings. Beers are from regional independents.
P (1)

North Waltham

Fox

Popham Lane, RG25 2BE (between village and A30)
11-11 (midnight Fri & Sat); 12-10.30 Sun
☎ (01256) 397288 thefox.org
Brakspear Bitter; West Berkshire Good Old Boy; 2 changing beers (sourced locally; often Ringwood) H
Lovely traditional country pub on the edge of the village and overlooking extensive farmland. The pub is divided into two – a popular restaurant and a public bar where food is also served (booking advisable). Local seasonal produce is featured where possible. Outside there is an extensive beer garden and a children's adventure play area. The Ushers signage remains on the rear of the pub.
QP (16)

Oakley

Barley Mow

19 Oakley Lane, RG23 7JZ
12-11.30 ☎ (01256) 782591 barleymowatoakley.com
Flowerpots Goodens Gold; Sharp's Doom Bar; 2 changing beers (sourced locally) H
An old-fashioned non-chain local pub in the heart of the picturesque village, serving well-kept and traditional ales including three from local brewers, the choice of which has increased since the removal of its tie via the market rent-only option. On Monday evenings a fish & chip van visits; you can either eat in the pub or have a beer while

waiting. A warm, family-oriented and dog-friendly hostelry, often used as a refreshment and meeting point for ramblers. Q ❀ ♣P (11)

Old Basing

Bartons Mill

Bartons Lane, RG24 8AE (follow signs to Basing House)
11-11; 10-11 Sat; 10-10.30 Sun ☎ (01256) 331153
bartonsmillpubanddining.co.uk/home
Wadworth IPA, Horizon, 6X, Swordfish; 1 changing beer (often Black Sheep) H
An attractively situated Wadworth house, once part of a still-existing water mill that overlooks the River Loddon and a water meadow. The pub is a short walk from the historic and picturesque ruins of Basing House and a large medieval tithe barn. The venue features traditional pub food and six Wadworth cask ales, plus one rotating guest ale, served seven days a week by friendly staff. Children are welcome, as is the occasional duck from the river! Conference facilities are available. ❀ ♿ P

Otterbourne

Otter

Boyatt Lane, SO21 2HW
11-11; 12-10.30 Sun ☎ (023) 8025 2685
theotterpub.co.uk
Hogs Back TEA; Otter Ale; Ringwood Razorback; Sharp's Doom Bar H
Popular, family-run pub, a short walk across the green from the main road bus stop, although Eastleigh/Winchester buses stop at the door. Stepping directly into the large bar, four real ales are always available. An extensive menu of home-made food is served in the adjoining restaurant (also available for family occasions) and in the bar area. Events include a Monday night quiz, Tuesday burger night and Sunday afternoon meat draw. Plentiful car parking adjoins the garden's seating area. Q❀ ♣P (1,E2)

Overton

Red Lion L

37 High Street, RG25 3HQ
12-3, 6-11; 12-10.30 Sun ☎ (01256) 773363
redlion-overton.co.uk
Bowman Swift One; Flowerpots Bitter; Sharp's Doom Bar H
Popular village pub that prides itself on well-kept local real ales and high-quality, freshly cooked food including specials. It is divided into three areas, including a main bar and snug with wood-burning stove. Near to the new Bombay Sapphire Distillery, the pub also offers an extensive gin menu. Outside there is a pleasant beer garden, partially covered patio area, separate function room with skittle alley available for hire, and a car park. The restaurant is closed Sunday evening and Monday. Q ❀ ♿♣P (76,86)

Park Gate

Village Inn

67 Botley Road, SO31 1AZ
11.30-11 (midnight Thu & Fri); 10-midnight Sat; 10-11 Sun ☎ (01489) 573223
House beer (by Black Sheep); 4 changing beers (often Fuller's, Harviestoun, Oakham) H
The Village Inn is a cosy, atmospheric Ember Inns pub, resembling a large house, offering great food alongside a selection of ales on five handpumps, four of which are rotating guest beers from the Ember portfolio. It is less than five minutes' walk from Swanwick train station. The pub has ticketed metered car parking Monday to Friday until 5pm, with parking charges refundable on bar purchases. ❀ ♿⇌P (28,28A)

Petersfield

Townhouse L

28 High Street, GU32 3JL
9am-11 (midnight Fri & Sat) ☎ (01730) 265630
petersfieldtownhouse.com
3 changing beers (sourced regionally; often Broken Bridge, Langham, Red Cat) H
A relatively small, modern bistro-style pub towards the eastern end of the town. It is furnished with plain wooden tables and chairs and a few comfortable armchairs and sofas. The floor has bare boards and the single bar has old taps for coat hooks. An additional upstairs bar also serves as a function room. At the rear is a small patio garden. The pub specialises in beers from small independent breweries. ❀ ⇌♣P (67)

Portsmouth

Apsley House

Auckland Road West, Southsea, PO5 3NY
3-11 (1am Fri); 12-1am Sat; 12-11 Sun ☎ (023) 9282 1294
St Austell Tribute; Sharp's Doom Bar; Timothy Taylor Landlord H
The pub is named in honour of the 1st Duke of Wellington, Arthur Wellesley, whose home on London's Hyde Park Corner was called Apsley House. Hidden in the back streets a short walk from the shops in Palmerston Road and Southsea Common, it is a traditional drinkers' pub with a single large U-shaped bar. The small south-facing patio to the front is popular in the warm summer months. ❀♣

Artillery Arms L

Hester Road, Milton, PO4 8HB
12-11.30 (midnight Fri & Sat) ☎ (023) 9273 3610
Ringwood Fortyniner; Triple fff Alton's Pride, Moondance; 3 changing beers (sourced locally; often Langham, Red Cat, Triple fff) H
A traditional two-bar locals' ale house with a friendly welcome for all. It has a large enclosed safe garden with play equipment for children (who are welcome until 7pm). No food is served except for rolls on match days. It is five minutes' walk from Fratton Park and can get busy before and after matches, but is friendly both to home and away fans. It supports many darts and pool teams, and has occasional live music on some Saturday nights. ❀♣P

Barley Mow L

39 Castle Road, Southsea, PO5 3DE
12 (11 Sat)-midnight; 12-11 Sun ☎ (023) 9282 3492
barleymowsouthsea.com
Fuller's London Pride; Gale's HSB; 6 changing beers (sourced nationally) H
Designed by AE Cogswell, although not typical of his style, this large, friendly community pub supports many events. It has both bar billiards and shove-ha'penny tables and a collection of board

games. There are pool, darts and golf teams, a chess league, weekly quiz, meat raffle, live music and monthly druid moots. The award-winning garden is a true gem. The lounge bar ceiling used to feature a painting of the Battle of Southsea. No entry after 11pm. (7,25)

Brewhouse & Kitchen

26 Guildhall Walk, Landport, PO1 2DD

11-11 (midnight Fri & Sat); 11-10.30 Sun
(023) 9289 1340

Brewhouse & Kitchen Sexton, Mucky Duck, Black Swan; 1 changing beer H

Distinctive from the outside with its Brewers' Tudor timber-clad Grade II-listed façade, you enter to the sight of gleaming copper and possibly brewing aromas; this pub constantly brews all of its own ale in a 2.5-barrel plant. Brew days where you become the brewer are offered, and takeouts of the beers are available. Food is served all day and the kitchen is open until 10pm (9pm Sun). Do not miss the Sunday roast dinners.

Hole in the Wall

36 Great Southsea Street, Southsea, PO5 3BY

4-11; 12-midnight Fri; 2-midnight Sat; 2-11 Sun
(023) 9229 8085 theholeinthewallpub.co.uk

Flowerpots Goodens Gold G**; 5 changing beers (sourced nationally)** H

The Hole may be one of the smaller pubs in Portsmouth but, as a genuine free house, it offers a wide range of beers from a varying selection of local and national breweries (check the website for the current beer range). Real ciders are usually available. It is open Saturdays from noon for Pompey home games. No admittance after 11pm, and dogs must be on leads. (7,23)

King Street Tavern

70 King Street, Southsea, PO5 4EH

12-3 (not Mon-Wed), 5-11; 12-3, 5-midnight Fri; 12-midnight Sat; 12-7 Sun (023) 9307 9568
kingstreettavernportsmouth.co.uk

Wadworth IPA, Horizon; 5 changing beers (sourced nationally; often Wadworth) H

A splendidly tiled exterior tempts you into a friendly pub and smokehouse. A good menu is available and most of the food is locally sourced, but this is definitely still a drinkers' pub, with up to seven well-kept ales and some craft keg and bottles. It does special food deals on a Monday night. A small sheltered patio is available for outdoor drinking in summer. It gets busy on Sundays for the award-winning lunches.
(7,25)

Lawrence Arms

63 Lawrence Road, Southsea, PO5 1NU

12-11.30 Mon; 2-11 (12.30am Fri); 11-12.30am Sat; 11-11 Sun (023) 9282 1280 lawrence-arms-portsmouth.co.uk

Harvey's Sussex Best Bitter; 5 changing beers (sourced nationally; often Flowerpots, Irving, Langham) H

A well-run Victorian street-corner pub, current local CAMRA Pub and Cider Pub of the Year. It always offers a warm welcome and a good range of ales and ciders. It has many TVs for sporting occasions, but they are usually muted until the sport begins. It gets busy on Portsmouth home match days. Most ales change almost daily, with usually at least one dark ale and one pale, hoppy one. Good-value toasties are available at all times.
(18)

Lord Palmerston

84-90 Palmerston Road, Southsea, PO5 3PT

8am-midnight (1.30am Fri & Sat) (023) 9272 8000

Fuller's London Pride; 9 changing beers (sourced nationally) H

A large Lloyds No.1, broken up into several areas. It uses the LocAle scheme as much as possible, with most of the ales coming from Hampshire and West Sussex. The usual good-value chain fare is served all day. It is just yards from Southsea Common and gets busy when festivals are held. It morphs into a nightclub on Friday and Saturday night when a DJ plays, and proof of age is required then, no matter how old you are.

Northcote Hotel

35 Francis Avenue, Southsea, PO4 0HL

12-midnight (1.30am Fri & Sat) (023) 9278 9888

Harvey's Sussex Best Bitter; Irving Invincible; Long Man American Pale Ale; Timothy Taylor Landlord; 1 changing beer (sourced locally; often Irving, Langham) H

A substantial two-bar pub in the back streets of Southsea a few minutes' walk from Albert Road. The public bar has a pool table and a small raised area with a dartboard. The smaller lounge has fitted seating round most of the walls and is decorated with memorabilia of the early days of cinema comedy, including Charlie Chaplin, Laurel and Hardy and the most famous of fictional detectives, Sherlock Holmes. (2,25)

Phoenix

13 Duncan Road, Southsea, PO5 2QU

10-midnight (1am Fri & Sat); 12-midnight Sun
(023) 9278 1055

Ringwood Fortyniner; 2 changing beers (sourced nationally; often Dark Star, Irving, Urban Island) H

This two-bar pub is a true community local. The public bar has memorabilia relating to Portsmouth Football Club, while the lounge is decorated with photographs of stars who have performed at the nearby Kings Theatre and some interesting images of the theatre itself. It also has an upright piano, a number of board games and a tabletop Space Invaders machine. A quirky patio garden separates the bars from the games room, once part of the Dock End Brewery. (2,25)

Porters

31-35 Albert Road, Southsea, PO5 2SE

12-midnight; 12-10.30 Sun (023) 9229 3474

Otter Ale; Sharp's Doom Bar; 3 changing beers (sourced nationally; often Dark Star, Staggeringly Good) H

A large single-bar pub divided into several drinking areas. The front is reminiscent of a shop with large plain windows. The floor is tiled throughout and the furniture is mainly bare wooden tables and chairs, with a small number of high stools at the bar. Altogether it has a modern but retro feel with painted boarded walls and candles. One handpump is used exclusively for beers from the Staggeringly Good Brewery. (2,25)

Rose in June

102 Milton Road, Milton, PO3 6AR

12-midnight (1am Fri & Sat) (023) 9282 4191
theroseinjune.co.uk

Fallen Acorn Twisted Oak; Gale's HSB; Irving Frigate; 3 changing beers (often Langham) H

A hub of the community, this is a large two-bar pub with a huge garden that is popular in summer. It

supports pool and darts teams and is five minutes' walk from Fratton Park, so gets busy on match days. There is a special deal on guest beers on Friday, and meat raffles and cash draws each weekend. No food is provided, except rolls on match days. Six ciders are always available. It holds a beer festival on the last weekend in June.
Q P

Sir Loin of Beef

152 Highland Road, Eastney, PO4 9NH
12-midnight (12.30am Fri & Sat) (023) 9282 0115
Gale's HSB; Titanic Plum Porter; 6 changing beers (sourced nationally)
Friendly street-corner local with eight ales on handpump and a good selection of bottled beers. This large, single-bar pub has a lot of naval memorabilia adorning the walls and a klaxon is used to call time. Quiz night is Thursday and there is live music and a meat raffle on Sunday lunchtime. If in Southsea, this little gem is a must.

Wave Maiden

36 Osborne Road, Southsea, PO5 3LT
6-11; 12-midnight Fri & Sat; 12-10 Sun (023) 9217 8878
3 changing beers (sourced nationally; often Franklins, Gun, Staggeringly Good)
An independent, family-owned establishment, focusing on artisan beer and cheese. Go to this premises for beer brewed for taste, not mass consumption, alongside a menu that offers delicious home-made cheese-based dishes, with vegan specials available. It is one of the few gravity stillages in the area, with a constant rotation of local and national ales, offering a welcoming atmosphere for beer lovers of all ages. (1,23)

Ringwood

Railway

35 Hightown Road, BH24 1NQ SU152048
11.30-11; 12-10 Sun (01425) 473701 therailway.co
House beer (by Ringwood); 4 changing beers (sourced nationally)
Friendly two-bar local pub, with a cosy snug and a good lounge, leading to a child-friendly enclosed garden. It is warm and welcoming, with a woodburner in the snug. As well as the Ringwood ale, there is a changing range of beers including craft keg and a good selection of gins (many local) and bag-in-box ciders. An interesting range of railwayana adorns the walls. A range of quality burgers is available, plus a selection of roasts on Sunday. Q P

Romsey

Old House at Home

62 Love Lane, SO51 8DE (NE of town centre)
11-11 (11.30 Fri & Sat); 12-10.30 Sun (01794) 513175
theoldhouseathomeromsey.co.uk
Fuller's London Pride; Gale's Seafarers Ale, HSB; 2 changing beers (sourced nationally; often Fuller's)
Just five minutes' walk from the town centre, Romsey's only thatched pub has lots of old-world charm. The single L-shaped bar with a separate dining area has beams, booths and a woodburner giving a comfortable ambience. Outside it has a large heated patio. Dating in part from the 17th century, this pub is popular with locals and visitors alike and the restaurant gets good reviews. Folk music sessions take place on a Monday night.
P

Star Inn

13 The Horsefair, SO51 8EZ (N of town centre)
12-11 (midnight Fri & Sat) (01794) 511165
Bowman Wallops Wood; St Austell Tribute; 2 changing beers (sourced locally; often Bowman)
A charming old local, originally the Strong's Brewery tap, now a free house. It is a dog-friendly pub, and within walking distance of the town centre on the road to Stockbridge. One large bar area, warmed by a log woodburner, generally serves four draught beers, of which normally three are local. It has a convivial atmosphere with much local involvement, and features an informal folk session on Wednesdays and live music on Saturday evenings. Other attractions include poker league on Thursdays and league darts on Tuesdays and Fridays. Accommodation comprises two double and two family rooms.

Selborne

Selborne Arms

High Street, GU34 3JR
11-3, 6-11; 11-11 Sat; 12-11 Sun (01420) 511247
selbornearms.co.uk
Bowman Swift One; Ringwood Fortyniner; 3 changing beers (sourced regionally; often Fallen Acorn, Hogs Back, Langham)
A traditional award-winning multi-roomed village pub with real fires and a friendly atmosphere, located at the foot of the zig-zag path carved by famous naturalist Gilbert White. Up to three guest beers come from local breweries. Beer bats offering three thirds of beer for the price of a pint are a useful innovation. Extensive menus showcase local and home-made produce, with vegetarian and gluten free options. The safe play area in the garden is popular with children.
Q P (38)

Shedfield

Wheatsheaf Inn

Botley Road, SO32 2JG (on A334)
12-11; 12-10.30 Sun (01329) 833024
flowerpotscheriton.co.uk/wheatsheaf
Flowerpots Perridge Pale, Bitter, Goodens Gold; 3 changing beers (sourced locally; often CrackleRock, Goddards, Palmers)
Friendly, popular, award-winning pub, serving all local beers (mostly from Cheriton's Flowerpots Brewery) direct from the cask, plus ciders from Westons. The pub is split between two rooms, warmed by a double-sided wood-burning stove. The side room has been extended to provide more seating and easy access to the beautiful rear garden. Home-cooked food is served every lunchtime and Tuesday/Wednesday evenings. Live music is hosted most Saturdays, and an annual beer festival on the late May bank holiday weekend. Q P (69)

Sherfield English

Hatchet Inn

Salisbury Road, SO51 6FP (on A27)
12-3, 5-11.30; 12-11.30 Fri-Sun (01794) 322487
hatchetinn.com

Bombardier Burning Gold; St Austell Tribute; Sharp's Doom Bar; 1 changing beer (sourced nationally) [H]
Easily found, this is the last pub in Hampshire on the A27. It is family run by Liz and the chef Lin, ably assisted by friendly, efficient staff. There are two bars: a square public and a long dining saloon, the end wall of which is a giant menu. People flock here for good-value home-made food. Mondays and Thursdays are fish and steak specials nights. Outside is a children's adventure playground. There is a beer festival in August.
Q ❀ ◑ ▲ ♣ P 🚌 (X7R) 🐾 📶

Silchester

Calleva Arms

The Common, RG7 2PH
11-11 (11.30 Fri & Sat); 12-11 Sun ☎ (0118) 970 0305
Fuller's Oliver's Island, London Pride; Gale's Seafarers Ale, HSB; 1 changing beer [H]
An attractive village pub opposite the common, named after the local Roman settlement of Calleva Atrebatum. A Fuller's establishment, it has five handpumps serving four regular Fuller's ales plus one guest ale which is often a Fuller's seasonal or a local real ale. There is a welcoming bar with a separate comfortable dining area; an excellent choice of bar and restaurant food is also served in the conservatory and the large garden in the summer months. ❀ ◑ ♣ P 🚌 (14) 🐾 📶

Soberton

White Lion

School Hill, SO32 3PF
11-11; 11-10 Sun ☎ (01489) 877346
thewhitelionsoberton.co.uk
Bowman Swift One, Wallops Wood; 1 changing beer (sourced nationally; often Bowman, Flowerpots, Triple fff) [H]
Well-appointed inn with a small village bar and larger restaurant. There are seats outside the pub, and a large village green close to the historic St Peter's church. Good-value food is served every day, with large roast dinners on Sunday. Most ales are from the Bowman Brewery, less than two miles away, and it has a good wine list. The village bar is a nice spot for a quiet pint after a walk in the local countryside. Q ❀ 🛏 ◑ 🍎 🐾

Southampton

Bar Marina

Unit 7A, Kemps Quay, Quayside Road, SO18 1AD
SU438131
3-10.30 (11 Fri); 12-11 Sat; 12-10.30 Sun
☎ (023) 8178 5486
4 changing beers (sourced locally) [G]
You feel comfortable as soon as you step through the door of this cosy bar, welcomed by friendly staff and an enthusiastic landlord. Located at Kemps Quay, this little gem is well worth seeking out. Two walls feature imposing pictures of Southampton's famous liners, the Queen Mary and the Queen Elizabeth. Local beers are gravity served. A great place to relax and watch the sun go down in summer. Q ❀ ⇌ (Bitterne) 🍎 🚌 🐾

Belgium & Blues

180 Above Bar Street, SO14 7DW
12-11 (midnight Fri & Sat); 12-10.30 Sun
☎ (023) 8022 5411 belgiumandblues.co.uk
4 changing beers (sourced regionally; often Broken Bridge, Vibrant Forest) [H]
A unique pair of Belgian-inspired bars – a brasserie/gin bar at street level and downstairs a bigger cellar bar with large group tables and two cosy side booths. Handpumps serve up to four changing ales (some unfined) and several ciders, and there is a range of Belgian and Belgian-style beers in kegs and bottles. Home-made food is also Belgian inspired. The bar features a blues DJ and live music at weekends and also holds brewery tap takeovers and tasting evenings. Q ◑ ⇌ 🍎 🚌 🐾 📶

Bitter Virtue

70 Cambridge Road, SO14 6US (jct with Alma Rd)
closed Mon; 10.30-8.30; 10.30-2 Sun ☎ (023) 8055 4881
bittervirtue.co.uk
2 changing beers (sourced regionally; often Bowman, Broken Bridge, Siren) [G]
Hidden in the back streets, but close to main roads, this world-class street-corner beer shop attracts customers from far and wide. It is now in its 21st consecutive year in the Guide, and Southampton's longest-standing entry. Over 1,000 beers and ciders in bottles and cans are stocked from Britain, Belgium, the US, and many other countries worldwide. Two cask beers and a draught cider are also available. The side wall of the shop is a community historical mural. Q 🍎 🚌 🐾

Bookshop Alehouse

21 Portswood Road, SO17 2ES
12-11
4 changing beers (sourced locally) [H]
Local CAMRA Pub of the Year and Wessex Region runner-up for 2017, having been converted from a bookshop in 2016 (books are still on sale!). Four handpumps serve a changing variety of mainly local ales; a fridge houses four bag-in-box ciders. It has no music, TV or games machines, so conversation rules here. There is no food but customers are encouraged to purchase food at the many local takeaways; plates and cutlery are provided. A wheelchair access ramp is available.
Q ♿ ⇌ (St Denys) ♣ 🍎 🚌 🐾 📶

Brewhouse & Kitchen

47 Highfield Lane, SO17 1QD
11-11 (midnight Fri & Sat); 12-10.30 Sun
☎ (023) 8055 5566
Brewhouse & Kitchen Speedwell, On Le Tiss, Walk the Line; 2 changing beers [H]
Part of the ever-growing Brewhouse & Kitchen chain, this family-friendly pub opened under its current guise in 2015. The old public bar now houses the 2.5 barrel (720 pint) brewery where all the pub's real ales are created. It serves regular core beers and two other changing ales – one seasonal and the other a one-off brew. It also has a large selection of bottled beers and craft kegs. Good-quality food is served from midday every day. ❀ ◑ ♿ 🍎 P 🚌 🐾 📶

Butcher's Hook

7 Manor Farm Road, SO18 1NN
closed Mon & Tue; 6-11 Wed & Thu; 4-11 Fri; 1-11 Sat; 2-10 Sun ☎ (023) 8178 2280 butchershookpub.com
4 changing beers (sourced nationally) [G]
The inspirational first micropub to grace the Southampton beer scene. It always has interesting and varying beers, sourced both locally and nationally, in the shape of four cask ales, gravity served, with five craft keg lines. The small interior

of the original Victorian butcher's shop, latterly a florist, always makes for a friendly and enjoyable atmosphere. Occasional beer-themed events and musical evenings plus the popular Butcher's Hook pie competition add to the community feel of this gem. Q (Bitterne) (7)

Caskaway

47 Oxford Street, SO14 3DP

closed Mon & Tue; 4-10 Wed-Fri; 12-10 Sat; 3-8 Sun

caskaway.pub

6 changing beers (sourced regionally) G

A cosy micropub, the Caskaway Tasting Rooms serves a selection of cask ales, plus ciders and perry, all on gravity. An eclectic variety of bottled, canned and craft keg beers also features. Bench seats run down each side of the room, where table service is offered. The theme is nautical, with flags, ropes and lifebelts on the walls. Pavement seating is available outside on the semi-pedestrianised Oxford Street. Local CAMRA Cider Pub of the Year 2018. Q

Freemantle Arms L

31 Albany Road, SO15 3EF

12-2.30, 5-8 (11 Tue & Wed); 12-11 Thu-Sat; 12-10 Sun

(023) 8077 2536 thefreemantlearms.co.uk

Sharp's Doom Bar; 4 changing beers (sourced nationally; often Fallen Acorn, Goddards, Red Cat) H

Proper back-street local with Victorian charm, close to the busy Shirley Road. Five cask ales are served, both from local and national breweries. The friendly staff welcome you into the single bar area, which is tastefully decorated with Southampton vistas and interesting old tools. The enclosed colourful garden is an oasis from the surrounding city. Cribbage is played regularly and most alternate Thursdays have quiz evenings. The pub holds an annual beer festival and hosts charity events. (Millbrook)

Guide Dog L

38 Earl's Road, SO14 6SF (corner with Ancasta Rd)

12-11; 12-10.30 Sun (023) 8063 8947

Dark Star American Pale Ale, Hophead; Flowerpots Goodens Gold; Red Cat Prowler Pale; 7 changing beers (sourced nationally; often Binghams, Siren, XT) H

Former CAMRA Wessex Pub of the Year, this gem is well worth seeking out. Eleven handpumps, of which seven always offer changing beers, make this a mecca for real ale fans. The Dog House is a Thai-themed back room where musical evenings are regularly staged, and on Thursday evenings the Thai landlady creates extremely popular Thai dishes. Within walking distance of St Mary's football stadium, all are welcome, giving this cosy pub a friendly atmosphere on match days.
Q (7,U6)

Hop Inn L

Woodmill Lane, SO18 2PH

12-11; 11-11.30 Fri & Sat; 12-10.30 Sun

(023) 8055 7723

Bowman Swift One; Gale's HSB; Greene King Abbot; Sharp's Doom Bar, Atlantic H

The proud overall winner of the 2017 Southampton in Bloom Mabs Cottel Trophy. Step into this welcoming 1930s residential two-bar pub and you will instantly feel at home. A long lounge with L-shaped bar sits to one side, the walls adorned with decorative plates and jugs contributing to the warm homely feel. The public bar, reached through a separate entrance, houses a games and sports bar with a jukebox. Popular folk music evenings are held on Wednesdays. Q P (16,7)

Junction Inn L

21 Priory Road, SO17 2JZ

11-11 (midnight Fri & Sat); 12-11 Sun (023) 8058 4486

junctionstdenys.co.uk

Greene King XX Mild, IPA, Abbot; 5 changing beers (sourced locally) H

Classic mid 19th-century pub retaining many preserved features including engraved windows and back-bar fittings. Now a Greene King Local Hero beer house, eight handpumped ales dispense the rare XX Mild and a number of local small brewery beers. Several ciders are served in summertime. It has an extensive food menu and is very much a hub of local activity with Friday quiz night, Sunday meat draw and plenty of live music. The nearby riverside boardwalk footpath leads towards St Mary's football ground.
(St Denys) (7)

Olaf's Tun

8 Portsmouth Road, SO19 9AA

closed Mon & Tue; 6-10; 4-11 Fri; 1-11 Sat; 1-9.30 Sun

(023) 8044 7887 olafstun.co.uk

4 changing beers (sourced nationally) G

Friendly, welcoming micropub offering a regularly changing selection of up to four gravity dispensed cask ales, plus two real ciders. The enthusiastic bar staff are knowledgeable on the beers served. The bright, airy feel helps the pub seem much bigger, and a ramp to the rear gives wheelchair access. Acoustic music evenings feature at least monthly. You may order in a takeaway and a nearby pizzeria delivers to the bar. Q (Woolston)

Park Inn

37 Carlisle Road, SO16 4FN

3-11; 12-11 Fri & Sat; 12-10.30 Sun (023) 8078 7835

theparkinn.co.uk

Wadworth IPA, 6X, Swordfish; 2 changing beers (sourced nationally) H

The epitome of a street-corner local, this early Victorian pub is tucked away just off the busy Shirley Precinct. Following a sensitive refurbishment in 2016, the distinctive public and lounge areas in what is now a single bar were retained. There is a paved outside seating area in front of the pub. Guest beers are from a Wadworth list. Generally, no food is available but on Fridays customers can choose from home-made Scotch eggs and a cheeseboard.

Platform Tavern L

Town Quay, SO14 2NY

12-11 (midnight Thu); 11.30-midnight Fri; 12-midnight Sat

(023) 8033 7232 platformtavern.com

Fuller's London Pride; Gale's Seafarers Ale; 3 changing beers (sourced locally) H

A bustling city pub, opposite the Isle of Wight and Hythe ferry terminals, with a rear entrance in historic Winkle Street. Three changing guest ales are usually from local small breweries. The decor incorporates part of the original city walls along with African art, batik panels and musical instruments. In a separate dining area home-cooked food is served daily; Sunday roasts are a speciality. Events include live music every week, three beer festivals each year and an Easter cider festival.

Rockstone

63 Onslow Road, SO14 0JL

12-midnight; 12-11 Sun (023) 8063 7256

therockstone.co.uk

7 changing beers (sourced regionally; often Dark Star, Flack Manor, Vibrant Forest) [H]

Increasingly popular LocAle-accredited pub, with up to seven varied real ales and up to two real ciders, served by knowledgeable and friendly staff. A fine selection of bottled beers, gins, rums and whiskies from around the world complements the beers. Occasional beer festivals are held. The building celebrated 175 years of selling beer in 2018. The increasingly popular and generous burgers include a Sunday Roast burger. Note the listed horse trough outside. (7,U6)

Witch's Brew

220 Shirley Road, SO15 3FL

closed Mon & Tue; 5-11; 4-11 Sat; 4-10 Sun

07403 871757 thewitchsbrewsouthampton.com

4 changing beers (sourced regionally) [G]

Previously a mysticism shop, it was converted into a micropub with ornamentation reflecting the witchcraft theme. The bar is at the back of the pub with interconnected snug rooms in front. A fenced-off front courtyard allows you to watch the bustle of the street. The welcoming landlady, who is keen to encourage conversation, adds to this friendly atmosphere. Up to four regularly changing cask ales are dispensed by gravity along with two bag-in-box ciders. Carryouts are available. **Q**

Southwick

Golden Lion

High Street, PO17 6EB

12-3, 5.30-11; 12-midnight Sat; 12-7 Sun

(023) 9221 0437

Suthwyk Old Dick, Skew Sunshine Ale; 4 changing beers (sourced locally; often Langham, Palmers, Triple fff) [H]

This free house is a central part of the village's annual D-Day celebration (Southwick D-Day Revival) in June, reflecting its part in the planning for the Normandy landings. Award-winning food is served in the separate dining room or in the bar. Beers are usually local. The house beer is named after the last brewer, Old Dick. His old brewhouse is now a museum in the car park. Live jazz is played on Tuesdays. **Q P**

Swanwick

Elm Tree Inn

Swanwick Lane, SO31 7DX

11-11 (1am Fri; midnight Sat); 11.30-11 Sun

(01489) 579818 elmtreeinn.co.uk

Flowerpots Bitter, Goodens Gold; 2 changing beers (sourced locally) [H]

Traditional two-bar free house serving up to four real ales, owned and run by the landlady. There is also an extensive restaurant serving lunch and evening meals. An annual beer festival held in May utilises the garden. There is ample car parking and Swanwick rail station is just over half a mile away. Nearby attractions include the yachting area of the river Hamble and Bursledon Brickworks Museum. **P** (28,28A)

Tichborne

Tichborne Arms

SO24 0NA (1¼ miles S of B3047) SU571304

11.45-3, 6-9.30 (11 Wed & Thu; 11.30 Fri); 11.45-11.30 Sat; 12-7.30 Sun (01962) 733760 tichbornearms.co.uk

Palmers Copper Ale; 2 changing beers (sourced locally; often Bath Ales, Bowman) [G]

Owned by the Tichborne estate, this is a proper thatched village pub with a comfortable old-world feel. Palmers Copper is the regular beer, with the two guest ales tending to come from Dorset or Somerset, all served on gravity. The imaginative upmarket food menu using locally sourced products gives it a well-earned reputation for quality food. A popular beer and music festival, with overnight camping and some motorhome parking, makes the August bank holiday a big hit. **Q P**

Titchfield

Wheatsheaf

1 East Street, PO14 4AD

12-11 (midnight Fri & Sat) (01329) 842965

wheatsheaftitchfield.co.uk

Flowerpots Bitter; Palmers IPA; 3 changing beers (sourced regionally; often Fallen Acorn, Hop Back, Red Cat) [H]

As Titchfield's only privately owned free house, this welcoming 17th-century pub continues to gain in popularity for its excellent selection of ales and high-quality food. An intimate bar with a real fire and a cosy snug to the back add to the friendly atmosphere. Food is available Monday to Sunday in the bar and separate restaurant. Steak night is Tuesday and roasts are served every Sunday. A popular beer festival is held summer and winter. **Q P** (X4)

Twyford

Bugle Inn

Park Lane, SO21 1QT (jct of High St and Park Lane)

11-11; 11-10.30 Sun (01962) 714888

bugleinntwyford.co.uk

Bowman Swift One; Flowerpots Bitter, Goodens Gold; Timothy Taylor Boltmaker, Landlord; 1 changing beer [H]

Modernised from a multi-roomed village pub, the interior is now one long bar. To the left is a cosy area with sofas around the fireplace, at the centre a lengthy bar with stools, and to the right a dining area. Five beers (occasionally including a seasonal variety) from three breweries are complemented by a large wine selection – over 10 by the glass. Although not quite a gastropub, the extensive menu sets it in that direction. Three high-quality double rooms are on offer. **Q P** (69,E1)

Warsash

Ferryman

2 Warsash Road, SO31 9HX

12-11 (11.30 Fri & Sat); 12-10.30 Sun (01489) 573088

4 changing beers (sourced nationally; often Adnams, Milk Street) [H]

In the centre of the village, this pub provides four changing real ales, an excellent restaurant and a separate function room. There is a decked area to the front used for beer and cider festivals, along with live music. The River Hamble and Southampton Water are close by. Buses running between Southampton and Fareham stop outside. P (X5)

West Tytherley

Black Horse

North Lane, SP5 1NF

closed Mon; 6-9 Tue; 12-3, 6-11; 12-7 Sun

(01794) 340308 theblackhorsepub.co.uk

Butcombe Adam Henson's Rare Breed; 2 changing beers (sourced regionally; often Andwells, Bowman, Ringwood)

A charming Grade II-listed village free house dating from the 17th century. The main bar has a substantial carved dark-wood fireplace that was already 150 years old when it was relocated from the nearby Norman Court manor house in 1830. Five handpumps serve three beers, and one or two ciders. Food is locally sourced and often includes proper pies on the specials board. Across the courtyard is a traditional skittle alley which can be hired for functions. Q P (37)

Weyhill

Weyhill Fair

Weyhill Road, SP11 0PP

11.30-3, 5.30-11; 11.30-11 Fri & Sat; 12-6 Sun

(01264) 773631 weyhillfair.com

Fuller's London Pride; Gale's Seafarers Ale, HSB; 2 changing beers (often Butcombe, Castle Rock, Wychwood)

A country-style pub three miles west of Andover, standing on the site of the historic Weyhill fairground. It serves meals every session using locally sourced ingredients where possible. The three regular Fuller's beers are usually supplemented by both a seasonal and a guest beer from the Fuller's portfolio. A popular outdoor music and beer festival is usually held in July. Closed Mondays winter. P

Whitchurch

Whitchurch Sports & Social Club

Winchester Road, RG28 7RB (S edge of town)

12-1.30 (not Wed), 7-11; 12-11 Sun (01256) 892493

Red Cat Prowler Pale; St Austell Proper Job; 1 changing beer

Tucked away opposite the tranquil Millennium Meadow, this club features two large bars open most lunchtimes, evenings and weekends, serving two real ales, usually local. Home to Whitchurch United Football Club, the venue is shared by the indoor bowling club whose impressive green can be viewed from the comfortable lounge bar. Events include quizzes, parties, cabarets, discos and live bands. Opens as a café most mornings from 7.30am (10am Sun). P (86)

White Hart Hotel

The Square, RG28 7DN

11-11 (midnight Fri & Sat); 12-10.30 Sun

(01256) 892900 whitehartholelwhitchurch.co.uk

Arkell's Wiltshire Gold, 3B, Moonlight

This 15th-century coaching inn is a centre of community life, with a lively public bar, pleasant dining area and a quiet restaurant/function room. Look for the decorated bollards outside; one commemorates author Charles Kingsley, who stayed here. Regular events include discos, bands and charity challenges. The right to demonstrate was won for the country in the 19th century in The Square outside. Q P (76,86)

Widley

George Inn

Portsdown Hill Road, PO6 1BE

11-11; 12-11 Sun (023) 9222 1097

the-george-inn.co.uk

Adnams Broadside; Fuller's London Pride; Greene King Abbot; Ringwood Razorback; Sharp's Doom Bar; 2 changing beers (sourced nationally; often Irving, Flowerpots, Langham)

Set on top of Portsdown Hill, the pub offers commanding views of Portsmouth and the Isle of Wight. It was once a stop on the Portsdown & Horndean Light Railway, although little trace of this remains. The single U-shaped bar is decorated with brewery memorabilia including a number of display cases full of beer bottles. The transport theme is maintained with an old bus stop sign affixed to one of the pillars on the bar. P

Winchester

Albion

2 Stockbridge Road, SO23 7BZ

12-11 (11.30 Fri & Sat); 12-10.30 Sun (01962) 867991

Flowerpots Perridge Pale, Bitter, Goodens Gold; 1 changing beer (sourced locally)

Small, oddly angled corner pub at the bottom of Station Hill, one of two now owned by the Flowerpots pub/brewery at Cheriton. Three of the four pumps are devoted to the Cheriton core beers and the fourth either to a seasonal or a guest small local brewery. There is no food service but there are snacks including pies and Scotch eggs. An ideal spot for a relaxing break in your train journey, sampling beer from Hampshire's (now) oldest independent brewery. Q

Black Boy

1 Wharf Hill, SO23 9NQ (just off Chesil St, B3404)

12-11 (midnight Fri & Sat); 12-10.30 Sun

(01962) 861754 theblackboypub.com

Alfred's Saxon Bronze; Flowerpots Bitter; 3 changing beers (sourced locally; often Bowman, Hop Back, Itchen Valley)

A multi-level collection of adjoining rooms set on a hilly slope, all served from a central bar. The five ales are always from small local breweries, and several ciders are usually offered. The eclectic decor is almost beyond description – collections of tools from many trades, scientific instruments, taxidermy, model aircraft... the list is endless! The pub menu offers plenty of choice, or for more formal dining there is the co-owned Michelin-starred Black Rat restaurant opposite. Q (4)

Fulflood Arms

28 Cheriton Road, SO22 5EF (jct with Western Rd)

12-2.30, 4.30-11; 12-midnight Fri & Sat; 12-11 Sun

(01962) 842996 thefulfloodarms.co.uk

Greene King IPA; Red Cat Prowler Pale; 6 changing beers (sourced locally; often Flowerpots, Red Cat)

A classic back-street local, the original dark-green tiled façade and etched windows remaining as evidence of this 19th-century pub's former Winchester Brewery ownership. Inside, a makeover has produced a smart and pleasant single bar divided into differing areas, with a wood-burning stove and comfy chairs, and a library. Quizzes and special events attract a loyal local following. There are patios outside for drinkers, front and rear. Q❀♣(4)

Hyde Tavern

57 Hyde Street, SO23 7DY

12.30-2 (not Thu), 5-11; 5-midnight Fri; 12.30-midnight Sat; 12-11 Sun ☎ (01962) 862592 hydetavern.co.uk

Flowerpots Bitter; Harvey's Sussex Best Bitter H; 4 changing beers (sourced locally; often Flowerpots, Red Cat, West Berkshire) H/G

An ancient listed building with a fine twin-gable frontage. Step down from street level into the small, low-ceilinged bar leading to a smaller back room and the cellar function room. Six beers, mostly local, always include a dark variety. There is no food service but takeaways may be ordered in (plates/cutlery provided for a small charge). Many activities take place including music groups, storytelling nights, a writers' circle and a Sunday quiz. Q❀♣

Old Vine

8 Great Minster Street, SO23 9HA

11-11; 11-10.30 Sun ☎ (01962) 854616 oldvinewinchester.com

Timothy Taylor Landlord; 3 changing beers (sourced locally; often Bowman, Flowerpots, Longdog) H

A vine-clad, 18th-century, Grade II-listed inn, with stunning views across to the cathedral. The single, cosy, oak-beamed bar has an adjoining restaurant serving home-cooked food using much local produce. A rear courtyard has a terrace, which is smoke-free, and an inviting courtyard garden room. Its medieval cellars are said to have two ghosts who haunt the premises. It has a strong commitment to LocAle. Q❀♣(1,69)

Queen Inn

28 Kingsgate Road, SO23 9PG

11-midnight ☎ (01962) 853898 thequeeninnwinchester.co.uk

Greene King IPA; Morland Old Speckled Hen H; 8 changing beers (sourced locally; often Broken Bridge, Flowerpots, Red Cat) H/G

A must-visit pub for real ale fans, with local ales in abundance, situated in the southern edge of town close to bus routes. Its own microbrewery produces a range of Queen Inn beers. The comprehensive food menu is sourced locally within a 15-mile radius. Six beers are on handpump, four on gravity. Outside is a large garden to the rear (including a barbecue area) and a seating area at the front. A beer festival is held on Mayday bank holidays. ❀P(1,69)

Wykeham Arms

75 Kingsgate Street, SO23 9PE

11-11; 11-10.30 Sun ☎ (01962) 853834 wykehamarmswinchester.co.uk

Flowerpots Goodens Gold; Fuller's London Pride; Gale's Seafarers Ale, HSB; 1 changing beer H

Lovely Georgian (1755) inn by Winchester's college and cathedral. Although a Fuller's pub, a local Flowerpots Brewery beer is always available. The jumble of interconnected rooms is served from one bar area and is totally crammed full with memorabilia, much of it Nelsoniana. High-quality food and accommodation (14 rooms) ensure the Wykeham is in virtually every guide. The tea rooms opposite belong to the same establishment. Q❀(1,69)

Wonston

Wonston Arms

Stoke Charity Road, SO21 3LS

closed Mon; 5-10; 12-10 Sat; 12-8 Sun ☎ 07909 993388

Bowman Yumi; Flowerpots Goodens Gold; 2 changing beers (sourced locally; often Bowman, Flowerpots, Red Cat) H

In the heart of the village, this true community pub is just a 15-minute walk from Sutton Scotney. Four real ales are served from local breweries, plus 160 gins. It opens Mondays for darts matches, a fish and chip van visits Tuesdays, curries are delivered Fridays, and a fishmonger visits on Thursday. Folk music takes place on the second and fourth Wednesdays. Jazz sessions, quizzes and a photography club also feature. CAMRA Regional Pub of the Year 2017 and local Pub of the Year 2018. Q❀♣P

Wootton

Rising Sun

Bashley Common Road, BH25 5SF (on B3058)

10-11; 10-10.30 Sun ☎ (01425) 610360 therisingsunbashley.co.uk

Flack Manor Flack's Double Drop; Morland Old Speckled Hen; 3 changing beers (sourced nationally; often Flack Manor, Hop Back, Otter) H

Located in the south-west of the New Forest, close to the A35, this is an excellent place to meet with family and friends. The front bar looks on to open forest, to the side is a large car park, and at the back a large garden with excellent children's play facilities. Up to five cask ales are complemented by draught cider in summer. Quality food is served, with locally sourced meats and other produce where possible. Dogs are welcome in hard-floor areas. ❀P(C32,C33)

Yateley

Dog & Partridge

105 Reading Road, GU46 7LR

12-11 (midnight Fri & Sat); 12-10.30 Sun ☎ (01252) 870648 dogandpartridgeyateley.co.uk

House beer (by Caledonian); 3 changing beers (sourced nationally; often St Austell, Theakston, Wychwood) H

Customers are assured of a friendly welcome in this pub at the heart of the local community next to the village green. It has an excellent reputation for quality cask ale, often including local brews, and home-made food. Sunday lunch is popular and booking is essential. Quiz night features on Monday and live music on Saturday. A pool table and dartboard are available, together with sport on Sky and BT. ❀♣P(2,3)

> Good ale is the true and proper drink of Englishmen. He is not deserving of the name of Englishman who speaketh against ale, that is good ale. **George Borrow, Lavengro**

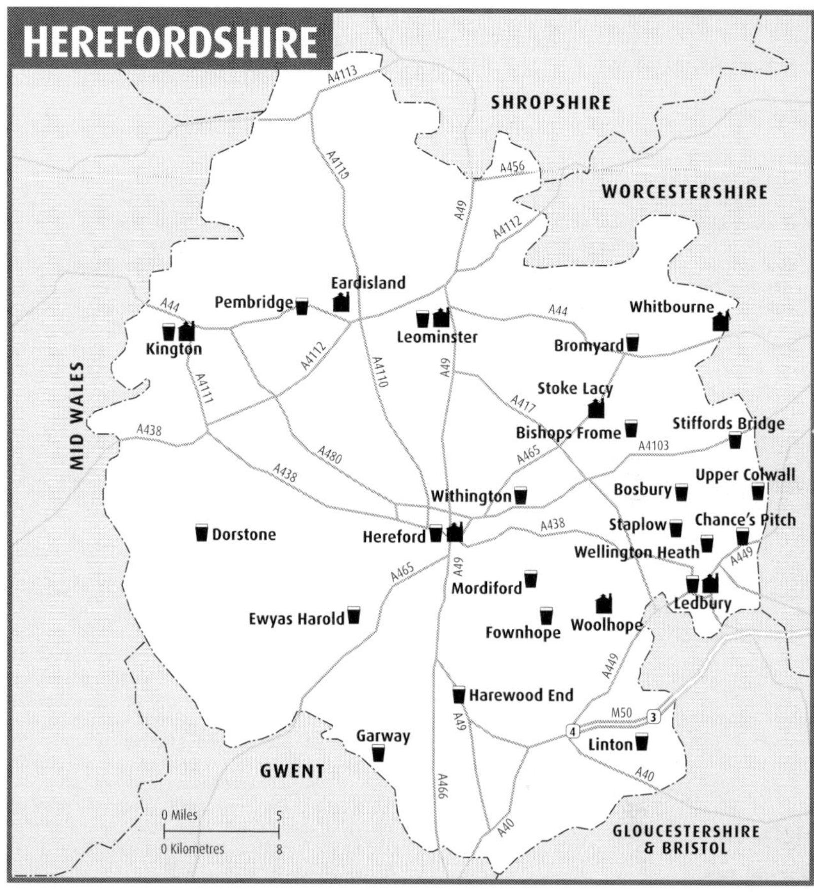

Bishops Frome

Chase Inn

4 Bridge Street, WR6 5BP (on B4214)
12-11 (midnight Thu); 12-1am Fri & Sat; 12-10 Sun
☎ (01885) 490358
Otter Bitter; Wye Valley Bitter, HPA; 1 changing beer (often Hobsons, Ludlow, Otter) Ⓗ
Imposing pub facing the village green. A main lounge bar, with two fine bay windows, divides into separate dining and drinking areas – the latter with a comfy corner sofa and woodburner. A public bar to the rear offers pool, darts and TV. Homely and friendly, with many original features, the pub also offers accommodation in five en-suite rooms. Traditional pub meals are available lunchtimes and evenings, with curry and pie nights every other week.

Green Dragon

WR6 5BP (in village, just off B4214)
5 (4.30 winter)-11; 4-11.30 Fri; 12-11.30 Sat; 12-6 Sun
☎ (01885) 490607 thegreendragoninn.com
Otter Bright; Purple Moose Cwrw Eryri/Snowdonia Ale; Timothy Taylor Golden Best; Wye Valley Bitter; 2 changing beers (sourced locally) Ⓗ
A warren of flagstone-floored rooms, genuine low beams and a fabulous inglenook fireplace are a treat for visitors to this 17th-century village inn. With six handpumps offering a range of local and regional beers, plus five local ciders and perries, it is no surprise the pub is a regular award winner. Bar meals are served Tuesday to Saturday evenings and lunchtimes Saturday and Sunday.
Q

Bosbury

Bell Inn

HR8 1PX (in village, on B4220)
12-2 (not Mon-Thu), 5-11; 12-9 Sun ☎ (01531) 640285
Otter Bitter; Wye Valley Butty Bach; 1 changing beer (often Swan, Unity Brew House, Welder) Ⓗ
A two-bar black-and-white half-timbered inn in a terrace opposite the imposing village church, the bells of which lend the place its name. The restaurant area (no food Sun eve and Mon) contrasts with a basic yet comfortable public bar, replete with grand fireplace, alcoves, books and

REAL ALE BREWERIES

Arrow Kington
Butchers Arms Woolhope
Hereford Hereford
Ledbury Ledbury
Odyssey Whitbourne
Simpsons Eardisland
Swan Leominster
Wobbly Hereford
Wye Valley Stoke Lacy

newspapers. A large garden features at the rear. Plenty of on-street parking is available.
Q🚼❀◐♣●🚌(417)🐾📶

Bromyard

Rose & Lion Ⓛ ✔

5 New Road, HR7 4AJ
⏲ 11-11 ☎ (01885) 482381
Wye Valley Bitter, HPA, Butty Bach Ⓗ
The Rosie is very much a traditional town pub, with a loyal following by locals. Two small original rooms are complemented by a further bar to the rear, plus a more contemporary annexe with accessible toilets and a pleasant garden. Furnished throughout in a modern but appropriate style, there is always a real buzz about the place. No food is available. Q🚼❀♿♣P🚆🚌(420)🐾

Chance's Pitch

Wellington Inn Ⓛ

WR13 6HW (on A449, near B4218 jct)
⏲ closed Mon; 12-3, 6.30-11; 12-3.30 Sun
☎ (01684) 540269 🌐 thewellingtoninnmalvern.co.uk
Goff's Tournament; 2 changing beers (often Gloucester, Lakehouse, Swan) Ⓗ
This is a much-extended, multi-level inn that majors on dining, but also happily caters for drinkers, with a choice of local ales. A comfortable and plainly decorated drinkers' bar area presents a traditional feel, with a lounge on the lower level offering views out across open country. Two restaurant areas to the rear serve a wide range of often locally sourced meals, from sandwiches to full à la carte. Q🚼❀◐P🐾📶

Dorstone

Pandy Inn Ⓛ

HR3 6AN (signed off B4348)
⏲ 12 (5 Mon)-11; 12-9 Sun summer; 5-11 (12 Fri & Sat); 12-9 Sun winter ☎ (01981) 550273 🌐 thepandyinn.co.uk
Sharp's Doom Bar; Wye Valley Butty Bach; house beer (by Grey Trees Ind Craft Brewers); 1 changing beer Ⓗ
Opposite the small village green, the Pandy has a history dating back to the 12th century. Although opened out, discrete areas give a welcoming feel, with timber-framing, exposed stone walls and a huge fireplace. The pub caters equally for drinkers and diners, with an interesting range of dishes, including vegetarian. Gwatkins and nearby Pips ciders are available in bottles. A quiz and curry night is hosted monthly (booking advisable), as well as regular themed evenings.
Q🚼❀◐♣●P🚌🐾📶

Ewyas Harold

Temple Bar Ⓛ

HR2 0EU (in village, just off B4347)
⏲ 11-3, 5-11.30; 11-1.30am Sat; 11-midnight Sun
☎ (01981) 240423 🌐 thetemplebarinn.co.uk
Ludlow Gold; Wye Valley Butty Bach; 2 changing beers (often Harviestoun, Hobsons) Ⓗ
The Temple Bar Inn has been extensively refurbished with a bar, games room, restaurant, outside seating area, function room and three en-suite rooms. Meals are served in the bar lunchtimes and early evenings and in the restaurant from 7pm and on Sunday lunchtimes. The restaurant menu changes weekly to include locally sourced seasonal ingredients, freshly prepared and cooked.
Q🚼❀🛏◐♿♣●P🚌(440)🐾📶

Fownhope

New Inn Ⓛ

HR1 4PE (in village, on B4224)
⏲ 12-3, 6-midnight; 12-midnight Sat & Sun
☎ (01432) 860350 🌐 thenewinnfownhope.co.uk
Hobsons Best; house beer (by Wye Valley); 1 changing beer (often Hobsons, Swan, Wood) Ⓗ
A true locals' pub at the heart of a thriving village community. The single room with exposed beams and light decor is divided into more discrete spaces by a central, bare-brick fireplace. Typical pub food is served every lunchtime with a roast on Sunday; evening specials may feature fish and chips, pies, steaks or curry. 🚼❀◐♿⛺♣P🚌(454)🐾📶

Garway

Garway Moon Ⓛ ✔

Garway Common, HR2 8RQ SO465227
⏲ 6-11 Mon & Tue; 11-2.30, 5-11 Wed-Fri; 11-11 Sat & Sun
☎ (01600) 750270 🌐 garwaymooninn.co.uk
Butcombe Adam Henson's Rare Breed; Wye Valley HPA; 2 changing beers (sourced locally; often Bespoke, Butcombe, Kingstone) Ⓗ
A remote, welcoming pub overlooking the village green and cricket pitch, with a lounge, public bar, separate snug/family room and garden with play area. The British pub food and grill menu is sourced locally where possible and is freshly prepared, with vegetarian options. Food evenings include Italian on Tuesday, curry Wednesday, surf and turf Thursday and roasts on Sunday. The last Friday of the month is open mic night, and the last Sunday quiz night. Four local ciders are available.
🚼❀🛏◐⛺♣●P🚌(412)🐾📶

Harewood End

Harewood End Inn Ⓛ ✔

HR2 8JT (on A49)
⏲ closed Mon; 12-3, 6-11; 12-3, 7-10.30 Sun
☎ (01989) 730637 🌐 theharewoodend.com
St Austell Tribute; 2 changing beers (sourced locally; often Purity, Welder) Ⓗ
An old roadside pub which in coaching days provided horses for the climb to Hereford. The compact and cosy bar with pool table leads out to a beer garden and two separate dining areas, featuring rustic-style panelling and a wealth of old enamel signs. An interesting menu of freshly prepared food is offered and booking is advised at weekends. Families are welcome. Accommodation is in five en-suite rooms.
Q🚼❀🛏◐♣P🚆🚌(33)🐾📶

Hereford

Barrels Ⓛ ✔

69 St Owen Street, HR1 2JQ
⏲ 11-11.30 (midnight Fri & Sat); 12-11.30 Sun
☎ (01432) 274968
Wye Valley Bitter, The Hopfather, HPA, Golden Ale, Butty Bach, Wholesome Stout; 1 changing beer (often Wye Valley) Ⓗ
No food, no gimmicks, but there are tons of character across five bars, plus a cobbled courtyard to the rear which hosts a charity beer and music

festival on the August bank holiday weekend. With the TV only turned on for major sports events, this is a pub where conversation and good times always hold sway.

Firefly

16 King Street, HR4 9BX

4-11; 12-1am Fri & Sat; 12-11 Sun ☎ (01432) 358252

4 changing beers Ⓗ

Dating from the 17th century, this small, much-altered, single-bar pub reopened in 2016 after a spell as a restaurant. At the trendier end of the spectrum, but with much original woodwork and floors, it is the younger sibling of its namesake in Worcester. It offers craft keg beers, an imaginative draught ale selection and real ciders, often local. Lunch and evening food menus are entirely vegan, with one of the beers usually vegan too. Live bands or a DJ feature on Friday and Saturday.

Gordon Bennetts

8 St Peters Street, HR1 2LE

11am-2am (3am Thu-Sat) ☎ (01432) 360250

Sharp's Doom Bar; Wye Valley Bitter, HPA, Butty Bach Ⓗ**; 2 changing beers (sourced regionally)** Ⓖ

This city-centre bar has been given a high quality refurbishment in a contemporary style, providing a relaxed environment for drinking late into the night. While the four regular ales are served via handpumps, there is the facility to serve up to eight more direct from casks housed in chilled cabinets. A mezzanine bar doubles as a function room. Live music at weekends.

Kington

Olde Tavern ★

22 Victoria Road, HR5 3BX

6.30-11.30; 5-midnight Fri; 12-midnight Sat; 12-11 Sun
☎ (01544) 231945

Hobsons Mild; 4 changing beers (often Ludlow, Three Tuns, Wye Valley) Ⓗ

One for the pub connoisseur – a real time warp. Behind a delightfully understated Victorian red-brick façade is this diminutive two-bar gem, with its original entrance lobby, serving hatches, flagstone floor and bench seating – plus a treasure trove of interesting keepsakes. It was once the pub for the (now closed) railway station. Pub teams root it firmly in the local community. A changing menu of freshly prepared food is served in the Out the Back restaurant Thursday to Monday evenings and weekend lunchtimes. QP

Oxford Arms Hotel

Duke Street, HR5 3DR

closed Mon; 12 (5 Tue & Wed; 4 Thu)-midnight
☎ (01544) 230322 the-oxford-arms.co.uk

Hobsons Town Crier; 2 changing beers Ⓗ

Located on the edge of the town centre, its 17th-century timber construction now hidden behind a Victorian frontage. The public bar is popular with locals and attracts a younger clientele with pool, darts and quoits. The large dining lounge doubles as a function room, staging occasional live music. Good locally sourced home-prepared food is served. The range of regularly changing local beers is added to during several annual beer festivals. A board in the dining lounge lists the winners of the 8-Peaks Challenge held in September during the Kington Walking Festival.
QP

> Beer makes you feel the way you ought to feel without beer. **Henry Lawson**

Ledbury

Prince of Wales

Church Lane, HR8 1DL

11-11 (10.30 Sun) ☎ (01531) 632250 powledbury.com

Eagle IPA; Ledbury Dark; Wye Valley HPA, Butty Bach; Young's Bitter; 2 changing beers Ⓗ

Hidden away in a picturesque cobbled alley leading up to the church, this 16th-century timber-framed pub boasts two bars, plus a discrete alcove where a folk jam session is held each Wednesday evening. It is a genuine community pub always bustling with locals and visitors. Orchard Pig draught cider is served, together with an extensive range of foreign beers. The bar meals are excellent value (booking advisable for the Sunday roasts).

Talbot Hotel

14 New Street, HR8 2DX

11-11 (midnight Fri & Sat) ☎ (01531) 632963
talbotledbury.co.uk

Wadworth IPA, 6X; Wye Valley Butty Bach; 1 changing beer (often Wadworth) Ⓗ

An outstanding black-and-white half-timbered hotel and bar dating back to the 1590s, with direct links to the Civil War. Various comfortably furnished seating areas, with hidden nooks and corners, surround a central bar-servery facing a splendid fireplace. The restaurant, with its superb wood-panelling, offers affordable fine cuisine featuring locally sourced ingredients, while snacks are available in the bar. The guest beer is from Wadworth's seasonal range or Red Shoot subsidiary. Last orders is 11pm Friday and Saturday.

Leominster

Chequers

63 Etnam Street, HR6 8AE

11-11 (midnight Fri & Sat); 12-10.30 Sun
☎ (01568) 612473

Wye Valley Bitter, HPA, Golden Ale, Butty Bach; 1 changing beer (often Wye Valley) Ⓗ

Probably the oldest pub in the town, with a fine timber-framed façade and interesting protruding gables. A wonderful unspoiled front bar was at one time two bars, but still has much charm, with a fine tiled floor, original fireplace, timbers and cosy window alcoves. To the rear is a more conventional lounge bar and dining area serving good-value meals, with a speciality pie menu and Sunday lunches. A quiz is held on alternate Wednesdays.
QP

Linton

Alma Inn

HR9 7RY (off B4221, W of M50 jct 3) SO659255

12-3 (not Mon), 6-11; 12-3, 7-10.30 Sun
☎ (01989) 720355 almainnlinton.co.uk

Butcombe Original; Ludlow Gold; Malvern Hills Black Pear; Oakham JHB; 1 changing beer (often Bespoke, Bristol Beer Factory) Ⓗ

Behind a plain façade is an award-winning pub of true pedigree. The convivial front bar with real fire contrasts with the rear pool room and a separate wood-panelled dining room. Hearty freshly prepared pub classics are offered, with seasonal specials, light bites and bar snacks. The pub hosts events including the nationally renowned Linton Music Festival in June and Summer Acoustic Sessions in August – both held in the extensive grounds along with accompanying beer festivals. Local CAMRA Pub of the Year 2017. Q♣P

Mordiford

Moon Inn

HR1 4LW (in village, on B4224)
12 (10 Mon)-11; 12-midnight Sat & Sun
(01432) 873067 mooninnmordiford.co.uk
Bombardier; Otter Amber; St Austell Proper Job; Timothy Taylor Landlord; 1 changing beer
A half-timbered and much-altered two-bar roadside village inn, the Moon started life as a farmhouse over 400 years ago. It benefits from its proximity to the Mordiford Loop – a well-known local walk – as well as the Rivers Lugg and Wye. Traditional locally sourced pub food is served, with a pie night on Wednesday. Quiz night is alternate Tuesdays. There is a children's play area in the garden, plus a camping and caravan site to the rear. ♣P (453)

Pembridge

Red Lion

High Street, HR6 9DS
12-midnight (01544) 388007
4 changing beers (often Hobsons, Purity, Wye Valley)
Sympathetically refurbished while retaining its original timbers, this pub has a large single bar screened off into what may be loosely described as drinking and dining areas. A small beer garden to the side backs onto the churchyard, with its distinctive medieval bell tower. Primarily a community pub, the Red Lion serves simple, good-value lunches and bar snacks made with locally sourced produce. The Thursday evening session specialises in steaks. ♣P

Staplow

Oak Inn

HR8 1NP (on B4214)
12-11 (10.30 Sun) (01531) 640954
oakinnstaplow.co.uk
Bathams Best Bitter; Ledbury Gold; Wye Valley Bitter; 1 changing beer
A stylishly renovated and well-run roadside country inn offering exceptional food, good beer and quality accommodation overlooking nearby hop yards. A contemporary public area neatly divides into three – a reception bar area with modern sofas and low tables, a snug and a main dining area featuring an open kitchen. At the rear is a further room with scrubbed tables. Such is the reputation of the Oak that booking is essential for food and accommodation. Q P (417)

Stiffords Bridge

Red Lion

WR13 5NN (on A4103)
12 (4 Mon)-11; 12-10.30 Sun (01886) 880318
Pitchfork Golden Ale; Wye Valley Butty Bach; 4 changing beers (often Malvern Hills, Purity, Salopian)
This multi-roomed roadside pub is as popular with out-of-town diners as it is with locals and drinkers. A survivor of multiple floods, it is characterised by modern flagstone floors, wood panelling, bare brick walls, cosy window alcoves and two large fireplaces with woodburners. There are pleasant and extensive gardens to the rear where events are hosted. Traditional locally sourced food dominates the menu. The guest beers are from breweries far and near, many unusual for the area. ♣P

Upper Colwall

Chase Inn

Chase Road, WR13 6DJ (off B4218, turning at upper hairpin bend signed British Camp) SO766431
12-3, 5-11; 12-11 Sat; 12-10.30 Sun (01684) 540276
thechaseinnmalvern.co.uk
Bathams Best Bitter; Courage Directors; 2 changing beers (often Malvern Hills, Prescott, Purity)
Two-bar free house hidden away in a quiet wooded backwater on the western slopes of the Malvern Hills. A former Herefordshire CAMRA Pub of the Year, with a genteel atmosphere, it is popular with walkers as well as regulars. It comprises a small lounge for dining (booking advisable at weekends) and a long, narrow public bar. A delightful manicured rear beer garden commands panoramic views across Herefordshire to the Welsh Hills. Q♣P (675)

Wellington Heath

Farmers Arms

Horse Road, HR8 1LS (in village, E of B4214)
closed Mon; 12-3, 5.30-11; 12-11 Sat; 12-10 Sun
(01531) 634776 farmersarmswellingtonheath.co.uk
Wye Valley HPA, Butty Bach; 2 changing beers (often Hillside, Salopian, Tiny Rebel)
Follow the signs carefully to find this pub in its dispersed rural community. The bar and main dining area are in the original 18th-century building, and on either side are more modern extensions housing a games room with pool table and a restaurant. The food ranges from burgers and pub classics to steaks and speciality dishes. Eight local draught ciders are available. A popular Beer & Beast festival is held each June or July. Open on bank holiday Mondays.
♣P (675)

Withington

Cross Keys

HR1 3NN (on A465 in Withington Marsh)
5-11; 12-11 Sat; 12-10.30 Sun (01432) 820616
Otter Ale; Wye Valley Butty Bach; house beer (by Wye Valley); 1 changing beer
Run by the same landlord for over 45 years, a long single bar here divides either side of a central servery into two drinking areas, with original beams, exposed stonework and comfortable bench seating along each wall, both book-ended by woodburners. A folk jam session is held on the last Thursday of each month. Filled rolls are available on Saturday. Q♣P (420)

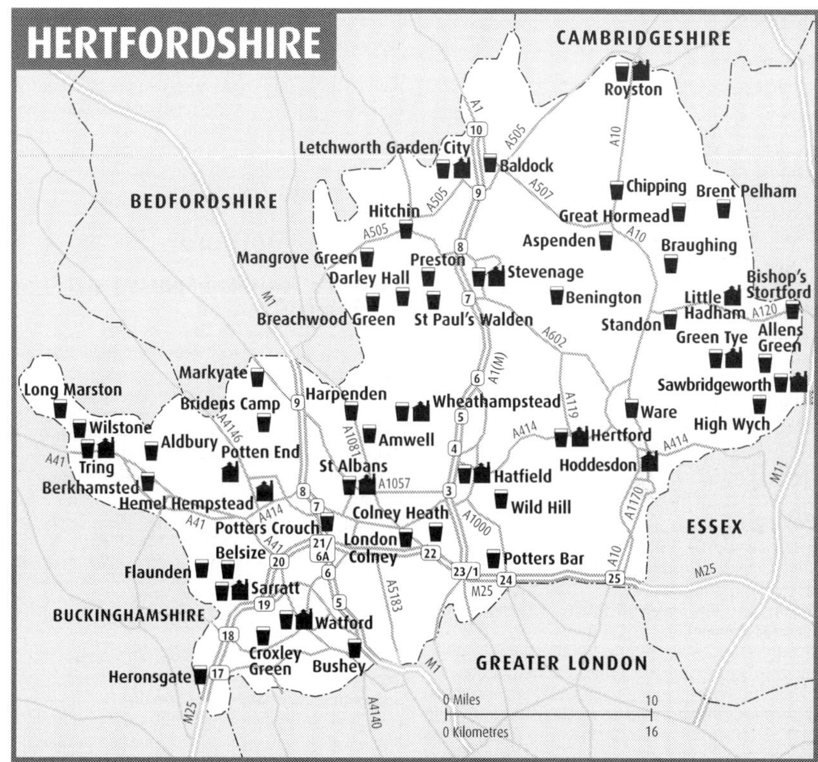

Aldbury

Valiant Trooper

Trooper Road, HP23 5RW

11-11; 10-11 Sat; 10-10.30 Sun ☎ (01442) 851203
valianttrooper.co.uk

Chiltern Beechwood Bitter; Tring Side Pocket for a Toad; 3 changing beers (sourced regionally; often Dark Star, Vale, XT)

Situated in the heart of the Chiltern Hills, the Trooper is a stunning 17th-century pub that retains the classic style and charm from that era. There is a lovely beer garden for the summer and a log fire for winter. It offers an outstanding selection of beers in excellent condition, from local breweries and further afield, and has a separate restaurant serving an array of classic British pub fare.
Q P (387)

Allens Green

Queen's Head

CM21 0LS TL455170

12-2.30 (not Mon & Tue), 5-11; 12-11 Sat; 12-10.30 Sun ☎ (01279) 723393 qhpub.co.uk

Fuller's London Pride; Mighty Oak Maldon Gold; 2 changing beers (sourced locally)

Popular village inn which was once closed but reopened by a group of locals. It is well worth seeking out for a constantly changing range of beers. Hot snacks are available unless the pub is busy. A frequent local CAMRA Pub of the Year over the past decade and current local and Hertfordshire CAMRA Cider Pub of the Year. Q P

Amwell

Elephant & Castle

Amwell Lane, AL4 8EA TL167131

12-11 ☎ (01582) 832175 elephantcastle.co.uk

Greene King IPA, Abbot; 3 changing beers (sourced nationally)

Hidden away in an attractive and peaceful setting, this deservedly popular, successful rural community pub dates from 1714 and has never forsaken real ale. The characterful front bar features terracotta tiles and a fireplace; the back bar has a 100-foot well. Outside are two large gardens. Lunches are served daily and evening meals Tuesday to Saturday. The pub hosts the local Amwell charity fundraising event in September each year. Q P

Aspenden

Fox

SG9 9PD TL360282

12-3, 6 (5 Fri)-11; 12-11 Sat; 12-9 Sun ☎ (01763) 271886 thefoxaspenden.co.uk

3 changing beers (sourced nationally)

The Fox is a pretty two-bar inn with a large fire for the winter and a spacious garden for the summer. Set in a tranquil village in East Hertfordshire, close to Buntingford, the pub has a pétanque team and is popular with the village cricket team. Guest beers come from Marston's or the SIBA list. There is a beer festival, usually in May. Charity quiz nights and themed food evenings are held regularly.
P

Baldock

Orange Tree

Norton Road, SG7 5AW

12-2.30, 4.30-11; 12-midnight Thu-Sat; 12-10.30 Sun
(01462) 892341 theorangetreebaldock.com

Greene King XX Mild, IPA, Abbot; 9 changing beers (sourced nationally)

Three-hundred-year-old, multi-roomed pub, home to many local clubs and societies. Nine guest ales are on offer from small breweries, always including two from the local Buntingford Brewery, plus five local real ciders. A huge malt whisky collection is also kept. Vintage beer bottles are on display. Good home-cooked food is served, with meats and sausages from the local, award-winning Chapman's Butchers. Quiz night is Tuesday, folk night Wednesday. Six Nations rugby is screened in all rooms and the pub can get crowded. P

Belsize

Plough

Dunny Lane, WD3 4NP

12-11 (10.30 Sun) (01923) 262261
theploughatbelsize.co.uk

Greene King IPA; St Austell Tribute; 1 changing beer (sourced nationally)

This free house was purpose-built for the Kings Langley Brewery in the 1840s. Located in the hamlet of Belsize between Chipperfield and Sarratt, it is in the style of a traditional English country pub with open log fires, comfy settees, a pleasant garden and a large rear car park. Food is served Wednesday to Sunday lunchtimes and Wednesday to Saturday evenings. Dogs are not allowed in the restaurant area. QP(352)

Benington

Lordship Arms

42 Whempstead Road, SG2 7BX

closed Mon; 12-3, 6 (7 Sun)-11 (01438) 869665
lordshiparms.com

Black Sheep Best Bitter; Crouch Vale Brewers Gold; Timothy Taylor Landlord; 6 changing beers (sourced nationally)

Under the same ownership and management for 25 years, this pub is a repeat winner of local and county CAMRA awards. The single bar is decorated with telephone memorabilia – some of the handpumps are even modelled on telephones. The lovely garden features floral displays to be enjoyed in the summer. Wednesday evening curries are popular. Lunchtime snacks are served until 2pm Monday to Saturday. There is a classic car gathering on the third Tuesday of each month April to September. Winter Sunday hours can vary; call to check. QP

Berkhamsted

Rising Sun

1 Canal Side, George Street, HP4 2EG (at lock 55 on Grand Union Canal)

12-11 (midnight Thu-Sat); 12-10.30 Sun
(01442) 864913 theriserberko.net

Tring Drop Bar Pale Ale; house beer (by Tring); 3 changing beers (sourced nationally)

The recipient of many well-deserved CAMRA awards, the Riser is a thriving canalside pub and a firm favourite of hikers, dog walkers and cyclists. It serves five well-kept real ales and 10-20 real ciders. The food range has recently expanded and now includes bar snacks such as pork pies and nachos, in addition to the renowned ploughman's. It hosts many popular events including quarterly beer festivals, weekly pub quiz nights, a monthly cheese club and folk music afternoons. (500,501)

Bishop's Stortford

Bishop's Stortford Sports Trust

Cricketfield Lane, CM23 2TD

5-11; 12-11 Sat & Sun (01279) 654463

3 changing beers (sourced locally; often Buntingford, Mauldons)

Visitors are welcome at this pub within a club – no membership required. The beer quality is driven by high turnover thanks to thirsty sports-playing members. Conversation flourishes in the comfortable seating area as the sports screens usually have the sound off. Outside drinking in summer comes with an attractive view. Easily reached from town via Chantry Road – turn left at the end to see the grounds on the right. P

Star

7 Bridge Street, CM23 2JU

11-midnight (2am Fri); 12-2am Sat; 12-10.30 Sun
(01279) 654211 thestar-bishopsstortford.co.uk

3 changing beers (sourced regionally)

A 17th-century town-centre pub catering for all ages. It is busy on Friday and Saturday evenings with a young crowd, and at other times attracts a cross-section of ages. Tuesday is quiz night. A quiet pint can be enjoyed on other evenings and at lunchtimes. Reasonably priced traditional pub food is freshly prepared throughout the day. Additionally, pizzas can be made to order at any time. Beers from regional and local breweries are offered on an ever-changing basis.

Braughing

Brown Bear

14 The Street, SG11 2QF

3-6 Mon (11 Tue); 12-11.30; 12-6 Sun (01920) 822157
brownbearbraughing.co.uk

3 changing beers (sourced nationally)

REAL ALE BREWERIES

3 Brewers of St Albans Hatfield
Ash Valley Green Tye
Bog Brew Stevenage (NEW)
Buntingford Royston
Farr Brew Wheathampstead
Foragers St Albans
Garden City Letchworth
Hadham Little Hadham
Mad Squirrel Potten End
McMullen Hertford
Mix Hemel Hempstead
New River Hoddesdon
Old Cross Hertford
Paradigm Sarratt
Pope's Yard Hemel Hempstead
Sawbridgeworth Sawbridgeworth
Tring Tring
Watling Street Watford
White Hart Tap St Albans

A pub since at least 1740, the Brown Bear has a public bar and a restaurant, both with impressive fireplaces – have a go at identifying the implements. The Thursday pub quiz, darts and pétanque teams, a large garden with a pizza oven, occasional outside bars and monthly live music mean there is something for everyone. A widely varying choice of three real ales is usually available. 🐴❀◐◑♣P🚌(331)🐾📶

Breachwood Green

Red Lion ✔

16 Chapel Road, SG4 8NU

◷ 12-11 (midnight Sat) ☎ (01438) 833123
🌐 redlionbreachwoodgreen.co.uk

Adnams Broadside; Greene King IPA; St Austell Tribute; 1 changing beer (sourced nationally) 🄷

The only pub in the village, the Red Lion attracts many locals and some visitors from further afield. It serves good home-made food and the guest beers are unusual for this area. There is a TV showing major sporting events and also a quiet dining area. The garden provides great views of the countryside and is a good vantage point to view the aircraft approaching Luton Airport. The pub is home to darts and dominoes teams and football and cricket sides. 🐴❀◐◑♣🍎P🚌🐾📶

Brent Pelham

Black Horse

SG9 0AP (down lane to right of church)

◷ closed Mon; 11.30-2.30 (not Tue), 5.30-11; 11.30-11 Sat; 11.30-7 Sun ☎ (01279) 778925
🌐 blackhorsebrentpelham.co.uk

Adnams Southwold Bitter; 2 changing beers (sourced nationally) 🄷

Reopened after a refurb in 2016, this much-extended pub has separate drinking and dining areas on many different levels. The focus is on food but drinkers are welcome too. An old pub, once frequented by farm workers, it now attracts walkers and cyclists. It has a huge garden for the summer, now with a barbecue. Take a walk down to the church to see the ancient stocks outside. 🐴❀◐◑P🐾📶

Bridens Camp

Crown & Sceptre 🄻

Red Lion Hill, HP2 6EY (from A4146 at Water End take Red Lion Lane up hill for ½ mile) TL044111

◷ 11-3, 5.30-midnight; 11-midnight Sat & Sun
☎ (01442) 234660 🌐 crownandsceptrepub.co.uk

Greene King IPA, Abbot; 4 changing beers (sourced regionally; often Tring, Vale) 🄷

The Crown & Sceptre is thought to date back to the mid-1800s, with a classic interior that includes a dark wood-panelled bar and roaring fire. Located in the quiet village of Bridens Camp, it provides a refreshing stop on a country walk. The home-cooked traditional pub food is excellent and reasonably priced. It boasts four handpumps serving a changing variety of local and regional ales. There is always a warm welcome from the locals. Q🐴❀◐◑♿P🚌(29)🐾📶

Bushey

Swan

25 Park Road, WD23 3EE

◷ 11-11; 12-10 Sun ☎ (020) 8950 2256
🌐 swanpubbushey.co.uk

Black Sheep Best Bitter; Greene King Abbot; Timothy Taylor Landlord; Young's Bitter 🄷

Historic, traditional pub just off the main high street with a single bar and four regular beers. A real gem, it has old photos and sporting mementos adorning the walls and two coal fires. The original jug-and-bottle window has been retained. Hot snacks are available at all times including toasties and pies. Pub games include darts, shut the box and board games. The Ladies is accessed from the garden via a side alley. ❀♣🚌(142,258)🐾📶

Chipping

Countryman

Ermine Street, SG9 0PG TL356319

◷ closed Mon-Thu; 12-11 Fri & Sat; 12-10.30 Sun
☎ (01763) 272721

3 changing beers (sourced nationally) 🄷

Built in 1663 and a pub since 1760, the Countryman has a one-bar split-level interior with an impressive fireplace. The bar front features some well-executed carvings dating from the 1970s, and obscure agricultural implements decorate the walls. The beer range varies, with three real ales (and a cider in summer) usually available. There are chickens in the garden. Note the limited opening hours. Q🐴❀🍎P🚌(331)🐾

Colney Heath

Crooked Billet 🄻

88 High Street, AL4 0NP

◷ 11-2.30, 4.30-11 Mon & Tue; 11-11 Wed-Fri; 12-11 Sat; 12-10.30 Sun ☎ (01727) 822128 🌐 thecrookedbilletpub.com

Sharp's Doom Bar; Tring Side Pocket for a Toad; Young's Special 🄷

Popular and friendly cottage-style village pub dating back over 200 years. A genuine free house, it stocks three beers from national, regional and micro breweries. A wide selection of good-value, home-made food is served lunchtimes and Friday and Saturday evenings. Summer barbecues and Saturday events are held occasionally. This is a favourite stop-off for walkers on the many local footpaths. Families are welcome in the bar until 9pm and in the large garden, where there is play equipment. 🐴❀◐◑♣P🚌(304)🐾

Croxley Green

Sportsman 🄻

2 Scots Hill, WD3 3AD (at A412 jct with the Green)

◷ 2-11; 12-11 Fri & Sat; 12-10.30 Sun ☎ (01923) 443360

Fuller's ESB; Oakham JHB; Sharp's Doom Bar; 4 changing beers (sourced nationally) 🄷

Welcoming, family-run community pub with up to seven real ales. Beers are varied and usually include a dark brew, with an emphasis on microbreweries – tasting trays are available. Pub games include darts and pool. The pub hosts a popular weekly quiz and live music on alternate Sunday afternoons, with a music jam on the last Sunday afternoon of the month. Community activities include a book group, men's and ladies' darts teams and a pool team. Croxley tube station is a 15-minute walk away. ❀♣P🚇🚌

Darley Hall

Fox

Darley Road, LU2 8PP
⏲ closed Mon; 12-11 ☎ (01582) 731366
🌐 thefoxdarleyhall.co.uk
Greene King IPA; Oakham Citra; 2 changing beers (sourced nationally) Ⓗ
Late 19th-century inn in a small hamlet close to Luton Airport. This double-fronted single-bar pub is first recorded as having a landlord in the 1891 census. It welcomes allcomers, whether drinking or dining. Outside is a walled family-friendly garden and a large mezzanine decking area linked to the excellent restaurant which overlooks the countryside. Local CAMRA Most Improved Pub 2017. ⛁❀◐◑P🚌🐾

Flaunden

Green Dragon ★

85 Flaunden Hill, HP3 0PP TL015008
⏲ 3-6 Mon; 12-6 Tue (10 Wed & Thu; 11 Fri); 12-6 Sun
☎ (01442) 832269 🌐 greendragonflaunden.co.uk
Fuller's London Pride, ESB; St Austell Tribute; Young's Bitter Ⓗ
This rural 17th-century pub, in good walking country, has been in the same family since 1932. The taproom, which was constructed in 1838 and has many interesting old photographs, features in CAMRA's Britain's Best Heritage Pubs. There is an enclosed garden at the rear and roadside seating. Traditional pub games including darts, dominoes, cribbage, shut the box and shove-ha'penny are played here. A log fire warms the main bar in the winter months. ⛁❀◐♣🍎P🐾

Great Hormead

Three Tuns

Pelham Road, SG9 0NT (off B1038)
⏲ closed Mon; 12-3, 6-11; 12-7 Sun ☎ (01763) 289405
Adnams Southwold Bitter; 2 changing beers (sourced nationally) Ⓗ
The Three Tuns is a 16th-century thatched pub with a new restaurant area added at the rear after a fire in 1996. The main bar has a lovely fireplace. Monthly quiz nights are popular. The food has a good reputation and Thursday night fish and chips often sells out. Adnams Bitter is a regular, with guest beers from local breweries Buntingford and New River. ⛁❀◐◑P

Green Tye

Prince of Wales 🄻

Green Tye, Much Hadham, SG10 6JP TL444184
⏲ 12-3, 5.30-11; 12-11 Sat; 12-9.30 Sun ☎ (01279) 842139
🌐 thepow.co.uk
Ash Valley Prince of Wales IPA; Wadworth 6X; 3 changing beers (sourced locally; often Ash Valley) Ⓗ
A traditional and friendly village local, whether you are a walker, cyclist, dog owner or just plain thirsty. The owner has established the Ash Valley Brewery at the back of the pub, making the Prince of Wales its brewery tap. Food includes sandwiches and great-value traditional pub grub. There is a small garden for fine weather. Beer festivals with a barbecue and entertainment are held in May and September. Q⛁❀◐♿🍎P🐾📶

Harpenden

Cross Keys ✔

39 High Street, AL5 2SD (opp war memorial)
⏲ 11.30-11; 12-10.30 Sun ☎ (01582) 763989
Farr Brew Our Greatest Golden; Rebellion IPA; Timothy Taylor Landlord Ⓗ
A regular entry in the Guide, located on the lower High Street, this two-bar pub has retained its traditional charm with a rare fine pewter bar top and flagstone floors. The original oak-beamed ceiling has tankards from past and present customers. In spring and summer, enjoy your pint in the secluded, attractive rear garden, and in autumn or winter savour your beer in front of the saloon bar's fire. Traditional home-cooked lunches are served Monday to Saturday.
Q⛁❀◐⇌♣🚌🐾📶

Oddfellows Arms 🄻 ✔

15 Leyton Green, AL5 2TG (2 mins' walk from High St)
⏲ 8am-11; 9am-10.30 Sun ☎ (01582) 766765
Bombardier; Young's Bitter; 2 changing beers (sourced nationally) Ⓗ
The pub reverted to its original name under new ownership in 2015 – for some while it had been known as The Oak Tree. It features a handsome new zinc bar top and a logburner. One handpump is dedicated to a beer from a Hertfordshire brewer. The extensive outdoor area has been redesigned with tiered patio-style areas, mostly covered, and is popular during the warmer months. Lunches and fresh coffee are available every day.
⛁❀◐♿⇌♣🚌📶

Hatfield

Horse & Groom

21 Park Street, AL9 5AT
⏲ 11.30-11 (midnight Fri & Sat); 12-10.30 Sun
☎ (01707) 264765 🌐 horseandgroom-oldhatfield.com
Greene King Abbot; Oakham JHB; Otter Bitter; 3 changing beers (sourced nationally) Ⓗ
In the heart of Old Hatfield, this supposedly haunted, 16th-century, Grade II-listed building is thought to house a priest hole. The former timber-framed and later brick-clad pub serves up to six real ales, hosting beer festivals during the year. Tuesday is bangers and mash night and Saturday is chilli and rice night – purchase an ale for a free portion. Enjoy Thai food on Friday evenings. Hatfield railway and bus stations are nearby via 'blood and guts alley'. Q⛁❀◐♿⇌♣🍎🚌🐾📶

Heronsgate

Land of Liberty, Peace & Plenty 🏆 🄻

Long Lane, WD3 5BS TQ023949
⏲ 12-11 (midnight Fri & Sat); 12-10.30 Sun
☎ (01923) 282226 🌐 landoflibertypub.com
8 changing beers (sourced nationally) Ⓗ
Welcoming, award-winning pub close to the M25, popular with walkers, cyclists, locals and real ale enthusiasts. Up to eight microbrewery beers are offered in a range of styles and strengths. Real cider, perry and a wide range of whiskies are also available, as are bottled beers. Beer festivals, tastings and other events are held throughout the year. Bar snacks are available all day. There is a large outside pavilion and garden for families.
❀♣🍎P🚭🚌(R2)🐾📶

Hertford

Black Horse 🄻 ✔

29-31 West Street, SG13 8EZ

12-11 (midnight Fri & Sat); 12-10.30 Sun
☎ (01992) 583630 theblackhorse.biz

6 changing beers (sourced nationally) 🄷

A community-focused, timbered free house, dating from 1642 and situated in one of Hertford's most attractive streets, near the start of the Cole Green Way. Six real ales from around Britain and Hertfordshire are on offer. Well-kept gardens include a separate and safe children's area. The interesting food menu features game and daily specials, and the pub has its own bakery. The pub has its own rugby team affiliated to the RFU. Handy for Hertford Town FC supporters.

Hertford Club

Lombard House, Bull Plain, SG14 1DT

12-11; 11-11 Sat; 12-10 Sun ☎ (01992) 421422
hertford.club

4 changing beers (sourced nationally) 🄷

Dating from the 15th century with later additions, Lombard House, on the River Lea, was built as an English Hall House and is one of the oldest buildings in Hertford. It has been the home of this private members' club since 1897. CAMRA members are welcome and may be signed in on production of a membership card. You will find three or four ever-changing beers and real cider, which in summer can be enjoyed in the delightful walled garden and riverside terrace.

Old Barge ✔

2 The Folly, SG14 1QD TL326128

11-11 (midnight Fri & Sat); 12-11 Sun ☎ (01992) 581871
theoldbarge.com

Marston's 61 Deep; 4 changing beers (sourced nationally) 🄷

A free house on Folly Island, pleasantly situated canalside on the River Lea, offering a good selection of ales – often including a dark brew – and a range of ciders and perries. Locally sourced home-cooked food is served all day. There is a popular Sunday night quiz. The Spring Fling music festival takes place on the second May bank holiday Monday. Look out for the annual duck race and the children's crayfish festival in August.

Old Cross Tavern 🏆 🄻

8 St Andrew Street, SG14 1JA

4.30-11; 4-midnight Fri; 12-midnight Sat; 12-10.30 Sun
☎ (01992) 583133 oldcrosstavern.com

Old Cross Gertcha!; Timothy Taylor Landlord; 4 changing beers (sourced nationally) 🄷

Superb town free house offering a friendly welcome. Up to six real ales, usually including a dark beer of some distinction, come from brewers large and small, including the pub's own microbrewery, and there is a fine choice of Belgian bottle-conditioned beers. Two beer festivals are held each year – one over the spring bank holiday, the other in October. No TV or music here, just good old-fashioned conversation. Home-made pork pies are available. Local CAMRA Pub of the Year 2018.
Q (395)

High Wych

Rising Sun

High Wych Road, CM21 0HZ

12-2.30 (not Tue & Thu), 5.30-11; 12-3, 6-11 Sat; 12-3, 7-10.30 Sun ☎ (01279) 724099

Courage Best Bitter; 4 changing beers (often Mighty Oak, Oakham) 🄶

This friendly village local has never used handpumps – a range of four or five beers is served on gravity, often from East Anglian breweries. Although recently refurbished, the original character has been preserved by means of a stone floor, attractive fireplace and wood panelling. Popular with locals and walkers, the pub holds a monthly quiz and an annual vegetable competition. Parking is in the village hall car park opposite. Q P (347)

Hitchin

Half Moon 🄻

57 Queen Street, SG4 9TZ

12-midnight (1am Fri & Sat); 12-11 Sun ☎ (01462) 453010

Adnams Southwold Bitter; Young's Bitter; 8 changing beers (sourced nationally) 🄷

This welcoming one-bar pub dates from the 18th century. The two house ales and eight ever-changing guest ales ensure a variety of beer styles is always on offer from a range of breweries near and far, alongside a choice of traditional ciders. Home-cooked food is served every day except Monday, with bar snacks always available. Twice-yearly beer festivals, regular quizzes and music nights are popular in this friendly community pub. Hertfordshire CAMRA Pub of the Year 2016.
P

Letchworth Garden City

Garden City Brewery & Bar 🄻

22 The Wynd, SG6 3EN

closed Mon-Wed; 12-10 Thu (11 Fri & Sat); 12-10 Sun
☎ 07932 739558 gardencitybrewery.co.uk

8 changing beers (sourced nationally) 🄶

Award-winning family-run brew-bar opened in 2016 in a former café on a charming pedestrianised street. All ales are served on gravity, usually four of the brewery's own Garden City beers and four guests. A large selection of local and other UK ciders is also available, and locally produced bar snacks. The paved beer garden has hay bale seating and a weatherproof awning. A regular events programme is hosted and the TV shows tennis and rugby. Two minutes from the town centre, five minutes from the station, with adjacent parking. County Cider Pub of the Year 2018. Q P

London Colney

Bull

Barnet Road, AL2 1QU

12-11 (midnight Fri & Sat) ☎ (01727) 823160
thebullatlondoncolney.co.uk

Fuller's London Pride; Jennings Cumberland Ale; 2 changing beers (sourced nationally) 🄷

A lovely old 17th-century timbered building near the River Colne, offering a range of real ales. It has a cosy lounge featuring an original fireplace and a large public bar with a dartboard and TV. Evening events include live music sessions on Saturdays.

Good-value home-made meals are served Monday to Saturday lunchtimes and evenings, with roasts on Sunday. Outside there is a children's play area. ❀◑♣P🚌🐾📶

Long Marston

Queen's Head

38 Tring Road, HP23 4QL
✪ 5-11 (10 Mon); 4-midnight Fri; 12-midnight Sat; 12-10 Sun
☎ (01296) 668368 🌐 queensheadlongmarston.com
Tring Side Pocket for a Toad Ⓗ/Ⓖ**; 3 changing beers (sourced nationally; often Tring)** Ⓗ
Now the only pub in the village, this traditional free house dates back over 500 years, with beamed ceilings and an open fire creating the impression you have stepped back in time. Recently purchased from Fuller's by locals, the pub has greatly improved its beer quality and choice. Quiz night on Tuesday and visits from the fish and chip van on Wednesday are popular with the regulars. There are monthly music evenings and an open mic night on Sunday.
🐎❀🛏◑P🚌(164)🐾📶

Mangrove Green

King William IV

LU2 8QE (follow directions to Cockenhoe on Luton Rd, then straight on to Mangrove Green via no-through-road) TL124239
✪ 11-11 (midnight Fri & Sat); 12-midnight Sun
☎ (01582) 728086 🌐 kingwilliamhotel.com
Sharp's Doom Bar; 3 changing beers (sourced nationally) Ⓗ
The King William IV is thought to date back to the 17th century and generations of local people and visitors have enjoyed a warm welcome here. Recently renovated, it is now a country inn and restaurant, situated in a quiet area facing the large village green. Blessed with views over open fields to the back, the Hertfordshire countryside only a step away. 🐎❀🛏◑♿🍎P🚌(88)🐾📶

Markyate

Local

42 High Street, AL3 8PA
✪ 6-10 Tue-Thu; 5-11 Fri & Sat; closed Sun & Mon
☎ 07787 171629
6 changing beers (often Chiltern, Rebellion, Tring) Ⓖ
This thriving High-Street micropub has been open for just over two years. It serves an an ever-changing range of six beers and up to six ciders on gravity, with occasional beer festivals. There are strictly no spirits, apart from premium gins at the weekend. Featuring a modern decor, the walls are lined with old photos, signs and great quotes. There is always a friendly welcome – no TVs or loud music. The bar is cash only. Q♿♣🍎🚌🐾📶

Potters Bar

Admiral Byng ✔

186-192 Darkes Lane, EN6 1AF (corner of Byng Drive)
✪ 8am-midnight (12.30am Thu-Sat) ☎ (01707) 645484
Adnams Broadside; Greene King Abbot; Ruddles Best Bitter; Sharp's Doom Bar; 8 changing beers (sourced nationally) Ⓗ
A friendly community Wetherspoon pub with a display of two model sailing ships and other memorabilia celebrating the exploits and death of Admiral Byng, who was executed for 'failing to do his utmost' to save Minorca from falling to the French in 1756. In summer the frontage of the pub is opened onto the street, with additional seating provided. There is a good choice of real cider.
🐎❀◑♿⇌♣🍎🚌(84,610)📶

Potters Crouch

Holly Bush ✔

Bedmond Lane, AL2 3NN (off B5183 at jct of Potters Crouch Lane and Ragged Hall Lane) TL116052
✪ 12-2.30, 6-11; 12-3, 7-10.30 Sun ☎ (01727) 851792
🌐 thehollybushpub.co.uk
Fuller's London Pride, ESB; Gale's Seafarers Ale Ⓗ
This charming wisteria-covered early 17th-century pub sits in rural surroundings. Attractively furnished throughout, it boasts large oak tables and period chairs. There are no jukeboxes, slot machines or TVs to disturb the drinker in any of the three pleasant drinking areas. The food menu is not extensive but is of high quality. Well-behaved children are welcome. The garden is ideal in summer. Q🐎❀◑♿P🚌(300,301)

Preston

Red Lion 🏆 L

The Green, SG4 7UD (on green at crossroads)
✪ 12-2.30 (3.30 Sat), 5.30-11; 12-3.30, 7-10.30 Sun
☎ (01462) 459585 🌐 theredlionpreston.co.uk
Fuller's London Pride; Young's Bitter; 3 changing beers (sourced nationally) Ⓗ
This attractive free house stands on the village green and was the first community-owned pub in Great Britain. It offers an ever-changing list of beers, many from small breweries. Fresh home-made food is served, often featuring locally sourced ingredients (no food Sun eve and Mon). The pub hosts the village cricket teams and fundraises for charity. Local CAMRA Pub of the Year 2018. Q🐎❀◑♣🍎P🚌🐾📶

Royston

Manor House ✔

14 Melbourn Street, SG8 7BZ
✪ 8am-midnight (1am Fri & Sat) ☎ (01763) 250160
Greene King Abbot; Ruddles Best Bitter; Sharp's Doom Bar; 3 changing beers (sourced nationally) Ⓗ
This Grade II listed former town house dates from the early 18th century, with the block on the left added late in the 19th century. The decorative iron railings at the front were removed during World War II. Royston Manor House was the name adopted in October 1948 for what later became known as The Manor House Club. This thriving Wetherspoon pub is full of character and personality, with local artwork adding interest.
🐎❀◑♿🍎🚌(331)📶

St Albans

Boot Inn L ✔

4 Market Place, AL3 5DG
✪ 12-midnight (1am Fri & Sat); 12-11.30 Sun
☎ (01727) 857533 🌐 thebootstalbans.co.uk
Oakham JHB, Citra; 6 changing beers (sourced nationally) Ⓗ
City-centre, Grade II listed, one-bar pub dating back to 1422 – a regular in the Guide, run by a long-serving licensee. The historic Clock Tower is outside

the front door and the Abbey and Verulamium Park are nearby. Unusually, the pub sign bears its phone number. Internal features include a low ceiling, real fire and wood flooring. Home-made food is all locally sourced, with evening meals Tuesday only. Families are welcome until 6pm.

Great Northern

172 London Road, AL1 1PQ

4-11; 12-12.30am Fri & Sat; 12-11 Sun (01727) 730867 greatnorthernpub.co.uk

Black Sheep Best Bitter; 3 changing beers (sourced nationally)

Originally called The Alma, the pub changed its name due to the nearby, now preserved, railway station – but alas, there are no longer any trains. Located next door to the Odyssey Cinema, this independent Grade II listed pub was reopened in 2015 after significant renovation. It has a pleasant contemporary feel and features a restaurant, bar area, snug and spacious garden The menu consists of innovative food alongside British classic dishes and Sunday roasts. Join the quiz on Tuesday night.

Lower Red Lion

34-36 Fishpool Street, AL3 4RX

12-11 (10 Sun) (01727) 855669 thelowerredlion.co.uk

Oakham JHB; 4 changing beers (sourced nationally)

Both bars in this classic Grade II listed pub have plenty of character and history. In a conservation area between the city centre and the site of Roman Verulamium, the pub stands in one of St Albans' most picturesque streets. The Lower Red was an early champion of CAMRA's values in the real ale revival movement and continues to stock quality real ales, ciders and perries. Home-made food is served lunchtimes and weekday evenings. B&B is also available. Q P

Mermaid

98 Hatfield Road, AL1 3RL

12-midnight (11 Mon & Tue); 12-10.30 Sun (01727) 845700

Oakham Citra; 5 changing beers (sourced nationally)

This friendly free house is one of the few remaining bare-boards pubs in St Albans. Customers can choose from Oakham Citra and five regularly changing ales plus a dozen ciders and perries and a range of Belgian beers. There are music nights on Wednesdays, with regular quizzes and events held in the garden and under cover during the spring and summer. Two beer festivals are hosted during the year, and a 50-plus cider/perry festival at the end of May. A regular winner of Hertfordshire CAMRA Cider Pub of the Year. P

Olde Fighting Cocks

16 Abbey Mill Lane, AL3 4HE

12-11 (midnight Fri & Sat); 12-10.30 Sun (01727) 869152 yeoldefightingcocks.co.uk

Farr Brew The Best Bitter, Black Listed IBA; Purity Pure UBU; 6 changing beers (sourced nationally)

The Fighters claims to be the oldest pub in England, dating from the late 8th century, though the current building was completed in 1485. Some original features remain including the low ceilings, a bread oven next to one of the open fireplaces and of course the cockpit. Up to 16 real ales are available in the summer months. Not to be missed following a visit to the Abbey and nearby Roman remains in Verulamium Park. Parking nearby can be difficult.

Robin Hood

126 Victoria Street, AL1 3TG

12-11 (11.30 Fri); 1-11.30 Sat; 1-11 Sun (01727) 856459 robin-hood-st-albans.co.uk

Harvey's Sussex Best Bitter; 2 changing beers (sourced nationally)

A friendly community pub, handy for St Albans City station. The large single bar has been significantly improved to provide a warm and comfortable environment. To the rear there is a large, pleasant beer garden. A constantly changing range of three or more well-kept guest real ales is available from around Britain, as well as a real cider or perry. Pickled eggs are a speciality. A rare home in the city for traditional table skittles.

Six Bells

16-18 St Michael's Street, AL3 4SH

11.30-11 (midnight Fri-Sun) (01727) 856945 the-six-bells.com

Oakham JHB; Timothy Taylor Landlord; Tring Ridgeway; 3 changing beers (sourced nationally)

A 16th-century timbered free house with three regular beers and three changing guests, one of which is always from a Hertfordshire brewer. Real cider is available during the summer. The pub is the only licensed premises within the walls of Roman Verulamium and is within walking distance of the city centre, Abbey, Verulamium Park and Museum. Quiz nights and live music sometimes feature. Good home-cooked food is served lunchtimes and evenings (not Sun eve). Outside there is a pleasant patio area. P (300,301)

White Hart Tap

4 Keyfield Terrace, AL1 1QJ

11-11; 12-11 Sun (01727) 860974 whiteharttap.co.uk

Castle Rock Harvest Pale; Sharp's Doom Bar; Timothy Taylor Landlord; Tring Side Pocket for a Toad; 3 changing beers (sourced nationally)

Welcoming, one-bar, back-street local featuring beers from Punch Taverns, three free of tie. It now brews occasional beers on the premises in various styles. Good-value, home-cooked food is served lunchtimes and Monday to Saturday evenings, with roasts on Sunday and monthly themed food nights. Quiz night is Wednesday. There is a public car park opposite the pub and a heated, covered smoking area outside. Barbecues are held in the summer and several beer festivals hosted throughout the year.

White Lion

91 Sopwell Lane, AL1 1RN

12-11 (01727) 850540 whitelionstalbans.co.uk

Adnams Broadside; Oakham JHB, Citra; St Austell Tribute; 3 changing beers (sourced nationally)

A sister pub to the White Hart Tap, this is a pleasantly laid-out hostelry within a 16th-century half-timbered frame. There is a small, friendly front bar and a larger main bar with alcoves. The large rear garden is a haven for drinkers in warm weather and boules, chess and Jenga are played here. Choose meals from an inviting menu of quality home-made food served every lunchtime and weekday evenings. Occasional open mic or live band sessions are hosted.

St Pauls Walden

Strathmore Arms

London Road, SG4 8BT TL193222
6-11 Mon; 12-2.30, 5-11 Tue-Thu; 12-11 Fri & Sat; 12-10.30 Sun (01438) 871654 thestrathmorearms.co.uk
Tring Side Pocket for a Toad; 4 changing beers (sourced nationally)
On the Bowes-Lyon estate, this pub has been serving drinkers since 1882, offering a constantly changing list of guest beers from obscure breweries. Unusual bottled beers are also available along with real ciders and perries. A regular in the Guide since 1981, the pub displays a full collection of the Good Beer Guide going back to 1976. It has a separate snug. Pizza and pasta evening is Wednesday and gourmet food nights are held on occasion (booking essential). Well known for fundraising locally. **Q P**

Sarratt

Cricketers

The Green, WD3 6AS TQ043992
10-11 (10.30 Sun) (01923) 270877
cricketers-sarratt.co.uk
Brunning & Price Original; 4 changing beers (sourced nationally)
Facing Sarratt Green and formerly three buildings, the pub has been tastefully modernised inside, with a number of seating areas. Drinkers are welcome and a range of five handpumps offers a changing selection of beers, with a focus on local breweries. Details of the beers are displayed on a blackboard. The menu offers interesting choices including pub classics and features local produce. Look for the wicket-shaped boot scrapers by the front door. **Q P** (352)

Sawbridgeworth

Bull

89 Cambridge Road, CM21 9BX
11-11; 12-9 Sun (01279) 722777
Fuller's London Pride
This pub offers just the one ale, but the turnover is rapid and local drinkers say it is consistently the best Pride they have tasted! Staff are welcoming at the popular local, with a comfortable interior adorned with beams and brasses. The small sports screens are unobtrusive, often with the sound off. Excellent Sunday lunchtime roasts are served. Bus services are frequent and the Bull is also walkable from Sawbridgeworth station. **Q P**

Old Bell

38 Bell Street, CM21 9AN
11-11 (midnight Thu & Sat; 1am Fri); 12-11 Sun
(01279) 725052
Adnams Broadside; Woodforde's Wherry; 1 changing beer (sourced nationally)
This 16th-century timber-framed pub boasts many exposed beams in the main bar. Situated among Bell Street's traditional village shops, it is cosy and friendly. There is a side bar where food is served and a popular courtyard and sunny garden with a children's play area for the summer. A quiz is hosted on Sunday evening and a ukulele jam session on Tuesday evening. Real cider and perry are always available. **P**

Standon

Star

62 High Street, SG11 1LB
12-3, 5-11; 12-11.30 Fri & Sat; 12-11 Sun
(01920) 823725 star-standon.co.uk
Greene King IPA, Abbot; 2 changing beers
Traditional 17th-century pub with exposed wooden beams. It has a separate sports-themed public bar and a quiet and comfortable saloon/restaurant. Food is classic pub grub with roasts on Sunday. Two guest beers are offered, at least one not from Greene King – usually from a small independent local brewer. **P** (331,386)

Stevenage

Standing Order

33 High Street, SG1 3AU
8am-midnight (11 Sun) (01438) 316972
Greene King IPA, Abbot; Sharp's Doom Bar; 5 changing beers (sourced nationally)
There is a keen focus on cask ale at this Wetherspoon pub, with many beers from microbreweries far and wide. Situated at the northern end of Stevenage Old Town, the building was a bank from the early 1960s to the late 1990s before it was converted to a pub by Wetherspoon in 2000, hence the name. **Q**

Tring

King's Arms

King Street, HP23 6BE (corner of Queen St and King St in middle of Tring Triangle) SP921111
12-2.30, 5.30 (5 Fri)-11.30; 12-11.30 Sat & Sun
(01442) 823318 kingsarmstring.co.uk
Tring Moongazing; 4 changing beers (sourced regionally; often Hook Norton, Leighton Buzzard, XT)
Affectionately known as the pink pub by its regulars because of its fuchsia exterior, the King's Arms is a classic back-street boozer with an attached dining-room, offering fantastic home-cooked cuisine, five real ales and a cider. Situated in the centre of Tring, the pub has a traditional interior with no music or TV, two real fires and a heated patio and canopies outside. Children are welcome at all times. **Q**

Robin Hood

1 Brook Street, HP23 5ED (jct with B4635/B486)
11.30-11 (11.30 Fri); 12-11.30 Sat; 12-11 Sun
(01442) 824912 therobinhoodtring.co.uk
Fuller's London Pride, ESB; 3 changing beers (sourced nationally; often Fuller's)
A classic, 16th-century Fuller's house offering well-kept beer and good pub food. On Sunday evenings you can also enjoy a Tip Khao Thai menu. Characterful features such as stoves and low ceilings create a cosy, country-pub ambience. Set at the foot of Tring's high street, with a heated patio and conservatory area, this pub has a lot to offer. **Q**

Ware

Brewery Tap

83 High Street, SG12 9AD
12-11.30 (10.30 Sun) (01920) 468549
brewerytapware.co.uk

Hardys & Hansons Olde Trip; 5 changing beers (sourced nationally) Ⓗ
Refurbished and stylish town-centre Grade II listed pub with six handpumps, featuring Greene King and local Hertfordshire beers. Three or four traditional ciders and perries are also available. Ware House Ale is a house beer brewed by Greene King. The long-closed cellar bar has been reopened and outside there is a heated courtyard. The all-day food menu comprises pies, sausages, paninis and pizzas. Old photographs and maps of Ware are an interesting distraction, and look for the one-penny wall. (331,383)

Crooked Billet

140 Musley Hill, SG12 7NL (via New Rd from High St)
5.30-11.30 (midnight Fri); 12-midnight Sat; 12-11.30 Sun
(01920) 462516
4 changing beers (sourced nationally) Ⓗ
Presided over by the same landlords for more than 20 years, this Guide perennial has stocked more than 600 different ales since it was acquired by Admiral Taverns. Utilising the local SIBA Direct Delivery Scheme, it offers a varying range of four or five beers including a mild, porter or stout. Two beer and cider festivals are held annually. This gem of a community pub has two small bars featuring TV sport, pool and darts. Carlisle United and Ware FC fans are assured of a warm welcome.
(395)

Waterside Inn

Bridgefoot, SG12 9DW
9am-11 (midnight Thu-Sat); 10-10.30 Sun
(01920) 468628 watersideinnware.co.uk
Adnams Ghost Ship; St Austell Tribute, Proper Job; 5 changing beers (sourced nationally) Ⓗ
Popular large town-centre pub located alongside the River Lea. The award-winning garden/patio is a summer suntrap where beers can be enjoyed against the backdrop of passing narrowboats. A fine bank of eight handpumps dispenses three regular and five guest ales including some local beers from Hertfordshire's New River, Farr and Tring breweries. Good-value food is served all day and the pub hosts a well-attended quiz on Wednesday evening.
P(395,331)

Watford

Wellington Arms

2 Woodford Road, WD17 1PA
11-11 (midnight Fri & Sat); 12-10.30 Sun
(01923) 220739 wellingtonarmshotel.co.uk
Fuller's London Pride; 2 changing beers (sourced locally) Ⓗ
Run by the same family for 28 years, this modernised free house has a focus on sports. Major football, rugby, cricket and golf matches are shown on various screens around the pub, with other events screened on request. The pub is conveniently located on a street corner between Watford Junction station and the town centre. Food is available and there is accommodation in 13 rooms. (Jct)P

West Herts Sports Club

8 Park Avenue, WD18 7HP (S of A412, nr town hall)
5-11; 4-11.30 Fri; 12-11 Sat; 12-10.30 Sun
(01923) 229239 westhertssportsclub.co.uk
Tring Side Pocket for a Toad; Young's Bitter; 3 changing beers (sourced nationally) Ⓗ
This members' bar is a regular winner of the Watford & District CAMRA Club of the Year award. The bar is decorated with sporting memorabilia and sporting events are shown on big screens. Real ciders are regularly on offer. A separate function room, home of the Watford Beer & Cider Festival, is available to hire. Show a CAMRA membership card or a copy of this Guide to gain entry up to four times a year. The bar can get busy on Watford FC match days. P

Wheathampstead

Swan

56 High Street, AL4 8AR
11.30-11.30 (11 Sun) (01582) 833110
theswanwheathampstead.co.uk
Greene King IPA; St Austell Tribute; 3 changing beers (sourced nationally) Ⓗ
Dating from the 16th century, this thriving and friendly traditional village inn has retained many interesting features including exposed beams and an inglenook fireplace. It has an upper bar with darts and TV Sport. A community pub popular with workers and walkers, dogs are welcome. Lunches are available every day, evening meals Monday and Friday. Wednesday is quiz night and bingo is hosted on the last Thursday of the month. The three guest ales come from the SIBA range.
P

Wild Hill

Woodman

45 Wildhill Road, AL9 6EA (between A1000 and B158)
TL264068
11.30-2.30, 5.30-11; 12-2.30, 7-10.30 Sun
(01707) 642618
Greene King IPA, Abbot; 4 changing beers (sourced nationally) Ⓗ
This superb inn is an unpretentious, friendly, rural community local. Ninety per cent wet-led, it thrives on and is a staunch supporter of real ale, with six beers including four guests. Lined oversized glasses are available on request. The large garden is ideal in summer. Good pub grub is served lunchtimes (no food Sun). Look for God's Waiting Room. Eleven-times winner of local CAMRA Pub of the Year and three times Hertfordshire CAMRA Pub of the Year. P

Wilstone

Half Moon

60 Tring Road, HP23 4PD
12-11 (10.30 Sun) (01442) 826410
Sharp's Doom Bar; Tring Side Pocket for a Toad; 2 changing beers (sourced locally; often Malt, Tring, XT) Ⓗ
Lovely old welcoming village pub, close to the Grand Union Canal, with an inglenook fireplace and beamed ceilings, adorned with horse brasses and old black and white pictures of the village and locals. The food is good, home-cooked fare and reasonably priced. Three or four beers are on offer, mostly from local breweries. A Scrabble night is held on the fourth Sunday of the month. A cottage provides self-catering accommodation.
QP(164)

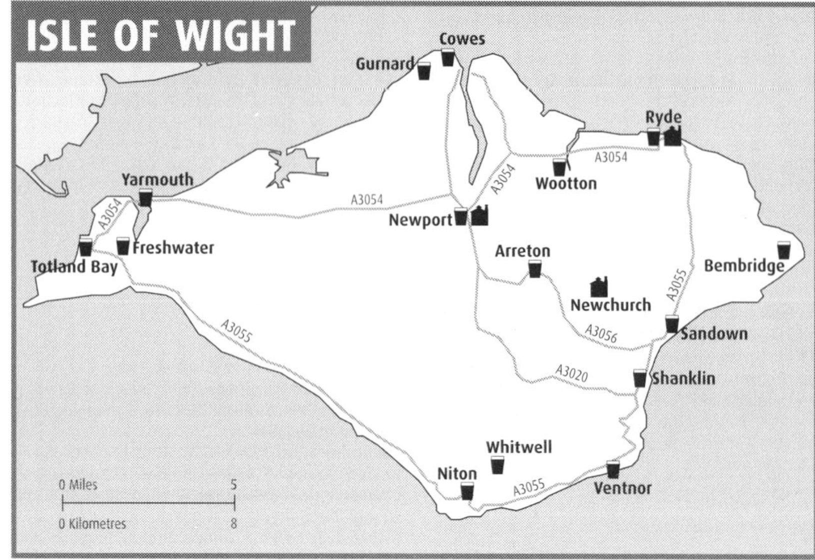

Arreton

Dairyman's Daughter L

Main Road, PO30 3AA SZ53258680
10-11; 10-10.30 Sun (01983) 539361
thedairymansdaughter.com
Ringwood Razorback, Fortyniner; 4 changing beers (sourced nationally) H
Arreton Barns Craft Village includes the Dairyman's, Shipwreck Centre and Maritime Museum and IW Studio Glass, all worth visiting, plus the 12th-century church of St George and the grave of the original Dairyman's Daughter. The pub provides up to six beers including local ales, plus a large selection of Island bottled beer in the old brewery. Breakfast, lunch and evening meals can be enjoyed indoors or in the garden. Tuesday is folk night and live music plays on Friday, Saturday and Sunday. P(8)

Bembridge

Old Village Inn

61 High Street, PO35 5SF
12-11 (midnight Fri & Sat); 12-10.30 Sun
(01983) 872616 yeoldevillageinn.co.uk
Thwaites Original; 3 changing beers (sourced nationally; often Butcombe, Greene King, West Berkshire) H
The Old Village Steak and Ale House is the latest addition to the Bembridge scene, specialising in local meat and fish dishes. A fine choice of real ales and selected wines is served in a refined and relaxed atmosphere alongside home-cooked lunchtime and evening meals. Live music plays on occasional Fridays and a popular quiz is held on the first Monday of the month. There is a patio area to the rear and a pétanque terrain. A pizza oven and outdoor covered area are recent additions. Q P(8)

Cowes

Anchor Inn L

1 High Street, PO31 7SA (opp Sainsbury's)
11-11 (midnight Fri & Sat); 12-10.30 Sun
(01983) 292823 theanchorcowes.co.uk
Fuller's London Pride; Goddards Fuggle-Dee-Dum; Wadworth 6X; 2 changing beers (sourced nationally) H
This High Street pub, originally The Three Trumpeters back in 1704, is close to the marina, tempting visiting yachtsmen for their first pint ashore. The recent conversion has integrated the stables and created a pleasant beer garden. A good selection of beer is on offer, with one Island ale and two guests always available. The varied food menu is served in prodigious quantities. Live entertainment is a regular feature. Accommodation is in seven comfortable rooms.
(1)

Cowes Ale House

5A Shooters Hill, PO31 7BE (up hill from Sainsbury's)
12-11 (midnight Fri & Sat); 12-10.30 Sun
(01983) 294027 cowesalehouse.co.uk
4 changing beers (sourced nationally) G
Ideally situated in the main street, the Ale House is small, friendly and sometimes crowded – like its sister pub, the Newport Ale House. Four real ales are usually on stillage in an ever-rotating selection – expect to find the occasional mild and porter. Bar snacks are available. There are many events during the week including a well-supported Irish night on Monday, the ever-popular quiz on Wednesday and live music Friday and Sunday. Q (1)

Freshwater

Red Lion L

Church Place, PO40 9BP (follow Hook Hill towards The Causway) SZ34508738
11-11 (01983) 754925 redlion-freshwater.co.uk
St Austell Proper Job; 3 changing beers (sourced nationally; often Adnams, Long Man, West Berkshire) H
Former three-bar coaching inn dating back to the 11th century, now converted to one large bar but still retaining much of its character. It is situated in the most picture-postcard area of Freshwater in the

church square and by the Causeway, and enjoys splendid views of the River Yar towards Yarmouth. The pub is noted for its fine food, with a daily changing blackboard menu featuring local produce (diners are advised to book ahead). May close earlier during the winter. Q❀◐P🚌(7,12)🐾📶

Gurnard

Portland Inn ✔

2 Worsley Road, PO31 8JN (opp church) SZ47909530
12-11 (10.30 Sun) ☎(01983) 243300
theportlandinn.co.uk
St Austell Tribute; Sharp's Doom Bar; 1 changing beer (sourced regionally; often Arundel, Goddards, Wadworth) H
Located at the entrance to Gurnard village, the pub has been completely refurbished and offers comfortable surroundings for drinkers and diners. The new publicans are passionate about creating a great local pub, with a focus on offering superb food and drink in a welcoming atmosphere. Weather permitting, head outside to enjoy drinks, lunch or supper in the pleasant garden. A good selection of cask ales often includes a beer from a local brewer. Q❀◐♿🚌(1,32)🐾📶

Newport

Bargeman's Rest 🏆 L

Little London Quay, PO30 5BS (signed from dual carriageway)
10.30-11 (10.30 Sun) ☎(01983) 525828
bargemansrest.com
Goddards Fuggle-Dee-Dum; Ringwood Razorback; 4 changing beers (often Marston's) H
This massive locally owned pub has previously been an animal feed store and a sail and rigging loft for the barge fleet that once used the river. The huge bar room provides intimate drinking areas and the nautical memorabilia, decor and ambience are what you would expect from a traditional, well-seasoned pub. The outdoor drinking area is only a few feet from the bustling River Medina. Beer and food are consistently good and the range is varied. Live entertainment features most nights. ❀◐♿P🚌🐾📶

Man in the Moon L ✔

16 St James Street, PO30 5HB
8am-12.30am (1.30am Fri & Sat) ☎(01983) 530126
Greene King Abbot; Sharp's Doom Bar; 5 changing beers (often Island) H
Opened in 2014, this impressive Wetherspoon conversion of the former Congregational Church maintains the character of the original while adding sympathetic extensions. The drinking and dining areas include an upstairs gallery and an outdoor area where dogs and children are welcome. Although a food-led pub, the beers are well kept, with a good selection of local ales featuring among the guests. You may find the excellent Island Brewery RDA here and often a cider on handpump. ❀◐♿🍎🚌📶

Newport Ale House L

24A Holyrood Street, PO30 5AZ
12-11; 11-midnight Fri & Sat; 12-10.30 Sun
☎ 07708 018051 newportalehouse.co.uk
5 changing beers (sourced nationally) G
The listed building has previously traded as a hairdresser, undertakers and posting house and stables. It is the Island's smallest pub, recalling the days when there were several such establishments in Newport. This is a hugely popular venue with all generations, where conversation comes easy – it can get crowded and noisy. Live music is hosted, often on a Sunday afternoon. The beer choice is always interesting and varied. No meals, but snacks are high-quality locally sourced pies, rolls and sandwiches. Q🍎🚌🐾

Niton

Joe's Bar L ✔

High Street, PO38 2AZ
11-11 ☎(01983) 730280
Dartmoor Jail Ale; Yates' Islander; house beer (by Yates'); 1 changing beer (often Rudgate, Titanic, Yates') H
Joe's Place is unique to the Island as it opened when the village pub closed for a while and has since become the hub of the village life with a post office, tea room and newsagent. The well-maintained cask ales, including beers from the local Yates' Brewery, attract an ever-increasing following from across the Island. There is a garden and patio outside. Booking is essential for feast-night Friday, and snacks and sandwiches are available. This gem is well worth a visit. Q❀◐🚌(6)

Ryde

Railway L

68 St Johns Road, PO33 2RT (by St Johns Station)
3-11; 12-midnight Sat & Sun ☎(01983) 611500
6 changing beers (often Heritage, Island) H
Refurbished to a high standard by the previous owner, the pub has retained the flagstone floors, beams and plenty of wood. For the horticulturally minded, note the ginkgo biloba tree in the garden, a species whose ancestry can be traced back over 200 million years. The train station is just yards away, bringing visitors from Portsmouth to enjoy the quality, ever-changing, competitively priced real ales. Quiz night is Tuesday and live music features on Friday. ❀♿⇌(St Johns)♣🍎🚌🐾

S Fowler & Co L ✔

41-43 Union Street, PO33 2LF (top of Union St)
7am-midnight (1am Fri & Sat); 8am-midnight Sun
☎(01983) 812112
Adnams Broadside; Fuller's London Pride; 8 changing beers (sourced nationally) H
Although not the most charismatic pub in the Wetherspoon chain, this converted drapery store offers a varied range of well-kept beers. The pub is in the centre of town, with a bus stop conveniently outside. The pub name was at the suggestion of the local CAMRA branch – not only is Fowler the name of the former store, but also that of the first local CAMRA chairman and revered early campaigner. The family-friendly food area is upstairs. Q◐♿⇌🍎🚌📶

REAL ALE BREWERIES

Goddards Ryde
Island Newport
Yates' Newchurch

Sandown

Castle Inn

12-14 Fitzroy Street, PO36 8HY (off High St)
11-11 (midnight Fri); 10.30-midnight Sat & Sun
(01983) 403169 sandowncastle.co.uk
Goddards Fuggle-Dee-Dum; Shepherd Neame Spitfire; Wadworth IPA; Wychwood Hobgoblin Gold; 2 changing beers (sourced locally; often Upham) H
The Castle is an excellent town freehouse and locals' pub with crib and two darts teams. Six real ales are on offer including the best from local breweries. There is a children's room at the back and a patio for warm weather. The TV is not allowed to intrude, but is turned on for special occasions. Happy hour (5-7pm nightly) is popular, as is the Sunday quiz. Beer festivals are held twice a year, usually featuring local ales and cider.
Q (3,8)

Culver Haven Inn

Culver Down, PO36 8QT (by Culver Down monument) SZ63258565
closed Tue; 10.30-11 (4 Mon) (01983) 406107
culverhaven.com
3 changing beers (often Goddards, Timothy Taylor, Wadworth) H
Surely one of the best pub views in the whole of Great Britain, perched on Culver Down overlooking Sandown Bay and Bembridge Harbour. The view back down the hill is also spectacular. Nearby is the Culver Battery (opened regularly by the National Trust), an impressive remnant of the Napoleonic Wars and built to protect Portsmouth. This cosy restaurant and pub offers an excellent and varied food menu, from snacks to full meals. Closed throughout February. Q P

Shanklin

King Harry's Bar

6 Church Road, PO37 6NU (edge of the Old Village)
12-11 (10 Mon); 12-10.30 Sun (01983) 863119
kingharrysbar.co.uk
Fuller's ESB; 3 changing beers (often Goddards, Shepherd Neame, Young's) H
Charming 19th-century thatched property with two established Tudor-themed bars, restaurants, decked gardens and the Chine walk, plus car parking front and rear. Up to three guest beers are offered, chosen for their originality. The long-established Henry VIII kitchen specialises in steaks to die for (the evening menu is available May-September only). Opening hours vary – the pub often stays open until midnight in summer.
Q P (3,2)

Totland Bay

Highdown Inn

Highdown Lane, PO39 0HY (W of Alum Bay on Old Road) SZ32348596
11-11 (9 Mon-Thu winter) (01983) 752450
highdowninn.com
3 changing beers (sourced nationally; often Marston's, Prescott, Upham) H
In an area once known as Highdown, this hospitable pub is an ideal base for walkers and cyclists alike. An interesting range of home-cooked food includes a seasonal variety of fresh local game, fish and vegetables served in good-sized portions. A children's menu is available and in summer food is served all day. B&B accommodation is offered in three comfortable rooms and there is a campsite a few hundred yards away. No buses serve the pub in winter.
Q P

Waterfront

The Beach, PO39 0BQ
10-11 (9pm winter) (01983) 756969
thewaterfront-iow.co.uk
Sharp's Doom Bar; 3 changing beers (sourced regionally; often Andwells, Dorset, Island) H
Pleasant and popular pub/restaurant beside the sea, enjoying excellent Solent views to Portland and beyond. The beer range has been extended in recent years – the ales are reasonably priced and constantly changing, including stouts and milds. There is an outside tented area and the pub is accessible from the cliff path as well as the promenade. Food includes a Sunday roast. No food is served 3-5pm on winter weekdays.
Q P (7,12)

Ventnor

Spyglass Inn

The Esplanade, PO38 1JX
10.30-11 (01983) 855338 thespyglass.co.uk
Ringwood Razorback, Fortyniner; 3 changing beers (sourced locally; often Andwells, Goddards, Yates') H
Nineteenth-century ex-guesthouse at the western end of Ventnor Esplanade in a superb position overlooking the English Channel. Wisely, the temptation has been avoided to knock all the rooms into one; instead they have been skilfully incorporated into the overall layout. The inn has considerable character and boasts a large collection of seafaring memorabilia. Local seafood is a speciality and there is a small beer festival every year. Regular entertainment is hosted most evenings and Sunday lunchtime, and families are welcome. P (3,6)

Volunteer

30 Victoria Street, PO38 1ES (50yds from bus terminal)
11-11 (midnight Fri & Sat); 12-midnight Sun
(01983) 852537
Courage Best Bitter; Goddards Ale of Wight; Young's Special; 2 changing beers (often Adnams, Goddards, Marston's) H
Built in 1866, this wonderful, traditional establishment is one of the smallest pubs on the island. No chips, no children, no fruit machines, no video games – just a pure adult drinking house and one of the few places where you can still play rings and enjoy a traditional games night. Up to five beers are available including a local brew. A former winner of local CAMRA Pub of the Year.
Q (3,6)

Whitwell

White Horse Inn

High Street, PO38 2PY SZ52007800
10-11 (10 Sun) (01983) 730375
whitehorseiow.co.uk
4 changing beers (sourced nationally; often Adnams, Goddards, Thwaites) H
Built in 1454, this stone building is considered to be the oldest established inn on the Isle of Wight. An extension to the side adds a family area and additional dining space. The remainder of the building is traditional, with intimate areas to the

rear. Four handpumps serve a changing range of beers and the excellent food menu is extensive. A large garden is fine for children on warmer days. Breakfast is served 10am-midday.
Q❀◐♿●P🚌(6)🐾📶

Wootton

Cedars

2 Station Road, PO33 4QU
11-11; 12-10.30 Sun ☎ (01983) 882593
cedarsisleofwight.co.uk
Fuller's London Pride; Gale's Seafarers Ale, HSB Ⓗ
In a prominent position at the top of Wootton High Street is this late Victorian two-bar village local. It is a large pub though, curiously, it has one of the smallest front doors on the Island. There is a children's room and a large garden with a play area. Smokers are spoilt as the outdoor smoking area is adapted from a beautiful Victorian outbuilding. An extensive food menu is offered, and the friendly bar staff ensure a welcoming atmosphere. Close to the steam railway station.
Q❀◐♿≈♣P🚌(4,9)🐾📶

Yarmouth

King's Head

Quay Street, PO41 0PB (opp ferry terminal)
11-11; 12-10.30 Sun ☎ (01983) 760177
thekingsheadyarmouth.co.uk
6 changing beers (sourced nationally; often Adnams, Timothy Taylor, Upham) Ⓗ
Ancient 16th-century town pub with a big open fire and an interesting collection of old Island prints and local photographs. Stone floors, low ceilings and cosy corners feature in abundance. Home-cooked food includes fresh fish, daily specials and a Sunday carvery. A selection of favourite beers is available, including local ales, with six in the summer and three in the winter. Beer festivals and quiz nights are hosted. ❀◐🚌(7)🐾📶

Portland Inn, Gurnard (Photo: Ronald Saunders/flickr CC BY-SA 2.0)

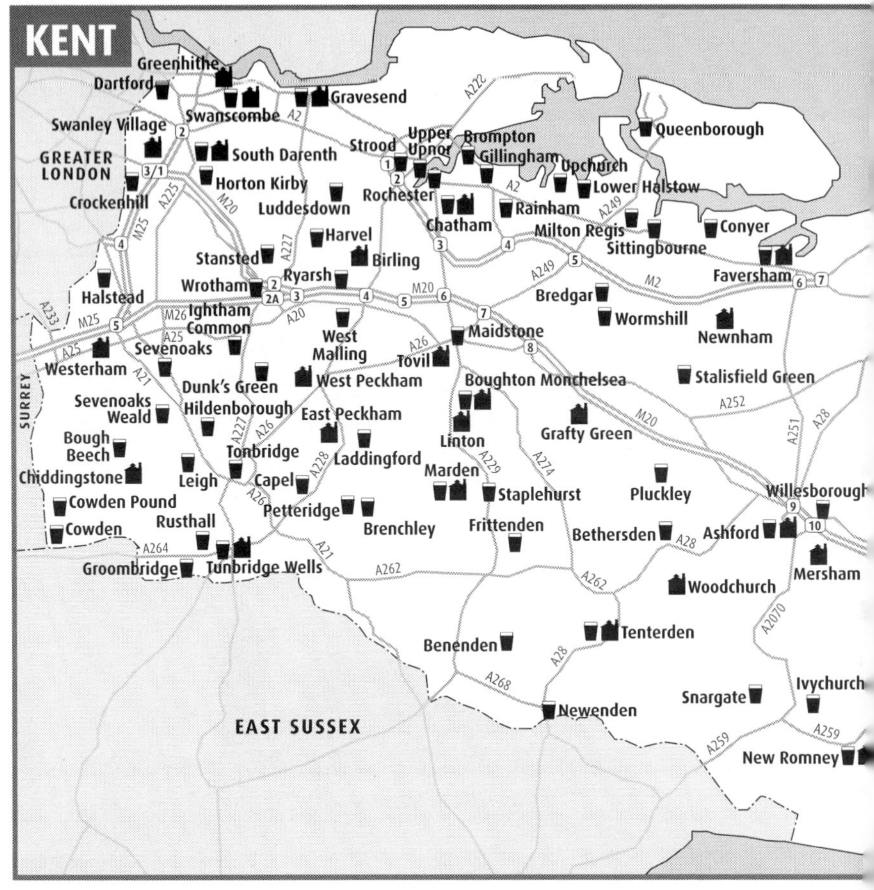

Ashford

County Hotel ✔

10 High Street, TN24 8TD (at lower end of High St)
✪ 8am-midnight (1am Fri & Sat); 8am-11 Sun
☎ (01233) 646891
Greene King Abbot; Ruddles Best Bitter; Sharp's Doom Bar; 4 changing beers (sourced nationally) Ⓗ
A spacious Wetherspoon pub in an 18th-century building in the centre of Ashford, with one bar with three separate seating areas. Originally red brick, the top floor and the parapet are now tile hung. Up to two real ciders are dispensed from polypins in the fridge. Food is available every day from 8am to 11pm; children are allowed in the dining area until 9pm. Summer and autumn national and international beer festivals and a summer cider festival are held. Q

Barfrestone

Wrong Turn Ⓛ

Pie Factory Road, CT15 7JG (2½ miles from Barfrestone jct off A2) TR261503
✪ closed Mon & Tue; 4-8 Wed; 2-7 Thu; 2-8 Fri; 12-8 Sat & Sun summer; closed Mon-Wed; 3-6.30 (8 Fri); 12-8 Sat; 12-6.30 Sun winter ☎ 07522 554118
Wantsum Black Prince; 2 changing beers (sourced locally) Ⓖ
Rural pub with a comfortable, country-style kitchen interior with wooden tables, chairs, sideboard and a wood-burning stove. Three real ales including a mild are usually on tap, primarily from Kent microbreweries, alongside real ciders from Kentish Pip and Westons. Snacks include pork pies, Scotch eggs and cheeseboards. Outside, there is a sheltered patio and garden. A pleasant 1½-mile walk from Shepherds Well railway station. Local CAMRA Pub of the Year 2016.
QP

Beltinge

Copper Pottle Ⓛ

84 Reculver Road, CT6 6ND
✪ closed Mon; 12-2, 6-9; 12-3 Sun ☎ 07710 001261
🌐 copperpottle.co.uk
Kent Session Pale; Ramsgate Gadds' No.5 Best Bitter Ale; 2 changing beers (sourced locally) Ⓖ
Originally a pet food shop, this friendly micropub has an attractive blue-tiled frontage. Drinks are dispensed from a temperature-controlled cellar via a small bar counter. Conversation is encouraged by the layout of high and low narrow tables, and the walls are decorated with amusing posters and postcards. Every six weeks there is a charity fundraising event which might either be a quiz, a food evening or barbecue. The south-facing garden is a good place to enjoy your drink. Q

Benenden

Bull

The Street, TN17 4DE

12-midnight; 12-11 Sun ☎ (01580) 240054

thebullatbenenden.co.uk

Dark Star Hophead; Harvey's Sussex Best Bitter; Larkins Traditional Ale; 1 changing beer (sourced locally) H

Imposing 17th-century free house beside the large and picturesque village green. The public bar is characterised by wooden floors, exposed oak beams and a large inglenook fireplace. A separate dining room serves locally grown produce although meals may also be taken in the public bar. Booking is advisable for the Friday fish and chips and Sunday lunchtime carvery (no food Sun eve). Early evening music sessions are held monthly on a Sunday. Q P (297)

Bethersden

George

The Street, TN26 3AG (off A28 between Ashford and Tenterden in centre of village)

12-midnight ☎ (01233) 820235

Harvey's Sussex Best Bitter; St Austell Cornish Best Bitter; 2 changing beers (sourced regionally) H

A two-bar free house in a picturesque Kentish village decorated with pictures of local life. The public bar is a survivor of what village inns used to be like, with wood panelling, hops over the bar, a wood-burning stove, pub games, jukebox and good conversation. Food is served except Monday lunchtime and Sunday evening, with carveries on Wednesday evening and Sunday lunchtime. A beer festival is held around St George's Day. Buses from Ashford and Tenterden stop outside. A proper village pub. P (2)

Birchington-on-Sea

Old Bay Alehouse

137 Minnis Road, CT7 9NS

closed Mon; 12.30-2, 5.30-9.30 (10.30 Fri & Sat); 12.30-4 Sun oldbayalehouse.co.uk

3 changing beers G

Fine micropub located an easy five-minute stroll from the beach at Minnis Bay, near Birchington. The bar counter on the right serves real ales and ciders on gravity dispense from a temperature-controlled cool room behind. Seating is at wall-

REAL ALE BREWERIES

Amazing Sandgate
Angels & Demons Capel-le-Ferne
Boutilliers Faversham
Breakwater Dover
Brew Buddies Swanley Village
Brumaison Marden
By The Mile Broadstairs
Canterbury Ales Chartham
Canterbury Brewers Canterbury
Caveman Swanscombe
Farriers Arms Mersham
Four Candles St Peters
G2 Ashford
Goacher's Tovil
Goody Herne
Hop Fuzz West Hythe
Hopdaemon Newnham
Iron Pier Gravesend (NEW)
Isla Vale Margate
Kent Birling
Larkins Chiddingstone
Mad Cat Faversham
Millis (Dartford Wobbler) South Darenth
Musket Linton
NauticAles Broadstairs
Nelson Chatham
No Frills Joe Greenhithe (NEW)
Northdown Margate (NEW)
Old Dairy Tenterden
Pig & Porter Tunbridge Wells
Ramsgate (Gadds') Broadstairs
Range Lympne
Ripple Steam Sutton
Rockin' Robin Boughton Monchelsea
Romney Marsh New Romney
Samphire Folkestone
Shepherd Neame Faversham
Stag Woodchurch
Swan West Peckham
Tír Dhá Ghlas Dover
Tonbridge East Peckham
Turnstone Whitstable
Wantsum St Nicholas at Wade
Westerham Westerham
Whitstable Grafty Green

mounted benches with high tables, plus some low tables and chairs. There are some comfy armchairs in the front window. The real ale selection always includes at least one local beer. Bar snacks are available and there are occasional pop up food events. Q (33,34)

Bough Beech

Wheatsheaf

Hever Road, TN8 7NU
11.30-11; 12-9 Sun (01732) 700100
wheatsheafboughbeech.co.uk
Harvey's Sussex Best Bitter; Larkins Traditional Ale; 2 changing beers (sourced locally; often Westerham) H
A splendid historic building from Tudor times, believed to have been a favourite of Henry VIII, which reopened in 2014 after refurbishment by the new owner, a director of Westerham Brewery. An impressive oak-beamed interior features large inglenooks and ancient artefacts, with several separate areas affording plenty of room both for drinkers and diners. Two Westerham beers are always on the bar. The pub enjoys a lovely terrace garden to the front and side of the building. Closed Mondays in winter. P (231,233)

Boughton Monchelsea

Beer Barn L

Campfield Farm, Haste Hill Road, ME17 4LR
closed Mon-Thu; 4-midnight Fri; 2-6 Sat; 12-5 Sun
(01622) 747106 rockinrobinbrewery.co.uk
Rockin' Robin Reliant Robin; 2 changing beers (sourced locally; often Rockin' Robin) H
Log cabin-style micropub within the Rockin' Robin brewery barn. Opening hours are extended during the summer months. Beers are priced at £3 per pint. Quiz nights are held on the first Friday of each month, duo/trio bands play on other Fridays, events, competitions and games are held on summer Saturdays, and a special Saturday party is held in July/August each year at an all-inclusive price for food, drinks and three bands.
P

Cock Inn L

Heath Road, ME17 4JD TQ776512
11-11; 12-9 Sun (01622) 743166
cockinnmaidstone.co.uk
Shepherd Neame Master Brew, Spitfire Gold; 2 changing beers (sourced nationally; often Shepherd Neame) H
A 16th-century coaching inn built to provide lodgings for Canterbury pilgrims, full of character, with oak beams and an inglenook fireplace. A large and varied menu complemented by real ales is served in both the bar and restaurant (no food Sun eve). There is a large patio area. Various board games are available. Near the Greensand Way, dogs and walkers are welcome.
Q P (59)

Bramling

Haywain L

Canterbury Road, CT3 1NB
7.30-11 Mon; 12-3, 6-11; 12-4 Sun (01227) 720676
thehaywainbramling.co.uk
Bombardier; Fuller's London Pride; 2 changing beers (sourced locally; often Goacher's, Ramsgate, Whitstable) H
Classic friendly country pub which features hop bines and a cosy snug. Traditional games include darts and bat and trap. There is a Monday quiz night, a Wednesday crib night, a cheese club on the last Sunday of the month, and jazz on the last Tuesday. Guest beers are usually from Kent breweries, and an annual beer festival is hosted over the spring bank holiday weekend in a marquee in the attractive garden. Excellent home-cooked food, using local produce, is served.
P (43)

Bredgar

Sun Inn

The Street, ME9 8EY
11-11 (01622) 884221 thesuninn.co.uk
Harvey's Sussex Best Bitter; Sharp's Doom Bar; Shepherd Neame Master Brew H
The Sun Inn has been a village hostelry since the early 1700s. The sizeable front bar area has a long bar separating it from the large restaurant space to the rear. A wide and varied food menu is offered. The bar has a real log fire. P

Brenchley

Halfway House L

Horsmonden Road, TN12 7AX (½ mile SE of village)
12-11; 12-10.30 Sun (01892) 722526
halfwayhousebrenchley.co.uk
Dark Star Hophead; Goacher's Fine Light Ale; Skinner's Betty Stogs; Westerham 1965 Special Bitter Ale; Young's Special; house beer (by Goacher's); 3 changing beers (sourced locally; often Hopdaemon, Musket, Tonbridge) G
A former coaching inn lying outside the village on the road to Horsmonden, this renowned free house serves the beers direct from cooled casks, along with Chiddingstone cider. Hops hanging from wooden beams in rooms arranged over many levels, farming and brewery memorabilia and open fires combine to provide a cosy, rustic ambience. Beer festivals are held over the Whitsun and August bank holidays in the garden which includes its own bar and a separate family area.
Q P (297)

Brompton

King George V

1 Prospect Row, ME7 5AL
12-11; 12-10.30 Sun (01634) 842418
kinggeorgevpub.co.uk
3 changing beers (sourced locally; often Mad Cat) H
An 18th-century free house with three connecting areas decorated with military memorabilia and a covered and heated smoking area outside. At least two beers feature, many from local microbreweries. The pub also sells an extensive range of Belgian draught and bottled beers, malt whiskies, rums and gins. Food is served every day; Sunday roasts are recommended. The pub also holds regular quiz and music nights. Three en-suite guest rooms are available.
(101,182)

Canterbury

Dolphin

17 St Radigund's Street, CT1 2AA
12-11 (midnight Thu-Sat) (01227) 455963
thedolphincanterbury.co.uk
Sharp's Doom Bar; Timothy Taylor Landlord; 1 changing beer (sourced locally; often Ramsgate) H
Friendly local decorated with 1950-1970 memorabilia, free of TV screens but with a comprehensive collection of board games. Pub food in generous portions is served, with roasts on Sundays. The attractive veranda is popular with diners, and there is a large suntrap garden, in which the Henri the H van sells rotisserie food. One handpump serves cider, and there is a wide range of beers on other pumps. Opening hours vary from month to month.

Eight Bells

34 London Road, CT2 8LN
3-11; 12-midnight Fri & Sat; 12-10.30 Sun
(01227) 454794
Young's Bitter, Special H
Small, traditional local dating from 1708 and rebuilt in 1902, retaining original embossed windows and decorated with memorabilia. There is live music fortnightly on Fridays, and a quiz, usually on the last Wednesday of the month. Five darts teams play every week and their trophies are on display. Food is served only on Sunday lunchtimes. There is an attractive small walled garden and a comfortable heated smoking area.
(West)

Foundry Brew Pub

White Horse Lane, CT1 2RU (just off High Street)
12-midnight (3am Fri & Sat); 12-11 Sun
(01227) 455899 thefoundrycanterbury.co.uk
Canterbury Brewers & Distillers Foundryman's Gold, Foundry Torpedo, Little Red Rye, Streetlight Porter; 2 changing beers (often Canterbury Brewers & Distillers) H
The home of Canterbury Brewers & Distillers, this 19th-century foundry is on two floors. There are usually six ales on sale, all of which are brewed on the premises. They also produce their own cider, vodka and gin and most of what they make is available to take away in bottles. Good-value pub food is served till 8pm (6pm Sun and Mon; 9pm Fri and Sat). There is a pleasant patio area.

New Inn

19 Havelock Street, CT1 1NP (off ring road near St Augustine's Abbey)
12-3, 5.30-11.30; 12-midnight Fri & Sat; 12-11.30 Sun
(01227) 464584 newinncanterbury.co.uk
7 changing beers (often Dark Star, Oakham, Ramsgate) H
Victorian back-street terraced house a few minutes' walk from the cathedral, St Augustine's Abbey, and the bus station. The main bar has a cosy woodburner and a jukebox. At the back is a long bright conservatory with newspapers and a range of board games. It has a large whisky selection and an interesting and ever-changing range of cask ales. Beer festivals are held on the Whitsun and August bank holiday weekends. Wheelchair access is through the attractive garden via Old Ruttington Lane. Q

Thomas Tallis Alehouse

48 Northgate, CT1 1BE
5-9.30 Mon; 2-11 Tue-Thu; 12-11 Fri & Sat; 12-10 Sun
(01227) 464952
3 changing beers (sourced locally; often Kent, Old Dairy, Ramsgate) G
Canterbury's first micropub-style ale house, located in a lovely 15th-century half-timbered building, part of the historic Hospital of St John. Three varied Kent beers from the cask are served, and many national and international beers in KeyKeg, bottles and cans, plus five or six Kentish ciders. One of the two front rooms has a log-burning stove. The rear snug has armchairs and a sofa. Generally, table service applies. Outside seating is available on the street. Q

Unicorn

61 St Dunstan's Street, CT2 8BS
11.30-11 (midnight Fri & Sat) (01227) 463187
unicorninn.com
4 changing beers (often Adnams, Hopdaemon, Shepherd Neame) H
Comfortable 1604 pub near the historic Westgate, with an attractive suntrap garden and garden bar. Bar billiards is played and a quiz, set by regular customers, is held every Sunday evening. One guest beer is often from one of several Kent microbreweries, and beer updates are posted on social media. There is a bottled beer list. Food is good value, with a two-meals-for-£12 special offer on selected meals. Sporting events (not Sky) are televised unobtrusively. Q

Capel

Dovecote Inn

Alders Road, TN12 6SU (½ mile W of A228 towards Tudeley)
12-3 (not Mon), 5.30-11; 12-10.30 Sun (01892) 835966
dovecote-capel.co.uk
Gale's HSB; Harvey's Sussex Best Bitter; 3 changing beers (sourced nationally; often Hop Back, Long Man, Wye Valley) G
Set in orchard country and attracting many walkers, the Dovecote recently celebrated its 20th consecutive appearance in this Guide. Ales and Westons Old Rosie cider are served direct from the cask, and a good selection of home-cooked dishes is available (no food Sun and Mon eves). The cosy interior features exposed red brickwork, oak beams decorated with local hops and a log fire, while customers may also enjoy the shaded patio and garden in warmer weather, when bat and trap is played. QP

Chatham

Thomas Waghorn

14 Railway Street, ME4 4HU
8am-midnight (1am Fri & Sat) (01634) 405422
Greene King IPA, Abbot; Sharp's Doom Bar; house beer (by Rockin' Robin); 4 changing beers (sourced locally; often Hopdaemon, Westerham, Whitstable) H
An establishment ideally situated in the heart of Chatham, just a short walk from both railway and bus stations. The manager is a keen real ale enthusiast and CAMRA member, which shows in the quality of the ales served. The pub has many nooks and crannies for you to while away the hours. Q

Coldred

Carpenters Arms 🄻
The Green, CT15 5AJ
5-9 (11 Fri & Sat); 7-11 Sun ☎ (01304) 830190
2 changing beers (often Ramsgate, Romney Marsh) 🄷
Overlooking the village green and duckpond, this 18th-century two-roomed pub is a real gem and well worth seeking out. It has been in the Fagg family for over a century, largely unchanged in the last 50 years and the centre of the local community, where conversation is king. At least two real ales are served and three real ciders, from Kentish Pip. Regular community events are hosted including quizzes and vegetable competitions. A beer festival is held in June. Q❀♣P

Conyer

Ship ✔
Conyer Quay, ME9 9HR
12-3, 6-11 (midnight Fri); 10-11.30 Sat; 10-9.30 Sun
☎ (01795) 520881 shipinnconyer.co.uk
Shepherd Neame Master Brew; 3 changing beers (sourced regionally; often Adnams, Old Dairy) 🄷
An 18th-century creekside pub with a nautical-themed interior. Bare floorboards and scrubbed pine tables add rustic charm, and a real fire adds character. On the Saxon Shore Way footpath, it is popular with walkers and cyclists, and is a 20-minute walk from Teynham railway station. Food is served in the main pub and in an upstairs dining room. A small courtyard garden overlooks the creek. Q❀♣P (8,344)

Cowden

Fountain ✔
30 High Street, TN8 7JG (1 mile N of A264)
12-3, 6-midnight (11 Tue); 12-11 Sun ☎ (01342) 850528
fountaincowden.com
Harvey's IPA, Sussex Best Bitter; 1 changing beer (sourced locally; often Harvey's) 🄷
Friendly village pub attracting locals, families, walkers and those in search of well-maintained beer. The original bar has been expanded to incorporate a bright conservatory restaurant without losing any of the features or traditional atmosphere that is its hallmark. A roaring log fire in winter and a pleasant rear suntrap garden for summer use add to the ambience. Harvey's beers and substantial food prove an attractive combination that rewards those venturing into this bucolic corner of west Kent.
Q❀♣P (234)

Cowden Pound

Queen's Arms ★ 🄻
Hartfield Road, TN8 5NP (on B2026 halfway between Edenbridge and A264)
5-7.30 (10.30 Tue; 9 Fri); 12-3 Sun
Larkins Traditional Ale 🄷**; 1 changing beer (sourced locally; often Larkins)** 🄶
Owned and operated by a local family, this is one of only three Kent pubs recognised as having a nationally important historic interior, the public bar having remained unaltered since the Victorian era. Larkins Trad may be accompanied by one of its seasonal beers, enjoyed alongside friendly locals in the ambience of the pub's old-world charm. Open fires are in both bars. Customers may bring their own food to share at the bar. No lager is served.
Q❀♣P

Crockenhill

Chequers ✔
Cray Road, BR8 8LP
11-11; 12-9 Sun ☎ (01322) 662132
chequerscrockenhill.co.uk
Courage Best Bitter; 3 changing beers (sourced nationally; often Hook Norton, Otter, Ringwood) 🄷
Friendly village local with the three rotating guest ales coming from a wide range of breweries. Lunches and evening meals, with daily specials, are served with discounts for the over-55s Monday to Wednesday lunchtimes. There is plenty of room for those who just wish to drink and chat, or darts may be played in a side area. Quiz night is on Monday and various events feature on other nights including live music. The hub of village life.
❀♣P (477)

Dartford

Dartford Working Men's Club 🄻 ✔
Essex Road, DA1 2AU
11-11; 12-10.30 Sun ☎ (01322) 223646
dartfordwm.club
Courage Best Bitter 🄷**; 14 changing beers (sourced regionally; often Caveman, Leatherbritches, Oakham)** 🄷/🄶
Past winner of the CAMRA National Club of the Year and regular regional winner, this modern club has 15 ales on handpump and several ciders on gravity. The club is home to the award-winning Dartford Folk Club on Tuesday evenings and has live music every Saturday and Sunday night. A popular quiz takes place on the first Wednesday of each month and live tribute acts usually on the last Friday of the month. CAMRA members are welcome as guests.
❀♣

Foresters
15/16 Great Queen Street, DA1 1TJ
11-11; 11-10.30 Sun ☎ (01322) 223087
Adnams Ghost Ship; Harvey's Sussex Best Bitter; 1 changing beer (sourced nationally; often Skinner's) 🄷
Five minutes' walk from the town centre is this pleasant, traditional back-street local. Quiet at lunchtime, it is busy in the evenings with men's and women's darts, pool and crib teams. It has a wood-burning fire at one end of the U-shaped single bar. The graveyard opposite contains the unmarked pauper's grave of famed steam pioneer Richard Trevithick, its approximate location being indicated by a plaque on the north wall.
❀♣P

Malt Shovel
3 Darenth Road, DA1 1LP
3 (12 Thu)-11; 12-midnight Fri; 12-11 Sat; 12-10.30 Sun
☎ (01322) 224381 maltshovelda1.co.uk
St Austell Tribute; Young's Bitter, Special; 2 changing beers (sourced nationally) 🄷
Attractive country-style building dating from 1673, five minutes' walk from the town centre. There are two separate bars, a small taproom with a low

ceiling featuring an 1880s Dartford Brewery mirror, and a larger saloon bar leading to a conservatory where meals are served Thursday to Sunday lunchtimes and Friday and Saturday evenings. A large beer garden is accessed from the conservatory. Popular quiz nights take place on Mondays and crib on Tuesdays. There is a small car park adjacent to the pub. Q P

Deal

Just Reproach

14 King Street, CT14 6HX

12-3, 5-9 Mon; 12-2, 5-9 (11 Fri); 12-11 Sat; 12-4 Sun

4 changing beers Ⓖ

A town-centre micropub with a welcoming ambience; its high benches and table service make for a friendly, convivial atmosphere. At least one beer is from a Kent brewery. Ciders are typically from Kent Cider Company and further afield. Wines are from the local Barnsole vineyard and further afield; gins and quality soft drinks are also sold. Snacks include pork pies and local cheese. No keg, no fruit machines, no music, and do not let your mobile phone ring! Q

Ship Inn

141 Middle Street, CT14 6JZ

11-midnight; 12-midnight Sun ☎ (01304) 372222

Dark Star Hophead; Ramsgate Gadds' No.7 Bitter Ale, Gadds' No.5 Best Bitter Ale; Timothy Taylor Landlord; 1 changing beer (often Dark Star, Ramsgate) Ⓗ

Just 10 minutes' walk from the town centre, this unspoilt, traditional pub is located in Deal's historic conservation area. Dark wooden floors and subdued lighting give a warm and comfortable atmosphere, complemented by the nautical theme. A wide variety of drinkers enjoy the good range of beers dispensed from the five handpumps. The pub has a small cosy rear bar overlooking a large patio garden, accessed by a staircase, with a covered smoking area.

Dover

Breakwater Brewery Taproom

St Martin's Yard, Lorne Road, CT16 2AA

closed Mon-Wed; 5-10 Thu; 4-10.30 Fri; 12-10.30 Sat; 2-10 Sun ☎ (01304) 700043 breakwater.beer

Breakwater Dover Pale Ale, Hellfire Corner, Mogul West Country IPA; 5 changing beers (sourced locally; often Breakwater) Ⓖ

Opened in December 2016, the brewery tap is located on the site of the Harding's Wellington Brewery which closed in 1890. Modern, well lit and furnished with chunky wooden furniture, it has a bar counter resembling a stone breakwater. Cask ales from the brewery are served on gravity along with real ciders from Duddas Tun. No food is available, however customers are welcome to bring their own. Tours of the brewery are possible by prior arrangement.

Eight Bells

19 Cannon Street, CT16 1BZ

8am-midnight (1am Fri & Sat) ☎ (01304) 205030

Greene King Abbot; Ruddles Best Bitter; Sharp's Doom Bar; 8 changing beers Ⓗ

The name of this popular and bustling Wetherspoon pub, situated on the precinct, is linked to the church opposite. It has a large open-plan room with a long bar and a raised restaurant area. At the front an enclosed seating area looks out on to the precinct. At least two ales are from Kent microbreweries. There are real ale offers on Monday. Q

Lanes

15 Worthington Street, CT17 9AQ

12-11 (6 Mon); closed Sun ☎ (01304) 213474

5 changing beers (sourced locally) Ⓖ

Friendly award-winning micropub near the pedestrian precinct, comfortably furnished and carpeted. Ciders, wines, a mead and soft drinks are from Kent producers. Five real ales, mostly from Kentish microbreweries, and over 10 ciders, are served on gravity from the temperature-controlled cellar room. You will not find keg beer, lager or piped music. Snacks can be brought in from the local deli and a feasting board is available with 48 hours' notice. Dogs on a lead are allowed, but no children. Q

Louis Armstrong

58 Maison Dieu Road, CT16 1RA

3-11; 7-11 Sun ☎ (01304) 204759

Hopdaemon Skrimshander IPA; 3 changing beers (sourced locally; often Old Dairy, Ramsgate, Westerham) Ⓗ

Down-to-earth pub and music venue which has featured live music for over 50 years. The large L-shaped bar and stage is surrounded by music posters, a large mirror and long bench seating. Real cider is from Duddas Tun. On Wednesday evening, good-value food and real ales from £3 a pint are served. There is a monthly charity quiz night. It has a pleasant beer garden and is easily accessible by bus. A public car park is opposite.

Mash Tun

3 Bench Street, CT16 1JH

closed Mon; 12-10; 12-4 Sun ☎ (01304) 219590

4 changing beers

Comfortable micropub on the edge of Dover's shopping precinct. Soft armchairs, a sofa, tables and chairs give a homely feel. A 200-year-old church pulpit forms the bar. On offer are a varying list of ales, including a gluten-free, unrefined Pilsner-style ale from Westerham, and a good range of ciders from rare and smaller cider makers. There is no food, but customers are welcome to bring their own or order a takeaway. It can open Monday by arrangement.

Thirsty Scarecrow

107 High Street, CT16 1EB

closed Mon; 12-10; 1-9 Sun ☎ 07454 934833

2 changing beers Ⓐ

Cider micropub which was previously the Corner Café, rustic and brightly furnished on two levels, linked by a small set of stairs. The chilled cellar room is on the upper level from which 20-25 ciders and perries and two KeyKeg ales are served. There is also a small selection of bottled beers. The ciders/perries major on Kentish cidermakers but many come from far and wide. Regular charity quiz nights and themed food events take place.

Dunk's Green

Kentish Rifleman

Roughway Lane, TN11 9RU (jct with Dunks Green Rd, 4 miles N of Tonbridge, off A227)
11.30-3, 6-11; 11.30-11 Fri-Sun ☎ (01732) 810727
thekentishrifleman.co.uk
Harvey's Sussex Best Bitter; 3 changing beers (sourced locally; often Tonbridge, Westerham, Whitstable) H
In the Kent Downs Area of Outstanding Natural Beauty, this 16th-century pub is a welcoming stop or overnight stay, especially when walking the Greensand Way. An attractive destination all year round, it provides a warming open fire in the winter, a pretty beer garden for summer, and has an enviable reputation for home-cooked, locally sourced food. It has a traditional wooden-beamed bar at the front of the pub decorated with historic rifles. The centre of village life, it hosts pub quizzes and local groups including an art club.
Q P (222)

Eastry

Five Bells

The Cross, CT13 0HX
11-11.30 (1am Fri & Sat) summer; 11-11 (1am Fri & Sat) winter ☎ (01304) 611188 thefivebellseastry.com
Greene King IPA; Wantsum Black Prince; 1 changing beer H
Traditional community pub in the heart of the village with a comfortable lounge bar and dining room. Ales served include a mild from the Wantsum Brewery. The old fire station, with historic memorabilia, serves as a sports bar and function room. The busy calendar features live music, quiz nights and an Easter beer festival. Home-made food is served all day, including a good-value two-course lunchtime menu Monday-Friday. The suntrap patio has a children's play area and pétanque pitch. P (81)

Faversham

Bear Inn

3 Market Place, ME13 7AG
10.30-11; 11.30-11 Sun ☎ (01795) 532668
bearinnfaversham.co.uk
Shepherd Neame Master Brew; 1 changing beer (sourced locally; often Shepherd Neame) H
A 16th-century pub in Faversham's historic market square. The traditional and historic interior has three separate bar areas running the length of the building. The lunchtime menu is popular. A general knowledge quiz is held on the last Monday of the month. The beer range often features either a seasonal Shepherd Neame beer or guests from another brewery. It is frequented by visitors to Faversham and locals alike. A small number of tables out the front of the pub are popular in summer. Q

Corner Tap

37 Preston Street, ME13 8PE
2-10.30; 12-10.30 Fri-Sun ☎ 07718 649995
Whitstable Native Bitter, East India Pale Ale, Kentish Reserve; 3 changing beers (sourced nationally; often Blue Monkey, Oakham, Rudgate) G
The Corner Tap, following the micropub concept, was converted from a former glazing shop and opened in 2016. It offers a range of drink options as well as beer. There are two rooms with some solid and comfortable furniture, including a lounge area with a Chesterfield and armchairs in the room at the rear. It also has air conditioning.
Q

Elephant

31 The Mall, ME13 8JN
closed Mon; 3-11; 12-11 Sat; 12-7 Sun ☎ (01795) 590157
House beer (by Hopdaemon or Mad Cat); 5 changing beers (sourced regionally; often Dark Star, Mad Cat, Rother Valley) H
Popular and characterful traditional pub close to the railway station. The five changing beers often include styles such as mild or stout, and are mainly from microbreweries. Local real cider, often from Kent Cider Company or Dudda's Tun, is on handpump. The pub has a log fire, a large enclosed garden and a newly refurbished and extended function room. Regular music nights feature. Dogs and children welcome.

Furlongs Ale House

6A Preston Street, ME13 8NS
4-10; 3-11 Fri; 12-11 Sat; 12-9 Sun ☎ 07747 776200
5 changing beers (sourced locally; often Canterbury Ales, Kent, Ramsgate) H
Faversham's first micropub, opened in late 2014. The beers drawn by handpump from the cellar to a small bar are mainly from Kent microbreweries, although others from across the UK also feature. It has wooden bench seating and solid tables, together with a raised floor area against the wall to assist the older generation. Kent wines, ciders and a selection of gins are also served. Q

Shipwrights Arms

Hollowshore, ME13 7TU (over a mile N of Faversham at confluence of Faversham and Oare creeks) TR017636
closed Mon; 11-3, 6-10; 11-11 Sat; 12-10 Sun
☎ (01795) 590088 theshipwrightsathollowshore.co.uk
Goacher's Real Mild Ale, Special/House Ale; Kent Prohibition; 3 changing beers (sourced locally; often Harvey's) G
Remote 300-year-old family-run free house with a jolly, welcoming old-style landlord, a good pub to relax in after a 45-minute walk across the marshes from Faversham. The wooden-clad building's interior reflects its nautical heritage, with many ornaments and pictures on display or tucked into nooks and crannies. The large rear garden is open spring to autumn, and it has outside seating at the front for all seasons. Opening hours are extended in summer, while in severe winter weather check ahead before travelling. Food is served lunchtimes Wednesday to Sunday. Q P

Finglesham

Crown Inn

The Street, CT14 0NA
12-11; 12-10 Sun ☎ (01304) 612555
thecrowninnfinglesham.co.uk
Dark Star Hophead; 2 changing beers H
Traditional village pub with a warm welcome and friendly atmosphere. One ale is usually from a microbrewery. There is quality home-made food lunchtimes and evenings, including a roast on Sunday. Eat in the bar or the restaurant, which

opens on to the pleasant garden. Occasional live music events take place, and bat and trap is played in summer. It has a children's play area. Buses are 5-15 minutes' walk, depending on the day and time. The magnificent Kentish barn is available for functions and weddings. Summer closing times may be extended. P (81)

Folkestone

Chambers

Radnor Chambers, Cheriton Place, CT20 2BB (off Hythe end of Sandgate Rd)
12-11 (1am Fri & Sat); closed Sun (01303) 223333
pubfolkestone.co.uk
Adnams Lighthouse; 5 changing beers (sourced regionally) H
Spacious cellar bar with six handpumps beneath a licensed coffee shop; beers include some from local breweries and at least two real ciders. A beer festival is held over the Easter weekend. Food, including Mexican, European and daily specials, is served except on Mondays and Friday evenings. It has a disco on Fridays and a quiz on the first Sunday of the month. There is live music on Thursday, usually with free admission.

Firkin Alehouse

20 Cheriton Place, CT20 2AZ
12-9 (10 Fri & Sat); 12-4 Sun 07894 068432
firkinalehouse.co.uk
4 changing beers (sourced regionally) G
Folkestone's first micropub, which moved from premises next door in late 2017. Up to four cask beers – usually one from a Kent microbrewery – and six ciders are served on gravity from a temperature-controlled cellar room. There is no lager, alcopops or spirits, but there is a limited wine selection. Bar snacks include pickled eggs, pickled onions and other basic fare. No music or pub games feature, just good company and conversation, making the Firkin a place to enjoy a good drink and relax. Q

Troubadour of Kent

61 Tontine Street, CT20 1JR
closed Mon; 4-9 Tue-Thu; 12-10.30 Fri & Sat; 12-5 Sun
07930 542441
4 changing beers (sourced locally; often Ramsgate) G
This micro pub opened in 2017 and has a small raised stage area for poetry readings, story-telling and live acoustic music. Beers are served from a cooled stillage area. There is no bar, just table service in true micropub tradition. High-backed bench seating with high tables is provided on the left-hand side of the pub, with low tables and seating on the right-hand side. Cider and fine wines are also on offer.

Frittenden

Bell & Jorrocks

Biddenden Road, TN17 2EJ TQ815412
12 (3 Mon & Tue)-11; 12-10.30 Sun (01580) 852415
thebellandjorrocks.co.uk
Black Sheep Best Bitter; Harvey's Sussex Best Bitter; 2 changing beers (sourced nationally; often Dark Star, Rother Valley, Tonbridge) H
A coaching inn dating from the early 18th century, very much the centre of the local community. Originally called the Bell, it gained its current name when the pub opposite, the John Jorrocks, closed in 1969. Among the historical memorabilia is a propeller blade from a German Heinkel bomber that was shot down just outside the village in 1940. Excellent food is served, and the stables at the rear hold a beer festival every April. Local CAMRA Pub of the Year 2018.

Knoxbridge

Cranbrook Road, TN17 2BT TQ788406
closed Mon; 12-9 (10 Fri & Sat); 12-6 Sun
(01580) 895374 theknoxbridge.co.uk
2 changing beers (sourced regionally; often Brumaison, Harvey's, Musket) H
Formerly the Hopbine Inn, which had been closed for several years, this roadside inn has been turned around by the current licensee in the last two years. It is a relaxed family-friendly pub serving great food cooked by a French chef, complemented by up to three changing ales that come from local breweries, as well as the occasional distant one. A beer festival is held on the weekend of St George's day, with a large number of military vehicles in attendance. P (5)

Gillingham

Frog & Toad

38 Burnt Oak Terrace, ME7 1DR
2-11; 12-11 Fri & Sat; 12-8 Sun (01634) 852231
2 changing beers (sourced nationally; often Black Sheep, Cotleigh, Shepherd Neame) H
A previous three-time winner of the local CAMRA Pub of the Year, this back-street local is only 10 minutes' walk from the railway station. In keeping with the frog theme, there is a treat to be found on the over-bar glass rack for the musically minded. A large patio garden at the rear has wooden bench tables and an outside bar. The pub hosts several beer festivals throughout the year, normally over bank holidays. Q

Past & Present

2 Skinner Street, ME7 1HD
12-7 (9 Thu; 11 Fri & Sat); 12-4 Sun 07725 072293
pastandpresentmicropub.co.uk
3 changing beers (sourced regionally) G
Medway's first micro, and current local CAMRA Pub and Cider Pub of the Year for the second consecutive year. Three ales and up to eight ciders are dispensed by gravity from a temperature-controlled room. It has an interesting display of closed Gillingham pubs (past) and Kent micropubs (present). It stages an Easter cider festival and an August bank holiday real ale festival. A rear decked area is a suntrap in the warmer months. No admittance to the pub after 10pm on Friday and Saturday. Q

Will Adams

73 Saxton Street, ME7 5EG
12.30-4 (not Mon-Fri), 7-11; 12.30-3, 7.30-11 Sun
(01634) 575902
3 changing beers (sourced nationally; often Adnams, Oakham, St Austell) H
Now in its 25th year in the Guide, this back-street corner pub is a former local CAMRA Pub of the Year, and is named after a local navigator of 1564. Three ales are usually served, more on Gillingham FC home match days. It also has three real ciders and a perry, plus up to 30 single malts for whisky

connoisseurs. Various games are provided, and it has pool and darts teams (and a doubles-only board). Sports events and football matches are screened. Away fans are always welcomed.

Gravesend

Compass Alehouse

7 Manor Road, DA12 1AA

closed Mon; 12-2 (not Tue & Wed), 5-9; 12-2, 5-10 Fri; 12-10 Sat; 1-6 Sun ☎ 07873 918545

4 changing beers (sourced nationally; often Iron Pier)

Enterprising micropub opened in 2014 in a former estate agents. It has a small front room with high bench seats and a smaller room off a little courtyard to the rear. Four varying real ales are on sale, often local and now regularly including beers from the associated Iron Pier Brewery. At least three ciders are sold, often from Kent producers. Convivial atmosphere and conversation are paramount – talking on mobile phones incurs a fine for charity. Q

Jolly Drayman

1 Love Lane, Wellington Street, DA12 1JA

12-11.30; 12-midnight Fri-Sun ☎ (01474) 352355

jollydrayman.com

Dark Star Hophead; St Austell Proper Job; Skinner's Betty Stogs; 2 changing beers (sourced nationally)

A cosy pub just to the east of the town on the site of the former Walker's Wellington Brewery, with quirky low ceilings and a relaxed atmosphere – no gaming machines and a TV that is muted. Daddlums (Kentish skittles) is played most Sundays and men's and women's darts teams are hosted. Lunches are served 12-3pm, plus Sunday meals in the restaurant 12-5pm. Live music is featured on the first Saturday of the month and themed food nights on the last Saturday. Tuesday is quiz night. P

Three Daws

7 Town Pier, DA11 0BJ

11-11 (1am Fri & Sat); 12-11 Sun ☎ (01474) 566869

threedaws.co.uk

6 changing beers (sourced locally; often Canterbury Ales, Dartford Wobbler)

Historic inn with stories of ghosts, press gangs, smugglers, secret tunnels and more. The back room and terrace offer views of the Thames and passing river traffic. The interior is divided into small rooms with photos and pictures of local interest and very few right angles. The range of real ales always includes some from breweries in Kent. Meals, using local ingredients, are served until 9pm every day. Live music is staged on Fridays, quizzes on Sundays and a beer festival in August.

Three Pillars

25 Wrotham Road, DA11 0PA (on A227 opp civic centre)

closed Mon; 2-10 Tue-Thu; 12-10 Fri & Sat; 12-4 Sun

☎ 07794 348529 threepillarsgravesend.co.uk

5 changing beers

A small cellar bar underneath the masonic hall, reached by steep steps to the right of the hall. Two carpeted front rooms lead to the brick-floored bar area. The ceilings are low throughout. At least five real ales and at least 10 ciders are served from a temperature-controlled room. Music at low volume is provided by radio or records. The masonic hall car park must not be used by patrons. Q

Groombridge

Crown Inn

Groombridge Hill, TN3 9QH (on village green)

12-3, 5.30-11; 12-11 Sat; 12-9 Sun ☎ (01892) 864742

thecrowngroombridge.com

Harvey's Sussex Best Bitter; Larkins Traditional Ale; 1 changing beer (sourced locally; often Brumaison)

Set in a pretty row of tile-hung cottages overlooking the village green and church, this historic family-run pub dates back to 1585 and is a popular stop-off for villagers, walkers, families and rock climbers. Food from the popular restaurant can be enjoyed in the main bar area or snug, surrounded by the pub's many original features including an inglenook fireplace, or in summer outside, using the front or rear seating. B&B is available in five characterful wooden-beamed bedrooms. Q P (291)

Halstead

Rose & Crown

Otford Lane, TN14 7EA

12-11.30; 12-10.30 Sun ☎ (01959) 533120

Larkins Traditional Ale; house beer (by Tonbridge); 4 changing beers (sourced nationally; often Cotleigh, Rudgate, St Austell)

Built in 1860, this flint-faced free house is a draw for the real ale enthusiast, having served nearly 150 different beers over the past three years. The front bar hosts darts and has a TV showing various sports events. The side bar, with log fire, provides space for dining, with home-cooked food served 12-3pm weekdays and 12-5pm weekends. A separate restaurant/function room is available and a quiz night is held on the last Sunday of the month. P (431,R5)

Harvel

Amazon & Tiger

Harvel Street, DA13 0DE

closed Mon; 4-11; 12-midnight Fri & Sat; 12-9.30 Sun

☎ (01474) 814705

3 changing beers (sourced locally; often Kent, Skinner's, Westerham)

Close to the North Downs Way and Pilgrims Way, this pub is popular with walkers. It was built in 1914, opposite the site of the original inn and designed to blend in with the village houses. It has two distinct bar areas where modern furnishings combine with wooden floors, plus separate dining and TV areas. The village cricket team can be watched from the garden. The good range of ales is mainly from west Kent and east Sussex. Fresh fish night is Thursday. Newly furnished holiday lets are available. Q P

Hastingleigh

Bowl Inn

The Street, TN25 5HU TR095449

closed Mon; 5-9 (10 Thu & Fri); 12-10 Sat; 12-9 Sun

☎ (01233) 750354 thebowlonline.co.uk

3 changing beers (sourced locally) Ⓗ
This lovingly restored listed village pub retains many period features, including a taproom used for playing pool and decorated with vintage advertising material. The lovely garden has a tame European eagle owl. A beer festival is held on August bank holiday Monday. Excellent sandwiches and baguettes are available at weekends. The pub will stay open if custom warrants it or if you phone ahead. Local CAMRA Pub of the Year in 2017 and again in 2018. Q

Herne

Butchers Arms

29A Herne Street, CT6 7HL (opp church)
closed Mon; 12-1.30, 6-9; 1-3 Sun ☎ 07908 370685
micropub.co.uk
Adnams Broadside; Oakham JHB; Old Dairy Copper Top; 2 changing beers (sourced locally; often Adnams, Ramsgate) Ⓖ
Britain's first micropub, opened in 2005, is a real ale gem and the inspiration for other micropubs. Once a butcher's shop, it still has the original chopping tables. There is seating for 12 customers and standing room for 20 – the compact drinking area ensuring lively banter. The range of beers changes frequently. Customers can also buy beer to drink at home. The pub has won many CAMRA awards and the landlord was voted one of CAMRA's top 40 campaigners. Q

Herne Bay

Bouncing Barrel

20 Bank Street, CT6 5EA
closed Mon; 12-2, 6-9; 12-11 Sat; 12-2 Sun
☎ 07777 630685
4 changing beers (often Goody Ales, Old Dairy, Ramsgate) Ⓖ
Welcoming micropub with bench seating for 20 customers around old workshop tables. The beer range changes regularly and is mainly from microbreweries, generally at least one from a Kent brewery. Local snacks are available. The pub is named after the bombs used in the Dam Buster raids, which were tested off the coast nearby. The pub has a mural of a bomber flying past the Reculver Towers. A small beer festival is held over the May Day weekend. Q

Parkerville

219 High Street, CT6 5AD
12-9; 1-4 Sun ☎ 07939 106172
House beer (by Four Candles); 3 changing beers (sourced locally) Ⓖ
Lively micropub in a former music store. The spacious front seating area has a corner bar and a small stage with a piano in the front window. The back bar has a TV screen for big events only. Beers usually come from local microbreweries, and there is an excellent range of artisan gins, plus other wines and spirits. Live music plays once a month, and the pub celebrates its birthday every 24 July with music and food. Q

Hildenborough

Plough

Leigh Road, TN11 9AJ (½ mile S of Hildenborough at Powdermills)
closed Mon & Tue; 12-11; 12-9 Sun ☎ (01732) 832149
theploughatleigh.com
Tonbridge Coppernob; 2 changing beers (sourced locally; often Kent, Rockin' Robin, Westerham) Ⓗ
Tucked down a rural lane, this classic 16th-century inn is well worth a detour. Gradually extended over the centuries, the interior ticks all the boxes. Sturdy low beams are decked with hop bines, and a large polished wooden plank table and stunning doubled-sided open fire dominate the bar room. The secluded garden with a stream is busy on sunny days. The pub is also popular for food and functions in the adjacent great barn. The owners are strong supporters of local breweries.
QP(210)

Horton Kirby

Bull

Lombard Street, DA4 9DF
12-11; 12-10.30 Sun ☎ (01322) 860341
thebullhortonkirby.com
Dark Star Hophead; 4 changing beers (sourced regionally; often Dark Star, Kent, Oakham) Ⓗ
Friendly and comfortable one-bar village local with a large garden affording views across the Darent Valley, within walking distance of Farningham Road railway station and close to the daytime 414 bus route. Real cider is served in summer, and there is an open mic night on the first Friday of each month. The pub hosts regular beer festivals in the garden, normally over the Whitsun and August bank holidays. (414)

Hythe

Potting Shed

160A High Street, CT21 5JR
closed Mon; 12-6 (7 Wed & Thu; 9 Fri & Sat); 12-4 Sun
☎ 07780 877226
4 changing beers (sourced regionally) Ⓖ
A former café converted into a micro-alehouse at the Folkestone end of Hythe High Street serving an interesting range of ales from around the country by gravity, although one ale is sometimes pulled through a handpump. There is usually one local Kentish beer from Hop Fuzz, and a range of three ciders is usually served from boxes. Limited bar snacks are available. It makes a good place to enjoy a drink and interesting conversation after visiting the High Street.

Ickham

Duke William

The Street, CT3 1QP
11-11 (midnight Fri & Sat); 10-10.30 Sun
☎ (01227) 721308 thedukewilliamickham.com
3 changing beers (sourced locally) Ⓗ
This attractive pub in a quintessentially English village is welcoming towards locals, diners and drinkers. Guest ales are mostly from local microbreweries. The pub has been recently renovated and is a welcome addition to former

Chef of the Year and ex-Gordon Ramsay restaurant head chef Mark Sargeant's portfolio. Events include live music, a resident magician on the last Friday night of each month, and food and drink festivals in the summer. The roaring log fire is welcoming in winter. (11)

Ightham Common

Old House ★

Redwell Lane, Redwell, TN15 9EE (half mile SW of Ightham village, between A25 and A227) TQ590558

7-11 (9 Mon & Tue); 12-3, 7-11 Sat & Sun

(01732) 886077 oldhouse.pub

6 changing beers (sourced locally; often Dark Star, Hopdaemon, Larkins) G

Kentish red-brick, tile-hung cottage located in a narrow isolated country lane. The public bar features a Victorian wood-panelled counter, parquet flooring and an imposing inglenook fireplace. The parlour is a quiet haven. Beers are dispensed by gravity, often from wooden casks, always including at least one bitter, a golden ale and a dark beer. Several ciders from Kent are always on offer. Identified by CAMRA as having a nationally important historic pub interior. Local CAMRA Pub of the Year 2018. QP

Ivychurch

Bell Inn

Ashford Road, TN29 0AL (signed from A2070 between Brenzett and Hamstreet, 2 miles from A259/A2070 roundabout at Brenzett) TR028275

12-11; 12-10.30 Sun (01797) 344355

thebellinnromneymarsh.co.uk

St Austell Trelawny; Sharp's Doom Bar, Atlantic; 2 changing beers H

A pretty 16th-century free house adjacent to St George's Church where a warm welcome awaits all who visit. The real ales have won the pub many awards, including local CAMRA Pub of the Year in 2016. During the colder months a wood-burning stove adds to the comfortable atmosphere. Well worth finding, The Bell is steeped in marshland history as it was once a base for smugglers the Romney Marsh Owlers. P(11)

Kingsdown

King's Head

Upper Street, CT14 8BJ

5-11; 12-3, 6-11 Sat; 12-10.30 Sun (01304) 373915

kingsheadkingsdown.co.uk

Goacher's Special/House Ale; 2 changing beers (often Ramsgate) H

Traditional 18th-century village pub with three beamed rooms surrounding the central bar. There is a dining/family room, a rear courtyard, skittle alley and smoking area. Local historical photos adorn the walls. In winter there is a log fire in the public bar. Cider is sold in the summer. Home-made food is served in the evenings and Saturday and Sunday lunchtimes. Events include quiz nights and a guitar club. (82)

Laddingford

Chequers

The Street, ME18 6BP TQ689481

12-3, 5-11; 12-11 Sat & Sun (01622) 871266

chequersladdingford.co.uk

Adnams Southwold Bitter; 3 changing beers (sourced nationally) H

Attractive, oak-beamed pub, dating from the 15th century, with one double letting room. It is the heart of village life, with a variety of events held, including a beer festival at the end of April. A roaring log fire keeps customers warm in winter, and the pub frontage is a sea of flowers in summer. Good food is served and, on Thursdays, a wide selection of sausage dishes is available. The large garden has children's play equipment. Buses stop outside. QP(23,25)

Leigh

Fleur De Lis

High Street, TN11 8RL

11-3, 6-11; 11-midnight Fri & Sat; 12-8 Sun

(01732) 832283 fleurdelis-leigh.co.uk

Greene King IPA; house beer (by Greene King); 2 changing beers (sourced nationally; often Timothy Taylor, Tonbridge, Westerham) H

Village pub tastefully refurbished in 2015 with two separate rooms, one offering dining around an open fire while the other smaller bar includes a TV showing BT sports. The Fleur is open from 10am Monday to Saturday for morning coffee, croissants and pastries. Meal choices include sandwiches and classic home-cooked pub dishes. Themed dining nights are organised every second Monday of the month and monthly quiz nights are held. P(210)

Lower Halstow

Three Tuns

The Street, ME9 7DY

12-11 (midnight Fri & Sat); 12-10.30 Sun

(01795) 842840 thethreetunsrestaurant.co.uk

Goacher's Real Mild Ale; 3 changing beers (sourced locally; often Caveman, Hop Fuzz, Wantsum) H

A true family village pub with a friendly, cheerful atmosphere and lively conversation. The owners actively support real ale, offering mainly Kentish ales and several local ciders, including Dudda's Tun. It has a good reputation for high-quality locally sourced food and has won many awards. A beer festival is held during the summer bank holiday and there are monthly quizzes. A log fire, sofa seating, brick walls and beams add character. It has a large garden with streamside decking. P(327)

Luddesdown

Cock Inn

Henley Street, DA13 0XB (1 mile SE of Sole Street Station) TQ664672

4-11; 12-11 Fri & Sat; 12-10.30 Sun (01474) 814208

cockluddesdowne.com

Adnams Lighthouse, Southwold Bitter, Broadside; Goacher's Real Mild Ale; Harvey's Sussex Best Bitter; St Austell Trelawny H

Traditional rural free house dating from 1713, under the same ownership since 1984, with two distinct bars, a large conservatory, a separate function room and a comfortable heated smoking area. It is the meeting place for many local clubs and societies. Traditional pub games are played including pétanque and bar billiards. There is a free quiz on Tuesday evenings devised and hosted by the landlord. Children are not permitted. Snacks such as pies and pasties are available at all times. Q❀♣P🐾

Maidstone

Cellars Alehouse 🄻

The Old Brewery, Buckland Road, ME16 0DZ (if front gates closed then use the rear via alley alongside railway)

closed Mon; 4.30-9 (11 Thu); 12-11 Fri & Sat; 12-6 Sun
☎ (01622) 761045 thecellarsalehouse.co.uk

5 changing beers (sourced nationally; often Burning Sky, Dark Star, Ramsgate) 🄶

Head down a flight of steps into what was formerly the barley wine cellar of the old Style & Winch brewery and a surprisingly spacious interior is revealed, with traditional high wooden seats and tables. The barrel-vaulted ceiling with original cast iron supports is adorned with pumpclips and hops. Real ales are served by gravity from the capacious cool room. Several real ciders and craft keg beers are also stocked. Regular events include quizzes, folk music, comedy and Meet the Brewer.
Q⇌♣🍎🚌

Flower Pot 🄻

96 Sandling Road, ME14 2RJ

12-11; 11-11 Sat; 12-10.30 Sun ☎ (01622) 757705
flowerpotpub.com

Goacher's Gold Star Strong Ale; 8 changing beers (sourced nationally; often Dark Star, Oakham) 🄷

A split-level street-corner ale house, a must-visit when in Maidstone. The upper bar has nine handpumps with ales mainly from microbreweries. Up to four ciders and perries are served directly from the container and there is a small selection of KeyKeg beers; all beers and ciders are listed on video screens. Maidstone United football ground is nearby. There are music nights every other Saturday and jam nights on Tuesdays. Beer festivals are held throughout the year. Kent CAMRA Pub of the Year 2017.
❀◐⇌♣🍎🚌(101,155)🐾

Olde Thirsty Pig 🄻 ✔

4A Knightrider Street, ME15 6LP

12-1am (2am Fri; 3am Sat) ☎ (01622) 299283
thethirstypig.co.uk

4 changing beers (sourced locally; often Mad Cat, Musket, Rockin' Robin) 🄷

Built in the 15th century and maybe the third-oldest building in Maidstone, it was originally a farmhouse within the estate of the archbishop's palace. It is Grade II listed, on two storeys, with original beams, low ceilings and tucked-away rooms. Outside there is a heated and covered courtyard area. The bar has four handpumps dispensing ales mainly from Kent microbreweries. Draught local cider is also stocked, along with many bottled beers, including several from abroad.
❀♣🍎🚌🐾

Society Rooms ✔

Brenchley House, Week Street, ME14 1RF

7am-midnight (1am Fri & Sat) ☎ (01622) 350910

Greene King Abbot; Ruddles Best Bitter; Sharp's Doom Bar; 7 changing beers (sourced nationally; often Old Dairy, Rockin' Robin, Wantsum) 🄷

A spacious Wetherspoon pub on the site of a former local newspaper printing works. The mainly glass external walls allow panoramic views of the pedestrian shopping street alongside. The large covered outside space is split into smoking and non-smoking areas. The name is taken from William Shipley, founder of the Royal Society of Arts and the Maidstone Society for Promoting Useful Knowledge, who is buried nearby. Beer is served from 9am. Q❀◐♿⇌♣🚌(101,155)

Swan 🄻

2 County Road, ME14 1UY (from Maidstone East station, past right of County Hall up slight hill)

4-11; 12-11 Fri; 11-midnight Sat; 12-10.30 Sun
☎ (01622) 681744 swanmaidstone.co.uk

Shepherd Neame Master Brew, Whitstable Bay Pale Ale 🄷

Welcoming traditional locals' pub dating back to 1840, two minutes' walk from Maidstone East railway station, opposite Maidstone prison. To the right is a lower level stone-flagged drinking area with a warming logburner, and to the left a bar area with darts and a TV (including BT Sports) which leads to the garden. The pub has local darts and quiz teams, fun quiz nights and occasional live music and karaoke. ❀◐⇌♣🚌(101,155)🐾

Marden

Marden Village Club 🄻

Albion Road, TN12 9DT

6-11; 12-3, 5-11 Fri; 12-3, 6-11 Sat; 12-3, 6.30-10.30 Sun
☎ (01622) 831427 mardenvillageclub.co.uk

Shepherd Neame Master Brew; 4 changing beers (sourced regionally; often Goacher's, Kent, Ramsgate) 🄷

Five real ales are now offered at this Grade II-listed club, a community hub; four change regularly and are generally from Kent microbreweries. Many members are followers of football and rugby on TV and are also involved in the club's snooker and darts teams; others simply enjoy the friendly ambience. Regularly voted CAMRA branch Club of the Year. Card-carrying CAMRA members are welcome but regular visitors will be required to join. ♿⇌♣🍎🚌(25)🐾

Stile Bridge 🄻 ✔

Staplehurst Road, TN12 9BH (on A229 just before jct with B2079)

11-11.30; 12-10.30 Sun ☎ (01622) 831236
thestilebridge.co.uk

Goacher's Special/House Ale; 4 changing beers (sourced nationally; often Dark Star, Musket, Rockin' Robin) 🄷

Five real ales and pub and drinking memorabilia greet visitors to this roadside hostelry. The bar has a wood-panelled dining area to the right and seating with a log fire to the left. There is a large function room at the rear plus an enclosed garden/patio area. Local cider makers and microbreweries are supported as well as a good selection of continental and US beers and lagers. Live music and comedy are featured several times each year.
❀◐🍎P🚌(5)🐾

Margate

Fez

40 High Street, CT9 1DS
12-10.30; 12-10 Sun
4 changing beers G

This eclectically furnished micropub which opened in 2015 has a mixture of high and low tables along with some raised bench seating. Brewery and fairground memorabilia adorn the walls while musical instruments are fixed on the ceiling. The small bar counter at the rear has a temperature-controlled cellar room from which cask ales and ciders are served on gravity dispense. A limited wine range along with a selection of soft drinks is also offered. (56)

London Tavern

Addington Street, CT9 1PN
closed Mon; 5-10; 4-11 Fri; 1-11 Sat; 12-9 Sun
07598 647753
3 changing beers H

An 18th-century hostelry with two single-storey extensions, formerly known as the Shakespeare Tavern then, from 1858 until the early 1990s, as the London Tavern, after which it was the Everybody's Inn. Situated across the road from the Theatre Royal, many famous thespians have agonised over their lines at this bar. It was taken over in July 2015 by new owners who reverted to the former name and gave the premises a complete and welcoming refit. Local CAMRA Pub of the Year 2017.

Two Halves

2 Marine Drive, CT9 1DH
3.15-10.30; 12-10.30 Fri; 12.30-10.30 Sat & Sun
07538 771904
3 changing beers G

Small, friendly, welcoming micropub with an incredible location on Margate's seafront. Beers are supplied from all regions of the country and regularly changed by a landlord who knows his ale. Whatever the weather this micropub has great aspects, either for sunsets out of the window or just for watching the world go by. The beer and cider are kept in immaculate condition in a large stillage room. Look out for the old-fashioned postcards in the loo! Local CAMRA Pub of the Year 2018. Q (56)

Milton Regis

Three Hats

93 High Street, ME10 2AR
12-11; 12-10.30 Sun (01795) 427645
3 changing beers (sourced nationally; often Dartmoor, Purity, St Austell) H

Friendly community local in historic Milton Regis. The open-plan interior has low beams and a large back lounge bar area. The spacious, attractive beer garden is popular in summer. The pub was instrumental in organising the annual Milton Regis Saffron Fair – this used to be a noted saffron-producing area. (347)

Minster-in-Thanet

Hair of the Dog

73 High Street, CT12 4AB
12-10 (11 Fri & Sat); 12-3 Sun 07885 362326
3 changing beers G

This micropub, previously a dog groomer's, provides a warm welcome on the village high street, usually offering three real ales and at least three ciders, all served from the cask in a cool room directly off the bar. The furniture is rustic, with a mix of high and low seating and tables, where one can play a mix of old games such as shove-ha'penny or try and crack some of the puzzles left out. Dogs are still welcome.
Q (11,42)

New Romney

Smugglers' Alehouse

10 St Lawrence Court, High Street, TN28 8BU
12-9 (9.30 Fri & Sat); 12-8 Sun 07581 230397
smugglersalehouse.co.uk
3 changing beers (sourced regionally) H

A welcoming micropub which opened in 2016 at the west end of the High Street. It was awarded runner-up local CAMRA Pub of the Year in 2017. You can relax, read the newspapers or join in with the conversations between customers and friendly staff. In addition to the changing real ales and ciders on offer, there is a selection of wines, spirits, tea, coffee and snacks (including pickled eggs). Well-behaved dogs on leads are welcome.
Q

Newenden

White Hart

Rye Road, TN18 5PN TQ834273
11-11; 12-11 Sun (01797) 252166
thewhitehartnewenden.co.uk
Harvey's Sussex Best Bitter; Rother Valley Level Best; 2 changing beers H

This historic 16th-century weatherboarded building includes old oak-beamed bars and an inglenook fireplace. The pub provides good-quality home-cooked food and has six en-suite rooms. Conveniently situated for the Kent and East Sussex Railway and several National Trust properties, it is also an ideal location for exploring the Rother Valley. A pub quiz is held on the first Monday of the month. P (2)

Petteridge

Hopbine

Petteridge Lane, TN12 7NE (1 mile E of Matfield)
12-2.30, 5-11; 12-11 Fri & Sat; 12-10.30 Sun
(01892) 722561
Long Man Best Bitter; Tonbridge Traditional Ale; 2 changing beers (sourced regionally; often Dark Star, Long Man) H

Picturesque tiled and weatherboarded gem with affable staff and a local clientele, perched on the junction of Petteridge and Tibbs Court lanes. Customers may be welcomed by a log fire and the aroma of fresh home-made pizza (not served Mon and Sun eves), baked in a wood-fired oven, before reaching the bar where Kent and Sussex beers are accompanied by a local cider such as Chiddingstone or Turners. It is a regular stopping place for ramblers taking advantage of the landscaped garden and patio. Q P (297,296)

Pluckley

Rose & Crown ✔

Mundy Bois Road, Mundy Bois, TN27 0ST (off the beaten track between Pluckley, Egerton and Smarden) TQ908455

12-11; 12-10.30 Sun ☎ (01233) 840048

theroseandcrownpluckley.co.uk

Harvey's Sussex Best Bitter; Whitstable Native Bitter; 1 changing beer (sourced nationally) H

Tile-hung 17th-century pub combining the warmth of a traditional Kentish country free house with a first-class restaurant, lying in farmland in the heart of the Weald of Kent. Many good walks are to be enjoyed nearby. The Village Bar is hop-entwined and has a welcoming fire; the Saloon also features an open fire. The 1989 Guinness Book of World Records named Pluckley the most haunted village in England, with 12 ghosts. P

Queenborough

Admiral's Arm ✔

West Street, ME11 5AD (in Trafalgar Court, 30yds left from crossroads of High St and Park Rd)

4.30-9; 12-11 Fri & Sat; 12-9 Sun ☎ (01795) 668598

admiralsarm.co.uk

4 changing beers (sourced locally; often Oakham, Pig & Porter, Ramsgate) H/G

Located in the historic heart of Queenborough, with a nautical theme, including local shipping maps which add much character, and frequented by locals and visitors alike. It has a good range of beers, ciders and gins, hosts regular quiz nights and cheese Sundays, and now also offers home-made pizzas Thursday, Friday and Saturday evenings and Saturday lunchtime. The warm and welcoming owners will happily serve beer direct from the cask or via handpump. Mobile phone calls must be taken outside. Local CAMRA Pub of the Year 2018. Q (334)

Rainham

Prince of Ales

121 High Street, ME8 8AN

closed Mon; 5.30-9.30; 12-10 Fri & Sat; 12-3 Sun

☎ 07982 756412 princeofales.co.uk

4 changing beers (sourced nationally; often Canterbury Ales, Kent, Ramsgate) G

On the outskirts of the town centre, this micropub is an ideal haven for those wishing to find both good quality beer and conversation. The wooden-benched bar area is divided into an open space to encourage discussion plus a number of booths if a degree of privacy is required. Cushions are available for your comfort in return for a charity donation. The beer garden can be a suntrap during warmer months. Q (132)

Ramsgate

Conqueror Alehouse

4C Grange Road, CT11 9LR (on corner of St Mildred's Rd)

closed Mon; 11.30-2.30, 5.30-9.30; 12-3 Sun

☎ 07890 203282 conqueror-alehouse.co.uk

3 changing beers G

A multi award-winning micropub, Thanet's first, a cosy place for gravity-dispensed ales, ciders and bottled beers. A former CAMRA national Pub of the Year finalist, since opening in 2010 it has always featured in this Guide. Although it underwent a major refurbishment in 2017, you can still find images of the paddle steamer the pub is named after, as well as memorabilia of local brewing history. Q

Montefiore Arms

1 Trinity Place, CT11 7HJ

12-2.30, 5.30-11; 12-11 Sat; 12-3, 7-10.30 Sun

☎ (01843) 593265 montefiorearms.co.uk

Ramsgate Gadds' No.7 Bitter Ale; 4 changing beers H

An award-winning traditional back-street local enjoying a good reputation with real ale drinkers in the Thanet area. The pub's name and sign are unique, honouring the great Jewish financier and philanthropist Sir Moses Montefiore, who lived locally for many years. Now under the personal control of Eddie Gadd of nearby Ramsgate Brewery, the pub showcases its beers along with changing guest ales and Biddenden cider.

NauticAles

347 Margate Road, CT12 6SG

4.30-10.30; 12-11 Sat; 12-9 Sun ☎ 07552 600919

House beer (by NauticAles); 3 changing beers G

This micropub opened in former office premises in the Northwood district in 2016 after several planning delays. It has a small L-shaped bar counter serving real ales and ciders on gravity dispense from stillage in a cooled cabinet on the back wall. Seating is mainly around low tables. It offers up to four ales including at least one NauticAles beer.

Rochester

Britannia Bar Café

376 High Street, ME1 1DJ (midway between Chatham town centre and Rochester Star Hill)

10-11 (9 Mon; midnight Fri & Sat); 12-10 Sun

☎ (01634) 815204

Goacher's Fine Light Ale; 2 changing beers (sourced nationally; often Caledonian) H

Stepping into this outlet is like walking into a haven of peace and calm. It is a one-bar pub with a small side room and a terraced garden at the rear evoking an atmosphere of tranquillity. Meals are catered for with both breakfast and lunch Monday to Saturday, plus Sunday lunch (prior booking advisable). Q (145)

Coopers Arms

10 St Margarets Street, ME1 1TL

12-11 (midnight Fri & Sat) ☎ (01634) 404298

thecoopersarms.co.uk

Courage Best Bitter; Young's Special; 4 changing beers (sourced regionally; often Canterbury Ales, Tonbridge, Westerham) H

A few minutes' stroll through historic Rochester behind the cathedral, this charming old inn dates from 1199 and is one of the oldest in Kent. The front bar is of interest, with an impressive beamed ceiling and fireplace. A passageway leads to a more modern rear bar and out to a garden which is busy in summer. Quiz night is Tuesday and live music plays on Sunday evening. Food is available, with both lunch and evening menus.

P

Flippin' Frog

318 High Street, ME1 1BT

closed Mon; 4-10 Tue; 3-11 Wed & Thu; 12-11 Fri & Sat; 12.30-9 Sun ☎ 07889 214000

5 changing beers (sourced locally; often Goody Ales, Kent, Old Dairy) G

A micropub with constantly changing ales, ciders and wines. Good food is served, prepared in an open kitchen so you can see it being cooked and smell the flavours of what you have ordered, but the selling of good quality ale is the priority. Art produced by local artists is on sale and adorns the walls. The pub has a pleasant atmosphere and a welcoming feel. Q

Man of Kent Ale House

6-8 John Street, ME1 1YN (200yds off A2 from bottom of Star Hill)

2 (3 Mon)-11; 2-midnight Fri; 12.30-midnight Sat; 12.30-11 Sun ☎ 07772 214315

Goacher's Gold Star Strong Ale; 9 changing beers (sourced locally; often Bexley, Ramsgate, Tonbridge) H

The outside of the pub depicts the name of an old Kent brewery, Style & Winch, whose beers have long been unavailable. However, the ale house carries on the tradition of selling beers from Kent together with local cider and foreign ales. There is live music during the week, and it is a great place for meeting with friends for nights out or for lazy afternoons.

Who'd Ha' Thought It

9 Baker Street, ME1 3DN

12-midnight ☎ (01634) 830144 whodha.co.uk

3 changing beers (sourced nationally; often Hardys & Hansons, Titanic) H

On a side street off Maidstone Road, this welcoming pub has a spacious wood-panelled main bar, with TVs showing sporting events and a log fire lit in winter. A small snug bar to the rear leads to a well-maintained garden. A selection of three changing ales is served. It holds a pub quiz once a month and murder mystery evenings. Occasional live music is staged. Bar snacks are available. (155)

Rusthall

Toad Rock Retreat

1 Upper Street, TN4 8NX

closed Mon; 12-3.30 (not Tue), 5.30-11; 12-10.30 Sun ☎ (01892) 520818 toadrockretreattunbridgewells.co.uk

Harvey's Sussex Best Bitter; 2 changing beers (sourced regionally; often Fuller's, High Weald, Tonbridge) H

Visitors drawn to the famous sandstone Toad Rock formation will be delighted to relax afterwards in this adjacent Retreat, where a good variety of substantial home-cooked food is served lunchtimes and evenings Wednesday to Sunday lunchtime. Choose between the dining area, the comfortable bar (separated by a double-sided open log fire from the plush snug complete with leather sofas), or the terrace and raised side garden. Monthly live music is performed on the last Tuesday night. P(281)

Ryarsh

Duke of Wellington

The Street, ME19 5LS

11-11; 12-10.30 Sun ☎ (01732) 842318

dukeofwellingtonryarsh.com

Harvey's Sussex Best Bitter; Kent Pale; 2 changing beers (sourced nationally; often Musket, St Austell) H

A 16th-century pub in the village centre, welcoming to ramblers. The main bar is to the left while the restaurant to the right features a varied menu. Fireplaces in both bars provide winter warmth. A covered and heated patio with tables opens on to the garden and overlooks the pétanque piste. In front, an area with tables provides additional space. A popular jazz music evening is held monthly on a Thursday. Quiz night is every other Sunday. QP(58)

St Peter's

Four Candles Alehouse

1 Sowell Street, CT10 2AT

5-11.30; 12-11.30 Sat & Sun ☎ 07947 062063

thefourcandles.co.uk

3 changing beers G

This former shop is firmly established on the local micropub scene and renowned for its friendly atmosphere. Seating is provided at high bench tables, while the beer is served from a cooled cabinet in an adjacent room. The pub has its own microbrewery in the cellar which supplies one-off beers to complement the offerings from other brewers. In the warmer weather benches outside provide for a superb suntrap. Q(56)

Yard of Ale

61 Church Street, CT10 2TU

5-11; 12-11 Sat & Sun ☎ 07790 730205

3 changing beers G

Attractive rustic stable converted into a unique micropub in a village location, adorned with hops and old riding equipment; the seating varies from high stools to straw bales, and there is a wood-burning stove for the colder months. It is family and dog friendly and has strong links to the community. The yard is a suntrap with plenty of seating, and a canopy and heaters for inclement weather. A wide-ranging selection of ales and cider is available. CAMRA National Pub of the Year finalist in 2016. Q

Sandgate

Inn Doors

96 Sandgate High Street, CT20 3BY

5-10 (11 Fri); 12.30-11 Sat; 12.30-5 Sun ☎ 07958 474473

inndoorsmicropub.co.uk

House beer (by Four Candles); 3 changing beers (sourced regionally) G

Micropub at the west end of Sandgate based on a 1930s living room, with a small bar and two-level seating. Beers are served from a cold room visible through a window. The landlord brews his own beers at the Four Candles Brewery in Broadstairs. Tasty snacks are available, and a large variety of gins. The pub hosts Bring Your Own Vinyl nights played on a vintage record player and holds monthly charity quiz evenings.
Q(16,102)

Ship Inn

65 Sandgate High Street, CT20 3AH (on A259)
11.30-11.30 (12.30am Fri & Sat) (01303) 248525
Dark Star Hophead; Greene King IPA, Abbot; Hop Back Summer Lightning; 2 changing beers (sourced regionally)
This narrow corner pub incorporating the Amazing Brewery fronts on to the High Street and backs on to the beach. Partly dating from 1798, it has a front bar and a back room plus a function room and a restaurant with sea views; upstairs there is a top deck for drinkers. Nautical maps and pictures reflect the landlord's naval and military interests. Biddenden cider is always available and an August bank holiday beer festival is held.
(16,102)

Sandwich

Crispin Inn

4 High Street, CT13 9EA
11-11 (midnight Fri & Sat); 12-10.30 Sun
(01304) 621967 sandwichpubs.co.uk
House beer (by Mad Cat); 3 changing beers (often Adnams)
Ancient public house by the medieval barbican and toll bridge. Low ceilings, wooden beams and brick walls provide a congenial ambience. Relax by the window and watch the world go by, or sit in the back courtyard overlooking the river. There's also a cosy snug if you want to get away from the crowds. Real cider is from Westons or Thatchers. A good range of home-made food and snacks usually features Caribbean specialities, for example goat curry. Regular live music events are held.

Sevenoaks

Anchor

32 London Road, TN13 1AS
11-3, 6-11; 10.30-midnight Fri; 12-4, 7-10.30 Sun
(01732) 454898 anchorsevenoaks.co.uk
Harvey's Sussex Best Bitter; Woodforde's Wherry; 1 changing beer (sourced locally; often Tonbridge, Westerham)
Friendly town-centre local, popular with all ages, run by jolly long-serving landlord Barry. Good-value home-cooked food is served lunchtimes throughout the week, with bar snacks in the evening. The guest ale is from a microbrewery and changes weekly. Regular live evening entertainment ranging from blues music to open mic nights and morris dancing is enthusiastically promoted.

Sevenoaks Weald

Windmill

1 Windmill Road, TN14 6PN
5-9 Mon; 12-11; 12-9 Sun (01732) 463330
Larkins Traditional Ale; 5 changing beers (sourced nationally; often Binghams, Dark Star, Rudgate)
By the village green, this former CAMRA national award finalist continues to be renowned for the quality of beer, cider, food and friendly service. Six Kentish ciders complement the ales, thoughtfully selected to provide a choice of strengths and styles, which can be sampled in three one-third-pint tasting glasses. Live music and themed dining nights take place weekly and an interesting array of dishes is served (no food Sun and Mon eves). A pleasant, flower-adorned patio garden is to the rear. Q (401,435)

Sittingbourne

Golden Hope

The Court House, 1 Park Road, ME10 1DR
8am-midnight (1am Fri & Sat) (01795) 476791
Greene King Abbot; Ruddles Best Bitter; Sharp's Doom Bar; 5 changing beers (sourced nationally; often Batemans, Shepherd Neame, Wantsum)
A Wetherspoon pub converted from the old magistrates' court and police station, which opened in 2015. Some original features remain, including the old cells now adapted into small dining areas. The name derives from a Thames sailing barge built on the nearby creek. There is one main bar area with several smaller seating areas, plus front and rear patios with smoking allowed on the rear one. Wheelchair access is via Park Road. Q

Paper Mill

2 Charlotte Street, ME10 2JN (N of Sittingbourne station, almost in Milton Regis at corner of Church St and Charlotte St)
12-2 (not Mon-Thu), 5-9; 12-9 Sat; 12-6 Sun
07927 073584 thepapermillmicropub.co.uk
3 changing beers (sourced regionally; often Dark Revolution, Goacher's, Salopian)
A popular one-room micropub close to Sittingbourne town centre and railway station with bench seating around four large wood tables. Local beers feature alongside national beers such as Blue Monkey and RedWillow and there is a range of Dudda's Tun ciders available. Occasional events such as Meet the Brewer and pub quizzes take place. Opening hours are flexible with advance notice. Local CAMRA Pub of the Year 2015-2017.
Q (334,347)

Red Lion

58 High Street, ME10 4PB
12-11 (1am Fri & Sat) (01795) 472706
3 changing beers (sourced nationally; often Fuller's, St Austell, Sharp's)
A large and welcoming coaching inn in Sittingbourne High Street which is steeped in history; it is believed that both Henry V and Henry VIII stayed here. A real fire separates the restaurant area from the bar, where dogs are welcome. It now serves excellent-quality food at lunchtime and dinner. Up to four beers are sold from the Ei Group range.

Snargate

Red Lion ★

TN29 9UQ (on B2080, 1 mile NW of Brenzett) TQ990285
closed Mon; 12-3, 7-10 (11 Fri & Sat); 12-4, 7-10.30 Sun
(01797) 344648
4 changing beers (often Goacher's)
This multi-room 16th-century smugglers' pub has been in the same family for over 100 years. The superb, unspoiled hostelry passed to the next generation in 2016 but is still universally known as Doris's, and is decorated with posters from the 1940s and the Women's Land Army. Four or five guest beers, at least one from Goacher's, are

served. A beer festival is held in June near the summer solstice and a mini festival in October. Identified by CAMRA as having a nationally important historic pub interior.
Q❀♣●P🚍(11B)🐾

South Darenth

Queen 🄻

58-62 New Road, DA4 9AR
⏲ 2-11; 12-11.30 Sat; 12-10.30 Sun ☎ (01322) 862430
Fuller's London Pride; Greene King Abbot; Kent Session Pale, Brewers Reserve 🄷
Community back-street terraced local within walking distance of the railway station. It was extended in 1998 to incorporate a former shop, and has two separate bars, one with a sports theme and adorned with memorabilia of London football teams, the other a traditional quieter saloon bar. It is a genuine free house, promoting beers from Kent Brewery. The pub has a garden/patio area and free bar food is available Sunday lunchtimes. Children are welcome until 8.30pm.
❀(Farningham Rd)♣●🚍(414)🐾

Stalisfield Green

Plough Inn 🄻

Stalisfield Road, ME13 0HY
⏲ closed Mon; 12-3, 6-11; 12-3, 5-11 Fri; 12-11 Sat; 12-6 Sun ☎ (01795) 890256 🌐 theploughinnstalisfield.co.uk
House beer (by Musket); 3 changing beers (sourced locally; often Musket, Old Dairy, Whitstable) 🄷
Grade II-listed family-run country pub serving local beers, wines and cider, high on the North Downs, two miles from Charing and close to the A20, with wonderful views over farmland. It does a seasonal and constantly changing food menu, with local ingredients whenever possible. Biddenden Bushels cider is served on handpump. The pub is frequented by walkers and cyclists. A family-friendly garden is popular in summer and the real fires add character. Q❀♿▲●P🚍(660)🐾

Stansted

Black Horse 🄻

Tumblefield Road, TN15 7PR (1 mile N of A20) TQ606620
⏲ 12-11 (10.30 Mon); 12-10.30 Sun ☎ (01732) 822355
🌐 theblackhorsestansted.co.uk
Larkins Traditional Ale; Young's Bitter; 2 changing beers (sourced locally; often Bexley, Tonbridge) 🄷
In the heart of the North Downs, not far from the M20, this large recently refurbished village free house is surrounded by rolling hills and woodlands, attracting ramblers and cyclists as well as locals. Traditional English meals, often using local produce, are served Tuesday to Sunday. Four real ales are normally on offer, with guests usually from local breweries. An extensive range of wines and bottled beers is also available. ❀♣P🐾

Staplehurst

Lord Raglan 🄻

Chart Hill Road, TN12 0DE (½ mile N of A229 at Cross-at-Hand) TQ786472
⏲ 12-3, 6.30-11; closed Sun ☎ (01622) 843747
Goacher's Fine Light Ale; Harvey's Sussex Best Bitter; 1 changing beer (sourced locally; often Musket, Tonbridge, Westerham) 🄷
A longstanding entry, this popular and unspoilt free house retains the atmosphere of a country pub from bygone days. The bar is hung with hops and warmed by two log fires and a stove. The large orchard garden catches the evening sun. Excellent snacks and full meals are always available. The guest beers change regularly, and Westons Perry and local Double Vision cider are also on the bar. A short walk from the Cross-at-Hand (No.5) bus stop on the A229. Q❀●P🐾

Strood

10:50 From Victoria 🄻

Rear of 37 North Street, ME2 4JJ (in railway arches at rear of Asda car park)
⏲ 4-9; 12-10 Fri & Sat; closed Sun ☎ 07941 449137
🌐 1050fromvictoria.co.uk
Dartford Wobbler; Old Dairy Blue Top; house beer (by Grainstore) 🄶**; 5 changing beers (sourced nationally)** 🄷/🄶
Justly popular micropub opened in 2015. The name relates to the Network Rail arch number, not a train time. Full of railway memorabilia and bric-a-brac, it has internal bench seating plus a large decked area outside which is pleasant on warm summer days. A logburner inside keeps everyone warm and cosy in the winter. There is always a choice of five real ales and five real ciders. No children allowed.
Q❀♿♣●P🚍(191)🐾

Swanscombe

George & Dragon 🄻

1 London Road, DA10 0LQ
⏲ 12 (4 Mon & Tue)-11; 12-10.30 Sun ☎ (01322) 386440
🌐 georgedragonswanscombe.co.uk
6 changing beers (sourced nationally; often Iron Pier) 🄷
This privately owned former Victorian coaching inn is a popular destination for good real ale and food. A horseshoe-shaped bar supports six handpumps with changing beers and six different ciders, plus selected whiskies and bottled beers from UK and international brewers. The restaurant is open Friday and Saturday lunchtimes and evenings, and Sunday lunchtimes for a traditional roast. Former local CAMRA Pub of the Year and Cider Pub of the Year 2017. Q❀♣●🚍🐾

Temple Ewell

Fox 🄻

14 High Street, CT16 3DU
⏲ 11.30-3.30, 6-11.30; 12-4, 7-11 Sun ☎ (01304) 823598
Exmoor Fox; Kelham Island Pride of Sheffield; 2 changing beers 🄷
Traditional village pub with a warm welcome for locals and visitors. Enjoy a good range of styles and strengths of real ales in the main bar or in one of the smaller rooms. A variety of events, quiz nights, curry nights and occasional music evenings keeps the pub busy. In June a charity beer festival is organised by the local Rotary Club. It has an attractive streamside garden with a skittle alley, and is close to Kearnsey Abbey gardens and public transport. ❀♣P🚍(15,68)🐾

Tenterden

Woolpack Hotel

26 High Street, TN30 6AP (on A28 in centre of town)
11-11 (1.30am Fri & Sat) (01580) 388501
thewoolly.com
Harvey's Sussex Best Bitter; Timothy Taylor Golden Best; 1 changing beer (sourced locally; often Old Dairy, Sharp's)
An early 15th-century coaching inn, originally the mayor's parlour. The magistrates' court once met here in this red-tiled building, while smugglers were sitting in the back room doing their trading. The pub name refers to the business that brought so much prosperity to this part of Kent. Excellent bar and restaurant food is available from the landlord's local farm, and it is a good place to stay for a short break in Tenterden. It hosts quiz evenings on alternate Mondays. It is close to the terminus of the heritage Kent & East Sussex Railway.

Tonbridge

Foresters Arms

51 Quarry Hill Road, TN9 2RT
3-11 Mon & Tue; 12-10 (1am Fri & Sat); 12-9 Sun
(01732) 361927 forestersarmstonbridge.co.uk
Shepherd Neame Whitstable Bay Pale Ale, Spitfire; 1 changing beer (sourced nationally; often Black Sheep, Shepherd Neame)
Recently revitalised, the Foresters has a bright and cheerful character. Wooden tables and seating by picture windows are enhanced by the addition of candles and cushions, while walls are decorated with photos of bygone Tonbridge, music posters, maps and striking images from around the world. One side is mainly devoted to sports and games with a TV, table football, pool and bar billiards. There is a front patio and a larger decked area to the rear. A selection of pizzas is served all day.

Humphrey Bean

94 High Street, TN9 1AP (near castle and river)
9am-midnight (1am Fri & Sat) (01732) 773850
Greene King Abbot; Ruddles Best Bitter; Sharp's Doom Bar; 6 changing beers (sourced regionally; often High Weald, Old Dairy, Tonbridge)
Ever-popular Wetherspoon house close to Tonbridge castle and the river Medway, with ample space and an extensive flower-adorned garden. The interesting range of six guest beers from local breweries illustrates the commitment to local real ales, enhanced by occasional organised brewery visits and events showcasing a brewery's beers. Ask for the current choice of ciders supplementing Westons Old Rosie, kept behind the bar. Food is served 7am (8am Sun)-11pm.

Tunbridge Wells

Fuggles Beer Café

28 Grosvenor Road, TN1 2AP (opp Tesco bus stop)
11.30-11; 12-10.30 Sun (01892) 457739
fugglesbeercafe.co.uk
Tonbridge Coppernob; 3 changing beers (sourced nationally; often Downlands Brewery, Gun, Wild Beer)
Award-winning café/pub with an excellent selection of well-kept cask ales alongside an extensive range of wines, gin, whisky and other spirits, plus real cider such as Turners or Dudda's Tun. Drink in or take away from a vast range of offerings from local, continental and national breweries. The contemporary setting varies in nature from relaxed to vibrant, according to the time of day. Charcuterie, toasted sandwiches and cheeses complement the beer, served by knowledgeable staff. Children are welcome until 7pm.

George

29 Mount Ephraim, TN4 8AA
12-11 (midnight Thu; 1am Fri & Sat) (01892) 539492
thegeorgepubtunbridgewells.co.uk
Long Man Best Bitter, American Pale Ale; 7 changing beers (sourced regionally; often Dark Star, Gun, Old Dairy)
This old Georgian coaching inn, a 10-minute walk up from the station, has now been developed inside to provide plenty of space and different seating areas. It is home to Fonthill, a microbrewery in operation since 2017; currently it only sells its beer in-house. Two ciders including Seacider are always available alongside the changing range of beers. Light bites are served every day beyond lunchtimes. There is a large secret courtyard garden at the back and additional seating at the front for warmer days.

Grove Tavern

19 Berkeley Road, TN1 1YR
11-midnight (01892) 526549 grovetavern.co.uk
Harvey's Sussex Best Bitter; Timothy Taylor Landlord; 2 changing beers (sourced nationally; often Dark Star, Wantsum)
Laying claim to be the oldest in Tunbridge Wells, this narrow, single-bar pub with a dartboard and pool table at either end dispenses well-kept beers that reward thirsty customers prepared to make the short climb up from the High Street. Friendly conversation and amiable dogs are a constant reminder that this is a neighbourhood tavern where the emphasis is on social interaction. A proper, traditional pub making its 16th consecutive appearance in this Guide.

Mount Edgcumbe

The Common, TN4 8BX
11-11 (11.30 Thu-Sat); 12-10.30 Sun (01892) 618854
themountedgcumbe.com
Harvey's Sussex Best Bitter; 3 changing beers (sourced regionally; often Dark Star, Old Dairy, Pig & Porter)
Within walking distance of the town centre and railway station, this pub, restaurant and hotel occupies a large Georgian house on the common surrounded by woods. Walkers and dogs are welcome in the garden, bar and in the adjacent internal 6th-century cave complete with comfy sofas and chairs. The extensive patio beer garden includes a play area overlooking sandstone rock formations and is popular in the warmer months. Quiz nights are organised on the second and fourth Sunday of each month.

Opera House

88 Mount Pleasant Road, TN1 1RT
9am-midnight (1am Fri & Sat) (01892) 511770

Greene King IPA, Abbot; Sharp's Doom Bar; 6 changing beers (sourced nationally; often Kent, Marston's, Old Dairy) Ⓗ
JD Wetherspoon has tastefully restored the old Opera House to its former glory, featuring the theatre circle, boxes and huge central chandelier. Located in the centre of town close to the Victoria shopping centre, the pub is a convenient place to take refuge from the shopping crowds. A wide range of guest ales is always stocked, sourced both locally and nationally. The stage bar provides the opportunity to eat or drink while imagining performing in such splendid surroundings.
Q🐴◑♿⇌🚌📶

Royal Oak Ⓛ
92 Prospect Road, TN2 4SY
⏲ 12 (3 Mon)-11; 12-9 Sun ☎ (01892) 542546
Harvey's Sussex Best Bitter; 4 changing beers (sourced regionally; often Dark Star, Gun, Tonbridge) Ⓗ
A wonderful traditional pub from a bygone era, dating back to 1735, with a strong community focus and an emphasis on live music. The pub was acquired by new owners in spring 2017 and has so far been sympathetically refurbished. Harvey's Sussex is a permanent cask beer, with up to five further offerings from Kent and Sussex and occasionally further afield. The beer is kept in first-class condition from a well-organised and clean cellar. Real cider from Biddenden or Lilley's is always available. Live bands play on Saturdays.
🐴❀◑⇌♣🍎P🚌(6,285)🐾📶

Tyler Hill

Tyler's Kiln ✔
27 Hackington Road, CT2 9NE
⏲ 11-11.30 (12.30am Fri & Sat); 11.45-11 Sun
☎ (01227) 471912 🌐 tylerskiln.co.uk
Harvey's Sussex Best Bitter; Shepherd Neame Master Brew; 2 changing beers (sourced locally; often Harvey's) Ⓗ
Community-focused village pub, refurbished to a high standard with innovative touches and a loyalty scheme. It is a pleasant place to drink and eat, with cosy armchairs and an open fire. Tiles from the nearby ancient kiln are displayed. A small range of groceries is sold. The separate TV room is comfortably furnished and a good place for children. The well-designed garden has a fountain and high-tech heating. Events include coffee mornings, live music and quizzes.
Q🐴❀◑♿P🚌(5)🐾📶

Upchurch

Brown Jug
76 Horsham Lane, ME9 7AP
⏲ 12-10 ☎ (01634) 366543
Harvey's Sussex Best Bitter; 2 changing beers (sourced nationally; often Greene King, Harvey's, Timothy Taylor) Ⓗ
A welcoming and popular community pub on the outskirts of the village. It is unpretentious, with good service and a friendly atmosphere. It was sold off by Shepherd Neame and is now a true free house with a strong liking for Harvey's of Lewes; Harvey's seasonal specials also feature. The food menu is predominantly Italian but also includes British classics. The spacious garden has an area of decking, and there is large car park. The pub is a popular stop-off for cyclists.
Q🐴❀◑♿♣P🚌(327)🐾📶

Upper Upnor

King's Arms
2 High Street, ME2 4XG
⏲ 11.30-midnight; 12-10.30 Sun ☎ (01634) 717490
🌐 kingsarmsupnor.co.uk
5 changing beers (sourced locally; often Tonbridge, Westerham) Ⓗ
This friendly local has a good choice of ales, ciders and perries as well as European bottled beers. Frequent beer festivals are held in the large garden. The restaurant has an excellent reputation for quality food. At the opposite end of the cobbled High Street are views over the River Medway and the old naval dockyard at Chatham. Upnor Castle is 100 yards down the street. Parking is available in the village car park nearby. Q🐴❀◑🍎P🚌(197)🐾

Tudor Rose
29 High Street, ME2 4XG
⏲ 12-11; 12-8 Sun ☎ (01634) 714175
🌐 tudorroseupnor.co.uk
Shepherd Neame Master Brew, Whitstable Bay Pale Ale; 2 changing beers (sourced nationally) Ⓗ
This inn lies down a narrow cobbled cul-de-sac and dates from the late 17th century. It has a large walled garden and is multi-roomed with a U-shaped bar. The extensive food menu offers a range of modern dishes, traditional favourites and vegetarian options, all freshly prepared on the premises. It is close to the historic Upnor Castle and the village car park at the far end of the High Street. Currently owned by brewers Shepherd Neame. Q🐴❀◑♣🚌(197)🐾📶

Walmer

Berry Ⓛ
23 Canada Road, CT14 7EQ
⏲ 11 (3 Tue)-11; 12-11 Thu; 11-11.30 Fri & Sat; 11.30-11 Sun
☎ (01304) 362411 🌐 theberrywalmer.co.uk
Dark Star American Pale Ale; Harvey's Sussex Best Bitter; Oakham Citra; 8 changing beers (often Ramsgate, Time & Tide) Ⓗ
This multi award-winning alehouse is located off Walmer seafront. The bar has a light and airy feel and at the back there is a pleasant patio. The welcome, service and quality of the ales and ciders reflects the landlord's enthusiasm. There is plenty of choice, with up to 11 cask ales, seven KeyKeg ales (many from Time & Tide), and up to 10 ciders. Three ale festivals are hosted annually. Entertainment includes darts, pool, a monthly quiz and live music. ❀♣🍎🚌🐾

Freed Man Ⓛ
329 Dover Road, CT14 7NX
⏲ 12-9 (10 Tue; 11 Fri & Sat); 12-8 Sun ☎ (01304) 364457
🌐 thefreed-man.co.uk
4 changing beers (sourced locally) Ⓗ
This offers everything for the discerning drinker in a micropub atmosphere. The decor is cosy and warm, with nautical memorabilia covering the reclaimed-wood walls. Up to four real ales, predominantly from local breweries, are served from the Victorian beer engine. Alongside these are real ciders, wines, selected spirits and authentic draught and

bottled European lagers. Food can be brought in and the staff will provide plates and cutlery. Regular events include a Thursday ladies' night and a monthly quiz night.

West Malling

Bull Inn

1 High Street, ME19 6QH

12-2.30, 4-11 Mon & Tue; 12-11 Wed-Sat; 12-10.30 Sun

(01732) 842753 thebullinnwestmalling.com

Timothy Taylor Landlord; Young's Bitter; 6 changing beers (sourced nationally; often Goacher's, Musket, Tonbridge) H

A welcoming village free house with wood panelling and a log fire. There is a focus on local beer and cider, with the cider on handpump. A terrace at the rear offers alfresco drinking. A quiz is held on Monday evenings and live music plays twice monthly on Saturdays. Good home-made pub meals are served throughout, with the left-hand bar for diners. Q (72,151)

Malling Jug

52 High Street, ME19 6LU (in a narrow alley opp Swan St between a funeral directors' and a hospice shop)

12-9; closed Tue (01732) 667832

themallingjug.co.uk

Kent Session Pale; 7 changing beers (sourced nationally; often Kent) G

Opened in 2017, this community micropub has a main drinking area with high and low level tables and, mostly, bench seating. The courtyard has further seating and access to the toilets. At least eight beers plus Turners cider are provided from the barrel by gravity. A chalkboard shows beers currently available or coming soon. There is also a selection of bottled beers. Service is to your seat at busy times. Beers are served as pints, halves or three third-pint samplers in oversized glasses. Pub snacks are sold.

Westgate-on-Sea

Bake & Alehouse

21 St Mildred's Road, CT8 8RE

12-2, 5-8 Mon; 12-2, 5.30-9 Tue-Sat; 12-2 Sun

07913 368787 bakeandalehouse.co.uk

5 changing beers G

Welcoming micropub down the alleyway between the Carlton Cinema and a bookmaker's – an oasis for the local real ale drinker. A selection of four different beers mainly from Kentish breweries is served straight from barrels kept in a temperature-controlled room, along with Kentish ciders. With seating for around 20 people, the small interior has been managed well, and has a welcoming, friendly atmosphere. Locally produced cheese and pork pies are also available. Q

Whitstable

Black Dog

66 High Street, CT5 1BB

12-11.30 (midnight Thu-Sat)

Kent Session Pale; 4 changing beers (sourced regionally; often Kent, Oakham, Triple fff) G

This attractive town-centre micropub has lush Victorian decor with a twist. The long narrow room is lined with high bench seating. There are five constantly changing real ales, from local and regional microbreweries, and up to 18 ciders and perries. The five handpumps on the bar counter are for decoration only, though they do show the beers available, which are dispensed by gravity from the cooled cellar room. There is a quiz on the first Wednesday of each month. Q

Handsome Sam

3 Canterbury Road, CT5 4HJ

6-10 Mon; 12-2, 6-10.30 (11 Fri & Sat); 12-3 Sun

07931 662081

4 changing beers (sourced regionally; often Dark Star, Mighty Oak, Skinner's) G

Popular micropub just outside the town centre and five minutes from the railway station. Named after the owner's late pet cat, the high-ceilinged pub has the original exposed beams. High tables, benches and stools provide seating, and hops adorn the two bay windows. There are three or more beers on the bar, always including a pale ale, a copper ale and a stronger ale, as well as eight ciders, wines, champagne, malt whiskies and other spirits, tea and coffee, and pub snacks.

Q

Ship Centurion

111 High Street, CT5 1AY

11-11 (11.30 Fri & Sat); 12-7 Sun (01227) 264740

Adnams Southwold Bitter; 4 changing beers (often Canterbury Ales, Old Dairy, Pig & Porter) H

A friendly and traditional town-centre pub with pictures of Whitstable in the bar and colourful hanging baskets adding to its charm in summer. A mild is always served and a Kentish beer. Home-cooked bar food often includes authentic German dishes, and there is a schnitzel on Saturdays (no food Sun). Live music plays on Thursday evenings (except in Jan). There is a summer cider festival and an October beer festival. Sky Sports is shown.

Willesborough

Blacksmiths Arms

84 The Street, TN24 0NA

12-11 (midnight Fri & Sat); 12-11.30 Sun

(01233) 623975 blacksmithsarmsashford.co.uk

Fuller's London Pride; 3 changing beers (sourced nationally) H

This 18th-century Grade II-listed family-friendly pub is on the outskirts of Ashford and just off junction 10 of the M20, offering a broad range of cask ales, wines and a changing food menu. There is a large terraced garden and children's play area, which provides a welcome break for those travelling to the continent. A footpath on the east side of the pub leads to the William Harvey Hospital. P

Wormshill

Blacksmiths Arms

The Street, ME9 0TU TQ878571

closed Mon & Tue; 7-11; 12-11 Sun (01622) 884386

3 changing beers (sourced regionally; often Arran, Westerham) H

A Grade II-listed, timber-framed, 17th-century village pub that was formerly three cottages. It is situated in rolling downland countryside near to the Pilgrims Way. It has a cosy bar with original brick floor, and is warmed in winter by an inglenook log fire. Beers feature from near and far with Scottish beers alongside local ales, often from Westerham Brewery. Well-cooked food is served in the restaurant. Clocks and various antique artefacts can be purchased. **Q**❀◑**P**🐾 ᯤ

Wrotham

George & Dragon

High Street, TN15 7AA

12-11; 12-10.30 Sun ☎ (01732) 884298
georgeanddragon.wrotham.net

Harvey's Sussex Best Bitter; 4 changing beers (sourced nationally; often Bath Ales, Timothy Taylor, Wychwood) H

A welcoming village local at the foot of the North Downs and close to the M20 junction with the A227. This comfortable single-bar pub, with a real fire, offers five real ales from regional and national breweries. Conversation is key here. Good food is served Monday to Wednesday lunchtimes, and Thai food features on Thursday and Friday evenings.
Q❀◑♿♣🚌(308)🐾 ᯤ

Old House, Ightham Common (Photo: Bob Steel)

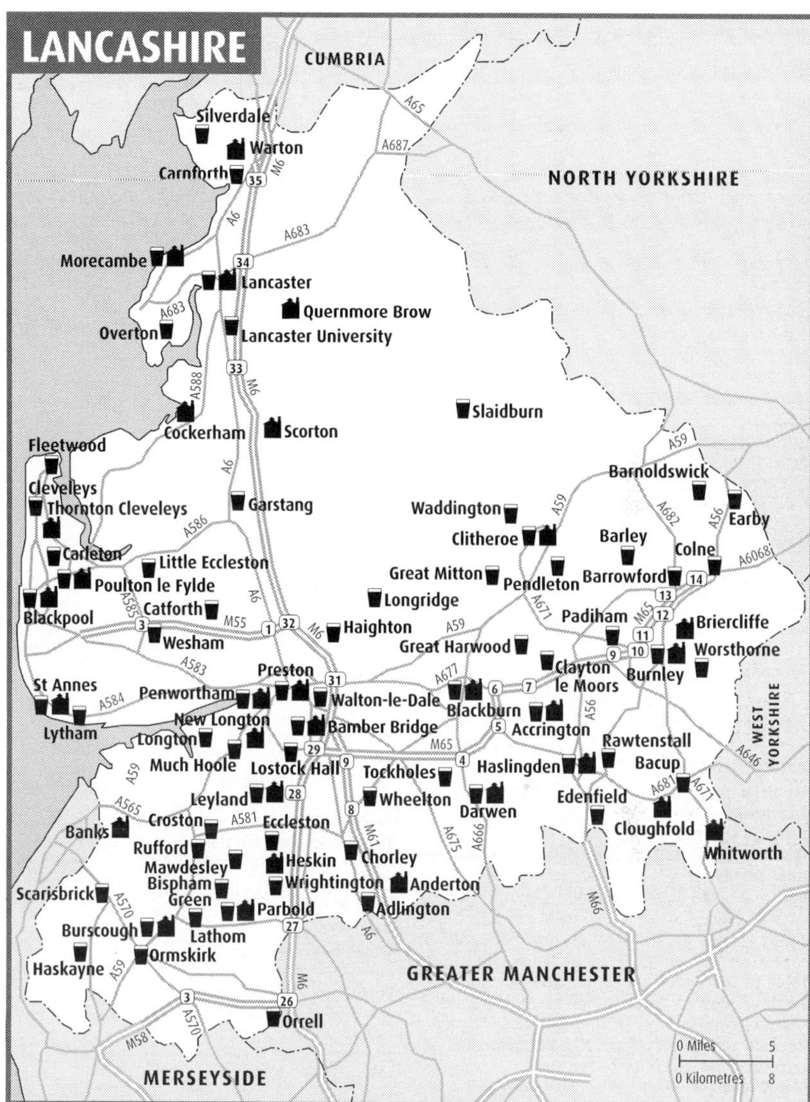

Accrington

Canine Club

45-47 Abbey Street, BB5 1EN

11-11 ☎ (01254) 233999

Tetley Bitter; 3 changing beers (sourced nationally; often Reedley Hallows, Worsthorne) Ⓗ

A large street-corner social club on a busy street. The central bar serves a comfortable lounge to the front and a traditional games room to the rear where snooker, pool and darts are played. There is a large upstairs function room. This popular club is welcoming to all and hosts live entertainment most weekends. The changing beer range usually includes a couple of east Lancashire brews and one from further afield.

Peel Park Hotel

Turkey Street, BB5 6EW

12-11.30 ☎ (01254) 235830

Tetley Bitter; 5 changing beers (sourced nationally) Ⓗ

A true free house at the foot of the Coppice and opposite the site of the old Accrington Stanley football ground, still used by Peel Park FC. Six beers are sold, mainly from smaller regional breweries. The warm and welcoming main bar is divided into split-level front, side and rear sections. There is a separate small pool room, and a smart rear room used for functions and meetings. Outside there is a pleasant garden area to the side of the pub.

P

Adlington

Spinners Arms

23 Church Street, PR7 4EX

12-midnight (1am Fri & Sat) ☎ (01257) 483331

Moorhouse's Pride of Pendle; Southport Dark Night; 5 changing beers (sourced regionally; often Abbeydale, George Wright, Oakham) Ⓗ

Known as the Bottom Spinners to differentiate it from the other Spinners Arms in the village. Built in 1838, the pub is welcoming and friendly, with a single bar serving three seating areas. There is a pleasant outdoor drinking area to the front. It has no pool table or gaming machine, just an open log fire. The bar menu offers home-cooked food with Sunday specials. Five alternating guest beers are served, often sourced from local breweries. Small functions are catered for. P (8A)

Bacup

Crown Inn

19 Greave Road, OL13 9HQ

5-11; 3-midnight Fri; 12-midnight Sat & Sun

(01706) 873982

Pictish Brewers Gold; 2 changing beers (sourced locally) H

Cosy traditional country pub with a large L-shaped bar and stone-flagged floors throughout. It was built in 1865 and once owned by Baxter's of Glentop Brewery. A welcoming coal fire adds warmth in the cooler months. There are always three beers on, usually sourced locally. Food is available most evenings and quiz nights are held on Wednesday and Sunday. On the second floor is a function room accommodating up to 35 guests. There is a patio beer garden to the front and beer festivals are held in July and October.
P (465)

Bamber Bridge

Withy Arms

Station Road, PR5 6QP

11-midnight (1am Fri); 10.30-1am Sat; 10.30-midnight Sun

(01772) 697706 withyarms.com

Ribble WA Bitter, Odd Job; 3 changing beers (sourced nationally) H

There is a small taproom to the right of the entrance while the open-plan main bar area has a slightly continental feel. An impressive bar counter features six handpumps. The two house beers from Ribble Brewery are contract brewed by an unnamed brewery to the pub's own recipe. The changing guest ales tend to be below 4.5% ABV and from microbreweries. Decked outdoor seating areas are front and back of the pub.

Barley

Pendle Inn

Barley Lane, BB12 9JX

12-11.30 (01282) 614808 pendle-inn.co.uk

Moorhouse's Pride of Pendle, Wainwright; 4 changing beers (sourced nationally; often Marston's) H

In the heart of Pendle Witch country and handy for the climb up Pendle Hill, this inn welcomes all with a fine selection of beers, good food in generous portions and warm rooms. There is a ramp for wheelchair access but toilets are not specially adapted. Popular with locals and visitors alike, it is also a dog-loving pub. The Clitheroe to Nelson bus stops nearby (not Sun).
Q P (66,67)

Barnoldswick

Barlick Tap Ale House

8 Newtown, BB18 5UQ

closed Mon & Tue; 4-9 Wed & Thu ; 4-10 Fri; 2-10 Sat; 2-8 Sun 07739 088846

5 changing beers (sourced nationally) H

This friendly one-room micropub was the first to be set up in the town and is just off the town square, two minutes from the main bus stop. With a choice of five changing cask beers, one of them will be a dark beer and one a LocAle. It has a large selection of continental bottled beers, and there are always two ciders, usually including Broadoak Pheasant Plucker. No music disturbs the place, and it is dog friendly. Events and tastings feature on occasion.
Q (M1)

Barrowford

Bankers Draft

143 Gisburn Road, BB9 6HQ

closed Mon & Tue; 4-9 Wed & Thu; 4-10.30 Fri; 2-10.30 Sat; 2-9 Sun 07739 870880

5 changing beers (sourced nationally) H

Former bank that is now a small and friendly micropub specialising in real ale and conversation, without loud music or TV. The five handpumps dispense rotating cask ales from national small brewers, offering a great variety of beer styles, from hoppy blondes and traditional bitters to dark

REAL ALE BREWERIES

3 Piers Poulton-le-Fylde (NEW)
Avid Quernmore Brow (NEW)
Beer Brothers Bamber Bridge
Big Clock Accrington
Bishop's Crook Penwortham
Bloomfield Blackpool
Bluestone Whitworth
Bowland Clitheroe
Chain House New Longton (NEW)
Chapel Street Poulton-le-Fylde
Crankshaft Leyland
Cross Bay Morecambe
Darkwave Preston
Doghouse Darwen
Farm Yard Cockerham
Fuzzy Duck Poulton-le-Fylde
Hop Vine Burscough
Hopstar Darwen
Hubsters Bamber Bridge
Lancaster Lancaster
Lytham St Annes
Mighty Medicine Whitworth
Moonstone Burnley
Moorhouse's Burnley
Northern Whisper Cloughfold
Old School Warton
Oscars Preston
Parker Banks
Priest Town Preston
Problem Child Parbold
Providence Bamber Bridge (NEW)
Reedley Hallows Burnley
Rivington Anderton
Rock Solid Blackpool
Rossendale Haslingden
Skippool Creek Thornton-Cleveleys
Snowhill Scorton
Third Eye Heskin (brewing suspended)
Three B's Blackburn
Thwaites Blackburn
West Coast Rock Blackpool (NEW)
Withnell's Bamber Bridge
Worsthorne Briercliffe

beers. There is also a good selection of bottled continental beers, with at least one real cider available. Q P (2)

Bispham Green

Eagle & Child

Malt Kiln Lane, L40 3SG
12-11; 12-10.30 Sun (01257) 462297
eagleandchildbispham.co.uk
Southport Golden Sands; Thwaites Original, Wainwright; 5 changing beers H
An 18th-century pub with eight handpumps including local ales; Southport Golden Sands is always available and a variety of guests from Prospect and Moorhouse's. This busy country pub has been Lancashire Dining Pub of the Year and is noted for its food. The huge beer garden, with its wildlife area and great views, hosts a beer festival on the first May bank holiday. Quiz night is every Monday. P

Blackburn

Black Bull L

Brokenstone Road, BB3 0LL (corner of Brokenstone Rd and Heys Lane) SD666247
closed Mon & Tue; 4-11; 12-11 Sat; 12-10.30 Sun
(01254) 581381 threebsbrewery.co.uk
Three B's Stoker's Slake, Bobbin's Bitter, Oatmeal Stout, Black Bull, Weavers Brew, Knocker Up; 2 changing beers H
In the heart of rural Lancashire, this is an independent family-run pub with a brewery attached. Eight handpumps serve a selection of Three B's ales including the exclusive Black Bull bitter. Try the popular three-beer sampler wedges. Built as a farmhouse in the 18th century, this venue was purchased by Robert Bell from Thwaites and transformed into a place for those who appreciate fine beer and friendly conversation. It has no jukebox, fruit machines or food, just a friendly, relaxing atmosphere. Q P

Drummers Arms L

65 King William Street, BB1 7DT
12-8 (11 Fri & Sat) 07341 565657 q-ale.co.uk
Three B's Stoker's Slake; 4 changing beers (sourced locally; often Big Clock, Cross Bay, Hopstar) H
Single-roomed bar opposite the town hall and on the edge of the main shopping area. The walls are adorned with breweriana and old pub signs. The bi-weekly Sunday free and easy music sessions are legendary. At other times expect a range of classic tracks from the eclectic jukebox. A strong supporter of LocAle, the majority of beers here are from Lancashire breweries, though a visitor from across the Pennines sometimes makes an appearance. It has a pleasant terrace at the front.

Hare & Hounds L

78 Lammack Road, BB1 8LA
4-11.30; 12.30-12.30am Sat; 12.30-11.30 Sun
(01254) 676724
Moorhouse's Blond Witch; 4 changing beers (sourced regionally; often Bowland, Reedley Hallows, Worsthorne) H
Former Whitbread estate pub rescued by the current landlord and backed by a passionate local community. It is adjacent to Old Blackburnians FC, and to Pleckgate and Lammack playing fields. Local breweries such as Reedley Hallows, Moorhouse's and Worsthorne feature regularly. The large, comfortable open-plan lounge is served from a bar with five handpumps. Popular quality live entertainment is put on at weekends, when the pub can get busy. P

Blackpool

Bar 19

19 Queen Street, FY1 1NL
11-4am; 10-4am Fri & Sat; 12-4am Sun (01253) 627986
4 changing beers (often Coach House, Holt, Lees) H
An oasis of real ale on one of Blackpool's main party streets, this uncomplicated, single-room bar may be a surprise choice for the Guide to some. Very much a locals' bar during the day with a large number of regulars, it becomes more of a nightclub as the night goes on. The four varying beers, all of exceptional quality, come from a wide choice of breweries both near and far. A beer festival is held each year in May. Local CAMRA Pub of the Year 2018. (North Pier)

Blackpool Cricket Club

Barlow Crescent, West Park Drive, FY3 9EQ (follow signs to Stanley Park)
4.30-11; 12-midnight Sat; 12-11 Sun (01253) 393347
blackpoolcricket.co.uk
Wainwright; 4 changing beers (sourced regionally) H
On the western edge of Stanley Park, within the cricket pavilion, this club is host to many sports teams, while several TVs show major sports fixtures. An upstairs room is available for social events. The club has its own squash courts and holds quiz and entertainment nights. There is now a ladies' cricket team. Many times local CAMRA branch Club of the Year, it holds an annual beer festival. Entry is free to all cricket games except Lancashire's. P (15,16)

Layton Rakes

17-25 Market Street, FY1 1ET
8am-midnight (1am Fri & Sat) (01253) 743710
Greene King Abbot; Ruddles Best Bitter; Sharp's Doom Bar; 5 changing beers (sourced regionally) H
Near to North Pier, this multi-floored Wetherspoon is popular with locals and tourists alike. It features a bar on each floor, with lift access to all floors, and a range of three regular and at least five changing guest beers and a small range of ciders. The pub, especially the ground floor, can get busy at weekends and during the main holiday season. Outdoor seating is available to the front and side and on the roof terrace.
(North Pier)

Pump & Truncheon

13 Bonny Street, FY1 5AR
10.30-11; 12-10.30 Sun (01253) 624099
thepumpandtruncheon.co.uk
6 changing beers (sourced nationally; often Cross Bay) H
Old-fashioned and welcoming free house, just off the Golden Mile, whose police-themed decor reflects the pub's proximity to the local police station. Up to six different guest beers can be on sale although at quiet times of the year the range may be reduced. A range of real ciders is also available. Dogs are especially welcome. Occasional live bands perform, and a roaring log fire is lit in winter. Home-made pizzas and foot-long sausages are available throughout the day.

Saddle Inn ✓

286 Whitegate Drive, FY3 9PH

10.30-11 (midnight Fri & Sat); 11-midnight Sun (01253) 767827 thesaddleblackpool.co.uk

Draught Bass; 5 changing beers (sourced nationally; often Lytham) H

A Blackpool institution, the building dates from about 1776 when it was owned by a saddler. Real fires are found in each of the two rooms off the main bar area, and walls feature many sporting prints. Food is normally served until 9pm daily. Two real ciders are usually available in the summer months.

Washington ✓

Topping Street, FY1 3AF

10.30-11 (midnight Fri & Sat); 11-11 Sun (01253) 620885

Greene King IPA; Morland Old Speckled Hen; Ruddles Best Bitter; 6 changing beers (sourced nationally) H

Town-centre pub, handy for the railway station. It is decorated with many pictures of Blackpool, the Golden Mile and and the illuminations. Divided into three rooms, it is popular with locals. The six guest beers come from brewers both near and far. There is an extensive menu of good-value food. Several screens show live sports and live bands perform on Saturday. (North)

Burnley

Bridge Bier Huis L

2 Bank Parade, BB11 1UH

closed Mon & Tue; 12-midnight Wed & Thu; 12-1am Fri & Sat; 12-11 Sun (01282) 411304 thebridgebierhuis.co.uk

Moorhouse's Premier Bitter; 4 changing beers (sourced regionally) H

An award-winning true free house with a large open-plan bar that has a logburner and a small snug to one side. It offers mainly microbrewery beers alongside a changing real cider. More than 60 foreign bottled beers are sold plus seven foreign beers on tap. Wednesday is quiz night and live music is hosted on occasional weekends. This welcoming pub opens 5pm Monday or Tuesday if Burnley FC are at home.

Ministry of Ale

9 Trafalgar Street, BB11 1TQ

closed Mon & Tue; 5-11 Wed & Thu; 12.30-midnight Fri & Sat; 3-11 Sun (01282) 830909

Moonstone Black Star Dark; 3 changing beers (sourced nationally) H

Home of the Moonstone Brewery which can be viewed in the front room of the pub. This small, friendly local places an emphasis on excellent beer and good conversation. One Moonstone beer is generally on sale alongside three rotating guests, usually from microbreweries. A popular quiz is held every Thursday night and the pub hosts regular photo exhibitions of old Burnley pubs. It will open if Burnley FC are at home on Monday or Tuesday evenings. Q(Manchester Road)(X43)

New Brew-m L

St James Row, BB11 1DR

12-8 Mon & Wed; closed Tue; 12-10 Thu-Sat; 12-6 Sun 07902 961426

6 changing beers (sourced nationally) H

Smart micropub in the centre of town which serves as the Reedley Hallows Brewery tap. At least one of its own beers is always on the bar alongside five others sourced nationwide using the head brewer's contacts from years in the trade. A limited range of foreign bottled beers and bottled ciders is also available. Comfortable seating around wooden hogsheads on the raised portion complements bench seating opposite the bar. Opens on Tuesday night if Burnley FC are at home. Q

Rifle Volunteer L

1 Smalley Street, BB11 3HH

2-11; 12-11 Sat; 12-10.30 Sun (01282) 453839

Draught Bass; 2 changing beers (sourced locally; often Reedley Hallows) H

The Vols is an award-winning pub and a rare outlet in this area for the iconic Draught Bass. This free house is a supreme example of the street-corner local. There is no jukebox to disturb the quiet ambience of this friendly pub where the emphasis is on good beer and conversation. Check out the gents' toilet for a rare example of Burnley-manufactured Ducketts urinals. QP(483)

Talbot L ✓

65 Church Street, BB11 2RU

5-midnight; 4-1am Fri; 12-1am Sat; 12-midnight Sun (01282) 412074 talbotburnley.co.uk

Moorhouse's Premier Bitter; Timothy Taylor Boltmaker; 6 changing beers H

A warm welcome awaits you at this large free house situated just off the town centre and dating back to the 1800s. The licensee is a real ale enthusiast and keen supporter of local breweries. Live music features every weekend. There are two pool tables plus large-screen TV for sports fans. Four well-appointed en-suite rooms are available for guests, who also have use of the private car park. P(M2,M3)

Burscough

Hop Vine L

Liverpool Road North, L40 4BY (on A59 in village centre)

10.30-midnight (12.30am Fri & Sat); 10.30-11 Sun (01704) 893799 thehopvinepub.co.uk

Timothy Taylor Landlord; house beer (by Hop Vine); 4 changing beers H

This spacious former coaching house is now a thriving community brewpub renowned for its friendly atmosphere and popular for the quality of its beer and food. The classic country pub interior has wood panelling and characterful wood flooring throughout and is decorated with historic local maps, photographs and vintage bottled ales. The Hop Vine Brewery operates from the attractive floral courtyard at the rear. Catering for all ages, it offers great value meals, live music and twice-yearly beer festivals.

Carleton

Castle Gardens ✓

Poulton Road, FY6 7NH

10-11 (midnight Fri & Sat) (01253) 890015

Moorhouse's White Witch, Wainwright; house beer (by Black Sheep); 6 changing beers (sourced nationally) H

There has been an inn on this site since about 1750. Extremely popular, it is now both a food-led destination and a local community venue. A weekly quiz is held. Despite basically comprising one room, there are lots of nooks and crannies should you wish for a quiet drink. A range of nine ales including six changing guests is available. There is a pleasant outdoor area to the side of the pub. (14)

Carnforth

Snug

Unit 6, Carnforth Gateway Building, LA5 9TR (at N end of former mainline up platform)
12-2 (not Mon), 5-9; 12-9 Sat; 1-4.30 Sun
☎ 07927 396861 thesnugmicropub.blogspot.co.uk
5 changing beers H
The area's first micropub. The only drinks are ale, cider, wine, a few soft drinks and at least 10 good-quality gins; the only food is a few light snacks. The only sounds are conversation and the roar of the passing trains. Decor is similarly stripped back: painted walls, bare floorboards and chunky tall tables. The eye is naturally drawn to a beautiful glazed wooden cabinet, where all the drinks are stored. Parking is on the station car park (a charge applies). Q

Catforth

Running Pump

Catforth Road, PR4 0HH
closed Mon; 4.30-10 Tue-Thu; 4-midnight Fri; 12-midnight Sat; 12-10 Sun ☎ (01772) 690265
Thwaites Original; house beer (by Pixie Spring/ Hopcraft); 3 changing beers (sourced nationally; often Elland, Wishbone) H
A 300-year-old building, this traditional country pub reopened in 2015 after refurbishment. Five ales are sold, three of which are from brewers far and wide. It is well known for its good food which is served throughout the pub, though there is also a separate dining room. Offering stunning views of the Pennine Fells, the pub is in a pleasant rural area. There is a water trough and pump, and an old horse stop with feeding cage outside.
Q P (77,77A)

Chorley

Ale Station

60 Chapel Street, PR7 1BS
closed Mon; 4-11 Tue-Thu; 3-12.30am Fri; 1-12.30am Sat; 2-11 Sun ☎ (01257) 368003
6 changing beers (sourced locally; often Hawkshead, Rock the Boat) H
A micropub conveniently near to both the bus and train stations. A modern-looking establishment with a wine-bar feel, this inviting pub offers a full range of drinks. Five changing real ales are served, increasing to six at weekends, mainly from north-western microbreweries, although expect to find others from far and wide. There are also two changing real ciders. Pictures of old Chorley adorn the walls. The pub may close earlier during the week if custom is insufficient. Q

Bob Inn

24 Market Place, PR7 1DA
10-6; closed Wed & Sun ☎ 07767 238410
3 changing beers (sourced nationally) H
A tiny bar housed in a market stall. With an adjacent unit now used as a lounge area, this is the smallest pub in the branch area. Outside seating is available during summer and drinkers often spill over into the market space. With three varying cask beers from smaller breweries, at least two ciders and a good selection of bottled beers, there is something for every taste. No food is served, but you are welcome to bring your own. Q

Malt 'n' Hops

50-52 Friday Street, PR6 0AA
12 (3 Mon)-11; 12-midnight Sat & Sun ☎ (01257) 260074
Bank Top Dark Mild; Irwell Works Marshmallow Unicorn; 7 changing beers (sourced nationally; often Fernandes, Moorhouse's, Rat) H
Converted from an old shop, the pub is handily situated for both the railway and bus stations. A single L-shaped bar on two levels, it has been recently redecorated and has a bright yet traditional feel. A genuine free house, there are up to seven guest ales usually from Lancashire and Yorkshire micros, with Rat, Ossett, Elland, Lancaster and Blackedge often featuring. Two regular dark beers are usually served and filled rolls and pork pies are often available. Local CAMRA Pub of the Year 2016-17.

Masons Arms

98 Harpers Lane, PR6 0HU
3-11; 12-midnight Fri & Sat; 12-11 Sun ☎ 07464 841589
5 changing beers (sourced locally; often Blackjack, Hawkshead, Marble) H
Tastefully modernised multi-room pub a short walk from the town centre and a recent convert to real ale. Beers are mainly from north-west micros and usually include a dark beer. A separate taproom and two distinct lounges, complete with wood-burning stoves, give distinctly different drinking areas. Light and airy, this is a cosy pub with a growing reputation for good beer.
(24,125)

Shepherds' Hall Ale House

67 Chapel Street, PR7 1BS
closed Mon; 2-10.30 Tue; 3-10.30 Wed & Thu; 2-11.30 Fri; 1-11.30 Sat; 3-10.30 Sun ☎ 07412 584907
5 changing beers (sourced nationally) H
The first micropub in Chorley, opening in 2014. Formerly a florist's shop, it has been tastefully converted and utilises fittings from other closed pubs in the town. In common with most micropubs, there is no TV or music. Up to five beers are served, mainly from microbreweries across the country, although a LocAle or two can be expected. Three ciders are usually served, although hidden from sight under the counter – check the chalkboard for details. Q

Clayton le Moors

Forts Arms

1 Lower Barnes Street, BB5 5TA
4-midnight; 2-2am Fri & Sat; 2-11 Sun ☎ (01254) 433713
4 changing beers (sourced regionally; often Bowland, Snaggletooth, Wishbone) H
Partially opened out in a modern style, yet still retaining a separate lounge, this corner pub boasts a large rear beer garden, popular with families in summer, and a two-floor function suite to the side where regular music events are held. Beers are mainly from the plethora of breweries in east Lancashire. Folk music sessions take place weekly and music, art and beer festivals are held twice a year. Handy for Mercer Park and a short walk downhill from the Leeds-Liverpool canal.
Q P

Cleveleys

Jolly Tars

154-158 Victoria Road, FY5 3NE

8am-midnight (12.30am Fri & Sat) (01253) 856042

Greene King Abbot; Ruddles Best Bitter; Sharp's Doom Bar; 7 changing beers (sourced nationally; often Bank Top, Coach House, Lancaster)

Opened in 2011, this Wetherspoon pub, a conversion from a former Kwik Save supermarket, is named after a highly popular nine-strong family team who entertained huge crowds locally during the '40s. It is a pleasant and welcoming environment in which to enjoy a quiet drink, with several secluded booths. A pleasant open-air drinking area is at the front. Real cider is available alongside the wide choice of local, national and regional ales.

Clitheroe

Ale House

12-14 Market Place, BB7 2DA

12-10 (midnight Fri & Sat) 07530 045365

thealehouseclitheroe.co.uk

5 changing beers (often Beer Monkey, Blackedge, Vocation)

Previously the old Tourist Information Office, this centrally located micropub is just a five-minute walk uphill from the rail and bus stations. As well as a continually changing range of five cask beers, it also offers a wide choice of bottled craft beers from around the world. The tasteful conversion now features three small rooms, two downstairs and one upstairs. Acoustic music sessions are held every fortnight as well as the occasional comedy night, Meet the Brewer and tap takeovers.

Bowland Beer Hall

Greenacre Street, BB7 1EB

11-11 (midnight Fri & Sat); 11-9 Sun (01200) 401035

holmesmill.co.uk/beer-hall

Bowland Pheasant Plucker, Gold, AONB, Hen Harrier, Buster IPA; 16 changing beers (sourced nationally)

A beer hall in a former mill in heritage-rich Clitheroe with many preserved industrial features. The huge circular bar has 42 handpulls and Bavarian-style communal tables. The Engine Room boasts a restored mill engine and smaller cosy tables. A huge glass wall faces into on-site Bowland Brewery. Casks, ciders and bottled beers change weekly. Food is served 12-9pm (7pm Sun), from small plates to crowd-pleasing classics. Monthly Frog and Bucket comedy nights take place, and Drink it Dry ales on Monday and Tuesday. The complex includes a food hall, bistro and hotel. Clitheroe Castle and museum are nearby.

New Inn

20 Parson Lane, BB7 2JN

11-11; 12-11 Sun (01200) 423312

Coach House Gunpowder Mild, Farrier's Best Bitter; Moorhouse's Premier Bitter, White Witch, Pride of Pendle, Blond Witch; 5 changing beers (sourced regionally; often Deeply Vale, Prospect, Worsthorne)

This gem of a pub can be found beneath the 12th-century castle and only a few minutes' walk from the bus and rail stations. Its quirky layout has a narrow corridor that leads to a cosy bar area, with four other rooms and a spacious beer garden at the rear. Guest beers are mainly from local breweries including Bowland, Prospect and Worsthorne. The back room hosts traditional Irish music sessions every alternate Sunday afternoon and a number of local groups meet here regularly.

Colne

Admiral Lord Rodney

Mill Green, BB8 0TA

4-midnight (2am Fri); 1-2am Sat; 1-midnight Sun

(01282) 219759 thelordrodney.co.uk

9 changing beers (sourced regionally; often Goose Eye, Ilkley, Reedley Hallows)

A much-loved and welcoming community pub in Colne's South Valley area, the old industrial heart of the town. The stone floor includes mosaics and there are beautiful tiles up the inner staircase. Set out in three rooms, the pub has become the meeting place for a number of clubs. Regular live entertainment takes place during evenings, plus local history and art displays. The recent refurbishment has brought open fires and some flagged flooring, plus much-improved outdoor seating and a separate smokers' area.

Boyce's Barrel

7 New Market Street, BB8 9BJ

closed Mon; 4-9; 1-9 Sat 07736 900111

5 changing beers (sourced nationally)

The first micropub in Colne and a member of the Micropub Association, offering five real ales. No music, no lager, just a great atmosphere and plenty of banter. Tastefully styled with tall polished wooden sleeper tables, it is reminiscent of a rail staging post. Ales are rotated often, with new beers put on the bar almost as soon as barrels runs dry. All ales are from non-local breweries, with a mild and a porter or stout always among the range. A pub that is sure to suit any real ale fan's tastes.

Wallace Hartley

35-37 Church Street, BB8 0EB

8am-11 (midnight Thu; 1am Fri & Sat); 8am-11.30 Sun

(01282) 857990

Greene King Abbot; Ruddles Best Bitter; 8 changing beers (sourced nationally; often Moorhouse's, Titanic, Worsthorne)

Named after the bandmaster of the ill-fated Titanic who was born in Colne, the building was originally a pub in the 1920s, later becoming a Greek restaurant, then opening in 2008 as a Wetherspoon. The wood-panelled interior is split into a number of seating areas and has a relaxed, friendly atmosphere. Ten ales are usually available including, of course, Titanic. The history of Wallace Hartley and old Colne decorate the walls. Close to the bus station and an uphill walk from the train station.

Croston

Wheatsheaf

Town Road, PR26 9RA

12-11 (midnight Fri); 10-midnight Sat; 10-11 Sun

(01772) 600370 wheatsheaf-croston.com

Robinsons Dizzy Blonde; 4 changing beers (often Hawkshead)

On the main road and overlooking the village green, this recently refurbished pub has a contemporary feel. It has a distinct area for dining as well as a comfortable drinking space with sofas and chairs. The large patio to the front holds an annual beer festival in October. Children are welcome. Food is served lunchtimes and evenings during the week and all day at weekends, with the pub opening at 10am for breakfast. P

Darwen

Number 39

39-41 Bridge Street, BB3 2AA

12-midnight 07531 425352

number39.darwenmusic.org.uk

Hopstar Dizzy Danny Ale, Dark Knight, JC, Lancashire Gold

The Hopstar Brewery tap where new brews are tried out, this classic single-roomed continental-style bar serves a variety of Hopstar beers and two ciders or perries. Bottled continental and world beers and draught Timmermans are also on offer. An eclectic range of background music plays and weekly live music sessions are held, usually Thursday night. Friday is tapas day and Sunday afternoon is the legendary apple, cheese and perry session. Close to the bus station. (1)

Earby

Red Lion

Red Lion Street, BB18 6RD

closed Mon & Tue; 5 (4 Fri)-11; 1-midnight Sat; 2-10.30 Sun

(01282) 843395

Naylor's Gold, Pinnacle Blonde; 2 changing beers (sourced locally; often Settle)

This is a true drinkers' delight, a traditional country local in a delightful village setting. The pub is owned by local people and a warm and friendly welcome awaits you from both the host and locals. Both rooms have been renovated with taste and on cold days the cosy lounge is heated with a woodburner. Close to Earby youth hostel and handy for the Pennine Way. Q

Eccleston

Greenhaus

276B The Green, PR7 5TF

4-11; 2-midnight Sat; 2-11 Sun 07725 185211

5 changing beers (sourced nationally)

Micropub and gin bar in what used to be the Grocer's on the Green store. Opened in October 2015 as the Cock T'Alehouse, it changed ownership and name in April 2017. The pub has a modern feel, light and airy. Up to five different cask ales are sold including at least one locally sourced. Parking can be difficult.

Edenfield

Rostron Arms

1 Market Place, BL0 0JZ

12-midnight; 12-11 Sun (01706) 824532

5 changing beers (sourced regionally; often Moorhouse's)

A large stone-built pub overlooking both Scout Moor and Dearden Moor, and just a short walk from Irwell Vale station on the East Lancs Heritage Railway. Built in the 19th century, it was one of three coaching inns in the town. There is a large bar area and a separate pool room. The pub has both darts and pool teams. P

Fleetwood

Royal Oak Hotel

171 Lord Street, FY7 6SR

12-midnight (1am Fri & Sat) (01253) 873486

Banks's Sunbeam; house beer (by Reedley Hallows); 6 changing beers (sourced locally; often Blackedge, Bowness Bay, Cross Bay)

Known locally as Dead 'Uns, this pub has gone from strength to strength after being rescued from closure in 2013. It still retains many original features. Up to eight beers are available, mainly from local brewers, and Westons Old Rosie cider is also on the bar. There is a function room for hire, and the Fleetwood Rock and Blues Club hosts live bands regularly. Dogs are allowed in the vaults, and away fans are welcome when playing Fleetwood Town.

Steamer

Queens Terrace, FY7 6BT

12 (11 Tue)-midnight; 11-midnight Thu (1am Fri & Sat)

(01253) 681001

7 changing beers (sourced nationally)

Impressive street-corner pub, one of Fleetwood's oldest, close to the town's market, the tram terminus and Knott End ferry. Seven changing beers are normally available along with one cider. There is a live singer every Tuesday afternoon and live bands every Friday and Saturday night. Food is served in a side room where you may be waited on by TV legend Syd Little.

Garstang

Crown

High Street, PR3 1FA

12-midnight (01995) 602152

Thwaites Original; Wainwright; 2 changing beers (often Thwaites)

A local in the town centre where a 2017 revamp has tartan fabrics blending with varnished wood. It has a single room with a corner devoted to pool and a trophy cabinet; other walls have photos of old Garstang. The sport TV is often on, and it has music on Saturday, disco or karaoke on Friday. A bowling green is at the rear.

Great Harwood

1B Tap

1B Glebe Street, BB6 7AA

closed Mon-Wed; 2 (4 Thu)-11

4 changing beers (sourced nationally)

Comfortable two-roomed bar opened in former office premises by three real ale enthusiasts, close to Towngate square and preservation area, on a side street opposite the post office. The main room, featuring plenty of beer-related displays, sells a changing and skillfully selected range of cask beers which usually includes a strong stout or porter. A side room, housing a separate bar specialising in gin and world beers, offers additional seating. Local CAMRA Pub of the Year for 2017. P

Great Mitton

Aspinall Arms

Mitton Road, BB7 9PQ

10.30-11; 10.30-10.30 Sun (01254) 826555

aspinallarmspub.co.uk

Brunning & Price Original; 5 changing beers (sourced regionally; often Acorn, Dent, Moorhouse's) Ⓗ
Large, multi-roomed riverside establishment catering mainly for diners. There has been a pub on this site since the 17th century. Six ales are usually available including the house beer. Beer miles are recorded for each ale, and a sample is placed in front of each handpull. Several real fires are lit in winter. The food is excellent, with a menu that changes daily, and the bar bites are great value. It has a huge garden with plenty to interest children of all ages, and welcomes cyclists and walkers. P (5)

Haighton

Haighton Manor

Haighton Green Lane, PR2 5SQ
11-11 (midnight Fri & Sat); 11-10.30 Sun
☎ (01772) 706350
House beer (by Phoenix); 6 changing beers (often Hawkshead, Moorhouse's, Worsthorne) Ⓗ
Refurbished and extended in September 2016, this former country house hotel and wedding venue is now a bustling pub with dining. Seven handpumps offer a varied range of real ales, including the house ale from Brunning & Price. Beers usually include a dark mild or stout, and there is a choice of real ciders. Quality locally sourced food is served as well as a selection of beer tapas. Stone walls, flagged and wooden floors, low-beamed ceilings and open fires add to the country house feel. Voted local CAMRA Cider Pub of the Year 2018. P

Haskayne

King's Arms Hotel

1 Delph Lane, L39 7JJ (near bridge where Leeds-Liverpool canal crosses A5147)
2-midnight; 12-midnight Sat & Sun ☎ (01704) 840033
Salopian Oracle; 4 changing beers (sourced regionally; often Martland Mill, Rock the Boat, Windmill) Ⓗ
The King's Arms is on the busy A5147 between Maghull and Scarisbrick, a real community inn with two rooms that have many attractive original features. There is a small beer festival over the August bank holiday weekend which includes a family fun day, including many quirky rural competitions. The pub runs occasional coach trips to local breweries and other interesting places. P

Haslingden

Griffin Inn

86 Hud Rake, BB4 5AF
2-midnight; 12-2am Fri & Sat; 12-midnight Sun
☎ (01706) 214021 rossendalebrewery.co.uk
Rossendale Floral Dance, Glen Top Bitter, Ale, Halo Pale, Pitch Porter, Sunshine; 1 changing beer Ⓗ
Situated on Hud Rake, this is a traditional community pub and also the home of the Rossendale Brewery on the floor below. The large bar has a separate area for pub games, and the large lounge has picture windows overlooking the local hills and valleys. On the hill facing the front sits the Halo panopticon. The pub is easily accessible but there is a steep uphill walk from main road bus stops. Q (464,X41)

Lancaster

Bobbin

8 Chapel Street, LA1 1HH
11-midnight (1 Thu-Sat) ☎ (01524) 32606
thebobbinlancaster.co.uk
Coniston Bluebird XB; York Guzzler; 4 changing beers (often Abbeydale, Skinner's, York) Ⓗ
Large mainly Victorian pub, though part 18th century and with a vaguely Edwardian decor, entirely open plan but divided up by raised areas and pillars. It is frequented by a goth/metal crowd (although they are by no means the only customers). It has an extremely eclectic jukebox, an open mic night on Mondays, live music on Thursdays and some Fridays, and a quiz Sundays. Close to the bus station.

Britannia

101 Ullswater Road, LA1 3PX
5-11; 12-midnight Sat; 12-10.30 Sun ☎ (01524) 63691
thebritannialancaster.co.uk
Borough Pale, Bitter; 3 changing beers (often Old School, Borough, Marston's) Ⓗ
This pub was renovated in 2012 in a mixture of green, dark red and beige, with slate and wood for hard wear areas, and has one large bar room and another cosy open-plan room. For all the new look, it is still definitely a suburban local. It majors in pizzas, has a quiz on Monday, and open mic night on Thursday. The men's toilet is wheelchair accessible. (10,18)

Golden Lion

33 Moor Lane, LA1 1QD
2-midnight (1am Fri; 2am Sat); 2-midnight Sun
☎ (01524) 842198 goldenlionpublancaster.co.uk
Butcombe Original; Castle Rock Harvest Pale; Moorhouse's Pride of Pendle; Theakston Best Bitter; 2 changing beers Ⓗ
The pub is reputed to have been the last drinking place of the Pendle witches in 1612. The present building may date from around 1818, and is included in the Pendle Trail. Also known as the Whittle, it is a popular pub with a friendly and relaxed atmosphere. It has a nice collection of old Lancaster photos inside with lots of pictures of old pubs. Live music takes place every other Saturday evening (alternating with a DJ), and an open mic session is held every Tuesday.

John o' Gaunt

53 Market Street, LA1 1JG
12-midnight ☎ (01524) 65356
Jennings Cumberland Ale; Lancaster Black; Titanic Plum Porter; Wychwood Hobgoblin; 3 changing beers (often Wychwood) Ⓗ
A handsome Victorian frontage, dating from 1871, hides a narrow pub in which the walls are crammed with a variety of objects collected by a former licensee – beer mats, jazz posters and photos of musicians (reflecting one of his enthusiasms). At lunchtime most of the customers are from nearby banks and offices, in the evening mostly regulars. There is music Mondays, Friday and Saturdays, and a quiz Thursdays.

Merchants

29 Castle Hill, LA1 1YN
11.30-11 (12.30am Fri); 11-12.30am Sat ☎ (01524) 66466
merchants1688.co.uk

House beer (by Old School); 7 changing beers (sourced regionally; often Allendale, Kirkby Lonsdale, Tirril) H
A converted wine-merchant's cellars built in 1688 with an extensive outdoor drinking area creating a peaceful haven from the hubbub of the city centre. The main drinking areas are in three separate tunnels, with a fourth forming the entrance and bar area. One tunnel is now a restaurant, while another is used for functions as required. There is a quiz night on Sundays. Look out for the stoneware bottles used in the construction of the cellar walls. The house beer, Castle Blonde, is brewed by Old School. Many board games are available, and there is live music until late every Saturday evening.

Sun ✔
63 Church Street, LA1 1ET
11-midnight; 11.30-1am Fri; 11-1am Sat; 11-11.30 Sun
(01524) 66006 thesunhotelandbar.co.uk
Lancaster Amber, Blonde, Black, Red; Wainwright; 5 changing beers (often Lancaster) H
Completely altered in 2004 and then extended next door in early 2005, the decor here combines a mixture of exposed stonework, wood panelling and solid furniture, with ambient candlelight in the evenings. The original pub has open space for vertical drinking; the extension is mostly furnished with old dining tables. Some original features remain, including stone fireplaces, one with a wood-burning stove, and a well. The pub is the primary outlet for Lancaster Brewery in the city. Outside is a peaceful courtyard with a heated and covered smoking area.

Three Mariners ✔
Bridge Lane, LA1 1EE (near Parksafe car park entrance)
12-midnight (1am Fri & Sat) (01524) 388957
Oakham Citra; Robinsons Wizard, Dizzy Blonde; 7 changing beers H
Commonly claimed to be the oldest pub in Lancaster, it certainly looks old, inside as well as out, but has suffered some rebuilding; it had a comprehensive revamp in 2004. The cellar is excavated at first-floor level. The pub is now a popular watering hole with a thriving local clientele. Home-cooked, reasonably priced food is available. It has limited parking. Bluegrass is a feature on Wednesdays, and folk on the first Friday of the month. Beacon is sold as Mariner's Gold.
Q

White Cross L ✔
Quarry Road, LA1 4XT (behind town hall, on canal towpath)
11.30-11 (12.15am Fri & Sat); 12-11 Sun (01524) 33999
thewhitecross.co.uk
Salopian Shropshire Gold; Sharp's Doom Bar; Timothy Taylor Landlord; 9 changing beers (sourced regionally; often Allendale, Settle, Tirril) H
A 1988 renovation of an old canalside warehouse with an open-plan interior and a light, airy feel. French windows open on to extensive canalside seating. There is a Tuesday quiz, and a beer and pie festival each April. It stands in the corner of an extensive complex of Victorian textile mills, now converted to other uses. The wide open spaces and decor makes it look like a circuit pub, but in fact much of the custom comes either from the residential areas up the hill or from the nearby workplaces including the Adult College.
P

Lancaster University

Graduate College Bar
Bailrigg, LA2 0PF (on pedestrian square in Alexandra Park; Graduate College is signposted)
7-11; 5-11.30 Fri (01524) 592824 lancaster.ac.uk/eat/graduate.php
4 changing beers (sourced nationally) H
The Graduate College bar is much pubbier and attracts a higher age range than the usual student watering hole. The choice of beer is good, with eight handpumps. There is a beer fest in June. Curry night is Friday, and open mic night alternates with live bands on Thursday. The university bars all have alternative names; this one is Herdwick. It has pork pies and pickled eggs for sale. Opening hours are reduced in vacations. (3,4)

Lathom

Ship Inn ✔
4 Wheat Lane, L40 4BX (take School Lane from Burscough, turn right after humpbacked bridge) SD452116
12-midnight; 12-11.30 Sun (01704) 893117
shipatlathom.co.uk
House beer (by Moorhouse's); changing beers (sourced regionally; often Black Sheep, Sharp's) H
A traditional country pub in an idyllic canalside location. The cosy central bar features a real fire and separates the two dining areas, which serve pub classics through to interesting and changing specials. There is a dog-friendly boot room complete with logburner. The pub is popular all year but especially in summer with its large beer garden. A highlight is the September Beer, Pie and Sausage Festival with over 40 handpulled ales.
P (337,3A)

Leyland

Gables ✔
2 Hough Lane, PR25 2SD
12-11.30 (midnight Fri & Sat) (01772) 493077
gablesleyland.co.uk
Robinsons Dizzy Blonde; Sharp's Doom Bar; Timothy Taylor Landlord; 3 changing beers (sourced nationally) H
A red-bricked former doctor's house in the town centre, converted to a pub in the 1950s. A central bar serves two distinct drinking areas. The vault has a pool table and TVs, while the comfortable lounge has walls decorated with pictures, plates and a collection of teapots. A large wooden decking area to the front provides a pleasant outside drinking area. Although a Punch house, three pumps are free of tie and often dispense beers from smaller breweries. P

Golden Tap Ale House L
1 Chapel Brow, PR25 3NH
closed Mon; 3-10; 2-11.30 Fri & Sat; 2-10 Sun
(01772) 431859
6 changing beers H
Located in a former shop, The Golden Tap opened its doors in 2016 and is a cosy one-roomed micropub (one of two in Leyland). Six changing cask ales are served, usually including two dark beers, from microbreweries far and wide, but usually at least one from the local region. No food is served other than a few snacks, but the pub is right in the heart of the town's fast food and takeaway area. Q (109,111)

Leyland Lion

60 Hough Lane, PR25 2SA

8am-11.30 (12.30am Fri & Sat) (01772) 643990

Greene King Abbot; Hawkshead Windermere Pale; Ruddles Best Bitter; Sharp's Doom Bar; house beer (by Moorhouse's); 6 changing beers

Opened in 2011, this conversion of a town-centre post office has recently been extended due to its popularity. Unusually for Wetherspoon, it features a central log fire. The pub's name commemorates one of the buses that made this town famous and which were built a few yards up the road. A good selection of guest beers is usually on the bar, often from local breweries, plus a real cider. The house beer, Leyland Lion, is brewed by Moorhouse's. Handy for the Commercial Vehicle Museum. Alcohol is served from 9am.

Market Ale House

33 Hough Lane, PR25 2SB

2-10 (11 Thu); 12-11 Fri & Sat; 1-8 Sun (01772) 623363

6 changing beers (sourced locally)

As the area's first micropub, it opened in 2013 in former shop premises, and at the time was Leyland's smallest pub. It is located at the entrance to the former Leyland Motors North Works, which now serves as the town's market hall. Six changing real ales come from local and national breweries. Changing ciders, wine and a few spirits are also served. Food is limited to Lancashire cheeses and pork pies. TV and music are absent. In summer tables are put on the wide pavement to create an outside drinking area. CAMRA branch Cider Pub of the Year 2016. **Q**

Little Eccleston

Cartford Inn

Cartford Lane, PR3 0YP

12-2 (not Mon), 5.30-9; 12-2, 5.30-10 Fri & Sat; 12.30-8.30 Sun (01995) 670166 thecartfordinn.co.uk

Hawkshead Lakeland Gold; Moorhouse's Pride of Pendle; Theakston Old Peculier; house beer (by Farm Yard)

Originally a 17th-century coaching inn, this multi award-winning pub, restaurant and boutique hotel is less than 10 minutes from the motorway, in an idyllic setting beside the River Wyre at the heart of rural Lancashire. The bar alcoves allow for informal dining while the River Lounge boasts panoramic riverscape views. A range of four cask beers is available, usually including a dark beer. A variety of draught continental lagers, bottled beers and ciders is also sold. Accommodation is offered in 15 luxury bedrooms. If coming from the north, do not forget your change for the toll bridge. **P**

Longridge

Hoppy Days

36A Derby Road, PR3 3JT

3-8 (9 Wed & Thu; 10 Fri); 1-10 Sat; 1-8 Sun 07772 901515

5 changing beers

A warm and friendly welcome awaits at this pleasant single-room micropub which opened in 2016. There are five handpumps serving frequently changing beers, often from small local microbreweries, in a range of strengths and styles, always including a dark ale. The beers are kept in perfect condition in a temperature-controlled area. There are also Belgian bottled beers, and wines, all served in a relaxed, convivial atmosphere. A no-swearing rule is enforced via a swear box. (1)

Tap & Vent

4 Towneley Parade, PR3 3HU

3-9 (8 Mon; 10 Fri); 2-10 Sat; 2-8 Sun (01772) 875781

4 changing beers

Opened in 2016, the Tap & Vent was the first micropub in Longridge. Situated in a row of shops on Towneley Parade, the pub has a welcoming, friendly atmosphere. Five handpumps serve a selection of four rotating cask ales, typically from microbreweries, with the fifth devoted to real cider. Craft keg and bottled beers plus fine wines and Prosecco are also available. A crafty free house encouraging the art of conversation. (1)

Longton

Dolphin

Marsh Lane, PR4 5JY

12-11; 11.30-11 Sun (01772) 612032

4 changing beers (sourced locally)

Isolated country pub, known locally as the Flying Fish, at the end of a lane on Longton Marsh, close to the Ribble Way. The cask ales can be found in the wood-floored public bar to the right of the main entrance. There is a restaurant in the rear conservatory and a large and varied menu covers everything from sandwiches to man v food challenges. Up to four handpulled real ales and a cider are available – a changing selection with an emphasis on local micros. Evening closing time is flexible dependent on trade. **P**

Lostock Hall

Anchor

Croston Road, PR5 5LA (300yds from B5254 alongside Preston-Blackburn railway line)

4.30-11.30; 4-midnight Fri; 12-midnight Sat; 1-11.30 Sun (01772) 335637

5 changing beers (sourced nationally)

Just a short distance from the Tardy Gate shopping area, this friendly community pub offers five changing cask ales which can be from across the country but are often from local breweries. In both spring and autumn a beer festival takes place (weather permitting) in marquees on a large grassy area adjacent to the pub. A traditional roast is available on Sundays only 3-5pm. **Q P**

Lytham

Craft House Beer Café

Clifton Street, FY8 5EP

closed Mon; 4-11 Tue; 2-11 Wed & Thu; 2-11.30 Fri; 1-11.30 Sat; 1-8 Sun (01253) 730512

3 changing beers (sourced regionally; often Cumbrian Legendary Ales, Hawkshead)

Formerly a bistro, this pub opened as Lytham's first micropub in the summer of 2016. The compact seating encourages conviviality and dog owners often add their animals into the social mix. There is an outside seating area on the pavement. A good range of world and British bottled beers is available, as is cider. Come and watch the world hurry by! **Q**

Taps ✓
12 Henry Street, FY8 5LE
11-11 (midnight Fri & Sat) ☎ (01253) 736226
thetaps.net
Greene King IPA; Moorhouse's Pendle Witches Brew; Morland Old Speckled Hen; Robinsons Dizzy Blonde; 6 changing beers (sourced nationally) H
A multi award-winning, longstanding Guide entry, The Taps continues to shine. A recent refurbishment has given it a more open aspect and broadened its appeal, lending a relaxed atmosphere with more seating. There is a TV for major sporting events only and a popular quiz on Monday evening. Food is home cooked from locally sourced ingredients. Children are welcome until 7.30pm, while dogs are permitted in an outdoor covered area.

Mawdesley

Red Lion L ✓
68 New Street, L40 2QP (on main road in centre of village)
12-11 (midnight Fri & Sat) ☎ (01704) 822208
redlion-mawdesley.com
Moorhouse's White Witch; 3 changing beers (often Hawkshead, Moorhouse's, Salopian) H
This small white-painted pub at the centre of the village is gaining a reputation for food, which is served in the attractive conservatory at the rear of the pub as well as in the lounge bar. There is a small public bar with a cosy real fire in winter. Guest beers are from the Enterprise list and change regularly. Regulars have a preference for pale and golden beers below 4% ABV and the beers served reflect this. P (347,337)

Morecambe

Eric Bartholomew ✓
10 Euston Road, LA4 5DD
8am-11 (midnight Fri & Sat) ☎ (01524) 405860
Greene King Abbot; Ruddles Best Bitter; Sharp's Doom Bar; 3 changing beers (often Cross Bay) H
Opened in 2004, this Wetherspoon pub is dedicated to Eric Morecambe (born Eric Bartholomew). The pub near the seafront functions on two levels, with an upstairs lounge and dining area. The long bar services an open-plan pub with pictures of 19th-century Morecambe and some artwork with a Morecambe and Wise theme. Some outside seating is at the front for smokers, but no drinking is allowed. Close to shops and a public car park. Q

Little Bare 🏆
23 Princes Crescent, LA4 6BY
closed Mon; 5-9 Tue-Thu; 3-9 Fri; 12-9 Sat; 12-6 Sun
☎ 07490 690179
5 changing beers H
A micropub opened in 2017 in a former off-licence and retaining the shop window. It features grey paint, bare floorboards and candles after dark, and follows the micropub formula: no food, no music, no machines. There is a second room down a corridor with extra seating and board games. A microgarden is planned, which may be open when you read this. (Bare Lane)

Morecambe ✓
25 Lord Street, LA4 5HX
12-11 ☎ (01524) 415239 themorecambehotel.co.uk
Cross Bay Halo; 4 changing beers H
The place to come if you want a choice of Cross Bay beers. Reopened in 2015 after renovation in contemporary style, it is light and airy, and has flagged floors and a variety of seating and tables. The bar is faced with unplaned wood, and has four rooms around a bar and a surprisingly spacious garden. Screens show videos of 20th-century Morecambe. For most of the day, food dominates. The name is not hubris: this was a coaching inn built long before there was a town called Morecambe.

Palatine ✓
The Crescent, LA4 5BZ (overlooking prom opp clock tower)
12-11 (midnight Fri & Sat) ☎ (01524) 410503
thepalatinemorecambe.co.uk
Lancaster Blonde; 3 changing beers (often Lancaster) H
An Edwardian seafront mid-terrace pub. The ground floor was completely transformed in late 2008 with much bare stone and woodwork. The bar room is quite small, with some intimate corners and music most evenings. An upstairs room is rather different. Cosy and carpeted, many of the fittings – leaded lights, shelving, fireplace – appear to be original. Enjoy the spectacular views across the Bay, especially at sunset. There are seats on the pavement in front.

Much Hoole

Th'owd Smithy Inn ✓
133 Liverpool Old Road, PR4 4GB
4 (12 Wed & Thu)-11.30; 12-midnight Fri & Sat; 12-10.30 Sun ☎ (01772) 614844
Moorhouse's White Witch; Robinsons Cumbria Way; 2 changing beers H
A traditional village pub in appearance, the interior has been completely opened out to create one large room for drinkers. Once the smallest of three pubs in the village, this is now the only survivor. It is located on the Liverpool Old Road which runs parallel to the main A59. Live music plays on Saturday, quiz night is Tuesday. Snacks are available. P (2)

Ormskirk

Court Leet ✓
4 Wheatsheaf Walk, L39 2XA
8am-12.30am (1am Thu-Sat) ☎ (01695) 579803
Greene King 1799; Ruddles Best Bitter; 10 changing beers (often Cross Bay, Moorhouse's, Weetwood) H
Opened in 2014, this Wetherspoon pub is in the centre of Ormskirk in a small courtyard area off Burscough Street. It has a large open-plan main bar area fitted out in a contemporary style. Virtually the entire upper floor is taken up by a fully exposed terrace which includes a no-smoking area. It is thought the pub occupies the site where the Court Leet met, which was responsible for running the town's affairs until 1876. A lift is available.

Cricketers 🏆 L
24 Chapel Street, L39 4QF
12-midnight; 12-11 Sun ☎ (01695) 571123
thecricketers-ormskirk.co.uk

Thwaites Nutty Black, Wainwright; 4 changing beers (sourced regionally; often Blackedge, Mobberley, Old School) Ⓗ
Close to Ormskirk town centre, the pub prides itself both on quality food and cask ales; the six cask ales come from local and regional breweries. The extensive food menu is served all day in its restaurant or bar area. Cricket memorabilia around its walls reflect its close relationship with Ormskirk cricket club, as does the successful Ormskirk Food and Drink Festival run each September, featuring over 60 cask ales. P (375,385)

Tap Room No.12

12 Burscough Street, L39 2ER
closed Mon; 11-11; 12-8 Sun ☎ (01695) 575907
Hawkshead Windermere Pale; 3 changing beers (sourced regionally) Ⓗ
Formerly a shop, this is now a single room bar featuring four regional cask ales – Windermere Pale and three changing brews – plus an extensive range of local and international bottled beers and craft beers on tap. There is a quiz every Wednesday, open mic on Thursday and live music Saturday and Sunday.

Orrell

Delph Tavern

Tontine Road, WN5 8UJ
11.30-11.30 (12.30am Fri & Sat) ☎ (01695) 622239
5 changing beers Ⓗ
Free house popular with locals and visitors that serves five varying ales with an emphasis on local breweries. Food is available daily and offers a balance of traditional pub classics alongside innovative street food. Live sports are shown on a number of unobtrusive screens while a vault area offers pool and darts. Weekly quiz nights are popular. The outside space offers a small play area as well as tables to enjoy food and drinks.
P

Overton

Ship

9 Main Street, LA3 3HD
closed Mon & Tue; 5-10 (11 Fri); 4-11 Sat; 3-10 Sun
☎ 07979 030196
4 changing beers Ⓗ
Restored in 2016 to Victorian basics (bar and fittings, decorative floor tiles). Traces of 20th-century alterations have almost vanished but there remain four quite distinct public rooms, one a games room. A space between two of them is occupied by a wood-burning stove, with upholstered bench seating around the walls and café-style tables in the middle. The white and beige walls display paintings for sale. No food is served except on special booked nights. Upstairs are two function rooms, one with famous displays of birds eggs. QP (5)

Padiham

Hare & Hounds

58 West Street, BB12 8JD
4-11; 12-midnight Sat; 12-10.30 Sun ☎ (01282) 545308
10 changing beers (sourced regionally) Ⓗ
An award-winning true free house rescued from pub company mismanagement, now thriving and selling an excellent choice of beers – four during the week rising to 10 at the weekend – alongside a changing real cider. Two rooms front the large bar, with a large separate room to one side where beer festivals are held. There are real fires in all rooms. A large beer garden to the rear and a small seating area to the front complete this warm friendly pub. Adjacent to Padiham FC and cricket club.
P (M2,152)

Parbold

Railway Hotel

1 Station Road, WN8 7NU
5-11; 12-11.30 Fri & Sat; 12-10.30 Sun ☎ (01257) 462917
railwayhotelparbold.co.uk
Tetley Bitter; 4 changing beers (sourced locally; often Hophurst, Problem Child, Prospect) Ⓗ
A former Marston's inn now privately owned, this non-food pub is frequented by locals, with the emphasis on excellent beer and hospitality. There is a central drinking area and two small rooms to either side. A coal fire adds to the ambience in winter together with comfy seats and sofas. There is a large-screen TV and pool table set back. The pub sells one regular beer, Tetley Bitter, and four changing locally sourced ales.
QP

Wayfarer Inn

1-3 Alder Lane, WN8 7NL
12-2, 5-10; 12-10 Sat & Sun ☎ (01257) 464600
wayfarerparbold.co.uk
Problem Child Good Spankin'; 5 changing beers Ⓗ
A country pub with a focus on dining, serving ale from six handpulls and a range of craft keg beers. Landlord and brewer Jonny Birkett is happy to show you around his on-site microbrewery, Problem Child Brewing. The pub has low beamed ceilings with cosy nooks and crannies. It is popular with walkers, being close to the Leeds-Liverpool Canal and Parbold Hill; suitable walks are shown on the website. It has a countryside beer garden with pleasant views. QP

Pendleton

Swan With Two Necks

Main Street, BB7 1PT (off A59 nr Clitheroe)
12-2.30 (not Mon), 6-11; 12-11 Sat; 12-8 Sun
☎ (01200) 423112 swanwithtwonecks.co.uk
5 changing beers (sourced regionally; often Prospect, Rat)
Britain's best pub in 2013 (CAMRA National Pub of the Year winner) and one that continues to regularly win awards. It is in the centre of the village and is very much the centre of village life, having been family run for over 30 years. A dark mild is always on one of the six handpulls, along with a real cider or perry. Third-of-a-pint beer bats are offered, and good-quality, reasonably priced meals. QP

Penwortham

Black Bull Inn

83 Pope Lane, PR1 9BA
11-11 (midnight Fri; 11.30 Sat); 12-11 Sun
☎ (01772) 752953 blackbull-penwortham.co.uk/ales
Robinsons Dizzy Blonde; Theakston Best Bitter, Lightfoot; 2 changing beers (sourced nationally) Ⓗ
Attractive cottage-style inn dating back to the early 1800s, which has managed to retain a village pub

atmosphere despite its location in a well-populated area. On entering, a narrow passageway leads through to a central bar serving a number of drinking areas including a separate public bar. It is a friendly community pub which actively supports local charities. It is also a Cask Marque Excellence award winner. One of the guest ales will be from the SIBA list and comes from a local brewery.
Q❀♣P🚌🐾

Poulton le Fylde

Old Town Hall ✔

5 Church Street, FY6 7AP

11-midnight (1am Fri & Sat); 12-11.30 Sun
☎ (01253) 892257

6 changing beers (sourced locally; often Kirkby Lonsdale, Moorhouse's, Rooster's) H

Originally a pub called the Bay Horse, for most of the 20th century it was used as council offices. TV screens cater for racing fans every day and football fans whenever there is a match on. The rear portion has a mural featuring former Blackpool footballers and a small stage area where bands play each Saturday. Last orders are called 30 minutes before closing time. ♿⇌♣🚌🐾

Poulton Elk ✔

22 Hardhorn Road, FY6 7SR

8am-midnight (1am Fri & Sat) ☎ (01253) 895265

Greene King Abbot; Ruddles Best Bitter; Sharp's Doom Bar; 7 changing beers (sourced nationally; often Bradfield, Phoenix, Saltaire) H

On the outskirts of the town centre, with a varied clientele, this busy, single-roomed pub is cleverly subdivided to provide a number of quieter areas. There is a terrace at the front and a suntrap dog-friendly beer garden with smoking shelters overlooking a large public car park at the rear. It is named after the nearby discovery of a 13,000-year-old elk skeleton accompanied by two spear points, the earliest evidence of people living in north-west England. ❀◑♿⇌🍏🚌

Thatched House ✔

30 Ball Street, FY6 7BG

11.30-11 (midnight Fri & Sat); 12-11 Sun
☎ (01253) 891063

Chapel Street Brewhouse Blonde, Cream Stout, Double Hopped; 7 changing beers (sourced regionally; often Bradfield, Rooster's, Saltaire) H

This place was built on the site of a thatched building at the start of the 20th century. Ten beers are on the bar, three from the Chapel Street Brewhouse, housed in the former stables at the back of the pub, and the remaining seven from a changing range. Wood-panelled throughout and decorated with pictures of past sporting heroes and often noisy with chatter, the pub is warmed in winter by log-burning stoves and a log fire.
Q❀⇌♣🚌🐾

Preston

Black Horse ★ ✔

166 Friargate, PR1 2EJ

11-11 (midnight Fri); 10.30-midnight Sat; 12-11 Sun
☎ (01772) 204855

Robinsons Dizzy Blonde, Unicorn, Trooper, Old Tom; 4 changing beers (sourced nationally) H

Classic Victorian Grade II-listed pub in the main shopping area close to the historic open market. With its tiled bar, walls and mosaic floor, it has a nationally important historic pub interior. The two front rooms with real log fires are adorned with Robinsons memorabilia and photos of old Preston. The famous hall of mirrors seating area is to the rear. Four Robinsons beers are served, with different guest beers coming from far and wide, supplied through Titanic. An upstairs function room is available to hire, plus there is a smoking terrace.
⇌♣🍏🚌🐾

Continental

South Meadow Lane, PR1 8JP

12-11 (12.30am Fri & Sat) ☎ (01772) 499425

House beer (by Fernandes); 6 changing beers (sourced nationally) H

Beside the River Ribble, the main railway line and Miller Park, the pub has a main bar area plus a lounge with a real fire in winter and a conservatory overlooking the garden. Live music and theatre regularly feature in a separate events space which is also used to house beer festivals. It has seven handpumps, with a cider and up to six microbrewery beers including the house ale from Fernandes and a dark beer. Freshly cooked meals are served daily except Monday. A two-times winner of local CAMRA Pub of the Year.
Q❀◑♿⇌🍏P🐾

Guild Ale House 🏆 L ✔

56 Lancaster Road, PR1 1DD

12-9.30 (10 Thu; 11 Fri & Sat); 12-10 Sun ☎ 07932 517444

7 changing beers (sourced locally; often Dark Star, Phoenix, Reedley Hallows) H

A larger than usual micropub opened in February 2016, the first in Preston, and a few doors away from Preston's Guild Hall complex. The main room has high and low level seating and the tall ceilings give a light and airy feel. A small lounge is tucked away to the rear of the bar and there is a comfortable lounge upstairs. Seven changing beers are on the bar, mainly local or from Yorkshire, and at least one dark beer, as well as a range of continental beers in keg and bottle. It has no jukebox, music, TV, or food, but live jazz or blues is played on Sunday afternoons.
Q❀♿⇌♣🍏🚌🐾

Mad Hatters

53 Fylde Road, PR1 2XQ

12-11 ☎ (01772) 379534

10 changing beers (sourced nationally) H

A genuine free house serving 10 guest beers from microbreweries. It has a comfortable single-room bar set back from Fylde Road at the side of the unrelated Ferret pub. There is a pool table and darts in the area behind the bar and three large sports screens. Live music ranging from jazz to blues plays five nights a week. An upstairs room is also available for hire. Although surrounded by university buildings, it is not primarily a student bar. It changed its name from Ale Emporium to Mad Hatters in February 2018.
◑♿♣🍏🚌(35,68)

Moorbrook

370 North Road, PR1 1RU

12-midnight ☎ (01772) 823302 🌐 themoorbrook.com

Thwaites Original; house beer (by Blackjack); 7 changing beers (sourced nationally) H

Now privately owned, this pub is where the West Lancs CAMRA branch was formed in 1973. It has a traditional style wood-panelled bar with two rooms off the main bar area. The beer garden to the rear is a sun trap. Food now includes authentic wood-fired pizzas. Seven guest beers are served from all over the country plus Thwaites Original. The house beer, Moorbrook Pale Ale, is brewed specifically for the pub by Blackjack of Manchester. The pub gets busy on Preston North End match days.

Old Vic

79 Fishergate, PR1 2UH
10-11 (midnight Fri); 11-midnight Sat; 12-11.30 Sun
(01772) 828519
Bombardier; 6 changing beers H
Opposite the railway station, and on bus routes into the city, this is a popular pub that can get busy at weekends. A number of TVs show sports events and this is a rare city-centre pub for darts enthusiasts. To the rear is an outdoor decked smoking area and a car park that is only available on Sunday and in the evenings. Seven handpumps offer a good range of beers, with local microbreweries usually represented. Real ale carryouts are available, as are third-of-a-pint taster paddles. Accepts CAMRA Wetherspoon's vouchers. P

Plungington Hotel

67 Lytham Road, Fulwood, PR2 3AR
12-11; 12-midnight Fri-Sun (01772) 712000
theplungingtonhotel.com
House beer (by Jennings); 4 changing beers H
Traditional family-friendly community pub with a large lounge and real fires, traditional pub games and a welcoming atmosphere. The pub has six handpumps in total, with two house beers by Caledonian and Jennings and four changing guest ales. Unusual beers from microbreweries are often available, plus real cider. It has possibly the largest beer garden in Preston. Live music and other events often feature. P(23)

Princess Alice

29-31 Cambridge Walk, PR1 7SL
4.30-11.30 (12.30am Fri); 12-12.30am Sat; 12-11.30 Sun
(01772) 823737
Lancaster Blonde; 3 changing beers H
Warm and friendly Victorian street-corner local in a redeveloped residential area. The ornate tilework reflects the former Matthew Brown brewery ownership. The interior has been modernised and opened out. A large number of TV screens show multiple (often sports) channels. The pub is only 10 minutes' walk from Deepdale stadium and is popular on match days. Beers are normally from small Lancashire breweries, often Lancaster, Snowhill and Wily Fox. P(23)

Twelve Tellers

14-15 Church Street, PR1 3BQ
8am-midnight (1am Thu; 2am Fri & Sat)
(01772) 550910
Greene King Abbot; Moorhouse's Pendle Witches Brew; Ruddles Best Bitter; Sharp's Doom Bar; 7 changing beers (sourced nationally) H
This is a conversion of what was the Trustee Savings Bank into a large, mostly open-plan pub with some small rooms and alcoves. It retains some features of its previous life, including its ornate ceiling and bank vaults. It has two extensively wood-panelled former boardrooms available for functions, and attractive toilets, especially the Ladies, which has retained original copper work. There is a large rear patio with smoking and no-smoking areas. Quiet until 5pm, DJs play from 10pm Thursday to Saturday. Expect bouncers on the door on weekend evenings when more formal dress is required.

Wellington

40 Glovers Court, PR1 3LS (down hill from Waterstones on corner, towards Avenham car park, on right)
11-midnight (1am Thu-Sat); 12-9 Sun (01772) 821288
wellingtoninn.co.uk
4 changing beers (often Brakspear, Marston's)
A busy city-centre pub with a small snug on the right and three other seating areas leading off from the bar. A conservatory and an extensive outdoor smoking area are to the rear, and it has a coal fire in winter. It was refurbished in 2017 to develop the outside areas. It now has a new menu, and can get busy lunchtimes. There are four handpumps with four changing beers, all from the extended Marston's range. Discounts are offered for students and pensioners. Quiz night is Tuesday.

Wheatsheaf

50 Water Lane, Ashton-on-Ribble, PR2 2NL
11-11 (11.30 Fri & Sat); 12-10.30 Sun (01772) 725917
5 changing beers (sourced nationally; often Moorhouse's) H
Victorian local on the way to Preston marina, a mile from the city centre, where beer prices are among the lowest in the area. It is big on TV sports, and live music plays Friday and Saturday nights. There is wheelchair access through the courtyard, which has outdoor seating with a TV screen, heating and a pizza oven. Five guest beers usually include at least one from Moorhouse's, otherwise they come from anywhere in the country.

Rawtenstall

Hop Micro Pub

70 Bank Street, BB4 8EG
10-midnight (9 Mon; 10 Tue & Wed); 11-9 Sun
07753 775150 hopmicropubs.com
Deeply Vale Hop; 5 changing beers H
A micropub with a big heart. On Rawtenstall's cobbled Bank Street, Hop conjures up a pleasant and congenial venue more reminiscent of the traditional local pub. It is spread across three levels, with a heated outdoor drinking area. With six handpulled cask ales, including the permanent Hop from Deeply Vale, as well as craft keg beers and ciders, there is always a fantastic choice. Close to the northern terminus of East Lancs Heritage Railway.

Rufford

Hesketh Arms

81 Liverpool Road, L40 1SB (on A59 at jct with B5246)
12-11 (midnight Fri & Sat) (01704) 821002
Moorhouse's White Witch, Pride of Pendle; 7 changing beers (sourced regionally; often Cross Bay, Phoenix, Reedley Hallows) H
A spacious former Greenall's inn on the A59, the Hesketh is now a free house serving up to six ales, mostly from local microbreweries. Set in a charming village, it is near to the National Trust property of Rufford Old Hall, the delightful St Mary's Marina, and the popular Mere Sands nature reserve. A large split-level establishment with

several dining areas, the pub serves good-quality food throughout the day. Monthly live entertainment and a Tuesday quiz attract a mixed clientele. Q P (2A,347)

St Annes

Fifteens at St Annes

42 St Annes Road West, FY8 1RF
11-11 (midnight Fri & Sat); 12.30-11.30 Sun
(01253) 725852
House beer (by Moorhouse's); 4 changing beers (sourced regionally)
Set in a former Lloyds Bank, this quirky pub is larger than it first appears. Eclectically decorated, it incorporate many of the bank's original features, including the vault, complete with safe, which is both comfortable and peaceful. Popular with locals and visitors alike, there is regular live music at weekends. Beers are mostly from local and regional brewers.

No.10 Ale House

10 Park Road, FY8 1QX
12-11 (midnight Fri & Sat) 07809 368682
5 changing beers (sourced locally; often Bank Top, Moorhouse's, Reedley Hallows)
Handy for the railway station and near to the shopping in St Anne's Square, this cosy and friendly micropub serves at least five beers, mainly from local and regional brewers, and a small range of ciders. Bar snacks are available. Decorated with retro Blackpool tourism posters and with no television, this pub is a little real ale haven. Opening times may vary, phone ahead to check if making a special visit. Q

St Annes Cricket Club

Vernon Road, FY8 2RQ (road access from Highbury Rd East)
4-11; 12-midnight Sat; 12-11 Sun (01253) 721849
stannescricketclub.org
Lees Bitter; 2 changing beers (sourced regionally)
A spacious modern clubhouse, popular in the local area, with views onto the pitch where Andrew Flintoff made his first team début at the age of 15. A full social calendar includes ladies' nights, live music and sportsmen's dinners as well as a summer beer festival with real ciders. Darts, snooker and dominoes teams play in local leagues. There is hard standing for caravans with facilities available. Food is served Saturday until 7pm and Sunday until 6pm. P (17,77)

Trawl Boat

36-38 Wood Street, FY8 1QR
8am-midnight (1am Fri & Sat) (01253) 783080
Greene King Abbot; Ruddles Best Bitter; Sharp's Doom Bar; 7 changing beers (sourced regionally; often Bank Top, Lytham, Moorhouse's)
The pub name recalls an old inn used by fishermen in what was then a sparsely populated area, well out of town. The original building still stands but is no longer a pub. A homely, friendly atmosphere greets locals and visitors alike. It can get busy at weekends and the designated family area is popular. Spacious outdoor seating is attractive in summer months. Seven changing guest beers and two real ciders are always on tap. Handy for shops, the railway station and the beach.

Victoria

Church Road, FY8 3NE
12-11 (midnight Thu-Sat) (01253) 721041
victoriahotel-lytham-stannes.co.uk
Draught Bass; Greene King IPA; 4 changing beers (sourced nationally)
This magnificent, late Victorian building was saved from demolition by local activists only a few years ago. It recently received a complete refurbishment. The main bar opens out into separate drinking and dining areas. There is a separate taproom and snooker room where community and pub sports are enjoying a revival. The big-screen TV is not too intrusive. Food is served all day.
P (11,68)

Scarisbrick

Heatons Bridge Inn

2 Heatons Bridge Road, L40 8JG (on B5242 by Leeds-Liverpool Canal)
12-midnight (01704) 840549
Moorhouse's Black Cat; 2 changing beers (sourced regionally; often George Wright, Wily Fox)
A canalside pub dating from 1837, when it served as offices for the Leeds and Liverpool freight services. It is traditional, with separate areas and home-cooked food. Pillbox beer is often served as a reminder of WWII. There is a lookout post outside. Twice-yearly military displays and annual classic bus services prevail, with themed beers for the occasion. This is a popular pub with families, walkers and cyclists, in an excellent rural setting, and it has a garden with a dining area.
(375)

Silverdale

Woodlands

Woodlands Drive, LA5 0RU
5-11.30; 12-midnight Sat; 12-11.30 Sun
(01524) 701655
4 changing beers
A large country house on an elevated site dating from about 1878 and converted to a pub with only minimal alterations. Most of the trade is provided by locals. The bar has a large fireplace as big as the counter and enjoys great views across Morecambe Bay. The beer pumps are in another room, with a list of the four available ales on the wall facing the bar. Home-made sandwiches are served at weekends. It stages a beer festival of 30 ales in October and has a quiz on the last Sunday of the month. To telephone the pub you need to ring twice. Q P

Slaidburn

Hark to Bounty

Townend, BB7 3EP
8am-11; closed Tue (01200) 446246
Theakston Best Bitter, Old Peculier; 2 changing beers (sourced regionally)
Parts of this ancient pub date from the 1300s, and it is ideally situated for walkers, cyclists and those touring rural Lancashire. There are always four real ales on offer and the food is proper pub grub. Check food service times before you arrive. Fish night is Friday. Real fires in winter make this a welcoming pub. Ask for the key to see the old courtroom on the first floor.
Q P (10)

Tockholes

Royal Arms

Tockholes Road, Rydal Fold, BB3 0PA

closed Mon; 12-11; 12-10.30 Sun (01254) 705373

4 changing beers (sourced regionally; often Hopstar) H

Traditional free house formed from two cottages knocked together. It is small but has a great atmosphere within its four back-to-back rooms, where the original stone walls, real fires and flagged and wooden floors have been retained. Beers are from local microbreweries. In the West Pennine Moors, close to Darwen Tower and adjacent to Roddlesworth Visitors Centre, it looks over moors, woods and reservoirs. Friendly staff welcome walkers, cyclists, ramblers and dogs alike, and offer a good food menu. Opening hours may vary in winter. Q P

Waddington

Lower Buck Inn

Edisford Road, BB7 3HU (behind parish church)

12-11 (01200) 423342 thelowerbuck.com

Bowland Hen Harrier; Moorhouse's Premier Bitter; Timothy Taylor Landlord; 3 changing beers (sourced regionally) H

A small and cosy traditional 18th-century stone-built pub in a lovely village steeped in history. Family friendly, this multi-roomed pub features several rooms with open fires and a flagged bar area. Food is served lunchtime and evenings (not Mon) and all day weekends. Popular with walkers, dogs are welcome and there is an outdoor seating area at the front looking across to the church. Accommodation is available in an adjoining cottage. Q P (66,67)

Walton-le-Dale

White Bull

109 Victoria Road, PR5 4BA

12-11.30 (midnight Fri & Sat); 12-12.30am Sun

Wainwright; 3 changing beers (sourced locally; often Cross Bay, Hopstar, Three B's) H

A true community local retaining the original multi-room layout with a bar area and lounge at the front, a games room with pool table and dartboard and a small lounge behind the bar. There is a small seating area on the paving at the front of the building. This cosy pub serves three guest beers, usually from local micros, and can get busy at weekends. P

Wesham

Stanley Arms

8 Garstang Road South, PR4 3BL

3 (12 Thu & Fri)-midnight; 11-midnight Sat; 10-midnight Sun (01772) 469495 stanleyarmswesham.co.uk

Sharp's Doom Bar, Atlantic; 2 changing beers (sourced nationally) H

A friendly street-corner pub close to Fox's biscuit factory and half a mile from the AFC Fylde Mill Farm complex. The open-plan layout was refurbished two years ago with a fine wooden bar at its centre. It has the longest-serving landlord in town and a benign resident ghost. A hub for many local activities, it extends a warm welcome to all. Open for breakfast and coffee from 10am on Sunday. (Kirkham & Wesham)

Wheelton

Red Lion

Blackburn Road, PR6 8EU (opp clock tower)

11-11 (11.30 Wed & Thu; 12.30am Fri & Sat) (01254) 659890 theredlionatwheelton.co.uk

Coniston Bluebird Bitter; Timothy Taylor Landlord; 7 changing beers (sourced nationally; often Durham, Hawkshead, Oakham) H

Built around 1826, this authentic pub reflects the former mill village it used to serve. Previously a Matthew Brown house, the bar retains the Lion Ales windows and a large stone lion at roof level above the door. It has a comfortable lounge with an open fire and a second room up a few steps. The single bar serves nine varying real ales from breweries large and small. P (24)

Worsthorne

Crooked Billet

1-3 Smith Street, BB10 3NQ

7 (6 Thu)-midnight; 4.30-1am Fri; 12-1am Sat; 12-12.30am Sun 07766 230175 crookedbilletworsthorne.co.uk

Tetley Bitter; Timothy Taylor Boltmaker, Landlord; 4 changing beers (sourced regionally; often Worsthorne) H

An award-winning true free house, this well-presented village pub has a beautiful wood and glass horseshoe bar serving both the main lounge area and snug, and acts as the Worsthorne brewery tap. Quiz nights are popular, as are Thai nights and soul nights. It has a large covered outdoor drinking area where you can enjoy the flower-bedecked exterior. Q P (2)

Wrightington

White Lion

117 Mossy Lea Road, WN6 9RE

10-11 (01257) 425977 thewhitelionlancs.co.uk

Jennings Cumberland Ale; Banks Amber; 6 changing beers H

This popular country inn has a good range of food and beers for diners and drinkers, with eight handpumps. The pub runs a Monday Club with drinks offers, a quiz on Tuesday, a poker league on Thursday, a monthly cocktail night and live music every Saturday. It is family friendly with board games and a large beach hut-themed garden area. It is also community orientated, running the village scarecrow festival and themed evenings throughout the year. Q P (113)

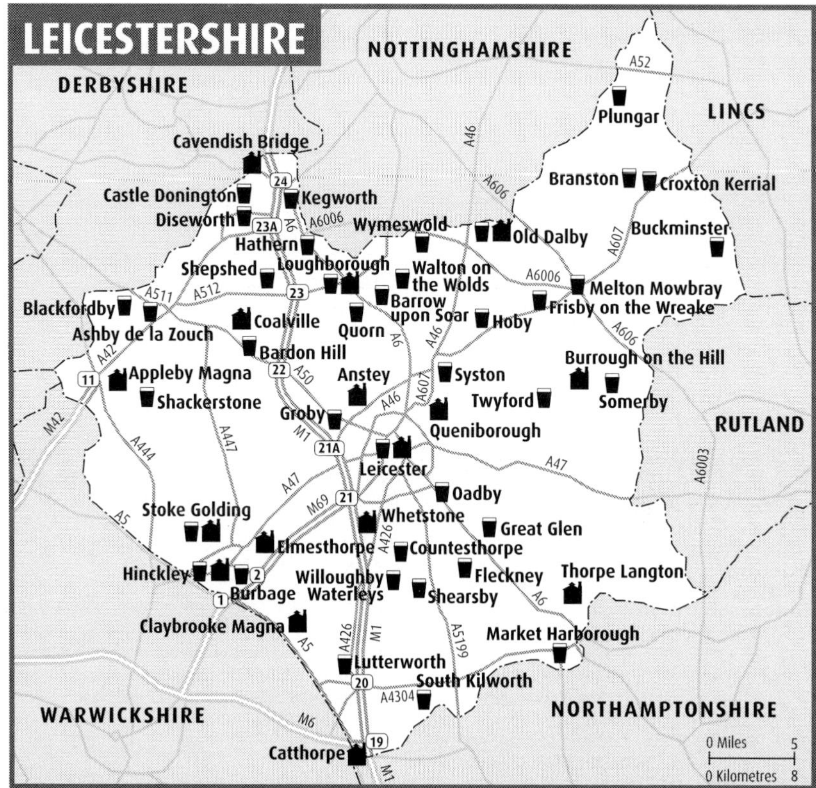

Everards Brewery closed July 2017 for relocation. Its beers are currently brewed by Joules and Robinsons

Ashby de la Zouch

Tap at No.76

76 Market Street, LE65 1AP

closed Mon; 4-11 Tue & Wed; 12-11 Thu (midnight Fri & Sat); 12-10 Sun thetapatno76.co.uk

Tollgate Ashby Pale; 6 changing beers Ⓗ

This micropub, on the high street, has a 'hipster' serving area and is a relatively recent addition to the Ashby scene. A Tollgate Brewery pub, it offers seven real ales – four handpump, three gravity. Third-pint tasting trays are available for those wishing to try the whole range of beers. Pork pies are served.

Bardon Hill

Birch Tree

Bardon Road, LE67 1TD

12-3, 5-11; 12-10.30 Sun ☎ (01530) 832134

Everards Tiger, Old Original; Morland Old Speckled Hen; 2 changing beers (sourced locally; often Everards, Titanic) Ⓗ

On a roundabout on the A511 (old A50), close to Bardon Hill Quarry on the southern outskirts of Coalville. This multi-roomed, family-friendly and beautifully decorated pub is as proud of its food as it is of its well-kept beer. Titanic Plum Porter is often available during the winter. Events are held throughout the year, including a mini steam rally.

P

Barrow upon Soar

Soar Bridge Inn

29 Bridge Street, LE12 8PN

12 (4 Mon)-11; 12-10.30 Sun ☎ (01509) 412686

Everards Tiger, Old Original; 4 changing beers (often Everards) Ⓗ

Situated next to the bridge that gave it its name, this pub is popular with walkers, boaters and drinkers. The large single-room interior divides into distinct areas, with a separate restaurant, function room and skittle alley. Outside there is a floodlit pétanque court, beer terrace and garden. Well-behaved dogs and children are welcome. Home-made food is available Tuesday to Sunday, with a different theme each evening.

Q P (K2,CB27)

Blackfordby

Black Lion

3 Main Street, DE11 8AB

3-11 (1am Fri); 12-1am Sat; 12-11 Sun ☎ (01283) 337551

theblacklionblackfordby.com

Draught Bass; 5 changing beers (sourced locally; often Blue Monkey, Derby) Ⓗ

Popular local in a quiet village in north-west Leicestershire, bought from Enterprise Inns and reopened in 2013 as a free house following a substantial refurbishment. Grade II listed with old beams and open fires, it has a lovely courtyard and covered smoking area. Guest beers are often sourced from small local breweries, and up to four ciders are on draught. Cheeseboards and ham and cheese cobs are available. Quiz night is the first Sunday of each month, jam night the last Wednesday. Q

Branston

Wheel Inn

Main Street, NG32 1RU

12-11; 12-8 Sun ☎ (01476) 870376

thewheelinnbranston.co.uk

Black Sheep Best Bitter; 2 changing beers H

This attractive stone-built 18th-century village pub houses a cosy bar with seating plus a larger restaurant with rustic tables and a real fire. The outdoor area is quiet and relaxing in the summer months, with traditional outbuildings used for beer festivals and live music. The Wheel boasts an extensive food menu using locally sourced ingredients where possible, including produce from the Belvoir Estate. Cask cider is usually available on the bar. A former local CAMRA Pub of the Year. Q P

Buckminster

Tollemache Arms

48 Main Street, NG33 5SA

closed Mon; 11-3, 6-11; 11-11 Sat; 12-5 Sun

☎ (01476) 860477 tollemache-arms.co.uk

Oakham JHB; 3 changing beers H

This beautiful building is at the heart of what was the Tollemache family estate, with the rows of stone buildings featuring heavily in this picturesque village. Three cask ales are available, including local offerings. The pub serves food lunchtimes and evenings, is family- and dog-friendly and popular with locals and tourists alike. P

Burbage

Burbage & District Constitutional Club

Church Street, LE10 2DE

11-2, 6-11; 11-11.30 Fri (11.45 Sat); 12-3, 7-11 Sun

☎ (01455) 615142 burbageconclub1911.com

Greene King Abbot; Marston's Saddle Tank; 3 changing beers (often Church End, Grainstore) H

Formerly the home of Prime Minister George Canning, the club was founded in 1911. This Grade II listed building, in the heart of the village, features a comfortable lounge with open fire, wheelchair access, garden, function room equipped with a skittle alley, snooker and pool tables, darts, dominoes, crib, chess and table tennis. Live music plays every Saturday night. Sandwiches and cobs are available. A frequent branch CAMRA Club of the Year and East Midlands Club of the Year in 2017.

Lime Kilns

Watling Street, LE10 3ED

12-3, 5.30-11; 12-11 Sat; 12-10.30 Sun ☎ (01455) 631158

limekilnsinn.co.uk

Black Sheep Best Bitter; Fuller's London Pride; Marston's Pedigree; St Austell Tribute; 2 changing beers (sourced locally) H

Situated alongside the Ashby Canal and the A5, the pub was originally an 18th-century coaching inn. It offers free garden-side moorings and a large canalside beer garden with a marquee. The first-floor lounge has canal views and an open fire in winter. A ground floor canalside stable bar, with a woodburner in winter, opens to the beer garden. The guest beers change regularly alongside seven real ciders, often from Thatchers and Westons. Traditional food is served, with special deals Monday to Thursday evenings. Local CAMRA branch Pub of the Year 2016. Q P

Castle Donington

Chequered Flag

32 Borough Street, DE74 2LA

closed Mon; 4-10.30 (11 Fri & Sat); 12-5 Sun

☎ 07841 374441

House beer (by Dancing Duck) G**; 6 changing beers** H

A thriving micropub in the heart of a busy street. It serves real ale straight from the cask, visible from a temperature-controlled cool-room cellar. A range of eight ciders and quality wines is also kept. Award-winning local pork pies and pickles can be enjoyed with your beer, subject to availability. Bus routes on the Skylink services make it accessible from Derby, Nottingham, Loughborough and Leicester. Q

Countesthorpe

Railway

128 Station Road, LE8 5TD

5-midnight; 3-midnight Fri; 12-midnight Sat & Sun

☎ (0116) 277 3551

Draught Bass; Greene King Abbot; Marston's Pedigree; 1 changing beer (sourced nationally; often Bradfield) H

Close to the site of Countesthorpe railway station which fell under the Beeching axe on New Year's Day 1962. A cul-de-sac near the pub is aptly named Beeching's Close and the gardens of nearby houses meet with the boundary of the old line. The interior was refurbished in 2017 and comprises a front lounge bar, which appears to be two rooms knocked into one, stretching the full width of the front elevation, and a similar-sized back public bar with skittles table and darts. P (85)

Croxton Kerrial

Geese & Fountain

1 School Lane, NG32 1QR

REAL ALE BREWERIES

Anstey Ale Anstey
Belvoir Old Dalby
Charnwood Loughborough
Co Pilot Whetstone
Dow Bridge Catthorpe
Elliswood Hinckley
Elmesthorpe Elmesthorpe (NEW)
Framework Leicester
Golden Duck Appleby Magna
Langton Thorpe Langton
Market Bosworth Stoke Golding
Mount St Bernard Coalville (NEW)
O'Brien Whetstone
Parish Burrough on the Hill
Pig Pub Claybrooke Magna
Q Queniborough
Shardlow Cavendish Bridge
West End Leicester

11-11; 12-10.30 Sun (01476) 870350
thegeeseandfountain.co.uk
5 changing beers H
This village inn reopened in 2016 after a long period of closure. With wood fires, a flagstone floor and rustic seating, it has a quiet, relaxed atmosphere. Dogs, children, cyclists and walkers are all welcome. Local breweries always feature on the five handpumps, plus guest beers from other local microbreweries, brewed lagers and three real ciders. B&B rooms are available and food is served every day. Occasional mini beer and cider festivals feature throughout the year, and regular live music nights. Local CAMRA Pub of the Year 2018.
Q P

Diseworth

Plough

33 Hall Gate, DE74 2QJ
11.30-11 (midnight Fri & Sat); 12-10.30 Sun
(01332) 810333 theploughdiseworth.com
Draught Bass; Marston's Pedigree; Timothy Taylor Landlord; 1 changing beer (often Wadworth) H
Situated in a village with many half-timbered buildings, this is a cosy, multi-roomed pub with parts dating back to the 13th century. Low-beamed ceilings and exposed brickwork are just some of the original features discovered during renovation work in the 1990s. There is an interesting display of old photographs of the area. Tasty home-made food is served. The spacious, well-presented beer garden is popular in summer. A former local CAMRA Village Pub of the Year. Q P

Fleckney

Golden Shield L

46 Main Street, LE8 8AN
4 (12 Wed & Thu)-11; 12-midnight Fri & Sat; 11.30-11 Sun
(0116) 240 2366 goldenshieldfleckney.co.uk
Greene King IPA, Abbot; St Austell Tribute; Timothy Taylor Landlord; 2 changing beers (sourced nationally; often Bradfield, Church End, Theakston) H
Village pub in the heart of Leicestershire offering six real ales, including ever-changing LocAles, microbrewery and regional beers. There is an L-shaped bar at the front and a restaurant at the rear. Home-cooked meals are served lunchtimes Wednesday to Sunday and evenings Wednesday to Saturday – Sunday lunches are always popular. A pétanque court is available and BT Sports is screened. P (44,49B)

Frisby on the Wreake

Bell Inn

2 Main Street, LE14 2NJ
closed Mon; 5-11; 12-11 Sat; 12-6 Sun (01664) 434736
thebellinnfrisby.co.uk
Charnwood Vixen; Hancock's HB; 1 changing beer (sourced nationally) H
A change of licensee saw the Bell reopen in 2017 after several recent periods of closure. It has regained popularity within the local community and does not rely on national brands for its ale range. The pub is clean and bright with simple decor. It has three rooms – a traditional wood-beamed front bar room, a dining area to the right of the entrance and a further room behind the bar.
P

Great Glen

Pug & Greyhound

14 London Road, LE8 9GF
11-midnight (0116) 259 2265
thepugandgreyhound.com
Sharp's Doom Bar; 3 changing beers (sourced nationally; often Framework, Langton, Nobby's) H
The oldest building in Great Glen, it dates mostly from the 18th century but partially from the 16th. On the road from London to the north that became the A6, it used to be a coaching inn and was called the Old Greyhound until 2015. The food menu ranges from steaks to pizzas. Breakfast is served until 11am. One of the guest beers is from a local brewery. P (X3,X7)

Groby

Stamford Arms L

2 Leicester Road, LE6 0DJ
10-11 (11.30 Fri & Sat) (0116) 287 5616
stamfordarms.co.uk
Everards Beacon Hill, Tiger, Old Original; house beer (by Everards); 3 changing beers (sourced nationally; often Brunswick) H
A fantastic pub that sells food, modernised in 2013 and continuing to develop into a great village inn. It has recently purchased the neighbouring Blacksmiths Cottage which is available as a holiday let or for overnight stays. It has six cask ales, rough ciders, craft beers and a gin selection second to none. The food is traditional with daily specials and pizza from the oven. Ideally located for Bradgate Park and the National Space Centre.
P

Hathern

Dew Drop

49 Loughborough Road, LE12 5HY (on A6)
12-3, 6-midnight; 12-3, 7-1am Fri-Sun (01509) 842438
Greene King XX Mild, Abbot; 1 changing beer H
Traditional two-roomed local with a long-serving landlord, in the centre of Hathern. It has a large bar and a small, well-upholstered, comfortable lounge with real fires. Do not miss a visit to the architecturally unspoilt toilets with their tiled walls and original features. A large range of malt whiskies is stocked and cobs are available at lunchtime.

Hinckley

Elbow Room Ale & Cider House L

26 Station Road, LE10 1AW (below Cineworld at The Crescent)
closed Mon; 2-11 Tue-Thu; 12-11.30 Fri & Sat; 12-7 Sun
07900 191388 elbowroomalehouse.co.uk
6 changing beers G
Family-run micropub decorated in an industrial style, offering a warm welcome and a great atmosphere. The ales and ciders are served by gravity directly from the cellar behind sliding glass doors. High quality wines, gins, whiskies, vodkas, world craft beers and lagers plus a range of soft drinks are available. Pork pies and Scotch eggs complement the drinks. There is no TV, jukebox or gaming machine as conversation is king. Children are welcome until 8pm. Local CAMRA Pub of the Year 2018. Q

New Plough Inn ✔

Leicester Road, LE10 1LS

4.45-11; 3-midnight Fri; 12-midnight Sat & Sun
☎ (01455) 615037 thenewploughinn.co.uk

Marston's Saddle Tank, Pedigree; 3 changing beers (often Jennings, Ringwood, Wychwood) H

Run by CAMRA members, this award-winning Victorian pub has old settles and a comfortable ambience. Sporting memorabilia reflect sponsorship of local cricket and rugby teams. Pub quizzes have raised over £100,000 for charity. Darts, dominoes, skittles, crib and shooting teams attract the local community, as does the Stables function room. Nearby, the Greyhound, home to Elliswood Brewery, is of historic interest, with a Blue Plaque honouring brewer William Butler. (159,1)

Pestle & Mortar L

81 Castle Street, LE10 1DA

2-11; 12-11 Fri & Sat; 12-10 Sun ☎ 07715 106876
thepestlehinckley.co.uk

Draught Bass; 6 changing beers (sourced locally) H

Since opening in 2015, Hinckley's first micropub has been awarded branch CAMRA Cider Pub of the Year 2016-18 and East Midlands Cider Pub of the Year 2016. Up to 22 changing real ciders are available, with Westons Old Rosie Rhubarb and Gwynt y Ddraig Farmhouse Scrumpy permanently on offer. Handpumps deliver up to six changing real ales from casks behind the bar. Cobs and pork pies are available. This comfortable, pleasantly quirky micropub satisfies a wide range of drinking tastes, with a friendly atmosphere. Q (8,X55)

Queen's Head

Upper Bond Street, LE10 1RJ

5-11 (midnight Fri); 12-midnight Sat; 12-6 Sun
☎ 07887 770038

4 changing beers H

A warm welcome awaits at this multi award-winning Victorian free house serving four ever-changing real ales. It has been sympathetically refurbished and features open fires and a Victorian range, helping to enhance a cosy atmosphere. A frequent local CAMRA Pub of the Year and three times one of CAMRA's top 200 pubs, it has featured in the Guide since 2013. Sorry, no children and no pets.

Hoby

Blue Bell L

36 Main Street, LE14 3DT

12-11 ☎ (01664) 434247 bluebell-hoby.co.uk

Everards Beacon Hill, Old Original, Sunchaser, Tiger; 2 changing beers (sourced nationally) H

A picturesque thatched village pub with a beer garden providing fine views across the Wreake Valley. The pub is usually busy, its exposed wooden beams and tiled floors with rug coverings giving it a cosy and pleasant feel. It is an ideal stopping off point for those seeking refreshment while walking the Leicestershire Round footpath. There is always a good range of Everards beers available, including its seasonal brews, and usually a guest ale or two. P

Kegworth

Red Lion

24 High Street, DE74 2DA

11.30-11; 12-10.30 Sun ☎ (01509) 672466
redlionkegworth.com

Adnams Southwold Bitter; Castle Rock Harvest Pale; Charnwood Vixen; Draught Bass; Gale's HSB; 4 changing beers (sourced locally; often Milestone) H

Georgian building standing on the 19th-century route of the A6, with four rooms served from one bar. There are bench seats and original features including coal fires. Eight cask ales, including Nutbrook The Mild Side, and real cider, are on offer, plus a good selection of malt whiskies. Food is served every lunchtime and weekday evenings. Outside is a large car park and garden plus a pétanque court and children's play area. En-suite accommodation is available. A frequent winner of local CAMRA awards. Q P

Leicester

Ale Stone

660 Aylestone Road, Aylestone, LE2 8PR

11-11 ☎ (0116) 319 2320

5 changing beers H

A sister pub to the Blue Boar in central Leicester, this micropub opened in a converted shop unit in July 2017. The nicely furnished interior has wooden benches and dados all round. Up to five real ales, plus four ciders and perries, are stillaged in a temperature-controlled glass-fronted 'cellar' behind the counter. Ham and cheese cobs and coffee are usually available. This and the Blue Boar are the only pubs in the city using oversize glasses to guarantee a full pint. Q

Ale Wagon

27 Rutland Street, LE1 1RE

11-11; 7.30-10.30 Sun ☎ (0116) 262 3330
alewagon.co.uk

Hoskins Hob Bitter, IPA H; house beer (by Hoskins) P; 4 changing beers (sourced regionally; often Hoskins) H

Run by the Hoskins family, this city-centre pub with a 1930s interior, including an original oak staircase, has two rooms with tiled and parquet floors and a central bar. The interior features photos of the former Queens Hotel which was across the road, this pub in the 1930s, and Hoskins Brewery. A function room is available to hire. Handy for the nearby Curve Theatre. Plans are underway to begin brewing on the premises.

Black Horse

65 Narrow Lane, Aylestone, LE2 8NA

11-11; 12-midnight Fri & Sat ☎ (0116) 283 7225

Everards Beacon Hill, Tiger, Old Original; 4 changing beers (sourced nationally; often Brunswick, Everards, Titanic) H

Sympathetically refurbished in 2018, this is a welcoming, traditional Victorian pub with a distinctive bar servery, set in a village conservation area on the city's edge. Up to eight real ales are offered alongside home-cooked food. Quiz night is Sunday and comedy features regularly. There is a large beer garden, and a skittle alley and function room available to hire. Beer festivals and community events are regularly hosted. Coaches are welcome by prior arrangement. The pub has a customer loyalty scheme. Q

Black Horse

1 Foxon Street, Braunstone Gate, LE3 5LT
12-midnight (11 Sun) (0116) 254 0446
Everards Beacon Hill, Sunchaser, Tiger, Old Original; 2 changing beers (sourced nationally) H
The only remaining traditional pub, home to a real community, in a street of youth-oriented bars. It has two rooms separated by a central bar, with wood-panelled walls and practical furniture providing a comfortable setting. There is live music four nights a week and a quiz night on Wednesday. The guest beers are sourced through Everards and the cider is Westons Old Rosie. A large roof terrace is popular for open-air drinking.

Blue Boar

16 Millstone Lane, LE1 5JN
11-11 (0116) 319 6230 blueboarleicester.co.uk
House beer (by Leatherbritches); 9 changing beers (sourced nationally) H
Light, airy single-room micropub, opened in 2016. It is named after the Blue Boar Inn where Richard III stayed before the Battle of Bosworth Field. The cellar is visible through a glass partition behind the bar. House beers are brewed by Exit 33 and Leatherbritches, and guest beers, including many rare brews, are sourced from microbreweries around the country. This and sister pub The Ale Stone are the only pubs in the city using oversized glasses to ensure customers get a full pint. Local CAMRA Pub of the Year 2018.
Q

Bowling Green

44 Oxford Street, LE1 5XW
10-1am (midnight Mon-Wed) (0116) 254 6496
greatukpubs.co.uk/thebowlinggreenleicester
Marston's 61 Deep; Wychwood Hobgoblin Gold; 4 changing beers (sourced nationally) H
One of the oldest pubs in Leicester, in 2015 it was given a makeover to return it to a more traditional pub. The load-bearing truss in the pub entrance area dates back to the 14th century. The front parts are old and beamed with panelling; the opened-out rear areas are modern, with music, games and sports TVs. The pictures and wall displays feature scenes of Leicester or bowling. There is an enclosed courtyard area at the rear.

Broood@VinQuatre

24 King Street, LE1 6RL
11-11 (7 Sun) (0116) 254 4228 broood.co.uk
Changing beers (sourced nationally) H
Located on Leicester's New Walk, VinQuatre opened in the 1980s. After many name changes it finally became Broood in December 2016. Seven real ales and eight ciders are offered. It holds many events – Monday vinyl night, Tuesday and Thursday quiz nights, resident blues band Sunday afternoon and open mic on the first Wednesday of each month. It also runs quarterly beer festivals. Meals include pizza and chicken, and there is a special lunchtime menu.

Criterion

44 Millstone Lane, LE1 5JN
3-9 Sun & Mon; 12 (3 Tue)-11 (0116) 262 5418
thecriterionleicester.com
Changing beers (sourced nationally; often Market Harborough, Tres Bien) H
A free house since 2003, leased to Market Harborough Brewery in 2016. The two-roomed pub offers up to 10 cask ales from microbreweries and regionals. Beer festivals are held regularly. Darts and dominoes are played. Quiz night is Wednesday, live music plays Thursday to Saturday. The pub hosts monthly comedy events and is a venue for Leicester Comedy Festival. Pizzas are available Monday to Saturday.

King's Head

36 King Street, LE1 6RL
12-midnight (0116) 254 8240
Black Country Bradley's Finest Golden, Pig on the Wall, Fireside; 7 changing beers H
A traditional one-room city-centre local owned by Black Country Ales. Twelve handpulls serve the regular beers, seven changing guest ales and two varying ciders. Its open fire and roof terrace make it popular throughout the year with real ale and cider enthusiasts. A range of bottles is offered. No meals are served, but filled cobs are often available. Seasonal beer festivals are held. Sky and BT Sports are screened.

Old Horse

198 London Road, LE2 1NE
11-11.30 (12.30am Fri; midnight Sat); 11-11 Sun
(0116) 254 8384 oldhorseleicester.co.uk
Everards Beacon Hill, Sunchaser, Tiger, Old Original; 4 changing beers (sourced nationally; often Everards) H
Nineteenth-century coaching inn, handy for dog walkers, students and sports supporters. The four guest beers change monthly. The addition of a cider bar serving eight handpulled ciders earned the pub local CAMRA Cider Pub of the Year in 2017 and 2018. Tasty, good-value food is served, including a Sunday carvery. Behind the building is the largest pub garden in town complete with children's play equipment. Regular quiz nights, karaoke and special events take place.
P

Real Ale Classroom

22 Allandale Road, Stoneygate, LE2 2DA
5-9 Mon; 4-10 Tue-Thu (11 Fri); 12-11 Sat; 1-4 Sun
(0116) 319 6998 therealaleclassroom.com
5 changing beers (sourced regionally; often Grainstore, Oakham) G
A classroom-themed micropub set up by career-change teachers in a converted shop in a suburban shopping street. The furniture includes reclaimed desks with original graffiti, and the beers are written up on a roller blackboard. Cask ales and ciders are served from a home-made chiller cabinet behind the high bar. A logburner warms the rear room. In both rooms seating around large tables encourages conversation between regulars and visitors. Bar snacks include local pork pies, a cheeseboard and charcuterie platter. Q

Rutland & Derby

21 Millstone Lane, LE1 5JN
12-11 (1am Fri & Sat); closed Sun (0116) 262 3299
therutlandandderby.co.uk
Everards Sunchaser, Tiger; 2 changing beers H
This pub has an open-plan interior with a contemporary ambience. The long servery bar is directly facing the front entrance, while off to the left is a lounge-style bar which in turn leads to a restaurant area on a raised level. Out back is a block-paved courtyard with a metallic spiral staircase leading up to a rooftop terrace. The food offering features uncomplicated, ethically sourced ingredients.

Salmon

19 Butt Close Lane, LE1 4QA (from Clock Tower walk down Churchgate; Butt Close Lane is second left)
11-11 (midnight Fri & Sat) ☎ (0116) 253 2301
Black Country Bradley's Finest Golden, Pig on the Wall, Fireside; 7 changing beers (sourced nationally) H
A small corner local with a U-shaped single-room interior, refurbished in 1992 in a bright traditional style. It has a friendly, welcoming atmosphere and a strong sports following. A Black Country Ales pub since 2016, 12 handpumps dispense the brewery's ales, guest beers and two real ciders. Lunchtime meals and a Sunday carvery are complemented by cobs, pork pies and Scotch eggs available throughout the day. Bus stations are nearby.
Q

West End Brewery

68-70 Braunstone Gate, LE3 5LG
5-11; 2-midnight Fri; 12-midnight Sat; 12-10 Sun
☎ 07875 745302
West End Stout, Copper, IPA; 3 changing beers H
Leicester's original brewpub opened in March 2016. The owner/brewer aims to produce innovative beers, and plans to increase the range over time. He likes to experiment with his recipes and takes on board customers' suggestions. Four house beers are available plus at least three guests from quality local microbreweries or from further afield. The brewery is behind the pub and can be visited by customers. Live music nights are hosted twice a month.

Western

70 Western Road, Westcotes, LE3 0GA
12-midnight (1am Fri & Sat) ☎ (0116) 254 5287
Steamin' Billy Tipsy Fisherman, Bitter, Skydiver; 4 changing beers (sourced regionally; often Charnwood, Everards, Leatherbritches) H
A traditional local in a residential location close to football and rugby grounds on the edge of the city centre, now surrounded by high-rise student flats. The bar and lounge are popular with a mixed clientele of all ages. Up to four guest beers are available, mainly from microbreweries. Old pub signs decorate the pub and beer garden. There are regular music and beer festivals and the pub is home to a theatre upstairs. A barbecue is held on Leicester City home match days.

Loughborough

Needle & Pin

The Rushes, LE11 5BE
closed Mon; 5-11 Tue-Thu; 3.30-11 Fri; 12-11 Sat; 12-10 Sun ☎ 07973 754236
4 changing beers H
A micropub in what was the old H&R Electronics shop. Beer is served downstairs in a continental-style bar with high stools. The upstairs room has a record player, board games and music. More than 50 continental and craft beers are stocked. Local CAMRA Pub of the Year 2018.

Organ Grinder

4 Woodgate, LE11 2TY
12-11 (midnight Fri & Sat); 12-10.30 Sun
☎ (01509) 264008
Blue Monkey BG Sips, 99 Red Baboons, Infinity, Guerrilla; 4 changing beers (sourced locally; often Blue Monkey) H
Previously known as the Pack Horse, bought by Blue Monkey in 2012, the pub has received a top-to-bottom renovation, uncovering lots of interesting original features. The new stable bar at the back reflects the pub's past life as a coaching inn. Eight cask ales are always available alongside a choice of four real ciders, sometimes a perry, and Belgian bottled beers. Bar snacks include an interesting range of pork pies. A former local CAMRA Pub of the Year.

Swan in the Rushes

21 The Rushes, LE11 5BE
11-11 (midnight Fri & Sat); 12-11 Sun ☎ (01509) 217014
Castle Rock Sheriff's Tipple, Harvest Pale, Elsie Mo; 6 changing beers (often Castle Rock, Charnwood) H
Traditional three-room Castle Rock pub comprising a quiet, traditionally styled lounge, a contemporary dining room and a lively bar with a jukebox. A constantly changing range of up to seven guest beers always includes a mild. Real cider, perry, a wide range of continental bottled and draught beers and a good choice of malt whiskies and country wines are also available. Upstairs is the Hop Loft function room and first-floor outside terrace. Q P

Tap & Mallet

36 Nottingham Road, LE11 1EU
7-midnight; 5-midnight Sat
Marston's Pedigree; 4 changing beers (sourced regionally; often Abbeydale, Charnwood, Salopian) H
Genuine free house with a regularly changing beer range including mainly seasonal brews from Abbeydale and Salopian. The interior has a large single room divided into two distinct drinking areas – a public bar with pool table, darts and boxed games, and a quieter lounge area that can be partitioned off for functions. Outside there is a large, secluded lawned garden, patio area and pets' corner. Q

White Hart

27 Churchgate, LE11 1UD
11-midnight; 12-11 Sun ☎ (01509) 236976
Draught Bass; Timothy Taylor Landlord; 3 changing beers (sourced locally; often Charnwood, Leatherbritches, Sarah Hughes) H
Reopened in 2013 as a free house after an extensive refurbishment, it has a secluded patio and beer garden to the rear. Changing guest beers are sourced from local breweries such as Leatherbritches and Charnwood. Sarah Hughes Dark Ruby is also a regular. Bar snacks and tapas are available until early evening. Live music plays on Friday evening and Sunday afternoon. Local CAMRA Pub of the Year 2016.

Lutterworth

Fox

34 Rugby Road, LE17 4BN (400yds from Whittle roundabout)
12 (5 Mon)-1am; 12-midnight Sun ☎ (01455) 550935
fox-lutterworth.co.uk
Draught Bass; Sharp's Doom Bar; 2 changing beers (sourced nationally; often Timothy Taylor, Wadworth) H
Described as the village pub in Lutterworth, The Fox is situated south of the town not far off the M1. It has a friendly atmosphere and a warm welcome for all. The open-plan interior is warmed by two real fires, which add to the ambience in cooler

months. Food is served lunchtimes, including roasts on Sunday. Thai food is available in the evening in the separate Sawasdee restaurant. Outside there is a lovely landscaped garden. Quiz night is Tuesday. (58,X44)

Real Ale Classroom

4 Station Road, LE17 4AP

closed Mon & winter Sun; 4-10 Tue-Thu; 3-11 Fri; 12-11 Sat; 2-8 Sun (0116) 319 6998 therealaleclassroom.com

10 changing beers (sourced nationally; often North Riding, Shiny) G

The Classroom is a micropub established in 2017 by two former teachers. It offers a constantly changing line up of ales, ciders and craft beer from renowned brewers nationally. The pub has a logburner for the winter and a fantastic beer garden to enjoy in the summer months. Friendly staff are knowledgeable about the drinks on offer, including excellent gin and spirits from local distillers. Q (X84,58)

Unicorn

29 Church Street, LE17 4AE (near church)

10.30-11 (midnight Fri & Sat); 12-11 Sun

(01455) 552486

Adnams Southwold Bitter; Draught Bass; Greene King IPA; 1 changing beer (sourced nationally; often Brains, Hobsons) H

Traditional street-corner local built in the early 1900s, situated in the town centre by the church. The main bar has an open fire, skittles table and dartboard used by teams in the local leagues. Sport is shown on TV. A smaller lounge doubles as a family room, with another small room used for diners. Vegetarian and children's dishes are available at reasonable prices. Lots of local photographs adorn the walls to peruse while enjoying your pint. P (8,X44)

Market Harborough

Beerhouse

76 St Mary's Road, LE16 7DX

closed Tue; 12 (6 Mon & Wed)-11; 12-10 Sun

(01858) 465317

8 changing beers (sourced nationally; often Hart Family, Tres Bien) P

Market Harborough's first micropub, set in a converted furniture shop behind the chip shop on St Mary's Road. The focus is very much on beer – no food, gaming machines or loud music. There are 20 taps for draught products – the first eight are used for cask ales, the rest for kegs and ciders. Monday is quiz night and occasional comedy nights, live music, vinyl nights and a book club are hosted. P

Melton Mowbray

Boat

57 Burton Street, LE13 1AF

4-11 Mon & Wed; 11-2.30, 4-11 Tue; 2-11 Thu (midnight Fri); 11-midnight Sat; 12-11 Sun (01664) 500969

Adnams Southwold Bitter, Bombardier; 1 changing beer (sourced nationally) H

A traditional single-roomed pub that takes its name from a canal basin that was once adjacent. The walls are wood panelled and decorated with old pictures of the town and a map of the old Melton-Oakham canal. The pub is always busy and popular with those who enjoy good conversation with their pint. A range-style fire gives plenty of warmth and adds to the atmosphere in winter. Branch CAMRA Pub of the Year 2017.

Gas Tap

11A Burton Street, LE13 1AE

closed Mon & Tue; 3 (4 Thu)-10; 2-10 Sat 07946 508251

4 changing beers (sourced nationally) G

The Gas Tap is Melton's first micropub – the single room has space for 25 customers. It is situated in a historic building known as The Old Club (Melton's first gentlemen's club), where frequent visitors included the Prince Regent. The beers are dispensed by gravity from a stillage to the left and rear of the room. Pictures on the wall offer an insight into how the building looked from 1870 to the present day. Q

Oadby

Cow & Plough

Gartree Road, LE2 2FB

11-11 (0116) 272 0852

Fuller's London Pride; Steamin' Billy Bitter, Skydiver; 4 changing beers (sourced regionally; often Abbeydale, Belvoir, Charnwood) H

Situated in a former farm building with a conservatory, the pub is decked out with breweriana. It is home to Steamin' Billy beers, named after the owner's now departed Jack Russell who features on the logo and pumpclips. A mild is always available and a real cider in the summer months. An annual beer festival is held. Former dairy buildings house a renowned restaurant. QP

Lord Keeper of the Great Seal

96-100 The Parade, LE2 5BF

7am-midnight (0116) 272 0957

Greene King Abbot; Ruddles Best Bitter; Theakston Best Bitter; 6 changing beers (sourced regionally) H

Named after Sir Nathan Wright, a local landowner who held this position in the 17th century, this typical Wetherspoon conversion of a row of shops stands on the site of Sandhurst Infants School. It features pictures of old buildings and industries of Oadby and a varied library of books. Regular beer festivals and charity events are held. Families are welcome until 9pm. (31,31A)

Old Dalby

Belvoir Alehouse L

Station Road, LE14 3NQ

10-9 (11 Thu-Sat); 12-6 Sun (01664) 823978

belvoiralehouse.co.uk

Belvoir Dark Horse, Whippling, Star Bitter, Beaver Bitter, Oatmeal Stout, Old Dalby H

The brick-fronted venue on the outskirts of the village incorporates a bar, function room and visitors' centre, with brewery tours available by arrangement. The spacious interior is filled with brewing artefacts, and has a traditional bar area, with room for long-alley skittles and a bar billiards table. Large internal windows provide views into the brewery. A full food menu is served daily, with the focus on wholesome food made with local produce. A range of regular and seasonal Belvoir Ales is served. A former local CAMRA Pub of the Year. P (23)

Plungar

Anchor

Granby Lane, NG13 0JJ

5-11; 12-3, 5-11 Fri; 12-11 Sat; 12-10.30 Sun

(01949) 860589

3 changing beers

This brick building in the heart of a small Leicestershire village dates from 1774, having previously served as the local courtroom. The pub has a large bar, lounge area and separate restaurant, plus an annexe housing the pool table, and an attractive beer garden. Up to three beers, including at least one local brew, are available in a range of styles. The pub is popular with locals and visitors, cycling groups, horse riders and anglers using the nearby fishing lakes.

Q P (24)

Quorn

Manor House

Woodhouse Road, LE12 8AL

12-11 (midnight Sat); 12-10 Sun (01509) 413416

themanorhouseatquorn.co.uk

Charnwood Salvation; Draught Bass; Timothy Taylor Landlord; 2 changing beers (often Leatherbritches)

Built in 1899 by the Great Central Railway, the Manor House was designed to serve passengers arriving at Quorn & Woodhouse Station, which it still does today – the preserved steam and diesel-hauled trains pass by 150 yards from the door. The building was refurbished in 2005 and now has an open-plan bar and award-winning restaurant, with a separate function/meeting room available to hire. A free house, two guest beers are available during the week and three at weekends.

Q P

Shackerstone

Rising Sun

Church Road, CV13 6NN

12-3 (not Mon), 5-11.30; 11.30-11.30 Fri-Sun

(01827) 880215 risingsunpub.com

Marston's Pedigree; Timothy Taylor Landlord; 2 changing beers

A traditional family-owned free house in the heart of the village near the Ashby Canal and the preserved Battlefield Railway. It has a wood-panelled bar serving traditional ales, a restaurant, a pool room with Sky Sports, a family-friendly conservatory and an attractive garden. The pub, popular with locals and visitors alike, is renowned for the quality and variety of its ales and serves good pub food – the ideal hub for visiting this rural part of Leicestershire. Q P

Shearsby

Chandlers Arms

Fenny Lane, LE17 6PL

closed Mon; 6-11 Tue-Thu; 12-3, 6-11 Fri & Sat; 12-7 Sun

(0116) 247 8384 thechandlersinshearsby.co.uk

Dow Bridge Acris; Belvoir Beaver Bitter; 4 changing beers (sourced regionally)

Quintessential village inn with a big reputation – the pub is a community hub for the village and welcoming to visitors. Its name derives from the building's original use as a tallow candlemaker's premises. The beer garden overlooks the village green from a high vantage point. Microbrewery beers are always on the bar, often locally sourced, including a stout or porter. Good food is available, but the owners see it as primarily a drinkers' pub.

> What care I how time advances: I am drinking ale today. **Edgar Allan Poe**

Shepshed

Black Swan

21 Loughborough Road, LE12 9DL

5-midnight Mon & Wed; 5-11.30 Tue; 12-midnight

(01509) 506222

Charnwood Vixen; Draught Bass; Greene King Abbot; Timothy Taylor Landlord

Multi-roomed pub situated in a prominent position close to the town centre, offering two guest beers alongside the regulars. An extremely good range of whiskies is also kept. The main room has two drinking areas, both with comfortable seating. A further small room can be used by families and is available to hire for functions. Wednesday is quiz night. Local events include the ukulele orchestra. Shepshed Dynamo football ground is nearby.

P

Horse Shepshed

196 Ashby Road West, LE12 9EF (on A512)

12 (4 Mon)-11 (01509) 507006

thehorseshepshed.co.uk

Charnwood Vixen; Greene King Abbot; Marston's Pedigree; 1 changing beer

The Horse, one of the oldest free houses in Shepshed, is traditionally built, with a restaurant and bar. In 2015 major extension work almost doubled the size of the premises, enabling a much greater emphasis on food. It has a feature fireplace with a wood-burning stove, and outside an alfresco dining area serving wood-fired oven-baked pizza. A good range of beers is available and the pub takes pride in serving freshly prepared food made on the premises using produce sourced within a five-mile radius of Shepshed. P

Somerby

Stilton Cheese

High Street, LE14 2QB

12-3, 6 (7 Sun)-11 (01664) 454394

stiltoncheeseinn.co.uk

Grainstore Ten Fifty; Marston's Saddle Tank; 3 changing beers (sourced nationally)

Late 16th-century pub built in local ironstone, ideally located on the Leicestershire Round to provide refreshment and a warm welcome to walkers. The cosy bar and adjoining room are decorated with a large collection of objects including a stuffed pike and a badger, adding to the welcoming atmosphere. Tall customers beware the large number of pumpclips on the low beam above the bar. Branch CAMRA Pub of the Year 2016.

Q P

South Kilworth

White Hart

Rugby Road, LE17 6DN

12-2.30 (not Mon-Wed), 5-11; 12-midnight Sat; 12-10.30 Sun (01858) 575416 thewhitehartsk.co.uk

3 changing beers (often Langton)

A classic village pub with low ceilings, exposed beams and a large fireplace with a wood-burning stove. Home-cooked food is available in the small restaurant, including the house speciality, chargrilled steak. Traditional games include darts, Northamptonshire skittles and pool. There is a large grassed drinking area outside. Nearby attractions include Stanford Reservoir and Stanford Hall, dating from 1697, which has a museum dedicated to aviator pioneer Percy Pilcher.

Stoke Golding

George & Dragon

Station Road, CV13 6EZ

closed Mon; 12-3, 6-11; 12-11 Fri & Sat; 12-10.30 Sun

(01455) 213268 churchendbrewery.co.uk/pubs

Church End Gravediggers Ale, What the Fox's Hat, Stout Coffin, Fallen Angel, Arthur's Wit; 3 changing beers (sourced locally; often Church End)

Renowned village local serving eight real ales from the Church End range and a real cider. Good home-cooked lunches feature local produce, and bar snacks, made on the premises, are always available. Each month, the second Tuesday is steak night and lunch is served on the last Sunday. Close to the historic Bosworth battlefield, the pub supports a number of clubs and societies, and is popular with walkers, cyclists and boaters from the nearby Ashby Canal. Q

Syston

Queen Victoria

76 High Street, LE7 1GQ

4-11; 12-midnight Fri & Sat; 12-10.30 Sun

(0116) 260 5750

Everards Beacon Hill, Sunchaser, Tiger, Old Original; 2 changing beers (sourced nationally)

A former coach house, the building is 200 years old. Everards has traded here since 1922. Three rooms have been knocked together to form the bar at the front, and there is a small room to the rear. At the back is a carvery restaurant and large garden. Entertainment features every other Saturday. Beer and cider festivals are held at Easter and in the summer. Guest beers are sourced through Everards and can include regional and microbrewery beers.

Syston & District Social Club

36 High Street, LE7 1GP

6-11; 11.30-midnight Fri & Sat; 11.30-11 Sun

(0116) 260 9086 systonsocial.weebly.com

Banks's Mild, Amber Ale; 4 changing beers (sourced regionally; often Brewsters, Castle Rock, Oakham)

Historically, this old building was a pub, the Bull's Head. It became a Labour club for a while, but is now an independent non-political members' club. It is home to many local societies and sports clubs including darts, skittles, chess and crib. The range of six beers includes four regularly rotating guests. Beer festivals are held in February and June. For entry, show a CAMRA membership card or a copy of this Guide. (5,5A)

Twyford

Saddle

10 Main Street, LE14 2HU

4-11; 12-11 Sat; 12-9.30 Sun (01664) 841108

thesaddletwyford.co.uk

Grainstore Cooking; Greene King IPA; 2 changing beers (sourced nationally)

Pleasant community pub opposite the 900-year-old village church. It has a small front bar and a longer room to the right with a pool table and dining tables. On the walls there are interesting framed documents relating to the pub's history. Behind the bar is a small function room and seated area. Food includes a choice of good-value pub favourites as well as a range of home-made pizzas and a Sunday carvery.

Walton on the Wolds

Anchor

2 Loughborough Road, LE12 8HT

5.30-11 Mon, Tue & Thu; 12-2.30, 5.30-11 Wed & Fri; 12-3, 5.30-11 Sat; 12-10.30 Sun (01509) 880018

Adnams Southwold Bitter; Fuller's London Pride; Timothy Taylor Landlord; 1 changing beer (often Charnwood)

The Anchor is situated in the centre of a small village within easy reach of Leicester and Nottingham via the A46. It is a popular venue for walkers who stop for a well-earned home-cooked lunch in front of the log fire. There is a menu to suit all tastes plus an extensive specials board. Outside is an elevated seating area to the front and a garden and large car park to the rear.

Q

Willoughby Waterleys

General Elliott

Main Street, LE8 6UF

closed Mon; 5.30-10 Tue (11.30 Wed); 11.30-2, 5.30-11.30 Thu; 11.30-2, 4.30-11.30 Fri; 11.30-11 Sat; 12-6 Sun

(0116) 247 8058

Draught Bass; Theakston Best Bitter; 1 changing beer (sourced nationally)

The pub is named after an 18th-century British Army officer, most noted for his successful defence of the garrison during the Great Siege of Gibraltar, which lasted from 1779 to 1783, during the American War of Independence. The L-shaped room has skittles and darts at one end, a public/lounge bar space in the middle and a snug area at the other end. It is conveniently situated for passing hikers on the Leicestershire Round and cyclists on Cycle Route 6.

Wymeswold

Three Crowns

45 Far Street, LE12 6TZ (opp church)

12-midnight (01509) 880011 thecatandwickets.com

Draught Bass; Sharp's Doom Bar; 2 changing beers (often Belvoir)

Reopened late 18th-century friendly village local featuring open fires, a beamed ceiling in the bar and a cosy split-level snug/lounge. Guest beers are usually from local breweries including Castle Rock, Belvoir or Nottingham. A good range of snacks and main meals is available lunchtimes and Thursday to Saturday evenings, including pizzas cooked in the newly installed oven. A function room and skittle alley are available to hire. There is a regular daytime bus service. Q

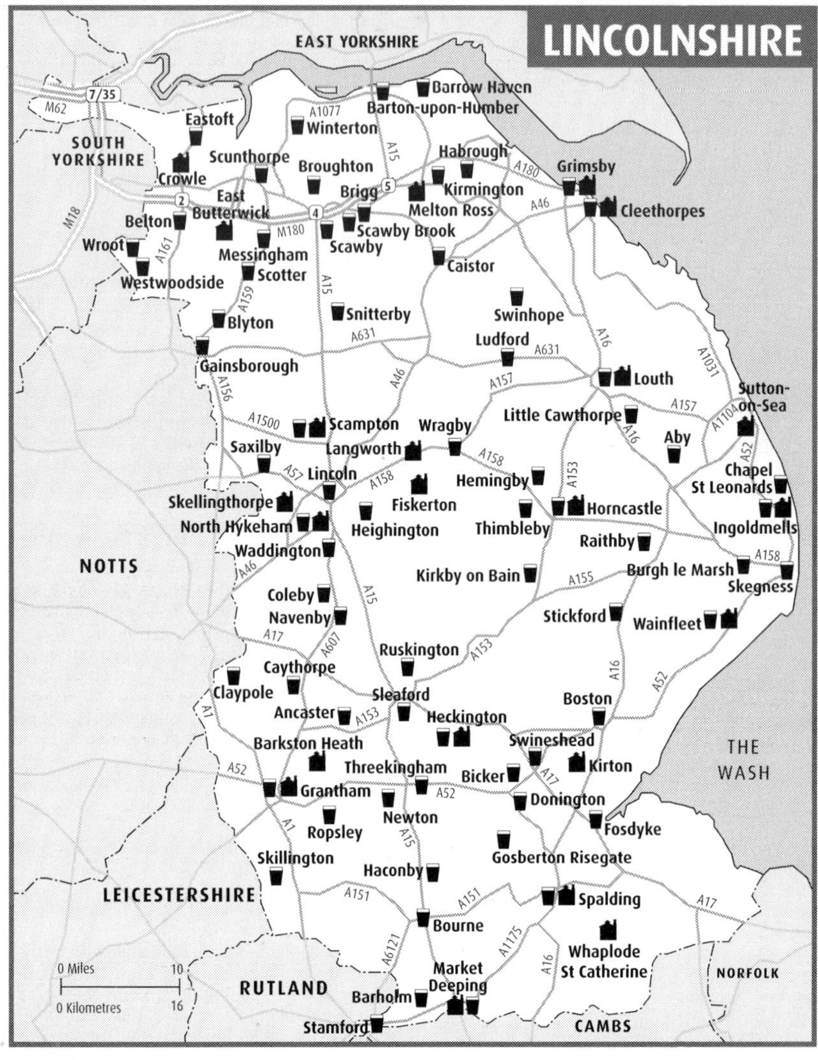

Aby

Railway Tavern

Main Road, LN13 0DR (off A16 via South Thoresby)

12-11.30 (01507) 480676 railwaytavern-aby.co.uk

2 changing beers (sourced nationally) H

A lovely rural inn which lies just outside the beautiful village of Aby. There is always a fine selection of carefully chosen real ales alongside a good home-cooked food menu. A real fire adds to the homely atmosphere at this welcoming pub. Closed on Tuesdays in November and between January and Easter.

Ancaster

Ancaster Social Club

Ermine Street, NG32 3PW

7-11; 12-10.30 Sun (01400) 230896

Bombardier; 2 changing beers (often Brewsters, Wood) H

In the heart of the village, this club hosts various sporting events on its playing fields. Sports include football, cricket and rounders. Inside, darts, pool and live sports are available. It has an airy conservatory and seating outside overlooking the sports field. A regular winner in the past, this excellent club has once again been voted local CAMRA Club of the Year.

Barholm

Five Horseshoes L

PE9 4RA

4 (1 Sat)-11; 12-10.30 Sun (01778) 560238

Adnams Southwold Bitter; Draught Bass; Oakham JHB; 3 changing beers (often Grainstore, Hopshackle) H

A classic 18th-century stone-built country pub, well known for supporting many charities. It comprises two bars, two cosy side rooms and a pool room. A real cider is served along with three permanent and three changing ales. Pizzas are available on Friday and Saturday evenings, while barbecues and live music in the large garden are a feature of the summer months. Q

ENGLAND

Barrow Haven

Haven Inn 𝕃

Ferry Road, DN19 7EX (approx 1½ miles E of Barrow-upon-Humber)

🕐 12-11 ☎ (01469) 530247 🌐 thehaveninn.co.uk

Timothy Taylor Landlord; 2 changing beers (sourced locally; often Axholme, Lincolnshire Craft Beers) Ⓗ

Built in 1730 as a coaching inn in the quiet north Lincolnshire countryside for travellers using the former ferry, the Haven has been renowned for hospitality, good food and drink, and comfortable lodgings ever since. Recently taken over but remaining full of character, a warm welcome awaits, with a bar, lounge and attractive conservatory, perfect for walkers from the Humber Bank to call in for a tasty pint. The well-appointed restaurant offers traditional dishes and seasonal specials. P

Barton-upon-Humber

Wheatsheaf ✔

3 Holydyke, DN18 5PS

🕐 12-11.30 (12.30am Fri & Sat); 12-11 Sun

☎ (01652) 633292

Moorhouse's White Witch; Theakston Best Bitter; Timothy Taylor Boltmaker; 1 changing beer (sourced nationally; often Lancaster) Ⓗ

Occupying a prominent position on the main road through the town, this friendly pub from Enterprise Inns dates back to the 18th century. It has an unspoilt, traditional atmosphere with a front bar, a small snug at the rear and a seating area for drinkers and diners. Four real ales and a real cider are served. A large beer garden to the rear makes for pleasant outdoor drinking.

Q P (350,450)

White Swan 𝕃

66 Fleetgate, DN18 5QD

🕐 closed Mon; 11-12.30am (11 Tue & Wed); 10.30-11.30 Sun

☎ (01652) 661222

3 changing beers (sourced regionally; often Black Sheep, Clark's) Ⓗ

This renovated 17th-century coaching inn was lcoal CAMRA Pub of the Year 2017. In a prominent position opposite the bus/train interchange, it offers all a warm welcome. Three changing cask ales are complemented by a rotating craft keg beer, two permanent Westons ciders and three additional changing real ciders. Diverse community groups meet here, some using the charming converted farrier shed in the spacious rear courtyard. Quiz night is Sunday, with a monthly vinyl night plus a Curiosity Shop.

Q P

Belton

Crown Inn 𝕃

Church Lane, DN9 1PA (behind All Saints church)

🕐 1-midnight; 12-1.30am Sat; 12-midnight Sun

☎ (01427) 872834

Bradfield Farmers Blonde; Brakspear Bitter; Jennings Cocker Hoop; Oakham Citra; 1 changing beer (sourced nationally; often Abbeydale, Lacons) Ⓗ

Difficult to find – behind All Saints church – but well worth the effort. This is a haven for the discerning drinker. The pub has two bars, one equipped for live music, and a games room. Four regular cask ales are featured along with a changing guest/house ale from the nearby Cuckoo Brewery, in which the licensee is a partner. A winner of several local CAMRA awards. No food is served.

P (399)

Bicker

Red Lion

Donington Road, PE20 3EF

🕐 closed Mon & Tue; 12-11; 12-7 Sun ☎ (01775) 821200

🌐 redlionbicker.co.uk

Adnams Southwold Bitter; Courage Directors; 1 changing beer (often Austendyke Ales) Ⓗ

A typical country inn with low beams and tiled floor and in a pleasant setting. Extensively and tastefully redecorated in 2015, it reopened after two years' closure. Welcoming and multi-roomed, it has a small bar, and is popular for dining, with a varied, extensive menu. The pub is known to date from at least 1665. P (59)

Blyton

Black Horse

93 High Street, DN21 3JX (on A159)

🕐 11.45-midnight ☎ (01427) 628277

🌐 blackhorseblyton.co.uk

3 changing beers (often Batemans, Milestone) Ⓗ

The Black Horse Inn has been a village pub for over 250 years. It is around four miles from Gainsborough and some 10 miles from Scunthorpe. In the last few years it has been given a new lease of life with a major building project, where great care has been taken to revitalise the inn as a traditional public house. P

Boston

Eagle

144 West Street, PE21 8RE

🕐 11-midnight ☎ (01205) 361116

Castle Rock Black Gold, Harvest Pale, Preservation Fine Ale, Screech Owl; 7 changing beers Ⓗ

Part of the Castle Rock chain, the Eagle is known as the real ale pub of Boston. This friendly two-roomed hostelry has an L-shaped bar with a large TV screen for big sports events. The small cosy

REAL ALE BREWERIES

8 Sail Heckington
Austendyke Spalding
Axholme Crowle/Grimsby
Bacchus ▪ Sutton-on-Sea
Batemans Wainfleet
Blue Bell ▪ Whaplode St Catherine
Brewster's Grantham
Cheeky Imp Skellingthorpe
Consortium ▪ Louth
Dark Tribe ▪ East Butterwick
Ferry Fiskerton
Firehouse Louth
Fuddy Duck Kirton
Greg's ▪ Scampton
Hopshackle Market Deeping
Horncastle ▪ Horncastle
Leila Cottage ▪ Ingoldmells
Lincolnshire Langworth
Lincolnshire Craft Melton Ross
Newby Wyke Grantham
Oldershaw Barkston Heath
Poachers North Hykeham
Willy's ▪ Cleethorpes

lounge has an open fire. The pub stocks a wide range of guest ales, and at least one cider. A function room upstairs is home to Boston Folk Club. Thursday is quiz night – allegedly the hardest in town. Q❀♿⇌♣🍎🚌🐾📶

Goodbarns Yard ✔

8 Wormgate, PE21 6NP

⏲ 11.30-11; 12-11 Sun ☎ (01205) 355717
🌐 goodbarnsyard.co.uk

Morland Old Speckled Hen; Timothy Taylor Landlord; 1 changing beer (sourced nationally) Ⓗ

In a cobbled medieval street which runs northwards away from the Boston Stump, parallel to the River Witham, this 700-year-old pub is popular for meals, with a busy restaurant. Old signs and pictures of Boston adorn the walls. A large garden with tables and covered patio areas overlooks the river. In winter, an open fire welcomes you inside. 🐎❀◐⇌📶

Bourne

Anchor

44 Eastgate, PE10 9JY

⏲ 3-11 (midnight Fri); 12-midnight Sat; 12-10.30 Sun
☎ (01778) 422347

House beer (by Dancing Duck); 4 changing beers (sourced regionally; often Nene Valley, St Austell, Thornbridge) Ⓗ

Traditional two-roomed locals' pub with a pretty patio by the banks of a tributary of the River Glen. It is strong on sports, with pool and darts played, Sky Sports on the TV and several sporting trophies on display, and raises funds for the local air ambulance service. The car park is small. It has been under new management and ownership since summer 2014, and serves up to six real ales. The house beer, Bourne Particular, is supplied by Dancing Duck. Local CAMRA Gold Award winner in July 2017. 🐎❀♿♣🍎P📶

Smith's 🄻

25 North Street, PE10 9AE

⏲ 10-11 (midnight Fri); 8.30am-midnight Sat; 8.30am-11 Sun
☎ (01778) 426819

Fuller's London Pride; Oakham JHB; 4 changing beers (often Hopshackle) Ⓗ

A successful conversion of an old grocery store into an atmospheric pub with exposed red brick walls throughout. The building is a warren of interconnecting rooms spanning three floors. The main bar usually serves six beers, mostly from independent brewers, as well as six ciders from all over the country. Outside there is a large patio and beer garden with a children's play area. There is an annual beer festival in summer and a cider and sausage festival in August. Q❀◐♿♣🍎🚌🐾📶

Brigg

Yarborough Hunt 🄻

49 Bridge Street, DN20 8NS

⏲ 11-11 Mon-Wed; 10-11.30 Thu; 11-midnight Fri; 10-midnight Sat; 11-10.30 Sun ☎ (01652) 658333

Greene King Abbot; Lincolnshire Craft Beers Best Bitter, Lincoln Gold, Bomber County; 3 changing beers (sourced nationally; often Jennings, Morland, Timothy Taylor) Ⓗ

Former Sergeants Brewery pub, built in the 1700s and retaining original features. It is simply furnished, with open fires in some of the cosy rooms, and has an enclosed, accessible beer garden. It offers an extensive range of wines, whisky and cider, with around eight craft and continental beers on tap. No food is served, but customers can bring their own sandwiches and other cold food. Q🐎❀♿⇌♣🍎🚌(4,95)🐾📶

Broughton

Red Lion

45 High Street, DN20 0HY (on main road in village)

⏲ 11-11 ☎ (01652) 659418 🌐 theredlionbroughton.co.uk

Sharp's Doom Bar; 3 changing beers (sourced regionally; often Lincolnshire Craft Beers, Oakham, Robinsons) Ⓗ

A village local sympathetically refurbished in 2017, comprising a small front bar, a sports bar with sports TV and pool to one side, plus a large central restaurant area. At the rear is a large function room. An extensive food menu operates from Tuesday to Sunday, with special meal nights throughout the week, and Sunday lunches. The permanent beer complements the two or three rotating guest ales. It features occasional live music plus themed nights. 🐎❀◐♿♣P🚌(4)🐾📶

Burgh le Marsh

Bell Hotel

45 High Street, PE24 5JP

⏲ 12-midnight ☎ (01754) 810318 🌐 bellhotelburgh.co.uk

Batemans XB, Gold; 1 changing beer (often Batemans) Ⓗ

The pub lives up to its name, with a large bell above the entrance doorway. Inside is an L-shaped bar with a substantial drinking area, which is popular with local groups. In addition to the hotel rooms, there are three self-catering cottages in the hotel grounds. Nearby is a fishing lake.
🐎❀🛏◐♿♣🍎P🚌🐾📶

Caistor

White Hart

21 South Street, LN7 6UB

⏲ 11-11 (midnight Fri & Sat) ☎ (01472) 851734
🌐 whitehartcaistor.co.uk

Black Sheep Best Bitter; Caledonian Deuchars IPA Ⓗ

A traditional-style country pub just off the market square in this historic market town. Very welcoming, it has two rooms: a small front bar mainly used for dining and a much larger L-shaped bar. There is outside seating to the rear of the pub and a couple of benches to the front. It has a good reputation for serving quality locally sourced food and has a vegetarian option.
🐎❀🛏◐♣🍎P🚌(53)

Caythorpe

Red Lion ✔

62 High Street, NG32 3DN

⏲ 12-3, 6-11; 12-3 Sun ☎ (01400) 272632
🌐 redlioncaythorpe.org.uk

2 changing beers (often Adnams)

A warm welcome awaits at this traditional village inn, sympathetically refurbished to create a comfortable, relaxing atmosphere. The excellent food menu is available both in the bar and restaurant. The well-kept real ales are complemented by a wide range of wines, spirits and soft drinks. Definitely worth a visit. ❀◐P🚌

Chapel St Leonards

Admiral Benbow

The Promenade, PE24 5BQ

10-7 (10.30 Fri & Sat); 10-8 Sun (01754) 871847

admiralbenbowbeachbar.co.uk

Black Sheep Best Bitter; 2 changing beers

A beach bar on the promenade whose opening times and facilities are dependent on the weather and are limited in winter. (Please see the website for current times.) Bar snacks and hot food are served. It has an outside seating area on the newly refurbished boat deck (Hispaniola), and provides picnic trays and plastic glasses to take your favorite ales on to the beach. Dogs are welcome on leads, with blankets and dog treats available. If the flag is flying it is open.

Claypole

Five Bells

95 Main Street, NG23 5BJ

11 (4 Mon & Tue)-11; 10-10.30 Sun (01636) 626261

Greene King IPA; 3 changing beers

Traditional village pub always offering four beers and two ciders. The guest ales are predominantly from local microbreweries, with small jars displaying the colour of the beers available. There is a large public bar and a small lounge and restaurant serving home-cooked food. Outside there is a spacious beer garden and children's play area. It has four en-suite rooms. A former local CAMRA Pub of the Year.

Q P

Cleethorpes

No.1 Pub

Railway Station, DN35 8AX

12-7.30 Mon; 1-midnight; 12-midnight Sat & Sun (01472) 696221

Batemans XXXB; Draught Bass; 6 changing beers (sourced regionally; often Axholme, Horncastle Ales)

Typical railway bar on Cleethorpes station. This popular local has a main bar with a smaller one off it overlooking the platform and is themed towards railway memorabilia, while there is a fair-sized seating area outside at the front. From the bar, customers can order quality real ales and locally sourced home-cooked food – check the Facebook page for daily specials. P

No.2 Refreshment Room

Station Approach, DN35 8AX

7.30am-12.30am (11 Mon; 11.30 Tue & Wed); 9am-midnight Sun 07905 375587

Hancocks HB; Rudgate Ruby Mild; Sharp's Doom Bar, Atlantic; 2 changing beers (sourced nationally)

Multiple CAMRA award-winning local – a small and cosy pub on the scenic riverfront station at Cleethorpes, with a reputation for quality ale and conversation. It serves both travellers and locals throughout the day, just the place for a refresher before or after your train journey or a walk on the beach. A covered smoking area is provided. A little gem.

Nottingham House

7 Seaview Street, DN35 8EU

12-11; 11.30-midnight Fri (1am Sat); 11.30-11 Sun (01472) 505150 nottinghamhousehotel.com

Oakham Citra; Tetley Bitter; Timothy Taylor Landlord; 4 changing beers (sourced regionally)

Popular traditionally styled pub with three rooms all accessible from the front bar and a cosy snug at the rear. All bars and toilets are on the ground floor. Cards and dominoes are available to play, and there is a separate restaurant upstairs which supplies bar meals to all the downstairs bars. The public bar shows sports matches on the TV. Well-behaved children and dogs are made welcome in this old coaching house. Q

Signal Box Inn

Lakeside Station, King's Road, DN35 0AG

11-11 (01472) 604657 cclr.co.uk/signalboxinn

4 changing beers (sourced nationally)

An original signal box, signed as the smallest pub on the planet, and part of the Cleethorpes Coast Light Railway. However, on any day with reasonable weather the beer garden is a great location for a pint or two. The site runs events such as the Real Ale and Blues and the Folk and Cider festivals. It tends to be open only at weekends from October, closes a week before Christmas, and reopens a week before Easter. A family-friendly pub. Q

Willy's

17 High Cliff, DN35 8RQ

11-11 Mon & Tue (midnight Wed & Thu; 2am Fri & Sat); 11-1am Sun (01472) 602145

Draught Bass; Willy's Original; 2 changing beers (sourced nationally)

Willy's is a seafront bar with views over the Humber Estuary to the Yorkshire coast. There is a microbrewery on the site where Willy's Original Bitter is brewed. The pub mainly operates from a downstairs bar; an upstairs bar is used if it becomes busy. Limited outdoor seating is available. It serves good-quality locally sourced home-made food.

Coleby

Tempest Arms

Hill Rise, LN5 0AG

4-8 Mon; 12-11 (midnight Fri & Sat); 12-8 Sun (01522) 810258 thetempestcoleby.co.uk

Brains Rev James; St Austell Cornish Best Bitter; Timothy Taylor Knowle Spring; 2 changing beers (sourced nationally)

A traditional village local perched on the edge of the Lincoln Cliff. A group of villagers bought the pub from Marston's in 2015, and the recent refurbishment has provided an extra dining area, allowing more room for drinking round the central bar. Enjoy panoramic views over the Witham Valley from the restaurant and the tables on the paved patio. Popular with walkers following the Viking Way and with cyclists. Q P (1)

Donington

Black Bull

7 Market Place, PE11 4ST

10-11.30 (01775) 822228

Batemans XB; Sharp's Doom Bar; 2 changing beers (often Brains)

Busy local just off the A52. Five handpumps feature two regular beers and occasionally two varying guest beers from small brewers as well as large regionals. The comfortable bar has low, beamed ceilings, wooden settles and a cosy fire in winter. The restaurant offers a good choice of reasonably priced evening meals; lunches are served in the bar. Tables in the car park are used for outdoor drinking. Buses run from Boston and Spalding (not Sun).

Eastoft

River Don Tavern

Sampson Street, DN17 4PQ (on A161)

3.30-11; 12-11 Sun (01724) 798040

theriverdoneastoft.co.uk

2 changing beers (sourced regionally; often Acorn, Rooster's)

Village local on a main road with an open-plan design comprising an L-shaped bar and a larger drinking and dining area. A separate restaurant is used for the popular Sunday carvery. The pub is traditionally styled with dark-wood ceiling beams, rustic furniture and vintage photographs. Two rotating guest beers are offered, one usually from Roosters, and there is a real cider in summer. Accommodation is available in outdoor lodges and in rooms in the pub itself.

P (356)

Fosdyke

Ship Inn

Moulton Washway, PE12 6LH

11.30-10 (11 Fri & Sat) (01205) 260764

shipinnfosdyke.com

Adnams Southwold Bitter; Batemans XB; 1 changing beer

Located just outside Fosdyke when travelling from Boston on the A17, next to the bridge. As its name suggests, this former Batemans pub is dedicated to all things maritime; maps, photographs, charts, model ships and artefacts of every description are in plentiful supply. The week's tidetable is also detailed on a blackboard. It is near to the busy Fosdyke marina and boaters and landlubbers are well catered for with excellent home-cooked food, good beer and a warm welcome. Q P

Gainsborough

Blues Club

Northolme, North Street, DN21 2QW

7-midnight; 5-1am Fri; 12-1am Sat; 12-midnight Sun

(01427) 613688

3 changing beers

The club has a bar area with several TVs showing sport, a quieter lounge and a large function room which hosts regular live entertainment (admission charges may apply). Two changing real ales are usually on the bar and details of forthcoming beers can be emailed to customers on request. CAMRA guests are always welcome on production of a membership card. (Central)

Eight Jolly Brewers

Ship Court, DN21 2DW

11-11 (1am Fri & Sat); 12-11 Sun

Dukeries A Ray of Sunshine; Full Mash Apparition; changing beers

The branch's flagship real ale haven, in the Guide since 1995, based in a 300-year-old Grade II-listed building. Six beers are on sale, always different, many from northern micros, but new breweries from all areas feature. Real cider and continental bottled beers are also sold. Fortnightly Wednesday quiz nights are staged. Customers bring in food to share Sunday lunchtimes. Q P (200)

Elm Cottage

138 Church Street, DN21 2JU

11-midnight; 12-midnight Sun 07590 806584

Changing beers

The pub is close to Gainsborough Trinity's football ground and The Blues Club. There are six beers on tap, some from the Marston's portfolio, but frequently from microbreweries. Good value lunchtime food and early evening meals are served Tuesday to Saturday, with Sunday lunch 12-5pm. The pub is popular with local amateur sports teams and weekly live music is featured.

Q P

Sweyn Forkbeard

22-24 Silver Street, DN21 2DP

8am-11 (10.30 Thu; midnight Fri & Sat) (01427) 675000

Greene King Abbot; Ruddles Best Bitter; Sharp's Doom Bar; 3 changing beers

This town-centre Wetherspoon is making itself one of the must-do pubs in town. Three rotating guest beers often feature some oddities for this part of the country. Customers can ask for their favourite beer and it frequently appears. The pub is named after the Danish King of England in 1013, whose son Canute is rumoured to have stopped the aegir (tidal bore). Good-value food is served until 10pm.

(Central)

Gosberton Risegate

Duke of York

106 Risegate Road, PE11 4EY

12 (6.30 Mon)-11; 11-3, 7-10.30 Sun (01775) 840193

Batemans XB; St Austell Tribute; 1 changing beer (sourced regionally)

A friendly pub and a longstanding entry in the Guide with a deserved reputation for value-for-money beers and food. As well as regular ales, guests come from a range of independent brewers. A wide choice of cooked food is served, with portions to suit the largest appetite. Local community life is supported through charities, sports teams and other social events. Visitors can expect an enthusiastic welcome from the two pub dogs. Q P

Grantham

BeerHeadZ

27 Watergate, NG31 6NS

1-11; 12-midnight Fri & Sat; 12-10 Sun (01476) 330274

beerheadz.biz

5 changing beers

The sign 'Fancy a pint of the unusual?' greets the customer outside this pub in the area of town dominated by St Wulfram's church spire. Since opening in 2016 the pub has sold almost 900 different cask beers. Continental and craft beers are also available. There is a free function room and customers are welcome to bring in their own food.

Q

Chequers

25 Market Place, NG31 6LR

12-midnight (2am Fri & Sat) (01476) 570149

Castle Rock Harvest Pale; 3 changing beers (often Oakham, Brewsters, Oldershaw)

A cosmopolitan and contemporary bar that features beers from Brewsters and Oldershaw supplemented with changing guest beers. Located on a paved side street off the High Street, known locally as Butchers Row, it has a relaxing atmosphere during the day and comes alive evenings and weekends. Q

Lord Harrowby

65 Dudley Road, NG31 9AB

3-11; 12-11 Sat; 1-11 Sun (01476) 563515

Oldershaw Heavenly Blonde; 4 changing beers

A friendly back-street community pub, one of the few in Grantham, with a bar and lounge with a real fire; it is how pubs used to be, with a dartboard in the corner and crib and dominoes played in leagues. At least two beer festivals with live music are held in the excellent enclosed area at the back. The landlord, a CAMRA member and real ale enthusiast, sources four changing guest beers and real cider to complement the Oldershaw Heavenly Blonde Q

Nobody Inn

9 North Street, NG31 6NU (opp Asda car park)

12-11; 12-10.30 Sun (01476) 565288

Sharp's Doom Bar; 5 changing beers (often Black Sheep, Newby Wyke)

The Nobody is famous for its hidden toilet door behind the bookcase. The pub sells beer from the award-winning Newby Wyke Brewery in Grantham. It gets lively at the weekends and when a big sporting event is taking place, but is also a pleasant place for a quiet drink with good bar staff. There is a downstairs room for meetings. Live music is staged during the year. Watch out for the giant spider.

Grimsby

Barge

Victoria Street, DN31 1NH

10-11 (2am Tue, Fri & Sat); 12-11 Sun (01472) 340911

thebargegrimsby.co.uk

Axholme Cleethorpes Pale Ale, Bombardier

As its name implies, this is an old converted grain barge that is berthed in the town centre near all bus routes. It has a slight list to starboard, but do not worry, it has been there for over 20 years! Afternoon trade is food oriented but evenings have more of a rock/student feel when the jukebox is turned on. There is a quiz on Monday nights with a free supper.

Spiders Web

180 Carr Lane, DN32 8LN

12-11 (midnight Fri & Sat) (01472) 692065

thespiderswebgy.co.uk

John Smith's Bitter; 3 changing beers (sourced nationally; often Leeds, Wainwright)

A typical estate pub about two miles from Grimsby in Old Clee. The pub has three rooms: the bar for pool and darts, a lounge and a music room. It also runs a weekly poker session and a quiz night. A beer garden is to the rear of the pub which contains a separate play area for children. It has ample car parking space. There is always a good selection of beer available served by welcoming staff. Q P (4)

Yarborough Hotel

Bethlehem Street, DN31 1JN

7am-midnight (1am Fri & Sat) (01472) 268283

Greene King Abbot; Kelham Island Easy Rider; Ruddles Best Bitter; 12 changing beers (sourced regionally)

Large open-plan establishment next door to Grimsby Town railway station serving 15 real ales from national brands through to more local ales from the Lincolnshire area. Like many in the Wetherspoon chain, it can be popular on its Tuesday steak night and again on Thursday curry night. Following a troubled past where it was under threat of demolition, the building has been restored to a grand hotel and a thriving pub in town. Q

Habrough

Station Inn

Station Road, DN40 3AP

11-11 (01469) 572896

3 changing beers (sourced regionally; often Caledonian)

Originally a hotel built in 1848 for the Great Grimsby and Sheffield Junction Railway, this community pub has tastefully decorated walls adorned with memorabilia from the days of steam. Live bands are featured once a month on Saturday and this, together with karaoke, theme nights and traditional pub games, makes for a lively environment. Three handpumps feature changing beers from regional brewers. An open fire adds warmth in cold weather. P

Haconby

Hare & Hounds

2 West Road, PE10 0UZ

12-2, 6-11 (10.30 Mon); 6-11 Tue; 12-11 Sat; 12-10.30 Sun (01778) 570521

Marston's EPA; 1 changing beer (often Wychwood)

This low-beamed inn built around 1600 has soft settees in the back room and is a popular dining hostelry. Walking groups frequent the pub, and there is live music on the first and second Sundays and third Monday in the month. Guest beers are from the Marston's stables, often alternating between a dark and a light ale. Nearby is the Primitive Baptist Methodist Chapel built in 1867 which must be one of the smallest in the land. Q P

Heckington

8 Sail Brewery Bar

Heckington Mill, Hale Road, NG34 9JW

closed Mon-Thu; 12-8 Fri; 12-4 Sat & Sun (01529) 469308 8sailbrewery.co.uk

3 changing beers (sourced locally)

Situated in part of the Heckington Windmill complex, this is a single-room brewery bar featuring a restored Victorian bar and church pew and Britannia bar seating. Usually three changing 8 Sail Brewery beers and occasional guest beers are on the bar. A selection of German bottled beers and local cider is also available. Beer festivals are held in mid July over Heckington Show weekend. On winter weekends it tends to close at 3pm. Q

Heighington

Butcher & Beast

High Street, LN4 1JS

12-11; 12-10 Sun ☎ (01522) 790386
Batemans XB, XXXB; 4 changing beers (sourced regionally) H
With welcoming staff, this old stone Batemans pub is in the centre of the village served by regular buses. An award-winning summer floral display adorns the exterior, while inside are photos of the old village. A separate restaurant serves fine food but does not impinge on the drinking area. Beer festivals, games, quizzes, meat raffles and charity events are popular. A new patio area is behind the pub. Dogs are welcome in non-food areas. Q P (2)

Hemingby

Coach & Horses

Church Lane, LN9 5QF (1 mile from A158 at Baumber)
6 (7 Mon & Tue)-11; 12-2.30, 7-11 Sat; 12-2.30, 7-10.30 Sun ☎ (01507) 578280
2 changing beers (sourced nationally) H
On the edge of a picturesque Wolds village a few miles from Cadwell Park race circuit, this traditional pub has been under the same ownership for over 25 years. The building dates from the 17th century, with a low-beamed ceiling and a welcoming real fire in winter months. The two handpumps serve a varied selection of beers. Award-winning food is available in the evenings from Wednesday to Saturday and at lunchtimes on Saturday and Sunday. Q P

Horncastle

King's Head

16 Bull Ring, LN9 5HU
12-11 ☎ (01507) 523360
Batemans XB, XXXB; 2 changing beers (sourced locally; often Batemans) H
A comfortable, cosy and friendly pub. Unusually for this locality, the building has a thatched roof, hence its local name, The Thatch. Three beers from Batemans are generally sold plus a guest. Reputedly the pub inspired an 00 gauge Hornby model, an example of which is displayed behind the bar. Summertime sees the pub resplendent with hanging baskets and it has been the winner of Bateman's Floral Display competition. Try spotting the pub cat, Rufus.

Old Nick's Tavern

8 North Street, LN9 5DX
closed Mon; 5-midnight (1am Fri); 2-1am Sat; 2-midnight Sun ☎ (01507) 526862 oldnickstavern.co.uk
4 changing beers (sourced locally; often Horncastle Ales) H
Built in 1752 as a coaching inn, this original building is now a town-centre pub with its own microbrewery, the home of Horncastle Ales. The place has been refurbished and incorporates the old pub sign and old photos of the pub. Live bands perform regularly. There are five handpumps, four of which usually serve ales from the Horncastle Brewery. The head brewster is the landlord's daughter. Currently no food is served.

Ingoldmells

Countryman L

Chapel Road, PE25 1ND
12-midnight; 12-3, 7-midnight winter ☎ (01754) 872268
Leila Cottage Leila's Lazy Days, Ace Ale, Lincolnshire Life, Leila's One Off H
The privately owned Countryman appears to be a modern building but it incorporates the early 19th-century Leila Cottage, which gives its name to the brewery behind the pub. A notorious smuggler, James Waite, used to reside here when Ingoldmells was a wild and lonely place, but he certainly would not recognise the current holiday coast, with Skegness, Butlin's and Fantasy Island nearby. Information boards give brewery, pub and beer information for visitors. The pub is on northern bus routes from Skegness. P

Kirkby on Bain

Ebrington Arms

Main Street, LN10 6YT
12-2 (not Mon), 6-11 ☎ (01526) 354560
ebringtonarms.com
Adnams Broadside; Batemans XB; Black Sheep Ale; Sharp's Doom Bar; Timothy Taylor Landlord; 1 changing beer (often Adnams) H
Attractive country pub close to the River Bain and dating from 1610. World War II airmen used to slot coins into the ceiling beams to pay for beer when they returned from missions over Germany; sadly, many of these coins are still in situ and make a unique memorial to the dead. The popular restaurant offers good food made with local produce (booking advised). There is a convenient caravan site within a mile of the pub. A folk club features on Monday evenings, except on the second Monday of the month, when there is a book club. Q P (65)

Kirmington

Marrowbone & Cleaver

High Street, DN39 6YZ
11.30-11 ☎ (01652) 688335
marrowboneandcleaver.com
Sharp's Doom Bar; house beer (by Batemans); 1 changing beer H
Following a period of closure, this village pub was refurbished and reopened by motorbike racer Guy Martin. The inside is adorned with racing memorabilia and also items from 166 Squadron. It is a family-run pub managed by Guy's sister, Sally. Although mainly food oriented, there are three handpumps. Drinkers are given a warm welcome as well as diners. The house beer was developed in a collaboration between Guy and Batemans Brewery. Q P

Lincoln

Adam & Eve Tavern

25 Lindum Road, LN2 1NT
12-11 (midnight Fri & Sat) ☎ (01522) 537108
adamandevelincoln.co.uk
Castle Rock Harvest Pale; Morland Old Speckled Hen; 2 changing beers (sourced nationally) H
With low beams and thick walls, this is reputedly the oldest tavern in Lincoln. The main bar has a number of alcoves, one with a dartboard. The front room, offering views of the medieval Pottergate and the cathedral, leads to a secluded beer garden. There are weekly music gigs and quiz nights, and sports matches are shown on two screens. The guest beers usually include a local brew, and it does good-value meals. P

Cardinal's Hat

268 High Street, LN2 1HW

12-11 (1am Fri & Sat) ☎ (01522) 527084

cardinalshatlincoln.co.uk

Adnams Mosaic; Lincolnshire Craft Beers Lincoln Gold; house beer (by Bad); 5 changing beers (sourced nationally; often Bad) H

Steeped in history, this Grade II-listed timber-framed building was an inn from the 15th to the 19th century. Restored in 1952, it became home to St John's Ambulance. In 2015 the building was sympathetically refurbished revealing a number of historical features. The many rooms lend themselves to a social gathering or a quiet drink in one of the snugs. The eight ales, four ciders and other drinks can be enjoyed with a menu of charcuterie and cheese-based platters.

Q

Golden Eagle

21 High Street, LN5 8BD

11-11 (11.30 Fri & Sat); 12-11 Sun ☎ (01522) 521058

Castle Rock Harvest Pale; Sharp's Doom Bar; house beer (by Castle Rock); 7 changing beers (sourced nationally) H

This friendly old two-roomed coaching inn has up to nine real ales and at least one real cider. The bar is a pleasant room but can get busy on match days, while the lounge is quiet, relaxed and cosy. Occasional beer festivals, usually in summer, and live music events plus port, whisky, or gin tasting nights take place. Friday is quiz night. Outside is an excellent beer garden with sheltered seating, lighting and heaters. A small function room can be hired. QP

Hop & Barley

417 High Street, LN5 8HX

5-11; 12-11 Fri & Sat; 12-10 Sun lincolnmicropub.co.uk

4 changing beers (sourced regionally) H

Lincoln's first micropub offers a changing selection of real ales and ciders. The walls and ceiling are adorned with an array of past pumpclips. The pub features a concrete bar and visible stillage. A friendly atmosphere awaits and it is a great place to meet new friends while enjoying a quiet pint. The venue benefits from being on a regular bus route and is a short walk from central bus and train stations. Q

Joiners Arms

4 Victoria Street, LN1 1HU

4-midnight; 3-12.30am Fri; 2-12.30am Sat; 4-10.30 Sun

☎ 07871 887459

5 changing beers (sourced nationally) H

Just off the city centre, the pub's deceptive early '60s-style exterior leads into a traditional interior. You enter a seating space with two steps up to the bar, which has five changing ales often from local breweries. A recently refurbished pool and darts area is to the left of the bar, and there is a bar billiards table, a real blast from the past. Music and quiz nights feature.

Jolly Brewer L

27 Broadgate, LN2 5AQ

12-11 (10 Mon; midnight Fri & Sat); 12-10 Sun

☎ (01522) 528583 jollybrewer.org

Welbeck Abbey Henrietta, Portland Black; 4 changing beers (sourced nationally) H

A characterful city-centre pub that attracts a diverse clientele. The decoration is Art Deco in style and a side room has reclaimed cinema seating. Live music is a major feature, with a weekly open mic session and bands at weekends. The jukebox is usually playing at other times. The large courtyard has a covered area where bands perform in summer. There is a dartboard and table football. Good-value, home-cooked meals are served.

P

Morning Star

11 Greetwell Gate, LN2 4AW

11-11; 12-11 Sun ☎ (01522) 514269

morningstarlincoln.co.uk

Bombardier; Ruddles Best Bitter; Sharp's Doom Bar; Timothy Taylor Golden Best; 2 changing beers (sourced regionally) H

In a building that has been in continuous use as a pub since 1791, this friendly local is much loved by its strong core of regulars and by visitors. The Lincoln Cathedral, Castle and Bailgate shopping area are all close by. The award-winning beer garden hosts live music in the summer, and winter nights can be spent by the fire in the cosy bar. A quiz night is held every Tuesday. QP

Ritz L

143-147 High Street, LN5 7PJ

8am-midnight (1am Fri & Sat) ☎ (01522) 512103

Greene King Abbot; Ruddles Best Bitter; Sharp's Doom Bar; 7 changing beers (sourced nationally) H

Close to the city's new transport hub, Ritz is split on two levels, having the family area on the lower tier and the bar on the top tier, accessible by lift for wheelchair visitors. The decor reflects its past use as a cinema/entertainment venue. It is popular on match days due to its proximity to Lincoln City FC's ground. It hosts monthly Meet the Brewer events on the last Thursday, and there is a twice-yearly beer festival. Q

Strugglers Inn L

83 Westgate, LN1 3BG

12-1am (11 Mon; midnight Tue & Wed); 12-11 Sun

☎ (01522) 535023 strugglers-lincoln.co.uk

Greene King Abbot; St Austell Tribute; Timothy Taylor Landlord; 7 changing beers (sourced nationally) H

Standing in the shadow of Lincoln Castle, the Struggs is a magnet for locals and visitors. The walls and ceiling of the main bar are covered in pumpclips from the 600-plus different beers served each year – the collection is now spreading to the small snug. Musicians play each Sunday teatime and occasional Saturday evenings. The sunken garden at the rear is a suntrap in the summer. Filled rolls and pork pies are available.

Q

Victoria

6 Union Road, LN1 3BJ

11-midnight (1am Fri & Sat); 12-midnight Sun

☎ (01522) 541000 victoriapub.net

Batemans XB; Castle Rock Harvest Pale; Timothy Taylor Landlord; 3 changing beers (sourced regionally) H

Celebrating 34 consecutive years in this Guide, the Victoria is an 1880s-built traditional two-room pub adjacent to the west gate of Lincoln Castle, one of the most historic parts of the city, and is popular with locals and tourists alike. An upstairs function room is available which hosts a board games group and folk club. Live music and a quiz are regular features. The outdoor seating area is a summer suntrap and there is a daily lunch menu.

Q

Little Cawthorpe

Royal Oak Inn (Splash)

Watery Lane, LN11 8LZ (through ford and turn left)
11-midnight (01507) 600750 royaloaksplash.co.uk
Black Sheep Best Bitter; Greene King IPA; 2 changing beers H

Known locally as the Splash because of the picturesque ford nearby, this 400-year-old inn is in its own large lawned gardens on the edge of the Lincolnshire Wolds near Louth. Four beers are regularly available, plus often a guest ale from a local brewery. Three restaurants cover most culinary requirements and themed evenings are popular. The en-suite rooms are often used by visitors to Cadwell Park or explorers of the Wolds. ♣P

Louth

Brown Cow ✔

133 Newmarket, LN11 9EG (jct of Church St)
5-11; 12-3 Fri; 12-11 Sat & Sun (01507) 605146
Black Sheep Best Bitter; Castle Rock Harvest Pale; Courage Directors; Fuller's London Pride; 1 changing beer H

Friendly town pub, an excellent community meeting place, with a good atmosphere and, most importantly, great beer. A free quiz is held every Sunday night and the local folk club meets here on a Tuesday evening. The popular bistro serves traditional home-cooked food, made with locally sourced products. Every Thursday is pie night, with a selection of different pies. Food is served Thursday to Sunday. Q♣P

Cobbles Bar

New Street, LN11 9PU (off Cornmarket)
10-midnight
Black Sheep Ale; Marston's Pedigree; 1 changing beer H

Traditional pub-style bar based in the centre of town with friendly staff. This small but accommodating venue has multiple personalities, from a bustling coffee shop serving light lunches to a busy pre-club local with DJ and live music at weekends. It has a good beer trade, with two contrasting cask ales, as well as a huge selection of exotic spirits. Wheelchair access is right through the front doors.

Consortium Micropub L

13C, D & E Cornmarket, LN11 9PY
closed Mon; 11-11 Tue; 3-7 Wed & Thu; 12-midnight Fri & Sat; 12-6 Sun (01507) 600754
theconsortiumlouth.co.uk
Changing beers

A micropub in a small courtyard 100 yards from the marketplace. Six real ales and one real cider are always on, changing every week. The pub has its own microbrewery upstairs producing, usually, three of the six ales supplied on the bar. The venue was opened in 2017 to give a wider selection of ales from Lincolnshire, Leicestershire, Nottinghamshire and Derbyshire, as well as other counties. Q

Gas Lamp Lounge L

13 Thames Street, LN11 7AD (bottom of Thames St)
5-11; 12-11 Sat & Sun (01507) 607661
sales12018.wixsite.com/firehousebrewery
1 changing beer H

A unique pub – one of only 22 in the UK lit by gas lamps. It has no music or bandits, just good pub traditions, serving four regular beers from the upstairs brewery, plus a guest beer. Benches are set along the canalside for enjoying a drink during the summer, while inside is a roaring logburner to sit beside in the winter months. Dogs are welcome. Q♣P

Olde Whyte Swanne ✔

45 Eastgate, LN11 9NP
11 (10 Wed)-11; 11-midnight Fri & Sat; 12-11 Sun
whyteswannelouth.co.uk
Rudgate Ruby Mild; 1 changing beer H

The oldest pub in a pretty market town. Established in the early 1600s, upon entering this Grade II-listed building you are met by traditional low-beamed ceilings and a real fire. Beyond this is another modern room which is used for dining. The bar offers a variety of beers and cider on handpump. Q

Wheatsheaf

62 Westgate, LN11 9YD
11-11 (01507) 606262
Batemans XB; Black Sheep Ale; Brains Bitter; Thornbridge Jaipur IPA; 1 changing beer H

A picturesque pub that lies close to Louth's historic St James' Church, which boasts the highest single spire of any medieval parish church in England and is visible for miles around. A good selection of real ales and tasty home-made food is served. Outside is a lovely beer garden and the pub is a popular meeting place for walkers. P

Ludford

White Hart L

Magna Mile, LN8 6AD
closed Mon & Tue; 11-11 (01507) 313489
4 changing beers (sourced nationally) H

A flagship ale pub where the licensees do their best to get as many ales behind the bar as possible. Formerly a coaching house dating from the 18th century, it is now a two-roomed village inn, close to the Viking Way and popular with hikers and ramblers. Four different guest beers are offered. The licensees pride themselves on selling real ale from microbreweries. All food is home made using ingredients from local suppliers. Meals are served lunchtimes and evenings. QP

Market Deeping

Vine Inn L

19 Church Street, PE6 8AN
4-11; 12-11 Fri-Sun (01778) 218622
Sharp's Doom Bar; house beer (by Hopshackle); 3 changing beers (often Courage, Lacons) H

Formerly a Charles Wells pub, now a free house, this small, friendly pub features oak beams and stone floors, with many 20th-century prints on the walls. There is a large patio at the rear. Five handpumps dispense two regular beers, one brewed especially for the pub by Hopshackle, plus a changing range of guests. Boxed real cider is sold. Free nibbles are provided Sunday lunchtime and early during the week. The TV is only used for major sporting events. P(101)

Messingham

Horn Inn

61 High Street, DN17 3NU

12-3 (not Mon-Wed), 5-11; 12-midnight Fri & Sat; 12-11 Sun ☎ (01724) 761190

Timothy Taylor Golden Best, Landlord; 2 changing beers (sourced regionally; often Adnams, Fuller's) Ⓗ

Popular village local thriving again since reopening in 2015. The open-plan design includes two areas for dining, with the remainder in a more traditional pub style. Meals are served at lunchtime from Thursday to Sunday, and in the evening from Wednesday to Saturday. Up to four real ales are on tap; two from Timothy Taylor are regulars and two are rotating guests. A Cask Ale Club and a pub quiz take place on a Monday evening, and live music is featured every Friday. 🐴❀◐♿P🚌📶

Pooleys

46 High Street, DN17 3NT

closed Mon; 6-11; 7-11 Sun ☎ 07860 799178

5 changing beers (sourced regionally; often Batemans, Oakham, St Austell) Ⓗ

Attractive village local, sympathetically styled with rustic furniture, vintage artefacts, signs and pictures. Only open in the evenings, it is popular with locals and visitors. It has three separate drinking areas with a mix of wooden and flagstone floors and real fires. A changing choice of five quality real ales is on the bar alongside a large selection of malt whiskies, gins and wines. Current real ales are listed on the pub's Facebook page. Q♿🚌🐾📶

Navenby

Lion & Royal

57 High Street, LN5 0DZ

12-11 (midnight Fri & Sat); 12-10.30 Sun ☎ (01522) 810368

Greene King Abbot, IPA; 3 changing beers Ⓗ

Welcoming brick and stone village pub with a flagged floor area in front of the bar plus an impressive fireplace. There is a separate pool room, and a function room upstairs. Live music is hosted on a Saturday evening, and a quiz night every Tuesday. Good-value pub food is served until 8pm. The bus stops are conveniently situated outside the pub. 🐴❀◐♿♣P🚌(1)🐾📶

Newton

Red Lion 🏆 L

Newton, NG34 0EE

closed Mon; 12-3, 5.30-11; 12-7 Sun ☎ (01529) 497256

🌐 redlionnewton.co.uk

3 changing beers Ⓗ

The Red Lion has been standing in this picturesque country village for over 300 years. With its roaring real fire and old-world charm, it welcomes you inside. The traditional village pub serves a range of real ales and a choice of home-cooked food. Local CAMRA Pub of the Year 2018. 🐴❀◐P

North Hykeham

Centurion ✔

Newark Road, LN6 8LB

11-11 (midnight Thu-Sat) ☎ (01522) 509814

Abbeydale Moonshine, Bombardier; Brakspear Bitter; house beer (by Black Sheep); 4 changing beers (sourced nationally) Ⓗ

Built in 1969, the aptly named Centurion is right on the old Roman Fosse Way, just south of Lincoln. Although family friendly and popular with diners, it is a proper pub which serves food, not a mere restaurant with a bar. Local regulars and visitors enjoy weekly quizzes, there is a convenient bus service, and it has ample parking on site, with more at the adjacent supermarket – you can shop then drop, right into the pub! 🐴❀◐♿P🚌📶

Raithby

Red Lion

Raithby Road, PE23 4DS

closed Mon; 12-2 (not Tue), 6-10; 12-2 Sun ☎ (01790) 753727

Batemans XB; Black Sheep Ale Ⓗ

Cosy village pub built around 1650, with beamed low ceilings in its many small rooms that surround the bar. Pictures of outdoor pursuits and old photographs adorn the walls. It sits in an attractive quiet village in the Wolds and is excellent for walking and cycling. The landlord has been known to provide plastic covers for the muddy boots of CAMRA trekkers. Q🐴❀🛏◐♿♣P🚌

Ropsley

Green Man

24 High Street, NG33 4BE

closed Mon; 11-11; 11-10.30 Sun ☎ (01476) 585897

🌐 green-man-ropsley.co.uk

Wainwright; 3 changing beers (sourced nationally; often Caledonian, Grainstore, Theakston) Ⓗ

Crowned local CAMRA Pub of the Year 2017, this 17th-century village pub has a growing reputation for innovative food, including exotic meats, locally sourced game and seafood. There is a relaxed tearoom area frequented by walkers and cyclists and a pleasant tranquil beer garden as well. Themed food and drink-matching evenings are held regularly. It is also renowned for an extensive bottled range. 🐴❀◐♣P🐾📶

Ruskington

Shoulder of Mutton

11 Church Street., NG34 9DU

12-midnight ☎ (01526) 832220

Bombardier; John Smith's Bitter; 2 changing beers (sourced regionally; often Sharp's) Ⓗ

A popular and thriving pub in the heart of the village attracting customers of all ages. It is one of the oldest buildings in Ruskington and was once a butcher's shop, hence the name. A few old meat hooks can still be seen in the wooden ceiling in the bar. Changes have been made in recent years but have not spoilt the essential character. Standing guard outside is Knight and Day, a sculpture from Lincoln's 2017 Knight's Trail. ❀⇌♣P🚌(31)🐾📶

Saxilby

Anglers ✔

65 High Street, LN1 2HA

11.30-11.30 (12.30am Fri & Sat); 12-11.30 Sun ☎ (01522) 702200 🌐 anglerspublichouse.com

Theakston Best Bitter; 3 changing beers Ⓗ

A convivial community pub that hosts crib, darts, dominoes, pool and football teams. Poker is played on Tuesday evenings, and two golf societies are run, while a boules court in the car park is popular. The lounge – no dogs allowed – has many old village photographs. No food is served, but a chippy is across the road. Moorings on the Fossdyke, Britains oldest canal, are close by. Beers are often from the Star Taverns range.
Q❀≠♣P🚌(100,106)🐾📶

Scampton

Dambusters Inn Ⓛ
23 High Street, LN1 2SD
closed Mon; 12-9.30 Tue (11 Wed & Thu; midnight Fri & Sat); 12-7.30 Sun ☎ (01522) 731333 dambustersinn.co.uk
Greg's Dambusters Ale, Scampton Ale; 5 changing beers (sourced nationally) Ⓗ
A village pub with a twist. It has a unique collection of RAF memorabilia, including one wall dedicated to the memory of the airmen who took part in the legendary dambusters' raid. A beer festival is held in May, around the date when 617 Squadron attacked the German dams. Sit in the rear garden and you may be treated to a display by the locally based Red Arrows. Two beers brewed by the landlord are always on the bar.
Q❀◐◑🍎P🚌(103)🐾📶

Scawby

Sutton Arms
10 West Street, DN20 9AN
11.30-midnight; 11.30-11 Sun ☎ (01652) 652430
suttonarmsscawby.co.uk
Sharp's Doom Bar; Theakston Best Bitter; 2 changing beers (often Great Newsome, Milestone) Ⓗ
A comfortable, traditionally styled village local. It has a central bar serving an open-plan dining area and separate dining room, together with a narrow snug to one side. The latter is mainly used for drinking, but meals can also be taken here. Renowned for its home-made food, an extensive menu is offered at lunchtimes and in the evening, with daily specials. Two regular real ales and two rotating guest beers are featured. Quiz night is on Sunday. ❀◐◑♿P🐾📶

Scawby Brook

King William IV ✔
Scawby Road, DN20 9JX
12-2, 5.30-11 ☎ (01652) 657106
Timothy Taylor Landlord; 2 changing beers (sourced regionally; often Everards, Hancocks) Ⓗ
Roadside village local, comfortably and attractively furnished with traditional stylings, open-plan in design and with a dining area to the rear and a small lounge and snug with TV at the front. It has a strong emphasis on food, with lunchtime and evening meals served every day, with daily specials. Three real ales are generally on tap, two of which are rotating guest beers, mainly from regional brewers. ❀◐◑♿P🚌🐾📶

Scotter

Sun & Anchor
54 High Street, DN21 3RX
3-11; 12-11 Sat; 12-10.30 Sun ☎ (01724) 763444
Bradfield Farmers Blonde; John Smith's Bitter; Ossett Yorkshire Blonde; 1 changing beer Ⓗ
A warm and inviting hostelry serving one regular and two guest ales. Traditional pub food, including a popular Sunday roast, is available. There is a darts and pool area and a large private beer garden with a children's play area. Local CAMRA Pub of the Year 2017. ❀◑♿♣P🚌🐾📶

White Swan
9 The Green, DN21 3UD
12-midnight; 11.30-midnight Fri-Sun ☎ (01724) 763061
whiteswanscotter.com
Black Sheep Best Bitter; Sharp's Doom Bar; 3 changing beers (often Thwaites) Ⓗ
In a village between Gainsborough and Scunthorpe, this is a privately run hotel, restaurant and bar which also caters for weddings and conferences. The Mucky Duck Bar has tables by the fire and still has the traditional ceiling beams which are untouched and give a feel of the building's coaching inn history. Q❀🛏◐◑P🚌📶

Scunthorpe

Berkeley Hotel ★
Doncaster Road, DN15 7DS (½ mile from end of M181)
11.30-2.30, 5-11; 12-11 Fri & Sat; 12-10.30 Sun
☎ (01724) 842333 theberkeleyscunthorpe.co.uk
Samuel Smith Old Brewery Bitter Ⓗ
A Samuel Smith's pub, opened in 1940, with an Art Deco interior recognised by CAMRA as having a nationally important historic interior. It has three internal drinking areas leading from the front reception: a main bar with real fire, a restaurant lounge and separate ballroom, plus a large public bar and beer garden with its own side entrance. It can get exceptionally busy on match days as Glanford Park football ground is a 15-minute walk away. The landscaped front entrance has a large car park. Q❀🛏◐◑♿P🚌📶

Blue Bell ✔
1-7 Oswald Road, DN15 7PU
8am-11 (1am Fri & Sat); 8am-midnight Sun
☎ (01724) 863921
Greene King Abbot, IPA; Ruddles Best Bitter; 5 changing beers (sourced regionally; often Acorn, Bradfield, Hop Studio) Ⓗ
Popular Wetherspoon town-centre pub, currently open plan on two levels. Twice-yearly beer festivals and an annual cider festival are supplemented by themed events such as Burns Night and Valentine's Day. There is a muted TV screen showing sports and news. Food is served all day to 11pm. It has a small beer garden with heaters for the use of smokers. A major expansion and refurbishment is planned for the end of 2018.
❀◐◑♿🍎🚌📶

Honest Lawyer
70 Oswald Road, DN15 7PG
11-11 (midnight Fri & Sat) ☎ (01724) 276652
honestlawyerbar.co.uk
Sharp's Atlantic; Timothy Taylor Landlord; 2 changing beers (sourced regionally; often Lincolnshire Craft Beers, Otter) Ⓗ
Recently redecorated small pub on the edge of the town centre. An upstairs restaurant holds themed events, and there is a small heated outside drinking area with tables at the front. Inside there is a side bar with high stools in front of the bar, with sofas and tables at the rear. It has a limited

menu of bar snacks. Two regular real ales are supplemented by two rotating guests. Sports TV is popular for live football matches.

Malt Shovel

219 Ashby High Street, Ashby, DN16 2JP
10-11 (midnight Fri & Sat) (01724) 843318
maltshovelashby.co.uk
Exmoor Gold; 4 changing beers (sourced regionally; often Elland, Kelham Island, Oakham) H
A distinctive high-street pub with a front beer garden overlooking the shopping area. The interior has a country-style, comfortably furnished, open-plan lounge, with a conservatory leading off to the beer garden. It is often busy at mealtimes, so booking is advisable. Quiz nights are on Tuesday and Thursday, with live music every other Saturday night. Attached is a members-only social and snooker club. Four permanently rotating guest beers from regional breweries are kept, with real ciders and perries served from the cellar.
Q

Skegness

Seathorne Arms

Seathorne Crescent, PE25 1RP
11-midnight (01754) 767797
2 changing beers (often Greene King, Morland) H
Set back from Roman Bank 15 minutes' walk from Butlin's, the pub has a big outside seating space, while the large interior has partitioned areas for dining, pub games, drinking and TV watching. It has a seasonal trade due to local caravan sites, and closes in January. The landlord operates a constantly rotating two-beer selection. The extensive food menu includes locally sourced meat.

Vine Hotel

Vine Road, PE25 3DB (off Drummond Rd)
11-11 (01754) 763018
Batemans XB, XXXB; 1 changing beer (often Batemans) H
A delightful building, one of the oldest in Skegness, dating from the 18th century and set in two acres of pleasant grounds. Inside are comfortable wood-panelled bars in which to enjoy a quiet pint or two after experiencing some of the noisier attractions and bustle of Skegness. Within striking distance of the Gibraltar Point National Nature Reserve, walking trails, beach and golf links, the inn has reputed Tennyson connections.
P

Skillington

Cross Swords

The Square, NG33 5HB
closed Mon; 12-2, 6-11; 12-8 Sun (01476) 861132
thecross-swordsinn.co.uk
2 changing beers (sourced nationally) H
Dating from the early to mid 18th century, this impressive stone-built pub commands a good position in the centre of the village and the current hosts have owned it since 1991. The bar area boasts a real fire. Ales are from regional and national breweries and quality pub food is served daily; the menu shows allergen information. There is a patio area with outside seating and it has three letting cottages. Q P

Sleaford

Carre Arms Hotel

Mareham Lane, NG34 7JP
11-11 (01529) 303156 carrearmshotel.co.uk
3 changing beers (often Marston's, Oldershaw, Springhead) H
A privately run hotel previously owned by Bass, adjacent to the Bass Sleaford Maltings complex which is now awaiting a regeneration scheme. It has a comfortable bar area with two rooms, offering three real ales which regularly change, featuring both larger regional and local breweries. Often a cider is on handpump. An extensive food menu is offered, served in the bar area or restaurant. There is a pleasant covered courtyard, ideal on inclement days. P

White Horse

Boston Road, NG34 7HD
11-11.30 (midnight Fri & Sat); 12-11 Sun
(01529) 968003
Bombardier; 2 changing beers (often Batemans, Horncastle Ales) H
On the junction of Carre Street and Boston Road, the pub serves the housing area along the Boston Road. It is one of the few remaining traditional locals' pubs in Sleaford, with wet sales only. The interior has been opened out into a single L-shaped room which still retains a cosy feel. Sports predominate, with both darts and pool teams.
P

Snitterby

Royal Oak

High Street, DN21 4TP (1½ miles from A15)
5-midnight; 12-midnight Sat; 12-9 Sun (01673) 818273
royaloaksnitterby.co.uk
Lees Bitter; Rooster's Buckeye; Theakston Best Bitter H**; 5 changing beers (sourced regionally; often Ferry Ales, Pheasantry)** H/G
A wet-led local community pub. Here beer is a backdrop to conversation, where you want to linger longer. With open fires and bare floorboards, it has up to eight handpulled ales, three ciders and a selection of quality beers including Brewdog Nanny State (0.5% ABV) to cater for all tastes. On three Fridays per month there are themed food nights. Outside there is bench seating overlooking a stream with a ford and an ancient weeping ash tree. Q P

Spalding

Olde White Horse

Churchgate, PE11 2RA
11.30-11; 12-10.30 Sun (01775) 766740
Samuel Smith Old Brewery Bitter H
An attractive white-painted early 17th-century building with a steep thatched roof, on the east river bank. The interior consists of several interconnected rooms with wood-panelled walls and a flagstone floor in the bar. A number of pictures and artefacts add interest. The convivial feel is enhanced when the large open fire is burning hot and cheerfully in the stone fireplace.
Q P

Priors Oven L

1 Sheep Market, PE11 1BH
closed Mon; 12-8 (9 Thu; midnight Fri & Sat)
6 changing beers G

The first micropub to open in Lincolnshire. The building has quite a history and is believed to be 800 years old and originally the prison of the local priory. Its more recent use was as a bakery and it became a pub in 2013. As well as the ground floor bar with its vaulted ceiling, a a recently opened gin bar is up a stone spiral staircase. Beers can be sampled in third-pint measures. Q≠⚈⊟

Red Lion Hotel ✓

Market Place, PE11 1SU

10-midnight ☎ (01775) 722869

redlionhotel-spalding.co.uk

Bombardier; Draught Bass; Greene King Abbot Ⓗ

The Red Lion is a carefully refurbished 18th-century family-run hotel. The cosy, comfortable and welcoming bar overlooks the marketplace. It is popular owing to its consistently well-kept range of cask ales, which the bar staff take great pride in serving in top condition. It is a rare outlet for Bass in the locality. On fine sunny days the experience is enhanced with tables and chairs outside beneath attractive floral displays.

Stamford

Jolly Brewer L

1 Foundry Road, PE9 2PP

11-midnight; 12-11.30 Sun ☎ (01780) 755141

thejollybrewer.com

Brewsters Marquis; Oakham JHB; 4 changing beers (sourced locally; often Baker's Dozen) Ⓗ

A locals' pub dating back to 1830 and twice local CAMRA Pub of the Year, the Brewer boasts a roomy split-level drinking area with open fires in the winter and a separate dining room. The car park and large patio host a beer festival in the autumn while pub games, including the World Pushpenny Championships, are a feature. Six handpumps dispense LocAles, national ales and the pub's own Baker's Dozen beers. The real cider is usually Old Rosie. Q (9,202)

King's Head

19 Maiden Lane, PE9 2AZ

closed Mon; 12-11; 12-5 Sun ☎ (01780) 753510

5 changing beers (sourced locally) Ⓗ

A compact 19th-century pub just off the High Street, this is a one-roomed house featuring a wood-burning stove and wooden-beamed ceiling as well as a pleasant patio area to the rear. The pub operates a one-barrel policy, with five constantly changing ales from the length and breadth of the country. Over 400 were promoted in the first two years of the scheme. Q

Tobie Norris

12 Saint Pauls Street, PE9 2BE

10-11 (midnight Fri & Sat); 12-10.30 Sun ☎ (01780) 753800

Fuller's London Pride; Oakham JHB Ⓗ**; 3 changing beers (sourced regionally; often Adnams)** Ⓗ/Ⓖ

The building, parts of which date back to 1280, was bought by Tobie Norris in 1617 and used as a bell foundry. Formerly the RAFA Club, it won CAMRA's Conversion to Pub Use Award for its transformation into a pub in 2007. It now has many small rooms with real fires, stone floors and low beams. Five handpumps serve beers from local and countrywide brewers. A former local CAMRA Pub of the Year. Q (202,203)

> Not all chemicals are bad. Without chemicals such as hydrogen and oxygen, for example, there would be no way to make water, a vital ingredient in beer.
> **Dave Barry**

Stickford

Red Lion Inn L

Church Road, PE22 8EP

closed Mon & Tue; 7-11 Wed & Thu; 4-11.30 Fri & Sat; 12-10.30 Sun ☎ (01205) 480395 redlionstickford.co.uk

Batemans XB; 1 changing beer (sourced locally; often 8 Sail, Horncastle Ales) Ⓗ

The pub name Red Lion, the most common in England, is frequently found hereabouts because it was a heraldic emblem of 14th-century John of Gaunt, Earl of Lancaster and Lord of the Manor at nearby Bolingbroke Castle. This cosy and friendly two-bar pub produces its own range of cider and holds an annual cider festival. Food is served evenings and Sunday lunchtime using local produce, and all pies are homemade. There are two en-suite letting bedrooms.

Q (113)

Swineshead

Green Dragon

Market Place, PE20 3LJ

5-11; 12-midnight Fri & Sat; 12-11 Sun ☎ (01205) 821381

Batemans XB; Theakston Traditional Mild; 3 changing beers (sourced regionally) Ⓗ

Years ago the pub was called the Green Dragon. Its fortunes gradually declined; it became run down and, despite a change of name, it eventually closed. New owners brought it back to life as a vibrant and thriving village local, successfully blending old and new to recreate a genuine community pub with an emphasis on beer and traditional pub games. Another change of ownership has now seen the pub revert to its original name. (K59)

Swinhope

Clickem Inn

Binbrook Road, LN8 6BS (on B1203)

12-3 (not Mon-Wed), 5-11; 12-11.30 Fri & Sat; 12-10.30 Sun ☎ (01472) 398253 clickem-inn.co.uk

Batemans XXXB; Timothy Taylor Landlord; house beer (by Pheasantry); 3 changing beers (sourced regionally; often Horncastle Ales, Rudgate, Springhead) Ⓗ

Set in the picturesque Lincolnshire Wolds and a popular stopping place for walkers and cyclists, the pub's name originates from the counting of sheep passing through a nearby clicking gate. It is renowned for its home-cooked food served in the bar and conservatory and it offers a choice of drinks, including six real ales and a traditional cider. The house beer is Terry's Tipple. There is pool, darts and a jukebox. Monday is quiz night. A covered, unheated area is provided for smokers.

Q P

Thimbleby

Durham Ox

Main Road, LN9 5RB

12-3, 6-11; closed Tue (01507) 527152
durhamoxpubthimbleby.co.uk
Batemans XB; Black Sheep Best Bitter; 1 changing beer (often Charnwood) H
Fine country inn over 200 years old and reopened in November 2013. This welcoming pub, with its beamed ceilings, cowshed bar and RAF corner, also has a large field at the rear for caravans and camper vans. There is an extensive menu serving local produce. The pub is named after a huge 18th-century ox which toured the country; at its largest it weighed 270 stone. P

Threekingham

Three Kings Inn

Saltersway, NG34 0AU
closed Mon; 12-3, 6-11; 12-3, 6-10.30 Sun
(01529) 240249 thethreekingsinn.com
Draught Bass; Timothy Taylor Landlord; 1 changing beer (sourced regionally) H
A classic country inn with charm and character. Its bright and comfortable lounge bar and panelled dining room serving locally sourced food are deservedly popular with locals and visitors. Guest beers are usually from independent brewers. There is a pleasant beer terrace and garden for the summer months. The pub's name refers to the slaying, by the Saxons, of three Danish chieftains in battle in 870 at nearby Stow; look for the effigies above the entrance. QP

Waddington

Three Horseshoes

High Street, LN5 9RF
3-11; 11-11 Sat; 12-11 Sun (01522) 720448
Theakston Best Bitter; 5 changing beers (sourced locally) H
In the heart of the village, the inn is next to the church and has easy access to Lincoln. The varied selection of five beers is often local, but smaller breweries from further afield are not ignored. Televised sport and a range of pub games provide a lively atmosphere. The smaller back room is usually quiet unless there is a big game on. Real fires give both rooms a cosy feel.
(1,13)

Wainfleet

Batemans Brewery Visitor Centre

Salem Bridge Brewery, Mill Lane, PE24 4JE
10-5 (9 Thu-Sat); 10-5 Sun; closed Mon & Tue winter
(01754) 882017
Batemans XB, Gold, Salem Porter, XXXB; 1 changing beer (sourced locally; often Batemans) H
Visiting Batemans Brewery provides the chance to experience their blend of 140-plus years of proud craft brewing tradition with their forward-thinking outlook. Mr George's Bar, within the attractive windmill, is the ideal venue to sample a range of the beers. Further entertainment is to be found with brewery tours, featuring the Theatre of Beers, and in the pleasant beer garden with its games. Opening days and times vary throughout the year – see the website for details. Usually closed in January. P(7)

Westwoodside

Carpenter's Arms

Newbigg, DN9 2AT (on B1396 in centre of village)
4-11.30; 2-11.30 Sat; 12-11.30 Sun (01427) 752416
Black Sheep Best Bitter; Caledonian Deuchars IPA; Sharp's Doom Bar; 2 changing beers (sourced nationally; often Brains, Wychwood) H
A popular community pub which is well supported by locals, hosting various community events and raising large amounts for charity. Up to five cask ales are available, with some original choices as guest ales. It is CAMRA friendly, with two welcoming and comfortable bars. A regular in this Guide since the present licensees took over in 2005, it is also winner of the local Haxey Hood game in 2018. P(399)

Winterton

George Hogg

25 Market Street, DN15 9PT
2-11 (midnight Fri); 12-midnight Sat; 12-11 Sun
(01724) 732270 thegeorgehogg.co.uk
Draught Bass; Lincolnshire Craft Beers Lincoln Gold; 2 changing beers (sourced regionally; often Black Sheep, York) H
Popular Grade II-listed marketplace pub. Award-winning and friendly, it has a large lounge/dining area and separate public bar, both with real fires. Good-value Sunday lunches are served. Further dining is available upstairs during busy times. Locally sourced guest beers are changed on a regular basis and there is an annual beer festival. It is a meeting place for local football teams and Scunthorpe United supporters' club.
QP(350)

Wragby

Ivy

Market Place, LN8 5QU
12-11 (midnight Fri & Sat) (01673) 858768
theivywragby.co.uk
Draught Bass; Black Sheep Best Bitter; 3 changing beers (sourced nationally) H
A village-centre pub with three separate areas including a restaurant. A wood-burning stove adds to the home-from-home feeling. There is always a varied selection of ales plus one real cider. Tasty, home-cooked food is served, including gluten-free options, and gluten-free bottled beers are also available. Sport is screened in the main bar area and there is a popular quiz on Sunday evening.
Q(50,56)

Wroot

Cross Keys

Main Street, DN9 2BT (centre of village)
5-11; 4-midnight Sat; 12-11 Sun (01302) 770231
Theakston Best Bitter; 2 changing beers (sourced regionally; often Eagle, Welbeck Abbey, Wychwood) H
A genuine village pub, popular and well served by locals in this small rural community. There are four separate rooms, and pub games are popular. Always a drinkers' pub, the beer range has expanded under the current licensee and now features up to four cask ales, with local breweries often showcased. The pub takes an active part in community events. QP

CAMRA's Essential Home Brewing

Andy Parker & Graham Wheeler

CAMRA'S essential guide to brewing exciting world beers at home.

Whether you're taking your first steps in home brewing, or you're a more experienced home brewer entering competitions or following a dream of brewing commercially, this book contains everything you need to know. From understanding and selecting your ingredients, through to equipment, the brewing process, and troubleshooting, this is a step-by-step guide to brewing your own great-tasting beer.

Featuring 30 exciting recipes from world-leading, innovative craft breweries, with hints and tips on adapting the brews to make them your own.

Written by Andy Parker, an award-winning home brewer who now owns and operates Berkshire-based microbrewery Elusive Brewing, and incorporating key text from acclaimed home brewing expert Graham Wheeler, CAMRA's *Essential Home Brewing* is the ultimate home brewer's guide.

RRP £11.99 **ISBN** 978-1-85249-351-6 **208 pages**

For this and other books on beer and pubs visit CAMRA's online bookshop at **www.camra.org.uk/books** or call **01727 867201**. Discounts are available for CAMRA members.

London index

*Shown on Inner London map

GREATER LONDON

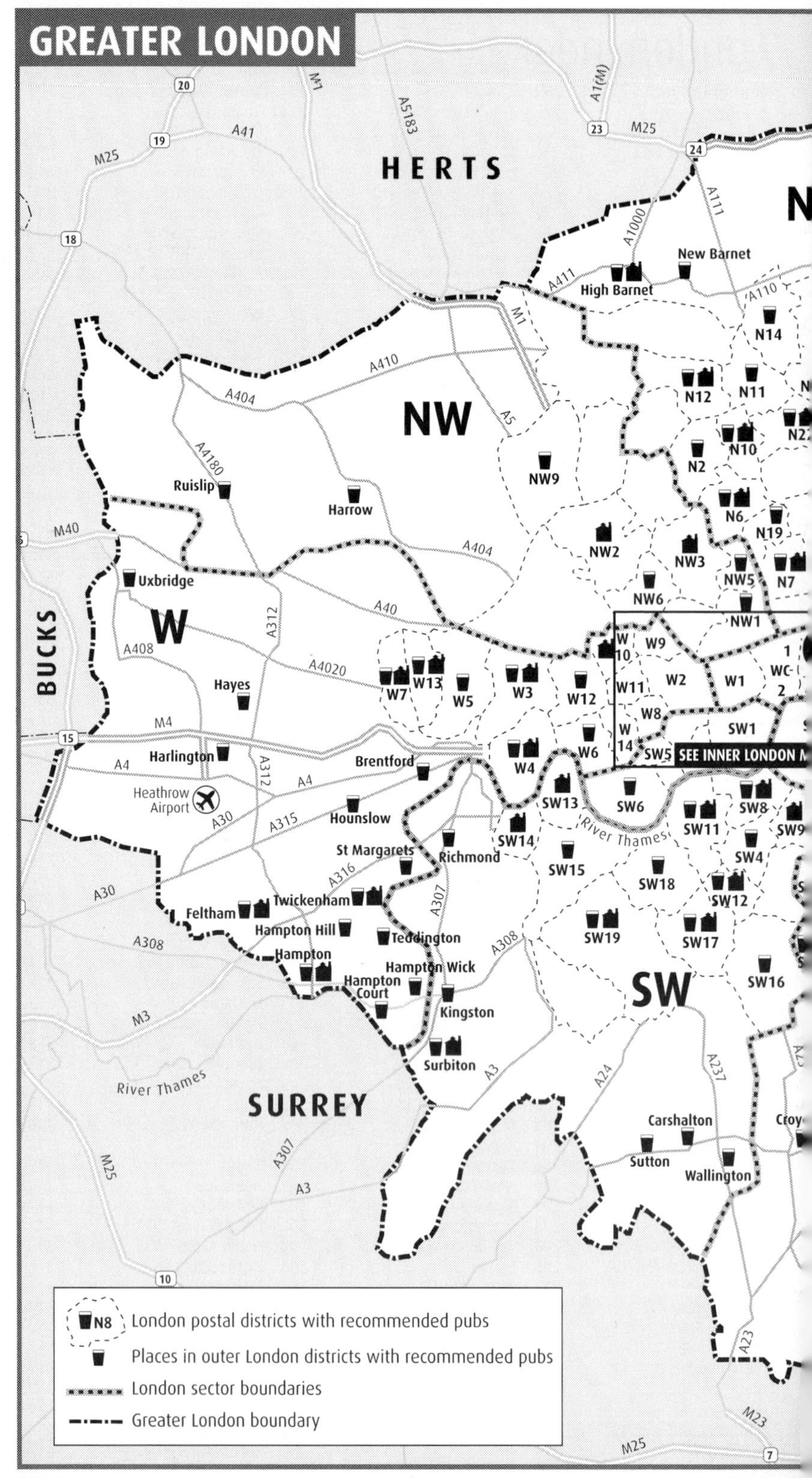

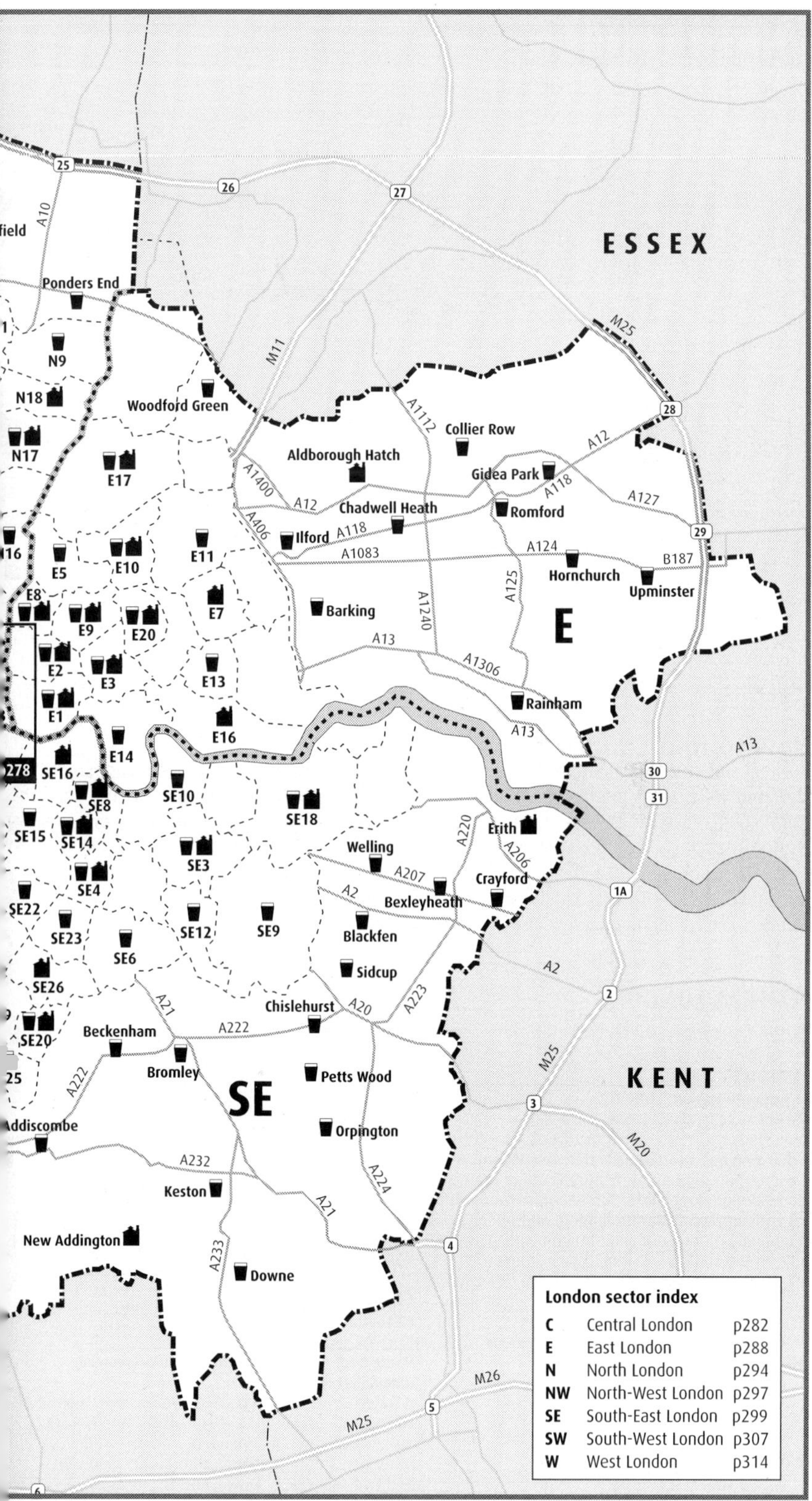

London sector index

C	Central London	p282
E	East London	p288
N	North London	p294
NW	North-West London	p297
SE	South-East London	p299
SW	South-West London	p307
W	West London	p314

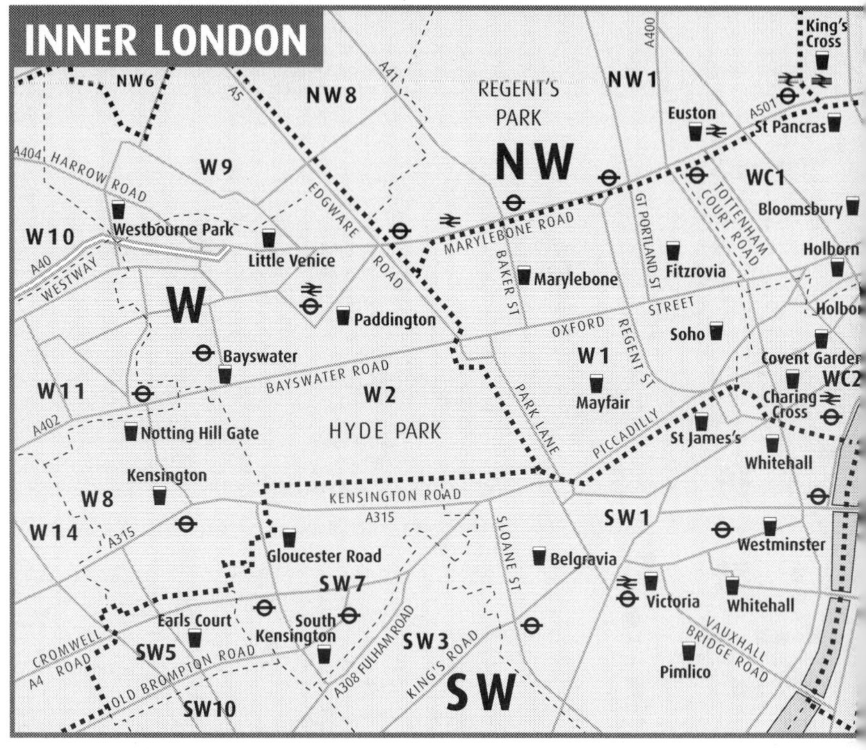

How to find London pubs

Greater London is divided into seven sectors: Central, East, North, North-West, South-East, South-West and West, reflecting postal boundaries. The Central sector includes the City (EC1 to EC4) and Holborn, Covent Garden and the Strand (WC1/2) plus W1, where pubs are listed in postal district order. In each of the other six sectors the pubs with London postcodes are listed first in postal district order (E1, E2 etc), followed by those in outer London districts, which are listed in alphabetical order (Barking, Chadwell Heath, etc) – see Greater London map. Postal district numbers can be found on every street name plate in the London postcode area.

CENTRAL LONDON

EC1: Clerkenwell

Exmouth Arms

23 Exmouth Market, EC1R 4QL

11-midnight (1.30am Fri & Sat; 11.30 Sun)

☎ (020) 3551 4772 exmoutharms.com

4 changing beers (often Dark Star, Revolution) H

A corner pub with a noteworthy Courage brewery tiled exterior, now part of the Barworks group. The bar is open plan with dim lighting and offers a wide range of draught and bottled beers, plus real cider in the summer. Standard pub grub and specialist burgers are served until 10pm (9pm Sun). There is an outside drinking area on the pavement. Music is played but there are no TVs.

♿ ≉(Farringdon) ⊖(Angel/Farringdon)

EC1: Farringdon

Jerusalem Tavern

55 Britton Street, EC1M 5UQ

12-11; closed Sat & Sun ☎ (020) 7490 4281

St Peter's Best Bitter, Mild, Golden Ale, Organic Best, Organic Ale, Grapefruit Beer A

Named after the medieval priory of St John of Jerusalem, the gatehouse of which is nearby, this sucessor to an older pub of the same name opened in 1996 in an 18th-century building. It appears mainly untouched, with wooden furniture and alcoves. The draught beer from St Peter's Brewery is all dispensed from taps in the wall behind the bar. Cooked food is available at lunchtime, bar snacks in the evening. Q

EC1: Hatton Garden

Craft Beer Co

82 Leather Lane, EC1N 7TR

12-11; closed Sun ☎ (020) 7404 7049

House beer (by Kent); changing beers (sourced nationally) H

A Grade II-listed traditional free house with a glass ceiling and a large Bass mirror. There are 14 cask ales, mainly from independent microbreweries, 21 other beers on tap, over 200 in bottles and cans and two real ciders. Downstairs is plenty of standing room with stools and tables around the

wall; extra seating is upstairs and the pavement outside provides a smoking area. Bar snacks include pies and Scotch eggs.
≠(Farringdon)⊖(Chancery Lane/Farringdon)

Olde Mitre ★ L ✓

1 Ely Court, Ely Place, EC1N 6SJ

11-11; closed Sat & Sun ☎ (020) 7405 4751

Fuller's Oliver's Island, London Pride; Gale's Seafarers Ale; 3 changing beers (often Clarkshaws, Sambrook's, Windsor & Eton) H

Hidden in an alley between Hatton Garden and Ely Place, there has been a pub on this site since 1546. Mainly dating from the 18th century, the current pub has two bars and an upstairs function room, reached by a narrow staircase. All are wood panelled, giving a traditional feel, and it has been identified by CAMRA as having a nationally important historic pub interior. A real cider is available. Bar snacks include a range of toasties.
Q≠(City Thameslink)⊖(Chancery Lane/Farringdon)

EC1: Old Street

Old Fountain L

3 Baldwin Street, EC1V 9NU

11 (12 Sat)-11; 12-10.30 Sun ☎ (020) 7253 2970

Fuller's London Pride; 7 changing beers (sourced regionally) H

A free house behind Moorfields Eye Hospital. The rear bar area is two steps up from the front. Eight handpumps serve a rotating range of cask ales, which are listed on the blackboard. Fourteen other beers on tap, a range of bottled beers and a changing real cider are served, and meals are available until 9pm (8pm Sun). There is a heated roof terrace for outdoor drinking. Major sporting events are shown. Background music is quiet.
≠⊖

EC1: Smithfield

Butcher's Hook & Cleaver

60-63 West Smithfield, EC1A 9DY

11-11; closed Sat & Sun ☎ (020) 7600 9181

Fuller's Oliver's Island, London Pride, ESB; Gale's Seafarers Ale; 1 changing beer H

Since Victorian times Smithfield has been London's largest meat market. This Fuller's pub, in a former bank and commercial premises, is close to the market and Bart's hospital. The interior is rather grand, with a part-tiled floor, wood panelling and chandeliers. Further seating is on a mezzanine. Twelve handpumps dispense four beers from the Fuller's range. Food is served 12-9pm. Music is played but there are no TVs.
≠(Farringdon)⊖(Barbican)

EC2: Liverpool Street

Hamilton Hall ✓

Street-level Concourse, Unit 32, Liverpool Street Station, EC2M 7PY

7am-11.30; 9am-10.30 Sun ☎ (020) 7247 3579

Greene King IPA, Abbot; Sharp's Doom Bar; 7 changing beers (sourced nationally) H

A pub based in a Grade II-listed building that used to be the ballroom of the Great Eastern Hotel. The main bar has 10 handpumps dispensing three standard Wetherspoon ales and seven rotating guests. Upstairs five of the same ales are available in a smaller, more comfortable bar. Food is served most of the day, starting with breakfast from 7am on weekdays. Given its location, the place can be busy. Train times are displayed on TV screens.
Q≠⊖

Magpie ✓

12 New Street, EC2M 4TP

11-midnight (11 Mon & Tue); 12-11 Sat; closed Sun ☎ (020) 7929 3889

Fuller's London Pride; St Austell Nicholson's Pale Ale; Sharp's Doom Bar; Truman's Runner; 6 changing beers (sourced regionally) H

A traditional pub with pictures of the area's history on the walls along with details of the building's previous use as an ambulance station. The pub serves 10 cask ales with five being guest ales from the Nicholson's seasonal list. Food is available until 9pm with pies a speciality, but children are only allowed on a Saturday. Owing to its proximity to Liverpool Street station it will be crowded during rush hour; there is a function room upstairs.
≠⊖

EC3: Gracechurch Street

Crosse Keys ✓

7-12 Gracechurch Street, EC3V 0DR

8am-11 (midnight Fri); 9am-11 Sat; 9.30am-6.30 Sun ☎ (020) 7623 4824

Fuller's London Pride; Greene King IPA, Abbot; Sharp's Doom Bar; changing beers H

Housed in a grandiose building that used to be the headquarters of a banking corporation, this Wetherspoon pub is named after a coaching inn that was nearby. Twenty-four handpumps dispense

the four regular ales and a range of rotating guests. These are listed on the screens above the bar and ordered by pump number. Food is available and there are three function rooms for hire. Popular with city workers, it can be busy at times.
Q⚭◐♿⇌(Cannon St/Fenchurch St)⊖(Bank/Monument)🍎🚌📶

Ship ✔

11 Talbot Court, EC3V 0BP

⏲ 11-11; 12-6 Sat; closed Sun ☎ (020) 7929 3903

Fuller's London Pride; St Austell Nicholson's Pale Ale; Sharp's Doom Bar; 6 changing beers (sourced nationally) Ⓗ

A narrow street surrounded by tall buildings leads off Gracechurch Street to this quaint pub with an intriguing history. Originally the Talbot, it was destroyed by the Great Fire of London. The single bar is split into two by the staff entrance. Both ends have a bank of handpumps and fonts. Above are glass panels, above and to the rear are mirrored panels; it feels like a gin palace from a bygone era. It has an extensive food menu.
◐⇌(Cannon St/Fenchurch St)⊖(Bank/Monument)🚌📶

Swan Tavern ✔

Ship Tavern Passage, 77/80 Gracechurch Street, EC3V 1LY

⏲ 11-10; closed Sat & Sun ☎ (020) 7929 6550

Fuller's Oliver's Island, London Pride; Gale's Seafarers Ale; 1 changing beer Ⓗ

This Fuller's house is a traditional, small City pub on two floors, just off Gracechurch Street. Four handpumps and two banks of fonts dispense ales and lagers downstairs. A narrow space for drinkers in front of the bar leads to an area with marble shelves and a few bar stools. Upstairs seating is limited to about a dozen stools with shelves, and there are a couple of tables to rest your drinks. Food is from local markets.
◐⇌(Cannon St/Fenchurch St)⊖(Bank/Monument)♣🚌

EC3: Tower Hill

Liberty Bounds ✔

15 Trinity Square, EC3N 4AA

⏲ 8am-midnight ☎ (020) 7481 0513

REAL ALE BREWERIES

40FT E8: Dalston
Affinity SE16: South Bermondsey
Alphabeta ▤ EC2: Liverpool Street
Anspach & Hobday SE1: Bermondsey
Barnet ▤ High Barnet
Beavertown N17: Tottenham Hale
Beerblefish N18: Upper Edmonton
Belleville SW12: Wandsworth Common
Bexley Erith
Big Smoke ▤ Surbiton
Block ▤ N1: Hoxton (NEW)
Brew By Numbers SE16: Bermondsey
Brewheadz N17: Tottenham Hale
Brewhouse & Kitchen ▤ EC1: Islington
Brewhouse & Kitchen ▤ N5: Highbury
Brick SE8: Deptford
Brixton SW9: Brixton
Brockley SE4: Brockley
Bullfinch SE24: Herne Hill
By The Horns SW17: Summerstown
Canopy SE24: Herne Hill
Cellar Boys SE14: New Cross Gate (NEW)
Clarkshaws SW9: Loughborough Junction
Craft Academy ▤ SE24: Herne Hill (NEW)
Crate E9: Hackney Wick
Cricklewood NW2: Cricklewood (NEW)
Cronx New Addington
Dragonfly ▤ W3: Acton
East London E10: Leyton
Enfield N18: Upper Edmonton
Essex Street ▤ WC2: Temple
Five Points E8: Hackney Downs
Fourpure SE16: South Bermondsey
Fuller's W4: Chiswick
Gorgeous ▤ N6: Highgate
Hackney E2: Haggerston
Hammerton N7: Barnsbury
Hop Stuff SE18: Woolwich
House ▤ N22: Wood Green (NEW)
Howling Hops ▤ E9: Hackney Wick
Husk E16: West Silvertown
Ignition SE26: Sydenham (NEW)
Jeffersons SW13: Barnes (NEW)
Kernel SE16: Bermondsey
Kew SW14: East Sheen
Laine ▤ E9: Hackney
Laine ▤ SW11: Battersea
London Beer Factory SE27: West Norwood
London Beer Lab SW9: Brixton
London Brewing ▤ N12: North Finchley
Long Arm ▤ EC2A: Old Street (NEW)
Magic Spells E10: Leyton
Maregade E9: Homerton
Marko Paulo ▤ W13: Northfields
Moncada NW2: Dollis Hill
Mondo SW8: South Lambeth
Muswell Hillbilly N10: Muswell Hill (NEW)
Oddly Hampton
One Mile End ▤ E1: Whitechapel/N17: Tottenham
Orbit SE17: Walworth
Partizan SE16: South Bermondsey
Portobello W10: North Kensington
Pressure Drop N17: Tottenham Hale
Pretty Decent E7: Forest Gate (NEW)
Project 88 ▤ NW2: Willesden Green (NEW)
Redchurch E2: Bethnal Green
Redemption N17: Tottenham
Reunion Feltham
Sambrook's SW11: Battersea
Signature Brew E10: Leyton
Small Beer SE16: South Bermondsey (NEW)
Solvay Society Aldborough Hatch
Southey SE20: Penge
Southwark SE1: Bermondsey
Spartan SE16: South Bermondsey (NEW)
St John at Hackney E8: Hackney (NEW)
St Mary's NW3: Primrose Hill (NEW)
Tap East ▤ E20: Stratford Westfield
Three Sods ▤ E2: Bethnal Green
Tiny Vessel Hampton (NEW)
Truman's E3: Hackney Wick
Twickenham Twickenham
Two Tribes N7: King's Cross
Ubrew SE16: Bermondsey
Volden Croydon
Weird Beard W7: Hanwell
Wild Card E17: Walthamstow
Wimbledon SW19: Colliers Wood
Zerodegrees ▤ SE3: Blackheath

Adnams Broadside; Fuller's London Pride; Greene King IPA, Abbot; Sharp's Doom Bar; 6 changing beers (sourced nationally) Ⓗ
A Wetherspoon pub in a grand building near the Tower of London. The interior is comfortably furnished and arranged over different levels. Both the downstairs and upstairs bars boast 12 handpumps but the range, up to six regular beers and six guest beers, remains the same on both. The food, served until 11pm, represents good value for the area. Wheelchair access is via the rear entrance. Dogs (except assistance dogs) are not admitted. The TVs are usually mute.
Q⚲◑♿⇌(Fenchurch St)⊖(Tower Gateway/ Tower Hill)●🚌📶

EC4: Cannon Street

Pelt Trader

Arch 3, Dowgate Hill, EC4N 6AP
12-11; closed Sat & Sun ☎ (020) 7160 0253
pelttrader.co.uk
6 changing beers (sourced nationally) Ⓐ
Under arches beside the new Cannon Street station, the glass-fronted exterior leads to a large but cosy U-shaped bar at the rear. Behind it, there is an array of taps and fonts, always offering a good choice; cask ale is dispensed from wall-mounted taps using air pressure. Given the design, it does not look or feel like an arch inside. Around the outer walls are ironing board-shaped tables with seating. A varied selection of home-made pizzas is offered. The name relates to the Skinners' Company hall, opposite. ⚲❀◑⇌⊖🚌🐾📶

Sir John Hawkshaw ✔

Cannon Street Station, Cannon Street, EC4N 6AP
7am-11.30 (midnight Thu & Fri); 8am-7 Sun
☎ (020) 3206 1004
Fuller's London Pride; Greene King IPA, Abbot; Sharp's Doom Bar; 3 changing beers Ⓗ
Sited by Platform 1 on the concourse and named after the station's co-designer, this modern, glass-fronted building, with a central door and outside seating, has a long, single, copper-topped bar located at the rear. Six handpumps and three banks of fonts serve a selection of ales, lagers, ciders and wines. To the left of the bar a screen displays up-to-date train information. The pub will be closed if the station is not open. Q⚲◑♿⇌⊖🚌📶

WC1: Bloomsbury

Calthorpe Arms

252 Grays Inn Road, WC1X 8JR
12 (11 Wed & Thu)-11.30; 11-midnight Fri; 11-11 Sat; 12-10.30 Sun ☎ (020) 7278 4732
Young's Bitter, Special; 3 changing beers (sourced nationally; often Young's) Ⓗ
Unusual double doors lead into this single-bar corner local. With no music and an unobtrusive corner TV, it is easy either to strike up a conversation at a bar stool or take one of the tables along the sides for more privacy. The upstairs dining room opens for lunch (12-2.30pm) but can be booked at other times. Evening meals are served 5.45-9.30pm. Young's bottle-conditioned beers are stocked plus a Young's seasonal and/or two guest beers. There is pavement seating outside. ❀◑⊖(Russell Sq)●🚌🐾

Lamb 🄻

94 Lambs Conduit Street, WC1N 3LZ
11-11 (midnight Thu-Sat); 12-10.30 Sun
☎ (020) 7405 0713 thelamblondon.com
Young's Bitter, Special; house beer (by Sharp's); 5 changing beers (often Redemption, Truman's, Wimbledon) Ⓗ
Beautifully preserved, Grade II-listed, and identified by CAMRA as having a regionally important historic pub interior, the Lamb has dark-blue upholstery, a small snug and etched-glass snob screens above the bar. The Empire Room bar and meeting room is upstairs. The glorious Victorian history of the pub and area is commemorated by a working polyphon (predecessor to the gramophone) and sepia prints of music hall players. Many of the guest beers are locally brewed, and real ciders are served from boxes. Behind is a small walled garden.
Q❀◑⊖(Russell Sq)●🚌📶

Marlborough Arms 🄻 ✔

36 Torrington Place, WC1E 7LY
12-11 (10.30 Sun) ☎ (020) 7636 0120
Greene King IPA; 7 changing beers (often Hammerton, Redemption, Sambrook's) Ⓗ
Commemorating the coat of arms first worn by the third Duke of Marlborough, John Churchill, this is a traditional pub perpetually busy with students, business people, tourists and locals from a surprisingly residential neighbourhood. A large open area surrounded by oak panelling and some fine features, with the bar pushed to one side, makes an easy area to fill with tables in regular formation but with a nod to informality and comfort in the small area beyond the bar.
⚲❀◑♿⇌⊖(Goodge St)●🚌🐾📶

Swan 🄻 ✔

7 Cosmo Place, WC1N 3AP
11-11 (midnight Fri); 12-10.30 Sun ☎ (020) 7837 6223
Greene King IPA, Abbot; Hammerton N1; 5 changing beers (often Harvey's, St Austell, Wimbledon) Ⓗ
Popular family-oriented pub among the tourist hotels on Southampton Row, close to Great Ormond Street Children's Hospital. There is a single long room, and tables in front on a pedestrian passage. Real cider is on handpump during summer and festivals. Pub grub and snacks are available until 10pm (9.30 Sun). A large-screen TV shows live sports events.
Q⚲❀◑♿⊖(Russell Sq)●🚌🐾📶

WC1: Holborn

Craft Beer Co

168 High Holborn, WC1V 7AA
12-midnight (1am Thu-Sat) ☎ (020) 7240 0431
15 changing beers (sourced nationally) Ⓗ
In the ancient parish of St Giles, whose church featured in several of Hogarth's works including Gin Lane, though its location on the north-eastern edge of Covent Garden will probably have a more modern resonance. On two levels, this, the sixth Craft Beer Co outlet, would be more at home in Beer Street, with its 15 pumps dispensing a range of beers from across the UK, while fridges boast over 200 bottles and cans. There are frequent tap takeovers and Meet the Brewer events.
⊖(Covent Garden/Holborn)🚌

Holborn Whippet

25-29 Sicilian Avenue, WC1A 2QH
12-11; closed Sun (020) 3137 9937
holbornwhippet.com
5 changing beers (sourced nationally) Ⓗ
This pub uses a flow-jet to pump the beer to the taps; a blackboard above shows what is on sale. Real ales come from the likes of Adnams, Bristol Beer Factory, Dark Star, Mighty Oak, Oakham, Redemption and other London breweries; many other draught beers are sold. It has a simple menu: pizza, bratwurst, barbecue wings, all nicely done. Decor is basic, with bare wooden floors, brown tiles and cream-painted walls; there is outside seating on Sicilian Avenue.

WC1: St Pancras

Queen's Head

66 Acton Street, WC1X 9NB
12-midnight (11 Sun & Mon) (020) 7713 5772
queensheadlondon.com
Redemption Trinity; 2 changing beers (sourced regionally) Ⓗ
Narrow, late Georgian premises off Gray's Inn Road, with a single bar, a smoking patio at the rear and benches in front. The piano is used for jazz and blues on Thursdays and late Sunday afternoons. Guest beers from microbreweries usually include a dark one. One handpump serves cider, with three more real ciders and a range of other draught and bottled beers. Sharing platters of snacks are on offer at this comfortable pub frequented by locals and the occasional tourist.
(King's Cross/St Pancras)

Skinners Arms

114 Judd Street, WC1H 9NT
12-11; closed Sun (020) 7837 6521
skinnersarmslondon.com
Greene King Abbot, IPA; 4 changing beers (sourced nationally) Ⓗ
Named after the City Livery Company and standing on a street named after a past Master of the Company, this traditional, quiet corner pub has essentially been converted to one bar, despite the signs on the doors and in the stained glass, of which there is quite a lot in the windows. There is a raised seating area on the left as you enter, and what was a separate room at the back is a large alcove with more seating.
(King's Cross/St Pancras)

WC2: Charing Cross

Harp

47 Chandos Place, WC2N 4HS
10.30-11.30 (midnight Fri & Sat); 12-10.30 Sun
(020) 7836 0291 harpcoventgarden.com
Dark Star Hophead, American Pale Ale; Fuller's London Pride; Harvey's Sussex Best Bitter; 5 changing beers (sourced nationally) Ⓗ
Small, friendly Fuller's pub that became a haven for beer choice as a free house under the management of the late, legendary, Binnie Walsh. Ciders and perries complement the fine range of real ales. The narrow bar is adorned with mirrors and portraits. There is no intrusive music or TV and a cosy upstairs room provides a refuge from the busy throng. Numerous awards include the CAMRA National Pub of the Year accolade for 2010.
Q

Lemon Tree

4 Bedfordbury, WC2N 4BP
12-11 (10.30 Sun) (020) 7831 1391
lemontreecoventgarden.com
Harvey's Sussex Best Bitter; St Austell Proper Job; 3 changing beers (often Otter, Portobello, Timothy Taylor) Ⓗ
This one-bar pub next to the stage door of the Coliseum is a favourite among locals, musicians and theatregoers. The Thai restaurant upstairs doubles as a function room. Look out for the pub's entrance, slightly set back. In the choice of guest beers there is an emphasis on London brews, by popular demand.

WC2: Covent Garden

Coach & Horses

42 Wellington Street, WC2E 7BD
11-11; 12-10.30 Sun (020) 7240 0553
Adnams Southwold Bitter; St Austell Tribute Ⓗ
A small, traditional independent pub with a strong Irish influence, used very much by locals, to which visitors make a beeline, along with theatre- and opera-goers. It has a fantastic collection of about 70 Irish whiskeys and gins, and Scottish whiskies. There are photographs of Gaelic football teams, and the sport of hurling also features, plus theatre posters. Note the beautiful engraved front windows. Q

Cross Keys

31 Endell Street, WC2H 9BA
11-11; 12-10.30 Sun (020) 7836 5185
crosskeyscoventgarden.com
Brodie's Bethnal Green Bitter, Old Street Pale Ale; Greene King London Glory; 2 changing beers (sourced nationally; often Brodie's) Ⓗ
Built in the mid-1840s when Endell (formerly Belton) Street was widened as part of clearing the St Giles's rookery (slum), an ornate façade reveals a long, welcoming bar, subdued lighting, comfortable banquette seating and tables and chairs. Copper kettles, pans, street signs, stuffed fish, framed pictures, Beatles memorabilia and a fine Truman, Hanbury, Buxton & Co mirror cover the walls. Families are welcome (over-12s only) until 7pm unless it is busy, but no dogs.

White Swan

14 New Row, WC2N 4LF
11-11 (11.30 Fri); 10-11.30 Sat; 12-10.30 Sun
(020) 3077 1129
St Austell Nicholson's Pale Ale; 6 changing beers (sourced nationally) Ⓗ
Grade II-listed, once owned by the London banking firm of Hoare & Co and formerly an O'Neills, this M&B Nicholson's pub is popular with Covent Garden tourists. It has been tastefully refurbished with a small bar; there is limited seating in the bar area but more room past a partition. The first-floor dining room can be booked for functions – note its contrasting fireplaces. Breakfast is served until 12pm (not Sun).
(Charing Cross)(Leicester Sq)

WC2: Holborn

Shakespeare's Head

Africa House, 64-68 Kingsway, WC2B 6BG
7am-midnight; 8am-1am Fri & Sat; 8am-midnight Sun
(020) 7404 8846

Fuller's London Pride; Greene King IPA; Sharp's Doom Bar; 6 changing beers (sourced nationally) Ⓗ
Large Wetherspoon bank conversion from 1998, named after a famous pub in the locality until the demolition of Wych Street over 100 years ago. It is usually busy with shoppers, tourists, local office workers and, during term time, students from the nearby London School of Economics. A convenient place for a couple of pints after a cultural sojourn at the British Museum. Q

WC2: Temple

Edgar Wallace

40 Essex Street, WC2R 3JF
11-11; closed Sat & Sun ☎ (020) 7353 3120
theedgarwallace.co.uk
Crouch Vale Brewers Gold; 7 changing beers (often Dark Star, Timothy Taylor) Ⓗ
Just off Fleet Street near the Royal Courts of Justice, this is a real gem of a one-room pub, with additional seating upstairs. The comfortable downstairs room, walls and ceiling covered with beer mats and old advertising signs, has a fine wooden bar offering a wide range of rotating ales. Good-value food is served all day (until 3pm Fri) and it is quiet; no music, laptops, mobiles and so forth are allowed. Q

Temple Brew House ✔

46 Essex Street, WC2R 3JF
12-11 (11.30 Thu; midnight Fri & Sat); 12-10.30 Sun
☎ (020) 7936 2536 templebrewhouse.com
Essex Street TemPAle; 5 changing beers (often Essex Street) Ⓗ
This basement bar, just off the Strand, is run by the City Pub Group and continues its development of microbrew pubs, joining the Bath Brew House and the Cambridge Brew House. The 5-barrel plant is visible from the bar, a single room with minimal decor, novel lighting and schoolroom-style furnishings, as well as some tables set aside for dining. Generally quiet during the day, it can get noisy in the evening. Q

W1: Fitzrovia

Queen Charlotte

43 Goodge Street, W1T 1TA
12-11 (11.30 Thu; midnight Fri & Sat); closed Sun
☎ (020) 7323 9361
3 changing beers (often By the Horns, Harbour, Sambrook's) Ⓗ
A big welcome awaits you in this small, single-bar corner pub, part of the Draft House group, with its bare wooden floors and simple furnishings. Changing offerings from Sambrook's and other local smaller breweries are sold in one-third and two-third pint measures as well as the usual halves and pints. Plenty of other interesting draught and bottled beers are also stocked. Cooked dishes, including speciality burgers, are served lunchtimes during the week and until 9pm on Saturdays; bar snacks, including giant pork scratchings, are otherwise available. (Goodge St)

Stag's Head

102 New Cavendish Street, W1W 6XW
11 (12 Sat)-11; 12-10 Sun ☎ (020) 7580 8313
Fuller's London Pride; Tring Side Pocket for a Toad; 1 changing beer (sourced locally; often Tring) Ⓗ
A smart, oak-panelled pub, offering a friendly welcome to regulars and visitors alike. Rebuilt in the late 1930s by brewers William Younger, it has a marvellous Art Deco exterior sporting a curved corner profile, and has been identified by CAMRA as having a regionally important historic interior. Vertical drinking is assisted by unusual peninsular shelf projections to the bar and elsewhere. Sun-lovers and smokers can relax on shaded benches outside. Traditional pub food is served lunchtimes only. (Gt Portland St)

W1: Marylebone

Carpenters Arms

12 Seymour Place, W1H 7NE
11-11; 12-10.30 Sun ☎ (020) 7723 1050
thecarpentersarmspub.co.uk
Harvey's Sussex Best Bitter; 5 changing beers (sourced nationally; often Portobello) Ⓗ
A sister pub to Southwark's Market Porter but with fewer beers, and a welcoming haven for escapees from the bustle of Oxford Street. TV sports and a dartboard add to the appeal for the regulars. A sensitive refurbishment has preserved the wall tiling and floor mosaics at the main entrance. Elsewhere is a display of woodworking tools. Snacks are mainly pork pies and Scotch eggs. (Marble Arch)

Golden Eagle

59 Marylebone Lane, W1U 2NY
12-11 (midnight Fri & Sat); closed Sun ☎ (020) 7935 3228
Fuller's London Pride; St Austell Tribute; 2 changing beers (often Adnams, Twickenham) Ⓗ
First licensed in 1842 and rebuilt in 1890, this single-bar pub is traditional in every way: small and cosy with smart decor, a fine etched bar-back mirror and leaded windows. It has been identified by CAMRA as having a regionally important historic pub interior. Landlady Gina Vernon and her family celebrated 25 years here in 2016. Piano singalongs on Tuesday, Thursday and Friday evenings maintain the timeless atmosphere. Real ales are quality, not quantity! Q(Bond St)

Thornbury Castle

29A Enford Street, W1H 1DN
12-11; closed Sat & Sun ☎ (020) 7402 2189
thornburycastle.uk.com
6 changing beers (sourced regionally) Ⓗ
A small, family-run pub in a side street near Marylebone station, with wood panelling throughout and a raised seating area at the back. There is a strong Rugby Union connection (Wasps) and the pub may open at weekends for big games on TV. Discerning drinkers will find it a worthwhile alternative to the more mainstream pubs in the area. Thai food is served. Q

W1: Mayfair

Clarence ✔

4 Dover Street, W1S 4LB
10-11 (midnight Fri & Sat) ☎ (020) 7491 3607
Fuller's London Pride; St Austell Nicholson's Pale Ale; Sharp's Doom Bar; 5 changing beers (sourced nationally) Ⓗ
Licensed in 1724 as the Coach & Horses, later named after the Duke of Clarence, who became King William IV in 1830. A smallish frontage belies a much larger area extending back, which

incorporates a beer library. The atmosphere is convivial, especially since M&B Nicholson's refurbishment in 2012; upstairs it has a pleasant, quieter bar. The pub is close to the Ritz Hotel in Piccadilly. ⊖(Green Park)

W1: Soho

Argyll Arms ★

18 Argyll Street, W1F 7TP

10-11.30 (midnight Fri & Sat); 10-11 Sun
(020) 7734 6117

Fuller's London Pride; St Austell Nicholson's Pale Ale; 6 changing beers (sourced nationally) H

A Victorian Grade II*-listed M&B Nicholson's house, identified by CAMRA as having a nationally important historic pub interior. Three snugs are separated by etched-glass partitions; note the remarkable Bass mirror. The bar-back is impressive and next to it is a rare survivor, a manager's office with more etched glazing. The magnificent saloon is decorated with ornate mirrors. Enjoy a reliable range of regular and guest ales on eight or more handpumps. ⊖(Oxford Circus)

Crown

64 Brewer Street, W1F 9TP

11-11 (11.30 Fri & Sat); 11-10.30 Sun (020) 7287 8420

St Austell Nicholson's Pale Ale; Truman's Runner; 3 changing beers (sourced nationally) H

A popular M&B Nicholson's pub on the site of the Hickford Rooms, London's main concert venue in the 1740s and 50s; a notice displays the history of the pub. The main bar, with its banquettes, is a welcome retreat from the bustling street. Children are welcome, with parents, in the upstairs dining room. Starting with breakfast, food is served daily until 10pm. The guest beers are often unusual choices. Q⊖(Piccadilly Circus)

Dog & Duck ★

18 Bateman Street, W1D 3AJ

11-11 (11.30 Fri & Sat); 12-10.30 Sun (020) 7494 0697

St Austell Nicholson's Pale Ale; Sharp's Doom Bar; 5 changing beers (sourced nationally; often St Austell, Sharp's) H

In the heart of Soho since 1897, this Grade II-listed Nicholson's outlet has been identified by CAMRA as having a nationally important historic pub interior. An elaborate mosaic depicts dogs and ducks, and wonderful advertising mirrors adorn the walls. The upstairs Orwell Bar can be hired for functions. The pub is small but so popular, especially with media people, that not only smokers have to drink outside. The bar has been extended towards the Frith Street door. ⊖(Tottenham Court Rd)

Lyric L

37 Great Windmill Street, W1D 7LU

11-11.30 (midnight Fri & Sat); 12-10.30 Sun
(020) 7434 0604 lyricsoho.co.uk

8 changing beers (sourced nationally) H

A small, independently owned bar just off Shaftesbury Avenue, bay fronted with a tiled, panelled interior, popular with local trade. Once two adjacent taverns, the Windmill and the Ham merged in the mid 18th century to form the Windmill & Ham, renamed in 1890 and rebuilt 16 years later. As well as other draught beers including London specialities, cask ales may include Big Smoke, Brodie's, Dark Star, Magic Rock, Marble, RedWillow, Redemption, Tiny Rebel or Thornbridge brews. ⊖(Piccadilly Circus)

Old Coffee House L

49 Beak Street, W1F 9SF

11-11; 12-11 Sun (020) 7437 2197

Brodie's Bethnal Green Bitter, London Fields Pale, Old Street Pale Ale; 3 changing beers H

A large but cosy pub, close to the buzz of Carnaby Street, with six handpumps offering a range of ales from Brodie's. First licensed as the Silver Street Coffee House, it was rebuilt in 1894 and is now Grade II-listed. The long bar and dark panelling are adorned with Watneys Red Barrel signage, brewery mirrors and sundry prints, posters, pictures and brassware. At lunchtimes you will find good-sized portions of pub grub, reasonably priced. ⊖(Piccadilly Circus)

Queen's Head L

15 Denman Street, W1D 7HN

11-11.30 (midnight Fri & Sat); 12-10.30 Sun
(020) 7437 1540 queensheadpiccadilly.com

Fuller's London Pride; Robinsons Trooper; 3 changing beers (often Dark Star, Gun, Sambrook's) H

A rare West End free house with plenty of vertical drinking space below and a restaurant upstairs. The traditional feel is enhanced by an attractive bar-back and wall mirroring downstairs and an unusual leather-fronted bar in the restaurant. With its real ales, good-value pies and other pub food, including snacks and cheeseboards at the bar, this is a popular pub before and after theatre visits. ⊖(Piccadilly Circus)

Star & Garter

62 Poland Street, W1F 7NX

11 (12 Sat)-11; closed Sun (020) 7437 9278

Fuller's London Pride; Greene King IPA; Shepherd Neame Spitfire H

A pub on one of the earliest sites to be developed in Poland Street; its name appears in 1825 in the Westminster victuallers' records. Formerly a Courage house, it had previously belonged to Style & Winch of Maidstone and the windows advertised Maidstone Ales. It has a small, cosy, wood-panelled bar with a matchboard ceiling. An additional bar upstairs is usually open on Thursday and Friday nights to cope with the throng. ⊖(Oxford Circus/Piccadilly Circus)

EAST LONDON

E1: Aldgate

Dispensary

19A Leman Street, E1 8EN

11.30-11; closed Sat & Sun (020) 7977 0486
thedispensarylondon.co.uk

Dark Star Hophead; 4 changing beers (often Adnams, Hogs Back) H

Erected in 1858, this stylish and welcoming pub was once the Eastern Dispensary Hospital, providing treatment and medicines to the poor of the East End. Extensively refurbished in 2013-14, it is now known for its ales and dining (booking advised). The number of cask ales on the five handpumps increases towards Friday. The main room has a lofty ceiling, and a dining balcony above the bar area. There are various rooms on its three floors. Closed Christmas and Easter. ⇌(Fenchurch St)⊖(Aldgate/Aldgate East)

E1: Spitalfields

Commercial Tavern

142-144 Commercial Street, E1 6NU

12-11 ☎ (020) 3137 9563

4 changing beers (often Burning Sky, Siren, Wild Beer) Ⓗ

A Grade II-listed pub with an eclectic interior, now part of the Barworks group. Wooden floors and furniture give a traditional feel. As well as the four rotating guest ales, there is a range of other draught beers and more than 60 bottled beers from a variety of countries. Sourdough pizzas are served all day. There is a function room upstairs. The smoking area is outside the front of the pub. ♿ ⇌(Liverpool St) ⊖(Liverpool St/Shoreditch High St)

Crown & Shuttle

226 Shoreditch High Street, E1 6PJ

11-11 (midnight Thu; 1am Fri); 12-1am Sat; 12-10.30 Sun ☎ (020) 7375 2905 crownandshuttle.com

4 changing beers (often Purity, Redemption, Vale) Ⓗ

Refurbished with bare floorboards, this place has exposed brickwork, a large colourful beer garden and a food truck. Usually three or four cask ales are served but the back room is dominated by large Meantime lager tanks. Catering for a broad clientele, it is quiet in the afternoons, noisier with a younger vibe in the evenings. It has Filthy Fanny's cocktail bar upstairs, a quiz on Tuesdays, and jazz on Sundays. The 'shuttle' in the name records part of the weaving kit used by local Huguenots. ⇌(Liverpool St/Shoreditch High St) ⊖(Shoreditch High St)

Pride of Spitalfields

3 Heneage Street, E1 5LJ

10-1am (2am Fri & Sat); 10-midnight Sun ☎ (020) 7247 8933

Crouch Vale Brewers Gold; Fuller's London Pride, ESB; Sharp's Doom Bar; 1 changing beer (sourced locally; often Truman's) Ⓗ

Welcoming and traditional East End two-roomed pub, just off busy Brick Lane. Food is served during the day, and there is a Sunday roast. This small and friendly local has a great atmosphere. Young and old mix well; often, when it is busy, customers spread onto the quiet street outside. Monday is vinyl night, there is a piano for singalongs, and Lenny the pub cat presides from his seat near the chimney. Sport is sometimes screened. ⊖(Aldgate East/Shoreditch High St)

Williams Ale & Cider House

22-24 Artillery Lane, E1 7LS

11-11 (midnight Thu-Sat); 12-10 Sun ☎ (020) 7247 5163 williamsspitalfields.com

Greene King IPA; house beer (by Greene King); 5 changing beers (often Crouch Vale, Hackney, Truman's) Ⓗ

A traditional pub a short distance from Liverpool Street station. At the front of the bar, seven handpumps serve two Greene King ales and five changing guest ales from local breweries. To the rear, six more serve Westons Old Rosie and five changing ciders. There is a dartboard, and board games are available. Food is served throughout the day. Children are welcome only at weekends. ⇌⊖(Liverpool St)

E1: Whitechapel

White Hart

1-3 Mile End Road, E1 4TP

11-midnight (1am Fri & Sat) ☎ (020) 7790 2894 the-white-hart.co.uk

6 changing beers (often One Mile End) Ⓗ

A friendly and popular refurbished Victorian pub with large windows, bare floorboards and plenty of seating (some out at the front). Beers are mainly from One Mile End Brewery, formerly located in the basement. Hospital Porter is named after the Royal London Hospital across the road; Joseph Merrick, the Elephant Man, spent the last few years of his life there. Good-value food is served afternoons and evenings. Quiz night is Tuesday. ♿⇌⊖(Bethnal Green/Whitechapel)

E2: Bethnal Green

Camel

277 Globe Road, E2 0JD

12-11 (10.30 Sun) ☎ (020) 3620 2333 thecamele2.co.uk

Adnams Broadside; Sambrook's Wandle Ale; 3 changing beers (often Five Points, Oakham, St Austell) Ⓗ

This small, refurbished Victorian pub has a single bar and a traditional feel. One of the changing guest beers usually comes from Five Points Brewery in Hackney. There is food throughout the day with a range of pies and mash, toasties and puddings. The distinctive exterior tiling gives a clue to the original brewery; the last one with a tie was Ind Coope. The pub is convenient for the Museum of Childhood and York Hall. ⊖

Carpenters Arms

73 Cheshire Street, E2 6EG

4 (12 Thu)-11.30; 12-midnight Fri & Sat; 12-11.30 Sun ☎ (020) 7739 6342 carpentersarmsfreehouse.com

Timothy Taylor Landlord; 2 changing beers (often Adnams, Purity) Ⓗ

Small back-street corner pub (apparently once owned by the Kray twins in the 1960s) of a type becoming rare in East London. Independently owned, it is comfortably furnished and tastefully decorated. Background music is just that and there are no TVs. Three real ales are served from a limited selection but a range of Belgian bottles is also available. Food from a varied menu is on offer from opening, with roasts on Sundays. ⊖(Bethnal Green/Shoreditch High St)

King's Arms

11A Buckfast Street, E2 6EY

12-11.30 (midnight Fri & Sat) ☎ (020) 7729 2627 thekingsarmspub.com

4 changing beers (often Five Points, Howling Hops, Siren) Ⓗ

Relaxed corner pub just off Bethnal Green Road, part of the Barworks group. No pumpclips are displayed, instead a large wallboard lists the beers and ciders; printed menus are also available daily. The focus is on local, UK and international artisanal beers, with simple cheese and meatboard snacks. Six handpumps dispense up to four cask ales and two ciders, with another 14 beers on tap and over 60 UK and imported bottled beers in the fridges. ♿⊖(Bethnal Green/Shoreditch High St)

E3: Bow

Eleanor Arms

460 Old Ford Road, E3 5JP
4-11; 12-11 Fri-Sun (020) 8980 6992
eleanorarms.co.uk
Shepherd Neame Master Brew, Whitstable Bay Pale Ale, Spitfire Gold, Spitfire; 2 changing beers (sourced nationally) H
This CAMRA award-winning pub has been run by the same three-person team for over 10 years, with occasional help from the customers. It is traditionally furnished, with wood panelling and an eclectic mix of pictures adorning the walls, and has a small beer garden at the back. The pub hosts regular live jazz every Sunday and disco every Friday and Saturday nights. There are traditional games and a monthly quiz. (8)

E5: Clapton

Crooked Billet

84 Upper Clapton Road, E5 9JP
4-11; 12-midnight Fri & Sat; 12-11 Sun (020) 3058 1166
e5crookedbillet.co.uk
5 changing beers (often Hammerton, Siren, Truman's) H
Transformed in 2013 and now a vibrant pub, where two entrances lead to a single large bar with three sides. London beers always feature on the five handpumps at the back; on the other two sides are another 21 fonts. The Monday night quiz is popular and sport is shown. Furniture is a mix of tables and chairs with some sofas. There is a large, well-equipped garden. The kitchen, visible from the bar, produces a changing selection of food.

E8: Hackney

Cock Tavern

315 Mare Street, E8 1EJ
12-11 (1am Fri & Sat); 12-10.30 Sun
thecocktavern.co.uk
8 changing beers (often Hackney, Howling Hops, Maregade) H
This excellent friendly and cosy pub, right in the centre of Hackney, stocks a generous selection both of real ales and ciders, and boasts eight handpumps for each. Bar snacks include a wide variety of pickled eggs. The cellar holds the Howling Hops brewery which contributes to the interesting selection of beers. The bar has a traditional feel, with wooden floorboards and furniture, and there is a tiny patio to the rear. (Downs) (Central/Downs)

Pembury Tavern

90 Amhurst Road, E8 1JH
4-11 (midnight Fri); 12-1am Fri & Sat (020) 8986 8597
Five Points Pale, Railway Porter; 10 changing beers (often Five Points, Milton) H
A large, open-plan pub with bare floorboards and mostly wooden furniture, with pool and bar billiard tables. The pub was bought by the Five Points Brewery in early 2018 as its taphouse. As part of the deal it will continue to sell a limited range of Milton ales along with guest ales from the independent London beer industry.
Q (Downs) (Central/Downs)

E9: Hackney Wick

Crate Brewery Bar & Pizzeria

Unit 7, White Building, Queen's Yard, White Post Lane, E9 5EN (down steps by canal bridge or through Queen's Yard)
12-11 (midnight Fri & Sat) 07834 275687
cratebrewery.com
Crate Golden, IPA; 3 changing beers (sourced regionally; often Crate) H
This opened in an old print factory in 2012 and has since expanded into a back area. The main brewery is now across the yard, with the original brewery still in use. The furniture is made locally from pallets, with the bar made from railway sleepers and bedspring lampshades. A large range of pizzas is available. No spirits are sold. Customers may use the boat moored on the River Lea. DJs entertain on Fridays, Saturdays and summer Sundays.

E9: Homerton

Adam & Eve

155 Homerton High Street, E9 6AS
4-11 (midnight Thu; 1am Fri); 12-1am Sat; 12-11 Sun
(020) 8985 1494 adamandevepub.com
East London Pale Ale; Five Points Railway Porter; 4 changing beers (often Hackney, Siren) H
A tile-fronted pub built in 1914 and refurbished in 2014, retaining some original features including wood panelling. It is much larger inside than it looks from the front. The bar extends to both sides of the pub and stretches back past an open kitchen and an L-shaped pool table to a garden. Much of the food is from Cornwall. Children are admitted until 8pm. It has sports TV, and DJs entertain on Friday and Saturday evenings.

Chesham Arms

15 Mehetabel Road, E9 6DU
4 (12 Fri & Sat)-11; 12-10.30 Sun (020) 8986 6717
cheshamarms.com
4 changing beers (sourced nationally) H
A back-street gem, bought and gutted by a property developer but reopened in 2015 after being listed as an Asset of Community Value and winning a landmark appeal case. The single bar is divided, in effect, into two rooms, and to the rear is an attractive garden with a heated smoking area. Occasional live music and cider festivals are planned. You can take your own food or have takeaways delivered. Local CAMRA Cider Pub of the Year 2018. (Hackney Central)

E10: Leyton

Leyton Orient Supporters Club

Matchroom Stadium, Oliver Road, E10 5NF
5-7.30, 9.30-11 Tue; 12-2.30, 5-8 Sat (020) 8988 8288
orientsupporters.org
Mighty Oak Oscar Wilde G**; 9 changing beers** H
Probably the best supporters' club bar for real ale in the country, it is the winner of numerous branch, regional and even national CAMRA awards. The busy bar, which is run by volunteers, is open on match days both before and after games, with nine beers available. It often holds brewery-themed evenings and also opens for the occasional televised match. The club reserves the right to check CAMRA membership on match days.

Leyton Technical

265B High Road, E10 5QN

4-11 (midnight Thu); 12-1am Fri & Sat; 12-11 Sun (020) 8558 4759 leytontechnical.com

Volden Session Ale; 7 changing beers (sourced nationally)

This pub retains many of the original features of the old Leyton Town Hall, dating from 1896, including chandeliers and marbled mosaic floors. Its many rooms are furnished in the typical Antic shabby-chic style. Owing to its proximity to Leyton Orient's ground it is particularly busy on match days. It features DJs on Fridays and Saturdays, live music on Sundays, a quiz on Wednesdays and other occasional events.

E11: Leytonstone

North Star

24 Browning Road, E11 3AR

4 (12 Sat)-11; 12-10.30 Sun (020) 8530 3197

East London Foundation Bitter; Oakham JHB; 4 changing beers (sourced nationally)

A comfortable two-bar local in Leytonstone Village conservation area, with historical photographs and steam train paintings adorning the walls. Service in the public bar is through a hatch. The garden is covered in winter. Thai food is available evenings (not Mon) and weekends, and there are wood-fired pizzas Thursday to Sunday evenings. Dogs are welcome in the saloon bar. Local CAMRA Community Pub of the Year 2018.

Northcote Arms

110 Grove Green Road, E11 4EL

2-11 (10.30 Mon; 11.30 Tue); 12.30-12.30am Fri; 12-1am Sat; 12-midnight Sun (020) 8518 7516 thenorthcotee11.com

4 changing beers (often Crate, East London, Signature)

Expect a warm welcome in this street-corner local. The central bar has five handpumps, one of which serves real cider. Choose between the settle-style benches or comfortable sofas. A small stage is overlooked by some pictures of drag cabaret artistes who entertain on Sunday evenings. Artisan pizzas are available Thursday to Sunday and pop-up street food Tuesday and Wednesday evenings.

(Leyton)

Red Lion

640 High Road, E11 3AA

12-11 (midnight Thu; 2am Fri & Sat) (020) 8988 2929 theredlionleytonstone.com

Sharp's Atlantic; Volden Session Ale, Pale Ale; 7 changing beers (sourced nationally)

This large single-bar Antic pub has a rustic feel with wooden floorboards and eclectic furniture. As well as the cask ales there is a real cider, a range of other draught beers and an interesting selection of bottles. The changing menu of home-cooked food includes vegetarian and vegan options. The large walled garden is now canopied. The impressive upstairs ballroom hosts music, comedy, film and dance events. There is a Monday quiz.

E11: Wanstead

George

155-159 High Street, E11 2RL

8am-midnight (12.30am Fri & Sat) (020) 8989 2921

Fuller's London Pride; Greene King IPA, Abbot; Sharp's Doom Bar; 8 changing beers (sourced nationally)

There has been a pub for hundreds of years on this site – the large, two-storey 1903 survivor with its etched windows is now the local Wetherspoon's. The 12 handpumps on the main bar are overseen by a large dragon. Pictures of old Wanstead and famous Georges are displayed on the walls. The upstairs bar does not serve real ale but can be reserved for larger groups. A garden and car park are to the rear. Q

E13: Plaistow

Black Lion

59-61 High Street, E13 0AD

11-11; 12-10.30 Sun (020) 8472 2351 blacklionplaistow.co.uk

Mighty Oak Captain Bob; 3 changing beers (sourced nationally)

This 18th-century wooden-beamed coaching inn, identified by CAMRA as having a historic interior of some regional importance, has an original cobbled courtyard, a function room in a converted outbuilding and a garden. The narrow main bar is where four ales are on offer. The smaller back bar is accessible by a separate door or through the main bar. Sports TVs can be viewed from all points. Home-cooked food and sandwiches are served weekday lunchtimes and evenings.

P

E14: Canary Wharf

Henry Addington

22-28 Mackenzie Walk, E14 4PH

11-11.30 (9.30 Sat); 11-6.30 Sun (020) 7719 1114

9 changing beers (sourced nationally)

Located below a modern office block by the side of Middle Dock, the pub is named after the man who, as Viscount Sidmouth, was Prime Minister (1801-04) and who allowed the original West India Docks to be built. Spacious, with a long bar and plenty of seating, it is popular at lunchtimes and after work. There are usually eight or nine cask ales on offer from the Nicholson's seasonal range, and the food is good value.

Ledger Building

4 Hertsmere Road, West India Quay, E14 4AL

9am-midnight; 9am-11 Sun (020) 7536 7770

Adnams Broadside; Fuller's London Pride; Greene King IPA, Abbot; Sharp's Doom Bar; 5 changing beers (often Portobello, Truman's, Twickenham)

In a building dating from 1800, this pub stands at the north-west corner of the former Import Dock. It takes its name from its original use, to house the ledgers of the West India Docks, and pictures of the area's history adorn the walls. A large single bar serves the standard Wetherspoon range, with five rotating guest ales featuring London breweries. Three further rooms provide plenty of space. The smoking area is in front of the pub.

Q (West India Quay)

E14: Limehouse

Craft Beer Co

576 Commercial Road, E14 7JD

⏲ 3.30-11 (midnight Fri); 12-midnight Sat; 12-10.30 Sun
☎ (020) 7790 2726
House beer (by Kent); 5 changing beers (sourced nationally) Ⓗ
A refurbished pub outside Limehouse station. Six cask ales are mainly from microbreweries, alongside 20 other draught beers and a large range in bottles. A limited food menu is available (no food Mon). Iron and wooden beams remain from the original building, now with bare walls and eclectic '60s furniture as well as a range of authentic pub mirrors. There is more seating upstairs and the roof garden is also a smoking area.

E17: Walthamstow

Bell

617 Forest Road, E17 4NE
⏲ 12-midnight (1am Fri & Sat); 12-11 Sun & Mon
☎ (020) 8523 2277 🌐 belle17.com
Sharp's Doom Bar; Timothy Taylor Landlord; 6 changing beers (sourced regionally; often Salopian) Ⓗ
A prominent landmark at the Forest Road junction with Chingford Road, this large Victorian pub, built in 1900, was refurbished in 2012. One bar serves all the rooms – most have been knocked through – and there is a beer garden to the side and behind. Tuesday quiz night and Sunday meals see the pub at its busiest. There is no TV but it is noisy. Children are welcome until 8pm; dogs are also admitted.

Chequers

145 High Street, E17 7BX
⏲ 5-11 (midnight Fri); 12-midnight Sat; 12-10.30 Sun
☎ (020) 8503 6401 🌐 chequerse17.com
4 changing beers (sourced nationally) Ⓗ
Dating from 1698 and originally used as a courtroom and meeting place, many rebuilds later the premises is now owned by Rose Pubs. Rotating ales are mainly from East London breweries. Food is served until 10pm (8pm Sun) and children are welcome until 8pm. Wheelchair access is via the side gate and staff will assist if asked. Sports TV is available, with live music on Friday and Saturday nights. (Central)

Coppermill

205 Coppermill Lane, E17 7HF
⏲ 11-11 (12.30am Fri & Sat) ☎ (020) 8520 3709
🌐 coppermillpub.co.uk
Fuller's London Pride; Sharp's Doom Bar; 2 changing beers (sourced nationally) Ⓗ
A small, traditional pub at the far end of Coppermill Lane, converted from an off-licence. The two guest beers come from the Heineken or Greene King lists and food is just bar snacks and crisps. Enjoy TV sports, quiz night on Sunday, live music Friday and Saturday and open mic night Monday. The W12 bus stops outside the pub and the entrance to Walthamstow Wetlands is 100 yards further down the lane. (St James St) (W12)

Mirth, Marvel & Maud

186 Hoe Street, E17 4QH
⏲ 4-11 (midnight Thu; 2am Fri); 12-2am Sat; 12-11 Sun
☎ (020) 8520 8636 🌐 mirthmarvelandmaud.com
6 changing beers (often East London, Volden) Ⓗ
In 2002 this 1931 cinema closed and in 2015 Antic reopened it as a pub. Original glass doors lead into a grand foyer where the ticket office is currently a cocktail bar. Behind, the downstairs bar serves a varying range of draught beers, boxed cider and bottles. To the left is the restored cinema and toilets while at the rear of the foyer two flights of stairs rise to a restaurant seating area. Local CAMRA Pub of the Year 2017. (Central)

Olde Rose & Crown

53-55 Hoe Street, E17 4SA
⏲ 10-11 (1am Fri & Sat); 12-midnight Sun
☎ (020) 8509 3880 🌐 yeolderoseandcrowntheatrepub.co.uk
6 changing beers (sourced nationally) Ⓗ
A spacious Victorian pub run by the same management team for over a decade and offering an attractive choice of real ales from many different breweries, with cider also on handpump and in boxes. Theatre, comedy, live music and a range of community activities set it apart from the rest. Alcoholic drinks are served from 12pm. Sunday roasts are its only food offering, though at times there may be pop-up catering outside. Local CAMRA Pub of the Year 2018.
(Central)

E20: Westfield Stratford City

Tap East

7 International Square, Montfichet Road, E20 1EE
⏲ 11-11; 12-10 Sun ☎ (020) 8555 4467 🌐 tapeast.co.uk
Tap East Tonic Ale; 5 changing beers (sourced nationally; often Tap East) Ⓗ
Often busy on match days owing to the proximity of the West Ham football ground, this brewpub within the Westfield shopping centre otherwise has a relaxed atmosphere, complete with comfortable sofas. The brewery is visible behind a glass door and windows. Three house beers are complemented by three guest beers, with an enticing excess of 100 international bottled beers on offer. The pub holds occasional beer festivals. Food is available all day.
(Stratford/Stratford Int)

Barking

Barking Dog

61 Station Parade, IG11 8TU
⏲ 8am-midnight ☎ (020) 8507 9109
Greene King Abbot; Ruddles Best Bitter; Sharp's Doom Bar; 6 changing beers Ⓗ
Busy town-centre Wetherspoon pub, close to Barking station and many bus routes, popular with locals and passing commuters alike. An impressive 12 handpumps serve up to six different beers of varying types and strengths, plus three or four periodically changing regular beers and two or three real ciders, including Old Rosie and Black Dragon. Food is served until 11pm, alcoholic drinks from 9am. Muted TV screens show rolling news and occasional sport.

Chadwell Heath

Eva Hart

1128 High Road, RM6 4AH (on A118)
⏲ 8am-12.30am (1am Fri & Sat) ☎ (020) 8597 1069
Adnams Broadside; Greene King Abbot; Ruddles Best Bitter; Sharp's Doom Bar; Truman's Runner; 4 changing beers (sourced regionally) Ⓗ
Large and comfortable split-level Wetherspoon pub, divided into several distinct drinking areas. The building dates from 1892 and used to be the

area police station. It is named after a local musical personality who was one of the longest-living survivors of the 1912 Titanic disaster; photographs and memorabilia are on display. Alcoholic drinks are served from 9am, food until 10pm. Muted TVs display subtitles. Q

Collier Row

Colley Rowe Inn

54-56 Collier Row Road, RM5 3PA (on B174)
8am-midnight ☎ (01708) 760633
Greene King IPA, Abbot; Sharp's Doom Bar; 4 changing beers H
Converted from two shops, the pub is close to six bus routes, giving easy access to and from Romford. Alongside the ales, there are two ciders on gravity dispense (usually Westons Old Rosie and Gwynt y Ddraig Black Dragon). It is often lively around the bar, but there are quieter alcoves at the rear. Alcoholic drinks are served from 9am. Steak night is particularly popular. Local CAMRA Pub of the Year 2016. (247,252)

Gidea Park

Gidea Park Micropub

236 Main Road, RM2 5HA (on A118)
12-11 ☎ (01708) 397290
6 changing beers (sourced nationally) G
Havering Borough and East London's second micropub opened in December 2017 in a former accountants' office after a planning appeal achieved a change of use to a pub. Four to eight real ales from microbreweries come straight from casks in the ground-floor cellar, together with real ciders, wines and gins. There are high and low tables and chairs and unusual 'spider' lighting. Please turn mobile phones to silent. Card payments are welcome. Note that the opening hours are liable to change. Q(174,498)

Ship

93 Main Road, RM2 5EL (on A118)
12-11 (midnight Thu-Sat) ☎ (01708) 741571
theshipgideapark.co.uk
Greene King IPA; Morland Old Speckled Hen; Sharp's Doom Bar; Timothy Taylor Landlord; 1 changing beer H
More than 250 year old, this Grade II-listed split-level pub has extensive dark-wood panelling, timber beams and huge fireplaces. The building is largely unchanged and has low ceilings in places – so duck or grouse! It is a family-run business. Quiz nights are held on Thursdays and there is live music on Saturdays. QP(174,498)

Hornchurch

JJ Moon's

48-52 High Street, RM12 4UN (on A124)
8am-11.30 (12.30am Fri & Sat) ☎ (01708) 478410
Greene King Abbot; Ruddles Best Bitter; Sharp's Doom Bar; 8 changing beers (sourced nationally) H
A busy Wetherspoon pub, popular with all ages, featuring a good variety of ales with an emphasis on breweries from London and the South-East. Watercolour paintings of local scenes provide the main decoration, with the usual local interest panels to the rear. Families are welcome until 6pm, and alcoholic drinks are served from 9am.
Q(Emerson Park/Hornchurch)

Ilford

Jono's

37 Cranbrook Road, IG1 4PA (on A123)
11-11 (midnight Thu; 1am Fri & Sat); 12-10.30 Sun
☎ (020) 8514 6676
Castle Rock Harvest Pale; St Austell Tribute H
A couple of minutes' walk from the station, Jono's is a converted shop with an unusual style. The front of the bar is in dark wood and the rear is half-timbered with a patch of thatch over the seating. Large-screen TVs show sports fixtures; it can be noisy at times. Friendly and efficient bar staff serve well-kept ales; Castle Rock beer is a rarity in East London. Thursday quizzes are held and live music performances at weekends.

Rainham

Phoenix

Broadway, RM13 9YW (on B1335)
11 (12 Sun)-11 ☎ (01708) 553700
the-phoenix-hotel.com
Courage Directors; Greene King Abbot; John Smith's Bitter; Sharp's Doom Bar; 1 changing beer H
Busy, spacious town pub close to Rainham station and convenient for the RSPB Rainham Marshes nature reserve. It has a public bar with dartboard and a saloon for dining. Poker is played on Wednesday; quizzes and live entertainment/music alternate on Thursday. There is also entertainment on Saturday and Sunday. The large garden has three aviaries, animals and a barbecue area. Family fun days are held every bank holiday Monday.
P

Romford

Moon & Stars

99-103 South Street, RM1 1NX
8am-11.30 (1am Fri & Sat) ☎ (01708) 730117
Greene King Abbot; Ruddles Best Bitter; Sharp's Doom Bar; 5 changing beers (sourced nationally) H
A Wetherspoon pub close to Romford station and buses, allowing children in the raised area at the rear until 6pm Friday and Saturday, later on other days. Real ciders including Old Rosie and Black Dragon are dispensed on gravity from glass containers in a cool cabinet behind the bar. Displays of local history are on the walls and assorted books on the shelves. It gets busy on Thursday and Friday evenings.
Q

Upminster

Upminster TapRoom L

1B Sunnyside Gardens, RM14 3DT (off B187, St Mary's Lane)
closed Mon; 4-11; 12-11 Sat; 12-10 Sun ☎ 07841 676225
Dark Star Hophead; 6 changing beers (sourced locally) G
Upminster and East London's first micropub opened in 2015 in a converted office, initially as a real ale snack bar before securing a change of use on appeal. Garlands of hops adorn the walls. Beers are served from casks in the cool cellar visible from the bar. Table service is optional. There is no parking available, so please use public transport. Set mobile phones to silent or pay a fee for charity. Open bank holiday Mondays. Local CAMRA Pub of the Year 2017 and 2018. Q

Woodford Green

Travellers Friend ✔

496-498 High Road, Woodford Wells, IG8 0PN (on slip road off A104)

12-midnight (11 Mon & Tue); 12-11 Sun

(020) 8504 2435 thetravellersfriendwoodford.co.uk

New River London Tap; St Austell Tribute; Timothy Taylor Landlord; 3 changing beers (often Adnams, New River)

In its fifth year under the ownership of two local families, this friendly, comfortable pub was completely refurbished and extended in 2017. The rare snob screens from the bar counter are now located above the bar-back. The original oak panelling was removed, restored and reinstated, but some had to be replaced. There are picnic tables at the front and in the side beer garden. At the rear is a small car park.

QP(20,179)

NORTH LONDON

N1: Angel

Angel ✔

3-5 Islington High Street, N1 9LQ

8am-midnight (020) 7837 2218

Greene King IPA; Sharp's Doom Bar; 6 changing beers (often Truman's, Twickenham, Windsor & Eton)

A large, modern, open-plan Wetherspoon conversion with some booths towards the back giving slightly more privacy. The adjacent tower was a part of the Angel (one of the first talkie cinemas) that was sadly mostly demolished. With the long-gone Philharmonic Hall (subsequently Grand Theatre), this was always a centre of popular entertainment. Its classic columns and caryatids can apparently be seen in the Museum of London.

N1: Hoxton

Wenlock Arms

26 Wenlock Road, N1 7TA

3-11 Mon; 12-11 (midnight Thu; 1am Fri & Sat)

(020) 7608 3406 wenlockarms.com

Dark Star Hophead, American Pale Ale; Mighty Oak Oscar Wilde; 7 changing beers (sourced nationally)

Local CAMRA Pub of the Year 2017, this free house was saved from closure by a vigorous local campaign. Regularly changing beers from across the UK, usually including a mild, come mostly from small and medium-sized breweries. With up to seven ciders and perries and a small snacks menu of toasties, Scotch eggs, sausage rolls and pickled eggs, this is a truly welcoming street-corner local with an international reputation. Jazz is played in the bar on Thursday night.

(Old St)

N1: Islington

New Rose

84-86 Essex Road, N1 8LU

12-11 (midnight Thu; 2am Fri & Sat); 12-10.30 Sun

(020) 7226 1082

5 changing beers (sourced nationally; often Redemption)

Spacious and friendly pub, traditional but quirky, in the heart of Islington. There is a changing range of five quality real ales, light through dark, many from the surrounding area, as well as American bottled beers and traditional cider. A tempting menu of pub favourites, from locally sourced ingredients, includes home-cooked pizzas and impressive Sunday roasts. Enjoy a pint in the small rear garden or on a bench at the front, or catch the big game on TV. (Essex Rd)

N1: King's Cross

Parcel Yard

Upper Level, King's Cross Station Concourse, N1C 4AP

7.30am-11; 9am-10.30 Sun (020) 7713 7258

parcelyard.co.uk

Butcombe Original; Fuller's Oliver's Island, London Pride, ESB; Gale's Seafarers Ale, HSB; 5 changing beers (often Fuller's, Wimbledon)

Large pub approached by stairs at the rear of the concourse, converted from the former station parcel office. It is used by local workers, commuters and for meetings; as well as bars on two levels there are semi-private rooms converted from offices (bookable) and an indoor balcony. It has no music; the decor is minimal and features rescued furniture. Food, starting with breakfast, is served until 10pm (9pm Sun). Wheelchair access is by lift and there are no smoking facilities.

(King's Cross/St Pancras)

N1: Pentonville

Craft Beer Co

55 White Lion Street, N1 9PP

4-11; 12-1am Fri & Sat; 12-10.30 Sun (020) 7278 0318

Kent Pale; 9 changing beers (sourced nationally)

Multi-room pub with a wooden bar displaying 10 handpumps, all serving beers from independent brewers. Green curtains and red carpet give some warmth to the main bar, which has two Victorian pillars, a wooden floor and raised tables and stools, all overseen by Winston Churchill. A cosy room, with settees and subtle lighting, is to the right as you enter, and there is a smaller room at the back. To the side is a small garden. (Angel)

N2: East Finchley

Bald Faced Stag ✔

69 High Road, N2 8AB

12-11 (midnight Fri & Sat) (020) 8442 1201

thebaldfacedstagn2.co.uk

Greene King IPA; 3 changing beers (often Old Dairy, Sambrook's, Truman's)

A short walk from the underground station – look out for the iconic rooftop stag emblem overlooking the High Road. The pub is popular with patrons from the local Phoenix cinema and has a large dining area with another smaller area, both of which are available for private functions. There is also a decked garden, built around an historic sycamore tree. A selection of board games can be played. P

N5: Canonbury

Snooty Fox

75 Grosvenor Avenue, N5 2NN

4-11 (1am Fri); 12-1am Sat; 12-10.30 Sun

(020) 7354 9532 snootyfoxlondon.co.uk

Otter Ale; 3 changing beers (sourced nationally)

A vibrant community pub with 1960s icons depicted throughout, serving up to four real ales and a real cider. The airy bar features a 45rpm jukebox and the patio offers pleasant outside drinking. A function room is available for local groups and private dining. The pub is well known for its ale and cider festivals, which attract people from far and wide. Its kitchen serves quality modern British food and an excellent Sunday roast.

N5: Highbury

Brewhouse & Kitchen

2A Corsica Street, N5 1JJ

11-11 (midnight Fri & Sat); 12-11 Sun ☎ (020) 7226 1026

4 changing beers (often Brewhouse & Kitchen)

This was once the tram shed at Highbury Corner, now refurbished and reopened with an in-house brewery. The company is continuing to expand, opening new outlets across the UK, but this location offers a lovely outdoor space at the front, a large interior to accommodate private parties, brewing classes in its academy and plenty of room to enjoy pub classics with a delicious twist. On Arsenal home match days it is only open to season ticket holders.
(Highbury & Islington)

N6: Highgate

Duke's Head

16 Highgate High Street, N6 5JG

12-midnight (1am Thu-Sat); 12-11.30 Sun

☎ (020) 8341 1310 thedukesheadhighgate.co.uk

8 changing beers (sourced nationally) H

Former coaching inn with a courtyard, reopened as a specialist beer house offering a large range of real ale and cider. Local brewer Hammerton is a fairly permanent presence but expect to find beers from around the country, such as Burning Sky, Magic Rock, Moor and Siren; usually at least a mild, a porter or stout, a pale and a best bitter are listed on a board behind the bar. Monthly pop-up kitchen rotations and tap takeovers take place.
(210,271)

N7: Holloway

Coronet

338-346 Holloway Road, N7 6NJ

8am-midnight ☎ (020) 7609 5014

Fuller's London Pride; Greene King Abbot; 6 changing beers (sourced nationally) H

Impressive Wetherspoon conversion of a cinema, the Savoy, designed by William Glen, that showed its last film in 1983 and now displays large prints of movie stars and former local entertainers, with an old projector the centrepiece of a raised dais towards the rear. Sometimes there are single brewery festivals. Expect plastic glasses and higher prices when Arsenal are playing at home. Tables (some under cover) are on the pavement and at the rear. Q (Holloway Rd)

N9: Lower Edmonton

Beehive

24 Little Bury Street, N9 9JZ

11.30-11.30 (1am Fri); 9am-1am Sat; 12-11 Sun

☎ (020) 8360 4358 thebeehivebhp.co.uk

Greene King IPA, Abbot; St Austell Tribute; house beer (by Greene King); 2 changing beers (often Enfield, New River) H

Tucked away in semi-detached suburbia, this imposing pub rebuilt in 1929 has a through bar offering pool and darts at one end and a dining area at the other. A collection of goats, chickens, rabbits, a pony, a donkey and a quail can be seen in the garden. Quiz night is Tuesday and live music is played most Saturday evenings. Lunches, dinners and Saturday breakfasts attract many customers.
P (329,W8)

N10: Muswell Hill

Mossy Well

258 Muswell Hill Broadway, N10 3SH

8am-1am (11.30 Mon; midnight Tue & Wed)

☎ (020) 8444 2914

Fuller's London Pride; Greene King IPA, Abbot; Sharp's Doom Bar; 8 changing beers (sourced nationally) H

A former Express Dairies tearoom and milk depot, but a pub since 1984, reopened by Wetherspoon's in October 2015, its name derived from the etymology of Muswell. Many internal features reflect its milky history. It is spacious inside, with a mezzanine floor and outdoor drinking areas at both front and back (closing at 9pm). Despite the size it can be packed. Four house beers are sold plus up to eight guests and one Westons cider, served from the fridge. Q

N11: Arnos Grove

Arnos Arms

338 Bowes Road, N11 1AN

9am-11.30 (midnight Fri & Sat); 9am-10.30 Sun

☎ (020) 8368 4456 arnosarms.com

3 changing beers (often Crate, One Mile End, Redemption) H

Emerging from the tube station, turn left and you cannot miss the large, imposing 1930s building, now imaginatively refurbished and with three handpumps prominently displayed as you enter. To the left is a dining area, with ample space elsewhere to sit and enjoy a beer or two. Bar billiards, table football, pinball and traditional board games will keep all entertained, young and old. Table tennis can be played in the garden.
(New Southgate) P

N12: North Finchley

Bohemia

762-764 High Road, N12 9QH

12-11 (midnight Thu; 1am Fri & Sat); 12-10.30 Sun

☎ (020) 8446 0294 thebohemia.co.uk

London Brewing Company Beer Street, 100 Oysters Stout, Skyline, Never Mind the Kent Hops; 1 changing beer (often London Brewing Company, Rooster's, Windsor & Eton) H

A lively brewpub with five handpumps each for ale and cider, the beers often brewed on the premises. It also stocks a large range of other draught and bottled beers and serves good food all day. Games include table tennis and table football. No admission after 11.30pm on Friday and Saturday boogie nights. Local CAMRA Pub of the Year 2016.
(Woodside Park) (125,263)

Elephant Inn

283 Ballards Lane, N12 8NR

11-11 (midnight Fri & Sat); 12-10.30 Sun

☎ (020) 8343 6110

Fuller's London Pride, ESB; 1 changing beer (often Fuller's, Long Man, St Austell) Ⓗ
Popular corner pub with fine wood panelling. There are three distinct drinking areas in a U shape: screens to the right show live sport; the left bar is TV-free for a more relaxed feel; the middle bar has raised tables and stools and the daily papers. Thai food from the restaurant upstairs can be eaten in the pub. At the front is a large patio with wooden seating and huge umbrellas.
♨❀◐◑♿⊖(West Finchley)♣🚌🐾📶

N13: Palmers Green

Alfred Herring ✔

316-322 Green Lanes, N13 5TT
⏲ 8am-11 (midnight Thu-Sat) ☎ (020) 3232 1083
Greene King Abbot; Ruddles Best Bitter; Sharp's Doom Bar; 7 changing beers (often East London Brewing, Redemption, Sambrook's) Ⓗ
A busy Wetherspoon shop conversion opened in 2006 in the heart of the Green Lanes shops, comprising a large open drinking and dining area with side booths. For the guest ales, the manager regularly obtains beers from the wide choice of London breweries. The pub is named after a local First World War soldier who was awarded the Victoria Cross for his heroic action in France in 1918.
Q♨◐◑♿⇌🍎🚌📶

N14: Southgate

New Crown ✔

80-84 Chase Side, N14 5PH
⏲ 8am-11.30 (12.30am Fri & Sat) ☎ (020) 8882 8758
Greene King IPA, Abbot; Sharp's Doom Bar; 5 changing beers (sourced regionally; often Portobello, Redemption, Sambrook's) Ⓗ
There was an Old Crown on Chase Side until its demolition in the 1960s, hence the name here for one of the older Wetherspoon pubs, close to the underground and bus stations. Pictures of Southgate from days gone by hang on the walls of the open-plan bar which offers a superb range of five guest real ales, with an emphasis on beers from London breweries. You can enjoy an ale from 9am. Q♨◐◑♿⊖♣🍎🚌📶

N16: Stoke Newington

Jolly Butchers 🄻

204 Stoke Newington High Street, N16 7HU
⏲ 4-midnight (1am Fri); 12-1am Sat; 12-11 Sun
☎ (020) 7249 9471 🌐 jollybutchers.co.uk
6 changing beers (sourced nationally) Ⓗ
A classic Art Deco-style bar boasting elaborate ironwork and glass, with a lively modern feel and the enviable status of being a true free house. Nine handpumps offer six different real ales, usually from microbreweries, and three ciders or perries. The beers are always changing but the website provides up-to-date pouring information. The beer is complemented by great food, served lunchtimes and evenings on weekdays and evenings at weekends. ❀◐◑⊖🍎🚌🐾📶

N17: Tottenham

Antwerp Arms 🄻

168-170 Church Road, N17 8AS
⏲ 12 (3 Mon & Tue)-11; 12-10.30 Sun ☎ (020) 8216 9289
🌐 antwerparms.co.uk
Redemption Pale Ale, Hopspur; 2 changing beers (sourced locally) Ⓗ
Tucked away in the historic and atmospheric Bruce Castle Park area is Tottenham's longest-established working pub. Serving local people since 1822, this Georgian building with beer garden faced demolition in 2013. It was saved from developers by the local community and CAMRA campaigners and is now operated as a community collective-owned pub, which will in effect be a permanent outlet for Redemption Brewery beers. Pub food is available at weekends.
♨❀◐◑⊖(White Hart Lane)♣P🚌🐾📶

N19: Upper Holloway

Shaftesbury Tavern 🄻 ✔

534 Hornsey Road, N19 3QN
⏲ 12-11 (12.30am Fri & Sat); 12-10.30 Sun
☎ (020) 7272 7950
Hammerton N1; 3 changing beers (often Fuller's, Sambrook's) Ⓗ
A nice old pub, identified by CAMRA as having a regionally important historic interior, comprehensively restored following a 2014 refurbishment, its former pool room becoming the restaurant area under a fine skylight. Outside is seating on a terrace at the front. Operated by Remarkable Pubs, it offers a beer range that varies most of the time. Food comes from a predominantly Thai menu with some pub classics such as fish and chips and sausage and mash. There is a Tuesday quiz.
♨❀◐◑♿⊖(Crouch Hill)🍎🚌🐾📶

N21: Winchmore Hill

Dog & Duck

74 Hoppers Road, N21 3LH
⏲ 12-11.30 (12.30am Fri & Sat) ☎ (020) 8886 1987
🌐 doganddduckn21.co.uk
Greene King IPA; Timothy Taylor Landlord; Young's Bitter; 1 changing beer (often Adnams) Ⓗ
Friendly one-bar pub, popular with locals and welcoming to visitors. The guest ale is often a seasonal tie, a sport-related beer or Adnams Ghost Ship. Sporting events are shown on a large-screen TV, local football teams meet and it hosts a golf society. A fortnightly quiz night is on Mondays, when you can enjoy a takeaway pizza. There is a pretty patio-style walled garden at the rear. A consistent entry in this Guide for 15 consecutive years, 28 in total. ❀♣🚌(W9)🐾📶

Little Green Dragon 🏆

928 Green Lanes, N21 2AD
⏲ closed Mon; 4-10; 12-10 Fri & Sat; 12-7 Sun
☎ (020) 8351 3530 🌐 littlegreendragonenfield.com
4 changing beers (often Dark Star, New River, Wantsum) Ⓖ
Formally a hairdressers', the area's first micropub was voted the local CAMRA Pub of the Year 2018. Beers are dispensed by gravity from the cool room; availability is regularly posted online. Takeaway containers and a varied selection of bottled beers are also on offer, along with up to seven ciders, five gins, some wines and soft drinks. Sofas, a church pew and bus seats create a cosy, friendly atmosphere. Interesting pub games can be played.
Q⇌🍎🚌(125,329)📶

Orange Tree

18 Highfield Road, N21 3HA

12 (2.30 Tue & Wed)-midnight (020) 8360 4853

Greene King IPA; 3 changing beers (often Hook Norton, New River, Redemption) H

Step back in time into this back-street local just yards from the New River walk. Toby jugs, decorated plates, pumpclips and sporting posters adorn the walls and shelves. Darts night is Wednesday, quiz night every other Thursday, there is a pool table and TVs show live sport. Enjoy a summer barbecue or a hearty Sunday lunch. With the well-kept ales, you will understand how the landlord has kept this pub in the Guide since 1995.

P(329)

N22: Wood Green

Prince

1 Finsbury Road, N22 8PA

4-11 (midnight Thu; 1am Fri); 12-1am Sat; 12-10.30 Sun (020) 8888 6698 theprincen22.co.uk

4 changing beers (sourced regionally; often House) H

A handsome two-roomed pub occupying a prominent corner site, brought back to life in 2016 with up to six regularly changing cask ales, nine other draught beers and a range of ciders. The beers come from small breweries across the UK and are listed on the pub's website as they change. Hot food comes from various pop-ups. An in-house brewery, House, was recently installed; cask beers available can include House Brewery Bitter at 3.8% ABV and Table Beer at 3.0% ABV.

(Alexandra Palace)

Enfield

Moon Under Water

115/117 Chase Side, EN2 6NN

8am-11 (10.30 Sun) (020) 8366 9855

Greene King IPA, Abbot; Ruddles Best Bitter; Sharp's Doom Bar; 6 changing beers (often Adnams, Redemption, Twickenham) H

Well-established Wetherspoon pub that used to be a dairy, within easy reach of both Enfield Chase and Gordon Hill stations. The L-shaped bar sports 10 handpumps, with real cider served from polypins. Look up while drinking and you will see exposed roof trusses, stained-glass windows and a mock balcony complete with library. The conservatory at the back adds to the light and airy ambience. The pub attracts all age groups; accompanied well-behaved children are welcome until 8.30pm.

(Chase)P(191,W9)

High Barnet

Olde Mitre Inne

58 High Street, EN5 5SJ

12-midnight (1am Fri & Sat) (020) 8449 5701

Adnams Southwold Bitter; Caledonian Deuchars IPA; Greene King Abbot; Timothy Taylor Landlord; 4 changing beers (often Five Points, Redemption, Tiny Rebel) H

The oldest coaching inn in Barnet, now free of tie, with beers from around the country served by efficient and well-trained staff. Oozing character and charm, it has been enhanced by sensitive and barely perceptible internal alteration. Family friendly – customers are requested to refrain from bad language – it has a large courtyard that can be heated and covered in winter. There is live music every Sunday evening. Local CAMRA Pub of the Year 2017 and several times previously.

Olde Monken Holt

193 High Street, EN5 5SU

12-midnight (11 Mon; 1.30am Fri & Sat) (020) 8449 4280

Greene King IPA, Abbot; Morland Old Speckled Hen; Timothy Taylor Landlord H

An historic pub at the north end of the High Street near the site of the 15th-century Battle of Barnet. It has wood panelling, exposed brickwork, a real fire and a patio garden safe for families. Barnet Council granted ACV status in 2017 and it remains popular with locals and newcomers alike. Regular entertainment includes a Thursday quiz, Friday DJ, Saturday live music, Sunday acoustic and occasional Irish traditional music. Widescreen TVs at the rear show sporting events.

(84/A,399)

New Barnet

Railway Bell

13 East Barnet Road, EN4 8RR

8am-midnight (1am Fri & Sat) (020) 8449 1369

Courage Directors; Greene King IPA, Abbot; Sharp's Doom Bar; Twickenham Naked Ladies; 5 changing beers (often Adnams, Sambrook's, Truman's) H

Built in the late 1800s following the arrival of the railway, this former Ind Coope house is one of the area's earliest Wetherspoon pubs. The rear has the feel of a huge conservatory and incorporates the kitchen servery. Ten real ales are almost always available. Popular and always busy, the pub welcomes families until 9pm; a pint can be enjoyed from 9am. The large patio to the side and rear helpfully includes a no-smoking area.

Ponders End

Picture Palace L

Howard Hall, Lincoln Road, EN3 4AQ

9am-11 (midnight Fri & Sat) (020) 8344 9690

Caledonian Deuchars IPA; Greene King Abbot; Sharp's Doom Bar; 4 changing beers (often 3 Brewers of St Albans, New River, Redemption) H

A former Wetherspoon conversion with an established management team. Some architectural features from the original 1913 cinema are preserved as well as fabulous murals of 1920s stars high above in the spacious main hall. TVs are kept silent; a huge screen drops down for major sport events. Two smaller areas to the front and the side are quieter. There is also an outside patio. Good-value food is served throughout the day.

(Southbury)P

NORTH-WEST LONDON

NW1: Camden Town

Constitution L

42 St Pancras Way, NW1 0QT

11-11.30 (midnight Fri); 12-midnight Sat; 12-10.30 Sun (020) 7380 0767 conincamden.co.uk

Dark Star Hophead; Sambrook's Junction Ale; 2 changing beers (sourced nationally; often Oakham, Sharp's) H

Founded in 1858, this dog- and family-friendly community pub is a welcome haven within

bustling Camden and its vibrant market area. Its award-winning patio terraced garden (four times Camden in Bloom finalist) has a pleasant south-facing outlook over the Regent's Canal. The downstairs cellar bar is host to live music and comedy events. Pool and darts are played and it has a large-screen TV. Weather permitting, there is occasional home-made street food outside.
(Camden Rd/Town)

Prince Albert

163 Royal College Street, NW1 0SG

11-11 (midnight Thu; 1am Fri & Sat); 11-10.30 Sun

(020) 7485 0270 princealbert.pub

4 changing beers (sourced nationally) H

A traditional Charrington tavern (1843), sensitively and tastefully refurbished, this comfortable, welcoming and charming pub retains the original horseshoe bar, wood panelling, leaded windows, stunning outdoor tiling and a pleasant garden. The first-floor restaurant area, or the whole pub, can be booked for private functions – check in advance if visiting on a Saturday. Quiz night is Tuesday and there is live acoustic music on Sunday, plus twice-yearly beer festivals. Happy hours are Monday to Friday 3-7pm and all day Saturday.
Q(Camden Rd/Town)

Tapping the Admiral

77 Castle Road, NW1 8SU

12-midnight (11 Mon & Tue); 12-10.30 Sun

(020) 7267 6118 tappingtheadmiral.co.uk

8 changing beers (sourced regionally) H

A popular and enjoyable community pub where friendly and knowledgeable staff offer a warm welcome. Eight handpumps deliver guest ales, mainly local. The menu is great British food including speciality home-made pies. A heated and covered beer garden is well designed and a nice feature. There is a popular Wednesday quiz and live traditional music on Thursday evenings. Look out for monthly tap takeovers and pop-up events. Local CAMRA Pub of the Year 2018.
Q(Kentish Town West)

NW1: Euston

Doric Arch

Euston Station Colonnade, 1 Eversholt Street, NW1 2DN

8am-11 (10.30 Sun) (020) 7383 3359

Fuller's Oliver's Island, London Pride, ESB; Gale's HSB; 4 changing beers (sourced nationally; often Fuller's) H

Up a flight of stairs, large picture windows in a raised area afford a view of the busy urban world below. Right next to Euston station, it is used extensively by commuters, aided by the train-times screen. Brewery and railway memorabilia adorn the walls. The excellent staff are helpful and informative about the ales, including guest beers from London and across the UK. Food is served all day, alcoholic drinks from 10am. Toilets are at basement level.
(Euston/Euston Sq)

Euston Tap

West & East Lodges, 190 Euston Road, NW1 2EF

12-11.30 (10.30 Mon); 11.30-11.30 Sat; 12-10 Sun

(020) 3137 8837 eustontap.com

12 changing beers (sourced nationally) H

Fronting the main station building, these impressive Grade II-listed Portland stone lodges, separated by a bus lane, are relics from the original 1830s station. Up to 12 changing beers are served, mostly from smaller breweries, and are pumped up to taps behind the bar. Small ground-floor spaces are augmented by large outside heated drinking areas as well as seating (and toilets) up the wrought-iron spiral staircases. The East Lodge opens later in the afternoon and offers traditional cider. (Euston/Euston Sq)

NW5: Kentish Town

Grafton

20 Prince of Wales Road, NW5 3LG

12-11 (midnight Fri & Sat); 12-10.30 Sun

(020) 7482 4466 thegraftonnw5.co.uk

Purity Mad Goose; Sambrook's Wandle Ale; 4 changing beers (sourced locally) H

Popular pub with beautiful Victorian features, combining a traditional feel with many contemporary touches and specialising in local cask beers. The spacious ground-floor horseshoe bar is partly tiled, with ample seating. Upstairs is a bar/function room (no real ale). It has an elegant, covered roof garden (closes 11pm). Knowledgeable and friendly bar staff will serve you. Quiz night is Tuesday and there are occasional open mic evenings, as well as the piano and board games.
(Kentish Town/Kentish Town West)

Lion & Unicorn

42 Gaisford Street, NW5 2ED

12 (10 Sat)-11; 12-10.30 Sun (020) 7267 2304

thelionandunicornnw5.co.uk

Young's Bitter; 3 changing beers (sourced regionally; often Redemption, Southwark, Twickenham) H

A popular community venue that is a great favourite, with its genuine homely feel, open fire and comfortable seating. Run by friendly management and staff as a Geronimo-branded gastropub, it offers a good-quality cask ale range featuring several local breweries. It has won local and regional awards for both front and back gardens. There are quizzes on Sunday. Above is the Lion and Unicorn Theatre; details of productions are available on the theatre's website.

Pineapple

51 Leverton Street, NW5 2NX

12-11 (midnight Fri & Sat); 12-10.30 Sun

(020) 7284 4631

Marston's Pedigree; 4 changing beers (sourced nationally) H

An authentic and friendly community pub, saved from closure by the locals, Grade II-listed and identified by CAMRA as having a regionally important historic interior, notable for its mirrors and splendid bar-back. The front bar, with comfortable seating around tables, leads through to an informal conservatory overlooking the patio garden. The food menu is Thai kitchen cuisine. Local beers can come from across London and, the pub being free of tie, the range changes regularly.
Q

Southampton Arms

139 Highgate Road, NW5 1LE

12-11 (midnight Fri & Sat); 12-10.30 Sun

thesouthamptonarms.co.uk

10 changing beers (sourced nationally) H

This pub does what it says on the sign outside: Ale, Cider, Meat. The multiple CAMRA award-winning venue has 18 handpumps on and behind the bar, serving almost equal amounts of cider and different beers from microbreweries across the UK. Snacks include pork pies, roast pork in baps, cheese and meat baps plus veggie options. Music is played on vinyl only and the piano is in regular use. Down at the back is a secluded patio.
❀◑⇌⊖(Gospel Oak/Kentish Town)●⊟

NW6: Kilburn

Sir Colin Campbell Ⓛ

264-266 Kilburn High Road, NW6 2BY
⏲ 4-midnight (1am Fri); 12-1am Sat; 12-12.30am Sun
☎ (020) 7693 5443 ⊕ thesircolincampbell.co.uk
Dark Star Hophead; 3 changing beers (sourced nationally) Ⓗ
This establishment was acquired in early 2017 and restored to its original beauty by three local people who run two other pubs. The lovely wood cladding was cleaned up, and two separate rooms around a central bar give a real feel of how traditional pubs used to be. Cask beer returned, with extras such as live traditional Irish music every Friday, Saturday and Sunday night. It also has a nice selection of bottled and canned beers. The upstairs room operates as a restaurant.
♞❀◑♿⊖(Brondesbury/Kilburn)♣●⊟🐾ᯤ

NW9: Colindale

Moon Under Water ✔

10 Varley Parade, Edgware Road, NW9 6RR
⏲ 8am-midnight ☎ (020) 8200 7611
Greene King Abbot; 4 changing beers (often Enfield, Sambrook's, Twickenham) Ⓗ
A large Wetherspoon pub converted from a Woolworths store in 1990. The rear is mainly for food, where well-behaved children are welcome; the front is a more traditional drinking and chatting area. Some of the changing beers will come from London breweries and the manager occasionally arranges Meet the London Brewer events. Many of the other beers on draught or in bottles are also London brewed. Silent TVs show either news or racing. ♞◑♿⊟(32,142)ᯤ

NW9: Kingsbury

J J Moons Ⓛ ✔

551-553 Kingsbury Road, NW9 9EL
⏲ 8am-midnight ☎ (020) 8204 9675
Greene King IPA, Abbot; 4 changing beers (sourced nationally) Ⓗ
Early (1988) Wetherspoon shop conversion, with silent TV screens featuring horse racing. A large, one-room establishment with low ceilings, lots of wood panelling, subdued lighting and a raised section at the rear, this is a rare outlet for real ale in this part of outer London. The name plays on the George Orwell Moon Under Water theme of some of the company's earliest pubs. Children permitted until 9pm. Q♞◑♿⊖⊟ᯤ

Harrow

Castle ★

30 West Street, HA1 3EF
⏲ 12-11 (midnight Fri); 10-midnight Sat; 10.30-11 Sun
☎ (020) 8422 3155
Fuller's London Pride, ESB; Gale's Seafarers Ale, HSB; 1 changing beer (sourced nationally; often Butcombe, Fuller's) Ⓗ
A lively and friendly Fuller's house, in the heart of historic Harrow-on-the-Hill. Built in 1901 and Grade II-listed, it has been identified by CAMRA as having a nationally important historic interior. Food is served until 9.30pm (8pm Sun); reservations are recommended for Sunday lunchtimes. Three real coal fires help to keep the pub warm and cosy in the colder months, and a secluded beer garden is popular during the summer. Harrow CAMRA Pub of the Year 2017. Q♞❀◑♿♣⊟(258,H17)🐾ᯤ

Moon on the Hill ✔

373-375 Station Road, HA1 2AW
⏲ 8am-midnight (12.30am Fri & Sat) ☎ (020) 8863 3670
Greene King Abbot; Sharp's Doom Bar; 4 changing beers (often Redemption, Sambrook's, Truman's) Ⓗ
Small, busy Wetherspoon pub close to Harrow-on-the-Hill station and served by numerous bus routes. A good-value food menu is available all day, making it popular with price-conscious regulars, office workers and students from the nearby University of Westminster. The pub gets extremely busy when there are sporting events on at nearby Wembley Stadium.
Q♞◑♿⇌⊖(Harrow-on-the-Hill)●⊟ᯤ

Ruislip

Hop & Vine Ⓛ

18 High Street, HA4 7AN
⏲ closed Mon; 12-2.30, 5-10; 12-11 Fri & Sat; 12-8 Sun
6 changing beers (sourced nationally; often Malt) Ⓖ
Cosy bar converted from a former café, opened in 2016. Seating is at low tables with chairs and benches. A small bar counter in the right-hand corner sells real ales and ciders on gravity dispense from a temperature-controlled cellar room behind it. Bottled beers, cans, wines and spirits are also on offer. Snacks include cheese and charcuterie-board options. There may be six or seven real ales at weekends and table service often applies. Local CAMRA Pub of the Year 2018. Q♞❀♿⊖♣●⊟🐾

SOUTH-EAST LONDON

SE1: Bermondsey

Simon the Tanner Ⓛ

231 Long Lane, SE1 4PR
⏲ 5-11 Mon; 12-11 (midnight Fri & Sat); 12-10.30 Sun
☎ (020) 7357 8740 ⊕ simonthetanner.co.uk
4 changing beers (often Redemption, Siren, Southwark) Ⓗ
In a quiet road just off busy Bermondsey Street, the Simon is a mid-terrace, modestly sized, Grade II-listed pub. A former Shepherd Neame outlet, it is now a free house. The real ales, which change regularly, are often from London breweries, and there is real cider. Food is along the lines of Scotch eggs and cheese and meat platters. A quiz is held on Tuesday evenings. Children are admitted until 7pm. ♞◑⇌⊖(London Bridge)●⊟🐾ᯤ

SE1: Borough

Royal Oak ✔

44 Tabard Street, SE1 4JU
⏲ 11 (12 Sat)-11; 12-9 Sun ☎ (020) 7357 7173
Harvey's Sussex XX Mild Ale, IPA, Sussex Best Bitter; 3 changing beers (often Fuller's, Gale's, Harvey's) Ⓗ

A charming back-to-basics drinkers' pub separated into two sections by the bar counter and an off-sales hatch. This was Harvey's brewery's first London tied house and is renowned for friendly and attentive service. The wide range of beers includes seasonal brews and, unusually for London, a mild, plus a changing guest Fuller's beer. The inventive and extensive food menu sources many ingredients from London markets. Regulars come from miles around to spend time here.
Q◖◗⇌(London Bridge)⊖♣🍎🚌

SE1: Borough Market

Market Porter

9 Stoney Street, SE1 9AA
⏲ 11 (12 Sat)-11; 12-10.30 Sun ☎ (020) 7407 2495
🌐 themarketporter.co.uk
Harvey's Sussex Best Bitter Ⓗ**; 10 changing beers** Ⓗ/Ⓐ
This classic, rustic pub next to the famous Borough Market still retains its traditional 6-8.30am weekday opening hours. A Guide regular, it serves up to 10 changing real ales plus four ciders, usually including a Westons. Adorning the walls, a vast array of pumpclips reflects the huge range of beers offered over the years. Popular with locals and visitors alike, it can get busy, with drinkers spilling out onto the street. An upstairs restaurant serves lunches. 🐎◖◗⇌⊖(London Bridge)🍎🚌

Old King's Head

King's Head Yard, 45-49 Borough High Street, SE1 1NA
⏲ 11-midnight (1am Fri & Sat); 12-midnight Sun
☎ (020) 7407 1550 🌐 theoldkingshead.uk.com
Harvey's Sussex Best Bitter; St Austell Tribute, Proper Job; Sharp's Doom Bar; 2 changing beers (often Harvey's) Ⓗ
A traditional pub down a narrow, cobbled lane off Borough High Street. Stained-glass windows hint at a bygone era and the pictures adorning the walls tell the story of a pub, and an area, that has a rich history. The layout inside is simple, with an L-shaped bar in one corner usually offering six real ales on handpump. The clientele is a mix of tourists, office workers and visitors to the nearby Borough Market. ◖◗♿⇌⊖(London Bridge)🚌📶

Rake

14 Winchester Walk, SE1 9AG
⏲ 12 (11 Fri; 10 Sat)-11; 12-8 Sun ☎ (020) 7407 0557
4 changing beers (sourced nationally) Ⓗ
On the edge of Borough Market, this small pub prides itself on offering a high-quality, varied beer selection, and over the years has become a real global destination for beer aficionados and brewers. Beers on four handpumps are complemented by a comprehensive range of bottles, mainly from North America and Europe, plus a small selection of wines and spirits. It holds periodic brewery tap takeovers and other themed beer selections. Q❀♿⇌⊖(London Bridge)🚌📶

SE1: Elephant & Castle

Elephant & Castle ✔

119 Newington Causeway, SE1 6BN
⏲ 12-midnight (1am Thu; 2am Fri & Sat) ☎ (020) 7403 8124
🌐 elephantandcastlepub.com
Volden Session Ale; 4 changing beers (sourced nationally) Ⓗ
Following closure in 2015 and a subsequent local campaign to save it, the pub was reopened by Antic in the summer of 2016. The interior is typical of their style, with an eclectic mix of furnishings and exposed services and pipework. There is also a large outdoor drinking area to the side of the building. ❀◖◗⇌⊖🚌

SE1: Waterloo

Hole in the Wall

5 Mepham Street, SE1 8SQ
⏲ 11-11 (11.30 Fri & Sat); 12-10.30 Sun ☎ (020) 7928 6196
Greene King IPA; Hogs Back TEA; Sharp's Doom Bar; Young's Bitter; 4 changing beers (often Sambrook's, Southwark, Truman's) Ⓗ
A short hop across the road from Waterloo railway station, this unusual free house enjoys the comforting rumble of trains overhead. A long-time real ale outlet from when this was rare in the area, it has a small, cosy front bar and a larger back bar showing sport on TV. Alongside the range of cask ales, good food is served all day. Folk music plays on Sunday evenings. The clientele is mixed and the pub gets busy when there is rugby at Twickenham. 🐎❀◖◗⇌⊖🍎📺🚌🐾📶

King's Arms Ⓛ

25 Roupell Street, SE1 8TB
⏲ 11-11; 12-10.30 Sun ☎ (020) 7207 0784
🌐 thekingsarmslondon.co.uk
Adnams Southwold Bitter; house beer (by Sharp's); 7 changing beers (sourced nationally) Ⓗ
Tucked away in a back street, this pub is worth seeking out although it gets busy in the early evenings. The two small rooms are separated by a central bar and drinking is also allowed outside at the front. Nine real ales usually include two or more from London breweries and at least one dark beer. To the rear is a Thai restaurant.
🐎◖◗⇌(Waterloo/Waterloo East)⊖🚌🐾📶

Waterloo Tap

Arch 147, Sutton Walk, SE1 7ES
⏲ 12-11 (11.30 Thu & Fri); 11-11.30 Sat; 12-10 Sun
☎ (020) 3455 7436 🌐 waterlootap.com
6 changing beers (often Hammerton, Siren, Titanic) Ⓐ
This fairly compact, modern sister pub to the Euston Tap is in a railway arch close to Waterloo Station and a short stroll from the South Bank, making it handy for visitors to the BFI IMAX and Royal Festival Hall complex. The cask beers are all dispensed from taps mounted on the copper bar-back. Details of the beers available are listed on a blackboard above the bar. 🐎♿⇌⊖🍎🚌🐾

SE3: Blackheath

Hare & Billet ✔

1a Eliot Cottages, Hare & Billet Road, SE3 0QJ
⏲ 12 (11 Sat)-11; 11-10.30 Sun ☎ (020) 8852 2352
🌐 hareandbillet.com
Greene King IPA; house beer (by Greene King); 6 changing beers (often Dark Star, Old Dairy, Sambrook's) Ⓗ
An inn of this name has existed on the site since at least 1732, though the current building dates from the 19th century. The decor is faux-Victorian in a contemporary style, with stripped natural-finish wood cladding and bare floorboards. There are up to eight real ales on handpump, including one from Greene King, plus Biddenden Bushels cider. In the

summer plastic glasses are available for outdoor drinking overlooking the open expanse of the heath. (380)

SE4: Brockley

Brockley Barge ✔

184 Brockley Road, SE4 2RR

8am-midnight (1am Fri & Sat) ☎ (020) 8694 7690

Greene King Abbot; Ruddles Best Bitter; Sharp's Doom Bar; 5 changing beers (often Hop Stuff, Rooster's, Tring) H

A former Courage public house, now part of the Wetherspoon chain, located a stone's throw from the station. The name derives from the Croydon Canal, which was situated where the railway line now runs. A popular, thriving hub whose clientele reflects the vibrant area, it is laid out in a semi horseshoe shape with a variety of seating areas. A small courtyard to the south side is well used in the summer. Q

Talbot L

2-4 Tyrwhitt Road, SE4 1QG

2-11; 12-midnight Fri & Sat; 12-10.30 Sun

☎ (020) 8692 2665 talbotpublichouse.com

Harvey's Sussex Best Bitter; 4 changing beers (sourced nationally; often Bedlam, Old Mill, Brockley) H

A fine Victorian suburban local on two floors, popular with all ages, families and dog owners. It has recently been tastefully redecorated inside and out, with large windows making the interior light and airy. A series of murals, highlighted with gilt, decorates the walls. An extensive, upmarket food menu includes vegetarian and vegan choices, with daily specials and meal deals on Mondays. The pub hosts regular live music, seasonal events and a weekly quiz.
Q (St Johns) (Elverson Rd)

SE5: Camberwell

Stormbird

25 Camberwell Church Street, SE5 8TR

4-midnight (1am Fri); 12-1am Sat; 12-midnight Sun

☎ (020) 7708 4460 thestormbirdpub.co.uk

Dark Star Hophead; 3 changing beers (often Bristol Beer Factory, Dark Star, Five Points) H

The sister pub to the Hermit's Cave across the road, offering a slightly more contemporary feel and attracting a mixed but generally younger crowd. There is a huge array of beers of all types on the bar, including four real ales on handpump and an extensive bottled beer selection. This range encompasses brews from the UK, continental Europe and the US. Draught beers are available in third-pint measures. (Denmark Hill)

SE6: Catford

Catford Bridge Tavern

Station Approach, Catford Bridge, SE6 4RE

4-11 (midnight Thu); 12-midnight Fri; 12-11 Sat & Sun

☎ (020) 8690 6759 catfordtavern.com

Southwark Bermondsey Best; 3 changing beers (often Brockley, Hop Stuff, Truman's) H

An imposing Tudor-style pub originally named the Railway Tavern. More recently, it survived a supermarket redevelopment threat and then a catastrophic fire in 2015. Reopened in 2017 after extensive renovation, the spacious interior has a long bar at the front and a dining area with open kitchen to the rear. A partially covered roof terrace overlooks the railway station. The four real ales are generally from independent London breweries. (Catford/Catford Bridge)

SE8: Deptford

Brookmill ✔

65 Cranbrook Road, SE8 4EJ

12-11 (midnight Fri & Sat) ☎ (020) 8333 0899

thebrookmill.co.uk

5 changing beers (often Brixton, Gipsy Hill, Wimbledon) H

Spacious Victorian corner pub, reopened under new management in 2016, sister pub to the Great North Wood in West Norwood. Much of the original exterior survives but the interior now has a more contemporary feel, with bare-board flooring and part-exposed brickwork. There is an outdoor area and also an upstairs function room. Good-quality food is served daily. The changing selection of real ales places an emphasis on local south London brews.
Q (St Johns) (Elverson Rd) (47,225)

Dog & Bell L ✔

116 Prince Street, SE8 3JD

12-11 (11.30 Fri-Sun) ☎ (020) 8692 5664

Fuller's London Pride; 5 changing beers (often Clarkshaws, Dent, Old Dairy) H

Traditional and welcoming pub down a side street a short stroll from the centre of Deptford. A Guide stalwart for over 30 years, it offers six real ales plus a selection of Belgian bottled beers, malt whiskies and simple, tasty meals. A lively bar and a real fire in winter greet a good mix of clientele including locals, cyclists and those strolling along the nearby Thames Path. Regular beer festivals are now held, often themed around the UK patron saints' days.
Q

Job Centre ✔

120 Deptford High Street, SE8 4NS

4-11 (midnight Thu & Fri); 11-midnight Sat; 12-11 Sun

☎ (020) 8692 6859 jobcentredeptford.com

Volden Session Ale; 3 changing beers (often Brixton, Brockley, Thornbridge) H

A welcome addition to the previously fairly sparse Deptford real ale pub scene, opened by Antic in 2014 and named after a former occupier. The spacious rectangular bar area has minimalist decor, including bare concrete flooring and exposed ducts and pipework. Music is often playing from a twin-deck turntable. The beer range has a mainly regional focus. The cider on handpump is frequently Westons. Food is varied and includes light bites and burgers.
(Deptford Bridge)

SE9: Eltham

Long Pond L

110 Westmount Road, SE9 1UT

5-10 Mon; 11.30-2.30, 5-10 (11 Thu & Fri); 11-3, 6.30-11 Sat; 12-2.30 Sun ☎ (020) 8331 6767

House beer (by Tonbridge); 5 changing beers (often Kent, Tonbridge, Wantsum) G

Micropub opened in 2014 in a former plumbers' merchants and named after the pond in nearby Eltham Park North. Six real ales, including Kent's, are available on gravity dispense from a rear chilled stillage room. In true micropub tradition, no lager or spirits are served but wine and Dudda's Tun real cider/perry are, plus bar snacks. Seating is mainly high benches and tables, though the rear snug features low tables and chairs. Winner of several local CAMRA awards. Q (B16)

Park Tavern

45 Passey Place, SE9 5DA

12-11 (020) 8850 3216 parktaverneltham.co.uk

8 changing beers (often Otter, Sambrook's, Shepherd Neame) H

Traditional Victorian pub with original Truman's Brewery tiled frontage and signage. The compact interior has an L-shaped bar with stylish lamps and chandeliers. The etched windows have elegant drapes, and decorative plates and pictures line the walls. Light background music is played. There is a well-kept, heated rear garden and further seating to the front and side. An impressive selection of whiskies and wine is available alongside the real ales. Q

SE10: Greenwich

Gate Clock

210 Creek Road, SE10 9RB

8am-midnight (1am Wed & Thu; 2am Fri & Sat)
(020) 8269 2000

Greene King IPA, Abbot; Sharp's Doom Bar; 5 changing beers (sourced nationally) H

A Wetherspoon pub, conveniently located for all the main Greenwich attractions including Greenwich Park, the Old Royal Naval College and the National Maritime Museum. It is a modest and contemporary building with drinking and dining set over two floors plus a small seating area outside. Customers are an international and occupational mix of students, city professionals, the retired, tourists and locals. (Cutty Sark)

Plume of Feathers

19 Park Vista, SE10 9LZ

12-11; 11-midnight Fri & Sat (020) 8858 1661
plumeoffeathers-greenwich.co.uk

Harvey's Sussex Best Bitter; Sharp's Doom Bar; 2 changing beers (sourced nationally) H

With parts dating from 1691, this cosy and quiet historic pub is near the northern entrance to Greenwich Park, close to the National Maritime Museum. The maritime location is reflected inside the bar with much memorabilia on display and interesting historical paintings. As well as bar meals, there is a separate restaurant to the rear, and also a pleasant garden area. The pub has a football team, the Plume Rockets, and a golf society. (Maze Hill)(Cutty Sark)

SE11: Kennington

Mansion House

48 Kennington Park Road, SE11 4RS

12-midnight (1am Fri & Sat) (020) 7582 5599

Oakham JHB, Inferno, Citra, Bishops Farewell; 1 changing beer (often Gale's, Oakham) H

Oakham Ales' only tied outlet in London, situated in a former cocktail lounge and piano bar. The contemporary design includes a stylish juxtaposition of materials and textures. During the summer, the glass frontage can be opened onto the outside seating area. One guest or seasonal Oakham beer complements the permanent range. Attentive staff also serve in the attached pan-Asian Oaka restaurant. Discounted cask beers are on the bar 5-7pm every evening.
(Elephant & Castle)

Old Red Lion

42 Kennington Park Road, SE11 4RS

4-11 (1am Fri); 12-1am Sat; 12-11 Sun
(020) 7735 4312 theoldredlion.com

4 changing beers (sourced regionally; often Volden) H

Grade II-listed twin-bar Antic pub with plenty of character, a fine example of the Brewers' Tudor style, as rebuilt by Hoare & Co in 1933. It has been identified by CAMRA as having a regionally important historic interior, with many original features including exposed wooden beams, fireplaces and low doors connecting the bars. In addition to four changing real ales, there are usually two varying real ciders. Often there is background music. Monthly quiz and folk music nights are held.
(Elephant & Castle)

SE12: Grove Park

Baring Hall Hotel

368 Baring Road, SE12 0DU

4-11 (midnight Fri); 12-midnight Sat; 12-11 Sun
(020) 8851 2184 baringhallhotel.com

Adnams Lighthouse; Caledonian Deuchars IPA; 4 changing beers (often Hawkshead, Mantle, Sambrook's, Volden) H

Dating from 1882 and designed by local architect Ernest Newton, the pub is named after Lord Baring, Earl of Northbrook. It was saved from demolition in 2012 by local campaigners and subsequently reopened by operator Antic. The current decor makes a feature of the scorched paintwork suffered in an earlier fire. A cosy and welcoming refuge opposite the station, and the only pub in the immediate vicinity.

SE14: New Cross

Royal Albert

460 New Cross Road, SE14 6TJ

4-midnight (1am Fri); 12-1am Sat; 12-midnight Sun
(020) 8692 3737 royalalbertpub.com

House beer (by Volden); 6 changing beers (often Burning Sky, Five Points, Moor) H

Grade II-listed Victorian pub with the original etched glass and bar-back, offering up to seven real ales and one real cider on handpump. Furnishings and decor are an eclectic mix, enhancing a convivial atmosphere, and the food is distinctive and enticing. There is a quiz on Monday evening, a DJ on Friday and live music on Sunday. This pub is popular with local academia.

SE15: Nunhead

Beer Shop London

40 Nunhead Green, SE15 3QF

closed Mon; 4-11 (11.30 Fri); 12-11.30 Sat; 12-8 Sun
(020) 7732 5555 thebeershoplondon.co.uk

3 changing beers (often Hop Stuff, Moor, Weird Beard) G

A former corner shop, haberdashery and, latterly, a recording studio. The knowledgeable staff serve a

varied selection of three real ales direct from the cask, along with an extensive range of bottled beers, plus wine, spirits and soft drinks. Boxed cider, from various producers, is also available, as are pub snacks. It hosts occasional events such as Meet the Brewer evenings. Note that January opening hours may vary.
(78,P12)

Ivy House

40 Stuart Road, SE15 3BE
12-11 (midnight Fri & Sat); 12-10.30 Sun
(020) 7277 8233 ivyhousenunhead.com
Brockley Pale Ale; Dark Star Hophead; Truman's Swift; 2 changing beers (sourced regionally; often Brick, Buxton, Tiny Rebel) H
Large 1930s former Truman's pub with its original wood-panelled interior, identified by CAMRA as having a regionally important historic interior. The building was saved in the nick of time from conversion to flats by being Grade II-listed and is now community owned. There are three bars, the largest of which features a stage hosting regular live music, continuing the venue's proud history of live entertainment. One ale, usually Truman's Runner, is sold at a discounted price.
Q (343,484)

SE15: Peckham

Beer Rebellion

129 Queens Road, SE15 2ND
12-11 (12.30am Fri & Sat) (020) 7732 7552
Dark Star Hophead; 3 changing beers (sourced nationally; often East London Brewing, Siren) H
Close to Queens Road station, this bar is in the style of a micropub, situated in former shop premises. The concrete walls and floor give a post-industrial feel. Lamps fashioned from jars, along with high tables and stools, add to the utilitarian ambience. Details of the range of varying real ales and cider are listed on a large chalkboard. There is limited outdoor seating on the pavement at the front.
(Queens Rd)

SE18: Plumstead

Old Mill

1 Old Mill Road, SE18 1QG
12-11 (11.30 Fri; midnight Sat); 12-10.30 Sun
(020) 3719 1499
6 changing beers (often Bexley, Goddards, Hop Stuff) H
On the north side of Plumstead Common, this pub was formerly an 18th-century windmill, the Grade II-listed tower of which still remains. The single L-shaped bar is sparsely furnished, including a pool table to the rear, leaving ample space for the frequent live music acts. Real ales change often, with those from local and regional independent breweries predominating. Two changing real ciders are also usually available. Lunchtime and evening meals are served except on Wednesdays.

SE18: Woolwich

Taproom L

15 Major Draper Street, SE18 6GD
4-11; 12-midnight Fri & Sat; 12-10 Sun (020) 8316 4413
taproomse18.com
4 changing beers (often Brew York, Bristol Beer Factory, Hop Stuff) H
Opened in 2015 as the first bar owned by the nearby Hop Stuff Brewery, this pub has a somewhat minimalist decor of bare wood and exposed brickwork. The bar area is furnished with stools and barrel tables, with a metal spiral staircase leading to an upper floor with conventional table seating. The varying real ale range usually includes at least one from Hop Stuff plus four from other local breweries. It also serves a good-quality, changing pizza menu.
(Woolwich Arsenal)

SE19: Gipsy Hill

Beer Rebellion

126 Gipsy Hill, SE19 1PL
2 (12 Sat)-11; 12-10 Sun (020) 8670 9034
East London Brewing Foundation, Cowcatcher H**; 3 changing beers (often Crate, East London Brewing, Saltaire)** H/P
Conveniently located opposite the railway station. Despite having the feel of a micropub in a parade of shops, this pub packs in everything you would expect in a full-sized version. The small ground-floor bar is supplemented by additional seating in the basement. Do not be put off by the keg-style taps located in a Welsh dresser; the top row dispenses cask ales and ciders pumped up from a cellar under the pavement. (322)

SE20: Penge

Moon & Stars L

164-166 High Street, SE20 7QS
8am-11 (020) 8776 5680
Dark Star Hophead; Greene King Abbot; Kelham Island Pale Rider; Ruddles Best Bitter; 12 changing beers (sourced nationally) H
Popular high-street Wetherspoon pub with the widest choice of real ale in the local branch area from 17 handpumps. A variety of real ale styles is always offered, usually including beers from London microbreweries. The pub has a large L-shaped bar with a Wizard of Oz theme which includes a huge sculpture of a lion. There are several alcoves suitable for small groups. Regular mini-festivals and other beer-related events are held, including Meet the Brewer evenings.
(Kent House) (Beckenham Rd)
P

SE22: East Dulwich

East Dulwich Tavern

1 Lordship Lane, SE22 8EW
12-midnight (1am Fri & Sat) (020) 8693 1316
eastdulwichtavern.com
Dark Star Hophead; Volden Session Ale; 4 changing beers (often Brick, Truman's, Twickenham) H
An imposing pub in a prominent corner position and the home of the Antic pub company. The interior is classic boozer but contemporised and alive with customers. Its upper storeys are now offices, although the first-floor masonic hall with its own bar opens occasionally for music and events, including a monthly film club. There is usually real cider during summer months, and good-quality food is on offer.

SE23: Forest Hill

All Inn One

53 Perry Vale, SE23 2NE
3-11.30; 2-1.30am Fri; 12-1.30am Sat; 12-11.30 Sun
(020) 8699 3311 allinnone.org.uk
3 changing beers (often Brockley, Southwark, Tiny Rebel)
A red-brick free house, still also known locally as the Foresters. The open-plan interior is surprisingly spacious and the gardens include a family area with children's play equipment. A separate restaurant room can be reserved for private functions. The changing beer is sourced from local south-east London and Welsh breweries. Wheat beers are among the good range of bottles. The Forest Hill Gin Club meets here.

Blythe Hill Tavern

319 Stanstead Road, SE23 1JB
11-11 (midnight Thu-Sat); 12-11 Sun (020) 8690 5176
blythehilltavern.org.uk/blythe-hill-tavern
Dark Star Hophead; Harvey's Sussex Best Bitter; 4 changing beers (sourced nationally; often Brockley, Dark Star, Ringwood)
A regular recipient of awards for beer and cider, this friendly Victorian local has an unusual three-bar layout which CAMRA has identified as a regionally important historic pub interior. Usually, six cask beers and up to 13 real ciders are available. In two of the bars TV screens show sporting events, especially horse racing. Traditional Irish music performances are on Thursday evenings and there are also regular poetry evenings. The pretty garden includes a children's play area.
Q (Catford/Catford Bridge)

Capitol

11-21 London Road, SE23 3TW
8am-midnight (1am Fri & Sat) (020) 8291 8920
Greene King Abbot; Ruddles Best Bitter; Sharp's Doom Bar; 5 changing beers (sourced nationally)
Grade II-listed and described as a rare surviving example of a 1920s cinema building, built in a neoclassical style, this Wetherspoon pub opened in 2001. The split-level, grand interior offers a range of seating areas, and there are also outdoor picnic benches. Recommended tours of the building's non-public areas occur at various times of the year, including London Open House weekend in September.

SE25: South Norwood

Shelverdine Goathouse

7-9 High Street, SE25 6EP
4-11 (midnight Thu); 12-midnight Fri & Sat; 12-11 Sun
(020) 8916 1001 shelverdinegoathouse.com
Volden Session Ale, Pale Ale; 4 changing beers (sourced nationally)
This modern pub has three distinct areas, all with large windows overlooking the High Street but decorated in different styles, with kitchen equipment, clocks (not accurate) and pictures. It is the nearest Antic pub to their Volden brewery in Selhurst. Some guest beers often come from other London breweries. A home-fans-only policy operates when Crystal Palace are playing. Quiz night is Monday. Live music events are held on alternate Fridays. (Norwood Jct)

SE27: West Norwood

Great North Wood

3 Knights Hill, SE27 0HS
12-11 (midnight Fri); 10.30-midnight Sat; 10.30-11 Sun
(020) 8766 0351 thegreatnorthwood.co.uk
4 changing beers (often Belleville, Cronx, Sambrook's)
A traditional Victorian pub on two floors, close to the railway station, extensively refurbished and rebranded as a pub and kitchen in 2014. Offering a wide range of food and real ale, it can be busy Fridays and at weekends; it is quieter but still with a friendly atmosphere through the week. The four cask beers tend to be from London brewers, usually including one or two from Sambrook's.

Addiscombe

Claret & Ale

5 Bingham Corner, Lower Addiscombe Road, CR0 7AA
11.30-11 (11.30 Thu; midnight Fri & Sat); 12-11 Sun
(020) 8656 7452
Palmers IPA; 5 changing beers (sourced nationally)
Small, privately owned and friendly free house around the corner from Addiscombe tram stop, boasting 31 years in this Guide. A community pub where conversation is king, it received a sympathetic makeover in 2016. The guest beers are mainly from microbreweries. See the unique board opposite the bar for beers on and coming next. Two draught ciders are always available, served from the cellar.

Beckenham

Bricklayers Arms

237 High Street, BR3 1BN
12 (11 Thu-Sat)-11; 12-10 Sun (020) 8402 0007
bricklayersarms.co
St Austell Tribute, Proper Job; Young's Special; 1 changing beer (sourced nationally)
Traditional local high-street pub providing a friendly welcome to a clientele of all ages. There is an open log fire in winter and a covered outdoor seating area with heaters and even a TV screen. The guest ales often reflect recommendations by customers. The pub was the local CAMRA branch Community Pub of the Year in 2016. Sunday hours apply on most bank holidays.
(Junction/Clock House) (Junction)

Bexleyheath

Furze Wren

6 Market Place, Broadway Square, DA6 7DY
8am-midnight (020) 8298 2590
Greene King Abbot; Ruddles Best Bitter; Sharp's Doom Bar; 7 changing beers (often Rockin' Robin, Twickenham, Westerham)
Spacious Wetherspoon pub named after the local bird also known as the Dartford Warbler. It is at the heart of the shopping area, with a wide clientele. Plenty of seating and large windows make it a great place to eat, drink and people-watch. The toilets are on the same level, a rarity for this chain. Local history panels are displayed throughout the pub. Alcoholic drinks are served from 9am, including Westons and Gwynt y Ddraig Black Dragon ciders. Q

Robin Hood & Little John

78 Lion Road, DA6 8PF
11-3, 5.30-11; 11-3, 7-11 Sat; 12-4, 7-10.30 Sun
(020) 8303 1128 robinhoodbexleyheath.co.uk
Adnams Southwold Bitter, Broadside; Bexley's Own Beer; Fuller's London Pride; Harvey's Sussex Best Bitter; Sharp's Doom Bar; 2 changing beers (often Shepherd Neame, Westerham) H
A back-street local dating from the 1830s, when it was surrounded by fields. Eight real ales are on offer, mostly from independent breweries including the Bexley Brewery. It has a good reputation for its home-cooked food at lunchtimes (no food Sun) with Italian specials, which can be eaten at tables made from old Singer sewing machines. Frequent local CAMRA Pub of the Year and regional winner three times. Over-21s only.
Q (B13)

Wrong 'Un

234-236 Broadway, DA6 8AS
8am-midnight (020) 8298 0439
Greene King Abbot; Ruddles Best Bitter; Sharp's Doom Bar; 5 changing beers (sourced nationally; often Hop Stuff, Shepherd Neame) H
Bexleyheath's first Wetherspoon pub, opened in 1994 in a single-storey former furniture store. The unusual pub name is an alternative expression for a googly – there are records of cricket being played in the locality since 1746. Westons Old Rosie cider is stocked. There are comfortable booths to sit in as well as an open-plan area. Alcoholic drinks are served from 9am and food until 11pm daily.
Q

Blackfen

Broken Drum

308 Westwood Lane, DA15 9PT
3-10; 12-10 Sat; 1-4 Sun 07803 131678
thebrokendrum.co.uk
3 changing beers (sourced nationally) G
One of Bexley's growing list of micropubs, opened in April 2015 and named after an inn in a Terry Pratchett novel. It sells real ale and cider on gravity from a stillage in a temperature-controlled room at the rear, viewable through its glazed door. Furnishings includes a settee in each of the bay windows and a variety of tables and chairs. Society for the Preservation of Beers from the Wood London Pub of the Year 2018.
Q P (51,132)

George Staples

273 Blackfen Road, DA15 8PR
11-11 (midnight Thu-Sat); 12-11 Sun (020) 8850 3181
Sharp's Doom Bar; 4 changing beers (sourced nationally) H
Originally the Woodman, built in 1845 and one of the first buildings in Blackfen. It was then demolished and rebuilt in 1931 when large-scale building began in the area. Refurbished in 2007 and renamed after the original landlord, it is now a large, comfortable single-roomed pub/sports bar with plenty of outdoor seating as well. A buy-five, get-one-free loyalty scheme is advertised.
P (51,132)

Bromley

Red Lion

10 North Road, BR1 3LG
11-11; 12-11 Sun (020) 8460 2691
redlionbromley.co.uk
Greene King IPA, Abbot; Harvey's Sussex Best Bitter; 2 changing beers (often Black Sheep, Jennings, Oakham) H
Traditional, well-kept pub in the quiet back streets just north of Bromley town centre. It is the only pub in the branch area to have featured in every edition of this Guide since the local branch was formed in 2011, and is well worth seeking out. Many original features include its tiling, and an extensive library dominates one wall. A range of good-value meals is served. Q (North)

Shortlands Tavern

5 Station Road, BR2 0EY
12-11.30 (midnight Fri & Sat); 12-11 Sun
(020) 8466 0202 theshortlandstavern.com
St Austell Tribute; 5 changing beers (often Brentwood, Dorking, Plain) H
Victorian gem of a pub which is part of the town, and conveniently located both for trains and buses, but far enough away from the main road to feel quite peaceful. You can be sure of a friendly and helpful welcome whether you are after the changing range of non-mainstream real ales, the food or one of the many activities including comedy nights, live music, a book club, a knitting group, painting classes and even bingo.
Q (Shortlands)

Star & Garter

227 High Street, BR1 1NZ
4-11 Mon; 12-11 (midnight Fri & Sat); 12-9 Sun
(020) 3730 9458
6 changing beers (often Bristol Beer Factory, Dark Star, Siren) H
A late 19th-century, Grade II-listed pub reopened in 2016 and serving real ale for the first time, following closure for more than two years. The building has been completely refurbished and now boasts eight handpumps, one of which often dispenses real cider. The real ales are usually non-mainstream, with local and regional microbreweries well represented. Customers are allowed to order in food from local takeaways. Local CAMRA Pub of the Year 2018.
Q (North)

Chislehurst

Imperial Arms

Old Hill, BR7 5LZ
12-11 (10.30 Sun) (020) 3605 7899
imperialarms.co.uk
Fuller's London Pride; Harvey's Sussex Best Bitter; Marston's Pedigree; 1 changing beer H
Cosy and inviting hillside pub with two bars. The Catherine Bar is named after the mistress of Napoleon III who stayed here when he was exiled to Chislehurst in 1870. The management are proud of their food – lobster and steaks being specialities – but reinforced their continuing commitment to real ale in 2016 with a fourth handpump that sometimes serves guest beers. Quizzes are held every Wednesday. Q (162,269)

Crayford

Penny Farthing

3 Waterside, DA1 4JJ

closed Mon; 12-3, 5-9.30; 12-10.30 Fri & Sat; 12-3 Sun
☎ 07772 866645 pennyfarthingcrayford.co.uk
4 changing beers (sourced nationally) G
The local CAMRA branch's second micropub, opened in 2014, is a haven of real ale near the banks of the River Cray. Ale and cider are dispensed direct from the cask in a cold room with a viewing window. A charity fine is levied should your mobile phone ring. Cider is usually from Dudda's, although Westons is also often available. Q

Croydon

Cronx L
Units 3 & 4, Boxpark Croydon, 99 George Street, CR0 1LD
11-10.30; 11-10 Sun ☎ (01689) 809093 thecronx.com
Cronx Standard, Kotchin; 2 changing beers (sourced locally) H
A modern micropub-sized bar located in Croydon's Boxpark development beside East Croydon station, accessed via Dingwall Road by the bus stop. Six handpumps serve a range of Cronx beers and normally two varying guests, with a real cider on occasion. The decor is simple but stylish, employing scaffolding and adapted beer casks and fonts. Plastic glasses will be used for customers taking their drinks out of the bar into the Boxpark complex. Food is available elsewhere in Boxpark itself. (East)

Dog & Bull ✔
24 Surrey Street, CR0 1RG
12-11 (11.30 Fri & Sat); 12-10.30 Sun ☎ (020) 8667 9718
dogandbullcroydon.co.uk
Young's Bitter, Special; 2 changing beers (sourced nationally) H
Historic Grade II-listed pub in the middle of Croydon's daily street market, with origins going back to the 16th century. The interior has a classic layout: an island bar with two adjoining rooms. It has an unexpected and attractive walled garden at the rear with bedding plants and seasonal baskets. During the summer there are regular barbecues, with beers served from a garden bar. An upstairs function room can be hired.
(East/West)(George St/Reeves Corner)(West)

George L ✔
17-21 George Street, CR0 1LA
8am-midnight (1am Fri & Sat) ☎ (020) 8649 9077
Burning Sky Plateau, Aurora; Ruddles Best Bitter; Sharp's Doom Bar; Thornbridge Jaipur IPA; 9 changing beers (often Surrey Hills, Tillingbourne) H
A converted shop, this town-centre pub is named after a former coaching inn in Croydon. The 17 handpumps are fully utilised. The pub has two bars, the rear one being slightly raised (a ramp allows access), with its six handpumps often showcasing beers from breweries such as Dark Star, Oakham, Saltaire and Thornbridge. The front bar has a wider mix of beers, including those from local breweries and the Wetherspoon national range.
(East/West)(George St/Reeves Corner)(West)

Green Dragon L ✔
58 High Street, CR0 1NA
11-11 (midnight Thu; 1am Fri & Sat); 12-10.30 Sun
☎ (020) 8667 0684
8 changing beers H
At the end of Croydon's famous Surrey Street Market, this recently refurbished Stonegate pub and former bank boasts eight real ale handpumps, eight craft keg lines and up to six boxed ciders. Beers are both from local and national breweries, and a range of British and foreign bottled beers is also available. The upstairs function room hosts regular events including a quiz on Mondays, poker on Tuesdays and monthly open mic sessions.
(East/West)(George St/Reeves Corner)(West)

Oval Tavern ✔
131 Oval Road, CR0 6BR
12-11 (midnight Fri & Sat) ☎ (020) 8686 6023
theovaltavern.co.uk
6 changing beers (often Cronx) H
Back-street family-friendly pub with a good reputation for live music, including jam sessions, acoustic acts and the occasional DJ. A quiz is held on Wednesdays. Tasty home-made food is served; the kedgeree and huge sausage rolls are especially recommended. There is a large garden and barbecue area to the rear. The decor is unusual; half-timbering creates an interesting interior with a rural atmosphere. The pub continues to improve and promote its range of cask ale, often featuring local beers. (East)

Royal Standard
1 Sheldon Street, CR0 1SS
12-midnight (11 Sun) ☎ (020) 8686 4288
Fuller's London Pride, ESB; Gale's HSB; 1 changing beer (often Dark Star) H
A street-corner local dwarfed by the adjacent Croydon flyover and multi-storey car park. This quiet retreat just south of the town centre offers a single bar with four different drinking areas, each with its own character. Football and rugby are often shown on the TV with the sound turned down.
Q(George St/Reeves Corner)

Skylark ✔
34-36 South End, CR0 1DP
8am-midnight (1am Fri & Sat) ☎ (020) 8649 9909
Fuller's London Pride; Greene King Abbot; Ruddles Best Bitter; Sharp's Doom Bar; Shepherd Neame Spitfire; 7 changing beers H
Spacious Wetherspoon pub in the restaurant quarter south of the town centre. The main bar is wood panelled with a raised library area to the rear. The decor includes pictures of nearby former Croydon Airport, London's first civil airport. A grand staircase at the rear leads to an upstairs bar offering a reduced range of beers, when open. Changing ales are mainly from microbreweries, often local ones. (South)

Spreadeagle
39-41 Katharine Street, CR0 1NX
11-11 (midnight Fri & Sat); 12-10.30 Sun
☎ (020) 8781 1134
Fuller's Oliver's Island, London Pride, ESB; Gale's HSB; 2 changing beers H
Large street-corner pub built in 1893 as a bank. The spacious interior boasts wood panelling, high ceilings, glass mirrors and an imposing staircase leading to two function rooms, one of them regularly used as a 50-seater theatre/cinema. As well as real ale from six handpumps, a good range of other draught and bottled beers is on offer. The pub has Fuller's Master Cellarman accreditation.

Quiz night is Sunday and a cinema club is held on Mondays in the theatre.
❀◑♿⇌(East/West)⊕(George St/Reeves Corner)⊖(West)🚌📶

Downe

Queen's Head L ✔

25 High Street, BR6 7US TQ432616
🕐 12-11 (11.30 Fri & Sat); 12-10.30 Sun ☎ (01689) 852145
🌐 queensheaddowne.com
Harvey's Sussex Best Bitter; 3 changing beers (often Adnams, Westerham) H
An attractive pub, dating from 1565 and named following a visit by Queen Elizabeth I. Though located in the centre of an historic village, it is less than 20 minutes by bus from Bromley or Orpington. Charles Darwin, a regular patron, lived at Down House, less than a mile away. Traditional and comfortable, with open fireplaces and several dining areas, the pub is popular with walkers and locals all year round. ❀◑♣●P🚌(146,R8)🐾📶

Keston

Greyhound ✔

Commonside, BR2 6BP TQ413646
🕐 11-11; 12-10.30 Sun ☎ (01689) 856338
🌐 greyhoundkeston.co.uk
Sharp's Doom Bar; Timothy Taylor Landlord; 4 changing beers (sourced nationally) H
A popular local with an enthusiastic and welcoming landlord, it overlooks the common and is on walking routes including the London Outer Orbital Path, but is also easily accessed by bus from Bromley. At the heart of village life, it details in the newsletter a crowded calendar of local events. Regular beer festivals are held, especially during the Easter weekend when up to 15 unusual beers are available. Local CAMRA Pub of the Year 2017.
Q❀◑♣●P🚌(146,246)🐾📶

Orpington

Orpington Liberal Club L

7 Station Road, BR6 0RZ
🕐 8 (7 Wed)-11; 6-11 Fri; 12-3, 7-11 Sat; 12-3, 8-10.30 Sun
☎ (01689) 820882 🌐 orpingtonliberalclub.co.uk
4 changing beers H
Friendly club that serves more than 200 different real ales annually, mainly from microbreweries. A range of real ciders and perries is on offer together with some local bottled and gluten-free beers. Live music nights are held in the adjoining hall. The club hosts and supports local charitable events including PDSA and Samaritans, and has won many local and regional CAMRA awards. A CAMRA or NULC membership card is required for entry.
Q❀⇌♣●P🚌🐾📶

Petts Wood

One Inn The Wood L

209 Petts Wood Road, BR5 1LA
🕐 closed Mon; 12-2.30, 5-9.30 (11 Fri); 11.30-11 Sat; 12-8 Sun ☎ 07799 535982 🌐 oneinnthewood.co.uk
House beer (by Tonbridge); 4 changing beers (often Kent, Old Dairy, Rockin' Robin) G
Dog- and family-friendly micropub, winner of several CAMRA branch awards, opened in 2014 in a former wine bar. Seating is on benches, and a large woodland backdrop dominates the left-hand wall. Beers are served directly from the casks in a glass-fronted cool room. Wine, gin and soft drinks are also available, together with a range of mainly locally produced snacks. Q⇌●🚌🐾

Sidcup

Hackney Carriage L

165 Station Road, DA15 7AA
🕐 3-10; 12-10.30 Fri & Sat; 12-8 Sun ☎ 07715 680727
🌐 thehackneycarriagemicropub.com
5 changing beers (often Dark Star, Reunion, Thornbridge) G
A welcome addition to the micropub scene. Emphasis on local beers and ciders, together with a Strong Beer Thursday promotion, give it a different feel from the other micropubs in the area. Ales and ciders are dispensed on gravity from a cool room behind the bar, together with local wines and a special brand of Kent gin. Seating is at wall-mounted high benches at high tables. Last orders are 30 minutes before closing time.
Q⇌●🚌🐾

Welling

Door Hinge L

11 Welling High Street, DA16 1TR
🕐 closed Mon; 3-9 (10 Fri); 12-10 Sat; 12-3 Sun
☎ 07956 845509 🌐 thedoorhinge.co.uk
3 changing beers (sourced nationally) G
A welcome breath of fresh air on the local pub scene and handy for the football ground, this was London's first permanent micropub. It opened in March 2013 in part of a former electrical wholesalers. Normally at least three beers are dispensed from within a glass-fronted cold room. The cosy bar encourages conversation among previous strangers. Cider comes from various sources. Q●🚌🐾

SOUTH-WEST LONDON

SW1: Belgravia

Antelope

22-24 Eaton Terrace, SW1W 8EZ
🕐 12-11 (11.30 Fri); 12-10 Sun ☎ (020) 7824 8512
Fuller's London Pride, ESB; Gale's Seafarers Ale; 2 changing beers (sourced nationally) H
Dating back to 1827, this Fuller's establishment spent several years as a Nicholson's pub until 2005. Original preserved features include etched-glass windows, a side room used as a snug and the central bar. This is very much an upmarket house, and the clientele consists mostly of local professionals. The pub plays cricket matches against the Churchill Arms (Notting Hill). The upstairs bar and side room can be hired for functions. Q◑⊖(Sloane Sq)🚌📶

Star Tavern L

6 Belgrave Mews West, SW1X 8HT
🕐 11 (10.30 Sat)-11; 12-10.30 Sun ☎ (020) 7235 3019
Fuller's London Pride, ESB; 3 changing beers (often Fuller's) H
Down a mews, near embassies and rich in the history of the powerful and famous, it is rumoured that the Great Train Robbery was planned here. Now it is a popular Fuller's pub where local residents, business people and embassy staff rub shoulders with casual visitors. Sometimes a special Fuller's beer can be found. Upstairs is a dining

room, also bookable for functions. The pub has featured in every edition of this Guide.
Q(Hyde Park Corner/Knightsbridge)

SW1: Pimlico

Cask Pub & Kitchen

6 Charlwood Street, SW1V 2EE
12-11; 12-10.30 Sun (020) 7630 7225
caskpubandkitchen.com
Dark Star Hophead; 9 changing beers (sourced nationally) H
Formerly the Pimlico Tram, it was converted to a beer destination by owners who have since acquired and modernised several more pubs in the South-East. Ten real ales come from many microbreweries such as Arbor Ales and Dark Star, and a vast range of bottled beers from the UK and around the world complements some unusual draught choices. Burgers feature on the weekday menu, with roasts on Sundays until late afternoon. A regular local CAMRA Pub of the Year finalist.
Q(Victoria)

SW1: St James's

Red Lion ★

2 Duke of York Street, SW1Y 6JP
11.30-11; closed Sun (020) 7321 0782
redlionmayfair.co.uk
Fuller's Oliver's Island, London Pride, ESB; Gale's Seafarers Ale; 2 changing beers (often Fuller's) H
Close to the upmarket shops in Jermyn Street, this is a deservedly celebrated little gem, identified by CAMRA as having a nationally important historic pub interior, in particular its spectacular Victorian etched and cut mirrors and glass. The Grade II-listed building dates from 1821 and was given a new frontage in 1871. With little space inside, visitors often spill out onto the pavement. Beware the precipitous steps down to the toilets! Food is served 11.30-4pm (5pm Sat).
Q(Green Park/Piccadilly Circus)

SW1: Victoria

Willow Walk

25 Wilton Road, SW1V 1LW
7am (8am Sat)-midnight; 8am-11 Sun (020) 7828 2953
Fuller's London Pride; Greene King IPA, Abbot; 9 changing beers (often Twickenham) H
A 1999 Wetherspoon conversion. This ground-floor pub extends back to Vauxhall Bridge Road from opposite Victoria Station's eastern side entrance. Some wood panelling, quite a low ceiling and subdued lighting create a warm atmosphere. One TV is usually switched off, the other silent. Friendly and attentive staff look after a mixed clientele including families. Prints on the walls give information on local history. Alcoholic drinks are sold from 9am.

SW1: Westminster

Buckingham Arms

62 Petty France, SW1H 9EU
11-11; 11-6 Sat & Sun (020) 7222 3386
buckinghamarms.com
Young's Bitter, London Gold, Special; 2 changing beers (often Young's) H
Once reportedly a hat shop, this pub opened in the 1720s as The Bell. Renamed The Black Horse in the 1740s, it was rebuilt in 1898 and renamed again in 1901. Substantially renovated in recent years, furnishings include a mix of modern and traditional seats and tables, high and low. The pub has appeared in every edition of this Guide and draws civil servants, visitors and the occasional member of parliament. Open on Sundays from the end of March through the summer.
(St James's Park)

Speaker

46 Great Peter Street, SW1P 2HA
12-11; closed Sat & Sun (020) 7222 1749
Dark Star Hophead; Timothy Taylor Landlord; house beer (by Adnams); 2 changing beers (sourced nationally) H
A friendly pine-panelled one-bar local decorated with parliamentary caricatures. Historically part of the Devil's Acre, a notorious slum next to the world's first public gas works, it dates from 1729 or earlier as The Castle, renamed The Elephant & Castle around 1800. The Speaker since 1999, it welcomes local estate residents and office workers, not to mention the occasional MP, with an attractive range of beers and hot bagels. No music, TV or children. Q(St James's Park)

SW1: Whitehall

Lord Moon of the Mall

16-18 Whitehall, SW1A 2DY
8am-11.30 (midnight Fri & Sat); 8am-11 Sun
(020) 7839 7701
Fuller's London Pride; Greene King IPA, Abbot; Sharp's Doom Bar; 7 changing beers (sourced nationally) H
A 1995 Wetherspoon conversion of a bank built in the early 1870s. The pale pink sandstone, dark-wood panelling, high ceilings and arched windows would still be recognisable to the Victorian clerks. Even the portrait of a youthful Tim Martin, the chain's founder, on the pub sign seems in keeping! Open plan, it welcomes children until 9.30pm in a family dining area to the rear. Meals start with breakfasts at 8am; alcoholic drinks are sold from 9am. Q(Charing Cross)

SW4: Clapham

King & Co

100 Clapham Park Road, SW4 7BZ
4-11 (midnight Thu; 1am Fri); 12-1am Sat; 12-11 Sun
(020) 7498 1971 thekingandco.uk
House beer (by London Beer Lab); 4 changing beers (sourced nationally) H
An innovative pub attracting a youngish clientele, offering an exciting range of beer styles from microbreweries throughout the UK, plus a non-mainstream real cider. One regular beer is brewed off-site by the staff. Regular events include Meet the Brewer nights, tap takeovers and a quiz on Mondays. Food now includes Sunday roasts, when booking is advisable.
(Common)

SW5: Earls Court

King's Head

17 Hogarth Place, SW5 0QT
10-11; 10-10.30 Sun (020) 7373 5239

Fuller's Oliver's Island, London Pride; 2 changing beers (often Fuller's, Windsor & Eton) Ⓗ
A 1937 rebuild of the oldest (circa 17th-century) licensed premises in the area, now a comfortable, friendly corner pub with a modernised interior, hidden away off the busy Earl's Court Road. Seating is a mixture of high stools around tall tables, dining tables and settees with low tables. There is usually a locally brewed guest ale alongside the Fuller's beers, with alcoholic drinks served from 11am. Food service starts with breakfast and continues to late evening. Quiz night is Monday.
(West Brompton)

SW6: Fulham

Durell Arms

704 Fulham Road, SW6 5SB
12-11 (1am Fri & Sat) ☎ (020) 7736 3014
durellarmsfulham.com
Greene King IPA; 3 changing beers (often Sambrook's, Sharp's, Wychwood) Ⓗ
Making a third consecutive appearance in the Guide, this spacious Greene King Metropolitan corner pub has an L-shaped drinking area and also a large rear room, with mouldings and mirrors giving an air of Victorian decadence (it can be hired for functions). There is a big screen for sporting events. Attractive local ales complement Greene King and national guests, and it is busy on Sundays for the excellent roast.
(Parsons Green)

King's Arms

425 New Kings Road, SW6 4RN
11-11; 12-10.30 Sun ☎ (020) 7371 9585
kingsarms-fulham.co.uk/home
Wadworth IPA, Horizon, 6X, Bishops Tipple, Swordfish; 1 changing beer (often Wadworth) Ⓗ
Following a £300,000 refurbishment, this pub reopened in 2016 as Wadworth's first in the capital. The large corner site at the north end of Putney Bridge has been divided into areas and comfortably and tastefully furnished with upholstered banquettes and chairs. A wide range of Wadworth's beers is offered. Food includes stone-baked pizzas and match day menus. There is a patio smoking area to one side.
(Putney Bridge)

SW6: Parsons Green

White Horse

1-3 Parsons Green, SW6 4UL
9.30am-11.30 (midnight Thu-Sat) ☎ (020) 7736 2115
whitehorsesw6.com
Harvey's Sussex Best Bitter; Oakham JHB; 6 changing beers (sourced nationally) Ⓗ
A destination Mitchells & Butlers pub that normally boasts five guest beers on handpump and an international selection of bottled beers. Regular beer and food matching events take place as well as four annual beer festivals, including the Old Ale Festival in late November when the Coach House, normally reserved for dining, has a stillage. The pub can get busy when Chelsea FC is playing at home, but the upstairs area is a good place to escape the crowds.
Q (22,424)

SW7: Gloucester Road

Queen's Arms

30 Queen's Gate Mews, SW7 5QL
12-11; 12-10.30 Sun ☎ (020) 7823 9293
thequeensarmskensington.co.uk
Sharp's Doom Bar; Timothy Taylor Landlord; 6 changing beers (sourced nationally) Ⓗ
Lovely corner mews pub, discreetly tucked away off Queen's Gate but well worth seeking out for its real ales and its large range of interesting draught and bottled beers, malt whiskies and other spirits. Note the unusual curved doors. The L-shaped room has wooden floors and panelling. The clientele reflects the location: opulent locals, students from Imperial College and musicians from, and visitors to, the nearby Royal Albert Hall. The food is of superior quality.

SW7: South Kensington

Anglesea Arms

15 Selwood Terrace, SW7 3QG
11-11; 11-10.30 Sun ☎ (020) 7373 7960
angleseaarms.com
Greene King IPA; 5 changing beers (often Sambrook's, Triple fff, Wimbledon) Ⓗ
A real ale stalwart from CAMRA's early years, this hostelry was built in 1827 and was a Meux tied house for more than a century. Now a Grade II-listed Greene King Metropolitan pub, it has the air of a country inn, with outside seating and an interior featuring a diverse collection of mirrors, prints, photographs and paintings. Alongside the range of real ales, the menu offers a variety of food at reasonable prices for the area.
Q

SW8: South Lambeth

Priory Arms

83 Lansdowne Way, SW8 2PB
5-11; 3-11 Sat; 3-10.30 Sun ☎ (020) 7622 1884
theprioryarms.com
5 changing beers (often Crouch Vale, Dark Star, Kent) Ⓗ
Award-winning and stylish free house with a modernised, split-level interior. Microbreweries are well supported here, and there is a good range of German and Belgian bottled beers. The pub hosts at least four beer festivals annually, including on the May and August bank holiday weekends and another, usually German-themed, in the autumn. The menu features Mexican dishes and burgers. Board games are available, while at the front is a small patio for smoking and outdoor drinking.
(Stockwell)

Surprise

16 Southville, SW8 2PP
12-midnight (1am Fri & Sat) ☎ (020) 7622 4623
Young's Bitter, Special; 1 changing beer (often Sambrook's, Young's) Ⓗ
Tucked away next to Larkhall Park, this small, L-shaped pub is the only building remaining from streets that were replaced by the park after WWII bomb damage. The back-room walls feature caricatures of regular customers, while the middle section has black and white photos of pubs in the old Young's estate. Outside there is a patio and boules (pétanque) pitch. Wednesday is poker night. The pub may close early on Sunday if quiet.
(Stockwell, Wandsworth Rd)

SW11: Battersea

Lighthouse

441 Battersea Park Road, SW11 4LR

12-11 (midnight Fri); 10-midnight Sat; 10-10.30 Sun

(020) 7223 7721 thelighthousebattersea.com

Sambrook's Wandle Ale; 3 changing beers (often Old Dairy, Twickenham)

Smart, popular pub, with fairy lights in the front windows, near the south-west entrance to Battersea Park, usually offering an interesting selection of ales for the area. Its strong emphasis on food attracts families, particularly at weekends, but drinkers are equally welcome. The uncluttered interior features various pictures of lighthouses. The rear covered patio has heaters, a big screen and two small booths. Board games are available and quiz night is Tuesday.

Sambrook's Brewery Tap Room

Unit 1 & 2 Yelverton Road, SW11 3QG

5-10.30 Thu & Fri; 12-10.30 Sat; closed Sun-Wed

(020) 7228 0598 sambrooksbrewery.co.uk

Sambrook's Wandle Ale, Pumphouse Pale Ale, Junction Ale, Powerhouse Porter

This cute little bar affords a bird's-eye view of a working brewery and offers an array of Sambrook's award-winning beers on four handpumps (typically, those listed above) plus another four taps. The full range of Sambrook's bottled beers is also available. Seating is varied, with some stools by the bar and some comfortable sofas at the far end. A pull-down TV screen shows major rugby games. Pizzas can be delivered from a nearby parlour. (Clapham Jct) (44,170)

SW11: Clapham Junction

Eagle Ale House

104 Chatham Road, SW11 6HG

4 (3 Fri; 12 Sat)-11; 12-10.30 Sun (020) 7228 2328

Surrey Hills Shere Drop; changing beers (often Downton, Hackney, Pilgrim)

Homely, traditional pub, a short uphill walk from Northcote Road, with a friendly welcome for all, regulars and visitors alike (and their canine companions). In recent years it has been at the heart of the Fair Deal For Your Local campaign. The Eagle has been the South-West London CAMRA Pub of the Year more than once, and several times the runner-up. Major sporting events are shown on four TV screens, including in the heated marquee in the garden. (319,G1)

Four Thieves

51 Lavender Gardens, SW11 1DJ

12-midnight (2am Fri & Sat); 12-10.30 Sun

(020) 7223 6927 fourthieves.pub

6 changing beers (often Dark Star, Laine)

Cavernous pub reopened in 2014 by the Laine Pub Company after major refurbishment and installation of a brewery; most of the cask beers are brewed on the premises. The layout comprises a main bar, split over two levels, the Boat House to the right that hosts music and comedy, an upstairs games room, and a gin yard with heated and covered areas. Attracting a young crowd, it can get busy at weekends.

SW12: Balham

Balham Bowls Club

7-9 Ramsden Road, SW12 8QX

4-11 (midnight Thu; 1am Fri); 12-1am Sat; 12-11 Sun

(020) 8673 4700 balhambowlsclub.com

Volden Session Ale; 3 changing beers (often By the Horns, Sambrook's, Twickenham)

Converted to a pub by Antic in 2006, this multi-roomed former club just off Balham High Road retains a traditional feel but is now more popular with young people. It has been identified by CAMRA as having a regionally important historic interior, featuring wood panelling, decorated with emblematic military shields and sporting paraphernalia. Guest beers may be from Volden but are typically from other London microbreweries. Live music entertains on Friday evenings.

SW15: Putney

Half Moon

93 Lower Richmond Road, SW15 1EU

12-11.30 (midnight Fri & Sat); 12-11 Sun

(020) 8780 9383 halfmoon.co.uk

Young's Bitter; 3 changing beers (often Twickenham, Wimbledon, Young's)

Renowned as a live music venue, the present pub was rebuilt in 1903, taking in some neighbouring cottages and so extending it to include what is now the soundproofed function room at the back where gigs take place. Since refurbishment in 2011 it has operated as part of Young's Geronimo chain of gastropubs, featuring meals all day until 10pm (9pm Sun) alongside a refreshing range of guest beers including local brews.

(Putney Bridge)

SW16: Streatham

Bull

498 Streatham High Road, SW16 3QB

12-11 (midnight Fri & Sat) (020) 8764 4003

thebullstreatham.co.uk

Young's Bitter, London Gold, Special; 1 changing beer (often Sambrook's, Young's)

A landmark Victorian pub opposite Streatham Common, now bright and modern and with more emphasis on food: the back bar has reverted to a restaurant area. The garden has its own bar (no real ale) and a burger shack, with much more seating including heated beach huts with TVs for major sporting events. A guest beer now often comes from the local Inkspot Brewery. Try the public bar for a quiet pint.

(Streatham/Streatham Common)

Pratts & Payne

103 Streatham High Road, SW16 1HJ

4-11 (2am Fri); 12-2am Sat; 12-11 Sun

(020) 8677 1664 prattsandpayne.com

Volden Session Ale; 6 changing beers (often Dark Star)

A large, high-ceilinged pub with a relaxed atmosphere and TV sports. Tables and chairs for dining are complemented by comfortable sofas and armchairs. Opened by Antic in March 2012, its name commemorates the former Pratts department store and the notorious former Streatham resident and hostess Cynthia Payne. Food is served Monday to Thursday evenings, all day Friday and Saturday, and until 8pm on Sunday.

Railway

2 Greyhound Lane, SW16 5SD

12-11 (midnight Thu; 1am Fri & Sat) (020) 8769 9448
therailwaysw16.co.uk

5 changing beers (sourced regionally; often Belleville, Redemption, Twickenham)

Across the road from Streatham Common station, this busy community pub showcases beers exclusively from London microbreweries, both cask and bottled. It hosts a quiz on Tuesday, music nights, and a popular comedy night in the large back room on the last Sunday of the month. There is seating outside and in the yard, where a farmer's market is held on the second and fourth Saturdays. Regularly in the top three of the local Pub of the Year ballot. (Common) (60,118)

SW17: Summerstown

By the Horns Brewery Tap

25 Summerstown, SW17 0BQ

closed Mon; 4-10 Tue & Wed; 4-11 Thu; 5-11 Fri; 12-10 Sat; 12-9 Sun (020) 3417 7338 bythehorns.co.uk

Changing beers (often By the Horns)

A brewery taproom and beer hall, open Tuesday to Sunday. Three cask beers are usually on, with other draught and bottled choices and occasional guests from other small breweries. There is plenty of space in the bar and the enclosed car park outside. Major sporting events shown on large projection TVs are popular (it is often advisable to reserve your place in advance). Brewery tours and private event hire are also offered. P

SW17: Tooting

Antelope

76 Mitcham Road, SW17 9NG

4-11 (midnight Thu; 1am Fri); 12-1am Sat; 12-11 Sun (020) 8672 3888 theantelopepub.com

Thornbridge Jaipur IPA; Volden Pale Ale; 4 changing beers (sourced nationally; often Adnams)

A cavernous Victorian pub restored by Antic in 2009. Around a panelled island bar, green-painted walls are decorated with taxidermy and china plates. At the back is a dining area and a huge separate room known as the Anchor Bar. The pub has real fires and serves popular Sunday roasts. There is a quiz on Mondays and live music on Thursdays and Sundays. (Broadway)

Wheatsheaf

2 Upper Tooting Road, SW17 7PG

11-midnight (1am Fri); 10-1am Sat; 10-11 Sun (020) 8672 2805 thewheatsheafsw17.com

5 changing beers (often Sambrook's, Wimbledon, Windsor & Eton)

Spacious, late Victorian pub on a prominent corner site at Tooting Bec crossroads. Of five handpumps in use, three or four are usually devoted to ales from London breweries. Saved from the threat of redevelopment in 2013 thanks to a local campaign, this has become a vibrant community pub. The interior features exposed brickwork and large pillars and arches, with a back room used as a restaurant. Look for the many black and white photographs of old Tooting. (Bec)

SW18: Earlsfield

Country House

2-4 Groton Road, SW18 4EP

12-11 (midnight Fri & Sat) (020) 8870 3204
thecountryhouseearlsfield.co.uk

Sambrook's Wandle Ale; Sharp's Doom Bar; 2 changing beers (often Sambrook's, Twickenham)

An unspoilt back-street boozer, traditionally known as The Fog, which has been identified by CAMRA as having a regionally important historic pub interior. Remarkably, the separate public bar, games room and lounge all survive. Pleasantly refurbished by Enterprise's Bermondsey Pub Co in August 2017, it has a mixed, friendly clientele. Meet the Brewer evenings are now occasionally held.

SW18: Southfields

Earl Spencer

260-262 Merton Road, SW18 5JL

4-11; 11-midnight Fri & Sat; 12-10.30 Sun
(020) 8870 9244 theearlspencer.com

Purity Pure UBU; Sambrook's Wandle Ale; Wimbledon Common PA; 1 changing beer

Winner of the 2016 Pub of the Year in the Wandsworth Business Awards, this is a gastropub with a no reservations policy, a sport-free oasis with no TVs and a quiet pub with no music. Open plan with some sofas, its walls display antique mirrors and old photographs. At the front is a comfortable covered terrace. It offers a popular Sunday lunch, and sells excellent Cuban cigars from a humidor – for smoking on the terrace only!
Q (39,156)

Pig & Whistle

479-481 Merton Road, SW18 5LD

12-midnight (11 Mon & Tue); 12-10.30 Sun
(020) 8874 1061 pigandwhistlesw18.co.uk

Young's Bitter, Special; 3 changing beers (often Sambrook's, Twickenham, Wimbledon)

Busy pub popular with families, refurbished in contemporary Young's style featuring stripped wood, high tables and picture windows bringing much light into the main bar area. Fortunately, the collection of miniature pigs has survived and the pub still offers its doggie menu. Humans can enjoy a pub menu with a South African influence. Chairs and tables in front of the pub and seating on astroturf and in hutlets at the rear offer an alfresco alternative. (Earlsfield) (156)

SW18: Wandsworth

Cat's Back

86-88 Point Pleasant, SW18 1NN

12-midnight; 12-10 Sun & Mon (020) 8617 3448
thecatsback.com

Harvey's Sussex Best Bitter, Old Ale; 2 changing beers

Harvey's first south-west London pub is an elegant, restrained refurbishment of a wonderful back-street local and a welcome survivor among the mass development of luxury riverside apartments that surround it. Four of Harvey's cask beers are usually available. The pub offers occasional live music (folk, jazz, classical) on Thursday evenings and a film show (also upstairs at 8pm) most Wednesdays. The food offering is excellent, especially Sunday lunch.

Roundhouse 🄻 ✔

2 North Side, Wandsworth Common, SW18 2SS
⏲ 12-11 (midnight Fri & Sat); 12-10.30 Sun
☎ (020) 7326 8580 🌐 theroundhousewandsworth.com
Sambrook's Wandle Ale; house beer (by XT) 🄷
This popular gastropub in a Victorian corner building retains an ornate entrance lobby among some original features. Excellent food and real ale attract a mainly young, affluent crowd and beer platters offer a third of each of five imported bottled beers. Booking is essential for the Monday night quiz as well as Sunday lunches. Rugby internationals are shown on terrestrial TV.
🐴❀◑⇌⊖(Clapham Jct)🍎🚌🐾📶

SW19: South Wimbledon

Sultan

78 Norman Road, SW19 1BT
⏲ 12 (3 Mon-Wed)-11; 12-midnight Fri & Sat
☎ (020) 8544 9323
Hop Back GFB, Summer Lightning; 3 changing beers (often Downton, Hop Back) 🄷
Hop Back's only London tied house, an attractive two-bar 1950s brick building identified by CAMRA as having a regionally important historic pub interior. Mostly carpeted, it has dark-wood walls, large tables with chairs, some fixed seating, and settees in the conservatory. Westons Country Perry and Wessex Dry Cider are available. Sandwiches are made to order. Enjoy three-day April and September beer festivals and early opening on bank holiday Mondays.
❀♿⇌(Haydons Rd)⊖(Colliers Wood/South Wimbledon)♣🍎P🚌📶

Trafalgar 🏆 🄻

23 High Path, SW19 2JY
⏲ 12-11 (midnight Fri & Sat) ☎ (020) 8542 5342
🌐 trafalgarfreehouse.co.uk
Downton Quadhop; Surrey Hills Shere Drop; 4 changing beers (sourced nationally; often Ascot, Coastal, Downton) 🄷
A narrow, one-bar street-corner house dating from the 1860s with a 1906 extension. Refurbished in 2014, it is mostly carpeted, furnished with farmhouse chairs and tables and Nelson memorabilia. Alongside the cask range are five guest ciders, often Lilley's, plenty of bottled and canned beers, and other beers on tap that may include KeyKeg choices. Cold and hot snacks (pot meals) are available until 10pm. There is often live music. ❀🚋(Morden Rd)⊖♣🍎🚌🐾📶

SW19: Wimbledon

Hand in Hand 🄻

7 Crooked Billet, SW19 4RQ
⏲ 11-11 (midnight Fri & Sat); 12-11 Sun ☎ (020) 8946 5720
🌐 thehandinhandwimbledon.co.uk
Courage Directors; Young's Bitter, Special; 5 changing beers (often Adnams, Portobello, Young's) 🄷
Celebrated dog-friendly ale house on the edge of Wimbledon Common with separate drinking areas and a variety of seating. At least three guest beers are usually sold, increasingly from local breweries. Children are welcome in the family room. This is a great place to eat, inside or on the front patio, with beer included in several recipes. There is poker on Monday, a quiz on Tuesday, and enthusiastic beer tastings and cellar tours are occasionally on offer.
Q🐴❀◑♿♣🚌(200)🐾

Carshalton

Hope 🏆 🄻

48 West Street, SM5 2PR
⏲ 12-11; 12-10.30 Sun ☎ (020) 8240 1255
🌐 hopecarshalton.co.uk
Downton New Forest Ale; Windsor & Eton Knight of the Garter; 5 changing beers 🄷
Traditional multi award-winning free house owned by a group of its regulars. Seven handpumps and several taps dispense a remarkable range of the country's finest beers served in measures from third-pints upwards. The well-trained and knowledgeable staff can advise you about the latest offerings. Good-value no-nonsense lunches are served until 3pm and pot meals until 10pm. CAMRA Greater London Pub of the Year 2017.
Q🐴❀◑⇌🍎P⊟🚌🐾📶

Sun 🄻

4 North Street, SM5 2HU
⏲ 11-11 (10 Mon; midnight Fri & Sat); 12-10 Sun
☎ (020) 8773 4549 🌐 thesuncarshalton.com
6 changing beers (sourced nationally) 🄷
This handsome and imposing Victorian pub was given a tasteful makeover several years ago and has not looked back since. Divided into several distinct areas, diners enjoy the excellent food and discerning drinkers a wide beer choice on six handpumps. In summer the large courtyard garden with its continental-style veranda is popular. The huge upstairs function room, available for hire, receives sunlight almost all day, hence the pub's name. 🐴❀◑⇌♣🚌🐾📶

Windsor Castle

378 Carshalton Road, SM5 3PT
⏲ 12-11.30 (midnight Fri & Sat); 12-11 Sun
☎ (020) 8669 1191 🌐 windsorcastlepub.com
Long Man Best Bitter; Shepherd Neame Kent's Best, Spitfire; 3 changing beers 🄷
Large pub on the crossroads to the west of the town centre. There is a variety of seating areas in the single bar and a popular restaurant area at one end. A courtyard at the rear leads to a function room and a garden. The staff are invariably friendly and welcoming. Alongside regular and seasonal beers from owning brewery Shepherd Neame, there are three changing ales from local and regional brewers. Regular live music features on Saturday nights.
🐴❀◑♿⇌(Beeches)P🚌(154,407)🐾📶

Kingston

Albion 🄻 ✔

45 Fairfield Road, KT1 2PY
⏲ 12-11 (11.30 Fri & Sat); 12-10.30 Sun ☎ (020) 8541 1691
🌐 thealbionkingston.com
10 changing beers (often Big Smoke)
The pub is one of a small chain which includes the Big Smoke Brewery, sharing a loyalty card scheme. An interesting array of handpumped beers and up to five changing ciders are on offer. Varnished wooden floors and comfortable wood-panelled seating areas run across the width of the pub and towards the back. Doors then lead to a large patio garden with heaters. Music is from an extensive collection of vinyl LPs. Home-cooked food is served (not weekday afternoons). 🐴❀◑♿⇌🍎🚌🐾📶

Boaters Inn

Canbury Gardens, Lower Ham Road, KT2 5AU (off A307 via Woodside Rd)
10-11 (020) 8541 4672 boaterskingston.com
Greene King IPA; 4 changing beers (sourced locally; often Twickenham)
Downstream from the town centre in a riverside location within Canbury Gardens, with moorings available by arrangement. A raised dining area overlooks the Thames, with a small balcony. The large garden features a barbecue in summer. Food in general is popular, particularly on Sundays when live jazz plays from 8pm. Boaters is also extremely busy during the annual dragon boat racing weekend. There is a Meet the Brewer session on the first Friday of the month. (65)

King's Tun

153-157 Clarence Street, KT1 1QT
8am-midnight (1am Fri & Sat) (020) 8547 3827
Greene King IPA, Abbot; Oakham Citra; Sharp's Doom Bar; 8 changing beers (often Loddon, Oakham, Surrey Hills)
A Wetherspoon pub since 1997 in the former Empire music hall, latterly a cinema, supermarket and shop. Two large bars on separate floors attract all during the day with a younger crowd in the evenings, frequently busy and with Friday and Saturday night discos from 9pm. Guest beers often come from local microbreweries. Ciders include Westons Old Rosie and Gwynt y Ddraig Black Dragon. Children are welcome until 9pm if eating. Alcoholic drinks are served from 9am.

Willoughby Arms

47 Willoughby Road, KT2 6LN
10.30-midnight; 12-midnight Sun (020) 8546 4236
thewilloughbyarms.com
Surrey Hills Shere Drop; Twickenham Grandstand Bitter; Weltons Horsham Pale; 4 changing beers (often Downton)
Friendly Victorian back-street local, divided into a sports bar with games and large-screen TV, and a quieter lounge area. It recently became free of tie. Beers are from smaller breweries nationally and pizzas and pies are cooked to order. Upstairs is a function room. The spacious garden includes a heated and lit smoking area with TV screen. Quiz nights are Sundays. A loyalty card operates from 6pm Sunday to Thursday. One or two beer festivals are held per year. Q (371,K5)

Richmond

Mitre

20 St Mary's Grove, TW9 1UY
3-11; 12-11 Sat; 12-9 Sun (020) 8940 1336
themitretw9.co.uk
Timothy Taylor Landlord; 7 changing beers (often Bristol Beer Factory, Thornbridge)
A traditional pub tucked away off Sheen Road, originally owned by Young's and now a free house. Simply furnished with wood flooring, a decked area at the front, benches to the side and a back patio, it has a number of leaded stained-glass windows featuring different colourful church mitres. Ten handpumps serve beers from independent brewers outside the M25 and three are dedicated to cider/perry. Food ordered from Basilico Pizza is delivered to the pub.
(North Sheen)

Roebuck

130 Richmond Hill, TW10 6RN
12-11 (midnight Fri); 11-midnight Sat; 12-10.30 Sun
(020) 8948 2329
Greene King IPA; 4 changing beers (often Purity, Surrey Hills, Thames Side)
Close to Richmond Park Gate, this 200-year-old pub overlooks the World Heritage view of Petersham Meadows and the River Thames. It is air-conditioned and carpeted except in front of the bar. One or two regular beers from Greene King, four frequently rotated guest beers and one real cider are augmented by another three handpumps in the summer. The outside terrace across the road can also be used by patrons. Food is available until 10pm (9pm Sun). (371)

Waterman's Arms

12 Water Lane, TW9 1TJ
11-11; 12-10.30 Sun (020) 8940 2893
Twickenham Naked Ladies; Young's Bitter, Special; 2 changing beers (often Sambrook's, Young's)
One of the oldest pubs in Richmond, dating back to at least 1660 and rebuilt in 1898, tucked away down a cobbled side street leading to the Thames. Retaining its Victorian two-bar layout, it is cosy and full of character, wood panelled throughout and with etched-glass windows. Traditional pub food, Sunday lunches and Thai specials are served daily. A Monday music club meets upstairs.
Q

Surbiton

Antelope

87 Maple Road, KT6 4AW
12-11 (11.30 Fri & Sat); 12-10.30 Sun (020) 8399 5565
theantelope.co.uk
Changing beers (sourced nationally; often Big Smoke)
Home of the Big Smoke Brewery, from which two or three beers are usually available. The spacious split-level interior has a real fire in winter. At the rear is a covered, heated and lit courtyard. Five changing ciders are usually on offer. Home-cooked food includes Sunday roasts. Two beer festivals are held annually. Popular with locals and commuters, it can be particularly busy evenings and weekends. Voted local CAMRA Pub of the Year since 2016.

Coronation Hall

St Marks Hill, KT6 4LQ
8am-midnight (1am Fri & Sat) (020) 8390 6164
Exmoor Gold; Greene King IPA, Abbot; Oakham Citra; Sharp's Doom Bar; 7 changing beers (often Oakham, Sambrook's, Windsor & Eton)
Across the road from Surbiton station, the building housing this Wetherspoon pub has had a variety of former uses including music hall, cinema, bingo hall and nudist club. The decor is themed on a mix of movie stars, film artefacts, the coronation of King George V and the planets. Guest beers change regularly, many from local microbreweries such as Thameside. Occasional local beer festivals are held. Westons Old Rosie and Orchard Pig Hogfather ciders are served. Q

Lamb

73 Brighton Road, KT6 5NF
12-11.30 (12.30am Thu-Sat) (020) 8390 9229
lambsurbiton.co.uk

Black Sheep Best Bitter; Hop Back Summer Lightning; Surrey Hills Ranmore; 1 changing beer (sourced regionally) H
Small, family-run free house, at the heart of the local community. Built in 1850 and formerly four separate rooms, it retains the original horseshoe-shaped bar. The changing beer is from a microbrewery, sometimes local, or a family brewery. Specialist cheeses are always available with cheeseboards on offer all day Friday to Sunday. Live music and other events are regularly held, including pop-up street food stalls in the garden.

Sutton

Moon on the Hill

5-9 Hill Road, SM1 1DZ
8am-midnight (1am Fri & Sat) (020) 8643 1202
Greene King Abbot; Ruddles Best Bitter; Sharp's Doom Bar; 7 changing beers (often Dark Star, Surrey Hills) H
Formerly the furniture depository of a department store, this is a popular and well-established Wetherspoon pub, conveniently situated for Sutton's main shopping area. It comprises a single bar with ample seating on three levels and a garden for those preferring to drink and eat alfresco. The guest beers are local whenever possible and mini beer festivals are held throughout the year. Draught ciders on offer come from different parts of the country.

Shinner & Sudtone L

67 High Street, SM1 1DT
12-11 Mon; 4-midnight Tue-Thu; 4-2am Fri; 12-2am Sat; 12-11 Sun (020) 8643 8395 shinnerandsudtone.com
Volden Session Ale; 2 changing beers (sourced nationally) H
In the shopping area of Sutton, this is a pub acquired by Antic and decorated in its familiar shabby-chic style. Its name combines that of a former department store nearby and an old name for Sutton. The long bar has tables and chairs either side of a central walkway, leading to a small raised area at the rear. Volden regular beers are served, and a board indicates beers waiting in the cellar. Quiz night is Tuesday.

Wallington

Wallington Arms L

6-16 Woodcote Road, SM6 0NN
4-11 (midnight Fri); 12-midnight Sat; 12-11 Sun
(020) 8773 0404 wallingtonarms.com
4 changing beers (often Twickenham, Volden, Wimbledon) H
A charming local next to the railway station, revived by the Antic pub company and popular with a large clientele. A Volden beer is usually on tap. The wood-panelled front bar is typically furnished in an interesting mixture of the plain and the elegant. To the rear is a large drinking and dining area. Wednesday is quiz night and the popular Ale Club is on Thursday. Check social media for live music events and open mic at weekends.

WEST LONDON

W2: Bayswater

Champion

1 Wellington Terrace, W2 4LW
12-11 (midnight Fri & Sat); 12-10.30 Sun
(020) 7243 6054 thechampionpub.co.uk
Adnams Ghost Ship; 4 changing beers (often Purity, St Austell, Thornbridge) H
The nearest pub to Kensington Palace, opposite the security-protected road on the northern side of Kensington Gardens. Built in 1838 and Grade II-listed, it was refurbished in 2004 and spruced up more recently by owners Mitchells & Butlers. In warm weather the front windows are often opened into the bar with its dining tables, chairs and standing area. A plush basement area leads on to a sunken beer garden, with patio heaters lit in cold weather.
(Notting Hill Gate/Queensway)

Leinster Arms

17 Leinster Terrace, W2 3EU
12-11 (midnight Fri & Sat); 12-10.30 Sun
(020) 7402 4670 theleinsterarmsbayswater.co.uk
Fuller's London Pride; 3 changing beers (sourced nationally) H
A Grade II-listed pub built in 1856 as the Scotch Stores and renamed 18 years later. The façade is impressive, the name extending across the arch to the adjacent mews. Inside is a fascinating collection of prints, portraits and paintings and a notable brewery mirror in the rear area. Beer mats and pumpclips on display attest to previous guest beers. Popular with tourists, it offers a loyalty card for regulars and locals.
(Paddington) (Queensway)

W2: Little Venice

Bridge House

13 Westbourne Terrace Road, W2 6NG
12-11 (11.30 Fri & Sat); 12-10.30 Sun (020) 7266 4326
thebridgehouselittlevenice.co.uk
Sharp's Doom Bar; Timothy Taylor Landlord; 2 changing beers (often St Austell, Thornbridge) H
Dating from 1848, the Bridge House beside the canal is now a lounge-style bar, ideal for a quiet afternoon drink. There is a good solid bar counter, wooden floor and panelling, with old mirrors (Bass and HD Rawlings' High Class Mineral Waters above the fireplace). A chandelier, pastel-painted walls, high tables and chairs, low easy chairs and tables and chairs complete the setting. The Canal Café Theatre is above the pub.
(Warwick Ave)

W2: Paddington

Mad Bishop & Bear

Upper Level, Paddington Station, W2 1HB
8am-11; 10-10.30 Sun (020) 7402 2441
Fuller's Oliver's Island, London Pride, ESB; 5 changing beers (sourced nationally; often Fuller's) H
Above the shopping complex just behind the station concourse, the traditional pub interior features a long bar, mirrors, prints and a rather grand chandelier, with train information screens and two TVs for sports. The raised area can be hired for events and there are café-style seats outside. It

may not be crowded even in the rush hour, but the bar may close early if football crowds are passing through.

Victoria ★

10A Strathearn Place, W2 2NH
11-11; 12-10.30 Sun (020) 7724 1191
Fuller's Oliver's Island, London Pride, ESB; 2 changing beers (sourced nationally; often Adnams, Fuller's)
There is plenty to admire in this Grade II-listed mid-Victorian inn, identified by CAMRA as having a nationally important historic interior: ornately gilded mirrors above a crescent-shaped bar, painted tiles in wall niches and numerous portraits of Queen Victoria. The walls display cartoons, paperweights and a Silver Jubilee plate. A recessed area at the back is furnished with a leather bench seat. Upstairs, via a spiral staircase, a library and Theatre Bar provide extra space. Tuesday is quiz night.
Q(Lancaster Gate/Paddington)

W3: Acton

George & Dragon

183 High Street, W3 9DJ
4-11 (midnight Thu; 1am Fri); 12-1am Sat; 12-10.30 Sun
(020) 8992 3712
2 changing beers (often Clouded Minds)
At the heart of the historic Acton town centre, this Grade II-listed pub has three bars of real character. From an atmospheric front bar, with a list of landlords dating back to 1759, go through into a heritage bar with exposed original features and then enter a cavernous and stylish back room and brewery. Two changing guest cask beers are served, and usually two real ciders.
(Central)

Red Lion & Pineapple

281 High Street, W3 9BP
8am-midnight (1am Fri & Sat) (020) 8896 2248
Greene King IPA, Abbot; Sharp's Doom Bar; 5 changing beers
A Wetherspoon pub formerly owned by Fuller's, originally two pubs which then combined. The larger room is home to the circular bar, surrounded by red and black tiles. The windows are large, with etched and stained tops, and the walls are decorated with photographs of old Acton. The smaller room is mainly for diners and families. There are four guest ales during the week, five at weekends. Alcoholic drinks are served from 9am.
Q(Town)

West London Trades Union Club

33-35 High Street, W3 6ND
7pm-midnight (020) 8992 4557 wltuc.com
2 changing beers (often Nelson)
A small, friendly club, run as a co-operative, which combines excellent beer with a busy cultural and social life. Two real ales are normally served from a variety of independent breweries. The Acton Community Theatre is upstairs, and the club hosts summer barbecues in the courtyard. The local CAMRA branch is an associate member; show a CAMRA membership card or this Guide for entry.
Q(Central)

W3: North Acton

Castle

140 Victoria Road, W3 6UL
11-11 (midnight Fri); 11.30-11 Sat; 12-10.30 Sun
(020) 8992 2027
Fuller's London Pride; 2 changing beers (often Fuller's)
A 1938 Fuller's pub built for industrial North Acton and Park Royal, but now among new housing, hotels and student accommodation. BBC rehearsal rooms were next door and are reflected in historic photographs in the bar. Usually busy with local workers on weekday evenings, the pub is quieter during the day and at weekends. Seating areas surround the island bar, and there is a family room and a paved garden. P

W4: Chiswick

Mawson Arms/Fox & Hounds

110 Chiswick Lane South, W4 2QA
9am-8; 10.30-5 Sat; closed Sun (020) 8994 2936
mawsonarmschiswick.co.uk
Fuller's Oliver's Island, London Pride, ESB; Gale's Seafarers Ale; 4 changing beers (often Fuller's, Gale's)
On a corner of the Griffin Brewery site, and its de facto brewery tap, the two externally displayed names of this welcoming Grade II*-listed pub are a legacy of once-separate licences for beer and spirits. Complementing the wide range of Fuller's beers, the emphasis is now on food, served from breakfast time until 7pm (with an 11am-noon break). Brewery memorabilia on the walls include ancestral portraits of the Fuller, Smith and Turner families. Q(Stamford Brook)(190)

Tabard

2 Bath Road, W4 1LW
12-11 (midnight Thu-Sat) (020) 8994 3492
Greene King IPA; 8 changing beers (often Greene King, Titanic, Truman's)
Built in 1880 as part of the Bedford Park estate, London's first garden suburb, this Grade II*-listed establishment has been identified by CAMRA as having a regionally important historic pub interior. Features include the swing sign originally painted by TM Rooke, interior tiling by William de Morgan and Walter Crane, and Arts and Crafts mirrors and pictures. One handpump serves cider. Saturday evening live music and a Wednesday quiz are usually in the dining area. Upstairs is an intimate fringe theatre.
(Turnham Green)

W5: Ealing

Grove

1 Ealing Green, W5 5QX
12-11 (020) 8567 2439 thegrovew5.co.uk
Greene King IPA; 5 changing beers (often Sambrook's, Southwark, Vale)
Large, single-bar Greene King pub, with many semi-private areas. The beer range focuses on local microbreweries from London and the Thames Valley, and occasional tap takeovers are held. The food offer is broad, and there is a dedicated restaurant area. The large, heated front and side garden is popular and overlooks historic Ealing Green and the Grade I-listed Pitzhanger Manor House. (Broadway)

Questors Grapevine Bar

12 Mattock Lane, W5 5BQ

7-11; 12-2.30, 7-10.30 Sun ☎ (020) 8567 0011
questors.org.uk/grapevine

Fuller's London Pride; 2 changing beers H

A friendly theatre club bar near the centre of Ealing and Walpole Park, run by enthusiastic volunteers. CAMRA members and Questors theatre ticket holders are also welcome. Guest beers include some from local breweries, beer festivals are held twice yearly and there are malt whisky tastings. Some books and the odd board game are available.
Q ♿ ⊖(Broadway)♣P

Sir Michael Balcon

46-47 The Mall, W5 3TJ

9am-11.30 (midnight Fri & Sat) ☎ (020) 8799 2850

Greene King IPA, Abbot; Sharp's Doom Bar; 4 changing beers (often Adnams, Hogs Back, Sambrook's) H

On the busy Uxbridge Road east of Ealing town centre, this became a Wetherspoon pub in 2008, named after the legendary film producer whose life and films form the basis of many of the wall displays. It is split level, with a raised area at the rear and a glass-covered area at the front for smokers. Q ♿ ⊖(Broadway)

W5: North Ealing

Greystoke

7 Queens Parade, W5 3HU

11-11 (midnight Fri & Sat) ☎ (020) 8997 6388

Greene King IPA, Abbot; 5 changing beers (often Truman's, Twickenham, Wimbledon) H

A spacious family dining pub built in typical 1930s style, with affordable hot food and a changing selection of mostly local real ales. The single open-plan bar is comfortably furnished. All major sporting events from around the world (including NFL) are shown. The name derives from the Greystoke estate which owned Hanger Hill for many years. Opposite North Ealing station.
♿ ⊖♣P(112,483)

W6: Hammersmith

Andover Arms

57 Aldensley Road, W6 0DL

12-11 ☎ (020) 8748 2155 theandoverarms.com

Fuller's London Pride; Gale's Seafarers Ale; 2 changing beers (often Fuller's) H

Hidden away in the back streets of Hammersmith, this popular and welcoming local is an enduring real ale champion with a rural feel about it. The attractive panelled bar counter, with its elaborate bar-back, separates two areas furnished with an assortment of dining tables and chairs. The kitchen offers a wide range of dishes lunchtimes and evenings. Quiz night is Sunday (9pm).
⊖(Ravenscourt Park)

Dove

19 Upper Mall, W6 9TA

11-11; 12-10.30 Sun ☎ (020) 8748 9474

Fuller's Oliver's Island, London Pride, ESB; 1 changing beer (often Fuller's, Gale's) H

A Grade II-listed pub dating from the 1740s, identified by CAMRA as having a regionally important historic interior. Overlooking the Thames, it is often crowded in summer. The likes of Dylan Thomas, Ernest Hemingway and Alec Guinness have enjoyed a pint or two here. Off the main bar, a tiny public bar holds the Guinness world record for the smallest bar area. The food service can be slow at busy times but is worth the wait.
⊖(Hammersmith/Ravenscourt Park)

Plough & Harrow

120-124 King Street, W6 0QU

8am-11.30 ☎ (020) 8735 6020

Greene King IPA, Abbot; Sharp's Doom Bar; 7 changing beers (sourced regionally) H

On the site of an inn established in 1419, and more recently a Rolls-Royce showroom, this light and airy Wetherspoon pub dates from 2002. It has a mixture of stone and carpeted floors and a long metal-topped bar with 10 handpumps, more than half devoted to the changing guest ales, many from microbreweries. There are several tables outside. Alcoholic drinks are served from 9am.
Q ♿⊖(Hammersmith/Ravenscourt Park)

W7: Hanwell

Dodo Micropub

52 Boston Road, W7 3TR

closed Mon; 12-2 (not Tue), 5-10; 12-10.30 Fri & Sat; 12-5 Sun ☎ (020) 8567 5959 thedodomicropub.com

5 changing beers (sourced locally) G

A classic micropub shop conversion which landed in Hanwell in January 2017. Up to five cask beers are served on gravity dispense from a temperature-controlled cellar room at the rear, along with cider and wine. Beers almost certainly include ones from local breweries. There is a small bar counter by the front door but table service is the order of the day here. Q

Fox

Green Lane, W7 2PJ

11-11; 12-10.30 Sun ☎ (020) 8567 4021
thefoxpub.co.uk

Fuller's London Pride; St Austell Proper Job; Timothy Taylor Landlord; 3 changing beers (sourced nationally) H

A wonderful back-street free house, as popular with walkers, cyclists and other nearby canal users as with locals. A good range of beers, with changing guest ales from independent breweries, is complemented by excellent, inexpensive food, including a popular Sunday lunch (booking recommended). Added to all this are two annual beer festivals and occasional jazz. Local CAMRA Pub of the Year on many occasions.
♿♣P(195,E8)

Grosvenor

127 Oaklands Road, W7 2DT

12-11; 9am-11 Fri; 12-10.30 Sun ☎ (020) 8840 0007

4 changing beers (often Sharp's, Truman's, Weird Beard) H

A traditional Edwardian local, refurbished in 2014 without losing its features and charm and identified by CAMRA as having a regionally important historic pub interior. There is a dining room section and a main bar, stocking a wide range of locally produced beers. Family friendly, it has a congenial atmosphere and promotes local events. Jazz night is the second Tuesday of every month and there is an open mic night on the fourth Tuesday. Local CAMRA Pub of the Year 2017.
♿♣

W8: Kensington

Elephant & Castle

40 Holland Street, W8 4LT

11-11; 12-10.30 Sun (020) 7937 6382

Fuller's London Pride; St Austell Nicholson's Pale Ale; Sharp's Doom Bar; 3 changing beers (sourced nationally) H

First licensed in 1865 as a beer house in what were two adjacent houses and tucked away north-east of Kensington Town Hall, this busy, cosy, wood-panelled Nicholson's pub with its rural feel is a welcome refuge from the hurly-burly of Kensington High Street. Guest beers are from the wide-ranging Nicholson's portfolio including its own-brand ales. Food, especially pies and sausages, is available all day except 4-5pm. Note the fine Charrington's bar-back.
(High St Kensington)

W8: Notting Hill Gate

Churchill Arms

119 Kensington Church Street, W8 7LN

11-11 (midnight Thu-Sat); 12-10.30 Sun
(020) 7727 4242

Fuller's Oliver's Island, London Pride, ESB; 1 changing beer (often Fuller's) H

A multi award-winning pub, identified by CAMRA as having a regionally important historic interior. Churchillian and Irish memorabilia are among the bric-a-brac, and numerous plaques commemorate former drinkers. With its well-kept Fuller's beers, it is deservedly popular. The Thai restaurant in the conservatory was one of the first to be found in a London pub. Outside, at busy times, drinkers stand on the pavement below the numerous hanging flower baskets. At Christmas, the tree decorations are quite something to behold. **Q**

Windsor Castle ★

114 Campden Hill Road, W8 7AR

12-11 (10.30 Sun) (020) 7243 8797
thewindsorcastlekensington.co.uk

Marston's Pedigree; Timothy Taylor Landlord; 4 changing beers (sourced nationally) H

This back-street 1830 corner pub contrasts an old-world feel that you might expect in a more rural setting with modern upmarket service and menu style. Grade II-listed, it has been identified by CAMRA as having a nationally important historic pub interior although the partitions between the four drinking areas and other wood panelling date from a 1933 refurbishment. Four of the real ales may rotate through some interesting brews. The beer garden to the rear boasts its own bar.
Q

W9: Westbourne Park

Union Tavern L

45 Woodfield Road, W9 2BA

12-11 (midnight Fri & Sat); 12-10.30 Sun
(020) 7286 1886

Five Points Pale; Fuller's London Pride; 3 changing beers (sourced locally; often Windsor & Eton) H

In a radical departure by Fuller's, this unbranded beer house offers cask ales from within 30 miles and, with only one exception, in London. The mainly young crowd enjoys reduced beer prices on Monday, various music nights and a Meet the Brewer event on the first Tuesday of the month. Good-value food is another attraction, with traditional Sunday lunches. The canalside terrace comes into its own on a warm, sunny day.

W12: Shepherds Bush

Defector's Weld L

170 Uxbridge Road, W12 8AA

12-midnight (2am Fri & Sat); 12-11 Sun
(020) 8749 0008 defectors-weld.co.uk

Young's Bitter, Special; 3 changing beers (often Redemption, Truman's, Twickenham) H

Since Young's took over this pub, it has continued to rotate local guest beers. The large horseshoe-shaped main bar has a welcoming mix of sofas, tables and chairs. An upstairs bar is available for hire. DJs play music Thursday to Sunday evenings (no admission after midnight Friday and Saturday). Only home fans are admitted on Queen's Park Rangers match days, but card-carrying CAMRA members not wearing team colours are welcome.
Q (Shepherd's Bush/Market)

W13: West Ealing

Forester ★

2 Leighton Road, W13 9EP

11-11.30 (midnight Wed & Thu; 1am Fri & Sat); 11-11 Sun
(020) 8567 1654 theforesterealing.com

Fuller's London Pride, ESB; 4 changing beers (often Fuller's, Gale's) H

Built in 1909 from designs by Nowell Parr for the Royal Brewery of Brentford and bought by Fuller's in 2012, this pub has been identified by CAMRA as having a nationally important historic interior. Thai and English food are available daily, except Sundays when the traditional carvery is served until 6pm. Wednesdays are quiz nights and Thursdays offer poker tournaments. Two guest beers are supplemented by others from Fuller's (often Gale's HSB), and two beer festivals are held annually. Local CAMRA Pub of the Year 2018.
(Northfields) (E2,E3)

Owl & The Pussycat L

106 Northfield Avenue, W13 9RT

4-10; 1-10.30 Fri & Sat; closed Sun markopaulo.co.uk

Changing beers (often Marko Paulo)

Unique to West London, this is a combination of microbrewery and pub in a former bookshop. Drinkers can view the brewing process while avid readers can browse through the beer-related books and magazines. All of six beers are brewed on the premises. The ciders are often from Oliver's if not home-produced. In this small, friendly environment, conversation is all-important.
Q (Northfields) (E2,E3)

Brentford

Express Tavern

56 Kew Bridge Road, TW8 0EW

11-11 (midnight Thu-Sat) (020) 8560 8484
expresstavern.co.uk

Big Smoke Solaris Session Pale Ale; Draught Bass; Harveys Sussex Best Bitter; 7 changing beers H

A local landmark since the 1800s, the building retains its illuminated external Bass signage. It has been identified by CAMRA as having a regionally important historic pub interior. The Chiswick Bar has 10 ale handpumps and a playable upright piano (music is also on vinyl LPs), while the Saloon

and Lounge Bar handpumps dispense five ciders and perries. At the rear is a beer garden with a covered and heated area.
(Kew Bridge)

Magpie & Crown

128 High Street, TW8 8EW
12-midnight (1am Thu-Sat) (020) 8560 4570
Butcombe Original; 5 changing beers (often Five Points, Marble, Oakham)
A traditional mock-Tudor free house. Six cask ales, one cider and one perry, as shown on a chalk display board, always include one golden, one dark and one bitter, usually from Manchester, Yorkshire and London breweries and served by enthusiastic and knowledgeable staff. The Magpie Chips and Burgers kitchen serves freshly cooked food. There is a pool table. Outside at the front are tables and a cycle rack; a patio at the back has a covered smokers' area.

Feltham

Moon on the Square

30 The Centre, High Street, TW13 4AU
8am-midnight (10.30 Sun) (020) 8893 1293
Bombardier; Courage Best Bitter; Greene King Abbot; Ruddles Best Bitter; 4 changing beers (often Reunion, Thames Side, Twickenham)
A busy real ale oasis that continues to flourish. The interior is early Wetherspoon's: split level with a central square spiral staircase featuring a half-size man suspended by wires from the ceiling riding a golden crescent moon, as well as wood panelling and glass-partitioned booths, with pictures and local history panels. Continually varying guest ales include local brews. Westons cider is also available. Food is served all day with alcoholic drinks from 9am. Families with children are welcome until 6pm.

Hampton

Jolly Coopers

16 High Street, TW12 2SJ
11-11 (midnight Fri & Sat); 12-10.30 Sun
(020) 8979 3384 squiffysrestaurant.co.uk
Caledonian Deuchars IPA; Courage Best Bitter; Hop Back Summer Lightning; 2 changing beers (often Hammerpot, Reunion, Thames Side)
A popular, traditional community pub, proud of its heritage; a wooden wall panel lists landlords from 1727 to the present owners, who took over in 1986. The small horseshoe bar features five handpumps with a guest beer from a local brewery often available. Walls are adorned with water jugs and local memorabilia, including some coopers' tools. An extensive menu of tapas and traditional food, including Sunday lunches (booking essential), is served in Squiffy's restaurant and, weather permitting, on the sun patio outside.

Hampton Court

Mute Swan

3 Palace Gate, KT8 9BN
11-11 (midnight Fri & Sat); 11-10.30 Sun
(020) 8941 5959
House beer (by St Austell); 5 changing beers (often Surrey Hills, Timothy Taylor, Wimbledon)
A friendly upmarket pub and restaurant opposite the Palace gates. A good selection of food can be eaten either in the upstairs restaurant or in the main bar. Bar bites are also served. The guest beers change frequently, real cider is often on handpump, and the range of whiskies and gins is extensive. Seating and tables are provided outside. There are no TV screens to spoil the atmosphere of this popular pub that draws locals and tourists alike. No prams allowed inside.

Hampton Hill

Roebuck

72 Hampton Road, TW12 1JN
11-11 (11.30 Fri & Sat); 12-4, 7-10.30 Sun
(020) 8255 8133 roebuck-hamptonhill.co.uk
St Austell Tribute; Sambrook's Junction Ale; Young's Bitter; 2 changing beers (often Hammerpot, Triple fff, Windsor & Eton)
Comfortable Victorian street-corner pub with screens dividing the single bar into various seating areas. An amazing array of bric-a-brac and other displays (framed banknotes, military memorabilia, model seaplanes, cigar-store Indian and the wickerwork Harley-Davidson) keeps growing but still does not detract from the comfort of the pub. The small garden has a gazebo for smokers and there is a garden room (available for hire) for cooler evenings. The real fire never goes out in winter. (Fulwell)

Hampton Wick

Foresters Arms

45 High Street, KT1 4DG
4-11 Mon; 12-11 (midnight Thu-Sat); 12-8.30 Sun
(020) 8943 5379 the-foresters.com
Fuller's London Pride; 3 changing beers (often Park, Twickenham, Wimbledon)
A small, traditional neighbourhood pub/hotel (but no breakfast), refurbished in 2017, with a reputation for good food (not Mon). A wide bottled-beer range complements the cask beers. The decor incorporates a fireplace, leather sofas and dark woodwork. The pub is part carpeted with a wooden floor in the centre bar area. There is also a small comfortable side room and a separate restaurant room. Outside seating is provided on the front corner pavement.

Harlington

White Hart

158 High Street, UB3 5DP
11-11 (11.30 Thu; midnight Fri & Sat); 12-11 Sun
(020) 8759 9608
Fuller's London Pride, ESB; 1 changing beer (often Fuller's, Gale's)
Large, Grade II-listed Fuller's pub standing proud at the north end of the village. The bar provides access to an open-plan area with soft seating, leading to a seated area favoured by diners. It was refurbished in 2009 to improve facilities and create the open feel it has now. Local history is the theme of the wall displays, enjoyed by regulars and visitors from nearby Heathrow Airport. Quiz night is Thursday. P

Hayes

Botwell Inn ✔

25-29 Coldharbour Lane, UB3 3EB
9am-midnight ☎ (020) 8848 3112
Greene King Abbot; Ruddles Best Bitter; Sharp's Doom Bar; 3 changing beers (often Adnams, Hogs Back, Windsor & Eton) H
A large Wetherspoon pub opened in 2000 following a shop conversion from furnishers S Moore and Son, with several areas for dining and drinking. There is a fenced paved area to the front and a patio at the rear with large market-type parasols with heaters. At least one Westons cider is stocked. Several beer festivals are held annually. Q ❀ ◑ ♿ ⇌(Hayes & Harlington)

Hounslow

Moon Under Water ✔

84-88 Staines Road, TW3 3LF (W end of High St)
9am-12.30am (1am Fri & Sat) ☎ (020) 8572 7506
Greene King Abbot; Ruddles Best Bitter; Sharp's Doom Bar; 5 changing beers (often Windsor & Eton) H
A 1991 Wetherspoon shop conversion in original style, still displaying many local history panels and photographs. It is a regular venue for the town's beer lovers, also attracting others from surrounding areas. Up to five guest ales are offered, both national and local, with more at festival times, when 10 handpumps are put to work. The cider is usually Westons Old Rosie, again with others during festivals. Q ❀ ◑ ♿ ⇌ ⊖(Central)

St Margarets

Crown

174 Richmond Road, TW1 2NH
11-11 (11.30 Fri & Sat; 10.30 Sun) ☎ (020) 8892 5896
crowntwickenham.co.uk
Harvey's Sussex Best Bitter; Oakham Citra; Surrey Hills Shere Drop; 1 changing beer (often Big Smoke, Twickenham) H
A large, spacious pub from about 1730 and Grade II listed, with a substantial refurbishment enhancing the Georgian heritage of the original building. The Victorian hall to the back of the pub has been opened up for dining and the courtyard garden attractively remodelled. Inside are various seating areas and three fireplaces, one with a real fire. Several windows and doors are original and listed. Food is served 12-9.30pm (10pm Fri & Sat).
❀ ◑ ♿ ⇌ P

Teddington

Masons Arms

41 Walpole Road, TW11 8PJ
12-11 (11.30 Fri & Sat); 12-10.30 Sun ☎ (020) 8977 6521
the-masons-arms.co.uk
Hop Back Citra; Sambrook's Junction Ale; 2 changing beers (often Andwells, Coastal, Kissingate) H
A small, friendly, back-street community free house, very much a beer drinkers' haven, as reflected in the array of bottles, pictures and pub memorabilia on display (including an infamous Watney's Party Seven). Guest beers change frequently, coming from a wide range of independent brewers nationwide. Carpeting and comfortable seating create a cosy atmosphere. There is a log-burning stove, a dartboard and a secluded rear patio. ❀ ♿ ⇌ ♣

Twickenham

Rifleman

7 Fourth Cross Road, TW2 5EL
12 (2 Mon & Tue)-11; 12-10.30 Sun ☎ (020) 8893 3836
theriflemantwickenham.co.uk
Butcombe Original; Dark Star Hophead; Timothy Taylor Landlord; Twickenham Naked Ladies; Young's Bitter; 1 changing beer (often West Berkshire) H
A traditional Victorian pub whose name commemorates riflemen billeted nearby in Napoleonic times. It has a small beer garden and front patio and is conveniently close to seven bus routes. No main meals are served but toasties are available until 7pm. Very much a community hub, with board games, TV sport and a lively open mic night on Thursday, it is a 15-minute walk from Twickenham Stadium and Harlequins rugby club.
❀ ⇌(Strawberry Hill) ♣ P

Sussex Arms ✔

15 Staines Road, TW2 5BG
12-11 (11.30 Fri & Sat); 12-10.30 Sun ☎ (020) 8894 7468
thesussexarmstwickenham.co.uk
Big Smoke Solaris Session Pale Ale; Twickenham Naked Ladies; changing beers (sourced nationally) H
A traditional pub with a real fire, now a firm favourite with beer lovers. Fifteen handpumps showcase independent UK breweries and six ciders and perries. Acoustic blues and Irish music feature regularly, and recorded music is played on vinyl LPs. Food includes Anthea's famous pies and much more. Every 10th pint of ale is free with the pub's loyalty card. Twice CAMRA Greater London Cider Pub of the Year and local CAMRA Pub of the Year.
❀ ◑ ⇌(Strawberry Hill) ♣

White Swan

Riverside, TW1 3DN
11-11 (10.30 Sun & Mon) ☎ (020) 8744 2951
whiteswantwickenham.co.uk
Sharp's Doom Bar; Twickenham Naked Ladies; 3 changing beers (often Fuller's, Kew, Reunion) H
A Grade II-listed building and award-winning traditional pub, built around 1690. Entry is via steps up to the first floor, with real fires and walls covered with rugby and other memorabilia. A small veranda/balcony and a triclinium (three-sided room with window seats) afford views of the river and Eel Pie Island. Directly opposite is a larger beer garden (tides permitting), right on the water's edge. A summer beer festival and an annual raft race are held. Q ❀ ◑ ⇌

William Webb Ellis

24 London Road, TW1 3RR
9am-10.30 (11.30 Fri & Sat) ☎ (020) 8744 4300
Fuller's London Pride; Greene King IPA, Abbot; Sharp's Doom Bar; 8 changing beers (often Oakham, Twickenham, Windsor & Eton) H
A large and spacious Wetherspoon pub in the centre of the home of English rugby, named after the alleged inventor of the game. Twelve handpumps are in constant use; real cider is available. The rear patio is open until 9pm, food is served all day and children are welcome until 8pm. A Monday ale club offers reduced prices and third-pint glasses. Silent screens show live news and sport. ❀ ◑ ♿ ⇌

Uxbridge

Good Yarn ✓

132 High Street, UB8 1JX

9am-midnight (1am Fri & Sat) ☎ (01895) 239852

Greene King Abbot; Ruddles Best Bitter; Sharp's Doom Bar; 4 changing beers (often Binghams, Oakham, Twickenham) Ⓗ

Opened in 1994 in the former Pearson's menswear shop in the town centre, this Wetherspoon pub has a long, narrow bar, the raised far end edged with shelves of old books. The front section boasts vintage framed advertisements for local businesses on the walls, and local old photographs can be found throughout. Alcoholic drinks are served from 9am. Opening hours may vary.

Queen's Head ✓

54 Windsor Street, UB8 1AB

10-11 (midnight Fri & Sat); 12-10.30 Sun

☎ (01895) 258750

Black Sheep Best Bitter; Greene King IPA; Morland Old Speckled Hen; 3 changing beers (sourced nationally; often Greene King, Sharp's, Wadworth) Ⓗ

A Grade II-listed mid-19th century pub that still retains its old charm, opposite the church, a few yards down from the tube station. The decorations and furnishings are traditional. It has bay windows, wooden floorboards, low ceilings, walls largely of exposed brick, and an irregularly shaped bar. On the walls are photographs related to royalty and a corner is dedicated to James Bond.

Forester, W13: West Ealing (Photo: Bob Steel)

GREATER MANCHESTER

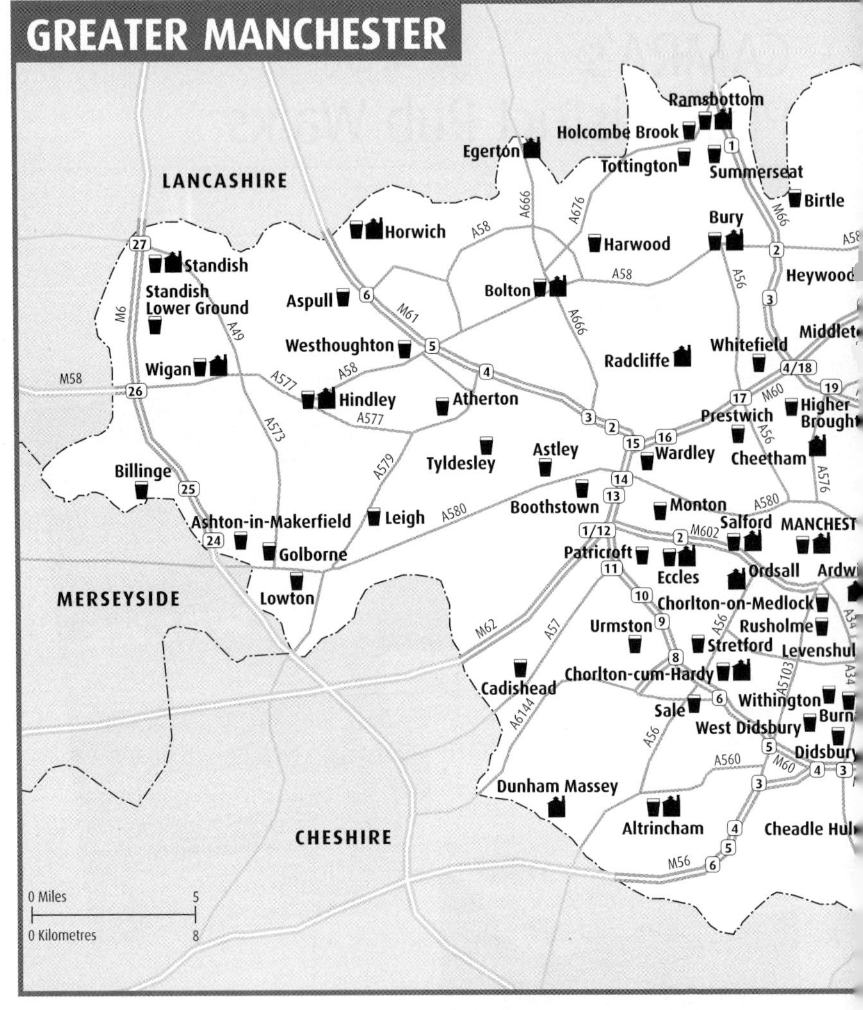

Altrincham

Cheshire Tap

36 Railway Street, WA14 2RE

5-midnight; 12-1am Fri & Sat; 12-midnight Sun

(0161) 929 7810

4 changing beers (sourced regionally; often Poynton, RedWillow, Robinsons)

Five minutes' walk from Altrincham Interchange, this is a long thin bar that backs on to Kings Court. Soft lighting, bare brick, a metal bar top and bare squirrel-cage filament lamps above the bar create a stylish laid-back feel to this modern bar. The four real ales on handpump are mostly from Cheshire. Cocktails are a speciality here.

Costello's Bar

18 Goose Green, WA14 1DW (alleyway from Stamford New Rd/opp Regent Rd, adjacent to new hospital)

12-11 (midnight Thu; 1am Fri & Sat) (0161) 929 0903

costellosbar.co.uk

Dunham Massey Big Tree Bitter, Dunham Dark; 5 changing beers (often Dunham Massey)

This small bar is in Altrincham's attractive and popular Goose Green behind the new hospital. It has a modern feel and is a favourite both for locals and visitors. The tap house for Dunham Massey Brewery, on the bar there are seven handpumps featuring a continually changing selection of beers from the brewery's 25 recipes. There are a large number of award certificates adorning the walls, reflecting the high regard the bar is held in.

Jack in the Box

Altrincham Market Hall, Market Street, WA14 1SA

closed Mon; 12-10 (6 Sun) 07917 792060

Blackjack JITB House Pale; 4 changing beers (sourced nationally)

Located inside the popular Altrincham Market House, part of the town's historic market, this is one of the Blackjack Brewery bars. Six handpumps on the bar sit alongside eight keg fonts. Blackjack beers are always available as well as a changing cider. The guest beers are sourced from local breweries such as Track and Squawk and others further afield. The casks are housed in a chilled 'cellar' behind the bar. There is now a sibling bar in Manchester city centre.

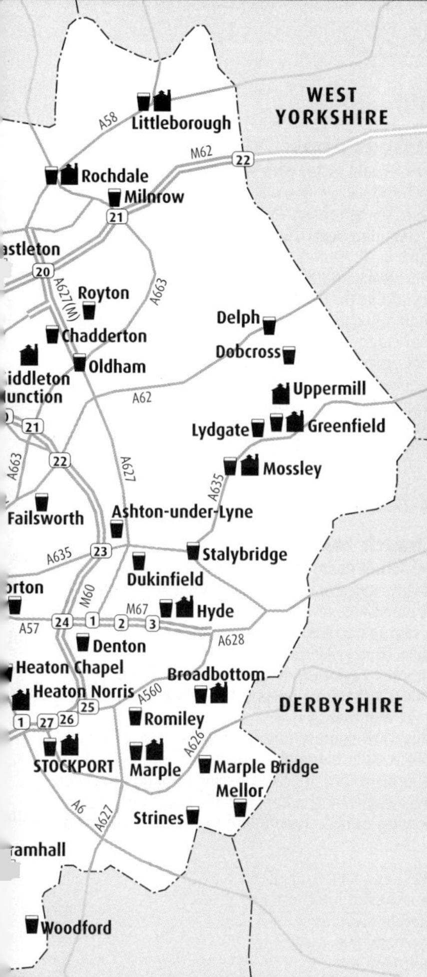

Pi

18 Shaws Road, WA14 1QU

11-11 (midnight Fri & Sat) ☎ (0161) 929 9098

abarcalledpi.com

Tatton Blonde; 2 changing beers (sourced nationally; often First Chop Brewing Arm, RedWillow, Saltaire) [H]

A contrast to the crowded neighbouring Altrincham Market, Pi is smaller, quieter, but still popular. The bar is situated on the ground floor and upstairs is a larger room with more tables and seating. Outside there are pavement tables with blankets for cooler times of year. Typically three real ales are on handpump, with guests sourced from micros or more established, but still small, breweries. Pieminister pies and mash are served until 10pm daily. The bar is a sibling to Pi (Chorlton).

Ashton-in-Makerfield

Caledonian Hotel

154 Bolton Road, WN4 8PF

5-11.30; 3-midnight Fri; 12-1am Sat; 12.30-11.30 Sun

☎ (01942) 727875

2 changing beers (sourced regionally) [H]

Large former Walker's free house built in 1897 with an open-plan lounge, a games room with large-screen TV and an upstairs function room. Prints of old Ashton are of interest. It hosts a popular quiz night on Thursday, open mic on Tuesday and artists in the lounge most Saturday evenings. Pool teams are based here. There are two guest beers available and it holds occasional mini beer festivals. P

Ashton-under-Lyne

Ash Tree

9-11 Wellington Road, OL6 6DA

8am-midnight ☎ (0161) 339 9670

Greene King Abbot; Ruddles Best Bitter; Sharp's Doom Bar; 4 changing beers (sourced regionally) [H]

Directly facing the Victorian Market Hall and square, this pub has become one of the premier real ale destinations in the town centre and is easily accessible by bus and train. Families are welcome in the lower level; above are the bar and lounge/dining area which leads to the rear entrance and outdoor smoking area. Wetherspoon's usual good value applies to the beers and food. Two real ale festivals are held each year. TVs operate with the sound off.

Dog & Pheasant

528 Oldham Road, OL7 9PQ

12-11 (11.30 Fri & Sat) ☎ (0161) 330 4894

Marston's Saddle Tank, Pedigree [H]**; 3 changing beers** [H]/[G]

Known as the Top Dog, this popular, friendly local near the Medlock Valley Country Park has been a regular in the Guide since 1992. It has a large bar serving three areas, plus another room at the front. The beer range is supplemented by three guest beers from the Marston's portfolio. A menu of good-value food includes vegetarian options. Quiz night is Thursday. P (409,419)

Aspull

Victoria

50 Haigh Road, WN2 1YA

3.30-midnight; 12-1am Sat & Sun ☎ 07548 178021

4 changing beers (sourced regionally) [H]

A traditional two-roomed local adjacent to the popular Haigh Country Park. A large lounge displays photographs depicting the history of Aspull and Haigh. Four handpulls dispense beers sourced from all over the UK, as well as two real ciders and over 30 gins mainly from handcrafted, small batch distilleries. Large-screen TVs cater for sports fans. Pool, darts and dominoes are played here. There is a small car park to the rear and on-street parking. Children are permitted until 8pm. Q P

Astley

Old Boat House

Higher Green Lane, M29 7JB

12-midnight ☎ (01942) 883300

oldboathouseastley.co.uk

Wainwright; 3 changing beers (sourced regionally) [H]

Situated on the towpath of the Bridgewater Canal, this place was originally built as stabling for horses that pulled the barges. A major refurbishment was carried out in 2016, opening up the pub to add more dining space. There are still areas for drinking though, particularly outside where there is plenty of seating near the canal. Live music features most weekends (see the website for details). (551)

Atherton

Atherton Arms

6 Tyldesley Road, M46 9DD

11.30-11 (midnight Fri & Sat); 12-11.30 Sun
(01942) 875996

Joseph Holt Bitter, Two Hoots; 1 changing beer (sourced regionally)

Traditional public house with a great atmosphere and good facilities, including a full-sized snooker table and a function room. The pub is known for its superb beer garden, which has TV screens and heaters. The beer is competitively priced and promotions change on a monthly basis. A wide range of events is hosted, with live entertainment at the weekend and most sports shown throughout the week. P (V2)

Pendle Witch

2-4 Warburton Place, M46 0EQ

12-midnight (2am Fri & Sat) (01942) 884537

Moorhouse's Black Cat, Premier Bitter, Pride of Pendle, Blond Witch, Pendle Witches Brew; 2 changing beers

A real gem hidden down a narrow alley. The entrance, part of a conservatory, leads to an open-plan bar that serves the full range of Moorhouse's beers plus guests. A large selection of Belgian bottled beers is also kept. The games area has a pool table and large-screen TV. Regular rock nights are hosted and occasional beer festivals are held. Food is served during the day, with a quiz night on Thursday. There is a well-kept garden for the summer. Parking is close by in the town centre. P (V2)

Billinge

Masons Arms

99 Carr Mill Road, WN5 7TY

2-11 (midnight Wed & Fri; 11.30 Thu); 12-midnight Sat; 12-11 Sun (01744) 603572 masonsarmsbillinge.co.uk

5 changing beers (sourced regionally)

Built in 1779 and run by the same family for over 200 years, the pub is well placed for walking or cycling in the local area. Five handpumps offer regularly changing guest beers alongside up to four real ciders. There is a smoking shelter with a logburner and a beer garden overlooking fields at the back. Dogs and children are welcome. Sky Sports is screened. Quiz night is Wednesday. Locally baked Burchall's pork pies are available Fridays only – be quick, they sell fast. P

Birtle

Church Inn

Castle Hill Road, BL9 6UH (straight up Castle Hill Rd, clearly signed or via bridle path from Pack Horse)

closed Mon; 12-2.30, 5-8.30 Tue & Wed; 12-8.30 Thu (9 Fri & Sat); 12-7.30 Sun (0161) 764 2857
thechurchinnbirtle.co.uk

Timothy Taylor Landlord; house beer (by Deeply Vale); 3 changing beers (often Black Sheep, Deeply Vale, Moorhouse's)

This 17th-century inn and former law court still keeps its traditional character despite a major refurbishment. It boasts excellent panoramic views over east Manchester towards Cheshire. There is seating outside with a large car park, and it is also

REAL ALE BREWERIES

Alphabet Manchester
Bank Top Bolton
Beatnikz Republic Manchester
Beer Nouveau Manchester: Ardwick
Blackedge Horwich
Blackjack Manchester
Bootleg Chorlton-cum-Hardy
Brewsmith Ramsbottom
Brightside Radcliffe
Chorlton Manchester: Ardwick
Cloudwater Manchester
Deeply Vale Bury
Donkeystone Greenfield (NEW)
Dunham Massey Dunham Massey
Dunscar Bolton
Epicurus Bolton (brewing suspended)
Federation Altrincham (NEW)
First Chop Eccles
Fool Hardy Stockport: Heaton Norris
Four Kings Hyde
Gasworks Manchester
Green Mill Broadbottom
Greenfield Greenfield
Hay Rake Littleborough
Hexagon Marple
Hogarths Bolton
Holy Well Egerton
Hophurst Hindley
Hydes Salford
Irwell Works Ramsbottom
Joseph Holt Cheetham
JW Lees Middleton Junction
Manchester Manchester
Marble Manchester
Martland Mill Wigan
Millstone Mossley
Northern Monkey Bolton
Origami Manchester: Ardwick
Outstanding Manchester: Ordsall
Phoenix Heywood
Pictish Rochdale
Pomona Island Salford (NEW)
Prospect Wigan
Ramsbottom Craft Bolton
Remedy Stockport
Rising Sun Mossley
Robinsons Stockport
Runaway Manchester
Saddleworth Uppermill
Serious Rochdale
Seven Bro7hers Salford
Silver Street Bury
Squawk Manchester: Ardwick
Stockport Stockport
Stubborn Mule Altrincham
Thirst Class Stockport
Track Manchester
Tweed Hyde
Wander Beyond Manchester
Watts Brewing? Stockport
Wigan Wigan (NEW)
Wily Fox Wigan
Windmill Standish

well worth making the 15-minute walk up from the bus stop. The pub has a cosy atmosphere with three interconnecting rooms and a separate restaurant. Excellent food is served which complements the top-quality ales, one of which is usually from the nearby Deeply Vale Brewery.

Bolton

Bank Top Brewery Tap

68-70 Belmont Road, Astley Bridge, BL1 7AN

12-11 (11.30 Fri & Sat) (01204) 302837
banktopbrewery.com

Bank Top Dark Mild, Flat Cap, Pavilion Pale Ale, Port O Call; 4 changing beers (sourced locally; often Bank Top)

The Tap, which has won numerous local CAMRA awards, is a popular two-roomed street-corner local. There are eight handpumps supplying ales from Bank Top Brewery, plus a guest beer. Up to six real ciders are also on offer in a pleasant environment, with great service, quiet music and an absence of distractions from TV, jukebox or gaming machine. A dartboard is situated in the vault and there is a large outdoor drinking area with a covered smoking shelter.

Bolton Ukrainian Social Club

99 Castle Street, BL2 1JP

3.30-11; 12-11 Sat & Sun (01204) 529258

3 changing beers (sourced locally; often Bank Top, Blackedge)

Large, imposing building to the east of town with a comfortable and well laid-out two-room bar. At least one of the three handpumps will have beers from Bank Top or Blackedge. Guests from further afield feature on the other two. The club is home to several societies including brass band, choir, chess and bagpipes. The annual Bolton CAMRA Beer Festival is held here in April. Local CAMRA Club of the Year 2011-2018. Q

Bunbury's

397 Chorley Old Road, BL1 6AH

1 (5 Mon & Tue)-10; 1-11 Fri & Sat 07952 344838
bunburys.co.uk

3 changing beers (sourced locally; often Brass Castle, Magic Rock, Rivington)

Named after a fictitious character in Oscar Wilde's play The Importance of Being Earnest and opened on Back to the Future Day in 2015, this cosy bottle shop with a bar serves the needs of an area of Bolton bereft of good beer. Bunbury's offers three ever-changing beers on handpump from local breweries such as Rivington, Holy Well and Northern Monkey, and from similar-sized breweries further afield. It also stocks a wide range of often rare bottled beers from around the world and a choice of craft beers. Q (125)

Elephant & Castle

4-10 Deansgate, BL1 1BR

9am-midnight Mon & Wed (1am Tue; 2am Thu; 3am Fri & Sat); 12-1am Sun (01204) 384544
theelephantandcastlebolton.co.uk

Bank Top Flat Cap, Pavilion Pale Ale; Moorhouse's Blond Witch; 2 changing beers (sourced nationally; often St Austell)

The Elephant & Castle is a large town-centre pub in the heart of Bolton's main nightlife area. Weekend evenings can be busy when the pub acts as a meeting point for revellers while DJs play tunes old and new. The host of large TV screens is also a magnet for football fans during big games. There are food theme nights and special offers during the week.

Great Ale at the Vaults

Vaults Below Market Place, BL1 2AL

11-11 (01204) 773458 greataleatthevaults.co.uk

4 changing beers (sourced locally)

This is the jewel in the crown of The Vaults, the arches below ground level of the former Market Hall development – a leisure venue with chain eateries, cinema and kids' play area. The long bar has four handpumps serving three guest beers and Vaults Bitter specially brewed by Outstanding Brewery using Australian hops. The beer is kept in glass-fronted chilled cupboards behind the bar. Paddles of three thirds of cask ale are available along with hot beverages and cold bar food. Q

Hen & Chickens

143 Deansgate, BL1 1EX

11-11; 12-11 Sun 07850 026681

5 changing beers (sourced locally; often Lancaster, Northern Monkey, Three B's)

The Hen & Chickens has long been one of the most pleasant and popular of town-centre pubs. The smart exterior and colourful floral displays brighten up this end of Deansgate. Inside there is a central horseshoe bar serving both sides of the pub. Although now open plan, the entrance doors lead on the left to the smaller vault with a comfortable raised seating area and on the right to the lounge which is used for dining.

Olde Man & Scythe

6-8 Churchgate, BL1 1HL

11-11 (12.30am Fri & Sat); 12-11 Sun (01204) 559060

Bank Top Flat Cap; Hop Back Summer Lightning; 2 changing beers (sourced locally)

This Grade II listed pub is reputedly the fourth-oldest in the country and sits near the parish church on historic Churchgate, site of a famous Civil War execution. Rebuilt in 1636 and modified in recent times, the pub retains some traditional features such as wooden beams, leaded windows and stone floors. There is a lively bar, a cosy snug and a separate room often used for jamming and open mic nights. At most times only the Thatchers cider is real.

Spinning Mule

Unit 2 Nelson Square, BL1 1JT

8am-midnight (1am Fri & Sat) (01204) 533339

Bank Top Flat Cap; Greene King Abbot; Phoenix Wobbly Bob; Ruddles Best Bitter; 7 changing beers (sourced nationally; often Acorn, Brightside, Leeds)

Opened in 1998, this large town-centre pub has an open-plan split-level interior with a separate comfortable dining area. It is named after Samuel Crompton's mule, a revolutionary invention in cotton spinning that made Bolton famous worldwide. The seven guest beer handpumps serve a range of ales from near and far. Two or three real ciders are usually available. Q

Boothstown

Royal Oak

20 Leigh Road, M28 1LZ

4-10.30 (11 Mon; 11.30 Fri); 1-midnight Sat; 1-10 Sun

Joseph Holt Bitter; Sharp's Doom Bar Ⓗ
This family-run pub is being turned around slowly with the help of the local community. It has three rooms – clockwise from entering, you will find a small lounge leading to a larger lounge with dance floor, then the vault with a real fire and games accessed via a small corridor. Pies are available behind the bar. Entertainment includes occasional live shows. A real gem. ♣🚌(34,553)🐾📶

Bramhall

Mounting Stone
8 Woodford Road, SK7 1JJ
🕓 4 (2 Wed & Thu)-10.30; 12-11 Fri & Sat; 12-10.30 Sun
☎ (0161) 439 7563 🌐 themountingstone.co.uk
Bollington Best, Long Hop; 4 changing beers (sourced locally) Ⓗ
The sister pub to Cheadle Hulme's Chiverton Tap, this is a cosy, friendly micropub right in the village centre. The former blacksmith's operates over two floors – ground and basement – with a small beer garden to the rear. The name derives from a local large stone that allowed riders to mount their horses. Alongside the Bollington beers are four from microbrewers, one a dark beer. Winner of a City Life Award for best pub in Greater Manchester.
Q🐴❀♿⇌🍎🚌🐾📶

Broadbottom

Harewood Arms Ⓛ ✔
2 Market Street, SK14 6AX
🕓 3-11 (midnight Fri); 2-midnight Sat; 12.30-11 Sun
☎ (01457) 762500
Green Mill Gold, Stellar, Chief, Old Git; 2 changing beers (sourced regionally) Ⓗ
This former Regional CAMRA Pub of the Year has gone from strength to strength since being bought by the current owners in 2013. Home of the Green Mill Brewery, it offers five regular Green Mill beers plus seasonals, guests and a rotating real cider. The pub has various seating areas and two real fires. For warmer days, there is a beer garden to the rear. Approximately five minutes' walk from Broadbottom railway station and on local bus routes. 🐴❀◑♿⛺⇌♣🍎▯🚌🐾📶

Burnage

Reasons to be Cheerful
228 Fog Lane, M20 6EL
🕓 closed Mon; 4.30-10 Tue; 3.30-11 Wed & Thu; 1.30-midnight Fri & Sat; 1.30-11 Sun ☎ (0161) 425 9678
3 changing beers (sourced locally) Ⓗ
Opened in 2017, this friendly modern beer café occupies former shop premises near Burnage railway station. Three handpulls generally serve a session strength beer, a stronger beer and a dark beer; eight taps serve keg or KeyKeg beers. Bottles and cans from independent brewers complete the picture. A partial wall divides two distinct seating areas in the narrow space. There are no TV screens and background music is discreet. The proprietors are passionate about beer and host regular event nights. Q❀⇌🚊🍎🚌🐾📶

Bury

Art Picture House Ⓛ ✔
36 Haymarket Street, BL9 0AY (opp metro/bus station interchange)
🕓 8am-midnight (3am Fri & Sat) ☎ (0161) 705 4040
Greene King Abbot; Moorhouse's Blond Witch; Ruddles Best Bitter; changing beers Ⓗ
A beautifully restored former 1920s cinema. This warm, friendly, town-centre pub is conveniently located opposite the bus/tram interchange. Seven handpumps offer ever-changing beers from near and far – the team of experienced bar staff are knowledgeable about the ales and happy to advise. There is a large seating area with booths and traditional seating on two levels. Food is available all day every day. It gets busy at lunchtimes on market days Wednesday and Friday, and Friday and Saturday evenings when its hosts a DJ and dancing. 🐴◑♿⇌(Bolton St ELR)🚊🚌📶

Clarence Ⓛ
2 Silver Street, BL9 0EX
🕓 11-11; 12-11 Sun ☎ (0161) 464 7404 🌐 theclarence.co.uk
Silver Street Session, One, Ruby, Ruby, Ruby, Ruby; changing beers (often Deeply Vale, Saltaire, Silver Street) Ⓗ
A gastropub with fine dining and excellent real ale. It has been lovingly and stylishly restored, recreating the pub 'as it was'. The basement houses the Silver Street microbrewery which brews only for the Clarence, the main brewery being at The Mill. Ever-changing guest ales are also sold. The ground floor contains the main bar, back to its former position, with the original black and white floor tiles. The restaurant is on the first floor and the cocktail bar on the second floor.
Q🐴◑♿⇌(Bolton St ELR)🚊🚌🐾📶

Lamb Ⓛ
533 Tottington Road, Woolfold, BL8 1UB (on B6213 from Bury)
🕓 4.30-11 (midnight Fri); 1-midnight Sat; 1-10.30 Sun
☎ (0161) 764 2714
Sharp's Doom Bar; 1 changing beer (sourced locally; often Deeply Vale, Ramsbottom Craft) Ⓗ
A well-run local with a reputation for being a friendly pub where all are welcome. The warm atmosphere is enhanced by an open fire in winter. The pub, originally a coaching house, was built in 1831. The landlord is keen on real ale with two pumps always in use, one permanent and one changing. Local microbreweries are promoted, mainly Deeply Vale and Ramsbottom Craft. A real cider is always available. 🐴❀♣🍎P🚌(469)🐾📶

Robert Peel Ⓛ ✔
10 Market Place, BL9 0LD
🕓 8am-midnight (1am Fri & Sat) ☎ (0161) 764 7287
Greene King Abbot; Ruddles Best Bitter; Sharp's Doom Bar; changing beers (often Brightside) Ⓗ
The Robert Peel is a well-established and popular pub in Bury's cultural quarter, named after the local mill owner and MP whose son became Prime Minister and founded the modern police force. The pub has the largest open public area in Bury. The decor celebrates other local worthies such as Richmal Crompton, the author of the Just William books. Six handpumps include three dedicated to the regular brews, the others dispensing frequently changing ales. Real cider is on three handpumps – two ever-changing guests and the house cider.
🐴◑♿⇌(Bolton St ELR)🚊🍎🚌🐾📶

Trackside Bar Ⓛ ✔
Bolton Street Station, BL9 0EY (platform 2 East Lancs Railway)

12 (11 Wed & Thu)-11; 11-midnight Fri; 9am-midnight Sat; 9am-11 Sun (0161) 764 6461
Outstanding Piston Broke; changing beers
The house beer from Outstanding is joined by up to 11 varying guest ales alongside craft keg. It also sells up to 10 real ciders or perries. The large outdoor seating area on the platform provides a lovely suntrap. There is also a covered heated space for those wanting a closer railway experience. (Bolton St ELR) P

Cadishead

Grocers
152A Liverpool Road, M44 5DD (close to Moss Lane)
closed Mon; 5-10 (10.30 Fri); 2-10 Sat; 2-9 Sun
07950 522468
3 changing beers (sourced regionally; often Cheshire Brewhouse, Dunham Massey, Track)
The first microbar to open in Salford is a conversion of a former grocer's shop, hence the name. There is no music nor TV, just friendly conversation. Table service is provided by the owner from a separate air-chilled room. Blackboards list the ales and ciders available. There is a small yard to the rear. Local CAMRA Pub of the Year in 2016.
Q (67,100)

Castleton

Blue Pits Inn
842 Manchester Road, OL11 2SP
12-midnight (01706) 632151
JW Lees Bitter, Dragon's Fire; 1 changing beer (sourced locally; often JW Lees)
The Blue Pits is a welcoming, friendly local in a former railway building once used as a mortuary. The building was fully refurbished by Lees in 2013 and now has three distinct drinking areas, offering a much warmer atmosphere than before. Cards and darts are played in the taproom and sport is shown on TV. There is a regular quiz night and karaoke. Of particular interest is the tiled mosaic of John Willie on the outside wall. Lees' seasonal ales are featured alongside bitter and Dragon's Fire.
P (17)

Old Post Office Ale House
858 Manchester Road, OL11 2SP
2-11; 12-1am Fri & Sat; 12-11 Sun
5 changing beers (sourced locally)
A community microbar, opened in 2016, free from music and TV, although there is a screen used for advertising and the odd TV programme. Quality locally brewed ales are on offer plus ciders and wines. There is no food but you are welcome to bring your own, with plates and cutlery provided. The Rochdale-bound bus stops outside the door.
Q (17)

Chadderton

Rose of Lancaster
7 Haigh Lane, OL1 2TQ
11.30-11 (11.30 Fri & Sat); 12-11 Sun (0161) 624 3031
roseoflancaster.co.uk
JW Lees Manchester Pale Ale, Bitter; 1 changing beer (sourced locally; often JW Lees)
A conservatory restaurant, lounge bar and thriving separate vault where sporting events are screened provide a great choice for the varied clientele. Drinkers and diners mix easily in the busy lounge and the management ensures swift and cheerful service. A chalkboard in the lounge details the number of pints of real ale sold each week. Outside, a covered patio with views to the rear of the Rochdale Canal is popular, weather permitting. Nearby bus and train links make for easy travel to this well-run and popular pub.
(Mills Hill) P (58,59)

Cheadle Hulme

Chiverton Tap
8 Mellor Road, SK8 5AU (off Station Rd)
4-10.30; 12-11 Fri & Sat; 12-10.30 Sun (0161) 485 4149
Bollington Best, Long Hop; 4 changing beers (sourced locally)
This friendly micropub opened in early 2015 in what was once Arthur Chiverton's draper's shop. Note the mosaic in the doorway and framed displays of drapery tools on the wall and bar. Six handpumps dispense two regular beers plus four varying ales from small breweries both local and further afield. Beer tapas (a selection of three third-pints) is available. An ever-changing real cider is served straight from the box. Voted regional CAMRA Pub of the Year runner-up in 2018.
Q

Chorlton-cum-Hardy

Chorlton Tap
533 Wilbraham Road, M21 0UE
4-11.30 (midnight Thu); 12-1am Fri & Sat; 12-11.30 Sun
(0161) 861 7576 barchorlton.co.uk
Wander Beyond Peak; 7 changing beers (sourced regionally; often Acorn, Magic Rock, Pictish)
A Chorlton institution specialising in cask beer for over 24 years and attracting the most diverse clientele in the area. Eight handpumps split over two sections of the bar focus on local breweries and the best micros from further afield. A range of up to six ciders and perries is kept in the fridge. Food is available until 8pm Thursday to Sunday with sandwiches, wraps, pies and pub classics such as fish and chips. Traditional roasts are served on Sunday. Monday is quiz night.

Dulcimer
567 Wilbraham Road, M21 0AE
4-12.30am (1.30am Fri); 12-1.30am Sat; 12-11.30 Sun
(0161) 860 6444 dulcimer-bar.co.uk
Wainwright; house beer (by Outstanding); 4 changing beers (sourced nationally; often Blackjack, Wild Beer)
Now operating for more than 10 years, this bar in the heart of Chorlton continues to serve a good range of beers. Its house beers are brewed by Outstanding. There are one or two bag-in-a-box ciders. Live acts perform on the first floor on Tuesday and Wednesday, and DJs play an eclectic mix of music Thursday, Friday and Saturday. Quiz night is Monday.

Font
115-117 Manchester Road, M21 9PG
11-12.30am (1am Fri & Sat) (0161) 871 2022
thefontbar.wordpress.com
8 changing beers (sourced nationally; often Mallinsons, RedWillow, Track)
Eight changing real ales are from local, regional and national microbreweries including RedWillow, Track, Squawk, Blackjack, Mallinsons, Kirkstall,

Arbor and more. Two guest ales are from JW Lees, either MPA, Stout, or their seasonal. The bar also features 16 keg lines with around eight for regularly changing guests, and between four and six traditional ciders, varying seasonally. Simple but hearty dishes including pizza and platters are served from the small open kitchen until 10pm daily. Local CAMRA Cider Pub of the Year four times in recent years. (86)

Pi

99 Manchester Road, M21 9GA

11-11 (12.30am Fri & Sat) (0161) 882 0000

abarcalledpi.com

Tatton Blonde; 3 changing beers (sourced regionally) [H]

Pi is a popular bar on the increasingly crowded northern part of Manchester Road. It celebrated its 10th anniversary in 2017 with a refurbishment and is a long-standing Guide entry. Pi offers four real ales and a guest cider or perry, all on handpump, alongside a selection of world beers on draught and an impressive menu of bottled beers from around the world. Food is a changing selection of Pieminister pies (with or without mash, peas and gravy), served until 11pm daily. Coffee, tea and cake are also available. (86)

Sedge Lynn

21A Manchester Road, M21 9PN

8am-11 (midnight Thu-Sat) (0161) 860 0141

Greene King Abbot; Moorhouse's Blond Witch; Phoenix Wobbly Bob; Ruddles Best Bitter; house beer (by Brightside); 7 changing beers (sourced nationally; often Acorn, Hawkshead, Kelham Island) [H]

Built by Norman Evans as a billiard hall for the temperance movement, this Grade II listed building with a barrelled roof and Art Deco styling is well worth a look. The toilets have recently undergone a sympathetic refurbishment. This Wetherspoon establishment provides a good selection of ales, often of local origin. The manager's aim is to ensure there is a range of light to darker beers always available on the 12 handpumps, including seven different guests. Q

Chorlton-on-Medlock

Sandbar

120-122 Grosvenor Street, M1 7HL (off Oxford Rd A34/B5117 jct)

12-midnight (1am Thu; 2am Fri & Sat)

sandbarmanchester.co.uk

Beartown Polar Eclipse; Facer's Clwyd Gold; Phoenix Arizona; 4 changing beers (sourced regionally) [H]

Originally two 18th-century town houses, this is now one of the longest-established bars on the university area beer scene. Quirky and bohemian, it is popular with students and university staff alike. There are regular exhibitions of photographs and paintings, and displays of old curios. The cask beers are usually local and are accompanied by modern British and European bottled, canned and kegged beers and a changing guest cider. Home-made pizzas are available at weekends. Payment is by card or Bitcoin.

(Oxford Rd) (Deansgate/Castlefield)

Delph

Royal Oak (Th' Heights)

Broad Lane, OL3 5TX (via Thame Lane, off main Delph-Denshaw road)

closed Mon; 7 (5 Thu & Fri)-11; 12-6.30 Sun

(01457) 874460

House beer (by Coach House); 3 changing beers (often Millstone) [H]

A 1767 stone-built pub on a pack horse route enjoying an elevated panoramic position overlooking the Tame Valley, in a popular walking area next to the Heights Chapel. The building comprises a cosy bar area with three rooms each with an open fire, and retains exposed wooden beams and a hand-carved stone fireplace. Local photographs of the inn decorate the walls.

Q P

Denton

Carters Arms

Stockport Road, M34 6AQ

4-11; 12-11 Sat & Sun (0161) 320 3752

Black Sheep Best Bitter; Box Steam Tunnel Vision; 2 changing beers (sourced regionally) [H]

Friendly local with two large open-plan rooms. A lounge-style room is to the left, which is regularly hired out for functions, and a traditional bar/games room to the right, with wood panelling and dark leather seating. The pool team plays on Wednesday, quiz night is Thursday, a live artist features on Friday, karaoke and a disco on Saturday. The Carters football team gathers post-match on Sunday. Accompanied children are welcome until 8pm. There is wheelchair access to the rear. Q P

Crown Point Tavern

16 Market Street, M34 2XW (in pedestrianised Denton Civic Square)

11-10 (11 Fri & Sat) (0161) 337 9615

thecrownpointtavern.co.uk

House beer (by Tweed); 5 changing beers (sourced locally) [H]

A micropub near the old post office and library. The house real ale, brewed by the nearby Tweed Brewery, is complemented by five changing guests, usually from breweries in Greater Manchester. A blackboard provides useful information about the ales on offer. A wide selection of bottled beers is also available. The pub has a community feel, with offers for senior citizens Monday to Friday, free nibbles on Sunday afternoon and its own football team.

Q

Lowes Arms

301 Hyde Road, M34 3FF

12-midnight; 10.30-midnight Sat & Sun

(0161) 336 3064 lowesarms.co.uk

4 changing beers (sourced locally) [H]

Built in 1824 to serve the then new Manchester Road, this thriving local features quality beers and good-value food. Beers from Conwy, unusual for the area, are regulars alongside three others, mainly from local micros. The lounge to the left is the main food area. Beer festivals are held in May, August and October. The pub has teams in local darts, dominoes and pool leagues. Breakfast club is Saturday and Sunday 10.30-midday.

P (201)

Didsbury

Fletcher Moss ✓

1 William Street, M20 6RQ (off Wilmslow Rd, A5145 via Albert Hill St)
12-11 (11.30 Thu; midnight Fri & Sat) ☎ (0161) 438 0073
Hydes Original, Lowry; 5 changing beers (sourced nationally; often Hydes) Ⓗ
Named after the alderman who donated the nearby botanical gardens to the village, this thriving community local is home to people of all ages and drinking tastes, usually engaged in lively conversation. The front encompasses three traditional snugs full of Hydes memorabilia and a collection of porcelain teapots, while the rear opens up into a conservatory, leading to an extensive outdoor seating area. There is a quiz every Tuesday and acoustic music on alternate Mondays. **Q**

Gateway ✓

882 Wilmslow Road, M20 5PG (jct Kingsway and Manchester Rd)
8am-11.30 (midnight Fri & Sat); 8am-11 Sun
☎ (0161) 438 1700
Greene King Abbot; Ruddles Best Bitter; house beer (by Brightside); 5 changing beers (sourced nationally) Ⓗ
This large, comfortable and extremely popular late-1930s roadhouse is conveniently located opposite the Parrs Wood leisure complex and public transport interchange. It has a central island bar surrounded by various drinking areas, with quieter spaces to the rear, giving customers real choice. What makes this Wetherspoon stand out from the crowd, however, is the enthusiastic manager and staff who have successfully created a real pub atmosphere and provide excellent beer.
Q(E Didsbury)**P**

Dobcross

Navigation Inn

21-23 Wool Road, OL3 5NS
12-3, 5-11 (midnight Fri); 12-11 Sat; 12-8 Sun
☎ (01457) 872418 thenavigationdobcross.co.uk
Millstone Tiger Rut; Timothy Taylor Boltmaker; 2 changing beers Ⓗ
Nestling in the idyllic rolling countryside of Saddleworth and close to the Huddersfield Narrow Canal, the Navigation was built in 1806 to slake the thirst of navvies cutting the Standedge Tunnel. A traditional family-run pub with an open-plan bar and an L-shaped interior, it serves four real ales alongside a varied choice of freshly prepared food. A daily specials menu is available and themed evenings are organised throughout the year. It is a venue for the popular Rushcart Festival in August.
QP(184,354)

Dukinfield

Angel

197 King Street, SK16 4TH
4-11; 3-midnight Fri; 12-midnight Sat; 12-11 Sun
☎ (0161) 830 0223
4 changing beers (sourced nationally) Ⓗ
A large red-brick pub on the main road close to the centre of Dukinfield. It is something of an oasis for real ale in the area. The pub features four regularly changing beers, nearly always from national microbreweries. There is a large, comfortable lounge, a good taproom and a function room available to hire. This is a pub to suit all tastes and age ranges. It can get busy when one of the local Premier League football sides is on TV.
P(330)

Eccles

Eccles Cross ✓

13 Regent Street, M30 0BP (opp Metrolink)
8am-midnight (1am Fri & Sat) ☎ (0161) 788 0414
Greene King Abbot; Ruddles Best Bitter; 5 changing beers (sourced regionally) Ⓗ
Named after a nearby stone cross, this Wetherspoon pub in the former New Regent cinema is smaller and has a more pub-like feel than most. A series of alcoves along one wall provides a degree of privacy for more intimate drinking while open-plan areas are more popular with older customers. Part of the original decor remains. Outside, the original brick and stone 1920s frontage is well maintained. The house beer, This Is Eccles, is brewed by Peerless.
Q

Lamb Hotel ★

33 Regent Street, M30 0BP (opp Metrolink)
11.30-11 (11.30 Fri & Sat); 12-11 Sun ☎ 07702 400292
Joseph Holt Mild, Bitter; 1 changing beer (sourced nationally) Ⓗ
A Grade II listed red-brick building dating from 1906, on CAMRA's National Inventory of Historic Pub Interiors. Most original features remain intact, including etched-glass doors and windows, polished mahogany and the original billiards room with its full-size table. Wood panelling and carved wooden fire surrounds adorn the four rooms and the spacious lobby adjacent to the bar. Karaoke features on Friday night and Sunday afternoon. The car park charge is refundable at the bar.
QP

Failsworth

Millgate ✓

Ashton Road West, M35 0ES
12-11 (11.30 Fri & Sat) ☎ (0161) 681 8284
themillgatepub.co.uk
JW Lees Bitter; 2 changing beers (often JW Lees) Ⓗ
Taking its name from the now demolished Failsworth Mill, this is now a traditional and family-friendly carvery pub. The main room is large and open plan with a separate vault bar/pool room. The building features a spacious dining area, a sizeable function room with its own bar and ample car parking. To the rear is the beer garden, complete with children's play area.
P

Golborne

Queen Anne

14 Bridge Street, WA3 3PZ
12-11 (10.30 Sun) ☎ (01942) 726922
queenanne-golborne.co.uk
2 changing beers (sourced regionally) Ⓗ
Tucked away on Bridge Street just off the East Lancs Road, the Queen Anne is handy for Haydock Park Racecourse and caters for pre-race parties. Home-cooked food is served in the bar and separate dining area, with early-bird specials on weekdays 3.30-7pm plus Sunday roasts. The beer garden is a real suntrap in the summer. **QP**(360)

Gorton

Vale Cottage

Kirk Street, M18 8UE (off Hyde Rd, E of jct Chapman St)
12-4, 7-11; 12-11.30 Fri & Sat; 12-11 Sun
(0161) 223 4568 thevalecottage.co.uk
Timothy Taylor Landlord; 2 changing beers (sourced nationally) H
Well hidden in the Gore Brook conservation area, the Vale Cottage has the feel of a country pub. Parts date from the 17th century, hence the low beamed ceilings, multiple drinking areas and reputed ghost. A relaxed, friendly atmosphere, where conversation predominates, is disturbed only by the lively, ever-popular quizzes (Tuesday general knowledge, Thursday music). Indulge in an excellent home-cooked meal in the garden to round off a visit or even partake in steak night on the last Thursday of the month.
Q(Ryder Brow/Belle Vue/Gorton) P

Greenfield

King William IV L

134 Chew Valley Road, OL3 7DD
12-midnight (1am Fri & Sat) (01457) 873933
Black Sheep Best Bitter; Tetley Bitter; 4 changing beers (sourced locally; often Donkeystone, Millstone, Pictish) H
Traditional stone-built pub comprising a central bar with log-burning fire and two side rooms. Six handpulled beers are available including two or three LocAles. Traditional food is served Wednesday to Sunday. Monday is quiz night which includes free supper and cash prizes. The outdoor cobbled area to the front has seating, heaters and a retractable awning, and is a welcome addition as a pleasant overspill area. There is a large car park to the rear. P(180,350)

Wellington Inn L

29 Chew Valley Road, OL3 7AF
3-9 Mon (11 Tue); 12-11; 12-9 Sun
Millstone Tiger Rut; Phoenix Arizona; Salopian Lemon Dream; Thwaites Nutty Black, Original; Wainwright; 1 changing beer (sourced locally; often Donkeystone) H
The Wellington is a family-owned village end-of-terrace free house with a friendly welcome. The building comprises a small bar area featuring seven handpulled cask ales, an attached main room popular with diners, and a side room with a dartboard, cribbage and dominoes. A varied menu of good-value home-made food including daily specials is available on Wednesday, Friday and Sunday. Pies, puddings and real chips are particularly popular, and fish on a Friday.
(180,350)

Harwood

House Without a Name L

75 Lea Gate, BL2 3ET
12-midnight (1.30am Fri & Sat) (01204) 433568
housewithoutaname.co.uk
Joseph Holt Bitter; Sharp's Doom Bar; 4 changing beers (sourced locally; often Holy Well, Northern Monkey) H
Locally known as the No Name, this cosy terraced venue was originally two cottages built in the 1830s, now sensitively modernised and refurbished retaining the flag floors and wooden beams. The main lounge has a bar servery with a blackboard beer listing, a large-screen TV and a real fire, and there is a small bar to the left. Simple bar food is served during opening hours. All premium TV sports channels are screened.
(480,507)

Heaton Chapel

Heaton Hops

7 School Lane, SK4 5DE (jct Manchester Rd)
closed Mon; 4.30-10 Tue; 1.30-10 Wed (11 Thu-Sat); 1.30-10 Sun (0161) 442 3541 heatonhops.co.uk
2 changing beers (sourced regionally) H
Since opening in 2015, this cosy and highly popular micropub has been collecting awards, including Manchester Food & Drink Craft Bar of the Year 2016 and Greater Manchester Beer Awards Best Bar 2017. Based in converted shop premises, with just two small rooms (the second is downstairs) and an outside drinking area, it is an intimate and hospitable place to have a drink. A range of bottle-conditioned beers is stocked.

Higher Broughton

Duke of York

97 Marlborough Road, Hightown, M7 4SP (opp Inghamwood Close)
11-11 (midnight Fri & Sat); 11-10.30 Sun 07827 850214
Joseph Holt Mild, Bitter H
This large Victorian-gothic pub was built in 1899 in an area of dense housing but managed to outlive this and escape the clearances of the 1970s. Now positioned on a quiet new estate, it still offers a glimpse of old Salford. A collection of rooms branches from a central bar, with lots of fine woodwork and etched glass. It hosts an enthusiastic darts team and some live music.
(42,135)

Hindley

Hare & Hounds

31 Ladies Lane, WN2 2QA
3-midnight; 12-midnight Fri & Sat; 12-11 Sun
(01942) 200370
5 changing beers H
This small but traditional pub is located between Hindley railway station and the town centre. It has a large, cosy lounge and a distinct bar/vault area. The lounge displays pictures from bygone Hindley and has a large-screen TV for sports. The pub has a darts team playing in the local league. Quiz night is Thursday. Beers are from Wigan Brew House along with other local breweries as well as from further afield.

Holcombe Brook

Hare & Hounds L

400 Bolton Road West, BL0 9RY (on A676, jct with Longsight Rd)
12-11 (midnight Thu-Sat) (01706) 822107
hare-and-hounds-bury.co.uk
10 changing beers H
This popular community pub goes from strength to strength. Its function room is used by various local groups to hold meetings and private parties. The pub supports a quiz team which competes in a local league. The licensee organises two beer festivals a year, around St Patrick's Day and

Halloween, when he sources beers from around the country and puts in extra handpumps on the bar. Food is served daily until 10pm. Sports TV (on mute) is shown around the bar.
(472,474)

Horwich

Bank Top Brewery Ale House

36 Church Street, BL6 6AD
12-11 (11.30 Fri & Sat) (01204) 693793
banktopbrewery.com
Bank Top Dark Mild, Flat Cap; 6 changing beers (sourced locally; often Bank Top)
The second Bank Top Brewery pub sits in a conservation area opposite Horwich Parish Church and alongside 18th- and 19th-century cottages associated with the area's history of textiles. It is an immaculate pub showcasing eight beers from Bank Top, always including Dark Mild, former Champion Mild of Britain, plus one ever-changing guest ale. Up to six real ciders and perries are also available, most kept cellar-cool. Walkers and their dogs are welcome. (125)

Brewery Bar

Moreton Mill, Hampston Street, BL6 7JH (just behind Old Original Bay Horse)
closed Mon & Tue; 4-11 Wed & Thu; 12-11.30 Fri & Sat; 12-9 Sun (01204) 692976 thebrewerybar.co.uk
7 changing beers (sourced locally; often Blackedge)
Upstairs bar serving seven changing cask beers from the award-winning Blackedge Brewery plus a range of real ciders. Converted from a former industrial premises and retaining some original features, comfortable settees and barrel tables with stools are now spread throughout a large drinking area. Generous food platters made from local ingredients are available. The brewery is visible downstairs through large glass windows as you enter. The toilets are on the ground floor and no lift is available. P

Crown

1 Chorley New Road, BL6 7QJ (on B6226, 200yds from A673)
11-11 (midnight Fri & Sat); 12-11.30 Sun 07827 850221
Joseph Holt Mild, IPA, Bitter, Two Hoots; 4 changing beers (sourced locally; often Blackedge, Bootleg)
A spacious, comfortable and popular landmark pub whose multi-room layout provides a home to many community activities. The separate pool and games room with its own bar hosts darts, dominoes and pool teams. Elsewhere are quiet drinking areas and a large sports TV. There is live entertainment on Saturday or Sunday evenings and home-cooked food is served every day. The Crown's location attracts outdoor enthusiasts stopping for a pint after enjoying the beautiful countryside of the neighbouring West Pennine Moors. QP(125,575)

Hyde

Cheshire Cheese

407 Stockport Road, Gee Cross, SK14 5RY
4-midnight; 12-midnight Sat & Sun (0161) 637 0233
John Smith's Bitter; Sharp's Doom Bar; 3 changing beers (sourced nationally)
Comfortable and welcoming pub with a loyal group of regulars. Beer is the thing here – there is no food. Three constantly changing guests (all over 4% ABV) from all over the country complement the two regular ales. The pub is a member of the Ossett Beer Excellence Club so there is every chance of finding an unusual Ossett beer here. An outside seated area to the front of the pub has a retractable canopy to protect customers in wet weather. Children are welcome until 8pm.
Q

Cheshire Ring Hotel

72-74 Manchester Road, SK14 2BJ
4-11; 12-11 Sat; 12-10.30 Sun 07917 055629
6 changing beers
One of the oldest pubs in Hyde and comprehensively overhauled several years ago by Beartown Brewery, but now a free house. Seven handpumps offer a range of ales from micros near and far in addition to ciders, perries and continental beers. A selection of bottled beers is also stocked. Home-made curries are available on Thursday evening, Sunday is quiz night. Opening hours vary with the season and closing time may be earlier on Monday and Tuesday. P(201)

Joshua Bradley

Stockport Road, SK14 5EZ
11-11 (midnight Fri & Sat); 12-10.30 Sun
(0161) 406 6776 thejoshuabradley.co.uk
Hydes Original; 4 changing beers (often Hydes)
The Joshua Bradley opened following an extensive renovation of Bamford Hall and is named after a former local mill manager. Although this is a food-oriented establishment there is plenty of space for beer drinkers in the imposing interior of the former mansion house. Hydes beers are on permanent offer as well as rotating guest ales including those from the Hydes Beer Studio range.
P(330)

Sportsman Inn

57 Mottram Road, SK14 2NN (exit Morrisons car park)
12-midnight (0161) 368 5000
Rossendale Floral Dance, Glen Top Bitter, Ale, Halo Pale, Pitch Porter, Sunshine
A regular in this Guide, with a full range of Rossendale Brewery ales plus a mild from Thwaites and real cider on a regularly changing basis. The upstairs is a Cuban restaurant, including tapas and vegetarian options. The pub is home to pool teams and also hosts matches for the local chess team. This former CAMRA Pub of the Region is popular with locals and retains its character. The rear patio includes a covered and heated smoking area.
P(201,202)

Leigh

Bobbin

38A Leigh Road, WN7 1QR
closed Mon; 5-11 Tue & Wed; 2-11 Thu (midnight Fri & Sat); 2-11 Sun
4 changing beers (sourced locally)
The Bobbin takes its name from the nearby sewing shop where it was originally established. It is a reasonably sized micropub comprising one room with a central bar and comfortable seating. Prices are competitive. The beers are generally from regional microbreweries, with up to four on offer at any one time, and a real cider is available.
Q

George & Dragon

7 King Street, WN7 4LP

11-11 (midnight Fri & Sat); 12-11 Sun ☎ (01942) 605214

2 changing beers (sourced regionally) H

A pub with a Tudor façade in the centre of Leigh near the bus station. The smartly furnished interior is divided into two areas – the upper part is mainly for drinking while the lower level has plenty of seating. There are many TV screens showing live rugby, horse racing and football, and there is a large outdoor seating area to the rear. Please note that children are not allowed. ❀♿P🚌

Levenshulme

Blue Bell 🏆

170 Barlow Road, M19 3HF (just to E of Cromwell Rd jct)

12-11 (10.30 Sun) ☎ (0161) 224 1723

Samuel Smith Old Brewery Bitter H

Smart Smith's house, which underwent a thorough and classy refurbishment around 2006. On the right is a spacious vault, and to the left are three further rooms – a large parquet-floored lounge that wraps itself around the bar counter, a smaller carpeted lounge and a snug. The pub is truly at the heart of the local area and is home to a variety of groups raising funds for community improvement projects. Regular events include a quiz night, hoy bingo and a knitting club. ❀(≉P🚌

Fred's Ale House ✔

843 Stockport Road, M19 3PW (opp Albert Rd)

4-midnight (11 Tue & Wed); 12-midnight Sat; 12-11 Sun ☎ (0161) 221 0297

Timothy Taylor Landlord; Wainwright; 4 changing beers (sourced regionally; often Blackjack) H

Set over three floors, this is part-bar, part-coffee shop, and art gallery. The neat yet narrow interior has the stylish bar set to the left, its size dictating that it is mostly standing room only on the ground floor apart from some seats at the front and rear. The spartan basement is a large drinking area-cum-gallery space, and can accommodate live gigs and acoustic acts. The upstairs lounge exudes warmth and intimacy with comfortable leather sofas and mood music. ❀()♿≉🍎🚌

Littleborough

Red Lion L

6 Halifax Road, OL15 0HB

2-midnight; 12.30-1am Fri & Sat; 1-midnight Sun ☎ (01706) 378195

JW Lees Bitter; Timothy Taylor Landlord; house beer (by Robinsons); changing beers (often Robinsons) H

Detached stone-built pub, nestling between the railway and canal, yet far older than both. There are four distinct rooms, each different in character. The main room is large and homely, the adjacent snug has comfortable high-backed chairs, and the final two rooms are for games and TV sport. Up to six guest beers supplement the two regulars and the house beer from Robinsons, while traditional ciders come from Thatchers and Westons. Quiz night is Tuesday. Happy hour is 2-7 Monday to Friday, 2-5 Saturday and Sunday, when beer is 40p off. Q♿≉♣🍎P🚌🐾

White House L

Blackstone Edge, Halifax Road, OL15 0LG

12-3, 6.30-midnight; 11-11 Sun ☎ (01706) 378456

thewhitehousepub.co.uk

Theakston Best Bitter; 3 changing beers H

The White House is situated where the Pennine Way crosses the A58 between Rochdale and Halifax. Built in 1691 as the Coach & Horses, the building is 1,300ft above sea level, giving panoramic views of the moors and valley below. It has two rooms, both with log fires. A family-run establishment for 30 years, it offers a warm and friendly welcome to all including walkers. Excellent food is served, all day on Sunday. There is a bus stop on the Rochdale to Halifax route outside the front door. Q❀()♿▲P🚌(X58)

Lowton

Travellers Rest ✔

443 Newton Road, WA3 1NZ

12-11 (10.30 Mon; midnight Fri & Sat); 12-10.30 Sun ☎ (01925) 293222 travellersrestlowton.com

Theakston Best Bitter; Wainwright; 2 changing beers H

Traditionally furnished pub/restaurant between Lowton and Newton-le-Willows. The Travellers Rest has a number of seating areas and a separate restaurant. There is also a bar area to the right as you enter for customers who just prefer to drink, with ales from Thwaites and Theakston. Outside there is a large garden and car park. A private room is available to hire for special occasions. Q❀()♿P🚌(34)🐾

Lydgate

White Hart Inn ✔

51 Stockport Road, OL4 4JJ

12-midnight (11 Sun) ☎ (01457) 872566

thewhitehart.co.uk

JW Lees Bitter; Timothy Taylor Golden Best, Boltmaker; 3 changing beers (often Ossett) H

A true free house in a classic stone building dating from 1788, commanding impressive views over the surrounding hills and Greater Manchester. The multi-room layout has log-burning stoves in the refurbished bar area and brasserie, plus a restaurant, function rooms and guest accommodation. Quality food is served daily in the pub and separate brasserie from an award-winning kitchen. Three regular handpulled beers are supplemented by three guests, including one from Ossett. The pub hosts a variety of events including themed dinners and wine tastings. Q❀🛏()♿P🚌(180,184)🐾

Manchester: City Centre

Angel

6 Angel Street, M4 4BQ (off Rochdale Rd)

12-midnight ☎ (0161) 833 4786

theangelmanchester.com

House beer (by Howard Town); 9 changing beers (sourced nationally) H

On what has become a busy junction on the outskirts of the Northern Quarter, the Angel prides itself on providing a full range of ales. The house ale, Angel, is an exclusive brewed by Howard Town. There are usually two ciders on handpump or in a box. Food is served both in the bar and in the upstairs restaurant when not being used for functions.

❀()≉(Victoria)🚊(Shudehill)🍎🚌🐾

Brink 🏆

65 Bridge Street, M3 3BQ
4-11 Mon (midnight Tue); 12-midnight Wed & Thu (1am Fri & Sat); 4-11 Sun ☎ (0161) 834 6346 🌐 brinkmcr.co.uk
5 changing beers (sourced locally)
This cosy single-room basement bar sets out to provide local ale for customers who enjoy good beer and good conversation. The bar boasts several changing cask and craft keg beers, all brewed within a 25-mile radius of nearby St Ann's Church. Up to four ciders from Dunham Press Cider are available. Local CAMRA Pub of the Year 2017.
(Salford Central)(St Peters Sq)

Café Beermoth

40A Spring Gardens, M2 1EN (entrance is on Brown St)
12-11.30 (12.30am Fri & Sat); 12-11 Sun
☎ (0161) 835 2049 🌐 beermoth.co.uk
7 changing beers (sourced nationally)
A modern bar situated in the heart of the city, just off the main shopping street. Hops overhang the bar, which boasts seven different cask beers and 10 keg fonts dispensing both British and international beers. Tap takeovers feature on occasion. A mezzanine floor provides extra space when busy below. There is an impressive display of bottles for sale, many using wild yeast, to the left of the glass-fronted cellar behind the bar area.
(Market St)

Cask

29 Liverpool Road, M3 4NQ
12-11 (midnight Fri & Sat); 12-10.30 Sun
☎ (0161) 819 2527
4 changing beers (sourced regionally; often Elland, Pictish)
In the heart of Castlefield, this deceptively deep pub holds a few gems. With beer on four handpumps, it usually offers a good range of flavours, including a dark. The selection of international beers is particularly impressive, both on fonts and in bottles. Although no food is provided, customers are permitted to bring their own, including takeouts from the excellent chippy next door.
(Deansgate)(Deansgate/Castlefield)

City Arms ✔

46-48 Kennedy Street, M2 4BQ (near town hall, next to Waterhouse pub)
12-11 (midnight Fri & Sat); 12-8 Sun ☎ (0161) 236 4610
Brightside Odin; Moorhouse's Pride of Pendle; Robinsons Dizzy Blonde; Titanic Plum Porter; 4 changing beers (sourced regionally)
A compact multi award-winning pub with two traditional rooms and many original features. The room facing the street contains the bar and is fairly basic with a dartboard; a smarter and cosier room is available at the back. Eight handpumps offer a full range of beer styles in excellent condition. Lunchtime food is served Monday to Friday only.
(Oxford Rd)(St Peters Sq)

Crown & Kettle

2 Oldham Road, M4 5FE (corner Great Ancoats St)
12-11 (midnight Fri & Sat); 12-10.30 Sun
☎ (0161) 236 2923
8 changing beers (sourced nationally)
This Grade II listed street-corner building has a large drinking area in front of the bar along with a small vault and a snug at the rear. The high ornate ceiling in the main bar is well worth seeing. Thursday is open mic and weekends occasionally feature live music. Beers from far and wide are served from the eight handpumps. There are regular tap takeovers and occasional beer festivals. Hot pies are available.
(Victoria)(Shudehill)

Gas Lamp

50A Bridge Street, M3 3BW
4-midnight Mon & Tue; 12-midnight Wed (1am Thu; 2am Fri & Sat); 12-midnight Sun ☎ (0161) 478 1224
🌐 thegaslamp.co.uk
4 changing beers (sourced nationally; often Pomona Island, Squawk, Track)
The Gas Lamp is an interesting pub. Housed in the former Manchester and Salford Children's Mission, it has an impressive frontage but the small doorway that leads down to the subterranean bar can easily be missed. The main bar area has Victorian glazed-brick walls and wooden flooring. A narrow passageway leads to a cosy back room. Quiet conversation prevails. The pub now has its own brewery in nearby Salford, Pomona Island.
(Salford Central)(St Peters Sq)

Grey Horse ✔

80 Portland Street, M1 4QX (jct Princess St)
11-midnight (1am Fri & Sat); 12-midnight Sun
☎ (0161) 228 2595
Hydes Old Indie, Original; 3 changing beers (sourced nationally)
Entered by steps from the street, this is a traditional single-roomed wood-floored pub set in the city centre on the edge of Chinatown. The fine and friendly Grey Horse is popular with locals and visitors, many from across Europe. It can get busy on match days for both Manchester teams. As well as the regular beers there are usually two from Hydes Beer Studio and a guest ale. There is 50p off cask ale on Monday.
(Oxford Rd)(St Peters Sq)(1,3)

Knott Bar

374 Deansgate, M3 4LY
12-11.30 (midnight Thu; 12.30am Fri & Sat)
☎ (0161) 839 9229 🌐 knottbar.co.uk
8 changing beers (sourced nationally; often Wander Beyond)
An award-winning stalwart of the Manchester beer scene, the Knott has had a major redecoration, losing the much-loved poster wall but creating a clean, fresh canvas. The multiple fonts have been relocated to a simple rear wall leaving the eight handpumps up front and proud. Regular beers are from Wander Beyond, invariably in a range of styles and strengths. Cider is served on handpump or from a box. The friendly staff will assist in your deliberations, if the need arises.
(Deansgate)(Deansgate/Castlefield)

Lass o' Gowrie ✔

36 Charles Street, M1 7DB (off Princess St)
12-midnight (1am Thu-Sat) ☎ (0161) 273 5822
🌐 thelassogowrie.com
Hardys & Hansons Olde Trip; Morland Old Speckled Hen; house beer (by Greene King); 5 changing beers (sourced locally)
This former Threlfall's house is a splendid Victorian glazed-tile building and is popular with students in term time. There is a snug tucked away for small informal gatherings and a larger function room upstairs. A beer bat can be ordered – three third-pints for the price of a pint. Quiz night is Thursday.

A former National Pub of the Year in John Smith's Great British Pub Awards. It is the site of Manchester's first pissoir, evidently depositing into the Medlock!
♨◐≹(Oxford Rd)⍾(St Peters Sq)♣⊟(50,147)ᯤ

Marble Arch Inn ★

73 Rochdale Road, Collyhurst, M4 4HY (corner Gould St)
⚙ 12-11 (midnight Fri & Sat) ☎ (0161) 832 5914
Marble Pint, Manchester Bitter, Lagonda IPA; 6 changing beers (sourced nationally; often Marble) Ⓗ
Home of Marble beers, this famous real ale pub is a 10-minute walk from the city centre. It serves Marble beers alongside two guests plus craft keg and bottled beers. The listed pub has many interesting features, with a mosaic sloping floor leading you inexorably to the bar and glazed-tile walls adding to the splendour of the interior. There is a plainer back room used as a restaurant, and a beer yard at the rear.
Q♨❀◐◗≹(Victoria)⍾(Shudehill)●⊟🐾ᯤ

Molly House

20 Richmond Street, M1 3NB (jct Sackville St)
⚙ 12-midnight (1am Wed & Thu; 2am Fri & Sat)
☎ (0161) 237 9329 🌐 themollyhouse.com
6 changing beers (sourced regionally) Ⓗ
A former tailor's shop behind Canal Street, opened as a bar and café in 2010. The name derives from the London molly houses of the Victorian era. On two levels, the decor is described as post-Victorian decadent shabby chic. The Tea Room has the cask bar. Upstairs is the Bordello and a sheltered outdoor terrace. The beer range specialises in ales from local brewers in a range of styles. Twenty different teas, specialist coffees and high-end spirits are also available.
❀◐◗≹(Piccadilly)⍾(Piccadilly Gardens)♣⊟(1,3)

Paramount ✔

33-35 Oxford Street, M1 4BH (jct Portland St)
⚙ 7am-midnight (1am Fri & Sat) ☎ (0161) 233 1820
Sharp's Doom Bar; 8 changing beers (sourced nationally; often Phoenix, Robinsons) Ⓗ
Named because of its location in Manchester's old theatre-land, old photos of now closed theatres and cinemas adorn the walls. This large and extremely popular Wetherspoon pub has a lively yet always controlled atmosphere. However, what really sets it apart is the enthusiasm of the team for the wide and interesting range of cask beers on offer. Changing guest ales are on the left set of handpumps and longer-term ales on the right.
♨◐◗♿≹(Oxford Rd)⍾(St Peters Sq)●⊟(1,3)ᯤ

Peveril of the Peak ★

127 Great Bridgewater Street, M1 5JQ
⚙ 12-11 (11.30 Thu; midnight Fri & Sat); 12-10.30 Sun
☎ (0161) 236 6364
Timothy Taylor Landlord; Titanic Plum Porter; 2 changing beers (often Brightside) Ⓗ
The Pev is a famous Manchester institution, still run by the city's longest-serving landlady. A splendid etched mirror hangs over the fireplace in the snug, commemorating the first 40 years of her tenure. The pub stands as a small triangular island of civilised drinking, shorn of the rest of the original terrace and surrounded by much taller office and apartment blocks. It is Grade II listed and has a glorious green-tiled exterior with more impressive tiling inside.
Q❀≹(Oxford Rd)⍾(St Peters Sq)♣⊟🐾ᯤ

Piccadilly Tap

8 Gateway House, Piccadilly Station Approach, M1 2GH (up station approach, off London Rd)
⚙ 12-11 Mon-Wed; 11-midnight Thu-Sat; 12-10 Sun
☎ (0161) 393 4168 🌐 piccadillytap.com
6 changing beers (sourced nationally; often Bristol Beer Factory, Marble, Moor Beer) Ⓗ
Opened in 2015 in a former shop unit in the iconic Gateway House, the bar is on the ground floor and features a standing room area with tall tables; upstairs is a seating area, table football and toilets. The six real ales and a number of craft ales are dispensed from taps at the back. A large beer and price list is on the wall to the right of the bar. Very handy for the trains.
♨❀≹(Piccadilly)⍾(Piccadilly)♣●⊟🐾ᯤ

Port Street Beer House

39-41 Port Street, M1 2EQ (opp Brewer St)
⚙ 4-midnight; 2-midnight Fri; 12-1am Sat; 12-midnight Sun
☎ (0161) 237 9949 🌐 portstreetbeerhouse.co.uk
7 changing beers (sourced nationally) Ⓗ
Seven cask beers are served here from some of the finest breweries in the British Isles, alongside a good range of contrasting worldwide keg beers, bottles and cans. With knowledgeable staff and regular tap takeovers, this is certainly one of the best beer emporiums in the city and a treat for beer novices and connoisseurs. Seating is also available upstairs, to the front and to the rear of the building in a small yard.
♨❀≹(Piccadilly)⍾(Piccadilly Gardens)
♣●⊟🐾ᯤ

Smithfield Market Tavern

37 Swan Street, Manchester, M4 5JZ (corner Coop St)
⚙ 4-11 Mon; 2-midnight; 12-midnight Sat; 12-11 Sun
6 changing beers (sourced nationally) Ⓗ
From old origins to new, Blackjack Brewery has established the Smithfield as a formidable presence on any beer connoisseur's radar. It offers a comprehensive range of six quality cask beers from breweries both local and far away, usually two from Blackjack, 10 keg taps and a good selection of bottles in the fridge. There are traditional old-fashioned pub games that are not out of place in this establishment. Music is hosted on Sunday afternoon.
≹(Victoria)⍾(Shudehill)♣●⊟🐾ᯤ

Marple

Beer Traders

113 Stockport Road, SK6 6AF
⚙ closed Mon; 3.30-11 Tue-Thu; 1.30-11 Fri & Sat; 1.30-10.30 Sun ☎ (0161) 427 0667 🌐 marplebeertraders.com
3 changing beers (sourced locally) Ⓗ
An interesting innovation for the area in that the business combines a bottle shop with a micropub, based in a converted shop premises. Three handpulls serve changing beers, normally from local micros. The aim is to have one traditional bitter, one darker beer and something hoppy. Three bag-in-box ciders are also available. Live music often features on Saturday evening. Opening times can vary – it may be worth checking prior to a visit. ❀≹●⊟🐾

Samuel Oldknow

22 Market Street, SK6 7AD
⚙ 1-10.30 (11 Fri); 11-11 Sat; 12-10 Sun ☎ 07766 301627

5 changing beers (sourced locally; often Brightside, Outstanding) Ⓗ
Named after a local mill owner who was responsible for much of the development of Marple and Mellor some 200 years ago, this is a somewhat quirky two-level bar in a converted shop. Six vintage-style handpulls dispense five changing real ales plus a real cider. The regular beers are from Brightside and Outstanding, complemented by guests from local micros. A range of bottled beers is also available to take away or to drink on the premises. Opening hours are subject to change. Q

Marple Bridge

Norfolk Arms

2 Town Street, SK6 5DS
12-11 (10.30 Sun) ☎ (0161) 427 8090
thenorfolkarms.co.uk
4 changing beers (sourced regionally; often Blackjack, Green Mill) Ⓗ
A recently refurbished stone-built pub in an attractive setting next to the Goyt river bridge. Comfortably furnished, it attracts a wide-ranging clientele by catering for all tastes. With four real ales usually from micros, the beer range is a good addition to the choice in the area. The atmosphere is warm and friendly, with good-value food available. Live music plays on Thursday and occasional beer festivals are held in the summer. Well served by public transport.
Q

Mellor

Oddfellows Arms

73 Moor End Road, SK6 5PT
closed Mon; 12-11 ☎ (0161) 449 7826
oddfellowsmellor.com
Marston's Pedigree; 3 changing beers (sourced regionally) Ⓗ
This elegant stone-built pub is tucked away in a dip in the road in the old part of the village. Inside, the smart but traditional ambience is enhanced by beams and flagged floors, with blazing real fires in winter. Guest beers are often sourced from micros such as Marble, Howard Town and Thornbridge. Sought-after food comes from a realistic menu with a gourmet twist. The 375 bus service passes the door but runs only infrequently.
P (375)

Middleton

Lancashire Fold

77 Kirkway, M24 1EP
12-11 ☎ (0161) 643 4198 lancashirefold.co.uk
JW Lees Manchester Pale Ale, Bitter; 1 changing beer (sourced locally; often JW Lees) Ⓗ
Built by Lees in 1961 in the estate style, the Fold is popular and busy. The pub boasts a large lounge, a small function room, a separate public bar and a recently refurbished outside drinking area. Seasonal beers are always available and occasionally other beers from the Lees range. Live football on screen is a big attraction and there is live music once a month. Food is home-cooked and hearty and parties can be catered for. Buses to Middleton and Oldham pass the pub for onward travel. P (415)

Ring o' Bells

St Leonards Square, M24 6DJ
5-midnight; 12-1am Fri & Sat; 12-11 Sun
☎ (0161) 654 9245
JW Lees Manchester Pale Ale, Bitter; 2 changing beers (sourced locally; often JW Lees) Ⓗ
A pub since 1831, the Ringers enjoys a fine elevated location opposite the medieval parish church within the conservation area above Jubilee Park. Visitors can enjoy stunning views across to Oldham and beyond, especially at night. Very much community focused, the pub hosts a unique Pace Egg play on Easter Monday and a Maypole event on the May bank holiday Monday. Weekly quizzes and occasional live music are well attended. There is an attractive beer garden to the rear and a covered smoking area. P (17)

Tandle Hill Tavern

14 Thornham Lane, M24 2SD (1 mile on unmetalled road from either A664 or A627)
closed Mon & Tue; 5-10 Wed & Thu (11 Fri); 12-10.30 Sat & Sun ☎ (0161) 376 4492
JW Lees Bitter; house beer (by JW Lees); 1 changing beer (sourced locally; often JW Lees) Ⓗ
A one-mile walk from either end of an unmade, potholed lane rewards the drinker with a neat little pub nestling among a number of farms. Popular with walkers, farmers and locals, dogs are welcome. There is a main bar area and a separate quiet side room, while a walled rear beer garden and benches to the front and side provide outdoor seating. Food is limited to toasties. The house beer, Bumpy Lane, is dry-hopped Lees Bitter. In adverse weather, or in winter, phone ahead to check opening times. Q

Milnrow

Waggon Inn

35 Butterworth Hall, OL16 3PE
12-11 (midnight Fri & Sat) ☎ (01706) 648313
Banks's Amber Ale; 2 changing beers Ⓗ
Built in 1782, this place, locally known as the Back Waggon, still retains many original features including mullioned windows. The building has been sympathetically refurbished but maintains a traditional ambience. An excellent food menu features daily specials, tapas and a Sunday roast, complemented by three beers from Marston's, two of which change on a monthly basis. Awarded Marston's National Pub of the Year in 2017, a warm welcome is always assured. Within easy walking distance of Milnrow's Metrolink stop and local bus services. P

Monton

Malt Dog

169 Monton Road, M30 9GS (opp Hawthorne Avenue)
5 (4 Wed & Thu; 1 Fri & Sat)-11; 1-10 Sun
☎ 07541 553646 maltdog.com
3 changing beers (sourced locally; often Blackjack, Brightside, Manchester) Ⓗ
A small but friendly pub converted from an old shop. The ground floor is open plan and upstairs is a spacious lounge which hosts live music twice a week, mainly jazz. A range of mostly German and Belgian draught beers is available plus a good number of bottled beers. A popular and thriving part of the Monton village scene. Local CAMRA Pub of the Year in 2017. Q

Mossley

Church Inn

82 Stockport Road, OL5 0RF
5 (4 Thu)-midnight; 4-1am Fri & Sat; 2-midnight Sun
4 changing beers (often Cross Bay, Greenfield) H
This corner terrace pub on the A670 takes its name from the nearby St John's Church. Now a free house, the traditional stone-built local has a comfortable lounge and bar that also serves the separate games room. Four handpumps dispense regularly changing cask beers. The verandah at the rear provides a commanding view down the Tame Valley. P(353)

Fleece

53 Stamford Street, OL5 0LN
12-midnight (1am Fri & Sat) ☎ (01457) 835487
House beer (by Tatton); 6 changing beers (sourced nationally; often Brightside, Grafton, Titanic) H
The Fleece is in Brookbottom, less than half a mile from the station, but much higher up. You will deserve a pint after the climb (or you could catch the bus). In 1890 the inn could accommodate three travellers, feed up to 50 and stable one horse. Today the visitor will find a tidy pub with a small vault area, an airy back room and a lounge. Cider or perry is always available. Dogs are welcome but horses perhaps less so.

Oldham

Ashton Arms

28-30 Clegg Street, OL1 1PL (opp Odeon cinema complex)
11.30-11 (11.30 Fri & Sat); 11.30-8.30 Sun
☎ (0161) 630 9709
6 changing beers (often Millstone, Pictish, Riverhead) H
Based across from the new town-centre cinema complex, this ever-popular free house is also just 100 yards from the Oldham Central Metrolink tram stop. The pub has an excellent range of four to six rotating beers, mainly LocAles and from local micros, but also from further afield. Traditional cider or perry is permanently available. The fridges contain a good selection of Belgian and German bottled beers. Good-value food is served weekdays until 6pm (5pm Fri), with pork pies and sandwiches at the weekend.

Carrion Crow

271 Huddersfield Road, OL4 2RJ
12-midnight ☎ (0161) 633 4490
6 changing beers (often Banks's, Jennings, Marston's) H
Originally a coaching inn dating from 1796 and refurbished in 2017, the Crow is an attractive, open-plan, popular pub. Six handpumps serve a range of cask ales from Marston's extended stable. Reasonably priced pub food is available. A community local, it hosts crib, darts, dominoes, football and quiz teams. All cask ales are discounted after 6pm on Monday. Thursday is quiz night followed by a light supper. There is live music at the weekend and regular beer festivals.
P(350)

Patricroft

Queen's Arms

Green Lane, M30 0SH (next to railway station, up ramp opp James Nasmyth Way)
7-11; 5-11 Fri; 12-midnight Sat; 12-11 Sun
☎ (0161) 789 2019
Thwaites Original; 1 changing beer (sourced nationally) H
The pub was built in 1828 for the arrival of the Liverpool & Manchester Railway in 1830. Originally named the Patricroft Tavern until 1857, the name changed after Queen Victoria's second visit to Salford. It has a vault on the left as you enter, a tiny snug to the right and a large lounge at the rear. It has twice won the local CAMRA branch Neil Richardson award for best-preserved traditional pub. QP(67,100)

Prestwich

Church Inn

40 Church Lane, M25 1AJ (nr St Mary's church)
12-midnight (11.30 Sun) ☎ (0161) 798 6727
156513.mrsite.com
Bombardier; Brightside Odin; 2 changing beers H
This venue offers up to four real ales including local beers, and provides lunchtime meals. There are rooms off the main bar area if you want a quiet drink, and a beer garden to the rear. An upstairs meeting room is used by local groups and is available to hire. A folk night is held every Friday and an open jam session on Tuesday evening. There are five en-suite bedrooms and car parking at the front. QP

Ramsbottom

Irwell Works Brewery Tap

Irwell Street, BL0 9YQ
closed Mon; 12-11 Tue-Thu (midnight Fri); 11-midnight Sat; 11-11 Sun ☎ (01706) 825019 irwellworksbrewery.co.uk
Irwell Works Tin Plate, Copper Plate, Costa Del Salford, Iron Plate; 4 changing beers (often Irwell Works) H
This small local is situated on the first floor above the Irwell Works Brewery, with a balcony for outside drinking. A range of Irwell's beers is served. The brewery prides itself on the brewing and sale of traditional beers made with predominantly English hops and barley. Food is served Friday to Sunday 12-5.30pm. The bar is decorated with old photographs of the Ramsbottom area. The pub is a short walk from the East Lancashire Railway, the local preserved railway. (472,474)

Major

158 Bolton Street, BL0 9JA
12-midnight ☎ (01706) 826777
Bank Top Flat Cap; 4 changing beers H
A regular in the Guide, this stone-built pub is on the main road into Ramsbottom. The building has two rooms – a central bar with TV and a main lounge featuring a large logburner. One regular and four guest beers are on handpump and real cider is available – Westons Old Rosie and Rosie's Pig. Good-value food is served. Live music features on the last Friday of each month.
P(472,474)

Rochdale

Baum

35 Toad Lane, OL12 0NU
11.30-11 (midnight Fri & Sat); 11.30-10.30 Sun
☎ (01706) 352186 thebaum.co.uk

7 changing beers Ⓗ
Situated in the Toad Lane conservation area, next to the Rochdale Pioneers Museum, the Baum is within easy reach of the tram and bus interchange. It is a former CAMRA National Pub of the Year, with a traditional frontage and interior, together with a conservatory and beer garden at the rear. Seven changing cask beers and a traditional cider are served, plus a wide selection of bottled beers and continental lagers. Good food matches the well-kept beers and is reasonably priced.

Flying Horse Hotel

37 Packer Street, OL16 1NJ
11.30-11 (1am Thu); 1.30-2am Fri; 10-2am Sat; 10-1am Sun ☎ (01706) 646412 theflyinghorsehotel.co.uk
Changing beers (sourced locally; often Phoenix, Pictish, Serious) Ⓗ
An impressive Edwardian stone free house situated in the town hall square. Built in 1691 and rebuilt in 1926, the building retains many original features including log fires. There is also accommodation, a function room for hire and a heated smokers' area outside. Ten cask ales are sold alongside four real ciders. Live music plays on Thursday, Friday and Saturday and live sport is screened. The home-made food menu features meat from the local butcher and pies made on the premises. Local CAMRA Pub of the Year in 2017.
P

Oxford

662 Whitworth Road, OL12 0TB
12-11 (10 Mon; midnight Fri & Sat); 12-10 Sun ☎ (01706) 345709 theoxfordpub.com
Wainwright; 3 changing beers (sourced nationally) Ⓗ
The Oxford is a well-patronised stone-built pub standing on the A671 Rochdale to Burnley road. Internally, the layout is open plan in two areas, namely for dining and drinking, although food is also served in the bar area. Good well-presented meals are available daily, cooked to order. Four real ales are on handpump – Wainwright is a permanent beer, with the other changing ales sourced from near and far. The beer garden at the rear has an excellent view of the nearby moors.
P (486)

Regal Moon

The Butts, OL16 1HB
9am-midnight (1am Fri & Sat) ☎ (01706) 657434
Elland 1872 Porter; Hawkshead Windermere Pale; Moorhouse's Blond Witch; Ossett Silver King; Ruddles Best Bitter; changing beers Ⓗ
A large and imposing former cinema in the town centre, refurbished after the 2015 Boxing Day flood. Thankfully, the mannequin organist remains on his perch above the bar. This is regularly the top-selling real ale establishment in the Wetherspoon estate, dispensing a wide variety of ales from local and West Yorkshire microbreweries. Five ciders are available, one from Westons, plus rotating guests. The open-plan interior splits into discrete drinking areas. The rear patio is for smokers. Close to the tram and bus interchange.
Q

Romiley

Jake's Ale House

27 Compstall Road, SK6 4BT
12.30-10 (11 Fri & Sat); 12.30-10.30 Sun ☎ 07927 076941
5 changing beers (sourced locally; often Poynton) Ⓗ
Romiley's first micropub, formerly a shop, has established itself in just over a year. The small front bar area has a relaxed atmosphere and there is a smaller room at the rear. The changing range of beers, often from local micros, is a welcome addition to the local scene. The pub is close to the railway station and good bus routes, and the Peak Forest Canal is a short walk away. Opening hours may vary. Q

Royton

Puckersley Inn

22 Narrowgate Brow, OL2 6YD (off A671 via Dogford Rd and Fir Lane)
12-midnight (1am Fri & Sat) ☎ (0161) 652 2834
JW Lees Supernova, Manchester Pale Ale, Bitter; 1 changing beer (sourced locally; often JW Lees) Ⓗ
This welcoming JW Lees local is a detached, stone-fronted pub situated on the edge of the green belt, with panoramic views over Royton, Shaw and Oldham. The building has a traditional vault, a comfortable lounge and a dining extension where children are welcome. An excellent range of well-prepared meals is served lunchtimes and evenings until 9pm (8pm Sun). Cosy corners provide plenty of space to chat and chill out over a pint or two. A garden area is available for warmer weather.
P (408)

Rusholme

Ford Madox Brown

Unit 1 Wilmslow Park, Wilmslow Road, M14 5FT (jct Hathersage Rd)
8am-midnight ☎ (0161) 256 6660
Greene King Abbot; Ruddles Best Bitter; Sharp's Doom Bar; house beer (by Hafod); 5 changing beers (sourced nationally) Ⓗ
This modern Wetherspoon pub is paradoxically named after the eminent Victorian Pre-Raphaelite painter (he lived nearby in Victoria Park), and built on the site of the old Rusholme Hall. It is handy for the curry mile, MRI hospital, Whitworth Gallery and university; although many of the clientele are students, it attracts a real cross-section of people. Although an open-plan pub, it has a warmer feeling than you might expect, the community feel enhanced by brewery visits and local events.
Q

Sale

JP Joule

2A Northenden Road, M33 3BR
8am-midnight (1am Fri & Sat) ☎ (0161) 962 9889
Greene King Abbot; Ruddles Best Bitter; Sharp's Doom Bar; 6 changing beers (sourced nationally; often Peerless, Phoenix, Weetwood) Ⓗ
Named after the famous physicist who was a resident of Sale for a time, this popular Wetherspoon pub is close to the tram station and on several bus routes. Set on two floors, with a bar on each, the pub offers a total of 13 handpumps featuring nine real ales (four are duplicated upstairs). Six beers are constantly changing and sourced nationally. Real ale and cider and perry festivals are held twice a year. Q

Salford

Eagle Inn

18 Collier Street, M3 7DW (opp Rolla St)
3-11 (1am Fri); 1-1am Sat; 1-11 Sun (0161) 819 5002
eagleinn.info
Bootleg Urban Fox; Joseph Holt Bitter, Two Hoots; 2 changing beers (sourced locally)
This hidden gem of a traditional back-street boozer is known to locals as the Lamp Oil. A Grade II listed building dating from 1902, there is a fine terracotta plaque of an eagle above the door – for years this was the only pub sign. There are three small rooms off a central corridor with a central bar. The attached cottage next door has been converted into a live music venue. Handy for Manchester Arena. Q (Central)

New Oxford

11 Bexley Square, M3 6DB (corner of Browning St)
12-midnight (0161) 832 7082 thenewoxford.com
16 changing beers (sourced regionally)
Situated just off the A6, this well-regarded pub attracts regulars as well as visitors from far afield. A multiple CAMRA award winner, it has 16 real ale and three real cider handpumps on a central bar that serves two rooms. Beers are sourced from around the region and change regularly. The pub also keeps a wide range of Belgian bottled beers. Occasional beer festivals are held.
(Central)

Salford Arms Hotel

146 Chapel Street, M3 6AF (corner Bloom St)
12-11.30 (1.30am Fri & Sat); 12-11 Sun
(0161) 288 8883 salfordarmshotel.co.uk
6 changing beers (sourced regionally)
The pub is on the main A6 into Manchester, over the road from Salford Central railway station and on major bus routes. With a pool table and a further side room creating extra space, this is a comfortable and welcoming establishment. A changing variety of ales is offered as well as a house beer by the local Blackjack Brewery. Lunchtime and evening meals are served. Accommodation is available in nine rooms.
(Central)

Stalybridge

Bridge Beers

55 Melbourne Street, SK15 2JJ
12-7 (9 Thu; 10 Fri & Sat); closed Sun & Mon
07948 617145 bridgebeers.co.uk
4 changing beers (sourced locally)
A combined micropub and bottle shop on the main pedestrianised shopping street in Stalybridge. A small entrance area leads to the bar which sits in front of a row of stillaged casks, of which four are generally in use. Beers are constantly changing and all locally sourced. The bottle display is opposite. Upstairs is a comfortable lounge. Last entry is one hour before closing. Q

Society Rooms

49-51 Grosvenor Street, SK15 2JN
8am-midnight (1am Fri & Sat) (0161) 338 9740
Greene King Abbot; Ruddles Best Bitter; Sharp's Doom Bar; changing beers (sourced nationally)
This Wetherspoon pub is named after the former Co-op store premises it occupies within the town centre. It has a large main area and two elevated sections either side of the entrance. Enthusiastic management and a strong focus on real ales (on 10 handpumps) have made this a favourite destination for local drinkers. Beer-oriented events such as Meet the Brewer nights and beer requests by customers have helped to boost the pub's reputation. Real cider is always available.

Station Buffet Bar ★

Platform 4, Stalybridge Railway Station, Rassbottom Street, SK15 1RF (access from station Platform 4)
12-11 Mon; 11-11 (midnight Fri & Sat) (0161) 303 0007
Changing beers (sourced regionally)
One of the few Victorian station buffet bars remaining and well worth missing a train for. A sympathetic refurbishment has allowed expansion of the food menu which includes home-cooked meals. Nine handpumps dispense a variety of beers, most of which are locally sourced, plus at least one real cider or perry. A good range of bottled beers is also available. Events include live music and Meet the Brewer nights. Monday is quiz night. On the Transpennine Real Ale Trail.
Q P

Wharf Tavern

77 Caroline Street, SK15 1PD
12-2, 7-11.30; 12-midnight Fri & Sat; 12-10 Sun
(0161) 338 2662
Lancaster Bomber; Wainwright
Canalside pub occupying a triangular plot next to the Huddersfield Narrow Canal. Opened as a beer house in 1850, it was taken over by Gartsides Brewery in 1922 and the stained-glass windows recall that era. A free house since 1981, this is a comfortably furnished, cosy locals' pub. No food is available but the fish and chip shop next door is under the same ownership and its food can be brought in (Mon-Fri only). Opening hours may vary due to functions.

White House

1 Water Street, SK15 2AG
12-11.30 (1am Fri & Sat); 12-11 Sun (0161) 303 2154
Hydes Original; 5 changing beers
Previously the Laughing Cavalier, this popular pub, close to both bus and rail stations, is semi open plan but retains four distinct drinking areas. Up to five guest beers from micros and Hydes Beer Studio complement the regular Original. Up to three real ciders are offered. A popular live music venue, a folk night is held every Thursday and bands play most Fridays and Saturdays. Sunday is quiz night. Food is available noon-6pm on Sunday only.
P

Standish

Albion Ale House

12 High Street, WN6 0HL
4-7 Mon; 3-10 Tue & Wed (11 Thu); 2-midnight Fri & Sat; 2-9 Sun (01257) 367897 albionalehouse.co.uk.
8 changing beers
The first micropub in Standish, located in a former shop right on the High Street, now well established with a loyal clientele and voted local CAMRA Community Pub of the Year 2017/18. Five cask ales are normally on offer, sometimes more, always including one dark beer. Snacks are also usually available. There is occasional live music and the pub holds beer festivals.
Q (362,113)

Hoot Standish

34A High Street, WN6 0HL

closed Mon & Tue; 11-11 (midnight Fri & Sat); 11-10.30 Sun
(01257) 806262

7 changing beers (sourced nationally) H

This modern-styled café/bar, with interesting accent lighting, a slate-tiled floor and modest silent TVs with subtitles, opened in January 2016. Varying local real ales are served alongside speciality coffees and Prosecco, which makes this venue popular with all age groups. Light bites and sandwiches are also served, and it has a wood-burning stove. Q

Standish Unity Club

Cross Street, WN6 0HQ

7.30-11 (midnight Fri & Sat) (01257) 424007
standishunityclub.com

Sharp's Doom Bar; 4 changing beers H

In the centre of Standish but tucked away so a little tricky to find, this popular club offers five real ales including one dark beer, often Titanic Plum Porter. The club is divided in two – a large function room and a bar area including the games room plus a quieter drinking area. A frequent winner of local CAMRA Club of the Year and last year runner-up Regional Club of the Year.
QP(362,113)

Standish Lower Ground

Crooke Hall Inn

Crooke Road, WN6 8LR

12-11 (01942) 236088

11 changing beers H

Very much the hub of the community, this large, multi-roomed canalside pub resides in a picturesque location just outside Wigan. Popular with locals and visitors alike, dogs and children (up to 9pm) are welcome. Home-made food features locally sourced ingredients where possible. There is a separate cellar bar ideal for functions and a large beer garden outside. Local CAMRA Community Pub of the Year 2014-2016. P

Stockport

Bakers Vaults

Market Place, SK1 1ES (jct Vernon St)

12-11.30 (1.30am Fri & Sat); 12-10.30 Sun
(0161) 480 9448

Robinsons Unicorn, Dizzy Blonde, Trooper, Old Tom; Titanic Plum Porter; 4 changing beers (sourced nationally; often Robinsons) H

Grade II listed marketplace house with high ceilings and feature arch windows. These give the gin palace-style interior a wonderfully spacious feeling, further enhanced by the well-stocked bar centrally positioned towards the back of the room. A small lounge area with sofas is to the bar's rear, providing a welcome retreat from the hustle and bustle of the main bar area. Live weekend jazz and blues adds to the buzz and vibrancy of this bohemian setting.

Blossoms

2 Buxton Road, Heaviley, SK2 6NU (at A6/A5102 jct)

12 (3 Mon & Tue)-midnight; 11-midnight Sat & Sun
(0161) 222 4150

Robinsons Unicorn H**, Old Tom** G**, Dizzy Blonde, Trooper, Double Hop; 1 changing beer (often Robinsons)** H

An excellent local pub with a vault, front lounge and cosy snug around the central bar. It was given a makeover recently by owner Robinsons, and is now one of the brewery's Ale Shrine pubs, with a striking decor and an air of elegance. At the rear, the now disused cobbled street sports benches for outside drinking, while the former outside toilet is now the smoking area. The pub offers excellent service and a warm welcome, and is well worth a visit. QP

Hope Inn

118 Wellington Road North, Heaton Norris, SK4 2LL (to N of Belmont Way)

12-11 (midnight Fri & Sat) (0161) 637 6191
thehopestockport.co.uk

Fool Hardy Ales Rou Shou, Risky Blond, Reckless Danger, Rash Dash; Outstanding 3.9; 6 changing beers (sourced nationally; often Fool Hardy Ales) H

Transformed in 2013 from a dead duck to a multi-beer free house that was awarded local CAMRA Pub of the Year in 2014. Home to the Fool Hardy Ales microbrewery, it comprises two large rooms – to the right is the cask ale side where 11 handpumps dispense a mix of house-brewed beers and changing guests, to the left is a room dedicated to foreign/keg beers and real ciders. Enjoy the pinball machine, pool table and a variety of board games. QP

Magnet

51 Wellington Road North, Heaton Norris, SK4 1HJ (jct Duke St)

4-11; 12-11 Fri-Sun (0161) 429 6287
themagnetfreehouse.co.uk

Salopian Oracle; 13 changing beers (sourced nationally; often Tiny Rebel) H

Family-run, award-winning pub focusing on quality and choice. It offers 14 handpumped beers alongside up to 12 craft keg beers, plus a large range of foreign bottles. The in-house microbrewery produces seasonal ales. Digital beer boards display all the available beers. On the left is a bustling vault leading to a lower pool room and a series of other rooms. Outside, there is a twin-storey beer terrace with seating. An upstairs room opens at weekends. A former local CAMRA Pub of the Year. QP

Olde Vic

1 Chatham Street, Edgeley, SK3 9ED (jct Shaw Heath)

5-11 yeoldevic.pub/en

6 changing beers (sourced nationally) H

Saved from closure in 2015 by a community buyout, a gentle renovation is currently in progress. The interior resembles a licensed version of the Old Curiosity Shop, containing a huge array of bric-a-brac and memorabilia, all presided over by larger-than-life host Steve. Details of the six ever-changing guest beers are displayed on the 'pumpotron' TV screen. A real fire makes this a cosy haven in winter. Last entry is usually 10.30pm. A regular in this Guide. Q

Petersgate Tap

19A St Petersgate, SK1 1EB (jct Etchells St)

closed Mon; 12 (4 Tue; 2 Wed)-11; 1-8 Sun
07925 078426 petersgatetap.com

Hawkshead Windermere Pale; 5 changing beers (sourced regionally) H

Opened in 2016 in former betting shop premises, this family-run bar is a welcome sign of the regeneration of the town's Market Place. Set over

two floors, downstairs the style is fairly modern with a continental feel to the bar area. Recycled oak-topped tables and a mix of seating sit under interesting posters and breweriana on the walls. Monthly events include a pop-up kitchen, live music and poetry and prose evenings. Local CAMRA Cider Pub of the Year 2018.
Q❀♿≋●🚌(300)🐾📶

Railway

1 Avenue Street, Portwood, SK1 2BZ (jct Gt Portwood St A560)
⏲ 12-11 (10.30 Sun) ☎ (0161) 429 6062
Outstanding Blond; Pictish Brewers Gold; Rossendale Floral Dance, Pitch Porter, Sunshine, Ale; 6 changing beers (sourced nationally) Ⓗ
Bustling street-corner house showcasing Rossendale and other local micros plus guests. A changing mild and real ciders are always stocked, plus a wide selection of Belgian, German and other bottled beers. Occasional beer and cider festivals also take place. A bar billiards table is well used, and the outside yard is a summer suntrap. A local CAMRA Pub and Cider Pub of the Year on numerous occasions. Q❀♣●🚌🐾📶

Remedy Bar & Brewhouse

10-11 Market Place, SK1 1EW (jct Mealhouse Brow)
⏲ closed Mon; 12-11.30 ☎ (0161) 477 1842
🌐 remedybarandbrewhouse.co.uk
6 changing beers (sourced regionally; often Remedy) Ⓗ
Overlooking the historic Market Hall, with views of historic St Mary's Church, this is a simple but inspired conversion of two shop units into an atmospheric steampunk-style bar. The pristine in-house brewing equipment is sited behind a glazed wall, producing occasional brews. Weekends will often feature live music. Since opening in 2015, Remedy has been a significant addition to the regeneration of the marketplace and the pub scene in Stockport Old Town. 🐴◖♿≋●🚌(300)🐾📶

Stretford

Sip Club Ⓛ

164A Barton Road, M32 8DP
⏲ closed Mon; 6-11 Tue-Thu; 5-midnight Fri; 2-11.30 Sat; 2-8 Sun ☎ 07903 310125
2 changing beers (sourced locally) Ⓗ
A club only in name – this is actually a small bar above an estate agent. The main lounge has sofas and easy chairs resembling the front room of a house. The bar is at the rear with two handpumps serving a range of local cask beers, stillaged and cooled under the bar. Snacks include locally sourced cheeses and pork pies. The bar's many activities include a knitting club, a quiz night and live music on Tuesday. 🐴🚏♣●🚌🐾📶

Strines

Sportsman Ⓛ

105 Strines Road, SK6 7GE (2 miles out of Marple on B6101)
⏲ 12-11 ☎ (0161) 427 2888 🌐 the-sportsman-pub.co.uk
Phoenix Spotland Gold; 4 changing beers Ⓗ
Splendid white pub standing alone overlooking the Goyt Valley, popular both with local drinkers and diners. The comfortable lounge has large picture windows giving superb views over the wooded valley to the hills beyond. A monumental fireplace accommodates a log fire in winter. There is a separate taproom. Five guest beers, mainly from micros, are available. Outside, a terrace and balcony are popular in summer. The pub is close to the Peak Forest Canal and Goyt Way Trail.
Q🐴❀◖◗♿⛺♣P🚌(358)🐾

Summerseat

Footballers Inn

28 Higher Summerseat, BL0 9UG
⏲ 12-midnight (1am Fri & Sat) ☎ (01204) 880008
Moorhouse's Blond Witch; Wainwright; 4 changing beers Ⓗ
A much-loved pub, earning its rightful place at the heart of the local community. Six real ales are on offer, four of them changing. It has an open-plan layout with three seating areas, a dartboard and three sports TVs. A beer garden and barbecue area have been built at the rear, giving great views towards the Pennines to the east. The pub is a shortish walk from Summerseat station on the preserved East Lancashire Railway. Dogs are welcome. ❀≋♣P🚌(477)🐾📶

Tottington

Dungeon Inn

9 Turton Road, BL8 4AW
⏲ 4-11 (midnight Fri); 12-midnight Sat; 12-10.30 Sun
Lancaster Bomber; Wainwright; house beer (by Thwaites); 3 changing beers Ⓗ
A traditional, family-friendly Thwaites pub. The building has a quiet front lounge with a real open fire in cold winter periods and a separate pool room off the main bar room. There is a beer garden at a lower level to the rear. Six handpumps serve regular and guest ales. On Monday all real ales are discounted to £2.90 a pint. There is live music every Saturday evening. Dogs are welcome until 7.30pm. Q🐴❀♣P▯🚌(469,480)🐾📶

Tyldesley

Union Arms

83 Castle Street, M29 8EW
⏲ 12-11 (midnight Fri & Sat); 12-10.30 Sun
☎ (01942) 870645
3 changing beers (sourced locally) Ⓗ
This family-friendly pub is very much part of the local community with regular charity events and occasional theme nights including live music. The interior is divided into a number of separate connected areas. The left side is the vault and the right is a lounge used for dining. There are usually three to four real ales including Wainwright, with good-value fresh home-cooked food served until 8pm and traditional lunch on Sunday until 6pm. Most sporting events are shown on TV.
🐴❀◖◗♣🚌(V2)🐾

Urmston

Flixton Conservative Club ✔

Abbotsfield, 193 Flixton Road, M41 5DF
⏲ 12-3, 6-11; 12-11.30 Fri & Sat; 12-11 Sun
☎ (0161) 748 2846 🌐 flixtonconservativeclub.co.uk
5 changing beers (sourced nationally; often Bank Top, Elland, Pictish) Ⓗ
National CAMRA Club of the Year 2018, this large suburban club offers a varied range of local, regional and national beers as well as a real cider.

In the upstairs function room there is usually a brewery takeover on the last Friday of the month with five handpumps serving a range of the guest brewer's offerings. There is a small charge for entry, with pie and peas thrown in. The club has a bowling green, four snooker tables and a darts room. ⇌(Chassen Rd)P(255)

Lord Nelson

49 Stretford Road, M41 9LG

11-11 (11.30 Fri; midnight Sat); 12-11 Sun

☎ 07827 850255

Joseph Holt Mild, Bitter, Two Hoots, IPA H

The Nellie, as it is known locally, is your classic Holt's suburban pub, although older than most of the examples in the Greater Manchester area. It caters for the basic essentials in life – a drink, a chat and sport on the many TV screens. Food is limited to the usual pub fare of nuts, crisps and snacks. The pub was recognised as part of the local CAMRA branch's 40th anniversary in 2017 for continuing to sell cask beer since its first appearance in the 1977 Guide. ⇌P

Prairie Schooner Taphouse L

33 Flixton Road, M41 5AW

4-10 Mon; 12-11 Tue-Thu; 12-midnight Fri & Sat; 12-10 Sun

prairie-schooner-taphouse.co.uk

4 changing beers (sourced locally; often Brightside, Dunham Massey, Outstanding) H

Opened in 2014, this larger-than-usual micropub has become an established part of the area's expanding real ale scene. Four cask ales, mainly local, are joined on the bar by six craft kegs. A fine selection of bottled beers is also available to either drink on the premises or take away. A hub for various community groups including the local home-brew and camera clubs, it also holds regular quiz and music nights. Q⇌(255)

Wardley

Morning Star

520 Manchester Road, M27 9QW (opp Bagot St)

12-11 (11.30 Fri & Sat) ☎ (0161) 727 8373

Joseph Holt Mild, Bitter, Two Hoots; 1 changing beer (sourced locally) H

Built in 1890, this imposing red-brick building is a good example of a community establishment. A smart and tidy pub, to the left is the traditional vault with darts, dominoes and TV. To the right is a small front room leading to a much larger lounge/dining room. A central bar serves all rooms. Check the boards for meal deals. The pub hosts a fortnightly Wednesday quiz night and Friday evening entertainment. A covered outside area is a real asset in summer. ⇌P

West Didsbury

Wine & Wallop

97 Lapwing Lane, M20 6UR (jct Palatine Rd)

11-11 (midnight Fri & Sat); 11-10.30 Sun

☎ (0161) 446 2464

Brightside Maverick IPA; First Chop Brewing Arm Hop; Howard Town Super Fortress; 5 changing beers (sourced nationally) H

This comfortable bar, previously a video shop and grocer's (you can still see tiling from its grocery days), is set over two floors. Upstairs you can sit on sofas gazing down on your fellow drinkers from the internal balcony. Downstairs, bare-boarded floors and part-plastered, wainscoted or bare-brick walls are adorned with occasional large mirrors. Feature chandeliers add softness and a degree of class to the decor. Guest beers are mainly from local breweries. CityLife Bar of the Year 2016 award winner.

Westhoughton

Beer School L

88 Market Street, BL5 3AZ

closed Mon & Tue; 12 (3 Wed & Thu)-11

☎ (01942) 396280 thebeerschool.co.uk

4 changing beers (sourced locally) H

A micropub that is decked out to look like a school, though school uniforms are not required! There is a wall with library wallpaper showing shelves of books, many tables and stools that will take you back to your old art room days, complete with a free-standing roller blackboard. The 'cellar' is on view behind the bar. Try before you buy is available. Large racks display the bottled beers for sale. Note that the toilets are upstairs. ⇌(540,715)

Whitefield

Eagle & Child

Higher Lane, M45 7EY

12-11 (midnight Fri & Sat) ☎ 07827 850229

Joseph Holt Mild, Bitter, Two Hoots; 1 changing beer (often Joseph Holt) H

A traditional black and white timber-fronted inn with a spacious lounge and vault served by a central bar. Food is served until 8pm daily, including Sunday roasts. A quiz and supper is run fortnightly. Live acts perform every Friday and live bands on alternate Wednesdays. Sky and BT Sports are shown on TVs. A large floodlit bowling green, which is available for hire, is open from April to September. QP(98,135)

Wigan

Anvil

Dorning Street, WN1 1ND

11-11; 12-10.30 Sun ☎ (01942) 239444

Bank's Mild; Brakspear Oxford Gold, Wainwright; 4 changing beers (sourced nationally) H

Popular town-centre pub with seven handpumps offering various guests beers, two real ciders, six draught continental ales and a range of bottled beers. At least one real cider is available. Several TV screens show sports action and the small snug contains the 'wall of fame' displaying numerous award certificates. There is a garden at the rear. Close to bus and railway access for the DW Stadium, the pub can be busy on match days. Over-18s only. ⇌(Wallgate/N Western)

Blundell's Café Bar L

90 Wigan Lane, WN1 2LF

6-11 Mon; closed Tue; 4-11 Wed & Thu; 2-11 Fri & Sat; 2-10 Sun ☎ 07810 396736

3 changing beers H

Situated just off the main road with reasonable parking outside and in side streets, this is a quiet haven for a pint of local ale, a fine coffee and simple snacks. The bar is often candlelit in the evening. Family-sized functions are usually held Monday through to Wednesday. QP

Doc's Symposium L

85 Mesnes Street, WN1 1QJ
closed Mon-Wed; 12-11 Thu-Sat; 1-10.30 Sun
(01942) 567765
Weetwood Cheshire Cat; 4 changing beers H
A warm welcome awaits you from the well-respected landlords at Wigan's first micropub. Five cask ales, European beers, ciders and bottled beers are available. The deli counter offers a wide range of light snacks and nibbles made from fresh ingredients daily. Situated within walking distance of Wigan town centre, this micropub has outdoor seating overlooking Mesnes Park. From March to the end of September it also opens Wednesday 4-7pm. **Q**

John Bull Chophouse

2 Coopers Row, Market Place, WN1 1PQ
4.30-11; 1-1am Fri; 12.30-1am Sat; 3-11 Sun
(01942) 242862 johnbullchophousewigan.co.uk
House beer (by Thwaites); 4 changing beers H
A vibrant and lively pub in a town-centre building over 300 years old which has been cottages, stables and a slaughterhouse in the past. It has been run by the same family for over 40 years. There are six handpumps serving Thwaites beers. Renowned for having the best pub jukebox in the north-west, this popular, quirky hostelry is on two floors with a pool table and seating outside. The toilets are upstairs. Closed Monday and Tuesday in winter. (Wallgate/N Western)

Raven Hotel

5 Wallgate, WN1 1LD
11-11 (1am Fri & Sat) (01942) 239764
theravenwigan.com
Tetley Bitter; 4 changing beers H
An early 1900s commercial hotel, virtually derelict before a tasteful renovation in 2012 that retained and restored many original features including tiles, panelling and windows. The retro interior is warmed by cosy coal fires in winter and with two unobtrusive TVs. It serves a varying range of real ales and cider on handpump, alongside good home-made pub food at a reasonable price. Loyalty cards are in operation and a Wednesday cask critics night offers discounts on real ale.
(Wallgate/N Western)

Tap 'n' Barrel L

16 Jaxon's Court, WN1 1LR
12-10 (midnight Fri); closed Tue; 12-12.30am Sat; 1-10 Sun
(01942) 386966 martlandmillbrewery.co.uk
Martland Mill Lancashire Loom; 4 changing beers (sourced regionally) H
Located adjacent to the bus station in a narrow shopping mews, this microbar is the brewery tap for Martland Mill. The main bar area is long and narrow, leading to a covered, heated, smoke-free garden, which hosts live music on Sunday afternoon. There is additional seating upstairs. Four real ciders are served from the fridge. Beer and cider are available in paddles of three third-pints. Occasional beer and sausage festivals are held. Local CAMRA Cider Pub of the Year 2017.
Q(Wallgate/N Western)

Wigan Central L

Arch No.1 & 2 Queen Street, WN3 4DY
12-11 (midnight Fri); 11-midnight Sat; 12-10.30 Sun
(01942) 246425 wigancentral.bar
House beer (by Prospect); 6 changing beers (sourced nationally) H
This two-roomed pub has a railway-themed interior with a live feed displaying arrival and departure times from both Wigan railway stations. The pub is owned by the nearby Prospect Brewery but sources real ales from all over, alongside continental bottled beers displayed in the 'library'. Live music plays on Sunday. Bar snacks are available. Local CAMRA Cider Pub of the Year 2016 and a runner-up in the National Pub of the Year competition in 2018. **Q**

Withington

Victoria

438 Wilmslow Road, M20 3BW (on B5093, jct Davenport Av)
12-11 (midnight Thu-Sat) (0161) 434 2600
Hydes Original, 1863, Lowry; 5 changing beers (sourced nationally; often Hydes) H
This busy, late 19th-century community pub with its period exterior and etched windows has been a Hydes house for 114 years. A more recent sensitive refurbishment has almost created separate rooms, giving the place a more intimate feel. However, along with the excellence of the beer, the overriding feature of the pub is the warm and friendly ambience the licensees and staff have created.

Woodford

Davenport Arms (Thief's Neck)

550 Chester Road, SK7 1PS (on A5102, jct Church Lane)
11-11; 12-10.30 Sun (0161) 439 2435
davenportarms.co.uk
Robinsons Unicorn, Dizzy Blonde, Old Tom, Wizard; 1 changing beer (often Robinsons) H
Characterful red-brick farmhouse-style pub which received a smart refurbishment in 2014 but retains a multi-roomed feel with real fires in winter. This is its 32nd consecutive year in the Guide, and the licence has now been in the same family for a mammoth 86 years. Excellent food is mostly home made, with some adventurous specials. Outside, the spacious forecourt and attractive garden, set well away from the road, are popular in summer, boasting impressive floral displays.
P(42B)

Noted ales

At one time or another nearly every county town in England of any size has been noted for its beers or ales. Yorkshire claims not only stingo but also Hull and North Allerton ales whilst Nottingham, Lichfield, Derby, Oxford and Burton have almost branded their ales. During the eighteenth century the fame of Dorchester beer almost equalled the popularity of London porter.
Frank A. King, Beer has a History, 1947

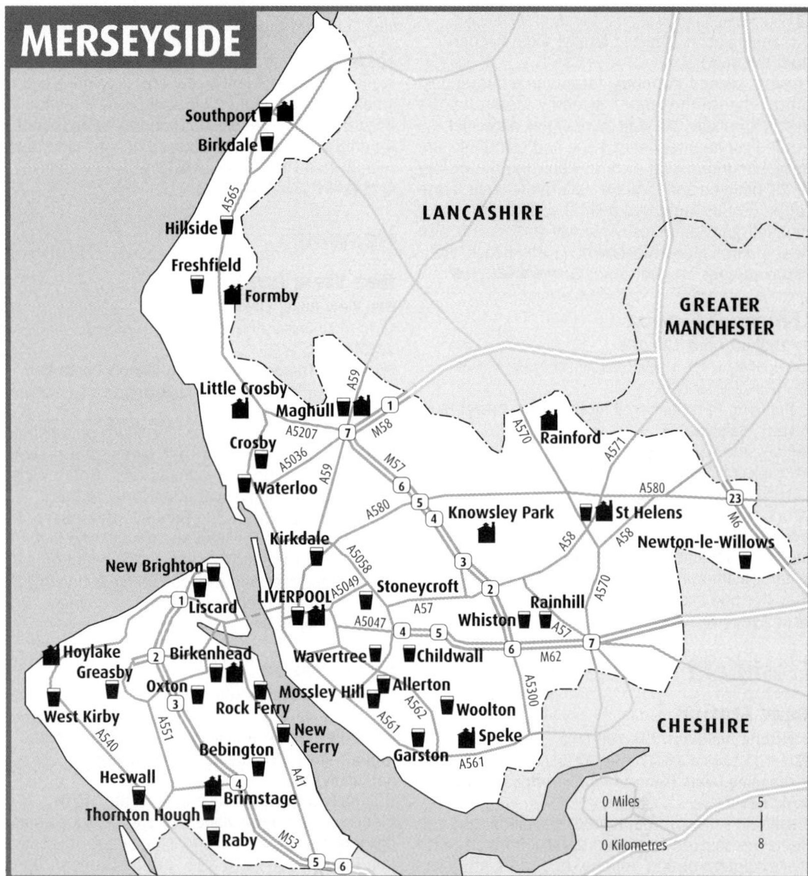

Bebington

Travellers Rest

169 Mount Road, CH63 8PJ

12-11 (11.30 Thu; midnight Fri & Sat) ☎ (0151) 608 2988

thetravsbebington.co.uk

Sharp's Doom Bar; Timothy Taylor Landlord; 4 changing beers (sourced nationally; often Brimstage, Fuller's) H

A former coaching inn, this cosy, popular pub is reputedly over 300 years old. Close to Storeton Woods, it has a country-pub feel and is decorated throughout with brasses and bric-a-brac. A central bar serves the main area and two side rooms. The guest ales are often from local microbreweries. At lunchtime the emphasis is on serving award-winning food, but in the evening this is very much a traditional pub. No evening meals Monday or Tuesday. Q (464,487)

Birkdale

Barrel House L

42 Liverpool Road, PR8 4AY

10-10.30 ☎ (01704) 566601

2 changing beers (often Parker, Salopian, Southport) H

The Barrel House is a micropub opened in 2014. A former newsagents, it still sells the daily paper. When a Sainsbury's supermarket opened over the road it changed business and became a beer shop. It is now an Aladdin's cave of wonderful bottled beers, wines, loose-leaf teas and speciality coffees. It also has two real ales on handpump, usually from local breweries such as Southport and Parker. Q (49,X2)

Birkenhead

Gallaghers Traditional Pub L

20 Chester Street, CH41 5DQ

12 (4 Mon)-11; 12-midnight Fri & Sat ☎ (0151) 649 9095

gallagherspubwirral.com

Brimstage Trapper's Hat Bitter; 5 changing beers (sourced regionally; often Hawkshead, Rat, Salopian) H

Multiple award-winning genuine free house close to the Mersey ferries, rescued after closure and refurbished in 2010. It is decorated with a range of military memorabilia and a collection of shipping images. Several ciders are always on offer. Good-value meals are served until 9pm daily (no food Mon). Live music plays every Sunday. Cheese night is the last Sunday of the month – bring your own cheese. (Hamilton Sq)

Crosby

Corner Post L

25 Bridge Road, L23 6SA

closed Mon; 4-9; 1-9 Sat; 1-7 Sun ☎ 07587 177453
4 changing beers (sourced locally; often Peerless, Rock the Boat) H
Crosby's second micropub, located in a former post office – hence the name – is easily spotted by the postbox outside. As well as real ales and cider, bottled continental beers, wine and soft drinks are available. Interesting pictures depicting the history of the building and local area adorn the walls. Close to the 53 bus route and a short walk from Blundellsands and Crosby railway station, it is also near the Iron Men attraction on Crosby beach. Well-behaved dogs are welcome. Q (53)

Liverpool Pigeon L

14 Endbutt Lane, L23 0TR
closed Mon; 4-9; 1-9 Sat; 1-5 Sun ☎ 07766 480329
liverpoolpigeon.co.uk
5 changing beers (sourced locally; often Bristol Beer Factory, Salopian) H
Merseyside's pioneering micropub is a fine example of the type, with real ales, ciders and bottled beers available but no spirits, alcopops, keg beers or music. The cask beers will usually include a local brew and often a dark beer. Locally made pies are available at the bar. The Liverpool Pigeon is named after an extinct bird from Polynesia – long may this one live. A former local CAMRA Pub of the Year. Q

Freshfield

Beer Station L

3 Victoria Buildings, L37 7DB (opp railway station)
3-9; 12-10 Fri & Sat; 12-9 Sun ☎ (01704) 807450
3 changing beers (sourced locally; often Neptune, Red Star) H
Freshfield's first micropub promotes all things local. Beers are sourced to showcase local brewers, with the exception of one 'foreign' beer a month from out of the region. A fridge with bottled beers adds to the variety. The few spirits stocked also have their provenance checked. Food comes in the form of local pies and nuts. The walls are decorated with work by local artists. Dogs are welcome on a lead.
Q

Greasby

Coach & Horses L

Greasby Road, CH49 3NG
12-midnight (11 Sun) ☎ (0151) 677 4509
coachandhorsesgreasby.co.uk
Butcombe Original; Peerless Triple Blonde; 1 changing beer (sourced nationally) H
Charming whitewashed traditional street-corner local, dating back nearly 300 years. Formerly a farmhouse where ale was brewed and sold from 1725, it became a pub in the 1820s. Three small cosy rooms with real warming fires for the winter surround a compact central bar, with the ambience of a small country local. There is a folk/acoustic jam session every Monday.
QP (437,88)

Irby Mill L

Mill Lane, CH49 3NT (on roundabout between Greasby and Irby)
12-11 (midnight Fri & Sat); 12-10.30 Sun
☎ (0151) 694 0194 irbymill.co.uk
Caledonian Deuchars IPA; 6 changing beers (sourced nationally; often Eagle, Peerless, Young's) H
Formerly a café, the pub was originally the house of the miller of the windmill on the site, and opened as a pub in 1982. With thick sandstone walls, low beams and a real fire, it comprises a small L-shaped, stone-floored bar and a lounge used mainly by diners. The pub has an excellent reputation for its locally sourced home-made food, with a menu to suit most tastes.
QP (88)

Heswall

Dee View Inn L

Dee View Road, CH60 0DH
12-11.30 (midnight Fri & Sat); 12-11 Sun
☎ (0151) 345 9165
Brimstage Trapper's Hat Bitter; Sharp's Doom Bar; Timothy Taylor Landlord; 2 changing beers (sourced nationally) H
Traditional local built in the late 1800s on a hairpin bend by the war memorial and famous mirror, with views over the Dee Estuary and close to the Wirral Way path. Offering a warm welcome, it has retained its character and friendly atmosphere. A popular quiz night is held on Tuesday and live music is a frequent attraction. Traditional home-cooked food is served (no food on Fri, no eve meals Sat or Sun). Children are welcome if dining.
P

Jug & Bottle L

13 Mount Avenue, CH60 4RH
12-11.30 ☎ (0151) 342 5535 the-jugandbottle.co.uk
Brains Rev James; Brimstage Trapper's Hat Bitter; Higsons Pale; 3 changing beers (sourced nationally) H
Originally a private house built in the 1870s, hidden behind the village hall and library a short distance from the main shopping street. This smart pub reopened in 2016 after a refurbishment. Open fires and various cosy areas create a warm and friendly atmosphere while, outside, the decking gives views towards the River Dee and North Wales. P

Hillside

Grasshopper L

70 Sandon Road, PR8 4QD
5-10.30; 2-10.30 Sat & Sun ☎ (01704) 569794

REAL ALE BREWERIES

Ad Hop Liverpool
Big Bog Speke
Brimstage Brimstage
Brooks Hoylake (NEW)
Connoisseur St Helens
Craft, The Southport
George Wright Rainford
Gibberish Liverpool (NEW)
Handyman Liverpool (NEW)
Higsons Liverpool (NEW)
Liverpool Craft Liverpool
Mad Hatter Liverpool
Melwood Knowsley Park
Neptune Maghull
Peerless Birkenhead
Red Star Formby
Rock the Boat Little Crosby
Southport Southport
Stamps Liverpool

8 changing beers (sourced regionally; often Bank Top, Salopian) Ⓗ
A micropub opened in 2016 in what was once a Martins Bank branch, situated in a row of shops just down the road from Hillside station. The pub's name comes from the old logo of Martins which was the grasshopper. Food can be ordered from a nearby takeaway and eaten in the pub. Four changing ciders are served. The pub hosts monthly meetings of CoLAPs (Coast of Lancashire Ale Preservation Society). Q❀♿⇌♣●P🚌🐾

Liscard

Lazy Landlord Ale House 🏆 Ⓛ
56 Mill Lane, CH44 5UG
4-10.30 Mon, Wed & Thu; closed Tue; 2-10.30 Fri; 12-10.30 Sat & Sun ☎ 07583 135616
Joseph Holt Bitter; 4 changing beers (sourced nationally; often Hawkshead, Oakham, Salopian) Ⓗ
Wirral's first micropub, opened in former shop premises in 2014, is run by the Henry brothers who are cask ale enthusiasts. Two small cosy rooms, decorated with large amounts of breweriana, local artworks and a small library, are served from the front bar. Mostly frequented by a more mature, discerning local clientele, the pub is a venue for meetings of local societies. The cider is usually from SeaCider. Awarded local CAMRA Pub of the Year in 2017 and 2018. Q♨♣●🚌(410,432)🐾

Liverpool: Allerton

Three Piggies
77-79 Allerton Road, L18 2DA
11-midnight; 10-midnight Sat & Sun ☎ (0151) 722 6510
threepiggies.co.uk
House beer (by Marston's); 3 changing beers (sourced regionally; often Hawkshead, Ilkley, Titanic) Ⓗ
Open plan with trestle tables, this bright, lively 'alehouse and canteen' opened in 2016. Unlike numerous other businesses in the area, the owner says it is not a restaurant. Food starts with brunch in the morning, after which there is an extensive, varied menu, from mains to light bites, plus coffee and cakes. A wide selection of craft beers is available. Last entry is 10.45pm, although the pub often stays open until midnight. ♨◑♿🚌(86)

Liverpool: Childwall

Childwall Fiveways Ⓛ ✔
179 Queens Drive, L15 6XS
8am-midnight ☎ (0151) 738 2100
Greene King Abbot; Robinsons Trooper; Ruddles Best Bitter; Sharp's Doom Bar; 4 changing beers (often Robinsons) Ⓗ
A former Higson's tied house, this large single-roomed pub opened as a Wetherspoon in 2010. Located in a leafy suburb, it has good motorway and public transport links. The refurbished interior is decorated with wood panelling, and outside there is a beer garden. A popular establishment, it can get busy, especially at weekends. The site was used for a water tank during WWII.
♨❀◑♿●P🚌(79,81)📶

Liverpool: City Centre

Augustus John Ⓛ
Peach Street, L3 5TX (off Brownlow Hill)
11.30-11; closed Sat & Sun ☎ (0151) 794 5507
5 changing beers (sourced nationally; often Peerless, Rock the Boat) Ⓗ
Opened in 1968 and run by the University of Liverpool, the Augustus John is an open-plan pub popular with students, lecturers and locals. The cask ales always come in a range of styles, and a large number of ciders are on offer – two on handpump and many more from the cellar. Pizza is served at all times, sport is shown and there is a jukebox. Closed over Christmas and New Year. Many times a CAMRA branch winner and a former regional Cider Pub of the Year. ◑♿♣●🚌(79)📶

Baltic Fleet Ⓛ
33a Wapping, L1 8DQ
12-11 (midnight Fri & Sat) ☎ (0151) 709 3116
balticfleetpubliverpool.com
6 changing beers (sourced locally; often Big Bog, Melwood) Ⓗ
This Grade II listed building is located near the Albert Dock. It has a distinctive flat-iron shape and the interior is decorated on a nautical theme. The existence of tunnels in the cellar has led to speculation that the pub's history may involve smuggling. It also originally had many doors to allow customers to escape the press gangs. The previous Wapping Brewery kit was removed from the cellar in 2017. It can get busy when events are on at the nearby Echo Arena. ❀◑⇌●🚌🐾📶

Belvedere Ⓛ
8 Sugnall Street, L7 7EB (off Falkner St)
12-11 ☎ (0151) 709 0303
4 changing beers (sourced regionally; often Melwood, Salopian) Ⓗ
Tucked away in the Georgian area of the city, close to the famous Philharmonic Hall and frequented by its orchestra members, this small two-roomed pub is a free house serving four rotating beers from – mainly local – microbreweries. Redeemed in 2006 from closure for housing development, this Grade II listed building retains original fixtures and interesting etched-glass features. With a mixed local clientele, it is a pub where various small cultural groups meet and good conversation thrives. Q❀●▯🚌🐾📶

Crown Hotel ★ Ⓛ ✔
43 Lime Street, L1 1JQ
8am-11 (midnight Fri & Sat); 10-midnight Sun
☎ (0151) 707 6027 thecrownliverpool.co.uk
Black Sheep Best Bitter; Greene King IPA; 6 changing beers (sourced nationally; often Timothy Taylor) Ⓗ
Grade II listed with a nationally important historic interior and ornate plasterwork ceilings, the building is noticeable for its Walker's Ales Warrington stucco frieze. Many original features are retained in the two downstairs rooms, including some impressive wood panelling and push bells. There is also an ornate glass dome above the staircase. Breakfast is served until noon, a wide menu of pub food until 10pm. Close to Lime Street Station and public transport links.
♨◑⇌🚌📶

Dispensary Ⓛ
87 Renshaw Street, L1 2SP
12-11 (midnight Fri & Sat) ☎ (0151) 709 2160
George Wright Mild; changing beers (often Fyne Ales, Ossett, Titanic) Ⓗ
This lively city pub, where the licensee's impeccable attention to beer quality is renowned, is a haven for real ale drinkers of all ages. Seven

handpumps serve an ever-changing choice of interesting microbrewery beers in a good range of both styles and strengths. A regular local beer, Mark's Mild, commemorates the much-missed barman who died in 2012. The attractive bar area has Victorian features, and there is a raised wood-panelled area to the rear. ≠🚌

Excelsior L ✔

121-123 Dale Street, L2 2JH (close to Birkenhead Tunnel entrance)

11-11; 12-11 Sun ☎ (0151) 236 0079

Brains Rev James; Robinsons Dizzy Blonde; Timothy Taylor Landlord; 3 changing beers (sourced locally; often Brimstage, Red Star, Rock the Boat) H

Large, comfortable corner pub on the edge of the business district. The main room has a three-sided bar with a series of distinct seating areas. There is a large room off the bar area which includes a raised seating area which can be hired for meetings or other functions. Three large-screen TVs show sports events, particularly football, but are mostly silent unless Liverpool or Everton are playing. ◐≠P🚌

Fly in the Loaf ✔

13 Hardman Street, L1 9AS

12-11 (midnight Fri & Sat) ☎ (0151) 708 0817

Okell's Bitter; 6 changing beers (sourced nationally; often Kirkstall, Okell's) H

A former bakery, the name comes from the slogan 'no flies in the loaf'. Owned by Isle of Man brewer Okell's, it serves its beers alongside a changing range of guests from around the country, many from microbreweries, and a good selection of foreign beers. The spacious interior has a light, airy frontage with contrasting wood-panelled areas towards the rear, and plenty of rugby league memorabilia. There is an attractive small on-street drinking area at the front and a function room upstairs. ◐♿≠🚌(86)

Grapes L

60 Roscoe Street, L1 9DW

1-12.30am (1.30am Thu-Sat) ☎ (0151) 709 3977

thegrapesliverpool.co.uk

8 changing beers H

This corner local dates back to 1804 and retains its original Mellors signage outside. There is a total of nine handpumps, with a large number of beers coming from local microbreweries such as Mad Hatter and Liverpool Craft. After a major refurbishment during the summer of 2016, stairs now lead to a partly sheltered patio area, atop the extension. Live jazz features every Sunday night from 9pm. ❀≠🍎🚌

Hard Times & Misery L

2B Maryland Street, L1 9DE

closed Mon; 4-10.30 (midnight Fri); 2-midnight Sat; 4-9 Sun ☎ 07595 588426 hardtimesandmisery.co.uk

3 changing beers (sourced locally; often Big Bog, Rock the Boat) G

Cosy hostelry next door to the Shisha bar on Maryland Street, downhill from the Hope & Anchor. The small room upstairs has more seating. Three or four, often local, cask ales are on gravity dispense in pins, plus a selection of bottled beers and craft keg. The bar also specialises in artisan gins and vodkas. Opening times may change during the year. There is 50p off a pint Tuesday to Thursday. Q≠🚌

Lime Kiln L ✔

Fleet Street, L1 4NR

9am-midnight (1am Thu; 2am Fri & Sat)

☎ (0151) 702 6810

Greene King Abbot; Ruddles Best Bitter; changing beers (often Peerless) H

On first impression, the decor and layout may appear not to offer much for the real ale drinker, but looks can be deceiving. Thanks to continued commitment by Wetherspoon's, real ale is well catered for, with at least one local beer usually available. Handpulls are in the downstairs bar only. Situated in the Concert Square area, the pub is a peaceful haven during the day. A Victorian warehouse occupied the site, which was home to manufacturing chemists, from the early 1900s to the 1950s. ◐♿≠🍎🚌

Lion Tavern ★ L ✔

67 Moorfields, L2 2BP

12-11 (11.30 Fri-Sun) ☎ (0151) 236 9768

theliontavernliverpool.co.uk

Moorhouse's Pride of Pendle; house beer (by Red Star); 6 changing beers (sourced nationally; often Red Star, Rock the Boat) H

Named after the locomotive that worked the Liverpool to Manchester railway, the Lion features exquisite artwork plus intricately etched and stained glass which bear testimony to its Grade II-listed status and its entry on CAMRA's National Inventory of Historic Pub Interiors. It was refurbished in 2017. Four beers are available from the SIBA list, usually including ales from local micros. The cider is from Westons. Lunchtime food is served and speciality pork pies are available at all times. ◐≠(Moorfields)🍎🚌

Pen Factory L

13 Hope Street, L1 9BQ

11-midnight; closed Sun & Mon ☎ (0151) 709 7887

pen-factory.co.uk

5 changing beers (sourced nationally; often Brimstage, Hawkshead, Titanic) H

The Pen Factory opened in 2015, brought to you by innovator of the original Everyman Bistro, entrepreneur Paddy Byrne. This large open-plan bistro-style establishment with a wood-burning stove and a small garden is a convivial place to drink and eat. Up to six handpumps include beers from smaller breweries such as Brimstage. The venue can be busy before or after productions at the nearby Everyman Theatre or Philharmonic Hall. Excellent food, not your average pub grub. ❀◐♿≠🍎🚌(86)

Peter Kavanagh's ★

2-6 Egerton Street, L8 7LY (off Catharine St)

12-midnight (1am Fri & Sat) ☎ (0151) 709 3443

Greene King Abbot; 4 changing beers (sourced nationally; often Castle Rock) H

On CAMRA's National Inventory of Historic Pub Interiors and situated in the Georgian era. The snugs feature murals by Eric Robinson on the walls and there are fine stained-glass windows with wooden shutters. The benches have carved armrests thought to be caricatures of Peter Kavanagh, the licensee for 53 years until 1950. These features were not adversely affected when the pub was expanded, firstly in 1964 into next door, then in 1977 into next door but one. Q🚌(86)🐾

Richard John Blackler

Units 1 & 2 Charlotte Row, L1 1HU

9am-midnight (1am Fri & Sat) (0151) 709 4802

Greene King Abbot; Ruddles Best Bitter; Sharp's Doom Bar; Wychwood Hobgoblin; 8 changing beers

This Wetherspoon pub is the ground floor of the former Blackler's department store which opened in 1908 and finally shut in 1988. The famous rocking horse from that store is in the corner. Close to the bus station, Saint John's shopping centre and Liverpool One, it is always busy – especially when Liverpool or Everton are playing at home – but it is a good place to take a break. The Beatles' George Harrison served his electrician's apprenticeship at Blackler's.

Roscoe Head

24 Roscoe Street, L1 2SX

11.30-midnight (11 Mon); 12-midnight Sun

(0151) 709 4365 roscoehead.co.uk

Tetley Bitter; Timothy Taylor Landlord; 4 changing beers (sourced regionally; often Rock the Boat)

One of the Magnificent Five pubs in every edition of the Guide. Conversation and the appreciation of real ale rule in this cosy four-roomed hostelry. Run by members of the same family for over 30 years, the name commemorates William Roscoe, a leading campaigner against the slave trade. Six handpumps feature national and local breweries. Since its sale by Punch Taverns to New River Retail in 2015 there has been concern over the future of the pub, with an active Save the Roscoe Head campaign. Q

Sanctuary

72 Lime Street, L1 1JN

closed Mon; 11-6 Tue; 12-11 (1am Fri & Sat)

(0151) 703 0116 sanctuarybar.co.uk

6 changing beers (often Big Bog, Robinsons, Titanic)

Opened in 2017, this free-of-tie pub is located next to Design 4 Life tattoo parlour and owned by the same couple. Themed as a run-down 1920s hotel, the pub has Art Deco lighting and long-abandoned suitcases on the well-stocked wooden beer cabinet where bottled beers are available to take away. A comfortable seating area has a pulpit in the centre of the bar and round tables. The beer range always includes at least one local ale and flight boards are available.

Ship & Mitre

133 Dale Street, L2 2JH (by Birkenhead Tunnel)

10-11 (midnight Thu); 9am-midnight Fri & Sat

(0151) 236 0859 theshipandmitre.com

Flagship Lupa, Sublime, Silhouette; 5 changing beers (sourced nationally; often Big Bog, Flagship)

The name derives from two previous incarnations, the Flagship and the Mitre. The 1930s Art Deco pub is partly hidden by the Queensway Tunnel entrance and the Churchill Way flyover. A changing array of 15 beers and real ciders is served by friendly and knowledgeable staff. There is also an impressive range of world beers. The pub now brews its own Flagship beers using the plant at Stamps Brewery in Crosby. The Ship in a Bottle shop is situated a five-minute walk away.

Thomas Rigby's

23-25 Dale Street, L2 2EZ

11.30-11 (0151) 236 3269

Okell's Bitter, IPA; 4 changing beers (often Kirkstall)

This multi-roomed, Grade II listed building, bearing the name of wine and spirit dealer Thomas Rigby, now supplies an extensive world beer range on draught and in bottles. The regular beers on handpump come from the pub's owner, Okell's. Good-value food including specials is served until early evening, with one room offering a friendly and efficient table service. The old coaching inn courtyard for outdoor drinking is shared with sister pub Lady of Mann.

Vernon Arms

69 Dale Street, L2 2HJ

12-11 (midnight Fri & Sat) (0151) 236 6132

Brains Rev James; house beer (by Stamps); 3 changing beers

Situated close to the business district, the Vernon retains the feel of a street-corner local. The single long-roomed bar serves three drinking areas including a back room with frosted-glass windows advertising the Liverpool Brewing Company. The main bar has wood panelling, several large columns and a small snug area. Real cider on handpull is unusual for the city centre. Live music plays on Friday and Saturday.

Ye Hole in ye Wall

4 Hackins Hey, L2 2AW (off Dale St)

12-11 (10.30 Sun) (0151) 227 3809

6 changing beers (sourced nationally; often Red Star)

A traditional side-street pub rumoured to be the oldest hostelry in the city, dating back to the start of Liverpool's maritime heyday in 1726. Wood panelling and stained glass abound. Built on the site of an old Quaker graveyard, there are tales of ghosts, and this old coaching house boasts at least two. The beer cellar is unusually on the first floor above the bar. Five guest beers are offered on rotation and may be from local and micro breweries. Q(Moorfields)

Liverpool: Garston

Masonic

35 Gladstone Road, L19 1RR

11-midnight (1am Fri & Sat); 12-midnight Sun

(0151) 280 0200

6 changing beers (sourced regionally; often Big Bog)

Community pub amid terraced houses with seven handpumps, one usually dispensing a cider. Beers are supplied directly, often by local breweries, and from around the country through brewery swaps. A supporter of local sports teams, horse racing and other sport are shown on TV. Live music plays Thursday to Sunday. There is a drinking area outside in front of the pub and a covered smoking area in the yard to the side. Real ale promotions are offered on Tuesday evenings. Beer festivals are held in January, May and September.

(82)

Liverpool: Kirkdale

Thomas Frost

177-187 Walton Road, L4 4AJ

8am-11.30 (0151) 207 8210

Greene King Abbot; Ruddles Best Bitter; Sharp's Doom Bar; 4 changing beers

This Wetherspoon pub occupies the ground floor of a Grade II listed building where draper Thomas

Frost moved into one of the six shops here in 1885 and, by 1910, had expanded his business into all the shops. Frost's department store was later built on the site. The pub is near both Everton and Liverpool grounds and gets busy on match days. It has a spacious open-plan layout with a large family area. No children permitted after 9pm.
(20,21)

Liverpool: Mossley Hill

Pi

106 Rose Lane, L18 8AG
11-11 (11.30 Fri & Sat) ☎ (0151) 222 0443
Tatton Blonde; 3 changing beers (sourced regionally) H
A café-style bar in premises that were previously a shop, near to Mossley Hill railway station. The guest beers are from smaller breweries in the region. A number of foreign beers are also on tap alongside dozens of bottled beers. A simple hot-food menu – comprising of real pies with sides – is available all day. Expansion into the shop next door has provided more space. (61,80)

Liverpool: Stoneycroft

Cask

438 Queens Drive, West Derby, L13 0AR
closed Mon; 4-9.30; 2-9.30 Sat & Sun ☎ 07747 034499
7 changing beers (sourced nationally; often Hawkshead) H
Comfortable, immaculate, one-roomed micropub that opened in 2015. It is located on Queens Drive (corner of Derby Lane), which acts like a Liverpool circular road. An interesting collection of breweriana includes some from Higsons. There are usually four beers on Tuesday and Wednesday, five on Thursday and up to seven from Friday. Cider and perry are dispensed direct from taps at the rear of the bar. Occasional special beers are kept in wooden pins, and bottled beers are stocked. Local CAMRA Pub of the Year 2016-2018.
Q (60,81)

Liverpool: Wavertree

Handyman Supermarket

461 Smithdown Road, L15 3JL
12 (3 Mon-Wed)-11.30 ☎ (0151) 222 7422
handymansupermarket.co.uk
House beer (by Handyman); 3 changing beers (sourced locally; often Handyman, Melwood, Red Star) H
A new brewpub opened in 2017 in a former hardware shop, hence the name. It has a large open-plan bar plus an events/function room at the rear. The brew plant is on the mezzanine above the bar. Handpumps serve the Handyman cask beers and there is a selection of bottled beers and craft keg on taps. The brewery beers are unfined. Many events are hosted, from live music to craft fairs.
(60,86)

Willow Bank

329 Smithdown Road, L15 3JA
12-11 (midnight Fri & Sat) ☎ (0151) 733 5782
willowbank-pub.co.uk
Castle Rock Harvest Pale; Greene King IPA, Abbot; Tetley Bitter; house beer (by Greene King); 3 changing beers (sourced nationally; often Big Bog) H
Vibrant, traditional, multi-room hostelry with the original public bar dating from the time it was a Walker's pub. It has a mixed clientele of shoppers and locals and is popular with students. Good-value food includes Sunday lunches. Up to eight different guest beers complement the regular ales. The real cider is Westons Rosie. Activities include a regular quiz night. Real ale night is Tuesday, and there are occasional beer festivals. Sports TV is shown on large screens on the roadside patio.
P (60,86)

Liverpool: Woolton

Gardeners Arms

101 Vale Road, L25 7RW
12-midnight (11.30 Sun) ☎ (0151) 428 1443
Fuller's London Pride; Greene King IPA; Marston's 61 Deep; Sharp's Doom Bar; 3 changing beers (sourced regionally; often Big Bog, Taylors) H
Friendly community village pub situated over the hill from Woolton village and separated from Menlove Avenue by blocks of flats. Guest beers regularly include a local Big Bog beer and a Welsh beer from Purple Moose, Heavy Industry or Cwrw Lal. A quiz is held on Tuesday evening. Woolton is famous as the home of the Beatles – their original name was The Quarrymen after the local school – and Eleanor Rigby's gravestone can be found in St Peter's churchyard. Q (76)

Maghull

Frank Hornby

38 Eastway, L31 6BR
8am-11.30 (midnight Fri & Sat) ☎ (0151) 520 4010
Phoenix Wobbly Bob; 9 changing beers (often Lancaster, Lytham, Moorhouse's) H
This Wetherspoon establishment is named after local man Frank Hornby, famous inventor of the Hornby train set. Unsurprisingly, samples of his work are on display in the pub including Meccano and Dinky Toys. Situated in a surburban street, the bar is spacious and light inside with a decked area outside at the front. A varied selection of guest ales is available including some from local microbreweries. Alcohol is served from 10am. No children after 10pm. Q P

New Brighton

Magazine Hotel

7 Magazine Brow, CH45 1HP
12-11 (11.30 Thu; midnight Fri & Sat) ☎ (0151) 630 3169
the-magazine-hotel.co.uk
Brimstage Trapper's Hat Bitter; Draught Bass; 3 changing beers (sourced regionally; often Big Bog, Brimstage, Higsons) H
This unspoilt multi-roomed, low-beamed pub with an attractive black and white frontage, dating from 1759, suffered from a fire in 2010 but has been restored without losing its unique character. Three rooms lead off the main central bar area with an open fireplace. Traditionally renowned for its Draught Bass, other beers are usually from local microbreweries. One changing real cider is kept. Overlooking Egremont Promenade, the pub has fine views over the River Mersey to Liverpool. The pub hosts biannual beer and cider festivals.
Q P (106,411)

Stage Door Tap

Queen's Royal, Marine Promenade, CH45 2JT
11-11; 11-10.30 Sun (0151) 691 0101
thequeensroyal.com
5 changing beers (sourced regionally; often Brimstage, Hawkshead, Phoenix)
A bright, airy, recently refurbished bar in the Queen's Royal Hotel, an imposing Victorian building close to the Floral Pavilion Theatre. In a seafront location overlooking Marine Promenade, Marine Lake and Fort Perch Rock, this free house is popular both with locals and day trippers. The enclosed drinking area outside affords superb views over Liverpool Bay. Good-value bar snacks and meals are served in the bar until 9pm (7pm Sun) and there is an adjoining restaurant.

Stanley's Cask

212 Rake Lane, CH45 1JP
11-midnight (11 Mon & Wed); 12-midnight Sun
(0151) 691 1093
5 changing beers (sourced nationally; often Caledonian, Robinsons, Theakston)
This ever-popular friendly local continues to thrive, due in no small part to the landlady who has a track record of serving quality beer. The five guest ales on offer often include seasonal beers from regional breweries and a beer from a local brewery. A traditional, single-roomed community local, it hosts various sports teams, quiz nights and regular popular live music including rock, blues and folk. (410,433)

New Ferry

Freddie's Club

36 Stanley Road, CH62 5AS
7-11; 5-11 Fri & Sat; 12-11 Sun
Brimstage Trapper's Hat Bitter; 1 changing beer (sourced locally; often Brimstage)
Comfortable two-roomed former club located in a quiet residential area near the end of a cul-de-sac a short walk from New Ferry shopping centre. Two ales from the local Brimstage Brewery are served from a single bar in the main room. The adjoining room features two full-size snooker tables and there are men's and women's darts teams. Monday is quiz night. **Q P**

John Masefield

70-72 New Chester Road, CH62 5AD
8am-midnight (0151) 644 4250
Greene King Abbot; Ruddles Best Bitter; 6 changing beers (sourced nationally; often Peerless)
Comfortable open-plan Wetherspoon venue in a former bicycle shop in the main shopping area. Named after the former poet laureate, who spent time in New Ferry as a young man, controversy surrounded the opening of the pub when locals suggested that the portrait on the sign looked more like Adolf Hitler – judge for yourself. The pub features Wetherspoon's meal deals, a Wednesday night quiz and regular vintage bus pub trips. At least one real cider is available.

Newton-le-Willows

Firkin

65 High Street, WA12 9SL
closed Mon-Wed; 5.30-11 Thu; 1-11.30 Fri & Sat; 1-10.30 Sun (01925) 225700 thefirkin.co.uk
8 changing beers (sourced locally)
A former shop, this small, friendly establishment dispenses a selection of eight real ales, including at least one dark beer, all sourced from micro or SIBA breweries. Two traditional ciders are also available. Small seating areas are to the front and rear, and pictures of Newton of old adorn the walls. Free of electronic noise, this is a place in which to engage in conversation with like-minded people and to make new friends. Over-18s only.
Q (34,22)

Oxton

Oxton Bar & Kitchen

2 Claughton Firs, CH43 5TQ
12-midnight (11 Mon; 11.30 Fri & Sat); 12-11 Sun
(0151) 651 2535 oxtonbar.co.uk
3 changing beers (sourced locally; often Brimstage, Peerless)
Situated in the centre of the attractive Oxton village among shops, bars and restaurants, this former John Smith's pub built in 1969 has been tastefully converted into a smart, comfortable, single-room lounge bar with an attractive outside seating area. There is a strong emphasis on quality food, ranging from sandwiches and snacks to full meals. Beers are usually from local microbreweries. **P** (492,495)

Raby

Wheatsheaf Inn

Raby Mere Road, CH63 4JH
11.30-11 (midnight Fri & Sat); 12-10.30 Sun
(0151) 336 3416 wheatsheaf-cowshed.co.uk
Black Sheep Best Bitter; Brimstage Trapper's Hat Bitter; Tetley Bitter; Thwaites Original; Titanic Plum Porter; Wainwright; 3 changing beers (sourced nationally; often Brimstage, Castle Rock)
An inn for 350 years, this is Wirral's oldest pub. The thatched building was rebuilt following a fire in 1611 and is reputed to be haunted by Charlotte, who died here. The walls are decorated with old photographs of Raby. The single bar serves three rooms and a restaurant in a converted cowshed. Lunch is served in the bar until 2pm, then snacks until 5pm. The restaurant is open evenings from 6pm Tuesday to Saturday. **Q P**

Rainhill

Skew Bridge Alehouse

5 Dane Court, L35 4LU
4 (2.30 Sat)-11; 2.30-10.30 Sun (0151) 792 7906
6 changing beers (often Big Bog, Connoisseur, Melwood)
A micropub in the centre of Rainhill village, the Skew Bridge offers a selection of six cask ales, four real ciders and two craft lagers. Locally sourced ales are complemented by beers from all over the UK. A good range of gins and single malt whiskies is also stocked. With no TV or music to distract customers, conversation is very much encouraged. A wide selection of board games is available.
Q P

Rock Ferry

Refreshment Rooms

2 Bedford Road East, CH42 1LS (off B5136, take Rock Lane East, then 4th right and over bridge)

⏲ 11.30-11 ☎ (0151) 644 5893 🌐 refreshmentrooms.info
House beer (by JW Lees); 2 changing beers (sourced locally; often Big Bog, Brimstage, Peerless) Ⓗ
Refurbished and reopened in 2012 under its original name, the pub was built in the 1880s for ferry passengers to Liverpool. Although the ferry terminal is long gone, this off-the-beaten-track establishment is well worth seeking out, with excellent views over the Mersey. One central bar services two rooms. The focus is on food, with excellent, reasonably priced meals served daily until 9pm. The house beer, 4% ABV HMS Conway, is from Lees and the cider is from Rosie's.
❀◐●♣🚌🐾 ᯤ

St Helens

Connoisseur Ales Tasting Room

Rear of Wolverhampton House, 121-125 Church Street, WA10 1AJ
⏲ 12-10 1st Sat of the month ☎ 07921 838831
Connoisseur; 8 changing beers Ⓗ
Cosy bar situated in the Connoisseur Ales Brewery serving a selection of beers brewed on-site. There is always a dark beer and all new and test brews appear here first. A large selection of bottle-conditioned beers is also available as well as fruit wines and mead. There is extra seating outside in the summer. The monthly open days are busy with a mix of locals plus out-of-town visitors. Proximity to the train and bus stations makes it an ideal place to start the real ale trail around town.
Q♿≋●P🚌🐾

Cricketers Arms

Peter Street, WA10 2EB
⏲ 12-midnight (1am Fri & Sat); 12-11.30 Sun
☎ (01744) 361846
13 changing beers (sourced regionally; often Ossett, White Rat) Ⓗ
The current CAMRA National Pub of the Year is part of the St Helens vibrant pub scene. A friendly, family-run, community inn, it has 13 handpumps offering at least one dark beer at all times, plus 10 ciders and a range of rum, brandy, whisky and gin. This traditional pub has just undergone a refurbishment and has two beer gardens and an outside bar used for regular beer festivals as well as private events. Darts and pool leagues are hosted as well as quiz nights and fundraising events for local charities. An on-site microbrewery is planned. Q❀♿♣●P🐾ᯤ

News Room

89 Duke Street, WA10 2JG
⏲ closed Mon & Tue; 5-11 Wed-Thu; 3-midnight Fri & Sat; 3-11 Sun ☎ (01744) 322129
3 changing beers (often Salopian) Ⓗ
A music-themed bar, The News Room offers three handpumps, craft beers and a wide range of foreign bottled beers as well as gins, rums and malt whiskies in stylish surroundings where conversation is encouraged. It has a warm and friendly, laid-back atmosphere, with music from the '60s, '70s and '80s playing on large screens. Themed music nights take place every six to eight weeks. ♿ᯤ

Phoenix

34 Canal Street, WA10 3LL
⏲ 2-11 (1am Fri); 12-1am Sat; 12-11 Sun ☎ (01744) 751850
Changing beers Ⓗ
An old community pub local to the town centre, the Phoenix welcomes families and pets. It has a comfortable large lounge and traditional bar with pool table and dartboard, and serves up to three cask ales plus ciders. Live music and quiz nights are hosted, and karaoke and sport can be watched on large screens in both rooms. ♿♣🐾ᯤ

Talbot Ale House

97 Duke Street, WA10 2JG
⏲ 12-1am (2am Fri & Sat); 12-midnight Sun
☎ (01744) 607578
3 changing beers (often George Wright) Ⓗ
This is a true community pub on the town-centre circuit with a traditional bar, games room and multi-functional lounge with a quiet room. The well-appointed beer garden adds extra drinking space. There are ales on 10 handpumps plus nine or more ciders, as well as a wide range of gins and malt whiskies. This sports-themed pub hosts many different games and quiz leagues, and karaoke on a Saturday night. Q❀♣●P🐾ᯤ

Turk's Head

Morley Street, WA10 2DQ
⏲ 2 (12 Sat & Sun)-11 ☎ (01744) 751289
Changing beers Ⓗ
This elegant pub a short walk from the town centre is a must for real ale lovers. It has a wide range of beers and ciders from around the country plus a large selection of gins and malt whiskies. The comfortable, quiet lounge is separated from the traditional bar with real fire by a pool room complete with piano. Home-made food is served Thursday to Sunday. Tuesday is quiz night and Wednesday is cheese night. A sheltered beer garden offers additional seating – pets are welcome here. ❀◗♣●ᯤ

Southport

Barons Bar

239 Lord Street, PR8 1NZ (on A565 opp Eastbank St)
⏲ 12-11 (midnight Fri & Sat) ☎ (01704) 534000
Moorhouse's Pride of Pendle; Tetley Bitter; house beer (by Moorhouse's); 6 changing beers (sourced regionally; often Lancaster, Moorhouse's, Southport) Ⓗ
An ornate baronial-style bar within the Scarisbrick Hotel complex, with a front lounge with chairs, tables and comfy settees overlooking the town's famous Lord Street. The bar has been a champion of real ale in Southport now for many years and has a varied selection of beers both local and national. One real cider is also available.
Q❀🛏♿≋●🚌🐾

Bottle Room

657 Lord Street, PR9 0AW
⏲ 12-10.30; 11-11 Fri & Sat ☎ (01704) 533054
Southport Sandgrounder Bitter, Golden Sands; 2 changing beers (sourced locally; often Southport) Ⓗ
Friendly café bar, formerly called the Inn Beer Shop, offering a huge selection of local, national and foreign bottled beers, real ciders and draught foreign lagers for takeaway or consumption on the premises. The bar now sports a second handpump. The interior is lined with bottles and continental-style seating, leading to a comfy area with games. Outside seating is on Lord Street. Dog-friendly, though it can get busy at weekends. ≋♣●🚌🐾ᯤ

Guest House

16 Union Street, PR9 0QE

11.30-11 (midnight Fri & Sat); 12-10.30 Sun

(01704) 537660 guesthouse-southport.blogspot.com

Butcombe Original; Ruddles Best Bitter; house beer (by Caledonian); 3 changing beers (often Phoenix, Salopian, Southport) H

Close to the station and Lord Street, this Grade II listed building has an impressive frontage and interior with three separate wood-panelled rooms. There is seating outside at the front and a courtyard area to the rear. The bar has 11 handpumps, one serving a local microbrewery beer, and also offers a wide range of malt whiskies. A quiet, traditional pub, it attracts a mixed clientele, with a quiz night on Thursday and acoustic folk club on the first and third Mondays of the month. Q

Peaky Blinders

589 Lord Street, PR9 0AN

10-midnight (1am Fri & Sat) (01704) 651881

thepeakyblinders.com

Robinsons Cumbria Way, Double Hop; Timothy Taylor Landlord; 2 changing beers (sourced regionally; often Martland Mill, Old School, Tatton) H

Peaky Blinders, named after the popular TV programme, opened in 2015 on the north end of Lord Street in what is now known as the Northern Quarter of Southport. The bar is in an old corner shop just up Seabank Road from the promenade. It is dog-friendly, with water bowls and doggy treats for four-legged friends. P

Phoenix

4-6 Coronation Walk, PR8 1RF

10-midnight (1am Sat) (01704) 513233

Sharp's Doom Bar; 2 changing beers H

A popular family-run sports pub at the top end of Lord Street. Free of tie, it is a favourite with real ale drinkers, and serves good food at reasonable prices. The pub has plenty of traditional games and hosts a poker night on Monday and Wednesday, darts on Tuesday, and live music on Friday. Football is shown on plasma TV screens scattered about the pub, with major fixtures shown on a large screen. A great family pub.

Sir Henry Segrave

93-97 Lord Street, PR8 1RH (on A565, S end of Lord Street)

8am-midnight (01704) 530217

Greene King Abbot; Moorhouse's Pendle Witches Brew; Phoenix Wobbly Bob; Ruddles Best Bitter; Sharp's Doom Bar; Wainwright; 6 changing beers (sourced regionally; often Lytham, Robinsons, Saltaire) H

Named after the former land speed world record holder who used to race on Southport flats, this is a spacious Wetherspoon pub with an attractive 19th-century exterior. The manager is a strong supporter of real ale and runs regular beer festival trips and occasional Meet the Brewer evenings. The 12 handpumps offer the best all-round choice of microbrewery beers in Southport – regular orders are placed with Phoenix, Saltaire, Titanic and Hawkshead. There is outside seating on the famous Lord Street. Q

Tap & Bottles

19A Cambridge Walk, PR8 1EN

12-11 (midnight Fri & Sat); 12-10.30 Sun

(01704) 544322

4 changing beers H

The Tap & Bottles is a micropub situated in the arcade between Chapel Street and Lord Street next to the Atkinson Centre. Four real ales may come from virtually any brewery, with a preference for north-west England beers. A huge range of bottles is also offered, but not all are real ale in a bottle. A small beer tapas menu is available all day. Pork pies and cheeseboards are served.

Q

Willow Grove

387-389 Lord Street, PR9 0AG (on A565)

8am-midnight (01704) 517830

Greene King Abbot H/G; **Moorhouse's Pendle Witches Brew; Phoenix Wobbly Bob; Ruddles Best Bitter; Shepherd Neame Bishops Finger; Wainwright; changing beers (often Bank Top, Parker, Saltaire)** H

The Willow Grove is a quiet Wetherspoon pub with an emphasis on real ale and food. It is situated on the town's famous Lord Street opposite the impressive 1920s war memorial. The interior is L-shaped with a long bar, cubicles and a mixture of furniture including comfy settees, chairs and tables. Ten handpumps dispense a choice of beers from breweries ranging from the local Parker to other micros to nationals. Q

Thornton Hough

Red Fox

Neston Road, CH64 7TL

10-11 (10.30 Sun) (0151) 353 2920

House beer (by Facer's and Phoenix); 7 changing beers (sourced locally; often Conwy, Neptune) H

Imposing building in its own extensive grounds dating from the 1890s, refurbished and reopened in 2014 as a smart gastropub serving quality food and well-kept beers. The front bar has the ambience of a friendly pub, with up to seven real ales and eight real ciders available. A smaller bar area at the back serves seating outside and a large lawned garden. House beers are Facer's 4% ABV Sunlight Blonde and Phoenix 3.8% ABV Brunning & Price Original Bitter. Q P (487)

Waterloo

Four Ashes

23 Crosby Road North, L22 0LD

closed Mon; 5-10 Tue-Thu; 4-10 Fri & Sat; 2.30-7.30 Sun

6 changing beers (often Liverpool Craft, Melwood, Wily Fox) H

Micropub with cask and bottled real ale from local breweries, continental bottled beers including alcohol-/gluten-free, premium vodkas, gins, wine and quality soft drinks. Tea and coffee are also served. Bar snacks include pork pies. Beers conditioning in the cellar are displayed on the wall and take-out containers are available. Waterloo is home to Gormley's Another Place cast-iron figures art installation on the estuary.

Q (Waterloo)

Stamps Too

99 South Road, L22 0LR (opp Waterloo station)

12-11 (midnight Thu-Sat) (0151) 280 0035

5 changing beers (sourced locally; often Brimstage, Oakham) H

A former local CAMRA Pub of the Year and CAMRA's original accredited LocAle pub. This friendly open-plan venue, where lively banter prevails at the bar, is the haunt both of real ale enthusiasts and live music fans. Five handpumps serve mainly local beers, from Brimstage, Southport and AllGates in particular, with occasional beers from further afield – a sixth handpump dispenses real cider. Bands and local musicians feature Thursday to Sunday. (53,133)

Volunteer Canteen ★

45 East Street, L22 8QR

2-11; 12-midnight Fri & Sat; 12-10.30 Sun

☎ 07891 407464

4 changing beers (sourced nationally) H

A cosy traditional pub in a Grade II listed terraced building, the Volly, as it is locally known, still provides table service. Nestling in the back streets of Waterloo, the pub dates from 1871 and, until the 1980s, was owned by Higsons, evidence of which can be seen etched into its windows. Small breweries around Merseyside and north Wales often supply guest ales. Pies, pâté, olives and nuts are served at all times. **Q** (53)

West Kirby

West Kirby Tap

Grange Road, CH48 4DY

12-11 (11.30 Fri & Sat) ☎ (0151) 625 0350

westkirbytap.co.uk

Spitting Feathers Thirstquencher; 7 changing beers (sourced nationally) H

Refurbished and reopened by Spitting Feathers brewery in 2014, this smart, modern bar features wood panelling, bare-brick walls and a high ceiling. The single bar has a small raised area and some discrete spaces. It is close to West Kirby's shops and transport connections, a short walk from the beach and convenient for trekkers to Hilbre Island. Eight handpumps dispense a varying range of beers plus a changing real cider.

Whiston

Beer EnGin

9 Greenes Road, L35 3RE

closed Mon; 4-9.30 (10 Fri); 2-10 Sat; 2-7 Sun

☎ 07496 616132

Changing beers H

Set among a row of shops, this unassuming-looking single-room micropub is a delight from the moment you walk in. The bar serves five real ales from local breweries plus craft beers, wines and a selection of unusual gins. With a warm welcome for all, including dogs, the pub has a laid-back, cosy atmosphere enhanced by impromptu music sessions. A selection of board games is available. Well worth the walk from the train station. Bank holiday hours may vary. **Q**

Baltic Fleet, Liverpool City Centre (Photo: Adrian Tierney-Jones)

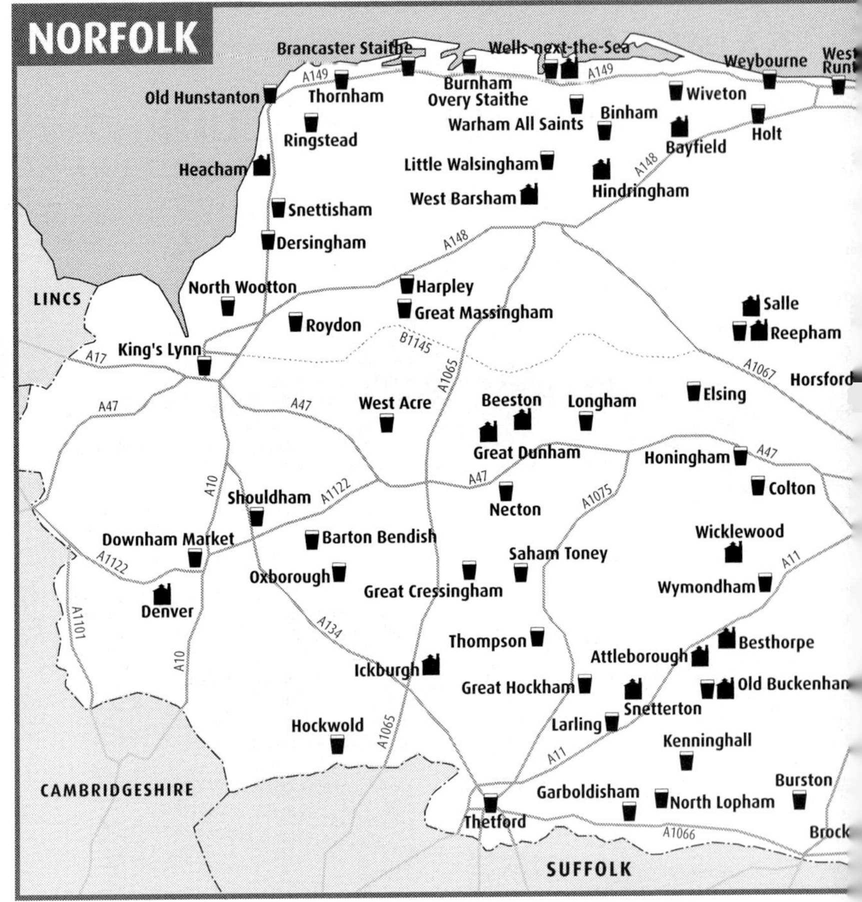

Banningham

Crown Inn

Colby Road, NR11 7DY (N of B1145, 1 mile E of A140)
12-11 (12.30am Fri & Sat) ☎ (01263) 733534
banninghamcrown.co.uk
Greene King IPA, Abbot; 4 changing beers
Traditional 17th-century free house overlooking the village green. The warm atmosphere of the original beamed bar interior is enhanced in winter by a log fire. Across seven handpumps, four feature guest beers from regional and micro breweries and one an artisan cider from a local producer. Popular for fine cuisine using local produce, the restaurant is open to the kitchen. The patio, garden and barbecue areas are ideal for summer alfresco dining. Regular events include quiz nights and music on Sundays. Winter opening hours may vary.
Q P (18)

Barton Bendish

Berney Arms

Church Road, PE33 9GF
12-11 ☎ (01366) 347995 theberneyarms.co.uk
Adnams Southwold Bitter; 2 changing beers
In a well-appointed quiet Norfolk village, this smartly presented old village pub is a quality establishment with energetic and friendly staff. The featured beer is often from the Moon Gazer range brewed by local Norfolk Brewhouse, plus the Adnams Southwold staple. In addition to the bar room, with a fire in the winter, there is a smart dining room and lovely garden with seating for summer. The adjacent renovated old stable block offers accommodation. Q P

Binham

Chequers Inn

Front Street, NR21 0AL
12-3, 6-11; 12-11 Fri & Sat; 12-10.30 Sun
☎ (01328) 830297 binhamchequers.co.uk
Adnams Southwold Bitter; Norfolk Brewhouse Moon Gazer Golden Ale; 3 changing beers
A traditional brick-and-flint village pub, the Chequers is a tremendously popular place both with locals and visitors, a friendly local with strong support from the surrounding community. The menu comprises a range of good wholesome fare (including vegetarian) at reasonable prices. There is an additional specials menu and regular themed evenings. One of the guests beers is from Norfolk Brewhouse, and others are sourced regionally, but often from Norfolk. In addition to the bar area, there are benches and tables both inside and outside, and a large garden to the rear.
P

Brancaster Staithe

Jolly Sailors

Main Road, PE31 8BJ

12-11; 12-10.30 Sun ☎ (01485) 210314

jollysailorsbrancaster.co.uk

Adnams Broadside; Woodforde's Wherry; 2 changing beers H

A cosy inn with several small drinking areas and two dining rooms, convenient for the Norfolk coast path and Brancaster Staithe harbour. It has a garden and play area, welcomes families and dogs, and has an ice cream hut. Brancaster beers are produced by a local brewery to the pub's recipes and at least one is always available. Food offerings include local seafood and stone-baked pizza, with the oven visible from the bar. Coasthopper buses stop outside. A beer and music festival takes place every June. Q ♣P

Brockdish

Old King's Head

50 The Street, IP21 4JY

closed Mon; 10-10 (11 Fri & Sat); 10-9 Sun

☎ (01379) 668843 kingsheadbrockdish.co.uk

Adnams Southwold Bitter; Humpty Dumpty Nord Atlantic, Red Mill; 2 changing beers (often Calvors Brewery, Wolf) H

A 16th-century beamed community pub with a friendly atmosphere. The pub reopened in 2015 with an added coffee shop (open from 10am) serving delicious home-made cakes, and bread at weekends. A family-friendly seating bar and a standing bar with woodburner both serve imaginative Italian food from noon, using locally sourced meats and ingredients where possible. Gluten-free meals and cakes are also available. Regular music events take place, usually on a Thursday. A gin club adds to the mix, with a choice of 150 gins. Local artists display work in the bars and a gallery. ♣P

Brooke

King's Head L

6 Norwich Road, NR15 1AB

12-11; 9.30-11 Sat & Sun ☎ (01508) 550335

kingsheadbrooke.co.uk

Adnams Southwold Bitter; Sharp's Doom Bar; 2 changing beers H

A 17th-century single-bar village inn with a more contemporary decor and furnishings. Run by two professional chefs, the pub offers food lovers an imaginative menu with many locally sourced

REAL ALE BREWERIES

All Day Salle
Ampersand Earsham
Barsham West Barsham (NEW)
Beeston Beeston
Blimey! Norwich (NEW)
Boudicca West Barsham
Buffy's Wicklewood
Bull of the Woods Kirby Cane (NEW)
Chalk Hill Norwich
Dancing Men Happisburgh
Elmtree Snetterton
Fat Cat Norwich
Fox Heacham
Golden Triangle Norwich
Grain Alburgh
Humpty Dumpty Reedham
Iceni Ickburgh
Lacons Great Yarmouth
Malt Coast Wells-next-the-Sea (NEW)
Neatishead Neatishead
Norfolk Brewhouse Hindringham
Oakwood Wells-next-the-Sea
Opa Hay's Aldeby
Panther Reepham
People's Thorpe-next-Haddiscoe
Poppyland Cromer
Redwell Norwich
S&P Horsford
St Andrews Norwich
Stumptail Great Dunham
Taylors Attleborough
Tindall Seething
Tipples Salhouse
Tombstone Great Yarmouth
Two Rivers Denver
Wagtail Old Buckenham
Waveney Earsham
Why Not Norwich
Wildcraft Buxton
Winter's Norwich
Wolf Besthorpe
Woodforde's Woodbastwick
Yaarbrew Hickling
Yetman's Bayfield

ingredients, and beer lovers a selection of four real ales, two of which are from local breweries such as Humpty Dumpty, Wolf, St Peter's and Woodforde's. Themed food evenings run from Monday to Friday, with breakfast served 9.30-11am at the weekend, and there is occasional live music, mainly on bank holidays. Q (88,87)

Broome

Artichoke

162 Yarmouth Road, NR35 2NZ

closed Mon; 12-3, 5-11; 12-11 Fri-Sun (01986) 893325

Adnams Southwold Bitter H, Broadside; Lacons Legacy G; Mauldons Micawber's Mild H; 6 changing beers G

A community-oriented village local made special by the people who run it. Delicious home-cooked food is served lunchtimes and evenings, which can be eaten in the separate dining area, the main bar near a roaring log fire, or in the garden in summer. A range of up to 10 beers is offered, with emphasis on local ales, dispensed either by handpump in the bar or by gravity from the taproom. The pub has around 100 malt whiskies. Open all day Tuesday-Friday from April to September.
Q P (580,588)

Burnham Overy Staithe

Hero

Wells Road, PE31 8JE

9am-11 (01328) 738334

theheroburnhamovery.co.uk

Adnams Southwold Bitter; Grain ThreeOneSix; Woodforde's Wherry H

Situated on the beautiful north Norfolk coast, this pleasant single-bar pub reopened two years ago after a complete refurbishment. The fresh and contemporary country-style interior includes many brass ornaments and items with naval connections. Food is available in the bar area, where dogs are welcome, or in the restaurant. There is also plenty of outdoor seating to take in the sea air.
P

Burston

Crown Inn

Mill Road, IP22 5TW (by crossroads in middle of village, on green)

12-11; 12-10.30 Sun (01379) 741257

burstoncrown.com

Adnams Southwold Bitter H/G; Greene King Abbot; 4 changing beers (often Adnams) H

Attractive 16th-century Grade II-listed pub featuring exposed beams, deep sofas, newspapers and a log fire blazing in the inglenook fireplace. There are two bars, one with a pool table and darts. Boules is played in the garden in summer. A small restaurant serves a mixed cuisine with locally sourced freshly cooked food (no food Sun eve or Mon). Booking is advisable. Live music takes place on Thursday evenings, and music and other entertainments regularly throughout the year, including a beer festival. The village is famous for the Burston School Strike that ran from 1914-1939.
Q P

Catfield

Crown Inn

The Street, NR29 5AA (in centre of village, S of A149, E of Stalham)

12-2.30, 7-11; 12-2.30, 5-11 Fri; 12-3, 7-midnight Sat; 12-6, 7-10.30 Sun (01692) 580128 catfieldcrown.co.uk

Greene King IPA; 3 changing beers H

This 300-year-old village inn, with its real fire, is a genuine focus for village life. Ales are usually from local breweries. The food includes home-made pub offerings, with fresh local ingredients used where possible. There is a separate function/dining room and a secluded rear garden for the summer. Accommodation is available in two holiday cottages. An annual beer festival is held in the summer, usually in July. Q P

Coltishall

Red Lion

77 Church Street, NR12 7DW

12 (4 Mon)-11 (01603) 736644

redlion-coltishall.co.uk

Sharp's Doom Bar; 2 changing beers H

A warm, friendly and comfortable establishment which dates from the 16th century. The intricate two-level pub has a separate dining area complemented by a café. In the cosy lower bar with logburner up to five real ales can be found, some from local and regional microbreweries. The pub also presses its own bottled cider from local orchards. The varied menu features specials and there are theme nights. Beer festivals are held at Easter and in late summer, and the pub even has its own taxi. Q P (29)

Colton

Norfolk Lurcher

High House Farm Lane, NR9 5DG (2 miles from S of A47 Norwich Southern bypass)

12-2.30 (not Tue), 6-11; 12-2.30, 6-10 Sun

(01603) 880794 the-norfolklurcher.com

4 changing beers H

A traditional and welcoming family owned and run country pub in the heart of the Norfolk countryside, yet only a short drive from Norwich. The landlord cellars his beers well, and always has four handpumps serving the best of local real ales, or you could try one of his 60 single malts. Large comfortable bar areas are complemented by the excellent Ugly Bug restaurant serving locally produced food. An extensive beer garden can be enjoyed on warmer days. There are monthly jazz evenings and eight en-suite bedrooms are available. Q P

Cromer

Red Lion Hotel

Brook Street, NR27 9HD (behind church on clifftop)

11-11 (01263) 514964 redlion-cromer.co.uk

6 changing beers H

Splendidly situated with views of Cromer pier and the sea, the 19th-century Red Lion has retained many of its original features including panelling, a Victorian tiled floor and open wood fires. The work of local artists decorates the walls of the two bar areas. Up to six guest ales are usually available, often from local breweries such as Humpty Dumpty, Beeston and Wolf. Beer festivals are held in the summer. The award-winning restaurant offers an extensive menu, and serves breakfast 7-10.30am. Q 🛏 ◐ ♿ ⇌ 🍎 P 🚌 🐾 📶

Dersingham

Coach & Horses ✔

77 Manor Road, PE31 6LN

12-11 ☎ (01485) 540391 🌐 thecoachpub.com

Woodforde's Wherry; 3 changing beers H

A 19th-century carrstone pub near Sandringham offering three changing guest ales plus one constant and a draught real cider, at reasonable prices. It is popular for home-made traditional meals. Entertainment includes quiz nights, a piano, a pool table and live music Friday nights and some Sundays. The large garden includes a children's play area. It has three en-suite B&B rooms. An October beer festival offers around 20 real ales plus five real ciders. Q ❀ 🛏 ◐ Ă 🍎 P 🚌 🐾 📶

Downham Market

Crown Hotel

12 Bridge Street, PE38 9DH

9.30am-11 ☎ (01366) 382322 🌐 crowncoachinginn.com

Adnams Southwold Bitter; Greene King IPA, Abbot; 2 changing beers H

An unspoilt 17th-century coaching inn at the heart of the town. Enter through a room with a lovely staircase to find a bar with a beamed ceiling and large fireplace serving a good selection of ales. There is a restaurant, which serves a range of meals and lighter bites, with roasts on Sunday, and a separate function room that caters for parties and weddings. There is plenty of outside seating. Accommodation is provided, with 18 rooms including family suites. Q ❀ 🛏 ◐ ⇌ P 🚌 📶

Elsing

Mermaid Inn

Church Street, NR20 3EA (opp St Mary's Church)

12-3 (not Mon), 6-11; 12-3, 6-10.30 Sun

☎ (01362) 637640 🌐 elsingmermaidinn.co.uk

Adnams Broadside; Woodforde's Wherry G**; 1 changing beer** H

Well-regarded rural pub with restaurant comprising a large bar and dining room, featuring a fire at one end and a pool table at the other. A good selection of ales is on offer dispensed by gravity. The menu includes the landlord's well-rated pies and curries together with several vegetarian options. Local groups and societies meet here regularly, while ramblers from further afield arrive via the 12-mile Wensum Way along the river Wensing. Two outdoor seating areas provide for pleasant summer drinking. ❀ ◐ ♿ P 🐾 📶

Fritton

Decoy Tavern

Beccles Road, NR31 9AB

11-11 ☎ (01493) 488277

2 changing beers H

Traditional country free house set back from the road between Beccles and Great Yarmouth, close to Fritton Lake and about a mile from Broads moorings on the River Waveney at St Olaves. There is a grassed beer garden to the side of the pub with seating. A wide range of home-cooked meals is available in the separate dining area. The beer selection varies but tends to feature two or three locally sourced real ales. The current landlords have been here for 30 years. ❀ ◐ ♣ P 🚌 (580) 🐾 📶

Garboldisham

Fox Inn L

The Street, IP22 2RZ

closed Mon-Thu; 5-10 Fri; 12-10 Sat; 12-5 Sun

☎ (01953) 688538 🌐 garboldishamfox.co.uk

Lacons Encore; Old Chimneys Great Raft Bitter; 4 changing beers (often Boudicca, Elmtree, Star Wing) G

A welcoming 17th-century coaching inn near Bressingham Gardens/Banham Zoo. Bought by the local community to run as a community pub, it reopened in 2016 and remains open while renovation continues. A collection of old jugs belonging to a lady who lived in The Fox several years ago is on display. Q ❀ ♣ 🍎 P 🐾

Geldeston

Locks Inn L

Locks Lane, NR34 0HS (around 800yds along track from Station Rd)

11-11 ☎ (01508) 518414 🌐 geldestonlocks.co.uk

Grain Redwood, Oak; 6 changing beers H

Geldeston's Locks is probably one of the most secluded pubs in Norfolk. It is accessible by a track across several marshes or by boat from the river Waveney. The pub has grown over the years as a great place for beer, food and a varied programme of events. It has been maintained to look as traditional as possible, with low wooden beams and an old-style bar. The outside seating covers a vast area all the way to the river. Q ❀ ◐ ♿ Ă ♣ 🍎 P 🐾

Gorleston

Dock Tavern L

Dock Tavern Lane, NR31 6PY (opp N side of Morrisons)

11-11; 12-11 Sun ☎ (01493) 442255

🌐 thedocktavern.com

Adnams Broadside; 3 changing beers H

As its name suggests, the Dock Tavern is close to the river, and not far from the main shopping area. It has been subject to flood damage many times and the various flood levels can be seen by the front door. The outside drinking area at the front has views of the river and docks. There is live music most weekends, and curry and quiz nights monthly, plus an annual charity music day. ❀ ◐ ♣ 🍎 🚌 🐾 📶

New Entertainer

80 Pier Plain, NR31 6PG

12-midnight ☎ (01493) 300022

Greene King IPA; 11 changing beers H

This traditional and unusual pub has a curved frontage with an interesting design and layout. There is a varied choice of beers on offer, including up to 10 guest real ales, many of which are locally brewed, as well as up to nine traditional ciders. The customers are as widely varied as the beers, with pool and darts available along with a monthly quiz. This free house is well worth seeking out; please note that the main entrance is on Back Pier Plain. CAMRA Pub of the Year 2018. ❀ ⇌ ♣ 🍎 🚌 🐾 📶

Oddfellows Arms

43 Cliff Hill, NR31 6DG
4-10.30 (11 Fri); 2-11 Sat & Sun ☎ 07876 545982
oddiesgy.co.uk
Lacons Encore, Legacy; St Austell Tribute; 1 changing beer Ⓗ
This quaint and friendly pub, the last remaining on Cliff Hill, comprises a U-shaped bar over two split-level rooms. The upper bar, which houses the pool table, dartboard and comfy seating, is where the live music is staged. The lower bar, considered the main bar area, has five handpumps, with two Lacons real ales and St Austell Tribute as the regular beer. There is also a selection of other quality beers. ❀♿P🐾📶

Great Cressingham

Olde Windmill Inn

Water End, IP25 6NN (off A1065 S of Swaffham)
11-11 ☎ (01760) 756232 oldewindmillinn.co.uk
Adnams Southwold Bitter, Broadside; Greene King IPA; 2 changing beers Ⓗ
The Windmill is a large rural pub and hotel, feeling cosy despite its size. Family run for three generations, it has a rolling range of beers, including house beer Windy Miller, mostly supplied by Purity. Real cider also features. Modern hotel accommodation is available in separate buildings behind the pub. The popular food menu has something for all tastes. Dining areas vary in size from a large conservatory to smaller, intimate rooms. Q❀◑◐♿⛺♣P🐾

Great Hockham

Eagle

Harling Road, IP24 1NP
12-2.30, 6-11 (11.30 Thu); 12-midnight Fri & Sat; 12-10.30 Sun ☎ (01953) 498893 hockhameagle.com
Adnams Southwold Bitter, Ghost Ship; Morland Old Speckled Hen; Woodforde's Wherry; 1 changing beer Ⓗ
Dating from the 1850s, this large pub is set in a picturesque village close to Thetford Forest, and welcomes families and dogs. Two bars divided by an open fire serve five real ales on handpump. Outdoor seating is provided at the front and in an enclosed brick-weave courtyard at the rear. The pub hosts three pool teams and a darts team in addition to a fortnightly quiz and other regular events. ❀◑◐♿♣P🚌🐾📶

Great Massingham

Dabbling Duck

11 Abbey Road, PE32 2HN
11-11; 11-10.30 Sun ☎ (01485) 520827
thedabblingduck.co.uk
Adnams Ghost Ship; Woodforde's Wherry, Nelson's Revenge; 1 changing beer Ⓗ
Set between two ponds at the heart of a lovely village, the pub features bar areas with roaring fires in the winter and a garden to enjoy in the summer. With ample room for those wishing to try one of the three or four beers on offer, there is also a popular restaurant (booking recommended). Accommodation is in six rooms and guides featuring details of local walks are available from the bar. ❀◑◐♣P🐾📶

Great Yarmouth

Avenue

43 Beatty Road, NR30 4BW
12-11; 11-midnight Fri & Sat; 12-10.30 Sun
☎ (01493) 843220 theavenuegreatyarmouth.co.uk
Adnams Ghost Ship; Sharp's Doom Bar; 1 changing beer Ⓗ
Built in 1929, this imposing Lacons mock-Tudor building is close to the racecourse. The interior, although somewhat opened up, still retains the original bar-back and most of the original three-room layout. The pub has recently been taken over by Heineken, which may vary the beer selection. There is a beer garden at the rear, food is served all day, and pool, darts and live sports TV are all available. ❀◑◐⛺♣P🚌(8)🐾📶

King's Arms

229 Northgate Street, NR30 1BG
12-10 (11 Wed & Thu; midnight Fri & Sat)
☎ (01493) 843736 thekingsarmsgreatyarmouth.co.uk
Adnams Broadside; Woodforde's Wherry; 1 changing beer Ⓗ
Rebuilt in the early 20th century, there has been a pub on this site near the Market Place since the 1600s. It has a large part-lawned enclosed beer garden outside with a children's playground and views of St Nicholas, the largest parish church in England. Food is served in the cosy restaurant lunchtimes and evenings. Barbecues are held through the summer, with a beer festival on the August bank holiday. Live music can be enjoyed most Saturday evenings. ❀◑◐⇌♣P🐾

Lichfield Arms

116-117 Lichfield Road, NR31 0AB
2-midnight; 12-midnight Sat & Sun ☎ (01493) 302959
2 changing beers Ⓗ
A traditional community pub, full of character and characters, consisting of a large, single U-shaped bar with numerous entrances from the street. At either end of the bar you have a dartboard and a pool table, with various board games also available. There is a patio and covered smoking area outside. The long-serving landlord, who has been at the pub for 30 years, offers two rotating guest ales. Well-behaved dogs are welcome.
❀♿♣🚌🐾📶

Mariners

69 Howard Street South, NR30 1LN (between Palmers and the Star Hotel)
12-midnight ☎ (01493) 331164
12 changing beers Ⓗ
Traditional two-bar flint-walled pub in the town centre which stocks up to 12 ales and several ciders/perries, with a range from all over the country. The pub decor has a maritime theme, with photos of different ships on the walls. In the winter you can enjoy your drinks while sitting next to a lovely open fire. Knowledgeable staff and great choice make it well worth the visit.
❀⇌♣P🚌🐾📶

Red Herring

24-25 Havelock Road, NR30 3HQ (off St Peters St and at back of Time & Tide museum)
12-3, 7-midnight; 12-midnight Sat & Sun ☎ 07876 644742
4 changing beers Ⓗ
The Red Herring gets its name from the fish that were cured in the nearby now-closed smokehouses, and is close to the impressive

medieval walls along with the award-winning Time and Tide museum. The pub hosts three changing beers with two ciders, and darts and pool are available. There is always a relaxing and friendly atmosphere here. ❀♣●▯🚌🐾

Tombstone Saloon 🏆

6 George Street, NR30 1HR (on NE corner of Hall Quay)
🕔 closed Mon-Wed; 12-midnight; 12-8 Sun ☎ 07584 504444
🌐 tombstonebrewery.co.uk
10 changing beers Ⓖ

Old West-style bar specialising in real ale and cider, operated by the local Tombstone Brewery sited at the rear of the premises. Staff are friendly and knowledgeable about beer, and there are usually up to six Tombstone real ales, plus four others from various breweries. Many buses stop outside the pub. George Street was once one of the main roads into Yarmouth. It is closed Monday-Wednesday in winter except December, and holds an annual Easter beer festival and occasional live music. East Norfolk CAMRA Pub of the Year 2018.
Q🐴⚟♣●▯🚌🐾

Happisburgh

Hill House Ⓛ

The Hill, NR12 0PW (off B1159, behind church)
🕔 12-11 ☎ (01692) 650004 🌐 hillhouseinn.co.uk
6 changing beers Ⓗ

A Grade II 16th-century former coaching inn in an attractive coastal village. It was a haunt of Sir Arthur Conan Doyle – the in-house brewery is named after his 'Dancing Men' story. The pub usually offers a range of up to six real ales and one cider, all from this brewery. Hot meals are available lunchtimes and evenings. A noteworthy beer festival is held each June offering over 120 real ales and ciders. Q🐴❀🛏◐◑⛺♣●P🐾📶

Harpley

Rose & Crown

Nethergate Street, PE31 6TW
🕔 12-11; 12-10.30 Sun ☎ (01485) 521807
Woodforde's Wherry; 4 changing beers Ⓗ

Just off the A148 King's Lynn to Fakenham Road, this attractive 17th-century pub offers guest ales from local breweries. It features open bar areas with a stylish and comfortable feel and has log fires in winter, while outside is an enclosed beer garden for summer drinking. There is an extensive menu serving excellent food, including one of the best Sunday roasts in the area. The unspoilt village provides pleasant walks and is close to Houghton Hall. Q🐴❀◐◑P🚌(X29)🐾📶

Hickling

Greyhound Inn Ⓛ ✔

The Green, NR12 0YA (in village, not by Broad)
🕔 12-11 ☎ (01692) 598306 🌐 greyhoundinn.com
Adnams Ghost Ship; 3 changing beers Ⓗ

A traditional village-centre pub with a welcoming atmosphere. The bar has an attractive open fireplace and an area where pub games and music events are staged. In addition to the regular beer there are three guests. The restaurant is popular for home-prepared meals using fresh local ingredients wherever possible. There is an outdoor covered area and an award-winning garden for alfresco summer dining. Social and community events are held regularly. Ideally situated near the north-east Norfolk coast and Hickling Broad.
Q❀◐◑♿⛺♣P🐾📶

Hockwold

Red Lion

114 Main Street, IP26 4NB
🕔 11.30-3, 6 (5 Sat)-11.30; 12-10.30 Sun ☎ (01842) 829728
🌐 redlionhockwold.com
3 changing beers Ⓗ

Traditional friendly village pub set on a green. The Red Lion was refurbished and reopened as a free house in 2012; it has a smart but comfortable interior – see how many toby jugs you can spot. A good selection of home-made food is served all week, with a carvery on Sunday and Tuesday lunchtimes. Thursday is steak night. There are regular well-supported quizzes and darts matches. Outside is a spacious garden with plenty of seating and a children's play area. 🐴❀◐◑♣P🐾

Holt

King's Head

19 High Street, NR25 6BN
🕔 11.30-11; 11.30-10.30 Sun ☎ (01263) 712543
🌐 kingsheadholt.org.uk
Greene King St Edmunds, London Glory; Norfolk Brewhouse Moon Gazer Golden, Moon Gazer Amber, Moon Gazer Ruby; Woodforde's Wherry Ⓗ**; 7 changing beers** Ⓖ

A Grade II-listed building in the centre of this delightful Georgian market town. The pub features two bars and a snug, a conservatory and a small outside drinking area. The beers change on a monthly basis, with most being sourced regionally, and there can be up to eight gravity-fed ales from the ale wall. There are also three bedrooms, two with self-catering kitchens.
Q🐴❀🛏◐◑♣🚌(X6)🐾📶

Honingham

Buck Ⓛ

29 The Street, NR9 5BL (centre of village)
🕔 11.30-11; 11.30-10 Sun ☎ (01603) 880393
🌐 thehoninghambuck.co.uk
Lacons Affinity, Encore; 2 changing beers Ⓗ

Dating back to 1789, this traditional one-bar village pub has a separate restaurant area with an emphasis on home-cooked food. It serves Lacons real ales since the brewery bought the pub in May 2015, and has slate floors, oak beams, a large fireplace and period furniture - it fits the image of a country pub. The excellent menu of unusual food freshly cooked to order makes it a great venue for eating. Q🐴❀🛏◐◑♿P🐾

Kenninghall

Red Lion ★ Ⓛ

East Church Street, NR16 2EP (opp parish church)
🕔 12-10 Mon; 10-11 Tue-Sat; 12-10 Sun ☎ (01953) 887849
🌐 redlionkenninghall.co.uk
Adnams Old Ale, Ghost Ship; Morland Old Golden Hen; Woodforde's Wherry Ⓗ

Dating from the early 16th century, this beautifully restored pub is recognised by CAMRA as having a nationally important historic interior for its pine-panelled snug (one of only two in East Anglia); adjacent is a 50-seater restaurant in the style of old stables. The good wholesome home-cooked menu includes fresh fish Fridays. Regular live music and other community events take place. It has four guest rooms including a linkable pair for families. Sunday brunch is 10am-3pm.

King's Lynn

Stuart House Hotel

35 Goodwins Road, PE30 5QX (up gravel drive off Goodwins Road)

6-11 (01553) 772169 stuart-house-hotel.co.uk

3 changing beers H

About a 10-minute walk across the park from the railway station, this hotel bar is open to anyone and has been a Guide regular for over 20 years. There are two or three beers on offer, usually from well-known breweries in the local area. A regular beer festival is staged in the large garden, usually in the last week in July, and occasional events such as live music and murder mystery evenings are held throughout the year. Although the bar is only open in the evening, it is often possible to arrange lunchtime opening if you contact the hotel.

Larling

Angel

NR16 2QU (1 mile SW from Snetterton racetrack, just off A11)

10-midnight; 11-11 Sun (01953) 717963

angel-larling.co.uk

Adnams Southwold Bitter; 4 changing beers H

Well known for its annual beer festival in August, the Angel offers a variety of real ales on handpump, including a mild. One real cider is on the bar plus a huge range of whiskies. The lounge and bar have open fires; the friendly atmosphere reflects the farming nature of the area. There is a dining room where the food is home-made and comes in impressive portions. The pub features B&B accommodation plus camping facilities.

Q

Lessingham

Star Inn L

Star Hill, NR12 0DN (just off main B1159, corner of High Rd and Star Hill)

closed Mon; 12-3, 6-11; 12-11 Sun (01692) 580510

thestarlessingham.co.uk

Adnams Southwold Bitter; Lacons Encore; Woodforde's Once Bittern; 1 changing beer G

Local CAMRA Rural Pub of the Year 2017, this is a traditional hostelry with a friendly atmosphere and a log fire in winter. Four ales, including one guest, are served from the cask, as are three ciders. It is popular for high-quality meals, with carefully sourced ingredients served in decent portions. Meals may be enjoyed in the bar, in a separate restaurant or in the spacious beer garden. Two en-suite double B&B rooms make this the perfect base to explore the north-east Norfolk coast and the Broads. A rural gem. Q (34)

Little Walsingham

Black Lion Hotel

Friday Market Place, NR22 6DB

11-11; 11-10.30 Sun (01328) 820235

blacklionhotelnorfolk.co.uk

Adnams Ghost Ship; Woodforde's Wherry; 2 changing beers H

This family-friendly pub with rooms, parts of which date back to the 15th century, is in the centre of Walsingham, a major pilgrimage centre famed for its religious shrines in honour of the Virgin Mary. The bar is relaxed with a slightly rustic feel, including oak beams, farm implements and old tractor seat stools. The food is all locally sourced and prepared on site (except the pies).

Q

Longham

White Horse

Wendling Road, NR19 2RD

11.30-2.30, 5-11; 11.30-midnight Sat; 11-10.30 Sun

(01362) 687464 longhamwhitehorse.co.uk

4 changing beers H

Quiet, attractive village pub with restaurant. The beer range, which can be as many as six, usually includes Oakham Bishop's Farewell and local brews such as Moon Gazer. The current landlord has traced his predecessors back to 1640, with names displayed on a glass panel in the bar. Beer festivals with live music are staged in August and December. It has a pleasant garden and outdoor seating area, while two doubles and a family room provide B&B. Various themed events and music take place through the year.

Q

Martham

King's Arms

15 The Green, NR29 4PL

12-11 (midnight Fri & Sat); 12-10.30 Sun

(01493) 749156

3 changing beers H

Previously owned by Adnams, and well before that by the original incarnation of Lacons, The King's Arms, in the centre of the village by the pond, has recently become a free house, serving up to five ales from local and less-local breweries. There is a nice garden out the back, a large car park, and food is served all day. A sloe gin competition is held annually.

Neatishead

White Horse L

The Street, NR12 8AD

11-11; 11-10.30 Sun (01692) 630828

thewhitehorseinnneatishead.com

Woodforde's Wherry; 6 changing beers H

Traditional Broadland village pub just a short walk from the moorings. A tasteful modernisation retains many original features. There are three drinking areas and log fires in winter. Of the seven real ales, six change frequently and are mainly from microbreweries across the UK, including from the in-house brewery. The pub also has a good range of craft keg beers. Excellent, reasonably priced meals are home prepared with local produce. There is a cosy, split-level restaurant. Beer festivals are held in spring and autumn.

Q

Necton

Windmill Inn

15-17 Mill Street, PE37 8EN

⌚ 11-3.30, 6-11; 11-11 Sat; 12-10.30 Sun ☎ (01760) 722057
🌐 thenectonwindmill.co.uk

Greene King IPA; 2 changing beers Ⓗ

The pub is next to the ground-floor remains of the former Necton windmill, hence the name. This is a friendly, family-run, two-bar pub with a large restaurant extension. There is a games room with a pool table. It serves regular Greene King IPA and a Beeston beer; there is also a varying guest, usually from Humpty Dumpty. The pub has a large rear beer garden and paved and decked areas at the front with tables. Bar meals and a full restaurant menu are on offer, with an excellent local reputation. **P**

North Lopham

King's Head ✔

16 The Street, IP22 2NE (2 miles N of A1066)
⌚ 11.30-3 (not Mon), 5-11; 11.30-midnight Sat; 12-10.30 Sun
☎ (01379) 688007 🌐 lophamkingshead.co.uk

Adnams Southwold Bitter; Star Wing Spire Light; 1 changing beer (sourced nationally; often Cotleigh, Elmtree) Ⓗ

A timber-framed and thatched 16th-century pub set back from the main road through the village. It has two bars: the public bar has a pool table and inglenook fireplace, and the comfortable saloon/dining room has a woodburner. The guest ale varies but is usually 4% ABV or more. The discounted guest ale on Saturday sells quickly. Food is served Wednesday to Saturday lunch and evening, plus Sunday lunch. It has a crazy golf course with free club and ball hire. Letting rooms and Wi-Fi are coming soon. **QP**

North Walsham

Hop In 𝕃

2 Market Street, NR28 9BZ
⌚ closed Mon; 12-10.30 (11 Fri & Sat); 12-10 Sun
☎ 07426 139417 🌐 thehopin.co.uk

6 changing beers Ⓖ

Norfolk's only (known) micropub, in a converted shop with beams and a bay window, with views down Market Street. Ales are served on gravity, there is real cider and wine also available, and always one dark beer. It has seating for about a dozen downstairs, and around 20 more upstairs. In keeping with the micropub philosophy, there is no Wi-Fi, music or machines, just good conversation! Owned and run by keen CAMRA members. **Q**

Orchard Gardens 𝕃 ✔

Mundesley Road, NR28 0DB
⌚ 3-midnight; 1-midnight Fri; 12-midnight Sat & Sun
☎ (01692) 405152 🌐 theorchardgardens.co.uk

Adnams Ghost Ship; 3 changing beers (often Lacons, Woodforde's) Ⓗ

A town pub combining local beers from breweries like Adnams and Lacons with friendly service. A games area and conservatory are a feature in this Victorian building with a large garden. Pool and darts teams are supported, and there is live sport on the large-screen TV, a weekly quiz and live music every Saturday. **P**

North Wootton

Red Cat Hotel

Station Road, PE30 3QH (road is opp All Saints church, at jct of N end of Nursery Rd and W end of Manor Rd)
⌚ 5-11; 12-2, 7-11 Sun ☎ (01553) 631244
🌐 redcathotel.co.uk

Adnams Southwold Bitter; 1 changing beer Ⓗ

Village local with a reputation for well-kept beer, albeit of limited range – a nicely decorated bar in a quiet location. Ask about the history of the namesake red cat – if you can believe it. It has attractive gardens for summer drinks, and is near National Cycle Route 1, the Sandringham Estate and the west Norfolk coast. **QP**(3)

Norwich

Alexandra Tavern

16 Stafford Street, NR2 3BB (on corner of Stafford St and Gladstone St, off Dereham Rd)
⌚ 12-11 (midnight Thu-Sat) ☎ (01603) 627772
🌐 alexandratavern.co.uk

Chalk Hill CHB, Gold, Tap Bitter; 2 changing beers Ⓗ

Popular, bustling and friendly, this pub is a real gem found just outside the city centre. The interior is brightly decorated, with the walls featuring pictures and articles of a nautical nature. The bar regularly has three Chalk Hill Brewery beers as well as guest ales. Food is served daily until 7pm with a good variety available, including a soup menu. There is a dartboard and plenty of board games to choose from, with children also welcome until 7pm. **Q**

Beehive 𝕃

30 Leopold Road, NR4 7PJ
⌚ 12 (4 Mon)-11; 12-midnight Fri & Sat ☎ (01603) 451628
🌐 beehivepubnorwich.co.uk

Fuller's London Pride; Green Jack Golden Best; Oakham Bishops Farewell; 4 changing beers Ⓗ

A traditional friendly local with knowledgeable staff, with two bar areas and a comfortable lounge bar with sofas. A popular beer garden is used all year round and hosts a beer festival with around 25 ales/ciders in late June. There is a function room upstairs with a pool table, and the pub has hockey, korfball, golf, darts and pool teams, a regular quiz, and folk music nights. Norfolk CAMRA Pub of the Year in 2015. **QP**

Coach & Horses

82 Thorpe Road, NR1 1BA
⌚ 11-11 (1 Fri & Sat) ☎ (01603) 477077
🌐 thecoachthorperoad.co.uk

Chalk Hill CHB, Dreadnought, Gold, Tap Bitter; 3 changing beers Ⓗ

Close to the station, this coaching inn, with its iconic balcony, is the home of the Chalk Hill Brewery and serves the full range of beers, along with Burnard's cider. A tour of the brewery is available by appointment. Excellent-value food is served. Sport, especially rugby, is shown on big screens, and the large fire is welcome in winter. Not far from football ground, it gets busy before matches. **P**

Coach & Horses

51 Bethel Street, NR2 1NR
⌚ 12-midnight ☎ (01603) 618522
🌐 thecoachandhorsesbethelstreet.co.uk

6 changing beers Ⓗ

Historic city-centre local near the Theatre Royal, the Forum and City Hall. It is a bright, welcoming bar with several separate seating areas including cosy alcove-style seats, which stocks a great range of local ales from brewers including Norfolk Brewhouse, Humpty Dumpty, Golden Triangle and Jo C's. The wholesome food menu is driven by the best of local produce. Ideal for a beer before or after the theatre, or any time of day. Try some celeb spotting too! Q🐎❀◐♣●🚌🐾📶

Duke of Wellington Ⓛ

91-93 Waterloo Road, NR3 1EG

12-11 (midnight Fri & Sat); 12-10.30 Sun

☎ (01603) 441182 🌐 dukeofwellingtonnorwich.co.uk

Fuller's London Pride [H]; Oakham JHB, Bishops Farewell [G]; Wolf Golden Jackal [H], Wolf in Sheep's Clothing; 15 changing beers [G]

Friendly pub with a changing range of guest ales to complement the permanent beers, the majority of which are served on gravity from a taproom behind the bar. The attractive award-winning enclosed rear garden/patio area accommodates a beer festival in late August, plus regular barbecues at weekends in summer. Events include monthly quiz evenings and folk music every Tuesday evening. Customers can bring their own food in or sample the filling and inexpensive pies and sausage rolls. ❀♿♣●P🚌(9A,16)🐾📶

Eaton Cottage Ⓛ

75 Mount Pleasant, NR2 2DQ

12-11 (midnight Fri & Sat) ☎ (01603) 453048

Fuller's London Pride; Wolf Golden Jackal; 4 changing beers [H]

A large and friendly local pub close to the shops in the Golden Triangle, with a number of seating areas inside and out, serving an interesting variety of ales from local breweries such as Elmtree and Wolf, plus beers from other UK breweries large and small. Sports are shown on TV but the screens do not dominate (except in one small area!). There is also a pleasant pergola-covered patio to one side of the pub. ❀♿♣🍺🚌(25)🐾📶

Fat Cat Ⓛ

49 West End Street, NR2 4NA

11-11 (midnight Fri & Sat) ☎ (01603) 624364

🌐 fatcatpub.co.uk

Adnams Southwold Bitter; Crouch Vale Yakima Gold [H]; Fat Cat Marmalade Cat [G], Bitter [H]; Greene King Abbot; Timothy Taylor Landlord; 20 changing beers [G]

A beer-lover's paradise that no visitor to Norwich should miss out on. Ales from the Fat Cat range are on the bar, plus about 10 regular and 20 guest beers from all over the UK, real ciders, and several craft keg beers. The Cat has been voted CAMRA National Pub of the Year twice. An amazing range of brewery memorabilia is displayed around the walls and alcoves of this traditional-style pub. Food is limited to good-value rolls and pies. An outstanding example of what a real ale pub should be, with excellent, friendly service. Q❀●🚌🐾📶

Fat Cat Brewery Tap 🏆 Ⓛ

98-100 Lawson Road, NR3 4LF

12-11 (midnight Fri); 11-midnight Sat; 11-10.30 Sun

☎ (01603) 413153 🌐 fatcattap.co.uk

Adnams Southwold Bitter [H]; Fat Cat Bitter [G], Honey Ale, Marmalade Cat [H]; Oakham Bishops Farewell; 16 changing beers [G]

Former Norfolk CAMRA Pub of the Year, with breweriana adorning the walls and ceilings. It is the home of the Fat Cat Brewery, with a wide range of other local and national ales, ciders and craft keg beers. Live music on Fridays and Sundays complements a variety of events held at the pub including tap takeovers, themed beer evenings, a monthly cycling club, a fortnightly quiz and a ladies' beer club. Food is largely confined to snacks but cheeseboards can be provided (with 24 hours' notice). Q❀♿♣●P🚌(11,11A)🐾📶

Jubilee Ⓛ ✔

26 St Leonards Road, NR1 4BL

12-11 (midnight Fri & Sat) ☎ (01603) 618734

Greene King IPA; Woodforde's Wherry, Sundew, Nelson's Revenge; 2 changing beers [H]

An attractive Victorian corner pub with a warm welcome. There is a choice of two bars, a comfortable conservatory and an enclosed patio garden. Many of the well-kept ales are local. This popular pub is at the heart of the community and caters for all tastes, from sports fans to those who enjoy local history talks, and has a village feel although it is within easy reach of the city centre. Occasional pop-up street food fairs are held. 🐎❀◐⇌♣🚌🐾📶

King's Arms

22 Hall Road, NR1 3HQ

11-11 (11.30 Fri & Sat); 12-11 Sun ☎ (01603) 477888

🌐 kingsarmsnorwich.co.uk

Batemans XB; 10 changing beers [H]

A friendly Batemans house to the south of the city, which serves an extensive and varied range of guest ales to complement the Batemans beers, usually including a stout or porter and a mild. Between three (in winter) and six (in summer) real ciders are also available. Customers can bring their own food from various nearby takeaways, with plates and condiments provided. Monthly quiz nights, poker evenings and live music feature. Busy on match days. 🐎❀♿♣●🚌(39)🐾📶

King's Head Ⓛ

42 Magdalen Street, NR3 1JE

12-midnight; 12-11 Sun ☎ (01603) 620468

🌐 kingsheadnorwich.com

14 changing beers [H]

Friendly and welcoming traditional-style two-bar pub which offers up to 14 quality real ales and one cider, but no keg beer. The house beer, KHB, is brewed by Winter's, while the changing beers are from all around the country, with a bias towards Norfolk micros. Local fresh eggs and honey are often available. There is no food except snacks, pork pies and pickled eggs, but you can bring your own, and plates and cutlery will be supplied. Bar billiards is well supported, with two teams in the local league. Q❀♣●🍺🚌🐾📶

Leopard Ⓛ

98-100 Bull Close Road, NR3 1NQ

12-11 (midnight Fri & Sat) ☎ (01603) 631111

5 changing beers [H]

A traditional single-bar corner local with a variety of changing ales from the smaller breweries, usually including at least one from Lacons. The house beer, Leopard Ale, is brewed specially by Tombstone. This friendly and welcoming pub has a clean and bright bar area which gives a spacious feel, plus a pleasant and quiet enclosed patio at the rear. Open mic events are held on the first Wednesday of the month, and food can be brought in. Q❀♿♣●🍺🚌(11,12)🐾📶

Lord Rosebery 𝕃

94 Rosebery Road, NR3 3AB

3-11; 12-midnight Sat; 12-10.30 Sun ☎ (01603) 414284

theroseberynorwich.co.uk

5 changing beers Ⓗ

A large pub between Angel Road and St Clement's Hill, tastefully decorated in a modern style with high ceilings and decorative lighting. It has up to five real ales from around the country, including a few locals, and a good range of spirits, especially gins, including its own infusion. There is a regular pub quiz on Tuesdays, excellent Sunday roasts, and evening meals from a varied menu. B&B accommodation is available upstairs.
❀🛏◑♿♣P⬚🚌(10)🐾📶

Murderers 𝕃

2-8 Timber Hill, NR1 3LB

10-11.30; 12-10.30 Sun ☎ (01603) 621447

themurderers.co.uk

Adnams Ghost Ship; Sharp's Doom Bar; Woodforde's Wherry; 7 changing beers Ⓗ

City-centre free house packed with character, beams and wood panelling. It is on several levels, with lots of little alcoves, and has been family-owned for 30 years. Up to 10 real ales are available from local micros and around the country, including the house ale brewed by Coors. It is popular with shoppers, office workers and the evening going-out scene alike. Its real name is The Gardener's Arms, but nobody knows it as that since a 19th-century landlord convicted of murdering his wife gave the pub its alternative name. A regular blues night takes place every Thursday. 🐴❀◐⚽🚌📶

Plasterers Arms 𝕃

43 Cowgate, NR3 1SZ

12-midnight (1 Fri & Sat) ☎ (01603) 387525

theplasterersarms.co.uk

10 changing beers Ⓗ

This is a friendly corner local with a wide range of microbrewery beers from around the country, specialising in new and exciting breweries. A variety of craft keg beers from near and far is also available, alongside a great range of bottled and canned beers. Regular tap takeovers and Meet the Brewer events are held. There is also sport, with a big screen for more important events, music from local bands and DJs on Sundays, pizza every weekday, and breakfast 10am-2pm at weekends.
Q◑♣⚽🚌🐾📶

Playhouse Bar

42-58 St George Street, NR3 1AB

10-midnight; 12-midnight Sun ☎ (01603) 612580

norwichplayhouse.co.uk/bar

4 changing beers Ⓗ

The bar serving the Norwich Playhouse theatre (so it can be crowded before performances and at the interval), with a large tree-shaded patio by the river. It serves three or four ales including a couple of locals and an eclectic selection of guests. The bar features a 3D cityscape on the ceiling, an unusual collection of objets d'art and comfortable seating. There are regular DJ sessions at weekends. A good-sized lounge is across the foyer. ❀♿📶

Plough

58 St Benedict Street, NR2 4AR

12-11 (midnight Fri & Sat); 12-10.30 Sun

☎ (01603) 661384 theploughnorwich.co.uk

6 changing beers Ⓗ

Popular pub in one of the city's oldest areas near the Norwich Arts Centre. One of three Grain Brewery-owned pubs, the six ales available are usually all from the brewery. The two-bar interior is fairly small, with wooden chairs and tables, and an open fire in winter. The large Mediterranean-style courtyard garden is a fine place to spend a summer's evening. Grain lager and craft beers are also sold, along with Vic's special sausage pie, and barbecues in the summer. ❀♣⚽🚌🐾📶

Ribs of Beef 𝕃 ✔

24 Wensum Street, NR3 1HY

11-11.30 (midnight Fri & Sat); 11-10.30 Sun

☎ (01603) 619517 ribsofbeef.co.uk

Adnams Ghost Ship; Oakham JHB; Wolf Golden Jackal; Woodforde's Wherry; 5 changing beers (sourced locally) Ⓗ

Traditional and well-decorated pub overlooking the River Wensum. A welcoming row of nine handpumps dispenses four regular ales and a selection from local and other micros, with foreign beers and real cider as well. The pub is popular with visitors and the kitchen offers a great selection of meals made with locally sourced ingredients. The atmosphere is relaxed and friendly, with a room downstairs, a tiny veranda over the river, and several outdoor tables at the rear. Just the place to watch the boats go by.
❀◐♿♣⚽🚌📶

Rose

235 Queens Road, NR1 3AE

3 (5 Mon)-11; 3-midnight Fri; 2-midnight Sat; 2-10.30 Sun

☎ (01603) 623942 theroseinnnorwich.co.uk

6 changing beers Ⓗ

Popular pub with a music theme including a snare drum table, cymbal and drum lights, and a full drum kit, plus murals on the walls of the smoking area/beer garden. The interior could be described as like your own funky front room, with wood floors, comfy sofas, board games and cards. The owner's passion for beer shows in the choice of six or more real ales from some of the most exciting microbreweries around the country, plus several real ciders, and a wide range of interesting canned and bottled beers. Bar billiards is played here.
❀🛏◑♿⚽🚌🐾📶

St Andrews Brewhouse ✔

41 St Andrews Street, NR2 4TP

11-midnight (11 Mon; 1 Fri & Sat); 11-11 Sun

☎ (01603) 305995 standrewsbrewhouse.com

St Andrews Grocers Ghost Pale Ale, Tombland Porter, Wensum Ale; 2 changing beers Ⓗ

Grade II*-listed building refurbished during 2015 in distressed industrial style, now a brewhouse and smokehouse restaurant with an eclectic food menu. The bar and microbrewery face St Andrews Street, while the restaurant has views of the ancient St Andrews Hall, home of the Norwich Beer Festival. Six handpumps dispense mostly house beers. Wensum Ale is gluten-free, with a couple of local guests or seasonal specials and sometimes a cider/perry, supplemented by a good range of craft beers. Upstairs rooms feature board games and views of the brewery fermentation tanks.
Q🐴❀◑♿♣⚽🚌🐾📶

Trafford Arms 𝕃 ✔

61 Grove Road, NR1 3RL

11-11 (11.30 Fri & Sat); 10-11 Sun ☎ (01603) 628466

traffordarms.co.uk

Adnams Southwold Bitter, Ghost Ship; Lacons Encore; 7 changing beers Ⓗ
This pub stands at the junction of Trafford Road and Grove Road, near the city centre, and continues to be a flagship for real ale in Norwich. The cask beer offering includes both regular and guest beers, often including a dark beer. High-standard pub food is available and there are special themed food evenings. The Valentine's beer festival continues to be a major attraction, as are the regular pub quizzes on the last Sunday of the month.
❀◑P🚌(38)📶

Vine 🄻

7 Dove Street, NR2 1DE
11-11; closed Sun ☎ (01603) 627362 🌐 vinethai.co.uk
Lacons Patriot; Oakham JHB; 2 changing beers Ⓗ
Norwich's smallest pub, just off the marketplace, serving up to four quality ales, mostly from local breweries, plus traditional Thai cuisine in an award-winning combination. Beer festivals are held in January and City of Ale week. The restaurant is upstairs, although customers often eat downstairs in the bar area, and functions are catered for outside normal opening hours on demand. Extra tables and chairs are set outside in the pedestrianised street. Q❀◑♣🚌

Whalebone ✔

144 Magdalen Road, NR3 4BA
12-11 (midnight Fri & Sat) ☎ (01603) 425482
🌐 whalebonefreehouse.co.uk
Adnams Southwold Bitter; Fuller's London Pride; Humpty Dumpty Little Sharpie; Oakham JHB, Citra; Wolf Golden Jackal; 2 changing beers Ⓗ
A community local with eight real ales, conveniently situated just to the south of Sewell Park. It has three separate areas: the original front and rear bars plus a newly refurbished area leading to a covered and heated terraced patio, which is popular and used for summer barbecues. The pub holds an annual beer festival in July and supports three cricket teams as well as a golf society. Bar snacks including locally sourced pork pies, Scotch eggs and sausage rolls are available daily, plus freshly made coffee, hot chocolate and tea.
❀♣P🚌(10,18)🐾📶

White Lion

73 Oak Street, NR3 3AQ
12-11 (11.30 Fri & Sat); 12-10.30 Sun ☎ (01603) 632333
Milton Dionysus, Justinian; 3 changing beers Ⓗ
Former East Anglian Cider Pub of the Year with over 20 varieties of cider and perry from near and far, also serving a range of beers from Milton Brewery and two or three guests, usually from non-local microbreweries. Food is varied and of excellent value, using traditional local produce – check the daily specials menu. An annual beer festival is held in the autumn, and bar billiards and darts are played. The traditional interior is split into three rooms, with a front and back bar and a games room to the side. Q❀◑♣🐾📶

Wig & Pen 🄻

6 St Martin at Palace Plain, NR3 1RN
11.30-11 (midnight Fri & Sat); 11.30-6.30 Sun
☎ (01603) 625891 🌐 thewigandpen.com
Adnams Southwold Bitter; 5 changing beers Ⓗ
Pretty beamed 17th-century free house with a spacious patio, immediately opposite the Bishop's Palace, and with an impressive view of Norwich cathedral spire. Six ales are always available, usually including two local beers. The small back room can be used for meetings. Good-quality food is served lunchtimes and evenings. The pub is a short walk from Tombland, where there are bus stands for several bus routes, and is an ideal starting or stopping place for a walk along the river.
Q❀🛏◑♿🚌📶

Old Buckenham

Ox & Plough

The Green, NR17 1RN (in centre of village overlooking green)
11-midnight; 12-midnight Sun ☎ 07887 691722
Adnams Southwold Bitter; Sharp's Doom Bar; 3 changing beers (often Hop Back, Oakham) Ⓗ
Family-friendly pub on one of the largest village greens in England, a community hostelry at the centre of local life. It has two open-plan drinking areas, one quiet without TV or electronic games machines. The garden at the front of the pub overlooks the green. Real ale is dispensed from three to five handpumps; as a member of the Oakham Academy it serves various changing Oakham ales. Bar snacks are available.
❀♿♣P🐾📶

Old Hunstanton

Ancient Mariner ✔

6 Golf Course Road, PE36 6JJ (within Le Strange Arms hotel complex)
11-11 ☎ (01485) 534411
Adnams Southwold Bitter, Broadside; 3 changing beers Ⓗ
Adjoining the Le Strange Arms Hotel, this popular pub consists of old barns and stables and includes a family room and restaurants. At least four ales are available. A large beer garden offers direct access to the beach and as Old Hunstanton is on the east coast facing west, there are superb views of spectacular sunsets over the sea from the decking at the rear. Q❀🛏◑♿P🚌🐾📶

Overstrand

White Horse 🄻

34 High Street, NR27 0AB
8am-11 ☎ (01263) 579237
🌐 whitehorseoverstrand.co.uk
Woodforde's Wherry; 5 changing beers Ⓗ
The White Horse is in the centre of this coastal village, a short walk from a sandy beach. Behind its Edwardian exterior lies a recently refurbished pub offering excellent beer as well as outstanding food and accommodation. A spacious modern bar serves up to six guest ales, usually from local Norfolk breweries such as Humpty Dumpty, Grain, Buffy's and Wolf. Outside is a large beer garden with play equipment, which also hosts occasional beer festivals in the summer. Breakfast is served 8-10am. Q❀🛏◑♿P🚌(5,36)🐾📶

Oxborough

Bedingfeld Arms

Stoke Ferry Road, PE33 9PS
11-11 (midnight Fri & Sat) ☎ (01366) 328300
🌐 bedingfeldarms.co.uk
Adnams Broadside; Woodforde's Wherry; 1 changing beer Ⓗ

A historic independent free house, refurbished throughout, providing high-quality beers, meals, service and accommodation. A central room with a bar and casual seating provide for chat, coffee and cakes. There are two separate public dining rooms in a smart but relaxed country style, and a private dining room. A patio area of local wood construction leads onto the large garden with outdoor seating. It is located by the village green and part-ruined church. The historic Oxborough Hall (National Trust) is adjacent. On Sundays, a roast dinner is available 12-8pm. Q🐎❀🛏◑♿♣P🐾📶

Poringland

Royal Oak 🄻

44 The Street, NR14 7JT (on the B1332)
⏲ 12-11 (midnight Fri & Sat) ☎ (01508) 493734
🌐 poringlandroyaloak.com
Adnams Southwold Bitter; Fuller's London Pride; Woodforde's Wherry; 5 changing beers 🄷
A comfortable country pub with woodburners and welcoming bar staff. The interior is divided into separate seating areas around the bar, one of which features memorabilia of the former RAF radar station which was nearby. An excellent selection of real ales and ciders is stocked. A wide range of community groups and clubs meets here and it holds three beer festivals and a cider festival each year, plus wine, whisky and gin tastings. There is a themed tea room and live music once a month. Q❀◑♿♣🍎P🚌🐾📶

Reepham

King's Arms 🄻

Market Place, NR10 4JJ
⏲ 11.30-3, 5.30-11; 11.30-11 Sat; 12-10.30 Sun
☎ (01603) 870345 🌐 kingsarmsreepham.com
Adnams Southwold Bitter, Ghost Ship; Greene King Abbot; Panther Golden Panther; Woodforde's Wherry; 1 changing beer 🄷
A former coaching inn, dating back to 1667, in the picturesque square of this small market town, with original beams, Norfolk brickwork and open fires. There are several comfortable drinking and dining areas, tables in front with views across the square, and five permanent real ales on sale, including at least one from the local Panther Brewery, plus a guest. The comprehensive menu is mostly sourced from nearby suppliers. Jazz bands play in the rear courtyard on summer Sundays. Dogs are welcome. Q🐎❀◑🚌🐾

Ringstead

Gin Trap Inn

6 High Street, PE36 5JU
⏲ 11-11 ☎ (01485) 525264 🌐 thegintrapinn.co.uk
Adnams Southwold Bitter; Woodforde's Wherry; 2 changing beers 🄷
The Gin Trap is at the end of this small village. This attractive-looking whitewashed village pub, dating back at least a couple of centuries, has an outside seating area at the front and an enclosed garden to the rear. There is a split-level bar area and a separate restaurant. Food is available throughout. In addition to the main menu, there are regular themed food evenings as well as live music nights. The main bar area has a log-burning stove, and also features a range of some 35 different gins. ❀🛏◑♿P🐾📶

Roydon

Union Jack

30 Station Road, PE32 1AW (off A148)
⏲ 4 (2 Mon)-midnight; 1.30-midnight Fri; 12-midnight Sat & Sun ☎ 07771 660439
4 changing beers 🄷
Popular with locals, this traditional village pub has twice been local CAMRA Pub of the Year. Four handpumps dispense a variety of ales, with beer festivals held over the Easter and August bank holidays usually featuring local breweries. There are occasional food nights, live music each month, regular bingo and quizzes, and weekly support for darts, crib and dominoes. Dogs are welcome. ❀🛏♣🍎P🚌(48)🐾

Saham Toney

Old Bell

1 Bell Lane, IP25 7HD
⏲ 11-11; 11-10.30 Sun ☎ (01953) 884934
Woodforde's Wherry; 3 changing beers 🄷
Next to a mere and near a medieval church, the Bell is a lovely old building which consists of a long bar room and restaurant heated by open fires, offering guest beers of good quality. There is always a friendly atmosphere. An annual Oktoberfest is staged alongside German-twinned Watton. The pub supports good causes both locally and nationally. Food is available daily from noon, with themed food events in the evening. ◑♿⛺♣P

Shouldham

King's Arms 🍷 🄻

The Green, PE33 0BY
⏲ 4.30-10.30 Mon; 12-3, 4.30-11 Tue-Thu; 12-11.30 Fri; 11.30-11.30 Sat; 12-10.30 Sun ☎ (01366) 347410
🌐 kingsarmsshouldham.co.uk
2 changing beers 🄶
Named the local CAMRA Pub of the Year again in 2018, completing a hat-trick of successes, this is a community-owned business which also includes a café open from 9.30am. The beer is served straight from the cask and two or three choices are usually available. Lined glasses are used and cider is often also on tap. Lots of community activities take place, from poetry evenings and live music to quiz nights. 🐎❀◑🍎P🚏🐾📶

Snettisham

Rose & Crown

Old Church Road, PE31 7LX (off B1440)
⏲ 11-11; 11-10.30 Sun ☎ (01485) 541382
🌐 roseandcrownsnettisham.co.uk
Adnams Broadside; Banks's Amber Ale; Marston's Pedigree; Woodforde's Wherry; 2 changing beers 🄷
A popular traditional village inn with cosy bars, exposed beams, a real fire and a dining room. Head through the narrow passage to find a larger bar and dining areas with a contemporary feel. It is well known for quality traditional and exciting local seasonal fare; the bars also remain popular with local drinkers. The garden and play area make it appealing to families. Accommodation is available for those who wish to remain longer in this beautiful area. Q🐎❀🛏◑♿♣P🚌🐾📶

Thetford

Albion 🄻 ✔

93-95 Castle Street, IP24 2DN (opp Castle Park and Hill)
🕒 12-11.30 (1.30am Fri & Sat) ☎ (01842) 338208
Greene King IPA; Woodforde's Wherry; 1 changing beer 🄷
A classic flint Norfolk town pub. The management team at the Albion has revitalised the pub, providing a warm welcome for all. Its refurbished interior has mellowed, featuring wherry-themed tables, giving a comfortable space to drink. The six handpumps offer a range of standards and more interesting choices. There is seating outside from where you can see the 1,000-year-old castle mound and its surrounding Iceni hill fort. Although food is not available you are welcome to order in from one of the food outlets in the town. ❀♿♣P

Black Horse 🄻

64 Magdalen Street, IP24 2BP
🕒 11-11; 12-11 Sun ☎ (01842) 762717
Adnams Southwold Bitter; Greene King IPA; Woodforde's Wherry; 2 changing beers 🄷
A welcome returnee to the Guide, the Black Horse offers five handpumps with a varying range. A good no-nonsense town pub, it stages a popular annual St George's Day festival. The food is home made and good both in quality and value, served in a small but pleasant dining area; it prides itself on its desserts. Look for the changing murals on the end wall. ❀◖◗♿P

Red Lion 🄻 ✔

Market Place, IP24 2AL
🕒 8am-11 (1am Fri & Sat) ☎ (01842) 757210
Adnams Broadside; Greene King IPA, Abbot; 3 changing beers 🄷
Situated on the market square once used by Captain Mainwaring and his men, the pub has a varied history – the wall outside still retains its original Lacons plaque, it was later a Portuguese restaurant, then became a Wetherspoon pub six years ago. The beer range is the usual fare, and well kept. It has a variety of dining and drinking areas plus an outdoor space for sunny days. The decor features much information about local history and attractions. 🐴❀◖◗⇌🍎 wifi

Thompson

Chequers Inn

Griston Road, IP24 1PX
🕒 12-3, 6.30-11; 11.30-11 Sun ☎ (01953) 483360
🌐 thompsonchequers.co.uk
Greene King IPA; Woodforde's Wherry; 1 changing beer 🄷
Situated in this tiny village outside Watton, the 16th-century inn has a steep thatched roof and timber-framed interior. When approaching the bar it helps to be 16th-century height to clear the beam! There are two rooms laid out for dining and a small area in which to drink. In the summer it is better to drink outside. The food is excellent, crafted by the chef/landlord from local produce. Modern accommodation is available. 🐴❀🛏◖◗♿P

Thornham

Lifeboat Inn

Ship Lane, PE36 6LT (signed from A149 Coast Road)
🕒 11-11; 12-10.30 Sun ☎ (01485) 512236
🌐 lifeboatinnthornham.com
5 changing beers 🄷
Busy pub just off the North Norfolk Coastal Path on the edge of the salt marshes, with a wide range of drinking areas, from the dark and cosy bar to the light and airy conservatory. There is an enclosed garden at the rear. It has been tastefully renovated while retaining the atmosphere of the smugglers' inn it undoubtedly was. Food is available in all areas and there is a separate large restaurant. Accommodation is in 12 rooms. Whatever the season or weather, this is a comforting place to enjoy a pint. Q🐴❀🛏◖◗P🐾 wifi

Thorpe Market

Gunton Arms 🄻 ✔

Cromer Road, NR11 8TZ (on W of A149 Cromer to North Walsham road, SE of Thorpe Market; look for hanging sign, lit at night)
🕒 12-11; 12-10.30 Sun ☎ (01263) 832010
🌐 theguntonarms.co.uk
Adnams Southwold Bitter, Broadside; Woodforde's Wherry; 1 changing beer 🄷
A fine country inn with magical vistas of Gunton Park and its deer herd. Tasteful decor with comfortable furnishings feature, and a log fire in winter. East Anglian ales predominate, with regular guests. First-class cuisine is served in two restaurant areas; several dishes are cooked on an open range in the vaulted main room. It has 16 luxurious rooms and suites, some with parkland views, to suit all tastes. There is a beer garden for alfresco dining, and a food and music festival is held in summer. Q❀🛏◖◗♿♣P🚌(4)🐾 wifi

Thurlton

Queen's Head 🄻

Beccles Road, NR14 6RJ
🕒 6-11 Mon; 12-3, 6 (5 Thu & Fri)-11; 12-midnight Sat; 12-10 Sun ☎ (01508) 548667 🌐 queensheadthurlton.co.uk
3 changing beers (often People's) 🄷
Recently refurbished community owned pub with three real ales available, including beers exclusively brewed by the nearby People's Brewery. Other locally brewed ales are also regularly available plus a selection from breweries further afield. The pub is family and dog friendly, children are permitted in the bar, and the village play area is to the rear, next to the car park. Excellent locally sourced food is served. It opens for breakfast Wednesday and Saturday, has a cosy log fire in winter, and an Easter beer festival. 🐴❀◖◗♿♣🍎P🚌(577)🐾 wifi

Thurne

Lion Inn

The Street, NR29 3AP (at end of Thurne Dyke)
🕒 12-11 ☎ (01692) 670796 🌐 thelionatthurne.com
6 changing beers 🄷
Large country pub in a remote village, near the River Ant, with a busy holiday trade from travellers and Broads cruisers in summer. Plenty of moorings are available nearby, and there is an amusement arcade for children and a large garden. It usually serves at least five real ales, a range of draught ciders, and a range of craft keg beers. It does bar meals and has a separate restaurant. Owned by the same people who transformed the White Horse at Neatishead. Q🐴❀◖◗♿♣🍎P🐾 wifi

Upton

White Horse [L]
17 Chapel Road, NR13 6BT
12-midnight ☎ (01493) 750696 ⊕ whitehorseupton.com
Woodforde's Wherry; 3 changing beers [H]
Traditional broadland pub dating from 1798, a five-minute walk from Upton Dyke Staithe and moorings. It was renovated in 2012 and is now owned by the local community – residents own shares. A community shop caters for locals and holidaymakers alike. Beers are usually from local breweries. Genuine pub food features strongly, and a new restaurant is planned for 2019. An annual beer, cider and perry festival takes place in July. ❀◖◗♿▲♣●P🐾

Warham All Saints

Three Horseshoes
The Street, NR23 1NL (2 miles SE of Wells)
11-11; 12-10.30 Sun ☎ (01328) 710547
Woodforde's Wherry [G]**; 5 changing beers** [H]
A real pub in every sense of the word, with the perfect atmosphere for a quiet drink and conversation. The interior comprises three connected rooms that are filled with a fascinating collection of antiques and pictures, including the traditional game of Norfolk twister. In winter months customers can warm themselves by a log fire in the main bar. The beer garden provides a quiet haven in the summer. The pub is renowned for good traditional cooking, featuring soups, pies and puddings. Q❀◖◗♿♣●P🐾

Wells-next-the-Sea

Lifeboat Inn
Station Road, NR23 1EA
closed Mon; 12-3, 6-11; 12-11 Sat & Sun
☎ (01328) 711735
Adnams Southwold Bitter, Ghost Ship, Broadside; 1 changing beer [H]
Comfortable two-bar locals' town pub, offering Danish/English B&B and a restaurant, which reopened in 2015 under Carsten Lund, and which stocks three or four ales, mostly from Adnams, and varieties of Danish schnapps. As well as home-cooked Sunday roasts there are Danish open sandwiches filled with meatballs or marinated herring. The pub, which has portraits of the different lifeboats that have served the town on its tables, began life as The Railway Inn in the 1840s. Live music features every two weeks and there is a monthly Thursday quiz. ❀◖◗●P🐾

West Acre

Stag [L]
Low Road, PE32 1TR
closed Mon; 12-3, 6.30-11; 12-3, 5-11 Fri
☎ (01760) 755395 ⊕ westacrestag.co.uk
3 changing beers [H]
This cosy pub is well worth finding at the east end of picturesque West Acre and is popular with locals, walkers, cyclists and riders. It is a strong supporter of local ales, maintaining a high standard with its three varying beers, and hosting excellent beer festivals. There is a popular monthly quiz on Sunday nights. The restaurant serves a variety of great-value freshly prepared meals using locally sourced ingredients. Q❀◖◗♿▲♣P

West Runton

Village Inn
Water Lane, NR27 9QP
11-11; 12-11 Sun ☎ (01263) 838000
⊕ villageinnwestrunton.co.uk
Adnams Ghost Ship; 4 changing beers [H]
A large pub a short distance from the beach, set in pleasant gardens in the centre of this quiet village. Up to six well-kept and mostly local ales are stocked and rotated. Excellent home-cooked meals can be enjoyed in the dining areas or outside, where the gardens can seat up to 200. In the 1970s rock bands such as Deep Purple played secret gigs at the Pavilion which was at the rear of the pub (sadly now demolished). Q❀◖◗♿🐾

Weybourne

Ship Inn ✔
The Street, NR25 7SZ
12-11; 11-midnight Fri & Sat; 11-11 Sun
☎ (01263) 588721 ⊕ theshipinnweybourne.com
4 changing beers [H]
In the heart of this attractive north Norfolk coastal village, the Ship has up to six cask ales from local brewers including Woodforde's, Humpty Dumpty, Beeston, Norfolk Brewhouse, Wolf, Grain and Panther, plus a range of bottled craft beers. House beer is from Greene King. Home-cooked food is available lunchtimes and evenings. There is a monthly quiz night, a pleasant enclosed garden in summer, the Coasthopper bus stops outside, and the Muckleburgh Collection of military vehicles is close by. ❀◖◗♿▲♣P🐾

Wiveton

Wiveton Bell [L]
The Green, Blakeney Road, NR25 7TL (on B1156)
12-11 ☎ (01263) 740101 ⊕ wivetonbell.co.uk
Norfolk Brewhouse Moon Gazer Golden Ale; Woodforde's Wherry; Yetman's Red; 1 changing beer [H]
The Bell has an L-shaped bar, a large conservatory which is mainly set up for food, and a stylish and spacious enclosed garden, with views to the church. Although food-led, there are always seats reserved for drinkers. A good selection of ales from local breweries is available. A pleasant walk can be had from the Bell, via the Three Swallows (or vice versa) to Cley about a mile away, around what was in medieval times the harbour. ❀◖◗▲P🐾

Wortwell

Bell
52 Low Road, IP20 0HH
12-10 Mon & Wed; 5-10 Tue; 12-11 Thu-Sat; 12-9 Sun
☎ (01986) 788025 ⊕ wortwellbell.pub
Otter Bitter; Purity Pure UBU; Upham 1st Drop; house beer (by Woodforde's); 3 changing beers [H]
A 17th-century coaching inn with two bars and an open fire. A fishing lake is nearby. Enthusiastic hosts, whose family were historically linked to the licensed trade, reopened the pub in 2015. They have rejuvenated this community local to its former glory, with regular village events, and have now added to the community feel with a small village shop and a small borrowing library based at the pub and open during pub hours. A regular beer festival is held. ❀◖◗▲♣●P(580)🐾

Wymondham

Feathers

13 Town Green, NR18 0PN

11-2.30, 7-11.30; 11-2.30, 6-midnight Fri; 11-2.30, 7-midnight Sat; 12-2.30, 7-10.30 Sun ☎ (01953) 605675

Adnams Southwold Bitter, Ghost Ship; Fuller's London Pride; 2 changing beers H

The Feathers dates from the 18th century. The interior consists of two main drinking areas with alcove areas served by one bar. The alcoves and walls are adorned with postcard collections, enamel signs and farming and rural memorabilia, including an old bike. There is a large well-furnished patio garden at the rear, and good-value food is available lunchtime and evenings. Folk evenings take place on the last Sunday of each month. Feathers Tickler is the popular house beer, brewed by Nethergate. **Q**

Green Dragon L ✔

6 Church Street, NR18 0PH (between Market St and Wymondham Abbey)

12-11 (midnight Fri & Sat); 12-10.30 Sun

☎ (01953) 607907 greendragonnorfolk.co.uk

5 changing beers H

A haunted half-timbered inn recognised by CAMRA as having a historic interior of regional importance, with an attractive beer garden. On the road to Wymondham's beautiful Abbey, this inn dates back to 1371. One bar serves the downstairs bar, a snug and restaurant area. The interior has beamed timbers and carved stone, and evidence of medieval construction methods. The rotating real ales are mostly from local or East Anglian breweries. Beer festivals take place in May and August, with live music. It serves excellent home-made food using locally sourced ingredients where possible. **Q**

Fat Cat, Norwich (Photo: Cath Harries)

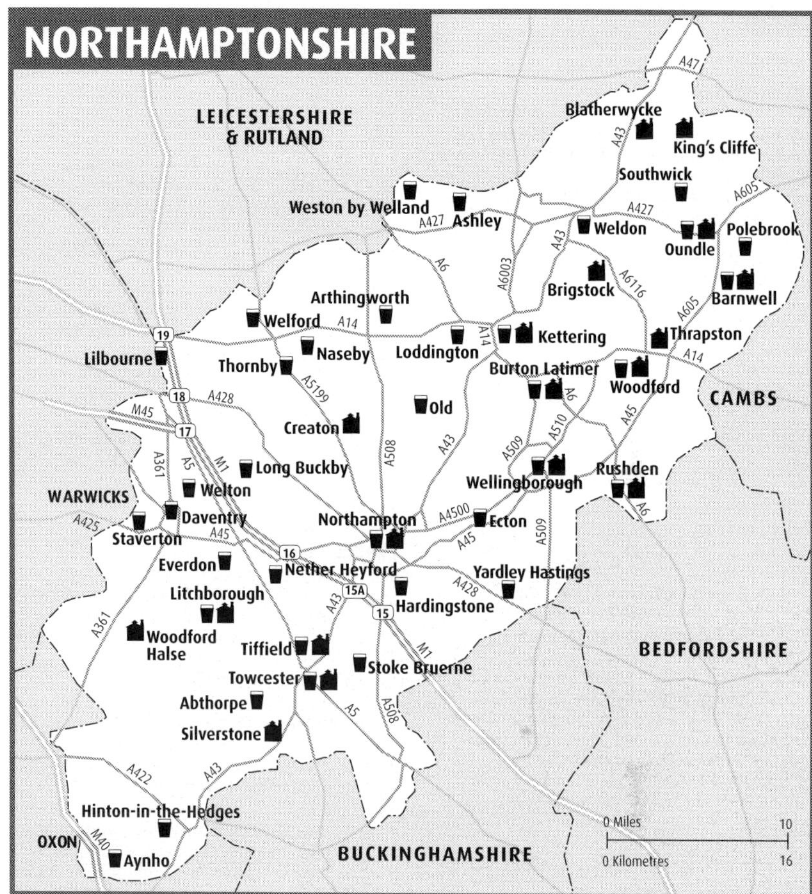

Abthorpe

New Inn

Silver Street, NN12 8QR (off Main St, left at church)
12-3 (not Mon & Tue), 5-11.30; 12-11.30 Fri & Sat; 12-11 Sun (01327) 857306 newinnabthorpe.co.uk
Hook Norton Hooky, Hooky Gold, Old Hooky; 1 changing beer (often Hook Norton)
This tranquil country hostelry is tucked away in a back street close to the green and church. It is a quintessentially English village pub built of local mellow sandstone complete with an inglenook fireplace with seating and low ceilings. Welcoming to visitors and locals alike, it serves good food including meats from the owner's farm, plus ales that are still brewed in the traditional way by Hook Norton – its seasonal beers feature as guests. Traditional pub games including darts and Northamptonshire skittles are played.

Arthingworth

Bull's Head

Kelmarsh Road, LE16 8JZ (A14 jct 2, off A508)
12-2.30, 6-11; 12-11 Sat & Sun (01858) 525637
thebullsheadonline.co.uk
Adnams Southwold Bitter; 2 changing beers (sourced locally; often Grainstore, Silverstone)
Popular red-brick village pub occupying a former farmhouse dating from the 19th century, featuring an opened-up bar with several cosy drinking areas and a restaurant to the front serving home-cooked fresh food from local producers. Ideal for ramblers and cyclists, this is the perfect place to finish a walk in the local area, or stay over in one of the annexe rooms. A beer festival is held over the Whitsun bank holiday on the suntrap patio. Sparklers can be removed on request. Q P

Ashley

George

21 Main Street, LE16 8HF (off B664)
closed Mon; 6-11 Tue-Thu; 12-2, 6-11 Fri; 12-11 Sat; 12-8 Sun (01858) 565411 thegeorgeatashley.co.uk
3 changing beers (sourced locally; often Langton, Nobby's, Phipps NBC)
Following a campaign by residents, this traditional 17th-century ironstone village pub has been saved from conversion into houses. It stands proud above a patch of grass at the roadside. The interior has been opened out although there are still two separate areas for dining and drinking. The pub serves three changing local ales from a number of microbreweries. The Coach House to the rear has been redecorated to a high standard with accommodation in six rooms.

Aynho

Great Western Arms 🄻 ✔

Station Road, OX17 3BP (on B4031)
✪ 11-11 ☎ (01869) 338288 🌐 great-westernarms.co.uk
Hook Norton Hooky, Old Hooky; 2 changing beers (sourced regionally; often Hook Norton) 🄷
Straddling the Northants and Oxfordshire borders and between the former Great Western Railway and Oxford Canal, this is an inviting country pub with a difference. The ivy-clad traditional pub is full of Great Western Railway and canal memorabilia, with the walls of the main bar and side restaurant displaying many photographs. Renowned for its food, outdoor seating alongside the canal is pleasant in the summer. Accommodation is offered in four individually decorated rooms.
❀🛏◐♿●P🚌🐾📶

Barnwell

Montagu Arms 🄻

PE8 5PH
✪ 6-11; 12-11 Sat & Sun ☎ (01832) 273726
Adnams Southwold Bitter; 3 changing beers 🄷
Overlooking the river and stone bridge, this 16th-century stone-built inn has a public bar at the front and a large restaurant to the rear. The car park is behind the inn and accessed via the village hall entrance. Also at the rear is a large play and camping area. There is wheelchair access from the rear to the restaurant only. The traditionally decorated bar area has original exposed wood beams on the ceiling and walls, and a large fireplace in the middle of the room.
Q❀◐♿⛺♣●P🚌🐾

Burton Latimer

Dukes Arms ✔

123 High Street, NN15 5RL (off A14 jct 10)
✪ 4-11; 2-11 Sat; 12-11 Sun ☎ (01536) 390874
3 changing beers (sourced nationally; often Acorn, Lacons)
For many years keg only, this revitalised pub has recently installed handpumps for real ale. A central U-shaped bar serves the opened-out rooms, with comfortable leather seating and more traditional seating in the small bay windows. The walls are adorned with vinyl LPs and a collection of books is available for customers to read. A wide selection of board games is available and there is a quiz every Sunday evening. There is no parking but a free car park is just across the road. ❀♣●🚌🐾📶

Daventry

Early Doors 🄻

3 Prince William Walk, NN11 4AB
✪ 12-9; closed Sun & Mon ☎ 07707 299959
🌐 earlydoorsdaventry.co.uk
Phipps NBC India Pale Ale 🄷**; 5 changing beers (sourced locally; often Gun Dog Ales, Towcester Mill)** 🄶
Tucked away down a narrow alley, this warm and welcoming micropub was the first in the county. The bar is simply decorated and made from reclaimed doors and weathered scaffolding planks. Beers are all on gravity and locally produced cider is made within one mile from Welton. Hand-made local pork pies are available although pubgoers are welcome to bring their own food which will be plated-up for a small charge being donated to charity. Local CAMRA Pub of the Year 2017.
Q♿●P🚌

Ecton

Three Horseshoes 🄻

23 High Street, NN6 0QA (off A4500)
✪ 7-midnight; 5.30-midnight Fri; 12-midnight Sat & Sun
☎ (01604) 407446
St Austell Trelawny, Proper Job; 2 changing beers (sourced nationally) 🄷
A whitewashed stone pub extended over many years, although the original pub is said to date from 1757. The name is taken from the forge that was originally on the site and where Benjamin Franklin's Uncle Thomas was the last of the family to work the family business. The traditional multi-room layout has been retained, with a separate bar and games area with Northants skittles and darts. Happy hour is 5.30-7.30pm Friday. ❀♣P🚌🐾📶

Everdon

Plough Inn 🄻

High Street, NN11 3BL (opp church)
✪ 12-11 ☎ (01327) 361606 🌐 theploughinneverdon.com
Greene King IPA; Gun Dog Ales Jack's Spaniels; Sharp's Doom Bar; 1 changing beer (sourced regionally) 🄷
Attractive and convivial early 18th-century Northamptonshire ironstone-built village pub with a small bar and flagstone floors. From the entrance lobby on two levels there is a small lounge, formerly two small rooms, which has a fairly modern counter and a working Rayburn woodburner. The plaster-over-stone walls remain. More interconnected rooms to the left include a snug with leather settees. This is a quaint and unusual pub – check out the garden and the Furrow outbuildings in summer. Q❀◐♿⛺●P🚌🐾📶

Hardingstone

Sun Inn 🄻 ✔

9 High Street, NN4 7BT

REAL ALE BREWERIES

Boot Town Burton Latimer
Brigstock Brigstock
Cotton End ▤ Northampton
Creaton Grange Creaton (NEW)
Digfield Barnwell
Frog Island Northampton
Great Oakley Tiffield
Gun Dog Woodford Halse
Hart Family Wellingborough
Hoppy Family Kettering (NEW)
King's Cliffe King's Cliffe
Maule Northampton
Merrimen Litchborough
Nene Valley Oundle
Nobby's Thrapston
Phipps Northampton
Potbelly Kettering
Purple Cow ▤ Kettering (NEW)
Rockingham Blatherwycke
Silverstone Silverstone
Three Hills Woodford
Towcester Mill Towcester
Weldon Rushden

11-11 (midnight Fri & Sat); 12-10.30 Sun
(01604) 700007 thesuninnhardingstone.co.uk
Courage Directors; 5 changing beers (sourced regionally; often Gun Dog Ales, Phipps NBC)
Friendly, attractive, whitewashed pub with a good atmosphere in the older part of the village. The interior is welcoming and cosy with soft lighting, a beamed ceiling, two character fireplaces and half-panelling separating the numerous drinking/dining alcoves which are all served by a side bar. Outside there is a courtyard with seating and a children's play area, and a barn bar used as a function room. Northamptonshire Food & Drink Rural Community Pub of the Year 2016-17. (7)

Hinton-in-the-Hedges

Crewe Arms

Sparrow Corner, NN13 5NF
12-11 (10.30 Sun) (01280) 705801
crewearmshinton.co.uk
Sharp's Doom Bar; Timothy Taylor Boltmaker; 1 changing beer (sourced nationally; often Vale)
Stone built and situated in a gully in the village, the Crewe Arms can be hard to find. The entrance is through the rear gravel car park. Four comfortably furnished rooms provide a relaxed environment. The pub's cellar, located in the main dining area, may have been part of a tunnel between the village manor and the local church. The pub has a choice of three real ales at weekends. Happy hour is 6-8pm Friday-Sunday. QP

Kettering

Piper

Windmill Avenue, NN15 6PS (nr Wicksteed Park)
11-3, 5-11; 11-11 Sat; 12-10.30 Sun (01536) 513870
thepiper.net
Castle Rock Harvest Pale; Fuller's London Pride; 4 changing beers (sourced nationally; often Potbelly)
Popular 1950s two-roomed pub which has been run by a CAMRA member for 28 years. There is a quiet lounge to the left, while to the right is a more lively bar/games room where a quiz is held on Sunday night. A beer festival is held on the third weekend of August. Nearby Wicksteed Park was one of Britain's first theme parks. An outdoor seating area is across the road from the pub.
QP

Three Cocks

48 Lower Street, NN16 8DJ (opp Morrisons)
12-11.30 (11 Sun) 07909 698798
Grainstore Ten Fifty; Mighty Oak Maldon Gold; 5 changing beers (sourced regionally; often Church End, Full Mash, Oakham)
A popular locals' town-centre pub comprising an L-shaped servery at the centre looking after the two main bar areas, furnished with comfortable armchairs and high-backed stools. On an upper level is a games area featuring Northants skittles and darts. A variety of CAMRA branch magazines is available to read while sampling the well-kept ales. Home to three skittles teams, also of interest are board games and monthly quiz and poetry reading evenings. Q

Lilbourne

Head of Steam

10 Station Road, CV23 0SX (just off Rugby Rd)
5-11.30; 12-3, 5-midnight Fri; 12-midnight Sat; 12-11 Sun
(01788) 860166 headofsteampub.co.uk
4 changing beers (sourced nationally; often Church End, Phipps NBC, Wye Valley)
You have to admire the landlord for turning his home into this superb village pub, which is very much a community hub, family-friendly and welcoming. The railway theme refers to the nearby disused Rugby to Peterborough line. Four well-kept beers can be found including a regular house beer from St Austell, along with locally sourced pork pies and freshly made rolls. The large garden at the rear is ideal for summer drinking. QP

Litchborough

Old Red Lion

4 Banbury Road, NN12 8JF (opp church)
4-8 Mon; 2.30-11; 12-11 Sat; 12-4 Sun (01327) 830064
oldredlionlitchborough.co.uk
Great Oakley Wagtail; house beer (by Grainstore); 1 changing beer (sourced regionally)
A traditional four-roomed stone-built village pub well worth seeking out, popular with walkers and cyclists on the Knightly Way. The bar has flagstone flooring and seats inside a large inviting inglenook. The snug to the rear of the bar is a comfy, casual room with double doors leading to a courtyard. The extension houses a restaurant and shop that sells local farm produce. A wide range of locally brewed bottled beers is stocked, often from Merrimen Brewery on the edge of the village.
QP

Loddington

Hare at Loddington

5 Main Street, NN14 1LA (on village loop)
closed Mon; 12-3, 5.30-11 (11.30 Fri); 12-11.30 Sat; 12-10.30 Sun (01536) 710337
thehareatloddington.com
Bombardier; Greene King Abbot; Sharp's Doom Bar; 1 changing beer (sourced locally; often Langton, Nobby's, Silverstone)
Set in a conservation area, the Hare is a listed building in this picturesque village built from local ironstone. It stands back in the middle of Main Street surrounded by listed houses, and has a pleasant front garden. Now more open, it comprises four areas – two are spread around the central bar and two are for dining, with good home-cooked food sourced from local producers. The guest beer is often from an established or county microbrewery. QP(35)

Long Buckby

Old King's Head

2 Harbidges Lane, NN6 7QL (off B5385)
closed Mon; 12-2.30, 5-11; 12-11 Fri & Sat; 12-10.30 Sun
(01327) 842680 oldkingsheadlongbuckby.co.uk
Everards Beacon Hill, Tiger; 4 changing beers (sourced regionally; often Everards, Phipps NBC, Titanic)
The fortunes of this charming 17th-century thatched pub continue to go from strength to strength under the continued stewardship of the tenants. It has two very different attractive bars, one with a small skittles and darts area, the other

with a restaurant, making it an interesting place to explore. Up to three guest ales are available along with three regulars from the Everards stable. Paintings by a local artist adorn the walls. Beer, cider and gin each merit separate festivals during the year. Q P (11,96)

Naseby

Royal Oak

Church Street, NN6 6DA (on B4036)

5-8.30 Mon; 12-2.30, 5-10.30 Tue-Thu; 12-11.30 Fri & Sat; 12-8 Sun ☎ (01604) 743077

Oakham Bishops Farewell; 4 changing beers (sourced nationally; often Oakham, Timothy Taylor, Towcester Mill) H

A revived rural village pub close to the Naseby Battlefield, scene of a key battle in the English Civil War in 1645. Now leased by Towcester Mill Brewery, two of its beers always feature on the bar. The main L-shaped room is divided into three areas with a real fire in the wall between the main bar and games room where Northants skittles and darts are played. The kitchen prepares reasonably priced pub classics, burgers and pizzas. Q P

Nether Heyford

Foresters Arms

22 The Green, NN7 3LE

5-11; 12-11 Fri & Sat; 12-10.30 Sun ☎ (01327) 340622

2 changing beers (sourced regionally) H

A double bay-fronted ironstone building opposite the village green. The current owner bought the pub in 2012 and has made many improvements. The interior is decorated with pictures and many pumpclips above the bar. Two regularly changing ales are always available, one sourced locally and the other often from one Welsh microbrewery or another. Two ciders are dispensed on gravity at the back of the bar. P (D3)

Northampton

Albion Brewery Bar

54 Kingswell Street, NN1 1PR (bottom of Bridge St hill)

5-10.30 Mon; 12-3, 5-11; 12-12.30am Fri & Sat; 12-3.30 Sun ☎ (01604) 946606 phipps-nbc.co.uk

Hoggleys Northamptonshire Bitter; Phipps NBC Red Star, India Pale Ale, Ratliffe's Celebrated Stout, Becket's Ale; 3 changing beers (sourced locally; often Phipps NBC) H

Phipps NBC returned to its roots in a Victorian brewery in the heart of Northampton in 2014, 40 years after Phipps' Bridge Street brewery closed. The brewery bar subsequently opened, with an oak and glass partition between the bar and brewery enabling the brewing process to be viewed. Almost all the bar fittings are reclaimed, with many coming from former Phipps pubs. There is much memorabilia to read and view. Eight handpumps serve six ales from the brewery including a Hoggleys beer plus a rotating guest, with the final pump reserved for a Northamptonshire cider. Q

Bold Dragoon

48 High Street, NN3 3JW (off A4500 at traffic lights)

12-11.30 (midnight Fri & Sat); 12-11 Sun ☎ (01604) 401221

Fuller's London Pride, ESB; Greene King IPA, Abbot; 3 changing beers (sourced regionally; often Phipps NBC, St Austell, Timothy Taylor) H

A popular and well-kept pub built in the 1930s on the site of a 19th-century inn that was demolished to enable road widening. The Bold is in the centre of the village, now absorbed into Northampton borough. This spacious pub has a lively bar, carpeted lounge, games room and superb conservatory restaurant serving a full menu. Seven beers are stocked, four permanent and three changing, usually from local and regional breweries. It has the welcoming atmosphere of a country pub in the town. P (1,X46)

Kingsley Park Working Men's Club

120 Kingsley Park Terrace, NN2 7HJ

12-11 (11.30 Fri); 11-11.30 Sat; 11-11 Sun ☎ (01604) 711002 kpwmc.co.uk

Fuller's London Pride, ESB; Greene King IPA; Sharp's Doom Bar; Tetley Bitter; 3 changing beers (often Great Oakley, Nobby's, Phipps NBC) H

Long-established, thriving working men's club on the main road in a residential area, founded in 1892 in a nearby street. There are eight handpumps serving five regular and three changing beers, overseen by an award-winning steward. Live music is hosted three nights a week and trips out are organised for members.

Lamplighter

66 Overstone Road, NN1 3JS

12-midnight (1am Fri & Sat); 12-11 Sun ☎ (01604) 631125 thelamplighter.co.uk

Nobby's Plum Porter; Oakham JHB; Phipps NBC India Pale Ale; Vale Gravitas; 4 changing beers (sourced regionally) H

A deservedly popular, traditional, street-corner pub just off the town centre attracting young and old alike. There is a roaring fire in the bar, a lovely snug and a heated courtyard. Four local and four guest beers are from established micros, along with a selection of bottled beers. Home-cooked food is served and children are welcome during mealtimes. The pub hosts open mic, discos, live music and quiz nights each week, and beer festivals throughout the year.

Malt Shovel Tavern

121 Bridge Street, NN1 1QF

11.30-11; 12-10.30 Sun ☎ (01604) 234212 maltshoveltavern.com

Frog Island Natterjack; Fuller's London Pride; Nethergate Priory Mild; Oakham Bishops Farewell; 10 changing beers (sourced nationally) H

Close to the town centre and opposite the Carlsberg brewery, this popular pub has won many awards over the past 20 or more years. Breweriana features everywhere, with real cider, LocAle, Belgian draught and bottled beers available. Two beer festivals are held each year on bank holidays with live bands. Home-made lunches are served all week. Blues bands play on Wednesday nights. The pub has a strong rugby following.

Olde England

199 Kettering Road, NN1 4BP (near racecourse)

12-midnight (11 Mon); 12-11 Sun ☎ (01604) 603799

Digfield Barnwell Bitter; Hop Back Summer Lightning G**; Marston's EPA; Ringwood Old Thumper** H**; Vale Gravitas; Wychwood Hobgoblin; changing beers**

(sourced regionally; often Nobby's, Phipps NBC, Potbelly) G
Converted end-of-terrace Victorian building on three floors with bars on two floors. The ground and first floors have a medieval theme with solid fuel burners. The cellar bar has a contemporary style and is more intimate. Up to 15 beers from local micros and regional breweries are served by gravity and handpump alongside 15 ciders. Various board games, cards and dominoes are provided. Live folk music plays on Thursday. A former local CAMRA Cider Pub of the Year and Northants Town Community Pub. Q

Pomfret Arms

10 Cotton End, NN4 8BS
12-midnight (11 Mon-Wed) ☎ (01604) 555119
pomfretarms.co.uk
Cotton End Aramis, Coffee Porter; Great Oakley Gobble; Hart Family No.3; 1 changing beer (sourced locally) H
With its own microbrewery, this town pub is situated on the south west side of the River Nene in Cotton End. Its small central bar contains six handpumps serving both the front opened-out room and rear bar. The brewery and a function room are in a separate building in the lovely beer garden. Two of the beers are usually Cotton End brews from the brewery itself or from the Hart Family sister brewery.

Road to Morocco

Bridgwater Drive, NN3 3AG
12-11 (midnight Fri & Sat); closed Sun ☎ (01604) 632899
Greene King IPA, Abbot; Theakston Old Peculier; 4 changing beers (sourced regionally) H
Run by a CAMRA member, this popular 1960s brick-built estate pub has a Moorish theme in some of the decor, reflecting its name. It has two connected but distinctly different rooms. The busy bar area can get especially lively when live sport is on TV, and is where darts and pool are played. The homely lounge is generally the quieter area for a drink. Quiz night is Tuesday.
P(5,9B)

St Giles Ale House

45 St Giles Street, NN1 1JF
closed Mon; 12-8 (10 Thu); 12-11 Fri & Sat; 12-7 Sun
☎ (01604) 636332
6 changing beers (often Framework, Grainstore)
Northampton's first and only micropub, opened in 2016 following conversion from retail premises. it specialises in real ale, real cider and a small number of craft/continental bottled beers. Ales are from around the country and tend to be new releases or from more obscure breweries. With no music, fruit machines or Wi-Fi, this is an ideal place for drinking and conversation. Q(5)

Old

White Horse

Walgrave Road, NN6 9QX
closed Mon; 12-3, 5-11 Tue-Thu; 12-11 Fri & Sat; 12-7 Sun
☎ (01604) 781297 whitehorseold.co.uk
3 changing beers (sourced locally; often Nobby's, Potbelly) H
A rustic country pub comprising two opened-out rooms with polished wooden floors and a real fire, and a small snug towards the rear. Upstairs is the Millstone room which can be used for functions and leads to the south-facing garden overlooking the church. The menu is relatively small, offering interesting, quality, home-cooked seasonal lunches and evening meals including pub classics and specials. Attractions are monthly live music and quiz nights and a weekly Tuesday pie night.
QP

Oundle

Ship Inn

18 West Street, PE8 4EF
11-11.45 (midnight Fri & Sat); 12-11 Sun
☎ (01832) 273918 theshipinn-oundle.co.uk
Nene Valley Blonde Session Ale; 3 changing beers (often Nene Valley) H
This Grade II listed pub is full of character with original beamed ceilings and the ghost of a former landlord. It has three bars with many small rooms adjoining, and a large function room available to hire for birthday celebrations and small weddings. Good food is served in all rooms. Accommodation is in two stone annexes and a small cottage to the rear. The rear car park is accessed through an archway off West Street.
QP(24,X4)

Polebrook

King's Arms

Kings Arms Lane, PE8 5LW
12-3, 6-11; 12-11 Sat & Sun ☎ (01832) 272363
kingsarmspolebrook.co.uk
Digfield Fools Nook, Barnwell Bitter; 3 changing beers H
Traditional stone-built thatched inn that can be accessed from doors at the front and rear off the car park. The pub is open plan with a main bar, three areas for diners and a small garden. Third-pint glasses allow the opportunity to taste a wider variety of beer. There is an annual themed beer festival mid-September and regular food and beer pairing evenings. Free tapas happy hour is 6-7pm Monday. QP

Rushden

Rushden Historical Transport Society

Station Approach, NN10 0AW (on ring road)
7.30-11 Mon & Tue; 6-11 Wed & Thu; 4.30-11 Fri; 12-11 Sat & Sun ☎ (01933) 318988 rhts.co.uk
Phipps NBC India Pale Ale; Salopian Golden Thread; 5 changing beers (sourced regionally; often Marston's, Phipps NBC, Woodforde's) H
This award-winning club occupies the former Midland Railway Station. The ladies' waiting room is now the bar, with gas lighting and walls adorned with enamel advertising panels, railway photos and many CAMRA awards. On the platform, carriages provide a meeting room, Northants skittles, and a buffet for the numerous open days held during the year when steam and diesel train rides are provided. A beer festival is held in September. Day membership is £1 except on open days. Q

Southwick

Shuckburgh Arms

Main Street, PE8 5BL
6-10 Mon; 12 (6 Tue)-11; 12-10 Sun ☎ (01832) 272044
shuckburghpub.co.uk

Brewster's Hophead; Wadworth 6X; 3 changing beers (sourced locally; often Digfield, Grainstore, Nene Valley) 🄷
Thatched stone-built pub in the village centre, serving five real ales. The bar area doubles as a restaurant and there is a small side room. To the rear is a covered outdoor area, car park, large garden and the village cricket pitch. The pub is run by the local community with shareholders and a small committee. It hosts the annual World Conker Championship in October and jousting in May. Popular well-priced food is available, including breakfast by arrangement. Q❀◐▲♣P🚌🐾📶

Staverton

Countryman 🄻 ✔
Daventry Road, NN11 6JH (on A425)
12-3, 6-11; 12-10 Sun ☎ (01327) 311815
thecountrymanstaverton.co.uk
Bombardier; Hook Norton Greedy Goose; 1 changing beer (sourced locally; often Church End) 🄷
This Guide regular is the last survivor of the three pubs that once served this lovely village close to Daventry. The long wooden-beamed bar serves four areas, and an open hearth fire between the rooms provides some seclusion. The enthusiastic landlord offers a good choice of ales, always including one local brew. There is also a wide choice of reasonably priced food, sourced locally whenever possible. Q❀◐♿P🚌(66)📶

Stoke Bruerne

Boat Inn ✔
Shutlanger Road, NN12 7SB
9am-11 ☎ (01604) 862428 boatinn.co.uk
Banks's Amber Ale; Jennings Cumberland Ale; Marston's Old Empire; Ringwood Boondoggle; Wychwood Hobgoblin; 2 changing beers (sourced nationally) 🄷
In a picturesque setting alongside the Grand Union Canal and opposite the National Canal Museum, the Boat Inn has been owned by the same family since 1877. The long, narrow, stone building has a thatched roof and a wonderful tap bar with interconnecting rooms with canal views, open fires, original stone floors and window seats. An adjoining room has Northants skittles. A canal boat is available to hire. A loyalty card scheme rewards regulars. Breakfast is served until 11am.
Q❀◐♿♣●P🚌(86)🐾📶

Thornby

Red Lion 🄻 ✔
Welford Road, NN6 8SJ (on A5199)
5-10 Mon; 12-3, 5-11 Tue-Thu; 12-11 Fri & Sat; 12-10 Sun
☎ (01604) 740238 redlionthornby.co.uk
6 changing beers (sourced regionally; often Adnams, Grainstore, Wadworth) 🄷
An impressive whitewashed village pub situated on the old A50 dating back more than 400 years. The compact bar has two drinking areas with a wood-burning open fire in the lounge. To the rear is the restaurant, which occupies two linked rooms, one heavily beamed. Accommodation is in a converted barn. A beer festival is held in late July. A local CAMRA award winner in 2016.
Q❀◐♿P🚌(60)🐾📶

Tiffield

George at Tiffield 🄻 ✔
21 High Street North, NN12 8AD (centre of village)
12-3, 6-11 Mon, Wed & Thu; 7-11 Tue; 12-midnight Fri; 12-11 Sat; 12-7 Sun ☎ (01327) 350587
thegeorgeattiffield.co.uk
Great Oakley Egret, Tiffield Thunderbolt; Vale Pale Ale; 2 changing beers (sourced regionally; often Vale) 🄷
A true community inn central to many village activities – the building dates from the 16th century, with Victorian additions when it became a public house. It has a cosy bar, games room with Northants skittles and a back room restaurant which can be booked for small functions. It is the tap for Great Oakley Brewery, just outside the village. A beer festival is held in October. A former local CAMRA Rural Pub of the Year.
❀◐♿▲♣●P🚌🐾

Towcester

Plough 🄻 ✔
96 Watling Street, NN12 6BT
12-11 (5 Sun) ☎ (01327) 352515
ploughinntowcester.co.uk
Bombardier; Eagle IPA; 1 changing beer (sourced nationally) 🄷
Situated in the centre of this racecourse town, in front of Bury Mount on which the town's Roman fort once stood. The pub has a cosy front bar with stone floors and a large bay window overlooking the main street, and a larger lounge bar/restaurant to the rear. A wide corridor runs from the front to the back, leading to a small outdoor drinking area. The Plough participates in the town's June music festival. No food on Monday. Q❀◐♿●🚌🐾📶

Towcester Mill Brewery Tap 🄻
Chantry Lane, NN12 6AD
5-10.30 (8 Mon); 3-11 Fri; 12-11 Sat; 12-8 Sun
☎ (01327) 437060 towcestermillbrewery.co.uk
Towcester Mill Mill Race, Bell Ringer, Black Fire, Roman Road; 4 changing beers (sourced locally; often Towcester Mill) 🄷
Popular and welcoming brewery tap in a historic Grade II listed mill dating from 1794, straddling the old mill race and adjacent to Bury Mount on which the town's fort once stood. The bar retains many original features including beams, stonework and a wooden floor, with a second room to cope with demand. Outside is a large garden alongside the mill. Local CAMRA Pub of the Year 2016, two guest ales from other local breweries and six ciders are available. Q❀♿●P🚌🐾📶

Weldon

Shoulder of Mutton 🄻
12 Chapel Road, NN17 3HP
3-10; 12-midnight Fri-Sun ☎ (01536) 601016
shoulderofmuttonweldon.co.uk
Weldon Cupola, Dragline, Galvy Stout, Roman Mosaics; 1 changing beer (sourced locally; often Weldon) 🄷
Large, two-roomed pub – a locals' bar at the front and a function room to the rear. The front bar was originally three rooms which have been made into one, with an open fire at one end. In 2016 the pub's microbrewery moved off-site to Rushden and was renamed the Weldon Brewery. The food menu includes home-made Serbian dishes alongside

traditional pub meals. Brewery tours can be arranged in advance which include transport and food back at the pub for up to eight people.
(X4)

Welford

Wharf Inn

NN6 6JQ (on A5199 by canal basin)
12-11 (01858) 575075
Grainstore Ten Fifty; Marston's Pedigree; Oakham Bishops Farewell; 3 changing beers (sourced locally)
This original ironstone building dates from 1814 and is situated at the end of the Welford cut on the Grand Union Canal, a few yards from the border with Leicestershire. The main room is segregated by an open fireplace between the two rooms. A smaller snug and back bar is occasionally used. Several walks can be started from here – a handy leaflet behind the bar provides details. Guest beers are always sourced locally or regionally. Local CAMRA Rural Pub of the Year 2017.
QP(60)

Wellingborough

Coach & Horses

17 Oxford Street, NN8 4HY (near Market Square)
12-11 (9 Mon); 12-6 Sun (01933) 441848
thecoachandhorseswellingborough.co.uk
12 changing beers (sourced nationally; often Abbeydale, Great Oakley, Phipps NBC)
A long-standing Guide entry, this popular town-centre local offers a constantly changing choice of 12 real ales and 12 ciders, including two or more local ales. The central bar serves three drinking areas, all adorned with breweriana. Traditional home-cooked food is available (no food Sun eve, Mon & Tue), with 40 different pies on the menu. A quiz is held on alternate Wednesdays. CAMRA East Midlands Leicestershire & Northamptonshire Pub of the Year 2016. Q

Little Ale House

14A High Street, NN8 4JU
closed Mon; 5-9 Tue; 12-9 Wed & Thu; 12-11 Fri & Sat; 12-5 Sun 07870 392011
7 changing beers (sourced regionally; often Castle Rock, Nene Valley, Potbelly)
A wonderfully friendly one-roomed micropub whose small size encourages interaction between guests and the landlady. Up to seven rotating real ales are served on handpump and gravity from local and other micro breweries. In addition, up to six draught ciders and a good selection of gins, single malt whiskies, wines and soft drinks are also stocked. Close to Jackson's Lane car park.
QP

Welton

White Horse

High Street, NN11 2JP (off A361 betwen Rugby and Daventry)
12-2 (not Mon & Tue), 5-11; 12-midnight Fri & Sat; 12-11 Sun (01327) 702820 thewhitehorsewelton.co.uk
Adnams Southwold Bitter; Oakham Bishops Farewell; Purity Pure Gold; 1 changing beer (sourced nationally)
A well-run 17th-century village pub serving excellent beers and locally produced Vale of Welton cider. It has two bar areas – the first, where children and dogs are welcome, has a logburner and steps leading down to a skittles area. The second is a lounge bar with a coalburner and an archway leading to the restaurant, which serves a wide variety of good, reasonably priced food. A canopied patio overlooks the large garden and decking area. P

Weston by Welland

Wheel & Compass

Valley Road, LE16 8HZ (off B664)
12-11 (10.30 Sun) (01858) 565864
thewheelandcompass.co.uk
Banks's Amber Ale; Greene King Abbot; Marston's Pedigree; 4 changing beers (sourced nationally; often Adnams, Everards, St Austell)
A rural pub in the picturesque Welland Valley which has recently been refurbished, opening up the entrance lobby and incorporating part of the former dining area, with flagstone floors, a woodburner and sofas. The outside drinking area offers good views across the valley and is an ideal playground for children. This is a popular stopping-off place for walkers on the Jurassic Way which runs close by. Good-value food includes lunchtime specials.
P

Woodford

Duke's

83 High Street, NN14 4HE (off A510)
12-11 (01832) 732224
Greene King Abbot; 7 changing beers (sourced nationally; often Digfield, Fuller's, Oakham)
Overlooking the village green, this community focused pub was a 17th-century manor. The Duke's was renamed in honour of the Duke of Wellington, who was a frequent visitor to the village. The interior includes a split main bar, lounge restaurant, rear room and an upstairs games room. The pub holds a May bank holiday beer festival and August bank holiday music festival, plus regular open mic, disco, karaoke and acoustic music nights. Traditional pub food is available.
P(16)

Yardley Hastings

Rose & Crown

4 Northampton Road, NN7 1EX
5-10 Mon; 12-11; 12-10 Sun (01604) 696276
roseandcrownbistro.co.uk
Greene King IPA, Abbot; house beer (by Hart Family Brewers); 3 changing beers (sourced nationally; often Adnams, Black Sheep)
An award-winning ironstone pub, extensively refurbished in olde-worlde style. The single large room retains stone-flagged floors and beamed ceilings, and has a small drinking area in the bay window. The emphasis is on traditional home cooking, with a daily changing menu and light meals served throughout the day. The house beer is from Hart Family. Board games are available and monthly music events are held. The landscaped gardens are wonderful in summer.
QP(41)

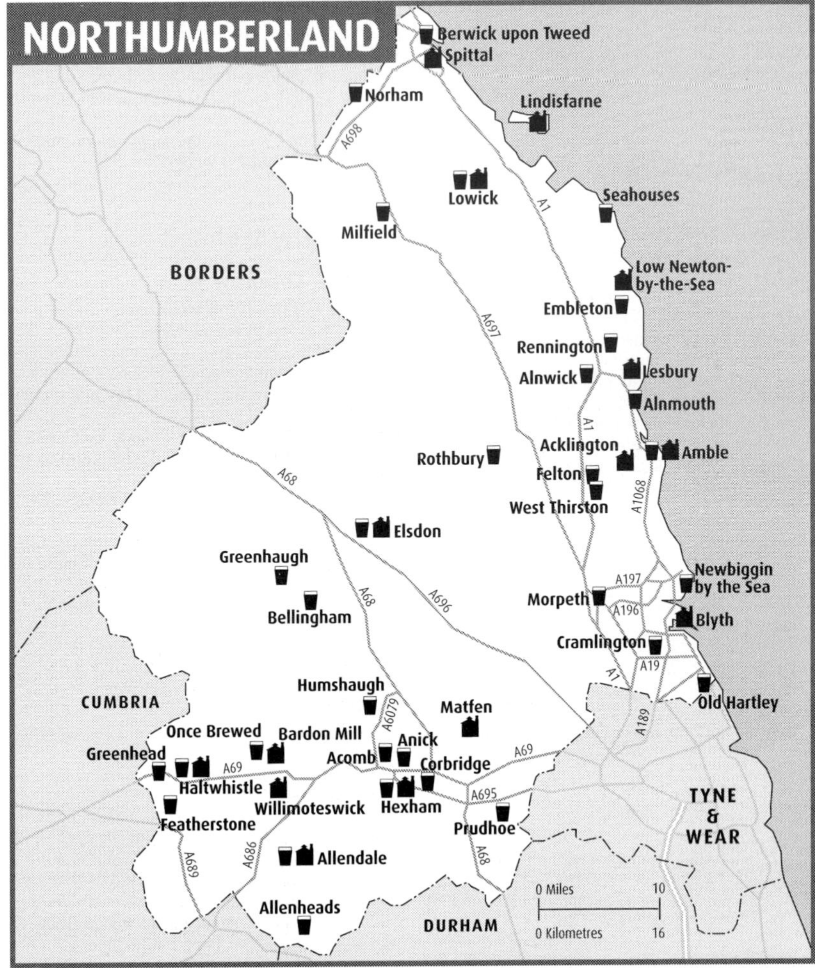

Acomb

Miners Arms

Main Street, NE46 4PW

5-11.30; 12-midnight Sat & Sun ☎ (01434) 603909
theminersacomb.com

Wylam Gold Tankard; 2 changing beers Ⓗ

Superb, traditional 1746 inn with an emphasis on real ale, served in oversized lined glasses. The pub hosts regular music and folk nights. The bar has a cosy feel and is divided by a central staircase. Energetic dogs provide a friendly welcome. The miners have long gone but their legacy lives on in this this family-run pub. (680)

Allendale

Golden Lion Hotel

Market Place, NE47 9BD

12-1.30am (1am Wed); 12-2.30am Fri-Sun
☎ (01434) 683225 goldenlionhotel.net

Timothy Taylor Landlord; Wylam Gold Tankard; 3 changing beers Ⓗ

Friendly and hospitable pub in the centre of town, patronised by locals and tourists. The walls are adorned with photographs of the annual tar barrel procession, an experience in itself, and landscapes of the surrounding area. Allendale's choir practise here on Tuesday evening, and live Irish music plays on the last Wednesday of the month. With two regular beers and three guests, some brewed in-house, there is always plenty of choice of local ales. Home-cooked food is available. The pub has a late licence at weekends. (688)

REAL ALE BREWERIES

Allendale Allendale
Beacon Brauhaus Lindisfarne
Bear Claw Spittal
Credence Amble
First & Last Elsdon (NEW)
Hawk Wing Lesbury
Hetton Law Lowick
Hexhamshire Hexham
High House Farm Matfen
Muckle Haltwhistle
North Blyth Blyth (brewing suspended)
Pit Top Willimoteswick (NEW)
Rigg & Furrow Acklington
Ship Inn Low Newton-by-the-Sea
Twice Brewed Bardon Mill (NEW)

Allenheads

Allenheads Inn

NE47 9HJ

4-11; 12-11 Sat; 12-10.30 Sun ☎ (01434) 685200
allenheadsinn.co.uk

Mordue Northumbrian Blonde; house beer (by Anarchy); 3 changing beers

Superb 18th-century rural inn with a public bar with a log fire, games room and dining room. On the Coast-to-Coast cycle route, it is popular with cyclists, ramblers and tourists. Good bar meals are available at a decent price. Originally the home of Sir Thomas Wentworth, the multi-roomed premises is bedecked with memorabilia and knick-knacks from a bygone age. The pub will open early on request for coach parties and other groups. P (688)

Alnmouth

Red Lion Inn

22 Northumberland Street, NE66 2RJ

11-midnight ☎ (01665) 830584 redlionalnmouth.com

4 changing beers

Charming, family-run, 18th-century coaching inn with a cosy lounge bar with attractive woodwork. The decked area at the bottom of the garden enjoys panoramic views across the Aln Estuary. Occasional live music plays – in the open air in summer. Guest beers usually include one local and two interesting brews from further afield. An annual beer festival is held in October. Open for breakfast from 9am, excellent en-suite B&B accommodation is available. Popular with tourists and locals. QP (x18)

Alnwick

John Bull Inn

12 Howick Street, NE66 1UY

5-11; 12-3, 7-11 Sat & Sun ☎ (01665) 602055
john-bull-inn.co.uk

5 changing beers

Many times local CAMRA Pub of the Year and a former Regional Pub of the Year, this 180-year-old inn thrives on its reputation as a back-street boozer. The landlord offers a wide range of cask-conditioned ales at varying ABVs, real cider, the widest range of bottled Belgian beers in the county and over 120 single malt whiskies. The darts team competes in the local league and the pub upholds the North-East tradition of an annual leek show. There is a cheese club on Saturday night.
Q

Tanners Arms

2-4 Hotspur Place, NE66 1QF

5-11 (midnight Fri); 12-midnight Sat; 12-10.30 Sun
☎ (01665) 602553

6 changing beers

Ivy-covered stone-built pub just off Bondgate Without and a short distance from Alnwick Garden. The rustic single room has a flagstone floor and tree beer shelf. A large fireplace provides added warmth in winter. Acoustic music nights feature regularly with open mic on the last Friday of the month. The ever-changing real ales frequently come from North-East and Scottish Borders microbreweries.

Amble

Masons Arms

Woodbine Street, NE65 0NH

4-11.30; 3-12.30am Fri; 12-11.30 Sat & Sun
☎ (01665) 799275 masonsarmsamble.co.uk

6 changing beers (often Credence)

This large, multi-roomed pub is situated on a corner at the south edge of the Northumberland coastal village of Amble. Five handpumps adorn the bar and dispense a range of local brewery beers, including ales from the Credence Brewery based in Amble. Regular quizzes are held and a function room is available. Boat trips to Coquet Island depart from the nearby harbour.

Anick

Rat Inn

NE46 4LN (follow signpost at Hexham roundabout)

12-11.30 (10.30 Sun) ☎ (01434) 602814 theratinn.com

4 changing beers

Superb 1750 country inn with spectacular views across the Tyne Valley. The pub has a welcoming and friendly ambience, with an open log fire and chamber pots hanging from the ceiling. It has an excellent reputation for good food prepared with locally sourced ingredients and appears in several food guides. Half portions are available for children. Bottled beers are stocked. The first Thursday of the month is singers/poetry night. Well worth the short taxi ride from Hexham rail station.
QP

Bellingham

Cheviot Hotel

Main Street, NE48 2AU

10-midnight (1am Fri & Sat) ☎ (01434) 220696
thecheviothotel.co.uk

4 changing beers

Friendly hotel on Main Street opposite the bus stop. A log-burning stove warms the bar area. Cask beer is available all year round including one ale supplied by High House Farm Brewery. There is plenty of outside seating at the front. Regular theme nights are hosted. Stay up to date with the monthly newsletter, The Sheep Dip.
P (680)

Berwick upon Tweed

Barrels Ale House

59-61 Bridge Street, TD15 1ES

12-midnight (11.30 Sun) ☎ (01289) 308013

5 changing beers

There is an Old Curiosity Shop-ambience to this pub, located in the old part of Berwick next to the original road bridge over the Tweed. The excellent real ale no doubt helps customers brave the 'dentist's chair' at the side of the bar. A downstairs bar is used by DJs and bands at weekends. Outside is a unique open drinking area surrounded by high walls. A former winner of CAMRA Pub of the Year.

Brown Bear

27 Hide Hill, TD15 1EQ

12-11 (1am Sat & Sun) ☎ (01289) 298258
Berwickbrownbear.co.uk

Hadrian Border Tyneside Blonde; house beer (by Cross Borders); 2 changing beers

The Brown Bear Inn is Berwick-upon-Tweed's most iconic pub. It was sold at auction by Enterprise Inns in 2016. Concerned about the future of this important Berwick landmark, local businessman Frank Flannigan bought the property to save it from possible permanent loss. A group of locals have helped bring it back to life as a vibrant social business showcasing everything good about Berwick. Q

Curfew

46A Bridge Street, TD15 1AQ
12-9 (10 Fri-Sun) 07842 912268
4 changing beers
Berwick's first micropub is located up a small lane which opens out into a large courtyard off Bridge Street. It has a small bar area with a bottle fridge to one side. The courtyard makes a pleasant outdoor drinking area in summer. The cellar is in the shed at the top of the yard. CAMRA Northumberland Pub of the Year in 2016 and 2018. Q

Pilot

31 Low Greens, TD15 1LZ
12-midnight; 11-midnight Sat; 12-11 Sun
(01289) 304214
Caledonian Deuchars IPA; 2 changing beers
This popular pub with friendly bar staff is well patronised by locals and sought out by train trippers who have heard about this gem. The stone-built end-of-terrace hostelry dates from the 19th century and has a regionally important historic interior. It retains the original small room layout and boasts several nautical artefacts over 100 years old. It is home to a darts team and hosts music nights.

Corbridge

Angel of Corbridge

Main Street, NE45 5LA
11-11; 12-11 Sun (01434) 632119
theangelofcorbridge.com
Cumberland Corby Ale; Hadrian Border Tyneside Blonde; Mordue Workie Ticket; Wylam Galatia; 2 changing beers
Superb former coaching inn dating from 1726 located on the main road with good transport links. Seven handpulls adorn the bar and a wonderful selection of malt whiskies is also kept. Family-friendly and with a reputation for good food, the pub is popular with tourists, ramblers and locals. A separate lounge area has comfy leather seating and outside is a relaxed seating area. The town has strong links with the Romans and Hadrian's Wall is nearby. QP

Cramlington

Plough

Middle Farm Buildings, NE23 1DN
11-11 (midnight Fri & Sat); 12-11 Sun (01670) 737633
Cullercoats Jack the Devil; Harviestoun Bitter & Twisted; 5 changing beers
Converted farm buildings in the old village make up this Sir John Fitzgerald outlet, which is arranged in the style of a traditional pub with separate bar and lounge areas. A function room is available upstairs where children are always welcome – under-18s are only permitted in the bar areas during the daytime. An excellent range of ales from local micros is on continual rotation here in addition to the local core range, backed by a commitment to bringing in the best beers from across the UK. QP

Elsdon

Bird in Bush

Village Green, NE19 1AA
closed Mon-Wed; 7-11.45 Thu; 4.30-11 Fri; 12-11 Sat; 12-10.30 Sun (01830) 520914
4 changing beers
This recently reopenend pub is currently installing a biomass boiler to provide hot water and heating to the property. There are plans for a microbrewery once funding has been raised, run by First and Last Brewery who set up Stu Brew at Newcastle University. Accommodation is available.
P

Embleton

Greys Inn

Stanley Terrace, NE66 3UZ
12-11 (10.30 Sun) (01665) 576983
5 changing beers
Pleasant, traditional pub in a lovely seaside hamlet, just a short walk to a wonderful beach. It has three open fires and a framed 1904 grocery list hangs on the wall. The pub is an excellent venue to enjoy a bite to eat washed down with a locally sourced real ale, sitting outside on the superb patio in good weather. It is home to a ladies' darts team, clay pigeon club and golf club.
(418,X18)

Featherstone

Wallace Arms

Rowfoot, NE49 0JF
5-11.30 (10.30 Mon); 3-11.30 Fri; 12-midnight Sat & Sun
(01434) 298921
4 changing beers
Cosy country pub warmed by real fires, with no jukebox or fruit machines to disturb the peace. Split over two levels and three rooms, it has a traditional bar area and various spaces. The welcoming landlady is always prepared to open early for groups of walkers, preferably if arranged in advance. Opening hours are reduced in winter – check ahead. QP

Felton

Fox's Den

Cellar 2, 4 Riverside, NE65 9EA
closed Tue; 6 (7 Mon)-10.30; 5-10.30 Fri & Sat
07707 703182
4 changing beers
This micropub is a welcome addition to the mid-Northumberland pub scene. Situated in the basement below the Running Fox bakery and café, it has its own door on the main street. It is the sister pub to the Office in Morpeth. Four handpumps serve ever-changing, mostly local, ales. Dogs are welcome and fussed over.
QP(X15)

Greenhaugh

Holly Bush Inn

NE48 1PW

4-midnight; 12-midnight Sat & Sun ☎ (01434) 240391
hollybushinn.net
High House Farm Nel's Best; 1 changing beer Ⓗ
Independently owned pub, over 300 years old and set in the heart of the Northumberland National Park and the Dark Sky Park, making it ideal for those with an interest in real ale and real stars. No TV and no mobile reception make for a peaceful drinking experience. The pub hosts informal jam sessions – bring your instrument if you like.
Q❀♿P

Greenhead

Greenhead Hotel
CA8 7HB
12-11 ☎ (016977) 47411
greenheadhotelandhostel.co.uk
Cumberland Corby Ale, Corby Blonde; 1 changing beer Ⓗ
Welcoming family hotel near the Roman wall, well patronised by locals, tourists and ramblers. Many a walker will have been cheered by the roaring log fire, usually lit when the weather gets cooler. Home-made food is served all day, with meals freshly prepared from locally sourced ingredients. A separate function room holds 120 people. The 685 bus stops on the A69 a short walk away.
❀P

Haltwhistle

Black Bull
Black Bull Lane, Market Square, NE49 0BL
3.30-10 (11 Fri); 12-11 Sat; 12-10 Sun ☎ (01434) 320463
theblackbullhaltwhistle.co.uk
Allendale Golden Plover; 5 changing beers (sourced nationally) Ⓗ
Warm, friendly, two-roomed inn close to Hadrian's Wall and popular with locals and ramblers. An open fire warms the low wood-beamed interior, with a wooden bar and horse brasses enhancing the traditional ambience. The pub is down a cobbled lane just off the marketplace in the centre of the town. Beers are available on six handpulls. Regular theme nights are hosted. Ring to check winter hours, and meal times can vary too.
Q❀⇌(685)

Milecastle Inn Ⓛ
North Road, NE49 9NN (on Military Rd parallel to Hadrian's Wall N of Haltwhistle)
12-11 ☎ (01434) 321372 milecastle-inn.co.uk
Big Lamp Bitter, Sunny Daze; 1 changing beer Ⓗ
This 1600s pub adjacent to Hadrian's Wall sells ale mainly from Newburn-based Big Lamp Brewery. Located a mile and a half north of Haltwhistle, the rural hostelry has a homely feel and is popular with ramblers and tourists. Food is home-made and locally sourced. There are also two comfy holiday cottages. The Hadrian's Wall bus stops outside April to September. Check ahead for winter opening hours. **Q❀P**

Hexham

Dipton Mill Inn Ⓛ
Dipton Mill Road, NE46 1YA
12-2.30, 6-11; 12-3 Sun ☎ (01434) 606577
diptonmill.co.uk
Hexhamshire Blackhall English Stout, Devil's Elbow, Devil's Water, Old Humbug, Shire Bitter, Whapweasel Ⓗ
The tap for Hexhamshire Brewery, now relocated to the beer garden, this small inn is run by real ale enthusiasts who brew their own excellent beers. Blackhall English Stout has proved so popular with drinkers that it has ousted Guinness. To complement the ales there is great home-cooked food – Saturday is curry night. A cosy atmosphere and warm welcome make this pub well worth seeking out. The large garden has a stream running through it and there is plenty of countryside to explore. **Q❀P**

Heart of Northumberland Ⓛ
5 Market Street, NE46 3NS
11-11.30 (11 Mon); 11-11 Sun ☎ (01434) 608013
thehearthexham.com
Timothy Taylor Landlord; 4 changing beers Ⓗ
Five handpumps, four selling local ales, adorn the bar in this recently refurbished and reopened, food-led pub. The single large room is divided almost in two near the end of the bar, with wooden floors throughout. A large open fire warms things nicely in the back room and another smaller fire keeps the front room cosy, too. Excellent food is served. **❀⇌♣**

Humshaugh

Crown Inn Ⓛ
NE46 4AG
12-11 ☎ (01434) 681231 crownhumshaugh.co.uk
5 changing beers Ⓗ
A traditional village pub located in the centre of the beautiful village of Humshaugh, five miles north of the market town of Hexham. The Crown has a homely charm, with a wood-burning stove, cask ales and traditional home-cooked food. Simple guest accommodation is offered in comfortable rooms, ideal for those wishing to explore Hadrian's Wall.

Lowick

Black Bull Ⓛ
Main Street, TD15 2UA
10-11 (midnight Sat) ☎ (01289) 388375
blackbulllowick.co.uk
4 changing beers Ⓗ
First licensed as a public house in 1817, it is believed that some of the building dates back to the mid-1600s, when it was part of a farm. The pub closed in 2014 after several years of brewery ownership and was declared an asset of community value in 2015 after campaigning by the locals. In the same year a family business created to support rural and community development in Northumberland acquired the freehold. The pub was totally refurbished and reopened as a country inn in early 2017. **❀P**

Milfield

Red Lion Inn Ⓛ
Main Road, NE71 6JD (in middle of village)
11-2, 5-11; 11-11 Sat & Sun ☎ (01668) 216224
redlionmilfield.co.uk
2 changing beers Ⓗ
A true local pub at the heart of the village, just eight miles inside the border, dating back to the

mid-1700s. Rescued by the current licensee from the tight grip of Scottish & Newcastle, the Red Lion is a proper free house, with many varied guest beers served through the third handpump. Freshly prepared food is available, with blackboards proudly displaying where the local produce is sourced. Home to the local leek-growing club.
Q P (267)

Morpeth

Electrical Wizard

11 New Market, NE61 1PS
8am-midnight (1am Fri & Sat) (01670) 500640
Greene King Abbot; Ruddles County; 4 changing beers
This pub, formerly a cinema, was refurbished by Wetherspoon in 2011 to a high standard. It is named after Dr Walford Bodie, the Electrical Wizard, who entertained packed audiences here in the cinema's early years. It has one long bar to the right on entering the pub, and comfortable seating throughout. Interesting electrical sculptures and pictures of old Morpeth adorn the walls. The pub participates in an annual local beer festival along with other local Wetherspoons.

Office

The Toll House, Castle Square, NE61 1YL
5-10.30; 2-10.30 Sat; 12-10.30 Sun 07957 721066
5 changing beers
Formerly the brewery tap for Acton Ales, The Office is a micropub with no music or games machines. It features five handpulls and three craft keg beers, all of local origin, and three real ciders served on gravity from the glass-fronted fridge opposite the bar. No food is available. Q

Tap & Spile

23 Manchester Street, NE61 1BH
12-2.30, 4.30-11; 12-11 Fri & Sat; 12-10.30 Sun
(01670) 513894
Everards Tiger; Greene King Abbot; Timothy Taylor Landlord; 5 changing beers
The pub is popular with locals, though all are welcome here. It has eight handpulls offering a good choice of ales, with local ales from Northumbrian breweries often available, alongside Westons Old Rosie cider. The bar area at the front of the building is usually busy, though there is a quieter, cosy lounge to the rear accessible from either side of the room. A traditional folk group plays on Sunday lunchtime. Close to the town's bus station. Q

Newbiggin by the Sea

Queen's Head

7 High Street, NE64 6AT
10-midnight (01670) 817293
2 changing beers
Single-room establishment, rebuilt in 1909, with the bar, lounge and snug all together. Some Edwardian features have been retained including the curved bar counter. The pub sells competitively priced real ales at advantageous opening times and displays an impressive ever-growing collection of guest beer pumpclips on the walls. One beer is usually available, two on Fridays, varying weekly. This no-nonsense pub is popular with locals and visitors alike.

Norham

Mason's Arms

17 West Street, TD15 2LB
12-11 (01289) 382326
themasonsarmsnorham.co.uk
4 changing beers (often Allendale)
The cosy wood-panelled public bar, with a real fire at its heart, is the hub of this pub. Photos of bygone Norham adorn the walls, along with collections of fishing gear and joinery tools, and an old Younger's brewery mirror. The area is popular with tourists – nearby are a ruined castle and the railway station museum. Close to the Tweed Cycle Way and 67 bus stop. (67)

Old Hartley

Delaval Arms

NE26 4RL (jct of A193/B1325 S of Seaton Sluice)
12-11 summer; 12-2.30, 4.30-10.30; 12-11 Fri-Sun winter
(0191) 237 0489 thedelavalarms.wordpress.com
4 changing beers
Multi-roomed Grade II listed building dating from 1748, with a listed WWI water storage tower (part of Roberts Battery) behind the beer garden. It is the first pub in Northumberland for those following the coastal route. Good-quality, affordable meals complement the beer, with guest ales coming from local micros. To the left as you enter there is a room served through a hatch from the bar and to the right a room where children are welcome.
Q P (308,309)

Once Brewed

Twice Brewed Inn

Miltary Road, Bardon Mill, NE47 7AN (on B6318 Military Rd)
11-11 (01434) 344534 twicebrewedinn.co.uk
House beer (by Twice Brewed); 3 changing beers (often Twice Brewed)
A excellent remote inn on the Military Road, with Hadrian's Wall, Steel Rigg and Vindolanda nearby, attracting walkers and tourists. It has a fully refurbished bar area and offers a wide range of bottled beers from around the world. Home-cooked food, locally sourced where possible, is available all day in both the bar and restaurant. B&B is offered in 18 en-suite bedrooms. The Twice Brewed Brew House started producing its own beers in 2017. Q P

Prudhoe

Wor Local

Front Street, NE42 5HJ
4-10.30; 3-10.30 Thu & Fri; 2-10.30 Sat & Sun
(01661) 598150 worlocalmicropub.com
4 changing beers
Wor Local (or Our Local if you are not a Geordie) is a micropub with room for around 40 customers. The layout of the bar, with its comfy seating, encourages conversation. There are lots of traditional pub and board games available. Four local beers in a variety of styles are offered, one always at a lower price. Real ciders are also

available. Pork pies and cheese are on sale along with crisps and nuts. A welcome addition to the area.

Rennington

Horseshoes Inn

6 Rennington Village, NE66 3RS

closed Mon; 12-3, 6.30-11 (01665) 577665
thehorseshoesrennington.co.uk

Hadrian Border Farne Island Pale Ale; 1 changing beer

Superb traditional family-run village pub dating from 1841, with its history detailed on the chimney breast. The bar is warm and friendly without TV or jukebox, with dry hops hanging over the serving area and a cosy log fire. The restaurant seats 50 and has an excellent reputation. A pleasant beer garden is at the front. The pub hosts a scarecrow competition every August bank holiday Saturday and is home to two darts teams. QP

Rothbury

Narrow Nick

High Street, NE65 7TB

5-10.30; 2-10.30 Sat & Sun 07707 703182

6 changing beers

In a Northumberland market town, this micropub opened in 2016 in a former clothes shop. The single room has the bar at one side, with a more recent wooden bar-back. Six handpumps sell a range of local brewery beers, and a large range of gins is stocked. The front windows feature Art Deco-style stained glass.

Seahouses

Olde Ship Inn

7-9 Main Street, NE68 7RD

11-11; 12-11 Sun (01665) 720200 seahouses.co.uk

Black Sheep Best Bitter; Courage Directors; Hadrian Border Farne Island Pale Ale; Morland Old Speckled Hen; Ruddles County; Theakston Best Bitter; 2 changing beers

This farmhouse, built in 1745, was converted to the licensed trade in 1812 and has a regionally important historic pub interior. Family-owned since 1910, the pub has three quality bars adorned with a veritable treasure trove of 19th- and 20th-century maritime memorabilia. Fully residential, it offers an interesting menu of fish, fresh crab meals and snacks. QP(418,X18)

West Thirston

Northumberland Arms

The Peth, NE65 9EE

11.30-11 (10.30 Sun) (01670) 787370
northumberlandarms-felton.co.uk

3 changing beers (often Allendale)

This fine stone-built pub was put up in the 1820s by Hugh Percy, 3rd Duke of Northumberland, as a coaching inn. The building has been lovingly restored in an eclectic style while remaining warm, comfortable and welcoming. Bare stone walls and real fires add to the ambience. A large function room caters for groups of up to 30. The beer range is predominantly from local breweries.
P(X15)

Miners Arms, Acomb

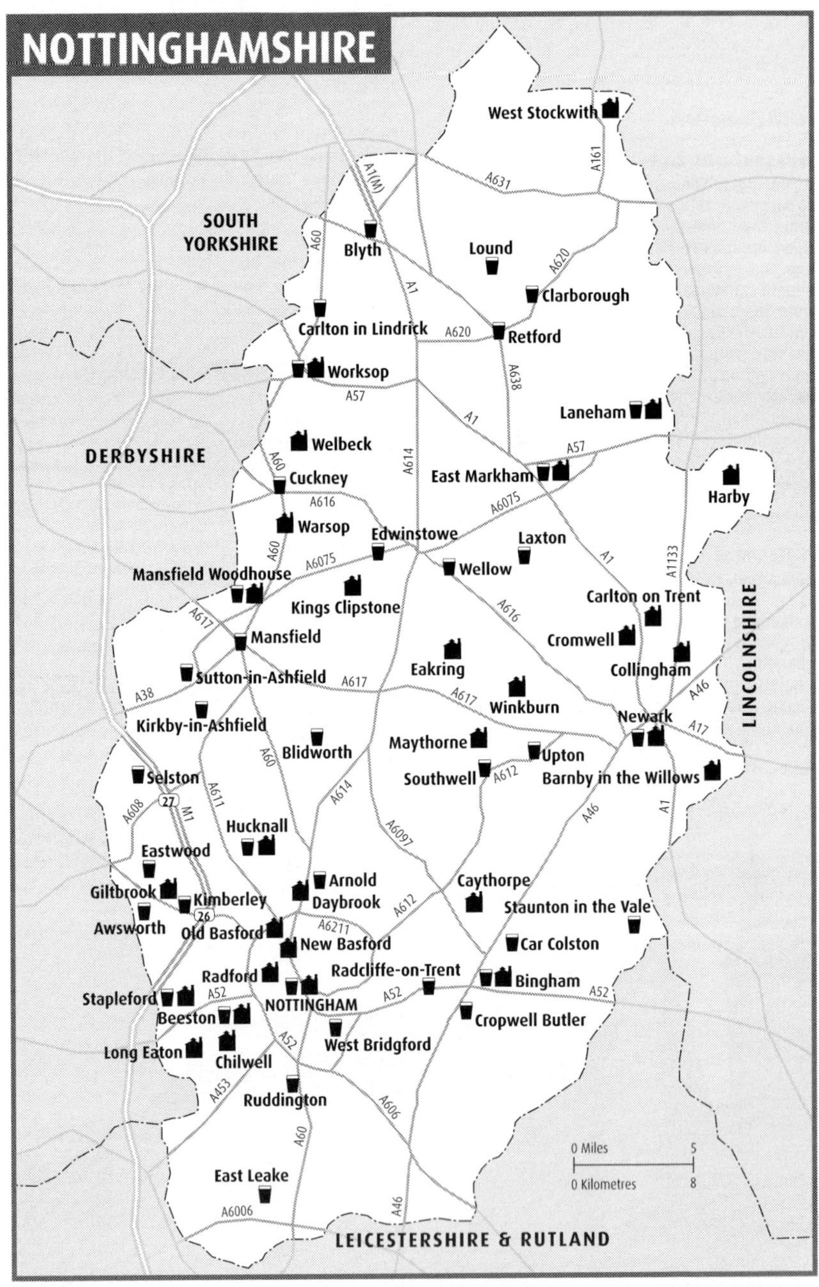

Arnold

Abdication L

89 Mansfield Road, Daybrook, NG5 6BH

closed Mon & Tue; 4-9.30; 2-6 Sun theabdication.co.uk

4 changing beers H

Built in 1936/37, this modern micropub is part of the Home Brewery Coronation Buildings opposite the gates of the former brewery, and was for many years a shop. The four cask ales, two KeyKeg beers and two ciders are from microbreweries, small producers or the on-site nanobrewery, and come in a mix of styles. An archway divides the single room, giving an appearance of a much larger area. Participants in the monthly quiz are grouped into teams by a raffle. **Q**

Robin Hood & Little John L

1 Church Street, NG5 8FD (on corner of Cross St)

12-11.30 (midnight Fri & Sat); 12-10.30 Sun

☎ (0115) 920 1054 therobinhoodandlittlejohn.co.uk

Everards Tiger; Lincoln Green Marion, Archer, Hood, Tuck; 10 changing beers H

Two-room Project William refurbishment between Lincoln Green and Everards breweries. The bar features Home Ales memorabilia, while the lounge has details of the pub's history and the local area. The rear courtyard has outdoor seating and a covered skittles alley. Along with 10 real ale pumps in each bar offering microbrewery beers, the real cider wall has eight taps dispensing ciders from small local producers and further afield.
🐎❀♿♣●🚌🐾📶

Awsworth

Gate Inn Ⓛ

Main Street, NG16 2RN
✪ 12-midnight ☎ (0115) 932 9821
7 changing beers Ⓗ
Deemed to be unviable and sold by the pub's former owners, The Gate reopened in 2010 as a free house and quickly established itself as a quality real ale outlet. A truly welcoming and friendly venue, this late 19th-century inn has a bar, lounge and rooftop sun terrace. The bar areas and snug were refurbished in 2017. Q🐎❀♿♣●P🚌🐾

Beeston

Crown Inn ★ Ⓛ

Church Street, NG9 1FY
✪ 12-11.30 (11 Sun) ☎ (0115) 967 8623
Blue Monkey Infinity; Brewsters Hophead; Dancing Duck Nice Weather; Nottingham Rock Ale Mild Beer; 9 changing beers Ⓗ
Nineteenth-century Grade II listed alehouse, acquired and sympathetically refurbished by Everards. Up to 14 ales and several real ciders and perries are served at this former East Midlands CAMRA Pub of the Year. An outside bar opens during the summer, extending the range to 22 beers. Inside, there are five distinct drinking areas including a snug and three-seat 'confessional', once used as a hideaway by the local vicar. Although busy, the pub retains a community feel, with a cosy atmosphere throughout. Substantial snacks are available. Q🐎❀♿⇌⚲♣●P🚌🐾📶

Star Inn Ⓛ

22 Middle Street, NG9 1FX
✪ 12-11 (midnight Thu-Sat) ☎ (0115) 854 5320
🌐 starbeeston.co.uk
10 changing beers (often Nottingham) Ⓗ
Former Shipstone's pub still with branded windows, restored beyond its former glory. The decor is tasteful and minimal with three separate rooms, complemented by a permanent marquee, sports/games room, spacious garden and patio outside. Visitors may recognise the bar, which featured in Boon and Auf Wiedersehen, Pet. Ten cask ales are on offer alongside a wide selection of whiskies and wines. Meals are served as well as a popular and extensive range of bar snacks. Families are welcome during the day.
🐎❀🛏◐♿⇌⚲♣●P🚌🐾📶

Victoria Hotel Ⓛ

85 Dovecote Lane, NG9 1JG
✪ 10.30-11 (midnight Fri & Sat); 12-11 Sun
☎ (0115) 925 4049 🌐 victoriabeeston.co.uk
Castle Rock Harvest Pale; Everards Tiger; Fuller's London Pride; 12 changing beers Ⓗ
Located alongside the platform of Beeston railway station, this restored Victorian masterpiece has mass appeal. Sixteen real ales are joined by real ciders and perries, an extensive whisky and wine list, and a renowned food menu. Taster trays of three third-pints are offered. Two distinct bars are complemented by a dining room and a covered, smoke-free seating area outside. VicFest is hosted in July in addition to beer festivals throughout the year. NUS discounts are available Sunday to Thursday. Q❀◐♿⇌⚲●P🚌🐾📶

Bingham

Horse & Plough Ⓛ

Long Acre, NG13 8AF
✪ 11-11 (midnight Fri & Sat) ☎ (01949) 839313
Castle Rock Harvest Pale, Preservation Fine Ale; 7 changing beers Ⓗ
Situated in the heart of a busy market town, this small pub is a former Methodist chapel with a traditional interior and flagstone floor. Up to nine cask ales and three ciders are available. A varied seasonal food menu is served in the bar and upstairs restaurant. Local CAMRA Pub of the Year in 2017, for the fourth time, and a former Cider Pub of the Year, the pub always offers a wide range of styles and strengths of real ale and cider, showcasing smaller producers alongside established favourites. 🐎◐♿⇌●🚌🐾📶

REAL ALE BREWERIES

Angel ▤ Nottingham
Bang the Elephant ▤ Long Eaton (NEW)
Beermats Winkburn (NEW)
Beeston Hop Beeston
Black Iris Nottingham: New Basford
Black Market ▤ Warsop
Blue Monkey Giltbrook
Brewhouse & Kitchen ▤ Nottingham
Castle Rock Nottingham
Cat Asylum Collingham (NEW)
Caythorpe ▤ Caythorpe
Double Top Worksop
Dukeries Worksop
Full Mash Stapleford
Good Stuff ▤ Nottingham: Daybrook
Grafton Worksop
Handley's ▤ Barnby in the Willows
Harby ▤ Harby
Idle ▤ West Stockwith
Kings Clipstone Kings Clipstone
Lenton Lane Nottingham
Lincoln Green Hucknall
Linear Bingham
Magpie Nottingham
Mallard Maythorne
Maypole Eakring
Milestone Cromwell
Navigation ▤ Nottingham
Neon Raptor Nottingham
Newark Newark
Nottingham ▤ Nottingham: Radford
Pheasantry East Markham
Prior's Well Mansfield Woodhouse
Reality Nottingham: Chilwell
Robin Hood Nottingham: New Basford
Scribbler's Stapleford
Shipstone's ▤ Nottingham: Old Basford
Springhead Laneham
Tom Herrick's Carlton on Trent
Totally Brewed Nottingham
Welbeck Abbey Welbeck

Blidworth

Black Bull

Main Street, NG21 0QH
8am-11.30 (midnight Fri & Sat) (01623) 490222
blackbullblidworth.co.uk
Blue Monkey BG Sips; Church End Goat's Milk; Prior's Well Citra; 2 changing beers
Recently refurbished family-owned pub offering a warm welcome to both locals and visitors. It has two large rooms – a bar and restaurant. Up to five rotating guest beers are available, three usually brewed in Nottinghamshire. The restaurant offers good traditional and more adventurous meals including vegetarian options and Sunday roasts. Ingredients are freshly sourced from local suppliers and the menu changes to reflect seasonal availability. It offers B&B in four rooms and opens from 8am for breakfast. P (141)

Blyth

Red Hart

Bawtry Road, S81 8HG (opp church)
2.30-11.30 Mon; 11.30-midnight (01909) 591221
redhart.co.uk
3 changing beers (sourced regionally)
An attractive village pub situated in the centre of Blyth with a lounge, taproom, separate dining room and outside seating area. The bar has a pool table and TV for sport. Food is served daily and three changing guest beers are available. The pub runs an annual beer festival in May from a bar in an outbuilding. The Red Hart is a recent winner of North Notts CAMRA Pub of the Season.
Q P (25,29)

Car Colston

Royal Oak

The Green, NG13 8JE
11.30-11 (01949) 20247 royaloakcarcolston.co.uk
Marston's 61 Deep; Ringwood Boondoggle; 2 changing beers
This country inn – a former hosiery factory – is on one of England's largest village greens. The pub has a cosy bar with comfortable seating and a real fire, a separate, generously sized restaurant and a function room. Four beers, all from the Marston's range but often less-heralded brews, are available. Food is served lunchtimes and evenings. There is a skittle alley to the rear, a beer garden and camping facilities. P

Carlton in Lindrick

Grey Horses Inn

The Cross, S81 9EW (in centre of old village)
12-11; 11-11 Sun (01909) 730252
Welbeck Abbey Henrietta, Portland Black; house beer (by Welbeck Abbey); 3 changing beers (sourced regionally)
The Grey Horses is within the conservation area here, and has a cosy front bar accessible from the street, a spacious lounge bar where excellent food is served and a large beer garden. It is the tap for Welbeck Abbey Brewery and its beers are rotated. The pub hosts an annual beer festival, usually in June. A warm welcome is assured.
Q P (21,22)

Clarborough

King's Arms

Main Street, DN22 9LN (centre of village on main road)
12-midnight (01777) 708845
3 changing beers (sourced locally)
A quiet pub run by real ale enthusiasts, well supported by locals and situated three miles from Retford. Two or three changing ales are on handpump, often from local breweries. Food is served and there is a separate restaurant. Seating is available outside. The pub supports local events and good causes. Q P

Cropwell Butler

Plough

Main Street, NG12 3AB
12-3 (not Mon), 5-11; 12-midnight Fri & Sat; 12-10.30 Sun
(0115) 933 3124 theplough-cropwellbutler.co.uk
Castle Rock Harvest Pale; 1 changing beer
Set in the heart of the village, this pub has a welcoming interior with real fires in both the bar and larger restaurant, and a large, picturesque beer garden. Three cask ales are available including one local beer. A full lunchtime and evening food service is provided. Regular quiz nights take place, often combined with themed food menus.
P (100)

Cuckney

Greendale Oak

Budby Road, NG20 9NQ
12-11 (1am Fri); 12-3, 6-1am Sat (01623) 844441
greendaleoak.co.uk
Everards Sunchaser, Tiger; 5 changing beers (sourced regionally; often Ashover, Castle Rock, Joule's)
The Greendale Oak is a traditional village pub which offers up to seven real ales, two from the Everards range and five guests. Set in the middle of the Welbeck Estate, parts of the building claim to date back to 600AD. A comprehensive food menu is served every day. Wednesday is quiz night and Thursday is fish market night. P

East Leake

Round RobINN

54 Main Street, LE12 6PG
closed Mon; 5-11 Tue-Thu; 4-11 Fri; 12-11 Sat & Sun
(0115) 778 8168
6 changing beers (sourced locally)
Micropub opened in 2015, serving six local beers on gravity. The single room accommodates up to 45 patrons – seating is a mixture of chairs, cushioned benches and high stools. A small outdoor area to the front offers alfresco drinking. Light bar snacks are served. A range of ciders and continental bottled beers is available.
Q (1)

East Markham

Queen's Hotel

High Street, NG22 0RE
12 (2 Mon)-11 (01777) 870288
Adnams Southwold Bitter; Everards Sunchaser, Tiger; 2 changing beers (sourced nationally)
This cosy pub has a friendly atmosphere enhanced by an open fire in winter. A single bar with five handpumps serves the lounge and dining areas.

Food ranges from hot and cold snacks to full home-cooked meals. There is a large garden area at the rear of the car park. The Queen's has received several local CAMRA awards.
Q (36,37)

Eastwood

Tap & Growler

209 Nottingham Road, Hill Top, NG16 3GS
4-9 Mon; closed Tue; 12 (4 Wed)-10.30; 12-10 Sun
tapandgrowler.co.uk
8 changing beers (sourced locally) H/G
In a row of shops, this micropub sells a range of mostly local real ales, five on handpump and up to five more on gravity. The pub gets its name from the growler beer jug – when the building was being renovated a ceramic lion was found and he is now proudly on display as 'the growler'. A pub quiz is held on Monday. Q

Edwinstowe

Forest Lodge

2-4 Church Street, NG21 9QA
11.30-3, 5.30 (5 Fri)-11; 12-3, 6-10.30 Sun
(01623) 824443 forestlodgehotel.co.uk
Bombardier; house beer (by Welbeck Abbey); 3 changing beers (often Acorn, St Austell) H
Based in the heart of Sherwood Forest, this 18th-century coaching inn is a free house offering a range of ever-changing guest beers including a house beer supplied by Welbeck Abbey. The high-class restaurant serves a wide choice of daily specials, and is proud to use local produce wherever possible. Private functions can be catered for. Accommodation is 4-star AA rated. Voted Best Mild Pub on the local mild trail in 2016.
QP

Hucknall

Station Hotel

Station Terrace, NG15 7TQ
12-11 (midnight Fri & Sat); 12-10.30 Sun
(0115) 963 2588 thestationhotelhucknall.co.uk
Lincoln Green Marion, Archer, Hood, Tuck, Buttermuch; Wychwood Hobgoblin; 13 changing beers H
An archetypal Victorian railway hostelry, originally completed for GNR in 1893 then subsequently owned by Nottingham's Home Brewery. It is now the brewery tap for Lincoln Green Brewery following an impressive and sympathetic refurbishment in 2017. The walls feature much railway memorabilia. Nineteen handpumps dispense an eclectic range of cask beers both from Lincoln Green and further afield, with one pump for real cider. Traditional pub games are played in a separate room. B&B accommodation is available.
P (141)

Kimberley

Cricketers Rest

4 Chapel Street, NG16 2NP
12-11.30 (12.30am Fri & Sat); 12-11 Sun
(0115) 938 3105
Castle Rock Harvest Pale; Sharp's Doom Bar; 4 changing beers (often Castle Rock) H
In Kimberley conservation area, this single-roomed pub with a small snug is close to the centre of town. Refurbished in 2016 after being sold by Greene King, it is now operated by Castle Rock. Handpumps dispense six cask ales, usually including the current Castle Rock seasonal beer. The ever-changing range of guest beers is mainly from local microbreweries. Unsurprisingly, cricket memorabilia is much in evidence. Snacks such as pork pies and jacket potatoes are available.
P

Roots Emporium

17 Nottingham Road, NG16 2NB
closed Mon & Tue; 5-10 Wed; 4-10.30 Thu & Fri; 12-10.30 Sat; 12-10 Sun 07864 572037 rootsemporium.co.uk
6 changing beers H
Converted from a furniture and gift shop, this small but spacious micropub opened late in 2016. It is open plan but has three separate drinking areas. The walls feature interesting memorabilia including items relating to the former Kimberley Brewery. A front patio area has been added. Beers are generally from microbreweries, always including at least one local brew. Q

White Lion

74 Swingate, NG16 2PQ
4-11.30; 12-11.30 Sat; 12-10.30 Sun (0115) 938 3193
whitelionswingate.co.uk
Black Iris Snake Eyes; Blue Monkey Infinity; Castle Rock Harvest Pale; Oakham Bishops Farewell; Sharp's Doom Bar H**; 3 changing beers** H/G
A community free house in a residential area, a short distance from the town centre. It was modernised throughout four years ago without detracting from its traditional two-roomed status. Eight cask beers are on handpump on the central bar, with guests mainly from local microbreweries. Sunday lunches are served and sandwiches available on request Friday to Sunday. Dogs are welcomed with treats. Opens 2pm on Friday in summer. QP (27)

Kirkby-in-Ashfield

Dandy Cock Ale House

184A Victoria Road, NG17 8AT
closed Mon & Tue; 5-10 Wed & Thu; 2-10.30 Fri; 12-10.30 Sat; 12-9.30 Sun 07854 054060 thedandycock.co.uk
4 changing beers (sourced locally) H
Micropub offering four real ales on handpull and up to six real ciders on tap. It has two small rooms with views into the cellar behind the bar. A range of wines and spirits is available including over 200 gins. Live acoustic music nights and other events are hosted. Dogs are welcome. There is on-street parking and a bus stop directly outside the front door. A local CAMRA Pub of the Year in 2018.

Regent

Kingsway, NG17 7BQ
8am-midnight (1am Fri & Sat) (01623) 687630
Courage Directors; Greene King Abbot; Ruddles Best Bitter; Shepherd Neame Spitfire; Wychwood Hobgoblin; 4 changing beers H
Converted from the former Regency cinema on the corner of Kingsway by Wetherspoon, this pub has a large open-plan format with a smaller separate dining area to the front. There is a big emphasis on cask ales, with up to 10 choices at any one time. The usual range of Wetherspoon meals is served all day every day and families are welcome.

Laneham

Bees Knees

Springhead Brewery, Robin Hood Site, Main Street, DN22 0NA (centre of village)
4-midnight; 3-midnight Fri; 12-midnight Sat & Sun
(01777) 228090 springhead.co.uk
Oakham Citra; Springhead Surrender, Outlawed, Leveller, Roaring Meg; 1 changing beer H
A popular country pub with three small rooms converted from a former shop on the Springhead Brewery site and well supported by locals. The interior has recently been refurbished. It offers four Springhead beers along with Oakham Citra and a rotating guest beer. Over 100 gins are also available. Excellent food is served (booking recommended). There is an adequate outside seating area. **Q P**

Laxton

Dovecote Inn

Cross Hill, NG22 0SX (centre of village)
11.30-3, 5.30-11; 11.30-11 Sat; 12-9 Sun
(01777) 871586 thedovecoteinnlaxton.co.uk
3 changing beers (sourced regionally) H
Laxton boats the last remaining working open-field farming system in the country. This traditional inn boasts four cosy dining areas (food is served daily) and a drinking space near the entrance. Three changing guest beers, often from local breweries, and a craft lager, are available. An annual beer festival is held. There is a large beer garden, and Laxton's Visitor Centre is accessed from the car park. **Q P** (33,36)

Lound

Bluebell Inn

Town Street, DN22 8RN (on main road through village)
5-11; 12-11 Sat; 12-10.30 Sun (01777) 818457
bluebellinnretford.co.uk
Black Sheep Best Bitter; Welbeck Abbey Harley; 1 changing beer (sourced locally) H
This traditional family-owned village pub with two rooms is gaining a growing reputation for high-quality food and beer. Black Sheep is always available alongside a Welbeck Abbey beer, usually Harley or Red Feather, plus a changing guest beer, often a local ale. There is a large car park and a fenced outside seating area where French boules is played in the summer on Wednesday and Sunday. Wednesday is quiz night. **Q P**

Mansfield

Bold Forester

Botany Avenue, NG18 5NF
11-11.30 (12.30am Fri & Sat); 12-11.30 Sun
(01623) 623970
Greene King IPA, Abbot; Hardys & Hansons Olde Trip; Morland Old Speckled Hen; 6 changing beers H
Hungry Horse-branded pub and restaurant. Up to 12 real ales are available, usually including six from Greene King and up to six guests. Food is served daily until 9pm. The spacious open-plan interior has large-screen TVs showing all major live sport. There is a covered smoking area outside with a TV. The enclosed beer garden is popular with families in the summer. Situated on the main road into Mansfield, it is well serviced by public transport and has a large car park. **P**

Brown Cow

31 Ratcliffe Gate, NG18 2JA
12-11 (midnight Fri & Sat) (01623) 645854
browncow-mansfield.co.uk
Everards Tiger; 9 changing beers (often Raw) H
Operated by Raw Brewery under the Project William scheme with Everards of Leicester. It has two separate bar areas and a function room upstairs. A range of up to 12 real ales and ciders is offered alongside a selection of world bottled beers. Regular beer festivals are hosted. Folk music features on a Tuesday night and a quiz on Wednesday. The pub is a short walk from Mansfield town centre bus and railway stations and has ample car parking. Local CAMRA Pub of the Year 2017. **Q P**

Railway Inn

9 Station Street, NG18 1EF
11-11 (01623) 623086
4 changing beers H
A stone's throw from the railway and bus stations, this community pub serves home-cooked foods and has two separate rooms for diners or those desiring a little privacy. Four real ales are available, at least one a local offering, and one or more real cider. A music night is held once a month. Outside there is a walled garden and smoking area. A former local CAMRA Pub of the Year.
Q

Widow Frost

41 Leeming Street, NG18 1NB
8am-midnight (1am Fri & Sat) (01623) 666790
Greene King Abbot; Ruddles Best Bitter; 4 changing beers H
A spacious open-plan pub not far from the town centre. It can get busy, especially at weekends, but families are welcome and there is usually a quiet corner to be found. The full range of Wetherspoon meals is served all day every day. Up to six real ales are available, plus real ciders, and Meet the Brewer events are held. Popular with visitors to the theatre just over the road. **Q**

Mansfield Woodhouse

Greyhound Inn

82 High Street, NG19 8BD
12-11 (midnight Fri & Sat); 12-10.30 Sun
(01623) 464403
Adnams Broadside; Caledonian Deuchars IPA; 3 changing beers (often Robinsons) H
Landlady Lynda has been at the Greyhound for 34 years and her achievements were recognised with a special award from CAMRA in 2017. The traditional two-room pub offers five beers along with one cider. Weekly activities include open the box, play your cards right, quiz night and card bingo. Pool, darts and dominoes are played in the public bar. Dogs are welcome in the taproom. No food, just bar snacks and lively conversation.
P

Well

Farmway, NG19 9BG
2.30-7.30 Thu & Fri; closed Sat-Wed (01623) 632393
priorswellbrewery.co.uk
Prior's Well Priory Gold, Prior's Pale, Resurrected; 2 changing beers (often Prior's Well) H
The Well is the brewery tap at Prior's Well Brewery. The Victorian bar is on a mezzanine level with four

handpulls dispensing beers from the Prior's Well range alongside a lager and a cider. The bar is open only Thursday and Friday afternoons, and the occasional Sunday, but will remain open later if busy. Children and dogs are welcome but this is a working brewery and supervision is advised. (11,12)

Newark

Flying Circus

53 Castle Gate, NG24 1BE
12-11 (midnight Fri-Sun) (01636) 302444
flyingcircuspub.com
4 changing beers
Reopened in its present incarnation in 2014, the pub walls are decorated with Monty Python quotes and brewery logos, and old aircraft are suspended from the ceiling. The four ever-changing cask ales are complemented by a wide range of keg, bottled and canned craft beers. More beers may be available when the pub holds one of its many special musical events, including some served by gravity from the Barrel House to the rear of the building.

Fox & Crown

4-6 Appleton Gate, NG24 1JY
10.30-11 (midnight Fri & Sat); 10-11 Sun
(01636) 605820
Castle Rock Harvest Pale, Preservation Fine Ale, Elsie Mo, Screech Owl; 5 changing beers
Popular, friendly, town-centre local opposite the parish church, busy with shoppers during the day. Six real ales, KeyKeg beers and over 100 bottled beers are available to drink in or take away. It has an open-plan layout with a central bar and three side rooms. The decor includes brewery pictures, posters, mirrors and old photos of Newark. Live music features on a Friday night.
Q (1,2)

Just Beer Micropub

32A Castle Gate, NG24 1BG (in Swan & Salmon Yard, off Castle Gate)
1-11; 12-midnight Fri & Sat; 12-10 Sun (01636) 312047
justbeermicropub.biz
4 changing beers
Micropub concentrating on cask ales, cider and perries. In February 2016 the milestone of 3,000 different beers from 1,000 different breweries was reached. World and unusual UK ales are available from the fridge. Snacks include locally sourced pork pies, cheeseboards and pork scratchings. Traditional pub games are played, including an annual cribbage tournament. Three beer festivals are held each year. A repeat local and regional CAMRA Pub of the Year award winner.
Q

Organ Grinder

21 Portland Street, NG24 4XF
12-11 (midnight Fri & Sat); 12-10.30 Sun
(01636) 671768 bluemonkeybrewery.com/organ-grinder-newark
Blue Monkey BG Sips, 99 Red Baboons, Infinity; 3 changing beers
Reopened in 2014 by the Blue Monkey Brewery, a display on the wall reveals it was previously known as the Horse & Gears. A no-nonsense beer-drinking pub, it offers a range of bar snacks to accompany the seven real ales from Blue Monkey. Bottled beers are also stocked. The Monkey Room is adorned with film and music posters with monkey and ape references. A covered smoking area is to the rear.

Prince Rupert

46 Stodman Street, NG24 1AW
11-11 (midnight Wed & Thu; 1am Fri & Sat); 12-11 Sun
(01636) 918121 kneadpubs.co.uk
Brains Rev James; Oakham JHB; 4 changing beers
Reopened in 2010, this historic pub dates back to 1452. Multi-roomed on two separate levels, exposed beams are evident and various interesting artefacts and brewery memorabilia decorate the walls and ceilings. The Nelson room has an open fire. An extensive lunchtime and evening food menu is available, with pizzas a speciality. A former local CAMRA Pub of the Year, it has featured in the Guide for eight consecutive years.
Q

Nottingham: Central

Crafty Crow

102 Friar Lane, NG1 6EB
12-11; 11-midnight Fri & Sat (0115) 837 1992
craftycrownotts.co.uk
8 changing beers (often Magpie)
Magpie Brewery's first pub, with eight handpulls serving microbrewery beers and a further four offering a good variety of real ciders. Maintaining a green ethos throughout, the majority of fittings are recycled or home-made – the sinks are made from beer casks with ex-keg fonts as taps. Snacks and light meals are served until 9pm, made from locally sourced produce. Situated on two levels, a side entrance leads directly to all facilities. Corvid birds feature strongly.

Hand & Heart

65 Derby Road, NG1 5BA
12-11 (midnight Fri & Sat); 12-10.30 Sun
(0115) 958 2456 thehandandheart.co.uk
Maypole Little Weed; house beer (by Dancing Duck); 6 changing beers (sourced locally)
The modern frontage and bar area hide the age of this pub – there are sandstone caves to the rear used as a dining space. A high-quality menu of both food and beer is offered, with eight mostly local beers on handpump, together with three real ciders or perries. The upstairs room has a separate bar for private functions, and there is a partially covered first-floor terrace overlooking the busy street below. Live music features on Sunday and Thursday.

Kean's Head

46 St Mary's Gate, Lace Market, NG1 1QA
11-11 (midnight Fri & Sat); 12-10.30 Sun
(0115) 947 4052
Castle Rock Harvest Pale; 5 changing beers
Owned by Castle Rock, this cosy one-room pub is opposite the imposing medieval St Mary's Church in Nottingham's historic Lace Market district. Named after the 19th-century actor Edmund Kean, it is popular with a diverse clientele and serves inventive, freshly prepared food from an ever-changing English and European menu. The guest beers always provide a varied choice of styles. There is also a wide selection of craft beers, along with three handpumps dispensing real cider.

King William IV

6 Eyre Street, Sneinton, NG2 4PB

2-11 Mon; 12-11 Tue & Wed (11.30 Thu), 11 midnight Fri & Sat ☎ (0115) 958 9864

Oakham Citra, Bishops Farewell; house beer (by Black Iris); 6 changing beers Ⓗ

Known widely as the King Billy, this Victorian gem on the edge of the city centre is close to the Motorpoint Arena. A family-run free house that oozes charm and character, it is a haven for real ale drinkers, with a choice of up to eight microbrewery ales from near and far, as well as real cider. Folk music is popular on Thursday night. A selection of rolls is always available. Q (43,44)

Lincolnshire Poacher

161-163 Mansfield Road, NG1 3FR

11-11 (midnight Thu & Fri); 10.30-midnight Sat; 12-11 Sun ☎ (0115) 941 1584

Castle Rock Harvest Pale, Elsie Mo, Screech Owl; Everards Tiger; Fuller's London Pride; 8 changing beers Ⓗ

Thirteen handpumps offer a wide selection of guest ales, mainly from microbreweries. A mild, stout or porter is always available alongside real ciders and perries, continental bottled beers and a good selection of whiskies. The food menu features locally sourced ingredients. Walls display artwork celebrating the pub's twinning with In de Wildeman bar in Amsterdam, and various memorabilia of local and international interest. Live music plays on Sunday and Wednesday. Q

Newshouse

123 Canal Street, NG1 7HB

12-11 (midnight Fri & Sat) ☎ (0115) 952 3061

Castle Rock Harvest Pale; 4 changing beers (sourced locally; often Totally Brewed) Ⓗ

In times past, newspapers would be read out here to inform the illiterate of elections at home and military victories overseas, hence the name. The walls are covered with framed front pages of local newspapers showing headlines going back over many years. The public bar has a large TV screen, dartboard, bar billiards and table skittles. The lounge has more comfortable seating. Light lunches are served and snacks at all times. Beers from the local Totally Brewed Brewery are almost always available.

Olde Trip to Jerusalem ★

Brewhouse Yard, NG1 6AD (off Castle Road)

11-11 (midnight Fri & Sat) ☎ (0115) 947 3171

triptojerusalem.com

Greene King IPA; Hardys & Hansons Olde Trip; Nottingham Extra Pale Ale; 6 changing beers Ⓗ

Famous pub at the bottom of Castle Road, built into the rock beneath Nottingham Castle. Several rooms on the ground and first floor are open to the public. Play ring the bull at quieter times in the back bar. The cursed galleon in the upstairs rock lounge is reputed to have claimed the lives of those who tried to clean it. Beer festivals are held in the enclosed courtyard. A cobblestone area outside the pub is popular on warmer days. Q

Organ Grinder

21 Alfreton Road, Canning Circus, NG7 3JE

12-11 (11.30 Thu; midnight Fri & Sat) ☎ (0115) 970 0630

Blue Monkey BG Sips, Infinity, Guerrilla; Sharp's Doom Bar; 5 changing beers Ⓗ

Previously the Red Lion, this pub was bought and refurbished by Blue Monkey Brewery. The single-roomed, multi-level pub boasts a wood-burning fire. To the rear is a small courtyard leading to a raised decked area and the first floor function room (where a TV is in occasional use). The full Blue Monkey range of beers is offered, as well as a guest and three real ciders or perries. No meals, but bar snacks such as Scotch eggs and pork pies are sold.

Sir John Borlase Warren

1 Ilkeston Road, NG7 3GD

11-11 (midnight Fri & Sat); 11-10.30 Sun ☎ (0115) 988 1889

Everards Tiger; 10 changing beers (often Lincoln Green) Ⓗ

An Everards Project William establishment with Lincoln Green, this pub is situated in the centre of Canning Circus. The lower bar area can be hired for private parties, and there is a small snug at the far end of the bar. Outside is a secluded, enclosed garden and a large rooftop patio – a quiet haven in the centre of a busy area. Tap takeovers are often held, when at least four handpumps showcase a single brewery. Q

Vat & Fiddle

Queens Bridge Road, NG2 1NB

11-11 (midnight Fri & Sat) ☎ (0115) 985 0611

Castle Rock Sheriff's Tipple, Black Gold, Harvest Pale, Preservation Fine Ale, Elsie Mo, Screech Owl; 5 changing beers Ⓗ

The tap for the adjoining Castle Rock Brewery, this 1937 Art Deco gem two minutes from the recently refurbished Nottingham rail station has 12 handpumps which serve at least seven from the Castle Rock range. There are always guest beers from near and far as well as a range of real ciders. The outside area to the rear features an impressive mural depicting Nottingham events. Hot food is served all week. Tasting trays of six third-pints are available.

Nottingham: East

Willowbrook

13 Main Road, Gedling, NG4 3HQ

10-11 (midnight Fri); 9am-midnight Sat; 9am-11 Sun ☎ (0115) 987 8596

Castle Rock Harvest Pale, Preservation Fine Ale, Elsie Mo; Morland Old Speckled Hen; house beer (by Castle Rock); 4 changing beers Ⓗ

Formerly a club, this pub was refurbished in late 2013, and again in 2015 due to a fire. The 14 handpumps often offer a mild, stout or porter, as well as a selection of three real ciders or perries. A small side room and entrance lounge lead to the bar, which opens to a rear room. Patio doors lead to a paved, secluded, no-smoking outdoor area. A good food menu is complemented by daily specials.

Nottingham: North

Doctor's Orders

351 Mansfield Road, Carrington, NG5 2DA

12 (4 Mon-Wed)-10.30 ☎ (0115) 960 7985

doctorsordersmicropub.co.uk

5 changing beers (sourced locally) Ⓗ

Compact beer emporium with two distinct areas, refurbished in 2015. A small square lounge leads to a corridor flanked on one side by a narrow raised seating area with benches, with a small bar and serving area at the rear. Beer and cider are served at your table from handpumps at the rear of the pub. While now owned by Magpie Brewery, the pub continues with its original ethos of providing a range of microbrewery beers in an intimate atmosphere. Q❀♿♣●🚌🐾📶

Fox & Crown

33 Church Street, Old Basford, NG6 0GA

12-midnight (1am Fri & Sat) ☎ (0115) 942 2002

thefoxandcrown.com

Shipstone's Original, Nut Brown, Gold Star; house beer (by Shipstone's); 2 changing beers H

This pub is the brewery tap for the adjacent Shipstone's (formerly Alcazar) Brewery and is decorated with a large Fox & Crown mural depicting Sherwood Forest in the 13th century featuring Robin Hood. Both front doors lead to a central bar with TVs, a dartboard and pool table on one side. This pub is popular with both locals and students and can get busy during the kitchen's opening hours as the Thai food is held in high regard. ❀♿♣P🚌🐾

Lion Inn

44 Mosley Street, New Basford, NG7 7FQ

12-11 (midnight Fri & Sat) ☎ (0115) 970 3506

thelionatbasford.co.uk

Castle Rock Harvest Pale; Draught Bass; 8 changing beers H

This free house has a large range of cask ales on handpump on a central bar, from both local and national breweries, alongside real cider and craft beer. The decor features bare brick walls and wooden floors. Its rustic charm and alehouse ambience have made it popular with locals and visitors. A large glass-covered well with a view down into the cellars below dominates. Outside are a large heated patio and spacious garden. Live music features regularly. ❀♿♣●P🚌📶

Nottingham: South

Embankment

282-284 Arkwright Street, The Meadows, NG2 2GR

11-11; 10-midnight Fri & Sat; 10-11 Sun

☎ (0115) 986 4502

Castle Rock Harvest Pale, Preservation Fine Ale, Elsie Mo; Fuller's London Pride; 6 changing beers (often Castle Rock) H

Originally one of the largest shops belonging to Boots the Chemist, where Jesse Boot had his office, this was home to the Boots Members' Social Club. The white mock-Tudor building has been restored, retaining the oak-panelled walls and stained-glass leaded windows. It is adjacent to Trent Bridge, close to three of Nottingham's well-known sports venues. A large range of real ales and ciders is available, both from the Castle Rock range and guest microbreweries, as well as a selection of craft beers. Q❀♿●P🚌🐾📶

Nottingham: West

Plough Inn

17 St Peter's Street, Radford, NG7 3EN

12-11 (midnight Wed & Thu); 12-10.30 Sun

☎ 07972 094425 nottinghambrewerytaphouse.co.uk

Nottingham Rock Ale Bitter Beer, Rock Ale Mild Beer, Legend, Extra Pale Ale; 4 changing beers H

Linked with the old Nottingham Brewery since 1887, the Plough is now the brewery tap for the company. The four regular beers come from the brewery as well as two of the four rotating guests. Four ciders are served. The present building, a 1932 two-room house with a central servery, is largely unchanged. This 'village pub in the city' has retained a local feel, offering real fires, a skittles alley and a popular quiz night. Q❀♿♣●P🚌🐾📶

Radcliffe on Trent

Chestnut

Main Road, NG12 2BE

12-11 (11.30 Fri & Sat) ☎ (0115) 933 1994

thechestnutradcliffe.co.uk

Fuller's London Pride; Oakham JHB; St Austell Tribute; 4 changing beers H

Well-regarded, cask beer-led village pub with a smart 1920s-style decor. Originally the Cliffe Inn, following a major refurbishment in 2006 it became The Horse Chestnut and in 2015 simply The Chestnut. Seven reasonably priced real ales are served including changing guests, one always a local brew. Quality home-made food, ranging from stone-baked pizzas to classic British dishes, is served in a relaxed, casual atmosphere. ❀♿●P🚌🐾📶

Yard of Ale

1 Walkers Yard, NG12 2FF (off Main Rd, between Costa and public car park)

5-11 Wed-Fri; 3-11 Sat; closed Sun-Tue

☎ (0115) 933 4888 yard-of-ale.business.site

6 changing beers H/G

This small, friendly micropub opened in 2016 in a former café and chocolate shop in the centre of the village. The premises are narrow, with access from the side. Up to seven guest ales always include at least one local brew and a dark ale. The pub features a separate gin bar known as Gin Within. Q●P🚌🐾

Retford

BeerHeadZ

3 Town Hall Yard, DN22 6DU (off Market Square, through arch to rear of 10 Green Bottles)

1-11.30; 12-11.30 Fri-Sun ☎ (01777) 949631

beerheadz.biz

5 changing beers (sourced regionally) H

A small, friendly pub serving five rotating guest beers, three ciders and a range of bottled beers. The ale is always in excellent condition and served in oversized glasses so you can be sure of a full pint. There are also a limited number of wines and spirits. BeerHeadZ has won several CAMRA awards including Nottinghamshire Pub of the Year 2016. Q♿●🚌🐾📶

Brew Shed

108 Carolgate, DN22 6ES (on Carolgate bridge opp masonic hall)

4-11; 1-11 Fri; 12-11 Sat & Sun

Shiny 4 Wood; 3 changing beers (sourced regionally) H

A small venue with four handpulled beers on the bar plus a variety of other drinks, some of which you would not expect to find in a pub of this size. There is a well-stocked fridge and a pleasing range of British bottled beers along with the continental selection. Real cider is also available. Harrisons Brewery is set to open on-site. Local CAMRA Pub of the Year 2018. Q ♣ P

Idle Valley Tap

Carolgate, DN22 6AS

1-midnight; 11-midnight Fri-Sun ☎ (01777) 948586

8 changing beers (sourced regionally) H

Originally the tap for Idle Valley Brewery, with its closure beers are now from elsewhere. The one-room pub was renovated in 2015 and has a pool table and dartboard away from the bar. The outside space has been put to good use, attracting large numbers in fine weather. ♿ ♣ P

Ruddington

Frame Breakers

High Street, NG11 6DT

11-11 (midnight Fri & Sat); 12-10.30 Sun

☎ (0115) 859 0060 theframebreakers.co.uk

Nottingham Rock Ale Mild Beer, Legend, Extra Pale Ale; house beer (by Nottingham); 2 changing beers (sourced locally) H

A large three-storey painted corner building. Inside, the open-plan layout features low wood beams and a decor with plenty of wood including a solid bar, plus tiled, wood and carpet flooring, settles and chunky furniture. Live music is confined to the rear. Run by Nottingham Brewery since 2015, a number of its beers are featured, including a dark brew. Food is served daily but not afternoons Monday to Wednesday.

Q ♿ P (3,10)

Selston

Horse & Jockey

Church Lane, NG16 6FB

12-3.30, 5-midnight; 12-6, 7-midnight Sun

☎ (01773) 781012

Greene King Abbot; Timothy Taylor Landlord H**; 4 changing beers** H/G

A drinkers' gem dating from 1664 with wooden bench seating, large open fires and flagstone floors. Up to six real ales are available, two served under gravity from casks on stone trestles. A real cider or perry is always available. A quiz is held on Sunday evening and a folk night every Wednesday. Look out for the Selstock Beer & Music Festival in July. A winner of many CAMRA awards including Pub of the Year. Q ♿ ♣ P

Southwell

Final Whistle

Station Road, NG25 0ET

12-11.30 ☎ (01636) 814953

Draught Bass; Everards Ascalon; 6 changing beers (often Oakham) H

Adjacent to the Southwell Trail, formerly an old railway line popular with walkers, this comfortable pub has a railway theme and features plenty of memorabilia. The rear garden is a mock station with a section of track. The bar has 10 handpumps serving two regular beers, six changing ales and two house beers brewed by Ashover Ales. Quiz nights are Tuesday and Sunday. Various bar snacks are available. Local CAMRA Pub of the Year 2017.

♿ ♣ P (28,100)

Stapleford

Horse & Jockey

20 Nottingham Road, NG9 8AA

12-11 (midnight Fri & Sat) ☎ (0115) 875 9655

horseandjockeystapleford.co.uk

Full Mash Horse & Jockey; 12 changing beers H

Known locally as The Jockey, this white-painted building with steps up to the front door has two rooms on split levels, each with a different ambience. Refurbished in 2012, it has become a real ale destination pub. A choice of 13 cask ales, including at least five LocAles, is offered, accompanied by local ciders and a range of whiskies. Pictures of local landmarks adorn the walls and whisky water jugs hang from the ceiling. There is no music, TV (other than for major sporting events) or games machines. A former CAMRA National Pub of the Year finalist. Q ♿ P

Staunton in the Vale

Staunton Arms

NG13 9PE

12-11 (midnight Fri & Sat); 12-10 Sun ☎ (01400) 281218

stauntonarms.co.uk

Castle Rock Harvest Pale; Draught Bass; 1 changing beer H

Two-hundred-year-old listed inn in the far north of the Vale of Belvoir, carefully restored to retain its original character. The large bar offers comfortable seating for drinkers and diners, with a further separate raised restaurant area. The pub serves freshly prepared meals lunchtimes and evenings and has built a reputation for good food. Three cask beers, one always a LocAle, are on the bar, and mini beer festivals are held regularly.

Q ♿ ♣ P

Sutton-in-Ashfield

Scruffy Dog

Station Road, NG17 5HF

closed Mon & Tue; 4-11 Wed-Fri; 12-11 Sat; 12-10.30 Sun

☎ (01623) 550826 thescruffydog.co.uk

7 changing beers (often Abbeydale, Froth Blowers, Thornbridge) H

Comfy sofas and a real fire on colder days welcome visitors to this dog-friendly pub. Superbly refurbished by the current owners, it has a small L-shaped bar and a large open-plan bar area, and its own small on-site brewery. Six beers are usually available, often from the Scruffy Dog Brewery range. The pub is closed on Monday and Tuesday except bank holidays. Q ♿ P

Speed the Plough

Mansfield Road, NG17 4HG

12-11; 12-midnight Fri; 12-1am Sat; 12-midnight Sun

☎ 07821 331173

Greene King Abbot; 2 changing beers (often Blue Monkey, Castle Rock) H

Three beers are usually available on handpump at this community pub, with two nationals and one local brew offered. A pleasant, enclosed garden is at the rear. The pub is dog and child friendly except Saturday evenings when a popular karaoke night is hosted. A range of homemade food is available including original recipe minced beef and onion pie and special quarter pounder burgers, plus steaks on request (every day except Sunday). The pub is a big supporter of armed forces charities.

♣ P

Upton

Cross Keys

43 Main Street, NG23 5SY

⏲ closed Mon; 12-3, 5-11.30 Tue-Thu; 12-11.30 Fri-Sun

☎ (01636) 813269

Mallard Duck 'n' Dive; 3 changing beers 🄷

This 16th-century pub is situated on the main route from Newark to Southwell. It serves excellent food at lunchtime and holds themed food evenings and events. Fish prepared by the French-born chef is a speciality and Sunday lunch is not to be missed. Home of Mallard brewery, two of its ales are always on handpump plus one guest, all in excellent condition. Locals enjoy the book club and dominoes. **Q🐎❀◐◑♣●P🚌🐾**

Wellow

Olde Red Lion 🄻

Eakring Road, NG22 0EG

⏲ 12-11 ☎ (01623) 861000 🌐 wellow.me/lion.htm

Bombardier; 2 changing beers (sourced locally) 🄷

This 400-year-old village pub is situated on the village green with its maypole, and participates in a large event on May Day. The traditional wood-beamed interior includes a restaurant, lounge and bar areas, with photographs and maps depicting the history of the village on the walls. Good food and three real ales are available – Bombardier and two rotating guest beers, usually LocAles. An annual beer festival is hosted. Close to Rufford Park, Sherwood Forest and Clumber Park.
Q🐎❀◐◑♣P🚌

West Bridgford

Poppy & Pint 🄻

Pierrepont Road, NG2 5DX

⏲ 9.30am-11; 10-11 Sun ☎ (0115) 981 9995

Castle Rock Sheriff's Tipple, Harvest Pale, Preservation Fine Ale, Screech Owl; 8 changing beers 🄷

Former British Legion Club converted in 2011 to become a Castle Rock pub. It has a large main bar with a raised part and a family area with a café bar (children welcome until 9pm). A large upstairs function room features a folk club and the beer garden overlooks a bowling green. Twelve handpumps dispense Castle Rock beers plus guests, often from new breweries. There are usually two real ciders and excellent food is served.
🐎❀◐◑♿●P🚌🐾📶

Stratford Haven 🄻

2 Stratford Road, NG2 6BA

⏲ 11-11 (midnight Thu & Fri); 10-midnight Sat; 10-11 Sun

☎ (0115) 982 5981

Adnams Broadside; Batemans XB; Castle Rock Harvest Pale, Elsie Mo, Screech Owl; Everards Tiger; 6 changing beers 🄷

A former pet shop, The Strat has a single central bar with extended seating at the back and a secluded snug to the right. Up to 12 cask ales plus a cider are available on handpump at any one time, including at least six from owner Castle Rock's portfolio. Guest ales are predominantly from microbreweries near and far. Themed food nights feature Monday to Thursday. Sunday is silent quiz night and new brew day the first Thursday of the month.
Q🐎❀◐◑♿●🚌🐾📶

Worksop

Fuggle's Chapter One

20 Park Street, S80 1HB

⏲ closed Mon-Wed; 12 (4 Thu)-11 ☎ 07813 763347

🌐 fugglebunnybrewhouse.co.uk

Fuggle Bunny Chapter 5 Oh Crumbs, Chapter 2 Cotton Tail, Chapter 8 Jammy Dodger, Chapter 4 24 Carrot 🄷

Opened in 2017 following a modern refurbishment, this L-shaped single-roomed little alehouse is now firmly established, attracting a cosmopolitan clientele. It serves quality real ales alongside specialised gins, spirits and wine. The real ales rotate but are all from the award-winning Fuggle Bunny Brew House at Halfway near Sheffield. **Q♿●🚌🐾**

Mallard 🄻

Station Approach, S81 7AG (on railway station platform, entrance from car park)

⏲ 12 (5 Mon; 4.30 Tue)-11; 11-11 Fri & Sat; 12-10.30 Sun

☎ 07973 521824

4 changing beers 🄷

Formerly the station buffet, this small, cosy pub offers a warm welcome. Four changing real ales are available – usually a dark beer, one from Double Top Brewery and two guests – plus two ciders, a selection of foreign bottled beers, country fruit wines and specialist gins. There is a room downstairs used on special occasions. Four beer festivals are held each year. Local CAMRA Pub of the Year. **Q⇌♣●P🚌🐾**

Station Hotel 🄻

Carlton Road, S80 1PS (opp railway station car park entrance)

⏲ 12-11; 11.30-11 Sat ☎ (01909) 474108

🌐 thestationhotelworksop.co.uk

5 changing beers (sourced regionally) 🄷

On the edge of the town centre, there is always a welcome in this pub. The long bar serves a lounge drinking area with a separate dining room attached, and there is a further small room suitable for meetings. A spacious and well-maintained garden with seating is to the rear. Five changing real ales are available, with a discount scheme for regulars. Food is served lunchtimes and evenings and accommodation is offered.
Q❀🛏◐◑♿⇌♣●P🚏🚌(5)🐾📶

Warm beer

It is said that the Maids of Honour of the Tudor Court, who we have seen were ale-ladies, if they cannot be called ale-knights, frequently liked their beer warm, and had it placed upon the hob of the grate 'to take the chill off'. It was therefore natural for their attendants to ask the question, 'From the hob or not from the hob?', which in process of time became 'hob or nob?'

John Bickerdyke, 1889

OXFORDSHIRE

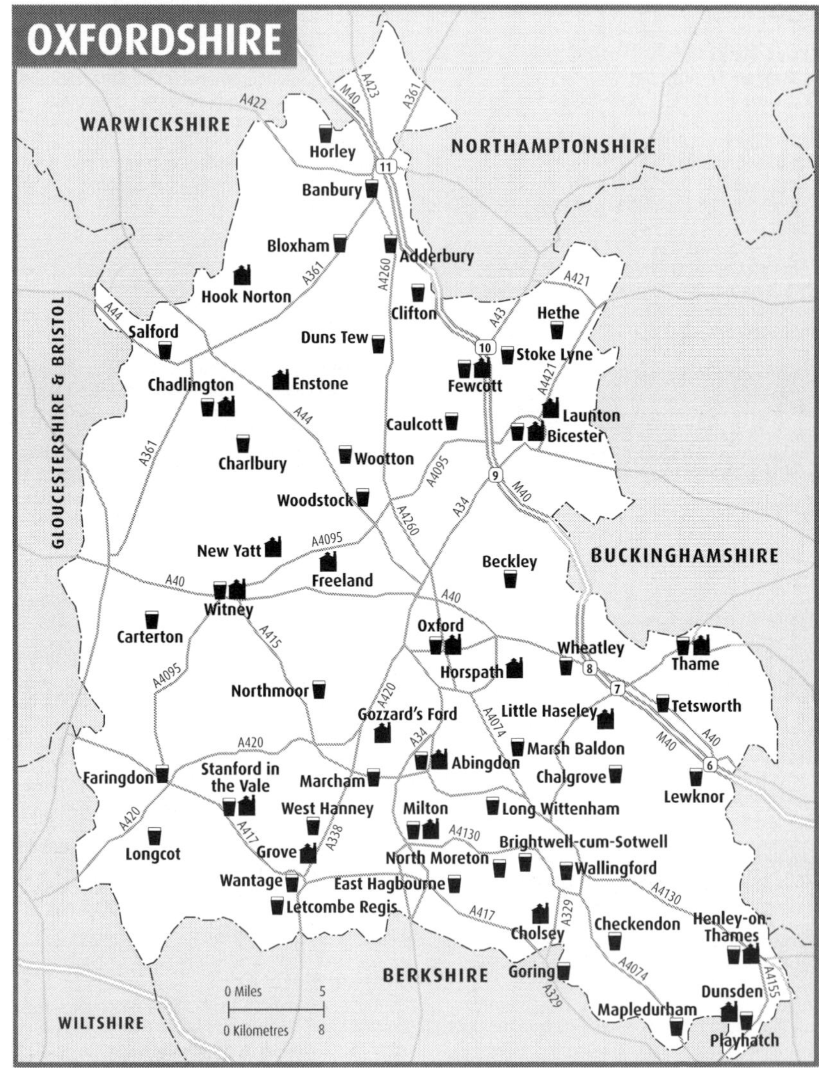

Abingdon

Brewery Tap 🄻 ✔

40-42 Ock Street, OX14 5BZ

11-11.30 (1am Fri & Sat); 12-11 Sun ☎ (01235) 521655
thebrewerytap.net

Loose Cannon Abingdon Bridge; 5 changing beers (sourced regionally; often West Berkshire) 🄷

Morland created a tap for its brewery in 1993 from three Grade II listed town houses. The brewery is no more but the pub, run by the same family since it opened, has thrived. It offers a diverse range of beers all sourced from within 40 miles, and hosts three beer festivals each year with ales from further afield. The pub has three rooms, two of them away from the bar, and a courtyard outside.
Q 🚌 ☕

Broad Face 🄻 ✔

30-32 Bridge Street, OX14 3HR

11-midnight (1am Thu-Sat); 11.30-midnight Sun
☎ (01235) 538612 broadfaceabingdon.co.uk

West Berkshire Good Old Boy; house beer (by Belhaven); 4 changing beers (sourced nationally; often Loose Cannon) 🄷

Deceptively large two-roomed pub near the river with a small outside seating area on Thames Street. It has had several short-lived changes of management but is now under a new landlord with an emphasis on real ale. The interior is nicely decorated, bright and welcoming. Traditional stories behind the unique pub name are written on the outside wall but omit the most likely explanation – that it was previously called the Saracen's Head and the sign was over-painted.
Q

Nag's Head on the Thames 🄻 ✔

The Bridge, OX14 3HX

11-11 (midnight Fri & Sat); 12-10 Sun ☎ (01235) 524516
thenagsheadonthethames.co.uk

Loddon Ferryman's Gold; house beer (by Caledonian); 5 changing beers (sourced regionally) 🄷

Set on an island in the Thames, this Grade II listed pub is split over two levels, with a large garden area next to the river and lovely views of the countryside and the town's historic buildings. A free house, it offers seven regularly changing beers, always including something local. Live music plays at weekends and some weekdays. Salter's Steamer cruises from Oxford stop nearby in summer. A three-times local CAMRA branch Town and Village Pub of the Year.

Narrows

25 High Street, OX14 5AA
8am-midnight (1am Fri & Sat) (01235) 467680
Greene King Abbot; Ruddles Best Bitter; 8 changing beers (sourced nationally) H
Wetherspoon converted the former post office in October 2013. The pub is named after this part of the High Street which during the 19th century was called The Narrow. The area at the front of the pub has a long bar with 10 handpumps offering an impressive range of real ales, some from local breweries. To the rear, the former sorting office and telephone exchange provides more space for drinkers and diners. Abingdon's was the last manual telephone exchange in England when it closed in 1975.

Adderbury

Bell Inn

High Street, OX17 3LS (off A4260)
12-3, 6-11; 12-midnight Fri & Sat; 12-10.30 Sun
(01295) 810338 thebelladderbury.co.uk
Hook Norton Hooky Mild, Hooky, Hooky Gold, Old Hooky; 2 changing beers (sourced locally; often Hook Norton) H
Back to its community-oriented best under the current stewardship, this gem at the heart of the village was justly awarded Hook Norton Brewery Pub of the Year in 2017, and six handpumps dispense ales from their portfolio. The spiritual home of the three village morris teams, it has a morris room with murals. A folk music session is held on Monday. The locally sourced bar menu and two bedrooms make it an ideal base for exploring the surrounding area.
Q (S4)

Coach & Horses

The Green, OX17 3ND
12-2.30 (not Mon), 6-midnight; 12-1.30am Fri & Sat; 12-midnight Sun (01295) 810422
coachandhorsesadderbury.co.uk
Wadworth IPA, 6X, Swordfish H
This early 18th-century Wadworth house was deservedly awarded the brewery's Community Pub of the Year in 2014. Three handpumps dispense ales from the Wadworth portfolio. Set in a prime location in this attractive ironstone village just off the A4260, it offers value-for-money good honest pub grub, with main meals from £3.50 and roasts on Sunday and Wednesday at £4! Ladies' darts and pool are played. There is an outside seating area overlooking the village green.
Q P (S4)

Banbury

Bailiff's Tap

4 Southam Road, OX16 2ED
closed Mon; 12-10 (8 Tue & Wed); 12-4 Sun
4 changing beers (sourced locally; often Byatt's, Phipps NBC, Towcester Mill) G
Banbury's first micropub opened in 2017. It is based in a former bailiff's office and serves an ever-changing variety of beers mostly from independent breweries, with three ciders also usually available. In its first year it offered 232 different beers, all served direct from barrels on stillages in the bar. A traditional snack selection includes pork pies and crisps. The lively front bar buzzes with conversation. Q

Exchange

49-50 High Street, OX16 5LA
8am-midnight (1am Fri & Sat) (01295) 259035
Greene King Abbot; Ruddles Best Bitter; Sharp's Doom Bar; 9 changing beers (sourced nationally) H
Now the only Wetherspoon bar in Banbury, The Exchange occupies an imposing split-level site in the former main post office and telephone exchange close to Banbury Cross. The walls abound with old photos and pictures of the building and surrounding area. It follows the usual Wetherspoon formula with several banks of handpumps offering a changing range of ales, normally including at least one local ale, in addition to the two regulars, real cider and a good-value food offering.

Three Pigeons

3 Southam Road, OX16 2ED
12-11 (midnight Fri & Sat); 2-11 Sun (01295) 275220
thethreepigeons.com
Purity Pure Gold; Sharp's Doom Bar; 2 changing beers (sourced nationally) H
Beautiful 17th-century thatched coaching inn on the main road through Banbury, close to the town centre, with a feature fireplace with a woodburner. There are two regular beers, usually Doom Bar and a Purity ale, and a fabulous courtyard outside with lovely flower beds, to enjoy them in. The pub is well respected for an interesting menu of high-quality food, and three luxury bedrooms make it a good base for a relaxing break.
Q P

REAL ALE BREWERIES

Amwell Springs Cholsey
Barn Owl Gozzard's Ford
Bell Street Henley-on-Thames
Bellinger's Grove
Bicester Bicester (NEW)
Brakspear Witney
Chadlington Chadlington
Church Hanbrewery New Yatt
Hook Norton Hook Norton
Little Ox Freeland
Loddon Dunsden
Loose Cannon Abingdon
LoveBeer Milton
Oxbrew Enstone (NEW)
Philsters Little Haseley
Pirate Fewcott
Shotover Horspath
Tap Social Movement Oxford
Thame Thame
Turpin Hook Norton
White Horse Stanford in the Vale
Wriggly Monkey Launton (NEW)
Wychwood Witney

White Horse

50-52 North Bar Street, OX16 0TH
2-10 Mon; 12-11 (midnight Fri & Sat); 12-10 Sun
(01295) 277484 whitehorsebanbury.com
Everards Tiger; Turpin Golden Citrus; 8 changing beers (sourced nationally; often Derby, Oakham, XT)
A warm and welcoming alehouse in an imposing building in the heart of Banbury. The White Horse serves an extensive range of up to 10 ales and a couple of ciders from its large L-shaped bar. A selection of home-made dishes, based on locally sourced ingredients, is freshly cooked to order. Alfresco drinking and dining can be enjoyed in the courtyard area to the rear. Regular events such as live music on Friday and a monthly pub quiz are organised. Q

Beckley

Abingdon Arms

High Street, OX3 9UU
closed Mon; 11-11 (9 Sun) (01865) 655667
theabingdonarms.co.uk
Shotover Prospect; XT Four; 2 changing beers (sourced regionally)
A lovely old pub with a fine garden affording great views across Otmoor. It has a small bar and separate dining area. The arms in question are of James Bertie (1653-1699) who was created 1st Earl of Abingdon in 1682. The Bertie family owned the village until 1919 when it was broken up and sold off in lots. The pub was put up for sale in 2016 and bought by a local group after a community share offer. Q P

Bicester

Angel

102 Sheep Street, OX26 6LP
12-11 (midnight Fri & Sat) (01869) 360410
theangelbicester.co.uk
6 changing beers (sourced regionally; often Banks's, Barnet)
A traditional pub in a good location. A log fire on cold days adds to the welcoming atmosphere. The Bottle Shop offers an extensive range of real and craft ales from local breweries and around the world. Bar snacks are limited but street food vendors serve food from the outdoor kitchen hatch at weekends in summer. There is a large seating area outside and a permanent marquee. The on-site Bicester microbrewery operates to seasonal demand. Q (North) P

Bloxham

Elephant & Castle

Humber Street, OX15 4LZ (off A361)
10-3, 6 (5 Fri)-11; 10-11 Sat; 12-11 Sun
(01295) 720383 bloxhampub.co.uk
Hook Norton Hooky; 2 changing beers (sourced nationally; often Hook Norton)
This 17th-century coaching inn is at the heart of many village activities and events. The courtyard hosts live music during the Bloxham Family Fun Day, and the sound of battens being thrown during a game of Aunt Sally is regularly heard during the spring and summer. Indoors there is a range of traditional pub games including bar billiards, darts and shove-ha'penny. Well-kept Hooky plus two guest ales are complemented by the full range of ciders from Westons. P (488,489)

Brightwell-cum-Sotwell

Red Lion

Brightwell Street, OX10 0RT (S off A4130)
12-3, 6-11; 12-11 Sat; 12-10.30 Sun (01491) 837373
redlionbrightwell.co.uk
Loddon Hoppit; West Berkshire Good Old Boy; 2 changing beers (sourced nationally)
A popular traditional thatched inn dating from the 16th century in a quiet village. It has a cosy bar featuring exposed beams and brickwork, leading to a restaurant area to one side. The recently extended rear courtyard garden is a summer suntrap. The beers and ciders are usually from local breweries, and good-quality pub food is served (no food Mon or Sun eve). Jazz evenings and charity quiz nights are held regularly. Local CAMRA Cider Pub of the Year 2016. P (X2)

Carterton

Siege of Orleans

5 The Giles Centre, Alvescot Road, OX18 3DH (down passage next to cycle shop)
3-11; 12-midnight Fri & Sat; 12-11 Sun (01993) 845663
siegeoforleans.co.uk
4 changing beers (sourced regionally)
Not so much a pub as a self-styled micro-alehouse, set in a former record shop, so on the small side. It has four handpumps dispensing mainly local ales from relatively unknown breweries alongside a selection of bottled beers from around the world and a real cider. The unisex toilets proved not to be to everyone's liking and now there is a Ladies upstairs. Regular retro games nights and competitions are hosted. P

Caulcott

Horse & Groom

Lower Heyford Road, OX25 4ND
closed Mon; 12-3, 6-11; 12-3, 7-10.30 Sun
(01869) 343257 horseandgroomcaulcott.co.uk
Black Sheep Best Bitter; Church End Goat's Milk; 3 changing beers (sourced nationally; often Church End, Goff's, Vale)
Lovely 16th-century coaching house with a cosy open fire in winter and a warm welcome whatever the season. Three guest ales are served, often from Church End, Goff's, Tring or Vale, along with Black Sheep Bitter. The French landlord/chef offers wonderful seasonal and locally sourced food, including Thursday steak night and Sunday lunch (booking advised), along with themed French evenings. A Bastille Day beer festival is held annually. Dogs are allowed in the beer garden (but not the bar). A Guide regular and a former local CAMRA Pub of the Year. Q P

Chadlington

Tite Inn

Mill End, OX7 3NY
11.30-11 (10.30 Sun) (01608) 676910
thetiteinn.co.uk
Sharp's Doom Bar; 2 changing beers (sourced nationally; often Chadlington, Cotswold Lion, Sharp's)
This welcoming country pub can be found in the beautiful Evenlode Valley. One regular and two guest ales are served, along with a Westons cider on handpump. The pub has exposed beams and

stonework, flagstone and oak boarded flooring, and an open fire. There is a lovely hillside beer garden where a peaceful pint can be enjoyed. Tite is old local dialect for spring – water runs under the pub and down the hill to the site of the Great Brook Run held each December. Good reasonably priced food is available in the comfortable bar and restaurant. Q P (S3,X9)

Chalgrove

Red Lion

115 High Street, OX44 7SS

11-3, 6-11.30; 12-11 Sun (01865) 890625

redlionchalgrove.com

Butcombe Original; Fuller's London Pride; 3 changing beers (sourced nationally; often Rebellion, West Berkshire) [H]

Church-owned, picturesque and friendly 16th-century village local. The interior is divided into several distinct areas and the pub is used by a wide cross-section of the community. It is popular for its menu of locally sourced and freshly made food. Up to three guest beers are often from small local breweries. You can drink outside in both front and rear gardens, while a real fire awaits inside in the winter months. Real Hitchcox cider in bottles is usually available during the summer.
Q P (T1)

Charlbury

Rose & Crown

Market Street, OX7 3PL

12-11 (1am Fri); 11-1am Sat (01608) 810103

roseandcrown.charlbury.com

Ramsbury Bitter; 7 changing beers (sourced nationally; often Dark Star, Kelham Island, Salopian) [H]

This popular traditional wet-sales-only pub is North Oxon's longest standing Guide entry at 32 years. Eight handpumps serve Ramsbury Bitter and seven ever-changing guests along with six traditional ciders and perries – one of the best selections in the area. Dark Star, Kelham Island, Salopian, Vale, Turpin, Wye Valley, Oakham and XT feature regularly, along with other breweries, both new and established. There is live music fortnightly and an annual beer festival in January. Real ale is £2.50 a pint on Monday. Local CAMRA Pub of the Year 2018. (S3,X9)

Checkendon

Black Horse

Burncote Lane, RG8 0TE (500yds along narrow lane NE from Checkendon-Stoke Row road) SU666841

12-2 (3 Sun), 7-11 (01491) 680418

Rebellion IPA; West Berkshire Mr Chubb's Lunchtime Bitter, Good Old Boy [G]

Buried in the Chilterns woods, the effort of finding this old-fashioned 350-year-old inn, which has been run by the same family for over 110 years, is rewarded by a choice of three excellent gravity dispensed beers. The two-roomed pub welcomes an eclectic mix of locals, walkers, horse riders and cyclists. Filled rolls at lunchtime are the only food available. The outside Gents are not to be missed. Outside seating is available. During the winter months the pub is closed Sunday evening and opening times may vary. Q P

Highwayman

Exlade Street, RG8 0UA

closed Mon; 12-3, 6-11; 12-11 Fri & Sat; 12-5 Sun

(01491) 682020 thehighwaymaninn-checkendon.co.uk

Fuller's London Pride; Loddon Hoppit; West Berkshire Good Old Boy [H]

The original building dates from 1625 but the inn now has a contemporary ambience while retaining the feel of a traditional pub, with two rooms for dining and a separate bar and drinking area with woodburner, beams and exposed brickwork. Three ales are on handpump – two from local microbreweries, always including Loddon Hoppit, the others occasionally seasonal beers. A large enclosed garden where numerous chickens roam is popular with families. Q P

Clifton

Duke at Clifton

Main Street, OX15 0PE

11 (5 Mon)-11; 11-9 Sun (01869) 226334

thecliftonduke.co.uk

Hook Norton Hooky; Turpin Golden Citrus; 2 changing beers (sourced regionally; often North Cotswold, Tring, XT) [H]

This 17th-century Grade II thatched country inn has been rejuvenated by the owners. The roaring fire in the inglenook fireplace and the superb garden make this a perfect setting to sample the award-winning ales, whatever the season. Fabulous food features on a locally sourced à la carte menu. Four guest rooms and a fully serviced campsite provide ideal accommodation. Walkers, wet dogs and wellies welcome. Q P (81)

Duns Tew

White Horse Inn

Daisy Hill, OX25 6JS

10-11 (10.30 Sun) (01869) 340272

dunstewwhitehorse.co.uk

3 changing beers (sourced nationally) [H]

This traditional 17th-century Hornton stone inn lies at the heart of the village and has a pleasant outside drinking area. It offers three ever-changing ales, imaginatively chosen from the Greene King guest beer list by the real ale loving landlord, usually with an ABV under 4.5%. Food is served daily and breakfast can be booked. A village night is held once a month. There are 11 en-suite letting rooms and wheelchair access from the car park at the rear. P

East Hagbourne

Fleur de Lys

30 Main Road, OX11 9LN

11.30-2.30, 6-11 (10 Mon); 11.30-11 Fri & Sat; 12-10 Sun

(01235) 813247 thefleurdelyspub.co.uk

Morland Original Bitter; 3 changing beers (sourced nationally) [H]

The Fleur de Lys is a family-friendly 17th-century pub situated in the rural village of East Hagbourne. It offers one regular beer from Morland and three nationally sourced guests. The large bar and dining area are comfortable and cosy, warmed by a large open fire. Live music evenings are hosted regularly. Outside is an extensive decked area with a separate beer garden where Aunt Sally is played in summer. No food is available on Monday or Sunday evenings. P

Faringdon

Swan

1 Park Road, SN7 7BP

4.30-midnight (2am Fri); 12-2am Sat; 12-midnight Sun
☎ (01367) 241480 swanfaringdon.co.uk

4 changing beers (sourced nationally; often White Horse) [H]

An attractive free house, the large, friendly, multi-level single bar has a small roadside patio for sunny afternoons. A selection of four constantly changing guest beers is complemented by two ciders on handpump. Third-pint glasses are available for the unsure. Popular music nights include live bands every Saturday, folk music and open mic nights twice monthly. There is also a regular quiz night. Q♣(66)

Fewcott

White Lion

Fritwell Road, OX27 7NZ

closed Tue; 4-11 Mon, Wed & Thu; 11-2, 4-midnight Fri; 12-midnight Sat; 12-9 Sun ☎ (01869) 346676

3 changing beers (sourced nationally; often Black Sheep, Pirate, Wadworth) [H]

A welcoming family-friendly free house, with the Pirate microbrewery on-site. Three constantly changing real ales are served along with four real ciders, and for gin lovers, two dozen gins. Sports fans can watch games on two TVs while enjoying their pint. The spacious beer garden is popular in summer, home to Aunt Sally and a large pirate play ship. A cider and pirate festival is held in August. A regular in the Guide, the pub is a former local CAMRA Cider Pub of the Year and Pub of the Year.
♣P(81)

Goring

Goring Social Club

1 High Street, RG8 9BA

6.30-11; 4.30-11 Fri; 12-11 Sat; 12-10.30 Sun
☎ (01491) 873105 goringsocialclub.co.uk

Hook Norton Hooky; 2 changing beers (sourced nationally) [H]

A splendid, welcoming, community-based establishment in the heart of the village. The club prides itself on both the quality and variety of its beer and last year over 70 different ales were dispensed from the constantly changing middle pump and the quarterly-changing third pump. Traditional pub games, TV and function rooms are available, and the club hosts regular quizzes, meat draws, bingo and cribbage evenings, and other community events. Entry is £1 with a CAMRA membership card. Local CAMRA Club of the Year multiple times including 2018.
(Goring & Streatley)♣P

Henley-on-Thames

Bird in Hand

61 Greys Road, RG9 1SB

12-2, 5-11; 12-11 Sat; 12-10.30 Sun ☎ (01491) 575775

Brakspear Bitter; Fuller's London Pride; Hook Norton Hooky Mild; 2 changing beers (sourced nationally; often Loddon, Rebellion, West Berkshire) [H]

A Guide regular for over 20 years, the Bird has flourished under the stewardship of the same family throughout. Two diferent guest beers complement three regulars. TVs show sporting events and the pub is home to darts and cribbage teams and hosts regular quiz nights. The family room leads to a delightful garden boasting a pond and aviary, and dogs on leads are welcome. Hot and cold snacks are available all day. A frequent winner of local CAMRA Pub of the Year.
Q♣

Hethe

Muddy Duck

Main Street, OX27 8ES

11-11 ☎ (01869) 278099 themuddyduckpub.co.uk

Hook Norton Hooky; Phipps NBC India Pale Ale; St Austell Tribute [H]; Timothy Taylor Landlord; 2 changing beers (sourced nationally; often Harvey's, Hawkshead, Skinner's) [H]/[G]

Saved from becoming a residential property in 2011, the pub was purchased and renovated by a local businessman. Retaining the previous landlord as its cellar expert, it serves quality real ale from three handpumps and two gravity-fed casks. The pub has a reputation for good food with seasonal menus, and offers an extensive wine list. There is a large garden area at the rear. An Aunt Sally team plays here in the summer season. Walkers are welcome. ♣P

Horley

Red Lion

Hornton Lane, OX15 6BQ

closed Mon; 6-11; 12-6 Sun ☎ (01295) 730427

Hook Norton Hooky; Purity Pure UBU; Sharp's Doom Bar [H]

This traditional village wet-sales-only pub is the focal point of the community, offering a friendly welcome to visitors, including walkers and well-behaved dogs. The garden provides a tranquil area for a summer evening's tipple. Three handpumped ales are served (four on special occasions). The annual beer festival for St George's Day has become a must with locals and visitors alike. Darts and dominoes are played, and a TV shows live sporting events. Local CAMRA Pub of the Year 2017.
♣P

Letcombe Regis

Greyhound Inn

Main Street, OX12 9JL

3.30-10 Mon; 10-11; 11-10 Sun ☎ (01235) 771969
thegreyhoundletcombe.co.uk

4 changing beers (sourced regionally; often Little Ox, North Cotswold, Ramsbury) [H]

Large, welcoming pub in the centre of the village, recently refurbished to a high standard. Inside is a single bar with dining areas and a formerly hidden inglenook fireplace. Locally sourced home-cooked food and four constantly changing handpumped beers are available. The garden has been relandscaped for outdoor dining during the summer months. Parking is available at the side of the building, as well as provision for tethering horses. Eight boutique en-suite bedrooms are now open. Within a couple of miles of the Ridgeway, the Greyhound provides a welcome place of refreshment for wayfarers.
Q♣P

Lewknor

Leathern Bottle

1 High Street, OX49 5TW (off B4009 near M40 jct 6)
11-2.30 (3 Sat), 5.30-11; 12-3, 7-10.30 Sun
(01844) 351482 theleathernbottle.co.uk
Brakspear Bitter; Marston's Pedigree; 1 changing beer (sourced nationally) H
This traditional old country pub, run by two generations of the same family for over 40 years, has featured in all but one edition of the Guide. It serves good home-cooked pub food using locally sourced produce, and also offers woodburners and a family-friendly garden. The guest beer comes from the Brakspear pubco approved list. The pub offers a warm welcome to all, including walkers from the nearby Ridgeway, with some of the best trails starting and finishing here. It is also a short walk from the Oxford Tube and the airline coach stop. Q P

Long Wittenham

Plough L

24 High Street, OX14 4QH
12-11 (01865) 407738 theploughinnlw.co.uk
Butcombe Original; 2 changing beers (sourced nationally; often Loose Cannon, West Berkshire) H
The Plough is a traditional Grade II listed family-friendly pub built in the 17th century in the village of Long Wittenham in rural south Oxfordshire. The large garden stretches down to the River Thames and has ample outdoor seating and a children's play area. There are two bar areas and a separate restaurant. One regular and two changing beers are available, from breweries and microbreweries mainly in the South-East. Each June, the pub hosts Wittfest, a music festival that raises money for charities. P

Longcot

King & Queen L

Shrivenham Road, SN7 7TL
12-2 (not Mon), 5-11; 12-2.30, 5-11 Sat; 12-2.30, 5-10.30 Sun (01793) 784348 longcotkingandqueen.com
Loose Cannon Gunners Gold; 2 changing beers (sourced nationally; often Oakham, Ramsbury, XT) H
This pub enjoys one of the best views of White Horse Hill and its famous 3,000-year-old chalk figure. The interior comprises an extensive, open-plan drinking area and, to one side, a restaurant serving organic meat and local produce. A good selection of beers from local breweries is complemented by two ciders on handpump. Q P (66)

Mapledurham

Packhorse L

Woodcote Road, RG4 7UG (on A4074)
11.30-11; 11.30-10.30 Sun (0118) 972 2140
homecountiespubs.co.uk/packhorse
Loddon Hoppit; West Berkshire Good Old Boy; 3 changing beers (sourced nationally) H
Originally a farm on the Mapledurham House estate dating from the 1600s, this Brunning & Price establishment is now a cosy pub and restaurant. The low-beamed bar has ample seating for drinkers and usually features local microbrewery beers. The larger restaurant area is furnished with bookcases and numerous prints and offers a wide-ranging good-value menu. A large secluded garden at the rear has a shaded seating area overlooking fields. There is 60p off a pint 5-7pm weekdays. Regular Meet the Brewer evenings are proving popular. Q P

Marcham

Crown L

1 Packhorse Lane, OX13 6NT
12 (5 Mon)-11; 12-midnight Fri & Sat; 12-10.30 Sun
(01865) 391735 thecrownmarcham.co.uk
Bombardier; Loose Cannon Abingdon Bridge; Sharp's Doom Bar; 3 changing beers (sourced nationally) H
Traditional friendly village local with a lively public bar and cosy dining room with its own bar, owned by Admiral Taverns. Additional handpumps have been fitted and three regular beers and three changing guests are usually available. The pub was designated a Grade II listed building in 1987. Marcham is home to Denman College, headquarters of the WI. P (S8,15)

Marsh Baldon

Seven Stars on the Green L

The Green, OX44 9LP
10-10 (11 Wed & Thu; midnight Fri & Sat); 10-7 Sun
(01865) 343337 sevenstarsonthegreen.co.uk
Fuller's London Pride; 3 changing beers (sourced locally; often Loddon, Shotover, White Horse) H
This old coaching inn reopened as a community-owned pub in 2013 with a refurbished main bar and a new function room/restaurant. It sits next to the village green, which claims to be the largest in Europe, and has a big garden for the summer. Three local ales are always available and good food is served including extensive gluten-free options. A former local CAMRA Town and Village Pub of the Year. Q P

Milton

Plum Pudding L

44 High Street, OX14 4EJ
11.30-2.30, 5-11; 11.30-midnight Fri & Sat; 12-10.30 Sun
(01235) 834443 theplumpuddingmilton.co.uk
Loose Cannon Abingdon Bridge; LoveBeer OG; house beer (by Ringwood); 1 changing beer (sourced nationally) H
Plum Pudding refers to the Oxford Sandy and Black pig, one of the older and rarer British breeds, which features on the menu. Regular live music is hosted, and two beer festivals are held each year. The house beer is Plum Pudding Best Bitter (3.8% ABV). Sitting in the pleasant walled garden, you would not know it, but you are only a couple of minutes from the busy A34. A Guide regular, the pub is a former local CAMRA Pub of the Year and Cider Pub of the Year in 2018. P

North Moreton

Bear at Home L

High Street, OX11 9AT (S off A4130)
12-3, 6-11; 12-11 Sat; 12-10 Sun (01235) 811311
bear-at-home.co.uk
Timothy Taylor Landlord; house beer (by West Berkshire); 2 changing beers (sourced locally) H
Friendly village local dating back to the 15th century with an open fire and plenty of tables for diners to enjoy the excellent pub food. There are

two regular beers – Landlord and Bear Beer (4% ABV), the latter brewed exclusively for the pub by West Berkshire – together with two changing guests. The Bear adjoins the village cricket ground and hosts a popular four-day beer and cricket festival at the end of July. P (94S)

Northmoor

Red Lion

Standlake Road, OX29 5SX

closed Mon; 12-3, 5.30-11; 11-11 Sat; 12-6 Sun
(01865) 300301 theredlionnorthmoor.com

Brakspear Bitter; Wychwood Hobgoblin; 2 changing beers (sourced locally; often Hook Norton, Loose Cannon, Vale) H

Traditional village inn with whitewashed stone walls, heavy oak beams, real fires and a large garden. Purchased by the local community from Greene King in 2014, the pub has gone from strength to strength ever since. The focus is on local produce, with a changing menu of home-cooked food, some of which is grown in the pub's kitchen garden. A selection of four local beers is available in the small bar alongside locally made soft drinks from Samuelsons of Witney.
Q P (18)

Oxford

Butchers Arms

5 Wilberforce Street, Headington, OX3 7AN (from centre of Headington, past the shark, first left, first right)

12-2.30, 4.30-11; 12-midnight Fri & Sat; 12-11 Sun
(01865) 742470 butchersarmsoxford.co.uk

Fuller's London Pride, ESB; Gale's Seafarers Ale; 2 changing beers (sourced nationally; often Fuller's) H

A friendly back-street late-Victorian red-brick pub – a little hard to find but worth searching out. It has one long room with the bar in the middle serving a good range of Fuller's beers, and a pretty paved courtyard garden outside. Traditional pub food includes light lunch options. The inn sign, a parody of the arms of the Worshipful Company of Butchers, and the motto, which means 'God gives us everything', are both of unknown origin.
Q

Castle

24 Paradise Street, OX1 1LD

11-11 (midnight Fri & Sat); 12-11 Sun (01865) 248990
thecastleoxford.co.uk

Hook Norton Hooky, Hooky Gold, Old Hooky; 3 changing beers (sourced nationally) H

Rebuilt in 1892 to a design by HG Drinkwater, the pub is now above the street after the realignment of Castle Street when the Westgate Shopping Centre opposite was first built. Some period features remain but the interior is modern with one long room and a pleasant half cellar. Purchased by Hook Norton in 2016 for its first venture into the city and extensively refurbished, it now offers a range of real ales, not all from Hook Norton. Q

Chequers

130A High Street, OX1 4DH

11-11 (11.30 Fri & Sat); 11-10.30 Sun (01865) 727463

St Austell Nicholson's Pale Ale; Thornbridge Jaipur IPA; 7 changing beers (sourced nationally; often Brakspear, Sharp's) H

Worth searching out down a passageway off the High Street, much of this Grade II listed pub dates back to the early 16th century when it was converted from a moneylender's tenement to a tavern, hence the name. Note the fine carvings, windows and the ceiling in the lower bar. There is an upstairs bar with three handpumps, and a cobbled courtyard provides alfresco drinking, dining and smoking space.
Q

Chester

19 Chester Street, OX4 1SN

12 (5 Tue)-11; 10-11 Sat; 12-10 Sun (01865) 790438

3 changing beers (sourced regionally; often Loose Cannon) H

A modern back-street pub off the Iffley Road built in 1898 and now opened out with boarded floors and powder-blue painted walls. The stud copperwork bar front is of interest, as are the brass light fittings, but the star of the show is some original Halls Brewery stained and leaded glasswork on the entrance surrounds. There is a large patio garden to the rear with an impressive tree. Opens early for breakfast on Saturday.
Q

Fir Tree

163 Iffley Road, OX4 1EJ

4-11; 12-2am Fri & Sat; 12-11 Sun (01865) 245290

5 changing beers (sourced nationally) H

Multi-level pub with a quiet snug at the back and a small patio garden and smoking area to the rear. There are some pavement tables at the front. The house speciality is pizza and a pop-up diner serves a vegan roast dinner on Sunday afternoon. The interior of this quirky pub still bears the scars of its days as a Morrells alehouse, with a whole bank of handpumps and a mishmash of finishes and artefacts.

Gardener's Arms

39 Plantation Road, OX2 6JE

12-2.30 (not Mon & Tue), 5-midnight; 12-11 Sun
(01865) 559814 thegarden-oxford.co.uk

4 changing beers (sourced nationally) H

Cosy pub down a narrow street off Woodstock Road. The small bar opens up to a spacious dining area, once two rooms, serving some of the finest vegetarian and vegan food in the city. At the rear is a large and pleasant garden as well as the outside toilets. A popular and relaxing place to eat and drink, and now free of tie. Quiz night is Sunday.
Q

Lamb & Flag

12 St Giles, OX1 3JS

12-11 (10.30 Sun) (01865) 515787

Palmers IPA; Skinner's Betty Stogs; Theakston Old Peculier; house beer (by Palmers); 3 changing beers (sourced nationally; often Tring, XT) H

Grade II listed building owned by the adjacent St John's College. Some of the profits from the pub support student scholarships. This is a classic city pub with no music, Wi-Fi or other distractions from friendly conversation. Beers from the South-West feature – the house beer Lamb & Flag Gold (4.5% ABV) is brewed by Palmers of Bridport. It is believed to be the setting for the inn in Thomas Hardy's novel Jude the Obscure and has other literary links. Q

Masons Arms

2 Quarry School Place, Headington Quarry, OX3 8LH
5 (7 Mon)-11; 12-11 Sat; 12-4, 7-10.30 Sun
(01865) 764579 themasonsarmshq.co.uk
Dark Star Hophead; Timothy Taylor Boltmaker; 3 changing beers (sourced nationally; often Loddon, Rebellion)
Family-run community pub hosting many pub games leagues, including bar billiards and Aunt Sally. The guest ales are varied and a wide range of bottled beers is stocked. The pub is home to the Headington beer festival in September. A heated decking area and garden lead to a function room. Multiple local CAMRA City Pub of the Year winner. P(H2)

Old Bookbinders

17-18 Victor Street, Jericho, OX2 6BT
12-11 (01865) 553549 oldbookbinders.co.uk
Greene King IPA; Morland Original Bitter; house beer (by Greene King); 3 changing beers (sourced nationally)
This family-run pub near the Oxford canal mixes a Victorian tavern with a French bistro. The Bookbinders Arms became the Old Bookbinders Ale House when sold by Morrells. Two rooms are served by a single bar and furnished in typical style with an eclectic mix of decor and bric-a-brac. Free monkey nuts are available from the barrel by the entrance. The outside of the pub featured on TV in the first episode of Inspector Morse as The Printer's Devil. Q(17)

Rose & Crown

14 North Parade Avenue, OX2 6LX (½ mile N of city centre, off Banbury Rd)
11-midnight (1am Fri & Sat) (01865) 510551
roseandcrownoxford.com
Adnams Southwold Bitter; Hook Norton Old Hooky; Shotover Scholar; 1 changing beer (sourced nationally)
Now a free house, this popular Victorian local on a vibrant north Oxford street is a time capsule with two small rooms and many original features. A friendly community pub, it has been run by the same landlords for over 30 years. No intrusive music or mobile phones are permitted. Its fame has even spread to Everest – see the photo on the wall. To the rear is a heated, covered patio. Children are welcome until 5pm. Q

St Aldates Tavern

108 St Aldate's, OX1 1BU
11.30-11 (midnight Thu & Fri); 11-midnight Sat; 11-11 Sun
(01865) 241185 staldatestavernoxford.co.uk
7 changing beers (sourced nationally; often Dark Star, Shotover, XT)
Not the original St Aldate's Tavern – that was at no. 61 – but there was an inn recorded at this site in the centre of town in 1397. The pub has been rebuilt at least once since then and was a coaching inn in the 18th century. It features up to seven well-kept real ales, with at least two often from local breweries. Good-quality, freshly cooked food is served all day using locally sourced ingredients where possible. Q

White Hart

12 St Andrews Road, Headington, OX3 9DL (opp church in Old Headington village)
12-11 (midnight Fri & Sat) (01865) 761737
thewhitehartheadington.com
Everards Sunchaser, Tiger; 3 changing beers (sourced nationally; often Bath Ales, Brunswick, Oakham)
Terraced, stone-built pub with a good selection of Everards ales. The interior is divided into three, with two small bars, and it has a large garden. Note the framed extract from a play The Tragi-comedy of Joan of Hedington by Dr William King of Christ Church, written in 1712 about the proprietor of a dishonourable ale house – thankfully the pub now has a much better reputation. The food is traditional and home made, with pies a speciality. Current local CAMRA City Pub of the Year and Pub of the Year 2018. P

White Rabbit

21 Friars Entry, OX1 2BY (alley between Magdalen St and Gloucester Green)
12-midnight (01865) 241177
whiterabbitoxford.co.uk
Shotover Scholar; 3 changing beers (sourced locally)
This pub reopened in 2012 as the White Rabbit following its closure as Oxford's premier rock pub, the Gloucester Arms. It is brighter and more spacious than before (although there is still not much room), with a central bar surrounded by three areas. Four real ales are on offer, three changing and all local. Bar snacks and panini are available and a wide range of hand-made pizzas, gluten-free on request.

Playhatch

Flowing Spring

Henley Road, RG4 9RB (on A4155)
closed Mon; 12-2.30, 5.30-11; 12-11 Sat & Sun
(0118) 969 9878 theflowingspringpub.co.uk
Fuller's London Pride, ESB; 4 changing beers (sourced nationally)
Sociable 18th-century country pub on the edge of the Chilterns. Now a free house owned by the former tenants, it features Fuller's London Pride and three or four varying beers. It serves home-made food with award-winning gluten-free, dairy-free, vegetarian and vegan options. Events include a monthly unplugged night, classic car and bike meets, murder mysteries, and beer and cider festivals in the summer and autumn. The pleasant covered balcony and large riverside garden are ideal for summer. Local CAMRA Pub of the Year 2018. P

Salford

Salford Inn

Lower End, OX7 5YW
closed Mon; 12-2.30, 6-11; 12-4 Sun (01608) 642631
thesalford.co.uk
Ruddles Best Bitter; 1 changing beer (sourced locally; often North Cotswold)
Welcoming one-room stone-built pub just off the A44 less than two miles from Chipping Norton, tastefully renovated and reopened in early 2016 under its new name, with a father and son team at the helm. Quality food, freshly prepared and locally sourced where possible, is served alongside two well-kept ales. There is a patio area for outside drinking and dining. Accommodation is available in three rooms and a nearby cottage.
QP

Stanford in the Vale

Stanford Social Club

Sheards Lane, SN7 8LW
8-11; 12-6 Sun ☎ (01367) 710734
stanfordsocialclub.net
2 changing beers (sourced nationally) H
Formerly known as The Working Men's Club, it was built in 1928 on donated land using volunteer labour, and later run by steward Fred 'Buster' Smith until his death in 1977, after which it was run by a group of 12 people as the Stanford Social Club. CAMRA Members are welcome on production of a CAMRA membership card and a contribution of 50p. Two constantly changing beers are served on handpump. Local CAMRA Club of the Year 2017 and 2018. ♣P

Stoke Lyne

Peyton Arms

OX27 8SD
closed Mon; 5-11; 12-7 Sat & Sun ☎ 07546 066160
Hook Norton Hooky, Old Hooky; 1 changing beer (sourced locally; often Hook Norton) G
Just two miles from junction 10 of the M40, enter here and step back in time. Up to three Hooky ales are served through a hatch, direct from casks. Simple filled rolls are usually available. Regular users of the pub include members of the local farming community looking to enjoy quality ales with great conversation. The bar area is for adults only; however, children are welcome in the garden. No dogs allowed. Weekday opening hours can vary. QP (81)

Tetsworth

Old Red Lion L

40 High Street, OX9 7AS
11-10 (midnight Fri); 11-5 Sun ☎ (01844) 281274
theoldredliontetsworth.co.uk
XT Four; 1 changing beer (sourced locally) H
The recently refurbished pub has a warm and friendly atmosphere with wood-burning stoves in the winter. Up to three well-kept real ales come from local breweries. Traditional pub food is served all day. The pub is a member of Brit Stops and allows motorhomes free overnight parking. It also serves as the village shop and offers B&B accommodation. Truly an asset of community value. Q♣P (275)

Thame

Cross Keys L

East Street, OX9 3JS
12-2, 5-11; 12-11 Sat; 12-10.30 Sun ☎ (01844) 218202
crosskeysthame.co.uk
XT Four; 7 changing beers (sourced nationally) H
Once almost lost forever, this pub was saved by the current tenants, who have transformed it from a failing keg-only pub into a drinkers' local. Serving a wide range of ales and ciders, the on-site Thame Brewery and other local breweries are often represented alongside breweries from around the country. At busy times, it is not uncommon for several beers to change during the evening. A regular local CAMRA Pub of the Year and Cider Pub of the Year. Q♣

James Figg L

21 Cornmarket, OX9 2BL
11-11; 12-10.30 Sun ☎ (01844) 260166
thejamesfiggthame.co.uk
Purity Mad Goose; Sharp's Doom Bar; Vale Best IPA; 1 changing beer (sourced locally) H
Former 17th-century coaching inn with an early-Georgian frontage. There is a choice of bars to the left or right as you enter. Dried hops hang down from the ceiling and sporting prints adorn the walls. The bar area opens out into a larger room complete with sofas, and a beer garden beyond. Nibbles are usually available on the bar to enjoy with your drink. Previously the Abingdon Arms, it is now renamed after Thame's very own 18th-century undefeated bare-knuckle boxing champion of England. Q♣P (280)

Wallingford

George Hotel L

25 High Street, OX10 0BS
11-11; 12-10.30 Sun ☎ (01491) 836665
Rebellion IPA; 2 changing beers (sourced locally; often Rebellion) H
A coaching inn dating from the 16th century and close to the town centre. This Peel Group hotel hosts various functions and is licensed for civil wedding ceremonies. Cask ales are available in the Tavern Bar, which has several separate areas, and can also be enjoyed in the spacious hotel courtyard, ideal for alfresco dining and drinking. Food ranges from bar snacks to fine dining from an à la carte menu in the bistro.
P

Wantage

Royal Oak L

Newbury Street, OX12 8DF (S of Market Square)
5.30-11; 12-2.30, 7-11 Sat; 12-2, 7-10.30 Sun
☎ (01235) 763129 royaloakwantage.co.uk
Wadworth 6X; West Berkshire Maggs' Magnificent Mild, Dr Hexter's Healer; 8 changing beers (sourced nationally) G
This multi award-winning street-corner pub is a mecca for the discerning drinker. The pub is the primary outlet for West Berkshire ales in the area – two carry the landlord Paul Hexter's name – together with 30 or more ciders and perries. All beers are served by gravity. Photographs of ships bearing the pub's name are displayed. The lounge features wrought-iron trelliswork covered in pumpclips. Many times a local CAMRA Pub of the Year and Cider Pub of the Year, including 2017 and 2018. Q♣

Shoulder of Mutton L

38 Wallingford Street, OX12 8AX (E of Market Square)
12-11 (midnight Fri & Sat); 12-10.30 Sun
10 changing beers (sourced nationally) H
Victorian corner pub close to the town centre with 10 constantly changing beers on handpump to suit all tastes. The sympathetically renovated interior comprises public and lounge bars, a cosy snug and a 'lay-by' leading to small courtyard and function room. A former CAMRA local, regional and county Pub of The Year. Q

West Hanney

Plough 𝕃 ✔

Church Street, OX12 0LN

⏲ closed Mon; 12-3, 6-11 (midnight Fri); 12-midnight Sat; 12-9 Sun ☎ (01235) 868987

🌐 theploughatwesthanney.co.uk

4 changing beers (sourced regionally; often Loose Cannon, St Austell, Shotover) Ⓗ

Picturesque, friendly, 16th-century thatched pub, opposite the church. Sold in 2015 by Punch Taverns to a local community group, it has been refurbished and now offers four changing beers. The cosy beamed and alcoved split-level bar has an open fire, and the separate dining room serves traditional British food. The hub of the community, most of the local clubs meet here from time to time. In summer Aunt Sally is played. 🐴❀◑◐♿⛺♣P🐾📶

Wheatley

Cricketers Arms 𝕃

38 Littleworth, OX33 1TR (walk W along Littleworth Rd from Wheatley)

⏲ 6-11; 5-11 Fri; 12-3, 6-11 Sat; 12-4, 7-10.30 Sun ☎ (01865) 872738 🌐 cricketers-arms.co.uk

Hook Norton Hooky; 2 changing beers (sourced locally) Ⓗ

A friendly, traditional free house, offering three cask ales from local breweries, often including darker beers. A range of local bottled beers is also available and real cider. Regular beer festivals are held in spring and autumn. A popular stop-off for walkers, and dogs and children are welcome. There is a frequent bus service to Wheatley (a 15-minute walk away) and the pub is on National Cycle Route 57. **Q**🐴❀◑◐♣🍎P🐾📶

Witney

Angel Inn 𝕃 ✔

42 Market Square, OX28 6AL

⏲ 10-11 (midnight Fri & Sat); 11-11 Sun ☎ (01993) 703238

Brakspear Oxford Gold; Wychwood Hobgoblin Gold, Hobgoblin; house beer (by Marston's) Ⓗ

A Grade II listed free house at one time owned by Joseph Early of the blanket manufacturing dynasty and a brewer. It has a fine front bar with low beams and a bay window with plenty of space for drinkers and diners beyond. Outside is a small paved and walled courtyard. It was said once to have had a cursed bar stool – thankfully no longer there. The beer range is mostly from Marston's – its Wychwood Brewery is just around the corner. One of the regular beers is sometimes replaced by a guest. ❀◑◐♣🚌(S1,S2)

Eagle Tavern 𝕃 ✔

22 Corn Street, OX28 6BL

⏲ 11-3, 5-midnight (2am Fri); 11-2am Sat; 12-midnight Sun ☎ (01993) 700121

Hook Norton Hooky, Hooky Gold, Old Hooky; Wychwood Hobgoblin; 1 changing beer (sourced locally; often Hook Norton) Ⓗ

The landlord has been running pubs in Corn Street for over 25 years, this one for over 10, and has won Hook Norton Pub of the Year and Best Kept Beer and Cellar several times. This Grade II listed pub has wood panelling and stone floors, and you can see the cellar through the window next to the bar. Friendly locals, welcoming staff and quality beer all add up to a must-visit pub. Wychwood Brewery is just across the road. **Q**❀♿♣🍎🚌(S1,S2)📶

Woodstock

Black Prince ✔

2 Manor Road, OX20 1XJ

⏲ 12-11 (9 Sun) ☎ (01993) 811530

🌐 theblackprincewoodstock.com

Loddon Hullabaloo; St Austell Tribute; 2 changing beers (sourced nationally; often St Austell, Vale) Ⓗ

Historic 16th-century pub in an attractive riverside location by the River Glyme, opposite Blenheim Palace. The garden and terrace offer a tranquil setting to enjoy a well-kept pint. You can choose from two regular ales and two changing guests, often from local breweries. Fresh well-cooked snacks and meals are available daily at reasonable prices. The open-plan interior boasts two ancient fireplaces and a French suit of armour. Aunt Sally is played, and families, walkers and well-behaved dogs are welcome. **Q**🐴❀◑◐♿♣P🚌🐾📶

Wootton

Killingworth Castle

Glympton Road, OX20 1EJ

⏲ 9am-11 ☎ (01993) 811401 🌐 thekillingworthcastle.com

6 changing beers (sourced locally; often Little Ox, North Cotswold, Yubberton) Ⓗ

This welcoming coaching inn on the ancient Worcester to London road dates from 1637. There is a small bar and dining area to the front with a wood-burning stove, and to the rear a larger restaurant serving award-winning food. Four handpumps offer two ales from sister brewery Yubberton and two guests from regionals and micros, available in tasting paddles of three third-pints to allow sampling of the range. Eight letting rooms are available. **Q**🐴❀🛏◑◐♣P🐾📶

Learned drinker

He was a learned man, of immense reading, but is much blamed for his unfaithfull quotations. His manner of studie was thus, he wore a long quilt cap, which came two or rather three inches at least over his eies, which served him as an umbrella to defend his eies from the light. About every three houres his man was to bring him a roll and a pot of ale to refocillate (refresh) his wasted spirits so he studied, and dranke, and munched some bread and this maintained him till night, and then he made a good supper.

An Oxford man, William Prynne (1600-69), as described by John Aubrey in Brief Lives, ed. John Buchanan-Brown, 2000

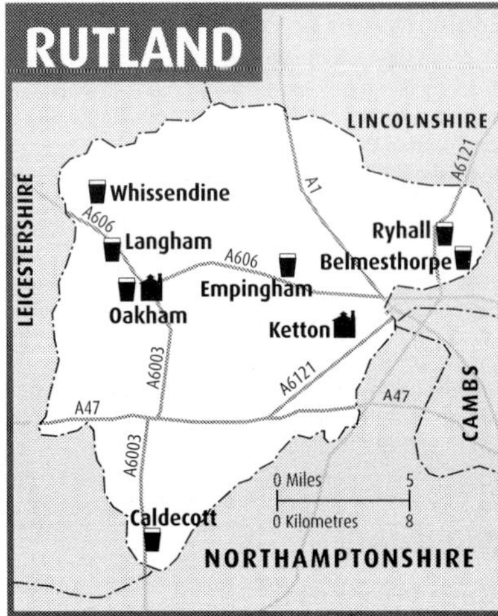

Belmesthorpe

Blue Bell

Shepherds Walk, PE9 4JG

12-2.30 (not Mon), 6-11; 12-2.30, 5-11 Fri; 12-11 Sat & Sun
(01780) 753081

Draught Bass; Grainstore Ten Fifty; Greene King IPA; Oakham Bishops Farewell; 1 changing beer (often Abbeydale)

Historic village pub with low ceilings, a roaring fire and stone walls all part of its charm. Six handpulls offer a wide range of well-kept guest beers, including at least one LocAle and a real cider. Dogs on leads are welcome in the bar area. Good honest home-made pub food is available Tuesday to Sunday lunchtimes (booking advisable). A former Rutland CAMRA Pub of the Year.
Q P

Caldecott

Plough Inn

16 Main Street, LE16 8RS

11-3.30 (not Mon-Fri), 6-11 (01536) 770284

Grainstore Rutland Bitter; Langton Angler; 2 changing beers

Welcoming traditional sandstone pub on the village green. The attractive open-plan interior incorporates a bar area, restaurant and relaxing snug space. There is a large garden to the rear and a terrace at the front. Beers are often from local breweries Grainstore in Rutland and Langton in nearby Leicestershire. **Q P**

Empingham

Empingham Cricket & Social Club

Exton Road, LE15 8QB

8-11 Wed; 8.30-midnight Fri; 1-3 Sun; closed Mon, Tue, Thu & Sat (01780) 460696 empinghamcsc.com

Magpie Best; 3 changing beers (often Great Heck, Greg's, Stockport)

Recently refurbished, the Cricket & Social Club is noted for the quality and variety of the ales served, many from microbreweries. Its opening hours are often dependent on sporting and other social events. An annual beer festival is held to coincide with the final matches of the Six Nations rugby in March. **Q P**

Langham

Wheatsheaf

2 Burley Road, LE15 7HU (N of Oakham on A606)

12 (5 Mon & Tue)-11; 12-midnight Fri & Sat
(01572) 869105 thewheatsheaf-langham.co.uk

Fuller's London Pride; Greene King Abbot; 2 changing beers (often Robinsons, Woodforde's)

A former Mann's pub now free of tie and serving beers from many breweries, micro and otherwise. It has an excellent reputation for food and can be extremely busy, particularly in the summer months. A children's menu is available.
Q P

Oakham

Lord Nelson

Market Square, LE15 6DT

11-11 (midnight Fri & Sat); 11-10.30 Sun
(01572) 868340

Castle Rock Harvest Pale; Fuller's London Pride; 2 changing beers

A new addition to the county's real ale circuit. Part of the Knead group of pubs, it is a characterful example of a pub in a traditional town. Alongside the quality beers, good home-cooked food is available daily. A regular quiz night is hosted.
Q

Ryhall

Green Dragon

The Square, PE9 4HH

12-2.30 (not Mon), 5-11; 12-11 Sat & Sun
(01780) 751999 thegreendragonryhall.co.uk

Greene King IPA; 3 changing beers (often Gun Dog Ales, Oakham, Springhead)

Former Melbourn's stone-built pub in the heart of the village. The main building is from the 17th century and is Grade II listed, with low ceilings and nooks and crannies creating a nice cosy feel. Superb home-cooked meals are served including the pub's speciality pizzas cooked in the pizza oven, available every evening. Local CAMRA Pub of the Year 2018. **Q** (202)

Whissendine

White Lion Inn

Main Street, LE15 7ET

12-3 (not Mon), 5-11; 12-11 Sat; 12-10.30 Sun
(01664) 474233 whitelioninn.com

Everards Tiger, Old Original; changing beers (often Brunswick)

Recently refurbished Everards pub next to the village brook with a restaurant and accommodation in eight rooms. There are 11 handpumps, with one dedicated to real cider. The landlord is a member of The Magic Circle and regularly entertains customers with his close-up magic. **Q**

REAL ALE BREWERIES

Baker's Dozen Ketton
Grainstore Oakham

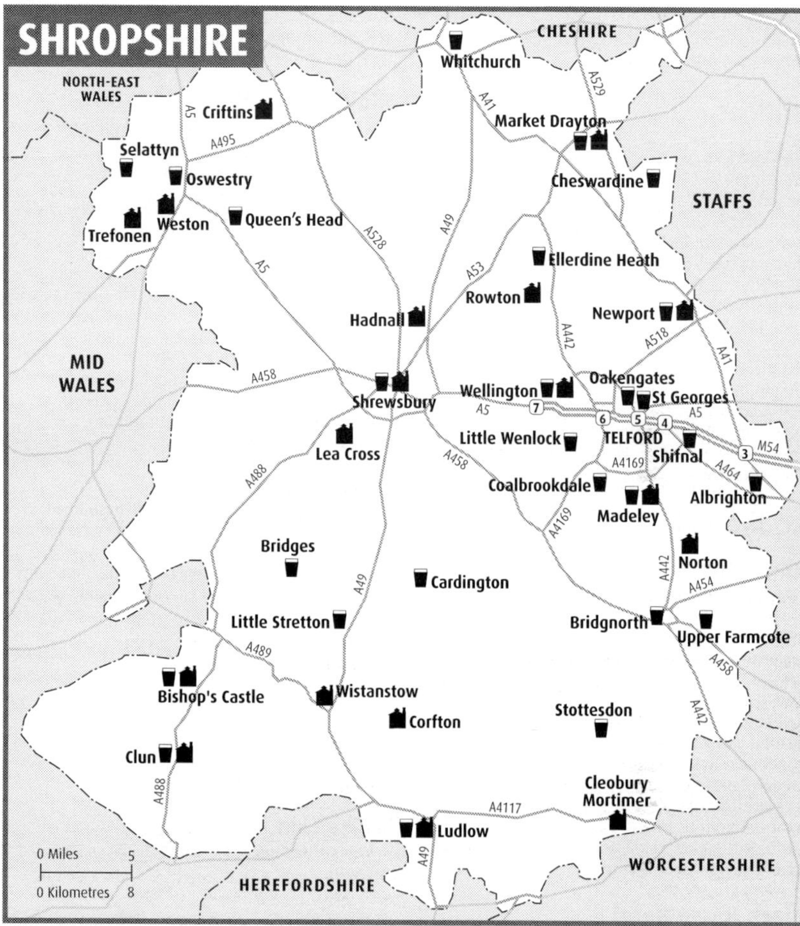

Albrighton

Platform Ale House 𝕃

Station Road, WV7 3FD

closed Mon-Wed; 5-11 Thu & Fri; 12-1am Sat; 12-6 Sun
☎ 07387 573922

Rowton Area 51; 4 changing beers (sourced locally) Ⓗ

Run by a group of local enthusiasts, this micropub opened in 2016 at Albrighton Station on the westbound platform of the Wolverhampton to Shrewsbury railway line. The building dates from 1849, the year after the railway, and the single-room interior is decorated in the original GWR colours. Children are allowed until 8pm and dogs are welcome. Beers on offer usually include a dark ale, and a real cider is on tap – tasters of three thirds are available. The pub can cater for private parties.

Bishop's Castle

Three Tuns Inn 𝕃

Salop Street, SY9 5BW

12-11; 12-10.30 Sun ☎ (01588) 638797
thethreetunsinn.co.uk

Three Tuns Rantipole, XXX, Stout, Cleric's Cure; 1 changing beer (often Three Tuns) Ⓗ

A truly historic pub, this is one of the Famous Four who were still brewing in the early 1970s. The brewery is now separately owned. Refurbished and enlarged, the pub has been extended into four rooms – on one side is the lounge, on the other, the ever-popular front bar leading to the central

REAL ALE BREWERIES

Battlefield Shrewsbury
Chapel Criftins
Clun Clun
Corvedale Corfton
Gorgeous Madeley
Hobsons Cleobury Mortimer
Hop & Stagger Norton
Joule's Market Drayton
Ludlow Ludlow
Offa's Dyke Trefonen
Plan B Newport
Rowton Rowton/Wellington
Salopian Hadnall
Six Bells Bishop's Castle
St Annes Lea Cross (NEW)
Stonehouse Weston
Three Tuns Bishop's Castle
Wood Wistanstow

snug and the extended oak-framed, glass-sided dining room. A function room is available for hire. Q🍴🌼◐◑⛺♣🚌(553)🐾📶

Bridges

Bridges 🄻

SY5 0ST (on back road from Shrewsbury to Bishops Castle via Longden)

⏲ 11-11 ☎ (01588) 650260 🌐 thebridgespub.co.uk

Three Tuns Rantipole, XXX, Stout, Cleric's Cure; 3 changing beers (sourced locally; often Three Tuns) 🄷

Formerly The Horseshoe, the pub is one of two tied houses belonging to the Three Tuns Brewery. A long, low building of some age, it nestles on the western edge of the Long Mynd on the banks of the River East Onny. Inside, there is a large dining area to the left, a bar area to the right, and beyond that a newly constructed room with a woodburner, used primarily for drinking. Six Three Tuns beers are regularly on offer. Walkers are welcome.

Q🍴🌼🛏◐◑⛺♣P🚌🐾📶

Bridgnorth

Black Boy 🄻

58 Cartway, WV16 4BG

⏲ 12-11 (10.30 Sun) ☎ (01746) 766497

House beer (by Gorgeous); 5 changing beers (sourced regionally; often Greene King, Salopian, Three Tuns) 🄷

Award-winning Grade II listed 17th-century alehouse, first licensed in 1790. It stands on the historic Cartway linking High Town with the quayside. Knowledgable staff can advise on the range of ales from Greene King, complemented by a choice from local breweries and the house beer by the Gorgeous Beer Co. A real cider and traditional bar snacks are also available.

🍴🌼⇌(SVR)♣🍎🚌🐾📶

Black Horse Hotel 🄻

4 Bridge Street, Low Town, WV15 6AF

⏲ 12-midnight (1am Thu-Sat); 12-11.30 Sun

☎ (01746) 762415 🌐 theblackhorsebridgnorth.co.uk

Bathams Best Bitter; Hobsons Town Crier; Three Tuns XXX; Wye Valley HPA; 3 changing beers (sourced nationally) 🄷

This popular Low Town free house has two bars serving four regular and three changing guest beers. Extended into the adjacent property in 2016, the front bar has a rustic feel and hosts regular live music. To the side is a wood-panelled lounge and conservatory, both with widescreen TVs for sporting events. Filled rolls are often available but no meals. The smoking area leads to a long courtyard. Car parking is accessed from Severn Street. 🍴🌼🛏⇌(SVR)♣P🚌🐾📶

King's Head 🄻

3 Whitburn Street, High Town, WV16 4QN

⏲ 11-11 (midnight Fri & Sat); 12-10.30 Sun

☎ (01746) 762141 🌐 thekingsheadbridgnorth.co.uk

Hobsons Twisted Spire, Town Crier; Wye Valley HPA; 2 changing beers (sourced nationally; often Kelham Island, Thornbridge, Three Tuns) 🄷

Historic Grade II listed coaching inn first established in the 16th century. Recently renovated, it features the original timber beams, flagstone floor, leaded windows and three roaring open log fires. Three regular local ales and two changing guests, quality food and friendly service are at the heart of this traditional local pub. Well-behaved dogs are welcome in the bar and lounge area.

🍴🌼◐◑♿⇌(SVR)🍎🚌🐾📶

Old Castle 🄻 ✔

10/11 West Castle Street, WV16 4AB (between Severn Valley Railway and town centre)

⏲ 11.30-11 (10.30 Sun) ☎ (01746) 711420

🌐 oldcastlebridgnorth.co.uk

Hobsons Town Crier; Sharp's Doom Bar; Wye Valley HPA, Butty Bach; 1 changing beer (sourced nationally; often Thwaites, Wye Valley) 🄷

A popular 17th-century pub, where the dining area at the front is separated from the bar by a real log fire. To the rear is a conservatory/games room with darts, pool and table football leading to a well-kept garden with excellent views. A well-balanced menu, including vegetarian and gluten-free options and a popular Sunday carvery, is offered. There is a small function room.

🍴🌼◐◑⇌(SVR)♣🚌(436)🐾📶

Railwayman's Arms 🄻

Severn Valley Railway Station, Hollybush Road, WV16 5DT (follow signs for SVR, pub is on Platform 1)

⏲ 11-11 (10.30 Sun) ☎ (01746) 760920 🌐 svr.co.uk

Bathams Best Bitter; Bewdley Worcestershire Way; Hobsons Mild, Best, Town Crier; 4 changing beers (sourced nationally) 🄷

A unique and popular pub owned by the Severn Valley Railway at Bridgnorth Station, licensed since 1861 and full of railway memorabilia. There are 10 handpumps, eight serving real ales from near and far, and two for real ciders. In summer a perry replaces one of the ciders. The platform drinking area is alongside the steam locomotives.

Q🍴🌼⇌(SVR)🍎P🚌(436,101)🐾📶

White Lion 🄻

3 West Castle Street, WV16 4AB (between town centre and SVR)

⏲ 11.30-11; 12-10.30 Sun ☎ (01746) 763962

🌐 whitelionbridgnorth.co.uk

Hop & Stagger Golden Wander; house beer (by Hop & Stagger); 3 changing beers (sourced regionally) 🄷

An 18th-century inn with two bars, offering a warm welcome to regulars and visitors. Murals by a local artist adorn the walls inside and out. Eight handpumps offer a selection of the pub's own Hop & Stagger beers plus LocAles, national beers and a cider. Snacks are available including the pub's famous Scotch eggs. Outside is a terrace and lawned garden. A regular venue for a story-telling group, folk club, quiz team and charity quizzes.

Q🍴🌼🛏⇌(SVR)♣🍎🚌(436,890)🐾📶

Cardington

Royal Oak

SY6 7JZ

⏲ closed Mon; 12-2.30, 6-11 Tue-Fri; 12-11 Sat; 12-11 (4 winter) Sun ☎ (01694) 771266 🌐 at-the-oak.com

Ludlow Best; Sharp's Doom Bar; 2 changing beers 🄷

The Royal Oak, dating back to the 15th century, is reputedly Shropshire's oldest continually licensed pub, and is the archetypal country inn. The single room is multi-functional with a bar, lounge and dining area, and has a relaxed ambience. It is low beamed and dominated by a large inglenook fireplace which provides a home for various interesting artefacts. A good choice of beers includes a mix of local and regional brews.

Q🌼◐◑⛺♣🍎P🚌(540)🐾📶

Cheswardine

Fox & Hounds 𝕃

High Street, TF9 2RS (opp church)
⏲ 12-11.30; 11.30-midnight Sat ☎ (01630) 661244
Joule's Blonde, Pale Ale, Slumbering Monk; 2 changing beers (sourced regionally; often Joule's) Ⓗ
A traditional inn in this beautiful village offering Joule's well-kept ales, also serving a good selection of quality traditional food, ranging from sandwiches and baguettes to full hearty meals. The decor is tasteful and the lobby door incorporates an original Joule's etched window. There is a pub garden which is a suntrap when it shines.
Q❀◑♿♣●P

Clun

White Horse Inn 𝕃 ✔

The Square, SY7 8JA
⏲ 12-midnight ☎ (01588) 418128 🌐 whi-clun.co.uk
Clun Loophole, Clun Pale, Citadel; Hobsons Best; Wye Valley Butty Bach; 2 changing beers (often Salopian) Ⓗ
Sixteenth-century inn and post house standing in the old market square at the centre of a timeless town, described by AE Housman as one of 'the quietest places under the sun'. Inside is an L-shaped bar with low beams and an adjoining dining room serving excellent, reasonably priced food. Outside is a secluded garden. The pub has its own nanobrewery which has now grown up. Rotating real ciders are stocked. Jam nights are held once a month. ❀◑Ʌ♣●

Ellerdine Heath

Royal Oak 𝕃 ✔

Hazles Road, TF6 6RL (midway between A442 and A53)
SJ603226
⏲ 12-11 ☎ (01939) 250300
Hobsons Best; Rowton Star Light; Wye Valley HPA; 3 changing beers (sourced locally; often Rowton, Salopian) Ⓗ
This long-standing Guide entry, also known as The Tiddly, is a hub of the local rural community, used by young farmers, shooting parties and folk groups. Rallies are also hosted. Features include a pool table, dartboard, real fires in both main rooms, a smoking shed and a marquee Easter to October. Food is served in the dining room – lunchtimes weekends only and evenings Wednesday to Sunday. Q❀◑♿Ʌ♣●P

Little Stretton

Green Dragon

Ludlow Road, SY6 6RE
⏲ 11.30-11.30 ☎ (01694) 722925
🌐 greendragonlittlestretton.co.uk
Draught Bass; Ludlow Gold; Wye Valley Butty Bach; 2 changing beers (often Hobsons, Wye Valley) Ⓗ
The pub is set in a picturesque location in the Shropshire Hills Area of Outstanding Natural Beauty, with an abundance of walks in the district. The L-shaped bar has a comfortable and welcoming feel and the pleasant, separate dining room is well used. A collection of wonderfully shaped clay pipes on the bar wall may well be of interest. The beer is mostly from local breweries, as is the cider (at the appropriate time of year).
❀◑♣●P(435)

Little Wenlock

Huntsman Inn

Wellington Road, TF6 5BH
⏲ 11-11 (10.30 Sun) ☎ (01952) 503300
🌐 thehuntsmanoflittlewenlock.co.uk
Greene King Abbot; house beer (by Ruddles); 3 changing beers (sourced regionally; often Hobsons, Wood, Wye Valley) Ⓗ
Set in the village not far from The Wrekin, this recently refurbished pub has two bars, one with a real fire where walkers and dogs are welcome. There is also a separate restaurant, also with a real fire. Food is served in all rooms, from bar snacks to full meals, including weekly three-course specials and Sunday roasts. Accommodation is provided in three en-suite rooms and a field for camping, including a camper van hook-up.
Q◑♿ɅP

Ludlow

Queens 𝕃

113 Lower Galdeford, SY8 1RU (just off town centre, opp Co-op)
⏲ 12-11 (midnight Fri & Sat); 12-10.30 Sun
☎ (01584) 879177 🌐 thequeensludlow.com
Hobsons Best; Ludlow Gold; Wye Valley Butty Bach; 1 changing beer (sourced locally; often Hobsons, Ludlow) Ⓗ
Named after Queen Victoria, this is a popular pub and café bar with a decent range of local ales. Look out for the guest beer offered at a competitive price. The light and airy L-shaped bar has three distinct areas, with the dining space down a short flight of steps. Bar meals are available, with local produce a proud boast. The large, enclosed patio garden has views toward Ludford. The monthly quiz is always well attended. ❀◑♿≷♣

Railway Shed 𝕃

Station Drive, SY8 2PQ
⏲ 10-5 (6 Fri); 11-4 Sun ☎ (01584) 873291
🌐 theludlowbrewingcompany.co.uk
Ludlow Best, Blonde, Gold, Black Knight, Boiling Well, Stairway Ⓗ
The brewery tap and visitor centre for the Ludlow Brewing Company and, as the name suggests, the building was once a transit depot for railway goods. An imaginative conversion, it is built on two levels, with two huge mash tuns on the upper level, and more comfortable seating and tables. On the ground floor there are hand-crafted timber tables and benches, together with a shop. Brewery visits are welcome and the centre is available for hire. Q❀♿≷●P

Rose & Crown

8 Church Street, SY8 1AP
⏲ 11-11 (midnight Fri & Sat); 11-10.30 Sun
☎ (01584) 875726 🌐 roseandcrowninnludlow.co.uk
Joule's Blonde, Pale Ale, Slumbering Monk, Old No.6; 2 changing beers (often Hobsons, Hop Back) Ⓗ
Hidden away in a courtyard, the Rose & Crown is probably Ludlow's oldest inn, possibly 12th century. Recent refurbishment has created a much larger pub with exposed beams and a fireplace. The Sun Room is open to the elements on one side and there is a garden area. A private room upstairs is available to small groups. Food is good honest pub grub such as bangers and mash or bubble and squeak. There is a carvery on Sunday.
❀◑♿≷

Market Drayton

Hippodrome

Queen Street, TF9 1PS

8am-midnight (11 Sun) (01630) 650820

Greene King Abbot; Ruddles Best Bitter; 3 changing beers (sourced locally; often Lymestone, Slater's, Titanic)

Originally Market Drayton's first cinema, it opened its doors to the public in 1927 and closed in 1966. After spells as a bingo hall and supermarket, it became a Wetherspoon pub in 2007, retaining some unique features of the original building. The usual food fare is served, but what makes this pub different is that it actively supports local breweries and regularly showcases their beers on the bar.

Red Lion

Great Hales Street, TF9 1JP

11-11 (midnight Fri & Sat) (01630) 652602

Joule's Blonde, Pale Ale, Slumbering Monk; 5 changing beers (sourced locally; often Joule's)

A previous winner of the CAMRA/English Heritage Pub Design Award, this Joule's brewery tap was previously a coaching inn built in 1623. Its unique features include the Mouse Room, a Robert Thompson-inspired function room featuring carved mice, and an illuminated well in the main bar. Log fires and oak beams create a comfortable atmosphere where locally sourced food can be enjoyed from an extensive menu, with the Joule's range of beers brewed at the adjacent brewery. QP

Sandbrook Vaults

4 Shropshire Street, TF9 3BY

5-11; 12-midnight Fri & Sat; 11-11 Sun (01630) 478405

Joule's Blonde, Pale Ale, Slumbering Monk; 1 changing beer (often Joule's)

You are guaranteed a warm welcome at this Joule's pub, originally built in 1653. It has a familiar easy-on-the-eye Joule's interior and well-kept ales from the brewery close by. Free hot food is available at the weekend (with an optional donation to charity). The pub hosts high-quality live acoustic music nights on Thursday and Sunday featuring regional bands. Q

Newport

New Inn

2 Stafford Road, TF10 7LX

12-11.30 (01952) 812295 thenewinnnewport.co.uk

Joule's Blonde, Pale Ale, Slumbering Monk; 2 changing beers (sourced locally; often Joule's, Ludlow, Wood)

Reopened in 2016 and expanded in typical Joule's style, including wood panels, flooring and decoration, while retaining original features and log fires. A large beer garden with plenty of benches and beautiful borders complements the look. A full range of Joule's beers is served plus seasonal craft beers and one frequently changing guest ale. An excellent menu offers fresh home-cooked food. Q

Oswestry

Bailey Head

Bailey Head, SY11 1PZ (in Market Square opp Guildhall)

12 (3 Mon)-11.30; 12-12.30am Sat; 12-10.30 Sun

baileyhead.co.uk

5 changing beers (sourced nationally; often Oakham)

Near the old castle, The Bailey Head is a free house which opened in 2016. Five constantly changing real ales, three KeyKeg beers and draught cider are on offer. Beers are sourced locally, regionally and nationally, usually from microbreweries. Locally produced, traditional food is served until 10pm. The market car park is close by. Events include Meet the Brewer and quiz nights.

Black Lion

Salop Road, SY11 2RJ (S of town centre on B4579)

6-11; 4.30-midnight Fri; 12-midnight Sat; 12-11 Sun

(01691) 652745 theblacklionoswestry.co.uk

Salopian Oracle; 4 changing beers (sourced locally; often Hobsons, Salopian, Wood)

Just inside the town's conservation area, this family-run establishment is a true community pub and has a warm and friendly atmosphere. It is home to sports teams and social groups, with plenty of TVs for sports fans and tasting boards for beer lovers. The central bar divides the pub into a comfortable lounge at the front and public bar at the rear. Well-kept ales from various local and regional brewers can be enjoyed.
QP

Plough

Beatrice Street, SY11 1QE (nr bus station)

12-midnight (1am Sat)

Greene King Abbot; Sharp's Doom Bar; 4 changing beers (often Adnams, St Austell, Timothy Taylor)

A plain pub with two downstairs areas, one including the bar, and an upstairs games room. The Plough is on the edge of the town centre, with its own parking. A good range of real ales is available. Special events, especially live music, often feature. Prices are reduced on Monday. P

Queen's Head

Queen's Head

West Felton, SY11 4EB (next to Montgomery Canal)

12-11 (01691) 610255

the-queens-head-oswestry.co.uk

Church End Fallen Angel; Stonehouse Station Bitter, Off the Rails

This pub is primarily a dining venue with a pleasant bar area (meals are served noon-9pm). All beers are locally sourced, and Sweeney Mountain real cider is available. There is an attractive conservatory and the front patio has views over the canal. QP (70)

Selattyn

Cross Keys ★

SY10 7DN

closed Mon & Tue; 6-midnight; 12-midnight Sun

(01691) 653347

Stonehouse Station Bitter; Three Tuns XXX; 1 changing beer (sourced locally)

This 17th-century gem has been a pub since 1840 and has a nationally important historic interior. It is situated in a village close to the Welsh border and Offa's Dyke. The cosy small bar with its quarry-tiled floor and real fire is probably the soul of the pub, although original features in other rooms are being carefully restored by the owners.
QP

Shifnal

Plough Inn

26 Broadway, TF11 8AZ
12 (4.30 Mon)-11; 12-10.30 Sun ☎ (01952) 463118
theploughinnshifnal.co.uk
Hobsons Mild, Best; 6 changing beers (sourced regionally; often Bathams, Sarah Hughes, Six Bells)
Traditional, family-run free house dating back to the 17th century, with exposed beams and tiled floors. Eight handpulled ales including at least one strong and one dark beer are on offer, together with two ciders and Belgian bottles. Hearty home-cooked meals are served (no food Mon). A huge suntrap beer garden proves popular in warm weather, and a function room is available to hire. Work from local artists is on display and available to buy. The weekly Wednesday quiz night is popular. Q

White Hart

High Street, TF11 8BH
12-11 ☎ (01952) 461161
Greene King Abbot; Holden's Black Country Mild; Salopian Shropshire Gold; Wye Valley HPA, Butty Bach; 4 changing beers (sourced regionally; often Enville)
Grade II listed, 17th-century, timber-framed free house. A community-oriented, family-run establishment, it has knowledgeable staff offering great service, and is noted for the lunchtime food menu (not available Sun). Nine handpumps serve a good range of local and regional beers, with real ciders also available. Outside, there is a large car park, beer garden and sunny, walled patio area. Traditional values and good conversation abound.
Q P

Shrewsbury

Abbey

83 Monkmoor Road, Monkmoor, SY2 5AZ
12-11 (midnight Fri & Sat) ☎ (01743) 236788
theabbeyshrewsbury.co.uk
Bombardier; Sharp's Doom Bar; 4 changing beers
A large refurbished pub with several alcoves and multiple fireplaces and a comfortable and calm ambience. The Abbey's publican is an ale enthusiast, running frequent Meet the Brewer sessions and several beer festivals a year. In between, he has expanded the range of guest ales and real ciders. Food is served until 10pm every evening. There are regular community events including quizzes, and occasional live music.
P (1)

Admiral Benbow

24 Swan Hill, SY1 1NF (just off Main Square)
5-11; 12-11 Sat; 7-10.30 Sun ☎ (01743) 244423
Battlefield 1066; Ludlow Gold; Six Bells Sixth Sense; 2 changing beers (sourced locally)
Spacious free house serving a range of Shropshire and Herefordshire beers plus a selection of ciders from Rosie's including Black Bart and Wicked Wasp. A good choice of Belgian, American and other foreign beers is also offered. A small room off the bar can be used for private functions, and there is a seating and smoking area outside at the rear. Children are not permitted. The admiral was a notorious 17th-century naval officer born in Shrewsbury. Q

Coach & Horses

23 Swan Hill, SY1 1NF
11.30-midnight (12.30am Fri & Sat); 12-11.30 Sun
☎ (01743) 365661
Salopian Shropshire Gold, Oracle; Stonehouse Station Bitter; 3 changing beers
Set in a quiet street off the main shopping area, the pub is a peaceful haven, with magnificent floral displays in summer. Victorian in style, it has a wood-panelled bar, a small side snug area and a large lounge where meals are served lunchtimes and evenings. Bar snacks are also available at lunchtimes. Cheddar Valley or Sweeney Mountain cider is dispensed on handpull.
Q

Cross Foxes

27 Longden Coleham, SY3 7DE (close to River Severn in suburb of Longden Coleham)
11-midnight (11 Sun) ☎ (01743) 355050
Draught Bass; Salopian Shropshire Gold; Three Tuns XXX; Worthington's Bitter
The pub has been a free house since its purchase from Mitchells & Butlers in the late 1980s, and run by the same family since 1985. It has one large, L-shaped room, with the bar and major drinking area on the large stroke, the smaller stroke occupied by the darts and a smaller drinking area. The main area has an efficient woodburner and the walls are adorned with sports trophies and a fine Bass mirror. Q

Dolphin

48 St Michaels Street, SY1 2EZ
12-11 (10.30 Sun) ☎ (01743) 247005
Joule's Blonde, Pale Ale; 3 changing beers
Part of the Joule's sponsored estate, this end-of-terrace ale house is within easy walking distance of the railway station. A sympathetic refurbishment has retained the traditional atmosphere, with wooden floors, internal gas lighting and open fires. A pub for the community, folk music is hosted on the first and third Thursdays of the month, quiz and open mic sessions on the second and fourth Thursdays. Newspapers are usually available. A cider, often Westons, is served.
Q

Montgomery's Tower

Lower Claremont Bank, SY1 1RT
8am-midnight (1am Wed & Thu; 2am Fri & Sat)
☎ (01743) 239080
Greene King IPA; Salopian Shropshire Gold; Wood Shropshire Lad; 4 changing beers (often Sadler's, Sharp's, Slater's)
Close to the Quarry Park and handy for Theatre Severn, this Lloyds No.1 offers a choice of two bars. To the left is a large open area rich in natural light, with a smoking area to the rear. The bar to the right provides quieter surroundings and subdued lighting, except on Friday and Saturday when there is a DJ. The walls display prints illustrating local history and famous Salopians.

Nag's Head

22 Wyle Cop, SY1 1XB
11.30-midnight; 10.30-1am Fri; 12-midnight Sun
☎ (01743) 362455
Hobsons Best; Sharp's Doom Bar; Timothy Taylor Landlord; Wye Valley HPA; 1 changing beer (often Titanic)
Situated on the historic Wyle Cop, the main features of this Grade II listed, timber-framed

building are best appreciated externally – in particular the upper-storey jettying and, to the rear, the timber remnants of a 14th-century hall house including a screened passage which provided protection from draughts (and now offers shelter for smokers). The old-style interior has remained unaltered for many years. The pub is said to be haunted and features on the Shrewsbury Ghost Trail. ❀≹♣🚌🐾

Prince of Wales 𝕃

30 Bynner Street, Belle Vue, SY3 7NZ

⏲ 5-midnight; 12-midnight Fri-Sun ☎ (01743) 343301
🌐 theprince.pub

Greene King IPA; Hobsons Mild, Twisted Spire; St Austell Tribute; Salopian Golden Thread; Wainwright; 1 changing beer (sourced locally; often Rowton, Wood) Ⓗ

Welcoming two-roomed community pub with a heated smoking shelter and a large suntrap deck adjoining a bowling green. The green is overlooked by a 19th-century maltings. Darts, dominoes and bowls teams abound. Beer festivals take place each year in February and May. Shrewsbury Town FC memorabilia adorn the building both inside and out, with some of the seating from the old Gay Meadow ground skirting the bowling green. Westons Rosie's Pig is on handpull.
Q❀♿♣●P🚌🐾

Salopian Bar 𝕃 ✔

Smithfield Road, SY1 1PW

⏲ 11-midnight (11 Tue); 11-11 Sun ☎ (01743) 351505

Hobsons Best; Oakham Citra; Salopian Oracle; 5 changing beers (often Oakham, Salopian) Ⓗ

A single-room pub popular with all age groups. The bar's management strives to increase, and vary, the beer, cider and perry range to satisfy public demand. Regular cider and perry are provided by Westons and Thatchers, and a good range of bottled beer, including gluten-free, is also served. Large-screen TVs show coverage of major sporting events. Live music features on Friday evening.
♿≹●🚌🐾📶

Three Fishes 𝕃

4 Fish Street, SY1 1UR

⏲ 11.30-3, 5-11; 11.30-11.30 Fri & Sat; 12-10.30 Sun
☎ (01743) 344793 🌐 realaleshrewsbury.co.uk

Stonehouse Station Bitter; Three Tuns Stout; Timothy Taylor Landlord; 2 changing beers (often Oakham, Salopian) Ⓗ

Fifteenth-century building standing in the shadow of two churches, St Alkmund's and St Julian's, within the maze of streets and passageways in the town's medieval quarter. Freshly prepared food is available lunchtimes and early evenings Monday to Saturday. The pub offers a range of up to five local and national ales, usually including some dark beers, and a choice of real ciders and perries.
Q◐≹♣●🚌🐾📶

Woodman 𝕃

32 Coton Hill, SY1 2DZ

⏲ 4-midnight; 12-midnight Sat & Sun ☎ (01743) 351007

Salopian Shropshire Gold; Wye Valley Butty Bach; 3 changing beers (sourced regionally; often Abbeydale, Ossett) Ⓗ

Half-brick and half-timbered black & white corner pub, originally 19th century but rebuilt in 1925. The wonderful oak-panelled lounge has two real log fires and traditional settles, and the separate bar has the original stone-tiled flooring, wooden seating, fire and listed leaded windows. The courtyard has a heated smoking area and seating.
Q❀≹♣●🚌🐾📶

Stottesdon

Fighting Cocks 𝕃

1 High Street, DY14 8TZ

⏲ closed Mon; 12-2.30, 5-11.30; 12-11.30 Sat; 12-11 Sun
☎ (01746) 718270 🌐 fightingcocks.co.uk

Ludlow Blonde; Wye Valley Bitter, HPA, Butty Bach; 1 changing beer (sourced regionally; often Hobsons, St Austell, Three Tuns) Ⓗ

Set in the heart of rural south Shropshire, this local CAMRA award-winning pub was first licensed in 1830. Recently refurbished, the traditional bar with log fire leads to two dining rooms where locally sourced food is served. Live music features most weekends. Outside is a patio area and lawned garden with a children's play area. Walkers and cyclists are welcome. A community shop and café/ function room are also on the premises.
❀◐♿⛺♣●P🐾📶

Telford: Coalbrookdale

Coalbrookdale Inn 𝕃

12 Wellington Road, TF8 7DX (between traffic lights opp Enginuity Museum)

⏲ 4-11; 12-11 Sat; 12-10.30 Sun ☎ (01952) 432166

Hobsons Mild, Town Crier; Sarah Hughes Dark Ruby Mild; Wye Valley HPA; 4 changing beers (sourced regionally; often Plan B, Thornbridge, Wye Valley) Ⓗ

A Victorian Grade II listed village inn close to the Ironbridge Gorge World Heritage Site. This cosy pub has three rooms, two with real fires, where dogs and families are welcome. A community local, it offers darts, dominoes, a guitar club on Monday, ukulele night on Tuesday, a fortnightly quiz on Wednesday and occasional community dining nights. Simple bar snacks are available.
❀⛺♣●P🚌(9)🐾📶

Telford: Madeley

All Nations 𝕃

20 Coalport Road, TF7 5DP (signed off Legges Way, opp Blists Hill Museum)

⏲ 12-midnight ☎ (01952) 585747

Hobsons Twisted Spire; 2 changing beers (sourced regionally; often Hobsons, Ludlow, Wye Valley) Ⓗ

Cosy, traditional, two-roomed 1832 brewhouse with wooden beams and a warm, inviting fire in winter. The walls are decorated with old photographs, and original Jackfield tiles adorn the fireplace. In a secluded setting in the Ironbridge Gorge World Heritage Site, the pub welcomes families and dogs, and has an outside courtyard with seating. The 10-barrel brewhouse brews on Mondays and the bar usually serves two of its beers. Newspapers are available and there is a book exchange. Quiz night is Monday and live bands play May to July. Q❀🛏⛺P🐾

Telford: Oakengates

Crown Inn 𝕃 ✔

Market Street, TF2 6EA

⏲ 12-11 ☎ (01952) 610888 🌐 crown.oakengates.net

Hobsons Twisted Spire, Best; Purity Bunny Hop; 10 changing beers (sourced nationally; often Burton Bridge, Joule's, Rudgate) Ⓗ

Traditional town pub, warmed by real fires in the winter. Cask Marque-accredited, a mild and a stout or porter are often on the bar. Two beer festivals are held the first weekend of May and October when the number of pumps rises to 34. A good range of foreign bottled beers is also kept. The pub is home to Telford Comedy Club and Telford Acoustic Club, and features live music and a monthly quiz night. Food includes tasty pies and pasties, plus takeaways from the neighbouring Indian restaurant. **Q🧸❀♿⇌♣🍎P🚌🐾📶**

Old Fighting Cocks 🄻

48 Market Street, TF2 6DU (nr bus and train stations)
🕘 3.30-11; 12-11.30 Fri & Sat; 12-10.30 Sun
☎ (01952) 615607
Everards Tiger; Hop & Stagger Golden Wander, Pure Amber; 3 changing beers (sourced nationally; often Green Duck, Oakham, Purple Moose) 🄷
Old coaching inn on the former Watling Street. Twelve handpulls showcase beers from the Hop & Stagger Brewery alongside ales from local and national breweries up and down the country. The front bar has a newly installed open fire, while two log-burning stoves warm the back rooms. You are welcome to bring your own food – plates and cutlery provided. Upstairs, a function room for 60 people is available to hire. **Q🧸❀♿⇌♣🍎🚌🐾📶**

Station Hotel 🄻

42 Market Street, TF2 6DU
🕘 11-11 (9 Mon); 12-11 Sun ☎ (01952) 612949
Bathams Best Bitter; 8 changing beers (sourced nationally; often North Riding, Oakham, Salopian) 🄷
The landlord specialises in Yorkshire pale ales, but also sources locally and nationally. There is a real fire in the front room where drinkers can enjoy home-made bar snacks, pizzas and a Wednesday night curry. The Shropshire fidgets are recommended. Beer festivals with up to 12 pumps are held in May, August and November. Cider is available in the summer. **Q❀⇌♣🍎🚌🐾**

Telford: St Georges

St Georges Sports & Social Club

Church Road, St Georges, TF2 9LU
🕘 5-11; 12-midnight Sat; 12-11 Sun ☎ (01952) 612911
🌐 stgeorgesclub.co.uk
Banks's Mild; 5 changing beers (sourced regionally; often Hobsons, Ludlow, Salopian) 🄷
Private members' club where the spacious lounge bar shows live sport on two screens and has views of the sports fields. Six handpulls dispense mostly regional beers. Home-cooked food is served, with a roast on Sunday. A large function room is available for weddings and parties, with a bespoke bar and on-site catering services. CAMRA members are welcome at all times. **🧸❀◐◑♿P🚌📶**

Telford: Wellington

Cock Hotel 🄻

148 Holyhead Road, TF1 2DL
🕘 4 (12 Thu)-11.30; 12-11.45 Fri & Sat; 12-11 Sun
☎ (01952) 244954 🌐 cockhotel.co.uk
Hobsons Mild, Best; 5 changing beers (sourced regionally; often Holden's, Six Bells) 🄷
A friendly and comfortable award-winning 18th-century coaching inn with eight handpulls dispensing mostly regional ales, including a dark beer and a real cider. The large main room has the bar and a fire in winter, while the smaller front room provides more seating. A rear semi-covered courtyard is used by smokers. Award-winning pork pies are served from the bar. B&B accommodation and a meeting room are available. There is no music or TV, just interesting conversation and good ales. **Q❀🛏♣🍎P🚌(4)🐾📶**

Pheasant Inn 🄻

54 Market Street, TF1 1DT
🕘 11-11 (midnight Fri & Sat); 12-10.30 Sun
☎ (01952) 260683
Everards Tiger; Rowton Ironbridge Gold, Area 51; 5 changing beers (sourced regionally; often Oakham, Rowton, Wye Valley) 🄷
Family-run Rowton Brewery Tap with nine handpulls on the bar, three devoted to Rowton's own ales. The traditional pub has a large single-room interior with individual alcoves. There is no electronic ephemera so conversation prevails. The large suntrap beer garden at the rear has a covered smoking area. You can enjoy home-made food Monday to Saturday 11am-4pm plus bar snacks at any time. Situated opposite the market and next to a large public car park. **Q❀◐♿⇌🍎P🚌🐾📶**

Upper Farmcote

Lion O'Morfe 🏆 🄻

WV15 5PS (½ mile from A458 signpost Claverley)
SO770919
🕘 12-11.30 ☎ (01746) 389935
Enville Ale; Hobsons Town Crier; Wye Valley HPA; 2 changing beers (sourced regionally) 🄷
A Georgian farmhouse until 1850, this friendly old pub is situated in the countryside a few miles east of Bridgnorth. A warm welcome is assured for regulars and visitors including walkers and cyclists. Bar snacks and light lunches are served 12-3pm. There are open fires in the winter and a beer garden for the summer, including a boules piste adjacent to the large car park. **Q🧸❀⛺♣🍎P🐾📶**

Whitchurch

Black Bear 🄻

High Street, SY13 1AZ
🕘 12-3, 6 (5 Fri)-11; 12-11 Sat; 12-10.30 Sun
☎ (01948) 663800 🌐 blackbearpub.co.uk
Purple Moose Ochr Tywyll y Mws/Dark Side of the Moose; Salopian Shropshire Gold; Stonehouse Station Bitter; 3 changing beers (often Hobsons, Reunion, Three Tuns) 🄷
A tastefully renovated black & white pub opposite the historic St Alkmund's Church at the top of the High Street. The ornate bar here has six handpulls serving a range of guest beers both from local and lesser-known national microbreweries, with pumpclips adorning the walls, ceiling and bar area. Cider is served on gravity. There are two separate dining areas and an upstairs meeting room. **Q❀◐◑🍎P🚌🐾**

> A fine beer may be judged with only a sip, but it's better to be thoroughly sure.
> **Czech proverb**

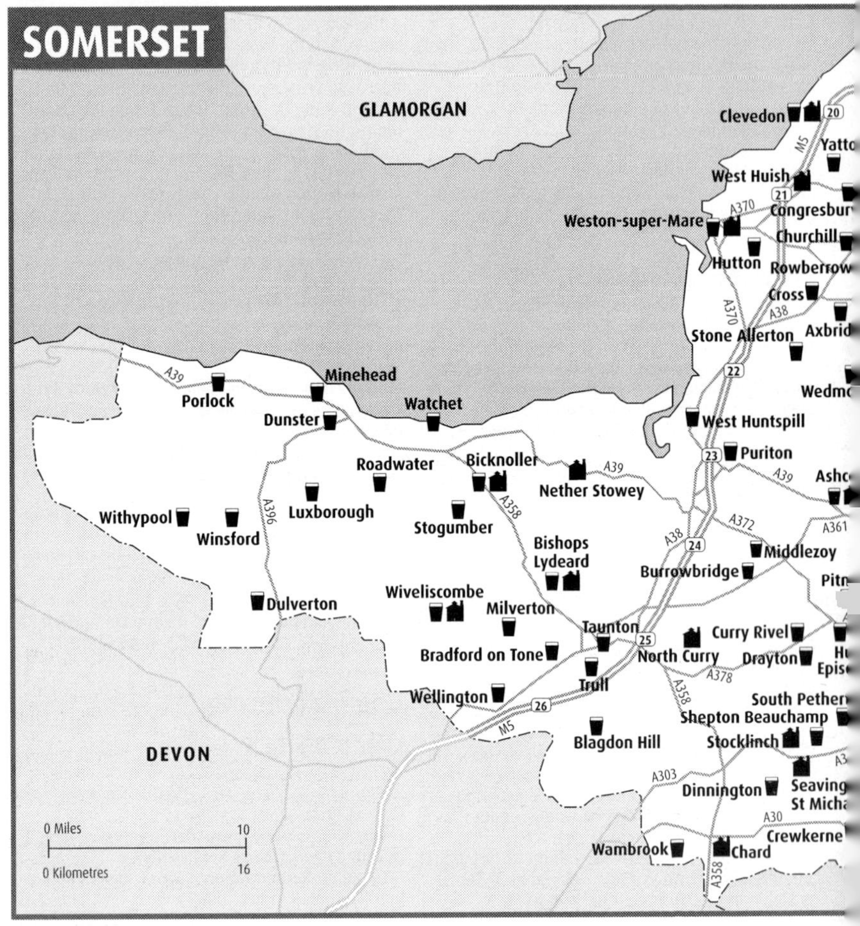

Ash

Bell Inn 𝕃

3 Main Street, TA12 6NS

12-11; 12-10 Sun ☎ (01935) 822727

thebellinnash.co.uk

Sharp's Doom Bar; 3 changing beers (sourced nationally; often Eagle, Exmoor, St Austell) Ⓗ

The Bell continues to be a warm, welcoming traditional pub with four ale handpumps and a real cider or two. A wide menu choice of locally sourced, home-cooked meals is served, featuring blackboard specials and a Sunday roast. Occasional live music nights and regular open mic nights are popular. The skittle alley doubles up as a function room. It is possible to camp at the pub by prior arrangement. Q❀◑♿⛺♣●P🚌(52)🐾

Ashcott

Ring o' Bells

16 High Street, TA7 9PZ (signposted off A39)

12-2.30, 7-11; 12-2.30, 7-10.30 Sun ☎ (01458) 210232

ringobells.com

2 changing beers (sourced regionally; often Cheddar Ales, Pitchfork, Teignworthy) Ⓗ

An 18th-century free house, in the same family ownership for 30 years. The pub comprises three traditional areas on split levels, with a separate restaurant. Old beams and fireplaces provide a warm ambience. There is a contrasting modern skittle alley/function room at the rear and an enclosed garden. Good home-cooked food is served, with meals and ales available to take away. Wilkins cider is on tap. It has regular live music and a monthly pub quiz night. Close to Ham Wall and Shapwick Heath nature reserves. ❀◑♿⛺♣●P🚌(29,75)🐾

Axbridge

Lamb ✔

The Square, BS26 2AP

11.30-11 (midnight Fri & Sat); 12-11 Sun

☎ (01934) 732253

Butcombe Original; 2 changing beers (often Butcombe) Ⓗ

Lovely Butcombe-owned Grade II-listed coaching house in the village square. Inside is a large low-beamed bar area with several smaller, quieter areas leading off it, where traditional pub games can be played. Outside drinking spaces are to the front, as well as to the rear via the courtyard. Several real ciders are sold and there is an interesting food menu. The National Trust's medieval King John's Hunting Lodge lies directly opposite, where Hanging Judge Jeffreys held court. Q❀◑♿♣●🚌(26,126)🐾

Batcombe

Three Horseshoes Inn

BA4 6HE (off Back Lane) ST69023908

11-3, 6-11; 11-11 Sat; 12-10.30 Sun ☎ (01749) 850359

thethreehorseshoesinn.co.uk

Butcombe Original; 3 changing beers Ⓗ

A 400-year-old country pub which has a spacious bar with an inglenook fireplace and beamed ceiling, a stunning dining room with a vaulted ceiling, and a lawned garden overlooked by the church tower. Food is from local suppliers. Open to all, it welcomes drinkers, foodies, walkers, children (with colouring books and games to keep them entertained) and dogs. Local cider is from Rich's. **Q**

Bath

Bath Brew House ✔

14 James Street West, BA1 2BX

12-midnight (1am Fri & Sat); 12-11 Sun

☎ (01225) 805609 thebathbrewhouse.com

James Street Gladiator, Emperor; 5 changing beers (sourced regionally; often Bristol Beer Factory, Castle Combe, James Street) Ⓗ

Refurbishment in 2013 saw the former Midland Hotel transformed into a City Pub Company brewpub. The on-site James Street Brewery produces two regular beers, the refreshing and malty Gladiator (3.9% ABV) and the hoppy, citrussy Emperor (4.4% ABV), and rotating seasonal beers. Five guests, usually from nearby micros, are complemented by four craft beers. A large L-shaped bar leads to a dining area and a good-sized beer garden. The upstairs room hosts sports TV, quizzes, comedy and the like.

Coeur de Lion ✔

17 Northumberland Place, BA1 5AR

11-11.30 (12.30am Sat); 12-6 Sun ☎ (01225) 463568

coeur-de-lion.co.uk

Abbey Bath Best, Bellringer; 2 changing beers (sourced nationally; often St Austell) Ⓗ

In a passageway opposite the Guildhall in the centre of town, this pub claims to be the smallest in Bath. With just four tables in the small bar, this may well be true. Traditional pub food is served at lunchtime. Seating capacity is increased in summer by placing tables outside. There is also an upstairs room used mainly for food. The pub's most unique feature is the fine stained-glass window that forms its frontage. **Q**

Cross Keys ✔

Midford Road, Combe Down, BA2 5RZ

12-3, 5-11; 12-midnight Fri & Sat; 12-11 Sun

☎ (01225) 832002 crosskeysbath.co.uk

Butcombe Original; Sharp's Doom Bar; 2 changing beers (sourced locally) Ⓗ

Historic inn dating from 1718 on the southern outskirts of the city, close to the beautiful Midford valley and popular with walkers. It features four ales, including guests often from a local brewery of the month range of ales. Highly recommended, gastro standard, home-made food is available at all sessions. The main bar on the left still has many original features and an open fire. The restaurant is on the right and split across three levels. Parking can be restricted. **P** (3,267)

REAL ALE BREWERIES

Abbey Bath
Albion Bath (brewing suspended)
Beat North Curry
Black Bear Wiveliscombe
Blindmans Leighton
Butcombe Wrington
Cheddar Cheddar
Cotleigh Wiveliscombe
Electric Bear Bath
Epic Beers (Pitchfork/3D Beers) West Huish (NEW)
Exmoor Wiveliscombe
Fine Tuned Somerton
Glastonbury Somerton
Glede Clevedon
Isle of Avalon Ashcott
James Street Bath
Milk Street Frome
Odcombe Odcombe
Patriot Bicknoller
Quantock Bishops Lydeard
Ralph's Ruin Bath
RPM Weston-super-Mare (brewing suspended)
Stocklinch Stocklinch
Stowey Nether Stowey
Tapstone Chard
Twisted Oak Wrington
Wild Beer Evercreech
Windy Seavington St Michael
Yeovil Yeovil

Griffin Inn

Monmouth Street, BA1 2AP
12-11; 12-10 Sun (01225) 420919
thegriffinbath.co.uk
Bristol Beer Factory Nova; Timothy Taylor Boltmaker; 4 changing beers (sourced regionally; often Bristol Beer Factory, Electric Bear) H
Grade II-listed inn refurbished in a modern minimalist style. The bar offers up to six real ales, many from regional microbreweries, and two draught ciders. A range of craft beers is also on tap. Local breweries hold tap takeovers on occasion. The two rooms provide ample space and reveal the internal fabric of this Georgian building. Popular with a varied clientele, it has an urban café-bar feel mixed with that of a friendly local. Four-star accommodation includes eight (mostly en-suite) bedrooms. Q

Old Green Tree ★

12 Green Street, BA1 2JZ
11-11; 12-6 Sun (01225) 448259
Butcombe Original; Pitchfork Golden Ale; house beer (by Blindmans); 3 changing beers (sourced locally) H
A classic, unspoilt pub in a 300-year-old building. The three oak-panelled rooms include a superb northern-style drinking lobby. Although the pub can get crowded, there is often space in the comfortable back bar. Guest beers are generally from local microbreweries, with a stout or porter usually on offer in the winter months. A local farmhouse cider is also available, along with a range of fine wines and malt whiskies. Winter Sunday hours may be extended. Q

Pig & Fiddle

2 Saracen Street, BA1 5BR
11-11.30 (midnight Fri & Sat); 12-10.30 Sun
(01225) 460868
Butcombe Original; Fuller's London Pride; 3 changing beers (sourced nationally; often Butcombe, Marble, Thornbridge) H
A large and busy town-centre pub with a varied clientele and a friendly atmosphere. One end is an old shop front, the other a courtyard with drinking benches and covered heaters. The decor is an esoteric collection of art displays and sports memorabilia. Up to three guest beers come from local breweries. Table football is played, and there are regular live music and open mic nights. The pub is popular with rugby fans and has several large TV screens.

Pulteney Arms

37 Daniel Street, BA2 6ND (on corner of Daniel St and Sutton St)
12-11 (midnight Thu-Sat); 12-10.30 Sun
(01225) 463923 thepulteneyarms.co.uk
Box Steam Piston Broke; Exmoor Ale; Skinner's Cornish Knocker; Timothy Taylor Landlord; 1 changing beer (sourced nationally) H
Tucked away near the end of Great Pulteney Street, the Pulteney Arms has been open since 1792. There are five gas light fittings (now sadly condemned) above the bar. The decor shows an emphasis on sport, particularly rugby. The cat symbol on the pub sign refers to the Pulteney coat of arms. The food menu is extensive and deservedly popular (no food Sun eves). The guest beer is usually from a national brewery. (Note winter hours: pub closed 3-5pm Monday-Thursday.)

Raven

6-7 Queen Street, BA1 1HE
11.30-11 (midnight Fri & Sat); 12-10.30 Sun
(01225) 425045 theravenofbath.co.uk
House beer (by Blindmans); 4 changing beers (sourced regionally; often Cotswold Lion, Moles) H
A busy 18th-century free house in the heart of Bath, voted the local CAMRA branch's Pub of the Year in 2018. The six ales include two brewed exclusively by Blindmans. Guest ales come from far and wide, with several mini beer festivals a year. The main bar and the quieter first-floor bar serve the same range of ales. Famous for its sausages and Pieminister pies, the Raven is one of the few pubs in Bath serving food on Sunday evening.
Q

Royal Oak

Lower Bristol Road, Twerton, BA2 3BW (on A36 at intersection with road to Windsor Bridge)
2-midnight; 12-1am Fri & Sat; 12-midnight Sun
(01225) 481409 theroyaloakbath.co.uk
Downton IPA; Ralph's Ruin Sirius, Dark Side of the Ralph; 5 changing beers (often Butts, Downton, Stonehenge) H
Two regulars from Butts Brewery, one from Downton, some from its own brewery, Ralph's Ruin, and up to five guest beers from microbreweries near and far are served here alongside an interesting range of ciders, perries and bottled beers. Live music is staged on Wednesday evenings and most weekends, while Tuesday is quiz night. It has a small secluded garden and a small park. Occasional beer festivals are held. Local CAMRA City Pub of the Year 2017.
P

Salamander

3 John Street, BA1 2JL
11-11 (midnight Fri & Sat); 11-10 Sun (01225) 428889
Bath Ales Special Pale Ale, Gem, Barnsey; St Austell Proper Job; 1 changing beer (sourced locally; often Bath Ales, Beerd) H
An 18th-century building, tucked away in a side street, that opened as a coffee bar in 1957 and got a pub licence five years later. Taken over by Bath Ales in around 2000 and revamped in the company's inimitable style, it looks and feels like a pub that has been there for a century or more. Wooden floorboards, wood panelling and subdued lighting add to the ambience of the ground-floor bar, created from several small rooms. A popular restaurant is upstairs.

Star Inn ★

23 Vineyards, BA1 5NA
12-2.30, 5.30-midnight; 12-1am Fri & Sat; 12-midnight Sun
(01225) 425072
Abbey Bellringer G**; Draught Bass; 3 changing beers (sourced nationally; often Adnams, Skinner's)** H
A main outlet for Abbey Ales, this classic town pub was fitted out by Gaskell and Chambers in 1928. Its four small rooms have benches around the walls, wood panelling and roaring fires. The smallest room has a single bench, called Death Row, while the pub itself, which dates from around 1760, is coffin shaped. Abbey Bellringer is served from the cask and complimentary snuff is available. Cheese night is every Thursday and live music features on Fridays from 8.30pm. Q

Bicknoller

Bicknoller Inn

32 Church Lane, TA4 4EL (off A358 SE of Williton)
11.30-3, 6-11; 11.30-11.30 Sat; 12-10 Sun
(01984) 656234 thebicknollerinn.co.uk
Palmers Copper Ale, Dorset Gold, 200, Tally Ho! H
Set in the centre of a delightful village, this Palmers Brewery pub has small rooms off the main bar and a restaurant at the back. There is a large courtyard outside for a pleasant summer tipple. Charity and themed nights feature on the events calendar. The pub runs two boules teams and five skittles teams. Fish and chips night is popular on a Tuesday. There is a TV for selected sporting events. Q P (28)

Bishops Lydeard

Bird in Hand

34 Mount Street, TA4 3LH (signposted off A358 Taunton to Minehead road)
12-11 (01823) 432090
Sharp's Doom Bar; 4 changing beers (sourced regionally; often Exmoor, Otter, St Austell) H
A free house that is very much a community pub at the centre of the village, and 10 minutes' walk from West Somerset Railway. Five ales are served, from local and South-West breweries. The slate-floored bar warmed by an open fire in winter leads to a dining area. Good locally produced and home-cooked food is served. The skittle alley hosts functions. Families and dogs are welcome in the pub and large garden. Sport is shown on the TV in the bar. Q P (28)

Quantock Brewery Tap

Westridge Way, Broadgauge Business Park, TA4 3RU (follow signs to West Somerset Railway WSR and shop can be found on left just before railway station)
10-5.30 (10 Fri & Sat); closed Sun (01823) 433812
Quantock Ale, QPA, Wills Neck, Nightjar; 2 changing beers (sourced nationally) H
Spacious brewery taproom showcasing brewery beers and guests from near and far. In addition to cask ales there is also a brewery shop for takeaway bottles and other brewery gifts. An annual beer festival takes place in July. Opening hours may vary to include Sundays and bank holidays when there are railway events (check Facebook for details). Street food is available Friday and Saturday evenings. Close to West Somerset Steam Railway. P (28)

Blagdon Hill

Lamb & Flag

TA3 7SL (4 miles S of Taunton on unclassified road via Trull)
5-10 Mon; 12-10.30; 12-11 Fri & Sat; 12-7 Sun
(01823) 421893 thelambandflag.com
Exmoor Ale; Quantock Wills Neck; St Austell Proper Job; 1 changing beer (sourced regionally) H
Dating from 1705, the pub can be found at the foot of Blagdon Hill and is a great location for walking, cycling and horse riding. It has undergone a recent refurbishment but still retains originality, with some 16th-century wooden beams, traditional furniture and a double-sided fireplace. You are assured of a friendly welcome here and fine locally sourced food is cooked to order. As well as the ales, there is an excellent collection of malt whiskies and gins. Q P

Bradford on Tone

White Horse Inn

Regent Street, TA4 1HF (off A38 between Taunton and Wellington)
12-3 (not Mon), 6.30-11; 12-3, 6-11 Fri & Sat; 11.30-10.30 Sun (01823) 461239 whitehorseinn.co
3 changing beers (sourced regionally; often Hanlons, Otter, St Austell) H
A friendly village freehold pub but also a local hub, housing the community-run local shop in the outbuildings. Real fires in winter warm both the bar and restaurant. Three beers are sourced locally and regionally and a real cider is available. The beautiful large garden hosts barbecues in summer and the excellent food comes from local suppliers and is home-cooked. Regular events include music and quiz nights. Closes at 5pm on a Sunday from October till April. P

Burrowbridge

King Alfred Inn

Burrow Drove, TA7 0RB (on A361, 9 miles from Taunton)
12-11; 12-9 Sun (01823) 698379 king-alfred.co.uk
Butcombe Adam Henson's Rare Breed, Original; Otter Amber; 1 changing beer (sourced nationally) H
A welcoming old-fashioned free house on the Somerset Levels north-east of Taunton, under the shadow of Burrow Mump, where allegedly King Alfred famously burnt the cakes. It is a perfect stopping-off point for walkers on the River Parrett Trail. Good locally sourced seasonal food includes excellent-value hearty weekday lunches and a Friday fish supper (no food Sun eves). Local ciders come from Burrow Hill and Parsons Choice. Quiz night is the first Tuesday of the month. Coaches are welcome by arrangement.
P (29)

Butleigh

Rose & Portcullis

Sub Road, BA6 8TQ (on crossroads at S side of village)
5.30-11 Mon; 12-3, 5.30 (5 Fri)-11; 12-3, 7-10 Sun
(01458) 850287 rose-and-portcullis.co.uk
Otter Bitter; 4 changing beers (sourced nationally; often Butcombe, Oakham, Timothy Taylor) H
A warm welcome awaits you at this blue lias stonework hostelry where you will find flagstone floors and real fires. There are some fascinating old pub games such as London five board (darts), Irish rings and Dutch shuffle board, which are great fun. It is very much a rugby pub, frequented by members of the local amateur club, who enjoy the rugby matches shown on TV. A beer festival is hosted in May. Closed Monday lunchtimes in the winter months. Q P (667)

Cheddar

White Hart

The Bays, BS27 3QN
10-midnight (1.30am Fri & Sat); 10-11.30 Sun
(01934) 741261 thewhitehartcheddar.co.uk
Butcombe Original; St Austell Tribute; 1 changing beer (often Cheddar Ales) H
A traditional country pub at the bottom of Cheddar Gorge in a quiet street just off the main road through the gorge. Its location, hidden away from the tourist attractions, means it can be more

relaxed than other pubs in the village. Good food is served daily from 10am, with a popular carvery on Sunday. There is a large upstairs function room and a pleasant garden to the side. ⚲❀◑⛺●P🐾ᯤ

Churchill

Crown Inn

The Batch, Skinners Lane, BS25 5PP (off A38, 400yds S of A368 jct)
11-11; 12-11 Sun ☎ (01934) 852995
the-crown-inn.co.uk
Bath Ales Gem; Butcombe Original; Otter Bitter; Palmers IPA; St Austell Tribute; 2 changing beers [G]
Long-time Guide regular and winner of many CAMRA awards, the pub is tucked away down a small lane yet close to the village centre. Several cosy rooms with stone-flagged floors are warmed by two log fires and offer an assortment of seating. Excellent food is provided at lunchtimes using local ingredients. Up to eight beers, usually local, are served on gravity. Outside drinking areas are to the front and rear. Families are welcome away from the bar itself. A classic, unchanged old pub; cash only, no cards. Q⚲❀◑⛺●P🚌(A2)🐾

Clevedon

Royal Oak ✔

35 Copse Road, BS21 7QN (behind ice cream parlour near pier)
12-11 (midnight Fri & Sat) ☎ (01275) 563879
theroyaloakclevedon.co.uk
Butcombe Original; St Austell Tribute; Sharp's Atlantic, Doom Bar; 1 changing beer [H]
Lively, friendly, mid-terrace pub close to the seafront and connected via an alley. It has a large front window and an unexpectedly spacious interior with many rooms. This community hub is home to cribbage and cricket teams. A winner of various awards, it hosts many events, including cooking competitions and dancing, ranging from morris men through belly dance to Zulus. There is a quiz on Monday and folk music on Wednesday. Thatchers cider is sold. Q⚲◑♣●🚌(X5,X6)🐾ᯤ

Congresbury

Plough

High Street, BS49 5JA (off A370 at B3133 jct)
11.30-2.30, 4.30-11; 12-2.30, 7-10.30 Sun
☎ (01934) 877402 the-plough-inn.net
Butcombe Original; St Austell Tribute [H]/[G]; Twisted Oak Fallen Tree [G]; 5 changing beers (sourced locally) [H]/[G]
Characterful village pub with flagstone floors and many original features, decorated with interesting local artefacts. Five guest beers, mainly from local breweries, are delivered from a row of old cask heads behind the bar. Up to 16 ciders are also stocked. Food is served lunchtime and evening, except Sunday evening, which is quiz night. The pub has real fires and a large garden. Mendip morris men meet here.
Q❀◑♿♣●P🚌(X1,353)🐾

Crewkerne

King William Inn

Barn Street, TA18 8BP (take A30 towards Chard and, at fringe of town, uphill, Barn St is on left)
5-midnight; 12-midnight Sat; 12-4 Sun ☎ (01460) 279615
3 changing beers (sourced nationally; often Bristol Beer Factory, Butcombe, Oakham) [H]
A short walk from the town centre towards Chard takes you to this traditional pub. The three changing guest ales are mainly from regional breweries but may also come from further afield. Beer festivals are held in May and at the end of September. There are happy hours on Monday and Wednesday, and for music lovers there is an acoustic night on the last Wednesday of each month. The TV has terrestrial and BT Sport.
⚲❀♣●P🚌🐾

Croscombe

George Inn

Long Street, BA5 3QH (on A371 between Wells and Shepton Mallet)
7.30-3, 6-11; 7.30-3, 5-midnight Fri; 7.30-midnight Sat & Sun ☎ (01749) 342306 thegeorgeinn.co.uk
House beer (by Blindmans) [H]; 3 changing beers (often Arbor, Cheddar Ales, Yeovil) [H]/[G]
Attractive 17th-century inn refurbished by the owner, serving at least four guest ales from West Country independents and hosting two beer festivals a year. Blindmans King George and George and Dragon are exclusively brewed for the pub. Four real ciders are stocked, with Hecks Kingston Black, Thatchers Cheddar Valley and Orchard Pig the regulars. It has a large main bar, a snug with a fireplace, a family room and a separate dining room. Food is home-cooked using locally sourced ingredients in the modern theatre kitchen. A skittle alley/meeting room is to the rear, and it has a large garden with a covered terrace.
Q⚲❀🛏◑♿♣●P🚌🐾ᯤ

Cross

New Inn ✔

Old Coach Road, BS26 2EE (on A38/A361 jct)
12-11 (midnight Fri & Sat) ☎ (01934) 732455
newinncross.co.uk
Otter Bitter, Ale; 4 changing beers [H]
A 17th-century roadside inn on the A38, close to the historic medieval town of Axbridge. It is popular for its extensive food menu served all day until 9pm (8pm Sun) and its beer festivals on Easter and August bank holidays. Four guest beers, often rare for the area, are usually available. There is a function room on the first floor. Families are welcome – dogs too. The large hillside garden with children's play facilities offers a fine view of the Mendip Hills and Somerset Levels. There is a small car park opposite. ⚲❀◑♣P🚌(126)🐾ᯤ

Curry Rivel

Firehouse

Church Street, TA10 0HE (Church St is off A378 Langport to Wrantage Road)
12-11; 11-10 Sun ☎ (01458) 887447
thefirehousesomerset.co.uk
Butcombe Adam Henson's Rare Breed, Original; 4 changing beers (often Exmoor, Oakham, Otter) [H]
This enticing village hostelry has been beautifully restored with a modern twist and yet is also packed with traditional charm. On the left when entering is the house bar which serves up to six real ales with four changing choices. In addition there is real cider from local producers. Leading off from the bar are five further sitting/dining areas

arranged over three floors, with wood-burning stoves in abundance. Well worth a visit in this delightful village. (54)

Dinnington

Dinnington Docks Inn

TA17 8SX (approx 3 miles E of Ilminster off B3168)
12-3, 5.30-11; 11.30-11 Fri & Sat; 12-10.30 Sun
(01460) 52397
Butcombe Original; Teignworthy Gun Dog; 1 changing beer (sourced regionally; often Otter, Teignworthy, Yeovil) H
This is very much a traditional country pub where the conversation will not be interrupted by fruit machines or music. The three cask ales are served in excellent condition and the meals are prepared to order from the blackboard menu above the fireplace. A garden with trestle tables can be found at the rear of the pub. There is an abundance of railway memorabilia including a spoof illustration of an old rail crossing outside. QP

Draycott

Cider Barn

Latches Lane Crossroads, Draycott Road, BS27 3RU
12-10 (11 Thu-Sat) (01934) 741837
3 changing beers H/G
Quirky, relaxing bar, café and takeaway cider and ale barn on the main A371 near Cheddar, where you can also buy coffee, tea and cakes, simple locally sourced home-cooked food and great little snacks (Somerset tapas!). Up to 13 real ciders and three usually local real ales are served, two on gravity. There is live music every other Sunday afternoon. The bar sometimes stays open until 11pm. Caravan electric hook-up and camping are available. QP(126)

Drayton

Drayton Crown

Church Street, TA10 0JY (in centre of village near church)
closed Mon winter; 11-11 (01458) 250712
thedraytoncrown.co.uk
Butcombe Original; Timothy Taylor Landlord; 2 changing beers (sourced nationally; often Butcombe, Fuller's) H
This pub has undergone a rather splendid two-year refurbishment but has retained character, with flagstone floors and beams. Locally sourced food is provided from a modern kitchen and there is a new skittle alley/function room. The outside area has been vastly improved with lots of seating, a large deck, increased parking capacity and a lawn area. There are four en-suite high-quality B&B rooms. Opens on a Monday in summer.
P

Dulverton

Bridge Inn L

20 Bridge Street, TA22 9HJ
11-11 (01398) 324130 thebridgeinndulverton.com
Exmoor Ale; 3 changing beers (sourced regionally; often Burning Sky, Butcombe, Dark Star) H
A warm, welcoming pub dating from 1845, in a delightful small town. As the name implies, it is close to a bridge crossing the River Barle upstream from its confluence with the River Exe. The pub has a cosy single-room bar with a wood-burning stove and an extended restaurant area. There is always an interesting selection of national cask ales, and bottled beers include a Belgian selection. Check on the website for restricted opening hours in winter.
QP

Dunster

Luttrell Arms Hotel

36 High Street, TA24 6SG
10-11.30 (01643) 821555 luttrellarms.co.uk
Exmoor Ale; Otter Amber; 2 changing beers (sourced locally) H
The hotel, with its 28 beautiful bedrooms, is on the site of three ancient houses dating back to 1443. The back bar has an open log fire and features some of the oldest glass windows in Somerset; there is also fine plasterwork on the lounge ceiling. You can dine in the à la carte restaurant or, if you prefer, order a bar snack. The view of Dunster Castle from the back garden is wonderful. Mini beer and cider festivals are held.
Q(28,198)

East Harptree

Castle of Comfort

Old Bristol Road, BS40 6DD (on B3134 just N of jct with B3135)
12-3, 6-11 (01761) 221321 thecastleofcomfort.co.uk
Butcombe Original; Sharp's Doom Bar; 1 changing beer H
Splendid sprawling, isolated inn on the Mendip Hills, within reach by car of both Cheddar Gorge and Wookey Hole caves, and 1½ miles from a campsite. The name is believed to derive from the time when the pub housed condemned criminals on their last night. A hostelry since 1684, it is popular for locally sourced, generously portioned food. One guest beer features regularly from the South-West and sometimes further afield. The child-friendly garden is busy in summer.
QP

Faulkland

Tucker's Grave ★

BA3 5XF
12-3 (not Mon), 6-11; 12-3, 6-10 Sun 07921 140638
tuckersgraveinn.co.uk
Butcombe Original G
A gem from a bygone age, with a nationally important historic pub interior, this pub was built in the mid 17th century and has changed little since. It was named after Tucker, who hanged himself close by and was buried at the crossroads outside, and featured in a song by The Stranglers. There is no bar; the beers and Thatchers cider are served from an alcove. Shove-ha'penny is played and there is a skittle alley. Camping is planned from summer 2018. QP

Frome

Griffin

Milk Street, BA11 3DB
5-11; 4-1am Fri; 3-1am Sat; 1-9 Sun (01373) 467766
fromegriffin.co.uk
Milk Street Same Again, Funky Monkey, The Usual, Beer; 2 changing beers (sourced nationally; often Milk Street) H

Situated in the part of Frome known as Trinity, the Griffin is the brewery tap for Milk Street Brewery, now located on the edge of town. A wide range of ales is produced along with seasonals and specials. The single bar retains original features such as etched windows and a wooden floor. Regular quiz nights and live music take place. The small garden is open all year. Food is limited to Wednesday world food nights and Sunday lunches.
❀◖◗P🚌(184)🐾📶

Three Swans

16-17 King Street, BA11 1BH
🕒 4.30-11; 12-11 Fri-Sun ☎ (01373) 452009
🌐 threeswans.pub
Abbey Bellringer; Butcombe Original; 1 changing beer (sourced regionally; often Butcombe) Ⓗ
A 17th-century, Grade II-listed, two-bar pub in the centre of Frome. Extensively refurbished in 2013, it has a comfortable and inviting feel, quirky and traditional. The interior is heated by traditional gas burners, while paintings and various ornaments adorn the walls. The back door leads out to a beautiful secluded courtyard. There is also an upstairs function room. Home-made pies are available on Fridays and at weekends, plus Sunday lunch. Expect a welcome from the friendly dogs.
🐎❀◖🚌🐾📶

Glastonbury

Hawthorns Hotel

8-12 Northload Street, BA6 9JJ (at bottom of Glastonbury High St turn into Northload St at Market Cross)
🕒 6-11 (11.30 Tue & Thu); 12-11.30 Fri & Sat; 12-11 Sun
☎ (01458) 831255 🌐 hawthornshotel.com
2 changing beers (often Fine Tuned, Glastonbury, Pitchfork) Ⓗ
Quirky hotel and bar in the centre of this historical town within walking distance of Glastonbury Tor and Glastonbury Abbey. A well-known music venue with an open mic session on a Tuesday, it also has a blues jam on a Sunday and regular music on Friday nights. It is famous for producing authentic curries from around the world and the Sunday carvery is popular. In May there is a well-supported beer festival with 20 ales and six ciders.
🐎❀🛏◖◗♣🍎P🚌🐾📶

Henstridge

Bird in Hand

Ash Walk, BA8 0QD
🕒 11-2.30, 5.30-11; 11-11 Sat; 12-10.30 Sun
☎ (01963) 362255
Butcombe Original; 2 changing beers (often Sharp's) Ⓗ
Old stone village pub with low ceilings, beams, a fireplace at each end of an attractive long bar, and a games room housing a TV. There is an adjoining skittle alley. Excellent-quality ales and good-value snacks make a visit to this friendly pub well worthwhile. At the heart of most village activities, this is a true community pub. It serves Thatchers cider on handpump and more cider in boxes. Local CAMRA Pub of the Year 2017. Q❀◖♣🍎P🚌(58)📶

Huish Episcopi

Rose & Crown ★ 𝕃

TA10 9QT (on A372 in village)
🕒 11.30-3, 5.30-10.30; 11.30-11.30 Fri & Sat; 12-10.30 Sun
☎ (01458) 250494
Teignworthy Reel Ale; 2 changing beers (sourced regionally; often Cheddar Ales, Hop Back, Otter) Ⓗ
Locally known as Eli's, this 17th-century pub has been in the same family for four generations. It has an unspoilt interior and so is on CAMRA's National Inventory of Historic Pub Interiors. Ales are served from a taproom with no bar counter and with old-fashioned lever pumps. Leading off the serving area are various rooms and drinking spaces. Regular quiz nights are held. The bus service is limited, but there are more options a short walk away in Langport. Q🐎❀◖◗⛺♣🍎P🐾📶

Hutton

Old Inn

Main Road, BS24 9QQ
🕒 11.30-11 (midnight Fri & Sat); 12-11 Sun
☎ (01934) 812336
Fuller's London Pride; Otter Bright, Head; St Austell Tribute; 1 changing beer Ⓗ
Genuine free house owned by a long-standing Guide landlord, and now a thriving local, right at the heart of the local community. The pub is extremely popular for its excellent and great-value food, particularly the Sunday carvery (booking advised). Food is served all lunchtimes and evenings except Sunday, which is quiz night. Dogs are welcome in the bar. The car park behind the pub is accessed by narrow one-way lanes either side. 🐎❀◖◗♿♣P🚌(4)🐾

Kelston

Old Crown ✔

Bath Road, BA1 9AQ (3 miles from Bath on A431)
🕒 12 (3 Mon)-11; 12-10 Sun ☎ (01225) 423032
🌐 oldcrownkelston.com
Butcombe Original; Draught Bass; 1 changing beer (often Butcombe) Ⓗ
In the countryside between Bristol and Bath, this attractive multi-roomed 18th-century coaching inn underwent a refurbishment in 2015, while retaining many original features such as the rare cash register handpumps, flagstone floors, open fires and settles. There are several areas in which to dine. A guest beer is occasionally available. In summertime, barbecues and live music events are occasionally held in the large, attractive garden. Take care crossing the busy road to the car park. Buses stop directly outside.
🐎❀🛏◖◗🍎P🚌(19,37)🐾📶

Keynsham

Old Bank

20 High Street, BS31 1DQ
🕒 10-11.30 (1.30am Fri & Sat) ☎ (0117) 904 6356
Severn Copper Ale; 3 changing beers Ⓗ
This Grade II-listed building was originally a coaching inn, then a branch of Westminster Bank, before becoming a pub again. It is a free house with one large room for drinking, and a covered, heated outdoor area at the back where the smokers go. There is a small car park to the rear, reached through a narrow archway. The landlord tries to have at least one dark, often strong, beer on at all times. The pub has a large TV screen for sport and can sometimes get lively on late weekend openings. ❀◖♿⇌♣🍎P🚌🐾📶

Litton

Litton

BA3 4PW

12-11; 12-10.30 Sun (01761) 241554 thelitton.co.uk

Bristol Beer Factory Nova; Cheddar Ales Potholer; Great Western Old Higby; 3 changing beers (often Cheddar Ales, Great Western, Twisted Oak) H

Large 15th-century village pub and restaurant reopened in March 2017 after being closed since summer 2014. The emphasis is on comfort without ruining the character of this lovely old building. The old part of the pub has been retained largely in its original format, with a separate whisky bar. At the right of the central bar is a restaurant area with a riverside terrace where you can take your drinks. Accommodation is available, accessed at the rear of the pub where there is accessible parking.

P

Lower Godney

Sheppey Inn

BA5 1RZ

12-3, 5.30-11; 12-midnight Sat; 12-11 Sun

(01458) 831594 thesheppey.co.uk

4 changing beers (sourced nationally; often Bristol Beer Factory, Dawkins, Glastonbury) H

A many-roomed, quirky pub with off-the-wall decoration including graphic arts, taxidermy and surreal ornaments, set in the wilds of the Somerset Levels, west of Wells. It has a good range of changing real ales, plus six or more craft beers from home and overseas, and up to 12 ciders on gravity. Outside the barn-like interior is a lovely terrace overlooking the River Sheppey, where otters have been spotted. The food is highly recommended. P

Luxborough

Royal Oak Inn

TA23 0SH (2½ miles from B3224 between Wheddon Cross and Raleghs Cross)

closed Mon; 12-11 (01984) 641498

theroyaloakinnluxborough.co.uk

Exmoor Ale; 3 changing beers (sourced nationally; often Butcombe, Cheddar Ales, Quantock) H

Voted by a national newspaper as one of the top 10 country pubs and set in the Brendon Hills, this ancient village inn has an original flagstone floor in the bar and a large inglenook fireplace. There is a second bar, a children's room and, to the rear, a dining room where you can enjoy meals freshly cooked using seasonal produce. If you wish to sit outside there is a sunny courtyard. Popular with locals and shooting parties. Q P

Lydford on Fosse

Cross Keys Inn

TA11 7HA (next to A37 between Yeovil and Shepton Mallet at traffic lights in village)

11.30-11; 12-11 Sun (01963) 240473

crosskeysinn.info

House beer (by Downton); 4 changing beers (sourced regionally; often Cheddar Ales, Pheasantry, Yeovil) G

Dating from 1759, this is a fine example of a traditional pub with flagstone floors, blue lias stonework and a wealth of beams. There is an open-plan area with two fireplaces at each end and a snug. Many events are organised such as live music, a beer festival, comedy nights and charitable events. Camping is available on-site with showers and toilets. Generally there are six ales on gravity available at weekends and between two and four during the week.

Q P (667)

Middlezoy

George Inn

42 Main Road, TA7 0NN (off A372, 1 mile NW of Othery, 5 miles E of Bridgwater)

closed Mon; 7-midnight Tue; 12-3, 6.30-midnight; 2-7 Sun

(01823) 698215 thegeorgeinnmiddlezoy.co.uk

St Austell Tribute; 2 changing beers (sourced regionally; often Fine Tuned, Otter) H

A warm welcome awaits you at this friendly 17th-century free house with stone-flagged floors, exposed beams and log fires. Excellent locally sourced food is served from Wednesday to Saturday. A private dining room seating 12 can be reserved. Somerset ciders from Thatchers and Farmer Jim's are on the bar. A beer festival is held over the Easter weekend. Accommodation is a recent addition. Occasional live music and regular bingo nights take place.

Q P (16)

Milverton

Globe

Fore Street, TA4 1JX (15 mins through country lanes from M5, jct 26 at Wellington)

12-3 (not Mon), 6-11; 12-3, 6-11.30 Fri & Sat; 12-3 Sun

(01823) 400534 theglobemilverton.co.uk

Otter Bitter; 3 changing beers (sourced regionally; often Exeter) H

Fifteenth-century former coaching inn set in an interesting village founded on the cotton industry, with a warm welcome for all. A locally sourced, varied and cooked-to-order food menu is available, complemented by themed food evenings. Parking is limited but there is a village car park 150 yards away. Real cider is served in the summer months only. There are two double bedrooms should you wish to night stop at this excellent family-run pub.

Q P (25)

Minehead

Kildare Lodge

Townend Road, TA24 5RQ (2 mins from town centre)

11-3, 6.30-11; 12-5 Sun (01643) 702009

kildarelodge.co.uk

St Austell Tribute; 3 changing beers (sourced regionally) H

This cracking locals' pub is close to Minehead town centre. The Grade II-listed building in the Arts & Crafts style has a bar, two lounges and a dining room. There are 12 en-suite rooms including a bridal suite with a four-poster bed. Two beer festivals are held every year with up to 20 beers to sample. The pub is in the local boules and quiz leagues. It is a great base for exploring Exmoor, Dunster and the coast.

Q P (28,198)

Old Ship Aground

Quay Street, TA24 5UL (beside Minehead harbour)

11-11 (midnight Fri & Sat) (01643) 703516

theoldshipaground.com

Ringwood Boondoggle, Fortyniner; Wychwood Hobgoblin; 2 changing beers (sourced nationally; often Cotleigh, Wychwood) H
Built in 1906 between the harbour and the lifeboat station, the pub has 12 letting rooms with fantastic views over the Bristol Channel. Exmoor National Park is only a 20-minute drive away and it is within walking distance of the town centre and the West Somerset Railway. The pub holds themed food nights through the week and a Sunday carvery. Beer festivals are staged and there is live music on a Friday night. (28,198)

Queen's Head Inn

Holloway Street, TA24 5NR
11-11 (midnight Wed-Sat) (01643) 702940
queensheadminehead.co.uk
Exmoor Gold; St Austell Tribute; house beer (by Hancocks); 5 changing beers (sourced nationally; often Draught Bass, Otter, St Austell) H
In a side street just off The Parade, this popular town pub sells up to eight ales including a house beer, Queen's Head, which is reasonably priced. There is an extensive food menu offering English and Thai food as well as a Wednesday and Sunday carvery. The spacious single bar has a raised seating area for dining and families. The pub features a skittle alley and games room at the back. Live music is staged on a Saturday.
(198,28)

Norton St Philip

Fleur de Lys

High Street, BA2 7LG
5-11; 11-midnight Fri & Sat; closed Sun (01373) 834333
fleurdelysnsp.co.uk
Wadworth 6X, Bishops Tipple; 1 changing beer (sourced nationally) H
An inn since 1584, the Fleur is a warm, welcoming pub. Its three main drinking and dining areas are served by a single bar. Old beams, stone walls and a log fire impart a cosy feeling, and look for the old hand-painted Wadworth's pub signs on the walls. At the rear is a much-used skittle alley where a number of local teams regularly play. The food offering is based mainly around pizzas, but other dishes are available. P

Pitney

Halfway House

Pitney Hill, TA10 9AB (on B3153 between Langport and Somerton)
11.30-3, 4-11; 11.30-11 Sat & Sun (01458) 252513
thehalfwayhouse.co.uk
Hop Back Summer Lightning; Otter Bright; Teignworthy Reel Ale; 6 changing beers (sourced regionally; often Cheddar Ales, Plain, Quantock) G
An outstanding pub serving eight to nine regional ales on gravity alongside many bottled beers and real ciders. The inside is traditional, with flagstone flooring, old solid wooden tables and benches, and three real fires. This busy pub deserves its many accolades and has featured in the Guide for 25 years, gaining the ultimate award of CAMRA National Pub of the Year in 1996. Superb home-cooked food includes a roast lunch served on Sundays. The website has a sample menu.
Q P (54)

Porlock

Ship Inn

High Street, TA24 8QD
11-midnight; 12-midnight Sun (01643) 862507
shipinnporlock.co.uk
Exmoor Beast; Otter Bitter; 6 changing beers (sourced regionally; often Otter) H
Known locally as the Top Ship, the bar is a gem with its flagstone floor, open fire and settle seating. It has changed little since featuring in RD Blackmore's novel Lorna Doone. The building dates from the 13th century and sits at the bottom of the notorious Porlock Hill that takes you up to Exmoor. Eight ales and a local cider are available and good food can be enjoyed in its restaurant or delightful three-tiered garden in summer.
Q P (10)

Priddy

Hunters Lodge

Hillgrove Road, BA5 3AR (on isolated crossroads 1 mile from A39 close to TV mast) ST549500
11.30-2.30, 6.30-11; 12-2, 7-11 Sun (01749) 672275
Butcombe Original; Cheddar Ales Potholer; 1 changing beer (often Butcombe) G
The landlord of this timeless, classic roadside inn has been in charge for 48 years. At a crossroads near Priddy, the highest village in Somerset, it is popular with cavers and walkers. Three rooms include one with a flagged floor, and all beer is served direct from casks behind the bar. Local cider is sold and the home-cooked food is excellent and exceptional value. A folk musicians' drop-in session is held on Tuesday evening. The garden is pleasant and secluded. Mobile phones are not welcome but dogs are. Q P

Queen Victoria Inn

Pelting Drove, BA5 3BA
12-11; 12-10.30 Sun (01749) 676385
thequeenvicpriddy.co.uk
Butcombe Original; 2 changing beers (often Fuller's, Butcombe) H
Creeper-clad inn, a pub since 1851, with four rooms that feature low ceilings, flagged floors and log fires. A wonderfully warm and relaxing haven on cold winter nights, it is popular during the Priddy Folk Festival in July and the annual fair in August. Reasonably priced, home-cooked food is a speciality. Children are welcome and there is a play area by the car park. Cheddar Valley and Ashton Still ciders are sold. May close briefly on some afternoons. Q P

Puriton

37 Club

1 West Approach Road, Woolavington Road, TA7 8AD (5 mins from jct 23 of M5 between Bridgwater and Wells)
4-11; 2-midnight Fri; 12-midnight Sat & Sun
(01278) 685190 37club.co.uk
Otter Amber, Ale; 3 changing beers (often Bath Ales, Exmoor, Glastonbury) H
Standing on the site of the former Royal Ordnance Factory, allocated the number 37, this is a large club offering a great many facilities to members and visitors. It has two bars and its multi-roomed layout incorporates a concert room, two skittle alleys, a dining room, a snooker room with five tables and, outside, a beer garden, fishing lake and football pitch. CAMRA members are welcome with

a membership card. The food menu includes a Sunday carvery for which booking is advisable. (75)

Radstock

Fromeway

Frome Road, BA3 3LG

closed Mon; 12-3, 6-11; 12-11 Sun (01761) 432116 fromeway.co.uk

Butcombe Adam Henson's Rare Breed H**; 2 changing beers (sourced nationally; often Timothy Taylor, Wadworth, Yeovil)** H/A

This friendly free house is now in its sixth generation of the same family. Emily and Andrew welcome you to a great selection of weekly changing ales. In the first year of their takeover they have provided over 100 different beers from all over the country. The food is emphasised with traditional classics as well as more contemporary dishes. The pub has an award-winning garden. Regular charity events, quiz nights and walks take place from month to month. P (768,178)

Rickford

Plume of Feathers

Leg Lane, BS40 7AH (off A368, 2 miles from A38)

12-11 (01761) 462682 theplumeoffeathers.com

Butcombe Adam Henson's Rare Breed, Original; Cheddar Ales Potholer; 1 changing beer (often Butcombe) H

This 17th-century building has been a pub since the 1800s. If approaching from Churchill, the left U-turn into Leg Lane is extremely tricky. The interior is divided into several areas including a restaurant with a real fire. The pub provides a pleasant and convenient base from which to walk, fish or explore the Mendips. It has a garden at the rear and a stream running along the front leading to a ford. A popular charity duck race takes place here in July. Car parking is limited. QP (791)

Roadwater

Valiant Soldier

TA23 0QZ (off A39 at Washford)

11.30-2.30, 6-11; 12-3, 6-11 Sun (01984) 640223 thevaliantsoldier.co.uk

Exmoor Ale; Sharp's Doom Bar; 1 changing beer (sourced regionally; often Cotleigh) H

The inn dates back to 1720 and is ideal for country walks and exploring nearby Exmoor and the old Mineral Line. Run by the same landlord for over 30 years, this vibrant locals' pub has quiz, pool, darts and nine skittles teams to see it through the winter months. It is set by a small river where you can relax and watch the ducks and, if you are lucky, kingfishers. Good-quality locally sourced food is served. P

Rode

Cross Keys

20 High Street, BA11 6NZ (on main street through village)

12-2.30 (not Mon), 5.30-11; 12-11 Sat; 12-10.30 Sun (01373) 830900 crosskeysrode.co.uk

Butcombe Original; 1 changing beer (sourced nationally; often Bristol Beer Factory, Oakham, Three Daggers) H

Reopened in 2004 after 10 years of closure, this was originally the brewery tap for the long-closed Fussell's Brewery and, more recently, a Bass depot. Sympathetically restored, it has succeeded in bringing back a strong village trade. A passageway featuring a deep well links two bars. There is also a large restaurant. The one or two guest beers can come from almost anywhere and encompass major brands, like London Pride, but more usually breweries otherwise unknown in the area. P

Rowberrow

Swan Inn

Rowberrow Lane, BS25 1QL

12-11; 12-10.30 Sun (01934) 852371

Butcombe Original; 2 changing beers (often Butcombe) H

Believed to date from around the late 17th century, this country pub made up of three knocked-through miners' cottages enjoys an attractive setting, nestling beneath the Dolebury Iron Age hillfort. A convenient stop for walkers on the Mendip Hills, the emphasis is on quality home-cooked food, but customers who just want a drink are welcome, and at least one guest beer is available, often from a brewery unusual for this area. The large beer garden, children's playground and car park are opposite. QP

Saltford

Bird in Hand

58 High Street, BS31 3EJ

11-11 (01225) 873335 birdinhandsaltford.co.uk

Butcombe Original; Sharp's Doom Bar; 2 changing beers H

A traditional 19th-century country inn set among stone dwellings at the bottom of the village high street, 400 yards from the A4 and close to the Bristol to Bath Railway Path and River Avon. It has a long L-shaped bar and a pleasant conservatory with fine views across the garden to the hills beyond. Quality food is served lunchtimes and evenings, all day at weekends, with gluten-free options. There is a pétanque piste in the garden. P

Shepton Beauchamp

Duke of York

North Street, TA19 0LW

4.30-11 Mon; 3.30-11 Tue & Wed; 12-11 Thu; 12-midnight Fri & Sat; 12-10.30 Sun (01460) 240314 thesheptonduke.co.uk

St Austell Tribute, Proper Job; Sharp's Doom Bar; 1 changing beer (sourced regionally; often Otter) H

A typical south Somerset village, with the inn, school, shop and church dominating the centre. The pub has a split-level interior which makes it somewhat unusual. Externally, a high pavement with benches gives a village overview and to the rear is a pleasant beer garden and letting rooms. This family establishment welcomes dogs on leads and children. It offers a Sunday carvery, nightly specials board, and breakfast 9-11am on the first Saturday of the month (no food Mon). Bingo nights are a regular feature. P

Somerton

White Hart Inn ✔

Market Place, TA11 7LX (centre of village)
9am-11; 9am-10.30 Sun ☎ (01458) 272273
whitehartsomerton.com
Bath Ales Gem; Cheddar Ales Potholer; Otter Amber; 1 changing beer (sourced locally; often Brotherhood) [H]
The White Hart has been trading as an inn in Somerton's market square since the 16th century. It has eight en-suite letting rooms and was named as one of the best affordable places to stay by The Sunday Times in 2017. The pub is much larger inside than you might at first envisage and there are plenty of tables for breakfast, lunch and dinner as well as coffee and cakes. It has a courtyard for alfresco dining and drinking.
(54,77)

South Cadbury

Camelot [L]

Chapel Road, BA22 7EX (just off A303 between Sparkford and Wincanton)
12-3, 5-11; 11-11 Fri & Sat; 12-10.30 Sun
☎ (01963) 441685 camelotpub.co.uk
Sharp's Doom Bar; house beer (by Wadworth); 2 changing beers (sourced regionally; often Glastonbury, Otter, Teignworthy) [H]
Surrounded by wonderful walks, with Cadbury Castle a short distance away, the pub is a favourite with ramblers. An informative display inside catalogues what is known of the local history and contains finds from the Hill Fort. Close to the A303 and well signposted, it makes an ideal stop-off for those travelling to or from the West Country. Dogs and children are welcome. Popular with diners, the pub provides breakfasts at weekends and a Sunday roast. Q P (1)

South Cheriton

White Horse ✔

Cabbage Lane, BA8 0BL
closed Mon; 12-3, 5-11; 12-11 Sat; 12-10.30 Sun
☎ (01963) 370394 whitehorsecheriton.co.uk
3 changing beers [H]
A 17th-century public house with a large selection of home-cooked meals, real ales and an extensive wine list. It has a variety of seating areas to suit customers' needs, from a formal dining space to casual seating in the bar and snugs. There is a large car park to the side of the pub and a fully fenced beer garden at the rear. Q P (58)

South Petherton

Brewers Arms [L] ✔

18-20 St James Street, TA13 5BW (½ mile off A303 in centre of village)
11.30-3, 6-11; 11.30-midnight Fri & Sat; 12-11 Sun
☎ (01460) 241887 the-brewersarms.com
Otter Bitter; 3 changing beers (sourced nationally; often Butcombe, St Austell, Thornbridge) [H]
Local CAMRA Pub of the Year 2016, this hostelry has appeared in 23 consecutive issues of the Guide. During this time almost 3,000 different ales have been served and documented. The Brewers is a hub of village life, a true community pub that keenly supports local events and charities. Beer festivals are held over both spring and summer bank holiday weekends, and there are regular live music and quiz nights. The adjoining Old Bakehouse Restaurant was acquired and successfully incorporated into the business some time ago. P (81)

Stogumber

White Horse Inn

High Street, TA4 3TA (turn left off A358 at Crowcombe)
12-2.30, 4.30-11; 12-11 Sat & Sun ☎ (01984) 656277
whitehorsestogumber.co.uk
Otter Bitter; St Austell Proper Job; 2 changing beers (sourced regionally; often Otter, Quantock) [H]
In a picturesque village near the Brendon Hills and close to the WSR steam railway, this traditional freehouse is a Grade II-listed building. Ales are from local and regional breweries. The bar has a friendly atmosphere with a cosy log fire, there is a courtyard garden, and the separate restaurant, originally the Market Hall, serves Somerset-produced food. The skittle alley doubles as a function room and hosts a music festival in September. Accommodation is reached via an outside stairwell. P

Stone Allerton

Wheatsheaf Inn

Notting Hill Way, BS26 2NH
closed Mon; 12-2, 6-11; 12-2 Sun ☎ (01934) 444333
Bristol Beer Factory Milk Stout; 2 changing beers (often Cheddar Ales, Twisted Oak) [G]
One of the only pubs in a wide area, it was reopened in 2014 after a long closure. The modern yet boutique interior, including old bookshelves, provides a comfortable and warm place to eat and drink. Only local products are sold, including an unusual lager selection; the cask ales are served by gravity and often come from Cheddar Ales and Twisted Oak breweries. The restaurant is popular, with all food produced in the on-site smokery. There are no electronic gaming machines, only quiet background music. Q P

Stratton-on-the-Fosse

White Post Inn

BA3 4QA
12-3, 5.30-11; 10-3, 5.30-11 Fri (11.30 Sat); 12-11 Sun
☎ (01761) 413394
Bath Ales Gem; Butcombe Original; 1 changing beer (sourced regionally) [H]
A popular community-based pub offering good real ale and three ciders. As well as the two regular beers, there is one guest that could be local or national. Traditional home-cooked food is served daily, lunchtime and evening. In winter months there is a welcoming real fire and, outside, a large, well-kept garden and children's play area.
P

Taunton

Bank

Middle Street, TA1 1SJ
11-11 (midnight Sat); closed Sun ☎ (01823) 257788
thebanktaunton.co.uk
3 changing beers (sourced nationally; often Arbor, Moor Beer, Oakham) [H]
Close to Somerset cricket ground, the Bank features three changing cask ales from small breweries. The pub has two floors: the ground is a cosy bar, and

upstairs is reserved for diners and has doors opening on to a terrace. Excellent food is prepared and can be described as modern British with an international influence. Bar meals reflect the quality of the main menu. ❀◑♿⇌●⊟❀ᯤ

Coal Orchard 🄻 ✔

30-32 Bridge Street, TA1 1UD (near to River Tone bridge in town centre)

8am-midnight ☎ (01823) 447330

Greene King Abbot; Ruddles Best Bitter; Sharp's Doom Bar; 4 changing beers (sourced regionally; often Dartmoor, Exmoor, Quantock) 🄷

North Town Wharf once stood behind this Wetherspoon house, next to the River Tone. Facing it was the Coal Orchard, the site of an orchard which became the landing place for Welsh coal. Latterly the pub was converted from a former hardware store. One of JDW's smaller premises, the frontage has Art Deco styling, and seating is arranged over a single open-plan level. There is a small garden and patio area at the rear. Q❀◑♿⇌●⊟ᯤ

Perkin Warbeck 🄻 ✔

22-23 East Street, TA1 3LP

8am-midnight (1am Fri & Sat) ☎ (01823) 335830

Greene King Abbot; Ruddles Best Bitter; Sharp's Doom Bar; changing beers (sourced nationally; often Butcombe, Exmoor, Otter) 🄷

This Wetherspoon pub is named after the man who claimed to be the rightful heir to the throne of England in 1497. Recently refurbished, it has one of the longest bars in the county and a splendid terrace at the rear. Somerset cricket memorabilia adorn the walls, as befits the pub's location a stone's throw from the cricket ground. An excellent range of ales and ciders is kept in excellent condition. ❀◑♿●⊟ᯤ

Racehorse Inn ✔

East Reach, TA1 3HT

12-4, 6-11 Mon; 12-11.30 (1am Fri; 2.30am Sat); 12-11 Sun ☎ (01823) 327513

St Austell Trelawny, Tribute, Proper Job; 1 changing beer (sourced nationally; often Dartmoor, Fuller's, Marston's) 🄷

Popular St Austell hostelry close to the town centre at the top of East Reach, a traditional community pub with front and rear bars and a small lounge with comfortable armchairs. Skittles and darts are played regularly, and there is live music every week, which is extremely popular. A large walled garden at the rear is ideal for a relaxing drink on those warm summer days. No food is served. ❀♿♣●⊟❀ᯤ

Ring of Bells 🄻

16-17 St James Street, TA1 1JS

11-11 ☎ (01823) 259480 theringofbellstaunton.com

5 changing beers (sourced nationally; often Arbor, Oakham, Quantock) 🄷

Town-centre pub close to the theatre and Somerset cricket ground, and therefore a favourite haunt of cricket fans. Wooden floored, there are two bar areas with open fires, a downstairs dining area, upstairs restaurant and a large outside courtyard. The five cask beers are from local, regional and national breweries. Excellent locally produced food is served, and booking is recommended. Sporting events are shown on a TV in the bar area. ❀◑⇌⊟❀ᯤ

Wyvern Social Club 🄻

Mountfields Road, TA1 3BJ (off South Rd, approx 1 mile from town centre)

6-11; 2-11 Sat; 12-3, 7-10.30 Sun ☎ (01823) 284591

wyvernclub.co.uk

Exmoor Ale; 2 changing beers (sourced regionally; often Exmoor, Quantock, St Austell) 🄷

For over 30 years this has been a great venue to drink real ales and now real cider. It is a members-only club with a visitors' licence; show a CAMRA membership card to be signed in as a guest. The club is the hub for the rugby, cricket and squash clubs who use the attached playing fields. It was joint CAMRA Somerset branch Club of the Year 2017. Its annual beer festival is in October. The bus routes given here are only relevant for Saturday daytime. ❀◑♿♣●P⊟(6,99)ᯤ

Trull

Winchester Arms

8 Church Road, TA3 7LG

12-3, 6.30-11; 12-4 Sun ☎ (01823) 284723

winchesterarmstrull.co.uk

4 changing beers (sourced regionally; often Cotleigh, Otter, St Austell) 🄷

Thriving community free house on the outskirts of Taunton, near the Blackdown Hills. A comfortable bar area is separated from a long dining space by a fireplace. The locally sourced home-cooked food is excellent (booking is advised at popular times). Streamside gardens, perfect for family and dogs, becomes the venue for entertainment and barbecues. The pub offers good-value accommodation. A popular quiz takes place on Sunday nights and there is occasional live music. Q❀◑♣●P⊟(97)❀ᯤ

Wambrook

Cotley Inn

TA20 3EN (from A30 W out of Chard, by toll house, take left fork and almost immediately left again; continue for just over 1 mile on narrow lane)

closed Mon; 12-3, 6-11; 12-3 Sun ☎ (01460) 62348

cotleyinnwambrook.co.uk

Otter Bitter; 2 changing beers (often Exeter, Exmoor, Otter) 🄶

A traditional country pub that is well worth finding. Inside the main entrance is a bar area with a welcoming wood-burning stove to greet you in the winter months. To the right of the bar is a challenging skittle alley and to the left you will find dining areas where you can sample the excellent food. Ales are served from gravity racking behind the bar. The pub is in a wonderful rural setting where sitting outside is a delight. Q❀◑♣●P❀

Watchet

Esplanade Club 🄻 ✔

5 The Esplanade, TA23 0AJ (opp marina)

12-3 (not Tue), 7-midnight; 12-midnight Fri-Sun ☎ (01984) 634518 esplanade-club.co.uk

House beer (by St Austell); 4 changing beers (sourced regionally; often Exmoor, Quantock, St Austell) 🄷

Built in the 1860s as a sailmaking factory and now home to the Boat Owners Association, the club is an archive of local history and memorabilia, with unique murals and even its own Tardis. There are great views over the marina and the Bristol

Channel. A busy music venue, live acts feature every weekend, open mic on the first Tuesday of the month and folk every fourth Wednesday. Winner of Somerset CAMRA Club of the Year four times. (28)

Pebbles Tavern

24 Market Street, TA23 0AN (in heart of Watchet, near museum)

11 (5 Wed)-11; 12-11 Sun (01984) 634737
pebblestavern.co.uk

3 changing beers (sourced nationally; often Otter, Stowey, Timothy Taylor)

A small, unique tavern that has won numerous CAMRA awards for Cider Pub of the Year, and in 2015 it was the national runner-up. As well as the ales, there can be up to 30 ciders, 60 gins, 24 rums and 64 whiskies. You are allowed to bring in your fish and chips from the shop next door. Poetry night is the first Tuesday of the month and regular music nights include folk, sea shanty, acoustic and jazz. (28)

Star Inn

Mill Lane, TA23 0BZ

12-3, 6.30-11 (01984) 631367 starinnwatchet.co.uk

House beer (by Exmoor); 3 changing beers (often Butcombe, Exmoor, Sarah Hughes)

This 16th-century pub has been in the Guide for over 15 years and was Somerset CAMRA branch Pub of the Year runner-up in 2018. It is renowned for its friendly staff and the congenial atmosphere. It has darts, quiz and boules teams and holds music nights in the summer. It also hosts port and cheese nights and is home to the Sunday night Bad Boys Club. Mick's beer tours have run over 80 trips from the pub.

Wedmore

New Inn

Combe Batch, BS28 4DU

12-2.30 (not Mon & Tue), 5-midnight; 12-midnight Fri-Sun
(01934) 712099 newinnwedmore.co.uk

Butcombe Original; 3 changing beers (sourced regionally; often Bath Ales, Exmoor, Otter)

This classic village inn is the centre for many local events including the famous annual turnip prize, conkers, spoof and penny chuffin'. The public bar, lounge and dining areas are complemented by a beer garden to the rear. A chalkboard lists forthcoming ales, mainly from the West Country, served from three handpumps and one on gravity. Traditional good-value home-cooked food is available. There is a skittle alley/function room, and winter skittles and darts provide a hive of activity. Q P (67)

Wellington

Dolphin

37 Waterloo Road, TA21 8JQ

4-11; 12-11 Sat; 12-10 Sun (01823) 665889
thedolphinwellington.co.uk

Otter Amber; 2 changing beers (often Exeter, Exmoor, Quantock)

Traditional town centre pub serving up to four local ales at weekends. Home-cooked food is served daily including pizzas to eat in or take away (with vegan and gluten-free varieties available). Live music is hosted twice a month, usually on Thursday or Saturday, as well as monthly themed food and charity nights. The colourful pub frontage features an unusual mural featuring handpumps depicting local breweries and wine bottles.
Q (22A)

Wellow

Fox & Badger

Railway Lane, BA2 8QG

11.30-3, 6-11; 11.30-11 Fri & Sat; 12-4 Sun
(01225) 832293 thefoxandbadger.com

Butcombe Original; 1 changing beer (sourced regionally; often Electric Bear, Flying Monk, Otter)

A popular unspoilt village local, with a single central bar decorated with hops. Up to three ales are on including two changing guests. Rustic furniture rests on flags and wooden floors, while there is a fine stone fireplace with a wood-burning stove. It gets busy in the evenings for its food, so book up if you wish to eat. It is a great destination for walkers and cyclists (close to National Cycle Route 244). Car parking can be a problem.
P (757)

Wells

Just Ales

38 Market Street, BA5 2DS

12-9 (11 Fri & Sat) (01749) 678480 justales.com

7 changing beers (sourced nationally; often Langham, Milk Street, Portobello)

Wells' first micropub, opened in 2016 by two beer enthusiasts in what was an old tea shop, just a few yards from the High Street. As well as up to seven ales on gravity, there are as many real ciders. The ales can come from any part of the country. The pub's emphasis is on providing a quiet, comfortable place for a pint and a natter with friends or strangers. Tea, coffee, sandwiches, jackets and toast are all available. Q

West Huntspill

Crossways Inn

Withy Road, TA9 3RA (on A38)

12-midnight (1am Fri & Sat); 12-11 Sun
(01278) 783756 thecrosswaysinn.com

6 changing beers (sourced regionally; often Exmoor, Pitchfork, St Austell)

This fabulous 17th-century inn is a well-deserved winner of Somerset CAMRA Pub of the Year in 2017 and 2018. It has several bar areas, a separate dining room and two log fires during winter, including an outside fireplace for smokers. There is also a skittle alley that can be used as a function room. Six ales, normally from the South-West, are stocked as well as real ciders from the cellar. A beer festival is held over the August bank holiday.
P (21)

Weston-super-Mare

Bear

66 Walliscote Road, BS23 1ED

1-11.30; 12-midnight Fri & Sat; 12-11 Sun
(01934) 641722 thebearinnweston.co.uk

4 changing beers (sourced regionally)

Spacious and comfortable pub a few minutes' walk from the seafront. It was formerly called the Balmoral, and reopened in 2012 with a new name after a period of closure. Beers can be unusual for the area, and come in a variety of styles. Live music

is popular every Saturday evening. There is a skittle alley, a refurbished function room at the back with a stage, and 23 en-suite rooms. Sport is occasionally shown on TV.
(5,7)

Brit Bar

118 High Street, BS23 1HP
12-1am (01934) 632629
5 changing beers H
Town-centre pub given a bright modern makeover while retaining the important traditional elements. Mondays to Wednesdays are gaming nights, with live music at weekends. Two or three changing beers are offered and it is not unusual for all to be dark beers, including stouts and porters. In September 2015 brewing commenced on-site, under the RPM Brewery label, and there is sometimes an RPM beer on the bar. Families are welcome in the covered, heated courtyard.

Criterion

45 Upper Church Road, BS23 2DY
12-11.45 (11 Mon); 11-1am Fri & Sat; 12-11 Sun
07538 753350
Courage Directors H**; St Austell Tribute; 3 changing beers** G
Genuine free house and traditional community pub, just off the seafront in the Knightstone area. Believed to be one of the oldest pubs in town, it has interesting local photos on the walls. Pub games feature strongly, with darts and table skittles, plus a quiz on Tuesday. Bar snacks are available, and filled rolls at lunchtime. Between three and five guest beers are sold, with all beer styles and local breweries well supported.
(1,4)

Off the Rails

Station Road, BS23 1XY (on railway station concourse)
7am-11; 8am-11 Sun (01934) 415109
2 changing beers H
This genuine free house, conveniently situated at the railway station, also serves as the station buffet. Two changing beers are served, often, but not always, from West Country microbreweries. There are also two local ciders, from Rich's and Thatchers. The landlord welcomes suggestions from his regulars as to which beers to stock. Two-pint carryout containers are handy for train travellers. Three TVs show sporting events, often silently. Karaoke frequently features at weekends. May close early when quiet. P

Regency

22-24 Lower Church Road, BS23 2AG
10-11.30 (midnight Fri & Sat); 10.45-11.30 Sun
(01934) 633406
Bombardier; Butcombe Original; Courage Best Bitter; Draught Bass; 1 changing beer H
Comfortable, friendly town-centre local, attracting a mixed clientele including students at lunchtime. The pub has pool, skittles and crib teams, but also offers a quiet refuge for conversation. The pool room with TV and jukebox is separate from the main bar area, and children are welcome here. Keenly priced home-cooked food is served lunchtimes, and it has Wednesday curry and Thursday grill evenings. There are patios to the front and rear. Pub outings feature, plus occasional live bands.

Wincanton

Nog Inn

South Street, BA9 9DL
10.30-11 (midnight Fri & Sat); 12-11 Sun
(01963) 32998 thenoginn.com
St Austell HSD; Sharp's Original; 2 changing beers (often Bath Ales, Otter, Plain) H
This attractive listed pub with a striking Georgian façade fronts a long, narrow building with parts dating back to the 16th century. A secluded sunny garden with covered seating can be found at the far end of the property. The guest ales are often seasonal and an extensive range of continental beers on tap is always available, as are real ciders. It serves home-cooked pub classics. Regular events on Thursday evenings include open mic and a quiz night. P (58)

Winsford

Royal Oak Inn

Halse Lane, TA24 7JE (turn left off A396 at Coppleham Cross N of Bridgetown)
11-3, 6-11 (01643) 851455 royaloakexmoor.co.uk
Exmoor Ale; Otter Amber H
An attractive thatched inn within Exmoor National Park. The village is noted for having been the birthplace of Ernest Bevin. The pub has won a number of awards for its food, and details of its locally sourced produce can be found on the website. The building also houses the Oak Shop and post office. The Winn Brook runs past the inn and over the ford that leads up to Exmoor and Tarr Steps. Summer hours are extended on Saturday and Sunday. QP

Witham Friary

Seymour Arms ★

BA11 5HF
11-3, 6-midnight; 12-midnight Sun (01749) 850742
Cheddar Ales Potholer; 1 changing beer (sourced locally) H
A hidden rural gem, this pub has probably changed very little over the last 50 or so years (apart from new loos!). Built in the 1860s as a hotel to serve the nearby Mid-Somerset GWR branch railway station, it was part of the Duke of Somerset's estate. Sadly, in the 1960s, Mr Beeching closed the station, and the hotel became a quiet country pub. Beer and cider are served from a glass-panelled hatch in the central hallway. QP

Withypool

Royal Oak Inn

TA24 7QP (W of B3223 between Dulverton and Exford at Comers Cross) SS847356
12-3 Mon; 12-3, 6-11 (01643) 831506
royaloakwithypool.co.uk
Exmoor Ale, Gold; 2 changing beers (sourced locally; often Exmoor) H
Set in a remote village, the pub has been providing great ale and food for over 300 years. It is larger than first appears. It has two bars and a dining room which are decorated with an interesting array of country pursuits memorabilia. It also has eight en-suite rooms. The pub will arrange shooting, riding and fishing locally. Although remote, beauty spots such as Tarr Steps, which is four miles away, are easily accessible. QP

Wiveliscombe

Bear Inn 🄻

8-10 North Street, TA4 2JY
⏲ 10.30-11 ☎ (01984) 623537
🌐 thebearwiveliscombe.co.uk
Black Bear Wivey Best, Bitter; 4 changing beers (sourced locally; often Exmoor, Otter) Ⓗ
This 17th-century former coaching inn is very much a community pub. The Cotleigh and Exmoor breweries are nearby and the on-site Black Bear microbrewery operates from the Bear Inn's outbuildings. A single bar serves two rooms, a children's area and garden. Good value meals and daily specials, using local produce where possible, are served. There is an excellent choice of ales and a strong commitment to real cider, with ciders from Sheppy and various other local producers. A real ale festival is held every August.
🛏❀⛕◑♿♣●P🚌(25)🐾📶

Yatton

Butchers Arms

31 High Street, BS49 4JD
⏲ 12-11; 12-10 Sun ☎ (01934) 838754
Butcombe Original; Twisted Oak Fallen Tree; 1 changing beer (sourced locally; often Bristol Beer Factory, Glede) Ⓗ
Reopened and refurbished after a period of closure, this traditional village pub is now free of tie. Mind your head as you go in – there are low ceilings throughout, with flagstones on the floor by the front bar and a feature bay window with a settle beneath. Up a step is the rear lounge bar and there is a beer garden beyond. The guest ale is normally from a local brewery such as Glede in Clevedon or Bristol Beer Factory. ❀◑🚌(W1)🐾📶

Yeovil

Quicksilver Mail ✔

168 Hendford Hill, BA20 2RG (at jct of A30 and A37)
⏲ 11-11 (midnight Fri); 10.30-midnight Sat; 12-10.30 Sun
☎ (01935) 424721 🌐 quicksilvermail.com
Butcombe Adam Henson's Rare Breed; St Austell Tribute; 1 changing beer (sourced nationally; often Bath Ales) Ⓗ
Large pub on the outskirts of town, with the same landlord for over 15 years. During this time he has built up a good reputation for food and the encouragement of live music. The pub name is unique and commemorates a high-speed mail coach service from Exeter to London which used to call here. There is a bar on one level and a restaurant area down a few steps. The skittles alley doubles as a function room.
❀⛕◑♣P🚌(40,99)🐾📶

Old Green Tree, Bath (Photo: Katie Button)

Historic Coaching Inns of the Great North Road

Roger Protz

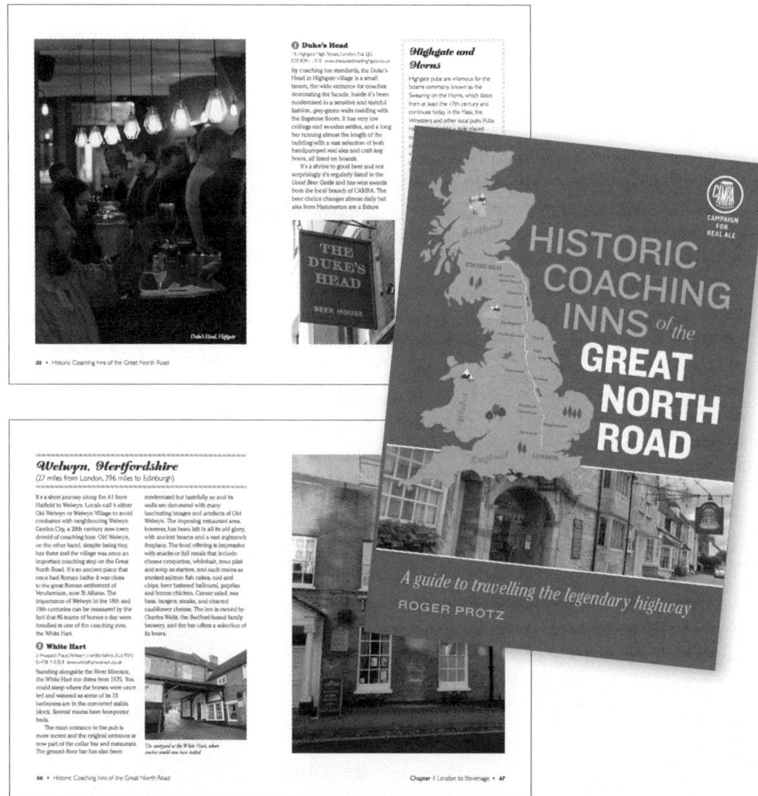

The Great North Road is part of British folklore, the Route 66 of Britain, except instead of gas stations and diners we have magnificent coaching inns, part of the living history of our islands. Taking in the history of these buildings as well as the literature that has celebrated them – from Charles Dickens through to J B Priestley – Roger Protz describes these coaching houses with an expert and discerning eye, producing not only a great pub guide but a gazetteer of the history and culture that are draped along this iconic road.

RRP £12.99 **ISBN** 978-1-85249-339-4 **224 pages**

For this and other books on beer and pubs visit CAMRA's online bookshop at **www.camra.org.uk/books** or call **01727 867201**. Discounts are available for CAMRA members.

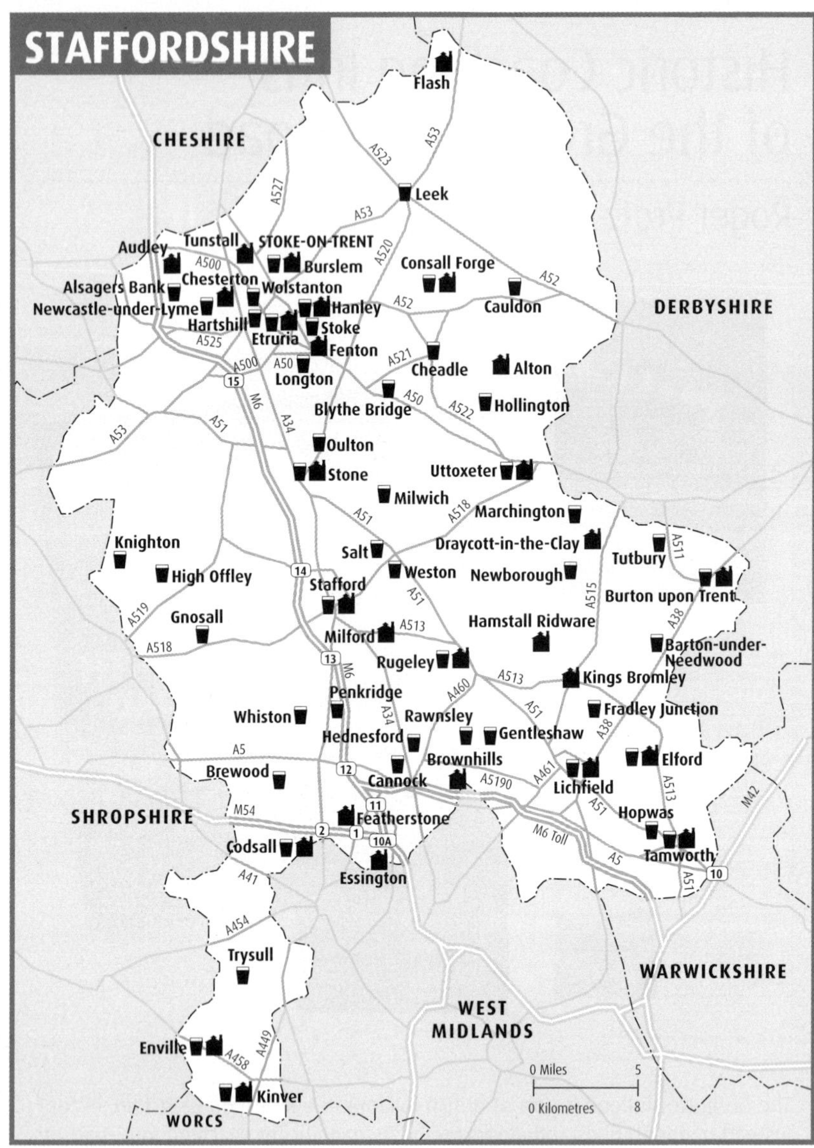

Alsagers Bank

Gresley Arms 𝕃

High Street, ST7 8BQ (on B5367)

12 (3 Mon-Wed)-11 ☎ (01782) 722469

gresleyarms.co.uk

8 changing beers (often Abbeydale, Marston's, Townhouse) Ⓗ

This traditional, popular free house, over 200 years old, has been in the same family for nearly 30 years and always offers a warm, friendly welcome. The landlord is enthusiastic about his real ale and eight perfectly kept beers are on the bar, including house beer Gresley Blonde. Eight ciders and perries are also served, plus delicious, affordable home-cooked food. The beer garden offers breathtaking views across nine counties, and is an ideal place to relax with a pint after a local walk.

P (1A)

Barton-under-Needwood

Barton Turns

3 Barton Turn, DE13 8EA (off B5016, ½ mile E of village, by Trent & Mersey Canal)

12-11; 11-11 Sat & Sun ☎ (01283) 480682

Marston's Pedigree, Wainwright; 1 changing beer (sourced nationally) Ⓗ

Friendly, traditional Victorian pub with an open-plan single room, still known by locals as The Vine, its former name. The beer garden at the rear has a sheltered decking area and lawn, and there are more outdoor drinking areas (with picnic tables) at the front of the pub and across the road by the side of the canal. Bar meals are served every day until 8.30pm. Boaters, cyclists and walkers are welcome. The pub is popular with TV sport fans, especially for Saturday afternoon horse racing and rugby. P (811,812)

Royal Oak ✔

74 The Green, DE13 8JD (½ mile S of B5016 via Wales Lane)
12-11.30 (12.30am Fri & Sat); 12-11 Sun
☎ (01283) 713852
Marston's Pedigree; 2 changing beers (sourced nationally) H/G
Bustling community local on the southern edge of the village, home to many traditional pub games teams. While parts of the building date back to the 16th century, the pub has only existed since the mid-1800s. Public bar and lounge customers are served from a central sunken bar below the level of the rest of the ground floor. A separate conservatory offers access to the garden. Beers are on handpump or by gravity, direct from the cask, on request. **Q** P (811,812)

Blythe Bridge

Crossways Micropub

246 Uttoxeter Road, ST11 9LY (close to crossroads, in centre of Blythe Bridge)
closed Mon-Wed; 12 (5 Thu)-10 ☎ 07376 259117
peakstonesrock.co.uk/micropub.htm
3 changing beers (sourced nationally; often Burton Bridge, Leatherbritches, Milestone) H
Opposite the library, this venue is just a five-minute walk from the local railway station. It is a no-nonsense, no-frills drinking establishment, selling two ales from the full range of the Alton-based Peakstones Rock Brewery, along with a changing guest ale. The pub is a chilled-out place, where chatting to the friendly locals is almost compulsory. Dogs are very welcome.
Q (6A)

Brewood

Swan Hotel ✔

15 Market Place, ST19 9BS
11.45-midnight ☎ (01902) 850330
Courage Directors; Salopian Lemon Dream; Wye Valley HPA; 3 changing beers (sourced locally; often Burton Bridge, Three Tuns, Weetwood) H
Characterful old coaching inn with low-beamed ceilings and seasonal log fires. Its village-centre location makes it convenient for the Shropshire Union Canal and the Staffordshire Way. Cosy snugs displaying early prints of the district flank the central bar which, unusually for the area, stocks nearly 80 malt whiskies and 20 gins from around the world. There is a traditional skittle alley upstairs which doubles as a function room and hosts a fun quiz on Sunday evenings. Major Freeview sporting events are shown. **Q** P (877,878)

Burton upon Trent

Burton Bridge Inn

24 Bridge Street, DE14 1SY (on A511, at town end of Trent Bridge)
12-2 (not Mon), 5-11; 12-2.30, 5-11 Thu; 11.30-11.30 Fri & Sat; 12-3, 7-11 Sun ☎ (01283) 536596
burtonbridgeinn.co.uk
Burton Bridge Golden Delicious, Sovereign Gold, Bridge Bitter, Burton Porter, Stairway to Heaven, Festival Ale; 1 changing beer (sourced locally) H
This 17th-century pub is the flagship of the Burton Bridge Brewery estate and fronts the brewery itself. It incorporates two rooms served from a central bar: a smaller front room with wooden pews and displaying many awards, brewery memorabilia and framed old maps of Burton, and a back room featuring oak beams and panels. A dining/function room and a skittle alley are upstairs. Meals are limited to monthly steak nights and fish nights on Tuesdays; see website for details. **Q**

Coopers Tavern ★

43 Cross Street, DE14 1EG (off Station St)
5-10 Mon: 5 (2 Thu)-11; 12-11.30 Fri & Sat; 12-10 Sun
☎ (01283) 567246
Draught Bass G; **Joule's Slumbering Monk** H; **7 changing beers (sourced regionally)** H/G
Classic 19th-century alehouse, once the Bass Brewery tap but currently part of the Joule's estate. The pub now features five linked rooms after a sympathetic refurbishment and expansion in early 2017, but the intimate inner taproom has retained its barrel tables and bench seating, where beer is served from a small counter by the cask stillage. Up to four changing ciders/perries plus fruit wines are also available. Impromptu folk music may feature on Tuesday evenings and live music some Sunday afternoons. **Q**

Crossing ✔

50 High Street, DE14 1JS (on N corner of jct with Worthington Way)
12-10 Mon & Tue (11 Wed & Thu; midnight Fri & Sat); 12-9 Sun ☎ (01283) 529902 thecrossingburton.co.uk
Dancing Duck Ay Up, Dark Drake; Draught Bass; Oakham Citra; Sharp's Doom Bar, Atlantic; 1 changing beer (sourced regionally) H

REAL ALE BREWERIES

Beowulf Brownhills
Blythe Hamstall Ridware
Brewhouse & Kitchen Lichfield (NEW)
Burton Bridge Burton upon Trent
Burton Old Cottage Burton upon Trent
Burton Town Burton upon Trent
Consall Forge Consall Forge
Crown Brewhouse Elford (NEW)
Dogbreath Kinver (NEW)
Enville Enville
Firs Codsall (NEW)
Flash Flash
Gates Burton Burton upon Trent
Grey Friars Featherstone (brewing suspended)
Heritage Burton upon Trent
Inadequate Stoke-on-Trent: Etruria (NEW)
Kinver Kinver
Lymestone Stone
Marston's Burton upon Trent
Marts Stoke-on-Trent: Hanley (NEW)
Morton Essington
Peakstones Rock Alton
Quartz Kings Bromley
RAN Stoke-on-Trent: Fenton
Roebuck Draycott-in-the-Clay (NEW)
Shugborough Milford
Slater's Stafford
Sunset Taverns Tunstall (NEW)
Tamworth Tamworth (NEW)
Titanic Stoke-on-Trent: Burslem
Tower Burton upon Trent
Townhouse Audley
Uttoxeter Uttoxeter
Vine Inn Rugeley
Weal Chesterton

Imposing, popular pub near the town centre, built in 1927 to replace an earlier 18th-century hostelry. Renamed several times over the last decade, it has been recently revived as a gastropub, its current name and logo derived from LS Lowry's 1961 painting Level Crossing, Burton-on-Trent, which features the pub. Comfortably furnished throughout, there is an L-shaped bar area at the front with an open log fire, plus a dining space to the rear overlooking the garden. Meals are served all day to 9pm (6pm Sun). P

Derby Inn

17 Derby Road, DE14 1RU (on A5121, 350yds N of jct with A511)

5 (12 Thu)-11; 12-midnight Fri & Sat; 12-10 Sun

07736 953206

Draught Bass; Timothy Taylor Boltmaker; 2 changing beers (sourced nationally)

Friendly Victorian two-roomed local, towards the northern edge of the town. Very much a community pub, it offers a step back in time to a more relaxed pace of life. It is popular with football supporters on match days as it is en route between the railway station and Burton Albion's Pirelli Stadium. Evening meals, with limited choice, are only available on Wednesdays, but pizzas are served at all times. Cheesy quiz night is Tuesday. P (V1,X38)

Dog Inn

5 Lichfield Street, DE14 3QZ (opp Burton College, near High St/New St jct)

12-11 (11.30 Fri & Sat) (01283) 517060

Black Country Bradley's Finest Golden, Pig on the Wall, Fireside; Draught Bass; 7 changing beers (sourced regionally)

Attractive half-timbered terrace pub near the town centre, dating back to the early 19th century. Purchased and refurbished by Black Country Ales in 2015, this radically revitalised pub offers an impressive selection of cask ales and ciders. Internally, a large, comfortable, square-shaped single room surrounds a central bar and features a wood-framed ceiling and wood panelling on the walls, plus three real fires and numerous framed old photographs of Burton. Available beers are listed on two boards on opposite sides of the room.

Elms Inn

36 Stapenhill Road, DE15 9AE (on A444)

12-11.30 (midnight Fri & Sat); 12-10.30 Sun

(01283) 535505 the-elms-burton.co.uk

Draught Bass; Marston's Pedigree; 2 changing beers (sourced nationally)

Lively local on the opposite bank of the River Trent from the town centre. Built as a private house in the late 19th century, this is one of Burton's original parlour pubs. Sensitively renovated, the small public bar, snug and a side room at the front are largely unchanged. In contrast, the lounge to the rear has been extended and refurbished in a modern style. Meals are available to 7pm Wednesday-Saturday, 3pm Sunday. Occasional live entertainment features.

Roebuck Inn

101 Station Street, DE14 1BT (on corner of jct with Mosley St)

12-11 (01283) 511213 roe-buck-inn.co.uk

Draught Bass; Greene King Abbot; Marston's Pedigree; Theakston Old Peculier; 2 changing beers (sourced regionally)

Friendly Victorian corner-terrace pub near the railway station, once the Ind Coope Brewery tap, opposite the former brewery. The original classic Draught Burton Ale was launched here in 1976. Inside, there is a long, narrow, single room with dark-wood panelling and the bar counter down one side. A small patio at the rear can be used for outdoor drinking, as well as a few tables and chairs at the front in summer. Live music plays early Sunday evenings.

Cannock

Linford Arms

79 High Green, WS11 1BN

8am-midnight (1am Fri & Sat) (01543) 469360

Greene King Abbot; Ruddles Best Bitter; Sharp's Doom Bar; 5 changing beers (sourced nationally; often Backyard, Beowulf, Salopian)

Established town-centre Wetherspoon pub serving eight real ales and ciders. Its name originates from the builders' merchants that formerly occupied the premises. It has a seating area on two floors, with quieter alcoves and a separate snug. Two ale festivals are held each year and local breweries feature regularly. It has often been a local CAMRA Pub of the Year finalist in recent years. With good bus and rail links, it is not to be missed if visiting Cannock.

Newhall Arms

81 High Green, WS11 1BN

12-10 (11 Wed & Thu; midnight Fri); 11-midnight Sat

07852 573042 thenewhallarms.co.uk

8 changing beers

Cannock's first micropub, owned and run by Kev and his sons Matt and Jay. This is a friendly place, with no loud music or TV, just good conversation and great beer. The pub is located in the centre of the town and the bar serves eight ales and two ciders; cobs are available as well as the usual snacks. The beers change all the time, sourced locally as well as nationally. A real gem. Q P

Cauldon

Yew Tree Inn

ST10 3EJ (turn left at Cross pub, Cauldon Lowe, approx 1 mile from jct)

12-3, 6-midnight; 12-midnight Sat & Sun

(01538) 309876 yewtreeinncauldon.co.uk

Burton Bridge Bridge Bitter; Rudgate Ruby Mild; 1 changing beer (sourced nationally; often Blue Monkey, Dancing Duck, McMullen)

On a quiet bend just outside Leek, this is possibly one of the most famous pubs in the country, and one of the few where even the local CAMRA committee would admit that the good real ale is the least of its attractions; the inside is stuffed to the brim with antiques, guns, pianos, penny farthings, a working pianola and so much more bric-a-brac that it is impossible to list it all here. The entrance is dominated by the eponymous yew tree. Q P (109)

Cheadle

Huntsman

The Green, ST10 1XS (at bottom of hill)
12-midnight ☎ (01538) 750502
thehuntsmancheadle.com
Marston's Pedigree; Sharp's Doom Bar; 4 changing beers (sourced regionally; often Joule's, Peakstones Rock, Sarah Hughes) H
Now a regular entry in this Guide, with two log fires and friendly bar staff, you can expect a warm welcome here. A good range of beers is on offer for the discerning real ale drinker. Recently refurbished with a rustic brickwork theme, traditional pub food is available, with excellent service. There are annual beer and cider festivals held in the beer garden to the rear. This is a great pub for families as well as those who enjoy a quiet pint. P

Codsall

Codsall Station

Chapel Lane, WV8 2EJ
11.30-11 (11.30 Fri & Sat); 12-10.30 Sun
☎ (01902) 847061
Holden's Black Country Bitter, Golden Glow, Special; 3 changing beers (sourced regionally; often Holden's, Salopian) H
Sensitively converted from the waiting room, offices and stationmaster's house, the Grade II-listed building comprises a bar, lounge, snug and conservatory and displays worldwide railway memorabilia. Steps lead to a drinking area outside with tables and benches overlooking the working platforms. Bar meals are served except Sunday and Monday; cobs and locally made pork pies are available all week. Beer festivals are held over the May and August bank holiday weekends.
QP(5,10B)

Crown Joule's

1 Wood Road, WV8 1DB
10.30-11 (11.30 Fri & Sat) ☎ (01902) 844876
thecrownjoules.pub
Joule's Blonde, Pale Ale, Slumbering Monk; 5 changing beers (sourced regionally; often Joule's) H
The oldest pub in Codsall was bought by Joule's and reopened in 2016 after a major refurbishment which transformed it into a slightly grand Edwardian-style pub with a modern twist; it features open fires, stained-glass windows, old beams and reclaimed furniture. The former function room, which in the '60s and '70s hosted a renowned jazz club, has been fitted out in the style of a library. The pub opens early for breakfast. Canine cuisine, with optional gravy, is available for dogs. QP(5,10B)

Firs Club

Station Road, WV8 1BX (entrance from shared Co-op car park off Station Rd)
7.30-11 (midnight Fri); 12-midnight Sat; 12-11 Sun
☎ (01902) 844674 thefirscodsall.com
3 changing beers (sourced locally; often Hobsons, Ludlow, Wye Valley) H
A previous CAMRA regional Club of the Year runner-up, the club contains a bar area, quiet lounge and sports lounge with pool table, dartboard and card table. Snooker tables are upstairs. Up to three guest ales, mainly local, are served. A beer festival is held in November and a cider and golden ales festival is staged in May. The large function room is available to hire. A pedestrian entrance in Wood Road is handy for the bus stop.
QP(5,10B)

Consall Forge

Black Lion

ST9 0AJ (off A522, follow signs to Consall Gardens then Nature Reserve on hairpin bend, go straight on, ignore No Vehicular Access sign, bottom of hill, left along track to car park)
12-11; 12-10.30 Sun ☎ (01782) 550294
blacklionpub.co.uk/index.html
Peakstones Rock Black Hole; 3 changing beers (sourced regionally; often Consall Forge, Falstaff, Lymestone) H
Not the easiest pub to find, The Black Lion is full of characters and rural charm; changing guest beers and a large range of real ciders feature on the bar. Food is typical pub grub, but arrive hungry, as the portions are generous. To get here, drive along a track to the pub car park or walk from Cheddleton or Froghall along the canal for about one hour. Regular beer festivals are staged, normally to coincide with a steam gala on the Churnet Valley Railway. QP

Elford

Crown Inn

The Square, B79 9DB (600yds E of A513) SK189106
6-11; 12-midnight Fri-Sun ☎ (01827) 383602
Burton Bridge Sovereign Gold; Draught Bass; 2 changing beers (often Crown Brewhouse) H
Welcoming, multi-room village pub, now home to the in-house Crown Brewhouse, launched in 2017. Beamed ceilings feature throughout the pub, with real fires creating a cosy glow. In the 18th century, the upstairs rooms were used as a courthouse. Darts and pool are hived off to a modern room at the side. The guest ale is often from Burton Bridge. It is advisable to book in advance for the good-quality food. No evening or Sunday bus service.
P

Enville

Cat Inn

Bridgnorth Road, DY7 5HA (on A458)
12-2.30 (not Mon), 5-11; 12-11 Fri & Sat; 12-6 Sun
☎ (01384) 872209 thecatinn.com
Enville Ale, Ginger Beer; 5 changing beers (sourced regionally; often Enville, Olde Swan, Salopian) H
A quiet community inn with low oak-beamed ceilings, this is a fine place to enjoy a quality pint of real ale and a bite to eat. Each room has a real fire and, throughout summer, hanging baskets adorn the beer garden and courtyard. House beers are from Enville Brewery, but the pub showcases guest beers both from regional and national breweries. A smaller selection of rotating real ciders is also kept. Local CAMRA Pub of the Year 2018.
QP

Fradley Junction

Swan Inn

Alrewas, DE13 7DN (by Trent & Mersey Canal, about 1 mile W of Fradley village) SK140140
12-11; 12-10.30 Sun ☎ (01283) 790330
Everards Beacon Hill, Sunchaser, Tiger, Old Original; 2 changing beers (sourced regionally) H

Inevitably known locally as the Mucky Duck, this late 18th-century, Grade II-listed, mid-terrace pub overlooks the junction of the Trent & Mersey and Coventry canals. The cosy public bar, which retains an old-fashioned charm, and a smaller lounge, are on opposite sides of a central serving area. There is a cellar room, with vaulted brick ceiling, down steps beyond the lounge. Guest beers are usually from Midlands microbreweries. Folk night is Thursday, open mic nights the second and fourth Sundays of the month. Boaters and walkers welcome. **Q P**

Gentleshaw

Olde Windmill

Windmill Lane, WS15 4NF SK051118
12-midnight ☎ (01543) 682468 yeoldewindmill.co.uk
Draught Bass; 3 changing beers (sourced nationally)
Welcoming 400-year-old country pub with smartly attired staff and equally sharp food and drink offerings. Free of tie, the two guest ales are usually interesting microbrews. The cosy bar is dog friendly, while the wood-panelled lounge offers freshly cooked meals including interesting specials. Both rooms feature old beams (some cleverly fake!) and open fires. A number of teams use the Crown bowling green. The pub is 100 yards from the stump of an old disused windmill.
Q P (62)

Gnosall

George & the Dragon

46 High Street, ST20 0EX
4-10.30; 2-10.30 Sat; 12-10.30 Sun ☎ 07779 327551
georgeandthedragongnosall.com
Holden's Golden Glow; Wood Shropshire Lad; 3 changing beers (sourced locally)
This lovely little pub opened in 2015 and soon received acclaim, winning the CAMRA branch Cider Pub of the Year 2016 and Pub of the Year 2016. The building dates from 1736, with a past life as a home, shop and off-licence. It has two rooms served by one bar. With no TV, no music and no bandits, it has a good old-fashioned appeal. Tasty home-made snacks are available at the bar but they do sell out fast. **Q (5)**

Hednesford

Bridge Inn

387 Cannock Road, WS11 5TD (on jct with Belt Rd)
12-11 (midnight Fri & Sat) ☎ (01543) 423651
Banks's Amber Ale; 6 changing beers (sourced nationally)
Located close to Cannock Chase, this real ale-based pub prides itself on a changing selection of ales as well as real cider. Food is served Thursday to Sunday, all produced on-site using only fresh local produce. The chips are triple-cooked and the burgers are from the pub's own special recipe. Theme nights and live music feature most Saturday nights, and pool and darts teams are also based at the pub. **P**

Cross Keys Hotel

42 Hill Street, WS12 2DN
12-midnight ☎ (01543) 879534
Draught Bass; Holden's Golden Glow; Salopian Oracle; Wye Valley HPA; 5 changing beers (sourced nationally; often Beowulf, Ludlow, Three Tuns)
A former coaching inn dating back to 1746 and serving up to eight real ales including several guests. Hednesford Town football club was originally based behind the pub and the licensee is an ex-player and is now assistant manager. Sporting and historic photographs decorate the walls, and monthly quiz nights are held. It is rumoured that the highwayman Dick Turpin stopped here on his famous ride to York. Local CAMRA Pub of the Year many times.
P

High Offley

Anchor Inn ★

Peggs Lane, Old Lea, ST20 0NG (by bridge 42 of the Shropshire Union Canal) SJ775256
closed Mon-Thu; 7-11 Fri & Sat; 12-3 Sun
☎ (01785) 284569
Wadworth 6X
An unspoilt example of a 19th-century canalside pub, built around 1830 on the Shropshire Union Canal, England's last narrow trunk canal. It has been run by the same family since 1870. The right-hand room has a quarry-tile floor, two high-back settles, a window bench and scrubbed tables, all of which create a timeless atmosphere. There is a large garden and camping on-site.
Q P

Hollington

Raddle Inn

Quarry Bank, ST10 4HQ
8am-2am ☎ (01889) 507278 raddleinn.com
Brains Rev James; Marston's Pedigree, Wainwright; Wychwood Hobgoblin; 1 changing beer (often Peakstones Rock)
Picturesque country pub overlooking Croxden Abbey and the beautiful moorlands countryside, just five minutes' drive from Alton Towers. The pub comprises three separate rooms: two for diners, plus a comfortable bar area for the passing imbiber. There is a large and relaxing beer garden outside, as well as ample car parking space. Accommodation is available in the six log cabins on-site, plus two cottages. There is a pool table and bouncy castle outside, and one of the guest beers will often be from the local Peakstones Rock Brewery. **Q P**

Hopwas

Coton & Hopwas Social Club

School Lane, B78 3AD (turn into School Lane opp Tame Otter; after 200yds bear left over the canal bridge)
5-11 (midnight Fri); 12-midnight Sat; 12-11 Sun
☎ (01827) 62684 cotonandhopwassocialclub.co.uk
Draught Bass; Wye Valley HPA, Butty Bach
A small CIU affiliated members' club – non-members are always welcome. Situated at the end of School Lane, its grounds are bordered by the Coventry Canal and Hopwas Woods. There is a pleasant bar plus a room for private functions. A regular programme of activities includes ladies' darts, karate, zumba and bingo. Thursday is folk club night and Sunday is charity quiz night. A popular summer beer festival draws crowds.
P

Kinver

Cross Inn

Church Hill, DY7 6HZ

12-11 (midnight Fri & Sat) ☎ (01384) 878481

Black Country Bradley's Finest Golden, Pig on the Wall, Fireside; 4 changing beers (sourced nationally; often Fixed Wheel, Oakham, Salopian)

A 19th-century pub near to the Staffordshire & Worcestershire Canal. It originally brewed its own beers but today operates as part of the Black Country Ales chain. The pub has a large L-shaped room with a log-burning fire. Cobs and snacks are served at the bar while hot pork sandwiches and 'grey paes' are available on weekends and bank holidays. Stourbridge buses stop nearby, but there is no service after 6pm or on Sundays. P (228)

Kinver Constitutional Club

119 High Street, DY7 6HL

12 (5 Mon & Tue)-11; 12-midnight Fri; 11.30-midnight Sat ☎ (01384) 872044 kinverconstitutionalclub.co.uk

Hobsons Best; Malvern Hills Black Pear; Olde Swan Bumble Hole Bitter; Three Tuns Cleric's Cure; Wye Valley Butty Bach; 9 changing beers (sourced locally; often Enville, Holden's, Kinver Brewery)

Popular club at the heart of Kinver High Street with a large snooker room at the rear and an open-plan bar area which has separate tables for diners. Card-carrying CAMRA members are welcome but will pay a higher price. It is a festival of beer every day, with over a dozen to choose from. Buses from Stourbridge stop nearby, but there is no service after 6pm or on Sundays. CAMRA branch Club of the Year 2008-18. P (228)

Plough & Harrow

82 High Street, DY7 6HD

4-11; 12-midnight Fri-Sun ☎ (01384) 872659

Bathams Mild Ale, Best Bitter

Affectionately nicknamed Steps, this characterful community pub is deservedly popular with locals, cyclists and walkers alike. The front bar sees locals and visitors intermixing and engaging in lively conversation while the plusher lounge is more comfortable. Note the usual Bathams breweriana and old advertising hoardings bedecking the walls. Snacks are available. P (228)

Knighton

Haberdashers Arms

Knighton, ST20 0QH (between Adbaston and Knighton) SJ753275

12.30 (7 Wed & Thu)-midnight; 12.30-1am Fri & Sat ☎ (01785) 280650 haberdashersarms.com

Rowton Moonstruck Mild, Bitter; 1 changing beer (sourced locally)

Built about 1840, this unusual, traditional country pub offers a warm and friendly welcome. The four compact rooms are served from a central bar. The pub hosts a range of events in its large garden including the annual Potato Club show and music festivals; see the Facebook page for details. The collection of oil lamps is not just for decoration – on Lamp Nights, electric lights are switched off and the lamps are lit, creating a relaxed atmosphere. QP

Leek

Earl Grey Inn

38 Ashbourne Road, ST13 5AT

3 (5 Mon)-11; 12-11.30 Fri & Sat; 12-11 Sun ☎ (01538) 372570

Whim Earl Grey Bitter; 4 changing beers (sourced nationally; often Blackjack, Great Heck, Marble)

Leek has become a mecca for CAMRA members from all over the west Midlands and the north of England, with this small, multi award-winning pub at the top of drinkers' must-visit lists. Now a regular entry in this Guide, it is run by joint licensees who are passionate and knowledgeable about the beer they sell from the five handpumps on the bar, including the house beer from local brewery Whim, plus two real ciders. Q

Fountain Inn

14 Fountain Street, ST13 6JR

12-midnight (1am Fri & Sat); 12-11.30 Sun ☎ (01538) 387205

Draught Bass; Falstaff Darkside; Salopian Oracle; St Austell Tribute; Thornbridge Jaipur IPA; 3 changing beers (sourced regionally; often Exmoor, Front Row, Wincle)

A magnificent bank of 10 handpulls greets the eye on entering this smart, well-appointed boozer. Constantly changing guests complement regular ale; two real ciders are also stocked. The experienced landlord prides himself on his beer quality, and the pub was voted local CAMRA Pub of the Year in 2017. Real fires, a suntrap beer garden and an almost full range of past Guides make this a must-visit when in the great pub town of Leek. Live music is an attraction on Sunday evenings. Accommodation is available.

Wilkes Head

15 St Edwards Street, ST13 5DS

12 (3 Mon)-midnight; 12-11 Sun ☎ 07976 592787

Whim Hartington Bitter, Hartington IPA, Flower Power; 2 changing beers (sourced nationally; often Broughton, Burton Bridge)

Regular house beers from local brewery Whim are complemented by an assortment of unusual and often stronger-than-average guests, plus a choice of real cider. An array of past CAMRA awards hanging proudly over the bar attests to why this is the longest continuous Guide entry in this great pub town. The now-famous live music events (dubbed Wilkstonbury) held over weekend slots in the summer months draw in an eclectic mix of local and internationally known musicians. QP

Lichfield

55 Wade Street

55 Wade Street, WS13 6HL

10-11; 10.30-11 Sun ☎ (01543) 415524 55wadestreet.com

Wye Valley HPA; house beer (by AJ's); 4 changing beers

Cosmopolitan bar and eatery where six real ales go head-to-head with cocktails, gins and craft beers. The interior has a bright, contemporary feel, while the front pavement area offers café-style drinking in fine weather. An all-day menu includes breakfast options. The staff are friendly and attentive. The pub is opposite the Garrick Theatre and the main bus station is conveniently nearby.

Beerbohm 🏆

19 Tamworth Street, WS13 6JP

11-11; closed Sun & Mon ☎ (01543) 898252

beerbohm.co.uk

4 changing beers (sourced nationally) Ⓗ

Classy, continental-style café-bar, whose brown and gold colour scheme is enhanced by gilded mirrors and globular chandeliers. An airy upstairs room offers views of the busy pedestrian street below. Four real ales are complemented by upmarket continental draft beers, plus a well-chosen range of foreign bottled beers. The ales can be sampled with a three-thirds paddle. Customers can bring their own food. The unisex toilets are upstairs. Q

Bitter-Suite

55 Upper St John Street, WS14 9DT

closed Mon & Tue; 5-10 Wed; 12-10 Thu; 12-11 Fri & Sat; 2-7 Sun ☎ 07852 179340 bittersuite-micropub.co.uk

Changing beers (sourced nationally; often) Ⓗ

After a gap of 30 years, the former Bridge Inn is once again serving beer. This simple micropub consists of two fairly large rooms, comfortably furnished. As there is no bar, drinks are brought to your table – make your choices from the chalkboard. Four real ciders are offered, plus gins and wines. There are cobs, pork pies and savoury eggs for the peckish. No music or TV allows for a convivial, conversational atmosphere.
Q

Duke of York

23-25 Greenhill, WS13 6DY

12-11.30 (12.30am Fri & Sat) ☎ (01543) 307313

Joule's Blonde, Pale Ale, Slumbering Monk; 4 changing beers Ⓗ

The plainish frontage of this Grade II-listed pub conceals a superb interior: aged beams, aromatic log fires and a rambling layout. The large split-level bar at the front is complemented by a roomy, comfortable lounge to the rear and a side room known as the Courtyard. A Joule's seasonal beer is usually one of the four changing ales, and a wide range of rums, whiskies and country wines is available. An annual beer festival is held.
QP

Horse & Jockey

8-10 Sandford Street, WS13 6QA

11.30-11; 11-11.30 Sat; 11-11 Sun ☎ (01543) 410033

Greene King Abbot; Holden's Golden Glow; Marston's Pedigree; Timothy Taylor Landlord; Wye Valley HPA; 3 changing beers Ⓗ

Local CAMRA Pub of the Year for 2017, this free house is a must on the growing Lichfield real ale circuit. The regular ales are joined by three guests, mainly from microbreweries. There is a cosy snug and a separate games room at the back of the large open-plan bar. Hot food is served 12-3pm Tuesday to Saturday, and a pork pie/cheeseboard selection is always available. Sport is shown on muted TV screens. A 21-plus policy applies.
P

Marchington

Dog & Partridge

Church Lane, ST14 8LJ (250yds along Church Lane from High St)

12-3, 6-11; 12-3, 5-midnight Fri; 12-midnight Sat; 12-11 Sun ☎ (01283) 820394

dogandpartridgemarchington.co.uk

Draught Bass; 3 changing beers (sourced locally; often Abbeydale, Gates Burton, Uttoxeter) Ⓗ

A gem of a village inn with Bass always available, plus a selection of local guest ales on several handpumps. Formerly a restaurant, the pub is split into four main indoor areas with open fires. Food is served lunchtimes and evenings. A pleasant beer garden to the rear is popular in the summer months. It is renowned locally for its weekly live music sessions and regular beer festivals. Parking is available to the side of the pub. Children are welcome. QP(402)

Milwich

Green Man

Sandon Lane, ST18 0EG (on B5027 in centre of village)

5 (12 Thu-Sat)-11; 12-10.30 Sun ☎ (01889) 505310

greenmanmilwich.com

Draught Bass; 5 changing beers (sourced nationally) Ⓗ

An old-fashioned community pub where the licensee has presided for more than a quarter of a century. The Green Man has also appeared in 25 consecutive editions of the Guide, so good beer is assured. There is a large garden to the rear where many events are held including a yearly free music festival. Good pub grub is served; the long single room is split into a bar area at the front with the rear set aside for dining. QP

Newborough

Red Lion

Duffield Lane, DE13 8SH (on B5234, at corner of jct with Yoxall Rd)

12-11 (midnight Fri & Sat); 12-10 Sun ☎ (01283) 576182

redlionnewborough.co.uk

Draught Bass; Marston's 61 Deep, Pedigree; 1 changing beer (sourced regionally) Ⓗ

Popular village local, built in the 17th century as a farmhouse and converted into a pub in the early 1800s. It is now the only pub in the village and an independently owned free house. There is a long, comfortable public bar, plus a smart two-section restaurant which incorporates the former snug and features a number of framed old local photographs. It has imaginative separate menus for main meals, bar snacks and children (no food Sun eve). Occasional themed food evenings and other events are held. P(402A,403)

Newcastle-under-Lyme

Bridge Street Ale House

31 Bridge Street, ST5 2RY

1-10; 12-11 Fri & Sat; 12-9 Sun ☎ (01782) 499394

6 changing beers (sourced nationally; often Coach House, Dorking, Rat) Ⓗ/Ⓖ

The first micropub in the area, the Bridge is a special place for regulars and newcomers alike. From Grum, the charismatic owner, and his hospitable staff, to the quirky decor, the pub oozes charm and appeal. There are four changing guest beers on handpull from various breweries, with more usually available straight from the barrel. An array of ciders also features, several exceptional rums adding to the individuality of this fantastic pub. A Newcastle real ale institution. Q

Hopinn

102 Albert Street, ST5 1JR
4-midnight; 12-midnight Sat; 12-11 Sun
(01782) 711121
Black Sheep Best Bitter; Draught Bass; Oakham Citra; 6 changing beers (sourced nationally; often Mallinsons, Northern Monk, Oakham)
This glorious three-roomed, family-owned free house has excelled since opening in 2014, winning the local CAMRA Pub of the Year on two occasions. The main focus is the nine real ales, showcasing an array of changing breweries as well as a few regulars. KeyKeg ales are also well represented, with five lines dispensing an abundance of quality flavours. Go in – you are guaranteed a warm welcome and wonderful tipple.

Hopwater Cellar

2 Bridge Street, ST5 2RY
12-8 (9 Fri & Sat); 12-4 Sun (01782) 713311
3 changing beers (sourced nationally; often Front Row, Twisted Barrel, Weal Ales)
Since opening in 2015, this bottle shop has flourished and now stocks an impressive range of 500 global beers plus bottled cider. Draught ale is dispensed from one handpump which has seen over 300 different beers from the UK since opening, in addition to the two KeyKeg pumps which usually offer some stronger beers. Dogs are welcome and there is even a dog beer available. The absence of music and TV allows for friendly conversation, which adds to a welcoming atmosphere. Q

Lymestone Vaults

Pepper Street, ST5 1PR
11-11 (midnight Fri & Sat); 12-10.30 Sun
(01782) 615801
Lymestone Stone Cutter, Stone Faced, Foundation Stone, Ein Stein, Stone the Crows; 4 changing beers (sourced regionally; often Facer's, Lymestone, Magpie)
Down a narrow road off the High Street, this multiple award-winning pub is the first of three Lymestone Brewery taphouses; there is always a good range of its beers, both on handpump and in bottles, plus a wide variety of guest ales. Brews from Stray Cat, Lymestone's affiliated brewery, can also be sampled, all in traditional yet modern surroundings with a log-burning stove and a variety of comfortable seating. The lunchtime menu offers hearty home-cooked food at good-value prices.

Wellers

3 Pepper Street, ST5 1PR
4-10 Mon & Tue; 3-10.30 Wed & Thu; 12-11 Fri & Sat; 1-7 Sun (01782) 698080
Weal Ales Weller Weal, Centwealial Milk Stout; 4 changing beers (often Derby, Slater's, Weal Ales)
Opening in 2016, this small pub is at the bottom of a narrow road off the High Street, and is the first tap for Weal Ales Brewery, based a few miles away in Chesterton. Smart, modern and comfortable inside, the pub is named after the legendary Paul Weller, as is the brewery's flagship beer. No food is served but customers are welcome to bring their own and eat it with a Weal or two.

Oulton

Brushmakers Arms

8 Kibblestone Road, ST15 8UW (500yds W of A520, 1 mile NE of Stone)
12-11 (midnight Wed & Sat; 1am Fri) (01785) 812062
Lancaster Bomber; Thwaites Original; 1 changing beer (sourced nationally)
Named after a now-extinct local industry, The Brush is a true community pub in a tiny village where the same licensee has been in situ for more than 27 years. It is an old-fashioned place where the bar is always busy, but there is a quiet comfy lounge off to one side and a suntrap seating and smoking area to the rear. It is pretty much a fixture in the Guide and a winner of many CAMRA branch awards for the consistency of the beer.
Q P (842A)

Penkridge

Star Inn

Market Place, ST19 5DJ (150yds from A449 along New Road)
12-11 (11.30 Thu; midnight Fri & Sat) (01785) 712513
thestarpenkridge.wixsite.com/home
Banks's Amber Ale; Marston's Pedigree, Wainwright; 3 changing beers
A one-room pub with a very welcoming, cosy feel, particularly on a cold winter's day. There are patio and seating areas outside. The pub is in the old Market Place and first traded in 1830. After becoming a private house and a shop, it was restored as a pub in 1981. It has become an important part of the town and community life, with an excellent choice of permanent and changing ales. Not to be missed on your travels around the area. Q P

Rawnsley

Rag

Ironstone Road, WS12 0QD
12-11; 12-10.30 Sun (01543) 277491
theragatrawnsley.co.uk
Castle Rock Harvest Pale; 4 changing beers (sourced nationally)
A free house with five ales on the bar; it now also has a brewery on-site, supplying the bar to the front. An award-winning 100-seat restaurant and seven en-suite rooms make this an ideal base for visiting local attractions such as Lichfield Cathedral, Trentham Village, Monkey Forest and Chasewater Light Railway. There is a bowling green at the rear. Regular summer barbecues are held.
Q P

Rugeley

Plaza

Horsefair, WS15 2EJ
9am-11.30 (12.30am Fri & Sat) (01889) 586831
Greene King Abbot; Ruddles Best Bitter; Sharp's Doom Bar; 7 changing beers (sourced locally; often Beowulf, Blythe, Salopian)
Previously a cinema dating from the 1930s, this spacious Wetherspoon pub retains much of the cinematic atmosphere and Art Deco flourishes of the period. The light and airy interior allows for three widely separated levels, accentuated by a large window area where the cinema screen once was; this leads to a drinking area outside with

balcony, terrace and lawned beer garden. Around seven guest ales are offered, with micros such as Salopian proving popular. The small car park is Pay & Display. Q P

Rusty Barrel

103 Fernwood Drive, WS15 2GS
closed Mon; 4-11; 1-11 Fri-Sun therustybarrel.co.uk
4 changing beers (sourced locally) H
The first micropub in this town, a single room establishment with a friendly atmosphere. The decor is simple painted brick with the ceiling adorned with pumpclips showing the vast array of beers that have been sold. There are four handpumps offering a varied selection of beers. At least five ciders are also available, plus a good choice of wines, gins and whiskies. Dogs are are welcome, as are children up to 7pm.
Q P (22,825)

Salt

Holly Bush Inn

Salt Road, ST18 0BX (turn W off A518 opp Weston Hall)
SJ959277
12-11 (01889) 508234 hollybushinn.co.uk
Adnams Southwold Bitter; Marston's Pedigree; 1 changing beer (sourced regionally; often Lymestone) H
The pub has antecedents possibly dating back to the 12th century; the current thatched building is said to date back to the early 17th century, though much altered over the years. It has a stellar reputation for its food, meaning that there is limited standing room for drinkers – most of the lounge, snug and bar area are set aside for diners.
P

Stafford

Bird in Hand

Victoria Square, ST16 2AQ (corner of Victoria Square)
12-11 (midnight Fri & Sat) (01785) 252198
Black Country Bradley's Finest Golden, Pig on the Wall, Fireside; 3 changing beers (sourced regionally) H
A welcoming and comfortable pub in Stafford town centre, refurbished in 2017. The venue has a traditional feel to it, with three rooms and open fires. It has a function room for private hire and also hosts live music on Sunday evenings. It boasts the largest beer garden in the town centre, and offers home-cooked food to complement the ales it serves, including a carvery on Sundays.

Floodgate Ale House

147 Newport Road, ST16 2EZ
closed Mon; 5-10 Tue-Thu; 2-11 Fri & Sat; 2-10 Sun
07917 885821
5 changing beers (sourced nationally) H
A one-room micropub with space for 45 people. There are plenty of tables and it is a good place for conversation. Up to five real ciders are sold and 30 whiskies. It is normally closed on Mondays, except for a monthly Tiny Pub Concert night. The walls are adorned with pumpclips that show the incredible range of beers that have been sold. Winner of the local CAMRA Urban Pub of the Year Award in 2017.
Q

Greyhound

12 County Road, ST16 2PU (off A34, opp jail)
4 (12 Sat)-midnight; 12-11 Sun (01785) 222432
greyhoundfreehousestafford.co.uk
Bradfield Farmers Blonde; 7 changing beers (sourced nationally) H
A short walk from the centre of Stafford, this two-room free house is well worth a visit. The pub dates from 1831 and a newspaper article from the day it opened can be seen above the bar. Today the pub offers a changing range of eight beers, often from the north-east, especially Yorkshire breweries; it also stocks a range of bottled ciders. The Greyhound has won several CAMRA branch awards including Pub of the Year. Q

King's Arms

11-12 Peel Terrace, ST16 3HD (off B5066 Sandon Rd)
12-11.30 (11 Mon-Wed) (01785) 246562
kings-arms-staffordshire.co.uk
Draught Bass; 3 changing beers (sourced nationally) H
Converted a long time ago from two terraced houses, it has been further opened up in more recent times but retains a separate snug and a bar, and has a surprisingly large garden. With two dartboards, it supports a number of darts teams who play Tuesday to Thursday, as well as a crib team on Thursday. A good turnaround of ales is complemented by a number of real ciders. There is regular live music (see the pub website for details) as well as beer and cider festivals.
(4,5)

Olde Rose & Crown

10 Market Street, ST16 2JZ
12-11 (midnight Fri & Sat); 12-10.30 Sun
(01785) 251343
Joule's Blonde, Pale Ale, Slumbering Monk; 2 changing beers (sourced locally) H
This comfortable Joule's house is right in the heart of Stafford and is much larger than it looks from the outside. Five handpumps serve Joule's ales and guests. Lunches are served Monday to Saturday and bar snacks using locally sourced ingredients are available all day. Next to the Gatehouse Theatre, the pub is a favourite of theatregoers and is frequented by cast members enjoying an after-show drink. An acoustic night is held every Wednesday, with a jazz and blues night monthly on Thursdays. Q

Picture House

14 Bridge Street, ST16 2HL
8am-midnight (1am Fri & Sat) (01785) 222941
Greene King Abbot; Ruddles Best Bitter; 4 changing beers (sourced nationally; often Slater's) H
A Wetherspoon conversion of a small 1914 provincial cinema. It retains many original and ornate features including the entrance foyer and projection room. Posters from the golden age of film adorn the walls. The pub is a cinemagoer's delight and on Wednesday nights at 9pm films are once again shown. A wide selection of real ales is served to a mixed clientele and the bar is often busy in the evenings. There is an outdoor drinking area overlooking the River Sow.
Q

Sun

7 Lichfield Road, ST17 4JX
12-11 (midnight Fri & Sat) (01785) 248361
thesunstafford.co.uk

Everards Tiger; Titanic Steerage, Iceberg, White Star, Captain Smith's Strong Ale; 6 changing beers (sourced nationally) H
A popular town-centre pub owned by Titanic Brewery. Twelve handpumps supply a constant choice of beers from Titanic's own range and others from around the country. A good choice of food is available, primarily from local sources, with different meal deals each night. Titanic and other shipping memorabilia are to be found throughout the pub. An outdoor drinking area with its own bar is great on warmer days. **Q**

Stoke-on-Trent: Burslem

Bull's Head

14 St John's Square, ST6 3AJ
3-11 (11.30 Wed & Thu); 12-midnight Fri & Sat; 12-11 Sun
(01782) 834153
Titanic Steerage, Iceberg, White Star, Plum Porter; 6 changing beers (sourced nationally) H
Titanic's brewery tap in Burslem, a 10-minute walk from Port Vale's ground; the pub opens at 11am on Vale home Saturdays and is welcoming to all supporters, home and away. This is a two-room pub with an island bar with up to 10 real ales on tap, as well as seven or more real ciders and perries, available straight from the cellar, alongside draught and bottled Belgian beers. Bar billiards, table skittles and a jukebox are in the bar. There is a large outside seating area at the rear. **Q**

Bursley Ale House

Wedgwood Place, ST6 4ED
12-11; 12-10.30 Sun (01782) 911393
5 changing beers (often Abbeydale, Blue Monkey, Charnwood) H
Smallish pub on two floors, run along the lines of a microbar; the cellar is on the ground floor to the right of the door. Five ales are served from handpumps off the bar and can be from a wide variety of breweries. There is a beer patio outside to the front. The regular curry and pint nights are always a big draw, with a real fire and friendly staff adding to the warm welcome. Two real ciders are stocked. (3,98)

Duke William

2 St John's Square, ST6 3AJ
12-11 (midnight Fri & Sat) (01782) 814809
dukewilliamburslem.co.uk
Greene King Abbot; Oakham Citra; Sarah Hughes Dark Ruby Mild; 5 changing beers (sourced nationally; often Abbeydale, Acorn, Salopian) H
An imposing mock-Tudor building in the heart of Burslem with a friendly, relaxed atmosphere. Since reopening in 2010 after a sympathetic refurbishment, this free house has become a popular haunt both for diners and drinkers. Original features remain, such as the horseshoe-shaped bar and its heated foot rail, bell pushes in the lounge, the serving hatch and leaded windows. The ground floor has a lounge and a snug, plus a large public bar; the splendid restaurant with its own bar is on the first floor.

Stoke-on-Trent: Etruria

Holy Inadequate

67 Etruria Old Road, ST1 5PE
4-11 (midnight Thu); 12-midnight Fri & Sat; 12-11 Sun
07771 358238
Joule's Pale Ale; 5 changing beers (sourced nationally; often Beartown, Burton Bridge, Hawkshead) H
Multiple award-winning free house just outside Hanley, an instant hit from the day it opened. The Holy is a proper drinkers' pub, with bare floorboards, bench seating, plus a variety of stools and chairs at the back. Delicious pork pies & scotch eggs are available all day. After what seemed like an age, the first beer from the on-site Inadequate Brewery appeared on the bar in June 2017; there is usually a stout or bitter from the range but this may vary as time goes on. A true classic. **P**

Stoke-on-Trent: Hanley

BottleCraft

33 Piccadilly, ST1 1EN
12-9 (10 Fri & Sat); 12-6 Sun (01782) 911819
bottlecraft.beer
12 changing beers (sourced nationally; often Brew by Numbers, Kernel, Partizan)
Modern but comfortable craft beer bar in the centre of Hanley, serving two traditional cask beers and ten KeyKeg ales. Friendly and enthusiastic staff are more than happy to help you with your beer choice. There is also a vast array of real ale and real cider in a bottle to tempt you; the upstairs room can be hired for functions. It moved to its new address in 2017; the previous establishment was located around a couple of corners. **Q**

Victoria Lounge Bar

5 Adventure Place, ST1 3AF (opp Hanley bus station)
10-11 (01782) 273530 thereardon.com
Draught Bass; Greene King Abbot; 4 changing beers (sourced nationally; often Blue Monkey, Brains) H
A gem of a pub run by the same family for 34 years. Customers can enjoy one of six changing real ales from all around the country while relaxing on a Chesterfield sofa. Beer styles are clearly shown to help you make your choice and the friendly staff are more than happy to advise and chat. It is the ideal place for pre-theatre drinks, meeting friends or waiting for your bus (Hanley bus station is opposite); a warm welcome and good beer are guaranteed. **Q**

Stoke-on-Trent: Hartshill

Greyhound

67 George Street, ST5 1JT
12-11 (11.30 Wed & Thu; midnight Fri); 11-midnight Sat; 11-11 Sun (01782) 635814
Everards Tiger; Titanic Steerage, Iceberg, White Star, Plum Porter; 4 changing beers (sourced nationally; often Nethergate, Portobello, Rooster's) H
A friendly, traditional pub boasting nine handpumps which showcase a selection of beers from the excellent local Titanic range plus an exciting and varying range of quality real ales catering to all tastes from across the UK. Very dog friendly, it has a warm, welcoming atmosphere and a cosy fire in winter. Bottled beers, real cider, country wines and craft beer are also served, as well as tasty bar snacks. Occasional live music from local groups features, and it has a regular, lively pub quiz on Sunday nights. **Q**

Sanctuary 🄻
493-495 Hartshill Road, ST4 6AA
closed Mon; 3-10 (11 Fri); 12-11 Sat; 3-8 Sun
☎ (01782) 437523
4 changing beers (often Backyard, Cross Bay, Lymestone)
A newcomer to the Stoke pub scene and a true sanctuary in every sense, this wonderful pub features four changing real ales, four varied real ciders and a choice of bottled beers plus wines and gins. Ales are both from local brewers and from further afield. Decorated in a cosy and eclectic style, including quirky features such as leather car seats and a rocking chair, this one-room pub feels like a home from home where all are made welcome. Q

Stoke-on-Trent: Longton

Congress Inn 🄻
14 Sutherland Road, ST3 1HJ (¼ mile from Longton bus and rail stations, opp police station)
2-11; 12-midnight Fri-Sun ☎ (01782) 763667
congressinnlongton.co.uk
Adnams Broadside; Castle Rock Sheriff's Tipple; Townhouse Styrian Pale, Gladstone Strong Ale; 5 changing beers (sourced nationally; often Acorn, Wadworth, Welbeck Abbey) 🄷
Friendly community pub with nine cask ales, two or three ciders and a large range of Belgian and Samuel Smith's bottled beers. There is a beer and cider festival every May. The pub is a Victorian building with sash windows, quarry tiles, high ceilings and a large display of breweriana, including original, restored Joule's signage on the delivery gates, with antique Joule's lighting hanging over them. A regular Guide entry, the pub also supports its local community, contributing to four charities.

Stoke-on-Trent: Stoke

London Road Ale House 🄻
241 London Road, ST4 5AA
3-10; 12-11 Fri-Sun ☎ (01782) 698070
6 changing beers (sourced nationally; often Burton Bridge, Coach House, Great Orme) 🄷
A short walk from Stoke town centre, this is a vibrant, convivial one-room pub where conversation is encouraged. London Road offers six changing high-quality real ales plus six rotating real ciders. Smaller breweries feature heavily and all beer styles are accounted for. These sit alongside an extensive bottled beer selection plus wines and spirits. Cheeses and pork pies are served, or bring your own food to eat with your beer. Tuesday is quiz night. Q (21,21A)

White Star 🄻
63 Kingsway, ST4 1JB (off Church St, close to King's Hall)
11-midnight; 12-11 Sun ☎ (01782) 848734
Everards Tiger; Titanic Steerage, Anchor Bitter, Iceberg, White Star, Plum Porter; 4 changing beers (sourced nationally; often Everards, Titanic) 🄷
This popular, multi award-winning pub is one of the renowned Titanic Brewery fleet, with a well-established reputation for the quality of its beers. Internally, the pub has a large, comfortably furnished split-level bar, with photos and information about the liner Titanic adorning the walls, adding to the atmosphere. With 10 handpumps, five Titanic beers are supplemented by Everards Tiger and four changing guests. A menu of fresh home-cooked food is served lunchtimes and evenings; a function room is also available. Q

Stone

Borehole
Unit 5, Mount Road Industrial Estate, Mount Road, ST15 8LL
12-10 (11 Fri & Sat) ☎ (01785) 813581
Lymestone Stone Cutter, Stone Faced, Foundation Stone, Ein Stein, Stone the Crows; 2 changing beers (sourced regionally) 🄷
The Borehole was originally an office for Bent's Brewery and has proved a hit since opening in 2015. Small and friendly, there are eight handpumps offering the majority of the Lymestone range plus guests. Children are welcome until 8pm, as are dogs, and the pub has won several dog-friendly awards. It is very much a LocAle pub as the casks are brought down the estate road direct from the brewery. A variety of bar snacks is available.
Q P (101)

Royal Exchange
26 Radford Street, ST15 8DA (on corner of Northesk St and Radford St)
12-11 (midnight Fri & Sat) ☎ (01785) 812685
Everards Tiger; Titanic Steerage, Iceberg, White Star, Plum Porter, Captain Smith's Strong Ale; 4 changing beers (sourced nationally) 🄷
A one-roomed corner pub with four distinct drinking areas and real fires at both ends. Ten real ales are sold alongside a real cider. The four changing beers are mainly from microbreweries. There are no TVs but acoustic music and quiz nights are hosted and the pub is home to a number of clubs including knitting, reading, gaming and photography. Light snacks, and lunches on Friday and Saturday, are made with local ingredients.
Q

Swan Inn 🏆
18 Stafford Street, ST15 8QW (on A520 near Trent & Mersey Canal)
12-1am (11 Mon; midnight Tue & Wed); 12-11 Sun
☎ (01785) 815570 swaninnstone.co.uk
House beer (by Coach House); 8 changing beers (sourced nationally) 🄷
A thriving free house in a carefully renovated Grade II-listed building, close to the Trent & Mersey Canal. With nine handpulls, The Swan serves as a permanent mini beer festival. It has a gin bar and a pleasant open rear area which is partially covered. Four real ciders and bottled varieties are sold. A long-running themed beer festival is held in July. Music evenings are Wednesday, Thursday and Saturday, often heavy rock and featuring nationally known acts. Strictly adults-only at all times.
(101)

Tamworth

King's Ditch 🄻
51 Lower Gungate, B79 7AS
closed Mon; 5-9 Tue & Wed; 5-10.30 Thu; 4-10.30 Fri; 12-10.30 Sat; 12-9 Sun ☎ 07989 805828 kingsditch.co.uk
6 changing beers 🄶
Tamworth's first micropub, opened in 2015. The single ground-floor room is simply decorated, with the novel feature of a TV screen showing the cellar.

There is an additional small drinking area upstairs. Up to six ales and 30 real ciders are served, with the pub having been a finalist in CAMRA's national Cider Pub of the Year competition for both 2016 and 2017. Simple snacks are available. Occasional beers festivals are held. Children are welcome until 7pm.

Market Vaults

7 Market Street, B79 7LU

3-10 Mon; 12-10 Tue; 12-11 Wed & Thu; 12-midnight Fri & Sat; 12-9 Sun (01827) 66552

Joule's Pale Ale; 7 changing beers (often Bathams, Sarah Hughes)

Traditional, historic town-centre pub close to the attractive town hall and Norman castle. The bar room at the front is partnered by a comfier lounge to the rear. In winter the pub is cheered by solid fuel stoves, while a suntrap walled garden at the back provides sanctuary on fine days. The seven guest beers change often, and a wide range of real ciders is available. Hot lunchtime food is served daily except Mondays. May close early if quiet.

Sir Robert Peel

13-15 Lower Gungate, B79 7BA

2 (4 Tue)-11; 12-11 Sat & Sun (01827) 300910

House beer (by Church End); 5 changing beers (often Salopian)

Popular town-centre free house which has featured in the last 15 editions of the Guide. Named after the town's historic statesman, the pub has benefited from the recent addition of a large beer garden at the rear, overlooked by the historic St Editha's Church. Attentive staff dispense up to five changing ales, plus four real ciders and a large selection of foreign bottled beers. The pub is lively at weekends, with the jukebox providing music to suit all tastes.

Tamworth Tap

29 Market Street, B79 7LR

closed Mon-Wed; 4-10.45 Thu & Fri; 12-10.45 Sat; 12-9 Sun 07712 893353

4 changing beers

Tamworth's first brewery in 70 years has its home in the centre of town. This former tourist information office houses both Tamworth Brewing Company and its taphouse. The four handpulls feature at least two Tamworth beers, with local microbrewery ales usually completing the lineup. Simple snacks are offered, plus a range of gins, wines and bottled beers. The historic courtyard terrace to the rear offers unique views of Tamworth Castle. Opening hours may change.

Trysull

Bell Inn

Bell Road, WV5 7JB

11.30-3, 5-11 (midnight Fri); 11.30-midnight Sat; 12-11 Sun (01902) 892871

Bathams Best Bitter; Holden's Black Country Bitter, Golden Glow; 3 changing beers (sourced regionally; often Burton Bridge, Enville, Ludlow)

A fine 18th-century building next to the village church. It has a small yet cosy bar, a pleasant lounge and a large dining room. An extensive food menu is available in the lounge and restaurant. There is a large patio area at the front which overlooks several picturesque residential properties. The pub is popular with walkers; the Staffordshire & Worcestershire Canal is 15 minutes away.

Tutbury

Cross Keys

39 Burton Street, DE13 9NR (E side of village, 300yds from A511)

closed Mon; 11-3, 5-11; 12-9 Sun (01283) 813677

Burton Bridge Draught Burton Ale; 3 changing beers (sourced regionally)

Privately owned 19th-century free house, overlooking the Dove Valley and providing a fine view of Tutbury Castle. The two split-level rooms, public bar and lounge, have a homely feel and are served from a similarly split-level bar. There is a separate large dining room to the rear (evening meals Tue-Sat, lunches Sun only). This is the only pub in the area which has offered Draught Burton Ale since its launch by Ind Coope in 1976 through to its 2015 reincarnation by Burton Bridge.

Uttoxeter

Horse & Dove

21 Market Place, ST14 8HY

3.30-10 (11 Thu); 12.30-11 Fri & Sat; 12.30-10 Sun (01889) 735942 horsendove.co.uk

6 changing beers (sourced locally; often Heritage, Titanic, Uttoxeter)

A warm welcome awaits visitors to the town's first micropub. It has a pleasant traditional decor with plenty of hard and soft furnishings ensuring a cosy but vibrant atmosphere. An excellent selection of up to six real ales, with many offerings from local breweries, plus a lengthy real cider list and a selection of gins, means all tastes are catered for. Snacks are served from the bar. Friendly staff and regulars ensure a pleasant and varied drinking experience.

Old Swan

Market Place, ST14 8HN

8am-midnight (1am Fri & Sat) (01889) 598650

Greene King Abbot; Ruddles Best Bitter; Sharp's Doom Bar; 3 changing beers (sourced locally; often Backyard, Lymestone, Slater's)

Centrally located close to the town's marketplace, this Wetherspoon pub attracts a varied clientele throughout the day. Up to six handpumps are in use at any one time with a varied choice of frequently changing local and national ales. A large open-plan seating area downstairs is supplemented with a quieter upper level to the rear. A small rear outdoor patio and separate smoking area are also provided. Food is served all day. Busy on race days.

Weston

Woolpack Inn

The Green, ST18 0JH (off A518)

11-11 (midnight Fri & Sat); 11.30-11 Sun (01889) 270238 woolpackpubweston.co.uk

Banks's Amber Ale; Marston's Pedigree; Ringwood Boondoggle; 2 changing beers (sourced nationally)

A popular community pub on the village green. Refurbished in 2017, it has oak beams (not all original) and lovely fireplaces. There is a big beer garden that is attractive in summer months. It was

originally a row of cottages and a blacksmith's shop before being converted. There is a decent choice of well-kept Marston's beers and it serves reasonably priced meals.
Q🍺❀◑◐♿♣P🚌(841)🐾📶

Whiston

Swan at Whiston

Whiston Road, ST19 5QH (in Penkridge, turn W off A449 at roundabout by Hodsons onto Bungham Lane, cross Cuttlestone Bridge and follow signs to Whiston) SJ895144
⏲ 5-9 Mon; 12-3, 5-11; 12-11 Sat; 12-10.30 Sun
☎ (01785) 716200 🌐 swanwhiston.co.uk
Holden's Black Country Bitter, Golden Glow; 4 changing beers (sourced nationally) Ⓗ
Although remotely situated, The Swan's high-quality, well-kept ales and superb food make this a thriving pub. Built in 1593, burned down and rebuilt in 1711, the oldest part today is the small bar housing an inglenook fireplace. The lounge features an intriguing double-sided log fire. Six acres of grounds include a children's play area, aviary and a large beer garden which get busy on summer evenings. The pub has a welcoming ambience. Q🍺❀◑◐⛺♣🍎P🚌(878,76)🐾📶

Wolstanton

Archer

21 Church Lane, ST5 0EH
⏲ 12-11 (midnight Fri & Sat) ☎ (01782) 740467
Greene King Abbot; Hop Back Citra, Summer Lightning; house beer (by Hop Back); 3 changing beers (often Hop Back, Six Bells, Weal Ales) Ⓗ
A busy neighbourhood pub with a mature clientele and a good early doors trade, with one large, rambling bar replete with nooks and crannies. There is a walled patio along the front of the pub for smokers. Called The New Smithy for around 15 years, in 2016 the landlord persuaded owners Hop Back to revert the pub to its previous name The Archer, much to the delight of the locals – a house beer is brewed under the same name. Q❀♣🍎P🚌

Wilkes Head, Leek (Photo: Bob Steel)

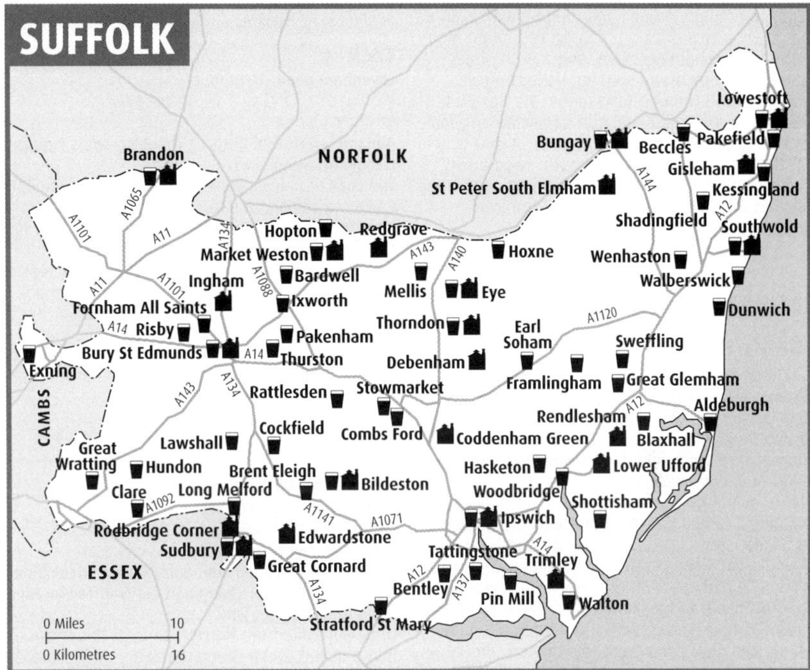

Aldeburgh

White Hart

222 High Street, IP15 5AJ

11.30-11; 12-10.30 Sun ☎ (01728) 453205

Adnams Southwold Bitter, Ghost Ship, Broadside; 3 changing beers (often Adnams)

Friendly single bar, formerly used as a public reading room, next to the town's renowned chippy. Drinkers can buy fish and chips from next door and eat them in the garden, weather permitting, with a drink from the bar. Live music features on occasion. Families are welcome to use the garden in the summer months, with a covered barbecue and wood-fired pizza oven in use Easter to mid-September.

Bardwell

Dun Cow

Up Street, IP31 1AA (approx 1 mile off A143 at Stanton)

11.30-2.30, 5-midnight; 12-midnight Sat; 12-10.30 Sun ☎ (01359) 250806

Greene King IPA; Young's Bitter; 3 changing beers

A traditional pub in a pleasant village set in the Suffolk countryside. The pub has two bars and offers speciality food nights. Six real ales are available at weekends. Outside is a covered smoking area and large family space in the garden. Parties and coaches are welcome if booked in advance. The picturesque restored village windmill is worth a visit and has occasional threshing open days. P

Beccles

Butchers Arms

51 London Road, NR34 9YT

4-midnight; 12-12.30am Fri & Sat; 12-midnight Sun ☎ (01502) 712243 mypub.org.uk

Woodforde's Nelson's Revenge; 5 changing beers (sourced nationally; often Green Jack, St Peter's, Woodforde's)

Situated opposite Beccles Cemetery, this popular pub serves up to six real ales. Live music, open mic evenings and charity events are hosted. The pub originally had separate lounge and public bars, both with bay windows, but is now open plan following a 1980s extension. The bar and real fire are in the original pub area, with more seating and pool tables in the extension. Customers are welcome to bring their own meals to eat on the premises. P(90)

Caxton Club

Gaol Lane, NR34 9SJ

12-1.30 (not Tue), 7-11; 12-2, 6.30-11 Fri; 12-11 Sat; 12-10.30 Sun ☎ (01502) 712829

4 changing beers (sourced nationally; often Green Jack, Greene King, Woodforde's)

Spacious club conveniently situated a short walk from train and bus stations and close to the town centre. All members and guests are warmly welcomed (a small charge is made to cover entertainment on Saturday evenings). It has a central bar, TV and darts room, and a snooker room. There is also a large function room, garden with children's play area and a bowling green. Four real ales and a large choice of real ciders are available. Guide dogs only are allowed.

Bentley

Case Is Altered

Capel Road, IP9 2DW

closed Mon & Tue; 12-2.30 (3 Sat), 6-11.30; 12-4, 7-10.30 Sun ☎ (01473) 805575 thecasepubbentley.co.uk

Adnams Southwold Bitter; 3 changing beers (sourced locally)

Local community owned and run pub with a single bar serving two drinking areas, a restaurant area with a wood-burning stove, and a pretty beer garden with plenty of seating. Various music evenings and themed food nights are hosted but there is no TV. Traditional pub games are available including darts, cards and dominoes. A quiz is held on the last Saturday of the month. Local artists' work is on display. Some of the produce used in the kitchen is now grown at home by the local community.

Bildeston

King's Head

132 High Street, IP7 7ED

closed Mon & Tue; 6-11.30 Wed & Thu; 4-11.30 Fri; 12-11.30 Sat; 12-10.30 Sun (01449) 741434

bildestonkingshead.co.uk

Kings Head Bildeston Best, Brettvale Gold; 4 changing beers (sourced locally) H

Home of the King's Head Brewery since 1996, the building's carved timbers indicate its history as part of a larger complex dating from around 1530. Now a single bar with a large, cosy inglenook fireplace, a friendly alehouse atmosphere has evolved, with food available at weekends only. There is a fully enclosed rear garden with a covered patio area, lawns and play equipment for children. The late May bank holiday beer festival is long established and popular.

Blaxhall

Ship

School Road, IP12 2DY

12 (11 Mon)-11.30 (01728) 688316

blaxhallshipinn.co.uk

Adnams Southwold Bitter; Woodforde's Wherry; 3 changing beers H

A cosy two-roomed 16th-century pub with a long reputation for traditional singing in the main bar. The menu offers a wide choice of home-made dishes and daily specials using locally sourced ingredients (book for breakfast from 10.30am in the summer months). Live entertainment includes folk music, bands and story-telling every week, and the pub hosts a Folk East stage during the festival weekend. Letting chalets are available beside the pub and camping at the nearby village hall is by arrangement.

Brandon

Ram

High Street, IP27 0AX

11-1am; 12-1am Sun (01842) 810275

Adnams Ghost Ship; Greene King Abbot, IPA Reserve H

Said to be one of the oldest surviving buildings in Brandon, this attractive Grade II listed building dates back 500 years in parts. A wonderful log fire greets you as you enter this friendly, family owned and run free house. It is home to regular club nights for the Iceni Car Club, Classic Vehicle Club, Model Engineering Club, Brandon Speakers Club and the Champions Poker League.

Brent Eleigh

Cock ★

Lavenham Road, CO10 9PB

12-4, 6-11; 12-11 Fri & Sat; 12-10.30 Sun

(01787) 247371

Adnams Southwold Bitter; 2 changing beers (sourced locally; often Adnams) H

The Cock remains a gem and has been identified by CAMRA as having a nationally important historic interior. It has two bars, the smaller one ideal for families. The landlady provides good food throughout opening times, including Sunday roasts, keeping visiting walkers and cyclists more than happy. Seating outside is ideal for watching the world go by. The pub has cats but well-behaved dogs are always welcome. Real cider comes from local suppliers. Q P (111)

Bungay

Green Dragon

29 Broad Street, NR35 1EE

11-midnight; 12-midnight Sat; 12-5 Sun

(01986) 892681 greendragonbungay.co.uk

Green Dragon Chaucer Ale, Gold, Bridge Street Bitter H**, Strong Mild** G**; 1 changing beer (sourced locally; often Green Dragon)** H

Originally called the Horse & Groom, this is the home of the Green Dragon Brewery and is located on the northern edge of town. The pub is a regular in the Guide and its ales are brewed in outbuildings next to the car park at the rear (brewery tours are available by appointment). Seasonal ales are often served. There is a public bar and a spacious lounge with a side room where families are welcome, leading to the garden.

Bury St Edmunds

Beerhouse

1 Tayfen Road, IP32 6BH

REAL ALE BREWERIES

Adnams Southwold
Brandon Brandon
Brewshed Ingham
Briarbank Ipswich
Calvors Coddenham Green
Cliff Quay Debenham
Deben Peninsular Rendlesham (NEW)
Dove Street Ipswich
Earl Soham Debenham
Green Dragon Bungay
Green Jack Lowestoft
Greene King Bury St Edmunds
Kings Head Bildeston
Little Earth Project Edwardstone (NEW)
Mauldons Sudbury
Mr Bees Trimley (NEW)
Nethergate Rodbridge Corner
Old Cannon Bury St Edmunds
Old Chimneys Market Weston
Shortts Thorndon
St Judes Ipswich
St Peter's St Peter South Elmham
Star Wing Redgrave
Station 119 Eye
Trinity Gisleham
Uffa Lower Ufford

⏲ 5-11; 12-11 Sat; 12-10 Sun ☎ (01284) 766415
🌐 burybeerhouse.co.uk
Brewshed Best; 7 changing beers (sourced nationally) [H]
Traditional beer house in an unusual semi-circular Victorian building (previously called the Ipswich Arms), handy for the railway station, and refurbished with a modern feel. Seven beer engines provide a selection of well-kept real ales. It also serves its own beers from the Brewshed Brewery, which is now located out of town and supplies the brewery's three other local pubs. Three real ciders are also available. Regular beer festivals and an annual cider festival are hosted. Major sporting events are shown on a big screen. ❀≥●P🚌🐾📶

Dove [L]

68 Hospital Road, IP33 3JU (5 mins' walk from town centre)
⏲ 5-11; 12-3, 6-11 Sat; 12-3, 6-10.30 Sun ☎ (01284) 702787
🌐 thedovepub.co.uk
Woodforde's Wherry [H]**; changing beers** [H]/[G]
No lager, TVs, pool or gaming machines here – the Dove is how pubs used to be, with a traditional, basic main bar and a parlour area. A back-street community free house, it is just five minutes from the town centre. Six ever-changing beers are on handpump alongside a good selection of real ciders, and the staff are knowledgable about the ales. Locally made pies and snacks are available. A former East Anglian CAMRA Regional Pub of the Year and local Cider Pub of the Year in 2018. Q❀♣●P🚌🐾

Oakes Barn

St Andrews Street South, IP33 3PH (opp Waitrose car park)
⏲ 11-11.30; 12-5 Sun ☎ (01284) 761592 🌐 oakesbarn.co.uk
Oakham JHB; Woodforde's Wherry; 4 changing beers (sourced nationally) [H]
A real ale free house and social hub near the town centre with some period features and historic links to the medieval town. Six real ales are always on including one dark beer alongside craft cider. Home-made food comprises lunchtime specials and snacks served all day. There is a covered smoking area outside and an open courtyard with seating. Regular events are held in the bar. An upstairs function room is available to hire. Local CAMRA Pub of the Year 2018. ❀(♿♣●🚌🐾📶

Rose & Crown ✔

48 Whiting Street, IP33 1NP (on corner of Whiting St and Westgate)
⏲ 11.30-11.30; 11.30-3, 7-11.30 Sat; 12-2.30, 8-11.30 Sun
☎ (01284) 755934
Greene King XX Mild, IPA, Abbot; 3 changing beers (sourced nationally) [H]
In sight of Greene King's Westgate Brewery, this is a traditional inn with two bars and a separate off-sales hatch. The present tenants have run the pub for over 30 years and it has been in the same family for over 40 years. Good-value wholesome food is served lunchtimes Monday to Saturday. Regular darts and crib matches and pub quizzes are held. Children are not allowed in the bars but are welcome in the garden. The pub is a Grade II-listed building within the conservation area of Bury St Edmunds, and has a regionally important historic pub interior. Q❀(♣🚌📶

Clare

Cock

3 Callis Street, CO10 8PX
⏲ 11.30-11; 11-11 Sun ☎ (01787) 277391
🌐 thecockinnclare.com
6 changing beers (often Nethergate) [H]
Grade II listed building dating from the early 15th century. A small brewery was located somewhere on-site in the late 19th century. The pub underwent major renovation in 2017 and now offers two ales from the local Nethergate Brewery alongside four guests. Good-quality food is served. Outside, there is a pleasant garden to the rear. A welcome new entry to the Guide and only a few doors down from the Globe. ❀()♿♣P

Globe

10 Callis Street, CO10 8PX
⏲ 5-11.30; 4-11.30 Fri; 11-11.30 Sat; 12-7 Sun
☎ (01787) 278122
Young's Bitter; 3 changing beers (sourced nationally) [H]
A phoenix risen from the ashes, the Globe reopened in 2013 after a two-year closure. Serving one well-kept regular beer and up to three changing guests, it is now a thriving local where beer and conversation dominate. Live music plays every other Saturday night and afternoon sessions every other Sunday. It has a separate pool room at the rear and a pleasant garden for summer drinking. No food is served. Just a few doors away from The Cock. Q❀♣P🚌🐾📶

Cockfield

Horseshoes Inn ✔

Stow's Hill, IP30 0JB
⏲ closed Mon; 12-3, 6-11 (11.30 Fri); 12-11 Sat; 12-6.30 Sun
☎ (01284) 828177 🌐 thehorseshoes-inn.co.uk
Adnams Southwold Bitter, Broadside; house beer (by Black Sheep); 1 changing beer (sourced nationally) [H]
A sympathetically refurbished thatched 14th-century building on the A1141 road to Lavenham. The large, long bar room is divided by a chimney breast into two areas, and there is a separate spacious dining area. The bar area features an exposed crown post and many original beams dating from 1350. Good-value meals are available, with speciality food nights. The hilltop beer garden enjoys fabulous views. Q❀()P🚌🐾📶

Combs Ford

Gladstone Arms [L]

2 Combs Road, IP14 2AP
⏲ 12-midnight (11 Sun) ☎ (01449) 771608
🌐 gladstonearms.co.uk
Adnams Southwold Bitter, Broadside; Crouch Vale Brewers Gold; Fuller's London Pride; Sharp's Doom Bar; Woodforde's Wherry [H]**; 4 changing beers** [H]/[G]
A large open-plan pub serving consistently good beer. The owners also run the Dove Street Inn in Ipswich. The two pubs share a similar beer range, with between 12 and 14 ales, including house beers brewed in Ipswich. Four or five ciders and a wide range of craft lagers, imported foreign beers and whiskies are also on offer. Good-value food is served with vegetarian options. Sports TV is screened and regular live music is hosted. A beer festival features over the Easter weekend. The garden at the rear is by the river.
Q❀()♿♣●P🚌🐾📶

Dunwich

Ship

St James Street, IP17 3DT
⏲ 11-11 ☎ (01728) 648219 🌐 shipatdunwich.co.uk
Adnams Southwold Bitter; 3 changing beers 🄷
Once a haunt of smugglers, this is now a great place to eat, drink, relax and get away from it all. The small public bar is simply furnished with wooden furniture and a woodburner. Comfortable, traditionally furnished rooms have views across the sea or nearby salt marshes. Beers are from local brewers and bottled local cider is available. There is an extensive food menu. The enormous garden has fruit trees including a 300-year-old fig. The beach is a short walk away. Beer festivals are held in March and September. 🐴❀🛏◐◑P🐾📶

Earl Soham

Victoria 𝕃

The Street, IP13 7RL
⏲ 11.30-3, 5.30-11; 11-3, 7-10.30 Sun ☎ (01728) 685758
Earl Soham Victoria Bitter; 2 changing beers (often Cliff Quay, Earl Soham) 🄷
A popular, traditional pub that has changed little over the years and still has an outside toilet, with two small bars and a prominent fireplace (now fitted with a woodburner). An ever-changing food menu with daily specials is offered lunchtimes and evenings, all home-cooked. The pub gets very busy at weekends, especially on sunny days when even a seat in the garden can be hard to find. Dogs and children are welcome. The Earl Soham Brewery was originally behind the pub.
Q🐴❀◐◑♣P🚌🐾📶

Exning

White Horse ✔

23 Church Street, CB8 7EH
⏲ 12-midnight ☎ (01638) 577323
🌐 whitehorseexning.co.uk
Changing beers 🄷
Mentioned in the Domesday Book, this fine free house has been run by the same family since 1935. A 300-year-old pub still retaining much original character, it comprises a public bar, cosy lounge and separate restaurant. At least 10 changing real ales are on offer each week, and a good choice of home-cooked food is served. Happy hour is 5.30-6.30pm, extended to 7pm on Friday. A private room can be hired. Q❀◐◑♣P🚌🐾

Eye

Queen's Head ✔

7 Cross Street, IP23 7AB
⏲ 11-11 ☎ (01379) 870153 🌐 queensheadeye.co.uk
Adnams Southwold Bitter, Broadside; 3 changing beers (often Batemans, Nethergate) 🄶
Dating from 1590, this is now the only pub remaining in this delightful north Suffolk town with many buildings of character and historic significance. The main bar has a wood-burning stove, Cross Street bar is a former butcher's shop, and there is also a snug bar. Beers are dispensed direct from casks (with water-cooling jackets) in the main bar. Traditional pub food and daily specials are served, including breakfast 8.30-10.30am. A community pub where families are welcome. 🐴❀◐◑♣🍎P🚌🐾📶

Fornham All Saints

Three Kings ✔

Hengrave Road, IP28 6LA
⏲ 12-11 (4 Sun) ☎ (01284) 766979 🌐 the-three-kings.com
Greene King IPA; 2 changing beers (sourced nationally; often Greene King, Morland) 🄷
Large 17th-century four-star coaching inn located in this pretty village, just two miles from the historic town of Bury St Edmunds. The pub caters for travellers with en-suite accommodation and offers good-quality food. Various themed food evenings and quiz nights are hosted. The pub's name refers to a legend that Kingsbury Hill (in Fornham St Genevieve) marks the grave of three kings. 🐴❀🛏◐◑♿♣P🐾

Framlingham

Station Hotel 𝕃

Station Road, IP13 9EE
⏲ 12-2.30, 5-11; 12-11 Sat; 11-2.30, 7-10.30 Sun
☎ (01728) 723455 🌐 thestationframlingham.com
Earl Soham Gannet Mild, Victoria Bitter, Brandeston Gold; 2 changing beers (often Earl Soham) 🄷
Cosy two-bar pub set in a former station buffet (the branch line closed in 1963). Beers and a guest cider are dispensed from a set of Edwardian German silver handpumps. It enjoys a good reputation for food, made with locally sourced ingredients and prepared on the premises. An ever-changing menu is displayed on chalkboards. On Sundays, brunch and beers are available from 11am. The garden bar has a wood-fired pizza oven. A beer festival is held over the third weekend in July. Children and dogs welcome. Q🐴❀◐◑🍎P🚌🐾📶

Great Cornard

Five Bells

63 Bures Road, CO10 0HU
⏲ 12-11 ☎ (01787) 379016
Adnams Broadside; Greene King XX Mild; 1 changing beer (sourced nationally) 🄷
A friendly free house situated near the church (home of the five bells) on the main Sudbury to Bures road. The main bar has a library and a piano. A separate small bar is home to a Tunisian restaurant. Outside is a large beer garden behind the car park. Pub games include bar billiards. An open mic session is hosted every third Thursday and karaoke every second Friday of the month. The home-made pies are legendary. A rare outlet for Greene King XX Mild. Q🐴❀◐◑♿♣P🚌🐾📶

Great Glemham

Crown

The Street, IP17 2DA
⏲ 12-3 (not Tue), 6-11; 12-6 Sun ☎ (01728) 663693
🌐 thecrowninnglemham.co.uk
6 changing beers (sourced locally) 🄷
Refurbished to a high standard, this multi-roomed pub has woodburners, traditional tiled floors and many lovely seating areas. Up to 10 beers are on offer during the busy summer months and at least four during quieter periods. Acoustic music sessions feature regularly. The pub hosts a local community lunch once a month and caters for private parties. All food is cooked on the premises, from bar snacks to an à la carte menu (no food Tue).
🐴❀◐◑♣🍎P🚌🐾📶

Great Wratting

Red Lion

School Road, CB9 7HA
⏲ 11-2.30, 5-11; 11-1.30am Sat; 12-3, 7-10 Sun
☎ (01440) 783237
Adnams Southwold Bitter, Broadside; 1 changing beer Ⓗ
A whale's jawbones frame the doorway to this village local dating from the 17th or 18th century, making an unusual and amusing entrance. Now a free house, this ex-Adnams pub offers good beer, quality food and conversation as its mainstay. Locals love this hostelry and are passionate supporters of the activities overseen by an enthusiastic landlord of long experience. Quiz nights and a darts league thrive here.
Q

Hasketon

Turk's Head

Low Road, IP13 6JG
⏲ 11-11 (midnight Fri & Sat); 11-8 Sun ☎ (01394) 610343
theturksheadhasketon.co.uk
Adnams Ghost Ship; Morland Old Speckled Hen; Woodforde's Wherry; 2 changing beers (sourced locally) Ⓗ
The pub has been much refurbished and extended in recent years but retains a cosy two-room timber-framed bar. The main area has a large fireplace with a woodburner, and there is a spacious restaurant and kitchen to the rear. Good food includes renowned Sunday lunches. Three to five beers are on handpump and change regularly. An annual beer festival is held in the summer. Events include quiz nights and themed food nights. The beautiful two-acre garden has pétanque pistes and a fireplace. P

Hopton

Vine

High Street, IP22 2QX
⏲ 3-11; 12-midnight Sat; 12-10.30 Sun ☎ (01953) 688581
Adnams Southwold Bitter, Broadside; Greene King IPA, IPA Reserve; 5 changing beers (sourced locally; often Colchester, Lacons, Wolf) Ⓗ
On the main road near the church, this village local has been revitalised since it was taken over by the current landlord in 2013. Nine ales including a selection of local and regional guests are offered at reasonable prices. There is a pool table in one of its three separate areas. A welcoming pub, popular with locals and visitors, and a former local CAMRA Pub of the Year. P (100)

Hoxne

Swan

Low Street, IP21 5AS
⏲ 12-11; 11-midnight Fri & Sat ☎ (01379) 668275
swaninnhoxne.co.uk
Adnams Southwold Bitter, Broadside; Timothy Taylor Landlord; Woodforde's Wherry Ⓖ
The Swan reopened in 2016 after temporary closure and is once again a thriving village local. The 15th-century building has a colourful history – it claims to be both the former home of the Bishop of Norwich and later a brothel. There is a large open fire in the main bar and a woodburner in the adjacent bar. The restaurant serves excellent home-cooked food, with an emphasis on local produce. To the rear is a large garden. An annual beer festival features in August. Buskers' night is Thursday. P

Hundon

Rose & Crown

20 North Street, CO10 8ED (centre of village)
⏲ closed Mon; 12-2 (not Tue), 6-10; 12-midnight Fri & Sat; 12-9 Sun ☎ (01440) 786261 hundon-village.co.uk/roseandcrown.html
Sharp's Doom Bar; 3 changing beers (sourced nationally; often Fuller's, Mauldons, St Austell) Ⓗ
A traditional country pub comprising two bars with open fires. Home-cooked food is available Thursday to Sunday including popular Sunday roasts. The deceptively large beer garden has a patio for alfresco dining leading to a lawned area with a stage. The outside bar is used for weddings, parties, an annual community music festival over the August bank holiday and other events. The morris men gathering on St George's Day is enjoyed by all. A proud winner of local CAMRA Community Pub of the Year in 2017.
P

Ipswich

Arcade Street Tavern

Arcade Street, IP1 1EX (behind corn exchange)
⏲ 10.30-3 Tue (11 Wed & Thu; midnight Fri; 1am Sat); closed Sun & Mon ☎ (01473) 805454 arcadetavern.co.uk
2 changing beers Ⓗ
A stylish and highly popular multi-roomed café bar with a traditional wooden interior, with an emphasis on craft and imported beers. Two handpumps dispense a variety of cask beers. There is no food in-house but the bar regularly hosts street-food Friday in conjunction with other local traders. There are heated seating areas outside and two function rooms upstairs – one used for product launches and tasting evenings. Artisan coffee is available. Q

Briarbank

70 Fore Street, IP4 1LB
⏲ 4-11; 12-11 Fri-Sun ☎ (01473) 284000
Briarbank Perpendicular, Old Spiteful; 3 changing beers (sourced locally; often Briarbank) Ⓗ
A smart and modern first-floor drinking bar which opened in 2013 above the Briarbank Brewery. The building was previously a bank. Many beers from the brewery are also available as craft keg. The bar frequently opens earlier, and for longer, in the summer months and provides seating outside if weather permits. Live music, often jazz, features twice monthly either in the bar or outside. Easter and summer beer festivals are hosted. The TVs are turned on for sport only. P

Dove Street Inn

76 St Helen's Street, IP4 2LA
⏲ 12-midnight (10.30 Sun) ☎ (01473) 211270
dovestreetinn.co.uk
Adnams Broadside; Crouch Vale Brewers Gold; Fuller's London Pride; Greene King Abbot Ⓗ**; changing beers (often Dove Street)** Ⓗ/Ⓖ
Popular multi-roomed inn with a large selection of real ales including milds, plus ciders and continental beers. Some ales are from its own brewery next door, where there is also a beer

shop. Home-cooked food and bar snacks are served at all times. Sports TV is shown in the conservatory. A covered and heated seating area outside hosts various events including three beer festivals. Well-behaved dogs and children are welcome. A sister pub to The Gladstone Arms in Combs Ford. Last admission is 10.45pm. (66)

Fat Cat

288 Spring Road, IP4 5NL
12-11 (midnight Fri & Sat) (01473) 726524
fatcatipswich.co.uk
Adnams Southwold Bitter H; Fuller's London Pride; Woodforde's Wherry; changing beers G
Ever popular, this small, multi-roomed drinking bar is free from background music and games machines. Up to 18 gravity beers are dispensed from the taproom and up to five ciders. Bar snacks include Scotch eggs and pasties cooked on the premises. An airy conservatory behind the main bar leads out to the pretty garden – the patio and garden provide extra space on sunny afternoons, with the occasional barbecue. Often voted the best pub in town by local CAMRA branch members. No children under 16. Q

Spread Eagle

1-3 Fore Street, IP4 1JW
closed Mon; 12-midnight (10.30 Sun) (01473) 421858
Grain Oak, Best Bitter, Redwood, Slate, Lignum Vitae; 1 changing beer (often Grain) H
Increasingly popular, this historic building was restored to a high standard a few years ago. Six real ales are on handpump, all from Grain, plus a selection of craft and imported beers and imported bottled beers. Some bar snacks are available and quality, locally roasted coffee. There is a secluded seating area outside. The pub is candlelit throughout on Tuesday evenings. The distinctive Grade II listed building is the sole survivor of four pubs that once stood at this busy road junction.
Q

Steamboat Tavern

78 New Cut West, IP2 8HW
12-11 (midnight Sat); 12-8 Sun (01473) 601902
thesteamboat.co.uk
4 changing beers H
Popular L-shaped bar in a historic riverside location, featuring live music and good food prepared on the premises. It has various drinking areas and a recently refurbished beer garden. Live music includes jazz on alternate Sundays and folk music on the third Thursday of the month. Occasional blues and punk music nights are held, and an annual folk music weekend – see the website for details. Suffolk songwriters play here monthly.

Thomas Wolsey

9-13 St Peters Street, IP1 1XF (300yds from bus station)
4.30-11.30 (1am Fri & Sat); closed Sun (01473) 210055
Adnams Ghost Ship; Crouch Vale Brewers Gold; Woodforde's Wherry; 1 changing beer H
Single-room lounge bar set in a historic Grade II listed building. It has a patio area to the side and two nicely furnished function rooms upstairs, used for a wide variety of events including story-telling nights, charity quizzes and meetings. A range of ales is available on draught plus over 25 bottled beers and 40 quality wines. Games are available including darts. Home supporters only on football match days.

Ixworth

Greyhound

49 High Street, IP31 2HJ
11.30-2.30, 6 (5 Fri & Sat)-11; 12-3, 7-11 Sun
(01359) 230887
Greene King XX Mild, IPA, Abbot; 2 changing beers (sourced nationally) H
Situated on the village's attractive high street, this welcoming traditional inn has three bars, one a lovely central snug. The heart of the building dates back to Tudor times. The pub is a rare outlet for Greene King XX Mild. Good-value lunches and early evening meals are served in the restaurant including a daily special. Dominoes, crib, darts and pool are played in leagues and for charity fundraising. Dogs and children are welcome.
QP

Kessingland

Sailors Home L

302 Church Road, NR33 7SB
12-11 (01502) 740245 sailorshome.co.uk
Adnams Southwold Bitter H; 6 changing beers (sourced locally; often Green Jack, Humpty Dumpty, Wolf) H/G
Located within easy reach of the shingle beach and with views of the North Sea, the pub is popular all year round with locals, walkers and holidaymakers alike. The interior comprises four rooms – one for diners, a games room, a side room and a large central bar area with TV screen. Four handpulled beers are available and up to three on gravity plus a changing real cider. Beer festivals are held in June and August. P(99)

Lawshall

Swan

The Street, IP29 4QA
closed Tue; 12-3, 5 (6 Mon)-10; 12-10 Sat & Sun
(01284) 828477 swaninnlawshall.com
5 changing beers (sourced nationally; often Adnams, Colchester, Woodforde's) H
Set in the heart of rural Suffolk, this is everything a country pub should be. The beautiful 18th-century thatched building was lovingly restored in 2013 and is crammed full of period features. On the menu you will find all the traditional pub classics and a few extra culinary delights. The large garden encourages children to play. A real ale festival is held in May. QP

Long Melford

Crown Inn

Hall Street, CO10 9JL
11-11; 12-10.30 Sun (01787) 377666
thecrownhotelmelford.co.uk
Adnams Southwold Bitter, Ghost Ship; 2 changing beers (sourced nationally) H
A busy family-run free house and cosy hotel set in the popular antiques centre of Long Melford. Two regular ales and two changing guests, together with real cider, are on handpump. A high-quality home-cooked menu is served in the spacious bar and separate restaurant. There is a large attractive patio garden for summer dining and drinking. Eleven comfortable bedrooms are available for those wishing to stay and explore this picturesque area. QP

Lowestoft

Norman Warrior

Fir Lane, NR32 2RB

11-11.30 (12.30am Fri & Sat); 12-11.30 Sun (01502) 561982 thenormanwarrior.co.uk

Greene King IPA; 4 changing beers (sourced nationally; often Greene King, Sharp's, Wolf) H

Popular twin-bar local situated between the town centre and Oulton Broad North railway station, with bus stops nearby and ample parking. It comprises a public bar where pool and darts are played and a comfortable lounge leading to a spacious restaurant serving home-cooked food daily. Outside is a large garden and terrace where a beer and cider festival with live music is held annually over the August bank holiday weekend. You will usually find a locally sourced guest ale here. QP(102)

Stanford Arms

Stanford Street, NR32 2DD

closed Mon; 4-midnight Tue-Thu; 3-1am Fri; 12-midnight Sat; 12-10 Sun (01502) 587444

12 changing beers (sourced locally; often Golden Triangle, Grain, Wolf) H

The open-plan L-shaped bar has a large array of handpumps serving beers mainly from East Anglia and up to six ciders on gravity. Brewery memorabilia adorn the walls. A woodburner has been installed near the patio doors leading to a courtyard garden, aviary and a wood-fired pizza oven (Friday is pizza night). Wednesday is usually speciality food night (booking required) and there is live music on Sunday afternoon. A CAMRA National Pub of the Year finalist two years running.

Triangle Tavern

29 St Peters Street, NR32 1QA

11-11 (midnight Thu; 1am Fri & Sat); 12-10.30 Sun (01502) 582711 green-jack.com

Green Jack Golden Best, Orange Wheat Beer, Trawlerboys Best Bitter, Lurcher Stout, Gone Fishing ESB, Ripper Tripel H**; 3 changing beers (sourced locally; often Crouch Vale, Green Jack, Oakham)** G

This lively town-centre tavern is the brewery tap for Green Jack Brewery. The parlour-style front bar is decorated with brewery memorabilia and CAMRA awards and hosts live music every Friday evening. A corridor leads to a back bar with a central pool table. Alongside the full Green Jack range are guest ales, real ciders and continental beers. Occasional beer festivals are held. Customers are welcome to bring their own food.

Market Weston

Mill

Bury Road, IP22 2PD

11-3 (not Mon), 5-11; 12-3, 7-11 Sun (01359) 221018

Adnams Southwold Bitter; Greene King London Glory; Old Chimneys Military Mild, Golden Pheasant; 1 changing beer (sourced nationally; often Fuller's, St Austell, Shepherd Neame) H

Striking white brick and flint faced inn standing at a crossroads on the main B1111. The landlady celebrated 20 years at the Mill in 2015. It is the closest outlet to Old Chimneys Brewery on the other side of the village and always has a good choice of its beers, complemented by a menu of home-cooked meals. QP

Mellis

Railway Tavern

Yaxley Road, IP23 8DU

closed Mon; 6-11 Tue-Thu; 4-midnight Fri; 12.30-midnight Sat; 12.30-11 Sun (01379) 783416

Adnams Southwold Bitter; Crouch Vale Brewers Gold; Greene King IPA; 1 changing beer H

Two-bar pub close to the mainline railway crossing point (the station is no longer in use) with two snug railway carriage booths and good views over the large village green. It has a covered and heated terrace outside and seating out on the common to the side of the pub. Lively and well-supported music events are offered, plus Ruby Tuesday curry nights and fish and chips on Friday. An annual beer festival with music is held on the last Saturday in July on the common. The bus service is limited. P

Pakefield

Oddfellows

6 Nightingale Road, NR33 7AU

11-11; 12-10.30 Sun (01502) 538415

Adnams Southwold Bitter; house beer (by Green Jack); 3 changing beers (sourced locally; often Green Jack, Lacons, Woodforde's) H

Situated close to the cliff top, the pub is popular with locals and walkers on the coastal heritage path. The interior comprises three open-plan areas including one for diners (booking advised), and sporting events are shown on TV screens. Up to five ales are available from local breweries. In summer, a popular beer festival is hosted on the green opposite the pub and, in January, a small winter festival features performances by the Old Glory Molly Dancers.

Pakenham

Fox

The Street, IP31 2JU

12-3 (not Mon & Tue), 5-11; 12-3, 5-11.30 Fri & Sat; 12-3, 6-11 Sun (01359) 230347 pakenhamfox.co.uk

Mighty Oak Kings; Woodforde's Wherry; 2 changing beers (sourced regionally) H

After a lengthy closure, The Fox reopened in 2016 following a full refurbishment, and celebrated becoming a free house for the first time in its history. Four real ales are available on handpump. Food includes Friday night pizza, Saturday night curry and traditional Sunday lunches. The pub hosts regular quiz nights. QP

Pin Mill

Butt & Oyster

Pin Mill Road, IP9 1JW

10-11; 9am-11 Sat & Sun (01473) 780764

Adnams Southwold Bitter, Ghost Ship, Broadside; 1 changing beer (often Adnams) G

Traditional 17th-century pub on the bank of the River Orwell with three separate rooms and a connecting corridor with flagstone floors. Famous for its setting, with fine views of the water, there is plenty of outdoor seating at the front, often used by diners during busy sessions. Inside, there are some high-backed settles and a large woodburner in the main bar area, making it cosy on cold winter days. Breakfast is available until 11.45am, weekends only. QP

Rattlesden

Five Bells

High Street, IP30 0RA

12-midnight (11 Sun) ☎ (01449) 737373

3 changing beers (sourced locally; often Earl Soham, Woodforde's) Ⓗ

Set on the high road through a picturesque village, this is a good old Suffolk drinking house – few of its kind still survive. Three well-chosen ales on the bar usually come direct from the breweries. The cosy single-room interior has a games area on a lower level and there is occasional live music. Pub games include shut-the-box and shove-ha'penny plus pétanque in the garden in summer. A motorcycle show is hosted in May. Q❀♣

Risby

Crown & Castle

South Street, IP28 6QU

12-3, 5 (6.30 Sat)-11; 12-3, 7-10.30 Sun

☎ (01284) 810393 crownandcastle.com

Adnams Southwold Bitter; 2 changing beers (sourced nationally) Ⓗ

This attractive flint-faced building opened as an inn and shop in the late 1800s and was sold by Greene King in 2014. The current licensees have run the pub for 16 years. A 120ft unrecorded well was discovered during alterations in recent times and is now a feature beneath a grille in the entrance lobby. The pub has classic back and front bars, with food served in both. The back bar is the public, dominated by games and conversation, and well-behaved dogs are allowed in here.

Q❀♣P

Shadingfield

Fox

London Road, NR34 8DD

12-11.30 (10.30 Sun) ☎ (01502) 575100

shadingfieldfox.co.uk

8 changing beers (sourced locally; often Lacons, Nene Valley, Wolf) Ⓗ

Just a short drive from Beccles, this charming and cosy rural inn dates from the 16th century. It has retained the original arched doors and carved fox heads on the beams. The central bar has comfortable seating, with a conservatory on one side and a restaurant on the other. Outside is a small garden and sun terrace. Two beer festivals are held each year, one over the Father's Day weekend and the other close to Guy Fawkes Night.

Q❀P (90)

Shottisham

Sorrel Horse

Hollesley Road, IP12 3HD

12-3, 6-11; 12-11 Sat; 12-10.30 Sun ☎ (01394) 411617

thesorrelhorse-shottisham.co.uk

Woodforde's Wherry; 2 changing beers Ⓖ

A former smugglers' inn, dating back to the 15th century, this picturesque thatched two-bar pub was bought by a local village consortium a few years ago. It retains a gravity stillage for beers. Food includes locally sourced dishes prepared on the premises, special themed evenings and Sunday morning breakfasts (9-11am). Music nights – folk or jazz – are held on the second and fourth Monday of the month and a quiz on Wednesday evening. The main bar now has a bar billiards table. Seats in the garden are popular on sunny days.

Q❀♣P

Southwold

Lord Nelson

42 East Street, IP18 6EJ

10.30-11; 12-10.30 Sun ☎ (01502) 722079

thelordnelsonsouthwold.co.uk

Adnams Southwold Bitter, Ghost Ship, Broadside; 2 changing beers (sourced locally; often Adnams) Ⓗ

Situated near the Sailors Reading Room Museum and a stone's throw from the sea, this busy and lively town-centre inn is popular both with locals and visitors to Southwold. It has three drinking areas, with children welcome in the side room, and a partly covered heated patio area to the rear. The main bar has a flagstone floor with an open fire in winter months and features much Nelson and other navy memorabilia. ❀

Stowmarket

King's Arms

Station Road, IP14 1RQ

11-11; 10.30-11 Sun ☎ 07852 497412

Woodforde's Wherry; 2 changing beers (often Adnams) Ⓗ

Multi-roomed hostelry, just a short walk from the railway station and town centre. Pub games are popular, and occasional live music and barbecues are hosted. Food includes snacks, stews, chilli and omelettes. The patio to the rear leads to a smoking room and various other spaces used for live music and private parties. There is a children's play area and dogs are welcome when the pub is not busy. Two or three beer festivals are held each year. The cider is usually Old Rosie. ❀♣P

Little Wellington

12 Stowupland Road, IP14 5AG

12-midnight (11 Sun) ☎ (01449) 614174

Greene King IPA; St Austell Tribute; 2 changing beers Ⓗ

A good local community pub, accessed via a short flight of steps up from street level. It has a central servery and a reputation for good-value Sunday lunches. It hosts regular live music on Saturday evening and occasional events such horse-racing evenings and private parties. The beer garden has a play area for children and pizzas are cooked outside in the summer. Convenient for the railway station, especially if travelling eastwards.

❀♣P

Royal William

53 Union Street East, IP14 1HP

11-11 (midnight Fri & Sat); 12-10.30 Sun

☎ (01449) 674553

Greene King IPA; 10 changing beers Ⓖ

An end-of-terrace back-street bar, tucked away down a narrow side street, a short walk from the town centre and railway station. Well supported by locals, it is worth seeking out. Ales are served by gravity dispense from the cellar behind the bar, with up to 10 beers and five ciders. There is a games room, home to regular dominoes, darts and crib matches, and a smoking area in the enclosed garden to the rear. Sport is shown on TV. Home-made bar snacks are available. A winner of many local CAMRA awards. ❀♣

Stratford St Mary

Swan ✔

Lower Street, CO7 6JR

closed Mon & Tue; 11-11 (10.30 Sun) ☎ (01206) 321244 stratfordswan.com

3 changing beers Ⓗ

The building is part of a historic former coaching inn dating from about 1520. It has a small, friendly bar retaining many historic features, several other wood-panelled rooms mainly used for dining, and a large garden to the rear. The pub has its own house brewery – brewing started in 2015 – with some beers now available on draught. A wide range of bottled beers is also available and an annual beer festival is held in summer.

Sudbury

Bay Horse

61-65 Melford Road, CO10 1JS

4-11; 12-midnight Fri & Sat; 12-11 Sun ☎ (01787) 377450 bayhorsesudbury.co.uk

Woodforde's Wherry; 8 changing beers Ⓗ

A traditional family-run free house with an impressive array of nine handpumps. Outside, there is a heated patio and a large rear garden overlooking the water meadows and River Stour. Filled baguettes are available and free food for sport lovers on Sundays. There are regular music sessions, a beer festival and five en-suite letting bedrooms. The pub is a short walk from the town centre.

Brewery Tap

21-23 East Street, CO10 2TP (200yds from marketplace)

11-11 (midnight Fri & Sat); 12-10.30 Sun ☎ (01787) 370876 blackaddertap.co.uk

Mauldons Moletrap Bitter, Suffolk Pride, Black Adder Ⓗ**; 7 changing beers (sourced nationally)** Ⓗ/Ⓖ

The Mauldons Brewery Tap is a haven for ale lovers. A good selection of the brewery's beers is always available complemented by a range of national and locally sourced ales, up to 10 at any one time, on both handpump and gravity. Hearty snacks are available at lunchtime including pies and sandwiches. Beer festivals are held in April and October and quiz, music and comedy nights are regular attractions in a pub where conversation dominates. Q

Sweffling

White Horse

Low Road, IP17 2BB

closed Tue-Thu; 7-11 Mon, Fri & Sat; 12-3, 7-11 Sun ☎ (01728) 664178 swefflingwhitehorse.co.uk

3 changing beers Ⓖ

A cosy, traditional two-room pub, warmed by a woodburner and wood-fired range. The owners have refurbished the building in an environmentally-friendly manner. Beers from local brewers are dispensed on gravity, served through a taproom door. Fair-trade, organic and locally produced bottled beers are also available, and cider too. Hot and cold bar snacks are sold. Pub games include bar billiards, darts, crib and board games, and live music features twice a month. Horse and trap rides are available in summer. A former CAMRA East Anglian Pub of the Year.

Q

Tattingstone

Wheatsheaf

Church Road, IP9 2LY

closed Mon; 12-3, 6-11 Tue-Thu; 12-midnight Fri & Sat; 12-9 Sun ☎ (01473) 805470 wheatsheaftattingstone.com

2 changing beers (sourced locally) Ⓖ

Comfortable open-plan single bar pub, fully refurbished by the current owners. It is located on the outskirts of a small village divided by the nearby Alton Water Park reservoir. Beers are usually from local brewers. Themed food nights and Sunday roasts are popular. Live music and quiz nights feature occasionally. The pub hosts local cribbage league matches and caters for parties and private events. There is a large garden to the side and plans for a conservatory and accommodation. Local CAMRA Pub of the Year.

Thorndon

Black Horse

The Street, IP23 7JR

closed Tue; 12-3, 5 (6 Sat)-11; 12-9.30 Sun ☎ (01379) 678523 theblackhorsethorndon.co.uk

Adnams Southwold Bitter; Shortts Strummer; 2 changing beers (sourced regionally; often Adnams, Earl Soham, Woodforde's) Ⓗ

Traditional oak-beamed country pub dating back to the 1600s with the same welcoming landlord for the last 12 years. The central bar has an inglenook fireplace with a log fire and two restaurant areas. A varied lunchtime menu includes a carvery and vegetarian options. Evening meals and takeaways are also available including curries, pasta and fish and chips. Dogs on leads are welcome in the main bar. A community shop staffed by volunteers operates from a separate unit in the car park.

Thurston

Fox & Hounds ✔

Barton Road, IP31 3QT

11.30-11 ☎ (01359) 232228 thurstonfoxandhounds.co.uk

Adnams Broadside; Greene King IPA; 4 changing beers (sourced nationally; often Cliff Quay, Green Jack, Tring) Ⓗ

A listed building, this popular local sits in the middle of the village a short walk from the railway station. The restaurant, serving good home-cooked food, is within the public bar area, separated by uplights from an original wall. There is a separate bar for pool and darts. Regular quiz nights and bingo feature, and on bank holidays and special occasions live music is hosted. A conker competition is held in the autumn.

Walberswick

Anchor ✔

The Street, IP18 6UA

11-11; 12-11 Sun ☎ (01502) 722112 anchoratwalberswick.com

Adnams Southwold Bitter, Broadside; 1 changing beer (often Adnams) Ⓗ

Situated in an idyllic coastal village, this bar and hotel caters for holidaymakers and locals alike. It has two cosy alcove areas heated by a fire on both sides, with a side room for families and a spacious restaurant serving local produce. The pub is accessible from Southwold via footbridge or ferry. As well as Adnams ales, an extensive range of global bottled beers and craft ales is stocked. Accommodation is available in the main building or in chalets in the garden. Q🝖❀⇔◐◑ ⅄P🐾ᯤ

Walton

Half Moon L

303 High Street, IP11 9QL

12-3 (not Mon), 5-11; 12-3, 5-midnight Fri; 12-11 Sat; 12-3, 7-11 Sun ☎ (01394) 285586

Adnams Lighthouse, Southwold Bitter, Broadside; 3 changing beers (often Adnams) Ⓗ

An excellent, traditional, two-bar local community pub with wood panelling and an open fire in the public bar in winter. A meeting place for local groups of all kinds, it has quiz nights, darts matches, cribbage and a selection of books to read. There are no gaming machines or music. The secure garden has a children's play area which has proved popular with families in the summer. Food is available lunchtimes only. Monthly folk nights are hosted as well as other live music on occasion. ❀◐♿♣P🚌🐾ᯤ

Wenhaston

Star Inn L

Hall Road, IP19 9HF

12-3, 6-11; 12-11 Sun ☎ (01502) 478240

wenhastonstar.co.uk

Adnams Southwold Bitter; 5 changing beers (sourced locally; often Colchester, Green Jack, Wolf) Ⓗ

Free house situated on the outskirts of the village, with fine views of the Blyth Valley. It has three small public rooms – the front bar is full of character with old enamel advertising signs. Good food is all home-cooked using local produce where possible. Beer festivals are held in the large lawned garden over the late May and August bank holiday weekends. The pub is popular with walkers and cyclists, and camping is available by prior arrangement. Q❀◐◑⅄♣P🚌(88A)🐾ᯤ

Woodbridge

Cherry Tree

73 Cumberland Street, IP12 4AG

7.30am-11; 9am-11 Sun ☎ (01394) 384627

thecherrytreepub.co.uk

Adnams Southwold Bitter, Ghost Ship, Broadside; Elgood's Black Dog; 5 changing beers (often Adnams) Ⓗ

Spacious family-friendly lounge bar/diner with a large central counter and several distinct seating areas. Nine beers are usually on offer and an annual summer beer festival is hosted. Food is locally sourced and home cooked, including some gluten-free options, and served all day every day, with breakfast until 11am. Board games and cards are available to play and a quiz is held on Thursday. The large garden has children's play equipment. Accommodation is offered in a converted barn. ❀⇔◐◑≈♣P🐾ᯤ

Old Mariner ✔

26 New Street, IP12 1DX

12-11 (10.30 Sun) ☎ (01394) 382679

theoldmariner.co.uk

Adnams Ghost Ship; Fuller's London Pride; Sharp's Doom Bar; Woodforde's Wherry; 1 changing beer Ⓗ

Traditional bar close to the town centre, with a lively front bar with scrubbed tables and a rear seating area leading to the garden with smoking area and a small car park. The back room can be booked for private parties. A good range of food, often gluten-free, is offered including tapas and sandwiches (no food Mon). The Sunday roast is very popular. Two beer festivals are held each year. Entertainment includes story-telling every other month, a quiz every other week and regular live music. ❀◐≈(Melton)♣P🚌🐾ᯤ

Olde Bell & Steelyard ✔

103 New Street, IP12 1DZ

12-3, 5-11.30; 11-12.30am Fri & Sat; 12-11 Sun ☎ (01394) 382933 yeoldebellandsteelyard.co.uk

Greene King IPA, Abbot; 2 changing beers (often Greene King) Ⓗ

Large multi-roomed pub with oak beams in two bars and a separate function room. The steelyard – a former cart weighbridge that dates from 1650 and still works – was on show at the Great Exhibition in 1851. Traditional games include bar billiards, chess and bar skittles. Live rugby is shown on TVs in the side-bar area. Good home-cooked food is served. To the rear of the building is a large heated and covered patio area and wheelchair access. ❀◐◑♿≈♣🚌🐾ᯤ

Spores for thought

Yeast is a fungus, a single cell plant that can convert a sugary liquid into equal proportions of alcohol and carbon dioxide. There are two basic types of yeast used in brewing, one for ale and one for lager. (The yeasts used to make the Belgian beers known as gueuze and lambic are wild spores in the atmosphere). It is often said that ale is produced by 'top fermentation' and lager by 'bottom fermentation'. While it is true that during ale fermentation a thick blanket of yeast head and protein is created on top of the liquid while only a thin slick appears on top of fermenting lager, the descriptions are seriously misleading. Yeast works at all levels of the sugar-rich liquid in order to turn malt sugars into alcohol. If yeast worked only at the top or bottom of the liquid, a substantial proportion of sugar would not be fermented. Ale is fermented at a high temperature, lager at a much lower one. The furious speed of ale fermentation creates the yeast head and with it the rich, fruity aromas and flavours that are typical of the style. It is more accurate to describe the ale method as 'warm fermentation' and the lager one as 'cold fermentation'.

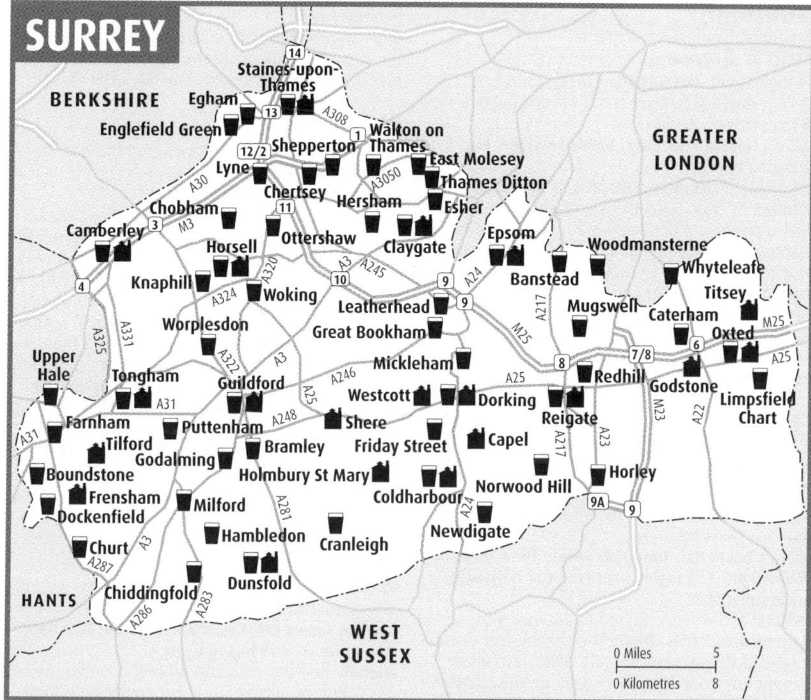

Banstead

Woolpack ✓

186 High Street, SM7 2NZ

11-11; 12-10.30 Sun ☎ (01737) 354560

thewoolpackbanstead.co.uk

Shepherd Neame Whitstable Bay Pale Ale, Spitfire, Bishops Finger; 2 changing beers H

The Woolpack has a single bar and a restaurant behind it. The frequently changing guest beers come from breweries in the South-East. Good food is available all day (not Sun eve); children are only allowed when dining. Weekly quizzes and monthly jazz afternoons are hosted, and an August bank holiday beer festival. Both the patio area at the front and the small garden at the back have smokers' umbrellas. The side entrance has a ramp for wheelchairs. P (16,17)

Boundstone

Bat & Ball L

15 Bat & Ball Lane, GU10 4SA (off Sandrock Hill Rd via Upper Bourne Lane) SU833444

11-11; 12-10.30 Sun ☎ (01252) 792108

thebatandball.co.uk

Dark Star Hophead; 4 changing beers (sourced locally) H

Once a tallyman's office where hop-pickers received (and spent) their earnings, this is now a genuine free house offering six interesting beers, mainly from adjoining counties, alongside excellent reasonably priced food. A family-friendly front room complements the cosy inner sanctum. The garden, with children's playground, hosts an annual charity beer festival. There is a quiz night every Tuesday, and the last Thursday in the month is open mic night. Q P (16,17)

Bramley

Jolly Farmer L

High Street, GU5 0HB

11-11; 12-11 Sun ☎ (01483) 893355 jollyfarmer.co.uk

Greene King IPA; 7 changing beers (sourced nationally; often Crafty, Langham) H

Privately owned traditional free house in the village centre. The characterful decoration and oak beams create a cosy, welcoming atmosphere. Good-quality food is served (booking is essential for the Sunday lunchtime carvery). The changing ales are from a rota of small breweries, several from Hampshire and Sussex, and usually include a dark beer in winter. Real cider is available in the summer months only. Dogs are welcome in the bar but not the restaurant. Easily accessible by bus at all times. P (53,63)

Camberley

Claude du Vall L ✓

77-81 High Street, GU15 3RB

8am-midnight (12.30am Wed; 1am Fri & Sat)

☎ (01276) 672910

Greene King Abbot; Ruddles Best Bitter; Sharp's Doom Bar; 4 changing beers (often Surrey Hills, Tillingbourne, Windsor & Eton) H

Located on the High Street close to the shopping area, station and bus stops, this large Wetherspoon pub attracts a variety of customers throughout the day. The long bar offers four guest ales at the entrance end, including at least one LocAle, and three regular ales and a real cider at the far end. The seating area is imaginatively divided into various large and small areas, some with lounge furniture.

Caterham

King & Queen [L]

34 High Street, CR3 5UA (on B2030)
11-11 (midnight Fri & Sat); 12-11 Sun ☎ (01883) 345438
kingandqueencaterham.co.uk
Fuller's London Pride, ESB; Gale's Seafarers Ale; 1 changing beer [H]
A friendly welcome awaits you at this popular community pub. Once three cottages, this 400-year-old building became an inn in the 1840s. It features a traditional public bar together with a beamed room with an inglenook fireplace. A side room has a dartboard and there is a rear patio outside which hosts occasional theatrical events. Portraits of King William and Queen Mary, after whom the pub is named, adorn the walls.
❀◐♣P

Chertsey

Olde Swan

27 Windsor Street, KT16 8AY
12-11 (midnight Fri & Sat) ☎ (01932) 562129
theoldeswanhotel.co.uk
Sharp's Doom Bar; Tring Side Pocket for a Toad; Wainwright; 1 changing beer (sourced nationally; often Fuller's) [H]
Refurbished when acquired by Mclean Inns, without spoiling its charm. The shabby-chic decor is intended to give drinkers and diners a mellow experience. Four ales are usually on offer and the food menu features stone-baked pizza, home-made burgers and sizzling steaks, while Friday is Mexican night. Accommodation includes double, twin and family rooms. Chertsey is handy for the M3 junction 11 and Thorpe Park.
❀◐⇌P (446,456)

Thyme at the Tavern [L]

20 London Street, KT16 8AA (jct of London St and Heriot Rd)
12-midnight (1am Fri & Sat) ☎ (01932) 429667
thymeatthetavern.co.uk
Courage Best Bitter; 5 changing beers (sourced locally; often Thames Side, Thurstons, Windsor & Eton) [H]
Family-run, dog-friendly free house, and local CAMRA Pub of the Year 2017. Alongside the Courage Best are up to five guest beers, mostly sourced locally. Regular beer festivals are held, usually on a LocAle or regional theme. An extensive food menu is available (no food Sun, Mon and Fri eves). Friday is live music night and there is a comfortable heated marquee in the rear courtyard. The pub is heavily involved in fundraising for local good causes.
❀◐♿⇌♣

Chiddingfold

Crown Inn [L]

The Green, Petworth Road, GU8 4TX
10-11; 12-10.30 Sun ☎ (01428) 682255
thecrownchiddingfold.com
Fuller's London Pride; 4 changing beers [H]
Originally a 14th-century alehouse, this attractive, Grade II* listed, timber-framed inn has a main bar area with a large inglenook fireplace. Wood beams feature throughout the open-plan layout, which divides into several distinct drinking and dining areas. The main dining space has wood panelling and stained-glass windows. Guest ales are generally from local breweries, particularly from West Sussex. The beer of the month is chosen by the regular customers. Booking is recommended for Sunday lunch. ❀◐♣P (71)

Chobham

White Hart [L]

58 High Street, GU24 8AA
11-11; 9am-11 Sat; 9am-10.30 Sun ☎ (01276) 857580
Brunning & Price Original; 4 changing beers (often) [H]
The White Hart is a lovely rambling building with interesting nooks and crannies, decorated with prints of paintings and early 20th-century photos and posters. Five ales are on handpump in a range of strengths and styles, always including Brunning & Price Original – the others could come from any of the many local breweries, with the distance from the pub prominently displayed. There are two restaurant areas and a less formal area for drinkers as you enter the pub. Q❀◐♿P (73)

Churt

Crossways Inn [L]

Churt Road, GU10 2JS
11-3, 5-11; 11-11 Fri & Sat; 12-4, 7-10.30 Sun
☎ (01428) 714323 weydonian.net/crossways
Arundel Sussex IPA; Courage Best Bitter; Hop Back Crop Circle [H]**; 4 changing beers** [G]
Friendly two-bar pub with a homely ambience. At the centre of village life, it is popular with local groups as well as customers from further afield including ramblers and cyclists. Guest beers are fetched from their casks in the cellar, usually including local ales and a stout or porter. Good-value food is served lunchtimes, plus fish and chips night on Wednesday (no food Sun).
❀◐♣P (19)

Claygate

Platform 3 [L]

Claygate Station, The Parade, KT10 0PB
closed Mon-Wed; 3-9 (9.30 Fri); 12.30-7 Sun; Jan-Apr closed Sat-Wed; 3-8.30 Thu & Fri ☎ 07802 316389
brightwaterbrewery.co.uk
3 changing beers (sourced locally; often Brightwater) [H]

REAL ALE BREWERIES

Antoine's Westcott
Ascot Camberley
Brightwater Claygate
Crafty Brewing Dunsfold
Dorking Capel
Felday Holmbury St Mary (NEW)
Frensham Frensham
Fuzzchat Epsom (NEW)
Godstone Godstone
Hogs Back Tongham
Leith Hill Coldharbour
Little Beer Guildford
Oxted Oxted
Pilgrim Reigate
Surrey Hills Dorking
Thames Side Staines-upon-Thames
Thurstons (Horsell) Horsell
Tilford Tilford
Tillingbourne Shere
Titsey Titsey (NEW)

The outlet for locally brewed Brightwater beers, housed in a former coal office at Claygate Station. A guest ale from another brewer is sometimes available. All seating is outside on the station forecourt under a gazebo, heated in winter. One of the smallest pubs in the UK, but well established as a focal point for the local community. Call before travelling to visit as opening is weather-dependent – bonus opening times are advertised on social media. Q (K3)

Coldharbour

Plough Inn

Coldharbour Lane, RH5 6HD

11.30-11; 12-9 Sun (01306) 711793 ploughinn.com

Leith Hill Crooked Furrow, Smiler's Happiness, Surrey Puma; Tillingbourne Falls Gold H

Home to the Leith Hill Brewery, this 17th-century inn is set in lovely countryside down narrow lanes close to Leith Hill, the highest point in south-east England. Excellent home-made food, featuring seasonal dishes alongside daily specials, uses local produce where possible and is available lunchtimes and evenings (not Sun eve). The pub is understandably popular with walkers and cyclists. The pub shop provides hot drinks and snacks alongside local produce (open 8am-6pm). Six en-suite letting rooms are available.
QP (50,433)

Cranleigh

Three Horseshoes

4 High Street, GU6 8AE (on B2128)

12-11 (01483) 276978

threehorseshoescranleigh.co.uk

Crafty Loxhill Biscuit G**; Harvey's Sussex Best Bitter; Timothy Taylor Boltmaker** H**; 5 changing beers** H/G

This two-bar 17th-century pub features an inglenook fireplace with a roaring wood fire in winter. The long gone Brufords Brewery used to stand behind the pub and some photos in the lounge bar show the building. Good home-made food is available each day (not Sun eve). The garden has children's play equipment. Five constantly changing guest beers are available, frequently served straight from the cask – check to see what is available. P

Dockenfield

Bluebell

Batts Corner, GU10 4EX (½ mile N of Dockenfield village) SU820410

12-3, 5.30-11; 12-11 Fri & Sat; 12-8 Sun summer; 12-3, 5.30-11; 12-11 Sat; 12-8 Sun winter (01252) 792801

bluebell-dockenfield.com

4 changing beers (sourced locally; often Frensham, Langham, Triple fff)

A 150-year-old hidden gem tucked away in a rural setting under a mile from Dockenfield village. The open-plan interior has a light, contemporary feel with three seating areas for both formal and informal dining as well as drinking, warmed by a real fire in the winter. The pub has a large garden and plenty of parking, and is a truly independent family-run establishment. The breweries are regulars and their beers rotate.
QP

Dorking

Cobbett's

23 West Street, RH4 1BY (on A25 one-way system eastbound)

12-8; 11-8.30 Fri; 10-8 Sat; 12-6 Sun (01306) 879877

cobbettsrealales.com

10 changing beers G

This excellent off-licence and micropub sells the largest choice of beer in Surrey. The bar, open from noon (earlier on Fri and Sat for off-sales only), is situated in a tiny back room, complete with garden. The beer range changes constantly, with up to six cask beers plus six KeyKegs served by knowledgeable staff. Hop monsters are popular. Hundreds of bottles and cans from Britain and beyond, plus two draught ciders, provide more choice. Q

Cricketers

81 South Street, RH4 2JU (on A25 one-way system westbound)

1-11 Mon; 12-11 (midnight Thu & Sat; 12.30am Fri) (01306) 889938 cricketersdorking.co.uk

Fuller's Oliver's Island, London Pride, ESB; 2 changing beers H

This small and well-run pub is justifiably a regular in the Guide. It has an excellent mix of customers, helping to create a lively atmosphere. The single bare-bricked L-shaped room is covered with old photographs and adverts. Rugby is popular – when England play it is standing-room only. The multi-level walled Georgian garden is the scene of the pub's May bank holiday and autumn beer festivals. On alternate Monday evenings a classic film is shown.

Lincoln Arms

Station Approach, RH4 1TF (just off A24 by station)

11-11 (midnight Thu-Sat); 11-10.30 Sun (01306) 882820 lincolnarms.co.uk

Sharp's Doom Bar; 3 changing beers H

Handy for both Dorking and Deepdene stations, this Victorian two-bar hotel retains some impressive period features. The front bar has two pool tables at one end and TVs showing live sport. The rear bar is usually quieter, with access to the outdoor patio area and smokers' shelter. At least one guest beer will be from a local brewer such as Dorking or Weltons, another may be from a larger regional brewery. The pub opens 7am (9am weekends) for breakfast. P

Dunsfold

Sun Inn

The Common, GU8 4LE

11-midnight (1am Fri & Sat); 12-11.30 Sun (01483) 200242 suninndunsfold.co.uk

5 changing beers (often Crafty, Firebird, Triple fff) H

Part of this inn is a converted coach house about 400 years old. The interior is cosy, with subdued lighting in the older part. Exposed wooden beams and an open log fire add to its charm and character. Darts is played. Casks ales alternate depending on season but there are some regular favourites. A varying seasonal food menu is available. There is plenty of outdoor seating in front of the building on an unfenced green. QP (42)

East Molesey

Bell ✔

4 Bell Road, KT8 0SS (off B369)

⌚ 11-11 (midnight Fri & Sat); 11-10 Sun ☎ (020) 8941 0400

🌐 bell-pub.co.uk

Greene King IPA, Abbot; Morland Old Speckled Hen; house beer (by Twickenham); 2 changing beers (sourced nationally; often Greene King) 🄷

Historic coaching inn with stone and wood floors, known locally as the Crooked House. It dates from 1460 and was later East Molesey's first post office. The walls are decorated with old photos of the area. The 18th-century highwayman Claude Duvalier hid from the Bow Street Runners here. Full of nooks and crannies, it is ideal for romantic liaisons. The large garden has a children's play area. Various TV screens show sport, which can be avoided if preferred. Quiz night is Tuesday. ❀◐◑♣P🚌(411)🐾📶

Egham

Egham United Services Club 𝕃

111 Spring Rise, TW20 9PE (close to A30 Egham Hill)

⌚ 12-11 (midnight Fri & Sat) ☎ (01784) 435120

🌐 eusc.co.uk

Rebellion IPA; Surrey Hills Ranmore; 3 changing beers (sourced nationally; often Burning Sky, Red Cat, Thames Side) 🄷

Once again local CAMRA Club of the Year and featuring in the Guide for the 11th consecutive year. A changing range of guest ales includes something dark, and a wide choice of ciders is available from the cellar. Three beer festivals a year showcase an eclectic range of ales, mostly from the newest micros around. Comfortably furnished with sports TV and free Wi-Fi, the club hosts live music most Saturday evenings. Show a copy of this Guide or CAMRA membership card for entry. ❀♿≠♣●P🚌📶

Englefield Green

Bailiwick 𝕃

Wick Road, TW20 0HN

⌚ 10-11; 9am-11 Sat & Sun ☎ (01784) 477877

Windsor & Eton Guardsman; house beer (by Phoenix); 2 changing beers (sourced locally; often Reunion, Thames Side) 🄷

After several incarnations, this is now a proper pub serving local ales, with a front bar leading through to a large dining area offering an extensive food menu. A small front patio overlooks the adjacent Windsor Great Park, where the landlord organises occasional rambles. Meet the Brewer evenings are proving popular. Dogs are welcome in the bar. Tea and coffee are always available. Q❀◐◑●P🐾📶

Happy Man 𝕃

12 Harvest Road, TW20 0QS (off A30)

⌚ 12-11.30 (midnight Fri & Sat); 12-10.30 Sun

☎ (01784) 433265

Hop Back Summer Lightning; 3 changing beers (sourced nationally; often Crouch Vale, Purity, Reunion) 🄷

In Victorian times two houses were converted to a pub serving workers building Royal Holloway College. Refurbished but virtually unchanged, this is a popular haunt for students and locals. Three changing guest ales are sourced from local and national breweries. Regular beer festivals are held on the rear patio, which has a heated marquee. Darts and quiz nights are hosted and food is available every day. A former local CAMRA Pub of the Year. ❀◐◑♣●🚌🐾

Epsom

Cricketers ✔

1 Stamford Green Road, KT18 7SR (off B280)

⌚ 10-11 (midnight Fri & Sat) ☎ (01372) 729384

🌐 thecricketersinnepsom.co.uk

4 changing beers (sourced locally; often Surrey Hills, Wimbledon) 🄷

Weatherboarded pub with a brick extension in an idyllic setting next to a pond with its waterfowl, opposite the cricket green. The building is 250 years old and was originally two cottages, becoming a pub in 1836. It is divided into two wood-floored bar areas, while to the rear is a split-level area used more for dining. Breakfast is served 10am-midday. ❀◐◑♿🚌(E9,E10)🐾📶

Jolly Coopers 𝕃 ✔

84 Wheelers Lane, KT18 7SD (off B280 via Stamford Green Rd)

⌚ 12-11 (8 Sun) ☎ (01372) 723222 🌐 jollycoopers.co.uk

Fuller's London Pride; 3 changing beers (sourced regionally; often Fuzzchat) 🄷

On the edge of Epsom Common, this pub is more than 200 years old. The interior is divided into two – a carpeted bar area to the left and another larger area with polished parquet flooring to the right used more for dining, but not exclusively so. The decor is modern, with painted walls. There is a large paved garden at the rear. The pub can get busy at weekends but is quieter during the week. A beer from Fuzzchat, brewed in an outbuilding, is often available. Varying cider is sold in the summer. Q❀◐◑♣●P🚌(E9,E10)🐾📶

Rifleman 𝕃

5 East Street, KT17 1BB (on A24)

⌚ 12-11 (midnight Fri & Sat); 12-10.30 Sun

☎ (01372) 721244 🌐 therifleman.co.uk

Greene King London Glory; house beer (by Hardys & Hansons); 3 changing beers (sourced regionally; often Hammerpot, Twickenham, Windsor & Eton) 🄷

Small corner pub in the shadow of a bridge carrying the railway to and from London. It is decorated in a traditional style with wood panelling and two fireplaces, but also has some modern features such as bare brickwork and high tables at the front. There is a pleasant garden to the rear, an oasis of calm close to central Epsom. The name comes from the Surrey Rifle Volunteers who trained nearby. Children are welcome until 6pm. A changing cider is available. ❀◐◑≠●🚌📶

Esher

Wheatsheaf 𝕃

40 The Green, KT10 8AG

⌚ 11-11 (11.30 Fri & Sat); 11-10.30 Sun ☎ (01372) 464014

🌐 wheatsheafesher.co.uk

Harvey's Sussex Best Bitter; Surrey Hills Shere Drop; 2 changing beers (often Twickenham, Wimbledon) 🄷

Imposing inn about 200 years old opposite Esher Green. This is a smart community pub where diners and drinkers alike are looked after with the same friendly service. Comfortably furnished throughout in a modern style, the original oak flooring in the main part has been retained and replicated in the extended areas. The bar area has an open fire. A bicycle rack is provided at the rear. Changing guest beers may be local. Local CAMRA joint Pub of the Year 2017. P

Farnham

Hop Blossom

50 Long Garden Walk, GU9 7HX (between Waitrose and Castle St) SU838469
12-11.30 (12.30am Fri & Sat); 12-11 Sun
☎ (01252) 710770 hopblossom.co.uk
Fuller's Oliver's Island, London Pride, ESB; Gale's Seafarers Ale; 1 changing beer (often Fuller's) H
A hidden gem in the heart of Farnham with a lovely welcoming feel and a log fire in winter. There are three distinct areas – the main bar, a conservatory and a back room. The wood flooring is very traditional and there is a mix of seating including some old pews. The pub can be very crowded during events in the town. Dogs are welcome, as are children during the day and early evening. No food on Sunday or Monday.
Q (4)

Jolly Sailor

64 West Street, GU9 7EH
12-11 (midnight Fri & Sat); 12-10.30 Sun
☎ (01252) 719139 jollysailorfarnham.com
Greene King London Glory, Abbot; Morland Old Speckled Hen; 5 changing beers (sourced locally; often Thurstons, Tillingbourne, Wild Weather Ales) H
Cosy pub with a nautically-themed interior and a mix of comfortable seating. Simple wooden flooring and an occasional log fire add to the homely ambience. There are usually four ales from Greene King breweries and four local ales. When the pub is not serving food you can order in a takeaway. A pub quiz is held on the second Tuesday of every month. P (65)

Friday Street

Stephan Langton Inn

RH5 6JR TQ12804559
closed Mon; 11-11; 11-7 Sun ☎ (01306) 730775
stephanlangton.pub
Tillingbourne The Source, AONB, Hop Troll; 1 changing beer (often Tillingbourne) H
Stephan Langton was a local man who became Archbishop of Canterbury and was involved in the writing of the Magna Carta. The pub is in a beautiful position, hidden away down narrow country lanes and surrounded by National Trust land. The bar is warmed by a real fire and is popular with walkers and cyclists. Excellent food including local game and fish is served in the bar and restaurant. To the rear is a large and attractive garden. Q P

Godalming

Star Inn

17 Church Street, GU7 1EL
11.30 (12 Mon)-11; 11.30-12.30am Fri; 11-12.30am Sat; 12-11 Sun ☎ (01483) 417717 thestargodalming.co.uk
Hardys & Hansons Olde Trip H**; 9 changing beers (sourced nationally; often Hardys & Hansons)** H/G
Dating from around 1830, the Star has a small public bar at the front, with the main room to the side leading to a patio garden and smoking area. There is a separate lounge with a bespoke cider bar, open Thursday to Sunday. Up to 10 real ales are stocked, some from the Greene King range. Beer festivals are held at Easter and Halloween. The pub is a regular winner of local and regional CAMRA cider awards

Great Bookham

Anchor

161 Lower Road, KT23 4AH (off A246 via Eastwick Rd)
11.30-11.30; 12-10.30 Sun ☎ (01372) 452429
Brakspear Bitter; Courage Best Bitter; Sharp's Doom Bar; 1 changing beer (often Tillingbourne) H
Historic Grade II listed inn dating from the 15th century. Low-beamed ceilings, wooden floors, exposed brickwork and an inglenook with a real fire in winter give the pub a traditional and homely feel. A charity quiz night is held every Tuesday (booking required) and a meat raffle on Sunday. There is a patio garden with a pond, and a heated smoking area at the front. Children under 14 are not allowed in the bar. Q P (479)

Guildford

King's Head

27 King's Road, GU1 4JW (on A320 Stoke Rd)
11-11 (11.30 Tue & Thu; midnight Fri & Sat); 12-10.30 Sun
☎ (01483) 568957 kingsheadguildford.co.uk
Fuller's Oliver's Island, London Pride, ESB; 2 changing beers (sourced nationally; often Butcombe, Fuller's) H
Built in 1860 as two cottages, which soon became a beer house, the pub is deceptively spacious after much enlargement and features service from both sides of a central bar. The full range of Fuller's beers including seasonals is available, as well as a guest beer usually from a smaller brewery, and cider on draught. Acoustic music features on Tuesday, quiz night on Wednesday, and open mic on Thursday. TV sport is screened in most areas. Noted for its attractive hanging baskets.
(London Rd) P

Robin Hood

38 Sydenham Road, GU1 3RT
12-11 Tue & Wed; 11-midnight Thu-Sat; closed Sun & Mon
☎ 07736 337770
6 changing beers (sourced nationally) H
Attractive small mid-Victorian street-corner pub which has been left isolated following housing clearance in the late '60s. The L-shaped bar offers a sanctuary from the nearby busy high street. There is an interesting choice of beers, usually from microbreweries within 25 miles. Good-value food is served all day Tuesday to Saturday. Occasional live music plays. (London Rd) P

Row Barge

7 Riverside, GU1 1LW
12-11 (midnight Fri & Sat) ☎ (01483) 570242
therowbargeguildford.com
Dartmoor Jail Ale; St Austell Tribute; 4 changing beers (often Hogs Back, Surrey Hills) H
Built in 1856 and extended for the post-war Bellfields Estate, this two-bar pub with pool room is a mile-and-a-half along the River Wey towpath from the town centre, close to the A320 Woking Road. Day and night moorings are available for customers and a cycle rack is provided. Poker night is Thursday, live music features on Friday and Saturday. Food is served until 7pm (5pm Sun).
P (3,34,35)

Royal Oak

Trinity Churchyard, GU1 3RR (behind Trinity Church)
12-11 (midnight Thu, 12.30am Fri & Sat); 12-10.30 Sun
(01483) 457144 royaloakguildford.co.uk
Fuller's Oliver's Island, London Pride; Gale's HSB; 2 changing beers (sourced nationally) H
Originally the rectory of Holy Trinity Church and the largest house in an early 17th-century terrace. It was converted to a pub in about 1870 with the two front sitting rooms becoming bars that have since been knocked into one. Comfortable seating helps to provide a homely atmosphere. The beer benefits from a cellar that is larger than the pub, and two changing guest beers are available.

Hambledon

Merry Harriers

Hambledon Road, GU8 4DR SU967391
11.30-3 (not Mon), 5.30-11; 12-3, 5.30-11 Wed & Thu; 11.30-midnight Fri & Sat; 12-8 Sun (01428) 682883
merryharriers.com
Crafty Loxhill Biscuit; Surrey Hills Shere Drop; 1 changing beer (sourced locally; often Firebird, Langham) H
Traditional country pub set in the Surrey Hills. The main bar has an inglenook fireplace, to the left is a small, quiet side room and to the right a restaurant/function room. All food except fish is sourced from within a 15-mile radius. Live music features monthly on a Saturday. Accommodation is available either in a converted barn or the camping field. Llamas can be admired from the garden or even walked! P

Hersham

Royal George

130 Hersham Road, KT12 5QJ (off A244)
11-11 (midnight Fri & Sat); 12-11 Sun (01932) 220910
theroyalgeorge-hersham.co.uk
Young's Bitter, Special; 1 changing beer (sourced regionally) H
The pub was built in 1964 – the name refers to a 100-gun ship from the Napoleonic Wars. It has one L-shaped bar with tartan carpet and upholstered banquette seating. A real fire adds to the comfortable atmosphere. It offers a menu featuring excellent Thai food alongside more traditional British fare (Mon-Sat), with a roast on Sunday lunchtime. There are paved outdoor seating areas to the front and rear for the warmer months. Quiz night is every Tuesday. P (555)

Horley

Farmhouse

Ladbroke Road, RH6 8PB
12-11 (01293) 782146 thefarmhousehorley.co.uk
Harvey's Sussex Best Bitter; 3 changing beers H
This Grade II listed building was originally a farmhouse and dates from the 17th century, with some more recent additions. It became a pub in 1985 – the bar is in the old farmhouse and retains many original features. Guest beers are mainly from national or regional brewers and change frequently. Food is available 12-9.30pm (8pm Sun). The large garden offers plenty of seating alongside play facilities for children. P (20)

Horsell

Crown

104 High Street, GU21 4ST
12-11 (midnight Fri); 11-midnight Sat (01483) 771719
6 changing beers (often Thurstons) H
Welcoming two-bar community local offering six real ales, three of which are brewed by Thurstons, who started brewing in the Crown and are now located next door. One beer will come from another local brewery. Behind the pub is a sturdy smokers' shelter and well beyond that a large garden with two pétanque pistes. There is a weekly quiz on Wednesday, and an annual beer festival in late May. P (48)

Knaphill

Garibaldi

134 High Street, GU21 2QH
12-11 (midnight Fri & Sat); 12-10.30 Sun
(01483) 473374 thegaribaldi-knaphill.co.uk
2 changing beers (sourced regionally) H
Enterprising pub on the edge of Knaphill. Its compact interior has exposed beams and wooden floors. Two or three changing cask ales are served, with regional beers favoured. A real cider is available direct from the cellar. Monday is real ale club night, with beers sold at a reduced price. There is a quiz on Sunday evening, as well as Tuesday curry night and Thursday steak night. Beer festivals are held in April and October.
P (91,34)

Royal Oak

Anchor Hill, GU21 2JH
12-11 (midnight Sat); 12-10.30 Sun (01483) 473330
royaloakknaphill.co.uk
5 changing beers (often Exmoor, Ringwood, Wye Valley) H
An attractive 17th-century building situated at the bottom of the hill and set back from the road. The five beers include one of premium strength and local breweries are well represented. Up to five ciders are also available. Behind the pub is a superb garden with a barbecue and children's play equipment. An annual cider and beer festival is held, live bands perform and the pub supports charity work for a Woking hospice.
P (91,48)

Leatherhead

Running Horse

38 Bridge Street, KT22 8BZ (off B2122)
11.30-11; 12-10.30 Sun (01372) 372081
running-horse.co.uk
Shepherd Neame Master Brew, Spitfire; Surrey Hills Ranmore; 1 changing beer (sourced regionally; often Shepherd Neame) H
Overlooking the River Mole, this Grade II* listed two-room pub, dating from 1403, features a real log fire, home-made food, an outside courtyard seating area plus a large back garden. The public bar has TV, pool table and dartboard, and the cosy lounge bar has low ceilings and exposed beams. Traditional pub games include bar skittles and shove-ha'penny, with a quiz night on Tuesday. Live jazz plays on Sunday lunchtime and live bands monthly, with a charity music event on May Day. Children are allowed until 9pm. Local CAMRA Pub of the Year 2018. Q P

Limpsfield Chart

Carpenters Arms

12 Tally Road, RH8 0TG (off B269)
12-11 Mon-Wed; 11-midnight Thu-Sat; 12-10.30 Sun
(01883) 722209 carpenterslimpsfield.co.uk
Westerham Finchcocks Original, British Bulldog, 1965 Special Bitter Ale; 2 changing beers
Located adjacent to the National Trust's Limpsfield Common, this Westerham Brewery tied house attracts both walkers and horse riders. The L-shaped bar has parquet flooring and a copper-topped bar, and the walls are adorned with an interesting collection of old photos and artwork. One side of the bar caters for diners enjoying the good home-made food on offer. There is a quiz on the first Sunday of the month.
P (594)

Lyne

Royal Marine

Lyne Lane, KT16 0AN
12-2.30, 5.30-11; closed Sat; 12-3 Sun (01932) 873900
royalmarinelyne.co.uk
Ruddles Best Bitter; Sharp's Doom Bar; 1 changing beer (sourced nationally; often Greene King)
The name of this rural pub commemorates Queen Victoria's review of her troops in 1853 on nearby Chobham Common. Royal Marine memorabilila, a collection of drinking jugs and other bric-a-brac are on display. Generous portions of home-cooked food are served Monday to Friday and Sunday lunchtime. Friday is bingo quiz night. Occasional beer festivals are held. **QP**

Mickleham

King William IV

4 Byttom Hill, RH5 6EL (behind Frascati restaurant)
11-11.30; 12-10.30 Sun (01372) 372590
thekingwilliamiv.com
Hogs Back TEA; Surrey Hills Shere Drop; 1 changing beer (sourced regionally; often Crafty, Dorking, Hammerpot)
A quaint, welcoming country pub nestled on a hillside. The main bar is homely with a log fire and there is a smaller bar to the front. An attractive outside terrace, with some tables under cover, enjoys stunning views over the Mole Valley. Good home-made food is served – book ahead for lunch, especially on summer weekends. Steep steps can make access difficult. A shared car park is on the A24 southbound. **QP** (465)

Running Horses

Old London Road, RH5 6DU (B2209)
11-11 (10.30 Sun) (01372) 372279
therunninghorses.co.uk
Brakspear Bitter, Oxford Gold; Fuller's London Pride; 1 changing beer (sourced nationally)
Large and attractive 16th-century, Grade II listed coaching inn. It is named after a run-off of The Derby in 1828 after there was a dead heat in the original race – racehorses were stabled here then. The main bar is dominated by a large fireplace where a real fire blazes away in winter. The pub is popular with walkers and cyclists. There are six letting rooms (dogs not allowed). The guest beer is supplied by Marston's. **Q** (465)

Milford

Refectory

Old Portsmouth Road, GU8 5HJ
10.30-11; 12-10.30 Sun (01483) 413820
Brunning & Price Original; Dark Star Hophead; Hogs Back TEA; 3 changing beers
A fascinating building of uncertain age with a very large open interior with plenty of exposed beams and several distinct areas. There are pretty fireplaces with roaring log fires in winter. Farming paraphernalia adorn the walls. The three guest beers are generally from local independent and micro breweries. Food is served 12-9.30pm (10pm Fri & Sat). **P** (70,71)

Mugswell

Well House Inn

Chipstead Lane, CR5 3SQ (off A217) TQ25845526
12-11 (01737) 830640
wellhouseinn.timewellspent.co.uk
Fuller's London Pride; Surrey Hills Shere Drop; 2 changing beers
Part of the local Time Well Spent group, the Well House originated as three cottages in the 1560s and became a pub in the 1950s. It is a rural gem with a secluded feel and has retained many original features. The garden contains St Margaret's Well which is mentioned in the Domesday Book. The three small bars each have a log fire and there is a conservatory to the rear. Food is served all day. Tuesday is quiz night. **P**

Newdigate

Surrey Oaks

Parkgate Road, Parkgate, RH5 5DZ (between Newdigate and Leigh) TQ20524363
11.30-11 (midnight Fri); 9am-11 Sat & Sun
(01306) 631200 thesurreyoaks.com
Surrey Hills Ranmore, Shere Drop; 9 changing beers
This attractive 16th-century inn is renowned for its commitment to good-quality real ale from microbreweries. Six handpumps, one of which offers a dark ale, alongside five KeyKeg beers and a dozen ciders and perries, provide great choice. The main bar features low beams, flagstones and an inglenook fireplace with log-burning stove. Excellent food served from an open kitchen includes home-made pizzas and daily specials. Outside is a large garden where the extremely popular late spring and August bank holiday beer festivals are held. **QP** (21,50)

Norwood Hill

Fox Revived

RH6 0ET
10.30-11 (10.30 Sun) (01293) 229270
foxrevived.co.uk
Surrey Hills Shere Drop; 5 changing beers
The pub has been greatly extended and updated by its new owners, Brunning & Price. There is a large and comfortable bar area as you enter. The restaurant is very popular for its wide-ranging menu served all day from noon. A Brunning & Price house beer is served alongside a number of local ales. Set on high ground, from the large garden there is a fine view to the north, with the North Downs and Box Hill ahead, rising towards Leith Hill in the west. **P** (22)

Ottershaw

Castle

220 Brox Road, KT16 0LW (signed off A320)
11-11 (midnight Fri); 12-10.30 Sun ☎ (01932) 872373
the-castle-ottershaw.co.uk
Harvey's Sussex Best Bitter; Sharp's Doom Bar; Timothy Taylor Landlord; 1 changing beer (sourced nationally; often Otter)
This attractive tile-hung pub has retained its two-bar layout. Built as a beer house in 1840, the building was extended in 1905 and a conservatory added to one side more recently. The rustic feel is enhanced with agricultural implements around the walls inside and out, and each bar has an open fire. The emphasis is on friendly conversation in a music-free environment. An extensive food menu is available seven days a week. Outside is a heated wooden gazebo. Q P (446)

Oxted

Crown Inn

53 High Street, Old Oxted, RH8 9LN (just off A25)
12-3 (not Mon), 5.30-11; 12-3, 5.30-midnight Fri & Sat; 12-10.30 Sun ☎ (01883) 717853
Fuller's London Pride; 3 changing beers (often Oxted)
Dating from the 17th century and reputedly haunted, this pub has two contrasting bars, each operating different hours (so check the other if one seems closed). The main bar is on the upper level. The pub has a number of interesting features including Victorian wood panelling and irregularly shaped windows. A selection of board games is available and live music is a regular feature. Home-cooked food is served Tuesday to Sunday. One of the guest ales is usually from Oxted Brewery. (410)

Puttenham

Good Intent

60-62 The Street, GU3 1AR
12-3, 6-11.30 (10.45 Mon); 12-11.30 Sat; 12-10.30 Sun ☎ (01483) 810387 thegoodintentpub.co.uk
Hogs Back TEA; Purity Pure Gold; Timothy Taylor Landlord; 3 changing beers (sourced nationally; often Jennings, Robinsons, Theakston)
A 16th-century inn situated in an attractive village on the North Downs Way. The bar has oak beams and an inglenook fireplace and is decorated with hops and hop-growing equipment. A varied food menu is served each session plus specials including burger night Tuesday, fish and chips night Wednesday and pie night winter Thursday (no food Sun eve and Mon). Popular with walkers and cyclists, the pub also has monthly sewing, darts, pool and quiz nights. Q P

Redhill

Garibaldi

29 Mill Street, RH1 6PA
4-11 (midnight Fri); 12-midnight Sat; 12-10.30 Sun ☎ (01737) 773094 thegaribaldiredhill.co.uk
4 changing beers
This single-room Victorian pub is to be found south of the town centre. It was saved from demolition in 2017 by a community group and is run on a not-for-profit basis with any money made put back into improving the pub. The four beers change frequently, always including a local ale. There is a dartboard, book corner, Sunday meat raffle and a fortnightly quiz on Thursday. Sport is shown on TV. (Earlswood)

Garland

5 Brighton Road, RH1 6PP (on A23 S of town)
12-11 (12.30am Fri & Sat); 12-10 Sun ☎ (01737) 764612
Harvey's IPA, Sussex Best Bitter, Armada Ale; 2 changing beers
Harvey's only tied house in Surrey, the Garland is a classic Victorian street-corner local less than five minutes' walk from the town centre. The two dartboards and bar billiards table are very popular. Good-value food is available weekday lunchtimes and Friday evening. There are usually two Harvey's seasonal beers available. Live music plays some Saturday evenings. A function room is available to hire. P

Sun

17-21 London Road, RH1 1LY (on A25 in town centre)
8am-midnight (1am Fri & Sat) ☎ (01737) 766886
Adnams Ghost Ship; Greene King Abbot; Ruddles Best Bitter; Sharp's Doom Bar; 5 changing beers
A modern town-centre pub a short walk from the railway and bus stations. The large bar room has a raised dining area, a few sofas and a corner allocated to families (children welcome until 6pm). An extensive menu of reasonably priced food is available all day. TVs show major sporting events but with the sound turned off. There is no garden, but there is a separate smoking area outside at the front. Q

Reigate

Bell Inn

21 Bell Street, RH2 7AD (on A217)
11-11 (midnight Thu-Sat); 12-10 Sun ☎ (01737) 244438
thebellreigate.co.uk
Greene King IPA, Abbot; 4 changing beers
This long, narrow pub is one of the oldest in town, with low ceilings, wooden floors and tables, and a comfortable and welcoming feel. The guest beers change frequently and are often from local microbreweries. Food is served 12-3pm and 6-9pm daily – the menu includes over a dozen varieties of burger sourced from local butchers. There is a selection of board games available. Note the old Ordnance Survey map on the pub ceiling.

Shepperton

Barley Mow

67 Watersplash Road, TW17 0EE (off B376 in Shepperton Green)
12-11 (10.30 Sun) ☎ (01932) 225326 themow.co.uk
Hogs Back TEA; Hop Back Summer Lightning; 3 changing beers (sourced locally; often Thames Side, Twickenham, Windsor & Eton)
Friendly community local in Shepperton Green to the west of the main village centre. Five handpumps serve two regular beers plus up to three usually local guest ales. Many pumpclips adorn the bar and beams. Entertainment includes jazz on Wednesday, a quiz night on Thursday, live rock or blues bands on Friday or Saturday night, and a traditional charity meat raffle on Sunday afternoon. Outside, there is a covered, heated patio area at the rear. P

Staines-upon-Thames

Beehive

35 Edgell Road, TW18 2EP

🕘 12-11 (midnight Fri & Sat) ☎ (01784) 452663

Courage Best Bitter; 1 changing beer (often Thames Side) 🄷

Unspoilt 19th-century two-bar community local. The saloon bar is wood panelled and the public bar has a pool table and darts. In keeping with the historical theme, the toilets are on an outside passage, but modern and warm. The regularly rotated guest beer is drawn mainly from a regional brewer, though more recently local micros have featured. Pickled eggs are available.
🚆♣🚌(458,570)

Bells

124 Church Street, TW18 4ZB (off B376)

🕘 12-11 (midnight Fri & Sat); 12-10.30 Sun

☎ (01784) 454240 🌐 thebellspub.co.uk

Young's Bitter, Special; 2 changing beers (often St Austell, Sharp's) 🄷

Friendly, comfortable, 18th-century pub opposite the historic St Mary's Church, close to the Thames Path and within easy walking distance of the town centre. Regular beers and seasonals from the Young's brand are available plus two guest ales. The Bells is noted locally for the quality of its food (no food Sun eve). The pleasant rear patio garden, with a large heated canopy, is especially popular in summer, attracting local workers and shoppers.
Q❀◑♿🚌

Wheatsheaf & Pigeon 🄻 ✔

Penton Road, TW18 2LL (corner of Wheatsheaf Lane and Penton Rd)

🕘 12-11 ☎ (01784) 452922

🌐 thewheatsheafandpigeon.co.uk

Bombardier; Fuller's London Pride; Otter Ale; 2 changing beers (sourced regionally; often Reunion) 🄷

Welcoming community local between Staines and Laleham, a short signposted walk from the Thames Path. Ales often include local micro beers or guests from the West Country. Good-value, interesting food is served every day (no food Sun or Mon eve). The pub is dog-friendly with water bowls provided. There is outside seating front and back, plus a covered area. Quiz night is Sunday and occasional beer festivals are held. A local bus stops in Laleham Road. Staines Town FC is nearby.
🐴❀◑♿♣P🚌(458,570)🐾📶

Thames Ditton

Red Lion

85 High Street, KT7 0SF

🕘 11-11 (midnight Fri); 10-midnight Sat; 10-10.30 Sun

☎ (020) 8398 8662

2 changing beers (sourced locally) 🄷

Situated near the church, this quirky, eclectically styled pub has a wooden floor, two open fireplaces, seating in a wide variety of styles and an island bar fronted by odd bits of wooden door panels. The original mottled leaded windows have mostly been retained. To the rear is a restaurant in the conservatory, where vinyl LPs are used as placemats (no food weekday eves). The courtyard is a suntrap in summer. 🐴❀◑♿P🚌(515)🐾📶

Tongham

White Hart 🄻 ✔

76 The Street, GU10 1DH

🕘 12-11 (10.30 Mon; midnight Fri & Sat); 12-10.30 Sun

☎ (01252) 782419 🌐 whiteharttongham.co.uk

Hogs Back TEA; 5 changing beers (sourced nationally; often Surrey Hills, Triple fff) 🄷

A family-run three-room village institution which attracts a wide cross-section of the local community. The middle room is listed, the rear bar is usually the liveliest. It offers up to seven real ales – the publican tries to keep one pump dedicated to a rotating dark beer – and a real cider. Live music sometimes features at weekends. No food on Monday. Q🐴❀◑♣🍎P🚌(3)🐾📶

Upper Hale

Alfred Free House

9 Bishops Road, GU9 0JA

🕘 5.30-11 (11.30 Fri & Sat); 12-11.30 Sun ☎ (01252) 820385

🌐 thealfredfreehouse.co.uk

3 changing beers (sourced nationally; often Three Castles) 🄷/🄶

This friendly local pub, tucked away in a residential area, features a bar area and a restaurant/function room. It offers up to three guest ales, and hosts two beer festivals a year in May and October. Live music features every month. Fresh home-made food, using locally-sourced ingredients, is available Thursday to Saturday evenings and Sunday lunchtime. Q🐴◗♿♣P🚌(5)🐾📶

Walton on Thames

Regent 🄻 ✔

19 Church Street, KT12 2QP (on A3050)

🕘 8am-midnight (1am Fri & Sat) ☎ (01932) 506379

Greene King Abbot; St Austell Tribute; Sharp's Doom Bar; 5 changing beers (often Hogs Back, Surrey Hills, Twickenham) 🄷

A pleasantly furnished town-centre former Wetherspoon pub in what was originally the Regent cinema in the 1920s, and more recently a furniture shop. It has a light interior with numerous TV screens. A long bar runs along the right-hand side and steps at the far end lead to a raised seating area. The walls are decorated with photos of old Walton plus Brooklands and Shepperton Studios. It has a relaxed and comfortable atmosphere, though it gets busy at weekends and is popular with students. Lilley's cider is sold.
🐴❀◑♿🍎🚌(461,564)📶

Whyteleafe

Radius Arms

205 Godstone Road, CR3 0EL (on A22)

🕘 closed Mon; 4-9.30 Tue-Thu; 12-10.30 Fri & Sat; 12-5 Sun

☎ 07514 916172

8 changing beers 🄷/🄶

This friendly and popular micropub opened in 2015. The walls are decorated with dried hops, bottles and pumpclips, and the tables were recycled from the Olympic Park in London. An ever-changing selection of cask-conditioned ales from around Britain is sold alongside four KeyKeg beers and up to 13 ciders and perries. Dominoes is played and there is a book library. The pub hosts occasional sausage-making and pickled onion competitions.
Q🚆(Whyteleafe/Upper Warlingham)♣🍎🚌🐾

Woking

Herbert Wells 🄻 ✔

51-57 Chertsey Road, GU21 5AJ

8am-midnight (1am Fri & Sat) ☎ (01483) 722818

Courage Best Bitter; Greene King Abbot; Hogs Back TEA; Sharp's Doom Bar; Wychwood Hobgoblin; 7 changing beers (sourced nationally) H

A wide range of up to seven guest beers, plus eight ciders and perries are available in this popular town-centre Wetherspoon, which is close to bus stops and the railway station and attracts a wide range of clientele including shoppers and office workers. The large open-plan bar is decorated with HG Wells-inspired features including an invisible man sitting in the window and its own time machine. A wealth of information about local history covers the walls of both the main bar and the smaller side room. **Q**

Woking Railway Athletic Club

Goldsworth Road, GU21 6JT (behind offices at E end of Goldsworth Rd) TQ003585

10.30-11; 11.30-10.30 Sun ☎ (01483) 598499

2 changing beers H

Friendly and lively social club tucked away near Victoria Arch, serving between two and four beers. One side of the bar is sports-oriented with darts, free-to-play pool and Sky Sports, while the other side is quieter. Children are welcome at all times and free Wi-Fi is available. Filled rolls are on sale on Saturday afternoon. Show a CAMRA membership card or a copy of this Guide for entry. Local CAMRA Club of the Year 2018.

Woodmansterne

Woodman ✔

Woodmansterne Street, SM7 3NL (on B278)

11-11 (midnight Fri & Sat); 11-10.30 Sun

☎ (01737) 371841 thewoodmanbanstead.co.uk

Sharp's Doom Bar; 3 changing beers H

The Woodman, an attractive building with a circular turret room, was built as an annexe to the local manor house in the early 1900s. Up to three guest beers, and often a cider in the summer, are available in this one-bar pub. Outside is a large and pleasant garden with a sandpit for children and a heated smoking area. Events including poker, quizzes, live music and barbecues are held and food is available all day. **P** (166)

Worplesdon

Fox Inn 🄻

Fox Corner, GU3 3PP

12 (4 Mon)-11; 12-midnight Fri & Sat ☎ (01483) 234024

foxinn.org

Skinner's Betty Stogs; 3 changing beers (sourced nationally; often Crafty, Thurstons, Young's) H

Convivial and welcoming free house rescued from closure by a local resident. The two separate bars have subdued lighting and low beams, and contain an eclectic collection of effects that make the rooms interesting without being cluttered. Outside is a patio and beyond that a substantial garden. Lunch is served daily except Monday, evening meals Thursday to Saturday. The menu changes daily. **Q** **P** (28)

Crown, Horsell (Photo: Tim Griffiths)

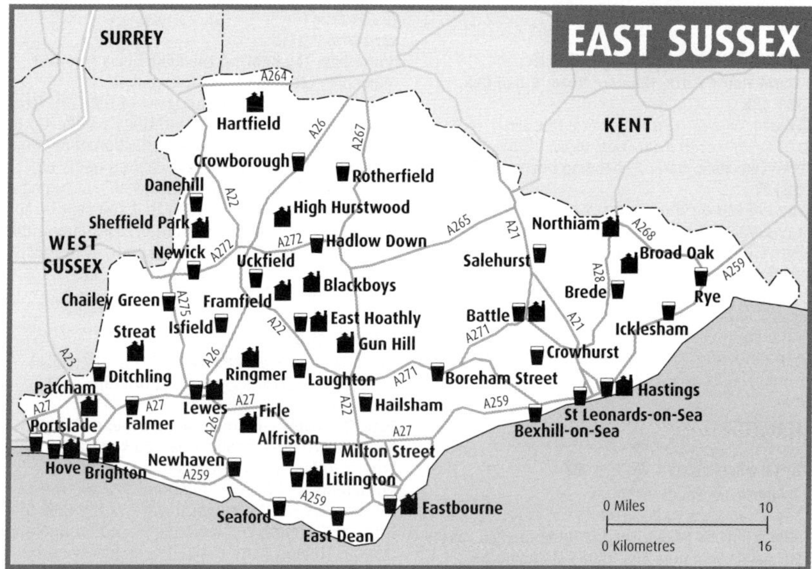

SUSSEX (EAST)

Alfriston

Olde Smugglers Inn

Waterloo Square, BN26 5UE

11 (12 winter)-11; 12-10.30 Sun (01323) 870241
smugglersalfriston.co.uk

Harvey's Sussex Best Bitter; 4 changing beers (sourced locally; often Long Man) H

Nestled in the South Downs this historic, friendly, cosy village pub was built in 1358 and still holds its character today, with its impressive dominating inglenook fireplace, oak beams and brick floor in the main bar area. Outside there is a large garden and patio area with picnic tables. Good-quality pub food is offered, often locally sourced. Several Sussex traditional themed nights are held throughout the year, and toad in the hole is played – an old Sussex game. Accommodation is offered in four rooms. Q

Battle

Squirrel

North Trade Road, TN33 9LJ

11-11; 12-10.30 Sun (01424) 772717
thesquirrelinn-battle.co.uk

Harvey's Sussex Best Bitter; 3 changing beers (sourced locally; often Battle) H

An 18th-century family-run traditional free house to the west of Battle in the heart of 1066 country. There are four handpumps over two bars dispensing only Sussex beers, including one from neighbouring Battle Brewery. Menus change frequently, reflecting seasonal availability of local produce. Meat is free range, with fish from the nearby Hastings day boats. The bar and restaurant areas offer ample seating while outside the large garden has plenty of tables and a children's play area. P (95)

Bexhill on Sea

Albatross Club (RAFA)

15 Marina Arcade, TN40 1JS (on seafront 200yds E of De La Warr Pavilion)

11-2.30, 7 (5 Thu)-11; 11-11 Fri; 12-5 Sun
(01424) 212916 bexhillrafa.co.uk

5 changing beers (sourced locally) H

A most welcoming, popular and friendly RAFA club, winner of National CAMRA Club of the Year in 2016 and runner-up in 2017, and a consistent winner of local and regional CAMRA awards. Local beers feature strongly here, from such as Three Legs, Gun and Rother Valley; other beers are nationally sourced. There are regular folk, jazz and quiz nights and meat raffles; additionally, the club stages popular public beer festivals. CAMRA members are always welcome to sample the range of quality ales on offer. No food on Monday.
Q (98,99)

Boreham Street

Bull's Head

The Strait, BN27 4SG

11.30-11; 11.30-7 Sun (01323) 831981
bullsheadborehamstreet.com

Harvey's Sussex Best Bitter; house beer (by Harvey's); 2 changing beers (often Harvey's) H

This 18th-century pub was the first ever Harveys tied house and is popular with locals, visitors and walkers. Harvey's regular and seasonal ales are offered including house beer Bull's Head Bitter plus a real cider, often Thatchers. Rustic and rural it features wooden flooring and furniture, outdoor seating and a spacious car park. A wide selection of home-cooked meals are served, with Sunday roasts particularly popular. The campsite at the rear belongs to the pub, offering toilet and shower facilities. Many local events are hosted including the Sussex Chopper club in July. The pub may close early Monday to Wednesday winter evenings if quiet. Q P (98)

Brede

Three Legs Brewery Tap

1 Burnt House Farm, Udimore Road, Broad Oak, TN31 6BX
closed Sun-Wed; 12-6.30 Thu; 12-8 Fri & Sat
07939 997622 thethreelegs.co.uk
Three Legs Pale, Dark; 2 changing beers (often Three Legs) H
Brewery tap on the premises of the Three Legs Brewery in a small industrial unit on a farm; the bar always has four ales on handpump and often additional ones from the cask. A selection of good-quality snacks is offered such as cheeses, cured meats and pickles. Seating is available inside and in the warmer weather outside too. Parking is next to the brewery but, like the bar, it gets busy in the evening. QP(2)

Brighton

Basketmakers Arms

12 Gloucester Road, BN1 4AD
11-11 (midnight Fri & Sat); 12-11 Sun (01273) 689006
Fuller's Oliver's Island, London Pride, Bengal Lancer, ESB; Gale's Seafarers Ale, HSB; 1 changing beer (sourced nationally; often Butcombe) H
A Guide regular for many years, the pub is a two-roomed gem in the heart of the North Laine area of the City and within half a mile of the Royal Pavilion. Popular with all ages, the Fuller's beers are complemented by locally sourced fish and meats, with vegetarian options. Plans are in place to relocate the kitchen in order to form an additional seating area.

Brighton Beer Dispensary

38 Dean Street, BN1 3EG
12-11 (midnight Fri & Sat) (01273) 710624
dizzygull.co.uk
4 changing beers (sourced nationally; often Arbor, Brighton Bier, Southey) H
Formerly the Prince Arthur, this pub is sandwiched between domestic terraced premises on a steep hill off the Western Road shopping area. Reopened in 2014, the bar usually has four changing beers and three ciders. A blackboard shows beers available with prices and ABVs. At the rear is a conservatory seating area, at the front a decked area for seating/smoking. A varied, locally sourced food menu is available with vegan options and Sunday roasts. Local CAMRA Pub of the Year 2017.

Brighton Bierhaus

161 Edward Street, BN2 0JB
12-midnight (01273) 686386 brightonbierhaus.com
5 changing beers (sourced locally; often Brighton Bier) H
Brewery tap for Brighton Bier serving up to five changing beers from its range and up to two ciders on handpump, plus around 15 craft beers, mostly on tap. Family (until 7pm) and dog friendly, it is close to the Royal Pavilion, Palace Pier, shops and restaurants. An extensive pizza menu is available via a local outlet. Live sport is shown on Wednesdays, with beer cocktails plus rock and roll DJs every second Sunday (see website for details).

Craft Beer Co

22-23 Upper North Street, BN1 3FG (short walk from Churchill Square shopping centre)
4-11 (1am Fri); 12-1am Sat; 12-10.30 Sun
(01273) 723736
House beer (by Kent); 4 changing beers (sourced regionally; often Kent, Pig & Porter) H
A simple, wood-floored pub, part of the Craft Beer Co group, selling cask ales and Lilley's cider. Up to 18 craft keg beers plus a large selection of national and international bottled and canned beers are also sold. Additional seating is upstairs, including a slightly secluded smaller area that can seat up to 10 people. Food is served from 5.30pm during the week and from midday at weekends, with roasts on Sundays. There is flatscreen TV for sports.

Evening Star

55-56 Surrey Street, BN1 3PB (200yds S of station)
12-11; 11.30-midnight Fri & Sat (01273) 328931
darkstarpubs.co.uk/eveningstar
Dark Star Hophead, American Pale Ale; 6 changing beers (sourced regionally; often Dark Star) H
What can be said about this pub that has not already been said? Brighton's real ale mecca for many years, it is the birthplace of the Dark Star Brewing Co and is conveniently placed for Brighton station. Though fairly basic, it is dearly loved by many Brightonians. Three or four Dark Star beers will always be found, together with three guests. There are continental beers on tap as well as a large range of bottled beers from around the world. Very popular and often crowded at weekends.

Hanover

242 Queens Park Road, Hanover, BN2 9ZB
3-11 (midnight Thu); 12-midnight Fri & Sat; 12-11 Sun
(01273) 679902 hanoverbrighton.co.uk
4 changing beers (sourced locally) H
An estate pub from circa 1927, since opened out but retaining its well-used function/meeting room. Although the place is quite large there are discrete areas with a variety of seating and tables. Part of the Indigo chain, it serves a range of Sussex ales plus a local cider on handpump. Food is served

REAL ALE BREWERIES

1648 East Hoathly
360° Sheffield Park
Bartleby's Brighton
Battle Battle
Beer Me Eastbourne
Beercraft Hove
Brewing Brothers Hastings
Brick House Patcham (brewing suspended)
Brighton Bier Brighton
Burning Sky Firle
Cellar Head Framfield
Engineer High Hurstwood
FILO Hastings
Franklins Ringmer
Gun Gun Hill
Hand Brighton
Harvey's Lewes
High Weald Hartfield
Holler Blackboys
Laine Brighton
Long Man Litlington
Loud Shirt Brighton (NEW)
Old Tree Brighton
Rectory Streat
Rother Valley Northiam
Three Legs Broad Oak

12.30-10pm, a feature of the bar area being the pizza oven. Sunday roasts are served midday-9pm. There is a quiz night on Tuesday and occasional live music. ❀ (21,23)

Lion & Lobster ✔

24 Sillwood Street, BN1 2PS (jct Bedford Sq and Bedford Place)

11-1am (2am Fri & Sat); 12-midnight Sun
☎ (01273) 327299 thelionandlobster.co.uk

Dark Star Hophead, American Pale Ale; Harvey's Sussex Best Bitter; Sharp's Doom Bar; 1 changing beer (sourced nationally; often Old Dairy) Ⓗ

North of Bedford Square is this impressive back-street pub, spacious inside with an upstairs restaurant and two-level terrace with bar. Closing times are generously late, with food served until 10pm (9pm Sun), and a late menu on Wednesdays, Fridays and Saturdays. Real cider is stocked in summer only. An eclectic mix of pictures and framed mirrors adorns the timber-panelled walls. With a wide range of customers, the pub blends a modern feel with a traditional atmosphere. The subdued lighting includes candles. ❀

Prince Albert

48 Trafalgar Street, BN1 4ED

12-midnight (12.30am Fri & Sat) ☎ (01273) 730499

5 changing beers (sourced locally; often Burning Sky) Ⓗ

A former Victorian hotel on the railway station's doorstep, this welcoming free house offers five changing mainly local ales plus a cider on handpump. There are several drinking areas off the main bar, with a large seating area on the pavement at the front and a smaller one at the rear. Portuguese food is served during the week, with a traditional roast on Sunday. There is live music most days. It has a Banksy-style mural on its gable. ❀

Southover

58 Southover Street, Hanover, BN2 9UF

3-midnight (1am Fri); 12-1am Sat; 12-midnight Sun
☎ (01273) 601419 thesouthoverbrighton.co.uk

5 changing beers (sourced locally; often 360 Degree Brewing, Gun) Ⓗ

Towards the top of a steep hill, this comfortably furnished corner-site pub is very dog friendly, with free biscuits and water available. It has two function rooms, one with a free ping-pong table. Usually, there are at least two Sussex-brewed real ales; a premium is charged on half pints. Pies are a feature of the menu, with Sunday roasts including vegetarian and vegan options. A board game night is held fortnightly on Sundays 6-10pm.
❀ (18,23)

Chailey Green

Five Bells

East Grinstead Road, BN8 4DA

11.30-11.30 ☎ (01825) 722259
thefivebellschailey.com

Harvey's Sussex Best Bitter; 3 changing beers (sourced locally; often Bedlam, Harvey's, Long Man) Ⓗ

Country pub on the A275 between Lewes and East Grinstead, popular with car enthusiasts. It has three gardens, with a smoking area to the front of the pub. The timber-fronted bar has carved moulded pilasters separating the shelving areas on the gantry, and there is a mixture of tiled and timber floors. Look out for the brass wall lanterns and the picture supposedly signed by Picasso. No food available on Mondays. Q❀P

Crowborough

Coopers Arms

Coopers Lane, TN6 1SN

12-2.30 (not Mon), 5-11; 12-11 Sun ☎ (01892) 654796

Larkins Traditional Ale; 3 changing beers (sourced nationally) Ⓗ

Something of a beer mecca, this cosy and welcoming Victorian local offers one permanent and three changing real ales, as well as a number of hand-picked craft keg beers. The owner goes to great lengths to seek out the unusual, both locally and from further afield. It has open fires in winter, wholesome pub grub and a secluded garden with great views that make it well worth the trip. Attending one of the regular beer festivals is a must. Open all day bank holidays.
Q❀P (29,29B)

Wheatsheaf ✔

Mount Pleasant, Jarvis Brook, TN6 2NF

12-11; 12-10.30 Sun ☎ (01892) 663756
wheatsheafcrowborough.co.uk

Harvey's Sussex XX Mild Ale, IPA, Sussex Best Bitter; 1 changing beer (often Harvey's) Ⓗ

The Wheatsheaf continues to maintain its local following with a full range of Harvey's beers and a traditional, cosy pub atmosphere. It offers open fires and wood-panelled walls in three separate small drinking areas. Regular music events are staged and the pub food is well regarded, especially the recent addition of a Tuesday steak night. The summer beer festival continues to be very popular. Q❀P (228,229)

Crowhurst

Plough Inn

1 Plough Lane, TN33 9AW

12-11 (10.30 Sun) summer; closed Mon; 5-10 Tue; 12-11 (10 Sun) winter ☎ (01424) 830310

Harvey's Sussex Best Bitter; Long Man Best Bitter; 3 changing beers (sourced locally) Ⓗ

Friendly rural local free house with views over the Sussex Weald; it has two real fires and gives a warm welcome to walkers. The owners have renovated the Plough and introduced a regularly changing menu, doing a fine job in turning the pub around. Up to five ales are offered, always including a LocAle in good condition. Excellent locally sourced food is served; the pub is a recent recipient of a local radio Best Eatery award.
Q❀♿▲P

Danehill

Coach & Horses

School Lane, RH17 7JF

12-3, 5.30-11; 12-11.30 Sat; 12-10.30 Sun
☎ (01825) 740369 coachandhorses.co

Harvey's Sussex Best Bitter; 1 changing beer (sourced locally; often Franklins, Long Man) Ⓗ

A traditional country pub built in 1847 and retaining many original features. The former adjoining stables have been converted to a restaurant serving high-quality locally sourced food. There are separate public and saloon bars with real fires and simple farmhouse-style furniture. It has a large garden to the front with a children's play area and a rear patio with extensive farmland views. Q❀◐♣●P🚌(270)🐾

Ditchling

White Horse

16 West Street, BN6 8TS

11-11 ☎ (01273) 842006 🌐 whitehorseditchling.com

Dark Star Hophead; Harvey's Sussex Best Bitter; 3 changing beers (sourced regionally) Ⓗ

This inn, which dates back to the 12th century, lies below the parish church in this picturesque and historic village. Its cellar leads to a network of tunnels under the village, thought to have been used for smuggling in times past. The accommodation can cater for weddings and birthday parties or as a stopover while walking the South Downs Way. Log fires in winter, excellent food and a varied choice of quality guest beers are certain to fortify the traveller. Q❀◐P🚌(167,168)🐾

East Dean

Tiger Inn

The Green, BN20 0DA

11-10.30 (11 Fri & Sat); 10-10 Sun ☎ (01323) 423209 🌐 beachyhead.org.uk/the-tiger-inn

Harvey's Sussex Best Bitter; Long Man Long Blonde; St Austell Tribute; 3 changing beers (sourced locally) Ⓗ

This quaint smugglers' inn dating from the 15th century is set in the South Downs, making it popular with walkers and cyclists. Nestling in the heart of the village facing the village green, there is ample outside seating from which to admire the idyllic scene. The main bar is full of charm and character, with wooden beamed ceiling, stone floor and log fire. There are two further side rooms; one is accessible by wheelchair from the side entrance. Freshly cooked food is available. Q❀◐♿♣●P🚌🐾

East Hoathly

King's Head

1 High Street, BN8 6DR

11 (12 Sun)-11 ☎ (01825) 840238 🌐 thekingshead.org

1648 Triple Champion, Signature; Harvey's Sussex Best Bitter; 1 changing beer (often 1648) Ⓗ

This Grade II-listed free house was converted over 250 years ago from the village school and remains the heart of the community, with its welcoming atmosphere, well-kept beers and good locally sourced food. Three beers from the adjoining 1648 Brewing Company are always on offer as well as Harvey's Best Bitter, plus a changing real cider usually from Kent or Sussex. There are two function rooms, a restaurant area and a tiered garden with a well at the rear. Q❀◐●P🚌(54)🐾

Eastbourne

Crown

22 Crown Street, Old Town, BN21 1PB

11-11 (midnight Fri & Sat); 12-11 Sun ☎ (01323) 724654

Dark Star Hophead; Harvey's Sussex Best Bitter; Shepherd Neame Spitfire; Wadworth 6X Ⓗ**; Young's Special** Ⓗ/Ⓖ**; 1 changing beer (sourced locally)** Ⓖ

A friendly local pub with two bars, both with log fires, and a separate pool room. Home-made bar snacks and beer discounts are offered every Sunday lunchtime, followed by meat raffles. Popular monthly themed quiz nights include complimentary hot buffets and there is occasional live music. A large enclosed rear garden has children's play equipment and regular summer barbecues. Recent honours from the local CAMRA branch include LocAle and Community awards and runner-up Pub of the Year. ❀♣🚌🐾

Dew Drop Inn

37-39 South Street, BN21 4UP

12-midnight (1am Fri & Sat) ☎ (01323) 723313

Greene King Abbot; Hardys & Hansons Olde Trip; 2 changing beers Ⓗ

Recent improvements to this cosy Little Chelsea pub have enhanced some of the interior space, back garden and toilet facilities without altering the character and atmosphere. It has an alternative feel, with a broad clientele and no TV or gaming machines. There is occasional live music or a DJ at weekends. A welcome spot for conversation, drink and food a short walk from the main town centre. The Greene King Local Heroes scheme provides a range of guest beers. ❀◐♿⇌🚌(3,3A)🐾

Eagle

57 South Street, BN21 4UT

11-11 (12.30am Fri & Sat) ☎ (01323) 417799

Harvey's Sussex Best Bitter; 4 changing beers (sourced regionally) Ⓗ

A classic town pub that seeks to cater for everybody, and so delivers pool, darts, sports on big screens, cosy big armchairs, bar stools, food, four changing guest beers, one draught cider and a warm welcome. Close to the station and major bus routes, it is located in the area known as Little Chelsea. An unusual roof beer garden is open during the summer. Pints are at a discounted price; this can apply to two halves of different beers bought simultaneously. ❀◐⇌♣●🚌🐾

Hurst Arms

76 Willingdon Road, Ocklynge, BN21 1TW

12-2 (not Mon), 5-11.30; 12-midnight Fri & Sat; 12-11.30 Sun ☎ (01323) 419440 🌐 thehurstarms.pub

Harvey's Sussex Best Bitter, Armada Ale; 4 changing beers (sourced locally; often Harvey's) Ⓗ

This classic Victorian pub, unusual in the area for not doing food, is in the heart of Ocklynge about a mile from the town centre. It has two bars, one a typical public bar with pool table, darts and jukebox, the other a comfortable quieter lounge. Three beers from Harvey's are usually on, plus the seasonals. Check the pub's website for its many events. ❀♿♣🚌🐾

London & County

46 Terminus Road, BN21 3LX

8am-midnight (1am Fri & Sat) ☎ (01323) 746310

Greene King Abbot; Ruddles Best Bitter; Sharp's Doom Bar; 3 changing beers (sourced nationally) Ⓗ

A town-centre Wetherspoon Lloyds No.1 bar, close to bus stops and the railway station. It has a large ground floor bar with dining areas, muted news screens and outside seating. A smaller upstairs bar also serves as a function room. Regular, guest and local ales feature on seven handpumps and three ciders are offered. All-day good-value food is served and music plays every night, with a DJ at weekends, when a smart casual dress code applies. ◐♿⇌●🚌

Victoria Hotel

27 Latimer Road, BN22 7BU (behind TAVR Centre from seaside)
closed Mon-Wed; 11.30-2, 6-9; 12-4 Sun
(01323) 722673 thevictoriaeastbourne.co.uk
Harvey's Sussex Best Bitter; house beer (by Harvey's); 1 changing beer (often Harvey's)
Traditional family-run local, close to the seafront. The large front bar has two TVs showing major sporting events, and features brewery memorabilia and Victorian portraits. The back bar has TV, dartboard, pool and toad in the hole tables. The secluded rear garden is available for barbecues and functions. All Harvey's seasonal beers are on offer, while good-value home-made food is served Thursday to Sunday lunchtimes and Thursday to Saturday evenings.

Falmer

Swan Inn

Middle Street, BN1 9PD (just off A27 in N of village)
closed Mon; 12-11; 12-10.30 Sun (01273) 681842
swanfalmer.co.uk
Palmers Tally Ho!; 4 changing beers (sourced regionally; often Downlands, Long Man, Palmers)
This is a traditional family-run free house in the village of Falmer near the universities. It has three bar areas and a barn available for functions. Good-value food is served at lunchtimes plus Thursday and Friday evenings. It gets very busy when Brighton & Hove Albion play at home. The pub opens at varying times on match days and also in the event of Monday evening games. There is a small courtyard area at the side of the pub.
Q P (28,29)

Hadlow Down

New Inn ★

Main Road, TN22 4HJ
6 (1 Wed)-11; 12-11 Sat & Sun
Harvey's IPA, Sussex Best Bitter; 1 changing beer (often Harvey's)
Step back in time to a village local where conversation is king. Although food does not feature, pork pies are usually available. The pub was rebuilt in 1885 by Southdown and East Grinstead Brewing Company on the site of a pub, also called the New Inn, that had burnt down. The pub still has the original back bar fittings – ceramic spirit casks and a panelled counter – hence its inclusion in CAMRA's National Inventory of Historic Pub Interiors. Q P (248)

Hailsham

George Hotel

3 George Street, BN27 1AD
8am-11 (midnight Fri & Sat) (01323) 445120
Greene King Abbot; Ruddles Best Bitter; Sharp's Doom Bar; 2 changing beers (sourced nationally)
A spacious town-centre Wetherspoon pub, comprising an L-shaped bar with a small raised alcove, plus an enclosed beer garden to the rear with more seating areas outside. Situated oppostite the Hailsham Pavilion, a classic Edwardian auditorium, the George has a range of reasonably priced ales, always including at least one LocAle. Local CAMRA Cider Pub of the Year in 2017 and 2018, up to four real ciders are stocked – two regular and two guests – served from a dedicated cool-room for optimum temperature. Brewery tours and Meet the Brewer events are planned for the coming year. Q

Hastings

Crown

64-66 All Saints Street, Old Town, TN34 3BN
11-11; 11-10.30 Sun (01424) 465100
thecrownhastings.co.uk
4 changing beers (sourced locally)
Just below the East Hill Country Park, this award-winning pub, with a vast crown sculpture above the door, will ensure drinkers and diners feel equally at home. The four real ales are from Kent and Sussex breweries and the produce for the regularly changing menu is locally sourced. The subdued paintwork, wooden floor and hand-made tables and chairs create a relaxed atmosphere. There are two open fires, the second one in a small snug at the side.

Dolphin

11-12 Rock-A-Nore Road, Old Town, TN34 3DW
11-11 (midnight Fri & Sat) (01424) 434326
dolphininnhastings.co.uk
Dark Star Hophead; Harvey's Sussex Best Bitter; Young's Special; 3 changing beers (sourced nationally)
An 18th-century traditional pub in Hastings Old Town. It is family run and has long links to the local fishing community - witness the memorabilia and old photographs that adorn the walls. There is a large veranda overlooking the famous fishermen's huts, and both food and drink can be enjoyed here while watching the various fishing activities. Fish comes from the Hastings fishermen and is delivered to the pub kitchen, straight from the beach or market. Q

First In Last Out

14-15 High Street, Old Town, TN34 3EY (near Stables Theatre)
12-11; 11-midnight Fri & Sat (01424) 425079
thefilo.co.uk
FILO Brewery Crofters, Churches Pale Ale, Old Town Tom, Gold; 1 changing beer (sourced regionally)
This popular pub in the heart of Hastings Old Town serves six cask beers, mainly from its own brewery, located nearby. The large single bar is warmed by a central open fire in winter, in which the booth seating is popular. Good food is served in the restaurant area at the back, Monday is tapas night and Thursday thali. Live music is on Tuesdays and Thursdays and jazz Sunday is once a month (check website for details). Q

Jenny Lind

69 High Street, Old Town, TN34 3EW
12-11 (midnight Fri & Sat) (01424) 421392
jennylindhastings.co.uk
Courage Directors; Long Man Long Blonde; Theakston Old Peculier; 7 changing beers (sourced nationally)
This Old Town pub is named after the singer known as the Swedish Nightingale who, it is reputed, stayed in Hastings in the 1880s. There are 10 handpumps in the main bar and up to four changing local real ciders. Well-attended music events are staged at weekends and the RX Shantymen sing every Thursday. There is a real fire and a bar billiards table in the rear bar. The pub has six letting rooms and a terraced garden to the rear.

White Rock Hotel

White Rock, TN34 1JU (opp pier)
10-11, 12-11 Sun (01424) 422240
thewhiterockhotel.com
4 changing beers H
Adjacent to the White Rock Theatre, this friendly hotel welcoming non-residents has a spacious contemporary bar, with ample seating and a seafront terrace. A new large downstairs bar is due to open in 2018. Four beers are offered, from various Sussex breweries, some of which are usually dark. Freshly prepared hot and cold food is available until 10pm. The guest rooms are en-suite, many with fantastic sea views, and some on the first floor have Juliet-style balconies.
QP

Hove

Blind Busker

75-77 Church Road, BN3 2BB
11-11 (midnight Fri & Sat); 12-10.30 Sun
(01273) 749110 blindbuskerhove.co.uk
Greene King Abbot; Ringwood Razorback; 4 changing beers (sourced regionally) H
A traditional pub at the eastern end of the main shopping centre. The pavement side and an indoor area are easily accessible but not the toilet. Upstairs is a bar area with small rooms, subdued lighting and music providing a good atmosphere for drinking, talking and eating. Food is cooked to order. Beers are well kept, with guests changing frequently. Prices are reduced all day on Tuesdays and lunch with a pint is available at a bargain price every day.

Neptune Inn

10 Victoria Terrace, BN3 2WB (on coast road E of King Alfred leisure complex)
12-1am (2am Fri & Sat); 12-midnight Sun
(01273) 736390 theneptunelivemusicbar.co.uk
Dark Star Hophead; Greene King Abbot; Harvey's Sussex Best Bitter; 2 changing beers (sourced regionally) H
No-frills single-bar Victorian pub close to the King Alfred centre and Hove seafront. A reclining figure of Neptune rests above the old Courage signage at the front. Five beers are on the bar, including two changing guests. Children are welcome until 8pm, and it is dog friendly. Live music features strongly, with blues or rock every Friday and jazz on Sundays (see website for details). (700)

Watchmaker's Arms

84 Goldstone Villas, BN3 3RU
closed Mon; 12-2, 5-9; 12-2, 5-11 Fri; 12-11 Sat; 12-3 Sun
(01273) 776307 thewatchmakersarms.co.uk
5 changing beers (sourced regionally; often Brighton Bier, Downlands, Hammerpot) G
Hove's first micropub opened in 2015 – the name comes from the discovery that the premises was a watchmaker's shop in 1889. That theme is carried throughout the pub, with clocks and watches on the walls alongside a large selection of pumpclips showing the range of beers served over the years. Beers are kept in a cool room at the rear of the pub, dispensed from the cask. A selection of sausage rolls is available together with real ciders.
Q(7,21)

Icklesham

Queen's Head

Parsonage Lane, TN36 4BL (opp village hall)
11-11; 12-10.30 Sun (01424) 814552
queenshead.com
Greene King Abbot; Harvey's Sussex Best Bitter; 4 changing beers (sourced locally; often Hardys & Hansons) H
Built in 1632 as two dwellings, the Queen's Head has been a pub since 1831 and in the Guide for over 30 years. It has open fires and a beer garden with fantastic views over the Brede Valley. Three changing ales and two ciders supplement three regular beers. Excellent, good-value home-made food is served daily. There is live music on Sunday afternoons and regular quizzes on Wednesdays (ring for dates). Occasional mini beer festivals with live music take place over bank holiday weekends.
P(100)

Isfield

Laughing Fish

Station Road, TN22 5XB (off A26 between Lewes and Uckfield)
11.30 (10 Thu)-10; 11.30-11 Fri & Sat (01825) 750349
thelaughingfish.co.uk
Greene King IPA; Hardys & Hansons Olde Trip; Long Man Best Bitter; 3 changing beers (sourced locally) H
Formerly the Half Moon, then the Station Hotel, this 1860s pub is next to the preserved Lavender Line. WWII brought the custom of Canadian troops, not without incident. In the 1950s it was the HQ of the District Angling Club, the probable origin of the present name. It combines the Greene King portfolio with guest beers from other Sussex breweries. It features good pub food and a range of games including bar billiards. A pub quiz is held on the first Sunday of each month.
P(29,29B)

Laughton

Roebuck Inn

Lewes Road, BN8 6BG
10-11; 12-11 Sun (01323) 811244
theroebuckinn.pub
Burning Sky Plateau; Harvey's Sussex Best Bitter; 3 changing beers (sourced locally) H
A 17th-century former coaching inn that has been extensively modernised in a steampunk style. The main bar area is open plan, with a smaller snug at the rear. There is accommodation and a large function room which can cater for parties and is used for occasional live music and theatre productions. The beer and food is usually sourced locally and includes good vegetarian options. The East Sussex pub game toad in the hole is played here. Open at 10am for breakfast.
QP

Lewes

Black Horse

55 Western Road, BN7 1RS
11-11; 12-10.30 Sun (01273) 473653
theblackhorselewes.co.uk
Burning Sky Plateau; Greene King Abbot; Morland Old Speckled Hen; house beer (by Greene King); 3 changing beers (sourced regionally; often Greene King) H

A traditional pub with large bay windows, towards the western end of town; the main bar has plenty of seating and a real fire plus pub games. There are two TVs showing most sporting events. The smaller, quieter back bar has further seating. The terrace at the rear of the pub is popular in the summer. Home-made food including vegan options is served lunchtimes and evenings. Friendly poker is played every Wednesday and a quiz is held on alternate Sundays.
(28,29)

Brewers Arms

91 High Street, BN7 1XN (near Lewes Castle)
10-11; 12-10.30 Sun (01273) 475524
brewersarmslewes.co.uk
Harvey's Sussex Best Bitter; 4 changing beers (sourced regionally)
Close to Lewes Castle, this genuine second-generation family-run free house has two contrasting bars – a quiet, comfortable one at the front and a back bar with a jukebox, pool table, darts and the old Sussex game of toad in the hole. It is popular on match days with Lewes FC, Brighton & Hove Albion and away fans alike. Traditional, good-value pub food is served daily until 8pm. Dogs are welcome. The exterior proclaims former owners Page & Overton, Brewers of Croydon.
Q (28,29)

Elephant & Castle

White Hill, BN7 2DJ (off Fisher St, near old police station)
11.30-11 (midnight Fri & Sat); 12-11 Sun
(01273) 473797 elephantandcastlelewes.com
Harvey's Sussex Best Bitter; 3 changing beers (sourced nationally)
A spacious pub with three rooms around a central bar. It has several big screens for sport, making it popular with Lewes, Brighton FC and away fans alike on match days. Good-value food is served lunch and evening including the famous Elly burger. It has a large selection of craft beer bottles and cans, which on Crafty Thursday are available to drink in at takeaway prices. It is also home to a number of clubs. (127,132)

Gardener's Arms

46 Cliffe High Street, BN7 2AN
11-11; 12-10.30 Sun (01273) 474808
Harvey's Sussex Best Bitter; 5 changing beers (sourced regionally; often Harvey's)
A traditional, genuine free house near Harvey's Brewery. It is a one-roomed pub with a wooden floor and central bar. Five changing guest ales are dispensed, generally from small breweries across the country, and a real cider is always available. It is popular with Lewes and Brighton FC fans on match days. Food consists of locally made pies and pasties. An Old and Dark beer festival is held in February. No children allowed, but dogs are especially welcome. (28,29)

Lansdown Arms

36 Lansdown Place, BN7 2JU
11-11 (01273) 470711
Harvey's Sussex Best Bitter; Timothy Taylor Landlord; 2 changing beers (sourced locally; often Gun, Long Man)
A small but often incredibly busy pub close to Lewes station and the new Depot cinema. Football match days are even busier, with supporters of both nearby Lewes FC and Brighton & Hove Albion FC. There are regular live music performance events. On entering, the eye is drawn to the Tree of Life and various artworks. Furnishings are spartan: wooden seats, church pews and old school chairs.

Lewes Arms

1 Mount Place, BN7 1YH
11-11 (midnight Fri & Sat); 12-11 Sun (01273) 473152
Fuller's London Pride; Gale's Seafarers Ale, HSB; Harvey's Sussex Best Bitter; 2 changing beers (sourced regionally; often Fuller's)
An historic pub in the heart of the county town, made up of three small rooms. You will find a real fire in winter, with a raised terrace and courtyard garden for the summer. Home-made food is served every day from noon. It is home to the world pea throwing championship, dwyle flunking matches, spaniel racing and other unusual events. A pantomime is held every March in the upstairs function room in aid of local charities. Dogs are welcome. Q (28,29)

Snowdrop Inn

119 South Street, BN7 2BU
12-midnight; 12-11 Sun (01273) 471018
thesnowdropinn.pub
Burning Sky Plateau; Harvey's Sussex Best Bitter; 4 changing beers (sourced locally; often Burning Sky)
On the outer edge of the Cliffe area of this historic town, the Snowdrop is a popular and welcoming free house serving six cask ales, one cider and four, often unusual, beers on KeyKeg. The pub has a central bar, with additional seating upstairs and two outside drinking areas. It is family friendly and serves good home-cooked food all day. It hosts a jazz night every Monday and music most Saturdays. A beer festival is held in October.
(28,29)

Litlington

Plough & Harrow

The Street, BN26 5RE
11.30-11; 12-10.30 Sun (01323) 870632
ploughandharrowlitlington.co.uk
Long Man Best Bitter; 4 changing beers (sourced locally; often Long Man)
A traditional English village local, dating back to the 17th century. The original part of the building, now a cosy snug, has been extended over the years to include a bar area and a family room/restaurant. Four handpumps usually serve beer from the local Long Man brewery, with the other two used for a guest ale and cider, often local too. Good-quality food is served daily. The pub makes an excellent stop for walkers in the South Downs.
P

Milton Street

Sussex Ox

BN26 5RL
11.30-3, 5.30-11; 11.30-11 Sat; 12-10.30 Sun; 11.30-11; 12-10.30 Sun summer (01323) 870840
thesussexox.co.uk
Long Man Best Bitter; 2 changing beers (sourced locally)
A popular free house with stunning views, at the foot of the South Downs between the picturesque villages of Alfriston and Wilmington. In the old bar three real ales, plus a local real cider, all on

handpump, are served by friendly staff. Other interconnected rooms and an outside decked terrace provide plenty of seating. Good-quality contemporary-style food is served, with many ingredients coming from the pub's owners' adjacent organic farm; the menu changes daily.
Q P

Newhaven

Hope Inn

West Pier, BN9 9DN
11-10.30 (midnight Wed, Fri & Sat) (01273) 515389
hopeinnnewhaven.co.uk
Harvey's Sussex Best Bitter; 2 changing beers (sourced regionally) H
A spacious pub at the far end of town, close to Newhaven Fort, with a covered balcony overlooking the harbour entrance. The interior has a timber-panelled beamed ceiling, timber-panelled bar, walls and polished timber floors. Look out for the stained-glass panels, the multitude of nautical themed pictures and the flag signals on the ceiling beams. Heed the sign warning you against feeding the pub dog. Quiz night is Wednesday. Home-cooked food is available every day. There is a raised patio smoking area at front. P

Newick

Crown Inn

22 Church Road, BN8 4JX
12 (3 Mon)-11; 12-10.30 Sun (01825) 723293
thecrownatnewick.co.uk
Harvey's Sussex Best Bitter; 1 changing beer (sourced regionally) H
This family-run free house is at the southern end of the village near the post office. The 121 bus stops just round the corner. There is a central bar with two smaller rooms off to either side and a pleasant garden to the rear. Good-value meals are served using local produce. With two other pubs on the village green, Newick is well worth a whole afternoon's stay, but do not miss the last bus!
P (31,121)

Portslade

Stag's Head

35 High Street, Old Portslade, BN41 2LH
12-3, 4.30-11; 12-11.30 Fri & Sat; 12-10.30 Sun
(01273) 416058
Harvey's Sussex Best Bitter; Long Man American Pale Ale; 3 changing beers (sourced nationally; often Brains, Goddards) H
This pub, originally the Bull, dates from the 16th century. It stands in the shadow of John Dudney's magnificent 1881 brewery to which it was allegedly linked by a tunnel fitted with rails to allow the rolling of barrels; the brewery was closed in 1930. The pub was enlarged in 1959 with the adjacent cottage becoming the saloon bar. The interior shows little sign of the pub's age, but some evidence of Watneyisation remains.
Q (1,1A)

Stanley Arms

47 Wolseley Road, BN41 1SS (on corner of Wolseley Rd and Stanley Rd)
4 (3 Thu & Fri; 12 Sat)-11; 12-10.30 Sun
(01273) 973531 thestanley.com
5 changing beers (sourced regionally; often Downlands, Long Man, Sharp's) H
An excellent street-corner local tucked away in a residential area, a genuine free house with a changing range of beers, ciders, British and foreign bottled beers. A large TV shows football, rugby and other sports. Three beer festivals are held in the spring, summer and autumn. The first Monday of the month, 7-9pm, is Cellar Night, with a reduced price for beers and free nibbles. Occasional live music plus weekly quiz and crib nights take place.
Q (2,46)

Rotherfield

King's Arms

High Street, TN6 3LJ
12-midnight; 12-10.30 Sun (01892) 853441
Harvey's Sussex Best Bitter; 2 changing beers (sourced locally) H
Busy and friendly 17th-century village local with separate comfy bars and restaurant, open fires and a large garden with panoramic views over the Sussex Weald. It has a reputation for excellent-quality food without being too gastro. The pub runs regular events including a summer beer and music festival, Halloween spectacular, and is a major contributor to the bonfire and firework night in October/November. P (252)

Rye

Standard Inn

The Mint, TN31 7EN
11-11 (midnight Fri & Sat); 12-10 Sun (01797) 225231
thestandardinnrye.co.uk
House beer (by Old Dairy); 3 changing beers (often Three Legs) H
A 15th-century inn, it is well positioned in a narrow street that meanders from the town centre to the riverside area. Recently refurbished, it is comfortable yet rustic, the exposed beams and quarry-tile floors giving a hint of an inn well used over many years. There are five en-suite rooms and a menu featuring typical English pub fare, locally sourced where possible. The house beer is by Old Dairy, and three varying Three Legs beers are offered. Q (100,101)

Ypres Castle Inn

Gun Garden, TN31 7HH (difficult to access from A259 although close to it; from Church Square is better)
12-11 (midnight Fri); 12-10.30 Sun summer; closed Mon; 12-11; 12-10.30 Sun winter (01797) 223248
yprescastleinn.co.uk
Old Dairy Copper Top; 4 changing beers (sourced locally) H
An attractive weatherboarded pub built in 1640 with fantastic views across Romney Marsh; the outside drinking areas include part of the top of the town ramparts. The Wipers has one large bar with an open fire and an adjoining room which can be used for functions. The cider is Biddenden Bushels, and the menu usually includes locally sourced seafood. Music is on Friday evenings and Sunday afternoons, while the large garden accommodates musical Wipers Weekends in August. The pub is closed winter Mondays.

St Leonards on Sea

Tower

251 London Road, Bohemia, TN37 6NB
11-11.30 (12.30am Fri & Sat); 11-11 Sun
(01424) 721773
Dark Star Hophead, American Pale Ale; 4 changing beers (sourced regionally)
A friendly welcome and a great selection of reasonably priced ales and ciders are guaranteed at this self-proclaimed proper boozer that truly lives up to the label. The main football and rugby matches are shown on HD TV screens and the pub also has a jukebox. There is a wood-burning stove adding to the convivial atmosphere. The Tower was local CAMRA Pub of the Year for three consecutive years.

Salehurst

Salehurst Halt

Church Lane, TN32 5PH (by church)
closed Mon; 12-11 (01580) 880620
salehursthalt.co.uk
Harvey's Sussex Best Bitter; 2 changing beers (sourced locally)
Established in 1837, this charming family-run pub is the heart of the village. Excellent real ales plus usually local ciders are served, and a quirky menu of exceptional fresh home-cooked food is available (booking advisable). On summer Wednesday evenings fresh-baked pizza is served from the wood-fired oven outside. The garden offers lovely views over the tranquil Rother Valley. This dog-friendly pub was local CAMRA branch Community Pub of the Year 2016. Q

Seaford

Old Boot Inn

16 South Street, BN25 1PE
10-11 (midnight Fri & Sat); 11-10.30 Sun
(01323) 895454
Harvey's Sussex Best Bitter; 4 changing beers (sourced regionally; often Dark Star, Harvey's, Thornbridge)
Deceptively large pub with three entrances, one in South Street and two in High Street. The South Street entrance has a large outside seating area; the one in High Street has wheelchair access. The pub is under the same ownership as the Gardener's Arms in Lewes. Food is served, with plenty of tables and a wide choice of roasts on a Sunday. There are six handpumps, with four changing guest beers and a real cider.

Wellington

33 Steyne Road, BN25 1HT
12-11 (midnight Fri & Sat); 12-10 Sun (01323) 899517
wellingtonseaford.com
Dark Star Hophead, American Pale Ale; Long Man Best Bitter; 7 changing beers (sourced nationally; often Moorhouse's, Springhead, Timothy Taylor)
Greene King supplies the ales but the pub boasts 10 handpumps serving local and national beers, imaginative food deals and B&B accommodation. It is on the former quayside in the old part of the town, close to the beach and town centre, handy for buses to Brighton and Eastbourne. The pub has three rooms, a small sports TV bar, a comfortable main bar, and a third room across the corridor. Dogs are welcome in the TV bar.
Q (12,12A)

White Lion Hotel

74 Claremont Road, BN25 2BJ
11-11 (01323) 892473 whitelionhotelseaford.co.uk
Harvey's Sussex Best Bitter; 4 changing beers (often Long Man)
The family-run White Lion Hotel has one traditional bar and one sports bar with wide-screen TV. There are five real ales from local breweries - Harvey's and Long Man together with guest ales from around the UK. The amenities include a function room, a conservatory restaurant and a patio/beer garden. Meals are served every day and include weekday lunchtime specials and steak nights on Wednesdays. Food is all locally sourced as far as possible. P

Uckfield

Alma Arms

65 Framfield Road, TN22 5AJ (on B2102)
11-11 (11.30 Fri & Sat); 12-10.30 Sun (01825) 762232
almaarmsuckfield.co.uk
Harvey's Sussex XX Mild Ale, Sussex Best Bitter; 2 changing beers (often Harvey's)
A Guide regular, this friendly two-bar Harvey's tied house is within easy walking distance of the town centre, station and buses. The main building, which dates from 1851, was named after the Crimean battle of the Alma in September 1854. At one time the pub was the brewery tap for Bourner's Lion Brewery which stood where the extension and car park is now. The regular cider is Weston's Rosie's Pig. There is no food on Monday or Tuesday.
Q P (31)

SUSSEX (WEST)

Alfold Bars

Sir Roger Tichborne

Loxwood Road, RH14 0QS (2 miles S of A281 towards Loxwood)
11-midnight; 12-11 Sun (01403) 751873
thetichborne.co.uk
Dark Star Hophead; Young's Bitter; house beer (by Firebird); 2 changing beers (sourced locally)
Located off the A281, this beautiful old country pub, whose origins date back to medieval times, is stunning. It oozes charm from the low ceilings, slate floors and inglenook fireplaces and has breathtaking views onto the South Downs. Helpful staff serve beers from local breweries on five handpumps. The atmosphere is friendly and the landlord is passionate about local ales and locally-sourced food. Q P

Amberley

Bridge Inn

Houghton Bridge, BN18 9LR (on B2139 just W of railway bridge at Amberley station)
11-11; 12-9 Sun (01798) 831619
bridgeinnamberley.com
Harvey's Sussex Best Bitter; Long Man Long Blonde; 1 changing beer (sourced nationally; often Timothy Taylor)
Close to Amberley Museum and Heritage Centre, the South Downs Way and Amberley railway station, this Grade II-listed inn serves three real ales. Inside is a single cosy bar, open log fires and a large dining area to the side, serving mainly locally

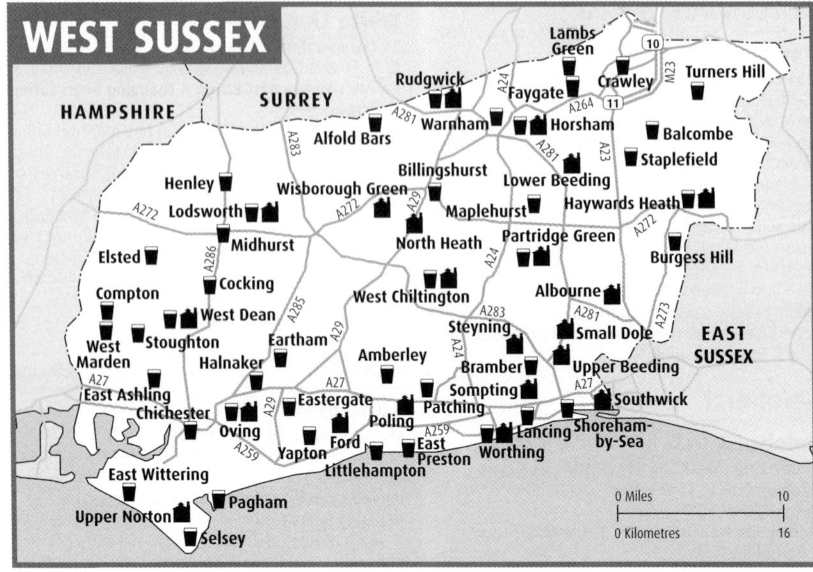

sourced home-cooked produce. There is a patio at the front and an attractive gated garden to the side. Q🐎❀◑≹●P🚌(73)🐾📶

Balcombe

Half Moon

Haywards Heath Road, RH17 6PA

⏲ 12-11 (10 Mon; midnight Fri & Sat); 11-9 Sun

☎ (01444) 811582

Harvey's Sussex Best Bitter; High Weald Chronicle; 1 changing beer (sourced regionally) Ⓗ

A small pub with tables in the lower part as you enter, and the bar beyond up a couple of steps. Food-led, this is north Sussex's first community-owned pub, with three handpumps. One normally has Harvey's Sussex Best, the other two dispense rotating guests, which are mainly local. It also serves a varied range of locally sourced meals. ◑≹●P📶

Billingshurst

King's Head 🄻

40 High Street, RH14 9NY

⏲ 11-11 (midnight Fri & Sat); 12-11 Sun ☎ (01403) 782012

Hogs Back TEA; 7 changing beers (sourced regionally; often Crafty Brewing, Greyhound) Ⓗ

Former Enterprise pub that is now a free house, enjoying a resurgence after many years out of the Guide, boasting a wide range of real ales from the eight handpumps. It is a large town-centre establishment dating from the 18th century, with plenty of space for drinkers and diners, and a great pub for watching sport. 🐎❀◑P🚆🚌🐾📶

Bramber

Castle Inn Hotel 🄻

The Street, BN44 3WE (just off A283, near S Steyning roundabout)

⏲ 11-11; 11-10.30 Sun ☎ (01903) 812102

🌐 castleinnhotel.co.uk

Downlands Bramber; Harvey's Sussex Best Bitter; Sharp's Doom Bar; 1 changing beer (sourced locally; often Dark Star, Riverside) Ⓗ

Set in a rural Sussex village, this historic inn has been called the Castle Inn Hotel since Victorian times, and there has been a coaching house or inn on the site since the early 13th century. The oldest part of the current building dates back to the 17th century. It is a family-run 3-star B&B and pub with good food and drinks on offer. There is a picturesque garden at the rear with a stream flowing through it. Q🐎❀🛏◑P🚌🐾📶

Burgess Hill

Quench Bar & Kitchen 🄻

2-4 Church Road, RH15 9AE

⏲ 9am-11 (12.30am Fri; 1am Sat); 10-10.30 Sun

☎ (01444) 253332 🌐 quenchbar.co.uk

Harvey's Sussex Best Bitter; 2 changing beers (sourced locally; often Downlands, Franklins, Pig & Porter) Ⓗ

Within sight of the railway station, this pub is at the top end of the town's original shopping street. It comprises a bar area together with a comfortable lounge. Quality local beers prevail, alongside a range of bottled beers, spirits, teas and espresso coffees. Occasional live music events and beer festivals are held. A limited number of tables and chairs are provided outside. All buses that serve Burgess Hill pass by the door. ◐≹🚌📶

Chichester

Bell Inn

3 Broyle Road, PO19 6AT (on A286 just N of Northgate)

⏲ 11.30-2, 5-midnight; 12-3, 7-11 Sun ☎ (01243) 783388

🌐 thebellinnchichester.com

3 changing beers (sourced nationally; often Hop Back, Sharp's, Triple fff) Ⓗ

Cosy and comfortable city local with a traditional ambience enhanced by exposed brickwork, wood panelling and beams. A rear suntrap garden has a covered smoking area heated by a chimenea in winter. The pub tends to become busiest after

10pm, when the nearby Festival Theatre empties out. The beer selection usually comprises two from the Enterprise range and one from a local micro, complemented by an extensive monthly changing food menu (no food Sun eve).
Q🚸❀◑♣P⊡🚌(60)🐾📶

Chichester Inn L

38 West Street, PO19 1RP (at Westgate roundabout)
⏲ 12-11.30 (midnight Fri & Sat); 12-9 Sun
☎ (01243) 783185 🌐 chichesterinn.co.uk
Harvey's Sussex Best Bitter; 3 changing beers (sourced regionally; often Dark Star, Langham, Vibrant Forest) H
Pleasant two-bar pub with a real fire in the front lounge surrounded by comfortable chairs, with a mix of seating and table types elsewhere. The larger public bar to the rear features regular live music on Wednesday, Friday and Saturday evenings. Outside is an attractive walled garden with a heated and covered smoking area. Four B&B rooms are available. Food includes Sunday lunches. There is a strong emphasis on LocAles.
❀🛏◑⇌♣●P🚌🐾📶

Dolphin & Anchor L ✔

5 West Street, PO19 1QF
⏲ 8am-midnight (1am Fri & Sat) ☎ (01243) 790280
Greene King Abbot; Ruddles Best Bitter; Sharp's Doom Bar; 6 changing beers (sourced nationally; often Arundel, Goldmark, Langham) H
Conversion of part of a historic city-centre hotel opposite the cathedral. Once two separate hotels, combined in 1910, the pub occupies the lower floor of what was The Anchor. This Wetherspoon venue is popular with young and old alike and is nearly always busy. It serves up to six changing beers, championing local microbreweries, and hosts Meet the Brewer evenings every two months or so. There is also a small courtyard to the rear for smoking and drinking. 🚸❀◑♿⇌●🚌📶

Eastgate ✔

4 The Hornet, PO19 7JG (500yds E of Market Cross)
⏲ 12 (11 Wed)-11; 10-12.30am Sat; 12-11.30 Sun
☎ (01243) 774877
Fuller's London Pride; Gale's Seafarers Ale, HSB; 2 changing beers (sourced nationally; often Adnams, Castle Rock, Fuller's) H
Welcoming town pub with an open-plan bar and tables for diners. Good-quality traditional pub meals are served daily. There is a heated patio garden to the rear, which is the venue for a beer festival in July. The pub attracts locals, holidaymakers and shoppers from the nearby market, with a warm welcome and traditional pub games such as darts, cribbage and pool. Music is turned up on Friday and Saturday late evenings, while live bands perform once a month.
❀◑♣🚌(51,700)🐾📶

Cocking

Greyhound

Cocking Causeway, GU29 9QH (on A286 between Cocking and Midhurst)
⏲ 11-11; 12-10.30 Sun ☎ (01730) 814425
🌐 thegreyhoundpub.com
4 changing beers (sourced regionally; often Greyhound, Hop Back, Long Man) H
Traditional free house close to the South Downs. The front bar is largely unspoilt and relaxing for both drinkers and diners. To the rear is a large modern conservatory restaurant offering locally sourced seasonal food. There are extensive gardens to both the front and rear, the latter with a large children's play area and patio for alfresco dining. The four beers are usually sourced from a mix of traditional regional brewers alongside more local micros from Sussex and Hampshire.
Q🚸❀◑♣🚌(60)🐾📶

Compton

Coach & Horses L

The Square, PO18 9HA (on B2146)
⏲ closed Mon; 12-3, 6-11; 12-9 Sun ☎ (023) 9263 1228
🌐 coachandhorsescompton.com
Greyhound Blonde Bird; Red Cat Prowler Pale; 3 changing beers (sourced locally; often Fallen Acorn, Red Cat, Triple fff) H
A 16th-century pub in a quiet, pleasant downland village, popular both with walkers and cyclists. The front bar, with internal wooden shutters and wooden floors, has a wood-burning stove at one end and an open fire at the other, while the oldest part of the pub at the rear is now used only occasionally for dining. An adventurous menu of high-quality food is served daily. The well-loved owners, David and Christiane Butler, have now been in charge for 34 years.
Q❀◑⛺♣●⊡🚌(54)🐾📶

Crawley

Brewery Shades L

85 High Street, RH10 1BA
⏲ 10-11.30 (1.30am Fri & Sat) ☎ (01293) 514255
Dark Star Revelation; Greene King Abbot; 8 changing beers H
Arguably the oldest building in Crawley High Street, dating back to the 1400s and complete with two active ghosts. The pub is wet-sales led. The licensee has a true passion for the trade, demonstrated by the inspired range of guest ales

REAL ALE BREWERIES

81 Artisan West Dean
Adur Steyning
Arundel Ford
Bedlam Albourne
Brew Studio Sompting (NEW)
Brolly Wisborough Green (NEW)
Chapeau Horsham (NEW)
Dark Star Partridge Green
Downlands Small Dole
Firebird Rudgwick
Goldmark Poling
Greyhound West Chiltington
Gribble ▮ Oving
Hammerpot Poling
Heathen Haywards Heath
Hepworth North Heath
Kissingate Lower Beeding
Langham Lodsworth
Lister's Ford
Pin-Up Southwick
Polarity Worthing
Ridgeway North Heath
Riverside Upper Beeding
Spencer's Upper Norton (NEW)
Top-Notch Haywards Heath
Two Tribes Horsham
Weltons Horsham

and cider which are always in excellent condition. The haunted upstairs room is now available for meetings. Good food is served during the day and evening – check the specials board.

Eartham

George

PO18 0LT (turn N off A27 at Crockerhill or W of Fontwell and proceed 2 miles to centre of village)
closed Mon; 11.30-11; 12-6 Sun (01243) 814340
thegeorgeeartham.com
House beer (by Otter); 3 changing beers (sourced locally; often Downlands Brewery, Gun, Langham)
A tastefully refurbished old village pub whose landlord's passion for the best of English, and especially Sussex, extends to the entire drinks and food menu. All changing beers are LocAle and always include one from Langham. Usually, one is a hoppy golden ale while another is a porter, old ale or mild. The food menu features locally sourced ingredients. Popular with walkers and cyclists, the pub holds a beer festival in its garden each April featuring LocAles and live music.
Q P (99)

East Ashling

Horse & Groom

PO18 9AX (on B2178 in village) SU820077
12-11; 12-6 Sun (01243) 575339
thehorseandgroomchichester.co.uk
Dark Star Hophead; Hop Back Summer Lightning; Long Man Best Bitter; Young's Bitter; 1 changing beer (sourced regionally; often Langham)
Between the South Downs and the sea, and an inn for over 200 years, this fine country free house has a compact bar featuring flagstones, settles, half-panelled walls and a lovely old range. Sympathetically extended, it remains unspoilt. The beers are meticulously presented and are sold at consistently good-value prices. A blackboard reveals the diverse, high-quality menu of hearty home-made dishes, all sourced locally (no food Sun eve). En-suite accommodation is dog friendly, some in a converted 17th-century oak-beamed flint barn. Q P (54)

East Preston

Clockhouse Bar

103-105 Sea Road, BN16 1NX (beach end of East Preston, opp village green)
12-11 (11.30 Fri & Sat); 12-10 Sun (01903) 788367
theclockhousebaranddeli.co.uk
St Austell Tribute; 2 changing beers (sourced locally; often Hammerpot)
This ex-bank, built in 1929, has plenty of character, complete with its own deli next door. A working clock above the pub serves as a war memorial, and in the pub itself there are many different types of clocks on the walls. There are cork-style tables and a raised level with comfy seating. The emphasis is on local beers, with a Hammerpot ale being a regular on one of three handpumps in use.
Q (700)

East Wittering

Shore

Shore Road, PO20 8DZ (50yds from sea)
11-11; 11-10.30 Sun (01243) 674454
theshorepub.co.uk
Castle Rock Harvest Pale; Dark Star Hophead; Hop Back Summer Lightning; Palmers Copper Ale, Dorset Gold; Sharp's Doom Bar; 1 changing beer (sourced regionally; often Dark Star)
Friendly beachside pub popular with the locals (particularly dog owners) and the many summer visitors. There are two main bars, a children's area and a fair-sized area for outside drinking as well as smoking. The good-quality lunchtime menu can be enjoyed either in the bar or restaurant, when extremely inviting dishes are on offer at fair prices. It has occasional live music – see the website for details. Q P (52,53)

Eastergate

Wilkes' Head

Church Lane, PO20 3UT (off A29 in old village, 350yds S of B2233 roundabout, just over 1 mile W of Barnham station) SU943053
12-11 (01243) 543380
Adnams Southwold Bitter; 5 changing beers (sourced nationally; often Langham, Long Man)
Small Grade-II listed red-brick pub, built in 1803 and named after 18th-century radical John Wilkes. There is a cosy lounge left of the central bar, and to the right a larger room with inglenook fireplace, flagstones and low beams, plus a separate restaurant. At the rear is a permanent marquee with seating plus a heated smokers' shelter and a large garden. There are five well-chosen changing beers, and regular beer festivals are held.
Q P

Elsted

Three Horseshoes

GU29 0JY (at E end of village)
11-2.30, 6-11; 12-3, 7-10.30 Sun (01730) 825746
Bowman Wallops Wood H/G; Flowerpots Bitter; Young's Bitter; 2 changing beers (sourced locally; often Langham)
Old and cosy rural inn divided into small rooms, including one reserved for dining and one with a blazing log fire in winter. Outside, the large, pleasant garden enjoys superb views of the South Downs. In summer there are five beers (mainly from local micros), and three in winter, all served by gravity from a stillage alongside the bar. Meals are substantial and of high quality. This is a popular and homely pub, which you will be reluctant to leave. Q P

Faygate

Frog & Nightgown

Wimland Road, RH12 4SS
5-10 Mon; 10.30-11; 12-7 Sun (01293) 852764
thefrogandnightgown.co.uk
Fuller's London Pride; 3 changing beers (sourced regionally; often Dark Star, Harvey's)
Coral and Ritchie bought the pub in 2015 and spent several months refurbishing it; it is now run by their son Lewis. Regular events including quiz nights, open mic nights, a classic car show, live music and wine tasting all feature. Street food is often available on a Friday night. It is known as the fastest pub in West Sussex due to its motorsport connections. P

Halnaker

Anglesey Arms

Stane Street, PO18 0NQ (on A285)
11-3, 5.30-11; 11-11 Fri & Sat; 12-7 Sun
(01243) 773474 angleseyarms.com
Harvey's Sussex Best Bitter; Young's Bitter; 2 changing beers (sourced locally; often Arundel, Bowman, Langham) H
Close to the Goodwood Estate, which owns the freehold, this Grade II-listed, family-run Georgian pub and dining room features a wood- and flagstone-floored public bar with a log fire, plus a comfortable restaurant renowned for good food made with local produce (reservation essential). Two local SIBA guest beers are usually on the bar. Dogs are welcome. The 2½-acre rear garden with pétanque court is popular for wedding receptions and classic car meetings as well as regular boules matches in summer. Q P (55,99)

Haywards Heath

Lockhart Tavern

41 The Broadway, RH16 3AS
12 (9 Sat)-11; 12-7 Sun (01444) 440696
Dark Star Hophead, American Pale Ale; 4 changing beers (sourced locally; often Dark Star) H
Centrally located café-style pub tied to the local Dark Star brewery; it is popular without being noisy. There is a bar area at the front with a wood-panelled dining area behind and a few picnic tables outside on a patio. Good food is served lunchtimes and evenings from a regularly changing menu. There are usually six handpumps for real ales plus a choice of wine, cans and bottles.

Henley

Duke of Cumberland

Henley Village, GU27 3HQ (off A286, 2 miles N of Midhurst) SU894258
11-11; 12-10.30 Sun (01428) 652280
dukeofcumberland.com
Harvey's Sussex Best Bitter; Langham Hip Hop; Timothy Taylor Landlord; 1 changing beer (sourced locally; often Langham) G
Stunning 15th-century inn nestling against the hillside in over three acres of terraced gardens with extensive views. The rustic front bar has scrubbed-top tables and benches, plus log fires at both ends, while to the rear is a dining extension that blends in perfectly with the original pub and offers much-needed additional space. A former local CAMRA Pub of the Year, this is a rural gem. May close winter Sunday evenings. Q P (70)

Horsham

Anchor Hotel

3 Market Square, RH12 1EU
11-11 (midnight Fri & Sat); 12-10.30 Sun
(01403) 250640
Greene King IPA; Long Man Best Bitter; 5 changing beers (often Westerham) H
This Taylor Walker pub is an impressive Victorian building in the heart of the town, comprising a large ground-floor room and balcony room, plus a heated courtyard to the rear. Freshly prepared great British pub food is served daily. There is an emphasis on local ales, complemented by the occasional festival featuring beers from around the country. It offers 10 per cent off ales for CAMRA members, and hosts a variety of entertainment including live music, comedy, DJs and quizzes.

Anchor Tap

16 East Street, RH12 1HL
closed Mon; 12-10.30 (11 Fri & Sat) (01403) 274542
Dark Star Hophead, Partridge Best Bitter, American Pale Ale; 4 changing beers (sourced regionally) H
Having been closed for 30 years, this pub was reopened in 2016 by Dark Star Brewing. A much-welcome addition to the town's drinking establishments, it is popular with customers both local and from afar. Refurbished in an early 20th-century style, there are six handpumps offering Dark Star beers, together with other ales from across the country, plus real cider. The back bar has 10 brews from Dark Star and other breweries. Bar snacks are served lunchtimes.

Beer Essentials

30A East Street, RH12 1HL
10-6 (7 Fri & Sat); closed Sun & Mon (01403) 218890
thebeeressentials.co.uk
Arundel Sussex Gold; 7 changing beers (sourced locally) G
A mecca for the connoisseur, this shop opened in Horsham following the demise of King & Barnes in 2000. Up to seven cask ales are served on gravity to take away in two- and four-pint containers, along with real cider and occasionally perry. The shop also stocks over 150 bottled beers from near and far. A popular beer festival is organised each September in the nearby Drill Hall. Every town should have a shop like this!

Black Jug

31 North Street, RH12 1RJ
11.30-11; 12-10.30 Sun (01403) 253526
Long Man Best Bitter; 6 changing beers (sourced locally; often Brains, Marston's, Robinsons) H
A large bustling town-centre pub, the Jug is something of a Horsham institution. It has a welcoming interior with bookshelves, pictures, a fire and friendly efficient staff. Two regular ales are available with rotating guests and a cider. Excellent food is served all day and the pub is equally popular as a venue to meet and chat with no intrusive music. It is close to the railway station and arts complex. It also has an extensive range of malt whiskies and gins. Q

Malt Shovel

15 Springfield Road, RH12 2PG
11-midnight (11 Mon; 1am Fri & Sat); 12-11 Sun
(01403) 252302
6 changing beers H
Close to the town centre, the pub has six handpumps on year round, plus two ciders and a mix of bottles/canned ales. Though with no regular ales, it has a focus on local beers and usually at least one dark ale. There is live music every Saturday night, as well as frequent open mic and jam events. The landlord takes great pride in his real ale and his friendly staff are equally proud. Good parking for a town-centre pub.
P

Piries Bar

Piries Place, RH12 1NY
11-midnight; 11-1am Fri-Sun (01403) 267846
piriesbar.co.uk

Burning Sky Plateau; 2 changing beers (sourced locally; often Long Man) Ⓗ
In a building dating from the 15th century with exposed original timber beams, the pub is tucked away down a narrow alley adjoining Horsham's Carfax. It comprises a small downstairs room, an upstairs lounge bar and a small modern extension in character with the building. Regular charity events are organised. Evenings here can be lively, with karaoke on Sunday, quiz night on Tuesday and occasional live music. With two cask ales always on, this bar is well worth a visit.

Lambs Green

Lamb Inn

RH12 4RG (2 miles N of A264)
11.30-3, 5.30-11; 11.30-11 Fri & Sat; 12-10.30 Sun
☎ (01293) 871336 thelambinn.org
Dark Star Hophead; Gale's HSB; 3 changing beers Ⓗ
Lovely old pub with a mixture of flagstones and wood floors interspersed with wrought-iron work, low-beamed ceilings and exposed brick walls. Furnishings include high-backed settles and soft sofas, and a real fire adds warmth in winter. This welcoming hostelry's friendly landlord and staff are committed to LocAle – all beers come from within 25 miles, and customers elect the guest beer. Lunchtime and evening food is served daily using quality home-made locally sourced ingredients.
Q P

Lancing

Stanley Ale House

5 Queensway, BN15 9AY (N of Lancing railway station)
12 (2 Mon)-10; 12-8 Sun ☎ (01903) 366820
thestanleyalehouse.com
Langham Arapaho Ⓗ**; 3 changing beers (sourced regionally; often Downlands)** Ⓖ
This former launderette opened as a welcoming, family-oriented ale house in 2014. Just 200 yards north of the railway station, near local shops, it offers up to four changing ales, plus ciders and craft beers. There is ample seating, both inside and out. Bar snacks are served, but you can bring in takeaways to eat. There is a weekly quiz and regular music nights. A variety of board games is available. Q

Littlehampton

New Inn

5 Norfolk Road, BN17 5PL (N from Sea Rd)
12-11 (midnight Fri & Sat); 12-10.30 Sun
☎ (01903) 713112 newinnla.co.uk
3 changing beers (sourced nationally) Ⓗ
Friendly community pub offering three changing ales, just a short walk from the beach. This traditional inn has two bar areas; the front bar has ample seating, a real fire and hosts weekly pub quizzes and regular charity events; the rear bar has a pool table and dartboard, as well as showing live sport. A free jukebox is a feature of Monday nights. There is a heated courtyard at the back.

Steam Packet

54 River Road, BN17 5BZ
closed Mon; 12-11; 12-10 Sun ☎ (01903) 715994
Downlands Best; 6 changing beers (sourced locally; often Bedlam, Fallen Acorn, Franklins) Ⓗ
A one-bar establishment with a pleasing light and airy bar which makes good use of the available floor space. It overlooks the harbour, is near the river footbridge, and is a short distance from where a cross-Channel steam packet ferry service operated from Littlehampton to Honfleur. Several guest ales are sold, and are mainly local, although it now sells some ales in pins, to give a greater variety. Fresh food is prepared on the premises, and vegetarians and vegans are catered for.
(700)

Lodsworth

Hollist Arms

The Street, GU28 9BZ (in village centre, 1 mile N of A272)
11-3.30, 5.30-11; 11-11 Sat ☎ (01798) 861310
thehollistarms.com
Dark Star Hophead; Timothy Taylor Landlord; 3 changing beers (often Langham) Ⓗ
Set in the village centre overlooking the green, complete with a chestnut tree planted in 1897 to mark Queen Victoria's diamond jubilee, the building was formed from two cottages in 1825. A small bar leads to a larger restaurant area serving home-cooked food all week. There is also a small snug with inglenook fireplace. At the rear the raised beer garden has a barbecue area, in the front there are seats on the green. The rear car park houses the village's community shop.
Q P

Maplehurst

White Horse

Park Lane, RH13 6LL
12-2.30 (not Mon), 6-11; 12-2.30, 6-11.30 Fri & Sat; 12-3, 7-11 Sun ☎ (01403) 891208 whitehorsemaplehurst.co.uk
Weltons Pride 'n' Joy; 4 changing beers Ⓗ
Under the same ownership for 35 years, this splendid and welcoming country pub has featured in the Guide 33 times. Popular with locals, cyclists and walkers, the cosy interior, with its unusually large wooden bar, boasts real fires and many interesting artefacts and bric-a-brac. While good honest pub fare is provided, the emphasis is on beer and conversation. Many local beers feature including a good selection of dark ales. Local JB cider is also stocked. Q P

Midhurst

Swan

Red Lion Street, GU29 9PB (opp church in old town)
12-midnight; 12-11.30 Sun ☎ (01730) 812853
theswaninn.pub
Harvey's Sussex Best Bitter; 1 changing beer (sourced locally) Ⓗ
This has now become a single-bar pub as the upstairs area has been given over exclusively to dining. It has a TV and silent quiz machines as well as a dartboard. During the week it may only be the Sussex Best that is stocked, but in spring, summer and at weekends there will additionally be at least one changing beer, all in great condition. Accommodation is in six en-suite rooms. There is limited public parking nearby.
Q (1,60)

Oving

Gribble Inn

Gribble Lane, PO20 2BP (at W end of village)
11-11; 12-11 Sun ☎ (01243) 786893 gribbleinn.co.uk
Gribble Sussex Quadhopper, Ale, Fuzzy Duck, Reg's Tipple, Plucking Pheasant, Pig's Ear H
Once home to a Miss Gribble, this attractive thatched cottage has been a traditional village pub for over 30 years and shares the premises with the Gribble Brewery. The full range of Gribble regular beers complemented by seasonals is always available. Cosy, with log fires in winter, home-made food is served in the bar/restaurant. In summer a large attractive garden offers occasional weekend barbecues, and the skittle alley can be used for functions. Q P (85,85A)

Pagham

Inglenook

255 Pagham Road, PO21 3QB
11-11 (midnight Fri & Sat) ☎ (01243) 262495
the-inglenook.com
Fuller's London Pride; Young's Special; 4 changing beers (sourced nationally; often Brighton Bier, Dark Star, Staggeringly Good) H
A 16th-century Grade II-listed hotel, restaurant and free house, owned and run by the Honour family for over 40 years. There is always a selection of excellent well-hopped real ales available from highly regarded microbreweries alongside local real ciders. The cosy bar areas have real fires and there is a large garden to the rear and a patio area at the front. Local CAMRA Pub of the Year 2015-2017. Q P (600)

Partridge Green

Partridge

Church Road, RH13 8GW (on B2135 at jct of High St and Church Rd)
12-11; 12-10.30 Sun ☎ (01403) 710391
Dark Star Hophead, Partridge Best Bitter; 4 changing beers (sourced nationally; often Dark Star) H
A former railway hotel, this is a spacious village pub and the Dark Star Brewing tap, offering up to six ales. It is near the brewery and adjacent to the popular Downs Link trail that follows the track bed of the disused Shoreham-by-Sea to Guildford railway line. The large, wood-panelled lounge has a huge fireplace. There is a pleasant patio area, garden and play area. The front bar has a display of local photographs, and pool and darts can be played here. Q P (17)

Patching

Fox

Old Arundel Road, BN13 3UU (on old A27, near Patching outside Worthing)
11-3, 6-11; 12-9 Sun ☎ (01903) 871299
thefoxpatching.co.uk
Harvey's Sussex Best Bitter; 4 changing beers (sourced regionally; often Arundel, Castle Rock, Hammerpot) H
A large pub alongside the old A27 where beautiful gardens make the perfect setting for outside dining and lazy lunches in the sun. There are lovely views over the West Sussex countryside. Dogs are warmly welcomed in any of the garden areas and there is a children's play area at the rear. A selection of local and national brews is stocked in the bar, and there is a restaurant area with a menu full of choices. Q P (9)

Rudgwick

King's Head

Church Street, RH12 3EB
11.30-11; 11-11 Sun ☎ (01403) 822200
kingsheadrudgwick.co.uk
Crafty Brewing Crafty One; 2 changing beers (often Harvey's, Morland) H
This 18th-century low-beamed pub can be found at the northern end of the village opposite the Norman church in a conservation area. There is a restaurant at one end of the pub and a bar with a wood-burning stove and leather sofas at the other. Food is freshly prepared and includes Italian dishes. The Downslink footpath passes nearby.
Q P

Selsey

Crab Pot

145 High Street, PO20 0QB (opp Lloyds Bank)
closed Mon; 12 (4 Tue & Wed)-9; 12-5.30 Sun
☎ 07834 226751
3 changing beers (sourced locally; often Broken Bridge, Downlands, Vibrant Forest) G
New micropub opened in 2017. Beers and ciders are served by gravity from a glass-fronted temperature-controlled stillage in the single bar. High wooden tables with steel-framed chairs create a typically convivial micropub atmosphere, and the walls have a selection of pictures featuring Selsey scenes. The pleasant rear garden area is larger than many others. Beers and ciders change regularly and are from within a 45-mile radius, gin and vodka are also locally sourced, and there is a carefully selected wine list. Regular live music features. Q (51)

Seal

6 Hillfield Road, PO20 0JX (on B2145, 600yds from sea)
10.30-midnight; 12-11 Sun ☎ (01243) 602461
the-seal.com
Dark Star Hophead; Young's Bitter; 4 changing beers (sourced nationally; often Hammerpot, Hop Back, Langham) H
A real community hub, family run for 44 years. It has a spacious public bar with a pool table at one end and a comfortable lounge with an extended restaurant featuring quality home-cooked food including locally caught fish (booking advised). It serves a good variety of guest beers, mostly from local micros. Acoustic live music often features on Sunday. The patio has seating and umbrellas to cater for smokers. Camping is available nearby at West Sands caravan park. The 13 en-suite B&B rooms are popular. Q P (51)

Shoreham-by-Sea

Duke of Wellington

368 Brighton Road, BN43 6RE (on A259)
12-11 (12.30am Fri & Sat) ☎ (01273) 441297
dukeofwellingtonbrewhouse.co.uk/home
Dark Star American Pale Ale; 6 changing beers (sourced regionally) H
A pub of contrasts because, on some nights, it is a quiet drinking emporium and, on others, packed to the gills with a ukulele band, the Wellington

Wailers, or a local group. What is consistent is the beer quality and range. Its pedigree is Dark Star and the original brewer has a small shrine of certificates together with copies of all past editions of this Guide in a display case. There are original Kemp Town Brewery windows.
♉❀⇌♣●⊟(2,700)🐾ᯤ

Marlipins ✔

38 High Street, BN43 5DA
⏲ 10-11 (12.30am Fri & Sat); 11-10.30 Sun
☎ (01273) 453772 🌐 themarlipins.co.uk
Fuller's London Pride; Harvey's Sussex Best Bitter; 2 changing beers (often Adnams, Sharp's) Ⓗ
A 17th-century town-centre pub, the name comes from the historic Norman building next door which now houses the town museum. Low background music does not detract from the conversation at the bar. A separate dining area at the rear leads on to a patio garden which is a suntrap in the summer. The pub features two regular beers plus two changing guests, live music every Friday and food deals during the week. It has a small pavement seating area. ♉❀⦅⦆⇌⊟🐾ᯤ

Old Star Ale & Cider House

Church Street, BN43 5DQ
⏲ 12-9 ☎ 07720 892767 🌐 oldstarshoreham.co.uk
4 changing beers (sourced locally; often Brighton Bier, Burning Sky, Gun) Ⓖ
A well-run micropub just off the High Street. At least four beers are dispensed, mainly from Sussex microbreweries, served direct from the casks on stillage behind the bar. Up to 12 bag-in-box ciders may also be available at any time. A cider festival is held over the autumn bank holiday. A complimentary cheeseboard is on offer every Saturday after 6pm. Q⇌♣●⊟(2,700)🐾ᯤ

Staplefield

Jolly Tanners Ⓛ ✔

Handcross Road, RH17 6EF
⏲ 11-3, 5.30-11; 11-11 Fri & Sat; 12-10.30 Sun
☎ (01444) 400335 🌐 jollytanners.com
Fuller's London Pride; Harvey's Sussex Best Bitter; changing beers Ⓗ
Independently run free house on the north corner of the cricket green which prides itself on providing a wide selection of real ales and cider, as well as tasty food made using local ingredients where possible. A range of beer styles, usually including at least two dark brews, is dispensed from the eight handpumps. It is a friendly place and well worth a visit. A roaring fire welcomes you in winter. Open mic night is Tuesday. Beer festivals are held regularly with an excellent range of beer to be enjoyed. Q♉❀⦅⦆♿⛺♣●P⊟(271)🐾ᯤ

Stoughton

Hare & Hounds Ⓛ

PO18 9JQ (off B2146, through Walderton) SU803115
⏲ 11-11; 12-10.30 Sun ☎ (023) 9263 1433
🌐 hareandhoundspub.co.uk
Dark Star Hophead; Long Man Best Bitter; Otter Amber; 1 changing beer (sourced locally) Ⓗ
Traditional country pub in a beautiful setting that makes it an ideal base for walking. The large dining room serves fresh local produce in comfortable surroundings with an open fire in winter. A separate public bar has pictures of vintage racing cars and its own open fire, popular with locals. The fires, stone-flagged floors and simple furniture create a wonderful atmosphere. Outside, the paved patio area complements a rear garden for dining and drinking. Two ciders are stocked.
Q❀⦅⦆♣●P🐾ᯤ

Turners Hill

Red Lion Ⓛ ✔

Lion Lane, RH10 4NU
⏲ 11-3, 5-11; 11.30-11 Sat; 12-10.30 Sun ☎ (01342) 715416
🌐 redlionturnershill.com
Harvey's Sussex XX Mild Ale, IPA, Sussex Best Bitter, Armada Ale; 2 changing beers (often Harvey's) Ⓗ
Still very much a village local, offering a warm welcome to all who enter, this is a split-level pub with a large inglenook fireplace. Good-value and high-quality lunchtime food is served. The pub has recently had a tasteful extension to the dining area. Children and dogs are welcome and there is a fortnightly quiz. The local CAMRA branch held its first meeting here in 1974.
Q♉❀⦅♿♣P⊟(84,272)🐾ᯤ

Warnham

Sussex Oak Ⓛ ✔

2 Church Street, RH12 3QW
⏲ 11-11; 11-10.30 Sun ☎ (01403) 265028
🌐 thesussexoak.co.uk
Dark Star Hophead; Timothy Taylor Landlord; 2 changing beers (sourced locally; often Hogs Back, Long Man) Ⓗ
Popular village pub with a separate dining area. Six handpumps dispense three regular beers and up to three guests; LocAle is actively supported. Two handpumps serve real cider and perry in the summer months. An extensive menu of high-quality, reasonably priced food is available. There is a large garden and dogs are welcome. Quiz nights are held fortnightly and jazz nights on the last Thursday of the month, with beer festivals on bank holidays. Q♉❀⦅⦆♿♣●P⊟(93)🐾ᯤ

West Chiltington

Five Bells Ⓛ

Smock Alley, RH20 2QX (approx 1 mile S of West Chiltington old village centre) TQ092171
⏲ 12-3, 6-11; 12-3, 7-10.30 Sun ☎ (01798) 812143
🌐 thefivebellsinn.com
5 changing beers (sourced nationally; often Harvey's, Jennings, Palmers) Ⓗ
A friendly village free house and a regular in the Guide. Dating from 1935, this former King & Barnes pub has been run by the same couple since 1983. Five handpumps are on what is probably Sussex's longest copper-top counter, serving local and regional ales, one usually a dark ale. There is also a large copper-hooded open fire. Locally sourced home-cooked food is served in the bar and large conservatory (no food Sun eve). CAMRA branch Country Pub of the Year 2016-2018.
Q❀🛏⦅⦆●P⊟(1,74)🐾ᯤ

West Marden

Victoria Ⓛ

PO18 9EN (just W of B2146 in village centre)
⏲ closed Mon; 12-2.30, 6 (5 Fri)-11; 12-11 Sat; 12-10 Sun
☎ (023) 9263 1330 🌐 victoriainnwestmarden.co.uk

Langham Hip Hop; 2 changing beers (sourced locally; often Bowman, Flowerpots, Langham) Ⓗ
Comfortable old rural inn at the heart of its tiny downland community. Cricket and bar billiards teams plus a golf society help maintain its local involvement, and many country pursuits including walking, riding and shooting are supported. Inside there are several intimate spaces in which to drink and dine, with a log-burning stove for cold evenings. The front garden has splendid views of surrounding hills. Changing beers come from mainly local breweries while beers at occasional festivals are from further afield.
Q❀◑♣P(54)

Worthing

Anchored in Worthing Ⓛ
27 West Buildings, BN11 3BS (close to seafront)
closed Mon; 12-9.30; 12-5.30 Sun ☎ (01903) 529100
anchoredinworthing.co.uk
3 changing beers (sourced locally; often Goldmark, Gun, Long Man) Ⓖ
Look for the Tardis-style entrance to Sussex's first micropub, where you can be assured of a warm welcome. High wooden tables are arranged so customers face each other and conversation quickly flows. On offer are three ales, ciders, perry and wine, all from local producers. The ceiling is adorned with pumpclips of the many ales sold since opening, while the walls have maps showing breweries and micropubs, plus CAMRA and local event information. CAMRA branch, county and area Pub of the Year 2017. Q♣

Brooksteed Alehouse Ⓛ
38 South Farm Road, BN14 7AE (100yds N of South Farm Road level crossing, 5 mins walk from Central station)
12-9.30 (8 Mon); 12-5 Sun ☎ 07484 840103
brooksteedalehouse.co.uk
House beer (by Arundel); 5 changing beers (sourced nationally; often Goldmark, Gun, North Riding) Ⓖ
Worthing's second micropub opened in 2014, with a change of ownership in 2017. There are usually five varying cask ales, four KeyKeg and up to five ciders/perry from local and national brewers, plus a range of bottled beers, wines and gin. Locally sourced pub snacks are available, and a cheeseboard on Sundays. It boasts stylish and quirky décor with comfortable areas and outdoor seating in the forecourt. Local CAMRA, Sussex and Regional Pub of the Year 2016. Regular events include other local businesses and the community.
Q≠♣(16)

Corner House Ⓛ ✔
80 High Street, BN11 1DJ (opp Waitrose)
12-11 (midnight Sat); 12-10.30 Sun ☎ (01903) 216463
cornerhouseworthing.co.uk
4 changing beers (sourced regionally; often Harvey's, Long Man, Shepherd Neame) Ⓗ
The Corner House occupies a prominent position at the town centre's eastern edge. The original pub, The Anchor, dates back to 1805 and was one of Worthing's oldest. It had an interesting history, but was rebuilt in 1895. The pub reopened in late 2015 under new ownership, with a new name, and quickly became popular. There is an emphasis on local suppliers for both food and drink. The large beer garden is popular all year round. Quiz night is Monday. ❀◑♿≠

Egremont Ⓛ
32 Brighton Road, BN11 3ED (short walk from seafront and town centre)
12-11 ☎ (01903) 600064 theegremont.co.uk
Harvey's Sussex Best Bitter; house beer (by Goldmark); 3 changing beers (sourced regionally; often Burning Sky) Ⓗ
Previously, when Worthing was its HQ, the English Bowls Association nicknamed this pub The Bowlers' Arms. Refurbished and reopened in 2015, it feels much lighter, brighter and more spacious, while retaining the lovely old doors and stained glass Kemp Town Brewery windows. Several different seating areas allow space for regular mini beer festivals, quizzes and weekend live music. A house beer is on tap, plus up to four other ales, and it has an extensive range of over 50 gins. ◑♣

Georgi Fin
54 Goring Road, BN12 4AD (on A259, N side, in Goring Road shops)
closed Mon; 12-2, 5-10; 12-10 Fri & Sat; 12-5 Sun
thegeorgifin.co.uk
4 changing beers (sourced regionally; often Franklins, Thornbridge) Ⓖ
This popular micropub opened in 2017. Named after the owner's children, it is located in a busy shopping parade. The interior has been redecorated and it has wooden tables and seats with scaffolding poles for legs. Unusually for a micropub, it has both ladies' and gents' toilets. The drinks are served from a purpose-built cold room and include four ales from local and national brewers, three traditional ciders, wines, plus a selection of English, Belgian and German bottled beers. Q≠

Green Man Ale & Cider House 🏆 Ⓛ
17 South Street, BN14 7LG (40yds N of West Worthing railway crossing)
12-9; 12-4 Sun ☎ 07984 793877
green-man-ale-and-cider-house.co.uk
6 changing beers (sourced regionally; often Goldmark, Gun, Wantsum) Ⓖ
This micropub opened in 2016 and quickly became popular. It serves up to six ales on gravity, seven ciders and a perry from Sussex and surrounding counties, as well as a selection of gins and tonics. There is always a friendly welcome from the owner, who will offer you a drink to suit your taste. The cool room is visible from the main drinking area, which has back-to-back high tables and chairs of a unique design, plus two armchairs. Local CAMRA Pub of the Year and Cider Pub of the Year 2018. Q≠♣

Hare & Hounds Ⓛ ✔
79-81 Portland Road, BN11 1QG
11-11 (11.30 Tue & Thu; midnight Fri & Sat); 12-11 Sun
☎ (01903) 230085 hareandhoundsworthing.co.uk
Exmoor Ale; Fuller's London Pride; Harvey's Sussex Best Bitter; St Austell Proper Job; 1 changing beer (sourced regionally; often Harvey's) Ⓗ
In the heart of Worthing, this 18th-century flint building became a pub in 1814, extending into the adjoining property in the 1990s. The large, wood-panelled U-shaped bar leads to the rear conservatory and heated and covered patio. Old prints focusing on hunting hang from the walls. There are five handpumps, serving local and national ales. Tuesday evenings feature live jazz and Saturday evenings live bands, while Sunday night has a music quiz. Q❀◑≠

Parsonage Bar & Restaurant 🄻 ✔

6-10 High Street, BN14 7NN (at S end of Tarring High St – not to be confused with High St Worthing)
✪ 12-10.30 (10 Mon; 11 Fri & Sat); 12-9 Sun
☎ (01903) 820140 🌐 theparsonage.co.uk
Burning Sky Plateau; Harvey's Sussex Best Bitter Ⓗ**; 2 changing beers (sourced nationally; often Downlands, Hammerpot, Harvey's)** Ⓗ/Ⓖ
This interesting Grade II-listed 15th-century building was originally three cottages. A quality restaurant since 1987, several years ago it added a handpump in the bar area serving a popular local bitter. There are now four pumps offering a selection of beer styles. Guest ales usually include a dark one, typically an old ale during winter. The secluded courtyard garden is great for the warmer weather. Q❀◐◑⇌●▯🚌(6,16)🐾📶

Selden Arms

41 Lyndhurst Road, BN11 2DB (about 5 mins from centre of town and 2 mins from Worthing Hospital on Lyndhurst Rd, opp gasometer)
✪ 11-11; 12-11 Sat & Sun ☎ (01903) 523361
🌐 seldenarms.co.uk
6 changing beers (sourced nationally; often Brighton Bier, Burning Sky, Gun) Ⓗ
This welcoming 19th-century free house is a Guide regular. Six handpumps serve a changing selection of local and national ales, one of which is always dark. There are also five craft beers, in keg, cans and bottles, plus an extensive range of around 80 bottled Belgian beers. A blackboard displays upcoming ales. Lunchtime food is served from Monday to Saturday, with curry Friday and Saturday evenings. The annual winter beer festival is in January. ◐◑⇌♣●🚌🐾📶

Yapton

Maypole 🄻

Maypole Lane, BN18 0DP (off B2132 ½ mile N of village, with pedestrian access across railway from Lake Lane, just over 1 mile E of Barnham station) SU978042
✪ 12-11 (midnight Fri & Sat) ☎ (01243) 551417
Dark Star Hophead; Lister's Best Bitter; 3 changing beers (sourced nationally; often Dark Star) Ⓗ
Small 18th-century flint-built free house of character hidden away from the village centre, down a narrow lane ending in a pedestrian crossing over the railway. The cosy, often lively lounge boasts two open fires and a row of six handpumps dispensing beers from independent brewers, while real cider is served from the cellar. There is also a traditional public bar with pool and darts, plus a skittle alley/function room with bar billiards. Lunchtime food is served Monday-Friday 12-4pm. Dogs are welcome.
Q🐴❀◐♿⛺♣●P🚌🐾📶

Coach & Horses, Compton (Photo: Bob Steel)

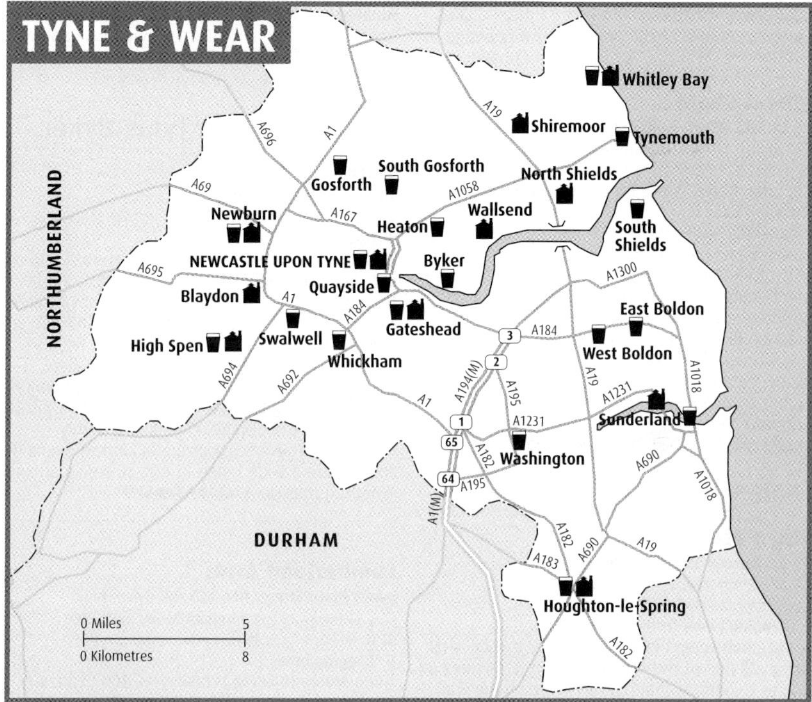

East Boldon

Grey Horse ✓

Front Street, NE36 0SJ

⏲ 11-midnight; 9am-midnight Sun ☎ (0191) 519 1796

🌐 greyhorseeastboldon.co.uk

6 changing beers Ⓗ

Distinctive mock-Tudor building with separate pleasant and comfortable lounge and bar areas and an upstairs function room. Up to six changing ales are available, from local and national breweries. Meals are served daily with themed nights during the week. There are large-screen TVs in the bar for football and other sports. A folk club meets on the first Thursday of every month and the Boldon History Society on the last Tuesday of the month. Q🛋❀◐◑♿⚐P🚌🐾📶

Gateshead

Central ★ Ⓛ

Half Moon Lane, NE8 2AN

⏲ 10-11 (10.30 Sun) ☎ (0191) 478 2543

8 changing beers Ⓗ

Marvellous mid 19th-century, Grade II listed, four-storey wedge-shaped building. It now comprises a revamped public bar, two function rooms and a rooftop terrace, and hosts regular live music. However, the main attraction is the magnificently restored Buffet (closed when quiet – ask to view), identified by CAMRA as having a nationally important historic pub interior. The style is circa 1900 with a great U-shaped carved counter and bar back, plasterwork frieze and panelling. 🛋◐◑♿⚐♣🍎🚌🐾📶

Old Fox Ⓛ

10-14 Carlisle Street, Felling, NE10 0HQ

⏲ 4-11; 12-11 Fri-Sun ☎ (0191) 442 9423

5 changing beers Ⓗ

Superb traditional community pub restored to its former glory by a previous landlord, now back in situ, and with a friendly welcome for all. The open fire gives the bar a homely feel. There is also a lounge and pool area; the pub has two teams, plus a patio area at the back. Monday is local buskers' night, Tuesday ladies' darts, Wednesday poker 'n' pool, Thursday quiz, Friday men's darts, Saturday live bands or disco/karaoke. A short walk from Felling Metro. 🛋❀⚐♣🚌🐾📶

Schooner Ⓛ

South Shore Road, NE8 3AF (just down from jct between Saltmeadows Rd and Neilson Rd, vehicular access only from E end of South Shore Rd)

⏲ 12-11 (10.30 Sun) ☎ (0191) 477 7404

🌐 theschooner.co.uk

6 changing beers Ⓗ

On the banks of The Tyne, the Schooner currently has six handpumps for cask ales and one for cider. The range changes regularly to showcase the best local and national ales and ciders. Home-cooked food is served through the week, with a traditional roast on Sunday. Live music plays every Sunday afternoon, some Saturday nights, and on many other occasions. 🛋❀◐♿⚐♣🍎P🚌(93,94)🐾📶

Station East Ⓛ

Hills Street, NE8 2AS

⏲ 12-11 ☎ (0191) 435 3389

Hadrian Border Farne Island Pale Ale, Grainger Ale, Secret Kingdom; 3 changing beers (often Hadrian Border) Ⓗ

Occupying the site of the former Gateshead East Station and Railway Hotel, the building is now stripped back and enlarged with much new structural work. Formerly a small pub, it is now open and spacious. There is a pleasant mezzanine floor above the main room and a further arched room to the rear below another railway bridge. A rear room is available for functions. Q♿🚉🚌

Wheat Sheaf 🄻

26 Carlisle Street, Felling, NE10 0HQ
5 (3 Thu; 12 Fri & Sat)-11; 12-10.30 Sun
☎ (0191) 597 2981
Big Lamp Bitter, Prince Bishop Ale, Sunny Daze; 1 changing beer Ⓗ
Welcoming street-corner pub owned by Big Lamp Brewery and patronised by a loyal band of regulars who often travel quite a distance to drink here. The pub features some original details, mismatched furniture and, when needed, real coal fires. The outdoor toilets have original Victorian urinals. There is a fortnightly Monday night quiz, traditional folk music featuring keen local musicians on Tuesday night and dominoes on Wednesday night. An original CAMRA clock keeps time behind the bar. Snacks are available. 🚉♣🚌🐾📶

High Spen

Wig's Place 🄻

49-51 Ramsay Street, NE39 2EJ
closed Mon-Wed; 3-9 ☎ (01207) 549333
wigsplace.co.uk
6 changing beers (often Wylam, TOPS) Ⓗ
A micropub spread over two rooms, named after the male half of the couple running it. Pictures of Wig as a young aspiring musician are on the wall. A true community pub, families are welcome and local groups use the comfy lounge bar for meetings. Ales are from the North-East and North Yorkshire. A very local ale from the neighbouring TOPS nanobrewery is usually on offer. Around five real ciders in boxes are also available. Bus links can be sparse, especially on Sunday. 🚌 (10A)

Houghton-le-Spring

Wild Boar ✔

Frederick Place, DH4 4BN
8am-midnight ☎ (0191) 512 8050
Greene King Abbot; Ruddles Best Bitter; 6 changing beers Ⓗ
Formerly a club, the Wild Boar was opened by Wetherspoon in 2011. Named after the Black Sabre boar on the crest of the former rector of Houghton, this open-plan pub offers well-priced ales and a good-value food menu. Its 10 handpulls serve a selection of national and local beers, as well as real cider. There is a quiz every Monday night and popular day trips are organised throughout the year (often during the spring and summer months). QP🚌📶

Newburn

Keelman 🄻

Grange Road, NE15 8NL
11-11; 12-10.30 Sun ☎ (0191) 267 1689
keelmanslodge.co.uk
Big Lamp Bitter, Keelman Brown, Prince Bishop Ale, Summerhill Stout, Sunny Daze; 1 changing beer Ⓗ
This tastefully converted, Grade II listed former pumping station is now home to the Big Lamp Brewery and the Keelman is the brewery tap. A conservatory restaurant serves excellent food and quality accommodation is provided in the adjacent Keelman's Lodge and Salmon Cottage. Attractively situated by Tyne Riverside Country Park, the Coast-to-Coast cycleway and Hadrian's Wall National Trail. ♿P🚌 (22,71) 📶

Newcastle upon Tyne: Byker

Cluny 🄻

36 Lime Street, NE1 2PQ
12-11 (10.30 Sun) ☎ (0191) 230 4474 thecluny.com
7 changing beers Ⓗ
Large, former industrial building converted into a pub, art gallery and two stage live music venue. The pub runs frequent themed beer festivals and always has a good selection of British and foreign draught and bottled products available. Freshly-cooked food is available daily. The art gallery shows work of all kinds, ranging from final degree shows to local independent established artists in all media, with the displays changing monthly. Popular live music sessions are held most evenings and include a wide range of British, European and American musicians. Q♿🚉🚌📶

Cumberland Arms 🄻

James Place Street, NE6 1LD (off Byker Bank)
3-11 (midnight Fri); 12-midnight Sat; 12-11 Sun
☎ (0191) 265 1725 thecumberlandarms.co.uk
6 changing beers Ⓗ
Three-storey building rebuilt over 100 years ago and relatively little changed since. It stands in a prominent position overlooking the lower Ouseburn Valley. The pub is home to traditional rapper sword dancers and folk musicians, the upstairs room is a music and comedy venue. A multiple winner of CAMRA regional Cider Pub of the Year awards, it generally offers up to 12 ciders and perries. Winter and summer beer festivals are held each year. Closing time may vary.
Q🚉♣P🐾📶

REAL ALE BREWERIES

Almasty Shiremoor
Anarchy Newcastle upon Tyne
Arcane Bridge Newcastle upon Tyne (suspended)
Big Lamp Newburn
Box Social Newburn
Brinkburn Street Newcastle upon Tyne
Cullercoats Wallsend
Darwin Sunderland
Dog & Rabbit Whitley Bay
Errant Newcastle upon Tyne
Firebrick Blaydon
Flash House North Shields
Great North Eastern Gateshead
Hadrian Border Newburn
Hop & Cleaver Newcastle upon Tyne
Maxim Houghton-le-Spring
Mordue North Shields
Newcastle Newcastle upon Tyne
Northern Alchemy Newcastle upon Tyne
Out There Newcastle upon Tyne
Stu Brew Newcastle upon Tyne
Tavernale Newcastle upon Tyne
Three Kings North Shields
TOPS (The Olde Potting Shed) High Spen
Two by Two Wallsend
Tyne Bank Newcastle upon Tyne
Whitley Bay Whitley Bay
Wylam Newcastle upon Tyne

Free Trade Inn

St Lawrence Road, NE6 1AP

11-11 (midnight Fri & Sat); 12-10.30 Sun
(0191) 265 5764

7 changing beers

Unique former S&N pub with wonderful views of the Tyne bridges and Newcastle and Gateshead quaysides. Up to nine beers and two ciders are available on the bar, with cellar runs willingly offered. Interesting ales come from far and wide including an extensive range of foreign bottled beers. Service is with a smile, friendly and knowledgable. The jukebox is classic and free. The beer garden is excellent. Local CAMRA Cider Pub of the Year 2017 and 2018. Q (Q3)

Tyne Bank Tap Room

375 Walker Road, NE6 2BS

closed Mon-Wed; 4-11 Thu; 12-midnight Fri & Sat; 12-8 Sun
(0191) 265 2828

14 changing beers (often Tyne Bank)

Tyne Bank's new brewery and taphouse has an industrial feel with open steel roof trusses on display. The bar is constructed from scaffolding planks and corrugated iron, continuing the theme. Downward-facing gas heaters provide interesting feature heating. The corner stage is used for live music and events. Up to eight real ales are served. The huge steel pipe keg fonts are unusual.
(Q3)

Newcastle upon Tyne: City Centre

Bacchus

42-48 High Bridge, NE1 6BX

11.30-midnight; 12-11 Sun (0191) 261 1008

6 changing beers

Formerly CAMRA Tyneside Pub of the Year for four years running, this smart city-centre pub boasts nine handpumps offering a range of changing guest beers, with one pump dedicated to cider. A seasonal house beer is brewed by Yorkshire Dales, and a large range of draught and bottled foreign beers is available. Photographs and posters showing the industries in which this region used to lead the world cover the walls.
(Monument)

Bodega

125 Westgate Road, NE1 4AG

12-11 (midnight Fri); 11-midnight Sat; 12-10.30 Sun
(0191) 221 1552

Big Lamp Prince Bishop Ale; Fyne Ales Jarl; Oakham Citra; house beer (by Almasty); 4 changing beers

Two fine stained-glass domes are the architectural highlights of the pub, which is popular with football and music fans. TVs show sporting events and the pub can be busy on match days. The interior offers a number of standing and seating areas with separate booths for more intimate drinking. A number of old brewery mirrors adorn the walls. Eight handpumps include beers from Oakham and Fyne Ales, alongside a good selection of foreign bottled beers. (Central)

Box Social

Arch 11, Forth Street, NE1 3NZ

12-midnight boxsocial.pub

Box Social Gentlemans Nectar Pale Ale; 3 changing beers (often Box Social)

Pleasant recently opened micropub, owned by Box Social Brewery, occupying the former site of the Split Chimp. The bar is constructed from scaffolding planks with a wooden bar back. There are 10 craft keg beer taps on the wall behind the bar and a colourful tap board provides details of what is on the handpumps and wall taps. A mezzanine floor gives extra seating to the rear. Q (Central)

Bridge Hotel

Castle Square, NE1 1RQ

11.30-11 (midnight Fri & Sat); 12-10.30 Sun
(0191) 232 6400

Anarchy Blonde Star; Sharp's Doom Bar; 7 changing beers

Large Fitzgerald pub situated next to Stephenson's spectacular High Level Bridge – the rear windows and patio have views of the city walls, River Tyne and Gateshead Quays. The main bar area, with many stained-glass windows, is divided into a number of seating areas with a raised section at the rear. Guest beers come from far and wide. What claims to be the oldest folk club in the country is among live music events hosted in the upstairs function room. (Central)

Fitzgeralds

60 Grey Street, NE1 6AF

11-midnight; 12-11 Sun (0191) 230 1350

Anarchy Blonde Star; 5 changing beers (sourced nationally)

Large, open-plan, friendly Sir John Fitzgerald pub in the city centre, now refurbished with six handpulls serving local and national beers. The pub is much bigger inside than it appears from the outside owing to its depth, with the bar situated towards the back. There is plenty of seating in various areas as well as a large standing area in front of the bar. The manager likes to offer an ale selection not found elsewhere locally, including an extensive range of bottled beers. Local CAMRA Pub of the Year 2017. (Monument)

Head of Steam

1 Neville Street, NE1 5EN

12-2am (3am Fri & Sat) (0191) 230 4236

6 changing beers (often Camerons)

Facing the central railway station, this is an unusual pub in that there is nothing on the ground floor. Upstairs is the main bar with six cask beers, three real ciders and a good selection of continental draught beers. Downstairs is one of the most popular music venues in the city centre, which has hosted early appearances from bands such as the Arctic Monkeys and Maximo Park (no draught beers here although there is an extensive range of cans and bottles). (Central)

Lady Greys

20 Shakespeare Street, NE1 6AQ

11-2am (0191) 232 3606 ladygreys.co.uk

Mordue Northumbrian Blonde; 7 changing beers

Close to the historic Theatre Royal and busy shopping areas, this pub, formerly The Adelphi, is a welcome addition to the city-centre real ale scene. Beers are mainly from local brewers Mordue, Hadrian Border, Allendale and Wylam, with guests from all over the country. Food is served all day. Recent refurbishment added two more handpumps for beer and two for real cider.
(Monument)

Newcastle Tap

Ground Floor, Baron House, 4 Neville Street, NE1 5EN
11-11 (midnight Thu & Fri; 1am Sat) (0191) 261 6636
tapnewcastle.com
8 changing beers G
Opened in 2017 on the ground floor of a former office block opposite Royal Station Hotel and Newcastle Central station. The single-room open-plan interior has beer casks and kegs displayed behind glass on a mezzanine above the bar. Cask beers are dispensed through handles in the bar-back rather than handpumps, there being no dispensers on the bar counter itself. A pizza menu is available all day. (Central)

Old George

Old George Yard, NE1 1EZ
11-11 (1am Thu; 2am Fri & Sat); 12-midnight Sun
(0191) 260 3035 oldgeorgeinnnewcastle.co.uk
Draught Bass; 6 changing beers H
Built in 1582, this historic pub is alleged to have been frequented by King Charles I and is a welcoming watering hole for customers who like a piece of old England. The corridors and stairs creak and the ambience is mostly original. A cabinet of five handpulls complements the traditional bar area, and a smaller bar has an additional three handpulls. Buskers' nights are Thursday and Sunday. In summer bands play regularly in the yard. (Monument)

Split Chimp

Arch 7, Westgate Road, NE1 1SA
3-10; 12-11 Fri & Sat; closed Sun splitchimp.pub
House beer (by Errant); 4 changing beers (sourced nationally) H
Newcastle's first micropub opened in 2015 in a recently refurbished railway arch behind Central station opposite the site of the former Federation Brewery. It relocated to a larger arch on Westgate Road in 2016. More spacious than some micropubs and split over two levels, six handpumps serve an ever-changing selection of real ales, with one dedicated to the house beer, Clever Chimp, from nearby Errant Brewery. Foreign bottled beers are also available. (Central)

Town Mouse Ale House

Basement, 11 St Mary's Place, NE1 7PG
2-10; 12-11 Fri & Sat; 12-8 Sun
townmousealehouse.co.uk
4 changing beers H
This micropub opened in 2017. The basement bar is located in a former coffee shop and has space for around 50 people. The bar area is to the front with another seating area to the rear. A large blackboard gives details of the four cask beers and larger range of keg and bottled beers. Local CAMRA Pub of the Year 2018. (Haymarket)

Trent House

1-2 Leazes Lane, NE1 4QT
12-11 (0191) 261 2154
9 changing beers H
Friendly and laid back, the Trent is popular with students. It is home to the best jukebox in town, featuring an eclectic mix of classic rock, jazz and electronica. There is an upstairs room with a pool table, and board games are available at the bar. The pub has a nightly happy hour 8-9pm, with cask ales priced at £2 per pint, and on the first Sunday of the month ales are just £1 between 5-10pm.
(Haymarket) (32,32A)

Tyneside Cinema Bar Café

Pilgrim Street, NE1 6QG
8-11 (midnight Fri & Sat); 10-11 Sun 0845 217 9909
House beer (by Wylam); 3 changing beers H
Part of Tyneside Cinema, the Bar Café is a large open-plan bar with its own curtained-off cinema screen. The bar has three handpumps serving a range of locally brewed cask ales including the house beer, 35mm from Wylam Brewery. Beers can be taken into cinema screenings. A tasty selection of cakes and pastries is also available. The cellar is in the vault of a former bank.
(Monument)

Wylam Brewery

Palace of Arts, Exhibition Park, NE2 4PZ
closed Mon-Wed; 5-11 Thu & Fri; 12-11 Sat & Sun
(01661) 853377 wylambrewery.co.uk
8 changing beers (often Wylam) H
Wylam's shiny new brewery and bar is situated in the Palace of Arts built for the 1929 North East Exhibition. Art Deco features are plentiful and massive internal doors have been retained. Industrial-style lights adorn the bar area and steel bookcases are filled with a selection of interesting old books. There is a pleasant outdoor drinking area. The bar has limited hours and there may be an admission charge during live events.

Newcastle upon Tyne: Gosforth

County

High Street, NE3 1HB
11-11; 12-10.30 Sun (0191) 285 6919
14 changing beers H
The large L-shaped bar with pleasant stained-glass windows on the main road frontage attracts a variety of visitors, from office workers to students, and can get very busy, especially at weekends. A separate quiet room at the back offers respite from the hustle and bustle of the main bar, and also doubles as a small meeting or function room. Several guest beers are available. P

Gosforth Hotel

High Street, NE3 1HQ
10-11 (midnight Fri & Sat) (0191) 285 6617
gosforthhotelnewcastle.co.uk
Anarchy Blonde Star; Mordue Workie Ticket; 6 changing beers H
Located on the corner of a busy junction at the top of the High Street, this is a stalwart of the lively Gosforth pub scene. Popular with a wide clientele, from nearby office workers to locals and students, the pub often gets very busy. The rear bar opens at 5pm Monday to Thursday and midday Friday to Sunday. A good range of local ales is always available.

Newcastle upon Tyne: Heaton

Chillingham

Chillingham Road, NE6 5XN
11-11 (midnight Fri & Sat); 12-11 Sun (0191) 265 3992
Anarchy Blonde Star; Sharp's Atlantic; 8 changing beers H
Close to Chillingham Road Metro station, this large two-roomed pub was extensively renovated, refurbished and reopened in 2016. It has a comfortable bar and lounge, with sport shown on TVs, appealing to the widest-possible clientele. The

food menu is popular with locals and visitors alike. An excellent choice of local microbrewery beers is offered – and look out for the bottled beer, whisky and wine of the month. A function room upstairs hosts regular quiz nights. ◐🚉♣🍎P🚌(62,63)📶

Newcastle upon Tyne: Quayside

Bridge Tavern 🄻

7 Akenside Hill, NE1 3UF
⏲ 12-midnight (1am Fri & Sat); 12-11 Sun
☎ (0191) 261 9966 🌐 thebridgetavern.com
7 changing beers 🄷
A popular pub with its own microbrewery – the Bridge Tavern's one-barrel plant brews a range of beers under the Tavernale name. Food ranging from bar snacks to buffets and full meals is prepared and cooked by a professional chef. There has been an alehouse on this site for over 200 years – the original building was demolished in 1925 and a new premises built following the construction of the town's most famous landmark, the Tyne Bridge. Children welcome until 7pm.
🐴❀◐◑♿⇌🚉(Central)🍎🚌🐾📶

Broad Chare 🄻

25 Broad Chare, NE1 3DQ
⏲ 11-11 (10 Mon) ☎ (0191) 211 2144
🌐 thebroadchare.co.uk
4 changing beers (often Wylam) 🄷
A warm welcome awaits in this cosy bar just off Newcastle's historic, bustling Quayside. Stripped floors and exposed brickwork help make this a comfortable, quiet place to relax in and enjoy a pint. Bar food is served all day and there is a restaurant upstairs if you wish to dine in style. The house beer is The Writer's Block from Wylam.
◐◑⇌🚉(Manors)🍎🚌(Q3)📶

Crown Posada 🄻

31 Side, NE1 3JE
⏲ 12 (11 Thu)-11; 11-midnight Fri; 12-midnight Sat; 12-10.30 Sun ☎ (0191) 232 1269
Allendale Pennine Pale; Hadrian Border Tyneside Blonde; 4 changing beers (often Hadrian Border) 🄷
An architecturally fine pub, on CAMRA's Regional Inventory of Historic Pub Interiors. Behind the narrow street frontage with its two impressive stained-glass windows lie a small snug, bar counter and a longer seating area. There is an interesting coffered ceiling, as well as local photographs and cartoons of long-gone customers and staff on the walls. Local small brewers are enthusiastically supported, with three regular local ales.
Q⇌🚉(Central)🚌📶

Hop & Cleaver 🄻

40 Sandhill, NE1 3JF
⏲ 5-1am; 12-1am Fri-Sun ☎ (0191) 261 1037
🌐 hopandcleaver.com
6 changing beers 🄷
Interestingly renovated pub now stripped back to the brickwork throughout, with a microbrewery in one room, leading through to the Red House next door. The food majors on smoked American-style meats and burgers, while the Red House features specialist pies, peas and mash. A good range of real ales is served from a bar with an open front. A courtyard offers covered seating and a smoking area. ◐◑♿⇌🚉(Central)🚌

Newcastle upon Tyne: South Gosforth

Brandling Villa 🄻 ✔

Haddricks Mill Road, NE3 1QL
⏲ 12-11 (midnight Fri & Sat) ☎ (0191) 284 0490
🌐 brandlingvilla.co.uk
10 changing beers 🄷
Large double-fronted establishment, keen to promote real ale, offering a constantly changing selection of 10 beers – also available in third-pint tasting glasses – plus two ciders on handpump. The manager organises various well-attended beer-related events, including brewery takeovers, local sausage and pie festivals, music, cinema and beer festivals. The house beer, Frank & Bird, is from Hadrian Border and is a special brew, not a rebadge. 🐴❀◐◑♿🚉♣🍎P🚌🐾📶

South Shields

Dolly Peel

137 Commercial Road, NE33 1SQ
⏲ 11-11 (midnight Thu-Sat); 11-10.30 Sun
☎ (0191) 427 1441
Timothy Taylor Landlord; 2 changing beers 🄷
Named after a local fishwife and smuggler whose husband and sons were press-ganged into the navy, this is a cosy, welcoming, street-corner local popular with a more mature clientele. The interior is divided into two areas – the bar and a quieter comfortable room to the rear. There are large-screen TVs for sporting events. Note the large picture depicting the history of Dolly Peel. Real ales are from national and local breweries.
Q🚉(Chichester)P🚌🐾

Marine 🄻

230 Ocean Road, NE33 2JQ
⏲ 11-11 (midnight Fri & Sat); 12-10.30 Sun
☎ (0191) 455 0280
4 changing beers 🄷
Large 1840s pub opposite Marine Park, close to the seafront. This free house offers four changing real ales and two real ciders. To the left of the bar are two raised areas with plenty of seating, and to the right is a games area. There is a function room upstairs. Unobtrusive background music plays. Pub food is served daily, including a traditional Sunday lunch. ◐◑🚉♣🍎P🚌(E1,516)🐾

Steamboat 🏆 🄻 ✔

Mill Dam, NE33 1EQ (follow signs for Customs House)
⏲ 12-11 (midnight Thu-Sat); 12-11.30 Sun
☎ (0191) 454 0134
9 changing beers 🄷
Under the same management for nearly 30 years, this multi award-winning pub has one of the largest selections of cask ales in South Shields. Nine handpumps dispense a range of beers from local and national breweries, and Meet the Brewer events and beer festivals take place throughout the year. The split-level bar and small lounge have a nautical decor. The pub is a short walk from bus stops, the Shields Ferry and Customs House Theatre. Q🚉🐾📶

Sunderland

Avenue

Zetland Street, Roker, SR6 0EQ (just off Roker Avenue)

12-11 (midnight Fri); 11-midnight Sat; 11-11 Sun
(0191) 567 7412 theavenue.pub
8 changing beers H
Fifteen minutes' walk from the Stadium of Light, this local pub hosts various themed nights throughout the week including music, bingo, football and a popular Thursday night quiz, often followed by a live band. The bar has six handpulls for ale and cider. There is a pool table and an upstairs games room with a snooker table and two dartboards. A function room with two handpulls provides extra space during busier periods and is available to hire. P (E1)

Chaplins
Stockton Road, SR1 3NR
10-11; 12-10.30 Sun (0191) 567 3562
Thwaites Original; 5 changing beers H
A city-centre pub with seven handpulls including a house ale brewed by Thwaites and a real cider. Good-value food is served daily. A quiz is held on Thursday evening and live music on Saturday. There is plenty of seating either side of the main entrance, as well as outside. Some tabletops depict scenes of Sunderland's heritage. Handy for public transport with Park Lane Interchange two minutes away.

Chesters L
Chester Road, SR4 7DR
10-11 (midnight Fri & Sat); 12-10.30 Sun
(0191) 565 9952
6 changing beers H
This popular pub just outside the city centre has a smart interior, with a large main bar and a more intimate area at the back. With six handpulls, there is always one beer from a local brewery as well as guest ales from other brewers, alongside a real cider. Meals are served all day. Outside is a pay car park (you can claim the charge back at the bar) and a large beer garden. A function room with private bar is also available. P

Cooper Rose
2-4 Albion Place, SR1 3NG
8am-midnight (12.30am Thu; 3.30am Fri & Sat)
(0191) 514 8530
Greene King Abbot; Ruddles Best Bitter; 3 changing beers H
Named after the Cooper Rose vaccinator used by Dr Henry Renney who lived in Albion Place in the 1890s, this Lloyd's No.1 bar opened in 2011. Beers vary on the long ground-floor bar and there is a smaller bar upstairs. Many photographs are displayed depicting local figures from Sunderland's past. Reasonably priced food is available from breakfast time until late.

Dun Cow ★ L
High Street West, SR1 3HA
11-11 (midnight Fri & Sat) (0191) 567 2262
Anarchy Blonde Star; Sharp's Doom Bar; 5 changing beers H
This Grade II listed building is an architectural gem and features on CAMRA's National Inventory of Historic Pub Interiors. It was a winner of two CAMRA/Historic England awards for restoration and conservation following a refurbishment in 2014. It offers real ale and cider on eight handpulls. Meals are served daily, and there is a Tuesday buskers' night and a Thursday quiz. The pub is next to the Empire Theatre and can get busy around performance times. Q

Fitzgeralds L
12-14 Green Terrace, SR1 3PZ
11.30-11 (11.30 Fri & Sat); 12-11 Sun (0191) 567 0852
Fyne Ales Jarl; 8 changing beers H
Part of the real ale-friendly Sir John Fitzgerald chain, this city-centre pub serves two regular beers complemented by up to eight guests. The pub comprises a large main bar offering a number of different seating areas and the smaller, quieter, nautically themed Chart Room. Meals are served all day from an extensive menu. Live music features on Tuesday and Sunday, and a quiz is held every Thursday evening.

Harbour View
Harbour View, Roker, SR6 0NU
10.30-11.30 (midnight Fri & Sat) (0191) 567 1402
6 changing beers H
The Harbour View is a modern local pub with six handpulls offering regularly changing beers chosen by local CAMRA members. A blackboard displays a tally of beers to date from 1 January – the aim is to offer in excess of 600 ales a year. A cask ale club is held every Wednesday evening. This is a relaxing pub for a drink, with additional seating outside to take in the sun. (E1,18)

Ivy House
7A Worcester Terrace, SR2 7AW
12-11 (midnight Fri & Sat) (0191) 567 3399
5 changing beers H
Tucked away but close to the Park Lane bus and Metro interchange, the Ivy House is well worth seeking out. Five ever-changing guest ales feature as well as a real cider and an extensive range of bottled international beers. Home-made pizzas and burgers are prepared in an open kitchen. There is a weekday happy hour from 5pm, themed meal nights and a Wednesday night quiz. Live music features on the second Saturday and last Sunday of the month. P

Museum Vaults L
33 Silksworth Row, SR1 3QJ
5-11; 3-midnight Fri; 12-midnight Sat; 12-10.30 Sun
(0191) 565 9443
3 changing beers H
Small former beer house on the edge of the city centre run by the same family for over 40 years. The single room is divided in two, both sides with open fires. The pub offers up to three cask beers, mostly from local breweries, and is a regular outlet for student brews from Brewlab in Sunderland. The real ale is complemented by a small range of bottled beers. P

Poetic License L
Roker Terrace, Roker, SR6 9ND
11-11 (1am Fri & Sat) (0191) 567 1786
poeticlicensebar.co.uk
Sonnet 43 Abolition, Athenaeum, Impressment, Seraphim, The Aurora H
A pub/restaurant with fine views of the mouth of the River Wear and the seashore. The decor is a blend of modern and traditional. Five of the Sonnet 43 core beers are usually available. A real ale club is hosted every Tuesday evening. Food is served daily, with meal deals Monday to Thursday. The venue is also home to a gin distillery, visible from the bar. Disabled access is to the left of the adjacent Roker Hotel reception.
P (18,E1)

Port of Call

1-3 Park Lane, SR1 3NX

11.30-11 (3am Fri & Sat) (0191) 514 5408

portofcall.co

Maxim Double Maxim; Thornbridge Jaipur IPA

Bar and eatery in a nautical themed building in a central location in the city. Set over three floors, the ground floor bar has two cask ale handpulls as well as a selection of international bottled beers. There are outside drinking areas on the first and second floors overlooking Park Lane. An extensive food menu is also available all day. Close to most city-centre buses and the Metro.

Ship Isis

26 Silksworth Row, SR1 3QJ

12-11.30 (midnight Fri & Sat); 12-11 Sun

(0191) 514 7684

8 changing beers

Restored to its original Victorian splendour by the former Jarrow Brewery, this is now a Camerons Head of Steam pub. Twelve handpumps offer nine cask beers and three real ciders, complemented by an extensive selection of bottled beers and a range of craft gins, served by knowledgable staff. Monday is quiz night, Wednesday is buskers' night and there is live music on Sunday. Just a short walk from the city centre, the Ship Isis has something for everyone.

William Jameson

30-32 Fawcett Street, SR1 1RH

8am-midnight (0191) 514 5016

Greene King Abbot; Ruddles Best Bitter; 6 changing beers

Sunderland's first Wetherspoon is in a former department store opposite the Winter Gardens in the heart of the city. All the usual features associated with the chain can be found in this busy corner pub, including good-value meals served all day. Twelve handpumps offer up to six guest beers and a cider to complement the regular range. The pub is a keen supporter of local brewers and holds twice-yearly beer festivals. Q

Swalwell

Sun Inn

Market Lane, NE16 3AL (just off roundabout at end of Front St)

11-11; 12-11 Sun

Marston's Pedigree; 2 changing beers

The Sun is situated in the heart of the historic village that spawned many internationally renowned engineers and industrialists, and of course the famous Swalwell cabbage. This truly no-nonsense community pub provides good company for locals and strangers alike. Sword dancers, darts, dominoes handicaps, a monthly pie competition and Saturday buskers' night all feature. Bar food and snacks are available, free on Sundays. There is a regular bus service from Newcastle.

Tynemouth

Tynemouth Lodge Hotel

Tynemouth Road, NE30 4AA

11-11; 12-10.30 Sun (0191) 257 7565

tynemouthlodgehotel.co.uk

Caledonian Deuchars IPA; Draught Bass; Mordue Northumbrian Blonde; 1 changing beer

This attractive externally tiled 1799 free house, next to a former house of correction, has featured in every issue of the Guide since 1983. The comfortable pub has a U-shaped lounge with the bar on one side and a serving hatch on the other, and is noted in the area for the quality of its Draught Bass. A popular stopping-off point for those completing the Coast-to-Coast cycle route. QP (1,1A)

Washington

Courtyard

Biddick Lane, NE38 8AB

11-11 (midnight Fri); 10-midnight Sat; 12-11 Sun

(0191) 417 0445 artscentrewashington.co.uk/courtyard.aspx

Timothy Taylor Landlord; 7 changing beers

Located within the Washington Arts Centre, this pleasant café/bar offers a warm welcome to drinkers and food lovers alike. Eight handpulled beers, two real ciders and a perry are available. An extensive range of food is served at lunchtime and early evening, including nightly specials. Quiz nights are held on Sunday and Thursday and a songwriters' night on Monday. Outdoor seating is within the spacious courtyard. Two popular beer festivals feature annually, on the Easter and August bank holidays. P

Sir William De Wessyngton

2-3 Victoria Road, NE37 2SY

7am-11 (midnight Fri & Sat); 8am-11 Sun

(0191) 418 0100

Greene King Abbot; Ruddles Best Bitter; 6 changing beers

This large open-plan Wetherspoon pub is a former snooker hall and ice cream parlour. It is named after a Norman knight and lord of the manor whose descendants later emigrated to the United States. The pub offers value-for-money beer and the usual well-priced Wetherspoon menu. The regular ales are complemented by up to four guests and at least two real ciders. Twice-yearly beer festivals are held. A large selection of local and international bottled beers is available. QP

Steps

47 Spout Lane, NE38 7HP

3.30-11; 12-11 Sat; 12-10.30 Sun (0191) 415 0733

5 changing beers

Opened in 1894 as the Spout Lane Inn, the pub was renamed The Steps in 1976. The small, comfortable and friendly single-room lounge bar is divided into two drinking areas and the walls are decorated with pictures of old Washington. Five varying beers are on offer, frequently from local microbreweries. Quizzes are held on Tuesday and Thursday nights, live entertainment features on the last Saturday of the month. Opening hours vary. QP (84)

West Boldon

Black Horse

Rectory Bank, NE36 0QQ (off A184)

11-11; 12-10.30 Sun (0191) 536 1814

Jennings Cumberland Ale; 1 changing beer

An old-fashioned pub with one small L-shaped bar and every available wall and shelf adorned with bric-a-brac. Note the assorted headgear hanging from the ceiling. Two handpulls offer Cumberland

Ale and a guest beer. With a popular restaurant serving high-quality food, the pub can get busy in the evenings and at weekends. ◑♿P🚌

Whickham

One-Eyed Stag 𝕃

5 The Square, NE16 4JB

⏲ 11.30-10.30 (11 Fri & Sat); 12-10 Sun ☎ 07811 261924

4 changing beers Ⓗ

A recent, welcome addition to the Whickham pub scene, this micropub has a tile-topped bar with four handpumps serving beer from local microbreweries. Blackboards adorn the wall behind the bar giving details of the beers and other drinks available. There is an interesting light fitting covering most of the ceiling and a wood-burning stove in an alcove. 🐾

Whitley Bay

Dog & Rabbit 𝕃

36 Park View, NE26 2TH

⏲ 12-10; 3-10 Sun ☎ 07944 552716

🌐 dogandrabbitbrewery.co.uk

4 changing beers Ⓗ

It is good to have this micropub, formerly a women's clothing shop, to add to the choice of drinking venues in Whitley Bay. It features a corner bar with four handpumps serving mostly local beers. The owner's microbrewery has now been installed on-site and brews Dog & Rabbit beers for the pub. Books, games and newspapers are available for those who want them, but the convivial atmosphere, with no music, no Wi-Fi and no sports TV encourages conversation among drinkers. **Q**🐴🚂🍎🚌🐾

Bridge Hotel, Newcastle upon Tyne: City Centre (Photo: Cat Button)

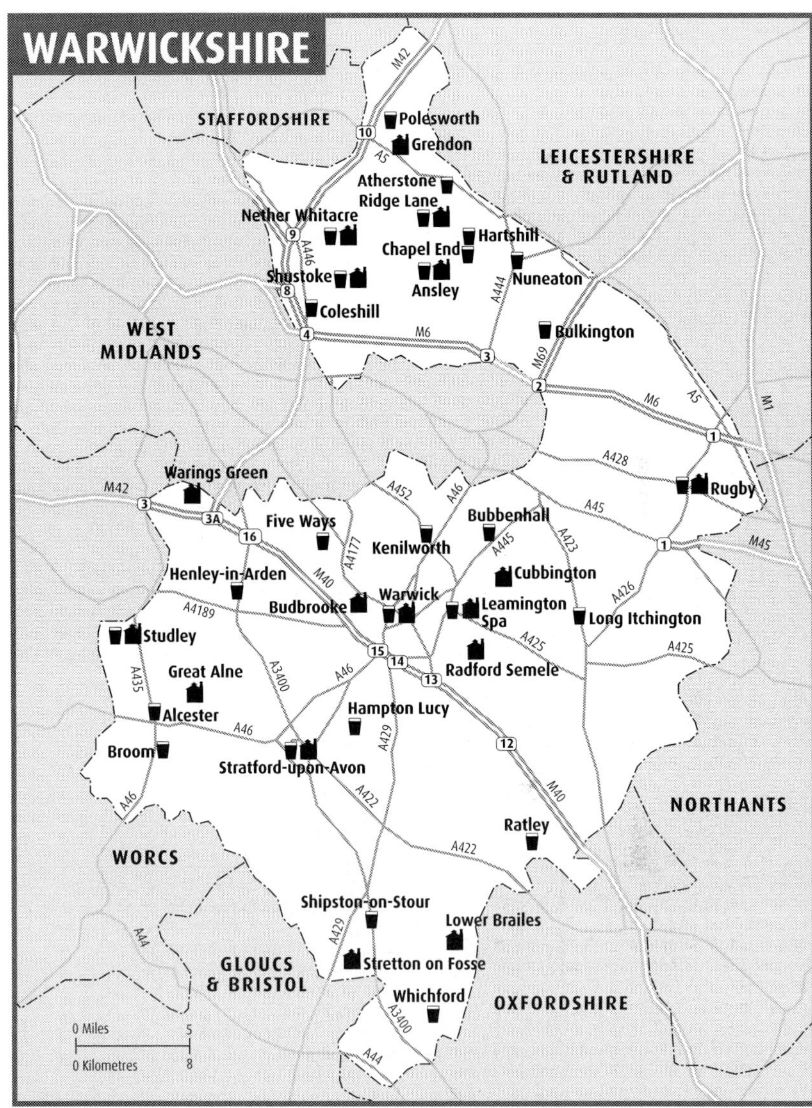

Alcester

Three Tuns

34 High Street, B49 5AB

12 (1 Mon-Thu winter)-11 ☎ (01789) 762626

thethreetunsalcester.com

Adnams Southwold Bitter; 5 changing beers (sourced regionally; often Bathams, Hobsons, Titanic) H

Nestled in the historic market town of Alcester this welcoming, single-bar pub retains the original beams, stone-flagged floors and sections of wattle and daub. No food, no loud music, but a relaxed atmosphere and a fantastic selection of real ales, fine wines and an array of ciders await you. There is also a varied range of malt whiskies and gins, plus Prosecco from the bottle and tap. The pub hosts monthly bake-off nights and ale, cider and whisky tasting nights. Small parties can be catered for.

Turk's Head

4 High Street, B49 5AD

12-11; 10-11 Sat; 12-10.30 Sun ☎ (01789) 765948

theturkshead.net

Wye Valley HPA; 3 changing beers (sourced regionally; often Salopian, Timothy Taylor, Tiny Rebel) H

A central location helps make this a popular place. The publican is a real ale enthusiast, staging beer festivals during the summer months, either from the garden bar or from the mobile bar outside the pub during Alcester's popular food festivals. Beers are from Cornwall, South Wales, Shropshire and Yorkshire to give an ever-changing range of styles and flavours. A busy dining pub, it finds the best-quality ingredients to deliver classic and modern pub dishes (booking advisable). Local CAMRA Pub of the Year 2018.

Ansley

Lord Nelson Inn

Birmingham Road, CV10 9PQ
12-11 (10 Sun) ☎ (024) 7639 2305
thelordnelsoninnansley.co.uk
Sperrin Ansley Mild, Head Hunter, Band of Brothers, Third Party, Thick as Thieves; 3 changing beers Ⓗ
This nautically themed pub has been run by the Sperrin family since 1974 and has featured in the Guide for 24 consecutive years. Nine handpulls dispense the pub's own Sperrin brews, ales from other breweries local and not so local, plus a real cider. There is an extensive food menu with meal nights and tribute nights hosted. The suntrap courtyard garden is a venue for beer festivals and barbecues.

Atherstone

Angel Ale House

24 Church Street, CV9 1RN
4-11 (midnight Fri); 12-midnight Sat; 12-10.30 Sun
☎ 07525 183056
Blythe Palmers Poison; Oakham Citra; 4 changing beers Ⓗ
Popular real ale flagship on the historic market square. It has a busy bar and a comfortable lounge to the rear, where children are allowed. Logburners feature in winter. Six real ales are offered, often local and usually including a dark beer. A good range of real ciders is also available. Music is via customer select-and-play from a large vinyl LP collection. There is a large free council car park to the rear. (48,65)

Broom

Broom Tavern

32 High Street, B50 4HL
12-3, 5-11; 12-11 Sat & Sun ☎ (01789) 778199
broomtavern.co.uk
North Cotswold Shagweaver; Purity Pure UBU; 2 changing beers (often Stratford upon Avon, Wye Valley) Ⓗ
A lovely brick and timber multi-room building which retains a great amount of character. It has been tastefully made over, while keeping the cosy snug and log fire in winter. Reopened by two experienced chefs with a good pedigree in the kitchen, it serves great food lunchtimes and evenings, made with local ingredients. Local beers are frequently found here alongside the Cornish contingents and at least one real cider. There is a choice of beer gardens.

Bubbenhall

Malt Shovel

Lower End, CV8 3BW
12-11 ☎ (024) 7630 1141
Greene King Abbot; 3 changing beers (sourced regionally; often Church End, Purity) Ⓗ
Friendly village free house in a 17th-century Grade II listed building, comprising a large L-shaped lounge bar at the front and a small public bar to the rear. Outside, there is a small patio at the front and a large walled garden and adjacent bowling green behind the spacious car park. The pub is popular for home-cooked food and holds regular fish nights and pie nights. Convenient for the nearby Ryton Pools Country Park. P (539)

Bulkington

Weavers Arms

12 Long Street, CV12 9JZ
4-midnight; 12-midnight Fri-Sun ☎ (024) 7631 4415
Draught Bass; 1 changing beer Ⓗ
Family-owned, two-roomed, traditional village pub converted from weavers' cottages. It has a wood-panelled games room, log-burning fireplace and a slate floor. Outside, the extensive, well-kept beer garden hosts barbecues in the summer. Children are welcome and private functions can be catered for. The Pork Pie Club, Weavers Walkers and Hillbilly Golf Society hold regular meetings here. The pub is well known for the quality of its Bass. Closing time may be after 11pm but no later than 1am. (56)

Chapel End

Salutation

Chancery Lane, CV10 0PB
1-11 (midnight Thu); 12-1am Fri & Sat; 12-10.30 Sun
☎ (024) 7704 7573
3 changing beers Ⓗ
This award-winning community pub makes a welcome return to the Guide after an absence of 30 years. It is sports-oriented, showing major football, rugby and boxing matches. Local history nights, quizzes and other events take place. Regular live bands are hosted and the pub stages occasional bus trips. Guest beers often come from Church End, Bass, Oakham and Castle Rock.
P

Coleshill

Green Man

68 High Street, B46 3AH
12 (4 Tue)-11; 12-10.30 Sun ☎ (01675) 463376
Draught Bass; M&B Brew XI; 2 changing beers Ⓗ
Hard-to-miss, white-painted, three-storey pub sitting on the main town crossroads. The old-fashioned interior features a busy bar and servery area, a comfy lounge to the rear and a quiet snug to the side. The decor is pleasantly dated and a display of 1980s beermats and the 1958 price list may make older drinkers feel nostalgic. There are TVs throughout but used with discretion. The two guest beers are from the Punch Finest Cask range.
P

REAL ALE BREWERIES

Atomic Rugby
Blue Bell Warings Green
Church End Ridge Lane
Church Farm Budbrooke
Clouded Minds Lower Brailes
Fizzy Moon Leamington (NEW)
Freestyle Shustoke
Merry Miner Grendon
North Cotswold Stretton-on-Fosse
Old Pie Factory Warwick
Purity Great Alne
Slaughterhouse Warwick
Sperrin Ansley
Stratford Upon Avon Stratford-upon-Avon
Warwickshire Cubbington
Weatheroak Studley
Whitacre Nether Whitacre (NEW)
Windmill Hill Radford Semele (NEW)

Five Ways

Case is Altered 🄻

Case Lane, CV35 7JD (off Five Ways Rd near A4141/ A4177 jct) SP225701

🕐 12-2.30, 6-11; 12-7.30 Sun ☎ (01926) 484206

Wye Valley Butty Bach; house beer (by Old Pie Factory); 3 changing beers (sourced locally) 🄷

A traditional unspoilt country pub with a bar and separate snug. The current landlady has been here for 33 years, taking over from her grandmother. The traditional bar billiards table still takes the old sixpences which have to be bought from the bar. Monday is cribbage night. Do not miss the Victorian print of a former Leamington brewer in the bar plus a clock from another old local brewer. There is even a propeller from a World War I fighter plane on the ceiling. **Q❀♿♣P**

Hampton Lucy

Boar's Head 🄻 ✔

Church Street, CV35 8BE

🕐 12-11 (midnight Fri & Sat); 12-10 (8 winter) Sun ☎ (01789) 840533 🌐 theboarsheadhamptonlucy.com

Ringwood Boondoggle; 4 changing beers (sourced locally; often North Cotswold, Slaughterhouse, Stratford upon Avon) 🄷

A friendly, popular village pub dating back to the 17th century. Originally built as a cider house, the present kitchen was once a mortuary. On a Sustrans route and close to the River Avon, it is frequented by cyclists, walkers and visitors to nearby Charlecote Park. Five real ales are served including at least two LocAles. The menu offers fresh, home-made food. The walled rear garden is popular in good weather. An annual themed beer festival is held in summer. **❀◐◑P**📶

Hartshill

Royal Oak 🄻 ✔

Oldbury Road, CV10 0TD

🕐 4-11; 12-midnight Fri & Sat; 12-11 Sun ☎ (024) 7639 6442 🌐 theroyaloakhartshill.co.uk

Draught Bass; 2 changing beers 🄷

A former Charles Wells pub and now a free house, the Royal Oak has been refurbished to give a good old-fashioned community feeling, with many pictures of old Hartshill on display. It offers a changing range of beers from breweries near and far, alongside a real cider. A garden at the rear accommodates live music and beer festivals during the summer months. Various events take place throughout the year. **🐎❀♣●🚌** (48)🐾📶

Henley-in-Arden

Three Tuns

103 High Street, B95 5AT

🕐 12 (3.30 Mon & Tue)-11; 12-10.30 Sun ☎ (01564) 792723

Fuller's London Pride; Sharp's Doom Bar, Atlantic; Wye Valley Butty Bach; 1 changing beer 🄷

An unpretentious 16th-century two-roomed inn with a single bar serving both areas. Popular with locals, this traditional drinkers' pub is usually busy and the atmosphere is always friendly. Five real ales are served in consistently good condition from the bar. Pub snacks plus home-made sausage rolls and cobs are usually available. Parking is on the main street outside the pub.
Q🐎♿⇌♣🚌 (X20)🐾📶

White Swan ✔

100 High Street, B95 5BY

🕐 12-11 (10.30 Sun) ☎ (01564) 792623

🌐 thewhiteswanhotel.com

Black Sheep Best Bitter; Purity Pure Gold; St Austell Tribute; Sharp's Doom Bar; 1 changing beer (often Purity) 🄷

An inn has existed on this site since 1352 – the current building was erected between 1550 and 1565. Locals claim to have seen a ghostly child roaming the area. The main bar is a cosy, attractive area with many exposed original beams and a real fire. Good-quality, home-cooked food is served to complement the excellently kept ales. The rear area is now a Stoneaged Steakhouse restaurant, serving food 6pm-9pm Monday to Saturday.
Q🐎❀🛏◐◑♿⇌P🚌 (X20)📶

Kenilworth

Green Man 🄻 ✔

Warwick Road, CV8 1HS

🕐 10-11 (midnight Fri & Sat) ☎ (01296) 863061

House beer (by Black Sheep); 9 changing beers (sourced nationally; often Purity) 🄷

Popular Ember Inn within walking distance of Kenilworth town centre. The central bar has two banks of five handpumps dispensing a range of permanent and changing beers. The house beer, Ember Ale, is brewed by Black Sheep. Good-quality food is available daily noon-10pm, plus brunch from 10am on Saturday and Sunday. There is an assortment of distinct seating areas and a pleasant patio. Ample parking is available and dogs are welcome. Public transport passes nearby.
🐎❀◐◑♿P🚌 (11,X17)🐾📶

Old Bakery 🏆 🄻

12 High Street, CV8 1LZ (near A429/A452 jct)

🕐 5.30-11.30; 5-11.30 Sat; 5-11 Sun ☎ (01926) 864111

🌐 theoldbakery.eu

Wye Valley HPA; house beer (by Byatt's); 2 changing beers (sourced regionally) 🄷

Located in the old part of Kenilworth near St Nicholas Church and Abbey Fields, this interesting two-roomed bar is set in an oak-beamed 400-year-old building. There are four ales served in a friendly atmosphere, without TV screens, music or noisy games machines. The house beer is from Byatt's, brewed locally. Wheelchair access is to the rear of the building. Accommodation is available in 14 en-suite rooms. Local CAMRA Pub of the Year 2018.
Q❀🛏♿P🚌 (11)📶

Virgins & Castle

7 High Street, CV8 1LY (A429/A452 jct)

🕐 11-11 (midnight Fri & Sat); 11-10.30 Sun ☎ (01926) 853737 🌐 virginsandcastle.co.uk

Everards Beacon Hill, Sunchaser, Tiger, Old Original; 1 changing beer (sourced regionally; often Everards) 🄷

Situated in the quaint old town and dating from the 16th century, this is reputed to be Kenilworth's oldest pub. It was here that the original Coventry & Warwickshire branch of CAMRA formed in 1974. The building has a split-level interior and characterful snug rooms. Diners enjoy English and Filipino cuisine (no food Sun eve). Popular beer and cider festivals are held in May and October. There is limited street parking but a public car park is nearby. Dogs are welcome except in the dining area. **🐎❀◐◑♿●🚌** (11)🐾📶

Leamington Spa

New Inn ✔

197 Leam Terrace, CV31 1DW
12 (4 Mon)-11 ☎ (01926) 422861
thenewinnleamington.co.uk
Eagle IPA; Greene King Abbot; Sharp's Doom Bar, Atlantic; 2 changing beers H
A traditional pub located in a Victorian terrace on the outskirts of Leamington Spa. The original pub has been extended into the next-door property. A central door opens directly on to the bar, with a seating area to the left and a games area to the right leading to an extension at the rear. Outside is a good-sized walled garden. Home-cooked food is available. A quiz is hosted fortnightly on a Wednesday. (63/64)

Woodland Tavern L ✔

3 Regent Street, CV32 5HW
12-midnight (1am Fri & Sat); 12-11.30 Sun
☎ (01926) 425868
Slaughterhouse Saddleback Best Bitter; Wychwood Hobgoblin; 2 changing beers H
Traditional Victorian street-corner pub situated close to the centre of Leamington Spa and enjoyed by locals and visitors alike. It has a public bar and a separate lounge, also used as a function room. The unique partially covered courtyard features murals depicting local references and jokes. On the side of the building is a large colourful mural showing a dray and horses delivering ale to the pub.

Long Itchington

Harvester L

6 Church Road, CV47 9PE (off A423 at village pond, then first left)
12-2.30, 6-11; 12-3, 7-10.30 Sun ☎ (01926) 812698
theharvesterinn.co.uk
Hook Norton Hooky; 2 changing beers H
This white-fronted pub is near the village pond, on the corner of the square. Inside is a main bar, a small drinking area and a restaurant specialising in good-value steaks. The beer range changes frequently, usually supporting smaller breweries. Real cider and a Belgian fruit beer are also available. The pub hosts a beer festival each May bank holiday. A large walled courtyard garden to the rear has a wood-fired pizza oven. Gruntfuttocks Speciality Pickles can be purchased to take home. (64)

Nether Whitacre

Dog Inn ✔

Dog Lane, B46 2DU SP232930
12-3, 6-11; 12-11 Sat & Sun ☎ (01675) 481318
Sharp's Doom Bar; Wye Valley Butty Bach; 3 changing beers (sourced nationally; often Castle Rock) H
A quintessentially English country pub, with a peaceful beer garden including a pets' corner. Inside, brass knick-knacks abound, and in winter two log fires add warmth. Easily missed is the elaborate carved frontage to the bar, including two pairs of stuffed jays. Full of character throughout, there are two separate dining rooms. The pub now offers ales from the on-site Whitacre Brewing Company, generally at weekends. Try-before-you-buy is offered on all ales. Complimentary bar nibbles are available on Sunday lunchtimes.
P

Nuneaton

Felix Holt L ✔

3 Stratford Street, CV11 5BS
8am-11 (midnight Fri & Sat) ☎ (024) 7634 7785
Byatt's Regal Blond; Greene King Abbot; Ruddles Best Bitter; Sharp's Doom Bar; changing beers H
Large Wetherspoon outlet in the town centre. The pub takes its name from a novel by George Eliot and the literary theme is reflected in the décor of books and pictures of local history. A good range of guest beers includes local ales, with Byatt's and Oakham often represented. Food is served 8am-10pm. There is a heated area for smokers.
Q

Horseshoes L

2 Heath End Road, CV10 7JQ
11-11 (midnight Fri & Sat); 12-11 Sun ☎ (024) 7767 5066
Everards Tiger, Old Original; 4 changing beers (sourced nationally) H
An Everards pub selling a large range of the brewery's own beers alongside a choice of guests plus cider and perries. The pub is close to the George Eliot Hospital and Coventry Canal, and has been refurbished to provide more room. The family-friendly venue is popular with diners and holds various themed food nights. Quiz night is Wednesday. There is a drinking area outside at the side of the building. QP

Lord Hop L

38 Queens Road, CV11 5JX
12-10 ☎ (024) 7798 1869
4 changing beers H
Town-centre micropub on two levels, with four or more real ales served on handpull or straight from the cask from both local and far-away breweries, plus two ciders or perries on handpull and up to six more in the chiller. Wine and soft drinks are also sold, and various snacks. CAMRA magazines are available to read. No under-18s, and assistance dogs only. Local CAMRA Pub of the Year and Cider Pub of the Year. Q

Polesworth

Bull's Head

Tamworth Road, B78 1JH (by canal bridge on B5000)
11-midnight (11.30 Sun) ☎ (01827) 898990
Sharp's Doom Bar; Wainwright; 1 changing beer H
Solidly traditional community local next to the canal. The L-shaped bar is generally busy but the small lounge through the archway tends to be quieter. There is plenty going on here including darts and bowls clubs, quizzes, raffles and sports screenings. One or two guest beers feature depending on the time of week. Aside from snacks for darts nights and other occasions there is no food, but the independent Indian restaurant upstairs is happy to fetch ale for you from downstairs. P

Ratley

Rose & Crown

Chapel Lane, OX15 6DS
12-3 (not Mon), 5-11; 12-11 Fri-Sun ☎ (01295) 678148
roseandcrown-ratley.co.uk
Bombardier; Otter Bitter; St Austell Tribute; 2 changing beers (sourced locally; often Prescott, Purity) H

ENGLAND

Tucked away at the bottom of an ancient village on the northern extremity of the Cotswolds escarpment, this 11th-century golden stone pub has a wealth of detail, with cosy log fires in winter and a suntrap garden in summer. High-quality food is served. Walkers, dogs, locals and visitors are all welcome. This friendly local is reputedly haunted by the ghost of a Roundhead soldier.
Q🍽❀◑⛺♣🚌🐾📶

Ridge Lane

Church End Brewery Tap Ⓛ

Ridge Lane, CV10 0RD (2 miles SW of Atherstone)
⏲ closed Mon & Tue; 6-11 Wed & Thu; 12-11 Fri & Sat; 12-10.30 Sun ☎ (01827) 713080 🌐 churchendbrewery.co.uk
Church End Poachers Pocket, Gravediggers Ale, What the Fox's Hat, Fallen Angel; 4 changing beers Ⓗ
This brewery tap is hidden from the road, with access signposted by a board positioned at the entrance. Eight handpulls serve the bar and vestry – beers change regularly but always include a mild. The ever-changing ciders are dispensed direct from the barrel. Under-18s are allowed in the vestry until 6pm, and there is a large meadow garden with ample seating. Entertainment includes an open mic night on the third Wednesday of the month. Q❀♿⛺🍎P🚌🐾📶

Rugby

Alexandra Arms Ⓛ

72-73 James Street, CV21 2SL (next to John Barford multi-storey car park)
⏲ 11.30-11.30 (1am Fri & Sat); 12-11.30 Sun
☎ (01788) 578660 🌐 alexandraarms.co.uk
Fuller's London Pride; 4 changing beers (sourced nationally; often Abbeydale, Atomic, Hook Norton) Ⓗ
Town-centre hostelry that is almost two pubs in one. The lounge has been refurbished and the fireplaces have been reinstated, providing a cosy atmosphere in the winter. Good-value pub food is served at lunchtimes. The popular large back bar accommodates a pool table and an excellent jukebox. Outside, the large rear garden hosts a beer festival in summer. The Atomic Brewery is at the back and its beers are available in the pub.
🍽❀◑♿🚆♣🍎🐾📶

Merchants Inn Ⓛ

5-6 Little Church Street, CV21 3AW
⏲ 12-midnight (1am Fri & Sat); 12-11.30 Sun
☎ (01788) 571119 🌐 merchantsinn.co.uk
Oakham Bishops Farewell; Purity Mad Goose; house beer (by Nethergate) Ⓗ**; 6 changing beers (sourced nationally)** Ⓗ/Ⓖ
This popular town-centre pub's walls and ceilings are adorned with an impressive range of pub and brewery memorabilia. Flagstone floors and an open fire greet you as you walk in. Traditional pub food is available Monday to Saturday lunchtime, including The Merchants' First XV burgers, plus the best Sunday lunch in town (served 12-5pm). Daily specials feature local seasonal produce. Rugby and cricket are shown on the big screen. Annual festivals include two for real ale and one apiece for cider, gin and Belgian and German beer.
🍽❀◑♿♣🍎▭🚌🐾📶

Raglan Arms

50 Dunchurch Road, CV22 6AD (on A426 nr gyratory and town centre)
⏲ 4-midnight (1am Fri); 12-1am Sat; 12-midnight Sun
☎ (01788) 544441
Greene King Abbot; Morland Old Golden Hen; house beer (by Greene King); 4 changing beers (sourced nationally; often Abbeydale, Newby Wyke, St Austell) Ⓗ
A warm, friendly, traditional pub with comfortable bar areas and a cosy snug. Three regular ales – Abbot, Old Golden Hen and Raglan Bitter – and four changing nationally sourced guests are complemented by two traditional ciders. The Raglan has an outside smoking area to the rear and dogs are welcome. The pub shows sporting events and has a skittles table for those who like to play.
🍽❀♣🍎P🚌🐾📶

Rugby Tap Ⓛ

3 St Matthews Street, CV21 3BY (adjacent to A426 gyratory)
⏲ 10-6 (10 Thu-Sat); 12-4 Sun ☎ (01788) 576767
🌐 rugbytap.co.uk
6 changing beers (sourced locally; often Byatt's, Church End, Phipps NBC) Ⓖ
The Rugby Tap off-licence and adjacent Tap Room micropub stock a large selection of draught and bottled ales and ciders, and a good range of imported beers. The Tap Room offers an environment that shuns electronic entertainment, promoting conversation in an intimate setting. Acoustic music is a regular feature on Thursday evening. The pub serves up to six LocAles and ciders and has a range of traditional pub snacks.
Q🍎🚌🐾📶

Seven Stars 🏆

40 Albert Square, CV21 2SH
⏲ 12 (4 Mon)-11; 12-midnight Fri & Sat; 12-10 Sun
☎ (01788) 535478 🌐 sevenstarsrugby.co.uk
Everards Tiger; Grainstore Ten Fifty; Oakham JHB; 9 changing beers (sourced nationally) Ⓗ
Quintessential back-street local with plenty of charm and character, offering a warm and friendly welcome. The interior displays plenty of Rugby Union memorabilia, and quiet background music makes conversation a delight. The bar boasts 14 handpumps, with mild and two ciders permanently on offer, and guest beers available alongside the Everards, Oakham and Grainstore regulars. The recently refurbished courtyard garden features a painted mural. Local CAMRA Pub of the Year 2017.
Q🍽❀🚆♣🍎🚌🐾📶

Squirrel Inn Ⓛ

33 Church Street, CV21 3PU
⏲ 12-11; 4-10.30 Sun ☎ (01788) 578527
4 changing beers (sourced nationally; often Dow Bridge, Marston's, Merry Miner) Ⓗ
Charming 18th-century town pub with old beams and low ceilings. This regular Guide entry has undergone sympathetic renovation, restoring and exposing its many historic features. Bric-a-brac around the walls and a good selection of table games add to the ambience. This free trade house provides a wide range of guest ales including a local ale. Live music forms part of the weekly calendar of events and established Rugby bands return for repeat performances. ♣🍎🚌🐾

Town & County Club

12 Henry Street, CV21 2QA
⏲ 12-4 (Tue only), 7.30-11; 11.30-5, 7.30-11 Sat; 12-5, 7.30-10.30 Sun ☎ 07931 661840

Church End Gravediggers Ale; Greene King IPA; 2 changing beers (sourced nationally; often Donnington, Otter, Timothy Taylor) ⓗ
This is the first appearance in the Guide for The Town & County, which has been trading since 1933. The small town-centre club is a local CAMRA award winner with four handpumps, two of which dispense changing guest ales. Regular events include Tuesday bingo, a monthly quiz, Sunday night rock DJ, occasional live music and coach trips. The club runs dominoes and skittles teams. CAMRA members are welcome and guests may be signed in. Q🐴♣P🚌🐾

Victoria Inn 🄻

1 Lower Hillmorton Road, CV21 3ST
⏲ 12 (4 Mon-Wed)-midnight ☎ (01788) 544374
🌐 downthevic.com
Atomic Strike, Half Life; Hook Norton Hooky; 7 changing beers (sourced nationally; often Abbeydale, Hop Studio) ⓗ
A traditional Victorian real ale pub owned by the Atomic Brewery with 10 handpumps offering rapidly changing ales. Real cider is also on handpull and a selection of foreign and craft beers is available. There is a bustling period lounge and a traditional bar with darts and pool. TV sport is regularly screened and quiz nights are held on Sunday and Wednesday evenings. Themed beer festivals feature twice a year. The railway station is less than a mile away. 🐴✿◐♣🍎🚌🐾📶

Shipston-on-Stour

Black Horse Inn 🄻

Station Road, CV36 4BT
⏲ 12-3 (not Mon), 6-11; 12-11 ☎ (01608) 238489
🌐 blackhorseshipston.com
Prescott Hill Climb; Wye Valley Butty Bach; 1 changing beer ⓗ
This stone-built 15th-century inn is the oldest pub and only thatched building in Shipston, with a licence that dates back to 1540. It has two rooms – the main bar is cosy and welcoming with a large inglenook log fireplace, the second bar has a log fire, wooden beams and a dartboard. Thai food is available. There is live music in the garden in summer and several beer and cider festivals are staged. Q🐴✿◐◑♣🍎P🚌🐾📶

Shustoke

Griffin Inn 🄻

Church Road, B46 2LB (on B4116 on sharp bend)
⏲ 12-2.30, 7-11; 12-11 Fri-Sun ☎ (01675) 481205
Freestyle Griffin Dark; Marston's Pedigree; Oakham Citra; Theakston Old Peculier; Wye Valley Butty Bach; 5 changing beers (sourced nationally; often Freestyle, Oakham) ⓗ
A real ale bastion for decades, this classic pub features beams and inglenook fireplaces with solid fuel stoves. The cosy atmosphere is unsullied by music or TV. Freestyle ales from the adjacent brewery usually feature among the five guest beers. There is always one real cider and up to four in summertime. A large, busy beer festival is the highlight of summer. Children are welcome in the conservatory, beer terrace and meadow-style garden. Home-cooked lunches are served (no food Sun). Q🐴✿◐⛺🍎P🐾📶

Plough 🄻 ✔

The Green, B46 2AN
⏲ 12-3, 5.30-11; 12-11 Fri & Sat; 12-10.30 Sun
☎ (01675) 481557 🌐 theploughinnshustoke.co.uk
Draught Bass; 4 changing beers ⓗ
Attractive community hostelry on the village green. Four guest ales usually include offerings from the landlord's fledgling brewery. The bar area with a real fire is compact and cosy, with games in a separate room. The pub is popular for food, so the rooms are generally busy with diners. There is a twittering aviary to the rear, while the front has a tidy beer terrace with greenery. Quiz night is the first Monday of the month. 🐴✿◐◑♿♣P🐾📶

Stratford-upon-Avon

Stratford Alehouse 🄻

12B Greenhill Street, CV37 6LF
⏲ 1-11; 2-9 Sun ☎ 07746 807966
🌐 thestratfordalehouse.com
4 changing beers (sourced nationally; often North Cotswold, Old Pie Factory, Stratford upon Avon) ⓗ
A family-run, one-bar micropub serving the finest real ales, ciders and wines. There is no loud music (except on live music nights), noisy children or gaming machines to distract you here – just a friendly welcome in a relaxing environment for drinking, chatting, making new friends or reading the newspapers. Snacks are served. Since opening in 2013, more than 900 different beers have made an appearance. Home to Stratford Folk Club on a Wednesday and live bands at the weekend. Local CAMRA Pub of the Year in 2016. Q♿🚆🍎🚌🐾

Studley

Weatheroak Tap House 🄻

21A High Street, B80 7HN (next to chippy)
⏲ 4-9 Mon; 12.30-10.30 (11 Fri); 12-11 Sat; 12-9 Sun
☎ (01527) 854433 🌐 weatheroakbrewery.co.uk
Weatheroak Bees Knees, Ale, Victoria Works, Keystone Hops; house beer (by Weatheroak); 1 changing beer (sourced locally; often Church End) ⓗ
This micropub with two small, cosy rooms opened in 2016 and is the outlet for the nearby Weatheroak Brewery. Basic snacks are available and there is a chip shop next door – you are welcome to bring in food to the pub. Off-sales from the nearby brewery are also available in various quantities. Q🍎🚌🐾📶

Warwick

Cape of Good Hope 🄻

66 Lower Cape, CV34 5DP (off Cape Rd)
⏲ 11-11 (1am Fri & Sat); 11-midnight Sun
☎ (01926) 498138 🌐 thecapeofgoodhopepub.com
Church Farm Harry's Heifer; Hook Norton Hooky; Wye Valley Butty Bach; 3 changing beers ⓗ
This historic 1798 alehouse on the Grand Union Canal welcomes canal users and locals alike. The original building on the waterside is now the front bar, with a modern extension to the rear. Internal decorations feature canal memorabilia, including interesting maps. Three permanent real ales along with three locally sourced guest beers are offered. The friendly staff are knowledgable and proud to serve local ales and foods. There is outside seating alongside the water next to a sometimes-busy double lock. 🐴✿◐◑♿⛺♣P🚌(G1)🐾📶

Oak

27 Coten End, CV34 4NT

1 (3 Mon)-midnight; 12-1am Fri-Sun (01926) 493774

Fuller's London Pride; 3 changing beers H

The Oak dates back to at least 1874. The building is long and narrow, with a small patio garden at the rear. The pub was refurbished in 2017 – the pool table was removed and more seating installed. The emphasis changed to sport on TV and music on a jukebox. Live music plays at the weekend. The house beer is London Pride. (X17)

Old Post Office

12 West Street, CV34 6AN

closed Mon; 12-9; 12-5 Sun 07765 896155

Slaughterhouse Saddleback Best Bitter; Young's Special H**; 4 changing beers** H/G

Warwick's first alehouse offers a friendly, relaxed atmosphere and traditional beers served on handpump and straight from the cask. Popular with real ale enthusiasts and local residents, the small bar is housed in a former shop just below the West Gate and within easy walking distance of Warwick Castle. It is decorated with a large collection of pub memorabilia and Batman hangs from the ceiling drinking a pint. No food is served but you are welcome to bring your own.

Punch Bowl

1 The Butts, CV34 4SS

closed Mon; 12-2.30, 5-11 (11.30 Thu); 12-11 Fri & Sat; 12-10 Sun (01926) 403846 punchbowlwarwick.co.uk

5 changing beers H

The building is an old coaching inn and hostelry dating back to the early 19th century. It has a large, open bar area on different levels – a raised area serves as a stage for popular music events held every Thursday evening and on special occasions. Sports events are shown on a large screen. The pub promotes real ale, with five changing guest beers available at all times. A blackboard behind the bar keeps a tally of all the different ales sold.
P (X17)

Thomas Lloyd

3-7 Market Place, CV34 4SA

8am-midnight (1am Fri & Sat) (01926) 475690

Greene King Abbot; Marston's Pedigree; Ruddles Best Bitter; 8 changing beers H

Located in Warwick's market square and named after local philanthropist Thomas Lloyd, this 19th-century building was formerly a Lloyds Bank until it became a Wetherspoon Lloyd's No.1 bar in 2002. Inside, there is a large open-plan area with a long bar to the right and a raised area to the left. Pictures showing the history of Warwick hang on the walls. Seating outside in the square catches the sun on late summer evenings.

Wild Boar

27 Lakin Road, CV34 5BU

12-11.30 (12.30am Fri & Sat); 12-10.30 Sun (01926) 499968 thewildboarwarwick.co.uk

Slaughterhouse Saddleback Best Bitter; 9 changing beers (often Everards, Slaughterhouse) H

Award-winning Project William community pub, close to the railway station. An end-of-terrace Victorian building, it has a bar, snug and separate beer hall which was formerly a skittle alley. The taphouse for Slaughterhouse Brewery, the on-site two-barrel microbrewery can be viewed from within the pub. Ten handpumps deliver Slaughterhouse, Everards and guest ales alongside two real ciders. Outside there is an attractive patio hop garden – the hops are used for Slaughterhouse's annual brew, the Green Hopper.
Q (X17)

Whichford

Norman Knight

CV36 5PE (2 miles E of A3400 at Long Compton, facing village green)

12-3 (not Mon), 6-11; 12-11 Fri & Sat; 12-6 Sun (01608) 684621 thenormanknight.co.uk

Hook Norton Hooky; Stratford upon Avon Stratford Gold, Stratford Mosaic, Malty Pig Bitter; 2 changing beers (sourced locally; often Stratford upon Avon) H

Stratford Upon Avon tap, with seven handpumps showcasing the brewery's fine ales alongside a locally sourced beer and local Grumpy Frog cider. It has two flagstone-floored rooms plus a restaurant serving excellent freshly prepared meals – seafood is a speciality. The beer garden overlooks the village green where classic cars gather on Thursday evenings in summer. Motorhomes are welcome and electric car charging sockets available, plus glamping pods. The pub hosts a monthly quiz night and regular live music. Local CAMRA Pub of the Year 2017. Q P

Case is Altered, Five Ways (Photo: Andrew Laycock)

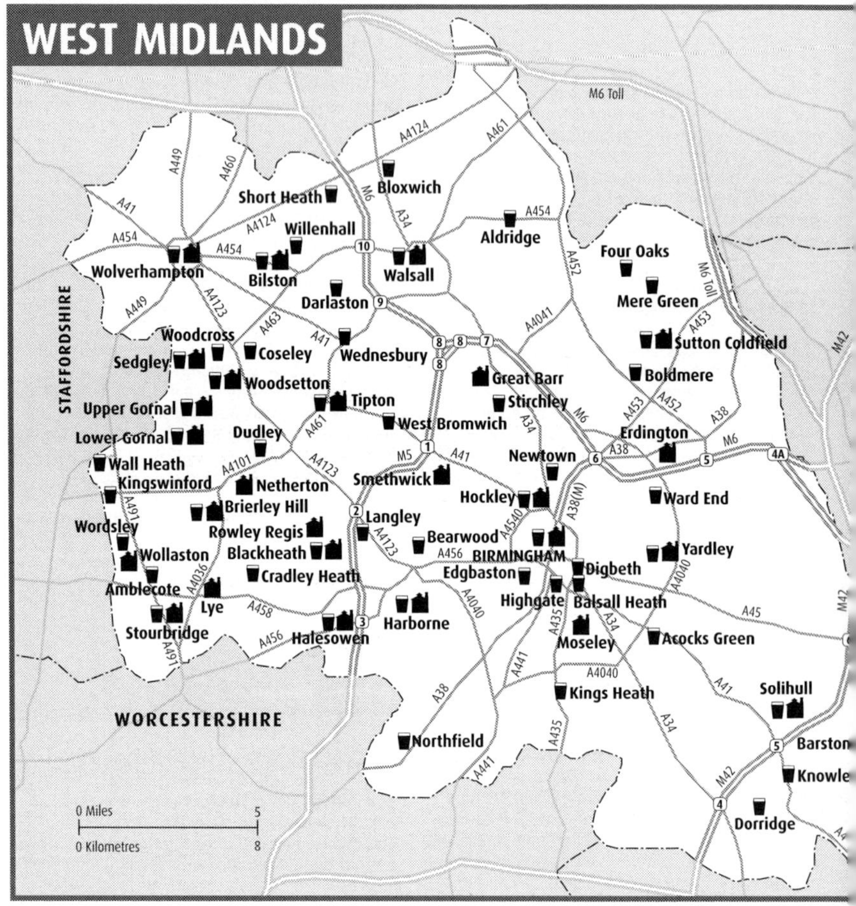

Aldridge

Turtle's Head

14 Croft Parade, WS9 8LY

closed Mon; 12-10 (10.30 Fri & Sat); 12-9 Sun

(01922) 325635 theturtleshead.co.uk

4 changing beers (sourced locally; often Backyard, Church End, Fixed Wheel)

Micropub with a warm welcome, opened in 2015, in the centre of Aldridge town. Four handpulls serve a range of ales from throughout the UK. No regular beers are sold, but the beer menu changes daily. Up to four real ciders are available, increasing to eight in the summer months. Food consists of various filled rolls as well as bar snacks. A selection of complimentary cheeses and pates is served up on Sundays. Dogs are very welcome.

Amblecote

Robin Hood

196 Collis Street, DY8 4EQ (on A4102 one-way street off Brettell Lane A461)

12 (4 Mon & Tue)-11; 12-midnight Fri & Sat

07436 793462

Bathams Best Bitter; Enville Ginger Beer; Holden's Golden Glow; Kelham Island Pale Rider; St Austell Proper Job; Wye Valley HPA; 4 changing beers (often Titanic)

Fine ales, quality food and a warm welcome – a fine traditional Black Country local. In 2015 the pub celebrated 160 years as a licenced house and it was local CAMRA Pub of the Year. The front rooms house a wonderful beer bottle collection including international and historic brews. The pub hosts occasional themed culinary nights. The LocAle scheme is emphasised, with many local beers always on sale. Q P

Barston

Bull's Head

Barston Lane, B92 0JU (on main street in village, opp church) SP2073378090

11-2.30, 5-11; 11-11 Fri & Sat; 12-11 Sun

(01675) 442830 thebullsheadbarston.co.uk

Adnams Southwold Bitter; Purity Mad Goose; Sharp's Doom Bar; 1 changing beer (sourced nationally)

This former coaching inn is a tranquil, unspoilt village local, always offering a friendly welcome. There are two comfortable bars with real fires and an intimate restaurant. Three regular ales are available, plus one changing guest. It offers a good-value standard menu and seasonal home-cooked specials. The beer garden is flanked by fields where the pub hosts the annual village fête

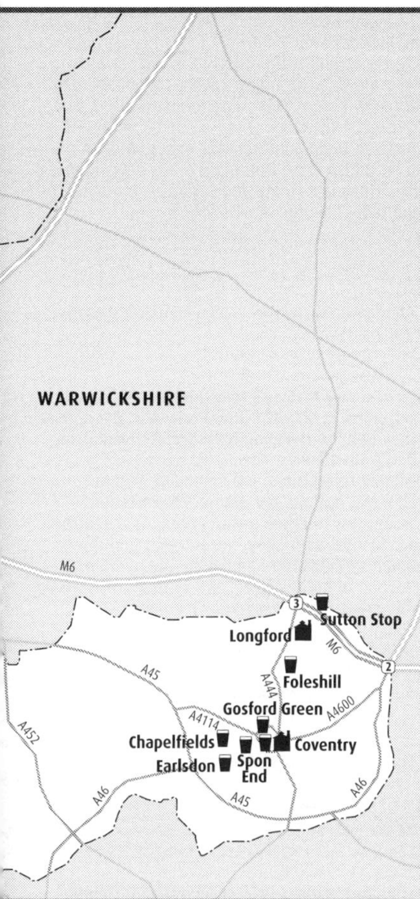

every August bank holiday. Local CAMRA Pub of the Year seven times and in this Guide for over 25 years. Q

Bearwood

Bear Tavern

500 Bearwood Road, B66 4BX

9am-11.30 (midnight Fri; 1am Sat); 10-11.30 Sun

(0121) 429 1184

Greene King IPA; 5 changing beers (sourced nationally; often Fixed Wheel, Purity, Titanic) H

Busy, open-plan, community pub around a central bar. Sports screens dominate throughout as live matches are often shown. Attentive staff serve an interesting range of nationally sourced real ales which are regularly advertised on Facebook. There is a large function room upstairs with a wooden floor. Affordable pub food is served throughout the week.

Bilston

Trumpet

58 High Street, WV14 0EP

12-4, 7.30-11.30 (01902) 493723

trumpetjazz.org.uk

Holden's Black Country Mild, Black Country Bitter, Golden Glow, Special H

Welcoming, one-room local with jazz, mainly traditional, featured seven nights per week and Sunday lunchtimes. Holden's award-winning ales and the music draw in customers from around the area. Music memorabilia of all styles and eras line the walls. A collection plate for the band is handed around when live music is being played. It is around a 10-minute walk from the bus and metro stations.

Birmingham: Acocks Green

Inn on the Green

2 Westley Road, B27 7UH

11-11 (midnight Fri); 10-midnight Sat & Sun

(0121) 708 0108

6 changing beers (sourced nationally; often Wye Valley) H

Run by a passionate landlord who is an active CAMRA member, with friendly and knowledgeable staff, this place has regular entertainment and shows live sports and live music on weekends. Excellent beer festivals are held four times a year. Four handpulls are in use during the week and six at weekends. The pub rarely has the same beers on twice, so it is a great place to find beers from new breweries and is well worth a visit. P

Birmingham: Balsall Heath

Old Moseley Arms

53 Tindal Street, B12 9QU (400yds off Moseley Rd)

REAL ALE BREWERIES

AJ's Walsall
Angel Halesowen
Backyard Walsall
Banks's Wolverhampton
Bathams Brierley Hill
Birmingham Birmingham
Black Country Lower Gornal
Blue Bear Smethwick
Brewhouse & Kitchen Sutton Coldfield
Burning Soul Birmingham: Hockley
Byatt's Coventry
Craddock's Stourbridge
Dhillon's Longford
Dig Birmingham (NEW)
Edmunds Birmingham
Fixed Wheel Blackheath
Fownes Upper Gornal
Froth Blowers Erdington
Green Duck Stourbridge
Holden's Woodsetton
Indian Great Barr
Moseley Moseley
Newbridge Bilston
Olde Swan Netherton
Ostlers Harborne (NEW)
Pig Iron Rowley Regis
Punchline Wolverhampton (NEW)
Red Moon Yardley (NEW)
Rock & Roll Birmingham: Hockley
Sadler's Lye
Sarah Hughes Sedgley
Silhill Solihull
Thousand Trades Birmingham (brewing suspended)
Toll End Tipton
Twisted Barrel Coventry
Two Towers Birmingham
Websters Wollaston

12-11 (midnight Fri & Sat) ☎ (0121) 440 1954
oldmoseleyarms.co.uk
Church End Goat's Milk; Enville Ale; Wye Valley HPA, Butty Bach; 1 changing beer (sourced nationally) Ⓗ
This is a traditional 19th-century pub; the left bar has an 80-inch screen for sport, the right bar has the jukebox. There is an upstairs room for functions, which has a pool table and hosts Sunday evening music; there are comfy sofas in the covered garden/smoking area. A superb tandoori menu is served weekday evenings and 1-10.45pm Sundays. There are regular beer festivals offering 16 ales and two ciders. Live music is upstairs every Sunday evening. (50)

Birmingham: City Centre

Gunmakers Arms

93 Bath Street, B4 6HG
12-midnight ☎ (0121) 236 8486 gunmakersarms.com
Two Towers Baskerville Bitter, Hockley Gold, Complete Muppetry, Chamberlain Pale Ale; 2 changing beers (often Two Towers) Ⓗ
This is the Two Towers Brewery tap, with the brewery next to the beer garden. The Grade II-listed pub is a small, traditional venue just a few minutes' walk from Snow Hill station and St Chad's metro. Six handpulls serve a range of Two Towers ales and occasional guest beers. The pub hosts a range of events from book readings to beer festivals. Traditional pub food, often incorporating Two Towers beers, is available noon-8pm.

Post Office Vaults

84 New Street, B2 4BA (entrances are on both New St and Pinfold St)
11-11 (midnight Fri & Sat); 12-11 Sun ☎ (0121) 643 7354
postofficevaults.co.uk
Hobsons Mild; house beer (by Kinver); 6 changing beers (sourced nationally) Ⓗ
Only a two-minute walk from the Stephenson Street entrance to New Street station and close to Victoria Square, this subterranean pub offers a range of eight traditional beers in excellent condition. At least 350 different bottled beers are available from all over the world, one of the largest ranges in the country. Serving 14 ciders and perries, the extremely knowledgeable staff will make your visit a pleasure. **Q**

Pure Craft Bar & Kitchen

30 Waterloo Street, B2 5TJ (5 mins from New St and Snow Hill stations)
11-11 (midnight Fri & Sat); 12-10 Sun ☎ (0121) 237 5666
purecraftbars.com
Purity Bunny Hop, Pure Gold, Mad Goose; 4 changing beers (sourced nationally; often Kirkstall, Rooster's, Tiny Rebel) Ⓗ
This bar was the first in the chain to open and is set in a traditional building with an industrial interior on Waterloo Street, in the centre of the business district. There are six cask and 16 craft beer lines plus a selection of 60 bottled craft beers. Gourmet food is served; all food is made with beer and the menu has been matched to the beers available (meals can be booked online). The walls are adorned with modern art.

Victoria

48 John Bright Street, B1 1BN
12-midnight (2am Fri & Sat) ☎ (0121) 633 9439
thevictoriabirmingham.co.uk
8 changing beers Ⓗ
The locally based Bitters n' Twisted chain has resurrected this 19th-century theatre bar next to the stage door of the Alexandra Theatre. It gets very busy before theatre performances and gigs at the nearby O2 Arena. Food is served with an American Deep South flavour and a twist on the classic British roast. Quiz night is Tuesday and music plays Thursday, Friday and Saturday. The pub is reportedly haunted.

Wellington

37 Bennetts Hill, B2 5SN (5 mins from New St and Snow Hill stations)
10-midnight ☎ (0121) 200 3115
thewellingtonrealale.co.uk
Black Country Bradley's Finest Golden, Pig on the Wall, Fireside; Oakham Citra; Purity Mad Goose; Wye Valley HPA; 10 changing beers (sourced nationally; often Froth Blowers, Titanic) Ⓗ
Recently refurbished and extended, with an additional upstairs bar and roof terrace beer garden, this multiple award winner is a veritable beer festival every day. Sixteen ales and three traditional ciders on handpump, and a wide selection of bottled beers and whiskies, are served to a varied clientele by knowledgeable staff. Regular quizzes, cheese nights and darts competitions are held. No food is served but you are welcome to bring your own; plates, cutlery and condiments are provided. **Q**

Birmingham: Digbeth

Spotted Dog

104 Warwick Street, B12 0NH
6-11; 3-1am Fri; 12-1am Sat; 12-midnight Sun
☎ (0121) 772 3822 spotteddog.co.uk
Castle Rock Harvest Pale; Holden's Black Country Mild; 2 changing beers (sourced nationally) Ⓗ
This is a traditional multi-roomed pub with an Irish feel. It is off the beaten track but well worth a trip. Excellent Holden's Mild is served at a competitive price. It has a large covered garden/smoking area with heaters and a barbecue area. Live traditional Irish music is staged Mondays, jazz nights on Tuesdays and blues nights on Thursdays. There is a mixture of sports on the large screen, especially rugby. Excellent Scotch eggs are served, including vegetarian and gluten-free versions.

Woodman ★

New Canal Street, B5 5LG (opp old Curzon St by Millennium Point)
11-11 (midnight Fri); closed Sun ☎ (0121) 643 4960
Castle Rock Black Gold, Harvest Pale; 6 changing beers (sourced nationally) Ⓗ
This environmentally friendly pub, recently refurbished, is Grade II-listed and on CAMRA's National Inventory of Historic Pub Interiors. There is a red-bricked tile and terracotta exterior, with an L-shaped bar inside, tiled above a wooden dado. A tiled lobby on Albert Street leads to an attractive small drinking area, with a hatch to the servery; there is also a real fire. The third room, quite plain, on the left now makes for a pleasant dividing area. Good food is served daily and quiz night is every Wednesday. **Q**

Birmingham: Edgbaston

Physician

Harborne Road, B15 3DH

10-11; 10-10.30 Sun (0121) 272 5900

Brunning & Price Original; Purity Mad Goose; Timothy Taylor Landlord; 3 changing beers (sourced regionally)

Large, historic, former BMI building used to house the vast Sampson Gangee Library for the History of Medicine, and recently converted into a pub. It is an upmarket establishment with several drinking and dining areas. A range of ales is available, often including a lot of local brews, and the pub is proud of its food, wine and spirits offering as well.

Birmingham: Harborne

Hop Garden

19 Metchley Lane, B17 0HT (100yds from High St, at back of M&S)

3-11 (midnight Fri); 12-midnight Sat; 12-11 Sun

07496 389166 hopgardenpub.co.uk

5 changing beers (sourced nationally)

Formerly called the Sportsman and recently reopened, it now serves five real ales from small and local breweries, seven craft beers and five craft ciders as well as real cider. It also has an interesting selection of bottled beers. The decor is original and eclectic. There is a large garden which will be growing hops in the future, hence the name. There will also be an entrance through the garden.

White Horse

2 York Street, B17 0HG

11 (12 Mon)-11.30; 11-12.30am Fri & Sat; 12-11.30 Sun

(0121) 427 8004 whitehorseharborne.com

Greene King Abbot; 9 changing beers (sourced nationally; often Bathams, Holden's, Three Tuns)

A much-improved and extended free house, just off the busy High Street. It has an island bar with a front snug and a rear heated area. There is a great emphasis on real ale, with an electronic beer board linked to its website. Regular live music nights are held on Fridays and Saturdays and there is a monthly open mic night on the last Wednesday. A basic food menu is served and a quiz night is held every Tuesday.

Birmingham: Highgate

Lamp Tavern

157 Barford Street, B5 6AH (500yds from A441 Pershore Rd near bottom of Hurst St)

1-11 (9 Mon & Wed); 1-7 Sun (0121) 688 1220

Hobsons Mild; 4 changing beers (sourced nationally; often Stanway)

This hidden gem of a pub, close to Digbeth and the Arcadian areas, has two excellent regular real ales – Hobson's Mild and one from the Stanway range – plus three wonderful changing guests (sometimes local). It has been run by the friendly Eddie Fitzpatrick for 24 years now. The pub has a homely feel; there is a folk club on Friday evenings and a jazz club on some Tuesday evenings. It has roadside parking only, but with good local bus routes nearby. Q

Birmingham: Hockley

1000 Trades

16 Frederick Street, B1 3HE

4-11 (midnight Thu & Fri); 12-midnight Sat; 12-10 Sun

(0121) 233 6291 1000trades.org.uk

4 changing beers (sourced nationally; often Titanic)

This delightful addition to the Jewellery Quarter has distinctive bare boards and brickwork, with full-width doors opening on to the pavement, giving this independent craft beer bar a distinctive atmosphere. There are four handpumps serving a changing range of beers, usually with at least one from a local micro. The cask offering is supported with five KeyKeg taps and an interesting range of bottled beers. The bar hosts kitchen residencies, meaning the food is characterised by evolving variety, often street food.

Burning Soul Brewery

Unit 1, Mott Street Industrial Estate, B19 3HE

closed Mon-Thu; 4-8 Fri; 1-8 Sat; closed Sun

(0121) 439 7253 burningsoulbrewing.com

Changing beers

There is an ever-changing list of smaller experimental pilot brews at this taproom, so they can capture at first-hand what people think of their beer; those liked most are brewed again and sold outside of the brewery. There is a pool table and tours are available on request. P

Jewellers Arms

23 Hockley Street, B18 6BW

10.30-11 (0121) 236 4402

Black Country Pig on the Wall, Fireside; 8 changing beers (often Black Country)

Refurbished and reopened by Black Country Ales in 2017, the pub has 10 real ales and two ciders and gets busy in the evenings. Food is limited to cobs. There is no separate bar as the pub is now all open plan. Electronic equipment is limited to a fruit machine. Parking is available at the side of the pub. There is a function room upstairs and a real fire at one end of the pub, lit daily in winter.

Red Lion

95 Warstone Lane, B18 6NG

10-midnight (2am Fri & Sat) (0121) 233 9144

theredlionbirmingham.com

Wye Valley Butty Bach; 3 changing beers (sourced nationally; often Bathams)

Traditional, two-roomed pub that is both rich in local heritage and modern art. There is a lively front bar and a cosy back lounge. A good-sized club room is upstairs and there is a sheltered patio and smoking area to the rear. An excellent extensive food menu is served all day, particularly at the Cow Club on Mondays. It has three changing guest beers and two changing ciders. There is a comedy night every third Monday and large screens show sporting events.

Rock & Roll Brewhouse

Unit 2, 60 Regent Place, B3 1UG

5-9 Fri; 1-7 Sat; closed Sun-Thu 07969 759649

Rock & Roll Brew Springsteen, Thirst Aid Kit; 1 changing beer (often Rock & Roll)

A small, quirky brewery taproom, bedecked with music memorabilia. There are usually three vegan-friendly ales available, always including a dark ale to start with. It is open every Friday evening and Saturday afternoon. The bar staff and their knowledge of beer is excellent; their other shared love is music and there is a playlist of what you are hearing on the wall. Hogan's cider is also available.

Rose Villa Tavern ★ ✓

172 Warstone Lane, B18 6JW

12-midnight (1am Fri & Sun); 11-1am Sat & Sun

(0121) 236 7910 therosevillatavern.co.uk

Sharp's Doom Bar; 4 changing beers H

Prominent red-bricked pub, now owned by the Bitters n' Twisted chain who also run the Victoria in Birmingham and the New Inn in Harborne. The Grade II-listed building is on CAMRA's National Inventory of Historic Pub Interiors. Inside there is beautiful tiling and stained-glass windows. It has five handpumps, serving a changing range of beers, and over a hundred different vodkas and an interesting cocktail menu. There are various forms of entertainment (quizzes, DJs) throughout the week.

Birmingham: Kings Heath

Kings Heath Cricket & Sports Club ✓

Charlton House, 247 Alcester Road South, B14 6DT

12-midnight (0121) 444 1913

kingsheathsportsclub.com

Wye Valley HPA, Butty Bach; 2 changing beers (sourced nationally) H

Welcoming sports club where CAMRA members are permitted entry on production of a membership card (maximum 10 visits per year). The club has two rooms; the comfortable lounge for relaxed drinking and the large room for watching sporting events on big screens and also housing two full-size snooker tables. The beer range always includes two rotating guest ales. Varying social events are held throughout the year, including live music. Q P

Birmingham: Newtown

Bartons Arms ★ ✓

144 High Street, B6 4UP

12-11; 12-10.30 Sun (0121) 333 5988

Oakham JHB, Inferno, Citra, Bishops Farewell; 2 changing beers (sourced nationally; often Oakham) H

A stunning red-bricked pub run by Oakham Brewery from Peterborough. The 1901 interior is Grade II*-listed and on CAMRA's National Inventory of Historic Pub Interiors. There are ornate Minton tiles throughout, including a central tiled staircase, original stained-glass windows and snob screens on the bar. Superb Thai food is served in the lounge. A range of Oakham Ales is available, with usually one guest and a cider. Quiz nights are on Mondays and regular music and beer festivals are held. P

Birmingham: Northfield

Black Horse ★ L ✓

Bristol Road South, B31 2QT (opp Sainbury's)

8am (1am Fri & Sat); 8am-midnight Sun

(0121) 477 1800

Greene King Abbot; Ruddles Best Bitter; Sharp's Doom Bar; changing beers (sourced nationally; often Adnams, Fuller's, Purity) H

Large inter-war mock-Tudor roadhouse, offering the only extensive real ale choice in this part of the city. It has transformed from being an undesirable local into a popular pub, serving consistently good-quality beer. Unusually for Wetherspoon's, this pub has a multi-room layout and bars on two levels. It still retains the original baronial hall entrance, but the bar has been tastefully refurbished with an etched-glass entrance door. There is a bowling green with original outbuildings to the rear. Q P

Birmingham: Stirchley

Wildcat Tap

1466 Pershore Road, B30 2NT

closed Mon & Tue; 5-11; 2-9 Sat; 2-6 Sun

stirchleywildcat.co.uk

3 changing beers (sourced nationally) G

A small independent pub, it offers three cask beers served via gravity dispense and two keg beers at most times, complemented by a selection of bottled craft beers, gin, whisky and soft drinks. If you are coming far for a drink, please check the pub is open beforehand by dropping an email to liam@stirchleywildcat.co.uk.

Birmingham: Ward End

Hornet

991 Alum Rock Road, B8 2LY

8am-11 (0121) 789 5920

Greene King IPA, Abbot; Sharp's Doom Bar; 2 changing beers H

Herbert Austin's famous motor works stood near this Wetherspoon pub, which bears the name of his famous Wolseley Hornet model, produced from 1930 until the mid-1970s. The usual selection of house beers and lagers is found and food is the standard Wetherspoon menu. It is somewhat smaller than the average Wetherspoon house and quite dimly lit. There are a few seats out front and it has a rear patio area.

Birmingham: Yardley

Sheldon Marlborough Cricket Club

Foliot Fields, B25 8RF

7-11; closed Wed; 3-11 Sat; 1-11 Sun (0121) 784 9191

smcc.co.uk

2 changing beers H

Here you will find a spacious family and pet-friendly environment, focused on the development and playing of cricket, with five senior teams and three junior teams playing throughout the week. The club has a relaxed atmosphere and runs events for fundraising including quiz nights, occasional beer festivals and fun days, which are always well worth attending. P (11)

Blackheath

Britannia ✓

124 Halesowen Street, B65 0ES

8am-midnight (1am Fri & Sat) (0121) 559 0010

Exmoor Gold; Greene King Abbot; Sharp's Doom Bar; 7 changing beers (sourced nationally; often Backyard, Kinver Brewery, Slater's) H

Bustling JD Wetherspoon outlet frequented by old and young alike. The pub is an open-plan, L-shaped design and was previously called the Traveller's Rest. Pictures placed throughout the pub depict local monuments and historic characters. Food is served all day, every day, and the bar sports 10 handpumps serving up to seven guest beers, often including Kinver and Backyard. The garden at the rear can be a peaceful retreat for a quiet drink.

Bloxwich

Wheatsheaf

35 Field Road, WS3 3JL

11-midnight ☎ (01922) 279799

Banks's Mild, Amber Ale; Wainwright; 3 changing beers (sourced locally; often AJ's, Sadler's) Ⓗ

Dating back to the 16th century, the Wheatsheaf is a five-minute walk from the town centre. The friendly staff aim to make visitors feel welcome as soon as they walk through the door. It has traditional pub games, with darts, dominoes, crib and pool teams based here. Friday and Saturday evenings feature live music. Food is limited to cobs. There is a TV showing terrestrial channels only.

Boldmere

Bishop Vesey

63 Boldmere Road, B73 5UY

8am-11 (midnight Fri & Sat) ☎ (0121) 355 5077

Greene King Abbot; Oakham Citra; Ruddles Best Bitter; Sharp's Doom Bar; 12 changing beers Ⓗ

Popular Wetherspoon which now has 18 consecutive years in the Guide. Since the last edition it has added more handpulls and a spacious rooftop garden. Up to 12 interesting guest beers are offered, many from local microbreweries, plus one changing real cider; little wonder that it is a frequent local CAMRA Pub of the Year. Home to a thriving darts team.

Brierley Hill

Black Horse

52 Delph Road, Delph, DY5 2TP

3 (12 Thu)-11; 12-midnight Fri & Sat; 12-11 Sun

☎ (01384) 673361

Enville Ale; Wye Valley Butty Bach, HPA Ⓗ

Following a refurbishment in 2016, the Black Horse offers a modern, stylish drinking environment. There is a mixture of high and low seating and a rectangular pillar in the heart of the pub, which is suitable for the standing drinker. There are numerous high definition flatscreen TVs showing sports fixtures on Sky and BT. At the rear of the pub there is a cosy, heated, sheltered extension with another TV. Here you will find the kitchen where fresh pizzas are prepared. P (287)

Vine

10 Delph Road, DY5 2TN

12-11; 12-10.30 Sun ☎ (01384) 78293

Bathams Mild Ale, Best Bitter Ⓗ

Unspoilt brewery tap with an ornately decorated façade proclaiming the Shakespearian quotation: 'Blessing of your heart, you brew good ale.' An elongated pub with a labyrinthine feel, the front bar is staunchly traditional, while the larger rear room has its own servery and dartboard. The homely lounge was partly converted from former brewery offices. Black Country lunches such as faggots and home-made pies are served weekdays, with generously filled rolls and pork pies at other times. Local CAMRA Pub of the Year 2016. Q P (X96)

Coseley

Old Chainyard

63 Castle Street, WV14 9DW

12-11 (11.30 Fri & Sat)

2 changing beers (sourced regionally; often Church End, Kinver, Salopian) Ⓗ

Lively single-roomed community pub serving two rotating cask beers, at least one of which is always from Salopian Brewery. It is a five-minute walk from Coseley train station and a three-minute walk from the A4123 – both of which offer direct links to Birmingham and Wolverhampton. The handpulls not in use will advertise beers that are currently resting in the cellar and coming soon. The manageress always sources beers that her regular customers approve of. P

Coventry: Chapelfields

Nursery Tavern

38-39 Lord Street, CV5 8DA (1 mile W of city centre, off Allesley Old Rd)

12-11.30 (midnight Fri & Sat); 12-11 Sun

☎ (024) 7667 4530

Fuller's London Pride; Otter Bitter; 4 changing beers (sourced nationally) Ⓗ

Opened as the Nursery Gardens in 1852, this mid-terrace community pub in the watchmaking quarter has been in the same hands for over 25 years. Conversation dominates in the two front rooms, which are served by a central bar. The back room is used for dining on Sunday lunchtimes, and hosts local societies, charity events and music nights. Beer festivals are held in the garden every June and December. Q

Coventry: City Centre

Earl of Mercia

18 High Street, CV1 5RE

8am-midnight (1am Fri & Sat) ☎ (024) 7643 3990

Greene King Abbot; Ruddles Best Bitter; Sharp's Doom Bar; 5 changing beers (sourced nationally) Ⓗ

Named after Leofric, Earl of Mercia, this well-established and bustling Wetherspoon is a conversion of a former bank building. Its location opposite the Council House and near the cathedral quarter ensures it attracts a good combination of workers, shoppers and families during the day and early evening. There is seating in the ground-floor bar area, mezzanine and pavement patio. It gets busy on Friday and Saturday nights with a mixed crowd. (8,9)

Gatehouse Tavern

44-46 Hill Street, CV1 4AN (close to Belgrade Theatre and Spon St, near jct 8 of ring road)

10-11; 12-11 Sun ☎ (024) 7663 0140

gatehousetavern.com

Draught Bass; Fuller's London Pride; 4 changing beers (sourced locally; often Byatt's, Church End, Twisted Barrel) Ⓗ

Built on the site of the former Leigh Mills Weaving Company gatehouse by the landlord, this is a longstanding entry in the Guide. With stained-glass windows portraying all Six Nations rugby teams, it is a very sports-oriented pub, with up to four screens showing major events. Uniquely, the pub has the only grassed beer garden within the city centre. Home-cooked food is offered, including breakfast from 10am. No food is provided on Saturday evenings or Sundays.

Golden Cross

8 Hay Lane, CV1 5RF

11-11 (midnight Fri; 1am Sat); 12-7 Sun
(024) 7655 1855 thegoldencrosscoventry.co.uk

House beer (by Caledonian); 3 changing beers (sourced nationally; often Byatt's, Warwickshire) H

A lucky survivor of the Blitz, this is one of Coventry's finest medieval buildings. Built in 1583, it was established as a pub around 1661 and recently sympathetically refurbished. It has a comfortable lounge downstairs and a more formal dining space upstairs at busy times. An excellent menu is served every day of the week, supplemented by a snack menu 12-3pm Monday to Friday. Live bands play upstairs every Saturday from 9pm, with open mic downstairs on Tuesdays from 8pm.

Old Windmill

22-23 Spon Street, CV1 3BA (in medieval Spon St, behind IKEA)

12 (4 Mon)-11.30 (024) 7625 1717

Morland Old Speckled Hen; Theakston Old Peculier; Timothy Taylor Landlord; 4 changing beers (sourced locally) H

An ancient building in this historic street, and one of the claimants to being the oldest pub in Coventry. It comprises several small rooms, the rearmost housing an old brewhouse from Victorian times, complete with a brick brewing kettle. A good selection of beers is available along with locally produced pork pies which are gaining an excellent reputation. The pub is still locally known as Ma Brown's in honour of an early 20th-century landlady.

Town Crier

Corporation Street, CV1 1PB (next to IKEA)

11-11 (1am Thu & Fri); 10-1am Sat; 11.30-6 Sun
(024) 7663 2317 towncriercoventry.co.uk

Jennings Sneck Lifter; Marston's Saddle Tank; 2 changing beers (sourced nationally; often Marston's) H

A 1980s pub built to a traditional style by Wolverhampton and Dudley Brewery, now part of the Marston's empire. It has one bar serving a large single room. In the busy heart of the city, it has a varied clientele, being popular with shoppers and workers alike. Guest beers are imaginatively sourced from the Marston's stable. There is often live music on Saturday evenings and a large screen is used occasionally for big sporting events.

Town Wall Tavern

Bond Street, CV1 4AH

12 (4 Mon)-11; 12-midnight Fri & Sat; 12-10 Sun
(024) 7622 0963

Adnams Southwold Bitter; Brains Rev James; Caledonian Deuchars IPA; Draught Bass; Theakston Old Peculier; 3 changing beers (sourced nationally; often Courage, Purity, Robinsons) H

One of the few remaining traditional locals in the city centre. Built around 1816, it is tucked away behind the Belgrade Theatre and now surrounded by new buildings. Frequented by actors, it can become busy immediately before and after performances. The bar and lounge are supplemented by the Donkey Box, a small snug at the front just big enough to hold a donkey. There is an imaginative locally sourced food offering (not available Mondays). No children.

Coventry: Earlsdon

City Arms

1 Earlsdon Street, CV5 6EP (on roundabout at centre of Earlsdon)

8am-midnight (1am Fri & Sat) (024) 7671 8170

Greene King Abbot; Ruddles Best Bitter; Sharp's Doom Bar; 7 changing beers (sourced nationally; often Byatt's, Grainstore, Purity) H

Prominent Wetherspoon pub in the centre of Earlsdon and an enthusiastic supporter of real ale. It has a large open-plan main room, a quieter smaller room at the rear and a part-covered outdoor area. The pub has a strong local following, but also attracts visitors from further afield due to its proximity to frequent bus services between the city centre and Warwick University. Additional outside seating is provided at the front of the pub. (5,11)

Coventry: Foleshill

Byatt's Brewhouse Bar

Unit 7-8, Lythalls Lane Industrial Estate, Lythalls Lane, CV6 6FL

4-9 Fri; 12-9 Sat; closed Sun-Thu (024) 7663 7996
byattsbrewery.co.uk

6 changing beers (sourced locally; often Byatt's) H

This bar opened in 2016 and is to the front of the brewery in a small industrial estate. The taproom has a ground-floor bar area and a mezzanine with beer-themed furniture. Handpumps dispense four to six changing beers from Byatt's range and one cider. Byatt's vegan-friendly, bottle-conditioned beers are also available, along with carryout containers. Opening hours are limited, but the bar also opens some Sundays prior to Wasps home fixtures at the nearby Ricoh Arena. P

Coventry: Gosford Green

Twisted Barrel Brewery & Tap House

Fargo Village, Far Gosford Street, CV1 5ED

closed Mon & Tue; 2-10 Wed & Thu; 12-midnight Fri & Sat; 12-10 Sun (024) 7610 1701 twistedbarrelale.co.uk

Twisted Barrel Beast of a Midlands Mild, God's Twisted Sister, Inspired, Sine Qua Non, Call of Korriban P**; 5 changing beers (often Twisted Barrel)** H/P

An expanded brewery and taphouse within the popular Fargo Village just outside the city centre. There are two handpumps on the bar, however KeyKegs are mostly used to hold the vast range of real ale brewed on the premises, which is dispensed via a wall of keg fonts. All of the brewery's beers are unfiltered and suitable for vegans. Visit the website for details of additional opening hours and special events. P

Coventry: Spon End

Broomfield Tavern

14-16 Broomfield Place, CV5 6GY (adjacent to rugby ground but hidden from main road)

4-midnight; 12-1am Fri & Sat; 12-midnight Sun
(024) 7663 0969

11 changing beers (sourced locally; often Church End, Froth Blowers, Hobsons) H

Now an established entry in the Guide, this is a local CAMRA Pub of the Year and Cider Pub of the Year 2018. The small bar is virtually filled with

handpumps dispensing up to 11 real ales. A further 15 ciders and perries are served on gravity. The pub has an L-shaped bar area and a small patio at the front. It also has a separate room used for local group meetings and live music at weekends.
Q

Coventry: Sutton Stop

Greyhound Inn

Sutton Stop, Hawkesbury Junction, CV6 6DF (off Grange Rd at jct of Coventry & Oxford canals)
11-11; 12-10.30 Sun ☎ (024) 7636 3046
Draught Bass; Greene King Abbot; 3 changing beers (sourced nationally; often Brains, Holden's, Kelham Island)
A canalside hostelry popular with locals and visitors alike. It is a four-times winner of the Godiva Award for best pub in Coventry and Warwickshire, and has been local CAMRA Pub of the Year several times. The venue dates from the 1830s and the front terrace overlooks a bustling canal junction. An extensive menu of freshly cooked food is offered, and beer festivals are held twice yearly. The Whippet Bar in the garden is open at weekends in the summer. Q P

Cradley Heath

Plough & Harrow

82 Corngreaves Road, B64 7BT
11-11 ☎ (01299) 638351
Banks's Mild; Ludlow Gold; Wye Valley HPA, Butty Bach; 2 changing beers (sourced nationally; often Abbeydale, Bristol Beer Factory, Kelham Island)
Traditional community pub, tastefully modernised to provide a pleasant, comfortable hostelry in the heart of the Black Country. Children are allowed until 9pm and dogs are welcome but must remain on a lead. Baguettes and cobs are available. Sports TV is a background feature and does not detract from an enjoyable drinking environment. The pub serves four regular beers and two changing beers (both above 5% ABV) that are all keenly priced. CAMRA branch Community Pub of the Year 2018.
QP(243)

Darlaston

Green Dragon

55 Church Street, WS10 8DY
12-11 (11.30 Fri); 11-midnight Sat ☎ 07707 101276
3 changing beers (sourced locally; often Backyard, Salopian)
Two-roomed pub just out of the town centre which has a local atmosphere, with old photos of the town and local pubs in the area. The staff are welcoming to all, with four changing beers on tap. It has a patio area at the back with a covered smoking shelter. There is live entertainment on Friday and Saturday night, with darts played during the week. (34)

Dorridge

Knowle & Dorridge Cricket Club

Station Road, B93 8ET (corner of Station Rd and Grove Rd)
5.30-10.30 (11 Fri); 12-11 Sat; 12-10.30 Sun
☎ (01564) 774338 knowleanddorridgecc.co.uk
3 changing beers (sourced nationally)
This established cricket club is set in an upmarket residential area. Visitors are welcome to try the varied range of up to three cask-conditioned ales, always in excellent condition and often from interesting breweries. There are no entry restrictions, but club members are able to purchase drinks at a reduced price. There is outside seating to watch top-class cricket in the Birmingham league. Bar snacks and filled rolls are usually available. CAMRA branch Club of the Year two years in succession. P(S2,S3)

Dudley

Malt Shovel

46 Tower Street, DY1 1NB (off Broadway, A459, opp Dudley College Evolve campus)
12-10.30 (midnight Fri & Sat) ☎ (01384) 252735
5 changing beers (sourced nationally; often Enville, Fixed Wheel, Oakham)
A former back-street Banks's pub which reopened in 2017 following an extensive but sympathetic refurbishment. Now a free house, this iconic town-centre boozer offers an eclectic range of both local and national cask and keg products in a stylish setting. The real ales include a mixture of local breweries (such as Fixed Wheel and Enville) plus national breweries (such as Oakham and Abbeydale). It does traditional Black Country pub snacks such as cobs, pork pies and scratchings. Live music plays fortnightly. P(1,126)

Four Oaks

Butlers Arms

444 Lichfield Road, B74 4BL
12-11 (midnight Fri & Sat); 12-10.30 Sun
☎ (0121) 308 0765 butlersarms.co.uk
4 changing beers
This attractive, family-run, suburban pub is geared towards dining, though drinkers are always made welcome. The interior decor is a colourful and striking mix of styles, with lamps, mirrors and curiosities, plus attractive leaded windows. The four guest ales vary but usually feature a Caledonian beer plus Greene King Abbot. The chalkboard menu is full of fish specials, with meat and vegetarian alternatives. A small beer terrace is to the front. Car parking charges apply.
QP

Crown

66 Walsall Road, B74 4RA
10-11 (midnight Thu-Sat) ☎ (0121) 323 2715
Marston's Pedigree; house beer (by Black Sheep); 6 changing beers
Attractive Ember Inn featuring tall chimneys and curvaceous gable ends at the two entrances. The pleasant seating area surrounding the pub has a variety of shrubs plus heated patio areas, while the comfortable interior features a log fire to the rear and several flaming gas fires. Good food is offered until 10pm. All cask ales are sold at a special price on Mondays, and regular Meet the Brewer nights are hosted. Car parking charges are refundable with purchases over £5. P(6)

Halesowen

Crafty Pint H'ales'owen

8 Wassell Road, B63 4JU

closed Mon; 4.30-10 Tue & Wed; 1-10 Thu; 1-11 Fri & Sat; 1-8 Sun ☎ 07823 880240

Wye Valley Butty Bach; 5 changing beers (often Fixed Wheel, Oakham, Salopian) H

This micropub, now occupying the adjacent building as well, is run by Andy, a local resident. He offers traditional ale, cider, wines and beverages plus pork pies in a small pub environment. No children are allowed after 7.30pm. Coffee is generally available into the evening during the week, along with crusty cobs and sausage rolls. Last orders on Sunday are 7.40pm. **QP**

Fixed Wheel Brewery Tap

Unit 9, Long Lane Trading Estate, Long Lane, Blackheath, B62 9LD

closed Sun-Thu; 4-10 Fri; 11-10 Sat ☎ 07766 162794
fixedwheelbrewery.co.uk

4 changing beers (sourced locally; often Fixed Wheel) H

A traditional taproom within the brewery and right next to the brewery kit, with a vibrant community atmosphere, where all people are friends of the brewery – you will soon be welcomed into the community. In addition to four cask beers, there are usually 12 KeyKegs and four rotating guest ciders on offer, together with bottle-conditioned beers brewed and bottled on site.
QP(241,140)

Swan

282 Long Lane, B62 9JY

12-midnight ☎ (0121) 559 5207

Black Country Bradley's Finest Golden, Pig on the Wall, Fireside; 8 changing beers H

Former local CAMRA Pub of the Year, this popular, comfortable pub was saved from the bulldozers in 2014 by local campaigners and Black Country Ales. The central bar serves two main drinking areas. Eleven ales and six real ciders are sold as well as a fine selection of gins. Regular beer festivals are held. A staircase leads to the toilets and gives access to the garden and smoking area to the rear. Parking is limited but there is adequate street parking nearby. **QP**(241,140)

Waggon & Horses

21 Stourbridge Road, B63 3TU (on main A458, ½ mile from bus station)

12-11 (11.30 Fri & Sat); 12-10.30 Sun ☎ (0121) 585 9699

Black Country Bradley's Finest Golden, Pig on the Wall, Fireside; 12 changing beers (sourced nationally) H

Former local CAMRA Pub of the Year, the Waggon dates from the 1850s and was recently refurbished by Black Country Ales, retaining many of its historical features. One long bar serves three main drinking areas. The main bar is very narrow, with a famous sloping floor. Fifteen handpulls serve three regular ales and 12 guests, and three real ciders are also available as well as cobs and snacks. There is no car park but there is adequate street parking nearby. **Q**(9)

Kingswinford

Cottage

534 High Street, DY6 8AW

12-11 (midnight Fri & Sat); 12-10.30 Sun
☎ (01384) 287133

Enville Ale; St Austell Tribute; 2 changing beers (sourced nationally; often Exmoor, St Austell, Wye Valley) H

Cosy former Scottish & Newcastle pub set on two levels. A carvery is available every day which also supplies the meat for delicious sandwiches and cobs. The layout is L-shaped and diners and drinkers intermingle throughout this spacious pub. Guest beers are always pale and sessionable. The frontage would not look out of place on a postcard and the interior is homely and inviting.
QP(205,255)

Knowle

Ale Rooms

1592 High Street, B93 0LF

12-11 ☎ (01564) 400040 alerooms.co.uk

7 changing beers (sourced nationally; often Church End, Silhill) H

A micropub in a converted shop (formerly a funeral director's) on the High Street, a welcome addition to the Knowle pub scene. It stocks at least one real ale from the local Silhill brewery, along with one from Church End and guests, plus real cider, and also offers wines and spirits, including speciality gins. Pieminister pies are available throughout opening times until 10pm, and there is free Wi-Fi. Local CAMRA Pub of the Year 2018.
(S3)

Langley

Old Dispensary

Causeway Green Road, B68 8LS (turn right off Wolverhampton Rd A4123 if heading S towards Harborne)

4-10 Mon-Wed; 11.30-11 Thu & Fri; 12-11 Sat; 1-10 Sun

Fownes Old Dispensary Ale; Wye Valley Butty Bach; 3 changing beers (sourced nationally; often Backyard, Burning Soul, Salopian) H

CAMRA branch Cider Pub of the Year 2018. Formerly the Oldbury Pharmacy, this one-time drugstore opened its doors in 2017 and is now a thriving free house serving five real ales and eight real ciders. It opens at 9am Monday to Friday for the sale of hot drinks, and is licensed to serve alcohol from 11.30am. Any deviation from advertised opening hours is displayed on Facebook. Scotch eggs and pork pies are available.
Q(49)

Lower Gornal

Chapel House

Ruiton Street, DY3 2EG

3 (12 Sat)-11; 11-10.30 Sun ☎ 07599 809579

Holden's Black Country Bitter, Golden Glow, Special; 1 changing beer (sourced locally; often Holden's) H

Typical Holden's pub, but smaller in size when compared to the rest of the estate. The façade has been stripped back to expose the original sandstone tiles, which is a wonderful sight. Inside, there is a real fire and fixed seating in an L-shape around the bar. Cobs are available. There is regular live music as advertised on the Facebook page.
(257)

Old Bull's Head

1 Redhall Road, DY3 2NU (at jct with Temple St, B4175)

12-11 (midnight Fri & Sat) ☎ (01384) 231616

Black Country Bradley's Finest Golden, Pig on the Wall, Fireside; 5 changing beers (often Downton, Loddon, Salopian) H

A late-Victorian pub with two separate rooms. The lounge is often hired for private functions, with in-house catering available. The Black Country Ales Brewery is at the rear. Large crusty cobs are served daily. It is a five-minute uphill walk from Gornal Wood bus station, where the number 27 and 257 buses stop. The 27 bus also stops outside going downhill (towards the bus station).
❀♣●P🚌(27,257)🐾📶

Red Cow

84 Grosvenor Road, DY3 2PR
4-midnight; 12-midnight Sat & Sun ☎ 07943 189351
Abbeydale Absolution; 8 changing beers (sourced nationally; often Holden's, Thornbridge, Wye Valley) Ⓗ
An early 19th-century hostelry in a cul-de-sac, which is part of Grosvenor Road. This thriving community pub supports several pub games teams. To the left is a large bar with a dartboard. The cosy lounge to the right is partly divided by a chimney with a wood-burning stove. A large garden is at the rear. The varying real ales are sourced both locally and nationally. It is a five-minute walk from the bus stop in Corncrake Road.
❀♣P🚌(257)🐾

Mere Green

Mare Pool ✔

297 Lichfield Road, B74 2UG (behind shops on E side of Lichfield Rd)
8am-midnight (1am Fri & Sat) ☎ (0121) 323 1070
Greene King Abbot; Ruddles Best Bitter; Sharp's Doom Bar; 5 changing beers Ⓗ
Suburban Wetherspoon whose name refers to one of the many pools which used to surround Sutton, and the watery theme includes hundreds of hanging glass droplets. The café-style seating around the frontage is complemented by a beer terrace to the side, accessed from inside the pub. There are occasional showings of big-screen sports. The guest ales often come from breweries from the region such as Titanic or Sadler's. Occasional Meet the Brewer evenings are staged.
Q❀◐♿P🚌📶

Sedgley

Beacon Hotel 🏆 ★

129 Bilston Street, DY3 1JE (on A463)
12-2.30 (3 Fri), 5.30-11; 12-3, 6-11 Sat; 12-3, 7-10.30 Sun
☎ (01902) 883380 🌐 sarahhughesbrewery.co.uk
Sarah Hughes Pale Amber, Sedgley Surprise, Dark Ruby Mild; 3 changing beers (often Bristol Beer Factory, Exit 33, Shiny) Ⓗ
In the shadow of the ancient Sedgley beacon, this old hotel has sat virtually unchanged for decades. It is a Grade II-listed building and has a nationally important historic pub interior. At its heart is a small central servery with hatches serving four rooms, including a family room. The Sarah Hughes Brewery lives in a tower out the back and supplies the pub. The Beacon lives up to its name: it shines. CAMRA branch Metropolitan Pub of the Year 2018.
Q❀P🚌(229,224)

Mount Pleasant

144 High Street, DY3 1RH (on A459)
6.30 (7 Mon & Tue)-11; 12-3, 7-10.30 Sun
☎ 07950 195652
9 changing beers (sourced nationally; often Church End, Oakham, Salopian) Ⓗ
Known locally as The Stump, this popular free house serves a selection of nine beers. It possesses a mock-Tudor frontage and a Tardis-like interior. The front bar is the first room off a long corridor. The lounge areas have an intimate feel, with two rooms on different levels housing various nooks and crannies and a real coal stove in each. It is on the main No.1 bus route, or a five-minute walk from the centre of Sedgley. Q❀♣P🚌(1)🐾

Short Heath

Duke of Cambridge

82 Coltham Road, WV12 5QD
12-11 ☎ (01922) 712038
Black Country Bradley's Finest Golden, Pig on the Wall, Fireside; 3 changing beers (sourced nationally) Ⓗ
A traditional, homely, welcoming pub converted from 17th-century cottages. The public bar has a solid-fuel woodburner and wooden beams. The quieter lounge has been tastefully refurbished. A rear room caters for darts and pool and is also used for functions and beer festivals. A quiz is held every other Wednesday. There is a beer garden at the rear of the pub. Q❀♿♣●🚌(41,69)🐾

Solihull

Fieldhouse ✔

10 Knightcote Drive, Monkspath, B91 3JU
11.30-11.30 (midnight Fri); 10-midnight Sat & Sun
☎ (0121) 703 9209
Purity Pure UBU; house beer (by Black Sheep); 4 changing beers (sourced nationally) Ⓗ
Part of the Ember Inns chain, this large, modern pub is tastefully decorated and comfortably furnished. It features three large fires (one real, two coal-effect) and pleasant patio areas. It normally serves six ales, with four guest ales from across the country, often unusual ones and changing frequently. Often busy, it attracts a wide age range. Quiz nights are Sundays and Tuesdays; on Mondays cask ales are discounted. The pub holds monthly tribute acts and occasional Meet the Brewer events. ❀◐♿P🚌(S15,5)📶

Pup & Duckling

1 Hatchford Brook Road, Olton, B92 9AG
closed Mon & Tue; 5-10; 12-3 Sun ☎ (0121) 247 8358
🌐 pupandduckling.co.uk
6 changing beers (sourced nationally; often Fixed Wheel, Thousand Trades, Twisted Barrel) Ⓗ
Solihull's first micropub, opened in 2016 in a vacant shop. Family run, it has added a garden area and another room to the initial two-room layout. Six rapidly changing real ales are on handpull, along with six ciders. The latest ales are listed on Facebook, but can sell out in an evening. Bar snacks are available and customers are welcome to bring in their own food from the nearby Chinese, Indian and fish and chip shop takeaways. Local CAMRA Pub of the Year 2017.
Q❀●🚌(73,957)🐾📶

Stourbridge

Badelynge Bar

Rufford Road, DY9 7ND (entrance is green door next to Base Studios on Rufford Rd)

⏲ 4-11 Fri; 1-7 Sat; closed Sun-Thu ☎ (01384) 377666
5 changing beers (sourced locally; often Green Duck) Ⓗ
Tap for the Green Duck Brewery located in a large converted industrial unit, which also houses the brewery. Light and airy, it has a unique atmosphere among Stourbridge pubs. The brewery is visible through a glass partition. Seating is plentiful. Cask ale is sold using a token system at four pints for £10, but is also available by the pint. The bar can be hired for functions, and regular beer festivals are held featuring many guest beers. It also plays host to Stourbidge Gin Bar, serving at least 80 gins at any one time. (287)

Barbridge
Victoria Passage, DY8 1DP (at end of Victoria Passage on Talbot St)
⏲ 10.30-11 (1.30am Fri & Sat) ☎ (01384) 379898
4 changing beers (sourced nationally; often Fixed Wheel) Ⓗ/Ⓖ
Opened in December 2015 in an old retail unit at the end of Victoria Passage behind the Rye Market, this is a busy, bustling bar appealing to all age ranges. Four ales are served, usually one from Fixed Wheel, from a chiller unit to the rear of the bar through handpulls at the end of the bar. Four KeyKegs, frequently at least one from Beavertown, and six real ciders are also available. Cobs are sold. P

Old Bank
38 High Street, DY8 1AD
⏲ 11-11 (12.30am Fri & Sat); 12-11 Sun ☎ (01384) 396079
9 changing beers (sourced nationally) Ⓗ
Beautiful converted building, once a bank, now a stylish pub, serving a variety of beverages. The bar comprises a large, high-ceiling ground floor and a mezzanine to the rear which can be reserved for functions. Expect to see food being served in the near future as a kitchen is being built downstairs. A separate server in the bar provides freshly made lunchtime snacks. Nine handpulls offer a wide range of ales, and in addition there are gin and champagne menus. P(250)

Red House Boutique
21-26 Foster Place, DY8 1EL
⏲ 11-11 (midnight Fri & Sat); 12-8 Sun ☎ (01384) 936430
Enville Ale; Holden's Golden Glow; Wye Valley HPA; 5 changing beers (sourced nationally; often Fixed Wheel, Three Tuns) Ⓗ
Large, single-bar free house near Stourbridge Interchange. Originally part of the Hogshead chain, this refurbished pub has returned to being an alehouse. Beers from Enville, Fixed Wheel and Three Tuns will usually be on tap, but may change from those listed. A range of KeyKegs is also kept. Snacks are sold at all times including gourmet Scotch eggs and flavoured scratchings. Fridges behind the bar are stocked with many bottles from around the world.

Royal Exchange
75 Enville Street, DY8 1XW (on A458 just off ring road)
⏲ 1 (12 Sat)-11; 12-10.30 Sun ☎ (01384) 396726
Bathams Mild Ale, Best Bitter Ⓗ
The busy, traditional bar is to the front and a newly extended small cosy lounge is to the rear, accessed through a side passage. A large beer garden to the rear has a heated smoking area. The bar is decorated with a small collection of whisky bottles and boxes, pewter tankards and foreign bank notes. The beer is served in handled glasses on request. Bathams XXX is on the bar in winter only. A public car park is directly opposite. QP

Waggon & Horses
31 Worcester Street, DY8 1AT
⏲ 12-11 (midnight Thu-Sat) ☎ (01384) 395398
Enville Ale, Ginger Beer; Holden's Golden Glow; 3 changing beers Ⓗ
Recent refurbishment has created a comfortable, welcoming alehouse. There is a small cask ale bar to the front with a narrow passageway leading to a larger rear bar. To the side is a cider bar with a small serving hatchway. Parking can be difficult in the narrow surrounding streets. Two or more real ciders are usually on sale.

Sutton Coldfield

Brewhouse & Kitchen
8 Birmingham Road, B72 1QD
⏲ 11-11 (midnight Fri & Sat) ☎ (0121) 796 6838
Brewhouse & Kitchen The Cup, Sutton Pale Ale, 004 Oaks, Black Belt, Marksman; 2 changing beers (often Brewhouse & Kitchen) Ⓗ
Spacious brewpub which is part of a small national chain. The real ales are made in the tidy brewery which is a prominent feature at the entrance. The decor is rustic wood and bare brick, with a variety of seating areas and an atmospheric open log fire. There is a streetside beer terrace; note its ironwork cup sign relating to a former name of the pub. The large beer garden to the rear features rustic cabins and wooden cask tables.

Duke Inn
12 Duke Street, B72 1RJ
⏲ 12-11 (midnight Fri & Sat); 12-10.30 Sun
☎ (0121) 355 1767 🌐 dukeinnsutton.co.uk
Brains Rev James; Caledonian Deuchars IPA; Greene King Abbot; Young's Bitter; 1 changing beer Ⓗ
This side-street boozer is a welcome break from the chain pubs of town. Regulars play darts in the main bar, which has a pale-wood gantry complete with mirrors and clock. A simple, small lounge to the rear is more cosy. The corridor abutting the bar features elaborate floor tiles, decorated mirrors and even a short panel of snob screens. Children are welcome in the grassy beer garden, an unusual feature in the area. One or two beer festivals are staged during the year. P

Tipton

Fountain
51 Owen Street, DY4 8HE
⏲ 11.30-11; 11-midnight Fri & Sat; 11-11 Sun
☎ (0121) 522 3606
Banks's Mild; Wye Valley HPA; 4 changing beers (often Castle Rock, Oakham, Wye Valley) Ⓗ
This canalside pub attracts gongoozlers, boaters, families and lovers of cask beer. Guest beers can include not only national mainstream brands such as Sharp's or Greene King, but also the odd Salopian and Oakham beverage. Lunchtime meals, such as beef 'n' onion pie, are served Monday to Friday. Snacks are available all week including cobs and pork pies. P

Rising Sun
116 Horseley Road, DY4 7NH (off B4517)
⏲ 12-11 (midnight Fri & Sat) ☎ (0121) 557 1940

ENGLAND

Black Country Bradley's Finest Golden, Pig on the Wall, Fireside; 7 changing beers (sourced nationally; often Coach House, Froth Blowers, Malvern Hills) H
Former CAMRA National Pub of the Year which reopened in 2013 following a refurbishment by Black Country Ales. It is an imposing Victorian hostelry with two distinct rooms warmed by open fires. It has a large yard at the rear with patio heaters and an outbuilding. There are seven changing guest beers plus the three BCA core beers and five traditional ciders. Cobs are available. It is a 10-minute walk from Great Bridge, which has frequent services to Dudley, West Bromwich and Birmingham. (22)

Tame Bridge

45 Tame Road, DY4 7JA (off A461)
12-11 (0121) 557 2496
Wye Valley HPA; 3 changing beers (sourced nationally; often Church End, Hop Back, Three Tuns) H
A reliable locals' pub with a trio of changing keenly priced guest ales. The front bar has an open coal fire above which there is a wall-mounted flatscreen TV showing live sport, teatime quiz shows and occasionally a music channel. The comfortable White Room at the rear is often occupied by families and has a smaller bar counter with a bell to catch the attention of the bartender. There is a 'coming soon' board and an accessible water closet for wheelchair users.
(74)

Upper Gornal

Britannia ★ L

109 Kent Street, DY3 1UX (on A459)
12-11; 12-10.30 Sun (01902) 883253
Bathams Best Bitter H
Dating to the early 19th century, this pub has a nationally important historic pub interior for the taproom at the rear with its wall-mounted handpulls. Service can be obtained from the front bar, itself a comfortable place to be. There is also a family and games room with TV. Behind the pub is the former brewhouse and garden. A selection of bar snacks is served. On the main No.1 bus route between Dudley and Wolverhampton.
(1)

Jolly Crispin

25 Clarence Street, DY3 1UL (on A459)
4 (12 Fri & Sat)-11; 12-10.30 Sun (01902) 672220
thejollycrispin.co.uk
Fownes Crispin's Ommer; 8 changing beers (sourced nationally; often Abbeydale, Fownes, Oakham) H
Once a shoemaker's house in the 18th century, this building has been a pub for 200 years. It sits on the top of the Black Country ridge, with distant views from the rear. Inside, the locals are friendly, the fires glow and dogs are welcome. The pub's house beer, Crispin's Ommer, comes from the on-site Fownes brewery. Real ales are complemented by different real ciders, and a cider festival is held in the garden in May/June in aid of charity.
P (1)

Wall Heath

Horse & Jockey

High Street, DY6 0HA
12-11 (midnight Fri & Sat) (01384) 298986
Banks's Mild, Amber Ale, Sunbeam; Enville Ale; 1 changing beer (often Jennings, Marston's, Wychwood) H
A busy community pub next to the infamous double island in Wall Heath. There is a large bar at the front of the pub and a comfortable, slightly smaller lounge at the rear. Outside seating can be found at the front where there is artificial turf. A dartboard is located in the bar and TV screens show all sports fixtures. P

Walsall

Black Country Arms L

High Street, WS1 1QW (in market, opp Asda)
11-11 (midnight Fri); 12-midnight Sat; 12-11 Sun
(01922) 640588 blackcountryarms.co.uk
Black Country Bradley's Finest Golden, Pig on the Wall, Fireside; 11 changing beers (sourced nationally) H
A large, imposing multi award-winning pub on three levels, part of which was originally the Green Dragon Inn that dated back to the 18th century. The place lay empty for 70 years until extensive refurbishment saw it reopen in 1987. The impressive bar boasts 16 handpumps serving up to 11 guest ales, mainly from microbreweries, with two real ciders always available. One changing craft beer is also stocked. Live music features frequently - check website for details. Booking is recommended for Sunday lunches.
P

Butts Tavern L

44 Butts Street, WS4 2BJ (200yds from Arboretum's Lichfield St entrance)
12-11 (01922) 629332 buttstavern.co.uk
Holden's Golden Glow; Wye Valley Butty Bach; 2 changing beers (often Castle Rock, Church End, Enville) H
Large community-based local with a spacious main bar including a small stage and a sports TV, complemented by a smaller bar at the rear with a pool table and darts facilities. A warm welcome is assured from the staff; there is an outside patio area for smokers. Local dominoes and crib teams are based here, and entertainment features on Friday and Saturday night. There are normally two guest beers, including one at 5% ABV or above, which accompany the regular ales.

Fountain Inn L

49 Lower Forster Street, WS1 1XB (off A4148 ring road)
12-2, 5-11; 12-midnight Fri & Sat; 12-11 Sun
(01922) 633307
Backyard The Hoard, Blonde; 6 changing beers (sourced nationally; often Holden's, St Austell) H
A family-run pub, this is the brewery tap for Backyard Brewhouse with up to eight real ales on the bar. It has a friendly atmosphere and welcoming staff. Bar snacks are available such as cobs and pork pies. Regular music events are held including vinyl nights, indie nights, classic rock, reggae, funk and soul nights. It also has monthly film nights on Mondays and drawing classes. Both rooms feature log fires. Q

Lyndon House Hotel L

9-10 Upper Rushall Street, WS1 2HA (between market and St Matthew's church)
11-11 (1am Fri & Sat); 12-11 Sun (01922) 612511
lyndonhousehotel.co.uk

Bathams Best Bitter; Burton Bridge XL Mild, Stairway to Heaven; Caledonian Deuchars IPA; Greene King Abbot; Holden's Golden Glow 🄷
Situated at the top of Walsall Market, the New Royal Exchange pub was, in 1995, incorporated into an adjoining Salvation Army hostel and leather factory. It now forms the luxurious Lyndon House Hotel. Its comfortable bar has an island counter and cosy corners with old wood and brickwork. With its function room, downstairs Sally Ann bar and outdoor terraces, the premises is unexpectedly spacious. It is popular with business people and is a slice of Walsall life. Live music is featured most Sunday afternoons, with tribute bands on Saturdays in a separate function room.
Q❀🛏◐◑♿P🚌(7,51)📶

Pretty Bricks 🄻

5 John Street, WS2 8AF (near magistrates court, off B4210)
⏲ 12-11 ☎ (01922) 612553
Black Country Bradley's Finest Golden, Pig on the Wall, Fireside; 7 changing beers (sourced nationally; often Salopian) 🄷
Small, friendly, cosy and comfortable pub dating from 1845. There is a front bar with a wood fire, a lounge, an upstairs function room and a small blue brick courtyard with a couple of benches. Originally called the New Inn, its current name derives from a part-glazed frontage. Great cobs and pork pies provide sustenance alongside the excellent range of ales. A folk night is held every second Thursday of the month. Q❀≹♣🍎🚌(301)🐾

Victoria 🄻

23 Lower Rushall Street, WS1 2AA
⏲ 12-11.30 (midnight Fri & Sat); 12-11 Sun
☎ (01922) 635866
Backyard Bitter; Church End Gravediggers Ale; Jennings Sneck Lifter; Lancaster Bomber; 3 changing beers (sourced regionally; often AJ's, Salopian) 🄷
Popular two-roomed pub, close to the town centre, dating from 1845. The former brewhouse is at the rear. Excellent Sunday lunches are served and great cobs are available on other days. Open mic and quiz nights are held regularly, plus Sunday evening live entertainment. A pool table is upstairs. There is a pleasant garden and smoking facilities to the rear. One real cider is permanently stocked. There is a large Pay & Display car park at the rear of the pub. 🐴❀◐≹♣🐾

Wednesbury

Bellwether ✔

3-4 Walsall Street, WS10 9BZ
⏲ 7am-midnight (1am Fri & Sat) ☎ (0121) 502 6404
Greene King Abbot; Oakham JHB; Ruddles Best Bitter; 7 changing beers (sourced nationally) 🄷
Near the main shopping area and market, this pub attracts a wide clientele. It has a large L-shaped room on a split level, with open-plan tables and chairs in front of the bar. There is more intimate seating at the rear, leading on to a split-level, tranquil garden area. The pub is decorated with historic events and characters associated with the town. Ten handpumps serve a large selection of guest ales. Q🐴❀◐◑♿🚆♣🍎🚌📶

Cottage Spring 🄻

106 Franchise Street, WS10 9RG
⏲ 3 (1 Thu)-11.30; 12-midnight Fri & Sat; 12-11.30 Sun
☎ (0121) 531 7191
Holden's Black Country Mild, Black Country Bitter, Golden Glow; 1 changing beer (sourced locally; often Holden's) 🄷
The front bar has photos of the pub and owners from yesteryear. Darts is played at one end while the lounge also has old-world prints and old-fashioned manufacturing devices; there is also a stage area in one corner. The bar features an old red phone box. Friday is quiz night, and live music takes place on Saturday nights and Sunday afternoons. Sunday lunches are served.
Q❀◐◑♣P🚌(34)

Olde Leathern Bottel

40 Vicarage Road, WS10 9DW (just off A461; bus 311 from Walsall is 5 mins' walk)
⏲ closed Mon; 4-11; 12-11.30 Sat; 12-11 Sun
☎ (0121) 505 0230 🌐 yeoldeleathernbottel.co.uk
3 changing beers (sourced nationally; often Exmoor, Wye Valley) 🄷
The front areas of the Bottel (bar and snug) are set in cottages dating from 1510, while a later extension contains a comfy lounge. The small snug is often used as a function room. The four rooms have many old photos and the bar displays a photo of the pub from 1887 and a map of Wednesbury from 1846. At the rear is a pleasant benched patio area with plant pots. There is a quiz on Sunday evenings. Q🐴❀◑♣P🚌(11)🐾📶

Queen's Head ✔

100 Brunswick Park Road, WS10 9QR
⏲ 12 (5 Mon)-11; 12-midnight Fri & Sat ☎ 07713 756570
🌐 queensheadwednesbury.com
Wye Valley HPA; 1 changing beer (often Backyard) 🄷
Enthusiastically run, this brick-built, twin-gabled pub provides a warm welcome to all. There are two rooms: the front bar has tables and booths and is popular with diners, while the side bar has a TV and dartboard. The home-made food, good beer and entertainment (frequent live bands and DJs) ensure that the Queen's Head is well supported by the local community. Tennis, football and water polo teams all meet here. Summer barbecues and the occasional beer festival also feature.
Q🐴❀◐◑♿♣🍎P🚌🐾📶

West Bromwich

Crown & Cushion

2 Lloyd Street, B71 4AT
⏲ 12-11 ☎ (0121) 553 4493
Castle Rock Harvest Pale; St Austell Tribute; 1 changing beer (sourced nationally; often Harviestoun) 🄷
Family-friendly hostelry run by a pleasant and welcoming landlady. It has an L-shaped single room interior and is popular in summer with visitors to nearby Dartmouth Park. As the pub is within easy walking distance of West Bromwich Albion's football ground, it can get busy on match days. However, away supporters are made welcome. A popular quiz night is held on a Thursday. 🐴❀♣P🚌(46)📶

Royal Oak 🄻 ✔

14 Newton Street, B71 3RQ (down side road off Hollyhedge Rd)
⏲ 2-11; 12-midnight Fri & Sat; 12-11 Sun ☎ (0121) 588 5857
St Austell Proper Job; Sharp's Doom Bar; Wye Valley HPA; 2 changing beers (sourced nationally) 🄷
Traditional back-street local with two small rooms. There are TVs showing sport in both rooms,

normally with their sound reduced. The bar on the left is adorned with West Bromwich Albion football club pictures and on the right is the quieter lounge. There is a terrace in the rear yard for smokers and two benches outside the front of the pub where you can bask in the summer. Parking is difficult, but use the neighbouring streets.

Three Horseshoes

86 Witton Lane, B71 2AQ

12-11 (0121) 556 4734

Black Country Bradley's Finest Golden, Pig on the Wall, Fireside; 10 changing beers (sourced nationally)

This refurbished hostelry was taken on by Black Country Ales in 2016 with 10 handpulls added. The one-roomed, spacious pub has been furnished in a traditional style but also has a TV and pool table to keep people entertained. The warm welcome provided by the staff makes you feel right at home. Bar snacks are served and there is a beer garden to enjoy the local atmosphere this pub provides. (79)

Vine

152 Roebuck Street, B70 6RD

11.30-2, 5-11; 11.30-11 Fri; 12-11 Sat; 12-10.30 Sun (0121) 553 2866 thevine.co.uk

2 changing beers (sourced nationally; often Backyard, Holden's, Otter)

From the street this building appears to be a traditional corner pub, but be prepared for a surprise. The traditional part consists of three small rooms off the corridor. Continue further in and the building opens up into a large dining area, where an extensive range of Indian meals is available together with British and vegetarian options, which are all excellent value. Two guest ales are regularly on tap. This popular establishment gets busy, especially when West Bromwich Albion are at home. (74,79)

Willenhall

Falcon

77 Gomer Street West, WV13 2NR (off B4464, behind flats)

12-11; 12-10.30 Sun (01902) 633378

Salopian Oracle; Skinner's Cornish Knocker; 3 changing beers (sourced nationally)

A two-roomed pub with a lively public bar and quieter lounge at the rear, a short walk from the town centre. Dating back to 1936, the Falcon has been in the same family for over 30 years. Old pub memorabilia adorn both rooms where keenly priced beers are served. There is a beer garden at the rear of the pub, and plenty of on-street parking. (529)

Malthouse

The Dale, New Road, WV13 2BG

8am-midnight (1am Fri & Sat) (01902) 635273

Burton Bridge Stairway to Heaven; Greene King IPA, Abbot; 8 changing beers (sourced nationally; often Backyard, Sadler's)

A large, family-friendly Wetherspoon pub in the centre of the town, adjacent to the Dale restaurant. The building was previously used as a cinema and bingo hall and is built on the site of an old maltings. It consists of an L-shaped drinking area with an external patio reached via a flight of steps. Although the pub does not have a car park, there is plenty of free parking close by.

Robin Hood

54 The Crescent, WV13 2QR (200yds from A462/B4464 jct)

12-11 (midnight Fri & Sat) (01902) 635070

Black Country Bradley's Finest Golden, Pig on the Wall, Fireside /; 6 changing beers (sourced nationally; often Salopian)

Black Country Ales-owned pub with an old-fashioned feel and welcoming, friendly staff. One central bar serves both drinking areas, with a large bar at the front and a more intimate lounge at the rear. The three permanent beers are supplemented by six changing guest beers from throughout the UK. Two real ciders are also sold. Bar snacks including cobs and pork pies are available throughout the day. A heated and covered smoking area is to the rear. A beer festival is held every July in the beer garden. P (529)

Wolverhampton

Chindit

113 Merridale Road, WV3 9SE

4-11 (midnight Fri); 12-midnight Sat; 2-11 Sun
07986 773487 thechindit.co.uk

Castle Rock Harvest Pale; Hop Back Summer Lightning; Wye Valley HPA; 2 changing beers (sourced locally; often Burton Bridge, Salopian, Three Tuns)

Originally built in the 1950s as an off-licence, the first landlord served in the Chindit Regiment in Burma in WWII and named it after his comrades. It is thought this is the only pub in the country honouring Major General Orde Wingate's special forces; their history is displayed on the wall in the lounge. The two-roomed pub has a small lounge, and in the large bar there is an original Wurlitzer jukebox stocking '60s and '70s 45s. P (3,4)

Claregate

34 Codsall Road, WV6 9ED

12-11; 12-10 Sun (01902) 754761
claregatepub.co.uk

Banks's Amber Ale, Sunbeam; 3 changing beers (sourced nationally)

Originally named the Fieldhouse, which itself replaced an earlier building, the mid-'70s saw the name changed and rooms amalgamated into two large areas. After being threatened with demolition, an active campaign in 2016 secured it a nomination as an Asset of Community Value and plans were cancelled. Then in 2017 a major refurbishment changed the pub to a Marston's Generous George brand. Although the emphasis is on dining, it offers a good selection of Marston's beers. A Tesco Express store is located in the large car park. P (5,5A)

Clarendon Hotel

38 Chapel Ash, WV3 0TN

11.30-11 (midnight Fri & Sat); 12-10.30 Sun
(01902) 420587 clarendonhotelpub.co.uk

Banks's Mild, Amber Ale, Sunbeam; Marston's Pedigree; Wainwright; Wychwood Hobgoblin Gold; 1 changing beer (sourced nationally)

Dating back to 1849, the Clarendon is located next to Banks's Park brewery, visitor centre and Marston's head office. There have been many extensions so what was once a small pub has grown considerably. It was purchased by Wolverhampton & Dudley breweries in 1896 from Brindley Brewery of Burton upon Trent. The last refurbishment in 2016 created a number of niches and seating areas which highlight the history of the breweries within the group. Upstairs, a large function room and the former boardroom are available for hire. The range of ales comes from the Marston's group breweries.

Combermere Arms

90 Chapel Ash, WV3 0TY (on A41 Tettenhall Rd)
12-3 (not Mon winter), 5-11; 12-midnight Fri & Sat; 12-10.30 Sun (01902) 421880
5 changing beers (sourced nationally; often Greene King) H
Grade II-listed building with original sash windows. A short walk or bus ride from the city centre, the pub comprises three charming rooms with cosy fireplaces, classic adverts and a comical Guinness cartoon series. A pub favourites menu is available weekday lunchtimes (not Mon). Cheese, pie and sausage tasting festivals are held annually and there is occasional live entertainment. Characterful features include the tree in the gents. One locally brewed beer and four from the Greene King portfolio are served. QP

Dog & Doublet

9 North Street, WV1 1RE
12-11 (1am Thu-Sat); closed Sun (01902) 423805
thedoganddoubletinn.co.uk
Ludlow Gold; Oakham Bishops Farewell; 4 changing beers (sourced nationally) H
City-centre pub near the Civic and Wulfrun halls, a mix of modern and traditional, with real fires and Chesterfield furniture on the right as you enter, while the rear is reserved for dining. Outside, there is a heated and covered patio, also used for taking meals. Regular music events are held including occasional jazz. The pub is Oakham brewery accredited, which allows it access to the brewery's limited special brews.

Great Western

Sun Street, WV10 0DJ
11-11; 11-10.30 Sun (01902) 351090
Bathams Best Bitter; Holden's Black Country Mild, Black Country Bitter, Golden Glow, Special; 3 changing beers (sourced regionally) H
A previous CAMRA National Pub of the Year near to the former low-level railway station. It attracts a varied clientele, including a rock-climbing club and railway groups. Plenty of railway and Wolverhampton Wanderers memorabilia is on display and cosy real fires blaze in the winter. Meals are served at lunchtime (not Sundays) and hot pork baps, gray pays and bacon, beef and vegetable stew are available every day until 10pm. A beer festival is held over November's remembrance weekend. QP

Hail to the Ale

2 Pendeford Avenue, Claregate, WV6 9EF (on Claregate Island)
closed Mon-Wed; 5-10 Thu & Fri; 12-10 Sat; 12-5 Sun
07846 562910 hailtothealemicropub.co.uk
4 changing beers (sourced locally; often Beowulf, Lymestone, Morton) H

> When you have lost your inns, drown your empty selves, for you will have lost the last of England.
> **Hilaire Belloc, The Four Men, 1912**

The West Midlands' first micropub, this welcoming one-room beer-focused bar was opened in 2013 by Morton Brewery, following a simple formula of good ale and conversation. Four handpulls serve at least one Morton beer and guest beers, usually from local microbreweries. Also on handpull and from the cellar are four ciders or perries. Locally sourced pies, cheese, sausage rolls and Scotch eggs are available along with fruit wines. It also opens 5-10pm on the last Wednesday of each month. QP(5,6)

Hogshead

186 Stafford Street, WV1 1NA
10-midnight (1am Fri); 10-2am Sat (01902) 717955
10 changing beers (sourced nationally) H
Large 19th-century city-centre pub with an attractive brick terracotta exterior. A stained-glass window above the entrance displays the original name, The Vine. One large single room is divided into separate areas, with wide-screen TVs showing sport and music videos throughout. It serves a range of 10 guest ales, often from local microbreweries, up to three changing ciders and five changing keg beers. The pub is popular with all age groups. There is a quiz on Wednesday evenings and games on Monday evenings.

Lych Gate Tavern

44 Queen Square, WV1 1TX (off Queen Square between Nationwide and Barclays banks by St Peter's church)
11-11 (midnight Fri & Sat) (01902) 399516
lychgatetavern.co.uk
Black Country Bradley's Finest Golden, Pig on the Wall, Fireside; 6 changing beers (sourced nationally) H
Friendly traditional city-centre pub, housed in one of the oldest timber-framed buildings in Wolverhampton. The Georgian frontage dates from 1726, while the timber-framed rear dates from about 1500. The bar area is reached by a short flight of stairs down from street level and there is a function room available for hire upstairs. Cobs are served, and customers may bring their own food, with plates and cutlery provided. All floors are accessible via a lift. Q

Posada

48 Lichfield Street, WV1 1DG
12-11 (1am Fri); 11.30-1am Sat; 12-6 Sun
Hobsons Town Crier; Sharp's Doom Bar; 3 changing beers (often AJ's, Salopian, Wye Valley) H
Victorian Grade II-listed city-centre pub with tiled walls, original bar fittings including rare snob screens, and little altered since 1900. It attracts a varied clientele and is quiet during the day but busy in the evening and weekends, especially when Wolverhampton Wanderers are at home. There is a courtyard to the rear with a smoking area. Cobs are available.

Royal Oak

70 Compton Road, WV3 9PH
11.30-11 (midnight Fri & Sat); 12-11 Sun
(01902) 422845 royaloakwolverhampton.co.uk
Banks's Mild, Amber Ale, Sunbeam; Wychwood Hobgoblin Gold; 3 changing beers (sourced nationally; often Jennings, Ringwood, Wychwood) H
Friendly local, a short walk or bus ride from the city centre, serving a wide range of changing real ales from Marston's. The bustling pub, with good sports coverage, hosts open mic evenings on Wednesdays

and live bands on Fridays and Saturdays (also Sunday afternoons in summer). Part of the community, the pub raises money for local and national charities, features a book swap library, and is the headquarters of Old Wulfrunians hockey club. Fresh cobs are available at the bar.
❀♿♣P (10,890)

Stile Inn

3 Harrow Street, Whitmore Reans, WV1 4PB (off Newhampton Rd East/Fawdry St)
11.30-11 (midnight Fri; 1am Sat) ☎ (01902) 425336
Banks's Mild, Amber Ale, Sunbeam; 1 changing beer (sourced nationally) H
A typical late Victorian street-corner pub, built in 1900, featuring a public bar, smoke room and snug. It is a true community local, with an emphasis on sports: darts and dominoes feature inside, Crown Green bowls take place on the unusual L-shaped green outside, and the pub gets very busy with Wolverhampton Wanderers fans on match days. Excellent-value food, including Polish dishes, is served all day. Friday is disco night and Saturday is karaoke. Sky and BT Sports are shown in all rooms. ❀♣ (5,6)

Swan

Bridgnorth Road, Compton, WV6 8AE (at Compton Island, on A454)
12-11 (11.30 Thu; midnight Fri & Sat) ☎ (01902) 754736
swanpubwolverhampton.co.uk
Banks's Mild, Amber Ale, Sunbeam; Marston's Old Empire; Wainwright; 3 changing beers (sourced nationally; often Brakspear, Jennings, Wychwood) H
Built around 1780, this Grade-II listed former coaching inn is close to the Staffordshire & Worcestershire Canal and Smestow Valley nature reserve, attracting locals, boaters, ramblers and cyclists. It comprises a lively bar full of local banter, a games room and a more sedate snug. It hosts charity dog shows, three beer festivals featuring ales from outside the Marston's range, and the local Pigeon Flyers Club meets here every week. A well-considered and sympathetic refurbishment was carried out in 2016. Q❀♣P

Woodcross

Horse & Jockey

Robert Wynd, WV14 9SB
12-11 (11.30 Fri & Sat) ☎ (01902) 662268
horseandjockeywoodcross.co.uk
Hobsons Twisted Spire, Town Crier; St Austell Tribute; 4 changing beers (sourced locally; often Backyard, Salopian, Three Tuns) H
Run by two CAMRA members, this friendly and thriving community pub comprises bar, large contemporary lounge with seasonal open fire, rear beer garden and a small smoking shelter at the front. Good-value, home-cooked food, including vegetarian options, is served daily until 8.30pm (6pm Sun). Tuesday is quiz night. Under-18s are allowed in the lounge area and garden until 8pm.
Q❀♣P

Woodsetton

Park Inn

George Street, DY1 4LW (on A457, 200yds from A4123)
12-11; 12-10.30 Sun ☎ (01902) 661279
Holden's Black Country Mild, Black Country Bitter, Golden Glow, Special; 3 changing beers (sourced nationally; often Oakham, Purple Moose, Salopian) H
Busy brewery tap which has been owned by the Holden family for more than a century. The bar has a chalkboard advertising up to three guest beers, and a large flatscreen TV showing BT Sport, although this is not intrusive. There is a raised dining area, a games room with a pool table, and a conservatory which is used for Dudley Winter Ales Fayre planning meetings. Pub grub is served all week except Sunday. ❀♣P (81,229)

Wordsley

New Inn

117 High Street, DY8 5QR (on A491)
12-11; 12-10.30 Sun ☎ (01384) 295614
Bathams Mild Ale, Best Bitter H
With an imposing three-storey Victorian façade, this is very much a locals' pub, and it has become extremely popular and is usually busy. An L-shaped bar serves a single room with a small annexe at one end, plus a patio area and newly refurbished garden outside. Children are not allowed in the pub. A variety of cobs is available.
❀♣P (256,257)

Queen's Head

129 High Street, DY8 5QS (on A491)
12-11 (midnight Fri & Sat) ☎ (01384) 402967
Black Country Bradley's Finest Golden, Pig on the Wall, Fireside; 6 changing beers (sourced nationally; often Fixed Wheel, Peerless, Swannay) H
Comfortable roadside pub on the main Stourbridge to Wolverhampton road. The layout echoes its multi-roomed past, although most of the walls have gone. The decor is cosy Victorian or Edwardian in style. It sells up to nine real ales, with three from the parent brewery, and a traditional cider. To the right is a bar-type area which has a large-screen TV and dartboard. The pub now sells food Wednesday to Sunday (book ahead for Sunday lunch).
❀♣P (256,257)

The importance of the pub

Perhaps the workman spends, night after night, more than he should on beer. Let us remember, if he needs excuse, that his employers have found him no better place and no better amusement than to sit in a tavern, drink beer (generally in moderation), and talk and smoke tobacco. Why not? A respectable tavern is a very harmless place; the society which meets there is the society of the workman; it's his life; without it he might as well have been a factory hand of the good old time – such as hands were 40 years ago; and then he should have but two journeys a day – one from bed to mill, and the other from mill to bed.

Walter Besant, As We Are and As We May Be, 1903

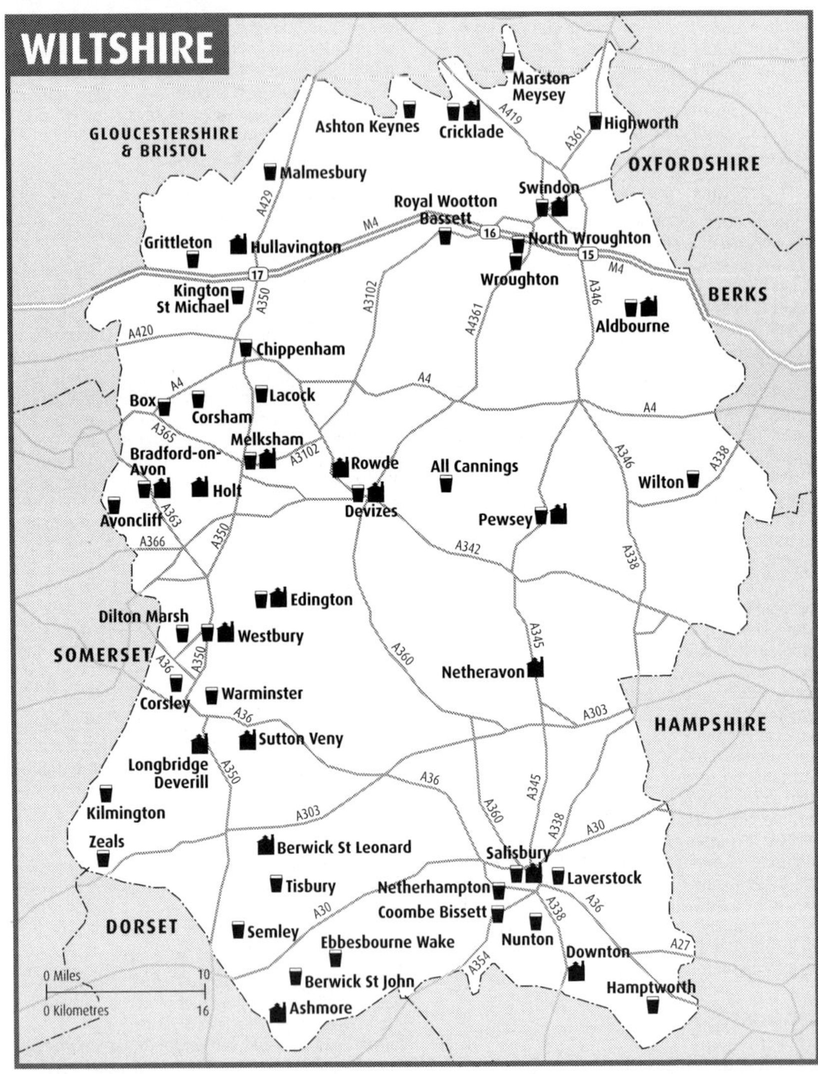

Aldbourne

Crown Hotel ✓

The Square, SN8 2DU

12-midnight (10.30 Sun) ☎ (01672) 540214

thecrownaldbourne.co.uk

Sharp's Doom Bar; Shepherd Neame Spitfire; Timothy Taylor Landlord; 2 changing beers Ⓗ

In the middle of the village opposite the duck pond, a Dalek stands guard outside. The Crown has a relaxed and pleasant atmosphere with two bars. The main bar is stylishly refurbished and has a welcoming fire during the colder seasons. The smaller bar shows films on Monday night. The restaurant serves freshly prepared food until 9.30pm. ❀🛏◑⛺♣🚌(46,48)🐾📶

All Cannings

King's Arms Inn

The Street, SN10 3PA

12-3 (not Mon), 6-11; 12-11 Sat & Sun ☎ (01380) 860328

kingsarmsallcannings.co.uk

Wadworth IPA, 6X; 1 changing beer Ⓗ

A genuine traditional pub serving good home-made food, with menus changing all the time and a daily specials board. Drinks include first-class Wadworth ales, guest beers and wine by the glass or bottle. An annual charity rock concert is held in the pub's camping field every May when the pub offers a greater range of Wadworth ales including a special concert ale. The bus service is limited. ❀◑⛺♣P🚌(101,102)

Ashton Keynes

White Hart ✓

High Road, SN6 6NX

6-10 Mon; 12-2.30, 6 (5 Fri)-11; 12-midnight Sat; 11.30-11 Sun ☎ (01285) 861247 thewhitehartashtonkeynes.com

Ramsbury Gold; house beer (by Stroud); 2 changing beers (sourced regionally; often Ramsbury, Wadworth) Ⓗ

Pretty Ashton Keynes bestrides the Thames in the far north of Wiltshire, close to the Gloucestershire border. It is known as 'the village of four crosses' – one of which stands to the south of the pub. Although essentially open plan, the White Hart's interior is divided into three distinct areas – a small bar with games and TV, the main narrow bar area with window benches, and the dining room. There is much bare stone. ❀◑♣P🚌(93)🐾📶

Avoncliff

Cross Guns

159-160 Avoncliff, BA15 2HB

⏲ 10-11 ☎ (01225) 862335 🌐 crossgunsavoncliff.com

Box Steam Golden Bolt; 4 changing beers (sourced nationally) [H]

A world away, yet only 12 minutes by rail from Bath, this 16th-century canalside inn is popular with walkers, cyclists and narrow-boaters. Overlooking the small village is the historic Avoncliff aqueduct where the Kennet & Avon Canal crosses the River Avon and the railway line. Features include an inglenook fireplace, priest hole, garden bar, weekend barbecues and a resident ghost. Live music plays every Tuesday. Beers can be from local breweries and from far and wide. Just 100 yards from Avoncliff station.

Q❀◑♿⛺⇌♣🍎🐾📶

Berwick St John

Talbot

The Cross, SP7 0HA

⏲ closed Mon; 12-2.30, 6-11; 12-4 Sun ☎ (01747) 828222

🌐 talbotinnberwickstjohn.co.uk

Sixpenny 6d Best Bitter; Wadworth 6X; house beer (by Ringwood); 1 changing beer (often Sixpenny) [H]

Set in a small, rural, peaceful village, The Talbot opened as a beer house circa 1832 despite vehement opposition from the local parson's wife. The building is predominantly stone built, with a long, low bar with beams and an inglenook fireplace. The more inquisitive visitor will find the dining room behind the inglenook. The pub is popular with walkers from the local downs and cyclists on the 160-mile Wiltshire Cycleway. There is no mobile phone signal but Wi-Fi is available.

Q❀◑P🐾📶

Box

Quarryman's Arms [L]

Box Hill, SN13 8HN (off A4 follow signs)

⏲ 10-11 (midnight Fri & Sat) ☎ (01225) 743569

🌐 quarrymans-arms.co.uk

Butcombe Adam Henson's Rare Breed, Original; Fuller's London Pride; 2 changing beers (sourced nationally; often Oakham, VOG) [H]

Originally miners' dwellings dating back 300 years, supporting the local Bath stone mines. There are three comfortable areas to enjoy a drink and locally sourced food – the snug, bar and the restaurant area overlooking the stunning valley towards Colerne and Bath. The beams are adorned with old pumpclips celebrating the range of beers served here over the years. The garden terrace also enjoys fine views. Four B&B rooms are available.

Q❀🛏◑♿⛺♣🍎P🚌(X31)📶

Bradford-on-Avon

Castle Inn

Mount Pleasant, BA15 1SJ

⏲ 9am-11; 10-10.30 Sun ☎ (01225) 865657

Three Castles Barbury Castle, Vale Ale; 4 changing beers (often Electric Bear) [H]

A popular, comfortable pub commanding splendid views across the town towards Salisbury Plain. The recent refurbishment by Flatcappers won it joint Best Refurbishment in the CAMRA Design Awards. A wide range of handpulled real ales is complemented by excellent food, served all day until 10pm. The three guest beers are usually sourced from microbreweries in Wiltshire and east Somerset. There is a good-sized garden at the front and children are welcome. Bed & Breakast is available, with four luxury double bedrooms. Local CAMRA Pub of the Year 2017.

❀🛏◑♿⛺⇌🍎P🚌(D1)🐾📶

Stumble Inn

Market Street, BA15 1LL

⏲ 7 (6 Thu; 5 Fri; 12 Sat)-11; closed Sun & Mon

☎ (01225) 862115 🌐 thestumbleinnboa.com

4 changing beers (sourced locally; often Cheddar Ales, Kettlesmith, Milk Street) [H]/[G]

A new micropub opened in 2017. Set on the ground floor of what was previously a local club in the centre of town, it has a main bar at the back with seating and a good-sized comfortable room at the front overlooking the main street. It offers a varying range of up to four beers, with two on handpump and two on gravity. Local brewers Kettlesmith sometimes have a tap takeover on Sunday. ⇌🚌🐾📶

Three Horseshoes

55 Frome Road, BA15 1LA

⏲ 11-11; 12-10.30 Sun ☎ (01225) 867856

3 changing beers (sourced regionally) [H]

The Horseshoes is a nice old coaching inn on the edge of the town centre next to the rail station. It comes complete with the old wooden door where the horses went through to the yard. Outside at the back is a small garden and terrace with seating. At

REAL ALE BREWERIES

Arkell's Swindon
Box Steam Holt
Brotherhood Westbury (NEW)
Dark Revolution Salisbury
Devitera Rowde (NEW)
Downton Downton
Flying Monk Hullavington
Gritchie Ashmore (NEW)
Hop Back Downton
Hop Kettle ▮ Cricklade/Swindon
Kettlesmith Bradford-on-Avon
Keystone Berwick St Leonard
Plain Sutton Veny
Ramsbury Aldbourne
Shed Pewsey
Stealth Melksham
Stonehenge Netheravon
Three Castles Pewsey
Three Daggers Edington
Twisted Westbury
Wadworth Devizes
Weighbridge ▮ Swindon
Wessex Longbridge Deverill
World's End ▮ Pewsey

the bar there are usually three constantly changing beers, often local. Live bands play at weekends. ❀⇌P🚌(D1)📶

Chippenham

Bridge House L ✔

Borough Parade, SN15 3WL (just off town bridge)
⏲ 8am-11 (1am Fri & Sat) ☎ (01249) 450980
Greene King Abbot; Ruddles Best Bitter; Sharp's Doom Bar; 4 changing beers (sourced nationally; often Box Steam, Flying Monk, Twisted) H
Modern purpose-built pub in the Borough Parade shopping centre, just off the high street. It adjoins the River Avon and has outside tables. Although one of the smaller Wetherspoons, it has an upstairs lounge away from the bar which also serves as a function room. In the bar is a panel celebrating US rock 'n' roll pioneer Eddie Cochran who was killed in a road accident at Chippenham while on tour in 1960. ❀◑♿⇌●P🚌📶

Old Road Tavern

Old Rd, SN15 1JA (over bridge from railway station)
⏲ 11-11.30 (12.30am Fri & Sat); 12-11.30 Sun
☎ (01249) 652094
Bath Ales Gem; Hop Back Summer Lightning; Otter Bitter; Wye Valley HPA; 2 changing beers (sourced nationally; often Adnams, Dartmoor, Moorhouse's) H
The pub has been a traditional community local since 1842. It has a large garden with plenty of seating, well used in the summer. A diverse mix of regulars ensures lively and friendly conversation. It hosts regular live music and comedy sessions and gets especially busy during the Chippenham Folk Festival at the end of May. The recently refurbished hall adjacent to the bar is available to hire for special occasions. ❀◐⇌♣🚌🐾📶

Three Crowns L

18 The Causeway, SN15 3DB (S of centre opp Kwik Fit)
⏲ 5-11; 12-midnight Fri & Sat; 12-11 Sun ☎ (01249) 449029
🌐 threecrownschippenham.co.uk
7 changing beers (sourced nationally; often Arbor, Slater's, XT) H
Friendly family-run 18th-century two-roomed waggoners' pub. Popular with locals and visitors, it has a large log fire in the winter. Seven continually changing beers include at least two dark ales, as well as four ciders and a perry, usually from local producers. Four seasonal beer festivals are held each year. A fortnightly pub quiz and other ad hoc themed nights are always lively. Dogs are welcomed with biscuits and water.
Q⇌♣●P🚌🐾📶

Coombe Bissett

Fox & Goose L

Blandford Road, SP5 4LE
⏲ 11-11; 12-10.30 Sun ☎ (01722) 718437
🌐 foxandgoose-coombebissett.co.uk
Sharp's Doom Bar; Sixpenny 6d Best Bitter; 1 changing beer (sourced nationally) H
An 18th-century coaching inn on the A354, three miles south of Salisbury. This popular community pub has a loyal village clientele and a welcoming atmosphere. Divided into a bar and restaurant, it offers an extensive food menu with ever-changing specials. There is a loyalty card scheme for regular diners. Outside, there are pleasant gardens to the rear. Q❀◑P🚌(20,29)🐾📶

Corsham

Flemish Weaver ✔

63 High Street, SN13 0EZ (next to town hall)
⏲ 11-11; 12-10.30 Sun ☎ (01249) 701929
4 changing beers (sourced nationally; often Marston's, Salopian, Wadworth) H
Extensively refurbished in 2017, the Flemish Weaver is an intriguing pub and full of character with many nooks and crannies. The garden is a pleasant and unexpected surprise. There is a focus on quality service and real ale, with four handpumps offering a regularly changing range. The building is in the oldest part of Corsham where you may notice locations from the TV series Poldark, some of which was filmed here.
❀◑♣🚌🐾📶

Corsley

Cross Keys Inn

Lye's Green, BA12 7PB
⏲ 12-3, 6-11; 12-11 Sun ☎ (01373) 832406
🌐 crosskeyscorsley.co.uk
Three Daggers Daggers Ale; 3 changing beers (sourced locally; often Box Steam, Moles, Twisted) H
This rural gem in the shadow of Cley Hill (famed for its UFO sightings) has a large open fire and a warm, welcoming atmosphere. A good selection of guest ales mainly sourced from local breweries is available, along with excellent bar food and restaurant meals. In 2016 the pub was taken over by a village consortium. It is in an excellent walking area, close to the Somerset border, and near Longleat House and Safari Park.
❀◑⛺♣●P🐾📶

Cricklade

Red Lion L

74 High Street, SN6 6DD
⏲ 12-11 (10.30 Sun) ☎ (01793) 750776
🌐 theredlioncricklade.co.uk
Hop Kettle Cricklade Ordinary Bitter, North Wall; Wadworth 6X; 6 changing beers (often Hop Kettle) H
Friendly, popular and comfortable inn, parts of which are quite ancient – the old Saxon town wall passes through the building. It is home to the Hop Kettle Brewing Co, which brews here and in Swindon. Ten real ales – two regular, four from Hop Kettle and four guests – are on handpump, plus real cider. A winter beer festival is held in February, a summer festival in June. Food is served 12-2.30pm and 6.30-9pm Monday to Saturday, 12-3pm on Sunday. There is a large garden at the back, and accommodation in five rooms.
Q❀🛏◑♿●🚌(51,53)🐾📶

Devizes

British Lion ✔

9 Estcourt Street, SN10 1LQ (opp Kwik Fit)
⏲ 11-11 (midnight Fri & Sat); 12-11 Sun ☎ (01380) 720665
🌐 britishliondevizes.co.uk
4 changing beers (sourced nationally; often Palmers, Plain, Stonehenge) H
The British has been ever-present in the Guide for over 20 years. An unpretentious free house with wooden floors, cosy settles and an eclectic group of talkative regulars, it is an essential port of call in town. There are four handpumps and the beers change frequently throughout the week – time it

right and you can savour eight different ales. The knowledgeable landlord is always pleased to offer his advice. Not to be missed. P (49)

Three Crowns

Maryport Street, SN10 1AG

10.30-11 (midnight Fri); 9am-midnight Sat; 11.30-10.30 Sun (01380) 722331 threecrownsdevizes.co.uk

Wadworth IPA, Horizon, 6X, Bishops Tipple, Swordfish H

Extensively modernised recently, but the pub retains the original beams of the historic 17th-century building. Located in the central town area, the Three Crowns is currently a flagship Wadworth brewery pub. It offers a minimum of five of the brewery's ales plus occasional guests, including Corvus for stout drinkers. An all-day menu includes breakfast, lunch and evening meals, and families are welcome. P

Vaults

28A St John's Street, SN10 1BN (opp town hall)

5-9; 12-9 Fri-Sun (01380) 721443

thevaultsdevizes.com

6 changing beers (sourced nationally; often Stealth) H

The Vaults maintains its high standards, with six handpumps usually offering two ales from Stealth Brewing Co plus regularly changing guests and ciders. A vast selection of bottles and tins from around the world is also stocked. Paddles are available – three third-pint glasses allow you to sample several ales at a time. It has a long, galley-style bar and a huge cellar used for events. Conversation rules here – there is no music or fruit machines but a great atmosphere. Q

Dilton Marsh

Prince of Wales

94 High Street, BA13 4DZ

5-11; 12-11 Fri-Sun (01373) 865487

powdiltonmarsh.co.uk

Otter Amber, Ale; St Austell Cornish Best Bitter, Trelawny; 1 changing beer (sourced regionally; often Bath, St Austell) H

A smart, friendly, local, refurbished in 2013. The layout comprises a bar, separate dining area and a skittle alley doubling as function room. There is a beer garden and a paved outdoor area to the side. The menu consists of traditional pub food including Sunday lunches. The guest beer can be from St Austell (HSD or Proper Job) but quite often comes from elsewhere and has included London Pride, Draught Bass and beers from local microbreweries such as Box Steam and Twisted.
P

Ebbesbourne Wake

Horseshoe

The Cross, SP5 5JF

closed Mon; 12-3, 6.30-11; 12-4 Sun (01722) 780474

thehorseshoe-inn.co.uk

Bowman Swift One; Flack Manor Romsey Gold; Otter Bitter; Red Rock Lighthouse IPA; 1 changing beer (sourced nationally) G

Unspoilt 18th-century pub in a remote rural setting at the foot of an old ox drove. This friendly pub has two small bars displaying an impressive collection of old farm implements, tools and lamps, plus a restaurant, conservatory and pleasant garden. Good local food is available Tuesday to Sunday and four or five beers are served direct from casks stillaged behind the bar. The original serving hatch just inside the front door is still in use. Real cider is usually available, often from Wessex or Orchard Pig. Q P (29)

Edington

Three Daggers

Westbury Road, BA13 4PG

8am-11; 9am-10.30 Sun (01380) 830940

threedaggers.co.uk

Three Daggers Daggers Blonde, Daggers Ale, Daggers Edge; 1 changing beer (often Three Daggers) H

This refurbished village pub is now the brewery tap for the eponymous brewery, situated in an adjacent farm shop. The pub has a main bar with three distinct drinking areas, leading into a seating area and a dining room. Two mirrors hide TV screens that are occasionally used for sporting events. At the rear is a lovely garden. Accommodation is available. Regular seasonal beers are brewed, and carryouts and bottles are available in the shop. Q P

Grittleton

Neeld Arms

The Street, SN14 6AP

12-3, 5.30-11; 12-midnight Sat; 12-11 Sun

(01249) 782470 neeldarms.co.uk

St Austell Tribute; Wadworth 6X; 1 changing beer (sourced locally; often Flying Monk, Otter, Ramsbury) H

The motto 'Proud to be a Pub' sums up this welcoming village inn perfectly. The long-established publican and team offer a good range of quality ales and locally sourced food to the pub's many regular and visiting customers. The 17th-century stone building housing the pub, restaurant and accommodation has a unique, rustic yet modern decor. The resulting ambience makes this deservedly busy hostelry one to linger in.
Q P (35)

Hamptworth

Cuckoo Inn

SP5 2DU

12-3, 5.30-11; 12-11 Fri-Sun (01794) 390302

Hop Back Summer Lightning; Palmers Dorset Gold; house beer (by Hop Back); 3 changing beers (sourced regionally) G

Friendly real ale pub in the Wiltshire countryside. All ales are served straight from the cask, alongside an extensive range of real ciders. The main room is square, encouraging conversation, and there are three further rooms. Outside is a large garden and dogs are welcome. Food choices include pies, jackets, rolls, soups and other warming bites, plus a fish and chips van on Friday. Music plays on alternate Thursdays and beer festivals are held in May and September. Local CAMRA Cider Pub of the Year 2017 and 2018. Q P

Highworth

Rose & Crown

19 The Green, SN6 7DB

9am-11 (midnight Fri & Sat) (01793) 764699

roseandcrownhighworth.co.uk

Sharp's Doom Bar, Sea Fury; 3 changing beers (sourced regionally; often Halfpenny) H
A free house since 2014, following a major facelift, this is one of the oldest pubs in Highworth. Cheerful and friendly staff add to the pleasant atmosphere. It has five handpumps, three serving changing guest ales. The lunch menu is good quality and value. Open mic and folk sessions are held once a month on a Monday. The garden has a boules pitch. Q P (7)

Kilmington

Red Lion Inn

BA12 6RP (on B3092 between Mere and Frome)
11-2.30, 5-8 (9 Thu & Fri); 12-6 Sun (01985) 844263
theredlionkilmington.co.uk
Butcombe Original; Wessex Stourton Pale Ale; 1 changing beer H
A warm and friendly traditional free house with a low-beamed, flagstoned front bar with cushioned walls and window seats, curved high-backed settle seats and woodburners. The larger back bar has tables for diners to enjoy the home-cooked food sourced from high-quality local food producers (some from the village itself). Thatchers Heritage cider completes the excellent drinks range. Dogs are welcome to join their owners in the front bar or in the large attractive garden which has fine views of White Sheet Hill. Opens on bank holiday Mondays. Q P

Kington St Michael

Jolly Huntsman

SN14 6JB
11.30-2.30, 6-11 (midnight Fri & Sat); 12-3, 7-10.30 Sun
(01249) 750305 jollyhuntsman.com
Flying Monk Elmers; Moles Best; 2 changing beers (sourced locally; often Goff's, Ramsbury) H
A former brewery situated on the village high street, this free house offers a warm and friendly welcome, with a large open fire in the winter. It serves a selection of locally brewed real ales and a choice of ciders, usually from regional suppliers. An excellent food menu is available lunchtimes and evenings, featuring a range of traditional fare and chef's specials, plus occasional themed evenings. Accommodation is en-suite. Q P (99)

Lacock

Bell Inn

The Wharf, SN15 2PJ (½ mile over bridge to Bowden Hill)
11-2.30, 5-11; 11-11 Sat; 12-10.30 Sun (01249) 730308
thebellatlacock.co.uk
House beer (by Great Western); 4 changing beers (sourced regionally; often Butts, Great Western, Plain) H
Renowned for its friendly welcome and superbly kept ales, this free house on the edge of the National Trust village of Lacock is popular with locals and visitors alike. Local CAMRA Pub of the Year on a number of occasions, it has an excellent reputation for the variety of ales served, quality food and all-round good value. Two beer festivals are held each year. The house beer, Beau Bell, celebrates the birth of the first child of the landlord and landlady. Q P

George Inn

4 West Street, SN15 2LH
11-11 (10.30 Sun) (01249) 730263
georgeinnlacock.co.uk
Wadworth IPA, Horizon, 6X, Swordfish; 2 changing beers (sourced nationally; often Oakham, Wadworth) H
This stone and timber pub situated near the centre of the beautiful National Trust village dates from the mid-14th century. Look for the original fireplace and dog-driven spit in the oak-beamed interior. A changing range of cider is available and good-quality meals using locally sourced ingredients. A beer festival is held in August and the Boxing Day barbecue is popular. Photographs and cuttings reflect the popularity of the village with film and TV programme makers.
Q P (X34)

Laverstock

Duck

Duck Lane, SP1 1PU
12-midnight; 12.30-midnight Sun (01722) 327678
theduckatlaverstock.co.uk
Hop Back Crop Circle, GFB, Summer Lightning; 1 changing beer (sourced locally) H
A busy community village pub serving traditional home-cooked food in a large, well-furnished, open-plan bar. Sunday lunches are popular so early booking is advisable. A variety of entertainment includes open mic nights, live music at weekends and themed barbecues. Families are welcome and there is full wheelchair access and facilities. Well situated for walkers on the Clarendon Way.
P (66,R6)

Malmesbury

Whole Hog

8 Market Cross, SN16 9AS
11-11; 12-midnight Fri & Sat; 12-11 Sun
(01666) 825845
Ramsbury Same Again; Stonehenge Pigswill; Wadworth 6X; Young's Bitter; 1 changing beer (sourced locally) H
Located between the 15th-century Market Cross and the Abbey in the oldest borough in England, this is a popular town-centre pub, serving well-kept ales and freshly prepared food. There is a diverse range of seating areas, from a former shop window overlooking the Market Square to cosy nooks and crannies. A pub central to the community with many regulars and equally welcoming to visitors looking for respite from sightseeing. Q

Marston Meysey

Old Spotted Cow

SN6 6LQ
11-11 (6.30 Sun) (01285) 810264
theoldspottedcow.co.uk
Otter Bitter; Skinner's Betty Stogs; 1 changing beer (sourced nationally; often Marston's) H
With large gardens and a cosy interior featuring beamed ceilings and log fires, this pub is popular with locals and visitors alike. There is a strong emphasis on good food sourced from local producers and suppliers. In the bar there are three real ale handpumps. The Thames Path is nearby, making the pub attractive to hikers, the source of

the River Thames is only a few miles away. A classic car show features in late May.
Q

Melksham

Bear

3 Bath Road, SN12 6LL

8am-midnight (1am Fri & Sat) (01225) 792690

Greene King Abbot; Ruddles Best Bitter; Sharp's Doom Bar; 2 changing beers (sourced nationally; often Exmoor, Prescott)

A spacious Wetherspoon pub with interesting local history storyboards adorning the walls, and a real fire in winter. Friendly and helpful staff serve a range of three regular ales and two or more guests, often including LocAle, as well as two ciders. A full range of food is always available, including the popular weekly steak, curry and fish nights. The large paved garden includes a smoking area. Frequent buses stop directly outside the pub.
Q P

Pig & Whistle

1 Woodrow Road, SN12 7AU

12-midnight (11 Mon); 12-11 Sun (01225) 705118

Sharp's Doom Bar; 2 changing beers (sourced nationally; often Box Steam, Eagle)

This relaxed and welcoming hostelry is the beating heart of the local community. The single large room has a main bar, snug and a pool table/TV area, with a comfortable and informal atmosphere. There is also a conservatory and, outside, a spacious garden. Real pub food includes a traditional Sunday lunch. Local charities are strongly supported. A great example of a friendly neighbourhood pub selling quality food and ales – just as it should be. **P**

Netherhampton

Victoria & Albert

Netherhampton Road, SP2 8PU

11-3, 5.30 (5 Sat)-11; 12-5 Sun (01722) 743174

victoriaandalbert.org

3 changing beers (sourced regionally)

A genuine classic English country inn, dating back to 1540 and little changed over the years. The beautiful, thatched building lies in the centre of the village opposite the church and is a focus of local life. Inside, it boasts flagstone floors, a log fire and original oak beams, while outside are a large covered patio and spacious garden. Snacks and full meals are available lunchtimes and evenings. A long-established family business and winner of numerous awards including local CAMRA Pub of the Year 2018. **Q P**

North Wroughton

Check Inn

79 Woodland View, SN4 9AA

12-11 (midnight Fri & Sat); 12-10.30 Sun

(01793) 331428 checkinnswindon.co.uk

Fuller's Oliver's Island, London Pride; 2 changing beers (sourced nationally; often Fuller's, Gale's)

This Fuller's pub is hidden away in a residential cul-de-sac next to the motorway on the edge of Wroughton. Photographs of old Wroughton decorate the walls. One seasonal beer complements the regular ales. Live music plays, mostly on the last Saturday of the month, with a blues session the second Sunday afternoon of the month. Quizzes also feature regularly. Beer and cider festivals are held in spring and over the summer bank holiday.
Q P (49)

Nunton

Radnor Arms

SP5 4HS

12-11 (01722) 329722

Sharp's Doom Bar; 2 changing beers (sourced nationally)

Built as a cottage in the mid-18th century, it became a pub in 1853 and is named after Lord Radnor whose descendants still own the nearby estate. The open-plan interior has low ceilings and various seating areas allowing for privacy. Two guest beers are available, one usually from Hop Back. Popular with diners, it offers an extensive family-friendly menu. The large open garden has a children's play area and leads down to the River Ebble. **Q P** (44,X3)

Pewsey

Shed Alehouse

20 North Street, SN9 5EX

closed Mon & Tue; 5-9.30 Wed & Thu; 4-10 Fri; 2-10 Sat; 1-5 Sun 07769 812643

5 changing beers (sourced regionally)

A former shop converted to a cosy award-winning micropub, the interior reflecting its name with a basic wood-panelled decor complete with tools. This is a free house with five handpumps serving a changing range of beers from local and regional brewers, often including Shed Ales from Pewsey, alongside four real ciders and a craft pilsner. There is not much space inside, so you soon get to know your fellow drinkers. No dogs allowed.
Q (X5)

Royal Wootton Bassett

Five Bells

Wood Street, SN4 7BD

12-3, 5-11.30; 12-midnight Fri-Sun (01793) 849422

Black Sheep Best Bitter; Fuller's London Pride; 4 changing beers (sourced nationally; often Sharp's, Timothy Taylor)

Dating from before 1841, this is a busy and cosy traditional thatched local with a beamed ceiling and open fires. The bar, which has now been extended, has seven handpumps for two regular beers, four guests and a cider. Food is served lunchtimes and Wednesday and Thursday evenings (booking recommended). The pub has darts and crib teams. Special events are held throughout the year including a beer festival in the summer.
Q P (55)

Salisbury

Duke of York

34 York Road, SP2 7AS

6.30-midnight; 6-midnight Fri; 4-midnight Sat; 1-11 Sun

(01722) 503872

Hop Back GFB; 4 changing beers (sourced locally)

A popular free house sporting mainly local beers and two or three traditional ciders. A pub for the community, the focus is on conversation, and an informal quiz is held on Sunday night. It is home to the Fisherton History Society who meet on the second Wednesday of the month, and hosts other events on occasion. Background music and videos play on TV. Opening times may be later so check ahead. ❀≹♣●🚌(R1)🐾ᯤ

Haunch of Venison ★

1 Minster Street, SP1 1TB

11-11 (midnight Fri & Sat); 11-10 Sun ☎ (01722) 411313
haunchpub.co.uk

Courage Best Bitter; Hop Back GFB, Summer Lightning; 1 changing beer (sourced nationally) Ⓗ

Known as one of Britain's finest old inns and identified by CAMRA as having a nationally important historic interior. Three small drinking areas downstairs and a dining room upstairs are all unique. Look for the original spirit taps, the floor tiles in the Commons and the mummified hand of a cards cheat in the Lords. An unmissable gem right in the heart of this historic city.

New Inn

41 New Street, SP1 2PH

12-11 (midnight Sat) ☎ (01722) 326662
newinn-salisbury.co.uk

Hall & Woodhouse Fursty Ferret, Tanglefoot; 1 changing beer Ⓗ

Originally several cottages, parts of the timber-framed building have been standing here since the 14th century, but it has only been used as a public house for around 200 years. There are two bars – one at the front and one at the rear used for dining. The changing beer is from Badger's seasonal range. A large well-kept garden extends to the Cathedral Close wall, with a fire pit used on weekend evenings.

Rai d'Or 𝕃

69 Brown Street, SP1 2AS

5-10 (11 Thu-Sat); closed Sun ☎ (01722) 327137
raidor.co.uk

2 changing beers (sourced locally) Ⓗ

Characterful 13th-century free house with a fascinating history. An inglenook fireplace and low ceilings make for an appealing ambience. Excellent, reasonably priced Thai food is complemented by two changing, usually local, beers. It can be busy at mealtimes, but drinkers are always welcome. There is a discount on food before 6.30pm. Local CAMRA Town Pub of the Year 2018, with 14 years in the Guide.

Rugby Club 𝕃

Castle Road, SP1 3SA

closed Mon; 7-11; 12-midnight Sat; 8-11 Sun
☎ (01722) 325317 salisburyrfc.org

Hop Back Crop Circle, GFB, Summer Lightning; 1 changing beer Ⓗ

Occupying a corner of the large club house, this cosy, refurbished lounge bar is open to the public. Retaining its sporting roots, the bar features rugby memorabilia. Two TVs generally show rugby or other sport. The function room bar is open at busy times such as match days. The three Hop Back ales are often joined by a Hop Back or Downton seasonal brew. Quiz night is Wednesday. A beer festival is held in May. There are camping facilities close by.

Village Freehouse 𝕃

33 Wilton Road, SP2 7EF

5-11; 12-11 Fri-Sun ☎ (01722) 329707

Downton Quadhop; 4 changing beers (sourced nationally) Ⓗ

A lively pub, handy for those arriving by train. Microbrewery beers are sourced from near and far, with customer requests welcomed. There is always at least one dark brew, either stout, porter or mild. Teams are fielded in the local crib, cricket and football leagues and a TV shows BT Sport, with the sound off much of the time. Filled rolls are available or you are welcome to bring your own food. Local CAMRA Pub of the Year three times.

Winchester Gate 𝕃

113-117 Rampart Road, SP1 1JA

3 (12 Thu-Sat)-11; 12-10 Sun ☎ (01722) 411529

House beer (by Wadworth); 4 changing beers (sourced nationally) Ⓗ

This free house, an inn since the 17th century, once provided for travellers at the city's east tollgate. Five handpumps offer ales that can be from all over the country but are mainly quite local. A real cider is also often available, particularly in summer months. Cider festivals in spring and summer complement three beer festivals throughout the year. A small terraced garden accommodates a pétanque terrain, with boules available. Live music features most weekends.

Wyndham Arms 𝕃

27 Estcourt Road, SP1 3AS

4.30 (12 Thu)-11.30; 12-midnight Fri & Sat; 12-11.30 Sun
☎ (01722) 331026

Hop Back Citra, Crop Circle, GFB, Summer Lightning; 2 changing beers Ⓗ

The birthplace of the Hop Back Brewery, now celebrating 32 consecutive years in the Guide. A traditional ale house, it has a single bar with six handpumps serving a selection of Hop Back ales including its seasonal offerings. There is also a fine selection of bottled beers and wines. Two small quiet rooms off the main bar area provide more seating. This is a pub for conversation, good-natured banter and fine ales. Local CAMRA Pub of the Year 2017. (R2,R6)

Semley

Benett Arms 🏆

Village Green, SP7 9AS (1 mile E of A350) ST891270

12-3, 5-11; 12-3, 5.30-11 Sat; 12-3, 5.30-10 Sun
☎ (01747) 830221 benettarms.co.uk

House beer (by Ringwood); 2 changing beers Ⓗ

A genuine free house sitting by the green and pond in a quiet village, with a single small bar and separate dining areas. The beer choice varies but there are usually three to choose from, either on handpump or direct from the cellar. The cider is from Bridge Farm. Excellent home-cooked food is available at all sessions. A warm welcome is extended to all, including families and dogs, in an area popular with walkers. Local CAMRA Pub of the Year 2016 and 2018. Q (84,247)

Swindon

Beehive ✔

55 Prospect Hill, SN1 3JS

12-midnight (1am Thu-Sat) ☎ (01793) 523187
bee-hive.co.uk

Hardys & Hansons Olde Trip; house beer (by Greene King); 4 changing beers (sourced regionally; often Greene King) Ⓗ
Built at a sharp corner on a hill, this multi-levelled, four-room pub has retained its quirky layout and charm. There is a map of Swindon in the 19th century on the rear room ceiling. A popular live music venue, it hosts performances on most Thursday and Friday evenings, and other nights too on occasion. The walls are often adorned with pictures and other artwork for sale. Locally sourced pies are available lunchtime until early evening. Poker night is Monday. ◑♣🚌🐾📶

Blunsdon Arms ✔

Lady Lane, SN25 2NA
10-midnight (12.30am Fri & Sat) ☎ (01793) 729801
St Austell Tribute; house beer (by Black Sheep); 6 changing beers (sourced nationally; often Bath Ales, Butcombe) Ⓗ
This Ember Inns pub opened in 2006 and has a large open-plan interior with lots of comfortable seating. The six guest beers rotate from a selection of 12 ales changing quarterly. There are also three real ciders. Food is served every day until 10pm. Quiz nights are Wednesday and Sunday, poker night every Monday. Live music features on the last Saturday of the month. A friendly welcome is assured from the pleasant staff.
❀◑♿♣●P🚌📶

Glue Pot

5 Emlyn Square, SN1 5BP
12 (4.30 Mon)-11; 11.30-11 Fri & Sat; 12-10.30 Sun
☎ (01793) 497420
Downton New Forest Ale; Hop Back Citra, Crop Circle, Entire Stout, Summer Lightning; 3 changing beers (sourced nationally; often Downton, Hop Back) Ⓗ
The Glue Pot is part of the historic Swindon Railway Village. The inside is basic with wooden bench seats. There are seven Hop Back or Downton ales, one guest, and nine real ciders. A range of sandwiches, wraps and subs is always available. There is a pub quiz on Wednesday night and a beer festival over the Easter weekend. Local CAMRA Cider Pub of the Year in 2016 and 2017.
Q❀≠●🚌🐾

Hop Inn L

7 Devizes Road, SN1 4BJ
12-11 (10.30 Mon); 12-midnight Fri & Sat; 12-10.30 Sun
☎ (01793) 976833 🌐 hopinnswindon.co.uk
House beer (by Ramsbury); 4 changing beers (sourced regionally) Ⓗ
A genuine free house and great example of the growing success of micropubs, this former shop has become a popular destination for real ale lovers. The small bar has one house beer from Ramsbury and four different guest ales, normally from smaller regional breweries. There are two changing real ciders. The inside is furnished in an eclectic style including chairs and tables made from reclaimed wood. Fresh pizzas are available Tuesday to Sunday evenings. Q◗♿♣●🚌 (12,15)🐾📶

Savoy L ✔

38-40 Regent Street, SN1 1JL
8am-midnight (1am Fri & Sat) ☎ (01793) 533970
Greene King Abbot; Ruddles Best Bitter; Sharp's Doom Bar; 10 changing beers (sourced nationally) Ⓗ
This lively and friendly town-centre pub is the oldest Wetherspoon in Swindon, converted from the foyer and ground floors of a 1930s cinema. Cinema photos and information from the era decorate the walls. It has a spacious interior on different levels, divided into separate areas. There is a TV screen in one corner, mainly silent. A large selection of well-kept beers is available and food is served 8am-11pm. Handy for the theatre, cinema, restaurants and shopping.
Q❀◑♿♣●🚌 (1,1A)📶

Weighbridge Brewhouse L ✔

Penzance Drive, SN5 7JL
12-11 (10 Sun) ☎ (01793) 881500
🌐 weighbridgebrewhouse.co.uk
Weighbridge Brinkworth Village, Best, Pooley's Golden; 2 changing beers Ⓗ
The Weighbridge Brewhouse is an upmarket brew- and gastropub in the former home of Archers Brewery and the GWR Weighbridge. It features a long, shiny bar with five handpumps dedicated to the real ale brewed on the premises. Seating in the bar is limited, but an upper level has more seating, a glass piano and a display of bottled beers. Live music plays Thursday to Saturday evenings. The modern open-plan restaurant serves freshly prepared food 12-2pm and 6-9.30pm (6-8pm Sun), booking advisable. Q❀◑♿P🚌 (1A,55)

Yates ✔

49-50 Bridge Street, SN1 1BL
10-11 (1am Fri & Sat); 11-10 Sun ☎ (01793) 484924
Bombardier; Wadworth 6X; Wychwood Hobgoblin; 3 changing beers (sourced nationally) Ⓗ
Large town-centre chain pub which unusually has a better-than-average interest in and sale of real ales and ciders. It can be very lively, especially at weekends. Essentially a sports bar, a number of TV screens show various sports throughout the week. Refurbished in the last couple of years, facilities are all on one level. ❀◑♿≠●🚌 (1,8)📶

Tisbury

Boot Inn L

High Street, SP3 6PS
12-2.30 (not Mon & Tue), 7-11; 12-3 Sun
☎ (01747) 870363
3 changing beers (sourced locally) Ⓖ
Fine village free house built of Chilmark stone, licensed since 1768. Run by the same landlord since 1976, locals and visitors alike are assured of a cordial welcome. A new coat of paint has freshened the interior, enhancing the friendly, relaxed atmosphere. It usually offers three ales and an additional beer is often available at weekends, all dispensed directly from casks behind the bar. Excellent food is served and there is a spacious garden. The third Tuesday of the month is quiz night, attracting a full house.
Q❀◑≠♣P🚌 (25,26)

Warminster

Fox & Hounds

6 Deverill Road, BA12 9QP
11-11 ☎ (01985) 216711
Wessex Warminster Warrior; house beer (by Wessex); 2 changing beers (sourced regionally; often Flack Manor, Otter, Palmers) Ⓗ
A friendly two-bar local – the main bar with a pool table and sports TV is at the rear, and a quiet snug bar is to the right of the entrance. There is a large skittle alley and function room at the back. Guest

real ales are usually from local and regional breweries. Regular ciders are from Thatchers and Rich's, plus up to five guests. Closing time may be later than 11pm. A local CAMRA multiple award-winning pub. Q❀♿♣●P🚌(50,55)🐾📶

Organ Inn ✔

49 High Street, BA12 9AQ

4-midnight; 12-midnight Sat; 4-11 Sun ☎ (01985) 211777
theorganinn.co.uk

3 changing beers (sourced regionally; often Plain, Stonehenge) Ⓗ

An inn until 1913, the Organ reopened as a pub in 2006. The welcoming interior comprises three rooms with a traditional feel, plus a snug, games room and skittle alley. The beer range constantly changes but will always include Organ Bitter (the brewery is a secret). The cider is mainly from Westons with guests. A beer festival is held in September. Bar snacks are interesting and there is an art gallery upstairs. Local CAMRA Rural Pub of the Year 2018. Q❀♿⇌♣●🚌🐾📶

Westbury

Hollies

55A Westbury Leigh, BA13 3SF

12-11 (midnight Fri & Sat); 12-10.30 Sun
☎ (01373) 864493 theholliesinn.com

Twisted Gaucho; 2 changing beers (sourced locally; often Box Steam, Twisted) Ⓗ

A handsome old red-brick village pub in the Westbury Leigh area of town. Inside there is plenty of comfortable seating in multiple areas including a separate dining room. An outlet for the local Twisted Brewery, at least two of its extensive range are on offer, and usually a guest from elsewhere. The food is highly rated and there is good-quality accommodation in three rooms. ❀🛏◐⇌(Dilton Marsh)P🚌🐾📶

Wilton

Swan L

SN8 3SS

12-3, 6-11; 12-11 Sat; 12-10.30 Sun ☎ (01672) 870274
theswanwilton.co.uk

5 changing beers (sourced regionally; often Flying Monk, Stonehenge, Plain) Ⓗ/Ⓖ

This popular village pub near lock 61 on the Kennet & Avon Canal has an open and attractive interior. Real ale dispense is a mixture of handpump and gravity – a beer board displaying the distance from the brewery underlines the pub's commitment to local produce. Good-quality food also uses local ingredients (no eve meals Sun). Themed food evenings include steak night on Tuesday. Crofton Beam Engines featuring one of the oldest working steam engines in the world is nearby.
❀◐P🚌(21,22)🐾📶

Wroughton

Carters Rest L ✔

57 High Street, SN4 9JU

5-11 (midnight Fri); 12-midnight Sat; 12-11 Sun
☎ (01793) 813841

Castle Rock Harvest Pale; Sharp's Doom Bar; 5 changing beers (often Ramsbury) Ⓗ

First mentioned in 1671, the inn was extensively altered in 1912/13 to give it a Victorian appearance, with large gables and high ceilings. Its name originates from the stables that used to be here, providing extra horses for the journey to Devizes market. A large building with two bars, this is a real ale destination also offering three regular ciders and a guest cider or perry. Quiz night is Thursday and the pub is dog-friendly.
❀♿♣●P🚌(9,81)🐾📶

Zeals

Bell & Crown

New Road, BA12 6NJ

closed Mon; 11-3, 5-11; 11-11 Fri & Sat; 12-3 Sun
☎ (01747) 840404 bellandcrown.com

3 changing beers (often Bristol Beer Factory, Otter, Palmers) Ⓗ

A fine-dining pub with a traditional bar with an open fire and real ales, equally popular with locals and visitors. The layout allows almost complete separation of the bar and dining areas. The beer choice changes regularly with West Country breweries always well represented. A constantly changing menu of fresh home-made food is prepared seven days a week by the chef landlord. The National Trust property of Stourhead is nearby. Q❀◐♿P🚌

King's Arms Inn, All Cannings

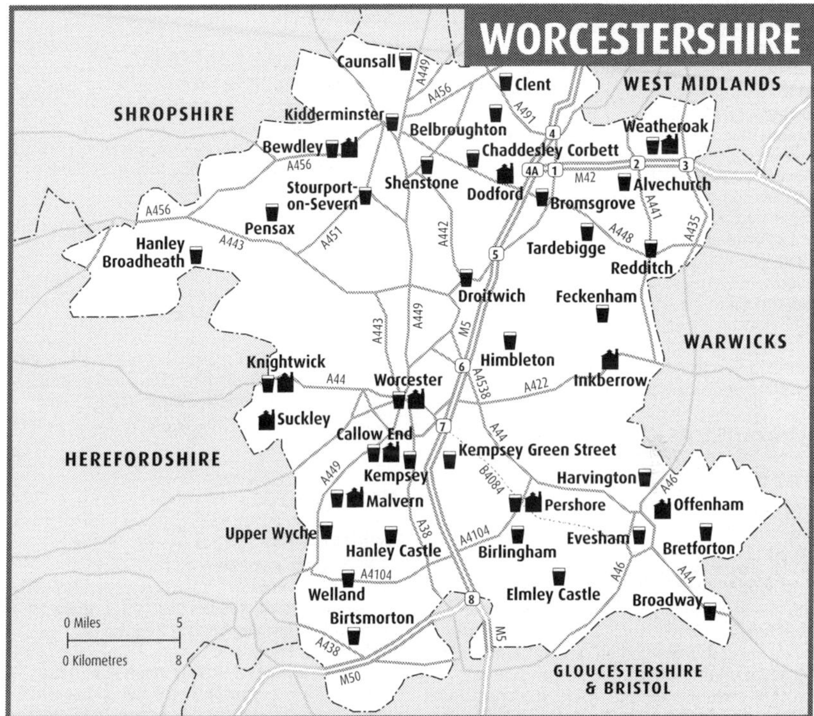

Alvechurch

Weighbridge 🄻

Scarfield Wharf, Scarfield Hill, B48 7SQ (follow signs to marina from village) SP022721
12-3, 7-11 (10.30 Sun) ☎ (0121) 445 5111
the-weighbridge.co.uk
House beer (by Weatheroak); 4 changing beers (often Wye Valley) 🄷
This cosy canalside pub is a regular local CAMRA Pub of the Year. It has two small lounges, a public bar and a pleasant garden. Good-value home-cooked food is served lunchtimes and evenings (no food Tue and Wed) and excellent Sunday lunches. A covered area outside can be used for functions. Its quality beer is served by enthusiastic and knowledgable staff. House beers are Weatheroak Tillerman's Tipple and Kinver Bargees Bitter. Changing guest beers include a mild, and real cider or perry is available. Spring and autumn beer festivals are held. Q❀◑⇌●P🚌(146)

Belbroughton

Holly Bush Inn

Stourbridge Road, DY9 9UG (on A491, nr jct 4 of M5)
11.30-11; 11.30-3, 6-11 Sat; 12-3, 7-10.30 Sun
☎ (01562) 730207
Hobsons Mild, Twisted Spire, Town Crier; 1 changing beer (sourced regionally; often Hobsons) 🄷
This popular pub was originally terraced cottages dating back to 1845. Excellent beers from the Hobsons range are served. The lively public bar hosts traditional games including cards and dominoes while two other areas, one with a real fire, are used for dining. Good food is served from a traditional menu. Thatchers cider is on handpump. Q❀◑♿●P🚌(318)🐾

Bewdley

Great Western 🄻

Kidderminster Road, DY12 1BY (near SVR station, walk past signal box and under viaduct)
11.30-11 ☎ (01299) 488828
Bewdley Worcestershire Way; Holden's Golden Glow; Morland Old Golden Hen; house beer (by Bewdley); 1 changing beer (sourced regionally; often Enville, Ludlow, Three Tuns) 🄷
The comfortable pub has a simple railway theme reminiscent of an earlier age. Overlooking the bar is an upper level from which to admire the decorative wall tiles. Pub snacks such as pork pies and cobs go with the concept of a traditional pub, and on the bar there are five real ales including regulars from Holden's and Bewdley, and two Westons ciders. Q❀♿⇌(SVR)♣●P🚌🐾

Mug House 🄻 ✔

12 Severnside North, DY12 2EE (150yds along Severnside North from river bridge)
12-11 (11.30 Fri & Sat) ☎ (01299) 402543
mughousebewdley.co.uk
Bewdley Worcestershire Way; Purity Mad Goose; Timothy Taylor Landlord; Wye Valley HPA; 1 changing beer (sourced locally; often Holden's, Salopian, Wye Valley) 🄷
On the side of the Severn, the Mug House is not to be missed. A friendly pub that welcomes locals and visitors alike, there are comfortable settles and a log fire in the lounge bar, and outside is a sun terrace with a glass-covered patio with grapevines and wisteria. It serves five well-kept beers from Bewdley, Purity, Wye Valley and Timothy Taylor, a changing guest and two ciders. An à la carte menu is available in the restaurant and meals in the bar at lunchtime. Q❀🛏◑♿⇌(SVR)●🚌🐾

Old Waggon & Horses 𝕃

91 Kidderminster Road, DY12 1DG (on Bewdley to Kidderminster road at Catchems End)
12-11; 11.30-11 Fri; 11.30-1am Sat ☎ (01299) 403170
waggonbewdley.co.uk
Banks's Mild; Bathams Best Bitter; Ludlow Gold; Wainwright; 2 changing beers (sourced locally; often Enville, Hobsons, Holden's) Ⓗ
Popular pub with a central bar serving three distinct areas. The small wooden-floored snug has a dartboard and the larger room a woodburner. There is a roll-down screen for major sporting events, but at most times conversation prevails. An old kitchen range adds to the cottagey feel. Pub food is available, plus a pie night and a tapas night once a month, and a carvery on Sunday. The attractive terraced flower garden is on many levels.
(SVR)P

Birlingham

Swan

Church Street, WR10 3AQ
closed Mon; 11.30-3, 6-11; 12-7 Sun ☎ (01386) 750485
theswaninn.co.uk
3 changing beers (often Flying Monk, Goffs) Ⓗ
A delightful thatched free house, tucked away at the end of a lane in a quiet village. The pub is food-oriented, with meals served in the conservatory overlooking the fine garden, and fresh fish a highlight on the specials menu. The pub has recently been modernised inside in a sympathetic manner in keeping with the historic building.
QP(382)

Birtsmorton

Farmers Arms

Birts Street, WR13 6AP (off B4208) SO790363
11 (12 Sun)-4, 6-midnight ☎ (01684) 833308
farmersarmsbirtsmorton.co.uk
Hook Norton Hooky, Old Hooky; 2 changing beers (sourced locally) Ⓗ
Grade II listed black-and-white village pub dating from 1480, found down a quiet country lane. The large bar area features a splendid inglenook fireplace while the cosy lounge has old settles and low beams. Good-value, home-made food is on offer daily (lunch until 2pm, eve meals until 9.30pm weekdays, 9pm Sun). A beer from a local independent brewer is often available. The spacious garden provides fine views of the Malvern Hills. QP(577)

Bretforton

Fleece Inn ★ 𝕃

The Cross, WR11 7JE
11-11 ☎ (01386) 831173 thefleeceinn.co.uk
Uley Pig's Ear Strong Beer; Wye Valley Bitter; 3 changing beers (often North Cotswold, Purity, Wye Valley) Ⓗ
Renowned 15th-century timber-framed village pub owned by the National Trust on the edge of the Cotswolds. It is recognised by CAMRA as having a nationally important historic pub interior, and houses a world-famous 17th-century pewter collection which can be viewed in one of the three main rooms. Morris dancers and music feature all year round, with entertainment evenings in the medieval barn. Local CAMRA Pub of the Year 2018.
Q

Broadway

Crown & Trumpet Inn 𝕃

14 Church Street, WR12 7AE (just off village green)
11-10.30 (11.45 Fri & Sat) ☎ (01386) 853202
crownandtrumpet.co.uk
Prescott Chequered Flag; Stanway Broadway Artist's Ale; Stroud Tom Long; Timothy Taylor Landlord; 2 changing beers (sourced locally; often Bath Ales, North Cotswold) Ⓗ
Picturesque 17th-century Cotswold-stone inn where the landlord has 33 years' experience as a Guide licensee. This hostelry has welcoming and friendly staff and an abundance of character, with oak beams, log fire and Flowers Brewery memorabilia. Good, honest, home-made local dishes are offered at reasonable prices alongside regular ales and guests plus ciders and perries. Entertainment includes midweek live jazz and blues nights. A former local CAMRA award winner.
QP

Bromsgrove

Golden Cross Hotel 𝕃

20 High Street, B61 8HH (S end of High St)
8am-midnight (1am Fri & Sat) ☎ (01527) 870005
Greene King Abbot; Ruddles Best Bitter; Sharp's Doom Bar; 9 changing beers (often Enville, Inveralmond, Prescott) Ⓗ
This stylish split-level Wetherspoon pub in the town centre was previously a hotel and coach house. It has 12 individual booths with interesting glass throughout. The permanent beers are complemented by a range of guest ales, many sourced locally. Beer festivals are held twice a year as part of the national programme. There is a pay & display car park at the rear, free after 7pm.
QP

Ladybird 𝕃

2 Finstall Road, B60 2DZ (on B4184 on corner of roundabout near station) SO969695
11-11; 12-10.30 Sun ☎ (01527) 878014
ladybirdinn.co.uk
Bathams Best Bitter; Sharp's Doom Bar; Wye Valley HPA, Butty Bach; 2 changing beers (often Malvern Hills, Purity, Salopian) Ⓗ
This popular local has a light, airy lounge, with a polished wooden floor, and is decorated with historic railway photographs. A function/meeting room is available on the first floor. Food is served in the pub every day, and Rosado's, a privately run

REAL ALE BREWERIES

Ambridge Inkberrow
Bewdley Bewdley
Boat Lane Offenham
Crafted Bewdley
Friday Beer Malvern
Hop Shed Suckley
Lakehouse Malvern
Malvern Hills Malvern
Pershore Pershore
Sociable Worcester
St George's Callow End
Teme Valley Knightwick
Weatheroak Hill Weatheroak
Wintrip Worcester
Woodcote Manor Dodford
Worcester Worcester

Italian restaurant, is on the same site, as well as a Travelodge. A token is needed to exit the car park.

Little Ale House

21 Worcester Road, B61 7DL (on corner of Station St)
12 (3 Mon-Wed)-10 07791 698641
7 changing beers (often Hobsons, Malvern Hills, Wye Valley) G
Bromsgrove's first micropub has a friendly and cosy atmosphere. All seven ales are served straight from the cask, and the house beer, Half Cut, is brewed by Woodcote Manor. A range of ciders and perries is also stocked and takeaway containers are available. Snacks include fresh rolls and Scotch eggs. A council car park is nearby and the bus station is parallel with the high street.
Q

Park Gate

Kidderminster Road, Park Gate, B61 9AJ
12-11 (midnight Fri & Sat) (01527) 272665
parkgateinn.co.uk
6 changing beers H
A functional but welcoming roadside inn with excellent views from the large, attractive gardens. It is a popular stop-off for weekend walkers and a selection of marked walks is displayed on the noticeboard in the car park. A range of snacks, including cobs with various fillings, pies and pickled eggs is available, alongside a choice of up to 10 different ales on the bar. A bus stop is near the pub. P (42)

Callow End

Old Bush

Upton Road, WR2 4TE (small lane off B4424) SO835497
12-3, 5-11.30; 12-midnight Fri & Sat; 12-11.30 Sun
(01905) 830792 old-bush.com
Butcombe Adam Henson's Rare Breed, Original; Hobsons Twisted Spire; 1 changing beer (sourced locally) H
Village local with a pretty black and white exterior recently rescued from closure by a strong local campaign and bought in 2017 by the landlord. The interior is cosy with a logburner. Food is served in the bar and a separate dining area. The large and attractively laid-out garden has country views and a play area for children. Events include regular live music, an annual blues festival and celebrations on firework night. P

Caunsall

Anchor Inn L

DY11 5YL (off A449 Kidderminster to Wolverhampton road)
11-4, 7-11; 11-3, 7-10.30 Sun (01562) 850254
theanchorinncaunsall.co.uk
Hobsons Best, Town Crier; Three Tuns XXX; Wye Valley HPA, Butty Bach H
Friendly village inn renowned for its five real ales, traditional ciders and especially its well-filled cobs. A central doorway leads into the bar with its original 1920s furniture and horse-racing memorabilia. Outside, the garden is a suntrap in summer, and this popular pub can get busy, especially at lunchtimes and weekends. Easily reached from the nearby canal, this gem is well worth stopping off for. Local CAMRA Pub of the Year finalist 2016-2018. Q P

Chaddesley Corbett

Swan L

High Street, DY10 4SD (along High St from A448) SO892737
11-11 (midnight Fri); 12-11 Sun (01562) 777302
theswanchaddesleycorbett.co.uk
Bathams Mild Ale, Best Bitter H
Characterful village pub dating from 1606 with an impressive lounge with a raised stage area for entertainment, a cosy side room with a real fire, and a traditional public bar. A recently extended food menu includes roasts, lasagne and fish and chips as well as filled rolls and pies. Live jazz is hosted on Thursday evening and open mic on the first Friday of the month. There is a large garden at the rear overlooking the beautiful local countryside. Guest still cider is available on handpull. The pub is popular with walkers and cyclists and is close to historic Harvington Hall.
Q P

Clent

Clent Club

Pool Furlong, DY9 9RE (¼ mile from central crossroads in Clent, in lane off Belbroughton Rd)
4.30-11 (10 Mon); 11-11 Fri & Sat; 12-10.30 Sun
(01562) 730279 clentclub.co.uk
Wye Valley HPA; 3 changing beers (often Holden's, Oakham, St Austell) H
This sizeable refurbished club is on the edge of Clent. It has a large, comfortable main room with the bar and a small side meeting room. TVs show major sports fixtures. Four ales and two real ciders are served. Snacks include filled rolls, pork pies and sausage rolls. The large rear grassed area hosts village events and has extensive views. Families and dogs are welcome. Show a copy of the Guide or a CAMRA membership card for entry. Local CAMRA Club of the Year 2018. P

Droitwich

Hop Pole L

40 Friar Street, WR9 8ED
12-11 (10.30 Sun) (01905) 770155
Malvern Hills Black Pear; Wye Valley HPA, Butty Bach; 2 changing beers H
Popular and unchanging 18th-century pub located at a dead end in the old part of Droitwich between the Norbury Theatre and the fire station. There is a separate pool room adjoining the bar and a heated patio area at the rear to accommodate smokers. Three locally sourced beers are usually available with an occasional guest. Good-value food is served at lunchtimes, and pub games and live music on some weekends ensure a convivial atmosphere.

Elmley Castle

Queen Elizabeth

Main Street, WR10 3HS
11 (5 Mon)-11; 11-8 Sun (01386) 710251
elmleycastle.com
4 changing beers (sourced locally; often Purity, Wye Valley) H
An old pub with a fresh, modern feel inside, named after Elizabeth I's visit to the village in August 1575. This is a community pub, owned by a group of local residents who rescued it from closure. The

bar has a flagstone floor, timber beams and a roaring fire. There is a comfortable lounge and a separate dining room. Themed food evenings are held regularly and two annual beer festivals on the May and August bank holidays.

Evesham

Red Lion

6 Market Place, WR11 4RE

11-11; 12-10.30 Sun ☎ (01386) 761688

2 changing beers (sourced locally; often North Cotswold) H

Closed for over 100 years, this historic town-centre local overlooking Evesham's market reopened in 2014. Two bars serve a large seating area and smaller snug with an inglenook fireplace, all decorated with knick-knacks, breweriana and old advertising. There is no TV or jukebox. Live music plays on Friday evening and Sunday afternoon. No food is served but you are welcome to bring in your own, with plates and cutlery provided. One real cider is always available, two in summer.

Feckenham

Rose & Crown

High Street, B96 6HS

11-3, 6-11; 12-11 Sat & Sun ☎ (01527) 892188

roseandcrownfeckenham.co.uk

Banks's Amber Ale; Brakspear Oxford Gold; 2 changing beers (often Marston's, Wye Valley) H

A welcoming family-run Grade II listed village pub near the church. It has a traditional bar, with up to four real ales and at least one real cider. Attentive staff serve food from a wide menu of pub classics in the cosy low-ceilinged lounge. The large enclosed beer garden at the rear is suitable for children. An annual beer festival is held over the August bank holiday. Parking is limited, but there is a free car park 200 yards away.

Hanley Broadheath

Fox Inn

WR15 8QS (on B4204 E of Tenbury Wells) SO671652

5-11; 3-12.30am Fri; 12-12.30am Sat; 12-10 Sun

☎ (01886) 853189

Bathams Best Bitter; Brakspear Oxford Gold; Joseph Herbert Smith Foxy Lady; 1 changing beer (often Hogarths) H

The main bar of this 16th-century black-and-white timbered free house is decorated with hops and has a large fireplace with a wood-burning stove. The panelled dining area is separated from the bar by wood beams. The games room has a pool table, TV and darts. Home-made food, including Sunday lunch, is available, with bar snacks at any time. One guest beer is usually from Hogarths Brewery in Bolton.

Hanley Castle

Three Kings ★

Church End, WR8 0BL (signed off B4211) SO838420

12-3, 7-11 (10.30 Sun) ☎ (01684) 592686

Butcombe Original; Hobsons Best; 3 changing beers (often Beowulf, Malvern Hills, Slater's) H

On CAMRA's National Inventory of Historic Pub Interiors, this unspoilt 15th-century country pub on the village green near the church has been run by the Roberts family since 1911. The three-room interior comprises a small snug with large inglenook, serving hatch and settle wall, a small side room, and Nell's Lounge with another inglenook, beams and its own entrance. Three guest ales are on offer, often from local breweries, plus Westons Old Rosie draught cider. Live music sessions feature regularly and a popular beer festival is held in November.

(363)

Harvington

Coach & Horses

Station Road, WR11 8NJ

5-midnight; 12-midnight Sat; 12-11.30 Sun

☎ (01386) 870249 coachandhorsesharvington.com

Greene King IPA; 4 changing beers (sourced nationally) H

CAMRA multi award-winning family-run country pub with a warm welcome, celebrating its 300-year anniversary in 2018. There is a logburner in the lounge and an open fire in the bar. Good-value food is prepared by the landlord. The recently refurbished function room doubles as a skittle alley and is available to hire for private functions. An annual beer festival is held in September. Local CAMRA Pub of the Year 2014-2017.

Himbleton

Galton Arms

Harrow Lane, WR9 7LQ (on edge of village)

12-2 (not Mon), 4.30-11; 11-11 Sun ☎ (01905) 391672

Banks's Amber Ale; Bathams Best Bitter; Wye Valley HPA; 1 changing beer (sourced locally) H

Splendid rural pub with a friendly welcome and popular with locals and visitors alike. The unspoilt interior is warmed by open fires and retains the original beams that divide up the space. The guest beer is often from a local brewery. Good-value food is served in two separate dining areas. The bar area shows sports TV.

Kempsey

Walter de Cantelupe

34 Main Road, WR5 3NA (on A38 next to post office)

closed Mon; 6-11 Tue-Thu; 5.30-11 Fri; 12-2.30, 5.30-11 Sat; 12-3, 5.30-9 Sun ☎ (01905) 820572

walterdecantelupe.co.uk

Timothy Taylor Landlord; Wye Valley Bitter; 2 changing beers H

A comfortable inn named after a 13th-century Bishop of Worcester, divided into three cosy drinking areas. Traditional but inventive food is served, made with local ingredients where possible. Events include a paella party in the attractive walled garden in June. Beers are served in lined glasses, including third pints, and a parish discount is available to local residents. The pub may open all day on summer weekends and winter hours may vary.

Kempsey Green Street

Huntsman Inn

Green Street, WR5 3QB (from A38 at Kempsey via Post Office Lane) SO868490

5-11; 12-11 Sat & Sun ☎ (01905) 820336

Bathams Best Bitter; Greene King IPA; Morland Original Bitter Ⓗ
A 300-year-old former farmhouse with exposed beams, this cosy and friendly multi-roomed local has a small main bar with a real fire to the front and a larger bar down steps. The separate restaurant serves reasonably priced home-cooked food. There is also a skittle alley with its own bar, an attractive garden and a large car park. Dogs are welcome in the bar and lounge. 🐴❀◑♣P🐾

Kidderminster

Beer Emporium & Cider House

Oxford Street, DY10 1AR (between railway station and town centre)
⏲ closed Mon & Tue; 4-10 Wed (11 Thu & Fri); 12-11 Sat; 12-8 Sun ☎ 07803 357362
4 changing beers (sourced nationally) Ⓖ
The single room micropub, furnished with a mixture of barrel furniture and low and high tables, is lively with the buzz of conversation. Table service is the norm. A chalkboard shows between four and six real ales sourced locally and from around the country. Four ciders and two perries, an interesting selection of bottled foreign beers, wines and soft drinks ensure there is something for everyone. Q🐴♿⇌(SVR)🍎P▯🚌🐾📶

King & Castle Ⓛ ✔

Comberton Hill, DY10 1QX (next to main line station and part of SVR terminus)
⏲ 10-11 (11.30 Sat); 11-11 Sun ☎ (01562) 747505
Bathams Best Bitter; Bewdley Worcestershire Way; Hobsons Mild, Town Crier; 4 changing beers (sourced regionally; often Enville, Exmoor, Malvern Hills) Ⓗ
Atmospheric recreation of a GWR terminus station bar and gateway to the Severn Valley Railway. Eight handpumps dispense beers from Hobsons, Bewdley and Bathams, with changing beers from regional and national breweries. Three still ciders are also available. Breakfast is served until 11am, then pub meals, cobs and snacks until 4pm. Bottled beers from Bewdley are available on trains, and pubs along the line are an attraction for locals and visitors using the railway.
Q🐴❀◐♿⇌(SVR)♣🍎P🚌🐾📶

Olde Seven Stars Ⓛ ✔

13-14 Coventry Street, DY10 2BG (not far from upper end of High St, facing Swan Centre)
⏲ 11-11 (11.30 Fri & Sat); 12-11 Sun ☎ (01562) 228641
6 changing beers Ⓗ
With six well-kept real ales and one draught cider, this historic town-centre family-friendly pub is well worth visiting. The front and rear bars display many old features from previous ages. It serves cobs and pork pies, and customers can bring their own food (there are plenty of takeaways nearby), with tableware and condiments provided. Live music plays on the last Friday evening of the month. The quiet rear garden is popular in summer. A former local CAMRA Gold Pub of the Year.
🐴❀♿♣🍎🚌🐾📶

Station Inn Ⓛ ✔

7 Farfield, DY10 1UG
⏲ 12-11 ☎ (01562) 569621 🌐 stationkidderminster.co.uk
Enville Ale; Holden's Golden Glow; Wye Valley HPA, Butty Bach; 1 changing beer (sourced locally; often Bewdley, Enville, Hobsons) Ⓗ
A friendly pub just a short walk from the railway station. Two rooms are served from a central bar and there is a large beer garden to the rear. Five handpulled ales always include one from Enville, Hobsons or Wye Valley. Good-value home-cooked food is available during the day, with traditional roast dinners on Sunday. The warm welcome, community atmosphere and excellent ales won it a local CAMRA Community Pub of the Year award and it was a Pub of the Year finalist in 2016 and 2017.
Q🐴❀◐♿⇌(SVR)♣P🚌🐾📶

Swan Ⓛ ✔

Vicar Street, DY10 1DE (opp town hall)
⏲ 10-7 (10 Thu; 1am Fri & Sat); 12-6 Sun ☎ (01562) 823008
🌐 swankidderminster.co.uk
Bewdley Sir Keith Park, Worcestershire Sway; St Austell Tribute; 3 changing beers (sourced nationally; often Purity, Sharp's, Wye Valley) Ⓗ
A one-room pub dating from 1865, serving six well-kept real ales including offerings from Bewdley Brewery and a changing real cider. The long, single room has quiet tables for dining towards the rear, while the front bar gets lively on rugby match days. Breakfast is available from 10am, followed by freshly prepared bar meals daytime Monday to Saturday. A beer festival is usually held over the August bank holiday.
🐴◐♿🍎🚌🐾📶

Weavers at Park Lane Ⓛ

40 Park Lane, DY11 6TG (opp Tesco)
⏲ 12-10 (11 Fri & Sat) summer; 4 (12 Wed & Thu)-10; 12-11 Fri & Sat; 12-7 Sun winter ☎ (01562) 742717
Hobsons Town Crier; Wye Valley Butty Bach; house beer (by Woodcote Manor); 3 changing beers (sourced regionally; often Backyard, Beowulf, Fixed Wheel) Ⓗ
Canalside pub with a beer garden overlooking the canal and moorings by the towpath, a short walk from the nearby bridge. There are six well-kept real ales including some sourced locally and others from further afield – sometimes more unusual brews – as well as eight ciders and perries. Hot meals are served until 7pm (not Mon & Tue), plus cobs and pork pies. Last orders are 20 minutes before closing. Local CAMRA Cider Pub of the Year 2018. Q🐴❀◑⇌(SVR)♣🍎P🐾📶

Weavers Real Ale House 🏆 Ⓛ

98 Comberton Hill, DY10 1QH (down hill from railway station)
⏲ 12-11 (10.30 Sun) ☎ (01562) 229413
Pig Iron Unbeweavable; Three Tuns XXX; Wye Valley Butty Bach; 5 changing beers (sourced nationally; often Bewdley, Fixed Wheel, Fownes) Ⓗ
A pub for conversation, this micropub is deceptively spacious inside, with bench seating along the sides and plenty of tables. Light and airy, the walls display pictures of old Kidderminster and beer memorabilia. It serves eight ales, four ciders and a perry on handpump, plus six craft beers. Cobs are always available. Just a short walk from the railway station, this is a convenient stop-off for a pint and a chat on the way into town. Local CAMRA Pub of the Year 2018 and National Pub of the Year finalist 2018. Q🐴♿⇌(SVR)🍎🚌🐾📶

Knightwick

Talbot Ⓛ

WR6 5PH (on B4197 400yds from A44 jct)
⏲ 8am-11 ☎ (01886) 821235 🌐 the-talbot.co.uk
Teme Valley T'Other, This, That Ⓗ**; changing beers (often Teme Valley)** Ⓖ

A 14th-century coaching inn with a large lounge bar, divided into two by a large fireplace and a separate taproom. The conservatory is especially fine in summer. The small wood-panelled restaurant serves an imaginative menu using local ingredients (6-9pm). The bar usually offers three or four beers from the Teme Valley Brewery behind the pub. There is a farmers' market outside on the second Sunday of the month. Beer festivals are held in April, June and early October (for green hop beers). Dogs and walkers are welcome.
Q (420)

Malvern

Great Malvern Hotel

Graham Road, WR14 2HN (by crossroads with Church St)
10-11; 11-10.30 Sun (01684) 563411
great-malvern-hotel.co.uk
Malvern Hills Black Pear; Wye Valley HPA, Butty Bach; 2 changing beers (often Friday Beer) H
Popular hotel public bar, a short walk from the Malvern Theatres complex, ideal for pre- and post-performance refreshment. The beer range usually includes something from Malvern's two breweries. Meals are served in the bar and the adjoining brasserie, including Sunday lunches. There is also a comfortable lounge with lots of sofas, fresh coffee and newspapers. Live music sessions are hosted weekly. The Great Shakes cellar bar has sport on TV and is available for hire. On-site parking is limited but there is plenty of public parking nearby.
P

Morgan

52 Clarence Road, WR14 3EQ
12-3, 5-11; 12-11 Fri & Sat; 12-10.30 Sun
(01684) 578575
Wye Valley Bitter, HPA, Butty Bach; 2 changing beers (sourced locally) H
Named after the town's Morgan car factory, this Wye Valley Brewery-owned premises has an open-plan interior divided into a games area for darts, a drinking space and a slightly raised seating area with comfy settees. The landscaped patio has ample seating, a fish pond and 'Them Organ' gates. Activities include a monthly book club and weekly quizzes. The pub is muzak-free and the TV is only turned on for major sporting events. Up to two guest beers come from the Wye Valley range.

Nag's Head

19-21 Bank Street, WR14 2JG (off Graham Rd at Link Top common)
11-11.15 (11.30 Fri & Sat); 12-11.15 Sun
(01684) 574373 nagsheadmalvern.co.uk
Banks's Amber Ale; Bathams Best Bitter; St George's Friar Tuck, Charger, Dragons Blood; Wood Shropshire Lad; 2 changing beers (often Otter, Ringwood) H
A free house serving beers from the owner's brewery, St George's in nearby Callow End, alongside others from all over the county, plus two draught ciders. Mismatched furniture, nooks and crannies, newspapers and foliage create a homely environment. Quality food is served in the bar and separate restaurant (open until 9pm Fri and Sat). Outside is a large covered and heated area to the front and a garden to the rear. Dogs are welcome and numerous. P (44)

Pensax

Bell

WR6 6AE (on Clows Top to Great Witley road S of Pensax)
12-2.30 (not Mon), 5-11; 12-10.30 Sun (01299) 896677
Exmoor Gold; Hobsons Best; 5 changing beers (sourced nationally; often Bewdley, Otter, Wye Valley) H
Seven well-presented real ales plus two local ciders adorn the bar here. There is a separate dining room and a snug where families are welcome. Renowned home-cooked meals are made using local seasonal ingredients. Wooden floors, hanging hops, open fires and pew seating give a true country feel. A former runner-up West Midlands Pub of the Year. Q P

Pershore

Pickled Plum

135 High Street, WR10 1EQ
12-11 (midnight Fri & Sat) (01386) 556645
pickledplum.co.uk
Brakspear Bitter; Dark Star Hophead; Wye Valley HPA, Butty Bach; 2 changing beers (often Purity) H
A large, smart pub with a modern, airy interior, divided into several areas, with exposed beams and real fires adding a cosy old-world charm. The bar serves up to six real ales including Dark Star, always features some local breweries, and has six real ciders. A three third-pint tasting option is offered. Food is available lunchtimes and evenings. The pub hosts a regular Sunday night quiz and an acoustic jam on the first Monday of the month.
P

Redditch

Black Tap Brew Pub

Church Green East, B98 8BP (near top of Church Green East opp fountain)
closed Mon; 4-11 Tue-Thu; 12-11 Fri & Sat; 12-6 Sun
(01527) 549997
4 changing beers (sourced locally) H
A converted office building conveniently located near the town centre, which originally opened as a brewpub, but is now a pub in its own right. The main bar has a roaring fire, adding to the warm, welcoming ambience. The beer range includes a good mix of styles, and a cider is usually available. A small side room can be booked and live music often plays at weekends.
(57,58)

Rising Sun

4 Alcester Street, B98 8AE (opp town hall)
8am-midnight (1am Fri & Sat) (01527) 62452
Greene King IPA, Abbot; Morland Old Speckled Hen; Sharp's Doom Bar; 4 changing beers H
Large open-plan town-centre pub in the Wetherspoon style with a raised seating area and booths, serving six to eight cask ales. Local histories of Redditch's manufacturing industries adorn the walls and a large metal horse and rider stands in the centre. The pub gets busy at lunchtimes and weekends. Outside, a glass canopy and café-style seating are ideal for people-watching (there is also a smoking area). Screens at both ends of the pub show news and sports.
P

Shenstone

Plough 🄻

DY10 4DL (off A450/A448) SO865735
12.30-3.30, 6-11; 12-11 Fri-Sun ☎ (01562) 777340
bathams.co.uk
Bathams Mild Ale, Best Bitter 🄷
A traditional rural village pub dating back to 1840. The long single bar serves both the lounge, complete with real fire, and public areas. A large enclosed courtyard/conservatory serves as an overflow area in which children are permitted. There is a small patio with seating to the front. Snacks include cobs and pork pies. Bathams Bitter and Mild are always available and the stronger Christmas brew of XXX is served briefly during the winter months. The Elizabethan Harvington Hall is nearby. Q P

Stourport-on-Severn

Black Star 🄻

Mitton Street, DY13 8YP (just off top end of High St)
12-11 (midnight Fri & Sat); 12-10.30 Sun
☎ (01299) 488838
Wye Valley HPA, Golden Ale, Butty Bach, Wholesome Stout; 1 changing beer (sourced nationally; often Exmoor, Rudgate, Wye Valley) 🄷
Next to the canal, the pub has a historic feel. The main bar has a real fire, low ceilings and cosy corners. An attractive beer garden with a shelter, tables and raised flower beds overlooks the canal. Moorings are just through the bridge towards the basins. The varied food menu includes doorstep sandwiches, baguettes, rib-eye steaks and everything in between. Four beers are from Wye Valley plus a guest and a cider. A runner-up for local CAMRA Pub of the Year 2018.

Swan

56 High Street, DY13 8BX
12-midnight (11 Sun) ☎ (01299) 877832
stourporttown.co.uk/the-swan
Brains Rev James; Butcombe Gold; Hobsons Old Prickly; Wainwright; 2 changing beers (often Bewdley, Salopian) 🄷
Former hotel with a large lounge bar decorated with vinyl LPs – this is a pub by day and a music venue by night. Six well-kept real ales grace the bar, along with a range of gins. At the back there is a tranquil, secluded garden. The integral Mimi's Bistro serves breakfast from 9am and Mediterranean specialities from a wood-fired oven during the day. Live music on most evenings has a loyal following. An interesting and unusual venue, well worth a visit. (3)

Tardebigge

Alestones

Unit 23 Tardebigge Court, B97 6QW
closed Mon-Wed; 5-9 Thu; 3-9 Fri; 12-9 Sat; 12-3 Sun
☎ (01527) 275254 alestones.co.uk
Woodcote Manor SSS; 3 changing beers 🄷
A well-maintained micropub, opened in 2016, which sits in a courtyard alongside several small independent shops and businesses. There are usually four beers available including a golden ale, a dark beer and a best bitter, plus real cider and perry. Although recently expanded, the pub retains its cosy, convivial atmosphere – but now there is room to stretch your legs. Local musicians play on Sunday and comedians perform once a month on a Thursday. Pub snacks are usually available.
Q P (43,42)

Upper Wyche

Wyche Inn 🄻

Wyche Road, WR14 4EQ (on B4218, follow signs from Malvern to Colwall)
12-11 (9 Mon); 11-11 Sat & Sun ☎ (01684) 575396
thewycheinn.co.uk
Wye Valley HPA; 3 changing beers (sourced regionally) 🄷
The highest pub in Worcestershire, this free house has panoramic views towards the Cotswolds. Ideally situated for hill walkers, it offers two bars – one with pool and darts, the other dedicated to drinking and dining. The range of real ales always features some from local breweries. Home-cooked food is served lunchtimes and evenings, with specials throughout the week including steak on Tuesday and Saturday. B&B accommodation and a holiday cottage are AA 4-star rated.
Q P (675)

Weatheroak

Coach & Horses 🄻

Weatheroak Hill, B48 7EA (Alvechurch to Wythall road) SP057740
11.30-11; 12-10.30 Sun ☎ (01564) 823386
coachandhorsesinn.co.uk
Holden's Golden Glow; Hook Norton Old Hooky; Weatheroak Hill Gold, Icknield Pale Ale, Impossible IPA, Cofton Common; 4 changing beers (sourced nationally; often Hobsons, St Austell, Wood) 🄷
Award-winning country free house with a traditional bar with a real fire and quarry-tiled floor, a modern lounge bar and a restaurant. Outside, the large garden is popular in the summer. Formerly a coach house, the pub has been in the same family for 50 years. Ten real ales are stocked from national and regional breweries including the on-site Weatheroak Hill. Polypins from the brewery are on sale to take away. Fresh rolls are always available. The pub is adjacent to Icknield Street Roman road. P

Welland

Marlbank Inn 🄻

Marlbank Road, WR13 6NA (on A4104 W of Welland) SO786404
12-midnight ☎ (01684) 310603 themarlbankinn.co.uk
Greene King Abbot; Wye Valley HPA 🄶; 3 changing beers (sourced nationally) 🄷
A sizeable pub in the countryside at the foot of the Malvern Hills. It has an interesting interior with two main rooms around a central bar. Live music nights and themed dinners feature regularly throughout the year, and the pub hosts party nights on St Patrick's Day, Halloween and New Year's Eve. The real cider is Westons Old Rosie. B&B is available and a camping and caravan site is adjacent with a children's play area. P

Worcester

Bull Baiters Inn

22 St Johns, WR2 5AH
12-2 (not Mon), 5.30-9.30; 12-9.30 Fri & Sat; 3-6 Sun
☎ (01905) 421579 bullbaiters.com

7 changing beers (sourced locally) Ⓗ
Worcester's only micropub, in the St Johns area of the city, a short walk across the river from the city centre. A small, single room housed in a former patisserie, it has bench seating and stools covered in replica hop pocket sacks. Up to seven ever-changing beers are available, mostly from local brewers, with eight ciders and perries, also locally sourced. Interesting pub games, including ringing the bull, can be played. Q♣

Cardinal's Hat

31 Friar Street, WR1 2NA
12 (4 Mon)-11; 12-10.30 Sun ☎ (01905) 724006
the-cardinals-hat.co.uk
Purity Mad Goose; 4 changing beers (sourced locally) Ⓗ
Worcester's oldest pub is a period building set in the heart of the city centre. The main bar at the front has a scrubbed wooden floor, beams and leaded windows. A stone-flagged, panelled passageway leads to a patio at the rear. The atmospheric back room features wood panelling, a stone-flagged floor, serving hatch and impressive fireplace with woodburner and dribbly candles. A small snug has views of the bustling old street outside. Folk night is the first Tuesday of the month. Imaginative bar snacks are available until 9pm.

Dragon Inn

51 The Tything, WR1 1JT (on A449, 300yds N of Foregate St Station)
4-11; 12-11 Fri & Sat; 12-10.30 Sun ☎ (01905) 25845
thedragoninnworcester.co.uk
Church End Goat's Milk, What the Fox's Hat, Fallen Angel; 5 changing beers (often Church End) Ⓗ
A Georgian building on the edge of the city centre run by Church End Brewery. The bar is towards the back while the front space offers the opportunity to watch the world go by. Behind the pub is a large, quiet patio area with a covered space in the old side passage. A changing variety of Church End beers is on the bar plus two guest ales from other small breweries. Pork pies and sausage rolls are always available. Q♣

Firefly

54 Lowesmoor, WR1 2SE
3 (12 Wed & Thu)-midnight; 12-1am Fri (2am Sat); 12-11 Sun ☎ (01905) 616996
5 changing beers (often Dark Star, Oakham, Tiny Rebel) Ⓗ
Once the old vinegar works' manager's Georgian residence, this is now a comfortable, stylish bar. It has five handpulls for beers and two for ciders – one usually from Snails Bank. The interior has soft furnishings, subtle lighting and an open fire. Downstairs is a cosy snug with bench sofas, upstairs is a bar that hosts live music. There is a paved, partially covered beer garden.

Lamb & Flag

30 The Tything, WR1 1JL
12-midnight ☎ (01905) 26894
Wye Valley HPA; 3 changing beers Ⓗ
A Worcester institution, this Two Crafty Brewers pub has a traditional feel but with a subtle urban twist. The popular community local is renowned for its niche activities such as backgammon, poetry reading and folk music. At the front is a no-frills saloon which caters for all tastes but can get rather noisy. The cosy lounge bar offers a bar menu. Upstairs is the SUGO Italian restaurant, serving proper Italian food freshly prepared by an Italian chef. The world conker championship is held here in early October. (Foregate St)♣

Paul Pry ★

6 The Butts, WR1 3PA
12-1am ☎ (01905) 28992
4 changing beers (often Dark Star, Gloucester) Ⓗ
An old town-centre market tavern with a well-preserved Grade II-listed interior. The main bar has a splendid ornate mahogany and etched glass bar back. The tiled passageway has a couple of steps leading to the toilets and more tilework. The beer garden is at the rear. Lunchtime food is served Wednesday to Sunday and bar snacks Friday and Saturday from 6pm. There is a record player and a selection of vinyl records, or you can bring your own. ♣

Plough

23 Fish Street, WR1 2HN (on Deansway)
12-11 (11.30 Fri & Sat); 12-10.30 Sun ☎ (01905) 21381
Hobsons Best; Malvern Hills Black Pear; 4 changing beers (sourced regionally; often Froth Blowers, Mighty Oak, Salopian) Ⓗ
A Grade II listed pub near the cathedral. There is a short flight of steps leading to a tiny bar with rooms leading off either side. The beers usually come from Worcestershire and the surrounding counties, but occasionally from small breweries further afield. Draught cider and perry are from Barbourne in the city. There is also a wide range of whiskies for the connoisseur. Outside is a small patio area. Rolls are available at weekends and when the cricket is on. ♣

Postal Order

18 Foregate Street, WR1 1DN
8am-midnight (1am Fri & Sat) ☎ (01905) 22373
Greene King Abbot; Ruddles Best Bitter; 10 changing beers (sourced nationally) Ⓗ
A classic Wetherspoon pub, formerly the old Worcester telephone exchange. It has one of the largest real ale sales in the chain's West Midlands region and a wide range of beers is served, with beer festivals throughout the year adding even more variety. A cider from local producer Barbourne and Old Rosie from Westons are always available plus two others. Good-value food is served daily 8am-11pm (alcohol from 9am). The volume on the TV may be turned up for important games. Q

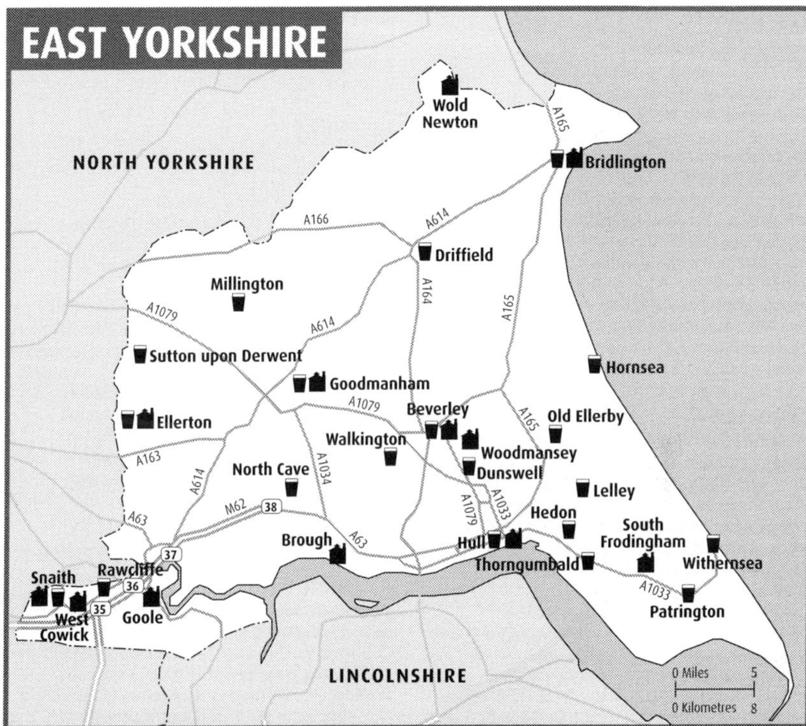

YORKSHIRE (EAST)

Beverley

Chequers Micropub L

15 Swaby's Yard, Dyer Lane, HU17 9BZ (off Saturday Market)

12-10 (11 Thu-Sat) ☎ 07964 227906

5 changing beers (sourced regionally; often Atom, Brass Castle, North Riding) H

Yorkshire's first micropub, set in a former baker's shop near the bus station. Local breweries are well represented on the bar plus micros from throughout the UK. Eight ciders/perries are sold but, typically for a micropub, no lager. There is no TV or loud music, making Chequers a place for real conversation, like pubs used to be. A selection of board games is available for customers. The cellar is above the bar. Q

Dog & Duck

33 Ladygate, HU17 8BH (on side street off Saturday Market adjacent to Brown's store)

11-4, 7-midnight; 11-midnight Fri & Sat; 11.30-3, 7-11 Sun ☎ (01482) 862419 bedandbreakfastbeverley.com

Black Sheep Best Bitter; John Smith's Bitter; Ossett Big Red Bitter; Timothy Taylor Boltmaker; 2 changing beers (sourced nationally) H

The pub was built in the 1930s and has been run by the same family for 45 years. It comprises three areas: a bar with a period brick fireplace and bentwood seating, a front lounge with an open fire, and a rear snug. The good-value, home-cooked lunches are popular. Guest accommodation is in six purpose-built self-contained rooms to the rear. It is dog-friendly after food service. Close to Beverley bus station.

Monks Walk L

19 Highgate, HU17 0DN

12-11; 12-10.30 Sun ☎ (01482) 864972

monkswalkinn.co.uk

5 changing beers (sourced locally; often Atom, Brass Castle, Yorkshire) H

Dating back to the 13th century and built as a merchant's warehouse, records show there was a brewery attached in the 19th century. There are two bars, the Minster and Monks Bar, divided by an open passageway, plus a dining room with exposed roof beams and an open fire. Conversation is encouraged at this genuine free house. Known as the George and Dragon until the 1980s, its sheltered beer garden has splendid views of the minster. Access to the car park is off Eastgate. QP

REAL ALE BREWERIES

Aire Heads Goole
All Hallows Goodmanham
Atom Hull
Bricknell Hull
Bridlington Bridlington
Crafty Little Brough (NEW)
East Yorkshire Woodmansey (NEW)
Gene Pool Hull
Great Newsome South Frodingham
Half Moon Ellerton
Old Mill Snaith
Spotlight West Cowick (NEW)
Twisted Angel Beverley (NEW)
Vision Hull (NEW)
Wold Top Wold Newton
Yorkshire Hull
Yorkshire Brewhouse Hull (NEW)

Sun Inn

1 Flemingate, HU17 0NP (adjacent to Beverley Minster)
⏲ 4-11 (12.30am Fri); 12-12.30am Sat; 12-10.30 Sun
☎ 07541 456215 🌐 suninnbeverley.co.uk
Black Sheep Best Bitter; Morland Old Speckled Hen; Timothy Taylor Boltmaker; York Guzzler; 1 changing beer (sourced nationally; often Robinsons) Ⓗ
The pub's medieval timber-framed building is set opposite the eastern front of Beverley's famous minster, so the view from the courtyard beer garden should not be missed. Formerly a Tap & Spile, the pub's stripped-back interior featuring bare brick walls reflects that style. It is a live music venue, with blues and rock bands on a weekend and folk sessions on Saturday teatimes; among other events there is a popular quiz on Thursdays. Sunday lunches are served 12-3pm.

Tiger Inn

97 Lairgate, HU17 8JG (nr Memorial Hall)
⏲ 12-11 (midnight Fri & Sat); 12-10.30 Sun
☎ (01482) 869040 🌐 tigerinnbeverley.co.uk
Black Sheep Ale; Timothy Taylor Landlord; Wainwright; 2 changing beers (sourced nationally; often Marston's, Wychwood) Ⓗ
Attractive Grade II-listed 18th-century building re-fronted in 1930s Brewers' Tudor style by the now defunct Darley and Co, which once owned several pubs in Beverley. It has a multi-roomed interior with a public bar, snug, dining room/lounge and function room, all retained during a major refurbishment in 2017. Many local clubs and societies meet here and folk music sessions are held on Friday evening. The large car park to the rear was once stables and outbuildings. Meals include a Sunday carvery.
QP

Bridlington

Board Inn

62 High Street, YO16 4QA
⏲ 3-11; 12-11 Fri (midnight Sat); 12-11 Sun
☎ (01262) 672087
Adnams Ghost Ship; Fuller's ESB; St Austell Proper Job; Tetley Bitter; Titanic Plum Porter; 2 changing beers (sourced nationally) Ⓗ
Located in Bridlington's Old Town, this lovingly restored historic inn dates back to the 18th century, with wood panelling, flagged and timber floors and four open fires. It has a multi-roomed interior with three comfortably furnished rooms and a snug upstairs. Music nights are hosted at weekends. To the rear, the new Taproom has been established in converted stables selling 10 craft beers. The restoration was Highly Commended in the CAMRA Pub Design Awards Refurbishment category. A real gem, not to be missed. QP

Marine Bar

North Marine Drive, YO15 2LS (1 mile NE of centre)
⏲ 12-11 (11.30 Sat) ☎ (01262) 675347 🌐 marinebar.net
John Smith's Bitter; Timothy Taylor Landlord; Wold Top Bitter; 2 changing beers (sourced regionally; often Daleside, Rooster's) Ⓗ
Large open-plan bar, part of the Expanse Hotel. Spectacular sea views are the perfect accompaniment to enjoying the home-cooked food served here daily. Attracting a good mix of regulars, a warm welcome awaits the influx of summer visitors. Two regional guest beers complement the three regular ales, with real cider also stocked. Ample parking is available along the promenade, where a land train operates during the summer. Local CAMRA 2017 Town Pub of the Year.
P(512,513)

Driffield

Butcher's Dog

24 Middle Street South, YO25 6PS
⏲ closed Mon; 12-11 (10 Tue & Wed); 12-10 Sun
☎ (01377) 254032 🌐 thebutchersdog.co.uk
5 changing beers (sourced locally; often Wold Top, Yorkshire Heart, Yorkshire) Ⓗ
One-room micropub that returns to traditional pub values with modern twists. Five real ales from local and regional breweries are served in oversized glasses or you can try tasting paddles, alongside a wide selection of real ciders, but no spirits. Customers are encouraged to rely on good conversation in an environment free from Wi-Fi and music. Simple bar snacks are served, including a cheeseboard on Sunday afternoons, but customers may bring their own food. Local CAMRA Town Pub of the Year for the last two years.
Q(121)

Mariners Arms

47 Eastgate South, YO25 6LR (on back street running parallel with Middle St)
⏲ 3-midnight; 12-midnight Sat & Sun ☎ (01377) 253708
Banks's Sunbeam; Jennings Bitter; Ringwood Boondoggle; 1 changing beer (often Ringwood) Ⓗ
A street-corner local well worth seeking out. The beer range is from the Marston's portfolio, as an alternative to the other breweries more commonly available in the town. Formerly part of the Hull Brewery estate, its four small rooms have now become two: a public bar and a more comfortable lounge. Live terrestrial broadcast sport is shown, and the pub fields various sports teams. The longstanding licensees enjoy a loyal following among locals and offer a friendly welcome to all visitors. P(121)

Dunswell

Ship Inn

Beverley Road, HU6 0AJ
⏲ 11.30-11 (11.30 Thu; midnight Fri & Sat); 12-11.30 Sun
☎ (01482) 859160 🌐 shipsquarters.co.uk
Great Newsome Frothingham Best; Hardys & Hansons Bitter; 2 changing beers (sourced regionally; often Great Newsome, Partners, Pennine) Ⓗ
Fronting the old Hull-Beverley road, this inn once served traffic on the nearby River Hull, and is decorated with nautical memorabilia including the bell from the shipwrecked Caroline. Log fires warm the convivial interior, which is partly divided to create a separate dining area with church pew seating. Former outbuildings have been developed to create en-suite accommodation in the Ships Quarters. The large garden has an outside bar and barbecue area for summer events. The pub maintains good links with the local primary school and church. P

Ellerton

Boot & Shoe

Main Street, YO42 4PB
⏲ 5.30-11; 4-midnight Fri & Sat; 12-11 Sun
☎ (01757) 288346

House beer (by Dark Horse); 2 changing beers (sourced nationally; often Dark Horse) Ⓗ
A welcoming country village inn of character, dating from the 17th century. The building wraps around a large tree and features low-beamed ceilings. There is a cosy bar area with exposed brick and an open fire, plus two intimate separate dining rooms. Three real ales are on offer in this free house, including two from Dark Horse Brewery. Food is served Friday and Saturday evenings and Sunday lunchtime (booking advisable). **Q◑♣P🐾**

Goodmanham

Goodmanham Arms 🏆 Ⓛ

Main Street, YO43 3JA (close to Wolds Way footpath)
🕐 11.30-midnight; 11.30-11 Sun ☎ (01430) 873849
🌐 goodmanhamarms.co.uk
All Hallows Peg Fyfe Dark Mild, Ragged Robyn, No Notion Porter; Hambleton Stallion Amber; Theakston Best Bitter; 3 changing beers (sourced regionally; often Oakham, Wold Top) Ⓗ
A unique village local with the All Hallows brewery attached. There are three log fires warming the bar, dining room and kitchen. The landlord's private motorcycle museum adds further interest. Hearty meals are served including a Gypsy Pot in the winter (no food Mon lunchtime). Folk nights are held every first, and blues/jazz/country every third, Thursday of the month, with further events on bank holidays. Local CAMRA Village Pub of the Year winner 2016 and 2017. **Q❀◑P**

Hedon

Hed'On Inn Ⓛ

7 Watmaughs Arcade, St Augustine Gate, HU12 8EZ
🕐 1-11 (11.30 Fri & Sat) ☎ (01964) 601100
🌐 hedoninn.co.uk
Black Sheep Best Bitter; Titanic Plum Porter; 4 changing beers (sourced nationally; often Great Newsome) Ⓗ
Micropub next to a car park at the end of a shopping arcade in the centre of this old market town, converted from a disused carpet shop office. The premises are tastefully decorated with recycled fittings. There are two regular and four changing beers covering the full spectrum of styles, together with three real ciders, bottled beers and a range of spirits and wines. Acoustic music sessions take place on Tuesday nights and Sunday afternoons, quiz and games on Wednesday nights. **Q♣P🚌**

Hornsea

Marine Hotel Ⓛ ✔

Marine Drive, HU18 1NJ
🕐 11-11 (11.30 Fri & Sat) ☎ (01964) 532183
Greene King IPA; 3 changing beers Ⓗ
Large two-roomed pub with a garden overlooking the beach and spectacular sea views. It offers a choice of four real ales, and meals are served every day 12-8pm. There is a quiz night on Thursday and occasional live music. Camper vans are accepted in certain circumstances. The pub is also the base of the local angling club. Dog-friendly in the bar. ❀◑♿♣P🚌🐾📶

Stackhouse bar

8a Newbegin, HU18 1AG
🕐 4-11; 2-11 Fri; 12-midnight Sat & Sun ☎ (01964) 534407
4 changing beers (sourced regionally; often Brass Castle, Great Newsome, Yorkshire) Ⓗ
Former shop converted to a micropub in 2014 with an interesting choice of regional ales and a large range of real ciders. Attracting a mixed clientele, customers are encouraged to engage in conversation. There is a separate function room. Although no food is provided, customers may bring in their own. Vaping is permitted.
♣🚌(240,246)🐾📶

Hull

Admiral of the Humber Ⓛ ✔

1 Anlaby Road, HU1 2NT
🕐 8am-midnight (1am Fri & Sat) ☎ (01482) 381850
Greene King Abbot; Ruddles Best Bitter; Sharp's Doom Bar; 6 changing beers (sourced nationally) Ⓗ
Following a £2.5m upgrade, the Admiral is now a Wetherlodge Hotel. A former paint and wallpaper shop, the site was previously connected to Hull's seafaring past. Now a large single room, mostly on one level, the building is ideally suited to those finding steps or stairs a problem. There is a large open-air rooftop garden for smokers and non-smokers alike (closes 10pm nightly). A designated area is set aside for diners during the day, and children are welcome until 6pm.
Q❀◑♿P🚌📶

Chilli Devil's Ⓛ

Manor Street, HU1 1YP
🕐 closed Mon; 12-midnight; 12-11 Sun ☎ (01482) 961666
4 changing beers Ⓗ
A small one-room pub in the heart of the city, with an extensive collection of photographs of Hull in bygone times on show. Cask ales and real cider only are served – no gas-assisted dispense is used; a selection of bottled beers meeting LocAle criteria is also available. Prior to becoming a licensee, the landlord was well known locally for his passion for all things related to chilli, which is reflected in his ever-changing chilli-based food menu.
Q◑🚌🐾

George Hotel 🏆 ✔

Land of Green Ginger, HU1 2EA
🕐 12-midnight ☎ (01482) 226373
Abbeydale Moonshine; Bradfield Farmers Blonde; Theakston Old Peculier; 4 changing beers (sourced regionally) Ⓗ
In the heart of the old town on Hull's most famous street, this one-roomed pub is of historic interest. The Georgian interior, featuring beamed ceilings, wood-panelled walls and pictures of old Hull, remains virtually unaltered. The fine glazed leaded windows have been retained and of note is reputedly the smallest pub window in England, dating from its former coaching days. Meals are served daily except Monday. Local CAMRA City Pub of the Year 2017. ♣🚌🐾

Head of Steam

10 King Street, Old Town, HU1 2JJ
🕐 11-11 (midnight Thu-Sat); 11-10.30 Sun
☎ (01482) 217236 🌐 theheadofsteam.co.uk
Camerons A-Hop-Alypse Now; Leeds Best; 4 changing beers (sourced regionally) Ⓗ
This is a single-roomed pub decorated with beer-related artefacts, whose large picture windows overlook Hull Minster and Trinity Square. An outdoor seating area is to the front of the premises and provides an ideal location to watch the world

go by. The cask ales constantly vary, often promoting new breweries, and are complemented by an extensive selection of craft products, reflecting the passion of the management team.
❀◑≡●🚌🐾

Hop & Vine L

24 Albion Street, HU1 3TG (250yds from Hull New Theatre and Central Library)
closed Sun & Mon; 11 (4 Tue)-11 ☎ 07507 719259
3 changing beers (sourced nationally; often Great Newsome, Isaac Poad, Wold Top) H
Atmospheric basement-bar free house serving three changing guest beers from Yorkshire's independent breweries. Unusual still ciders and perries are also stocked and some continental bottled beers. Oversized lined glasses are used. A selection of freshly prepared food including home-baked bread is served until 9pm. It was former CAMRA National Cider Pub of the Year and four-times Yorkshire Regional winner. Shove-ha'penny, cribbage and shut the box games are available.
◑Å≡♣●🚌🐾

Larkin's L

48-52 Newland Avenue, HU5 3AE (near jct of De Grey St)
11-11 (11.30 Fri & Sat) ☎ (01482) 440991
larkinsbar.co.uk
Wold Top Wold Gold; 2 changing beers (sourced regionally; often Abbeydale, Gene Pool, Great Newsome) H
One-roomed café-bar, named after poet Philip Larkin; it was once two shops and can still be partitioned for small private functions. A good selection of home-cooked food is served every day including specials. There is a paved area to the front and a newly extended family-oriented beer garden to the side and rear. Beer festivals with live music from local acts are usually held over bank holiday weekends during spring and summer.
Q❀◑♿🚌🐾

Lord Nelson

163 Endike Lane, HU6 7UA (3 miles N of city centre)
1-11; 12-midnight Fri & Sat; 12-11 Sun ☎ (01482) 801844
3 changing beers (sourced nationally; often Adnams, Backyard, Wadworth) H
Comfortable, friendly estate pub with traditional appeal, north of the city centre. It is easily accessible by bus and a short walk from main Hull to Beverley road. The main bar features a blue and white tiled fireplace, walls of half-brick/half-wood cladding and a display of rugby shirts on the ceiling. The pub supports various sports clubs from the local estate. There is a pool room and the back bar/function room has a dance floor and stage used for karaoke/discos at weekends.
❀♣P🚌(115,5)🐾

Minerva Hotel L

Nelson Street, HU1 1XE
11.30-11.30 (midnight Fri & Sat) ☎ (01482) 210025
minerva-hull.co.uk
Tetley Bitter; 5 changing beers (sourced regionally; often Atom, Revolutions, Yorkshire) H
Overlooking the Humber estuary and Victoria Pier, this famous pub, built in 1829, is a great place to watch the ships go by. Photos and memorabilia are a reminder of the area's maritime past. The central bar serves various rooms including a tiny three-seat snug. The former brewhouse was converted to provide an additional drinking area and is available for functions. Connected to The Deep visitor attraction by a footbridge at the mouth of the River Hull. ❀◑🚌(16)

Olde White Harte ★ ✔

25 Silver Street, HU1 1JG (in alley between Silver St and Bowlalley Lane)
11-midnight ☎ (01482) 326363 yeoldewhiteharte.com
Theakston Best Bitter, Old Peculier; house beer (by Caledonian); 3 changing beers (sourced nationally) H
Historic pub in a 17th-century merchant's house, with strong connections to the English Civil War, hidden down an alley near Hull's old town. The existing ground-floor interior dates back to a major refurbishment in 1881, which was an idealised re-creation of an old English inn, complete with massive inglenook fireplaces and stained-glass windows. The first floor features the Plotting Parlour, which is available for meetings and functions. There is also a heated courtyard providing an all-weather outdoor drinking area.
❀♣🚌

Pave L ✔

16-20 Princes Avenue, HU5 3QA
11-11 (11.30 Fri & Sat) ☎ (01482) 333181
pavebar.co.uk
Tetley Gold; Theakston Best Bitter; 3 changing beers (sourced regionally; often Great Yorkshire, Saltaire, Scarborough) H
The original pavement café in this popular area of the city, this continental-style bar attracts a diverse range of customers. As well as the regular ales, there are three guest ales, usually regional and including one stout, and a varied range of European draught and bottled beers. Home-cooked food including vegetarian and gluten-free options is served daily. Complimentary live music is provided on Tuesday evenings and Sunday afternoons. A changing Westons cider is sold.
❀◑♿≡(Interchange)●🚌

St John's Hotel

10 Queens Road, HU5 2PY
12-11.30 (midnight Tue & Thu; 12.30am Fri & Sat)
☎ (01482) 341013 stjohnshull.com
Marston's 61 Deep; Wainwright; 3 changing beers (sourced nationally; often Brakspear, Courage, Young's) H
Grade II-listed classic street-corner local that boasts one of the least-altered interiors in the city, now identified by CAMRA as having a regionally important historic pub interior. The front corner public bar complements a quiet back room, with original bench seating. A basic larger room accommodates the pool table and is home to regular beer festivals. It is a community local, with two darts teams, a football team and the Oddfellows cricket league which hosts quiz nights in the winter. Open mic night is Tuesday.
Q❀♿♣●P🚌🐾

Three John Scotts L ✔

Lowgate, HU1 1AA
8am-midnight (1am Fri & Sat) ☎ (01482) 381910
Greene King Abbot; Ruddles Best Bitter; Sharp's Doom Bar; 7 changing beers (sourced regionally; often Great Newsome) H
Originally an Edwardian post office, this open-plan Wetherspoon features modern decor and works of art. The name derives from three successive 19th-century vicars of St Mary's Church opposite. The pub has established a broad customer base

appealing to a wide clientele. Up to 10 real ales and two real ciders are on the bar. Children are welcome up to 9pm. There is a large rear courtyard seating area which is a great suntrap in the summer.

Whalebone

165 Wincolmlee, HU2 0PA

12-midnight (11 Tue & Wed); 12-11 Sun ☎ 07506 868461

Half Moon Old Forge Bitter; Rudgate Viking; 5 changing beers (sourced regionally; often Abbeydale, North Riding, Rat)

The local CAMRA branch's multi award-winning City Pub of the Year and Cider Pub of the Year, and Yorkshire Regional Pub of the Year runner-up for 2016. It is a rare gem, sited within the old Greenland whaling trading area. Licensed since 1791, the current building dates from 1890, and has been a free house since 2002. Photos celebrating the city's sporting heritage and bygone Hull pubs adorn the saloon bar walls. Artefacts showcasing the whaling industry can be viewed in the quiet room (formerly the pub's brewery). An old illuminated Moors' & Robson's Brewery sign hangs outside. Q

Lelley

Stag's Head Inn

Main Street, HU12 8SN

12-midnight ☎ (01482) 891460

Black Sheep Ale; 3 changing beers (sourced locally; often Crafty Little Brewery, Great Newsome, Wold Top)

A 200-year-old pub on the edge of the village and at the heart of the local community. The interior comprises a main bar where four real ales are served, a restaurant with home-made food prepared from local produce, and a separate games room. The well-maintained garden makes for a pleasant experience, especially in summer. Families are welcome, as well as dogs, and the pub has a designated dining area for visitors with their pets. Q P

Millington

Gait

Main Street, YO42 1TX

closed Mon; 6.30-11 Tue-Thu; 12-3, 6.30-11 Fri; 12-4, 6-11 Sat; 12-3, 6-11 Sun ☎ (01759) 302045

gait-inn-millington.co.uk

Black Sheep Best Bitter; Tetley Bitter; Theakston Best Bitter; 2 changing beers (sourced locally; often Great Yorkshire, Half Moon, Wold Top)

A delightful Yorkshire Wolds pub that provides a warm welcome (in winter by means of a wood-burning stove) both to locals and to the many walkers enjoying the attractions of Millington woods and pastures. The idiosyncratic bar is filled with a range of ornaments and local pictures. Sit at kitchen-style tables to enjoy hearty, home-made food served from an extensive menu. It has three regular beers and at least one guest, when surveyed, all from Yorkshire. The annual beer festival offers up to 35 beers. P

North Cave

White Hart

20 Westgate, HU15 2NJ

4-11 (midnight Fri & Sat) ☎ (01430) 470940

whitehartnorthcave.co.uk

House beer (by Great Newsome); 2 changing beers (sourced regionally; often Great Newsome, Theakston, Wold Top)

This traditional village pub is a credit to the community it serves. There is a long bar to the side and rear while the quieter front bar has comfortable seating and is where you will find the three real ales. The name of the house beer, 1776, provides an insight to the history of the pub. Open fires are lit during winter months, adding to the home comforts. Walkers and dogs are welcome. Third-pint taster trays are now available. A popular stopping off point for Beverley races.
Q P (155)

Old Ellerby

Blue Bell

Crabtree Lane, HU11 5AJ

closed Mon & Thu; 7-11.30 (midnight Fri & Sat); 12-6, 8-11.30 Sun ☎ (01964) 562364

Great Newsome Sleck Dust; Tetley Bitter; 2 changing beers (sourced regionally; often Great Newsome)

A 16th-century inn with an L-shaped bar and a single room divided into distinct areas, including a snug to the right and a rear pool area where children are welcome until 8.30pm. The pub has a strong community focus and is home to several darts and dominoes teams. Two guest beers in winter increase to three in summer. Outside there is a fishing pond and bowling green together with a sun terrace. It is popular with walkers (wipe your boots please) and dog friendly. Q P

Patrington

Amy's Bar & Kitchen

8 Westgate, HU12 0NB

9am-11.30 (6 Mon & Tue); 12-10 Sun ☎ (01964) 631593

Sharp's Atlantic; 3 changing beers (sourced regionally; often Rooster's, York)

Open since 2016, this is a family-run micropub in the heart of an attractive Holderness village. It focuses on regularly changing cask ales and is always keen to support local breweries, complemented by a changing range of ciders. Home-cooked food is served from 9am. Occasional music and open mic events are held.
Q (76)

Rawcliffe

Jemmy Hirst at the Rose & Crown

26 Riverside, DN14 8RN (from village green turn N on Chapel Lane)

6-midnight; 5-midnight Fri; 12-midnight Sat & Sun ☎ (01405) 831038 jemmyhirst.freeservers.com

Timothy Taylor Landlord; 4 changing beers (sourced locally; often Abbeydale, Ossett, Wold Top)

A free house in the heart of the village, well known regionally and winner of numerous local CAMRA awards, including Pub of the Year eight times. It has been in the Guide continuously since 2004. There is always a warm, friendly welcome from the owners Simon and Jane, and Bruno the dog. Book-lined walls and many artefacts give a homely atmosphere. You can sample five real ales and a traditional cider here. P (88,401)

Snaith

Brewers Arms Hotel 𝕃

10 Pontefract Rd, DN14 9JS (on A645 near petrol station)

✪ 9am (5.30 Mon)-11.30; 9am-midnight Sat; 9am-9 Sun ☎ (01405) 862404 🌐 thebrewersarms.co.uk

Old Mill Traditional Bitter, Blonde Bombshell; 2 changing beers (sourced locally; often Old Mill) Ⓗ

This recently renovated pub has retained its original features, although lightened and brightened in a modern style. Oak beams are in evidence, as well as four fireplaces. It has one large main bar, with oak casks behind the bar for decoration. Two regular handpulled beers are served, four in summer. The six bedrooms have been refurbished to a high standard. Q🚸❀🛏◑♿⇌♣P🚌 (400) 📶

Sutton upon Derwent

St Vincent Arms 𝕃

Main Street, YO41 4BN

✪ 11.30-3, 6-11; 12-3, 6.30-10.30 Sun ☎ (01904) 608349 🌐 stvincentarms.co.uk

Fuller's London Pride; Greene King IPA; Theakston Old Peculier; Timothy Taylor Landlord; York Guzzler; 2 changing beers (sourced nationally) Ⓗ

Former winner of many local CAMRA awards, this pretty white-painted village free house on a bend in the road has been family owned and well run for many years. A long-time supporter of Fuller's beers, it has a consistent but large ale range. The bar, featuring a large Fuller, Smith & Turner mirror, is popular with locals. Another small bar with a serving hatch leads to the dining rooms. Excellent food is served. Q🚸❀◑P

Thorngumbald

New Royal Mail 𝕃

Sorting Room, Main Road, HU12 9LN (behind café)

✪ 4-11; 2-11 Sat & Sun

Brakspear Bitter; Theakston Best Bitter; Wainwright; 3 changing beers (often Great Newsome) Ⓗ

This pub commemorates a previous hostelry, now lost, that had the same name. Many of the fixtures are made from materials taken from the earlier Royal Mail pub when it was demolished. A small, intimate venue has been created, catering for a diverse range of customers. Promotional prices are offered on Tuesdays. The window boxes are spectacular. Q❀♣●P🚌📶

Walkington

Barrel Inn

35 East End, HU17 8RX

✪ 4.30-midnight (1am Fri); 12-1am Sat; 12-midnight Sun ☎ 07550 078833

Lancaster Bomber; Wainwright; 1 changing beer (sourced regionally) Ⓗ

Friendly drinkers' local in a quiet three-pub village, and one of only two Thwaites pubs in East Yorkshire. The interior comprises a front bar with log fire and beamed ceiling; a step leads to a connecting lounge, also with a log fire. To the rear is a secluded cottage-style garden. Families and dogs are welcome throughout. Although essentially a quiet pub, major Premier League football matches and some other sporting events are shown. Thursday is quiz night. 🚸❀♣🚌🐾

Ferguson Fawsitt Arms 𝕃

East End, HU17 8RX

✪ 11-11 ☎ (01482) 882665

Black Sheep Best Bitter; Wold Top Wold Gold; 3 changing beers (sourced locally; often All Hallows, Great Newsome) Ⓗ

Originally the village blacksmith's, the pub known locally as The Fergie was granted its first licence in 1866. It has three distinct areas: a traditional bar with logburner, a quieter lounge area, and a modern coffee shop to the rear. The pub is primarily food-oriented, with traditional locally sourced home-cooked food served every day. However, there is always a warm welcome for the casual drinker, be they local or from further afield. 🚸❀🛏◑♿P🚌📶

Withernsea

Old Boat Shed 𝕃

2 Seaside Road, HU19 2DL

✪ closed Mon; 1-midnight; 12-midnight Sat & Sun ☎ 07975 539539

4 changing beers (sourced regionally; often Great Newsome, Isaac Poad, Wold Top) Ⓗ

Originally built in 1881 to house the Withernsea lifeboat station before it was decommissioned in 1913, this building was virtually derelict when the current owners took over. Following 11 months' hard work, the micropub opened in 2016. Four cask ales and six real ciders are served in this community-focused bar, where conversation is actively encouraged in preference to loud music or TV. A selection of unusual board games such as shove-ha'penny and bar skittles is available. Q🚸❀♿▲♣●▯🚌 (76,129) 🐾

YORKSHIRE (NORTH)

Aldbrough St John

Stanwick 𝕃 ✔

High Green, DL11 7SZ (1 mile from B6275)

✪ closed Mon & Tue; 12-3, 5.30-11 Wed-Fri; 12-3, 6-11 Sat; 12-9 Sun ☎ (01325) 374258 🌐 thestanwick.co.uk

Daleside Bitter; Great North Eastern Rivet Catcher; 2 changing beers (sourced locally) Ⓗ

In a picturesque village on one of the country's largest village greens, this multi award-winning, welcoming 19th-century inn has two bars: one for drinkers and one for the two excellent restaurants, where locally sourced food is served six days a week (closed Mon). It was local CAMRA Country Pub of the Year 2017 and 2018. The brewery tap for the village's Mithril Ales, one of its beers is always featured. Cricket, quoits and darts are supported. Takeaway fish and chips are served Wednesday 5.30-8pm, roast baguettes Sunday 2-5pm, and there is a food theme night on the last Friday of the month. Q🚸❀◑♿♣P🚌 (29) 🐾📶

Appletreewick

Craven Arms 𝕃

BD23 6DA

✪ 12-11; 12-10.30 Sun ☎ (01756) 720270 🌐 craven-cruckbarn.co.uk

Dark Horse Craven Bitter, Hetton Pale Ale, Night Jar; Theakston Best Bitter, Old Peculier; Wharfedale Blonde; 1 changing beer (sourced regionally) Ⓗ

Dating from 1548, this multi-roomed free house has stone-flagged floors, oak beams and gas lighting. The bar features an original Yorkshire range while the cosy taproom has an open fire and ring the bull. A snug behind the bar leads to the cruck barn, built in 2006 using traditional techniques. This can be hired for functions and hosts occasional events including music and a beer festival in October. Two additional guest beers are added in summer. Accommodation is in three shepherd's huts. Q P (74A)

Arncliffe

Falcon Inn

BD23 5QE

12-3, 6.30-11; 12-11 Fri & Sat; 12-10.30 Sun

(01756) 770205 thefalconinnskipton.co.uk

Timothy Taylor Boltmaker H/G; 1 changing beer (sourced locally) H

Unspoilt traditional Dales pub-cum-hotel nestled next to the village green, the original Woolpack in Emmerdale Farm. Eschewing modern gimmickry, the last significant changes to the pub interior took place in the 1950s. Timothy Taylor Boltmaker is served from the cask via a jug or on handpump. A second pump offers a changing guest from a local brewery. Loved by visitors from near and far, the pub is also well supported by Dales folk. Evening meals are available if booked 24 hours in advance. Q

Austwick

Game Cock

LA2 8BB (on Horton road)

11.30 (3 Mon)-11 (015242) 51226

gamecockinn.co.uk

Thwaites Nutty Black, Original; Wainwright; 1 changing beer H

Cosy, multi-roomed pub with the emphasis on good food. The old-fashioned bar, used mainly for drinking, has a warming real fire and is decorated with cartoons and old photos. Popular with locals, hikers and cyclists, it can be quite intimate, with conversation involving the whole room. There are two cosy snugs behind the bar, and the dining rooms extend into the small south-facing conservatory. Food specials include French night Wednesday, steak night Thursday, fish & chips Friday and Sunday roasts.

Q P (581)

Aysgarth

George & Dragon

DL8 3AD (on main A684 between Hawes and Leyburn)

12-11 (01969) 663358

georgeanddragonaysgarth.co.uk

Black Sheep Best Bitter; Theakston Best Bitter; house beer (by Yorkshire Dales); 1 changing beer (sourced locally) H

One of the Yorkshire Dales' most famous natural features, the famous Aysgarth falls on the River Ure, lie less than a mile away from this attractive 17th-century coaching inn. Drinkers are welcome in its cosy, wood-panelled bar which serves up locally brewed real ales, while for diners there is a separate restaurant. En-suite accommodation is also offered. An outside drinking area has great views of the stunning surrounding Wensleydale countryside. Q P

Beck Hole

Birch Hall Inn ★

YO22 5LE (approx 1 mile N of Goathland)

11-11 (01947) 896245 beckhole.info

Black Sheep Best Bitter; North Yorkshire Beckwatter; 1 changing beer H

Unspoilt family-run rural gem, resting among a hamlet of cottages, run by the same licensee, an accomplished fine artist, for 38 years. A winner of multiple CAMRA awards, it only serves beers from Yorkshire. It comprises the Big Bar and the Small Bar, which sandwich a sweet shop. Pleasant outdoor drinking facilities overlook the Murk Esk. The house beer, Beckwatter, is brewed organically by North Yorkshire. Sandwiches, pies, beer cake and traditional sweets are always available. Hours change during winter. Q

Beckwithshaw

Smith's Arms

Church Row, HG3 1QW

11-11; 12-10 Sun (01423) 504871

Black Sheep Best Bitter; Greene King IPA; 3 changing beers H

A Chef & Brewer food-led pub in an 18th-century inn that, as the name suggests, was once a blacksmith's forge. In a quiet hamlet to the south-west of Harrogate, the pub comprises an L-shaped bar area and a separate restaurant. An excellent menu with many seasonal dishes is available throughout the day in both the restaurant and bar. The five handpumps serve two permanent beers and three widely sourced guest ales.

P

Bilbrough

Three Hares

Main Street, YO23 3PH

closed Mon; 12-2.30, 5.30-11; 12-11 Sat; 12-9 Sun

(01937) 918005 thethreeharesinn.co.uk

Bilbrough Top Beer; Hambleton Stud Blonde; Timothy Taylor Landlord; 1 changing beer (sourced regionally; often Ossett, Theakston) H

A comfortable and inviting village pub and the unofficial tap for the local Bilbrough Top Brewery. The four real ales are chosen in conjunction with the locals and a regular gluten-free beer is available. The combination of traditional pub food, a short yet interesting dining menu, plus a regular quiz night and live music, makes this an all-round community hostelry that attracts locals and regulars from further afield. A generous outdoor area works well in the summer. Q P

Bishopthorpe

Ebor

46 Main Street, YO23 2RB

11-midnight; 12-11.30 Sun (01904) 706190

Samuel Smith Old Brewery Bitter H

Officially haunted and with 16th-century origins, this pub is uniquely the only tenanted Samuel Smith's property. Landlord of 37 years Gordon Watkins provides a welcoming ambience, quality Old Brewery Bitter, and an extensive home-cooked menu (Whitby fish a speciality) including vegetarian options, lunchtimes and evenings (no food Sun eve). With two separate bars and a family atmosphere, the Ebor is at the heart of the local

NORTH YORKSHIRE

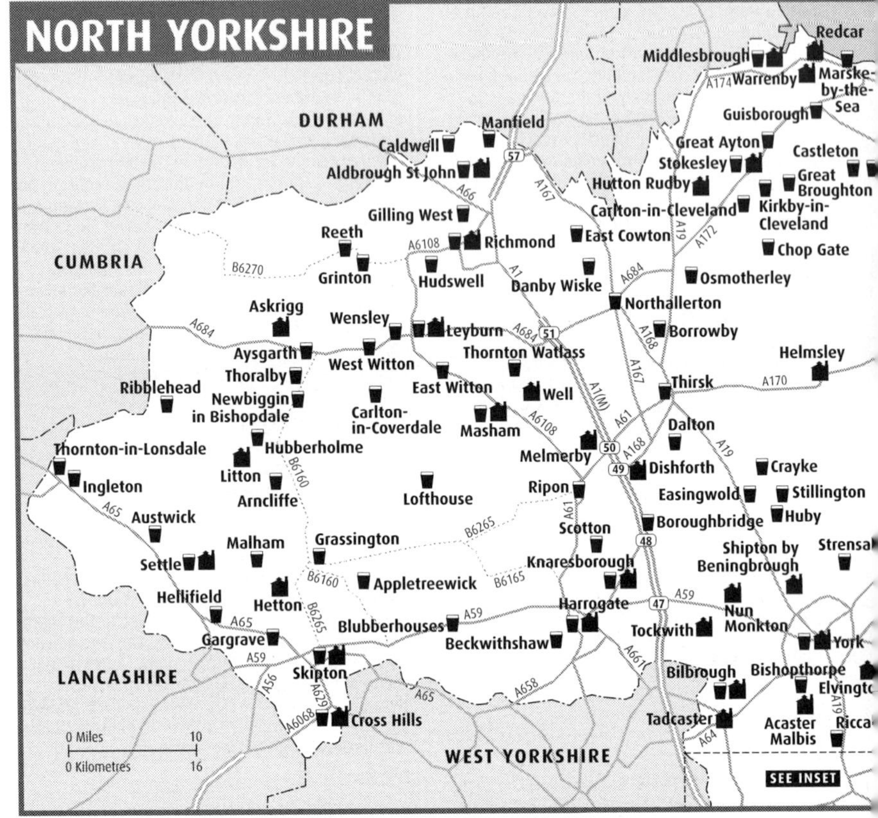

community, and it has a large beer garden. Children and dogs welcome.
⛀❀◑♿▲♣P🚌(11)🐾ᯤ

Marcia 🄻 ✔

29 Main Street, YO23 2RA

⏲ 11-midnight; 12-11 Sun ☎ (01904) 706185

🌐 themarciayork.co.uk

Leeds Pale; Ossett Yorkshire Blonde; Rooster's Yankee; Timothy Taylor Landlord; 2 changing beers (sourced locally; often Half Moon, Treboom, York) 🄷

Welcoming and popular village local with a landlord passionate about real ale. Six handpumps dispense three permanent and three rotating real ales (mainly LocAle). An annual summer beer and cider festival is held in the large rear garden, which has a children's play area. A good range of food is served every day in the bar and in the large restaurant/conservatory. The pub has a relaxed and friendly atmosphere, with games and occasional live music. Quiz night is Wednesday.
Q⛀❀◑♿▲♣P🚌(11)🐾ᯤ

Blubberhouses

Hopper Lane Hotel

Skipton Road, LS21 2NZ

⏲ closed Mon; 12-11; 12-10.30 Sun ☎ (01943) 880010

🌐 hopperlanehotel.co.uk

3 changing beers 🄷

A family-owned establishment on the main A59 Harrogate to Skipton road above Fewston Reservoir. Double fronted and stone built, the original three front rooms are pleasantly decorated and furnished; beyond are dining areas set out with tables and chairs. The front rooms have open fires and the original stone flags remain by the front door. An old glass-covered well is an unusual feature in the lounge by the left-hand room, which is furnished with leather settees and chairs.
⛀❀🛏◑♿♣P🐾ᯤ

Boroughbridge

Black Bull Inn

6 St James Square, YO51 9AR

⏲ 11-midnight; 12-11 Sun ☎ (01423) 322413

John Smith's Bitter; Timothy Taylor Boltmaker; 1 changing beer 🄷

Nestling in a corner of the market square, this 13th-century inn is immaculately kept and comfortably furnished, popular with locals and tourists alike. A Grade II-listed gem, it has a resident ghost. Three drinking and dining areas include a small cosy snug and a larger bar with open fires and good-value beers. A wide range of bar meals is served and there is a separate restaurant. A local CAMRA Pub of the Year.
Q🛏◑▲♣P🚌(22)🐾ᯤ

Borrowby

Wheatsheaf Inn 🄻

YO7 4QP (800yds from A19)

⏲ 5.30-11; 12-10.30 Sun ☎ (01845) 537274

Daleside Bitter; 2 changing beers (sourced locally) 🄷

A well-kept and welcoming free house in a rambling, attractive village a short hop from the busy A19 trunk route and on the edge of the North Yorkshire moors. The cosy public bar features a low-beamed ceiling and a splendid canopied fireplace, showing its 17th-century origins and giving a traditional feel, particularly in winter. There is a small dining room and a further drinking area to the rear. Themed food nights feature regularly. The two guest beers are usually from Yorkshire microbreweries. **Q⛟❀◗♣P🐾📶**

Brompton by Sawdon

Old Post Office Tavern 🄻

High Street, YO13 9DP

⏲ closed Mon & Tue; 5-9 Wed-Fri; 12 (4 winter)-9 Sat; 2 (4 winter)-7 Sun ☎ (01723) 850202

🌐 oldpostofficetavern.co.uk

4 changing beers (sourced regionally; often Great Newsome, North Riding, Three Brothers) 🄷

Opened in 2015, this is a recent addition to the Scarborough area rural pub scene, located on the A170 Scarborough to Pickering road. This former village post office has been converted into a cosy single-room pub which encourages good old-fashioned conversation. Quiz night takes place on the second Sunday of each month. Four regularly changing beers are offered, predominantly from Yorkshire microbreweries, together with a choice of real ciders. Open on bank holiday Mondays 12-7pm. **Q⛟◗♿⛺♣🍎🚌**(128)**🐾**

Burn

Wheatsheaf 🄻

Main Road, YO8 8LJ

⏲ 12-11 (midnight Fri & Sat) ☎ (01757) 270614

🌐 wheatsheafburn.co.uk

5 changing beers (often Brown Cow, Great Heck, Ossett) 🄷

Traditional country pub serving a varied range of guest beers mainly from Yorkshire breweries. A narrow entrance leads to the bar, a small room to the left and a spacious lounge with a huge open fire to the right. There is a collection of artefacts from bygone days and memorabilia of 578 and 431 Squadrons stationed at Burn in WWII. Food is served every lunchtime and Wednesday to Saturday evenings. Regular beer festivals, a popular Sunday quiz night and occasional live entertainment take place.
Q⛟❀◐◗♣P🚌(476,405)**🐾📶**

REAL ALE BREWERIES

Ainsty Acaster Malbis
BAD Dishforth
Bad Seed Malton
Beer Monkey Skipton
Bilbrough Top Bilbrough
Black Sheep Masham
Brass Castle Malton
Brew York York
Brown Cow Barlow
Captain Cook Stokesley
Crooked Church Fenton (NEW)
Daleside Harrogate
Dark Horse Hetton
Great British Breworks 🍺 Pickering
Great Heck Great Heck
Great Yorkshire 🍺 Cropton
Hambleton Melmerby
Harrogate Harrogate
Helmsley Helmsley
Hop Studio Elvington
Jolly Sailor 🍺 Selby
Lady Luck 🍺 Whitby (NEW)
Little Black Dog Carlton
Littondale 🍺 Litton (NEW)
Mithril Aldbrough St John
Naylor's Cross Hills
North Riding (Brewery) Scarborough
North Riding (Brewpub) 🍺 Scarborough
North Yorkshire Warrenby
Pennine Well
Redscar 🍺 Redcar
Richmond Richmond
Rooster's Knaresborough
Rudgate Tockwith
Ryedale Cross Hills (brewing suspended)
Samuel Smith Tadcaster
Scarborough Scarborough
Settle Settle
Taylor Illingworth Middlesbrough (NEW)
Theakston Masham
Three Peaks Settle
Treboom Shipton-by-Beningbrough
Turning Point Kirkbymoorside (NEW)
Wainstones/Bay Hutton Rudby
Wensleydale Leyburn
Whitby Whitby
York York
Yorkshire Dales Askrigg
Yorkshire Heart Nun Monkton

Burythorpe

Bay Horse

Main Street, YO17 9LH
⏲ 11.30-11.30 ☎ (01653) 658302
🌐 thebayhorseburythorpe.co.uk
Hambleton Stallion Amber; 7 changing beers (sourced locally; often All Hallows) Ⓗ
Reopened in 2016 following an extensive renovation, the former modern interior has been totally transformed, restoring it to an authentic-looking pub from the past. Full of character, with a number of small rooms, it serves real ales from All Hallows Brewery, situated at its sister pub (Goodmanham Arms, Goodmanham), and many guest beers including a good selection of local real ales. Lunch is served daily 12-2pm.
Q❀◐♣●P🚌🐾📶

Caldwell

Brownlow Arms

DL11 7QH
⏲ 5.30-11; 12-11 Sat & Sun ☎ (01325) 718471
🌐 brownlowarms.co.uk
Timothy Taylor Landlord; 2 changing beers Ⓗ
Set in a quiet village, this could be described as the perfect country inn. It boasts a fine dining restaurant as well as two cosy bars, accompanied by open log fires, where you are guaranteed to find some welcoming locals. It serves three cask ales (up to six in summer), always including Timothy Taylor Landlord, with the others changing all the time but regularly from the Yorkshire Dales – requests are welcome. There is a huge choice of home-cooked food to accompany your ale.
Q🐴❀◐♿P🐾📶

Carlton-in-Cleveland

Blackwell Ox Inn

TS9 7DJ (800yds E of A172)
⏲ 11.30-11 ☎ (01642) 712287 🌐 blackwellox.co.uk
4 changing beers Ⓗ
Set in a beautiful area on the northern edge of the North York Moors, with the same licensee for 30 years, this very popular, multi-roomed village inn is as renowned for its fine beers as it is for its Thai food. Look out for the lunchtime and early-doors food offers. But you do not have to eat; four handpumps provide an eclectic range of beers in various styles. The garden has an extensive well-designed children's play area. Q🐴❀◐P🚌(89)

Carlton-in-Coverdale

Foresters Arms 𝕃 ✔

DL8 4BB
⏲ 12-2 (not Mon), 6-11; 12-2, 6-midnight Fri; 12-midnight Sat; 12-4, 7-11 Sun ☎ (01969) 640272
🌐 forestersarms-carlton.co.uk
5 changing beers (sourced locally; often Black Sheep, Timothy Taylor, Wensleydale) Ⓗ
Well worth seeking out, this 250-year-old free house is named after the Foresters Friendly Society. This pretty village on the Dales cycle route is convenient for the Forbidden Corner fantasy maze (advanced booking essential). In community ownership since 2011, the pub's low-beamed ceilings and open fire contribute to its character, with wooden settles fashioned from pews from the former village church. There is always a guest ale plus changing beers from Black Sheep, Timothy Taylor and Wensleydale breweries.
Q🐴🛏◐♿♣P🐾📶

Castleton

Eskdale Inn 𝕃

Langburn's Bank, YO21 2EU (next to Castleton Moor railway station, 500yds N of village centre) NZ684085
⏲ 12-11 ☎ (01287) 660333 🌐 theeskdalecastleton.co.uk
Black Sheep Best Bitter; Tetley Bitter; Theakston Old Peculier; 2 changing beers Ⓗ
Wedged between the Esk Valley railway and the River Esk, this imposing former Victorian station hotel offers a friendly welcome. The casks sit in a cool cellar directly beneath the five handpumps (three in winter), and well away from the roaring fire. The guest beers are often chosen by the locals themselves and are usually something more interesting. A good-value food menu is served. The pub hosts darts and pool teams. Two letting bedrooms are available.
Q🐴❀🛏◐♿⇌♣●P🍷🐾📶

Chop Gate

Buck Inn 𝕃

Chop Gate, TS9 7JL (on B1257, between Stokesley and Helmsley)
⏲ 12 (5 Mon-Wed)-9 ☎ (01642) 778334
🌐 the-buck-inn.co.uk
3 changing beers Ⓗ
Set amid a walkers' paradise and close to the route of Wainwright's Coast-to-Coast walk, this picturesque family-run village pub offers a truly Yorkshire/Teutonic twist. Three locally sourced beers and seven draught German lagers, brewed under the 503-year-old purity laws, are served, together with real home-made food, again half Yorkshire/half German. There are six en-suite bedrooms, some designated dog-friendly, while free camping is offered to those campers who also choose to dine here. Check winter opening hours.
Q🐴❀🛏◐⛺♣P🐾📶

Church Fenton

Fenton Flyer 𝕃 ✔

Main Street, LS24 9RF
⏲ 5-11 Mon-Wed; 4-midnight Thu & Fri; 12-midnight Sat; 12-11.30 Sun ☎ (01937) 558137
Rooster's Yankee; 4 changing beers (sourced regionally; often Ilkley, Leeds, Ossett) Ⓗ
Friendly village pub with pictures of the nearby WWII airbase which is now a commercial airport. The beers here are chosen from the SIBA list and are often LocAle. Live music features on the first Friday of each month, it has a monthly Saturday disco with karaoke, and a quiz night on Wednesday raising money for local charities. There is a Sky and BT Sports TV in the main bar and an adjacent games room with a pool table and darts. Beer festivals are held in June and November.
🐴❀⛺♣P🚌(492)🐾📶

Cliffe

New Inn 𝕃

York Road, YO8 6NN
⏲ 2-11; 12-midnight Fri & Sat; 12-10.30 Sun
☎ (01757) 633888

Theakston Best Bitter; 5 changing beers (sourced regionally; often Half Moon, Small World, Sunbeam)
Now established as a superb example of how a village local can also be a real ale emporium, this award-winning pub is a delight to visit. It is comfortable, two-roomed and serves five guest beers – almost always local and certainly from Yorkshire. Blazing log fires for cosy winter drinking are complemented by a shady beer garden for summer. The annual beer festival is held every August, ramping up the number of ales served alongside live local music and a traditional barbecue. ♣P

Crayke

Durham Ox

Westway, YO61 4TE
11-11; 11-10.30 Sun ☎ (01347) 821506
thedurhamox.com
Black Sheep Best Bitter; Theakston Best Bitter; Timothy Taylor Boltmaker
While the emphasis is on quality dining, the beer is not an orphan. There is a dedicated drinkers' bar which caters for locals, cyclists and walkers, with plenty of heat from the fires in winter. The atmosphere is subdued and reserved but the staff are approachable and friendly, as befits this beautiful village which has this pub at its heart. Q P

Cropton

New Inn

Cropton Lane, YO18 8HH (leave A170 at Wrelton and follow signs for Cropton)
11-11 (midnight Fri & Sat) ☎ (01751) 417330
newinncropton.co.uk
Great Yorkshire Pale, Classic, Golden; 3 changing beers (sourced locally; often Great Yorkshire)
A family-run pub on the edge of the North Yorkshire Moors National Park, the New Inn is the tap for the Great Yorkshire Brewery (formerly Cropton Brewery). A perfect base for walking and cycling, it offers good food in the bars, conservatory or restaurant, and B&B or camping accommodation. Many real ales are on the bar, and a legendary beer festival is held every November. Other festivals and music events are put on during the year. A positive and chatty pub, it is dog- and rambler-friendly. Q ♣P

Cross Hills

Gallagher's Ale House

1-3 East Keltus, BD20 8TD (village centre)
closed Mon & Tue; 3-10 Wed & Thu; 1-11 Fri; 12-11 Sat; 12-8 Sun ☎ 07834 456134
5 changing beers (sourced nationally)
This popular micropub, established in 2015, is in what used to be Gallagher's bookmaker's. The five changing beers usually include a dark brew, a pale bitter and a strong or speciality beer. The cellar can be viewed through a window to the left of the bar. No electronic music or TV disturbs the conversation. Parking is available adjacent to the Co-op store round the corner. The phone number is shared with the Beer Engine in Skipton. Q (M4,66)

Dalton

Jolly Farmers Inn

Brookside, YO7 3HY
4-11; 12-midnight Sat & Sun ☎ (01845) 578053
John Smith's Bitter; 1 changing beer
A large local in the heart of a working village. The three rooms offer drinking, dining and pub games, with sports TV in the bar and the games room. Various pub games league teams are supported by the regulars. Accommodation is available across the courtyard from the main building in what were formerly outbuildings. The village is conveniently located close to the A1M and the A19 near the foot of the North York Moors escarpment.
♣P

Danby

Duke of Wellington

West Lane, YO21 2LY (300yds N of railway station)
12-2.30 (not Mon), 7-11; 12-11 Fri-Sun ☎ (01287) 660351
dukeofwellingtondanby.co.uk
Daleside Bitter; Whitby Saltwick Nab; 1 changing beer
This 18th-century inn, and previous CAMRA branch Pub of the Year, is set in idyllic countryside, close to the popular Moors National Park Centre and equally popular traditional bakery. The inn was used as a recruiting post during the Napoleonic Wars, with a cast-iron plaque of the first Duke, unearthed during restorations, hanging above the fireplace. All beers are from Yorkshire, with cider and perry served Easter to October. The kitchen offers traditional British home-cooked meals at their best, using local produce. Q ♣

Danby Wiske

White Swan

DL7 0NQ (approx 3 miles N of Northallerton off A167)
12-11 ☎ (01609) 775131
thewhiteswandanbywiske.co.uk
4 changing beers (sourced locally)
A much-appreciated inn on the 192-mile Coast-to-Coast route, this village green pub offers a warm welcome to walkers and locals alike. The opened-out interior features a stone floor and wood-burning stoves, and is home to the local sword dancers. Two ciders and a perry are usually available. Food is served April to October and geared to walkers' needs, with lunchtime snacks and hearty evening meals using much locally sourced produce (booking is advisable). Winter hours may vary and are much more limited (closed Mon and weekend afternoons, open eves only Tue-Fri). Q ♣P

Easingwold

George Hotel

Market Place, YO61 3AD
11-11 ☎ (01347) 821698 the-george-hotel.co.uk
Black Sheep Best Bitter; Timothy Taylor Boltmaker; 1 changing beer (sourced regionally)
In a fine Georgian town of many pubs, this is one not to miss, either for its beer or food. Try the others but you will find yourself drifting back to this traditional yet unstuffy country hotel. If you can bag the bay window you will have an excellent view of the town's bustle. A longstanding favourite and rightly so. Q P

East Cowton

Beeswing

Main Street, DL7 0BD
5-11; 11.30-11 Fri-Sun (01325) 378349
thebeeswing.weebly.com
4 changing beers H
Traditional country village pub with two bars, a pool room and a highly rated restaurant. Named after a locally bred champion racehorse, there are numerous racing references. It has up to four varying beers from breweries countrywide and one real cider. Real fires create a relaxing atmosphere. The staff are welcoming, and the pub supports the local community with regular music and quizzes.
Q P

East Witton

Cover Bridge Inn

DL8 4SQ (½ mile N of village on A6108)
11-midnight; 12-11 Sun (01969) 623250
thecoverbridgeinn.co.uk
Black Sheep Best Bitter; Theakston Old Peculier; Timothy Taylor Landlord; 5 changing beers (sourced locally) H
A splendidly traditional Dales inn where numerous CAMRA awards tell their tale. The River Cover runs along the foot of the attractive garden and play area, near its confluence with the River Ure. Fathom out the door latch and you will be able to enjoy the warm welcome in the unspoilt public bar, with its eight beer pumps and giant hearth, or sit in the tiny lounge or pleasant beer garden. There is a choice of locally brewed beers and guests from further afield, plus two real ciders and perry. Q P (159)

Egton

Wheatsheaf Inn

YO21 1TZ
closed Mon; 11.30-2.45, 5.30-11; 11.30-11 Sat & Sun
(01947) 895271 wheatsheafegton.com
Black Sheep Best Bitter; Timothy Taylor Landlord; 2 changing beers H
Winner of many CAMRA awards, this Grade II-listed 19th-century pub serves four Yorkshire beers. The pub is now in its 19th year in the Guide, and remains under the stewardship of a licensee with over 30 years of continuous Guide recognition. Church pews, country collectables and a roaring range add to the ambience. The grassy area to the front and the boules terrain to the rear are ideal for summer drinking. The renowned first-class restaurant always features local meat, fish and game. Q P (99)

Egton Bridge

Horseshoe Hotel

YO21 1XE
11.30 (11 Mon & Tue)-3, 6-11; 12-11 Sun
(01947) 895245 egtonbridgehotel.co.uk
Bradfield Farmers Blonde; Theakston Best Bitter; 2 changing beers H
Secluded and unspoilt 18th-century gem located in a horseshoe-shaped hollow and accessed either by road, from the railway station, or from walking over the stepping stones across the River Esk. Old-fashioned settles, a large fire and angling memorabilia adorn the bar, while picnic tables, on a large raised grassy bank, make outdoor drinking a pleasure. Four handpumps feature some interesting beers. The menu and specials board are locally sourced and represent good value. Accommodation is in eight letting bedrooms.
Q P (99)

Filey

Cobbler's Arms

2 Union Street, YO14 9DZ
closed Mon; 4-10; 12-10 Sat; 12-9 Sun (01723) 512511
Wainwright; 4 changing beers (sourced regionally; often Isaac Poad, Milestone) H
Micropub in the centre of Filey. It was originally a private residence before becoming the cobbler's shop from which it takes its name. The front bar area encourages conversation and there is a second smaller snug to the rear which is available for meetings free of charge. Four changing guest ales are served alongside seven real ciders. Families and dogs are welcome. There is a regular quiz on a Tuesday night and live music occasionally. Q

Star Inn

23 Mitford Street, YO14 9DX
12-midnight (1am Fri & Sat) (01723) 512031
thestarfiley.co.uk
Black Sheep Ale; Bradfield Farmers Blonde; Theakston Best Bitter; 3 changing beers (sourced nationally) H
The Star Inn is just off the Filey town centre and has a large main room and separate restaurant/ function room. Three regular beers and three rotating guests are offered. Freshly cooked meals are served lunchtimes and evenings (except Mon). Live entertainment features occasionally. Pub teams participate in a local pool league. Smokers are catered for both front and rear of the building, while parking is provided behind the pub. Local CAMRA runner-up Rural Pub of the Year 2016.
P (121)

Gargrave

Masons Arms

Marton Road, BD23 3NL (on road over River Aire to railway station off A65)
12-midnight (11 Wed) (01756) 749304
masonsarmsgargrave.co.uk
Tetley Bitter; Timothy Taylor Boltmaker; Wainwright; 1 changing beer H
This attractive village pub is in a quiet residential location opposite St Andrews Church, between the railway station and the River Aire. With its low oak-beamed ceilings, it offers a comfortable and relaxing environment both for drinkers and diners. A strong supporter of local sports teams, the pub has its own Crown Green bowling green. Accommodation is in six en-suite rooms alongside the pub, making it a great base for exploring the southern Dales. Lockable cycle storage is available for residents.
Q P (580,210)

Gilling West

White Swan

51 High Street, DL10 5JG (1 mile W of Scotch Corner, off A66)
12-11; 9am-11 Sat (01748) 825122
thewhiteswan.co

2 changing beers Ⓗ
A historic coaching inn, recently modernised, with a bar, restaurant and rooms. An open fire, courtyard garden and traditional beams continue the tradition, while a granite bar, tin tables and modern rooms bring this charming village pub into the present. It serves real ales from a local microbrewery, Mithril, who brew the house beer, The Swan, as well as craft lagers, and it has an extensive wine and gin menu. The kitchen specialises in steaks, seafood and Yorkshire tapas, doing all of its own butchery in-house, and sources its famous steaks from a local Yorkshire farm. It has a modern pool room, and there is regular live music. Q (29)

Grassington

Foresters Arms

20 Main Street, BD23 5AA
11-midnight (1am Fri & Sat) ☎ (01756) 752349
forestersarmsgrassington.co.uk
Black Sheep Best Bitter, Riggwelter; Tetley Mild, Bitter; Timothy Taylor Landlord; 1 changing beer (sourced locally; often Timothy Taylor, Wharfedale) Ⓗ
Just off the cobbled town square, the Foresters is a lively inn, popular with locals and visitors alike. The main bar and pool/TV area are to the left and further seating to the right leads to a separate dining room. Accommodation is available in seven en-suite rooms and fishing permits for the local River Wharfe can be bought at the pub. There is a quiz on Mondays. It has secure cycle storage for staying guests. CAMRA branch Community Pub of the Year 2017. (72,72B)

Great Ayton

Royal Oak Hotel

123 High Street, TS9 6BW (in centre of village opp High Green)
10-11 (midnight Fri & Sat); 11.30-11 Sun
☎ (01642) 722361 royaloakgreatayton.co.uk
Theakston Old Peculier; Timothy Taylor Landlord; Wainwright; 1 changing beer Ⓗ
A warm welcome is extended to locals and visitors alike at this extensive 18th-century Grade II-listed building and former coaching inn. Always busy, the pub is equally famed for its four beers as well as its food, where breakfast, lunch and dinner are all served, together with various different offers on food throughout the week. There is also a takeaway service. An enclosed courtyard to the rear, a function room and four en-suite bedrooms are all available. Q (28,81)

Great Broughton

Bay Horse

88 High Street, TS9 7HA (at S end of village)
11.30-3, 5.30-11; 11.30-11 Sat; 12-11 Sun
☎ (01642) 712319 thebayhorse-greatbroughton.co.uk
Camerons Strongarm; Jennings Sneck Lifter; 2 changing beers Ⓗ
Visitors and locals alike enjoy the welcoming hospitality offered by friendly bar staff at this spacious village country inn, situated beneath one of the northern entrances to the North York Moors. While the emphasis is on good-value, freshly prepared, home-cooked meals, drinkers are also especially well catered for. In addition to Strongarm and Sneck Lifter, which the pub is renowned for having served for many years, two changing beers, from the Marston's stable, are also sold. Q P (89,X89)

Great Heck

Bay Horse

Main Street, DN14 0BE (S of A645 between Pontefract and Snaith)
3-10 (midnight Thu & Fri); 12-midnight Sat; 12-10 Sun
☎ (01977) 661125 bayhorsegreatheck.co.uk
Old Mill Traditional Bitter; 1 changing beer (sourced locally; often Old Mill) Ⓗ
An Old Mill tied house, the Bay Horse is a cosy, inviting and traditional pub in a remote country hamlet, serving well-kept ales from the Old Mill Brewery. The bar is divided into three distinct areas, with dining rooms at each end and a central lounge near the bar. It has comfortable seating and a log-burning fire. Interesting artefacts and pictures decorate the walls and oak beams, adding to the ambience. Food is served in the evening, as well as lunches on Sunday. Q P

Grinton

Bridge Inn

DL11 6HH (on B6270, 1 mile E of Reeth)
12-11.30; 12-11 Sun ☎ (01748) 884224
bridgeinn-grinton.co.uk
Jennings Cumberland Ale; Wainwright; 3 changing beers (sourced nationally; often Marston's) Ⓗ
A friendly, well-run historic inn, close to a crossing of the River Swale as its name suggests, lying beneath the towering hills of Fremington Edge and Harkerside. It has a comfortable lounge, a wood-panelled bar and two restaurant rooms offering home-made food, and is a haven for walkers and cyclists on the Coast-to-Coast and Inn Way walks and Dales Cycle Way; a Youth Hostel is half a mile up the hill. Guest beers are from the Marston's range. May close early at quiet times.
Q P (30)

Grosmont

Crossing Club

Co-operative Building, Front Street, YO22 5QE (opp NYMR car park – ring front door bell)
8-11 ☎ 07766 197744
5 changing beers Ⓗ
Set amid beautiful scenery in the Esk Valley, this recent CAMRA branch Club of the Year is located opposite the NYMR/Esk Valley railway stations in what was the village Co-op's delivery bay. Converted by dedicated villagers into a railway-themed private members' club 20 years ago, a warm welcome always awaits CAMRA members. The five handpumps have now served over 1,200 different beers. For railway enthusiasts, both steam and diesel memorabilia adorn the walls. Opening hours are extended during NYMR galas. Q

Guisborough

Monk

27 Church Street, TS14 6HG (at E end of Westgate)
closed Mon; 11.30-3, 5-11.45 Tue & Wed; 11.30-11.45 Thu-Sat; 12-11 Sun ☎ (01287) 205058
5 changing beers Ⓗ
This hostelry is directly opposite Gisborough Priory, which was razed to the ground by King Henry VIII in

1540. The pub is aptly named as, legend has it, the 12th-century Black Monk made use of the tunnel, discovered during recent renovations, for his nefarious nighttime activities. The access stairs to the tunnel are now on view. This contemporary pub/cocktail lounge is now an upmarket addition to the town's social life and attracts a discerning clientele. Five rotating beers and a real cider are served. ♿🍎🚌(5,X93)🐾📶

Harrogate

10 Devonshire Place

10 Devonshire Place, HG1 4AA

3-midnight; 12-midnight Fri-Sun ☎ (01423) 202356

10devonshireplace.com

Timothy Taylor Boltmaker; 8 changing beers H

Cosy old pub that was rescued, restored and renovated in 2014; the original semicircular counter with its stained-glass canopy has been refurbished and is complemented by a newly installed reclaimed floor. Ten handpumps serve local cask ales and a cider, and flights of thirds are offered. A well-stocked range of interesting bottled beers and cans is available which can be drunk on or off the premises. 🚂🍎🐾📶

Coach & Horses

16 West Park, HG1 1BJ

11-11; 12-10.30 Sun ☎ (01423) 561802

thecoachandhorses.net

Daleside Bitter; Tetley Bitter; Timothy Taylor Landlord; 5 changing beers H

A busy traditional pub popular with locals and visitors by Harrogate's famous Stray. The counter is surrounded by snugs and alcoves, creating a cosy atmosphere inside. Tables and chairs are provided outside for customers in summer, while window boxes create a spectacular display and add year-round colour. The pub offers a guest beer range and serves excellent meals at lunchtime as well as holding themed evenings. Many of these, together with a popular Sunday night quiz, have raised a considerable amount of money for a local children's hospice. Q🚂🚌📶

Harrogate Tap

Station Parade, HG1 1TE

11-11 (midnight Fri); 10-midnight Sat ☎ (01423) 501644

harrogatetap.co.uk

11 changing beers (often Harrogate, Rooster's) H

Just off Platform 1 of Harrogate station is this impressive transformation of a neglected railway building into a fine pub of similar style to the Tapped Brew Company's other bars at York and Sheffield. Comprising a long bar room and a separate snug, the decor features dark wood panelling, a tiled floor and tasteful Victorian-style fittings. A diverse range of cask ales is available on 12 handpumps, with one devoted to cider. These are complemented by craft kegs and bottled world beers. Bar snacks are also available. ♿🚂🍎🚌🐾

Little Ale House

7 Cheltenham Crescent, HG1 1DH

2-9 (10 Thu & Fri); 12-10 Sat; 1-7 Sun ☎ (01423) 391996

alehouseharrogate.co.uk

5 changing beers H

A popular micropub, comprising one room with the counter at the back. As in many other micropubs, the beers are kept cool in a glass cabinet to one side. Five handpumps dispense cask beers while four KeyKeg taps are mounted behind the counter; local artisan gins are also available. There is also a pleasant drinking yard at the rear. Selected sporting events are sometimes televised in the cellar, and it hosts live music and other events. Q🚂🍎🚌🐾📶

Major Tom's Social

The Ginnel, HG1 2RB

12-11.30 (1am Fri & Sat) ☎ (01423) 566984

majortomssocial.co.uk

House beer (by Rooster's); 3 changing beers H

An unusual café bar housed upstairs from a vintage clothes and record shop. It provides a changing selection of beers, pizzas and artworks, and is simply furnished and decorated in a mix of styles to suit the eclectic customers. The artwork on display is for sale. The four handpumps dispense a variety of ales, usually from a range of smaller breweries; there are also interesting keg beers, and bottles and cans from the UK, US and Europe. 🚂🐾📶

North Bar Harrogate

2D Oxford Buildings, Cheltenham Parade, HG1 1DA

8am-11 (midnight Fri); 9am-midnight Sat; 10-11 Sun ☎ (01423) 520772

3 changing beers H

A shop conversion to form a modern bar; a second downstairs room houses a photo booth and there is a small function room upstairs. Three handpumps provide a varying choice of cask beers while there are numerous keg taps and fridges with bottles sourced from the UK, the US and Europe. Some of the beers in each style are from North Bar's own brewery in Leeds, while others come from local favourites including Rooster's. 🚂🚌🐾

Old Bell ✔

6 Royal Parade, HG1 2SZ

12-11; 12-10.30 Sun ☎ (01423) 507930

Hawkshead Windermere Pale; Theakston Best Bitter; Timothy Taylor Boltmaker; 4 changing beers (often Okell's, Rooster's) H

Recently refurbished to a mixed response, the building became a pub in 1999 on the site of the Blue Bell Inn. Seven handpumps offer a changing range of beers including a varied choice of guests, usually including one from Okell's (who own the Market Town Tavern group), a Rooster's and a dark beer. The side room has a collection of Farrar's Harrogate Toffee memorabilia and upstairs is a well-regarded restaurant. Q🚂

Starling Independent Beer & Coffee House 🏆 L

47 Oxford Street, HG1 1PW

9am-10 (11 Thu-Sat); 9am-9 Sun ☎ (01423) 531310

starlinghgte.co.uk

Black Sheep Best Bitter; Hawkshead Windermere Pale; 4 changing beers (often Rooster's) H

A modern bar and coffee shop in a converted retail outlet also serving stone-baked pizzas. It has a modern look, with whitewashed stripped-back brickwork. One wall has a mural of a murmuration of starlings in homage to the owners. The pallet-fronted counter holds six handpumps with a range of (mainly) Yorkshire beers offering a good mix of styles and strengths. In addition to the two regular beers, one pump will have a changing beer from Rooster's. 🚂🚌🐾📶

Swan ✔

17 Devonshire Place, HG1 4AA

12-11; 12-10.30 Sun ☎ (01423) 524587

7 changing beers (often Okell's, Rooster's, Timothy Taylor)
Formerly known as the Black Swan and then the Swan on the Stray, this Market Town Taverns pub was refurbished in a modern style and reopened in 2016. Seven changing real ales are stocked, most from Yorkshire brewers and owners Okell's from the Isle of Man. There is a beer garden at the rear and well-behaved children and dogs are welcome until 8pm. P

Hellifield

Black Horse Hotel

Main Road, BD23 4HT
12-11; 5 (4 Fri)-11; 12-11 Sat & Sun winter
(01729) 851402
4 changing beers
Large rambling village pub, a popular venue for dining and drinking. The spacious main lounge has large settees and coffee tables surrounded by more conventional seating. Note the collection of musical instruments. There is also a taproom, accessed off the main A65, and a small dining room suitable for meetings and family gatherings. Paved areas either side of the building offer ample outdoor seating. Four changing real ales are available, often from local breweries. It also does a Sunday carvery. P (580)

Hubberholme

George Inn

Kirk Gill, BD23 5JE (opp church, 1 mile NW of Buckden)
4-10.30 Mon; closed Tue; 12-10.30 Wed-Sun summer; 6-10.30 Mon; closed Tue; 12-2.30, 6-10.30 Wed-Fri; 12-10.30 Sat; 12-5 Sun winter (01756) 760223
thegeorge-inn.co.uk
Black Sheep Best Bitter; Theakston Best Bitter; 2 changing beers (sourced locally; often Dark Horse, Naylor's)
Supposedly a favourite haunt of JB Priestley, this Grade II-listed whitewashed building dates from the 1600s and boasts mullioned windows, heavy oak beams and flagstone floors. A lighted candle on the bar denotes that it is open and is associated with the Hubberholme Parliament, an annual auction for letting church land. George of the George (the owners' Jack Russell) eagerly greets visitors! Booking for food is advisable. Closes for a short annual holiday around the end of January.
Q P

Huby

Mended Drum

Tollerton Road, YO61 1HT
5-11.30; 4-12.30am Fri; 12-12.30am Sat; 12-11.30 Sun
(01347) 810264 themendeddrumhuby.blogspot.co.uk
Black Sheep Best Bitter; 5 changing beers (sourced locally; often Bad Seed, Hop Studio, North Riding)
You need to make an effort to get to Huby, but once inside this pub it is well rewarded. This is a destination pub, but what a destination! Bright, lively and dedicated to real ale is a fitting description both of the pub and its staff. With a better beer range than many big city pubs (plus an excellent bottle range to take home if constrained by driving) there is never a dull moment. The food is excellent and served in Yorkshire portions.
P (x30)

Hudswell

George & Dragon

DL11 6BL
11-3, 5-11; 11-11 Sat & Sun (01748) 518373
georgeanddragonhudswell.co.uk
Rudgate Ruby Mild; Wensleydale Falconer Session Bitter; 3 changing beers (sourced locally)
This homely, two-roomed village inn became a media celebrity in 2017 when CAMRA named it as its National Pub of the Year. Rescued from closure and refurbished after a successful community buy-out in 2010, it now features its own library, shop, allotments and other local facilities, as well as great food, Yorkshire-brewed beers and a selection of nearly 70 whiskies. A large beer terrace to the rear offers stunning panoramic views over the Swale Valley. Open all day bank holidays.
Q P (32)

Ingleton

Masons

New Road, LA6 3HL
11.30-11; 12-10.30 Sun (015242) 42040
masonsismoran.co.uk
Black Sheep Best Bitter; Sharp's Doom Bar; 3 changing beers
Early Victorian building on the busy main road away from the centre of this popular tourist village. Extensively refurbished in 2016, it is now a true family-run free house. A small bar counter serves a long drinking space of linked areas with light and airy decor. Live music features but not yet regularly. P (80)

Kirk Smeaton

Shoulder of Mutton

Main Street, WF8 3JY (follow signs from A1)
12-midnight; 11.30-midnight Sun (01977) 620348
Black Sheep Best Bitter; 1 changing beer (sourced regionally; often Theakston)
A welcoming, traditional village pub convenient for the Went Valley and Brockadale Nature Reserve, and popular with walkers and the local community. The beer quality is superb, coming directly from the brewery. It is an award-winning free house and comprises a large lounge with open fires and a cosy dark-panelled snug. The spacious beer garden has a covered and heated shelter for smokers and there is ample parking. Quiz night is Tuesday.
Q P (409)

Kirkby-in-Cleveland

Black Swan

Busby Lane, TS9 7AW (800yds W of B1257) NZ539060
12-midnight (01642) 712512
Bradfield Farmers Blonde; Sharp's Doom Bar; Timothy Taylor Landlord; Wainwright; 1 changing beer
Nestling at the foot of the Cleveland Hills, at the crossroads of this ancient village, this warm and cosy free house comprises a bar, an adjacent pool room, a lounge/restaurant, a pleasant conservatory and also a patio seating area. A genuine welcome is always afforded from the friendly staff. Four regular beers, together with a changing guest beer, are dispensed, while good-value meals are served from a comprehensive restaurant menu, including daily specials and bar meals. P (89)

Knaresborough

Blind Jack's

19 Market Place, HG5 8AL
5-11; 3-11 Fri; 12-11 Sat; 12-10.30 Sun ☎ (01423) 869148
Black Sheep Best Bitter; 6 changing beers Ⓗ
A multi-roomed pub with bare-brick walls, wooden floorboards and panelling. It is an award-winning ale house and provides a focal point both for locals and the many visitors who appreciate the excellent selection of ales and cosy ambience. The beer range usually includes ales from BAD Company Brewery at Dishforth as well as beers from other small Yorkshire breweries, and also a range of craft kegs. The pub has been listed in the Guide since 1993. **Q** (1)

Cross Keys

17 Cheapside, HG5 8AX
4-11; 12-midnight Fri & Sat; 12-11 Sun ☎ (01423) 863562
Jennings Bitter; Ossett Yorkshire Blonde, Big Red Bitter, Silver King; Rat White Rat; 3 changing beers (sourced regionally; often Rat) Ⓗ
A former Tetley's house, refurbished by Ossett Brewery in its trademark style of stone-flagged floors, bare-brick walls and stained glass. This traditional pub serves four regular beers and and two guests, one of which is usually a dark beer or stout from either a microbrewery or from one of the other breweries within the Ossett company. Thursday is quiz night and a live band plays on most Saturday nights. Lunches are served on Sundays. (1)

Half Moon

1 Abbey Road, HG5 8HY
5-11; 4-11 Fri; 12-11 Sat & Sun ☎ (01423) 313461
4 changing beers Ⓗ
A popular watering hole down from the town at river level, this recently restored independent free house, with bare-brick walls, a real fire and wood-burning stove, provides a welcoming atmosphere. Four handpumps dispense a varying range of beers, one of which is usually from the local Rooster's Brewery. The pub hosts a popular quiz every Tuesday at 8pm, and a grazing menu of boards and light snacks is available every evening until 10pm. Dogs are welcome in the outdoor area. (22)

Mitre Hotel

4 Station Road, HG5 9AA (opp railway station)
12-11 ☎ (01423) 868948
Black Sheep Ale; Okell's Manx Pale Ale; Timothy Taylor Boltmaker; 3 changing beers Ⓗ
The Mitre offers a modern split-level bar, a side function room and another in the basement, along with a beer garden with views of the local church. There are six handpumps serving beers mainly from Yorkshire and including some from the town's own Rooster's Brewery. There is accommodation available in four en-suite rooms and food is served every day. Dogs are welcome. (1)

Lastingham

Blacksmiths Arms

Anserdale Lane, YO62 6TN
11.30-11.30 ☎ (01751) 417247
blacksmithsarmslastingham.co.uk
Saltaire Blonde; Theakston Best Bitter; 1 changing beer (sourced regionally; often Daleside, Rudgate) Ⓗ
Pretty stone inn in a conservation village, opposite St Mary's Church famous for its 11th-century crypt. The interior comprises a cosy bar with a York range lit in winter, a snug and two dining rooms. Excellent-quality food, including local game dishes, is served alongside interesting guest beers. A secluded beer garden is to the rear. This remote pub is popular with locals, walkers and shooting parties. Sorry, no dogs. **Q**

Lealholm

Board Inn

Village Green, YO21 2AJ
9am-midnight (2am Fri & Sat) ☎ (01947) 897279
theboardinn.com
3 changing beers Ⓗ
Overlooking the Esk, this family-run 17th-century pub is at the heart of village life. Three beers, four ciders and 60 whiskies are served. It comprises a locals' bar, a lounge/restaurant, and a riverside patio where an Easter beer festival is held. The food is virtually all traceable to within a mile of the pub. The licensees air-cure their own hams, keep hens, ducks and livestock, and have salmon fishing rights. A recent winner of local CAMRA Community Pub and Cider Pub awards.
Q (99)

Leavening

Jolly Farmers

Main Street, YO17 9SA
5.30-midnight (1am Fri); 12-1am Sat; 12-midnight Sun
☎ (01653) 658276 thejollys.co.uk
Timothy Taylor Landlord; York Guzzler; 3 changing beers (sourced locally; often Brass Castle, Half Moon, Wold Top) Ⓗ
A 17th-century pub on the edge of the Yorkshire Wolds between York and Malton. The multi-room interior retains old-world cosiness in two small bars, a games/family room and separate dining room. It is community focused, with meetings, charity events, darts and quiz leagues, occasional live music and beer festivals. Varied guest beers come from independent breweries. It serves an extensive menu of quality food including locally caught game dishes in season (no food Mon or Tues eve). A beer festival is held every June, a gin festival every August bank holiday.
Q **P**

Leyburn

Golden Lion

Market Place, DL8 5AS
11-11 ☎ (01969) 622161
John Smith's Bitter; Wensleydale Semerwater Summer Ale, Coverdale Gamekeeper; 1 changing beer (sourced locally) Ⓗ
A traditional market-town pub facing onto the main square of this busy and attractive Dales centre, a short walk from the revived Wensleydale Railway with its steam trains in summer. The comfortable main bar area is opened out and largely wood-panelled, with a real fire at each end, and there is a separate dining room to the rear, particularly popular for the Sunday carvery. Tables outside are great for eating and drinking in fine weather.

Lofthouse

Crown Hotel

Thorpe Lane, HG3 5RZ

12-3, 7-11; 12-3, 7-10.30 Sun ☎ (01423) 755206

Black Sheep Best Bitter; Theakston Best Bitter; 1 changing beer (sourced locally) H

A traditional Dales pub and hotel in the Nidderdale Area of Outstanding Natural Beauty. It is a short way uphill from the main part of the village on a road with spectacular views. There is an unusual panelled entrance corridor leading to a traditionally furnished comfortable bar decorated with local pictures, maps and brassware; a more formal dining room is reached through the bar. There is no cellphone coverage inside the pub and no payment by card.

Loftus

Station Hotel

Station Road, TS13 4QB (100yds S of A174)

3-11; 12-11.30 Sat & Sun ☎ (01287) 640373

2 changing beers H

This once-bustling railway hotel is now a free house. The last passenger train left in 1953 – the overgrown platform is still in-situ. The licensee, a keen musician and local independent councillor, has served best/premium bitters for 27 years, and anything under 4% ABV generally meets with the locals' disapproval. The pub comprises a cosy bar, a lounge and a function room where live music plays on Thursdays and Saturdays. Fans of particularly eccentric railway memorabilia are well catered for. (X4,5)

Malham

Lister Arms

Gordale Scar Road, BD23 4DB

8am-11 ☎ (01729) 830444

Lancaster Bomber; Thwaites Nutty Black; Wainwright; 3 changing beers (sourced locally; often Dark Horse, Naylor's, Settle) H

Substantial stone-built Grade II-listed inn dating from 1723 or earlier, overlooking the green. The tiled entrance hall opens to the stone-flagged main bar with separate areas to left and right and a dining room/restaurant beyond. The large secluded garden at the rear has ample comfortable seating. Food is served all day with breakfast/brunch on offer before midday and the main menu available thereafter. Home-made cakes and cream teas are also to be had. Malham can get busy in weekends and school holidays.

P

Malton

Blue Ball

14 Newbiggin, YO17 7JF

12-midnight ☎ (01653) 690692

Tetley Bitter; Timothy Taylor Landlord; 1 changing beer (sourced locally) H

A Grade II-listed pub dating from the 16th century, named the Blue Ball in 1823, identified by CAMRA as having a regionally important historic pub interior. The low front elevation hides a maze-like interior with the frontward cosy bar, compact servery and linking corridor retaining most of the pub's historical flavour. A smoking area is located at the rear of the pub. Home-cooked food is available daily (except Wed). The Blue Ball Folk Club meets on the second Tuesday of each month.

Q P (843)

Brass Castle Brewery Tap House

10 Yorkersgate, YO17 7AB

closed Mon; 4-9; 12-10 Fri & Sat; 12-8 Sun

☎ (01653) 698683 brasscastle.co.uk

2 changing beers (sourced locally; often Brass Castle) H

Formerly a temperance hotel in the town centre, Malton's newest hostelry is a short walk from the railway station. The single-roomed bar is tastefully designed in a rustic style, with one wall partially adorned with barrel staves. Two regular changing cask ales are offered together with six craft keg ales. An extensive range of bottled beers is also available. Snacks may be purchased at the bar. There is a smoking/drinking area to the rear of the premises and an upstairs seating area.

Q

New Malton

4 Market Place, YO17 7LX

11.30-11; 12-10.30 Sun ☎ (01653) 693998

thenewmalton.co.uk

3 changing beers H

Situated in the busy market place, this Grade II-listed building, formerly tea rooms, has been sensitively renovated. The large single-room interior is divided into three distinct drinking and dining areas. Three handpumps dispense varying beers mainly originating from Yorkshire breweries. Meals are served from midday throughout the week. There is a small area at the front for alfresco drinking. Children and dogs are welcome.

Q

Manfield

Crown Inn

Vicars Lane, DL2 2RF (500yds from B6275)

4-11.30; 10.30-11.30 Fri; 12-11.30 Sat & Sun

☎ (01325) 374243

Draught Bass; Village White Boar; 7 changing beers H

Local CAMRA Country Pub of the Year 14 times, and previously Yorkshire Pub of the Year, this 18th-century inn is in a quiet village. It has two bars and a games room. A mix of locals and visitors create a friendly atmosphere. Up to six guest beers from microbreweries with occasional ciders or perry are available. Two seasonal beer festivals are held. There is a real log fire in the main bar.

Q P (29)

Marske-by-the-Sea

Clarendon

88-90 High Street, TS11 7BA

11-11 (11.30 Fri-Sun) ☎ (01642) 490005

Black Sheep Best Bitter; Camerons Strongarm; Theakston Old Peculier, Best Bitter; 2 changing beers H

A recent local CAMRA award winner, the Middle House is a popular one-room locals' pub, where little has changed since the 1970s. Six beers are served from the mahogany island bar, a rarity on Teesside. The walls are adorned with interesting photographs of yesteryear. There is no TV/jukebox, no pool table, no children – just locals indulging in convivial conversation. There is no food either, but tea and coffee are available. Q P (X3,X4)

Masham

Bay Horse

5 Silver Street, HG4 4DX
12-11 (midnight Fri & Sat) (01765) 688297
bayhorseatmasham.co.uk
Black Sheep Best Bitter; Morland Old Speckled Hen; Theakston Best Bitter; 2 changing beers (sourced nationally; often Greene King, Morland) H
Friendly, recently refurbished pub welcoming tourists and locals alike with a range of ales unusual to Masham, although both the town's breweries are represented. As well as the front bar there is a dining area up a short flight of steps and a rear garden. Cask ends and pipework form a feature in the main front bar. A wide variety of home-cooked food is served, with ingredients coming from local suppliers.

Bruce Arms

3 Little Market Place, HG4 4DY
9am-11 (01765) 689372
Black Sheep Best Bitter; Theakston Best Bitter; 2 changing beers (sourced locally; often Theakston) H
A traditional pub tucked away in a side street off the market place. This is a whitewashed building with an interior of partly exposed stone, ceiling beams and wood, with bench seating throughout. It has one room that appears to have been created out of three smaller ones. There is a large TV plus a selection of games machines and a dartboard; there is also a pleasant rear garden.

White Bear

Wellgarth, HG4 4EN
11-midnight (01765) 689319
thewhitebearhotel.co.uk
Caledonian Deuchars IPA; Theakston Best Bitter, Black Bull Bitter, XB, Old Peculier; 1 changing beer H
Theakston's only pub, the White Bear offers food, drink, accommodation and conference facilities. There is a large dining area to one side and a small cosy taproom to the other serving almost the full range of Theakston beers. The pub hosts a popular three-day beer festival in late June with over 30 beers on offer. During the war the pub was a victim of bombing and was derelict for many years before being renovated to a high standard.
P (159,144)

Middlesbrough

Dr Phil's Real Ale House

10 Pilkington Buildings, Roman Road, Linthorpe, TS5 6DY (100yds N of The Crescent and Roman Road jct)
1-10 (11 Fri); 12.30-11 Sat; 12.30-8 Sun 07883 072389
drphilsrealalehouse.co.uk
4 changing beers H
The first micropub in the area is situated among a terrace of shops in the leafy suburbs of Linthorpe, a mile south of the town. It was opened in 2013 by an enthusiastic CAMRA member and soon became a branch multi award-winner. The five-yards-square space accommodates an eclectic mix of drinkers, who have a choice of four changing beers, together with cider/perry. Over 800 different beers have been served. Often, a cask does not even manage to last the day.
Q (11,17)

Infant Hercules

84 Grange Road, TS1 2LS (just S of Cleveland Centre and N of university campus)
1-10 (11 Fri & Sat) 07980 321626
3 changing beers H
One of several micropubs in the town's original solicitors' quarter, all located in a series of parallel streets of Victorian terraced houses, close to the law courts and the university. The pub is named after Gladstone's description of the town in 1862, after he had witnessed the rapid expansion of the area's steel furnaces and shipbuilding industries. Three interesting beers are served on a try-before-you-buy basis, and third-pint tasting bats are available. Regular CAMRA local branch award winner. Q

Sherlock's

7 Baker Street, TS1 2LF (between Cleveland Centre and university campus)
11-11; 12-11 Sun 07789 277364
3 changing beers H
A continuing part of the town's burgeoning micropub revolution, and now in its fourth year of operation, Sherlock's is one of several micropubs located on Baker Street, with some, but not all, having a Sir Arthur Conan Doyle connotation. Though small, the pub is friendly and full of character. Three beers are served to a wide clientele. The pub is the venue of Teesside University's Real Ale Society (TURAS). Not surprisingly, it can get busy on match days.

Newbiggin in Bishopsdale

Street Head Inn

DL8 3TE
11-3 (not Mon & Tue), 6-midnight (01969) 663282
thestreetheadinn.co.uk
John Smith's Bitter; Theakston Best Bitter; Wensleydale Semerwater Summer Ale H
This modernised but homely 17th-century inn lies in a remote but delightful location and is popular with those exploring the local Dales countryside. It attracts much of its trade from the nearby caravan site and former YHA bunk barn, now owned by the pub. Home-cooked food is served both in the bar, with its impressive fireplace, and in the separate restaurant, and a carvery is offered on Sundays. The pub has its own en-suite accommodation and dogs and children are welcome. P

Northallerton

Oddfellows Arms

251 High Street, DL7 8DJ (off main part of High St behind parish church)
4-11 Mon; closed Tue; 12-midnight; 12-11 Sun
(01609) 259107 theoddies.uk
Beer Monkey Blonde Rogue; Pennine Hair of the Dog; 1 changing beer (sourced locally) H
Hidden behind the parish church by the cemetery gates, the Oddies does not appear to be on the High Street, despite its address. In fact it is a thriving back-street community pub, handling a mainly local trade, and is popular with darts players, TV football fans and church bell ringers. Refurbished in a simple but traditional style with an open-plan interior, there is a games room upstairs and a secluded beer garden to the rear.

Stumble Inn

4 Garthway Arcade, DL7 8NS (in pedestrian arcade off High St next to Grovers shop)

closed Mon; 4.30-9.30 (11 Fri); 12-11 Sat; 2-8 Sun
07817 568042
5 changing beers (sourced locally)
A small, cosy and friendly micropub in a shopping arcade between the town's High Street and main Applegarth car park, offering a warm welcome. It serves a selection of local ales, craft beers and up to 20 real ciders, and staff are keen to offer tasting advice and guidance. With no music, gaming machines, Wi-Fi, children or sports TV, there is just good old-fashioned chat plus a quiz on the last Sunday of the month. Seasonal beer and cider festivals also feature. Q

Tithe

2A Friarage Street, DL6 1DP (just off High St near hospital)
12-11 (midnight Fri & Sat) (01609) 778482
Okell's Manx Pale Ale; Timothy Taylor Boltmaker; 5 changing beers (sourced regionally)
Part of the real-ale-championing Market Town Taverns chain, this is a pleasant town-centre bar. There is a strong commitment to cask beer, and numerous continental and speciality beers are also available, plus a good range of gins. Decor is simple, with wooden floors throughout, and often the only sound is the buzz of conversation. Upstairs, a brasserie is open most evenings. Children are welcome during the daytime.
Q

Osgodby

Wadkin Arms

Cliffe Road, YO8 5HU
12-11 (midnight Fri & Sat) (01757) 702391
wadkinarms.co.uk
Brown Cow White Dragon; Sharp's Doom Bar; Theakston Best Bitter; house beer (by Tetley); 1 changing beer (sourced nationally; often Marston's, Theakston)
A true community pub at the heart of the village, with five handpumps dispensing ales largely sourced from Yorkshire breweries. The Wadkin has a homely feel, with open fires and a friendly welcome, and is home to locals and visitors alike. The nearby Transpennine Cycle Trail sees cyclists and walkers visiting in the summer months, and a local bus service passes too. You will see much evidence of CAMRA sympathies on display. Bar meals are available throughout the week except Monday and Tuesday. P(4)

Osmotherley

Golden Lion

6 West End, DL6 3AA (in village centre, 1 mile E of A19)
12-3 (not Mon & Tue), 5-11; 12-midnight Sat; 12-11 Sun
(01609) 883526 goldenlionosmotherley.co.uk
Timothy Taylor Landlord; 3 changing beers (sourced locally)
An old inn set in the centre of a picturesque village on the edge of the North York Moors National Park and at the start of the long-distance Lyke Wake Walk. Popular with hikers, casual visitors and locals, much of the focus is on high-quality locally sourced food, but drinkers are always made welcome. The view from the drinking tables outside makes them in demand on fine days. Regularly changing beers are from local Yorkshire breweries, and a beer festival takes place each November. Dogs are welcome. Q(80,89)

Pickering

Bay Horse

8 Market Place, YO18 7AA
11.30-11.30 (midnight Sat); 12-11.30 Sun
(01751) 472526 bayhorsepickering.co.uk
Bradfield Farmers Blonde; Camerons Strongarm; Greene King Abbot; Tetley Bitter
A Grade II-listed local, handy for the nearby North Yorkshire Moors Railway. The quiet front bar boasts an open fire and window seats, with an impressive display of fishing flies, courtesy of Pickering Fishery Association. The large multi-level bar at the rear has a pool table and hosts live entertainment on occasional weekends. Freshly cooked meals are served lunchtimes and early evenings (not Tue), with a carvery on Sundays. There is a partially covered smoking/drinking area to the rear, adjacent to the beer garden.

Sun Inn

136 Westgate, YO18 8BB (on A170, 400yds W of traffic lights in town centre)
4-11; 12-midnight Fri & Sat; 12-11 Sun (01751) 473661
thesuninn-pickering.co.uk
Helmsley Yorkshire Legend; Tetley Bitter; 4 changing beers (sourced regionally; often Daleside, Hadrian Border, Saltaire)
Friendly local CAMRA Rural Pub of the Year, close to the steam railway. Four ales are offered (three from Yorkshire micros) and several traditional ciders. A cosy bar with a real fire leads to a separate room, ideal for families and special events, where local artists display their work. The large beer garden is used for the annual beer festival in September. Regular events include fortnightly acoustic music, charity quizzes and monthly vinyl nights. It is open from noon on Easter Monday. Dogs (on leads), children and walkers are welcome.

Reeth

Buck Hotel

DL11 6SW
11-midnight (01748) 884210 buckhotel.co.uk/index
Black Sheep Best Bitter; Timothy Taylor Landlord; Wensleydale Semerwater Summer Ale, Coverdale Gamekeeper; house beer (by Tetley)
At the top of the green in the centre of this attractive Swaledale village, this 18th-century former coaching inn, known as the top house, retains its beamed ceilings, open fire and even an ice house. Home-cooked food is offered along with five cask ales and six real ciders. Quoits is a popular summer activity, with three teams based here, along with two darts teams. During winter, beer and cider choice and opening hours may be reduced. (30)

Ribblehead

Station

Ingleton, LA6 3AS (on B6255 near B6479 jct)
11-midnight (015242) 41274
stationinnribblehead.co.uk
5 changing beers
Built at the same time as the nearby viaduct (1874), this is a welcome refuge in a bleak spot in the midst of superb walking country. During the day, the main bar room is laid out for diners while the smaller room has the pub games and sports TV. A surprisingly large number of locals frequent the

plainly furnished bar. It enjoys a good train service – times are above the bar counter. There is a bunk barn next door and wild camping behind. The house ale, Tet, is not one beer but the name applied to a number of different ales according to season. (830)

Riccall

Greyhound

82 Main Street, YO19 6TE

12-midnight (11 Sun) summer; 3 (12 Sat)-midnight; 12-11.30 Sun winter (01757) 249101

thegreyhoundriccall.co.uk

Tetley Bitter; Theakston Best Bitter, Old Peculier; 4 changing beers (sourced regionally; often Ossett, Rooster's, Rudgate)

Four miles north of Selby you will find the Greyhound, a welcoming inn in the heart of this historic village. This family-run pub dates back to the late 1800s and nowadays has up to seven cask beers on the bar. It is popular with locals and visitors alike, many who come to enjoy River Ouse walks and the Transpennine cycle trail. The large beer garden can get busy on warmer days. Food is available daily except Saturday. Check the website for winter opening hours and meal times.

Richmond

Holly Hill Inn

Sleegill, DL10 4RJ

11-11 (midnight Fri & Sat); 11-10.30 Sun

(01748) 884210 holly-hill-inn.co.uk

Black Sheep Best Bitter; Sharp's Doom Bar; Timothy Taylor Landlord; 1 changing beer

A pleasant but strenuous walk half a mile south from the town centre, this popular pub lies beyond the castle, across the River Swale and high above it. The bar is set on two levels separated by a stone chimney breast with a cast-iron stove, while there is a large extension in the style of a baronial hall with impressive fireplace, used as a restaurant and function room. Quiz night is Wednesday.
Q P (30)

Ripon

One-Eyed Rat

51 Allhallowgate, HG4 1LQ

5-11; 12-11 Fri & Sat; 12-10.30 Sun (01765) 607704

oneeyedrat.com

7 changing beers

A family-run hostelry that is well known and highly regarded for the quality of its ales; it has been in this Guide for over 25 years. The narrow frontage belies a long interior with traditional seating and an open fire. Seven changing real ales and a real cider are served, invariably including a dark ale and a stronger beer. Sarah Hughes Dark Ruby from the Black Country is sometimes available. The pub hosts regular live music and holds two beer festivals a year. Q (36)

Robin Hood's Bay

Bay Hotel

The Dock, YO22 4SJ (at end of a steep road, down towards bay from top car park; less able-bodied guests can be dropped off by car)

11-11 (01947) 880278 bayhotel.info

Caledonian Deuchars IPA; Theakston Lightfoot, Best Bitter; Wainwright

Magnificent Grade II-listed 1822 building and the finish line for Alfred Wainwright's Coast-to-Coast 192-mile walk, with the pub's bottom bar named in his honour, and from where the Dock patio can be accessed. Situated at the sea water's edge, with superb panoramic views, a friendly welcome awaits regulars, visitors, their children and their dogs. Four handpulls and an extensive good-value home-cooked menu are available. Access to this part of the village is not easy for the less mobile.
(X93)

Saltburn-by-the-Sea

Saltburn Cricket, Bowls & Tennis Club

Marske Mill Lane, TS12 1HJ (next to leisure centre)

8-midnight (1am Fri & Sat); 11.30-3, 8-midnight Sun

(01287) 622761 saltburn.play-cricket.com

2 changing beers

Visitors are made most welcome at this local CAMRA branch multi award-winner, now celebrating 23 years of continuous Guide recognition. It is a private sports club, run by an enthusiastic steward, and is well supported by the local community. It is also the watering hole for the local diving club. The balcony, ideal for those lazy summer afternoons, overlooks the cricket field. On match day Saturdays the club opens at 2pm. Two changing beers are served, often not even lasting the evening. P (X3,X4)

Scarborough

Cellars

35-37 Valley Road, YO11 2LY

12-midnight; 12-11.30 Sun summer; 4-11; 12-midnight Sat; 12-11.30 Sun winter (01723) 367158

scarborough-brialene.co.uk/cellars.htm

Bradfield Farmers Blonde; Camerons Strongarm; Daleside Monkey Wrench; 3 changing beers (sourced nationally; often Rooster's)

Scarborough's most frequent Guide entry, this family-run pub was converted from the cellars of a Victorian town house. Six handpumps dispense guest beers from micros. Locally sourced home-cooked food is available lunchtimes and evenings, with Sunday lunches always popular. Quiz night is Tuesday, open mic night is Wednesday, local acoustic acts play on Thursday, and Saturday is live music night. The patio fronting the pub is popular in summer. Children and dogs are welcome.
P (64)

North Riding Brewpub

161-163 North Marine Road, YO12 7HU

12-midnight (1am Fri & Sat) (01723) 370004

northridingbrewpub.com

6 changing beers (sourced nationally; often North Riding Brewery, North Riding Brewpub)

Scarborough's only brewpub, serving at least six continually changing beers from local and microbreweries around the UK, always including one or more North Riding ale together with beers brewed at the pub. These are complemented by three craft keg beers from around the world and an extensive range of craft bottled beers. The pub has a public bar and quiet lounge, both with real fires. Quiz night is Thursday. Local CAMRA Town Pub of the Year 2017. Q (9,9A)

Scarborough Borough Council Employees Welfare Club

Dean Road, YO12 7QS

7-midnight; 11-12.30am Fri & Sat; 12-3, 7-11.30 Sun
(01723) 364593

3 changing beers (sourced locally; often North Riding Brewery)

Close to the town centre, this club comprises a large bar area with adjacent snooker room and a function room upstairs with capacity for 200 people. Three changing guest cask ales are offered. Club teams participate in local snooker, darts and dominoes leagues. The club is family friendly, with CAMRA members welcome subject to signing in. An outdoor drinking/smoking area is at the side. Local CAMRA Club of the Year 2017.
Q (8,8A)

Scholars Bar

6 Somerset Terrace, YO11 2PA

4-midnight; 12-midnight Sat & Sun (01723) 372826

Hambleton Nightmare Porter; 5 changing beers (sourced regionally; often North Riding Brewery, Ossett)

A warm, friendly atmosphere prevails at this town-centre pub at the rear of the main shopping centre. It is a former CAMRA Town Pub of the Year runner-up and 2017 Town Cider Pub of the Year runner-up. The large front bar is dominated by TV screens showing major sporting events, with a smaller games area to the rear. Five rotating guest beers, usually from Yorkshire microbreweries, are served, plus numerous ciders and perries. The Thursday night quiz is popular, with a first prize of 28 pints.

Tap & Spile

94 Falsgrave Road, YO12 5AZ

4-midnight; 12-midnight Sat; 12-11 Sun
(01723) 507666

Black Sheep Best Bitter; Camerons Strongarm; Theakston Old Peculier; Timothy Taylor Landlord; 1 changing beer (sourced nationally)

Sympathetically restored Grade II-listed public house, not far from the town centre, serving five cask ales. There are two main rooms plus a small snug where local memorabilia are displayed. This thriving local has a friendly atmosphere and is a venue for live music, with Sunday afternoons particularly popular. TV sports are shown in one bar. A beer garden is situated at the rear. Dogs are welcome in the taproom. P

Valley Bar

51 Valley Road, YO11 2LX

12-midnight (1am Thu-Sat) (01723) 372593
valleybar.co.uk

Dark Star Hophead; 4 changing beers (sourced nationally; often Scarborough)

The pub, recently relocated adjacent to the original cellar bar, is a large room divided into several drinking areas. Of note is the remarkable décor utilising antique furniture components. Four guest beers are offered, usually including one or more from Scarborough Brewery. Up to 10 real ciders and perries are served as well as a selection of Belgian bottled beers. There is also a pool room together with a separate function room. Accommodation is available. (64)

Scotton

Guy Fawkes Arms

Main Street, HG5 9HU

12 (4 Mon)-11 (01423) 868400
guyfawkesarms.co.uk

Black Sheep Best Bitter; 3 changing beers

Popular village pub which was rescued from closure in 2013 by two local families. The L-shaped interior features a cosy lounge area, part-flagged, part-carpeted, with a mix of traditional and modern furniture and a real fire in winter. A separate dining room occupies one end and a raised seating area is at the other with its own mini-library. Guy Fawkes lived in the village and there are several related items displayed. Complementing the regular Black Sheep Bitter are three changing guests from Yorkshire breweries.
P (22)

Selby

Giant Bellflower

47A Gowthorpe, YO8 4HF

8am-midnight (1am Fri & Sat) (01757) 293020

Greene King Abbot; Ruddles Best Bitter; 6 changing beers (sourced nationally; often Adnams, Rudgate, Sharp's)

Named after a flower associated with a local 17th-century botanist, and converted from a furniture showroom, this modern and spacious pub is completely different from all the others in Selby. Artefacts and pictures from Selby's past complement the light and airy interior, and the pub is deceptively large despite its small frontage, with an enormous stainless steel bar taking pride of place. Offering a typical Wetherspoon range of keenly priced beers, real ciders and LocAles, it is an important addition to the town's pub scene.

Settle

Golden Lion

Duke Street, BD24 9DU

10-11 (01729) 822203

Lancaster Bomber; Thwaites Nutty Black, Original; Wainwright; 3 changing beers (sourced locally; often Kirkby Lonsdale, Saltaire, Settle)

Built around 1670, this former coaching inn has two comfortable high-ceilinged rooms for drinking. The main bar has wood panelling, a grand staircase and a huge fireplace. The Lion's Den is accessed from the bar or via the so-called dwarf door off the street. The separate dining area, refurbished in January 2018, is bright and colourful. Outside seating is in the yard to the side of the pub. Tuesdays feature jazz and there are twice-monthly folk sessions on Thursdays.

Talbot Arms

High Street, BD24 9EX

12-11 (01729) 823924 talbotsettle.co.uk

Settle Mainline; Theakston Best Bitter; 4 changing beers (sourced regionally; often Beer Monkey, Settle, Wishbone)

Just off the square, this family-run free house, claiming to be the oldest pub in town, offers a welcoming and friendly atmosphere. In winter a stove glows in the large stone feature fireplace to the left, with a pool table, dartboard and dominoes tables beyond providing a base for teams in local leagues. A pleasant terraced beer garden is at the rear. The three to five guest beers are usually from Cumbria, Lancashire or Yorkshire. Good-value food is served 12-8pm all week.

Skipton

Beer Engine

1 Albert Street, BD23 1JD
closed Tue; 12-10 (8 Mon; 11 Fri & Sat) ☎ 07834 456134
5 changing beers (sourced nationally)
Well-established micropub in a tiny street between the town centre and the canal. Five handpumps dispense a variety of beers; there is always one blonde/pale ale and one dark beer, plus a character beer. A still cider and a fruit cider are also on tap alongside a selection of bottled beers and wines. The beers are stored in refrigerated cabinets behind the bar. The ambience is friendly and welcoming, and closing time can be flexible. Well-behaved dogs welcome. Q

Boat House

19 Coach Street, BD23 1LH
12-10 ☎ (01756) 701660
5 changing beers (sourced regionally)
Tucked out of the way, access is through an arch from Coach Street or via the canalside path. The bar is light and airy, with picture windows looking onto the canal basin, and the decor is canal-themed. A cobbled outdoor drinking area offers the opportunity to enjoy a beer while watching the boats go by. An old-style stove keeps the bar warm in winter. One dark beer is usually on tap.

Narrow Boat

36-38 Victoria Street, BD23 1JE (alleyway off Coach St near canal bridge)
12-11 ☎ (01756) 797922
Ilkley Mary Jane; Okell's Bitter; Timothy Taylor Landlord; 5 changing beers
The eight handpumps dispense a varied selection of beers and there should always be one to suit most tastes; there is usually a dark beer and a good range of continental bottled and draught beers, plus up to three ciders or perries. The premises are spread over two rooms, with an upstairs gallery and function room and a covered outside drinking/smoking area. Note the somewhat unusual interpretation of the Leeds-Liverpool canal map in a mural. Well-behaved dogs welcome.

Snaith

Yorkshire Ales

Selby Road, DN14 9HT (on edge of Market Place)
4-midnight (10 Mon & Tue); 2-midnight Sat; 2-10 Sun
☎ (01405) 860603 yorkshireales.co.uk
Brown Cow White Dragon; 4 changing beers (sourced regionally; often Brew York, Brown Cow, Little Critters)
A pub that promotes beers brewed by independent Yorkshire microbreweries. The building dates back to 1750 and has seating for 80 over two floors plus the beer garden. Food is snacks only, but artisan chefs and street food vendors are booked regularly. Music is background volume and there are no TVs, thus promoting the art of conversation. Local cycling and photography clubs meet regularly and the weekly quiz is popular.
Q (401)

Staithes

Cod & Lobster Inn

High Street, TS13 5BH (at end of High St)
10-11 ☎ (01947) 840330 codandlobster.co.uk
4 changing beers
Superbly positioned at the seawater's edge in this sleepy picturesque fishing village, the large single-room open-plan pub offers three changing beers alongside the house beer, Old Jack's Tipple, named after a locally filmed children's TV character. Good-value traditional meals are served. On sunny days, a pleasant patio, directly overlooking the chilly sea, becomes popular. However, during high tides, combined with easterly winds, you are advised to use the roadside door or risk getting wet.

Stillington

White Bear

Main Street, YO61 1JU
5.30-8.30 Mon; 12-2, 5.30-9; 12-2, 6-9 Sat; 12-5 Sun
☎ (01347) 810338 thewhitebearinn-york.co.uk
Leeds Pale; 3 changing beers (sourced regionally; often Helmsley, Hop Studio, Rudgate)
If you want to try regularly changing beers from small and medium-sized Yorkshire breweries, this is an excellent choice. The multi award-winning pub is the beating heart of the village and is becoming accustomed to visitors from far and wide. Turn right for a traditional taproom bar and left for an unpretentious restaurant bar, but turn up or miss out. P (40)

Stokesley

White Swan

1 West End, TS9 5BL (at W end of town, 150yds beyond shops)
11-midnight (1am Fri & Sat); 11-11.30 Sun
☎ (01642) 041046
Captain Cook Black Porter, Endeavour, IPA, Navigator, Slipway, Sunset
Home of the Captain Cook Brewery, this friendly 18th-century pub, winner of many local CAMRA branch awards, is in a pretty market town, serving at least six Captain Cook beers, usually more, plus two ciders, from 12 handpulls. Beer festivals are held during Easter and in October. Quiz night is Wednesday, while music night is Thursday. The sheltered outdoor drinking area overlooks the brewery, which is behind the pub. Over-18s only. Dogs are welcome. (81,89)

Strensall

Ship

23 The Village, YO32 5XS
12-11 (midnight Fri & Sat) ☎ (01904) 490302
theshipinn-strensall.co.uk
Timothy Taylor Landlord; 3 changing beers (sourced regionally)
Popular family-run village pub near the River Foss, offering four real ales, occasionally a real cider, and restaurant food. Open all day and late at the weekend, it is popular with walkers, cyclists and caravanners in summer, with outside seating and a children's play area at the rear. Families and dogs are welcome. Regular events are held including music, quizzes and an annual spring beer festival. The bus stop from York is just across the road.
P

Thirsk

Black Swan

9 Front Street, Norby, YO7 1BG

4-midnight; 12-midnight Sat & Sun ☎ (01845) 525333

Black Sheep Ale; house beer (by Theakston); 2 changing beers (sourced locally)

A community free house lying a few hundred yards north of the town centre and close to Thirsk's impressive parish church on the Northallerton road. Although it mainly serves a growing nearby housing area to the rear, it is welcoming to all. The comfortable interior has been opened out into a single room but it retains three distinct drinking areas, with sports TV frequently showing.

Little 3

13-15 Finkle Street, YO7 1DA

11.30-11; 12-10 Sun ☎ (01845) 523782

littlethree.co.uk

5 changing beers (sourced nationally; often Theakston)

Old, low-beamed pub of character just off the Market Place claiming a history from 1214. It is a warren of nooks and crannies, all decorated in mock half-timbering, with an impressive fireplace in the main bar. Originally the Old Three Tuns, it was renamed to avoid confusion with the nearby Three Tuns. Regularly changing guest beers are from local and national brewers. Food is served in the upstairs bistro and there is live music every Thursday.

Thixendale

Cross Keys

YO17 9TG

6-11; 12-3, 6-11 Fri & Sat; 12-3, 7-10.30 Sun

☎ (01377) 288272

Tetley Bitter; 2 changing beers (sourced locally; often Great Newsome, Half Moon, Wold Top)

This single-room hostelry appears on a map dated 1851. It has been run by the same landlord for over 30 years. At the heart of five dry valleys, it is popular with walkers, including those on the Wolds Way and, though remote, is well worth seeking out. The two guest beers come from independent breweries and are usually not more than 4% ABV. Children are welcome in the beer garden. Good-value, traditional home-cooked food is served. Accommodation is in the adjoining converted stable. Q

Thoralby

George Inn

DL8 3SU (on a small lane off village centre)

6.30-11; 12-2, 6.30-11 Sat & Sun ☎ (01969) 663256

thegeorgeinnthoralby.com

3 changing beers (sourced locally)

Dating from 1732, this small, off-the-beaten-track inn lies tucked away in a small village just off the B6160 Bishopsdale road. The interior has been opened up into a single room but retains two distinct halves, and is cosy and comfortable, with a particularly impressive stone fireplace with a stove at one end. Beers are usually from local Yorkshire brewers and home-cooked food is offered. Separate apartments offer accommodation. Opens 7pm in the winter. Q P

Thornton Watlass

Buck Inn

Village Green, HG4 4AH

11-11 ☎ (01677) 422461 buckwatlass.co.uk

Black Sheep Ale; Theakston Best Bitter; 2 changing beers

Overlooking the village green, this traditional country inn features a cosy bar room with a real fire, a lounge/dining room and a large function room known as the Long Room. The new owners have redecorated, brightening the place up but retaining the village pub atmosphere. Local beers are a favourite here and excellent meals are available. The number and range of beers are likely to vary a little according to the season; the guest ales are usually from Yorkshire. P

Thornton-in-Lonsdale

Marton Arms

Ingleton, LA6 3PB (¼ mile from A65/A687 jct)

2-11 ☎ (015242) 42204 martonarms.co.uk

Black Sheep Best Bitter; Theakston Best Bitter; Timothy Taylor Boltmaker; 2 changing beers (sourced regionally)

In a hamlet with a parish church, old stocks and little else, the pub relies almost entirely on tourists. Behind the 1679 datestone and old oak door, a flagged passage leads to a modern bar with a recent refurbishment and a huge selection of gin. It has an attractive little garden and is 10 minutes on foot from the start of the Waterfalls Walk.

P (80,581)

Thornton-le-Dale

New Inn

The Square, YO18 7LF

12-11; 12-10.30 Sun ☎ (01751) 474226

the-new-inn.com

Theakston Best Bitter; 2 changing beers (sourced nationally)

Family-owned Grade II-listed inn, restored to create the feel of yesteryear. Dating to around 1720, this former coaching inn overlooks the medieval village stocks and market cross. It is an ideal touring base for the North Yorkshire moors, Dalby Forest, Ryedale and the coast. The pub prides itself on freshly cooked food, with a wide range of specials. The large main room is separated into a drinking and dining area. A smoking/drinking space is located at the rear. En-suite accommodation is available. Dogs are welcome away from dining areas.

Q P (128,840)

Ugthorpe

Black Bull Inn

Postgate Way, YO21 2BQ

12-2 (not Mon & Tue), 6-11 ☎ (01947) 840286

blackbullwhitby.co.uk

Theakston Old Peculier; 1 changing beer

A warm welcome is assured at this Grade II-listed traditional, pantiled country inn, where photographs of yesteryear adorn the walls. This comfortable, family-run establishment comprises a main bar, snug, restaurant and a games room. The guest beers complement the Old Peculier, and change weekly. Portions of the home-cooked food are such that going home hungry is not an option.

Drinkers and diners travel from far and wide for the impressive Sunday lunch carvery, for which booking in advance is advised. Q

Wensley

Three Horseshoes

DL8 4HJ (on A684)
11-11; 11-10.30 Sun (01969) 622327
thethreehorseshoeswensley.co.uk
Theakston Best Bitter; house beer (by Yorkshire Dales); 2 changing beers (sourced locally) H
This old and traditional country pub on the A684 is full of atmosphere, with its small bar and dining room both featuring low beams and real fires. Outside there is a terraced beer garden offering glorious views across Wensleydale, and forming a real suntrap on fine days. Wholesome and very reasonably priced lunchtime and evening meals are available Tuesday to Sunday. Regular beer from Yorkshire Dales Brewery, real cider and perry are served. QP

West Haddlesey

George & Dragon

Main Street, YO8 8QA
5-midnight (1am Fri); 2-1am Sat; 12-10.30 Sun
(01757) 228198 thegandd.co.uk
Brown Cow White Dragon; 2 changing beers (sourced regionally) H
Privately owned free house with enthusiastic support for local microbreweries. It has low ceilings, a cosy bar with a real fire, a TV showing sporting events, a separate room for diners and an attractive outside decked area for summer days. Food is served evenings (not Sun to Tue) as well as Sunday lunch. Beer festivals are held outdoors in April on the weekend closest to St George's Day (23 April) and the end of October, close to Halloween (31 Oct). QP

West Witton

Fox & Hounds

DL8 4LP (on A684)
12-3, 6-midnight; 12-midnight Sat & Sun
(01969) 623650 foxwitton.com
Black Sheep Baa Baa; Theakston Best Bitter; 3 changing beers (sourced locally; often Salamander, Yorkshire Dales) H
This welcoming, Grade II-listed and family-run free house is full of character. A real community local, it has a down-to-earth bar and games room popular with locals and visitors alike. Good-value meals are served all week, with a roast on Sundays, and the dining room boasts an inglenook fireplace with a quaint stone oven. Once a rest house for 15th-century Jervaulx Abbey monks, it has a pleasant patio at the rear; beware the tight entry to the car park. P

Whitby

Black Horse

91 Church Street, YO22 4BH (on E side of swing bridge on way to Abbey steps, close to marketplace)
11-11; 12-10.30 Sun (01947) 602906
the-black-horse.com
5 changing beers H
Former CAMRA branch award winner, this little multi-roomed gem, dating from the 1600s, offers a warm welcome. The frontage, with its frosted glass, together with one of Europe's oldest public serving bars, was built in the 1880s and remains largely unchanged. Beer is dispensed from five handpumps. Snuff, tapas, olives, Yorkshire cheeses and hot drinks are always available, while hot lunches are served during the winter months. The cider is Westons Rosie's Pig. Accommodation is in four bedrooms. Q (X93,840)

Dolphin Hotel

Bridge Street, YO22 4BG (on E side of swing bridge)
8.30am-midnight (01947) 821455
thedolphinwhitby.co.uk
6 changing beers H
Originally known as the Custom House Coffee House, this large and prominent harbourside building was developed into a public house in 1823 and then rebuilt in 1912 to its present form. The pub provides the complete package of six local and national beers on a try-before-you-buy basis, real cider, good-value food, sports TVs, a patio overlooking the harbour, six bedrooms fitted with king-size beds, live music Tuesdays and weekends, and even a friendly welcome for your dog.
(X93,840)

Endeavour

66 Church Street, YO22 4AS (on E side of swing bridge, close to an award-winning fish & chip shop)
12-11 (01947) 603557 endeavourpub.co.uk
4 changing beers H
Cosy and friendly one-room 1935 pub named after the ship in which James Cook made his voyages to the Antipodes. The warming fire and pleasant conversation add to the welcome from an enthusiastic licensee, who serves 140 different beers annually. Four handpumps, Yorkshire tapas bar snacks and permission to bring your own fish & chips into the pub, all make for a relaxing visit. Folk/Irish music both on Friday evenings and Sundays are well supported, and it gets manic during Goth weekends.
Q (X93,840)

Little Angel

18 Flowergate, YO21 3BA (200yds W of swing bridge, and 200yds N of railway/bus stations)
12-midnight (1am Fri & Sat) (01947) 820475
littleangelwhitby.co.uk
6 changing beers H
Just off the main tourist route and up a slight incline, locals and visitors alike are afforded a genuine friendly welcome at this extremely popular pub where, it is rumoured, the remains of the castle form part of the structure. Large-screen sports TVs, live music, outside drinking and even a horse mount, for those requiring this facility, complement the six beers served to three separate rooms from a central bar. CAMRA local branch Best Whitby Pub for three years running.
(X93,840)

Station Inn

New Quay Road, YO21 1DH
10-midnight; 10-11.30 Sun (01947) 603937
stationinnwhitby.co.uk
Camerons Strongarm; Ossett Yorkshire Blonde, Silver King; Timothy Taylor Boltmaker; Whitby Jet Black; 3 changing beers H
Next to the harbour and marina, this popular and recently refurbished multi-roomed pub offers a warm welcome. The enthusiastic licensees ensure

that the eight beers, including three guests, always encompass a superb range of varying styles, while cider and fruit wines mean there is something for everybody. Opposite the bus station and NYMR/Esk Valley railway station, the pub has become the discerning traveller's waiting room. Live music features three evenings a week. A recent local CAMRA Pub of the Year. (X93,840)

York

Blue Bell ★

53 Fossgate, YO1 9TF

11-11 (midnight Fri & Sat); 12-10.30 Sun
(01904) 654904

Bradfield Farmers Blonde; Kelham Island Best Bitter; Rudgate Ruby Mild; Timothy Taylor Landlord; 3 changing beers (sourced locally; often Half Moon, Ilkley, Rooster's)

With a nationally important Grade II* historic interior (1903), this small Edwardian pub has a central bar supplying two small rooms and, in summer, the side corridor. It can get full so it has a strict no-groups policy, and entry may be restricted at busy times. Permanent beers are complemented by a great range of rotating guests. Bar snacks and pork pies are served. It has a comparatively new landlord, and enjoys a friendly and welcoming atmosphere. Q

Brew York Tap Room

Unit 6, Enterprise Complex, Walmgate, YO1 9TT

closed Mon & Tue; 6-11 Wed & Thu; 4-11 Fri; 12-11 Sat; 12-10 Sun (01904) 848448 brewyork.co.uk

Brew York Jarsa, Maris the Otter, Viking DNA; 5 changing beers (sourced locally; often Brew York)

The tap room for Brew York is inside the brewery and the active process can be seen. The range of regular, seasonal, experimental and collaboration beers offers a different taste at each visit from this multiple award-winning brewery. Seating is inside by the brew tanks and outside in the beer garden by the River Foss. Frequent beer festivals with live music take place. The possibility of a large expansion into the next-door maltings will provide further facilities and food offerings.

Brigantes

114 Micklegate, YO1 6JX

12-11; 12-10 Sun (01904) 675355

Okell's Manx Pale Ale; 9 changing beers (sourced nationally; often Black Sheep, Brass Castle, Great Heck)

Welcoming Market Town Taverns pub in a smart Georgian building just inside the city walls on Micklegate. Ten ales are on the bar, at least one dark, featuring good Yorkshire brews and interesting guests from across the UK, plus a wide range of keg and bottled beers. At least one real cider is stocked and the Wall of Cider festival features in October. High-quality food is served, with a dining area on the ground floor. The function room upstairs is available for meetings and events. The pub is dog friendly and wheelchair accessible throughout. Q

Eagle & Child

9 High Petergate, YO1 7EN

11-11 (midnight Thu-Sat) (01904) 631536
eagleandchildyork.co.uk

Leeds Pale, Yorkshire Gold, Best, Midnight Bell; 4 changing beers (sourced regionally; often Brass Castle, Camerons, Track)

Former restaurant converted to a pub in 2015. It is set over three floors with several different rooms and a patio area at the rear. The four beers from Leeds Brewery are joined by an increasingly good range of interesting guest beers. It also has a wide choice of keg beer. There are regular music nights and other events, and the rooms on the upper floors can be booked for private functions. Dogs are welcome downstairs.

House of the Trembling Madness

48 Stonegate, YO1 8AS

10.30-midnight; 11-midnight Sun (01904) 289848
tremblingmadness.co.uk

3 changing beers (often Brass Castle, Thornbridge, Wilde Child)

Small but stunning medieval drinking hall with a beamed timber roof and lots of character, including a collection of stuffed animals, above a bottled beer shop in the centre of York. Three ever-changing real ales, two real ciders, a wide range of keg and bottled beers from around the world and tasty food are available here. Bottles from the shop can be drunk on the premises for a small corkage fee. The bar can get busy at weekends.

Maltings

Tanners Moat, YO1 6HU

11-11; 12-10.30 Sun (01904) 655387 maltings.co.uk

Black Sheep Best Bitter; Treboom Yorkshire Sparkle; York Guzzler; 4 changing beers (sourced nationally; often Bad Seed, Hop Studio, Wilde Child)

A popular pub close to the station. The cask ales from microbreweries, both local and from further afield, change regularly. At any one time customers can choose from seven real ales and four traditional ciders. The three permanent beers are from Black Sheep, Treboom and York breweries. The four changing beers always include a beer from Rooster's. An extension has provided more seating and a small outside area, while maintaining the original character.

Phoenix

75 George Street, YO1 9PT

12-11 (11.30 Fri & Sat); 12-10.30 Sun (01904) 656401
phoenixinnyork.co.uk

Timothy Taylor Landlord; Wold Top Bitter; 3 changing beers (sourced regionally; often Hop Studio)

An independently run pub with a regionally important historic pub interior, where a friendly welcome always awaits. Relax in the traditional pub atmosphere without the noise of gaming machines, TVs or jukebox, and enjoy your pint while reading a selection of newspapers or playing a game of bar billiards. In the winter months you can warm to a real log fire in the front room, while the beer garden overlooking the ancient city walls is a delight in summer. The pub hosts regular jazz nights and quizzes. Q

Rook & Gaskill

12 Lawrence Street, YO10 3WP

4-11.30 (12.30am Thu-Sat) (01904) 533105
rookandgaskillyork.co.uk

Castle Rock Harvest Pale; 8 changing beers (sourced nationally; often Bad Seed, Great Heck, Raw)

Just outside Walmgate Bar, this pub focuses on good-quality beer and cider at competitive prices, and is popular with locals, beer enthusiasts and the university community. A large range of carefully chosen cask ales is served through eight handpulls, plus up to three real ciders. In addition there are up to 20 craft beers and rare lagers. Food includes home-made burgers and wood-fired pizzas. There is a quiz on Thursdays. Local CAMRA Pub of the Year and Cider Pub of the Year 2018. ❀◗♣●🚌🐾📶

Slip Inn 🄻

Clementhorpe, YO23 1AN

⏲ 4-11.30; 1-midnight Fri; 12-midnight Sat; 12-11 Sun ☎ (01904) 621793 🌐 theslipinnyork.co.uk

Leeds Pale; Rudgate Ruby Mild; Timothy Taylor Boltmaker; 2 changing beers (sourced regionally; often Great Heck, Revolutions, Ridgeside) 🄷

Close to the river, this independent and unpretentious free house is a thriving community local with two bars, a snug, a sheltered courtyard and a beer garden to the rear. The pub hosts regular battle of the brewery events and several beer festivals each year, including one run jointly with The Swan just up the road. It supports traditional pub games such as darts, dominoes and cribbage. ♘❀♣🚌(11)🐾📶

Swan ★ 🄻

16 Bishopgate Street, YO23 1JH

⏲ 4-11 Mon-Wed; 3-11.30 Thu; 12-midnight Fri & Sat; 12-10.30 Sun ☎ (01904) 634968 🌐 theswanyork.co.uk

Tetley Bitter; Timothy Taylor Landlord; house beer (by Treboom); 3 changing beers (sourced regionally; often Half Moon, Revolutions, Salamander) 🄷

Just outside the city walls, this is a thriving traditional street-corner pub that became free of tie in autumn 2017. With a traditional West Riding-style drinking lobby, two bars and a snug, it is cosy, comfortable and unspoilt. Grade II-listed, it has a nationally important historic interior, plus a covered and heated beer garden to the rear. It hosts an annual beer festival jointly with The Slip Inn nearby and often serves beer from the wood. ❀♣●🚌(11)🐾

Waggon & Horses

19 Lawrence Street, YO10 3BP

⏲ 3-11; 12-11.30 Fri & Sat; 12-10.30 Sun ☎ (01904) 637478 🌐 waggonandhorsesyork.com

Batemans XB, XXXB; Oakham Citra; 4 changing beers (sourced nationally; often Ossett, Rooster's, Titanic) 🄷

A multi-roomed family-run pub owned by Batemans. The bar area and front room have TVs showing BT Sport. The two rooms at the back are quieter and used by various local groups to hold meetings. There is a free bar billiards table and a selection of board games. Good-value accommodation is also available. ❀🛏♿♣●🚌🐾📶

York Tap

Railway Station, Station Road, YO24 1AB

⏲ 10-11 (11.45 Fri & Sat); 11-11 Sun ☎ (01904) 659009 🌐 yorktap.com

18 changing beers (sourced nationally; often Anarchy, Tapped Sheffield, Thornbridge) 🄷

Situated on York railway station, this stunning Grade II*-listed Edwardian building has a circular wooden bar selling 18 cask beers plus two ciders or perries. The ornate ceiling, Art Deco stained-glass windows and ceiling domes create an award-winning backdrop. Regularly changing beers are chosen from a wide selection of Britain's finest breweries, with some from its own Tapped Brewery usually available. All styles and strengths of beers are represented. ❀♿⇌●🚌🐾

YORKSHIRE (SOUTH)

Arksey

Plough Inn 🄻

2 High Street, DN5 0SF (behind church)

⏲ 7 (6.30 Thu)-11; 12-2, 6.30-11 Fri; 12-3.30, 6.30-11 Sat; 12-3.30, 7-11 Sun ☎ (01302) 872472 🌐 arkseyplough.co.uk

Old Mill Blonde Bombshell; house beer (by Hilltop); 1 changing beer (sourced locally; often Abbeydale, Hilltop, White Rose) 🄷

A friendly, multi-roomed village free house featuring beers from small independent breweries. The lounge, which is heated by a log-burning stove, has horse harnesses and brasses on display along with photographs of the village, some depicting floods of long ago. Reasonably priced bar meals are served on Thursday, Friday and Saturday evenings, also at Saturday lunchtime, and the excellent Sunday lunch is popular. A general knowledge quiz is held on Sunday. Q♘❀◖◗♣🚌(64,64A)📶

Armthorpe

Wheatsheaf 🄻

Church Street, DN3 3AG

⏲ 5-11 Mon; 12-11.30; 12-5, 7-11 Sun ☎ (01302) 835868

Black Sheep Best Bitter; Purity Pure UBU; Sharp's Atlantic; 1 changing beer (sourced nationally; often Adnams, Purple Moose, Skinner's) 🄷

A roadside pub serving excellent beers and a variety of good-quality food. Donna and Colin make you feel welcome, and there is plenty of entertainment here including darts, dominoes and pool. Food is served Tuesday to Saturday lunchtimes and evenings, plus a popular carvery on Sundays. It has a good-sized outside drinking area at the front. Sunday is quiz night. Q♘❀◖◗♿♣●P🚌(81,82)🐾📶

Auckley

Eagle & Child ✔

24 Main Street, DN9 3HS

⏲ 11.30-11 (11.30 Fri & Sat); 12-10.30 Sun ☎ (01302) 770406 🌐 eagleandchildauckley.co.uk

Acorn Barnsley Bitter; Black Sheep Best Bitter; Timothy Taylor Landlord; 2 changing beers (sourced regionally; often Milestone, Springhead, Welbeck Abbey) 🄷

A much-loved pub on the main road in the village and winner of numerous CAMRA awards. Dating from the early 19th century, it has real character. There are two bars, one with a TV, the other quieter with tables for bar meals. The separate restaurant is decorated with photographs of local historic interest, and the home-cooked meals have a deserved reputation. Recently voted Doncaster's Best Pub by TRAX FM listeners. It is only one mile from Robin Hood Airport. Q♘❀◖◗♣P🚌(57)🐾📶

Barnsley

Arcade Alehouse 🏆 🄻

31 The Arcade, S70 2QP

⏲ closed Mon-Wed; 12-10; 12-8 Sun ☎ 07843 930974

6 changing beers (sourced regionally; often Geeves, Two Roses) 🄷

Barnsley's first micropub, a tiny one-up, one-down venue owned by Two Roses Brew Co. It is set in the lovely Victorian Arcade and was previously a cake

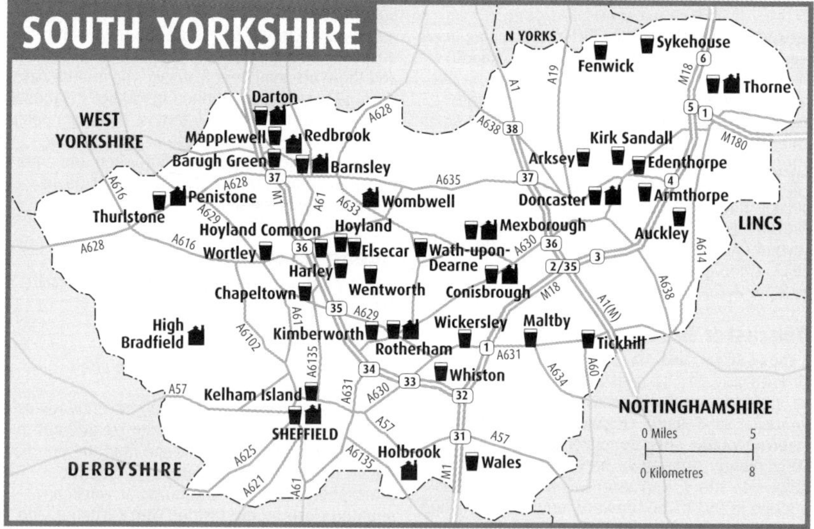

shop. The bar serves up to six real ales and up to four real ciders – most are local or regional. A large choice of craft beers is also available. The staff are welcoming and knowledgeable on the cask beers on offer. Q≠🍎🚌🐾📶

Old No.7 𝕃

7 Market Hill, S70 2PX

11-midnight (11 Mon & Tue); 11-11 Sun

☎ (01226) 244735 🌐 oldno7barnsley.co.uk

Acorn Barnsley Bitter, Blonde; 6 changing beers (sourced nationally; often Acorn) Ⓗ

The pub offers two bars – the main one upstairs is open each day while the one downstairs opens Friday and Saturday evenings, and is also home to a couple of beer festivals each year. The two bars offer a range of up to eight real ales from Acorn Brewery and other microbreweries, a choice of real ciders and perries, and a wide selection of craft and continental beers. ≠♣🍎🚌🐾📶

Silkstone Inn 𝕃 ✔

64 Market Street, S70 1SN

8am-midnight (1am Fri & Sat) ☎ (01226) 320860

Greene King Abbot; Ruddles Best Bitter; Sharp's Doom Bar; 4 changing beers (sourced nationally) Ⓗ

This popular JD Wetherspoon pub offers a good turnover of excellent real ales, including beers requested by the regulars. Outside is a seating forecourt with a no-smoking area. Inside, the dark-themed décor emphasises the coal seam on which Barnsley sits. The large one-roomed bar has plenty of snugs dotted around its central fireplace, creating a cosy feel. Q🐴❀◐♿≠🍎📶

Barugh Green

Crown & Anchor 𝕃

Barugh Lane, S75 1LL (on B6428)

11.30-11.30 (midnight Thu; 1am Fri & Sat)

☎ (01226) 387200 🌐 thecrownandanchor.com

7 changing beers (sourced nationally; often Bradfield, Great Heck, True North) Ⓗ

Known locally as The Whitehouse, this large pub is the Barnsley outpost of the True North portfolio. Seven handpulls – three always serving True North beers, the others ales from anywhere in the country – ensure that there are styles to suit all drinkers, along with a good selection of bottled world beers and a lengthy list of gins. The food menu changes often but the good pies are a constant. 🐴❀◐♿♣🍎P🚌🐾📶

Conisbrough

Hilltop 𝕃

Sheffield Road, DN12 2AY (on main A630)

12-11.30 (10 Mon & Tue); 12-midnight Sat & Sun

☎ (01709) 868811 🌐 thehilltophotel.co.uk

Hilltop Classic Bitter, Blonde, Stout, Porter Ⓗ

A traditional free house on the Rotherham side of Conisbrough, offering a relaxed and friendly atmosphere, serving four real ales from its own on-site brewery. Family run, it is split into a public bar and lounge area serving lunches and evening meals. Quiz night is on a Wednesday and includes supper. On Thursday evenings there are panel games. A regular in this Guide since 2014. Q🐴❀◐♣🍎P🚌(X78)🐾📶

Darton

Old Co-op Ale House 𝕃

28 Church Street, S75 5HG

closed Mon; 5-10; 2-10 Fri; 12-10 Sat & Sun

☎ 07718 974622

Timothy Taylor Landlord; house beer (by Two Roses); 6 changing beers (sourced nationally; often Two Roses) Ⓗ

A new micropub in the heart of Darton, in a former Co-op building, which has been tastefully refitted into a large open bar with exposed stonework and a wood-burning fire. The bar serves up six changing handpulled beers, including the house beer, Grumpy's Ale. There are also three real ciders and 10 lines of draught craft beers, plus a large spirit collection. Very dog friendly. Q♿≠♣🍎🚌🐾

Doncaster

Corner Pin 𝕃

145 St Sepulchre Gate West, DN1 3AH (5 mins walk from railway station)

12-11; 12-midnight Sun ☎ (01302) 340670
Leeds Pale; Stancill Barnsley Bitter; 4 changing beers (sourced locally; often Dukeries, Geeves, Stancill) H
Multi award-winning traditional pub close to the railway station and the Transport Interchange. Beers, in a variety of styles, are mainly from small independent breweries. Food is served weekend afternoons and there is a popular Sunday lunch. It has a public bar and separate lounge inside, and an outside drinking area with a small bar for occasional mini beer festivals. It is the winner of several CAMRA awards including Pub of the Year 2017. Lined glasses are used.
(71,73A)

Doncaster Brewery Tap

7 Young Street, DN1 3EL
closed Mon; 5-11; 12-11 Fri & Sat; 12-5 Sun
☎ (01302) 376436 doncasterbrewery.co.uk
Doncaster Sand House, Cheswold; 4 changing beers (sourced locally; often Doncaster) H
Conveniently situated in the town centre, down a quiet side street, Doncaster Brewery Tap was opened in 2014. The brewery, originally launched in 2012, was relocated to the rear and provides up to six beers, all served from handpumps into lined glasses. This welcoming pub also offers a range of six traditional ciders and perries. There is always something different going on in the Tap, from quiz night on Tuesday, to spoken word night on Thursday, to ukulele singalongs. Q

Draughtsman Alehouse

Station Court, DN1 1PE
10-9; 9am-9 Sat; 10-6 Sun ☎ 07999 874660
thedraughtsmanalehouse.co.uk
3 changing beers (sourced regionally; often Exit 33, Thornbridge) H
Located on Platform 3B of Doncaster Station and opened in 2017, this bar is the project of one man, Russell Thompson, who now runs it himself with assistance from his sons. The former Victorian buffet bar stood empty for 18 years. Real ales are changed regularly and come from regional brewers. Baguettes and locally made pies are usually available. Do be sure to inspect the fantastic Victorian wall tiles and mounted draft drawings of steam locomotives. Q(29)

Leopard

2 West Street, DN1 3AA (less than 5 mins walk from railway station)
10-10 (11 Mon); 10-11 Fri; 10-11.30 Sat; 12-9 Sun
☎ (01302) 739460 leopard-doncaster.co.uk
5 changing beers (sourced regionally; often Oakham, Ossett) H
This street-corner local close to the town centre has been a regular CAMRA award winner over the years. It has a superb tiled frontage recalling its days as a Warwicks and Richardsons house. There are two distinct rooms downstairs and a large one upstairs that regularly hosts rock and pop gigs. The pub serves a range of afternoon and early evening food to go with the five real ales usually on offer.
QP(71,72)

Plough ★

8 West Laith Gate, DN1 1SF (close to Frenchgate shopping centre)
11-11 (midnight Fri & Sat); 11-4, 7-11.30 Sun
☎ (01302) 738310
Acorn Barnsley Bitter; 2 changing beers (sourced regionally; often Moorhouse's, Ossett, Shipstone's) H
Known as the Little Plough, this is a friendly haven for anyone wishing to escape the town-centre bustle. CAMRA friendly, three real ales are served and there are mini beer festivals. The interior dates from 1934 and is mentioned in CAMRA's National Inventory of Historic Pub Interiors. There is a public bar at the front and a lounge at the rear. The frontage has recently been refurbished and a new pub sign painted by locally based artist David Venables. Q

Queen (Crafthouse & Kitchen)

1 Sunny Bar, DN1 1LY (on corner of Sunny Bar and Market Place)
closed Mon; 12-11; 11-midnight Fri & Sat
☎ (01302) 562908
5 changing beers (sourced nationally; often Hopjacker, Siren, Steel City) H
Old established marketplace pub, recently revived under new ownership. An interior created out of unusual boarding sets the scene, and the pub has drawn many new customers to sample the atmosphere, real ales and music at weekends. Situated close by the historic Corn Exchange and bustling market, this is a welcome addition to the town's real ale scene. Five changing real ales are on the bar, plus two real ciders typically from Gwynt y Ddraig or Celtic Marches.
Q(15)

Edenthorpe

Eden Arms

Eden Field Road, DN3 2QR (adjacent to Tesco)
11.30-11 (midnight Wed, Fri & Sat) ☎ (01302) 888682

REAL ALE BREWERIES

Abbeydale Sheffield
Acorn Wombwell
Blue Bee Sheffield
Bradfield High Bradfield
Chantry Rotherham
Concertina Mexborough
Dead Parrot Sheffield (NEW)
Don Valley Mexborough (NEW)
Doncaster Doncaster
Exit 33 Sheffield
Fuggle Bunny Holbrook
Geeves Barnsley
Hilltop Conisbrough
Hopscotch Craft Sheffield (NEW)
Imperial Mexborough
Jolly Boys Redbrook
Kelham Island Sheffield
Little Critters Sheffield
Lost Industry Sheffield
Loxley Sheffield (NEW)
Mitchell's Hop House Sheffield
Neepsend Sheffield
Old Vault Thorne (NEW)
On the Edge Sheffield
Penistone Penistone
Regather Sheffield
Sentinel Sheffield
Sheffield Sheffield
Stancill Sheffield
Tapped Sheffield
Toolmakers Sheffield
True North Sheffield
Two Roses Darton
White Rose Mexborough

Abbeydale Moonshine; house beer (by Black Sheep); 3 changing beers (sourced nationally; often Black Sheep, Marston's, Thornbridge) H
A fine, modern, busy estate pub built in the late 1980s. Attractive and comfortable, it is one of the area's most CAMRA-friendly pubs. On Mondays all cask ales are generously discounted the whole day. Five real ales are usually on offer, including Ember Inns Pale Ale, brewed by Black Sheep, with a display at the entrance informing customers about present and future cask beers. It has a large outside drinking area. Meet the Brewer evenings are popular, and it is notable for good-quality meals. Q❀P(87,8)

Elsecar

Crown Inn

22 Hill Street, S74 8EL
12-midnight (1am Fri & Sat) ☎ (01226) 361488
3 changing beers (sourced regionally; often Abbeydale, Acorn, Bradfield) H
Community pub in the picturesque village of Elsecar. A recent refurbishment has seen a new bar and the opening up of the main room. The TV here usually shows football. The lounge to the rear leads to a large conservatory area which overlooks the garden and children's play area. Various local groups meet here. Close to the Elsecar Heritage Centre and train station. ❀♣P

Maison du Biere

Wath Road, S74 8HJ (in Elsecar Heritage Centre, Unit 15)
closed Mon & Tue; 12-9 (7 Wed); 12-7 Sun
☎ (01226) 805255 maisondubiere.com
Changing beers (sourced nationally)
This popular beer shop and tap is in the heart of the historic heritage centre, serving up over 400 bottled and canned beers and ciders, with 10 lines of craft/draught beers and real ales and many real ciders. The knowledgeable staff can navigate you on a taste experience. The tap is popular with locals and visitors alike. There are lots of monthly events in the heritage centre.
❀♣P

Fenwick

Baxter Arms

Fenwick Lane, DN6 0HA (between Askern and Moss)
11.30 (5.30 Mon)-11 ☎ (01302) 702671
Theakston Best Bitter; 2 changing beers (sourced regionally; often Bradfield, Ossett, York) H
A warm welcome is assured in this award-winning free house, run by the same family for over 25 years. Popular with customers from far and near, this is truly a rural gem and well worth seeking out. The beers are from small independent breweries, and reasonably priced food, sourced locally, is served all day. Outside there is ample parking and seating. Wednesday is quiz night. Local CAMRA district Pub of the Year 2017.
Q❀♣P

Harley

Horseshoe

9 Harley Road, S62 7UD (off A6135 on B6090, 1 mile from Wentworth)
4-11 (10 Mon); 2-11 Sat; 12-10.30 Sun ☎ (01226) 742204
thehorseshoeharley.co.uk
Bradfield Farmers Blonde; 3 changing beers H
Popular village street-corner local in the same family for many years. Guest beers change regularly, ensuring their quality, with ales often coming from local breweries. It is home to football and pool teams. A carvery is held 12-3pm Sunday; book to avoid disappointment. The Horseshoe has been the hub of the local community for well over a century and is handy for walking around the Wentworth estate, for the Needles Eye, and for Elsecar Heritage Centre. Can be busy when the pool team has a home fixture. ❀♣(44)

Hoyland

Knave & Kestrel

23 King Street, S74 9JU
closed Mon, Tue & Thu; 5-11 Wed & Fri; 4-11 Sat; 4-10 Sun
☎ 07983 482638
Elland Nettlethrasher; Stancill Stainless; 3 changing beers (sourced regionally) H
This converted shop on the Hoyland one-way system opened in 2017 and has been delighting drinkers with its rapidly changing ale selection ever since. There is a front room with high tables and stools and a compact back room with bench seating and a fire. Live music features on occasion. It has a separate gin menu. Toilets are up steep stairs. Opening hours may vary so check before visiting. P

Hoyland Common

Keys

Sheffield Road, S74 0PY
12-11 (11.30 Fri & Sat); 12-10.30 Sun ☎ (01226) 824437
thekeyshoyland.co.uk
3 changing beers (sourced regionally) H
This large pub is close to junction 36 of the M1, and is popular with diners and drinkers alike. Three cask beers are available, with a good gin selection for the non-beer drinkers. It offers a full restaurant menu with regular specials nights. The pub hosts a couple of beer festivals each year, with live music from local acts. ❀P

Tap & Brew

9 Hoyland Road, S74 0LT
1-11; 12-11 Fri-Sun ☎ (01226) 824614
6 changing beers (sourced regionally) H
Converted from a Victorian tea shop in 2017, but retaining its fine overmantel and fireplace, this micropub has quickly become popular, stocking a selection of bottled beers and a range of gins alongside its regularly changing cask beers and cider. Food includes sandwiches, jacket potatoes, cheeseboards and pie and peas. Afternoon teas are also available. Board games and local history books abound. Open mic night is the first Sunday of the month, with occasional live music. ❀♣

Kimberworth

Manor Barn

109 Church Street, S61 1EP
4-11 (midnight Fri); 11.30-midnight Sat & Sun
☎ (01709) 551089 manorbarnrotherham.co.uk
3 changing beers (often Bradfield, Moorhouse's, Purity) H
Tasteful conversion of a barn in the grounds of the listed former Kimberworth Manor, which can be viewed to the rear of the car park. New tenants took over in 2016 following an uncertain time for

the pub. Real ale was reinstated, with three handpumps dispensing changing beers from national and microbreweries. This proved popular, as have the open mic and quiz nights. The food is home cooked from a varied menu. A large upstairs function room can accommodate 120 people. P

Kirk Sandall

Glasshouse

1 Doncaster Road, DN3 1HP (opp station)
11.30-11; 12-midnight Fri & Sat ☎ (01302) 884268
glassh.co.uk
3 changing beers (sourced nationally; often Don Valley, Old Mill, Wychwood) H
Large, modern roadside pub – the name refers to the nearby Pilkington Glass factory. Extensively refurbished in recent years, the interior is spacious, with varied seating and a separate function suite. Large TV screens are found throughout the pub. Three regularly changing cask ales are always available, with locally brewed beers often featured. Beer prices are generally lower than the local average. P

Maltby

Queen's Hotel

Tickhill Road, S66 7NQ
8am-midnight (1am Thu-Sat) ☎ (01709) 812494
Greene King Abbot; Ruddles Best Bitter; 4 changing beers H
Former residential hotel completely refurbished and reopened by Wetherspoon after a lengthy period of closure. Now firmly established, this spacious pub has an attractive family dining area offering typical Wetherspoon value-for-money food and drink. The reopening of the Queen's led to a much-needed raising of the profile of real ale in this small satellite town. Handy for Coronation Park next door, Roche Abbey and the shops. P (X1,10)

Mapplewell

Old Bakery

16 Blacker Road, S75 6BN
closed Mon & Tue; 6-9; 2-11 Fri & Sat; 2-9 Sun
☎ 07541 660287
6 changing beers (sourced regionally) H
This is a popular micropub in the heart of the real ale corridor of Mapplewell. The pub is in a converted bakery, which still has the working ovens in the bar area, with changing local and regional beers on tap. It has an extensive beer garden at the rear. Weekly and monthly events including quiz nights and vinyl music takeovers make this a popular destination. Q P

Talbot Inn

Towngate, S75 6AS
12-11 (11.30 Wed); 11.30-midnight Fri & Sat; 11.30-11 Sun
☎ (01226) 385629 thetalbotmapplewell.co.uk
4 changing beers (sourced locally; often Acorn, Magic Rock, Two Roses) H
A 17th-century coaching house, popular with diners, serving meals in the bar and the 1776 restaurant upstairs. The bar has an extensive beer and wine list to complement any food offerings, and always has four different beers. This pub is accredited to a buy-local policy and has received numerous awards. It is the official tap for the Two Roses brewery, and wider locals like Acorn and Magic Rock provide regular guest beers here. Q P (1,97)

Mexborough

Imperial Brewery Tap

Arcadia Hall, Cliff Street, S64 9HU (opp bus station)
closed Mon & Tue; 4.30-12.30am; 12-12.30am Sat; 12-10 Sun ☎ (01709) 584000
Imperial Bitter, Blonde, Bees Knees, Stout; 2 changing beers (sourced nationally; often Great Heck, Raw, Revolutions) H
This friendly brewery tap has a large main bar with a cosy lounge area plus a separate games/function room. Eight handpumps dispense quality Imperial ales, which may include seasonal specials and one-off brews, as well as guest beers. A real cider is sometimes available. There is entertainment most nights with a live band on Friday, Saturday and Sunday evenings, featuring music for a wide range of tastes. Thursday is acoustic open mic night and Wednesday is karaoke night. (220,221)

Rotherham

Bluecoat

The Crofts, S60 2DJ (behind town hall, off Moorgate Rd, A618)
8am-midnight (1am Fri & Sat) ☎ (01709) 539500
Greene King IPA, Abbot; Kelham Island Pale Rider; 7 changing beers (sourced locally) H
Originally a charity school, opened in 1776, it became a Wetherspoon pub in 2001. It is a Guide regular, with up to 10 real ales on offer, which are listed on a screen at the end of the bar. At least two real ciders or perries are served from bags behind the bar. Special brews from local breweries feature and regular Meet the Brewer nights are held. Winner of local CAMRA Pub of the Year five times. P

Cutler's Arms

29 Westgate, S60 1BQ
12-10 (11 Wed & Thu; 1am Fri & Sat); 2-10 Sun
☎ (01709) 382581 cutlersarms.co.uk
Chantry New York Pale, Iron & Steel Bitter, Diamond Black Stout; house beer (by Chantry); 2 changing beers (sourced locally; often Chantry) H
Originally dated 1825, the pub was rebuilt in 1907 and, following a period of closure, restored to its original Edwardian splendour by Chantry Brewery, reopening in 2014. It retains some some Art Nouveau windows, tiling and the original curved bar counter with elegant dividing screen. Grade II and ACV listed, it has a regionally important historic pub interior. A full range of Chantry beers is dispensed on eight handpumps, plus two real ciders or perries. Live music features strongly at weekends. Snacks are offered. It gets busy on Rotherham United home match days. Q

New York Tavern

84 Westgate, S60 1BD (at jct of Coke Lane)
12-11 (midnight Fri & Sat) ☎ (01709) 375596
newyorktavern.co.uk
Chantry New York Pale, Iron & Steel Bitter, Diamond Black Stout; house beer (by Chantry); 2 changing beers (sourced locally; often Chantry) H

A pub since 1856, it reopened in September 2013 as a real ale-led venue, renamed after a pub that was demolished when the nearby ring road was built. At least six Chantry beers are served plus two real ciders or perries, all at very competitive prices. A large selection of foreign bottled beers, pickled eggs and snuff is available. Rotherham United memorabilia adorn the walls. The jukebox has an eclectic selection of music. Local CAMRA Town Pub of the Year 2016-2018.

Rhinoceros

35-37 Bridgegate, S60 1PL

8am-11 (midnight Fri & Sat) ☎ (01709) 361422

Greene King Abbot; Marston's Saddle Tank; 5 changing beers

Busy town-centre venue with a single room on one level and booths down one side. Many local pictures decorate the walls – look for one explaining the origins of the name. The usual good-value Wetherspoon fare is on offer, and the beer quality and range have improved recently. Several real ciders and perries are also available. It can be very busy in the afternoon, early evening and on Rotherham United match days. Close to the minster, Bridge Chapel and the bus station.

Stag

111 Wickersley Road, Broom, S60 4JN (on A6021)

11-midnight (11 Mon & Tue); 10-midnight Sat & Sun ☎ (01709) 838929

4 changing beers (often Bradfield, Exmoor)

Much-improved popular suburban roadhouse on a busy roundabout. The good-value real ales often come from local microbreweries. A conservatory area leads to an extensive garden with a covered raised space. Sports are popular at the pub. Originally a coaching house that stood on its own on a main route between Rotherham and Bawtry, it acted as the centre of operations for the local Home Guard during WWII. The pub was refurbished in March 2017 and a single room created. It may start serving food again shortly. P(X1,19)

Sheffield: Central

Bath Hotel ★

66-68 Victoria Street, S3 7QL

12-11 (midnight Fri & Sat); closed Sun ☎ (0114) 249 5151 beerinthebath.co.uk

Thornbridge Wild Swan; 6 changing beers (sourced regionally; often Thornbridge)

A careful restoration of the 1930s interior gave this two-roomed pub a CAMRA Conservation Pub Design award and it is recognised as having a nationally important historic interior. The bar lies between the tiled lounge, a small corridor drinking area and the cosy well-upholstered snug. There are usually three Thornbridge beers and three guests on handpump. Regular live music features and a weekly quiz on Thursday. Light snacks are available. Q

Devonshire Cat

49 Wellington Street, S1 4HG

12-2am ☎ (0114) 279 6700 devonshirecat.co.uk

Abbeydale Moonshine, Absolution; 9 changing beers (often Abbeydale)

With 12 handpumps adorning the bar and over 100 beers from around the world, the Dev Cat is a great place for the discerning drinker. Now operated by Abbeydale Brewery, there are usually up to six of its beers on offer as well as a number of interesting guests. A recent refurbishment has created a central island bar with various seating areas around. The menu ranges from light snacks through to full meals, served all day to 9pm (8pm Sun). (West Street)

Dog & Partridge

56 Trippet Lane, S1 4EL

12-11 (11.30 Fri & Sat); 12-10 Sun ☎ (0114) 270 6156

Black Sheep Best Bitter; 3 changing beers (sourced locally; often Abbeydale, Blue Bee, Stancill)

Behind an impressive Gilmour's Brewery frontage and dating from 1796, here is a comfortable multi-roomed pub served by a central bar. To the right of the entrance is a spacious taproom with dartboard, and on the left a smaller seating area. Behind the servery is a cosy snug with a hatch for service, and at the rear the lounge often features live music. The three changing beers are usually from local breweries. (City Hall)

Head of Steam

103-107 Norfolk Street, S1 2JE

11-midnight (12.30am Thu-Sat) ☎ (0114) 272 2128

Camerons Strongarm; 5 changing beers (sourced regionally; often Abbeydale, Leeds, Thornbridge)

A pub for some 20 years, this former bank was acquired by Camerons Brewery in 2015 and after extensive refurbishment reopened as part of the Head of Steam chain in 2016. Behind the imposing frontage, the large single room is served by a central island bar, with a separate seating area at the rear leading onto an outside drinking area in Tudor Square. In addition to the brewer's own beers, the six handpumps usually dispense beers from independents in Yorkshire and the North-East. (Cathedral)

Red Deer

18 Pitt Street, S1 4DD

12-midnight (1am Fri & Sat); 12-11 Sun ☎ (0114) 272 2890 red-deer-sheffield.co.uk

Blue Bee Reet Pale; Moorhouse's Pride of Pendle; Welbeck Abbey Portland Black; 5 changing beers (sourced regionally)

A genuine, traditional local in the heart of the city. The small frontage of the original three-roomed pub hides an open-plan interior extended to the rear with a gallery seating area. As well as the impressive range of eight cask beers, including five guest ales, there is also a selection of continental bottled beers. Meals are served lunchtimes and evenings daily. The popular quiz is held Tuesday night, and an upstairs function room is available for bookings. Q(West St)

Rutland Arms

86 Brown Street, S1 2BS

12-11 (midnight Fri & Sat) ☎ (0114) 272 9003 therutlandarmssheffield.co.uk

Blue Bee Reet Pale; 6 changing beers (sourced regionally; often Blue Bee, Geeves)

Occupying a corner site in the Cultural Industries Quarter and near Sheffield's main railway station, the pub has operated as a free house since 2009. The comfortable interior provides ample seating either side of the central entrance, and the wall displays include photos of old Sheffield pubs. Most of the guest beers come from local and regional microbreweries, together with specials from Blue Bee. Food is served throughout the day to 9pm (6pm Sun).

Sheffield Tap ★

Platform 1B, Sheffield Station, Sheaf Street, S1 2BP
11-11; 10-midnight Fri & Sat ☎ (0114) 273 7558
sheffieldtap.com
Thornbridge Jaipur IPA; 9 changing beers (sourced nationally; often Tapped Sheffield)
Opened in 2009, this was originally the First Class refreshment room for Sheffield Midland Station, built in 1904. After years of neglect, the main bar area has been the subject of an award-winning restoration retaining many original features. Further seating has been provided in the entrance corridor and to the right of the bar. Usually three beers are from the on-site Tapped Brewery, opened in 2013 in the impressive former dining room. The brewery can be viewed behind a glass screen. Q

Sheffield: Chapeltown

Commercial

107 Station Road, S35 2XF
12-11 (midnight Fri & Sat) ☎ (0114) 246 9066
thecommie.co.uk
Abbeydale Moonshine; 7 changing beers (sourced nationally; often Durham, Neepsend, White Rose)
This friendly well-established free house provides six guest beers, including a porter or stout, together with at least one real cider. Built in 1890 by long-closed Strout's Brewery, a central island bar serves the games room, lounge and taproom. Beer festivals are held in May and November, while monthly tutored whisky tastings take advantage of the extensive range. There is a rear outdoor area, and an upstairs function room with regular folk sessions. No meals Sunday evening.
(Chapeltown) P (265,31A)

Sheffield: Kelham Island

Bar Stewards

163 Gibraltar Street, S3 8UB
closed Mon; 5.30-11; 5-11 Fri; 2-11 Sat; 2-9 Sun
☎ 07525 095123 thebarstewards.uk
4 changing beers (sourced nationally; often Arbor, Blue Bee, North Riding Brewery)
Opened in a shop unit in July 2017, this is a modern bar and bottle shop, and a welcome addition to the Kelham Island circuit. The four well-chosen cask beers are from independent producers and often include a local ale. The bar is available for private hire, as is a mobile bar service.
(Shalesmoor)

Fat Cat

23 Alma Street, S3 8SA
12-11 (midnight Fri & Sat) ☎ (0114) 249 4801
thefatcat.co.uk
Kelham Island Best Bitter, Pale Rider; Timothy Taylor Landlord; 8 changing beers (sourced nationally; often Kelham Island)
Opened in 1981, this is the pub that started the real ale revolution in the area. Beers from around the country are served alongside those from the adjacent Kelham Island Brewery. Vegetarian and gluten-free dishes feature on the menu (food is 12-3pm and 6-8pm during the week, 12-7pm Saturday, 12-3pm Sunday). The walls are covered with many awards presented to the pub and brewery. Beer festivals are held every August and at various other times. Monday is curry and quiz night. Q (Shalesmoor) P

Harlequin

108 Nursery Street, S3 8GG
12-11 (11.30 Thu & Fri; midnight Sat) ☎ (0114) 249 4181
theharlequinpub.wordpress.com
Exit 33 Blonde, Northern Best; 8 changing beers (often Exit 33)
Operated by Exit 33 Brewing, the Harlequin takes its name from another former Ward's pub just round the corner, now demolished. The large open-plan interior features a central bar with seating on two levels. There are two regular and usually four other beers from Exit 33, as well as guests from far and wide, with the emphasis on microbreweries. A large range of real ciders is also available. Wednesday is quiz night and there is live music at weekends.
(Castle Square)

Kelham Island Tavern

62 Russell Street, S3 8RW
12-midnight ☎ (0114) 272 2482 kelhamtavern.co.uk
Acorn Barnsley Bitter; Bradfield Farmers Blonde; Pictish Brewers Gold; 9 changing beers (sourced nationally; often Abbeydale, Brass Castle, North Riding Brewery)
Twice CAMRA National Pub of the Year and regular regional and local winner, this small gem was rescued from dereliction in 2002. Twelve handpumps dispense an impressive range of beers, always including a mild, a porter and a stout. In the warmer months you can relax in the pub's multi award-winning beer garden. Regular folk music features on Sunday evenings and quiz night is Monday. No meals Sunday.
Q (Shalesmoor)

Shakespeare's Ale & Cider House

146-148 Gibraltar Street, S3 8UB
12-midnight (1am Fri & Sat) ☎ (0114) 275 5959
shakespeares-sheffield.co.uk
Abbeydale Deception; Stancill Barnsley Bitter; 8 changing beers (sourced nationally; often Bad Seed, Blue Bee, North Riding Brewery)
Originally built in 1821, it reopened as a freehouse in 2011 following a refurbishment including incorporation into the pub of the archway to the rear yard. The central bar serves three rooms including the extension and there is a further room across the corridor. The eight handpumps have featured over 5,000 different beers over the last seven years, and over 100 whiskies are also stocked. There is regular live music, and beer festivals are held twice a year.
Q (Shalesmoor)

Wellington

1 Henry Street, S3 7EQ
3-11; 12-midnight Fri & Sat; 12-11 Sun ☎ (0114) 249 2295
Neepsend Blonde; 4 changing beers (sourced regionally; often Neepsend)
A traditional two-roomed local opened as a free house in 1993. Now part of the small Sheaf Inns group of pubs, it is the brewery tap for the nearby Neepsend Brewery. Sympathetically refurbished following the recent takeover, the rooms are comfortably furnished and welcoming. The seven handpumps feature at least three Neepsend beers and up to three changing guests, mainly from micros, together with a real cider. An extensive range of malt whiskies is also on offer.
Q (Shalesmoor)

Sheffield: North

Blake Hotel

53 Blake Street, Upperthorpe, S6 3JQ

12-11.30 (midnight Fri & Sat) ☎ (0114) 233 9336

Neepsend Blonde; 5 changing beers (sourced regionally; often Blue Bee, Neepsend)

This community pub, at the top of a steep hill (pedestrian handrails provided), reopened in 2010 after being closed for seven years. Although it has been extensively restored, it retains many Victorian features, including etched windows and mirrors, and there is a large decked garden to the rear. The pub has probably the largest selection of whiskies in Sheffield and a growing range of rums and other spirits. No electronic games, TV or jukebox. Q(Langsett)

Forest

Rutland Street, Neepsend, S3 9PA

12-midnight ☎ (0114) 275 0183

5 changing beers (often Toolmakers, White Rose)

Tap for the adjacent Toolmakers Brewery, with a selection of the brewery's beers always available on four handpumps. This welcoming and popular pub brings both local customers and visitors from further afield who are frequenting the nearby Valley of Beer. It was refurbished and had an exterior facelift in 2016. Karaoke takes place on Friday, live entertainment on Saturday and open mic nights on Wednesday and Sunday. (Shalesmoor)P

Gardeners Rest

105 Neepsend Lane, Neepsend, S3 8AT

3-11; 12-midnight Fri & Sat; 12-11 Sun ☎ (0114) 272 4978

thegardenersrest.com

Sheffield Crucible Best, Five Rivers, Blanco Blonde; 5 changing beers (sourced nationally)

Recently taken over by the Gardeners Rest Community Society, this friendly pub acts as the brewery tap for the nearby Sheffield Brewery. There are also at least four guest beers from independent breweries nationwide. To the rear is a conservatory leading to a beer garden overlooking the River Don. The cosy Dram Shop includes a restored bar billiards table. There is live music at weekends and regular festivals throughout the year. Q(Infirmary Rd)

Hillsborough Hotel

54-58 Langsett Road, Hillfoot, S6 2UB

2-10 Mon; 12-11 (midnight Fri & Sat) ☎ (0114) 232 2100

Acorn Barnsley Bitter; Tapped Mojo; 5 changing beers (sourced nationally)

Privately owned 4-star hotel with six en-suite rooms, providing beer from a wide range of independent breweries. There are regular themed events, with a quiz on Tuesdays, live bands at weekends and folk music sessions on the second and fourth Sundays in the month. The conservatory at the rear offers extensive views over the Don Valley, and a function room is also available. Q(Langsett)

Wisewood Inn

539 Loxley Road, Loxley, S6 6RR

12-midnight; 12-11.30 Sun ☎ (0114) 233 4310

wisewoodinn.co.uk

5 changing beers (often Acorn, Bradfield, Stancill)

The main bar has three rooms (including one for pool) and below is the cellar bar, which is available for hire. A large garden to the rear overlooks the Loxley Valley. The five handpumps invariably include some beers from local breweries (for example Abbeydale, Acorn, Bradfield, Exit 33 and Stancill). Also there are eight key taps, often featuring Beavertown and Thornbridge. The extensive food menu includes continental sausages, pizzas and tapas. Adjacent to the cellar bar is the Loxley Brewery, which commenced production in spring 2018.
P(61,62)

Sheffield: South

Ale House

187 Fraser Road, Millhouses, S8 0JP

closed Mon; 4-11; 3-11 Sat ☎ (0114) 274 5515

Saltaire Blonde; 5 changing beers (sourced nationally; often Bad Seed, Dancing Duck, Whitby)

A warm and friendly welcome awaits within this 1960s estate pub, which has been transformed in recent years into a real ale haven. Visitors are treated to six handpulled beers, always including one from Saltaire, and a well-chosen changing range from small breweries across the country, often breweries popular with the pub's loyal regulars. Food is served Friday evenings, and traditional music and food events are held throughout the year. P(86,96)

Beer Engine

17 Cemetery Road, Highfield, S11 8FJ

4-11; 12-midnight Fri & Sat; 12-11 Sun ☎ (0114) 272 1356

beerenginesheffield.com

Neepsend Blonde; 5 changing beers (sourced nationally; often Bad Seed, Exit 33)

A multi-roomed pub well refurbished in 2015 and deservedly popular. A generous choice of high-quality drink offerings is provided for its wide clientele. The five changing handpulled beers come from an interesting mix of microbreweries in Sheffield and across the country. Excellent tapas-style food is served each evening (except Sun) plus Friday and Saturday lunchtimes. A traditional roast is available on Sunday. The large beer garden has a covered area.

Broadfield

452 Abbeydale Road, Nether Edge, S7 1FR

11.30-midnight (1am Fri & Sat); 11.30-11 Sun

☎ (0114) 255 0200 thebroadfield.co.uk

Abbeydale Moonshine; True North Best Bitter; 7 changing beers (sourced nationally; often Abbeydale, Arbor, Ilkley)

Dating from 1896, the Broadfield's 2012 refurbishment provided two distinct areas around a horseshoe bar. On one side is a large, interestingly laid-out drinkers' room, while opposite is a similarly sized room with tables set for diners. It is extremely popular for its excellent food (pies a speciality), its selection of nine cask ales and its wide range of beers, wines and spirits. The pub has a large beer garden at its rear.

Brothers Arms

106 Well Road, Heeley, S8 9TZ

12-11 (midnight Fri & Sat) ☎ (0114) 258 3544

Bradfield Farmers Blonde; house beer (by Abbeydale); 6 changing beers (sourced nationally)

A classic, traditional local. Although the interior is open plan it is designed so the various seating and games areas all feel individual and cosy. The pub's name reflects its association with locally well known parody ukulele band The Everly Pregnant

Brothers, and live music is hosted every Monday evening, supplemented by folk sessions on the third Sunday. The bar features eight real ales with two regular beers and six changing guests, together with a real cider.

Sheaf View

25 Gleadless Road, Heeley, S2 3AA

11.30-11.30 (12.30am Fri & Sat) ☎ (0114) 249 6455

Neepsend Blonde; 7 changing beers (sourced regionally; often Neepsend, Pictish, Saltaire) H

A 19th-century pub near Heeley City Farm, the Sheaf experienced a chequered history before becoming a real ale oasis since reopening as a free house in 2000. The walls and shelves are adorned with assorted breweriana and provide an ideal background for good drinking and conversation. A wide range of international beers, together with malt whiskies and a real cider, complements the eight reasonably priced real ales. A busy pub, especially on Wednesday quiz night and Sheffield United match days. QP

White Lion

615 London Road, Heeley, S2 4HT

4-midnight (1am Fri); 12-1am Sat; 2-11 Sun
☎ (0114) 255 1500 whitelionsheffield.co.uk

Abbeydale Moonshine; Tetley Bitter; Wychwood Hobgoblin; house beer (by Kelham Island); 8 changing beers (sourced nationally) H

This Grade II-listed pub has been respectfully refurbished over the years. A tiled central corridor links a number of delightful small rooms and leads to the larger rear concert room. A wide selection of cask-conditioned beers always includes one gluten-free and one vegan option, and the pub is also proud of its selection of whiskies. It hosts many community events and has live music every night except Wednesday, which is quiz night.

Sheffield: West

Beer House

623 Ecclesall Road, Sharrow, S11 8PT

12-11

6 changing beers (sourced nationally; often Blue Bee, Exit 33, Hopjacker) H

Sheffield's first micropub opened in a small former shop unit in late 2014. The front room has level access from the street and contains the bar with its bank of six handpumps displaying a changing range of beers, mainly from microbreweries, with local breweries well represented. The rear room has seating focused around the fireplace, and there is a quiz on Wednesday evening. Q

Hallamshire House

49 Commonside, S10 1GF

4-11.30; 2-12.30am Fri; 12-12.30am Sat; 12-11.30 Sun
☎ (0114) 266 4466

Thornbridge Wild Swan, Jaipur IPA; house beer (by Thornbridge); 5 changing beers (sourced locally; often Thornbridge) H

Operated by Thornbridge Brewery, and known locally as The Tardis, the pub has two small comfy rooms at the front, and leading from the bar area are a large lounge and a snooker room. There is a courtyard drinking space downstairs with ample seating and soft furniture in a covered area. Quiz night is on Monday, and some Saturdays there is live music or a DJ. Q (95)

Itchy Pig Ale House

495 Glossop Road, Broomhill, S10 2QE

3-11; 12-11 Fri & Sat, 3-10.30 Sun ☎ (0114) 327 0780
theitchypig.co.uk

5 changing beers (sourced regionally; often Abbeydale, Exit 33) H

A cosy, friendly micropub with a relaxed atmosphere and a continental feel. The whitewashed walls are decorated with porcine-themed artwork, hop sacks and dried hops. There is craftsman-standard carpentry including a bar made from Victorian-era doors, with a glass-covered bar top formed from many two pence coins set in resin. A wide range of pork scratchings is available. Q

Rising Sun

471 Fulwood Road, Nether Green, S10 3QA

12-11 (11.30 Fri & Sat) ☎ (0114) 230 3855
risingsunsheffield.co.uk

Abbeydale Deception, Moonshine; 10 changing beers (sourced regionally; often Abbeydale, Ulverston) H

This pub is a large suburban roadhouse operated by local brewer Abbeydale. There are two comfortably furnished rooms with a log-burning fire between the main bar and the glass-roofed extension, which also has glass panels in the end wall. A range of Abbeydale beers is always served, with up to six guests mainly from micros, dispensed from the impressive bank of 13 handpumps. Quizzes are on Sunday and Wednesday evenings. The Sunfest beer festival is in July.
QP (120,83a)

University Arms

197 Brook Hill, Broomhall, S3 7HG

11-11 (midnight Fri); 12-11 Sat; closed Sun
☎ (0114) 222 8969

Kelham Island Pale Rider H**; Welbeck Abbey Red Feather** H/G**; house beer (by Acorn); 5 changing beers (sourced regionally)** H

Owned by the University of Sheffield, this former staff club has an open-plan lounge with a bar at one end adjacent to a small alcove seating area, and a conservatory leading to the large garden. There is additional seating upstairs with separate rooms for snooker and darts. The guest beers are mostly local and there are regular beer festivals. Entertainment includes a quiz on Tuesday and an open mic night on Wednesday.
(51,52)

Sykehouse

Old George Inn

Broad Lane, DN14 9AU (on main road, in centre of village)

12-midnight; 11.30-midnight Sun ☎ (01405) 785635

Tetley Bitter; 2 changing beers H

Multi-roomed village pub selling guest beers sourced nationally and often from breweries rarely featured in the local area. The building is over 200 years old and includes a lounge with an open fire, a restaurant and a games room. Excellent food is served throughout, and the Sunday carvery is particularly popular. Outside there is a camping field, a patio where barbecues are held in summer, and a large playground with a bathing pool and helter skelter. P

Thorne

Old Vault
Market Place, DN8 5DP (follow A614)
3-11 (midnight Fri); 12-midnight Sat; 12-11 Sun
☎ (01405) 947180
4 changing beers (sourced regionally; often Hilltop, Nightjar, Wold Top) H
Popular micropub with its own recently opened brewery, conveniently situated in the town's marketplace. Two Old Vault beers are always on offer, plus up to four different guest beers. Real cider is also occasionally available. There are regular live music events most Saturdays, with outside events also organised from time to time. Open mic and jam night is held on the last Thursday of every month, and quiz night is Sunday. Q♣ (87,88a)

Windmill
19 Queen Street, DN8 5AA
2-11 (midnight Fri); 12-midnight Sat; 12-11 Sun
☎ (01405) 812866
Kelham Island Pale Rider; Timothy Taylor Landlord; 2 changing beers (sourced regionally; often Abbeydale, Castle Rock) H
Friendly community pub comprising a smart lounge with conservatory at the side and linked by an archway to another room with a pool table. Good-natured conversation is the order of the day. Up to four real ales from small independent breweries are sold. Outside there is a large beer garden with play equipment and ample parking. The pub is close to the town centre on a street parallel to the main road. Q♣P (87,86)

Thurlstone

Crystal Palace
Towngate, S36 9RH (just round corner from war memorial)
5-midnight (1am Fri); 12-1am Sat; 12-midnight Sun
☎ (01226) 766331
Acorn Barnsley Bitter; Jolly Boys Golden Best; 1 changing beer (sourced locally; often Acorn, Jolly Boys) H
A small bar separates the lounge and public bar of this community pub which also has a small games area. Situated off the main A628 that runs through this rural village, it was saved from closure after being bought from a pub company. Following the purchase, the new management decided to introduce real ales and over the last four years the pub has gained high accolades. ♣P

Huntsman
136 Manchester Road, S36 9QW (on main A628 through village)
5-11; 3-midnight Fri; 12-midnight Sat; 12-10.30 Sun
☎ (01226) 764892 huntsmanthurlstone.co.uk
Black Sheep Best Bitter; Timothy Taylor Landlord; 4 changing beers (sourced nationally) H
The positioning of this village local on the main east-west Pennine route (A628 towards Woodhead) provides an interesting mixture of regular customers and passing trade. Genuine and friendly meeting, drinking and talking are this pub's lifeblood. Throw in old-fashioned pub games, LocAle and a seriously dog-friendly attitude, and it just should not be passed by. Food is served Tuesday evening and Sunday lunchtime only. You will not find a jukebox or TV, but Wednesday evening is live music night. Q♣

Tickhill

Scarbrough Arms
Sunderland Street, DN11 9QJ (on A631 near Buttercross)
12-11; 12-10.30 Sun ☎ (01302) 742977
John Smith's Bitter; Timothy Taylor Boltmaker; 2 changing beers (sourced locally; often Chantry, Kelham Island, Welbeck Abbey) H
A deserving Guide entry since 1990, this three-roomed stone-built pub has won several CAMRA awards over the years. Originally a farmhouse, the building dates back to the 16th century although it has undergone structural changes since then. The snug is a delight with its barrel-shaped furniture and real fire; there is also a rejuvenated front lounge with logburner and a traditional rear bar. An outbuilding doubles as a covered smoking area and an extension for beer festivals.
Q♣P (22,205)

Wales

Duke of Leeds
16 Church Street, S26 5LQ (off A618 into School Rd, opp parish church)
12-11 ☎ (01909) 515490 thedukeofleeds.co.uk
Theakston Old Peculier; 3 changing beers (sourced regionally; often Abbeydale) H
The former coaching inn of the Duke of Leeds, the pub is more than 300 years old. It reopened in 2015 following refurbishment after a period of closure. Four real ales are on the bar including one from Abbeydale Brewery. The bar opens into three other areas where drinks and meals can be taken. Popular with walkers, it has outdoor drinking spaces with views of the village. Parking is provided behind the pub, while buses travel along the main Wales road nearby. The food menu is extensive and freshly cooked to order.
P

Wath-upon-Dearne

Wath Tap
49 High Street, S63 7QB
12-11 ☎ (01709) 872150 wathtap.co.uk
6 changing beers (sourced locally; often Fernandes, Geeves, Ossett) H
The area's first micropub, opened in a former butcher's shop in 2016. Six real ales from local breweries are sold, plus five real ciders. These are listed on chalkboards and prices are very reasonable. Very welcoming, it can be busy at the weekend. The former walk-in cold store is now the cellar and there are tables outside. Food may be brought in from the surrounding takeaways. Local CAMRA Pub of the Year 2017 and 2018.
Q♣

Wentworth

George & Dragon
85 Main Street, S62 7TN (set back from road on B6090)
11-11 (11.30 Thu; midnight Fri & Sat) ☎ (01226) 742440
Theakston Old Peculier; 7 changing beers (sourced nationally; often Bradfield, Chantry, Geeves) H
In a picturesque and popular village, this free house offers up to eight ales from local, regional and national brewers. The pub has a car park and patio with a large grassed area at the rear containing a children's adventure playground,

marquee and craft shop. The home-cooked food is popular. This local, licensed since 1804, is handy for walking to historic Wentworth Woodhouse and Hoober Stand. It can also be accessed through the rear garden from the parish church.
Q P (44,227)

Rockingham Arms

8 Main Street, S62 7TL
11-11 (midnight Fri & Sat); 11-10.30 Sun
(01226) 742075
Black Sheep Best Bitter; Theakston Old Peculier; 5 changing beers (sourced regionally) H
Country pub dating from 1814, situated in a picturesque village. There are three rooms and a large function/dining room plus a barn for events. It serves up to seven real ales, and guest ales may be local or from further afield. Close to historic Wentworth Woodhouse and the Fitzwilliam Follies, the pub has accommodation across the road in converted cottages. An extensive range of home-cooked meals is offered. It features a bowling green plus a patio and gardens for summer drinking. Q P (44,227)

Whiston

Chequers Inn

Pleasley Road, S60 4HB (on A618, 1½ miles from M1 jct 33)
12 (4 Mon & Tue)-11; 12-11.30 Fri & Sat
(01709) 829168 thechequerswhiston.co.uk
Bradfield Farmers Blonde; Tetley Bitter; Theakston Best Bitter; house beer (by Greene King); 1 changing beer (sourced nationally) H
Next to a 13th-century thatched barn in the heart of old Whiston, this friendly local dates from 1933. One side of the bar acts as a taproom, with a split-level lounge to the right. There is seating at the front, plus a raised garden. The renowned food is home cooked by chefs. Quiz nights are held on Tuesday and Thursday. Occasional discos, live music and scooter club meets also feature. It has a dartboard and pool table.
P (27,29)

Hind

285 East Bawtry Road, S60 4ET (on A631)
11.30-midnight; 10-midnight Sat & Sun (01709) 532490
Abbeydale Moonshine; Tetley Bitter; house beer (by Black Sheep); 3 changing beers (sourced nationally; often Fyne Ales, Kirkstall, St Austell) H
Large roadhouse on the M1/M18 link road, built for Mappins Brewery of Rotherham in 1936. Since refurbishment the interior has been opened out, creating good wheelchair access. There are extensive gardens and a patio to the rear. The former snooker room upstairs is being converted to a function room. Guest beers are from the Ember Inns portfolio, and are cheaper on Mondays. There is also a cask club. Daytime, evening and takeaway food is popular. Q P

Wickersley

Three Horseshoes

133 Bawtry Road, S66 2BW (on A631)
10-11 (midnight Fri & Sat) (01709) 739240
greatukpubs.co.uk/threehorseshoeswickersley
Black Sheep Best Bitter; Fuller's London Pride; 6 changing beers (sourced locally; often Dukeries, Partners, Welbeck Abbey) H
Standing back from the busy M1/M18 link road, this mock-Tudor pub in the centre of the village reopened in February 2016 following refurbishment. It now boasts eight real ales. The six guest beers may be sourced locally or further afield and usually include a stout or porter. The upstairs room is used for a variety of functions and live acts. Regular beer festivals are held. The food menu includes breakfast, lunch and dinner. P

Wickersley Old Village Cricket Club

Northfield Lane, S66 2HL (opp Northfield primary school, down driveway beside pitch)
5-10 (11 Wed, Fri & Sat); 12-10 Sun (01709) 700536
Chantry New York Pale; 3 changing beers (often Bradfield, Moorhouse's, Robinsons) H
Popular cricket club open to the public. Comfortably appointed and friendly, it has recently been refurbished and extended. Its large lounge offers a more peaceful location for a quality beer than the local pubs. CAMRA members are more than welcome for a good-value, well-kept pint, and of course you could always watch the cricket. Opening hours are likely to be extended when home matches are on and it can get busy. Local CAMRA branch Club of the Year 2016-18.
P (10)

Wortley

Wortley Men's Club

Reading Room Lane, S35 7DB (in centre of village at back of Wortley Arms pub)
2-11; 12-11 Sat & Sun (0114) 288 2066
wortleymensclub.co.uk
Timothy Taylor Landlord; 2 changing beers (sourced nationally) H
Multiple CAMRA award-winning club, including national and local Club of the Year, in a pretty rural village near to Wortley Hall and gardens. With an opulent exterior and interior, features include exposed timber frames, ornate ceilings, wooden panelling and a real fire. Guest ales are from local and national breweries, and a guest cider is stocked. The club runs an annual beer festival in July. Show your CAMRA membership card or a copy of this Guide on entry. Q P (23,23A)

YORKSHIRE (WEST)

Ackworth

Boot & Shoe

Wakefield Road, WF7 7DF (on A638)
3 (2 Thu)-midnight; 12-midnight Sat; 12-10.30 Sun
(01977) 610218
Sharp's Atlantic; 4 changing beers (sourced regionally) H
A busy, non-food pub that dates back to the late 16th century and is one of seven real ale establishments in Ackworth. An extensive refurbishment in 2015 has retained the iron range and the delightful semi-circular vestibule and stone-flagged floors throughout. The Boot has maintained its reputation for live music (Friday and Saturday 9pm, Sunday 5.30pm) and the popular open mic on Tuesday evening. Three large screens show Sky Sports. The village cricket field is behind the pub. P

ENGLAND

Masons Arms 🄻

Bell Lane, WF7 7JD (turning off A628 by defunct railway bridge)

4-midnight; 1.30-1am Fri; 12-1am Sat; 12-midnight Sun

☎ 07966 501827

Bradfield Farmers Blonde, Farmers Brown Cow; 2 changing beers (sourced regionally) 🄷

A Grade II-listed former coaching house dating from 1682 built of locally quarried stone. The central bar serves the main room, pool room and smaller lounge. There are log-burning fireplaces in both the main rooms that were discovered 15 years ago during a sensitive refurbishment. Live music on Saturdays (9pm) and Sundays (4-6.30pm), games night on Tuesdays (9pm) and quiz night on Thursdays are all well attended by locals and visitors alike. ♣P

Altofts

Robin Hood 🄻

10 Church Road, WF6 2NJ (from Normanton town centre take road over railway into Altofts, continue through Lee Brigg, then High Green Rd and left on to Church Rd)

12-11 (midnight Fri & Sat) ☎ (01924) 892911

robinhoodaltofts.co.uk

Acorn Barnsley Bitter; 5 changing beers (sourced locally; often Tarn 51) 🄷

Locally owned free house/brewpub at the top end of the village, with a large new patio area seating 70 people. The Tarn 51 microbrewery is on-site next to the patio. This village pub is within easy reach of the Pennine Trail and Aire & Calder Navigation, and only a mile from Stanley Ferry Marina. ♣P

Alverthorpe

Alverthorpe WMC 🄻

111 Flanshaw Lane, WF2 9JG (on road from Alverthorpe to Flanshaw)

2-11; 1-11 Fri; 1-1.30am Sat; 12-11 Sun

☎ (01924) 374179

6 changing beers (sourced locally) 🄷

Multi-roomed CIU-affiliated club with a cosy interior and unusual stained-glass features. A selection of guest ales is sold, mainly from local micros. This venue is a regular winner of local CAMRA awards. Live entertainment features on Saturday and Sunday, while snooker and darts are among the traditional games. It has sporting teams and also a floodlit bowling green. ♣P

New Albion

2 Flanshaw Lane, WF2 9JH (from behind County Hall take Cliffe Lane which leads to Batley Rd, continue to traffic lights in Alverthorpe centre, left onto Flanshaw Lane and pub is on right)

12-11 (midnight Fri & Sat) ☎ (01924) 376946

5 changing beers (sourced regionally) 🄷

Traditional multi-roomed free house including a raised area comprising sofas and easy chairs. There

REAL ALE BREWERIES

Anthology Leeds (NEW)
Beer Ink Huddersfield
BEEspoke Shipley
Bingley Wilsden
Blue Square Leeds: Morley
Bosun's Horbury Bridge
Bradford Bradford
Bridge Holmbridge (brewing suspended)
Bridgehouse Keighley
Briscoe's Otley
Burley Street Leeds
Cap House Batley
Chin Chin South Kirkby
Cobbydale Silsden
Copper Dragon Silsden
Eagles Crag Todmorden
Elland Elland
Empire Slaithwaite
Fernandes Wakefield
Five Towns Wakefield
Frisky Bear Leeds: Morley
Ghost Baildon
Golcar Golcar
Goose Eye Bingley
Halifax Steam Hipperholme
Hamelsworde Hemsworth
Haworth Steam Cleckheaton
Hogs Head Sowerby Bridge
Horbury Ossett
Horsforth Leeds: Horsforth (NEW)
Hungry Bear Leeds
Ilkley Ilkley
Junction Baildon
Kirkstall Leeds: Kirkstall
Leeds Leeds: Holbeck
Legitimate Industries Leeds
Linfit Linthwaite
Little Valley Hebden Bridge
Lord's Golcar
Magic Rock Huddersfield
Mallinson's Huddersfield
Meanwood Leeds: Meanwood (NEW)
Mill Valley Cleckheaton
Milltown Milnsbridge
Morton Collins Wakefield
New Inn Liversedge
Nightjar Mytholmroyd
Nook Holmfirth
North Leeds
Northern Monk Leeds: Holbeck
Old Spot Cullingworth
Ossett Ossett
Outgang Kinsley
Partners Hightown
Quirky Leeds: Garforth
Rat Huddersfield
Revolutions Whitwood
Ridgeside Leeds: Meanwood
Riverhead Marsden
Salamander Bradford
Saltaire Shipley
Small World Shelley
St Oswald's Guiseley (NEW)
Stod Fold Halifax
Summer Wine Honley
Sunbeam Leeds
Tapped Leeds
Tarn51 Altofts (NEW)
Three Fiends Meltham
Three Valleys Todmorden (NEW)
Tigertops Wakefield
Timothy Taylor Keighley
Vocation Hebden Bridge
Wetherby Wetherby (NEW)
Wharfedale Ilkley
Wilde Child Leeds
Wishbone Keighley

WEST YORKSHIRE

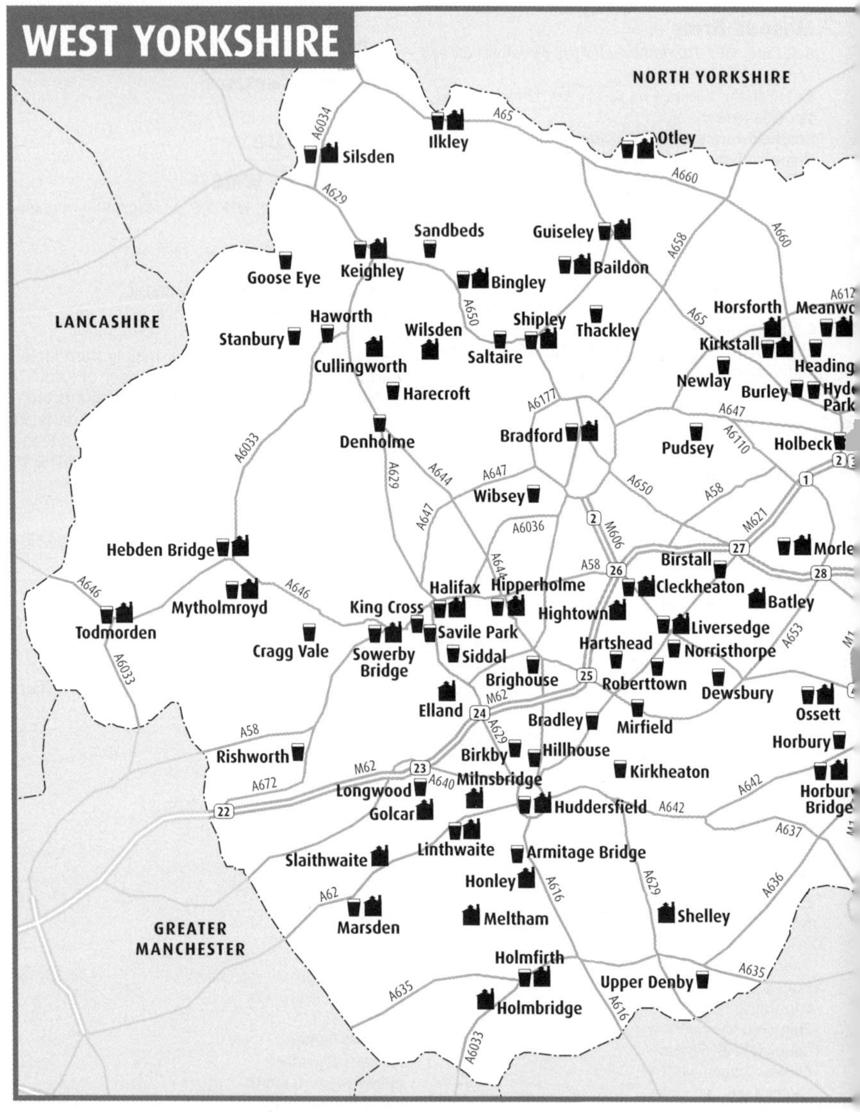

is a large, award-winning decking and seating area which is a suntrap, enhanced with many attractive planters. BT Sports is available to armchair enthusiasts in two of the four rooms. Wednesday is quiz night. Five rotating guest beers and a traditional cider are stocked at all times.
❀♣P

Armitage Bridge

Armitage Bridge Monkey Club

Dean Brook Road, HD4 7PB

7-11 Mon, Wed & Thu; closed Tue; 5-midnight Fri; 4-11 Sat; 12-10 Sun ☎ (01484) 522370 monkeyclub.co.uk

Goose Eye Bitter; 2 changing beers (often Empire, Tetley)

Recently refurbished and air-conditioned, this thriving little club in the hamlet of Armitage Bridge serves two guest beers. The annual Monkeyfest held in early July is very popular and is now into its 12th year. A regular local CAMRA Club of the Year and well worth seeking out.
❀♣P (324,388)

Baildon

Bull's Head Inn

6 Westgate, BD17 5ES

12-11.30 Mon; 11-11 ☎ (01274) 976416

Goose Eye Chinook Blonde; Saltaire Blonde; Sharp's Doom Bar; Tetley Bitter; 2 changing beers (sourced nationally; often Small World)

This two-roomed establishment with log fires has a warming ambience and is a popular village local where visitors, and well-behaved dogs, are always welcome. Photos of Baildon adorn the walls. Independent guest beers are always offered alongside the four regular real ales. Sunday and Tuesday evenings are quiz nights, occasional music nights are held, and piped background music is

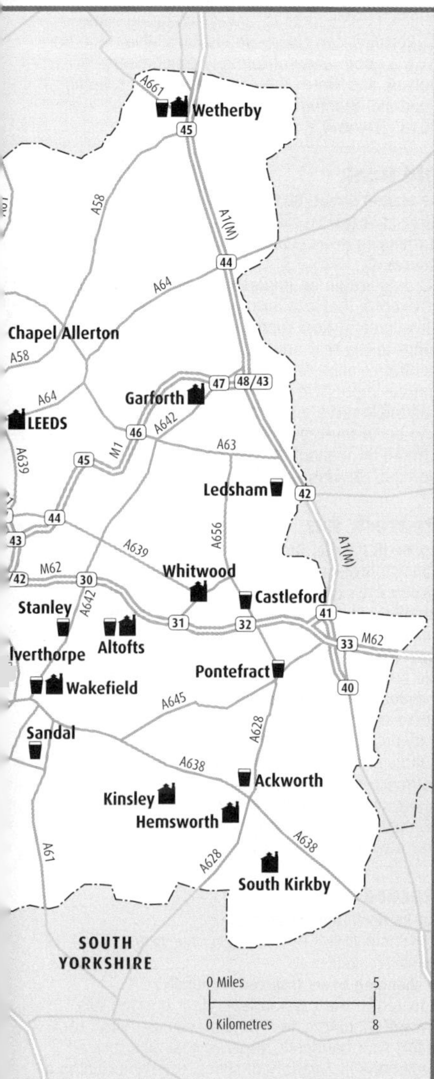

often played. The separate taproom houses darts and dominoes. It is a pub frequented by a clientele of all ages.

Junction L

1 Baildon Road, BD17 6AB (on A6038/B6151 jct)
12-midnight (1am Fri & Sat) ☎ (01274) 582009
Fuller's ESB; Junction Blonde; Tetley Bitter; 3 changing beers (sourced nationally) H
This popular three-roomed local comprises a lounge, public bar and a games area. The three regularly available beers, usually including one from the in-house Junction Brewery, are complemented by three guest ales. Cider and foreign bottled beers are also sold. Food is served on Friday lunchtimes only. Sports events on TV are popular, quiz nights are held on Tuesdays and Thursdays, and a musicians' jamming session on Sunday nights. A regular beer festival occurs at the end of July.

Bingley

Chip N Ern

73 Main Street, BD16 2JA
4-midnight; 12-midnight Sat; 12-11 Sun
☎ (01274) 985501
Bingley Goldy Locks Blonde; Bridgehouse Blonde, Aired Ale, Porter; Goose Eye Chinook Blonde; 2 changing beers (sourced regionally) H
Centrally located on Bingley's Main Street, this friendly micropub opened in 2015, and has quickly established itself as a popular addition to the local beer scene. The wood-panelled ground floor bar has a distinctive range of decorations. Additional seating is available in the upstairs gin bar. The seven cask ales include a varying range from Bingley, Bridgehouse, Goose Eye and other guest breweries. There are also up to five ciders dispensed from the taps at the back of the bar.

Foundry Hill

Wellington Street, BD16 2NB (opp railway station)
4-11 (1am Fri); 12-1am Sat; 2-11 Sun ☎ (01274) 566144
foundryhillbar.co.uk
5 changing beers (sourced nationally) H
A modern basement pub that comprises a small bar area and an adjacent larger room. There is a focus on selling a varying range of up to five good-quality real ales, sourced both regionally and nationally. The real ale styles tend to include a pale, two golden, one bitter/amber and one dark beer. Closing time may vary depending upon demand. Dogs are permitted, and children are welcome until 7pm.

Platform 1¾ L

1 Burrage Street, BD16 1GH (close to railway station)
3-10; 12-11 Fri-Sun ☎ 07561 195586
8 changing beers (sourced regionally) H
This single-room pub in the town centre off Chapel Lane opened in 2017. The interior seating is zoned and includes some unusual recycling. Eight handpulls serve two regular house beers (a bitter and a blonde) and up to six varying guest beers. Two of the real ales are also available directly from the cask. Lagers and an extensive range of ciders are also offered. Closing time may vary depending upon demand.

Birkby

Magic Rock Brewery Tap L

Willow Park Business Centre, Willow Lane, HD1 5EB
closed Mon; 4-10; 1-11 Fri; 12-11 Sat; 12-9 Sun
magicrockbrewing.com
Magic Rock Hat Trick, Ringmaster; 3 changing beers (sourced locally; often Magic Rock) H
The Tap opened in 2015. It sells up to five cask beers from the brewery, with Ringmaster and Hat Trick doubling up on busy match days. Less than 10 minutes' walk from the town centre, the Tap itself is housed in a 1,700 square foot area to the far end of the brewery, with a view directly into it. Street food outlets are laid on every weekend. Regular events include brewery tours on Saturdays at 3pm and 4pm, week night tasting (book ahead), as well as exhibitions and festivals, all of which definitely make the Tap worth a visit.

Birstall

Horse & Jockey 🏆 L ✔

97 Low Lane, WF17 9HB (on A643 near village centre)
12-11.30 Sun-Tue; 4-11.30 Wed; 12-midnight Thu; 12-1am Fri & Sat ☎ (01924) 472559
Bradfield Farmers Blonde; Jennings Cumberland Ale, John Smith's Bitter; Sharp's Doom Bar; 2 changing beers (sourced nationally; often Naylor's, Revolutions, Rudgate) H
A country-style pub licensed from the 1750s. The open-plan bar is split into four areas, with half-panelled walls and beamed ceilings. Darts, dominoes and pool are played, and on Thursdays there is a music and knowledge quiz. Guest beers come mainly from independent breweries, local where possible. One of the seven pumps serves real cider. Outside, the patio has a beautiful, award-winning flower display. Last admission is 11pm. ❀♣●P🚌📶

Bradford

Corn Dolly L

110 Bolton Road, BD1 4DE
11.30-11; 12-10.30 Sun ☎ (01274) 720219
corndolly.pub
Everards Tiger; Moorhouse's White Witch; Timothy Taylor Boltmaker; 5 changing beers (sourced nationally; often Durham, Kelham Island, Rooster's) H
An award-winning free house run by the same family for over 25 years, close to the city centre and Forster Square railway station. Previously called the Wharfe, due to its location near to the former Bradford Canal, it first opened its doors in 1834. An open-plan layout incorporates a games area to one end. Good-value food is served weekday lunchtimes. It has a friendly atmosphere and is popular before Bradford City matches. A collection of pumpclips adorns the beams.
❀(♿≉♣P🚌(640,641)

Fighting Cock 🏆 L

21-23 Preston Street, BD7 1JE (close to Grattans, off Thornton Rd)
11.30-11; 12-10.30 Sun ☎ (01274) 726907
Ilkley Mary Jane; Theakston Old Peculier; Timothy Taylor Golden Best, Boltmaker, Landlord; 7 changing beers (often Naylor's, Newby Wyke, Wishbone) H
A drinkers' paradise in an industrial area, this multi award-winning pub is 20 minutes' walk from the city centre and close to bus routes along Thornton Road and Legrams Lane. A large beer garden opposite the pub was added in 2015 and summer beer festivals now take place. Twelve real ales are usually on sale, including at least one dark beer. A choice of real ciders and foreign bottled beers is offered. Good-value lunches are served Monday to Saturday. ❀(●🚌🐾📶

Jacobs Beer House L

14 Kent Street, BD1 5RL (by Jacobs Well roundabout at end of Hall Ings)
4-10 (11 Thu); 12-11 Fri & Sat; 2-8 Sun ☎ (01274) 394479
Half Moon Dark Masquarade; Wychwood Hobgoblin; 8 changing beers (sourced nationally; often Salamander, Stancill, Sunbeam) H
Refurbished and reopened in 2013, this pub was formerly known as Jacobs Well, dating from about 1830. The layout is open plan but with a rustic feel and a snug to the side of the bar. Nine handpulls offer a changing range of beers from local and regional independents, always featuring some darker ales. Ten ciders are also available, together with a good range of foreign bottled beers. Sit outside and watch the city bustle while supping good ale. Bradford CAMRA Cider Pub of the Year 2018. ❀≉●🚌📶

Old Bank

69 Market Street, BD1 1NE (near City Hall)
10-11 ☎ (01274) 738218
4 changing beers (sourced nationally; often Coach House) H
Located within an impressive building in Bradford city centre that was formerly a bank, this pub has a large ground-floor room, with a semi-enclosed room to the rear finished with oak woodwork and neutral colours. An additional seating area upstairs has an impressive classical style to it. Four handpulls serve a beer from Coach House Brewery and up to three guests. Good-value meals are offered throughout the day. Sections of the pub can be hired. ♘()♿≉🚌📶

Peacock Bar

25 North Parade, BD1 3JL
11-10.30 (1am Fri & Sat); 12-10.30 Sun ☎ 07979 182599
peacockbar.co.uk
Bradfield Farmers Blonde; Thornbridge Jaipur IPA; 1 changing beer (sourced nationally) H
Opened in 2016, this Indian-themed bar offers real ale and Indian street food with a twist. Three handpumps serve real ale while a further two serve cider. There are two permanent beers and a varying guest ale. Traditional Indian meals and snacks are available on the ground floor. There is a further room upstairs with a large TV showing BT Sport, also available for meetings and functions. Free curries are offered on Wednesday evenings. It has outside pavement seating. ()≉●🚌

Record Café

45-47 North Parade, BD1 3JH
11-11 (midnight Fri & Sat); 12-11 Sun ☎ (01274) 723143
therecordcafe.co.uk
4 changing beers (sourced regionally) H
Located in the city's independent quarter, this award-winning café-style bar sells ale, vinyl and ham! Four handpulls dispense real ales sourced regionally in a variety of styles, usually including a dark beer. Real cider and perry are offered, and there are seven craft keg beers from independent brewers on tap. Food is served in a charcuterie style specialising in hams and cheeses from Spain. Meanwhile, in the upstairs mezzanine area, it is possible to browse and purchase vinyl records.
♘❀()♿≉●🚌🐾📶

Sparrow Bier Café L

32 North Parade, BD1 3HZ
11-11 (midnight Thu-Sat); 12-11 Sun ☎ (01274) 270772
4 changing beers (sourced regionally) H
This busy café-bar in Bradford's popular independent quarter is simply furnished in a minimalist style. A large main bar is complemented by a basement with additional seating. Four changing cask ales are offered plus at least two real ciders and a varied selection of international draught and bottled beers. Deli-style sandwiches and platters are available, while pies and peas are served for free prior to Bradford City FC home matches, when the pub can be extremely busy. ❀≉●🚌🐾📶

Wallers Brewery

Upper Millergate, BD1 1SD

11-midnight; 9.30am-2am Fri & Sat 07850 572771

sunbridgewells.com

3 changing beers (sourced locally; often Bosun's, Saltaire)

Located on the lowest level, this pub is accessed from the central core of the Sunbridgewells retail complex and from the Ivegate entrance. It comprises a bar area to one end and seating areas in two rooms with brick-vaulted ceilings. Up to three real ales are offered. Food bought from elsewhere in the complex can be brought in. Evidence of the building's history is displayed – it was the 2017 winner of the LABC Building Excellence Awards.

Bradley

White Cross

2 Bradley Road, HD2 1XD (on A62, 3 miles from Huddersfield centre, at Leeds Rd/Bradley Rd crossroads)

11.45-11 (midnight Fri & Sat); 12-10.30 Sun

(01484) 425728

St Austell Tribute; Wainwright; 3 changing beers

This friendly Bradley pub by the Leeds Road roundabout has been in the Guide for 15 years. It has been serving the community since about 1806 and still retains its Bentley Yorkshire Breweries green-tiled entrance and windows. The dining area and lounge sit either side of the central bar, where two regular beers are supported by up to three varied guests (including one dark). You will always get a warm welcome in this popular and cosy pub. No food Saturday. P

Brighouse

Market Tavern

2 Ship Street, HD6 1JX

closed Mon & Tue; 12 (2 Wed & Thu)-10 07908 698360

6 changing beers (often Abbeydale, Salopian, Vocation)

A single-storey former pork pie factory next to the canalside open-air market has been transformed into a micropub. There is seating in the bar, in a small snug by the entrance, and in a sheltered outside drinking area. At least one dark beer and a choice of real ciders including Thistly Cross cider are available at all times. Appropriately, pork pies are among the snacks served. Open bank holiday Mondays. Q

Millers Bar

47 Briggate, HD6 1EB (past market and across bridge)

11-11 (midnight Fri & Sat); 12-11 Sun (01484) 968144

themillersbar.co.uk

Stod Fold Blonde; Timothy Taylor Landlord; 5 changing beers (often Magic Rock, Track Brewing Co)

Formerly The Black Swan, Millers Bar reopened at the end of 2014 after an extensive refurbishment. It caters both for locals and town-centre visitors, and families are also welcome during food service times. While there is an upstairs restaurant for more formal occasions, a good range of home-made meals and bar snacks is available in the bar areas. The beer garden makes the most of the canalside location. The real ale range normally includes at least one dark beer. P

Red Rooster

123 Elland Road, HD6 2QR (on A6025 towards Elland)

4-11; 12-midnight Fri & Sat; 12-10.30 Sun

07825 128682

Abbeydale Moonshine; Oakham Citra; Saltaire Blonde; 6 changing beers (often Oakham, Salopian)

Half a mile from Brighouse town centre, it is well worth the walk to this longstanding and excellent free house. Formerly known as The Wharf, the alehouse was purpose built around 1900 for the adjacent coal wharf which served much of western Yorkshire. Three wharfmen's cottages still stand alongside the pub by the red beck. Locally sourced pie and peas are available at all times, as is fresh ground coffee. Bitter and dark beers are always on tap. Q P (571,564)

Castleford

Glass Blower

15 Bank Street, WF10 1JD (rear is also accessible from Aire St car parks off road by Allinson flour mill)

8am-midnight (1am Fri & Sat) (01977) 520390

Greene King Abbot; Ruddles Best Bitter; Sharp's Doom Bar; 6 changing beers

Characterful former post office converted by Wetherspoon. It offers four guest beers, usually including one dark and one special from a microbrewer. The name refers to the town's history of glass bottle making, with some examples on display. Locally born sculptor Henry Moore is represented via reproductions adorning the walls. It is a popular venue for families and rugby fans on match days. Regular Meet the Brewer events and brewery visits are arranged. Children are welcome in the family area.

Griffin Inn

Lock lane, WF10 2LB (10 mins from town centre on A656)

11-1am (01977) 731706

3 changing beers (sourced regionally)

Traditional refurbished two-roomed free house with a separate lounge and bar, close to the town centre and Castleford Tigers rugby ground. Family and dog friendly, it is next to the Aire & Calder Canal, where moorings are available. Food is served on Wednesday evenings, Saturday lunchtime (11-2pm) and Sunday lunchtime (12-3pm winter, 12-4pm summer). Voted the local CAMRA branch Most Improved Pub in 2017. P

Junction

Carlton Street, WF10 1EE (enter Castleford on A655; pub is on corner with Carlton St at top of town centre)

2-9 (11 Thu); 12-midnight Fri; 12-11.30 Sat; 12-9 Sun

(01977) 277750 thejunctionpubcastleford.com

6 changing beers

A rejuvenated pub handy for bus and train stations, specialising in beers in the landlord's own wooden casks. Up to six guest ales are available in the wood from enterprising local brewers, and it stages an annual Easter Woodfest beer festival. The large horseshoe-shaped bar is kept warm with open fires, with a stove-heated snug available for functions. Folk night is on the last Sunday of each month and a live band on Friday evenings. Q

Cleckheaton

Rose & Crown

6 Westgate, BD19 5ET (on A643, W off A638)
12-11; 12-10.30 Sun (01274) 861530
9 changing beers (sourced locally; often Empire, Ossett, Salamander)
A cosy town-centre pub with a five-barrel microbrewery producing quality beers under the Whitechapel and Haworth Steam brands. It was recently refurbished to a high specification, with lots of woodwork in the three rooms, plus comfortable seating and attractive features. Great-quality food is served lunchtimes and evenings. A good choice of mainly local beers is available, including some brewed here beyond the sheltered patio, dark beers being especially popular. The bus station is a three-minute walk.

Cragg Vale

Robin Hood

Cragg Road, HX7 5SQ (on B6138 1½ miles S of Mytholmroyd)
3-11; 12-11 Fri-Sun (01422) 885899
Timothy Taylor Boltmaker, Landlord; 4 changing beers (sourced regionally; often Mallinsons, Small World, Vocation)
Compact and welcoming two-roomed split-level local, set in the scenic wooded Cragg Valley, an ideal location for investigating the history of the infamous Cragg Vale Coiners. There is a cosy fire in the winter. Food is served Friday to Sunday (telephone to check times). The pub is customer led and guest ales are usually from West Yorkshire breweries. Real cider is sometimes available.
Q (900,901)

Denholme

New Inn

Keighley Road, BD13 4JT (on A629)
closed Mon-Wed; 5-11 Thu & Fri; 4-11 Sat & Sun
Tetley Bitter; 3 changing beers (sourced regionally; often Empire, Phoenix, Saltaire)
A warm welcome is assured in this cosy free house which sits high on the hillside alongside the A629 Keighley-Halifax road with stunning views over the Aire Valley. Three rotating guest ales are regularly sourced from regional breweries. The pub has a semi open-plan layout but retains a multi-room feel, warmed by real fires. A conservatory extension houses a pool table. For the energetic, the Great Northern walking/cycling trail is nearby.
P (67,68)

Dewsbury

Leggers

Calder Valley Marina, Mill Street East, WF12 9BD (off B6409; follow brown signs to canal basin)
11-11 (midnight Fri & Sat); 11-10.30 Sun
(01924) 488153 leggersinn.co.uk
Abbeydale Moonshine; Jennings Cumberland Ale; Saltaire Blonde; 4 changing beers (sourced nationally; often Dark Star, Leeds, Oakham)
A hidden gem in a former stable hayloft overlooking the canal basin. A large decked area welcomes cyclists and walkers, while inside, the interesting bar has a unique décor. A raging fire warms while you study the beer blackboard, but watch out for the low beams. The large function room hosts live music and annual beer festivals. Local pie and peas are a speciality plus good simple pub food, with gluten-free dishes available to order. Guest beers always include a dark brew.
P

West Riding Refreshment Rooms

Dewsbury Railway Station, Wellington Road, WF13 1HF
11 (12 Mon)-11; 11-midnight Fri; 10-midnight Sat
(01924) 459193
Black Sheep Best Bitter; Timothy Taylor Landlord; 7 changing beers (sourced nationally; often Brass Castle, Magic Rock, Vocation)
Multi award-winning pub in a Grade II-listed station building. The eclectic range of nine real ales always includes many colours and flavours. Real cider and a range of speciality bottled beers are also sold. Live music plays outside in summer and occasional beer festivals are held. Good meals are served daily plus pizzas until 8pm and curry on Wednesday teatimes. The pub is a mainstay of the Transpennine Rail Ale Trail, hence Saturdays can be busy. There are monthly Meet the Brewer sessions.
P

Goose Eye

Turkey Inn

BD22 0PD (village centre) SE028406
closed Mon; 12-2, 4-11 Tue; 12-11; 12-10 Sun
(01535) 681339 theturkeyinn.com
Goose Eye Bitter, Chinook Blonde; Timothy Taylor Golden Best, Landlord; 6 changing beers (sourced nationally)
Friendly, historic pub in a tiny hamlet approached by steep roads or a riverside footpath. Three snugs all have real fires to keep out the winter chill. It has a pool table, holds a quiz night on Wednesday, and hosts occasional live music and special theme nights. Food is served Wednesday to Sunday. Up to six guest beers are usually on the bar. A good base for exploring the surrounding countryside.
P

Guiseley

Coopers

4-6 Otley Road, LS20 8AH
12-11 (midnight Fri & Sat) (01943) 878835
Okells Bitter; Rooster's Yorkshire Pale Ale; Timothy Taylor Landlord; 5 changing beers (sourced regionally; often North Riding, Tapped, Thornbridge)
A light, modern, airy bar/diner converted from a former Co-operative store. It has a bar with a separate dining area and an upstairs function room. Eight ales are served, generally from Yorkshire or northern micros, with a dedicated dark beer pump and a large selection of continental beers in bottle and on tap. A diverse range of meals is available until 9pm. The large upstairs function room hosts regular music events and a monthly comedy club, and also provides extra dining space.
Q

Guiseley Factory Workers Club

6 Town Street, LS20 9DT
1-11 (midnight Fri); 11.30-midnight Sat; 11-11 Sun
(01943) 874793 guiseleyfactoryworkersclub.co.uk
Tetley Bitter; 3 changing beers (sourced locally; often Acorn, Salamander, Saltaire)

A three-roomed club founded over 100 years ago by the Yeadon and Guiseley Factory Workers Union. It is multi award-winning and was National CAMRA Club of the Year in 2009. The bar serves both the lounge and the concert room and has changing guest ales from micros and independents. There is also a snooker room and a small outdoor drinking area. Varied musical acts perform on Friday and Saturday nights and the club hosts many local organisations. CAMRA members are welcome with this Guide or a membership card. ❀⇌♣P🚌🐾ᯤ

Halifax: King Cross

Wainhouse Tavern ✔

Upper Washer Lane, Pye Nest, HX2 7DR (take Edwards Rd off Pye Nest Rd)

⏲ 4-10; 12-11 Fri & Sat; 12-10.30 Sun ☎ (01422) 339998

Wychwood Hobgoblin Gold; house beer (by Thwaites); 3 changing beers (sourced locally; often Mallinsons, Rudgate, Small World) Ⓗ

No two windows are alike in this unique-looking pub, built in 1877 as a home to industrialist JFE Wainhouse, whose name is associated with the nearby Tower. A lounge occupies the front of the premises, while up a few steps is a much larger room having as its focal point a long bar counter. Traditional home-cooked food is available in the evenings and at weekends.
❀◐♣P🚌(579,560)🐾ᯤ

Halifax: Savile Park

Big Six

10 Horsfall Street, HX1 3HG (off A646 Skircoat Moor Rd at King Cross)

⏲ 4-11; 3.30-11 Fri; 12-midnight Sat & Sun

☎ (01422) 350169

Old Mill Traditional Bitter; 4 changing beers (sourced regionally) Ⓗ

Characterful hidden gem in a row of terraces comprising two houses knocked together, adjacent to the Free School Lane recreation ground. The emphasis in this friendly pub is on good beer and conversation. Four rotating guest ales from regional or microbreweries are served alongside the regular beer, plus a large range of gins and malt whiskies. It has a regionally important historic pub interior with a through corridor separating the bar and cosy snug from the games room and the two lounges. A popular quiz night is held on Mondays. Q❀♣●🚌(577)🐾

Halifax: Siddal

Cross Keys

3 Whitegate, HX3 9AE

⏲ 3-11; 12-11 Fri-Sun ☎ (01422) 300348

8 changing beers (sourced regionally; often Half Moon, Mallinsons, Wishbone) Ⓗ

This 17th-century pub has a real traditional feel. The bar area is split into a snug in front of the bar and two rooms divided by an original inglenook fireplace. There is also a separate taproom and a display of old pub signs from the pub. Walkers and cyclists are welcome and two letting rooms are available. Live music is a feature on Sundays. Eight changing ales and European lagers are sold.
Q🐎❀🛏♣●🚌(542,555)🐾ᯤ

Halifax: Town Centre

Alexandra

17 Alexandra Street, HX1 1BS

⏲ 4-9 Mon; 12-10 (11 Thu); 2-11.30 Fri & Sat; 2-10 Sun

☎ 07712 172088

2 changing beers (sourced regionally) Ⓗ

Very much a micropub, set on two levels. The downstairs is decorated with wall-to-wall bottles of beer – all are for sale, the range is extensive, and many are bottle-conditioned. The friendly staff know how to keep their beer and there are always two different cask ales. The Lantern next door is owned by the same people; there you will find a further four cask-conditioned ales. Q⇌🚌🐾

Grayston Unity

1-3 Wesley Court, HX1 1UH

⏲ closed Mon; 4-10 (11 Thu); 12-11.30 Fri & Sat; 1-10 Sun

☎ 07807 136520

Elland Nettlethrasher; Goose Eye Chinook Blonde; 4 changing beers (sourced regionally; often Brew York, Marble, Torrside) Ⓗ

This micropub is opposite Halifax's town hall in a listed Grade II building. There is a café-style seating area in front of the bar, a side room with comfy chairs, and a vestibule leading to an outside seating area. It is officially the UK's smallest music venue and hosts music nights, quizzes and local history talks. Sundays has an Ale of the Day offer. Cutlery is provided if you bring your own food. Open 1-10pm on bank holiday Mondays.
🐎❀⇌♣🚌🐾ᯤ

Pump Room Micropub Ⓛ

33 Northgate, HX1 1UR

⏲ 4-10 Mon & Tue; 12 (2 Wed)-11; 12-10 Sun

☎ 07808 147575

5 changing beers (sourced regionally; often Bingley, Mallinsons, Vocation) Ⓗ

Modern-style bar discreetly situated in a row of shops facing the top of Halifax bus station. The bar is small in size, with additional seating in a similar room below. Despite this, many hundreds of beers have featured since opening, and it has a changing choice from many different breweries including seasonal beers. Occasionally single-brewery ranges feature. Q🐎⇌●🚌🐾ᯤ

Square Chapel Café & Bar

10 Square Road, HX1 1QG

⏲ 12-11 ☎ (01422) 349422 🌐 squarechapel.co.uk

4 changing beers (sourced nationally) Ⓗ

The Café & Bar is in an impressive modern structure which has been recommended for a Design Council award. It is situated between the original Grade II-listed Square Chapel and the historic Piece Hall. It acts as the foyer for the arts centre, where you can enjoy live music, family shows, films, workshops and other exciting events. The long bar sells four real ales along with a cider. It also serves good-value, high-quality seasonal food.
🐎❀◐♿⇌●🚌ᯤ

Victorian Craft Beer Café 🏆

18-22 Powell Street, HX1 1LN

⏲ 11-11; 12-10 Sun 🌐 victorian.beer

8 changing beers Ⓗ

This bar is behind the Victoria Theatre and is an ideal venue for a quick pint before or after a show. The Café is on two levels and there are many atmospheric secluded seating areas lit at night by candlelight. The tiled bar is on the ground floor and offers eight real ales and two ciders, as well as 12 craft beers on tap. An extensive range of bottled Belgian beers is also available.

Harecroft

Station Hotel

122 Lane Side, BD15 0BP (on B6144)

4-midnight; 12-midnight Sun (01535) 272430

Timothy Taylor Landlord; 2 changing beers (often Pennine, Settle)

In the heart of a small village between Bradford and Haworth, this homely community pub is named after a station on the long-gone Great Northern Railway. It comprises two linked rooms with real fires and a games room. A jazz/swing band plays on Monday nights, as does the local pool team. The local bus runs until early evening Monday to Saturday. P(727)

Hartshead

Hartshead

86 Prospect Road, WF15 8AY

5-11; 12-midnight Sat & Sun (01274) 873365

thehartshead.co.uk

3 changing beers (sourced regionally; often Abbeydale, Moorhouse's, Saltaire)

An attractive club in a rural location, founded in 1895. The layout is open plan, featuring a large horseshoe bar, comfortable seating and a small stage regularly used for live music (including resident band Blondhart). Open mic sessions are hosted on Fridays plus a quiz night on Wednesdays, and there is a full-size snooker table. The friendly community club, popular with walkers and ramblers, also serves non-members and has carefully chosen guest beers. There are good views from the small beer garden. The regular beer is currently Scotts 1816. P(229,259)

Haworth

Fleece Inn

67 Main Street, BD22 8DA

11-11 (11.30 Fri & Sat); 11-10.30 Sun (01535) 642172

fleeceinnhaworth.co.uk

Timothy Taylor Golden Best, Boltmaker, Knowle Spring, Landlord, Ram Tam; 1 changing beer (often Timothy Taylor)

Stone-built coaching inn on Haworth's famous cobbled Main Street, with spectacular views over the Worth Valley and close to the KWVR historic heritage railway. A cosy room to the right and a dining area offer quiet alternatives to the busy bar. Locally sourced food and accommodation are available. Cyclists are welcome and there is safe bicycle storage for guests. The beer garden is three storeys up from the bar, on the roof. A Timothy Taylor tied house, popular with tourists and locals alike.

King's Arms

2 Church Street, BD22 8DR

11.30-10 (midnight Fri & Sat) (01535) 645197

kingsarmshaworth.co.uk

House beer (by Bridgehouse); 2 changing beers (sourced nationally; often Bridgehouse)

A 17th-century former manor house at the top of Main Street, the King's sells five Bridgehouse beers renamed after Bronte family members, plus occasional guests. It has an L-shaped bar area and is on two levels, with a separate quieter area to the rear. It is decorated with pale-painted wood panelling, some exposed stonework and timber, with tiled/laminate flooring. On Cask Ale Club Mondays, all cask ales are served at a discount. Other events are Curry Club Tuesdays and Steak Night Thursdays. (B1,B2)

Hebden Bridge

Drink?

15 Market Street, HX7 6EU

closed Mon; 11-9; 11-5 Sun (01422) 844366

2 changing beers (sourced nationally; often Blackjack, Northern Whisper, Sunbeam)

Specialist bottle shop and sampling room with a small bar to the rear and a secluded upstairs lounge. It has minimalist decor but exhibits works by local artists. The two handpumps dispense a range of rotating pale and hoppy beers from northern independent breweries. The knowledgeable owner is from a brewing background. A wide range of bottled beers, some of which are bottle-conditioned, are available to take away or drink on the premises.
Q(590,592)

Fox & Goose

7 Heptonstall Road, HX7 6AZ (at traffic lights on jct of A646 and Heptonstall Rd)

12 (2 Mon)-11; 12-1am Fri & Sat (01422) 648052

foxandgoose.org

Pictish Brewers Gold; 5 changing beers (sourced nationally; often Elland, Salamander, Wishbone)

West Yorkshire's first community co-operative pub has a single bar serving three flagstone-floored rooms. The main bar is warmed by a roaring log fire in winter. The left-hand room is often used for live music, while the room to the right has a dartboard. There is a welcoming inclusive feel and a varied clientele. At least one vegan beer and one dark ale are always available. Do not miss the upstairs hillside beer garden with great views. Quiz night is Monday. Q(590,592)

Old Gate Bar & Restaurant

1-5 Old Gate, HX7 8JP

10-midnight; 10-11 Sun (01422) 843993

oldgatehebden.co.uk

Moorhouse's Pendle Witches Brew; Saltaire Cascade Pale Ale; Vocation Heart & Soul; 6 changing beers (sourced regionally; often Abbeydale, Marble)

Smart, modernised inn and restaurant on two floors with an impressive long copper-topped bar. Ten handpumps dispense the biggest selection of real ales in the town plus one rotating cider. Quality food is served all day. An eclectic mix of furniture and the large picture windows make it an ideal spot for relaxing with a pint and observing the comings and goings of Hebden's diverse and colourful population. At least one dark beer is always on and in summer another cider is added.
Q

Hillhouse

Slubbers Arms

1 Halifax Old Road, HD1 6HW (off A641)

4-11; 3-11 Fri & Sat; 2-11 Sun (01484) 429032

Timothy Taylor Boltmaker, Landlord; 3 changing beers (often Great Heck, Partners, Potbelly)

A former Timothy Taylor hostelry with a heritage of over 150 years. The pub features a lounge with a horseshoe bar, a games room and a quiet room ideal for small private gatherings. Outside is a patio area with seating. Good-value pub food is served on Saturdays and match day lunchtimes. It has a designated mild pump and was voted local CAMRA branch Mild Pub of the Year in 2017. Opens at noon on Saturday match days, when it gets particularly busy. Q

Hipperholme

Travellers Inn

53 Tanhouse Hill, HX3 8HN (off A58)
12-11.30 Mon-Wed; 11-midnight Thu-Sat; 11-11 Sun
(01422) 202434
Ossett Pale Gold, Yorkshire Blonde, Silver King, Excelsior; 4 changing beers (sourced locally; often Fernandes, Rat, Salamander)
Opposite the site of the former railway station, this 18th-century local has taken in adjoining cottages to create a series of distinct spaces. Well-behaved children and dogs on leads are welcome until 7pm. Thursday is quiz night. A covered and heated yard is provided for smokers. A dark brew is always available among the guest ales from Ossett group breweries, along with beers from microbreweries.

Holmfirth

Nook (Rose & Crown)

7 Victoria Square, HD9 2DN (down alley behind Barclays bank)
11.30-midnight (01484) 682373
thenookbrewhouse.co.uk
Nook Baby Blond, Best, Blond, Oat Stout; 3 changing beers (often Nook)
The Nook (properly, the Rose & Crown), dating from 1754, is a well-known real ale pub in the village and has been dispensing beers from its own adjacent brewhouse since 2009. There are occasional guest beers and Pure North ciders. Home-cooked food is served daily. It has well-attended folk evenings every Sunday, and real ale festivals on the weekend before Easter and the August bank holiday. A popular pub for all age groups, the log fire is particularly welcoming on cold winter nights. Under the same management, the next door Tap House also has a restaurant.

Horbury

Cricketers Arms

22 Cluntergate, WF4 5AG (in a right fork off High St at its lower end)
4-11; 12-midnight Fri & Sat; 12-11 Sun (01924) 267032
Bosun's Blonde; Timothy Taylor Landlord; 6 changing beers
On the edge of the town centre, this former Tetley's house is now a genuine free house, and enjoys a frequent bus service to Wakefield, Ossett and Dewsbury. Poker night is Monday, quiz night is Wednesday and open mic night is on the second Sunday of each month. Beer festivals are staged in late May (Yankee Fest) and mid October (Oktoberfest). P

Horbury Bridge

Bingley Arms

221 Bridge Road, WF4 5NL (on A642 by bridge over River Calder, facing viaduct)
12 (4 Mon & Tue)-11; 12-10.30 Sun (01924) 272838
Ossett Silver King; 5 changing beers (sourced regionally)
This pub, built in 1822, is bordered by the River Calder and the Aire & Calder Navigation Canal. It has its own moorings and is named after the Earl of Bingley who funded the building of the canal. Inside, it has two rooms, both with open fires, and is reputed to be haunted. The good-sized beer garden is home to the resident donkey, Nellie. Functions are catered for and there is folk music on Thursday evening. P

Huddersfield

Corner

5 Market Walk, HD1 2QA
11-11 (midnight Fri & Sat); 12-10 Sun
thecornerhudds.co.uk
Mallinsons Wappy Nick; house beer (by Mallinsons Brewing Co); 4 changing beers (sourced nationally; often Mallinsons, Outstanding, Squawk)
With the brewing pedigree of Tara and Elaine at Mallinsons and the award-winning front of house persona of Sam Smith, something special was expected when this Mallinsons tap opened in 2016. Those expectations have been fully realised. Seven cask ales are on offer, two Mallinsons and five rotating guests, always including a dark beer. At least five real ciders and food seven days a week are also available. The light, modern bar is on the first floor, with a function room on the second floor.

Grove

2 Spring Grove Street, HD1 4BP
2-11 (midnight Thu); 12-midnight Fri & Sat; 12-11 Sun
(01484) 430113 thegrove.pub
Marble Pint; Oakham Citra; Saltaire Blonde; Thornbridge Jaipur IPA; 16 changing beers (often Hawkshead, Mallinsons, Northern Monk)
This pub is the antithesis of all that is mass market, with artwork, a snack range and live music that are unusual, to say the least. However, it is the array of 31 beers, lagers and a real cider that set it apart, including a confusion-inducing 19 handpulled ales. Ranging from table beers through IPAs to imperial stouts, there is something for all. In addition there is a superb menu of 200-plus bottled beers and a comprehensive spirits range. The area's must-visit pub. Q

King's Head

St George's Square, HD1 1JF (on left when exiting station)
11.30-11; 12-11 Sun (01484) 511058
Bradfield Farmers Blonde; Magic Rock Ringmaster; Timothy Taylor Golden Best, Landlord; 6 changing beers (sourced regionally; often Abbeydale, Oakham, Pictish)
Situated in the Grade I-listed railway station, the King's Head has been restored with great care, winning a railway heritage award. Features include a beautiful tiled floor, wood panelling and wood-burning stoves. Ten handpumps serve top-quality competitively priced beers from local breweries and from further afield. A mild and a dark beer are always available and there is real cider on

handpump. Live music plays on Sunday afternoons. A Huddersfield institution with a friendly welcome for all.

Rat & Ratchet

40 Chapel Hill, HD1 3EB (on A616, just off ring road; car park at rear)
3-midnight (11 Mon); 12-midnight Fri & Sat; 12-11 Sun
(01484) 542400
Ossett Yorkshire Blonde, Silver King; Rat White Rat, King Rat; 8 changing beers (sourced regionally; often Acorn, Fernandes, Riverhead) H
Multi award-winning pub owned by Ossett but with its own on-site Rat microbrewery. The 12 handpumps offer ales from a range of breweries, always including two dark beers, alongside a good selection of ciders and perries. The large open-plan main area still retains the feel of separate rooms. A further room at the back leads to an outside drinking area. There is a dartboard and a pinball machine. A popular quiz is held on Wednesdays, and live bands perform on occasional Sundays. P

Sportsman ★

1 St John's Road, HD1 5AY
12-11; 11-midnight Fri & Sat (01484) 421929
Timothy Taylor Boltmaker; 7 changing beers (sourced regionally; often Mallinsons) H
This 1930s pub, with a 1950s refit by Hammonds (note the windows), has won a CAMRA English Heritage Conservation Pub Design award. The superb curved bar has eight handpumps including a dedicated Mallinsons beer pump. A dark beer is usually on the bar, along with two ciders, one from Pure North. The central bar has a parquet floor and an interesting wooden entrance. The two rooms off are regularly used by groups such as the poker, poetry and music clubs. Popular Meet the Brewer nights are held on the last Tuesday of the month.

Vulcan

32 St Peters Street, HD1 1RA
9am-1am (2am Fri; 2.30am Sat) (01484) 302040
Theakston Best Bitter; Wainwright; 5 changing beers (sourced nationally; often Bosun's, Bradfield, Marston's) H
Run by the same landlord for over 25 years, this town-centre pub has a local feel and generous opening hours. Six handpumps include guest beers often from local brewers, with Mallinsons and Bosun's featuring regularly. Bargain-priced lunches, popular with shoppers, are served every day, and free food is available on Friday teatimes. There are daily morning happy hours and the pub caters for enthusiasts of pool, karaoke and televised horse racing. Live bands feature every Sunday evening. It can be busy on match days.

Ilkley

Crescent Inn

Brook Street, LS29 8DG (within the Crescent Hotel)
12-11 (midnight Fri & Sat) (01943) 811250
thecrescentinn.co.uk
Goose Eye Bitter; Ilkley Mary Jane; Saltaire Blonde; house beer (by Ghost); 4 changing beers (sourced regionally; often Saltaire) H
Refurbished in 2011, this pub is on the ground floor of a town-centre building that has been a hotel since 1861. The single-room interior is traditionally but comfortably furnished and features original plasterwork and decorations. Eight real ales, comprising four regulars and four guests, are always on offer, usually sourced from local breweries. Bar meals are available until 9.30pm, with meal deals during the week. There are fully accessible disabled facilities but the rear door provides best access.

Flying Duck

16 Church Street, LS29 9DS (on A65)
12-11 (12.30am Thu-Sat) (01943) 609587
wharfedalebrewery.com/the-flying-duck
Wharfedale Black, Blonde, Best; house beer (by Wharfedale); 5 changing beers (sourced regionally; often Dark Horse) H
Originally constructed as a farmhouse in 1709, this is reputed to be Ilkley's oldest pub building. Substantially refurbished and reopened in late 2013, the Grade II-listed pub retains many original features such as York stone, oak flooring, beamed ceilings, internal stonework and mullioned windows. Up to nine real ales and two real ciders are stocked. Wharfedale Brewery is located to the rear and tours can be arranged. The first-floor function room includes a bar.

Keighley

Brown Cow

5 Cross Leeds Street, BD21 2LQ
4-11; 12-10.30 Sun
Timothy Taylor Golden Best, Landlord; 5 changing beers H
The ethos of this award-winning free house is quality, beer choice and customer comfort. A family-run community local, it is children and dog friendly. The interior is adorned with local breweriana and the back room can be booked for private functions and meetings. It offers five guest ales, usually from local micros, typically including a dark beer and one beer at a higher strength. A no-bad-language policy is in force. P

Lord Rodney Bar & Kitchen

Church Street, BD21 5HT
11.30-11 (2am Fri & Sat); 12-10 Sun (01535) 603053
lordrodney.co.uk
Timothy Taylor Golden Best, Boltmaker, Knowle Spring, Landlord; 1 changing beer (often Timothy Taylor) H
On the site of Keighley's oldest pub, the Olde Red Lion, the Lord Rodney is next to the parish church and offers a splendid view along North Street. A Timothy Taylor-managed house, it is a bright and modern town-centre pub. A variety of furniture from tall stools to armchairs surrounds the bar in the long single room, warmed by a real fire. A separate eating area leads to a heated beer garden at the rear. Look out for the seasonal Taylor Made cask and bottle range.

Kirkheaton

Yeaton Cask

4 Town Road, HD5 0HW
4-11 (9 Mon); 12-11 Thu; 12-11.30 Fri & Sat; 12-10.30 Sun
07796 641003
Wainwright; 5 changing beers H
Formerly The Junction, this award-winning free house was bought by the current owner in 2010. Beautiful furniture and flooring with the backdrop of striking exposed stonework give a traditional yet

contemporary feel. Two permanent ales are on the bar as well as the house beer from a secret West Yorkshire microbrewery. Five changing guests are sourced countrywide, always including a dark beer. Food is not served but there is complimentary bar food daily. A highly rated beer festival is held in October. Q≿♣⊟(262)🐾ᯤ

Ledsham

Chequers Inn L

Claypit Lane, LS25 5LP

⏲ 11-11; 12-6 Sun ☎ (01977) 683135

🌐 thechequersinn.com

Leeds Best; Theakston Best Bitter; Timothy Taylor Landlord; house beer (by Brown Cow); 1 changing beer (sourced locally; often Brown Cow, Stod Fold) H

A classic 16th-century country pub popular for its good food and Yorkshire beers, close to the oldest parish church in Yorkshire and handy for Fairburn Ings RSPB reserve. The entrance, past the stepped garden area, is through a stone-flagged yard. A passageway inside opens up at the bar and divides into rooms at either side with low beams and open fires. These in turn each lead to another cosy room complete with local photographs and other memorabilia. Q❀◐▶P⊟(175,405)ᯤ

Leeds: Burley

Cardigan Arms ★

364 Kirkstall Road, LS4 2HQ

⏲ 12-11 (1am Fri & Sat) ☎ (0113) 898 0288

Kirkstall Pale Ale, Three Swords, Dissolution IPA, Black Band Porter; 4 changing beers (sourced regionally; often Kirkstall, Track, Wylam) H

Built in 1896, this is a classic Grade II-listed Victorian pub with four rooms off an L-shaped bar area. Reopened in 2017 as a Kirkstall Brewery pub after a sensitive refurbishment, its fine woodwork, etched glass and ornamented ceilings are now displayed in their full glory. There are future plans to develop the first-floor function room and maybe restore the derelict former Cardigan Arms Brewery which is in the back yard of the pub.
Q◐▶⇌♣⊟🐾ᯤ

Leeds: Chapel Allerton

Regent L ✔

15-17 Regent Street, LS7 4PE

⏲ 12-11 (midnight Thu-Sat) ☎ (0113) 293 9395

Kirkstall Three Swords; Leeds Pale; Tetley Bitter; 5 changing beers (sourced locally; often Elland, Moorhouse's, Ossett) H

Two-roomed stone-built Victorian pub in the heart of Chapel Allerton keeping a traditional village atmosphere. Three permanent and five changing beers usually from Yorkshire or Lancashire are served by an enthusiastic landlord and friendly knowledgeable staff in a pleasant environment. Customers can be assured of a warm welcome. Quiz nights are held Mondays and Thursdays and there are occasional theme nights. TVs show sporting events and food is served until 8.30pm. Dogs are welcome in the public bar.
≿❀◐▶♣P⊟🐾ᯤ

Leeds: City Centre

Duck & Drake L ✔

43 Kirkgate, LS2 7DR

⏲ 10-11 (midnight Fri & Sat); 11-11 Sun ☎ (0113) 245 5432

🌐 duckndrake.co.uk

Brains Bitter; Rooster's Yankee; Saltaire Blonde; Theakston Old Peculier; Timothy Taylor Landlord; 10 changing beers (sourced locally; often Elland, Salamander, York) H

A fine example of a two-roomed Victorian corner pub retaining some original features. Wood-floored throughout, some of the floorboards have survived 200 years of trade. The central bar, with 15 handpumps, sits in between and serves both rooms. There is live music most nights from a small stage in the corner of the front room, which features a mural on the back wall depicting many blues and rock legends and is decorated with various music memorabilia. May close early on nights when a band is not on. ❀⇌●⊟🐾ᯤ

Foleys Tap House L

159 The Headrow, LS1 5RG

⏲ 12-11; 11-1am Fri & Sat; 12-10 Sun ☎ (0113) 242 9674

🌐 mrfoleysleeds.co.uk

York Guzzler, Centurion's Ghost Ale; 10 changing beers (sourced locally; often Abbeydale, Rooster's, York) H

Busy city-centre pub usually with four beers from York Brewery's range plus up to eight guest beers. A wide range of real ciders and perries along with draught and bottled beers from around the world are also available. The building is an impressive edifice built of Portland stone and was previously owned by the Pearl Assurance Company. The interior is on several levels with a variety of seating. The rear room can be hired for functions.
♿⇌●⊟🐾ᯤ

Head of Steam L

13 Mill Hill, LS1 5DQ

⏲ 11-midnight (1am Fri & Sat); 12-11 Sun

☎ (0113) 243 6618 🌐 theheadofsteam.co.uk/pub?pub=14

Camerons Strongarm; 8 changing beers (sourced locally; often Leeds, Northern Monk, Timothy Taylor) H

Single-roomed pub with a high ceiling and a central island bar surrounded by drinking areas with a variety of seating. The walls are decorated with breweriana. On the bar are nine handpumps, serving beers mainly from Yorkshire and the North-East. Complementing this are many international beers on draught and, in the fridges behind the bar, an extensive array of beers in bottles and cans, especially focusing on beers from Belgium and the United States. ⇌●⊟🐾ᯤ

North Bar L

24 New Briggate, LS1 6NU

⏲ 11-2am (1am Mon & Tue); 12-midnight Sun

☎ (0113) 242 4540

5 changing beers (sourced locally; often Kirkstall, Magic Rock, North) H

North Bar has been a pioneer of the Leeds beer scene since 1997. The quality cask ales are supported by a wonderful range of draught and packaged beers from the UK and far beyond. Often a champion of new brewers, North is always moving forward. The staff here are friendly and knowledgeable. This is a narrow bar and seating area, with wood featuring heavily in the design. Two of the five cask ales are permanently from North Brewing and Kirkstall Brewery. Bar food such as pork pies and cheese platters are available.
◐▶⇌●⊟

Reliance

76-78 North Street, LS2 7PN
12-11 (midnight Fri & Sat); 11-10.30 Sun
(0113) 295 6060 the-reliance.co.uk
House beer (by Acorn); 3 changing beers (sourced locally; often Rooster's)
Glass-fronted high-ceilinged corner local with three areas; the rear raised section is usually for diners. The two main drinking areas are bare-boarded, furnished with mix and match furniture and linked by a mini slope. Real ale is the focus, but there are some classic bottled and other imaginative draught beers too. It is not just a modern pub but also a wine shop and charcuterie; food is served most of the time including some of the best bar snacks you could hope for.

Scarbrough Hotel

Bishopgate Street, LS1 5DY
10-midnight (1am Fri & Sat); 10-10.30 Sun
(0113) 243 4590
St Austell Nicholson's Pale Ale; Tetley Bitter; 5 changing beers (sourced regionally; often Adnams, Great Heck, Vocation)
A busy ale house conveniently close to Leeds railway station. The building dates from 1765 and became a pub in 1826. It is named after Henry Scarbrough, the first owner of the pub, though it was then known as the King's Arms. At either end of the long bar are comfortable seating areas. The selection of guest ales is both from local breweries and a wide variety of others around the country.

Tapped Leeds

51 Boar Lane, LS1 5EL
11-11 (midnight Thu; 1am Fri & Sat) (0113) 244 1953
tappedleeds.co.uk
13 changing beers (sourced regionally; often Tapped)
A modern bar consisting of one room with the long bar to the right of the entrance and brewing equipment along the left-hand wall. Tapped Brewing Company real ales are usually brewed at Tapped's sister pub on Sheffield station. Signs above the bar give details of the beers available. There are no handpumps but the lower set of taps on the back wall dispense the real ale. A wide range of other draught, bottled and canned beers is also served.

Templar

2 Templar Street, LS2 7NU
11-11 (midnight Fri & Sat) (0113) 243 0318
Tetley Bitter; 7 changing beers (sourced locally; often Bradfield, Greene King, Kirkstall)
Community local in the city centre. The pub has a fine exterior with green and cream glazed Burmantoft tiles. The bowing courtier logo can be seen in the leaded window panes from the time it was a Melbourne Brewery pub. The interior is adorned with wooden panelling, still with the old service bells in place. There are large-screen TVs throughout showing a range of sporting events. Guest beers range from local ales to ones from further afield.

Town Hall Tavern

17 Westgate, LS1 2RA
11.45-11 (10 Mon); 12-11 Sat; 12-8 Sun
(0113) 244 0765 townhalltavernleeds.co.uk
Timothy Taylor Dark Mild, Golden Best, Boltmaker, Knowle Spring, Landlord, Ram Tam
Timothy Taylor's Champions Club gastropub, comprising a single room with open alcoves to the left and right of the door. A semicircular bar is along the left-hand wall. The left-hand alcove is perhaps best for drinking only, and is complete with circular copper-topped tables and old photographs of Leeds. Dining tends to be to the rear. May close early if quiet, especially on Mondays.

Veritas Ale & Wine Bar

43 Great George Street, LS1 3BB
11-11; 12-7 Sun (0113) 242 8094
Kirkstall Pale Ale; Okell's Manx Pale Ale; Timothy Taylor Boltmaker; 3 changing beers (sourced locally; often Kirkstall, Rooster's)
Part of the Market Town Taverns local chain, with an L-shaped open-plan layout. The pub has an modern, continental café-style design with separate areas and levels. Opposite the bar, the large front windows afford a fine view of George Gilbert Scott's classic Leeds General Infirmary over the road. The guest beers are mainly from local breweries. Other beers from around the world are also sold, both in bottle and on draught.
Q

Wapentake

92 Kirkgate, LS2 7DJ
7.30am-11 (9 Mon); 10-11 Sat; 10-9 Sun
(0113) 243 6248
Sharp's Atlantic; 3 changing beers (sourced locally; often Nomadic, Northern Monk, Sunbeam)
Referring to a parcel of land in northern England, as far as dedication to local produce and community goes, the pub's name could not be more apt. This little bar and bakery has many strings to its bow. It makes its own bread and cakes, serves meals using locally sourced ingredients and, of course, has a good range of real ales and other beers, predominantly from Leeds and Yorkshire. Wapentake is welcoming, with a locally customised piano, a sports TV upstairs and friendly bartenders.

Whitelock's Ale House ★

Turk's Head Yard, LS1 6HB (off Briggate)
11-midnight (1am Fri & Sat); 11-11 Sun
(0113) 245 3950 whitelocksleeds.com
Ilkley Mary Jane; Kirkstall Pale Ale; Theakston Best Bitter, Old Peculier; Timothy Taylor Landlord; 6 changing beers (sourced locally; often Acorn, Great Heck, Saltaire)
Described by John Betjeman as the very heart of Leeds, Whitelock's dates from 1715 and occupies a long, narrow yard. The interior is unchanged from 1895 and is a feast of mirrors, woodwork, stained glass and a fine faience bar. A varied beer selection is offered from local and national breweries. Its sister bar, The Turk's Head, is in the same building just down the yard and offers two real ales on handpump and a number of other draught beers.

Leeds: Headingley

Arcadia Ale House

34 Arndale Centre, Otley Road, LS6 2UE (corner of Alma Rd)
12-11 (0113) 274 5599
Okell's Manx Pale Ale; Timothy Taylor Boltmaker; 6 changing beers (sourced locally; often Elland, Ilkley, Rooster's)

This cleverly converted former bank is now a well-established and multi award-winning pub. The bar has ground-floor rooms plus an upstairs mezzanine level. Unusual modern décor features a chandelier formed of foreign beer crates and a fine mural of Headingley over the bar area. Eight real ales are offered along with a range of canned, bottled and draught foreign and UK beers, plus a rotating cider. Children, large groups and fancy dress are not permitted. Q♿●🚌🐾📶

Leeds: Holbeck

Cross Keys L

107 Water Lane, LS11 5WD

12-11 (midnight Fri & Sat); 12-10.30 Sun

☎ (0113) 243 3711 🌐 the-crosskeys.com

North Prototype; 3 changing beers (sourced locally; often Kirkstall, North, Rooster's) H

Set south of the River Aire in the area known as Holbeck Village, the Cross Keys is part of the North Bar pub group. The ground floor has a food-oriented area to the left and a more traditional drinking area to the right with four handpumps. Upstairs is a function room which is available to hire and has two handpumps. To the rear is a courtyard drinking area. There is also a good selection of both British and international bottled beers. ❀◑♿⇌🚌🐾📶

Grove Inn L

Back Row, LS11 5PL

11-midnight ☎ (0113) 244 2085

🌐 thegroveinnleeds.co.uk

Daleside Blonde; 7 changing beers (sourced regionally; often Acorn, Moorhouse's, Settle) H

Classic West Riding pub which was originally situated at the end of a row of houses but is now hidden away among modern offices. Eight real ales from local and regional breweries are available, with service to both the public bar and corridor. There are two small side rooms and the Concert Room to the rear which hosts a variety of music six nights a week including, every Friday since 1962, reputedly the oldest folk club in the world. ❀◐⇌♣●🚌🐾📶

Midnight Bell L

101 Water Lane, LS11 5QN

11.30-11 (midnight Fri & Sat); 12-11 Sun

☎ (0113) 244 5044 🌐 midnightbell.co.uk

Leeds Pale, Yorkshire Gold, Best, Midnight Bell; 3 changing beers (sourced locally; often Camerons, Rooster's) H

An award-winning pub in the regenerated area to the south of the River Aire known as the Holbeck Urban Village, which caters for office workers, discerning drinkers and diners, who can enjoy the Leeds Brewery range of beers in a relaxed atmosphere. To the rear of the building is a pleasant courtyard area which in warmer weather is served from the bar via a hatch. The upstairs area is more food-oriented. Real cider is added in the summer months. ⛵❀◑♿⇌🚌🐾📶

Leeds: Hyde Park

Brudenell Social Club L

33 Queen's Road, LS6 1NY

12-11 (midnight Fri & Sat) ☎ (0113) 275 2411

🌐 brudenellsocialclub.co.uk

Kirkstall Pale Ale, Three Swords; 3 changing beers (sourced locally; often Ossett, Partners) H

The Brudenell's website states it is a lively and fun-loving venue that embraces music and art under a wide and diverse umbrella that has no boundaries. It is a mainstay of the Leeds music scene, but it is not just about music; facilities include a lounge and games room with snooker and pool tables, darts, table football, pinball machine and TVs showing live sport. It is also a venue for local groups with interests such as photography, films or origami. ❀◑♿⇌♣●P🚌(56)🐾📶

Leeds: Kirkstall

Kirkstall Bridge Inn L

12 Bridge Road, LS5 3BW

12-11.30 (12.30am Fri & Sat) ☎ (0113) 278 4044

🌐 kirkstallbridge.co.uk

Kirkstall Pale Ale, Three Swords, Dissolution IPA, Black Band Porter; 4 changing beers (sourced regionally; often Sunbeam, Thornbridge, Wylam) H

Located on one bank of the River Aire and reopened in 2013 as a Kirkstall Brewery pub, this inn is now a treasure archive, with walls hung with traditional brewery mirrors and advertisements. There is bench seating, wooden upholstered chairs plus wooden tables, all conveying a spirit of tradition. This is a pub firmly rooted in the community, with its annual bonfire and fireworks packing the pub, car park and garden area to the rafters. The August bank holiday Kirkstapalooza is a must-visit locally. ❀◑♣P🚌🐾📶

Leeds: Meanwood

East of Arcadia L ✔

607 Meanwood Road, LS6 4HQ

11.30-11 (midnight Fri & Sat); 12-11 Sun

☎ (0113) 275 5488

Okell's Manx Pale Ale; Timothy Taylor Boltmaker; 6 changing beers (sourced regionally; often Kirkstall, Ridgeside, Thornbridge) H

This modern bar occupies a prominent corner position with Monk Bridge Road, in the heart of Meanwood. The open-plan design, which follows the sweep of tall windows curving around the pub, is on one level but with contrasting areas. Rotating real ales often come from Ridgeside, and bottled, canned and draught foreign and UK beers are also offered. One real cider is normally sold and there is a summer cider festival. Live music takes place on Thursday and Sunday evenings plus a quiz night on Wednesdays. ⛵◑♿●🚌(51,52)🐾📶

Leeds: Newlay

Abbey Inn L

99 Pollard Lane, LS13 1EQ (vehicle access from B6157 only)

12-11 ☎ (0113) 258 1248 🌐 abbeyinn.org

Leeds Pale; Marston's 61 Deep; 6 changing beers (sourced locally; often Kirkstall, Ossett, Revolutions) H

This historic ale house nestles between the River Aire and the canal towpath. A celebrated community pub, the Abbey showcases a selection of predominantly local ales, with pumps dedicated to dark ale and real cider. It bustles with friendly locals throughout the week, and has folk night on Tuesday, a music quiz on Wednesday, live music on Saturday and quizzes Thursday and Sunday. Ample seating outside attracts dog walkers and cyclists, and large annual events, including a beer and music festival, draw a crowd. P

Linthwaite

Sair

139 Lane Top, HD7 5SG (top of Hoyle Ing, off A62)
3-11; 12-11 Fri & Sat; 12-10.30 Sun (01484) 842370
Linfit Bitter, Gold Medal, Special, Swift, Autumn Gold, Old Eli H
A traditional multi-roomed stone building with a central bar and real fires. High on the edge of the Colne Valley, The Sair has been home to Linfit Brewery since 1982. The beer range is the ultimate in LocAle, with up to 10 beers unique to the pub, including three dark brews, and real cider from Pure North. It is a popular community venue providing a welcome for all – locals, visitors, walkers and their dogs alike. A former CAMRA National Pub of the Year. **Q**

Liversedge

Black Bull

37 Halifax Road, WF15 6JR (on A649, close to A62)
12-midnight (1am Fri & Sat) (01924) 403779
Ossett Pale Gold, Yorkshire Blonde, Big Red Bitter, Silver King, Excelsior; 4 changing beers (sourced nationally) H
Ossett Brewery's first pub. The five rooms each have unique, skilfully honed styles, including one dubbed the Chapel which has a high ceiling and reminders of local industrial heritage. A covered area by the stream outside adds to the choices. Nine handpumps always include a mild or dark ale, plus good guest beers from the group and from wide-ranging independents. The Black Bull is a popular, sociable community local with a warm welcome. Quiz night is Tuesday. **P**

Longwood

Dusty Miller Inn

2 Gilead Road, Longwood, HD3 4XH
5-11; 4-midnight Fri; 12-midnight Sat; 12-11 Sun
07946 589645 dustymillerlongwood.com
Milltown Platinum Blonde, Black Jack Porter, Weaver's Bitter; Timothy Taylor Landlord; 3 changing beers (often Elland, Newby Wyke, Phoenix) H
This pub is operated by local brewery Milltown as its first brewery tap. The cosy open plan interior has three distinct areas. Local historic photographs adorn the walls and stone floors dominate. From its outside benches there are great views up the Colne Valley. It is dog friendly and a haven for walkers. Seven real ales are served showcasing the Milltown brews, while three changing guests and a dark beer are always on offer. Snacks are locally made pies with chutney. **Q** (356)

Marsden

Riverhead Brewery Tap

Peel Street, HD7 6BR
12-midnight (01484) 844324
theriverheadmarsden.co.uk
Ossett Yorkshire Blonde, Silver King; Riverhead Butterley Bitter, March Haigh, Redbrook Premium; 5 changing beers H
A brewpub since 1995, now owned by Ossett Brewery and welcoming to all. The brewery is visible from the bar – beers do not get more LocAle than this. Ten ales are dispensed, four from the on-site brewery, two from Ossett, plus guests. A dark beer is almost always available and occasionally a real cider. A popular stop on the Real Ale Rail Trail, Saturdays are extremely busy. There is a riverside terrace for alfresco drinking and an upstairs bar with comfy seating. **P** (185)

Mirfield

Flowerpot

65 Calder Road, WF14 8NN (over river, 400yds S of railway station)
12-12.30am (1.30am Fri & Sat); 12-midnight Sun
(01924) 496939
Ossett Yorkshire Blonde, Big Red Bitter, Silver King, Excelsior; 4 changing beers (often Acorn, Marston's, Riverhead) H
An 1807 pub with a typically sensitive, tasteful restoration by Ossett Brewery, having an impressive tiled flowerpot as the centrepiece. There are real fires in each of the four inviting rooms. The riverside terrace is popular in good weather. Eight ales are offered from Ossett, Rat, Riverhead, Fernandes and independents, including a mild or stout, plus a rotating cider. Local farm shop Haigh's supplies five different pies with peas, served until 4pm Monday to Saturday. There is a Tuesday quiz. **Q P** (262)

Navigation Tavern

6 Station Road, WF14 8NL (next to Mirfield railway station)
11.30-11; 12-11 Sun (01924) 492476
Caledonian Deuchars IPA; John Smith's Bitter; Theakston Black Bull Bitter, Lightfoot, XB, Old Peculier; 3 changing beers (sourced nationally) H
A canalside free house with the same host for 20 years, serving eight or more beers, including five from Theakston plus up to four guests at weekends, all at keen prices. The pub features on the Transpennine Rail Ale Trail and holds occasional renowned beer festivals. It hosts Saturday night entertainment and active sports and pool teams. A large function room and en-suite B&B with stairlift are available, and winter comfort is aided by a large wood-burning fire. **P**

Old Colonial

Dunbottle Lane, WF14 9JJ (off A644 up Church Lane, 1 mile NE of station)
12-2 (not Mon-Wed), 5-11; 12-midnight Sat; 12-11 Sun
(01924) 496920 theoldcolonial.webplus.net
4 changing beers (sourced regionally; often JW Lees, Recoil) H
Former club with fascinating colonial memorabilia offering a cosy retreat with sofas around the fire. There is a Royal British Legion memorial in the prize-winning garden and local charities are well supported. The spacious conservatory is popular for functions and meetings. Three to five guests, including a dark ale from the likes of Thwaites, Lees, Marston's and small brewers, are on the bar. Meals are served Thursday to Saturday, plus an excellent-value traditional roast Sunday lunchtime. **P** (202,205)

Morley

Oscar's Bar

2A Queen Street, LS27 9DG

5-11; 2-11 Sat; 2-10.30 Sun
2 changing beers (sourced locally; often Nomadic) H
On the corner of Queen Street and Brunswick Street, this is a small, friendly bar, also home to the Frisky Bear Brewery, and named after a previous owner's cat. Two handpumps supply beers from mainly Yorkshire breweries. More draught beers plus bottles, cans and an array of gins are also available. The single wooden-floored room has seating for up to 17 people, with two high and two low tables, plus stools along the window.

Mytholmroyd

Dusty Miller

Burnley Road, HX7 5LH
12-11 (01422) 885959 dustymillerinn.co.uk
Elland Nettlethrasher; Goose Eye Chinook Blonde; 3 changing beers (sourced regionally; often Elland, Howard Town, Marston's) H
Built in 1760, this former coaching inn has a rich history, mainly associated with the Cragg Vale Coiners who reputedly held regular meetings here. The Grade II-listed building, originally a farmhouse, with an adjoining barn, is open as a drinking venue seven days a week. The entrance to the pub, from the main Burnley Road, leads to the stone-flagged bar area, with a comfortable lounge alongside.
Q P

Norristhorpe

Rising Sun

254 Norristhorpe Lane, WF15 7AN (almost ½ mile off A62)
12-11.30 (12.30am Fri & Sat) (01924) 400190
norristhorperisingsun.co.uk
Acorn Barnsley Bitter; Saltaire Blonde; 5 changing beers (sourced locally; often Bradfield, Partners, Timothy Taylor) H
The village local, under family ownership, is tastefully decorated, featuring a light and spacious bar and cosy lounge areas with exposed brickwork and real fires. The beer range is mainly from Yorkshire but with guests from local and national sources. Every Tuesday there is a popular quiz with prizes; also occasional live music. There is a large, well-maintained beer garden with plenty of seating and extensive views over the valley towards Mirfield and Emley Moor. P

Ossett

Old Vic

47 Manor Road, WF5 0AU (Manor Rd is a left turn from B6128 at S end of Ossett, or a right turn from The Green near Ossett School)
4-11; 12-midnight Fri & Sat; 12-11 Sun (01924) 273516
Fuller's London Pride; Ossett Pale Gold, Yorkshire Blonde, Silver King, Excelsior; 2 changing beers (often Abbeydale) H
Friendly local pub, previously known as the Victoria, a 10-minute walk from Ossett town centre. Fresh home-cooked food is served. Two varying guest beers and an alternating stout or porter complement the regular well-kept beers. Taken over a couple of years ago by Ossett Brewery, this pub has undergone a renaissance. It holds a beer festival in November featuring beers from every brewery in the local CAMRA branch area. P

Tap

2 The Green, WF5 8JS (from town centre turn left on to Queen St, which becomes The Green)
12-3 (midnight Thu-Sun) (01924) 272215
Ossett Pale Gold, Yorkshire Blonde, Big Red Bitter, Silver King, Excelsior; 3 changing beers H
Formerly known as the Mason's Arms, the pub was bought by Ossett Brewery and is now its brewery tap. Alongside three regular beers from Ossett, there is usually a special or seasonal from the Ossett group, a regular Fuller's beer and four guest ales. A real wood fire and stone-flagged floors give the pub an old-fashioned feel. Closing times are those permitted by the pub's licence.
Q P

Otley

Junction Inn

44 Bondgate, LS21 1AD
11-11 (11.30 Thu; midnight Fri & Sat); 12-11 Sun
(01943) 463233
Hambleton Stud Blonde; Robinsons Dizzy Blonde; Theakston Best Bitter, Old Peculier; Timothy Taylor Boltmaker, Landlord; 5 changing beers (sourced regionally; often Acorn, Adnams, Saltaire) H
A solid-looking stone-built pub on a prominent street corner site on the approach from Leeds. To the front, roadside tables allow for outdoor drinking. Eleven real ales are stocked, along with a real cider and a wide range of malt whiskies. There is a central fireplace, and comfortable fixed seating runs around the walls. A collection of farming implements hangs from the ceiling and on the walls are pictures of old Otley and enamel brewery signs.

Old Cock

11-13 Crossgate, LS21 1AA
11-11 (01943) 464424 theoldcockotley.co.uk
Ilkley Mary Jane; Theakston Best Bitter; Timothy Taylor Landlord; 6 changing beers (sourced locally; often Bradfield, Briscoe's, Great Heck) H
This genuine free house has already won multiple local CAMRA awards. It was painstakingly converted from a former café to create a pub that feels like it has been there many years. There are two low-ceilinged rooms downstairs with stone-flagged floors, and a further room upstairs. The guest ales are mostly from local breweries. At least two real ciders are also sold, plus a range of foreign beers. Frequent beer festivals are held. No admittance to under-18s. Q

Pontefract

Carleton

Hardwick Road, WF8 3PQ (on A639 1 mile S of town centre)
11-11 (midnight Fri & Sat) (01977) 703797
Greene King IPA; house beer (by Greene King); 8 changing beers H
A popular estate pub that now offers 10 well-kept cask ales not just from the Greene King stable, although the house beer is brewed by Greene King to the landlady's recipe. Plenty of outdoor seating is available round the side and to the rear. It gets busy at weekends, with the locals enjoying sport on the many TV screens. Beer festivals and Meet the Brewer evenings are held on occasion.
P

Pudsey

Fleece

100 Fartown, LS28 8LU
12-11 (0113) 236 2748 fleecepudsey.co.uk
Tetley Bitter; Timothy Taylor Golden Best, Landlord; 2 changing beers (sourced locally; often Elland, Ossett, Pennine)
A multi award-winning venue, this pub has built a reputation for exceptionally well-kept ales, among the best in Leeds. Here you are assured of a warm welcome in a friendly environment. A comfortable, traditional pub with community at its heart, it is decorated with film and music memorabilia from a golden era. Quizzes and games feature regularly. The pleasant outdoor space is ideal for the pub's annual summer beer festival. One of the two guest ales will be a pale beer. P

Rishworth

Booth Wood Inn

Oldham Road, HX6 4QU (on A672 towards jct 22 of M62) SE034170
12-10 (11 Fri & Sat) (01422) 825600
boothwoodinn.co.uk
Joseph Holt Bitter; 4 changing beers (sourced locally; often Bradfield, Pennine, Salopian)
A traditional family country pub and restaurant close to the scenic Yorkshire Moors, on the A672. It is open plan with a large central bar and two restaurant areas featuring beams and stone-flagged floors. Food is home-made and freshly prepared each day, with frequently-changing daily specials in addition to the main menu. There is always a good selection of carefully sourced real ales. P(560)

Roberttown

New Inn

Roberttown Lane, WF15 7NP
3-11.45 (10.30 Mon; 11 Tue); 12-11.45 Fri & Sat; 12-10.30 Sun (01924) 402069 thenewinnroberttown.com
Abbeydale Moonshine; Leeds Best; house beer (by Mallinsons); 3 changing beers (sourced nationally; often New Inn)
A traditional village local, popular with all ages. It is the brewery tap for the New Inn brewery, with one of the family's beers always on. There is a snug with comfy chairs, and a function room available for hire. The Wednesday quiz is popular, along with the occasional Sunday race day. An annual beer festival is now well established, featuring rare beers. Guest ales are from local and national sources. P(229,253)

Saltaire

Cap & Collar

4 Queens Road, BD18 4SJ
closed Mon; 5-10 Tue-Thu; 4-11 Fri; 1-11 Sat; 1-6 Sun
4 changing beers (sourced regionally; often Northern Monk, Saltaire, Wishbone)
Popular micropub with an open-plan café-style layout accommodating up to 35 customers. A beer garden and smoking area are at the rear. Four handpulls deliver a wide range of beers, many regional. Real cider is served on draught and there is a good selection of bottle-conditioned ales. Meet the Brewer and tap takeover events are held regularly and a homebrew club also meets here. Live music can be heard on Sunday afternoons and occasional evenings. Pub snacks are served.
Q

Fanny's Ale & Cider House

63 Saltaire Road, BD18 3JN (on A657)
12 (5 Mon)-11; 12-midnight Fri & Sat (01274) 591419
Timothy Taylor Golden Best, Landlord; 6 changing beers (sourced regionally; often Bingley, Bridgehouse, Naylor's)
Near the UNESCO World Heritage Site of Saltaire village and the historic Salts Mill, this cosy pub is popular with residents and visitors alike. Extensions into adjacent buildings have increased seating capacity downstairs and added wheelchair access, although there are stairs and narrow passageways within. A comfortable seating area is located upstairs. Two regular ales, up to six guests and real ciders are offered. The gas-lit lounge is adorned with breweriana and real fires add nicely to the welcome.

Hop

199 Bingley Road, BD18 4DH
12-midnight (01274) 582111 thehopsaltaire.co.uk
Ossett Yorkshire Blonde, Big Red Bitter, Silver King, Excelsior; 4 changing beers (sourced regionally; often Black Sheep, Rat)
This place is next to the main A650 road and built within an old tram depot, originally constructed in 1904. The premises are part of Ossett Brewery and feature a large open-plan main room with a horseshoe bar and an upper mezzanine dining area. The large outdoor seating area is popular in good weather. Excellent food from snacks to full restaurant meals are served; wood-fired pizzas are prepared in view of the main bar area. Local CAMRA Pub of the Year 2016. P

Sandal

Star

Standbridge Lane, WF2 7DY (near Asda on A6186 which links A61 and A636)
12-midnight (01924) 255254
6 changing beers (sourced regionally; often Morton Collins)
A cosy inn dating from 1821 with a streamside beer garden. It was recently leased from Enterprise Inns by the Morton Collins Brewery and the brewery itself has recently moved to the pub. It serves one or two of its own beers plus four or five guest ales mainly from local breweries. It is a welcoming, relaxed and dog-friendly pub with an open-plan layout and open fires in winter.
QP(110)

Sandbeds

Airedale Heifer

Bradford Road, BD20 5LY
11.30-11 (01274) 515870 theairedaleheifer.co.uk
Bridgehouse Blonde, Aired Ale, Porter, Holy Cow; 2 changing beers (often Bridgehouse)
An extensive roadside pub with a substantial food presence, many dishes featuring the brewery's beers. It is the tap for Bridgehouse Brewery situated in the car park behind. The pub is named after a famous cow of the early 1800s, the heaviest in the UK (see the statue at the front). The open-plan layout has a single L-shaped bar and there is a sizeable south-facing garden with patio heaters.

Children are welcome until 8pm, later if dining. Brewery tours can be arranged.
❀◐♿P🚌(662)🐾📶

Shipley

Fox Ⓛ

41 Briggate, BD17 7BP
⏲ 10.30-11 (midnight Fri & Sat); 12-10.30 Sun
☎ (01274) 594826 🌐 thefoxshipley.co.uk
BEEspoke Plan Bee, Shipley Stout; 4 changing beers (sourced regionally; often Great Heck, Small World) Ⓗ
An independent, single-roomed café-style bar, simply but smartly furnished featuring recycled church pews. Small but friendly and welcoming, it serves six handpulled ales, including one from the in-house BEEspoke microbrewery. Real ciders, often including one from a local producer, are sold, as is a wide range of international bottled beers. It is handy when waiting for trains at the nearby station as the times are displayed on a monitor. Live music plays every Tuesday and Wednesday evening, and often on a Saturday night.
❀◐♿≠●🚌🐾📶

Silsden

Counting House Ⓛ

23 Kirkgate, BD20 0AJ
⏲ closed Mon & Tue; 3-10.30 Wed; 3-11 Thu; 11-11 Fri & Sat; 11-10.30 Sun ☎ (01274) 405644
Dark Horse Hetton Pale Ale; 3 changing beers (sourced regionally; often Bingley, Saltaire) Ⓗ
Silsden's latest drinking venue opened in 2016 in part of an old bank. A brightly decorated café bar with a welcoming atmosphere, it has exposed brickwork, feature light fittings and multiple clocks and mirrors. The L-shaped drinking/dining area has plenty of small tables and small standing areas at the bar and by the door. The three guest beers change weekly and are usually from local suppliers. A small but varied menu of fresh, home-cooked food is served all day. ◐🚌(62,903)🐾📶

King's Arms Ⓛ ✔

Bolton Road, BD20 0JY
⏲ 12-midnight (11 Mon) ☎ (01535) 653216
Black Sheep Best Bitter; Saltaire Blonde; 5 changing beers (sourced nationally; often Rudgate, Wishbone) Ⓗ
Award-winning bustling community pub, run by the same couple since December 2003, with music nights (Tue and Thu), quiz nights (Wed), and a pool table combining to make it a great place to visit. Partitions divide the main bar into three distinct areas, each with its own feel. Westons cider and four to six guest beers from near and far (usually including a darker beer) provide something for all tastes. Regular buses between Keighley and Ilkley stop close by. ❀♣●P🚌(62,903)🐾📶

Sowerby Bridge

Firehouse Ⓛ

1 Town Hall Street, HX6 2QD
⏲ closed Mon; 4.45-11 (11.45 Fri); 12-11.45 Sat; 12-10.30 Sun ☎ (01422) 832586 🌐 firehousesowerbybridge.co.uk
Moorhouse's Pride of Pendle; Vocation Heart & Soul; 3 changing beers (sourced regionally; often Dark Star, Hawkshead, Saltaire) Ⓗ
Close to the bridge crossing the River Calder in the centre of Sowerby Bridge, this prominent building, dating from 1874, is a popular venue for those who like to eat out with the option of a traditional pint. The family-run outlet has built a reputation for food and real ale, in particular pizza cooked in an open oven, and for its tapas menu. Three guest beers are served, with at least one from a local or regional brewer. ◐♿≠●🚌(560,579)📶

Hog's Head Brew House & Bar Ⓛ

1 Stanley Street, HX6 2AH
⏲ 3-11; 12-midnight Fri & Sat; 12-11 Sun ☎ (01422) 836585
🌐 hogsheadbrewhouse.co.uk
Hogs Head 6 To 8 Weeks, White Hog, Hoppy Valley, Old Schnozzler; 3 changing beers (often Phoenix, Salopian, Vocation) Ⓗ
Close to the centre of Sowerby Bridge, the venue is in an 18th-century former malthouse which has been extensively renovated. The brewery is at the back of the building and can be viewed from the bar area. Five core Hogs Head beers are available as well as guest ales. There is plenty of seating in the huge, sprawling bar area where snacks are also served. Q♿≠🚌🐾📶

Jubilee Refreshment Rooms Ⓛ

Station Road, HX6 3AB (on railway station)
⏲ 9.30am-10; 9am-10 Sat; 12-9 Sun ☎ (01422) 648285
🌐 jubileerefreshmentrooms.co.uk
3 changing beers (often Bingley, Goose Eye, Mallinsons Brewing Co) Ⓗ
Located in the only surviving part of the 1876 station building, the bar serves three changing local beers and offers a pleasant place to while away the time. Refreshments are available from the morning hours, alcohol is served from noon onwards, and hot food noon-1.30pm. The walls are adorned with interesting railway and brewery-related memorabilia, and events and talks take place frequently. Trains depart regularly for Leeds and Manchester. Q❀♿≠P🐾📶

Shepherd's Rest ✔

125 Bolton Brow, HX6 2BD (on A58 towards Halifax)
⏲ 3-11; 12-11.30 Fri & Sat; 12-11 Sun ☎ (01422) 831937
Ossett Pale Gold, Yorkshire Blonde, Silver King; Rat White Rat; 4 changing beers (often Phoenix) Ⓗ
Built in 1877 and halfway up Bolton Brow out of Sowerby Bridge, this friendly local was purchased by Ossett Brewery in 2005. From the entrance steps a triangular area leads to the bar, which faces a cosy lounge with a large brick-arched fireplace. To the left is a comfortable seating area with flagged floor, leading to an enclosed outside area. A selection of pork pies is always available. Monday is dominoes league night, while Tuesday is quiz night, with free supper for entrants.
Q❀≠♣🚌🐾📶

Stanbury

Wuthering Heights Inn Ⓛ ✔

Main Street, BD22 0HB (in village centre)
⏲ 12-11 ☎ (01535) 643332 🌐 thewutheringheights.co.uk
Moorhouse's Blond Witch; Theakston Best Bitter; 2 changing beers (sourced regionally; often Abbeydale, Bingley, Bradfield) Ⓗ
A popular, friendly local dating from 1763. Warmed by logburners, the traditional main bar has photographs showing the history of the village and provides an internet terminal for customers' use. The cosy dining room has a Bronte theme. A third room hosts regular folk music gatherings and can be booked for parties and meetings. The rear

garden has spectacular views down the Worth Valley and there is a separate camping area (no caravans). Well-behaved dogs and children are welcome. There is a quiz every Thursday.

Stanley

Graziers Inn

116 Aberford Road, WF3 4NN (on A642 at bottom of hill after hospitals, near jct with road to Stanley Ferry)
12-midnight; 12-11 Sun ☎ (01924) 200283
Abbeydale Moonshine, John Smith's Bitter; 2 changing beers (sourced regionally; often Black Sheep, Theakston) H
The pub dates from 1890 and is a deserved entry in the Guide, having consistently served high-quality beers for a number of years. Traditional and welcoming, the pub boasts numerous rooms separated from a central bar. Copper-topped tables and a real fire in winter add to the atmosphere. There are many pictures of old Stanley adorning the walls. **QP**

Thackley

Black Rat

530 Leeds Road, BD10 8JH
4-9; 3-10 Fri & Sat; 2-9 Sun ☎ 07920 061671
4 changing beers (sourced regionally; often Bingley, Eyes, Small World) H
Previously a florist's shop, this micropub (with capacity for aroud just 15 people) opened in 2016. A friendly welcome is assured and there is a cosy atmosphere. As there is no music, TV or games machines, conversation and banter are key. The pub offers a varying selection of four real ales, primarily from Yorkshire breweries. Also offered are two craft keg ciders, four boxed ciders and two craft lagers, along with a range of artisanal gins. **Q**

Todmorden

Pub

3 Brook Street, OL14 5AJ
12-9 (10 Fri & Sat) ☎ (01706) 812145
4 changing beers (sourced locally; often Eagles Crag) H
Todmorden's first micropub opened June 2017 in a former café close to the market. The décor – exposed stone walls, reclaimed wood bar – enhances the simple layout, making the most of the limited space, with 20 seats downstairs, and a further 12 up a flight of steep stone steps also accessing the toilets. Six handpumps serve a changing range of five beers and one cider. Full tasting notes are on a chalkboard by the stairs. Over 30 UK-distilled gins are stocked.
Q(590,592)

Upper Denby

George Inn

114 Denby Lane, HD8 8UE
5-10.30; 12-11.30 Fri & Sat; 11.30-10.30 Sun
☎ (01484) 861347 thegeorgeinn-upperdenby.co.uk
Tetley Bitter; Timothy Taylor Landlord; 1 changing beer (often Acorn, Empire, Small World) H
A family-run village local going from strength to strength since becoming a free house in late 2012, and a former winner of local CAMRA Rural Pub of the Year. The hostelry hosts regular pie and pea walks, with a reward of home-made food at the end. Other entertainment includes jazz on a Thursday and folk on the first and third Mondays, as well as occasional traditional singarounds. Walkers and dogs are welcome, and families until 8.30pm.
QP

Wakefield

Black Rock

19 Cross Square, WF1 1PQ (between Bull Ring and top of Westgate)
11-11 (midnight Sat); 12-10.30 Sun ☎ (01924) 375550
Oakham Citra; Tetley Bitter; 4 changing beers (sourced regionally) H
A small frontage with an arched, tiled façade leads into this compact city-centre local with a warm welcome and comfy interior including photographs of old Wakefield. The Rock stands as one of the few proper pubs left in the middle of the clubs and bars of Westgate and is popular with drinkers of all ages looking for a real pint. Customers are encouraged to suggest beers, with four regularly changing guest ales on offer. There is a free function room for private use. **Q**

Fernandes Brewery Tap & Bier Keller

5 Avison Yard, Kirkgate, WF1 1UA (turn right approx 100yds S of George St/Kirkgate jct near Scartop Pine)
4-11 (11.30 Thu); 12-12.30am Fri & Sat; 12-11 Sun
☎ (01924) 386348
10 changing beers (sourced regionally; often Fernandes, Ossett) H
Owned by Ossett Brewery, the Fernandes Brewery operates in the cellar. It has 11 handpulls with two dedicated to dark beers. There are four Fernandes beers, two Ossett, one from the Marston's group and three guest beers, plus draught cider. The Bier Keller opens 6-midnight Friday and Saturday and has premier foreign beers on draught plus an Ossett beer and a cider on handpump. A quiz takes place on Wednesday evening, folk music on the first and open mic on the third Sunday of each month. **Q**

Harry's Bar

107B Westgate, WF1 1EL (turn right from Westgate station, cross road at traffic lights and pub is at back of car park on right)
5-midnight; 4-1am Fri & Sat; 12-midnight Sun
☎ (01924) 373773
House beer (by Five Towns); 7 changing beers (often North Riding) H
A small, one-roomed pub set in an alleyway just off Westgate. A real fire and a bare-brick and wood interior plus vintage sporting pictures enhance this small, cosy venue. It enjoys a fantastic view of Wakefield's famous 99-arch viaduct – if only steam trains were a regular feature. There is also a selection of bottled Belgian beers to add to the temptation. **QP**

Hop

19 Bank Street, WF1 1EH (in cobbled street off Westgate almost opp Theatre Royal)
4-11 (midnight Thu); 12-2.30am Fri & Sat; 12-10.30 Sun
☎ (01924) 367111 thehopwakefield.com
Ossett Yorkshire Blonde, Big Red Bitter, Silver King, Excelsior; Rat White Rat; 4 changing beers H

Converted into a venue for music and conversation, this Georgian building retains bare-brick walls, fireplaces and other original features along with an extension which includes an open fire. The main bar has nine handpumps, one reserved for a dark beer, as well as a selection of bottled Belgian and American beers. Open mic night is on Monday, a quiz on Tuesday and live music on Thursday, Friday and Saturday. Kebabs are served on Friday and Saturday nights. Rooms are available for hire (midweek only). ❀♿⇌●🚌

Wakefield Beer Exchange L

14 Bull Ring, WF1 1HA (at top of Westgate; bar is almost on jct with Wood St)

11-11 (midnight Fri & Sat) ☎ (01924) 339913

wakefieldbeerexchange.com

6 changing beers (sourced locally; often Revolutions) H

In a short time the pub has become one of the most popular in Wakefield. It has bare boards and minimalist furnishings, with paintings from local artists adorning the walls. A friendly welcome is assured for all, with cask beer drinkers getting a choice of straight or dimple glasses. Frequent Meet the Brewer nights take place, Hang the DJ (last Wednesday of the month) and a monthly quiz. Pie and peas with a pint of Revolutions beer is available at all times. ♿⇌♣●🚌🐾

Wakefield Labour Club L

18 Vicarage Street, WF1 1QX (at top of Kirkgate, round corner from Wakey Tavern)

7-11 (midnight Fri); 11-midnight Sat; 7-midnight Sun

☎ (01924) 215626 theredshed.org.uk

5 changing beers (sourced regionally) H

The Red Shed is a secondhand army hut that has been extensively refurbished, and is home to many union, community and charity groups. It holds a quiz night on Wednesday, occasional live music on the second Saturday and an open mic folk music night on the last Saturday of each month. There are three rooms, two of which can be hired for functions. An extensive collection of union plates and badges is displayed over the bar and numerous CAMRA awards adorn the walls.

Q♿⇌(Kirkgate/Westgate)♣P🚌🐾

Wetherby

Mews Ale & Wine Bar ✔

16 Bank Street, LS22 6NQ

12-11; 12-10 Sun ☎ (01937) 580201

Ilkley Mary Jane; Okell's Bitter; Timothy Taylor Landlord; 3 changing beers (sourced regionally; often Brass Castle, Kirkstall, Rooster's) H

Tucked away down Bank Street, Mews is part of the Market Town Taverns pub group. It serves a good selection of regional and local ales and has a reputation for good-quality food. Along with the six handpumps on the bar are a good range of draught and bottled beers plus a selection of gins. Wood-floored with a variety of seating inside, it has a paved outdoor drinking area to the side with plenty of tables and chairs. ❀♿P🚌🐾

Wibsey

Hooper Micropub L

209 High Street, BD6 1JU

closed Mon; 4.30-10.30; 4-11.30 Fri; 2-11.30 Sat; 2-9 Sun

thehoopermicropub.co.uk

5 changing beers (sourced regionally; often Bingley, Bridgehouse, Mallinsons) H

Opened on Christmas Eve 2015, this cosy, friendly, split-level micropub has quickly established itself with local people in this urban village. The bar is on the upper level and there is comfortable seating in the lower part. The five handpulls offer a varying selection of beers that are primarily from the Yorkshire region but with the occasional beer from further afield. Photographs of old Wibsey provide interest in an otherwise minimalist décor.

Q♣🚌🐾

Red Rooster, Brighouse (Photo: Bob Steel)

CAMRA's Wild Pub Walks

Daniel Neilson

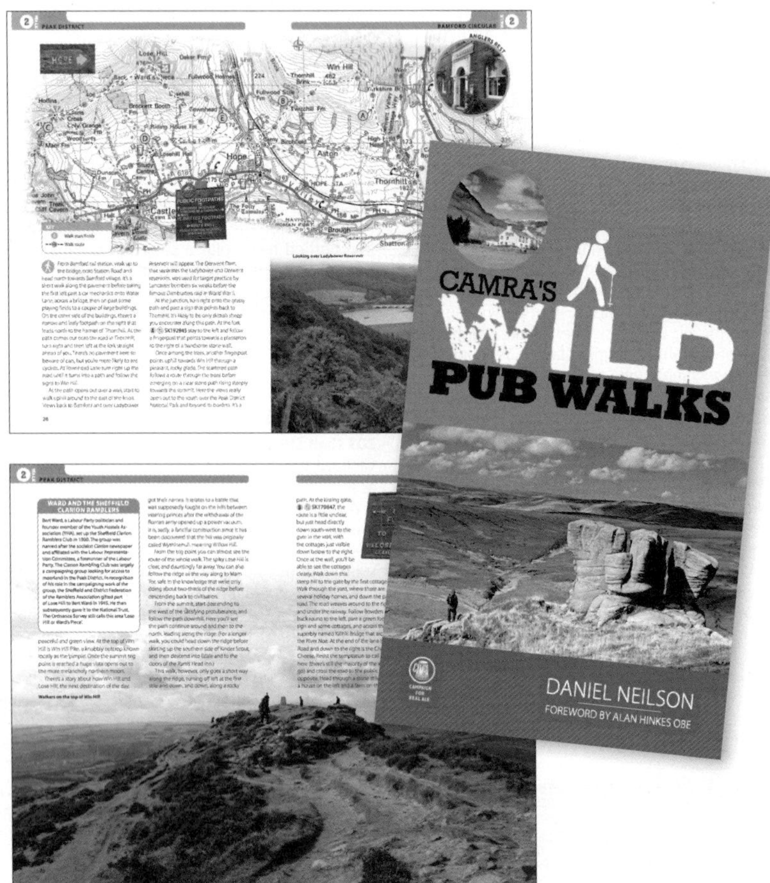

CAMRA's *Wild Pub Walks* brings you some of the most beautiful walks among the hills and mountains of the British Isles, each with one or more great pubs at journey's end. The book is aimed at the large market of hill walkers who enjoy long days out followed by some refreshing beer in a welcoming pub. The areas covered are: England – the Peak District, Lake District, Yorkshire Dales and North York Moors; Scotland – the Highlands and Borders; Wales – Snowdonia, the Brecon Beacons and Mid Wales. The walks vary in the level of challenge, from long walks in lower-lying areas to Grade 1 scrambles.

RRP £11.99 **ISBN** 978-1-85249-340-0 **192 pages**

For this and other books on beer and pubs visit CAMRA's online bookshop at **www.camra.org.uk/books** or call **01727 867201**. Discounts are available for CAMRA members.

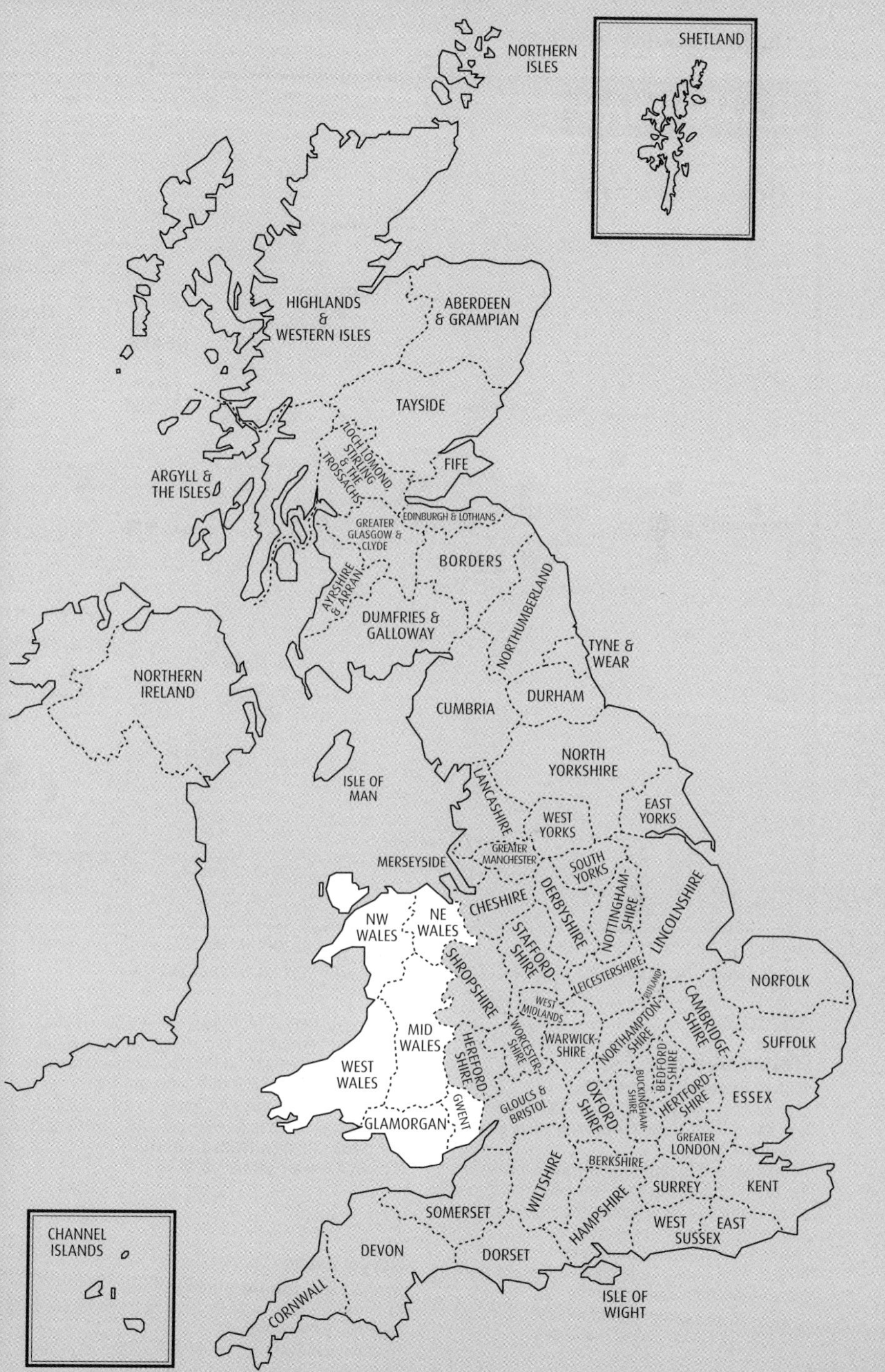

NORTHERN ISLES
SHETLAND
HIGHLANDS & WESTERN ISLES
ABERDEEN & GRAMPIAN
TAYSIDE
LOCH LOMOND, STIRLING & THE TROSSACHS
FIFE
ARGYLL & THE ISLES
EDINBURGH & LOTHIANS
GREATER GLASGOW & CLYDE
BORDERS
AYRSHIRE & ARRAN
DUMFRIES & GALLOWAY
NORTHUMBERLAND
TYNE & WEAR
NORTHERN IRELAND
DURHAM
CUMBRIA
NORTH YORKSHIRE
ISLE OF MAN
LANCASHIRE
WEST YORKS
EAST YORKS
GREATER MANCHESTER
MERSEYSIDE
SOUTH YORKS
CHESHIRE
DERBYSHIRE
NOTTINGHAM-SHIRE
LINCOLNSHIRE
NW WALES
NE WALES
STAFFORD SHIRE
SHROPSHIRE
LEICESTERSHIRE
RUTLAND
NORFOLK
WEST MIDLANDS
CAMBRIDGE-SHIRE
MID WALES
HEREFORD SHIRE
WORCESTER-SHIRE
WARWICK-SHIRE
NORTHAMPTON-SHIRE
BEDFORD-SHIRE
SUFFOLK
WEST WALES
BUCKINGHAM-SHIRE
HERTFORD-SHIRE
ESSEX
GWENT
GLOUCS & BRISTOL
OXFORD SHIRE
GLAMORGAN
GREATER LONDON
BERKSHIRE
WILTSHIRE
SURREY
KENT
SOMERSET
HAMPSHIRE
WEST SUSSEX
EAST SUSSEX
CHANNEL ISLANDS
DEVON
DORSET
CORNWALL
ISLE OF WIGHT

Wales

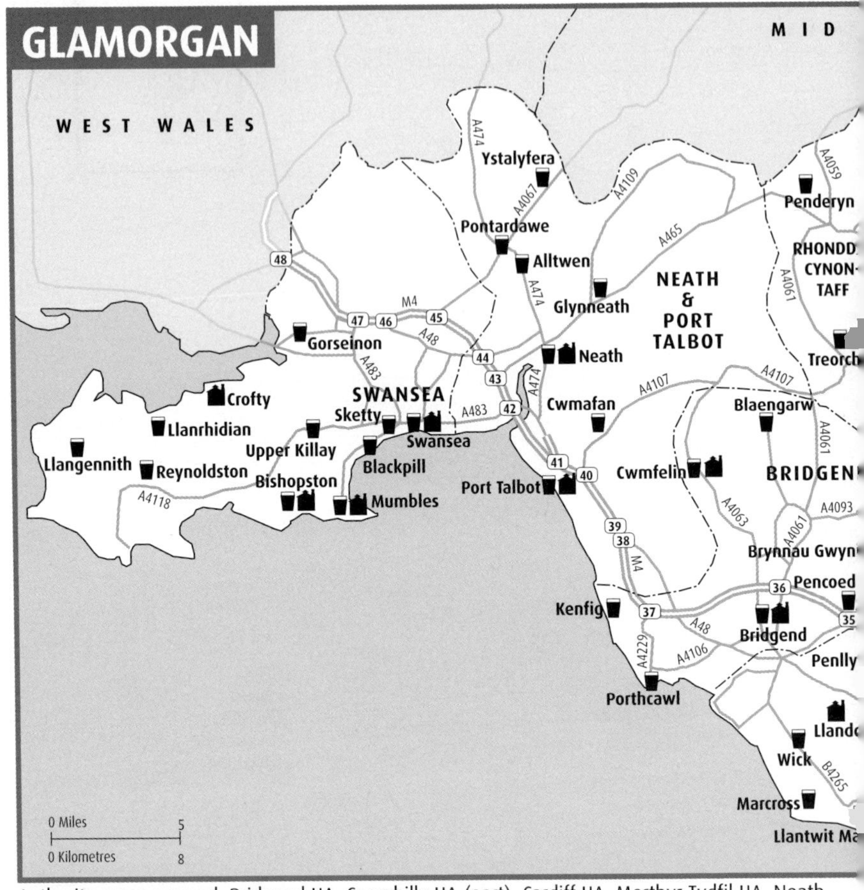

Authority areas covered: Bridgend UA, Caerphilly UA (part), Cardiff UA, Merthyr Tydfil UA, Neath & Port Talbot UA, Rhondda, Cynon & Taff UA, Swansea UA, Vale of Glamorgan UA

Aberdare

Whitcombe Inn

Whitcombe Street, CF44 7DA

12-midnight (11.30 Sun) (01685) 875106

Wye Valley Butty Bach; 2 changing beers (sourced nationally)

Traditional and friendly street-corner local, close to the town centre. The front bar backs on to a pool room at the rear. Sport sometimes plays on the TV, and there are projector screens for major events. Children are welcome until 9pm. Live music is hosted occasionally. Approximately a mile from the picturesque Dare Valley Country Park, which accommodates campers and touring vans, and offers great walks.

Aberthin

Hare & Hounds

Aberthin Road, CF71 7LG

12 (3 Mon & Tue)-midnight; 12-1am Fri & Sat
(01446) 774892 hareandhoundsaberthin.com

Hancocks HB; Wye Valley HPA; 2 changing beers (sourced regionally; often Evan Evans, Glamorgan)

A characterful pub whose cosy public bar with its traditional stone walls, wooden beams and log fire is the focal point where the locals gather. The dining area serves high-quality nouvelle cuisine, with some ingredients grown by the chef. A full menu is also available in the bar. The guest ales are mainly sourced locally, the ciders are from Llanblethian Orchards and Apple County. Outside, the beer garden has its own bar and, occasionally, live music. There is limited parking.
Q P (321)

Alltwen

Gwyn Arms

Gwyn's Place, SA8 3AJ

4-midnight; 12-midnight Sat & Sun 07754 716444

Wye Valley Butty Bach

Traditional independently owned village local, high up on the side of the picturesque Swansea Valley. Recently refurbished, retaining its old wooden fittings, conversation is the norm in the absence of games machines, and the TV is always set at a low volume. Darts is popular and there is a separate games area for the pub's teams. Live music features at weekends and an open guitar jam session on Wednesdays. There is plenty of scope for walkers and cyclists in this central location, the National Cycle Path 43 is nearby. A welcome refuge away from the busier town-centre pubs in nearby Pontardawe. Q (256)

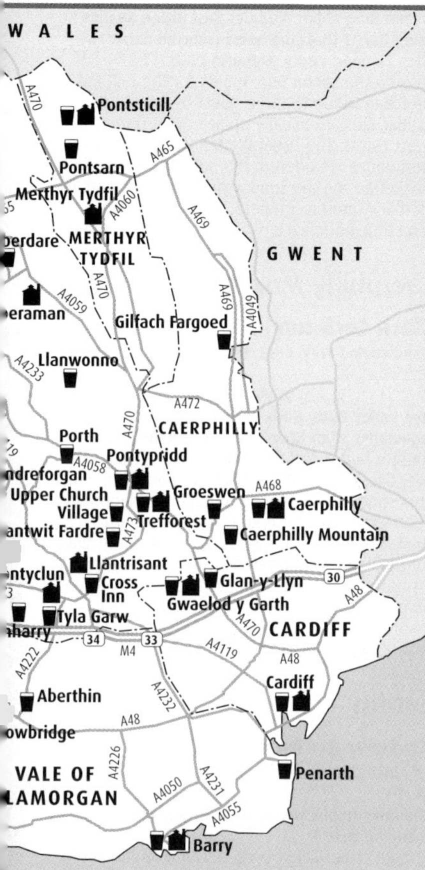

Barry

Barry West End Club 🄻

54 St Nicholas Road, CF62 6QY

⏲ 1-11.30; 12-midnight Sat & Sun ☎ (01446) 735739

🌐 barrywestendclub.webs.com

Wychwood Hobgoblin; Wye Valley HPA, Butty Bach; 2 changing beers 🄷

Many times local CAMRA Club of the Year, this establishment is housed in a large multi-floored red-brick building overlooking the old harbour. Visitors are welcome and CAMRA members are treated as honorary club members. Home to cricket, football, snooker and skittles teams as well as chess, scuba diving and fishing clubs, among others, there is always something going on here. Two beer festivals a year, live music at the weekend and pub grub including the amazing sandwiches help make it a must-visit.
Q🐎❀◑♿≋♣🍎🚌📶

Bishopston

Joiners Arms 🄻

50 Bishopston Road, SA3 3EJ

⏲ 3-10.30 Mon & Tue; 11.30-11; 12-11 Sun

☎ (01792) 232658 🌐 thejoiners.info

Marston's Pedigree; Swansea Bishopswood Bitter, Three Cliffs Gold, Original Wood; Theakston Best Bitter; 2 changing beers (sourced nationally) 🄷

Situated in the heart of the village, this 1860s free house remains popular with locals and visitors. Home of the Swansea Brewing Company, whose beers are showcased here, the pub has two bars and holds beer festivals and occasional music events, usually around public holidays. Good-value food is served lunchtimes and evenings (except Mon and Sun eve). The pub has won several local CAMRA awards over the years. There is a small car park. 🐎❀◑♣P🚌(14)🐾📶

Valley ✔

41 Bishopston Road, SA3 3EJ (on main road in village)

⏲ 11.30-11 ☎ (01792) 234820

🌐 valleyhotelbishopston.co.uk

Courage Best Bitter; 3 changing beers (sourced nationally; often Sharp's) 🄷

Traditional family-run country pub set in the heart of this pleasant village. A large porch area (which doubles as a convenient bus shelter) leads to a split-level bar and dining area, with exposed beams, a hearth and large open fire. A wide variety of home-cooked meals using local ingredients is served daily and a Sunday lunch take-away service is available. Live music plays on occasion.
🐎❀◑♿♣🍎P🚌(14)🐾📶

Blackpill

Woodman ✔

120 Mumbles Road, SA3 5AS (opp Blackpill Lido)

⏲ 12-11; 11.30-10.30 Sun ☎ (01792) 402700

4 changing beers (sourced nationally; often Greene King, Mumbles, Tomos Watkin) 🄷

REAL ALE BREWERIES

Arcadian Cardiff (NEW)
Bang-On Bridgend
Bont Bridgend (NEW)
Borough Arms Neath
Boss Swansea
Brains Cardiff
Brewhouse & Kitchen 🛢 Cardiff (NEW)
Bullmastiff Cardiff
Cerddin 🛢 Cwmfelin
Cold Black Label Bridgend
Crafty Devil Cardiff
Crafty Dragon Pontsticill (NEW)
Cwm Rhondda Treorchy
Dog's Window Bridgend (NEW)
Glamorgan Llantrisant
Gower Crofty
Grey Trees Aberaman
Hopcraft Pontyclun
Lines Caerphilly (brewing suspended)
Mabby's 🛢 Treforest (NEW)
Mountain Hare 🛢 Brynnau Gwynion
Mumbles Swansea
Neath Port Talbot
Pilot 🛢 Mumbles
Pipes Cardiff
Swansea 🛢 Bishopston
Tomos A Lilford Llandow
Tomos Watkin Swansea
Twin Taff Merthyr Tydfil (NEW)
Twt Lol Pontypridd
Violet Cottage 🛢 Gwaelod y Garth
VOG Barry
Well Drawn Caerphilly
West by Three Swansea
Zerodegrees 🛢 Cardiff

This historic pub and restaurant dating back to 1819 has been attractively refurbished. The deceptively spacious establishment, with its various nooks and alcoves, is situated on the main seafront road and the entrance to the beautiful Clyne Gardens. Popular with both families and diners, the pub also welcomes those only seeking liquid refreshment. A constantly changing range of guest ales is offered. There are seating areas outside and a small beer garden. ☺❀◐◑♿P🚌🐾📶

Blaengarw

Blaengarw Hotel

The Strand, CF32 8AA

11.30-11; 11-midnight Fri & Sat; 11-10.30 Sun

☎ (01656) 870287

1 changing beer (often Evan Evans, Glamorgan, Rhymney) Ⓗ

Nicely refurbished, large street-corner local at the heart of the community. Just one carefully chosen changing cask beer is on sale along with a couple of ciders. The public bar is popular for sports TV and hosts pool and darts league teams, and there is a fine jukebox. Meals are available in the lounge/dining room noon-8pm Tuesday and Thursday; Sunday lunches (until 3pm) are also popular. The famous Welsh hymn Calon Lan was written upstairs. ☺❀◐◑♿♣🍎🚌📶

Bridgend

Coach

37 Cowbridge Road, CF31 3DH

11.30-11; 12-10.30 Sun

Wye Valley Butty Bach Ⓗ**; 5 changing beers (often Grey Trees, Thornbridge, Tiny Rebel)** Ⓗ/Ⓖ

An incredible commitment to real ale, cider and independent producers has been the basis for the running of this pub since the current owners took it on. Basically furnished but comfortable, there is an art wall for local artists to display their work. Outings and events run from the pub, including open mic nights, and two beer festivals a year – all the goings on are to be found on the pub's lively Facebook page. ☺❀⇌♣🍎🚌(303,X2)🐾📶

Brynnau Gwynion

Mountain Hare

Brynna Road, CF35 6PG

4 (5 Mon)-11; 3-midnight Fri; 12-midnight Sat; 12-10.30 Sun ☎ (01656) 860453 🌐 mountainhare.co.uk

Mountain Hare Gold; Wickwar BOB; 2 changing beers (sourced nationally; often Glamorgan, Mountain Hare, St Austell) Ⓗ

The Mountain Hare is a typical Welsh village pub and has featured in the Guide for more than 10 years. The licensee and brewer began brewing on-site in 2014 and one of his two beers is always available. The pub has been in the same family for over 40 years and boasts a traditional public bar, games room and a lovely old stone-walled lounge. Sport is often on TV in this rugby lovers' pub. Q☺❀◑♣🍎P🚌(64,404)🐾📶

Caerphilly

Malcolm Uphill ✔

89-91 Cardiff Road, CF83 1FQ

8am-midnight (1am Fri & Sat) ☎ (029) 2076 0720

Greene King Abbot; Ruddles Best Bitter; Sharp's Doom Bar; 3 changing beers (sourced nationally; often Exmoor, Purity, Saltaire) Ⓗ

Busy Wetherspoon pub, handy for the rail and bus interchange. Up to three guest beers and three regular ales are usually on sale, plus one or two guest ciders. The usual Wetherspoon deals and promotions are offered. The pub can be crowded at weekends and the Sunday quiz is always popular – the back room is a quieter area. A separate accessible entrance is available. Q☺◐◑♿⇌🍎🚌📶

Caerphilly Mountain

Black Cock Inn Ⓛ

Waunwaelod Way, CF83 1BD (off A469, along Ffordd Waenwaelod)

12-11 (10.30 Sun) ☎ (029) 2088 0534

Wye Valley Butty Bach; 2 changing beers (sourced regionally; often Grey Trees, St Austell) Ⓗ

Country pub easily accessed from the main road over Caerphilly Mountain. Its two bars have a rustic atmosphere, one serving an adjacent dining area. Beers are well kept and a good range is usually available, including at least one from south Wales. Lunches and evening meals are popular (booking for the evening and Sunday is recommended). Dogs are welcome in the corner bar, which features a wood-burning stove. There is a large car park. Q❀◐◑♿🍎P🐾📶

Cardiff

Andrew Buchan

29 Albany Road, Roath, CF24 3LH

11-11

Rhymney Hobby Horse, Dark, Bitter, Export; 1 changing beer Ⓗ

A main-street community bar in a multi-cultural suburb which has forged links with the local musical and artistic communities. Frequent acoustic music sessions take place and the pub features exhibitions by local artists. One of a handful of pubs run by Rhymney Brewery, it now offers bag-in-box real cider and perry, frequently from Llanblethian Orchards. A real fire adds to the cosy ambience in winter. ❀♿⇌(Cathays)🍎🚌🐾📶

Chapter Arts Centre

Market Road, Canton, CF5 1QE (off Cowbridge Rd East behind Iceland store)

10-11; 12-12.30am Fri; 12-midnight Sat; 10-10.30 Sun

☎ (029) 2030 4400 🌐 chapter.org

Ringwood Boondoggle; 5 changing beers (sourced nationally) Ⓗ

Arts centre and cinema complex situated in a converted Victorian school, just off a busy main road. The open-plan bar has plenty of seating, and there is additional space in a covered area outside. The five guest beers come from across the UK, usually from small independent breweries, as well as a local ale. A number of fridges contain an impressive range of bottled beers from continental producers, with the accent on German beers. Occasional beer festivals are held. ☺❀◐◑♿⛺P🚌(17,18)📶

City Arms Ⓛ ✔

10-12 Quay Street, CF10 1EA

12-midnight (2am Fri & Sat); 12-10 Sun

☎ (029) 2064 1913

Brains Bitter, SA, Rev James Ⓗ**; 7 changing beers** Ⓗ/Ⓖ
A traditional pub in the heart of Cardiff's real ale and music district. Just off Westgate Street, it is in the shadow of the Principality Stadium and gets particularly busy on match days. The central three-sided bar separates the two drinking areas. Six traditional ciders and perries are served from the centre of the bar area, and craft keg beers are also on sale. The guest beers can originate from almost anywhere in the UK, with the accent on smaller breweries. ❀♿⛺⇌♣●🚌🐾ᯤ

Cricketers

66 Cathedral Road, CF11 9LL
⏲ 11.30-11 ☎ (029) 2034 5102 🌐 cricketerscardiff.co.uk
Evan Evans Welsh Pale Ale, Cwrw, Warrior; 2 changing beers (often Evan Evans) Ⓗ
The only pub run by Evan Evans in the area. A former Victorian town house, it is set in the Cathedral Road conservation area, close to the cricket stadium. Popular on match days, the open-plan interior is divided by a half-width wall into two distinct areas. A large rear yard is a popular suntrap in summer months. Award-winning meals are served and a jazz supper night takes place on the last Thursday of the month. Q🐎❀◐♿⛺🚌ᯤ

Discovery 🄻

Celyn Avenue, Lakeside, CF23 6EH
⏲ 12-11 Mon (11.30 Tue-Thu; 12.30am Fri & Sat); 12-11 Sun
☎ (029) 2075 5015
Sharp's Doom Bar; 5 changing beers (often VOG) Ⓗ
A spacious contemporary pub in a residential area close to the north end of Roath Park Lake. The public bar has the feel of a locals' bar, with a large-screen TV, dartboard and access to a covered outdoor area. The larger lounge/dining area serves a regularly changing variety of blackboard menu food. A large, impressive function room extension is available for private hire. There are usually five different beers on offer, with the accent on local breweries. 🐎❀◐♿⇌(Heath)♣P🚌(54)🐾ᯤ

Flute & Tankard

4 Windsor Place, CF10 3BX
⏲ 12-midnight (11 Sun) ☎ 07870 289735
🌐 thefluteandtankard.com
3 changing beers (often Brew Monster) Ⓗ
You will find this pub just off the eastern end of Queen Street, one of Cardiff's main shopping streets. Comfortable and quiet, it is just the ticket for anyone wanting a break from the hustle-bustle of city-centre activity. You can sample a choice of three real ales, mainly from independent breweries within a 50-mile radius. Enjoy the live jazz in the upstairs function room Tuesday and Wednesday evenings. Q❀⇌(Queen St)●🚌

Four Elms

1 Elm Street, CF24 3QR
⏲ 10-11; 11-midnight Sat; 12-11 Sun ☎ (029) 2046 2120
Felinfoel Double Dragon; 3 changing beers (often Boss, Evan Evans, Grey Trees) Ⓗ
Street-corner locals' pub off Newport Road east of the city centre. The front public bar is popular with the regulars, who are always happy to start a conversation. The rear area is a converted skittle alley with a small bar, open on busy periods. This leads to a large garden popular with younger patrons. The beers are supplemented by three real bag-in-box ciders. A good menu of reasonably priced pub food is served all day. ❀◐♣●🚌ᯤ

Gatekeeper ✔

9 Westgate Street, CF10 1DD
⏲ 8am-midnight (2am Fri & Sat) ☎ (029) 2064 6020
Greene King Abbot; Ruddles Best Bitter; Sharp's Doom Bar; 5 changing beers Ⓗ
Formerly a theatre, then auction rooms, this is now a Wetherspoon pub close to the Principality Stadium and Cardiff Castle. As well as the regular beers, a range of guest ales, often local, is available, alongside a choice of real ciders and perries. One downstairs bar services the two lower drinking areas, while another bar (not always open) serves the balcony public area. An elevator connects all areas. 🐎❀◐♿⛺⇌(Central)●🚌ᯤ

Grange 🏆

134 Penarth Road, CF11 6NJ
⏲ 12-11 (11.30 Fri & Sat); 12-10.30 Sun ☎ 07767 062126
5 changing beers Ⓗ
A real community pub, this former Brains house has been brought back to life by the team that operates the award-winning Lansdowne pub. The Grange has rapidly gained popularity under its new management regime. A central serving area divides the two bars. It has a recently refurbished skittle alley. The decor is tidy, if on the functional side, but the accent on quality real ales, cider and food has earned the pub the local CAMRA branch's Pub of the Year award for 2018.
🐎◐⇌(Grangetown)♣●🚌

Hopbunker

Kingsway, CF10 5AF
⏲ 12-11; 11-midnight Fri & Sat; 11-11 Sun
☎ (029) 2039 8889
Changing beers (sourced regionally; often Pixie Spring/Hopcraft) Ⓗ
Multi award-winning basement bar opposite Cardiff Castle offering the widest choice of real ales in the area – up to 15 are available at competitive prices. It is the tap for Hopcraft so expect to find a few examples of the brewery's beers on the bar. In addition, there is a bank of taps serving a range of keg beers, and a selection of up to 15 bag-in-box real ciders, all changing frequently. Monday is quiz night. ⇌(Queen St/Central)●🚌ᯤ

Lansdowne

71 Beda Road, Canton, CF5 1LX
⏲ 12-11 (11.30 Fri & Sat); 12-10.30 Sun ☎ (029) 2022 1312
5 changing beers (often Grey Trees, Tiny Rebel) Ⓗ
Former run-down hotel west of the city centre – the upper floors were converted into flats and the ground floor transformed into an award-winning pub. It has three distinct areas, with a fairly basic but bright and attractive decor and plenty of woodwork. Real ales are sourced from local microbreweries. There is also traditional cider and at least one keg beer from a local craft brewery. Good-quality food is served including award-winning Sunday lunches.
🐎❀◐♿⇌(Ninian Park)♣●🚌(96,X2)🐾ᯤ

Pen & Wig 🄻 ✔

1 Park Grove, CF10 3BJ
⏲ 11.30-midnight (1am Fri & Sat); 11.30-11.30 Sun
☎ (029) 2037 1217 🌐 penandwigcardiff.co.uk
8 changing beers (sourced nationally) Ⓗ
Formerly a large Victorian terraced residence, just off the city centre and near the university. The clientele is a mix of young professionals and office workers lunchtimes and after work, then students later in the evening. It offers a beer range from

WALES

local, regional and national breweries, plus some craft keg offerings. Two ciders are also available. Regular Meet the Brewer events and brewery takeovers are held. The large garden includes a covered section and a smokers' area.
❀◑◐≠(Queen St)●🚌

Queen's Vaults ✔

29 Westgate Street, CF10 1EH

10-11 (midnight Fri & Sat); 11-11 Sun ☎ (029) 2022 7966

Felinfoel Double Dragon; 5 changing beers Ⓗ

A busy pub on Cardiff's Westgate Street strip offering good-value drinks and meals. There is a raised lounge/dining area at the front and pool tables and dartboards towards the rear. TVs show live sport and can be quite noisy, although frequently the volume is muted and replaced by rock music. Guest beers can be from anywhere but are often from microbreweries. A former local CAMRA Cider Pub of the Year, with up to six ciders and perries regularly available.
❀◑◐♿⛺≠♣●🚌📶

St Canna's Ale House

42 Llandaff Road, CF11 9NJ

4-11; 12-11.30 Sat; 12-10.30 Sun ☎ 07890 106449

4 changing beers (often Grey Trees, Tiny Rebel, Untapped) Ⓗ

Micropub in a former corner shop, just off Cowbridge Road East. Up to six real ales are on cooled gravity stillage and four real ciders. The pub was founded to build community spirit and hosts regular activities such as tap takeovers and street food events. It has a piano and traditional board games to play. The yard, reached via a second room, has a covered smoking area.
Q❀♣●🚌(17,18)

Tiny Rebel

26 Westgate Street, CF10 1DD

12-2 ☎ (029) 2039 9557 🌐 urbantaphouse.co.uk

8 changing beers (often Tiny Rebel) Ⓗ

This popular city-centre pub is opposite the Principality Stadium. There are several rooms, upstairs and downstairs, decorated in Tiny Rebel brewery's unique style, with some available for private hire. The pub hosts regular quizzes, bring your own vinyl, Americana and board game nights, and occasional brewery tap takeovers. Eight handpumps offer four Tiny Rebel beers and a range of independent brewery beers from across the UK. There are four further handpumps for ciders and perries. A former local CAMRA Pub of the Year winner. ❀◑◐♿⛺≠♣●🚌🐾📶

Cowbridge

1 Town Hall Square

1 Town Hall Square, CF71 7DD

11.30-11 🌐 1townhallsquare.com

Wye Valley Butty Bach Ⓗ**; 3 changing beers (sourced nationally)** Ⓗ/Ⓖ

A new addition to the local beer scene, this small pub is aimed squarely at the ale enthusiast. The bar has a seating area off it while upstairs are another two rooms. Being so compact, expect it to be crowded at busy times. The decor is traditional with exposed stonework, tiled and wooden floors, and low beams. The entrance courtyard is a nice suntrap. No food is served but customers are welcome to bring their own.
❀♣●🚌(X2,321)🐾📶

Edmondes Arms

Cardiff Road, CF71 7EP

4-11; 12-midnight Sat; 4-10.30 Sun

Hancocks HB; Wye Valley HPA; 1 changing beer (sourced nationally; often Glamorgan) Ⓗ

Dating from 1899, this three-roomed pub has a strong local following. The building is of brick and local limestone with an unspoilt interior featuring stained-glass panels in the windows, wood panelling and other original features. The main bar and games room have wooden floors and open fires. There is a separate cosy lounge to the rear leading to a small patio area outside. Live bands play most Saturday evenings. Q❀♣🚌(X2,321)📶

Vale of Glamorgan Inn

51 High Street, CF71 7AE

11.30-11 (midnight Fri & Sat); 12-11 Sun
☎ (01446) 772252

Draught Bass; Hancocks HB; Sharp's Atlantic; Wye Valley HPA, Butty Bach; 1 changing beer (sourced nationally; often Borough Arms, Grey Trees, VOG) Ⓗ

Popular single-room pub in the centre of town. The wooden-floored bar area has a warming range fire, and recent work has added a flagstone floor to the rear area plus more seating around another stove. Outside is an attractive enclosed beer garden with a separate covered and heated smoking area. An annual beer festival coincides with the town's food and drink festival in May. Good-value home-made food is served 12-2.15pm (no food Sun). A former local CAMRA Pub of the Year.
Q🐎❀◑●🚌(X2,321)🐾📶

Cross Inn

Cross Inn Hotel ✔

Main Road, CF72 8AZ

12-11 ☎ (01443) 223431

Hancocks HB; Sharp's Doom Bar; Wye Valley HPA; 1 changing beer (sourced nationally) Ⓗ

Traditional unspoilt terrace pub on the old course of the A473. It has a convivial atmosphere and is popular with locals and visitors alike. Immaculately clean throughout, the main area is divided into a bar with flagstone floor and a comfortable lounge area. Well-kept beers are offered in excellent condition. Sunday lunches are popular (booking recommended) and regularly curry nights are held.
Q❀◑♿♣P🚌📶

Cwmafan

Brit Pub Ⓛ

London Row, SA12 9AH

5-11 Mon; 11.30-11 Tue-Thu (midnight Fri & Sat); 11.30-10.30 Sun ☎ (01639) 680247 🌐 thebrit.wales

Morland Old Speckled Hen; 3 changing beers (sourced locally; often Borough Arms, Grey Trees, Mumbles) Ⓗ

Dating back to 1845, this pub offers a warm welcome to drinkers, diners, backpackers, locals and tourists. A selection of up to four real ales and cider, mostly sourced locally, is available. It has a bunkhouse and award-winning food, not to mention a picturesque riverside beer garden. Music jam sessions feature regularly. A beer festival is held in summer. A gem found nestled in the beautiful Afan Valley, quirkiness mixes with tradition in this establishment.
Q🐎❀🛏◑◐♿●P🚌(83)🐾📶

Cwmfelin

Cross Inn 🏆

Masteg Road, CF34 9LB

11.45-midnight (1am Fri & Sat); 11-midnight Sun

(01656) 732476

Cerddin Solar, Cascade; 3 changing beers (often Cerddin) Ⓗ

Home to the Cerddin Brewery, this is a must-visit pub. As well as five cask beers from the brewery it also offers the bottle-conditioned range alongside eight real ciders. The traditional two-roomed Valleys pub has strong community links. The Tuesday night quiz raises money for the local food bank. Bar snacks are available. It has friendly locals and knowledgeable staff. Situated between Maesteg and Bridgend, buses stop at the front door and the railway station is within walking distance. Local CAMRA Pub of the Year 2018.
Q (Garth) (71)

Gilfach Fargoed

Real Ale Farm (RAF)

Gilfach Fargoed Fawr Farm, Cardiff Road, CF81 8NY

7-11 Mon (midnight Tue); closed Wed; 7-midnight Thu; 6.30-midnight Fri & Sat; 12-8 Sun 07837 006276

Felinfoel Double Dragon; 5 changing beers (sourced nationally; often Grey Trees, Salopian, VOG) Ⓗ

Award-winning club, offering the best range and quality of beer for miles, with up to five guest ales and two ciders or perries, selected for flavour and interest and which come from breweries both local and further afield. The building pre-dates the industrial age and has a complex history. Numerous charity events and the occasional beer festival are hosted. Visitors are welcome but must be signed in. The short walk from Gilfach Fargoed station presents a modest but energetic climb.
Q P (50)

Glan-y-Llyn

Fagins Ale & Chop House

9 Cardiff Road, CF15 7QD

3-11 Mon; 12-11.30; 12-10.30 Sun (029) 2081 1800

3 changing beers (sourced nationally; often Bragdy Twt Lol, Dark Star, Grey Trees) Ⓗ/Ⓖ

Friendly free house north of Taffs Well, where both gravity and handpump dispense can be found. The handpulled beers often include some from nearby Bragdy Twt Lol and Dark Star. Gravity beers tend to be well-hopped styles. Bottled ciders are from Gwynt y Ddraig. Good-value pub food is served (no food Mon). The logburner is most welcome on winter days. Live music plays on occasion. The pub is well served by bus and is a 15-minute walk from Taffs Well railway station.
Q (26,132)

Glynneath

Dinas Rock Hotel

High Street, SA11 5AP

5 (4 Fri)-11; 1-midnight Sat; 12-11 Sun (01639) 720105

2 changing beers (sourced regionally; often Glamorgan, Grey Trees) Ⓗ

Traditional local in the centre of the village which has been refurbished following a short period of closure. The two wood-burning stoves and original stone walls make for a cosy atmosphere. Live rugby is popular on TV, especially Six Nations and Ospreys games. The real cider is hand-produced by one of the pub's regular patrons. A welcome refuge in an area where real ale can be hard to find. Q (8,X55)

Gorseinon

Mardy Inn ✔

117 High Street, SA4 4BR

8am-midnight (1am Fri & Sat) (01792) 890600

Greene King Abbot; Ruddles Best Bitter; Sharp's Doom Bar; 4 changing beers Ⓗ

This modern Wetherspoon establishment opened in 2013 following a major refurbishment of a former traditional high-street pub. It has a large single bar with several TVs for news and sport, and an adjoining airy extension overlooking the furnished patio area. Some interesting pictures of old Gorseinon adorn the walls, depicting the town and its inhabitants in years gone by. A good selection of local and national beers can be enjoyed in the beer garden. P

Groeswen

White Cross Inn

CF15 7UT (overlooking Groeswen Chapel)

4-midnight; 12-midnight Fri-Sun (029) 2085 1332

4 changing beers (sourced nationally) Ⓗ

This cosy stone pub is well worth finding. Six handpumps dispense four changing beers and two ciders. The beer range offer a diverse choice of modern and traditional styles, regularly including a dark ale. Small and emerging breweries often feature, many unusual for the area. The back room hosts meetings including the Beer Bellies gathering with visiting brewers and beer industry speakers. Occasional beer festivals are held. Road access is narrow. A highly commended pub in the local CAMRA Pub of the Year awards for 2018.
P

Gwaelod y Garth

Gwaelod y Garth Inn

Main Road, CF15 9HH

10-11; 12-10.30 Sun (029) 2081 0408

gwaelodinn.co.uk

Dark Star American Pale Ale; Wye Valley Bitter; 4 changing beers (often Dark Star, Thornbridge) Ⓗ

A stone-built, multi award-winning village local. On the extreme outskirts of Cardiff and on the lower slope of Garth Mountain, in the village centre, it is frequented by locals as well as cyclists and walkers. Expect to find at least one beer from the on-site Violet Cottage Brewery, complementing a varying range of real ales which can originate from anywhere across the UK. There is a games room downstairs and an upstairs restaurant which serves high-quality meals. Q P (26B)

Hendreforgan

Griffin Inn

CF39 8YL (from Tonyrefail on A4093, turn down lane after Gilfach Goch village sign)

7 (6 Fri)-11; 12-11 Sat & Sun (01443) 670379

Brains SA; 1 changing beer (sourced locally; often Glamorgan) Ⓗ

Recognised by CAMRA as one of the Real Heritage Pubs of Wales, the Griffin has been in the same family for over 50 years. It can be difficult to find, but persistence pays off and it is well worth the effort. The Brains SA is always superb quality. The decor is worth a look in itself, featuring oak furniture, gleaming brasses and a splendid Victorian counter with an 1870 till. A heartfelt welcome is assured. Q (150,172)

Kenfig

Prince of Wales

CF33 4PR

4-8 Mon; 12-11 (01656) 740356 princekenfig.co.uk

Draught Bass; Sharp's Doom Bar; Worthington's Bitter G; 1 changing beer (sourced regionally) H

A heritage award-winning inn dating from the 15th century and steeped in local history. Visitors can expect three quality ales on gravity, good locally sourced food and a warm welcome. Family-friendly and popular with dog walkers, the pub is comfortable and cosy. Outside there is a stunning view over Kenfig Nature Reserve. The Draught Bass is renowned throughout the local area and outsells all the pub's lagers combined. Guest beers and cider are occasionally available.
Q P (63B)

Llangennith

King's Head

SA3 1HX

12-11 (01792) 386212 kingsheadgower.co.uk

Gower Brew 1, Gold; 3 changing beers (often Gower) H

A row of three 17th-century stone-built cottages, the pub offers quality 4-star accommodation, with some rooms pet-friendly. It is situated at the western end of the Gower Peninsula, a short distance from the sandy stretches of Llangennith Beach. Ales from nearby Gower Brewery are available (up to six in summer) plus a cask cider. An impressive variety of home-made food is served, with dishes inspired by fresh local produce. An annual beer festival is held in October and a themed fancy dress event over the August bank holiday. P (116)

Llanharry

Fox & Hounds

Llanharan Road, CF72 9LL

12-11 (midnight Fri & Sat) (01443) 222124
foxandhoundsllanharry.co.uk

4 changing beers (sourced nationally; often Glamorgan, Oakham, Salopian) H

A mix of old and new, traditional construction materials combined with modern furnishings, result in a pub well worth a visit. The stone-built inn is family owned and offers a good selection of varying guest beers, usually about four in number. It has a growing reputation for high-quality food. Bottled ciders are usually available. There is a large car park beside the pub.
Q P (64,404)

Llanrhidian

Dolphin Inn

Mill Lane, SA3 1EH (just off B4295 N Gower Rd)

4.30-11 Mon; 6-11 Tue; 1-11 Wed-Sat; 12-11 Sun summer; 4.30-11 Mon, Wed & Thu; 1-11 Fri & Sat; 12-10.30 Sun winter
(01792) 391069

Exmoor Gold; Fuller's London Pride; 1 changing beer (sourced nationally; often Glamorgan) H

Cosy village pub dating from the 18th century on the north side of Gower next to a 13th-century church, with stunning views of the estuary from the lovely beer gardens. The characterful single room is warmed by a solid fuel stove. A limited range of hot and cold meals is available. There is a children's play area at the rear with an enclosure for rabbits and poultry to roam. Quiz night is Sunday. Check ahead for afternoon opening times.
Q P (116,115)

Greyhound Bar & Grill

Oldwalls, SA3 1HA (1 mile W of Llanrhidian on B4295)

11-11 (01792) 391027 greyhoundgower.com

Draught Bass; Gower Gold, Power; 2 changing beers H

Traditional 19th-century inn with a welcoming atmosphere. It is the spiritual home of the Gower Brewery, with a wide range of the brewery's ales on offer at the bar. An extensive home-cooked bar menu is served every day, with Sunday lunches always popular (served 12-2.30pm). Outside at the rear is a large beer garden with a children's play area and wonderful views over the Gower countryside. The pub hosts the Great Gower Beer Festival in June, with camping available.
P (116)

Llantwit Fardre

Bush Inn

Main Road, CF38 2EP

4-midnight (1am Thu); 3-1am Fri; 12-1am Sat; 12-midnight Sun (01443) 203958

Hancocks HB; 2 changing beers (sourced nationally) H

Bustling village pub on the old course of the A473. The interior is semi open plan, featuring exposed stone walls and timber. Two guest beers tend to be from larger Welsh independent breweries. Quizzes are hosted on Tuesday and Wednesday, and a music jam on Thursday. A band often plays on Saturday, when the pub can get busy.

Ship Inn

Crown Hill, CF38 1BH (100yds off A473)

11-11 (01443) 202341

Greene King Abbot; Wickwar BOB H

Traditional one-bar pub in a semi-rural location, convenient for the local foot and cycle path. Outside is a large terrace with seating and a children's play area. The pub is popular for its food, served in the bar and separate restaurant (booking advisable). Options include vegetarian dishes and healthy summer specials plus a Sunday roast.
P (90)

Llantwit Major

King's Head

East Street, CF61 1XY

11.30-11.30 (midnight Fri & Sat); 11.30-10.30 Sun
(01446) 792697

Brains Bitter; 1 changing beer (often Belhaven, Brains) H

A family-run town-centre pub, in the Guide for the 20th consecutive year. The two-bar inn has a strong local following and the stone-floored public bar is popular for darts and pool. The comfortable lounge features wood panelling and an eclectic mix of furnishings, and leads to the patio beer garden. The two bars each have large-screen TVs for sport. Guest beers come from both local and national brewers. Thursday night karaoke is popular. QP

Llantwit Major Rugby Club

Old Market, Boverton Road, CF61 1XZ
4.30-11 (midnight Fri); 12-midnight Sat; 11-11 Sun
(01446) 792276 llantwitmajor.rfc.wales
Sharp's Doom Bar; 2 changing beers (often Wadworth, Wye Valley)
A friendly and vibrant community club where visitors are welcome – dogs too, in the players' bar. The big-selling Doom Bar and two changing guest ales are excellent value for money. There is a small patio area which is popular in summer and some covered seating at the side for smokers. The club has a cosy lounge bar and a function room, which holds up to 120 people, available for hire.
P

Old Swan Inn

Church Street, CF61 1SB
12-11 (10.30 Sun) (01446) 792230
Draught Bass; 4 changing beers (sourced nationally; often Milton, Springhead, VOG)
The town's oldest inn, overlooking the historic St Illtyd's Church and opposite the town hall. There is a popular front bar and a modern restaurant at the back, with excellent food served in both. It boasts an ever-changing range of four or five ales, often sourced from local brewers. Cider is occasionally available, more so in summer. Beer festivals are held in spring and summer featuring local bands. The town car park is nearby.
QP

Tudor Tavern

Church Street, CF61 1SB
12-11.30 (1am Fri & Sat); 12-10.30 Sun (01446) 794562
thetudorcf61.co.uk
Hancocks HB; Wye Valley HPA
The Tudor is a typical old town-centre pub, frequented by locals of all ages. Its small windows and sunken floor help to create a cosy atmosphere and a lived-in feel. There is a large pool area, popular with younger customers, a cosy bar area and a restaurant space. The food is good, typical pub fare. The friendly licensees have proved their commitment to real ale, winning the local CAMRA branch's Most Improved Pub award for 2018.
(303)

Llanwonno

Brynffynon Hotel

CF37 3PH (opp church) ST030955
12-11 (6 Mon); 12-10.30 Sun (01443) 790272
brynffynonhotel.com
3 changing beers (sourced nationally)
Set on top of the ridge between the urban Cynon and Rhondda Fach valleys, this tranquil country inn is well worth the effort to seek out. The lounge has a timeless atmosphere with its relaxing leather couches and log-burning fire. The dining room serves food of an excellent standard (booking advised), including cream teas. Three guest beers are available, and beer festivals are held throughout the year. A patio offers views of the forest and ancient churchyard. QP

Marcross

Horseshoe Inn

CF61 1ZG
12-2.30 (not Mon), 6-11; 12-11 Sat; 12-10.30 Sun
(01656) 890568 theshoesmarcross.co.uk
Sharp's Atlantic; Wye Valley Butty Bach; 2 changing beers (often Gower, VOG)
The Shoes is a beautiful 19th-century pub in the hamlet of Marcross. It usually has a range of three ales, one a Welsh brew. The food menu offers good pub fare. The bar is cosy on cold winter nights, with a large logburner, while the beer garden is a delight on summer afternoons. The pub is convenient for spectacular coastal walks, taking in the nearby Nash Point lighthouse.
QP(303)

Mumbles

Mumbles Ale House

2 Dunns Lane, SA3 4AA
4-9; 12-11 Thu-Sun 07971 194838
7 changing beers (sourced nationally; often Bluestone, Glamorgan, Mantle)
Wales' first micropub, this intimate bar is on the ground floor of a terraced house just off the main road, and has become popular as a pub for conversation. It offers a regularly changing real ale range – no keg beers here – along with real cider, wine, limited spirits and soft drinks, all listed on a large blackboard alongside the bar. Traditional bar snacks are available. Local CAMRA Pub of the Year in 2016. Q(2,3)

Park Inn

23 Park Street, SA3 4DA
4-11; 2-11 Sat & Sun (01792) 366738
5 changing beers (sourced regionally; often Evan Evans, Mumbles, Tiny Rebel)
The convivial atmosphere in this small establishment in a village side street attracts discerning drinkers of all ages. Five handpumps dispense a varied range of beers, with particular emphasis on independent breweries from Wales and the west of England. Alongside a fine display of pumpclips are pictures of old Mumbles and its pioneering railway. A popular quiz is held on Thursday, with occasional music at weekends.
Q(2,3)

Pilot Inn

726 Mumbles Road, SA3 4EL
12-11 (midnight Fri & Sat) 07897 895511
thepilotofmumbles.co.uk
Draught Bass; 6 changing beers (sourced nationally; often Pilot)
Welcoming and friendly local on the seafront at Mumbles and home to the Pilot Brewery. Seven ales are always available, usually including up to three rotating beers brewed on site. A wide range of bottled ciders is also kept and hot drinks are served. This historic pub, built in 1849, is next to the coastal path and popular with lifeboatmen, locals, walkers, cyclists and, of course, real ale fans. Local CAMRA Pub of the Year 2018.
Q(2B)

Victoria Inn

21 Westbourne Place, SA3 4DB
3-11; 12-11.30 Sat; 12.30-11 Sun 07704 373787
Brains Rev James; Draught Bass; Gower Gold

Traditional back-street corner local in the heart of Mumbles, dating from the mid 19th century. Now decorated in a modern but comfortable style, it retains some original features of historic interest including a well in the bar area – the source of water in the days when the pub brewed its own beer. Live sport is often shown and live music plays regularly. Although no food is served you are welcome to bring your own.

Neath

Borough Arms

2 New Henry Street, SA11 1PH (off Briton Ferry road, near Stockhams Corner roundabout)

4.30-9 Mon (11 Tue & Wed); 4-11 Thu & Fri; 12-11 Sat; 12-4 Sun ☎ (01639) 644902 boroughbreweryneath.com

4 changing beers (sourced locally; often Borough Arms, Butcombe, Evan Evans) [H]

The home of the Borough Brewery, this pub is cosy and welcoming. The Borough beer names generally have a steelworks theme, paying homage to the area's industrial past and the landlord's ties to the Margam steelworks. Favourites include Full Blast, Puddlers Peril and Nut Red Coke. One of the few remaining good back-street pubs, it can be difficult to find but is well worth seeking out. Q

David Protheroe

7 Windsor Road, SA11 1LS

8am-midnight (1am Fri & Sat) ☎ (01639) 622130

Greene King Abbot; Ruddles Best Bitter; Sharp's Doom Bar; 5 changing beers (sourced nationally; often Brains, Glamorgan, Mumbles) [H]

Situated opposite Neath railway station and a short walk from the bus terminus, this popular town-centre venue is a typical Wetherspoon pub. The building is the former Neath Police Station and is named after the town's first policeman. It has an open-plan interior with a family area at the rear. Welsh pub classics feature on the familiar food menu.

Penarth

Golden Lion

69 Glebe Street, CF64 1EF

10-11 (midnight Fri & Sat); 12-10.30 Sun ☎ (029) 2070 1574

4 changing beers (often Grey Trees, Pixie Spring/Hopcraft, VOG) [H]

A genuine locals' pub with a reputation for some of the best-kept quality real ale in the area. Three or four beers from Welsh breweries are usually available, along with good-value food. The pub can sometimes be loud and lively with its popular jukebox and numerous sports TVs, and football and darts teams are among the regular customers. The small beer garden is a delight in warmer weather, with artificial grass and wall paintings depicting Penarth.

Pilot

67 Queen's Road, CF64 1DJ

12-11 (midnight Fri & Sat) ☎ (029) 2071 0615

4 changing beers (often Dukeries, Milton, VOG) [H]

The Pilot has a growing reputation for high-quality food, wine and beer. Ales are chosen from a selection from some of the best Welsh breweries, alongside more unusual offerings from around the country. Five handpumps offer up to four quality cask ales alongside a real cider. There is pleasant seating outside at the front for warm weather, and the rear restaurant area with its log-fired stove is comfortable in winter. Q

Windsor

95 Windsor Road, CF64 1JE

11-11.30 (10.30 Sun) ☎ (029) 2070 8675

Brains Bitter, Rev James Gold, Rev James; 3 changing beers (sourced nationally; often Bath Ales, St Austell) [H]

Recently refurbished to a high standard, and with an emphasis on quality dining, the Windsor serves six real ales – three from the Brains portfolio and three guest beers, often national. The pub offers a relaxing environment, with a cosy front area with comfortable seating, a long dining/drinking space opposite the bar, and further tables to the rear. It is popular with families for Sunday lunch.

Pencoed

Little Penybont Arms

11 Penybont Road, CF35 5PY

3 (12 Fri & Sat)-11; closed Tue ☎ 07734 767937

4 changing beers (often Grey Trees, Mumbles, VOG) [G]

A cosy micropub converted from a café, offering up to four changing beers on gravity, 20-plus ciders and 15-plus single malt whiskies. The Steak & Stamp restaurant two doors down, formerly the post office, is under the same ownership and serves the same range of drinks. In the pub, excellent bar snacks are available including pork pies, nuts and home-made pork scratchings. A quiz and pizza night is held on Wednesday. Since opening, the pub has built up a strong local following. Q

Penderyn

Red Lion

Church Road, CF44 9JR

12-3 (not Mon), 6-11; 12-11 Sat; 12-10.30 Sun ☎ (01685) 811914 redlionpenderyn.com

Brains Rev James; Draught Bass; Fuller's ESB; Gower Gold; 2 changing beers (sourced nationally) [G]

Family-owned drovers' inn on the edge of the Brecon Beacons National Park, with parts dating back to the 12th century. Between six and 10 beers dispensed on gravity are usually available, with Fuller's ESB a favourite. The beer range may change on occasion. Up to five real ciders and perries are also served, with some from local producer Bragdy Brodyr. Two log fires keep the pub cosy during the colder months. There is a considerable focus on meal service, with a menu of high-quality traditional home-cooked food (booking essential). Q P

Penllyn

Red Fox

CF71 7RQ

12-11 ☎ (01446) 772352 redfoxinn.co.uk

Hancocks HB; Wye Valley HPA; 2 changing beers (sourced nationally) [H]

A warm welcome is guaranteed at this friendly, professionally run village local. Within the thick stone walls, a stone-floored main bar area with a log fire and a separate restaurant can be found. Outside, an attractive patio to the front and a large

enclosed garden with children's play area to the rear are excellent places to enjoy the warmer weather with a good pint and a quality meal. Quiz night is the last Thursday of the month.
Q

Pontardawe

Pontardawe Inn

123 Herbert Street, SA8 4ED
12-11.30 (midnight Fri & Sat) ☎ (01792) 447562
pontardaweinn.co.uk
Banks's Sunbeam; Marston's Pedigree; Ringwood Fortyniner; 4 changing beers (sourced nationally; often Gower, Jennings, Mumbles)
Originally a drovers' pub on the route to Neath, the Gwachel sits beside the picturesque River Tawe and is well worth the short walk from the town centre. Live music is prominent on Friday and Saturday evenings, and seasonal beer and music festivals are held. Good food is served from a varied menu. The landscaped garden at the rear is a welcome addition in the summer. CAMRA branch Pub of the Year on numerous occasions.

Pontsarn

Aberglais Hotel

CF48 2TS (between Trefechan and Pontsticill) SO043098
10.30-11 ☎ (01685) 377344 aberglais.com
3 changing beers (sourced nationally; often Grey Trees, Sharp's)
Rescued from the shell of a building, the Aberglais is in a picturesque setting on the route to Pontsticill Reservoir and Morlais Castle. The landlord was instrumental in the restoration of this gem, having run a nearby pub for many years. Good food and regularly changing guest beers are available. Holidaymakers, hikers and cyclists are welcome, and there is a play area for children. The pub is midway along Sustrans Taff Trail Route 8 between Cefn Coed and Pontsticill.

Pontsticill

Red Cow

CF48 2UN (middle of Village)
11-11 (8.30 Mon; 9.30 Tue); 11-10 Sun ☎ (01685) 387775
Wye Valley Bitter; 2 changing beers (sourced locally; often Crafty Dragon, Grey Trees)
Impressive tranquil stone-built village pub at the southern edge of the Brecon Beacons National Park. Pontsticill Reservoir is nearby, with the dam providing a less strenuous route for those walking or cycling from the nearby Brecon Mountain Railway. This is an ideal lunchtime stop when touring the Beacons, with scenic paths and trails nearby. The beer range focuses predominantly on locally produced brews, often including ales from Crafty Dragon Brewery, just a few doors away. A popular quiz is held on Wednesday evening.
Q

Pontypridd

Bunch of Grapes

Ynysangharad Road, CF37 4DA (off A4054)
11-1am (midnight Sun) ☎ (01443) 402934
bunchofgrapes.org.uk
8 changing beers (often Dark Star, Oakham, Salopian)
Fairly close to the town centre, this popular and award-winning pub dates from the 19th century and attracts a diverse clientele. Four local beers are augmented by six constantly changing guests from far and wide, plus two ciders or perries. The highly acclaimed separate restaurant serves locally sourced food. Numerous events include beer, cider and cheese festivals, in addition to themed nights and a weekly quiz on Tuesday.
QP

Llanover Arms

Bridge Street, CF37 4PE (opp N entrance to Ynysangharad Park, off A470)
11-11 ☎ (01443) 403215
3 changing beers (sourced nationally)
Built around 1794 to serve thirsty boatmen working the newly opened Glamorganshire Canal, this historic free house has been in the same family for over a century. Three rooms are linked by a central passageway, each room with its own regulars. The canal is long gone, though Ynysangharad Park and the famous town bridge and museum are close by, as is the Taff Trail path.
QP

Patriot Bar

25B Taff Street, CF37 4UA
12-midnight ☎ (01443) 407915
Rhymney Best, Bevans Bitter, Export; 1 changing beer (often Rhymney)
A Rhymney Brewery tied house, this is a popular no-frills bar, fondly known locally as the Wonky Bar. The ales are well kept – the changing beer is usually Hobby Horse or Dark. Prices are reasonable and rapid turnover promotes quality. The central location on Taff Street makes it easy to find, and it is just a short walk from the rail and bus stations.

Port Talbot

Lord Caradoc

69-73 Station Road, SA13 1NW (on main shopping street)
8am-midnight (1am Fri & Sat) ☎ (01639) 896007
Greene King Abbot; Ruddles Best Bitter; Sharp's Doom Bar; 7 changing beers (sourced regionally; often Brains, Glamorgan, Mumbles)
A comfortable Wetherspoon pub with a relaxed atmosphere, the Lord Caradoc is situated on the main shopping street and easily accessible from Parkway railway station and the bus terminus. The choice of beers is open to suggestion from regular customers, with a wide range always available. The pub has a spacious open-plan layout, plus an outdoor space for drinkers at the rear. It is family-friendly throughout and has a strong local following.

Porth

Rheola

Rheola Road, CF39 0LF
2-midnight; 1-1am Fri; 12-1am Sat; 12-midnight Sun
☎ (01443) 682633
Rhymney Best, Dark, Bitter, Export
A Rhymney Brewery tied house, this friendly local sells a range of good-value Rhymney beers. A large, detached building, it is situated at the confluence of the two Rhondda rivers, and is well served by both rail and bus. The bar features a

jukebox, pool table and dartboard, and is often quite lively, whereas the comfortable lounge will provide a quiet haven and only tends to get busy at weekends. Activities include a quiz night and whist night. (132)

Porthcawl

Lorelei Hotel

36-38 Esplanade Avenue, CF36 3YU

5-11 Mon; 12-1.30, 5-11 Tue; 12-11 Wed-Sat; 12-10.30 Sun

(01656) 788342 loreleihotel.co.uk

Draught Bass; Rhymney Export; 3 changing beers (often Boss, Grey Trees, VOG)

Near the seafront and the Grand Pavilion, this is the 20th year the Lorelei has been in this Guide. Good-quality and good-value food is served evenings (except Mon) and Sunday lunchtime. Four draught beers are available plus cider in summer. Beer festivals are held twice a year on Grand National and Halloween weekends. Built around the end of the 19th century, during World War I it was two separate buildings – one used as a hospice for injured soldiers. Q

Reynoldston

King Arthur Hotel

Higher Green, SA3 1AD (on village green)

10-11 (01792) 390775 kingarthurhotel.co.uk

Felinfoel Double Dragon; Gower Gold; Sharp's Doom Bar; 2 changing beers (often Glamorgan, Tiny Rebel)

Traditional family-owned hotel and acclaimed wedding venue, situated at the foot of Cefn Bryn in beautiful Gower, overlooking the village green. There is covered outdoor seating by the pub entrance and a large seating area on the green itself. The cosy, atmospheric main and rear bars are welcoming to drinkers and diners, serving home-cooked food made with local produce. Main meals and bar snacks are available all day, breakfasts for non-residents 8-11am. P

Sketty

Vivian Arms

104 Gower Road, SA2 9BZ (Sketty Cross, jct of A4118 and A4216)

11.30-11 (midnight Fri & Sat); 12-11 Sun

(01792) 516194

Brains Bitter, Rev James Gold, SA, Rev James; 1 changing beer

Situated on the main crossroads in Sketty, The Vivs attracts a wide range of customers young and old. The spacious pub has a mixture of seating areas, and plenty of TV screens throughout show live sport. Popular for family dining, a carvery is served on Sunday. Live music plays on Friday and occasionally Saturday. A general knowledge quiz is held on Sunday and a music quiz on Wednesday. A small meeting room provides extra seating, and there is an outdoor space. (20,21)

Swansea

Bank Statement

57/58 Wind Street, SA1 1EP

8am-midnight (1am Wed & Fri; 2am Sat)

(01792) 455477

Sharp's Doom Bar; 5 changing beers (sourced nationally; often Boss, Exmoor, Fuller's)

A former Midland Bank, sympathetically transformed by Wetherspoon, while retaining its original ornate interior. Trading as a Lloyds No.1, the pub is at the heart of the city's popular bar quarter and has a large ground floor with plenty of seating. Attracting all ages, it is busy throughout the week as well as at the weekend. Sport is shown on its many screens. A selection of bottled beers is available including real ales.

Bryn-y-Mor Hotel

16 Brynymor Road, SA1 4JQ

11-11.30 (midnight Fri & Sat); 12-11 Sun

(01792) 466650

Greene King IPA; 3 changing beers (sourced nationally; often Greene King)

Large pub, popular both with students and locals, served by a single bar offering five real ales (four during the summer months), with two from local breweries. Food is served daily from a comprehensive menu, with daily specials. There is an emphasis on sport and several TV screens are positioned around the bar area. A quiz features on Sunday, live music on Friday night.

Cockett Inn

Waunarlwydd Road, Cockett, SA2 0GB (just off A4216; take bus 12/13 to Elphin Crescent and walk down hill to pub)

11.30-11 (01792) 588748

Brains Bitter, SA Gold; 1 changing beer (sourced nationally; often Brains)

Recently refurbished, this large friendly pub has a lounge/dining area and bar at the front, and traditional pub games at the rear. Local history items and pictures adorn the room with several reminders of past generations of local and Welsh celebrities. Quiz night is Sunday and there is a karaoke night on the third Wednesday of the month. It has a community focus, and charity fundraising events are organised regularly.

No Sign Bar

56 Wind Street, SA1 1EG

11-11 (midnight Wed & Thu; 1am Fri & Sat); 12-11 Sun

(01792) 465300 nosignwinebar.com

Gower Gold; 3 changing beers (sourced nationally; often Butcombe, Mumbles, Tiny Rebel)

Historic narrow bar established in 1690, formerly known as Mundays Wine Bar and reputedly a regular haunt of Dylan Thomas. Architectural clues from various periods of the pub's past remain, some dividing the interior into separate areas. Quality food and wine are available, and up to five real ciders. Live music features in the bar on Friday, Saturday and often Sunday evenings. Bands also play in the Vault basement later at night.

Potters Wheel

85-86 The Kingsway, SA1 5JE

8am-midnight (1am Thu-Sat) (01792) 465113

Adnams Broadside; Fuller's London Pride; Ruddles Best Bitter; Sharp's Doom Bar; 6 changing beers (sourced nationally)

A city-centre Wetherspoon outlet with a long sprawling bar area offering various seating arrangements, attracting customers of all ages and backgrounds. An interesting selection of guest beers is kept, with a commitment to local breweries. Real cider is always available. Photographs on the walls feature local dignitaries associated with the area's industrial past, particularly the ceramics and pottery industries. Look for the CAMRA board and beer suggestion box.

Queen's Hotel

Gloucester Place, SA1 1TY (near Waterfront Museum)
11-11 (11.30 Sat); 12-11 Sun (01792) 521531
Theakston Best Bitter, Old Peculier; 2 changing beers (sourced nationally; often Fuller's, Glamorgan, Shepherd Neame) H
This vibrant free house is near the Dylan Thomas Theatre, City Museum, National Waterfront Museum and marina. The walls display photographs depicting Swansea's rich maritime heritage. The pub enjoys strong local support and home-cooked lunches are popular. Evening entertainment includes live music on Saturday, a Sunday quiz and bingo on Wednesday. This is a rare local outlet for Theakston Old Peculier in addition to a seasonal guest beer often from a local microbrewery.

Uplands Tavern

42 Uplands Crescent, SA2 0PG
11-11 (midnight Fri & Sat) (01792) 458242
Greene King IPA; 2 changing beers (sourced nationally; often Caledonian, Greene King) H
Although situated in the heart of Swansea's student quarter, the Tav continues to attract regulars from all walks of life. It is another former haunt of Dylan Thomas, commemorated in a separate snug area. The spacious single-room pub has a deserved reputation for the quality and variety of its live music at weekends, and hosts an open mic night on Monday. Tuesday is quiz night. There is a large heated outdoor drinking area at the front.

Westbourne

1 Brynymor Road, SA1 4JQ
11-11 Mon (11.30 Tue-Thu; midnight Fri & Sat); 12-11 Sun
(01792) 476637 westbourneswansea.com
Greene King Abbot; Sharp's Doom Bar; 4 changing beers H
Located on the western fringe of the city centre, this street-corner pub has a single split-level bar with various drinking areas including a heated terrace outside. An iPad ordering service is available at several tables. Four to six ales are always available – customers are able to request a particular beer on the pub's website. A lively quiz is held on Tuesday evening. The food is popular and booking is advised for Sunday lunch.
(2,3)

Trefforest

Otley Arms

Forest Road, CF37 1SY (on gyratory system)
11-midnight (1am Fri & Sat); 12-midnight Sun
(01443) 402033 theotley.co.uk
7 changing beers (sourced regionally; often Grey Trees, Oakham, Wylam) H
Recently renovated, the Otley enjoys a varied clientele, and is particularly popular with students from the nearby university during term time. Beers are widely sourced but always from independent brewers and come in a wide range of styles to cover all bases. Traditional food is of a high standard. Live music plays on the last Friday of the month, and also features at the Oct-O-Bar beer festival. The pub is well served by buses and trains.
(90,100)

Rickards Arms

61 Park Street, CF37 1SN
11-midnight; 12-11 Sun (01443) 402305
3 changing beers (sourced nationally) H
The pub has a core of local loyal adherents and is also a favourite with students and staff from the nearby university. It has several atmospheric areas within, including a vaulted cellar and dining area upstairs. Famed for its good-value bar food, the breakfasts are a notable feast. Three guest beers are available, one usually local and two national.
(90,100)

Treorchy

Pencelli Hotel

Pencae Terrace, CF42 6HL
closed Mon; 4-11 Tue; 6-11 Wed; 2-midnight Thu & Fri; 12-12.30am Sat; 12-11 Sun (01443) 775181
7 changing beers (sourced nationally; often Glamorgan, Salopian, Tiny Rebel) H
The Pencelli is an excellent and most welcoming community hostelry, with two large rooms served by a central bar offering a superb range of beers and ciders. A cosy log fire adds warmth in winter. The pub has a strong musical following and hosts live bands Thursday to Saturday and bank holidays. Easily reached by bus and train, there is also ample parking opposite. Local CAMRA Pub of the Year 2016-2018 and Cider Pub of the Year 2018.

Tyla Garw

Boar's Head

Coedcae Lane, CF72 9EZ (600yds from A473 over level crossing)
4-10 Mon; 12-11; 12-10 Sun (01443) 225400
8 changing beers (sourced nationally; often Dark Star, Oakham, Salopian) H
The pub has five rooms – bar, lounge, dining room, central bar and a recently added coffee lounge called Piglets. There is a large beer garden with a marquee for special events all year round. Up to eight changing real ales are available, plus a small selection of keg beers. Booking is advised for Sunday lunch. The direct walking route to Pontyclun railway station cuts through a small industrial area. **Q** **P**

Upper Church Village

Farmers Arms

St Illtyd Road, CF38 1EB
3-11 Mon-Wed; 12-midnight Thu-Sat; 12-10.30 Sun
(01443) 205766
Brains Rev James; 2 changing beers (sourced nationally; often Eagle, Greene King) H
Comfortable village local with one large bar, and a pleasant split-level beer garden and patio outside. The changing beers often include choices rarely found in the area. A popular quiz night is hosted on Tuesday, but beer and conversation are the main attractions. Traditional pub food and a logburner add to the appeal. **P** (90)

WALES

Upper Killay

Railway Inn L

553 Gower Road, SA2 7DS

☼ 12-11 (10.30 Sun) ☎ (01792) 203946

Swansea Deep Slade Dark, Bishopswood Bitter, Three Cliffs Gold, Original Wood; 1 changing beer Ⓗ

A classic locals' pub set in woodlands in the Clyne Valley. The adjacent former railway line forms part of Route 4 of the National Cycle Network. Two small rooms at the front comprise the main snug and bar, with a larger lounge at the rear. In winter the fire in the lounge provides welcome warmth and cheer. Traditional cider and at least one guest beer are kept alongside the Swansea Brewing Company beers. A large area outside hosts occasional barbecues and music events.
Q❀♣●P🚌

Wick

Star Inn

Ewenny Road, CF71 7QA

☼ 12 (5 Mon)-11.30; 12-10.30 Sun ☎ (01656) 890080

🌐 thestarinnwick.co.uk

Glamorgan Cwrw Gorslas/Bluestone Bitter; 2 changing beers (often Brecon, Evan Evans, St Austell) Ⓗ

Originally three farm cottages, the interior comprises a traditional bar with pew seating, a lounge/diner with flagstone flooring – both with log-burning fires – and an upstairs pool/function room. The landlady, her staff and locals make this a pleasant place to visit and will fill you in on some of the pub's history. Excellent food is available – the meat is supplied by an award-winning local farm butcher just a few hundred yards away. Well-behaved dogs on leads are welcome but only in the bar. Q❀◐♣●P🚌(303)🐾📶

Ystalyfera

Corner House Café Bar L

70 Commercial Street, SA9 2HS

☼ 9am-midnight; 1-1am Sat; 12-10.30 Sun

☎ (01639) 849420

3 changing beers (sourced locally; often Glamorgan, Gower, Grey Trees) Ⓗ

This traditional village pub has been tastefully refurbished and is now an open-all-day meeting place, with morning coffee and a lunchtime café to complement the pub's licensed trade (alcohol served from 11am weekdays). The ground floor is a large open area ideal for the enjoyment of real ales and cider, and also hosts occasional live entertainment. The basement area is used for playing darts. ●🚌(X50)🐾

Wern Fawr L

47 Wern Road, SA9 2LX

☼ 2-5, 7 (6.30 Fri)-11; 12-3, 7-11 Sat; 12-11 Sun

☎ (01639) 843625

9 Lives Amber, Dark, Gold; 1 changing beer (sourced locally; often Glamorgan, Grey Trees) Ⓗ

Small pub with a separate bar and lounge, run by the same family for three generations. The bar displays a collection of bricks plus mining, industrial and domestic items from the locality, making it a must-visit for historic pub enthusiasts. Occasional live music plays. The pub has a unique character and a strong local following. ❀🚌(X50)🐾📶

Pilot Inn, Mumbles

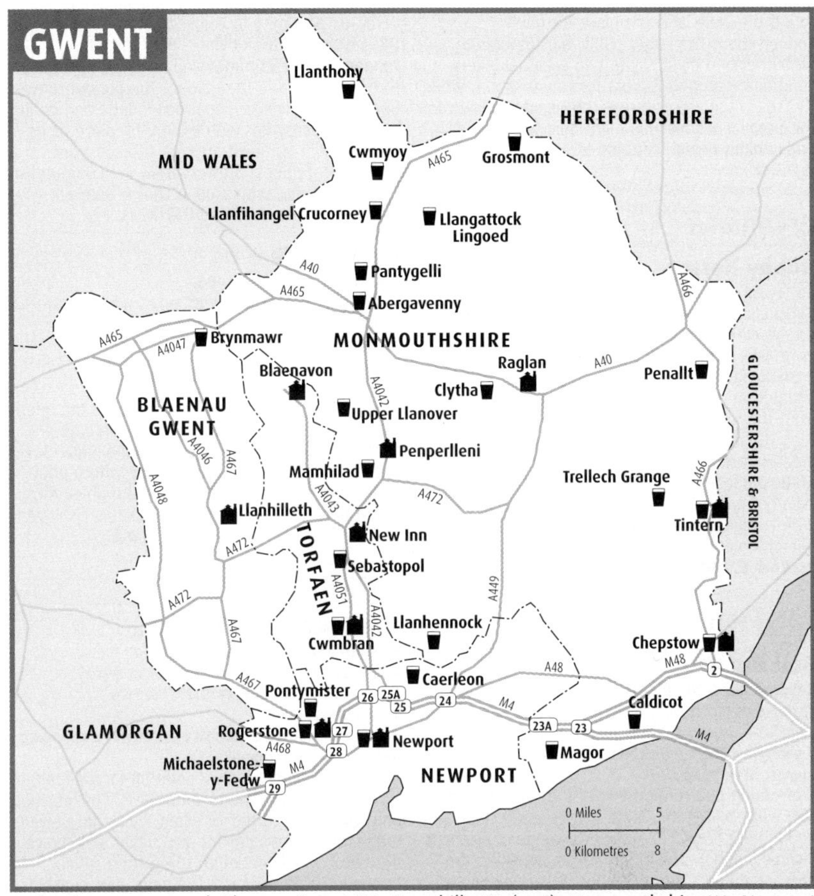

Authority areas covered: Blaenau Gwent UA, Caerphilly UA (part), Monmouthshire UA, Newport UA, Torfaen UA

Abergavenny

Cantreff Inn

61 Brecon Road, NP7 7RA

closed Mon; 12.30-11 ☎ (01873) 855799

cantreffinn.co.uk

Grey Trees Diggers Gold; Wye Valley Butty Bach; 1 changing beer (often Grey Trees) H

The only permanent outlet for Grey Trees beers in the Abergavenny area. This Victorian pub is marked by low ceilings and stone-flagged floors. There is a separate dining room, serving meals Thursday to Sunday. At the rear is a nice garden area which is a suntrap on warm summer days. A large wall mirror and a 19th-century clock – which chimes regularly on the hour but not always with the correct number of chimes – add character to the bar.

Grofield L

Baker Street, NP7 5BB

5-11 Mon; 11-11.30 ☎ (01873) 858939 grofield.com

Rhymney Bitter; Sharp's Doom Bar; 1 changing beer (sourced nationally; often Untapped, Wadworth) H

Family-run free house just off the main shopping street and opposite the cinema. The licensee has been in the trade for many years. There are two darts teams and a lively Sunday night quiz. Cooked meals are served lunchtimes and Thursday to Saturday evenings until 7.30pm. The garden is a popular suntrap in the summer months and home to an annual beer and music festival.

(47)

Station Hotel

37 Brecon Road, NP7 5UH

5 (2 Wed & Thu)-11; 1-11.30 Fri; 12-11.30 Sat; 11.30-11 Sun ☎ (01873) 854759

Draught Bass; Rhymney Bitter; Wye Valley HPA; 1 changing beer (sourced nationally) H

Featuring in CAMRA's Real Heritage Pubs of Wales, the Station is a fine example of a traditional two-room local. The small lounge has benches running

REAL ALE BREWERIES

Anglo Oregon Newport (NEW)
Baa Chepstow
Brew Monster Cwmbran (NEW)
Kingstone Tintern
Mad Dog Penperlleni
Red Dragon New Inn (NEW)
Rhymney Blaenavon
Tiny Rebel Rogerstone
Tudor Llanhilleth
Untapped Raglan

round the walls and is a place for quiet conversation. The larger public bar features a logburner and divides into two areas. Drinkers congregate around the bar for conversation, while the space towards the rear comes into its own for the popular Wednesday night quiz and regular Friday night music featuring local musicians.
♣P🚌🐾

Brynmawr

Hobby Horse

30 Greenland Road, NP23 4DT

closed Mon; 12-3 Tue; 12-3, 7-11 Wed & Thu; 12-3, 6.30-11.30 Fri; 12-midnight Sat; 11-10.30 Sun
☎ (01495) 310996

2 changing beers Ⓗ

Situated in a residential area five minutes' walk from the town centre, this pub has a strong local feel. The main front room leads to a small drinking area in front of the bar. A short corridor by the side of the bar leads to the restaurant, which also has its own entrance. The large front patio is very popular with families. The two ales on sale are usually from microbreweries, one often from a local brewery.
❀♿♣P🚌🐾

Caerleon

Bell Inn ✔

Bulmore Road, NP18 1QQ

closed Mon & Tue; 12-11 (midnight Fri & Sat); 12-10.30 Sun
☎ (01633) 420613 thebellinncaerleon.co.uk

3 changing beers (sourced nationally; often St Austell, Wye Valley) Ⓗ

Welcoming pub reminiscent of the hostelries of old, with solid stone walls, low-beamed ceilings and a great fireplace. An eclectic range of artefacts includes quirky artwork displayed alongside the more traditional pub trappings. This is a popular dining venue which also caters for those just wanting to relax with a drink. The real ales are mainly, but not always, well-known brands, and there is an impressive choice of ciders and perry.
❀♣P🚌🐾

White Hart ✔

28 High Street, NP18 1AE

2-11; 12-11.30 Fri & Sat; 12-11 Sun ☎ (01633) 430999

Greene King Abbot; 2 changing beers (sourced nationally) Ⓗ

A village favourite with pleasant front and rear areas linked by a stand-up drinking space alongside an impressive central bar open on three sides. The decor features well-maintained polished wood panelling and the rear room has an attractive trophy cabinet set into the wall. Some old mirrors promote popular drinks of their day. The competitively priced Abbot Ale is accompanied by two guest ales which reside on the front counter alongside Westons Old Rosie cider.
❀♣🚌🐾

Caldicot

Castle Inn

64 Church Road, NP26 4HW

closed Mon; 12-11 (midnight Fri & Sat); 12-7 Sun
☎ (01291) 420509 thecastleinncaldicot.com

2 changing beers (sourced nationally; often Greene King) Ⓗ

Given its proximity to Caldicot Castle Country Park, the castle links are obvious, with miniature cannons by the entrance and an impressive play fort for children in the garden. The pleasant low beamed interior has a spacious lounge and dining area and a cosy bar with a large fireplace as its focal point. Two guest ales are sourced from national or regional brewers from the Ei Group list. Food is popular, with a good choice from an extensive menu. ❀♿P🚌(X74)

Cross Inn ✔

1 Newport Road, NP26 4BG

12-11 (midnight Fri & Sat) ☎ (01291) 409042

Sharp's Doom Bar; 2 changing beers (sourced nationally) Ⓗ

Thriving pub with an often lively main bar which hosts live bands. A central partition with a wall-mounted TV above a fireplace separates the open-plan bar from a more secluded section with another comfortable seating area on a higher level at the rear. A small snug is quieter with a pool table. Two guest ales accompany the ubiquitous Doom Bar. Note the array of pumpclips displayed above the bar. ❀♿♣P🚌(X74)🐾

Chepstow

Chepstow Athletic Club Ⓛ

Mathern Road, Bulwark, NP16 5JJ (off Bulwark Rd)

7-11 (11.30 Fri); 12.30-midnight (11.30 winter) Sat; 12-5 (summer only), 7-11 Sun ☎ (01291) 622126
chepstowac.co.uk

Brains SA; St Austell Cornish Best Bitter; 2 changing beers (sourced regionally) Ⓗ

This friendly club is a focal point for local people of all ages, including sports enthusiasts. Conversation only gives way to the TV when Wales are playing rugby. Ultra-consistent for ale quality and choice, the two guest beers often come from small breweries across the UK. The patio suits sunshine supping while a large upstairs room sports a bar with cask ale. Good value for money enhances the popularity of the Athy. Visiting CAMRA members are particularly welcome. ❀♿♣P🚌(73,X74)

Five Alls

Hocker Hill Street, NP16 5ER

12-11 (midnight Thu-Sun) ☎ (01291) 622528

3 changing beers (sourced regionally; often Butcombe, Robinsons) Ⓗ

An old pub built in 1849 on a cobblestone street with a superb sign above the entrance depicting the Five Alls. A pub of character, the interior retains most of the original layout with some touches of modernity. The emphasis here is on rock music, with a digital jukebox and live music, ideal if you like to relax listening to classic rock tracks. It has a pinball machine and free pool on Sunday and Monday. ❀♣🚌🐾

Queen's Head 🏆 Ⓛ

Moor Street, NP16 5DD

closed Mon; 5-11 Tue-Fri; 12-2.30, 5-11 Sat; 2-8 Sun
☎ 07793 889613

8 changing beers (sourced regionally; often Gower, Grey Trees, Untapped) Ⓖ

Welcoming micropub that has achieved local CAMRA recognition. An eclectic range of furniture provides comfort while you sup your drink and absorb the atmosphere. Chatter and laughter dominate – there is no obtrusive noise from TV or electronic games here – and you cannot help but be drawn into friendly conversation with other drinkers. The ale and cider range is mainly sourced from Wales although occasional themed weeks are held with ales from other regions. Gwent CAMRA Town Pub of the Year 2016-18. Q

Clytha

Clytha Arms

Groesonen Road, NP7 9BW (on B4598 old road between Abergavenny and Raglan)

12-3.30 (not Mon), 6-11; 12-11 Fri-Sun (01873) 840206 clytha-arms.com

Brecon Three Beacons; Untapped Sundown; Wye Valley Bitter; 3 changing beers (sourced regionally) H

Multi award-winning pub, ever-present in this Guide for over a quarter of a century. It is well known for its food as well as the range and quality of its beers – six are usually on offer at any one time. Since the Untapped Brewery opened along the road the pub has become an unofficial brewery tap. Extensive lawns are lovely for sitting out on warm days, while the rear garden is ideal for the annual cider and perry festival.
Q P (83)

Cwmbran

John Fielding

1 Caradoc Road, NP44 1PP

8am-midnight; 7-1am Fri & Sat (01633) 833760

Greene King Abbot; Ruddles Best Bitter; Sharp's Doom Bar; 2 changing beers H

John Fielding, masquerading as John Williams, was a local war hero who won the Victoria Cross at the Battle of Rorke's Drift (1879) in the Zulu Wars. The pub proudly maintains links with former local servicemen of today and is a Wetherspoon community award winner. A popular all-day venue, it adds to Cwmbran's shopping and entertainment experience with its package of competitively priced food and drinks. The regular ales are supplemented by two guests often sourced from local Welsh breweries. Q P

Mount Pleasant

Wesley Street, Old Cwmbran, NP44 3LX

4-7 Mon; 12-11 (midnight Fri & Sat) (01633) 712176

2 changing beers (sourced regionally; often Kingstone) H

The Mount attracts a good mix of regulars who come in just for a drink, and others who come for a meal as well. A community hub in Old Cwmbran, its interior is modern and comfortable. There are broadly three areas – the main section in front of the bar, a smaller area to the right and a raised area on the left, mainly used for dining. The two handpumps serve ales primarily from Welsh breweries, with the Tintern-based Kingstone particularly popular. P (6)

Cwmyoy

Queen's Head

NP7 7NE SO311221

10.30-2, 6-9 Mon; 6-9 Tue; closed Wed & Fri; 12-2, 6-9 Thu; 11-3 Sat; 12-4 Sun (01873) 890241

Kingstone Classic H

An old stone-built pub whose heavy wooden beams and stone-flagged floors reflect its antiquity. The same landlord has run the pub for the last 40 years – the longest serving licensee in Gwent. Do not be deterred by the limited opening hours – this pub is well worth a visit. The beautiful and serene landscape surrounding it belies the fact that it is only a couple of miles from the A465 Abergavenny to Hereford road. Q P

Grosmont

Angel Inn

NP7 8EP

6-10.30 Mon; closed Tue; 6-11 Wed; 12-3, 6-11 Thu & Fri; 12-11 Sat; 12-6 Sun (01981) 240646 grosmont.wales/the-angel-inn

Butcombe Adam Henson's Rare Breed; Wye Valley Butty Bach; 2 changing beers (sourced regionally) H

Perched high, almost on England's border, The Angel really is the village hub. The guitars on the wall reflect the influence of music on the pub's life. Live music can be heard here on a monthly basis. The traditional bar, to the left as you walk in, has a rustic charm, with a selection of wooden tables, attractive benches and settles, as well as hop-decorated beams. Opening times may vary – check before visiting. P

Llanfihangel Crucorney

Skirrid Inn

Hereford Road, NP7 8DH

11.30-2.30 (not Mon), 5.30-11; 11.30-11 Sat; 12-5 Sun (01873) 890258 skirridmountaininn.co.uk

2 changing beers (sourced nationally; often Wye Valley) H

An ancient pub, where Owain Glyndwr is said to have rallied his troops, and the infamous Judge Jeffries hung people for alleged involvement in the 17th-century Monmouth Uprising. Named after the local mountain, the pub is in the centre of the village, bypassed by the A465. The village marks the start of the beautiful valley that makes its way through the Black Mountains to Llanthony, and the whole area is therefore popular with walkers and lovers of the outdoors. Q P (X3)

Llangattock Lingoed

Hunter's Moon Inn

NP7 8RR SO361201

12-11 (01873) 821499 hunters-moon-inn.co.uk

Wye Valley HPA H/G, **Butty Bach** H; **1 changing beer (sourced regionally)** H/G

Dating from the 13th century when it housed workers for the neighbouring church, this pub remains a haven for walkers on Offa's Dyke. It is very much the social hub of the village and serves a wide range of excellent food throughout the day. In the traditional flagstone-floored bar an owl gazes down at you from beneath a bright hunter's moon. Summer visitors can enjoy the attractive seating area outside overlooking the grounds of the adjacent church. Q P

Llanhennock

Wheatsheaf

NP18 1LT ST353927

11 (2 Sat)-11; 12-4, 8-11 Sun (01633) 420468

Fuller's London Pride; 2 changing beers (sourced regionally) H

A Guide fixture for over 30 years, The Wheatsheaf has probably remained almost unchanged over that time. The main bar is to the right, with a slightly smaller and cosier bar to the left. The walls of both are festooned with old photographs, bric-a-brac and memorabilia. Outside, there are views of the hills miles away both front and back, plus a secluded garden. Boules is played seriously in the car park. There is usually a beer from a local brewery on sale. 🐎❀◐▲♣P🐾📶

Llanthony

Half Moon

NP7 7NN (200yds past abbey) SO286279

⏲ 12-3, 6-11; 12-3 Wed; 12-11 Fri-Sun summer; 6-11 Fri; 11-11 Sat; 11-5 Sun winter ☎ (01873) 890611

🌐 halfmoon-llanthony.co.uk

Wye Valley Butty Bach; 1 changing beer (sourced regionally; often Wye Valley) Ⓗ

Situated near the romantic ruins of Llanthony Abbey and surrounded by miles of outstandingly beautiful countryside in the heart of the Black Mountains, this is a truly remote pub that continues to serve its scattered rural community. A recent repaint of the exterior walls uncovered and restored the name of Facey's Brewery, who supplied beer until it closed in 1950. Ten basic but comfortable bedrooms provide accommodation for walkers and those seeking the solitude of this truly spectacular area. Q🐎🛏◐◑▲♣P🐾📶

Llanthony Priory Hotel

Mill Farm, NP7 7NN SO288279

⏲ closed Mon; 12-3, 6-11; 11-11 Sat; 11-5 Sun ☎ (01873) 890487 🌐 llanthonyprioryhotel.co.uk

Felinfoel Double Dragon; 1 changing beer (sourced regionally) Ⓗ

A truly remarkable bar situated in what was once the abbot's vaulted cellars in a remote and hauntingly beautiful monastic ruin. Deserted by the monks even before the Dissolution, the remains are not surprisingly Grade I listed and the well-maintained grounds are now a stunning beer garden. The proximity of Offa's Dyke Path and glorious walking country makes this a popular spot within the Brecon Beacons National Park for walkers, day trippers and real ale drinkers. Q🐎❀🛏◐◑▲P

Magor

Wheatsheaf Ⓛ ✔

The Square, NP26 3HN

⏲ 10-11 (midnight Fri & Sat); 12-11 Sun ☎ (01633) 880608

4 changing beers (sourced regionally; often Rhymney, Sharp's) Ⓗ

A community-focused pub with a traditional internal layout including a public bar, lounge and restaurant. Low beams and exposed stonework add to the pub's character, and it is a popular venue in the area. The publican's genuine passion for real ale is evident, with every effort made to offer an interesting choice of styles within its permitted range. The ales are sourced from national, regional and local breweries – the pub is a staunch supporter of local produce. 🐎❀◐◑♿♣P🚌(62,74)🐾📶

Mamhilad

Horseshoe Inn ✔

Old Abergavenny Road, NP4 8QZ

⏲ 12-3, 5-11; 11.30-midnight Fri-Sun ☎ (01873) 880542

🌐 horseshoeinn.org

Sharp's Atlantic; Tiny Rebel Cwtch; house beer (by Mad Dog); 1 changing beer (sourced regionally) Ⓗ

This welcoming 200-year-old pub has an outside drinking area giving fine views of the surrounding hills, where you can drink to the sound of bleating sheep. The bar with its slate floor retains the cosy feel of a country pub and attracts walkers seeking refreshment. The food has a fine reputation with an appetising menu. The guest ales, which sit alongside the locally brewed house ale, are usually interesting for the area, while real cider is also served. Q🐎❀◐◑▲🍎P🐾📶

Michaelstone-y-Fedw

Cefn Mably Arms ✔

CF3 6XS

⏲ 12-midnight (10.30 Sun) ☎ (01633) 680347

🌐 cefnmablyarms.com

Butcombe Gold; Wye Valley HPA, Butty Bach Ⓗ

Popular local pub a couple of miles from the A48 at Castleton. It is slightly off the beaten track, with no public transport, and a good 20-minute walk from the A48. The pub is mainly laid out for diners, but has a selection of well-kept ales available. The garden/smoking area is reached through the cwtch – an additional dining area next to the bar. Opening times are reduced between November and Easter, so check with the pub before visiting. Q🐎❀◐◑P🐾📶

Newport

Godfrey Morgan Ⓛ ✔

158 Chepstow Road, Maindee, NP19 8EG

⏲ 8am-midnight (1am Fri & Sat) ☎ (01633) 221928

Brains SA; Greene King Abbot; Ruddles Best Bitter; Sharp's Doom Bar; 2 changing beers (sourced nationally; often Oakham, Wychwood) Ⓗ

Named after the 1st Viscount Tredegar, a survivor of the Charge of the Light Brigade, this large, open-plan Wetherspoon pub was once a cinema, and has numerous photos of erstwhile stars with local connections dotted around the walls. As well as the Wetherspoon regulars, two guest ales are available, and two ciders on gravity are served from the fridge. The main entrance is on the busy Chepstow Road, with the main bar area up steps at the rear which also gives access to a small car park. Q🐎❀◐◑♿🍎P🚌📶

McCann's Rock 'n' Ale Bar Ⓛ

10 High Street, NP20 1FQ

⏲ 12-11 (3am Fri & Sat) ☎ (01633) 253648

Robinsons Trooper; 1 changing beer (sourced regionally; often Cotleigh, Untapped) Ⓗ

Newport heavy metal mecca the Hornblower was sadly demolished at the end of 2017, but its spirit lives on in McCann's, which has much of its memorabilia. The main bar is long and narrow, with a raised stage at the back for the Saturday evening bands. There is a smaller lounge/function room downstairs. A pizzeria was installed in February 2018 selling pizzas and burgers (Wed-Sun), with the same hours as the pub. Cider is sold from polypins. ❀◐◑⇄♣🍎🚌📶

Olde Murenger House

52-53 High Street, NP20 1GA

⏲ 12-11; 12-3, 7.30-10.30 Sun ☎ (01633) 263977

Samuel Smith Old Brewery Bitter Ⓗ

Although of Tudor origin, this very popular local institution provides a snapshot of Newport's Victorian past thanks to the sympathetic attentions of Samuel Smith's brewery. Behind the leaded windows lies a characterful interior of dark wood and high-back settles, with old brewery scenes, images and characters of Newport past and present dotted around its walls. The long-serving management team provide a welcoming pub environment where drinking, chatting, laughter and good dining are the order of the day.

St Julian Inn

Caerleon Road, NP18 1QA

11.30-11.30 (midnight Fri & Sat); 12-11 Sun
(01633) 243548 stjulian.co.uk

Bombardier; Young's Bitter; 2 changing beers (sourced regionally; often Bath Ales, Ludlow, Wye Valley)

A well-run pub worth visiting before or after taking in the Roman tourist attractions of nearby Caerleon. It enjoys a wonderfully scenic location perched above the River Usk, with commanding views of the river, countryside and Caerleon from the outdoor balcony. A central bar attends to the needs of customers who can make themselves at home in a choice of areas for drinking and dining. Light, hoppy guest ales go down well here.

Tiny Rebel

22-23 High Street, NP20 1FX

12-11 (1am Fri & Sat) (01633) 973934

Tiny Rebel Fubar, Cwtch; 4 changing beers (sourced nationally; often Tiny Rebel)

Newport's most exciting beer venue has a wide appeal, particularly with younger drinkers who eagerly savour both the real ales and new wave keg beers. Tiny Rebel is one of Britain's most innovative breweries and this modern, attractive outlet is where it showcases its regular ales and new brews, plus beers from other like-minded breweries, sometimes with collaborative brews. Tasty burgers and pizzas can be chosen from a creative menu. When busy upstairs, the downstairs Cwtch lounge offers quieter surroundings.

Pantygelli

Crown Inn

Old Hereford Road, NP7 7HR

12-2.30 (not Mon), 6-11; 12-3, 6-11 Sat; 12-3, 6-10.30 Sun
(01873) 853314 thecrownatpantygelli.com

Draught Bass; Rhymney Best; Wye Valley HPA; 1 changing beer (sourced regionally; often Grey Trees, Kingstone, Monty's)

A perennially popular pub and restaurant. Family run, the warmth of the welcome is as important as the high quality of the beers and food. As a result, the faithful band of regulars are joined by visitors who often come from miles around, such is the pub's reputation. On warm days the flower-decked patio is extremely popular, with distant views over to The Skirrid mountain. Inside there are exposed beams and a stone-flagged floor, creating a characterful ambience. P

Bread is the staff of life, but beer is life itself. **Traditional**

Penallt

Boat Inn

Lone Lane, NP25 4AJ

12-11 (01600) 712615 theboatpenallt.co.uk

Wye Valley Butty Bach; 2 changing beers (sourced regionally; often Butcombe, Goff's, Wickwar)

This handsome old riverside pub in steeply wooded scenery attracts walkers, travellers and locals drawn by its magnificent location. One handy route is to park in England and cross into Wales via a footpath alongside the old railway bridge. Your reward is well-kept gravity-served ales (changing beers are often from Bespoke, Butcombe, Goffs or Wickwar) and up to 20 ciders, plus wholesome food. The interior comprises two simply furnished rooms, while outside, the garden, patio and riverside terrace are perfect on sunny days. Closed Tuesday winter. P (69)

Pontymister

Commercial Inn

Commercial Street, NP11 6BA

11 (10 Sat)-11.30; 12-11.30 Sun (01633) 612608
thecommercialpontymister.com

3 changing beers (sourced nationally; often Brains)

The pub of choice for local real ale lovers, with two interesting beers always available, and popular with sports fans, with up to five (often muted) TV screens dotted about. Excellent and reasonably priced food is served throughout the day. There is a large verandah/smoking area at the front and disabled access at the side. On the main street through Pontymister and within easy walking distance of buses and the local railway station. (56,151)

Rogerstone

Tiny Rebel Brewery Bar

Wern Industrial Estate, Wern Terrace, NP10 9FQ (off Chartist Drive)

closed Mon; 12-10 (1am Fri); 9am-1am Sat; 9am-11 Sun
(01633) 547378

6 changing beers (sourced locally)

Impressive new-build bar and dining area, with a shop on-site. A wide range of Tiny Rebel beers in cask, keg, bottles and cans is available. The bar has views of the brewery from the restaurant, while the front opens out on to a large south-facing verandah. The now familiar Tiny Rebel logo dominates the wall above the bar and is flanked by examples of merchandise available for purchase from the brewery shop. P

Sebastopol

Open Hearth

Wern Road, NP4 5DR

12-1am (2am Fri & Sat); 12-midnight Sun
(01495) 763752 theopenhearth.wales

Wye Valley HPA; 4 changing beers (sourced nationally; often Brains, Dartmoor, Sharp's)

Popular pub beside the Monmouthshire & Brecon Canal with a loyal local following and also attracting a passing trade of walkers, cyclists and boaters. The canalside entrance leads to an intimate bar with a cosy side room – there is also a lounge/dining room and function room. Outside, the towpath and decked seating areas are popular in fine weather. The ale range of nationally known brands changes regularly, while a comprehensive food menu is available 12-9pm (until 4pm Sun). ❀◑♣P🚌(X24)🐾📶

Sebastopol Social Club

Wern Road, NP4 5DU (on corner of Wern Rd with Austin Rd)

12-11 (midnight Fri & Sat); 12-10.30 Sun

☎ (01495) 763808 🌐 sebastopolsocial.org.uk

Glamorgan Welsh Pale Ale; 3 changing beers (sourced regionally; often Grey Trees) Ⓗ

One of the flagship award-winning clubs selling real ale in Wales, the club is comfortably furnished throughout and caters for a variety of indoor sports and functions. Live entertainment is hosted at the weekend and large screens show big sporting events. The real ale range is from popular south Wales breweries plus one or two guests generally from the West Country. CAMRA members are welcome (subject to entry rules). ❀♿♣P🚌(X24)🐾📶

Tintern

Anchor Inn

NP16 6TE (off A466 at Tintern Abbey)

11.30 (11 Fri)-11; 11.30-10.30 Sun ☎ (01291) 689582

🌐 theanchortintern.co.uk

Kingstone Tewdric's Tipple; Wye Valley HPA; 1 changing beer (sourced regionally; often Bath Ales, Butcombe, Otter) Ⓗ

Despite some redevelopment of the interior, the Anchor oozes with the rich history of this beautiful valley, at one time pounding with industry and at another solemnly and silently monastic. The local Cistercian monks made their cider here and their massive press is still the centrepiece of the bar. Kingstone and Wye Valley ales are usually available and enjoy high turnover, as this large pub has gained a burgeoning reputation for its tasty ales and excellent food. Muddy boots and pets are welcome. ❀◑P🚌(69)🐾📶

Wye Valley Hotel

Monmouth Road, NP16 6SQ

11-3, 6-11; 12-3, 6.30-10.30 Sun ☎ (01291) 689441

🌐 thewyevalleyhotel.co.uk

Wye Valley HPA, Butty Bach; 1 changing beer (sourced locally; often Kingstone) Ⓗ

Here is a fine place to pause, drink and stay, whatever the weather in this beautiful valley, with a friendly welcome from the long-established owners. Two Wye Valley beers often complement a guest ale from the nearby Kingstone Brewery. The comfortable single bar has a multi-angled shape matching the distinctive 1920s pub itself, while an array of commemorative beer bottles lines a shelf around the entire room. Home-cooked meals are available both in the bar and the traditional restaurant. ❀◑♿P🚌(69)🐾📶

Trellech Grange

Fountain Inn

NP16 6QW SO503011

closed Mon; 4-11 (9.30 Tue); 12-11 Sat; 12-9 Sun

☎ (01291) 689303 🌐 fountaininntrellech.co.uk

Glamorgan Cwrw Gorslas/Bluestone Bitter; Wye Valley Butty Bach; 1 changing beer (sourced locally; often Kingstone) Ⓗ

Well worth the effort to find, the Fountain is a tribute to its enterprising owners. Even in bleak midwinter you can rely on its opening times, two real fires and its ales, while in summer it is a rural idyll with its garden and cooling brook. Two regular ales are usually joined by one from Kingstone or Rhymney breweries. Appealing menus and midweek darts, quiz and cribbage evenings help keep this venerable pub popular all year round. ❀◑P🐾

Upper Llanover

Goose & Cuckoo

NP7 9ER (at end of Llanover village follow hand-written signs to the Goose) SO292073

closed Mon; 11.30-3, 7-11 Tue-Thu; 11.30-11 Fri & Sat; 12-10.30 Sun ☎ (01873) 880277

🌐 gooseandcuckooinn.wales

Rhymney Bitter; Untapped Border Bitter; 1 changing beer (sourced regionally) Ⓗ

The Goose has a reputation of being difficult to find, but leave the A4042 at the sign marked Upper Llanover, follow the signs to the pub, and you will discover it at the top of the hill on the right-hand side. Its comfortable interior has a flagged stone floor with attractive benches and chairs. As befits a pub belonging to a bygone age, the use of mobile phones is discouraged. Three local beers and a wide range of whiskies are served. Gwent CAMRA Country Pub of the Year 2018. Q❀◑♣P🐾

Kitchen of an inn

In the evening we reached a village where I had determined to pass the night. As we drove into the great gateway of the inn, I saw on one side the light of a rousing kitchen fire beaming through a window. I entered, and admired for the hundredth time that picture of convenience, neatness, and broad honest enjoyment, the kitchen of an English inn. It was of spacious dimension, hung around by copper and tin vessels, highly polished, and decorated here and there with a Christmas green. Hams, tongues, and flitches of bacon were suspended from the ceiling; a smoke-jack made its ceaseless clanking behind the fireplace, and a clock ticked in one corner. A well-scoured deal table extended along one side of the kitchen, with a cold round of beef, and other hearty viands upon it, over which two foaming tankards of ale seemed mounting guard. Travellers of inferior order were preparing to attack this stout repast, while others sat smoking or gossiping over their ale, on two high-backed oaken settles beside the fire.

Washington Irving, Travelling at Christmas, 1884

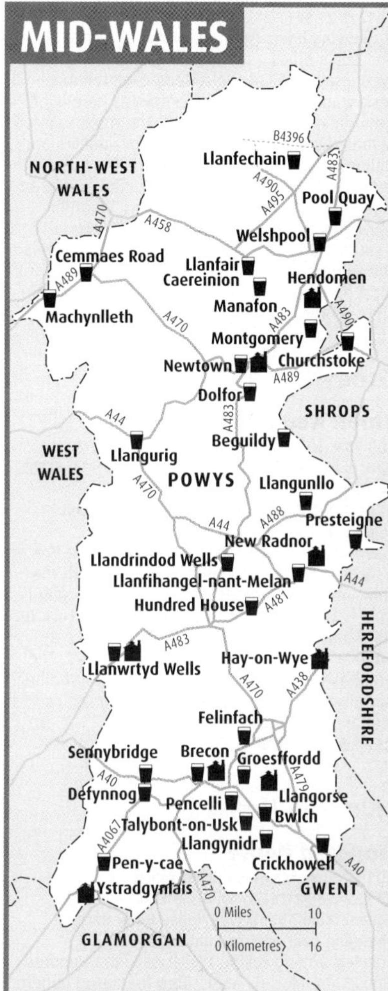

Authority area covered: Powys UA

Beguildy

Radnorshire Arms

LD7 1YE

closed Mon; 12-2, 6-11 (midnight Fri & Sat); 12-3.30, 7-11 Sun ☎ (01547) 510634

Ludlow Gold; Stonehouse Station Bitter Ⓗ

The Radnorshire Arms dates back to the 16th century and was probably a drovers' pub at one time. There is a cosy bar with an inglenook, an intimate dining area and a pleasant garden area to the side. The beers are from Ludlow and Stonehouse breweries. The pub is popular with diners. There are separate menus for lunchtimes and evenings as well as Sunday lunches and daily specials. Q P

Brecon

Brecon Tap

6 Bulwark, LD3 7LB

11-11 (midnight Fri & Sat); 12-11 Sun ☎ (01874) 623888

breconinns.co.uk

Brecon Three Beacons, Copper Beacons, Gold Beacons; 4 changing beers (sourced regionally) Ⓗ

In a prime town-centre location, this is a contemporary-style bar giving a light and airy feel, with comfortable seating throughout and walls lined with bottle-filled shelves. Three or four varying guest ales are sold, often from English apparent, sometimes further afield. There is also an interesting range of international and UK craft ales, plus simple food-good-value pies, gum including sugar free chewing and the like. Bottled beers, wines, spirits and local artisan craft produce are available for off-sales. Q

Bwlch

New Inn

Brecon Road, LD3 7RQ (on A40 between Brecon and Crickhowell)

5-11; 12-11 Sat; 12-8 Sun ☎ (01874) 730215

beaconsbackpackers.co.uk

Felinfoel Double Dragon; Wye Valley Butty Bach; 2 changing beers (sourced regionally; often Grey Trees, Salopian, Tiny Rebel) Ⓗ

Lively and cosy village pub popular both with locals and visitors. A comfortable dining area sits to the side of the stone-flagged public bar, with armchairs and settles arranged around a huge fireplace. Two interesting guest ales supplement the two regulars, and good-value home-cooked food is available weekend evenings and lunchtimes. The pub is an excellent base for exploring the Brecon Beacons and Black Mountains, with bunkhouse accommodation available. Local branch CAMRA Pub of the Year 2017 and 2018, and for South Wales in 2017. Q P (43,X43)

Cemmaes Road

Dovey Valley Hotel ★

SY20 8JZ

5-11 ☎ (01650) 511335

1 changing beer (sourced locally; often Cwrw Cader, Evan Evans, Monty's) Ⓗ

This gem of a pub was built to serve the nearby railway. Boasting a nationally important historic pub interior, it comprises a cosy main bar and a snug room with traditional features from the 1870s, including the original slate floors and Edwardian tiled fireplace (with log fires in winter). It is furnished with a mix of mirrors, brewery memorabilia and other eclectic items. Live music sessions take place on occasion.
Q P (X85)

Churchstoke

Horse & Jockey

SY15 6AE

12 (4.30 Mon & Tue)-11 ☎ (01588) 620060

2 changing beers (sourced regionally) Ⓗ

REAL ALE BREWERIES

9 Lives Ystradgynlais
Brecon Brecon
Heart of Wales Llanwrtyd Wells
Lithic Llangorse
Lucky 7 Hay on Wye
Monty's Hendomen
Radnorshire New Radnor
Wilderness Newtown (NEW)

A prominent stone-built pub on the edge of the village, offering a changing range of guest ales, and up to nine real ciders and perries during the summer. The public bar is wooden beamed with a pool table, darts and a bar billiards table. The lounge is carpeted, with comfortable armchairs and wall seating. There is a stone fireplace with a wood-burning stove. A large well-appointed restaurant is off the lounge.
(81)

Crickhowell

Bear Hotel

High Street, NP8 1BW

10-11; 11-10.30 Sun (01873) 810408

bearhotel.co.uk

Brains Rev James; Sharp's Doom Bar; 2 changing beers (sourced regionally) H

Originally a 15th-century coaching inn, this is now an award-winning hotel. The multi-roomed bar enjoys grand surroundings with exposed beams, wood panelling, fine settles and an eclectic selection of furnishings and decorations. The two bar rooms have exposed fireplaces, as does one of the side rooms. Food is excellent, with a varied menu featuring much local produce. The hotel is an ideal base for exploring the surrounding Black Mountains and Brecon Beacons National Park.
QP(43,X43)

Defynnog

Tanners Arms

LD3 8SF (on A4067)

5-midnight; 12-midnight Fri-Sun (01874) 638032

tannersarmspub.com

5 changing beers H/G

Family-run country pub known for its warm welcome, set in a delightful village in the Brecon Beacons National Park. It has traded continuously since 1870 but the original buildings – cottages for workers at the nearby tannery – date from circa 1806. A selection of real ciders is usually on offer alongside home-cooked food. A number of beer and cider festivals are held throughout the year. A multiple local CAMRA award winner.
P(T6)

Dolfor

Dolfor Inn

SY16 4AA

12 (6 Mon & Tue)-11; 12-midnight Fri & Sat

(01686) 626531 thedolforinn.com

Ludlow Gold; 3 changing beers (sourced locally; often Clun, Six Bells, Wye Valley) H

A former drovers' inn, this stone-walled, wooden-beamed rural pub has an intimate restaurant room with an inglenook fireplace. The bar area has settles and a low ceiling creating a cosy atmosphere. Adjacent to the well-stocked bar is a popular games area. For larger parties there is a room converted from the old stable block. The pub has gained a good reputation locally for its food and is handy for walkers on the Kerry Ridgeway path. P(T4)

Felinfach

Griffin L

LD3 0UB (just off A470 3 miles NE of Brecon)

12-11.30 (01874) 620111

4 changing beers (sourced locally) H

The pub's ethos – the simple things in life done well – says it all. A welcoming country inn, restaurant and rooms, the emphasis here is on good beer and excellent food. The multi-roomed layout allows for discrete areas for drinking and dining. The huge fireplace between the bar and the main dining area dominates in winter, while an Aga lurks in a side room, providing warmth throughout. On the outskirts of the Brecon Beacons, the large garden affords superb views of the surrounding mountains. Beers are sourced from local breweries. Accommodation is in seven en-suite rooms. QP(39,T4)

Groesffordd

Three Horseshoes

LD3 7SN (just off B4558)

12-3 (not Mon), 5-11; 12-11 Fri-Sun (01874) 665672

threehorseshoesgroesffordd.co.uk

St Austell Tribute; 2 changing beers (sourced regionally) H

Busy village-centre inn in the heart of the Brecon Beacons, boasting superb views from both the front and rear outdoor seating areas. The pub is only a 10-minute walk from the Brynich Lock on the Monmouthshire & Brecon Canal and is a popular stop for boaters and other visitors. The emphasis here is very much on food, but the beers are always varied and interesting. Brynich caravan site and the Brecon YHA are nearby.

Hundred House

Hundred House

LD1 5RY (on A481 near Builth Wells)

12-2, 5.30-11; 11-11 Sat & Sun (01982) 570231

Greene King Abbot; Wye Valley Butty Bach; 1 changing beer (sourced nationally) H

Located among rolling Welsh hills, the Hundred House Inn takes its name from the Saxon hundred, which was an administrative area. At one time a drovers' inn, this is now a traditional pub, well patronised by the local farming community. There is a lounge, locals' bar, pool room with TV (for rugby), restaurant area and beer garden. The pub is welcoming and friendly – afternoon closing times are flexible depending on custom.
QP

Llandrindod Wells

Arvon Ale House L

Temple Street, LD1 5DP

closed Mon & Tue; 4-10 Wed & Thu (11 Fri & Sat); 4-10 Sun

07477 627267

5 changing beers (sourced regionally) H

A welcome addition to the Llandrindod pub scene, this micropub offers sensibly priced beers sourced from Wales, the borders and the Midlands, plus at least four real ciders. Formerly shop premises, the pub is small and perfectly formed. It is a proper alehouse for the quiet enjoyment of beer with no distractions. Snacks are available. All-comers folk music sessions are held on the second and fourth Sunday of the month. Wales CAMRA Pub of the Year 2017. Q(T4)

Middleton Arms

Tremont Road, LD1 5EB (corner of Trefonen Lane)
11-3, 5-11.30 Mon; 12-3, 5-11.30 Tue; 2-11.30 Wed; 5-11.30 Thu; 11-1am Fri; 11-12.30am Sat; 11-11.30 Sun
(01597) 822066
Worthington's; 2 changing beers (sourced regionally) H
A friendly street-corner local at the north end of town on the road to Newtown, named after one of the town's Victorian developers. The guest beer changes weekly. The pub supports four darts teams as well as pool and dominoes teams, and screens sports channels on TVs. There is an enclosed drinking area outside and families and dogs are welcome. **Q** (461,T4)

Llanfair Caereinion

Goat Hotel

High Street, SY21 0QS (off A485)
11-11 (midnight Fri & Sat) (01938) 810428
thegoathotel.co.uk
3 changing beers (sourced locally; often Stonehouse, Wood) H
Excellent 300-year-old beamed coaching inn with a welcoming atmosphere which attracts both locals and tourists. The plush lounge, dominated by a large inglenook and open fire, has comfortable leather armchairs and sofas. There is a dining room serving home-cooked food and a games room to the rear. The choice of real ale always includes one from Wood Brewery. Beware the low-beamed entrance to the gents.
Q **P** (87)

Llanfechain

Plas-yn-Dinas Inn

SY22 6UJ (off B4393)
closed Mon & Tue; 12-2.30, 5-11; 12-11 Sat; 12-10.30 Sun
(01691) 829055 plasyndinas.co.uk
3 changing beers (sourced locally; often Monty's, Purple Moose, Stonehouse) H
Early 18th-century, Grade II listed public house which started life as a courthouse. Following a lengthy closure and a complete makeover, the Plas reopened in 2015. The interior features wooden beams and supports and has a number of handsome drinking spaces – the front area has tiled floors while the rear restaurant/lounge is carpeted. Outside is a patio with benches and a garden. Note the bottle collection from old Shropshire breweries. **Q** **P** (72,74)

Llanfihangel-nant-Melan

Fforest Inn

LD8 2TN (jct A44 and A481)
closed Mon; 12-11 (01544) 350526 theforest.co.uk
3 changing beers (sourced nationally) H
Built in the 16th century as a drovers' inn, the pub is steeped in history and retains many original features – alongside some modern – providing a comfortable and welcoming environment. Three regularly changing real ales are served in summer (two in winter). The food menu features fresh local produce and delicious home-made puddings all day Tuesday to Sunday. Well-behaved dogs are welcome in the bar and, subject to prior arrangement, in the guest rooms. Open seven days a week July and August. **Q** **P** (461)

Llangunllo

Greyhound L

LD7 1SP (on B4356 off A488)
closed Mon & Tue; 4.30-11 Wed & Thu (2am Fri); 2-2am Sat; 2-11 Sun (01547) 550400
2 changing beers (sourced regionally; often Broughs, Six Bells) H
This unique 16th-century inn, set in picturesque countryside, is the first stop on the Glyndwr's Way long-distance trail. The beers are usually from Broughs and Six Bells breweries, and the cider is Westons Family Reserve. Beer festivals are held on the May and August bank holidays and regular music sessions are hosted. You are welcome to bring your own food. Opening times are approximate – ring the doorbell any time after midday and with luck you will be served.
Q **P**

Llangurig

Black Lion Hotel

SY18 6SG
closed Mon; 6-11 (midnight Fri); 12-3, 6-midnight Sat; 12-3, 6-11 Sun (01686) 440223 llangurig.org.uk
2 changing beers (sourced nationally; often Greene King, Hardys & Hansons) H
Built originally as a shooting lodge, the Black Lion was first licensed in 1633, and rebuilt as a hotel in the late-19th century. The interior is divided into two bars and a conservatory, with wood beams and low ceilings. The first bar serves as the games area, with a pool table, dartboard and seating around the bar. The lounge/dining area has wall seating, a stone fireplace and settles. There is a side room with comfortable armchairs.
Q **P** (X75,525)

Llangynidr

Red Lion

Duffryn Road, NP8 1NT (off B4558)
12-11 (01874) 730223 theredlionpowys.co.uk
Rhymney Best; 2 changing beers (sourced regionally) H
Popular village local, situated away from the main road, with a warm welcome for walkers, boaters, families and dogs – the Monmouthshire & Brecon Canal is a short walk away. The beer range changes regularly and good-value home-cooked food is served in the bar. A separate games area, outside seating and children's play area make this a pub for all. Regular quiz nights and live music also feature.
P (43,X43)

Llanwrtyd Wells

Neuadd Arms Hotel L

The Square, LD5 4RB
11-midnight (2am Fri & Sat) (01591) 610236
neuaddarmshotel.co.uk
Felinfoel Double Dragon; Heart of Wales Irfon Valley Bitter, Aur Cymru, Welsh Black, Noble Eden Ale; 4 changing beers (sourced locally) H
This large Victorian hotel serves as the tap for the Heart of Wales Brewery. The Bells Bar features a large fireplace and an eclectic mix of furniture. The bells, formerly used to summon servants, remain on one wall, along with the winners' boards from some of the town's unusual competitions. The lounge bar is more formal. The hotel takes part in

the town's annual events, including a major beer festival over two weekends in November. There is a good range of real ciders.

Machynlleth

Dyfi Forester

4 Heol y Doll, SY20 8BQ

11-11 ☎ (01654) 703239

2 changing beers (sourced regionally; often Evan Evans, Wood, Wye Valley)

The Foz is situated halfway between the railway station and the bustling centre of Machynlleth. This friendly down-to-earth free house has a welcoming central bar with jukebox, pool and dartboards. Pub games are played with enthusiasm here and sometimes all-day pool and darts events are hosted. The original stained glass can still be found in the quirky exterior. Outside, there is a patio to the rear.

White Lion

Heol Pentrerhedyn, SY20 8DN

11 (10 Wed)-11; 12-11 Sun ☎ (01654) 703455

whitelionhotel.co.uk

6 changing beers (sourced nationally; often Black Sheep, Cwrw Cader, Sandstone)

This town-centre hotel is conveniently situated with a bus stop outside. The main room is a large, comfortable open-plan lounge with an inglenook fireplace. This is flanked by a separate dining area and a small rear snug. Piped music can be loud at times and live music features occasionally. The pub is particularly busy at weekends. There is an annual beer festival on the late-May bank holiday in the large scenic beer garden. Real cider is available in the summer months.

Manafon

Beehive Inn

SY21 8BL

7-11; 12-3, 7-11 Sat & Sun ☎ (01686) 651007

Battlefield Saxon Gold; Stonehouse Station Bitter

A timbered black-and-white Rhiw Valley local in the heart of the village, established in the 1650s as a drovers' inn with original beams and settles throughout. It was originally a lot smaller – other rooms have been brought into pub use over the years. The room on the right was once a butcher's. There is a caravan park at the rear with the river running beside the large beer garden. The adjacent church creates a peaceful backdrop amid pleasant scenery.

Montgomery

Crown Inn

Castle Street, SY15 6PW

11-11 ☎ (01686) 668533

Brains Rev James; Wye Valley Butty Bach; 1 changing beer (sourced regionally; often Three Tuns)

Traditional local in a town that once supported a multitude of hostelries. The pub is home to a large number of local sports teams. The public bar is long and quite narrow with a pool and games area at the rear. It has a small snug opposite the public bar with a large array of trophies in it. There are benches outside for the warmer weather. Beware of the low beams in the bar area. Handily located for Monty's brewery visitor centre.

(71,81)

> Give my people plenty of beer, good beer and cheap beer, and you will have no revolution among them.
> **Queen Victoria**

Dragon Hotel

Market Square, SY15 6PA

11-11 (10.30 Sun) ☎ (01686) 668359 dragonhotel.com

4 changing beers (sourced regionally; often Monty's)

Dating from the mid-1600s, this former coaching inn has a distinctive Tudor black-and-white half-timbered frontage. The bar has been relocated to the rear of the hotel, giving more space to its clientele. There are patio areas outside to the front and rear for alfresco drinking. The hotel boasts an indoor swimming pool and a large function room.

(71,81)

Newtown

Railway Tavern

Old Kerry Road, SY16 1BH (off A483)

11-2, 5-midnight Mon; 11-midnight Tue; 11-2, 7-midnight Wed & Thu; 11-1am Fri & Sat; 11-midnight Sun

☎ (01686) 626156

3 changing beers (often Clun, Stonehouse, Three Tuns)

This is the 24th consecutive year in the Guide for the Tavern. Two guest beers from Welsh or Shropshire regional or small breweries are always on offer. The pub hosts darts and dominoes, and can get crowded on match nights. The interior is essentially divided in two – a lower bar area and a rear area with benches around the walls. Outside toilets are located through the passageway. Note the poster listing over 50 pubs that once operated in Newtown.

Sportsman

17 Severn Street, SY16 2AQ (off A483)

closed Mon; 12-10 Tue (11 Wed & Thu; 11.30 Fri & Sat); 12-10 Sun ☎ (01686) 623978

Monty's Old Jailhouse, MPA, Sunshine, Masquerade, Mischief; 3 changing beers (sourced nationally; often Brains, Robinsons, Wychwood)

Monty's taphouse, with up to five of the brewery's beers alongside up to three guest ales and a varying number of ciders. The pub is divided into three areas – a snug with comfortable wall seating, a main bar area with a wood-burning stove and a rear tiled games area with pool table, TV and darts. There is a patio at the rear for summer drinking. A former local CAMRA Pub of the Year and Welsh Cider Pub of the Year.

Pencelli

Royal Oak

LD3 7LX

12-11 (10.30 Sun) ☎ (01874) 665396

Brains Rev James; 2 changing beers (sourced regionally)

A first-timer in this Guide, the Royal Oak is a comfortable and friendly family-run pub in a quiet village alongside the Monmouthshire & Brecon Canal. New owners have extended the opening times which has proved popular. The regular ale is supplemented with two or three others, often from

Welsh independents or Wye Valley. The pretty garden next to the canal is a delight on a sunny day. Popular with walkers, cyclists and boaters, with moorings adjacent to the garden.
Q P

Penycae

Ancient Briton

Brecon Road, SA9 1YY (on A4067 N of Abercrave)
12-midnight ☎ (01639) 730273 ancientbriton.co.uk
Draught Bass; Wye Valley Butty Bach; 8 changing beers (sourced nationally; often Hop Back, Oakham, Salopian) H
Attractive country inn situated on the main Swansea to Brecon road. It makes an ideal base for walkers, cyclists and cavers exploring the Brecon Beacons National Park, offering hotel accommodation plus full camping and caravanning facilities at the rear. An impressive array of 15 handpumps dispenses up to eight ever-changing real ales and three real ciders. A winner of local CAMRA Pub of the Year on numerous occasions including 2018. P (T6)

Pool Quay

Powis Arms

SY21 9JS
12-11 (midnight Fri & Sat) ☎ (01938) 590255
3 changing beers (sourced regionally; often Brecon, Wye Valley) H
This 18th-century coaching inn is located in what was once a major port on the River Severn before the demise of water transport. Locally known as the Quay, it was saved from closure in 2007 when Powis Estates tried to convert it to housing. It has a main bar with beams and a stone-tiled floor, a snug with armchairs, and a restaurant. The large beer garden at the front enjoys fine views.
Q P

Presteigne

Royal Oak

High Street, LD8 2BB
4-11; 12-11 Fri-Sun ☎ (01544) 260842
royaloakpresteigne.co.uk
3 changing beers (sourced locally; often Ludlow, Salopian, Wye Valley) H
A simple family-run community pub dating back to 1823 with a central bar and a separate dining area at a higher level. There are three beers (two in winter), usually sourced from local breweries. It is a popular place for good pub food – lunches are served Friday to Sunday, evening meals Wednesday to Saturday. There is live music once a month and an occasional quiz fundraising for a local charity. Q (46)

Sennybridge

Usk & Railway Inn

High Street, LD3 8RS
11 (5 Mon & Tue)-11; 12-11 Sun ☎ (01874) 636101
uskandrailwayinn.com
3 changing beers H
New to the Guide, this small but comfortable inn is on the main road in the centre of the village. The unpretentious bar has a separate dining area and usually offers a choice of three real ales, including some unusual for the area. Food ranges from pub favourites to lighter snacks, featuring local produce. There are six refurbished bedrooms for weary travellers along the A40. P (T6)

Talybont-on-Usk

Star Inn

LD3 7YX (on B4558 between Brecon and Crickhowell)
5-11; 12-11 Sat & Sun ☎ (01874) 676635
thestarinntalybont.com
4 changing beers (sourced regionally; often Brecon, Dark Star, Grey Trees) H
Traditional village pub tucked in alongside the Monmouth & Brecon Canal, popular with both locals and visitors. Two separate rooms with stone floors and log fires link to a small central bar, which usually offers up to four ales from local and regional breweries. The pub appeals particularly to boaters on the canal and walkers and cyclists taking advantage of the forest trails accessible from the village. The sunny garden is a popular spot when the weather is good.
(43)

Welshpool

Pheasant Inn

43 High Street, SY21 7JQ
1-11; 12-midnight Fri & Sat; 12-11 Sun ☎ (01938) 553104
2 changing beers (often Ludlow, Salopian, Three Tuns) H
The Pheasant is a Grade II listed building in a terrace of 18th-century former town houses. Much modified internally, it has one long room with a wooden floor, comfortable seating at the far end, and a pool table and dartboard. To the rear is a door leading to an outside drinking and smoking area. A third guest beer is often available at weekends; the beers are usually from small or regional breweries.

The soul of beer

Brewers call barley malt the 'soul of beer'. While a great deal of attention has been rightly paid to hops in recent years, the role of malt in brewing must not be ignored. Malt contains starch that is converted to a special form of sugar known as maltose during the brewing process. It is maltose that is attacked by yeast during fermentation and turned into alcohol and carbon dioxide. Other grains can be used in brewing, notably wheat. But barley malt is the preferred grain as it gives a delightful biscuity / cracker / Ovaltine note to beer. Unlike wheat, barley has a husk that works as a natural filter during the first stage of brewing, known as the mash. Cereals such as rice and corn / maize are widely used by global producers of mass-market lagers, but craft brewers avoid them.

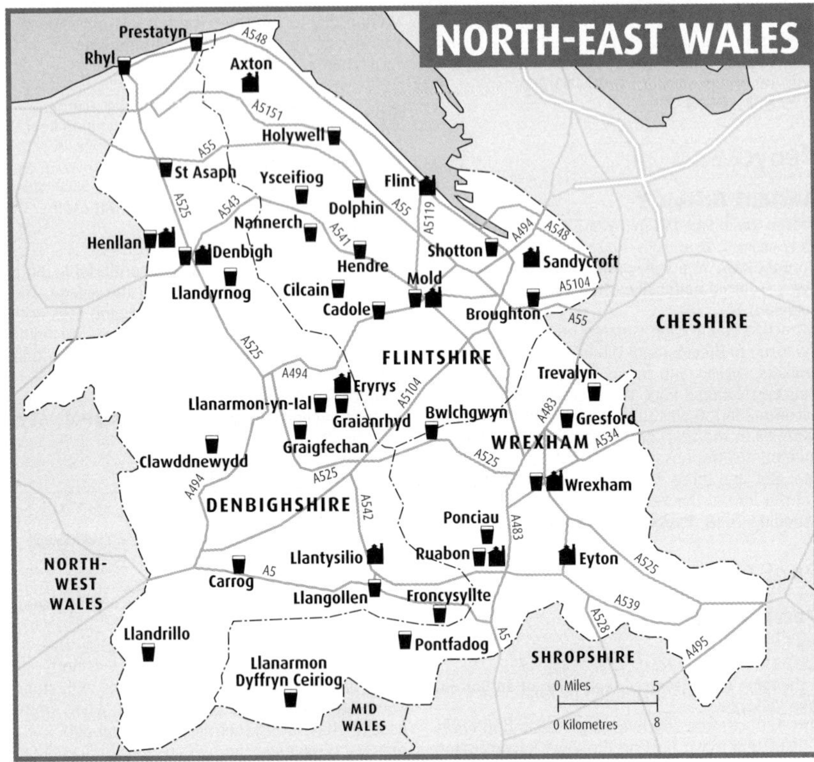

Authority areas covered: Denbighshire UA, Flintshire UA, Wrexham UA

Broughton

Offa's Dyke ✔

Broughton Hall Road, CH4 0QN

12-11 (midnight Thu; 1am Fri & Sat) ☎ (01244) 520133

offasdyke-hotel.co.uk

Greene King IPA; 4 changing beers (sourced nationally; often Brains, St Austell) Ⓗ

This popular Greene King-owned modern estate pub has served the needs of the Broughton community for more than 40 years. Meals are served in the large family-friendly lounge. In the livelier public bar you will find TV sport, and regular pool and poker nights are held. There is a spacious beer garden at the rear. Quiz nights are Thursday and Sunday. Two or three beers are available during the week and up to five at weekends.

Bwlchgwyn

King's Head Inn 🄻

Ruthin Road, LL11 5UT

closed Mon & Tue; 5-11 (midnight Fri); 12-midnight Sat; 12-11 Sun ☎ (01978) 753089

2 changing beers (sourced locally; often Big Hand) Ⓗ

Well-presented and friendly free house standing on the main road through one of the highest villages in Wales. It reopened in 2017 after an impressive refurbishment. The bar offers two locally sourced beers on handpump. A large woodburner features in the front room and a second is situated in the small side room which also has comfortable banquette seating.

Cadole

Colomendy Arms

Village Road, CH7 5LL (off A494 Mold-Ruthin road)

7-11 Mon-Wed; 6-11 Thu; 4-11 Fri; 2-11 Sat & Sun

☎ (01352) 810217

5 changing beers Ⓗ

A wonderful pub in the middle of the village, run by the same family for 30 years and featuring in the Guide for most of that time. It has two cosy rooms warmed by real fires and festooned with local history and photographs. Conversation is king here. Five varying beers come from far and wide. Be aware that the Black Sheep clock keeps dubious time. The Loggerheads Country Park is close by.

Q❀♣P

REAL ALE BREWERIES

Axiom Wrexham
Axton Axton
Big Hand Wrexham
Bragdy Dinbych Denbigh
Buzzard Denbigh
Dovecote Denbigh
Facer's Flint
Hafod Mold
Heavy Industry Henllan
Iâl Eryrys
Llangollen Llantysilio
Loka Polly Mold
Magic Dragon Eyton
McGivern Ruabon
Sandstone Wrexham
Top Rope Sandycroft (NEW)

Carrog

Grouse Inn

LL21 9AT (on B5437, off A5 at Llidiart Y Parc)
12-midnight ☎ (01490) 430272
thegrouseinncarrog.co.uk
JW Lees Bitter, John Willie's; 1 changing beer H
This friendly family-run pub was originally a farm and brewhouse. It has a single bar serving several rooms, including a games room with a pool table. Generous home-cooked food is served in most areas of the pub. There is a large covered patio area outside with splendid views of the Dee Valley, Berwyn Mountains and the 1660 Carrog Bridge. Carrog station on the Llangollen-Corwen railway is a short walk away. **Q**

Cilcain

White Horse

Ffordd Y Llan, CH7 5NN (signed from A451 Mold-Denbigh road)
12-3 (not Mon), 6-11; 12-11 Sat; 12-10.30 Sun
☎ (01352) 740142
2 changing beers (sourced nationally) H
A picturesque and cosy village pub with a separate quarry-tiled public bar with a set of antique beer engines. The original building dates from the early 19th century and was extended around 1940, creating a lounge of two rooms with distinctive fireplaces. A further extension in 1980 up a few steps to the rear created a dining area. Beers generally rotate but some may serve longer stints. Close to the Clwydian mountain range, the pub attracts many walkers. **Q P** (14C)

Clawddnewydd

Glan Llŷn Inn

Ruthin Road, LL15 2NA (on B5105)
5-11; 12-midnight Fri & Sat; 12-9 Sun ☎ (01824) 750754
clawddnewydd.org.uk/theglanllyninn
2 changing beers (sourced locally) H
This pub is now owned and run by the community, and a warm welcome awaits. Dating in parts back to the 16th century, it has been refurbished to include a lounge area with a real fire and a stove, a dining room and a separate public bar. Another extension provides an additional dining area and space for the community shop. The Sunday carvery is popular. Two changing beers are always from Welsh brewers. **Q P**

Denbigh

Y Goron Fach

6 Crown Lane, LL16 3SY (by town hall)
4-10 Thu-Sat; closed Sun-Wed
4 changing beers (sourced locally; often Buzzard, Dovecote, Heavy Industry) H
A small micropub opened in November 2016 in a former hairdresser's by the local Denbigh Brewery. A single area with room for around 25 people, there are high chairs around the walls and a couple of tables. Pumps are room-side and serve four local changing beers. The Little Crown (what the pub's name means) is just off Crown Square where the closed Crown Hotel once was. **Q**

Dolphin

Glan yr Afon Inn

Milwr, CH8 8HE
12-11 ☎ (01352) 710052 glanyrafoninn.com
Facer's Flintshire Bitter, Landslide; 1 changing beer H
First opened in the 16th century, this pub is situated in an elevated position with views of the Dee Estuary and the Wirral Peninsula. It has four separate seating areas and a dining room, with a real fire to keep you warm on cold days. Walkers and dogs are welcome. The pub is built above the historic Milwr Tunnel and there is information about this mine drainage network inside the inn. **Q P**

Froncysyllte

Aqueduct Inn

Holyhead Road, LL20 7PY
12-11 ☎ (01691) 777118
4 changing beers (sourced nationally; often Hafod, Peerless, Stonehouse) H
Friendly roadside free house standing beside the busy A5. Inside it is a simple three-roomed affair with a small central bar, games room to the side and a comfortable lounge with wood-burning stove. Food includes very popular Sunday lunches. There is some garden seating to the side and the rear verandah offers panoramic views, not least of the Llangollen Canal as it approaches the world-famous Pontcysyllte Aqueduct. Additional parking is down the lane and passing bikers are welcome. **P** (64)

Graianrhyd

Rose & Crown

Llanarmon Road, CH7 4QW (on B5430 off A5104)
4-11; 12-11 Sat; 12-10.30 Sun ☎ (01824) 780727
theroseandcrownpub.co.uk
Black Sheep Best Bitter; 2 changing beers H
A traditional early 19th-century pub with a strong local following. The long bar serves two rooms – the main room has an open fire, copper-topped tables and a vast array of pumpclips. Guest beers are usually from local breweries. Popular with tourists, walkers and fell runners keen to fuel up on post-race chip baps following the local Dash in the Park. **Q P** (2)

Graigfechan

Three Pigeons Inn

LL15 2EU (on B5429 about 3 miles from Ruthin)
closed Mon; 5-11; 12-11 Sat; 12-10 Sun
☎ (01824) 703178 threepigeonsinn.co.uk
Sharp's Doom Bar; 3 changing beers H
Fine old drovers' inn with parts originating from the 12th century. The interior is tastefully decorated, retaining the original features and open log fires. An extensive lounge area has a sports room to one side and a large dining area to the other. Cellars are ideal for keeping the cask ale that is still, on occasion, served in jugs. An outdoor area to the rear has great views over the Vale of Clwyd. Regular live music and other special events are hosted. A campsite is adjacent.
P (76)

Gresford

Griffin Inn

Church Green, LL12 8RG

⏲ 4 (5 Tue; 7.30 Wed)-11.30; 4-11 Sun ☎ (01978) 855280

Adnams Southwold Bitter; Courage Best Bitter; 1 changing beer (sourced nationally; often Moorhouse's, Weetwood) [H]

Friendly community pub built on a site that was a hostelry for pilgrims in the 14th century. The irregularly shaped open-plan bar area displays a variety of interesting pictures on the walls. A lawned area to the side has views of the 15th-century All Saints Church whose bells are one of the Seven Wonders of Wales. The landlady has been working behind the bar since 1973. Beers are sourced from the Punch Taverns list.

Q≋❀♣P🚌(1)🛜

Pant-yr-Ochain [L]

Old Wrexham Road, LL12 8TY (E from A483 follow signs to The Flash)

⏲ 11-11 (10.30 Sun) ☎ (01978) 853525

Purple Moose Cwrw Eryri/Snowdonia Ale; Stonehouse Off the Rails; Timothy Taylor Landlord; Weetwood Eastgate; house beer (by Phoenix); 4 changing beers (sourced regionally; often Big Hand, Castle Rock, Mobberley) [H]

Impressive 16th-century dower house which retains many historic features and sits beside a small lake within extensive gardens. The central room, dominated by a large double-fronted bar, leads to a variety of seating areas including a garden room, a small snug behind the period inglenook fireplace, and the patio and lawn outside. Hugely popular with diners, food is served all day. Five regular beers are supplemented by four guests, often local, and draught cider, plus perry in summer. Q≋❀◐♿♣🍎P🐾🛜

Hendre

Y Dderwen (The Oak) [L]

Denbigh Road, CH7 5QE (on A541)

⏲ 7-11 (midnight Fri & Sat) ☎ (01352) 741466

2 changing beers [H]

A roadside pub with a central bar serving two rooms, both with ceilings adorned with impressive collections of pottery. Up to four cask ales are available from a variety of north Wales microbreweries, too many to list. This 300-year-old pub has a strong community focus, hosting a range of social activities including folk nights and Welsh singing. It is popular with walkers and visitors to the nearby Clwydian hills. Q≋❀♿⛺♣P🚌🐾

Henllan

Llindir Inn [L]

Llindir Street, LL16 5BH

⏲ 5 (12 Thu)-11; 12-midnight Fri & Sat; 12-11 Sun ☎ (01745) 812188

Heavy Industry Electric Mountain; 6 changing beers (sourced locally; often Heavy Industry) [H]

Rambling 13th-century Grade II listed thatched inn. On entry you are welcomed by a long bar room with an inglenook fireplace and a comfortable TV lounge. Three steps take you up to another bar and a further three steps to a pleasant restaurant. The interior retains its character with old beams, tiled floors, copper and brassware. This is also the home of Heavy Industry Brewing situated close by and serves up to six cask beers. Q≋❀◐♣P🚌(6)🐾🛜

Holywell

Market Cross ✔

9-11 High Street, CH8 7LA

⏲ 8am-midnight (1am Fri & Sat) ☎ (01352) 717800

Ruddles Best Bitter; Sharp's Doom Bar; 3 changing beers (often Big Bog, Purple Moose) [H]

Converted in 2011 from a large retail outlet, this small Wetherspoon pub is named after the obelisk of the same name that stood outside. There are many pictures of local interest on the walls remembering Holywell and the Greenfield Valley in times gone by. The standard Wetherspoon beer range is complemented by three guest ales, usually including a brew from Purple Moose or Big Bog, plus a real cider in summer.

Q≋◐♿🍎🚌(X11,11)🛜

Llanarmon Dyffryn Ceiriog

Hand at Llanarmon

LL20 7LD (end of B4500 from Chirk)

⏲ 11-11 (12.30am Fri & Sat); 12-11 Sun ☎ (01691) 600666

🌐 thehandhotel.co.uk

2 changing beers (sourced regionally; often Stonehouse, Weetwood) [H]

Cosy free house standing in a scenic location at the head of the delightful Ceiriog Valley and marked by a giant hand sculpture. There are usually two real ales available, often from local breweries, which can be enjoyed in front of a roaring fire during winter months. Food and accommodation are both of a high standard (it is advisable to book at busy times). Dogs are welcome and the pub is popular with cyclists, walkers and tourists.

Q≋❀🛏◐♿♣P🚌(64)🐾🛜

Llanarmon-yn-Ial

Raven Inn [L]

Ffordd-Rhew-Ial, CH7 4QE (signed 500yds W of B5430)

⏲ closed Mon; 5-10.30 (11 Fri); 12-11 Sat; 12-9 Sun ☎ (01824) 780833 🌐 raveninn.co.uk

3 changing beers (sourced locally) [H]

Community-run by volunteers since 2009, this delightful old pub continues to go from strength to strength. There is a friendly and inviting ambience from the moment you enter. The bar serves two discrete carpeted areas and a tiled area. The three guest beers are from local breweries, usually including one from sister enterprise Cwrw Ial Brewery. Excellent locally sourced home-cooked food is served Thursday to Sunday. Three self-catering bedrooms are available.

Q≋❀🛏◐♿♣🍎P🚌(2)🐾🛜

Llandrillo

Dudley Arms Hotel

High Street, LL21 0TL

⏲ 6-11; closed Tue; 12-midnight Sat; 12-10.30 Sun ☎ (01490) 440223 🌐 dudleyarms.wales

Stonehouse Station Bitter; 1 changing beer (sourced locally) [H]

Traditional early 18th-century Welsh village inn nestling within the Berwyn mountains. The owners have carried out extensive refurbishment to create a pub full of charm with many period features and exposed oak beams. There are several discrete areas including a lounge, dining area and pool room with stone walls, tiled floors and cosy fires. The guest beer is always from a local brewery. B&B

accommodation is available upstairs and in an adjacent refurbished cottage.
Q🐎❀🛏◑◗⛺♣P🚌(T3)🐾📶

Llandyrnog

Kinmel Arms 🄻

Waen, LL16 4HN
⏲ 12-3, 5-11 (9.30 Mon & Tue); 12-11 Sat; 12-5 Sun
☎ (01824) 790291 🌐 kinmelarms.com
Thwaites Original; 3 changing beers (often Buzzard, Heavy Industry, Marston's) 🄷
A warm and traditional pub on the edge of the Clwydian Range and close to Offa's Dyke path and Moel Arthur hill fort. The front bar area features a large woodburner. There is a separate dining space, children's play area and games room. Opening times are subject to change so check before visiting. Q🐎❀◑◗♿⛺♣P🚌(76)🐾📶

Llangollen

Chainbridge Hotel 🄻

Berwyn, LL20 8BS (off B5103)
⏲ 9am-11 ☎ (01978) 860215 🌐 chainbridgehotel.com
Stonehouse Station Bitter; 2 changing beers (sourced locally; often Stonehouse) 🄷
Situated in a picturesque location between the Llangollen Canal and River Dee, close to the Horseshoe Falls, the pub enjoys excellent views of the river, surrounding wooded hills and the Llangollen Heritage Railway. It can be reached by bus or steam train to Corwen, then across the restored pedestrian chainbridge. It is also a pleasant, half-hour stroll along the canal towpath from the centre of Llangollen. Up to three ales are typically from Stonehouse or other local breweries.
Q🐎❀🛏◑◗♿⇌P🚌(T3)🐾📶

Corn Mill

Dee Lane, LL20 8PN (on town side, W of River Dee bridge)
⏲ 11-11; 11-10.30 Sun ☎ (01978) 869555
Facer's DHB (Dave's Hoppy Beer); house beer (by Phoenix); 3 changing beers (sourced nationally) 🄷
A splendidly converted flour mill incorporating the water wheel, with a series of open-plan rooms spread over three levels with bars on the first two floors. A large outside decking area has unparalleled views across the raging River Dee to the restored steam railway station. Six pumps serve five beers and one cider. Changing beers often include local micros. It is primarily a restaurant, with the drinking area confined to the ground-floor bar and outside areas.
Q🐎❀◑◗♿⛺⇌🍎🚌(5,T3)🐾📶

Ponsonby Arms 🄻

Mill Street, LL20 8RY (near steam railway)
⏲ closed Mon; 12-midnight summer; closed Mon; 5-midnight Tue-Thu; 3-midnight Fri; 12-midnight Sat; 3-midnight Sun winter ☎ (01978) 447985
Bollington Long Hop; Elland 1872 Porter; Ulverston Flying Elephants; 3 changing beers (sourced nationally; often Elland, Salopian, Saltaire) 🄷
Just north-east of Llangollen bridge, this welcoming independent free house is run by the same owners as the nearby Sun Inn. An extensive beer garden overlooks the river. Up to six beers and two ciders are available, with Ulverston and Bollington regularly represented. A free ticket for the adjacent council car park can be obtained at the bar. Opening hours may vary so please check ahead if travelling.
Q🐎❀◑◗⛺⇌♣🍎P🚌(5,T3)🐾📶

Sun Inn 🄻

49 Regent Street, LL20 8HN (E of town centre)
⏲ closed Mon; 7-2am (3am Fri & Sat) ☎ (01978) 860079
5 changing beers (often Bollington, Ulverston) 🄷
Free house fronting the A5 across the River Dee from its sister pub, the Ponsonby Arms. The stone-flagged bar room has two open fires and a games area with pool and table football. A quieter back room can be reached via a seating area outside. Wednesday to Saturday evenings feature live music. Five changing ales plus a changing cider are available. Opening hours may vary from time to time; check ahead if travelling.
❀⛺⇌♣🍎🚌(5,T3)🐾📶

Mold

Fat Boar 🄻

17 Chester Street, CH7 1EG
⏲ 11.30-11 (midnight Fri & Sat); 12-10.30 Sun
☎ (01352) 759890 🌐 thefatboar.co.uk
House beer (by Stonehouse); 2 changing beers (sourced locally; often Big Hand, Stonehouse) 🄷
A welcome addition to Mold town centre for real ale, the pub reopened as The Fat Boar in 2015 following a tasteful and contemporary refurbishment. A further refurbishment in 2017 added a large conservatory and additional seating outside at the rear of the building. There is a bar and seating area on the ground floor and also a large, pleasant restaurant, mostly on the upper floor. Guest beers are usually from north Wales breweries. 🐎❀◑◗♿🚌📶

Glasfryn 🄻

Raikes Lane, CH7 6LR (off A5119 ½ mile N of Mold)
⏲ 11-11 (10.30 Sun) ☎ (01352) 750500
🌐 glasfryn-mold.co.uk
Hobsons Best; Phoenix Brunning & Price Original; Purple Moose Cwrw Eryri/Snowdonia Ale; 6 changing beers 🄷
Near Theatre Clwyd and set in its own grounds opposite the civic centre, this large upmarket pub and restaurant was once the residence for circuit judges attending the nearby court. The walls are covered with many interesting and unusual pictures. Food predominates and is served all day in three dining areas. A total of nine handpumps supply national and local beers. There are extensive views over the surrounding countryside from the large beer garden.
Q🐎❀◑◗♿P🚌(28)🐾📶

Mold Alehouse 🏆 🄻

Unit 2, Earl Chambers, Earl Road, CH7 1AL
⏲ closed Mon & Tue; 2 (4 Thu & Fri)-10; 4-9 Sun
☎ (01352) 218188 🌐 moldalehouse.co.uk
4 changing beers (sourced locally) 🄷
Established in 2016 and one of the first of its type in North Wales, this micropub sets the standards for others to follow. It is centrally situated in a Grade II listed building opposite Daniel Owen Square – named after the renowned Welsh novelist and home to Mold museum and library. An arched entrance leads to a single room with a central column. No food, spirits or music, just real ale and cider, plus a good selection of craft beers.
Q🍎🚌🐾📶

WALES

Nannerch

Cross Foxes

Village Road, CH7 5RD
closed Mon; 6-11; 12-10.30 Sun (01352) 741464
nannerch.com
3 changing beers (sourced locally; often Big Hand, Buzzard, Cwrw Ial) H
This delightful village pub close to the church was built in 1780 and originally also served as a pub and butcher's – the meat hooks still remain over the bar. The entrance leads to a main bar with a large fireplace. Off this is another small bar, a lounge and a function room. Three pumps serve changing beers, usually sourced locally. Beer festivals are held in March and October.
P

Ponciau

Colliers Arms

Chapel Street, LL14 1SE (off B5426)
7 (5 Wed-Fri; 2 Sat)-11; 1-10.30 Sun
Facer's Flintshire Bitter; 3 changing beers (sourced regionally) H
This splendid free house on a narrow terraced street is a rare cask ale outlet for the area. The front room has a slate floor, comfortable bench seating, stools and small cast-iron tables. There is also a tiny snug area and a rear room with a pool table and jukebox. To the rear is a pleasant decked area and lawn. The four handpumps often feature beers from local micros. Public parking is available nearby. (3,3E)

Pontfadog

Swan Inn

Llanarmon Road, LL20 7AR (on B4500 next to post office)
11-11 (01691) 718273
3 changing beers (sourced nationally; often Big Hand, Conwy) H
Welcoming village free house in the scenic Ceiriog Valley which has been revitalised since new owners took over in 2017. The cosy red-tiled bar room, favoured by the locals, features a central fireplace which separates the TV and darts area from the servery. High-quality home-cooked food is available in the recently extended dining room, which leads to a pleasant outdoor area. Up to three cask beers, often from local independent breweries, are available.
P (64,65)

Prestatyn

Archies

151 High Street, LL19 9AS
5-11 Mon; 12-midnight; 12-11 Sun (01745) 855657
archiesbar.co.uk
Facer's Flintshire Bitter; 2 changing beers (often Axton) H
A town-centre café bar with a modern interior and a decking area at the front where you can watch the world go by on fine days. The bar is the only outlet for beers from Axton Brewery which is under the same ownership, although they may not always be available. Food is served all day Tuesday to Saturday and 12.30-4pm Sunday. Opening hours may be reduced during the winter months.

Halcyon Quest Hotel

17 Gronant Road, LL19 9DT (on A547 just E of town centre)
3-11 (midnight Fri); 12-midnight Sat; 12-11 Sun
(01745) 852442 halcyonquest-hotel.com
Facer's Flintshire Bitter; 3 changing beers (sourced nationally) H
A longstanding supporter of cask beer, the HQ, as it is known, is located at the southern end of town. It has just one room packed with sporting and other memorabilia, including a rowing boat suspended from the ceiling dedicated to JR Hartley of fly-fishing fame. The extensive garden patio at the rear has a covered area and is popular for drinking in the summer months. P (35,36)

Rhyl

Cob & Pen

143 High Street, LL18 1UF
11-11 (midnight Fri & Sat); 12-11 Sun (01745) 350446
Banks's Mild; Marston's 61 Deep, Pedigree; 2 changing beers H
Respected and welcoming pub serving drinks and lunchtime meals from a central bar. It has a number of themed seating areas, all decorated imaginatively in recognition of the local heritage. Televised sports events are shown on several large screens. A weekly acoustic night is a popular attraction, as are darts, pool and dominoes. This is one of the few local pubs serving cask-conditioned mild. Located close to the bus and railway stations.

Sussex

20-26 Sussex Street, LL18 1SG
8am-midnight (1am Fri & Sat) (01745) 362910
Greene King Abbot; Ruddles Best Bitter; 3 changing beers H
Located in a building that has been both a Wesleyan Chapel and an Old Comrades Club, this is an established Wetherspoon outlet, situated in the pedestrianised town centre. There are illustrated panels throughout detailing different aspects of the history of the town and surrounding area. Beers from new microbreweries are sometimes available but usually the ales are national and regional brews. Alcohol is served from 9am.
Q

Ruabon

Bridge End Inn

5 Bridge Street, LL14 6DA
5-11; 4-11 Fri; 12-11 Sat & Sun (01978) 810881
mcgivernales.co.uk
8 changing beers (sourced nationally; often Ossett, Rat, Salopian) H
Welcoming local in a dip close to the railway station with three low-ceilinged rooms and a covered outdoor drinking area. This traditional pub has won numerous awards since it was revitalised by the McGivern family in 2009, including the ultimate accolade of CAMRA National Pub of the Year in 2011. The changing range of eight ales will usually include a brew from the on-site McGivern brewery when it is operational. Families and well-behaved dogs are welcome in the lounge.
QP

St Asaph

Swan Inn 🄻

The Roe, LL17 0LT (just off A55 jct 27 on the A525)
12-midnight (11 Sun) ☎ 07535 452427
2 changing beers (often Conwy, Dovecote) 🄷
A roadside pub on the outskirts of St Asaph situated in a row of terraces with a predominantly local trade. There is a front bar area and a games room to the rear leading to an extensive garden. Two changing beers include at least one local brew. The pub supports pool and darts teams in local leagues. ❀♣🚌(51)🐾📶

Shotton

Central Hotel ✔

2-4 Chester Road West, CH5 1BX
8am-midnight (1am Fri & Sat) ☎ (01244) 845510
Greene King Abbot; Ruddles County; 3 changing beers (sourced nationally) 🄷
A local landmark built in the early 1920s beside the railway station. It had a major refurbishment in 2008 and reverted back to its original name. The interior is typical Wetherspoon mock-Edwardian, with a large single bar partially separated into three similarly furnished areas. Three changing guest beers are served alongside the two standard ales. At the front is an open seating area overlooking the street. There are regular Meet the Brewer evenings. ♘◑♿⇌P🚌📶

Trevalyn

Griffin

Rossett Road, LL12 0ER (at Butchers Arms pub in Rossett branch right, signposted Holt; continue for approx 1 mile)
12-11 (midnight Fri & Sat); 11-10.30 Sun
☎ (01244) 570515 🌐 griffininn-trevalyn.co.uk
2 changing beers (sourced regionally) 🄷
This cosy, attractive whitewashed local, said to be 400 years old, stands in the heart of the village about a mile from Rossett. The golden griffin on the wall is particularly eye catching. Look out for Phil, the bearded dragon. Outside is a grassed garden with trestles and to the rear a Camping and Caravanning Club site open all year. Unusual fabricated handpumps dispense ales from the Marston's stable. ♘❀Ⲁ♣P🐾📶

Wrexham

Elihu Yale ✔

44-46 Regent Street, LL11 1RR
8am-midnight (1am Thu-Sat) ☎ (01978) 366646
Greene King Abbot; Ruddles Best Bitter; Sharp's Doom Bar; 5 changing beers (sourced nationally) 🄷
Formerly the Majestic Cinema, this popular Wetherspoon town-centre pub is within walking distance of both the railway and bus stations. It serves three regular beers plus at least five guests, one of which will be from a Welsh brewery, and up to two real ciders. There are various seating areas in the large single room, with a quieter area towards the front. Families are welcome until 10pm. Quiz night is Wednesday, poker night Sunday. Q♘◑♿⇌(Central/General)🍎🚌📶

Fat Boar 🄻

11 Yorke Street, LL13 8LW
12-11 (midnight Fri & Sat); 12-10.30 Sun
☎ (01978) 354201 🌐 thefatboarwrecsam.co.uk
4 changing beers (sourced locally; often Big Hand, Hafod) 🄷
A sister pub to the one of the same name in Mold, this stripped-down establishment has a clean and bright feel with ceiling beams and exposed brick walls. It comprises a large L-shaped bar/lounge downstairs and a restaurant upstairs with a display of hanging potted plants. Up to four handpumps usually dispense beers from local microbreweries. There is a large, stylish beer garden and smoking area at the rear. ◑⇌🚌📶

Royal Oak

35 High Street, LL13 8HY
12-midnight (1am Fri & Sat) ☎ (01978) 364111
Joule's Blonde, Pale Ale, Slumbering Monk; 2 changing beers (sourced nationally) 🄷
A Grade II listed building with a long and narrow interior. The real fire, wood panelling and etched brewery mirrors around the bar create a comfortable ambience – and the mounted eland antelope head is impossible to miss. Three beers from Joule's plus up to two changing guest ales are available. The small beer garden on the roof is open April to September. No food is available but you are welcome to bring your own. Darts and traditional pub games are played.
Q❀♿⇌(Central/General)♣🍎🚌🐾📶

Ysceifiog

Fox ★

Village Road, CH8 8NJ (signed from B5121)
4-11; 1-11 Sat & Sun ☎ (01352) 720241
🌐 foxinnysceifiog.co.uk
Banks's Amber Ale; Brains Rev James; 2 changing beers (sourced nationally) 🄷
Built around 1730, the Fox is set in an area of outstanding natural beauty and is well worth seeking out. The interior comprises four small rooms, two of them for dining. There is a slate-floored drinking lobby and a tiny front bar with a sliding door that takes you back to the 1930s. A choice of four beers is available. A children's playground is adjacent to the outside drinking area. Identified by CAMRA as having a nationally important historic interior, this is a rare classic.
Q♘❀◑♣P🐾📶

Your shout

We would like to hear from you. If you think a pub not listed in the Guide is worthy of consideration, please let us know. Send us the name, full address and phone number (if known). If a pub in the Guide has given poor service, we would also like to know. Write to Good Beer Guide, CAMRA, 230 Hatfield Road, St Albans, Herts, AL1 4LW or email **gbgeditor@camra.org.uk**

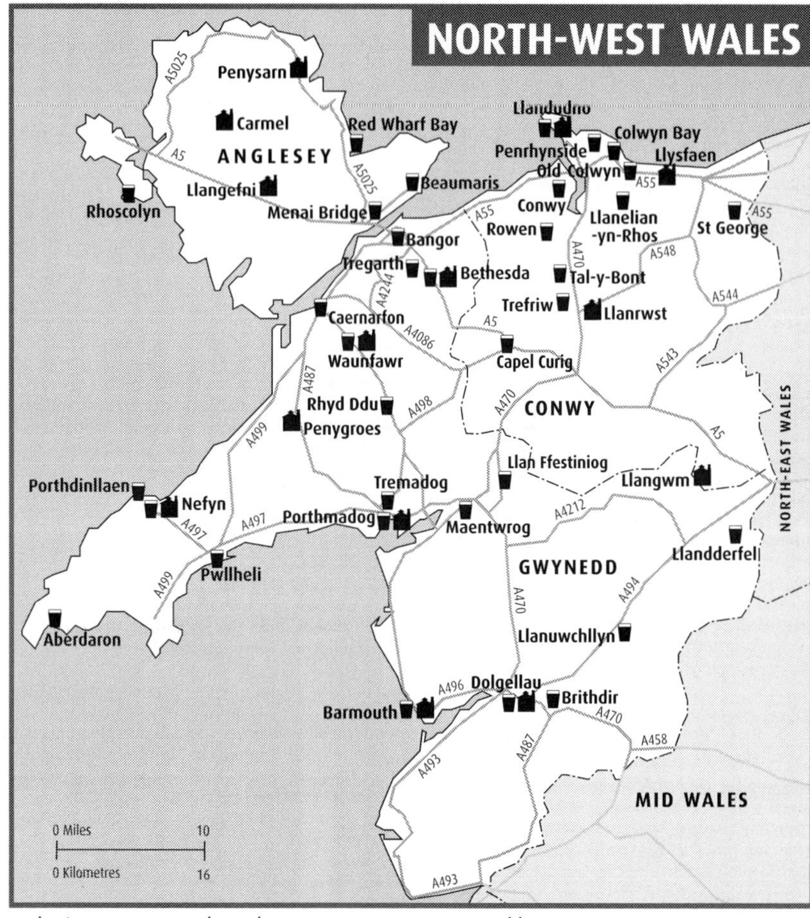

Authority areas covered: Anglesey UA, Conwy UA, Gwynedd UA

Aberdaron

Ty Newydd

LL53 8BE

11-midnight (10.30 Sun) (01758) 760207

gwesty-tynewydd.co.uk

Purple Moose Calon Lan; 2 changing beers (sourced locally)

The hotel is situated at the centre of a picturesque and historic village at the end of the Llŷn Peninsula. Beers are from two local breweries. Freshly caught Bardsey lobster and crab are on the menu, as well as afternoon teas. Eleven en-suite bedrooms are available, with stunning sea views. The Wales coastal footpath passes through the village. Bus services run from Pwllheli. Q

Bangor

Patricks

59 Holyhead Road, LL57 2HE

11-2am (2.30am Wed & Thu; 3am Fri & Sat)

(01248) 353062 patricksbar.com

4 changing beers (sourced regionally)

Situated in upper Bangor, this lively Irish-themed bar is popular with both the locals and students of Bangor University. Numerous TVs display sporting events. There are usually two locally sourced ales and one regional beer on the bar. Note the late opening hours for sport and late-night drinking. On the bus route towards the Menai Straits and near the railway station.

Barmouth

Royal Hotel

LL42 1AB

12-11 (midnight Sat) (01341) 280455

4 changing beers

Located beneath the main hotel with access from the main road, the hotel has had a major structural refurbishment including the kitchens. The pub is on two levels, with the main bar next to the entrance, and the lower level primarily for playing pool. There is a beer garden to the rear. Beers are usually from Welsh breweries but occasionally come from just over the border.

Beaumaris

Castle Court Hotel

Castle Square, LL58 8DA

12-11 (01248) 810078 castlecourtbeaumaris.co.uk

Facer's This Splendid Ale; 1 changing beer (sourced regionally)

Situated in the centre of this historic town and overlooking the castle, the guest house was originally called the White Lion Hotel. The owners have renovated the reception and dining areas. It has a small beer garden to the rear, but in spring and summer the courtyard outside the entrance provides more seating. Facer's Splendid Ale is always available plus one guest beer from a small independent brewery. Lunchtime meals are served 12-3pm during school holidays only.

Bethesda

Y Sior

35-37 Carneddi Road, LL57 3SE

7-midnight; 5-1am Fri; 1-1am Sat; 1-midnight Sun

(01248) 600072

4 changing beers (sourced locally) H

A friendly locals' pub in the village of Carneddi just outside Bethesda. A few minutes' drive from the A5, there is plenty of parking nearby. Free of tie, the pub offers a variety of ales from the Marston's range as well as locally brewed beers. There are views across the valley to the local slate quarry, which has the longest zip wire in Britain. Q

Brithdir

Cross Foxes

LL40 2SG (jct of A470 and A487)

11-midnight (01341) 421001

Cwrw Cader Gold; 2 changing beers (sourced regionally) H/G

A refurbished Grade II listed building situated near the foot of Cader Idris mountain and four miles from the historic town of Dolgellau. Beers are usually from Cader Ales and other local microbreweries. Breakfast is served from 8am and meals are available all day until 9pm. Dogs are welcome in the bar area. The hotel has Welsh Tourist Board 5-star grading. Bus service T2 passes by, but please check times.

QP(T2)

Caernarfon

Bar Bach

Tan y Bont, LL55 2NF (behind Caffi Maes)

11.30-1.30am

3 changing beers (sourced regionally) H

Under the looming shadow of Caernarfon's imposing castle lies the self-proclaimed smallest bar in Wales. Part of Caffi Maes, its narrow entrance is found around the corner. A charmingly intimate bar, it does indeed occupy a small area but it is deceptive in that the bar leads to another longer room on a lower level. Plenty of exposed stonework, a small fireplace and dark-wood furniture give it a lived-in feel. Q(WHR)

Black Boy Inn

Northgate Street, LL55 1RW

11-11 (11.30 Fri & Sat); 12-10.30 Sun (01286) 673604

black-boy-inn.com

Draught Bass; 5 changing beers (sourced regionally) H

The pub is set within the town walls between the marina and castle. This historic town, a World Heritage Site, is well worth a visit, ending with a welcome pint at the Black Boy. The public bar and small lounge are warmed by roaring fires. Good-value food is served and the guest beer usually comes from Purple Moose. There is a drinking area outside on the traffic-free street. Local CAMRA Pub of the Year 2018. (WHR)P(5)

Tafarn Y Porth

5-9 Eastgate Street, LL55 1AG (just off Bangor Rd near Barclays Bank)

9am-midnight (01268) 662920

Big Bog Bog Standard Bitter; Draught Bass; Greene King Abbot; Ruddles Best Bitter; 5 changing beers (sourced nationally) H

Friendly, welcoming Wetherspoon pub opposite the town walls and close to the castle. It has a large open-plan interior and a spacious, partly covered courtyard outside with plenty of seating. The real ale range often includes a beer from the Big Bog Brewing Company in Waunfawr, just a few miles away. The pub's location is handy for the Welsh Highland Railway.

Q(WHR)(5)

Capel Curig

Tyn-y-Coed Inn

Holyhead Road, LL24 0EE

3-11; 12-11 Fri & Sat; 12-10.30 Sun (01690) 720331

tyn-y-coed.co.uk

Purple Moose Cwrw Eryri/Snowdonia Ale, Cwrw Madog/Madog's Ale; 2 changing beers (sourced regionally) H

A spacious old multi-roomed pub with a hotel extension. To mark its historic past on the coaching route, the Tyn-y-Coed has a majestic stagecoach opposite the entrance on the A5. It is popular with outdoor enthusiasts owing to its location in the Snowdonia National Park, with welcoming log fires in winter. Locally sourced ales and a good selection of whiskies are available. Dogs are admitted on leads. P

Colwyn Bay

Bay Hop

17 Penrhyn Road, LL29 8LG

closed Mon; 2 (4 Tue & Wed)-10; 4-8 Sun

thebayhop.co.uk

5 changing beers (sourced regionally) H

This micropub and bottle shop opened in 2016, making a welcome addition to the Colwyn Bay drinking experience. Two large barrel tables are available for vertical drinkers and attractive high-backed wooden settles for those who prefer to sit down. Five ciders and perries are offered from a fridge behind the bar. Third-pint glasses and two-

REAL ALE BREWERIES

Anglesey Brewhouse Llangefni (NEW)
Anglesey Brewing Carmel
Cader Dolgellau
Conwy Llysfaen
Druid Penysarn (brewing suspended)
Geipel Llangwm
Great Orme Llandudno
Llŷn Nefyn
Lleu Penygroes
Myrddins Barmouth
Nant Llanrwst
Ogwen Bethesda
Purple Moose Porthmadog
Snowdonia Waunfawr
Wild Horse Llandudno

WALES

pint take-away cartons are available. Snacks include pies from local butchers. Thursday is cheese night, live music plays on Sunday. Local CAMRA Pub of the Year 2017 and 2018. Q

Pen-y-Bryn

Pen-y-Bryn Road, LL29 6DD

11-11; 12-10.30 Sun (01492) 533360
penybryn-colwynbay.co.uk

Purple Moose Cwrw Eryri/Snowdonia Ale; house beer (by Phoenix); 4 changing beers (sourced regionally) H

Spacious, open-plan pub with large bookcases, old furniture and real fires during the winter. The walls are decorated with photographs and memorabilia from the local area. Panoramic views of the Bay of Colwyn and the Great Orme can be admired from the terrace and garden. Food is served throughout the day. A boardroom-style function room for celebrations and meetings has been created in the cellar, opening onto the garden.
Q P (23)

Station

Abergele Road, LL29 8BP

11-11; 12-11 Sun (01492) 532818
thestationcolwynbay.co.uk

3 changing beers (sourced regionally) H

Large town-centre pub originally built around 1870 and reopened in 2015 by the management team from the successful Albert in Llandudno, following an extensive modern refurbishment and change of name. Food is served throughout the day. Beers are displayed on blackboards near the bar, with third-pint glasses available. With many tables overlooking the street, it is handy for a quick drink while waiting to travel home from the adjacent bus stop.

Conwy

Albion Ale House ★

Upper Gate Street, LL32 8RF

12-11 (midnight Fri & Sat) (01492) 582484
albionalehouse.weebly.com

8 changing beers (sourced regionally; often Conwy, Great Orme, Nant) H

Multi-room heritage pub superbly refurbished by the current owners. Each room retains original 1920s features and several have wonderful fireplaces. There is no music or TV, just pleasant conversation. The pub is managed by four local brewers – Conwy, Great Orme, Nant and Purple Moose – and showcases their beers as well as guests. There are up to 10 ciders and a good selection of wines and malt whiskies. CAMRA awards include branch and Welsh Pub of the Year.
Q (5,19)

Bank of Conwy

1 Lancaster Square, LL32 8HT

9am-11 (midnight Fri & Sat) (01492) 573741
bankofconwy.com

4 changing beers (sourced regionally) H

The Bank of Conwy is a modern continental-style craft beer bar which opened in 2015 in a Grade II listed former bank. It uses many fittings from the original building – the bar used to be the counter and the manager's officer is now a snug with a fire. The basement, which was formerly the vault, is available for private hire. Breakfast is served 9am-noon. Tuesday is jam night, Wednesday and Friday are music nights. (5,19)

Erskine Arms

Rosehill Street, LL32 8LD

11.30-11 (01492) 593535 erskinearms.co.uk

Black Sheep Bitter; Conwy Clogwyn Gold; Timothy Taylor Landlord; 2 changing beers (sourced regionally; often Heavy Industry) H

Reopened in 2017 following a major refurbishment, the pub's name was changed back to the Erskine Arms – the family name of the owners. It was previously The Malt Loaf, in keeping with its sister pub The Cottage Loaf in Llandudno. The Georgian former coaching inn has two distinct dining areas, one on an upper floor, and there is a snug to the left and an outside drinking area. The decor includes traditional wooden features, rugs, open fires and pictures on the walls portraying local history.

Liverpool Arms

Lower Gate Street, LL32 8BE

12-11 (11.30 Fri & Sat); 12-10 Sun (01492) 573393
liverpoolarmsconwy.net

Draught Bass; 2 changing beers (sourced regionally) H

This small one-roomed historic quayside pub is popular with locals and visitors alike because of its unique location built against the medieval town walls, with an outside seating area overlooking the Conwy quay and Deganwy on the far shore. Locally sourced beers are often available. It has been CADW Grade II listed since May 1970 for 'its special architectural interest as a commercial building retaining definite 19th-century character, with earlier origins that make it the earliest surviving quayside building in the town.'
(5,19)

Dolgellau

Torrent Walk Hotel

Smithfield Street, LL40 1AA

11-midnight (01341) 422858

Purple Moose Cwrw Eryri/Snowdonia Ale; Wychwood Hobgoblin; 3 changing beers (sourced nationally) H

An 18th-century hotel in the narrow streets of the town centre, retaining most of its multi-roomed interior and old fireplaces, although the bar fittings date from circa 1970. Note the Coffee Room etched panel in the door from the lobby to the room on the right. A real cider is always served and up to five ales, mostly from local breweries. An ideal base for walking in the Cader Idris area.

Llan Ffestiniog

Y Pengwern

Church Square, LL41 4PB

7-11.30; 5-midnight Fri; 12-midnight Sat & Sun
(01766) 762200 pengwern.org.uk

Purple Moose Cwrw Eryri/Snowdonia Ale; 1 changing beer H

This community-run hostelry was formerly an old drovers' inn. It has one regular beer from Purple Moose and guests from other local breweries such as Big Bog, Cwrw Llŷn and Heavy Industry. The pub holds a beer festival over the August bank holiday with around 20 beers. An ideal stop-off for walkers in the local area, and there is a bus stop right outside. Q P

Llandderfel

Bryntirion Inn

LL23 7RA (on B4401 4 miles E of Bala)
11-11; 12-11 Sun (01678) 530205
bryntirioninn.co.uk

Purple Moose Cwrw Eryri/Snowdonia Ale; 1 changing beer (sourced locally)

Dating back to 1695, this former hunting lodge and coaching inn overlooks the Dee Valley. The cosy and comfortable bar area with a log fire is open all day. There are a number of other rooms to accommodate diners and families including a large function room for special events. There is also a small covered and heated courtyard at the rear. The guest beer varies and may be from a local or national brewer. Two en-suite guest rooms are available upstairs. Q P (T3)

Llandudno

Albert

56 Madoc Street, LL30 2TW
11-11; 12-10.30 Sun (01492) 877188
albertllandudno.co.uk

5 changing beers (sourced regionally)

Just off the town centre and close to the railway station, this popular pub-restaurant has a contemporary decor with a range of interesting photographs and pictures on display. It offers five handpulled ales on rotation from local and independent breweries and a range of meals throughout the day. Current beers are clearly displayed on blackboards above and beside the L-shaped bar, with third-pint glasses available. There is a heated and covered verandah with seating at the front. Q

Links Hotel

77 Conwy Road, LL30 1PN
12-11 (10.30 Sun) (01492) 879180
linkshotelllandudno.co.uk

JW Lees Manchester Pale Ale, Bitter, Dragon's Fire; 1 changing beer (often JW Lees)

The Links is a family pub with large rooms and good car-parking facilities off the A470, enjoying a consistent local trade and also popular with holidaymakers. It was purpose-built in 1898 near two golf courses, hence the name. It reopened in 2017 following a lengthy and extensive refurbishment. The conservatory is used for dining and as a function space, and there is an enclosed outdoor play area adjacent to the patio decking. Third-pint taster glasses are available.
Q P (5)

Snowdon

11 Tudno Street, LL30 2HB
12-11 (11.30 Fri & Sat) (01492) 872166
the-snowdonhotel.co.uk

Draught Bass; house beer (by Coach House); 3 changing beers (sourced regionally)

One of the oldest pubs in Llandudno, just off the town centre and near the tram station, it offers four beers, including the house beer, Coach House Blue Sky, with tasters of three thirds for the price of a pint. The main lounge has leather sofas and features a Snowdon mirror above the fireplace. The small side snug with dartboard, displays autographed celebrity photographs. The pavement side garden, with fine views of the Great Orme, has won Llandudno in Bloom for its floral display.
(Great Orme) (5,12)

Tapps

35 Madoc Street, LL30 2TL
12-11 (9 Mon; 10 Tue & Wed); 12-10 Sun
(01492) 870956

Conwy Welsh Pride; 4 changing beers (sourced regionally)

This micropub opened in October 2017 in a former cake shop and has an open-plan bar at the front with a small snug to the rear. Welsh beer is to the fore and there is a large bottled beer selection. Vinyl music is played on an old record player. One of the tables is a chessboard that transforms into a backgammon or card table, other board games are provided and there are books to borrow.

WALES

Llanelian-yn-Rhos

White Lion Inn

LL29 8YA
closed Mon; 11.30-3, 6-11; 11.30-4, 5-11.30 Sat; 12-10.30 Sun (01492) 515807 whitelioninn.co.uk

Marston's 61 Deep; 2 changing beers (sourced regionally)

A regular in the Guide for more than 20 years, this 16th-century inn situated in the hills above Old Colwyn, offers a warm welcome. Gracing the entrance are two white stone lions, leading into the bar area with slate-flagged flooring and large comfortable chairs around the log fires. Decorative stained glass is mounted above the bar in the tiny snug. The restaurant serves delicious home-cooked food. Jazz night is Tuesday, quiz night Thursday.
Q P

Llanuwchllyn

Eagles Inn (Tafarn Yr Eryrod)

Llanuwchllyn, LL23 7UB
11-11 (midnight Thu-Sat); closed Sun (01678) 540278
yr-eagles.co.uk

6 changing beers (sourced locally; often Cwrw Cader, Purple Moose)

A friendly welcome awaits visitors to this little gem – an old stone-built village local opposite the church. The bar also doubles as a shop which is open all day. It retains plenty of historic features including a wonderful stone floor. The adjacent restaurant serves highly rated locally produced food. The patio garden has good mountain views. It is a 10-minute walk to Llanuwchllyn station on the Bala Lake Railway. Opening times and beer range are reduced in winter.
(Bala Lake) P (T3)

Maentwrog

Grapes Hotel

LL41 4HN (on A496 near A487 jct)
12-midnight (01766) 590365
grapeshotelsnowdonia.co.uk

Purple Moose Cwrw Eryri/Snowdonia Ale; Sharp's Doom Bar; 1 changing beer (sourced locally)

A former coaching inn, this hotel dates back to the 17th century and overlooks the Vale of Ffestiniog. The interior comprises a lounge, public bar, verandah and large dining room; outside there is a sheltered beer garden to the rear. Most of the beers are sourced locally. The railway station nearby at Rhyd is on the Ffestiniog line. The village is an ideal base for visiting this beautiful area.
Q P

Menai Bridge

Liverpool Arms ✔

St George's Pier, LL59 5EY

12-2, 5-11.30; 12-11.30 Fri-Sun ☎ (01248) 712453

Facer's Flintshire Bitter; Purple Moose Cwrw Eryri/Snowdonia Ale H/G, Ochr Tywyll y Mws/Dark Side of the Moose; 1 changing beer H

Refurbished to a high standard, the Livvy has four cask ales on offer and serves good-quality home-cooked food. This nautically-themed pub is frequented by locals, students in term time and the local sailing fraternity. A short walk takes you beneath the famous suspension bridge and it is close to the quay for local tourist boats. The Anglesey and Welsh Coast footpaths are nearby.

Nefyn

Bragdy Llŷn

Ffordd Dewi Sant, LL53 6EG

12-5; closed Sun ☎ (01758) 721981 cwrwllyn.cymru

Bragdy Llŷn Brenin Enlli, Cwrw Glyndwr, Seithenyn; 1 changing beer (sourced locally) H

A friendly bar located within the Cwrw Llŷn Brewery, open to the public all year round. Closing time may be later on Friday and Saturday depending on customer demand. Brewery tours are available on request which include a short film and tasters of the core range of ales. Near the coast and the National Trust village of Porthdinllean. P

Old Colwyn

Red Lion

385 Abergele Road, LL29 9PL

5-11; 4-midnight Fri; 12-midnight Sat; 12-11 Sun ☎ (01492) 515042

House beer (by Marston's); changing beers (sourced nationally) H

This free house, which serves up to five guest ales from independent and national brewers, has an L-shaped lounge featuring a real coal fire, antique brewery mirrors and other memorabilia. There is also a traditional public bar with a pool table, dartboard and TVs. To the rear is a Victorian-style covered and heated smoking conservatory. The real ale club held every Thursday offers nine beers at reduced prices. The pub sign is worth a look.

Q (12,13,14)

Penrhynside

Penrhyn Arms

Pendre Road, LL30 3BY

5 (4 Thu)-11; 4-midnight Fri; 12-midnight Sat; 12-11.30 Sun

Banks's Amber Ale; 4 changing beers (sourced regionally) H

Reopened in 2017 following a major refurbishment, this welcoming free house offers up to four guest beers, concentrating on new breweries and new beers. The spacious single-room L-shaped bar has pool, darts and a wide-screen TV. To the rear is a conservatory with views of the cliff face behind. As well as its quality ales, the pub is renowned for its range of real ciders and perries. Thursday is cheese night. Live music plays on Saturday.

Porthdinllaen

Ty Coch Inn

LL53 6DB (access by foot only)

closed Mon-Thu; 12-6 Fri & Sat; 12-5 Sun ☎ (01758) 720498 tycoch.co.uk

Bragdy Llŷn Brenin Enlli; Purple Moose Cwrw Ysgawen/Elderflower; 1 changing beer (sourced regionally) H

The building, in an iconic position on the beach at beautiful Porthdinllaen, opened as a pub in 1842 to serve the local fishermen. It is now rated one of the top 10 beach bars in the world. The single open-plan room is served by a central bar. It can only be reached on foot either along the beach or across the golf course. Parking is available at the NT car park or the golf clubhouse. Check for out-of-season opening times.

Porthmadog

Australia

31-35 High Street, LL49 9LR

12-11 (midnight Fri & Sat) ☎ (01766) 515957

Purple Moose Cwrw Eryri/Snowdonia Ale, Cwrw Ysgawen/Elderflower, Cwrw Glaslyn/Glaslyn Ale, Ochr Tywyll y Mws/Dark Side of the Moose; 2 changing beers (sourced locally) H

A pub since 1864, The Australia has become the Purple Moose Brewery taphouse. Most of its core real ale range is available as well as seasonal and special occasion beers. It is situated in the centre of town next to the bus stops. Two rooms are served by a long wooden bar with eight handpumps. There is a small outdoor seating area at the back. Near the Ffestiniog & Welsh Highland Railways station. Local CAMRA Pub of the Year 2016.

Royal Sportsman Hotel

131 High Street, LL49 9HB

12-11 (10 Sun) ☎ (01766) 512015

Purple Moose Cwrw Eryri/Snowdonia Ale, Cwrw Glaslyn/Glaslyn Ale; Sharp's Doom Bar H

Built in 1862 as a staging post for coaches on the turnpike road to Porthdinllaen, the hotel is situated near the centre of town and the railway station for the Cambrian Coast railway. With a welcoming real fire, Gelerts Bar is a comfortable place to enjoy a drink or a bar meal, and is popular with both locals and tourists. It hosts a popular quiz on Sunday evening. Also convenient for visiting the Ffestiniog & Welsh Highland Railways. P

Spooner's Bar

Harbour Station, LL49 9NF

9am-11; 12-10.30 Sun ☎ (01766) 516032 festrail.co.uk

Purple Moose Cwrw Eryri/Snowdonia Ale; 5 changing beers (sourced nationally) H

Spooner's beer range varies, but there are always at least two ales from the local Purple Moose Brewery. Situated in the terminus of the world-famous Ffestiniog & Welsh Highland Railways, steam trains are outside the door most of the year. Food is served every lunchtime, evening meals Tuesday to Saturday, but check first out of season. A former local CAMRA Pub of the Year award winner. Q (Ffestiniog & WHR)

Pwllheli

Pen Cob ✔

Station Square, LL53 5HG

⏲ 7am-11 ☎ (01758) 704970
Greene King Abbot; Ruddles Best Bitter; 4 changing beers Ⓗ
Wetherspoon pub opened in 2013 opposite the railway station at the start/end of the scenic Cambrian Coast Line. Formerly a Bon Marche shop, it has been tastefully refurbished and is now a light and airy venue popular with people of all ages. It gets especially busy with locals and tourists at weekends and during the holiday season. The area is popular for sailing. ♘◐◑♿⇌🚌ᯤ

Red Wharf Bay

Ship Inn ✔

LL75 8RJ (off A5025 between Pentraeth and Benllech)
⏲ 11-11 (10.30 Sun) ☎ (01248) 852568
🌐 shipinnredwharfbay.co.uk
Adnams Broadside; Brains SA; 2 changing beers Ⓗ
Red Wharf Bay was once a busy port exporting coal and fertilisers in the 18th and 19th centuries. Previously known as the Quay, the Ship enjoys an excellent reputation for its bar and restaurant, with meals served lunchtimes and evenings. It gets busy with locals and visitors in the summer. The garden has panoramic views across the bay to south-east Anglesey. The resort town of Benllech is two miles away and the coastal path passes the front door.
Q♘❀◐◑♿P

Rhoscolyn

White Eagle

LL65 2NJ (off B4545 signed Traeth Beach)
⏲ 12-3, 6-11; 12-11 Sat; 12-10.30 Sun ☎ (01407) 860267
🌐 white-eagle.co.uk
Marston's 61 Deep, Pedigree; Weetwood Ambush; 2 changing beers Ⓗ
Saved from closure by new owners, this pub has been renovated and rebuilt with an airy, brasserie-style ambience. It has a fine patio enjoying superb views over Caernarfon Bay and the Llŷn Peninsula to Bardsey Island. The nearby beach offers safe swimming with a warden on duty in the summer months. The pub is also close to the coastal footpath. Excellent food is available lunchtimes and evenings, all day during the school holidays.
Q♘◐◑♿⛺♣P

Rhyd Ddu

Cwellyn Arms

LL54 6TL
⏲ 11-11 ☎ (01766) 890321 🌐 snowdoninn.co.uk
Conwy Welsh Pride; 5 changing beers (sourced regionally) Ⓗ
A traditional Welsh country inn, in a fabulous situation in the village of Rhyd Ddu at the foot of Snowdon. The pub's boast that it has nine real ales nine days a week is only slightly exaggerated. There are usually four handpulls in use, dispensing ales from local breweries. The lovely log fire makes the pub cosy and welcoming after a walk on Snowdon, or after a ride on the nearby Welsh Highland Railway. ❀🛏◐◑♿⛺P🚌🐾

Rowen

Ty Gwyn ✔

High Street, LL32 8YU
⏲ 4-11 (1am Fri); 12-11 Sat; 12-10 Sun ☎ (01492) 650232
JW Lees Bitter; 2 changing beers (often JW Lees) Ⓗ
Community village inn in an idyllic setting with a warm welcome for locals and visitors alike. There are two walled gardens, one with a river running by. The comfortable lounge has horse brasses and old pictures on the walls, and there is a small restaurant area serving good food made with locally sourced ingredients. Traditional Welsh singing features on Friday evenings, live entertainment most Saturdays and charity quiz nights on occasion. Opening times may vary seasonally. ♘❀◐◑⛺♣P🚌(19A)🐾ᯤ

St George

Kinmel Arms

LL22 9BP
⏲ closed Mon; 11-11 (11.30 Fri & Sat); 11.30-8 Sun
☎ (01745) 832207 🌐 thekinmelarms.co.uk
Thwaites Original; 1 changing beer (sourced regionally) Ⓗ
Seventeenth-century former coaching inn on the hillside overlooking the sea. A central bar serves a large combined drinking and dining area with a real log fire in one corner and a spacious conservatory dining area at the rear. The guest beer often comes from a local brewery, and it stocks a selection of Belgian and continental beers. The pub has a reputation for good food, and luxury accommodation in four comfortable suites.
Q❀🛏◐◑♿P🐾ᯤ

Tal-y-Bont

Y Bedol Ⓛ

Conway Road, LL32 8QF
⏲ closed Mon; 5-10 (11 Wed; midnight Fri); 12-midnight Sat; 12-10 Sun ☎ (01492) 660164
Purple Moose Cwrw Ysgawen/Elderflower; 2 changing beers (sourced locally) Ⓗ
A traditional country pub on the main route down the west side of the Conwy Valley. It reopened in 2016 following a lengthy closure and refurbishment by the new owners, with the small bar to the back. It is popular with families, walkers and other outdoor enthusiasts, and has a large, attractive beer garden to the side and rear. Food and real ales are sourced with the emphasis on local suppliers. Opening times may vary seasonally.
♘❀◐◑P🚌(19)🐾ᯤ

Trefriw

Old Ship Ⓛ

LL27 0JH
⏲ closed Mon; 12-3, 6-10.30 Tue-Thu; 12-3, 5-11 Fri; 12-11 Sat & Sun ☎ (01492) 640013 🌐 the-old-ship.co.uk
Banks's Amber Ale; 2 changing beers (sourced regionally) Ⓗ
Dating from the 16th century, this former customs house is now a busy village local with a grassed area leading towards the River Conwy. A small central bar serves an L-shaped lounge with an open fire, brass ornaments and pictures of historic and nautical interest. The separate dining room features an inglenook fireplace and offers home-cooked food. This genuine free house keeps a good range of guest beers from regional and local breweries such as Conwy, Great Orme and Nant.
Q❀◐◑P🚌(19)

WALES

Tregarth

Pant Yr Ardd

LL57 4PL

2-midnight Mon; 4-midnight Tue-Thu, 4-1am Fri; 12-1am Sat; 12-midnight Sun ☎ (01248) 605546

Conwy Surfin' IPA; Hafod Hopper; 1 changing beer (sourced regionally) Ⓗ

This pub divides into two rooms on either side of the bar. The walls are adorned with pictures of the village from the past. A free house, the ales are mostly from local breweries, but sometimes national beers are available. The beer garden is adjacent to the car park over the road. The inn has been an integral part of the village community for generations and you are assured of a warm welcome here. ❀P

Tremadog

Union Inn ✔

7 Market Square, LL49 9RB

12-2, 5.30-12.30am (11 Sun) ☎ (01766) 512748

union-inn.com

Big Bog Bog Standard Bitter; Great Orme Atlantis; Purple Moose Cwrw Eryri/Snowdonia Ale Ⓗ

Friendly local situated in the village square, with two separate cosy bars and a restaurant at the rear. The pub has a policy of using locally sourced produce, and the ale range mainly features local beers. Children are welcome and there are board games available. Excellent food is served in the bar and restaurant. Tremadog was the birthplace of Thomas Edward Lawrence (Lawrence of Arabia) in 1888. Frequent bus services pass the building.

Q❀♿(1A,T2)

Waunfawr

Snowdonia Park

Beddgelert Road, LL55 4AQ

11-11 (10.30 Sun) ☎ (01286) 650409

snowdonia-park.co.uk

Snowdonia Trithro, Gold, Carmen Sutra, Cais, Dark and Delicious, Welsh Highland Bitter Ⓗ

Home of the Snowdonia and Big Bog breweries, this is a popular pub for walkers, climbers and families, with children's play areas inside and out. Meals are served all day. The pub adjoins Waunfawr station on the Welsh Highland Railway – stop off here before continuing on one of the most scenic sections of narrow-gauge railway in Britain. There is a large campsite adjacent on the riverside. A frequent local CAMRA Pub of the Year.

Q❀♿(WHR)♣P

Black Boy Inn, Caernarfon (Photo: Nelo Hotsuma/flickr CC BY 2.0)

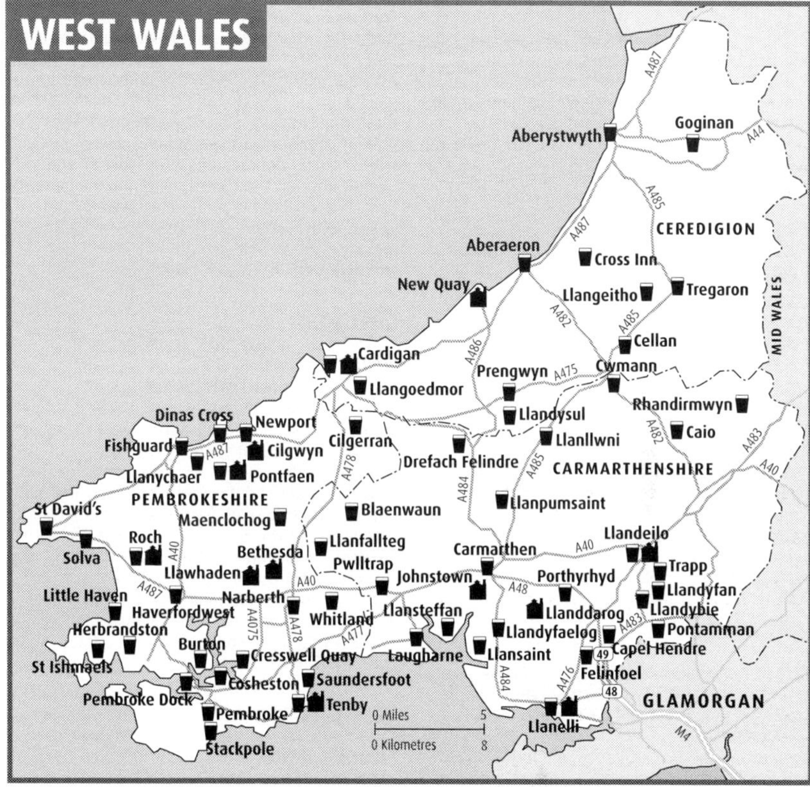

Authority areas covered: Carmarthenshire UA, Ceredigion UA, Pembrokeshire UA

Aberaeron

Cadwgan Inn

10 Market Street, SA46 0AU (off A487, overlooking harbour)

12 (5 Mon)-11; 12-midnight Fri & Sat; 12-5 Sun

(01545) 570149

Hancocks HB; 2 changing beers (sourced nationally; often Bluestone, Evan Evans, Oakham) H

Named after the last ship to be built in this attractive Regency planned town, this old-fashioned single-bar pub offers a friendly welcome and lively conversation. It is popular for its sports coverage, mainly rugby and racing. The guest beers are chosen from a wide range of small and regional breweries. Gwynt y Ddraig bottled ciders are available. There is a colourful hidden garden at the rear, and the small pavement drinking area at the front is a suntrap. Opposite is a free but busy harbourside public car park. (T1,T5)

Aberystwyth

Glengower Hotel

3 Victoria Terrace, SY23 2DH (on seafront at N end of promenade)

12-11 (01970) 626191 glengower.co.uk

Mantle Rock Steady; Wye Valley Butty Bach; 3 changing beers (sourced regionally; often Cwrw Cader, Evan Evans, Purple Moose) H

Excellent coastal views of Cardigan Bay can be enjoyed from the suntrap front terrace at this newly refurbished seafront hotel. The central front bar is the main drinking area, with a logburner for the winter months. There is also a quieter dining area and a large rear games room. An annual beer festival and raft race are held over the May bank holiday weekend. Food is locally sourced wherever possible. Up to five ciders come from Gwynt y Ddraig, plus regional guests.
Q (03)

Hen Orsaf

26 Alexandra Road, SY23 1LN

8am-midnight (1am Fri & Sat) (01970) 636080

Greene King Abbot; Ruddles Best Bitter; Sharp's Doom Bar; 6 changing beers (sourced nationally; often Purple Moose) H

An award-winning conversion of Aberystwyth's 1924-built ex-GWR railway station. This excellent Wetherspoon pub offers up to six guests, with a beer from Purple Moose always available on the purple handpump. A varied selection of light and dark beers is usually stocked. The ciders are from Westons and Gwynt y Ddraig. The usual Wetherspoon policies and promotions apply. Trains, buses and taxis are all adjacent. Outdoor drinking is on the old station concourse with direct access to the town's railway station.

Ship & Castle

1 High Street, SY23 1JG

2 (4 Mon)-midnight; 2-1am Fri & Sat 07773 778785

Wye Valley HPA, Butty Bach; 3 changing beers (sourced nationally; often Oakham, Salopian, Tiny Rebel) H

The town's flagship pub offers microbrewery guests from the UK and Ireland. Small amounts of excellent beer in other formats are also on offer including craft, keg, bottles and cans, plus real cider and perry from Gwynt y Ddraig. A five-pump platter of third-pint measures is available. Midweek beer festivals in spring and autumn offer extended choice. The well-considered décor reflects the pub's name and history. The venue can be very busy on rugby days, but is welcoming at all times. ⛺≠♣●P🚌🐾

Blaenwaun

Tafarn Yr Oen

SA34 0JD

4-midnight ☎ (01994) 448899

4 changing beers (often Evan Evans, Greene King) H

Known locally as The Lamb, this down-to-earth little pub, warmed by a woodburner, has a historic Buckley's Brewery connection. The staff are perfect hosts and the locals enjoy regaling visitors with tales, tall and true. Darts and pool are played, and wellies and dogs are welcome. Set in a remote and idyllic area, the pub is well worth a visit. There are plenty of parking spaces and a campsite half a mile away. Q⛺♣P🚌(221,230)🐾

Burton

Jolly Sailor ✔

SA73 1NX

11.30-3, 5-11.30 summer; 11.30-3, 6-11 winter
☎ (01646) 600378 jollysailorburton.co.uk

Brains Rev James; Draught Bass; Morland Old Speckled Hen H

Overlooking the River Cleddau and in the shadow of the toll bridge that traverses it, there has been a public house here for over 150 years. It was from this point that travellers would come to Burton to cross by rowing boat to Pembroke Dock. They would leave their supply donkeys outside the Jolly Sailor until their return. The large family- and food-oriented pub has a huge garden with a children's play area and an aviary. Winter opening times can vary – check ahead. P

Caio

Brunant Arms

Church Street, SA19 8RD (off A482 near Pumsaint Gold Mines)

closed Mon; 12.30-3 (not Tue), 6-10; 12.30-10 Fri (11 Sat); 12-3 Sun ☎ (01558) 650483

2 changing beers (sourced locally; often Evan Evans) H

Friendly village pub on a historic drovers' route opposite an interesting church where a legendary Welsh wizard is buried. One real ale is sold in winter, two in summer. A hub for local societies and pool and darts teams, live music is hosted on occasion. The central bar serves a games room and seating areas divided by movable pews, warmed by a wood fire. Excellent food is served and the pub attracts caravanners, Caio Forest walkers and horse trekkers. Children's games and rare quoits can be played. Q⛺♣●P🚌

Capel Hendre

King's Head Hotel L

Waterloo Road, SA18 3SF

4-11 Mon; 11-2.30, 5-midnight; 11-3, 5-11 Sun
☎ (01269) 842377

Glamorgan Cwrw Gorslas/Bluestone Bitter, Jemimas Pitchfork; 2 changing beers (sourced regionally; often Bluestone) H

A village pub tucked away just three miles from junction 49 of the M4, and a couple of miles from the former mining town of Ammanford. The interior comprises a main bar and dining room, with a sliding door leading to a separate snug. Outside there is a pleasant garden and a large car park. Two or three real ales are sourced from Wales, with Glamorgan, Bluestone and Neath breweries often represented.
●P🚌(128,129)🐾

Cardigan

Grosvenor

Bridge Street, SA43 1HY SN177459

11-11 ☎ (01239) 613792

Greene King Abbot; Sharp's Doom Bar; 1 changing beer (sourced nationally) H

Situated on the edge of the town centre next to Cardigan Castle and the River Teifi, this large pub offers a good choice of ales, including a selection of bottled beers. The large open-plan bar/lounge provides various areas to relax, eat and drink, and there is an extra room upstairs for dining and functions. Good-value food is served lunchtimes and evenings every day. An outdoor patio area overlooks the river and the revamped quay.
♣●🚌🐾

Carmarthen

Friends Arms

Old St Clears Road, SA31 3HH

11-11 (midnight Fri & Sat) ☎ (01267) 234073

Mantle MOHO; Thornbridge Jaipur IPA; 4 changing beers (sourced locally; often Castle Gate, Mantle, Thornbridge) H

Excellent local hostelry half-a-mile west of the town centre with a cosy and friendly atmosphere and a warm welcome, enhanced by two open fires. Popular with sports fans, it has Sky and BT Sports, plus darts. Four real ales are usually offered. The pub has its own microbrewery which regularly produces good beer. An outbuilding on two floors has function rooms for meetings and parties. Local CAMRA Pub of the Year in 2017. ●🚌🐾

Stag & Pheasant

34 Spilman Street, SA31 1LQ

12-11 (midnight Sat) ☎ (01267) 232040

House beer (by Marston's); 1 changing beer (sourced nationally; often Marston's) H

REAL ALE BREWERIES

4Four Bethesda (brewing suspended)
Bluestone Cilgwyn
Caffle Llawhaden
Castlegate Johnstown
Coles Family Llanddarog
Evan Evans Llandeilo
Felinfoel Llanelli
Friends Arms Johnstown
Gwaun Valley Pontfaen
Harbwr Tenby Tenby
Mantle Cardigan
Penlon Cottage New Quay
Tenby Tenby
Victoria Inn Roch

A busy locals' pub with a warm and friendly atmosphere on the main thoroughfare in Carmarthen, making it a popular venue for tourists and locals. The pub boasts an excellent beer garden with heaters at the rear. There is always a choice of two real ales from Marston's – Fortyniner or Hobgoblin Gold – and another Marston's guest. This is a popular venue for watching sporting events, with two large TV screens.

Yr Hen Dderwen

47-48 King Street, SA31 1BH
8am-midnight (1am Sat) (01267) 242050
Greene King IPA, Abbot; 8 changing beers (sourced nationally; often Castlegate, Glamorgan, Gwaun Valley) H
Named after the local legend of Merlin and an ancient oak which is depicted throughout the premises. Local Welsh ales are always available alongside a good selection of beers from around the world. A range of bottled and canned craft ale is also kept. There are beer festivals in the spring and autumn and a cider festival in the summer. The pub also hosts Meet the Brewer sessions throughout the year. Food is served all day.
Q P

Cellan

Fishers Arms

SA48 8HU (on B4343) SN596482
4-11; 2-11 Sat & Sun (01570) 422895
1 changing beer H
This friendly pub dates back to 1580, with a single bar divided into a flagstoned and beamed area and a lounge area with a large woodburner. A large-screen TV shows BT and Sky Sports and the games room offers pool and darts. Good-value home-made food is served in the rear dining room. Real cider is available during the summer months. The garden at the back has a children's play area.
P (585)

Cilgerran

Masons Arms

Cwnce, SA43 2SR
1 (4 Mon)-11; 12-11 Fri & Sat; 11-11 Sun 07989 990461
Hancocks HB; Sharp's Doom Bar; 1 changing beer (often Mantle) H
The Masons, also known as The Rampin, was thought to have opened in 1836. It is a small, cosy and friendly village pub with an open fire (an old kitchen range). Many local characters can be found here and a great atmosphere awaits your visit. Three real ales are on offer, one changing regularly, usually from a local brewery. Various charity events are held during the year along with an occasional musical evening. Winter opening times may vary – check ahead. P

Cosheston

Brewery Inn

SA72 4UD
closed Mon; 12-3, 6-11; 12-11 Sat; 12-6 Sun
(01646) 686678 thebreweryinn.com
Brains Rev James; Coles Family Cwrw Blasus; 1 changing beer H
This Grade II listed free house was once accommodation for monks, with its own brewhouse in outbuildings behind (brewing ceased in 1889). The light and airy stone-built inn has a traditional slate floor and beamed ceiling. To one side is a cosy area for drinkers to enjoy a chat in front of the log fire. Ingredients for the extensive menu are sourced locally, including fresh fish. The pub has a solid reputation for good food and ales.
Q P

Cresswell Quay

Cresselly Arms

SA68 0TE
12-11 (01646) 651210
Sharp's Doom Bar H**; Worthington's Bitter** G**; house beer (by Caffle); 2 changing beers (sourced locally; often Bluestone, Mantle)** H
Situated on the Cresswell River, this 250-year-old ivy-covered hostelry is a throwback to the Victorian age. The homely farm kitchen interior, where a roaring fire burns in the hearth, is a haven for locals and visitors alike. Accessible by boat from the Milford Haven estuary at high tide, the pub also lies on a series of interesting walking routes. The house beer from Caffle is complemented by Worthington's Bitter dispensed from the barrel by jug. Q P (361)

Cross Inn (Llanon)

Rhos yr Hafod Inn

SY23 5NB (at B4337/B4577 crossroads)
5-11; closed Sun (01974) 272644
2 changing beers (sourced regionally; often Bluestone, Evan Evans, Mantle) H
This friendly, family-run pub offers an ever-changing range of guest ales and a warm welcome. A choice of drinking areas includes the front bar, popular in the early evening with lively locals, and the comfortable rear bar. Sunny days can be enjoyed in the roadside drinking area or in the large rear garden. A traditional turntable and vinyl collection are available for customers to peruse. There is ample parking both sides of the pub. Varied events are held throughout the year.
P

Cwmann

Cwmann Tavern

SA48 8DR SN582473
closed Mon; 4-11; 12-11 Sun (01570) 423861
cwmannetavern.co.uk
2 changing beers (sourced nationally) H
A former coaching inn dating from the 1600s, within easy walking distance of the town of Lampeter. The stone floors and low beams help create a cosy atmosphere. The varied menu (available evenings only in the week) includes pub favourites, interesting specials and vegetarian options. There is a folk night every Thursday and a 'not so high stake' poker night every Friday.
P

Dinas Cross

Freemasons Arms

Spencer Buildings, SA42 0UW (on A487 coast road midway between Fishguard and Newport)
12-2.30 (not Mon), 4-11; 12-midnight Fri & Sat; 12-11 Sun
(01348) 811674
Gower Gold; 1 changing beer (often Coles Family, Harbwr Tenby) H

Traditional sea captains' meeting place in the Pembrokeshire National Park. This pub is conveniently placed for those who like to visit attractive beaches, walk the coastal path or enjoy sailing. It also has the advantage of being on a main bus route. Tastefully refurbished while retaining its original character, the main bar with a cosy open fire has a dining area at the side. Please check winter opening times before venturing forth. Q P (T5)

Drefach Felindre

John Y Gwas

SA44 5XG SN354383

5-11; 4-midnight Fri; 12-midnight Sat; 12-11 Sun

(01559) 370469

2 changing beers (sourced regionally; often Bluestone, Brains, Shepherd Neame) H

Early 19th-century village tavern with a striking yellow and black livery, attracting locals and tourists alike with snugs, a wood-burning stove, quality beer and cider, and a warm welcome, especially for dogs. Two ales are generally offered, and a wide variety of bottled beers and ciders. A beer festival, showcasing more than 10 different ales, is held over the August bank holiday weekend. Basket meals are available most evenings, bar meals on Friday and Saturday evenings. P (460)

Red Lion

SA44 5UH (in centre of village 1 mile off A484 Llandysul to Newcastle Emlyn road) SN354388

4-11 (midnight Fri & Sat); 12-10 Sun (01559) 371677

redlionwales.co.uk

Mantle Cwrw Teifi H

Located in this small village near the National Wool Museum, a warm welcome is assured at this 19th-century pub, which has been renovated in recent years. It is mostly open plan but with a separate dining room and a large outside drinking area. Community-focused, it hosts regular fundraising events for charity. The car park is small but there is on-street parking. The original tiled entrance porch is worthy of note. Q P (460)

Felinfoel

White Lion Inn

Parkview, SA14 8BH (on A476)

closed Mon; 12-11 (01554) 776644

Gower Gold; 4 changing beers (sourced nationally) H

A family-friendly split-level hostelry with defined drinking and dining spaces as well as a function room. There are no handpumps visible as the beer is dispensed from a draught system piped from the back wall of the bar. There are covered and open drinking areas outside. A good-value carvery is offered. Quiz nights are Sunday and Wednesday. National cycle and walking paths to the Swiss Valley and beyond are nearby. There is ample parking on the roadside.

Fishguard

Royal Oak Inn

Market Square, SA65 9HA

11-11 (01348) 218632

Brains Rev James; Glamorgan Jemima's Pitchfork; 1 changing beer (sourced locally; often Bluestone) H

This Grade II listed building is famous for its place in history – a French invasion attempt on the west coast of Wales in 1797 was thwarted by the locals in the Battle of Fishguard, known as 'the last invasion of Britain'. A peace treaty was signed between the British and the French in the Royal Oak's bar area. The pub has now reopened following a few uncertain years, sparingly decorated with exposed stone and wooden beams, but with little reference to its past history. Q

Goginan

Druid Inn

SY23 3NT (on A44 6 miles E of Aberystwyth)

12-midnight (1am Fri & Sat) (01970) 880650

Mantle MOHO; Wye Valley Bitter; 3 changing beers (sourced nationally; often Purple Moose, Wood) H

A very welcoming pub celebrating its 43rd year in the Guide. The dining room and pool room flank an L-shaped main bar where dogs are welcome. Up to four real ales and four ciders are served, plus interesting bottles and craft beers on draught. Occasional music nights (sometimes with acts of more-than-local renown) and beer festivals are hosted. Food is popular and high quality. Buses run until early evening Monday to Saturday. A pub-owned B&B can be found next door. Wales CAMRA Pub of the Year 2017. P (525,X47)

Haverfordwest

Pembroke Yeoman

11 Hill Street, SA61 1QQ

11-11 (01437) 762500

Draught Bass; 1 changing beer (sourced nationally) H

A little off the beaten track, conversation rules at this local pub, though there is a well-stocked jukebox should it flag. Guest ales come from small breweries and change often. Food is served in generous portions on special themed evenings. Known as the Upper Three Crowns until the 1960s, the pub's name was changed in recognition of the local yeomanry headquarters nearby. Q (301)

William Owen L

6 Quay Street, SA61 1BG

8am-midnight (1am Fri & Sat) (01437) 771900

Greene King IPA, Abbot; Sharp's Doom Bar; 5 changing beers (sourced regionally; often Bluestone, Caffle, Harbwr Tenby) H

Pembrokeshire's first and so far only Wetherspoon pub occupies a handsome 19th-century building, formerly a shop, hotel and restaurant, with a spacious extension to the rear. It was reputedly built in 1856 for Joseph Thomas, a corn and manure merchant, by local architect William Owen. It has also been a saddler's and more recently the Wilton House Hotel. Beer from one of the county's breweries is regularly available. The pub offers the chain's standard menu and promotional deals, and opens from 8am for breakfast. Q

Herbrandston

Taberna Inn L

SA73 3TD (3 miles W of Milford Haven)

12-11 (01646) 693498 taberna.org.uk

Caffle Drop Squint; Purple Moose Ochr Tywyll y Mws/ Dark Side of the Moose; 1 changing beer (sourced nationally) Ⓗ
Designed and built in 1963 by a local carpenter and builder with an eye to the area's then rapidly developing oil and petrochemical industry. A bus (service 300) is available from Milford Haven and the marina for visitors and crews looking for a choice of real ales. Local, regional and national beers are available alongside Westons and Moles Black Rat ciders. The pub maintains a list of all the guest beers sold throughout the year. A former local CAMRA Pub of the Year.
Q🔥🛏◑♿⛺🍎P🚉🚌(300,315)

Laugharne

New Three Mariners Inn 𝕃
Victoria Street, SA33 4SE
3-11 (midnight Fri); 12-1am Sat; 6-11 Sun
☎ (01994) 427426 🌐 newthreemarinersinn.co.uk
1 changing beer (often Evan Evans)
The building is located in the centre of Laugharne and only yards from its early 11th-century castle. Dylan Thomas lived in this historic town for a number of years and he and his wife Caitlin are laid to rest in the graveyard of St Martin's Church. The pub moved to its current site when the original ale house opposite was converted to a carpentry shop. Popular with locals, it hosts a weekly quiz night.
🔥❀🛏◗♿⛺♣P🚌🐾📶

Little Haven

Saint Bride's Inn 𝕃
St Brides Road, SA62 3UN
11-midnight ☎ (01437) 781266 🌐 saintbridesinn.co.uk
Brains Rev James; Hancocks HB; 2 changing beers (sourced regionally; often Bluestone, Brecon) Ⓗ
Little Haven is a quaint old fishing village in a conservation area of the Pembrokeshire Coast National Park. This family-run pub in the centre of the village is open all year round, selling a range of Welsh, often Pembrokeshire, ales. It is noted for the ancient well in the cellar. The attractive interior includes a separate dining area, and there are heaters on the patio in the pretty suntrap garden for outdoor drinking. Q🔥❀◑⛺P🚉🚌(311,400)📶

Llandeilo

Cottage Inn
Pentrefelin, SA19 6SD (on A40, 3 miles W of Llandeilo)
10.30-11 ☎ (01558) 824645 🌐 cottageinnbandb.co.uk
3 changing beers (sourced regionally; often Glamorgan) Ⓗ
A popular family-run local community pub on the A40. Dating back to the 1850s, it was formerly a coaching inn and a drovers' hostelry. Sky TV is available and the pub gets busy when major sporting events are screened. It has a separate restaurant/function room. At the rear is a spacious covered smoking area, garden and a large car park with caravanning and camping space. Two or three guest real ales are offered. It has B&B accommodation. Q🔥❀🛏◑♿⛺P🚌🐾📶

Salutation Inn 🏆
33 New Road, SA19 6DF
12-11 (10.30 Sun) ☎ (01558) 824255
Gower Gold; Sharp's Atlantic; Timothy Taylor Landlord; 2 changing beers (sourced nationally; often Mantle) Ⓗ
A locals' pub near the town centre. The landlord is a cask beer enthusiast and friendly staff dispense five rapidly changing ales. The interior is divided into two areas, with a pool table on one side and a wood fire on the other. Live music often features at weekends. There is a garden and function area to the rear. The pub hosts a beer festival in the summer. ❀♿⇌♣🚌🐾📶

White Horse
Rhosmaen Street, SA19 6EN
11-11; 12-10.30 Sun ☎ (01558) 822424
Evan Evans Best Bitter, Cwrw, Warrior; 2 changing beers Ⓗ
Grade II listed coaching inn dating from the 16th century. The tap for the local Evan Evans Brewery, this multi-roomed hostelry is popular with all ages. There is a small outdoor drinking area to the front and a large council car park to the rear with access to the pub down a short flight of steps. A covered area is available for smokers with its own TV showing sport. A former local CAMRA Pub of the Year winner. ⇌🍎🚉🚌(103,X13)🐾

Llandybie

Ivy Bush
18 Church Street, SA18 3HZ (100yds from church)
12-midnight (11 Mon); 11-midnight Sat & Sun
☎ (01269) 850272
Timothy Taylor Landlord; 1 changing beer (sourced regionally; often Exmoor) Ⓗ
This friendly local, modernised several years ago, has a single bar with two comfortable seating areas. Pub games and quizzes are held weekly and a large-screen TV shows sport. Timothy Taylor Landlord is usually joined by at least one regularly changing guest beer. The local birdwatching group holds its meetings here. The railway station nearby is on the scenic Heart of Wales line.
🔥❀⇌♣🍎P🚉🚌(103,X13)📶

Red Lion Hotel
6 Llandeilo Road, SA18 3JA (near railway station)
12-3, 6-11; 12-11 Sat; 12-8 Sun ☎ (01269) 851202
🌐 redlionllandybie.com
2 changing beers (sourced regionally; often Gower, Timothy Taylor) Ⓗ
Former coaching inn dating back to 1786 in parts with an old painted coat of arms inside the main front door. The family-run pub serves food and quality beers in a convivial atmosphere. There is a comfortable enclosed seating area for drinking, and food is served in separate dining areas. There are benches in the garden at the rear. Handy for the railway station on the popular Heart of Wales line.
🔥❀◑⇌🍎P🚌📶

Llandyfaelog

Red Lion
SA17 5PP (300yds off A484)
11-midnight ☎ (01267) 267530
🌐 redlionllandyfaelog.co.uk
3 changing beers (sourced regionally; often Butcombe, Evan Evans, Glamorgan) Ⓗ
This family-run village hostelry can truly be described as at the heart of the community. It has a separate annexe staging concerts and functions for

WALES

the surrounding area, and hosts the local choir practice evenings. The large public bar, with darts and a pool table, is complemented by a restaurant and a separate family room. Food is served throughout the bar and restaurant.
Q (198,X12)

Llandyfan

Square & Compass

SA18 2UD (between Ammanford and Trapp)
4.30 (12 Sat summer)-11; 12-10.30 Sun
(01269) 850402
Tomos Watkin Old Style Bitter; 2 changing beers (sourced locally) H
Originally the village blacksmith's, this 18th-century building was converted to a pub in the 1960s. Nestling on the western edge of the Brecon Beacons National Park, it enjoys magnificent local views and plenty of walking opportunities. A traditional family hostelry, it has a wonderful rustic charm and offers a warm, friendly welcome. Usually two, occasionally three, guest beers are available, at least one from a local brewery. Opening hours vary in winter – ring ahead to check.
Q P

Llandysul

Porth Hotel

Church Street, SA44 4QS SN418407
12-11 (5.30 Sun) (01559) 362202 porthhotel.co.uk
2 changing beers (sourced locally) H
Set on the banks of the River Teifi, this 17th-century coaching inn is now a family-run village hotel with a bar, restaurant and function room. The public rooms still retain the original oak beams and panels. Beers from the local Castle Gate Brewery are regularly featured alongside ales from other Welsh breweries such as Brecon, Glamorgan, Coles and Gower. An ideal location close to walks and fishing. P

Llanelli

York Palace

51 Stepney Street, SA15 3YA (opp Town Hall Square Gardens)
8am-midnight (1am Sat) (01554) 758609
Greene King Abbot; Ruddles Best Bitter; 8 changing beers (often Glamorgan, Gower, Tomos Watkin) H
A refurbished former picture palace retaining much of the original decor, offering a good selection of beers from around the world including bottled and canned craft ale. It also boasts a varied selection of boxed and bottled real ciders, occasionally also on handpull. There are beer festivals in the spring and autumn, and a cider festival in summer. The pub hosts Meet the Brewer sessions throughout the year. Food is served all day. Q

Llanfallteg

Plash

SA34 0UN (off A40 at Llanddewi Velfrey)
12 (4 Mon & Tue)-11; 3-9 Sun (01437) 563472
theplashinn.co.uk
Wye Valley Butty Bach; 2 changing beers H
At the centre of village life, this terrace-style cottage pub and garden has been an inn for more than 180 years and visitors are made welcome. It holds a quiz night on Tuesday, a regular folk night and a number of other special nights. The guest beers are usually from small, independent breweries. Home-made food, using locally sourced ingredients, includes specials on Wednesday, Friday and Saturday. An accessible entrance is to the rear. A former local CAMRA Pub of the Year.
Q P

Llangeitho

Three Horseshoe Inn

SY25 6TW
5.30-11; 12-2 Sun (01974) 821244
2 changing beers (sourced regionally; often Harbwr Tenby, Mantle) H
Friendly pub situated in a pretty village with historic connections to the Methodist revival in the 1700s. It has a main bar, games room and separate dining area also used for functions and events. An attractive outside seating area overlooks the village square and is a lovely place to enjoy a beer in the evening sun. Excellent-value, home-cooked meals are served, with a special offer menu on Wednesday. Pool and darts are played and there is a jukebox, plus a big screen for major sporting events. P

Llangoedmor

Penllwyndu

SA43 2LY (on B4570 4½ miles from Cardigan) SN240458
12 (3 Mon)-11; 11-11 Sat & Sun (01239) 682533
Hancocks HB; 2 changing beers (sourced regionally; often Brains) H
Old-fashioned ale house standing at an isolated crossroads where Cardigan's evildoers were once hanged – the pub sign is worthy of close inspection. The cheerful and welcoming public bar retains its quaintness, with a slate floor and inglenook with wood-burning stove. Good home-cooked food including traditional favourites is available all day in the bar and the separate restaurant. Live music plays on the third Thursday evening of the month.
P

Llanllwni

Talardd Arms

SA39 9DX SN487392
12-2.30, 6-11 (01559) 395633 talardd.co.uk
1 changing beer (sourced regionally; often Evan Evans) H
There are records of this old inn dating back to 1626, when drovers would stop for refreshments for man and beast before driving their livestock over Llanllwni Mountain on their way to markets over the border. Sympathetically modernised, Tafarn y Talardd continues to offer a traditional warm and friendly welcome. Live music, quizzes and film nights are organised most Mondays.
P

Llanpumsaint

Railway Inn

SA33 6BU (by old railway bridge on main road through village)
closed Mon; 4.30-11 Tue-Thu; 4-11 Fri; 12-11 Sat; 12-10 Sun (01267) 253643
2 changing beers (sourced nationally; often Bluestone (Pembrokeshire), Greene King) H

The Railway is at the centre of the village next to the old railway line – although the railway has long since gone. The restaurant has been refurbished and the pub is now a thriving hub for villagers and visitors. Food is served each evening except Sunday, with lunches on Saturday and Sunday. Good home cooking using local Welsh ingredients comes highly recommended, including a fine selection of desserts. P (215)

Llansaint

King's Arms

13 Maes yr Eglwys, SA17 5JE
closed Mon & Tue; 6.30-11 Wed-Fri; 12-11 Sat & Sun ☎ (01267) 267487
Glamorgan Jemima's Pitchfork; Young's Special; 1 changing beer (often Glamorgan) [H]
A former local CAMRA Pub of the Year, this friendly village hostelry has been a pub for more than 200 years. Situated near an 11th-century church, it is reputedly built from stone recovered from the lost village of St Ishmaels. There is live music every Thursday and a TV/big screen for major sporting events. Good-value home-cooked food is served (book ahead, especially Sunday). Carmarthen Bay Holiday Park is a few miles away.
P (198)

Llansteffan

Castle Inn

The Square, SA33 5JG
12 (5 Wed)-11; 12-10.30 Sun ☎ (01267) 241225
thecastleinnpub.com
Castle Gate Towy Gold; Evan Evans Welsh Pale Ale; Sharp's Doom Bar; house beer (by Evan Evans) [H]
The Castle continues to be a traditional pub committed to real ale. The interior has been completely redecorated and the toilets renovated while keeping the open-plan layout and plenty of cosy corners. Bar snacks are available from an uncomplicated menu. The pub hosts a number of local community groups, and has an outside seating area overlooking the village square where locals and tourists mingle.
Q (227)

Llanychaer

Bridge End Inn

SA65 9TB (on B4313, 2 miles SW of Fishguard)
4-9 Mon & Tue; 12-11 ☎ (01348) 872545
Mantle Rock Steady, Cwrw Teifi, Dark Heart [H]**; 1 changing beer (sourced locally; often Bluestone, Evan Evans)** [H]/[G]
Known locally as The Bont, this friendly country pub, over 150 years old, nestles in the beautiful Gwaun Valley at a bridging point across the river. The cosy bars with log fires serve mainly local real ales. The dining room is housed in the smithy, once run as a complementary business to the inn, and features an external water wheel. Home-made food is served daily, with Sunday lunches particularly popular. Check ahead for winter hours and food service. Q P (345)

Maenclochog

Globe Inn

SA66 7LE
4-11; 12-11 Sat; 7-10 Sun ☎ (01437) 532269
1 changing beer (sourced regionally; often Brecon, Gower, Harbwr Tenby) [H]
In the 19th century Maenclochog was an important trading centre for slate from nearby quarries, and held a monthly livestock market – because of this trade there were once 19 public houses in the village. The Globe, run by the same family for over 150 years, is now the only survivor, and has become the social centre for villages in the surrounding area. P

Narberth

Dragon Inn

5 Water Street, SA67 7AT
9am-11 (12.30am Fri & Sat) ☎ (01834) 860257
Marston's Pedigree; 2 changing beers (sourced nationally; often Jennings, Wychwood) [H]
This public house is in an attractive market town 10 miles north of Tenby, with a prominent place in Welsh mythology. It has a split-level bar leading to dining areas. The whitewashed walls display horse racing photographs. Narberth railway station is a mile from the town centre. Visit the Landsker Visitor Centre to find out more about this fascinating area.

Newport

Golden Lion

East Street, SA42 0SY (on A487 at E end of village)
12-midnight (11 Sun) ☎ (01239) 820321
goldenlionpembrokeshire.co.uk
Bluestone Bedrock Blonde; Sharp's Doom Bar; Worthington's White Shield; 1 changing beer (sourced nationally; often Wainwright) [H]
Situated in an area of outstanding natural beauty close to the Pembrokeshire Coast Path, this is one of the town's sociable locals and is reputed to have its own resident ghost. A number of internal walls have been removed to create a spacious open-plan bar area, with distinct sections helping to retain a cosy atmosphere. Locally caught fish and Welsh Black beef are specialities, served in the bar and restaurant. Car parking space is available on the opposite side of the road.
Q P (T5)

Royal Oak

West Street, SA42 0TA
11-midnight ☎ (01239) 820632
theroyaloaknewport.co.uk
Felinfoel Best Bitter; Gower Gold; 1 changing beer (sourced nationally) [H]
A warm welcome awaits you at The Royal Oak, a traditional Welsh country pub which retains all the charm and atmosphere of its roots, with oak beams, a tiled bar area and many original features. As well as the quality real ales, the pub is renowned for its Sunday roasts, curries and fish and chips. A pensioners' lunch is served on Tuesday.
Q P

Pembroke

Old King's Arms

Main Street, SA71 4JS
11-11 ☎ (01646) 683611 oldkingsarmshotel.co.uk
Felinfoel Double Dragon; Marston's Old Empire; 2 changing beers (sourced locally; often Bluestone, Evan Evans) [H]

WALES

This former coaching inn is allegedly the oldest inn in Pembroke, dating from around 1520. The hotel's Kings Bar is a small room with exposed stone walls, beams and a real fire. It has four handpumps serving local, regional and national beers. There is a separate lounge with a dining area, and a restaurant with room for larger groups. It prides itself on featuring locally sourced meat and fish products on the menu. Q P

Pembroke Dock

First & Last

London Road, SA72 6TX (on A477)
10-1am (1.30am Thu-Sat) (01646) 682687
Brains Rev James; Worthington's White Shield; 1 changing beer (sourced nationally; often Skinner's) H
Friendly single-bar local pub run by the same family for more than 50 years. Formerly the Commercial, it acquired its more distinctive name in 1991 to reflect its edge-of-town location. The walls display an eclectic mix of photos and prints. The guest beer can be from anywhere, local or national, and the food is traditional pub fare. There is a popular quirky Sunday evening quiz. It is handy for the Cleddau Bridge, giving easy access to Haverfordwest, and close to the historic naval dockyard and Irish Ferries. Q P

Station Inn

Hawkestone Road, SA72 6HN
10.30-2.30, 6.30-11; 12-2.30, 7-11 Sun (01646) 621255
3 changing beers (sourced nationally; often Otter) H
Housed in the town's only railway station, where trains depart for Carmarthen, Swansea and, on summer Saturdays, far-off Paddington. This town-centre pub is close to both the Irish Ferries terminal and Pembrokeshire Coastal Path. Meals are excellent value (no lunches Mon, evening meals Wed-Sat only). Three real ales are generally on sale, with Young's Bitter a frequent visitor and a new beer every Tuesday. The June beer festival offers around 20 beers. Live music is performed on Saturday evenings. P (349)

Pontamman

Red Kite Inn

89 Pontamman Road, SA18 2JD (just over 1 mile N of Ammanford on main A474 towards Neath)
5-10 Mon (11.30 Tue-Fri); 12-11.30 Sat; 12-10 Sun
(01269) 597177 theredkiteinnammanford.co.uk
2 changing beers (sourced regionally; often Morland, Timothy Taylor, Wye Valley) H
A family-run pub with a warm and charming atmosphere. Previously known as The Perrivale, it reopened as The Red Kite Inn (or Y Barcud Coch in Welsh). Two or three real ales are usually available, often sourced from Welsh breweries. There are a number of quiet corners and a separate restaurant. Meals are served evenings Wednesday to Saturday, and Sunday lunch. P

Pontfaen

Dyffryn Arms ★

SA65 9SE (off B4313)
11-11 (01348) 881305
Draught Bass G
A timeless gem to be treated with respect. This much-loved pub, a reminder of how country inns might once have looked, is the hub of life in a secluded valley whose cultural traditions include a long history of farmhouse brewing. There is no bar counter – beer is still served by the jug through a sliding serving hatch. Conversation is the main form of entertainment. A regular in the Guide for many years, the pub is on CAMRA's National Inventory of Historic Pub Interiors. Q P

Porthyrhyd

Mansel Arms

Banc y Mansel, SA32 8BS (on B4310 between Porthyrhyd and Drefach)
4-11 (8 Tue); 3-11 Sat; 12-4 Sun (01267) 275305
2 changing beers (sourced regionally) H
Friendly 18th-century former coaching inn with wood fires in each room. The original limestone flags have been broken up and used in the fireplace, and low beams have been added to create atmosphere, with numerous jugs hanging from them in the bar. There is a saloon bar and separate restaurant serving home-cooked food. Beers are varied and come from local and national brewers. Bus 129 runs Monday to Saturday. Q P (129)

Prengwyn

Gwarcefel Arms

SA44 4LU (on crossroads of A475 and B4476) SN424442
4-11; 12-11 Sat & Sun (01559) 363126
Sharp's Doom Bar; 1 changing beer (sourced nationally) H
A traditional country inn with a friendly atmosphere where everyone is welcome, including families and dogs. Situated at the junction of five roads, three miles north of Llandysul, the pub has a main bar with a wood-burning stove, cosy seating, a pool table and a dartboard. A separate restaurant area, which caters for functions and parties, offers evening meals and Sunday lunches. The beer garden and large car park are to the rear. P

Pwlltrap

White Lion

SA33 4AT
10.30-11; 11-10.30 Sun (01994) 230370
Courage Directors; Greene King Abbot; Shepherd Neame Bishops Finger; Young's Bitter; 1 changing beer (sourced locally) H
This roadside pub, just outside St Clears, is warm and welcoming with a real fire in winter. It has an old-world charm with oak beams and panelled walls, and boasts a large restaurant serving good food. Pool and darts are played and a large-screen TV shows regular sporting fixtures. The pub organises a range of events throughout the year. Two cask beers are available in winter, four in summer. Q P (224,322)

Rhandirmwyn

Royal Oak L

SA20 0NY
closed Mon; 12-2, 6-11; 12-2 Sun (01550) 760201
theroyaloakinn.co.uk
3 changing beers H
Remote stone-flagged inn with excellent views of the Towy Valley and close to an RSPB bird sanctuary. Originally built as a hunting lodge for

the local landowner, it is now a focal point for community activities and popular with fans of outdoor pursuits. The village shop is alongside. Two or three guest beers are offered and the good wholesome food is recommended. There are panoramic views from the beer garden at the side of the pub. Five times local CAMRA Pub of the Year. Q P

Roch

Victoria Inn

SA62 6AW (on A487)
11.30-11 (01437) 710426 thevictoriainnroch.com
Victoria Inn NewgAle, Fine & Dandy; 1 changing beer (sourced locally)
This brewpub with views across St Brides Bay is a little gem and a warm welcome is assured. The inn was established in 1851, although parts are older, and it has retained much of its olde-worlde charm, with beamed ceilings and low doorways. Food is available daily except Monday. For those in a hurry there is a beer carry-out service – the house ale is Fine & Dandy. Curry and a pint night is Friday. Live music features occasionally.
Q P (411)

St David's

Farmers Arms

14-16 Goat Street, SA62 6RF (down hill to left of square)
11-midnight (01437) 721666 farmersstdavids.co.uk
Brains Rev James; Felinfoel Double Dragon; house beer (by Hancocks); 2 changing beers (sourced nationally; often Evan Evans, Sharp's, Wychwood)
A traditional city pub comprising three rooms – the top bar, mainly for dining, the smaller Coxswains room, which is the social meeting place for the St David's lifeboat crew, and the Glue Pot bar, where the locals tend to gather around the fire. Outside, the patio offers views of the cathedral and has a seasonal bar. Winter opening times vary so please check before you visit. Q

St Ishmaels

Brook Inn

Brookside, SA62 3TE
closed Tue; 12-11 (1am Fri & Sat) (01646) 636277
brookinnpembs.co.uk
Hancocks HB; 1 changing beer
The Brook has been the village pub at the heart of the community since the 1880s. Previously brewery-owned, it became a free house when it was purchased by the current owner in 2014. The pub is in the centre of the village on the National Trails Pembrokeshire Coast Path, with stone-flagged floors and exposed brick walls adding to a comfortable ambience. It is reputed to be haunted by Gladwys and Tom who may or may not pull you a pint! P (315)

Saundersfoot

Royal Oak Inn

Wogan Terrace, SA69 9HA
10-11 (01834) 812546
theroyaloaksaundersfoot.co.uk
Courage Best Bitter; Sharp's Doom Bar; 4 changing beers (sourced nationally; often Courage, Mantle)
An old pub and restaurant in the centre of town offering a wide selection of real ales. On entering the pub, to the right is a cosy drinkers' bar where locals and visitors are made welcome. To the left is another bar and a further dedicated restaurant with an extensive menu. Food is available throughout the day during the summer months. At the front is a heated terrace with sea and harbour views.
Q (381)

Solva

Royal George

13 High Street, SA62 6TF
3 (2 Fri)-11; 11.30-11 Sat & Sun (01437) 720002
theroyalgeorgesolva.co.uk
Marston's Pedigree; Ringwood Boondoggle
Set on the main road to St David's in Upper Solva, this friendly imposing community pub commands stunning views over St Bride's Bay. The one-roomed bar has a busy, homely feel with rugby memorabilia on the walls. The furniture is both rustic and eclectic which adds to the ambience. In winter a guest beer is only available on big occasions. A beer festival is held at least once a year. Chinese food is cooked to order, 12-9.30pm weekends. P (411)

Stackpole

Stackpole Inn

Jasons Corner, SA71 5DF (on B4319)
12-3, 6-11; 12-11 Sat; 12-4 Sun (01646) 672324
stackpoleinn.co.uk
Brains Rev James; Felinfoel Best Bitter, Double Dragon; 1 changing beer (sourced regionally; often Mantle)
Set just three miles south of the historic town of Pembroke, this is a multi award-winning pub in the Pembrokeshire Coast National Park. The Stackpole has a restaurant that focuses on local seafood dishes and offers superb B&B accommodation. It is a short walk to the beautiful Pembrokeshire Coast Path and when visiting you can also explore the Stackpole Estate, Bosherston Lily Ponds, the amazing Barafundle Bay and Broad Haven beach.
P

Tenby

Buccaneer Inn

St Julian Street, SA70 7AS
11-12.30am (11 Sun) (01834) 842273
Harbwr Tenby MV Enterprise, North Star, RFA Sir Galahad; 1 changing beer (sourced regionally; often Glamorgan)
The Buccaneer is in a quaint street which links the town square to the harbour and beaches. The bar area is large but has a cosy feel with beams, stove and Tenby memorabilia adorning the walls. A sunny walled beer garden is to the rear, with heating for those chilly evenings. The pub is the brewery tap for the adjacent Tenby Harbour Brewery, offering its full range of beers. There is a good range of craft beers and Welsh ciders. Food is served all day with locally sourced produce including fresh fish on the menu.

Hope & Anchor

St Julian Street, SA70 7AS
11-midnight (10.30 Sun) (01834) 842131

Felinfoel Double Dragon; Harbwr Tenby MV Enterprise Ⓗ, North Star Ⓖ, Caldey Lollipop; Sharp's Atlantic; 2 changing beers (sourced nationally; often Bluestone, Mantle) Ⓗ
Welcoming pub set in the old town on the way down to the harbour. The medieval town walls can be seen nearby. Food is important here and specials supplement the standard menu. The convivial atmosphere and interesting local décor make it an excellent place to relax over a beer. Up to four guest beers are sourced mainly from Welsh breweries including Evan Evans, Mantle and Purple Moose, while Wye Valley sometimes sneaks over the border. Ciders include Westons Old Rosie and Somerset Tree Shaker West Country Cider.

Trapp

Cennen Arms

SA19 6TP (follow signs to Trapp from Llandybie)
12-3 (not Mon), 5.30-midnight; 12-10.30 Sun
☎ (01558) 822330 cennenlodge.co.uk
Joule's Slumbering Monk; 1 changing beer (sourced regionally) Ⓗ
The welcoming landlord has consistently delivered quality food and real ale here for more than 18 years. The pub has two main bars, one sharing a historic glass bar screen with the cosy snug, and three separate dining areas. There are also tables outside. The regular beer is Joule's Slumbering Monk, and another ale on handpump is often available. A good selection of food is served lunchtimes and evenings. The pub is the starting point for some pleasant walking routes.
Q P

Tregaron

Talbot

The Square, SY25 6JL
11-11 (10.30 Sun) ☎ (01974) 298208 ytalbot.com
4 changing beers (sourced regionally; often Ludlow, Mantle, Purple Moose) Ⓗ
A former drovers' inn of immense character in an unspoilt town on the edge of the Cambrian Mountains. It has a cosy front bar with a real fire, a beamed and flagstoned snug with an inglenook fireplace, a rear bar with TV and a contemporary restaurant. Two or three real ales are available in winter, four in summer, and three real ciders. Quality food includes locally reared meat and tempting desserts. The beautiful landscaped rear garden has fine views and a memorial to a circus elephant reputedly buried here.
Q P (585,588)

Whitland

Station House Hotel

St Johns Street, SA34 0AP
9am-1am (2am Fri & Sat); 10-midnight Sun
☎ (01994) 240556 stationhousewhitland.co.uk
Courage Directors; 2 changing beers (often Sharp's, Wye Valley) Ⓗ
A smile and a warm welcome are always on tap at this friendly hostelry. Very much a locals' pub for all ages, there is something for everyone here, with pool and darts teams and bingo on Sunday evening. There is plenty of space including a small room for people looking for a quiet corner. The outside drinking area is partly under cover. Car parking is to the rear and the railway station is close by. P

Friends Arms, Carmarthen

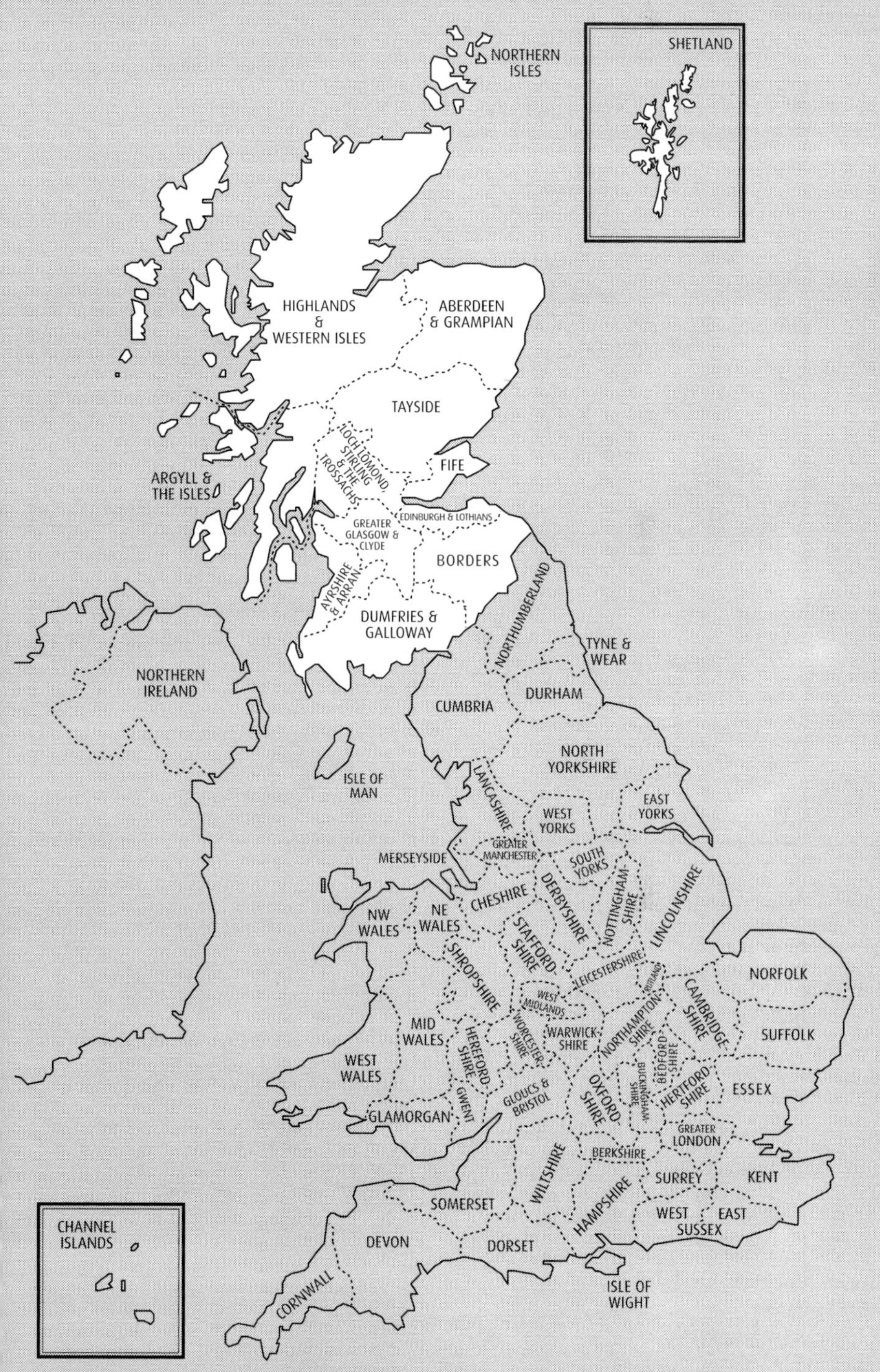

NORTHERN ISLES
SHETLAND
HIGHLANDS & WESTERN ISLES
ABERDEEN & GRAMPIAN
TAYSIDE
LOCH LOMOND, STIRLING & THE TROSSACHS
FIFE
ARGYLL & THE ISLES
EDINBURGH & LOTHIANS
GREATER GLASGOW & CLYDE
BORDERS
AYRSHIRE & ARRAN
DUMFRIES & GALLOWAY
NORTHUMBERLAND
TYNE & WEAR
NORTHERN IRELAND
DURHAM
CUMBRIA
NORTH YORKSHIRE
ISLE OF MAN
LANCASHIRE
EAST YORKS
WEST YORKS
GREATER MANCHESTER
MERSEYSIDE
SOUTH YORKS
LINCOLNSHIRE
CHESHIRE
DERBYSHIRE
NOTTINGHAMSHIRE
NW WALES
NE WALES
STAFFORDSHIRE
SHROPSHIRE
LEICESTERSHIRE
RUTLAND
NORFOLK
CAMBRIDGESHIRE
WEST MIDLANDS
MID WALES
HEREFORDSHIRE
WORCESTERSHIRE
WARWICKSHIRE
NORTHAMPTONSHIRE
BEDFORDSHIRE
SUFFOLK
WEST WALES
BUCKINGHAMSHIRE
OXFORDSHIRE
HERTFORDSHIRE
ESSEX
GWENT
GLOUCS & BRISTOL
GLAMORGAN
GREATER LONDON
BERKSHIRE
WILTSHIRE
SURREY
KENT
SOMERSET
HAMPSHIRE
WEST SUSSEX
EAST SUSSEX
CHANNEL ISLANDS
DEVON
DORSET
CORNWALL
ISLE OF WIGHT

Scotland

ABERDEEN & GRAMPIAN

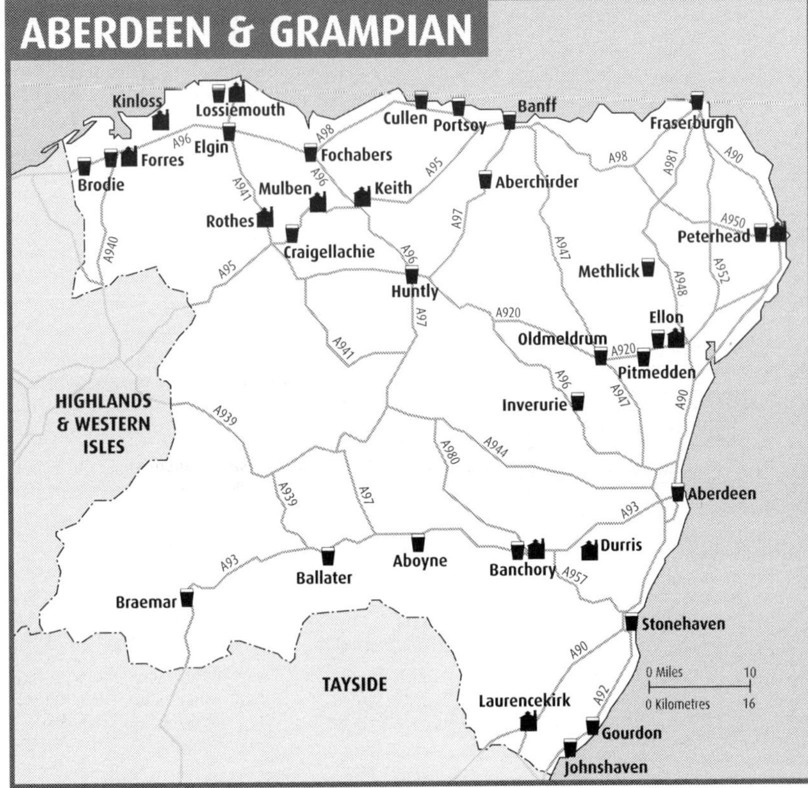

Authority areas covered: Aberdeenshire UA, City of Aberdeen UA, Moray UA

Aberchirder

New Inn

79 Main Street, AB54 7TB

12 (5 Mon)-12.30am; 12-11 Sun ☎ (01466) 780633

newinnaberchirder.co.uk

Windswept Wolf Ⓖ; 4 changing beers (sourced nationally; often Caledonian, Hambleton, Orkney) Ⓗ

Traditional, welcoming inn with wood-burning stoves, candlelit areas and a vintage atmosphere, offering a good selection of quality ales from local and national breweries, often featuring Hambleton beers. A separate dining area provides locally sourced home-made food prepared by the owner/chef – the pork pies are highly recommended. Families are welcome in the dining room until 9pm (booking recommended). Dogs are permitted in the bar but should be kept on a lead at busy times.

Q P (301)

Aberdeen

Aitchies Ale House

10 Trinity Street, AB11 5LY (across road from Union Square shopping centre)

8am-10 (11 Fri & Sat); closed Sun ☎ (01224) 581549

Orkney Dark Island Ⓗ

This small corner bar is the closest real ale outlet to the city rail/bus stations and the Union Square shopping complex. Family owned, it retains the flavour of an old-fashioned Scottish pub with service second to none and bar staff wearing traditional white aprons. Food is best described as basic Scottish pub grub, including roast beef stovies. Just one ale is available, Dark Island, which it has served for many years. A good selection of whiskies includes Bell's special editions.

Q

Archibald Simpson ✔

5 Castle Street, AB11 5BQ (E end of Union St)

8am-midnight (1am Fri & Sat); 9am-midnight Sun

☎ (01224) 621365

Caledonian Deuchars IPA; Greene King Abbot; Sharp's Doom Bar; 9 changing beers (sourced nationally; often Lerwick, Orkney, Windswept) Ⓗ

The former local headquarters of Clydesdale Bank, this Wetherspoon is in a magnificent granite building designed by local architect Archibald Simpson. It has a pillared entrance and retains

REAL ALE BREWERIES

7 Durris
Brew Toon Peterhead (NEW)
BrewDog Ellon
Burnside Laurencekirk
Deeside Banchory
Keith Keith
Quiet Banchory
Rothes Rothes
six°north Laurencekirk
Spey Valley Mulben
Speyside Craft Forres
Windswept Lossiemouth
Wooha Kinloss

many original architectural features – the main room is a central hall with a high ceiling and additional seating areas to the sides. The long bar has up to 12 handpumps offering a variety of beers, frequently from Scottish breweries. The usual beer festivals and Meet the Brewer nights are held. There is a narrow outside drinking area on the pavement on Union Street corner.

Carriages

101 Crown Street, AB11 6HH (below Brentwood Hotel)
4.30-midnight; 11-midnight Fri & Sat; 5.30-11 Sun
(01224) 595440 brentwood-hotel.co.uk
6 changing beers (sourced nationally; often Orkney, Swannay, Windswept) H

A mirrored downstairs bar in the basement of the Brentwood Hotel with lots of comfortable couches and seating areas. A winner of several local CAMRA awards, it offers up to six changing ales, usually a mix of national brands and Scottish microbrews, with tasters offered if undecided. Lunchtime meals are available in the bar, and the adjoining restaurant serves good food in the evening. Railway and bus stations are close and easily reached by descending the stairs from nearby Crown Terrace to Bridge Street. P

Grill ★

213 Union Street, AB11 6BA
10-midnight (1am Fri & Sat); 12.30-midnight Sun
(01224) 573530 thegrillaberdeen.co.uk
Harviestoun Bitter & Twisted; Inveralmond Ossian; 3 changing beers (sourced regionally; often Fyne Ales, Orkney, Windswept) H

With an exquisite interior redesigned in 1926 and remaining largely unchanged since, this is the only pub listed on CAMRA's National Inventory of Historic Pub Interiors in the area. For men only until 1975 when outlawed by legislation, a ladies' toilet was eventually provided in 1998. Situated across from the Music Hall, musicians often visit during concert breaks. Five ales are mainly from Scottish breweries, and the pub also has a huge selection of whiskies. Bar snacks such as stovies and pies are available. Local CAMRA Pub of the Year 2016.

Justice Mill

423 Union Street, AB11 6DA
8am-midnight (1am Fri & Sat); 9am-midnight Sun
(01224) 252410
Caledonian Deuchars IPA; Greene King Abbot; 3 changing beers (sourced nationally; often Harviestoun, Spey Valley, Windswept) H

Long, narrow, dark Wetherspoon outlet with some raised seating near the bar and booths at both the main entrance and at the rear entrance on Justice Mill Lane, hence the name of the pub. The quieter family-friendly atmosphere changes to a louder one favoured by many of its younger clientele in the evenings, with DJs at weekends. The pub has two statement art pieces – a statue of an upside down man and a fire behind glass. Alcohol is served from 11am.

Krakatoa

2 Trinity Quay, AB11 5AA (facing quayside at bottom of Market St)
2-midnight (3am Fri & Sat) (01224) 587602
krakatoa.bar
Windswept Weizen; 11 changing beers (sourced regionally; often Cromarty, Spey Valley, Windswept) P

This historic harbourside bar, formerly The Moorings and then rebranded as Krakatoa, changes character from a friendly, laid-back local to a raucous rock bar on weekend evenings, when there may be a cover charge. The eclectic jukebox is popular with the varied clientele. A wide selection of Scottish ales is served on up to 12 American-style fonts to the far left of the bar, and a varied selection of Belgian beers and ciders is also available. A multiple local CAMRA City Pub of the Year winner and branch winner in 2018.

Prince of Wales

7 St Nicholas Lane, AB10 1HF (in lane opp Marks & Spencer)
10-midnight (1am Fri & Sat) (01224) 640597
princeofwales-aberdeen.co.uk
8 changing beers (sourced nationally; often Cromarty, Swannay, Windswept) H

Refurbished in late 2016, the Prince is one of the oldest bars in town and features in Scotland's True Heritage Pubs, with possibly the longest bar counter in the city. It has a friendly atmosphere and a large following of regulars. It offers eight ales, mainly from Scottish breweries and from the owners Belhaven/Greene King, plus three craft beers. Sunday is folk music night and a prize quiz is held on Monday. A quiet pub, conversation is the only background noise. Good-value food is served daily until 9pm including filled rolls. Q

Queen Vic

126 Rosemount Place, AB25 2YU (10 mins' walk from W end of Union St along Rose St)
12-midnight (1am Fri & Sat); 12.30-midnight Sun
(01224) 638500 pbdevco.com/queenvic.html
Caledonian Deuchars IPA; Timothy Taylor Landlord; 2 changing beers (sourced nationally; often Harviestoun, Speyside Craft, Windswept) H

A cosy one-room locals' lounge bar slightly off the beaten track in a converted shop in a highly populated tenement area. Sporting events are frequently shown, when it gets extremely busy and noisy. Four cask ales are available including interesting guests often picked by the locals, alongside an extensive range of locally brewed bottled beers. Occasional Meet the Brewer nights are hosted, with cheeses to match the beers. A popular quiz is held on Monday evening and live bands play occasionally at weekends. Snacks include sandwiches, wraps and local Big Beefys Biltong. (3)

St Machar Bar

97 High Street, Old Aberdeen, AB24 3EN
11-midnight; 12.30-11 Sun (01224) 483079
adamsfamilypubs.com
Caledonian Deuchars IPA; 2 changing beers (sourced regionally; often Caledonian, Inveralmond, Wychwood) H

Located in the photogenic and historic Old Aberdeen conservation area amid the university buildings and close to King's College, this friendly and historic pub is frequented by academia and locals alike. A splendid mirror from the long-gone local Thomson Marshall Aulton Brewery and one from the original Devanha Brewery adorn the walls. Up to three guest beers, frequently from Scottish micros, are available alongside a selection

SCOTLAND

of whiskies and gins. The bar is home to a darts team, university football team and rugby team. Flippin' Bun & Wing food is served. (20)

Under the Hammer

11 North Silver Street, AB10 1RJ (off Golden Square)
5-11 (midnight Wed & Thu); 4-1am Fri & Sat; closed Sun
(01224) 640253
Cromarty Happy Chappy; Fyne Ales Jarl; 2 changing beers (sourced nationally; often Cromarty, Fyne Ales) H
Located in a quiet side street near Golden Square just minutes from Union Street, this popular pub is in a basement next to Milne's auction house – hence the name. It is convenient for the Music Hall and His Majesty's Theatre. Guest beers come from a wide variety of Scottish breweries including Fyne Ales and Cromarty. Unobtrusive background music plays. Works by local artists displayed on the walls are for sale if they take your fancy. Opens on the first Sunday of the month 5pm-midnight for an open mic session. Q

Aboyne

Boat Inn

Charleston Road, AB34 5EL (N bank of River Dee next to Aboyne Bridge)
11-11 (midnight Fri & Sat) (01339) 886137
theboatinnaboyne.co.uk
3 changing beers (sourced nationally; often Belhaven, Deeside) H
Popular riverside inn with a food-oriented lounge. Junior diners (and adults) may request to see the model train, complete with sound effects, traverse the entire pub at picture-rail height upon completion of their meal. The public bar has a recess at the back for musicians on live music nights. The local Rotary Club regularly meets here. Three ales are served in summer, usually two in winter, with one regular beer from Belhaven and another from the local Deeside Brewery. Breakfast is served 7.30-11.30am. QP

Ballater

Alexandra Hotel

12 Bridge Square, AB35 5QJ
11-2.30, 5-midnight; 11-midnight Fri; 11-midnight Sun
(01339) 755376 alexandrahotelballater.co.uk
Cairngorm Trade Winds; 2 changing beers (sourced regionally; often Cairngorm, Inveralmond) H
Originally built as a private home in 1800 and becoming the Alexandra Hotel in 1915, this smart refurbished lounge bar is popular with locals for bar suppers and regular bar drinkers too. It is easily spotted when entering Ballater from the east side. Ales are mostly from Cairngorm and Inveralmond. A handy stop-off on your way to Braemar for the Highland Games or on a visit with the royals at Balmoral. P

Glenaden Hotel

6 Church Square, AB35 5NE
11-1am (midnight Mon-Wed) (01339) 755488
3 changing beers (sourced regionally; often Burnside, Loch Lomond, Windswept) H
Situated on the far side of the picturesque town square, this small hotel displays a prominent external sign for its Barrel Lounge. It now serves three beers in busy periods, usually Scottish, mostly from Burnside, Windswept and Loch Lomond. Darker ales are apparently favoured by the locals. A large function suite is at the rear of the hotel. QP

Banchory

Ravenswood Club (Royal British Legion)

25 Ramsay Road, AB31 5TS (up Mount St from A93 then second right)
11-11 (midnight Fri & Sat) (01330) 822347
banchorylegion.co.uk
2 changing beers (sourced nationally) H
Large British Legion club with a comfortable lounge adjoining the pool and TV room and a spacious function room well used by local clubs and societies as well as members. Darts and snooker are popular and played most evenings. The two handpumps offer excellent value and the beer choice is constantly changing, with ales consistently the best quality in the village. An elevated terrace has fine views of the Deeside hills. Show a copy of this Guide or your CAMRA membership card for entry. P

Banff

Market Arms

5 High Shore, AB45 1DB
11-midnight (1am Fri & Sat) (01261) 812261
1 changing beer (sourced nationally; often Harviestoun, Kelburn, Timothy Taylor) H
This fine building is one of the oldest in historic Banff, dating back to 1585. It is worth stepping out the back to take a look at the courtyard, which retains many original features. The long public bar has several fine examples of historic brewery and distillery mirrors. A changing beer is available, usually from a Scottish microbrewery.

Braemar

Moorfield House Hotel

19 Chapel Brae, AB35 5YT (signposted from village centre)
4-10 (11 Fri); 3-11 Sat; 1.30-9 Sun (01339) 741244
moorfieldhousehotel.com
4 changing beers (sourced regionally; often Cairngorm, Orkney, Strathbraan) H
Small family-run hotel – the current owners took over in 2016 – overlooking the Highland Games ground at the edge of this historic village and close to the new heritage centre. Opening hours vary depending on the season and the weather – check ahead if you are travelling. If required, meals can be arranged outside official times by prior arrangement. Four varying ales are served, sometimes three in winter. The local ukulele club meets here on Friday nights. QP

Brodie

Old Mill Inn

IV36 2TD (on main A96 between Forres and Nairn)
11.30-11; 11.45-10.30 Sun (01309) 641605
oldmillinnbrodie.com
5 changing beers (sourced regionally; often Speyside Craft, Swannay, Windswept) H
This gem is a spacious family-friendly pub restaurant with a cosy fireside area, smart dining

room, function room and a charming conservatory with views of the old watermill and garden. Up to five ales are available, mainly from Scottish micros. An excellent range of food is served with specials changing daily. A full restaurant menu is served along with light lunches and traditional Scottish high teas. Live Scottish/Irish instrumental music plays on Sunday evening. Brodie Castle is nearby and Brodie Countryfare is opposite. A beer festival is held in June. Q♿P(10,10A)

Craigellachie

Copper Dog (Craigellachie Hotel)

Victoria Street, AB38 9SR

12-11 (1am Fri & Sat) ☎ (01340) 881204

craigellachiehotel.co.uk/copper-dog

3 changing beers (sourced locally; often Spey Valley, Windswept) Ⓗ

Situated in a beautiful village, the impressive Victorian building boasts picturesque views across the forests and mountains, and is next to the Fiddich and Spey rivers. The bar is beneath the hotel and while mostly given over to dining, it has a cosy, dimly lit area dedicated to drinking. There are over 800 whiskies in the Quaich Bar, with tasting sessions available. It can be busy, especially during whisky festivals. If you wish to eat here, booking is recommended.
♿P(36)

Highlander Inn

10 Victoria Street, AB38 9SR (on A95, opp post office)

12-11 (12.30am Fri & Sat) ☎ (01340) 881446

whiskyinn.com

3 changing beers (often Rothes, Spey Valley, Windswept) Ⓗ

Picturesque whisky and cask ale bar on Speyside's Whisky Trail, close to the Speyside Way. Popular with tourists, walkers and fishermen, it is very busy during whisky festivals and the tourist season. Twinned with the Highlander Whisky Bar in Tokyo, it offers a fine selection of malts including many from Japan. Three ales are served, two in winter. CRAC (Craigellachie Real Ale Club) meets on the first Wednesday of the month and its members help to choose the guest ales. An outside decked area is a delight on a sunny afternoon.
♣P(36)

Cullen

Three Kings

17-21 North Castle Street, AB56 4SA

closed Mon-Wed; 12-2, 5-12.30am; 12-2, 5-11 Sun

☎ (01542) 840031

3 changing beers (often Cairngorm, Orkney, Windswept) Ⓗ

Close to an impressive, but now defunct, railway viaduct, this small, family-run pub was converted over 40 years ago from 150-year-old railway workers' cottages. A low-beamed roof and real fire help to create a cosy atmosphere on colder days. The pub continues as before, with the same owners, after a proposed sale in November 2017 fell through. There is a large outdoor drinking area complete with pétanque courts. Up to three beers are served, mainly from Scottish micros. Four letting rooms have their own kitchen and other facilities. Q(35)

Elgin

Drouthy Cobbler ✔

Shepherd's Close, 48A High Street, IV30 1BU

10-12.30am (1.30am Fri & Sat) ☎ (01343) 596000

thedrouthycobbler.co.uk

Harviestoun Bitter & Twisted; Inveralmond Ossian, Lia Fail; 2 changing beers (sourced nationally; often Inveralmond) Ⓗ

A small, long, elegant pub named after John Shanks, who was a shoemaker and an important figure in the conservation of Elgin Cathedral. Breakfast is served from 10am and meals are available most of the day. Real ales are from Scottish microbreweries, and many local bottled beers are also on offer. A growing whisky collection stands at around 100, alongside a large gin and cocktail selection. There are benches outside in the lane with awnings and heaters. Alcohol is served from 11am. Q♿♣

Muckle Cross ✔

34 High Street, IV30 1BU

8am-midnight (1am Fri & Sat); 9am-11.45 Sun

☎ (01343) 559030

Caledonian Deuchars IPA; Greene King Abbot; Sharp's Doom Bar; 4 changing beers (sourced regionally; often Windswept) Ⓗ

Typical small Wetherspoon pub converted from what was once a bicycle repair shop, then a Halfords branch. The pleasant long room has ample seating and a family area. Deservedly popular, it can be busy, particularly at weekends. Eight handpumps offer a wide range of beers from national and Scottish microbreweries, often including one from Windswept. The pub also stocks a wide range of malt whiskies. A Scottish beer festival, world beer festival and cider fest are usually held annually. Breakfast is from 8am, alcohol is served from 11am. Q♿

Ellon

Tolbooth

21-23 Station Road, AB41 9AE (across road from public library)

12-11 (midnight Thu; 12.30am Fri & Sat); 12.30-11.30 Sun

☎ (01358) 721308

Greene King Abbot; 2 changing beers (sourced regionally; often Cairngorm, Cromarty, Strathbraan) Ⓗ

A large pub, popular with all ages, close to the centre of the town and just a short walk from the bus stops on Market Street. There are separate seating areas on split levels as well as an airy conservatory with barrel tables. One Scottish and one English guest ale are usually available. No food is served. Several National Trust Scotland properties are nearby. ♿♣

Fochabers

Grant Arms Hotel

42 High Street, IV32 7DX

4-12.45am; 2-1.45am Fri; 11-1.45am Sat & Sun

☎ (01343) 820202 thegrantarms.co.uk

Caledonian Deuchars IPA Ⓗ

Situated on the main street of Fochabers, which is now much quieter due to the bypass around the village, this large, friendly bar is popular with locals and a younger clientele at the weekend. A seating area at the far end of the bar separates drinkers from the jukebox, darts and pool. The decor is an eclectic mix of football and angling memorabilia, Vettriano prints and Banksy street art. Several large TVs cater for sporting fans. Golfers are looked after superbly with great-value courses in close proximity. (10,305)

Forres

Mosset Tavern

Gordon Street, IV36 1DL
11-12.30am (1.30am Fri & Sat); 12-midnight Sun
(01309) 672981 mossettavern.com
6 changing beers (sourced locally; often Speyside Craft, Swannay, Windswept)
Described as 'the country pub in the heart of Forres', this smart, extremely popular Scottish lounge bar/restaurant is situated next to the Mosset burn and pond, with swans and ducks. Friendly, efficient staff serve ale from a single handpump in the lounge and five in the spacious, comfortable public bar, where there are pool tables and large screens showing sport. A large function room is also available, home to the Foot Tapper beer festival in April. Live music plays on Friday evening, and there is a pub quiz every Tuesday.
P (10,10A)

Red Lion

2-6 Tollbooth Street, IV36 1PH
11-12.30am (1.30am Fri & Sat); 12-12.30am Sun
(01309) 672716
2 changing beers (sourced nationally)
Dating from 1838 and known locally as The Beastie, this is one of the longest-established real ale outlets in the north of Scotland. A popular venue with good food, the modern and smart lounge bar offers two beers from the Belhaven list, which can be brought through to the public bar. The public bar has a pool table and is of architectural interest, with a rare mirror from Campbell & Co's Argyll Brewery, established 1710. Live music plays on Saturday night.
(10,10A)

Fraserburgh

Elizabethan Bar & Lounge

36 Union Grove, AB43 9PH (10 mins' walk from A90)
10-1am (01346) 510464
3 changing beers (sourced regionally; often Cairngorm, Kelburn, Windswept)
Set in the middle of a housing estate, with a mock-Tudor exterior, the large bar and lounges are in three distinct sections, with sport on TV in two of them. The bar has a formidable reputation for offering a wide range of quality ales sourced from throughout the country – which has helped boost CAMRA membership numbers in the area – and also features well over 200 malts, the largest collection in the area. P

Gourdon

Harbour Bar

William Street, DD10 0LW
11-midnight (1am Fri & Sat); 12.30-midnight Sun
(01561) 361337 harbourbargourdon.co.uk
1 changing beer (often Deeside, Strathbraan)
Harbourside howff with traditional seafaring decor. It has a public bar, a smaller taproom with bar stools and a separate pool room with additional seating. The single handpump usually dispenses beer from the Strathbraan range or occasionally from Deeside. The bar is next door to the locally renowned Quayside Restaurant & Fish Bar and handy for the Maggie Law Maritime Museum.
(107)

Huntly

Crown Bar

4 Gordon Street, AB54 8AJ
11-11 (11.30 Sat); closed Sun (01466) 792244
Windswept Blonde, Wolf; 1 changing beer (sourced locally; often Keith)
Situated just off the main square in the centre of Huntly, the bar was taken over in 2017 by the legendary Harry Halkett, late of the Clifton Bar in Lossiemouth and then the short-lived Imperial in Elgin. The pub has an original open, airy public bar and a small lounge at the rear where the ale can be found. Beer is served on KeyKeg and can be classed as real ale – Windswept brews are all unfined and unfiltered. Toasties are available.
(10)

Inverurie

Gordon Highlander

West High Street, AB51 3QQ
9am-11.30 (1am Fri & Sat) (01467) 626780
Sharp's Doom Bar; 4 changing beers (sourced nationally; often Cairngorm, Inveralmond, Strathaven)
A fine Wetherspoon conversion of a splendid Art Deco building which used to be the Victoria Cinema. The name refers to a locomotive built at the now defunct Inverurie Locomotive Works and there are many references to this throughout the pub. The famous Gordon Highlander Regiment also features prominently, with displays and a large mural. The books on the shelves are free to read and take home, with donations welcome. There are at least three guest ales and two real ciders, and the usual Wetherspoon beer festivals feature. Alcohol is served from 11am.
(10,37)

Johnshaven

Ship Inn

3 Castle Street, DD10 0ER
12-midnight (1am Fri & Sat); 12.30-midnight Sun
(01561) 362257
1 changing beer (often Strathbraan)
While the pub may appear closed, check for the small light in the window near the door or just do battle with the door latch. First licensed in 1763, this well-worn howff offers a warm welcome and beers from the Strathbraan range. The public bar has a traditional coastal decor with a mixed-fuel stove and bar counter water founts. Children are permitted in the adjacent lounge, complete with a pool table. Dogs are allowed throughout. The Ship Inn is a proud sponsor of the local Shipwreck Charity Walk. (107)

Lossiemouth

Skerry Brae Hotel

Stotfield Road, IV31 6QS
12-11 (midnight Fri & Sat) (01343) 812040
skerrybrae.co.uk
Windswept Blonde, APA

Modern lounge bar with commanding views across the championship golf course, West Beach and the Moray Firth – spacious outside decking and a large conservatory enhance the viewing experience. It is the perfect spot to enjoy a sunny day at the coast. The 19-bed hostelry serves hearty food all day and two beers from the local Windswept Brewery. A decent selection of malt whiskies is also available. The bar may close afternoons Monday to Thursday in winter. Q P (33A,33C)

Methlick

Ythanview Hotel

Main Street, AB41 7DT

11-2.30, 5-11; 11-2.30, 4.30-1am Fri; 11-12.30am Sat; 12-11 Sun (01651) 806235 ythanviewhotel.co.uk

2 changing beers (sourced regionally; often Fyne Ales, Swannay, Windswept) H

Traditional inn in the village centre, home to the MCC (Methlick Cricket Club) at Lairds nearby. Log fires warm both the lounge bar at the front and the friendly sports-themed public bar at the rear. The pub is famous for the owner's special chicken curry, and Thursday's steak night is popular. Meals are served all day at weekends. Live music and quiz nights take place on most Saturdays. Beers are exclusively from Scottish micros. Haddo House, Tolquhon Castle and Pitmedden Garden are nearby. P (290,291)

Oldmeldrum

Redgarth

Kirk Brae, AB51 0DJ (outskirts of village, signposted off A947)

11-3, 5-11 (11.45 Fri & Sat); 12-11 Sun (01651) 872353 redgarth.com

3 changing beers (sourced locally; often Cromarty, Fyne Ales, Swannay) H/G

This renowned local inn has imposing views over the eastern Grampian mountains. A winner of many local CAMRA awards and CAMRA branch Country Pub of the Year 2018, it retains a strong reputation for its imaginative choice of beers, sourced from many Scottish microbreweries. During occasional Brewers in Residence evenings, the three handpumped ales may be supplemented by many more on gravity. A successful blend of popular family restaurant and marvellous real ale pub, it is appreciated by a dedicated core of regulars. P

Peterhead

Cross Keys

23-27 Chapel Street, AB42 1TH

7am-11 (midnight Thu; 1am Fri & Sat); 9am-11 Sun (01779) 483500

Greene King Abbot; Sharp's Doom Bar; 3 changing beers (sourced nationally) H

A typical Wetherspoon outlet in the centre of a bustling port, close to the local museum where you can learn about the town's maritime history. The pub is named after the chapel dedicated to St Peter that previously stood on the site. The long single room has the bar towards the front and a large seating area at the rear. A sheltered and heated area outside caters for hardy souls and smokers. Children are welcome until 8pm if dining. Q

Pitmedden

Craft Bar

Tarves Road, AB41 7NX

11-11 (midnight Fri & Sat); 12-11 Sun (01651) 842049

2 changing beers (sourced regionally; often Orkney, Spey Valley, Strathbraan) H

A one-room corner pub opened in 2017 and run by a local CAMRA member. Old church pews provide seating for some of the tables around the walls and other tables have bench seating. Up to two ales from varying breweries are supplemented by KeyKeg beers from Windswept (Aurora, Weizen and Wolf). There is also a comprehensive range of bottled and canned beer in the fridge. There are plans to serve snacks in the near future. Q

Portsoy

Shore Inn

Church Street, AB45 2QR (overlooking harbour)

11-11 (midnight Thu; 1am Fri & Sat); 12-1am Sun (01261) 842831

2 changing beers (sourced locally; often Spey Valley, Windswept) H

Cosy, comfortable, coastal howff with a warm welcome in winter and scenic outdoor views in summer. The pub overlooks the oldest harbour on Moray coast which was recently a location for the remake of Whisky Galore. The L-shaped room with low ceilings is a fine example of a nautical bar.

Stonehaven

Marine Hotel

9-10 Shorehead, AB39 2JY (overlooking harbour)

11-midnight (1am Fri & Sat) (01569) 762155 marinehotelstonehaven.co.uk

Timothy Taylor Landlord; house beer (by six°north); 4 changing beers (sourced regionally; often Burnside, Cairngorm, Windswept) H

Now the only outlet in the six°north empire that serves real ale, this is a former Scottish CAMRA Pub of the Year and a multiple branch winner. The small harbourside hotel features simple wood panelling in the bar and a rustic lounge with an open fireplace. Seating outside offers a splendid view of the harbour. One ale from six°north is served plus several Belgian beers and up to 18 craft keg beers. Historic Dunnottar Castle is one mile south and an open-air bathing pool one mile north.

Ship Inn

5 Shorehead, AB39 2JY (on harbour front)

11-midnight (1am Fri & Sat) (01569) 762617 shipinnstonehaven.com

2 changing beers (sourced regionally; often Strathbraan) H

Built in 1771, this harbour-front hotel has a maritime-themed, wood-panelled bar featuring a mirror from the defunct Devanha brewery, and a seating area outside overlooking the water. Two beers are offered, at least one from a Scottish microbrewery, and an extensive range of malt whiskies is stocked. A modern restaurant with panoramic harbour views is adjacent to the bar – food is served all day at the weekend. Accommodation is available in 11 guest rooms.

ARGYLL & THE ISLES

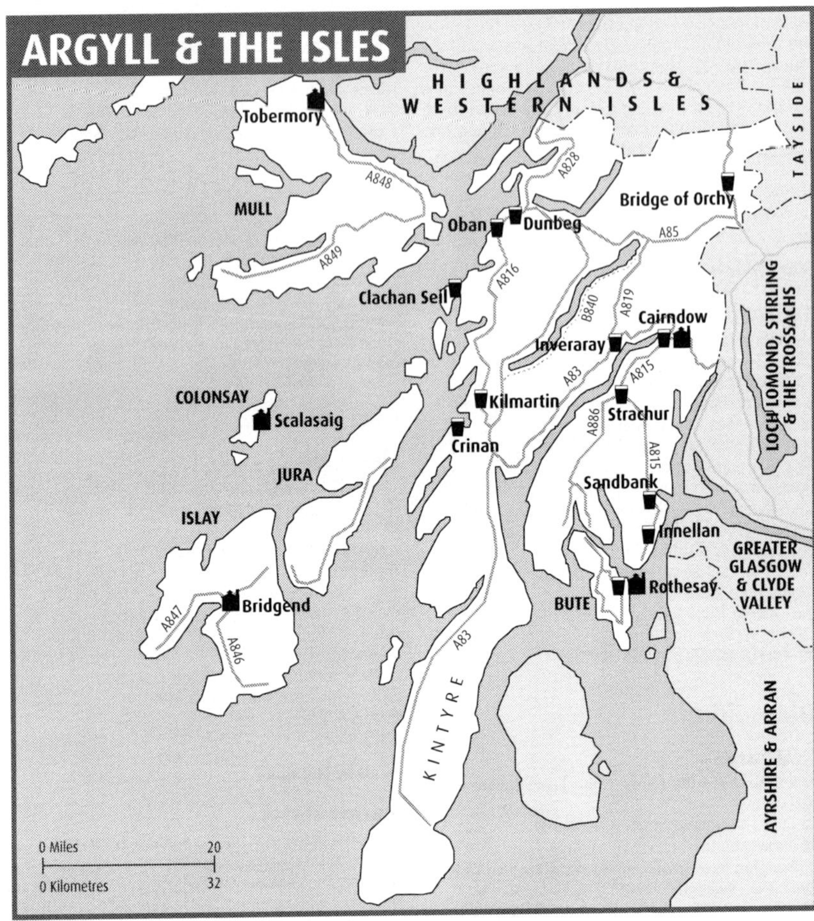

Authority area covered: Argyll & Bute UA

Bridge of Orchy

Bridge of Orchy Hotel

PA36 4AD

7-10 summer; 8-9 winter ☎ (01838) 400208

bridgeoforchy.co.uk

Harviestoun Bitter & Twisted; 1 changing beer (sourced regionally; often Harviestoun) Ⓗ

Prominent hotel on the A82 heading north before it climbs up to Rannoch Moor. It is a popular stopping-off place on the West Highland Way and at times gets busy with walkers – some of whom take advantage of the accommodation in the hotel itself, the annexe behind or the bunkhouse. The front bar looks across the road to the mountain beyond while the restaurant behind enjoys panoramic views across and down Glen Orchy.

P (915)

Cairndow

Fyne Ales Brewery Tap 🄻

Achadunan, PA26 8BJ (up side road at head of Loch Fyne)

10-6 ☎ (01499) 600120 fyneales.com/brewery-tap

Fyne Ales Jarl; 4 changing beers (sourced locally) Ⓗ

The Tap is situated in a converted barn which formed part of the original farm complex where the brewery was set up. Along with a selection of cask beers, the full range of bottled beers is always available. When the Argyll weather permits, seating in the courtyard allows visitors to view the spectacular scenery and spot red deer roaming the slopes. Meat produced on the farm is available for sale and used to fill the excellent hot pies.

QP

Stagecoach Inn 🄻

PA26 8BN (on slip road off A83)

11-11 (1am Fri & Sat; midnight Sun) ☎ (01499) 600286

cairndowinn.com

2 changing beers (sourced regionally; often Fyne Ales, Loch Lomond) Ⓗ

Old inn nestling in tall trees beside Loch Fyne at the foot of Glen Kinglas, providing a welcome resting place before the long ascent over the Rest and Be Thankful. The restaurant, converted from stables, enjoys fine views over the loch and leads through

REAL ALE BREWERIES

Argyll Tobermory: Isle of Mull
Bute Rothesay: Isle of Bute
Colonsay Scalasaig: Isle of Colonsay
Fyne Cairndow
Islay Bridgend: Isle of Islay

an archway to a small, cosy bar with a pool table in an alcove. Attractive views can also be enjoyed from the lochside garden. Good food is served until 9pm. Check ahead for opening times in winter. (926,976)

Clachan Seil

Tigh-an-Truish Inn

PA34 4QZ

11 (12 Sun)-11 summer; 5-8 Mon; closed Tue & Wed; 5-9 Thu; 11-11 Fri & Sat; 12-9 Sun winter (01852) 300242
tigh-an-truish.co.uk

2 changing beers (sourced nationally; often Fyne Ales, Orkney)

Eighteenth-century whitewashed inn by the Atlantic Bridge linking Seil island with the mainland. The translation of the pub name from Gaelic means 'the house of trousers' – staff will be happy to tell the story of how it got its name. The welcoming wood-panelled bar is warmed by a stove in winter and the walled garden is a delight in warmer weather. In 2018 a major extension added a separate restaurant and conservatory. Check winter hours before travelling any distance. QP (418)

Crinan

Crinan Seafood Bar

Crinan Hotel, PA31 8SR (at most westerly point of Crinan Canal)

12-11 (01546) 830261 crinanhotel.com

2 changing beers (sourced locally; often Fyne Ales)

The Seafood Bar is within the Crinan Hotel situated on the coast at the most westerly end of the Crinan Canal, possibly Britain's most beautiful shortcut. It sells highly recommended fresh local produce including of course seafood landed on the quayside. Large portions of fish and chips are particularly good value, perfect after sailing, walking or just watching the yachts entering or leaving the canal. In winter there may be only one beer available. P

Dunbeg

Wide-Mouthed Frog

PA37 1PX (approx 2 miles W of Connel Bridge in Dunstaffnage Marina car park)

11-11; 12.30-11 Sun (01631) 567005
widemouthedfrogofficialsite.co.uk

3 changing beers (sourced regionally; often Fyne Ales, Orkney)

In the grounds of Dunstaffnage Marina, this hotel bar and restaurant is frequented by yachtsmen and landlubbers alike. In 2017 it increased the number of handpumps and opened all year round. An outside seating area is available to enjoy the local scenery and in the season watch the yachts coming and going. If you choose to eat, good meals are served sourced from local produce, in particular fresh locally caught seafood. P

Innellan

Osborne

44 Shore Road, PA23 7TJ

11.30-midnight (1am Fri & Sat) (01369) 830820
theosborneinnellan.co.uk

St Austell Tribute; 2 changing beers (sourced nationally)

This whitewashed seafront hotel a few miles south of Dunoon was built in 1869 and has been completely refurbished in the past few years. The comfortable bar has a pool table to one side and a cosy lounge with a log fire. At the front a conservatory acts as the dining room and provides excellent views across the Firth of Clyde. Any good weather can be enjoyed in a small outdoor area to one side. (489)

Inveraray

George Hotel

Main Street East, PA32 8TT

11-midnight; 12-midnight Sun (01499) 302111
thegeorgehotel.co.uk

2 changing beers (sourced regionally)

Formerly two private houses, they were combined to form this attractive hotel in 1860 by the Clark family, who are still the owners – the sixth generation are currently managing it. The restaurants and bars have been restored but retain the original ambience with an abundance of dark wood, flagstone floors throughout and four roaring log and peat fires. Food has an emphasis on quality local produce, and the beers are mainly local too, served both in the main restaurant and lively public bar to one side. QP (926,976)

Kilmartin

Kilmartin Hotel

PA31 8RQ (on A816 10 miles N of Lochgilphead)

12 (5 winter)-11; 11-1am Fri (midnight Sat); 12-11 Sun (01546) 510250 kilmartin-hotel.com

3 changing beers (sourced regionally; often Belhaven, Loch Lomond, Orkney)

Homely family-run 19th-century hotel with a narrow bar complete with inglenook fireplace. Situated in the centre of the village, the hotel is an excellent base to explore the surrounding area of Kilmartin Glen, which is one of the world's most important archaeological landscapes of Neolithic and Bronze Age remains – over 800 monuments can be found within a six-mile radius. Good food and a great range of whiskies complement the real ales. There is a pool room to the rear. P (423)

Oban

Corryvreckan

The Waterfront Centre, Railway Pier, PA34 4LW

7am-midnight (1am Fri & Sat) (01631) 568910

Caledonian Deuchars IPA; Greene King Abbot; Sharp's Doom Bar; 6 changing beers (sourced nationally)

Excellently located Wetherspoon pub named after the famous whirlpool between Jura and Scarba. It lies alongside the fishing boat berth, next to both the rail station and ferry terminal and with views across Oban Bay. With a wood-panelled roof, the interior is open and spacious, enlivened by much nautical ephemera including a cast of a sea eagle. Opening time is 7am for breakfast but you will need to wait until at least 11am to sample the ale.

Oban Inn

1 Stafford Street, PA34 5NJ

11-1am (01631) 567441

3 changing beers (often Caledonian, Fyne Ales)

SCOTLAND

Formerly an 18th-century coaching inn, this traditional corner local by the old harbour pier was shut for many years before it reopened in late 2016. The public bar remains unspoilt and retains its dark-wood panelling and stone floors of Easdale slate. Maritime artefacts decorate the walls, and banknotes from many nations cover the wooden beams. The upstairs lounge features a collection of stained glass panels reputedly from an Irish monastery.

Rothesay: Isle of Bute

Black Bull Inn

West Princes Street, PA20 9AF (opp harbour)
11-11 (midnight Fri & Sat); 12.30-11 Sun
(01700) 502366
3 changing beers (sourced regionally) H
A pleasant ferry trip from Wemyss Bay rail station brings you to this well-known landmark, situated opposite the marina and within walking distance of all amenities including the Victorian toilets. The pub has two bars and a front and rear entrance. It is always busy with yachtsmen and others looking for a meal. Real ales are usually from the local Bute Brewing as well as other Scottish microbreweries.

Sandbank

Holy Loch Inn L

Springfield Place, PA23 8PJ (on A815 at jct with Shore Rd)
12-11 (01389) 706903
2 changing beers (sourced regionally) H
Attractive whitewashed pub across from a small marina and handy for the Gourock Western ferry from Hunters Quay. Now refurbished, it has a welcoming, light and airy feel with a lively public bar and a lounge with dining tables. Meals concentrating on local produce can be enjoyed throughout. Both rooms are presided over by stags shot nearby at the start of the last century. Beers come mainly from the Kelburn, Bute and Skye breweries. **QP**

Strachur

Creggans Inn L

PA27 8BX (on A815 at N end of village)
11-11; 12-11 Sun (01369) 860279
creggans-inn.co.uk
2 changing beers (sourced locally) H
Dating from the middle of the 19th century, this longstanding Guide entry sits on the east shore of Loch Fyne where the steamboat linked Strachur with Inveraray. MacPhunn's Bar, named after a half-hung sheep rustler of yore, is comfortable with a real fire and plenty of room for dining. The exploits of the local shinty team are recorded around the walls and a pool table provides entertainment on winter evenings. The changing cask beers usually come from Fyne Ales. There is a separate restaurant and accommodation is available. **QP** (484,486)

Bridge of Orchy Hotel, Bridge of Orchy (Photo: Andrew Bowden/flickr CC BY-SA 2.0)

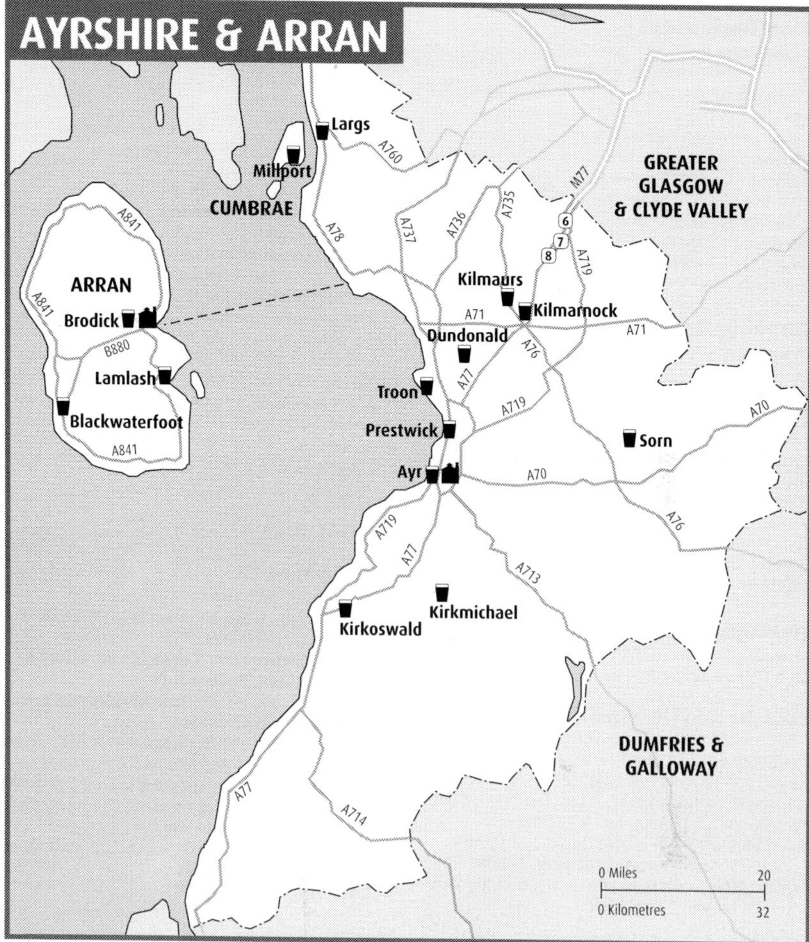

Authority areas covered: East Ayrshire UA, North Ayrshire UA, South Ayrshire UA

Ayr

Abbotsford Hotel

14 Corsehill Road, KA7 2ST

10-12.30am (midnight Sun) ☎ (01292) 261506

abbotsfordhotel.co.uk

3 changing beers (often Fyne Ales, Hop Back, Wainwright) H

A fine Scottish baronial-style building just under a mile south of Ayr town centre, a 20-minute walk from the railway station. The seafront is five minutes' walk away, with golf courses, parks and Burns attractions nearby. The delightful and aptly named Copper Bar has the real ale. There is a pleasant dining room and a games room with TV showing sports. Book ahead for meals.

P (57,361)

Chestnuts Hotel

52 Racecourse Road, KA7 2UZ (on A719 1 Mile S of centre)

10-11 (12.30am Fri & Sat) ☎ (01292) 264393

chestnutshotel.com

3 changing beers (sourced nationally) H

The real ales are offered in The 19th Hole, a delightful oak-beamed hall with an interesting history. The hotel welcomes both locals and visitors. Excellent food is available in the bar and separate restaurant. Open log fires add to the comfortable atmosphere in winter and a pleasant beer garden is popular when the weather allows.

P (9)

Geordie's Byre

103 Main Street, KA8 8BU (N of centre, in Newton area, over river towards Prestwick)

11-11 (midnight Thu-Sat); 12.30-9.30 Sun

☎ 07837 063877

4 changing beers (often Fyne Ales, Kelburn) A

CAMRA award-winning 18th-century pub serving up to four guest ales that come from far and wide. It is one of the few Scottish pubs using traditional Scottish tall founts. A wide selection of malt whiskies and rums is also available. Handy for several local bus routes. Q

REAL ALE BREWERIES

Arran Brodick: Isle of Arran

Ayr Ayr

Glen Park Hotel L

5 Racecourse Road, KA7 2DG
10-midnight; 12-midnight Sun ☎ (01292) 263891
Ayr Leezie Lundie, Jolly Beggars; 2 changing beers H
This comfortable lounge bar, in an attractive 1860s B-listed Victorian building, is the brewery tap for Ayr Brewing Company who brew in the rear of the building. The guest ales usually include a seasonal from the brewery. Beers are usually also available to take away from a new shop/bar at the rear of the dining room. Bar and restaurant meals are served daily except Monday.
P (9)

Smoking Goat

2A Academy Street, KA7 1HS
closed Mon; 12-12.30am (1am Fri & Sat)
☎ (01292) 857137 thesmokinggoat.com
3 changing beers H
Basement bar at the entrance to a lane opposite Ayr town hall. There are three handpumps dispensing changing beers from Ayr Brewing Co, Fyne Ales and Williams Bros. The full menu is available Wednesday to Saturday, plus roast dinners on a Sunday. The pub hosts a quiz night on Tuesday and DJ nights Thursday to Saturday.

Wellingtons Bar

17 Wellington Square, KA7 1EZ
11-12.30am; 12-midnight Sun ☎ (01292) 262794
welliesbar.weebly.com
3 changing beers (often Fyne Ales, Kelburn) H
A large Wellington boot advertises the location of this basement bar. Close to the seafront, bus station and local government offices, it attracts tourists and office workers alike. The Wednesday evening quiz is popular and weekend entertainment includes live music or a DJ on Saturday and an acoustic session on Sunday evening. The three changing ales constantly vary between brewers.

Blackwaterfoot: Isle of Arran

Kinloch Hotel

KA27 8ET (on W coast)
12-midnight ☎ (01770) 860444 bw-kinlochhotel.co.uk
Ayr Uisge Dubh; 1 changing beer (often Ayr, Marston's, Theakston) H
Sitting in a quiet rural village where the only thing you can escape from is peace and quiet itself, it offers coastal comfort and spectacular scenery. Fabulous local food includes fish and seafood. It has 37 bedrooms, a restaurant, three refurbished bars and a variety of facilities including a heated indoor swimming pool. A beer festival is held in August.
♣P

Brodick: Isle of Arran

Ormidale Hotel

Knowe Road, KA27 8BY (off A841 at W end of village)
4-midnight; 12-12.30am Sat; 12-midnight Sun
☎ (01770) 302293 ormidale-hotel.co.uk
Arran Guid Ale; 1 changing beer (often Arran, Ayr, Belhaven) A
This large red sandstone hotel with a small bar and spacious conservatory is set in seven acres of grounds. Beers are served from traditional Scottish tall founts on the boat-shaped bar, with Arran Blonde often available in summer. Home-cooked meals are recommended. Discos and folk nights are held. Accommodation is available all year round. ♣P (322,324)

Dundonald

Auchans

29-31 Main Street, KA2 9HH (on B730)
10-11 (12.30am Thu-Sat) ☎ (01563) 851472
theauchans.co.uk
2 changing beers (often Ayr, Kelburn, Sulwath) H
Friendly family-run restaurant bar with a varied choice of food appealing to all tastes, including snacks, tapas and pizza. The restaurant is to the rear and the comfortable and attractive lounge bar is next to the car park, with views of the historic castle. The two beers on handpump change regularly and tend to come from local and regional breweries. Dundonald is at the end of the historic smugglers' trail from Troon. Live jazz plays on the first Sunday of the month. Q P (10,110)

Kilmarnock

First Edition ✔

50 Bank Street, KA1 1HA
9am-11 (1am Fri & Sat); 11-11 Sun ☎ (01563) 528833
firsteditionkilmarnock.co.uk
Caledonian Deuchars IPA; 3 changing beers (often Arran, Harviestoun, Strathaven) H
This place is in the historic core of Kilmarnock. The large modern pub serves food all day in bright surroundings. Four ales are usually available, often including one from a Scottish regional brewer. There are 16 TV screens showing sports, and a DJ features Friday to Sunday evenings.

Kilmaurs

Weston Tavern

27 Main Street, KA3 2RQ
11-midnight (1am Thu-Sat) ☎ (01563) 538805
westontavern.co.uk
1 changing beer (often Ayr Brewing, Kelburn) H
Housed in the former manse of reformist minister David Smeaton, a contemporary of Robert Burns, this classic country pub and restaurant has a tiled floor, stone walls and a wood-burning fire. It sits beside the Jougs, a former jailhouse and tollbooth. A single pump dispenses ale from a rotating list of local breweries. The pub holds regular live music and quiz nights. ♣P

Kirkmichael

Kirkmichael Arms

3-5 Straiton Road, KA19 7PH
12-midnight (12.30am Fri & Sat) ☎ (01655) 750200
kirkmichaelarms.co.uk
2 changing beers H
A friendly country pub with a lounge bar and separate dining room. Two handpumps dispense an Ayr Brewing Co beer plus a guest. This is a pub serving excellent food made with locally sourced produce where possible. Small functions can be catered for. Well placed for Galloway Forest Park to the south, walkers and dogs are welcome.
Q ♣ (358,361)

Kirkoswald

Souter's Inn

47 Main Road, KA19 8HY

9am-11 (midnight Fri & Sat) ☎ (01655) 760653

soutersinn.com

Strathaven Witches Brew, Tam's IPA Ⓗ

A thatched building built on the site of the school that Robert Burns attended. Across the road in the graveyard lie the bodies of Tam o' Shanter, Souter Johnnie, Hugh Roger (Burns' teacher) and his grandparents. Souter Johnnie's Cottage is almost adjacent and Culzean Castle is close by. Both the ales are from Strathaven Brewery. The home-made ice-creams are fantastic, likewise the breakfasts. P (60)

Lamlash: Isle of Arran

Pierhead Tavern

Shore Rd, KA27 8JN

11-midnight (1am Fri & Sat) summer; 12-midnight (1am Fri & Sat) winter ☎ (01770) 600418 thepht.co.uk

3 changing beers (often Kelburn, Loch Lomond, Williams Bros) Ⓗ

Saved by new owners from conversion into flats, this famous village local is now open again. Three handpumps serve a variety of rotating ales from breweries such as Ayr, Inveralmond, Cairngorm and Orkney, in addition to local Arran ales in the summer season. The pub grub is all home made and chef's specials change weekly. There is a pool table at one end of the bar. Karaoke is hosted every second Friday. (323)

Largs

JG Sharps Bar

34-36 Nelson Street, KA30 8LW (turn off seafront at Nardini's; on corner with Boyd St)

11-midnight (1am Fri & Sat); 12.30-midnight Sun ☎ (01475) 675515 jgsharps.co.uk

Sharp's Doom Bar; 1 changing beer Ⓗ

This is a large traditional pub with several drinking areas and an open fire in the bar area. Good-quality pub meals are served lunchtimes and Friday to Sunday evenings. Games and sport on TV are in evidence and there is occasional live music. The beer garden outside has space for smokers. Q

Paddle Steamer

Gallowgate Street, KA30 8LX (on promenade nr Calmac ferry terminal)

8am-midnight (1am Fri & Sat) ☎ (01475) 686441

Greene King Abbot; Sharp's Doom Bar; 4 changing beers (often Kelburn, Strathaven) Ⓗ

Seafront Wetherspoon's outlet with a nautical theme. It has a feature fire in the centre of the bar area and a viewing window to the cellar. Large windows give views across to Bute and Cumbrae. Six of the 12 handpumps are usually in use, and potentially more in summer. Handy for the Cumbrae ferry and, in summer, the paddle steamer Waverley. Licensed from 11am.

Millport: Isle of Cumbrae

Fraser's Bar

7 Cardiff Street, KA28 0AS

11-midnight (1am Thu-Sat) ☎ (01475) 530518

2 changing beers (often Kelburn) Ⓗ

Well maintained and tidy, this pub caters for visitors to the island as well as locals. Buses meet every ferry from Largs and terminate just across the road. Two handpumps serve mostly light-coloured ales, usually including one from a local brewery. Good-value pub food is available lunchtimes and early evenings. Children are welcome in the rear lounge until 8pm. There is an open fire in the main bar. Local CAMRA Pub of the Year 2018. Q (320)

Prestwick

Prestwick Pioneer

87 Main Street, KA9 1JS

8am-midnight (12.30am Fri & Sat) ☎ (01292) 473210

Greene King Abbot; Sharp's Doom Bar; 8 changing beers Ⓗ

Modern Wetherspoon outlet named after the first Scottish Aviation Pioneer built in 1947 at the nearby international airport. It has an airy feel with a light-wood decor, and features photos of early Open Golf Championships at Prestwick and of Elvis at the nearby airport, the only place in the UK that he stepped foot on. Ten handpumps serve local and national ales and food is available all day. Licensed from 10am.

Sorn

Sorn Inn

35 Main Street, KA5 6HU

closed Mon; 12-2.30, 6-10 (midnight Fri); 12-midnight Sat; 12-10 Sun ☎ (01290) 551305 sorninn.com

1 changing beer (often Orkney) Ⓗ

The inn is the major community hub for the residents of the conservation village of Sorn. It has an award-winning restaurant with a menu that offers a mix of fine dining and brasserie-style food, featuring locally sourced produce. The cosy bar has one handpump and a selection of bottled ales. It offers accommodation in four rooms with en-suite facilities. P (X50,X76)

Troon

Bruce's Well

91 Portland Street, KA10 6QN

12-midnight; 11-1am Fri & Sat ☎ (01292) 311429

Morland Original Bitter; 1 changing beer (often Greene King) Ⓗ

A friendly, spacious and comfortable lounge bar, close to the town centre and a short walk from the station. The guest ales come from the Belhaven list and change regularly. Unusually, the cellar is in a temperature-controlled room off the main bar area. A number of TVs show sport with the volume turned down.

McKay's

69 Portland Street, KA10 6QU

10-12.30am (midnight Sun) ☎ (01292) 737372

3 changing beers (often Fyne Ales, Inveralmond, Stewart) Ⓗ

Popular town-centre bar with a large well-furnished beer garden which is busy in summer. The ale range varies but beers are usually from Scottish breweries. The bar hosts various food specials nights including burgers and steak. Local dominoes competitions are held here. Local CAMRA Pub of the Year 2017.

SCOTLAND

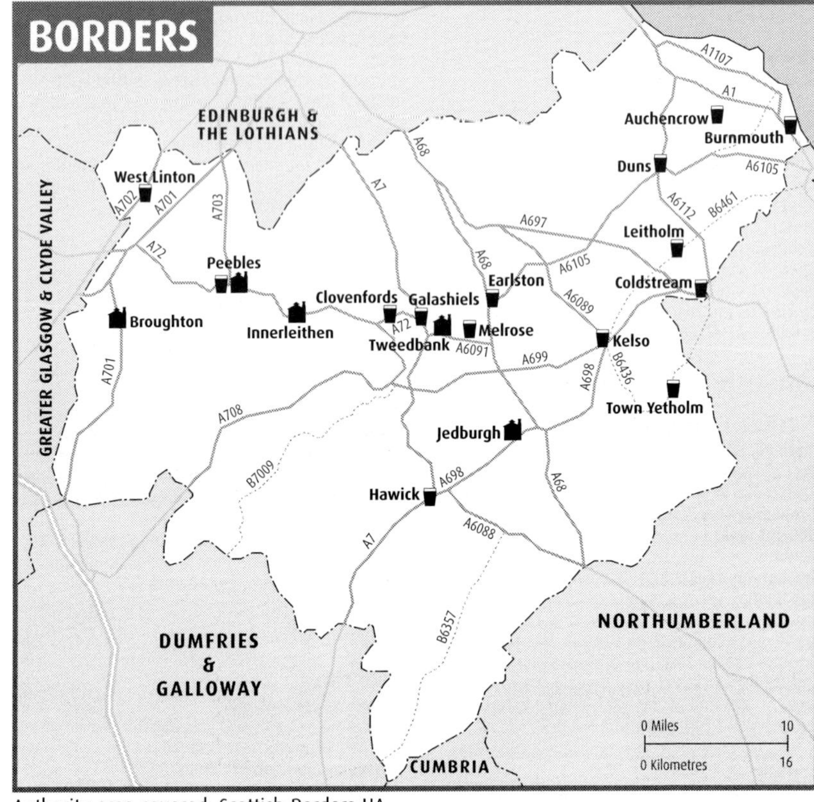

Authority area covered: Scottish Borders UA

Auchencrow

Craw Inn

TD14 5LS (signed from A1)

12-2.30, 6-11 (midnight Fri); 12-midnight Sat; 12-11 Sun

(01890) 761253 thecrawinn.co.uk

2 changing beers (sourced nationally; often Arbor, Swannay, Tempest) H

A friendly 18th-century listed country inn where good banter with the locals is guaranteed. New management in 2017 has introduced fresh ideas about beer and food. The real ales (three in summer) are usually from smaller breweries, as can be seen from the many pumpclips festooning the beams. The bar has a wood-burning stove and tables for dining and drinking. Excellent home-cooked food is served in both the bar and restaurant. Children are permitted but the pub is not family-oriented. Q P (34)

Burnmouth

First & Last

Upper Burnmouth, TD14 5SL

12-11 (1am Fri & Sat); 12.30-11 Sun (01890) 781306

thefirstandlastpub.co.uk

2 changing beers (sourced regionally; often Campbells, Inveralmond, Loch Lomond) H

This comfortable and welcoming pub is frequented by locals and travellers on the adjacent A1. The bar area, with a real fire and sports TV, is decorated with old photographs and nautical artefacts. It is carpeted throughout, and has a small dance floor in the dining/function area. Meals are served all day. Children are allowed but the pub is not family-oriented. Handy for a walk down the steep hill to the charming little harbour at Lower Burnmouth.

P

Clovenfords

Clovenfords Hotel

1 Vine Street, TD1 3LU

11-11 (1am Fri & Sat); 12-11 Sun (01896) 850203

2 changing beers (sourced nationally; often Campbells, Sharp's, Stewart) H

Set in the heart of an old vineyard village with a striking white statue of Sir Walter Scott outside, this family-run hotel offers quality food and drink. Families are very welcome. It has a conservatory restaurant – meals are served all day Saturday and Sunday. Old photos adorn the walls, reflecting the hotel's literary history. It is now home to the village shop, set up in conjunction with Pub is The Hub. Opening times may vary in winter.

Q P (62)

REAL ALE BREWERIES

Born in the Borders Jedburgh
Broughton Broughton
Campbells Peebles (NEW)
Freewheelin' Peebles
Old Worthy Broughton
Tempest Tweedbank
Traquair House Innerleithen

Coldstream

Besom ✔

75-77 High Street, TD12 4AE
11-midnight (1am Fri & Sat); 12.30-midnight Sun
☎ (01890) 882391 🌐 besom-inn.co.uk
Greene King IPA; 1 changing beer (sourced nationally; often Firebrick, Hetton Law, Campbells) H
One of the first and last pubs in Scotland, this three-roomed gem has remained relatively unchanged since it was built in the 1890s and revamped circa 1910. The cosy bar retains its original counter and gantry, while the diverse range of memorabilia, bookshelves and sofa seating gives the feel more of a living room than a pub. The lounge (where families are welcome) leads to a room dedicated to the history of the Coldstream Guards. The menu features freshly-cooked, regional dishes sourced locally.
Q (67,904)

Duns

Black Bull Hotel

15 Black Bull Street, TD11 3AR (between town square and A6109)
11-midnight (1am Fri & Sat); 12-midnight Sun
☎ (01361) 883379 🌐 blackbullhotelduns.co.uk
3 changing beers (sourced regionally; often Born in the Borders, Firebrick, Tempest) H
This family-run 200-year-old hotel is well worth seeking out. The cosy wood-panelled bar is popular with locals while the lounge is well suited to families. The restaurant specialises in fresh local produce, with an intimate, relaxed, candlelit atmosphere. The secluded beer garden is lovely in good weather, with a gazebo and play area. The bedrooms are named after local historical figures. No food is available on Mondays or winter Sundays. P (60,260)

Earlston

Red Lion ✔

The Square, TD4 6DB
11-11 (midnight Fri); 9am-11 Sat & Sun
☎ (01896) 848994 🌐 redlionearlston.co.uk
2 changing beers (sourced regionally; often Born in the Borders, Harviestoun, Orkney) H
Dating from the 1800s, this former coaching inn stands well back from the main street in this small town. Upgraded over the past few years, the pub boasts a spacious bar with a huge fireplace and open fire, and a pool table in the far corner. Food is served all day in the bar and attractive dining room, including breakfast on Saturday and Sunday. A children's menu and games are provided. Alcohol is sold from 11am. P

Galashiels

Hunters Hall ✔

56 High Street, TD1 1SE (N end of centre)
8am-midnight (1am Thu-Sat) ☎ (01896) 759795
Caledonian Deuchars IPA; Greene King Abbot; Sharp's Doom Bar; 2 changing beers (sourced nationally; often Broughton, Knops, Stewart) H
A Wetherspoon pub originally built as a church that morphs into a Lloyds No.1 pub in the evenings. The single room is set on two levels, with the main part having bare stone walls and some booth seating. Several displays by local artists, many depicting the Gala area, help to make up for the lack of natural light. Popular with families and students, food is served all day from 8am. Note: alcohol is not served until 11am. Q

Ladhope Inn ✔

33 High Buckholmside, TD1 2HR (on A7, ⅓ mile N of centre)
4-11 (midnight Thu; 1am Fri); 11-1am Sat; 12-11 Sun
☎ (01896) 752446
2 changing beers (sourced regionally; often Born in the Borders) H
Very much a community hub, this is a comfortable, friendly local with a vibrant Borders atmosphere. Originating circa 1792, it has been altered considerably over the years. Now a single room, it is decorated with a large inked map of the Galashiels area, and has a wee alcove with a golfing theme. Three TVs ensure the pub is busy during sporting events. Excellent home-made soup is served on Sunday. Live music is hosted on occasion. Children are not allowed. There may only be one real ale at quiet times.

Hawick

Exchange Bar (Dalton's)

1 Silver Street, TD9 0AD (off SW end of High St)
11-11 (1am Fri & Sat); 12.30-11 Sun ☎ (01450) 376067
2 changing beers (sourced regionally; often Born in the Borders, Kelburn, Orkney) H
Tucked away between St Mary's Kirk and the Heart of Hawick Heritage Centre, the pub used to overlook the Corn Exchange, hence the name – however, a previous owner was called Dalton and that name has stuck. It is a Victorian gem with original dark-wood panelling and ornate cornice work. The bar is popular with locals and there is a comfy lounge used for parties, Friday karaoke, Sunday folk sessions and music nights. Children are not admitted.

Kelso

Cobbles Freehouse & Dining

7 Bowmont Street, TD5 7JH (off NE side of town square)
11.30-11 (1am Fri); 11-midnight Sat; 12-11 Sun
☎ (01573) 223548 🌐 thecobbleskelso.co.uk
2 changing beers (sourced locally; often Tempest) H
Diners and drinkers are equally well catered for at this long-established gastropub. The bright and welcoming interior includes a cosy bar on the right and a dining area to the left, with food served throughout. There is a menu to suit all tastes including children's, available lunchtime and evening during the week, all day at the weekend. The handpumps are dedicated solely to Tempest beers – two at most times, occasionally three. Please ask before bringing in your dog.

Rutherfords

38 The Square, TD5 7HL
12-10 (11 Fri & Sat) summer; 3-10; 12-11 Fri & Sat; 12-10 Sun winter ☎ 07803 208460 🌐 rutherfordsmicropub.co.uk
4 changing beers (sourced nationally; often Firebrick, Fyne Ales, Stewart) G
At the time of writing, this tiny shop conversion is the only micropub serving real ale in Scotland. With no TV or music to distract, it is the ideal place to visit for a friendly chat or to play board games. All four real ales are served directly from the cask and

third-pint paddles are available. A selection of locally produced charcuterie, pies and cheeses is served all day. Winter hours apply from November to March, when cider may not be available. Children are welcome until 3pm. CAMRA Borders Pub of the Year 2018.

Leitholm

Plough Inn

Main Street, TD12 4JN

closed Mon; 12-10 (11 Fri & Sat) summer; closed Mon & Wed; 12-3, 5.30 (6 Thu)-10; 12-3, 6-11 Sat; 12-10 Sun winter (01890) 840408 theploughinnleitholm.co.uk

2 changing beers (sourced nationally; often Born in the Borders, Hetton Law)

Set in the main street of a quiet village, this former ailing pub has been transformed into a charming family-run inn. The wood-floored bar is decorated and furnished to create a bright, modern and welcoming ambience. A massive clock dominates the fireplace. Full meals are served evenings and Sunday lunchtime, with a café-style menu at other times. Open daily throughout the year for accommodation. P

Melrose

Burt's Hotel

Market Square, TD6 9PL

11-2.30, 5-11; 12-2.30, 6-11 Sun (01896) 822285 burtshotel.co.uk

Born in the Borders Game Bird; Timothy Taylor Landlord; 1 changing beer

An elegant family-run hotel with colourful window boxes providing a striking appearance in summer. The lounge bar decor reflects the country sporting interests of many of its clientele. The focus is unashamedly on food, which is very good in both the bar and restaurant. Those visiting solely for a drink may find space limited. Children are allowed but this pub is not family-oriented. Awarded the CAMRA Edinburgh and SE Scotland Real Ale Quality Award in 2017. QP

Peebles

Bridge Inn (Trust)

Portbrae, EH45 8AW

11-midnight (1am Thu-Sat); 12-midnight Sun (01721) 720589

Fyne Ales Jarl; 3 changing beers (sourced nationally; often Born in the Borders, Stewart, Tempest)

Cheerful, welcoming pub also known as The Trust and once called the Tweedside Inn. The bright, comfortable bar is decorated with jugs, bottles, pictures of old Peebles and displays relating to outdoor pursuits. There is a cosy corner with a logburner and a small room to the rear. The suntrap patio overlooks the river and hills beyond. The gents has superb old fittings. Children are not admitted. CAMRA Scotland & Northern Ireland Pub of the Year 2017 and runner-up local CAMRA Pub of the Year 2018. (X62)

County Inn

35 High Street, EH45 8AN

12-midnight (1am Thu-Sat) (01721) 720595 countyhotel-peebles.co.uk

5 changing beers (sourced nationally; often Belhaven, Greene King)

Past refurbishments blend well with original features in this circa 18th-century inn. The main room is a large space with a high ceiling, subdivided into intimate areas in a variety of styles. There is also a cosy library room with wood-panelled walls and a real fire, and an intriguing sunken room with a barrel-vaulted ceiling. At the front is a smaller bar area, also with a real fire. Meals are served all day and there is a children's menu. Closing time may be earlier in winter. (X62)

Cross Keys

Northgate, EH45 8RS

7am-midnight (1am Fri & Sat) (01721) 723467

Caledonian Deuchars IPA; Kelham Island Pale Rider; Sharp's Doom Bar; 2 changing beers (sourced nationally; often Broughton, Cairngorm, Harviestoun)

This old coaching inn is now a Wetherspoon pub and hotel. The pleasant, rambling, wood-panelled main area has low ceilings, and furnished booths with a mix of tables and chairs and benches. The serving area is tucked away to the left of the entrance and has high tables and chairs. Steps lead up to the excellent beer garden. Food is available all day from the Wetherspoon menu, and alcohol is served from 11am (noon Sun). Q(X62)

Town Yetholm

Plough Hotel

High Street, TD5 8RF

11-midnight (1am Fri & Sat) (01573) 420215 theploughhotelyetholm.co.uk

2 changing beers (sourced regionally; often Belhaven, Born in the Borders, Broughton)

A friendly inn dating from 1710 at the heart of a rural village, which is a haven for walkers with the Pennine Way, St Cuthbert's Way and the Scottish National Trail all nearby. A large wood-burning stove dominates the bar, where the locals are happy to chat. There is also a separate lounge and an attractive little dining room. Lunchtime meals are not always served at quiet times. Enjoy the beer garden in summer. P(81)

West Linton

Gordon Arms Hotel

Dolphinton Road, EH46 7DR (on A702)

11-midnight (1am Fri & Sat); 12-11 Sun (01968) 660208 thegordon.co.uk

4 changing beers (sourced nationally; often Black Sheep, Freewheelin', Stewart)

Situated in a picturesque village on the road from Edinburgh to Biggar. The large L-shaped, airy bar has stone walls and cornicing more reminiscent of an Edinburgh pub than a village local. There is a roaring log fire in winter and you can relax in comfortable seating. Meals including a children's menu are served in the bar, restaurant and covered outdoor area, and are available all day on Sunday. P

DUMFRIES & GALLOWAY

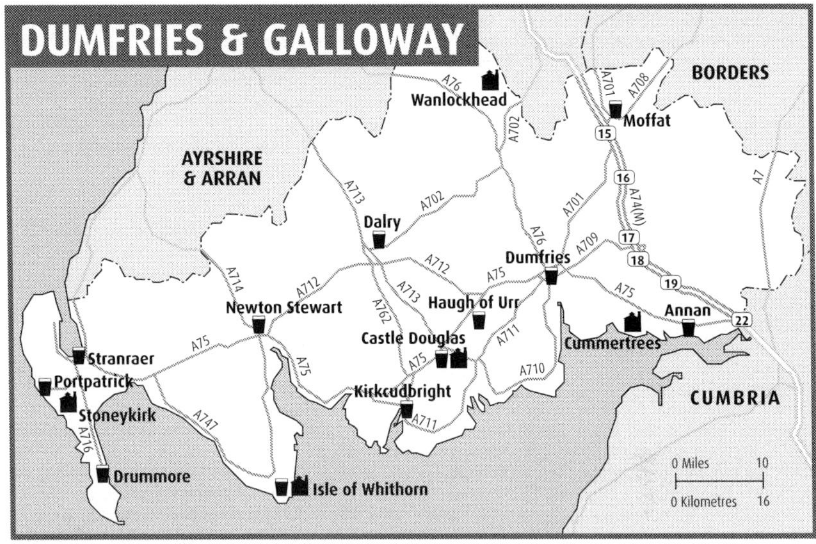

Authority area covered: Dumfries & Galloway UA

Annan

Blue Bell Inn

10 High Street, DG12 6AG

11-11 (midnight Thu-Sat); 12.30-11 Sun

(01461) 202385

Caledonian Deuchars IPA; 3 changing beers (sourced nationally; often Andrews Ales, Kelburn, Strathaven) Ⓗ

Former coaching inn dating from 1770 where Hans Christian Andersen is said to have stayed. The Blue Bell was part of the Gretna State Management Scheme from 1917 to 1972 when it was owned by the government. The pub is home to many community activities along with annual beer and cider festivals. The red sandstone building houses some traditional features, notably the panelled interior and rear stables. The gents has a panelled ante-room, tiled inner room and original Shanks urinals. P (79,383)

Castle Douglas

Sulwath Brewery Tap Room

209 King Street, DG7 1DT

11-6; closed Sun (01556) 504525

sulwathbrewers.co.uk

4 changing beers (sourced locally; often Sulwath) Ⓗ

The visitor centre for Sulwath Brewery is a showcase for the brewery's beers although not all may be cask conditioned. At times there may be guest beers from elsewhere. One draught cider, usually from Westons, is also stocked. Dried hop bines decorate the walls and old wooden casks of various sizes provide some of the furniture. Brewery tours are available and there is an annual beer festival. QP

Dalry

Clachan Inn

8-10 Main Street, DG7 3UW

12-midnight (01644) 430241 theclachaninn.co.uk

2 changing beers (sourced regionally; often Ayr, Fallen, Fyne Ales) Ⓗ

The Clachan has a reputation for excellent food, cosy, well-equipped bedrooms and a welcoming atmosphere. The menu is varied with excellent daily specials, and the kitchen makes use of local produce including organic lamb and venison. The pub has an attractive traditional main bar, a relaxing lounge bar and a separate restaurant – both bars have wonderfully warming open log fires in winter. A handy stop for walkers on the Southern Upland Way. Local CAMRA Pub of the Year 2018. QP (520,521)

Drummore

Clashwhannon

DG9 9QE (on A716 S from Stranraer)

12-midnight summer; 4 (12 Fri-Sun)-11 winter

(01776) 840632 clashwhannon.co.uk

2 changing beers (often Fyne Ales, Hadrian Border, Portpatrick) Ⓗ

This friendly and relaxing bar serves the adjacent caravan park and is open all year round. Demand from visitors and locals alike has seen the emergence of real ale in this remote location close to the Mull of Galloway. There is a bar area plus a large family room and restaurant where local produce is served at reasonable prices. Three handpumps are used in summer, one in winter. Music and variety events feature during the summer. P (407)

Dumfries

Cavens Arms

20 Buccleuch Street, DG1 2AH

11-midnight (11 Mon & Tue); 12-11 Sun

(01387) 252896

REAL ALE BREWERIES

Andrews Cummertrees
Five Kingdoms Isle of Whithorn
Lola Rose Wanlockhead
Portpatrick Stoneykirk
Sulwath Castle Douglas

Fyne Ales Jarl; Morland Old Speckled Hen; Swannay Orkney IPA; 4 changing beers (sourced nationally) Ⓗ
Busy food-oriented pub, popular with diners for its range of good-value meals. A separate restaurant space has been created to cope with demand at peak times. Drinkers are welcome in the bar area but seating can be limited during food service times. Guest ales are from a wide range of breweries including some rarely seen in this locality. There are regular charity quizzes and other theme nights. Local CAMRA Pub of the Year 2017.

Coach & Horses

66 Whitesands, DG1 2RS
closed Mon; 11-11 (midnight Sat); 12.30-11 Sun
☎ 07746 675349
Belhaven 80/- Ale Ⓗ
A small, lively former coaching inn overlooking the River Nith. Situated next to the Tourist Information Centre, the pub is handy for local attractions. The small bar can feel cramped but service is always quick. The bar features a flagstone floor with a warming open fire during the colder months. There is a great atmosphere in this gem of a pub, enhanced on regular live music nights. Winter opening times may vary. P

New Bazaar

39 Whitesands, DG1 2RS
11-11; 12-8 Sun ☎ (01387) 268776
Theakston XB; 3 changing beers (sourced nationally; often Fuller's, Greene King, Timothy Taylor) Ⓗ
Former coaching inn beside the River Nith with an attractive airy bar featuring a splendid Victorian gantry displaying an impressive malt whisky collection. The cosy lounge provides a quiet retreat and has a warming coal fire in winter. A small room is available for meetings. The pub is a favourite with football supporters attending nearby Palmerston Park and is ideally situated for car parking, local buses and tourist attractions. Winter opening times may vary. P

Riverside Bar

Dock Park, DG1 2RY
12-11 (midnight Thu; 1am Fri & Sat); 12.30-11 Sun
☎ (01387) 254477
Morland Old Speckled Hen; 3 changing beers (sourced nationally; often Cairngorm, Fallen, Orkney) Ⓗ
The Riverside Bar is now an established venue on the Dumfries real ale scene. Comfortable and friendly, it has seating on two levels and a large conservatory. Two outside seating areas include a terrace with open views over the Dock Park and down to the River Nith. The pub is accessible from the St Michaels area near Robert Burns Mausoleum or from Dock Park. Guest beers can be sourced from local brewers as well as from further afield. P

Robert the Bruce ✔

81 Buccleuch Street, DG1 2AB
8am-midnight (1am Fri & Sat) ☎ (01387) 270320

> How easy can the barley-bree
> Cement the quarrel.
> It's aye the cheapest lawyer's fee
> To taste the barrel.
> **Robert Burns**

Caledonian Deuchars IPA; Greene King Abbot; Sharp's Doom Bar; Thornbridge Jaipur IPA; 2 changing beers (sourced nationally) Ⓗ
This former Methodist church, sensitively converted by Wetherspoon in 2001, has a relaxed atmosphere and is a popular meeting place in the town centre. There is a pleasant outside seating area to the rear. The pub stands near the site where Robert the Bruce killed John Comyn in 1306 in an incident linked to Scotland's fight for independence. The food menu offers a range of good-value meals all day, every day. Alcohol is served from 11am. P

Tam o' Shanter

113-117 Queensberry Street, DG1 1BH
11-11 (midnight Fri & Sat); 12-10 Sun ☎ (01387) 267880
Broughton Clipper IPA, 6.2 IPA; 4 changing beers (sourced nationally; often Andrews Ales, Broughton, Sulwath) Ⓗ
Established in 1630, this 17th-century coaching inn with a connection to Robert Burns has been a mainstay of the Dumfries beer scene for many years. It is a small traditional pub with a main bar and a couple of quiet cosy rooms including a games area behind. An upstairs room hosts live music and other functions. It is well positioned just off the High Street. Two of the guest beers are usually from local breweries. P

Haugh of Urr

Laurie Arms Hotel

11-13 Main Street, DG7 3YA
12-2, 5-11 (9 Mon & Tue); 12-11 Sat & Sun
☎ (01556) 660246 haugh-of-urr.co.uk
4 changing beers (sourced nationally; often Caledonian, Fyne Ales, Strathaven) Ⓗ
Welcoming family-run pub and restaurant in a charming, quiet village, popular for its range of beers and freshly cooked food featuring local produce. It has a good village pub atmosphere, enhanced on winter nights by a warming log fire in the bar. Up to four beers are available depending on the season, mainly from independent breweries. National Cycle Route 7 passes nearby. A former local CAMRA award winner. Winter opening times may vary. P(501)

Isle of Whithorn

Steam Packet Inn ✔

Harbour Row, DG8 8LL (on B7004 from Whithorn)
11-11 (12.30am Fri & Sat) summer; 11-11 (midnight Fri & Sat); 12-11 Sun winter ☎ (01988) 500334
thesteampacketinn.biz
Morland Old Speckled Hen; 8 changing beers (often Five Kingdoms, Fyne Ales, Kelburn) Ⓗ
Traditional and historic family-run hotel overlooking the harbour, welcoming to all including families and pets. The public bar has stone walls and a multi-fuel stove, and there are pictures of the village and maritime events throughout. Four guest ales from a wide variety of breweries, and up to four ales plus bottle-conditioned ales from the in-house brewery, Five Kingdoms, are available in both bars. The extensive food menu features local produce and includes a Sunday hot buffet and various themed food nights. QP(415)

Kirkcudbright

Masonic Arms

19 Castle Street, DG6 4JA

12-midnight; 12.30-midnight Sun ☎ (01557) 330517

2 changing beers (sourced nationally; often Black Sheep, Caledonian, Wainwright) H

This friendly pub in the town has been a firm favourite with real ale enthusiasts for many years. The tables and bar fronts are made from old malt whisky casks from Islay's Bowmore Distillery. There is a smaller back bar and a garden with a smoking area. A wide selection of more than 50 malt whiskies and over 60 gins is available, as well as a good range of world beers.

Q ♿ P (431,502)

Selkirk Arms Hotel ✔

High Street, DG6 4JG

11-11 ☎ (01557) 330402 selkirkarmshotel.co.uk

3 changing beers (sourced nationally; often Fyne Ales, Sulwath, Timothy Taylor) H

Refurbished 18th-century hotel with a restaurant, bistro and lounge bar, renowned for locally sourced food, highlighted by the menus and photos of suppliers on the walls. The large garden area with tables is popular in summer. Robert Burns wrote his famous Selkirk Grace at the hotel in 1794. Kirkcudbright is notable for its artistic heritage and houses a number of interesting galleries and museums. One or two real ales are available in winter, three in summer.

Q ♿ P (431,502)

Moffat

Black Bull Inn

Church Gate, DG10 9EG

11-11 ☎ (01683) 221150 theblackbullmoffat.co.uk

Theakston Black Bull Bitter; 1 changing beer (often Andrews Ales, Sulwath) H

Recently reopened under new ownership following extensive renovations. The open-plan bar and dining area is light and airy with a small snug away from the restaurant. This historic hotel dating from 1568 is the oldest building in Moffat still in use and possibly one of the oldest hotels in Scotland. It was a centre for government troops during the time of the Covenanters and a visiting place for Robert Burns during his time as an excise officer.

Star Hotel

44 High Street, DG10 9EF

11-11 (midnight Thu-Sat); 12-11 Sun ☎ (01683) 220156

famousstarhotel.co.uk

2 changing beers (sourced regionally; often Sulwath, Greene King) H

The Famous Star Hotel is recognised in the Guinness Book of Records as the narrowest detached hotel in the world. The building is 20 feet wide and 162 feet long but feels much bigger due to the clever use of internal space. It has been run by the same family for over 30 years and offers excellent service. Moffat is a good base for exploring the Southern Uplands.

♿ P

Newton Stewart

Creebridge House Hotel

Minnigaff, DG8 6NP (on B7079, E of river)

12-2.30, 6-midnight ☎ (01671) 402121

creebridge.co.uk

2 changing beers (sourced nationally) H

This traditional country house hotel close to the town centre is set in three acres of gardens and woodland next to the River Cree. It offers two Greene King ales and occasional guests from the Belhaven and Greene King list. A choice of excellent food is available including locally sourced meat, game and fish, served in the top-class restaurant and adjacent informal brasserie. The bar and lounge areas have real fires. Dominoes league night is Tuesday and occasional quiz nights and charity events are held.

♿ P (X75,430)

Portpatrick

Crown Hotel

9 North Crescent, DG9 8SX

11-midnight (1am Fri & Sat); 12-midnight Sun

☎ (01776) 810261 crownhotelportpatrick.com

2 changing beers (often Eagle, Hadrian Border, Portpatrick) H

Hotel overlooking the picturesque and historic Portpatrick harbour with views on a clear day across to Ireland. The large comfortable bar area at the front of the building is adorned with fine pictures and ornaments and warmed by an open fire. Two regularly changing ales are available from across the UK, including the local Portpatrick Brewery. Live music plays on Friday and Saturday nights, featuring both local and visiting musicians and groups. Local CAMRA Pub of the Year 2017.

♿ ♣ (367)

Stranraer

Grapes

4-6 Bridge Street, DG9 7HY

11-11.30 (midnight Thu-Sat); 12.30-11.30 Sun

☎ (01776) 703386 thegrapes1862.co.uk

2 changing beers (often Portpatrick) H

Popular historic public bar, with an impressive mirror and gantry, which has altered little in over 50 years. It has a refurbished snug bar downstairs, an upstairs Art Deco lounge/function room, and a courtyard area with seating. Local musicians play in the public bar most Friday evenings, and touring American-style bands often perform upstairs. There is a strong commitment to real ales sourced both locally and from all over the UK. Mini beer festivals are held twice yearly. ♣

Ruddicot Hotel

London Road, DG9 8AJ

4-12.30am; 12-1am Sat & Sun ☎ (01776) 706192

theruddicothotel.co.uk

1 changing beer (often Strathaven) H

A welcome return to form for a previous Guide stalwart. This small hotel is handy for the town centre, Wigtownshire Rugby Club and Stair Park, home of Stranraer FC. It has a good-sized comfortable lounge and offers a selection of malt whiskies in addition to the single changing real ale. A popular quiz night is held every second Monday. Conveniently situated for the Cairnryan ferry ports a few miles away. P (500)

SCOTLAND

EDINBURGH & THE LOTHIANS

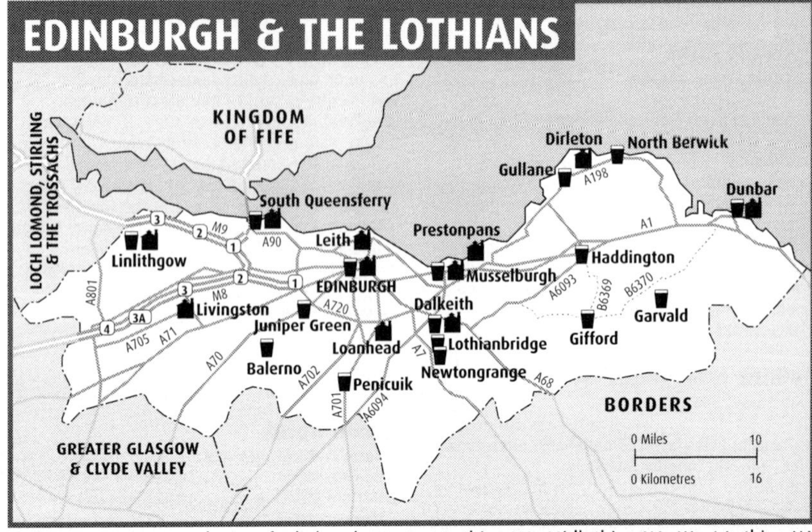

Authority areas covered: City of Edinburgh UA, East Lothian UA, Midlothian UA, West Lothian UA

Balerno

Grey Horse

20 Main Street, EH14 7EH (off A70, in pedestrian area)
11-11 (midnight Fri & Sat); 12-11 Sun (0131) 449 2888
greyhorsebalerno.com
Fyne Ales Jarl; 4 changing beers (sourced regionally; often Alechemy, Orkney, Stewart) [H]

The cosy public bar retains some original features with wood panelling and a fine Bernard's mirror. The lounge is furnished with tables and chairs and offers a gastropub-style menu as well as Chinese street food options (no food Mon). There is one folk evening each month, often on a Sunday. Dogs are allowed in the bar. May not open until noon in winter. Q

Dalkeith

Blacksmith's Forge

5 Newmills Road, EH22 1DU
8am-midnight (1am Fri & Sat) (0131) 561 5100
Caledonian Deuchars IPA; Greene King Abbot; Sharp's Doom Bar; 4 changing beers (sourced regionally; often Broughton, Stewart, Strathaven) [H]

Large open-plan Wetherspoon pub divided into several differently styled areas with a mix of tables and chairs, high tables and booths with bench seating. Changing real ales are often from Scottish breweries. Families are welcome until 10pm for meals, which are available all day. Alcohol is served from 11am (12.30pm Sun).
Q

Dunbar

Volunteer Arms

17 Victoria Street, EH42 1HP (near swimming pool)
12-11 Mon-Wed; 11-midnight Thu; 11-1am Fri & Sat; 12.30-midnight Sun (01368) 862278
volunteerarmsdunbar.co.uk
2 changing beers (sourced nationally; often Harviestoun, Orkney, Tryst) [H]

Close to Dunbar harbour, this is a friendly, traditional locals' pub. The cosy wood-panelled bar is decorated with lots of fishing and lifeboat-oriented memorabilia. The two real ales are often from smaller breweries. Upstairs is a restaurant serving an excellent, good-value range of food including a children's menu, with an emphasis on seafood. Meals are available all day, newspapers are provided and there is live music on Wednesday. Dogs must be on a lead.

Edinburgh: Central

Abbotsford Bar & Restaurant ★

3-5 Rose Street, EH2 2PR (city centre)
11-11 (midnight Fri & Sat) (0131) 225 5276
theabbotsford.com
6 changing beers (sourced regionally; often Cromarty, Fyne Ales, Swannay) [H]/[A]

A traditional Scottish bar featuring a magnificent island bar and gantry in dark mahogany that have been fixtures since 1902. The ornate plasterwork and corniced ceiling are outstanding and highlighted by concealed lighting. There is an extensive food menu, available all day in the bar. Children over five are permitted in the restaurant upstairs, where real ale can be ordered from downstairs. Q (Waverley)

Beehive Inn

18-20 Grassmarket, EH1 2JU (in Old Town)
11-11 (midnight Fri); 11-1am Sat (0131) 225 7171
beehiveinn-edinburgh.co.uk
5 changing beers (sourced nationally; often Belhaven, Greene King) [H]

A large three-floored multi-roomed pub built on the site of a 16th-century inn. Upstairs is the condemned cell door from the old tollbooth. The large beer garden has good views up to the castle. On Friday and Saturday evenings there is a lively atmosphere with a DJ providing music. The real ales have a Scottish bias, with three from Belhaven/Greene King. Meals are served all day. Although not family-oriented, children are allowed until 8pm if dining.

Blue Blazer

2 Spittal Street, EH3 9DX (SW side of centre)
11-1am; 12.30-1am Sun (0131) 229 5030
theblueblazer.co.uk
Stewart Pentland IPA Ⓐ; 7 changing beers (sourced regionally; often Cromarty, Edinbrew, Kelburn) Ⓗ
Two-roomed pub with wooden floors, high ceilings and old brewery window panels giving an old-fashioned feel, complemented by candles in the evening. The pub specialises in real ales from smaller Scottish breweries. Snacks are available all day. Close to theatres and cinemas, the pub stays open later in August and December. Children are not admitted.

Booking Office

17 Waverley Bridge, EH1 1BQ
6am-midnight (1am Fri & Sat) (0131) 558 1003
Caledonian Deuchars IPA; Greene King Abbot; Stewart Jack Back; 9 changing beers (sourced nationally; often Exmoor, Kelburn, Knops) Ⓗ
This single-storey building was erected in 1898-1900 and operated as Waverley Station Parcels Office until around 1988. In 2016 it opened as an attractive, modern Wetherspoon pub. Very close to Waverley Station and Princes Street, it is popular with travellers and shoppers alike. Food is available all day. Alcohol is served from 9am (11am Sunday).
(Waverley)

Bow Bar

80 West Bow, EH1 2HH (Old Town, off Grassmarket)
12-midnight; 12.30-11.30 Sun (0131) 226 7667
thebowbar.co.uk
Fallen Oddysey; Stewart 80/-; Tempest Cascadian; 5 changing beers (sourced nationally; often Cromarty, Swannay) Ⓐ
A re-creation of a classic Scottish one-roomed ale house, dedicated to traditional Scottish air pressure dispense and upright drinking. The real ales can be from anywhere in the UK and beer festivals are held in January and July along with frequent tap takeovers. Gourmet pies are available 12-4pm. Children are not admitted.
Q(Waverley)

Café Royal ★

19 West Register Street, EH2 2AA (off E end of Princes Street)
11-11 (midnight Thu; 1am Fri & Sat) (0131) 556 1884
caferoyaledinburgh.co.uk
House beer (by Broughton); 6 changing beers (sourced regionally; often Belhaven, Kelburn, Stewart) Ⓗ
One of the finest Victorian pub interiors in Scotland, dominated by an impressive oval island bar with ornate brass light fittings, with magnificent ceramic tiled wall murals of innovators made by Doulton from pictures by John Eyre, and with sporting windows in the adjacent Oyster Bar/Restaurant. The real ales are mainly from Scottish breweries. Meals are served all day. Children are only allowed in the restaurant. Q(Waverley)

Guildford Arms

1 West Register Street, EH2 2AA (off E end of Princes St)
11-11 (midnight Thu-Sat) (0131) 556 4312
guildfordarms.com
Bombardier; Fyne Ales Jarl; Orkney Dark Island; Stewart Pentland IPA; Swannay Orkney IPA; 4 changing beers (sourced nationally; often Alechemy, Fallen, Loch Lomond) Ⓗ
A large pub built in the golden age of Victorian pub design. There is a large standing space around the canopied bar plus extensive seating areas. The diverse range of real ales includes many from Scottish micros, and real cider is occasionally available. Bar snacks are on offer 3-9pm. Children over five are allowed in the noteworthy upstairs gallery restaurant. (Waverley)

Halfway House

24 Fleshmarket Close, EH1 1BX (up steps opp Waverley Station Market St entrance)
11-11 (midnight Fri & Sat) (0131) 225 7101
4 changing beers (sourced nationally; often Broughton, Stewart, Strathbraan) Ⓗ
Cosy, characterful bar hidden halfway down an Old Town close. Railway memorabilia decorates the interior of this small, often busy, bar. At the front are tables with window seats and stools. The rear area has more comfortable semicircular booth seating where children may be allowed if the pub is quiet. There are usually four interesting real ales from smaller Scottish breweries. Meals and bar snacks are served all day. The bar may stay open until 1am during busy times of year.
(Waverley)

Haymarket

11-14A West Maitland Street, EH12 5DS (W edge of centre)
11-midnight (1am Fri & Sat) (0131) 228 2537
Caledonian Deuchars IPA; St Austell Nicholson's Pale Ale; 8 changing beers (sourced nationally; often Inveralmond, Stewart, Thornbridge) Ⓗ
On the busy corner of the Haymarket, an island bar here overlooks a large central area with a raised mezzanine floor to one side and arches leading through to a restaurant. Twelve real ale handpumps dispense a varied and interesting range. Food is served all day from the Nicholson's menu. Children are permitted if dining.
(Haymarket)

Jolly Judge

7 James Court, 493 Lawnmarket, EH1 2PB (Old Town)
12-midnight (11 Tue & Wed); 12-11 Sun
(0131) 225 2669 jollyjudge.co.uk
3 changing beers (sourced nationally; often Burning Sky, Knops, Tiny Rebel) Ⓗ
Comfortable bar with an attractive painted ceiling hidden down an Old Town close just off the Royal

REAL ALE BREWERIES

Alechemy Livingston
Barney's Edinburgh
Belhaven Dunbar
Bellfield Edinburgh
Black Metal Edinburgh
Caledonian Edinburgh
Campervan Edinburgh
Cross Borders Dalkeith
Edinbrew Livingston
Eyeball Dunbar
Ferry South Queensferry
Hanging Bat Edinburgh
Hurly Burly Musselburgh
Kentwood Prestonpans
Knops Dirleton
Krafty Brew Linlithgow
Pilot Leith
Stewart Loanhead
Top Out Loanhead

SCOTLAND

Mile. This is a welcome spot for refreshment after visiting the castle. There are steps down to the entrance, as was common in the past. The real ales are usually from smaller breweries UK wide. This is one of Edinburgh's top pubs for cider, selling a varying selection of three types. Dogs are permitted after 3pm, but no children inside. (Waverley)

Monty's

185 Morrison Street, EH3 8DZ (W edge of centre)
4-11 Mon; 12-midnight; 12-1am Fri; 12.30-midnight Sun
(0131) 629 1104 montys.bar

Fyne Ales Jarl; Timothy Taylor Landlord; 4 changing beers (sourced nationally; often Alechemy, Cross Borders, Oakham) H

Busy street-corner bar favoured by a younger clientele, but welcoming to all. The wood-panelled interior has large windows and a varied range of comfortable seating. There is also an upstairs area with cosy seating. Cask ale is featured on the bar counter with keg beer consigned to the back wall, along with impressive laddered back-lit glass spirit shelves. Children are not allowed. (Haymarket)

Thomson's Bar

182-184 Morrison Street, EH3 8EB (W edge of centre)
12-11.30 (midnight Thu & Sat; 1am Fri); 4-11.30 Sun
(0131) 228 5700 thomsonsbaredinburgh.co.uk

Caledonian Deuchars IPA; Fyne Ales Jarl H**; 4 changing beers (sourced nationally; often Alechemy, Oakham, Swannay)** H/A

Superb single-roomed bar modelled on the style of Glasgow architect Alexander 'Greek' Thomson. The walls are decorated with rare mirrors, adverts and point of sale material from long-forgotten breweries. The bar is a member of Oakham Ales' Oakademy, and up to six, often hoppy, real ales are served from a variety of breweries. No food is served on Sunday and only pies on Saturday. Children are not admitted. Q(Haymarket)

Edinburgh: North

Cumberland Bar

1-3 Cumberland Street, EH3 6RT (New Town)
12-midnight Mon-Wed (1am Thu-Sat); 12-11 Sun
(0131) 558 3134 cumberlandbar.co.uk

Caledonian Deuchars IPA; Fyne Ales Jarl; Jennings Cumberland Ale; 2 changing beers (often Alechemy, Cairngorm, Harviestoun) H

Elegant, traditional New Town pub with a half-wood-panelled interior enhanced by dark green leather seating. Exquisite brewery mirrors hang beside framed, decorative and illustrative posters. The corridor between the front drinking area and the cosy area at the back is flanked by a small snug and another side room. Meals are served all day (until 7pm Sun). Children are allowed although this pub is not family oriented. Q

Dreadnought

72 North Fort Street, Leith, EH6 4HL (2 miles N of centre)
5-11.30; 2-1am Fri & Sat; 2-midnight Sun
07876 351535 dreadnoughtleith.com

4 changing beers (sourced nationally; often Brass Castle) H

A welcoming one-roomed pub with big picture windows, a high ceiling with plaster cornicing, sports TV screens and an attractive old-fashioned bar gantry. The Brass Castle beers are all vegan. No food is prepared on site but pizza can be ordered 5-10pm from Origano. CAMRA Edinburgh Pub of the Year 2018.

Kay's Bar

39 Jamaica Street West, EH3 6HF (New Town, off India St)
11-midnight (1am Fri & Sat); 12.30-11 Sun
(0131) 225 1858 kaysbar.co.uk

Caledonian Deuchars IPA; Fyne Ales Jarl; Theakston Best Bitter; 4 changing beers (sourced nationally; often Cross Borders, Stewart, Tryst) H

A cosy and convivial pub offering an impressive range of real ales. It also specialises in malt whisky, with a large selection behind the bar. Lunches consist mainly of traditional Scottish fare. Children are not admitted. Dogs are not permitted 12-2.30pm. Q

Malt & Hops

45 The Shore, Leith, EH6 6QU (1½m N of centre)
12-11 (midnight Wed & Thu; 1am Fri & Sat); 12.30-11 Sun
(0131) 555 0083 barcalisa.com

Hadrian Border Tyneside Blonde; 7 changing beers (sourced nationally; often Fallen, Hadrian Border, Swannay) H

Single-roomed, old-fashioned bar by the Water of Leith dating from 1747. The walls are bedecked with mirrors, prints and beer related artifacts. The wide variety of real ales has an emphasis towards smaller breweries. Bar snacks including toasties are always available. Children are permitted until 6pm.

Stockbridge Tap

2-4 Raeburn Place, Stockbridge, EH4 1HN (under a mile N of centre)
12-11.30 (midnight Wed & Thu; 12.30am Fri & Sat); 12.30-1.30am Sun (0131) 343 3000

Swannay Island Hopping; 6 changing beers (sourced nationally; often Alechemy, Cross Borders, Cromarty) H

A multi CAMRA award-winning specialist real ale house, the pub offers unusual and interesting ales from all over the UK and holds occasional beer festivals. The L-shaped room, with a bright bar area, boasts mirrors from lost breweries including Murray's and Campbell's. Cold snacks are served outside of main food times. Children are not admitted. Closing time may be a little earlier if quiet. Local CAMRA runner-up Pub of the Year 2018.

Teuchters Landing

1C Dock Place, Leith, EH6 6LU (2 miles N of centre)
10.30-1am (0131) 554 7427 aroomin.co.uk/teuchters-landing-bar-edinburgh

Fyne Ales Jarl; Inveralmond Ossian; Timothy Taylor Landlord; 3 changing beers (sourced regionally; often Cromarty, Swannay, Tempest) H

Once the waiting room for the Leith to Aberdeen ferry, the attractive front bar has a wood-panelled ceiling edged with tiles featuring Scottish place names from Teuchterland. To the rear are smaller rooms and a large conservatory extension opening out onto a pontoon floating on the Water of Leith. The varied food menu, available all day, features meals served in mugs. An excellent selection of malt whiskies is available. Children are allowed in the back rooms. Alcohol is served from 11am.

Windsor

45 Elm Row, EH7 4AH (under 1 mile N of centre)
12-1am (midnight Mon & Tue); 12.30-midnight Sun
(0131) 556 4558 windsoredinburgh.co.uk
Caledonian Deuchars IPA; 4 changing beers H
This late-Victorian locals' bar retains a traditional look and fine ceiling cornices but is now brighter and more open plan. Comfortable green leather armchairs and bench seating complement the extensive wood panelling. The three changing real ales come from a range of Scottish and north-east English breweries. Simple bar snacks are served. Children are not admitted.

Edinburgh: South

Bennets Bar ★

8 Leven Street, EH3 9LG (SW edge of centre)
12-1am (0131) 229 5143
bennetsbaredinburgh.co.uk
Caledonian Deuchars IPA; Harviestoun Schiehallion; Orkney Red MacGregor P**; 4 changing beers (sourced regionally; often Stewart)** H/P
One of the city's top pub interiors in a Grade B listed building, this is quintessential late-Victorian Edinburgh pub architecture, from the Jeffrey's Brewery etched door panels and window screens to the snug and magnificent gantry which houses a top-class range of malts and spirit barrels. Daytime food is typically pub grub but in the evening a restaurant-style menu is available. Children are permitted until 8pm. Q

Cask & Barrel (Southside)

24-26 West Preston Street, EH8 9PZ (1 mile S of centre)
12-midnight (1am Fri); 11-1am Sat (0131) 667 0856
Caledonian Deuchars IPA; Swannay Orkney Best; Tryst Drovers 80/-; 5 changing beers (sourced nationally; often Cross Borders, Fyne Ales, Loch Lomond) H
Modern re-creation of a Scottish city or tenement bar. The single room, with windows front and back, is divided by a horseshoe bar with a dark-wood gantry adorned with decorative wooden casks. Sport is screened on multiple TVs with the sound off. A good place to try real ales from interesting breweries UK-wide. Children are not admitted.

Cloisters Bar

26 Brougham Street, EH3 9JH (SW edge of centre)
12-midnight (1am Fri & Sat); 12.30-midnight Sun
(0131) 221 9997 cloistersbar.com
Stewart Pentland IPA, Holy Grale; 7 changing beers (sourced nationally; often Alechemy, Swannay, Thornbridge) H
Established in 1995 in the former All Saints Parsonage, many traditional features have been maintained in this warm and friendly bar. The real ales are generally from interesting breweries UK wide. Frequent beer festivals and Meet the Brewer events are held. The wide range of single malt whiskies, gins and rums does justice to the outstanding gantry. Meals are freshly prepared (no food Mon or Sun eve). Under-16s are not admitted.
Q

Dagda Bar

93-95 Buccleuch Street, EH8 9NG (under a mile S of centre)
12.30-1am; 1-1am Sun (0131) 667 9773
4 changing beers (sourced regionally; often Oakham, Orkney, Tryst) H
Small ground-floor bar in an 18th-century tenement terrace, in the heart of a university area. A stone-flagged floor surrounds the large rectangular counter which takes up at least a third of the room. The colourful, mirrored gantry blends with the cornice, the joins blurred by an extensive collection of pumpclips. Children are not admitted.

Edinburgh: West

Golden Rule ✔

30 Yeaman Place, EH11 1BT (1 mile W of centre)
12-midnight (1am Fri & Sat); 12.30-midnight Sun
(0131) 229 3413 goldenruleedinburgh.co.uk
Stewart Jack Back; 4 changing beers (sourced nationally; often Drygate, Magic Rock, Stewart) H
A split-level Victorian tenement bar close to the Union Canal and the Fountain Park entertainment complex. The pub is a real ale showcase, with a great selection from breweries around the UK. The upstairs bar is pleasantly furnished with bench seating, tables and stools. The downstairs bar comes into its own at weekends, but real ale has to be carried down the steps. There is live music most Saturday evenings and a quiz on Tuesday evening. Children are not admitted.

Roseburn Bar ✔

1 Roseburn Terrace, EH12 5NG (1½ miles W of centre)
9am-11 (midnight Thu-Sat); 11-11 Sun
(0131) 337 1067 roseburnbar.co.uk
Caledonian Deuchars IPA; Fyne Ales Jarl; 2 changing beers (sourced nationally) H
A traditional pub that is popular with locals. It boasts high ceilings and a largely wooden interior, with interesting mirrors and period photos on the walls. There are numerous comfortable booths along the walls and two separate lounge areas. Three TVs show sporting events, though the volume is typically kept low. Live music plays on Friday and Saturday evenings. Close to Murrayfield for rugby and Tynecastle for football. Children are not admitted. Winner of the CAMRA Edinburgh 2017 Real Ale Quality Award.

Garvald

Garvald Inn

EH41 4LN
closed Mon; 12-11 Tue-Thu (midnight Fri & Sat); 12.30-7.30 Sun (01620) 830311
1 changing beer (sourced regionally; often Stewart) H
A family-run 18th-century pub in a pretty village by the Lammermuir Hills. The bar is cosy and welcoming with half-panelled walls, a crimson colour scheme and an exposed stone wall with a large wood-burning stove. The inn is popular for food, served in both the bar and tiny dining room, the dinner menu being particularly impressive. Families are welcome, with a children's menu, garden play area and toys provided. Live music plays on occasion. Q P

Gifford

Tweeddale Arms Hotel

High Street, EH41 4QU
11-11 (1am Fri & Sat) (01620) 810240
tweeddalearmshotel.com

SCOTLAND

Hop Back Summer Lightning; 1 changing beer (sourced regionally; often Broughton, Knops, Stewart) H
Clad in traditional black and white and sitting opposite the village green, this hotel can be identified by its coat of arms sign suspended on wooden posts. The cosy locals' bar, with wood-burning stove in winter, is where you will find the handpumps. The larger former lounge bar is set up for meals, but there is also an elegant hotel lounge across the corridor. Food is served all day Saturday and also Sunday, extending till 9pm in summer.
(123)

Gullane

Old Clubhouse

East Links Road, EH31 2AF (W end of village, off A198)
11-11 (midnight Thu-Sat) ☎ (01620) 842008
oldclubhouse.com
Caledonian Deuchars IPA; Timothy Taylor Landlord; 2 changing beers (sourced nationally) P
There is a colonial touch to this pub, with views over the golf links to the Lammermuir Hills. The half-panelled walls are decorated with historic memorabilia and stuffed animals. Food features highly and is served all day – the varied menu, which includes a children's menu and simple snacks, is supplemented with daily specials.
(X24,124)

Haddington

Golf Tavern

5 Bridge Street, EH41 4AU
11-11 (midnight Thu; 1am Fri & Sat) ☎ (01620) 822327
golftavernhaddington.co.uk
1 changing beer (sourced regionally; often Broughton, Stewart, Tryst) H
A traditional locals' bar nestling behind the Waterside Bistro on the eastern side of the River Tyne. The public bar has a pool table and dartboard. Only one of the two handpumps on the U-shaped bar is used. The spacious lounge acts mainly as a popular restaurant and function room. Food, renowned for its generous portions, is available all day Saturday and until 7pm on Sunday.

Juniper Green

Juniper Green Inn

542 Lanark Road, EH14 5EL
11-midnight (11 Mon & Tue); 12.30-11 Sun
☎ (0131) 458 5395
Caledonian Deuchars IPA; Timothy Taylor Landlord; 2 changing beers (sourced nationally; often Black Isle, Hadrian Border, Orkney) H
Well-appointed, single-room lounge bar in a late-1800s building, with a strong community spirit. The mahogany bar counter has a more modern gantry designed to match. Pictures of the old Balerno branch line provide interest. The varied food menu includes meal deals (no food Sun, light meals only Mon). Children over 12 are permitted if dining.
Q

Linlithgow

Four Marys ✔

65-67 High Street, EH49 7ED
11-11 (11.30 Wed & Thu; 1am Fri & Sat); 12.30-11 Sun
☎ (01506) 842147 fourmarys-linlithgow.co.uk
Belhaven St Andrew's Ale; Caledonian Deuchars IPA; 6 changing beers (sourced regionally; often Fyne Ales, Swannay) H
A stone's throw from Linlithgow Palace, birthplace of Mary Queen of Scots, the building dates back to around 1500 and is named after the Queen's ladies-in-waiting. The building has had several changes of use over the years – at one time it was a chemist's run by the Waldie family whose most famous member, David, helped establish the anaesthetic properties of chloroform in 1847. Local CAMRA Pub of the Year 2018. Q

Linlithgow Tap

111 High Street, EH49 7AB
11-11 (midnight Wed & Thu; 1am Fri & Sat)
☎ (01506) 843590
Fyne Ales Jarl; Orkney Dark Island; 4 changing beers (sourced regionally; often Belhaven, Inveralmond, Kinneil) H
Situated a short distance west of Lithgae Cross and formerly known as the Footballers & Cricketers Arms, the pub underwent a makeover in 2015 and introduced six real ale taps. The stained-glass panels of footballer and cricketer have been replaced by clear glass windows, with a window depicting a footballer to the side. The pub has an island bar and there is a map of old Linlithgow on the ceiling. Snacks are available, and music plays on Friday and Saturday nights.

Platform 3 L ✔

1A High Street, EH49 7AB
10.30-midnight (1am Fri & Sat); 12.30-midnight Sun
☎ (01506) 847405 platform3.co.uk
Stewart Pentland IPA; 2 changing beers (sourced regionally; often Cairngorm, Harviestoun, Tryst) H
Small, friendly hostelry on the railway station approach, originally the public bar of the hotel next door and renovated in 1998 as a pub in its own right. Two Scottish beers are served in addition to Stewart's Pentland IPA. Dogs are welcome, with biscuits 'on tap'. A live train departures board keeps travellers informed. Alcohol is served from 11am (12.30pm Sun).

Lothianbridge

Sun Inn

EH22 4TR (on A7, near Newtongrange)
8am-11 (midnight Fri & Sat) ☎ (0131) 663 2456
thesuninnedinburgh.co.uk
2 changing beers (sourced regionally; often Alechemy, Kelburn, Stewart) H
Well-appointed award-winning gastropub overlooked by the impressive 23-span Waverley Line viaduct. The front area is for dining, the decor a mix of exposed stone, papered walls, wooden floors and carpets. To the rear is a more modern bar area for drinkers and a coffee shop/function room. Meals are served all day on Sunday until 7pm and breakfast and afternoon tea are available during the week. The bar may close earlier if quiet. Alcohol is available from 11am.
P (29,339)

Musselburgh

David MacBeth Moir ✔

Bridge Street, EH21 6AG (opp The Brunton)

8am-11 (midnight Thu & Sun; 1am Fri & Sat)
(0131) 653 1060
Caledonian Deuchars IPA; 4 changing beers (sourced nationally)
Wetherspoon pub named after a local physician and writer, set in a former cinema dating back to 1935. Many original features have been beautifully restored, and the vast single-room bar is filled with Art Deco cinema-themed artefacts. The long bar counter offers a good mix of real ales and ciders. Food is available all day. Alcohol is served from 11am (12.30pm Sun).

Levenhall Arms

10 Ravensheugh Road, EH21 7PP (B1348, 1 mile E of centre)
12-11 (midnight Thu; 1am Fri & Sat); 12.30-midnight Sun
(0131) 665 3220
Inveralmond Ossian; 2 changing beers (sourced regionally; often Knops, Sonnet 43, Strathaven)
A three-roomed hostelry dating from 1830 and close to the racecourse. The lively, cheerfully decorated public bar is half-timber-panelled and carpeted. Dominoes is popular here and there is a TV for sporting events. A smaller area leads off, with a dartboard and pictures of old local industries. The pleasant lounge has a hardwood floor and comfortable seating. Winner of the local CAMRA 2017 Real Ale Quality Award and runner-up local CAMRA Pub of the Year 2018.

Volunteer Arms (Staggs)

81 North High Street, EH21 6JE (behind The Brunton)
12-11 (11.30 Thu; midnight Fri); 11-midnight Sat; 12.30-11 Sun (0131) 665 9654 staggsbar.com
Oakham JHB, Bishops Farewell; 4 changing beers (sourced nationally; often Fyne Ales, Loch Lomond, Swannay)
Superb pub run by the same family since 1858. The bar and snug are traditional, with wooden floors, wood panelling and mirrors from defunct local breweries. The more modern lounge opens at the weekend. The real ales, mostly pale and hoppy but often one darker, change regularly. Local CAMRA Pub of the Year 2018. Children are permitted until 7pm.

Newtongrange

Dean Tavern

80 Main Street, EH22 4NA
11-11 Mon; 9am-11 (midnight Fri & Sat); 10-11 Sun
(0131) 663 2419 deantavern.co.uk
1 changing beer (sourced regionally; often Born in the Borders)
Superb pub run by trustees on Gothenburg principles, with profits returned to the local community. The light and spacious bar was designed to help miners recover from their day in darkness, with roof lights in a high ceiling supported by arched iron beams. There is also the Lamp Room restaurant and a function room. Meals are available all day. Children are permitted until 8pm if dining. Alcohol is served from 11am (12.30pm Sun).

North Berwick

Nether Abbey Hotel

20 Dirleton Avenue, EH39 4BQ (on A198 under a mile W of centre)
9am-11 (midnight Thu; 1am Fri & Sat) (01620) 892802
netherabbey.co.uk
Knops East Coast Pale; 3 changing beers (sourced nationally; often Stewart, Timothy Taylor, Williams Bros)
Busy, family-run hotel in a stone-built villa with a bright, contemporary, open-plan interior. The Fly Half Bar is in a split-level glass extension; large folding doors open out on to the patio. Real ales are often from Scottish breweries – sparklers can be removed on request. The upper central area is an award-winning restaurant. The Nethers is famous for its good, freshly cooked and locally sourced food, available all day Friday to Sunday. Alcohol is served from 11am.

Ship Inn

7-9 Quality Street, EH39 4HJ
11-11 (1am Thu-Sat) (01620) 890699
thistlestreetbar.co.uk/ship-inn
Fyne Ales Jarl; Harviestoun Schiehallion; 1 changing beer (sourced nationally; often Greene King, Orkney, Stewart)
Friendly and often lively bar at the leafy east end of the town centre. The spacious open-plan interior offers a wide variety of seating and tables. The bar area has pine floorboards, a mahogany counter, a dark-stained wood gantry and a framed pumpclip display. To the side and rear is a quieter carpeted area. The pub is popular for food, with good vegetarian options, served all day until 8pm. Sparklers are happily removed on request.

Penicuik

Navaar House Hotel

23 Bog Road, EH26 9BY (just W of centre)
12 (3 Mon)-midnight (01968) 672683
navaarhouse.co.uk
1 changing beer (sourced regionally; often Fyne Ales, Stewart, Swannay)
A lively pub with a strong community spirit, situated in an old private house once belonging to Professor James Cossar Ewart, where he conducted his world-famous work known as the Pennycuik Experiments. The large bar is open plan with a log/coal stove, a pool table and TV screens. A pleasantly decorated restaurant serves locally sourced food, throughout the day on Saturday and Sunday. Children are permitted in the restaurant and garden. The bar opens at 3pm Monday to Friday.

South Queensferry

Ferry Brewery Tap Bar & Shop

Bankhead Farm Steading, Bankhead Road, EH30 9TF (just off B924, SE of Hawes Pier out of town)
closed Mon; 10-5 (7 Fri & Sat); 12-5 Sun
(0131) 331 1851 ferrybrewery.co.uk
4 changing beers (sourced locally)
The only brewery in Queensferry since 1851, with some of its beers brewed from historic recipes that follow the original manuscripts of earlier brewers. A changing range of Ferry Brewery ales is served on four handpumps and seasonal beers are brewed for festivals such as the Loony Dook, Ferry Fair and Christmas. The small Tap Bar and shop is warm and friendly, with welcoming staff, great conversation and a relaxed atmosphere. Children are welcome. Q P (43,x43,63)

SCOTLAND

GREATER GLASGOW & CLYDE VALLEY

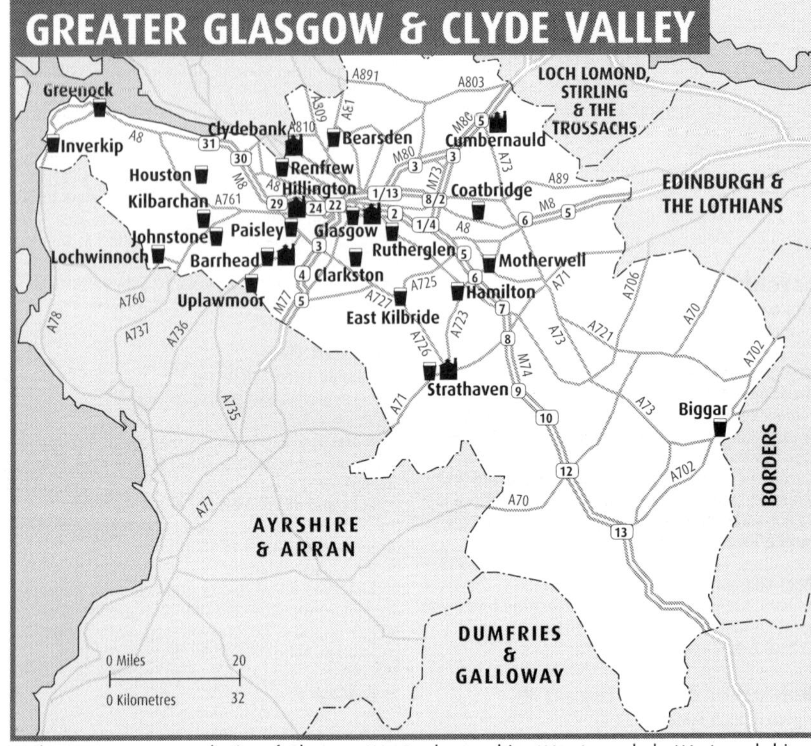

Authority areas covered: City of Glasgow UA, Dunbartonshire UAs, Inverclyde UA, Lanarkshire UAs, Renfrewshire UAs

Barrhead

Cross Stobs Inn

2-6 Grahamston Road, G78 1NS (jct of B771/B774)
11-11 (midnight Thu & Sat; 1am Fri); 12.30-11 Sun
☎ (0141) 881 1581 crossstobsinn.co.uk
2 changing beers (often Kelburn)
Eighteenth-century coaching inn on the road to Paisley. The public bar has a real coal fire and retains much of its original charm with antique furniture and service bells. The spacious lounge is mostly used for dining and leads to an enclosed garden to the rear. There is also a drinking area outside at the front. A pool room and function suite are situated off the public bar.
P (54,101)

Bearsden

Burnbrae

281 Milngavie Road, G61 3EA
7am-11 (midnight Fri); 8am-11 Sat & Sun
☎ (0141) 942 5951
6 changing beers (sourced nationally; often Greene King)
Relatively recently built but old-world-style family-friendly pub restaurant with real fires and oak beams within a quiet, residential setting. The interior is open plan with several distinct areas mostly for dining, but there is space around the bar for drinkers. The licensee runs a mini festival every Easter with a stillage set up in the bar. Alcohol is served from 11am (12.30pm Sun).
P (60A)

Biggar

Crown Inn

109-111 High Street, ML12 6DL
11-1am ☎ (01899) 220116 thecrownbiggar.co.uk
6 changing beers (sourced nationally)
Attractive long-established inn in the centre of a small market town situated in rolling hills just north of the Southern Uplands. The bar is in front of you as you enter, displaying six handpumps offering a wide range of ales. The large single room is divided into smaller open spaces, with a comfortable mix of ancient and modern decor and artefacts. There is live music every second Friday and a beer festival twice a year. (191)

Elphinstone Hotel

145 High Street, ML12 6DL
11-1am ☎ (01899) 220044 elphinstonehotel.co.uk
2 changing beers (sourced regionally; often Broughton, Fyne Ales)
A coaching inn with a history going back over 400 years in the centre of this small market town. Four handpumps are to be found in the public bar, the Elph, but the choice is limited at quiet times. The L-shaped bar offers a range of seating and there is a pool table towards the rear. (191)

Clarkston

White Cart

61 East Kilbride Road, G76 8HX
11.30-11; 12-10 Sun ☎ (0141) 644 2711

Greene King IPA; 2 changing beers (sourced nationally) Ⓗ
A friendly welcome awaits you at this large, bright and spacious Chef & Brewer pub. The emphasis is on food service but there are four handpumps offering three guest beers and a cider. A patio at the front is popular in the summer and there is an area for families inside. An added bonus is the roaring fire in winter.
♞❀◐♿⇌(Busby)●P🚌🐾📶

Coatbridge

Vulcan ✔
181 Main Street, ML5 3HH (jct with Dunbeth Rd)
⏲ 8am-midnight (1am Fri & Sat) ☎ (01236) 437972
Greene King Abbot; 5 changing beers (sourced nationally; often Broughton, Kelburn, Stewart) Ⓗ
A compact Wetherspoon pub at the end of the main street close to the town centre. The Vulcan was CAMRA Lanarkshire Pub of the Year in 2017, the second time it has claimed the honour in three years. The name comes from the first iron-build ship to reflect the area's industrial past. The five changing beers are usually from small Scottish brewers. A quiz night is held on the first Thursday of the month. Alcohol is available from 11am.
♞❀◐♿⇌(Sunnyside)P🚌📶

East Kilbride

Hay Stook Ⓛ ✔
26 Princes Avenue, G74 1JU
⏲ 8am-midnight ☎ (01355) 244323
Caledonian Deuchars IPA; Greene King Abbot; 4 changing beers (sourced nationally; often Jaw) Ⓗ
This Wetherspoon pub is situated at the Brouster Gate entrance in Princes Mall, the largest indoor mall in Scotland, which makes it handy for shoppers and for the nearby cinema complex. The staircase up to the toilets neatly divides the room, with the bar area to one side and family area to the other. It has a small beer garden at the side overlooking the Mall entrance. Scottish beers are well represented among the four guests. Alcohol is available from 11am. ♞❀◐♿⇌●🚌📶

Glasgow

Babbity Bowster
16-18 Blackfriars Street, Merchant City, G1 1PE
⏲ 11-midnight; 12.30-midnight Sun ☎ (0141) 552 5055
🌐 babbitybowster.com
3 changing beers (sourced regionally; often Fyne Ales) Ⓗ
A unique establishment just off the High Street, which has been providing the services of pub, café, restaurant and hotel for more than 30 years. The bar room has plain, functional tables with some wall seating, and in winter offers the radiance and aroma of a peat fire. Three handpumps serve Scottish ales, some from local breweries, usually pale amber at around 4% ABV. In summer the garden has barbecues and boules. Excellent food is Scottish with a touch of French.
Q❀🛏◐⇌(High St)🚋🚌

Blackfriars Ⓛ
36 Bell Street, Merchant City, G1 1LG
⏲ 11-midnight; 12.30-midnight Sun ☎ (0141) 552 5924
🌐 blackfriarsglasgow.com
5 changing beers (sourced nationally) Ⓗ
Popular Merchant City bar attracting a varied clientele finding their own niche in either the corner overlooking the streets, the central bar room or the quieter dining area to the rear. Five handpumps dispense at least one beer from the local Kelburn Brewery plus some Scottish ales and others from further afield. There is a good selection of foreign beers in bottle and draught and a variety of tasty food – try the smoked haddock goujons. Live music plays on Sunday and Tuesday nights.
◐♿⇌(High St)🚋🚌📶

Bon Accord Ⓛ
153 North Street, Charing Cross, G3 7DA
⏲ 11-midnight; 12.30-midnight Sun ☎ (0141) 248 4427
🌐 bonaccordpub.com
Caledonian Deuchars IPA, Edinburgh Castle 80/-; 8 changing beers (sourced nationally; often Lawman Brewing Company) Ⓗ
One of the pioneers of the real ale scene in Glasgow, the Bon has long been known for its commitment to good beer. It has appeared in many editions of the Guide and last year celebrated its 20th consecutive entry. The bar has 400 malt whiskies on offer and an online shop so they can be ordered ahead and collected from the bar. A seating area at the rear hosts quiz, poker and live music nights.
♞❀◐♿⇌(Charing Cross)🚋●🚌📶

Clockwork Beer Co Ⓛ ✔
Cathcart Road, Mount Florida, G42 9HB
⏲ 11-midnight ☎ (0141) 649 0184
🌐 clockworkbeercompany.co.uk
Clockwork Original Amber, Cartside Red, Craft Lager, Oregon IPA; 4 changing beers (sourced regionally; often Clockwork) Ⓐ
Eight varying Clockwork ales, ranging widely in style, along with two guests, greet the visitor to this spacious brewpub. Seating is spread around the walls, leaving a large area for upright drinking, handy when events at nearby Hampden Park stadium pack out the pub. Sport is shown on several screens, there is open mic on Monday, a quiz night on Thursday and live music on the last Friday of the month. A table service dining area is opposite the bar.
♞❀◐♿⇌(Mount Florida)P🚌📶

Counting House ✔
2 St Vincent Place, G1 2DH
⏲ 8am-midnight ☎ (0141) 225 0160
Caledonian Deuchars IPA; Greene King Abbot; Sharp's Doom Bar; changing beers (sourced nationally) Ⓗ
Large corner Wetherspoon pub with windows overlooking St Vincent Street and George Square to City Chambers. It started life as the city head office for the Bank of Scotland around 1870. At least 10 beers including constantly changing guests, and often real cider, are available on the three-sided

REAL ALE BREWERIES

Clockwork 🛢 Glasgow
Drygate 🛢 Glasgow
Jaw Hillington
Kelburn Barrhead
Late Night Hype Clydebank (NEW)
Lawman Cumbernauld
Merchant City Glasgow (NEW)
Shilling 🛢 Glasgow
Strathaven Strathaven
WEST 🛢 Glasgow

counter. These may be drunk in the impressive, opulent glass-domed central area or taken to several side rooms, all with their own character. The pub holds regular Meet the Brewer sessions and has a good range of bottled beers. (Queen St)

Crossing the Rubicon

372 Great Western Road, Woodlands, G4 9HT (just E of Kelvin Bridge)

12-midnight; 11-midnight Sat & Sun (0141) 337 3111 crossingtherubicon.com

3 changing beers (sourced regionally)

A modern craft beer pub serving a range of cask and keg beers alongside a selection of pizzas. The interior is divided, with high tables and chairs around the bar and a raised area to one side with more tables and chairs. The pub is set back from the road allowing plenty of pavement seating. Details of all the beers are clearly displayed and the knowledgeable staff will let you know which ones are from KeyKeg.

Drum & Monkey

91-93 St Vincent Street, G2 5TF (Renfield St jct)

12-11 (midnight Fri & Sat) (0141) 221 6636

St Austell Nicholson's Pale Ale; 6 changing beers (sourced nationally; often Inveralmond)

Upmarket Nicholson's pub handy both for Central and Queen Street stations. This former bank dating from 1924 has an opulent marble and wood-panelled interior and an ornate ceiling. The large central bar featuring nine handpumps is often busy, particularly with the after-work crowd in the early evening. There are two raised seating areas and a dining and function room at the rear. Toilets are down a spiral staircase. Food is served all day until 9.30pm. (Central)

Drygate

85 Drygate, Dennistoun, G4 0UT (off John Knox St)

11-midnight (0141) 212 8815 drygate.com

Drygate Pale Duke, Seven Peaks; 2 changing beers (sourced nationally; often Drygate)

Situated on the historic Wellpark Brewery site, this brewpub offers numerous cask, keg and bottled beers, firmly positioned towards the craft beer market and younger drinkers. Lively with an industrial aesthetic, there are two bars over the ground and first floors, an outside terrace and a panoramic view of the brewery. Food is served throughout the day – the menu varies from modern British to street-inspired. Live music and comedy feature regularly in the upstairs beer hall. (High St)P

Henglers Circus

351-363 Sauchiehall Street, Charing Cross, G2 3HU

8am-midnight (0141) 331 9810

Greene King Abbot; Sharp's Doom Bar; 12 changing beers (sourced nationally)

To the west of the city centre, this Wetherspoon pub concentrates on real ales in a very competitive area. The L-shaped bar is usually fairly busy at lunchtime for meals and in the evenings, especially the weekend, when older drinkers mix with the local student crowd enjoying a drink before going on to nearby clubs. Staff are keen to supply what the customers request so there are both the regular ales and an eclectic mix of guests available. Q(Charing Cross)

Inn Deep

445 Great Western Road, Hillhead, G12 8HH

12-midnight (11 Sun) (0141) 357 1075 inndeep.com

3 changing beers (sourced nationally; often Williams Bros)

Inn Deep is built into arches along the river walkway beside the former railway station and in the shadow of Kelvin Bridge. Access is down from a doorway on the main road or from the walkway. Two arches provide ample space for eating and drinking, with a wall of taps pouring an abundance of craft beers. Ample outdoor seating is also available with a heated area in a third arch and benches beside the river. (20,6)

Laurieston Bar ★

58 Bridge Street, Tradeston, G5 9HU

11-11; 12.30-11 Sun (0141) 429 4528

Fyne Ales Jarl; 2 changing beers (sourced locally; often Fyne Ales, Jaw)

Unchanged in decades, this pub is owned and run by two brothers, whose family has been in the pub trade for generations. It is among Glasgow's friendliest pubs, situated just south of the Clyde from Central Station and handy for some excellent curry houses. The horseshoe bar is surrounded by formica-top tables and walls covered in vintage photographs, mirrors, memorabilia and the occasional painting. Dogs are very welcome. Listed on CAMRA's National Inventory of Historic Pub Interiors. (Central)

Mulberry St

778 Pollokshaws Road, Strathbungo, G41 2AE

11-11 (midnight Fri & Sat); 12.30-11 Sun (0141) 424 0858 mulberry.st

Harviestoun Bitter & Twisted; 2 changing beers (sourced locally; often Fyne Ales)

This community pub, named after a street in New York, in the conservation area of Strathbungo, is conveniently placed near to Queens Park. It has an excellent bistro attached offering a varied menu and meals are also served in the cosy, comfortable bar. In summertime there is a beer garden on the pavement which is popular in good weather. The third guest beer is usually only available in summer. (Queens Park)

Pot Still

154 Hope Street, G2 2TH

11-midnight (0141) 333 0980 thepotstill.co.uk

4 changing beers (sourced regionally)

Cosy family-run bar, famous for its impressive selection of malt whiskies since 1981. Not far from both main rail stations, it hosts a steady flow of visitors from all over the world seeking drams from rare labels and an education. Four handpumps dispense Scottish beers, some from brewers unusual for Glasgow. Pub food includes various pies, sandwiches and soup, often vegan-friendly, all made in-house. If the main bar room is busy, a mezzanine corner offers a retreat. (Central)

Raven

81-85 Renfield Street, G2 1LP

12-11 (midnight Thu-Sat) (0141) 332 6151 theravenglasgow.com

3 changing beers (sourced nationally)

Opened in 2014 and handy for bus and rail stations, the Raven is a popular, modern pub close to shops, restaurants, theatres and cinemas. It has a split-level bar with a separate restaurant and a function room and bar on the mezzanine. There are three real ales, often from Scottish breweries, as well as a wide range of keg craft and bottled beers. Meet the Brewer nights are held regularly. Food is served all day. (Queen St)

Sir John Moore

260-292 Argyle Street, G2 8QW
7am-midnight; 8am-midnight Sat & Sun
(0141) 222 1780
8 changing beers (sourced nationally) H
Close to Central Station's lower level Hope Street exit, this busy Wetherspoon pub is a convenient place to wait for a train. Converted from several shops, it has a number of distinct areas on different levels and covered seating on the street. The beer selection usually includes a couple of local brews. It is named after a Glasgow-born soldier whose likeness was cast from brass cannons and whose statue was the first to be unveiled in George Square in 1819. (Central)

Sir John Stirling Maxwell

136-140 Kilmarnock Road, Shawlands, G41 3NN
8am-midnight (0141) 636 9024
Caledonian Deuchars IPA; Greene King Abbot; 7 changing beers (sourced nationally; often Kelburn) H
Popular Wetherspoon pub at the far end of Shawlands Arcade in what used to be Safeways supermarket. It is named after the former owner of the nearby Pollok House and Country Park, and furnished with bookcases plus pictures and stories of local historic figures. There is a quieter area up three steps at the back which is popular with families. At least six beers are served from the 10 handpumps. Alcohol is available from 11am. (Pollokshaws E)

Sloans

Argyll Arcade, G2 8AG (off Argyll St)
11-midnight (1am Fri & Sat) (0141) 221 8886
sloansglasgow.com
Caledonian Deuchars IPA; 3 changing beers (often Kelburn) H
One of Glasgow's oldest pubs, Sloans began life as a coffee house in 1797. It was remodelled in 1900 and retains many features including the tiled entrance off Argyll Arcade and the grand mahogany staircase leading to the restaurant and ballroom. The bar is on the ground floor with a bistro serving good pub food. A wide range of activities and events is hosted including film nights, ceilidhs, quiz nights, folk music, musical bingo and meetings of the Scottish Macaroni Appreciation Club. (Argyle St)

State Bar

148 Holland Street, Charing Cross, G2 4NG (just off Sauchiehall St, opp Henglers Circus)
11-midnight (0141) 332 2159
House beer (by Stewart); 6 changing beers (sourced nationally; often Oakham) H
A local CAMRA Pub of the Year for the last four years, this popular town-centre establishment gets busy at lunchtimes and weekends. It has a traditional island bar offering changing ales, often rarely seen in Glasgow, including at least one from Oakham. Its proximity to the King's Theatre is reflected in old pictures and show bills displayed round the walls. There is a blues session on Tuesday in the main bar and a comedy club downstairs on Saturday.
(Charing Cross)

Tennents

191 Byres Road, Hillhead, G12 8TN
10-11 (midnight Thu-Sat) (0141) 339 7203
thetennentsbarglasgow.co.uk
Caledonian Deuchars IPA; Draught Bass; Fuller's London Pride; Harviestoun Afterglow; Marston's Pedigree; Timothy Taylor Landlord; 4 changing beers (sourced nationally) H
Since opening in the 1880s, Tennents has been at the heart of the community and although the pub has undergone many refurbishments it has kept its traditional character. The large open bar with a small lounge to one side is frequented by many locals and not a few staff and students from the neighbouring university. The pub offers many regular and guest beers and a good-value range of food at all times. Several TV screens show mainly sports. Alcohol is served after 11am.

Three Judges

141 Dumbarton Road, Partick, G11 6PR
11-midnight (0141) 337 3055 threejudges.co.uk
8 changing beers (sourced nationally) H
Situated on a corner at the bottom of a tenement at Partick Cross, the Three Judges is one of the West End's best-known pubs. Over the past three decades it has served many different ales both from local breweries and from around the country, and last year it celebrated 25 years in the Guide. There are usually eight beers and a cider on offer, displayed on a chalkboard. Pork pies are available and other food can be brought in.
Q(Partick)

Greenock

James Watt

80-92 Cathcart Street, PA15 1DD
8am-midnight (1am Fri & Sat); 9am-midnight Sun
(01475) 722640
Greene King Abbot; Sharp's Doom Bar; 4 changing beers H
Situated across the road from Greenock Central Station and 200 yards from the bus station, this large open-plan Wetherspoon, in a former post office, is named after one of Greenock's famous sons who improved steam engine technology and has the SI unit of power named after him. The chain's standard value-for-money food is available all day and beer festivals are hosted at various times throughout the year. This pub is an oasis in a beer desert.

Hamilton

George Bar

18 Campbell Street, ML3 6AS
12-midnight (1am Fri); 12.30-midnight Sun
(01698) 424225
3 changing beers (sourced nationally; often Strathaven) H
This traditional, family-run pub is situated in a pedestrianised area just off the inner ring road in the town. The single bar room is decorated with hundreds of pumpclips celebrating many of the beers enjoyed over the years. Three handpumps offer ales from near and far, often including the nearby Strathaven Brewery. Tasty home-cooked meals are available until 6pm. In warmer weather café-style seating provides extra space outside.
(Central)

SCOTLAND

Houston

Fox & Hounds 𝕃

South Street, PA6 7EN

9am-midnight (1am Fri & Sat) ☎ (01505) 808604

foxandhoundshouston.co.uk

Kelburn Goldihops; 4 changing beers Ⓗ

Established in 1779, this iconic village pub reopened in December 2015 under new ownership and has been refurbished while retaining many traditional features. Downstairs is the quiet Vixens Bar Lounge and Stables Restaurant, with the Hunters Bar, a sports bar with TV and games, upstairs. Five handpumps downstairs offer beers from across the UK. The old Houston Brewery area is now an open kitchen. Q

Houston Inn

North Street, PA6 7HF

11-midnight (1am Fri & Sat) ☎ (01505) 614315

houston-inn.com

1 changing beer (sourced regionally; often Kelburn) Ⓗ

Friendly village inn with an L-shaped bar area warmed by a log fire and a separate restaurant. There is a weekly quiz night each Wednesday and poker nights on Tuesday and Wednesday. A variety of food, drink and music-themed events is also run throughout the year. Only a short drive from Glasgow, the large restaurant offers flavoursome traditional food made with locally sourced ingredients. P

Inverkip

Inverkip Hotel

Main Street, PA16 0AS

11-11 (11.30 Thu-Sat); 12.30-11 Sun ☎ (01475) 521478

inverkip.co.uk

Fyne Ales Jarl; 1 changing beer (sourced regionally; often Fallen, Fyne Ales) Ⓗ

Small family-run hotel located in the heart of a conservation village and just a short walk from the large Inverkip Marina, making it an ideal staging post for those just messing about on the river or passing through on the way to Largs and the Ayrshire coast. Food options range from snacks to special occasion dining. Battle of the Brewer nights are extremely popular. P (578,580)

Johnstone

Callum's 𝕃

26 High Street, PA5 8AH

11-midnight (1am Fri & Sat); 12.30-midnight Sun

☎ (01505) 322925

Kelburn Pivo Estivo, Jaguar; 5 changing beers (often Orkney) Ⓗ

> There is not a brewer who doesn't doctor his beer with something or other. Really something is in it. Four glasses made a Brooklyn man shoot down Dr Duggan in cold blood. Beer made a New York husband put a hole through his wife with a 22-calibre defender. Murder is in it. Who drinks lager beer is too apt to swallow the murder with it.
>
> **Elisha Chenery MD, 1889**

An oasis in a real ale desert, this is a popular town-centre pub offering a friendly welcome and a comfortable atmosphere. A large TV screen shows sporting events. The lounge is set for dining, with themed nights including curry on Thursday. Occasional live music features at weekends. Three regular beers are offered alongside four changing guests. (36,38)

Kilbarchan

Habbies Bar & Grill ✔

25 New Street, PA10 2LN

11-midnight (1am Fri & Sat); 12.30-midnight Sun

☎ (01505) 706606

3 changing beers (sourced locally) Ⓗ

Busy local pub within a conservation village and close to the famous Weaver's Cottage owned by the National Trust. Ales are from the Punch Taverns list. Both the bar and the separate Weaver's restaurant have been refurbished to a high standard. The open fire is a feature – look for Piper Habbie on the wall to the right of the fireplace. Live music plays most Saturday and Sunday nights. The beer garden is popular in summer. P (38)

Lochwinnoch

Brown Bull

32 Main Street, PA12 4AH

12-11 (midnight Fri & Sat); 12.30-11 Sun

☎ (01505) 843250

Harviestoun Bitter & Twisted; 3 changing beers (sourced regionally) Ⓗ

This village pub is a family-run free house more than 200 years old and popular with locals and visitors alike. Quiz night is Tuesday and live music features every second Sunday. An ever-changing choice of four ales is offered, mainly from Scottish breweries. At the rear is a quirky outdoor seating area and garden. The popular upstairs restaurant uses local produce and bar meals are also available. Located close to Lochwinnoch RSPB nature reserve and Castle Semple visitor centre. Q

Motherwell

Brandon Works ✔

Merry Street, ML1 1JS

8am-midnight (1am Fri & Sat) ☎ (01698) 210280

Caledonian Deuchars IPA; Greene King Abbot; changing beers (often Loch Lomond, Strathaven) Ⓗ

This busy town-centre bar, handy for buses and the main train station, is named after the works that previously occupied this site, in a town once known as Steelopolis. There are 10 handpumps with at least three guest beers available, often from local breweries. Motherwell's past is illustrated in the prints lining the walls on the upper level, depicting the long-gone industries and labour and trade union heritage. Alcohol is available from 11am.

Paisley

Bull Inn 🏆 ★ ✔

7 New Street, PA1 1XU

11-11 (1am Fri & Sat) ☎ (0141) 849 0472

4 changing beers (sourced regionally; often Kelburn, Lerwick, Loch Lomond) Ⓗ

Established in 1901 and identified by CAMRA as having a nationally important historic interior, this is the oldest inn in Paisley. The pub retains many original features including stained-glass windows, three small snugs and a spirit cask gantry, and boasts the only original set of spirit cocks left in Scotland. Four changing guest ales are from the likes of Kelburn, Jaw, Loch Lomond, Orkney, Stewart, Strathaven and Lerwick breweries. Live sport is shown on large screens in the main bar and in the snugs. Local CAMRA Pub of the Year 2018.

Last Post

2 County Square, PA1 1BN

8am-midnight (0141) 849 6911

Caledonian Deuchars IPA; Greene King Abbot; Sharp's Doom Bar; 6 changing beers H

Large Wetherspoon pub converted from the town's main post office. Open-plan in design on two levels, there is plenty of seating and good wheelchair access. The standard Wetherspoon food menu is served and six guest ales are usually available. Next to Gilmour Street railway station and close to the bus station, it is handy for a pint between trains or buses. (9,36)

Sandpiper

Glasgow Airport, PA3 2SW

5-9 (0141) 842 7858

Greene King Abbot; 4 changing beers H

Positioned on the ground floor, in the public area of the airport, The Sandpiper is ideal if you are looking for an ale before heading through security, waiting for family or friends arriving on an incoming flight or, if you are a plane spotter, in need of refreshment. With six handpumps you are spoiled for choice and can relax watching one of the many TV screens showing 24-hour news and sporting events. Opening hours are slightly longer in the summer season. Q P

Wee Howff

53 High Street, PA1 2AN

11-11 (11.30 Wed & Thu; 1am Fri; 12.30am Sat); 12.30-11 Sun (0141) 887 8299

2 changing beers (sourced nationally; often Kelburn) H

The Wee Howff has appeared in 25 editions of this Guide and is a little piece of heaven in an otherwise crowded area of cheap drinking establishments. A small traditional pub with a loyal regular clientele, the Howff offers up to three guest ales from all four corners of Britain from a quarterly rotating list. It has an open mic night on the first Monday of each month and a pub quiz every Thursday. The jukebox caters for even the most eclectic of tastes. (9,36)

Renfrew

Lord of the Isles

Unit 21 Xscape, Kings Inch Road, PA4 8XQ

8am-midnight (1am Fri & Sat) (0141) 886 8930

Caledonian Deuchars IPA; Greene King Abbot; Sharp's Doom Bar; 3 changing beers (sourced nationally) H

Large, purpose-built Wetherspoon establishment attached to the Soar leisure complex with its cinema, ski slope and rock-climbing at the Braehead shopping centre. The walls display photographs depicting the history of industry on the River Clyde. The outside seating area is a suntrap on summer days. Food is available all day and three ever-changing guest ales are on handpump. A short stroll allows you to view the ships docked at Yarrow Shipyard. P

Steam Wheeler

1 Row Avenue, G51 4SY

11-11 (10.30 Sun) (0141) 886 3995

steamwheelerpubbraehead.co.uk

Marston's Pedigree; 1 changing beer (sourced regionally) H

Modern Marston's chain family-friendly pub-restaurant, close to Braehead shopping centre and the King George V Dock, with good access to the M8 motorway. While the focus is on carvery meals, served all day, Marston's Pedigree is always on handpump and occasionally other beers from the Marston's range. Dogs are welcome in the beer garden. P

Rutherglen

An Ruadh Ghleann

40-44 Main Street, G73 2HY

8am-11.45 (midnight Fri & Sat) (0141) 613 2370

Caledonian Deuchars IPA; Greene King Abbot; 7 changing beers (sourced nationally) H

Contemporary Wetherspoon pub at the west end of the high street of one of the oldest royal burghs in Scotland. The small shop frontage leads to a long narrow room brightened up by large windows down one side. The bar is towards the middle. At the far end the room opens up, with windows providing a view of the cellar and the split-level garden and smoking area. Alcohol is served from 11am. Q

Strathaven

Weavers

1-3 Green Street, ML10 6LT

11-midnight Mon; 4.30-midnight Tue & Wed (1am Thu); 11-1am Fri & Sat; 2-1am Sun 07749 332914

4 changing beers (sourced nationally; often Strathaven) H

A family-run pub which takes its name from the traditional trade of the town. It acts as a community hub and is home to local clubs and groups, and supports the nearby Strathaven Brewery. The contemporary single-room bar, with a cosy space around the fire, is decorated with photographs of film and pop stars, and attracts a clientele who enjoy conversation. A frequent winner of local CAMRA Pub of the Year. (254,256)

Uplawmoor

Uplawmoor Hotel

66 Neilston Road, G78 4AF (off A736)

11-10 (11 Thu; midnight Fri & Sat) (01505) 850565

uplawmoor.co.uk

2 changing beers (sourced locally; often Kelburn) H

In a tranquil village setting, the building dates back to the 18th century. It was originally a coaching inn used by travellers and customs officers chasing smugglers en-route between Glasgow and the south-west coast of Scotland. Today the hotel continues to offer travellers the opportunity to relax and explore. The interior is rustic and cosy, with a public bar, pool room and lounge bar. The beer is from the local Kelburn Brewing. P (395,X44B)

SCOTLAND

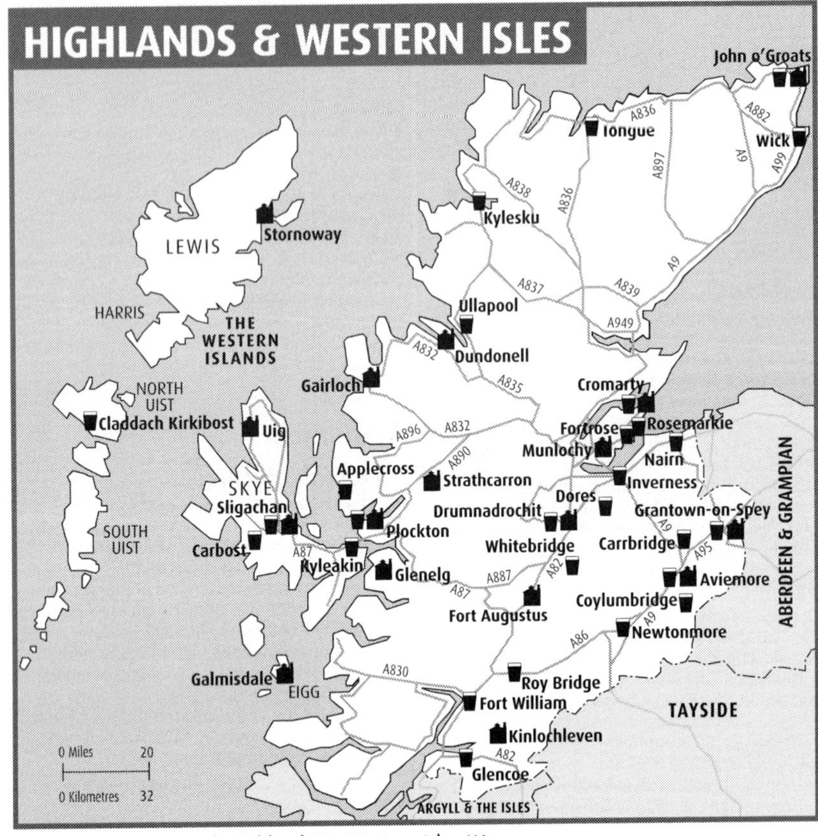

Authority areas covered: Highland UA, Western Isles UA

Applecross

Applecross Inn

Shore Street, IV54 8LR NG70974444
11-midnight (1am Fri); 12.30-11.30 Sun
(01520) 744262 applecross.uk.com/inn
2 changing beers (sourced locally; often An Teallach, Applecross, Isle of Skye)
This remote multi award-winning iconic inn is reached by a hair-raising road over the highest vehicular ascent in Britain or by a longer scenic coastal route and is well worth the journey. Various beers are served in rotation, joined by ales from the new local micro. Renowned for its local seafood and venison, with a massive chalkboard menu, the pub is a must for foodies.

Aviemore

Old Bridge Inn

23 Dalfaber Road, PH22 1PU
12-midnight (1am Fri & Sat) (01479) 811137
oldbridgeinn.co.uk
Cairngorm Stag, Trade Winds; Caledonian Deuchars IPA
Close to the gently flowing River Spey, this gem of a pub is worth seeking out and is an ideal place to relax after a busy day on the hills, or even just touring in the area. Booking is recommended for the restaurant with a quality menu using produce with low food-miles. Local entertainment is hosted most nights, and there is a selection of games and books to pass away the time over a pint. Handy for the Strathspey Steam Railway.

Winking Owl

123 Grampian Road, PH22 1RH (at N end of village)
12-11; 11-1am Fri & Sat; 12.30-11 Sun (01479) 812368
thewinkingowl.co
Cairngorm Stag, Trade Winds, Wildcat; 3 changing beers (sourced locally; often Cairngorm, Caledonian)
The Winky, reputedly the oldest hostelry in Aviemore, has been the brewery tap for the Cairngorm Brewery, half-a-mile away, since 2014. An innovative partial brewery tie means that Caledonian beers are also available. The menu has something for everyone, including children. Access to the bar on the first floor is via steps, but staff are more than happy to help if assistance is required. There are benches outside for hardy folk.

Carbost: Isle of Skye

Old Inn

IV47 8SR (on B8009) NG379318
11-1 (12.30am Sat); 12.30-11.30 Sun (01478) 640205
theoldinnskye.co.uk
3 changing beers (often Cuillin, Isle of Skye)
On the shores of Loch Harport, the Old Inn nestles on the tideline. Outside, trestle tables take

advantage of the views that Skye is famous for – there can be no better place to enjoy a pint. Three handpumps offer beers from the two Isle of Skye breweries. The pub is busy all year round with an eclectic mix of outdoor folk, and those touring Skye or visiting the Talisker Distillery close by. Seafood is top of the menu, most of it coming from the loch. Q P

Carrbridge

Cairn Hotel

Main Road, PH23 3AS (off A9 on B9153 to N of village)
12-midnight (1am Fri & Sat); 12.30-midnight Sun
(01479) 841212 cairnhotel.co.uk
3 changing beers (sourced regionally; often Cairngorm, Cromarty, Orkney)
The licensee is passionate about the beer he selects for his three handpumps and the Cairn is popular with loyal locals and the many visitors to the area. As well as the regular ales, a Two Thirsty Men beer makes an occasional appearance. The excellent pub grub is also a draw, as is the open fire on cooler days. The Cairn is the community hub of the village and can be busy when porridge-making or chainsaw-carving events are on. P

Claddach Kirkibost: North Uist

Westford Inn

HS6 5EP (2½ miles NW of Clachan on A865) NF7751066195
12-11 (midnight Fri; 1am Sat); 12.30-11 Sun
(01876) 580653
Isle of Skye Red; 2 changing beers (sourced regionally; often Fyne Ales, Isle of Skye)
The owners took on the Westford Inn in 2015 and have turned around its fortunes. Now very much the hub of the community, it hosts live music and an annual beer festival. A second Skye ale is on rotation in winter, with three ales in summer, as well as a range of bottled beers. Good-quality pub food is served. Although probably one of the most remote pubs in the Guide, it is well worth making the effort to visit. Q P

Coylumbridge

Hilton Coylumbridge (Woodshed Bar)

PH22 1QN
11-1am; 12.30-1am Sun (01479) 810661
hiltonaviemore.com
Cairngorm Trade Winds; 1 changing beer (sourced locally; often Cairngorm)
Within walking distance of Aviemore, the Woodshed Bar is set apart from the main hotel and is open to all, with ample parking. The entrance is reached by a raised walkway onto a decked area, with seating in warmer weather. On cold days the spacious interior offers comfort and a warm log fire. Two handpumps dispense the regular ale and a seasonal offering from Cairngorm Brewery. Simple pub grub is available all day and a barbecue on summer nights. P (31,37)

Cromarty

Cromarty Arms

Church Street, IV11 8XA
11-midnight; 12.30-11 Sun (01381) 600230
cromartyarms.com
Cromarty Happy Chappy; 1 changing beer (sourced locally; often Cromarty)
The Cromarty Arms is a family-run pub providing B&B accommodation and delicious home-made bar meals. A traditional music session is held on the second Friday of every month. Two handpumps are in use in summer, with beers from the Cromarty Brewery situated less than three miles away. Just opposite is NTS Hugh Miller's Cottage and Cromarty Courthouse, and in the firth you can see the oil rigs. From here you can take the seasonal four-car ferry over to Nigg. Q P

Dores

Dores Inn

IV2 6TR (on B862) NH59753476
closed Mon winter; 11-11 (midnight Fri & Sat)
(01463) 751203 thedoresinn.co.uk
4 changing beers (sourced regionally; often Cairngorm, Cromarty, Inveralmond)
Set on the shores of the north-east end of Loch Ness, the location offers excellent Nessie-spotting opportunities, and is popular all year round – a must-stop, just for the views. The cosy wood-finished bar has up to four handpumps offering ales from a selection of local and regional independents and occasionally an English ale. During the summer, a second OutDores Inn bar opens in the beer garden. Great food is available all day. Tea and coffee are served from 10am. A free minibus service is provided to/from Inverness. Q P

Drumnadrochit

Benleva Hotel

Kilmore Road, IV63 6UH (signed 800yds from A82) NH513295
11-midnight (1am Fri & Sat); 12.30-midnight Sun
(01456) 450080 benleva.co.uk
Hanging Tree First Light, After Dark, Hangmans IPA; 1 changing beer (sourced nationally)
This 300-year-old former manse is a popular, friendly village inn near Loch Ness. The sweet chestnut outside was once a hanging tree. Four handpumps dispense ales from the pub's own Hanging Tree Brewery and others in rotation from Scottish and UK breweries. Good home-made classic food features locally-sourced produce.

REAL ALE BREWERIES

An Teallach Dundonell
Black Isle Munlochy
Cairngorm Aviemore
Cromarty Cromarty
Cuillin Sligachan: Isle of Skye
Dun Glenelg (NEW)
Hanging Tree Drumnadrochit (NEW)
Hebridean Stornoway: Isle of Lewis
Isle of Skye Uig: Isle of Skye
John o'Groats John o'Groats
Laig Bay Galmisdale: Isle of Eigg
Nessie Fort Augustus
Old Inn Gairloch
Plockton Plockton
River Leven Kinlochleven
Strathcarron Strathcarron
Two Thirsty Men Grantown-on-Spey

Entertainment includes live music once a fortnight and occasional quiz nights. The pub hosts the famous Loch Ness Beer Festival in September. Handy for Urquhart Castle and all the Loch Ness attractions. ♞❀🛏◐⛺♣P🚌🐾📶

Fort William

Ben Nevis Inn Ⓛ

Achintee Road, Claggan, PH33 6TE (1½ miles from Spar shop at Claggan Rd) NN12477293
✪ 12-11 summer; winter hours vary ☎ (01397) 701227
🌐 ben-nevis-inn.co.uk
3 changing beers (sourced locally; often Cairngorm, Isle of Skye, River Leven) Ⓗ
Traditional stone-built barn at the start of the Ben Nevis mountain path, popular with outdoor enthusiasts. The small bar counter has three handpumps offering beers from local breweries. The interior, with long beer hall-style tables and a beckoning stove, is a warm, informal and friendly setting, an ideal venue for the regular live music. The hearty menu changes daily and is available until 9pm. Bunkhouse accommodation sleeps 24 people. Check ahead for opening hours in winter. Q❀🛏◐♿⛺P

Great Glen ✔

104 High Street, PH33 6AD (S end of pedestrianised area)
✪ 7am-midnight (1am Fri & Sat) ☎ (01397) 709910
Adnams Broadside; Caledonian Deuchars IPA; house beer (by Strathaven); 8 changing beers (sourced nationally) Ⓗ
Purpose-built in 2013, with a spacious and modern interior, this Wetherspoon pub is named after the 78-mile Great Glen (An Gleann Mor), the geological feature that runs up to Inverness. The decor is very much linked to local attractions, businesses and people. Up to 10 handpumps offer mostly local and regional beers, and the usual guests. An outside seating area is reached by an internal staircase. Alcohol is served from 11am (noon Sunday). ♞❀🛏◐♿≷P🚌📶

Grog & Gruel Ⓛ ✔

66 High Street, PH33 6AE (in pedestrianised area)
✪ 12-midnight; 12.30-midnight Sun summer; 12-11.30 Mon-Wed (12.30am Thu-Sat); 5-11.30 Sun winter
☎ (01397) 705078 🌐 grogandgruel.co.uk
6 changing beers (sourced locally; often Loch Lomond, River Leven) Ⓗ
The Grog is busy throughout the year and has justifiably featured in the Guide since 1997. A real draw for ale enthusiasts, it offers a combination of up to six beers from local breweries, including River Leven, and regional breweries, plus a great food menu. The upstairs restaurant opens in the evening to provide more tables. What better place to end the 96-mile walk along the West Highland Way? Entertainment is hosted most evenings and there is an annual beer festival. ♞◐⛺≷🍎🚌🐾📶

Fortrose

Anderson

Union Street, IV10 8TD (on high street)
✪ 4-11.30; closed Sun-Tue winter ☎ (01381) 620236
🌐 theanderson.co.uk
3 changing beers (sourced nationally; often Cromarty, Inveralmond) Ⓗ
Not only is owner Jim Anderson a beer writer, but he fanatically keeps his real ale in tip-top condition in the natural cellar. Three handpumps offer mostly Scottish ales and a fourth dispenses real cider. More than 100 Belgian and 30 Mikkeller bottled beers are also kept as well as approaching 300 malts. The multi award-winning kitchen has a well-deserved reputation for foodie excellence. Quiz, music, film and knitting nights are weekly regulars, complemented by mini beer festivals and special food nights. Closed November to early December. Q♞❀🛏◑♿⛺♣🍎P🚌🐾📶

Glencoe

Clachaig Inn Ⓛ ✔

Glencoe, PH49 4HX (3 miles SE of Glencoe village, off A82) NN12705668
✪ 10-11 (midnight Sat); 12.30-11 Sun ☎ (01855) 811252
🌐 clachaig.com
10 changing beers (sourced locally; often Cairngorm, Orkney, River Leven) Ⓗ
Isolated amid breathtaking scenery, the Clachaig has been a regular in the Guide since 1984. This real ale stronghold has a forest of handpumps in its three open-plan bars offering mainly Scottish beers to suit all tastes. Although quieter during the day, it is busy in the evening when walkers and climbers descend to slake thirsts and fill hungry stomachs with hearty fare after a day out on the hills. Superlatives abound, as do the wood-burning stoves that keep the place warm and cosy. ♞❀🛏◐♿♣P📶

Grantown on Spey

High St Merchants

74-76 High Street, PH26 3EL (S side of High St)
✪ closed Mon; 10-5 (10 Fri & Sat); 10-4 Sun
☎ (01479) 872246 🌐 thehighstmerchants.com
Two Thirsty Men Spey IPA, No.74 Ⓗ
High St Merchants is a small café and brew bar in the capital of Strathspey, offering a warm and friendly welcome in a relaxing ambience. The beers are from the Two Thirsty Men brewery situated just out the back – this is as LocAle as you can get! The walls are adorned with work by local artists. Q♞❀◐P🚌

Inverness

Black Isle Bar Ⓛ

68 Church Street, IV1 1EN
✪ 11-1am ☎ (01463) 229920 🌐 blackislebar.com
Black Isle Yellowhammer, Red Kite; 4 changing beers (sourced locally; often Black Isle) Ⓟ
Opened in 2016, the bar has grown in popularity, offering up to six real ales and 20 font beers. Two big screens show the beer menu, with prices for pints, halves and thirds. The open-plan bar area offers a mix of seating including comfy sofas. Upstairs is a secret garden with upcycled cable drums, pallet tables and stools under a cover of reclaimed corrugated iron. Other than pizza prepared on site, sides, salads and soups are available. Q🛏◐♿≷P🚌📶

Castle Tavern Ⓛ

1 View Place, IV2 4SA (top of Castle St)
✪ 11-1am (12.30am Sat); 12-midnight Sun
☎ (01463) 718178 🌐 castletavern.pub

6 changing beers (sourced regionally; often Cromarty, Isle of Skye, Windswept) 🄷
A five-minute walk from the centre of town will take you to the Castle Tavern, a pub popular with tourists visiting the castle opposite – and locals who know their beer. The impressive covered canopy area is always busy, even in winter, with fine views along the River Ness. Inside, six handpumps offer a changing selection of beers and styles from Scottish independents, and a few LocAles. Bar meals are available all day and there is a restaurant upstairs for evening meals.

Clachnaharry Inn
17-19 High Street, IV3 8RB (on A862 Beauly road)
11-11 (midnight Thu; 1am Fri & Sat); 12-11 Sun
☎ (01463) 239806 clachnaharryinn.co.uk
Fyne Ales Jarl; Harviestoun Bitter & Twisted; Inveralmond Ossian; 1 changing beer (sourced nationally; often Cairngorm, Greene King, Timothy Taylor) 🄷
The Clach has featured in the Guide for more than 30 years and is the place where many have discovered the joys of real ale. The 17th-century coaching inn is a must-visit pub, with a warm welcome for all. The bar oozes heritage, with an open fire on cooler days. Food is available in the bar area and the quieter dining area. On warmer days, the view from the terrace over the Caledonian Canal sea locks and Beauly Firth with Ben Wyvis beyond never fails to satisfy. Wednesday is quiz night, Scottish music jam on Thursday. Q P (28,28A)

King's Highway
72-74 Church Street, IV1 1EN (towards N end of Church St)
7am-1am ☎ (01463) 251830
Adnams Broadside; Caledonian Deuchars IPA; Fuller's London Pride; Greene King Abbot; Sharp's Doom Bar; 5 changing beers (often An Teallach) 🄷
Conveniently situated just a few minutes from the main shopping area, bus and train stations, King's Highway is an ideal place to meet up. It is busy from 7am onwards, with customers taking advantage of its breakfast, tea and coffee. Like many Wetherspoon pubs, it offers good-value fare throughout the day and is popular with a wide clientele including families. Up to 10 real ales are available, generally Scottish, with many local to the Highland area. Alcohol is served from 11am. A Wetherlodge provides accommodation.

MacGregor's
109-113 Academy Street, IV1 1LX (on corner of Academy St & Friars Lane)
11-1, 3-12.30am; closed Mon winter ☎ (01463) 719629
macgregorsbars.com
2 changing beers (sourced locally; often Cromarty, Spey Valley, Swannay)
A newcomer to Inverness in 2017 and an instant hit, offering an insight into Scottish history, culture, food and drink. Two handpumps offer different beers from local breweries and you never know what is going to be on until you get there. There is also an extensive collection of bottled beers to choose from. The main bar is in one area while a second is reached by a short corridor. The bar is a brainchild of musician Bruce MacGregor of Blazin' Fiddles, who is a regular attendee, particularly on a Sunday afternoon. P

Number 27
27 Castle Street, IV2 3DU
11-11 (12.30am Fri & Sat); 12.30-11 Sun
☎ (01463) 241999
4 changing beers (sourced regionally; often Speyside Craft, Windswept) 🄷
This popular city-centre bar-restaurant has four handpumps plus a large bottle and keg range including continental brews. A good selection of malt whiskies is also stocked. The venue has a reputation for good food – lunches range from sandwiches to light bites while the evening menu features traditional main courses made with locally sourced ingredients including venison and steak.

John o' Groats

Seaview Hotel
County Road, KW1 4YR (at A99/A863 jct) ND380727
11-midnight (1am Fri & Sat); 12-midnight Sun
☎ (01955) 611220 seaviewjohnogroats.co.uk
John o' Groats Swelkie; 1 changing beer (sourced locally; often John o' Groats) 🄷
The family-run Seaview Hotel has got to be the most northerly pub on the UK mainland and is the tap for nearby John o' Groats Brewery. The 26 rooms are well used by End to Enders, either beginning the John o' Groats to Lands End (JoGLE) route or ending (LEJoG) the 838-mile journey by road or 1,200 miles on foot. Rooms are in the hotel itself, the cottage or the annexe over the road. Meals are served throughout the day.
P

Kyleakin: Isle of Skye

Saucy Mary's
Main Street, IV41 8PL (from Skye Bridge, take first left at roundabout into Kyleakin, pub is approx 500yds on right)
11.30-1am ☎ (01599) 537062 saucymarys.com
Isle of Skye Red, Black; 1 changing beer (sourced locally; often Isle of Skye) 🄷
The bar overlooks the waterfront at Kyleakin, close to where the old ferry landing point was, now bypassed by the Skye Bridge. Two handpumps normally offer Skye Red and Black during the season, but occasionally a different Isle of Skye beer may be available. With a mission to deliver warm, comfortable and clean accommodation, the pub is an excellent place to stay if touring Skye and the Lochalsh area, and offers plenty of bunkhouse and guest house accommodation. The restaurant offers fresh meals using Scottish produce.
P

Kylesku

Kylesku Hotel
IV27 4HW (⅓ mile from A894) NC229337
11 (12.30 Sun)-11; closed Dec to mid-Feb
☎ (01971) 502231 kyleskuhotel.co.uk
Isle of Skye Red; Orkney Dark Island; 2 changing beers (sourced regionally; often Isle of Skye, Orkney) 🄷
Kylesku Hotel offers spectacular views of the loch and mountains. The hotel entrance is adorned with awards for its food over the years – this is a foodies' paradise. The crystal clear waters yield all the seafood, the venison is wild and the lamb and beef are also local (food served 8am-9pm). Four handpumps dispense the ales alongside an

SCOTLAND

excellent selection of bottles. On the North Coast 500 route, accommodation tends to be booked months in advance. Q🐴✿🛏◑♿P🚌🐾📶

Nairn

Braeval Hotel Ⓛ ✔

Crescent Road, IV12 4NB (E end of town, near beach)
⏲ 12-11 (midnight Fri & Sat) summer; 4-10; 12-midnight Fri & Sat; 12-10 Sun winter ☎ (01667) 452341
🌐 braevalhotel.co.uk

9 changing beers (sourced nationally; often Cairngorm, Cromarty, Orkney) 🄷

The family-run hotel's Bandstand Bar has up to nine handpumps offering an excellent selection of local and regional Scottish ales, with the occasional English brew. Live music plays every weekend. The biggest independent beer festival in the Highlands is held here after Easter with around 150 ales and 10 ciders, alongside excellent live music. The Seaview Restaurant offers fine food and great views. Winner of CAMRA Highland Pub of the Year three times. Q🐴✿🛏◑♿⛺⇌(10,11)♣●P🚌📶

Newtonmore

Glen Hotel Ⓛ

Main Street, PH20 1DD (S of village)
⏲ 11-11; 12.30-11 Sun ☎ (01540) 673203
🌐 theglenhotel.co.uk

4 changing beers (often Cairngorm, Caledonian) 🄷

This is the first of what now totals 200 real ale pubs as you enter the CAMRA branch area travelling north up the A9. The Glen was a trailblazer in what was a real ale desert – it now offers up to four handpumps featuring Cairngorm, Caledonian and guest beers, plus real cider in the summer. Good honest pub grub is served in the comfy bar, restaurant and outside on trestle tables. Quiz nights and a games room make this a popular evening retreat for locals and visitors alike.
🐴🛏◑♿⛺⇌P🚌📶

Plockton

Plockton Hotel ✔

41 Harbour Street, IV52 8TN NG80293343
⏲ 11-midnight; 12.30-11 Sun ☎ (01599) 544274
🌐 plocktonhotel.co.uk

5 changing beers (sourced regionally; often Cromarty, Fyne Ales, Swannay) 🄷

Plockton was the setting for TV's Hamish Macbeth, which is a draw for visitors to this pretty village, many of whom arrive by train on the picturesque Kyle Line. The bar proudly offers four handpumps dispensing both local and regional beers as well as a tempting food menu featuring locally sourced seafood, beef and venison. Take your beer onto the terrace and from the shade of the palm trees watch the tide. A real ale and gin festival is held in May. Closed throughout January. Q🐴✿🛏◑♿P▯🚌📶

Rosemarkie

Plough Inn ★

48 High Street, IV10 8UF (on A832)
⏲ closed Mon winter; 11-midnight (1am Fri & Sat); 12-midnight Sun ☎ (01381) 620164

Cromarty Happy Chappy; 1 changing beer (sourced locally; often Cromarty) 🄷

Identified by CAMRA as having a nationally important historic pub interior, this distinctive old country inn in a pretty village is built with the local red sandstone and is unmissable with its distinctive leaning gable. Inside, it has a cosy wood-lined bar and an ancient marriage stone lintel dated 1691 over the fireplace. Two handpumps offer beers from the Cromarty brewery, less than six miles away. There are trestle tables outside in a small enclosed suntrap grassed area, and the walls of the pub give off their heat long after the sun has moved round. Q🐴✿◑♿⛺♣P🚌🐾📶

Roy Bridge

Stronlossit Inn Ⓛ ✔

Main Street, PH31 4AG (on A86) NN27228117
⏲ 11-11.45 (1am Thu-Sat); 12.30-11.45 Sun
☎ (01397) 712253 🌐 stronlossit.co.uk

4 changing beers (sourced locally; often Cairngorm, Isle of Skye, Orkney) 🄷

The location of the Stronlossitt makes it attractive to those keen on the outdoors, and with the railway station just over the road, you can abandon the car and arrive by train from Fort William or London. The train can also take you for a day trip to Corrour to walk around Loch Ossian. Four handpumps spoil real ale fans, with beers from local Scottish breweries – more real ale is thought to be sold here than keg. Great food is available all day as well as rooms for all budgets.
Q🐴✿🛏◑♿⛺⇌●P🚌📶

Sligachan: Isle of Skye

Sligachan Hotel (Seumas' Bar) Ⓛ

IV47 8SW (jct of A87/A863) NG485298
⏲ 10-11 ☎ (01478) 650204 🌐 sligachan.co.uk

Cuillin Eagle Ale, Old Bridge, Black Face; 1 changing beer 🄷

Home to the Cuillin Brewery, the Sligachan Hotel has served mountaineers, walkers and lovers of the wild Highland scenery for nearly 180 years and has been in the same family for the last 100 years. The hotel opens March to the end of October, with the larger Seumas' Bar open May to September, where up to four ales are available in season, usually from Cuillin but sometimes from elsewhere. Over 370 Scottish malts are also on offer, 90 on optics. 🐴✿🛏◑♿⛺P🚌🐾📶

Tongue

Tongue Hotel

IV27 4XD (on A838 ½ mile from A836) NC590568
⏲ 12-11 (1am Fri & Sat); 12.30-11 Sun ☎ (01847) 611206
🌐 tonguehotel.co.uk

1 changing beer (sourced regionally; often Orkney)

This former hunting lodge is in a village on the north coast of the Scottish Highlands on Route 500. There are two bars, the Falcon in the main hotel and the Brass Tap to the rear, open March to October, named because of the brass tap set into the bar – a drop of water from it to 'let the dram breathe'. A large choice of whisky and gin is available alongside the Orkney brews. Lining the walls is an impressive selection of stuffed animals and birds. Q🐴🛏◑♿♣P🚌🐾📶

Ullapool

Morefield Motel Ⓛ

North Road, IV26 2TQ (just off A835)
⏲ 12-11 ☎ (01854) 612000 🌐 morefieldmotel.co.uk

3 changing beers (sourced locally; often An Teallach, Cairngorm) 🄷
The family-friendly and homely Morefield Motel is a popular place to stay for those exploring the spectacular west coast, or overnighting to catch the ferry to the Western Isles. Ullapool is a pretty fishing village and you can be assured that fresh seafood takes centre stage. The bar is open to all, with three handpumps featuring Scottish beers including at least one from An Teallach. A well-attended beer festival is held in October.
Q❀🛏◐♿▲♣P🚌🐾📶

Whitebridge

Whitebridge Hotel 🄻

IV2 6UN (on B862 SE of Loch Ness) NH487152
🕐 12-11 summer; 12-2, 5-11; 12-11 Sat & Sun winter
☎ (01456) 486226 🌐 whitebridgehotel.co.uk
3 changing beers (often Cairngorm, Cromarty, Orkney)
Built in 1899 and located on the quiet east side of Loch Ness, this 2-star hotel has fishing rights on three local lochs. Inside, the attractive pitch pine-panelled bar has a welcoming wood-burning stove. An adjacent room has a pool table and also a separate area for dining. Three ales are usually available, one or two in winter. The traditional pub food is all home cooked. The hotel has a green tourism policy. **Q❀🛏◐♿♣P🚌🐾📶**

Wick

Mackays Hotel (Cocktail Bar) 🄻

1 Ebenezer Place, Union Street, KW1 5ED (close to bridge)
🕐 11-11 ☎ (01955) 602323 🌐 mackayshotel.co.uk
1 changing beer (sourced locally; often John o' Groats) 🄷
Mackays Hotel is in the Guinness Book of Records as being on the shortest street in the world – the front door of the bistro is the only building. In the bar it has just one handpump, serving either Swelkie or Duncansby from John o' Groats Brewery 16 miles away. Wick is a pretty town and a convenient stopping-off point on the way to John o' Groats, or a base to explore the landscape and features of Caithness's sometimes wild but stunning coast and hinterland. **Q🛏◐♿▲⇌P🚌**

View from Plockton Hotel, Plockton (Photo: Simon Urry)

KINGDOM OF FIFE

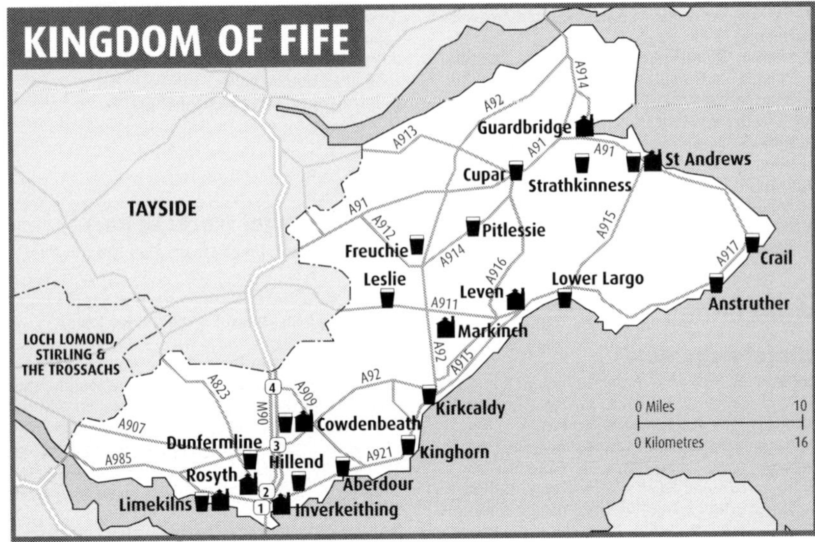

Authority area covered: Fife UA

Aberdour

Foresters Arms

35 High Street, KY3 0SJ

11-midnight (1am Fri); 10-1am Sat ☎ (01383) 860809

forries.co.uk

4 changing beers (sourced nationally; often Caledonian, Redcastle, Stewart) Ⓗ

Situated in the centre of the village, convenient for the railway station, castle, beaches and harbour. Bingo is played every Sunday afternoon and there is a monthly quiz. It has a jukebox and a pool table. The pub serves breakfast and lunchtime meals, and is a popular stop-off for walkers on the Fife Coastal Path. A repeat winner of local CAMRA Pub of the Year. (7)

Anstruther

Boathouse ✔

28 Shore Street, KY10 3AQ

12-11 (midnight Fri & Sat) ☎ (01333) 312105

at-the-shore.co.uk

House beer (by Eden Mill); 2 changing beers (sourced nationally; often Adnams) Ⓗ

Fomerly an 18th-century coaching inn, the Boathouse can be found in the middle of town by the harbour. It has two main rooms – the main bar area and a bistro where you can enjoy fresh locally prepared meals while taking in views of the sea. Three ales are on offer including the house ale, Harbour Craft. At the back of the bar is a games area with a pool table. Accommodation is offered in three en-suite rooms.
(X60,95)

Ship Tavern

49 Shore Street, KY10 3AQ

11-midnight (1am Fri & Sat); 12.30-midnight Sun
☎ (01333) 310347

2 changing beers (sourced nationally) Ⓗ

Right on the harbour front next door to the fishery museum, this traditional pub is a popular meeting place for fishermen, locals and visitors to the waterfront. The bar has all the character you would expect from a historic fishing village inn. Two ever-changing ales come from regional or national brewers. Sit back, relax and enjoy the views across the harbour. Q (X60,95)

Cowdenbeath

Woodside Hotel L

109 Broad Street, KY4 8JR

11-midnight; 12.30-midnight Sun ☎ (01383) 511598

woodsidehotelcowdenbeath.co.uk

1 changing beer (often Beath, Sharp's, Swannay) Ⓗ

Large single-roomed bar with two handpumps serving ales from local and north of England microbreweries in lined glasses. One side of the room has a pool table and dartboard, and four plasma screens show sport. A warm, friendly atmosphere prevails, with live entertainment at the weekend. A separate lounge is available for functions. Outside, a covered, decked area with seating is a lovely suntrap in summer.
P

Crail

Golf Hotel ✔

4 High Street, KY10 3TD

11-11 (midnight Sat & Sun) ☎ (01333) 450206

thegolfhotelcrail.com

3 changing beers (sourced nationally) Ⓗ

The Golf Hotel is a listed 16th-century coaching inn in a picturesque village in the East Neuk of Fife. The historic bar dates back to 1721, making it one of

REAL ALE BREWERIES

Beath Cowdenbeath
Brew Shed Limekilns
Craft Originale Markinch
Eden St Andrews Guardbridge
Inner Bay Inverkeithing
Kingdom Rosyth
Luckie Leven
St Andrews St Andrews

the oldest in Scotland. The room retains the original low-beamed ceiling, wooden floor and a 16th-century fireplace with a marriage lintel over it bearing the initials of the original owners. Relax with a beer in the garden or enjoy a meal in the restaurant after walking the coastal path. ❀⇆◐P🚌(95)🐾📶

Cupar

Boudingait 𝕃

43 Bonnygate, KY15 4BU

🕐 11-11 (midnight Thu; 1am Fri & Sat); 11-midnight Sun
☎ (01334) 654681 🌐 theboudingaitcupar.co.uk

2 changing beers (sourced regionally; often Eden Mill, Orkney) Ⓗ

A wee gem hidden off Main Street in Cupar. This bustling family-friendly outlet is traditionally decorated with a rustic feel. Two handpulls feature a variety of regional and local ales from Eden Mill and Orkney breweries. Meals are served daily and a loyalty card is available. A quiz night features weekly, live music fortnightly, and bingo every Sunday evening. ◐&≠🚌📶

Dunfermline

Commercial Inn 𝕃

13 Douglas Street, KY12 7EB

🕐 10-11 (midnight Fri & Sat) ☎ (01383) 733876

7 changing beers (sourced nationally; often Beath, Eden Mill) Ⓗ

A warm, welcoming hostelry in a historic building dating back to the 1820s and just a short walk from the High Street across from the old post office. This classic wood-panelled pub has a homely feel, with good food and friendly service attracting an eclectic clientele. A great variety of ales is available on seven handpulls as well as a real cider. Local CAMRA Pub of the Year on a number of occasions and a Scottish Pub of the Year finalist. ◐≠🍎🚌📶

East Port Bar

7 East Port, KY12 7JG

🕐 11-11 (midnight Fri & Sat); 12-11 Sun ☎ (01383) 736678

4 changing beers (sourced nationally; often Born in the Borders, Orkney, Timothy Taylor) Ⓗ

The East Port Bar is a terrific place to visit during a day out in Dunfermline. This busy town-centre bar has cosy sofas and booths in which to enjoy a drink or two. The interior features wood panelling and a wood bar and gantry, with soft background music usually playing. Value-for-money food is served at lunchtime. Sport from football to golf is shown on plasma screens. ❀◐&≠🚌📶

Freuchie

Albert Tavern

2 High Street, KY15 7EX

🕐 5-midnight; 12-1am Fri & Sat; 12.30-midnight Sun
☎ 07876 178863 🌐 alberttavern.wixsite.com/albert

5 changing beers (sourced nationally; often Elland, Mallinsons, Phoenix) Ⓗ

A cosy local with a low-beamed ceiling reminiscent of an English village pub. The small bar has five handpumps with an ever-changing choice of ales from microbreweries from Devon to Orkney. The lounge hosts various events such as a malt whisky club and is busy during rugby internationals. The village is renowned for its cricket team, once national village champions. A multi award-winning local CAMRA Pub of the Year and twice the Scottish Pub of the Year winner. Q❀🍎🚌🐾

Hillend

Hillend Tavern 🏆 𝕃 ✔

37 Main Street, KY11 9ND

🕐 4-midnight; 3-midnight Fri; 1-midnight Sat & Sun
☎ (01383) 415391 🌐 hillendtavern.co.uk

4 changing beers (sourced nationally; often Eden Mill, Fyne Ales, Timothy Taylor) Ⓗ

A small, welcoming pub with two real fires. This hidden gem not far from Dalgety Bay has a spacious room at the back and a large covered area outside. At the heart of the village community, the Hillend offers a wide variety of traditional events, live music, TV sport such as rugby, quizzes and karaoke. Four handpulls dispense a wide range of local, regional and national ales. Local CAMRA Pub of the Year 2017 and 2018. ❀≠🚌(7,87)🐾

Kinghorn

Crown Tavern 𝕃 ✔

55-57 High Street, KY3 9UW

🕐 11-midnight (1am Fri & Sat); 12-midnight Sun
☎ (01592) 890340

2 changing beers (sourced nationally; often Craft Originale, Tryst) Ⓐ

A lively two-roomed local, also called the Middle Bar, situated in a pleasant coastal village. It has attractive stained-glass windows and high ceilings featuring ornate plasterwork. TVs screens show a wide variety of sporting events and a pool table can be found to the rear. Two real ales are served through a pair of tall fonts, alongside two real ciders. The pub hosts a Sunday quiz. Current local Cider Pub of the Year. ≠♣🍎🚌(7)🐾📶

Kirkcaldy

Betty Nicols

297 High Street, KY1 1JL

🕐 12-8.30 (11 Thu; midnight Fri); 11-midnight Sat; 1-8 Sun
☎ (01592) 642083 🌐 bettynicolsbarandbistro.co.uk

2 changing beers (sourced regionally; often Broughton, Fyne Ales) Ⓗ

A longstanding real ale venue in the town of Kirkcaldy, serving quality drinks in a relaxing and comfortable atmosphere. The traditional bar attracts people of all ages with a good range of beers, while the modern bistro serves lunchtime meals and afternoon teas (booking required). Live music plays every Thursday, and a well-attended quiz is held on the first Tuesday and third Thursday of the month. ◐&≠🚌🐾📶

Harbour Bar

471-475 High Street, KY1 2SN

🕐 11-3 (not Mon & Tue), 5-midnight; 11-midnight Fri & Sat; 12-midnight Sun ☎ (01592) 264270

6 changing beers (sourced nationally; often Fyne Ales, Mallinsons, Saltaire) Ⓗ

The building dates from around 1870 and became a pub in 1924. Featured in Scotland's True Heritage Pubs and Grade C listed it retains a rare jug bar. Six handpulls serve up to 20 changing real ales from microbreweries all over the UK, along with a real cider. Celebrating 25 consecutive years in the Guide in 2018, the pub is a previous winner of local CAMRA and Scottish Pub of the Year. Q🍎🚌🐾

Leslie

Burns Tavern

184 High Street, KY6 3DB

11-midnight (1am Fri & Sat); 12.30-midnight Sun

☎ (01592) 741345

Timothy Taylor Landlord; 1 changing beer (sourced nationally; often Kelburn, Stewart) H

A friendly two-roomed local pub in a small former paper-making town, north of Glenrothes. The public bar is split-level with the bar on the lower level and a pool table on the upper. The spacious lounge hosts karaoke on Saturday, folk music on Sunday and a quiz on Thursday. Unusually for the area, Timothy Taylor Landlord is always on handpump. Q❀▲♣P🚌(39A)🐾

Limekilns

Ship Inn L

Halketts Hall, KY11 3HJ

10-11 (midnight Fri & Sat); 11-11 Sun ☎ (01383) 872247

3 changing beers (sourced nationally; often Blue Monkey, Brew Shed, Kent) H

The first pub in Fife to be accredited on the LocAle 2017 scheme for stocking Brew Shed ales, brewed in Limekilns. Three guest beers are available from microbreweries throughout the UK. Set on the River Forth, the pub has excellent views across the water. The bar has a cosy alcove to the left, and ship memorabilia on the walls. Meals are served lunchtimes, with fish and seafood the speciality (booking is essential). Q❀◐P🚌(6)

Lower Largo

Railway Inn L

1 Station Wynd, KY8 6BU

11-midnight (1am Thu-Sat) ☎ (01333) 320239

railwayinnlargo.co.uk

5 changing beers (sourced nationally; often Born in the Borders, Eden Mill) H

This friendly and traditional village pub has been established in Lower Largo, close to the picturesque harbour, since 1749. The current owners took over in 2013. The small two-roomed interior is warmed by a cosy real fire. Situated near the East Neuk section of the Fife Coastal Path, it is a firm favourite with ramblers, dog walkers and locals. Bar snacks are available. Five handpumps serve beers from all over the UK. Q❀🚌(95)🐾

Pitlessie

Village Inn

Cupar Road, KY15 7SU

12-2.30, 5-11 (midnight Thu); 12-midnight Fri; 12-11.30 Sat; 12-11 Sun ☎ (01337) 830595 pitlessievillageinn.com

2 changing beers (sourced nationally) H

A family-run business with a warm ambience in the bar and restaurant, serving great-value freshly produced meals and using the best seasonal produce from around Scotland. The former coaching inn is decorated with pictures of the maltings that were once opposite. A lovely real fire adds warmth to the wood-panelled, stone and plaster-walled bar. The room has a corner bar with bar stools and a separate seating area for bar meals or drinks. Two varying ales are offered. ◐●P🚌

St Andrews

Central Bar L ✔

77 Market Street, KY16 9NU

11 11.30 (midnight Fri & Sat); 12.30-11.30 Sun

☎ (01334) 478296 centralbar-standrews.co.uk

Eden Mill Blonde, Shipwreck IPA; 6 changing beers (sourced nationally; often Belhaven, Strathaven) H

As the name suggests, this large bar is centrally located in the town of St Andrews. A Greene King outlet, it has a Victorian-style island bar, large windows and ornate mirrors. A good mix of students, tourists and locals adds to the character of the pub. Live sport is shown on TV and bar meals are available all day. A wide selection of ales is dispensed from eight handpulls including local beers from Eden Mill. ❀◐♿🚌

Criterion L ✔

99 South Street, KY16 9QW

10-midnight (1am Fri & Sat) ☎ (01334) 474543

criterionstandrews.co.uk

Caledonian Deuchars IPA, Edinburgh Castle 80/-; 2 changing beers (sourced nationally; often Eden Mill, St Andrews) H

A cracking family-run pub at the seaward end of South Street. Relax with a few drinks and watch life go by in this bustling university town. Oak-panelled walls are adorned with photographs of St Andrews in days gone by. The pub is renowned for its home-made locally sourced meals and its legendary Cri Pie, available all day. Background music plays and the TV shows live sport. Weekly open music nights and the Sunday quiz are popular with visitors. ❀◐●🚌🐾

St Andrews Brewing Co L

177 South Street, KY16 9EE

11-midnight ☎ (01334) 471111

standrewsbrewingcompany.com

4 changing beers (sourced nationally; often Fyne Ales, St Andrews) H

This craft brewpub showcases a wide range of St Andrews Brewing Co beers in cask, keg and bottle, with 18 taps available – four dedicated to cask ales, two to STABCO ales, plus guest ales and a craft cider. Third-pint glasses are available. The pub is popular with students, tourists and visitors alike, with drinking areas downstairs by the fireplace or upstairs in the beer hall. Q❀◐♿♣●🚌🐾

Strathkinness

Tavern at Strathkinness

4 High Road, KY16 9RS

5-11; 12-1am Fri & Sat; 12-midnight Sun

☎ (01334) 850085 strathkinnesstavern.co.uk

2 changing beers (sourced nationally; often Cromarty, Strath Mash) H

The Tavern, owned and run by the same family for the past decade, is at the heart of the village and well known for its welcoming hosts, great food and cracking ales. The pub has recently started Strath Mash Brewing, an on-site microbrewery, and its ales are often on sale. Quiz nights and folk evenings are regular events. There is seating outside at the front of the building with lovely views over the river estuary. Q❀◐▲♣P🚌(64,64A)

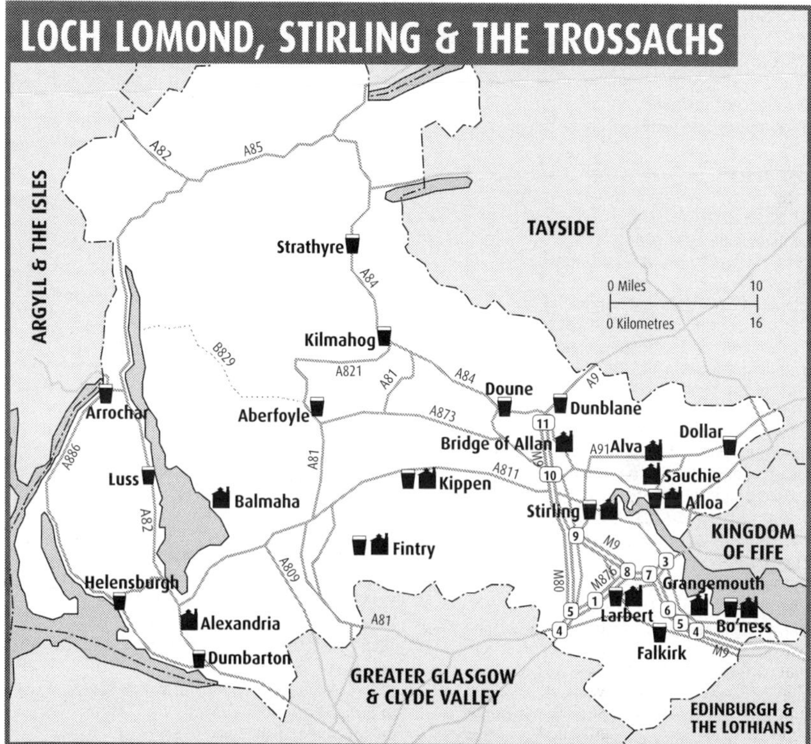

Authority areas covered: Argyll & Bute UA (part), Clackmannanshire UA, Falkirk UA, Stirling UA, West Dumbartonshire UA

Aberfoyle

Forth Inn ✓

Main Street, FK8 3UQ

10am-midnight (1am Fri & Sat) ☎ (01877) 382372

forthinn.com

Harviestoun Schiehallion; 4 changing beers (sourced regionally; often Belhaven, Cairngorm, Fallen) H

This 100-year-old inn is situated by the River Forth within the Trossachs National Park. The cosy wood-panelled bar is decorated with old photographs of the area and is a magnet for tourists and locals alike. The innovative landlord is proud to serve only Scottish ales from up to eight handpumps, with third-pint taster glasses available, and wholesome food featuring locally sourced produce. There is a separate dining room and a 'baronial' dining hall. Licensed from 11am. Q❀◑♿P (C11)

Alloa

Bobbing John ✓

46 Drysdale Street, FK10 1JL

8am-midnight (1am Fri & Sat); 8am-11 Sun

☎ (01259) 222590

Caledonian Deuchars IPA; Greene King Abbot; Sharp's Doom Bar; 2 changing beers (often An Teallach, Black Wolf) H

The pub is in a traditional three-storey sandstone building, purpose-built in 1895 for the Alloa Co-operative Society. Its name refers to Alloa-born John Erskine who created industrial Alloa, developing the town as a coal-mining centre. He was twice Secretary of State for Scotland under Queen Anne; however, his frequent changes of political allegiance earned him the nickname 'Bobbing John'. Much of the building's original stone has been retained and a Victorian shop front reintroduced. Alcohol is served from 11am. ❀◑♿

Arrochar

Village Inn ✓

Shore Road, G83 7AX (down A814 from A83 jct)

11-11 (midnight Fri & Sat); 12-11 Sun ☎ (01301) 702279

villageinnarrochar.co.uk

5 changing beers (sourced nationally; often Fyne Ales, Loch Lomond Brewery) H

Attractive pub set back from the road, originally built in 1827 as the local manse. Its position on the shore of Loch Long allows it excellent views across to the Cobbler and Arrochar Alps, especially from

REAL ALE BREWERIES

Balmaha Balmaha
Black Wolf Stirling
Devon Sauchie
Fallen Kippen
Fintry Fintry
Harviestoun Alva
Hybrid Grangemouth
Kinneil Bo'ness
Loch Lomond Alexandria
Tryst Larbert
Wash House Bridge of Allan
Williams Bros Alloa

the garden seating in the front. The large open log fire and hardwood floor and fittings give the public bar a cosy, welcoming ambience. Food is available all day and served throughout the pub, not just in the adjacent restaurant.
P (926,976)

Bo'ness

Corbie Inn

84 Corbiehall, EH51 0AS
12-11; 12.30-11 Sun (01506) 825307
corbieinn.co.uk
Changing beers (sourced nationally) H
This pub opened in 2011 and has been handcrafted by the owners. Six ales are usually on handpump, including one from the Kinneil Brew Hoose at the back of the premises. An ideal refreshment stop after a visit to the Bo'ness & Kinneil Railway or the Bo'ness Motor Museum, the pub is also handy for the Hippodrome, Scotland's oldest purpose-built picture house. It is a community venue and involved in local charity projects. Local CAMRA Pub of the Year 2017. **Q P**

Dollar

King's Seat

19-23 Bridge Street, FK14 7DE (on main street in centre of village)
4-midnight; 12-1am Fri & Sat; 12-midnight Sun
(01259) 742515 kingsseat.com
Fyne Ales Jarl; Harviestoun Bitter & Twisted; 4 changing beers (sourced nationally; often Fuller's, Harviestoun) H
Cosy, friendly bar with a separate American restaurant, in a quaint old village. Up to six ales and real cider are on offer during the summer, along with bar snacks. Dogs and children are welcome and there are tables and chairs outside for warmer weather. Occasional barbecues and live folk music are hosted. There are many great walks and attractions nearby. Local CAMRA Pub of the Year 2017. **Q**

Doune

Red Lion Inn

Balkerach Street, FK16 6DF
12-midnight (1am Fri & Sat); 12.30-midnight Sun
(01786) 842066 redlion-doune.com
1 changing beer (often Stewart) H
Dating from the mid-1700s, this traditional pub was acquired by the current landlord in 2010. It retains much of its original character including quirky bar stools depicting local trades. The bar has just one handpump serving locally sourced ales from central Scotland. Pub food is served in the bar, courtyard, restaurant and function room (no food Mon & Tue). Doune Castle, Blair Drummond Safari & Adventure Park and Argaty Red Kites are within easy reach. **Q P** (59)

Dumbarton

Captain James Lang

97-99 High Street, G82 1PH
8am-midnight (1am Fri & Sat) (01389) 742112
Greene King Abbot; 4 changing beers (sourced nationally; often Loch Lomond) H
Attractive conversion of a former Woolworths store in an Art Deco-style building on the High Street. One long room stretches from the main entrance through to the beer garden at the rear overlooking the River Leven. The pub is named after a local paddle steamer captain and is decorated with local ephemera reflecting the shipbuilding heritage of the town. The regular beers are supported by guests both from local micros and national breweries. Alcohol is served from 11am.
(Central)

Dunblane

Riverside

Stirling Road, FK15 9EP
8am-midnight (1am Fri & Sat); 9am-midnight Sun
(01786) 823318 theriversidedunblane.co.uk
Caledonian Deuchars IPA; house beer (by Harviestoun); 2 changing beers (sourced regionally; often Orkney, Strathaven, Tryst) H
Visit the Riverside for a healthy or hearty breakfast, a coffee and a home-bake beside the wood-burning stove, fantastic food with the family in the restaurant, or a glass of wine or a local beer with friends in the bar or on the terrace. There is a play area for children. The pub is close to Dunblane Cathedral and overlooks the Allan Water. Alcohol is served from 11am. A previous winner of local CAMRA Pub of the Year.

Tappit Hen

Kirk Street, FK15 0AL
11-midnight (1am Fri & Sat) (01786) 825226
thetappithen-dunblane.co.uk
Belhaven IPA; 4 changing beers H
A traditional single-room pub with the interior split up by wooden dividers. It is a cosy meeting point for local people as well as a delightful discovery for visitors. It hosts a weekly folk music night on a Tuesday and a real ale festival once or twice a year. Fundraising events in support of local charities are held regularly at this hospitable and generous community venue.

Falkirk

Carron Works

Bank Street, FK1 1NB
8am-midnight (1am Fri & Sat) (01324) 673020
Greene King Abbot; Sharp's Doom Bar; 3 changing beers H
An excellent Wetherspoon venue in a converted cinema with helpful staff dispensing the chain's guest beers. Centrally situated with a spacious interior, it is popular with locals and CAMRA members. It holds frequent beer festivals and is keen to promote real ale. The standard Wetherspoon menu is available all day. Licensed from 9.30am (11am Sunday).
(Grahamston)

Fintry

Fintry Inn

23 Main Street, G63 0XA
12-midnight (1am Fri & Sat); 12.30-midnight Sun
(01360) 860224 thefintryinn.co.uk
2 changing beers (sourced locally) H
The Fintry Inn was established in 1750 and has a long tradition as a country pub. Since 2012, it has been owned and managed by the Fintry Inn Collective whose aim is to ensure that the traditional values of the village pub are maintained

for the whole community. A full restaurant service is available along with ales from the Fintry Brewing Co based at the rear of the pub.

Helensburgh

Ashton

74 West Princes Street, G84 8UG

11-midnight; 11-1am Fri & Sat (01436) 675900

Belhaven IPA; 2 changing beers (sourced nationally)

A warm welcome awaits at this genuine local where the bar has been tastefully modernised and decorated with a nautical theme while retaining its original charm. During the work a set of tiles depicting scenes from Sir Walter Scott's Waverley novels was revealed. There is a small room for playing darts. A changing selection of ales from Scottish microbreweries is supported by quality English beers. Live music is a regular Saturday night feature. (Central) (1B,316)

Henry Bell

19-29 James Street, G84 8AS

8am-midnight (1am Fri & Sat) (01436) 863060

Greene King Abbot; Sharp's Doom Bar; changing beers (sourced nationally; often Loch Lomond)

Close to the recently revamped town centre and esplanade, this sympathetic conversion of an old furniture showroom is a busy and popular venue attracting both locals and visitors. At the heart of the town, it has now established itself as an important real ale outlet in the area and a wide range of ales from across Britain can be found here. The interior is in the style of Charles Rennie Mackintosh and the walls are adorned with TVs in homage to Helensburgh-born John Logie Baird. Alcohol is served from 11am.
Q (Central) (1B,316)

Kilmahog

Lade Inn

FK17 8HD

12-11 (1am Fri & Sat); 12.30-10.30 Sun (01877) 330152
theladeinn.com

House beer (by Tryst)

A pleasant, friendly pub in a handy spot on the Trossachs Trail to Loch Katrine, next to the multi-use path from Callander to Ben Ledi and beyond. Hearty wholesome food is an attraction. The three house beers are by Tryst Brewery. The Scottish Real Ale Shop, with its tremendous range of bottled ales, is next door. Scottish folk music features at weekends. Phone ahead to check opening hours in January and February. QP (C60)

Kippen

Cross Keys

Main Street, FK8 3DN

12-3, 5-11 (midnight Fri); 12-midnight Sat; 12-11 Sun
(01786) 870293 kippencrosskeys.com

House beer (by Fallen); 2 changing beers (sourced locally; often Fallen)

A traditional and comfortable old coaching inn with a rustic feel – the oldest of its kind in Stirlingshire. It is situated within the Loch Lomond & the Trossachs National Park, with Stirling only minutes away, and is ideal as a stopover whether travelling north or south. Popular with walkers, cyclists and golfers as well as the locals, it has low ceilings, wood-panelled walls, a wood floor and log fires in winter. The beer garden has great views in summer.
QP (B12,C12)

> I never drink water. I'm afraid it will become habit-forming. **W C Fields**

Larbert

Station Hotel

2 Foundry Loan, FK5 4AW

12-11 (midnight Thu; 1am Fri); 11-1am Sat; 12.30-11 Sun
(01324) 557186 thestationhotellarbert.co.uk

5 changing beers (sourced nationally; often Cairngorm, Greene King, Strathaven)

A popular local situated next to the railway station and on a regular bus route. The pub prides itself on the support it gives to a number of community groups. Three to five cask ales are usually on offer and efforts are made to provide a variety of local, regional and national ales. Large-screen TVs show sporting events. The Station is a sponsor of CAMRA's Larbert Real Ale Festival in nearby Dobbie Hall. P (6,7)

Luss

Loch Lomond Arms Hotel

G83 8NY

11-11; 12.30-11 Sun (01436) 860420
lochlomondarmshotel.com

3 changing beers (often Loch Lomond)

Take the High Road to the lovely village of Luss and enjoy some time in this well-renovated establishment. Situated close to the banks of Loch Lomond, there is much to do in the surrounding area. The premises are reachable by buses from Balloch and Helensburgh. Ales are provided by Loch Lomond Brewery and good freshly prepared local food is served. QP (302,305)

Stirling

No.2 Baker Street

2 Baker Street, FK8 1BJ

11-midnight (1am Fri & Sat) (01786) 448722
no2bakerstreet-stirling.co.uk

Belhaven 80/- Ale; Greene King Abbot; 2 changing beers

City-centre pub popular with locals, students and tourists. The single room has plenty of seating and tables, all on street level, and more seating outside for when the weather is good. Music, poker or quiz nights are held most evenings and it can get busy. A Belhaven-managed house, it has eight handpumps, with four or five usually serving Belhaven, Greene King and Scottish microbrewery ales.

Portcullis Hotel

Castle Wynd, FK8 1EG (adjacent to castle esplanade)

11-11 Mon & Tue; 11.30-midnight Wed-Sat; 11.30-11 Sun
(01786) 472290 theportcullishotel.com

2 changing beers (sourced regionally; often Isle of Skye, Orkney)

Popular pub at the top of town, originally the old grammar school building. Exposed stone walls and an open fireplace with ornate surround create a warm welcome in the heart of old Stirling. Frequented by tourists and supported by locals, the pub is renowned for its food and regularly

SCOTLAND

changing selection of Scottish ales from the far north and west. Always busy, diners are advised to reserve a table. Q P

Settle Inn

91 St Marys Wynd, FK8 1BU

3-midnight (1am Fri & Sat) (01786) 463403

3 changing beers (sourced nationally) H

Warm, friendly and atmospheric inn popular with a mixed clientele of locals, students and tourists. Situated on a route descending from Stirling Castle, the Settle Inn was built in 1733 and is the oldest pub in Stirling. The pub lives up to its name – settle down in front of the cosy fire and you may not want to leave, ghosts or no ghosts. There is music on Monday, Wednesday, Friday and Saturday evenings, and a quiz on Sunday. It opens at midday in the summer months - please phone ahead to confirm.

Strathyre

White Stag

Main Street, FK18 8NA

3-midnight; 1-1am Sat, 1 midnight Sun

(01877) 384224 thewhitestagfk18.uk

3 changing beers (sourced locally; often Inveralmond, Tryst) H

Cosy, popular pub, serving meals in the bar or bistro, with an emphasis on local produce. The beers are mainly Scottish. The raised beer garden enjoys panoramic views. Accommodation is available and dogs and children are permitted in the bar. Hill walking, fishing, golf and watersports are all close at hand, and Stirling, Callander and the Trossachs are within easy travelling distance. Opening hours are reduced in winter – it is advisable to check ahead before traveling. Local CAMRA Rural Pub of the Year 2018.

Q P (C60)

Riverside, Dunblane (Photo: Gary Holcroft)

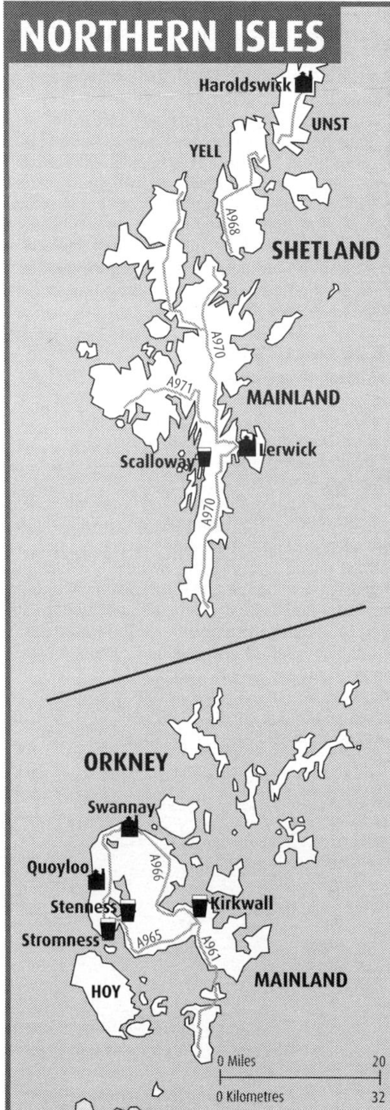

Authority area covered: Highland UA

Kirkwall: Orkney

Auld Motorhoose

26 Junction Road, KW15 1AB

11-midnight (1am Fri & Sat) (01856) 871422 auldmotorhoose.co.uk

Swannay Scapa Special H

A welcoming and friendly motor-themed pub with a single bar room, with lots of motoring memorabilia and car parts scattered throughout. The jukebox tends to blast out rock classics. There is regular live music, mainly at weekends, and the Moho is one of the venues for the Orkney Rock Festival. Outside, the patio has a smoking area. It is the sister bar to the Torvhaug in Bridge Street and convenient for the bus station nearby. CAMRA Northern Isles Pub of the Year 2016.

(X1)

Bothy Bar (Albert Hotel)

Mounthoolie Lane, KW15 1HW (lane connecting Junction Lane and Bridge St)

11-midnight Mon-Wed (1am Thu-Sat); 12-midnight Sun 0800 050 9037 hotelorkney.co.uk

Orkney Corncrake; Swannay Scapa Special; 2 changing beers (sourced locally; often Orkney, Swannay) H

Reconstructed following a fire about 12 years ago using much of the original materials, the Bothy has more space than previously and is a popular town-centre local handy for buses, North Isles ferries and the shops. Frequented by locals, after-work drinkers and as part of the weekend circuit, it has several intimate alcoves, and a roaring fire in the corner is welcoming in colder months. Historic St Magnus Cathedral is close by. A premium is paid when buying half pints.

Helgi's Bar

14 Harbour Street, KW15 1LE (by harbour)

11-midnight (1am Thu-Sat); 12.30-midnight Sun (01856) 879293 helgis.co.uk

Swannay Scapa Special; 2 changing beers (sourced locally; often Swannay) H

Converted from a former shipping office, this small smart bar has the look of a modern café with a local stone floor and wood panelling. Bar meals are available all day and special food nights are held where food is matched with ales. Regular music sessions and a Thursday quiz night also feature. Set on the harbour front where seafood is landed daily, this is a handy place to fill in time before island hopping on the many ferries to outlying parts. A former CAMRA Northern Isles Pub of the Year.

St Ola Hotel

Harbour Street, KW15 1LE

11-11.30 (midnight Thu); closed Fri; 10-1am Sat; 10-midnight Sun (01856) 875090 stolahotel.co.uk

Swannay Scapa Special; 1 changing beer (sourced locally; often Orkney, Swannay) H

Built on the site of the Inns of Sinclair dating back to the 14th century, the Ola is a solid building with a traditional appearance overlooking the harbour. The friendly and welcoming pub has a public bar at the front complete with a roaring fire in winter and a larger, recently refurbished lounge to the rear where food is served. An extensive range of whiskies is available alongside the ales. A music session is held on the last Sunday afternoon of the month. Joint CAMRA Northern Isles Pub of the Year 2018.

Scalloway: Shetland

Scalloway Hotel

Main Street, ZE1 0TR

11-11 (01595) 880444 scallowayhotel.com

Scapa Special; 1 changing beer (often Lerwick) H

Harbourside hotel in the centre of the village with tremendous views. Refurbished a few years ago, it has a small lounge bar where sport is sometimes shown and an award-winning restaurant. It is the

REAL ALE BREWERIES

Lerwick Lerwick: Shetland
Orkney Quoyloo: Orkney
Swannay Swannay: Orkney
Valhalla Haroldswick: Unst

SCOTLAND

keyholder for the neighbouring Scalloway Castle, a listed ancient monument. The Scalloway Museum is also close by, providing an interesting insight into life in the village through the ages. Both loch and sea fishing can be arranged, and there are 9-hole and 18-hole golf courses within three miles.

Stenness: Orkney

Standing Stones Hotel

KW16 3JX (on A965)
12-midnight (1am Fri & Sat) ☎ (01856) 850449
standingstoneshotel.co.uk
Swannay Scapa Special H
Set back from the main Stromness to Kirkwall road, this is a modern hotel with an open-plan lounge primarily focused on diners but welcoming to drinkers. The bar menu features handpicked local Orkney produce when in season. From the gardens you can look across to the Loch of Stenness and see the heart of Neolithic Orkney. Accommodation is offered in 17 en-suite rooms. The Standing Stones of Stenness, Ring of Brodgar and Maeshowe are all nearby.

Stromness: Orkney

Ferry Inn

10 John Street, KW16 3AD (across from ferry terminal)
9am-midnight summer; 4-11 (11.30 Fri); 9am-11.30 Sat; 9.30am-11 Sun winter ☎ (01856) 850280 ferryinn.com
Orkney Corncrake; Swannay Sneaky Wee Orkney Stout, Orkney IPA; 2 changing beers (sourced locally; often Orkney, Swannay) H
The Ferry reopened in March 2018 following refurbishment including a new kitchen and revamped bedrooms. An easy walk from the harbour front, it is handy for buses to Kirkwall and the ferry from Scrabster. It is popular with locals and visitors, including divers who come to Orkney to explore the sunken German fleet at Scapa Flow. Various attractions nearby include the Ring of Brodgar and Skara Brae village. Annual folk and blues festivals are held, with a marquee erected outside complete with an ale pump.

Stromness Hotel

15 Victoria Street, KW16 3AA (directly opp pier head)
12-midnight (1am Fri & Sat); 12.30-11 Sun; closed Jan & Feb ☎ (01856) 850298 stromnesshotel.com
Orkney Corncrake; Swannay Scapa Special; 2 changing beers (sourced locally; often Orkney, Swannay) H
On the first floor of this imposing hotel, which was used as an Army HQ during WWII, you will find the Hamnavoe Lounge, with windows and a small balcony giving commanding views of the harbour. In winter a roaring fire and comfy seating welcome the visitor and there is a separate whisky bar with over 100 bottles to choose from. The Flattie Bar downstairs, open all year round, is complete with a 'flattie' hanging from the ceiling (a small boat, unique to Stromness – see picture below) and serves a Swannay ale. Jazz, blues and beer festivals are held throughout the year.

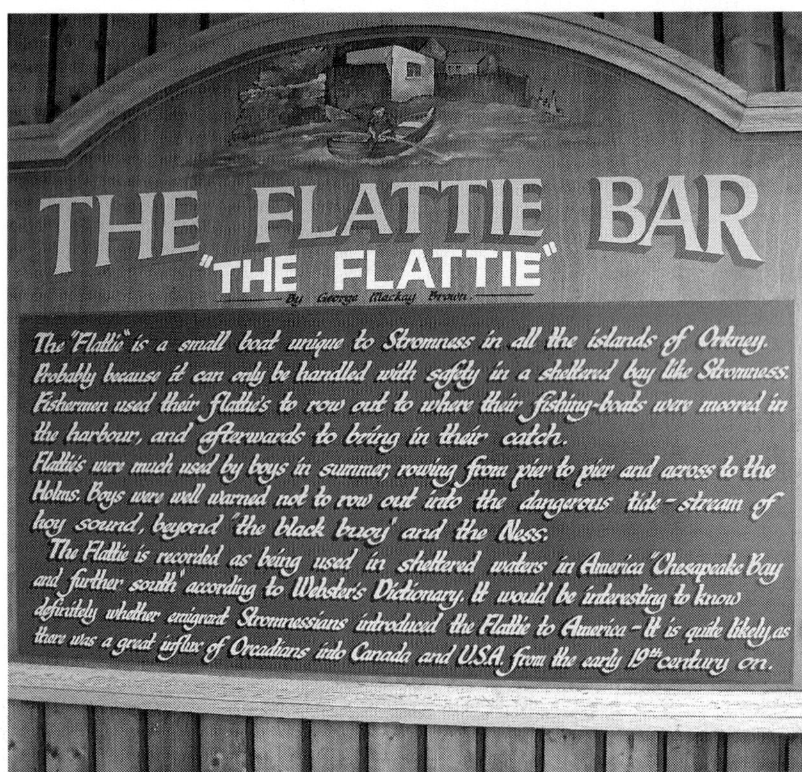

Stromness Hotel, Stromness: Orkney (Photo: summonedbyfells/flickr CC BY 2.0)

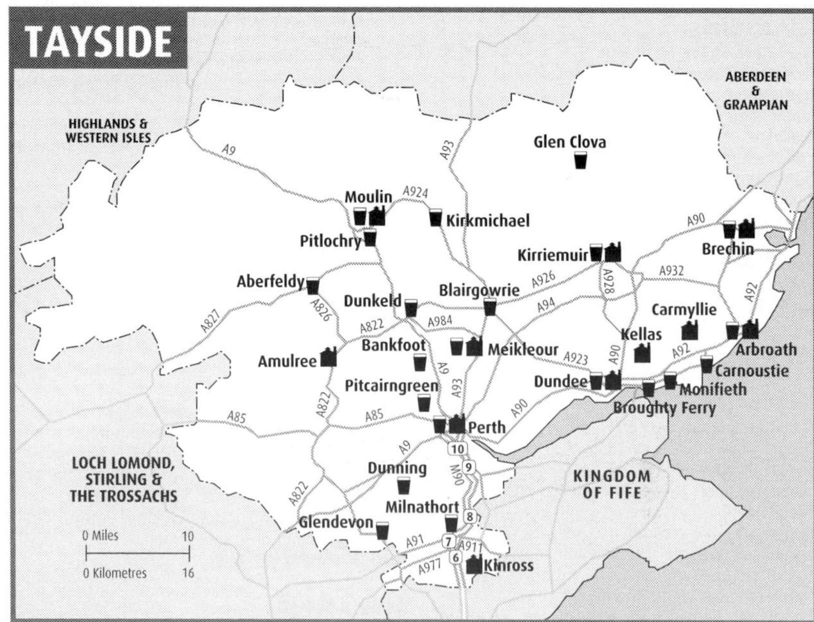

Authority areas covered: Angus UA, City of Dundee UA, Perth & Kinross UA

Aberfeldy

Ben Lawers Hotel

Loch Tay, PH15 2PA

11-11 (01567) 820436 benlawershotel.co.uk

3 changing beers (often Strathbraan)

In the heart of one of Scotland's most beautiful and accessible unspoilt areas, this small hotel offers some of the most fabulous views over Loch Tay. One handpull serves an ever-changing Inveralmond ale, with a taster happily provided. Staff are welcoming and good food and accommodation are available. The hotel is a popular stop-off for walkers.

Arbroath

Corn Exchange

14 Olympic Centre, Market Place, DD11 1HR

8am-midnight (1am Fri & Sat) (01241) 432430

Caledonian Deuchars IPA; Greene King Abbot; Sharp's Doom Bar; 3 changing beers

Located just off the High Street, this Wetherspoon pub occupies a 19th-century former corn exchange. Although it is largely open plan there are a number of booths providing some privacy. A varied selection of real ales is always available. Boat trips offering fishing or a visit to the 200-year-old Bell Rock lighthouse are available from the nearby harbour.

Bankfoot

Bankfoot Inn

Main Street, PH1 4AB

12-2 (not Mon & Tue), 6-11; 12-2, 5-12.30am Fri; 12-12.30am Sat; 12-midnight Sun (01738) 787243 bankfootinn.co.uk

3 changing beers

The hotel has a public bar and a small lounge bar with an adjoining restaurant, warmed by two real fires in winter. The owners are real ale enthusiasts and strongly committed to local breweries. Two ale fests are held each year. Good food is served lunchtimes and evenings Wednesday to Sunday. Quality live folk music features every Wednesday evening. There is outdoor seating at the front and rear of the building. A former local CAMRA Pub of the Year.

Blairgowrie

Ericht Alehouse

13 Wellmeadow, PH10 6ND

1.30-11 (01250) 872469

6 changing beers

Classic town-centre pub with a friendly atmosphere, close to the River Ericht. There are two seating areas inside separated by a well-stocked bar plus an outdoor area. A wide range of ever-changing ales and ciders is stocked, served in lined glasses, alongside a dozen Scottish gins. No food is served but customers are welcome to bring their own. A winner of local CAMRA Pub of the Year several times over the past decade.

REAL ALE BREWERIES

71 Dundee (NEW)
Dalrannoch Meikleour
Inveralmond Perth
Kirrie Kirriemuir
Law Dundee
Lion's Lair Arbroath (brewing suspended)
Loch Leven Kinross
MòR Kellas
Moulin Moulin
Park Brechin
Redcastle Carmyllie
Strathbraan Amulree

Fair o' Blair

25-29 Allan Street, PH10 6ND

8am-11 (12.30am Thu-Sat; midnight Sun)
(01250) 871890

Greene King Abbot; 4 changing beers (sourced locally) H

A Wetherspoon pub situated in The Wellmeadow at the centre of the town, with the grassy triangular plot hosting markets and outdoor entertainment. The pub promotes CAMRA's LocAle scheme by getting in beers from breweries within a 30-mile radius. The building is on two levels with wheelchair access to the lower area, and has a small beer garden to the rear.

Brechin

Caledonian

43 Southesk Street, DD9 6DZ

closed Mon & Tue; 5-10 Wed & Thu; 4.30-11.30 Fri; 3-11.30 Sat; 3-11 Sun (01356) 624345

3 changing beers (sourced nationally; often Inveralmond) H

Named after the privately run railway whose terminus is opposite, The Caledonian features a large bar and dining area. The extensive use of wood creates a warm and inviting interior. Inveralmond provides the regular ales, alongside guest beers sourced by the landlord on trips to Hampshire. A wide range of continental bottled beers is also offered. Live folk music on the last Friday of the month is popular. Opening hours are extended in summer.

Broughty Ferry

Fisherman's Tavern

10-16 Fort Street, DD5 2AD

11-midnight (1am Thu-Sat) (01382) 775941
fishermanstavern-broughtyferry.co.uk

5 changing beers (sourced nationally) H

Licensed since 1857, this famous hostelry was originally three fishermen's cottages, later converted into a small hotel, and now recently refurbished. The bar is to the right of the entrance, and a snug is to the left, leading to the dining room/lounge, warmed by a real fire. The lounge to the rear has wheelchair access from Bell's Lane. An annual beer festival is held in late May. A Belhaven/Greene King-managed house, the ales come from Scottish and English breweries.

Jolly's Hotel

43A Gray Street, DD5 2BJ

7am-midnight (1am Fri & Sat) (01382) 734910

Caledonian Deuchars IPA; Greene King Abbot; 2 changing beers H

Closed for several years, this 25-room hotel was bought by Wetherspoon and reopened in early 2014 after a major refit. There are two large areas, one for drinking and dining, the other principally for dining. Many handpulls serve a wide selection of ales, popular with a mixed clientele of all ages. TVs are usually muted. The outdoor patio area has a number of tables.

Royal Arch

285 Brook Street, DD5 2DS

11-midnight (1am Fri & Sat); 12.30-midnight Sun
(01382) 779741

Caledonian Deuchars IPA; 3 changing beers (sourced nationally) H

A popular locally owned pub in the centre of the Ferry. There are three TVs in the public bar for the many sports fans, and good-quality meals are served in the Art Deco lounge. Three handpulls dispense ales from local brewers as well as from all over Britain. The gantry in the public bar was rescued long ago from the demolished Craigour Bar in Dens Road, and the exterior was refurbished in 2014.

Carnoustie

Aboukir Hotel

38 Ireland Street, DD7 6AT

9am-midnight (1am Fri & Sat); 10-midnight Sun
(01241) 852149 aboukir.co.uk

2 changing beers (sourced nationally) H

This well-established locally owned hotel is at the eastern end of the main street in this famous golfing town. Food is available in both the bar and the Gable restaurant. Folk musicians play on Wednesday evening. In fine weather enjoy a drink on the verandah or in the garden.
P (53)

Stag's Head

61 Dundee Street, DD7 7PN

12-11 (01241) 858815

2 changing beers H

This friendly pub has a good-sized bar and a lounge/function area where local musicians play regularly. It is home to a number of games and sports teams including some very skillful dominoes players! The ale is very well looked after.

Dundee

Bank Bar

7-9 Union Street, DD1 4BN

11-midnight (10 Mon & Tue); 12.30-7 Sun
(01382) 205037

4 changing beers H

A former bank with bare-board floors, wooden furnishings and a series of alcoves with tables, in the tradition of older Scottish city pubs. A collection of themed pictures decorates the walls. Two or three ales are usually available and food is served until 7pm every day. Quality live music features on most Friday and Saturday nights.

Counting House

67-71 Reform Street, DD1 1SP

8am-midnight (01382) 225251

Greene King Abbot; 4 changing beers H

Now a Wetherspoon pub, this impressive building first opened as a bank in 1856 and was once a branch of the Royal Bank of Scotland. It was originally designed by George Angus, then modified by William Scott and reconstructed by Robert Gibson in the 1930s. Customers entered his new-look bank via a revolving door, crossed a terrazzo marble floor and were served at handsome mahogany counters topped with shiny bronze grilles. A great city-centre venue in which to enjoy a few ales.

Phoenix

103 Nethergate, DD1 4DH

11-midnight (01382) 200014

Caledonian Deuchars IPA; Timothy Taylor Landlord; 3 changing beers Ⓗ

One of Dundee's oldest pubs, this traditional inn has a great atmosphere. Subdued lighting, sturdy wooden tables and chairs, green leather benches and a rare Ballingall Brewery mirror give the place character. Five ales are on offer, and excellent pub food at conservative prices. The location is handy for the Rep Theatre, Dundee Contemporary Arts and Bonar Hall. Warm and cosy, like pubs used to be. (73)

Speedwell Bar (Mennies) ★

165-167 Perth Road, DD2 1AS

11-11; 12.30-11 Sun ☎ (01382) 667783 speedwell-bar.co.uk

3 changing beers Ⓗ

Built in 1903 for James Speed, the bar is known as Mennie's after the family who ran it for more than 50 years. The L-shaped bar is divided by a part-glazed screen and has a magnificent mahogany gantry and counter, dado-panelled walls and an anaglypta Jacobean ceiling. It has two sitting rooms, separated by a glass screen. There are usually three ales to choose from, alongside a selection of Belgian bottled beers and around 150 malt whiskies. You can take in your own food. Local CAMRA Pub of the Year 2017. (73)

Dunkeld

Perth Arms

High Street, PH8 0AJ

11-11 ☎ (01350) 727270

Strathbraan Due South, Head East Ⓗ

This cosy one-room establishment on the High Street serves a mix of locals and tourists. The friendly pub has been in the same family for almost 50 years. Real ale arrived here in 2012 and the bar now sports two handpulls. There is a beer garden at the back with an area for smokers.

Dunning

Kirkstyle Inn

Kirkstyle Square, PH2 0RR

12-3 (not Mon), 5-midnight; 12-midnight Wed-Sat; 12-10 Sun ☎ (01764) 684248 thekirkstyleinn.co.uk

2 changing beers (sourced nationally) Ⓗ

Traditional village inn dating from 1760 overshadowed by the impressive Norman steeple of St Serf's Church, home to the ancient Dupplin Cross and other Pictish relics. One or two ales in the cosy public bar come from a variety of Scottish independents, as well as English and Welsh regional breweries. There is a separate restaurant. Around a mile west of the village stands a 20-foot high stone cross, a memorial to Maggie Wall who was burned here as a witch in 1657.

Glen Clova

Glen Clova Hotel

DD8 4QS

11-11 (1am Fri & Sat); 12-11 Sun ☎ (01575) 550350 clova.com

2 changing beers (sourced regionally) Ⓗ

Situated near the head of one of Scotland's most beautiful glens, the hotel is popular with walkers after a day on the hills. The bar has a large log-fired stove and plenty of character. Two handpumps supply the ales, usually from Scottish breweries. Local food, including lamb and venison, is served in both the bar and adjoining restaurant. The hotel offers a range of accommodation from bunkhouse to en-suite room to self-catering luxury lodge. A summer beer festival is held in the field opposite. P

Glendevon

Tormaukin Hotel

FK14 7JY

11-11 ☎ (01259) 781252 tormaukinhotel.co.uk

Harviestoun Bitter & Twisted; 1 changing beer Ⓗ

This 18th-century drovers' inn is on the Yetts o' Muckhart to Gleneagles road in a peaceful setting surrounded by the Ochil Hills. It has a comfortable, relaxed atmosphere, with an open fire in winter. Lunch and dinner are served daily featuring fresh seasonal produce, with local venison a speciality. Soup, sandwiches, scones and snacks are available throughout the day. There will usually be a choice of ales on offer. Q

Kirkmichael

Strathardle Inn

PH10 7NS (on A924)

11-11 ☎ (01250) 881224 strathardleinn.co.uk

3 changing beers (sourced regionally) Ⓗ

Small, friendly hotel with a bar room with a coal fire and horse brasses around the mantelpiece. The historic coaching inn, dating back to the late 1700s, has a 700-yard fishing beat on the River Ardle which flows in front of the building. The Cateran Trail is also nearby and the Southern Highlands, Glenshee ski slopes, Deeside and Angus Glens are all within reach. Up to three ales are available from Scottish micros, and good lunches and evening meals are served. P

Kirriemuir

Airlie Arms

St Malcolm's Wynd, DD8 4HB

11-midnight (1am Fri & Sat); 12.30-1am Sun ☎ (01575) 218080 airliearms.net

2 changing beers (sourced regionally; often Eden Mill, Redcastle) Ⓗ

After many years left closed and in poor condition, this large, B-listed, 18th-century establishment was substantially renovated and reopened in 2015 by the local Ewart family. Real ale has made a welcome appearance, with two handpulls on the bar dispensing a good selection of beers. Food is served at most times in the bar and in the restaurant at weekends.

Meikleour

Meikleour Hotel

PH2 6EB

11-11 ☎ (01250) 883206 meikleourarms.co.uk

2 changing beers

Originally a coaching inn and posting house dating back to 1820, this country inn has an informal bar with a flagstone floor and a comfortable lounge/dining room with a log fire in an Adam-style fireplace. Up to three ales are available including the house beer from Inveralmond. Excellent food is served made with locally sourced ingredients. Outside is a beer garden and nearby is the famous

SCOTLAND

world's tallest beech hedge which was planted in 1745 and now stands 100ft high and a third-of-a-mile long.

Milnathort

Village Inn

36 Wester Loan, KY13 9YH

2-11 (midnight Fri); 12-midnight Sat; 12.30-11 Sun
(01577) 863293

3 changing beers (sourced nationally) H

Friendly local with a semi open-plan interior featuring classic brewery mirrors and local historic photographs. The comfortable lounge area has low ceilings, exposed joists and stone walls, and the bar area is warmed by a log fire. At the rear is a games room with a pool table. This pub has been family-owned since 1985 and usually serves three beers from Scottish and, often, English breweries. Milnathort links some great cycling routes through the Ochils, via Burleigh Castle, to the more leisurely Loch Leven Heritage Trail. (23)

Monifieth

Milton Inn

Grange Road, DD5 4LU

closed Mon; 12-2.30, 5-11 Tue-Thu; 12-midnight Fri & Sat; 12-11 Sun (01382) 532620 themiltoninn.co.uk

3 changing beers (sourced nationally) H

The only premises in Monifieth serving real ale, which it does with a passion. There are usually three beers to choose from, alongside good home-made food at fair prices. The pub is set back from the road, with large gardens and a sunny decked area to the rear providing a nice sheltered spot for a pint in the fresh air, or to enjoy a barbecue. Entertainment features regularly. P

Moulin

Moulin Inn

11-13 Kirkmichael Road, PH16 5EH

11-11 (01796) 472196 moulininn.co.uk

Moulin Light, Braveheart, Ale of Atholl, Old Remedial H

First opened in 1695, the inn is the oldest part of the Moulin Hotel, situated within the village square of an ancient crossroads, just east of Pitlochry. Full of character and charm, it is traditionally furnished and has two log fires. A good choice of home-prepared local fare is available, along with four Moulin beers, brewed in the old coach house behind the hotel. There is an area outside for dining and drinking in good weather. An ideal base for outdoor pursuits, with several marked walks nearby. Q P

Perth

Cherrybank Inn

210 Glasgow Road, PH2 0NA

11-11 (12.30am Thu-Sat); 12-midnight Sun
(01738) 624349 cherrybankinn.co.uk

Inveralmond Ossian; 4 changing beers (sourced regionally; often Inveralmond) H

This 250-year-old former drovers' inn is a popular watering hole and stopover for travellers. Ales from Inveralmond and other Scottish independents are dispensed from six handpulls in the multi-roomed public bar or the larger L-shaped lounge, with views up to a woodland walk. Good bar lunches and evening meals are served. The inn has seven well-appointed en-suite rooms, and golf can be arranged for residents. P (7)

Green Room

97 Canal Cres, PH2 8HX

12-11 (12.30am Thu; 1.30am Fri & Sat); 12-midnight Sun
(01738) 248121 thegreenroomperth.com

6 changing beers

This establishment has three bars, one with six handpulls, plus a large selection of bottled beers from around the world. Live entertainment plays seven nights a week, which pulls in plenty of customers. A must-visit venue in Perth for ale enthusiasts, in a convenient city-centre location near to the railway station. Local CAMRA Pub of the Year 2018.

Greyfriars

15 South Street, PH2 8PG

2.30-11 Mon-Wed; 12-12.30am Thu-Sat; 12-11 Sun
(01738) 633036 perth-bars.co.uk

Inveralmond Lia Fail; 3 changing beers (often Inveralmond) H

Compact city-centre lounge bar selling up to four ales, often including an Inveralmond beer. Good-value lunches are served in the bar and a small seating area upstairs. The pub takes its name from the former Greyfriars monastery. Nearby attractions include a Victorian theatre, art gallery, museum and concert hall. This may well be the smallest lounge bar in the Fair City but it has an enviable reputation among locals and visitors as one of the friendliest.

Pitcairngreen

Pitcairngreen Inn

PH1 3LP

10.30-11 (midnight Fri & Sat) (01738) 583022
pitcairngreeninn.co.uk

2 changing beers (sourced locally) H

A fairly large establishment with several different areas including a snug warmed by an open log fire. The inn has a real enthusiasm for good beer, served on three handpulls, and this is the finest place in Tayside to enjoy real ciders and perries, presented professionally and with passion. The car park is just across the road. Local CAMRA Cider Pub of the Year. Q P (14,15)

Pitlochry

Old Mill Inn

Mill Lane, PH16 5BH

11-11; 11-midnight Sat & Sun (01796) 474020
theoldmillpitlochry.co.uk

Strathbraan Due South, Head East; 2 changing beers H

Built in the 19th century as a mill, and with a mill wheel still driven by the stream, customers can sit beside it during outdoor drinking weather. This is a well-run family-owned establishment in the town centre. The large bar serves a varied selection of guest ales with usually three or four on, including the regular beers from local microbrewery Strathbraan. P

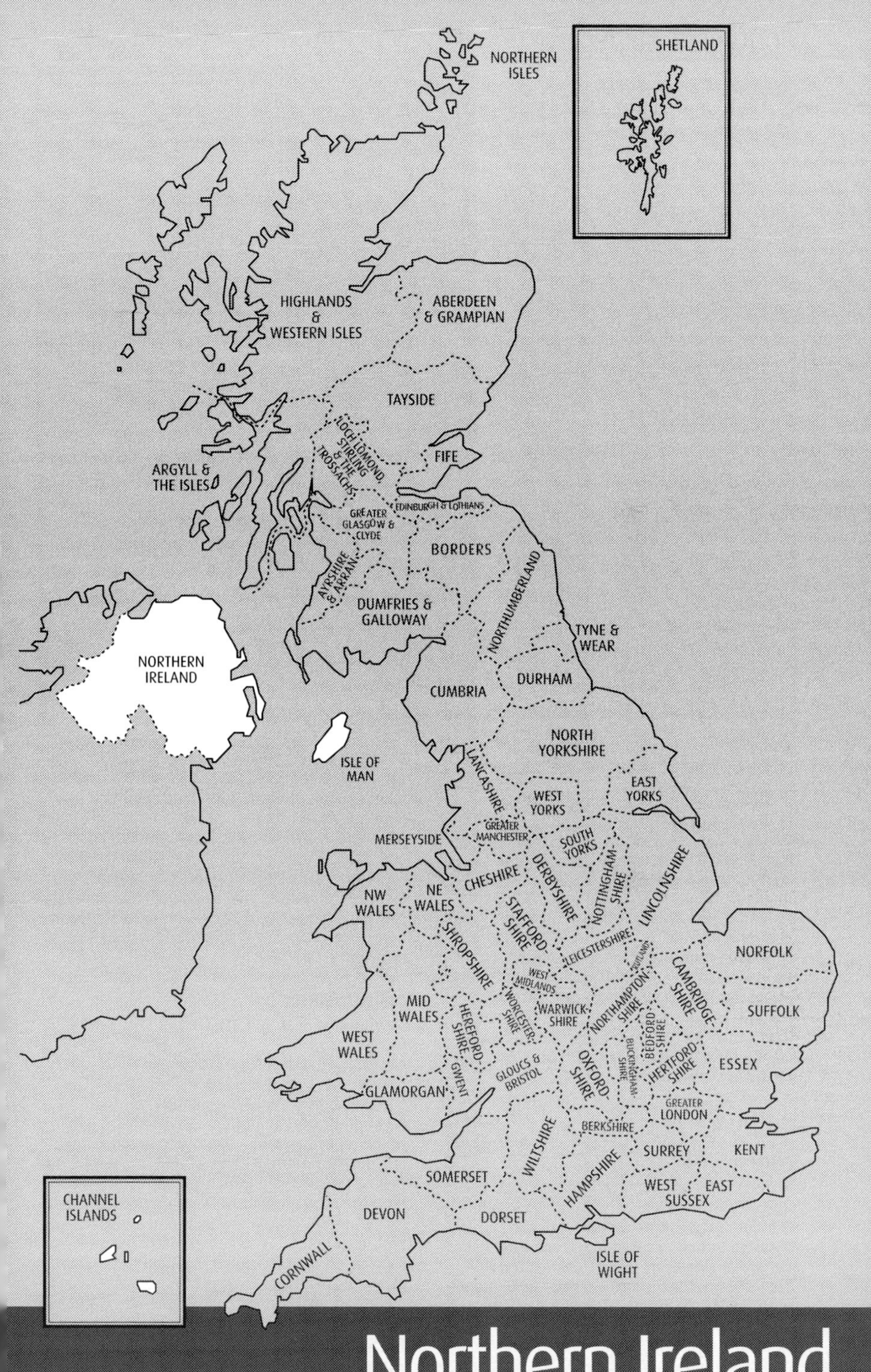

Northern Ireland Channel Islands Isle of Man

NORTHERN IRELAND

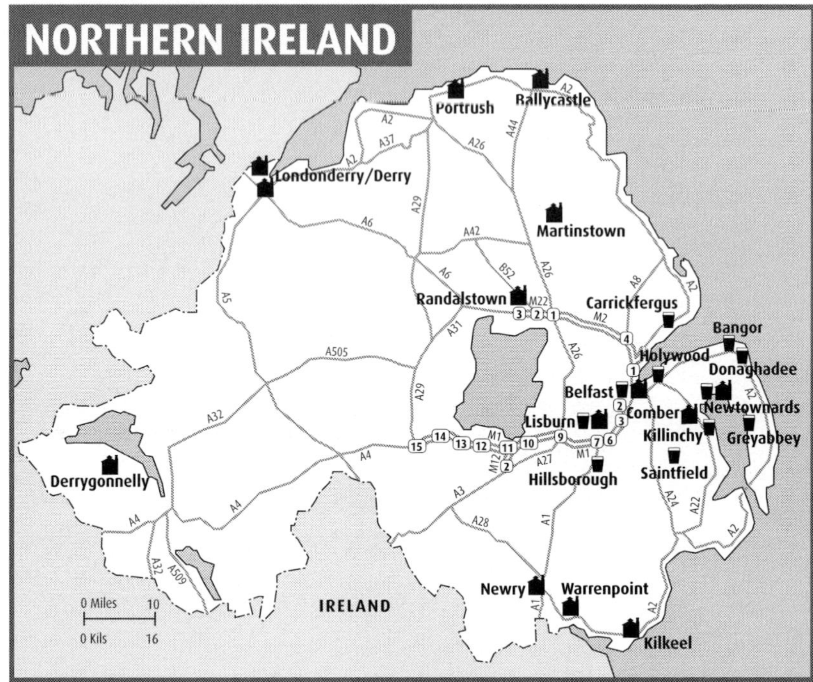

Bangor

Jenny Watts

41 High Street, BT20 5BE

11.30-11 (1am Wed-Sat); 12.30-midnight Sun

(028) 9127 0401 jennywattsbar.com

Sharp's Doom Bar H

Bangor's oldest public house, Jenny Watts retains a traditional feel inside, with a central bar, stone walls and flooring. It has been selling real ale for some years, with one handpump usually dispensing Sharp's Doom Bar or an ale from Hilden. Good food is available every day. Live music features Wednesday to Friday evenings and on Sunday there is jazz in the afternoon. Ruby's Lounge upstairs host '80s and '90s nights, and at the back is a beer garden. Q

Belfast

Crown ★

46 Great Victoria Street, BT2 7BA (opp Europa Hotel and Great Victoria St station)

11.30-11; 12.30-10 Sun (028) 9024 3187

St Austell Nicholson's Pale Ale; Whitewater Belfast Ale; 3 changing beers (sourced nationally) H

The Crown is known for its outstanding interior which looks even better now the gas lights have been restored. It is also a top spot for real ale, with six handpumps serving Nicholson's Pale Ale and local ales from Mourne Mountains and Whitewater breweries. Three guests vary, especially during the regular beer festivals. Upstairs is the Crown dining rooms where there are three more handpumps. A former local CAMRA Pub of the Year. Q

Errigle Inn

312-320 Ormeau Road, BT7 2GE

11.30-1am; 10-midnight Sun (028) 9064 1410

errigle.com

8 changing beers (sourced locally) H

The Errigle Inn has become a real ale and craft beer haven in recent years. The Oak Lounge has five handpumps focusing on local breweries, with beers from Hilden, Whitewater, Farmageddon, Knockout and Bullhouse frequently available along with some from Shepherd Neame. There are also tap takeovers and occasional beers from the wood. The Lounge is a quiet back bar where ale and food can be enjoyed in peace. Current local CAMRA Pub of the Year. Q

John Hewitt

51 Donegal Street, BT1 2FH (100yds from St Anne's Cathedral)

11.30-1am; 12-1am Sat; 7-midnight Sun

(028) 9023 3768 thejohnhewitt.com

1 changing beer (sourced nationally) H

Named after the poet John Hewitt, this is a busy single-room bar with a large snug in one corner. It is different from most bars in that it is run by the Belfast Unemployed Resource Centre, and profits fund the centre's work. It is also a popular venue for live music, charity evenings and art exhibitions. High-quality food is served at lunchtime with specials on the blackboard. A single handpump dispenses Shepherd Neame beers or an occasional guest such as Hercules Belfast Pale Ale. Q

McHughs

29-31 Queens Square, BT1 3FG (near Albert Clock)

12-1am; 12-11 Sun (028) 9050 9999

mchughsbar.com

Whitewater Maggie's Leap IPA H

Housed in Belfast's oldest building, McHughs is a lively pub with several different drinking and dining areas. The main public bar has a handpump exclusively dispensing ales from Whitewater Brewery. Next to it is the old bar where wall paintings depict scenes from Belfast's history. Good food is served in the restaurant upstairs as well as in the bars. Music is a regular feature – often folk or traditional – while the basement hosts a variety of acts. Q(Central)

Sunflower

65 Union Street, BT1 2JG

12-midnight (1am Fri-Sat); 5-11 Sun (028) 9023 2474 sunflowerbelfast.com

1 changing beer (sourced locally)

This corner bar was renovated five years ago and is now a lively, welcoming public house. The emphasis is on quality beer sourced mainly from local breweries – the handpump offers a variety of beers from Hilden. This is also one of the few bars that has replaced Ireland's best-known stout with a local one from Hercules brewery. There is music seven days a week and the beer garden is a popular attraction. Pizza is available Thursday to Saturday evenings. Q

Carrickfergus

Central Bar

13-15 High Street, BT38 7AN (opp Castle)

8am-midnight (1am Fri & Sat) (028) 9335 7840

Greene King Abbot; Sharp's Doom Bar; 3 changing beers (sourced nationally)

Lively market-town community local with a loyal clientele. This Wetherspoon pub has a ground-floor public bar of robust character and a quieter family-friendly first-floor loggia-style sitting room with exposed timber trusses, affording fine views from its many windows over Belfast Lough and the adjacent 12th-century castle. Handpumps on both levels serve two house beers and three guest ales, usually from mainland micros, or seasonal specials from various breweries. Alcohol is served from 11.30am (12.30pm Sun). Q(563)

Donaghadee

Moat Inn

102 Moat Street, BT21 0ED

11.30-11.30; 12.30-10 Sun (028) 9188 3297 moatinn.co.uk

Whitewater Belfast Ale; 1 changing beer (sourced locally)

A long-established hostelry conveniently located close to landmarks of the Ards Peninsula. It offers a public bar, lounge, Henry's Bistro and beer garden. The bar is compact though comfy and populated with jolly locals. There are two handpumps, with beers mainly from Whitewater Brewery. Very good food is available in the lounge and bistro. Sport is very popular in the area and the bar can be busy at times. Q(7)

Greyabbey

Wildfowler Inn

1 Main Street, BT22 2NE (6 miles S of Newtownards on A20)

5-9 Mon-Wed; 4-11 Thu & Fri (midnight Sat); 1-10 Sun (028) 4278 8234 wildfowlerinn.co.uk

1 changing beer (sourced locally)

The Wildfowler is a restaurant with a small public bar situated on the east coast of the Ards Peninsula. It has a country-style traditional tiled and stone floor, exposed oak beams and stained-glass windows. The quality fresh and seasonal food is locally sourced. A single handpump in the bar offers a changing variety of ales from Ards Brewing Company, which is less than two miles away. QP

Hillsborough

Hillside

21 Main Street, BT26 6AE

12-11.30 Mon-Wed (11.45 Thu; 12.30am Fri; 12.45am Sat); 12-11 Sun (028) 9268 9233 hillsidehillsborough.co.uk

Hilden Nut Brown, Twisted Hop

The Hillside is a bar and restaurant in Hillsborough, about 12 miles from Belfast. Inside there are a number of drinking and dining areas, with two handpumps in the front bar. Beers are mainly from Hilden Brewery including a new house ale, Hillside Embers. The annual beer festival is popular, and the bar hosts local groups such as Hillsborough's bell ringers and a variety of musical acts. It is notably dog-friendly. Q(38,238)

Holywood

Dirty Duck Ale House

3 Kinnegar Road, BT18 9JN

12-11 (1am Thu-Sat); 12.30-11 Sun (028) 9059 6666 thedirtyduckalehouse.co.uk

3 changing beers (sourced nationally; often Inveralmond, Sharp's, Shepherd Neame)

The Dirty Duck is a two-times winner of local CAMRA Pub of the Year. The single-room bar has a restaurant upstairs and good food is served throughout. Three regularly changing real ales are available including the house beer, Dirty Duck Ale, brewed by Hilden. There is much to admire here – a great view over Belfast Lough, a roomy beer garden, a collection of pumpclips, plastic ducks and a corner in honour of golfer Rory McIlroy. Q

Killinchy

Daft Eddy's

Sketrick Island, BT23 6QH (2 miles N of Killinchey at Whiterock Bay)

11.30-11.30 (1am Fri); 12-10.30 Sun (028) 9754 1615 dafteddys.co.uk

1 changing beer (sourced locally)

Set in glorious surroundings, this old favourite has been renovated with a new log cabin-style public bar inside the restaurant, while the old public bar

REAL ALE BREWERIES

Ards Newtownards
Barrahooley Craft Martinstown
Boundary Belfast
Bullhouse Newtownards
Dopey Dick Derry
Farmageddon Comber
Fermanagh Derrygonnelly
Glens of Antrim Ballycastle
Hercules Belfast
Hilden Lisburn
Hillstown Randalstown
Knockout Belfast
Lacada Portrush
Mourne Mountains Warrenpoint
Northbound Derry
Station Works Newry
Walled City Londonderry
Whitewater Kilkeel

has been replaced with The Islands coffee bar. The restaurant continues to serve quality local food, with oysters and lobster among the specialities. An alfresco dining area has also been added. The single handpump has recently been serving a variety of beers from Farmageddon Brewery. Q♉◑◗♿P

Lisburn

Tap Room

Hilden House, Grand Street, Hilden, BT27 4TY (5 mins walk from Hilden railway halt)

⏲ closed Mon; 12-2.30, 5.30-9; 12-3 Sun ☎ (028) 9266 3863

🌐 taproomhilden.com

Hilden Nut Brown; 1 changing beer (sourced locally; often Hilden) Ⓗ

Hilden Brewery is about one and a half miles from the centre of Lisburn City. The Taproom is adjacent to the main brewhouse in the courtyard of the Scullion's Georgian mansion. There are usually two ales from the brewery accompanying the locally sourced cuisine. As a licensed restaurant, alcohol is only available with a meal. The venue also hosts weddings and other functions including a popular annual beer festival. Q♉◑◗♿⇌🚌(325H)

Tuesday Bell ✔

4 Lisburn Square, BT28 1TS

⏲ 8am-11 (midnight Thu; 1am Fri & Sat) ☎ (028) 9262 7390

Greene King Abbot; Sharp's Doom Bar; 2 changing beers (sourced nationally) Ⓗ

The Tuesday Bell is a two-floor pub now well established in the city centre, close to the bus station. It is a popular location for eating and drinking, especially at the weekend. There are five handpumps downstairs and three upstairs offering a changing range of beers to complement the two regulars. Local ales from Hilden and real cider are occasionally available. Alcohol is served from 11.30am (12.30pm Sun). Q♉◑◗♿⇌♣●P🚌📶

Newtownards

Spirit Merchant ✔

54-56 Regent Street, BT23 4LP (next to bus station)

⏲ 8am-11 (midnight Thu; 1am Fri & Sat) ☎ (028) 9182 4270

Greene King Abbot; Sharp's Doom Bar; 2 changing beers (sourced nationally) Ⓗ

In some ways this is a regular Wetherspoon but it manages to retain the feel of the local pub it replaced. The single bar has five handpumps offering the regular beers and up to two changing guests – the ale is kept in good order by the manager and her dedicated staff. There is a large heated courtyard/beer garden at the side. Alcohol is available from 11.30am (12.30pm Sun). Q♉❀◑◗Å🚌(7)

Saintfield

White Horse

49-53 Main Street, BT24 7AB

⏲ 11.30-1am; 12-10 Sun ☎ (028) 9751 1143

🌐 whitehorsesaintfield.com

Whitewater Copperhead, Maggie's Leap IPA Ⓗ

The White Horse stands out among the buildings in the main street of the historic town of Saintfield. Formerly a coaching inn, it is now a modern pub with bar, lounge and dining areas. Food is very much to the fore with a pizza restaurant downstairs and a bistro upstairs. Although no longer owned by Whitewater Brewery, its ales are still available, usually on two handpumps. A former winner of local CAMRA Pub of the Year. Q❀◑◗♿🚌(15,215)

Crown, Belfast (Photo: Reading Tom/flickr CC BY 2.0)

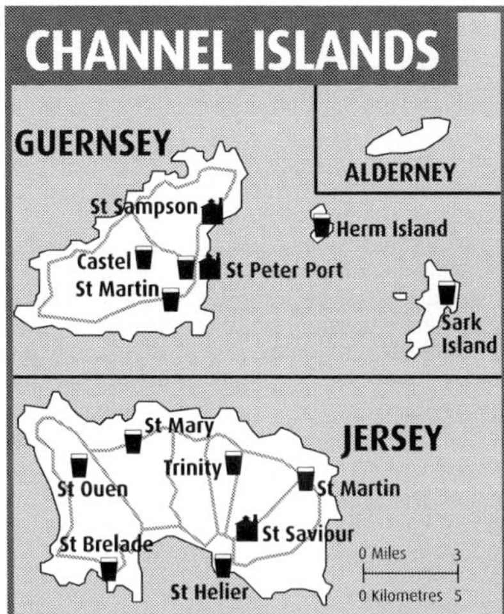

GUERNSEY

Castel

Fleur du Jardin ✔

Kings Mills, GY5 7JT

10.30-11.45 ☎ (01481) 257996 fleurdujardin.com

2 changing beers Ⓗ

A building of unique charm with two bars – one traditional, small and cosy, attached to the restaurant, the other renovated in a more contemporary style to create a comfortable, relaxing area to enjoy a beer. A door from here leads to a large covered patio and out to the garden. Menus in both the bar and restaurant feature fresh local produce. The car park can be busy during the summer months. Q&P

Rockmount Hotel

Cobo, GY5 7HB

10.30-midnight (12.45am Fri & Sat) ☎ (01481) 252778 therocky.gg

5 changing beers

The pub, overlooking Cobo beach, has a taproom with sport on TV and a large lounge bar. The lounge has an emphasis on food, serving lunchtime and evening meals, but there are comfy chairs near the fire for drinkers. Five handpumps offer a changing range of beers and you can also try a tasting paddle of different ales. Q

Herm Island

Mermaid Tavern ✔

GY1 3HR (travel Trident ferry from St Peter Port to Herm then follow signs)

11-10.30; 12-10.30 Sun ☎ (01481) 750050 herm.com/mermaid

House beer (by Liberation); 2 changing beers Ⓗ

A short trip by ferry from Guernsey takes you to Herm. A large courtyard acts as a suntrap in the summer while in winter an open fire creates a cosy atmosphere. Real ale and cider festivals are held twice a year. The house beer is 4.2% ABV Herm Island Gold. A trip to Herm to discover the island's tranquillity and outstanding natural beauty is a must for any visitor to Guernsey. Guernsey CAMRA Pub of the Year 2016.

St Martin

Captain's Hotel ✔

La Fosse, GY4 6EF

11-11 (midnight Fri & Sat); 12-4 Sun ☎ (01481) 238990 thecaptainshotel.co.uk

Butcombe Original; Sharp's Doom Bar Ⓗ

In a secluded location down a country lane, this is a popular locals' pub with a lively, friendly atmosphere. It has a small, raised area in front of the bar furnished with a sofa to make a comfy zone. Good-quality meals can be eaten in the bar or bistro area, or you can take away a pizza. A meat draw is held on Friday. The car park to the rear fills up quickly. P

Les Douvres Hotel

La Fosse, GY4 6ER

10.30-12.30am ☎ (01481) 238731 lesdouvres.com

Black Sheep Best Bitter; Timothy Taylor Landlord; 2 changing beers Ⓗ

Former 18th-century manor house, set in private gardens in St Martin near the south coast, two and a half miles from St Peter Port, with cliff walks and a tiny fishing harbour. A well-maintained, changing range of beers is offered on two handpumps, and seasonal real cider. Excellent meals are served in the bar and separate restaurant. Live music features on Friday nights and occasional Wednesdays. The venue is popular with locals and visitors. P

St Peter Port

Cock & Bull

Lower Hauteville, GY1 1LL

11-12.45am; closed Sun ☎ (01481) 722660 cockandbullguernsey.com/home

5 changing beers Ⓗ

Just up the hill from the town church, the pub has five handpumps providing a changing range of beers, and real cider in the summer months. Seating is on three levels, with a pool table in the lower level. Live music features throughout the week, with open mic on Tuesday, Irish on Thursday, baroque once a month on Monday, and on Saturday a silent set – gentle music that will not hinder conversation. A meat draw is held on Friday. The pub only opens on Sunday when rugby is on.

Cornerstone L

2 La Tour Beauregard, GY1 1LQ

11-12.30am; 12-11 Sun ☎ (01481) 713832

White Rock Wonky Donkey; 6 changing beers Ⓗ

The Cornerstone has a small bar area to the front and further seating to the rear, with a large screen for sporting events. White Rock beer is always on handpump together with a varying range of other ales – check on Facebook for current brews. Gluten-free beer in bottles is stocked and gluten-free meals are available with advance notice. There is a meat draw on a Sunday.

REAL ALE BREWERIES

Liberation St Saviour: Jersey
Randalls St Peter Port: Guernsey
White Rock St Sampsons: Guernsey

ISLANDS

Duke of Normandie Hotel (Pickled Pig)

Lefebvre Street, GY1 2JP (through arch close to jct of High St with Smith St)
11-12.45am (11 Sun) ☎ (01481) 721431
dukeofnormandie.com
2 changing beers Ⓗ
The Pickled Pig is on the ground floor of this town-centre hotel just off the High Street. The comfortable bar has been newly refurbished and has three rooms with different seating areas. There is an emphasis on dining, but you are welcome to come in just for a drink. Gluten-free beer is available in bottles and gluten-free food is on the menu. There is a courtyard garden for alfresco drinking and dining.

Golden Lion

7 Market Street, GY1 1HF
10-12.30am; 12-11 Sun ☎ (01481) 726634
thegoldenlion.gg
White Rock Wonky Donkey; 10 changing beers Ⓗ
Town-centre pub opposite the former Market. This is the second White Rock Brewery pub in Guernsey. One room with a long bar offers up to 10 real ales, usually including three from White Rock. The pub has the modern feel of a craft-beer bar. Live music plays on occasion in the downstairs bar. The first floor has been renovated and is now the Lions Den, open in the evenings and available for private hire. Gluten-free beer in bottles is available.

Red Lion

Les Banques, GY1 2RX (on seafront to N of St Peter Port)
11-11 (midnight Fri & Sat) ☎ (01481) 724042
3 changing beers Ⓗ
On the outskirts of St Peter Port, the Red Lion has two bar areas – a seafront lounge overlooking Belle Greve Bay to the front and a public area at the rear. Large-screen TVs show sport in both bars – just ask if there is something you would like to view. Meat draws are held on Friday and Saturday evenings. A changing variety of beers is offered on handpump and gluten-free beer in bottles. Real cider is available in the summer months. The pub is on several bus routes and on the cycle route between St Peter Port and St Sampson.

Ship & Crown

North Esplanade, GY1 2NB (opp Crown Pier car park on seafront)
10-12.45am; 12-12.45am Sun ☎ (01481) 721368
Liberation Ale; 3 changing beers Ⓗ
A traditional local in the heart of the town, in the same family for 34 years, with fantastic views of the harbour, neighbouring islands and Castle Cornet. A popular pub in which to enjoy a pint and a good-value meal, friendly and welcoming staff add to the appeal for locals, yachtsmen and tourists. The walls are decorated with photos of local shipwrecks, Guernsey and the pub under German occupation. All major sports events are shown in a friendly and lively atmosphere.

JERSEY

St Brelade

Old Smugglers Inn

Le Mont du Ouaisne, JE3 8AW
11-11 ☎ (01534) 741510 oldsmugglersinn.com
Draught Bass Ⓗ**; Greene King Abbot** Ⓖ**; 2 changing beers** Ⓗ
Perched on the edge of Ouaisne Bay, the Smugglers has been the crown jewel of the Jersey real ale scene for many years. Steeped in history, dating back to when pirates came to enjoy an ale or two here, it is set within granite-built fishermen's cottages with foundations reputedly from the 13th century. Up to four ales are available including one from Skinner's, and mini beer festivals are regularly held. The pub is known for its good food including fresh daily specials.
Q P (12,12A)

St Helier

Forum

13 Grenville Street, JE2 4UF
11-11 ☎ (01534) 768105
Liberation Herculius; 2 changing beers Ⓗ
On the outskirts of town, the pub is named after the cinema that once stood opposite. It has a modern interior but with a classic feel and includes a number of brass plaques taken from the old Royal Court building. Three real ales are always available, and a large range of real ciders. Upstairs is a sports bar with darts, pool and football tables, and sports TV. A former local CAMRA Pub of the Year. (3)

Lamplighter

9 Mulcaster Street, JE2 3NJ
11-11 ☎ (01534) 723119
8 changing beers Ⓖ
A traditional pub with a modern feel. The gas lamps that gave the pub its name remain, as does the original antique pewter bar top. An excellent range of up to eight real ales is available – the largest selection on the island – including one from Skinner's. All real ales are served direct from the cellar. A real cider is sometimes also on offer. Winner of local CAMRA Pub of the Year in 2016 and many times previously.

St Martin

Royal

La Grande Route de Faldouet, JE3 6UG
11-11 ☎ (01534) 856289 randallsjersey.com
Draught Bass; 1 changing beer Ⓗ
Originally a coaching inn, this large country-style hostelry is located at the centre of St Martin with sizeable public and lounge bars, a restaurant area and a spacious alfresco area. The interior features traditional furnishings, cosy corners and a real fire in colder months. Owned by Randalls Brewery, it serves guest ales from the Marston's, Sharp's and Skinner's stables. Quality food is popular with locals and visitors alike, with a good menu available lunchtimes and evenings until 8.30pm (no food Sun eve). The garden features a children's play area. P

St Mary

St Mary's Country Inn

La Rue des Buttes, JE3 3DS
11-11 ☎ (01534) 482897 liberationgroup.com
Liberation Ale, IPA; 1 changing beer (often Butcombe) Ⓗ
An archetypal country inn from the outside, this 17th-century farmhouse is opposite the 13th-

century parish church. The interior is contemporary with a main bar and an extensive dining area. The Liberation brews are joined by a guest ale. Reasonably priced good food is available daily. The inn has a comfortable and relaxed atmosphere, with seating outside at the front and rear for when the sun shines. The north coast is a half-hour walk away, including the Devil's Hole blow hole. P(7,27)

St Ouen

Farmers Inn

La Grande Route de St Ouen, JE3 2HY

10-11; 11-11 Sun (01534) 485311

Draught Bass; 2 changing beers H

Situated in the hub of St Ouen, near the war memorial and parish hall, the rustic Farmers Inn is a typical country pub offering up to three ales as well as a locally made cider when available (usually April to July). Traditional pub food is served in generous portions. Best described as a friendly community local, there is a good chance of hearing Jersey French (Jerriais) spoken at the bar. There is outside seating at the front of the pub. P(8,9)

Moulin de Lecq

Le Mont de Ste Marie, JE3 2DT

11-11 (01534) 482818 moulindelecq.com

House beer (by Liberation) H**; 2 changing beers (often Greene King)** G

A free house on the island offering a range of real ales, the Moulin is a converted 12th-century watermill situated in the valley above the beach at Greve de Lecq. The waterwheel is still in place and the turning mechanism can be seen behind the bar. A large restaurant adjoins the mill and can be hired for functions. The children's play space and a barbecue area are used extensively in the summer. There is a pool table in the second floor games room. QP(9,12)

Trinity

Trinity Arms L

La Rue es Picots, JE3 5JX

10-11; 11-11 Sun (01534) 864691

Liberation Ale H

Sporting the parish's ancient symbol of the Trinity, this 1976-built pub is modern by Jersey country pub standards but has plenty of character. Owned by Liberation Group, it is central to and popular within village community life. It has a public bar and restaurant where food is served lunchtimes and evenings. There is seating outside, a children's play area and car parking. Breakfast is served from 10am. Close to Jersey Zoo. P(4)

SARK

Sark

Bel Air Inn

Harbour Hill, GY10 1SB (top of Harbour Hill)

10-11.45 (01481) 832052

Shepherd Neame Spitfire; 1 changing beer (sourced locally) H

The Bel Air Inn serves a selection of traditional ales and ciders, and is a favourite pub among locals and tourists alike, with food being served all day. There is a large sheltered beer garden for sunny days and a cosy fire for when it is cold outside. Open every day all year round. On summer weekends there is live music and barbecues. Families and dogs welcome.

Hops: the essential flavouring

Hops are famous for adding bitterness to beer. But this remarkable perennial climbing plant – a member of the hemp family, Cannabinaceae – also contains acids, oils and resins that impart delightful aromas and flavours to beer.

These can be detected in the form of pine, spice, sap and tart, citrus fruit. Fruit is often similar to lemon and orange, while some English hop varieties give powerful hints of apricots, blackcurrants and damsons. American hop varieties, the Cascade in particular, are famous for their grapefruit aroma and flavour.

Many British brewers now use hops from mainland Europe – such as Styrian Goldings from Slovenia and Saaz from the Czech Republic – that have been developed primarily for lager brewing. They impart a more restrained aroma and flavour, with a gentle, resinous character. Lager hops used in ale brewing are usually added late in the copper boil to give a fine aroma to the finished beer.

Kent is often thought of as the main hop-growing area of Britain but in 2004 it was overtaken by Herefordshire. The main hop varieties used in cask beer production are the Fuggle and Golding, but First Gold, introduced in the 1990s, is now a major variety. First Gold was one of the first dwarf or hedgerow hops that grow to only half the height of conventional varieties. As a result they are easier to pick, are less susceptible to disease and aphid attack, and therefore use fewer agri-chemicals. In 2004, a new hop variety called Boadicea was introduced: it is the first aphid-resistant hop and therefore needs fewer pesticides. The hop industry is working on trials of new varieties that need no pesticides or fertilisers and should gain Soil Association approval as organic hops.

CAMRA's Home-Brewing Problem Solver

Erik Lars Myers

Real ale and other craft beers have become increasingly popular over the past few years, and as a result more people have been compelled to try making their own homebrew. However, while the concept behind making beer is simple, the execution can at times seem complex and confusing. The key to bridging the gap between brewing in theory and practise is being able to spot the signs of trouble and know how to respond. CAMRA's *Home-Brewing Problem Solver* provides the information you need to nip problems in the bud – and, better still, to avoid them in the first place.

RRP £12.99 **ISBN** 978-1-85249-347-9 **224 pages**

For this and other books on beer and pubs visit CAMRA's online bookshop at **www.camra.org.uk/books** or call **01727 867201**. Discounts are available for CAMRA members.

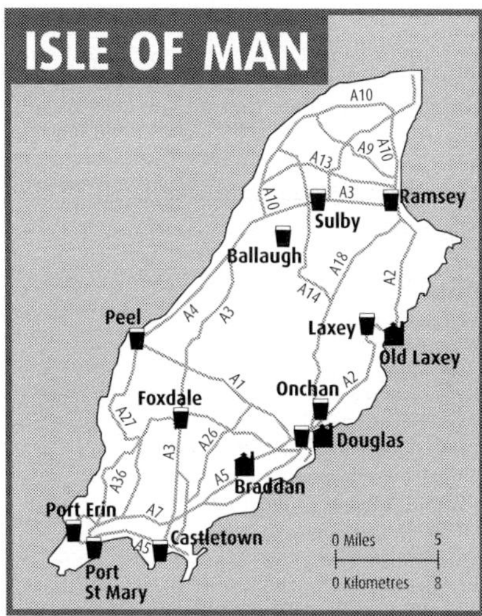

Ballaugh

Raven ✔

The Main Road, IM7 5EG

⏲ 12-11 (midnight Fri & Sat) ☎ (01624) 896128

Okell's Bitter; house beer (by Okell's); 2 changing beers (sourced nationally) Ⓗ

Renowned village-centre pub situated on the world-famous TT motorbike circuit adjacent to Ballaugh Bridge. Following some sympathetic refurbishments, the Raven retains a comfortable main bar, an intimate dining area and a separate games room for pool and darts. There are seating areas outside for the summer months and for watching the races. Rarely for the island, a house brew, Ravens Claw, is permanently available. Q❀◑♿♣P🚌(5,6)🐾📶

Castletown

Castle Arms ✔

The Quay, IM9 1LD

⏲ 12-11.30 (12.30am Fri & Sat) ☎ (01624) 824673

Okell's Bitter; 3 changing beers (often Okell's) Ⓗ

An attractive and historic pub, The Castle Arms is also known as The Glue Pot. It is next to Castletown harbour beneath the walls of Castle Rushen and handy for other heritage attractions. Two small ground-floor rooms have nautical and Manx motor-racing themes. The patio is ideal for watching quayside vessels and waterfront wildlife. This is the only pub in the British Isles to feature on a banknote (to the left of Castle Rushen on the Manx £5 note). Q❀⛺≹♣🚌(1,2)🐾📶

Sidings

Victoria Road, IM9 1EF (next to railway station)

⏲ 11.30-11 (midnight Fri & Sat) ☎ (01624) 823282

Bushy's Castletown Bitter, Ruby (1874) Mild, Bitter; Okell's Bitter; 8 changing beers (sourced nationally) Ⓗ

The Sidings, a former railway ticket office, comprises three distinct lounges, a bar area, a light and airy lounge mainly for dining and live music, and a refurbished games and TV room. There is an extensive beer garden and smoking area at the rear. Fourteen handpumps line the bar, with four for Manx ales, and a wide range of bitters is sourced from all over the UK. The pub is ideally placed to wait for a bus or a train.
Q❀◑≹♣P🚌🐾📶

Douglas

Albert Hotel ✔

3 Chapel Row, IM1 2BJ

⏲ 10-11 (11.45 Fri & Sat); 12-11 Sun ☎ (01624) 673632

🌐 albertiom.com

Bushy's Bitter; Okell's Bitter; 2 changing beers (sourced locally) Ⓗ

The nearest real ale pub to the sea terminal, The Albert is an unspoilt local with many regulars, plus darts and pool teams. It has a traditionally laid out central bar and dark-wood panelling, with a pool table in one room and interesting historic pictures of Steampacket boats in the other. Sport is often on TV but never loud enough to spoil conversation. The drinks are competitively priced – the resident beers include those from local breweries Okell's and Bushy's. Q≹♣🚌🐾📶

British Hotel ✔

North Quay, IM1 4LB

⏲ 12-11 (2am Fri & Sat) ☎ (01624) 616663

Okell's Bitter; 5 changing beers (often Okell's) Ⓗ

This attractive pub on the quayside in Douglas was orginally designed by noted Victorian architect Armitage Rigby in the Arts and Crafts style. The interior has undergone a sympathetic and stylish makeover. The building itself is spacious, with plenty of seating both inside and out and an impressive function room upstairs. This is a busy and thriving venue with an appetite for fun.
◑≹🍎📶

Hooded Ram

North Quay, IM1 4LH

⏲ 11-midnight (1am Fri & Sat) ☎ (01624) 612464

🌐 hoodedram.com

Hooded Ram Amber Ram, Black Pearl Oyster Stout; 6 changing beers (often Hooded Ram) Ⓗ

The Hooded Ram has a contemporary, yet rustic, traditional feel and offers a range of innovative ales. Formerly Clinch's Bar and Grill, which once housed the historic Clinch's brewery, it has been substantially refurbished. The bar has up to six real ales from Hooded Ram and a cider by the Manx Cider Co. There is comfortable seating and TVs for the sporting crowd, plus a back room for diners. Unusually, a particularly fine shuffleboard can be found in the main lounge area. ♨◑≹♣🍎🚌📶

Horse & Plough ✔

Isle of Man Business Park, Bradden, IM2 2QZ

⏲ 12-11 (midnight Fri & Sat) ☎ (01624) 626060

Okell's Manx Pale Ale, Bitter; 2 changing beers Ⓗ

A modern Heron & Brearley pub with a relaxed ambience serving the Isle of Man Business Park and nearby housing estate. The spacious interior comprises a large conservatory, a smaller dining area, a comfortable lounge with TVs showing sport, and a quieter raised area. The pub is a popular venue for functions and offers in-house catering for

REAL ALE BREWERIES

Bushy's Braddan
Hooded Ram Douglas
Okell's Douglas
Old Laxey 🛢 Old Laxey

formal occasions as well as good-value pub dining. Occasional live music events and regular quizzes are hosted.

Old Market Inn

Chapel Row, IM1 2BJ

9am-11

2 changing beers (often Bushy's)

Under the same ownership for many years, The Market has one of the smallest bars on the island, serving two separate rooms. What it lacks in size is more than made up for in character, and few pubs like this remain in the British Isles. Two ales, often from Bushy's, are served in this very friendly hostelry, where the visitor is almost bound to end up in conversation with other drinkers. In close proximity to the bus station and ferry terminal, it makes a great waiting room. **Q**

Prospect Hotel

Prospect Hill, IM1 1ET

12-11 (midnight Fri & Sat); closed Sun (01624) 616773

Okell's Manx Pale Ale, Bitter; 6 changing beers (often Okell's) H

Opened in 1857, the pub is in the finance sector of the island's capital. The law courts are in close proximity and the walls feature many pictures of luminaries of the law profession. Following refurbishment in 2017 there are now eight handpumps in two banks of four on separate bars. Real cider and perry are occasionally available. Wednesday is quiz night. The Library area to the rear of the building is also now back in use.

Queens Hotel

Queens Promenade, IM2 4NL

12-midnight (1am Fri & Sat) (01624) 674438

Okell's Bitter; 3 changing beers H

One of just a few remaining pubs situated on Douglas promenade, the refurbished Queens is popular with visitors and locals alike. There is a great view of Douglas Bay, ferries and trams from the terrace, which has plenty of seating under heated awnings. Inside there are three distinct areas, one with a pool table, two with low-volume TVs featuring sport. Pub grub is served seven days a week and there is live music at the weekend.

Q

Rosemount Hotel

Woodbourne Road, IM1 3HH

12-11 (midnight Fri & Sat) (01624) 618500

Okell's Bitter H

The Rosemount is a huge pub with plenty of character. There are three large rooms, each with their own personality and attracting a different clientele. The welcome is always friendly and the service exceptionally good. Entertainment includes karaoke on Sunday and live music on Friday or Saturday night. For some years the pub tried offering several real ales at the same time but demand was limited and in 2016 it returned to stocking Okell's Bitter alone, which is notably well kept. **Q**(2)

Rovers Return

11 Church Street, IM1 2AG

12-11 (midnight Fri & Sat) (01624) 676459

Bushy's Ruby (1874) Mild, Bitter; 5 changing beers H

The Rovers is a fascinating pub, with handpumps fashioned from fire hoses, a traditional coal fire, and a shrine to Blackburn Rovers in a back room. The interior comprises an almost warren-like series of rooms, frequented by a truly eclectic and loyal clientele. Famously large food portions are available at lunchtimes, and rare and unusual guest ales complement the Bushy's regular and seasonal ales. Real cider is also always on sale. The pub is worth seeking out, tucked away down a narrow street directly behind Douglas town hall.

Terminus Tavern

Strathallan Crescent, IM2 4NR

12-11 (midnight Fri & Sat) (01624) 624312

Okell's Bitter; 3 changing beers (often Okell's) H

Located next to the starting point for the seasonal Manx Electric Railway and horse trams, The Terminus has a comfortable, spacious front bar with alcoves around its large front windows. There is also a side bar for pool and darts, and a large outside seating area with views across Douglas Bay. This award-winning pub is popular for dining throughout the year, but nevertheless retains a local focus. **Q**(MER)**P**

Woodbourne Hotel

Alexander Drive, IM2 3QF

12-midnight (01624) 676754

Okell's Bitter; 4 changing beers H

Large three-bar Victorian local in a residential area within walking distance of Douglas centre. What was once the gents-only bar is now used to promote cask ale, offering a range of Okell's beers alongside several guests. The Woody is a popular, friendly pub with a varied clientele and boasts a genuine community spirit, with a proud record of charity fundraising. A regular pub quiz is held on Sunday evening, and there is a separate pool room, also used for meetings and live music.

Q

Foxdale

Baltic Inn

1 Glentramman Terrace, IM4 3EE

4-midnight; 2-midnight Fri & Sat (01624) 801305

balticinn.pub

Okell's Manx Pale Ale, Bitter H

Quiet, cosy local, with one main room divided into separate seating areas. A roaring real fire in winter adds to the atmosphere. Real ales on handpump supplement bottled Okell's IPA, Maclir and Hooded Ram beers. There are some fascinating historic photos on the walls of Foxdale during the mining boom. This friendly village pub continues to thrive following new ownership and a sympathetic refurbishment, and is well worth a visit.

Q

Laxey

Bridge Inn

6 New Road, IM4 7BE

12-11 (midnight Fri & Sat) (01624) 862414

Bushy's Bitter; 2 changing beers (sourced nationally) H

Popular and lively local pub in the centre of the village. The Bridge has been refurbished but retains its friendly atmosphere and continues to serve an excellent pint. A stout, porter or dark mild ale is usually among the beers. It offers occasional live music, wide-screen TV and a pool table. In 1897, after the Snaefell mining disaster in which 20 men perished, the cellar area was used as a temporary morgue. There are rumours of a resident ghost. ❀🛏◖⛺≹♣🍎🚌🐾📶

Queen's Hotel

New Road, IM4 7BP

⏲ 12-11 (midnight Fri & Sat) ☎ (01624) 861195

Bushy's Bitter; Hooded Ram Amber Ram; 1 changing beer (sourced nationally) Ⓗ

A large open-plan pub a quarter of a mile south of the village centre. The walls feature many photographs of the TT motorbike races and the surrounding area. The pub hosts live music on at least a monthly basis, and has pool, darts and TV for sport. There is an extensive beer garden overlooking the Manx Electric Railway tracks and a porch with seating where you can finish your drink while waiting for your bus. 🛏≹♣🍎P🚌(3,13)

Onchan

Manx Arms ✔

Main Road, IM3 1BE

⏲ 12-11 (midnight Fri-Sun) ☎ (01624) 675484

Okell's Manx Pale Ale, Bitter; 1 changing beer (sourced nationally) Ⓗ

Traditional village pub on the main road with two separate bar areas with pub games including pool, darts and dominoes, and large-screen TVs for sport. Live music features most Saturday evenings as well as an occasional karaoke night. There are attractive heated patios at the front and rear for smokers and a substantial car park. The regular real ale is from Okell's with a seasonal or guest beer usually available, as well as four real ciders.
Q❀♿♣🍎P🚌(3,23)🐾📶

Peel

Creek Inn ✔

Station Place, IM5 1AT (by harbour)

⏲ 10-midnight (12.30am Fri & Sat) ☎ (01624) 842216

🌐 thecreekinn.co.uk

Okell's Bitter; Sharp's Doom Bar; changing beers (often Hooded Ram) Ⓗ

Traditional and popular harbourside pub, with plenty of outdoor seating on the edge of the picturesque harbour. The lounge bar has a nautical theme, with etched-glass screens featuring sailing ships separating the cosy seating areas, and there is also some interesting beer memorabilia on display. A large selection of local, national and small brewery real ales is on offer, plus real cider. The comprehensive food menu includes locally caught Manx queenies (queen scallops) and locally cured kippers. Live music features at the weekends. 👶❀◖◗⛺♣🍎🚌(5,6)🐾📶

Marine Hotel

Shore Road, IM5 1AH

⏲ 10-midnight ☎ (01624) 842337 🌐 marinehotelpeel.co.uk

Okell's Bitter; 3 changing beers (sourced locally) Ⓗ

The Marine Hotel overlooks the beach and historic Peel Castle. It has two bar areas, one a traditional drinking corridor, and a lounge area. There is also a large restaurant at the rear, which can be accessed via a separate entrance, serving excellent, value-for-money meals seven days a week. The landlord is a staunch supporter of local breweries and cider producers, though guest ales from all over the UK are often available. 👶◖◗♣🍎🚌(5,6)🐾📶

White House Hotel 🏆 ✔

2 Tynwald Road, IM5 1LA (150yds from bus station)

⏲ 11-midnight ☎ (01624) 842252

Bushy's Ruby (1874) Mild, Bitter; Okell's Manx Pale Ale, Bitter; 2 changing beers (sourced nationally) Ⓗ

The White House, run by the same family for many years, features a public bar area, a separate pool room and a larger room for TV sport and live music at the weekend. There is also a cosy snug accessed internally via a sliding door, decorated with nautical memorabilia. The 2018 Isle of Man CAMRA Pub of the Year, this establishment now regularly stocks a Hooded Ram beer, and has long supported the island's growing cider market.
Q❀⛺♣🍎P🚌(5,6)🐾📶

Port Erin

Bay Hotel

Shore Road, IM9 6HL

⏲ 12-11 (midnight Fri & Sat); 12-11.30 Sun

☎ (01624) 832084

Bushy's Castletown Bitter, Ruby (1874) Mild, Bitter, Old Bushy Tail; house beer (by Bushy's); 2 changing beers (sourced nationally) Ⓗ

Bushy's flagship pub is on one of the best beaches on the island. Beach concerts featuring local bands and a promenade patio help make The Bay a great venue. The interior comprises three traditional rooms, including a public bar, a quiet room, and a dining area. A good range of Bushy's brews is usually available, including the Bushy's house brew, Bay IPA. Uniquely, this pub has been both local CAMRA Pub and Cider Pub of the Year.
Q👶❀◖◗♿≹♣🍎🐾📶

Port St Mary

Albert Hotel

Athol Street, IM9 5DS

⏲ 11-midnight (1am Fri & Sat); 12-midnight Sun

☎ (01624) 832118

Bushy's Bitter; Okell's Bitter; 2 changing beers (sourced nationally) Ⓗ

A hidden gem in the heart of this coastal village, The Albert boasts impressive views over the harbour. It has a public bar with games area, a cosy lounge bar complete with wood-burning stove, and an overflow area of tables and seating. Immaculately decorated and furnished, the walls are adorned with many paintings by local artists who frequent the pub. Isle of Man CAMRA Pub of the Year 2016. Q❀🛏♣P🚌(1,2)📶

Railway Station Hotel

Station Road, IM9 5LF

⏲ 5-11; 12-1.30am Fri; 12-2am Sat; 12-11 Sun

☎ (01624) 832494

Bushy's Bitter, Old Bushy Tail; Okell's Bitter; 1 changing beer (often Okell's) Ⓗ

In a picturesque rural location, the pub is on the steam railway station platform, convenient for rail and bus travellers. The beer garden is now complete, along with a secure and safe children's playground. The Sports Bar features live music most weekends and has a pool table. Four guest bedrooms are available. Q❀🛏♿≹♣🍎P🚌📶

Shore Hotel

Shore Road, Gansey, IM9 5LZ

⏲ 12-11 (midnight Fri & Sat) ☎ (01624) 832269

🌐 theshore.im

ISLANDS

Bushy's Old Bushy Tail; Okell's Bitter; 1 changing beer (sourced nationally) Ⓗ
A prominent building with stunning views over Gansey or Carrick Bay. Refurbished with ship timbers and door panelling, the Shore has comfy sofas and many interesting photographs, including one of the Bee Gees. There is also some nostalgic signage, and the gents is worth a look, too. The separate restaurant offers good food featuring fresh local produce. There is sheltered seating outside and a play area for children. The weekly quiz night is Tuesday.
(Colby Level)P

Ramsey

Mitre

16 Parliament Street, IM8 1AP
10-11 (1am Fri & Sat; midnight Sun) ☎ (01624) 813045
Okell's Bitter; house beer (by Okell's); 2 changing beers (sourced locally) Ⓗ
Built in 1840 as a hotel, with entrances on both sides and an excellent view of the quayside. The interior has been much refurbished in recent years but retains its comfortable seating and friendly atmosphere. Live music is hosted in the Harbour Bar upstairs, where food is served and the real ale is located. The basement Schooner Bar is only open on Friday and Saturday evenings. The Mitre is believed to be the only pub to serve Okell's Jough, as well as a changing guest ale from Hooded Ram and Bushy's. (Plaza)♣(3,3A)

Trafalgar Hotel

West Quay, IM8 1DW
11-11 (12.15am Fri & Sat); 11.30-11 Sun
☎ (01624) 814601
Moorhouse's Black Cat; Okell's Bitter; house beer (by Holt); 2 changing beers (sourced nationally) Ⓗ
Traditional twin-room pub situated on the harbour behind the main shopping street. The real ale range includes guests sourced from all over the UK. Friendly, welcoming and always busy, it is particularly popular during TT week. It is just around the corner from spectacular views of the races and not far from the electric tram terminus. A local CAMRA Pub of the Year finalist on several occasions. Q(Plaza)♣

Sulby

Ginger Hall

Ballamanagh Road, IM7 2HB
12-midnight (11 Sun) ☎ (01624) 897231
gingerhallhotel.com
Bushy's Castletown Bitter; Okell's Bitter; 1 changing beer (sourced nationally) Ⓗ
The Ginger Hall on the TT Course has been repainted white, and a window features black and white pictures of motorcycle riders. Inside there is a warm welcome in the bar, with a real fire and an impressive beer engine which dispenses two local real ales and guests that change every Thursday. Be careful not to spill your beer while admiring the huge TT map on the ceiling. The restaurant also offers food to take away. ♣P

All hands to the pumps

British beer is unique and so are the methods used for serving it. The best-known English system, the beer engine operated by a handpump on the pub bar, arrived early in the 19th century. It coincided with and was prompted by the decline of the publican brewer and the rise of commercial companies that began to dominate the supply of beer to public houses. In order to sell more beer, commercial brewers and publicans looked for faster and less labour-intensive methods of serving beer.

In The Brewing Industry in England, 1700-1830, Peter Mathias records that 'most beer had to be stored in butts in the publicans' cellars for the technical reason that it needed an even and fairly low temperature, even where convenience and restricted space behind the bar did not enforce it. This meant, equally inevitably, continuous journeying to and from the cellars by the potboys to fill up jugs from the spigots: a waste of time for the customer and of labour and trade for the publican. Drawing up beer from the cellar at the pull of a handle at the bar at once increased the speed of sale and cut the wage bill.'

The first attempt at a system for raising beer from cellar to bar was patented by Joseph Bramah in 1797. But his system – using heavy boxes of sand that pressed down on storage vessels holding the beer – was so elaborate that it was never used. But his idea encouraged others to develop simpler systems. Mathias writes: 'One of the few technical devices of importance to come into the public house since the publican stopped brewing his own beer was the beer engine. It was, from the first, a simple manually operated pump, incorporating no advances in hydraulic knowledge or engineering skill, similar in design to many pumps used at sea, yet perfectly adapted to its function in the public house.'

By 1801, John Chadwell of Blackfriars, London, was registered as a 'beer-engine maker' and soon afterwards Thomas Rowntree in the same area described himself as a 'maker of a double-acting beer-machine'. By the 1820s, beer engine services had become standard throughout most of urban England and Gaskell & Chambers in the Midlands had become the leading manufacturer, employing more than 700 people in their Birmingham works alone.

The Breweries

Breweries overview

Do you care where your beer comes from?

Today's beer drinkers want a story. In many ways, the idea of provenance in beer is not a new one – people like to drink local. Historically, beers from Burton, Leeds and Tadcaster were revered. Scottish drinkers would look to brewers in Edinburgh, the Welsh would turn their eye to Cardiff, and in Ireland's north, brews from Belfast were sought out. But a generation ago the industry changed and consolidation saw most local brewers disappear.

The importance of provenance

Now we can all drink local once again. The British brewing renaissance means we all live within a few miles of not just one brewery, but several. There are more than 1,750 brewers in the UK and that number is seemingly growing weekly. Along with all these British beers, a huge array of world 'craft' beers can also be found in pubs, beer taps and beer fridges.

However, following this increase in the popularity of craft beer and a number of brand acquisitions and buyouts of independent craft breweries by national and global brewers, many beer drinkers now want to be sure of who is brewing the beer they drink.

A survey of more than 1,000 beer drinkers commissioned by SIBA, the Society of Independent Brewers, found 6 out of 10 people cared who brewed their beer and more than two-thirds (69%) thought it would be useful to see a logo on beer clips, bottles and cans to show if a beer has been brewed by a truly independent craft brewer, rather than by a global beer company. More than half (54%) went even further and said that they would be more likely to drink a beer which carried a craft brewer logo.

SIBA's Assured scheme identifies breweries that are truly independent

The 'Assured Independent British Craft Brewer' initiative allows SIBA member brewers who are relatively small, fully independent, and brewing quality beer to use an 'Assured' seal on their beer products and point of sale marketing material to help them stand out from beers from other brewers.

The research also showed that half of beer drinkers (50%) were now drinking 'local craft beer', with this number rising to 61% for 25–34 year olds, suggesting a healthy future for this important British manufacturing industry.

SIBA spokesman Neil Walker said 'What this survey clearly shows is that consumers care whether the beer they are drinking was brewed by a truly independent British craft brewer or not – it's all about provenance, transparency and not misleading the consumer'.

Drinking local

For drinkers who want to support their local brewing economy, CAMRA's LocAle is an initiative that promotes pubs stocking locally-brewed real ale. The scheme builds on a growing consumer demand for quality local produce and an increased awareness of 'green' issues.

The CAMRA LocAle scheme was created in 2007 by CAMRA's Nottingham branch, which wanted to help support the tradition of brewing within Nottinghamshire following the demise of local brewer. Many CAMRA branches are now participating in the LocAle scheme, which has accredited hundreds of pubs that regularly sell at least one locally-brewed real ale.

Five Points brewery owner Ed Mason, who has run a bar at CAMRA's Great British Festival, said: 'I believe that consumers value provenance and want to support local and independent breweries. Many consumers don't realise that what looks like an independent local craft beer on the bar can often be owned by one of the global lager brands.

'As an industry, we truly independent craft brewers need to be vocal in championing provenance.'

CAMRA also believes that consumers should be given access to information to enable them to make informed choices about which beers to drink. There is currently no agreed definition of 'craft' beer, either in the UK or abroad. Currently, large global brewers, who produce beer in huge quantities, can market their products as 'crafted' to boost sales – riding the wave of the popularity of 'craft beer' for many drinkers. The discerning customer should have confidence that the beer they've chosen is indeed local and artisan, rather than just the product of clever marketing.

Global investment and buyouts

With more people than ever drinking more discerningly, and choosing full-flavoured, quality beer from independent British and international craft breweries, 'craft' beers have never been in

In 2018, North London brewer Beavertown sold a large stake of its business to global beer giant Heineken for an undisclosed sum

greater demand. It is therefore no surprise that this has attracted the attention of the global brewers, who have been actively buying out previously independent breweries and trying to get their own slice of this growing sector.

In June 2018, Beavertown brewery, of Tottenham, London, confirmed it had sold a minority stake of its business to international brewer Heineken. The amount of the investment was not confirmed, however, the financial boost will enable the ambitious Beavertown to complete the build of a £40-million new brewery and visitor site – Beaverworld – in North London.

In July 2018, Australian brewer Lion, a subsidiary of Japanese brewer Kirin, bought a 100 per cent stake in Bermondsey-based London brewer Fourpure, for an undisclosed sum.

These deals, following on from previous buyouts of once independent craft breweries such as that of Camden Town by ABInBev (the makers of Budweiser), London Fields by Carlsberg, and Anchor Brewing – one of the USA's first craft breweries – by Japanese giants Sapporro, have brought into focus the need for transparency in the beer world.

Regulation and innovation

Proposed new rules for the sale of higher strength beers and ciders damage producers and restrict consumer choice.

The proposed guidance from the Portman Group would limit non-resealable bottles and cans of beer and cider to no more than four units of alcohol. However, the proposals would not apply to the sale of wine, despite its much higer ABV, and packaging in similar sized containers.

The Portman proposals would apply to a 6.5% ABV speciality beer at sold in a 750ml bottle yet would not apply to a 14% wine sold in exactly the same bottle and quantity.

There are many traditional and speciality beer and cider styles where a higher alcohol content is integral to the character of that style. Such styles include stronger IPAs, barley wines and farmhouse ciders. CAMRA says the rationality of the current proposed definition is unclear and the outcome is entirely illogical.

'The proposals as set out discriminate against beer and cider drinkers, discriminate against speciality beer and cider types and will potentially have an anti-competitive effect by encouraging retailers and producers to drop speciality beer types from smaller producers,' says CAMRA.

Brewing – it's as easy as making bread

Whatever their size and commercial pressures, brewers are committed to taking naturally-grown raw materials to make beer. And in doing so they often pride themselves on minimizing their impact on the environment.

However, one brewer, Toast Ale, is thinking outside the loaf by using unsold bread. The bread to make the beer comes from all the leftover bread we don't buy. It seems around 12 million loaves are sold each day, but less than half get eaten. And, worse than that, tens of thousands of loaves a day are left on supermarket shelves. Food waste is a scourge of the 21st century.

Since 2016, Toast Ale has been taking a small proportion of our unsold bread that is perfectly safe for human consumption. It's sliced, dried and crushed into crouton-sized pieces. They then boil it with hops, cool it and add yeast. It's then fermented and bottled. The result is a perfectly drinkable beer. Who knows, one day it could be even bigger than sliced bread.

Toast brewery is highlighting and combating the issue of food waste by using unsold bread to create a range of beers

How to use the Breweries section

This section lists breweries operating in the United Kingdom, the Isle of Man and the Channel Islands. Breweries are listed in alphabetical order. They include independent companies (regional, family, micro-brewers and brewpubs), national brewers and global groups. If a brewery owns more than one site, these are cross-referenced. Within each brewery entry, regular beers are listed in increasing order of strength. Websites should be consulted when breweries produce occasional or seasonal beers that are available for less than six months of the year. We mention when breweries produce bottle-conditioned beers but do not list or evaluate them: for further information, see CAMRA's *Good Bottled Beer Guide*.

KEY TO BREWERY ENTRIES

BREWERY SYMBOLS

Brewpub: a pub that brews beer on the premises.

Cyclops: the brewery uses the Cyclops system for describing beers to consumers.

CAMRA tasting notes, supplied by a trained CAMRA tasting panel. Beer descriptions that do not carry this symbol are based on more limited tastings or have been obtained from other sources.

A CAMRA Beer of the Year in 2017.

One of CAMRA's Beers of the Year 2018: a finalist in the Champion Beer of Britain competition held during the Great British Beer Festival in London in August 2018, or in the Champion Winter Beer of Britain competition held earlier in the year.

Serve with tight sparkler: the brewery's beers can be acceptably served through a 'tight sparkler' attached to the nozzle of the beer pump, designed to give a thick collar of foam on the beer.

Do not serve with tight sparkler: the brewery's beers should NOT be served through a tight sparkler. CAMRA is opposed to the growing tendency to serve southern-brewed beers with the aid of sparklers, which aerate the beer and tend to drive hop aroma and flavour into the head, altering the balance of the beer achieved in the brewery. When neither symbol is used it means the brewery in question has not stated a preference.

Brewery tours available: check with individual breweries for details.

Brewery shop: beer available to take away. Check opening hours in advance.

RAIB **Real Ale in a Bottle:** the brewery produces bottle-conditioned beer (known by CAMRA as Real Ale in a Bottle).

♦ **Seasonal beers:** the brewery produces seasonal beers in addition to its regular range.

V **Vegan:** the brewery produces vegan beers (check with brewery for further details. Not all beers produced may be vegan).

GF **Gluten free:** the brewery produces gluten-free beers (check with brewery for further details. Not all beers may be gluten free).

ABBREVIATIONS

OG Stands for Original Gravity, the measure taken before fermentation of the level of 'fermentable material' (malt sugars and added sugars) in the brew. It is only a rough indication of strength and is no longer used for duty purposes.

ABV Stands for Alcohol by Volume, which is a more reliable measure of the percentage of alcohol in finished beer. Many breweries now only disclose ABVs but the Guide lists OGs where available. Often the OG and the ABV of a beer are identical, i.e. 1035 and 3.5 per cent. If the ABV is higher than the OG, i.e. OG 1035, ABV 3.8, this indicates that the beer has been 'well attenuated' with most of the malt sugars turned into alcohol. If the ABV is lower than the OG, this means residual sugars have been left in the beer for fullness of body and flavour: this is rare but can apply to some milds or strong old ales, barley wines and winter beers.

SIBA Indicates a member of the Society of Independent Brewers.

IFBB Indicates a member of the Independent Family Brewers of Britain.

NOTE: The Breweries section was correct at the time of going to press and every effort has been made to ensure that all regularly-available cask-conditioned beers are included.

The Breweries

The breweries listed in this section include micro, small, family, regional, national and global companies. Please use the Beer index (p1001) to help locate beers.

1648 SIBA

Old Stables Brewery, Mill Lane, East Hoathly, East Sussex, BN8 6QB
☎ (01825) 840830 🌐 1648brewing.co.uk

⊗ The 1648 brewery, set up in the old stable block at the King's Head pub in 2003, derives its name from the year of the deposition of King Charles I. One pub is owned and more than 40 outlets are supplied. ‼ ♦ RAIB

Hop Pocket (OG 1039, ABV 3.7%)

Triple Champion (OG 1041, ABV 4%)
A chestnut-coloured traditional ale, deeply flavoured and full bodied.

Signature (OG 1044, ABV 4.4%)
Pale, light, crisply refreshing ale with a bitter aftertaste.

Laughing Frog (OG 1052, ABV 5.2%)
Dark golden-coloured, full-bodied ale. Lightly hopped with a full malty flavour.

22 Bake & Brew SIBA

Platform 22, Station Road, Torphins, AB31 4JF
☎ (01339) 882807 ✉ david@platform22.co.uk

Brewery adjacent to Platform 22 café/bar. No real ale.

3 Brewers of St Albans SIBA

The Potato Shed, Symonds Hyde Farm, Symonds Hyde Lane, Hatfield, Hertfordshire, AL10 9BB
☎ (01707) 271636 ☎ 07941 854615
🌐 3brewers.co.uk

⊗ Launched in 2013 by three brewers from St Albans who turned a potato shed into an eight-barrel brewery. Spent malt becomes compost for the farm. Its range of seven beers is supplied to beer and wine merchants in the local area. ‼

Dark Mild (OG 1036, ABV 3.6%)
Dark ruby in colour this smooth and creamy mild combines a malty sweetness with a touch of liquorice bitterness to make a well-balanced ale.

Golden English Ale (OG 1038, ABV 3.8%)
A light golden-coloured refreshing ale with a subtle citrus flavour and a hint of sweetness.

Classic English Ale (OG 1040, ABV 4%)
Deep amber in colour with a light, hoppy aroma and a rich, rounded malty taste balanced by subtle hoppiness to give a clean, smooth and refreshing ale.

Blonde (OG 1042, ABV 4.2%)
A light golden-coloured ale with a hoppy aroma and a refreshing smack of fruity citrus flavours.

Ruby English Ale (OG 1043, ABV 4.3%)

IPA (OG 1046, ABV 4.6%)
Golden-coloured IPA with a clean, dry finish.

Special English Ale (OG 1048, ABV 4.8%)
A robust and full-bodied premium ale made with a deep copper colour and a hint of berries. Well-balanced and smooth.

3 Piers (NEW)

19 Cocker Avenue, Poulton Industrial Estate, Poulton-le-Fylde, Lancashire, FY6 8JU ☎ 07977 469326
🌐 3piersbrewery.com

Brewing began in 2017 using a 15-barrel plant. A wide range of beers is produced and delivered direct all over the UK. ‼ ♦

Northern Monkey (ABV 3.8%)
An amber-coloured beer brewed with a range of three hops to produce a pleasant session ale.

Golden Smiler (ABV 4%)
A crisp, golden-coloured ale with a fresh flavour.

Old Station Porter (ABV 4.5%)
A rich, dark porter that packs a punch.

West Coast Blonde (ABV 4.6%)
Pleasantly-hopped golden ale with a citrus bite.

Central Citra (ABV 5%)
A fresh IPA with a great hit of hops.

360° SIBA

Unit 24b, Bluebell Business Estate, Sheffield Park, East Sussex, TN22 3HQ
☎ (01825) 722375 🌐 360degreebrewing.com

⊗ Brewing began in 2013 using a six-barrel plant. Beers are available across Sussex, the South East, and London. ‼ ♦

Pale (ABV 3.9%)
A full-flavoured, zesty golden ale.

Best (ABV 4.2%)
A traditional, copper-coloured best bitter. Brewed with Kentish hops to produce an aromatic ale with a clean bitterness.

American Pale Ale (ABV 5%)
A contemporary pale ale, heavily hopped to produce intense tropical fruit flavours and a long bitter finish.

3D Beer

See Epic Beers

40FT

Bootyard, Abbot Street, Dalston, London, E8 3DP

Office: The Printhouse, 18-20 Ashwin Street, Dalston, London, E8 3DL 🌐 40ftbrewery.com

40FT began brewing in 2015. It is a six-barrel microbrewery, located in a 40-ft shipping container in a disused car park close to Ridley Road Market. Beers are produced for its brewery tap room as well as pubs, bars, restaurants and off licences.

#alesnotdead (OG 1045, ABV 4.5%)
An amber-coloured, hoppy ale.

THE BREWERIES

4Four

Sarngwm, Bethesda, SA67 8HG
☎ (01834) 474440 ☎ 07789 186503 🌐 4four.beer

4four began brewing in 2016 using a 2.5-barrel plant. Steve and Christie have had a passion for real ale for more than 12 years in their CAMRA award-winning pub and wanted to turn their hand at producing it themselves. Beers are music themed. Brewing is currently suspended. ♦RAIB

4Ts

Unit 20, Manor Industrial Estate, Lower Wash Lane, Latchford, Warrington, Cheshire, WA4 1PL
☎ (01925) 747463 ☎ 07917 730184
🌐 4tsbrewery.co.uk

Brewing returned to Warrington in 2015. Beers are usually available in the Tavern, Warrington. ‼♦

Pale Ale (OG 1037, ABV 3.7%)
Pale, refreshing session ale, well-balanced with spicy hop notes.

APA (OG 1040, ABV 4%)
An American-style pale ale, hoppy with spicy and citrus hints throughout and a hint of bitterness at the end leaving a burst of citrus flavour.

WSB (Warrington Special Bitter) (ABV 4.2%)
An English bitter with a malty base. Crisp and refreshing with aromas of blackcurrant and citrus.

IPA (OG 1046, ABV 4.6%)
A hoppy beer with hints of citrus and passion fruit and a punch of bitterness.

Pilsner (ABV 4.8%)
A Czech-style Pilsner. Earth and fresh bread aromas with hints of honeysuckle followed by malty sweetness and a pleasing bitterness.

Stout (OG 1050, ABV 5%)
A smooth, well-balanced stout with biscuit, chocolate and burnt notes to start and hoppy, flowery tones at the end.

Big Daddy IPA (ABV 7.2%)
A double IPA. Clean and crisp with an intense resinous, citrus and grapefruit aroma.

7

16 Woodlands Park, Durris, AB31 6BF ☎ 07890 814636 🌐 7reasonstobrew.co.uk

Brewing began in 2016 using a four-barrel plant.

71 (NEW) SIBA

36-40 Bellfield Street, Dundee, DD1 5HZ
☎ (01382) 203133 🌐 71brewing.com

Brewing began in 2016.

8 Sail SIBA

Heckington Windmill, Hale Road, Heckington, Lincolnshire, NG34 9JW
☎ (01529) 469308 ☎ 07866 183479
🌐 8sailbrewery.co.uk

8 Sail Brewery was established in 2010 and operates on a six-barrel brew plant. The brewery nestles in the shadow of Heckington Windmill, Britain's only eight-sailed windmill, from where the brewery takes its name. The mill is now working and helping to mill malted grain for the brewery. The brewery shop stocks bottle-conditioned beers alongside local ciders. The front of the brewery has been converted into a Victorian-style bar. 🛒♦RAIB

8 Sail Ale (OG 1040, ABV 3.8%)
A refreshing, traditional English pale ale.

Windmill Bitter (OG 1040, ABV 3.8%)
An amber-coloured session bitter with a good blend of malt and hops.

Blonde (OG 1042, ABV 4%)

Millwright (OG 1042, ABV 4%)
A mild with rich, dark flavours lightly balanced with hops. The aroma is chocolate with a dry roast and liquorice flavour.

Fenman (OG 1043, ABV 4.1%)

Rolling Stone (OG 1044, ABV 4.3%)

King John's Jewels (OG 1045, ABV 4.5%)

Millstone (OG 1046, ABV 4.5%)
A premium bitter with a good blend of malt and hops.

Windy Miller (OG 1047, ABV 4.6%)
A rich, dark, smooth-flavoured stout brewed with a generous amount of oat malt.

Damson Porter (OG 1053, ABV 5%)
Damsons have been added to give a full-bodied fruitiness to the rich, complex flavours. The aroma is bitter with caramel tones. Flavour is malty, slightly fruity with a bitter finish.

Victorian Porter (OG 1053, ABV 5%)
An aroma of berries, sour fruits and roasted malts and deep, intense, chocolaty flavours give this dark-coloured beer a rich and full-bodied flavour.

Old Colony – Deacon John Ales (OG 1052, ABV 5.3%)

Black Widow (OG 1054, ABV 5.5%)
A strong, dark ruby mild. Dark malt and liquorice flavours dominate.

John Barleycorn IPA (OG 1053, ABV 5.5%)

81 Artisan

The Courtyard, Crowshall Farm, Chilgrove Road, West Dean, West Sussex, PO18 9HP
☎ (01243) 527444 ☎ 07990 035736
🌐 81artisan.com

Brewing began in 2017 using a 10-barrel plant.

9 Lives

Unit 303, Ystradgynlais Workshops, Trawsffordd Road, Ystradgynlais, SA9 1BS ☎ 07743 559736
🌐 9livesbrewing.co.uk

◎9 Lives was established in 2017 by Robert Scott, formerly the brewer at the now defunct Bryncelyn Brewery, using the same six-barrel plant. ‼♦RAIB

Amber (OG 1039, ABV 3.9%) ◈
Pale amber in colour with a hoppy aroma. A refreshing, hoppy, fruity flavour with balancing bitterness; a similar lasting finish. A beer full of flavour for its gravity.

Dark (OG 1040, ABV 4%) ◈
Dark brown in colour with an inviting aroma of malt, roast and fruit. A gentle bitterness mixes

roast with malt, hops and fruit, giving a complex, satisfying and lasting finish.

Gold (OG 1045, ABV 4.5%)
An inviting aroma of hops, fruit and malt, and a golden colour. The tasty mix of hops, fruit, bitterness and background malt ends with a long, hoppy, bitter aftertaste. Full-bodied and drinkable.

Pale (OG 1045, ABV 4.7%)
A light amber-coloured ale with a citrus hop aroma and tropical fruit flavour. Hoppy with a dry bitter finish.

Special (OG 1050, ABV 5%)
A fruity pale ale, deceptively drinkable for its strength. Sweetish but not cloying.

Black Mass (OG 1065, ABV 6.7%)
A strong black stout with complex roast flavours and a lasting bitter finish.

A-B InBev UK

Porter Tun House, 500 Capability Green, Luton, Bedfordshire, LU1 3LS
☎ (01582) 391166 inbev.com

No real ale.

Abbey SIBA

Abbey Brewery, Camden Row, Bath, BA1 5LB
☎ (01225) 444437 abbeyales.co.uk

Founded in 1997, Abbey Ales was the first brewery in Bath for over 50 years. It supplies more than 80 regular outlets within a 20-mile radius. It operates four pubs in Bath. !! ♦

Somerset Ale (OG 1038, ABV 3.8%)
An amber-coloured, full-bodied, malty ale with hints of caramel balanced with a hoppy and floral finish.

Bath Best (OG 1040, ABV 4%)
A good balance of malt and hops. Sweet to the nose with a bitter finish.

Bellringer (OG 1042, ABV 4.2%)
A notably hoppy ale, light to medium-bodied, clean-tasting, refreshingly dry, with a balancing sweetness. Citrus, pale malt aroma and dry, bitter finish.

Abbey Grange

See Llangollen

Abbeydale SIBA

Unit 8, Aizlewood Road, Sheffield, South Yorkshire, S8 0YX
☎ (0114) 281 2712 abbeydalebrewery.co.uk

Since starting in 1996, Abbeydale Brewery has grown steadily; it now produces upwards of 200 barrels a week, and recent investment has enabled further growth. ♦

Daily Bread (OG 1037, ABV 3.8%)
A classic copper-coloured English bitter. Well-balanced with a smooth finish.

Deception (OG 1043, ABV 4.1%)
A pale-coloured beer with aromas of elderflower and grapes. Strong citrus flavours. Long-lasting bitter finish.

Moonshine (OG 1041.2, ABV 4.3%)
A well-balanced pale ale with a full hop aroma and pleasant grapefruit traces.

Absolution (OG 1050, ABV 5.3%)

Abernyte

South Latch Farm, Abernyte, Perthshire, PH14 9SU
☎ 07827 715915 abernytebrewery.com

Brewing began in 2016. No real ale.

Abington

Buckingham Garden Centre, Tingewick Road, Buckingham, MK18 4AE abingtonales.com

Started by Peter Brown as a home brewery, commercial production began in 2016 in 50-litre batches at the family garden centre in Buckingham. Beer is sold in bottles at the garden centre and at the Beer Grill, Northampton. RAIB

Abstract Jungle

Unit 14, Bailey Brook Industrial Estate, Amber Drive, Langley Mill, NG16 4BE ☎ 07481 849332

Office: 2 Manor Farm Mews, Brinsley, Nottinghamshire, NG16 5AG
simon@abstractjunglebrewery.co.uk

Set up in 2016 by experienced head brewer Simon King, Abstract Jungle is a husband-and-wife team. A range of five core beers is brewed on a custom-built six-barrel plant along with occasional beers that stretch the boundaries of modern day brewing. Its tap house is the Bunny Hop, Langley Mill. !!

Foolish (OG 1040.5, ABV 3.9%)
An easy-drinking session pale ale.

Pride (OG 1040, ABV 3.9%)
Crisp and clean pale ale with a low, mellow bitterness and a tropical aroma.

Jackal (OG 1043, ABV 4.2%)
Traditional-style porter with a subtle spicy aroma.

Easy American Brown (OG 1045, ABV 4.4%)
Biscuit, caramel and chocolate notes with subtle hop flavours.

Restless (OG 1045, ABV 4.5%)
A hoppy ale. Resinous and fruity.

Casual (OG 1048, ABV 4.6%)
A bold, complex stout using unrefined chocolate with a hint of blueberries.

Sturdy (OG 1054, ABV 5.6%)
A classic, hoppy IPA. Pine resinous and citrus fruits.

Abyss (NEW) SIBA

Unit 12, Squires Farm Industrial Estate, Palehouse Common, Framfield, East Sussex, TN22 5RB
☎ (01825) 840561 ☎ 07919 445345
abyssbrewing.co.uk

Small-scale brewing started in Lewes in early 2017 but moved to Framfield in late 2017 to a larger eight-barrel plant. Beers are only available in KeyKeg at present. ♦V

THE BREWERIES

Acorn SIBA

Unit 3, Aldham Industrial Estate, Mitchell Road, Wombwell, Barnsley, South Yorkshire, S73 8HA
☎ (01226) 270734 acorn-brewery.co.uk

Acorn was set up in 2003 with a 10-barrel expanding to a 20-barrel plant when the brewery moved to larger premises and currently has a 160-barrel a week capacity. All beers are produced using the Barnsley Bitter yeast strain, dating back to the 1850s. !! ♦ RAIB

Yorkshire Pride (OG 1037, ABV 3.7%)
This session beer is golden in colour with pleasing fruit notes. A mouthwatering blend of malt and hops create a fruity taste which leads to a clean bitter finish.

Barnsley Bitter (OG 1038, ABV 3.8%)
This brown-coloured bitter has a smooth, malty bitterness throughout with notes of chocolate and caramel. Fruity, bitter finish.

Blonde (OG 1040.5, ABV 4%)
A clean-tasting, golden-coloured hoppy beer with a refreshing bitter and fruity aftertaste.

Barnsley Gold (OG 1041.5, ABV 4.3%)
This golden ale has fruit in the aroma with a hoppy and fruity flavour throughout. A well-hopped, clean, dry finish.

Old Moor Porter (OG 1045, ABV 4.4%)
A rich-tasting porter, smooth throughout with a hint of chocolate and liquorice.

Gorlovka Imperial Stout (OG 1058, ABV 6%)
This black stout is rich and smooth and full of chocolate and liquorice flavours with a fruity, creamy finish.

Ad Hop

18 Severs Street, Liverpool, L6 5HJ ☎ 07957 165501

Ad Hop started life in 2014 at the Clove Hitch pub, moving a couple of times before ending up in much larger premises in 2017 where a 5.5-barrel plant was added to its existing 2.5-barrel one. The brewery specialises in innovative beers. ♦ RAIB

Merseyful (OG 1037, ABV 4.2%)
A rich bitter with a fruity nose.

Enigma (OG 1051, ABV 5.2%)
A single-hopped IPA with fruity hop notes.

Adnams SIBA

Sole Bay Brewery, East Green, Southwold, Suffolk, IP18 6JW
☎ (01502) 727200 ☎ 07787 151311
adnams.co.uk

The company was founded by George and Ernest Adnams in 1872. About 50 pubs are owned around East Anglia and outpost in London and there is national distribution. Beers are from a 300-barrel plant within the confines of the present site. !! ♦

Lighthouse (OG 1037, ABV 3.4%)
A quaffable beer with bitterness predominating.

Southwold Bitter (OG 1037, ABV 3.7%)
Aromas of toffee apple, caramel and sulphur. Taste is a complex mix of malt toffee and roast bitterness with hops. Malty bitter and apple flavours linger into the aftertaste.

Mosaic (OG 1041, ABV 4.1%)
Tropical fruit nose, intensely fruity flavour with complex hop characteristics, which linger in the aftertaste.

Old Ale (OG 1044, ABV 4.1%)
Aromas of malt and soft cheese, leading into malty and sweet flavours with fruit berries and vanilla. Caramel and roast finish.

Ghost Ship (OG 1046, ABV 4.5%)
A pale ale with an assertive pithy bitterness, biscuit flavours and fresh citrus aroma.

Broadside (OG 1049, ABV 4.7%)
Rich, malty aroma with blackberries and dried fruit. Rich and full flavours of malt and fruit, with roast and caramel notes and subtle hops. Well-balanced, long-lasting aftertaste.

Adur

Brick Barn, Charlton Court, Mouse Lane, Steyning, West Sussex, BN44 3DG
☎ (01903) 867614

Office: 2 Sullington Way, Shoreham-by-Sa, West Sussex, BN43 6PJ adurvalleycoop.com

Adur Brewery, nestled in the heart of the South Downs, was launched in 2008 on a 5.5-barrel plant, marking the return of brewing to the Adur Valley after an interval of nearly 100 years. The brewery was sold to the Adur Valley Co-Operative Ltd in 2012, including the Adur Brewery name and recipes. A large part of the output is sold as bottle-conditioned beer. !! ♦ RAIB

Ropetackle Golden Ale (OG 1036, ABV 3.4%)
A light, golden ale with an initial sweetness and delicate aroma balanced by a dry finish.

Hop Token: Amarillo (OG 1040, ABV 4%)
An amber-coloured bitter with notes of peach and grapefruit in both aroma and taste, a good bitterness and a long, dry finish.

Hop Token: Summit (OG 1040, ABV 4%)
Hints of tangerine in the aroma and flavour.

Velocity (OG 1044, ABV 4.4%)
Traditional best bitter with a hoppy aroma and a hint of marmalade in the taste.

Black William (OG 1055, ABV 5%)
A rich, black stout with dark chocolate aromas and roasted flavours.

Robbie's Red (OG 1050, ABV 5.2%)
A strong ale with an aroma of malt and hops. Slight initial sweetness leads to complex flavours including smoky orange peel and a satisfying bitterness which persists in the long finish.

Affinity

Railway Arch 7, Almond Road, South Bermondsey, London, SE16 3LR ☎ 07904 391807
affinitybrewco.com

Established in 2016 using a 2.5-barrel plant, Affinity moved from Tottenham to South Bermondsey in 2017. Beers are mainly available in KeyKeg but cask-conditioned beers are available.

Ainsty SIBA

Manor Farm, Intake Lane, Acaster Malbis, North Yorkshire, YO23 3UJ

☎ (01904) 703233 ☎ 07983 604989
🌐 ainstyales.co.uk

Established in 2014 as a cuckoo brewery, its own 10-barrel brewery opened in 2016 in the ancient York and Ainsty Wappentake, a few miles south-west of York. Homegrown hops are used in the beers, which can be found in York, across Yorkshire and as distant as the South of England. !! ♦

Angel (ABV 3.7%)
An easy-drinking session pale ale with a refreshing, clean and smooth finish.

Flummoxed Farmer (ABV 4%)
A blonde ale with a grapefruit and tropical nose, giving a refreshing and slightly hoppy, dry finish.

Bantam Best (ABV 4.2%)
Slightly sweet with a crisp bitter finish.

Assassin (ABV 4.9%)
Oatmeal stout with a smooth and slightly sweet finish.

Aire Heads

Unit 4d, Rawcliffe Road Industrial Estate, Lidice Road, Goole, East Yorkshire, DN14 6XL ☎ 07842 141584
🌐 aireheadsbrewery.com

Aire Heads began brewing in 2017. It is owned by lifelong friends Ben Pindar and Lee Lawrence, who have turned their passion into a profession. The brewery has 30 regular outlets and produces eight core beers alongside a range of special ales. !! ♦

Airelequin (ABV 3.5%)
An amber-coloured session ale with a rich hop flavour.

Aire-Brained (ABV 3.7%)
Session pale ale with gentle hop bitterness and fruit, pine and earthy flavours.

A Reet Gud Middl'n (ABV 4%)
Traditional Yorkshire bitter. Dark amber in colour, malty and with traditional English hops to deliver a bitter, fruity and floral finish.

Vintage Vixen (ABV 4%)
Dark amber in colour, rich malt with a big toffee finish.

Grain Disorder (ABV 4.5%)
An intensely-hopped American-style IPA. Sweet at first and then bitter with a big fruity finish.

Rye & Aire (ABV 4.5%)
A rye beer with a complex hop profile. Straw-coloured and dry on the palate with spicy and citrus fruit tastes.

Beyond a Shadow of a Stout (ABV 5%)
A dark, smoky stout with hints of chocolate, molasses and lashings of liquorice followed by a bittersweet finish.

The Tsar (ABV 7.5%)
A Russian Imperial stout with coffee. Rich molasses, chocolate, a strike of hop bitterness and a big coffee finish.

AJ's

Unit 12, Ashmore Industrial Estate, Longacre Street, Walsall, West Midlands, WS2 8QG ☎ 07860 585911
✉ ajs-ales@hotmail.com

AJ's was established in 2015 and use a four-barrel plant with three fermenting vessels and a cool room. Black Country pubs, local wholesalers and Wetherspoon outlets are supplied. ♦

Blackjack Mild (ABV 3.6%)

Stuck on Blondes (ABV 3.9%)

Best Bitter (OG 1040, ABV 4%)

Go-a-ld (ABV 4.1%)

SPA (OG 1042, ABV 4.2%)

Stuck in the Mud (ABV 4.3%)

Ruby (OG 1044, ABV 4.4%)

IPA (ABV 4.6%)

Stuck in the Doghouse (ABV 4.7%)

Albion

5 Milton Avenue, Bear Flat, Bath, BA2 4QZ
☎ (01225) 480465 🌐 albionbrewing.co.uk

Picobrewery established in 2016 brewing up to four regular beers and one-off specials. All output is bottle conditioned and available at local restaurants and speciality beer shops. Brewing is currently suspended. ♦RAIB

Alcazar

See Shipstone's

Aldwark Artisan (NEW)

Lydgate Farm, Aldwark, Derbyshire, DE4 4HW
☎ (01629) 540720 ✉ sales@aaabrewery.co.uk

Housed in an old milking shed on a rural working farm, this 10-barrel plant produced its first beers in 2017 using water from the farm's own borehole. ♦

Alechemy SIBA

Unit B, 1 Gregory Road, Kirkton Campus, Livingston, EH54 7DR
☎ (01506) 413634 ☎ 07748 156973
🌐 alechemy.beer

Dr James Davies, a keen traditional brewer and chemist, started brewing in 2012. A 12-barrel plant is used. New beers are being produced regularly. Beers can be found in shops and pubs across the UK. ♦RAIB

Charisma (OG 1036, ABV 3.5%)

Starhopper (OG 1036, ABV 3.5%)

Ritual (OG 1042, ABV 4.1%)
Well-balanced golden ale. A strong hop character, balanced by malt and fruit with a long, dry finish.

Photon (OG 1043, ABV 4.2%)
A pale ale with lots of American hops.

Five Sisters (OG 1045, ABV 4.3%)
Flavoursome tawny-coloured beer with excellent balance of malt, hops and fruit plus hints of roast and caramel. Lingering distinctive finish.

10 Storey Malt Bomb (OG 1049, ABV 4.5%)
Modern take on a traditional 80/- using 10 different malts.

Bad Day at the Office (OG 1047, ABV 4.5%)

Citra Simcoe (ABV 4.5%)

Damona (OG 1056, ABV 5.3%)

Secret Citra (OG 1056, ABV 5.7%)

Ales of Scilly

2b Porthmellon Industrial Estate, St Mary's, Isles of Scilly, TR21 0JY
☎ (01720) 423233 alesofscilly.co.uk

Opened in 2001, Ales of Scilly is the most south-westerly brewery in Britain. Several island pubs are supplied, plus a number of outlets on the mainland and beer festivals across the country. Special one-off beers are produced in celebration of significant island events. ‼ ♦

Schiller (OG 1038, ABV 3.9%)

Challenger (OG 1039, ABV 4.2%)
Amber-coloured best bitter with a faint malt and hop nose. A refreshing, light beer with apricot flavours throughout and gentle malty bitterness.

Alfred's

Unit 6, Winnall Farm Industrial Estate, Easton Lane, Winchester, Hampshire, SO23 0HA
☎ (01962) 859999 ☎ 07980 483124
alfredsbrewery.co.uk

Alfred's is a 3.5-barrel brewhouse opened by Steve and Isabelle Haigh in 2012. Steve previously brewed for three other renowned Hampshire breweries. In 2018 production was moved to a larger nearby site after the installation of a nine-barrel state-of-the-art brewhouse. Deliveries are made to pubs within 15 miles of Winchester. ‼ ♦

Saxon Bronze (OG 1038, ABV 3.8%)
Crisp, light and hoppy straw-coloured session ale with citrus notes.

Winchester Pale Ale (ABV 4.5%)
Pale golden-coloured beer with tropical and stone fruit flavours.

All Day

Salle Brewery Barns 14-16, Salle Moor Hall Farm, Wood Dalling Road, Salle, Norfolk, NR10 4SB
☎ (01603) 327656 ☎ 07825 604887
alldaybrewing.co.uk

Located in former farm buildings, the brewery has established its own hop yard, to be self-sufficient in 13 traditional varieties of hop. Hops are frozen and used to produce a range of green hop beers throughout the year. A tap room and shop are open at weekends and other ad hoc hours. Organic cider is also produced. A changing range of beers is available. ♦ RAIB

All Hallows

Main Street, Goodmanham, East Yorkshire, YO43 3JA
☎ (01430) 873849 goodmanhamarms.co.uk

Abbie Logozzi, landlady of the Goodmanham Arms, started brewing in 2012 in outbuildings behind the pub. The ex-Goodmanham Brewery Buildings were purchased and a five-barrel plant installed. The brewery name comes from the adjacent 12th-century All Hallows Church. Local legendary characters are used in the naming of some of the beers. Brews are supplied to the pub, its sister pub, the Bay Horse at Burythorpe. ♦

Allendale SIBA

Allen Mill, Allendale, Northumberland, NE47 9EA
☎ (01434) 618686 allendalebrewery.com

Established in 2006, the brewery is a state-of-the-art 20-barrel plant in a historic lead smelting mill, which formed the centre of the mining industry of the area during the industrial revolution. Many of the beer names reflect this and the local area. ‼ ♦

Wagtail Best Bitter (OG 1037, ABV 3.8%)
Amber-coloured bitter with spicy aromas and a long, bitter finish.

Golden Plover (OG 1039, ABV 4%)
Light, refreshing, easy-drinking blonde beer with a clean finish.

Pennine Pale (OG 1040, ABV 4%)
Pale ale brewed with American hops for a full, fruity aroma and flavour and a refreshing citrus finish.

Wayfarer (OG 1045, ABV 4.4%)
Single hop pale ale. Fruity and soft bitter taste.

Wolf (OG 1053, ABV 5.5%)
Full-bodied, red-coloured ale with bitterness in the taste giving way to a fruity finish.

Wilderness (OG 1058, ABV 6.5%)
A full-bodied West Coast-style IPA with citrus and tropical aromas, full of flavour and refreshing bitterness.

AllGates

See Wigan

Almasty

Unit 11, Algernon Industrial Estate, New York Road, Shiremoor, NE27 0NB
☎ (0191) 253 1639 almasty.co.uk

Opened in 2014, this two-man operated 10-barrel plant produces an ever-changing range of unfined, unfiltered beers. A barrel ageing programme is also in place. Twice yearly open days are held (in spring and summer). Pumpclips are made from screen-printed, hand-sawn logs. The brewery tap is the Free Trade Inn, Byker, while the beers are supplied nationwide. ‼ ♦

Alnwick

See Cumberland and Daleside

Alphabet SIBA

99 Northern Western Street, Ardwick, Manchester, M12 6JL
☎ (0161) 272 6532 alphabetbrewing.co.uk

Alphabet began brewing in 2014 and is situated in Manchester city centre under railway arches. It has an 1,344-barrel capacity with a new 15-barrel kit and 11 fermenting vessels. It focuses mainly on keg/KeyKeg beers, which are unflitered and unpasteurised. The brewery also cans its own beers on site. A brewery tap is open every Saturday (12-10pm). A new bar in Chorlton opened in 2018.

Alphabeta

Pittcue, 1 The Avenue, Devonshire Square, London, EC2M 4YP
☎ (020) 7324 7770

Alphabeta is a small in-house brewery contiguous with the Pittcue restaurant. A wide range of small-batch beers is available. ♦

Altarnun SIBA

Inner Trenarrett, Altarnun, Launceston, Cornwall, PL15 7SY
☎ (01566) 86069

Formerly known as Penpont, Altarnan began brewing in 2008 and has steadily increased its range and production since then. The award-winning brewery currently uses a 25-barrel plant with an eight-barrel plant for special brews. Beers are available in pubs across Cornwall. Beer is also brewed under the Firebrand Brewing Co label. ‼ ♦ RAIB

St Nonna's (OG 1037, ABV 3.7%)
Tawny-coloured session bitter with floral nose and balanced malt and hop bitterness throughout with roast and sweet notes. Bitter finish.

Cornish Arvor (OG 1040, ABV 4%)
Gold-coloured bitter with malt and hop aroma. Full-flavoured malt balanced by resinous and earthy hop bitterness. Rising dry and bitter finish.

Creation Pale Ale (OG 1039.2, ABV 4.2%)
Gold-coloured bitter with hop aroma. Quite hoppy taste with sweet peach, citrus zing and roast malt. Bitter, slightly dry finish.

Shipwreck Coast (OG 1044, ABV 4.4%)
Gold-coloured beer with a citrus aroma. Assertive lemon citrus hop notes with malt taste and finish with bitterness and fruits. Faint dryness.

Roughtor (OG 1047, ABV 4.7%)
Copper-coloured strong bitter with malt and citrus hop aroma. Hop bitterness balanced by malt, plum and marmalade. Bitter, dry finish.

Beast of Bodmin (OG 1046.5, ABV 5%)
Tawny-coloured strong bitter with malt aroma. Smooth roast malt, chestnuts and complex fruits in the mouth. Refreshing malty, bitter finish.

Stormer IPA (OG 1046.7, ABV 5.2%)
A full-bodied, American-style IPA.

Brewed under the Firebrand Brewery name:

Big Hop, Little Beer (OG 1035, ABV 3.6%)
A golden-coloured malty ale with a fruity aroma and taste.

Cross Pacific Pale Ale (ABV 4%)
A pale ale with a malty taste giving way to a burst of hop flavour.

Graffiti IPA (ABV 5%)
A smooth, malty body leads to a hoppy, fruity finish.

Amazing

Ship Inn, 65 High Street, Sandgate, Kent, CT20 3AH
☎ (01303) 248525

Amazing was set up in 2016 using a four-barrel plant and is situated at the Ship Inn, Sandgate. The pub and local beer festivals are supplied. The brewery can be viewed from inside the pub. ‼

Amber SIBA

Unit 7, Outram Business Centre, Whiteley Road, Ripley, Derbyshire, DE5 3QL
☎ (01773) 512864 amberales.co.uk

Amber Ales began production in 2006 on a five-barrel plant from the Firkin brewpub chain. Around 100 outlets are supplied in the Derby/Nottingham/Chesterfield area, further afield via distributors. ‼ ♦ RAIB V

Sunrise (ABV 3.8%)

Chocolate Orange Stout (OG 1040, ABV 4%)

Original Black Stout (OG 1040, ABV 4%)
Traditional stout made with a complex blend of malts to give a full-flavoured, smooth and easy-drinking ale with a subtle hop aroma.

Barnes Wallis (OG 1040, ABV 4.1%)
An easy-drinking IPA-style bitter, copper-coloured with a full malt flavour.

Revolution (OG 1047, ABV 4.5%)
Spicy golden ale with a touch of rye and a hoppy, citrus-packed flavour explosion.

Dambuster (OG 1051, ABV 5.5%)

Imperial IPA (OG 1058, ABV 6.5%)
Traditional IPA with a substantial malty base and a big hop profile.

Ambridge

Unit 2a, Priory Piece Business Park, Priory Farm Lane, Inkberrow, Worcestershire, WR7 4HT
☎ (01386) 792191 ☎ 07500 046391
ambridgebrewery.co.uk

Ambridge commenced brewing in 2013, initially for the family pub, the Bulls Head in Inkberrow. Later that year they acquired the Wyre Piddle Brewery and relocated it to the outskirts of the village. The beers from both breweries continue to be brewed. On-demand brews supplement the core range, and some small-run bottling is carried out. ‼ ♦ RAIB

Sticky Dog (OG 1040, ABV 4%)
Smooth and easy-drinking, citrus hop aroma with a refreshing finish.

Honey Bunny (OG 1043, ABV 4.2%)
Full-flavoured, honey infused ale; smooth with hints of honey.

WPA (Worcestershire Pale Ale) (OG 1043, ABV 4.2%)
A premium pale ale with an good balance of hops and malt. Hops carry on from the taste to a bittersweet finish.

Citra (OG 1044, ABV 4.4%)
Light and refreshing single-hopped beer with a zesty lemon and lime bitter finish.

Mosaic (OG 1044, ABV 4.4%)

Citralicious (OG 1046, ABV 4.6%)

Jester (OG 1048, ABV 4.8%)
Single-hopped beer with a punchy aroma of grapefruit and tropical fruits. Pale gold in colour with a delicate bitter finish.

Ampersand SIBA

Camphill Farm, Middle Road, Earsham, Norfolk, NR35 2AH ☎ 07791 086689 🌐 ampersandbrew.co

A small batch brewery established in 2017 and based on a family farm in South Norfolk.

Amwell Springs

Westfield Farm House, Cholsey, Oxfordshire, OX10 9LS ☎ 07812 396619 ✉ gibbo_seven@hotmail.com

Brewing began in 2017 on a 70-litre plant using water from a spring in the farmhouse grounds. Unfined bottle-conditioned beers are produced which are sold directly from the brewery. RAIB V

An Teallach

Camusnagaul, Dundonnell, Garve, IV23 2QT ☎ (01854) 633306 ✉ ataleco1@yahoo.co.uk

An Teallach was formed in 2001 by husband-and-wife team David and Wilma Orr, on the family croft on the shores of Little Loch Broom, Wester Ross. More than 60 pubs are supplied. !! ♦

Beallach Na Ba (OG 1038, ABV 3.8%)
Golden-amber-coloured citrus hoppy brew with some background malts.

Beinn Dearg Ale (OG 1044, ABV 3.8%)
A well-balanced, malty, hoppy, sweetish beer with a long, malty bitter aftertaste.

Ale (OG 1042, ABV 4.2%)
A pint in the Scottish 80/- tradition. Plenty of malt in the nicely-balanced bittersweet taste.

Crofters Pale Ale (OG 1042, ABV 4.2%)
Refreshing mix of citrus hops and malt.

Suilven (OG 1043, ABV 4.3%)
A refreshing yellow-coloured brew with plenty of citrus fruits and hops throughout.

Kildonan (OG 1044, ABV 4.4%)
Plenty of fruit and a good smack of bitterness in this golden ale.

Anarchy SIBA

Unit A1, Benfield Business Park, Newcastle upon Tyne, NE6 4NQ ☎ 07702 810111 🌐 anarchybrewco.com

Originally a 10-barrel plant based on the outskirts of Morpeth, the brewery moved to new premises in 2018, upgrading to a 30-barrel plant with a taproom. Run by an enthusiastic team producing a range of hand-crafted beers and lagers with big, bold flavours. !! ♦ RAIB

Smoke Bomb (OG 1043, ABV 3.9%)
Unfined and unfiltered bitter with a light, smoky nose and Bavarian smoked ham and citrus flavours matched with dark, smooth toffee malts.

Blonde Star (OG 1041, ABV 4.1%)
Lemon, grapefruit and passion fruit hop flavours combine with pale malts to give a crisp and fresh, light-bodied session ale.

Citra Star (OG 1041, ABV 4.1%)
Citrus, grapefruit, lemon, lime and passion fruit hop flavours give a clean, crisp, light-bodied ale.

Boot Boys (OG 1049, ABV 5%)
A brown-coloured ale with rich caramel malt flavours and a nutty finish.

Urban Assault (OG 1050, ABV 5%)
Medium-bodied, light red-coloured ale with heavy notes of lemon, orange and passion fruit in the flavour, followed by a bitter finish.

Crime Scene (OG 1056, ABV 5.5%)
Fruit-flavoured, medium-bodied, amber-coloured beer with a long-lasting bitter aftertaste.

Anti-Venom (OG 1057, ABV 6%)
A strong IPA with tropical fruit notes.

Quiet Riot (OG 1063, ABV 6.6%)
Kiwi fruit, lime and orange zest flavours combine to give a big bitterness balanced with sweet malts.

Sublime Chaos (OG 1075, ABV 7%)
Liquorice, chocolate and caramel flavoured breakfast stout infused with Ethiopian Guji coffee beans backed with dark malts.

Knuckle Dragger (OG 1075, ABV 8.3%)
A double IPA with big tropical fruit flavours and resinous hops.

Andrews

1 Railway Cottages, Cummertrees, Annan, DG12 5QG ☎ (01461) 700387 ☎ 07785 613321 🌐 andrews-ales.co.uk

Andrews Ales began brewing in 2011 and is situated at the family home in Cummertrees. Brewing capacity is three barrels. ♦

Supus Lupus (OG 1036, ABV 3.6%)
A straw-coloured session ale with a light, zesty finish.

Cummertrees Pale Ale (OG 1040, ABV 4%)
Full-bodied, IPA-style beer, refreshingly clean and crisp.

Into the Darkness (OG 1046, ABV 4.3%)
Dark-coloured, full-bodied stout made with chocolate and black malts and hopped with classic British hops.

Andwells

Andwell Lane, Andwell, Hampshire, RG27 9PA ☎ (01256) 761044 🌐 andwells.com

Brewing commenced in 2008 on a 10-barrel plant. The brewery relocated and expanded in 2011 to an idyllic riverside location with a new bespoke 20-barrel plant. Beer is distributed within a 40-mile radius to Hampshire, Surrey, Wiltshire, Berkshire, Greater London and the Isle of Wight. More than 200 outlets are supplied. !! ♦

Resolute Bitter (OG 1038, ABV 3.8%)
An easy-drinking session bitter. A malty aroma, leads into an initially malty flavour with some bitterness and sweetish finish.

Gold Muddler (OG 1039, ABV 3.9%)
Light golden-coloured standard bitter. Aroma of hops and malt; characteristics carried into flavour with solid bitterness and dry, biscuity finish.

Red Mist (ABV 4.1%)
Pale brown-coloured best bitter brewed for Red Mist Leisure. Predominantly bitter, with a malty backbone and a dry bitter finish.

King John (OG 1042, ABV 4.2%)
Malty best bitter, low in hops with short initial bitterness and underlying sweetness, leading to some dryness in the finish.

Ruddy Darter (OG 1047, ABV 4.6%)
A chestnut-coloured ale with a hoppy, spicy aroma and a full-bodied and fruity taste with a dry finish.

Angel

Angel, 7 Stoney Street, Nottingham, NG1 1LG
☎ (0115) 948 3343 angelmicrobrewery.com

Situated inside one of Nottingham's oldest pubs, the Angel Microbrewery is a 2.5-barrel plant nestled in the tap room. Beers are only available in the pub. Vegan and gluten-free beers are planned.

Angel Ales SIBA

62a Furlong Lane, Halesowen, West Midlands, B63 2TA ☎ 07986 382919 angelales.co.uk

Angel Ales began commercial brewing in 2011 and is expanding outlets. The brewery building has been a chapel of rest, a coffin makers' workshop and a pattern makers before becoming a brewhouse. Beers are produced using organic materials where possible, and all stouts are vegan-friendly. ♦RAIB V

Angel Ale (OG 1042, ABV 4.1%)
Ultra pale and intensely-hopped bitter with a citrus nose and a lingering bitter finish.

Ginger Stout (OG 1048, ABV 4.8%)
A stout produced using fresh ginger root.

Angels & Demons SIBA

Great Cauldham Farm, Cauldham Lane, Capel-le-Ferne, Kent, CT18 7HQ
☎ (01303) 255666 fantasticbeer.co.uk

Brewing began in 2016 using a 20-barrel plant. The brewery produces two ranges of beers, the McCanns range of traditional ales and the Angels & Demons range of more experimental brews.

49 Horses (ABV 2.8%)

Bombay Social (ABV 3.8%)

Racing Tiger (ABV 4.2%)

Panama Jazz (ABV 4.8%)

ADH Me (ABV 5.2%)

Goldilocks is Dead (ABV 5.3%)

Black Taxi to the Moon (ABV 5.4%)

Brewed under the McCanns brand name:

Harry Hop (ABV 3.7%)

Grahams (ABV 4.2%)

Hockley Soul (ABV 4.2%)

Angles SIBA

Unit 54, Culley Court, Peterborough, Cambridgeshire, PE2 6WA ☎ 07500 362007 angles-ales.uk

A highly qualified microbiologist and an Exciseman with a passion for real ales and lagers got together to found Angles Ales with the objective to brew with only natural ingredients in a traditional style.

Anglesey Brewhouse (NEW)

Unit 1, Cefn Uchaf Rostrehwfa, Llangefni, LL77 7AQ
☎ 07748 650368 angleseybrewhouse.co.uk

Microbrewery established in 2017 in the centre of Anglesey by a former home brewer. Currently producing one bottle-conditioned beer, largely sold direct from the brewery. A five-gallon plant is used but there are plans for expansion. RAIB

Anglesey Brewing

Chwaen Ddu, Carmel, LL71 7DE
☎ (01248) 717734
angleseybrewingcompany.co.uk

Brewing began in 2014 in Llanbadrig as Bragdy'r Bwthyn, producing bottle-conditioned beers. In 2017 the brewery relocated to Carmel under the Anglesey Brewing Co name and cask production began. Beers are mostly sold at events and outlets across Anglesey. RAIB

APA (OG 1040, ABV 4%)

Golden Ale (ABV 4.4%)

Amlwch Old Porter (OG 1056, ABV 5.6%)

Anglo Oregon (NEW)

3 Traston Lane, Newport, NP19 4RR
aobrewingco@gmail.com

Brewing takes place in a residential double garage using a 100-litre plant. Only bottle-conditioned beers are produced. RAIB

Animal

See XT

Anspach & Hobday

118 Druid Street, Bermondsey, London, SE1 2HH
☎ (020) 8617 9510 anspachandhobday.com

Anspach & Hobday began brewing in 2014 using a one-barrel plant, upgrading to 2.5 barrels later that year. In 2016 the brewery was upgraded again to a seven-barrel plant. It is based in a railway arch in Bermondsey. The vegan-friendly beers are available bottle-conditioned, in KeyKeg and increasingly in cask. A taproom is open at weekends. RAIB

The Smoked Brown (OG 1061, ABV 6%)
Smoked nose with traces of coffee. Flavour has damsons, toffee, dark chocolate, an underlying smoked character and lasting dry roastiness.

The Porter (OG 1062, ABV 6.7%)
Black/brown-coloured beer with roasted notes throughout with caramel, dark fruit and hops in the flavour and finish, which is slightly dry.

The Stout Porter (OG 1080, ABV 8.5%)

Anstey Ale

46a Albion Street, Anstey, Leicestershire, LE7 7DE
☎ 07960 776843 stuartslessor@me.com

Anstey Ale Brewery started as a one-barrel garage plant in 2015 brewing on a part-time basis. In 2017 it became full time and upgraded some of the brewery equipment. It moved to new premises later in 2017 and increased its plant size to 2.5 barrels. There are plans to open an on-site bar.

Daydreamer (ABV 3.7%)

THE BREWERIES

A pale ale with a smooth mouthfeel and a spicy, floral, grapefruit character.

Back Yard Bitter (OG 1046, ABV 4.7%)
Traditional English hopped, copper-coloured bitter.

Darkroom (OG 1048, ABV 4.7%)
Well-rounded, triple-hopped stout made with six grain types.

Milk Stout (OG 1062, ABV 4.8%)
Sweet, black and full-bodied stout with roast flavours and a slightly smoked finish.

Nook IPA (OG 1051, ABV 5%)

Anthology (NEW)

6 Bankfield Terrace, Leeds, West Yorkshire, LS4 2RE
anthologybrewing.co.uk

Established in 2018, Anthology is a small batch brewery based in Leeds.

Antoine's

The Garden Shed at 25 Ashley Road, Westcott, Surrey, RH4 3QJ ☎ 07545 828589 antoine@1beer.co.uk

Tiny brewery which produces occasional KeyKegs in a variety of styles.

Appleby

The Brewery at the Stables, Morland House, Morland, Cumbria, CA10 3AZ
☎ (01931) 714348 applebybrewery.co.uk

Established by Fred Mills in 2015, the brewery outgrew its original premises in Appleby within a year and moved to a former horse stable in an Eden Valley village in 2016. The beers are available at selected pubs across Cumbria, but mainly in the Eden Valley area. !! ♦ RAIB

Senior Moment (OG 1039, ABV 3.9%)

Vanya Yam (ABV 4%)
Amber-coloured IPA with a malty taste and a hoppy, citrus finish.

Mid Life Crisis (OG 1042, ABV 4.2%)

Middle Aged Spread (OG 1052, ABV 5.2%)
A rich, dark stout; nutty, chocolaty and lightly-hopped.

Applecross

c/o Applecross Inn, Shore Street, Applecross, IV54 8LR
☎ (01520) 744262 applecross.uk.com/inn

A microbrewery co-funded by 14 stakeholders. Brewing is currently suspended.

Arbor SIBA

181 Easton Road, Easton, Bristol, BS5 0HQ
☎ (0117) 329 2711 arborales.co.uk

Founded in 2007, Arbor has a brew length of 20 barrels and 10 fermenting vessels. Willing to experiment, more than 300 beers have been produced. The current range reflects modern tastes and leans towards hoppy pale ales and IPAs plus some interesting red and dark ales. ♦ RAIB V

Pocket Rocket (OG 1038, ABV 3.7%)

Shangri La (OG 1040, ABV 4.2%) ◆
Yellow-coloured best bitter with a hoppy aroma, light malt and tropical fruit on the palate and a clean, refreshing bitter finish.

Oz Bomb (OG 1045, ABV 4.7%) ◆
Hop forward nose. Citrus and tropical fruit flavours with a powerful bitterness, which lingers in the aftertaste.

The Devil Made Me Brew It (OG 1056, ABV 5.5%) ◆
A velvety speciality beer in stout style. Floral and citrus hops in the aroma, coffee and slightly burnt toffee flavours – sweet but with a bitter finish.

Why Kick A Moo Cow (OG 1052, ABV 5.5%) ◆
A strong, amber-coloured ale with malt and hops on the nose, flavours of tropical fruit and a dry bittersweet aftertaste.

Yakima Valley (OG 1067, ABV 7%) ◆
A strong, full-bodied IPA. Hoppy and very fruity. Sweetness is well balanced with bitterness, lasting into a soft bitter aftertaste.

Arcadian (NEW)

Bridge Studios, 454 Western Avenue, Cardiff, CF5 3BL
arcadianbrewing.com

Arcadian began brewing in 2018 using a 2.5-barrel brew plant. All beers are unfiltered and unpasteurised and available in keg and bottle.

Arcane Bridge

Arch 5, King Edward Bridge, Newcastle upon Tyne, NE1 3TQ ☎ 07932 774745 arcanebridge@aol.com

Brewing began in 2016 using a 5.5-barrel plant, supplying local outlets within a 20-mile radius. A tasting bar is located on the premises (please ring for opening hours). Brewing is currently suspended.

Archerfield

See Knops

Archers

See Evan Evans

Ards

34b Carrowdore Road, Newtownards, Co Down, BT22 2LX ☎ 07515 558406
ardsbrewing@blackwood34.plus.com

Ards began brewing in 2011 using a 100-litre plant. A five-barrel plant is now in operation, allowing cask production in addition to the increasing range of bottle-conditioned and KeyKeg beers. Very much a local brewery with beers generally only supplied within a 15-mile radius. RAIB

Rockin' Goose (OG 1044, ABV 4.4%)

BallyBlack (OG 1046, ABV 4.6%)

Hip Hop (OG 1050, ABV 5%)

Cardy Man (OG 1051, ABV 5.1%)

Pig Island (OG 1052, ABV 5.2%)

Argyll

Unit 8a, Baliscate Industrial Estate, Tobermory, Isle of Mull, PA75 6QA
☎ (01688) 302821
✉ isleofmullbrewing@btinternet.com

Argyll Breweries was formed in 2010 following the merger of Oban Bay and Isle of Mull breweries, continuing to trade under those names. A small brewing plant now supports the Isle of Mull beers in Tobermory, primarily producing bottles but some cask-conditioned ale is still available.

Brewed under the Isle of Mull Brewery name:

Island Pale Ale (OG 1038, ABV 3.9%)

Galleon Gold (OG 1041, ABV 4.1%)

Red Monk of Iona (OG 1042, ABV 4.2%)

Terror of Tobermory (OG 1045, ABV 4.6%)

Brewed under the Oban Bay Brewery name:

Kilt Lifter (ABV 3.9%)

Skinny Blonde (ABV 4.1%)

Ginger Jakey (ABV 4.2%)

Skelpt Lug (ABV 4.2%)

Fair Puggled (ABV 4.6%)

Arkell's SIBA IFBB

Kingsdown, Swindon, Wiltshire, SN2 7RU
☎ (01793) 823026 arkells.com

Arkell's Brewery was established in 1843 by John Arkell and the Arkell family still brew beer in the original Victorian Brewhouse every day. The brewery owns nearly 100 pubs across Wiltshire, Gloucestershire, Oxfordshire, Berkshire and Hampshire. In 2018 a brewery shop and visitor centre was opened on site. !! ♦

Wiltshire Gold (OG 1038, ABV 3.7%)
A light golden-coloured ale with a sweet, malty flavour. The use of traditional hops give the beer a mellow floral hop aroma followed by a distinctive hoppy taste.

3B (OG 1040, ABV 4%)
A medium brown-coloured beer with a strong, sweetish malt/caramel flavour. The hops come through strongly in the aftertaste, which is lingering and dry.

HOPeration IPA (OG 1041, ABV 4.2%)
A powerfully hoppy beer with a smooth, rounded finish.

Bee's Organic (OG 1045, ABV 4.5%)
A golden ale with a hint of organic honey and a light, fresh taste.

Moonlight (OG 1046, ABV 4.5%)
An auburn-coloured beer with a warm, toasty aroma and distinctive citrus hoppy flavour.

Arran SIBA

Cladach, Brodick, Isle of Arran, KA27 8DE
☎ (01770) 302353

Office: 100 Wellington Street, Glasgow, G2 6DH
arranbrewery.com

The brewery opened in Brodick in 2000 using a 20-barrel plant with water sourced from the nearby mountains. Around 400 outlets around the UK are supplied direct. Beers are also produced under the Devil's Dyke Brewery name. Gluten-free beers can be produced on request. !! ♦ RAIB

Guid Ale (OG 1038, ABV 3.8%)
A golden-coloured, refreshing session ale with a delicate balance of malt and fruit.

Dark (OG 1042, ABV 4.3%)
A well-balanced malty beer with plenty of roast and hop in the taste and a dry, bitter finish.

Sunset (OG 1042, ABV 4.4%)
A mid-amber-coloured summer ale, light perfumed aroma, good balance of malt, fruit and hops with a pleasant, dry finish.

Blonde (OG 1048, ABV 5%)
A hoppy beer with substantial fruit balance. The taste is balanced and the finish increasingly bitter. An aromatic strong bitter that drinks below its ABV.

Brewery Dug (OG 1055, ABV 5.5%)
An American-style IPA with a refreshing citrus body and a dry lemon zest bitter finish.

Brewed under the Devil's Dyke Brewery name:

Devil's Blonde (ABV 4%)

Pale Ale (ABV 5%)

Arrow

c/o Wine Vaults, 37 High Street, Kington, Herefordshire, HR5 3BJ
☎ (01544) 230685 ✉ deanewright@yahoo.co.uk

Brewer Deane Wright built this five-barrel brewery at the rear of the Wine Vaults and started brewing in 2005. The Wine Vaults is the only pub outlet for Arrow Bitter.

Bitter (OG 1042, ABV 4%)

Art Brew SIBA

Art Brew Barn, Brightwater Farm, Sutcombe, Devon, EX22 7QE ☎ 07881 783626
✉ artbrewdorset@googlemail.com

Brewing started in 2008 on a five-barrel plant near the Jurassic Coast. In 2016 the brewery relocated to a new site in Devon with a brewery tap using a 2.5-barrel plant. In addition to its core ales a rolling programme of beers is also produced. ♦ RAIB V

Baby Anarchist (OG 1034, ABV 3.2%)

Pale (OG 1034, ABV 3.2%)

Outsider Ale (OG 1042, ABV 4.4%)

Milk Stout (OG 1045, ABV 4.5%)

Ab6 (OG 1045, ABV 4.6%)

Ginger & Chilli IPA (OG 1055, ABV 6%)

Love or Nothing (OG 1055, ABV 6%)

Orange IPA (OG 1055, ABV 6%)

Anarchist Party Bitter (OG 1068, ABV 7.2%)

Artisan

See Evan Evans

Artisan Brewing

See Pipes

THE BREWERIES

Arundel SIBA

Unit C7, Ford Airfield Industrial Estate, Ford, Arundel, West Sussex, BN18 0HY
☎ (01903) 733111 🌐 arundelbrewery.co.uk

Founded in 1992, Arundel Brewery is the historic town's first brewery in 70 years. A brewery shop opened in 2014 by the quayside with a good selection of beers, both its own and from other breweries. The brewery also brews for the Bison Crafthouse, Brighton. !! ♦

Black Stallion (OG 1037, ABV 3.7%)
A dark mild with well defined chocolate and roast character. The aftertaste is not powerful but the initial flavours remain in the clean finish.

Castle (OG 1038, ABV 3.8%)
A pale tawny-coloured beer with fruit and malt noticeable in the aroma. The flavour has a good balance of malt, fruit and hops, with a dry, hoppy finish.

Maltravers Session IPA (ABV 4.2%)
An easy-drinking session IPA with a powerful hop character.

Sussex Gold (OG 1042, ABV 4.2%)
A golden-coloured best bitter with a strong floral hop aroma. The ale is clean-tasting and bitter for its strength, with a tangy citrus flavour. The initial hop and fruit die to a dry and bitter finish.

Sussex IPA (OG 1045, ABV 4.5%)
Formerly known as Heritage IPA. A special bitter with a complex roast malt flavour leading to a fruity, hoppy, bittersweet finish.

Hirondelle Coffee Milk Stout (ABV 5%)
A rich, smooth coffee milk stout, brewed using Edgcumbes coffee beans.

Wild Heaven (OG 1052, ABV 5.2%)
An American-style pale ale; full-flavoured with strong grapefruit, orange and lime notes resulting in a lingering, dry, bitter finish.

Smokehouse (ABV 6%)
A rich, smooth beer with subtle smoky overtones.

Ascot SIBA

Unit 5, Compton Place Business Centre, Surrey Avenue, Camberley, Surrey, GU15 3DX
☎ (01276) 686696 🌐 ascotbrewing.co.uk

Ascot started production in 2007 on a four-barrel plant in a small industrial unit. The brewery has successfully expanded over the years and 2017 saw the brewery with new owners. !! ♦ RAIB

Starting Gate (OG 1038, ABV 3.8%)
A pale brown-coloured session bitter with malt flavours present throughout. Dry with a lasting sharp and bitter finish.

Gold Cup (OG 1039, ABV 4%)
A lemon aroma leads to a dry, bitter taste, with more citrus flavours. Hoppy finish with a hint of sweetness.

Final Furlong (OG 1042, ABV 4.2%)
A best bitter with balancing biscuity malt sweetness. Some citrus fruitiness and a clean, hoppy aftertaste.

5-4 Favourite (OG 1047, ABV 4.6%)
Some grapefruit in the aroma, with hop and bitterness in the taste and plenty of balancing biscuit in the aroma and aftertaste.

Anastasia's Stout (OG 1049, ABV 5%)
Burnt coffee aromas lead to a roast malt flavour in this black beer. Notably fruity throughout, with a bittersweet aftertaste.

Yankee (OG 1049, ABV 5%)

Ash Valley

Prince of Wales, Green Tye, nr Much Hadham, Hertfordshire, SG10 6JP
☎ (01279) 842139 ☎ 07966 474730
🌐 thepow.co.uk

The brewery is part of the Prince of Wales pub in Green Tye, run by the landlord. Most of the beer is sold at the pub and occasional CAMRA beer festivals, and a small amount is swapped with other brewers. A micro pilot brewery is used to produce one-off experimental beers all year round.

Ashley Down

c/o 15 Wathen Road, St Andrews, Bristol, BS6 5BY
☎ (0117) 983 6567 ☎ 07563 751200
✉ ashleydownbrewery@gmail.com

Ashley Down began brewing in 2011 using a 5.5-barrel plant in the owner's garage. It suffered a major fire in 2017. The owner has brewed occasionally using spare capacity at other breweries and hopes to restart brewing in a new location soon. ♦RAIB

Ashover SIBA

Unit 1, Derby Road, Clay Cross, Derbyshire, S45 9AG
☎ 07803 708526 🌐 ashoverbrewery.com

Brewing began in 2007 on a 3.5-barrel plant in the garage of the cottage next to the Old Poets' Corner, Ashover. Since its acquisition of a 10-barrel brewery in the neighbouring village of Clay Cross in 2015, Ashover now brews at both sites. The brewery serves local freehouses across Derbyshire and further afield as well as the Poets' Corner and Brown Ales pub groups. !! RAIB

Light Rale (OG 1038, ABV 3.7%)
Light in colour and taste, with initial sweet and malt flavours, leading to a bitter finish and aftertaste.

Font (OG 1037, ABV 3.8%)

Poets Tipple (OG 1041, ABV 4%)
Complex, tawny-coloured beer that drinks above its strength. Predominantly malty in flavour, with increasing bitterness towards the end.

Littlemoor Citra (OG 1041, ABV 4.1%)

The Fabrick (OG 1042, ABV 4.4%)
Golden ale with a soft, fruity flavour and well-bodied mouthfeel.

Rainbows End (OG 1045, ABV 4.5%)
Slightly smooth, bitter, golden-coloured beer with an initial sweetness. Grapefruit and lemon hop flavours come through strongly as the beer gets increasingly dry towards the finish, ending with a bitter, dry aftertaste.

Red Lion (OG 1044, ABV 4.6%)
A full-bodied red-coloured ale with well-balanced malt complementing the fruitiness born from an abundance of American hops.

Coffin Lane Stout (OG 1050, ABV 5%)

Excellent example of the style, with a chocolate and coffee flavour, balanced by a little sweetness. Finish is long and quite dry.

Butts Pale Ale (OG 1055, ABV 5.5%) ◆
Pale and strong yet easy-drinking golden-coloured bitter. Combination of bitter and sweet flavours mingle with an alcoholic kick, leading to a warming yet bitter finish and aftertaste.

Milk Stout (OG 1060, ABV 6%)
Smooth, rich chocolate roasted essences with hints of coffee and caramel.

Atlantic

Treisaac Farm, Treisaac, Cornwall, TR8 4DX
☎ (01637) 880326 🌐 atlanticbrewery.com

⊗ Specialist microbrewery producing organic and vegan ales. All ales are unfiltered and finings-free. There are nine core brews including four food-matched dining ales developed with Michelin chef Nathan Outlaw. Casks are supplied locally and to London, with bottle-conditioned beers available nationally. ♦ RAIB V

Azores (OG 1042, ABV 4.2%) ◆
Unfined golden ale. Citrus and resinous hops dominate the aroma and taste with tropical fruits. Refreshing bitter and dry finish.

Earl Grey PA (OG 1045, ABV 4.5%) ◆
Cloudy, amber-coloured organic speciality ale. Hop aroma leads to powerful citrus fruit flavours becoming intense. Fairly bitter and dry.

Elderflower Blonde (OG 1045, ABV 4.5%)
A golden-coloured pale ale with floral elderflower throughout.

Mandarina Cornovia (OG 1045, ABV 4.5%) ◆
Pale gold-coloured beer with added orange peel. Assertive citrus hop aroma with crisp bitter lemon, peach and orange flavours.

Masala Chai PA (OG 1045, ABV 4.5%)
Classic Indian roadhouse spices and black tea tannins in this pale session ale.

Simcotica (OG 1044, ABV 4.5%)
Vibrant passion fruit and grapefruit throughout this balanced pale ale.

Gold (OG 1043, ABV 4.6%) ◆
Golden-coloured speciality beer with added ginger. Light aroma of malt. Refreshing hop bitter flavour dominated by strong, zingy ginger.

Blue (OG 1045, ABV 4.8%) ◆
Smooth, rich porter with heavy roast malt aroma and taste. Smoky liquorice, bitter coffee and chocolate flavours with sweet fruit.

Honey Ale (OG 1046, ABV 4.8%)
A smooth, well-balanced, golden-coloured honey beer.

Red (OG 1047, ABV 5%) ◆
Ruby-coloured strong bitter with natural cloudiness. Complex nutty malt, bitterness and light roast followed by hedgerow fruits. Long bittersweet finish.

Fistral (OG 1048, ABV 5.2%) ◆
Full-flavoured, copper-coloured wheat beer. Sweet, stone-fruit flavours blend with biscuit malt and citrus hops. Malt finish with hops and dryness.

Atlas

See Orkney

Atom SIBA

Unit 4, Food & Tech Park, Malmo Road, Sutton Fields Industrial Estate, Hull, East Yorkshire, HU7 0FY
🌐 atombeers.com

⊗ Atom is a collaboration between Allan Rice and Sarah Thackray, set up in 2013 in a modern industrial unit north-west of Hull city centre. The 10-barrel brewing equipment, which came from Oban Ales, is supplemented by a fermentation and conditioning capacity of 180 barrels. ‼♦

Schrodingers Cat (OG 1035, ABV 3.5%)

Blonde Ale (OG 1040, ABV 4%)
A fresh, smooth, easy-drinking pale ale with citrus notes.

Camomile (OG 1042, ABV 4.2%)
An easy-drinking ale with a floral aroma.

Pale Ale (OG 1045, ABV 4.5%)

Dark Alchemy (OG 1049, ABV 4.9%)
A complex malt bill with bitterness and aroma from cardamom and coriander but no hops creating a porter rich in body, smooth and brimming with character.

India Pale Ale (OG 1056, ABV 5.6%)
A thirst-quenching IPA with lots of malt and big juicy hops.

Atomic

c/o Alexandra Arms, 72-73 St James Street, Rugby, Warwickshire, CV21 2SL
☎ (01788) 576194 ☎ 07986 983984

Office: 1 Lower Hillmorton Road, Rugby, Warwickshire, CV21 3ST 🌐 atomicbrewery.com

Originally set up in 2006, the brewery stands in the garden of the Alexandra Arms in Rugby. ‼♦

Strike (OG 1039, ABV 3.7%)
A pale golden ale with a sharp, fruity aroma and a good, sharp bitter finish.

Fission (OG 1040, ABV 3.9%)

Scientist (OG 1039, ABV 3.9%)
Light on the palate with an intense hoppy and fruity, peachy flavour.

Spectrum (OG 1040, ABV 4%)
Pale golden in colour with a huge grapefruit nose and aroma.

Dark Matter (OG 1041, ABV 4.1%)
A dark-coloured, well-hopped ale with hints of chocolate and a good bitter finish.

Fusion (OG 1042, ABV 4.1%)
A golden-coloured ale with a citrus, hoppy aroma and a good bitter finish.

Half Life (OG 1051, ABV 5%)
A golden-coloured premium IPA with a citrus nose to finish.

Aurora

Unit 6, Gallows Industrial Park, off Furnace Road, Ilkeston, Derbyshire, DE7 5EP ☎ 07740 783631

Aurora was established in 2016 and joint owner Mark Derbyshire, formerly of Hardy & Hanson's, brews on a 10-barrel plant. Many local outlets as well as a few further away are supplied direct. The brewery swaps beers with other breweries throughout the UK, many of which can be found in its micropub, the Ilson Tap. ♦

Light Show (OG 1040, ABV 3.9%)
A refreshing, hoppy pale ale.

Ilkeston Pale Ale (OG 1041, ABV 4.1%)
A traditional old English pale ale brewed using traditional English hops, light amber in colour.

Constellation (OG 1043, ABV 4.2%)
Amber-coloured best bitter. Slight sweet initially giving way to a powerful bitterness and refreshing hoppy finish.

Solar Storm (OG 1046, ABV 4.5%)
A hoppy pale ale brewed using American hops with a citrus punch.

Big Dark (OG 1051, ABV 5.3%)
A rich stout with chocolate and liquorice aromas, which lead to a smooth, rich taste.

Mosaic (OG 1052, ABV 5.3%)
Single hop American-style pale ale with citrus and tropical fruit flavours.

Austendyke

The Beeches, Austendyke Road, Weston Hills, Spalding, Lincolnshire, PE12 6BZ ☎ 07866 045778

Austendyke Ales began brewing in 2012 using a seven-barrel plant. The brewery is operated on a part-time basis by brewer Charlie Rawlings and business partner Nathan Marshall, who handles sales. The brewery owns and runs its micropub, the Prior's Oven, Spalding.

Long Lane (OG 1039, ABV 4%)

Sheep Market (OG 1040, ABV 4%)

Bakestraw Bitter (OG 1041, ABV 4.1%)

Holbeach High Street (OG 1045, ABV 4.5%)

Hogsgate (OG 1050, ABV 5%)

Autumn (NEW)

8 East Cliff Road, Spectrum Business Park, Seaham, County Durham, SR7 7PS 🌐 autumnbrewing.co.uk

Autumn produce keg and bottled gluten free beers. No real ale. **GF**

Avid (NEW) SIBA

Red Moss Farm, Quernmore Brow, LA2 0QW ☎ 07814 206881 🌐 avidbrewing.co.uk

Avid is based in Quernmore, near Lancaster, and is capable of producing 150 casks per week. It currently supplies pubs, cafés, festivals and private parties throughout the North West.

Bitter (OG 1042, ABV 3.8%)
A traditional bitter with soft biscuit and caramel flavours with a crisp finish.

Golden Ale (OG 1042, ABV 3.9%)
A light, golden-coloured session ale using traditional English hops.

American Pale (OG 1042, ABV 4%)
A strongly-flavoured and bitter ale with floral and citrus notes.

New Zealand Pale (OG 1042, ABV 4%)
A well-balanced pale ale with lingering flavour and bitterness, and gooseberry aromas.

Milk Stout (OG 1046, ABV 4.5%)
Well-balanced, smooth, sweet stout with a hint of smokiness.

IPA (OG 1046, ABV 5%)
Traditional IPA with strong resin hop flavours and bitterness balanced by sweet malt.

Whisky Vanilla Stout (OG 1046, ABV 7.4%)
A well-balanced stout with vanilla added to soften the finish.

Axholme SIBA

7 Lakes Country Park, Wharf Road, Crowle, Lincolnshire, DN17 4JS
☎ (01724) 781804 ☎ 07551 910040

Office: The Church, King Edward Street, Grimsby, Lincolnshire, DN31 3JD 🌐 axholmebrewing.co.uk

Brewing began in 2012 in Scunthorpe using a 2.5-barrel plant. The brewery is now housed at a four-barrel exhibition brewery at 7 Lakes Country Park in Crowle. Beers are distributed nationwide. Due to rapid expansion in 2018 a new 15-barrel brewery at a second site in Grimsby came on stream. ♦RAIB

Best Bitter (OG 1038, ABV 3.8%)
Traditional English bitter; malty fruitcake flavours dominate with a peppery hop finish.

Cleethorpes Pale Ale (OG 1041.5, ABV 4.2%)
A refreshing pale ale with crisp citrus hops and a sweet undertone from sea buckthorn berries.

Lightning Pale Ale (OG 1041.3, ABV 4.3%)
A refreshing pale ale, hoppy with a n explosion of fresh citrus flavour notes.

Special Reserve (OG 1066, ABV 7.2%)
Amber-coloured old ale with flavours of brandy and dried fruits.

Axiom

Unit 4a, Wrexham Enterprise Park, Ash Road, North Wrexham Industrial Estate, Wrexham, LL13 9JT
☎ 07544 280353 🌐 axiombrewing.co.uk

Axiom was established in 2014 on a self-built four-barrel plant. Brewing only takes place occasionally.

Axton

Pentre Lane, Axton, CH8 9DH
☎ (01745) 855657 ☎ 07756 636415

Office: Archies Bar, 151 High Street, Prestatyn, LL19 9AS ✉ jamesmcgeown@live.co.uk

Axton commenced brewing in 2015 on a 1.5-barrel plant, supplying only the brewery tap at Archies Bar, Prestatyn. It specialises in one-off brews at the rate of about a dozen each year.

Aylesbury

83 Bicester Road, Aylesbury, Buckinghamshire, HP19 9AZ
☎ (01844) 239237 🌐 aylesburybrewhouse.co.uk

⊗ Established in 2011 at the Hop Pole as a sister brewery to Vale (qv). One-off beers are brewed on a weekly basis using a 12-barrel kit. ‼ ♦

Ayr

5 Racecourse Road, Ayr, KA7 2DG
☎ (01292) 263891
info@ayrbrewingcompany.com

Ayr began brewing in 2009 on a five-barrel plant and is located at the Glenpark Hotel. As well as the hotel around 50 other outlets are supplied throughout Scotland and England. ♦ RAIB

HipHopopotamus (OG 1039, ABV 3.8%)
Dry-hopped pale ale with caramel malts, bitter oranges and green hops.

Leezie Lundie (OG 1037.5, ABV 3.8%)
A pale golden-coloured session ale with hints of grapefruit and a dry, lingering finish.

Jolly Beggars (OG 1041, ABV 4.2%)
A complex best bitter with plenty of character and a lingering malty aftertaste.

Rabbie's Porter (OG 1042.5, ABV 4.3%)
Robust, full-bodied porter with well-balanced toffee, fruity maltiness and a slightly smoky finish.

Fair Jennys Jig (OG 1044, ABV 4.4%)

Burning Gull (OG 1048, ABV 5%)
A strong bitter with toffee, caramelised oranges and grapefruit on the palate leading to a creamy, rich bitter finish.

Betty and the Gardens (OG 1049.5, ABV 5.2%)
A blonde ale with hints of pineapple, passion fruit and strawberries leading to a smooth, fruity finish.

B&T SIBA

The Brewery, Shefford, Bedfordshire, SG17 5DZ
☎ (01462) 815080 banksandtaylor.com

⊗ Banks & Taylor – now just B&T – was founded in 1982. It produces 13 regular beers, plus monthly specials and occasional beers, in an industrial unit close to the town centre. There are five tied houses. ‼ ♦

Two Brewers Bitter (OG 1036, ABV 3.6%)
Bronze-coloured bitter with citrus hop aroma and taste and a dry finish.

Plum Mild (OG 1038, ABV 3.8%)
A rich, dark mild with a strong malty aroma and hints of plum flavour on the tongue, fruity plum finish.

Shefford Bitter (OG 1038, ABV 3.8%)
A pale brown-coloured beer with a light hop aroma and a hoppy taste leading to a bitter finish.

Shefford Dark Mild (OG 1038, ABV 3.8%)
A dark-coloured beer with a well-balanced taste. Sweetish, roast malt aftertaste.

Golden Fox (OG 1041, ABV 4.1%)
A golden, hoppy ale, dry tasting with a fruity aroma and citrus finish.

Black Dragon Mild (OG 1043, ABV 4.3%)
Black in colour with a toffee and roast malt flavour and a smoky finish.

Dunstable Giant (OG 1044, ABV 4.4%)
Tawny-coloured bitter with a subtle blend of malt and hops.

Dragon Slayer (OG 1045, ABV 4.5%)
A golden-coloured beer with a malt and hop flavour and a bitter finish. More malty and less hoppy than is usual for a beer of this style.

Edwin Taylor's Extra Stout (OG 1045, ABV 4.5%)
A complex black-coloured beer with a bitter coffee and roast malt flavour and a dry bitter finish.

Fruit Bat (OG 1045, ABV 4.5%)
A warming straw-coloured beer with a taste of apricots and a bitter finish.

SPA (Shefford Pale Ale) (OG 1045, ABV 4.5%)
A well-balanced beer with hop, fruit and malt flavours. Dry, bitter aftertaste.

SOD (OG 1050, ABV 5%)
SOS with caramel added for colour.

SOS (OG 1050, ABV 5%)
A rich mixture of fruit, hops and malt is present in the taste and aftertaste of this beer. Predominantly hoppy aroma.

Baa SIBA

Unit 4, Station Road Industrial Estate, Chepstow, NP16 5PF baabrewing.com

Located adjacent to Chepstow railway station, the brewery was established in 2015 using an eight-barrel plant with five fermenters and a bright beer tank. ‼

Baa B-Q Blonde (ABV 3.7%)
A light golden ale with a refreshing hint of fruity sweetness and a mild malty taste.

Best Bitter (ABV 4%)
Well-balanced with fruity, floral and aromatic hop notes and a smooth, mellow maltiness followed by crisp bitterness.

Hopping (ABV 4.2%)
A double-hopped ale with a light, refreshing taste.

Two Bridges (ABV 4.5%)
Smooth and full-bodied with a gentle citrus hoppy palate.

IPA (ABV 5%)

Bacchus

Bacchus Hotel, 17 High Street, Sutton-on-Sea, Lincolnshire, LN12 2EY
☎ (01507) 441204 bacchushotel.co.uk

Bacchus began brewing in 2010 and now has a two-barrel plant supplying the Bacchus Hotel. ‼ RAIB

Backyard SIBA

Unit 8a, Gatehouse Trading Estate, Lichfield Road, Brownhills, Walsall, West Midlands, WS8 6JZ
☎ (01543) 360145 tbb.uk.com

Backyard began brewing in 2008 and expanded in 2012 to a 12-barrel plant brewing up to 50 barrels a week. Two pubs are owned: the Fountain, Walsall and the Saddlers Arms, Solihull. A half-barrel experimental plant is also in operation and a tap house is open every Friday (1-8pm). ‼ ♦

Bitter (OG 1038, ABV 3.8%)
A blonde ale, slightly sweet with hints of tangerine and fruit salad.

The Hoard (OG 1040, ABV 3.9%)

Refreshing, dry golden ale. Light malt flavour with hint of lemon on the palate.

Blonde (OG 1041, ABV 4.1%)
Citrus and pine aroma with a dry, crisp and hoppy taste.

Americana (ABV 4.3%)
Light, fruity pale ale with powerful orange and lemon aromas and malty biscuit, fruity hops and vanilla flavours.

Gold (OG 1045, ABV 4.5%)
Golden-coloured bitter with tropical hop notes.

IPA (OG 1049, ABV 5%)
Intense floral, herbal aroma. Strong, rich, fruity bitterness.

Antipodean (OG 1052, ABV 5.6%)
Full-bodied pale ale. Complex flavours of exotic fruits, apricot and pine with an undercurrent of spicy cedar and oak.

BAD SIBA

Unit 3, North Hill Road, Dishforth, North Yorkshire, YO7 3DH
☎ (01423) 324005 🌐 wearebad.co

Brewing commenced in 2014, originally using a 13-barrel plant, since upgraded to cope with demand. Monthly specials often incorporate seasonal ingredients and the brewery also produces more experimental brews. !! ♦

Pale Aura (ABV 3.8%)
Fruity and slightly bitter, hop-packed with notes of tangerine, mango, grapefruit and pineapple.

Love Over Gold (ABV 4.1%)
A blonde ale, light and hoppy, well-balanced with grapefruit and grassy notes.

Wild Gravity (ABV 5.2%)
An IPA with a malty backbone and tropical hop flavours.

Dark Necessities (ABV 5.5%)
Dark, rich milk stout with hints of cherry, chocolate, coffee and almond.

Bad Seed

Unit 6, 7 Rye Close, York Way Industrial Estate, Malton, North Yorkshire, YO17 6YD
☎ (01653) 695783 🌐 badseedbrewery.co.uk

Launched in 2013 by James Broad and Chris Waplington, the four-barrel brewery was increased to a 12-barrel plant in 2016. Brewing 2-3 times a week the beers are unfined and unfiltered. !! ♦ V

Kiwi (ABV 3.8%)

Dalliance (ABV 4%)

Session IPA (ABV 4%)

Badger

See Hall & Woodhouse

Baker's Dozen

Unit 5, Ketton Business Estate, Pit Lane, Ketton, PE9 3SZ
☎ (01780) 238180 🌐 bakersdozenbrewing.co.uk

Brewing takes place on a five-barrel plant installed in 2015 by the owners of the Jolly Brewer, Stamford, where the beers are always available. ♦ V

Jentacular (OG 1033, ABV 3.5%)

Magic Potion (OG 1035, ABV 3.8%)

Stamford Pale (OG 1037, ABV 4%)

System of a Brown (OG 1038, ABV 4.1%)

Straight Outta Ketton (OG 1040, ABV 4.5%)

Electric Landlady (OG 1044, ABV 5%)

Bale

Janie Craig Cottage, Liddaton, Devon, EX20 4AD
☎ 07540 283014 🌐 baleale.com

Bale Ale is a nanobrewery established in 2016 situated near Dartmoor National Park. Only bottle-conditioned beers are produced at present. RAIB V

Ballard's

See Greyhound

Balmaha

Oak Tree Inn, Balmaha, G63 0JQ
☎ (01360) 870357 🌐 oak-tree-inn.co.uk

Balmaha began brewing in 2012 using a one-barrel plant. !! ♦

Bang the Elephant (NEW)

17 Craig Street, Long Eaton, Nottinghamshire, NG10 1ET ☎ 07539 652055
✉ bangtheelephantbrewing@hotmail.com

Bang the Elephant is a nanobrewery currently based at the owner's house. It is looking to cuckoo brew until suitable premises are found. Beers are inspired by neo-Victorian steampunk and are crafted in small batches. V

Bang-On SIBA

Unit 3, George Street, Bridgend Industrial Estate, Bridgend, CF31 3TS
☎ (01656) 760790 🌐 bangonbrewery.beer

Established in 2016, this five-barrel plant produces a variety of unique beers, the majority of which are vegan-friendly. An on-site tap room offers tours and brew day experiences. A bespoke beer service is offered where beers are available with personalised labels. !! ♦ V

Doris (OG 1031, ABV 3.4%)
A Session IPA with a fruity and fragrant palate.

Cariad (OG 1039, ABV 4.1%)
An easy-drinking, fresh, crisp session Welsh ale.

Arthur (OG 1039, ABV 4.4%)
Amber-coloured ale, lightly-hopped with a floral and berry aroma.

Trev (OG 1053, ABV 4.8%)
A ruby-coloured IPA with subtle hoppy notes.

Bank Top SIBA

The Pavilion, Ashworth Lane, Bolton, BL1 8RA

☎ (01204) 595800 🌐 banktopbrewery.com

Bank Top was established in 1995. Since 2002 the brewery has occupied a Grade II-listed tennis pavilion housing an 11-barrel plant. Bank Top Brewery Estates was formed in 2010 and now owns two pubs, Bank Top Brewery Tap and Bank Top Ale House. !! ♦

Barley to Beer (OG 1036, ABV 3.6%)
A pale bitter with a citrus lemon and herbal finish.

Sweeneys (OG 1038, ABV 3.8%)
An amber-coloured bitter with a bold, crisp flavour and a delicate, slightly spicy aroma.

Bad to the Bone (OG 1040, ABV 4%)
A tan-coloured beer with floral qualities and delicate citrus notes.

Dark Mild (OG 1040, ABV 4%)
Dark brown-coloured beer with a malt and roast aroma. Smooth mouthfeel with roast malt and hops prominent throughout.

Flat Cap (OG 1040, ABV 4%)
Amber-coloured ale with a modest fruit aroma leading to a beer with citrus fruit, malt and hops. Good finish of fruit, malt and bitterness.

Pavilion Pale Ale (OG 1045, ABV 4.5%)
A yellow-coloured beer with a citrus and hop aroma. Big fruity flavour with a peppery hoppiness; dry, bitter yet fruity finish.

Port O Call (OG 1050, ABV 5%)
Dark brown-coloured beer with a malty, fruity aroma. Malt, roast and dark fruits in the bittersweet taste and finish.

Banks's

Park Brewery, Wolverhampton, West Midlands, WV1 4NY
☎ (01902) 711811 🌐 bankssbeer.co.uk

Banks's was founded as a firm of maltsters in 1840, commencing brewing in 1874; and moved to the current Park Brewery the following year. It became the principal brewery of the Wolverhampton & Dudley Breweries, founded in 1890 by an amalgamation with two other local companies. Several other breweries were later acquired, notably Hanson's of Dudley in 1943, which continued brewing until 1991. Following the takeover of Marston's of Burton on Trent in 1999, W&DB subsequently adopted this name for the PLC in 2007. Whilst continuing to produce the original Banks's Mild & Bitter beers for which they gained fame throughout the Midlands, many new beers have been developed; notably Sunbeam, which was introduced in 2011 to coincide with the 10th anniversary of Wolverhampton's city status. In recent years, Marston's PLC has taken on contract brewing of several well-known national ales, many being produced at the Banks's site. These include Tetley Bitter, for Carlsberg; and the principal Thwaites' brands, which were brewed under licence from 2014; and purchased outright by Marston's the following year. Under the terms of the purchase of Thwaite's principle brands Marston's were required in 2016 to drop the Thwaite's name from all advertising. As a result Wainwrights & Lancaster Bomber carry no brewery name at point of sale. Part of Marston's PLC. !! ♦

Mild (OG 1036, ABV 3.5%)
An amber-coloured, well-balanced, refreshing session beer.

Amber Ale (OG 1038, ABV 3.8%)
A pale brown-coloured bitter with a pleasant balance of hops and malt. Hops continue from the taste through to a bittersweet aftertaste.

Sunbeam (OG 1042, ABV 4.2%)
Zesty golden-coloured beer with refreshing gooseberry and grapefruit citrus hops prominent. A vibrant hop aroma leads to a long, clean finish.

Brewed under the Mansfield brand name:

Cask Ale (OG 1038, ABV 3.9%)
A copper-coloured bitter with fruity notes, subtle hop aromas and a restrained bitterness.

Contract brewed for Carlsberg:

Tetley Mild (OG 1034, ABV 3.3%)

Tetley Bitter (OG 1035, ABV 3.7%)
A classic dry northern session bitter. A distinct hop character prevails with a subtle clove-like note.

Tetley Gold (OG 1041, ABV 4.1%)
A straw-coloured golden ale. A dry, refreshing citrus/herbal hop character predominates.

Contract brewed for Marston's:

Wainwright (OG 1042, ABV 4.1%)
Refreshing golden ale with gentle bitterness and a sweet lemon hop finish.

Lancaster Bomber (OG 1044, ABV 4.4%)
Full-bodied, deep amber-coloured beer with a raisin-like sweetness and a noticeable dry hop character.

Barefaced (NEW)

9 Norwich Avenue, Bournemouth, Dorset, BH2 5TG
☎ 07435 157767 🌐 barefacedbrewing.co.uk

Barefaced was started in 2017 by two friends, Nick Horne and Tom Cooper, in one of their garden sheds in Wimborne. Since then their beers have become so popular that they now brew in larger premises in Bournemouth, with a new 3.5-barrel plant. The small batch production allows for production of a core range as well as developing seasonal brews as part of the Jekyll & Hyde series. !! ♦ RAIB

Big Bang Blueberry Cream Ale (ABV 4.4%)
A speciality ale with added blueberries.

So You've Travelled (ABV 4.4%)

Heartbreak Stout (ABV 5.4%)
Stout with plenty of bitterness.

Boil or Bust (ABV 6.2%)

Sucker Punch Saison (ABV 6.4%)
A spicy wheat beer.

Barlow

Units 5 & 6, Shippen Rural Business Centre, Church Farm, Barlow, Derbyshire, S18 7TR
☎ (0114) 360 3676 ☎ 07976 884703
🌐 barlowbrewery.co.uk

Brewing started in 2009 on a self-built 2.5-barrel plant located in farm outbuildings. Expansion to five-barrel capacity was completed in 2014. Beers are supplied to the Hare & Hounds in Barlow and other local outlets. The brewery acquired its first pub, the Tap House, Brampton in 2014. ♦ RAIB

Heath Robinson (OG 1039, ABV 3.8%)

THE BREWERIES

A traditional dark bitter with a malty background and a balanced, bitter finish.

Betty's Blonde (OG 1042, ABV 4%)
A light golden-coloured beer, hopped for subtle citrus and passion fruit flavours with a clean, crisp finish.

Beyond the Pale (OG 1042, ABV 4%)
A well-balanced, straw-coloured pale ale; floral aroma with a light citrus grapefruit taste and a hint of lemons. A light bitter finish.

Carnival Ale (OG 1042, ABV 4%)
A light, golden-coloured pale ale with a citrus finish.

Dark Horse (OG 1043, ABV 4.2%)
A dark-coloured bitter with a coffee aroma.

Black (OG 1051, ABV 5%)
A dark-coloured ale with strong roast and malty flavours and a well-balanced, bitter finish.

Three Valleys IPA (OG 1052, ABV 5%)
An American-style IPA bursting with tropical fruit and citrus flavours, clean bitter finish.

Wakatu (OG 1050, ABV 5%)
A golden-coloured IPA with floral aromas and notes of fresh lime zest and citrus.

Jolly Roger (OG 1053, ABV 5.2%)
A robust porter; smooth and dark. Coffee and chocolate flavours with a warming finish.

Full Monty (OG 1067, ABV 6.5%)
A strong, full-flavoured IPA. Golden in colour with complex passion fruit, citrus and mandarin orange flavours and a warming alcoholic finish.

Anastasia (OG 1076, ABV 7.5%)
Strong, dark and smooth with complex malt flavours, chocolate, coffee and a hint of fruit.

Barn Owl

Buildings Farm, Faringdon Road, Gozzard's Ford, Oxfordshire, OX13 6QH ☎ 07724 551086

⊗ Located in a spacious barn on a farm just outside Abingdon, brewing began in 2016 using a four-barrel plant. Beers are often to be found in the Black Horse in Gozzard's Ford and other local free trade outlets.

Golden Gozzard (OG 1040, ABV 4%)
A light, refreshing golden ale with soft bitterness and a fruity finish.

Gozzard's Guzzler (OG 1044, ABV 4.4%)
A dark-coloured best bitter with a sweetish nose and fruity tones.

Old Scruttock's Dirigible (ABV 5%)

Barnaby's

The Old Stable, Hole Farm, Staverton, Devon, TQ11 0LA
☎ (01803) 762730 🌐 barnabysbrewhouse.com

Soil Association-certified organic brewery established in 2016. No real ale.

Barnard Castle (NEW)

Quaker Yard, rear of 24 Newgate, Barnard Castle, Durham, DL12 8NG

Brewing commenced in 2017 on a 3.6-barrel plant situated in one of the many yards that feature in Barnard Castle. A number of local outlets are supplied including the nearby Old Well Inn, which acts as the brewery tap. The beers are named after local themes.

Deliberation (ABV 3.7%)

Mechanical Swan (ABV 4.5%)

Peg Powler (ABV 5.6%)

Barnet

Black Horse, 80 Wood Street, High Barnet, Hertfordshire, EN5 4BW
☎ (020) 8449 2230 🌐 blackhorsebarnet.co.uk

⊗ The brewery opened in 2013 using a 2.5-barrel plant located behind the Black Horse pub. The brand name is now owned by the Oak Tavern pub chain. Brewing takes place two or three times a week using recipes from long since closed breweries. The beers are supplied mainly to the Black Horse, but small quantities may be found in other local pubs.

Barney's SIBA

Summerhall Brewery, 1 Summerhall, Edinburgh, EH9 1PL ☎ 07512 253660 🌐 barneysbeer.com

The only microbrewery in Edinburgh's city centre, Barney's Beer was founded in 2010 and now brews on the site of the original 1800s Summerhall brewery. Summerhall is Edinburgh's centre for the arts and science. ‼ RAIB

Vital Juices (ABV 3.8%)

Extra Pale (OG 1040, ABV 4%)

Red Rye (OG 1044, ABV 4.5%)
A copper-coloured beer with a clean, crisp, dry and fruity taste.

Volcano IPA (OG 1049, ABV 5%)
An American-style pale ale erupting with hops.

Barngates SIBA

Barngates, Cumbria, LA22 0NG
☎ (01539) 436575 🌐 barngatesbrewery.co.uk

Barngates was established in 1997 to supply only the Drunken Duck Inn. It became a limited company in 1999. Expansion over the years plus a new purpose-built 10-barrel plant in 2008 means it now supplies more than 150 outlets throughout Cumbria, Lancashire and Yorkshire. ‼ ♦

Pale (OG 1036, ABV 3.3%)
A well-balanced, fruity, hoppy bitter with plenty of flavour for its strength.

Cat Nap (OG 1037, ABV 3.6%)
Pale beer, unapologetically bitter, with a dry astringent finish.

Cracker (OG 1038, ABV 3.9%)
A full-bodied, hoppy beer with some balancing sweetness and fruit. There is plenty of taste in this brown beer. Cleverly constructed.

Brathay Gold (OG 1042, ABV 4%)
A sweet, rich aroma is followed by plenty of fruit and hops, then a long bitter finish.

Goodhew's Dry Stout (OG 1045, ABV 4.3%)
The inviting roast aroma leads to an easy-drinking, full-bodied and well-balanced roasty stout.

Tag Lag (OG 1044, ABV 4.4%)
This traditional bitter is full on: fruit, noble hops, malt balance, good body with a crisp, clean finish.

Red Bull Terrier (OG 1048, ABV 4.8%)
An assertive roasty red-coloured beer with full mouthfeel. Initial sweetness and luscious fruit, give way to a lingering bitter finish.

Barrahooley Craft

122 Glenravel Road, Martinstown, BT43 6QL
barrahooleybrewery.com

Located in the heart of the Glens of Antrim, Barrahooley started brewing in 2014 producing a range of bottle-conditioned beers. RAIB

Barsham (NEW)

Estate Office, West Barsham, Norfolk, NR21 9NR
(01328) 864459 07760 551056
barshambrewery.co.uk

Barsham Brewery purchased Jo C's Brewery business in 2017 and continues to brew the beers to Jo Coubrough's recipes. Maris Otter is grown on site and a private bore hole supplies water for the brewery. Jo is still on board as consultant. ♦

Oaks (ABV 3.6%)
An amber-coloured, easy-drinking bitter with a balanced hop finish.

Brewed under the Jo C's Brewery brand name:

Norfolk Kiwi (OG 1038.5, ABV 3.8%)
Yellow-coloured, hop dominated bitter. Citrus notes vie with bitterness to add depth. Quick, slightly astringent finish.

Bitter Old Bustard (OG 1045, ABV 4.3%)
A mixture of malt and caramel on the nose is joined by a dark fruitiness in the flavour. Quick finish.

Knot Just Another IPA (OG 1052, ABV 5%)

Bartleby's

Coachwerks, 19 Hollingdean Terrace, Brighton, East Sussex, BN1 7HB
(01273) 275012 07518 485342
bartlebysbrewery.com

Bartleby's began trading in 2014 in Brighton. Since opening it has expanded its distribution to local pubs and has established an on-site shop with home deliveries by veloelectric tricycle. An on-site venue is used for music, community events and art shows. !! ♦

Barum SIBA

c/o Reform Inn, Pilton High Street, Pilton, Barnstaple, Devon, EX31 1PD
(01271) 329994 barumbrewery.co.uk

Barum was established in 1996 by Tim Webster, and is housed in a conversion attached to the Reform Inn that acts as the brewery tap and main outlet. Distribution is exclusively within Devon. !! ♦ RAIB

Original (OG 1044, ABV 4.4%)
A smooth, tawny-coloured best bitter. A malt and fruit aroma leads to fruity, hoppy tastes into a short-lived bitter finish.

EPA (OG 1046, ABV 4.6%)
Pale golden-coloured ale with citrus/grapefruit notes throughout. Clean dry finish.

Breakfast (OG 1048, ABV 5%)
Copper-coloured, malty premium bitter with a floral nose and bittersweet finish.

Batemans SIBA IFBB

Salem Bridge Brewery, Mill Lane, Wainfleet, Lincolnshire, PE24 4JE
(01754) 880317 bateman.co.uk

Bateman's Brewery is one of Britain's few remaining independent family-owned and managed brewers. Established in 1874, it has been brewing award-winning beers for four generations. All 62 tied and managed houses serve cask-conditioned beer. !! ♦

XB (OG 1037, ABV 3.7%)
A well-rounded, smooth, malty beer with a blackcurrant fruity background. Hops flourish initially before giving way to a bittersweet dryness that enhances the mellow malty ending.

Gold / Yella Belly Gold (OG 1039, ABV 3.9%)
A golden-coloured, refreshing beer with a citrus flavour and aroma.

Salem Porter (OG 1048, ABV 4.8%)
A black-coloured beer with a complex mix of chocolate, liquorice and cough elixir.

XXXB (OG 1048, ABV 4.8%)
A brilliant blend of malt, hops and fruit on the nose with a bitter bite over the top of a faintly banana maltiness that stays the course. A russet-tan brown classic.

Bath

Hare Brewery, Southway Drive, Warmley, Bristol, BS30 5LW
(0117) 947 4797 bathales.com

Established in 1995, Bath Ales was taken over by St Austell in 2016. Bath Ales and subsidiary Beerd brands are still brewed as before on the same site, but a new brewery in the headquarters building became operational in 2018. Seven venues are operated in the Bristol/Bath area, all serving cask ale and one of which brews its own beer. ♦ RAIB

Special Pale Ale (OG 1039, ABV 3.7%)
Hoppy, pale golden-coloured session bitter. Light citrus aroma with bittersweet flavours and a bitter aftertaste. Some samples may have a hint of caramel.

Prophecy (OG 1040, ABV 3.9%)
Fruity, pine-like aroma, light colour and crisp bitter finish.

Gem (OG 1042, ABV 4.1%)
Pale brown-coloured best bitter with sweet fruit and malt flavours and a hint of caramel. Little aroma but a balanced taste with a short bitter finish.

Barnsey (OG 1045, ABV 4.5%)
A dark brown-coloured old ale with a grainy mouthfeel. Malt, dark fruits and toffee flavours combine to provide sweetness before a lingering bitter finish.

Platform 3 (OG 1044, ABV 4.5%)

A refreshing IPA with tropical fruit aromas, hints of citrus honey flavours, and a long bitter finish.

Lansdown (ABV 5%)
A West Coast-style pale ale with tropical grassy, lemon, lime and pine flavours.

Brewed under the Beerd brand name:

Monterey (OG 1040, ABV 3.9%)
A West Coast-style pale ale brewed with American-sourced hops. Pine and tropical fruits on the nose, more pine on the tongue followed by a quick, sharp bitter finish.

Silver Tip (OG 1046, ABV 4.7%)
A refreshing pale ale with a fruity aroma and a flavour that has hints of white wine. A fresh, quick bitter finish.

Bathams IFBB

Delph Brewery, Delph Road, Brierley Hill, West Midlands, DY5 2TN
☎ (01384) 77229 ⊕ bathams.com

A classic Black Country small brewery established in 1877. Tim and Matthew Batham represent the fifth generation to run the company. The Vine, one of the Black Country's most famous pubs, is also the site of the brewery. The company has 10 tied houses and supplies around 30 other outlets. Batham's Best Bitter is delivered in 54-gallon hogsheads to meet demand. ♦

Mild Ale (OG 1036.5, ABV 3.5%)
A fruity, dark brown-coloured mild with malty sweetness and a roast malt finish.

Best Bitter (OG 1043.5, ABV 4.3%)
A pale yellow-coloured, fruity, sweetish bitter, with a dry, hoppy finish. A good, light, refreshing beer.

Battle

The Calf House, Beech Farm, North Trade Road, Battle, East Sussex, TN33 0LL
☎ (01424) 772838 ⊕ battlebrewery.co.uk

Located on a working farm close to the iconic abbey in the heart of 1066 Country, Battle Brewery commenced brewing in 2016. ♦V

Conquest (OG 1043, ABV 4.1%)

Black Arrow (OG 1045, ABV 4.5%)

Abbey Pale (OG 1050, ABV 5%)

Battledown SIBA

Dowdeswell Park, London Road, Cheltenham, Gloucestershire, GL52 6UT
☎ (01242) 693409 ☎ 07734 834104
⊕ battledownbrewery.com

Battledown was established by Roland and Stephanie Elliot-Berry in 2005, joined by Ben Jennison-Phillips the following year. The brewery relocated to new premises in 2016 and supplies around 250 outlets. !! ♦ RAIB

Pale Ale (OG 1037, ABV 3.8%)
A refreshing aroma and sharp but smooth taste, leaving a dry, hoppy aftertaste which lingers on the palate.

Amber Ale (OG 1041, ABV 4.2%)
A deep golden-coloured beer, the malts evident but giving way to the triple hop addition giving a spicy and slightly citrus finish.

Original (OG 1046, ABV 4.6%)
A rich, amber-coloured ale. A malty aroma and taste with a deep, full-bodied fruit and malt texture leaving a well-rounded, mellow aftertaste.

Four Kings (OG 1066, ABV 7.2%)

Battlefield

See Tunnel

Battlefield (Shrewsbury) SIBA

Harlescott Lane, Shrewsbury, SY1 3AH
☎ (01743) 465000 ⊕ battlefieldbrewery.co.uk/

Battlefield Brewery began brewing in 2015 using a 25-hectolitre plant. It is located in the famous Battlefield area of Shrewsbury. !!♦

Saxon Gold (OG 1038, ABV 3.8%)
A golden ale with a subtle orangey marmalade aroma on the nose, crisp maltiness with touches of soft hops, yet offers a full, well-rounded finish.

1403 (OG 1043, ABV 4.3%)
A light, dry and crisp ale. Slight malt backbone with a subtle citrus/apricot note. The dry hop finish gives a lingering grapefruit and slight floral flavour.

1066 (OG 1045, ABV 4.5%)
A smooth, easy-drinking ale with rich malt and striking hop aromas.

Archers (OG 1049, ABV 4.9%)
A smooth, strong pale ale full of clean malt flavours with a hoppy finish.

Sabut Jung (ABV 5.8%)

Bay

See Wainstones

Bays SIBA

Aspen Way, Paignton, Devon, TQ4 7QR
☎ (01803) 555004 ⊕ baysbrewery.co.uk

Bays Brewery opened in 2007 in an old steel fabrication unit in Paignton using a 20-barrel plant. The brewery delivers to many pubs, hotels and restaurants in the south-west and further afield. !! ♦

Topsail (OG 1040, ABV 4%)
A tawny-coloured session bitter with complex aroma. Malty, bitter taste leading to a long, dry and refreshing aftertaste.

Gold (OG 1042, ABV 4.3%)
Smooth, golden ale. Light aroma and taste of hops, malt and caramel. Lingering hoppy aftertaste.

Trunk Ale (ABV 4.5%)

Devon Dumpling (OG 1048, ABV 5.1%)
Strong ale, easily drinkable. Light aromas of hops and fruit continue through taste and lingering aftertaste.

Beacon Brauhaus

Pilgrims Coffee, Falkland House, Marygate, Lindisfarne, TD15 2SJ

☎ (01289) 389109 🌐 pilgrimscoffee.com

Nanobrewery situated on Holy Island, the first brewery to be based there in around 500 years. Local outlets are supplied. RAIB

Bear Claw

Unit 3, Meantime Workshops, Spittal, Northumberland, TD15 1RG ☎ 07919 276715 🌐 bearclawbrewery.weebly.com

Bear Claw began brewing in 2012 using a two-barrel plant, producing a variety of mainly highly-hopped cask-conditioned ales and many bottle-conditioned beers, including continental styles. Beers are available in the Green shop and Curfew pub in Berwick upon Tweed. RAIB

Beartown

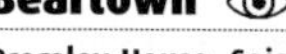

Bromley House, Spindle Street, Congleton, Cheshire, CW12 1QN
☎ (01260) 299964 🌐 beartownbrewery.co.uk

Beartown began brewing in 1994 and uses a 25-barrel plant. It supplies more than 250 outlets. It recently joined forces with Manning Brewers (qv), also of Congleton. !! ♦

Best Bitter (OG 1037, ABV 3.7%)
A copper-coloured session beer with a full palate of malt and crisp hops.

Bear Ass (OG 1040, ABV 4%)
Dark ruby-coloured, malty bitter with a good hop nose and fruity flavour with a dry, bitter, astringent aftertaste.

Ginger Bear (OG 1040, ABV 4%)
The flavours from the malt and hops blend with the added bite from the root ginger to produce a thirst-quenching blonde ale.

Kodiak Gold (OG 1040, ABV 4%)
Hops and fruit dominate the taste of this crisp, yellow-coloured bitter and these follow through to the dryish aftertaste. Biscuity malt also comes through on the aroma and taste.

Bearskinful (OG 1042, ABV 4.2%)
Biscuity malt dominates the flavour of this amber-coloured best bitter. There are hops and a hint of sulphur on the aroma. A balance of malt and bitterness follow through to the aftertaste.

Bearly Literate (OG 1045, ABV 4.5%)
Golden-coloured pale ale. Floral scented and packed with the flavours of summer fruits and lemon, ending with a smooth dryness.

Polar Eclipse (OG 1048, ABV 4.8%)
Classic black, dry and bitter stout, with roast flavours to the fore. Good hop on the nose follows through the taste into a long, dry finish.

Black Bear (OG 1050, ABV 5%)
Dark ruby-coloured strong mild ale. Subtle roast and malt flavours fill the taste, complemented by a mellow sweetness.

Bruins Ruin (OG 1050, ABV 5%)
Deep copper-coloured premium ale. Full of malty character and a palate of sweet, smooth, fruity flavours.

Beat SIBA

Old Coach House, Church Road, North Curry, Somerset, TA3 6LH ☎ 07821 132297

Office: 11 Sydenham Hill, Bristol, BS6 5SL
🌐 beatales.com

Beat Ales has been remarketed as Beat Brewery. It is brewing in North Curry at present, but has plans to move to Bristol, where the office is based. Beer names reflect the owners musical inspiration, taking in different genres. Music can be played from the pumpclips. ♦RAIB

Raver (OG 1034, ABV 3.8%)
A light pale ale, clean and hoppy with citrus aromas.

New Wave (ABV 4.5%)
A golden ale with fruit flavours of tangerine, melon and apricot.

Metal Head (OG 1042, ABV 4.8%)
A blend of six malts giving flavours of vanilla, chocolate and blackcurrant.

Rocka (OG 1044, ABV 5.3%)
Huge citrus and tropical fruit notes combined with a touch of pine and spice.

Funk (ABV 5.5%)
A dry-hopped IPA with a huge amount of tropical hop flavours and a simple malt base.

Cosmic Pop (ABV 6%)
Hop flavours of grapefruit, lemon and pine are offset against a dark malt centre in this black IPA.

Beath SIBA

54 Foulford Road, Cowdenbeath, KY4 9AS ☎ 07792 369678 🌐 beathbrewing.com

Beath began brewing in 2016, originally with a 20-litre capacity upgraded to 100-litre within a few months. There are plans for a further expansion. RAIB

Mad World (ABV 4%)

Are You With Me (ABV 4.5%)

Ella Ella Ella (ABV 4.5%)

Funky Town (ABV 5%)

Beatnikz Republic SIBA

Unit 15, Redbank Court, Green Quarter, Manchester, M4 4HF ☎ 07825 077832 🌐 beatnikzrepublic.com

Beatnikz Republic is a microbrewery brewing out of a railway arch near Manchester Victoria Station. Beers are available unfined in KeyKeg, can and cask. There are plans to open a bar in central Manchester. !!

Citra Pale (ABV 3.8%)

Beavertown SIBA

Units 17 & 18, Lockwood Industrial Park, Mill Mead Road, Tottenham Hale, London, N17 9QP
☎ (020) 8525 9884 ☎ 07976 984173
🌐 beavertownbrewery.co.uk

Beavertown began brewing in 2014. Beers are mostly sold in KeyKeg, can and keg without filtration or pasteurisation. Real ale is produced on a small plant. The brewery is open to visit (food,

THE BREWERIES

music and games available) most Saturday afternoons. ♦ RAIB

Beckstones

Upper Beckstones Mill, The Green, Millom, Cumbria, LA18 5HL
☎ (01229) 314900 🌐 beckstonesbrewery.co.uk

On the site of an 18th-century mill, with its own water supply, this five-barrel operation continues to win awards. Beer names have connections to the long-closed Millom Iron Works or local characters; the brewer designs the distinctive pump clips. ♦

Leat (OG 1036, ABV 3.6%)
A refreshing golden-coloured bitter with tangy fruit and a rising hop finish.

Barley Blonde (ABV 3.7%)
Full-flavoured, beautifully-balanced, emphatically fruity hoppy beer.

Black Dog Freddy Mild (OG 1038, ABV 3.9%)
A full-bodied, beautifully-balanced ruby-coloured dark mild, replete with fruit and roast malt.

Border Stones (OG 1040, ABV 4.1%)
An old-fashioned-style, tawny-coloured bitter with a sweet start, some bitter notes and plenty of aftertaste.

Iron Town (ABV 4.1%)
Creamy sweet brown ale full of well-balanced fruit and hop.

Rev Rob (OG 1044, ABV 4.6%)
A golden-coloured beer with a pronounced grapefruit aroma and taste. The hoppy bitterness lasts through to the aftertaste.

Bedlam SIBA

Albourne Farm, Shaves Wood Lane, Albourne, West Sussex, BN6 9DX
☎ (01273) 978015 ☎ 07801 822645
🌐 bedlambrewery.co.uk

The brewery, named after Bedlam Street, the Roman road that once ran through the adjacent countryside, has been brewing in the shadow of the South Downs since 2012. The Bull in Ditchling serves as the taphouse. ‼ RAIB

Benchmark (OG 1040, ABV 4%)
A classic English amber-coloured best bitter, full of roasted barley malts and bittering hops.

Golden (OG 1042, ABV 4.2%)

Beer Bores

Pixtons Green, Ashwicke, Gloucestershire, SN14 8AL
☎ 07790 715464 🌐 thebeerbores.co.uk

Mark Hempleman-Adams, Paul Clarke-Dabson and Marshall Ewart established Box Steam Brewery in 2004, before selling the business in 2007. However, Mark and Paul missed brewing so much that they set up a three-barrel microbrewery in 2015. Plans are in place to increase capacity with a new six-barrel plant and to distil their own West Country gin. Brewing is currently suspended. ♦

Beer Brothers SIBA

335 Ranglet Road, Walton Summit Centre, Bamber Bridge, Lancashire, PR5 8AR ☎ 07921 519129
🌐 beerbrothers.co.uk

Brewing began in 2015. The brewery moved in 2017 and expanded to a 10-barrel European-style brew plant. It has its own brewery tap, open Friday and Saturday from 12pm. ‼

Gold (OG 1037, ABV 3.8%)

IPA (OG 1035, ABV 3.8%)
A full-bodied, full-flavoured and hoppy IPA.

True Brit (OG 1042, ABV 3.8%)
A smooth, amber-coloured, full-bodied malty session ale.

Milk Stout (OG 1058, ABV 4.2%)
A dark, sweet and creamy ale, smooth on the palate with a gentle bitterness from the dark roasted barley.

Hop Chocolate (OG 1056, ABV 4.3%)
Full-bodied and well-balanced with notes of roasted coffee and dark chocolate. Made with real cocoa.

Beer Engine SIBA

Newton St Cyres, Devon, EX5 5AX
☎ (01392) 851282 🌐 thebeerengine.co.uk

The Beer Engine was established in 1983 and is the oldest working microbrewery in Devon. The brewery is visible downstairs in the pub through multiple viewing windows. Several outlets are supplied, as well as local beer festivals. ‼♦

Beer Ink

Plover Road Garage, Plover Road, Lindley, Huddersfield, West Yorkshire, HD3 3PJ
☎ (01484) 655262 ☎ 07739 754816

The Beer Ink Brewery Company is based in Lindley and opened in 2015 using an eight-barrel plant. It specialises in barrel-aged beers. A small on-site brewery tap opened in 2016. ♦

Avant Garde (OG 1041, ABV 4%)

Pin Up (OG 1040, ABV 4%)

Flagship (OG 1050, ABV 5%)

Noire (OG 1050, ABV 5%)

Two Faced (OG 1075, ABV 7.5%)

Beer Me

Belgian Café, 11-23 Grand Parade, Eastbourne, East Sussex, BN21 3YN
☎ (01323) 729967 🌐 thebelgiancafe.co.uk

Beer Me was launched in 2014 by the owners of the Belgian Café in Eastbourne, building on 10 years in the catering industry. It uses a 2.5-barrel plant and produces continental-style beers which are served direct from the brewery. ‼♦

Beer Monkey SIBA

Units 3 & 4, Enterprise Way, Airedale Business Park, Skipton, North Yorkshire, BD23 2TZ
☎ (01756) 701289 🌐 beermonkeybrewco.com

The Beer Monkey Brew Co has taken on the mantle of brewing real ales in Skipton at its modern brewery on the southern edge of town. Brewing takes place on a 30-barrel plant using water from its own borehole. The four permanent beers are supplemented with various limited edition ales.

Bitter Revival (ABV 3.9%)

Blond (ABV 3.9%)
A blonde beer with citrus flavours and aroma.

Evolution Pilsner (ABV 4%)
Straw-coloured premium Pilsner-style ale.

Uncle Monk's IPA (ABV 4.5%)
Full-bodied best bitter. Malty and nutty with an orange citrus edge, leading into a bittersweet finish.

Beer Nouveau

75 North Western Street, Ardwick, Manchester, M12 6DY beernouveau.co.uk

Beer Nouveau was established in 2014. Expansion from a small kit in the owner's garage to a railway arch and then doubling in size by taking on an adjoining arch has enabled an expanded range of beers including many one-offs. Beers based on historic recipes are reproduced and a barrel-ageing programme has been introduced. RAIB

Beer Refinery

Chapel Court Enterprise Centre, Wervin Road, Wervin, Chester, CH2 4BP 07939 875308
enquiries@thebeerrefinery.co.uk

The Beer Refinery is a partnership of 10 engineers, some homebrewers and some just beer lovers with a locally-built four-barrel plant. They are not reliant on the brewery for an income so are able to brew the beers they want to drink rather than the ones they think will sell the best.

Beerblefish SIBA

Unit 6, Georgiou Business Park, Second Avenue, Upper Edmonton, London, N18 2PG 07594 383195
beerblefish.co.uk

Beerblefish began brewing in 2015. It brews a wide variety of styles and experiments with new hops and malts. RAIB

Holy Smoke (OG 1034, ABV 3.1%)
An amber-coloured ale with a light smoky flavour.

ESB (OG 1048, ABV 4.8%)
A darker ale with a rich malt finish.

Black Beerblefish (OG 1053, ABV 5.2%)
A mellow stout using chocolate malts.

Bloodletter (OG 1050, ABV 5.2%)
A red-coloured IPA with a hint of citrus.

1892 (OG 1065, ABV 7.2%)
An IPA based on an 1890s recipe with a hint of modern aroma hops.

Beercraft

Watchmaker's Arms, 84 Goldstone Villas, Hove, East Sussex, BN3 3RU beercraftbrighton.co.uk

Beercraft Brighton is a 100-litre pilot kit based out of the Watchmaker's Arms micropub in Hove. Brewing started in 2016 with different beers being produced each time. There are plans for expansion to a full-size plant.

Beerd

See Bath

Beermats (NEW) SIBA

New Yard, Winkburn, Nottinghamshire, NG22 8PQ
(01636) 639004 beermatsbeer.co.uk

Brewing began in 2017 on the Winkburn Estate in old dairy buildings using a 10-barrel kit. The brewery was established by three friends with experience in the trade. Beers are named around the theme of the humble beermat. V

Charismatic (OG 1039, ABV 3.8%)

Pragmatic (OG 1039, ABV 3.8%)

Format (OG 1040, ABV 3.9%)

Teammates (OG 1040, ABV 3.9%)
A citrus pale ale.

Soulmate (OG 1043, ABV 4.2%)
A golden-coloured fruity ale.

Diplomat (OG 1047, ABV 4.6%)
A smooth chocolate stout.

Ultimate (OG 1050.5, ABV 4.9%)
A fruity red-coloured ale.

BeerRiff (NEW)

Pilot House Wharf, Swansea, SA1 1UN 07897 895511 beerriffbrewing.com

The proprietors of Pilot Brewery, Mumbles set up this four-barrel brewery in 2017, mainly producing beer in keg and can. All beers are unfined and unfiltered. No real ale. **V**

BEEspoke

Fox, 41 Briggate, Shipley, West Yorkshire, BD17 7BP
(01274) 594826 thefoxshipley.co.uk

Brewing began in 2015 in the cellar of the Fox pub using a one-barrel plant. Four regular beers are produced along with monthly specials. Beers are available in the pub and at local beer festivals.

Beeston SIBA

Fransham Road Farm, Beeston, Norfolk, PE32 2LZ
(01328) 700844 07768 742763
beestonbrewery.co.uk

The brewery was established in 2006 in an old farm building using a five-barrel plant. Brewing water comes from a dedicated borehole and raw ingredients are sourced locally whenever possible.
RAIB

The Squirrels Nuts (OG 1035, ABV 3.5%)
Cherry, chocolate and vanilla aroma. A malt and cherry sweetness comes to the fore but quickly fades. Short finish.

Worth the Wait (OG 1041, ABV 4.2%)
Hoppy throughout with a growing dryness. Complex and grainy with fruit notes, malt and understated bitterness.

THE BREWERIES

Stirling (OG 1045, ABV 4.5%)
Rich, malty, red-coloured bitter with toffee notes.

The Dry Road (OG 1048, ABV 4.8%)

Village Life (OG 1047, ABV 4.8%)
Copper-coloured with a nutty character. Malty throughout, a bittersweet background gives depth. Strong toffee apple finish.

On the Huh (OG 1048, ABV 5%)
A fruity raisin aroma. A bittersweet maltiness jousts with caramel and roast. A dry hoppiness adds to a strong finale.

Old Stoatwobbler (OG 1065, ABV 6%)

Contract brewed for Brancaster Brewery:

Best (ABV 3.8%)
A refreshing session ale with a touch of citrus on the finish.

Malthouse Bitter (ABV 4.2%)
A mid amber-coloured ale with a malty character and distinct bitterness on the finish.

Beeston Hop

Gwenbrook Avenue, Beeston, Nottingham, NG9 4BA
beestonhop.co.uk

A nanobrewery launched in 2015 producing mainly bottle-conditioned beers. Cask beers are occasionally produced for festivals using capacity at other breweries. The beers are unfined, unfiltered and unpasteurised. RAIB V

Belhaven

Brewery Lane, Dunbar, EH42 1PE
(01368) 862734

Office: Spott Road, Dunbar, EH42 1RS
belhaven.co.uk

Belhaven brewery is one of the oldest brewing sites in Scotland. Established in Dunbar in 1719, it brews beers made with water from its own well and local Scottish barley. Part of Greene King PLC. !!

60/- Ale (OG 1030, ABV 2.9%)
A fine example of a Scottish light. This bittersweet, reddish-brown-coloured beer is dominated by fruit and malt with a hint of roast and caramel, and increasing bitterness in the aftertaste.

IPA (OG 1038, ABV 3.8%)
A golden ale with refreshing floral and citrus tones produced by a well balanced fusion of malt and hops giving a clean, crisp flavour.

80/- Ale (OG 1040, ABV 4.2%)
One of the last remaining original Scottish 80 Shillings. Malt is the predominant flavour characteristic, though it is balanced by fruit and a little hop. A complex ale, true to the 80/- style.

Black (OG 1041, ABV 4.2%)
A smooth, balanced stout with malty body and roast notes of dark chocolate and coffee.

St Andrew's Ale (OG 1046, ABV 4.9%)
A bittersweet beer with lots of body. The malt, fruit and roast mingle throughout with hints of hop and caramel.

Bell Street

57-59 Bell Street, Henley-on-Thames, Oxfordshire, RG9 2BA
(01491) 570200 bellstreetbrewery.co.uk

Bell Street Brewery opened in 2013 at the rear of Brakspear pub company's Bull on Bell Street. A four-barrel plant is used. The beers are sold at the pub and through the Brakspear estate. ♦

Brakspear Special (OG 1043, ABV 4.3%)
Tawny-coloured, full-bodied beer with a well-balanced aroma and a hint of sweetness which gives way to a dry hop bitterness.

Belleville

36 Jaggard Way, Wandsworth Common, London, SW12 8SG 07712 298273
bellevillebrewing.co.uk

Belleville began brewing in 2012. It was formed by a group of parents who met in the playground of a local primary school and specialises in American-style beers. Its nearby taproom is open Friday-Sunday. !!♦

Northcote Blonde (OG 1042, ABV 4.2%)
Smooth dark golden ale with biscuity character and a trace of hoppy bitterness. Fruit is pineapple, orange and mixed citrus.

Picnic Session IPA (ABV 4.4%)

Commonside Pale Ale (OG 1050, ABV 5%)
Full-flavoured, amber-coloured beer with hops and fruit throughout. Initial palate is sweet but bitterness develops, particularly in the finish.

Thames Surf IPA (OG 1057, ABV 5.7%)
Strong amber-coloured IPA with citrus, hops, honey caramel and spicy notes. There is a long-lasting, faintly hoppy, bitter finish.

Bellfield

46 Stanley Place, Edinburgh, EH7 5TB
(0131) 656 9390 bellfieldbrewery.com

Founded by two coeliacs, Bellfield Brewery is the UK's first dedicated gluten-free microbrewery, with the first beers launched in 2016. Accredited by Coeliac UK. ♦GF

Lawless Village IPA (ABV 4.5%)

Bellinger's SIBA

Station Road, Grove, Oxfordshire, OX12 0DH
(01235) 772255 bellingersbrewery.co.uk

Established in 2011 by the late Mike Bellinger and now run by his nephew and son-in-law, Bellinger's is a five-barrel plant producing mainly bottled beer with the occasional cask-conditioned ale. All beers, when available, are sold in the garage forecourt shop and other local farm shops. !! ♦RAIB

Original Bitter (OG 1040, ABV 4.1%)
A light and refreshing, easy-drinking beer with a delicate malt flavour.

Arnhem (ABV 4.4%)

Cavalry (OG 1045, ABV 4.6%)
A malty, robust bitter.

IPA (OG 1050, ABV 5%)
Gently hoppy with a lingering bitter taste.

Gallipoli Stout (OG 1053, ABV 5.3%)
A stout with a big chocolate taste.

Belvoir SIBA

Crown Park, Station Road, Old Dalby, Leicestershire, LE14 3NQ
☎ (01664) 823455 🌐 belvoirbrewery.co.uk

Belvoir (pronounced 'beaver') Brewery was set up in 1995 by former Shipstone's and Theakston's brewer Colin Brown. Long-term expansion has seen the introduction of a 20-barrel plant that can produce 50 barrels a week. There is also a visitor centre incorporating brewery memorabilia, a bar, restaurant and shop (open seven days a week). Around 150 outlets are supplied direct. !! ♦ RAIB

Dark Horse (OG 1034, ABV 3.4%)

Whippling (OG 1037, ABV 3.6%)

Star Bitter (OG 1039, ABV 3.9%)
Reminiscent of the long-extinct Shipstone's Bitter, this mid-brown-coloured bitter lives up to its name as it is bitter in taste but not unpleasantly so.

Gordon Bennett (OG 1041, ABV 4.1%)
Light chestnut-coloured beer with a biscuity character and a pleasant hop finish.

Beaver Bitter (OG 1043, ABV 4.3%)
A light brown-coloured bitter that starts malty in both aroma and taste, but soon develops a hoppy bitterness. Appreciably fruity.

Old Dalby (OG 1050, ABV 5.1%)
A rich, smooth ruby red-coloured strong ale with pleasant hop character.

Contract Brewed for Hoskins Brothers:

Hob Bitter (OG 1040, ABV 4%)

IPA (OG 1040, ABV 4%)

Contract Brewed for Steamin' Billy:

Tipsy Fisherman (OG 1036, ABV 3.6%)
Traditional light amber-coloured bitter, mellow crisp flavour with hoppy aftertaste, quaffing ale that tastes more robust than its strength suggests.

Bitter (OG 1043, ABV 4.3%)
Light golden-coloured English bitter with a pronounced floral flavour and aroma followed by a lingering hop aftertaste.

1485 (OG 1050, ABV 5%)

Skydiver (OG 1050, ABV 5%)
Mahogany-coloured beer with a good balance of malty sweetness and hop bitterness.

Bendigo

See Robin Hood

Beowulf

Forest of Mercia, Chasewater Country Park, Pool Lane, Brownhills, Staffordshire, WS8 7NL
☎ (01543) 454067 ☎ 07714 291226
🌐 beowulfbrewery.co.uk

Beowulf Brewing Company is based at the Chasewater County Park. Its beers appear as guest ales predominantly in the central region, but also across the country. !! ♦ RAIB

Beorma (OG 1038, ABV 3.9%)
A perfectly balanced session ale with a malty hint of fruit giving way to a lingering bitterness. Background spice excites the palate.

Chasewater Bitter (OG 1043, ABV 4.4%)
Golden-coloured bitter, hoppy throughout with citrus and hints of malt. Long mouth-watering, bitter finish.

Chase Buster (OG 1045, ABV 4.5%)

Dark Raven (OG 1048, ABV 4.5%)
dark in colour with apple and bonfire in the aroma, sweet and smooth like liquid toffee apples with a sudden bitter finish.

Swordsman (OG 1045, ABV 4.5%)
Pale gold-coloured, light fruity aroma, tangy hoppy flavour. Faintly hoppy finish.

Folded Cross (OG 1045, ABV 4.6%)
Malt and caramel aromas and tastes with hints of fruity biscuits are nudged aside by the robust hops which give a lingering bitter edge.

Hurricane (OG 1041, ABV 4.6%)

Dragon Smoke Stout (OG 1048, ABV 4.7%)
Black with a light brown creamy head. Tobacco, chocolate, liquorice and mixed fruity hints on the aroma. Bitterness fights through the sweet and roast flavours and eventually dominates. Hints of a good port emerge.

Finn's Hall Porter (OG 1049, ABV 4.7%)
Dark chocolate aroma, after dinner mints, coffee and fresh tobacco. Good bitterness with woodland hints of autumn. Long late bitterness.

Heroes Bitter (OG 1046, ABV 4.7%)
Gold in colour, malt aroma, hoppy taste but sweetish finish.

Mercian Shine (OG 1048, ABV 5%)
Amber to pale gold in colour with a good bitter and hoppy start and a hint of nutmeg. Plenty of caramel and hops with background malt leading to a good bitter finish with caramel and hops lingering in the aftertaste.

IPA (OG 1067, ABV 7.2%)

Killer Stout (OG 1080, ABV 7.3%)
Dark, smooth bitter with dark chocolate and coffee hints in the aftertaste.

Bere

Homefield, Bere Alston, Devon, PL20 7JA
☎ (01822) 840382 🌐 berebrewery.co.uk

Established in 2016 by growers Jerry and Buffy on their smallholding on the Bere Peninsula in the Tamar Valley. The brewery produces bottle-conditioned beers using hops grown on the holding, with a 1.3-barrel plant and a 50-litre small batch kit. Building on its horticultural background, the brewery is working towards being self-sufficient in hops from 2019. Beers are sold at Tavistock Farmers' Market, by arrangement from the brewery, and at the Olde Plough Inn, Bere Ferrers. ♦ RAIB

Bespoke SIBA

Unit 5, The Mews, Mitcheldean, Gloucestershire, GL17 0SL
☎ (01594) 546426 🌐 bespokebrewery.co.uk

⊗ Brewing commenced in 2012 on a 5.5-barrel plant on the site of the former Wintles Brewery,

THE BREWERIES

which closed in the early 1900s. In 2014 capacity was increased to 12 barrels. Speciality-labelled bottles are offered for celebratory occasions. An on-site brewery tap opens Friday and Saturday. !! ♦

Saved by the Bell (OG 1037, ABV 3.8%)
A light, refreshing session bitter with a spicy hop bite and a light floral aroma.

Golden Rule (OG 1041, ABV 4%)
A light golden-coloured session ale with a subtly refreshing and fruity finish.

Running the Gauntlet (OG 1046, ABV 4.4%)
Full malty flavoured bitter with rich roasted undertones balanced with good hop bitterness with spicy blackcurrant aromas.

Going Off Half-Cocked (OG 1043, ABV 4.6%)
A spicily-hopped, golden-coloured pale ale.

Money for Old Rope (OG 1050, ABV 4.8%)
Classic stout with rich, dry flavours of malt and grain with deep hop bitterness.

Over a Barrel (OG 1052, ABV 5%)
A richly-coloured, fruity strong ale with generous peppery finish.

Betteridge's SIBA

Coopers Barn, The Dene, Hurstbourne Tarrant, Hampshire, SP11 0AG ☎ 07771 966058
betteridgesbrewery.co.uk

Microbrewery trading since 2014 using a 2.5-barrel plant. The founder and brewer, Mark Betteridge, brews four core beers using principally English hops and traditional floor-malted barley. Beers are supplied to beer festivals, private events and to a growing number of pubs in the Test Valley area and occasionally further afield. RAIB

Old Chap (ABV 3.8%)
An easy-drinking, amber-coloured session bitter with good malt flavour.

Jenny Wren (ABV 4.2%)
A dark golden-coloured, single-hopped beer. Initial fruit in aroma and taste leads to a bitter finish.

Private Sector (ABV 4.2%)
A full-flavoured, amber-coloured ale.

Serious Black (ABV 4.2%)
A complex stout with coffee and chocolate notes and roast flavours but with some underlying sweetness from added lactose.

Bewdley SIBA

Unit 7, Bewdley Craft Centre, Lax Lane, Bewdley, Worcestershire, DY12 2DZ
☎ (01299) 405148 bewdleybrewery.co.uk

Bewdley began brewing in 2008 on a six-barrel plant in an old school. This was upgraded to a 10-barrel plant in 2014. Beers are brewed with a railway theme for the nearby Severn Valley Railway. The brewery has an on-site tap and shop. Element gin is also produced. ♦RAIB

Worcestershire Way (OG 1036, ABV 3.6%)
Refreshing golden ale with a citrus, feintly orange peel aroma, leads to a balanced hop, malt and grapfruit taste and a lingering hoppy finish.

Old School (OG 1038, ABV 3.8%)
Pale copper in colour. A traditional English ale with a hoppy finish.

Jubilee (OG 1043, ABV 4.3%)
Pale in colour, fruit and citrus aroma, sweet malt with underlying citrus taste.

Sir Keith Park (OG 1045, ABV 4.5%)
Pale amber in colour, full, fruity and balanced flavour followed by a long hoppy finish.

2857/Worcestershire Sway (OG 1050, ABV 5%)
Complex amber-coloured bitter, also known as Worcestershire Sway. Fragrant malty aroma, well-balanced, slightly sweet malt and hops with hints of toffee and marmalade, malt with citrus and meadow grass finish.

William Mucklows Dark Mild (OG 1060, ABV 6%)
Dark in colour, malty, sweetish fruity flavour with slight liquorice finish.

Bexar County

8 Belgic Square, Padholme Road, Peterborough, Cambridgeshire, PE1 5XF ☎ 07934 722584
bexarcountybrewery.com

Bexar was established in 2012, brewing an ever-changing range of American-style beers. ♦

Poquito Pequeno (OG 1040, ABV 3.5%)

Prospect (OG 1048, ABV 4.5%)

Phantasmagorical (OG 1075, ABV 7.4%)

Bexley SIBA

18 Manford Industrial Estate, Erith, Kent, DA8 2AJ
☎ (01322) 337368 bexleybrewery.co.uk

Opened in 2014, brewers Cliff and Jane Murphy produce regular, seasonal and experimental brews as well as selling own-brand beer mustard. The premises also houses a chilli jam producer. A pub, the Bird & Barrel, opened in 2018. !! ♦RAIB

Session Golden Ale (OG 1042, ABV 3.6%)

Session Ruby Ale (OG 1042, ABV 3.7%)

Session Pale Ale (OG 1044, ABV 3.8%)
Refreshing beer with a zesty, citrus flavour. Limited sweetness and some bitterness in the taste.

Golden Acre (OG 1042, ABV 4%)
Smooth golden ale with citrus aroma. Flavour is of grapefruit, hops and a strong bitterness, continuing in the dry, fruity finish.

Bexley's Own Beer (OG 1044, ABV 4.2%)
Pale brown-coloured beer with a balance of fudge, floral hop, stone fruit and some bitterness growing in the dry finish.

Redhouse Premium (OG 1042, ABV 4.2%)
Copper-coloured best bitter with roast and sweet orange marmalade. Dry finish with a touch of chocolate in finish and aroma.

Bianca Road

19 Page's Walk, Bermondsey, London, SE1 4SB
☎ (020) 7732 2587 biancaroad.com

Brewing began in 2016. No real ale.

Bicester (NEW)

Angel, 102 Sheep Street, Bicester, Oxfordshire, OX26 6LP
☎ (01869) 360410 theangelbicester.co.uk

Brewing commenced in 2017 in an outhouse behind the Angel, Bicester. Beers are supplied solely to the pub.

Big Bog SIBA

74 Venture Point West, Evans Road, Speke, Merseyside, L24 9PB
☎ (0151) 558 0290 🌐 bigbog.co.uk

Big Bog was established in 2011. The brewery, which used to share its site with the Snowdonia Parc brewpub, underwent rapid expansion in 2013. In 2016 it moved to its present location in Speke, using a custom-built plant with a 10-barrel brew length. The brewery now has its own licenced bar and is open to the public. ♦

Bog Standard Bitter (OG 1035, ABV 3.6%)
A light-coloured session ale with medium bitterness and a refreshing hoppy, malty finish.

Mire (OG 1035, ABV 3.8%)
A tawny-coloured session ale with fruity notes.

Blonde Bach (OG 1037, ABV 3.9%)
A light-coloured quaffing ale with citrus/grapefruit notes.

Hinkypunk (OG 1039, ABV 4.1%)
A well-hopped beer with intense citrus notes.

Stog (OG 1040, ABV 4.1%)
A milk stout with a creamy, bittersweet taste.

Welsh Pale Ale (OG 1041, ABV 4.2%)
Copper-coloured classic ale with a medium bitterness and dry finish.

Morast (OG 1041, ABV 4.3%)

Swampy (OG 1046, ABV 4.7%)
Ruby red in colour with a robust bitterness that is offset by a slightly sweet finish owing to the inclusion of Muscovado sugar in the recipe.

Will o the Wisp (OG 1045, ABV 4.7%)
A golden-coloured ale with a strong, fruity and hoppy taste.

Bayou (OG 1047, ABV 5%)
American-style pale ale; intensely hoppy.

Quagmire (OG 1058, ABV 6%)
A strong but deceptively easy-drinking ale. Mid-brown in colour with a medium to high bitterness.

Big Clock

Grants, 1 Manchester Road, Accrington, Lancashire, BB5 2BQ
☎ (01254) 393938 🌐 thebigclockbrewery.co.uk

Brewing commenced in 2014. A 6.5-barrel plant is used.

Big Drop

c/o 5a Frascati Way, Maidenhead, Berkshire, SL6 4UY
🌐 bigdropbrew.com

Established in 2016 this company contract brews low-alcohol bottled beers of no more than 0.5% ABV at a variety of breweries around the country. No real ale.

Big Hand SIBA

Unit A1, Abbey Close, Redwither Business Park, Wrexham, LL13 9XG
☎ (01978) 660709 ☎ 07946 514238
🌐 bighandbrewing.co.uk

Big Hand began brewing in 2013 and operates from a 10-barrel plant on the outskirts of Wrexham. Now well established in the North Wales brewing scene, it has won many awards in recent years. ‼ ♦

Seren (OG 1037, ABV 3.7%)
Pale, full-flavoured and hoppy with a fruity aroma and taste.

Pendragon (OG 1039, ABV 3.9%)

Little Monkey (OG 1039, ABV 4%)
A malty mild, mahogany in colour, with a dry roasty taste. Some initial sweetness balanced by hoppy bitterness in the finish.

Super Tidy (OG 1040, ABV 4%)
A light-coloured session pale ale.

Bastion (OG 1041, ABV 4.2%)
A dry, malty best bitter, mahogany in colour with a full mouthfeel. Biscuity flavours and faint roast notes feature throughout.

Palewulf (OG 1042, ABV 4.2%)

Appaloosa (OG 1045, ABV 4.5%)

Spectre (OG 1045, ABV 4.5%)
A dry oatmeal stout.

Havok (OG 1049, ABV 5%)
A powerfully-hopped American-style IPA with strong and tangy citrus fruit bitterness throughout.

Big Lamp

Grange Road, Newburn, Newcastle upon Tyne, NE15 8NL
☎ (0191) 267 1689 🌐 biglampbrewers.co.uk

Big Lamp started in 1982 and relocated in 1997 to a 55-barrel plant in a former water pumping station. It is the oldest microbrewery in the North-east of England. Around 160 outlets are supplied and two pubs are owned, one of which (the Keelman) is attached to the brewery. ‼ ♦ RAIB

Sunny Daze (OG 1036, ABV 3.6%)
Golden-coloured, hoppy session bitter with a clean taste and finish.

Bitter (OG 1039, ABV 3.9%)
A clean-tasting bitter, full of hops and malt. A hint of fruit with a good, hoppy finish.

Lamplight Bitter (OG 1042, ABV 4.2%)
Crisp, light, refreshing ale with a dry aftertaste.

Summerhill Stout (OG 1044, ABV 4.4%)
A rich, tasty stout, dark in colour with a lasting rich roast character. Malty mouthfeel with a lingering finish.

Prince Bishop Ale (OG 1048, ABV 4.8%)
A refreshing, easy-drinking bitter. Golden in colour, full of fruit and hops. Strong bitterness with a spicy, dry finish.

Premium (OG 1052, ABV 5.2%)
Hoppy ale with a good bitter finish.

Keelman Brown (OG 1057, ABV 5.7%)
A full-bodied ale with a hint of toffee.

Big Smoke SIBA

Antelope, 87 Maple Road, Surbiton, Surrey, KT6 4AW

☎ (020) 8339 9721 ☎ 07859 884190
🌐 bigsmokebrew.co.uk

⊗ Big Smoke is a purpose-built brewery established in 2014 in courtyard buildings behind the Antelope pub, Surbiton. The five-barrel brew kit is used twice weekly. Beers can be found in the Antelope and the Sussex Arms in Twickenham, the Lyric in Soho, the Express in Brentford and occasionally in other local pubs and at beer festivals. ♦V

Solaris Session Pale Ale (ABV 3.8%)
Unfined golden ale with bitter grapefruit flavour, some malt and a long, dry bitter finish. Hoppy, fruity nose.

Dark Wave Porter (ABV 5%)
Creamy, black porter with a dry roasty bitter character balanced by a caramelised sweetness.

Electric Eye Pale Ale (ABV 5%)

Underworld Milk Stout (ABV 5%)
Sweet, smooth stout with hints of chocolate and coffee in the aroma and taste coupled with toasted nuts and vanilla.

Biggar

Queens Arms Courtyard, Biggar Village, Cumbria, LA14 3YG
☎ (01229) 474335 🌐 biggarbrewing.co.uk

This 2.5-barrel brewery, an independent co-operative of several shareholders, opened in 2015 in the courtyard of the Queens Arms in Biggar Village on Walney Island. The beer names are themed on Barrow's shipbuilding heritage, and the brewery logo features a representation of Barrow's dockside cranes, a strong visual motif of the town's history.

Mikasa (OG 1035, ABV 3.6%)

Vanguard (OG 1041, ABV 3.8%)

Oriana (OG 1039, ABV 4%)

Bilbrough Top

St. James House, Main Street, Bilbrough, North Yorkshire, YO23 3PH

Brewing began in 2016 using a six-barrel plant.

Top Beer (ABV 3.9%)

Billericay SIBA

Essex Beer Shop, 54c Chapel Street, Billericay, Essex, CM12 9LS
☎ (01277) 500121 ☎ 07788 373129
🌐 billericaybrewing.co.uk

Billericay Brewing opened at its present site in 2014, using a 4.5-barrel plant. A micropub and beershop are next door. ‼ ♦RAIB

Zeppelin (OG 1037, ABV 3.8%)
Easy-drinking session ale with slight smoky notes.

Blonde (OG 1040, ABV 4%)

Dickie (OG 1041, ABV 4.2%)
A well-balanced, amber-coloured ale with biscuit notes.

Vanilla Woods (OG 1042, ABV 4.2%)

Woody's Wag (OG 1042, ABV 4.2%)

Rhythm Stick (OG 1047, ABV 4.8%)
Hoppy, rich ale with caramel flavours.

Sex & Drugs & Rock & Roll (OG 1050, ABV 5%)

Chapel Street Porter (OG 1059, ABV 5.9%)
Rich, dark porter with chocolate and coffee flavours.

Chilli Porter (OG 1059, ABV 5.9%)

Mayflower Gold (OG 1064, ABV 6.5%)

Binghams SIBA

Unit 10, Tavistock Industrial Estate, Ruscombe, Berkshire, RG10 9NJ
☎ (0118) 934 4376 🌐 binghams.co.uk

⊗ Binghams began brewing in 2010, producing 40 firkins in each batch. The brewery is situated in an industrial unit on the site of a former brickworks – hence the name of one of the beers. Head brewer Chris Bingham is a member of the local branch of CAMRA and had extensive experience in homebrewing and a local brewery prior to starting up. ‼ RAIB

Twyford Tipple (OG 1040, ABV 3.7%)
Tawny-coloured bitter with a good balance of malt and hops in the flavour and a citrus hop finish.

Brickworks Bitter (OG 1047, ABV 4.2%)
Chestnut-coloured best bitter with a sweetish, malty nose. Hops balance the maltiness to give a well-rounded flavour with a slightly nutty hint and a sweet, earthy aftertaste.

Coffee Stout (OG 1056, ABV 5%)
A mellow beer with dark malts that complement the coffee flavour.

Doodle Stout (OG 1056, ABV 5%)
A blend of dark malts provide a complex character.

Ginger Doodle Stout (OG 1056, ABV 5%)
A dark stout with a subtle hint of ginger, which rounds off the bitterness.

Hot Dog Chilli Stout (OG 1056, ABV 5%)
Doodle Stout with a hint of chilli to provide a warm glow on the aftertaste.

Space Hoppy IPA (OG 1052, ABV 5%)
Pale golden in colour and packed with hops to create a complex flavour and a long citrus finish.

Vanilla Stout (OG 1052, ABV 5%)
Infused with vanilla pods that complement the dark malts to create a smooth-drinking, dark stout.

Bingley SIBA

Unit 2, Old Mill Yard, Shay Lane, Wilsden, West Yorkshire, BD15 0DR
☎ (01535) 274285 🌐 bingleybrewery.co.uk

Bingley is a small, family-run brewery that opened in 2014 using a six-barrel plant. It is located in a rural setting in the village of Wilsden, part of Bingley Rural Ward. Beers are distributed coast to coast and as far south as Derby. ‼

Goldy Locks Blonde (ABV 4%)
Blonde beer with a refreshing citrus aroma and delicate toffee aftertaste.

Azacca (ABV 4.1%)
A slightly bitter beer with citrus, mango and pine notes in the flavour and aroma.

Session IPA (ABV 4.2%)
A session IPA with sharp citrus and spicy notes.

Steady State (ABV 4.2%)
A smooth caramel/toffee flavour with a floral, sweet aroma and a tinge of elderberry.

Centennial (ABV 4.4%)
Golden-coloured beer with a subtle malty base, hoppy aroma and delicate floral, tangy aftertaste.

Tri State (ABV 4.5%)
A triple-hopped, American-style pale ale with flavours of citrus, pine and spice. A bitter and tart, dry finish.

1848 Stout (ABV 4.8%)
Creamy stout with hints of chocolate and liquorice and a pleasant bitter finish.

Birch Cottage (NEW)

Birch Cottage, Wilne Road, Sawley, Derbyshire, NG10 3AP ☎ 07966 757407
✉ birchcottagebrewery@outlook.com

Birch Cottage is a nanobrewery established in 2018 brewing small batch beers.

Birchover

Red Lion, Main Street, Birchover, Derbyshire, DE4 2BN
☎ (01629) 650363 🌐 red-lion-birchover.co.uk

The enthusiastic Sardinian born brewery/pub owner started brewing in 2016 at the Red Lion pub, Birchover. The brewery was upgraded in 2017 to a five-barrel plant. Several of the core beers are named after local landmarks in and around the adjacent Stanton Moor. ♦

Birmingham SIBA

Unit 15, Stirchley Trading Estate, Hazelwell Road, Birmingham, B30 2PF ☎ 07717 704929
🌐 birminghambrewingcompany.co.uk

Birmingham Brewing Co was established in 2016 and is based in a small unit on a trading estate outside the city. !! ♦

Pale Brummie (ABV 4%)

Bitter Brummie (ABV 4.1%)

Bishop Nick SIBA

33 East Street, Braintree, Essex, CM7 3JJ
☎ (01376) 349605 🌐 bishopnick.com

Bishop Nick was launched in 2011 by Nelion Ridley, a member of the family that started Ridley's brewery near Chelmsford in 1842. In 2013 a new brewery was established in Braintree using a 20-barrel plant. ♦ RAIB

Ridley's Rite (OG 1036, ABV 3.6%)
A classic bitter with a floral aroma and a subtle but long-lasting bitter aftertaste.

Heresy (OG 1041, ABV 4%)
Refreshing golden ale with a spicy bitterness before the hops set about delivering the citrus and floral notes.

1555 (OG 1043, ABV 4.3%)
Full-bodied, rich, tawny-coloured ale, sweet nutty taste underlined by ginger and fruit.

Martyr IPA (OG 1049, ABV 5%)
A full-flavoured ale with a spicy, floral bitterness supported by a sweet, malty backbone.

Divine (OG 1051, ABV 5.1%)
A dark amber-coloured beer with a warming malt aroma. Well-balanced with a mellow hoppiness and spicy, nutty and caramel notes.

Bishop's Crook

51 Woodcroft Close, Penwortham, Lancashire, PR1 9BX ☎ 07516 478003
🌐 bishopscrookbrewery.com

A small brewery based at the home of one of the owners, it started brewing commercially in 2013 and currently has just a handful of regular outlets. Due to construction work the brewery was out of action for a lengthy period in 2017-2018.

Galaxy (OG 1037, ABV 3.7%)
A pale ale with citrus and distinct passion fruit flavours.

Winding Staircase (OG 1038, ABV 3.8%)
A golden ale with a slight malty taste and having tangerine overtones.

Initiate (OG 1040, ABV 4%)
A golden ale with strong citrus and tropical fruit flavours.

Lancashire's Invaders (OG 1042, ABV 4.2%)
A refreshing amber-coloured ale, well hopped and providing a burst of grapefruit, lemon and pine.

Bitter End

See Tirril

Black Bear

c/o Bear Inn, 8-10 North Street, Wiveliscombe, Somerset, TA4 2JY
☎ (01984) 623537 🌐 blackbearbrewery.co.uk

Originally established in 2014 at the Northbrook Arms, East Stratton, Hampshire, before relocating to the Bear Inn, Wiveliscombe, Somerset in 2015. Five beers are currently regularly brewed for the pub and a small but growing number of other local outlets. ♦

Black Brook

See Loka Polly

Black Country

Rear of Old Bulls Head, 1 Redhall Road, Lower Gornal, West Midlands, DY3 2NU
☎ (01384) 401820

Office: 69 Third Avenue, Pensnett Trading Estate, Kingswinford, DY6 7FD 🌐 blackcountryales.co.uk

Brewery located at the rear of the Old Bulls Head. Brewing on the site began in the 1830s and continued until 1934, recommencing in 2002. In 2012 much of the brewing equipment was replaced or refurbished. Its sister company, Black Country Inns/Taverns, own 35 pubs across the West Midlands. Beers are also brewed under the Thomas Guest Brewing Company name. !! ♦

Bradley's Finest Golden (OG 1040, ABV 4.2%)
A straw-coloured quaffing beer with a bold citrus hop aroma, fruity, balanced sweetness and a lingering, refreshing aftertaste.

Pig on the Wall (OG 1042, ABV 4.3%)
A refreshing chestnut brown-coloured beer with a complex flavour of light hops giving way to a bittersweet blend of roasted malt. Suggestions of chocolate and coffee undertones.

Fireside (OG 1047, ABV 5%)
A well-rounded premium bitter, amber in colour, clean in taste leading to a pleasant, dry finish.

Black Dog

See Hambleton

Black Falls

See Neath

Black Flag

Unit 4D, Bridge Road Industrial Estate, Goonhavern, Cornwall, TR4 9QL
☎ (01872) 858004 🌐 blackflagbrewery.com

Black Flag began brewing in 2013 using an eight-barrel plant. Much use is made of New Zealand and American hops. ♦RAIB

Chameleon (OG 1038, ABV 3.8%)
Golden ale. Grassy and floral hops dominate throughout. Punchy lemon citrus flavour with apricot and peaches. Bitter and crisp finish.

Fang (OG 1040, ABV 4%)
Golden ale with powerful citrus hop aroma. Refreshing with lemon, orange, mango and grapefruit throughout. Long, bitter, hoppy finish.

Naughty Pilchard (OG 1040, ABV 4%)
Copper-coloured bitter with malt aroma. Dominant biscuit malt flavour with a sharp bite of crisp hops. Short malty, bitter finish.

Crab Claw (OG 1050, ABV 5%)
Red-coloured strong bitter with intense hop fruit nose. Powerful citrus hop flavour, lightly bittersweet. Dry hop and sweet finish.

Galaxy & Amarillo Pale Ale (OG 1055, ABV 5.5%)
Malty golden ale with mango and orange hops throughout.

Mosaic IPA (OG 1055, ABV 5.7%)
Smooth, easy-drinking golden ale with heady citrus hop nose. Powerful grassy and citrus hop flavours throughout, with mango fruit and bitterness.

White Cross IPA (OG 1057, ABV 5.7%)
Amber-coloured strong bitter with hop nose. Robust hop bitterness balanced by sweetness and malt. Fruit flavours emerge. Long, bitter finish.

Black IPA (OG 1060, ABV 6%)
Smooth coffee and chocolate maltiness with a punchy, hoppy finish.

Export Stout (OG 1063, ABV 6.3%)

Captain Haddock (OG 1056, ABV 6.5%)
Smooth Belgian-style ale with vibrant mango and banana notes and a prolonged rich finish.

Black Hole SIBA

Unit 3a, Old Hall Mill Business Park, Alfreton Road, Little Eaton, Derbyshire, DE21 5EJ
☎ (01283) 619943 ☎ 07812 812953
🌐 blackholebrewery.co.uk

Black Hole was established in 2007 using a 10-barrel plant in the former Ind Coope bottling stores in Burton-on-Trent but moved to its current location in 2017 when the original site owners evicted all the tenants. Around 600 outlets, mainly in the Midlands, are supplied direct, and many more via wholesalers. The brewery was bought by the owners of Mr Grundy's Brewery (qv) in 2014. !!♦

Golden Ale (OG 1040, ABV 3.8%)
A session beer with a clean, crisp finish of hoppy dryness and a touch of astringency. It has an amber glow and a malt and spicy hop aroma.

Cosmic (OG 1044, ABV 4.2%)
Almost golden in colour with an initial malt aroma. The complex balance of malt and English hops give lingering tastes of nuts, fruit and dry, hoppy bitterness.

Supernova (OG 1048, ABV 4.8%)
Pure gold in colour. Like marmalade made from Seville oranges and grapefruit the aroma mimics the sweet start but gives in to the hops which deliver a dry, lingering bitter finish.

Milky Way (OG 1059, ABV 6%)
Honey and banana nose advises the sweet taste but not the sweet, dry, spicy finish of this wheat beer.

Brewed for Small Beer:

Lincoln Imperial Ale (OG 1036, ABV 3.8%)

Black Horse

See Consortium

Black Iris SIBA

Unit 1, Shipstone Street, New Basford, Nottingham, NG7 6GJ
☎ (0115) 979 1936 ✉ blackirisbrewery@gmail.com

Black Iris began brewing in 2011 using a six-barrel plant behind the Flowerpot pub in Derby. It expanded to a brand new 10-barrel plant in 2014 and relocated to premises in Nottingham. !!♦

Snake Eyes (OG 1038, ABV 3.8%)
Golden-coloured ale with intense hoppy aroma and taste with a lingering bitter finish.

Bleeding Heart (OG 1044, ABV 4.5%)
Red rye malty ale balanced with roast and hops and a bitter finish.

Endless Summer (OG 1041.9, ABV 4.5%)
Golden in colour with a tropical citrus fruit presence throughout, from aroma to aftertaste with a gentle bitter finish.

Better the Devil You Know (OG 1053, ABV 5.5%)
Pale, citrus IPA with big fruity aromas and a lingering bitterness.

Black Isle

Old Allengrange, Munlochy, IV8 8NZ
☎ (01463) 811871 🌐 blackislebrewery.com

Black Isle Brewery was set up in 1998 in the heart of the Scottish Highlands. It expanded substantially in 2011 with a new brewhouse and bottling line. All beers are organic with Soil Association certification. !!♦V

Yellowhammer (OG 1038, ABV 3.9%) ◆
A refreshing, hoppy golden ale with light hop and peach flavour throughout. A short bitter finish.

Red Kite (OG 1042, ABV 4.2%) ◆
Tawny-coloured ale with light malt on the nose and some red fruit on the palate. Slight sweetness in the taste.

Heather Honey (OG 1045, ABV 4.6%) ◆
Very sweet honey flavoured brew.

Porter (OG 1046, ABV 4.6%) ◆
A hint of liquorice and burnt chocolate on the nose and a creamy mix of malt and fruit in the taste.

Blonde (OG 1046, ABV 5%)

Hibernator (OG 1068, ABV 7%) ◆
Strong tasting warming, malty, fruity, dark brown brew.

Black Lodge

4 Kitchen Street, Baltic Triangle, Liverpool, L1 0AN
☎ 07565 299879 blacklodgebrewing.co.uk

Small-batch and one-off brewery producing beers in keg, bottle and can formats that can be drunk in its own Tap Room. No real ale.

Black Market

The Workman's, 43 High Street, Warsop, Nottinghamshire, NG20 0AE ☎ 07824 363373

Beers first appeared from Black Market in 2016. The 2.5-barrel plant is situated in the basement of its brewery tap, the Workman's.

Black Metal

Unit 4, 6b Dryden Road, Loanhead, EH20 9LZ
☎ (0131) 623 3411 ☎ 07711 295385
blackmetalbrewery.com

Black Metal Brewery was established in 2012 by two old friends – metalheads and inspired brewers. Equipment was shared with Top Out (qv) brewery but it has now moved next door to its own site. ♦RAIB

Will-o'-the-Wisp (OG 1060, ABV 6%)

Blood Revenge (OG 1066, ABV 6.6%)

Yggdrasil (OG 1066, ABV 6.6%)

Black Paw

Unit 4, Westgate Road, Bishop Auckland, County Durham, DL14 7AX
☎ (01388) 602144 ☎ 07557 020664
blackpawbrewery.co.uk

Black Paw began brewing in 2011 using a 12-barrel plant and now supplies pubs across the North-east of England. Brewing is currently suspended. ♦

Black Rock SIBA

Unit 6c, Empire Way, Tregoniggie Industrial Estate, Falmouth, Cornwall, TR11 4SN
☎ (01326) 379477 blackrockbrewing.com

Black Rock began brewing in 2013, producing just one beer. It now has a core range of six beers, which are available in the brewery's first pub, the Small Ship, Falmouth plus a number of other local outlets. Relocation to larger premises within Falmouth is planned. ♦RAIB

Endless IPA (ABV 3.8%) ◆
Gold-coloured bitter with assertive fruity hop aroma and taste. Refreshing bitter citrus flavour followed by hints of caramel and summer fruits.

Pale Ale (OG 1042, ABV 4.2%) ◆
Pale gold-coloured best bitter. Balance of earthy malt and bitter hop flavours. Apricot and lime in the mouth. Long bitter finish.

Mean High Water (ABV 4.4%)

Deep (OG 1048, ABV 5%) ◆
Faintly sulphurous malt and light hop aroma. Strong malt and grassy hop bitterness with sweet tropical fruit. Bitter, dry finish.

Black IPA (OG 1058, ABV 6%) ◆
Black porter with pronounced roast malt from aroma to the long finish. Light bitterness with smoky stone fruit and toffee.

Sealegs (ABV 8.5%)

Black Sheep SIBA

Wellgarth, Masham, North Yorkshire, HG4 4EN
☎ (01765) 689227 blacksheepbrewery.co.uk

Established in 1992 by Paul Theakston, a member of Masham's famous brewing family. It is situated in the former Wellgarth Maltings and uses the traditional Yorkshire Square fermenting system. The company supplies around 600 free trade outlets, with national exposure through pubcos and wholesale channels, but owns no pubs. Production is 75% cask with the remainder bottled. Paul has now handed over operations to his sons. !! ♦

Best Bitter (OG 1038, ABV 3.8%) ◆
A hoppy and fruity beer with strong bitter overtones, leading to a long, dry, bitter finish.

Golden Sheep (OG 1039, ABV 3.9%)
A balanced blonde beer with a dry and refreshing bitterness. Light golden in colour with fresh citrus fruit flavours and a clean, crisp finish.

Baa Baa (ABV 4%)
A juicy pale ale with a generous hoppy tone and subtle zesty twang but low in bitterness.

Holy Grail (ABV 4%)
A fresh, zesty golden ale with a long, crisp finish. Clean and refreshing.

Ale (OG 1044, ABV 4.4%)
A premium bitter with robust fruit, malt and hops.

Riggwelter (OG 1059, ABV 5.9%) ◆
A fruity bitter with complex underlying tastes and hints of liquorice and pear drops leading to a long, dry, bitter finish.

Brewed for Ember Inns:

Pale Ale (ABV 4%)

Black Storm

See Hadrian Border

Black Tor SIBA

Unit 5, Gidley's Industrial Estate, Christow, Exeter, Devon, EX6 7QB
☎ (01647) 252120 blacktorbrewery.com

THE BREWERIES

This independent, family-run brewery is located on the eastern edge of the beautiful Dartmoor National Park, and has been under the current family ownership since 2015. Several changes of ownership and brewery name have occurred since brewing began on-site in 1998, with the present Black Tor name being established in 2013. ♦

Pride Of Dartmoor (OG 1040, ABV 4%)
This mid-brown-coloured session bitter has a gentle floral aroma and pleasant taste.

Raven (OG 1042, ABV 4.2%)

Devonshire Pale Ale (OG 1044, ABV 4.5%)

Black Wolf SIBA

Unit 7c, Bandeath Industrial Estate, Throsk, Stirling, FK7 7NP
☎ (01786) 817000 blackwolfbrewery.com

Established in 2005, and now owned by VC2 Brands, the brewery is located in a former torpedo factory on the shores of the River Forth. In 2014 the brewery changed its name from Traditional Scottish Ales to Black Wolf Brewery and rebranded its range of beers. ♦

Nevis (OG 1040, ABV 4%)

RoK (OG 1040, ABV 4%)

Florida Black (OG 1045, ABV 4.5%)

Glencoe (OG 1045, ABV 4.5%)

William Wallace (OG 1045, ABV 4.5%)

Lomond Gold (OG 1050, ABV 5%)

Valente's Double Espresso (OG 1060, ABV 6%)

Blackbeck SIBA

Blackbeck Inn, Blackbeck, Cumbria, CA22 2NY
☎ (01946) 841661 blackbeckbrewery.co.uk

A five-barrel brewery, established in 2009 and owned by a father-and-daughter team, producing handcrafted ales using English malts and hops. Beers have fairground themed names. ♦

Blackedge SIBA

Moreton Mill, Hampson Street, Horwich, BL6 7JH
☎ (01204) 692976 ☎ 07795 654895
blackedgebrewery.co.uk

Blackedge Brewery, established in 2011, has expanded from a five to a 10-barrel plant, visible through a viewing window on the ground floor beneath the brewery bar. !! ♦ RAIB

Session (OG 1038, ABV 3.5%)
A golden-coloured session bitter, surprisingly full bodied with a grapefruit flavour and aroma.

Zinc (OG 1038, ABV 3.5%)
A refreshing blonde ale with citrus notes.

Hop (OG 1039, ABV 3.8%)
Generously-hopped ale with a clean, dry and refreshing citrus, floral flavour.

Brewers Gold (ABV 3.9%)
A single-hopped blonde ale with spicy, blackcurrant and lemon flavours and a delicate citrus aroma.

Dark Mild (ABV 3.9%)
Lightly-hopped ale with a smooth caramel, chocolate flavour and a hint of liquorice and blackcurrant.

Black (OG 1047, ABV 4%)
A velvety stout with intense roasted barley flavours and rich undertones of chocolate and coffee with a liquorice finish.

Cascade (ABV 4%)

Pike (OG 1042, ABV 4%)
A pale ale with plenty of sweet citrus hop flavour.

West Coast (ABV 4.1%)
A golden ale with a clean, fresh flavour of tropical fruit and grapefruit. Hints of floral aroma.

American Pale Ale (OG 1043, ABV 4.2%)
Light, hoppy beer made with intense citrus hop aromas.

Platinum (OG 1046, ABV 4.4%)
Blonde ale with a clean, citrus flavour and sweet citrus aroma.

Blonde (OG 1046, ABV 4.5%)
Full-flavoured, full-bodied blonde ale with a clean, crisp fruit-like flavour and aroma.

Ginger (ABV 4.5%)
A golden ale brewed with fresh ginger to give a spicy orange and ginger flavour.

Dark Rum (OG 1045, ABV 4.6%)
Dark, rich porter with roasted coffee and chocolate flavours, hints of liquorice and finished with sweetness from dark rum.

IPA (OG 1047, ABV 4.7%)
Full-bodied, full-flavoured and well-balanced hoppy and intensely citrus beer with a grapefruit aroma.

Black Port (OG 1045, ABV 4.9%)
Black beer with a malty, fruity aroma. Rich with chocolate and dark fruits to taste and a slightly drier finish.

Blackened Sun

3 Heathfield, Stacey Bushes, Milton Keynes, Buckinghamshire, MK12 6HP ☎ 07963 529859
blackenedsunbrewing.co.uk

Blackened Sun began brewing unpasteurised, unfiltered beers in 2017, available in KeyKegs and bottles. ♦RAIB

Hedone Saison (ABV 3.6%)
A saison with a spicy, fruity yeast character and notes of citrus and berries from the hops.

Crossover Pale Ale (ABV 4.2%)
Citrus/tropical hop flavours with a spicy yeast character.

Collision ESB (Extra Special Belgian) (ABV 4.7%)
A malty, spicy, fruity beer.

Blackhill SIBA

Unit 14, Stella Gill Industrial Estate, Pelton Fell, Chester-le-Street, County Durham, DH2 2RG ☎ 07905 788286 blackhillbrewery.com

Blackhill began brewing in 2012 using spare capacity at Geltsdale Brewery. In 2013 it moved to its own premises in Stanley using a 10-barrel plant before relocating again in 2018. Beers are named after Durham coal mining seams and are available on rotation. !! ♦

Blackjack SIBA

36 Gould Street, Manchester, M4 4RN
☎ (0161) 819 2767 🌐 blackjack-beers.com

Blackjack began brewing in 2012 on a 4.5-barrel plant, expanding to a 10-barrel plant in 2017. Beers are widely available across the North West and in specialist beer outlets nationally. It brews a large range of regular beers from pale ales to specialist styles, many using Belgian and farmhouse yeasts. Glassworks Drinks, a distribution business specialising in craft breweries, is also owned. ♦RAIB

Mosaic Light (ABV 3.6%)
A punchy, hoppy beer for it's strength.

Pokies (OG 1036, ABV 3.6%)
A pale session ale with grapefruit, citrus and punchy floral aromas and a good, clean bitterness.

Shuffled Deck (OG 1039, ABV 3.9%)
Aromas are marmalade with pine and grapefruit. Flavours are woody with sweet citrus and bitter grapefruit, with a dry finish.

Bramling Cross (OG 1040, ABV 4%)
Amber-coloured beer with hops and tart fruit in aroma and taste. Good bitterness throughout.

You Bet (ABV 4%)
A heavily-hopped pale ale with a varying hop profile in each brew.

Dead Man's Hand (ABV 4.1%)

Jabberwocky (ABV 4.1%)

New Deck (OG 1042, ABV 4.2%)
A crisp, hoppy ale with a satisfying finish.

First Deal (OG 1044, ABV 4.4%)
A ruby-coloured ale with a dried fruit aroma and flavours of berries and earthy malts. A spicy, bitter finish.

Rabbit Hunt (ABV 4.5%)

Small Saison (OG 1042, ABV 4.5%)
A spicy, dry ale.

Double Bluff (OG 1048, ABV 4.8%)
An amber-coloured ale with full aroma and bitter notes.

Schafkopf (OG 1050, ABV 5%)
German-style witbier with lemongrass and ginger.

Stout (OG 1050, ABV 5%)
Aroma is roasted malts and chocolate syrup. Flavour is similar with a hint of maple syrup and light bitter hops. Finish is slightly fruity.

Aces High (OG 1055, ABV 5.5%)
Aroma has some ripe citrus notes of melon and orange. Flavour is sweet with mild grass and pine along with more ripe tangerine and melon.

Black Maria (OG 1057, ABV 5.8%)
A dark-coloured, hoppy ale with a light body.

Four of a Kind (OG 1060, ABV 6.2%)

Brewed for Jack in the Box, Altrincham:

House Pale (ABV 4%)

Blackpit

Blackpit Farm, Silverstone Road, Stowe, Buckinghamshire, MK18 5LJ 🌐 blackpitbrewery.co.uk

Brewing began in 2017 in a converted stable yard on Blackpit Farm, one mile south of Silverstone. ♦

Best (ABV 3.4%)
An amber-coloured bitter with a malty and slightly hoppy flavour.

Cloud Nine (ABV 3.9%)
A blonde beer with hints of lemon zest and pine kernels.

Loosehead (ABV 4.2%)
Mid to light brown in colour with butterscotch and a touch of barley sugar on the nose.

Goshawk (ABV 4.4%)
A chestnut-coloured bitter with earthy and malty flavours.

Sky Rocket (ABV 5.5%)
An amber-coloured, American-style IPA. It has an aromatic nose with hints of nettles and elderflower and an earthy flavour leading to a long, lingering finish.

Blimey! (NEW)

Branksome House, 166 St Clements Hill, Norwich, NR3 1RS ☎ 07775 788299
✉ adriankbryan@googlemail.com

Brewing began in 2017.

Infamy (OG 1040, ABV 4%)

Son of Pale Face (OG 1040, ABV 4%)

The Pale Face (OG 1045, ABV 4.5%)

First Born IPA (OG 1052, ABV 5.2%)
An American-style IPA with notes of citrus and tropical fruit.

Blindmans SIBA

Talbot Farm, Leighton, Somerset, BA11 4PN
☎ (01749) 880038 🌐 blindmansbrewery.co.uk

Established in 2002 in a converted milking parlour and purchased by its current owners in 2004, this five-barrel brewery has its own water spring. The range of ales is regularly on tap at the Cornerhouse, Frome. !!♦

Buff (OG 1036, ABV 3.6%)
Amber-coloured, smooth session beer.

Golden Spring (OG 1040, ABV 4%)
Fresh and aromatic straw-coloured beer.

Mine Beer (OG 1042, ABV 4.2%)
Full-bodied, copper-coloured, blended malt ale.

Icarus (OG 1045, ABV 4.5%)
Fruity, rich, dark ruby-coloured ale.

Block (NEW)

Wenlock Arms, 26 Wenlock Road, Hoxton, London, N1 7TA
☎ (020) 7608 3406

Block is a microbrewery in the cellar of the Wenlock Arms.

Bloomfield

Bloomfield Brewhouse, 47 Ansdell Road, Blackpool, FY1 6PW
☎ (01253) 693219 🌐 bloomfield-brewhouse.co.uk

Brewing began in 2015. The beers are finished on site using wort from a third-party brewery.

Rich, well-balanced stout with hints of coffee and chocolate leading to a bitter finish.

Blue Anchor SIBA

50 Coinagehall Street, Helston, Cornwall, TR13 8EL ☎ (01326) 562821 spingoales.com

15th-century thatched brewpub, the oldest continuously brewing plant in the country. Home of the famous Spingo ales, which are made with water from the pub's well. !! ♦ RAIB

Blue Bear SIBA

Unit 5, Empire House, 11 New Street, Smethwick, West Midlands, B66 2AJ ☎ (0121) 565 5622 ✉ info@bluebearbrewery.com

Blue Bear brewery, formerly in Worcestershire, relocated to an industrial unit in Smethwick on the outskirts of Birmingham. The nine-barrel plant produces a selection of beers, most of it under contract for the now defunct Highgate & Davenports brewery of Walsall. ♦

Contract brewed under the Highgate & Davenports brand name:

Dark Mild (OG 1036.8, ABV 3.4%)
Smooth, deep brown-coloured, traditional mild with a low bitterness and noticeable sweetness. It has a slightly caramel/roasted, low fruit and hop flavour and smooth aftertaste.

Bath Row Pale Ale (OG 1038, ABV 3.9%)

Original Bitter (OG 1041.8, ABV 4.2%)
Bright, copper-coloured premium ale with a good balance between malt and fruity bitterness.

Davenports Red Baron (OG 1046, ABV 4.8%)
Complex, dry-hopped, deep copper-coloured ale with a rich malty, toffee and biscuity flavour. Bitter with a strong, hoppy taste.

Davenports Imperial IPA (OG 1048, ABV 5.2%)
Bright golden-coloured beer with a vibrant bitter, hoppy and malty taste. A hoppy aroma with robust fruity and citrus flavours.

Blue Bee SIBA

Unit 29-30, Hoyland Road Industrial Estate, Sheffield, South Yorkshire, S3 8AB ☎ 07375 659349 bluebeebrewery.co.uk

Originally established in 2010, this independently-owned ten-barrel brewery supplies beer to the free trade throughout Yorkshire and the East Midlands, although it is occasionally seen further afield. Regularly produces collaborative beers with other breweries. ♦

Hillfoot Best Bitter (OG 1039, ABV 4%)
Traditional dark chestnut-coloured, fruity best bitter.

Reet Pale (OG 1038, ABV 4%)
Pale with floral and citrus flavours leading to a dry bitter finish.

Triple Hop (OG 1041, ABV 4.3%)

American 5 Hop (OG 1043, ABV 4.5%)

Ginger Beer (OG 1043, ABV 4.5%)
A pale ale with the addition of fiery ginger.

Tempest Stout (OG 1048, ABV 4.8%)

Blue Bell

Cranesgate South, Whaplode St Catherine, Lincolnshire, PE12 6SN ☎ (01406) 504300 ☎ 07788136663 thebluebell.net

Founded in 1998 behind the Blue Bell pub, the brewery is now back under the ownership of the pub after several years as a separate business. Beers are only available at the pub and to private customers. !! ♦ RAIB

Blue Bell Brewhouse

Warings Green Rd, Warings Green, B94 6BP ☎ 07922 554181 ✉ rnrbrewhouse@outlook.com

A two-barrel plant set up in 2013 by Mark Shepherd to resurrect on-site brewing at the Blue Bell Cider House (brewing ceased in 1968). Brewster Lynn Crossland, who joined in 2014, continues the tradition of female brewers in the original brewhouse, producing solely for the Blue Bell and local festivals. The brewery likes to experiment with unusual flavours, and using ingredients foraged from local hedgerows. ♦ V

Blue Monkey SIBA

10 Pentrich Road, Giltbrook Industrial Park, Giltbrook, Nottinghamshire, NG16 2UZ ☎ (0115) 938 5899 bluemonkeybrewery.com

Blue Monkey was established in 2008 as a 10-barrel plant but moved in 2010 to a bigger site to meet increasing demand. It now brews around 15,000 pints a week to supply more than 200 local outlets and selected national distributors. The name stems from a nickname for the blue flames that used to rise from the chimneys of Stanton Ironworks, which was a prominent local foundry. !!

Chimp Chim-in-Nee (ABV 3.8%)

BG Sips (OG 1041, ABV 4%)
Pale golden-coloured hoppy beer. Very fruity and bitter.

Funky Gibbon (OG 1042, ABV 4.1%)
Tawny-coloured, malty ale, dried fruit aroma and a gentle bitter finish.

99 Red Baboons (OG 1042, ABV 4.2%)
Red in colour with a malty fruitiness. Not overly hoppy.

Howler (OG 1046, ABV 4.5%)

Infinity (OG 1045.7, ABV 4.6%)
Golden ale packed with Citra hops.

Chocolate Guerilla (OG 1052, ABV 4.9%)

Guerrilla (OG 1052, ABV 4.9%)
A creamy stout, full of roast malt flavour and a slightly sweet finish.

Bonobo (OG 1052, ABV 5.3%)

Ape Ale (OG 1052, ABV 5.4%)
Intensely-hopped strong golden ale with dry bitter finish.

Blue Square

c/o MSS City Mills, Peel Street, Morley, Leeds, West Yorkshire, LS27 8QL
☎ (0113) 238 0382 ☎ 07950 567341
bluesquarebrewery.com

Established in 2016, Blue Square brews once a week on a four-barrel plant. It produces beers on a rotational basis in a split level building that is part of a mill complex.

Morley Rocket Session Ale (ABV 3.8%)

Moonlight Blonde (ABV 4%)
A blonde ale with a slight biscuit malt taste and dry hop finish.

Super Nova Pale Ale (ABV 4.3%)
An amber-coloured beer with a hint of lemon.

Abyss Dark Porter (ABV 4.8%)
A re-creation of a Victorian dark porter using six different malts, with an English hop finish.

Polaris IPA (ABV 5.1%)
A hoppy IPA with a slight citrus flavour.

Blueball

The Old Bakery, 31-33 Ashridge Street, Runcorn, Cheshire, WA7 1HU
☎ (01928) 775628

Blueball began brewing in 2010. After a short closure in 2017 the brewery re-opened and continues to brew the beers listed. Owner Alex Haycraft has entered into a collaboration business arrangement with Heavy Industry Brewery (qv) by opening a bar called STR (Society LTD Taprooms, Runcorn) in the brewery building. Beers are also available in the free trade and at Kash 22 Bar, Frodsham.

Indie Girl (OG 1036, ABV 3.8%)
A pale golden-coloured beer with citrus and tropical fruit aromas. The finish is clean and dry with a long, hoppy aftertaste.

Gold Digger (ABV 4%)

Communion (OG 1040, ABV 4.1%)

Ruby O'Reilly (OG 1040, ABV 4.3%)

Penny Black (OG 1045, ABV 4.5%)

Spank (OG 1059, ABV 6%)

Bluestone (Lancashire)

Unit 6, Daniel Street Industrial Estate, Whitworth, Lancashire, OL12 8BX
☎ (01706) 853009 ☎ 07802 792536
bluestonebrewery.co.uk

Bluestone is a small 3.5-barrel brewery using traditional methods including 'double dropping' fermentation. Brewing takes place mainly at the weekend.

Quarrymans Stout (OG 1041, ABV 4%)

EPA (English Pale Ale) (OG 1042, ABV 4.2%)
A traditional dry pale ale with strong malt and hop flavours.

Night Hops Stout (OG 1043, ABV 4.2%)
Dark, dry stout with a good hop flavour through the roasted malt, liquorice and spice.

AKA (Amber Kitchen Ale) (OG 1043, ABV 4.4%)
Based on an old recipe this is a brown-coloured ale with a caramel and liquorice malty flavour.

Spodden Pilsner (OG 1048, ABV 4.4%)
A full-bodied, full-flavoured, golden-coloured Pilsner.

Bluestone (Pembrokeshire) SIBA

Tyriet, Cilgwyn, Newport, Pembrokeshire, SA42 0QW
☎ (01239) 820833 bluestonebrewing.co.uk

A family-run business established in 2013 on a working hill farm in the Preseli Hills within the Pembrokeshire Coast National Park. The 10-barrel brewery has been installed in a renovated 200-year-old stone barn, which also doubles as a visitor facility and office, with the surrounding yard becoming an events venue throughout the summer months. The brewery uses water from a private supply, which filters down through the Preseli Hill. Numerous local outlets are supplied as well as wholesalers around the UK. !! ♦ RAIB

Rockhopper (OG 1039, ABV 3.9%)
Classic amber-coloured bitter with a light malt base and a spicy fruitiness from the hops.

Bedrock Blonde (OG 1040, ABV 4%)
A straw-coloured ale with creamy, soft malt flavours.

Elderflower Blonde (OG 1040, ABV 4%)
Straw-coloured, delicately-hopped ale finished with a delicate hint of elderflower.

Crystal Ruby (OG 1042, ABV 4.2%)
A balanced combination of rich malty flavours with a touch of caramelised grain on top.

Hammerstone IPA (OG 1044, ABV 4.5%)
A fruity, effervescent and refreshing modern IPA.

Moonstone (OG 1046, ABV 4.6%)
Full-bodied dark porter. Spicy bitterness complements its chocolate and nut flavours.

Rocketeer (OG 1046, ABV 4.6%)
A traditional, full-bodied bitter with a rich malty base.

Fossil Fuel (OG 5, ABV 5%)

Blythe SIBA

Blythe House Farm, Lichfield Road, Hamstall Ridware, Staffordshire, WS15 3QQ
☎ (01889) 504661 ☎ 07483 248723
blythebrewery.co.uk

Blythe began brewing in 2003 using a 2.5-barrel plant in a converted barn. 15 outlets are supplied direct. !! ♦ RAIB

Bagot's Bitter (OG 1040, ABV 3.8%)
Amber in colour with a fruit start and sweetness which develops to a smooth, bitter finish. A lightly-hopped, easy-drinking beer.

Ridware Pale (OG 1042, ABV 4.3%)
Bright and golden-coloured with a bitter floral hop aroma and citrus taste. Good and hop-sharp, bitter and refreshing. Long, lingering bite with ripples of citrus across the tongue.

Staffie (OG 1044, ABV 4.4%)
Hoppy and grassy aroma with hints of sweetness from this amber-coloured beer. A touch of malt at the start is soon overwhelmed by hops. A full, hoppy, mouth-watering finish.

Palmers Poison (OG 1045, ABV 4.5%) ◆
Refreshing dark-coloured beer. Tawny but light headed. Coffee truffle aroma, pleasingly sweet to start but with a good hop mouthfeel.

Johnsons (OG 1056, ABV 5.2%) ◆
Black in colour with a thick head. Refreshingly hoppy and full bodied with lingering bitterness of chocolate, dates, coal smoke and liquorice.

Boat Lane

Unit 3, Streamside Business Park, Boat Lane, Offenham, Worcestershire, WR11 8RS
☎ (01386) 48212 🌐 boatlanebrewery.co.uk

A microbrewery established in 2017 in a small village near Evesham.

Bog Brew (NEW) SIBA

On the Green, 11 High Street, Stevenage, Hertfordshire, SG1 3BG ☎ 07973 573040
🌐 bogbrew.co.uk

⊠ Paul Clinton started brewing as a hobby, then began brewing for his restaurant, On the Green, in 2017. Currently using a 1.5-barrel plant, there are plans for expansion. Beers are available in the restaurant, at local beer festivals and at free houses around Hertfordshire and Bedfordshire. !! RAIB V

Barking Spider (OG 1039, ABV 3.8%)
An easy-drinking session ale with hints of chocolate and coffee.

Bottoms Up (OG 1039, ABV 3.8%)
An easy-drinking, mid gold-coloured ale with pear and grapefruit notes.

Porter Potty (OG 1040, ABV 4.1%)
A deep, dark-coloured stout with hints of chocolate and a rich, silky mouthfeel.

Pail Ale (OG 1049, ABV 5.3%)
An IPA with peppery, citrus hop notes, a bitter, long-lasting finish and a crisp mouthfeel.

2Mhaard Blonde Ale (OG 1043, ABV 5.4%)
A saison-style blonde ale with classic sour notes from the Belgian yeast strain. Dry and crisp with hints of sage and pepper.

Bombs Away (OG 1057, ABV 6.3%)
A complex double IPA with peppery, citrus and fruity notes.

Bohem

Unit 5, Littleline House, 41-43 West Road, Tottenham, London, N17 0RE
☎ (020) 8617 8350 ☎ 07999 014294
🌐 bohembrewery.com

Traditional Bohemian lagers brewed by Czech expats in North London. Beers are supplied to local outlets, including its own nearby taproom. No real ale.

Bollington SIBA

Adlington Road, Bollington, Cheshire, SK10 5JT
☎ (01625) 575380 🌐 bollingtonbrewing.co.uk

⊠ Bollington began brewing in 2008 with the Vale Inn, Bollington, as the brewery tap. The Park Tavern, Macclesfield, and the Cask Tavern, Poynton, are also owned. Around 40 outlets are supplied direct. !! ◆ RAIB

Chinook & Grapefruit (OG 1036, ABV 3.6%)
Fresh grapefruit zest and juice paired with punchy hops.

Ginger Brew (OG 1041, ABV 3.6%)
A classic ginger bitter with a hoppy bitter flavour and a smooth taste with fresh root ginger added at the end.

White Nancy (OG 1038, ABV 3.6%)
A pale-coloured bitter with a good hoppiness and light body.

Long Hop (OG 1039, ABV 3.9%)
Pale lager-style bitter with fruity, refreshing hops.

Best (OG 1041, ABV 4.2%)
A hoppy bitter. Clean and crisp with a light golden colour and a refreshing bitter aftertaste.

Dinner Ale (OG 1042, ABV 4.3%)
Deep copper-coloured beer with a fresh, slightly fruity nose and a dry, hoppy finish.

Oat Mill Stout (OG 1049, ABV 5%)
An oatmeal stout with a hoppy, bitter taste, keeping the sweetness in check.

Eastern Nights (OG 1056, ABV 5.6%)
A pale gold-coloured, well-balanced IPA with a modest hop content.

Bond Brews

Units 3 & 4, South Barns, Gardeners Green Farm, Heathlands Road, Wokingham, Berkshire, RG40 3AS
☎ (01344) 775450 🌐 bondbrews.co.uk

⊠ Bond Brews was established in 2015 using a six-barrel plant. Beers are delivered to pubs within a 30-mile radius. Brewery experience days available by arrangement with the brewer. !! ◆ RAIB

Goldi-hops (OG 1039, ABV 3.9%)
A refreshing amber-coloured pale ale with a malty and delicately citrus nose, followed by a bitter flavour and a long, dry, bitter finish.

Best of British (OG 1040, ABV 4%)
A tawny-coloured best bitter with malt and fruit on the nose, dry fruity flavours balancing the bitterness, followed by a touch of blackcurrant in the aftertaste.

Bengal Tiger (OG 1043, ABV 4.3%)
A pale golden-coloured IPA with a hoppy, fruity aroma. The initially fruity flavour leads to an earthy bitterness and a long, dry, bitter finish.

Railway Porter (OG 1045, ABV 4.5%)
An easy-drinking, dark brown-coloured porter with a reddish tint. It has a subtle toasty maltiness with a gently-lingering fruity finish.

Bont (NEW)

7 Maes y Piod, Bridgend, CF31 5FJ 🌐 bontbrew.com

Bont Brew was started by Dr Jan Kletta and his family in 2017 in Bridgend, South Wales. Jan is a local GP and brews on his day off. The brewery is based in a converted garage. Beer is mostly sold in bottles at local farmers markets and brewery events; and is available online from the brewery.

Boot

12 Boot Hill, Repton, Derbyshire, DE65 6FT
☎ (01283) 346047

Office: 11 The Green, Willington, DE65 6BP
🌐 thebootbeer.co.uk

An eight-barrel brewery installed at the rear of the Boot Inn, Repton, home of the eponymous public school, during 2015. The brewery supplies the three pubs within the group and a number of free trade outlets. ‼ ♦ RAIB

Repton Cross (OG 1039, ABV 3.7%)
An easy-drinking ale with subtle roasted malt and earthy, floral hops followed by delicate citrus notes. Smooth in the mouth with a dry finish and hint of bitter.

Clod Hopper (OG 1041, ABV 3.9%)
Hints of caramel in this citrus hop dominated golden ale that has a soft, refreshing and lasting finish.

Bitter (OG 1045, ABV 4.3%)

Tuffer?s Old Boots (ABV 4.6%)
A velvety rich porter exuding notes of dark fruit, hazelnut and coffee with cocoa in the finish.

IPA (OG 1050, ABV 4.8%)
A strong, amber-coloured, full-bodied bitter packing fruity and floral hops and toasty malt flavour.

ReBoot (OG 1051, ABV 5.2%)
Refreshing beer with citrus and floral aromas balanced by a malty backbone. Smooth hop flavours linger in the finish.

Beast (OG 1067, ABV 6.6%)
Full-bodied and rounded with a rich dark chocolate and caramel character.

Boot Town

Copper Kettle Brewing, Bosworths Garden Centre, 110 Finedon Road, Burton Latimer, Northamptonshire, NN15 5QA
☎ (01536) 725212 🌐 boottownbrewery.co.uk

A microbrewery established in 2017 and based on the old Copper Kettle Brewery site, producing an ever-changing range of beers.

Bootleg IFBB

Horse & Jockey, 9 The Green, Chorlton-cum-Hardy, M21 9HS ☎ 07774 937910
🌐 bootleg-brewingco.com

Nestled within the old brewery tower of a 200-year-old village inn, the microbrewery produces a range of regular beers. An innovation has been the use of home-grown hops to produce a green-hopped ale. Some beers may be brewed at Joseph Holt (qv) when a larger volume is required. ‼ ♦

Bootlegger

Bootlegger, 3 Amersham Hill, High Wycombe, Buckinghamshire, HP13 6NQ
☎ (01494) 525457 🌐 thebootleggerpub.co.uk/brew-co

A small-scale brewery operating out of the Bootlegger pub in High Wycombe. It currently produces five bottle-conditioned beers. RAIB

Born in the Borders SIBA

Lanton Mill, Jedburgh, TD8 6ST
☎ (01835) 830495 ☎ 07802 416494
🌐 borninthebordеrs.com

Born in the Borders Brewery is Scotland's original plough-to-pint brewery, and started brewing as Scottish Borders Brewery in 2011 using barley from its own farm. Beyond its core range of ales, recent projects include the brewery's 'Wild Harvest' initiative, which sources locally foraged ingredients for its ales. The brewery has recently launched a visitor centre, offering brewery tours, a café/restaurant and retail units featuring Borders beer, produce and food. ‼ ♦

Foxy Blonde (OG 1037.5, ABV 3.8%)
Brewery-grown barley and a complex mixture of hops combine to create a golden ale bursting with citrus and floral flavours.

Game Bird (OG 1039.5, ABV 4%)
An amber-coloured ale with a good balance of malty sweetness and late summer fruit with a long and easy finish.

Holy Cow (OG 1041, ABV 4.2%)
Hints of dark malt combine with a long floral finish.

Gold Dust (OG 1041.5, ABV 4.3%)
A light-coloured IPA with a big burst of aroma hops.

Dark Horse (OG 1044, ABV 4.5%)
A classic dark ale with overtones of coffee and chocolate and a surprisingly spicy finish that lingers on the tongue.

Borough (Cheshire)

33 Earle Street, Crewe, Cheshire, CW1 2BG
☎ (01270) 254999
✉ info@borougharmscrewe.co.uk

A two-barrel brewery opened in 2005 to supply the pub but with beers occasionally available at festivals. Brewing is currently suspended pending the appointment of a new brewer. ‼ ♦

Borough Arms SIBA

Unit 5, Tonmawr Business Park, Neath, SA10 9UU
☎ (01639) 644902 ☎ 07577 461915

Offfice: Borough Arms, 2 New Henry Street, Neath, SA11 2PH 🌐 boroughbreweryneath.com

Opened in 2014, the brewery was built by the landlord Kevin Davies in a converted outbuilding at the rear of the Borough Arms, Neath. By 2016 the brewery had expanded to 10 barrels and relocated to a nearby industrial estate. The original kit remains at the pub but is used for experimental brews only. Beers are named primarily after the local coal and steel industry. ‼ RAIB V

Iron Runner (OG 1042, ABV 4.3%)
Best Bitter with a roasted nutty aftertaste.

IPA (OG 1044, ABV 4.4%)
Strong-tasting with a crisp, clean mouthfeel.

Full Blast (OG 1050, ABV 4.7%)
Golden-coloured, fruity, zesty ale .

Nut Red Coke (OG 1051, ABV 4.9%)
A chestnut-coloured ale with malt overtones.

Boss SIBA

176 Neath Road, Landore, Swansea, SA1 2JT
☎ (01792) 450978 ☎ 07825 525735
bossbrewing.co.uk

The brewery was established in 2015 in Llamsamlet by Roy Allkin and Sarah John, using a 10-barrel plant. It relocated in 2017 to larger premises opposite the Liberty Stadium in Swansea, which now includes an on-site brewery tap – the Brewery Bar. 250 outlets are supplied, with bottles and cans distributed to national retailers. In a further trade expansion exports to France and Germany commenced in 2017. A bar named Copper is also owned in Swansea city centre.
!! ♦ RAIB

Blonde (OG 1040, ABV 4%)
Aromas of pine forest, exotic spice and grapefruit peel followed by tastes of grapefruit, resinous pine and a clean bitterness to finish.

Blaze (OG 1045, ABV 4.5%)
A floral, herbal aroma gives way to a zingy citrus, spicy flavour.

Bix (ABV 4.6%)
A wheat beer brewed with orange peel and coriander seeds.

Bare (OG 1050, ABV 5%)
Lager-style beer; lemony zest with a malty biscuit undertone, hints of caramel leading to a clean, spicy finish.

Black (OG 1050, ABV 5%)
Aromas of roasted coffee and warm chocolate, with flavours of fire roasted nuts, toffee and chocolate.

Brave (OG 1055, ABV 5.5%)
Initial tropical fruit cocktail, elderflower and rose, with a grapefruit, citrus, pine kick to finish.

Bosun's

Unit 20, Wakefield Commercial Park, 97 Bridge Road, Horbury Bridge, West Yorkshire, WF4 5NW
☎ (01924) 671881 ☎ 07703 535735
bosunsbrewery.co.uk

The first brew was produced in 2013 by a father-and-son team who have both served in the armed forces. The regular beers are produced on a 10-barrel plant with some given military themed names. !! ♦

Tell No Tales (OG 1038, ABV 3.8%)

Blonde (OG 1039, ABV 3.9%)

Maiden Voyage (OG 1039, ABV 3.9%)

Down the Hatch (OG 1040, ABV 4%)

King Neptune (OG 1043, ABV 4.3%)

IPA (OG 1056, ABV 5.6%)

Botley

Botley Mills, Mill Hill, Botley, Hampshire, SO30 2GB
☎ (01489) 784867 ☎ 07909 337212
botleybrewery.com

Botley Brewery was established in 2010 and uses a five-barrel plant. A recently added small bar next door, appropriately named the Hidden Tap, serves three of its ales Thursday to Saturday.
♦ RAIB

Hampshire Bitter (OG 1038, ABV 3.8%)
Yorkshire-style, amber-coloured session bitter.

Pommy Blonde (ABV 4.3%)

English IPA (ABV 5.1%)

Stinger Porter (ABV 5.2%)

Bottle Brook

Church Street, Kilburn, Derbyshire, DE56 0LU
☎ (01332) 880051 ☎ 07971 189915

A sister brewery to Leadmill (qv), Bottle Brook was established in 2005 using a 2.5-barrel plant on a tower gravity system. New World hops are predominantly used. The core range of beers is supplemented by one-off brews.

Columbus (OG 1040, ABV 4%)

Heanor Pale Ale (OG 1041, ABV 4.2%)

Roadrunner (OG 1047, ABV 4.8%)

Mellow Yellow (OG 1054, ABV 5.7%)

Rapture (OG 1058, ABV 5.9%)

Sand in the Wind (OG 1060, ABV 6.1%)

Boudicca

The Old Store, Walsingham Road, West Barsham, Norfolk, NR21 9NP
☎ (01328) 863854 ☎ 07864 321732
boudiccabrewing.co.uk

Established in 2015, Boudicca Brewery moved to its current premises on an estate in North Norfolk in 2017. It is an award-winning, independent brewery exclusively producing vegan beers, supplied to free trade outlets across East Anglia, including cafés, delis and off licences. ♦ RAIB V

Queen of Hops (OG 1036.5, ABV 3.7%)
A refreshing pale ale with a soft, rounded aroma, grassy and fruity with hints of marmalade. On the palate it has a tangy and fruity hit of hops with some underpinning of malt and bitterness.

Three Tails (OG 1036.5, ABV 3.9%)
Amber-coloured bitter with a touch of peppery spiciness in the hop character.

Golden Torc (OG 1039.5, ABV 4.3%)
Subtle on the nose, hops start to come through in the mouth and grow in the lasting finish.

Spiral Stout (OG 1045, ABV 4.6%)
A full-bodied stout with undertones of coffee and dark chocolate and an aroma of dark autumnal berries. A lingering dry roast finish with a hint of smoke.

Prasto's Porter (OG 1053.5, ABV 5.2%)
Dark fruit and hops on the nose, with hints of roast malt and smoke. Full-bodied in the mouth. A dry, subtle smoky finish with fruit and hop notes.

Boundary

Unit A5, 310 Portview Trade Centre, Newtownards Road, Belfast, BT4 1HE boundarybrewing.coop

Boundary is a cooperative brewery based in Belfast, established in 2014. A taproom is open to the public. ♦

APA (OG 1035, ABV 3.5%)

Export Stout (OG 1070, ABV 7%)

IPA (OG 1070, ABV 7%)

Bournemouth

See Sandbanks

Boutilliers

The Hop Shed, Macknade Fine Foods, Selling Road, Faversham, Kent, ME13 8XF ☎ 07743 372434
🌐 boutilliers.com

Founded in 2016, Boutilliers is a small brewery specialising in left-field brews. Its beers are mainly bottled, but two are also available in cans, with more planned; cask-conditioned ales are supplied to a few local pubs.

Bowland SIBA

Holmes Mill, Greenacre Street, Clitheroe, Lancashire, BB7 1EB
☎ (01200) 443592 🌐 bowlandbrewery.com

Founded in 2003, this family-run business uses a 30-barrel plant together with a nanobrewery for experimental brews. The site features a beer shop and beer hall with 42 handpumps featuring beers from Lancashire and beyond. !! ♦ RAIB

Pheasant Plucker (OG 1038, ABV 3.7%)
A copper-coloured bitter with rounded blackcurrant flavours and a malty aftertaste.

Gold (OG 1039, ABV 3.8%)
A hoppy, golden-coloured bitter with intense grapefruit flavours and aromas.

AONB (Ale of Outstanding Natural Beauty) (OG 1040, ABV 4%)
A straw-coloured, refreshing ale with a delicate gooseberry flavour and aroma.

Hen Harrier (OG 1040, ABV 4%)
The malty start belies what comes next: fruity, sweet, hoppy bitter with a long-lasting finish comprising of all the previous elements.

Buster IPA (OG 1046, ABV 4.5%)
Well-balanced, medium-bodied IPA with tropical undertones.

Bowman SIBA

Wallops Wood, Sheardley Lane, Droxford, Hampshire, SO32 3QY
☎ (01489) 878110 🌐 bowman-ales.com

Brewing started in 2006 in converted farm buildings. The brewery supplies more than 100 outlets. A new 40-barrel plant came on stream in 2013, which is now working alongside the original 20-barrel plant. Bowman also brew the Suthwyk Ales range of beers. !! ♦ RAIB

Swift One (OG 1038, ABV 3.8%)
Easy-drinking bitter, well balanced with sweet maltiness leading to a bittersweet finish and slightly dry, hoppy aftertaste.

Yumi (OG 1039, ABV 3.9%)
A fairly bitter beer, rich amber in colour, brewed using only English hops.

Wallops Wood (OG 1040, ABV 4%)
No particular flavour dominates this well-crafted beer. Malt flavours throughout balanced by toffee notes, sweetness and slightly dry finish.

Contract brewed for Suthwyk Ales:

Old Dick (OG 1038, ABV 3.8%)
Pleasant, clean-tasting pale brown-coloured bitter. Easy-drinking and well-balanced.

Liberation (OG 1042, ABV 4.2%)
Light-coloured ale with a soft, berry fruit flavour.

Skew Sunshine Ale (OG 1046, ABV 4.6%)
An amber-coloured beer. Initial hoppiness leads to a fruity taste and finish.

Palmerston's Folly (OG 1050, ABV 5%)
A clear wheat and barley beer. Slightly dry with a hint of honey in the aftertaste.

Bowness Bay SIBA

Unit 10, Castle Mills, Aynam Road, Kendal, Cumbria, LA9 7DE ☎ 07885 171210
🌐 bownessbaybrewing.co.uk

Bowness Bay Brewery moved to Kendal in 2015, increasing capacity from five to 15 barrels. The original five-barrel plant is used for small experimental brews. The brewery now has its own tap house, the Factory Tap. !! ♦

Amazon Amber (OG 1038, ABV 3.8%)
A golden brown-coloured ale with a sweet, grainy mouthfeel and a fruity nose, continues with some hop and a bitter finish.

Swift Best (OG 1044, ABV 3.8%)
A tawny-coloured bitter where caramel sweetness dominates, leading to a gentle bitter finish.

Swallow Gold (OG 1039, ABV 3.9%)
A golden ale with smooth floral hints of apricot, lime and peach.

Swan Blonde (OG 1039, ABV 4%)
A sweet, malty start with a finish dominated by hop bitterness.

Swan Black (OG 1046, ABV 4.6%)
Stout-like beer with a fruity, raisin middle, grainy mouthfeel and roast bitter finish.

Tern IPA (OG 1043, ABV 5%)
Well-balanced IPA with some sweet malt and fruit to balance the lingering hoppy finish.

Box Social SIBA

18 Riverdale Court, Newburn, NE15 8SG
☎ (0191) 267 1295 ☎ 07803 791761
🌐 boxsocial.pub

Launched in 2015, this family-run brewery has a licence and is open to the public most days (12-9pm). In 2016 it opened a micropub-cuterie based in Forth Street, Newcastle. !! ♦ RAIB

Gentlemans Nectar Pale Ale (ABV 4.2%)

Kaffir (ABV 4.2%)

India Brown Ale (ABV 5.6%)

Campfire Porter (ABV 7%)
Porter with toasted marshmallow, coffee, vanilla, cocoa and lactose.

Box Steam SIBA

15 The Midlands, Holt, Wiltshire, BA14 6RU
☎ (01225) 782700 🌐 boxsteambrewery.com

The brewery was founded in 2004 and boasts a Fulton steam-fired copper, hence the name. New

THE BREWERIES

ownership since 2006 meant expansion and increased capacity with the brewery moving to larger premises in Holt in 2011. Two pubs are owned and more than 100 outlets supplied. !! ♦

Golden Bolt (OG 1037.5, ABV 3.8%)
A straw-coloured bitter with a slightly dry, hoppy aftertaste.

Tunnel Vision (OG 1040.5, ABV 4.2%)
A well-rounded, light amber-coloured bitter. Clean-tasting with a slight bitterness on the finish.

Piston Broke (OG 1045, ABV 4.5%)
A fine, full-bodied golden ale with a refreshing hoppy, citrus palate and a subtle fruit-hop aroma.

Boxcar (NEW)

Arch 221, Ponsford Street, Homerton, London, E9 6JU
boxcarbrewery.co.uk

Boxcar is a small batch brewery based in Homerton. No real ale.

Brack'N'Brew

Brackenrigg Inn, Watermillock, Cumbria, CA11 0LP
☎ (01768) 486206 brackenrigginn.co.uk

Brewing started in 2015 in a converted 16th-century stable overlooking Ullswater. Brewing takes place three times a week on a four-barrel plant.

Bradfield SIBA

Watt House Farm, High Bradfield, South Yorkshire, S6 6LG
☎ (0114) 285 1118 bradfieldbrewery.co.uk

Established in 2005, Bradfield is a family-run business, based on a working farm in the Peak District using pure Millstone Grit springwater. The direct delivery distribution area covers the North of England from Northumberland to Northampton, East to West Coast. Beer is also supplied to outlets outside this area. The Nag's Head in nearby Loxley, has been the brewery tap since 2009. In 2018 the brewery obtained the King & Miller, Deepcar, as its second pub. ♦ RAIB

Farmers Bitter (OG 1039, ABV 3.9%)
A traditional copper-coloured malt ale with a floral aroma.

Farmers Blonde (OG 1041, ABV 4%)
Pale, blonde beer with citrus and summer fruit aromas.

Farmers Steel Cow (OG 1045, ABV 4.5%)

Farmers Stout (OG 1045, ABV 4.5%)
A dark stout with roasted malts and flaked oats and a subtle, bitter hop character.

Farmers Sixer (OG 1058, ABV 6%)

Bradford SIBA

22 Rawson Road, Westgate, Bradford, West Yorkshire, BD1 3SQ
☎ (01274) 379054 bradfordbrewery.com

The brewery was established in 2015, seeing the return of brewing to Bradford city centre for the first time in 60 years. It is based in converted former factory buildings and uses a 10-barrel plant. The beers are available at the on-site taphouse, where a feature glass wall allows visitors to view the brewery in operation. Beers are available throughout Yorkshire and Lancashire. It recently opened an off-site pub, the Exchange Alehouse in Bradford. !! ♦

Hockney Pale (ABV 3.6%)
Sweet maltiness balances with fresh citrus flavours and floral and peppery hop notes.

Northern Soul (ABV 3.8%)
A traditional Yorkshire golden-coloured bitter, well-balanced and smooth with a subtle bitterness.

Broadford Blonde (OG 1043, ABV 4.2%)
Light and refreshing with herbal and spicy hops complementing a subtle malt profile.

Brains IFBB

Dragon Brewery, Pacific Road, Cardiff, CF24 5HJ
☎ (029) 2040 2060 sabrain.com

Brains was established in 1882 at the Old Brewery, moving to the former Hancock's brewery site in 1999. The Craft Brewery remains in the Central Quay development area and will be enhanced with a pub and visitor's centre, while the brewery and head office relocated to Cardiff Bay in mid 2018. The company has remained in family ownership and runs more than 270 pubs throughout Wales, the Midlands and the West Country. It is heavily involved in sponsoring charities and Welsh sport. ♦

Dark (OG 1035.5, ABV 3.5%)
A tasty, classic dark brown-coloured mild, a mix of malt, roast, caramel with a background of hops. Bittersweet, mellow and with a lasting finish of malt and roast.

Bitter (OG 1036, ABV 3.7%)
Amber-coloured with a gentle aroma of malt and hops. Malt, hops and bitterness combine in an easy-drinking beer with a bitter finish.

Rev James Gold (OG 1041, ABV 4.1%)

SA (OG 1042, ABV 4.2%)
A mellow, full-bodied beer. Gentle malt and hop aroma leads to a malty, hop and fruit mix with a balancing bitterness.

SA Gold (OG 1042, ABV 4.2%)
A golden beer with a hoppy aroma. Well-balanced with a zesty hop, malt, fruit and balancing bitterness; a similar satisfying finish.

Rev James Rye (OG 1043, ABV 4.3%)

Rev James (OG 1045.5, ABV 4.5%)
A faint malt and fruit aroma with malt and fruit flavours in the taste, initially bittersweet. Bitterness balances the flavour and makes this an easy-drinking beer.

Contract brewed for Molson Coors:

M&B Brew XI (OG 1036, ABV 3.6%)

Hancock's HB (OG 1037, ABV 3.7%)

Worthington's Bitter (OG 1037, ABV 3.7%)

Brakspear

Eagle Maltings, The Crofts, Witney, Oxfordshire, OX28 4DP
☎ (01993) 890800 brakspear-beers.co.uk

Brakspear beers have been brewed in Oxfordshire since 1779. They continue to be traditionally crafted at the Wychwood Brewery (qv) in the historic market town of Witney using the original Victorian square fermenters and the renowned 'double drop' fermenting system. Part of Marston's PLC. !! ♦ RAIB

Bitter (OG 1035, ABV 3.4%)
A classic copper-coloured pale ale with a big hop resins, juicy malt and orange fruit aroma, intense hop bitterness in the mouth and finish, and a firm maltiness and tangy fruitiness throughout.

Oxford Gold (OG 1040, ABV 4%)
A full-flavoured, fruity golden ale with a zesty aroma.

Brampton SIBA

Units 4 & 5, Chatsworth Business Park, Chatsworth Road, Chesterfield, Derbyshire, S40 2AR
☎ (01246) 221680 bramptonbrewery.co.uk

The original Brampton Brewery closed in 1955. In 2007 a new brewery was established, and brewing commenced on an eight-barrel plant. Two tied houses are situated close to the brewery. !! ♦ RAIB

Golden Bud (OG 1037, ABV 3.8%)
Crisp and refreshing golden bitter with a pleasant balance of citrus, sweetness and bitter flavours. Light and easy to drink.

1302 (OG 1040, ABV 4%)
A sweet-tasting pale ale.

Griffin (OG 1040, ABV 4.1%)
A pale-coloured, slightly-sweet summer ale.

Best (OG 1041, ABV 4.2%)
Classic, drinkable bitter with a predominantly malty taste, balanced by caramel sweetness and a developing bitterness in the aftertaste.

Impy Dark (OG 1047, ABV 4.3%)
Strong roasted coffee aroma and a rich flavour of vine fruit and chocolate combine to make this a tasty mild ale.

Jerusalem (OG 1046, ABV 4.6%)
The rich and roasted malt notes defy the pale colour in this special bitter.

Tudor Rose (OG 1045, ABV 4.6%)
A well-balanced and creamy pale ale with a good hop nose.

Wasp Nest (OG 1049, ABV 5%)
Strong and complex with malt and hop flavours and a caramel sweetness.

Speciale (OG 1056, ABV 5.8%)
An IPA-style ale, the fruity hoppiness is balanced by the residual sweetness.

Brancaster

See Beeston

Brandon SIBA

76 High Street, Brandon, Suffolk, IP27 0AU ☎ 07876 234689 brandonbrewery.com

Brandon started brewing in 2005 on the site of an old dairy situated on the Suffolk-Norfolk border. Beers are based on traditional styles which include unique recipes and incorporate locally-sourced ingredients. !! RAIB

Old Rodney (OG 1040, ABV 4%)
Damson jam aroma precedes a flavoursome balance of malt, fruit and hops in this tawny-coloured best bitter. Gently fading finish.

Saxon Gold (OG 1040, ABV 4%)
A pale, golden-coloured beer with a subtle aroma of hops. The taste is a clean, crisp mix of spice and bitter fruits with a dry, hoppy finish.

Molly's Secret (OG 1041, ABV 4.2%)
A pale ale based on an old recipe.

Royal Ginger (OG 1041, ABV 4.2%)
A refreshing summer ale with a distinctive mix of malt and hoppy spice, balanced with a gentle ginger flavour and finish.

Rusty Bucket (OG 1044, ABV 4.4%)
Aromas of figs and malt with dried fruit, and flavours of malt and hops, leading to a bitter, biscuity aftertaste. A well-balanced, traditional brown-coloured best bitter.

Dragon Fire (ABV 4.5%)
A dark-coloured golden ale, smooth on the tongue with initial strong malt flavours giving way to sweet fruit hints of blackberry and a crisp, sharp finish.

Grumpy Bastard (OG 1045, ABV 4.5%)

Slippery Jack (OG 1045, ABV 4.5%)
A dark brown-coloured stout. Complex but well-balanced flavours of roasted grain and hop bitterness. Dry with a lingering, pleasantly bitter finish.

Brewer's Droop (ABV 5%)
A full-flavoured stronger golden ale with a lightly roasted, smooth body. Floral and citrus hop notes impart a rounded orange aroma and flavour with an enduring, pleasant, warm finish.

Branscombe Vale SIBA

Branscombe, Devon, EX12 3DP
☎ (01297) 680511 branscombevalebrewery.co.uk

The brewery was set up in 1992 in cowsheds at the back of a farm owned by the National Trust, overlooking the sea at Branscombe. The brewery owners converted the sheds, digging their own well. In 2008 a new 25-barrel plant was shoehorned in through the roof to increase capacity. ♦ RAIB

Mild (OG 1036, ABV 3.7%)
A bittersweet mild with vanilla flavours.

Branoc (OG 1038, ABV 3.8%)
Amber-coloured session bitter. Hops and malt throughout with good bitterness in taste and aftertaste.

Golden Fiddle (OG 1040, ABV 4%)
Effervescent golden ale with a citrus and butterscotch aroma with hints of peach and grapefruit and a dry finish.

Summa This (OG 1040, ABV 4.2%)
Amber in colour with digestive biscuit notes and a floral hop.

BVB Best Bitter (OG 1045, ABV 4.6%)
Red/brown-coloured beer with a fruity aroma and taste, and bitter, dry finish.

Summa That (OG 1049, ABV 5%)
Light golden-coloured beer with a clean and refreshing taste and a long, hoppy finish.

Harbinger (OG 1100, ABV 9.2%)
A smooth and moreish barley wine.

Brass Castle SIBA

10a Yorkersgate, Malton, North Yorkshire, YO17 7AB
☎ (01653) 698683 ☎ 07740 336851
brasscastlebrewery.co.uk

The brewery is based in the centre of Malton with a 12-barrel plant, having begun life in 2011 on a one-barrel kit in the owner's garage. It has an on-site taproom with up to eight beers available for on and off sales. ‼ ♦RAIB GF V

Session Mini IPA (OG 1038, ABV 3.6%)

Hoptical Illusion (OG 1043, ABV 4.3%)
A gluten-free, hoppy pale ale bursting with tropical, citrus and pine notes.

Misfit (OG 1043, ABV 4.3%)

Bad Kitty (OG 1061.5, ABV 5.5%)
A chewy chocolate vanilla dream of a porter.

Sunshine (OG 1061, ABV 5.7%)

Breakwater

Former Factory Site, St Martin's Yard, Lorne Road, Dover, Kent, CT16 2AA
☎ (01304) 700043 ☎ 07979 867045
breakwater.beer

Breakwater is a brewery and tap room established in 2016 behind Buckland Corn Mill in former industrial premises and on the site of the former Wellington Brewery. ♦RAIB

HMS Minnow (ABV 2.8%)

Dover Pale Ale (ABV 3.5%)

Hellfire Corner (ABV 4.1%)

Castle on the Hill (ABV 4.4%)

Cowjuice Milk Stout (ABV 4.4%)

Mogul West Country IPA (ABV 5.6%)

Brecon SIBA

8a Brecon Enterprise Park, Brecon, LD3 8BT
☎ (01874) 620800 brewconbrewing.co.uk

Established in 2011 by Buster Grant, a range of cask, keg and bottled beers is produced. ‼

Three Beacons (OG 1030, ABV 3%)
A low ABV, American-style pale ale. Golden in colour, full-bodied and hoppy.

Welsh Beacons (OG 1037, ABV 3.7%)
A Welsh pale ale, golden-coloured with a gentle floral bitterness.

Dark Beacons (OG 1038, ABV 3.8%)
A full-flavoured yet light and refreshing Welsh dark beer.

Copper Beacons (OG 1041, ABV 4.1%)
A copper-coloured best bitter, smooth and well-balanced with fruit and hop flavours.

Gold Beacons (OG 1042, ABV 4.2%)
A deep golden ale with soft, well-defined bitterness balanced by a blend of malts.

Orange Beacons (OG 1043, ABV 4.3%)

Red Beacons (OG 1050, ABV 5%)
A premium red-coloured ale, complex, smooth and well-hopped.

Mind Bleach (ABV 10%)

Brentwood SIBA

Calcott Hall Farm, Ongar Road, Brentwood, Essex, CM15 9HS
☎ (01277) 200483 brentwoodbrewing.co.uk

Since its launch in 2006 Brentwood has steadily increased its capacity and distribution, relocating to a new purpose-built brewery unit in 2013 with a visitor centre. Seasonal and special beers are also available including more unusual beer styles under the Elephant School brand name. ‼ ♦RAIB

BBC2 (OG 1030, ABV 2.5%)
Full-bodied, mid-brown-coloured bitter with a dry, tropical citrus flavour.

IPA (OG 1039, ABV 3.7%)
A lightly-hopped, pale session beer.

Marvellous Maple Mild (OG 1038, ABV 3.7%)
Dark brown-coloured mild with a hint of maple syrup.

Legacy (ABV 4%)
Easy-drinking pale ale with citrus notes.

Best (OG 1042, ABV 4.2%)
A traditional, light-coloured best bitter with a well-rounded flavour and aroma.

Gold (OG 1043, ABV 4.3%)
A heavily-hopped, golden ale with a fruity taste and bitter finish.

Hope & Glory (ABV 4.5%)
A full-bodied, red-coloured premium bitter. Well-balanced with full malt flavours and light hops coming through in the flavour, leaving a lingering bitterness.

Lumberjack (ABV 5.2%)
A strong, slightly sweet, full-bodied bitter with a rounded, hoppy finish.

Chockwork Orange (OG 1067, ABV 6.5%)
A deep chocolate, malty beer brewed with oranges.

Brewed under the Elephant School brand name:

Cheru Kol (ABV 4.5%)
A fig and rosemary Belgian-style beer.

Sombrero (ABV 4.5%)
A chia and passion fruit saison.

Porter in A Storm (ABV 4.9%)
A chocolate and cranberry porter.

Brew Buddies

Unit 14, Highlands Farm Business Park, Highlands Hill, Swanley Village, Kent, BR8 7NA ☎ 07962 369717
brew-buddies.co.uk

Established by two friends in 2015, Brew Buddies operates on a six-barrel plant. The brewery supplies free trade outlets in Kent and the South East, while distribution further afield is via a wholesaler. ‼

Brew By Numbers

79 Enid Street, Bermondsey, London, SE16 3RA
☎ (020) 7237 9794 ☎ 07528 684105
brewbynumbers.com

Brew By Numbers is a small brewery established in 2012, specialising in saisons and hop-forward pale beers, all bottled on site. Most beers undergo secondary fermentation and conditioning in bottle and keg, but hop-forward styles are conditioned and carbonated in tank. All beers are named by a four digit number, the first two digits denoting style and the second denoting recipe. The latest releases are served in its taproom. RAIB

Brew Foundation 

c/o Wincle Brewery, Toll Barn, Wincle, Cheshire, SK11 0QE
☎ (0114) 282 3098 ☎ 07545 618894

Office: 18 Jarrow Road, Sheffield, S11 8YB
thebrewfoundation.co.uk

A father-and-son brewery, currently using spare capacity at Wincle Brewery (qv). Beer is distributed both east and west of the Pennines.

Pop (ABV 3.6%)
A session pale ale with tropical hop notes.

Little Bitter That (ABV 3.8%)

Hops & Dreams (ABV 4%)
A session IPA with a citrus, floral and tropical hoppy flavour and aroma.

Laughing Water (ABV 4.3%)
A fruity, tropical pale ale with a subtle citrus base.

First Light (ABV 4.6%)

Janet's Treat Porter (ABV 4.8%)
Brewed in collaboration with Wincle Brewery. A cherry flavour balanced against chocolate malt bitterness with a subtle dark cherry aroma.

Hop & Glory (ABV 4.9%)

Bitter That (ABV 5%)

Brew Monster (NEW) SIBA

Unit C, Avondale Business Park, Avondale Road, Cwmbran, NP44 1XE ☎ 07772 869856
brewmonster.co.uk

Brew Monster was established in 2017 after attracting backing from local investors. The focus is on IPAs with a monster naming theme.

Leviathan IPA (ABV 4%)

Daemon Red IPA (ABV 4.6%)

Tiamat IPA (ABV 5%)

Mephisto IPA (ABV 5.5%)

Brew Shack

Dairy Building, Manor Farm, Sixpenny Handley, Dorset, SP5 5NU ☎ 07580 120258
thebrewshack.co.uk

Brewing began in 2015 on a 1.5-barrel plant in purpose-built premises, later upgraded to 4.5 barrels. In 2018 the brewery moved to larger premises on a working farm in Sixpenny Handley. Experimental and seasonal beers are planned to complement the regular range. ♦

Amber Gambler (OG 1040, ABV 4%)
Medium-bodied, well-balanced, hoppy amber-coloured session bitter.

Pale Ale (OG 1045, ABV 4.5%)

Eight Grain Porter (OG 1050, ABV 5%)

5 a Day IPA (OG 1055, ABV 5.5%)

Sump Oil Stout (OG 1060, ABV 6%)

Brew Shed

Wellheads House, Sandilands, Limekilns, KY11 3JD
☎ 07484 727672 brewshedbeers.wordpress.com

Brewing began in 2016 in a tiny brewery behind the owner's house, the first brewery in Limekilns since 1849. Brew Shed Beers revives a tradition of local breweries serving the neighbourhood.

Brew Studio (NEW)

39 Meadowview Road, Sompting, West Sussex, BN15 0HU ☎ 07890 978350
ianthomasventon@gmail.com

Brew Studio started off as a 0.5-barrel nanobrewery in 2017 and has recently upgraded to a 2.5-barrel plant. Around 20 outlets are supplied direct. !! V

Mic Drop Extra Pale (OG 1038, ABV 3.7%)
A light and zesty pale ale.

Acoustic Session Pale Ale (OG 1040, ABV 4%)
A hop-forward ale with rich citrus flavours.

Unplugged APA (OG 1044, ABV 4.5%)
A smooth and tropical, hoppy American-style pale ale.

Showtime Roasted Dark Chocolate Porter (OG 1048, ABV 4.6%)
A rich and complex porter with a dark malt profile.

Headliner IPA (OG 1050, ABV 5%)

Brew Toon (NEW) SIBA

72a St Peter Street, Peterhead, AB42 1QB
☎ (01779) 476211 brewtoon.com

Established in 2017, beers are brewed in small batches in the nautical town of Peterhead. An on-site café/bar is open all week. !!

Brew York SIBA

Unit 6, Enterprise Complex, Walmgate, York, YO1 9TT
☎ (01904) 848448 brewyork.co.uk

Established in 2016, Brew York was born out of two friends passion for beer and brewing. The brewery is located within York's historic city walls, a 15 minute walk from the station. A unique tap room with riverside beer garden has been constructed alongside the brewhouse. !! ♦

Jarsa (ABV 3.7%)
Refreshing session pale ale with hints of orange and sherbet.

Maris the Otter (ABV 3.9%)
Classic English bitter with smooth bitterness and a good body.

Keras (ABV 4.1%)
An American-style session pale ale with fresh citrus and pine notes.

Little Eagle (ABV 4.5%)
Session IPA with big hop flavour and creaminess.

X-Panda (ABV 4.5%)

Brew York (ABV 4.9%)

Refreshing and light beer, citrus with a hint of blackcurrant.

Viking DNA (ABV 5%)
Strong coffee and chocolate notes encased in smooth smokiness.

Haast's Eagle (ABV 5.9%)
A pale ale packed full of hops. Subtle, delicate fruit and floral notes.

Big Eagle (ABV 6.5%)
West Coast-style IPA with big citrus flavours and a resinous finish.

BrewBoard (NEW) SIBA

Unit B3, Button End Industrial Estate, Harston, Cambridgeshire, CB22 7GX ⊕ brewboard.co.uk

Brewing began in 2017 using a 30-hectolitre brew plant. No real ale. !!

BrewDog

Balmacassie Industrial Estate, Ellon, AB41 8BX ☎ (01358) 724924 ⊕ brewdog.com

Established in 2007 by James Watt and Martin Dickie. Most of the production goes into bottles and keg. In 2016 a KeyKeg initiative began, described as 'real ale for modernists', which has now been expanded to include more beers. !!

Dead Pony (OG 1040, ABV 3.8%)

5am Saint (OG 1048, ABV 5%)

Brewers Folly (NEW)

Ashton Farm House, Stanbridge, Dorset, BH21 4JD ⊕ brewersfolly.co.uk

Brewing began in 2017 using a 1.4-barrel plant.

Brewheadz

Unit 16a, Rosebery Industrial Park, Rosebery Avenue, Tottenham Hale, London, N17 9SR ⊕ brewheadz.com

Established in 2016, Brewheadz is an independent microbrewery in Tottenham Hale, producing unpasteurised and unfiltered beers. The range is currently available in KeyKegs and bottle-conditioned from some speciality pubs, beer shops and online retailers. A tap room is open on Saturdays. RAIB

Brewhouse & Kitchen SIBA

Bedford: 115 High Street, Bedford, MK40 1NU ☎ (01234) 342931

Bournemouth: 154 Commercial Road, Bournemouth, Dorset, BH2 5LU ☎ (01202) 055221

Bristol: 31-35 Cotham Hill, Bristol, BS6 6JY ☎ (0117) 973 3793

Cardiff (NEW): Sophia Close, Pontcanna, Cardiff, CF11 9HW ☎ (029) 2037 1599

Cheltenham: Unit 7, The Brewery, St Margaret's Road, Cheltenham, GL50 4EQ ☎ (01242) 509946

Chester: Forest House, Love Street, Chester, CH1 1QY ☎ (01244) 404990

Dorchester: 17 Weymouth Avenue, Dorchester, DT1 1QY ☎ (01305) 265551

Gloucester Quay: Unit R1, St Anne Walk, Gloucester, GL1 5SH ☎ (01452) 222965

Highbury: 2a Corsica Street, Highbury, London, N5 1JJ ☎ (020) 7226 1026

Islington: 5 Torrens Street, Angel, London, EC1V 1NQ ☎ (020) 7064 9943

Lichfield (NEW): 1 Bird Street, Lichfield, WS13 6PW ☎ (01543) 224740

Milton Keynes (NEW): 7 Savoy Crescent, Milton Keynes, MK9 3PU ☎ (01908) 049032

Nottingham: Trent Bridge, Nottingham, NG2 2GS ☎ (0115) 986 7960

Poole: 3 Dear Hay Lane, Poole, Dorset, BH15 1NZ ☎ (01202) 771246

Portsmouth: 26 Guildhall Walk, Portsmouth, Hampshire, PO1 2DD ☎ (023) 9289 1340

Southampton: 47 Highfield Lane, Southampton, SO17 1QD ☎ (023) 8055 5566

Southbourne: 147 Parkwood Road, Southbourne, Dorset, BH5 2BN ☎ (01202) 055209

Sutton Coldfield: 8 Birmingham Road, Sutton Coldfield, West Midlands, B72 1QD ☎ (0121) 796 6838

Wilmslow: 6-12 Swan Street, Wilmslow, Cheshire, SK9 1HE ☎ (01625) 441850 ⊕ brewhouseandkitchen.com

Brewing started in 2013 in Portsmouth, the first in the growing Brewhouse & Kitchen chain. There are now 19 brewpubs, with more planned, each producing its own particular range of beers and with its brewery on open display in the bar area. Local freehouses and beer festivals can be supplied. Carry outs and brewery experience days are available at all venues.

Brewing Brothers

Imperial, 119 Queens Road, Hastings, East Sussex, TN34 1RL ⊕ brewingbrothers.org

⊗ Brewing began in 2016 behind the bar of the Imperial, Hastings, using a 2.5-barrel plant. A wide range of brother themed beers has been brewed to date. ♦

BrewSaurus (NEW)

2 Powys Place, Dinas Powys, CF64 4LB ☎ 07538 545491 ✉ brewsaurus@gmail.com

One of Wales' smallest breweries was established in 2017 and produces tiny batch runs on its 100-litre system. Beers can be made to order if required. No real ale.

Brewshed SIBA

Place Farm, Ingham, Suffolk, IP31 1NQ ☎ (01284) 848066 ⊕ brewshedbrewery.co.uk

⊗ Brewshed began brewing in 2011 using a five-barrel plant in buildings located behind the Beerhouse, one of its pub outlets. It's now located in the nearby village of Ingham, using a 12-barrel plant, which has resulted in greater capacity and a wider beer range. ♦

Pale (OG 1040, ABV 3.9%)

Best (OG 1044, ABV 4.3%)

Route 84 (ABV 4.4%)

Vanilla Porter (OG 1047, ABV 4.7%)
A traditional brown/black-coloured, smooth porter with a complex, layered malt character balanced with traditional hops and a soft vanilla finish.

American Blonde (OG 1055, ABV 5.5%)

Brewshine

4 Littledale, Kendal, Cumbria, LA9 7SG ☎ 07817 873997 🌐 brewshine.co.uk

Brewing began in 2014 using a nine-gallon plant situated in a garage in Kendal. There are plans for expansion.

Silly Billy (OG 1038, ABV 3.8%)
A smooth, copper-coloured bitter with balanced flavours and a caramel finish.

Billonde (OG 1040, ABV 4%)
A refreshing beer with a light citrus, fruity flavour.

Billy Goat Ale (OG 1040, ABV 4%)
Dark amber in colour with a rich, malty taste and a dry, caramel-chocolate finish.

Billyonaires Gold (OG 1040, ABV 4%)
A light, refreshing beer with a citrus fruity flavour.

Brewsmith SIBA

Unit 11, Cuba Industrial Estate, Ramsbottom, BL0 0NE ☎ (01706) 829390 🌐 brewsmithbeer.co.uk

Brewsmith is a 10-barrel microbrewery established in 2014 by the Smith family – James, Jennifer and Ted. It produces a range of cask and bottle-conditioned ales in traditional British beer styles. !! ♦ RAIB

Mosaic (ABV 3.5%)

Amarillo (ABV 3.8%)
Light golden-coloured beer with floral, citrus and orange tones.

Bitter (OG 1039, ABV 3.9%)
A pale-coloured session bitter. Moderate bitterness, pronounced floral/citrus hop aromas.

Pale Ale (OG 1042, ABV 4.2%)
A refreshingly bitter and hoppy pale ale.

Anvil Ale (OG 1045, ABV 4.5%)
Full-bodied, dark-coloured bitter with pine and fruit aromas.

APA (ABV 5%)
Pale ale made with American hops. Resinous pine, grapefruit and floral aromas.

Oatmeal Stout (OG 1052, ABV 5.2%)
A full-bodied, richly-textured stout.

IPA (OG 1060, ABV 6%)
Rich mouthfeel, big hop aromas, long and dry bitter finish.

Brewster's SIBA

Unit 5, Burnside, Turnpike Close, Grantham, Lincolnshire, NG31 7XU ☎ (01476) 566000 🌐 brewsters.co.uk

Brewster is the old English term for a female brewer and Sara Barton is a modern example. Originally established in the Vale of Belvoir in 1998, moving to Grantham in 2006, Brewster's produces a range of traditional and innovative beers with two regularly-changing ranges; Women of Wonder (4.8% ABV) and WhimsicAles (4.0% ABV). !! ♦

Hophead (OG 1036, ABV 3.6%)
An amber-coloured beer with a floral hop character. Hops predominate before yielding to grapefruit in the lasting dry finish.

Marquis (OG 1038, ABV 3.8%)
A well-balanced and refreshing session bitter with maltiness and a dry, hoppy finish.

Aromantica (OG 1042, ABV 4.2%)
An amber-coloured beer with a slightly sweet, nutty flavour. Tropical hop notes and aromas of lime and passion fruit with a long aromatic finish.

Hop a Doodle Doo (OG 1043, ABV 4.3%)
A copper-coloured ale with a rich, full-bodied mouthfeel and fruity hop character.

Decadence (OG 1044, ABV 4.4%)
A golden ale with a hint of malt sweetness. Passion fruit and grapefruit aromas on the nose. First taste gives a complex zesty hop palate leading on to a fresh herby finish.

Aromatic Porter (OG 1045, ABV 4.5%)
A rich, roasty porter with citrus and tropical fruit hop flavours.

Stilton Porter (OG 1049, ABV 4.9%)
A rich, roasty, malty porter balanced with spicy rich hop flavours.

Briarbank SIBA

70 Fore Street, Ipswich, Suffolk, IP4 1LB ☎ (01473) 284000 🌐 briarbank.org

The Briarbank Brewing Company was established in 2013, and is situated on the site of the old Lloyds Bank on Fore Street. The brewery is a small two-barrel plant. The bar above offers the range of beers. !! ♦

Brick SIBA

Units 13-14, Deptford Trading Estate, Blackhorse Road, Deptford, London, SE8 5HY ☎ 07747 787636 🌐 brickbrewery.co.uk

Established by owner and former homebrewer Ian Stewart in 2013. Due to continued expansion, the brewing operation relocated from Peckham to larger premises in nearby Deptford in 2017. The original Peckham railway arch site is retained as an expanded taproom. Numerous local and regional outlets are supplied. Frequent one-off and collaboration brews are produced. ♦

Kinsale (ABV 4%)
Fruity, tawny-coloured best bitter with a little nutty roast character and hops throughout. Sweetish with a little honey on the palate.

Peckham Pale (ABV 4.5%)
A light golden ale with fruit, floral notes typical of a North American-style pale ale.

Blenheim Black (OG 1053, ABV 5.3%)
Roasted notes throughout with black cherry and blackcurrant and a trace of hops. Finish is bitter, dry with some malt.

Brick House

Patcham, East Sussex, BN1 8HQ ☎ 07708 384604 ✉ brickhousebrewingco@gmail.com

Brick House has grown organically from humble homebrewing beginnings and plans to continue in this vein. Brewing is currently suspended. RAIB

Bricknell

Bricknell, Hull, East Yorkshire, HU5 4ET ☎ 07729 722953 🌐 bricknellbrewery.co.uk

Small scale commercial brewing has continued since 2015 with an emphasis on quality. Everything is hands on; growing Fuggles hops, brewing, bottling and labelling to produce 150 litres of hand-crafted, bottle-conditioned, vegan-friendly beers, following 19th-century recipes, once or twice a week. RAIB V

Bridge

Bridge, Woodhead Road, Holmbridge, West Yorkshire, HD9 2NQ
☎ (01484) 687652 ☎ 07970 779762

Brewing began in 2014 using a 2.5-barrel plant, in premises at the Bridge pub, Holmbridge. The brewery produces beers for the pub and also for its companion pub, Brambles, Holmfirth. Brewing is currently suspended.

Bridgehouse SIBA

Airedale Heifer, Bradford Road, Sandbeds, Keighley, West Yorkshire, BD20 9LY
☎ (01535) 601222

Office: Unit 1, Aireworth Mills, Aireworth Road, Keighley, BD21 4DH 🌐 bridgehousebrewery.co.uk

Bridgehouse began brewing in 2010 using a 10-barrel plant. The brewery purchased the recipes and branding of Old Bear Brewery in 2014 and moved into its premises in Keighley. In 2015 the brewery relocated again to its present address behind the Airedale Heifer pub in Sandbeds, which it also operates. A bespoke 15-barrel brewery is used and the site includes a visitor centre. !! ♦

Pale Bandit (ABV 3.6%)

Tequila Blonde (OG 1038, ABV 3.8%)
Refreshing blonde ale, initially sweet with hints of lime, finishing with a slight tingling aftertaste.

Blonde (OG 1040, ABV 4%)
A strong, fruity aroma with a sharp burst of grapefruit on the tongue and a touch of sweetness in the background. Bitter finish.

Aired Ale (OG 1042, ABV 4.1%)
Brown-coloured beer with a malty aroma. Malt, hops and fruit in equal balance with lingering fruitiness in a long bitter finish.

Porter (OG 1045, ABV 4.5%)
Dark brown-coloured beer with red hints. Aromas of malt and liquorice lead to coffee and wine fruit flavours, which carry through to a dry finish.

Holy Cow (OG 1057, ABV 5.6%)
Light brown-coloured strong ale with juicy malt and full hop flavour, citrus overtones. Light hop aroma and a bitter, slightly astringent finish.

Bridgetown

Albert Inn, Bridgetown Close, Totnes, Devon, TQ9 5AD
☎ (01803) 863214 🌐 albertinntotnes.com/bridgetown-brewery

Bridgetown started brewing in 2008 on a two-barrel plant in the outbuildings of the Albert Inn, Totnes. !! ♦ RAIB

Bridlington

Pack Horse, 7 Market Place, Bridlington, East Yorkshire, YO16 4QJ
☎ (01262) 603502

The brewery, founded in 2014 in the grounds of the Telegraph Inn, Bridlington, is now based in the beer garden of the Pack Horse, Bridlington. Beers are generally to be found on the bar of the Pack Horse and at local beer festivals.

Briggs Signature

c/o Unit 1, Waterhouse Mill, 65-71 Lockwood Road, Huddersfield, West Yorkshire, HD1 3QU ☎ 07427 668004 🌐 briggssignatureales.weebly.com

Nick Briggs, a member of the brewing team at Mallinson's and former head brewer at Elland, has branched out on his own, producing his first brew on the Mallinson's plant. Now producing various regular rotating, modern, hop-forward beers. RAIB

Northern Soul (OG 1038, ABV 3.8%)
Pale bitter with a citrus and zesty aroma.

Brighton Bier

Unit 10, Bell Tower Industrial Estate, Roedean Road, Brighton, East Sussex, BN2 5RU
☎ (01273) 567374 🌐 brightonbier.com

Brighton Bier was established in 2012. It operates a 15-barrel brewery close to the centre of the city and also owns the Brighton Bierhaus pub, Brighton. Beers are available throughout the UK and exported to Europe and Asia.

Brighton Bier (ABV 4%)

West Pier (OG 1042, ABV 4%)

Freshman (ABV 4.5%)

Grand Havana (ABV 5%)

No Name Stout (ABV 5%)

South Coast IPA (ABV 5%)

Downtown Charlie Brown (ABV 6%)

Old Skool (ABV 6.5%)

Imperial Freshman (ABV 7%)

Brightside SIBA

Unit 10, Dale Industrial Estate, Radcliffe, M26 1AD
☎ (0161) 725 9644 ☎ 07870 207442
🌐 brightsidebrewing.co.uk

Brightside began brewing in 2009 in the back of the family bakery and moved to its present location in 2014. At the start of 2017 the brewery introduced a second arm – Wildside Beers, which are usually one-off beers brewed in small batches. ♦ GF V

Odin Blonde (OG 1038, ABV 3.8%)
A fresh, light-bodied blonde ale with a fruity, citrus flavour and moderately bitter finish.

Our Town Pale Ale (OG 1040, ABV 4%)

A copper-coloured modern pale ale brewed with amber and roast barley, which strike a balance between honeyed orange citrus fruits and malt.

B-Side Gold (OG 1042, ABV 4.2%)
A refreshing session ale, pale golden in colour with a mild bitterness and vibrant fruity hop flavour.

Best Bitter (OG 1043, ABV 4.3%)
A mid-amber-coloured bitter with subtle fruit and citrus flavours as well as earthy and spicy notes.

Academy Ale IPA (OG 1044, ABV 4.5%)
A moderately malty base allows the hops to shine through.

Manchester Skyline Gold (OG 1045, ABV 4.6%)
A full-flavoured golden ale with fresh, fruity, floral aromas and moderate bitterness.

Maverick IPA (OG 1047, ABV 4.8%)
An American-style IPA with bold grapefruit and floral aromas, finishing with a clean, refreshing bitterness.

Topaz IPA (OG 1049, ABV 5%)
A light-amber coloured beer with delicate caramel and light, toasty malt notes. Tropical hop overtones with fresh, resinous aromatics.

Brightwater SIBA

9 Beaconsfield Road, Claygate, Surrey, KT10 0PN
☎ (01372) 462334 ☎ 07802 316389
brightbrew.co.uk

Established in 2013 at Claygate in Surrey, Brightwater is a five-barrel brewery producing traditional beers. The range is available at its brewery tap, Platform 3, outside Claygate Station, and other Surrey and South London pubs.

Little Nipper (OG 1033, ABV 3.3%)
A rather thin hoppy bitter with a hint of a citrus taste and a bitter, slightly dry finish.

Top Notch (OG 1035, ABV 3.5%)
Citrus notes dominate the aroma of this mid-brown-coloured bitter. It has a reasonably well-balanced taste with some bitterness in the finish.

Ernest Pale IPA Bitter (OG 1037, ABV 3.7%)

Daisy Gold (OG 1040, ABV 4%)
Golden-coloured ale with a moderate tropical fruit hoppy character and some balancing malt, leading to a bittersweet finish.

Wild Orchid (OG 1040, ABV 4%)
Dark-coloured oatmeal porter enhanced with a Madagascan vanilla pod in each cask giving the beer fragrant vanilla undertones.

All Citra (OG 1043, ABV 4.3%)
Bitter with bite due to the hops resulting in a distinctly citrus flavour.

Lip Smacker (OG 1043, ABV 4.3%)

Coal Porter (OG 1049, ABV 4.9%)
A classic porter with a delicate hazelnut flavour and a clean hop taste.

Brigstock

7 Park Walk, Brigstock, Northamptonshire, NN14 3HH
☎ (01536) 373428 brigstockbrewhouse.co.uk

Philip Wilks began brewing in 2012 on a small 52-litre plant using local spring water. Sales are direct to the public through markets, events and from the brewery. RAIB

Brimstage SIBA

Home Farm, Brimstage, Merseyside, CH63 6HY
☎ (0151) 342 1181 ☎ 07870 968323
brimstagebrewery.com

Brewing started in 2006 on a 10-barrel plant in a redundant farm dairy in the heart of the Wirral countryside. This is Wirral's first brewery since the closure of the Birkenhead Brewery in the late 1960s. Around 60 outlets are supplied across the Wirral, Merseyside, Cheshire and North Wales. ‼♦

Sandpiper Light Ale (OG 1036.5, ABV 3.6%)
A well-balanced session beer, light and refreshing with tropical fruit flavours.

Trapper's Hat Bitter (OG 1037.5, ABV 3.8%)
Gold-coloured with a complex bouquet. It provides a mouthful of fruit zest with hints of orange and grapefruit. A refreshingly hoppy session brew.

Rhode Island Red Rye (OG 1039, ABV 4%)
Red-coloured, smooth and well-balanced malty beer with a good dry aftertaste. Some fruitiness in the taste.

Elderflower Wheat (ABV 4.1%)
A light, refreshing wheat beer brewed with dried elderflower. It has a delicate vanilla and honey-like aroma.

Scarecrow Bitter (OG 1041, ABV 4.2%)
Orange marmalade in colour, this well-balanced session brew has a distinct citrus fruit bouquet and a bitter finish.

IPA (OG 1055.5, ABV 6%)
A modern IPA with a floral aroma and dry bitter finish.

Brinkburn Street SIBA

3 Hume Street, Newcastle upon Tyne, NE6 1LN
☎ (0191) 260 0688

Office: Quayside i4, Ouseburn Building, Albion Row, Newcastle upon Tyne, NE6 1LL
brinkburnbrewery.co.uk

Brewing began in 2015, much influenced by West Coast US beer styles. Citrus flavours and highly-hopped bitterness is a feature of many of its beers. The brewery relocated to a new site in 2018, which also incorporates a brewery tap.

Fools Gold Session (ABV 3.8%)

The Pursuit of Hoppiness Session (ABV 3.9%)

Byker Brown (ABV 4.8%)

Briscoe's

16 Ash Grove, Otley, West Yorkshire, LS21 3EL
☎ (01943) 466515 ✉ briscoe.brewery@talktalk.net

The brewery was launched in 1998 by microbiologist/chemist Dr Paul Briscoe in the cellar of his house with a one-barrel brew length. Dr Briscoe is currently producing one brew per week on his original plant, several beers are produced on an irregular basis.

Otley Gold (OG 1040, ABV 3.9%)

Bristol Beer Factory SIBA

Unit A, The Old Brewery, Durnford Street, Ashton, Bristol, BS3 2AW
☎ (0117) 902 6317 bristolbeerfactory.co.uk

THE BREWERIES

⊗ A 30-barrel micro-brewery in a part of the former Ashton Gate Brewing Co, which closed in 1933. 50 outlets are supplied and output and brewing capacity are steadily increasing. A brewery visitor centre opened in 2016. !! ♦ RAIB

Nova (OG 1040, ABV 3.8%)
Citrus hop aroma to this straw-coloured, light-bodied and very bitter session ale. Hop-led taste with lemon fruit and pale malt following into a bitter hop aftertaste.

Fortitude (ABV 4%)
Amber-coloured ale with light malt and a hop nose, mildly fruity flavours balanced with hop bitterness and a short, dry finish.

Seven (OG 1043, ABV 4.2%)
Mid-brown-coloured best bitter with a fruity aroma. Balanced malt and hops with hints of fruit and caramel flavours. Malt and bitterness remain on the aftertaste.

Milk Stout (OG 1049, ABV 4.5%)
Very sweet, full-bodied black stout with lactose creaminess. Finishes with smoky roast bitterness.

Independence (OG 1046, ABV 4.6%)
Strong, hoppy aroma and initial flavour. Sweet fruitiness follows, leading to a bitter hoppy finish. Well-balanced with impressive flavour for its strength.

Britman

The Stables, Atelier Suite, Burton Manor, Burton, Cheshire, CH64 5SJ ☎ 07925 875836 ⊕ burtonmanorgardens.org.uk/whats-here/britman-craft-beers/

Britman is a small, quirky independent brewery established in 2013. It brews to the Reinheitsgebot German purity law, and produces vegetarian-friendly beers. The brewery has been recognised by the Sustainable Restaurants Association as a sustainable product; all spent grain is sent to happy pigs locally. ♦

Best Bitter (OG 1044, ABV 4.5%)
Smooth, light and pleasantly bitter.

London Porter (OG 1043, ABV 4.5%)
Dark-coloured, hoppy and slightly bitter with a treacle and coffee aftertaste.

Golden Ale (OG 1044, ABV 4.6%)
A true golden ale, hoppy and slightly bitter with a mild, sweet aftertaste.

Brixton SIBA

Arch 547, Brixton Station Road, Brixton, London, SW9 8PF
☎ (020) 3609 8880 ⊕ brixtonbrewery.com

Located in a railway arch in central Brixton, the brewery opened in 2013. The bulk of the production is currently bottled, but cask-conditioned ales feature as occasional guests in several pubs in the Brixton area. Beers are generally named after places in Brixton. In 2017 Heineken UK invested in the company in order to expand production. A move to Loughborough Junction is planned. !! ♦ RAIB

Reliance Pale Ale (OG 1042, ABV 4.2%)
Tropical notes and a little malt are noticeable in this refreshing amber-coloured beer. A gentle bitterness grows on drinking.

Effra Ale (OG 1045, ABV 4.5%)
Dry, copper-coloured best bitter with peppery hops and fruit in flavour and bitter finish. A little caramel malt provides balance.

Atlantic APA (OG 1054, ABV 5.4%)
Hops and strong aroma of flowery hops, melon and citrus. Biscuit, grapefruit and melon flavours, with a little bitterness. Dry, complex finish.

Electric IPA (OG 1065, ABV 6.5%)
Sweet biscuit balances the bitterness in this golden ale. Strong citrus, passion fruit, melon with spicy hop flavours. Dry, hoppy aftertaste.

Brockenhurst (NEW)

Balmer Lawn Hotel, Lyndhurst Road, Brockenhurst, Hampshire, SO42 7ZB ⊕ balmerlawnhotel.com

A microbrewery located in the grounds of the Balmer Lawn Hotel & Spa.

Brockley SIBA

31 Harcourt Road, Brockley, London, SE4 2AJ
☎ 07814 584338 ⊕ brockleybrewery.co.uk

Established in 2013 by a group of local beer enthusiasts who installed a five-barrel plant in a converted builder's workshop. The brewery concentrates on supplying outlets within a six-kilometre radius. A bar is open on Fridays and Saturdays. ♦

Golden Ale (OG 1038, ABV 3.8%)
Gold-coloured beer with fruit and hoppy aroma. Ripe melon and pineapple notes. Bitter, hoppy finish.

Pale Ale (OG 1041, ABV 4.1%)
Light-drinking, hoppy, amber-coloured beer with caramelised citrus, lychee and floral hops becoming more spicy in the long bitter finish.

Porter (OG 1043, ABV 4.3%)
Roast malt with a hint of blackcurrant becoming more hoppy and bitter late in the taste and aftertaste.

Red Ale (OG 1048, ABV 4.8%)
Smoky aroma on this well-balanced, sweet, fruity red-coloured ale with a growing spiciness overlaid with dry roasted bitter character.

Brodie's

Office: Unit 40, 4 Lammas Road, Fairways Business Park, London, E10 7QT ☎ 07828 498733
⊕ brodiesbeers.com

⊗ Established in 2008 by James Brodie, beers are brewed using spare capacity at Rhymney Brewery (qv) in South Wales. !! ♦ RAIB

Broken Bridge

Unit 5, Lycroft Farm, Upper Swanmore, Hampshire, SO32 2QQ ☎ 07555 771257

Office: 2 Frys Cottage, Frys Lane, Meonstoke, Hampshire, SO32 3NL
✉ richard@brokenbridgebrewing.co.uk

⊗ Brewing began in 2016 in a small farm industrial unit. The brewery is a one-man operation using a 2.5-barrel plant and four fermenters, giving an annual capacity of around 500 barrels. Many one-off brews complement a diverse core range, intended to test new concepts and ingredients. Distribution is to free houses and Hampshire's many micropubs. ♦RAIB

Broken Biscuit (ABV 4%)
A brown-coloured porter with a chocolate digestive flavour.

Tessellate (ABV 4%)

Hygge (ABV 4.2%)

It's 5 O'Clock Somewhere (ABV 5%)
An American-style pale ale using modern hops and crisp, spicy rye malt.

Revolver (ABV 6%)
An unfined, hazy, single-hop IPA.

Brolly (NEW)

No. 5 Kiln Industries, Fittleworth Road, Wisborough Green, West Sussex, RH14 0ES ☎ 07720 847017
🌐 brollybrewing.co.uk

Brolly was established in 2017 by keen homebrewer Brook Saunders. Beers are available in local pubs and at the brewery's on-site bar (open Friday-Sunday). !! ♦RAIB V

New England Pale Ale (OG 1037, ABV 3.6%)
A smooth, juicy session pale ale.

Lowfold Wissy (OG 1037, ABV 3.8%)
A smooth session ale with layered malts and hops forming a balanced, earthy and floral traditional Sussex bitter.

Chub IPA (OG 1041, ABV 4.3%)
A well-balanced, American-style IPA. Clean and fresh with citrus flavours. Unfined and slightly hazy.

C.O.W. (OG 1048, ABV 4.8%)
A pale ale with citrus flavours of melon, lychee and lemon. Malted oats give this beer a smooth mouthfeel.

Natural Spring Water (OG 1051, ABV 5%)
A New England-style IPA with a varying hop profile.

Brooks (NEW)

17 Birkenhead Road, Hoylake, Merseyside, CH47 5AE
🌐 brooks-brewhouse.co.uk

A nanobrewery producing bottle-conditioned beers. RAIB

Brotherhood (NEW) SIBA

Oakfield Business Centre, Northacre Industrial Park, Westbury, Wiltshire, BA13 4WF
☎ (01373) 823250 🌐 brotherhood.co.uk

This 10-barrel brewery was founded in 2016 by three brothers in Westbury, just south of Bath. A growing number of local outlets are supplied. !!♦

Session Pale Ale (OG 1038, ABV 3.8%)
Thirst-quenching pale ale with a pleasant citrus and spice nose and a hint of grapefruit.

Dry Hopped Pale Ale (OG 1040, ABV 4%)
A refreshingly bitter golden ale with floral flavours and a big floral hop aroma.

Mango Pale Ale (OG 1042, ABV 4.2%)
A sweet, easy-drinking, fruity beer with strong mango flavours.

American Red (OG 1044, ABV 4.5%)
Citrus notes of orange and tangerine are topped off with huge kick of zesty grapefruit.

GIPA (OG 1050, ABV 5.2%)
A tangy bitter with strong grapefruit flavours imparted by the hops.

IPA (OG 1053, ABV 5.6%)
A fruity, floral IPA with hints of pine nuts.

Broughton SIBA

Main Street, Broughton, ML12 6HQ
☎ (01899) 830345 🌐 broughtonales.co.uk

Founded in 1979, Broughton Ales was then one of the first microbreweries. Broughton has developed since then and though more than 60% of production goes into bottle for sale in Britain and abroad, it retains a sizeable range of cask ales. All beers are suitable for vegetarians. !! ♦

Pale Ale (ABV 3.6%)

Hopopotamus (OG 1038, ABV 3.8%)

Greenmantle (OG 1038, ABV 3.9%)
A dark-coloured, bittersweet ale with a pleasant hop aftertaste.

Clipper IPA (OG 1042, ABV 4.2%)
A light-coloured, crisp, hoppy beer with a clean aftertaste.

Merlin's Ale (OG 1042, ABV 4.2%)
A well-hopped, fruity flavour is balanced by malt in the taste. The finish is bittersweet, light but dry.

Dark N'Cloudy (OG 1046, ABV 4.4%)

Exciseman's 80/- (OG 1046, ABV 4.6%)
A traditional 80/- cask ale. A dark, malty brew. Full-bodied with a good hop aftertaste.

Jeddart Justice (OG 1046, ABV 4.7%)

Dark Dunter (OG 1050, ABV 4.8%)
Bursting with oatmeal and chocolate aromas complemented by dark roasted malts and a rich aftertaste.

Proper IPA (OG 1050, ABV 5%)

6.2 IPA (OG 1060, ABV 6%)
With quadruple the hops of a typical IPA, this dark chestnut brown-coloured beer has a bold citrus aroma and a biscuit bitter aftertaste.

Old Jock (OG 1070, ABV 6.7%)
Strong, sweetish and fruity in the finish.

Brown Cow

Brown Cow Road, Barlow, North Yorkshire, YO8 8EH
☎ (01757) 618947 🌐 browncowbrewery.co.uk

Brewing since 1997, Brown Cow has won awards at many festivals. Keith and Sue Simpson operate a six-barrel plant at its maximum capacity of 17 barrels per week. Handcrafted cask beers brewed using traditional methods are delivered direct from the brewery. ♦RAIB

Sessions (OG 1033, ABV 3.6%)
A pale, hoppy session beer with a refreshing finish and citrus notes in the aftertaste.

White Dragon (OG 1039, ABV 4%)
A pale, aromatic beer with a good level of bitterness, citrus undertones and a clean finish.

Captain Oates Mild (OG 1044, ABV 4.5%)

A dark mild with a complex mix of malts and oats. Well-balanced with undertones of coffee and chocolate.

Mrs Simpsons Thriller in Vanilla (OG 1049, ABV 5.1%)
A rich porter brewed with fresh vanilla pods complementing the dark malts.

Broxbourne

See Fallen Angel

Brumaison SIBA

Unit 7, Crest Industrial Estate, Pattenden Lane, Marden, Kent, TN12 9QJ ☎ 07831 704089 brumaison.beer

The name Brumaison came about from ideas to set up in a small village in France. However, Peter and Caroline decided to keep their 'Brewing Maison' in England after another brewery got there first. Trading since 2016 using a 10-barrel plant, Peter started brewing full time in 2017.

BB Traditional Ale (OG 1036, ABV 3.6%)
Easy-drinking traditional English bitter with plenty of malt and subtle hop flavour.

GB Golden Blonde Ale (OG 1042, ABV 4.4%)
Refreshing ale with the bitterness of a golden ale and the fruit spice of a blonde.

Bullion (OG 1041, ABV 4.5%)

Beulter (OG 1043, ABV 4.6%)

1770 (OG 1054, ABV 4.7%)
Dark brown-coloured London porter with reddish hues. Full malt flavour with hints of coffee and chocolate.

Brunning & Price

See Phoenix & Tombstone

Brunswick SIBA

1 Railway Terrace, Derby, DE1 2RU ☎ 07534 401352 brunswickbrewingcompany.co.uk

Derby's oldest brewery, it is a 10-barrel tower plant built as an extension to the Brunswick Inn in 1991. Bought by Everards in 2002, the brewery is now run separately yet in conjunction with the pub. It supplies the Brunswick Inn, Everards, wholesalers and the free trade within 100 miles. Brunswick also swaps with other breweries. Beers are also produced under the Engine Shed Project brand name. !! ♦ RAIB

White Feather (OG 1038, ABV 3.6%)
Pale yet full-bodied session beer, easy drinking with a citrus twist.

Triple Hop (OG 1040, ABV 4%)
Straw-coloured ale with a bitter astringency.

The Usual (OG 1042, ABV 4.2%)
A traditional English malty best bitter, smooth with hints of toffee.

Railway Porter (OG 1045, ABV 4.3%)
A classic dark-coloured porter, lightly-hopped with chocolate and coffee notes.

Rocket (OG 1047, ABV 4.7%)
A New World IPA with citrus, apricot and mango flavours.

Black Sabbath (OG 1058, ABV 6%)
A strong, dark-coloured ale with finely balanced flavours of liquorice, coffee and chocolate.

Brewed under the Engine Shed Project brand name:

Ubiquitous (OG 1058, ABV 6%)

Brythonic

Tyersall Annexe, The Hudnalls, St Briavels, GL15 6RT ☎ 07766 652837 doug.morgan@hotmail.co.uk

One of the new breed of nanobreweries, having begun brewing in a Bristol suburb on a small scale in 2015. The brewery relocated to the Gloucestershire/Welsh border village of St Briavels. Beers can be found at the Doghouse, Coleford. RAIB

Raven (OG 1048, ABV 5.3%)

Spark (OG 1048, ABV 5.3%)

Buccaneer

Sycamore House, Sutton Quays Business Park, Sutton Weaver, Cheshire, WA7 3EH buccaneerbreweryltd@gmail.com

Buccaneer began brewing in 2016. Beers are usually named with a pirate theme.

Buckland (NEW)

Higher Thornhill Head, Bideford, Devon, EX39 5NU ☎ (01805) 601625 ☎ 07882 019255 thebucklandbrewers.co.uk

Brewing began in 2016. The brewery specialises in Belgian-style bottle-conditioned beers, which are supplied to around 24 local outlets including pubs, restaurants and farm shops. RAIB

Bucks Star

23 Twizel Close, Stonebridge, Milton Keynes, Buckinghamshire, MK13 0DX ☎ (01908) 590054 bucksstar.beer

A solar-powered brewery, Bucks Star opened in 2015 using a 10-barrel, purpose-built plant. Only organic malt is used and no sugars or syrups are added. The beers are distributed to local pubs, restaurants and garden centres. !! RAIB

No. 1 (OG 1040, ABV 4%)
A deep golden-coloured beer with a good balance between malt and hops. It has a light, dry and refreshing character with a lingering bitter finish.

Waltone (OG 1041, ABV 4%)
A refreshing wheat beer with a strong, distinctive taste.

Magiovinum (OG 1045, ABV 4.5%)
A dark, sweet stout.

Mideltone Pils (OG 1051, ABV 5%)
A unusually dark lager with a balanced hop aroma and flavour.

Bude SIBA

Unit 14c, Kings Hill Industrial Estate, Bude, Cornwall, EX23 8QN

☎ (01288) 359937 🌐 budebrewery.co.uk

Originally established near Launceston in 2011, the brewery moved to Bude to start brewing under the Bude name in 2014.

Neet Light Ale (OG 1037, ABV 3.7%)
Smooth, amber-coloured bitter with assertive and lasting bitterness. Malt, citrus and pine resin flavours. Dryness rises in the finish.

Porthbud (OG 1040, ABV 4%)
Pale brown-coloured bitter with crisp marmalade and lemon hop flavours and dominant bitterness. Hints of malt, honey and tropical fruits.

Haven (OG 1042, ABV 4.2%)
Amber-coloured best bitter with a hop aroma. Hop bitterness dominates taste persisting into the finish, balanced by light malt and fruit.

Summerleaze (OG 1047, ABV 4.7%)
Refreshing copper-coloured strong bitter. Malt with stone fruit flavours balanced by hops. Distinct bitterness and dryness becoming dominant in the finish.

Black Rock (OG 1051, ABV 5.1%)
Dark red-coloured porter with malt aroma. Sweet malt with a hint of roast and bitter flavour with stone fruits throughout.

Buffy's SIBA

Church Lane, Wicklewood, Norfolk, NR18 9QH
☎ (01953) 606962 🌐 buffys.co.uk

Established in 1993, Buffy's brewing capacity is 20 barrels. The brewery owns two pubs, the Wicklewood Cherry Tree, close to where the brewery has recently relocated, and the Foulden White Hart. Barley for all brewing is grown in Norfolk. Around 100 outlets are supplied. ♦RAIB

Norfolk Terrier (OG 1038, ABV 3.8%)
A strong, plummy aroma leads into a sweet, malty beginning. Caramel notes add depth to a long, fruity finish.

Beagle (OG 1040, ABV 4%)

Mild (OG 1042, ABV 4.2%)
Complex with a smooth but grainy feel. Caramel and blackcurrant initially bolster the heavy malt influence. Short, malty finish.

Polly's Folly (OG 1043, ABV 4.3%)
Well-balanced with a definitive malty spine. Elderberry notes and a long, dry, bittersweet finale.

Hopleaf (OG 1044.5, ABV 4.5%)
A gentle hop nose. Strawberries mingle with the hops as the malt gently subsides to leave a bittersweet, dry finish.

Mucky Duck (OG 1044, ABV 4.5%)
Roasted malt throughout with a sweet fruitiness giving depth without becoming dominant. Chewy mouthfeel and lingering finish.

India (OG 1046, ABV 4.6%)

Norwegian Blue (OG 1049, ABV 4.9%)
Nutty caramel aroma. A well-balanced mix of malt and bitterness with caramel, hops, and sweetness. Strong, increasingly bitter finish.

Ale (OG 1055, ABV 5.5%)

Bull Lane

See Stables

Bull of the Woods (NEW)

Brook Farm, Kirby Cane, NR35 2PJ
☎ (01508) 518080 ☎ 07833 702658
✉ info@botwbc.co.uk

Brewing began in 2017.

Bullards

See Redwell

Bullfinch

Arches 886 & 887, Rosendale Road, Herne Hill, London, SE24 9EH ☎ 07899 795823
🌐 thebullfinchbrewery.co.uk

Bullfinch began brewing in 2014 using a 2.5-barrel plant. Production is mainly keg but cask and bottle-conditioned beers are available. !! RAIB

RosendAle (OG 1039, ABV 3.8%)
A traditional bitter with earthy hop notes.

South Eastern Bloc Stout (OG 1060, ABV 5.2%)
Roasty nose and flavour with chocolate, earthy, plum notes. The finish is dry with some dark roast bitterness.

Bullhouse

10 Greengraves Road, Newtownards, Northern Ireland, BT23 5AG ☎ 07562 702825

Bullhouse was set up in 2016 by beer enthusiast and homebrewer William Mayne. It has since expanded from a 2.5-barrel plant to a custom-built 1,000-litre brewhouse with a fermentation capacity of 25,000 litres per year. RAIB

Bullmastiff SIBA

14 Bessemer Close, Leckwith, Cardiff, CF11 8DL
☎ (029) 2066 5292

Office: Units 7-8, Curran Road Industrial Estate, Cardiff, CF10 5DF ✉ bob.bullmastiff@live.co.uk

The brewery was purchased by the present owners following the retirement of the founders Bob and Paul Jenkins. The beers, which replicate the former owners' recipes as a condition of brewery purchase, are available in South-east Wales with the Bears Head, Penarth, serving as the informal brewery tap. The owners have recently secured an interest in the Traders Tavern, Cardiff, and some of the beers are featured there. ♦

Slobberchops (OG 1046, ABV 4.6%)

Welsh Red (OG 1048, ABV 4.8%)

Olde Snarler (OG 1053, ABV 5.1%)

Son of a Bitch (OG 1062, ABV 6%)
A complex, warming amber-coloured ale with a tasty blend of hops, malt and fruit flavours, with increasing bitterness.

Special Reserve (OG 1068, ABV 6.5%)

Bumbling

See Xtreme

Buntingford

Greys Brewhouse, Therfield Road, Royston, Hertfordshire, SG8 9NW
☎ (01763) 250749 ☎ 07851 743799
⊕ buntingfordbrewery.com

⊗ Brewing commenced on the current site in 2005 and has expanded to a capacity of around 60 barrels per week. Two regular beers are brewed year round alongside seasonal/occasional brews and various themed specials. The beers are brewed using water from an on-site well and all liquid waste is treated in a reed bed. The brewery is located on a conservation farm and there is a wide variety of bird life visible from the doors of the brewhouse, often including rare and endangered species. ♦

Twitchell (OG 1038, ABV 3.8%)

Polar Star (OG 1045, ABV 4.4%)

Burley Street

Fox & Newt, 7-9 Burley Street, Leeds, West Yorkshire, LS3 1LD
☎ (0113) 245 4527 ⊕ burleystreetbrewhouse.co.uk

Burley Street Brewhouse is in the cellar of the Fox & Newt pub where the first brewery was installed by Whitbread in the 1980s. The freehold was purchased by the current owners and brewing recommenced in 2010 and then again, after a two-year break, in 2015 by the team from the Whippet Brewing Company. The Pack Horse at Woodhouse is the only other outlet supplied.

Burning Sky SIBA

Place Barn, The Street, Firle, East Sussex, BN8 6LP
☎ (01273) 858080 ⊕ burningskybeer.com

⊗ Burning Sky started brewing in 2013 using a 15-barrel plant, based on the Firle Estate in the South Downs. It is owned and run by Mark Tranter (ex-Dark Star head brewer). The brewery has its own yeast strains suited to the beer styles. It specialises in pale ales and Belgian-inspired farmhouse beers and has an extensive barrel-aging programme. RAIB

Plateau (OG 1035, ABV 3.5%)
Pale gold in colour with a crisp malt edge and sharp bitterness.

Aurora (OG 1056, ABV 5.6%)
A premium strength pale ale with a juicy malt backbone and big citrus and tropical hop flavours.

Devil's Rest IPA (OG 1070, ABV 7%)

Burning Soul

Unit 1, 51 Mott Street, Hockley, Birmingham, B19 3HE
☎ (0121) 439 1490 ☎ 07793 026624
⊕ burningsoulbrewing.com

Established in 2016 by Chris Small and Richard Murphy, who chose the name Burning Soul to reflect their passion for beer and brewing, it's a five-barrel full mash brewery with an on-site brewery tap. !! ♦

Low Clarity (ABV 3%)

Mosaic Session IPA (ABV 4.5%)

Citra Amarillo Sour (ABV 5%)

Mount Olympus (ABV 5.2%)
Yellow in colour with a crisp hop aroma. Aromatic hops in the taste with resinous flavours and a long bitter finish.

OCT IPA (ABV 6.7%)
Pale gold-coloured beer with a fruity hop aroma and a long, hoppy, bitter aftertaste.

Belgian IPA (ABV 6.8%)

Coconut Porter (ABV 6.9%)
Dark brown-coloured beer with coconut in the aroma. A good balance of malt and hops in the taste leading to a fruity aftertaste.

Burnside SIBA

Laurencekirk Business Park, Laurencekirk, AB30 1EY
☎ (01561) 377316 ⊕ burnsidebrewery.co.uk

Burnside began brewing in 2010 using a 2.5-barrel plant and by 2012 had expanded to a 10-barrel plant. Since then the focus has been to establish the brand and range of cask-conditioned ales locally and to develop a range of bottle-conditioned beers. Further expansion is planned. !! ♦ RAIB

Black Katz (OG 1036, ABV 3.6%)

No 1 Pale Ale (OG 1036, ABV 3.6%)

3-BULLZ (OG 1038, ABV 3.8%)

Mad Dogz (OG 1038, ABV 3.8%)
Slight mix of roasted malt and citrus hop session brew.

Golden X (OG 1042, ABV 4.1%)

Wild Rhino (OG 1045, ABV 4.5%)

Chieftains Export (OG 1048, ABV 4.6%)

India Pale Ale (OG 1049, ABV 4.8%)
Full on citrus hop aroma declining through the taste.

After Dark (OG 1050.5, ABV 5%)
A double chocolate oatmeal stout.

M-PIRE (OG 1052, ABV 5.2%)
Sweetish peachy hoppy brew. Very warming.

Stealth (OG 1058, ABV 6%)
A full-bodied, rich, dark ale.

Burnt Mill (NEW)

Unit 10, Woodlands Dairy, Badley, Suffolk, IP6 8RS
⊕ burntmillbrewery.com

Brewing began in 2016 in a former dairy shed. Beers are available in KeyKegs and cans.

Burscough

See Hop Vine

Burton Bridge SIBA

24 Bridge Street, Burton upon Trent, Staffordshire, DE14 1SY
☎ (01283) 510573 ⊕ burtonbridgebrewery.co.uk

The brewery was established in 1982 by Bruce Wilkinson and Geoff Mumford and owns five pubs in the local area, including its CAMRA award-winning brewery tap. More than 300 outlets are supplied direct. ‼ ♦ RAIB

Golden Delicious (OG 1037, ABV 3.8%)
A Burton classic with sulphurous aroma and well-balanced hops and fruit. An apple fruitiness, sharp and refreshing start leads to a lingering, mouth-watering bitter finish with a hint of astringency. Light, crisp and refreshing.

Sovereign Gold (OG 1040, ABV 4%)
Sweet caramel aroma with a grassy hop start with malt overtones. Fresh and fruity with a bitterness that emerges and continues to develop.

XL Bitter (OG 1039, ABV 4%)
Another Burton classic with sulphurous aroma. Golden with fruit and hops and a characteristic lingering aftertaste hinting of toffee apple sweetness.

XL Mild (OG 1040, ABV 4%)
Black treacle initial taste after liquorice aroma. Sweet finish with a touch of bitterness.

Bridge Bitter (OG 1041, ABV 4.2%)
Gentle aroma of malt and fruit. Good balanced start finishing with a robust hop mouthfeel.

Burton Porter (OG 1044, ABV 4.5%)
Chocolate aromas and sweet smooth taste of smoky roasted grain and coffee.

Damson Porter (OG 1044, ABV 4.5%)
Faint roast, caramel and dark fruit nose. Cough mixture and Blackjack beginning. Uncomplicated profile with a fractious mix of bitter fruitiness and yeasty maltiness.

Draught Burton Ale (OG 1048, ABV 4.8%)
Fruity orange aroma leads to hoppy start, hop and fruit body then fruity aftertaste. Dry finish with fruity hints.

Bramble Stout/Top Dog Stout (OG 1049, ABV 5%)
Smoky aroma with a fruit hint. Roast start with briar dry fruit emerging then a sharp dark fruit taste emerges to balance the burnt effect with a sweetish, dry, blackberry finish.

Stairway to Heaven (OG 1049, ABV 5%)
Golden-coloured bitter. A perfectly balanced beer. The fruity and hoppy start leads to a hoppy body with a mouthwatering finish.

Festival Ale (OG 1054, ABV 5.5%)
Caramel aroma with plenty of hop taste balanced by a full-bodied malty sweetness.

Thomas Sykes (OG 1095, ABV 10%)
A sweet shop aroma. Rich, fruity, spirit tastes – warming and dangerously drinkable.

Burton Old Cottage SIBA IFBB

Unit 10, Eccleshall Business Park, Burton upon Trent, Staffordshire, DE14 1PT
☎ (01283) 542656 🌐 oldcottagebeer.co.uk

The brewery was originally installed in the old Heritage Brewery. When the site was taken over it moved to a modern industrial unit. The brewery was sold in 2005 and again in 2017. ‼♦

Oak Ale (OG 1044, ABV 4%)
Tawny-coloured, full-bodied bitter. A sweet start with balanced fruit gives way to a slight roast taste with some caramel for interest. A dry, hoppy finish satisfies the palate.

Chestnut (OG 1042, ABV 4.2%)
A dark-coloured session ale with a touch of bitterness and a pleasant, full aftertaste.

Stout (OG 1047, ABV 4.7%)
Roast aroma with background fruit, roast tastes with gentle sweetness. Bitterness develops surprisingly from the sweet start to leave a sharp-edged mouthfeel. Roast throughout with a malt background.

Pastiche (OG 1050, ABV 5.2%)
A smooth, balanced ale with a complex taste and aroma.

Halcyon Daze (OG 1050, ABV 5.3%)
Tawny-coloured and creamy with touches of hop, fruit and malt aroma. Fruity taste and finish.

Burton Road

See Mobberley

Burton Town

Unit 8, Falcon Close, Burton upon Trent, Staffordshire, DE14 1SG
☎ (01283) 510839 🌐 burton.town

Open since 2015, Burton Town is run by head brewer Steve Haynes from converted premises off Hawkins Lane. Currently using a six-barrel plant, there are plans for expansion. An on-site tap is open to the public on Saturdays and before Burton Albion home games. ‼

Swan/Albion (OG 1040, ABV 3.9%)
A pale ale with layers of toasted malt and a balanced hop finish.

Scorned Woman (OG 1040, ABV 4%)

Modwena (OG 1052, ABV 4.8%)
A velvety oatmeal stout with chocolate notes.

Thomcat (OG 1051, ABV 5.1%)
An unfined, amber-coloured beer with a strong citrus hop aroma. Citrus hop flavours with a hint of biscuity malt.

Burton IPA (OG 1054, ABV 5.6%)
A traditional, strong IPA. Full-flavoured with a hint of toffee and a long-lasting, bittersweet finish.

Burtonwood

Bold Lane, Burtonwood, Cheshire, WA5 4TH
☎ (01925) 220022 🌐 thomashardybrewery.co.uk

Thomas Hardy's only brewery was acquired by Molson Coors in 2015. Currently producing no real ale, and operating solely as a contract brewer.

Bushy's SIBA

Mount Murray Brewery, Mount Murray, Braddan, Isle of Man, IM4 1JE
☎ (01624) 661244 🌐 bushys.com

Launched in 1986 as a brewpub, Bushys relocated in 1990 when demand outgrew capacity. Bushys goes one step further than the Manx Pure Beer Law preferring the German Reinheitsgebot (Pure Beer Law). ‼♦

Castletown Bitter (OG 1035, ABV 3.5%)
A light, golden-coloured beer full of floral and citrus hints. A refreshing session beer.

Ruby (1874) Mild (OG 1035, ABV 3.5%)
Classic full-bodied malty ruby mild with sweet caramel flavours throughout, and well-balanced hops.

Bitter (OG 1038, ABV 3.8%)
A traditional malty and hoppy beer with good balance. The fruit lasts through to the bitter finish.

Norseman (OG 1040, ABV 4.2%)
Pilsner-style beer, lightly-hopped and refreshing.

Old Bushy Tail (OG 1045, ABV 4.5%)
A red-coloured beer with a pronounced hop and malt aroma. Slightly sweet and malty on the palate with distinct orange tones. The finish is malty and hoppy with a hint of toffee.

Red (OG 1047, ABV 4.7%)
Mahogany-coloured beer with a full mouthfeel, traditional, dry, hoppy bitterness and a rich, dark fruit aroma.

Butchers Arms

Butchers Arms, Woolhope, Herefordshire, HR1 4RF
☎ (01432) 860281 butchersarmswoolhope.com

Founded in 2016 in a building adjacent to the 17th century Butchers Arms.

Butcombe SIBA

Cox's Green, Wrington, Somerset, BS40 5PA
☎ (01934) 863963 butcombe.com

Originally established in 1978, Butcombe moved to a purpose-built brewery with a 150-barrel plant in 2005. The brewery was bought by the Jersey-based Liberation Group for a reported £15m in 2015. Around 500 outlets are supplied direct and similar numbers via wholesalers and pub companies. Butcombe opened a new distribution centre with a bottling line in Bridgewater in 2018. The brewery has an estate of around 20 managed and 20 tenanted pubs. !! ♦

Adam Henson's Rare Breed (OG 1038, ABV 3.8%)
Subtle aroma of unripe fruit with sulphurous hints. Malty flavour is masked by dry bitterness, which continues into the finish.

Original (OG 1039, ABV 4%)
A brown-coloured bitter with little aroma. Sweet and malty taste with faint fruit notes. The hop gradually asserts itself leaving a slightly bitter finish.

Gold (OG 1045, ABV 4.4%)
Amber-coloured golden ale with light aroma of fruit and hops, leading to well-balanced flavours of malt, pale fruit and hops. Bitter aftertaste.

Bute

15-17 Columshill Street, Rothesay, Isle of Bute, PA20 0DN
☎ (01700) 504260 ☎ 07980 259511
butebrewco.co.uk

Situated in the centre of Rothesay on the Isle of Bute, brewing began in 2015. Beers are supplied to several local outlets, and further afield. Beer festivals are also supplied. !!

Scalpsie Blonde (OG 1038, ABV 3.8%)

Red (OG 1042, ABV 4.2%)

The Maids (OG 1043, ABV 4.3%)

Butts

Northfield Farm, Wantage Road, Great Shefford, Berkshire, RG17 7BY
☎ (01488) 648133 buttsbrewery.com

The brewery was set up in a converted barn in 1994. In 2002 the owners took the decision to become dedicated to organic production; all the beers brewed use organic malted barley and organic hops and are certified by the Soil Association. ♦ RAIB

Jester (OG 1036, ABV 3.5%)
A pale brown-coloured session bitter with a hoppy aroma and a hint of fruit. The taste balances malt, hops, fruit and bitterness with a hoppy aftertaste.

Traditional (OG 1040, ABV 4%)
A pale brown-coloured bitter that is quite soft on the tongue with hoppy citrus flavours accompanying a gentle bittersweetness. A long, dry aftertaste is dominated by fruity hops.

Barbus Barbus (OG 1046, ABV 4.6%)
Golden ale with a fruity hoppy aroma and a hint of malt. Hops dominate taste and aftertaste, accompanied by fruitiness and bitterness, with a hint of balancing sweetness.

Buxton SIBA

Units 4 A & B, Staden Business Park, Staden Lane, Buxton, Derbyshire, SK17 9RZ
☎ (01298) 244200 ☎ 07754 015743
buxtonbrewery.co.uk

Set up in 2009 as a five-barrel plant, Buxton now uses a 20-barrel plant. Its brewery tap is in Buxton and there is a tasting room at the brewery with views of the Derbyshire countryside. A wide range of small-run beers are brewed throughout the year. ♦ RAIB

SPA (Special Pale Ale) (OG 1041, ABV 4.1%)
A fruity session IPA.

Buzzard

Unit 3, Vale Park, Colomendy Industrial Estate, Denbigh, LL16 5TA ☎ 07972 202880
buzzardbrewery.co.uk

Brewing commenced in 2013 on a 2.5-barrel plant in a former farm building. The brewery has now relocated to Denbigh to larger premises. 30-50 pubs are supplied within a 30-mile radius. ♦

Buzzard Session Ale (BSA) (OG 1037, ABV 3.6%)

Craigmill Gold (ABV 3.7%)
A complex golden ale with a lingering hoppy aftertaste.

Hoppin' Buzzard (OG 1038, ABV 3.9%)

Village Bitter (OG 1039, ABV 3.9%)
A malty session bitter with a dry taste and subtle hop characteristics, leading to a bitter finish.

Bwncath (OG 1042, ABV 4.2%)

Pale of Clwyd (OG 1042, ABV 4.2%)
A light and fruity best bitter with a sweetish initial taste and a hoppy, dry finish.

1492 (OG 1043, ABV 4.3%)

Ebony (ABV 4.4%)

Oatmeal stout with a rich chocolate coffee aroma, hints of dried fruit and a dry, satisfying, hoppy finish.

Triple C (OG 1044, ABV 4.5%)

Vale Ale (OG 1045, ABV 4.5%) ◆
A dark-brown-coloured best bitter, smooth and malty with a dry, hoppy finish.

Golden Buzzard (OG 1045, ABV 4.7%)

Bwthyn

See Anglesey

By The Horns SIBA

Unit 25, Summerstown, London, SW17 0BQ
☎ (020) 3417 7338 ⊕ bythehorns.co.uk

⊗ By the Horns began brewing in 2012 using a 5.5-barrel plant, since upgraded to a 12-barrel. It is located in an industrial unit near Wimbledon Stadium. The brewery tap is open six days a week (Tue-Sun) and hosts regular events.

Stiff Upper Lip (OG 1038, ABV 3.8%) ◆
A classic amber-coloured bitter, well-balanced with hops to the fore and a hint of citrus. Dry bitter finish.

Hop Air Balloon (ABV 4.2%)
A session IPA bursting with citrus and passion fruit notes.

Mayor of Garratt (OG 1042, ABV 4.3%) ◆
Amber-coloured best bitter with sweet biscuit and orange fruit flavour. Long, dry finish with some bitterness and peppery hop.

Diamond Geezer (OG 1049, ABV 4.9%) ◆
Malty, hoppy, red-coloured ale with blackcurrant, citrus and faint roast notes. Bitterness develops and builds in the aftertaste.

Lambeth Walk (OG 1051, ABV 5.1%) ◆
Well-balanced black porter with hops and a little fruit throughout. The roasted bitterness is complemented by the malt notes.

By The Mile

22 Detling Avenue, Broadstairs, Kent, CT10 1SL
☎ 07900 954680 ✉ jon@bythemilebrewery.co.uk

⊗ By the Mile began brewing in 2016 in domestic premises. RAIB

Byatt's SIBA

Unit 7-8, Lythalls Lane Industrial Estate, Lythalls Lane, Coventry, CV6 6FL
☎ (024) 7663 7996 ⊕ byattsbrewery.co.uk

Byatt's was established in 2011. In 2016 it expanded to a 12-barrel plant, still located on the north side of Coventry, just two doors down from the old brewery. A brewhouse bar is open on Saturdays and some Sundays. Beers are supplied across the region. !! ♦ RAIB

XK Dark (OG 1038, ABV 3.5%) ◆
Liquorice aroma, soft smoky tastes. Sweet but giving hoppy sides.

Coventry Bitter (OG 1039, ABV 3.8%)

Platinum Blonde (OG 1039, ABV 3.9%)

Big Cat (OG 1042, ABV 4%)

Brewhouse Best (OG 1040, ABV 4.1%)
Chestnut-coloured ale. Rich malt, toffee flavour with a balanced bitter finish.

Phoenix Gold (OG 1043, ABV 4.2%)

Urban Red (OG 1047, ABV 4.5%)

Regal Blond (OG 1053, ABV 5.2%)

Cader SIBA

Unit 4, Marian Mawr Enterprise Park, Dolgellau, LL40 1UU
☎ (01341) 388080 ☎ 07546 272372
⊕ caderales.com

Cader Ales was founded in 2012 by a husband-and-wife team. It was expanded in 2013 to its present five-barrel capacity and is situated close to the centre of the picturesque market town of Dolgellau. Beer is supplied to the licensed trade in North and Mid-west Wales. !!

Cwrw Cregennan (ABV 3.8%)
A golden ale with citrus notes and a soft malt flavour, enhanced by a little local honey.

Gold (OG 1038, ABV 3.8%)
A light, hoppy golden ale with a subtle aroma of honey, lemon and tarragon.

Machlyd Mawddach (ABV 3.9%)
A light and refreshing ale with added kaffir lime giving a fruity, citrus aroma.

Idris Bitter (OG 1041, ABV 4.1%)
Traditional bitter with caramel and spicy notes.

Tallyllyn Pale Ale (OG 1044, ABV 4.4%)
A classic IPA, refreshingly bitter, citrus floral notes.

Red Bandit (OG 1050, ABV 5%)
A warm ruby-coloured ale based on a traditional recipe, with spicy berry aromas.

Caffle

The Old School, Llawhaden, SA67 8DS
☎ (01437) 541 502 ⊕ cafflebrewery.co.uk

⊗ Caffle began brewing in 2013 using a four-barrel plant producing ale in small batches, mainly for the local market. Each year a green hop ale is produced using Pembrokeshire grown hops via Caffle's hop co-op. !! RAIB

Skirp Gold (OG 1039, ABV 3.8%)
Golden ale with fruity, spicy aromas. Bitter grapefruit flavour.

Quay Ale (OG 1044, ABV 4%)
An amber-coloured ale, caramel with a light hoppy citrus flavour. Balanced slightly to the malty side.

Sholly Amber (OG 1044, ABV 4%)
Light chestnut in colour with a good malt/hop balance.

Sprilly Maid (OG 1044, ABV 4%)
Light chestnut-coloured beer infused with rosemary to give a slight ginger finish.

Kift Blonde (OG 1044, ABV 4.3%)
Straw-coloured ale with citrus and floral notes, flavoured with nettle tips.

In The Grip (OG 1052, ABV 4.7%)
Ruby-red in colour, malty caramel, slightly sweet, warming.

Skaddly Puck (OG 1048, ABV 4.8%)
IPA using a blend of hops to give a distinctive hoppy, citrus flavour.

Drop Squint (OG 1052, ABV 5.2%)
Light golden in colour, smooth, clean-tasting with honey, malt and biscuit flavours.

Cairngorm SIBA

Unit 12, Dalfaber Industrial Estate, Aviemore, PH22 1ST
☎ (01479) 812222 cairngormbrewery.com

Cairngorm brews using a 20-barrel plant. Now with its own bottling line, it supplies the free trade as far south as the central belt and nationally via wholesalers. In 2016, in partnership with the Cobbs Group, it bought the brands of the Loch Ness Brewing Co and now brews selected beers under the Loch Ness brand name. ‼ ♦

Nessies Monster Mash (OG 1040, ABV 4.1%)
A traditional bitter with plenty of bitterness and strong malt flavour and a fruity background. Lingering bitterness in the aftertaste with diminishing sweetness.

Stag (OG 1040, ABV 4.1%)
A best bitter with plenty of roast and hop throughout. This tawny-coloured brew also has plenty of malt in the lingering bittersweet aftertaste.

Trade Winds (OG 1043, ABV 4.3%)
A citrus fruity hop and elderflower nose following on through to the bittersweet finish.

Black Gold (OG 1044, ABV 4.4%)
Roast malt dominates throughout, slight smokiness in aroma leading to a liquorice and blackcurrant background taste giving it a background sweetness. Very long, dry bitter finish.

Gold (OG 1044, ABV 4.5%)
Fruit and hops to the fore with a hint of caramel in this sweetish brew.

Highland IPA (OG 1049, ABV 5%)
Refreshing, light-coloured, citrus-hopped IPA.

Wildcat (OG 1049.5, ABV 5.1%)
A full-bodied, warming strong bitter. Malt predominates but there is an underlying hop character through to the well-balanced aftertaste.

Brewed under the Loch Ness Brewery brand name:

SaaziNess (ABV 4.5%)

HoppyNess (ABV 5%)

LochNess (ABV 5.1%)

Caledonian

42 Slateford Road, Edinburgh, EH11 1PH
☎ (0131) 337 1286 caledonianbeer.com

The brewery was founded by Lorimer and Clark in 1869 and was sold to Vaux of Sunderland in 1919. In 1987 the brewery was saved from closure by a management buy-out and became independent. The brewery was purchased by S&N in 2004 and became part of Heineken in 2008. Guest beers, sometimes of an unusual style, are produced for occasions throughout the year, and there is a rolling programme of special beers covering each of the seasons. A pilot brewery 'Wee George' named after the founding father George Lorimer, was opened in 2015 to allow small scale brews of new recipes. ‼ ♦

Deuchars IPA (OG 1039.5, ABV 3.8%)
Golden-coloured session ale with hop aroma and dry bitter finish. Balanced, with malt adding body and fruit a balancing sweetness.

Edinburgh Castle 80/- (OG 1042.4, ABV 4.1%)
A predominantly malty, brown-coloured beer with soft roast and caramel throughout. Fruit gives sweetness, typical of a Scottish 80/-.

Brewed for Heineken:

John Smith's Bitter (ABV 3.5%)

Calverley's SIBA

23a Hooper Street, Cambridge, CB1 2NZ
☎ (01223) 312370 ☎ 07769 537342
calverleys.com

This small central Cambridge brewery was started in 2013 by Sam Calverley and his brother Tom. The one-barrel plant is located in an old industrial unit close to the city centre. The major part of production is sold on the premises, but beer festivals and local pubs are supplied on demand. ‼

Blonde (ABV 3.7%)

Porter (ABV 5%)

Calvors SIBA

Home Farm, Coddenham Green, Suffolk, IP6 9UN
☎ (01449) 711055 calvorsbrewery.com

Calvors Brewery was established in 2008 and brews three craft lagers, as well as cask-conditioned beers. RAIB V

Lodestar Festival Ale (OG 1038, ABV 3.8%)
A rich, straw-coloured beer with a gentle sweetness and honey aroma.

Smooth Hoperator (OG 1040, ABV 4%)
An easy-drinking pale ale with a background sweetness.

Cambridge

Cambridge Brew House, 1 King Street, Cambridge, CB1 1LH
☎ (01223) 858155 thecambridgebrewhouse.com

Brewing began in 2013 on an on-site microbrewery in the Cambridge Brew House. ♦

Camden Town

Unit 1, Navigation Park, Morson Road, Ponders End, London, EN3 4NQ
☎ (020) 7485 1671 camdentownbrewery.com

No real ale. Bought by A-B InBev in 2016. A modern, automated brewhouse situated in five railway arches underneath Kentish Town West railway station with an on-site brewery tap. A second brewery in Ponders End opened in 2017. ‼

Camerons

Lion Brewery, Stranton, Hartlepool, County Durham, TS24 7QS
☎ (01429) 852000 cameronsbrewery.com

⊛Camerons was founded in 1865 and is once again family owned. The brewery has an estate of more than 70, including the Head of Steam pubs. Beers are also contract brewed for Copper Dragon Brewery. ‼ ♦

Strongarm (OG 1041, ABV 4%)
A well-rounded, ruby-red-coloured ale with a distinctive, tight creamy head; initially fruity, but with a good balance of malt, hops and moderate bitterness.

A-Hop-Alypse Now (ABV 4.3%)
A golden-coloured beer with a citrus aroma and satisfying hop flavour.

Road Crew (ABV 4.5%)
An American-style pale ale packed full of hoppy citrus and blackcurrant flavours.

Campbells (NEW) SIBA

Unit 9, Southpark Industrial Estate, Peebles, EH45 9ED
☎ 07899 653151 🌐 campbells-brewery.com

⊗Campbells was established in 2017 in Peebles, supplying pubs in the Borders, Edinburgh and the Lothians. The brewery has three fermentation vessels, using local malt from East Lothian, and has also invested in a bottling plant, which has an initial capacity of 3,000 bottles per week. ‼

Flintlock Golden Ale (OG 1035, ABV 3.7%)
A session ale with a fruity, citrus hop flavour.

Gunner (OG 1039, ABV 4.3%)
A well-balanced, crisp blonde ale.

Campervan SIBA

Bonnington Business Centre, 112 Jane Street, Edinburgh, EH6 5HG
☎ (0131) 553 3373 ☎ 07786 566000
🌐 campervanbrewery.com

Campervan began brewing in 2016 in a private garage but also in a 1973 VW campervan, hence the name. The van is used as a mobile sales outlet at beer festivals and other outdoor events. It expanded to a new 10-barrel facility in Edinburgh in 2017. A tap room is open on Fridays and Saturdays.

Blonde Voyage (OG 1038, ABV 3.8%)

All Shook Up (OG 1040, ABV 4%)

Mutiny on the Bounty (OG 1042, ABV 4.2%)

Canopy SIBA

Arch 1127, Bath Factory Estate, 41 Norwood Road, Herne Hill, London, SE24 9AJ
☎ (020) 8671 9496 ☎ 07792 463386
🌐 canopybeer.com

⊗Canopy started brewing in 2014 and opened a tap room in 2015. ‼♦RAIB

Sunray Pale Ale (ABV 4.2%)
Unfined, zesty, fruity refreshing golden-coloured pale ale with a building bitter hoppiness.

Tall Trees Session IPA (ABV 4.2%)
A session IPA with grapefruit notes.

Champion Kolsch (ABV 4.5%)
A crisp, fresh and light Kolsch-style beer.

Brockwell IPA (ABV 5.6%)
Smooth and well-rounded IPA with a tropical fruit hop flavour.

Canterbury Ales SIBA

Unit 7, Stour Valley Business Park, Ashford Road, Chartham, Kent, CT4 7HF
☎ (01227) 732541 ☎ 07944 657978
🌐 canterbury-ales.co.uk

⊗Brewing commenced in 2010. An eight-barrel plant is used. ‼♦

The Wife of Bath's Ale (OG 1038, ABV 3.9%)
A golden-coloured beer with strong bitterness and grapefruit hop character, leading to a long, dry finish.

The Reeve's Ale (OG 1040, ABV 4.1%)

The Miller's Ale (OG 1044, ABV 4.5%)

Canterbury Brewers SIBA

Foundry Brew Pub, White Horse Lane, Canterbury, Kent, CT1 2RU
☎ (01227) 455899 🌐 thefoundrycanterbury.co.uk

⊗Canterbury Brewers started brewing in the Foundry Brewpub (formerly a Victorian foundry) in the heart of Canterbury in 2011. The eight-barrel plant is purpose-built. Popular events are held there including the Kent Green Hop Festival (late Sep/early Oct). A wide range of spirits is now distilled in the brewpub and three ciders are produced. ‼♦RAIB V

Cap House

444-446 Bradford Road, Batley, West Yorkshire, WF17 5LW
☎ (01924) 479909 ☎ 07981 858270
🌐 caphousebrewery.co.uk

⊛Cap House began in 2011 using a 2.5-barrel plant as a joint venture between Peter Lister, who has a plastics business at the location, and Gary Wardman of the Reindeer Inn in Overton, which is the brewery tap. ♦

Miners a Pint (OG 1038, ABV 3.8%)
A tangy session bitter with a smooth mouthfeel balanced by a toffee undertone and a deep, dry finish with lingering fruit notes.

Hey Blondie (OG 1044, ABV 4.2%)

Hoppylicious (OG 1040, ABV 4.2%)
A light, hoppy beer with a well-balanced, fruity taste. Refreshing citrus and grapefruit flavours for a bittersweet finish.

Captain Cook

White Swan, 1 West End, Stokesley, North Yorkshire, TS9 5BL
☎ (01642) 714985

Office: Unit 9, Terry Dicken Industrial Estate, Station Road, Stokesley, TS9 7AE

⊛The Captain Cook Brewery is located behind the 18th-century White Swan pub. The brewery, which started in 1999, uses a four-barrel plant. Under new ownership from July 2017. ♦

Navigator (OG 1040, ABV 4%)
A light ale with a hint of grapefruit and spruce.

Sunset (OG 1040, ABV 4%)

A smooth, light ale with hints of citrus flavours.

Slipway (OG 1042, ABV 4.2%)
A light-coloured, full-flavoured, hoppy ale with a smooth malt aftertaste.

Endeavour (OG 1043, ABV 4.3%)
Brown-coloured ale with a bitter finish.

Black Porter (OG 1044, ABV 4.4%)
Chocolate notes and dominant roast flavours lead to a dry, bitter finish.

APA (OG 1047, ABV 4.7%)
Fruity, well-bittered American-style pale ale.

IPA (OG 1051, ABV 5.1%)

Carlisle SIBA

Unit 2, 12a Kingstown Broadway, Kingstown Industrial Estate, Carlisle, Cumbria, CA3 0HA
☎ (01228) 532928 ☎ 07423 595921

Office: Spinners Arms, Cummersdale, Carlisle, CA2 6BD thespinnersarms.org.uk

Carlisle Brewing Company is a family-run brewery established in 2013. Initially using a 2.5-barrel plant in a shed behind the owner's freehouse, by 2015 it had expanded to a 10-barrel plant in an industrial unit. Beer is available in the Spinners Arms and other local outlets. !! ♦

Pale Ale (OG 1039, ABV 3.8%)
A traditional pale ale, light and crisp with biscuit tastes.

Spun Gold (OG 1043, ABV 4.2%)
A reddish golden-coloured beer with a sweet taste followed by hops to complement the balanced finish.

Flaxen (OG 1042, ABV 4.5%)
A blonde ale, well-balanced with a hoppy bouquet.

Magic Number (OG 1045, ABV 4.5%)
A premium bitter, soft and smooth with caramel and toffee flavours.

Nut Brown (OG 1048, ABV 4.7%)
Sweet, mild and characterful amber-coloured ale with predominately nutty and roast flavours make for a long, quaffable strong ale.

Oatmeal Stout (OG 1048, ABV 4.7%)
An oatmeal stout with a soft mouthfeel and coffee, chocolate and smoky aromas.

The Carlisle Experiment (ABV 5.6%)

Carlsberg-Tetley

Jacobson House, 140 Bridge Street, Northampton, NN1 1PZ
☎ (01604) 668866 carlsberg.co.uk

International lager brewery, which, while brewing no real ale, is a major distributor of cask beer. The Tetley-owned real ales are brewed under contract by Marston's.

Castle SIBA

Unit 9a-7, Restormel Industrial Estate, Liddicoat Road, Lostwithiel, Cornwall, PL22 0HD ☎ 07880 349032
castlebrewery.co.uk

The brewery was established in 2007 using a one-barrel plant. It was re-equipped in 2016 with a new 200-litre plant. All brews are unfined, and are suitable for vegans. The brewery carries out its own bottling, and some for other breweries. ♦ RAIB V

Golden Gauntlet (OG 1038, ABV 4%)
Light, golden-coloured bitter with a gentle fruity nose. Heavy malt and bitter taste dominate the fruity hop, persisting into the finish.

Cornish Best Bitter (OG 1040, ABV 4.2%)

Once a Knight (OG 1048, ABV 5%)

Castle Combe

See Flying Monk

Castle Eden

8 East Cliff Road, Spectrum Business Park, Seaham, SR7 7PS
☎ (0191) 581 5711 ☎ 07768 044484
castleedenbrewery.com

Using the name of the former Castle Eden Brewery having acquired the intellectual rights and recipes, a new 20-barrel commercial plant was installed in 2015 along with a bottling/kegging plant. Besides its own brand production, the brewery also contract brews, including for HB Clark Brewery (Clark's). ♦

Ale (ABV 4.2%)
Light, creamy golden ale with an initial sweet surge of flavour followed by a slightly bitter aftertaste.

Brewed under the Merrie City brand name:

Atlantic Hop (OG 1040, ABV 4%)

Cascadian (OG 1040, ABV 4%)

Crystal Gold (OG 1042, ABV 4.2%)

Contract brewed for HB Clark Brewery:

Classic Blonde (OG 1039, ABV 3.9%)

English Pale Ale (ABV 4%)

Castle Rock SIBA

Queensbridge Road, Nottingham, NG2 1NB
☎ (0115) 985 1615 castlerockbrewery.co.uk

Castle Rock was established in 1998. From small beginnings, the brewery now has a capacity of 360 barrels per week, distributed through its estate of 25 pubs and further afield via wholesalers. Regular beers produced include a core range of four and a variety of yearly seasonals and specials, which include four Nottinghamian Celebration Ales a year and the 2.0 range, which is unfined, vegan-friendly and embraces modern brewing techniques. The brewery occasionally produces unfined, vegan friendly, experimental beer under the banner of Traffic Street Specials. !! ♦ RAIB V

Black Gold (OG 1037, ABV 3.8%)
A dark ruby mild. Full-bodied and fairly bitter.

Harvest Pale (OG 1037, ABV 3.8%)
Pale yellow-coloured beer, full of hop aroma and flavour. Refreshing with a mellowing aftertaste.

Preservation Fine Ale (OG 1044, ABV 4.4%)
A traditional copper-coloured English best bitter with malt predominant. Fairly bitter with a residual sweetness.

Sherwood Reserve (OG 1045, ABV 4.5%)

An earthy yet smooth-tasting dark stout with a smoked roastiness through to a roast bitter finish

Elsie Mo (OG 1045, ABV 4.7%)
A strong golden ale with floral hops evident in the aroma. Citrus hops are mellowed by a slight sweetness.

Midnight Owl (OG 1055, ABV 5.5%)
Black IPA with roast malts, fruity hops and a slightly sweet finish.

Screech Owl (OG 1055, ABV 5.5%)
A classic golden-coloured IPA with an intensely hoppy aroma and bitter taste with a little balancing sweetness.

Castlegate SIBA

Unit 13, Cillefwr Industrial Estate, Johnstown, SA31 3RB
☎ (01267) 468150
✉ castlegatebrewery@outlook.com

Castlegate began brewing in 2015 as a one-man operation. RAIB

Best Bitter (OG 1044, ABV 4.4%)

Towy Gold (OG 1044, ABV 4.4%)

Merlins Own (OG 1052, ABV 5.2%)

Castor SIBA

30 Peterborough Road, Castor, Cambridgeshire, PE5 7AX
☎ (01733) 380337 castorales.co.uk

This three-barrel brewery, established in 2009, is located in a specially converted outhouse in the garden of the founder brewer. Several local outlets feature the beers as well as many national beer festivals. !! ♦ RAIB

Roman Gold (OG 1037, ABV 3.7%)
Golden-coloured session bitter imparting refreshing citrus and fruit notes.

Hopping Toad (OG 1040, ABV 4.1%)
A light golden-coloured bitter, the pale malt balance by hops giving a refreshing citrus, flowery finish with a fruity aftertaste.

Salters Tree (OG 1043, ABV 4.3%)
Biscuit malt giving sweetness balanced by hops for a bitter finish.

Old Scarlet (OG 1045, ABV 4.6%)
A complex grain bill produces a ruby-coloured, malty beer balanced by subtle hops.

Cat Asylum (NEW)

12 Besthorpe Road, Collingham, Nottinghamshire, NG23 7NP
☎ (01636) 892229 ☎ 07773 502653
cat-asylum.com

Established in 2017, Cat Asylum is a microbrewery specialising in historic recipes from Britain and around the world. RAIB

Caveman

The Cave (below The George & Dragon), 1 London Road, Swanscombe, Kent, DA10 0LQ ☎ 07769 710665 cavemanbrewery.co.uk

Caveman began brewing in 2012 and moved to its current site beneath the George & Dragon pub in 2013 using a four-barrel plant. It is named for the local discovery in the 1930s of skull fragments from a Palaeolithic human, then the oldest remains found in the UK. Beers can be found nationwide through various wholesalers with direct supply to London, Kent and parts of Sussex. ♦ RAIB

Palaeolithic (OG 1038, ABV 3.8%)
A pale ale with some slight malt sweetness.

Neolithic (OG 1041, ABV 4.1%)
A hoppy pale ale with a straightforward malt character that lets the citrus, grapefruit and pine flavours shine through.

Neanderthal (OG 1044, ABV 4.4%)
Full of roast and caramel malt flavours and traditional Kent hops.

Cavedweller (OG 1059, ABV 5.8%)
A rich, full-bodied porter. Chocolate and coffee notes come through in the malt and dark berry flavours from the hops.

Caythorpe SIBA

c/o Black Horse, 29 Main Street, Caythorpe, Nottinghamshire, NG14 7ED
☎ (0115) 966 4933 ☎ 07807 583724

Office: Trentham Cottage, Boat Lane, Hoveringham, Nottinghamshire, NG14 7JP
caythorpebrewery.co.uk

Established in 1996 using a 2.5-barrel plant in a building at the rear of the Black Horse pub, the brewery upgraded to a six-barrel plant in 2010. !!

Cellar Boys (NEW)

c/o White Hart, 184 New Cross Road, New Cross Gate, London, SE14 5AA
☎ (020) 7277 6655

Originally brewing in the cellar of the White Hart pub, the plant is still in use but most of production is now brewed using spare capacity at Bianca Road Brew Co (qv).

Cellar Head SIBA

Unit 16, New Place Farm, Pump Lane, Framfield, East Sussex, TN22 5EQ
☎ (01825) 890078 cellarheadbrewing.com

Cellar Head is a microbrewery in the heart of the Weald countryside. ♦ RAIB V

Sub Three (ABV 2.7%)

Session Bitter (ABV 3.5%)

Amber (ABV 4%)

Golden Ale (ABV 4.3%)

Single Hop Pale Ale (ABV 4.6%)

India Pale Ale (ABV 5%)

Celt Experience

See Evan Evans

Cerddin SIBA

c/o Cross Inn, Maesteg Road, Cwmfelin, CF34 9LB

☎ (01656) 732476 ☎ 07949 652237
🌐 cerddinbrewery.co.uk

Established in 2010 using a 2.5-barrel plant in a converted garage adjacent to the owner's pub, now enlarged to a four-barrel plant. Beer is usually only available in the pub. ‼ ♦ RAIB

Cerne Abbas SIBA

Black Hill Barn, Sherborne Road, Cerne Abbas, Dorset, DT2 7SJ ☎ 07506 303407

Office: The Mill House, Mill Lane, Cerne Abbas, Dorset, DT2 7LB 🌐 cerneabbasbrewery.com

⊗ Established in 2014 by Vic Irvine and Jodie Moore. Operating a five-barrel plant, the beers are made as naturally as possible using local, chalk-filtered water. Many seasonal beers are produced, occasionally using locally-sourced barley and interesting non-conventional ingredients. Also contract brews beers for Dt Ales, Upwey, for sale in the Royal Standard Inn. ♦

Responsibly (OG 1035, ABV 3.2%)

Ale (OG 1040, ABV 3.8%)
A triple-hopped, well-balanced, tawny-coloured ale with a full mouthfeel and refreshing finish.

Blonde (OG 1042, ABV 4.2%)

Watercress Warrior (OG 1042, ABV 4.5%)
A pale ale made using local watercress; crisp with distinct spicy and mineral tones.

Gurt Stout (OG 1058, ABV 6.2%)
Silky smooth, full-bodied and rich stout.

Chadlington

Chapel Road, Chadlington, Oxfordshire, OX7 3LZ ☎ 07931 482807 🌐 chadlingtonbrewery.com

Chadlington began brewing in 2015 on an occasional basis. Beers are supplied to the local area. Increased production on new kit is due to commence.

Golden Ale (OG 1040, ABV 4%)
A light, fruity and refreshing golden ale.

Oxford Blonde (OG 1041, ABV 4%)
A blonde beer with light citrus notes and a crisp, dry finish.

Chain House (NEW)

20 Brookdale, New Longton, Lancashire, PR4 4XL ☎ 07732 688121 🌐 chainhousebrewingco.uk

Brewing began in 2017. There is limited availability of the beers at present but there are plans for expansion.

Lit by Gas (OG 1038, ABV 3.8%)
Tropical fruit flavours and aroma.

Two Coffins (OG 1057, ABV 5.7%)
An American-style IPA with fruity and citrus aromas.

Chalk Hill

Rosary Road, Norwich, NR1 4DA ☎ (01603) 477078 🌐 thecoachthorperoad.co.uk

⊗ Chalk Hill began production in 1993 on a 15-barrel plant. It supplies local pubs and festivals. ‼ ♦

Tap Bitter (OG 1036, ABV 3.6%)
Well-balanced with a light, hoppy character in both aroma and taste. Malt provides contrast. Short dry and bitter finish.

CHB (OG 1042, ABV 4.2%)
Yeasty aroma with malt and hop. Light biscuity airs flow over malt and floral hoppiness. Good balance, gentle finish.

Gold (OG 1043, ABV 4.3%)
A light, hoppy nose. Grapefruit, banana and hops mingle in a well-balanced beginning. The finish develops a growing bitterness.

Dreadnought (OG 1049, ABV 4.9%)
Red brown-coloured beer with a malty, sulphurous nose. Malty with fruit and nut notes. Full-bodied with a long finish.

Chantry SIBA

Units 1 & 2, Callum Court, Gateway Industrial Estate, Parkgate, Rotherham, South Yorkshire, S62 6NR ☎ (01709) 711866 ☎ 07815 727285 🌐 chantrybrewery.co.uk

Brewing returned to Rotherham with the opening of Chantry in 2012 using the latest brewing technology in a 20-barrel state of the art plant built by Sheffield-based Moeschle UK. ‼

Iron & Steel Bitter (OG 1040, ABV 4%)
Chestnut-coloured, complex spicy flavours of dark fruits with a clean finish. An easy-drinking Yorkshire session Bitter.

Steelos (ABV 4.1%)
A well-balanced pale ale. Fresh and easy-drinking with light, subtle aromas of sweet orange, apricot and blackcurrant.

Full Moon (ABV 4.2%)
Pale ale with a delicate balance of lemon, blackberry, pine and grapefruit.

Diamond Black Stout (OG 1045, ABV 4.5%)
Full-bodied dry stout with a bitter finish, spicy with hints of liquorice and dark berries.

Kaldo (ABV 5.5%)
An English pale ale, well-balanced with a subtle citrus taste and hints of orange and grapefruit.

Chapeau (NEW)

Unit 8, Redkiln Close, Horsham, West Sussex, RH13 5QL ☎ (01403) 252459 🌐 chapeaubrewing.com

⊗ Chapeau Brewing is a microbrewery based in Horsham, West Sussex. Beers are available direct from the brewery and in local pubs.

Slip Stream (ABV 3.5%)
Amber-coloured session bitter. Caramel malt flavours with a zesty bitter finish.

Routeur (ABV 4%)

Summit (ABV 4%)
Golden-coloured pale ale with a passion fruit aroma.

Open Road (ABV 4.5%)
Milk stout with rich roasted coffee and chocolate aromas, lactose sweetness balanced by dark malts and a hoppy finish.

Hard Yards (ABV 4.6%)

Best bitter with a strong malt profile and a hint of chocolate, fruit finish.

Chapel

Dinesfield, Chapel Lane, Criftins, Shropshire, SY12 9LZ
☎ (01691) 690412 ☎ 07928 682174
chapelbrewery.co.uk

Chapel began brewing in 2013 using a one-barrel plant behind the owner's bungalow. In 2016 the brewery moved to larger premises across the road. Occasional specials are brewed for festivals.

Angels Share (OG 1040, ABV 4%)

Miracle (OG 1044, ABV 4.4%)

Babylon (OG 1048, ABV 5%)

Chapel-en-le-Frith

5 Market Place, Chapel-en-le-Frith, Derbyshire, SK23 0EW ☎ 07951 524003
timboothman@aol.com

Opened in 2016, this is a small operation located at the rear of Chapel-en-le-Frith Post Office. The brewing kit consists of a single 200-litre capacity integrated system supplemented by a 60-litre trial kit. Beers are available in bottles and five-litre minicasks from Chapel-en-le-Frith and Whaley Bridge Post Offices. Casks are available from a limited number of local outlets.

Siena (OG 1041, ABV 4.1%)
A crisp, light ale hopped to give a unique balance of flavour and aroma.

Busted Monkey (ABV 4.6%)

Isambard (ABV 4.6%)

Leningrad (OG 1052, ABV 5%)
A strong, ruby-coloured ale full of malt character.

Elysium Amber Ale (OG 1056, ABV 5.4%)
A full-bodied, rich, sweet and malty amber-coloured ale with a clean, crisp bitter finish.

Acadian (OG 1057, ABV 5.6%)
An IPA with a delicate malt character and a crescendo of tropical citrus fruit hop flavours.

Hoppy as Funk (OG 1055, ABV 5.8%)
A light ale with a strong malt backbone, finished with a perfect blend of citrus flavour hops.

Sinamarian Black IPA (OG 1060, ABV 6%)
A smooth, dry black IPA with rich roast flavours and hints of chocolate, finished with tropical fruit flavour hops.

Chapel Street

Thatched House, Ball Street, Poulton-le-Fylde, Lancashire, FY6 7BG
☎ (01253) 891063 thatchedhousepoulton.co.uk

This four-barrel plant is situated in the coach house of the award-winning Thatched House pub in Poulton-le-Fylde and has been brewing since 2014. The beers are mostly available in the pub, at a few local outlets plus selected beer festivals.

Chapter

Unit 2a, Sutton Quays Business Park, Clifton Road, Sutton Weaver, Cheshire, WA7 3EH ☎ 07791 516948
Office: 38 Swanlow Lane, Winsford, CW7 1JE
chapterbrewing.co.uk

Chapter Brewing was established in 2016 using a 10-barrel brew plant. It produces diverse 'fictional beers' inspired by literature. ♦RAIB

Bread & Circuses (OG 1041, ABV 3.8%)
An easy-drinking, malt-forward session pale ale.

Temos Tanta (OG 1046, ABV 4.3%)
Marmalade flavours abound from the curacao peel used in this session pale ale.

Parabola (OG 1048, ABV 4.7%)
Punchy American-style pale ale bursting with hop freshness.

Dead Man's Fist (OG 1056, ABV 5.5%)
Smoked porter with black pepper for a fiery hit after a gentle, sweet smokiness.

As Lazarus (OG 1058, ABV 6.2%)
Big, bold IPA. Brewed using a different aroma hop each time.

Charnwood SIBA

22 Jubilee Drive, Loughborough, Leicestershire, LE11 5XS
☎ (01509) 218666 ☎ 07872 651561
charnwoodbrewery.co.uk

Charnwood is a family-run 10-barrel brewery established in 2014 in a former mozzarella factory. Beers are available in many local pubs. The front of the brewery has been fitted out as a shop, bar and reception area, with large glass windows giving a good view into the brewery. !! ♦

Salvation (OG 1038, ABV 3.8%)
A light, refreshing golden-coloured beer with tropical fruit, citrus, and floral flavours.

Vixen (OG 1040, ABV 4%)
A well-balanced, copper-coloured best bitter with subtle hints of honey, spice and hedgerow fruits. A fruity nose and finish.

Checkstone

First & Last Inn, 10 Church Street, Exmouth, Devon, EX8 1PE
☎ (01395) 263275

Checkstone Brewery, named after the Checkstone reef outside the Exe Estuary, is a one-barrel plant inside the First & Last pub, Exmouth, established in 2016. Like the brewery, the beers are named after various sea features around Exmouth. ♦

Cheddar SIBA

Winchester Farm, Draycott Road, Cheddar, Somerset, BS27 3RP
☎ (01934) 744193 cheddarales.co.uk

Established in 2006 in the heart of the Mendips, Cheddar Ales has expanded capacity to enable it to brew up to 100 barrels a week. Production is split approximately 75% cask-conditioned ale with the remainder bottle conditioned. Its bottling plant produces around 120,000 bottles annually. Around 450 outlets are supplied including pubs, clubs and off trade. !! ♦RAIB

Bitter Bully (OG 1038.5, ABV 3.8%)
Light session bitter with flowery hops on the nose and a dry, bitter finish.

THE BREWERIES

Gorge Best (OG 1040, ABV 4%) ◆
Malty bitter with caramel and fruit notes followed by a short, bittersweet aftertaste.

Potholer (OG 1043.5, ABV 4.3%) ◆
A well-balanced golden ale with fruit and sweetness throughout and some bitterness to finish.

Hardrock (OG 1044, ABV 4.4%)
Light gold-coloured, hoppy pale ale with spicy, herbal notes and a floral, citrus finish.

Totty Pot (OG 1044.5, ABV 4.5%) ◆
Roasted malts dominate this smooth, well-flavoured porter. Hints of coffee and rich fruits follow with a well-balanced bitterness.

Crown & Glory (OG 1045, ABV 4.6%)

Goat's Leap (OG 1054.5, ABV 5.5%)

Cheeky Imp

The Old Dairy, Monson Farm, Jerusalem Road, Skellingthorpe, Lincolnshire, LN6 4RP ☎ 07884 022236 🌐 cheekyimp.com

Brewing began in 2015 in Waddington using a 0.5-barrel plant. The brewery relocated and upgraded to a 2.5-barrel unit in Skellingthorpe in 2017. Emphasis is on quality and the brewer is developing collaborations with several landlords in the Lincoln area. RAIB

Chelmsford (NEW)

2 Brewery Fields, Church Street, Great Baddow, Essex, CM2 7LE ☎ 07972 145611 🌐 blueshackbeers.com

Chelmsford was established in 2017 by a former homebrewer who used to brew in a little blue shack at the end of his garden. RAIB

Blueshack Bitter (ABV 3.8%)
A floral, malty bitter.

Blueshack Pale Ale (ABV 3.8%)
A hoppy, zesty pale ale.

Port Jackson (ABV 4%)
A smooth, malty, dark-coloured ale.

Cheshire Brew Brothers

See Oaks

Cheshire Brewhouse SIBA

Units 5 & 6, Daneside Business Park, Riverdane Road, Congleton, Cheshire, CW12 1UN
☎ (01260) 274788 🌐 cheshirebrewhouse.co.uk

Cheshire Brewhouse was established in 2012 using a five-barrel plant, expanding in 2014 to a 10-barrel one. The business has taken over adjacent premises and an on-site brewery tap opened in 2016. ‼♦

Cheshire Gap (ABV 3.8%)

Cheshire Set (ABV 4%)

Engine Vein (ABV 4.2%)
A traditional copper-coloured, hoppy best bitter.

Lindow (ABV 4.5%)
A lighter take on stout, malty and easy-drinking with a hint of espresso and dark chocolate balanced with vine fruits.

DBA (ABV 4.6%)
A Burton-style bitter. Strong and malty with a peppery hop finish.

Dane'ish (ABV 5%)

Chiltern SIBA

Nash Lee Road, Terrick, Buckinghamshire, HP17 0TQ
☎ (01296) 613647 🌐 chilternbrewery.co.uk

Founded in 1980, Chiltern was one of the first microbreweries in the country and is the oldest independent brewery in Buckinghamshire and the Chiltern Hills, growing from a capacity of five to its present 10-barrel plant. Now run by the second generation of the Jenkinson family, George and Tom, it supplies around 100 outlets including its own brewery tap, the Farmers' Bar, at the historic King's Head in Aylesbury. ‼♦RAIB GF

Pale Ale (OG 1037, ABV 3.7%) ◆
An amber-coloured, refreshing beer with a slight fruit aroma, leading to a good malt/bitter balance in the mouth. The aftertaste is bitter and dry.

Black (OG 1040, ABV 3.9%)
Dark treacle tones, hints of roast barley and beautifully hopped. Rich, smooth flavours abound leading to a light, rewarding finish.

Beechwood Bitter (OG 1043, ABV 4.3%) ◆
This pale brown-coloured beer has a balanced butterscotch/toffee aroma, with a slight hop note. The taste balances bitterness and sweetness, leading to a long bitter finish.

Chin Chin

Unit 53F, Lidgate Crescent, Langthwaite Grange Industrial Estate, South Kirkby, West Yorkshire, WF9 3NS ☎ 07896 253650
✉ david@chinchinbrewing.co.uk

Chin Chin was established in 2016 by brothers David and Andrew Currie. Brewing began on a one-barrel plant based in a domestic garage, relocating to larger premises in 2018. An expanding range of small batch brews is supplied across Yorkshire and to beer festivals nationwide. ‼

Chorlton

69 North Western Street, Ardwick, Manchester, M12 6DX 🌐 chorltonbrewingcompany.com

Founded in 2014 by Londoner Mike Marcus, lack of available space means that, despite the name, the brewery is in fact based in Ardwick. Mike is passionate about sour beers and yeast experiments inspired by classic European beer styles. RAIB V

J Church

See Potbelly

Church End SIBA

Ridge Lane, Warwickshire, CV10 0RD
☎ (01827) 713080 🌐 churchendbrewery.co.uk

The brewery started in 1994 in an old coffin shop in Shustoke. It moved to its present site in 2001 and has expanded over the years, it currently operates a 24-barrel purpose-built plant. Many one-off specials and old recipe beers are produced.

Beers are available at the Brewery Tap, Ridge Lane, and its sister pubs, the George & Dragon, Stoke Golding and the Dragon Inn, Worcester. ‼ ♦ RAIB

Poachers Pocket (OG 1036, ABV 3.5%)

Cuthberts (OG 1038, ABV 3.8%)
A refreshing, hoppy beer, with hints of malt, fruit and caramel taste. Lingering bitter aftertaste.

Goat's Milk (OG 1038, ABV 3.8%)

Gravediggers Ale (OG 1038, ABV 3.8%)

What the Fox's Hat (OG 1044, ABV 4.2%)
A beer with a malty aroma and a hoppy, malty taste with some caramel flavour.

Vicar's Ruin (OG 1044, ABV 4.4%)
A straw-coloured best bitter with an initially hoppy, bitter flavour, softening to a delicate malt finish.

Stout Coffin (OG 1046, ABV 4.6%)

Fallen Angel (OG 1050, ABV 5%)

Church Farm SIBA

Church Farm, Budbrooke, Warwickshire, CV35 8QL
☎ (01926) 411084 ☎ 07939 607027
churchfarmbrewery.co.uk

Brewing began in 2012. A new 20-barrel gas fired plant was commissioned in 2016 to meet growing demand. Beers are brewed from local ingredients, some of the barley is grown on the farm and the water comes from its own well. Outlets across Warwickshire and South Midlands are supplied direct as well as local beer festivals. ♦ RAIB

Pale Ale (OG 1041, ABV 3.8%)
Lightly-hopped, easy-drinking, golden-coloured bitter with a tangy finish.

Ren's Pride (OG 1044, ABV 4%)
An amber-coloured best bitter with a slightly sweet taste. The distinctive initial flavour comes from a complex array of malts.

Brown's Porter (OG 1042, ABV 4.2%)
A porter with a smooth coffee taste and a long-lasting, creamy aftertaste.

Harry's Heifer (OG 1044, ABV 4.2%)
A light amber-coloured best bitter with slight floral notes.

IPA (OG 1052, ABV 5%)
Light amber-coloured hoppy IPA. Easy-drinking but full of flavour. Slight citrus fruit and toffee notes.

Church Hanbrewery

Unit F2, New Yatt Business Centre, New Yatt, Oxfordshire, OX29 6TJ
☎ (01993) 774986 ☎ 07907 272617

Office: Tithe Barn South, Church Hanborough, OX29 8AB churchhanbrewery.com

Brewing commenced in 2016 on a small scale until later that year when a 2.5-barrel plant came on stream. RAIB

Ale X IPA (ABV 4.5%)
A powerful and complex IPA with citrus, pine, spice and herbal notes.

RAUK (ABV 5%)
Inspired by Rauchbier (smoked lager) from Bamberg.

Red Beetter (ABV 5%)
Brown-red in colour from a small amount of organic beetroot juice. Malty and smooth, with low hop aroma and a balanced hop bitterness.

Bluenette (ABV 5.5%)
A porter with a smoothness that comes from the addition of Scottish rolled oats, a delicate sweetness from organic honey and rich, roasted chocolate flavours.

Mat Black (ABV 5.5%)
A black IPA with a strong lemon and herbal hop aroma and the smoothness of a stout.

Ciren

Twelve Bells, 12 Lewis Lane, Cirencester, GL7 1EA
☎ (01285) 652230 ☎ 07702 489589

A microbrewery at the rear of the Twelve Bells pub in Cirencester. The brewer is the owner Steve and brewing commenced in 2012. Steve sold the brewery in 2016, but bought it back in 2017. ‼ ♦

City of Cambridge

See Wolf

Clanconnel

PO Box 316, Craigavon, Co Armagh, BT65 9AZ
☎ 07711 626770 clanconnelbrewing.com

Beers are contract brewed by the Rye River Brewery in Co Kildare in the Republic of Ireland under the McGraths Craft Beer brand. No real ale.

Clark's

See Castle Eden

Clarkshaws SIBA

Arch 497, Ridgway Road, Loughborough Junction, London, SW9 7DT ☎ 07989 402687
clarkshaws.co.uk

Clarkshaws is a small brewery established in 2013 focusing on using ingredients sourced in the UK and on reducing beer miles. The beers are suitable for vegetarians and are accredited by the Vegetarian Society. All beers are unfined and may be hazy. Some beers are brewed on a Clarkshaws-owned brewing kit inside the Bexley Brewery site.

Gorgon's Alive (OG 1040, ABV 4%)
Unfined golden-coloured beer with spicy hops throughout. The flavour has hints of orange and peach with a dry bitterness.

Phoenix Rising (OG 1040, ABV 4%)
Tawny-coloured beer with a creamy toffee nose. Bananas, pineapple, hops and caramel flavours. Dry, short, fruity biscuit finish.

Strange Brew No. 1 (OG 1040, ABV 4%)
Easy-drinking, yellow-coloured ale. Flavour is of peppery hops, tropical fruits and biscuit sweetness with a trace of bitterness.

Coldharbour Hell Yeah Lager (ABV 5.3%)
Hops and mango notes that are also present on the flavour with some butterscotch. Dryish palate.

Hellhound IPA (OG 1056, ABV 5.5%)

Spiced and citrus notes in this unfined amber-coloured beer with a bitterness in the flavour and finish, which is dry.

Clavell & Hind (NEW)

The Old Haulage Yard, Old Cirencester Road, Birdlip, Gloucestershire, GL4 8JL
☎ (01542) 238050 🌐 clavellandhind.co.uk

Clavell & Hind is a 20-barrel brewery based in the Cotswold countryside. A tap room is open Friday afternoon and Saturday daytime.

Coachman (ABV 3.8%)
A golden-coloured ale with a perfect balance of citrus and marmalade hops and fresh ginger.

Blunderbus (ABV 4.2%)
An explosion of citrus and tropical hops.

Rookwood (ABV 4.4%)
A smooth blend of aromatic malts and dark hops.

Clearsky

See Hilden

Clearwater

Unit 1, Little Court, Manteo Way, Gammaton Road, Bideford, Devon, EX39 4FG
☎ (01237) 420492 🌐 clearwaterbrewery.co.uk

⊗ Established in 1999, Clearwater is a 10-barrel brewery regularly supplying more than 250 outlets across the South-west and nationally with its 'Devon's Own' labelled beers. Beers are also available at the brewery tap, the Champ, Appledore. !! ♦ RAIB

Expedition Ale (OG 1037.3, ABV 3.5%)
A traditional-style, brown-coloured ale with hints of blackcurrant. Well-balanced and hoppy with a bitter finish.

Real Smiler (OG 1037, ABV 3.7%)
A golden-coloured, crisp and hoppy session beer.

Broad Reach (OG 1039, ABV 4%) ◆
Fruity aroma leads to crisp and fruity yet bitter taste. The aftertaste continues a balanced sweet fruit bitterness, which is slightly dry.

Mariners (OG 1042.9, ABV 4.2%)
Pale gold in colour. Clean, crisp and hoppy with a fresh grapefruit zestiness and lingering hint of bitterness.

Proper Ansome (OG 1041, ABV 4.2%)
Full-flavoured, dark-coloured and malty beer.

Voyager (OG 1043, ABV 4.5%)
A fruity beer, copper in colour with a grape aroma and nutty taste. A light bitterness to end.

Artists Rifles (OG 1048.4, ABV 5%)
A refreshing, hoppy, crisp pale ale with spicy notes.

Cliff Quay

Unit 1, Meadow Works, Kenton Road, Debenham, Suffolk, IP14 6RT
☎ (01728) 861213 🌐 cliffquay.co.uk

⊗ Cliff Quay was established in 2008 by former Wychwood brewer Jeremy Moss and John Bjornson (owner of the Earl Soham Brewery) in part of the historic Tolly Cobbold brewery in Ipswich. In 2012 the brewery relocated to Debenham, a small, picturesque market town, due to redevelopment of the former brewery site. Now re-established alongside Earl Soham brewery, with shared shop and offices. !! 🛒 ♦

Bitter (OG 1034, ABV 3.4%) ◆
Pleasantly drinkable, well-balanced, malty, sweet bitter with a hint of caramel, followed by a sweet/malty aftertaste. A good flavour for such a low gravity beer.

Anchor Bitter (OG 1040, ABV 4%)

Black Jack Porter (OG 1042, ABV 4.2%) ◆
Unusual dark-coloured porter with a strong aniseed aroma and rich liquorice and aniseed flavours, reminiscent of old-fashioned sweets. The aftertaste is long and increasingly sweet.

Tolly Roger (OG 1042, ABV 4.2%) ◆
Well-balanced, highly drinkable, mid-gold-coloured summer beer with a bittersweet hoppiness, some biscuity flavours and hints of summer fruit.

Tumblehome (OG 1047, ABV 4.7%) ◆
Aroma of marzipan and dried fruit. Flavour reminiscent of Amaretto, leading to a short, bitter, slightly spicy aftertaste.

Sea Dog (OG 1053, ABV 5.5%)
A strong, hoppy beer with fragrant, punchy hops. Bursting with flavours of lemon and grapefruit with a full maltiness in contrast.

Dreadnought (OG 1065, ABV 6.5%)

Clockwork

1153-1155 Cathcart Road, Glasgow, G42 9HB
☎ (0141) 649 0184 🌐 clockworkbeercompany.co.uk

Established in 1997. The beers are stored in cellar tanks where fermentation gases from the conditioning vessel blanket the beers (but not under pressure). A wide range of ales, lagers and specials is produced. Most beers are naturally gassed while the Craft Lager is pressurised. The establishment parted ways with its previous managing company, Maclays, and in 2014 the pub underwent a full refurbishment. !! ♦

Clouded Minds

Unit 5b, Brailes Industrial Estate, Winderton Road, Lower Brailes, Warwickshire, OX15 5JW ☎ 07530 998149 🌐 cloudedminds.co.uk

Brewing began in 2013 using spare capacity at various breweries around London and Derbyshire. In 2015 the brewery moved to its own site near Banbury using a 10-barrel plant. The London area is mainly supplied but also some outlets in Birmingham, Nottinghamshire, Warwickshire and Oxfordshire. Wholesalers also distribute the beers more widely. RAIB

N29 (OG 1036, ABV 3.7%)
A citrus pale ale brewed with a small percentage of rye malt.

N253 (OG 1037, ABV 3.9%)
American-style pale ale with fruit and resin notes.

99 steps (ABV 4%)

N18 (OG 1038, ABV 4%)
A pale ale with mild citrus, pine and resin notes.

Luppol (OG 1040, ABV 4.2%)

A hoppy and refreshing beer with a good bitter finish.

Clout Stout (OG 1048, ABV 4.5%)
Velvet mouthfeel with an aroma of roasted malts, cocoa, dried fruits and figs. Mildly sweet and sour with a smoky and bitter finish.

Hazelnutter (OG 1048, ABV 5%)
Well-balanced, smooth, American-style brown-coloured ale brewed with organic Italian hazelnuts.

Elisir (OG 1052, ABV 5.3%)
Caramel and biscuit taste from the malts balanced by a generous amount of American hops. Very fruity.

Black Pike (OG 1057, ABV 6.1%)
A highly-hopped black IPA.

Dolce Vita (OG 1058, ABV 6.2%)
A West Coast American-style IPA; fruity and mildly spicy with a dry finish.

Double Clout Stout (OG 1064, ABV 6.6%)
A complex fusion of coffee, cocoa, liquorice, dark fruit and burnt sugar.

Cloudwater

Units 7-8, Piccadilly Trading Estate, Manchester, M1 2NP
☎ (0161) 661 5943 🌐 cloudwaterbrew.co

Cloudwater commenced brewing in 2015, specialising in creating and brewing modern, seasonal and special one-off brews, along with collaborations in conjunction with other micro and regional brewers both in the UK and internationally. Regular cask ale production ceased in 2017 but cask beers are still available for beer festivals and as one-offs. Its Barrel Store Tap Room is open Wednesday to Sunday. ‼♦

Clun SIBA

White Horse Inn, The Square, Clun, Shropshire, SY7 8JA
☎ (01588) 640021 🌐 whi-clun.co.uk

Formerly a tiny brewery, capacity was increased to 2.5 barrels in 2010. Established behind the White Horse in Clun, beers are produced for the pub and, increasingly, the local trade. ♦

Loophole (OG 1035, ABV 3.5%)
A dry, crisp, light-coloured beer with a hoppy flavour.

Clun Pale (OG 1040, ABV 4.1%)
A pale-coloured, clean-tasting bitter.

Solar (OG 1043, ABV 4.3%)

Solstice (ABV 4.8%)
A fruity, smooth ale with a hint of elderflower.

Citadel (OG 1065, ABV 5.9%)
Golden in colour, the rich and fruity malt flavours are met head on by intense hop bitterness and aroma which give rise to a long-lasting, dry finish.

Co Pilot

Unit 4, Sam Brown Industrial Units, Dog and Gun Lane, Whetstone, Leicestershire, LE8 6LJ ☎ 07342 040567 ✉ martinjallsopp@gmail.com

⊗ Blencow Brewery was established in 1998 at the Exeter Arms in Barrowden, Rutland. In 2005 Martin Allsopp bought the pub and brewery and renamed the latter as Barrowden. In 2016 Martin sold the pub and relocated the brewery to an industrial unit on the outskirts of Leicester, adopting the name Co Pilot. ♦

Pilot (OG 1028, ABV 2.6%)

Beech (OG 1040, ABV 3.8%)

Own Gear (OG 1040, ABV 4%)

Hop Gear (OG 1046, ABV 4.4%)

Coach House SIBA

Wharf Street, Howley, Warrington, Cheshire, WA1 2DQ
☎ (01925) 232800 🌐 coachhousebrewery.co.uk

Established in 1991 by three former employees of Greenall Whitley brewery, Coach House was bought by Martin Bailey in 2015. The 40-barrel plant produces up to 240 barrels per week. ♦

Coachman's Best Bitter (OG 1037, ABV 3.7%)
A well-hopped, malty bitter, moderately fruity with a hint of sweetness and a peppery nose.

Gunpowder Mild (OG 1037, ABV 3.8%)
Biscuity dark mild with a blackcurrant sweetness. Bitterness and fruit dominate with some hints of caramel and a slightly stronger roast flavour.

Honeypot Bitter (OG 1037, ABV 3.8%)
A medium-bodied, golden-coloured bitter. Brewed with Cheshire honey which adds a silkiness to the beer.

Farrier's Best Bitter (OG 1038, ABV 3.9%)
A smooth, tawny-coloured beer, slightly sweet but with rich hop flavours.

Cromwells Best Bitter (OG 1040, ABV 4%)
Amber-coloured, well-balanced beer with a smooth, clean-hopped finish.

Blonde (OG 1041, ABV 4.1%)
A thirst-quenching blonde ale with hints of citrus and grapefruit.

Cheshire Gold (OG 1042, ABV 4.1%)
A pale golden-coloured beer with a pine lemon crispness.

Dick Turpin (OG 1042, ABV 4.2%)
Malty, hoppy pale brown-coloured beer with some initial sweetish flavours leading to a short, bitter aftertaste. Sold under other names as a pub house beer.

ClIPAty Hop (OG 1043, ABV 4.3%)
A light-coloured IPA with a hoppy aroma and flavour but a well-balanced, malty finish.

Flintlock Pale Ale (OG 1044, ABV 4.4%)
A pale golden-coloured beer, light on the palate with a touch of sweetness in the finish.

Innkeeper's Special Reserve (OG 1045, ABV 4.5%)
A dark-coloured, full-flavoured bitter. Quite fruity, with a strong, bitter aftertaste.

Postlethwaite (OG 1045, ABV 4.6%)
A distinctive dry and fruity pale ale. Traditionally dry hopped to give a fine hop aroma.

Blueberry Classic Bitter (OG 1050, ABV 5%)
A wonderful, straw-coloured beer with a light, hoppy aroma and a distinct blueberry aftertaste.

Posthorn Premium (OG 1050, ABV 5%)

A rich, straw-coloured, smooth premium ale. A robust, malty palate and well-balanced bitterness with a complexity of flavours.

Blunderbus (OG 1053, ABV 5.3%)
A dark-coloured ale with a full malty flavour.

Brewed for 16 Hospitality:

16v9 (OG 1041, ABV 4.1%)
Flavours and aroma of tropical fruit with a well-balanced bitter aftertaste.

Coastal SIBA

Unit 20, Cardrew Trade Park South, Cardrew Way, Redruth, Cornwall, TR15 1SW
☎ (01209) 212613 ⊕ coastalbrewery.co.uk

⊗ Launched in 2006 by Alan Hinde, Coastal operates a six-barrel plant and supplies pubs all around England. It has a brewery tap on site, with Coastal beers on draught, plus a bottle shop offering a range of speciality beers, including its own. The brewery may relocate during the currency of this guide. ♦RAIB

Cornish Bronze (OG 1037, ABV 3.7%)

Hop Monster (OG 1038, ABV 3.7%)
Powerfully hoppy golden ale with grassy grapefruit and marmalade flavours. Quite sweet, somewhat dry. Rising dryness and bitterness in the finish.

Handliner (OG 1040, ABV 4%)
Red-coloured bitter with faintly roasted malt aroma. Smoky malt taste balanced by hop bitterness and gentle dryness, finishing bitter.

Merry Maidens Mild (OG 1040, ABV 4%)
Smooth, black-coloured mild with roasted malt, charcoal, liquorice and stone fruits fading slowly to a refreshing, dry, bitter finish.

Angelina (OG 1042, ABV 4.1%)
Golden ale with delicate floral aroma. Grassy, citrus hops with sweet grapefruit, marmalade and apricot throughout. Crisp, dry, fruity finish.

Golden Hinde (OG 1044, ABV 4.3%)
Golden ale with orange marmalade aroma. Apricot and citrus fruit flavours with dominant bitter and grassy hop. Refreshing long finish.

Pier Porter (OG 1043, ABV 4.3%)
A wholesome, full-bodied porter. Heavy malt flavour gives way to a malt character.

Poseidon Extra (OG 1046, ABV 4.5%)
Yellow-coloured golden ale. Orange and lemon aroma. Strong bitterness and grassy hops with dominant grapefruit. Long bitter and dry finish.

Cornish Cascade (OG 1050, ABV 5%)
Golden ale with hoppy aroma. Strong citrus hop taste, bitter and fruity with sweet malt. Long bitter and dry finish.

Cornish Honey Cascade (OG 1050, ABV 5%)

Cornish Porter (OG 1050, ABV 5%)
Smooth, black-coloured porter with powerful roast malt aroma and moderate fruit. Strong smoky charcoal roast malt flavour with bitterness.

St Pirans Porter (OG 1060, ABV 6%)
A traditional, full-bodied porter using seven different malts. Roasty, toasty malt notes mix with abundant hops.

Erosion (OG 1077, ABV 7.5%)
Dark brown in colour, heavy and alcoholic with roast malt aroma. Powerful sweet roast malt dominates flavours, with smooth dark chocolate, nuts and spices.

Kernow Imperial Stout (OG 1090, ABV 9%)
This full-flavoured, warming dark stout bursts with molasses and roast malts. Roast caramel adds to the dry stout finish.

Cobbydale

Red Lion, 47 Kirkgate, Silsden, West Yorkshire, BD20 0AQ
☎ (01535) 930884 ☎ 07965 569885
⊕ cobbydalebrewery.co.uk

Brewing began in 2017 at the Red Lion, Silsden. Originally only brewing one beer, others are now brewed on an occasional basis.

Cocksure SIBA

Unit 3, Great Leaze Farm, Oldbury Lane, Oldbury-on-Severn, BS35 1RF ☎ 07787 453222
⊕ cocksurebrewing.com

Established in 2017, this ten-barrel brewery is located in the Severn Vale, near Thornbury. Occasional beers, one-offs and collaborations brews with other breweries complement the core range. ♦RAIB V

Amber Session (OG 1038, ABV 3.9%)
A delicate malt platform provides sweetness and richness and the hops give a citrus, pine and spicy aroma.

Pale (OG 1042, ABV 4.2%)
A fruity pale ale with complex flavours.

Session IPA (OG 1046, ABV 4.8%)
A golden-coloured beer with tropical aromas of watermelon, pear and blueberries.

Cold Brew Stout (OG 1046, ABV 5%)
A smooth, rich and chocolaty stout with cold-infused coffee added to the brew.

IPA (OG 1056, ABV 6.5%)

Colchester SIBA

Viaduct Brewhouse, Unit 16, Wakes Hall Business Centre, Wakes Colne, Essex, CO6 2DY
☎ (01787) 829422 ⊕ colchesterbrewery.com

⊗ Set up in 2012 by three friends, Tom Knox, Roger Clark and Andy Bone, using the double drop process. Popular during the early 20th century this process requires additional brewing vessels in a two-tier system resulting in clean beer with pronounced flavours. !! ♦RAIB

AKA Pale (OG 1039, ABV 3.7%)
A mildy-hopped pale ale. Fresh and fruity.

Metropolis (OG 1040.5, ABV 3.9%)
A golden-coloured, hoppy beer. Full-flavoured with a long, spicy finish.

Jack Spitty's Smuggler's Ale (OG 1041.5, ABV 4%)
Golden-coloured, easy-drinking ale. Full of hop flavor with delicate bitterness and a light aroma.

Colchester No. 1 (OG 1042.5, ABV 4.1%)
A classic, copper-coloured English best bitter.

Red Diesel (OG 1043.5, ABV 4.2%)
Red-coloured best bitter. Well-balanced with a long, rich finish.

Brazilian Coffee & Vanilla Porter (OG 1048, ABV 4.6%)

Cat's Whiskers (OG 1050, ABV 4.8%)
Smooth-drinking, full-bodied cream stout with a slight sweetness.

Old King Coel London Porter (OG 1052, ABV 5%)
Rich, dark, old-fashioned porter brewed with brown malt.

Cold Black Label

Guardian House, 5 Squire Drive, Brynmenyn Industrial Estate, Bridgend, CF32 9TX
(01656) 728081 coldblacklabel.co.uk

Beginning as a wholesale drinks company, Cold Black Label extended its portfolio to include a range of cask-conditioned beers that were contract brewed at other breweries. In 2018 it commissioned a six-barrel plant so all beers are now brewed in-house.

Glyder Fawr (ABV 4%)
Dark golden-coloured ale with a smooth, malty, rounded finish.

Guardian (ABV 4.1%)
Rich, bronze-coloured bitter with a balance of hoppy and tangy citrus flavours.

Harlech Castle (ABV 4.4%)
Deep golden brown in colour with toffee notes.

Red Beast (ABV 4.4%)
Smooth, ruby-coloured beer with a fresh citrus aroma and well-hopped character.

Bwlch Passage (OG 1044, ABV 4.5%)
Pale-coloured, aromatic brew with a refreshing tang and clean finish.

Uncle Phil's Ale (OG 1042.5, ABV 4.5%)
Pale amber-coloured ale with a full, malty flavour and clean, refreshing bitterness to finish.

Chirk Castle (ABV 4.6%)
A golden-coloured ale with subtle citrus tones.

Miner's Ale (OG 1045.5, ABV 4.6%)

Crib Goch (ABV 5%)
Dark-coloured brew with a punch of robust flavours. A full-bodied blend of dark coffee and chocolate notes.

Nutty Ale (ABV 5%)
Dark ruby-coloured beer with a rich, nutty, complex finish.

Cold Town (NEW)

8-10 Dunedin Street, Edinburgh, EH7 4JB
(0131) 221 9978

A Signature Pubs venture that began brewing lager in 2018. No real ale.

Coles Family

White Hart Thatched Inn & Brewery, Llanddarog, SA32 8NT
(01267) 275395 thebestpubinwales.co.uk

The brewery is based at the ancient White Hart Inn, built in 1371, which historically had a brewery on site. Brewing started again in 1999 on a nine-gallon plant. A one-barrel plant was fitted in 2000 and in 2012 the brewery was opened to the public. Cider is also produced. ♦

Collyfobble (NEW)

Peacock, Hackney Lane, Barlow, Derbyshire, S18 7TD
(0114) 289 0611 collyfobblebrewery.com

Collyfobble began brewing in 2018. !! RAIB

Colonsay SIBA

The Brewery, Scalasaig, Isle of Colonsay, PA61 7YT
(01951) 200190 colonsaybrewery.co.uk

Colonsay began brewing in 2007 on a five-barrel plant. Beer is mainly bottled or brewery conditioned for the local trade. RAIB

Concertina SIBA

9a Dolcliffe Road, Mexborough, South Yorkshire, S64 9AZ
(01709) 580841 concertina@btconnect.com

Concertina started in 1992 in the cellar of a club once famous as the home of a long-gone concertina band. The plant produces up to eight barrels a week for the club and other occasional direct outlets and the wider trade, via beer wholesalers. !! ♦

Club Bitter (OG 1038, ABV 3.9%)
A fruity session bitter with a good bitter flavour.

Bengal Tiger (OG 1043, ABV 4.6%)
Light amber-coloured ale with an aromatic hoppy nose followed by a combination of fruit and bitterness.

Concrete Cow

59 Alston Drive, Bradwell Abbey, Milton Keynes, Buckinghamshire, MK13 9HB
(01908) 316794 07889 665745
concretecowbrewery.co.uk

Concrete Cow opened in 2007 on a 5.5-barrel plant. The beers are named after aspects of local history. The brewery supplies pubs, farmers' markets, local shops and restaurants. English single malt whisky is also available. !! ♦ RAIB

Pail Ale (OG 1036, ABV 3.7%)

Fenny Popper (OG 1039, ABV 4%)
A light-coloured, zesty ale.

Cock 'n' Bull Story (OG 1041, ABV 4.1%)
A dark amber-coloured, malty beer.

Cloven Hoof (OG 1045, ABV 4.5%)
A dark-coloured vanilla stout flavoured with natural vanilla pods.

Old Bloomer (OG 1045, ABV 4.7%)
A dark ruby-coloured strong bitter.

Coniston SIBA

Coppermines Road, Coniston, Cumbria, LA21 8HL
(01539) 441133 conistonbrewery.com

A 10-barrel plant started in 1995 behind the Black Bull Inn in Coniston, it now brews 40 barrels a week and supplies numerous outlets locally and nationally. Some bottle-conditioned Coniston beers are brewed using Ridgeway Brewery (qv). !! RAIB

Oliver's Light Ale (OG 1035, ABV 3.4%)
A fruity, hoppy, straw-coloured bitter with plenty of flavour for its strength.

THE BREWERIES

Bluebird Bitter (OG 1036, ABV 3.6%) ◆
A yellow-gold-coloured, predominantly hoppy and fruity beer, well-balanced with some sweetness and a rising bitter finish.

Asrai (OG 1039, ABV 4%) ◆
Crisp on the palate, a gently-hopped beer with a full-bodied finish.

Bluebird Premium XB (OG 1040.5, ABV 4.2%) ◆
Well-balanced, hoppy and fruity golden-coloured bitter. Bittersweet in the mouth with dryness building.

Old Man Ale (OG 1040.5, ABV 4.2%) ◆
Delicious fruity, wine-like beer with a complex, well-balanced richness.

Special Oatmeal Stout (OG 1045, ABV 4.5%) ◆
A well-balanced, easy-drinking stout, fruity with a balanced ratio of malt to hop bitterness. A good starting point for novice stout drinkers.

K7 (OG 1045, ABV 4.7%) ◆
Balance,d fruity, hoppy bitter, plenty of body and a long, hoppy, bitter finish.

Thurstein Pilsner (OG 1044.5, ABV 4.8%) ◆
True to style; mild but unusually sweet, with a hoppy fruitiness.

Blacksmiths Ale (OG 1047.5, ABV 5%) ◆
A tawny-coloured ale which holds both roastiness and fruitiness in a pleasing balance.

Infinity IPA (OG 1055, ABV 6%) ◆
High impact strong bitter. Fruity aromas persist in the powerful but well-balanced hoppiness and sweetness with nothing being lost in the finish.

No. 9 Barley Wine (OG 1087.5, ABV 8.5%) ◆
Hops and alcohol dominate with appropriate sweetness and fruit on the tongue. A full-bodied and beautifully balanced beer.

Connoisseur

(Rear of) Wolverhampton House, 121-125 Church Street, St Helens, Merseyside, WA10 1AJ ☎ 07921 838831 🌐 connoisseurales.com

Launched in 2014 by a family team of award-winning licencees, the brewery was run by Mark Yates until his death in 2017. The torch has now been passed to son Kevin who has reinvigorated the range with a selection of new recipes to complement existing brews. Tasting days with free brewery tours are held monthly.

Bloody Mild (ABV 3.7%)
Well-balanced dark mild with aromatic hops.

The Usual (ABV 3.8%)
A traditional ale making use of all English ingredients giving this beer its characteristic bitterness.

Ruby Ruby Ruby Ruby (ABV 4.1%)
A well-balanced, ruby-coloured, malty ale.

Phi (ABV 4.2%)
All American hops provide big bitterness atop a crisp and smooth blend of pale malts.

Lucem Light Ale (ABV 4.3%)
A hoppy ale with a distinctive nose and floral citrus taste.

Sparkling WIT (ABV 4.6%)
Complex malt flavours and a hint of chocolate with a hoppy aroma.

Bûte Noir Dry Stout (ABV 5%)
Full-flavoured dry stout with coffee, chocolate and a hint of smoke. A delicate molasses and spice nose.

Ex Terra Lupus IPA (ABV 5.6%)
A clean, crisp IPA with a well-balanced hop profile.

Consall Forge

3 Railway Cottages, Consall Forge, Staffordshire, ST9 0AJ

A one-barrel brewery set in the heart of the Staffordshire Moorlands adjacent to the Churnet Valley Railway. The Black Lion at Consall Forge is a regular outlet.

Dark Ruby Mild (OG 1050, ABV 5.2%)

Equilibrium (OG 1054, ABV 6%)
Traditional stout with flavours of coffee and molasses.

Consett Ale Works SIBA

Grey Horse Inn, 115 Sherburn Terrace, Consett, County Durham, DH8 6NE
☎ (01207) 591540 🌐 thegreyhorse.co.uk

The brewery opened in 2006 in the stables of a former coaching inn at the rear of the Grey Horse, Consett's oldest pub. The name commemorates the historic Consett Steel Works that closed in 1980. The brewery expanded in 2007 to cope with demand. More than 100 outlets are supplied direct. !! ♦

Steel Town Bitter (OG 1039, ABV 3.8%)

Steelworkers Blonde (OG 1040, ABV 4%)

White Hot (OG 1040, ABV 4%)

Cast Iron (OG 1040, ABV 4.1%)

Consett Stout (OG 1045, ABV 4.3%)

Men of Steel (OG 1045, ABV 4.3%)

Red Dust (OG 1045, ABV 4.5%)

Consortium

Consortium, 13c Cornmarket, Louth, Lincolnshire, LN11 9PY ☎ 07717 201724
🌐 theconsortiumlouth.co.uk

Formerly known as the Black Horse Brewery, Consortium is a new venture for owner Tony Hawkins. It is based above the Consortium Tasting Lounge, which is probably the smallest pub in Lincolnshire. !! ♦

Conwy SIBA

Unit 2, Ty Mawr Enterprise Park, Tan y Graig Road, Llysfaen, LL29 8UE
☎ (01492) 514305 🌐 conwybrewery.co.uk

Conwy started brewing in 2003 and was the first brewery in Conwy for at least 100 years. In 2013 it increased capacity and moved to bigger premises in Llysfaen with its own brewery tap. Monthly seasonals are available as well as the West Coast range showcasing American-style beers. Around 100 outlets are supplied. !! ♦ RAIB

Clogwyn Gold (OG 1037, ABV 3.6%) ◆
A full-flavoured golden ale featuring strong citrus fruit flavours throughout. Hoppy bitterness dominates the full mouthfeel and lasting finish.

Welsh Pride (OG 1040, ABV 4%)
A clean-tasting, malty bitter. Fruit in aroma and taste with a crisp, grainy mouthfeel and a lingering, hoppy, bitter aftertaste.

Beachcomber Blonde (OG 1042, ABV 4.2%) ◆
A pale-coloured beer with a citrus taste, initially sweetish with delicate hoppiness in the lingering bitter finish.

Honey Fayre (OG 1044, ABV 4.5%)
Golden-coloured best bitter with a hint of honey sweetness, balanced by an increasingly hoppy, bitter finish.

Rampart (OG 1045, ABV 4.5%) ◆
A dark-coloured, fruity beer with a sweetish initial taste. Fruit flavours accompanied by the underlying hoppiness continue into the bittersweet aftertaste.

Copper Dragon

Lee Mills, St Pauls Way, Silsden, West Yorkshire, BD21 4QW
☎ (01756) 243243

After a period of being contract brewed at Cameron's (qv) in Hartlepool, Copper Dragon has moved back to Yorkshire with a new bespoke brewery in Silsden. The beers are available at its own Cross Keys, East Marton, as well as across Yorkshire and further north.

Best Bitter (OG 1036, ABV 3.8%) ◆
A traditional Yorkshire bitter with a malty aroma and a hoppy, bitter taste with hints of fruit and a bitter finish.

Golden Pippin (OG 1037, ABV 3.9%) ◆
This golden ale has a citrus aroma and flavour. The dry, bitter astringency increases in the aftertaste.

Silver Myst (OG 1040, ABV 4%)
Pale-coloured, Pilsner-style ale. Crisp, smooth and refreshing.

Scotts 1816 (OG 1041, ABV 4.1%) ◆
This best bitter is fruity and malty with a bitter finish. Look for hints of nuts, tropical fruits and vanilla in the aroma and taste.

Brewed under the Recoil brand name:

Back to Best (ABV 3.8%)

Blonde Avenger (ABV 3.9%)

Collision (ABV 4%)

Corinium

Unit 1a, The Old Kennels, Cirencester Park, Cirencester, Gloucestershire, GL7 1UR ☎ 07716 826467 🌐 coriniumales.co.uk

⊗ Corinium Ales was established in 2012. The one-barrel plant relocated to newly refurbished ex-dog kennels in Cirencester. The award-winning beers are mainly available bottle-conditioned and make up the brewer's 'Roman Collection' but cask-conditioned production of the beers is increasing. Plans are in place to double capacity during the currency of this guide. !! ♦ RAIB

Gold I (OG 1043, ABV 4.2%)
An easy-drinking, fruity ale with a mellow blend of malt and hops and a soft bitter finish.

Plautus V (OG 1042, ABV 4.5%)
Fruity pale ale bursting hops.

Bodicacia IV (OG 1045, ABV 4.7%)
A full-bodied pale ale with a long-lasting citrus finish.

Centurion II (OG 1051, ABV 4.7%)
A rich, malty stout with toasty chocolate undertones. Lightly-hopped leaving a well-rounded aftertaste.

Ale Caesar III (OG 1050, ABV 5%)
A well-hopped IPA with a tropical fruit aroma balanced with a pleasing bitterness.

Corless (NEW)

c/o Station Road, Scorton, Lancashire, PR3 1AN
☎ 07983 563917

Brewing began in 2018 using spare capacity at Farm Yard Ales (qv).

Cornish Chough SIBA

Trethvas Farm, Lizard, Cornwall, TR12 7AR
☎ (01326) 290908 🌐 choughbrewery.com

⊗ Cornish Chough, the most southerly brewery on the UK mainland, commenced brewing in 2011 at its present location on Trethvas Farm, Lizard village. The brewery has its own borehole and draws water from between two seams of serpentine rock. !! RAIB

Kynance Blonde (OG 1039, ABV 4.2%) ◆
Refreshing golden ale with a strong citrus hop taste and assertive bitterness. Marmalade, lemon and peach flavours. Very hoppy finish.

Cadgwith Crabber (OG 1043, ABV 4.3%) ◆
Smooth amber-coloured best bitter. Biscuit malt balanced by zesty hop bitterness and mixed fruits. Gentle malt, fruity and dry finish.

Fire Raven (OG 1047, ABV 4.7%) ◆
Black porter with roast malt aroma. Velvety roasted barley with bitter chocolate, coffee and light nutty malt. Bitter roast finish.

Lizard Storm (OG 1048, ABV 4.8%) ◆
Strong bitter with dominant malt aroma. Assertive malt and resinous hop bitterness with fruits and coffee. Lingering bitter hop finish.

Kilcobben IPA (ABV 5%) ◆
Smooth amber-coloured strong bitter. Crisp citrus hop bitterness balanced by biscuit malt with dried and tropical fruits. Bitter hoppy finish.

Cornish Crown SIBA

End Unit, Badger's Cross Farm, Badger's Cross, Penzance, Cornwall, TR20 8XE
☎ (01736) 449029 ☎ 07870 998986
🌐 cornishcrown.co.uk

⊗ Cornish Crown began brewing in 2012 on a six-barrel plant and is based on a farm high above Mounts Bay. It was established by the brewer and landlord of the Crown Inn in Penzance, which acts as the brewery tap. Beer is available in local outlets and can be found as far away as the Southampton Arms in London. RAIB

Golden (OG 1038, ABV 4%)

Causeway (OG 1041, ABV 4.1%) ◆
Amber-coloured best bitter. Gentle biscuit malt throughout balanced by earthy hop bitterness and soft fruit hints. Bitter, faintly dry finish.

One Hop One Grain (OG 1041, ABV 4.1%) ◆

Gold-coloured best bitter with hops dominant from aroma to finish. Assertive bitter flavour with citrus fruits and faint maltiness.

Helter Skelter (OG 1042, ABV 4.2%)

Honeyfuggle (OG 1043, ABV 4.5%) ◆
Yellow-coloured speciality honey beer. Initial sweet honey and malt then oranges, lemons, tropical fruits and hop bitterness. Long, bittersweet finish.

SPA (OG 1048, ABV 4.8%) ◆
Heavily-hopped, golden-coloured strong bitter with citrus peel, marmalade and hints of sweet malt. The finish is long, bitter and dry.

Porter (OG 1053, ABV 5.2%) ◆
Dark-coloured vanilla porter with roast malt aroma. Creamy bitter chocolate, liquorice, plum and black cherry, laced with cream. Burnt coffee aftertaste.

IPA (OG 1055, ABV 5.5%) ◆
Amber-coloured IPA with hop aroma. Powerful, earthy hop bitter and persistent malt flavours. Kaleidoscope of fruitiness. Long bitter finish.

Red IPA (OG 1057, ABV 5.9%) ◆
Tawny-red-coloured speciality beer. Powerful malt and liquorice flavours, followed by resinous hop, citrus and vine fruits. Long, dry, fruity finish.

Corvedale SIBA

Sun Inn, Corfton, Shropshire, SY7 9DF
☎ (01584) 861239 🌐 home.btconnect.com/thesuninncorfton/corvedale.html

Brewing started in 1999 behind the pub. Landlord Norman Pearce is also the brewer and uses only British malt and hops, with water from a local borehole. Beers are brewed for the pub and wider distribution. !! ◆ RAIB

Dale Ale (OG 1040, ABV 4%)
Aromas of smoky molasses and dates with fruity, nutty, toffee tastes.

Fuggles Gold (OG 1042, ABV 4.2%)

Golden Dale (OG 1043, ABV 4.2%)

Katie's Pride (OG 1040, ABV 4.3%)

Norman's Pride (OG 1043, ABV 4.3%)
An amber-coloured beer with a refreshing, slightly hoppy taste and a bitter finish.

Farmer Rays Ale (OG 1045, ABV 4.5%)
A clear, ruby-coloured bitter with a smooth, malty taste.

Oatmeal Stout (OG 1045, ABV 4.5%)

Pax Ale (OG 1045, ABV 4.5%)

Dark & Delicious (OG 1045, ABV 4.6%)
A dark ruby-coloured beer with hops on the aroma and palate and a sweet aftertaste.

Cosmic (NEW)

13 Glaisdale Road, Fishponds, Bristol, BS16 2HY
✉ cosmicbrewingco@gmail.com

Brewing began in 2018 in the Fishponds area of Bristol. Owner and brewer, Pete Livingstone, predominantly uses American hops and yeast to produce American beer styles. ◆ V

Buck (OG 1040, ABV 4%)

Jack Rabbit (OG 1050, ABV 5%)

Plead the Fifth (OG 1052, ABV 5.4%)

Porterhouse Rock (OG 1061, ABV 5.4%)

$5 Shake (OG 1060, ABV 6%)

NEIPAlm (OG 1072, ABV 6.6%)

Cotleigh SIBA

Ford Road, Wiveliscombe, Somerset, TA4 2RE
☎ (01984) 624086 🌐 cotleighbrewery.com

Established in 1979, Cotleigh is based in the historic town of Wiveliscombe. It supplies direct to 750 pubs, 200 retailers and selected wholesalers and is contracted to supply Co-op in the South West region. A visitor centre is now established and available for functions. Monthly events include folk, jazz, open mike and curry nights. !! ◆ RAIB

Harrier (OG 1035, ABV 3.5%)
A light, golden-coloured beer with a delicate floral, fruity aroma and a refreshing, sweet, slightly hoppy finish.

Tawny Owl (OG 1038, ABV 3.8%) ◆
Well-balanced, tawny-coloured bitter with malt and fruity aroma, major malt taste followed by hop fruit, developing to a satisfying bitter finish.

IPA (OG 1039, ABV 3.9%)

25 (OG 1040, ABV 4%)
A pale golden-coloured beer with a fresh aroma and fruit-filled finish.

Commando Hoofing (OG 1040, ABV 4%)
A pale golden-coloured beer, refreshing and slightly sparkling.

Golden Seahawk (OG 1042, ABV 4.2%) ◆
Well-hopped golden ale with flowery hop aroma and fruity hop flavour, clean mouthfeel, leading to a dry, hoppy finish.

Barn Owl (OG 1045, ABV 4.5%) ◆
Mid-brown-coloured beer with a well-balanced malt and hop aroma; a smooth, full-bodied taste where hops dominate, balanced by malt.

Honey Buzzard (OG 1045, ABV 4.5%)
A honey-infused beer with a smooth, creamy and chocolate palate offering a subtle bittersweet finish.

Old Buzzard (OG 1048, ABV 4.8%)
A dark-coloured ale with roasted chocolate malt giving a dry, nutty flavour. The finish is dry, smoky and smooth.

Cotswold SIBA

College Farm, Stow Road, Bourton-on-the-Water, Gloucestershire, GL54 2HN
☎ (01451) 824488 ☎ 07760 889100
🌐 cotswoldbrewco.uk

An independent producer of craft lager and speciality beers. The brewery was established in 2005 and expanded in 2010. More than 150 outlets are supplied, mainly in the Cotswolds and London. !! ◆ RAIB

Cask (OG 1040, ABV 4%)
A copper-coloured, well-hopped, easy-drinking ale.

Cotswold Lion SIBA

Grain Store 5, Dowmans Farm, Coberley, Gloucestershire, GL53 9QY

☎ (01242) 870164 🌐 cotswoldlionbrewery.co.uk

⊗ Brewing began in 2012 using a 10-barrel plant located in a grain store on a farm in the Cotswolds. RAIB

Shepherd's Delight (OG 1036, ABV 3.6%)
A light, crisp ale, full of citrus flavours.

Hogget (OG 1039, ABV 3.8%)
A copper-coloured best bitter. Fruit, light on the citrus with a hint of spice.

Best in Show (OG 1042, ABV 4.2%)
Plenty of blackberry fruit with a hint of honey.

Golden Fleece (OG 1044, ABV 4.4%)
An IPA with Jamaican fruit flavours.

Drover's Return (OG 1050, ABV 5%)
A strong, ruby-coloured bitter with malt notes shining through.

Cotton End

Pomfret Arms, 10 Cotton End, Northampton, NN4 8BS
☎ (01604) 765544

⊗ Established in 2015, Cotton End Brewery is located in the garden of the Pomfret Arms, Northampton. A one-barrel plant, it brews specialist beers on sale at the pub as well as other local outlets.

Standard, Isn't It? (OG 1035, ABV 3.5%)
An amber-coloured session ale. Slight bitter notes and a hoppy finish.

Aramis (OG 1043, ABV 4.3%)
A pale-coloured, single-hopped ale. Refreshing with a slight bitterness.

Conker Classic Celebration Ale (OG 1043, ABV 4.3%)
A refreshing, amber-coloured ale with a good balance of sweet and bitter.

Goldings Pale Ale (OG 1046, ABV 4.6%)
A light, refreshing, golden-coloured, hoppy ale. Crisp and fruity.

Orange Wheat (ABV 4.8%)
A light and refreshing clear wheat beer made with freshly squeezed orange juice and orange zest.

Spiced Wheat Beer (OG 1047, ABV 4.8%)
A light, refreshing clear wheat beer infused with lemon grass and ginger for a zesty finish.

Coffee Porter (OG 1056, ABV 5.2%)
Dark-coloured and strong with a treacle taste using freshly filtered coffee.

Double Oat Stout (OG 1058, ABV 6%)
A thick and creamy strong double stout made with rolled oats. Chocolate and toffee flavours.

Country Life SIBA

The Big Sheep, Abbotsham, Devon, EX39 5AP
☎ (01237) 420808 ☎ 07971 267790
🌐 countrylifebrewery.co.uk

⊗ Country Life is based at the Big Sheep tourist attraction. The brewery offers a beer show and free samples in the shop during the peak season (Apr-Oct). A 15.5-barrel plant was installed in 2005, making Country Life the biggest brewery in north Devon. Around 100 outlets are supplied. !! ♦ RAIB

Old Appledore (OG 1037, ABV 3.7%)

Reef Break (OG 1039, ABV 4%)
A gentle, sweet, malty beer.

Shore Break (OG 1042, ABV 4.4%)

Black Boar/Board Break (OG 1044, ABV 4.5%)
Complex, well-balanced aromas. Unusual dry bitter hop taste leading to softer aftertaste with unexpected roasted malt and caramel.

Golden Pig (OG 1046, ABV 4.7%)

Country Bumpkin (OG 1058, ABV 6%)
A malty, full-flavoured, smooth ale.

CrackleRock

The Old Cooperage, High Street, Botley, Hampshire, SO30 2EA ☎ 07733 232806 🌐 cracklerock.co.uk

⊗ CrackleRock began brewing in 2014 at the Old Cooperage in the centre of Botley with experienced head brewer Andy Ingram. In 2015 the Taproom bar opened (Thu-Sun). !! ♦

Crackerjack (OG 1039, ABV 3.8%)
Full-flavoured, clean-tasting, light and hoppy ale with slight citrus notes.

Fire Cracker (OG 1043, ABV 4.2%)
Well-balanced traditional English bitter.

Gold Rush (OG 1046, ABV 4.5%)
A slightly sweet, premium golden ale with a full, deep, malty flavour and good hop balance.

Dark Destroyer (OG 1490, ABV 4.9%)
A rich, strong, dark-coloured, smooth porter. A little caramel but not too burnt, well balanced with chocolate malt.

Crafty Shag (OG 1050, ABV 5%)
A smooth, strong, full-bodied, well-balanced ale.

Craddock's

Duke William, 25 Coventry Street, Stourbridge, West Midlands, DY8 1EP
☎ (01384) 440202 🌐 craddocksbrewery.com

⊗ Craddock's began brewing at the rear of the Duke William pub in Stourbridge, though the brewing is now also carried out in the courtyard of the Stable Bar, Bridgnorth. It is an eight-barrel plant selling exclusively to its four pubs; the Duke William and the Plough & Harrow, Stourbridge, the King Charles, Worcester, and the Talbot, Droitwich. !! ♦ RAIB

Craft, The

29a Part Street, Southport, Merseyside, PR8 1HY
☎ 07870 160934 🌐 thecraftbrewery.com

The Craft is a small-batch, independently owned microbrewery producing vegan-friendly, unfined, hand-crafted ales using traditional techniques. ♦

Crafty Gold (OG 1045, ABV 4%)
A smooth single malt beer with slight fruit flavours and a refreshing finish.

Crafty Ale (OG 1055, ABV 4.5%)
A rich, dark-coloured ale with chocolate undertones and a malty finish.

Crafty IPA (OG 1055, ABV 4.5%)
A full-flavoured IPA, slightly bitter with citrus notes and a clean, dry finish.

Crafty Devil (OG 1062, ABV 5%)

A dark-coloured, rich, traditional porter with a hint of cherry.

Crafty Smoke (OG 1064, ABV 5%)
A pale ale with a pleasant smoky aftertaste.

Craft Academy (NEW)

Florence, 131-133 Dulwich Road, Herne Hill, London, SE24 0NG florencehernehill.com

The Florence Brewery is run by an on-site brewing team, the Craft Academy. Craft Academy was set up by Greene King in 2016 as an apprentice-led scheme offering young people the chance to learn the art of brewing. Beer is only available in the pub.

Craft Originale

1 Tofthill, Markinch, KY7 6HN ☎ 07790 172708
john@craftrigins.co.uk

Small scale brewing began in 2017.

Crafted

Unit 3c, Bewdley Business Park, Long Bank, Bewdley, Worcestershire, DY12 2TZ
☎ (01299) 269382 ☎ 07851 862254
craftedbrewing.co.uk

Set up in 2016, the brewery uses a five-barrel plant from Woodbury Brewery in Worcestershire. Beers are currently only available in the local area.

White Goose (OG 1036, ABV 3.8%)
Toffee aromas, fruity, smooth bitterness with a sweet, dry finish.

The Revolution (OG 1039, ABV 4%)
Honey, pine aromas, light toffee and caramel flavours.

Wyre (OG 1048, ABV 5%)
Amber-coloured strong bitter, apricot and light citrus aromas with a smooth and light fruity taste.

Crafty Beers

The Stables, Hall Farm, Stetchworth, Cambridgeshire, CB8 0TY
☎ (01223) 813938 craftybeers.co.uk

Crafty Beers are brewed by Robert Beardsmore in an old stable building situated between Cambridge and Newmarket. Brewing started in 2012 at the Carpenters Arms, Great Wilbraham. The move to larger premises in 2016 was made to increase brewing capacity. Beer is available at a number of pubs in and around Cambridge. RAIB

Mild Mannered (OG 1040, ABV 3.5%)
Dark mild with a pleasant balance of sweet malt and tempered bitterness.

Carpenter's Cask (OG 1038, ABV 3.8%)
A well-balanced, amber-coloured brew with biscuit malt character giving way to hops on the palate and long finish.

Sixteen Strides (OG 1037, ABV 3.8%)
Generously-hopped pale ale with plenty of citrus aroma.

Wilbraham (OG 1042, ABV 4.1%)
Amber-coloured ale with rich malt flavours and good balancing bitterness. Subtle hop aroma with earthy hop notes.

Sauvignon Blonde (OG 1043, ABV 4.4%)
An aromatic golden ale.

Crafty Brewing SIBA

Thatched House Farm, Loxhill, Dunsfold, Surrey, GU8 4BW
☎ (01483) 276300 ☎ 07702 305595
craftybrewing.co.uk

Opened in 2014 and situated on Luke Herman's family farm behind Dunsfold aerodrome, Crafty's base has a historic connection with the Canadian troop presence during WWII. The five-barrel plant supplies more than 175 pubs across the region plus local events and markets. RAIB

Loxhill Biscuit (OG 1038, ABV 3.8%)
Golden-coloured bitter which belies its strength. Initial malty aroma and taste with a dry bitter finish.

Dark Sessions (OG 1040, ABV 4%)
A light-bodied, dark-coloured beer with hints of chocolate and orange.

Dunsfold Best (OG 1040, ABV 4%)
A deep red-coloured English bitter, with initial toffee and caramel aromas, which leads to a slightly vinous flavour and a sweetish taste. The finish is shorter but with the caramel notes still present.

Five Hop (OG 1040, ABV 4%)
An IPA with heady aromas of mango and citrus.

Crafty One (OG 1042, ABV 4.2%)
Golden-yellow-coloured beer. Tropical fruits aroma leads to a full bitterness with a dry finish.

Hop Tipple (OG 1042, ABV 4.2%)
A dry-hopped beer with aromas of tropical fruits.

Crafty Devil

Ninian Park Road, Cardiff
☎ (029) 2021 8099 ☎ 07766 014550
craftydevilbrewing.co.uk

Crafty Devil began brewing in 2014. It currently only produces bottled, canned and keg beers but cask-conditioned beer can be arranged by special request, particularly for local events. !!

Crafty Dragon (NEW)

8 Castell Morlais, Pontsticill, CF48 2YB

Crafty Dragon began brewing in 2017 and is situated within the Brecon Beacons National Park.

Crawshay's Bitter (ABV 4.4%)
A pale-coloured bitter with citrus notes.

Crafty Little (NEW) SIBA

Building 40, British Aerospace Business Park, Saltgrounds Road, Brough, East Yorkshire, HU15 1EQ
☎ (01482) 661393 thecraftylittlebrewery.co.uk

Crystalbrew Ales Ltd, now trading as the Crafty Little Brewery, is an East Yorkshire family-run business. !! RAIB

ChamALEon (OG 1036, ABV 4%)

Red Tale (OG 1042, ABV 4.5%)

Well-balanced beer with toasted malt notes, earthy undertones and a light burst of passion fruit, pine and forest berries.

Black Ryeno (OG 1043.5, ABV 4.6%)
Well-balanced and delicate with lightly toasted liquorice, citrus and stone fruit flavours coming through.

Perky Porter (OG 1046, ABV 4.8%)
Slightly sweet, a velvety rich roasted coffee porter.

Wolf Bite APA (OG 1048, ABV 4.8%)
An intense blend of refreshing fruit, heady with citrus, a touch of pine and a powerful, lingering aftertaste.

Contract brewed for Dicks Brewery:

Big Head Bitter (OG 1043, ABV 4%)

Crafty Monkey (NEW)

Benknowle Farm, Elwick, TS27 3HF
🌐 craftymonkey.beer

Brewing commenced in 2018 on a plant supplied by Oban Ales.

New Gold Dream (ABV 4.1%)

New Era (ABV 4.7%)

Crafty Pint

c/o Half Moon, 130 Northgate, Darlington, County Durham, DL1 1QS
☎ (01325) 469965 ☎ 07804 305175

The Crafty Pint Brewery was established in 2013 in the cellar of the Half Moon in Darlington. Originally a 10-gallon brew length, it was upgraded to a one-barrel plant in 2015. One-off beers are produced solely for the pub with a few other outlets being occasionally supplied. ♦

Crankshaft

17e Boxer Place, Leyland, Lancashire, PR26 7QL
☎ 07827 289200 🌐 crankshaftbrewery.co.uk

Crankshaft was launched in 2016, brewing from home on a 0.5-barrel plant. It moved to new premises in 2017 using a 2.5-barrel plant due to demand. The beers are regularly available at local micropubs and beer festivals and in bottles at specialist outlets and local markets. ♦

Propshaft (OG 1038, ABV 3.8%)
A pale golden-coloured session beer. English hops give the ale a refreshing, grassy, earthy taste.

Crankcase (OG 1046, ABV 5%)

Ribble Red (OG 1047, ABV 5%)

Dryveshaft (OG 1054, ABV 5.2%)

Leyland Tiger Cub (OG 1052, ABV 5.5%)

Leyland Badger (OG 1058, ABV 5.8%)
Caramelised treacle toffee flavour and a dry taste with a hint of hops. Plenty of body and a smooth mouthfeel.

Sumners Steam (OG 1068, ABV 6.6%)

Crate

Unit 7, White Building, Queens Yard, Hackney Wick, London, E9 5EN ☎ 07834 275687
🌐 cratebrewery.com

Crate is a brewery and pizzeria opened in 2012 and situated in a canalside former print factory. RAIB

Best Bitter (OG 1045, ABV 4.3%)
Brown-coloured beer with roast and berry fruitiness. Sweetness and biscuit character is offset by bitterness that lingers with roast notes.

Stout (OG 1057, ABV 5.7%)
Slightly smoky nose with blackcurrant fruit. Caramelised toffee and liquorice flavour that lingers. Black roast notes throughout.

Creaton Grange (NEW)

Old Wash House, Creaton Grange, Grooms Lane, Creaton, Northamptonshire, NN6 8NN ☎ 07943 595829 🌐 creatongrangeales.co.uk

Microbrewery started in 2017 and based in a converted disused building on a family farm in rural Northamptonshire.

Pheasant Tale (OG 1038, ABV 3.8%)

Credence SIBA

Unit 16b, Coquet Enterprise Park, Amble, Northumberland, NE65 0PE
☎ (01665) 715855 🌐 credencebrewing.co.uk

Credence began brewing in 2015. A barrel aging programme is being established and a new trade counter is the first step in opening up the brewery to the public. Around 100 outlets are supplied direct. ♦RAIB

Revolving Session Pale (ABV 3.6%)

Blonde (ABV 4%)

Clearwater (ABV 4.2%)

Liberty (ABV 4.2%)

Porter (ABV 4.4%)

White Session IPA (ABV 4.8%)

Elemental IPA (ABV 5.5%)

Cricklewood (NEW)

Cotswold Gardens, Cricklewood, London, NW2

Brewing commenced in 2016 at the brewer's home. RAIB

Croft (NEW)

32 Upper York Street, Stokes Croft, Bristol, BS2 8QN
☎ 07480 624212 🌐 croftales.com

Croft began brewing in 2017 in a former faggot factory in Bristol's vibrant Stokes Croft area, from which the brewery takes its name. The brewery also serves as a tap room, which holds regular tasting events and launches of its seasonal ales, which are often accompanied by DJs and pop-up food vendors. !! ♦V

BS2 (OG 1042, ABV 4%)
Hazy, unfined golden ale with a grassy hop aroma, clean yet slightly sweet citrus flavours and a balanced, somewhat dry bitter finish.

Beast (OG 1042, ABV 4.2%)
Traditional-style best bitter, dark brown in colour with a good balance of malt and hops.

Backjump (OG 1046, ABV 4.5%)

THE BREWERIES

Classic English pale ale with aromas of citrus and spice.

Westide (OG 1045, ABV 4.5%)
Refreshing, distinctive pale ale with pine notes and a long citrus finish.

Deep Red (OG 1055, ABV 5.5%) ◆
Hoppy, red-coloured ale combining rye with sweetish malt and pine notes on the palate, finishing with a lingering bitterness.

Uproar (OG 1056, ABV 5.6%)
English IPA, spicy and aromatic with earthy notes.

Cromarty

Davidston, Cromarty, IV11 8XD
☎ (01381) 600440 ⊕ cromartybrewing.co.uk

Cromarty began brewing in 2011 in a purpose-built brewhouse. Additional fermenters were installed in 2014 and again in 2015 to meet demand. ‼ ♦

Atlantic Drift (OG 1035, ABV 3.5%) ◆
Good golden amber-coloured beer with a grapefruit hop flavour throughout.

Hit the Lip (OG 1037, ABV 3.8%) ◆
A good mouth-puckering grapefruit hoppy brew with a dry finish.

Happy Chappy (OG 1040, ABV 4.1%) ◆
A golden ale with plenty of hop character. Floral citrus hop aroma with a good bitter taste, which increases in aftertaste.

Kowabunga (OG 1046, ABV 4.6%) ◆
Refreshing, golden-coloured, peachy, hoppy brew.

Red Rocker (OG 1048.5, ABV 5%) ◆
Red-coloured rye speciality hop monster with a malty background leading to a bitter finish.

Rogue Wave (OG 1052, ABV 5.7%) ◆
Easy-drinking, strong, peachy, hoppy bitter.

Ghost Town (OG 1058, ABV 5.8%) ◆
Classic dark roasted malty porter with blackcurrant and liquorice background.

AKA IPA (OG 1067, ABV 6.7%) ◆
Strong IPA with a smooth, citrus hoppy taste.

Cronx SIBA

Unit 6, Vulcan Business Centre, Vulcan Way, New Addington, CR0 9UG
☎ (01689) 809093 ☎ 07793 974395
⊕ thecronx.com

⊗ Cronx began brewing in 2012 and is the first commercial brewery in the area since 1954. ‼ ♦

Standard (ABV 3.8%) ◆
Easy-drinking, brown-coloured bitter with sweetish fudge and spicy hoppiness notes throughout. A malty bitter finish with a dryness that remains.

Kotchin (ABV 3.9%) ◆
Grapefruity beer with pleasant hoppy notes. A little sweetness is balanced by a crisp bitter finish that grows on drinking.

Nektar (ABV 4.5%) ◆
Full-bodied, dark gold-coloured best bitter. Peach with citrus, sweet biscuit and floral hops, gently fade in the lingering bitter finish.

Entire (ABV 5.2%) ◆
Dark brown-coloured porter with chocolate roast notes in the aroma, flavour and finish. The fruit character is of caramelised raisins.

Crooked (NEW)

Units 12-15, The Garages, Leeds East Airport, Church Fenton, LS24 9SE ☎ 07890 526505
⊕ crookedbrewing.co.uk

Steve, Andy, Hudson and Mark started brewing in 2017. Beers are available in a number of city centre bars in York and Leeds.

Spokes (ABV 4%)
A session beer with a subtle blend of orange and grapefruit hop notes.

The Lash (ABV 4.4%)
A pale ale with juicy hop notes.

Rufus (ABV 4.8%)
A naturally hazy, hoppy, red-coloured ale.

Cropton

See Great Yorkshire

Cross Bay

White Lund Industrial Estate, Morecambe, Lancashire, LA3 3PT
☎ (01524) 39481 ⊕ crossbaybrewery.co.uk

Cross Bay commenced brewing in 2011 on a 28-barrel brew plant. In 2017 it rebranded its core range introducing a couple of brand new ales. An on-site brewery tap room opened in 2018. The beers are widely available around North-west England. ‼ ♦

Halo (OG 1037, ABV 3.6%) ◆
A crisp and hoppy, pale-coloured bitter.

Vesper (ABV 3.8%)
Bright tropical fruit flavours from American hops dominate this crisp and smooth beer.

RIPA (ABV 4%)

Sunset Blonde (OG 1043, ABV 4.2%) ◆
Sweet and fruity best bitter with a rising bitter finish.

Zenith (OG 1050, ABV 5%) ◆
Gentle bitterness and fruity sweetness with some astringency in the finish.

Cross Borders SIBA

28-1, Hardengreen Industrial Estate, Dalkeith, EH22 3NX
☎ (0131) 629 3990 ⊕ crossborders.beer

⊗ Established in 2016 by two friends, Jonathan Wilson and Gary Munckton. The brewery features an on-site tap (phone for opening hours). ♦

Pale (OG 1040, ABV 3.8%)
Notes of mint and lemon on the nose with a balanced citrus bitter finish.

Heavy (OG 1054, ABV 4.1%)
A malt-forward ale with a slight hoppy bite to the finish.

Porter (OG 1045, ABV 4.2%)
A porter with a roasted, smooth mouthfeel. Flavours of coffee, chocolate and subtle spice come through in the finish.

IPA (OG 1044, ABV 4.5%)
Aromas of pear and pineapple on the nose, followed by a resinous pine, bitter finish.

BRAW (OG 1055, ABV 5.2%)
A juicy, refreshing pale ale with citrus and tropical notes.

Crossed Anchors SIBA

c/o Grapevine, 2 Victoria Road, Exmouth, Devon, EX8 1DL
☎ (01395) 222208 ☎ 07843 577608
crossedanchors.co.uk

Crossed Anchors was established in 2015, with the beer initially produced using spare capacity at another brewery. In 2016 a six-barrel plant became operational in the old stables of the Grapevine in Exmouth town centre. Beers are available across Devon and the South-west, as well as in the Grapevine. ♦

CSH (OG 1038, ABV 3.8%)
A yellow-coloured beer with a hoppy aroma, less bitter in taste than expected.

Bitter Exe (OG 1041, ABV 4%)
A bitter beer, deep brown in colour with a light citrus aroma and taste and hints of marmalade.

Three Cs Gold (OG 1040, ABV 4.3%)
Pale gold-coloured beer with a strong hop aroma. Well-balanced and easy-drinking with a hoppy bitterness.

American Pale Ale (OG 1045, ABV 4.6%)
A copper-coloured ale with a citrus hop and stone fruit aroma. The fruit and hops continue in the taste and aftertaste.

Weisse Guy (OG 1047, ABV 5%)
A naturally hazy German-style wheat beer. It has an aroma of banana and lemon, with a crisp malty taste with a hint of cloves and a long finish.

Crouch Vale SIBA

23 Haltwhistle Road, South Woodham Ferrers, Essex, CM3 5ZA
☎ (01245) 322744 crouchvale.co.uk

Founded in 1981 by two CAMRA enthusiasts, Crouch Vale is now well established as a major player in Essex brewing, having moved to larger premises in 2006. The company is also a major wholesaler of cask ale from other independent breweries, which it supplies to more than 100 outlets, as well as beer festivals throughout the region. A tap room opened on the brewery site in 2016. One tied house, the Queen's Head in Chelmsford, is owned. !! ♦ RAIB

Blackwater Mild (OG 1037, ABV 3.7%)
A dark-coloured bitter rather than a true mild. Roasty and very bitter towards the end.

Essex Boys Best Bitter (OG 1038, ABV 3.8%)
Full-bodied, traditional-style, mid-brown-coloured best bitter.

Brewers Gold (OG 1040, ABV 4%)
Pale golden ale with a striking citrus nose. Sweet fruit and bitter hops are well matched throughout.

Yakima Gold (OG 1042, ABV 4.2%)
A golden-coloured ale with earthy hop notes.

Amarillo (OG 1050, ABV 5%)
A premium golden ale with a lasting spicy and orange flavour.

Crown (NEW)

Crown, Green End, Little Staughton, Bedfordshire, MK44 2BU
☎ (01234) 376260 thecrownstaughton.com

Brewing began in 2017 in a building behind the Crown public house in Little Staughton. The brewery is owned and run by the landlord of the Crown with the beers only being produced for the pub. ♦

Crown Brewhouse (NEW)

The Square, Elford, Staffordshire, B79 9DB
☎ (01827) 383602 ✉ bluecatsup@hotmail.com

A one-barrel brew plant, established in 2017 and housed in a former store room attached to the Crown pub. The pub and a limited number of local outlets are supplied.

Crystalbrew

See Crafty Little

Cuillin

Sligachan Hotel, Sligachan, Isle of Skye, IV47 8SW
☎ (01478) 650204 ☎ 07795 250808
cuillinbrewery.com

The five-barrel brewery opened in 2004 and is situated in central Skye at the foot of the Cuillin mountains. The water from the Cuillins provides a distinctive colour and taste to the ales. Beers are available on site at the Sligachan Hotel and at several other pubs and hotels on the Isle of Skye. The brewery is open by appointment only in winter (Nov-Mar). !! ♦

Cullercoats SIBA

Westfield Court, 19 Maurice Road Industrial Estate, Wallsend, Tyne & Wear, NE28 6BY ☎ 07837 637615

Office: 17 St Oswins Avenue, Cullercoats, NE30 4PH
cullercoatsbrewery.co.uk

Established in 2011 with brewing taking place twice a week. The brewery champions English hops. ♦ RAIB

Shuggy Boat Blonde (OG 1039, ABV 3.8%)
A refreshing, fruity blonde ale.

Lovely Nelly (OG 1039, ABV 3.9%)
A full-bodied, amber bronze-coloured session beer with a biscuit malt flavour balanced by a smooth hop bitterness.

Jack the Devil (OG 1045, ABV 4.5%)
A rich, dark chestnut-coloured ale with a good balance of malty nuttiness and fresh hop aroma.

Grace Darling Gold (OG 1050, ABV 5%)

Rocket Brigade (OG 1054, ABV 5.5%)
An English pale ale, strong and bitter yet easy drinking.

Cumberland

See Great Corby

Cumbrian Legendary SIBA

Old Hall Brewery, Hawkshead, Cumbria, LA22 0QF
☎ (01539) 436436 🌐 cumbrianlegendaryales.com

First established in 2003, the brewery is located in an idyllic position in a renovated barn on the shores of Esthwaite Water. The success of Loweswater Gold has meant the brewery is thriving. ‼♦

Esthwaite Bitter (OG 1038.5, ABV 3.8%)
Robust, refreshing bitter with plenty of hops, lasting well into the finish.

Langdale (OG 1040, ABV 4%)
Fresh grapefruit aromas with hoppy, fruity flavours and crisp long hop finish, make for a well-balanced beer.

Grasmoor Dark Ale (OG 1043, ABV 4.3%)
Dark-coloured, fruity beer with complex character and roast nutty tones leading to a short, refreshing finish.

Loweswater Gold (OG 1041, ABV 4.3%)
A dominant fruity body develops into a light bitter finish. A beer that belies its strength.

American Invasion (OG 1047, ABV 5%)
Well-balanced, gold-coloured beer with big hop impact and long fruity finish.

Cwm Rhondda

Fforch Farm, Cemetery Road, Treorchy, CF42 6TF
☎ (01443) 777491 🌐 cwmrhonddaales.co.uk

Cwm Rhondda is a family-run brewery situated on a farm in the Rhondda Valley. Brewing commenced in 2015 on a 2.5-barrel plant using the brewery's own spring water, which gives a unique taste to the ales. Expansion to the brewery, an online shop and a farm shop in a nearby village are planned.

Shwmae But (OG 1039, ABV 3.8%)

Boyo (OG 1044, ABV 4.5%)

Tommy Box (OG 1044, ABV 4.5%)

Afon Aur (OG 1046, ABV 4.6%)

Daleside SIBA

Camwal Road, Starbeck, Harrogate, North Yorkshire, HG1 4PT
☎ (01423) 880022 🌐 dalesidebrewery.com

Daleside opened in the mid-1980s before moving to larger premises in 1992. Further expansion has resulted in a 20-barrel plant. The brewery delivers direct to a range of outlets including pubs, restaurants and farm shops from Newcastle to Chesterfield as well as nationally via wholesalers. ♦

Bitter (OG 1039, ABV 3.7%)
Pale brown in colour, this well-balanced, hoppy beer is complemented by fruity bitterness and a hint of sweetness, leading to a long, bitter finish.

Blonde (OG 1040, ABV 3.9%)
A pale golden-coloured beer with a predominantly hoppy aroma and taste, leading to a refreshing hoppy, bitter but short finish.

Old Leg Over (OG 1043, ABV 4.1%)
Well-balanced, mid brown-coloured, refreshing beer that leads to an equally well-balanced, fruity, bitter aftertaste.

Square Rigger IPA (ABV 4.5%)
Light amber-coloured IPA with a floral aroma.

Monkey Wrench (OG 1055, ABV 5.3%)
Premium deep chestnut red-coloured ale with a spicy fruit aroma and warming spicy flavour.

Dalrannoch

Unit 16, The Old Dairy, Meikleour, PH2 6FB
🌐 dalrannochbrewing.co.uk

Brewing began in 2016 using a five-barrel plant.

Dan's

See Wander Beyond

Dancing Cows

Sadlers Farm Workshops, Lower Pennington Lane, Lymington, Hampshire, SO41 8AL
☎ (01590) 676071 ☎ 07952 639465
🌐 dancingcows.co.uk

Dancing Cows is a small-batch brewery and distillery close to Ancient Causeway and Pennington & Keyhaven Nature Reserve, sourcing local grains, hops, herbs and spices. Operated by the former owner of Bowland Brewery in Lancashire and inspired by a trip to Lake Michigan to bring a fresh outlook on brewing. New recipes are being developed constantly. ‼ ♦RAIB

Lighthouse (OG 1038, ABV 3.8%)
A golden ale with grapefruit hop flavours and aromas.

Pony (OG 1040, ABV 4%)
A traditional amber-coloured ale with rounded fruit flavours and good malt characteristics.

Admiral (OG 1045, ABV 4.5%)
A traditional best bitter with subtle orange hop notes.

Dancing Duck SIBA

1 John Cooper Buildings, Payne Street, Derby, DE22 3AZ
☎ (01332) 205582 ☎ 07581 122122
🌐 dancingduckbrewery.com

Dancing Duck was established in 2010 by Rachel Mathews using a 10-barrel brew plant. Its name comes from the local greeting 'ay up me duck'. The Exeter Arms in Derby is the brewery tap. ♦

Ay Up (OG 1040.5, ABV 3.9%)
A session pale ale with subtle malt and floral notes matched with citrus hop, rounded off with a slightly dry finish.

Waitangi (OG 1041.3, ABV 4%)
An easy-drinking, crisp, clean pale ale. Subtle malt character is balanced with zesty lemon and lime hops.

Ginger Ninja (OG 1042, ABV 4.1%)
Well-balanced, refreshing ale with citrus hop notes and a subtle ginger flavour.

Nice Weather (OG 1042, ABV 4.1%)
Copper-coloured, fruity ale packed full of flavour. Blackberry, strawberry and floral rose notes in perfect balance with a malt character. A refreshing summer thirst quencher, it's fruit salad in a glass

22 (OG 1044.1, ABV 4.3%)

A well-balanced best bitter with good malty flavour and dark fruit notes offset by a strong hop and clean finish.

DCUK (OG 1042, ABV 4.3%)
A pale ale with a fruity aroma and juicy citrus flavour with hints of orange, mango, lemon and pine.

Dark Drake (OG 1051, ABV 4.5%)
Malty, caramel, liquorice flavours combine in a smooth-drinking, velvety oatmeal stout with a freshly roasted coffee finish.

Waddle It Be? (OG 1045.2, ABV 4.5%)
Pale ale with a complex mouthfeel and intense fruity flavours of oranges, peaches and blackcurrants with a spicy black pepper kick.

Gold (OG 1046.5, ABV 4.7%)
A modern IPA with powerful hoppy bitterness and aroma balanced with strong malt notes.

Amberillo (OG 1047.2, ABV 4.8%)
An easy-drinking, amber-coloured ale. Earthy aromatic hops are balanced with biscuit malt flavours leading to a spicy, peppery finish.

Indian Porter (OG 1051.8, ABV 5%)
Smoky bonfire flavours with a spicy hop and pleasant warming afterglow.

Seduction (OG 1051.3, ABV 5.2%)
A ruby-coloured, malty beer. Dark, fruity flavours are followed by a lingering powerful hop taste.

Abduction (OG 1053, ABV 5.5%)
A myriad of tropical flavours in balance with a good level of hoppy bitterness, a malty character and clean finish.

Duck a l'Orange (ABV 6.4%)

Dancing Man SIBA

Wool House, Town Quay, Southampton, Hampshire, SO14 2AR
☎ (023) 8083 6666 ⊕ dancingmanbrewery.co.uk

⊗ Dancing Man began brewing in 2011 in the Platform Tavern. In 2015 the brewery moved to the historic Wool House, the only surviving freestanding medieval building in Southampton, in order to expand and include an on-site bar and restaurant. One-off and rare brews are available throughout the year. !! ♦ RAIB

Congo Driftwood (OG 1042, ABV 4.2%)
A modern pale ale with the addition of fresh mango and papaya, which deliver unique tropical flavours.

Fiddler's Jig (OG 1047, ABV 4.8%)
A rich malt body with fruity hop flavours.

Last Waltz (OG 1052, ABV 5.3%)
A black IPA with an intense hoppy nose, tropical fruit notes, a smoky roasted malt flavour and a dry bitter finish.

Big Casino (OG 1056, ABV 5.7%)
Pine and citrus fruit aroma with a warming malt body and a smooth bitterness with juicy hop flavours.

Pole-Axed IPA (ABV 6.7%)
An IPA with strong, hoppy flavours, sweet caramel notes and balanced bitterness.

Dancing Men

Hill House Inn, The Hill, Happisburgh, Norfolk, NR12 0PW
☎ (01692) 650004 ☎ 07818 038768
⊕ hillhouseinn.co.uk

⊗ Brewing began in 2014 at the 16th-century Hill House Inn on Happisburgh's fast-eroding clifftop. The microbrewery is named in honour of a famous Sherlock Holmes story written by Sir Arthur Conan Doyle after he visited the pub in 1903. The five-barrel plant was acquired from Bees Brewery after its partial destruction during the tidal surge events in Walcott in 2013. New recipes have been crafted using exclusive hops and barley including locally-grown Norfolk varieties. !! ♦

Dark Horse SIBA

Coonlands Laithe, Hetton, North Yorkshire, BD23 6LY
☎ (01756) 730555 ⊕ darkhorsebrewery.co.uk

Dark Horse began brewing in 2008. The brewery is based in an old hay barn within the Yorkshire Dales National Park. Around 50 outlets are supplied direct.

Craven Bitter (OG 1038, ABV 3.8%) ◆
Well-balanced bitter with biscuity malt and fruit on the nose continuing into the taste. Bitterness increases in the finish.

Blonde Beauty (OG 1040, ABV 3.9%)

Hetton Pale Ale (OG 1041, ABV 4.2%) ◆
Golden, well-balanced, full-bodied, with hoppy bitterness on the palate overlaying a malty base and a spicy citrus character.

Night Jar (OG 1042, ABV 4.2%) ◆
A malty, fruity bitter in aroma and taste. Caramel and dark fruits lace the finish.

Dark Revolution SIBA

Unit 3-5, Lancaster Road, Salisbury, Wiltshire, SP4 6FB
☎ (01722) 411179 ⊕ darkrevolution.co.uk

Dark Revolution started commercial brewing in 2015 using a one-barrel plant; the owner had been home-brewing for the previous decade. It upgraded to a 15-barrel brew plant in 2017 retaining the smaller plant for trial brews and short runs. An on-site taproom is also now open. Barrel aging is a speciality. ♦ RAIB

So.LA (ABV 4.5%)

Velveteen (ABV 4.8%) ◆
A smooth, rich, black-coloured stout, served unfined. Noticeable malt and roast in the taste with balanced bitterness through to the finish.

Deviant (ABV 5.6%)

ViPA (ABV 6%)

Dark Star

22 Star Road, Partridge Green, West Sussex, RH13 8RA
☎ (01403) 713085 ⊕ darkstarbrewing.co.uk

⊗ The Dark Star Brewing Co is named after a Grateful Dead song and was established in the cellar of the Evening Star in Brighton back in 1994, moving to its current home in Partridge Green in

2010. Owned by Fuller's, the 45-barrel plant produces a wide range of beers. !! ♦ RAIB

The Art of Darkness (OG 1040, ABV 3.5%)
Roast flavours with a hint of sweetness. Fruity and spicy hop flavours add balance.

Hophead (OG 1040, ABV 3.8%)
A golden-coloured bitter with a fruity, hoppy aroma and a citrus bitter taste and aftertaste. Flavours remain strong to the end.

Partridge Best Bitter (OG 1042, ABV 4%)

Espresso (OG 1048, ABV 4.2%)
A rich, black-coloured beer with added freshly ground Arabica coffee beans.

American Pale Ale (OG 1048, ABV 4.7%)

Festival (OG 1052, ABV 5%)
A bronze-coloured bitter with a smooth mouthfeel and freshness.

Original (OG 1052, ABV 5%)
A dark-coloured, strong and bitter beer.

Revelation (OG 1057, ABV 5.7%)

Dark Tribe SIBA

Dog & Gun, High Street, East Butterwick, Lincolnshire, DN17 3AJ
☎ (01724) 782324 darktribe.co.uk

Situated on the banks of the River Trent in the Dog & Gun pub, this 2.5-barrel brewing plant produces beers for the pub and local outlets. The award-winning brewery has been established since 1996. A range of one-off beers is produced throughout the year. !! ♦

Darkplace (NEW) SIBA

6a Wheelers Yard, Colyton Business Park, Colyton, Devon, EX24 6DT
☎ (01297) 551583

A microbrewery established in 2017 using a four-barrel plant. The brewer is frequently trialling new recipes and the majority of current production is bottle-conditioned. All beers are unfiltered, unfined and unpasteurised. An on-site brewery bar is planned. RAIB

Darkwave

52-54 Aqueduct Street, Preston, Lancashire, PR1 7RE
☎ 07970 110459 darkwave-ale@outlook.com

Previously known as Arkwright's, brewing began at the rear of the Real Ale Shop on Lovat Road in 2010 using a 2.5-barrel plant. In 2014 the plant was upgraded to a 10-barrel plant and moved to the current premises. Darkwave are now producing a range of modern artisan beers, always unfined and vegan. ♦V

Dartmoor SIBA

The Brewery, Station Road, Princetown, Devon, PL20 6QX
☎ (01822) 890789 dartmoorbrewery.co.uk

Formerly named Princetown, Dartmoor Brewery was established in 1994 and is the highest brewery in England at 1,465 feet above sea level. In 2006 the brewery moved to a purpose-built building and in 2012 capacity was increased to 360 barrels a week by the addition of another 60-barrel fermenter with a further increase in 2013. All beer is brewed using Dartmoor and Devon-grown barley. !! ♦

Dartmoor Best (OG 1037, ABV 3.7%)
An amber-coloured ale with a dry hop citrus fruit character.

IPA (OG 1039.5, ABV 4%)
There is a flowery hop aroma and taste with a bitter aftertaste to this full-bodied, amber-coloured beer.

Legend (OG 1043.5, ABV 4.4%)
Complex beer full of aromas and flavours. Malt and caramel dominate balanced in an aftertaste of bitter hops. Well-rounded.

Jail Ale (OG 1047.5, ABV 4.8%)
Stronger session ale with complex notes dominated by malty sweet bitterness. Well-rounded caramel and fruit with a pleasant aftertaste.

Darwin SIBA

1 West Quay Court, Sunderland Enterprise Park, Sunderland, SR5 2TE
☎ (0191) 549 9450 darwinbrewery.com

Established in 1994, Darwin Brewery is based in purpose-built premises in Sunderland with a 3.5-barrel brew plant. The brewery supports students on Brewlab brewing courses at the university, who produce many unique specialist and international beers, often available locally. A range of established Darwin beers is also produced, some based on analysis of historic recipes or student initiatives. !! ♦ RAIB

Dawkins SIBA

Unit 2, Lawnwood Industrial Units, Lawnwood Road, Easton, Bristol, BS5 0EF
☎ (0117) 955 9503 dawkinsales.com

The established Dawkins Taverns group of independent Bristol pubs bought the Somerset-based Matthews Brewery in 2009. New premises in Easton, Bristol, opened in 2015 with a 20-barrel plant. The brewery distributes to its own five pubs and directly to another 80 outlets in the area. A sister company was set up in Edinburgh in 2017, reviving the long-defunct 'Steel Coulson' brewing name for a bar in Leith with an on-site microbrewery planned. !! ♦ RAIB

Bristol Blonde (OG 1036, ABV 3.8%)
Pale yellow-coloured ale. Citrus aroma. Refreshing lemon taste with grassiness, which fades to astringent bitterness.

Bristol Best (OG 1040, ABV 4%)
Copper-coloured bitter with malty aroma and taste. Hints of apple. Astringent aftertaste.

Tremendous Delicious (OG 1042, ABV 4.2%)
Amber-coloured ale with a malty base balanced with soft apple fruit and a background hop bitterness that lingers in the aftertaste.

Bristol Gold (OG 1043, ABV 4.4%)
Golden ale with a slightly spicy fruit aroma and flavour.

Easton IPA (OG 1041, ABV 4.4%)

Hazy golden yellow-coloured unfined ale. Hop and ripe apple aroma. Slightly sour citrus on the palate. Dry and bitter aftertaste.

Resolution IPA (OG 1046, ABV 5%) ◈
Naturally hazy golden yellow-coloured beer with aromas of tropical fruit. Flavours of grapefruit and lemon continue into the bitter finish.

Dead Parrot (NEW)

44 Garden Street, Sheffield, South Yorkshire, S1 4BJ

New brewery established in 2018. An on-site taproom is planned.

Bohemia (ABV 3.7%)

Aurornis XUI (ABV 4.6%)

Deben Peninsular (NEW)

9 Rendlesham Mews, Rendlesham, Suffolk, IP12 2SZ
☎ 07825 670865 🌐 redwalds.co.uk

Nanobrewery a few doors down from the owner's micropub, Redwalds Ale House.

Deeply Vale

Unit 25, Peel Industrial Estate, Chamberhall Street, Bury, BL9 0LU
☎ (0161) 761 7334 ☎ 07736 936973
🌐 deeplyvalebrewery.com

Deeply Vale is a family-run business established in 2012 using a 2.5-barrel plant. The brewery's name immortalises the Deeply Vale area near Bury, famed for legendary 1970s music festivals. Beers are distributed to upwards of 150 regular outlets within a 40-mile radius of Bury. ♦RAIB

Equilibrium (OG 1036, ABV 3.8%)
A well-balanced golden ale. A malty base topped with just the right amount of bitterness to complement its satisfying aroma.

Session (ABV 3.9%)
A pale ale with a buttery biscuit base.

Citra Storm (OG 1038, ABV 4%)
A refreshing pale ale bursting with lemon and grapefruit flavours and aromas.

Ripper (OG 1038, ABV 4%)
A pale ale with a clean, fresh taste and hints of peaches and apricots.

Deeply Best (ABV 4.2%)
A well-balanced best bitter with a fruity aroma and crisp, malty finish.

Deeply Blonde (OG 1043, ABV 4.5%)
An easy-drinking golden ale with a citrus and tropical fruit explosion.

DV8 (OG 1050, ABV 4.8%)
Smooth, easy-drinking breakfast stout with hints of coffee and liquorice.

All American (ABV 5%)
American-style IPA delivering a powerful tropical fruit kick.

Brewed for Church Inn, Birtle:

Church (OG 1041, ABV 4.2%)

Brewed for the Hop, Rawtenstall:

Hop (OG 1036, ABV 3.8%)
A pale golden-coloured session bitter with complex flavours.

Deeside

The Steading, Lochton of Leys, Banchory, AB31 5QB
☎ (01330) 825598 🌐 deesidebrewery.co.uk

First established in 2005, a change of ownership and location in 2012 led to substantial growth in the Scottish retail sector as well as export markets in Europe, USA, the Middle East and Asia, while maintaining its independent status. RAIB

APA (OG 1038, ABV 3.8%) ◈
Light, citrus, hoppy session ale.

Blonde (OG 1038, ABV 3.8%) ◈
Grapefruit hoppy bitter with a slight malt background.

Macbeth (OG 1042, ABV 4.1%) ◈
Roasted malt and hops coming through in the taste in this best bitter.

80/- (OG 1048, ABV 4.5%) ◈
Sweet, malty brew in the traditional Scottish 80/- style.

IPA (OG 1054, ABV 5.2%) ◈
Slightly sweet with a mix of malt and hops and a slight raspberry background.

Denbigh

Crown Workshop, Crown Lane, Denbigh, LL16 3SY
☎ (01745) 817021 ☎ 07850 687701
🌐 bragdybinbych.co.uk

Brewing commenced in 2012 at the rear of the Hope & Anchor pub. The brewery relocated in 2015 to a dedicated brewhouse in the town. A micropub next to the brewery, Y-Goron-Fach, is owned. ♦RAIB

Dent SIBA

Hollins, Cowgill, Dent, Cumbria, LA10 5TQ
☎ (01539) 625326 🌐 dentbrewery.co.uk

Dent was set up in 1990 in a converted barn next to a former farmhouse in the Yorkshire Dales National Park. In 2005 the brewery was completely refurbished and capacity expanded. One pub is owned. More than 150 outlets are supplied direct. !!

Golden Fleece (OG 1035, ABV 3.7%) ◈
Light, hoppy and fruity with a bitter aftertaste.

Station Porter (OG 1042, ABV 3.8%) ◈
A veritable malt feast for the beer's strength. A complex porter ending with roast highlights.

Aviator (OG 1039, ABV 4%) ◈
This amber-coloured ale is characterised by citrus, caramel and hop flavours that evolve into a bitter finish.

Rambrau (OG 1042, ABV 4.5%)
A clean, crisp and refreshing cask-conditioned lager.

Ramsbottom Strong Ale (OG 1042, ABV 4.5%) ◈
A well-balanced, malty best bitter.

Kamikaze (OG 1047, ABV 5%) ◈
Hops and fruit dominate this full-bodied, golden-coloured, strong bitter with a dry bitterness growing in the aftertaste.

T'owd Tup (OG 1056, ABV 6%) ◈
A rich, full-flavoured, strong stout with a coffee aroma. The dominant roast character is balanced by

THE BREWERIES

a warming sweetness and a raisiny, fruitcake taste that lingers on into the finish.

Derby SIBA

Masons Place Business Park, Nottingham Road, Derby, DE21 6AQ
☎ (01332) 365366 ☎ 07887 556788
derbybrewing.co.uk

A family-run microbrewery, established in 2004 in the old Masons paintworks varnish shed by head brewer Trevor Harris, founder and former brewer at the Brunswick Inn, Derby (qv). The business has grown over the years and four pubs are now owned around Derby. More than 400 outlets are supplied including major retailers. In addition to the core range there are at least three new beers each month. ‼ ♦

Hop Till You Drop (OG 1039, ABV 3.9%)
A blonde beer with fruity overtones and a dry finish.

Triple Hop (OG 1041, ABV 4.1%)
A well-balanced, triple-hopped, classic pale ale.

Business As Usual (OG 1044, ABV 4.4%)
An easy-drinking, copper-coloured beer; well-balanced, smooth and malty with a satisfying finish.

Double Mash (OG 1046, ABV 4.6%)
A well-balanced, ruby-coloured beer, crafted using the double mash brewing process.

Penny's Porter (OG 1046, ABV 4.6%)
A rich, dark-coloured, robust beer with a fine hop balance.

Old Friend (OG 1047, ABV 4.7%)
A classic, well-rounded beer, balanced and full bodied.

Dashingly Dark (OG 1048, ABV 4.8%)
A smooth, dark-coloured beer with complex flavours and a chocolate roasted finish.

Mercia IPA (OG 1050, ABV 5%)

Old Intentional (OG 1050, ABV 5%)
A full-bodied, malty premium beer, rich chestnut in colour. Well-balanced with a delicate, sweet aroma and a smooth finish.

Quintessential (OG 1058, ABV 5.8%)
Complex and well-rounded with extraordinary fruit and citrus flavours.

Derventio SIBA

The Brew Shed, Darley Abbey Mills, Darley Abbey, Derbyshire, DE22 1DZ
☎ (01332) 380199 ☎ 07975 944242
derventiobrewery.co.uk

Established in 2005 and commercial brewing in 2006 at Trusley Brook Farm, Derventio moved to a Grade I listed mill complex in 2011, which is part of the Derwent Valley Mills World Heritage site. A six-barrel brew plant is used. It is one of the founder members of the Derbyshire Brewers Collective. Spent grain goes to a local farmer. A popular 'Day with the Brewer' is available, by prior arrangement. ‼ ♦

Minerva (OG 1036.8, ABV 3.8%)

Gold (OG 1040.7, ABV 4.2%)
A pale-coloured bitter with subtle character and an outstanding hoppy finish with lemon and pine notes.

Hoplite (ABV 4.2%)

Brutus (OG 1043.6, ABV 4.5%)
Dark-coloured ale; smooth with a long, bitter finish.

Civitas (ABV 4.8%)

Cleopatra (OG 1048.4, ABV 5%)
A complex beer with a hint of apricot.

Spartan (ABV 5.3%)

Barbarian Stout (OG 1053.3, ABV 5.5%)
Dark-coloured, smooth stout with a lingering finish and subtle hop character.

Lucretius (ABV 5.5%)
A cherry flavoured stout.

Derwent

Units 2a-2c, Station Road Industrial Estate, Silloth, Cumbria, CA7 4AG
☎ (01697) 331522 derwentbrewery.co.uk

Derwent was set up in 1996 in Cockermouth and moved to Silloth in 1998. Owners Mark and Allie Johnston bought the brewery in 2013. ♦RAIB

Cote Light (OG 1034, ABV 3.6%)

Carlisle State Bitter (OG 1036, ABV 3.7%)
Malty, biscuity, hoppy beer with a gold colour.

W&M Mild (OG 1036, ABV 3.7%)

Parsons Pledge (OG 1039, ABV 4%)
Amber-coloured ale with a biscuity tang and a slightly fruity finish.

Blonde (OG 1039, ABV 4.2%)

Hudson Bay (OG 1043, ABV 4.2%)

Reaper (OG 1042, ABV 4.3%)

Mutineer (OG 1043, ABV 4.4%)

W&M Pale Ale (OG 1042, ABV 4.4%)
A sweet, fruity, hoppy beer with a bitter finish.

Marshall Port Stout (OG 1054, ABV 5.2%)

Deviant & Dandy (NEW)

Arch 165, Nursery Road, Homerton, London, E9 6PB
deviantanddandy.com

Deviant & Dandy began cuckoo brewing in 2017. In 2018 it commenced production on its own premises. No real ale.

Devil's Dyke

See Arran

Devitera (NEW)

The New Bakery, High Street, Rowde, Wiltshire, SN10 2PL ☎ 07800 823383 devitera.co.uk

Brewing began in 2017 using a four-barrel brew plant. The brewery is named after the Latin 'ad divisas', meaning boundaries and 'terra', meaning land, and is inspired by the beautiful Wiltshire landscape. It currently brews six vegan-friendly beers generally available bottle-conditioned although the occasional cask is provided to local beer festivals and pubs. RAIB V

Devon

Mansfield Arms, 7 Main Street, Sauchie, FK10 3JR (01259) 722020 devonales.com

Established in 1992 to produce cask ales for the Mansfield Arms, Sauchie, Devon is the oldest operating brewery in the county. A second pub, the Inn at Muckhart, was purchased in 1994 and the only beers sold there are from the Devon Ales brewery. The brewery also sells beer to the open market. !!

Original (70/-) (OG 1038, ABV 3.8%)
A full-bodied session ale with a prominent malty flavour and distinct hoppiness.

IPA (OG 1042, ABV 4.2%)

Thick Black (OG 1042, ABV 4.2%)

Pride (OG 1046, ABV 4.8%)

Devon Earth SIBA

Buckfastleigh, Devon 07927 397871

Office: 7 Fernham Terrace, Torquay Road, Paignton, Devon, TQ3 2AQ info@devonearthbrewery.co.uk

Devon Earth was launched in 2008 on a 2.5-barrel plant located on the banks of the River Dart on the edge of Dartmoor and is run on a part-time basis. It supplies beer festivals, pubs and clubs in the Torbay area and supports local charity events. ♦

Devon Earth (OG 1042, ABV 4.2%)
A light, refreshing ale with a satisfying bitter finish.

Grounded (OG 1047, ABV 4.7%)
A well-rounded traditional session ale.

Lost in the Woods (OG 1052, ABV 5.2%)
A dark-coloured, full-flavoured porter with roasted malt flavours and a touch of liquorice.

Devon's Own

See Clearwater

DEYA

33-34 Lansdown Industrial Estate, Gloucester Road, Cheltenham, Gloucestershire, GL51 8PL (01242) 269189 07887 537356 deyabrewing.com

DEYA Brewing Company was established in 2016. It brews innovative, hop-forward beers, all of which are unfiltered, unfined and unpasteurised and available in keg and cans, with occasional casks. Twice weekly taproom events are held. Expansion plans are underway and a range of sour beers is being developed. !!

Dhillon's SIBA

14a Hales Industrial Estate, Rowleys Green Lane, Longford, West Midlands, CV6 6AL (024) 7666 7413 dhillonsbrewery.com

Originally named Lion Heart, the brewery was established in 2014. It relaunched as Dhillon's in 2016 with a new range of beers. A five-barrel plant is used. The main focus is on bottled beer but cask-conditioned ales are also brewed. Its brewery tap is open Friday evenings as well as before rugby and football matches at the nearby Ricoh Arena. ♦

Golden Pale Ale (ABV 3.8%)

Amber (OG 1048, ABV 4.5%)

Mild (ABV 4.5%)

Stout (ABV 4.5%)

Dark Ruby (ABV 5.1%)

Red IPA (ABV 6.2%)

Dicks

See Crafty Little

Dig (NEW)

43 River Street, Digbeth, Birmingham, B5 5SA (0121) 773 2111 digbrewco.com

Dig Brew Company is a craft brewing project founded by Oliver Webb and Peter Towler of Mad O'Rourkes Pie Factory. The brewery and taproom is housed within a repurposed industrial unit in Digbeth, Birmingham.

Digfield SIBA

Lilford Lodge Farm, Barnwell, Northamptonshire, PE8 5SA (01832) 273954 digfield-ales.co.uk

Digfield Ales started brewing in 2005 on a five-barrel plant, which was later expanded to seven barrels. Increased demand led to a move to larger premises in 2012, still in the Barnwell area. A reed bed effluent system has been installed and brewing capacity increased to 15 barrels with new equipment. More than 40 free houses are supplied. ♦

Fools Nook (OG 1037, ABV 3.8%)
The floral aroma, dominated by lavender and honey, belies the hoppy bitterness that comes through in the taste of this golden ale. A fruity balance lasts.

Chiffchaff (OG 1038, ABV 3.9%)
An amber-gold-coloured pale ale with a distinct hoppy aroma.

Barnwell Bitter (OG 1039, ABV 4%)
A fruity aroma introduces a beer in which sharp bitterness is balanced by dry, biscuity malt.

Old Crow Porter (OG 1042, ABV 4.3%)
A rich, full-bodied porter with a balanced roasted malt finish.

Shacklebush (OG 1044, ABV 4.5%)
This amber-coloured brew begins with a balance of malt and hop on the nose which develops on the palate, complemented by a mounting bitterness. Good dry finish with lingering malt notes.

Mad Monk (OG 1047, ABV 4.8%)
Fruity beer with bitter, earthy hops in evidence.

Dog & Rabbit

Dog & Rabbit Micro Brew Pub, 36 Park View, Whitley Bay, Tyne & Wear, NE26 2TH 07944 552716 dogandrabbitbrewery.co.uk

The Dog & Rabbit Brewery was established in 2015 and relocated to new premises as a micro brewpub in 2016. Expansion took place in 2017 due to demand. RAIB

THE BREWERIES

Dog's Window (NEW)

8 Nant-Yr-Adar, Llangewydd Court, Bridgend, CF31 4TY ☎ 07929 292930
✉ info@dogswindowbrewery.com

Dog's Window is a small batch brewery, established in 2018. It has a core range of eight beers plus an ever-changing range of limited edition brews. ♦RAIB

Dogbreath (NEW)

52 Hyde Lane, Kinver, Staffordshire, DY7 6AF
☎ 07729 121362 🌐 dogbreathbrewery.co.uk

Brewing began in 2016 using a 350-litre brew plant. Production is mainly bottled although a small number of cask-conditioned ales are available. **V**

Doghouse

Unit 6, Watery Lane Industrial Estate, Watery Lane, Darwen, Lancashire, BB3 2EB
☎ (01254) 366338 ☎ 07860 913679
🌐 doghousebrewery.co.uk

First brewed in 2016 having purchased the equipment from the brewery of the same name based in the Isle of Man.

UPA (ABV 4%)

Bitter (ABV 4.2%)

Pale Ale (ABV 4.6%)

Columbus Brown (ABV 5%)
Modern brown-coloured ale packed with hops bringing both a bitterness kick and a strong resin aroma.

IPA (ABV 5.5%)

Dominion

c/o Chicken Sheds, Upp Hall Farm, Salmons Lane, Coggeshall, Essex, CO6 1RY ☎ 07931 120806
🌐 dominionbrewerycompany.com

Dominion was established in 2012 by Andy Skene, renting the premises and Pitfield brand names from the founder of Pitfield, Martin Kemp. All Pitfield beers are certified organic by the Soil Association and vegan by the Vegan Society. The Pitfield range of beers is more traditional and include historic recipe beers, while Dominion beers are more experimental. In 2018 Andy began cuckoo brewing at Red Fox Brewery (qv). RAIB **V**

Woodbine Racer (OG 1042, ABV 4.2%)

Woodbine Racer Turbo (ABV 6.2%)
A malty, sweet beer with a juicy bitterness and an orange aroma.

Yukon Gold (OG 1090, ABV 9.7%)

Mad Trappiste (OG 1095, ABV 10%)
A Belgian Trappist-style, red-coloured ale, aged in cognac casks and deliberately soured to result in a beer with a complex flavour.

Brewed under the Pitfield Brewery brand name:

Bitter (OG 1036, ABV 3.7%)

Lager (OG 1037, ABV 3.7%)

Chococino Dark Beer (OG 1038, ABV 4%)

Shoreditch Stout (OG 1040, ABV 4%)

Eco Warrior (OG 1043, ABV 4.5%)
Golden ale with a vivid, citrus hop aroma. The hop character is balanced with a delicate sweetness in the taste, followed by an increasingly bitter finish.

Red Ale (OG 1046, ABV 4.8%)
Complex beer with a full, malty body and strong hop character.

1850 London Porter (OG 1048, ABV 5%)
Full-flavoured, dark-coloured ale dominated by coffee and forest fruits. The finish is dry but not acrid.

N1 Wheat Beer (OG 1048, ABV 5%)

1837 India Pale Ale (OG 1065, ABV 7%)
A strong IPA, hoppy with a floral aroma.

Sovereign IPA (OG 1066, ABV 7%)

Imperial Chocolate Stout (OG 1070, ABV 7.3%)
A traditional stout with overtones of chocolate.

Contract brewed for Billericay Brewery:

A Mild With No Name (OG 1055, ABV 5.5%)

Don Valley (NEW) SIBA

Unit 3, Canalside Industrial Estate, Glasshouse Lane, Mexborough, South Yorkshire, S64 9HU
☎ (01709) 580254 ☎ 07766 203585
🌐 donvalleybrewery.co.uk

The brewery was established in 2016 and is based in an old rustic building alongside the Don Navigation in Mexborough. !!♦

Hitchcock (OG 1037, ABV 3.8%)

Watson (OG 1037, ABV 3.8%)

Ribblehead (OG 1039, ABV 4%)

Gongoozler (OG 1044, ABV 4.5%)

Doncaster

7 Young Street, Doncaster, South Yorkshire, DN1 3EL
☎ (01302) 376436 ☎ 07770 958394
🌐 doncasterbrewery.co.uk

Established in 2012 and initially based at an industrial unit in Kirk Sandall, Doncaster, the brewery moved to new premises in the centre of Doncaster in 2014 and opened a micropub tap room. ♦

Sand House (OG 1038, ABV 3.8%)

Cheswold (OG 1042, ABV 4.2%)

Gold Cup (OG 1045, ABV 4.5%)

First Aviation (OG 1050, ABV 5%)

Donkeystone (NEW) SIBA

Units 17-18, Boarshurst Business Park, Boarshurst Lane, Greenfield, OL3 7ER
☎ (01457) 238710 🌐 donkeystonebrewing.co.uk

Donkeystone is a 10-barrel brewery set up in 2017 at the edge of the Peak District National Park featuring an on-site brewery tap. Former homebrewers Richard Thomas and Stephen James use a custom-built stainless steel plant supplied by Oban Ales. !!

Hoppinsesh (OG 1041, ABV 3.7%)
A crisp, clean, hoppy session beer.

Bray (OG 1040, ABV 4%)

Deep amber-coloured bitter with a residual malty sweetness and fruity hops.

Bad Ass Blonde (OG 1042, ABV 4.1%)
A crisp, light, hoppy blonde ale.

DPA (OG 1053, ABV 4.7%)
An American-style pale ale with citrus, grapefruit and pine flavours.

Javanilla (OG 1057, ABV 5%)
A coffee and vanilla stout with a rounded and complex flavour.

DAPA Donkey (OG 1068, ABV 6.9%)
A full-bodied, bitter, American-style pale ale with a malt backbone.

Donnington

Upper Swell, Stow-on-the-Wold, Gloucestershire, GL54 1EP
☎ (01451) 830603 🌐 donnington-brewery.com

Thomas Arkell bought a 13th-century watermill in 1827 and began brewing on the site in 1865; the waterwheel is still in use. Thomas's descendant Claude owned and ran the brewery until his death in 2007, supplying 20 outlets direct. It has now passed to Claude's cousin, James Arkell, also of Arkells Brewery, Swindon (qv). RAIB

BB (OG 1035, ABV 3.6%)
A pleasant, amber-coloured bitter with a slight hop aroma, a good balance of malt and hops in the mouth and a bitter aftertaste.

Donnington Gold (OG 1041, ABV 4%)
A golden ale with a citrus flavour followed by a rounded malt finish.

SBA (OG 1045, ABV 4.4%)
Malt dominates over bitterness in the subtle flavour of this premium bitter, which has a hint of fruit and a dry, malty finish.

Dopey Dick

Skeoge Industrial Estate, Derry, BT48 8SE
☎ (028) 7141 8920 ✉ dopeydickderry@gmail.com

A microbrewery founded by the proprietors of the Grand Central Bar in Londonderry.

Dorking SIBA

Aldhurst Farm, Capel, Surrey, RH5 5HJ
☎ (01306) 877988 🌐 dorkingbrewery.com

Dorking started brewing in 2008 at premises in Dorking. In 2017 production moved to a new, larger site in Capel with a 30-barrel brew plant capable of producing 35,000 pints per week. Beers can be found in Surrey, West Sussex and South London. !! ♦

Washington Gold (OG 1042, ABV 3.8%)

Pilcrow Pale (OG 1043, ABV 4%)

Smokestack Lightnin' (OG 1043, ABV 4%)

DB One (OG 1043, ABV 4.2%)
Hoppy best bitter with underlying orange fruit notes. Some balancing malt sweetness in the taste leads to a dry bitter finish.

Black Noise (OG 1045, ABV 4.5%)

Lunar White (OG 1045, ABV 4.6%)

Red India (OG 1052, ABV 5%)

Buffalo Buffalo (OG 1050, ABV 5.1%)

Dorset SIBA

Unit 7, Hybris Business Park, Warmwell Road, Crossways, Dorset, DT2 8BF
☎ (01305) 777515 🌐 dbcales.com

Founded in 1996, Dorset Brewing Company started in Hope Square, Weymouth, which was once the home of the Devenish and Groves breweries. In 2010 it moved to purpose-built premises near Dorchester. Here spring water is used in its state-of-the-art brewing equipment. Beers are available in local pubs and selected outlets throughout the South West. !!♦

Dorset Knob (OG 1039, ABV 3.9%)
Complex bitter ale with strong malt and fruit flavours despite its light gravity.

Jurassic (OG 1040, ABV 4.2%)
Clean-tasting, easy-drinking bitter. Well balanced with lingering bitterness after moderate sweetness.

Origin (ABV 4.4%)
A clean, fruity, citrus IPA with a hoppy, sweet finish.

DBC (ABV 4.5%)
Rich, copper-coloured ale with plum and burnt toffee notes and a citrus finish.

Yachtsman (OG 1048, ABV 4.7%)
A pale golden-coloured beer with hints of vanilla and honey in the aroma and aftertaste.

Durdle Door (OG 1046, ABV 5%)
A tawny hue and fruity aroma with a hint of pear drops and good malty undertone, joined by hops and a little roast malt in the taste. Lingering bittersweet finish.

Double Top

Unit 4, Kilton Terrace, Worksop, Nottinghamshire, S80 2DQ ☎ 07973 521824

Office: Mallard, Station Approach, Carlton Road, Worksop, S81 7AG 🌐 doubletopbrewery.co.uk

Double Top procured a 2.5-barrel plant in 2012, with fermenting capacity for 7.5 barrels a week. This was expanded to a five-barrel plant in 2015 with a fermenting capacity of 20 barrels. It caters for its brewery tap, the Mallard on Platform 1 of Worksop railway station, and for regional beer festivals and free houses. !!♦

Nelson Mild (OG 1037, ABV 3.5%)
A traditional dark mild with a delicate balance of malts.

Golden Arrow (OG 1038, ABV 3.9%)
A golden ale with citrus notes.

History Maker (OG 1039, ABV 3.9%)

Adonis (OG 1042, ABV 4.3%)
A pale bitter with a dry, biscuity finish.

Bad Boy (OG 1047, ABV 4.6%)
A sweet-tasting, chestnut-coloured bitter.

Citra Tip (OG 1050, ABV 5.2%)

Madhouse (OG 1053, ABV 5.2%)

Old Stoneface (OG 1058, ABV 6%)
A black-coloured stout with treacle flavours.

Double-Barrelled (NEW)

Unit 20, Stadium Way Industrial Estate, Reading, Berkshire, RG30 6BX ⊕ doublebarrelled.co.uk

Brewing began in 2018 on a new 15-barrel plant focusing on stouts, sours and sessionable beers.

Dove Street SIBA

82 St Helens Street, Ipswich, Suffolk, IP4 2LB
☎ (01473) 211270 ☎ 07880 707077
⊕ dovestreetbrewery.co.uk

⊠ Dove Street began brewing in 2011 using a 2.5-barrel plant in a garage opposite the Dove Street Inn. The pub, its sister pub and beer festivals are supplied. !!

Underwood Mild (OG 1033, ABV 3.2%)
Dark-coloured, traditional, thirst-quenching mild, fresh and spicy.

Gladstone Guzzler (OG 1037, ABV 3.6%)
Easy-drinking, light-coloured bitter with a hoppy flavour.

CITRA (Can I Try Real Ale) (ABV 3.8%)
A pale-coloured beer with a dry citrus flavour.

Incredible Taste Fantastic Clarity (OG 1041, ABV 4%)
Golden-coloured, hoppy session beer; clean, clear and crisp.

Dove Elder (OG 1042, ABV 4.1%)
A speciality beer with elderflower notes.

Apples & Pears (OG 1043.5, ABV 4.2%)
A pale-coloured beer with hints of orchard fruits.

Ed Porter (OG 1046.5, ABV 4.5%)
A dark-coloured, dry porter with hints of smoke and chocolate.

Thirsty Walker (OG 1047, ABV 4.6%)

Dovecote

Unit 2, Denbigh Enterprise Centre, Colomendy Industrial Estate, Denbigh, LL16 5TA
✉ dovecote.brewery@gmail.com

⊠ Also known as Bragdy Colomendy, named after the industrial estate where it is located. Owner and head brewer Richard Green commenced brewing in 2017 on a five-barrel plant previously used at the former Frodsham brewery. A brewery bar is planned. RAIB

Dove Dark (OG 1034, ABV 3.6%)
A dark-coloured, full-flavoured ale with subtle hints of toasted nuts, chocolate and liquorice on the palate, leading to a creamy, caramel malt finish.

Dove Ale (OG 1038, ABV 4%)

Dove From Above (OG 1040, ABV 4.2%)
A gold-coloured IPA with aromas of pine and tropical fruits and a fresh citrus finish.

Dove Down Under (OG 1045, ABV 4.8%)
A light amber-coloured ale with a huge mouthful of grapefruit and peppery pine needle flavours. Well-balanced with caramel malts.

Dove Pale (OG 1044, ABV 4.8%)

Dow Bridge SIBA

2-3 Rugby Road, Catthorpe, Leicestershire, LE17 6DA
☎ (01788) 869121 ⊕ dowbridgebrewery.co.uk

Dow Bridge commenced brewing in 2001 and takes its name from a local bridge where Watling Street spans the River Avon. The brewery uses English whole hops and malt with no adjuncts or additives. More than 50 outlets are supplied direct. !! ♦ RAIB

Bonum Mild (OG 1035, ABV 3.5%)
Complex, dark brown-coloured, full-flavoured mild with strong malt and roast flavours to the fore and continuing into the aftertaste, leading to a long, satisfying finish.

Acris (OG 1037, ABV 3.8%)

Centurion (OG 1039, ABV 4%)
Copper-coloured, well-rounded best bitter. Good balance of malt and hops in the flavour.

Legion (OG 1041, ABV 4.1%)
Golden hoppy ale. A good balance of malt and fruity hop on the nose and palate.

Ratae'd (OG 1041, ABV 4.3%)
Tawny-coloured, full-bodied beer with bitter hop flavours against a grainy background, leading to a long, bitter and dry aftertaste.

Dark (OG 1042, ABV 4.4%)
A strong, dark-coloured, full-bodied ale with roast malt giving hints of chocolate.

Gladiator (OG 1046, ABV 4.5%)
Ruby chestnut-coloured, well balanced beer. Smooth and malty but with a bitter, dry finish. Some fruit aroma and slight toffee sweetness.

Fosse Ale (OG 1046, ABV 4.8%)
Well-balanced premium beer with caramel and burnt toffee flavours leading to a hoppy, dry finish.

Praetorian Porter (OG 1048, ABV 5%)
Dark-coloured, rich, full-bodied porter. Slightly sweet with hoppy undertones.

Onslaught (OG 1049, ABV 5.2%)
A deep ruby-coloured strong ale. A good balance of fruit and hops with rich flavours and aroma.

Downham Isle (NEW)

1 Matthew Wren Close, Little Downham, Cambridgeshire, CB6 2UL
☎ (01353) 699695 ☎ 07732 927479
⊕ downhamislebrewery.co.uk

Downham Isle began brewing in 2016. The brewery is situated in the heart of fen country, three miles from Ely. Beers can be found in Ely, the village bar in Little Downham and at local farmers' and craft markets.

Downlands SIBA

Unit Z (2a), Mackley Industrial Estate, Small Dole, West Sussex, BN5 9XE
☎ (01273) 495596 ⊕ downlandsbrewery.com

A 10-barrel brewery set up in 2012 distributing beers across the South-east of England. ♦

Root Thirteen (OG 1033, ABV 3.6%)
Crisp, light golden ale that layers floral zesty aromas over a grapefruit and citrus flavour.

Best (OG 1042, ABV 4.1%)
A traditional and interesting malty, fruity best bitter.

Bramber (OG 1047, ABV 4.5%)

Powerfully-hopped American-style amber-coloured ale.

Black Seven Four (OG 1074, ABV 7.4%)

Downton SIBA

Unit 11, Batten Road, Downton Industrial Estate, Downton, Wiltshire, SP5 3HU
☎ (01725) 513313 ⊕ downtonbrewery.com

Downton was set up in 2003. The brewery has a 20-barrel brew length and produces around 1,500 barrels a year. Around 100 outlets are supplied direct. Eight regular beers are produced together with speciality and experimental beers. The brewery has no pub estate but offers an off-site mobile bar service and an online shop. A bar and sales are available on site. RAIB

New Forest Ale (OG 1037, ABV 3.8%)
An amber-coloured bitter with subtle aromas leading to good hopping on the palate. Some fruit and hoppiness in the aftertaste.

Quadhop (OG 1038, ABV 3.9%)
Pale golden-coloured session beer, initially hoppy on the palate with some fruit and a strong hoppiness in the aftertaste.

Elderquad (OG 1039, ABV 4%)
Golden yellow-coloured bitter with a floral, fruity aroma leading to a good well-hopped taste with hints of elderflower. Dryish finish with good fruit and hop balance.

Honey Blonde (OG 1041, ABV 4.3%)
Straw-coloured golden ale, easy drinking with initial bitterness giving way to slight sweetness and a lingering balanced aftertaste.

Nelson's Delight (OG 1044, ABV 4.5%)
An amber-coloured bitter full of hoppy character and a rich resinous aroma. Underlying sweetness and strength provided by the addition of navy rum.

Dark Delight (OG 1053, ABV 5.5%)
A strong, dark brown-coloured best bitter. Malt and roast in the aroma and on the palate initially, giving way to a balanced lingering aftertaste with noticeable hoppiness.

Chocolate Orange Delight (OG 1052, ABV 5.8%)
A speciality old ale with pronounced chocolate and orange flavours.

IPA (OG 1063, ABV 6.8%)
Golden yellow-coloured strong bitter with good balance of hops and fruit, slight sweetness and some malt notes, all through to the aftertaste.

Dowr Kammel

Deaconstowe, Lower Lank, Cornwall, PL30 4PW
☎ 07774 427635

Office: 9 Tregarne Terrace, St Austell, Cornwall, PL25 4DD ✉ dowrkammell@btinternet.com

Brewing began in 2016. A small number of local free houses are supplied.

Blisland Gold (ABV 3.6%)
Light golden ale with a strong citrus aroma. Dominant citrus and grassy hops with faint fruit sweetness. Very bitter and fairly dry finish.

Amber Rambler (ABV 4%)

Devil's Jump (ABV 4.6%)
Balanced, golden-coloured best bitter with malt and hops aroma. Assertive malt and bitterness in the mouth with smooth, zesty lemon hops.

Delank Dynamite (ABV 5.1%)
Dark brown-coloured porter with a roast malt aroma. Smooth roast, bitter coffee and malt flavours. Hints of stone fruit, finishing dry.

Brewards Droop IPA (ABV 6%)
Golden-coloured IPA with citrus aroma. Overpowering citrus hop with bitterness, balanced by malt and strong orange fruit through to the end.

Big Cat (ABV 7.7%)

Brewed for the Blisland Inn, Blisland:

Blisland Dark (ABV 3.5%)

Dragonfly

George & Dragon, 183 High Street, Acton, London, W3 9DJ
☎ (020) 8992 3712 ☎ 07788 859450
✉ dragonflybrewery@gmail.com

Brewing began in 2014 with a Chinese-built brewing kit installed in the back bar of the George & Dragon. The pub is supplied along with other outlets in the same pub group. ♦

Draycott (Cambridgeshire)

Low Farm, 30 Mill Road, Buckden, Cambridgeshire, PE19 5SS
☎ (01480) 812404 ☎ 07740 374710
⊕ draycottbrewery.co.uk

The brewery is located in an old farm complex and was set up by Jon and Jane Draycott in 2009. Only bottle-conditioned beers are produced. RAIB

Draycott (Derbyshire) SIBA

Draycott Brewing Co, Draycott Brewing Co, Dale Abbey, Derbyshire, DE7 4PS ☎ 07834 728540
✉ draycottbrewingcompany@yahoo.co.uk

Microbrewery established in 2014, supplying local pubs and beer festivals. Relocation to new premises in 2015 saw beer range and capacity increased. A tap house in Draycott village is also operated.

Top of the Hops (OG 1042, ABV 3.8%)
A single hop pale ale with a good hop/malt balance.

Lamb & Flag (ABV 4%)
A traditional porter with chocolate and coconut notes in the background.

Butcher's Bitter (OG 1042, ABV 4.2%)
A traditional bitter with caramel notes and a hint of nut.

California Steam Beer (OG 1042, ABV 4.2%)
American-style, red-coloured beer. Dry and refreshing with a hint of citrus.

Heisenberg Principle (OG 1042, ABV 4.2%)
Traditional dark-coloured ale. Toasted flavour with a good hop balance.

Kentucky Common Ale (OG 1042, ABV 4.2%)
American-style, amber-coloured bitter with big flavours.

Piano Man Blues (ABV 4.2%)

An American-style, ruby-coloured ale with malty tones and a clean, hoppy taste and finish.

Obsidian (ABV 4.5%)

Tap House Tipple (OG 1042, ABV 4.5%)

Minnesota North Star American Red Ale (ABV 4.7%)
A complex American-style, red-coloured bitter.

Christmas In July Chocolate/Coconut Porter (ABV 5%)
A traditional porter with chocolate and coconut notes in the background.

Irish Red Ale (ABV 5%)
Traditional, fruity, Irish-style, red-coloured ale.

Driftwood SIBA

Driftwood Spars Hotel, Trevaunance Cove, St Agnes, Cornwall, TR5 0RY
☎ (01872) 552591 🌐 driftwoodsparsbrewery.co.uk

Brewing since 2000 on a custom-built five-barrel plant, the brewery has since expanded to incorporate additional fermentation and conditioning capacity plus a brewery shop and visitor centre with annual production now standing at 1,300 barrels. Monthly specials are produced for selected circulation only. Besides the pub, other outlets and beer festivals are supplied. !! ♦ RAIB GF

Bawden Rocks (OG 1037, ABV 3.8%)
Refreshing bitter with floral hop aroma. Balanced biscuit malt and hop bitterness with orange, apple and plum notes. Bitter finish.

Blackheads Mild (OG 1037, ABV 3.8%)
Dark mild with coffee aroma. Silky, smoky roast malt, raisins and liquorice flavours persist to the finish with dry bitterness.

SPARS (OG 1038, ABV 3.8%)
Bitter, copper-coloured session beer with balance of sweet malt and earthy hops, plum and orange flavours. Bitterness rises in the finish.

Blue Hills Bitter (OG 1039, ABV 4%)
Refreshing pale brown-coloured bitter. Strong bitterness and resinous hops balanced by biscuit malt and fruit hints. Long bitter and flowery finish.

Booskor (OG 1042, ABV 4.2%)
Smooth, red-coloured mild with roast malt throughout. Sweetness, toffee apples, roast nuts and stone fruits. Low hop bitterness. Malty, sweet finish.

Forest Blond (OG 1044, ABV 4.3%)
Golden-coloured beer with modest malt and grassy hop flavours. Bittersweet fruitiness, elderflower and perfumed esters. Short bitter hop finish.

Sundrift (OG 1046, ABV 4.5%)
Copper-coloured best bitter packed full of fruit and hop flavours with malt and spices. Bitter finish with persistent sweet malt.

Bolster's Blood (OG 1049, ABV 4.8%)
Full-bodied, dark brown-coloured porter. Coal smoke and peaty malt flavour with dark chocolate and dried fruits. Bitterness and burnt malt persist.

Red River Rye (OG 1048, ABV 4.8%)
Tawny-coloured speciality rye beer. Clean-tasting sweet malt with spicy hops and hedgerow fruits. Lasting malty, peppery and malty finish.

Lou's Brew (OG 1049, ABV 5%)
Golden-coloured beer with strong lemon and grapefruit flavours, bitterness and dryness throughout. Long, tangy finish with hop bitterness fading.

JSB (OG 1050, ABV 5.2%)
Full-flavoured, copper coloured strong bitter with perfumed hop aroma. Assertive bitterness, woody malt and spicy hops. Marmalade and pears. Long, bitter finish.

Alfie's Revenge (OG 1060, ABV 6.5%)
Red-coloured, strong old ale with malt, sweet fruit aroma and flavours, balanced by spicy hop bitterness. Malt and fruit finish.

Drone Valley SIBA

Unstone Industrial Complex, Main Road, Unstone, Derbyshire, S18 4AB ☎ 07794 277091
🌐 dronevalleybrewery.com

Community-owned five-barrel brewery that began brewing commercially in 2016. The brewery is entirely volunteer operated and welcomes new members and investors. Profits go to local good causes. Regular open days are held throughout the year. ♦ RAIB

Dronny Bottom Bitter (ABV 3.7%)

Gosforth Gold (ABV 4%)
A pale straw-coloured beer with a full body for its strength. Well-balanced with a citrus hop finish.

Dronfield Best (ABV 4.3%)

Coal Aston Porter (ABV 4.5%)
Traditional, smooth, fruity porter.

Unstone Oatmeal Stout (ABV 4.5%)
A smooth, light stout with flavours of roasted barley.

Fanshaw Blonde (ABV 4.8%)

Stubley Stout (ABV 5%)

IPA (ABV 5.2%)
Traditional IPA, deep amber in colour with a rich malt base. Well-hopped, giving a full mouthfeel and dry bitter finish.

Drop the Anchor

Christchurch Emporium, Bridge Street, Christchurch, Dorset, BH23 1DY ☎ 07806 789946
🌐 droptheanchorbrewery.co.uk

Neil Hodgkinson began brewing in 2017 using a 2.5-barrel plant situated in the loft area of the Christchurch Emporium. Beer is available in a number of local pubs and a small bar and shop is situated in the brewery (open Fri-Sun). All beers are unfined. ♦ RAIB

Silent Stones (ABV 4.7%)
A hoppy, IPA-style, amber-coloured ale.

Tucktonia (ABV 4.7%)
A fruity pale ale.

Priest Hole Porter (ABV 4.9%)
A rich porter with prominent chocolate notes.

Fusee Chain (ABV 5%)
Full-flavoured, amber-coloured, American-style IPA.

Druid

4 Dinorben Terrace, Penysarn, LL69 9YR
✉ alan@druidbrewery.co uk

A new microbrewery in the north of the Isle of Angelsey. The brewery is fitted into an 18th-century cottage that was built to house miners working in the historic copper mines of the nearby Parys Mountain. It is also the home of the brewery's owners. The beers and ciders are made in a purpose-built brew room. Brewing is currently suspended. RAIB

Drygate SIBA

85 Drygate, Glasgow, G4 0UT
☎ (0141) 212 8810 drygate.com

Restaurant, bar and microbrewery, Drygate is a joint venture of Tennent's and Williams Bros, though operationally independent. The on-site brewery began production in 2014. !! ♦ RAIB

DT

See Cerne Abbas

Dukeries

Carlton Forest Distribution Centre, Unit 6, Blyth Road, Worksop, Nottinghamshire, S81 0TP
☎ (01909) 731171 ☎ 07584 305027
dukeriesbrewery.co.uk

Founded in 2012 and located in the heart of the Dukeries in Nottinghamshire using a five-barrel plant. The brewery tap is located at 18 Newcastle Avenue, Worksop, serving five rotating ales. ♦

Elsi Pale (OG 1036, ABV 3.6%)
Traditional chestnut-coloured bitter with slight nutty flavour mixed with hints of fruit, leading to a dry bitter finish.

Blonde (OG 1038, ABV 3.8%)
Blonde ale with citrus notes and low level bitterness ensuring a clean, crisp feel throughout.

A Ray of Sunshine (OG 1041, ABV 4.2%)
Tropical fruits throughout with a clean, fresh feel on the palate.

Castle Hill (OG 1041, ABV 4.2%)
Well-hopped bitter balanced throughout offering soft malt flavours with a smooth, mellow bitter finish.

De Lovetot (OG 1041, ABV 4.2%)
Golden-coloured pale ale with a citrus fruit aroma and feel, leading to a bitter finish.

Lime Tree Porter (OG 1043, ABV 4.4%)
Porter with a lightly smoky taste, some liquorice and a malt sweetness. Nose has peat and liquorice with a hint of sweetness. Gentle bitterness with hints of citrus.

Mining Stout (OG 1044, ABV 4.5%)
A dark-coloured ale bursting with robust, rich flavours leading to a well-balanced, dry finish.

Farmers Branch (OG 1047, ABV 5%)
A pale-coloured strong ale, zesty with fresh, clean, citrus notes.

Chapmans Map (OG 1051, ABV 5.2%)
Chestnut-coloured ale with a creamy head. Nose is cinnamon and cloves, caramel, biscuit and a slight hint of coffee. Taste is strong biscuit, lots of malt sweetness. Gentle bitterness to finish.

Wersheshope Gold (OG 1051, ABV 5.2%)
Golden-coloured ale with a light body. Nose has orange marmalade and limes. Taste is bitter orange marmalade, lime and slightly grassy hops.

Gunsmoke (OG 1050, ABV 5.5%)
Russet brown-coloured beer with hints of chocolate and liquorice. A soft, dry finish.

Bess of Hardwick (OG 1052, ABV 5.7%)
An American-style pale ale with floral, citrus flavours and herbal characteristics.

Dun (NEW)

Corrary Farm, Glen Beag, Glenelg, IV40 8JX
☎ (01599) 522333 dunbrewing.co.uk

Established in 2018, this four-barrel brewery is named after the two neighbouring Iron Age Brochs (forts) – Dun Telve and Dun Trodden. Using its own spring water and organic ingredients, the ales are unfiltered and naturally carbonated. Beers are only available locally at present. RAIB

Dunham Massey

100 Oldfield Lane, Dunham Massey, WA14 4PE
☎ (0161) 929 0663 dunhammasseybrewing.co.uk

Opened in 2007, Dunham Massey brews traditional North-western ales using only English ingredients. Around 30 outlets are supplied direct, along with the brewery tap, Costello's Bar, Altrincham. A sister brewery, Lymm (qv), opened in 2013 with Costello's Bar in Stockton Heath tied to both breweries. ♦ RAIB

Castle Hill (OG 1036, ABV 3.5%)
Session pale ale with aromas of grapefruit and tropical fruits.

Walker's Bitter (OG 1036, ABV 3.5%)

Little Bollington Bitter (OG 1037, ABV 3.7%)
Straw-coloured light ale with malt and citrus fruit taste and a dry, bitter finish.

Chocolate Cherry Mild (OG 1040, ABV 3.8%)
Dark chocolate, coffee and liquorice notes with a dry, bittersweet cherry flavour.

Dunham Dark (OG 1040, ABV 3.8%)
Dark brown-coloured beer with a malty aroma. Fairly sweet with malt, some roast, hop and fruit in the taste and finish.

Big Tree Bitter (OG 1041, ABV 3.9%)
Golden-coloured, full-bodied bitter with a good balance of hops and malt.

Obelisk (OG 1040, ABV 3.9%)
Light and hoppy, but not too bitter, with hints of citrus and grapefruit.

Dunham Milk Stout (OG 1051, ABV 4%)
A classic, full-bodied, sweet stout with a creamy, roast malt character.

Landlady (OG 1040, ABV 4%)
A biscuity, dry ale, with a spicy hop finish.

Dunham Stout (OG 1046, ABV 4.2%)
A creamy, full-bodied English stout with a classic bitter, burnt, dark roast flavour.

Stamford Bitter (OG 1045, ABV 4.2%)
A golden, full-bodied bitter with a complex blend of hops giving a slightly dry finish.

THE BREWERIES

Deer Beer (OG 1047, ABV 4.5%)
A clean, full-bodied, malty ale with a hint of toffee and a distinct hop finish.

Cheshire IPA (OG 1047, ABV 4.7%)
A fairly strong, pale-coloured, hoppy and bitter IPA.

Dunham Porter (OG 1056, ABV 5.2%)
A classic old-style English porter; creamy, full-bodied and packed with flavour.

East India Pale Ale (OG 1062, ABV 6%)

Dunham Gold (OG 1070, ABV 7.2%)
A Belgian-style ale. Strong, light and fruity with a hoppy finish.

Dunscar SIBA

Unit 12, Dunscar Bridge Business Park, Blackburn Road, Bolton, BL7 9PQ
☎ (01204) 563516 dunscarbridge.co.uk

Brewing began in 2009. In 2012 a 27-barrel plant was installed in a new brewery within the business park at Dunscar Bridge, Bolton. The brewery supplies individual pubs across the North-west and North-east, both direct and through close collaboration with wholesale distributors LWC. !!

Gold (ABV 3.8%)
A light, refreshing session ale with notes of new mown hay and hints of sweet pear to finish.

Monroe Blonde (ABV 3.8%)
A blonde session ale, slightly sweet and spicy on the palate.

Sessh! (ABV 3.8%)
A rich, malty session ale. Notes of freshly baked bread with a hoppy foretaste. Hints of tropical mango and papaya in the aftertaste.

Black IPA (ABV 4%)
A refreshing ale with notes of coffee in the finish.

Stout (ABV 4%)
A smooth, dark brown-coloured stout with hints of chocolate and oak.

Bitter (ABV 4.1%)
A mellow, full-bodied, crisp best bitter with delicate floral hop notes.

IPA (ABV 4.9%)
A fruity IPA with hints of citrus and notes of toasted biscuit.

Blissful Blonde (ABV 5%)
A refreshing, smooth blonde ale with a crisp, dry, apple taste to finish.

Durham SIBA

Unit 6a, Bowburn North Industrial Estate, Bowburn, County Durham, DH6 5PF
☎ (0191) 377 1991 durhambrewery.co.uk

Established in 1994, County Durham's oldest brewery has a portfolio of around 40 beers, some permanent, some on rotation and with new beers appearing regularly. Beers are available throughout the North-east. !! RAIB V

Magus (OG 1036, ABV 3.8%)
Pale malt gives this brew its straw colour but the hops define its character, with a fruity aroma, a clean bitter mouthfeel, and a lingering dry, citrus-like finish.

Citra Nova (OG 1039, ABV 3.9%)
Massive hop bouquet with a lively, fresh grapefruit bitterness.

Pale Ice (OG 1039, ABV 3.9%)
A refreshing and bitter pale ale with a floral aroma.

Apollo (OG 1040, ABV 4%)
A hoppy, American-style pale ale. Full-bodied and refreshing with grapefruit notes.

Black Velvet (OG 1040, ABV 4%)
A dark-coloured ale with rich coffee and roast flavours.

White Gold (OG 1040, ABV 4%)
A floral hop aroma and grapefruit taste.

White Amarillo (OG 1041, ABV 4.1%)

Columbus IPA (OG 1042, ABV 4.2%)
Full- bodied, hoppy, American-style IPA. Peachy aroma with a big grapefruit taste.

White Velvet (OG 1042, ABV 4.2%)

Evensong (OG 1050, ABV 5%)

White Stout (OG 1072, ABV 7.2%)
A pale-coloured stout. Full-bodied and strong with a massive floral and resinous character.

Dynamite Valley

Unit 5, Viaduct Works, Frog Hill, Ponsanooth, Cornwall, TR3 7JW
☎ (01872) 864532 ☎ 07775 570235
dynamitevalley.com

Dynamite Valley was set up in 2015 following a successful crowdfunding campaign. The brewery is located near a historic gunpowder site near Falmouth. Beers are influenced by European and US beer styles and all are unfined. V

Gold Rush (OG 1040, ABV 4%)
Smooth, gold-coloured bitter with a light malt nose. Malt dominates throughout with bitterness, honey, lemon and apricot flavours. Long, malty, bitter finish.

Kennall Vale Pale (ABV 4.3%)
A session ale with lemon and peach flavours.

TNT IPA (OG 1048, ABV 4.8%)
Robust, amber-coloured, American-style IPA with malt and fruity hop aroma. Heavy hop bitter taste with sweet toffee apples and malt balance.

Black Charge (OG 1050, ABV 5%)
Creamy black-coloured stout in the sweet oatmeal style. Powerful roast coffee and dark chocolate throughout. Malt presence and hints of prunes.

Prospector (OG 1052, ABV 5.2%)

Big Bang (ABV 5.3%)
A dark-coloured, Belgian-style IPA.

Eagle

Havelock Street, Bedford, MK40 4LU
☎ (01234) 272766 eaglebrewery.co.uk

Eagle Brewery was founded as Charles Wells in Bedford in 1876 and remained in family hands until May 2017 when the brewery and its brands were sold to Marston's (qv) for £55 million and renamed. Wells itself had expanded rapidly, merging its brewing and brands with Young's of Wandsworth, London, in 2006: the brands became wholly owned by Wells in 2014 while Young's concentrated on its pub estate. In 2007 Wells bought the Courage brands from Scottish & Newcastle —now Heineken —and in 2011 added the former McEwan's brands, giving it a presence in the Scottish market. Marston's plans to maintain production at the Eagle Brewery in Bedford while Wells will build a new brewery. Marston's will supply the Wells pub estate with beers from the Eagle Brewery and from the other Marston's Breweries portfolios. Part of Marston's PLC. ‼ ♦

IPA (OG 1035, ABV 3.6%)
A refreshing, amber-coloured session bitter with pronounced citrus hop aroma and palate, faint malt in the mouth, and a lasting dry, bitter finish.

Brewed under the Bombardier brand name:

Pale Ale (OG 1033, ABV 3.6%)
A golden-coloured pale ale with a hoppy aroma and notes of grapefruit and honey, balanced with a gentle, sweet maltiness and a dry finish.

Bombardier (OG 1041, ABV 4.1%)
A heavy aroma of malt and raspberry jam. Traces of hops and bitterness are quickly submerged under a smooth, malty sweetness. A solid, rich finish.

Burning Gold (OG 1037, ABV 4.1%)
Zesty aromas lead to a dry, crisp flavour with more than a hint of citrus on the palate and a smooth, lasting finish.

Brewed under the Courage brand name:

Best Bitter (OG 1038, ABV 4%)
Full-bodied beer with a bitter and fruity palate.

Director's (OG 1043, ABV 4.8%)
A rich, fruity and full-bodied, chestnut-coloured classic ale.

Brewed under the Young's brand name:

Bitter (OG 1034, ABV 3.7%)
This light-drinking, amber-coloured bitter has citrus initially on the palate with sweet malt and a hint of hops that linger into a slightly dry and bitter finish.

London Gold (OG 1037, ABV 4%)
A dark gold-coloured beer with a smooth mouthfeel. Citrus and malt in the low aroma, coming through more strongly on the palate and aftertaste with a little peach. Dry finish.

Special (OG 1043, ABV 4.5%)
Pale brown in colour, this rounded best bitter has citrus throughout plus some slight creamy toffee, which balances the bitterness that grows in the aftertaste.

Eagles Crag

Unit 21, Robinwood Mill, Todmorden, West Yorkshire, OL14 8JA
☎ (01706) 810394 ⊕ eaglescragbrewery.com

Eagles Crag is named after and overlooked by a prominent landmark, famous in local folklore. It is a brand new eight-barrel plant situated in a former textile mill, built over the River Calder. Commercial brewing began in 2017 and the two founders both have over 30 years of brewing experience. Beers are delivered direct to 60 outlets in Lancashire and Yorkshire. ♦V

Pale Eagle (OG 1041, ABV 3.8%)
Easy-drinking, well-balanced pale ale. Light citrus notes offset by a touch of sweetness, giving a smooth, bitter finish.

The Eagle's Feather (OG 1036, ABV 3.8%)
An amber-coloured bitter. Piny, floral hop flavours with balanced maltiness leads to a refreshing taste.

Eye of the Eagle (OG 1040, ABV 4.3%)
An amber-coloured, traditional best bitter with malt and fruit to the fore, lingering dry finish.

The Eagle Has Landed (OG 1048, ABV 4.6%)
An amber-coloured best bitter with a good balance of fruit and malt. Moderate bitterness with a lingering malty finish.

Golden Eagle (OG 1049, ABV 4.7%)
A fruity, full-flavoured golden ale. Hoppy bitterness dominates the full mouthfeel and lasting finish.

Eagle of Darkness (OG 1050, ABV 5%)
Refreshing dark brown-coloured porter. A subtle blend of chocolate malt and raisin-like fruit develops into a mellow, sweet aftertaste.

Bald Eagle (OG 1062, ABV 6.9%)
A big IPA with plenty of bittering; hoppy citrus aromas with plenty of fruit, balanced by the malt flavours.

Earl Soham SIBA

Meadow Works, Cross Green, Debenham, Suffolk, IP14 6RP
☎ (01728) 861213 ⊕ earlsohambrewery.co.uk

Earl Soham was set up behind the Victoria pub in 1984 and continued there until 2001 when the brewery relocated, moving again in 2013 to Debenham. Around 30 outlets are supplied and two pubs are owned. ‼ ♦RAIB

Gannet Mild (OG 1034, ABV 3.3%)
A well-balanced mild, sweet and fruity flavour with a lingering, coffee aftertaste.

Victoria Bitter (OG 1037, ABV 3.6%)
A light, fruity, amber-coloured session beer with a clean taste and a long, lingering hoppy aftertaste.

Elizabeth Ale (OG 1040, ABV 4.2%)
A rich premium beer with a clean bitter taste.

Sir Roger's Porter (OG 1042, ABV 4.2%)
Roast/coffee aroma and berry fruit introduce a full-bodied porter with roast/coffee flavours. Dry roast finish.

Albert Ale (OG 1045, ABV 4.4%)
Hops dominate every aspect of this beer, but especially the finish. A fruity, astringent beer.

Brandeston Gold (OG 1045, ABV 4.5%)
A sharp, clean flavour; malty/hoppy and heavily laden with citrus fruit. Malty finish.

Earth Ale (NEW)

c/o Unit 12, Platts Eyot, Hampton, London, TW12 2HF
☎ 07508 553546 ⊕ earthale.com

Earth Ale is a microbrewery that forages for wild ingredients that are then infused through its beers. Founder Alex Lewis is a Michelin-trained chef with nine years of professional kitchen experience and four years brewing experience. All beers are available unfiltered and bottle-conditioned. Beers are brewed using spare capacity at Oddly Beer (qv). ♦RAIB

East London SIBA

Unit 45, Fairways Business Centre, Lammas Road, Leyton, London, E10 7QB

THE BREWERIES

☎ (020) 8539 0805 ⊕ eastlondonbrewing.com

⊗ The East London Brewing Company is an award-winning 10-barrel brewery established in 2011 by a husband-and-wife team. ♦RAIB

Orchid Vanilla Mild (OG 1040, ABV 3.6%)
Delicate vanilla on nose and flavour. Fruity overtones coupled with cocoa dark roast character that is present in the finish.

Pale Ale (OG 1042, ABV 4%)
Amber-coloured best bitter with spicy hops, bitter lemon, tropical fruits and biscuit that are there in the dry aftertaste.

Foundation Bitter (OG 1044, ABV 4.2%)
Well-balanced, brown-coloured best bitter with fresh green fruity hop in aroma and flavour with caramelised pineapple. Short, bitter marmalade finish.

Nightwatchman Dark Premium Bitter (OG 1046, ABV 4.5%)
Dark ruby-brown-coloured, complex best bitter. Peach, caramelised fruit, toffee balanced by bitter, nutty and roasted malt flavours. Dry aftertaste.

Cowcatcher American Pale Ale (OG 1045, ABV 4.8%)
Fruity, hoppy, rich golden ale with honey sweetness, mango and hints of passion fruit lingering in the dry bitter finish.

Jamboree (OG 1048, ABV 4.8%)
Golden-coloured strong bitter with grassy and woody hop aroma. Flavour has spice with kiwi and sweet biscuit. Dry bitter finish.

Quadrant Oatmeal Stout (OG 1063, ABV 5.8%)
Smooth, rich oatmeal stout with liquorice, mocha and caramelised fruit. Roasted coffee aroma. A dry, slightly roasty bitter finish lingers.

East Yorkshire (NEW) SIBA

2a, The Courtyard, Tokenspire Business Park, Hull Road, Woodmansey, East Yorkshire, HU17 0TB
☎ (01482) 873382 ☎ 07456 063670
⊕ eastyorkshirebeer.co.uk

East Yorkshire Beer Company is a family-run, licenced brewery with a local and environmentally friendly ethos. Ingredients are sourced as locally as possible, grains malted in Bridlington and Castleford and UK hops used where possible. Spring water is drawn from an underground aquifer. Beers are named after Hull and East Yorkshire pubs. ‼

Top House Mild (OG 1041, ABV 3.8%)

King Billy Bitter (OG 1045, ABV 4.2%)

Earl de Grey IPA (OG 1047, ABV 4.5%)

Full Measure English Porter (OG 1049, ABV 4.5%)

Star of the West Pilsner (OG 1046, ABV 4.6%)

Eccleshall

See Slater's

Eden

See Eden River

Eden River SIBA

Hawksdale House, Hartness Road, Penrith, Cumbria, CA11 9DB
☎ (01768) 210565 ☎ 07729 677692
⊕ edenriverbrewco.uk

Originally named Eden Brewery, a name change to Eden River occurred in 2018. Set up in 2011, the brewery is run by Jason Hill, assisted by Linda and Chris. The five-barrel plant was located at historic Brougham Hall but moved in 2017 to premises on a Penrith industrial estate. ‼♦RAIB

Best (OG 1039, ABV 3.8%)
A traditional bitter with a hoppy beginning, a malty, bittersweet middle and a gentle finish.

Fuggle (OG 1039, ABV 3.8%)
Initially sweet, a gently-hopped pale beer with a more bitter finish.

Blonde Knight (OG 1040, ABV 4%)

Dynamite (OG 1040, ABV 4%)
Distinctive American-style pale ale, hoppy with a good aroma and flavour.

Atomic Blonde (OG 1041, ABV 4.1%)
The initially inviting aroma of hops is followed by an intense hop flavour with some fruitiness.

Gold (OG 1042, ABV 4.2%)
Gentle fruity and honey aromas to start leading to a well-balanced sweet beer with a lasting hoppy finish.

First Emperor (OG 1046, ABV 4.6%)
Fruity beer with balanced malt and hops and a hint of butterscotch combining to a rich bitter finish.

Eden St Andrews SIBA

Main Street, Guardbridge, KY16 0UU ☎ 07786 060013 ⊕ edenbrewerystandrews.com

The brewery was established in 2012 using a five-barrel plant in part of the former Guardbridge paper mills. In 2014 a new 20-barrel plant and distillery was installed. ‼ RAIB

St Andrews Blonde (OG 1040, ABV 3.8%)

19th (OG 1041, ABV 3.9%)

Clock Brew (OG 1045, ABV 4.3%)

1882 Lager (OG 1048, ABV 4.5%)

Seggie Porter (OG 1053, ABV 5.5%)

Shipwreck IPA (ABV 6%)
Tropical fruit aroma with a floral hop character, which leads to a hoppy body. A good bitterness develops alongside ripe, fruity notes, mellowing into a gentle, sweet finish.

Edinbrew SIBA

Unit 5, Knightsridge East Industrial Estate, Livingston, EH54 8RA ☎ 07736 680755 ⊕ edinbrew.beer/index

Edinbrew opened in 2015 within a small industrial estate in the Knightsridge area of Livingston. The brewery, operated by Ross Hamilton, who trained at the Milestone Brewery, uses a 5.5-barrel plant. ‼

Little Monster (OG 1040, ABV 3.7%)

70/- (OG 1039, ABV 3.8%)

The Good Stuff (OG 1039, ABV 3.9%)

Black Current (OG 1043, ABV 4.2%)

CommRed (OG 1043, ABV 4.2%)

Luxury IPA (OG 1041, ABV 4.2%)

Friendly Fire (OG 1045, ABV 4.3%)

85 Shilling (OG 1043, ABV 4.6%)

Super Stout (ABV 4.6%)

Industrial (OG 1054, ABV 5%)
Traditional IPA with a soft fruit and gentle malt taste.

Monster (OG 1065, ABV 5.7%)

Edinburgh Beer Factory (NEW) SIBA

Unit 15, Bankhead Industrial Estate, 7 Bankhead Crossway North, Edinburgh, EH11 4EQ
☎ (0131) 442 4562

Brewing began in 2015. No real ale.

Edmunds

Edmunds Brewhouse, 106-110 Edmund Street, Birmingham, B3 2ES
☎ (0121) 200 2423 edmundsbrewhouse.co.uk

Brewing began in 2015 at Edmunds Brewhouse in the heart of Birmingham's financial district. Beers are only available in the pub.

Eight Arch SIBA

Unit 3a, Stone Lane Industrial Estate, Wimborne, Dorset, BH21 1HB
☎ (01202) 889254 ☎ 07554 445647
8archbrewing.co.uk

Brewing commenced in 2015 on a five-barrel plant situated in a unit on a small industrial estate on the outskirts of Wimborne. It has recently expanded to a six-barrel plant. Local pubs and clubs are supplied. A brewery bar opens on Fridays 4-8pm. !! ♦ RAIB

Square Logic (ABV 4.2%)
A golden ale with a tangerine character.

Trefoil (ABV 4.5%)

Easy Life (ABV 5%)

Corbel (ABV 5.5%) ◆
Strong golden ale with hops dominating yet balanced with bitterness.

Layer Cake (ABV 6%)
A dark-coloured, fruity beer.

Electric Bear SIBA

Unit 12, Maltings Trading Estate, Locksbrook Road, Bath, BA1 3JL
☎ (01225) 424088 electricbearbrewing.com

Electric Bear began brewing in 2015 using a purpose-built 15-barrel plant, expanding capacity in 2016 and 2018. Its brewery tap showcases a selection of the range, including exclusive one-offs. All beers are unfiltered, unfined and unpasteurised. !! ♦ RAIB

Werrrd! (ABV 4.2%)
A well-balanced, session-strength, American-style pale ale.

Drop (ABV 4.3%)
A hoppy ale with a jam/marmalade malt base.

NZ Pale (OG 1046, ABV 4.5%)
An easy-drinking session ale with citrus flavours.

Inspector Remorse (ABV 4.7%)

Howdy Ho (ABV 5.1%)

Livewire (OG 1051, ABV 5.4%)

Above the Clouds (ABV 6.2%)

Elephant School

See Brentwood

Elgood's SIBA

North Brink Brewery, Wisbech, Cambridgeshire, PE13 1LW
☎ (01945) 583160 elgoods-brewery.co.uk

The North Brink brewery was established in 1795. Owned by the Elgood family since 1878, the fifth generation are now involved in running the business. Elgood's has approximately 30 tied pubs within a 50-mile radius of the brewery and a substantial free trade. Lambic style beers are produced using the brewery's old open cooling trays as fermenting vessels. Off sales are available all year round from the shop in the brewery office when the visitor centre is closed. !! ♦

Black Dog (OG 1036.8, ABV 3.6%) ◆
Black/red-coloured mild with liquorice and chocolate. Dry roasty finish.

Cambridge Bitter (OG 1037.8, ABV 3.8%) ◆
Fruit and malt on the nose with increasing hops and balancing malt on the palate. Dry finish.

Golden Newt (OG 1041.5, ABV 4.1%) ◆
Golden ale with floral hops and sulphur aroma. Floral hops and a fruity presence on a bittersweet background lead to a short, muted hoppy and fruity finish.

Elixir

Office: 2.1 Merchiston Place, Edinburgh, EH54 9BX
☎ 07760 330122 elixirbrew.com

Elixir Brew Company is an award-winning experimental brewery that produces beers using New World hops, unusual ingredients and novel techniques. Established in 2012, Elixir beers are produced at a variety of breweries throughout the UK, including frequent collaborations with the host brewers.

Elland SIBA

Units 3-5, Heathfield Industrial Estate, Heathfield Street, Elland, West Yorkshire, HX5 9AE
☎ (01422) 377677 ellandbrewery.co.uk

Orginally formed in 2002 as Eastwood & Sanders by the amalgamation of the Barge & Barrel and West Yorkshire Breweries, the company was renamed Elland in 2006 to reinforce its links with the town. The brewery has a capacity of 50 barrels (200 firkins) a week with further expansion planned. !! ♦ RAIB

White Prussian (OG 1039, ABV 3.9%) ◆
A straw-coloured, lightly-flavoured, easy-drinking and refreshing lager-style speciality beer.

Blonde (OG 1041, ABV 4%)
Creamy, yellow-coloured, hoppy ale with hints of citrus fruits. Pleasantly strong bitter aftertaste.

Beyond the Pale (OG 1042, ABV 4.2%)
Gold-coloured, robust, creamy beer with ripe aromas of hops and fruit. Bitterness predominates in the mouth and leads to a dry, fruity and hoppy aftertaste.

Nettlethrasher (OG 1044, ABV 4.4%)
Smooth, amber-coloured beer. A rounded nose with some fragrant hops notes followed by a mellow nutty and fruity taste and a dry finish.

1872 Porter (OG 1065, ABV 6.5%)
Creamy, full-flavoured porter. Rich liquorice flavours with a hint of chocolate from roast malt. A soft but satisfying aftertaste of bittersweet roast and malt.

Elliswood SIBA

Unit 3, Southways Industrial Estate, Coventry Road, Hinckley, Leicestershire, LE10 0NJ
☎ (01455) 635239 ☎ 07795 954392

Office: 24 Leicester Road, Hinckley, Leicestershire, LE10 1LS elliswoodbrewery.co.uk

Founded in 2013 by Tracy Ellis and Phil Woodward and taken over in 2016 by Darren and Louise Lavender, who continue to brew using the David Porter 5.5-barrel system with a capacity to brew twice weekly. Beers are available across the Midlands.

Flaming Star (OG 1039, ABV 3.8%)

X Porter (OG 1038, ABV 4%)
Rich, smooth porter with coffee undertones.

Barrel of Laughs (OG 1042, ABV 4.2%)
Copper-coloured, well-balanced ale with a spicy vanilla undertone. Slight bitterness all the way through with a sweet, pleasant aftertaste.

Just One More (OG 1042, ABV 4.2%)
A citrus beer with blackberry and grapefruit undertones.

Black Rose (OG 1045, ABV 4.5%)
A mild porter with a subtle chocolate aftertaste.

Fosse 107 (OG 1047, ABV 4.5%)
IPA with a crisp finish and bitterness.

Nelson's Right Arm (OG 1044, ABV 4.5%)
A mahogany-coloured beer, spicy with heavy hints of autumn fruits.

Royal Standard 1485 (OG 1047, ABV 4.8%)
A deep red-coloured bitter with a sweet toffee taste and caramel undertones.

Legless (OG 1048, ABV 4.9%)
Easy-drinking, gold-coloured beer. Full-bodied with undertones of blackberry and spice.

Elmesthorpe (NEW)

Church Farm, Station Road, Elmesthorpe, Leicestershire, LE9 7SG ☎ 07754 321283

Brewing began in 2017.

Elmtree SIBA

Snetterton Brewery, Snetterton Brewery, Snetterton, Norfolk, NR16 2JU
☎ (01953) 887065 ☎ 07939 549241
elmtreebeers.co.uk

Established in 2007, Elmtree brews on a six-barrel plant. More than 120 free trade outlets are supplied direct. Bespoke beers for individual pubs are also brewed. !! ♦ RAIB V

Burston's Cuckoo (OG 1038, ABV 3.8%)
Gentle malt airs. Biscuity sweet beginning with delicate lime hints. Full-bodied, short, sweet finish.

Bitter (OG 1041, ABV 4.2%)
A well-balanced, copper-coloured, crisp beer. The early malt notes give way to a distinctively complex hop finish.

Norfolk's 80 Shilling Ale (OG 1044, ABV 4.5%)
Roast malt and caramel provide balance to an inherent hoppy bitterness. A mix of well-balanced flavours. Finish becomes chewy.

Dark Horse Stout (OG 1050, ABV 5%)
Solid coffee and malt aroma. A cornucopia of vanilla, dark chocolate and roast with a sweet foundation. Long, strong finale.

Golden Pale Ale (OG 1048, ABV 5%)
Full-bodied with a swirling malty aroma. Lime fruit adds depth to the sweet malty character. Short sweetening finish.

Nightlight Mild (OG 1057, ABV 5.7%)
A heavy mix of liquorice, roast and malt infuses aroma and first taste. A sweet spiciness slowly develops.

Elusive

Unit 5, Marino Way, Hogwood Lane Industrial Estate, Finchampstead, Berkshire, RG40 4RF ☎ 07917 541718 elusivebrewing.com

Established in 2016, Elusive is a five-barrel brewery located on the Hampshire/Berkshire border.

Sphere of Destiny (OG 1044, ABV 4.4%)

Level Up (OG 1051, ABV 5%)

Overdrive (OG 1054, ABV 5.5%)

Spellbinder (OG 1060, ABV 6%)
A porter with notes of dark fruits and a hint of coffee.

EMAL

See Powderkeg

Empire SIBA

The Old Boiler House, Unit 33, Upper Mills, Slaithwaite, West Yorkshire, HD7 5HA
☎ (01484) 847343 ☎ 07966 592276
empirebrewing.com

Empire Brewing was set up 2006 in a mill on the bank of the scenic Huddersfield Narrow Canal, close to the centre of Slaithwaite. In 2011 the brewery upgraded from a five-barrel to a 10-barrel plant. Beers are supplied to local free houses and through independent specialist beer agencies and wholesalers. !! ♦ RAIB

Golden Warrior (OG 1039.5, ABV 3.8%)
Pale-coloured bitter, quite fruity with a sherbet aftertaste, moderate bitterness.

Strikes Back (OG 1041, ABV 4%)

Pale golden-coloured bitter with a hoppy aroma and good hop and malt balance with a citrus flavour.

Valour (OG 1042.5, ABV 4.2%)

Longbow (OG 1043, ABV 4.3%)

Imperium (OG 1050, ABV 5.1%)

Emsworth Brewery

Rear of 16 West Street, Emsworth, Hampshire, PO10 7DY ☎ 07717 510294
theemsworthbrewery.co.uk

Michael and Hilary Bolt began their family-run brewery in 2011 on a 2.5-barrel plant, obtained from Oban Ales, in a shed behind an antiques shop in Emsworth. ♦RAIB

Slipper (OG 1040, ABV 3.9%)

Wayfarer (OG 1042, ABV 4.1%)

Fairfield (OG 1042, ABV 4.2%)

Emsworth Brewhouse

26 Scratchface Lane, Bedhampton, Hampshire, PO9 3NG ☎ 07828 799885
theemsworthbrewhouse.co.uk

Launched in 2015, the Emsworth Brewhouse originally used a half-barrel plant but upgraded in 2016. In 2017 the brewery was sold and moved to its new location near Havant.

Mainsail (OG 1038, ABV 3.8%)
A floral aroma with hints of citrus peel and tangerine and a refreshing crisp taste.

Flotilla (OG 1044, ABV 4.4%)
A dark amber-coloured ale with fruity malt flavours. Hints of sultana in the finish.

Wodehouse (OG 1048, ABV 4.8%)
A rich, dark chestnut-coloured ale with a smooth, full-bodied taste and a slight hint of Christmas cake.

Enfield SIBA

Unit 17a, Eley Road, Upper Edmonton, London, N18 3BB
☎ (020) 8807 1533 enfieldbrewery.co.uk

Brewing began in 2015, initially only offering bottled and keg beers. Cask-conditioned production began in 2017. The brewery uses its own well water. RAIB

Engine Shed Project

See Brunswick

Engineer

Garage at Russetts, Burnt Oak Road, High Hurstwood, East Sussex, TN22 4AE ☎ 07841 669096
theengineerbrewery.co.uk

A tiny garage-based brewery that provides variety rather than volume to a small number of local pubs and retail outlets, as well as beer festivals and special events.

Dark Mild (OG 1035, ABV 3%)
Subtle roasted malt, smooth, light and easy drinking.

English Pale Ale (OG 1044, ABV 4.2%)
Session pale ale with refreshing citrus notes.

Milk Stout (OG 1051, ABV 4.2%)
Light milk stout with a little more hop character than typical for the style.

Dunkel (OG 1050, ABV 4.5%)
Malty, dark-coloured lager.

Golden Ale (OG 1045, ABV 4.5%)
Delicate fruit flavours from a blend of hops.

Altbier (OG 1051, ABV 5%)
Rich caramel and biscuit malt body balanced with a moderate and lingering bitterness.

US Amber Ale (OG 1049, ABV 5%)
Caramel maltiness with a subtle hop character.

Imperial Stout (OG 1072, ABV 6.8%)
Robust roasted malts and assertive bitterness smoothed off with real chocolate.

Ennerdale SIBA

Chapel Row, Rowrah, Cumbria, CA26 3XS
☎ (01946) 862977 ☎ 07918 626652
ennerdalebrewery.co.uk

Ennerdale started brewing in 2010 as a 10-barrel brewery in a converted barn. In 2016 the brewery moved to larger premises with plans for expansion. Beers are distributed throughout the north of England and south Scotland. !!♦

Blonde (OG 1039, ABV 3.8%)
A sweet, fruity, light-coloured beer with gentle bitterness.

Darkest (OG 1044, ABV 4.2%)
Sweet, roasty, black-coloured mild with a fruity, hoppy flavour.

Wild Ennerdale (OG 1043, ABV 4.2%)
Amber in colour with a fruity base and spicy finish yielding a good hop aroma and well-rounded bitterness.

Enville SIBA

Coxgreen, Hollies Lane, Enville, DY7 5LG
☎ (01384) 873728 envilleales.com

Enville Brewery is sited on a picturesque Victorian, Grade II-listed farm complex, using natural well water, traditional steam brewing and a reed and willow effluent plant. Enville Ale is infused with honey and is from a 19th-century recipe for beekeeper's ale passed down from the former proprietor's great-great aunt. !!♦

LPA (Light Pale Ale) (OG 1039, ABV 4%)
Traditional session bitter; dry and golden with a mellow, hoppy flavour.

Nailmaker Mild (OG 1041, ABV 4%)
A well-defined hop aroma and underlying caramel sweetness give way to a dry finish.

Simpkiss (OG 1039, ABV 4%)
Caramel smooth start, caramel body with sweet malt and hop bite. Fruity hop finish.

Cherry Blonde (OG 1042, ABV 4.2%)
A light blonde bitter, delicately infused with essence of cherry to produce a Belgian-style fruit beer. A dry, hoppy and refreshing bitter finish.

Saaz (OG 1042, ABV 4.2%) ◈
Golden-coloured, lager-style beer. Lager bite but with more taste and lasting bitterness. The malty aroma is late arriving but the bitter finish, balanced by fruit and hops, compensates.

White (OG 1041, ABV 4.2%) ◈
Yellow-coloured with a malt, hops and fruit aroma. Hoppy but sweet finish.

Ale (OG 1044, ABV 4.5%) ◈
Sweet, malty aroma and taste, honey becomes apparent before bitterness finally dominates.

Old Porter (OG 1044, ABV 4.5%) ◈
Black-coloured with a creamy head and sulphurous aroma. Sweet and fruity start with touches of spice. Good balance between sweet and bitter, but hops dominate the finish.

Ginger Beer (OG 1045, ABV 4.6%) ◈
Golden-coloured ale with gently gingered tangs. A drinkable beer with no acute flavours but a satisfying aftertaste of sweet hoppiness.

Brewed for the Stourton Brewing Co:

American Pale Ale (OG 1043, ABV 4.3%)
A classic American-style pale ale, creamy, smooth and bursting with citrus hops.

Epic Beers (NEW)

The Brewery, West Huish, BS24 6RR
☎ (01934) 384044 ⊕ pitchforkales.com / 3d-beer.com

⊗ Epic Beers was formed in 2017 after the demise of RCH Brewery by several former employees, brewing on the existing plant in the same premises. Beers are brewed under the Pitchfork Ales brand, which offers traditional British beers, while more modern styles are available under the 3D Beer brand name. !! ♦

Brewed under the 3D Beer brand name:

Hop Gun (OG 1043, ABV 4.3%) ◈
Pronounced hoppy aroma. Pale fruit balance the hoppiness on the tongue, leading to a dry and bitter finish.

Beer-Zinga (OG 1049, ABV 5%) ◈
Powerfully hopped with a citrus aroma. Refreshing bitterness on the palate, finishing with a lingering, dry yet balanced bittersweet aftertaste.

Brewed under the Pitchfork Ales brand name:

Goldbine (OG 1039, ABV 3.8%)
Grassy hops on the nose of this light-bodied golden ale precede a notably dry hop taste and increasingly bitter finish.

PG Steam (OG 1039, ABV 3.9%) ◈
Light malt and faint hop aroma. Pale fruit combines with dry bitterness in the flavour, before a lasting dry aftertaste.

Pitchfork (OG 1043, ABV 4.3%) ◈
Some hops on the nose, flavours combine hoppy bitterness with hints of fruit leaving a lasting dry and bitter aftertaste

Old Slug Porter (OG 1046, ABV 4.5%)
Smoky, full-bodied porter with dark fruits and roast malts, leaving a short, bitter, dry aftertaste.

Epicurus

11 Bow Street, Bolton, BL1 2EQ ☎ 07577 674377
⊕ epicurus-brewery.com

Formerly known as Hornbeam Brewery, it was taken over in 2016 by new owners, James Thompson and Nick Taylor, and completely rebranded as Epicurus in 2017 with a range of seven core beers, some using popular Hornbeam recipes. Brewing is currently suspended pending a move to Bolton. ♦RAIB

Errant

Arch 8, King Edward Bridge, off Pottery Lane, Newcastle upon Tyne, NE1 3TQ ☎ 07736 333303
⊕ errantbrewery.com

⊗ Brewing began in 2015 in an old Victorian railway arch. A range of speciality beers is available seasonally or on request. ♦

Essex Street

46 Essex Street, Temple, London, WC2R 3JF
☎ (020) 7936 2536 ⊕ templebrewhouse.com

Opened in 2014 within the Temple Brew House pub. Beers are neither filtered nor pasteurised. The City Pub Group also operates sister brewpubs in London, Bath, Bristol, Cambridge and Norwich. !! ♦ GF V

Evan Evans SIBA

The New Brewery, 1 Rhosmaen Street, Llandeilo, Carmarthenshire, SA19 6LU
☎ (01558) 824455 ⊕ evanevansbrewery.com

⊗ Evan Evans opened in 2004. The range of brands produced includes Evan-Evans, J Buckley Brewer, which focusses on hop flavour, Artisan, which is a US-style craft beer brand, and Fire-Island, which specialises in organic and gluten free beers. In 2016 the Celt Experience brand was acquired and its production moved to Llandeilo. Beers may also appear under the Archers brand name. As well as bottling its own beers, bottling is also undertaken for several other independent breweries and cider producers. !! ♦ GF

BB/Best Bitter (OG 1036, ABV 3.6%)
A light, malty character with a dry hop palate.

WPA (Welsh Pale Ale) (OG 1040, ABV 4%)
A golden ale with hints of tropical fruits and a malty finish.

Cwrw (OG 1043, ABV 4.2%)
Rich, malty flavour and a distinct fruity palate.

Britannia Celebration Ale (ABV 4.6%)
Dark amber-coloured ale with a rich malt, fruity hedgerow berry finish.

Warrior (OG 1046, ABV 4.6%)
Full-bodied and malty with a fruity flavour and dry hop finish.

Brewed under the Celt Experience brand name:

Castro Mosaic (ABV 3.9%)
A dry-hopped American-style pale ale infused with lemon peel to create a tropical fruit palate and citrus aroma.

Chieftain (ABV 4.3%)

A complex malt flavour balanced with citrus aromas.

Silures (ABV 4.6%)
A powerfully-hopped beer with tropical fruit flavours.

Brewed under the J Buckley Brewer brand name:

Original Best (ABV 4.4%)
A rich, malty bitter with a fruit aroma.

Everards

Office: Devana Avenue, Optimus Point, Glenfield, Leicester, LE3 8JS
☎ (0116) 201 4100 🌐 everards.co.uk

Everards was established in 1849 by William Everard and remains an independent family-owned company. It has a pub estate of more than 170 tenanted houses throughout the Midlands. It plans to move its brewing operation to a new site, Everards Meadows, but this cannot go ahead until sale of the Castle Acres site is complete. For the duration of this edition of the Guide its beers will be produced by what it calls Pub Partners. Robinson's (qv) of Stockport will brew Tiger and Beacon Hill while Joules (qv) of Market Drayton will produce Old Original, Sunchaser and limited edition beers. The new brewery will have a capacity of 15,000 barrels a year.

Exe Valley SIBA

Land Farm, Silverton, Devon, EX5 4HF
☎ (01392) 860406 🌐 exevalleybrewery.co.uk

Exe Valley was established as Barron's Brewery in 1984. The brewery is located in a converted barn overlooking the Exe Valley and Dartmoor hills. Locally sourced malt and English hops are used, along with the brewery's own spring water. Around 100 outlets are supplied within a 45-mile radius of the brewery. Beers are also available nationally via wholesalers. ♦RAIB

Bitter (OG 1036, ABV 3.7%)
Mid-brown-coloured bitter, pleasantly fruity with underlying malt through the aroma, taste and finish.

Darkest Devon (OG 1038, ABV 3.9%)

Barron's Hopsit (OG 1040, ABV 4.1%)
Straw-coloured beer with strong hop aroma, hop and fruit flavour and a bitter hop finish.

Dob's Best Bitter (OG 1040, ABV 4.1%)
Delicate aroma, well-balanced taste with malt, hops and sweet fruit continuing into a bitter, hoppy aftertaste.

Fryer's Thirst (OG 1041, ABV 4.3%)
A golden-coloured ale with a fruity/malty aroma. Well-balanced with a good body and a dry, hoppy bitter finish.

Devon Glory (OG 1046, ABV 4.7%)
Mid-brown-coloured, fruity-tasting beer with a sweet, fruity finish.

Mr Sheppard's Crook (OG 1046, ABV 4.7%)
Smooth, full-bodied, mid-brown-coloured beer with a malty fruit nose and a sweetish palate leading to a bitter, dry finish.

Exeter Old Bitter (OG 1046, ABV 4.8%)
Mid-brown-coloured old ale with a rich, fruity taste, slightly earthy aroma and bitter finish.

It's Phil's Ale (OG 1046, ABV 4.8%)
Deep golden-coloured beer with intense hop flavours and a long, dry bitter aftertaste.

Exeter SIBA

Unit 1, Cowley Bridge Road, Exeter, Devon, EX4 4NX
☎ (01392) 259059 🌐 exeterbrewery.co.uk

Exeter began brewing in 2003 and is the largest brewery in the city, supplying more than 600 outlets in Devon, Cornwall, Dorset and Somerset. It moved to its present site in 2012, having outgrown its previous location. !! ♦RAIB

Lighterman (OG 1036, ABV 3.5%)
A light copper-coloured ale, fruity malt flavour with a traditional bitter finish.

Avocet (OG 1038.5, ABV 3.9%)
Fruity and sweet from nose to aftertaste. Slight maltiness balances pineapple. Light session ale.

'fraid Not (OG 1040, ABV 4%)
A golden-coloured, hoppy beer. A distinct clean citrus bitterness and lasting dry finish.

Ferryman (OG 1041, ABV 4.2%)
Classic copper-coloured session ale. Well-balanced, sweet malt flavour. Crisp bitter finish.

County Best (OG 1045, ABV 4.6%)
Premium best bitter. Rich malt, fruity flavour. Smooth, bittersweet finish.

Darkness (OG 1050, ABV 5.1%)
Full-bodied stout. Roasted malt dominates the aroma. Complex taste with roast chocolate. Hints of liquorice in a bitter finish.

Exit 33

Unit 7, 106 Fitzwalter Road, Sheffield, South Yorkshire, S2 2SP
☎ (0114) 270 9991 🌐 exit33.beer

This eight-barrel brewery was founded in Sheffield in 2008 as Brew Company but rebranded in 2014. The brewer is also a joint partner at the Harlequin pub. Regular house beers are brewed for local pubs. Beers are available nationally. ♦

Blonde (OG 1038.8, ABV 4%)
A blonde session ale. Easy-drinking, light and fruity.

Thirst Aid (OG 1038.8, ABV 4%)
A light session ale with a juicy hop-forward flavour.

Mosaic (OG 1039.7, ABV 4.1%)

Northern Best (OG 1040.7, ABV 4.2%)
A premium bitter with a smooth, malty base and rich flavour.

Hop Monster (OG 1043.6, ABV 4.5%)
Golden ale with resinous pink grapefruit, biting citrus and soft floral characters. A hoppy and long bitter finish.

Stout (OG 1048.4, ABV 5%)
A dark-coloured traditional stout. The initial flavour hints of cocoa followed by delicate coffee and molasses with a silky, thick mouthfeel.

Exmoor SIBA

Golden Hill Brewery, Old Brewery Road, Wiveliscombe, Somerset, TA4 2PW
☎ (01984) 623798 🌐 exmoorales.co.uk

Somerset's largest independent brewery was founded in 1980 in the old Hancock's brewery, which closed in 1959. In 2015 Exmoor moved to new and larger premises within 100 yards of the original site, thus doubling brewing capacity. Around 250 outlets in the South-west are supplied and others nationwide via wholesalers and pub chains. ‼♦

Ale (OG 1039, ABV 3.8%)
Mid-brown-coloured, medium-bodied session bitter. Mixture of malt and hops in the aroma and taste lead to a hoppy, bitter aftertaste.

Fox (OG 1043, ABV 4.2%)
Slight maltiness on the tongue is followed by a burst of hops with a lingering, bittersweet aftertaste.

Gold (OG 1045, ABV 4.5%)
Golden-coloured best bitter with balance of malt and fruity hop on the nose and palate with sweetness following. Bitter finish.

Stag (OG 1050, ABV 5.2%)
A pale brown-coloured beer with a malty taste and aroma, and a bitter finish.

Beast (OG 1066, ABV 6.6%)
A dark-coloured beer similar to a strong porter with a complex, long aftertaste.

Eyam (NEW)

Unit 5a, Eyam Hall Craft Centre, Main Road, Eyam, Derbyshire, S32 5QW ☎ 07976 432682 eyambrewery.com

Brewing began in 2017 using a 1.5-barrel plant producing keg and bottle-conditioned beers. Most output goes to its shop and events but 10 local outlets are also supplied. ‼ RAIB V

Eyeball

The Works, Implement Road, West Barns, Dunbar, EH42 1UN ☎ 07764 606510 eyeballbrewing.co.uk

Eyeball Brewing was established in 2016 by James Dempsey, who developed a passion for lager while travelling through Germany. Inspired, he built a brewery in his home and began to experiment. Now housed in a new brewery on the East Lothian coast, Eyeball produces three lagers in cask, keg and bottle. V

Black (OG 1048, ABV 4.9%)

Yellow (OG 1048, ABV 4.9%)

Orange (OG 1060, ABV 6.5%)

Eyes SIBA

Manor Farm, Intake Lake, Acaster Mablis, York, North Yorkshire, YO23 3UJ ☎ 07837 898749

Office: 54 Eden Crescent, Leeds, West Yorkshire, LS24 2TW eyesbrewing.

Brewing began in 2016 using spare capacity at Ainsty Ales in York. Eyes is the first wheat-focused brewery in the UK. There are plans for moving to full production in its own brewery in the Leeds area. Brews a constantly evolving range of ales.

Fable (NEW)

c/o George's Brewery, Common Road, Great Wakering, Essex, SS3 0AG fablebrewery.com

A cuckoo brewery specialising in vegan beers. V

Genesis Pale Ale (OG 1038, ABV 3.8%)

Facer's

A8-9, Ashmount Enterprise Park, Aber Road, Flint, CH5 5YL ☎ 07713 566370 facers.co.uk

Facer's is the oldest brewery in Flintshire. Sales average some 30 barrels per week to around 100 outlets in North Wales and North-west England. Established in 2003 by ex-Boddingtons head brewer Dave Facer, the brewery now has three employees. ‼♦

Mountain Mild (OG 1035, ABV 3.3%)
A fruity dark mild, not too sweet, with underlying roast malt flavours and a full mouthfeel for its low ABV.

Clwyd Gold (OG 1034, ABV 3.5%)
Clean-tasting session bitter, mid-brown in colour with a full mouthfeel. The malty flavours are accompanied by increasing hoppiness in the bitter finish.

Flintshire Bitter (OG 1035, ABV 3.7%)
Well-balanced session bitter with a full mouthfeel. Some fruitiness in aroma and taste with increasing hoppy bitterness in the dry finish.

Abbey Blonde (OG 1037, ABV 4%)

Abbey Original (OG 1038, ABV 4%)
A sweetish golden-coloured beer with a good hop and fruit aroma, juicy taste and a dry hoppy finish.

Abbey Red (OG 1038, ABV 4%)
A darker version of Abbey Original, copper-coloured with a sweet, malty taste and a bittersweet aftertaste.

North Star Porter (OG 1042, ABV 4%)
Dark-coloured, smooth, porter-style beer with good roast notes and hints of coffee and chocolate. Some initial sweetness and caramel flavours followed by a hoppy bitter aftertaste.

Sunny Bitter (OG 1040, ABV 4.2%)
An amber-coloured beer with a dry taste. The hop aroma continues into the taste where some faint fruit notes are also present. Lasting dry finish.

DHB (Dave's Hoppy Beer) (OG 1041, ABV 4.3%)
A dry-hopped version of This Splendid Ale with some sweet flavours also coming through in the mainly hoppy, bitter taste.

This Splendid Ale (OG 1041, ABV 4.3%)
Refreshing, tangy best bitter, yellow in colour with a sharp, hoppy, bitter taste. Good citrus fruit undertones with hints of grapefruit throughout.

Landslide (OG 1047, ABV 4.9%)
Full-flavoured, complex premium bitter with tangy orange marmalade fruitiness in aroma and taste. Long-lasting hoppy flavours throughout.

Fallen

Station House, Kippen, FK8 3JA ☎ 07507 862167 fallenbrewing.co.uk

Fallen began brewing in 2014 using a 10-barrel plant. ♦RAIB

Fallen Acorn SIBA

Unit 7, Clarence Wharf Industrial Estate, Mumby Road, Gosport, Hampshire, PO12 1AJ
☎ (023) 9307 9927 fallenacornbrewing.co

Investment firm Just Develop It in Hampshire bought Oakleaf Brewery in 2016. The brewery was renamed Fallen Acorn and went into full production later that year. Ed Anderson remains head brewer. !! ♦ RAIB

Twisted Oak (OG 1040, ABV 4%)
A traditional mid-brown-coloured bitter with an initial malty flavour leading to a long hoppy finish.

Black Hearted (ABV 4.7%)

Hole Hearted (OG 1048, ABV 4.7%)
Amber-coloured with a strong floral hop aroma continuing into the flavour, with some malt, leading to a long, bittersweet finish.

Double Tide (ABV 5%)

Expedition IPA (OG 1053, ABV 5.5%)
Initially dry and bitter. Full-flavoured and complex marmalade/aniseed notes to follow, which leaves a lingering bitterness on the palate.

Fallen Angel SIBA

Unit 12c, Reeds Farm Estate Office, Roxwell Road, Writtle, Essex, CM1 3ST fallenangelbrew.co.uk

Formerly known as the Broxbourne Brewery, a name change to Fallen Angel occurred in 2017. Brewing began in 2013 using a 12-barrel plant. A 15-barrel plant has been in operation since the brewery's move from Hertfordshire to Essex in 2015. RAIB

Ginger Beer (OG 1035, ABV 4%)
Traditional ginger beer with a strong, sweet taste and smooth finish.

Cowgirl Gold (OG 1045, ABV 4.2%)

Angry Ox Bitter (OG 1047, ABV 4.8%)

Fire in the Hole (OG 1046, ABV 4.9%)
A milder chilli beer brewed using fresh chillies.

Black Death (OG 1052, ABV 5.2%)
A jet black stout infused with Naga chilli.

Falstaff

24 Society Place, Normanton, Derby, DE23 6UH
☎ (01332) 342902 ☎ 07947 242710
falstaffbrewery.co.uk

Attached to the Falstaff freehouse, the brewery dates from 1999 but was refurbished and re-opened in 2003 under new management. Themed special beers are produced all year round, including exclusive specials for the Babington Arms, Derby. ♦

Famous Railway Tavern

58 Station Road, Brightlingsea, Essex, CO7 0DT

The brewery started life as a kitchen-sink affair in 1998. In 2012 the brewery was completely refurbished; a two-barrel plant is used to create a selection of dark beers suitable for vegetarians. !!

Farm Yard SIBA

Gulf Lane, Cockerham, Lancashire, LA2 0ER
☎ (01253) 799988 ☎ 07717 081170
farmyardales.co.uk

Situated on a family-run farm, this 10-barrel plant began brewing in 2017 and will feature a canning plant from late 2018. The tap overlooks the brewery. Aiming to be completely sustainable, the mineral water used is sourced from its own borehole with all waste returned for use on the farm. The brewery supplies local pubs. Beer names are all farm themed. !! ♦

Holmes Stead (OG 1033, ABV 3.4%)
Easy-drinking ale with a caramel and biscuit flavour.

TVO 54 (OG 1036, ABV 3.7%)
Blonde beer, clean and crisp in malt with fruity aromas.

Haybob (OG 1041, ABV 3.9%)
A golden-coloured session beer, malty with hints of caramel.

Sheaf (OG 1040, ABV 4.1%)

Hoof (OG 1042, ABV 4.3%)

Chaff (OG 1046, ABV 4.6%)
A session IPA full of New World hops.

Gulf IPA (OG 1057, ABV 5.8%)
A premium IPA with a tropical and pine aroma.

Farmageddon

25 Ballykeigle Road, Comber, BT23 5SD ☎ 07885 442307 farmageddonbrewing.com

Co-operative brewery, formed in 2014. All beers are unfiltered with no preservatives and are suitable for vegans. ♦ RAIB V

California Common (ABV 4%)
Initial malt sweetness balanced by bitterness, light toffee notes followed by a lingering secondary citrus bitterness hit that is refreshing rather than overwhelming.

Gold Pale Ale (ABV 4.2%)
A light but well-hopped pale ale.

IPA (ABV 5.5%)
A big, hoppy American-style IPA.

Mosaic IPA (ABV 6.3%)
A light-bodied, straw-coloured, dry IPA. Expect tropical fruit, citrus and resinous pine backed up with a lasting bitterness.

Farmer's

See Maldon

Farr Brew SIBA

Unit 7, The Courtyard, Samuels Farm, Coleman Green Lane, Wheathampstead, Hertfordshire, AL4 8ER
☎ 07734 857881 farrbrew.com

Farr Brew began brewing in 2014. The beers proved popular necessitating a move to a brand new 10-barrel brewery in 2016. Ecological and environmental concerns are at the forefront of everything Farr Brew creates. The brewery now cultivates some of its own hops. A micropub and bottle shop, the Reading Rooms, opened in Wheathampstead in 2018. !! ♦

Chief Jester (OG 1036, ABV 3.6%)

A light amber-coloured session ale with flavour notes of grapefruit and tropical fruits.

Our Greatest Golden (OG 1041, ABV 4.1%)
A golden ale with a well-rounded but not overpowering hoppiness.

Our Most Perfect Pale (OG 1042, ABV 4.2%)
A powerful pale ale packed full of tropical and citrus flavours with a crisp bitter finish.

The Best Bitter (OG 1042, ABV 4.2%)
A dark-coloured, traditional bitter with a hint of caramel.

Black Listed IBA (OG 1045, ABV 4.5%)
Smoky, powerfully-hopped Indian black ale with a well-rounded, punchy flavour.

Our Most Potent Porter (OG 1050, ABV 5%)
A complex porter made with locally-sourced honey. A deep chocolaty nose and a rich, fruity, hoppy flavour.

Farriers Arms

The Forstal, Mersham, Kent, TN25 6NU
☎ (01233) 720444 thefarriersarms.com

Brewing commenced in 2010 in this brewpub owned by a consortium of villagers. ‼♦

Fat Belly

c/o Cottage Inn, Lynton, Devon, EX34 6NR
☎ (01598) 753496 thecottageinnlynton.co.uk

Established in 2016 using a 3.5-barrel plant at the rear of the Cottage Inn. Beers are available in the pub plus a growing number of other local outlets. Further beers are planned. ♦RAIB

Fat Cat

Fat Cat Brewery Tap, 98-100 Lawson Road, Norwich, NR3 4LF
☎ (01603) 788508 ☎ 07795 633368
fatcatbrewery.co.uk

Fat Cat Brewery was founded by the owner of the Fat Cat free house in Norwich. Brewing started in 2005 at the Fat Cat's sister pub, the Fat Cat Brewery Tap, under the supervision of former Woodforde's owner Ray Ashworth. ‼♦RAIB

Fat Pig

Railway Arches 17 & 18, St Thomas Court, Exeter, Devon, EX4 1AJ ☎ 07909 520580
fatpig-exeter.co.uk

Brewing commenced in 2013 using a 2.5-barrel plant to supply the Fat Pig pub and its sister pub, Tabac in Exeter. It is run as an experimental brewery, constantly playing with combinations of malts, hops and temperatures to improve the range of beers and push the boundaries. Grain liquor is also produced for its in-house gin and whisky distillery. The brewery relocated to its current address in 2018. ♦V

Pigmalion Bitter (OG 1039, ABV 3.9%)
Modern, golden-coloured session ale, with a citrus finish.

Pigasus Brown Ale (OG 1040, ABV 4%)
Classic brown-coloured ale with a refreshing, slightly sweet finish.

Ham 69 ESB (OG 1042, ABV 4.2%)
A spicy, dark-coloured ale with a bitter edge.

John Street Ale (OG 1043, ABV 4.3%)

Phat Nancys IPA (OG 1044, ABV 4.4%)
Pale amber in colour with a hoppy and fruity taste, leading to a spicy bitter aftertaste.

Faultline (NEW)

Office: 25 Ashley Road, Westcott, Surrey, RH4 3QJ

Cuckoo brewery set up in 2018 by Antoine Josserand and Matt Gillam. Brewing has mainly taken place on the Leith Hill Brewery (qv) plant.

Faversham Steam

See Shepherd Neame

Federation (NEW)

48 Greenwood Street, Altrincham, WA14 1RZ
☎ (0161) 696 6870 conclubuk.com

Located in the Con Club, a pub with restaurant that was formerly Altrincham Working Mens Conservative Club, this is a small 2.4-barrel plant that began brewing in 2017. Beer is only available in the pub.

Felday (NEW)

Royal Oak, Village Green, Holmbury St Mary, Surrey, RH5 6PF eldaybrewery.co.uk

Brewing began in 2017 on a custom-made plant next to the Royal Oak pub car park. Almost all of the beer is supplied to the pub. ♦

Felinfoel SIBA

Farmers Row, Felinfoel, Llanelli, SA14 8LB
☎ (01554) 773357 felinfoel-brewery.com

Founded in the 1830s, the company is still family-owned and is now the oldest brewery in Wales. The present buildings are Grade II*-listed and were built in the 1870s. It supplies cask ale to half its 84 houses, though some use top pressure dispense, and to approximately 350 free trade outlets. ‼♦

IPA (OG 1036, ABV 3.6%)

Celtic Pride (OG 1045, ABV 3.9%)
A light, golden-coloured premium ale with a bright, clean flavour and citrus overtones.

Double Dragon (OG 1042, ABV 4.2%)
This pale brown-coloured beer has a malty, fruity aroma. The taste is also malt and fruit with a background hop presence throughout. A malty and fruity finish.

Stout (OG 1048, ABV 5%)
A Welsh stout created with a subtle blend of chocolate malt giving a predominantly roast barley flavour and a rich, creamy head.

Fell

Unit 27, Moor Lane Business Park, Flookburgh, Cumbria, LA11 7NG
☎ (01539) 558980 ☎ 07967 503689
fellbrewery.co.uk

⊗ Fell Brewery was founded in 2012 by homebrewer Tim Bloomer and friend Andrew Carter, brewing beers inspired by their travels in the US and Belgium. Originally a five-barrel plant it recently expanded to 12 barrels.

Ghyll (OG 1035, ABV 3.7%) ◆
A yellow-coloured, hoppy session bitter with a long, drying, bitter finish.

Robust Porter (OG 1051, ABV 4.8%) ◆
Roast dominates throughout; fruit comes through on drinking, with a dry and bitter finish.

Tinderbox IPA (OG 1059, ABV 6.3%)
A strongly-hopped IPA with an initial sweetness leading to a lingering bitter aftertaste.

Fellows

2 Leopold Walk, Cottenham, Cambridgeshire, CB24 8XS
☎ (01954) 250262 ⊕ fellowsbrewery.co.uk

⊗ Fellows began production in 2010 though brewer Mark Burton had been developing recipes for a year or so before. Five regular beers are available with plans for a series of special ales. Beers are increasingly visible in the local free trade. ♦

Cambridge Fellow (OG 1038, ABV 3.8%)
A golden-coloured session ale; light and clean-tasting.

Gulping Fellow (OG 1042, ABV 4.2%)
A dry bitter finish complements the spicy hop character of this well-balanced best bitter.

Burton Snatch (OG 1048, ABV 4.8%)
Blonde ale with a citrus aroma and refreshing mouthfeel. A hint of wet leather completes the finish.

Jolly Fellows (OG 1050, ABV 5%)
Full-bodied, clean-tasting premium bitter.

Clever Fellow (OG 1052, ABV 5.2%)
Malt loaf and toffee flavours combine with back of the tongue bitterness to achieve a balanced richness.

Fermanagh

Old Pals, 75 Main Street, Derrygonnelly, BT93 6HW
☎ (028) 6864 1254 ✉ gordyfallis@hotmail.com

Now known as Fermanagh Beer Company but still using the Inishmacsaint brand, this small-scale brewery has been producing a range of bottle-conditioned beers since 2009. RAIB

Fernandes

5 Avison Yard, Kirkgate, Wakefield, West Yorkshire, WF1 1UA
☎ (01924) 291709 ⊕ ossett-brewery.co.uk

Opened in 1997 and housed in a 19th-century malthouse, Ossett Brewing Company purchased the brewery and tap in 2007 but independent brewing continues. Around 90 different beers are brewed each year. The tap sells Fernandes and Ossett beers as well as guest ales; the former are more widely available through Ossett's supply chain. !! ♦

Malt Shovel Mild (OG 1038, ABV 3.8%)
A dark, full-bodied, malty mild with roast malt and chocolate flavours, leading to a lingering, dry, malty finish.

Polaris (OG 1041, ABV 3.9%)
A golden-coloured session beer with resinous, hoppy grapefruit flavours.

Ale to the Tsar (OG 1042, ABV 4.1%)
A pale-coloured, smooth, well-balanced beer with some sweetness leading to a nutty, malty and satisfying aftertaste.

Black Voodoo (OG 1050, ABV 5.1%)
Smooth, full-bodied, black-coloured stout with a chocolate, orange, vanilla flavour coming through.

Ferry Ales SIBA

Ferry Hill Farm, Ferry Road, Fiskerton, Lincolnshire, LN3 4HU ☎ 07790 241999 ⊕ ferryalesbrewery.co.uk

Ferry Ales Brewery (FAB) began brewing in 2016 using a five-barrel brew plant, situated just outside Fiskerton, Lincoln. ♦

Just Jane (ABV 3.8%)

Spirit of Jane (ABV 3.8%)

Witham Shield (ABV 4.5%)

49 SQN (ABV 4.9%)
A pale amber-coloured beer, well-balanced with a malt and fruity, citrus hop flavour.

Smokey Joe (ABV 4.9%)
A classic porter with a hint of smokiness in the finish.

Ferry Brewery SIBA

Bankhead Farm Steading, Bankhead Road, South Queensferry, EH30 9TF
☎ (0131) 331 1851 ⊕ ferrybrewery.co.uk

The first brewery in South Queensferry since 1851, Ferry Brewery was established in 2016 by Mark Moran and has an on-site tap room. Its beers combine traditional and historic beer recipes with a contemporary twist as well as modern-style beers. ♦ RAIB

Ferry Fair (OG 1038.8, ABV 4%)
Refreshing, dry pale ale with a moderate bitterness, rich in colour and well-balanced.

Smokey Jack (OG 1040, ABV 4%)
A brown-coloured ale with smoked flavours and aromas, well-balanced bitterness with a fruity but slightly spicy note.

40/- Fine (OG 1040.7, ABV 4.2%)
An easy-drinking ale with aromas of malt, light hops and fruit to complement its smooth and creamy texture.

Ferry Crossing (OG 1043.6, ABV 4.5%)
A light, hoppy, crisp, fruity blonde ale.

Ferry Witches Brew (OG 1043.6, ABV 4.5%)
A well-balanced, copper-coloured ale with a hoppy flavour.

Three Bridges (OG 1043, ABV 4.5%)
Hoppy IPA, strong on citrus flavours and aroma.

Ferry Stout (OG 1055, ABV 4.9%)
Black in colour and rich with a roasted malty flavours and aroma of coffee and chocolate. A balanced bitter finish.

Thomas Miller 1785 (OG 1054.2, ABV 5.5%)

A smooth, smoky, bitter coffee porter with a sweet liquorice finish and aromas of smoke and coffee.

Fierce

Unit 46, Howe Moss Avenue, Dyce, AB21 0GP
☎ (01224) 729131 🌐 fiercebeer.com

Initially started by an enthusuastic homebrewer, the brewery re-located to a factory unit in 2016. No real ale.

Fierce & Noble (NEW)

25 Mina Road, Bristol, BS2 9TA
☎ (0117) 955 6666 🌐 fierceandnoble.com

This eight-barrel microbrewery was established in 2017 by the owner of a small café chain in Bristol, to supply beer to his cafés. There is a licensed tap room on site. RAIB

Noble Bitter (OG 1038, ABV 3.7%)

Fierce Pale Ale (OG 1042, ABV 4.2%)

FILO

The Old Town Brewery, Torfield Cottage, 8 Old London Road, Hastings, East Sussex, TN34 3HA
☎ (01424) 420212 🌐 filobrewing.co.uk

The brewery at the First In Last Out public house was established in 1985, with the current owners taking over in 1988. In 2011 the brewery relocated two minutes' walk away, remaining in the Old Town. The First In Last Out (FILO) is still supplied direct together with pubs throughout Sussex and Kent. !! ♦

Crofters (OG 1037, ABV 3.8%)

Churches Pale Ale (OG 1042, ABV 4.2%)

Old Town Tom (OG 1044, ABV 4.5%)

Gold (OG 1050, ABV 4.8%)

Fine Tuned SIBA

Unit 16, Wessex Park, Bancombe Road, Somerton, Somerset, TA11 6SB
☎ (01458) 897273 ☎ 07872 139945
🌐 finetunedbrewery.com

Established in Langport, Somerset in 2016, but relocated to its current site in 2017. ♦ RAIB

Langport Bitter (OG 1040, ABV 4%)

Rack & Roll (OG 1041, ABV 4%)

Sunshine Reggae (OG 1043, ABV 4.2%)
A refreshing and hoppy American-style pale ale.

Fintry SIBA

Fintry Inn, 23 Main Street, Fintry, G63 0XA
☎ (01360) 860224 ☎ 07833 662820
✉ bill@fintrymusos.co.uk

Fintry Brewing was established in 2013 in premises at the Fintry Inn. After expansion in 2015 it now uses an eight-barrel plant. The beers are always available in the Fintry as well as throughout Stirlingshire and selected outlets in Glasgow and Southern Scotland. !! ♦

Clachertyfarlie (OG 1039, ABV 3.9%)

Cort-ma-Law (OG 1041, ABV 4.1%)

Dunmore Pale Ale (OG 1041, ABV 4.2%)

Firebird SIBA

Old Rudgwick Brickworks, Lynwick Street, Rudgwick, West Sussex, RH12 3UW
☎ (01403) 823180 🌐 firebirdbrewing.co.uk

Firebird began brewing in 2013 and has grown rapidly with new beers, new vessels, an extended warehouse and an expanded team of five people. !! ♦ RAIB

Heritage XX (OG 1041, ABV 4%)

No. 79 (OG 1043, ABV 4.3%)
A pale-coloured, full-bodied and fruity golden ale.

Old Ale XXXX (OG 1045, ABV 4.5%)
A smooth, bittersweet, dark-coloured ale with hints of roasted chocolate.

Paleface APA (OG 1053, ABV 5.2%)
A zesty, aromatic, American-style pale ale.

Firebrand

See Altarnun

Firebrick SIBA

Units 10 & 11, Blaydon Business Centre, Cowen Road, Blaydon, Tyne & Wear, NE21 5TW
☎ (0191) 447 6543 🌐 firebrickbrewery.com

Firebrick began brewing on a 2.5-barrel plant in 2013, expanding to a 15-barrel plant in 2014. Beers are mostly available in pubs within the Tyne & Wear area and a few outlets further afield. ♦

Blaydon Brick (OG 1038, ABV 3.8%)

Coalface (OG 1039, ABV 3.9%)

Elder Statesman (OG 1043, ABV 3.9%)

Tyne 9 (OG 1039, ABV 3.9%)

Pagan Queen (OG 1040, ABV 4%)

Trade Star (OG 1041, ABV 4.2%)

Stella Spark (OG 1043, ABV 4.4%)

Toon Broon (OG 1046, ABV 4.6%)

Wey-Aye PA (OG 1058, ABV 5.8%)

Firehouse

13 Thames Street, Louth, Lincolnshire, LN11 7AD
☎ (01507) 608202 ☎ 07961 772905
🌐 firehouse-brewery.co.uk

Firehouse was founded by Jason Allen in 2014 in the village of Manby using a 2.5-barrel plant. In 2016, along with Louise Darbon, the Fulstow Brewery in Louth was purchased and the brewery was relocated there. Beers from the Fulstow range are also produced. Beers are available in the free trade and from the bar located at the brewery, the Gas Lamp Lounge. ♦

Mainwaring's Mild (ABV 3.6%)
A dark-coloured, malty mild based on a wartime recipe.

Marsh Mild (ABV 3.8%)
Traditional ruby red-coloured mild with a rich roast, full-bodied flavour.

FGB (ABV 3.9%)

Northway IPA (OG 1042.5, ABV 4.2%)
An IPA with a clean citrus flavour and a dry finish.

Woodman Pale Ale (ABV 4.4%)
Pale yellow-coloured, fruity, sweetish session bitter with a dry hoppy finish.

Pride of Fulstow (OG 1044, ABV 4.5%)
Premium English pale ale with a full-bodied flavour and rich mouthfeel.

Wobbly Weasel (ABV 4.9%)
Complex ale, rich and fruity in the mouth. Intense bittersweet finish.

Lincolnshire Country Bitter (ABV 5.1%)
A smooth, full-bodied, dark-coloured ale with fruity flavours. Intense bitter aftertaste that lingers.

Firs (NEW)

Station Road, Codsall, Staffordshire, WV8 1BX
☎ (01902) 844674 thefirscodsall.com

Beers are brewed on-site in the CAMRA award-winning Firs club and are exclusive to the club. ♦

First & Last (NEW) SIBA

Bird in Bush, Village Green, Elsdon, NE19 1AA
☎ (01830) 520804 ☎ 07757 286357
firstandlastbrewery.co.uk

First & Last was established in 2016 by Red Kelly, a founder member of Stu Brew (qv) in Newcastle upon Tyne. It was upgraded to a five-barrel plant in 2018, relocating from Rochester to the Bird in Bush, Elsdon. Other outlets in Northumberland and the Scottish Borders are supplied.

First Chop SIBA

B2, Barton Hall Business Park, Hardy Street, Eccles, M30 7NB ☎ 07970 241398
firstchopbrewingarm.com

Brewing began at Outstanding Brewery (qv) in Bury in 2012 before transferring to Salford in 2013. The brewery relocated again to Eccles in 2017 with increased capacity. It specialises in producing gluten-free beers. **GF**

AVA (OG 1034, ABV 3.5%)

POD (ABV 4.2%)

SYL (OG 1064, ABV 6.2%)

Fish Key SIBA

Unit 4, Granite Quay, Looe, Cornwall, PL13 1DX
☎ 07814 019250 fishkeybrewingcompany.com

Fish Key started production in 2016. Five local outlets are supplied at present. RAIB

Hop2It (OG 1039, ABV 4%)
Yellow-coloured ale with citrus hop aroma. Overpowering grassy citrus hop flavour with grapefruit, pith and robust bitterness. Finish becomes dry.

Brew.T (OG 1043, ABV 4.4%)
Amber-coloured best bitter with hop aroma. Assertive grassy hop flavour balanced by dry malt. Bitterness and dryness rise in the finish.

Hip Hop (OG 1044, ABV 4.5%)

RIPA (Red IPA) (OG 1049, ABV 4.9%)
Pale brown-coloured strong bitter with malt and toffee aroma. Assertive malt and sweet caramel flavour with bitterness and light fruit.

Great White (OG 1050, ABV 5%)

Fisher's SIBA

Unit 8, Central Park Business Centre, Bellfield Road, High Wycombe, Buckinghamshire, HP13 5HG
☎ 07789 007876 fishersbrewingcompany.com

Established in 2013 brewing at home and at Ubrew (qv), owner and brewer Mike Fisher expanded to a six-barrel plant in 2017 to begin brewing commercially in earnest. Beers are supplied to an ever-increasing number of local pubs and restaurants, and nationally via SIBA's Beerflex scheme. !! RAIB

Blonde Ale (ABV 3.5%)

Red Ale (ABV 4%)

Smoked Porter (ABV 4.4%)

APA (ABV 4.8%)

Five Kingdoms SIBA

Steam Packet Inn, Harbour Row, Isle of Whithorn, DG8 8LL
☎ (01988) 500334 thesteampacketinn.biz

Five Kingdoms was established in 2015 by Alastair Scoular, owner of the Steam Packet Inn, using a 2.5-barrel plant. It is situated in the harbourside village of Isle of Whithorn, the most southerly point of the Wigtownshire peninsular in Galloway and a tourist and sailing hotspot. The pub, selected beer festivals and a few local outlets are supplied. ♦RAIB

Five Points SIBA

3 Institute Place, Hackney Downs, London, E8 1JE
☎ (020) 8533 7746 fivepointsbrewing.co.uk

Five Points commenced brewing in 2013 on a 10-barrel plant. Based in a railway arch under Hackney Downs Railway Station, the brewery takes its name from the five-way junction where Dalston Lane, Amhurst Road and Pembury Road meet, the Five Points. RAIB

Pale (OG 1044, ABV 4.4%)
Strong, fruity, bitter, golden-coloured ale with citrus and tropical fruit fading in the aftertaste where the bitterness lingers.

Railway Porter (ABV 4.8%)
Roasted black malt throughout creating a dry roasted finish softened by a treacly sweetness. Some caramelised fruit and peppery hops.

Brick Field Brown (ABV 5.4%)
Complex dark brown-coloured beer. Fruit dominates the flavour with nutty chocolate and some sweet toffee character. Long, dry bitter aftertaste.

Hook Island Red (ABV 6%)
Treacle notes on nose and flavour linger in the dry bitterness, which builds on drinking. The mouthfeel is creamy.

Five Towns

651 Leeds Road, Outwood, Wakefield, West Yorkshire, WF1 2LU
☎ (01924) 781887
✉ malcolmbastow@googlemail.com

Five Towns began production on a 2.5-barrel plant in 2008 and mostly supplies outlets in Yorkshire. ♦RAIB

Mi Usual (ABV 3.7%)

Middle Un (ABV 4.6%)

Owt'll, Do (ABV 4.6%)
An easy-drinking mild with added rum.

Nowt (ABV 6.7%)
A full-bodied stout with an intense roasted malt and coffee flavour.

One at t' End (ABV 6.7%)
An American-style IPA with tropical, citrus and grapefruit flavours.

Summat Else (ABV 7.2%)
An IPA with a strong tropical fruit nose, biscuit malt with gooseberry flavour and a hoppy maple syrup aftertaste.

Fixed Wheel SIBA

Unit 9, Long Lane Trading Estate, Long Lane, Blackheath, West Midlands, B62 9LD ☎ 07766 162794 fixedwheelbrewery.co.uk

Set up in 2014 by cycling and brewing enthusiasts Scott Povey and Sharon Bryant, this full mash brewery is situated on a trading estate on the Blackheath/Halesowen border. It brews three times a week using an eight-barrel plant. !! ♦RAIB

Through & Off (OG 1038, ABV 3.8%)
A session IPA concentrating on big, fruity hops.

Chain Reaction Pale Ale (OG 1042, ABV 4.2%)
An American-style pale ale with orange and citrus flavours.

Century Gold (OG 1048, ABV 4.8%)
A bright golden ale with a big hop presence, firm lemon bitterness and an orange aroma.

Blackheath Stout (OG 1050, ABV 5%)
Full-bodied, fruity stout with an oaky bitterness and a smooth, creamy, dark fruits finish.

Mild Concussion (OG 1055, ABV 5.5%)
Ruby in colour with a creamy head. Aroma is red fruit with a rich, balanced taste and satisfying finish.

No Brakes IPA (OG 1059, ABV 5.9%)
An American-style IPA with upfront fruity citrus flavours. Malt adds some balance to the hops with a touch of sweetness.

Fizzy Moon (NEW)

Fizzy Moon, 35 Regent Street, Leamington, Warwickshire, CV32 5EE
☎ (01926) 888715 fizzymoonbrewhouse.com

Fizzy Moon is a bar and microbrewery in the heart of Leamington, brewing a range of small batch beers. Expansion is planned. ♦

Flack Manor SIBA

8 Romsey Industrial Estate, Greatbridge Road, Romsey, Hampshire, SO51 0HR
☎ (01794) 518520 flackmanor.co.uk

Flack Manor commenced brewing in 2010 using a 20-barrel plant purchased from Canada. The brewery employs the 'double drop' method of fermentation. Beers are supplied to local outlets within approximately 30 miles of Romsey, and may also be found in Wetherspoon pubs. !! ♦RAIB

Flack's Double Drop (OG 1037, ABV 3.7%)
A classic amber-coloured session bitter. Hops, malt and some bitterness in the taste, with more hop and some malt in the finish.

Flack Catcher (OG 1045, ABV 4.4%)
A well-balanced, amber-coloured best bitter with some fruit aroma throughout with good hop bitterness in the balanced taste and finish.

Hedge Hop (OG 1050, ABV 4.9%)
Amber-coloured best bitter, some fruit and hop in the aroma with biscuit malt balanced with fruit and spice flavours right through the taste.

Flagship

c/o Ship & Mitre, 133 Dale Street, Liverpool, L2 2JH
☎ (0151) 236 0859

Launched in 2016, the Ship & Mitre Brewing Co rebranded as Flagship Beer in 2017, and primarily supplies the iconic city centre pub, the Ship & Mitre, with some sales locally and nationally. Beers are brewed using spare capacity at other breweries. ♦RAIB

Sublime (OG 1036, ABV 3.7%)
This light, session pale ale has a hoppy citrus tang.

Lupa (OG 1037, ABV 3.8%)
A blend of citrus peels and hops for a sweeter, balanced pale.

Silhouette (OG 1048, ABV 4.5%)
Dry Irish-style stout with plenty of roasted, toasted richness.

Jar (OG 1047, ABV 4.7%)
Warm, sweet, light-bodied and roasted. Not bitter, not heavy.

Century (OG 1046, ABV 5%)
A West Coast-style IPA with a solid bitterness and juicy hops.

Flash

Moss Top Farm, Moss Top Lane, Flash, Staffordshire, SK17 0TA ✉ flashbrewery@hotmail.com

The brewery is located high in the Peak District and was founded by two friends who brew on a part-time basis. All natural ingredients are used including spring water and seaweed finings which make the beer suitable for vegans. Due to the altitude, a brick boiler was found and is used in the brewing process rather than electrical equipment. Three bottle-conditioned beers are produced and are sold at Leek Market, which is the only sales outlet. RAIB V

Flash House

Unit 1a, Northumberland Street, North Shields, NE30 1DS ☎ 07481 901875
flashhousebrewing.co.uk

Flash House was set up by Jack O'Keefe in 2016. There are plans to extend the brewery and taproom to open every weekend.

Tiny Dancer Pale Ale (OG 1051, ABV 5.4%)

Flipside SIBA

c/o Black Horse, 29 Main Street, Caythorpe, Nottinghamshire, NG14 7ED
☎ (0115) 987 7500 ☎ 07958 752334

Office: Old Volunteer, 35 Burton Road, Carlton, Nottinghamshire, NG4 3DQ flipsidebrewery.co.uk

Andrew and Maggie Dunkin established their six-barrel brewery in an industrial unit in Colwick in 2010, expanding to 12 barrels in 2013 in a larger adjacent unit. The brewery opened its own tap, the Old Volunteer, Carlton, in 2014. In 2016 it relocated again to share the plant at Caythorpe Brewery (qv). ♦ RAIB

Sterling Pale (OG 1039, ABV 3.9%)
Golden ale with a citrus aroma and hoppy taste, leading to a bitter and peppery finish.

Dark Denomination (OG 1041, ABV 4%)
Well-rounded, mildly-hopped beer. Chocolate and Caramel malt combined delicately with blackcurrant hop flavours.

Bitcoin (OG 1041, ABV 4.1%)

Copper Penny (OG 1043, ABV 4.2%)
An easy-drinking session bitter. Light brown-coloured, moderately bitter but with good hop flavours, ending with a hint of tangerine.

Golden Sovereign (OG 1043, ABV 4.2%)
A golden-coloured session ale. Refreshingly bitter with dry biscuit flavours, American hops are added to produce a pleasant citrus and grapefruit flavour in the finish.

Franc in Stein (OG 1043, ABV 4.3%)
Golden ale with a floral hop aroma, leading to a hoppy and bitter finish.

Random Toss (OG 1044, ABV 4.4%)
A refreshing pale ale with lemon and lime tropical fruit flavours.

Kopek Stout (OG 1046, ABV 4.5%)
Full-bodied, dark-coloured stout with a coffee aroma and assertive roast flavours throughout and a balanced bitterness.

Flipping Best (OG 1046, ABV 4.6%)
Brown-coloured, malty, strong bitter with lasting malt, bitterness and subtle hop flavours.

Dusty Penny (OG 1052, ABV 5%)
A full-bodied porter. Bursting with chocolate and caramel malt flavours, rounded off with bitterness provided by traditional English Hops.

Clippings IPA (OG 1062, ABV 6.5%)
A traditional IPA, golden in colour with crushed gooseberry and bitter white wine hop flavours.

Russian Rouble (OG 1072, ABV 7.3%)
Strong, dark-coloured stout with balanced malt, roast and fruit flavours.

Flowerpots SIBA

Brandy Mount, Cheriton, Hampshire, SO24 0QQ
☎ (01962) 771534 flowerpotscheriton.co.uk

Flowerpots began production in 2006. The brewery is in a pretty Hampshire village, and stands across the car park from the pub of the same name. Its beers are supplied direct to the Flowerpots, its two sibling pubs, and many other local outlets. ♦

Perridge Pale (OG 1035.5, ABV 3.6%)
Pale-coloured, easy-drinking golden ale. Honey-scented with high hops, grapefruit and bitterness throughout. Crisp with some citrus notes.

Bitter (OG 1038, ABV 3.8%)
Dry, earthy hop flavours balanced by malt. Good bitterness with some hop in aroma and sharp, bitter finish. Refreshing bitter.

Goodens Gold (OG 1046, ABV 4.8%)
Complex, full-bodied golden ale, bursting with hops and citrus fruit and a snatch of sweetness, leading to long dry finish.

Flying Monk SIBA

Unit 1, Bradfield Farm, Hullavington, Wiltshire, SN14 6EU
☎ (01666) 838553 flyingmonk.beer

Established in 2014 in a former farm building near Malmesbury, Flying Monk uses a 20-barrel plant, supplies more than 400 outlets regionally, and utilises national wholesalers and retail contracts. It uses only the best local ingredients including barley grown on its landlord's farm and English hops from Worcestershire. Its first pub opened in 2017, the Flying Monk Tavern, Chippenham. Castle Combe Brewery merged with Flying Monk in 2017. ♦

Elmers (OG 1040, ABV 3.8%)
A refreshing session beer with floral and citrus aromas, followed by an encouraging bitter finish.

Pendulum Pale Ale (OG 1037, ABV 3.8%)
Well-hopped, full-bodied, golden-coloured bitter.

Habit (OG 1045, ABV 4.2%)
An amber-coloured, traditional English best bitter with a contrast of sweet and bitter flavours.

Jackdaw (OG 1045, ABV 4.3%)

Birdman (OG 1049, ABV 4.6%)
A refreshing, pale golden-coloured premium bitter, well-hopped to give a full-bodied flavour.

Fool Hardy SIBA

Hope Inn, 118 Wellington Road North, Heaton Norris, SK4 2LL
☎ (0161) 637 6191 foolhardyales.co.uk

Martin and Samantha Wood bought the Hope Inn in 2012 and installed the brewery in the cellar. The beers first went on sale in 2013. In 2014 the brew kit was upgraded, almost doubling capacity to 4.5 barrels. Beers are supplied to the free trade, local pubs and festivals. !! ♦ RAIB

Jack's Ripper (OG 1034, ABV 3.4%)
A dark-coloured oatmeal stout; smooth and complex.

Rhidonkulous (OG 1037, ABV 3.7%)

THE BREWERIES

An pale-coloured, triple-hopped session ale with zesty citrus notes.

Rash Dash (OG 1038, ABV 3.8%)
Pale brown-coloured beer with a hoppy aroma, a balance of hops and malt in the taste and good bitterness throughout.

Ravenous Romp (OG 1038, ABV 3.8%)

Rendezvous #5 (OG 1037, ABV 3.8%)
A full-flavoured golden ale with fresh citrus notes and aroma.

Retro Chique (ABV 3.9%)
A golden-coloured, fruity, easy-drinking bitter.

Rise (ABV 3.9%)
A clean, easy-drinking, refreshing pale ale. Quite hoppy and fruity.

Rival Blond (OG 1039, ABV 4%)
An pale blonde session ale, hoppy and zesty. Distinct fruit hop flavours.

Rude Vagablond (OG 1041, ABV 4.2%)

Rou Shou (OG 1042.4, ABV 4.3%)
A clean-drinking, sweet, refreshing pale ale with a strong floral aroma and elderflower hop notes.

Risky Blond (OG 1042, ABV 4.4%)
An easy-drinking golden ale with a good balance of hops, subtle hints of citrus and a well-rounded finish.

Oozy Rat in a Sanitary Zoo (ABV 5%)
A hoppy and well-balanced IPA.

Reckless Danger (OG 1054, ABV 5%)
A sweet-tasting beer with bitterness shining through. A clean, hoppy finish and moderate aftertaste.

Riptide (ABV 5%)

Russian Roulette (OG 1049, ABV 5%)
A crisp, hoppy, distinctive and bitter IPA.

Rankenstein (ABV 5.5%)
A golden-coloured, American-style pale ale with a hoppy taste and aroma.

Foragers

Verulam Arms, 41 Lower Dagnall Street, St Albans, Hertfordshire, AL3 4QE
☎ (01727) 836004 the-foragers.com

Brewing began in 2015. Four base beers are brewed with different wild ingredients added throughout the year.

Force

Unit 2, Global Business Park, Wilkinson Road, Cirencester, Gloucestershire, GL7 1YZ
☎ (01285) 719495 forcebrewery.com

Force Brewery was established in 2014 using a four-barrel gravity-fed brew plant. At present the brewery is not open to the public as it undergoes significant restructuring and only bottle-conditioned beers are being produced. RAIB

Forge SIBA

Wilderland, Woolley, Cornwall, EX23 9PW
☎ (01288) 331669 ☎ 07837 487800
forge-brewery.co.uk

This multi-award-winning brewery was set up near Bideford in Devon by Dave Lang, who commenced brewing in 2008 using a five-barrel plant. The brewery relocated to Cornwall in 2017. ♦RAIB

Discovery (OG 1039, ABV 3.8%)
Gold-coloured bitter bursting with hops from start to finish. Some subtle hints of fruit to the discerning palate too.

Hartland Blonde (OG 1040, ABV 4%)
A golden ale with a light, straw hop aroma. Moderate hop with gentle fruit, malt and bitterness in the mouth.

Litehouse (OG 1042, ABV 4.3%)
Golden in colour, hints of elderflower with a citrus bite.

IPA (OG 1044, ABV 4.5%)
A light, hoppy beer with grapefruit and citrus notes.

Rev Hawker (OG 1046, ABV 4.6%)

Tamar Source (OG 1046, ABV 4.6%)
An amber-coloured beer with complex hop notes.

Handsome (OG 1048, ABV 5.1%)
A light brown-coloured, well-balanced, hoppy beer.

Four Candles SIBA

1 Sowell Street, St Peters, Kent, CT10 2AT ☎ 07947 062063 thefourcandles.co.uk

Based in the cellar of the micropub of the same name, Four Candles uses a 2.5-barrel plant and produces up to 10 nine-gallon casks with each brew. Never brewing the same ale twice, the brewery supplies the micropub, which is named after the well known Two Ronnies sketch. !!

Four Kings

Unit 15g, Newton Moor Industrial Estate, Lodge Street, Hyde, SK14 4LD ☎ 07951 699428
fourkingsbrewery.com

Four Kings is a six-barrel brewery established by five friends with a mutual love of beer. Brewing began in 2016 using only British ingredients. Regular events are held at the brewery, which boasts an in-house bar. Beers can be found in Hyde, Denton and Glossop. !! RAIB

Gold (ABV 4%)
Golden-coloured beer with a long finish, hop bitterness and tart fruit flavours.

IPA (ABV 4%)
Pale in colour with a fresh, hoppy aroma and a malty, hoppy flavour. An intense bitterness leads to a long, dry finish.

Bitter (ABV 4.5%)
Bitter taste with a slight sweetness and moderate bitter finish with a toffee in the aftertaste.

Porter (ABV 5.2%)
A rich, chocolaty porter. Bitter taste with a slight sweetness and moderate bitter finish with roasted coffee in the aftertaste.

Fourpure SIBA

22 Bermondsey Trading Estate, Rotherhithe New Road, South Bermondsey, London, SE16 3LL

☎ (020) 3744 2141 🌐 fourpure.com

Fourpure began brewing in 2013. Beers are available in cans and kegs, unfiltered, unpasteurised and unfined. Special bottle-conditioned beers are also available. In 2018 the brewery was bought by Lion of Australia, part of Kirin of Japan. RAIB

Fowey

Unit 3F, ¾ Restormel Industrial Estate, Liddicoat Road, Lostwithiel, Cornwall, PL22 0HD
☎ (01208) 871385 ☎ 07443 504644

Office: Pawton Mill, St Breock, PL27 7LH
🌐 foweybrewery.co.uk

Fowey began brewing in 2016, initially producing bottle-conditioned beers only. It relocated to a larger unit on the same industrial estate in 2017, allowing for a new seven-barrel plant and production of cask-conditioned ales. ♦RAIB

Sawmills Session IPA (OG 1045, ABV 4.5%)

Lerryn Blond (OG 1048, ABV 4.8%)

Lostwithiel Amber (OG 1048, ABV 4.9%)

Readymoney Pale Ale (OG 1051, ABV 5.2%)

Golitho Falls IPA (OG 1069, ABV 7%)
A strong bitter with malt flavour dominating the hops.

Fownes SIBA

25 Clarence Street, Upper Gornal, West Midlands, DY3 1UL ☎ 07790 766844

Office: 42 The Ridgeway, Sedgley, DY3 3UR
🌐 fownesbrewing.co.uk

The brewery was established in 2012 by James and Tom Fownes in premises to the rear of the Jolly Crispin in Upper Gornal. It expanded to a three-barrel plant in 2014. Beers are available in the Jolly Crispin and a number of free houses in the Midlands. ‼♦RAIB

Elephant Riders (OG 1040, ABV 4%)

Gunhild (OG 1041, ABV 4%)
Pleasant earthy aroma with hints of blackcurrants and honey. Pear drops and caramel with some malt and blackcurrant flavour. Dry, malty aftertaste.

Crispin's Ommer (OG 1038, ABV 4.1%)

Frost Hammer (OG 1047, ABV 4.6%)
Pine resin, nutmeg, malt, lemon and floral aroma. Dry mouthfeel with coffee, sweet malt and grapefruit flavours. Grapefruit and hoppy aftertaste.

Firebeard's Old Favourite No. 5 Ruby Ale (OG 1051, ABV 5%)
Malty, fresh earth, rhubarb and some coffee in the aroma. Dark chocolate and plum dominate the flavour with hints of malt and coffee. A pleasant dryness in the aftertaste.

King Korvak's Saga (OG 1058, ABV 5.4%)
Pear drop and cocoa aroma with hints of coffee. Coffee, toasted malt, blackcurrant and slight cocoa taste with rich malty tones in the aftertaste.

Fox

22 Station Road, Heacham, Norfolk, PE31 7EX
☎ (01485) 570345 🌐 foxbrewery.co.uk

Based in an old cottage adjacent to the Fox & Hounds pub, Fox Brewery was established in 2002 and now supplies around 30 outlets as well as the pub. All the Branthill beers are brewed from barley grown on Branthill Farm and malted at Crisps in Great Ryburgh. A hop garden next to the brewery, trialled during 2009, has been enlarged. ‼♦RAIB

Fox Meadow (NEW)

23 Courtauld Road, Braintree, Essex, CM7 9BD
☎ 07932 420708 🌐 foxmeadow.net

Fox Meadow is a small batch nanobrewery in Braintree, brewing just two firkins at a time.

Foxfield SIBA

Prince of Wales, Foxfield, Cumbria, LA20 6BX
☎ (01229) 716238 🌐 princeofwalesfoxfield.co.uk

Foxfield is a 4.5-barrel plant in old stables attached to the Prince of Wales. Several other outlets are supplied. Tiger Tops in Wakefield is also owned. The beer range constantly changes. ‼♦V

Framework

The Old City Depot, 72-74 Friday Street, Leicester, LE3 6HR
☎ (0116) 262 4037 🌐 frameworkbrewery.com

Framework Brewery is located in the old heart of Leicester city centre and was established in 2016. A six-barrel brew plant is used. The brewery's first tap house opened in 2018 in Leicester. ‼♦RAIB V

Jackpin Pale Ale (ABV 3.9%)

Sinker Stout (ABV 4%)
Silky smooth, rich stout with a complex caramel maltiness underneath fresh hop notes.

Winder Wheat Beer (ABV 4.6%)
Floral and citrus aromas and flavours with a subtle pine and mint character.

Friday Street Session IPA (ABV 4.9%)
A session IPA with a citrus hop hit.

Franklins SIBA

Highfields Farm, The Broyle, Ringmer, East Sussex, BN8 5AR
☎ (01273) 814447 🌐 franklinsbrewery.co.uk

Owned by Steve Medniuk, Franklins has recently moved to a new site in Ringmer in order to aid expansion. A 10-barrel brew plant is currently used. Beers are also brewed under the Hastings Brewery name. Beers are available throughout the South East, London and beyond. ‼

English Garden (OG 1042, ABV 3.8%)

Mumma Knows Best (OG 1043, ABV 4.1%)
A refreshing traditional English best bitter, rich in mango, lemon and earthy pine notes.

Resurrection Stout (ABV 5.3%)

Citra IPA (OG 1056, ABV 5.5%)
Single-hopped IPA bursting with citrus and lychee flavours and aroma.

North Shore IPA (ABV 5.5%)

Smoked Porter (OG 1052, ABV 5.5%)

A rich, intense porter made with oatmeal. Added chillies accentuate the smokiness and provide a touch of heat.

Freedom SIBA

1 Park Lodge House, Bagots Park, Abbots Bromley, Staffordshire, WS15 3ES
☎ (01283) 840721 🌐 freedomlager.com

No real ale. Freedom specialises in producing hand-crafted English lagers, all brewed in accordance with the German Reinheitsgebot purity law. ‼ 🛒

Freestyle

Church Road, Shustoke, Warwickshire, B46 2LB
☎ (01675) 481205 🌐 griffininnshustoke.co.uk

Griffin Inn started brewing in 2008 in the old coffin shop adjacent to the pub. In 2017 the brewery was updated to a modern, more efficient 2.5-barrel plant. At this time the name was changed to Freestyle though the business is still owned by the Pugh family who run the Griffin. Beers are available for the free trade as well as selling through the pub. ‼ ♦

Griffin Dark (ABV 3.8%)
Dark-coloured mild with a roasty palate and a long, dry finish.

Griffin Pale Ale (ABV 3.8%)
Crisp and hoppy with a rich, fruity malt finish.

Shawbury Blonde (ABV 4.2%)

Yeti IPA (ABV 4.5%)
A hoppy pale ale with a fruity finish.

Black Magic Woman (ABV 4.8%)

Muzungu (ABV 5.5%)
Light gold-coloured ale with a hoppy, bitter taste, malty body and sweet finish.

Freewheelin'

Peebles Hydro, Innerleithen Road, Peebles, EH45 8LX
☎ 07802 175826 🌐 freewheelinbrewery.co.uk

Freewheelin' began brewing in 2013 and is based in Peebles. It is located in a former joiners shed in the grounds of the Peebles Hydro Hotel. Local spring water is used in the brewing process. ‼ ♦

Blonde (OG 1040, ABV 3.8%)

IPA (OG 1043, ABV 4.2%)

Dizzy Blonde (OG 1045, ABV 4.3%)

Ruby (OG 1046, ABV 4.4%)

Stout (OG 1047, ABV 4.4%)

Frensham

The Old Dairy, Pierrepont Home Farm, The Reeds, Frensham, Surrey, GU10 3BS
☎ (01252) 793956 ☎ 07505 798380
🌐 frenshambrewery.co.uk

⊗ Set in the Surrey countryside, Frensham is a microbrewery situated in a 17th-century restored barn on a working dairy farm. A tap room opened in 2017. 🛒 ♦

Soul (OG 1038, ABV 3.8%)
A light, floral session beer with biscuit orange notes.

Rambler (OG 1039, ABV 3.9%)
A golden-coloured session ale, fruity hops with an oak edge give rise to a satisfying bitterness.

Silent Flight (ABV 4.2%)
A ruby-coloured ale with some bitterness and a spicy, floral aroma.

Forager (OG 1045, ABV 4.5%)
Rich, copper-coloured ale. A complex floral aroma with subtle vanilla oaks, offset with a caramel, spicy hop balance. Lingering bitter finish.

Friday Beer SIBA

Unit 4, Link Business Centre, Malvern, Worcestershire, WR14 1UQ
☎ (01684) 572648 🌐 thefridaybeer.com

Founded in 2011, the Friday Beer Co primarily produces bottle-conditioned ales, selling across the Three Counties. Available cask-conditioned in a small number of local pubs. ‼ 🛒 RAIB

Jubilee (OG 1034, ABV 3.1%)

Summer Hill Blonde (OG 1043, ABV 4.3%)
Pale golden ale with hints of pineapple and blackcurrant.

Pinnacle (OG 1046, ABV 4.5%)

Black Hill Stout (OG 1052, ABV 4.7%)
A smooth, sweet stout full of complex malty flavours.

Friday Gold (OG 1054, ABV 5.6%)
Refreshing golden ale with a smooth texture and slight citrus taste.

Friends Arms

Old St Clears Road, Johnstown, SA31 3HH
☎ (01267) 234073 🌐 thefriendsarms.co.uk

⊗ Friends Arms Brewery opened in 2011 on the premises of the Friends Arms, a traditional local community pub, which acts as the brewery tap.

Frisky Bear

Oscars Bar, 2a Queen Street, Morley, Leeds, West Yorkshire, LS27 9DG 🌐 friskybear.com

Established in 2016 using a one-barrel plant. Capacity was increased in 2018 with the addition of extra fermenters. Oscar's Bar is the main outlet but beers are available around West Yorkshire.

Grizzly Bear (OG 1042, ABV 4.5%)

Frog Island SIBA

The Maltings, Westbridge, St James Road, Northampton, NN5 5HS
☎ (01604) 587772 🌐 frogislandbrewery.co.uk

Established in 1994, Frog Island specialises in beers with personalised bottle labels, available by mail order. The brewery changed hands in 2013 and again in 2017. It is now run by Graeme Swanson. ‼ ♦ RAIB V

Best Bitter (OG 1038, ABV 3.8%) ◆
Blackcurrant and gooseberry enhance the full malty aroma with pineapple and papaya joining on the tongue. Bitterness develops in the fairly long hop finish.

Shoemaker (OG 1043, ABV 4.2%) ◆

An orangey aroma of fruity hops is balanced by malt. Citrus and hoppy bitterness last into a long, dry finish. Amber colour.

Natterjack (OG 1048, ABV 4.8%) ◆
Deceptively robust, golden and smooth. Fruit and hop aromas fight for dominance before the grainy astringency and floral palate give way to a long, dry aftertaste.

Croak & Stagger (OG 1054, ABV 5.6%) ◆
The initial honey/fruit aroma is quickly overpowered by roast malt then bitter chocolate and pale malt sweetness on the tongue. Gentle, bittersweet finish.

Front Row SIBA

Unit 1, Hopkins Close, Greenfield Farm Industrial Estate, Congleton, Cheshire, CW12 4TR
☎ (01260) 289055 ☎ 07861 718673
frontrowbrewing.co.uk

After starting operations on a 2.5-barrel plant in 2012, Front Row expanded to an eight-barrel plant in 2014 to meet demand. Beers are available locally and also nationally through brewery swaps and wholesalers. ‼◆

Crouch (OG 1039, ABV 3.8%)

LOHAG (Land of Hops & Glory) (OG 1036, ABV 3.8%)

Sin Bin (OG 1042, ABV 4.2%)

Pause (OG 1049, ABV 4.5%)

Pride (ABV 4.6%)

Collapsed (OG 1051, ABV 5.6%)

Froth Blowers SIBA

Unit P35, Hastingwood Industrial Park, Wood Lane, Erdington, West Midlands, B24 9QR ☎ 07966 935906
frothblowersbrewing.com

Froth Blowers began brewing in 2013. The brewery now has the capacity to brew 20 barrels at a new site only metres away from its original. ◆

Piffle Snonker (OG 1038, ABV 3.8%) ◆
Straw coloured. Aroma is almost jammy with a little malt and hop. Taste is well balanced with a slightly hoppy aftertaste.

Bar-King Mad (OG 1042, ABV 4.2%)

Wellingtonian (OG 1043, ABV 4.3%)

John Bull's Best (OG 1044, ABV 4.4%)
A golden-coloured, balanced bitter, using traditional British malts and hops.

Gollop With Zest (OG 1045, ABV 4.5%)
A blonde beer with a floral start and citrus finish.

Hornswoggle (OG 1050, ABV 5%)
A full-bodied blonde beer with a floral nose and sweetish start, soon replaced by a dry and satisfying bitterness

Fuddy Duck

Unit 12, Kirton Business Park, Willington Road, Kirton, Lincolnshire, PE20 1NN ☎ 07881 818875
thefuddyduckbrewery.co.uk

Small brewery based in Kirton near Boston, where brewing commenced in 2016.

Pale Ale (ABV 4%)
Golden ale with a grapefruit citrus flavour.

American Red Ale (ABV 4.5%)

Blonde Ale (ABV 4.5%)
A blonde ale with flavours and aromas of banana and clove.

Dark Porter (ABV 4.5%)
Porter with flavours of chocolate and liquorice.

German Ale Altbier (ABV 4.5%)

Biere de Garde (ABV 6.5%)

Fuggle Bunny SIBA

Unit 1, Meadowbrook Park Industrial Estate, Station Road, Holbrook, South Yorkshire, S20 3PJ
☎ (0114) 248 4541 ☎ 07813 763347
fugglebunny.co.uk

Fuggle Bunny was established in 2014 by a husband-and-wife team. The plant, originally obtained from Flipside Brewery, has since expanded and can now brew 24 barrels per week. Beers are delivered direct within a 40-mile radius of the brewery and available nationally through wholesalers. Its first pub opened in Worksop in 2017. ‼

Chapter 5 Oh Crumbs (OG 1038, ABV 3.8%)
Amber-coloured beer with hints of spice, cedar and pine. Sweet caramel and biscuity flavours give a distinctive finish.

Chapter 9 La La Land (ABV 3.9%)
An American-style pale ale, refreshingly tropical with citrus and passion fruit flavours and a fresh floral aroma.

Chapter 2 Cotton Tail (OG 1040, ABV 4%)
Fruity aromas of lychees and citrus with a dry, hoppy finish.

Chapter 6 Hazy Summer Daze (OG 1042, ABV 4.2%)
Tropical tastes with mango, lime, apricot, melon, lychees and grapefruit. Fresh floral aromas.

Chapter 8 Jammy Dodger (OG 1045, ABV 4.5%)
A ruby-coloured ale with hints of blackcurrants, liquorice and caramel and a malty undertone.

Chapter 1 New Beginnings (OG 1049, ABV 4.9%)
Amber-coloured classic bitter with a sweet edge of honey and spice leading to a dry, hoppy aftertaste.

Chapter 3 Orchard Gold (OG 1050, ABV 5%)
Golden ale with hints of spice and honey and an earthy undertone.

Chapter 7 Russian Rare-Bit (OG 1050, ABV 5%)
Dark-coloured, complex, malty beer a twist of chocolate, coffee and liquorice aromas.

Chapter 4 24 Carrot (OG 1060, ABV 6%)
Aromas of citrus and blackberry with a spicy blanket of malt-flavoured hoppiness.

Full Mash

17 Lower Park Street, Stapleford, Nottinghamshire, NG9 8EW
☎ (0115) 949 9262 fullmash.net

Brewing commenced in 2003 and has grown steadily since, with a gradual expansion in outlets and capacity. ◆

Horse & Jockey (OG 1039, ABV 3.8%) ◆

THE BREWERIES

Easy-drinking golden ale with moderate hoppy aroma and finish.

Seance (OG 1041, ABV 4%)
Predominantly hoppy golden-coloured beer, with a refreshing bitter finish.

Illuminati (OG 1043, ABV 4.2%)
Gently-hopped golden ale with initial hops and bitterness giving way to a short bitter finish.

Wheat Ear (OG 1043, ABV 4.2%)
Pale-coloured, clear wheat beer; fruity and aromatic.

Warlord (OG 1045, ABV 4.4%)
Amber-coloured beer with an initial malt taste leading to a dry bitter finish.

Apparition (OG 1046, ABV 4.5%)
A pale-coloured hoppy bitter brewed with Brewers Gold hops.

Nevermore (OG 1047, ABV 4.6%)
Well-rounded stout with soft roast chocolate flavours.

Manhattan Pale (OG 1053, ABV 5.2%)
Refreshing, pale-coloured, American-style IPA with a complex citrus aroma and big hop finish.

Bhisti (OG 1063, ABV 6.2%)
Strong IPA with a kick of bitterness.

Fuller's SIBA

Griffin Brewery, Chiswick Lane South, Chiswick, London, W4 2QB
(020) 8996 2000 fullers.co.uk

Fuller, Smith and Turner's Griffin Brewery has stood on the same site in Chiswick for more than 360 years. The partnership from which the company now takes its name was formed in 1845 and members of the founding families are still involved in running the company today. At the end of 2005 Fuller's announced an agreed acquisition of Hampshire brewer George Gale. The company now operates 388 pubs and hotels. Fuller's stopped brewing at the Gale's Horndean site in 2006 and all the brands, including some seasonals, are now brewed at Chiswick. Dark Star Brewery in Partridge Green, Sussex, was purchased in 2018. !! ♦ RAIB

Oliver's Island (OG 1039, ABV 3.8%)
Well-balanced golden ale with fruity aroma and flavour. Gentle bitter hoppiness balances a sweet, malty character and short finish.

London Pride (OG 1040.5, ABV 4.1%)
Well-balanced, smooth best bitter with orange citrus fruit, malt and hops in aroma and flavour, which linger into a slightly bitter aftertaste. Honey and toffee develop as the beer matures.

ESB (OG 1054, ABV 5.5%)
Bitter orange marmalade with hops, creamy toffee and some raisins are all present in this multifaceted strong, brown-coloured bitter. A satisfying long, bitter, dry finish balanced by a malty sweetness.

Brewed under the Gale's brand name:

Seafarers Ale (OG 1036.8, ABV 3.6%)
A pale brown-coloured bitter, predominantly malty, with a refreshing balance of fruit and hops that lingers into the aftertaste where a dry bitterness unfolds.

HSB (OG 1050, ABV 4.8%)
Dates and dried fruit with some spicy hops in the nose adding to the caramelised orange and treacle in the flavour of this smooth, brown-coloured beer. Malty throughout with a bittersweet finish.

Fulstow

See Firehouse

Fuzzchat (NEW)

Jolly Coopers, 84 Wheelers Lane, Epsom, Surrey, KT18 7SD
(01372) 723222 fuzzchatbrewery.co.uk

Fuzzchat is Epsom's first brewery in more than 90 years. Housed behind the Jolly Coopers, it used to be an old blacksmith's cottage, recently restored after being derelict for several years. A Fuzzchat is anyone born on Epsom Common. !! RAIB

Fuzzy Duck SIBA

18 Wood Street, Poulton Industrial Estate, Poulton-le-Fylde, Lancashire, FY6 8JY 07904 343729
fuzzyduckbrewery.co.uk

Fuzzy Duck was established in 2006. It relocated to Poulton-le-Fylde later that year, expanding capacity to an eight-barrel plant. The brewery delivers over a wide area of North-west England and Yorkshire. !! ♦ RAIB

Golden Cascade (OG 1038, ABV 3.8%)
Golden-coloured ale brewed with a citrus flavour and floral aroma.

Mucky Duck (OG 1042, ABV 4%)
Dark-coloured stout, slightly sweet with chocolate and coffee notes from the roasted malt.

Pheasant Plucker (OG 1042, ABV 4.2%)
Amber-coloured beer with a slightly spicy taste and citrus finish.

Ruby Duck (OG 1053, ABV 5.3%)
Dark ruby-coloured beer with a rich, full body and complex fruit flavours.

Fyne SIBA

Achadunan, Cairndow, PA26 8BJ
(01499) 600120 fyneales.com

Fyne Ales has been brewing since 2001 and is situated at the head of Loch Fyne. In 2012 an on-site brewery tap was added. Expansion has allowed for the production of experimental brews. FyneFest runs annually, celebrating local fare and showcasing other breweries. !! ♦ RAIB

Jarl (OG 1038, ABV 3.8%)
A light, golden-coloured ale with strong citrus notes.

Maverick (OG 1040.5, ABV 4.2%)
Full-bodied, roasty, tawny-coloured best bitter. It is balanced, fruity and well-hopped.

Hurricane Jack (OG 1042.5, ABV 4.4%)
Smooth golden ale with deep citrus flavours, which mellow to a lingering citrus bitter finish.

Vital Spark (OG 1042.5, ABV 4.4%)
A rich, dark-coloured beer that shows glints of red. The taste is clean and slightly sharp with a hint of blackcurrant.

Avalanche (OG 1043.5, ABV 4.5%)

This true golden ale starts with citrus hops on the nose. Well-balanced with good body and fruit, balancing a refreshing hoppy taste. It finishes with a long, bittersweet aftertaste.

Highlander (OG 1046, ABV 4.8%) ◈
Full-bodied, bittersweet ale with a good dry hop finish. In the style of a heavy although the malt is less pronounced and the sweetness ebbs away to leave a bitter, hoppy finish.

Sublime Stout (OG 1067, ABV 6.8%)
A stout with a hint of liquorice in the aftertaste.

Superior IPA (OG 1070, ABV 7.1%)
An IPA with aromas of apricot and pine resin and a dusty, hoppy bitterness.

G2 SIBA

Unit 5, Ashford Works, Brunswick Road, Cobbs Wood, Ashford, Kent, TN23 1EH
☎ (01233) 630277 🌐 g2brewing.com

Commercial brewing began in 2015. Currently a two man operation, outlets are supplied across Kent and London.

Orion Session (ABV 3.8%)

Sail Blonde (OG 1038, ABV 4.2%)

Plough IPA (OG 1040, ABV 4.4%)

Southern Cross Premium (OG 1044, ABV 4.8%)

Gadds

See Ramsgate

Gale's

See Fuller's

Gaol SIBA

The Old Lock Up, 46 North End, Wirksworth, Derbyshire, DE4 4FG ☎ 07981 220734
✉ sales@gaolales.co.uk

A small brewery established in 2015. Currently producing up to two barrels a week.

Jailbird (OG 1039, ABV 4%)

Black Maria (OG 1044, ABV 4.1%)
Traditional-style porter with a complex, strong malt taste and hints of wood smoke and chocolate.

Jailbreak (OG 1044, ABV 4.5%)
Traditional copper-coloured English bitter with a dry, balanced taste and caramel notes.

Strong Arm of the Law (OG 1052, ABV 5.1%)
A dark-coloured, strong ale with roasted malt and hints of dark fruits, liquorice and chocolate.

On Parole (OG 1055, ABV 5.2%)
A traditional stout with added cocoa nibs to give an extra chocolate bitterness to complement the roast barley.

No Prisoners (OG 1052, ABV 5.7%)
Strong IPA-style ale with a pleasant hoppy taste and a hint of spice and citrus flavours.

Garden City

22 The Wynd, Letchworth, Hertfordshire, SG6 3EN
☎ 07932 739558 🌐 gardencitybrewery.co.uk

A brewbar established in 2016 using a 2.5-barrel plant, serving a selection of its own ales plus guests on gravity.

Gasworks

First Street, Manchester, M15 4FN

Gasworks is a six-barrel brewpub from the team behind Dockyard, opened in 2016. It supplies Gasworks Tap, Dockyard, Salford Quays and Dockyard, Spinningfields.

Gates Burton

Reservoir Road, Burton upon Trent, Staffordshire, DE14 2BP
☎ (01283) 532567
✉ gatesburtonbrewery@talktalk.net

The Gates Burton Brewery was established in 2011 using a one-barrel plant. This has now expanded to a three-barrel plant. !! ♦

Reservoir (OG 1048, ABV 4.6%) ◈
Pale brown in colour with a malty aroma and roast hint. Caramel and malt lead to a sweet hop balanced taste. Hops arrive late on the palate to urge another mouthful.

GBA (Gates Burton Ale) (OG 1048, ABV 4.8%)
Amber-coloured ale with a floral aroma and sweet finish.

Damn (OG 1050, ABV 5%)
Smooth-drinking with chocolate malt tones. Delicately hopped with a subtle, sweet finish.

Reservoir Gold (OG 1075, ABV 7.5%)
Full-bodied, amber in colour, balanced with roast barley and subtly hopped. Smooth with a sweet finish.

Geeves SIBA

Unit 12, Grange Lane Industrial Estate, Carrwood Road, Stairfoot, Barnsley, South Yorkshire, S71 5AS
☎ 07859 039259 🌐 geevesbrewery.co.uk

Geeves began brewing in 2011 using a 5.5-barrel plant with recipes developed when the owners lived on a narrow boat. !! ♦ RAIB

Rococo (OG 1037, ABV 3.6%)
A smooth, dark mild with a hint of chocolate. Aromas are cocoa, dark fruits and berries with a subtle but lingering bitter finish.

Evolver (OG 1037, ABV 3.8%)
A light, single-hopped pale ale.

Renaissance (OG 1040, ABV 4.1%)
A red-coloured ale packed with sweet malts giving flavours of dark fruits and molasses. The hops give spicy earthiness, lemon citrus and hints of floral apricot and peach.

Aurelian (OG 1043, ABV 4.2%)
A golden ale with sweet, tangy orange citrus hop flavours and a refreshingly crisp and bitter finish.

Captain Gingerbread (OG 1043, ABV 4.3%)
A naturally hazy wheat beer infused with ginger. Spicy and refreshing with a hint of citrus.

Clear Cut (OG 1044, ABV 4.4%)
An extra pale ale with bags of American hops for a real citrus kick.

Oaty McOatface (ABV 4.5%)

THE BREWERIES

A rich, full-bodied stout packed with malted oats to create a smooth and silky mouthfeel balanced by a lightly spicy hop character.

Smokey Joe Stout (OG 1050, ABV 5%)
A rich, bold stout with flavours of black coffee, dark chocolate and a lingering smokiness. A combination of hops gives a spicy, oaky finish.

Fully Laden (OG 1060, ABV 6%)
A strong IPA with a juicy, citrus, sweet floral taste and aroma with a satisfying bitterness.

Geipel SIBA

Pant Glas, Llangwm, LL21 0RN
☎ (01490) 420838 ☎ 07549 526287 🌐 geipel.co.uk

Geipel commenced brewing in 2013 producing classic German-style, unpasteurised and unfiltered beers in keg, KeyKeg and bottle form. RAIB

Aloha from Bala (OG 1047, ABV 4.4%)

Pilsner (OG 1046, ABV 4.6%)

Golden Gate (OG 1050, ABV 5%)

Dunkelweizen (OG 1057, ABV 5.4%)

Zoigl (OG 1053, ABV 5.4%)

Hefeweizen (OG 1054, ABV 5.6%)

Bock (OG 1066.9, ABV 6.5%)

Gene Pool

Unit 6, 23 Arthur Street, Hull, East Yorkshire, HU3 6BH
☎ 07760 669157 🌐 genepoolbrewing.com

Father and son enterprise, hence the brewery's name, established in 2016 using a two-barrel brew plant currently brewing twice a week.

Primordial Ooze (OG 1044, ABV 4.3%)

DN Ale (OG 1044, ABV 4.5%)

Helix (OG 1050, ABV 5%)

Genetic Code (OG 1060, ABV 5.8%)

George Samuel

Spennymoor ☎ 07840 892751
🌐 georgesamuelbrewingcompany.co.uk

A small, two-barrel brewery originally set up at the Duke of Wellington pub in the small village of Welbury near Northallerton, and named after the brewer's two sons. It has now moved to a private address in Spennymoor and supplies a small number of outlets around County Durham and the North-east.

By George She's Got It (OG 1036, ABV 3.6%)
Blonde session ale ale with a hoppy punch.

Tower Bitter (OG 1038, ABV 3.8%)

Brew It Again Sam (OG 1042, ABV 4.2%)

New Horizon (OG 1042, ABV 4.2%)

Harvey (OG 1052, ABV 5.2%)

George Wright

See under W

George's SIBA

Common Road, Great Wakering, Essex, SS3 0AG
☎ (01702) 826755 ☎ 07771 871255
🌐 georgesbrewery.com

George's Brewery and Hop Monster Brewing Company (qv) are owned by the same brewer, using the same plant. George's concentrates on traditional styles and Hop Monster on the more unusual. !! ♦RAIB

Wallasea Wench (OG 1036, ABV 3.6%)
Pale copper-coloured, easy-drinking ale with a smooth mouthfeel.

Wakering Gold (OG 1038.5, ABV 3.8%)
Bursting with fresh hop aroma; a refreshing blend of English and American hops.

8-Bit Bitter (OG 1040, ABV 4%)

Best (OG 1041, ABV 4%)
Copper-coloured session bitter with a big hop flavour.

Cockleboats (OG 1040, ABV 4%)

Empire (OG 1040, ABV 4%)

Figaro (OG 1038.5, ABV 4%)
Pale ale with a tropical fruit taste and floral aroma.

Broadsword (OG 1047, ABV 4.7%)
Ruby/copper-coloured with a malty, smooth start and a well-balanced dry finish.

Brewed under the Hop Monster Brewery name:

Rakau (ABV 4.2%)

Snake Oil Stout (OG 1048, ABV 5%)

Ghost

Unit D, Tong Business Centre, Otley Road, Baildon, West Yorkshire, BD17 7QD
☎ (0113) 418 2002 🌐 ghostbrew.co.uk

Ghost Brew Co is the creation of Steve Crump and James Thompson.

Wraith (ABV 3.8%)

Spectre (ABV 4.4%)

Phantom (ABV 5.3%)

Gibberish (NEW)

15 Caryl Street, Liverpool, L8 5AA

Gibberish is a brewpub that opened in 2017 in Liverpool's Baltic Triangle.

Gipsy Hill SIBA

Unit 11, Hamilton Road Industrial Estate, 160 Hamilton Road, West Norwood, London, SE27 9SF
☎ (020) 8761 9061 🌐 gipsyhillbrewing.com

Founded in 2014, Gipsy Hill is a small, independent microbrewery producing mainly for the local market in London. A tap room is open to the public at weekends. No real ale. ♦RAIB

Wayfarer (ABV 4.6%)
Well-balanced porter with dark roast and spicy hop aroma. Roast continues in the taste, with sweetness balanced by bitterness.

Glamorgan SIBA

Unit J, Llantrisant Business Park, Llantrisant, CF72 8LF ☎ (01443) 406080 🌐 glamorganbrewingco.com

This family owned and run brewery moved to its present site in 2013. Production capacity was increased in 2017 and again in 2018. The brewery tap is open for special events and tours and the brewery shop is open daily. Direct deliveries are made throughout Wales and distributed further afield by selected wholesalers and breweries. ♦

Cwrw Gorslas/Bluestone Bitter (OG 1040, ABV 4%)
A well-rounded bitter delivering softly roasted undertones to a malty body complemented by a smooth and robust hoppiness from nose to finish.

Welsh Pale Ale (OG 1042, ABV 4.1%)
A crisp pale ale, light gold in colour, full of bright citrus aromas and flavours. Finishes dry, fruity and hoppy.

Jemimas Pitchfork (OG 1044, ABV 4.4%)

Thunderbird (OG 1045, ABV 4.5%)

Glastonbury

Unit 11, Wessex Park, Somerton Business Park, Somerton, Somerset, TA11 6SB ☎ (01458) 272244 🌐 glastonburyales.com

Glastonbury Ales was established in 2002 on a five-barrel plant. In 2006 the brewery changed ownership and moved to Somerton, enlarging capacity to a 20-barrel plant. Cider is also produced. ‼ ♦ RAIB

Mystery Tor (OG 1040, ABV 3.8%)
Golden-coloured bitter with floral hop and fruit on the nose and palate, sweetness giving way to a bitter hop finish. Full-bodied.

Lady of the Lake (OG 1042, ABV 4.2%)
Full-bodied, amber-coloured best bitter with hops balanced by fruity malt flavour and a hint of vanilla. Clean, bitter hop aftertaste.

Love Monkey (OG 1042, ABV 4.2%)
Golden ale loaded with zesty fruity hops and a variety of malts.

Black As Yer 'At (OG 1043, ABV 4.3%)

Hedge Monkey (OG 1048, ABV 4.6%)
A well-rounded, deep amber-coloured bitter. Malty, rich and hoppy.

Golden Chalice (OG 1048, ABV 4.8%)
A powerful golden-coloured ale with a good balance of malt and fragrant hops, a robust bitterness and lingering bittersweet finish.

Thriller Cappuccino Porter (OG 1050, ABV 5%)
Dark-coloured, richly roasted porter with hints of coffee.

Glede SIBA

Unit 1, Tweed Road Trading Estate, Clevedon, Somerset, BS21 6RR ☎ 07802 702367

Founded in the Chilterns by Howard Tucker in 2016 as Red Kite, the brewery relocated to Clevedon in 2017, changing its name to Glede. ♦

Glen Affric

Units 2 & 3, Lightbox, Knox Street, Birkenhead, Merseyside, CH41 5JG ☎ 07742 020275

Office: 53 Wood Street, Ashton-under-Lyne, OL6 7NB 🌐 glenaffricbrewery.com

Established in 2016, a small batch brewery producing only keg beers. ‼

Glens of Antrim

10 Murlough Road, Ballycastle, BT64 6RG ☎ (028) 2076 9696

Small, family-run brewery founded in 2014 producing bottle-conditioned beers. ♦ RAIB

Globe

144 High Street West, Glossop, Derbyshire, SK13 8HJ ☎ (01457) 852417 🌐 globepub.co.uk

Globe was established in 2006 by Ron Brookes on a 2.5-barrel plant in an old stable behind the Globe pub. Grandson Toby now has a major role in the brewery under the watchful eye of Ron. The beers are mainly for the pub but special one-off brews are produced for beer festivals. ♦

Gloucester SIBA

Fox's Kiln, West Quay, The Docks, Gloucester, GL1 2LG ☎ (01452) 668043 ☎ 07503 152749 🌐 gloucesterbrewery.co.uk

Situated in the historic Gloucester Docks, brewing began in 2011. The brewery expanded into larger premises in the docks area to cope with increased demand while retaining and sympathetically restoring its original converted stables site for experimental brews and a bar named Tank. The full range of beers is regularly available in pubs throughout Gloucestershire and beyond. ‼ ♦ RAIB V

Session Pale (OG 1037, ABV 3.7%)
A pale ale with a fresh, zingy fruit taste and citrus hop aroma.

Gold (OG 1040, ABV 3.9%)
A golden ale with a crisp, fruity and bitter taste and aroma of luscious tropical fruit.

Cascade (OG 1042, ABV 4.2%)
Best bitter with a full-bodied, fruity and bitter taste and aroma of bold, spicy and floral hops.

Session IPA (OG 1045, ABV 4.5%)
A resinous and full-bodied taste and aroma of juicy tropical fruit.

Six Malt Porter (OG 1045, ABV 4.5%)
A full-bodied, smooth porter with aromas of roasted malt and dark fruits.

West Coast Red (OG 1048, ABV 4.8%)
An American-style, red-coloured ale with a full-bodied, fruity, bitter taste and aroma of bold, spicy and floral hops.

Goacher's

Unit 8, Tovil Green Business Park, Burial Ground Lane, Tovil, Kent, ME15 6TA ☎ (01622) 682112 🌐 goachers.com

A traditional brewery that uses only malt and Kentish hops for all its beers. Phil and Debbie Goacher have concentrated on brewing good wholesome beers without gimmicks. Two tied houses and around 30 free trade outlets in the mid-Kent area are supplied. Special is brewed for sale under house names. ‼♦

Real Mild Ale (OG 1033, ABV 3.4%) ◆
A rich mild with moderate roast barley and a generous helping of chocolate malt.

Fine Light Ale (OG 1036, ABV 3.7%) ◆
A pale, golden brown-coloured bitter with a strong, floral, hoppy aroma and aftertaste. A hoppy and moderately malty session beer.

Special/House Ale (OG 1037, ABV 3.8%)

Best Dark Ale (OG 1040, ABV 4.1%) ◆
Dark in colour but light and quaffable in body, this ale features hints of caramel and chocolate malt throughout.

Crown Imperial Stout (OG 1044, ABV 4.5%) ◆
A good, well-balanced, roasty stout, dark in colour and bitter with just a hint of caramel and a lingering creamy head.

Gold Star Strong Ale (OG 1050, ABV 5.1%) ◆

Goddards SIBA

Barnsley Farm, Bullen Road, Ryde, Isle of Wight, PO33 1QF
☎ (01983) 611011 ⊕ goddardsbrewery.com

⊗ Anthony Goddard established what is now the oldest active brewery on the Isle of Wight in 1993. Originally occupying an 18th-century barn, a new brewery was built in 2008, quadrupling its capacity, which has since been further increased. Goddard's remain a locally-focused business distributing ales on the Isle of Wight and the easily accessible counties of southern England. ♦

Ale of Wight (OG 1037, ABV 3.7%)
An aromatic, fresh and zesty pale-coloured beer.

Starboard (ABV 4%)

Wight Squirrel (OG 1042.5, ABV 4.3%)
A russet-coloured best bitter with an initial dry taste on the palate.

Fuggle-Dee-Dum (OG 1047, ABV 4.8%) ◆
Brown-coloured strong ale with plenty of malt and hops.

Godstone SIBA

Flower Farm, Oxted Road, Godstone, Surrey, RH9 8BP
☎ 07791 570731

Office: 3 Willow Way, Godstone, Surrey, RH9 8NQ
⊕ thegodstonebrewers.com

⊗ The Godstone Brewers was established in 2015 using a one-barrel plant but moved to larger premises on a farm in Godstone with a five-barrel plant. Beers are named with local themes. Local outlets are supplied. Fresh Beer Fridays take place each week in the farm tearooms with a larger event held each quarter. ♦RAIB

Not So Black & White (ABV 3.7%)
A creamy, amber-coloured ale with fruity and refreshing hops.

Trenchman's Hop (OG 1041, ABV 3.8%)
A pale-coloured bitter with good balance of malt and hops.

Pondtail Pale (OG 1044, ABV 4.1%)
Pale ale with lemon and grapefruit flavours without being overpoweringly hoppy.

Junction 6 (ABV 4.2%)
Refreshing pale ale with a mandarin and orange character.

Oishi (ABV 4.2%)
A smooth-tasting ale with a refreshing citrus character.

Rusty's Ale (ABV 4.4%)
Traditional malty best bitter made exclusively from English hops.

Buzz (ABV 4.7%)
Dry honey ale retaining a lime blossom character.

Bitter Entropy (ABV 5.3%)
Malty caramel flavours dominate a sweeter ale with hint of added rye.

Polly Paine's Porter (OG 1070, ABV 6.5%)
Full-bodied and complex porter with caramel, coffee and chocolate notes.

Goff's SIBA

9 Isbourne Way, Winchcombe, Gloucestershire, GL54 5NS
☎ (01242) 603383 ⊕ goffsbrewery.com

⊗ Goff's is a family concern that has been brewing cask-conditioned ales since 1994. The ales are available regionally in more than 200 outlets and nationally through wholesalers. ♦

Jouster (OG 1040, ABV 4%) ◆
A tawny-coloured ale with a light hoppiness in the aroma. It has a good balance of malt and bitterness in the mouth, underscored by fruitiness, with a clean, hoppy aftertaste.

Tournament (OG 1038, ABV 4%) ◆
Dark golden in colour with a pleasant hop aroma. A clean, light and refreshing session bitter with a pleasant hop aftertaste.

White Knight (OG 1046, ABV 4.7%) ◆
A well-hopped bitter with a light colour and full-bodied taste. Bitterness predominates in the mouth and leads to a dry, hoppy aftertaste.

Golcar

60a Swallow Lane, Golcar, West Yorkshire, HD7 4NB
☎ (01484) 644241 ☎ 07970 267555
⊕ golcarbrewery.co.uk

Golcar started brewing in 2001 and production has increased from 2.5 barrels to five barrels a week. The brewery owns one pub, the Rose & Crown at Golcar, and occasionally supplies other outlets in the local area. ‼

Dark Mild (OG 1034, ABV 3.4%) ◆
Dark mild with a light roasted malt and liquorice taste. Smooth and satisfying.

Town End Bitter (OG 1039, ABV 3.9%) ◆
Amber-coloured bitter with a hoppy, citrus taste. Fruity overtones and a bitter finish.

Pennine Gold (OG 1038, ABV 4%)
A hoppy and fruity session beer.

Guthlac's Porter (OG 1047, ABV 5%)

Golden Duck SIBA

Unit 2, Redhill Farm, Top Street, Appleby Magna, Leicestershire, DE12 7AH ☎ 07846 295179
🌐 goldenduckbrewery.com

Golden Duck began brewing in 2012 using a five-barrel plant. It is run by the father-and-son team of Andrew and Harry Lunn. Beers have a cricket-related theme and are always available in Mushroom Hall, Albert Village. ♦RAIB

LFB (Lunns First Brew) (OG 1043, ABV 4.3%)
Traditional, golden-coloured, hoppy session ale with citrus overtones.

Wristy Fitzy (OG 1046, ABV 4.6%)
Deceptively smooth and rich chestnut-coloured ale. Hoppy but with slight malty overtones.

Lunnys No. 8 (OG 1048, ABV 4.8%)
Hoppy bitter with a fruity and lasting aroma.

Golden Triangle SIBA

Unit 9, Watton Road Industrial Estate, Norwich, NR9 4BG
☎ (01603) 757763 ☎ 07976 281132
🌐 goldentriangle.co.uk

⊗ Golden Triangle, named after an area of Norwich, has been brewing modern, hop-forward ales on a 10-barrel plant since 2011. The brewery moved to its current address in 2012, and continues to add new beers to its range. Beers are mainly found in pubs across Norwich. ♦

City Gold (OG 1038, ABV 3.8%) ◆
A lemony hop aroma introduces a mix of citrus, hop, and bitterness. Finish develops a dry astringency.

Mosaic City (OG 1038, ABV 3.8%)

Centropolis (OG 1039, ABV 3.9%)

Citropolis (OG 1039, ABV 3.9%)
Light, refreshing and zesty with citrus hop notes and fruity aroma.

Bonny's Gold (OG 1040, ABV 4%)
Golden ale with a citrus hop profile.

Hoptriptic (OG 1040, ABV 4%)

Black Hops IBA (OG 1047, ABV 4.6%) ◆
Intense hop and cherry aroma. Complex mix of malt, cherry and bitterness dominated by hops. Challenging, increasingly bitter ending.

Red Square (OG 1046, ABV 4.6%)
A red-coloured ale with a well-balanced, complex flavour and strong hoppy finish.

Shenanigans (ABV 5%)
A rich, velvety oatmeal and milk stout with coffee and chocolate notes.

Hop Lobster (OG 1053, ABV 5.5%)
A strong golden ale with plenty of citrus hop character.

Goldmark SIBA 👁

Unit 23, The Vinery, Arundel Road, Poling, West Sussex, BN18 9PY
☎ (01903) 297838 ☎ 07900 555415
🌐 goldmarks.co.uk

⊗ Ex-biochemist and homebrewer Mark Lehmann began commercial brewing in 2013 using an 11-barrel plant. ‼RAIB

Ebony Mild (OG 1035, ABV 3.5%)
Black-coloured, spicy mild with hints of chocolate, coffee and toffee.

Liquid Gold (OG 1040, ABV 4%)
A refreshing, full-bodied, golden-coloured beer with bursts of fruit and citrus.

Phoenix (OG 1041, ABV 4.1%)
A brown-coloured ale with hints of toffee, caramel and a smooth hop finish.

Red IPA (OG 1043, ABV 4.3%)

American Hop Idol (OG 1040, ABV 4.4%)
A pale ale using six American hop varieties balanced with roasted malt.

Warrior (OG 1046, ABV 4.6%)
A brown-coloured ale with hints of honey and caramel, ending with a smooth hop note.

Black Lion Porter (OG 1048, ABV 4.8%)
A rich, smooth, black-coloured porter with chocolate hints and coffee notes to finish.

Vertigo Craft Lager (OG 1048, ABV 4.8%)

Good Chemistry

Unit 2, William Street, St Philips, Bristol, BS2 0RG
☎ (0117) 903 9930 🌐 goodchemistrybrewing.co.uk

⊗ Good Chemistry was established in 2015 in a warehouse in St Philips, Bristol by Bob Cary and Kelly Sidgwick, using a 10-barrel plant. As the name suggests, all brewery and beer logos have a scientific theme. Frequent brewery open days are held. RAIB

Natural Selection (OG 1038, ABV 4%)
An American-style pale ale with a light, malty base, refreshing hoppy taste and a dry finish.

Kokomo Weekday (OG 1044, ABV 4.3%)
A session-strength IPA full of tropical flavours of pineapple, passion fruit and mango.

Good Stuff

Abdication, 89 Mansfield Road, Daybrook, Nottingham, NG5 6BH 🌐 theabdication.co.uk

A nanobrewery located inside the Abdication micropub. Capacity is 0.5 barrels so occasional beers can only be found at the pub and local beer festivals.

Goodall's

The Lodge, 88 Crewe Road, Alsager, ST7 2JA
☎ (01270) 873669
✉ goodalls.brewery@hotmail.co.uk

Goodall's began brewing in 2010 at the Lodge in Alsager using a 2.5-barrel plant. Mainly seasonal ales are brewed. ‼♦

Goody SIBA

Bleangate Brewery, Braggs Lane, Herne, Kent, CT6 7NP
☎ (01227) 361555 🌐 goodyales.co.uk

Goody Ales began brewing in 2012 using a 10-barrel plant. A wood-burning boiler is used to heat the water for the brews using wood from its copse, thereby minimising the use of non-renewable fuel. An on-site bar and shop, the Cathedral, is now open (limited hours). ♦RAIB GF V

Good Evening (OG 1034, ABV 3.4%)
A smooth, dark mild with a tinge of chocolate.

Genesis (OG 1035, ABV 3.5%)
A dark ruby-coloured ale with a full flavour and lasting bitter finish.

Good Health (OG 1038, ABV 3.6%)
A honey-coloured golden ale with a fresh, hoppy finish and undertones of zesty orange.

Good Life (OG 1040, ABV 3.9%)
Fresh-tasting pale ale bursting with citrus flavours and a host of hops.

Good Heavens (OG 1042, ABV 4.1%)

Good Sheppard (OG 1045, ABV 4.5%)
Deep amber-coloured ale with a warm vanilla twist on the palate and a soft feel on the tongue.

Goodness Gracious Me (OG 1047, ABV 4.8%)
Robust, hoppy IPA with a citrus flavour.

Good Lord (OG 1050, ABV 5%)
Rich porter with a smooth roasted coffee tinge and silky bitter finish.

Goose Eye SIBA

Unit 5, Castlefield Industrial Estate, Crossflatts, Bingley, West Yorkshire, BD16 2AF
☎ (01274) 512743 ⊕ goose-eye-brewery.co.uk

Goose Eye is a family-run brewery supplying 60-70 regular outlets, mainly in North and West Yorkshire and Lancashire. The beers are available through national wholesalers and pub chains. The brewery moved to a new custom-built brewery in 2017, which has enabled it to increase production. ♦

Springwell (OG 1036, ABV 3.6%)

Barm Pot Bitter (OG 1038, ABV 3.8%)
Bitter, hop and fruit flavours dominate this golden-coloured session bitter, over a malty base. Increasingly dry and bitter finish.

Bitter (OG 1038, ABV 3.9%)
Traditional Yorkshire brown-coloured session bitter, well-balanced malt and hops with a pleasingly bitter finish.

Blackmoor (OG 1040, ABV 4%)

Chinook Blonde (OG 1042, ABV 4.2%)
An increasingly tart bitter finish follows assertive grapefruit hoppiness in the aroma and tropical flavours in this satisfying brew.

Golden Goose (OG 1045, ABV 4.5%)
A straw-coloured beer, light on the palate with a smooth and refreshing hoppy finish.

Over & Stout (OG 1052, ABV 5.2%)
A full-bodied stout with roast and malt flavours mingling with hops, dark fruit and liquorice on the palate. Look also for tart fruit on the nose and a growing bitter finish.

Pommies Revenge (OG 1052, ABV 5.2%)
Golden-coloured, strong bitter combining grassy hops, a cocktail of fruit flavours, a peppery hint and a hoppy, bitter finish.

Gorgeous Beer SIBA

Unit 16, Tweedale Court, Madeley, Shropshire, TF7 4JZ
☎ (01952) 583656 ⊕ gorgeousbeer.co.uk

Brewing was established in 2016 by a small group of real ale enthusiasts. A 10-barrel plant is used, supplying three core beers plus seasonals to the free trade. A one-barrel plant is used for trial brews. ♦

Golden Bitter (OG 1034.5, ABV 3.8%)

Blonde Ale (OG 1046.5, ABV 4.8%)
Smooth-tasting with a slightly citrus bitterness.

Porter (OG 1051, ABV 5.5%)
Sweet, malty and dark-coloured porter.

Gorgeous Brewery

Bull, 13 North Hill, Highgate, London, N6 4AB
☎ 07754 925562 ⊕ gorgeousbrewery.com

Formerly the home of London Brewing (qv), Gorgeous inherited the brewing kit on the purchase of the pub in 2017. At the beginning of 2018 a newly built brewhouse at the rear of the pub came on stream.

Gower SIBA

Unit 25, Crofty Industrial Estate, Crofty, SA4 3RS
☎ (01792) 850681 ⊕ gowerbrewery.com

Established in 2011 on a five-barrel brew plant at the Greyhound Inn in Llanrhidian, Gower moved to a new 20-barrel brewery in Crofty in 2015. ‼ ♦

Brew 1 (OG 1039, ABV 3.8%)
Honey-coloured ale with a pronounced floral aroma.

Best Bitter (OG 1045, ABV 4.5%)
A traditional, honey-coloured ale with a full-bodied, balanced malty flavour and crisp, lingering bite of hop.

Gold (OG 1045, ABV 4.5%)
Thirst-quenching golden ale, refreshing citrus flavours and aromas.

Rumour (OG 1050, ABV 5%)
Strong ruby-coloured ale with complex tastes and aromas produced by a delicate mix of malts and hops.

Power (OG 1052, ABV 5.5%)
A strong, hoppy IPA.

Grafton SIBA

Walters Yard, Unit 4, Claylands Industrial Estate, Worksop, Nottinghamshire, S81 7DW
☎ (01909) 476121 ☎ 07436 282779

Office: 8 Oak Close, Crabtree Park Estate, Worksop, S80 1BH ⊕ graftonbrewing.co.uk

Grafton is a 12-barrel brewery established in 2007. The brewery tap is the Grafton Hotel, Worksop. In 2017 the brewery took over the operation of the former Hale's Brewery, which was based in an adjacent unit, but utilised the Grafton plant, and now produces Hale's beers as a sub-brand within its portfolio. ‼♦

Framboise (OG 1038, ABV 4%)
Golden ale with a raspberry aroma and taste, leading to a sweet and slightly bitter finish.

Silhouette (OG 1038, ABV 4%)
A pale-coloured beer, the addition of vanilla pods gives a unique vanilla flavour.

Lady Julia (OG 1041, ABV 4.3%)
A golden ale. Wheat and barley produce a crisp beer with a floral hop aroma.

Bananalicious (OG 1043, ABV 4.5%)
Mid brown-coloured ale with a banana and toffee aftertaste.

Lady Catherine (OG 1043, ABV 4.5%)
Well-balanced with a malty, slightly sweet biscuit flavour.

Lady Ruby (OG 1043, ABV 4.5%)
A ruby-coloured ale made with cherries. Hint of cherries on the nose, on the palate a bitter start which finishes with a cherry bomb on the back of the tongue.

Apricot Jungle (OG 1046, ABV 4.8%)
A fruity, golden-coloured beer with honey, apricot and almond notes. The sweetness is balanced by hop bitterness.

Blondie (OG 1046, ABV 4.8%)
A strong, golden-coloured beer. The aroma is dominated by characteristic citrus notes. Hops and fruit on the palate are balanced by malt, leading to a hoppy finish with soft fruit flavours.

Mint Chocolate Stout (OG 1046, ABV 4.8%)
Dark-coloured ale brewed with chocolate malt and mint which gives a mint chocolate flavour.

Caramel Stout (OG 1048, ABV 5%)
A black-coloured ale with caramel and dark roast notes.

Coco Loco (OG 1048, ABV 5%) ◆
Dark-coloured, smooth-drinking ale infused with coconut, gentle bitterness.

Grain SIBA

South Farm, Tunbeck Road, Alburgh, Norfolk, IP20 0BS
☎ (01986) 788884 ⊕ grainbrewery.co.uk

Grain Brewery was launched in 2006 by Geoff Wright and Phil Halls in a converted dairy in the Waveney Valley. It upgraded to a 15-barrel plant in 2012. Four pubs are owned, the Plough and the Cottage, both in Norwich, the Spread Eagle, Ipswich, and the Corn Hall Bar, Diss. !! ♦ RAIB

Oak (OG 1038, ABV 3.8%) ◆
A balanced mix of malt and hops with marmalade overtones. A hint of molasses in the short, sharp ending.

ThreeOneSix (OG 1039, ABV 3.9%) ◆
Strong citrus notes throughout. Tangerine, lemon and lime mix with a solid hoppy base. A well-balanced bitter finish.

Best Bitter (OG 1042, ABV 4.2%) ◆
Brazil nut and malt introduce this well-balanced complex bitter. Bittersweet caramel notes flourish before a gently tapering malty finish.

Redwood (OG 1043, ABV 4.3%) ◆
Heavy blackcurrant airs give way to a rich, fruity bitterness with malt overtones. Copper-coloured, crisp and satisfying.

Slate (OG 1060, ABV 6%) ◆
Coffee, caramel and plum on the nose. Dried fruit and sweet maltiness dominate a creamy roast background. Long, strong finish.

Lignum Vitae (OG 1065, ABV 6.5%) ◆
Solidly orangy and hoppy throughout. Imposing oily character with a definite marmalade bias. A bittersweet blast enlivens the towering finale.

Grainstore SIBA

Station Approach, Oakham, LE15 6RE
☎ (01572) 770065 ⊕ grainstorebrewery.com

Grainstore, the smallest county's largest brewery, has been in production since 1995, founded by Tony Davis and Mike Davies. After 45 years in the industry Tony decided to retire, handing the reins to his son, William. More than 200 outlets are supplied. !!♦

Rutland Bitter (OG 1032, ABV 3.4%)

Rutland Panther (OG 1034, ABV 3.4%) ◆
This reddish-black-coloured mild punches above its weight with malt and roast flavours combining to deliver a brew that can match the average stout for intensity of flavour.

Cooking (OG 1036, ABV 3.6%) ◆
Tawny-coloured beer with malt and hops on the nose and a pleasant grainy mouthfeel. Hops and fruit flavours combine to give a bitterness that continues into a long finish.

Red Kite (OG 1038, ABV 3.8%)
A malty, sweet beer with a good body.

Stoney Ford Sheepmarket Supernova (OG 1040, ABV 3.8%)

Rutland Osprey (OG 1040, ABV 4%)
A refreshing, light golden-coloured beer with a complex, mellow flavour and a floral aroma and smooth bitterness.

Stoney Ford PE9 Paradise Pale (OG 1041, ABV 4%)

Steelback IPA (OG 1042, ABV 4.2%)

Stoney Ford All Saints Almighty (OG 1044, ABV 4.2%)

Triple B (OG 1042, ABV 4.2%) ◆
Initially hops dominate over malt in both the aroma and taste, but fruit is there too. All three linger in varying degrees in the sweetish aftertaste of this brown-coloured brew.

GB Best (OG 1043, ABV 4.3%)
A pronounced floral aroma and flavour.

Ten Fifty (OG 1050, ABV 5%) ◆
Pungent banana and malt notes on the nose. On the palate, rich malt and fruit is joined by subtle hop on a bittersweet base. Dry malt aftertaste with some fruit.

Rutland Beast (OG 1053, ABV 5.3%)
A strong mild with a complex flavour made up of a combination of chocolate/coffee notes and those of raisins and autumn fruits.

Nip (OG 1073, ABV 7.3%)
A smooth, warming barley wine with a malty sweetness balanced by hop bitterness. Raisins and winter fruit are the dominant flavor notes.

Grampus

Grampus Inn, Lee Bay, Devon, EX34 8LR
☎ (01271) 862906 ⊕ thegrampus-inn.co.uk

Grampus was established in 2014 at the back of the Grampus Inn by Bill Harvey, the owner. It is a small plant using traditional brewing methods, but combining some unique and unusual ingredients.

At present most of production is sold through the pub with just a few casks going to local pubs and beer festivals. ♦RAIB

Granite Rock

Unit 19, Kernick Road Industrial Estate, Penryn, Cornwall, TR10 9EP
☎ (01326) 379251 ☎ 07436 817974
🌐 graniterockbrewery.co.uk

Granite Rock was established in 2013 as a brewery and homebrew shop. Located on an industrial estate in Penryn, the two-barrel plant currently supplies the free trade in west Cornwall. ‼ ♦RAIB

Penryn Company Pale Ale (OG 1040, ABV 4%)
Tawny-coloured bitter with fruity hop and malt nose. Assertive bitterness, resinous hops, roast malt with stone fruit traces. Dry finish.

Summer Solstice (OG 1040, ABV 4%)
Golden ale with a floral grapefruit aroma. Refreshing essences of oranges, lemons and grapefruit. Assertive bitterness throughout with some dryness.

Granite IPA (OG 1040, ABV 4.3%)
Aroma of orange and grapefruit with a bitter citrus finish.

Penryn Pride (OG 1042, ABV 4.5%)
A red/brown-coloured ale with malt, coffee and chocolate notes; strong hopping ensures the malt does not overwhelm this flavoursome beer.

Driller IPA (OG 1055, ABV 5.1%)
Aroma of apricots and orange peel; full-on citrus and mixed peel hop flavour balanced against toffee/caramel notes.

Bronescombe's Vision (OG 1048, ABV 5.2%)
Well-balanced, red-coloured, strong bitter with malt and hop aroma. Strong malt flavour, hop bitterness, some sweetness. Refreshing bitter, dry finish.

Glasney College Porter (OG 1050, ABV 5.4%)
Black-coloured porter with roast malt aroma. Full-bodied taste of creamy coffee and dark chocolate, liquorice and pear drops. Light finish.

Grasmere (NEW)

Lake View Country House, Lake View Drive, Grasmere, Cumbria, LA22 9TD
☎ (01539) 435572 🌐 grasmerepub.com

Brewing began in 2017 in old farm buildings at Lake View Country House. Beers are available at its nearby taproom and restaurant, the Good Sport.

Grasshopper

Unit F2, Langley Bridge Industrial Estate, Linkmel Road, Langley Mill, Derbyshire, NG16 3RZ
☎ (01773) 530224 ☎ 07968 818866
🌐 grasshopperbrewery.co.uk

Grasshopper commenced brewing in 2017 using a 10-barrel plant.

Knee High (OG 1041, ABV 3.8%)

Nymph (OG 1044, ABV 4.2%)

Cricket (OG 1046, ABV 4.5%)

Devil's Horse (OG 1049, ABV 4.8%)

Great British Breworks

The Brew House, Black Swan, 18 Birdgate, Pickering, North Yorkshire, YO18 7AL
🌐 blackswan-pickering.co.uk/breworks

Brewing started on a permanent basis in the rear yard of the Black Swan in 2016, using a 2.5-barrel plant. ♦

Great Corby SIBA

The Green, Great Corby, Cumbria, CA4 8LT
☎ (01228) 560899 🌐 greatcorbybrewing.co.uk

Established in 2009 with a bespoke 10-barrel plant, the brewery was situated in a building at the heart of the village, previously the farriers shop from 1833. The brewery was purchased by American brewer Alltech in 2015 and moved across the village green to a former honey factory in 2017. The former brewing site at the Forge is to become a visitor centre. ‼♦

Corby Ale (OG 1038, ABV 3.8%)
A fruity session beer with sweetness leading to gentle bitterness in the aftertaste.

Corby APA (ABV 4%)
A light-bodied, amber-coloured American-style pale ale, strong on grapefruit and stone fruit flavours with a hint of vanilla in the aroma.

Corby Blonde (OG 1042, ABV 4%)
Melon fruity hoppiness gives a light, refreshing drink.

Lakeland Summit (OG 1040, ABV 4%)

Corby Stout (OG 1044, ABV 4.5%)
Fruity aroma, sweet roast middle and dry finish.

Corby Fox (OG 1048, ABV 4.6%)
A pleasing brown-coloured ale with a slight bitter finish.

Great Heck SIBA

Harwinn House, Main Street, Great Heck, North Yorkshire, DN14 0BQ
☎ (01977) 661430 ☎ 07723 381002
🌐 greatheckbrewery.co.uk

Great Heck began production in 2008 in a converted slaughterhouse. The brewery moved across the road to a converted cottage in 2012 and now produces its regular beers on a 15-barrel plant with capacity for 45 barrels per week. ‼♦

Chopper (OG 1037, ABV 3.8%)
Pale-coloured session beer with a hoppy hit.

Dave (OG 1038, ABV 3.9%)
A dark-coloured session bitter with a roasty taste.

Mercy (OG 1039, ABV 3.9%)

Navigator (OG 1039, ABV 3.9%)
Traditional, mahogany-coloured session bitter with subtle exotic hop aromas.

Trafalgar (ABV 4%)

Blonde (OG 1043, ABV 4.3%)
A well-balanced blonde ale with a zesty finish.

Voodoo Mild (OG 1043, ABV 4.3%)
Rich, black-coloured mild bursting with flavour from the roasted malts.

Christopher (OG 1043, ABV 4.5%)
A clean-drinking, dry, moderately-bittered pale ale with a big hop aroma.

Divine Intervention (ABV 4.5%)

Hapi (ABV 4.5%)

Mount Hood (OG 1043, ABV 4.5%)

Amish Mash (OG 1045, ABV 4.7%)
A cloudy wheat beer with yeasty notes of banana and clove and fruity hop flavours.

Treasure IPA (OG 1045, ABV 4.8%)
Smooth, golden-coloured IPA with moderate bitterness and distinctive tropical fruit notes.

Shankar IPA (OG 1055, ABV 5.9%)
A pale-coloured, hoppy, fruity beer with a clean, zesty finish.

Black Jesus (OG 1060, ABV 6.5%)

Yakima IPA (OG 1070, ABV 7.4%)
Deep golden in colour and low in bitterness balanced by luscious fruity hop flavours and aromas.

Great Newsome SIBA

Great Newsome Farm, South Frodingham, East Yorkshire, HU12 0NR
☎ (01964) 612201 🌐 greatnewsomebrewery.co.uk

Nestled in the Holderness countryside, Great Newsome began brewing in 2007 in renovated farm buildings. A range of beers is now brewed using barley from the farm and brewing can be seen from a viewing area. Expansion into another farm building increased capacity in 2018. Beer is distributed throughout the UK and overseas. ‼ ♦

Sleck Dust (OG 1037, ABV 3.8%)
Straw-coloured, refreshingly bitter session beer with floral aroma and subtle dry finish.

Ploughman's Pride (OG 1042, ABV 4.2%)
Easy-drinking, moderately-bittered ale, deep chestnut in colour. Malty with liquorice tones.

Pricky Back Otchan (OG 1042, ABV 4.2%)
Golden-coloured bitter with nutty, toffee aroma. Complex with mild citrus notes.

Frothingham Best (OG 1042, ABV 4.3%)
Dark amber-coloured best bitter. Fruit and nut aroma with hop resin and peach notes leading to a sweetish finish.

Holderness Dark (OG 1042, ABV 4.3%)
Dark-coloured, strong mild. Chocolate malt and hazelnut notes with a hint of sweetness in a long, satisfying finish.

Jem's Stout (OG 1044, ABV 4.3%)
Dark-coloured, smooth beer with smoky, roasted malt flavours and aroma.

Liquorice Lads Stout (OG 1044, ABV 4.3%)
Black-coloured stout flavoured by real liquorice.

Great North Eastern SIBA

Contact House, Wellington Road, Dunston, Gateshead, NE11 9HS
☎ (0191) 447 4462 ☎ 07514 787483 🌐 gnebco.com

Brewing began in 2016 on a 10-barrel plant. In 2017 the brewery expanded into the adjacent premises and a tap and shop has now opened, with an events space for live entertainment. Beers are available throughout the North-east. ♦

Claspers Citra Blonde (OG 1038, ABV 3.8%)
A light pale ale with strong citrus notes.

Gold (OG 1039, ABV 4%)
A single-hopped golden ale with pungent hop flavours.

Rivet Catcher (OG 1039, ABV 4%)
A light, smooth golden-coloured bitter with subtle fruity hops.

Joblings Swinging Gibbet (OG 1041, ABV 4.1%)
A copper-coloured, well-balanced beer with a good hop aroma and fruity finish.

Minnikins Stout (OG 1045, ABV 4.6%)
A rich, creamy stout with a long, lingering liquorice and pale chocolate finish.

Westoe IPA (OG 1044.5, ABV 4.6%)
A pale golden ale with a soft malt character and refreshingly complex hop aroma.

Great Oakley SIBA

Ark Farm, High Street South, Tiffield, Northamptonshire, NN12 8AB
☎ (01327) 351759 🌐 greatoakleybrewery.co.uk

Award-winning brewery established in 2005 in Great Oakley, relocating to Tiffield in 2012. It is run by Guy Jenkins who took over in 2017. More than 60 outlets are supplied, including the George, Tiffield, which is the brewery tap. ‼ ♦ RAIB

Welland Valley Mild (OG 1037, ABV 3.6%)

Egret (OG 1038, ABV 3.8%)

Wagtail (OG 1040, ABV 3.9%)

Wot's Occurring (OG 1040, ABV 3.9%)
A golden-coloured session bitter with a subtle hop finish.

Tiffield Thunderbolt (OG 1043, ABV 4.2%)

Harpers (OG 1044, ABV 4.3%)
Traditional mid-brown-coloured bitter with a malty taste and slight hints of chocolate and citrus in the finish.

Gobble (OG 1045, ABV 4.5%)
Straw-coloured with a pleasant hop aftertaste.

Delapre Dark (OG 1047, ABV 4.6%)
A dark-coloured, full-bodied ale made from five different malts.

Abbey Stout (OG 1051, ABV 5%)

Tailshaker (OG 1051, ABV 5%)

Great Orme SIBA

Builder Street, Llandudno, LL30 1DR
☎ (01492) 330680 🌐 greatormebrewery.co.uk

Great Orme began brewing in 2005 on a five-barrel plant, situated in the Conwy Valley. It moved to larger premises in the Victorian seaside town of Llandudno, within sight of the Great Orme, from which the brewery takes its name. It now brews on an 18-barrel plant. Around 100 outlets are supplied. ‼ ♦

Welsh Gold (OG 1036, ABV 3.6%)
A pale brown-coloured malty session bitter with a dry taste. Some hoppy flavours develop in the bitter aftertaste.

Welsh Black (OG 1042, ABV 4%)
Smooth-tasting, dark-coloured beer with roast coffee notes in aroma and taste. Sweetish in flavour and having some characteristics of a mild ale with hoppiness also present in the aftertaste.

Celtica (OG 1045, ABV 4.5%) ◈
Yellow in colour with a zesty taste full of citrus fruit flavours. Some initial sweetness followed by peppery hops and a bitter finish.

Red Dragon (OG 1045, ABV 4.5%) ◈
A light brown-coloured best bitter with a sweet malty taste accompanied by faint fruit notes and peppery hops in the finish.

Ynys Mon (OG 1045, ABV 4.5%) ◈
A copper-coloured malty best bitter with a smooth, sweetish taste and satisfying finish

Great Western SIBA

Stream Bakery, Bristol Road, Hambrook, Bristol, BS16 1RF
☎ (0117) 957 2842 🌐 gwbrewery.co.uk

Great Western is a 12-barrel brewery set up in 2008 by Kevin Stone in a former bakery. The property has been renovated resulting in a bespoke showpiece brewery retaining many of the building's original features. The brewery owns a single pub – the Rising Sun, Frampton Cotterell – and 500 outlets are supplied. !! ♦

HPA (OG 1040, ABV 4%) ◈
Hoppy, yellow-coloured bitter with zesty citrus flavours and hints of tropical fruit, leading to a moreish bittersweet finish.

Maiden Voyage (OG 1040, ABV 4%) ◈
An amber-coloured bitter with a light aroma of malt and fruit, which continues to the palate before leading to a strong bitter finish.

Bees Knees (OG 1041, ABV 4.2%) ◈
Golden-coloured beer, bitter with malt nose and flavour and some honey. Lasting astringent bitter aftertaste.

Exhibitionist (OG 1044, ABV 4.5%)
Deep copper-coloured beer, full-bodied with a fruity taste.

Classic Gold (OG 1044, ABV 4.6%) ◈
Golden ale with subtle aromas of pale malt and fruits. Citrus fruits with balanced hop and malt character with a lingering bitter finish.

Old Higby (OG 1045, ABV 4.8%) ◈
Full-bodied, malty bitter with roast notes on the nose. Hints of fruit flavour give way to a bitter hop finish with some astringency throughout.

Moose River (OG 1047, ABV 5%) ◈
Light citrus aroma, delicate hop taste with long-lasting bitter finish.

Great Yorkshire

Cropton, North Yorkshire, YO18 8HH
☎ (01751) 417330
🌐 thegreatyorkshirebrewery.co.uk

In 2012 Cropton Brewery rebranded as Great Yorkshire for its export markets. Beers are available throughout Yorkshire and nationally through wholesalers. !! ♦ RAIB

Yorkshire Pale (OG 1038, ABV 3.8%)
A light, smooth pale ale with flavours of mango and pineapple.

Yorkshire Classic (OG 1043.5, ABV 4%)
Chestnut-coloured beer with a smooth, malty taste balanced with complex biscuity flavours.

Yorkshire Golden (OG 1045, ABV 4.2%)
A refreshing, golden-coloured beer with hints of caramel and a honey-like sweetness.

Yorkshire Blackout (OG 1051, ABV 5%)
An old-style porter with chocolate and vanilla flavours.

Green Dragon

Green Dragon, 29 Broad Street, Bungay, Suffolk, NR35 1EF
☎ (01986) 892681

The Green Dragon pub was purchased in 1991 and the rear converted to a brewery. In 1994 the plant was expanded and moved to a converted barn. The doubling of capacity allowed the production of a larger range of ales. !! ♦

Chaucer Ale (OG 1037, ABV 3.8%)

Gold (OG 1045, ABV 4.4%)

Bridge Street Bitter (OG 1045, ABV 4.5%)

Strong Mild (OG 1054, ABV 5.5%)
A ruby-coloured ale. Plum and dark chocolate on the nose with a rich, smooth taste full of dark malt notes.

Green Duck SIBA

Unit 13, Gainsborough Trading Estate, Rufford Road, Stourbridge, West Midlands, DY9 7ND
☎ (01384) 377666 🌐 greenduckbrewery.co.uk

Green Duck began brewing in 2012 and relocated to its present site in Stourbridge in 2013. Experimental beers are brewed alongside a core range. The brewery has an on-site brewery tap, the Badelynge Bar, where the brewing equipment is visible through a glass partition. Private events and quarterly beer festivals are hosted. !! ♦

Duck & Cover (OG 1041, ABV 4%) ◈
Pale gold in colour with a tropical aroma derived from Mosaic hops. Refreshing with a dry pine and resin aftertaste.

Duck Blonde (OG 1042, ABV 4.2%) ◈
Gold-coloured with a sharp, fruity aroma. Lots of passion fruit in the taste. Aftertaste is balanced with fruit sweetness and hops.

Sitting Duck (OG 1045, ABV 4.5%)
A hoppy and straw-like pale ale.

Duck Under (OG 1050, ABV 5%)
A strong malt backbone with an intense hop flavour delivers a well-balanced drink with a bitter citrus finish.

Duck & Dive (OG 1056, ABV 5.9%) ◈
Amber-coloured with a fruity aroma. Citrus hop and spicy orange peel sweetness in the taste with a long bitter finish.

Green Jack SIBA

Argyle Place, Love Road, Lowestoft, Suffolk, NR32 2NZ
☎ (01502) 562863 ☎ 07902 219459
🌐 green-jack.com

After 10 years at Oulton Broad, Green Jack moved to the Triangle Tavern, Lowestoft in 2003 and then to a nearby 35-barrel plant in 2009. One pub is owned and more than 150 outlets supplied. !! ♦ RAIB

Golden Best (OG 1037, ABV 3.8%)

Orange Wheat Beer (OG 1041, ABV 4.2%)
Marmalade aroma with a hint of hops, leading to a well-balanced blend of sweetness, hops and citrus with a malt background. Mixed fruit flavours in the aftertaste.

Trawlerboys Best Bitter (OG 1045, ABV 4.6%)
Tawny-coloured beer with aroma of apple, sultana and malt plus hints of caramel and hops. Rich fig and plum base with malt and roast overtones. Strong finish with a sticky mouthfeel.

Lurcher Stout (OG 1046, ABV 4.8%)
Pleasant malt, roast and fruit aromas. Blackberry, raisin and port flavours. Long, dry bitter roast finish.

Rising Sun (OG 1047, ABV 4.8%)

Red Herring (OG 1048, ABV 5%)

Gone Fishing ESB (OG 1052, ABV 5.5%)

Mahseer IPA (OG 1056, ABV 5.8%)

Ripper Tripel (OG 1074, ABV 8.5%)

Baltic Trader Export Stout (OG 1092, ABV 10.5%)

Green Mill SIBA

Harewood Arms, 2 Market Street, Broadbottom, SK14 6AX ☎ 07967 656887 greenmillbrewery.com

Green Mill started brewing in 2007 on a 2.5-barrel plant and moved in 2010 to the Cask & Feather in Rochdale. The brewery relocated again in 2013 to the Harewood Arms in Broadbottom. A number of occasional beers are brewed. Around 40 outlets are supplied. ♦

Gold (OG 1035, ABV 3.6%)

Chief (OG 1041, ABV 4.2%)

Citrus Snap (OG 1040, ABV 4.2%)
A copper-coloured bitter with citrus notes.

Old Git (OG 1040, ABV 4.2%)
A complex, well-hopped pale ale.

Talisman (OG 1040, ABV 4.2%)
A straw-coloured golden ale with tropical fruit notes.

Flavia (OG 1042, ABV 4.5%)
A blonde beer with a fresh hop aroma and a clean, dry finish.

Northern Lights (OG 1045, ABV 4.5%)

Big Chief (OG 1052, ABV 5.5%)

Greene King

Westgate Brewery, Westgate Street, Bury St Edmunds, Suffolk, IP33 1QT ☎ (01284) 763222 greeneking.co.uk

Greene King has been brewing in the market town of Bury St Edmunds since 1799. It brews its beers using water drawn from artesian chalk wells below its brewhouse as well as local East Anglia malt. !! ♦ RAIB

XX Mild (OG 1035, ABV 3%)
A dark mild with a sweet and roast flavour.

IPA (OG 1036, ABV 3.6%)
Hop-infused fruit cake aromas. Complex flavours of malt, caramel and hop with both sweetness and bitterness. A lingering mellow aftertaste with blackberries.

London Glory (OG 1041.1, ABV 4%)
Full-flavoured, rich and fruity.

IPA Gold (OG 1041, ABV 4.1%)
A golden ale with a blend of tropical fruits, mango and spicy notes.

St Edmunds (OG 1038.6, ABV 4.2%)
A golden-coloured beer with an intense hop aroma and fruity character.

Abbot (OG 1049, ABV 5%)
Strong malt, toffee and caramel aromas. Rich, malty, caramel flavours with vine fruit and a little hop bite. Heavy, sweet finish with a subtle hint of bitterness in the aftertaste.

IPA Reserve (OG 1055.5, ABV 5.4%)
A full-bodied, amber-coloured ale. Grapefruit and orange citrus tones combine with the floral and herbal hop notes and lead to a dry bitter finish.

Mighty Moose (ABV 5.6%)

Brewed for the Taylor Walker pub chain:

1730 (ABV 4%)

Brewed under the Hardys & Hansons brand name:

Bitter (OG 1038, ABV 3.9%)
A balance of sweetness and bitterness that combines with a subtle hop character. A distinctive beer with a full finish.

Olde Trip (OG 1043, ABV 4.3%)
A rich toffee flavoured beer with a fruity character and a clean, bitter finish.

Brewed under the Morland brand name:

Original Bitter (OG 1039, ABV 4%)
A subtle malt and fruit character and a pronounced bitter finish.

Old Golden Hen (OG 1038.6, ABV 4.1%)
Light golden-coloured beer brewed with tropical fruit notes.

Old Speckled Hen (OG 1045, ABV 4.5%)
Smooth, malty and fruity with a short finish.

Brewed under the Ruddles brand name:

Best Bitter (OG 1037, ABV 3.7%)
An amber/brown-coloured beer, strong on bitterness but with some initial sweetness, fruit and subtle, distinctive hop. Dryness lingers in the aftertaste.

County (OG 1043, ABV 4.3%)
Sweet, malty and bitter with a dry and bitter aftertaste.

Brewed under the Tolly Cobbold brand name:

English Ale (OG 1033.6, ABV 2.8%)
Amber-coloured ale brewed using a complex mix of hops to offer balanced bitterness with strong tropical notes.

Greenfield SIBA

Unit 8, Waterside Mills, Greenfield, OL3 7NH ☎ (01457) 879789 ☎ 07716 239883 greenfieldbrewery.co.uk

Greenfield was launched in 2002 and is situated in an old spinning mill next to the River Chew on the edge of the Peak District National Park. Spring water from the National Park is used for brewing. It is open to the public and supplies beer to more than 100 outlets. New owner Tony Pye took over in 2017. !! ♦

THE BREWERIES

Black 5 (OG 1041, ABV 4%)

Silver Owl (OG 1042, ABV 4%)
An amber-coloured beer with aromas of citrus fruits and hints of vanilla.

Thirst Born (OG 1041, ABV 4.1%)
Floral citrus aroma with malt and hops. Citrus, peach and floral malt flavours.

Dobcross Bitter (OG 1041, ABV 4.2%)
A full-bodied, amber-coloured beer with lemon flavours and a dry finish.

Copper Caskade (OG 1042, ABV 4.3%)
Full-bodied, single hop, copper-coloured beer with citrus and fruit tones in the finish.

Genesis (OG 1046, ABV 4.6%)

Greenodd

Ship Inn, Main Street, Greenodd, Cumbria, LA12 7QZ ☎ 07782 655294
greenoddbrewery@yahoo.co.uk

Established in 2010 at the Ship Inn on a two-barrel plant. The majority of production goes to the Ship with the remainder going to the local free trade. ‼♦

Greg's

Dambusters Inn, 23 High Street, Scampton, Lincolnshire, LN1 2SD
☎ (01522) 730123

Greg's is a microbrewery launched in 2013 on the premises of the Dambusters Inn. ♦

Grey Friars

Featherstone Hall Farm, New Road, Featherstone, Staffordshire, WV10 7NW
☎ (01785) 840093 ☎ 07966 361443

Office: 17 Cranbrooks, Wheaton Aston, ST19 9PZ
greyfriarsbrewery.co.uk

Established in 2014 and using equipment originally from Upham Brewery in Hampshire, the three-barrel plant is installed in a barn, formerly used as a snooker room and which still contains the original wood panelling. Brewing is currently suspended.

Grey Trees SIBA

Unit 5-6, Gasworks Road, Aberaman, CF44 6RS
☎ (01685) 267077 greytreesbrewing.com

Grey Trees began brewing at the Red Cow Inn in 2011 on the outskirts of Aberdare and relocated to its present location in 2013, upgrading to a 10-barrel plant. It supplies an increasing number of local outlets, as well as those in other parts of South Wales. There are a number of open nights throughout the year (see website for details). ‼ ♦ RAIB

Caradogs (OG 1038, ABV 3.9%)
Copper in colour with a crisp flavour and dry finish.

Black Road Stout (OG 1040, ABV 4%)
A dark-coloured, smooth stout with delicate roasted flavours and a bittersweet aftertaste.

Diggers Gold (OG 1040, ABV 4%)
A modern golden ale with fresh citrus aromas and a subtle bitterness.

Drummer Boy (OG 1042, ABV 4.2%)

Jagar Weizen (OG 1046, ABV 4.5%)
A Bavarian-style wheat beer with banana and clove notes.

Valley Porter (OG 1046, ABV 4.6%)
Warming and rich with notes of dark fruits, coffee, chocolate and hazelnuts.

JPR Pale (OG 1046, ABV 4.7%)

Afghan Pale (OG 1054, ABV 5.4%)

Greyhound SIBA

Watershed, Smock Alley, West Chiltington, West Sussex, RH20 2QX ☎ 07973 625510
greyhoundbrewery.co.uk

Established in 2015 by husband-and-wife team Nick and Sarah Allen, Greyhound is a 7.5-barrel brewery. In 2017 the brewery took over production of Ballard's Brewery beers, and continue to make its traditional ales alongside the Greyhound range. There are plans to open a brewery tap and expand to a new site. ‼♦RAIB

Good Ordinary Bitter (OG 1038, ABV 3.8%)
A classic session bitter with a nutty flavour and subtle bitterness.

Blonde Bird (OG 1039, ABV 3.9%)
A refreshing pale ale with a well-rounded, dry finish and subtle, fresh lemon aroma.

Amber Eyes (OG 1040, ABV 4.2%)
A rich, well-balanced, golden-coloured ale with complex floral aromas, rounded light biscuit malt flavours and a bitter finish.

B-46 (OG 1044, ABV 4.6%)
A rich, dark amber-coloured ale with a good balance of warm biscuity malt flavours moving towards toast and blackberry. A clean, hoppy finish.

White Bird (ABV 5.2%)
A cloudy, light straw-coloured beer with hints of spice and bitter orange.

Brewed under the Ballard's Brewery name:

Best Bitter (ABV 4.2%)
Amber-coloured ale with a malty aroma. A good balance of fruit and malt in the flavour gives way to a dry, hoppy aftertaste.

Nyewood Gold (ABV 5%)
Bronze-coloured premium ale with malty barley sugar and spicy hop aromas. A smooth, creamy flavour with soft fruits throughout and a balanced finish.

Gribble

Gribble Inn, Oving, West Sussex, PO20 2BP
☎ (01243) 786893 gribbleinn.co.uk

Established in 1980 using a five-barrel plant, the Gribble Brewery is the longest-serving brewpub in the Sussex area, independently owned and run by the licensees since 2005. A number of local outlets are supplied. ♦

Sussex Quadhopper (OG 1043, ABV 4%)
A full-flavoured beer with lots of hops.

Ale (OG 1041, ABV 4.1%)

Fuzzy Duck (OG 1045, ABV 4.3%)

Reg's Tipple (OG 1050, ABV 4.5%)
A smooth, nutty flavour with a pleasant aftertaste.

Plucking Pheasant (OG 1052, ABV 5.2%)

Pig's Ear (OG 1058, ABV 6%)

Wobbler (OG 1058, ABV 7.2%)

Griffin

See Freestyle

Gritchie (NEW)

Ashgrove Farm, Ashmore, Wiltshire, SP5 5AW
☎ (01747) 828996 🌐 gritchiebrewingcompany.co.uk

⊗ Brewing commenced in 2017 in converted farm buildings on the Ashcombe Estate. A 20-barrel brew plant is used with estate-grown barley and water from an on-site borehole. Local outlets are supplied. ‼

English Lore (OG 1040, ABV 4%)
Pale-coloured beer with caramel and slight citrus flavours. Floral, honey and orange marmalade hop notes.

GT

Unit 5, The Old Aerodrome, Chivenor Business Park, Braunton, Devon, EX31 4AY
☎ (01271) 267420 ☎ 07909 515170 🌐 gtales.co.uk

⊗ GT Ales was established in Barnstaple in 2013, producing only bottle-conditioned beers, before relocating to larger premises in Braunton in 2015. All five regular award-winning ales are now available in cask. More than 30 local outlets are supplied. ‼ ♦ RAIB

Thirst of Many (OG 1043, ABV 4.2%)
Amber-coloured best bitter with a slight caramel and fruity taste, good medium hop finish and a slight malty aftertaste.

North Coast IPA (OG 1045, ABV 4.3%)
American-style IPA with a strong, fruity aroma, sweet taste and hints of tropical fruits.

Blonde Ambition (OG 1044, ABV 4.5%)
Pale gold in colour with good hop and citrus/gooseberry notes and a floral aroma.

Dark Horse (OG 1048, ABV 4.5%)
Smooth, slightly sweet mouthfeel. Fruity taste with hints of blackcurrant and a slight coffee bitterness in the finish.

Battleaxe (OG 1046, ABV 4.7%)
A red-coloured ale with a fruity aroma with apricot and peach notes. Some woody aromas with a fruity medium hop finish.

Crimson Rye'd (OG 1048, ABV 4.8%)
A red-coloured ale with a strong, fruity, malty taste and fruity hop finish.

Gun SIBA 👁

Hawthbush Farm, Gun Hill, East Sussex, TN21 0JY
☎ (01323) 700200 ☎ 07900 683355
🌐 gunbrewery.co.uk

⊗ Gun Brewery is located on a beautiful 140-acre organic mixed farm in the Sussex Weald. It generates much of its own power from a 15-kW solar array and heating comes from a wood-powered boiler. Spent grains keep the local livestock happy and all the water used for brewing comes from the brewery's own spring. More than 30 outlets are supplied. RAIB V

Scaramanga Extra Pale (OG 1038, ABV 3.9%)
A pale session ale with a hoppy finish.

Parabellum Milk Stout (OG 1057, ABV 4.1%)
A rich, jet black-coloured milk stout with well-balanced coffee, vanilla and chocolate notes and a full malt base.

Project Babylon Pale Ale (OG 1044, ABV 4.6%)
An American-style pale ale. Vibrant and refreshing with citrus notes and a dry finish on the palate.

Base Ejection Smoked Rye (OG 1046, ABV 4.7%)
A pale ale with a good balance of spiciness from the rye and subtle smokiness from the malts.

Velo Dog (OG 1051, ABV 5.5%)

Zamzama IPA (OG 1060, ABV 6.5%)
A modern IPA with a rounded malt body and an avalanche of hops.

Gun Dog SIBA

Unit 5b, Great Central Way, Woodford Halse, Northamptonshire, NN11 3PZ
☎ (01327) 264095 ☎ 07834 374751
🌐 gundogales.co.uk

Gun Dog is a family-run brewery established in 2012. A six-barrel plant is used to brew modern crafted ales with a nod to brewing traditions of the past. Beers are available in a number of pubs and shops locally. ‼ ♦ RAIB

Jack's Spaniels (OG 1038, ABV 3.8%)
A well-balanced, floral, refreshing blonde ale.

Scrum Dog (OG 1040, ABV 4%)
An amber-coloured beer with a taste of fruit and hops.

Booze Hound (OG 1042, ABV 4.2%)
A copper-coloured IPA with a slightly sweet taste and a hoppy bitter twist.

Lord Barker (OG 1042, ABV 4.2%)
Rich, dark-coloured, smooth stout with a chocolate nose, well-rounded taste in the mouth and a clean finish.

Bad to the Bone (OG 1045, ABV 4.5%)
A light brown-coloured bitter with a fruity nose, biscuit malt flavour and a bitter finish.

Yankee Poodle (OG 1047, ABV 4.7%)
A golden-coloured beer with a citrus hop aroma, citrus bitter flavour and a bitter finish.

Gwaun Valley

Kilkiffeth Farm, Pontfaen, SA65 9TP
☎ (01348) 881304 🌐 gwaunvalleybrewery.co.uk

Gwaun Valley began brewing in 2009 on a four-barrel plant in a converted granary. The brewery offers views of the Preseli Hills and has a campsite, a holiday cottage and pitches for five caravans. Folk music sessions are held every Saturday evening. Each year a bluegrass festival is held at the brewery over a July weekend. ‼

Farmhouse Ale (OG 1040, ABV 4%)
A malty ale with a smooth, balanced character.

Golden Bitter Ale (OG 1040, ABV 4%)
A smooth bitter ale with a strong, hoppy flavour and a crisp finish.

Light Ale (OG 1040, ABV 4%)
Refreshing, easy-drinking ale with citrus undertones and a clean finish.

St Davids Special (OG 1040, ABV 4%)
A light, fruity beer with a refreshingly citrus flavour.

Valley Brew (OG 1040, ABV 4.1%)
Double-hopped bitter ale with a mellow taste and balanced sweetness.

Blodwen (OG 1043, ABV 4.3%)
Creamy, full-bodied bitter, ruby red in colour with a hint of caramel.

Cascade (OG 1043, ABV 4.3%)
Refreshing, clear, hoppy pale ale.

Calon Lan (OG 1044, ABV 4.5%)
Rich and malty with a bittersweet aftertaste.

King of the Road (OG 1045, ABV 4.5%)
A full-bodied, smooth classic light chestnut-coloured ale with a well-balanced finish.

Pembrokeshire Best Bitter (OG 1045, ABV 4.5%)
A full-flavoured, malty bitter ale with a delightfully hoppy finish.

Pembrokeshire Pirates (ABV 4.5%)
A smooth, hoppy, mid chestnut-coloured ale with a nutty finish.

Gyle 59 SIBA

The Brewery, Sadborow Estate Yard, Thorncombe, Dorset, TA20 4PW
☎ (01297) 678990 ☎ 07508 691178 ⊕ gyle59.co.uk

⊗ Gyle 59 is a 10-barrel brewery that began commercial production in 2014. Bottling takes place on site with bottles being available by mail order. A brewery bar is open Saturdays by prior appointment. ‼ ♦ RAIB V

Take It Easy (OG 1029, ABV 2.5%)

Freedom Hiker (OG 1038, ABV 3.7%)

Thoroughbred (OG 1037, ABV 3.7%)
A pale-coloured session beer with a citrus flavour.

Legless Liz (ABV 3.8%)

Toujours (OG 1042, ABV 4%)

Vienna Session Lager (ABV 4.2%)

Brad's Coffee Stout (OG 1045, ABV 4.5%)
A gentle stout with a subtle coffee aroma and taste.

Caribbean Cocktail (OG 1042, ABV 4.5%)

Halcyon Daze (OG 1046.5, ABV 5%)

Pale & Bitter (OG 1046, ABV 5%)

IPA (OG 1050, ABV 5.3%)

Dorset Gipa (OG 1050, ABV 5.4%)
A ginger-infused IPA.

Dark & Bitter (OG 1054, ABV 5.8%)

Starstruck (OG 1060, ABV 6.6%)
A fruity porter enhanced by the addition of star anise.

The Favourite (OG 1060, ABV 6.6%)

Double IPA (OG 1063, ABV 7.3%)

Contract brewed for Lyme Regis Brewery:

Cobb (OG 1039, ABV 3.9%)
An amber/brown-coloured bitter with a full flavour and a fruity hop finish.

Lyme Gold (OG 1042, ABV 4.2%)
A pale ale, easy drinking with a refreshing citrus aroma.

Rebel (OG 1041, ABV 4.2%)
A light, ruby-coloured ale with a malted biscuit aroma and a pleasant fruity flavour.

Dorset Pearl (OG 1041, ABV 4.3%)
Traditional English pale ale. Crisp, floral and refreshing.

Town Mill Best (OG 1045, ABV 4.5%)
A reddish brown-coloured bitter with a fruit and nut flavour.

Black Ven (OG 1050, ABV 5%)
A dark brown-coloured porter with a pronounced depth of flavour enhanced by the blackcurrant fruitiness of the hops.

Revenge (OG 1052, ABV 5.3%)
A traditional IPA with a well-balanced hop and spiced fruit flavour.

Hackney SIBA

Arch 358, Laburnum Street, Haggerston, London, E2 8BB
☎ (020) 3489 9595 ⊕ hackneybrewery.co.uk

⊗ Founded in 2011, Hackney Brewery is the oldest brewery in the area. Weekly cask-conditioned specials are available locally. RAIB

Golden Ale (OG 1041, ABV 4%) ◆
Perfumed hops, honey and fruit balanced by a dry, pleasant bitterness that builds as the fruit and hops diminish.

Best Bitter (OG 1044, ABV 4.4%) ◆
Pale brown-coloured beer with a sweet citrus aroma and full, smooth mouthfeel. Citrus and floral hops on the palate.

American Pale Ale (OG 1045, ABV 4.5%)

Hadham SIBA

Unit 6C, Hadham Industrial Estate, Church End, Little Hadham, Hertfordshire, SG11 2DY
☎ (01279) 771916 ☎ 07770 766376
⊕ hadhambrewery.co.uk

⊗ Hadham began brewing in 2015 with a 10-barrel plant, using its own spring water found on site. Outlets are supplied within a 25-mile radius of the brewery.

18ct Golden Ale (OG 1038, ABV 3.7%)
Golden ale with a light citrus and fresh hop character; crisp and lightly bitter with some sweetness developing.

First Brewed (OG 1042, ABV 4%)
Reddish-coloured best bitter. Fruity, bitter body with caramel notes and a full finish.

Hadrian Border SIBA

Unit 5, The Preserving Works, Newburn Industrial Estate, Shelley Road, Newburn, NE15 9RT
☎ (0191) 264 9000 ⊕ hadrian-border-brewery.co.uk

Based in Newburn near Newcastle-upon-Tyne using a 40-barrel plant, the brewery can produce up to 200 barrels per week. Beer is delivered directly to the area between Edinburgh, North Yorkshire, Carlisle and the East Coast. Beers are also available nationally through wholesalers. A three-barrel plant is used for experimental craft brews. !! ♦ RAIB GF

Tyneside Blonde (OG 1039, ABV 3.9%)
Refreshing blonde ale with zesty notes and a clean, fruity finish.

Farne Island Pale Ale (OG 1040, ABV 4%)
A copper-coloured bitter with a refreshing malt/hop balance.

Secret Kingdom (OG 1042, ABV 4.3%)
Dark-coloured, rich and full-bodied, slightly roasted with a malty palate ending with a pleasant bitterness.

Coast to Coast (OG 1043, ABV 4.4%)
Light amber-coloured and hoppy beer with a good malt balance.

Reiver's IPA (OG 1043, ABV 4.4%)
Golden-coloured bitter with a clean citrus palate and aroma with subtle malt flavours breaking through at the end.

Northumbrian Gold (OG 1044, ABV 4.5%)
Light golden-coloured ale with a biscuit malt flavour countered with floral and aromatic hops.

Grainger Ale (OG 1045, ABV 4.6%)
A pale-coloured ale, well-balanced with a refreshing bitter finish.

Ouseburn Porter (OG 1052, ABV 5.2%)
Traditional robust porter, made with chocolate and black malt. Distinct bitter coffee finish.

Contract brewed for Black Storm Brewery:

Bitter (ABV 4.3%)

Porter (ABV 5.2%)

IPA (ABV 5.5%)

Hafod

Old Gas Works, Gas Lane, Mold, CH7 1UR ☎ (01352) 750765 ☎ 07901 386638 🌐 welshbeer.com

Hafod began brewing in 2011 on a small scale and moved to new premises in 2014, retaining the original kit for low volume brewing. A number of speciality beers using ingredients from the local upland areas and heathlands are also produced on a limited basis. !! ♦ RAIB

Sunrise (OG 1037, ABV 3.8%)
A pale and refreshing golden ale with citrus fruit bitterness evident throughout and a mouthwatering astringent finish.

Hopper (OG 1040.5, ABV 4.3%)
A full-flavoured session bitter with a mouthwatering taste of peppery hops and a lasting dry finish.

Moel Fenlli (OG 1045, ABV 4.4%)
A speciality golden ale made with heather honey.

Landmark (OG 1046, ABV 4.6%)
Copper-coloured and malty with a juicy mouthfeel. Fruit and faint roast flavours also feature in the taste.

Clwydian Black (OG 1047, ABV 4.7%)
A stout with sweet chocolate and coffee notes.

Big Red (OG 1055, ABV 5.5%)

Empyre (OG 1061, ABV 6.1%)

Hairy Brewers

Venture Garage, Belper Road, Holbrook, Derbyshire, DE56 0SX ☎ 07415 209489 🌐 hairybrewersales.co.uk

Hairy Brewers Ales was established in 2015, with the first brew being released in 2016. The eight-barrel plant was born from two bearded friends and their love for fine ale, with six years of experience already in the brewing trade. Beers are available in the Derbyshire area with an increasing demand further afield.

Hair of the Dog (ABV 3.8%)
Traditional English bitter with a good balance of malt and hops. Full-bodied and rich on the palate, the malt gives a gentle caramel aroma with a spiced aromatic bitter finish.

Blonde Bombshell (ABV 4.3%)
Well-balanced, pale straw-coloured ale. Floral aroma leading to a citrus taste blast and a thirst-quenching bitter finish.

Belper Beast Cherry Porter (ABV 4.8%)

Fear the Beard (ABV 5%)
A rich, golden-coloured ale with a good balance of malt and hops. A gentle floral aroma and a soft, smooth sweetness lead to a bittersweet finish.

Devils Whiskers (ABV 5.2%)

Dead Beard IPA (ABV 5.5%)
Rich golden ale with a grapefruit, mango aroma and a soft, smooth sweetness leading to a crisp, dry, hoppy bitter grapefruit finish.

Hair Raiser IPA (ABV 7.3%)

Hal's (NEW)

22a Woodmancote, Dursley, Gloucestershire, GL11 4AF ☎ 07765 890946 🌐 halsales.uk

Hal's is a one-barrel microbrewery established in Dursley in 2016, producing a number of small-batch beers. ♦

HHH (ABV 3.6%)

Mick's Mild (ABV 3.8%)

What Sony's Avin (ABV 4.2%)

Gold (ABV 4.4%)
A classic golden ale with a slightly sweet finish.

Blackjack (ABV 4.5%)
A blackcurrant and vanilla stout.

New Inn Chestnut Bitter (ABV 4.6%)
A well-balanced, malty, brown-coloured ale.

Hale (NEW)

39a Markfield Road, Tottenham Hale, London, N15 4QA 🌐 hale.beer

Hale is a small batch brewery inside a shipping container, originally the home of Affinity Brewing (qv). No real ale.

Hale's

See Grafton

Half Moon SIBA

Forge House, Main Street, Ellerton, East Yorkshire, YO42 4PB

☎ (01757) 288977 ☎ 07741 400508
halfmoonbrewery.co.uk

Established in 2013 by Tony and Jackie Rogers, the brewery is based in the original blacksmith's forge next to their house. A five-barrel plant is used. ♦

Dark Masquarade (OG 1040, ABV 3.6%)
Rich, warm and smoky ruby-coloured ale packed with dark chocolate and liquorice flavours.

Old Forge Bitter (OG 1040, ABV 3.8%)
Bright amber-coloured bitter with soft spiced lemon and honey flavours.

F'Hops Sake (OG 1039, ABV 3.9%)
Pale-coloured session bitter with a fruity and hoppy aftertaste.

Golden Chance (ABV 4.2%)
A golden-coloured bitter with a complex hoppy finish.

Robustus Lunum (OG 1045, ABV 5%)
A dark-coloured stout with espresso and treacle notes. Initial sweetness develops into a dark honeycomb flavour and a smoky bitter finish with a lingering touch of liquorice.

Lunar (OG 1047, ABV 5.5%)
A refreshing, golden-coloured bitter with an intense hop aroma, a fine malt flavour and hints of caramel followed by a floral hop aftertaste.

Contract brewed for Suddaby's:

Golden Chance (ABV 4.2%)

Halfpenny

Crown Inn, High Street, Lechlade, Gloucestershire, GL7 3AE
☎ (01367) 252198 halfpennybrewery.co.uk

Halfpenny was established in 2008 on a four-barrel plant at the Crown at Lechlade, visible in a glazed outbuilding. Beers are mainly brewed for the pub but some appear in the local free trade. Brewing is currently suspended. RAIB

Halifax Steam

The Conclave, Southedge Works, Brighouse Road, Hipperholme, West Yorkshire, HX3 8EF ☎ 07506 022504 halifax-steam.co.uk

Brewing since 1999, the five-barrel plant supplies only the brewery tap, the Cock o' the North. It is now reputedly the oldest brewery in Calderdale. A range of permanent beers and around 200 different rotating beers are brewed, including the only rice beers in the country. 10-12 Halifax Steam beers are available in the pub at any one time, plus occasional guests on a fair trade basis. ♦

Hall & Woodhouse (Badger) IFBB

Bournemouth Road, Blandford St Mary, Blandford Forum, Dorset, DT11 9LS
☎ (01258) 452141 hall-woodhouse.co.uk

Hall & Woodhouse has been brewing in the heart of the Dorset countryside since 1777. As one of the leading independent brewers in the UK, Hall & Woodhouse is well known for its range of award-winning ales brewed under the Badger brand and its estate of around 200 pubs across the south of England. The brewery, owned and run by the seventh generation of the Woodhouse family, brews with Dorset spring water filtered through the Cretaceous chalk downs and drawn-up 120 feet from its own wells. Badger cask ales are available exclusively in Hall & Woodhouse public houses. !! ♦

Badger Best Bitter (OG 1037, ABV 3.7%)
Well-balanced bitter with malt caramel sweetness and hop fruitiness.

Fursty Ferret (OG 1041.5, ABV 4.1%)
Easy-drinking best bitter with sweet bitterness that lingers into a dry aftertaste with a hint of orange.

Tanglefoot (OG 1047, ABV 4.9%)
Relatively sweet-tasting and deceptive, given its strength. Pale malt provides caramel overtones and a bittersweet finish.

Hambleton SIBA

Melmerby Green Road, Melmerby, North Yorkshire, HG4 5NB
☎ (01765) 640108 hambletonales.co.uk

Established in 1991 on the banks of the River Swale in the Vale of York, after several moves Hambleton now occupies purpose-built premises. Capacity is 100 barrels a week with a monthly special supplementing the core range. Village Brewer, Black Dog and Wharfe Brewery beers are contract brewed and a bottling line handles brands for other brewers. The King Billy, Ripon, is the brewery tap. !! ♦ GF

Session Pale (OG 1036, ABV 3.6%)
A pale-coloured bitter with a good balance of malty and refreshing citrus notes leading to a mellow, dry, tangy finish.

Stallion Amber (OG 1041, ABV 4.2%)
A premium bitter, moderately hoppy throughout and richly balanced in malt and fruit, developing a sound and robust bitterness, with earthy hops drying the aftertaste.

Stud Blonde (OG 1042.5, ABV 4.3%)
A strongly bitter beer with rich hop and fruit. It ends dry and spicy.

Nightmare Porter (OG 1050, ABV 5%)
Strong roast malts dominate but hoppiness rears out of this complex blend.

Contract brewed for Black Dog Brewery:

Whitby Abbey Ale (OG 1037.5, ABV 3.8%)

Schooner (OG 1041.5, ABV 4.2%)

Rhatas (OG 1045, ABV 4.6%)

Contract brewed for Village Brewer:

White Boar (OG 1037.5, ABV 3.8%)

Bull (OG 1039, ABV 4%)

Contract brewed for Wharfe Beers:

Verbeia (ABV 3.6%)

Tether Blond (ABV 4.1%)

Hamelsworde

41b Kirkby Road, Hemsworth, West Yorkshire, WF9 4BA ☎ 07530 669332 hamelsworde.co.uk

The brainchild of enthusiastic homebrewer Dan Jones, his beers were originally brewed using a 50-litre boiler in a converted garage. A one-barrel plant was installed in 2013, which has now been moved into a converted shop with a tap house at the front. ‼ ♦ RAIB

Spanish Stout (OG 1045, ABV 4.2%)
A traditional stout with strong roasted flavours and a sweet liquorice taste complemented by aniseed.

Haley's Comet (OG 1047, ABV 4.5%)
A fresh ale with a citrus aroma and taste.

Jumping Pirate (OG 1051, ABV 4.9%)
A light golden-coloured ale in a Bavarian style with floral, pine and citrus notes.

Colin Brown Ale (OG 1054, ABV 5.2%)
A deep amber/red-coloured ale. A fruity hop aroma leads on to a malty, nutty bittersweet flavour with a long, dry aftertaste.

Scalded Shoulder (OG 1054, ABV 5.2%)
A golden-coloured wheat beer with coriander and orange notes.

Cherokee America IPA (OG 1063, ABV 6%)
A copper-coloured IPA with a strong, fruity hop aroma.

Hammerpot SIBA

Unit 30, The Vinery, Arundel Road, Poling, West Sussex, BN18 9PY
☎ (01903) 883338 hammerpot-brewery.co.uk

Hammerpot started brewing in 2005 using a five-barrel plant, which was upgraded to 10 barrels in 2011. The brewery supplies as far as London and Southampton. ♦ RAIB V

Shooting Star (OG 1037, ABV 3.8%)
A chestnut-coloured bitter with malt, toffee, citrus and dark fruit flavours. A citrus/floral hop aroma with a rounded, balanced aftertaste.

Mosaic Pale (OG 1038, ABV 4.1%)
A crisp, hoppy, fruity pale ale with hints of lemon, peach, mango and pine.

Pale Ale (OG 1038, ABV 4.1%)
A light-bodied, golden-coloured, tangy pale ale with a balance of sweet malted barley and a full, fresh hop flavour.

Red Hunter (OG 1043, ABV 4.3%)
A dark ruby-coloured ale with a full-bodied, rich, sweet, slightly vinous malt character, lightly balanced with English hops.

Brighton Belle (OG 1044, ABV 4.6%)
An American-style pale ale with fresh floral hop notes, spicy orange, crisp grapefruit and a hint of caramel.

Bottle Wreck Porter (OG 1047, ABV 4.7%)
A traditional pitch black-coloured porter with coffee, chocolate and rich roast malt flavours.

Hammerton SIBA

Unit 8 & 9, Roman Way Industrial Estate, 149 Roman Way, Barnsbury, London, N7 8XH
☎ (020) 3302 5880 hammertonbrewery.co.uk

Hammerton began brewing in London in 1868. It ceased to brew in the late 1950s and the brewery was later demolished. In 2014, a member of the Hammerton family decided to resurrect the family name in brewing. A 15-barrel plant is used. RAIB

N1 (OG 1044, ABV 4.1%)
Refreshing, smooth pale ale. Honey, some citrus and pineapple flavours, fading in the finish where a spicy, hoppy bitterness builds.

Life on Mars (OG 1045, ABV 4.6%)
Ruby-coloured ale with roast, toffee and fruit aroma. Peppery hops, nutty, roasty flavour with dark bitter marmalade. Dry, lingering finish.

N7 (OG 1052, ABV 5.2%)
Cocoa throughout with a pleasant sweetness, balanced by a lingering dark-roast dryness and a raisin fruitiness. A trace of liquorice.

Pentonville Oyster Stout (OG 1057, ABV 5.3%)
Liquorice and fruit on the palate. Dry finish with a little dark roast character and a touch of caramelised fruit.

Hand SIBA

33 Upper St James's Street, Kemptown, Brighton, East Sussex, BN2 1JN ☎ 07508 814541
handbrewpub.com/brew

Founded in 1989, the brewery is the smallest commercially operating tower brewery in the world. Originally operating under the Kemptown Brewery name before being used as a gypsy brewery by Brighton Bier for four years. Now operating as the Hand Brew Co since 2016. Around 10 other outlets are supplied. ‼

Handley's

Willow Tree, Front Street, Willow Tree, Front Street, Nottinghamshire, NG24 2SA
willowtreebarnby.co.uk

Handley's began brewing in 2011 on a 0.5-barrel plant installed behind the Willow Tree pub. Beer is mostly sold in the pub, with at least two being on pump at all times, and can occasionally be found at local beer festivals. ♦

Handsome SIBA

Bowstone Bridge Garage, Bowston, Cumbria, LA8 9HD
☎ 0344 848 0888 handsomebrew.co.uk

Originally Houston Brewery in Renfrewshire, it was re-established as Handsome in 2016 in the Lake District. It is situated on the River Kent in an old MOT garage, formerly the blacksmith's for James Cropper's paper mills.

Handyman (NEW)

461 Smithdown Road, Liverpool, L15 3LJ
☎ (0151) 222 7422 handymansupermarket.co.uk

Handyman Brewery is based within the Handyman Supermarket. For years this was a hardware store but has now been refurbished into the Handyman Pub, which opened in 2017. Its 400-litre brew kit is situated on a mezzanine floor above the bar. ♦

Hanging Bat

c/o 133 Lothian Road, Edinburgh, EH3 9AB
☎ (0131) 229 0759
hangingbatbrewco.tumblr.com

Brewing began in 2012 from within the Hanging Bat bar using a 50-litre brew kit from the United States.

Hanging Tree (NEW)

Benleva Hotel, Kilmore Road, Drumnadrochit, IV63 6UH

Hanging Tree began brewing in 2017 using a two-barrel brew plant in an old bothy in the grounds of the Benleva Hotel. Named after the 400-year-old chestnut tree growing in the garden, which was used as a hanging tree. Beers are available in the pub and a few other local outlets.

Hanlons SIBA

Hill Farm, Half Moon Village, Devon, EX5 5AE
(01392) 851160 hanlonsbrewery.com

Hanlons, one of Devon's largest brewers since 2013, supply a range of award-winning ales nationwide. The purpose-built brewery also has a shop, bar and restaurant. !! ♦

Firefly (OG 1038, ABV 3.7%)
Malty and fruity light bitter. Hints of orange in the taste.

Dry Stout (OG 1043, ABV 4.2%)
A dark-coloured, malty, well-balanced stout with a dry, bitter finish and plenty of roast and fruit flavours up front.

Yellow Hammer (OG 1041, ABV 4.2%)
Golden ale dominated by hops and fruit throughout. Sweetness develops through to a lingering aftertaste.

Brewers Blend (OG 1045, ABV 4.5%)

Port Stout (OG 1048, ABV 4.8%)
Strong, black-coloured, speciality ale. Mild coffee and chocolate with fruity port notes.

Stormstay (OG 1050, ABV 5%)
Tawny-coloured and full-bodied. Caramel with hints of malt on the nose. Triumvirate of malt, caramel and hops develop into lingering bitterness.

Happy Valley

73 & Pizza, 73 Oxford Road, Macclesfield, SK11 8JG
(01625) 618360 happyvalleybrewery.co.uk

Happy Valley was established in 2010 using a 2.5-barrel plant located in Bollington. In 2018 the brewery was sold and relocated to Macclesfield. !! ♦

Harbour SIBA

Trekillick Farm, Kirland, Bodmin, Cornwall, PL30 5BB
(01208) 832131 07870 305063
harbourbrewing.com

Harbour is an innovative brewery founded on the outskirts of Bodmin in 2011. Brewed using local spring water, the regular beers are established in an increasing number of outlets. A new 30-barrel plant was installed in 2016. ♦

Light (OG 1037, ABV 3.7%)
Yellow-coloured golden ale with a citrus hop aroma. Dominant zesty citrus hops with some pineapple and pear drops. Long, hoppy finish.

Daymer Extra Pale (ABV 3.8%)

Amber (OG 1037.5, ABV 4%)
Pale brown-coloured bitter with a floral hop aroma and malt. Biscuit malt throughout with apple, peach and plum, balanced by hops.

Cornish Bitter (ABV 4%)

New Zealand Gold (ABV 4.2%)
Golden ale with a light hop nose. Strong pine needle hop flavour. Bitter, sweet and dry throughout.

Ellensberg (ABV 4.3%)
Amber-coloured golden ale with a powerful citrus aroma. Strong grapefruit citrus hop flavour which fades to leave a long, bitter finish.

Session IPA (OG 1043, ABV 4.3%)

India Brown Ale (OG 1049, ABV 4.9%)
Smooth, copper-coloured strong bitter. Heavy body and balanced sweet malt and bitter hop flavour, with plums, prunes and some butterscotch.

IPA (OG 1048.5, ABV 5%)
Amber-coloured IPA with powerful citrus hop aroma and taste. Marmalade, red grapefruit and orange flavours with assertive bitterness.

Cascadia (ABV 5.2%)

Light No. 2 (ABV 5.2%)

Antipodean IPA (ABV 5.5%)

Little Rock IPA (ABV 5.5%)

Porter (OG 1055, ABV 5.5%)
Smooth, creamy, black-coloured porter with roast malt aroma. Malty, smoky and sweet followed by a bitter tang. Sweet finish.

Pale (OG 1059, ABV 6%)
Golden ale with powerful citrus hop aroma. Intense citrus hop flavour with marmalade, orange and bitterness. Hoppy, slightly dry finish.

Harbwr Tenby SIBA

Sargeants Lane, St Julian Street, Tenby, SA70 7BU
(01834) 845797 harbwr.wales

Brewing commenced in 2015 on a five-barrel plant in an outbuilding of the Buccaneer Inn, Tenby. Beers are available in the pub, at the nearby Hope & Anchor and further afield. A mezzanine bar area is available for tastings, tapas and tours. !! ♦

MV Enterprise (OG 1040, ABV 4%)
A citrus pale ale with spicy herbal bitterness finished with a floral, zesty aroma.

North Star (OG 1042, ABV 4.2%)
Smooth, malty, amber-coloured ale blending herbal bitterness and finishing with a spicy blackcurrant and lemon aroma.

Caldey Lollipop (OG 1044, ABV 4.5%)
Hoppy, golden-coloured IPA with hints of pine and grapefruit, blended with hop aromas.

RFA Sir Galahad (OG 1046, ABV 4.6%)
A complex malt character with a rich ruby red colour. Cedar, grapefruit and floral hop aromas.

Harby

Bottle & Glass, 5 High Street, Harby, Nottinghamshire, NG23 7EB
(01522) 703438
email@bottleandglassharby.com

Harby Brewstore is a four-barrel malt extract brewery established in 2015 and located at the Bottle & Glass in Harby. Most output goes to the three pubs in the small Wig & Mitre pub group; the

Wig & Mitre, Lincoln, Caunton Beck, Caunton and the Bottle & Glass itself.

Hardys & Hansons

See Greene King

Haresfoot SIBA

Global Infusion Court, Nashleigh Hill, Chesham, Buckinghamshire, HP5 3FE
☎ (01494) 790783 🌐 haresfoot.com

Established in Berkhamsted in 2014, the move to the current site in 2017 brought brewing back to the town of Chesham after an absence of 60 years. As well as the regular beers, a range of short run, limited edition beers under the Crafty Hare brand are brewed using a dual-channel 12- and 2.5-barrel plant. Beers can be found across the Chiltern area and London. !! ♦

Sundial Golden Ale (OG 1038, ABV 3.8%)
A refreshing, light golden ale with generous late hopping leading to an undercurrent of exotic fruits.

Lock Keeper's Launch Ale (OG 1039, ABV 3.9%)
A complex blend of malts with a hoppy edge and delicate fruit notes, leading to a long, bittersweet aftertaste.

Stardust (OG 1042.5, ABV 4.2%)
A red-coloured beer with fruit and floral aromas and a nutty sweetness rounded off with a crisp finish.

Conqueror's Premium Bitter (OG 1043, ABV 4.4%)
A full-bodied bitter with roasted barley creating a chestnut-coloured ale with a lingering malty taste and rounded bitter finish.

Totem American IPA (OG 1042, ABV 4.5%)
American-style IPA with citrus flavours and hop aromas all perfectly balanced by subtle malt character.

Harrogate SIBA

Unit 7, Hookstone Centre, Hookstone Chase, Harrogate, North Yorkshire, HG2 7HW ☎ 07774 891664 🌐 harrogatebrewery.co.uk

Established in 2013, the brewery also uses the names Spa Town Ales and It's Quicker By Ale on its logo and pumpclips. The brewery has a capacity of four barrels and brews several times each week.

Pale (OG 1040, ABV 4.2%)

Cold Bath Gold (OG 1042, ABV 4.4%)

Pinewoods Pale Ale (OG 1042, ABV 4.4%)
Pale-coloured beer with citrus hop flavours.

Plum Porter (OG 1048, ABV 4.8%)
Porter made with plums from a local allotment.

Vanilla Porter (OG 1048, ABV 4.8%)
Rich porter made with vanilla pods.

Kursaal Porter (OG 1054, ABV 5.4%)
A rich, bittersweet porter with espresso, liquorice and chocolate flavours.

Hart

See Oscars

Hart Family

The 1833 Brewery, 21 Nene Court, The Embankment, Wellingborough, Northamptonshire, NN8 1LD
☎ (01933) 228324 ☎ 07891 212476
🌐 hartfamilybrewers.com

Hart Family Brewers was established in 2012 using an eight-barrel plant. It is owned and operated by Rob and Sarah Hart, who are indulging their passion after a combined 25 years in the drinks industry. Recent expansion, including a third fermenter, gives weekly production of up to 38 barrels. !! ♦ RAIB

House Beer (OG 1036, ABV 3.6%)

Harts No. 1 (OG 1043, ABV 4.1%)
A tawny-coloured premium bitter with fruity, malty aromas and grassy citrus notes. Fresh and fruity on the palate with spicy bitterness and citrus, hay-like aromas on the refreshing finish.

Harts No. 9 (OG 1044, ABV 4.3%)
A golden-coloured beer, light and refreshing with spicy grapefruit aromas. Fresh and light on the palate with pithy grapefruit flavours supported by biscuity malt.

Harts No. 3 (OG 1047, ABV 4.7%)
A fruity, ruby-coloured beer with full malty, spicy aromas. Full and forward on the palate with rounded, rich malty flavours supported by gentle spicy hoppiness,

Harts No. 8 (OG 1052, ABV 5%)
A dark-coloured beer with bold toasted fruit aromas and hints of espresso. Full and warming roasted fruit and molasses flavours balanced by bitter coffee, chocolate and spice aromas over a long finish.

Pale (OG 1052, ABV 5%)
Strong bitter beer. Biscuity malt complemented by an orange-scented bitterness.

1833 India Pale Ale (ABV 6.6%)
An amber-coloured beer with a honey malt and orange marmalade hop aroma, a strong malt, marmalade and spice taste, with a dry bitter finish.

Hart of Stebbing

White Hart, High Street, Stebbing, Essex, CM6 3SQ
☎ (01371) 856383 ✉ nickeldred@hotmail.com

The brewery was established in 2007 by Nick Eldred, who is also the owner of the White Hart pub where the brewery is based. At present only the White Hart and local beer festivals are supplied. ♦

Hartshorns

Unit 4, Tomlinsons Industrial Estate, Alfreton Road, Derby, DE21 4ED ☎ 07830 367125
🌐 hartshornsbrewery.com

Hartshorns began brewing in 2012 using a six-barrel plant installed by brothers Darren and Lindsey Hartshorn. In 2015 the brewery acquired its first pub, the Little Chester Ale House, Derby.

Ignite (OG 1039, ABV 3.9%)

Highgate (OG 1044, ABV 4.3%)
Smooth, easy-drinking, pale copper-coloured ale. Well-balanced malt sweetness with fruity hop flavour and a well-rounded bitterness.

Porter (OG 1045, ABV 4.5%)

THE BREWERIES

Brooklyn Nights (OG 1052, ABV 5.4%)
A punchy American-style, brown-coloured ale with a complex malt base, a hoppy aroma and a clean, dry finish.

Shakademus (OG 1052, ABV 5.4%)
A full-bodied premium golden ale with a citrus hop bite.

Apocalypse (OG 1055, ABV 6.2%)
Easy-drinking golden ale with a clean bitter finish. Refreshingly crisp and packed with hop character.

Harvey's IFBB

Bridge Wharf Brewery, 6 Cliffe High Street, Lewes, East Sussex, BN7 2AH
☎ (01273) 480209 harveys.org.uk

Established in 1790, this independent family brewery operates from the banks of the River Ouse in Lewes. A major development in 1985 doubled the brewhouse capacity and subsequent additional fermenting capacity has seen production rise to more than 38,000 barrels a year. There is also a microbrewery on site used to brew special beers including replicating old Lewes Brewery recipes using the County Town Beers name. Harveys supplies real ale to all its 48 pubs and 550 free trade outlets in the south-east. There are plans to re-establish a microbrewery on site, which will be used to brew special beers including replicating old Lewes Brewery recipes using the County Town Beers name. !! ♦ RAIB

R (ABV 2.8%)

Sussex XX Mild Ale (OG 1030, ABV 3%)
A dark copper-brown in colour. Roast malt dominates the aroma and palate leading to a sweet, caramel finish.

IPA (OG 1033, ABV 3.5%)

Sussex Wild Hop (OG 1037, ABV 3.7%)

Sussex Best Bitter (OG 1040, ABV 4%)
Full-bodied, brown-coloured bitter. A hoppy aroma leads to a good malt and hop balance and a dry aftertaste.

Old Ale (OG 1043, ABV 4.3%)

Olympia (OG 1042, ABV 4.3%)

Armada Ale (OG 1045, ABV 4.5%)
Hoppy, amber-coloured best bitter. Well-balanced fruit and hops dominate throughout with a fruity palate.

Harviestoun SIBA

Alva Industrial Estate, Alva, FK12 5DQ
☎ (01259) 769100 harviestoun.com

Harviestoun has grown from one-man brewing in a bucket in the back of a shed in 1983 to a 60-barrel, multi-award-winning brewery today. With a reputation for experimentation, the brewery adds around eight to ten short-run seasonals to its core range. !! ♦ RAIB

Bitter & Twisted (OG 1039, ABV 3.8%)
Refreshingly hoppy beer with fruit throughout. A bittersweet taste with a long bitter finish. A golden-coloured session beer.

Old Engine Oil (OG 1045, ABV 4.5%)
Notes of dark chocolate, creamy coffee, burnt toast and sweet caramel.

Schiehallion (OG 1048, ABV 4.8%)
A Scottish cask-conditioned lager. A hoppy aroma, with fruit and malt, leads to a malty, bitter taste with floral hoppiness and a bitter finish

Harwich Town

See Red Fox

Hattie Brown's

Unit 1, The Sidings, Victoria Avenue Industrial Estate, Swanage, Dorset, BH19 1AU
☎ (01929) 439075

Office: Square & Compass, Worth Matravers, BH19 3LF
hattiebrownsbrewery.co.uk

Hattie Brown's began brewing in 2014 at the Wessex brewery. In 2015 it moved to its present location. It is owned by the manager of the Square & Compass, Worth Matravers, and partner, Jean, the brewer.

HBA (OG 1039, ABV 3.8%)
Well-balanced, copper-coloured ale. Lightly malted.

Moonlite (OG 1039, ABV 3.8%)
Hoppy pale ale with strong citrus notes and a big finish.

Hopsworth (ABV 4.4%)

Scarlet (ABV 4.5%)
Bright red-coloured, lightly-hopped ale made using beetroot.

Dog on the Roof (ABV 6%)
A dark golden-coloured ale with a fruity finish.

Hawk Wing SIBA

Unit E, Hawkshill Business Park, Lesbury, Northumberland, NE66 3PG

Brewing began in 2012 as VIP Brewery, using a five-barrel plant to serve the owner's pub, the Village Inn in Longframlington, and the local free trade. In 2018 the brewery changed its name to Hawk Wing.

One (ABV 4.3%)

Hawkshead

Mill Yard, Staveley, Cumbria, LA8 9LR
☎ (01539) 822644 hawksheadbrewery.co.uk

The brewery takes its name from the village in which it was founded in 2002. It outgrew its original barn and moved to Staveley in 2006 to a purpose-built 20-barrel brewery. Capacity has been increased several times since, a new micro packaging plant added and the Beer Hall, the brewery tap, developed as a showcase for real ale. Pubs are supplied directly throughout the north and further afield to selected outlets. In 2017 Hawkshead signed a deal with Halewood International that will triple capacity. Packaged beers will be sold globally but founder Alex Brodie and his team remain in control of draught beer production. !! ♦ RAIB

Iti (OG 1036, ABV 3.5%)
A beer packed with grapefruit aroma and taste. Beautifully balanced with a long-lasting, hoppy bitter finish.

Windermere Pale (OG 1036, ABV 3.5%)
Crisp and fruity, yellow-coloured beer with hints of melon and grapefruit and a strong bitter aftertaste.

Bitter (OG 1037, ABV 3.7%)
Well-balanced, thirst-quenching beer with fruit and hops aroma, leading to a lasting bitter finish.

Red (OG 1042, ABV 4.2%)
An impressive colour for this richly flavoured beer; lots of fruitiness and good hop flavour with a lingering aftertaste.

Lakeland Gold (OG 1043, ABV 4.4%)
Fresh, well-balanced fruity, hoppy beer with a clean bitter aftertaste.

Dry Stone Stout (OG 1044, ABV 4.5%)
Black-coloured, dry, bitter stout with an astringent, roast finish.

Great White (OG 1048, ABV 4.8%)
A spiced wheat beer served cloudy. Brewed with coriander seeds and Seville orange peel.

Brodie's Prime (OG 1048, ABV 4.9%)
Complex, dark brown-coloured beer with plenty of malt, fruit and roast taste. Satisfying full body with a clean finish.

Cumbrian Five Hop (OG 1050, ABV 5%)
A robust, hoppy bitter with citrus hops and a fruity middle.

Lakeland Lager (OG 1045, ABV 5%)

NZPA (OG 1056, ABV 6%)
A hoppy bitter with a sweet, fruity taste and a resounding dry bitter finish.

IPA (OG 1065, ABV 7%)
A modern IPA, amber in colour, with huge hop flavours.

Haworth Steam

Rose & Crown, 2 Westgate, Cleckheaton, West Yorkshire, BD19 5ET
(01535) 646059 07974 483310
haworthsteambrewery.co.uk

Established in 2011, the five-barrel brewery is located at the Rose & Crown, Cleckheaton, this being the main outlet for the beers along with the Haworth Steam Bistro, Haworth. Beers are also sold under the Whitechapel brand.

Hay Rake

Rake Tapas Bar, Blackstone Edge Old Road, Littleborough, OL15 0JX
(01706) 379689 07775 792684
hereforthebeer.co.uk/hay-rake

Mark Wickham, the landlord of the Rake Tapas Restaurant, resurrected the Hay Rake microbrewery in 2013. The Rake brewed its own beer during the reign of Queen Victoria but stopped in 1901. Beers are available in the restaurant, occasionally the nearby White House and at local beer festivals.

Haywood Bad Ram SIBA

Callow Top Holiday Park, Buxton Road, Sandybrook, Ashbourne, Derbyshire, DE6 2AQ
(01335) 344020 07974 948427
callowtop.co.uk/ccallow-top-brewery

Established in 2003, the brewery was based in a converted barn but a new brewery and bottling plant became operational in 2012. One pub is owned (on site) and several other outlets are supplied. !! RAIB

Thoroughbred Bad Ram (OG 1038, ABV 3.8%)
A refreshing, straw-coloured ale with a crisp bite and spice and flowery notes.

Dr Samuel Johnson (OG 1044, ABV 4.5%)
A slightly fruity and refined spicy flavour.

Callow Top Imperial IPA (OG 1050, ABV 5.2%)
A full-bodied, rich ale with a fruity and slightly citrus aftertaste.

Healey's

Wellington Inn, Main Street, Loppergarth, Cumbria, LA12 0JL
(01229) 582388

Healey's began brewing in the Wellington in 2012 using a custom-made 2.5-barrel stainless steel plant, which can be viewed through full-length windows in the pub. A range of different beer styles is brewed, available in more than 15 pubs.

Heaney Farmhouse

c/o Boundary Brewing, Portview Trade Centre, Newtownards Road, Belfast, BT4 1HE
heaneyfarmhousebrewing.com

Founded in 2014. Bottled beers are currently brewed at Boundary (qv) in Belfast while its brewhouse project is underway at a farm in Bellaghy, Co Londonderry. No real ale.

Heart of Wales

Stables Yard, Zion Street, Llanwrtyd Wells, LD5 4RD
(01591) 610236 heartofwalesbrewery.co.uk

The brewery was set up with a six-barrel plant in 2006 in old stables at the rear of the Neuadd Arms Hotel. Beers are brewed using water from the brewery's own borehole. Cambrian Heart Ale was commissioned by and is brewed for the Cambrian Mountains Initiative, inspired by the Prince of Wales, which aims to promote and support rural producers and communities in the region.
!! ♦ RAIB V

Heathen

Grape & Grain, 51 The Broadway, Haywards Heath, West Sussex, RH16 3AS
(01444) 456217 07825 429428
heathenbrewers.co.uk

Located in the basement of the Grape & Grain off-licence and delicatessen, brewing began in 2014 using a full mash, two-barrel plant. Local outlets and beer festivals are supplied. !! ♦ RAIB

ISA (OG 1040, ABV 3.9%)

Farmhouse (OG 1048, ABV 4.7%)

Pale (OG 1050, ABV 5.3%)

West Coast (OG 1049, ABV 5.4%)

Hoppler Effect (OG 1058, ABV 5.8%)

Sussex Genie (OG 1065, ABV 6.5%)

THE BREWERIES

Heathton

c/o Old Gate, Heathton, Shropshire, WV5 7EB

This brewery is planned to be resurrected at the Old Gate pub, but its three beers are produced at present in three different breweries, and served only in the Old Gate. Brewing is currently suspended.

Heavy Industry SIBA

The Old Slaughterhouse, Denbigh Street, Henllan, LL16 5AR
☎ (01745) 814655 ☎ 07813 024161
heavyindustrybrewing.com

Established in 2012, Heavy Industry is an award-winning brewery using a 10-barrel plant situated in an old slaughterhouse in the village of Henllan. !! ♦

Diawl Bach (OG 1036.5, ABV 3.8%)
Citrus fruit flavours feature strongly in this uncompromising, hoppy bitter. The acerbic, tart taste continues long into the aftertaste.

Electric Mountain (OG 1036.5, ABV 3.8%)
A full-bodied session bitter, dry and well-balanced with a satisfying hoppy finish.

Nelsons Eye (OG 1041, ABV 4.4%)
Heavily hopped with a strong, sharp bitter taste. Citrus fruit notes, mainly grapefruit, in the aroma and palate continue into the hoppy, bitter aftertaste.

Forza! (OG 1041.5, ABV 4.5%)
Pronounced tropical fruit flavours are accentuated by a balanced, smooth bitterness.

Freak Chick (OG 1042, ABV 4.5%)
A well-balanced, dark-coloured best bitter, initially sweet with caramel undertones complemented by hoppy bitterness in the aftertaste.

77 (OG 1046, ABV 4.9%)
A strong bitter with a powerful smack of fruit and hops. Tangy fruit flavours and hoppy bitterness feature strongly in the aroma, taste and finish.

Collaborator (OG 1046, ABV 5%)
A smooth and satisfying, dark-coloured, hoppy beer. The juicy malty taste is quite roasty and leads to a dry, hoppy aftertaste.

Pigeon Toed Orange Peel (OG 1048.5, ABV 5.2%)
A naturally hazy half wheat beer with a strong orange fruit aroma and taste and a tangy, hoppy, bitter finish.

Nos Smoked Porter (OG 1055.5, ABV 5.5%)
This, well-hopped, dark-coloured porter has a smoky taste mingling with coffee and roast notes.

Hebridean

10 Shell Street, Stornoway, Isle of Lewis, HS1 2BS
☎ (01851) 700123 hebridean-brewery.co.uk

Hebridean relocated its 14-barrel brew plant just around the corner to new premises in 2016 and now includes and on-site bar and shop. 70% of its output is bottled, with the rest cask-conditioned.

Celtic Black Ale (OG 1036, ABV 3.9%)
A dark-coloured ale balancing aromatic hops combined with a subtle bite and pleasantly smooth caramel aftertaste.

Clansman Ale (OG 1036, ABV 3.9%)
Lightly-hopped and subtly bitter.

Seaforth Ale (OG 1042, ABV 4.2%)
A light, quaffable beer with a delicate nose. A complex mixture of biscuity malt and fruit in the taste leads to a lasting, bittersweet finish.

Islander Strong Premium Ale (OG 1044, ABV 4.8%)
A malty, fruity strong bitter drinking dangerously below its ABV.

Berserker Export Pale Ale (OG 1068, ABV 7.5%)
This malty, fruity winter warmer is packed full of flavour, with toffee apple and caramel notes right through to the long, satisfying aftertaste.

Heidrun

Inn House Brewery, 449 Great Western Road, Glasgow, G12 8HH hello@valhallasgoat.com

A small batch brewery with beers contract brewed by Drygate Brewery (qv). RAIB

Heineken Royal Trafford

Royal Brewery, 201 Denmark Road, Manchester, M15 6LD

No real ale.

Helm Bar

Ellerholme, Appleby-in-Westmorland, Cumbria, CA16 6JG ☎ 07736 364478 helmbarbrews.com

Inspired by a passion for strong, distinctive beers from the US Pacific North West and Belgium, Helm Bar currently brews small batch beers using the highest quality grain and hops. RAIB

Jabberwock (ABV 5.2%)

Ghost Tractor (ABV 5.3%)
Robust porter with a hint of vanilla.

Jub Jub (ABV 5.5%)

Bandersnatch (ABV 6%)
American-style IPA; mid brown in colour, bitter and dry-hopped.

Vorpel Blade (ABV 6.4%)

Helmsley SIBA

18 Bridge Street, Helmsley, North Yorkshire, YO62 5DX
☎ (01439) 771014 ☎ 07525 434268

Located within the North York Moors National Park, brewing began in 2014. The brewery has a viewing gallery, tasting room and brewery tap. Local pubs are supplied. !! RAIB

Yorkshire Legend (ABV 3.8%)
Dark-coloured, toasted bitter combining floral and berry notes together with caramel and malt flavours.

Striding the Riding (ABV 4%)
Straw-coloured, refreshing beer. Subtly-hopped with pine and citrus notes.

Howardian Gold (ABV 4.2%)
Golden ale with bursts of zesty lemon and sweet floral aromas.

Honey (ABV 4.5%)

H!PA (ABV 5.5%)

Hemlock (NEW)

37 Main Street, Hemington, Derbyshire, DE74 2RB
☎ 07791 057994 ✉ hembrew@yahoo.com

Established in 2015, this two-barrel plant is located in the outbuildings of a 17th century thatched cottage. It currently supplies ales to pubs in the local area and the occasional beer festival. ‼

Hoptimystic (OG 1040, ABV 4.1%)
Copper-coloured, highly-hopped pale ale with lemon/lime rind bitterness to finish.

California Dreaming (OG 1042, ABV 4.3%)
A pale ale with a refreshing fruity and crisp hoppiness.

Hepworth SIBA

Stane Street, North Heath, West Sussex, RH20 1DJ
☎ (01403) 269696 hepworthbrewery.co.uk

Hepworth's was established in 2001. 274 outlets are supplied. Originally situated in Horsham, a new brewery site in North Heath opened in 2016. Its organic status is ratified by the Soil Association. ‼ ♦RAIB

Traditional Sussex Bitter (OG 1035, ABV 3.5%)
A fine, clean-tasting, amber-coloured session beer. A bitter beer with a pleasant fruity and hoppy aroma that leads to a crisp, tangy taste. A long, dry finish.

Pullman First Class Ale (OG 1041, ABV 4.2%)
A sweet, nutty maltiness and fruitiness are balanced by hops and bitterness in this easy-drinking, pale brown-coloured best bitter. A subtle bitter aftertaste.

Prospect Organic (OG 1045, ABV 4.5%)

Classic Old Ale (OG 1046, ABV 4.8%)
A traditional-style, rich porter with a variety of roasted malts balanced with sweetness and hop bitterness.

Iron Horse (OG 1048, ABV 4.8%)
There's a fruity, toffee aroma to this light brown-coloured, full-bodied bitter. A citrus flavour balanced by caramel and malt leads to a clean, dry finish.

Hercules

Unit 5b, Harbour Court, Heron Road, Sydenham, Holywood, Belfast, BT3 9HB
☎ (028) 9036 4516 ✉ niall@herculesbrewery.com

The original Hercules Brewing Company, founded in the 19th century, was one of 13 breweries in Belfast at the time. The company has been re-established to produce small batch brews using old brewing traditions. Its output is all under the Yardsman brand name.

Yardsman IPA (OG 1043, ABV 4.3%)

Yardsman Lager (OG 1048, ABV 4.8%)

Yardsman Belfast Pale Ale (OG 1056, ABV 5.6%)

Hereford

88 St Owen Street, Hereford, HR1 2QD
☎ (01432) 342125 ✉ jfkenyon@aol.com

Hereford began life as the Spinning Dog Brewery in 2000, changing its name in 2010. After a period as primarily a brewpub, in 2017 it began to expand its distribution to pubs in Herefordshire and Pembrokeshire. ‼ ♦RAIB

Herefordshire Owd Bull (OG 1039, ABV 3.9%)
A session beer with an abundance of hops and bitterness. Dry with a citrus aftertaste.

Dark (OG 1040, ABV 4%)
A dark-coloured, malty mild with a hint of bitterness and a touch of roast caramel.

HLA (Herefordshire Light Ale) (OG 1040, ABV 4%)
A crisp, light, refreshing ale made with Herefordshire hops.

Celtic Gold (OG 1045, ABV 4.5%)
A bright gold-coloured best bitter, full of fruit and blackcurrant flavours.

Mutley's Revenge (OG 1048, ABV 4.8%)
A strong, smooth, hoppy beer, amber in colour. Full-bodied with a dry, citrus aftertaste.

Mutts Nuts (OG 1050, ABV 5%)
A dark-coloured, strong ale. Full-bodied with a hint of a chocolate aftertaste.

Heritage SIBA

National Brewery Centre, Horninglow Street, Burton upon Trent, Staffordshire, DE14 1NG
☎ (01283) 777006
heritagebrewingcompany.co.uk

Heritage Brewing Company (formerly William Worthington's Brewery) was established in 2015 by Planning Solutions Limited, operators of the National Brewery Centre (NBC). They purchased the 25-barrel brewery and nearby bottling plant from the previous owners, Molson Coors. The team has set out to utilise the resources, history and knowledge available at the NBC to breathe new life into heritage beers, including those produced 10-15 years ago by the former Museum Brewing Co. ‼ ♦RAIB

Victoria Ale (OG 1034, ABV 3.8%)
Full-flavoured but light ale, rich amber in colour.

Charrington Oatmeal Stout (OG 1041, ABV 4%)

Offilers' Best Bitter (OG 1038, ABV 4%)
Amber-coloured best bitter with a light hop finish.

St Modwen Golden Ale (OG 1040, ABV 4.2%)
Refreshing but not too bitter with a subtle malted wheat biscuit taste.

Charrington IPA (OG 1046, ABV 4.5%)
Deep amber-coloured IPA with a pleasant hoppy bite leading to a smooth, malty flavour and a balanced, lingering bitterness.

Heritage Gold (OG 1044, ABV 4.8%)
Clean, refreshing, golden-coloured beer, lightly hopped.

Masterpiece IPA (OG 1055, ABV 5.6%)
Fruity nose which continues through the taste with a hoppy fruity finish. Hints of orange and apple.

Hermitage

Heathwaite, Slanting Hill, Hermitage, Berkshire, RG18 9QG
☎ (01635) 200907 ☎ 07980 019484
hermitagebrewery.co.uk

Brewing began in 2013 using a 0.5-barrel plant. The owner, Richard Marshall, taught food science at degree level and has been brewing his own beers for more than 40 years. Bottle-conditioned beers are sold in local shops and post offices. Casks are supplied to some independent pubs as well as local beer festivals. New beers are frequently introduced. RAIB

Tom Herrick's

The Stable House, Main Street, Carlton on Trent, Nottinghamshire, NG23 6NW ☎ 07877 542331
✉ tomherricksbrewery@hotmail.com

Tom Herrick installed his bespoke 2.5-barrel stainless steel brewery at the front of his premises during 2014 and began small scale commercial brewing the following year. The brewery is only operated on a part-time basis with output going to festivals and local pubs.

Bomber Command (OG 1045, ABV 4.2%)
A pale copper-coloured ale, full-bodied and malty with a delicate, well-balanced hop profile.

Hesket Newmarket SIBA

Old Crown Barn, Back Green, Hesket Newmarket, Cumbria, CA7 8JG
☎ (01697) 478066 🌐 hesketbrewery.co.uk

Founded in 1988, and bought by a co-operative in 1999 to preserve a community amenity. All the beers are named after Cumbrian fells, except for Doris' 90th Birthday Ale. !! ♦

Haystacks (OG 1037, ABV 3.7%)
Light, easy-drinking, thirst-quenching blonde beer.

Skiddaw Special Bitter (OG 1037, ABV 3.7%)
An amber-coloured session beer, malty throughout. Well-balanced with a dry finish.

Red Pike (OG 1038, ABV 3.8%)
A dark red-coloured ale with a complex malty backbone but plenty of hop flavour giving notes of resin and pine as well as some citrus and fruit.

Black Sail (OG 1042.1, ABV 4%)
A sweet stout with roast flavours.

Helvellyn Gold (OG 1039, ABV 4%)
Complex, hoppy and fruity beer with malt presence and a refreshing finish.

High Pike (OG 1042, ABV 4.2%)
A traditional-style bitter; fruity with a dry finish.

Doris' 90th Birthday Ale (OG 1045, ABV 4.3%)
A fruity premium ale.

Scafell Blonde (OG 1043, ABV 4.4%)
A hoppy, sweet, fruity, pale-coloured bitter.

Brim Fell (OG 1047, ABV 4.5%)
A light copper-coloured IPA. Fruity, citrus hop bitterness balanced by residual sweetness from the malt.

Catbells Pale Ale (OG 1050, ABV 5%)
Golden ale with a good balance of fruity sweetness and bitterness, almost syrupy but with an unexpectedly dry finish.

Old Carrock Strong Ale (OG 1060, ABV 6%)
Reddish brown-coloured strong ale, vine-fruity in flavour with slightly astringent finish.

Hetton Law

Hetton Law Farm, Lowick, Northumberland, TD15 2UL
☎ (01289) 388558 ☎ 07889 457140
🌐 hettonlawbrewery.co.uk

Brewing began in 2015 using a 2.5-barrel plant. Run by retired dentists Judith and Nicholas Grasse, it uses local spring water and locally grown malt, which gives the beers a distinctive character. ♦

Hetton Howler (ABV 4.2%)

Hetton Harlot (ABV 4.8%)

Hexagon

PO Box 174, Marple, SK6 9BR ☎ 07903 264243
🌐 hexagonbrew.co.uk

Hexagon was founded in 2015 and is run by a husband-and-wife team. The brewery produces small batch bottle-conditioned beers supplying bars and bottle shops locally and in Manchester. There are plans for expansion. RAIB

Hexhamshire SIBA

Dipton Mill Road, Hexham, Northumberland, NE46 1YA
☎ (01434) 606577 🌐 hexhamshire.co.uk

Hexhamshire is Northumberland's oldest brewery and is run by the same family since it was founded in 1993. The Brooker family also run the brewery tap, the Dipton Mill. Outlets are supplied direct and via the SIBA Beerflex scheme.

Devil's Elbow (OG 1036, ABV 3.6%)
Amber-coloured brew full of hops and fruit, leading to a bitter finish.

Shire Bitter (OG 1037, ABV 3.8%)
A good balance of hops with fruity overtones, this amber-coloured beer makes an easy-drinking session bitter.

Blackhall English Stout (OG 1040, ABV 4%)
A pleasant, bitter beer with a strong roast malt flavour.

Devil's Water (OG 1041, ABV 4.1%)
Copper-coloured best bitter, well-balanced with a slightly fruity, hoppy finish.

Whapweasel (OG 1048, ABV 4.8%)
An smooth, hoppy beer with a fruity flavour. Amber in colour, the bitter finish brings out the fruit and hops.

Old Humbug (OG 1055, ABV 5.5%)

High House Farm SIBA

Matfen, NE20 0RG
☎ (01661) 886192 🌐 highhousefarmbrewery.co.uk

The brewery was founded in 2003 by a Brewlab graduate on a working farm, with visitor centre, brewery shop and function room. This has now expanded to include a restaurant and wedding venue. More than 350 regional outlets are supplied. !! ♦

Sundancer (OG 1036, ABV 3.6%)

Pullet Please (OG 1037, ABV 3.7%)
A pale golden-coloured, refreshing ale with a delicate grapefruit nose and a crisp, dry finish.

Auld Hemp (OG 1038, ABV 3.8%)
Tawny-coloured ale with hop, malt and fruit flavours and a good bitter finish.

Nel's Best (OG 1041, ABV 4.2%)

Golden-coloured, hoppy ale full of flavour with a clean, bitter finish.

Matfen Magic (OG 1046.5, ABV 4.8%) ◆
Well-hopped, brown-coloured ale with a fruity aroma. Malt and chocolate overtones with a rich, bitter finish.

High Peak

41a Market Street, Chapel-en-le-Frith, Derbyshire, SK23 0HP ☎ 07936 174364 🌐 highpeakbrewco.com

High Peak is a microbrewery based in Chapel-en-le-Frith on the edge of the Peak District that specialises in hand-crafted, unfined, unfiltered and unpasteurised beers in small batches of 600 litres. There is no core range of beers as set recipes are not followed.

High Weald SIBA

Unit 24, Bassetts Manor, Butcherfield Lane, Hartfield, East Sussex, TN7 4LA ☎ 07836 291430

Office: 23 Hermitage Road, East Grinstead, RH19 2BP 🌐 highwealdbrewery.co.uk

Established in 2013, High Weald Brewery has grown from its home-brew origins to a four-barrel, purpose-built plant, which moved to Hartfield in 2017. The brewery supplies local (and not so local) free houses, shops and festivals.

Chronicle (OG 1038, ABV 3.8%)

Greenstede (OG 1040, ABV 4%)

Mosaic Pale (OG 1044, ABV 4.2%)

Charcoal Burner (OG 1043, ABV 4.3%)
A traditional English stout with a velvety smoothness.

Off the Chart (OG 1049, ABV 5%)

Higsons (NEW)

62-64 Bridgewater Street, Liverpool, L1 0AY ☎ (0151) 305 1292 🌐 h1780tapstill.co.uk

Established in 2017 in the Baltic Triangle area of Liverpool, the 30-barrel plant can be seen from the Higsons 1780 tap pub.

Pale (ABV 3.8%)

Amber (ABV 4.1%)

Hilden

Hilden House, Hilden, Lisburn, Co Antrim, BT27 4TY ☎ (028) 9266 0800 🌐 hildenbrewery.co.uk

Established 1981, Hilden is Ireland's oldest independent brewery. Now in the second generation of family ownership, the beers are widely distributed across the UK. The beers are regularly available in Wetherspoon outlets in Northern Ireland. ‼ ♦

Nut Brown (OG 1038, ABV 3.8%)

Ale (OG 1038, ABV 4%) ◆
An amber-coloured beer with an aroma of malt, hops and fruit. The balanced taste is slightly slanted towards hops, and hops are also prominent in the full, malty finish.

Barney's Brew (OG 1043, ABV 4.2%)
A wheat beer spiced with cardamom, coriander and black pepper.

Irish Stout (OG 1043, ABV 4.3%)

Scullion's Irish (OG 1045, ABV 4.6%)
An amber-coloured ale, initially smooth with a slight taste of honey that is balanced by a long, dry aftertaste.

Twisted Hop (OG 1047, ABV 4.7%)

Halt (OG 1058, ABV 6.1%)
A premium Irish red-coloured ale with a malty, mild hop flavour.

Contract brewed for Clearsky Brewing:

Fulcrum (ABV 4.5%)

Prism Red (ABV 4.5%)

Rowlock (ABV 4.5%)

Tidefall (ABV 4.5%)

Hill Island

Unit 7, Fowlers Yard, Back Silver Street, Durham, DH1 3RA ☎ 07740 932584 ✉ hillisland73@gmail.com

Established in 2002, the brewery name is a literal translation of Dunholme from which Durham is derived. It is situated in the Fowlers Yard complex by the banks of the River Wear. Beers can be crafted exclusively for individual pubs. A pop up bar regularly operates at weekends throughout the year (excluding Jan) from its premises. ‼ ♦

Peninsula Pint (OG 1036.5, ABV 3.7%)
Hoppy blonde ale with a zesty aroma.

Bitter (OG 1039, ABV 3.9%)
A reddish gold-coloured bitter with pronounced caramel flavor and zesty bitterness.

Stout for the Count (OG 1040, ABV 4%)
A traditional, full-bodied stout with roast coffee flavors and a clean hop bitterness.

Neptune's Gold (OG 1042, ABV 4.2%)
Subtle bitterness balanced with hop flavours and a hint of tropical fruit.

Cathedral Ale (OG 1042, ABV 4.3%)
Ruby red-coloured ale with hints of roast malts and a crisp bitterness.

THAI PA (OG 1043, ABV 4.3%)
An IPA brewed with lemongrass.

Griffin's Irish Stout (OG 1045, ABV 4.5%)
A traditional Irish-style stout. Black in colour and bitter.

Hillfire SIBA

23 Edison Road, Aylesbury, Buckinghamshire, HP19 8TE ☎ (01296) 338521 🌐 hillfirebrewing.com

Hillfire commenced brewing in 2016 using a 2.5-barrel plant. Sole owner and CAMRA member Neil Coxhead brews once a week.

3C (OG 1038, ABV 3.9%)

Lakewood Pale (OG 1041, ABV 4.2%)
A hoppy blonde beer with a clean, crisp, citrus flavour.

California Gold (OG 1043, ABV 4.3%)
A well-balanced, golden-coloured beer with subtle citrus and resin notes and hints of biscuit malt.

THE BREWERIES

Nighthawk (OG 1050, ABV 5%)
An American-style stout with dark roasty malt and a distinctive hop character.

Hillside SIBA

Holly Bush Farm, Ross Road, Longhope, Gloucestershire, GL17 0NG
☎ (01452) 830222 hillsidebrewery.com

A six-barrel plant in a reconstructed farm dairy that started in 2011. A 60 metre bore hole produces pure water rich in minerals ideally suited to brewing. The regular beers are supplemented by limited run specials that explore different styles and flavours. An on-site brewery tap, the Hop Barn, is now open, which holds monthly events and can be hired privately. !! ♦ RAIB

Over the Hill (OG 1042, ABV 3.5%)
Full-bodied, single-hopped dark mild with a cocoa and roast malt character.

Pinnacle (OG 1038, ABV 3.8%)
A well-balanced session beer with a fresh, fruity finish.

Legless Cow (OG 1043, ABV 4.2%)
A well-balanced, full-flavoured best bitter. Rich caramel flavours with a smooth, citrus hop finish.

HCL (OG 1038, ABV 4.3%)
A clean, crisp lager with a subtle honey flavour and refreshing peach, zesty finish.

Legend of Hillside (OG 1046, ABV 4.7%)
A traditional English IPA with a subtle honey flavour and strong hop finish.

Summit Ruby Ale (OG 1050, ABV 4.9%)
Packed with rich, malty flavours, deep caramel notes and hints of chocolate and toffee to finish.

Hillstown

128 Glebe Road, Randalstown, BT41 3DT
hillstownbrewery.com

Brewing began in 2014 in a converted barn on a farm in Randalstown producing bottle-conditioned beers. ♦ RAIB

Hilltop

Sheffield Road, Conisbrough, South Yorkshire, DN12 2AY
☎ (01709) 868811 ☎ 07947 146746
thehilltophotel.co.uk

Established in 2016, Hilltop Brewery is a 3.5-barrel plant situated in the outbuildings of the Hilltop Hotel in Conisbrough. Beers are available in the hotel and other local outlets. !! ♦ RAIB

Hippy Killer

c/o Whippet Inn, 21 Tamworth Street, Lichfield, WS13 6JP ☎ 07858 753653

Paul Hudson, owner of the Whippet micropub in Lichfield, began commercial brewing in 2016. He currently uses spare capacity at Merry Miner Brewery (qv) in Warwickshire. Beer is mainly available at the micropub but can occasionally be found in the free trade.

Lowrider (OG 1040, ABV 4%)
A pale ale with citrus notes and a dry bitter finish.

Filthy Juicebox (OG 1042, ABV 4.2%)
A golden ale with rounded tropical fruit notes.

Sleeping with Trash (OG 1050, ABV 5%)

Hobsons SIBA

Newhouse Farm, Tenbury Road, Cleobury Mortimer, Shropshire, DY14 8RD
☎ (01299) 270837 hobsons-brewery.co.uk

Established in 1993 in a former sawmill, Hobsons relocated to a farm site with more space in 1995. A second brewery, bottling plant and a warehouse have been added along with significant expansion to the first brewery. Beers are supplied within a 50-mile radius. The brewery has an on-site wind turbine and utilises environmental sustainable technologies where possible. !! RAIB

Mild (OG 1034, ABV 3.2%)
A classic mild. Complex layers of taste come from roasted malts that predominate and give lots of flavour.

Twisted Spire (OG 1036, ABV 3.6%)
Vibrant blonde beer with a sweet floral aroma bringing bursts of refreshing flavour and a crisp, dry finish.

Best (OG 1038.5, ABV 3.8%)
A pale brown-coloured, medium-bodied beer with strong hop character throughout. It is consequently bitter, but with malt discernible in the taste.

Old Prickly (OG 1042, ABV 4.2%)
Pale ale full of hop flavour with floral and citrus notes and a lingering but subtle bitterness.

Town Crier (OG 1044, ABV 4.5%)
A full-flavoured, crisp golden ale with a hint of sweetness complemented by subtle hop flavours, leading to a dry finish.

Hogarths SIBA

Hogarths, 37-41 Churchgate, Bolton, BL1 1HU
☎ (01204) 386964

Microbrewery located in the old kitchen of a Bolton pub of the same name. Beers are available in the pub, other Amber Taverns up and down the country and at beer festivals.

Beer Street (ABV 3.8%)
A session ale with a good hop balance.

Liberty (ABV 3.8%)
A light, fruity bitter.

The Bruiser (ABV 4%)

Enraged Musician (ABV 4.2%)

Hoggleys

See Phipps

Hogs Back SIBA

Manor Farm, The Street, Tongham, Surrey, GU10 1DE
☎ (01252) 783000 hogsback.co.uk

This traditionally-styled brewery, established in 1992, boasts an extensive range of award-winning ales. The shop sells all the brewery's beers and related merchandise plus over 400 beers and ciders from around the world. In 2014 the brewery planted hops on neighbouring farmland, restoring the ancient Farnham White Bine variety. ‼ ♦ RAIB

HBB (OG 1039, ABV 3.7%)
Biscuity aroma with some hops and lemon notes. Well-balanced, plenty of hop in the mouth with a long-lasting, dry bitter aftertaste.

Surrey Nirvana (OG 1039, ABV 4%)
A well-balanced, golden-coloured beer with a bittersweet balance and strong citrus aroma.

TEA (OG 1044, ABV 4.2%)
A tawny-coloured best bitter with toffee and malt present in the nose. A well-rounded flavour with malt and a fruity sweetness.

Hop Garden Gold (OG 1048, ABV 4.4%)
Full-bodied with an aroma of malt, hops and fruit. Hoppy bitterness grows in an increasingly dry aftertaste with a hint of sweetness.

Rip Snorter (OG 1052, ABV 5%)
Well-balanced, sweet and malty bitter. Red brown in colour with a moderate bitterness that grows in the aftertaste.

Hogs Head

1 Stanley Street, Sowerby Bridge, West Yorkshire, HX6 2AH
☎ (01422) 836585
hogsheadbrewpub@outlook.com

The Hogs Head Brewery opened in a huge 18th-century former malthouse at the end of 2015. The eight-barrel brewhouse is situated at the back of the accompanying bar with the copper and stainless steel brewing vats on display at the back of the building. Almost all of the production is sold on the premises with occasional casks being provided to beer festivals. ♦

Holden's SIBA IFBB

George Street, Woodsetton, West Midlands, DY1 4LW
☎ (01902) 880051 holdensbrewery.co.uk

A family brewery spanning four generations, Holden's began life as a brewpub in 1915. Continued recent expansion enables 21 tied pubs. ‼ ♦

Black Country Mild (OG 1037, ABV 3.7%)
A good, red/brown-coloured mild; a refreshing, light blend of roast malt, hops and fruit, dominated by malt throughout.

Black Country Bitter (OG 1039, ABV 3.9%)
A medium-bodied golden ale; a light, well-balanced bitter with a subtle, dry, hoppy finish.

Golden Glow (OG 1045, ABV 4.4%)
A pale golden-coloured beer with a subtle hop aroma plus gentle sweetness and a light hoppiness.

Special (OG 1052, ABV 5.1%)
A sweet, malty, full-bodied, amber-coloured ale with hops to balance in the taste and in the good, bittersweet finish.

Holler

19-23 Elder Place, Brighton, East Sussex, BN1 4BZ
☎ 07786 830368 hollerbrewery.com

Holler was established in 2017. V

Cheat Mode (ABV 3.8%)
Fruity, easy-drinking pale ale.

Brass Hand (ABV 4.2%)
A clean-tasting golden ale with an oaky, fruity bitterness.

Heavy Lifting (ABV 4.2%)
Double-hopped stout with a smooth combination of chocolate and coffee with sweet, tropical hop notes.

Mr Best (ABV 4.4%)

Fog Cutter (ABV 4.5%)
A session IPA with a citrus hop hit but smooth, sweet, biscuity notes.

Loot (ABV 5.5%)
A New England-style IPA with juicy peach notes.

Hollow Stone

See Shipstone's

Holsworthy

Unit 5, Circuit Business Park, Clawton, Devon, EX22 6RR
☎ (01566) 783678 ☎ 07879 401073
holsworthyales.co.uk

Holsworthy Ales began brewing in 2011 using a six-barrel plant, serving the local rural community. ‼ ♦ RAIB V

Mine's a Mild (OG 1035, ABV 3.5%)
A traditional English mild with a rich, malty taste.

Paler Shade of Ale (ABV 3.6%)

Original (ABV 3.8%)
A well-rounded session ale with a good bitterness and some fruity, hoppy notes.

Sunshine (OG 1040, ABV 4%)
Smooth golden ale. Hops overwhelm all else. Hints of fruit. Fresh and bitter hoppy aftertaste.

Boom! (ABV 4.2%)
A hoppy beer with a spicy finish.

Green Hop (ABV 4.3%)

Muck 'n' Straw (OG 1044, ABV 4.4%)
Hops dominate with hints of malt in aroma and taste. Well-balanced with slight dryness in the aftertaste.

Okey Smokey (ABV 4.5%)
A rich, full-flavoured, ruby-coloured ale with a warming smokiness on the nose.

Make Me Hoppy (OG 1046, ABV 4.7%)

Tamar Black (OG 1048, ABV 4.8%)
Dark-coloured stout with hints of liquorice and coffee. A complex mix full of malt, roast, fruit, hops and caramel.

Dark Bomb (OG 1050, ABV 5%)
Pleasant porter. Smoky chocolate aroma. Caramel throughout with complex sweet flavours of liquorice, malt and chocolate. Short, bittersweet, dry finish.

Hop on the Run (ABV 5%)
An American-style IPA packed full of vibrant hops.

Proper Lager (ABV 5%)

Old Market Monk (OG 1059, ABV 6.1%)
A Belgian-style ale with hints of coriander and a smooth finish.

Joseph Holt SIBA IFBB

The Brewery, Empire Street, Cheetham, Manchester, M3 1JD
(0161) 834 3285 joseph-holt.com

Joseph Holt, a family brewery, was founded in 1849 by Joseph and Catherine Holt and has remained in the family for six generations. 128 tied pubs are supplied in Manchester and the North-west plus more than 500 outlets nationally.

Mild (OG 1033, ABV 3.2%)
A dark brown/red-coloured beer with a fruity, malty nose. Roast, malt, fruit and hops in the taste, with strong bitterness for a mild, and a dry malt and hops finish.

IPA (OG 1038, ABV 3.8%)
Golden-coloured bitter with biscuity malt, hops and restrained lemony notes. Dry, bitter finish.

Bitter (OG 1040, ABV 4%)
Copper-coloured beer with malt and hops in the aroma. Malt, hops and fruit in the taste with a bitter and hoppy finish.

Two Hoots (OG 1043.8, ABV 4.2%)
A light, refreshing, well-balanced golden ale with a fruity, zesty taste.

Holy Well

4 Barnfield Close, Egerton, Bolton, BL7 9UP 07949 179338 holywellbrewing.com

A nanobrewery specialising in small batch brews celebrating different styles and traditions. These are sold mostly in bottle-conditioned form at local farmers markets plus a few local outlets. The owners have strong links with Halliwell, an ancient township of Bolton whose name derives from the original Holy Well. RAIB

Home Ales

See Oldershaw

Hooded Ram SIBA

Shepherd's Lodge, Leigh Terrace, South Quay, Douglas, Isle of Man, IM1 5AL
(01624) 612464 hoodedram.com

Brewing began in 2013 on a 2.5-barrel plant. Expansion in 2014 saw an increase to a 10-barrel plant with a 100-litre pilot plant added in 2016. Beers are available across the island. A tied pub in the old Clinch's Brewery building on the North Quay in Douglas has opened next door to the Hooded Ram Beer & Spirits store, from which all beer and merchandise are available. The brewery relocated in 2017 to larger premises and increased production. Two further pubs have opened in Wolverhampton and Birmingham. At the Isle of Man TT the brewery holds a multi-bar festival on Douglas Promenade. !! ♦ RAIB

Rams Head Bitter (OG 1037, ABV 3.7%)
A classic, amber-coloured English bitter with a balanced hop and malt mouthfeel.

Amber Ram (OG 1038, ABV 4.3%)
A well-balanced, amber-coloured session ale.

Jack the Ram Stout (OG 1044, ABV 4.7%)
Roast dominates the aroma and taste, with bitterness coming through in the finish. Plenty of body from the sweetness and fruit make this an easy-drinking stout.

Liberty East Coast Ales (OG 1044, ABV 4.8%)

Mosaic Single Hop Pale Ale (OG 1044, ABV 5%)
A notably hoppy aroma gives a clear indication of what is to come. The hop led taste is complemented with plenty of fruitiness, underlying sweetness, bitterness and a touch of malt, all of which are well matched.

Hook Norton SIBA IFBB

Brewery Lane, Scotland End, Hook Norton, Oxfordshire, OX15 5NY
(01608) 737210 hooky.co.uk

One of the finest examples of a Victorian tower brewery and the oldest independent brewery in Oxfordshire, Hook Norton has been brewing since 1849. The current premises were built in 1900 and still house much of the original machinery, including a 25hp steam engine, which operates occasionally. Shire horses are used to make deliveries to local pubs in Hook Norton and the surrounding area. Remaining family-owned, it combines its brewing heritage with a modern approach. The boardroom and Cellar Bar are available for hire. Customers can spend a day brewing their own beer. !! ♦ RAIB

Hooky Mild (OG 1033, ABV 2.8%)
A chestnut-coloured, easy-drinking mild. A complex malt and hop aroma give way to a well-balanced taste, leading to a long, hoppy finish that is unusual for a mild.

Hooky (OG 1036, ABV 3.5%)
A classic golden-coloured session bitter. Hoppy and fruity aroma followed by a malt and hops taste and a continuing hoppy finish.

Hooky Gold (ABV 4.1%)
A pale-coloured, crisp beer with a hoppy character. A fruity aroma and a pleasant light taste.

Old Hooky (OG 1048, ABV 4.6%)
A strong bitter, tawny in colour. A well-rounded fruity taste with a balanced bitter finish.

Hop & Cleaver

44 Sandhill, Newcastle upon Tyne, NE1 3JF
(0191) 261 1037 hopandcleaver.com

Established in 2014 the brewery is situated in the Hop & Cleaver pub, where the brewing equipment is on view. Its constantly changing beer range is supplied solely to the pub. ♦

Hop & Stagger SIBA

Unit 1, The Old Cow Shed, Astol Farm, Norton, Shropshire, TF11 9EW
(01952) 730737 07487 898151
hopandstaggerbrewery.co.uk

Hop & Stagger began brewing in 2012 having set up a 2.5-barrel plant at the White Lion Inn in Bridgnorth. Initially brewing a range of bitters and occasional seasonal ales exclusively for the White Lion, it has now moved to larger premises in rural Shropshire. ♦

Simpson's Original (OG 1038, ABV 3.6%)

Golden Wander (OG 1042, ABV 4.1%)

A crisp, pale golden ale with fruity notes and a lightly hoppy finish.

Pure Amber (OG 1045, ABV 4.5%)
A light amber-coloured, zesty ale.

Hop Back SIBA

Units 22-24, Batten Road Industrial Estate, Downton, Wiltshire, SP5 3HU
☎ (01725) 510986 🌐 hopback.co.uk

Founded in 1987, Hop Back owns 10 pubs and distributes nationally. The flagship beer, Summer Lightning, has won numerous CAMRA awards. **!! ♦ RAIB GF V**

GFB (OG 1035, ABV 3.5%)
A light gold-coloured, refreshing session bitter. The hoppy aroma leads to bitterness initially, lasting through to the finish with some fruit.

Citra (OG 1040, ABV 4%)
Pale yellow almost straw coloured ale with lemon and grapefruit on the aroma and taste, rapidly developing a balanced hoppy aftertaste.

Fugglestone (OG 1040, ABV 4%)
A dark copper-coloured beer with a full, slightly sweet, malty palate and a fresh, spicy citrus hoppiness.

Crop Circle (OG 1041, ABV 4.2%)
A pale yellow-coloured best bitter with a fragrant hop aroma, complex hop, fruit and citrus flavours with a balanced hoppy, bittersweet aftertaste.

Taiphoon (OG 1041, ABV 4.2%)
A clean-tasting, light, fruity beer with hops and fruit on the aroma, complex hop character and lemongrass notes in the taste, slight sweetness balanced with some astringency in the aftertaste.

Entire Stout (OG 1044, ABV 4.5%)
A smooth, rich, ruby-black-coloured stout with strong roast and malt aromas and flavours, with a long bittersweet and malty aftertaste.

Summer Lightning (OG 1048, ABV 5%)
Golden-coloured strong bitter with a hoppy aroma and slightly astringent bitterness in the taste, balanced with some fruit sweetness in the dry aftertaste.

Hop Fuzz SIBA

Unit 8, Riverside Industrial Estate, West Hythe, Kent, CT21 4NB ☎ 07730 768881 🌐 hopfuzz.co.uk

Hop Fuzz was started by two friends in 2011 and situated on an industrial estate next to the Royal Military Canal at West Hythe. In 2016, the brewery tap, Unit Number One, opened at the entrance to the estate. ♦

Yellow Zinger (OG 1038, ABV 3.7%)

Martello (OG 1038, ABV 3.8%)

Blacksmiths (OG 1042, ABV 4.2%)

Northern Star (OG 1044, ABV 4.4%)
An amber-coloured ale with honey notes.

Bullion (OG 1050, ABV 5%)

Hop Kettle

Cricklade: Red Lion, 74 High Street, Cricklade, Wiltshire, SN6 6DD
☎ (01793) 750776

Swindon: Unit 4, Hawksworth Industrial Estate, Newcombe Drive, Swindon, Wiltshire, SN2 1DZ
☎ (01793) 490556 🌐 hopkettlebrewery.co.uk

Brewing began in 2012 using a one-barrel plant. The brewery is situated in a stone barn behind the Red Lion Inn, Cricklade. A four-barrel plant followed, which now supplies the pub, with the smaller plant used for experimental brews. A further 10-barrel plant came on stream in 2016 in an old Royal Mail warehouse in Swindon. ♦

Cricklade Ordinary Bitter (ABV 3.8%)

Chameleon (ABV 4%)

North Wall (OG 1043, ABV 4.3%)

Brewed at the Swindon plant:

Loadstar (OG 1041, ABV 4.3%)
An English pale ale, a complex combination of bright fruits, spice and pine.

Rising Star (OG 1048, ABV 4.8%)

East Star (OG 1052, ABV 5%)

Red Star (OG 1051, ABV 5.2%)

Evening Star (OG 1053, ABV 5.5%)

Hop Monster

See George's

Hop Shed SIBA

Old Chicken Shed, Stocks Farm, Suckley, Worcestershire, WR6 5EQ
☎ (01886) 884110 ☎ 07484 688026
🌐 hopshed.co.uk

Originally named Unity Brew House, brewing began in 2016 using a 10-barrel plant. It is the only brewery in the UK located on a commercial hop farm. Based in an old chicken shed, the beers are named after breeds of chicken. An on-site bar is open on Fridays and Saturdays.

Buckeye Session Bitter (ABV 3.4%)
Easy-drinking, copper-coloured beer with subtle fruity hop flavours.

Sebright Golden Ale (ABV 3.8%)
Straw-coloured ale with fruity hop aromas and flavours.

Silkie Amber Ale (ABV 4.2%)
Medium-bodied ale with a pleasant bitterness and gentle, citrus hop aroma.

Frizzle British IPA (ABV 4.5%)
Golden in colour with a fruity, floral hop aroma and a significant hoppy bitterness.

Hop Studio SIBA

3 Handley Park, Elvington Industrial Estate, York Road, Elvington, North Yorkshire, YO41 4AR
☎ (01904) 608029 🌐 thehopstudio.co.uk

Founded in 2012 the Hop Studio brews on a 10-barrel plant in an industrial unit just outside York. Some barrel-aged specials are produced. Outlets in Yorkshire are supplied direct and the rest of the UK via wholesalers. ♦ RAIB

Blonde (ABV 3.5%)
Refreshing pale blonde ale with gooseberry, grapefruit and citrus aromas and flavours.

Bitter (ABV 3.9%)

Pale (ABV 4%)
A pale-coloured session ale. Grapefruit, lemon and tropical fruit tastes linger into a dry finish.

Pilsner (ABV 4.3%)

Porter (ABV 4.3%)
A dark-coloured porter. Intense chocolate, malt, vanilla and berry flavours.

Gold (ABV 4.5%)
Juicy, easy-drinking golden ale with a soft, rounded bitterness and citrus, peach and tropical fruit flavours.

India (ABV 5%)

XS (ABV 5.5%)
Strong, complex, chestnut-coloured ale. Spicy dark fruit flavours. Malty and bitter with hints of floral and citrus aroma.

Avenoir (ABV 6%)
Rich, velvety oatmeal stout. Coffee, chocolate and oat, with subtle blackcurrant and cherry flavours.

Chocolat (ABV 8.5%)

Hop Stuff SIBA

7 Gunnery Terrace, Cornwallis Road, Woolwich, London, SE18 6SW
☎ (020) 8854 9509 ☎ 07850 086461
hopstuffbrewery.com

Hop Stuff began brewing in 2013. After huge success with crowd funding it moved to a new 65-hectolitre brewhouse in 2018 and is increasing its chain of taprooms from two to eight by the end of 2019. ♦

APA (Arsenal Pale Ale) (ABV 3.8%)

Fusilier (OG 1041, ABV 4.3%)
Biscuity, malty best bitter with spicy hop notes. Finish is sweetish, slightly dry with a faint bitterness. Rich, smooth mouthfeel.

Renegade IPA (OG 1056, ABV 5.6%)
Smooth, dark gold-coloured IPA with a grapefruit and spiced hops aroma and flavour. Warm, lingering finish that is bitter and dry.

Hop Vine

c/o Hop Vine, Liverpool Road North, Burscough, Lancashire, L40 4BY
☎ (01704) 893799 ☎ 07920 002783
mikejulie6465@gmail.com

Hop Vine began brewing in 2017 using the four-barrel plant of the defunct Burscough Brewery. It is situated in old stable buildings in the courtyard to the rear of the Hop Vine. Beer is usually only supplied to the pub and the Legh Arms, Mere Brow. ♦

Hop Yard

c/o The Yard, Lewes Road, Forest Row, East Sussex, RH18 5AA
☎ (01342) 824272 hopyardbrewing.co.uk

Hop Yard began brewing in 2014 using a 100-litre brew plant. However, its cask-conditioned beers are now brewed using spare capacity at Westerham Brewery (qv). Beers are only available at its on-site brewery bar.

Golden Ale (OG 1050, ABV 5%)

Hopburst

80 Grange Road, Darlington, DL1 5NP
☎ (01325) 787912 ☎ 07929 007509
hopburstbrewing.com

Focussing on small batch ales, commercial brewing began in 2016. A micropub is planned.

Hopcraft

Unit C1, Coed Cae Lane Industrial Estate, Pontyclun, CF72 9HG ☎ 07814 255943 hopcraftbrewing.co.uk

Originally known as Pixie Spring, Hopcraft began brewing in 2011 in the Wheatsheaf, Llantrisant. In 2012 there was a joining of forces with Gazza Prescott of Steel City Brewing and a move to the present 12-barrel plant. The brewery opened the Hopbunker, a cellar bar in the centre of Cardiff, in 2015. ♦

Hopdaemon SIBA

Unit 1, Parsonage Farm, Seed Road, Newnham, Kent, ME9 0NA
☎ (01795) 892078 hopdaemon.com

Tonie Prins originally started brewing in Tyler Hill near Canterbury in 2000 and moved to a new site in Newnham in 2005. The brewery currently supplies more than 100 outlets. !! ♦ RAIB

Golden Braid (OG 1039, ABV 3.7%)
A refreshing, golden-coloured session bitter with a good blend of bittering and aroma hops underpinned by pale malt.

Incubus (OG 1041, ABV 4%)
A well-balanced, copper-hued best bitter. Pale malt and a hint of crystal malt are blended with bitter and slightly floral hops to give a lingering hoppy finish.

Skrimshander IPA (OG 1045, ABV 4.5%)
An aromatic copper-coloured pale ale with a refreshing taste and fruity finish.

Green Daemon (OG 1048, ABV 5%)
A golden-coloured beer with tropical fruit aromas and a crisp, clean finish.

Leviathan (OG 1057, ABV 6%)
A strong, ruby-coloured ale with spicy hop aromas and a rich, malty finish.

Hope Springs

Courtfield, Bacombe Lane, Wendover, Buckinghamshire, HP22 6EQ ☎ 07793 132829

Commercial brewing began in 2016. Bottle-conditioned beers are produced on an occasional basis in small batches on a 25-litre kit. Brewing is currently suspended. RAIB

Hophurst SIBA

Unit 8, Hindley Business Centre, Unit 8, Hindley Business Centre, Hindley, WN2 3PA
☎ (01942) 522333 hophurstbrewery.co.uk

Hophurst Brewery was started in 2014 by Stuart Hurst, whose passion for producing craft ales combined with 20 years of supporting businesses and re-skilling unemployed people created a unique social enterprise brewery that employs people over the age of 50 and guides them through their training programme in the Wigan area. A microbar in Ashton-in Makerfield opened in 2018. ♦

2 Rounds of 6 Before Breakfast (OG 1035, ABV 3.5%)
A refreshing beer with tropical fruit and citrus flavours.

Flaxen (OG 1038, ABV 3.7%)
A pale-coloured golden ale with a fresh, earthy hop aroma. Hints of honey in the taste and a long, refreshing finish.

Mellors (OG 1039, ABV 3.8%)
A citrus blonde ale with hop flavours of lemon and blackcurrant.

Campfire (OG 1042, ABV 3.9%)
A dark mild with a smoky, malty taste. Aromas of roasted coffee and chocolate.

Twisted Vine (OG 1041, ABV 4.1%)
A hoppy, American-style, amber-coloured ale with citrus hoppy aromas of grapefruit and passion fruit.

Cosmati (OG 1042, ABV 4.2%)
A hoppy, citrus golden ale with unique flavours of blueberry, citrus and tropical fruit.

Arlo (OG 1047, ABV 4.7%)
An American-style pale ale packed with fruity hops giving flavours of mango, grapefruit and tropical fruit.

Debonair (OG 1052, ABV 4.9%)
A robust stout with flavours of roasted coffee, liquorice and a pleasant bitter aftertaste.

Incognito (OG 1054, ABV 4.9%)
A black IPA with blueberry and tropical fruit flavours.

Hopjacker

Dronfield Arms, 91 Chesterfield Road, Dronfield, Derbyshire, S18 2XE ☎ 07841 487247 hopjacker.co.uk

Established in 2015 in the old restaurant space beneath the Dronfield Arms. Hopjacker specialises in unfined, vegan-friendly, hop-forward beers. ‼ V

The Long Con (OG 1037, ABV 3.8%)
Light copper in colour with masses of hops giving floral and pine notes to complement the subtle malt backdrop.

Pyrites (OG 1038, ABV 4.1%)
Easy-drinking golden ale with berry notes and a balanced yet lingering bitterness.

Beer House Pale (OG 1039, ABV 4.2%)
Hoppy pale ale with stunning tropical flavours and a citrus finish.

The Grifter (OG 1043, ABV 4.6%)
Rich, smooth and chocolaty oatmeal stout.

Hoppy Family (NEW)

Harcourt Street, Kettering, Northamptonshire, NN16 0RS ☎ 07986 019579 hfbrewery.com

Microbrewery established in 2017 brewing a range of bottled-conditioned beers using ingredients such as blueberries, raspberries and chillies. RAIB

Hopscotch Craft (NEW)

442 Manchester Road, Sheffield, South Yorkshire, S10 5DR ☎ 07828 869313 drinkhopscotch.co.uk

Hopscotch Craft began brewing in 2018, set up by lifelong friends Mark and Joe, who have been homebrewing for many years. A four-barrel plant is used. The beers are regularly available in an increasing number of Sheffield pubs, and direct from the brewery. ♦RAIB V

Stout (OG 1045, ABV 4.1%)
A stout with smoky, treacle notes.

Brown Ale (OG 1040, ABV 4.2%)
Brown-coloured ale with subtle fruit and nut flavours.

New England IPA (NEIPA) (OG 1042, ABV 4.6%)
IPA with passion fruit flavours and a light sourness.

Pale (OG 1044, ABV 4.8%)
Pale ale with orange notes and a bitter finish.

IPA (OG 1045, ABV 5.3%)
An IPA with honey and pineapple notes.

Hopshackle

Unit F, Bentley Business Park, Blenheim Way, Northfields Industrial Estate, Market Deeping, Lincolnshire, PE6 8LD ☎ (01778) 348542 hopshacklebrewery.co.uk

Hopshackle was established in 2006 using a five-barrel plant. A 10-barrel plant was installed in 2015. More than 40 outlets are supplied direct. ‼♦RAIB

Simarillo (OG 1037, ABV 3.8%)
Burnished gold in colour with an aroma of citrus and soft fruits. The taste is tangy fruit with blackberry, plum and pineapple.

Zen (OG 1037, ABV 3.8%)
Brown-coloured, traditional, full-flavoured bitter. Malty and fruity with a bittersweet finish.

American Pale Ale (OG 1042, ABV 4.3%)
An amber-coloured ale with a fruity, zesty aroma. The taste is citrus hop with background gooseberry and lychees and a dry bitter finish.

Hopnosis (OG 1050, ABV 5.2%)
Golden-coloured beer with a strong aroma of sweet malt and fruit. The taste is of strong citrus and tropical fruits with a dry finish.

Hopstar SIBA

Unit 9, Rinus Business Park, Grimshaw Street, Darwen, Grimshaw Street, BB3 2QX ☎ 07933 590159 hopstarbrewery.co.uk

Hopstar first brewed in 2004 on a 2.5-barrel plant and expanded in 2010 to a new unit with a six-barrel plant. More than 100 outlets are supplied around Lancashire and the Greater Manchester area. The brewery tap is Number 39 in Darwen. ‼♦RAIB

Chilli (OG 1039, ABV 3.8%)

Dizzy Danny Ale (OG 1039, ABV 3.8%)

Dark Knight (OG 1041, ABV 3.9%)

Off T'Mill (ABV 3.9%)

Smokey Joe's Black Beer (OG 1041, ABV 3.9%)
A black-coloured beer, slightly smoky with a chocolate finish.

Darwen Spitfire (ABV 4%)
A best bitter with caramel notes.

JC (OG 1041, ABV 4%)

Lancashire Gold (OG 1041, ABV 4%)

Lush (OG 1041, ABV 4%)

Saaz Blonde (OG 1038, ABV 4%)

Horbury

The Brewhouse, Healey Road, Ossett, West Yorkshire, WF5 8ND ☎ 07970 299292

Following the closure of Bob's Brewing Co, Horbury Ales took over the plant in 2016.

Horncastle

Old Nicks Tavern, 8 North Street, Horncastle, Lincolnshire, LN9 5DX
☎ (01507) 526862 horncastleales.co.uk

Brewing began in 2014 using a 3.75-barrel plant. The brewery is situated in Old Nicks Tavern with beer available in the pub plus other Lincolnshire outlets. It has its own bottling plant and a beer in box scheme is also available for pre-ordering. !!

Midnight Tempter (OG 1036.5, ABV 3.6%)
Smooth, roasted flavours with a hoppy edge.

Damned Deceiver (OG 1038, ABV 3.8%)
Smooth, rich, chestnut-coloured beer with a full body.

Wicked Blonde (OG 1039, ABV 3.9%)

Angel of Light (OG 1039.5, ABV 4%)
Light, malty beer with a nutty aftertaste.

Lilith's Lust (OG 1040.5, ABV 4.1%)
Traditional red-coloured bitter, malty and full bodied.

Satan's Fury (OG 1040.5, ABV 4.1%)
Full-bodied, fruity IPA with a dark golden colour.

Dragon's Flame (ABV 4.3%)
Light chestnut-coloured, smooth bitter with hints of vanilla and spice.

Sacrificed Soul (OG 1042, ABV 4.3%)
Chestnut-coloured, full-bodied bitter with caramel flavours and a slightly sweet edge.

Lucifer's Desire (OG 1046, ABV 4.8%)
Deep golden-coloured beer with citrus flavours and a hoppy aftertaste.

Hornes SIBA

19b Station Road, Bow Brickhill, Buckinghamshire, MK17 9JU
☎ (01908) 647724 hornesbrewery.co.uk

A purpose-built six-barrel brewery established in 2015 and producing a range of beers called Triple Goat after the three goats kept in a paddock at the brewery. There is no shop, but beers can be purchased at the brewery. ♦RAIB

Featherstone Amber Ale (OG 1037, ABV 3.6%)
A robust traditional bitter with a soft, fruity finish.

Dark Fox (OG 1039, ABV 3.8%)
A rich, malty, brown-coloured beer with burnt notes and a lasting, dry bitter finish.

Triple Goat Pale Ale (OG 1039, ABV 3.9%)
Easy-drinking, golden-coloured beer, bitter with hints of grapefruit.

Ryestone (OG 1042, ABV 4%)
A deep ruby-coloured rye ale with a spicy and fruity flavour.

Triple Goat Porter (OG 1047, ABV 4.6%)
Dark brown-coloured, sweet and fruity giving way to a lasting bitterness with hints of liquorice.

Triple Goat IPA (OG 1049, ABV 5%)
Deep golden-coloured beer, well-balanced with notes of orange and a touch of spice.

Horsforth (NEW)

Horsforth, Leeds, West Yorkshire ☎ 07854 078330
horsforthbrewery.co.uk

Brewing began in 2017 in the owner's garage and takes place twice a week on a one-barrel plant. There are plans for expansion. RAIB V

Blonde (OG 1037, ABV 3.8%)

Pale (OG 1042, ABV 4.8%)

Centennial (OG 1045, ABV 5.1%)

Simcoe (OG 1045, ABV 5.1%)

Aubretia (OG 1053, ABV 5.5%)

Night Ryder (OG 1055, ABV 5.5%)

Hoskins Brothers

See Belvoir

House (NEW)

Prince, 1 Finsbury Road, Wood Green, London, N22 8PA
☎ (020) 8888 6698

Brewing began in 2017 in the Prince public house in Wood Green. Beers are available in the pub at all times as well as a few other local outlets.

Howard Town SIBA

Hawkshead Mill, Hope Street, Glossop, Derbyshire, SK13 7SS
☎ (01457) 869800 howardtownbrewery.co.uk

Established in 2005, this eight-barrel, award-winning brewery moved to its current location in 2007. An on-site bar caters for members' evenings and open days. !! ♦RAIB

Mill Town Mild (OG 1038, ABV 3.5%)
Dark in colour and lightly hopped with hints of toffee and coffee.

Longdendale Lights (OG 1039, ABV 3.9%)

Monk's Gold (OG 1040, ABV 4%)
A golden-coloured session ale with subtle orange notes.

Wren's Nest (OG 1041, ABV 4.2%)
Citrus and floral hops dominate this uncompromising bitter.

Super Fortress (OG 1044, ABV 4.4%)
Well-balanced, chestnut-coloured premium bitter with malty caramel notes and fruity hops.

Dark Peak (OG 1064, ABV 6%)
Strong and dark in colour with a hint of liquorice and a warming rum kick.

Howling Hops

Unit 9a, Queen's Yard, White Post Lane, Hackney Wick, London, E9 5EN
☎ (020) 3583 8262 howlinghops.co.uk

Brewing began in 2012. Originally brewing at the Cock Tavern in Hackney, a new plant opened in 2015 in Hackney Wick. Beers are available at the on-site tap room, the Tank Bar, the Cock and occasionally in local free houses and at beer festivals. RAIB

Hubsters SIBA

Kenyons Farm, Gough Lane, Bamber Bridge, Lancashire, PR5 6AR
☎ (01772) 837655 ☎ 07725 057028
hubstersbrewery.co.uk

Hubsters started brewing commercially in 2017 using a five-barrel plant. The four regular beers are supplemented by seasonal and one-off brews and are available from a number of outlets in the local area. RAIB

Hop Session (ABV 3.6%)
Easy-drinking session ale with a balanced hop and malt profile.

Hop On (ABV 3.8%)
Full-bodied bitter with a sweet and spicy aftertaste.

Hopscotch (ABV 4%)
A light ale with the refreshing taste of tropical fruits and a citrus hop aroma.

Tribute (ABV 4%)
Dark oak-coloured, smooth, sweet ale with a slightly smoky finish.

Sarah Hughes

Beacon Hotel, 129 Bilston Street, Sedgley, West Midlands, DY3 1JE
☎ (01902) 883381 sarahhughesbrewery.co.uk

Traditional Black Country Victorian tower brewery, taken over by Sarah Hughes in 1921. Brewing ceased in the 1950s and recommenced in 1987. The original grist case and rare open-topped copper give a unique character to the brews. The Beacon Hotel is the brewery tap. !! ♦

Pale Amber (OG 1038, ABV 4%)
A well-balanced beer, initially slightly sweet but with hops close behind.

Sedgley Surprise (OG 1048, ABV 5%)
A bittersweet, medium-bodied, hoppy ale with some malt.

Dark Ruby Mild (OG 1058, ABV 6%)
A dark ruby-coloured, strong ale with a good balance of fruit and hops, leading to a pleasant, lingering hops and malt finish.

Humpty Dumpty SIBA

Church Road, Reedham, Norfolk, NR13 3TZ
☎ (01493) 701818 ☎ 07843 248865
humptydumptybrewery.co.uk

Established in 1998, this 11-barrel, award-winning brewery continues to grow and expand its range of beers. !! ♦ RAIB

Little Sharpie (OG 1039, ABV 3.8%)
Solid malty character throughout with an initial caramel boost. Grainy mouthfeel matches an increasingly bitter finish. Tart hoppy finale.

Lemon & Ginger (OG 1041, ABV 4%)
An amber-coloured, crisp ale with a ginger and lemon tang.

Swallowtail (OG 1041, ABV 4%)
Full-bodied marmalade and biscuit aroma with matching beginning. Grainy texture is enhanced by solid bitter notes flowing onward.

Ale (OG 1042, ABV 4.1%)
A hoppy vanilla fudge edge in both nose and taste. Malt provides balance as a gentle bitterness quickly recedes. Lengthy finish.

Broadland Sunrise (OG 1043, ABV 4.2%)
Rolling malt bouquet with tangerine notes. Well-balanced mix of malt, tangerine, gentle bittersweet hoppiness and caramel. Refreshing bitter finish.

Red Mill (OG 1045, ABV 4.3%)
A peppery redcurrant nose and grainy mouthfeel. Bittersweet base with vine fruit adding depth and gravity. Long, sherry-like finish.

Reedcutter (OG 1045, ABV 4.4%)
A sweet, malty beer; golden hued with a gentle malt background. Smooth and full-bodied with a quick, gentle finish.

Cheltenham Flyer (OG 1047, ABV 4.6%)
A full-flavoured, golden-coloured, earthy bitter with a long, grainy finish. A strong hop bitterness dominates throughout. Little evidence of malt.

EAPA (East Anglian Pale Ale) (OG 1047, ABV 4.6%)
Amber gold-coloured with an orange marmalade nose. A bittersweet caramel beginning slowly dries out as malty nuances fade away.

Hungry Bear

10-14 Stonegate Road, Leeds, West Yorkshire, LS6 4HY
☎ (0113) 274 0241 thehungrybear.co.uk

Hungry Bear began brewing in 2013 in the upstairs rooms of the Hungry Bear restaurant. A wide range of ales is produced in batches of about 70 litres, which are bottled and conditioned on site and supplied to the restaurant and also on sale from the off licence facility on the premises. !! RAIB V

Hunters SIBA

Bulleigh Barton Farm, Ipplepen, Devon, TQ12 5UA
☎ (01803) 873509 ☎ 07540 657115
huntersbrewery.com

Hunters began brewing in 2008. The award-winning brewery has a 60-barrel brew length and 4,000 gallon fermenting capacity. A bottling, labelling and packing plant means it can turn out 3,000 bottle-conditioned beers per hour; this, coupled with a dedicated conditioning room, is enabling Hunters to bottle for others as well as itself. !! ♦ RAIB

Old Charlie (OG 1038, ABV 3.8%)
Good malt feel in the mouth, dry, tangy bitter finish.

Crispy Pig (OG 1042, ABV 4%)
Speciality beer with a hint of apples. Refreshingly sharp and hoppy.

THE BREWERIES

Half Bore (OG 1040, ABV 4%) ◈
Light in colour and body. Malt dominates from start to finish. Lots of flavour and slightly flowery.

Devon Dreamer (OG 1042, ABV 4.1%) ◈
Amber-coloured best bitter with hop aroma and undertones of caramel. Hops in the taste and slight bitterness develops later.

Pheasant Plucker (OG 1044, ABV 4.3%)
Full-flavoured with a bittersweet finish.

Premium (OG 1048, ABV 4.8%)
A zesty, refreshing, well-balanced ale

Royal Hunt (OG 1055, ABV 5.5%) ◈
An easy-drinking strong ale. Malt dominates, with rich roast and caramel tones bursting through.

Black Jack (OG 1062, ABV 6%)
Triple-hopped stout made with Devon honey.

Full Bore (OG 1070, ABV 6.8%)
A malty ale made with Devon honey.

Hurly Burly

15 Wedderburn Terrace, Musselburgh, EH21 7TJ
☎ (0131) 665 8135

Office: 15 Glenorchy Road, North Berwick, EH39 4PH
🌐 hurlyburlybrewery.co.uk

Small, family-run brewery producing bottle-conditioned ales in the brewer's back kitchen. RAIB

Hurns

See Tomos Watkin (under W)

Husk

Unit 58a, Railway Arches, North Woolwich Road, West Silvertown, London, E16 2AA
☎ (020) 7474 3827 ☎ 07803 271160
🌐 huskbrewing.com

Brewing in West Silvertown, along the Royal Docks, since 2015. The first brewery in the area now has its taproom open every Friday and Saturday. RAIB

Milk Stout (OG 1050, ABV 5.1%)
Dark roast and chocolate milk stout given a silky feel with the addition of oats.

Pale Ale (OG 1050, ABV 5.1%) ◈
Light citrus, hoppy, bready aroma. Taste is slightly sweet, balanced with lemon peel, slight spiciness and tangerines becoming more bitter.

Mandarin & Earl Grey IPA (ABV 5.5%)
A light malt base, loaded with hops and infused with Earl Grey tea.

Hybrid SIBA

Unit 14c, Abbotsinch Road Industrial Estate, Grangemouth, FK3 9UX ✉ piker@blueyonder.co.uk

Hybrid began brewing in 2016 using a 10.5-barrel dual train brewplant, allowing for two different beers to be brewed at a time. 40 outlets are supplied direct.

Hydes IFBB

The Beer Studio, 30 Kansas Avenue, Salford, M50 2GL
☎ (0161) 226 1317 🌐 hydesbrewery.com

Hydes Brewery has been in the Manchester area since 1863, in 2012 it relocated to Salford's Media City area. The new plant brews four traditional beers and over fifty seasonal beers (three or four each month). 15 recipes are brewed under the banner of The Beer Studio, 12 are marketed as Provenance, reflecting different international beer styles. New for 2018 is the Kansas Avenue Brewing Co brand. ‼♦

1863 (OG 1033.5, ABV 3.5%) ◈
Lightly-hopped, pale brown-coloured session beer with some hops, malt and fruit in the taste and a short, dry finish.

Old Indie (OG 1033.5, ABV 3.5%) ◈
Dark brown/red in colour with a fruit and malt nose. Tastes include biscuity malt and green fruits, with a satisfying aftertaste.

Original (OG 1036.5, ABV 3.8%) ◈
Pale brown-coloured beer with a malty nose, malt and an earthy hoppiness in the taste, and a good bitterness through to the finish.

Lowry (ABV 4.7%)

Iâl SIBA

Pant Du Road, Eryrys, CH7 4DD ☎ 07956 440402
🌐 cwrwial.com

Cwrw Iâl Community Brewery is run as a social enterprise assisted by EU funding with all profits used for local community projects. The 10-barrel plant brews a core range as well as regular specials. It supplies outlets along the North Wales coast and in the North-west. ♦

Pocket Rocket (OG 1040, ABV 4%)
A pale session IPA.

Kia Kaha! (OG 1043, ABV 4.3%) ◈
A dry, bitter beer, gold in colour with a fruity aroma leading to a good hoppy taste and finish.

Lager (OG 1043, ABV 4.3%)
Crisp and clean, unfiltered, unpasteurised session lager.

Limestone Cowboy (OG 1045, ABV 4.5%) ◈
A copper-coloured best bitter, malty with faint roast notes and fruit flavours. Hops dominate in the dry bitter finish.

The Apache Line (OG 1050, ABV 5%)
An IPA with big mango fruit aromas, with a smooth bitterness and tropical fruits notes.

Pothole Porter (OG 1054, ABV 5.1%) ◈
A rich and fruity porter with a smooth mouthfeel and good roast notes in aroma and taste.

Iceni

Foulden Road, Ickburgh, Norfolk, IP26 5HB
☎ (01842) 878922 ☎ 07949 488113
🌐 icenibrewery.co.uk

The Iceni brewery is situated on the edge of the Thetford Forest, in the Brecklands area of Norfolk. The brewery is owned by Brendan Moore who set it up in 1995. ‼♦RAIB

Fine Soft Day (OG 1038, ABV 4%) ◈
Golden-hued with toffee notes throughout. A creamy, lightly-hopped backdrop softly sinks into a pleasant sweetness.

Idle

White Hart Inn, Main Street, West Stockwith, Nottinghamshire, DN10 4EY
(01427) 892672 07949 137174
theidlebrewery.co.uk

The brewery began production in 2007 and is situated in a converted stable at the back of the White Hart Inn, which Brian Cooper, the brewer, now owns. !!♦

Golden Crown (OG 1038, ABV 3.8%)

Dog (OG 1041, ABV 4.2%)
A copper-coloured ale, moderately hoppy with a good balance of malt and hops leading to a bitter finish.

Sod (OG 1041, ABV 4.2%)
Light golden-coloured ale which has a deep, fruity aroma and a well-balanced, hoppy bitterness.

Tongue (OG 1041, ABV 4.2%)

Black & Tan (OG 1042, ABV 4.3%)

Black Abbot (OG 1044, ABV 4.6%)
A black-coloured, strong ale with deep roasted notes.

Idle Landlord (OG 1044, ABV 4.6%)
A dark brown-coloured, full-bodied ale with a malty flavour and a caramel/coffee finish.

Ignition (NEW)

44a Sydenham Road, Sydenham, London, SE26 5QX
(020) 8852 4100 ignition.beer

Ignition is a South London brewery which employs and trains people with learning disabilities to brew beer. Beers are available bottle-conditioned in the London area. RAIB

Ilkley SIBA

The New Brewery, Ashlands Road, Ilkley, West Yorkshire, LS29 8JT
(01943) 604604 ilkleybrewery.co.uk

Ilkley brewery was founded in 2009 and now produces up to 160 barrels per week. It continues to expand, having aquired new units on the same site in 2016 and 2017. Further expansion in 2018-2019 will increase capacity by 40%. The brewery holds regular events and tours. !!♦RAIB

Mary Jane (OG 1036, ABV 3.5%)
A crisp, pale ale with citrus aromas.

Blonde (ABV 3.9%)

Ruby Jane (ABV 4%)

Fireside (ABV 4.2%)
A smoky porter.

Pale (ABV 4.2%)

Rombald (ABV 4.6%)
American-style, amber-coloured ale with crisp and fruity hop flavours.

Hanging Stone (ABV 5%)
Rich and creamy, with a bitter finish of forest fruits and coffee.

Crossroads IPA (ABV 5.4%)
Aromas of orange rind and citrus peel with dry, spicy finish.

Imperial

Arcadia Hall, Cliff Street, Mexborough, South Yorkshire, S64 9HU
(01709) 584000 07428 422703
imperialclub@hotmail.co.uk

Brewing began in 2010 using a six-barrel tower brewery system located in the basement of the Imperial Club, Mexborough. Beer is available in the club as well as local outlets. !!♦RAIB

Bitter (OG 1039, ABV 3.9%)

Blonde (OG 1040, ABV 4%)

Darkness (OG 1040, ABV 4%)

Bees Knees (OG 1043, ABV 4.2%)

Hop Bomb (OG 1042, ABV 4.2%)

IPA (OG 1052, ABV 5.5%)

Stout (OG 1054, ABV 5.8%)

Inadequate (NEW)

Holy Inadequate, 67 Etruria Old Road, Etruria, Stoke-on-Trent, ST1 5PE
(01782) 915170

Brewing began in 2017 in a building to the side of the Holy Inadequate pub.

Incredible SIBA

214-224 Broomhill Road, Brislington, Bristol, BS4 5RG
07780 977073 incrediblebrewingcompany.com

This microbrewery specialises in producing small batches of beer using a 2.5-barrel plant. It was established in 2014 by head brewer Stephen Hall with the aim of promoting experimental beers and traditional recipes. !!♦RAIB V

Milk Stout (OG 1044, ABV 4.4%)

Pale Ale (OG 1043, ABV 4.4%)

Amber Ale (OG 1052, ABV 5.2%)

Black IPA (OG 1056, ABV 5.6%)

Grapefruit IPA (OG 1054, ABV 5.6%)

Indian Pale Ale (OG 1063, ABV 6.6%)
This IPA has a robust maltiness and is powerfully hopped.

Independent Lakeland

See Strands

Indian

119b Baltimore Trading Estate, Baltimore Road, Great Barr, B42 1DD
(0121) 296 9000 indianbrewery.com

This six-barrel brewery, established in 2005 as the Tunnel Brewery at the Lord Nelson Inn, relocated to the picturesque stable block at Red House Farm in 2011. In 2015 the owners of Tunnel Brewery went their separate ways, with Mike Walsh retaining the brewery and renaming it the Indian Brewery. Later that year the Indian Brewery was sold to new owners and relocated to the outskirts of Birmingham. !!

Summer (ABV 4%)
A full-flavoured beer with distinct citrus hop notes.

IPA (ABV 4.9%)
A well-rounded IPA with citrus punch and tropical fruit flavours.

Bombay Honey (ABV 5%)
A blonde beer brewed with real honey.

Peacock (ABV 5%)
Vibrant amber-coloured ale with sweet mellow and spiced berry flavours.

Indigenous

Peacock Cottage, Main Street, Chaddleworth, Berkshire, RG20 7EH
☎ (01488) 505060 🌐 indigenousbrewery.co.uk

⊗ An occasional and informal microbrewer for many years, Kevin Brady established Indigenous in 2014, increasing production using a 2.5-barrel plant. Availability is restricted to local pubs, shops and an increasing number of regional beer festivals. ‼ ♦ RAIB

Baldrick (ABV 3.4%)
A smooth mild ale that delivers plenty of malty flavours.

Forager's Gold (OG 1038, ABV 4%)
A crisp golden ale. Smooth and refreshing with caramel notes.

Summer Solstice (OG 1042, ABV 4.1%)
A straw-coloured pale ale with a fresh, hoppy aroma coupled with a subtle bitterness and a long, dry finish.

Billy No Mates (OG 1050, ABV 4.2%)
A well-hopped, American-style pale ale with a slightly hazy appearance, good malt balance and a slightly bitter finish.

Frisky Mare (ABV 4.2%)
A generously-hopped, golden-coloured ale with notes of gooseberry, grape and floral accents, leading to a long, dry finish.

Monocle (OG 1049, ABV 4.5%)
A smooth stout with a malty aroma and slightly dry finish.

Nutcracker (ABV 4.5%)
A brown-coloured ale that delivers a good mix of roasted malts and fruity hops.

Old Cadger (OG 1046, ABV 4.5%)
Rich malts and fruity hops combine to produce a balanced, full-flavoured beer.

Moonstruck (OG 1051, ABV 4.8%)
A porter with plenty of chocolate and coffee notes, complemented by a subtle bitterness and smooth finish.

Nosey Parker (OG 1058, ABV 5.5%)
A strong ruby-coloured mild with a sweet malty base and a hint of hops.

AMMO Belle (OG 1055, ABV 5.6%)
A well-hopped, American-style pale ale that delivers lots of fruity notes, a floral aroma and a moderately dry finish.

Double Warp (ABV 5.8%)
A rich, dark-coloured, full-flavoured stout with plenty of deep chocolate notes and a hint of spice.

Inishmacsaint

See Fermanagh

Inkspot

Office: 42 Fox Hill, London, SE19 2XE ☎ 07747 607803 🌐 theinkspotbrewery.com

Inkspot began cuckoo brewing in 2012. A brewplant is due to come on stream in Streatham during the currency of this guide.

Inner Bay SIBA

Seacliffe Villa, Hill Street, Inverkeithing, KY11 1AB 🌐 innerbay.co.uk

Brewing began in 2016. Inner Bay is a family-run brewery using traditional ingredients and methods producing bottle-conditioned beers in small batches. RAIB

INNformal

Five Bells, Baydon Road, Wickham, Berkshire, RG20 8HH
☎ (01488) 657300 🌐 fivebellswickham.co.uk

⊗ INNformal was established in 2015 in a purpose-built building behind the Five Bells pub in Wickham. A bore hole in the pub garden supplies water for the 2.5-barrel plant. A secondary 0.5-barrel kit is used for experimental brews. Beers are supplied mainly to the Five Bells and the John O'Gaunt, Hungerford. ‼ ♦

Innis & Gunn

See Inveralmond

Instant Karma

4 John Street, Clay Cross, Derbyshire, S45 9NQ
☎ (01246) 250366 🌐 instantkarmabrewery.co.uk

Instant Karma began brewing in 2012 using a five-barrel plant with a brew length of 15 barrels per week. The brewery is part of the Rykneld Turnpyke brewpub.

Interbrew UK

Porter Tun House, Capability Green, Luton, Bedfordshire, LU1 3LS
☎ (01582) 391166

Interbrew (Magor): Magor Brewery, Magor, NP26 3DA

Interbrew (Samlesbury): Cuerdale Lane, Samlesbury, PR5 0XD

UK subsidiary of A-B InBev. No real ale.

Intrepid SIBA

Unit 12, Vincent Works, Brough, Derbyshire, S33 9HG
☎ (01433) 621851 ☎ 07870 777594

Based in the Hope Valley in the Peak District, Intrepid commenced brewing in 2014 using an eight-barrel plant. ‼ ♦

Explorer (OG 1038, ABV 4%)
A refreshing blonde beer with fruity aromas and a crisp, dry finish.

St Bernard (OG 1044, ABV 4.4%)
A malty ale with oak and vanilla aromas and caramel and biscuit flavours.

Porter (OG 1049, ABV 4.8%)

A traditional porter but using modern hops for a less bitter finish.

Traveller (OG 1049, ABV 5.4%)
American-style IPA with a fruity flavour and bitter finish.

Inveralmond

22 Inveralmond Place, Perth, PH1 3TS
☎ (01738) 449448 inveralmond-brewery.co.uk

Established in 1997, Inveralmond was the first brewery in Perth for more than 30 years. Around 250 outlets are supplied. In 2016, Innis & Gunn, the Edinburgh company that specialises in oak-aged beers, bought Inveralmond following a successful crowdfunding scheme that raised £3 million. I&G had planned to build a new brewing operation but decided instead to buy the Perth brewery, where the current 30-barrel plant will be expanded, with a new maturation plant for the I&G beers. I&G makes no real ale but the Inveralmond range will continue. ‼♦

EPA (ABV 3.8%)

Ossian (OG 1042, ABV 4.1%)
Well-balanced best bitter with a dry finish. This full-bodied, amber-coloured ale is dominated by fruit and hop with a bittersweet character although excessive caramel can distract from this.

Lia Fail (OG 1048, ABV 4.7%)
A dark-coloured, robust, full-bodied beer with a deep malty taste. Smooth texture and balanced finish.

Daracha (ABV 5.2%)
An oak matured, ruby-coloured Scotch ale.

Rascal London Porter (OG 1056, ABV 5.6%)

Iron Pier (NEW)

Units 6 & 7, May Industrial Estate, May Avenue, Northfleet, Gravesend, Kent, DA11 8RU
ironpier.beer

Iron Pier Brewery was established in 2017 using a 15-barrel plant. It takes its name from the oldest iron pier in existence residing on the River Thames at Gravesend. An on-site tap room offers the brewery's beers plus other local brews.

American Pale (ABV 3.7%)
A refreshing, light-bodied pale ale. Fruity, crisp and smoothly bitter.

Perry St Pale (ABV 3.7%)
A refreshing, light-bodied pale ale with tones of fruit and a smooth bitterness.

Bitter (OG 1040, ABV 4%)
A traditional English bitter with smooth bitterness, dark fruit and toffee flavours plus honey and spice hop notes.

English Pale (OG 1040, ABV 4.1%)
A hoppy pale ale with herbal, floral and fruit notes.

Porter (OG 1052, ABV 5.3%)
Rich porter with notes of chocolate and coffee. Balanced bitterness with dark fruit flavours in the finish.

Irving SIBA

Unit G1, Railway Triangle, Walton Road, Portsmouth, Hampshire, PO6 1TQ
☎ (023) 9238 9988 irvingbrewers.co.uk

Established in 2007 by former Gale's brewer Malcolm Irving using a 15-barrel plant. Around 120 outlets are supplied in Hampshire, Sussex and Surrey with beers available further afield through beer swaps with other breweries. Speciality beers may be ordered for festivals. ‼♦

Frigate (OG 1039, ABV 3.8%)
Satisfying session bitter. Hoppy, with a floral aroma and initial sweetness, leading to bitterness and a smooth, slightly dry finish.

Type 42 (OG 1042, ABV 4.2%)
A robust best bitter with a deep ruby red hue balancing sweet hedgerow berry notes with a long, roasted malt finish and a deep bitterness.

Admiral Stout (OG 1042.5, ABV 4.3%)
Well-balanced stout with plenty of fruit and roast together with pleasant hint of coffee. A short bitter finish.

Invincible (OG 1048, ABV 4.6%)
Tawny-coloured strong bitter. Sweet and fruity with underlying maltiness throughout and gradually increasing dryness, contrasting with the sweet finish.

Iron Duke (OG 1053, ABV 5.3%)
A refreshing, well-balanced, strong IPA. Hoppy – but not overly so.

Irwell Works SIBA

Irwell Street, Ramsbottom, BL0 9YQ
☎ (01706) 825019 irwellworksbrewery.co.uk

Irwell Works started brewing in 2010 in a building dating from 1888 that once housed the Irwell Works steam, tin, copper and iron works. It now houses a six-barrel plant. The brewery tap is on the first floor and hosts regular live music events. ‼♦GF

Lightweights & Gentlemen (OG 1031, ABV 3.2%)
Light, refreshing pale ale with some fruitiness and a hoppy, bitter finish.

Breadcrumbs (ABV 3.6%)
A light, session pale ale. Good bitterness followed by a spicy hoppiness.

Tin Plate (OG 1033, ABV 3.6%)
A traditional dark mild with a rich, creamy flavour and slight bitterness to contrast.

Copper Plate (OG 1036, ABV 3.8%)
Traditional Northern bitter. Copper-coloured with a satisfying blend of malt and hops and a good bitterness.

Costa Del Salford (OG 1039, ABV 4.1%)

Steam Plate (OG 1042, ABV 4.3%)
A golden-coloured best bitter with medium bitterness balanced by a slight sweetness.

Iron Plate (OG 1043, ABV 4.4%)
Roast malt in the aroma is joined by hop and a toasty bitterness in the taste and finish.

Marshmallow Unicorn (ABV 4.4%)
A dark-coloured, creamy milk stout.

Mad Dogs & Englishmen (OG 1052, ABV 5.5%)
A strong pale ale. Little sweetness for its strength and a strong hop character make this a smooth and easy drinking.

THE BREWERIES

Isaac Poad SIBA

Office: Axholme Croft, Chapel Street, Cattal, York, North Yorkshire, YO26 8DY
☎ (01423) 358114 🌐 isaacpoad.co.uk

Established in 2016, this is a subsidiary of a long established grain merchant known for supplying malting barley to many local maltsters. Currently using spare capacity at another local brewery pending the construction of its own plant, the emphasis is on using local Yorkshire malt and only British hops. ♦

No. 86 Golden Ale (OG 1008, ABV 3.6%)

1863 Best Bitter (OG 1009, ABV 3.8%)

No. 84 India Pale Ale (OG 1009, ABV 4.5%)
A powerful IPA with a huge hop aroma.

Isca SIBA

Court Farm, Holcombe, Devon, EX7 0JT ☎ 07773 444501 🌐 iscaales.co.uk

Established in a disused milking parlour in 2009, Isca has developed a large range of ales. Seasonal and special brews are often available at beer festivals, including outside of the region. ♦RAIB V

Citra (OG 1038, ABV 3.8%)
Light, refreshing beer with a grapefruit aroma leading to a dry bitter finish.

Dawlish Summer (OG 1038, ABV 3.8%)

Golden Ale (OG 1038, ABV 3.8%)

Dawlish Bitter (OG 1042, ABV 4.2%)

Glorious Devon (OG 1044, ABV 4.4%)

Gold (OG 1045, ABV 4.5%)
Golden-coloured beer, hoppy with a dry bitter finish.

Holcombe White (OG 1045, ABV 4.5%)
Cloudy wheat beer with hints of banana, oranges and spice.

Dawlish Pale (OG 1050, ABV 5%)

Black IPA (OG 1060, ABV 6%)

Devon Pale (OG 1068, ABV 6.8%)

Isla Vale

17 Westbrook Gardens, Margate, Kent, CT9 5DJ
☎ (01843) 292451 ☎ 07980 174616
🌐 islavalealesmiths.co.uk

Isla Vale was established in 2014 from a residential address in Westbrook (Margate). Along with its core range, specially commissioned beers are brewed for the Wheel Alehouse, Birchington, and the London Tavern, Margate. Outlets are supplied locally and across the South-east of England. ♦

Golding Delicious (OG 1038, ABV 3.8%)
A light, copper-coloured session ale with a slight malty sweetness.

Hopping Mad (OG 1042, ABV 4%)
A traditional session bitter, hoppy with complex aromas and malty flavours.

Two Halves (OG 1040, ABV 4%)

Ninkasi Pale Ale (OG 1045, ABV 4.5%)
A hoppy pale ale with added elderflower.

Big Red Beer (OG 1046, ABV 4.6%)
A red-coloured session beer; fruity with a hint of honey.

Cock-A-Snook (OG 1045, ABV 4.6%)
A dark gold-coloured session ale with a good hop aroma and hints of fruit.

Natural Blonde (OG 1046, ABV 4.7%)
A refreshing blonde ale, initial floral notes with a lasting hoppy bitterness throughout.

Befuggled (OG 1052, ABV 5.2%)
A rich, malty ale with plenty of hops.

IPA (OG 1058, ABV 5.5%)
A hint of fruit with an intense hoppy aroma and flavour.

Island SIBA

Dinglers Farm, Yarmouth Road, Newport, Isle of Wight, PO30 4LZ
☎ (01983) 821731 🌐 islandbrewery.co.uk

Island Brewery is the realisation of Tom Minshull's ambition to brew real ales to complement the existing family-owned drinks distribution business. Brewing commenced in 2010 using a 12-barrel brewery. More than 100 outlets are supplied direct. ‼♦

Nipper Bitter (OG 1038, ABV 3.8%)
Straw-coloured, light and refreshing with a good balance of malt and hops.

Wight Gold (OG 1040, ABV 4%)
Golden brown in colour with rounded malt and hops throughout.

Yachtsmans Ale (OG 1042, ABV 4.2%)
Chestnut-coloured ale with a rich, malty mouthfeel and hop aroma.

Wight Diamond (OG 1046, ABV 4.4%)

Wight Knight (OG 1045, ABV 4.5%)

Vectis Venom (OG 1048, ABV 4.8%)
Malty, dark ruby-coloured ale with an easy-drinking and underlying smooth characteristic.

Earls RDA (OG 1052, ABV 5%)
Rich stout with a classic espresso aftertaste.

Islay SIBA

The Brewery, Islay House Square, Bridgend, Isle of Islay, PA44 7NZ
☎ (01496) 810014 🌐 islayales.beer

The only brewery on an island famous for its malt whiskies, Islay Ales started brewing in 2004 and continues to use a four-barrel plant. Situated in converted farm buildings including a visitor centre and shop. ‼ ♦RAIB

Finlaggan Ale (OG 1039, ABV 3.7%)
A mid brown-coloured beer with a gentle, rounded bitterness and a fresh, fruity and hoppy flavour.

Black Rock Ale (OG 1040, ABV 4.2%)
A red-coloured beer with a soft, nutty flavour, a robust body and a floral, grassy and herbal nose.

Saligo Ale (OG 1044, ABV 4.4%)
A golden ale with a rounded bitterness and a refreshing citrus, lemon and grapefruit nose and taste.

Angus Og Ale (OG 1045, ABV 4.5%)

Isle of Avalon SIBA

Stagman Lane, Ashcott, Somerset, TA7 9QW
☎ (01458) 210050 ☎ 07809 056855
avalonwholesaleandbrewing.co.uk

Brewing began in 2008. Isle Of Avalon is a five-barrel plant brewing for the parent company Avalon Wholesale, and occasionally for one-off events and local supply.

Isle of Mull

See Argyll

Isle of Purbeck SIBA

Manor Road, Studland, Dorset, BH19 3AU
☎ (01929) 450227 isleofpurbeckbrewery.com

Founded in 2003, the brewery is situated in the grounds of the Bankes Arms Hotel, overlooking Studland Bay on the Jurassic Coast. A 10-barrel plant is used. The core beers are available nationwide via exchange swaps with other small breweries and at local beer festivals. ♦RAIB

Purbeck Best Bitter (OG 1036, ABV 3.6%)
A classic malty best bitter with rich malt aroma and taste and smooth, malty, bitter finish.

Force Four (OG 1040, ABV 4%)
A smooth-drinking beer packed with sweet roasted malt flavours and subtle spicy hop notes.

Fossil Fuel (OG 1040, ABV 4.1%)
Amber-coloured bitter with a complex aroma and a hint of pepper; rich malt dominates the taste, leading to a smooth, dry finish.

Solar Power (OG 1043, ABV 4.3%)
Tawny-coloured ale. Well-balanced flavours combine to provide a strong bitter taste but short, dry finish.

Studland Bay Wrecked (OG 1044, ABV 4.5%)
Deep red-coloured ale with a slightly sweet aroma reflecting a mixture of caramel, malt and hops that lead to a dry, malty finish.

Purbeck IPA (OG 1047, ABV 4.8%)
Mid-brown-coloured beer with hop/malt balance in the flavour and a long, dry aftertaste.

Isle of Skye SIBA

The Pier, Uig, Isle of Skye, IV51 9XP
☎ (01470) 542477 skyeale.com

The Isle of Skye Brewery was established in 1995. Originally a 10-barrel plant, it was upgraded to 20 barrels in 2004. Further expansion is planned. !! ♦

Skyelight (OG 1038, ABV 3.8%)
A slightly hoppy nose leads to a powerful hop and fruit taste and a sharp finish.

Tarasgeir (OG 1040, ABV 4%)
The peat roasted barley dominates giving a mellow peaty whisky taste.

Tiny Angels (OG 1040, ABV 4%)

YP (Young Pretender) (OG 1039, ABV 4%)
A refreshing, amber-coloured, hoppy grapefruit bitter. Some sweetness in the taste but continuing into a lingering bitter finish.

Skye Red (OG 1041, ABV 4.2%)
A light, fruity nose with a hint of caramel leads to a hoppy, malty, fruity flavour and a dry, bittersweet finish.

Skye Gold (OG 1041.5, ABV 4.3%)
Porridge oats are used to produce this speciality beer. Nicely balanced, it has a refreshingly soft lemon, bitter flavour with an oat background.

Skye Black (OG 1044, ABV 4.5%)
Full-bodied with a malty richness. Malt holds sway but there are plenty of hops and fruit to be discovered in its varied character. A delicious Scottish old ale.

Skye IPA (OG 1046, ABV 4.5%)
Well-balanced with a good malty background and complemented with hops.

Blaven (OG 1047, ABV 5%)
A well-balanced, strong, amber-coloured bitter with kiwi fruit and caramel in the nose and a lingering, sharp bitterness.

Skye Blonde (ABV 5.5%)
Citrus hoppy brew with some caramel sweetness.

Cuillin Beast (OG 1066, ABV 7%)
A winter warmer; sweet and fruity. Plenty of caramel throughout with a variety of fruit on the nose.

Itchen Valley SIBA

Unit D, Prospect Commercial Park, Prospect Road, Alresford, Hampshire, SO24 9QF
☎ (01962) 735111 itchenvalleybrewery.com

Established in 1997, Itchen Valley moved to new premises in 2006 with a 20-barrel plant. More than 350 pubs are supplied, with wholesalers used for further distribution. !! ♦RAIB

Pride of the Valley (ABV 3.8%)
An easy-drinking session bitter. Hazel-coloured with orange, coffee and honey notes.

Hampshire Rose (OG 1042, ABV 4.2%)
An amber-coloured ale. Fruit and hops dominate the taste throughout, with a good mouthfeel.

New Hampshire (ABV 4.3%)
A light, refreshing American-style pale ale. Hoppy with flavours of peach, pear and citrus.

Pure Gold (OG 1046, ABV 4.8%)
Aromatic hoppy, strong bitter. Golden-coloured, with initial maltiness and grapefruit counterbalanced with some sweetness, leading to a dry finish.

James Street

City Pub Company, 14 James Street West, Bath, BA1 2BX
☎ (01225) 805609

Office: City Pub Company Plc, Essel House, 2nd Floor, 29 Foley Street, London, W1W 7TH
thebathbrewhouse.com

The James Street Brewery opened in 2013 and is owned by the City Pub Company, which owns several other pubs around the country. The compact brewery is on the ground floor of the Bath Brewhouse, with the fermenting vessels and conditioning tanks on the first floor. The company's other pub, the Cork, Bath, is also supplied. !! ♦

THE BREWERIES

Jaw SIBA

Unit 9, The Centre Point, 67b Montrose Avenue, Hillington Industrial Estate, Hillington, G52 4LA ☎ (0141) 237 5840 jawbrew.co.uk

Brewing began in 2014. RAIB

Drop (OG 1042, ABV 4.2%)

Surf (OG 1043, ABV 4.3%)

Drift (OG 1047, ABV 4.6%)

Wave (OG 1048, ABV 4.7%)

Jeffersons (NEW)

Brew Shed, 84 Verdun Road, Barnes, London, SW13 8AX jeffersonsbrewery.co.uk

Brewing began in 2017 at this nanobrewery in Barnes, London.

Jennings

Castle Brewery, Cockermouth, Cumbria, CA13 9NE ☎ (01900) 820362 jenningsbrewery.co.uk

Jennings Brewery was established as a family concern in 1828 in the village of Lorton. The company moved to its present location in 1874. Pure Lakeland water is still used for brewing, drawn from the brewery's own well. Part of Marston's PLC. !! ♦

Bitter (OG 1035, ABV 3.5%)
A malty beer with a good mouthfeel that combines with roast flavour and a hoppy finish.

Cumberland Ale (OG 1038, ABV 4%)
A deep golden-coloured, hoppy beer with a dry aftertaste.

Cocker Hoop (OG 1044, ABV 4.6%)
Full-bodied, complex bitter beer with plenty of hops and a rising bitter finish.

Sneck Lifter (OG 1051, ABV 5.1%)
A strong, dark brown-coloured ale with a complex balance of fruit, malt, sweet and roast flavours through to the finish.

Jesus College (NEW)

Jesus College, Cambridge, CB5 8BL

In-house brewery for Jesus College at the University of Cambridge. Beers are produced for college use only and are not available to the general public.

Jo C's

See Barsham

John o'Groats

County Road, John o'Groats, KW1 4YR ☎ (01955) 611220 ☎ 07825 729680 johnogroatsbrewery@gmail.com

Brewing began in 2015 using a four-barrel plant. !!

Swelkie (ABV 4%)

Duncasby (ABV 4.5%)

Deep Groat (ABV 4.8%)

John Smith's

See under S

John Thompson

See under T

Jolly Boys SIBA

Unit 16a, Redbrook Business Park, off Wilthorpe Road, Redbrook, South Yorkshire, S75 1JN ☎ 07808 085214 jollyboysbrewery.co.uk

Jolly Boys started brewing using spare capacity at another brewery in early 2016. Brewing began on its own plant later the same year. One pub in Wakefield is owned. !! ♦

Jolly Collier Stout (OG 1035, ABV 3.5%)

Blonde (OG 1041, ABV 4%)

Golden Best (OG 1042, ABV 4.5%)

Jolly Collier Porter (OG 1052, ABV 5%)

Jolly IPA (ABV 5.8%)

Jolly Sailor SIBA

Olympia Hotel, 77 Barlby Road, Selby, North Yorkshire, YO8 5AB ☎ (01757) 707564 jollysailorbrewery.uk

Jolly Sailor is a family-owned microbrewery situated in the quaint market town of Selby. A six-barrel plant is used. ♦

Bullseye Bitter (OG 1039, ABV 3.8%)

Jolly Gold (OG 1039, ABV 3.9%)

Jolly Stout (OG 1050.4, ABV 4.5%)

Jollyboat SIBA

Coach House, Buttgarden Street, Bideford, Devon, EX39 2AU ☎ (01237) 424343

Established in 1995, the brewery is named after a sailor's leave vessel and all the beers have a nautical theme. Most outlets supplied are in Devon. !! ♦

Mainbrace (OG 1042, ABV 4.2%)
Pale brown-coloured beer with a rich, fruity aroma and a bitter taste and aftertaste.

Plunder (OG 1049, ABV 4.8%)
Red/brown-coloured beer with an aromatic nose, a good balance of malt, hops and fruit present throughout leading to a bitter finish.

Joseph Holt

See under H

Joule's SIBA

The Brewery, Great Hales Street, Market Drayton, Shropshire, TF9 1JP ☎ (01630) 654400 joulesbrewery.co.uk

Re-established in 2010, following a break of 40 years, Joule's is situated in Market Drayton and uses its own mineral water. It runs a collection of

40 pubs across Shropshire, Staffordshire and Cheshire. ‼♦

Blonde (OG 1038, ABV 3.8%)
Light, refreshing and aromatic, this well-balanced blonde ale delivers a crisp, clean palate coupled with a pleasing aroma of citrus fruit.

Pale Ale (OG 1042, ABV 4.1%)
Full-bodied and well-balanced with a pleasant bitter finish.

Slumbering Monk (OG 1045, ABV 4.5%)
Full bodied with a complex malt and nut character, this bright copper-coloured ale has hints of caramel which give a round, soft smoothness to the palate.

Contract brewed for Everards Brewery:

Sunchaser (OG 1038, ABV 4%)
A golden brew with a sweet, lightly-hopped character. Some citrus notes to the fore in a quick finish that becomes increasingly bitter.

Old Original (OG 1050, ABV 5.2%)
Full-bodied, mid-brown-coloured strong bitter with a pleasant rich, grainy mouthfeel. Well-balanced flavours, with malt slightly to the fore, merging into a long, satisfying finish.

Junction

1 Baildon Road, Baildon, West Yorkshire, BD17 6AB
☎ (01274) 582009 ☎ 07539 923744
andydoug48@gmail.com

Junction is a microbrewery established in 2012 in the cellar of the Junction pub in Baildon, brewing around 300 gallons a week. Beer is sold in the pub and other local outlets. RAIB

Keep

Village Inn, The Cross, Nailsworth, Gloucestershire, GL6 0HH ☎ 07963 200768 paul@dropinpubs.com

After a break of 96 years, brewing returned to Nailsworth in 2004 at the Village Inn. The pub and brewery were sold in 2016 to Paul Sugden and Adam Pavey, who changed the brewery name from Nailsworth to Keep Brewing. Expansion is planned. ♦RAIB

Keith SIBA

Unit R, Isla Bank Mills, Keith, AB55 5DD
☎ (01542) 488006 keithbrewery.co.uk

Formerly known as Brewmeister and established in 2012, the brewery was renamed Keith Brewery in 2015. Beer is mainly available in bottles in selected specialist off-licenses but cask-conditioned beer is available to a few outlets and beer festivals. The Brewmeister brand name is kept for export-only orders. ♦RAIB

Herr Keith (OG 1044, ABV 4.5%)
Cloudy white/yellow-coloured wheat beer with hints of coriander.

Larger Keith (OG 1048, ABV 4.5%)

Pale Keith (OG 1048, ABV 5%)
Grapefruit hoppy bitter.

Stout Keith (OG 1048, ABV 5%)
Coffee stout made with chocolate and coffee beans.

Sir Keith (OG 1096, ABV 10.1%)
Slightly sweet but hoppy with a fruity aroma and complex malty character.

Kelburn SIBA

10 Muriel Lane, Barrhead, G78 1QB
☎ (0141) 881 2138 kelburnbrewery.com

Kelburn is an award-winning family business established in 2002. ‼♦

Sunriser (OG 1034, ABV 3.4%)
A well-balanced, hoppy, refreshing beer with a touch of rye and a blend of hops giving a long-lasting biscuit and grapefruit finish.

Goldihops (OG 1038, ABV 3.8%)
Well-hopped session ale with a fruity taste and bitter finish.

Pivo Estivo (OG 1038, ABV 3.9%)
A pale-coloured, dry, citrus hoppy session ale.

Misty Law (OG 1040, ABV 4%)
A dry, hoppy, amber-coloured ale with a long-lasting bitter finish.

Red Smiddy (OG 1040, ABV 4.1%)
This bittersweet ale predominantly features an intense citrus hop character that assaults the nose and continues into the flavour, balanced perfectly with fruity malt.

Regnitz (OG 1042, ABV 4.4%)

Dark Moor (OG 1044, ABV 4.5%)
A dark-coloured, fruity ale with undertones of liquorice and blackcurrant.

Jaguar (OG 1043, ABV 4.5%)
A golden-coloured, full bodied ale with undertones of grapefruit and a long-lasting citrus, hoppy aftertaste.

Cart Noir (OG 1046, ABV 4.8%)

Cart Blanche (OG 1048, ABV 5%)
A golden-coloured, full-bodied ale. The assault of fruit and hop camouflages the strength of this easy-drinking ale.

Kelchner (NEW) SIBA

Unit D, The Sidings, Station Road, Ampthill, Bedfordshire, MK45 2QY ☎ 07508 305754
kelchnerbrewery@gmail.com

Brewing began in 2018 using a six-barrel brew plant. ‼RAIB

Local is Lekker (ABV 3.9%)

Ampthill Gold (ABV 4.1%)
Subtle biscuit flavours with a delicate hop aroma.

Ampthill IPA (ABV 4.5%)
A pale-coloured ale with a well-balanced hoppy and malty character.

After Dark (ABV 4.8%)
A black IPA with dense citrus, coffee and chocolate notes and a dry, resinous finish.

Kelham Island SIBA

23 Alma Street, Sheffield, South Yorkshire, S3 8SA
☎ (0114) 249 4804

Office: Prospect House, 17 Alma Street, Sheffield, S3 8RY kelhambrewery.co.uk

Opened in 1990 behind the Fat Cat pub, the brewery moved to new purpose-built premises in

1999. The old building is used as a visitor centre, and there is a separate brewery shop together with offices and a function room in nearby Prospect House. !! ♦ RAIB

Best Bitter (OG 1038, ABV 3.8%)
Classic amber-coloured Yorkshire bitter with spicy, earthy aromas and a sweet, refreshing, malty finish.

Pride of Sheffield (OG 1040.5, ABV 4%)
A full-flavoured, amber-coloured bitter.

Easy Rider (OG 1041.8, ABV 4.3%)
A straw-coloured beer with a sweetish flavour and delicate hints of citrus fruits. A beer with hints of flavour rather than full bodied.

Riders on the Storm (OG 1045, ABV 4.5%)
A robust, golden-coloured pale ale with berry notes and slight roasted notes.

Pale Rider (OG 1050, ABV 5.2%)
A full-bodied, straw-coloured pale ale with a good fruity aroma and a strong fruit and hop taste. Its well-balanced sweetness and bitterness continue in the finish.

Keltek SIBA

Candela House, Cardrew Way, Redruth, Cornwall, TR15 1SS
☎ (01209) 313620

Office: Unit 5, Kernick Business Park, Annear Road, Penryn, TR10 9EW ⊕ keltekbrewery.co.uk

Keltek, meaning 'Celtic' in Cornish, was founded in 1997 by Stuart Heath. It started life as a 2.5-barrel plant in Stuart's disused stable block on the Roseland Peninsula but several moves and expansions means it is now based in Redruth and has the capacity to brew more than 250 barrels a week. In 2013 Keltek acquired four pubs in south-west Cornwall, becoming only the second brewery in Cornwall to own its own estate of public houses. In 2016 Keltek acquired a further two pubs, bringing the estate to six pubs. ♦ RAIB

Even Keel (OG 1034, ABV 3.4%)
Pale brown-coloured session bitter. Refreshing malt and hop taste with apple, plum and pear drops. Gentle dry and bitter finish.

Golden Lance (OG 1038, ABV 4%)
Gold-coloured bitter with light fruity aroma. Grassy citrus hops, apples, malt and hints of elderflower and butterscotch. Long bitter finish.

Magik (OG 1040, ABV 4%)
Amber-coloured bitter with gentle malt and hop aroma. Malty with balancing resinous hop bitterness and various fruits. Bitter citrus hop finish.

Phoenix (OG 1045, ABV 4.5%)
Golden-coloured best bitter. Powerful fruity hops with high bitterness but backed with solid malt, which lingers well on the finish.

Wayward Knight (OG 1045, ABV 4.5%)

King (OG 1049, ABV 5.1%)
Pale brown-coloured, strong bitter with malt and citrus hops aroma. Biscuit malt balanced by hop bitterness and hints of fruits.

Gatekeeper (OG 1056, ABV 5.6%)
Rich, malty porter made with foraged kelp.

Beheaded (OG 1068, ABV 7.5%)
Smooth, brown-coloured, strong old ale. Christmas pudding with port wine. Smoked peat, figs and plums. Sweet, fruity finish, lightly dry.

Kendal

Tanners Yard, Kendal, Cumbria, LA9 4DH
☎ (01539) 733803 ⊕ burgundyswinebar.co.uk

Kendal Brewing Company was established in 2011. Brewing is currently suspended. !!

Kennet & Avon

See Stealth

Kent SIBA

The Long Barn, Birling Place Farm, Stangate Road, Birling, Kent, ME19 5JN
☎ (01634) 780037 ⊕ kentbrewery.com

Kent Brewery was founded in 2010 by Toby Simmonds (ex-brewer from Dark Star) and Paul Herbert. Originally brewed at Larkins, a 10-barrel plant has been in operation at the Birling site since 2011. More than 300 outlets are supplied direct, mainly throughout Kent, Sussex and London. ♦ RAIB

Session Pale (OG 1037, ABV 3.7%)
A light and hoppy session beer with hints of citrus and elderflower.

Black Gold (OG 1040, ABV 4%)

Pale (OG 1040, ABV 4%)

Cobnut (OG 1041, ABV 4.1%)
A well-hopped, dark-coloured beer with nutty flavours.

KGB (Kent Golding Bitter) (OG 1041, ABV 4.1%)

Single Hop (ABV 4.5%)
A strong citrus flavour and aroma.

Prohibition (ABV 4.8%)

Brewers Reserve (OG 1050, ABV 5%)
A strong hop flavour of citrus and resin.

Kentwood

Prestoungrange Gothenburg, 227-229 High Street, Prestonpans, EH32 9BE
⊕ kentwoodbrewery.wordpress.com

A microbrewery was installed at the award-winning pub, the Prestoungrange Gothenburg, in 2004. In 2015 the Kentwood Brewery took ownership of the five-barrel plant. Visitors to the pub are able to see the brewing process through windows separating the brewery and the main bar. Beers from the traditional Fowler's Ales range are also produced under the 'Kentwood at the Goth' label.

Keppels (NEW) SIBA

The Workshops, Little Stambridge Hall Lane, Rochford, Essex, SS4 1EW ☎ 07912 251278
⊕ keppelsbrewery.co.uk

Keppels was established in 2016, initially collaborating with Billericay Brewing Co (qv). In 2018 it moved to its own premises. ♦

Tipsy Crow Stout (ABV 5%)

A dark-coloured, strong stout with a smoky flavour. Thin liquorice taste with a mild bitterness.

Kernel SIBA

Arch 11, Dockley Road Industrial Estate, Dockley Road, Bermondsey, London, SE16 3SF
☎ (020) 7231 4516

Office: 01 Spa Business Park, Spa Road, London, SE16 4QT 🌐 thekernelbrewery.com

Kernel was established in 2010 by Evin O'Riordain and moved to larger premises in 2012 to keep up with demand. The brewery produces bottle-conditioned and keg beers, and has won many awards for its wide, ever-changing range. Bottles are available from the brewery on a Saturday as well as a selection of pubs around the country. RAIB

Keswick SIBA

The Old Brewery, Brewery Lane, Keswick, Cumbria, CA12 5BY
☎ (01768) 780700 🌐 keswickbrewery.co.uk

Keswick, owned by Sue Jefferson, began brewing in 2006 using a 10-barrel plant on the site of a brewery that closed in 1897.The brewery is set up to be environmentally friendly using sheeps wool insulation in the vessels and reducing its environmental impact. Outlets include Middle Ruddings Hotel in Braithwaite, the Dog & Gun, Keswick, and many other Lakeland pubs. !! ♦

Gold (OG 1035, ABV 3.6%)
Simple, slightly sweet, light ale with some bitterness in the finish.

Bitter (OG 1036, ABV 3.7%)
Gentle bitter with hints of roasted malt and a sweetness which fades.

Icknield (OG 1036, ABV 3.7%)

Park Your Thirst (OG 1038, ABV 3.9%)

Thirst Run (OG 1041, ABV 4.2%)
A well-balanced, golden-coloured beer that maintains its fruitiness from start to finish.

Thirst Quencher (OG 1042, ABV 4.3%)

Special (OG 1047, ABV 4.8%)
Full malt flavour with notes of chocolate and roast barley.

Thirst Celebration (OG 1065, ABV 7%)

Kettlesmith SIBA

Unit 16, Treenwood Industrial Estate, Bradford-on-Avon, Wiltshire, BA15 2AU
☎ (01225) 864839 🌐 kettlesmithbrewing.com

⊗ Kettlesmith is an independent microbrewery established in 2016. It brews modern interpretations of a wide variety of beer styles, drawing inspiration from its background in America and England, as well as a love of Belgian beer. !! ♦ RAIB

Outline (OG 1040, ABV 3.8%)
An amber-coloured session ale with hints of chocolate and molasses, balanced with floral and pine hops.

Faultline (OG 1043, ABV 4.1%)
A hoppy pale ale with resinous floral citrus notes of grapefruit.

Plotline (OG 1047, ABV 4.4%)
Flavours of dark chocolate, rich coffee and roast barley, with fruity hops.

Fogline (OG 1046, ABV 4.7%)
A Belgian-style ale with hints of clove and honey and a subtle, tart finish.

Coastline (ABV 4.9%)
Honey-like malt sweetness balanced with flavours of tangerine and lemon zest in this lager.

Ridgeline (OG 1051, ABV 5%)
A rich and powerful, American-style rye ale. The peppery, nutty rye malt is balanced by juicy, resinous hops.

Timeline (OG 1055, ABV 5.4%)
Hop-driven IPA with malty undertones. The hops combine for herbal, berry and citrus flavours.

Skyline (OG 1051, ABV 5.6%)
A Belgian saison-style beer; spicy and earthy with hints of orange and lemon with a refreshing, tart finish.

Kew

477 Upper Richmond Road West, East Sheen, London, SW14 7PU
☎ (020) 8878 9415 🌐 kewbrewery.co.uk

⊗ Established in 2015, Kew is a family-run, independent brewery situated less than a mile from, and inspired by, the world-famous Royal Botanic Gardens at Kew. !! ♦ RAIB

Botanic (OG 1038, ABV 3.8%)
Chocolate, grapefruit, juniper and unripe apricots in aroma and flavour where some toffee provides sweetness. Peppery, dry bitter finish.

Green (& Black) (OG 1040, ABV 3.9%)
Smooth milk stout with chocolate notes throughout. Some cherry in the sweet flavour and a bitterish roasty finish.

Nightshade (OG 1045, ABV 4.2%)
Chilli porter with cacao nibs creating a smooth balance. Earthy hops, chocolate and fruity flavours. Dry, roasty, lingering chilli finish.

Petersham Porter (OG 1045, ABV 4.3%)
Dark chocolate character in the aroma and flavour, which is malty with toffee, treacle and blackberry notes. Dry bitter finish.

Richmond Rye (OG 1045, ABV 4.3%)
Dark gold-coloured beer with typical tart rye aroma and flavour. Earthy hops, orange and honey flavours. Dry, spicy, hoppy finish.

Sandycombe Gold (OG 1040, ABV 4.4%)
Smooth, crisp golden ale with sweet biscuit and hints of cassis. Aftertaste starts sweetish but then a lingering dryness develops.

Pagoda Pale (OG 1052, ABV 4.5%)
Unfined dark gold-coloured beer with biscuit sweetness balancing the citrus fruit and dryness that builds in a long bitter finish.

Keystone SIBA

Old Carpenters Workshop, Berwick St Leonard, Wiltshire, SP3 5SN
☎ (01747) 820426 🌐 keystonebrewery.co.uk

⊗ Set up in 2006 with a 10-barrel plant, the brewer aims to be as sustainable and efficient as possible, brewing traditional southern English-style beers using local ingredients whenever possible. The beers are available in the brewery-run Benett Arms, Tisbury. Around 150 other outlets are also supplied. ‼ ♦

Bedrock (OG 1035, ABV 3.6%)
Copper-coloured bitter, hops and malt in the aroma, followed by fruit and bitterness in the taste. Long, lingering aftertaste.

Large One (OG 1041, ABV 4.2%)
Copper-coloured, malty best bitter, fruit and bitterness to the fore initially, long fruit and bitter hop flavours to the finish.

Kiln SIBA

Office: 1st Floor, 30 Church Road, Burgess Hill, West Sussex, RH15 9AE ☎ 07800 556729
thekilnbrewery.co.uk

Kiln brewery was set up by two friends in 2014. Following a search for new premises, it has joined forces with Missing Link Brewery (qv).

Mischief Maker (OG 1038, ABV 3.8%)
A fresh-tasting bitter with hints of fig and black pepper and a slightly fruity aroma.

Boardwalk (OG 1046, ABV 4.5%)
A refreshing, pale-coloured ale with a citrus aroma, light malt and spicy taste and a pleasing green fruit finish.

Bricks & Porter (OG 1052, ABV 5.6%)
A berry aroma, followed by cherry skin, sweet dark chocolate and coffee underpinned by a little smokiness.

King Alfred

11 Mill Rise, Bourton, Dorset, SP8 5DH
☎ (01747) 840967 ✉ kingalfredales@aol.com

⊗ King Alfred is a 0.5-barrel garage brewery that started production in 2012. It currently brews about once a month. A few local pubs and beer festivals are supplied.

871 (OG 1043, ABV 4.3%)
Mid brown-coloured, malty bitter with balanced hop flavours.

Saxon Gold (OG 1048, ABV 4.8%)
Mid gold-coloured bitter with prominent hop flavours and aroma.

King Street SIBA

Riverside House, Welsh Back, Bristol, BS1 4RR
☎ (0117) 405 8948

Office: The City Pub Company Plc, Essel House, 2nd Floor, Foley Street, London, W1W 7TH
kingstreetbrewhouse.co.uk

⊗ The King Street Brew House is owned by the City Pub Company, which owns several pubs around the country. The compact brewery is on the ground floor, with the fermenting vessels and conditioning tanks in the basement. It also supplies the company's other pub in Bristol, the Prince Street Social. ‼ ♦ RAIB

Kingdom

12 Jutland Street, Rosyth, KY11 2ZL
✉ joe.vettese@thekingdombrewery.com

Kingdom Brewery is run by the husband and wife team of Joe and Lois Vettese. It is situated in Joe's garage where he produces occasional small batch runs of beer.

King's Cliffe

Unit 10, Kingsmead, Station Road, King?s Cliffe, Northamptonshire, PE8 6YH ☎ 07843 288088
kcbales.co.uk

⊗ In 2014, exactly 100 years after the last brewery in King's Cliffe ceased brewing, village resident Jeremy O'Neill set up this new venture. It currently produces five barrels a week. ‼ ♦

5C (OG 1038, ABV 3.8%)
A light bitter with a balanced taste of malt and hops and a refreshing bitter finish.

No. 10 (OG 1040, ABV 4%)
Amber-coloured beer with a clean, malty taste and a long bitter finish.

66 Degrees (OG 1046, ABV 4.6%)
Amber-coloured beer with a floral aroma, a balanced taste of malt and hops, and a long bitter finish.

Kings Clipstone

Keepers Bothy, Kings Clipstone, Nottinghamshire, NG21 9BT
☎ (01623) 823589 ☎ 07790 190020
kingsclipstonebrewery.co.uk

Located in the heart of Sherwood Forest, Kings Clipstone began brewing in 2012 using a five-barrel plant. The owners, David and Daryl Maguire, produce a range of core beers plus one-off brews and seasonals. Beers are available nationwide to freehouses, festivals and wholesale markets. ♦

Palace Pale (OG 1036, ABV 3.6%)
A light, crisp golden ale with a refreshing taste.

Hop On (OG 1039, ABV 3.8%)
A pale, refreshing session beer with a fruity hop aroma.

Amazing Gazing (OG 1040, ABV 4%)
A red-coloured, easy-drinking bitter with a floral aroma.

Tabaknakas (OG 1041, ABV 4.1%)
A golden ale with overtones of spiced berries and floral characteristics.

Moonbeam (OG 1042, ABV 4.2%)
A chestnut-coloured bitter with a full flavour and well-rounded finish.

Sire (OG 1043, ABV 4.2%)
A well-rounded beer with a clean bitter finish.

Royal Stag Stout (OG 1045, ABV 4.5%)
Dark-coloured stout with roasted and dark chocolate malts.

Queen Bee (OG 1051, ABV 5.1%)
A ruby red-coloured, strong ale, classically rich and smooth.

Kings Head

Kings Head, 132 High Street, Bildeston, Suffolk, IP7 7ED
☎ (01449) 741434 bildestonkingshead.co.uk

Kings Head has been brewing since 1996 in an old cart lodge at the back of the pub. Under new ownership since 2008, the 2.5-barrel plant brews fortnightly. !! ♦

Kingstone

Tintern, NP16 7NX
☎ (01291) 680111 kingstonebrewery.co.uk

Kingstone Brewery is located in the Wye Valley close to Tintern Abbey. Brewing began on a four-barrel plant in 2005. Special brews are marketed under the Hapax Brewing Co label. !! RAIB

Tewdric's Tipple (OG 1038, ABV 3.8%)
An ale with a dry, bitter character and tangy core.

Challenger (OG 1040, ABV 4%)
A smooth, richly-hopped ale with a malty nose and toffee undertones.

Gold (OG 1040, ABV 4%)
A straw-coloured, smooth ale with citrus notes and a balanced, hoppy finish.

Llandogo Trow (OG 1042, ABV 4.2%)
A ruby red-coloured ale with a smooth, fruity finish.

Premium Stout (OG 1044, ABV 4.4%)
A smooth, rich stout with a bitter finish.

Classic (OG 1045, ABV 4.5%)
A balanced, hoppy, dry ale with a floral nose and a smooth, well-balanced finish.

1503 (OG 1048, ABV 4.8%)
A deep chestnut red-coloured beer, lightly-hopped and bursting with complex, rich flavours.

Abbey Ale (OG 1051, ABV 5.1%)
An amber-coloured, full-flavoured ale. The hoppy edge is balanced by a smooth, malty richness.

Humpty (OG 1058, ABV 5.8%)
An IPA with a slightly sweet, floral nose, a balanced level of malt supporting the hops and finally a subtle but slightly citrus finish.

Kinneil

84 Corbiehall, Bo'ness, EH51 0AS ☎ 07789 204008 kinneilbrew.co.uk

Kinneil began brewing in 2011 using a 2.5-barrel plant. The brewery is adjacent to the Corbie Inn but separately owned.

Wonderfu' Jake (OG 1037, ABV 3.6%)

Katie Wearie's (OG 1039, ABV 3.8%)

Wayfinder (OG 1038, ABV 3.8%)

Pennvael Amber (OG 1042, ABV 4%)

Kincardine Sunset (OG 1042, ABV 4.1%)

Caer Edin Dark (OG 1044, ABV 4.2%)

Kinver SIBA

Unit 1, Britch Farm, Rocky Wall, Kinver, Staffordshire, DY7 5NW ☎ 07715 842676 kinverbrewery.co.uk

Established in 2004, Kinver produces a wide range of different beer styles including one-off specials. The brewery relocated in 2012 to a new 10-barrel plant on the edge of Kinver due to increased demand. Around 30 outlets are supplied direct including several in Kinver. !! ♦ RAIB

Light Railway (OG 1038, ABV 3.8%)
Straw-coloured session beer. A fruity and malty start quickly gives way to well-hopped bitterness and lingering hoppy aftertaste.

Cavegirl Bitter (OG 1040, ABV 4%)
A pale straw-coloured, well-balanced bitter.

Edge (OG 1041, ABV 4.2%)
Amber-coloured with a malty aroma. Sweet, fruity start with a hint of citrus marmalade in the spicy edged malt; lasting hoppy finish that is satisfyingly bitter.

Noble (OG 1043, ABV 4.5%)
Fruity hop aroma. Fruity start then the grassy hops give a sharp bitter finish with malt support.

Maybug (OG 1045, ABV 4.8%)
A light beer brewed with German hops.

Half Centurion (OG 1047, ABV 5%)
A golden-coloured best bitter; malty before the hop takes command to give a balanced, hoppy finish and provide the great aftertaste.ô

Black Ram Stout (OG 1048, ABV 5.2%)
A full-bodied, roasty, dark-coloured stout.

Khyber (OG 1054, ABV 5.8%)
Golden-coloured, strong bitter with a hop bite that overwhelms the fleeting malty sweetness and drives through to the long, dry finish.

Over the Edge (OG 1068, ABV 7.5%)
Amber look, barley sugar aroma. Sweet sticky start, hop sharp and sugary. Warming and mind numbing sensational liquid. Long bitter finish.

Kirkby Lonsdale SIBA

Unit 2F, Old Station Yard, Kirkby Lonsdale, Cumbria, LA6 2HP
☎ (01524) 272221 ☎ 07793 149999
kirkbylonsdalebrewery.com

Kirkby Lonsdale is a family-run business established in 2009 on a six-barrel plant. In 2016 a further six-barrel plant was installed in its new brewery tap, the Royal Barn, Kirkby Lonsdale. !! ♦

Crafty Mild (OG 1036, ABV 3.6%)
A typical mild with powerful malty aromas and some caramel, which follows through in the taste and finish.

Tiffin Gold (OG 1036, ABV 3.6%)
A full-flavoured, grapefruit, hoppy and bitter beer with a dry finish.

Stanley's Pale Ale (OG 1038, ABV 3.8%)
Hops dominate this sweet and fruity, well-balanced beer.

Ruskins Bitter (OG 1039, ABV 3.9%)
A tawny-coloured bitter with a distinctive aroma of fruit and malt. The clean, hoppy flavour is well-balanced with fruity sweetness leading to a sustained bittersweet finish.

Singletrack (OG 1040, ABV 4%)
Crisp citrus hops predominate in a well-balanced beer with a pleasant bitter finish.

Pennine Ambler (OG 1040, ABV 4.1%)

THE BREWERIES

Radical Red (OG 1042, ABV 4.2%) ◆
Malty beer with a caramel sweetness that is balanced by a bitter finish.

Monumental Blonde (OG 1045, ABV 4.5%) ◆
Distinctly hoppy, a fruity, sweet, pale-coloured, full-bodied bitter.

Jubilee Stout (OG 1055, ABV 5.5%) ◆
Rich, well-balanced stout with malt. A long aftertaste retains this complexity and is surprisingly refreshing.

Imperial Dragon (OG 1080, ABV 8.2%)

Kirkstall SIBA

100 Kirkstall Road, Leeds, West Yorkshire, LS3 1HJ
☎ (0113) 898 0280 🌐 kirkstallbrewerycompany.com

The brewery was established in 2011 a few yards from the original Kirkstall Brewery beside the Leeds-Liverpool canal. Nearby Kirkstall Abbey, which had its own brewhouse, and lost local industries are the inspiration for the beer names. The range can be sampled in the Kirkstall Bridge Inn, the brewery tap. !! ◆

Pale Ale (OG 1040, ABV 4%)
A session pale ale with floral, citrus and herbal hop character, backed by a malty and balanced finish.

Three Swords (OG 1045, ABV 4.5%) ◆
Pithy grapefruit flavours characterise this light-coloured golden ale, plenty of hops from the start to the lingering finish.

Dissolution IPA (OG 1050, ABV 5%) ◆
Full-flavoured – hops lead the charge with bitter fruit just behind.

Black Band Porter (OG 1055, ABV 5.5%) ◆
Dark-coloured, smooth and complex. Sumptuous fruit cake flavours, hints of malted chocolate, coffee and liquorice plus occasional smokiness.

Kirrie

Bon Scott Brewery, 8 Bon Scott Place, Kirriemuir, DD8 4LD ☎ 07855 808975 🌐 kirrie-ales.co.nf

Established in 2014, Kirrie Ales is situated in the picturesque town of Kirriemuir, birthplace of JM Barrie, creator of Peter Pan, and gateway to the Angus Glens. The brewery space measures only 8 by 9 feet. RAIB

Fruity Wee Blonde (OG 1037, ABV 3.8%)
American-style IPA with lots of grapefruit and other citrus flavours but not overly dry and bitter.

Hoppy Daze (OG 1039, ABV 4%)
Well-balanced classic IPA session beer.

Red from the Shed (OG 1044, ABV 4.5%)
Scottish 80/- with subtle fruity notes on the finish.

Thrums Best (OG 1044, ABV 4.5%)
Well-balanced bitter with hints of orange on the finish.

Kissingate

Pole Barn, Church Lane Farm Estate, Church Lane, Lower Beeding, West Sussex, RH13 6LU
☎ (01403) 891335 ☎ 07909 975664
🌐 kissingate.co.uk

Kissingate Brewery was founded in 2010 by husband-and-wife team Gary and Bunny Lucas. Current production capacity is eight barrels. The brewery building is a converted barn set in a wooded valley near the village of Mannings Heath. It has a taproom and minstrels gallery. The brewery is available to hire for private events. !! ◆

Storyteller (OG 1036, ABV 3.5%)

Sussex (OG 1040, ABV 4%)

Moon (OG 1045, ABV 4.5%)
A golden-coloured beer with light roasted malt flavours, late autumn apples and a lingering hop bitterness.

Old Tale Porter (OG 1045, ABV 4.5%)

Pernickety Pale (OG 1045, ABV 4.5%)

Mandarina Red (OG 1048, ABV 4.8%)
A complex, red-coloured IPA with multiple flavour layers of malt and prominent citrus fruits. Pine and citrus bitter finish.

Chennai (OG 1050, ABV 5%)

Smelter's Stout (OG 1052, ABV 5.1%)

Power Blue (OG 1058, ABV 5.5%)

Mary's Ruby Mild (OG 1064, ABV 6.5%)
Deep ruby-coloured mild, gentle aromas of well-aged port, intense malt flavours and a light, floral hop aftertaste.

Six Crows (OG 1068, ABV 6.6%)
A rich, dark and decadent stout with intense notes of molasses, oak and woodsmoke.

Knockout

Unit 10, Alanbrooke Park, Alexander Road, Belfast, BT6 9HB

Founded in 2009 by Joseph McMullan, Knockout produces a range of bottle-conditioned beers. Each brew is usually in small 900-litre batches. RAIB

Knops SIBA

The Walled Garden, Archerfield Estate, Dirleton, EH39 5HQ ☎ 07949 879147 🌐 knopsbeer.co.uk

Knops began brewing in 2010 under contract. In 2013 it moved to new premises on the Archerfield Estate at Dirleton on the East Lothian coastline with an 11-barrel plant. Beers are based on modern interpretations of traditional styles and are bottled in-house. Cask-conditioned beers are available in Eastern Scotland and the Glasgow area. !! RAIB

East Coast Pale (OG 1039, ABV 3.8%)

Musselburgh Broke (OG 1045, ABV 4.5%)
Full malt flavour with a clean, brisk finish.

California Common (OG 1048, ABV 4.6%)
A deep golden-coloured ale with a clean hop finish and light toffee notes followed by a lingering bitterness.

India Pale Ale (OG 1047, ABV 5%)
Light, golden-coloured ale with a citrus and apricot aroma. Well balanced by a smooth, honeyed malt backbone.

Black Cork (OG 1066, ABV 6.5%)
A dark-coloured, intense beer with a prominent chocolate/coffee bitterness and hop aroma.

Contract brewed for Archerfield Fine Ales:

Golden Ale (OG 1039, ABV 3.8%)

Dark Ale (OG 1046, ABV 4.7%)

India Pale Ale (OG 1047, ABV 5%)

Krafty Brew

Star & Garter, 1 High Port, Linlithgow, EH49 7AB
☎ 07763 873596 kraftybrew.com

A small brewery with six Braumeister systems specialising in 'brew it yourself' and own label products. A range of bottle-conditioned beers is also sold under the Krafty brand name. Some cask-conditioned beer is available at the brewery's pub, Woodland Creatures, Leith. RAIB

Lacada

7a Victoria Street, Portrush, BT56 8DL
☎ (028) 7082 5684 lacadabrewery.com

Lacada was established in 2015 and produces its Salamander series alongside three core beers. RAIB

Giant's Organ (OG 1045, ABV 4.5%)

Sorley Boy's Stash (OG 1045, ABV 4.5%)

Stranded Bunny (OG 1045, ABV 4.5%)

Lacons SIBA

Falcon Brewery, Main Cross Road, Great Yarmouth, Norfolk, NR30 3NZ
☎ (01493) 850578 lacons.co.uk

Lacons Brewery has a rich history dating back to 1760 but was closed by Whitbread in the 1960s. It relaunched in 2013 and the Falcon Brewery is now nestled in a courtyard in Great Yarmouth. Beers are available across East Anglia and use the original Lacons yeast. A range of 'Heritage' seasonal ales is also produced, based on the brewery's original recipes from the archives. !! ♦ RAIB

Encore (OG 1038, ABV 3.8%)
Strong citrus and hop notes throughout. A balanced, hoppy bitter beginning. Full-bodied with a heavy mouthfeel. Strong bitter finish.

Patriot (OG 1038, ABV 3.8%)
A powerful hop presence from the nose to the long, dry finish. Citrus notes and malt give balance and depth.

Falcon Ale (OG 1042, ABV 4.2%)
Complex,with malt, caramel, hop and plum vying for supremacy. Both smooth and grainy with a well-rounded, bittersweet finale.

Legacy (OG 1043, ABV 4.4%)
Strong grapefruit aroma. Well-balanced mix of malt, citrus and bittersweet hoppiness. Full-bodied with a lemony malt finish.

Affinity (OG 1046, ABV 4.8%)
A bouncy citrus nose. Orange notes soar over an astringent hoppiness softened by a gentle malt background. A growing hop finish.

Audit (OG 1072, ABV 8%)
This strong, dark copper-coloured barley wine has a prominent flavour of berry fruit, laced with pronounced spice. The finish is warming, smooth and sweet.

Lady Luck (NEW)

Little Angel, 18 Flowergate, Whitby, North Yorkshire, YO21 3BA
☎ (01947) 602899 ☎ 07920 282506
ladyluckbrewery.com

Lady Luck is a 0.5-barrel brewery situated at the back of the Little Angel, Whitby. Brewing began in 2018 and takes place twice a week. Beers are also available in the Dolphin and Whitby Way, Whitby.

Laig Bay

Galmisdale, Isle of Eigg, PH42 4RL
laigbaybrewing.com

Laig Bay began brewing in 2014.

I am the Eiggman (ABV 4%)

Cleadale 80/- (ABV 4.5%)

Charadail Pale Ale (ABV 5.5%)

Independence IPA (ABV 602%)

Laine

Brighton: North Laine Bar & Brewhouse, 27 Gloucester Place, Brighton, East Sussex, BN1 4AA
☎ (01273) 683666

Battersea: Four Thieves, 51 Lavender Gardens, London, SW11 1DJ ☎ (020) 7223 6927

Victoria Park: People's Park Tavern, 360 Victoria Park Road, London, E9 7BT ☎ (020) 8533 0040

Laine launched its first brewery in 2012, in Brighton, using a five-barrel plant based within the North Laine pub, which is owned by the drinkinbrighton pub group. The brewing equipment and process can be viewed from the bar. In 2013 a sister brewery was opened in Acton, London (now closed). Since then two more Laine breweries have been established in London, in Hackney (2014) and Battersea (2015). The beer range varies in each establishment. !!

Lakehouse

Lake House, Peachfield Road, Malvern, Worcestershire, WR14 3LE ☎ 07532 440634
lakehousebrewery.com

Lakehouse was established in 2016 by Dan Frost and Graeme Gordon on a 2.5-barrel plant. Situated below the Malvern Hills, within the grounds of a country house and fishing lake, from which it takes its name. Beers can be found at food & drink festivals and Farmers' Markets as well as in trade outlets. RAIB

Amber Session Ale (OG 1038.5, ABV 3.9%)
Light, sweet and refreshing session ale.

Citrus Pale Ale (OG 1039.5, ABV 4%)
A light, refreshing pale ale with punchy citrus notes.

Cherry-Chocolate Porter (OG 1063, ABV 5.5%)
A soft and fruity speciality beer with a sweet chocolate influence. Brewed using fresh cherries.

Lancaster SIBA

Lancaster Leisure Park, Wyresdale Road, Lancaster, LA1 3LA
☎ (01524) 848537 lancasterbrewery.co.uk

Lancaster began brewing in 2005. The brewery moved to new premises in 2010 and installed a larger 60-barrel brewing plant. As well as the regular beers, seasonal beers are brewed under the T'ales from the Brewhouse name. ‼ ♦ V

Amber (OG 1037, ABV 3.6%) ◆
Amber malt flavours lead to an increasingly astringent bitter finish.

Blonde (OG 1041, ABV 4%) ◆
A pale-coloured, gently-hopped, easy-drinking, mild bitter with an astringent finish.

Black (OG 1045, ABV 4.5%) ◆
A satisfying and robust, roast bitter beer with hints of sweet fruitiness.

Red (OG 1047, ABV 4.8%) ◆
Sweet start with lasting roast malts leads to satisfying bitter finish.

Landlocked

Handle Bar, 54a King Street, Alfreton, Derbyshire, DE55 7DD ☎ 07845 609585
✉ brewhousemike@gmail.com

Landlocked began brewing in 2014 using a five-barrel plant in outbuildings behind the Beehive Inn, Ripley. In 2016 it moved to the Handle Bar, Alfreton, which is now the brewery tap. The beers can also be found in other local pubs. ♦ RAIB

Chapel Hill Pale (OG 1036, ABV 4%)
Golden ale brewed with a touch of honey.

Island IPA (OG 1044, ABV 4.7%)

A & E (OG 1064, ABV 7.4%)

Langham SIBA

Old Granary, Langham Lane, Lodsworth, West Sussex, GU28 9BU
☎ (01798) 860861 🌐 langhambrewery.co.uk

Langham Brewery was established in 2006 in an 18th-century granary barn and is set in the heart of West Sussex with fine views of the rolling South Downs. It is owned by Lesley Foulkes and James Berrow who brew and run the business. The brewery is a 10-barrel steam-heated plant and more than 200 outlets are supplied. ‼

Halfway to Heaven (OG 1035, ABV 3.5%)
A chestnut-coloured beer with a balanced biscuit maltiness and citrus and fruit hop character with a hint of spice.

Saison (OG 1039, ABV 3.9%)
A zesty, unfined, saison-style beer; light and well-hopped.

Hip Hop (OG 1038, ABV 4%)
A clean, crisp blonde beer. The nose is loaded with floral hop aroma while the pale malt flavour is overtaken by a dry and bitter finish.

Sundowner (OG 1042, ABV 4.2%)
A deep golden-coloured beer. The nose has tropical fruit, pineapple and citrus notes with a smooth maltiness in the background. There is a balanced dry and bitter finish with a floral hop aroma.

Best (OG 1043, ABV 4.5%)
A tawny-coloured classic best bitter with well-balanced malt flavours and bitterness.

Arapaho (OG 1046, ABV 4.9%)

LSD (Langham Special Draught) (OG 1049, ABV 5.2%)
An auburn-coloured beer with rich, complex flavours and a deep red glow. The sweet maltiness is balanced with spicy hop aromas and a dry finish.

Black Swallow (OG 1055, ABV 6%)

Langton SIBA

Grange Farm, Welham Road, Thorpe Langton, Leicestershire, LE16 7TU
☎ (01858) 540116 ☎ 07840 532826
🌐 langtonbrewery.co.uk

Established in 1999 in outbuildings behind the Bell Inn, East Langton, the brewery relocated in 2005 to a converted barn at Thorpe Langton, where a four-barrel plant was installed. Further expansion in 2010 and 2016 significantly increased capacity. ‼ ♦ RAIB

Caudle Bitter (OG 1039, ABV 3.9%) ◆
Copper-coloured session bitter that is close to a pale ale in style. Flavours are relatively well-balanced throughout with hops slightly to the fore.

Inclined Plane Bitter (OG 1042, ABV 4.2%)
A straw-coloured bitter with a citrus nose and long, hoppy finish.

Hop On (OG 1044, ABV 4.4%)
A premium bitter, deep chestnut colour with a good balance of flavours and aroma.

Bowler Strong Ale (OG 1048, ABV 4.8%)
A strong, traditional ale with a deep red colour and hoppy nose.

Bullseye (OG 1050, ABV 4.8%)
Dark-coloured stout with flavours of liquorice and chocolate.

Larkins SIBA

Larkins Farm, Hampkins Hill Road, Chiddingstone, Kent, TN8 7BB
☎ (01892) 870328

Larkins brewery was founded by the Dockerty family in Rusthall in Kent in 1986, on the site of the original Royal Tunbridge Wells Brewery. In 1988 the brewery relocated to Larkins Farm in Chiddingstone. All beers include hops grown on the farm itself. The brewery delivers direct to around 40-50 pubs and restaurants within a 20-mile radius. ‼ ♦

Traditional Ale (OG 1035, ABV 3.4%)
Tawny in colour, a full-tasting hoppy ale with plenty of character for its strength.

Pale (ABV 4.2%)
Pleasantly hoppy pale ale with a soft fruity rather than astringent aftertaste.

Best (OG 1045, ABV 4.4%) ◆
Full-bodied, slightly fruity and unusually bitter for its gravity.

Late Night Hype (NEW)

Unit 17, Andrew Court, South Douglas Street, Clydebank, G81 1PD
☎ (0141) 261 1278 🌐 latenighthypebrewing.com

Late Night Hype is owned and operated by two friends. Around 25 outlets are supplied direct. There are plans for expansion. RAIB

Lennox Amber (OG 1037, ABV 3.4%)

Dulce Stout (OG 1046, ABV 4%)

Clydebank Pale (OG 1039, ABV 4.6%)

Foudoo Pale (OG 1050, ABV 6%)

Boomtang IPA (OG 1056, ABV 6.7%)

Laverstoke Park

Laverstoke Park, Overton, Hampshire, RG25 3DR

A bottle-conditoned beer is contract brewed for Laverstoke Park by an unnamed brewery.

Law

Unit 17, Mid Wynd, Dundee, DD1 4JG ☎ 07893 538277 🌐 lawbrewing.co

Law was established in 2016 and is named after Dundee's most distinctive landmark; the volcano-like slopes of the Law.

Optimistic Sound Pale Ale (ABV 4.2%)

Cherry Red Stout (ABV 5.2%)
An intensely rich and smooth stout with chocolate cherry notes.

Rude Boy Juice (ABV 5.2%)
A Jamaican ackee and grapefruit/pineapple infused IPA with fruit notes.

Lawman

Craigmarloch, Cumbernauld
☎ (0141) 212 9570 ☎ 07872 525762
🌐 lawmanbrew.co.uk

Lawman began brewing in 2015 using a five-barrel brew plant located in an industrial unit near Cumbernauld town centre. ♦

Pixel Bandit (OG 1040, ABV 4%)
A session pale ale with a citrus aroma and flavours of lemongrass and tangerine.

Steadfast KûÑln-ish Bier (OG 1044, ABV 4.4%)
A session beer with an elderflower twist.

Onyx (OG 1048, ABV 4.8%)
A full-bodied stout with a clean coffee bitterness and dark chocolate finish.

Horizon APA (OG 1052, ABV 5.2%)
A deep golden-coloured, American-style ale ale packed with tropical fruits and pine.

Weatherall IPA (OG 1064, ABV 6.4%)
A modern, full-flavoured IPA with a complex orange marmalade bitterness.

Leadmill

Unit 3, Heanor Small Business Centre, Adams Close, Heanor, Derbyshire, DE75 7SW ☎ 07971 189915
✉ leadmill@fsmail.net

⊗ Set up in Selston in 1999, Leadmill moved to Denby in 2001 and again in 2010 to Heanor. A sister brewery to Bottle Brook (qv), the brewery tap is at the Old Oak, Horsley Woodhouse. ♦

Langley Best (OG 1036, ABV 3.6%)

Mash Tun Bitter (OG 1036, ABV 3.6%)

Old Oak Bitter (OG 1037, ABV 3.7%)

B52 (OG 1050, ABV 5.2%)

Slumdog (OG 1058, ABV 5.9%)

Leafy Hollow

Ferkins Barn, Lower Burlone, Washaway, Cornwall, PL30 3AJ ☎ 07592 310182
✉ leafyhollowbrewery@yahoo.com

This nanobrewery was established in 2015 and brews bottle-conditioned beers by hand-crafting without machinery, using traditional methods and containing no modern chemicals. RAIB

Leatherbritches

Brewery Yard, Tap House, Annwell, Smisby, Derbyshire, LE65 2TA ☎ 07976 279253
🌐 leatherbritches.co.uk

The brewery, founded in 1993 in Fenny Bentley, has relocated and expanded over the years, moving to its current address in 2011 where it effectively took over the existing Tap House Brewery (established 2010) but continued to brew the latter's beers. Since 2015, however, Tap House beers have become re-badged Leatherbritches products. !! ♦ RAIB

Goldings (OG 1036, ABV 3.6%)
A light, golden-coloured beer with a flowery hoppy aroma and bitter finish.

Lemongrass & Ginger (OG 1036, ABV 3.8%)
Pale, hoppy ale infused with lemongrass and ginger. Crisp and refreshing.

Ashbourne Ale (OG 1040, ABV 4%)
A pale-coloured bitter with a crisp, lasting taste.

Dr Johnson (ABV 4%)
A chestnut-coloured, smooth, well-rounded, malty bitter.

Scoundrel (OG 1040, ABV 4.1%)
Full-bodied porter with a well-rounded, sweet finish.

Dovedale (OG 1044, ABV 4.4%)
A copper-colouredr bitter with a crisp finish.

Ginger Helmet (OG 1047, ABV 4.7%)
A pale-coloured bitter, well-hopped with a hint of ginger in the finish.

Hairy Helmet (OG 1047, ABV 4.7%)
A pale-coloured bitter, well-hopped but with a sweet finish.

Ashbourne IPA (OG 1047, ABV 4.9%)
Pale ale with a flowery, hoppy aroma and a strong bitter finish.

Bespoke (OG 1048, ABV 5%)
Full-bodied, well-rounded premium bitter.

Stouter (OG 1049, ABV 5.2%)
A stout with coffee and vanilla notes.

Scary Hairy (OG 1057, ABV 5.9%)
Pale-coloured and hoppy, a stronger version of Hairy Helmet.

Scary Hairy Export (OG 1064, ABV 7.2%)
Strong, pale-coloured bitter with a dry bitter finish.

Ledbury SIBA

Gazerdine House, Hereford Road, Ledbury, Herefordshire, HR8 2PZ
☎ (01531) 671184 ☎ 07957 428070
🌐 ledburyrealales.co.uk

Established in 2012, Ledbury Real Ales uses hops grown in Herefordshire and Worcestershire with other materials sourced locally where possible. The beers are sold mainly within a 15-mile radius of the brewery. ‼♦

Bitter (OG 1038, ABV 3.8%)
A traditional, copper-coloured beer with a noticeably bitter start. Hints of spice and citrus in the finish.

Dark (OG 1039, ABV 3.9%)
A chocolate and coffee start with a smooth, mellow finish with notes of spice, marmalade and honey.

Gold (OG 1040, ABV 4%)
A well-balanced, golden-coloured bitter with a honey and fruit finish.

Dr Rudi's Extra Pale (OG 1041, ABV 4.1%)
A light beer with a slight bitter finish.

Leeds SIBA

3 Sydenham Road, Holbeck, Leeds, West Yorkshire, LS11 9RU
☎ (0113) 244 5866 🌐 leedsbrewery.co.uk

Production began in 2007 using a 20-barrel plant with capacity doubling in 2018 together with the introduction of a bottling line. One of the largest independent brewers in the city, it uses a unique strain of yeast originally used by a defunct West Yorkshire brewery. Beer is supplied direct as far as South Yorkshire, Lancashire, the North East and North Lincolnshire. In 2016 Camerons of Hartlepool (qv) bought the Leeds' pub estate. Beers are also brewed for Suddaby's. ♦

Pale (OG 1037.5, ABV 3.8%)
Hops and fruit, sometimes citrus or lemon, last through to the bitter, dry, hoppy finish. Light gold in colour.

Yorkshire Gold (OG 1040, ABV 4%)
Plenty of zesty citrus flavours, a wallop of hops and a long-lasting bitter finish make this a refreshing beer.

Best (OG 1041, ABV 4.3%)
There is a pleasing mix of malt and hops in this smooth, amber-coloured, bittersweet beer.

Midnight Bell (OG 1047.5, ABV 4.8%)
A full-bodied strong mild, deep red to dark brown in colour. Chocolate and strong malt flavours are present throughout.

Contract brewed for Suddaby's:

Double Chance (ABV 3.8%)
Full-bodied, medium-hopped bitter with a fruity yet bitter finish.

JW Lees IFBB

Greengate Brewery, Middleton Junction, M24 2AX
☎ (0161) 643 2487 🌐 jwlees.co.uk

Family-owned since its foundation by John Lees in 1828, the brewery has a tied estate of around 150 pubs, mostly in north Manchester, Cheshire, Lancashire and North Wales. The vast majority serve cask beer. The current head brewer is a family member. A new in-house microbrewery came on stream in 2018. ‼

Dark (OG 1032, ABV 3.5%)
A dark brown-coloured beer with a malt and caramel aroma. Creamy mouthfeel, with malt, caramel and fruit flavours and a malty finish. Becoming rare.

Supernova (OG 1035, ABV 3.5%)

Manchester Pale Ale (OG 1038, ABV 3.7%)
Yellow in colour, with malt, hops and a good bitterness throughout.

Bitter (OG 1037, ABV 4%)
Copper-coloured beer with malt and fruit in aroma, taste and finish.

Dragon's Fire (OG 1037, ABV 4%)

Game On (OG 1042, ABV 4.2%)

Stout (OG 1041, ABV 4.2%)

Founder's (OG 1041, ABV 4.5%)
A well-balanced, full-bodied premium bitter.

Gold (OG 1045, ABV 4.5%)

Moonraker (OG 1073, ABV 6.5%)
A reddish-brown-coloured beer with a strong, malty, fruity aroma. The flavour is rich and sweet, with roast malt, and the finish is fruity yet dry.

Left Handed Giant SIBA

Unit 8-9, Wadehurst Industrial Park, St Philips Road, St Philip's, Bristol, BS2 0JE 🌐 lefthandedgiant.com

Originally launched in 2015 as a cuckoo brewery using spare capacity at other local breweries, Left Handed Giant has operated since 2017 using its own 15-barrel plant in premises shared with Big Beer Distribution. The head brewer, Richard Poole, is a former homebrewer who previously had hisown nanobrewery, Rocket Science. ♦RAIB

Legitimate Industries

10 Weaver Street, Leeds, West Yorkshire, LS4 2AU
🌐 legitimateworldwide.com

Founded in 2016 using a 30-barrel plant, the brewery produces mainly keg beer but a limited amount of cask-conditioned beer is available.

Leigh on Sea (NEW) SIBA

35 Progress Road, Leigh-on-Sea, Essex, SS9 5PR
☎ (01702) 817255 🌐 leighonseabrewery.co.uk

Established in 2017 to produce vegan-friendly beer, which is unfiltered, unpasteurised, and unfined. Initially brewing on a one-barrel kit, Leigh on Sea rapidly progressed to a 10-barrel plant. The names of the beers are based on Leigh's rich maritime heritage. The brewery has its own licenced taproom.

Legra Pale (OG 1038, ABV 3.8%)
A light, fresh, session golden ale with a clean citrus flavour.

Six Little Ships (OG 1042, ABV 4.2%)

Two Tree Island Red (OG 1045, ABV 4.5%)
A spicy, red-coloured ale with a well-balanced blend of malt and hops.

Crowstone (OG 1055, ABV 5.5%)
A dark-coloured beer with rich, malty notes and a New World hop hit.

Cockle Row Spit (OG 1056, ABV 5.6%)
A strong, full-flavoured, hoppy beer with a strong hop aroma.

Leighton Buzzard SIBA

Unit 31, Harmill Industrial Estate, Grovebury Road, Leighton Buzzard, Bedfordshire, LU7 4FF ☎ 07538 903753 🌐 leightonbuzzardbrewing.co.uk

The first brewery to operate in Leighton Buzzard for over 100 years. Established in 2014 by local CAMRA member and homebrew enthusiast Jon d'Este-Hoare, the first beers were upscaled versions of his homebrews. ‼ ♦

Cuckoo (OG 1039, ABV 3.8%)
A traditional British malty bitter.

Narrow Gauge (OG 1040, ABV 3.9%)
A golden ale with a dry bitter taste and crisp citrus finish.

Restoration Ale (OG 1049, ABV 4.6%)
A mid brown-coloured beer, fruity and refreshing.

Rebel Yell (OG 1053, ABV 5%)
A black IPA with an initial smooth malty richness followed by sharp, dry hops.

Black Buzzard (OG 1061, ABV 5.8%)
A complex, robust porter brewed with six malts.

Leila Cottage SIBA

Countryman, Chapel Road, Ingoldmells, Lincolnshire, PE25 1ND
☎ (01754) 872268
✉ countryman_inn@btconnect.com

Brewing began in 2007. The brewery is situated at the Countryman pub – Leila Cottage was the original name of the building before it became a licensed club and more recently a pub. The history of the Countryman and the brewery is on display in the pub. ‼ RAIB

Leith Hill

c/o Plough Inn, Coldharbour Lane, Coldharbour, Surrey, RH5 6HD
☎ (01306) 711793 🌐 ploughinn.com

Leith Hill was established in 1996 at the Plough Inn and was moved to converted storerooms at the rear in 2001, increasing capacity to 2.5 barrels in 2005. New owners took over in 2016. ‼

Lenton Lane SIBA

Unit 5g, The Midway, Lenton Industrial Estate, Nottingham, NG7 2TS ☎ 0333 003 5008
🌐 lentonlane.co.uk

Lenton Lane began brewing in 2014 under the name Frontier, after taking over the brewing plant at the Flower Pot pub in Derby. Lenton Lane changed its name in 2016 and relocated to a purpose-built brewery in Nottingham using a 10-barrel plant. ♦ RAIB

Bluebird (OG 1035, ABV 3.8%)

Atlas Stout (OG 1039, ABV 4.2%)
Classic, full-bodied, dry stout with roast and chocolate notes.

Gold Rush (OG 1037, ABV 4.2%)
Zesty, golden-coloured, crisp ale.

Pioneer (OG 1039, ABV 4.3%)
A crisp, golden-coloured pale ale with a hoppy punch and dry finish.

Outpost (OG 1041, ABV 4.5%)

SM&SH (Single Malt & Single Hop) (OG 1039, ABV 4.5%)

Calibration (ABV 4.8%)
A zesty, citrus-tasting, crisp beer.

American Pale Ale (OG 1050, ABV 5.3%)
A hazy, hoppy pale ale.

Explorer IPA (OG 1051, ABV 5.5%)
A strong, hoppy IPA. Heavily-hopped with citrus fruit notes and a clean, bitter finish.

Lerwick SIBA

Staneyhill, North Road, Lerwick, Shetland, ZE1 0QA
☎ (01595) 694552 ☎ 07738 948336
🌐 lerwickbrewery.co.uk

Lerwick Brewery was established in 2011 using a 12-barrel plant and sits at the very edge of the North Atlantic. Originally only brewing keg beer, a cask-conditioned range was launched in 2015.

Shetland Pale Ale (ABV 3.8%)
Malt and citrus hops with a slight background sulphur taste.

Azure (ABV 4.3%)
Refreshing, grapefruit/peachy, hoppy, golden bitter.

IPA (ABV 5%)
Grapefruity, hoppy bitter with a slight biscuit background.

Tushkar (ABV 5.5%)
Dark brown-coloured, liquorice, roasted, malty stout.

Liberation

Tregar House, Longueville Road, St Saviour, Jersey, JE2 7WF
☎ (01534) 764089 🌐 liberationgroup.com

The Liberation Brewery is located at Longueville, just outside St Helier using a 40-barrel and an eight-barrel plant. Its multi-award-winning flagship beer, Liberation Ale, is now regularly seen on the mainland, as well as on the other Channel Islands. 68 pubs are owned with around two-thirds of these serving cask ale. In 2016 Liberation, including Butcombe (qv), was bought by Caledonia Investments. ‼ ♦

Ale (OG 1039, ABV 4%)
Golden-coloured beer with a hint of citrus on the nose.

IPA (OG 1047, ABV 4.8%)
Traditional IPA with a citrus hop flavour and a crisp, balanced finish.

Lincoln Green SIBA

Unit 5, Enterprise Park, Wigwam Lane, Hucknall, Nottingham, NG15 7SZ
☎ (0115) 963 4233 ☎ 07748 111457
🌐 lincolngreenbrewing.co.uk

Anthony Hughes established the Lincoln Green Brewing Company in 2012 using a 10-barrel plant. The brewery takes its name from the colour of dyed woollen cloth associated with the legend of Robin Hood. ♦ RAIB

Marion (OG 1038, ABV 3.8%)
Subtly-hopped golden ale with a citrus aroma and a dry bitter finish.

THE BREWERIES

Archer (OG 1040, ABV 4%) ♦
Citrus golden ale with American hops and a moderately bitter finish.

Hood (OG 1042, ABV 4.2%) ♦
Tawny-coloured ale with balanced hops and bitterness.

Tuck (OG 1047, ABV 4.7%) ♦
Full-bodied and rich, dark-coloured ale with roast and malt flavours throughout.

Lincolnshire SIBA

George, 15 Main Road, Langworth, Lincolnshire, LN3 5BJ
☎ (0845) 094 5784 ☎ 07508 554890
lincolnshirebrewingco.co.uk

An events company that operates mobile bars, in 2014 it started brewing for its own bars and has since expanded into the free trade. An eight-barrel plant brews both cask and bottle-conditioned beers, with bottling carried out in-house. Beers can be found at local fairs, shows, markets and free houses and nationally via wholesalers. ♦RAIB

Great Tom (OG 1037, ABV 3.7%)
A dark-coloured ale with chocolate and coffee on the nose. A fruity, malty mouthfeel with a long but soft bitter finish.

Yeast Coast Blonde (ABV 3.7%)
Easy-drinking blonde ale, zesty with a clean, fresh finish.

Don't Be Bitter (OG 1040, ABV 4%)
A bitter with a tropical fruit nose and roast malt flavours.

Impaled Up (OG 1040, ABV 4%)
A traditional IPA with a lively hop character and malt flavourings followed by an intense bitterness.

Spicy Sausage (OG 1041, ABV 4.1%)
An amber-coloured ale with a sharp bitterness and dry finish.

1215 Magna Carta Ale (OG 1043, ABV 4.3%)
A fruity nose with fruit ebbing away to leave malt flavours. A fruity aftertaste and gentle bitterness in the throat.

Friendly Rottweiler (OG 1045, ABV 4.5%)
A light, crisp ale with a subtle hoppy taste.

Medicinal Purposes (OG 1045, ABV 4.5%)
A satisfying stout with malt chocolate flavours.

Cheeky Imp (OG 1046, ABV 4.6%)
A malty ale with caramel notes, hoppy aromas and a slightly sweet taste.

Angry Rottweiler (OG 1060, ABV 6%)

Lincolnshire Craft SIBA

Race Lane, Melton Ross, Lincolnshire, DN38 6AA
☎ (01652) 680001 lincolnshirecraftbeers.com

Lincolnshire Craft Beers is the company formed by Mark Smith who bought the Tom Wood Brewery in 2017. It continues to brew the Tom Wood range of beers on the 60-barrel Melton Ross plant. ♦

Tom Wood's Best Bitter (OG 1035.5, ABV 3.5%) ♦
A good citrus, passion fruit hop dominates the nose and taste, with background malt. A lingering hoppy and bitter finish.

Lincoln Gold (OG 1041, ABV 4%)
Pale-coloured bitter with a fruity aroma and slightly zesty flavour but retaining malt characteristics.

Tom Wood's Bomber County (OG 1046, ABV 4.8%) ♦
An earthy malt aroma but with a complex underlying mix of coffee, hops, caramel and apple fruit. The beer starts bitter and intensifies to the end.

Linear

Bingham, Nottinghamshire, NG13 8EU linear.beer

Small-scale 50-litre brewery, which started production in 2016 and is located at the owner's house. Currently supplying three local pubs, with the rest of production bottle-conditioned. Limited capacity prevents the supply of cask beers to other outlets. RAIB

Lines SIBA

Unit 2e, Pontygwindy Estate, Caerphilly, CF83 3HU
☎ (029) 2085 0706

Office: 23 Jim Driscoll Way, Cardiff, CF11 7JA
linesbrewco.com

Lines has been formed out of the remains of the former Celt Experience brewery after it ceased trading. All beers are new recipes and names but at present there is no permanent range. Brewing is currently suspended although other breweries use the plant.

Linfit

Sair Inn, 139 Lane Top, Linthwaite, Huddersfield, West Yorkshire, HD7 5SG
☎ (01484) 842370

A 19th-century brewpub that started brewing again in 1982. The beer is only available at the Sair Inn.

Lion's Lair

2 Lochlair Farm Cottage, Arbroath, DD11 2RF
brewhouse@lionslairbrewery.co

Brewing began in 2015 but is currently suspended.

Lister's SIBA

The Old Dairy, Ford Lane, Ford, West Sussex, BN18 0DF
☎ (01903) 739117 ☎ 07775 853412
listersbrewery.com

Brewing began in 2012 using a 0.25-barrel kit. The brewery relocated in 2014 and expanded to a five-barrel plant. Lister's donates 5p from every pint and bottle sold to the Battersea Dogs & Cats Home.

Best Bitter (ABV 3.9%)

Golden Ale (ABV 4.1%)

Limehouse Porter (ABV 4.1%)

American Pale Ale (ABV 4.2%)

IPA (ABV 4.3%)

Special (ABV 4.6%)

Lithic SIBA

Ty Newydd Farm, Llangorse, LD3 7UA ☎ 07542 425408 🌐 lithicbrewing.com

Brewing began in 2016 at the premises of the former Redstone Brewery. Producer of small batch craft beers, mainly in bottles and cans although some cask-conditioned beer is available.

Little Beer SIBA

Building 3, 14-15 Midleton Road, Guildford, Surrey, GU2 8XW
☎ (01483) 497201 ☎ 07941 061241
🌐 littlebeer.co.uk

Little Beer Corporation is a Guildford-based 10-barrel brewery, the first to open there since Friary Meux closed in the 1970s. It is run by Jim Taylor, alongside around 400 local shareholders. !! RAIB

Little Haka (OG 1035, ABV 3.5%)
An easy-drinking session ale. Predominantly bitter but with with a good malt character and light hoppy tones.

Little Geyser (OG 1036, ABV 3.6%)

Little Vienna (OG 1038, ABV 3.8%)
A Vienna-style lager. An initially malty aroma leads to fruitiness in the tasty with a good hoppiness and a dry, spicy finish.

Little Kahuna (OG 1039, ABV 3.9%)

Little Smooth (OG 1050, ABV 3.9%)

Little Black Dog SIBA

Carlton Towers Brewery, Carlton Towers, Carlton, North Yorkshire, DN14 9LZ ☎ 07495 026173
🌐 littleblackdogbeer.com

Established in 2015, a small batch, family-run brewery based in the village of Carlton in North Yorkshire. All beer is unfined, unpasteurised and unfiltered.

Yorkshire Bitter (ABV 3.8%)
A traditional bitter, with malty notes of toffee over a light chocolate and biscuit base. Lightly-hopped giving delicate floral aromas and a light bitter finish.

India Pale Ale (ABV 3.9%)
A session pale ale with a delicate citrus nose over a light caramel base. A good bitter finish.

New World Pale Ale (ABV 4%)

American Pale Ale (ABV 4.1%)
A light amber-coloured pale ale, brewed with all American hops giving a citrus flavour with a thirst-quenching bitterness.

Black IPA (ABV 4.5%)

Oatmeal Stout (ABV 4.5%)
A creamy, dark-coloured stout. Flavours of chocolate and coffee are prominent without the dry, burnt, roasted flavour of a traditional stout.

Little Critters SIBA

80 Parkwood Road, Sheffield, South Yorkshire, S3 8AG
☎ (0114) 276 3171

Office: Horizon House, 2 Whiting Street, Sheffield, S8 9QR 🌐 littlecrittersbrewery.com

A small batch, family-owned microbrewery, opened in 2016. It runs two pubs in Sheffield; the Fox & Duck, Broomhill, and the Doctor's Orders. Pubs are supplied throughout Yorkshire and the East Midlands.

Little Hopper (OG 1038, ABV 3.6%)
Golden-coloured session ale with a malty, refreshing finish.

Blonde Bear (OG 1040, ABV 4.2%)
Smooth blonde ale with a balanced taste and tropical notes.

Shire Horse (OG 1043, ABV 4.3%)
A chestnut-coloured best bitter with strong flavours of bread and toffee and a floral nose.

Sleepy Badger (OG 1043, ABV 4.5%)
Stout brewed with locally sourced honey.

White Wolf (OG 1048, ABV 5%)
A refreshing, light-coloured beer with bitterness and a citrus finish.

Chameleon Series (OG 1052, ABV 5.5%)
Single-hopped pale ale with versions brewed simultaneously, strong bitter finish.

Nutty Ambassador (OG 1059, ABV 6%)
Smooth stout with a hazelnut nose, supported by coffee and chocolate notes for a well-balanced taste.

C Monster (OG 1060, ABV 6.5%)
Citrus IPA made with American hops, lime leaves and fresh citrus peel for a bold, refreshing taste.

King Crow (OG 1068, ABV 7.2%)
Smooth stout with a strong coffee taste brewed with espresso coffee from a local café.

Little Earth Project (NEW)

Edwardstone, CO10 5PX
☎ (01787) 211118 🌐 littleearthproject.com

Established as Mill Green Brewery in 2008, becoming Little Earth Project in 2016. The brewery is built on the site of an old stable behind the White Horse Inn, Edwardstone. A 'green' brewery, it has its own borehole for brewing water, it was built using local wood, reclaimed bricks, sheeps wool and lime plaster. The brewing liquor is heated using bio and solar power and it has a 3,000 litre storage tank that is constantly heated by solar panels topped up by a wood boiler. Malting barley and hops are grown nearby.

Little Giant (NEW)

Unit 3, Stoke View Business Park, Fishponds, Bristol, BS16 3AE
☎ (0117) 939 2589 🌐 littlegiantbrewery.co.uk

A microbrewery established in the Fishponds area of Bristol in 2017. No real ale. !!

Little London SIBA

Unit 6b, Ash Park Business Centre, Ash Lane, Little London, Hampshire, RG26 5FL
☎ (01256) 533044 ☎ 07785 225468
🌐 littlelondonbrewery.com

Brewing began in 2015 using a six-barrel plant. Three fermentation vessels ensure a production capability of 60 firkins per week, with capacity for expansion.

Doreen's Dark (OG 1035, ABV 3.2%)
Treacle-coloured beer with a creamy head, hints of liquorice and coffee and a dry finish.

Red Boy (OG 1036, ABV 3.7%)
A light, well-balanced session bitter with a delicate hop aroma and subtle hop flavours on the palate.

Hoppy Hilda (OG 1039, ABV 3.8%)

Pryde (OG 1040.5, ABV 4.2%)
A fruity, dark amber-coloured best bitter with caramel and toffee aromas and spicy hop notes.

Ash Park Special (OG 1048, ABV 4.9%)
A tawny-coloured ale with malt and raisin on the nose. Slightly sweet with a long finish.

Little Ox SIBA

Unit 6, Wroslyn Road Industrial Estate, Freeland, Oxfordshire, OX29 8HZ
☎ (01993) 881941 ☎ 07730 496525

Office: 25 Castle Road, Wootton, OX20 1EQ
littleoxbrewery.co.uk

Little Ox began production in 2016 using a 10-barrel plant. Beer is regularly supplied to the White Horse, Stonesfield, plus other local pubs, shops and off licences. ♦

Oddbod (OG 1040, ABV 4%)
A bitter with a malty backbone and a floral, bitter finish with hints of orange marmalade.

Wipeout (OG 1042, ABV 4.2%)
A zesty, pale gold-coloured ale, generously hopped, giving a full-bodied, fruity flavour with citrus and tropical notes.

Filthy Rich (OG 1044, ABV 4.5%)
A porter combining chocolate and roasted malts to give a rich, smooth body balanced with hops. Finishes smooth and creamy with berry notes.

Little Valley SIBA

Unit 3, Turkey Lodge Farm, New Road, Cragg Vale, Hebden Bridge, West Yorkshire, HX7 5TT
☎ (01422) 883888 littlevalleybrewery.co.uk

Little Valley began brewing in 2005 on a 10-barrel plant. All beers are organic and vegan, and Radical Roots uses Fairtrade ingredients. Around 300 outlets are supplied. Several beers are contract brewed for Suma Wholefoods. ♦RAIB V

Withens Pale (OG 1037, ABV 3.9%)
Creamy, light gold-coloured, refreshing ale. Fruity hop aroma, flavoured with hints of lemon and grapefruit. Clean, bitter aftertaste.

Radical Roots (OG 1037, ABV 4%)
Full-bodied speciality ale. Ginger predominates in the aroma and taste. It has a pleasantly powerful, fiery and spicy finish.

Cragg Bitter (OG 1039, ABV 4.2%)
Tawny-coloured best bitter with a creamy mouthfeel. Malt and fruit aromas move through to the palate which is followed by a bitter finish.

Dark Vale (ABV 4.5%)
Dark brown-coloured speciality beer. Dark roast and fruit blend with flavours of vanilla to create a smooth, mellow porter.

Hebden's Wheat (OG 1043, ABV 4.5%)
A pale yellow-coloured, creamy wheat beer with a good balance of bitterness and fruit, a hint of sweetness but with a lasting, dry finish.

Stoodley Stout (OG 1044, ABV 4.8%)
Dark brown-coloured, creamy stout with a rich roast aroma and luscious fruity, chocolate, roast flavours. Well-balanced with a clean bitter finish.

Tod's Blonde (OG 1045, ABV 5%)
Bright yellow-coloured, smooth beer with a citrus hop start and a dry finish. Fruity, with a hint of spice.

Moor Ale (OG 1051, ABV 5.5%)
Tawny in colour with a full-bodied taste. It has a strong malty nose and palate with hints of heather and peat-smoked malt. Well-balanced with a bitter finish.

Python IPA (OG 1055, ABV 6%)
Amber-coloured, creamy beer with a complex bitter fruit palate subtly balanced by a malty sweetness, leading to a strongly lingering bitter aftertaste.

Littleover SIBA

Unit 9, Robinson Industrial Estate, Shaftesbury Street, Derby, DE23 8NL
☎ (01332) 987100 ☎ 07449 586811
littleoverbrewery.co.uk

Littleover was established in 2015 using a six-barrel plant.

Gold (OG 1038, ABV 3.8%)
Golden-coloured session ale with a subtle hoppy aroma.

Apex Amber (OG 1040, ABV 4.1%)

Epiphany Pale Ale (OG 1040, ABV 4.1%)

The Panther Oatmeal Stout (OG 1049, ABV 4.2%)

Crest (OG 1044, ABV 4.4%)
Malty, chestnut-coloured best bitter with a clean fresh taste and a light, fruity aroma.

Dazzler IPA (OG 1043, ABV 4.5%)

Hollow Legs Pale Ale (OG 1050, ABV 5.2%)

Littondale (NEW)

Queens Arms, Litton, North Yorkshire, BD23 5JQ
☎ (01756) 770096 queensarmslitton.co.uk

The former Littondale Brewery started brewing in 2003 but ceased operation in 2014. In 2018 brewing recommenced at the Queens Arms, Litton, on a four-barrel plant.

Liverpool Craft SIBA

10 Love Lane, The Railway Arches, Liverpool, L3 7DD
☎ (0151) 236 9400 liverpoolcraftbeer.com

Brewing began in 2011 using a 10-barrel plant. Work is undergoing on new premises in the Baltic Triangle area of Liverpool. The brewery owns the rights to use the name of the old Higson's Brewery. ♦RAIB

Camel IPA (ABV 4.8%)

Little Albion (ABV 4.8%)

Mork (ABV 5%)

Lizard

The Old Nuclear Bunker, Pednavounder, Coverack, Cornwall, TR12 6SE
☎ (01326) 281135 🌐 lizardales.co.uk

⊗ Launched in 2004, Lizard Ales is now based at former RAF Treleaver, a massive disused nuclear bunker in the countryside near Coverack on the Lizard Peninsula. Specialising in bottle-conditioned ales, it mainly supplies west Cornwall. !! RAIB

Llangollen SIBA

Abbey Grange Brewing Ltd, Abbey Grange Hotel, Horseshoe Pass Road, Llantysilio, LL20 8DD
☎ (01978) 861916 🌐 llangollenbrewery.com

Brewing began in 2010 on a 2.5-barrel plant. The brewery was updated and upgraded in 2014 to a 10-barrel plant. !! RAIB

Lleu

Unit 9, Penygroes Industrial Estate, Penygroes, LL54 6DB ☎ 07724 902532 🌐 bragdylleu.cymru

Brewing began in 2014 using a 1.25-barrel plant. The beer reflects the Welsh folklore tales of the Mabinogi in both name and character. Capacity was upgraded to 5.5 barrels in 2016 to meet demand. !!

Blodeuwedd (OG 1036, ABV 3.6%)

Lleu (OG 1040, ABV 4%)
Full-bodied ale with a good mouthfeel and a lasting, satisfying hoppy aftertaste.

Gwydion (OG 1047, ABV 4.7%)
A dark chestnut-coloured bitter. Malty with a subtle hop character and lasting aftertaste.

Llŷn

Uned 6, Fford Dewi Sant, Nefyn, LL53 6EG ☎ 07792 050134 🌐 cwrwllyn.com

Cwrw Llŷn began brewing in 2011. In 2016 it moved to a new purpose-built 15-barrel plant that includes a shop, tap house and a visitor's gallery for tours. Beer is also contract brewed for the Old Market Brewery in Caernarfon. !! ♦

Y Brawd Houdini (OG 1040, ABV 3.5%)
A pale ale with citrus notes.

Brenin Enlli (OG 1041, ABV 4%)
A fruity bitter, the initial malty taste leads to a hoppy, bitter aftertaste.

Cwrw Glyndwr (OG 1041, ABV 4%)
A full-bodied and well-balanced, amber-coloured beer, quite fruity with a good hoppy finish.

A55 (ABV 4.2%)

Seithenyn (OG 1042, ABV 4.2%)
A fruity golden ale with a tangy citrus taste and a dry, hoppy finish.

Tria Hon (ABV 4.2%)

Porth Neigwl (OG 1044, ABV 4.5%)

Blonde (ABV 5.2%)

Genius (ABV 5.2%)

Loch Leven SIBA

The Muirs, Kinross, KY13 8AS

Based opposite the Green Hotel in Kinross, the brewery started production in 2017. Brewing plant and casks have been acquired from the former Loch Leven Brewery in Fife.

Loch Lomond SIBA

Unit 5, Block 1, Lomond Industrial Estate, Alexandria, G83 0TL
☎ (01389) 755698 ☎ 07891 920213
🌐 lochlomondbrewery.com

Established in 2011 by Fiona and Euan MacEachern, Loch Lomond is the first brewery to be established in the area. !! ♦

Bonnie 'n' Bitter (OG 1036, ABV 3.6%)
An easy-drinking blonde ale with citrus flavours and a full, rounded bitterness.

West Highland Way (OG 1037, ABV 3.7%)
A light ale with fruity flavours.

Bonnie & Blonde (OG 1040, ABV 4%)
A light, refreshing ale with a well-rounded citrus flavour.

Southern Summit (OG 1040, ABV 4%)
A highly-hopped blonde ale with a fresh, fruity palate. Hints of grapefruit and lemon, which lead to a crisp, light bitter finish.

The Ale of Leven (OG 1045, ABV 4.5%)
An amber-coloured ale with a spicy, citrus aroma and a well-rounded bitterness.

Bonnie 'n' Clyde (OG 1046, ABV 4.6%)
An amber-coloured ale with a big citrus hit on the nose that follows through to the rich, bitter finish.

Silkie Stout (OG 1050, ABV 5%)
A black-coloured stout with chocolate-orange spicy notes.

Kessog Dark Ale (OG 1052, ABV 5.2%)
Dark-coloured ale with warm, spicy flavours.

Bravehop Amber IPA (OG 1060, ABV 6%)
IPA with up-front hop bite and lots of sweetness to give balance.

Bravehop Dark IPA (OG 1060, ABV 6%)
A black IPA with upfront hop bite balanced with roasted malt and a long, dry bitter finish.

Loch Ness

See Cairngorm

Loddon SIBA

Dunsden Green Farm, Church Lane, Dunsden, Oxfordshire, RG4 9QD
☎ (0118) 948 1111 🌐 loddonbrewery.com

⊗ This family-run brewery was established in 2002 in a brick-and-flint barn that was originally a grain store. The custom-built 17-barrel plant typically produces 120 barrels per week and supplies more than 700 outlets far and wide. Popular open evenings are held quarterly and Beer Club members' evenings twice yearly. !! ♦

Hoppit (OG 1036.2, ABV 3.5%)
Hops dominate the aroma of this drinkable, light-coloured session beer. Malt and hops create a balanced taste and a pleasant bitterness carries through to the aftertaste.

Reading Best (OG 1041.5, ABV 4%)

A dark golden-coloured best bitter with a smooth but nutty body and a lingering bitter aftertaste.

Hullabaloo (OG 1043.8, ABV 4.2%)
A hint of fruit in the initial taste develops into a balance of hops and malt in this well-rounded, medium-bodied bitter with a bitter aftertaste.

Ferryman's Gold (OG 1045.8, ABV 4.4%)
Golden-coloured ale with a strong hoppy character throughout, accompanied by fruit in the taste and aftertaste.

NOTUS (OG 1048.1, ABV 4.7%)

Forbury Lion (OG 1056.5, ABV 5.5%)
A malty IPA with a strong, complex hop finish.

Loka Polly

Holland Farm, Blackbrook, Mold, CH7 6LU
☎ (01244) 940621 ☎ 07460 215571
lokapolly.co.uk

Established in 2016 inside the stable of an old horse called Polly as Black Brook Brewery and re-branded in 2018, Loka Polly concentrates on keg and canned beer widely distributed via wholesalers although some cask-conditioned beer is supplied to local outlets. The beer range changes constantly.

Lola Rose

Wanlockhead Inn, Wanlockhead, ML12 6UZ
☎ (01659) 74535 ☎ 07500 663405
lola-rose-brewery.co.uk

Lola Rose is based in the family-run Wanlockhead Inn, situated in the scenic Lowther Hills of the Scottish Lowlands. Local outlets only are supplied at present. ♦RAIB

London Beer Factory SIBA

Unit 4, 160 Hamilton Road, West Norwood, London, SE27 9SF
☎ (020) 8670 7054 ☎ 07760 290489
thelondonbeerfactory.com

The London Beer Factory started brewing in 2014 using a 20-barrel plant. Local outlets are supplied. A tap room is open to the public at weekends.

Beyond the Pale (ABV 4.2%)
Easy-drinking, unfined pale ale with some malt and fruit to provide balance. Slightly bitter aftertaste.

Chelsea Blonde (ABV 4.3%)
Grapefruit dominates the flavour and aroma with trace of spiciness and a dry bitterness balanced by a little honey sweetness.

Sayers Stout (ABV 4.5%)
Copper-coloured bitter with a pleasant malty aroma, soft, well-balanced taste and a dry aftertaste that continues into the finish.

Paxton Pale Ale (ABV 5%)

London Beer Lab SIBA

Arch 41, Nursery Road, Brixton, London, SW9 7DT
☎ (020) 8001 6552 londonbeerlab.com

Started as a bottle shop, brewing workshop and homebrew supplies outlet, London Beer Lab began commercial brewing in 2015. Initially offering only KeyKeg and bottled beers, it now offers some cask-conditioned ales. Originally sharing facilities with Clarkshaws (qv), it now brews on its own equipment in Brixton.

Tip Top Citra (ABV 5%)
A pale ale with a slightly sweet malt base.

London Brewing SIBA

Bohemia, 762-764 High Road, North Finchley, London, N12 9QH
☎ (020) 8446 0294 londonbrewing.com

London Brewing Co began brewing in 2011 at the Bull in Highgate using a 2.5-barrel plant. In 2014 it acquired its second pub, the Bohemia in North Finchley, at which brewing began in 2015 in a new 6.5-barrel brewhouse. The Bull was sold in the summer of 2016 to concentrate all production at the North Finchley site. Beer is now supplied widely beyond the Bohemia itself. ♦

Beer Street (OG 1042, ABV 4%)
Well-balanced, coppery brown-coloured best bitter with the hoppy bitterness underpinned by the caramelised malt character. Fruit is present throughout.

100 Oysters Stout (OG 1049, ABV 4.6%)
Sweet dark treacle and soft citrus fruit tastes in this smooth stout. Finish is dry roast with a little bitterness.

Skyline (OG 1053, ABV 5.3%)
Pale brown-coloured beer with a honey sweetness and a some soft fruit notes. Sweetness is balanced by a bitter dryness.

Never Mind the Kent Hops (OG 1056, ABV 5.5%)
A smooth, brown-coloured beer with spicy hops on the palate, lingering in the dry finish, which is slightly bitter. There is a sweet toffee character throughout.

London Fields

365-366 Warburton Street, London Fields, London, E8 3RR
☎ (020) 7524 7174 londonfieldsbrewery.co.uk

Brewing was suspended for some years but London Fields was purchased by Carlsberg UK in 2017. Refurbishment began in early 2018 with plans for the brewery to be on stream later that year. Beers are currently being brewed using spare capacity at Truman's Brewery (qv) and other local breweries until its own plant is on stream.

London Road Brew House

London Road Brew House, 67-75 London Road, Southampton, Hampshire, SO15 2AB
☎ (023) 8098 9401 ☎ 07399 999947
londonroadbrewhouse.com

Brewing commenced in 2017 in the London Road Brew House using a six-barrel plant. Beer is brewed for the pub, the City Pub Co estate and the trade.

Athena (OG 1040, ABV 3.8%)
A pale-coloured session bitter with hints of grapefruit, a floral aroma and medium bitterness.

Tame Impala (ABV 4%)

Kodiak (OG 1042, ABV 4.2%)

Lonesome (NEW)

36 Streatham Vale, Streatham, London, SW16 5TD

Lonesome began brewing in 2017 producing small batch bottled beers.

Long Arm (NEW)

Long Arm, 20-26 Worship Street, London, EC2A 2DX ☎ (020) 3873 4065 🌐 longarmpub.co.uk

Microbrewery that opened in 2017 as a sister brewery to the Long Arm Brewery in South Ealing. Run by the ETM Group, beers are available on site and at other pubs in the group. The South Ealing brewery closed in 2017 and all beers are now brewed at the Shoreditch site.

Long Man SIBA

Church Farm, Litlington, East Sussex, BN26 5RA ☎ (01323) 871850 ☎ 07976 777992 🌐 longmanbrewery.com

⊗ Long Man began brewing in 2012 using a 20-barrel stainless steel plant. Hops and grain are sourced locally with a view to using homegrown barley, as well as a traditional strain of Sussex yeast. ‼

Long Blonde (OG 1039, ABV 3.8%)
A light-coloured golden ale with a distinctive hoppy aroma and crisp, clean bitterness on the finish.

Best Bitter (OG 1040, ABV 4%)
Well-balanced with a complex, bittersweet, malty taste, fragrant hops and a long, deep finish.

Copper Hop (ABV 4.2%)

Old Man (OG 1048, ABV 4.3%)
Dark-coloured beer with soft malt notes of coffee and chocolate combined with a pleasant light hoppiness.

Sussex Pride (OG 1045, ABV 4.5%)
A classic strong pale ale. Bronze-coloured with a fruity nose and full, round flavours.

American Pale Ale (OG 1046, ABV 4.8%)
A triple-hopped, American-style pale ale with a pleasant citrus fruit aroma and robust bitterness.

Longdog SIBA

Unit A1, Moniton Trading Estate, West Ham Lane, Worting, Basingstoke, Hampshire, RG22 6NQ ☎ (01256) 324286 ☎ 07827 618733 🌐 longdogbrewery.co.uk

⊗ Longdog was established in 2011 using a six-barrel plant. The name is inspired by the owner's lurcher. ‼ ♦ RAIB

Bunny Chaser (OG 1036, ABV 3.6%)
A mid copper-coloured session bitter with plenty of malt in the mouth and a big hit of bitterness.

Golden Poacher (OG 1039, ABV 3.9%)
A fruity nose with plenty of hops, balanced by a malty sweetness in the flavour. The hops build to a faint astringent finish.

Red Runner (OG 1041, ABV 4.2%)
A fruity and hoppy, mahogany-coloured best bitter.

Kismet (OG 1045, ABV 4.5%)
A pale ale with assertive hop bitterness, flavour and aroma coming from a blend of fragrant American hops.

Lamplight Porter (OG 1048, ABV 5%)
Splendid porter, smoky and drier than many, with strong roast flavours giving way to a blackberry taste and slightly vinous finish.

Longhill

Longhill Cottage, Whitstone, Cornwall, EX22 6UG ☎ (01288) 341466

⊗ Longhill began brewing in 2011 using a 0.5-barrel plant, upgraded in 2012 to a four-barrel plant to meet demand. The beers are named with a wind theme. Eight outlets are supplied direct.

Whistler (OG 1038, ABV 3.8%)
Smooth, pale brown-coloured bitter with little aroma. Gentle balance of caramel malt, bitter hops and sweet fruit. Slowly fading bittersweet finish.

Westerly (OG 1040, ABV 4%)
Copper-coloured best bitter with malt and toffee aroma. Mainly malt and caramel flavour. Light finish with malt, fruit and bitterness.

Gale Force (OG 1048, ABV 4.8%)
Copper-coloured, strong bitter. Malt and almonds aroma. Malty flavours with toffee and nuts. Short, malty, dry finish with stone fruit.

Hurricane (OG 1048, ABV 4.8%)
Smooth, initially sweet with a full, rounded bitter aftertaste. Distinct fruity and earthy flavours.

Loose Cannon SIBA

Unit 6, Suffolk Way, Abingdon, Oxfordshire, OX14 5JX ☎ (01235) 531141 🌐 lcbeers.co.uk

Brewing began in 2010 using a 15-barrel plant, reviving Abingdon's brewing history after the Morland Brewery closed in 2000. Beers can be found in an increasing number of local pubs, and within 50 miles of the brewery. Popular brewery evenings take place on the first Tuesday of the month. ‼ ♦

Gunners Gold (OG 1034.5, ABV 3.5%)
Golden-coloured, easy-drinking session ale with a subtle peach flavour.

Abingdon Bridge (OG 1041, ABV 4.1%)
Full-flavoured and smooth with well-rounded hop bitterness and a floral aroma.

Detonator (OG 1044, ABV 4.4%)
Dark chestnut-coloured ale, malty and slightly sweet with hints of tropical fruit.

Porter (OG 1054, ABV 5%)
Moderately sweet with hints of dark chocolate and a smooth espresso finish.

India Pale Ale (OG 1053, ABV 5.4%)
Balanced floral aroma and fruity taste with a smooth bitter kick and a real warming quality.

Lord Conrad's

Unit 21, Dry Drayton Industrial Estate, Scotland Road, Dry Drayton, Cambridgeshire, CB23 8AT ☎ 07736 739700 🌐 lordconradsbrewery.co.uk

⊗ Lord Conrad's was established in 2007 and moved to Dry Drayton in 2011 using a 2.5-barrel plant. One permanent outlet is supplied, the Black

THE BREWERIES

Horse, Dry Drayton, along with other local free houses and beer festivals. The brewery adheres strongly to 'green' principles, using low energy systems, recycled materials and local ingredients. !! V

Zulu Dawn (OG 1037, ABV 3.5%)

Hedgerow Hop (OG 1039, ABV 3.7%)
An amber-coloured ale made with locally picked hops and supporting the RSPB.

Her Mages Tea (OG 1038, ABV 3.8%)
A light ale infused with Earl Grey tea.

Lickety Split (OG 1038, ABV 3.8%)
Sweet, malty, brown-coloured ale, light but not overly hoppy.

Tangerine Dream (OG 1038, ABV 3.8%)
A gold-coloured ale heavily infused with tangerine and bitter orange.

Spiffing Wheeze (OG 1040, ABV 3.9%)
A pale-coloured ale with lemongrass and a peppery bitterness.

Big Bad Wolf (OG 1042, ABV 4%)
A pale-coloured ale with citrus and pine hints in the taste.

Conkerwood (OG 1044, ABV 4%)
Dark-coloured porter with hints of liquorice.

Fools Gold (OG 1042, ABV 4%)
A pale gold-coloured ale with subtle pear and watermelon notes.

Gubbins (OG 1040, ABV 4%)
An old English ale brewed with a hint of warming spice.

Lobster Licker (OG 1043, ABV 4.2%)
A red-coloured, malty bitter with strong hoppy undertones.

Slap N'Tickle (OG 1042, ABV 4.3%)

Zulu (OG 1047, ABV 4.5%)

Horny Goat (OG 1048, ABV 4.8%)
A bitter brewed with nettles.

Pheasant's Rise (OG 1050, ABV 5%)
Smoky, woody traditional strong ale.

Stubble Burner (OG 1050, ABV 5%)
A straw-like beer with a good earthy nose and a well-balanced fruity bitterness.

Lord's

Unit 15, Heath House Mill, Heath House Lane, Golcar, West Yorkshire, HD7 4JW ☎ 07976 974162
lordsbrewing.com

Established in 2015, Lord's is the brain child of three brothers-in-law, Ben, John and Tim. A picturesque 19th-century mill houses their eight-barrel plant, large tap room and gift/bottle shop. ♦ RAIB

1895 Golden Ale (OG 1036, ABV 3.8%)
Crisp, pale-coloured bitter with citrus notes and a good malt character.

Tithe House Bitter (OG 1037, ABV 3.9%)
Light copper-coloured bitter with subtle malt flavours balanced by English hops. It has a soft malt and caramel base with a mellow pine and grapefruit flavour.

Expedition Blonde (OG 1038, ABV 4%)
Pale-coloured and delicately hopped. Refreshing, with citrus notes.

The Bandon Car Porter (OG 1048, ABV 4.8%)
Irish-style porter. Subtle roast flavour, chocolaty with a sweet toasty finish.

Mount Helix West Coast Pale (OG 1047, ABV 5%)
American-style ale bursting with citrus, pine and floral overtones, which give way to a lightly toasted crisp malt base.

Havelock IPA (OG 1055, ABV 5.9%)
A hoppy IPA with a touch of coriander seed and a hint of curacao orange peel.

Lost + Found SIBA

12-13 Ship Street, Brighton, East Sussex, BN1 1AD
lostandfoundbrewery.com

Brewing began in 2016. No real ale.

Lost & Grounded SIBA

Barley Mow, 91 Whitby Road, Bristol, BS4 4AR
☎ (0117) 332 7690 lostandgrounded.co.uk

Lost Industry

14a Nutwood Trading Estate, Sheffield, South Yorkshire, S6 1NJ
☎ (0114) 231 6393 lostindustrybrewing.com

Lost Industry is run by a family of beer enthusiasts and was established in 2015. A wide range of beer styles is brewed with no core range, although favourites may be repeated from time to time. A barrel aging programme began in 2018. Spare brewing capacity is utilised by Steel City (qv).

Loud Shirt (NEW) SIBA

Unit 5, Bell Tower Industrial Estate, Roedean Road, Brighton, East Sussex, BN2 5RU
☎ (01273) 087077 loudshirtbeer.co.uk

⊠ The brewery was set up by two old friends, Martyn and Mike. Established in 2017 using a 10-barrel plant. Regular monthly events are held at the brewery, look out for its psychedelic van at festivals. Around 30 outlets are supplied direct. RAIB V

Euphoria Red IPA (OG 1047, ABV 4.8%)
A malty IPA with a hint of blackcurrant.

Flowerpower Blonde (OG 1049, ABV 5.1%)
A mellow wheat beer with elderflower.

Psychedelic IPA (OG 1049, ABV 5.1%)
Bold citrus flavours from the late hopping.

Hallucination Brune (OG 1053, ABV 5.3%)
A Belgian-style, complex, malty beer.

Ecstasy Stout (OG 1065, ABV 6.6%)
A rich, chocolaty stout.

LoveBeer SIBA

95 High Street, Milton, Oxfordshire, OX14 4EJ
☎ 07889 455845 lovebeerbrewery.com

Established in a garage in 2013, LoveBeer's original 0.5-barrel plant grew to six barrels in 2017. The brewery supplies local pubs including the Plum Pudding, Milton, as well as beer festivals and farm shops. RAIB

Doctor Roo (OG 1038, ABV 3.7%)
A well-balanced, light pale ale with a zesty tropical flavour.

Molly's Malt (OG 1041, ABV 4%)
A well-hopped, amber-coloured ale with a caramel biscuit aroma and hints of citrus.

OG (OG 1042, ABV 4.1%)
A pale ale brewed with a light citrus flavour and hints of tropical fruit or rose petals.

Mild Rover (OG 1045, ABV 4.5%)
A mild ale with caramel and toffee notes and a floral hint.

Bonnie Hops (OG 1048, ABV 4.6%)
A hoppy pale ale with full-flavour American hops.

Hair of the Doug (OG 1053, ABV 5.1%)
A pale ale brewed with a hint of ginger and caramel.

Purdy Peculiar (OG 1056, ABV 5.4%)
A smooth, dark-coloured and smoky stout with hints of molasses and black treacle.

Monty's Jem (OG 1058, ABV 5.6%)
A traditional, full-bodied ale with a good hop flavour and a hint of lime or mandarin.

Lovibonds

Rear of 19-21 Market Place, Henley-on-Thames, Oxfordshire, RG9 2AA
☎ (01491) 576596 lovibonds.com

Lovibonds was founded by Jeff Rosenmeier in 2005 and is named after Joseph William Lovibond, who invented the Tintometer to measure beer colour. The beers are unfiltered and unpasteurised. In 2017 brewing moved from the kit at Old Luxters Brewery (qv) to a purpose-built brewery on the outskirts of Henley, which has a steam-heated mash tun and copper. ‼

Loxley (NEW)

539 Loxley Road, Sheffield, South Yorkshire, S6 6RR
☎ (0114) 233 4310 loxleybrewery.co.uk

Loxley Brewery is based in the cellar of the Wisewood Inn using a six-barrel plant. Brewing commenced in 2018. Two core beers are brewed at present with others evolving as more brews occur.

Luckie

Unit 4, Block 5, Banbeath Industrial Estate, Leven, KY8 5HD ☎ 07979 364906 luckie-ales.com

Luckie Ales was established in 2009 and is an artisan microbrewery specialising in handcrafted Scottish beers and historic British ales. Brewing moved to Markinch in 2012, operating on a one-barrel plant. The brewery was sold in 2016, and relocated to new premises in Leven. Bottle conditioned beers are available from specialist beer retailers in Edinburgh and Fife. RAIB

Lucky 7

Hay On Wye, HR3 5AW
☎ (01497) 822778 ☎ 07815 853353
lucky7beer.co.uk

Producer of small-batch craft and bottled beers, mainly sold through local stockists in Hay on Wye, Hereford and Cardiff.

Ludlow SIBA

The Railway Shed, Station Drive, Ludlow, Shropshire, SY8 2PQ
☎ (01584) 873291
theludlowbrewingcompany.co.uk

Established in 2006, the brewery occupies a converted railway sidings shed. Beers are produced using a 20-barrel plant. The premises also function as a brewery tap, visitor centre and events area. ‼

Best (OG 1037, ABV 3.7%)
A golden amber-coloured, well-balanced session beer with a banana, pineapple and toffee aroma and a resinous, dry finish.

Blonde (OG 1040, ABV 4%)
A well-hopped, aromatic, pale blonde ale.

Gold (OG 1041, ABV 4.2%)
A yellow-coloured ale with a papaya, pineapple and lemon aroma and a soft, full-bodied, creamy taste.

Black Knight (OG 1045, ABV 4.5%)
A ruby black-coloured stout with a smoky, liquorice aroma and sweet, roasted nutty flavour.

Boiling Well (OG 1046, ABV 4.7%)
A chestnut-coloured beer with a grassy aroma of autumn fruit with and a full-bodied sweet then dry taste.

Stairway (OG 1048.5, ABV 5%)
A honey-coloured beer with a grassy, citrus floral aroma and a sharp, sweet, full-bodied taste.

Luna

See White Horse

LWC

Beers brewed under the Gray's brand. See Marston's

Lydbrook Valley (NEW)

Forge Row, Lydbrook, Gloucestershire, GL17 9NP
☎ (01594) 860310

Brewing commenced in 2018 in the Forge Hammer pub in Lydbrook. Alison and Andrew Jopson use full mash to produce beers for sale in the pub.

Lyme Regis

See Gyle 59

Lymestone SIBA

The Brewery, Mount Road, Stone, Staffordshire, ST15 8LL
☎ (01785) 817796 ☎ 07891 782652
lymestonebrewery.co.uk

Lymestone commenced brewing in 2008. Based in the old Bents Brewery, it brews on a 10-barrel plant. A family-run business, daughter Sarah has joined the brew team as one of the UK's youngest brewsters at 24 years old. The brewery delivers in a 50-mile radius, works with National wholesalers and owns three pubs. ‼ ♦ V

Stone Cutter (OG 1037, ABV 3.7%)

THE BREWERIES

Hoppy and grassy aroma, clean, sharp and refreshing. A hint of caramel to start then intense bitterness emerges with a good bitter aftertaste and touch of mouthwatering astringency.

Stone Faced (OG 1040, ABV 4%)
Subtle citrus and toffee flavours balanced by a hoppy aroma and bitter finish.

Foundation Stone (OG 1047, ABV 4.5%) ◆
An IPA-style beer. Faint biscuit and chewy, juicy fruits burst on to the palate then the spicy hops pepper the taste buds to leave a dry bitter finish.

Ein Stein (OG 1052, ABV 5%)
A pale, citrus, hoppy ale.

Stone the Crows (OG 1056, ABV 5.4%) ◆
A rich, dark-coloured beer. Fruit, roasts and hops abound to leave a deep lingering bitterness.

Abdominal Stoneman (OG 1072, ABV 7%)
A powerfully-hopped, American-style pale ale.

Lymm

18 Bridgewater Street, Lymm, Cheshire, WA13 0AB
☎ (0161) 929 0663 🌐 lymmbrewing.co.uk

Lymm is a small, family-run brewery, launched in 2013. Located in an old post office, the brewing equipment is downstairs in what used to be the mess rooms with a brewery tap upstairs in what was the sorting office/post office counter. A sister brewery to Dunham Massey (qv), a joint bar opened in 2013, Costello's Bar, Stockton Heath. ♦

Bitter (OG 1040, ABV 3.8%)
A light, refreshing, medium-bodied session bitter with a good balance of malt and hops.

Bridgewater Blonde (OG 1041, ABV 4%)
Light, delicate, hoppy, subtle and refreshing.

Heritage Trail Ale (OG 1046, ABV 4.5%)
An easy-drinking, well-balanced best bitter, fruity with a light crisp hop.

IPA (OG 1048.5, ABV 4.8%)
Traditional hoppy pale ale with hints of tropical fruit.

Dam Strong Ale (OG 1071, ABV 7.2%)
Belgian-style ale. Strong, malty and fruity with a dry finish.

Lytham SIBA

8 Cambell's Court, Lord Street, St Annes, Lancashire, FY8 2DF
☎ (01253) 725440 🌐 lythambrewery.co.uk

Lytham is a well-established, family-run brewery that began brewing in 2007. !!♦

Amber (OG 1037, ABV 3.6%)
A traditional malty beer using English hops.

Blonde (OG 1038, ABV 3.8%) ◆
Smooth golden ale with a dry finish.

Gold (OG 1042, ABV 4.2%)
A golden-coloured beer with a fruity aroma and lasting bitter finish.

Royal (OG 1044, ABV 4.4%)
A full-bodied English ale with a crisp, fruity aroma and a smooth, dry finish.

Stout (OG 1046, ABV 4.6%)
Dark-coloured, rich, roasty, full-bodied stout. Roasted barley blends with the sweet, fruity flavours.

IPA (OG 1054, ABV 5.6%)
A pale-coloured bitter with a fresh, sweet, hoppy flavour leading to a long, dry finish.

McColl's

Unit 4, Randolph Industrial Estate, Evenwood, DL14 9SJ
☎ (01388) 417250 🌐 mccollsbrewery.co.uk

Brewing commenced in 2017 using a 20-barrel plant. Outlets are supplied across the North-east and further afield. A brewery tap is open on the last Friday and Saturday of each month.

Golden Ale (OG 1040, ABV 3.8%)
Delicate, light malt and citrus hop flavours with lemon and floral aromas building to soft bitterness and a medium dry finish.

Best Bitter (OG 1045, ABV 4.4%)
Rich and resinous malts with spicy marmalade hop flavours and deep citrus aromas leading to an assertive bitterness counter balanced by a sweet body.

Pale Ale (OG 1044, ABV 4.5%)
Smooth, full-bodied pale ale with light spicy notes leading to citrus and soft fruit aromas.

IPA (OG 1050, ABV 5%)
Full-bodied IPA with earthy, rich hop flavours and punchy citrus and grapefruit aromas. Well balanced with a firm bitterness and lingering dry finish.

McGivern

c/o Bridge End Inn, 5 Bridge Street, Ruabon, LL14 6DA
☎ (01978) 810881 ☎ 07891 676614
🌐 mcgivernales.co.uk

The brewery was established in 2008 and was originally based at the brewer's home in Wrexham but moved in 2011 to the award-winning Bridge End Inn in Ruabon using a 2.5-barrel plant. ♦

McMullen SIBA IFBB

26 Old Cross, Hertford, SG14 1RD
☎ (01992) 584911 🌐 mcmullens.co.uk

McMullen, Hertfordshire's oldest independent brewery, was founded in 1827 – its famous brew, AK, is traceable back into the 19th century. The 'Authentic Heritage' tag promotes its core beers. Additional seasonal ales are produced throughout the year, sometimes produced under the Rivertown Brewing name. A new microbrewery supplements the main plant. All 125 tied pubs, spread across South-east England, serve cask beer. !!♦

AK (OG 1035, ABV 3.7%) ◆
A pleasant mix of malt and hops leads to a distinctive, dry aftertaste that isn't always as pronounced as it used to be.

Cask Ale (OG 1039, ABV 3.8%)
A well-balanced ale with subtle biscuity malt and citrus hop flavours.

Country Bitter (OG 1042, ABV 4.3%) ◆
A full-bodied beer with a well-balanced mix of malt, hops and fruit throughout.

IPA (OG 1047, ABV 4.8%)
A strong bitter with deep, rich flavours created with specially kilned amber malts.

Mabby's (NEW)

Mabby Brew Pub & Kitchen, Forest Road, Treforest, CF37 1SY
☎ (01443) 402033

New brewery in the cellar of the Otley Arms supplying the pub and a few other local outlets. The name is derived from a partnership between brewer Matt Otley and his wife Gabby.

Macclesfield

76 Brown Street, Macclesfield, Cheshire, SK11 6RY
maccbrew.co

A small-batch 100-litre brewery producing bottled beers using seasonal ingredients. No core range.

Mad Cat SIBA

Brogdale Farm, Brogdale Road, Faversham, Kent, ME13 8XZ
☎ (01795) 597743 ☎ 07960 263615
madcatbrewery.co.uk

Established in 2012 by Peter Meaney in a refurbished cold store using an eight-barrel plant. Beers are distributed to local pubs. Bottles and polypins are available from the brewery and Peter often attends local markets and events. **!! ♦**

Red Ale (ABV 3.9%)

Crispin Ale (ABV 4%)

Golden IPA (ABV 4.2%)

Platinum Blonde (ABV 4.2%)

Emotional Blackmail (ABV 4.5%)

Jet Black Stout (ABV 4.6%)

Mad Dog

Shed 4, Unit 9, Park Farm, Plough Road, Penperlleni, NP4 0AL ☎ 07703 731197 maddogbrew.co.uk

Brewing began in 2014 based at the brewer's home in Cwmbran. The brewery relocated in 2015 expanding to a brew length of five barrels. An upgrade to larger premises on the same site later the same year has enabled a significant increase in production capacity.

Third Eye Blind (ABV 3.8%)
A pale ale with tropical and citrus hop flavours.

Now in a Minute (ABV 4.2%)
A traditional Welsh red-coloured ale with flavours of sweet chocolate and citrus.

Stouty McStoutface (ABV 4.5%)
Full-bodied, smooth stout with chocolate and roast flavours.

Bohemian Hipster (ABV 4.9%)
Pale ale with lemongrass and pine flavors.

It's All Propaganda (ABV 5%)
A black IPA with no roast flavour but full of lemon, coconut and grapefruit, finishing on a spicy note.

Mad Hatter

Unit 1, Palmer Hill Building, 15-37 Caryl Street, Liverpool, L8 5SQ ☎ 07474 797450
madhatterbrewing.co.uk

Mad Hatter began brewing in 2013. Most of its output is in bottled or keg form althogh cask-conditioned beers make an occasional appearance at beer festivals.

Mad Scientist

c/o the Quakerhouse, 2-3 Mechanics Yard, Darlington, DL3 7QF
☎ (01325) 245052

Brewing commenced in 2017 on a half-barrel plant situated in the cellar of the Quakerhouse.

Mad Squirrel SIBA

Unit 19, Boxted Farm, Berkhamsted Road, Potten End, Hertfordshire, HP1 2SG
☎ (01442) 256970 madsquirrel.uk

Based on the outskirts of Hemel Hempstead, brewing began in 2004. Formerly called Red Squirrel, the company changed name in 2017 to coincide with the installation of a larger brew kit. Beer is distributed to venues throughout the South-east, including to its own chain of venues, Tap & Bottleshop. **!! ♦ RAIB**

Hopfest (OG 1037.5, ABV 3.8%)
A pale golden ale with a floral/citrus aroma and elderflower notes.

Mister Squirrel (OG 1040, ABV 4%)
A chestnut-coloured bitter, lightly-hopped with a creamy texture. Hints of caramel and vanilla complement the slightly hoppy and malty overtones.

De La Creme (OG 1046, ABV 4.5%)
A smooth milk stout, full-bodied with hints of caramel, cream and chocolate.

$umo (OG 1046, ABV 4.7%)
An American-style pale ale with tropical fruit notes and some bitterness.

London Porter (OG 1052, ABV 5%)
Dark brown/black-coloured porter with a good balance of chocolate and roasted barley. Full-bodied on the palate with bittersweet liquorice, rich chocolate flavours and a creamy finish.

Roadkill (OG 1060, ABV 6.5%)
Based on an American-style IPA, yellow-coloured, unfiltered, unpasteurised and containing wheat and oats, the hop varieties used in Roadkill change with every batch and so will the flavour.

Madrigal

The Manor House, Manor Green, Lynmouth, Devon, EX35 6EN ☎ 07857 560677 madrigalbrewery.co.uk

The brewery was established in 2014 in the village of Combe Martin. It relocated to larger premises in Lynmouth in 2016 to help meet increased demand. **!! ♦ RAIB V**

Garland (OG 1036, ABV 3.5%)
A wheat beer with tropical fruit notes.

Surfer Rosa (OG 1036, ABV 3.6%)

Burning House (OG 1042, ABV 4%)

THE BREWERIES

A dark brown-coloured speciality beer with a smooth mouthfeel and a gradual smoke and hop finish.

Fossil (OG 1043, ABV 4%)

Hanged Man (OG 1042, ABV 4.2%)
Well-rounded stout made with raw cacao nibs. A smooth, soft taste with slight spicy notes.

Severed Hand (OG 1043, ABV 4.3%)

Monkey's Fist (OG 1048, ABV 5%)
Smooth, dark-coloured old ale with strong fruit and roast from start to lingering, slightly sour finish. Heavy, sweet but satisfying.

North Coast Voodoo (OG 1050, ABV 5%)
An aromatic IPA with a fruity aroma and a gradual hop finish.

Wheatear (OG 1048, ABV 5.1%)
Wheat beer made with fresh ginger and coriander.

Magic Dragon

Plassey Brewery, Eyton, LL13 0SP
☎ (01978) 781675 magicdragonbrewing.com

Originally named Plassey then New Plassey, brewing began in 1985 on the 250-acre Plassey Estate. New owners in 2017 have renamed to Magic Dragon Brewing. Pubs, restaurants and hotels are supplied across North Wales, Shropshire, Cheshire and beyond. ♦

Border Bitter (ABV 3.8%)

Eyton Gold (ABV 4%)

American Dragon (ABV 4.2%)

Eyton Bitter (ABV 4.5%)

Magic Rock SIBA

Units 1-4, Willow Lane, Huddersfield, West Yorkshire, HD1 5EB
☎ (01484) 649823 magicrockbrewing.com

Magic Rock began brewing in 2011. The brewery is located about half a mile walk from Huddersfield town centre on an industrial estate. The site also houses a tap room and distribution centre. ♦RAIB

Hat Trick (OG 1041, ABV 3.7%)
A complex malty body combined with fruity hops makes for a refreshing bitter.

Ringmaster (OG 1038, ABV 3.9%)
Pale ale with a floral/grassy aroma and citrus hops.

Inhaler (OG 1044, ABV 4.5%)
A pale ale with an abundance of hops producing a fruity beer that is low in bitterness.

Rapture (OG 1044.5, ABV 4.6%)
Full-bodied, red-coloured ale with grapefruit and pine aromas and a rich, malty body.

Common Grounds (OG 1063, ABV 5.4%)
Sweet toffee, rich fruit and chocolate flavours with notes of vanilla and hazelnut.

High Wire (OG 1051, ABV 5.5%)
Pale ale with mango, lychee and grapefruit flavours.

Dark Arts (OG 1057, ABV 6%)
Chocolate, liquorice, blackberry and fig flavours with a long, roasted bitter finish.

Magic Spells

24 Rigg Approach, Leyton, London, E10 7QN
☎ (020) 3475 1781 ☎ 07740 428952
magicspellsbrewery.co.uk

Magic Spells is an independent brewery located in East London, owned and operated by Jas Hare. Brewing takes place on a 10-barrel plant with a half-barrel kit used for experimental brews. RAIB

Magpie SIBA

Unit 4, Ashling Court, Ashling Street, Nottingham, NG2 3JA ☎ 07419 991310 magpiebrewery.com

Launched in 2006 using a six-barrel plant, the brewery upgraded to 17.5-barrels in 2017. Only British hops and malt are used in the core range, with the Wanderlust range taking more worldly influences and ingredients. ♦V

Hoppily Ever After (OG 1035, ABV 3.8%)
Golden-coloured bitter, gently-hopped with biscuit malt flavours and a bitter finish.

Best (OG 1040.7, ABV 4.2%)
A malty, traditional, pale brown-coloured best bitter with balancing hops giving a bitter finish.

Raven Stout (OG 1044, ABV 4.4%)
Dark-coloured stout with roast coffee aroma and taste leading to a dry bitter finish.

Thieving Rogue (OG 1042, ABV 4.5%)
A hoppy golden ale with a long-lasting, bitter finish.

Jay IPA (OG 1048.6, ABV 5.2%)
Mature hops, citrus fruit nose with a balance of hops and malt in the mouth with a smooth, hoppy aftertaste.

Maldon SIBA

Stable Brewery, Silver Street, Maldon, Essex, CM9 4QE
☎ (01621) 851000 maldonbrewing.co.uk

Established in 2002, this family-run brewery is tucked away behind the 14th-century Blue Boar Hotel. The six-barrel plant is at full production serving more than 50 outlets including the brewery's micropub on the High Street. ♦RAIB

Farmer's IPA (OG 1036, ABV 3.6%)
A crisp IPA based on an old Ridley's recipe.

Drop of Nelson's Blood (OG 1038, ABV 3.8%)
An easy-drinking bitter. A tot of brandy is added to each cask.

Hotel Porter (OG 1041, ABV 4.1%)
A classic stout with a smoky tang.

Pucks Folly (OG 1038, ABV 4.2%)
A pale golden ale with a spicy character and pineapple in the aroma and taste.

Farmer's Golden Boar (OG 1050, ABV 5%)
An amber-coloured ale with a hoppy aroma.

Dark Horse (OG 1064, ABV 6.6%)
A chestnut-coloured bitter, smooth but with spice in the finish.

Mallard

Unit A, Maythorne, Nottinghamshire, NG25 0RS
☎ 07811 193930 stevenhussey@tiscali.co.uk

⊛Mallard is a 2.25-barrel brewery run by Steve Hussey and Alison Ryan, brewing for their own pub, the Cross Keys in Upton, and local outlets in and around the county. ‼♦RAIB

Duck 'n' Dive (OG 1039, ABV 3.7%) ◆
A bitter, pale golden-coloured beer with a dry finish.

Greet Ale (OG 1037, ABV 3.7%)
A copper-coloured, traditional, malty ale. Pleasantly bitter on the palate.

Golden Duck (OG 1039, ABV 3.9%)

Quacker Jack (OG 1040, ABV 4%)
Copper-coloured bitter with a well-balanced hop/malt bitterness.

Feather Light (OG 1040, ABV 4.1%) ◆
A straw-coloured lager-style beer with a hoppy taste and aroma.

Duckling (OG 1041, ABV 4.2%) ◆
A dry-hopped golden ale. Very bitter; hops dominate in the aroma and aftertaste.

Specduckular (OG 1042, ABV 4.2%)
A refreshing golden ale full of fruity hops with a malty undertone.

Mallinson's

Unit 1, Waterhouse Mill, 65-71 Lockwood Road, Huddersfield, West Yorkshire, HD1 3QU
☎ (01484) 654301 ☎ 07850 446571
drinkmallinsons.co.uk

⊛Mallinsons Brewing Co was originally set up in 2008 on a six-barrel plant by CAMRA members Tara Mallinson and Elaine Yendall. The company moved to new premises in 2012 with a 15-barrel plant and speciailises in hop-forward and single hop beers. Its first tap house, the Corner, opened in Huddersfield in 2016. ‼♦RAIB V

Malt SIBA

Collings Hanger Farm, 100 Wycombe Road, Prestwood, Buckinghamshire, HP16 0HP
☎ (01494) 865063 maltthebrewery.co.uk

⊗ Family-owned brewery, founded in 2012 using a 10-barrel plant. Based on a dairy farm in the heart of the Chiltern Hills, it has sustainability built into its brewing with spent grains going to feed the pigs on the farm and spent hops being composted. In-house deliveries are made to trade and direct customers in six surrounding counties. National distribution is through leading distributors and wholesalers. ‼♦RAIB V

Missenden Pale (OG 1035, ABV 3.6%)
Light amber-coloured, hoppy session ale.

Golden Ale (OG 1038, ABV 3.9%)
Light and refreshing with a citrus finish.

Starry Nights (OG 1040, ABV 4%)
Light and fruity amber-coloured ale.

Anniversary Ale (OG 1043, ABV 4.4%)
Dark amber-coloured, classic-style bitter with a smooth finish.

Voyager (OG 1048, ABV 5%)
Amber-coloured IPA with aromatic hop notes.

Malt Coast (NEW)

Branthill Farm, Wells-next-the-Sea, Norfolk, NR23 1SB ☎ 07881 378900 maltcoast.com

Brewing began in 2016.

Malvern Hills SIBA

15 West Malvern Road, Malvern, Worcestershire, WR14 4ND
☎ (01684) 560165 malvernhillsbrewery.co.uk

⊗ Founded in 1998 in an old quarrying dynamite store and an established presence in the Three Counties, Birmingham and the Black Country. Seasonal and special beers are directed more by ad-hoc requests from publicans rather than a planned brewery timetable apart from green-hopped beers in September. ‼♦

Beacon Gold (OG 1036, ABV 3.7%)

Feelgood (OG 1037, ABV 3.8%)
A light bitter with a floral spicy aroma.

Malvern Spring (OG 1040, ABV 4.2%)

Black Pear (OG 1042, ABV 4.4%) ◆
A sharp citrus hoppiness is the main constituent of this golden-coloured best bitter that has a long, dry aftertaste.

Manchester

66 North Western Street, Manchester, M12 6DX
☎ (0161) 273 6167 manchesterbrewing.co.uk

Set up by two friends in 2016 in a railway arch in the Ardwick district of Manchester,an eight-barrel plant is used. Local pubs and beer festivals are supplied. ♦

Factory Pale Ale (OG 1040, ABV 4%)

King Cotton (OG 1043, ABV 4.2%)

Some Might Say (ABV 4.4%)

Cuts Like a Buffalo (OG 1045, ABV 4.5%)

Pick Me Up Coffee Porter (OG 1050, ABV 4.7%)
An easy-drinking porter spiked with cold brew coffee after fermentation.

Mad Carew (OG 1055, ABV 5.9%)

Manning SIBA

Lower Overton Farm, Overton, Congleton, Cheshire, CW12 3QW ☎ 07946 278018
manningbrewers.co.uk

A family-owned and run brewery using only British hops, opened in 2015. It has recently joined forces with the established Beartown Brewery (qv), also of Congleton.

Woah Man (ABV 3.8%)
A clean-drinking session pale ale with a floral aroma.

Man Up! (ABV 4%)
A bronze-coloured, malty session beer.

Cave-Man (ABV 4.2%)
A well-balanced bitter with a refreshing hop character and blackberry aromas. Caramel-coloured with a crisp bitter finish.

Mantle SIBA

Unit 16, Pentood Industrial Estate, Cardigan, SA43 3AG
☎ (01239) 623898 ☎ 07552 609909
mantlebrewery.com

Mantle began brewing in 2013 using a 10-barrel plant. Engineer Ian Kimber and his scientist wife Dominique, formerly homebrewers, have built a sound reputation for consistent quality. More than 200 outlets are supplied direct with wider distribution via selected wholesalers. !! ♦

Rock Steady (OG 1038, ABV 3.8%)

MOHO (OG 1041.5, ABV 4.3%)
A well-balanced, aromatic Welsh pale ale.

Cwrw Teifi (OG 1045, ABV 4.5%)
Full-bodied, malty best bitter with a well-balanced hop finish.

Dark Heart (OG 1052, ABV 5.2%)
Rich, dark-coloured and smooth porter with a hint of spice.

Marble SIBA

41 Williamson Street, Manchester, M4 4JS
☎ (0161) 819 2694 marblebeers.com

Originally based at the Marble Arch pub in 1997, Marble Beers now brews at a larger, 12-barrel plant in a nearby unit, producing vegetarian beers in both core and speciality ranges. it supplies its own three pubs and more than 70 other outlets. Speciality ranges for 2018/2019 include a hop-forward pale series and two sour beer series. ♦

Pint (OG 1038.5, ABV 3.9%)
Pale yellow in colour with a citrus aroma. Hop, fruit and bitterness in the taste, with a dry finish.

Manchester Bitter (OG 1040.5, ABV 4.2%)
Yellow-coloured beer with a fruity and hoppy aroma. Hops, fruit and bitterness on the palate and in the finish.

Tuckerlovsky (ABV 4.7%)

Lagonda IPA (OG 1047, ABV 5%)
Golden yellow-coloured beer with a spicy, fruity nose. Fruit, hops and malt in the mouth, with a dry fruitiness continuing into the bitter aftertaste.

Earl Grey IPA (OG 1065, ABV 6.8%)
An IPA with a citrus fruit aroma, smooth texture and hop notes complemented by bergamot and a light tannic finish.

Maregade

Arch 214, Ponsford Street, Homerton, London, E9 6JU
maregade.com

Microbrewery originally based in the basement of the Cock Tavern in Hackney, it moved to its present address in 2017. ♦V

Session IPA (OG 1047, ABV 4.4%)

Vanilla Milk Stout (OG 1054, ABV 4.5%)

Blonde Pale (OG 1047, ABV 4.8%)

Amber (OG 1049, ABV 4.9%)

Pale (OG 1051, ABV 5.2%)

Market Bosworth

Unit 10, Willow Farm Business Centre, Stoke Golding, Leicestershire, CV13 6EU
☎ (01455) 377855 marketbosworthbrewery.co.uk

The brewery was set up by Jon Skinner in 2016 as a natural progression from his homebrew retail business. Rich Brine joined in partnership in 2017 and the kit was doubled in size to two barrels to meet demand. Its two main outlets are the Gate Hangs Well, Carlton, and the Horse & Hockey, Congerstone. ♦

Stout (ABV 4.2%)
Dark-coloured stout with roasted notes.

Best Bitter (ABV 4.8%)
Dark copper-coloured ale with a malty mouthfeel and a lingering bitter finish.

Porter (ABV 5%)

Pale Ale (ABV 5.2%)
Golden-coloured ale with buckets of punchy, bitter hops and citrus aromas.

Marko Paulo

Owl & The Pussycat, 106 Northfield Avenue, Northfields, London, W13 9RT
☎ (020) 8810 0880 markopaulo.co.uk

A 1.25-barrel brewpub opened in 2016 in a former bookshop by two ex-teachers, it produces unfiltered and unpasteurised beers. The beer travels about 20 feet from mash tun to glass. Cask-conditioned beers are complemented by a wide range of traditional European-style keg beers.

Marlpool

5 Breach Road, Marlpool, Derbyshire, DE75 7NJ
☎ (01773) 711285 ☎ 07963 511855
marlpoolbrewing.co.uk

Marlpool was set up by brothers Andy and Chris McAuley in 2010 using a 2.5-barrel plant situated in an old slaughterhouse. The majority of the beer is sold through its own micropub built into the old butcher's shop attached to the brewery. The remainder is sold to reputable outlets. Marlpool's bottle-conditioned beers are only available at the micropub. !! ♦ RAIB

Blind Boris (OG 1038, ABV 3.5%)

Otters Pocket (OG 1040, ABV 4%)

Scratty Ratty (OG 1044, ABV 4.4%)
A lightly-hopped pale ale with a bitter, dry finish.

Frank (OG 1045, ABV 4.5%)

Derbyshire Classic (OG 1048, ABV 4.8%)

Black Oss (OG 1058, ABV 5.4%)

Marston's SIBA

Shobnall Road, Burton upon Trent, Staffordshire, DE14 2BW
☎ (01283) 531131 marstons.co.uk

Marston's has been brewing cask beer in Burton since 1834 and the current site is the home of the only working Burton Union fermenters, housed in rooms known as the Cathedral of Brewing. Burton Unions were developed in the 19th century to cleanse the new style of pale ale yeast. Only Pedigree is fermented in the unions but yeast from the system is used to ferment the other Marston's branded beers. In 2016 a small 2.5-barrel nanobrewery was installed within the DE14 visitors centre. Beers from this nanobrewery are available locally. Marston's continues to take contract brewing, and brews the iconic cask beer Draught Bass on behalf of AB Inbev. !! ♦ RAIB

EPA (OG 1036, ABV 3.6%)

61 Deep (OG 1038, ABV 3.8%)
Light amber-coloured ale with intense tropical fruit aroma. Sweet tropical start with hints of spice. Hoppy bitterness overcomes the fruit and leaves a pleasant mouthfeel.

Saddle Tank (OG 1037, ABV 3.8%)
Overwhelming sulphurous aroma supports a scattering of hops and fruit with an easy-drinking sweetness. The taste develops from the sweet middle to a satisfyingly hoppy finish.

Pedigree (OG 1043, ABV 4.5%)
Pale brown in colour with a sweet hoppy aroma. Malt with a dash of hop flavours give a satisfying tasty finish.

Old Empire (OG 1057, ABV 5.7%)
Sulphur dominates the gentle malt aroma. Malty and sweet to start but developing bitterness with fruit and a touch of sweetness. A balanced aftertaste of hops and fruit leads to a lingering bitterness.

For AB InBev:

Draught Bass (OG 1043, ABV 4.4%)
Hints of caramel in aroma and taste, lightly hopped for a short bitter finish.

Martland Mill SIBA

Unit 5, Otterwood Square, Martland Mill, Wigan, WN5 0LF
☎ (01942) 665656 martlandmillbrewery.co.uk

Established in 2014, Martland Mill Brewery is a family-run business based just outside of Wigan town centre using a six-barrel plant. Beers are available throughout the North-west region, as well as at the brewery tap, the Tap 'n' Barrel, Wigan. !! ♦

Chonkin Feckle (OG 1038, ABV 3.8%)
A golden yellow-coloured ale with a citrus hop aroma, floral notes and a pine finish.

Spinner's Gold (OG 1038, ABV 3.8%)
A well-balanced golden ale with a pleasant citrus taste and a hint of spiciness.

Clogmaker (OG 1043, ABV 4%)
A rich, golden-coloured, full-bodied ale with a refreshing fruity flavour and an hint of cedar and honey.

Lancashire Loom (OG 1046, ABV 4%)
A light golden ale bursting with a real fruit punch of grapefruit, lychees and lemon and a slight floral note.

D Day Dodger (OG 1046, ABV 4.1%)
Brown in colour with subtle malty aroma. Malt dominates throughout, with hop notes. Initial sweetness gives way to a bitter, dry finish.

Bomber's Blonde (OG 1053, ABV 4.4%)
A blonde ale with an intense hoppy aroma and a crisp, refreshing citrus taste, leading to a slightly dry finish.

George 'n' Dragon (OG 1052, ABV 4.8%)
A smooth, full-bodied ale with honey flavours and a well-balanced pine hop aroma.

Marts (NEW)

Marts Brewhouse & Tap, 66-68 Piccadilly, Hanley, Stoke-on-Trent, ST1 1HX ☎ 07709 110251

Brewing began in 2018.

MASH SIBA

Middle Barn, Burcot Farm, East Stratton, Hampshire, SO21 3DZ
☎ (01962) 795023 mashbrewery.com

Brewing began in 2013 using a one-barrel plant. A 10-barrel plant was installed in 2014. RAIB

Pale (OG 1035, ABV 3.8%)
A pale ale with a subtle aroma and long bitter finish.

Copper (OG 1037, ABV 3.9%)
A copper-coloured beer with fruity, peachy aromas and a dry bitter flavour.

Gilt (OG 1038, ABV 4.1%)
Golden ale with citrus orange aroma and spice. Dry bitter finish.

Amber (OG 1042, ABV 4.3%)
A well-balanced beer with floral aromas.

Ruby (OG 1045, ABV 4.8%)
Red-coloured ale with a malty, full-bodied finish.

Chocolate Stout (OG 1047, ABV 5%)
A rich, black-coloured stout with roasted malt and burnt coffee flavours. Dark chocolate is added during the brew.

Matlock Wolds Farm SIBA

South Barn, Cavendish Road, Farm Lane, Matlock, Derbyshire, DE4 3GZ
☎ (01629) 697989 ☎ 07852 263263
woldsfarm.co.uk

This family run brewery started in 2014 using a 50-litre kit and after expansions in 2015 and 2017 the now five-barrel plant is now housed in a converted barn at the owners 17th-century farm. Beers are available at many local outlets. ♦ RAIB V

The Bitter End (OG 1030, ABV 3.4%)
Ruby-coloured ale with a rich malty background. Earthy, grassy flavours. Notes of chocolate, nuts and pine with a long bitter finish.

Apogee (OG 1033, ABV 3.8%)
Amber-coloured ale with fruit and citrus aromas. Flavours include orange and grapefruit combined with a light bitterness.

Simcoe (OG 1033, ABV 3.8%)
Aromas of pine and apricot with earthy, citrus flavours. Hints of tropical fruit lead to a strong bitter finish.

High Tor (OG 1035, ABV 4%)
A pale-coloured bitter with a dry, hoppy finish.

Riber Gold (OG 1038, ABV 4.3%)
Traditional golden ale with floral and apricot aromas, hints of tropical fruit and a complex finish.

100cc (OG 1042, ABV 4.9%)
Well-rounded, light chestnut-coloured ale with a malty aroma complemented by orange and pine.

Huge citrus flavours with orange and lemon coming through a good hop bitterness.

Classic Porter (OG 1042, ABV 4.9%)
Full-bodied, dark-coloured porter with a chocolate aroma and a hint of vanilla. Full of roasted malt, coffee and a lingering bitterness.

Mauldons SIBA

Black Adder Brewery, 13 Church Field Road, Sudbury, Suffolk, CO10 2YA
☎ (01787) 311055 mauldons.co.uk

The Mauldon family started brewing in Sudbury in 1795. The brewery with 26 pubs was bought by Greene King in the 1960s. The current business, established in 1982, was bought by Steve and Alison Sims in 2000. They relocated to a new brewery in 2005, with a 30-barrel plant that has doubled production. One pub is owned and around 200 outlets are supplied. !! ♦ RAIB

Micawber's Mild (OG 1035, ABV 3.5%)
Light, easy-drinking mild. Malty smoothness with a rich roast flavour turns into a caramel liquorice aftertaste.

Moletrap Bitter (OG 1038, ABV 3.8%)
Plum and toffee on the nose. A good balance of malt, hops and fruit, leading to an increasingly bitter aftertaste.

Christies Golden Ale (OG 1040, ABV 3.9%)
A light golden-coloured, hoppy refreshing beer.

Silver Adder (OG 1042, ABV 4.2%)
Light, fruity aroma, dry hoppiness and citrus fruit with rich honey in the taste, and a long, fruity, sweet aftertaste. Refreshing and well-balanced.

Blackberry Porter (OG 1048, ABV 4.8%)
A full-bodied, black-coloured porter with balanced hop aroma and a rich blend of chocolate and roast flavours, giving way to a subtle sweet fruit finish.

Suffolk Pride (OG 1048, ABV 4.8%)
A full-bodied, copper-coloured beer. A bubblegum nose leads to a spicy taste, with mild astringency in the aftertaste.

Black Adder (OG 1053, ABV 5.3%)
Malty, roasty aroma leads to a well-balanced, full-bodied beer, malty with roast and dark soft fruit overtones.

Maule SIBA

Rothersthorpe Trading Estate, Northampton, NN4 8JH
maulebrewing.com

Brewing began in 2014 on a self-built plant. Production is mainly unfiltered keg and bottle-conditioned beers, but cask-conditioned ales are occasionally produced for festivals. The beers are available from various local stockists as well as featuring on the London craft beer scene. RAIB

Maxim SIBA

1 Gadwall Road, Rainton Bridge South, Houghton-le-Spring, DH4 5NL
☎ (0191) 584 8844 maximbrewery.co.uk

Rising from the ashes of Sunderland brewer Vaux, Maxim was set up with a 20-barrel plant in Houghton-le-Spring in 2007. More than 100 outlets are supplied direct and two pubs are owned. !! ♦

Lambtons (OG 1039, ABV 3.8%)
A smooth golden ale with citrus and hoppy flavours.

Samson (OG 1040, ABV 4%)
A traditional, chestnut-coloured best bitter with a caramel taste and a balanced bitterness.

Ward's Best Bitter (OG 1040, ABV 4%)
A tawny-coloured best bitter with a sweet, toasted biscuit flavour. Slightly hoppy, slightly fruity.

Swedish Blonde (OG 1042, ABV 4.2%)
A smooth, pale-coloured beer. Refreshingly hoppy with complex grapefruit flavours on the palate.

Double Maxim (OG 1048, ABV 4.7%)
A smooth, brown-coloured ale with a fruity, caramel, malty, nutty taste and a hint of sweetness.

Raspberry Porter (OG 1050, ABV 5%)

Maximus (OG 1062, ABV 6%)
Ruby-coloured, full-bodied premium ale. Sweet with liquorice, caramel and dark fruit flavours.

Maypole

North Laithes Farm, Wellow Road, Eakring, Nottinghamshire, NG22 0AN ☎ 07971 277598
maypolebrewery.co.uk

The brewery opened in 1995 in a converted 18th-century farm building. After changing hands in 2001 it was bought by the former head brewer, Rob Neil, in 2005. ♦

Midge (OG 1035, ABV 3.5%)
A hoppy pale ale with a lasting bitter finish.

Little Weed (OG 1037, ABV 3.8%)
Deep golden in colour with a subtle bitterness.

Celebration (OG 1038, ABV 4%)
Amber-coloured traditional English ale with slightly nutty overtones.

Gate Hopper (OG 1040, ABV 4%)
Golden ale with a floral aroma and lingering hoppy bitterness.

Hop Fusion (OG 1040, ABV 4.2%)

Major Oak (OG 1042, ABV 4.4%)
A well balanced red-coloured, full-bodied bitter. Hints of fruit and burnt malt.

Wellow Gold (OG 1044, ABV 4.6%)
Refreshing blonde ale with citrus flavours on the nose and aftertaste.

Meantime

Lawrence Trading Estate, Blackwall Lane, East Greenwich, London, SE10 0AR
☎ (020) 8293 1111

Office: Norman House, 110-114 Norman Road, London, SE10 9EH meantimebrewing.com

Founded in 2000, Meantime brews a wide range of continental-style beers. Two pubs are owned. In 2010 the brewery relocated to larger premises in Greenwich. Taken over by SABMiller in 2015 and now owned by Asahi UK. No real ale. !! ♦ RAIB V

Meanwood (NEW)

8a Stonegate Road, Meanwood, Leeds, West Yorkshire, LS6 4HY themeanwoodbrewery.com

⊗ The Meanwood Brewery was started by brothers Baz and Graeme Phillips in 2017 and focusses on brewing beer styles from around the world. A tap room opened in Leeds in 2018. !! ♦ RAIB V

Herald (OG 1038, ABV 3.9%)

Black Goddess (OG 1049, ABV 4.9%)
A rich porter with flavours of biscuit, chocolate, caramel and liquorice.

Heroic (OG 1046, ABV 5%)
An English IPA with earthy, floral and honey hop flavours against a strong but not overpowering malt backbone with a touch of caramel.

Shapeshifter (OG 1054, ABV 5.1%)
A steam beer with a bold malt body.

Melbourn

All Saints Brewery, All Saints Street, Stamford, Lincolnshire, PE9 2PA
☎ (01780) 752186

No real ale. A famous Stamford brewery that opened in 1825 and closed in 1974. It re-opened in 1994 and is owned by Samuel Smith of Tadcaster (qv). !!

Melwood SIBA

7 Stanley Grange, Knowsley Park, Merseyside, L34 4AR
☎ (0151) 214 3340 ☎ 07545 265283
melwoodbeer.co.uk

Melwood began brewing in 2013 using a five-barrel plant in an old dairy that used to house the Cambrinus Brewery. In 2016 the brewery moved to bigger premises in nearby old kennels on the Knowsley Estate. ♦

Lovelight (OG 1038, ABV 3.8%)
A light, hoppy blonde ale with a crisp, biting flavour.

Father Ted (ABV 4.2%)
A traditional English bitter with floral flavours.

High Time (ABV 4.3%)

Knowsley Blonde (OG 1043, ABV 4.3%)
Crisp, refreshing pale ale with a fresh hoppy aroma and a pleasant bitter taste.

Moondance (ABV 4.3%)

Stanley Gold (ABV 4.3%)
A well-balanced, complex beer with a crisp, hoppy flavour and citrus aroma.

Merchant City (NEW) SIBA

Block 5, Unit 1, Oakbank Trading Estate, Glasgow, G20 7LU
☎ (0141) 258 1661

Office: Unit 10, Italian Centre, 168 Ingram Street, Glasgow, G1 1DN merchantcitybrewing.com

Brewing began in 2017 using a 12-barrel plant. 25 outlets are supplied direct plus specialist off-licences across central Scotland.

American Pale Ale (OG 1045, ABV 4.7%)
A pale ale with citrus aromas, refreshing bitterness, and orange and lemon peel flavours from an infusion of tea.

Vienna Lager (OG 1049, ABV 5%)
A dark-coloured, European-style lager with toasted malt flavours and hoppy aroma.

IPA (OG 1055, ABV 5.8%)
Bold citrus hop character, crisp bitterness and a robust malt body.

Merlin SIBA

3 Spring Bank Farm, Congleton Road, Arclid, Cheshire, CW11 2UD
☎ (01477) 500893 ☎ 07812 352590
merlinbrewing.co.uk

Established in 2010 using an eight-barrel plant in a farm unit just outside Sandbach. The beers are principally supplied to outlets within a 30-mile radius. Brewing uses renewable energy from solar panels and wind power, and spent grain and hops are used on the farm. !! ♦ RAIB

Merlin's Gold (OG 1038, ABV 3.8%)
Light golden ale with rounded floral citrus flavours.

Excalibur (OG 1039, ABV 3.9%)
A light-coloured session ale. Bitter, hoppy flavours are accompanied by a faint sweetness.

Spellbound (OG 1040, ABV 4%)
A full-flavoured bitter, light chestnut in colour with a dry finish.

Avalon (OG 1041, ABV 4.1%)
A pale ale with grapefruit, lemon and spicy hop flavours.

The Wizard (OG 1042, ABV 4.2%)
A hoppy, bitter, golden-coloured ale with generous hints of grapefruit flavour.

Dark Magic (OG 1048, ABV 4.8%)
A strong, full-bodied dark mild with a caramel aftertaste.

Dragonslayer (OG 1056, ABV 5.6%)

Merrie City

See Castle Eden

Merrimen SIBA

Unit 12, Litchborough Industrial Estate, Northampton Road, Litchborough, Northamptonshire, NN12 8JB
☎ (01327) 831308 ☎ 07763 494673
merrimen.co.uk

Merrimen commenced brewing on an eight-barrel plant in 2013. All beers are named on a 'Merri' theme. Outlets include JD Wetherspoon, SIBA, pubs and off-licences in Northampton, Coventry, Warwick and surrounding areas. ♦ RAIB

Merri One (OG 1035, ABV 3.6%)
A light amber-coloured ale with medium bitterness, combining three spicy hops.

MPG (Merrimen's Pure Gold) (ABV 3.7%)

Hail Merri (OG 1036, ABV 3.8%)
Deep amber in colour with a fruity, floral and malty aroma and a biscuit, bitter taste with a dry finish.

Merri Weather (OG 1038, ABV 4%)
Rich, golden-coloured beer. Hoppy and refreshing.

Merri-ness (ABV 4.4%)
A floral nose with a hint of toffee and berries. Citrus and pomegranate flavours and a gentle bitterness.

Be Merri (OG 1042, ABV 4.5%)

Premium amber-coloured bitter with roasted chocolate malt and a smooth, rounded taste.

Merry Miner

Unit 20-21, Grendon House Farm, Grendon, Warwickshire, CV9 3DT ☎ 07811 932721 ⊕ merryminerbrewery.com

Brewing began in 2010, based in farm buildings on the outskirts of the village of Grendon. The brewery and beers are named after the brewer's former occupation. It also brews under the name of Morgans. Hippy Killer Brewing Company (qv) also brew on the premises. In 2018 Hippy Killer bought the brewery. !! ♦

Miners Best Bitter (OG 1035, ABV 3.7%)
A pale, smooth, traditional best bitter with a crisp bitter aftertaste.

Davy's Lamp (OG 1038, ABV 4%)

Cap Lamp (OG 1039, ABV 4.2%)
Mid gold-coloured beer with a refreshing, crisp bitterness.

Going Underground (OG 1041, ABV 4.4%)

Pit Pony (OG 1041, ABV 4.5%)

Coal Face Porter (OG 1045, ABV 5%)
Ruby-coloured porter with a honey and chocolate malt finish.

Mersea Island

Rewsalls Lane, East Mersea, Essex, CO5 8SX ☎ 07970 070399 ⊕ merseabrewery.co.uk

⊗ The brewery was established at Mersea Island Vineyard in 2005. It supplies several local pubs on a guest beer basis as well as beer festivals. It holds its own festival of Essex-produced ales over the four-day Easter weekend. RAIB

Mersea Mud (OG 1036, ABV 3.8%)
An easy-drinking mild ale with a refreshingly malty flavour.

Yo Boy! (OG 1038, ABV 3.8%)
A hoppy session bitter with a long-lasting bitterness on the finish.

Gold (OG 1043, ABV 4.4%)
A refreshing, golden-coloured Pilsner-style ale.

Monkeys (OG 1044, ABV 4.4%)
Sweet, lightly smoky and lightly roasted in aroma, while having smoky, fruity and light herbal flavours.

Skippers (OG 1047, ABV 4.8%)
A dark amber-coloured best bitter with a good malty flavour and smooth hop bitterness.

Oyster Stout (OG 1048, ABV 5%)
A traditional stout made with local oysters.

Middle Earth

Rowditch Inn, 246 Uttoxeter New Road, Derby, DE22 3LL ☎ 07504 304564

Office: 53 Springfield Road, Etwall, DE65 6JZ ⊕ mebrewco.com

⊗ Middle Earth was set up utilising spare capacity at the Rowditch Inn, Derby. Operations are currently suspended but the brewer (Steve Twells) intends to resume as soon as personal circumstances permit.

Mighty Medicine

Unit 4, Daniel Street, Whitworth, Lancashire, OL12 8BX ☎ (01706) 558980 ⊕ mightymedicine.com

Established in 2016 this brewery is committed to using the finest ingredients to produce an eclectic range of beers. A tap room is attached to the brewery.

Stunning Blonde (ABV 3.9%)
Easy-drinking, fruity blonde ale.

Greedy Boy (ABV 4%)

Madchester Cream (ABV 4.2%)
Creamy and smooth pale ale.

Magic Malt (ABV 4.5%)
A malty and hoppy, red-coloured ale.

Mighty Oak

14b West Station Yard, Spital Road, Maldon, Essex, CM9 6TW ☎ (01621) 843713 ⊕ mightyoakbrewing.co.uk

⊗ Mighty Oak was formed in 1996 and has expanded considerably following a move to Maldon in 2001. Current capacity is 8,000 barrels a year following the acquisition of two adjacent buildings and enlarged plant. Some 450 outlets are supplied. A popular free festive beer tasting day takes place each year in early December. !! ♦

Oscar Wilde (OG 1039.5, ABV 3.7%)
Roasty dark mild with suggestions of forest fruits and dark chocolate. A sweet taste yields to a more bitter finish.

Captain Bob (OG 1039.5, ABV 3.8%)
A traditional deep amber-coloured bitter with a fruity and hoppy aroma. A slight sweet maltiness balances an easy going bitterness, followed by hints of gooseberry, elderflower and grape in the finish.

Maldon Gold (OG 1039.5, ABV 3.8%)
Pale golden ale with a sharp citrus note moderated by honey and biscuity malt.

Jake the Snake (OG 1041, ABV 4%)
Pale golden-coloured quaffing ale with a subtle floral hop aroma and balanced maltiness.

Old Man and the Sea (OG 1045, ABV 4.1%)
Rich, black-coloured, creamy stout with flavours of espresso coffee, dark chocolate and a hint of dark fruit.

Kings (OG 1042.6, ABV 4.2%)
A deep golden-coloured beer bursting with hoppy fruitiness. Orange, nectarine and passion fruit flavours lasting into the finish.

Mile Tree SIBA

Mile Tree Lane, Wisbech, Cambridgeshire, PE13 4TR ☎ 07858 930363 ⊕ thesecretgardentouringpark.co.uk

Mile Tree began brewing in 2012 using a five-barrel plant. Local outlets and beer festivals are supplied. ♦ RAIB

Adventurer (OG 1040, ABV 4%)
Golden-coloured, full-flavoured beer with a ripe, generous fruitiness and a fresh light hop character.

Wellstream (OG 1049, ABV 4.9%)

Ruby brown-coloured, full-bodied, malty beer with a deep bittersweet finish.

Milestone SIBA

Great North Road, Cromwell, Nottinghamshire, NG23 6JE
☎ (01636) 822255 milestonebrewery.co.uk

Established in 2005, Milestone currently brews on a 12-barrel plant. More than 150 outlets are supplied. ‼ ♦RAIB

Best Bitter (OG 1037, ABV 3.7%)

Liberty Ale (OG 1037, ABV 3.7%)

Lion Bitter (OG 1038, ABV 3.8%)

Sherwood Pale Ale (OG 1039, ABV 3.9%)

Classic Dark Mild (OG 1040, ABV 4%)

Shine On (OG 1039, ABV 4%)
Straw-coloured session ale with floral and citrus notes.

Azacca Gold (OG 1042, ABV 4.2%)

Loxley Ale (OG 1042, ABV 4.2%)
Golden-coloured brew with a subtle hint of honey.

Black Pearl (OG 1043, ABV 4.3%)

Crusader (OG 1044, ABV 4.4%)
Belgian-style blonde beer with a zesty, clean finish.

Rich Ruby (OG 1044, ABV 4.5%)
Rich, smooth, creamy, Celtic red-coloured ale.

American Pale Ale (OG 1046, ABV 4.6%)
A blond, hoppy citrus ale.

Olde English (OG 1049, ABV 4.9%)
Full-bodied winter warmer with a pleasing nutty finish.

Raspberry Wheat Beer (OG 1055, ABV 5.6%)
Continental-style ale infused with fresh fruit.

Milk Street SIBA

Frome Brewing Co, Unit L13, Marshall Way, Commerce Park, Frome, Somerset, BA11 2FB
☎ (01373) 467766

Office: Griffin, 25 Milk Street, Frome, BA11 3DB
milkstreetbrewery.co.uk

Milk Street was established in 1999 behind the Griffin pub in Frome. In 2016 the brewery relocated to an industrial unit having outgrown the cramped facilities behind the pub and increased its capabilities to 60 barrels. Beer is supplied direct to its own estate of two pubs and other local outlets. Wholesalers are used to distribute the beers further afield. ‼♦

Same Again (OG 1039, ABV 3.9%)

Funky Monkey (OG 1040, ABV 4%)
Copper-coloured ale with fruity flavours and aromas. A dry finish with developing bitterness and an undertone of citrus fruit.

Ra (OG 1041, ABV 4.1%)
An American-style pale ale with clean citrus and bold floral hops.

Taiheke (OG 1043, ABV 4.3%)
A pale-coloured New Zealand wheat beer with citrus and tropical notes.

The Usual (OG 1045, ABV 4.4%)
Aromas of pear drops and orange marmalade give way to a well-rounded fruitiness and hints of caramel in the taste. The slight sweetness is balanced by a dry, bitter, grainy finish, with hints of raspberry.

Zig-Zag Stout (OG 1046, ABV 4.5%)
A dark ruby-coloured stout with characteristic roastiness and dryness with bitter chocolate and citrus fruit in the background.

Gulp IPA (OG 1048, ABV 4.8%)
A session beer with a pleasant lemon and citrus aroma and a full mouthfeel with good hop balance. The finish has a clean bitterness with spicy and blackcurrant notes.

Beer (OG 1049, ABV 5%)
A blonde ale with musky hoppiness and citrus fruit on the nose, while more fruit surges through on the palate before the bittersweet finish.

Mill Valley SIBA

Woodroyd Mills, South Parade, Cleckheaton, BD19 3AF ☎ 07565 229560
millvalleybrewery.co.uk

Brewing began in 2016. Initially using a three-barrel plant, since upgraded to 4.5 barrels. More than 40 outlets are supplied as well as numerous beer festivals. The on-site brewery tap hosts regular events. ‼V

Luddite Ale (ABV 3.8%)

Mill Bitter (ABV 4%)

Panther Ale (ABV 4%)
A hoppy, fruity, citrus ale.

Mill Blonde (ABV 4.2%)

The Dukes IPA (ABV 4.2%)
A light pale ale with a hoppy, bitter taste and citrus finish.

Black Panther (ABV 4.6%)

Millis (Dartford Wobbler) SIBA

Dartford Wobbler Brewery, St Margaret's Farm, St Margaret's Road, South Darenth, Kent, DA4 9LB
☎ (01322) 866233 dartfordwobbler.com

John and Miriam Millis started with a 0.5-barrel plant at their home in Gravesend. Demand outstripped the facility and Millis moved in 2003 to its current location – a former farm cold store – using a 10-barrel plant. It supplies around 40 outlets within a 50-mile radius. ♦RAIB

Curiously Dark (OG 1036, ABV 3.6%)
A dark mild with a roasted malt flavour and some background fruit notes, leading to a dry aftertaste.

Guinea Guzzler (OG 1037, ABV 3.7%)
An amber-coloured session beer with a malty, fruity taste and dry finish.

Penny Red (OG 1039, ABV 3.9%)
A burnished red-coloured beer that has pungent hop notes, a dry finish and a malty base.

Peddlars Best (OG 1040, ABV 4%)
A copper-coloured bitter with floral fruit notes and an oaky, dry flavour to finish.

Golden Wobbler (OG 1041, ABV 4.1%)
A pale golden-coloured malty beer with complex citrus and lightly-spiced flavours.

Dartford Wobbler (OG 1043, ABV 4.3%)
A full-bodied, russet brown-coloured premium bitter with a dark malt profile, fruit notes and a dry finish.

Thieves & Fakirs (OG 1043, ABV 4.3%)
A dark-coloured porter with a full-bodied malt and hop base and a long, dry aftertaste.

Country Wobbler (OG 1048, ABV 4.8%)
Bold flavours of malt and hops with a long, clean and dry finish.

Platinum Blonde (OG 1039, ABV 4%)
A pale-coloured, hoppy session bitter.

Tigers Tail (OG 1042, ABV 4.1%)

Slubbers Gold (OG 1040, ABV 4.2%)
A pale golden-coloured bitter, well-balanced with a lingering, hoppy finish.

Black Jack Porter (OG 1049, ABV 4.5%)

Weaver's Bitter (OG 1040, ABV 4.5%)

Milton SIBA

Pegasus House, Pembroke Avenue, Waterbeach, Cambridgeshire, CB25 9PY
☎ (01223) 862067 🌐 miltonbrewery.co.uk

The brewery has grown steadily since it was founded in 1999. In 2012 it moved to larger premises in the village of Waterbeach. It now operates pubs in Cambridge and Norwich through a sister company. In 2016 a separate brand, Beach Brewery, was created to market unpasteurised and unfiltered keg beers. **!!**

Minotaur (OG 1035, ABV 3.3%)
A dark ruby-coloured mild with liquorice and raisin fruit throughout. Light dry finish.

Dionysus (OG 1037, ABV 3.6%)
Yellow-coloured bitter with a good balance of biscuity malt and citrus hop. Some malt and hops linger on long, dry aftertaste.

Justinian (OG 1039, ABV 3.9%)
Straw-coloured bitter with pink grapefruit hop character and light malt softness. Dry finish.

Pegasus (OG 1043, ABV 4.1%)
Malty, amber-coloured, medium-bodied bitter with faint hops. Bittersweet aftertaste.

Sparta (OG 1043, ABV 4.3%)
A yellow/gold-coloured best bitter with floral hops, kiwi fruit and balancing malt softness which fades to leave long, dry finish.

Medusa (OG 1047, ABV 4.6%)

Minerva (OG 1046, ABV 4.6%)
A powerful hop punch and satisfying bitterness.

Nero (OG 1050, ABV 5%)
A complex, black-coloured beer comprising a blend of milk chocolate, raisins and liquorice. Roast malt and fruit completes the experience.

Cyclops (OG 1055, ABV 5.3%)
Deep copper-coloured ale with a rich, hoppy aroma and full body; fruit and malt notes develop in the finish.

Marcus Aurelius (OG 1075, ABV 7.5%)
A powerful, black-coloured brew brimming with raisins and liquorice. Big balanced finish.

Brewed under the Beach Brewery brand name:

Waikiki (OG 1061, ABV 6%)
Generous quantities of bergamot oranges make for a refreshing beer.

Mills

c/o Salutation Inn, Ham, Gloucestershire, GL13 9QH
☎ 07848 922558

Office: Jumpers Lane Yard, Berkeley, GL13 9BW
✉ millsbrewing@gmail.com

Mills was established in Berkeley in 2016 by Genevieve Kaye and Jonny Mills. Wort is produced in multiple locations, which is then fermented in wooden vessels at its premises in Berkeley using 100% wild yeasts and bacteria from the local surroundings. The Lambic-style beers are mostly available in bottles (bottle conditioned). RAIB

Millstone SIBA

Unit 4, Vale Mill, Micklehurst Road, Mossley, Lancashire, OL5 9JL
☎ (01457) 835835 🌐 millstonebrewery.co.uk

Established in 2003 by Nick Boughton and Jon Hunt, the brewery is located in an 18th-century textile mill and uses an eight-barrel plant. More than 30 regular outlets are supplied. ♦

Vale Mill (OG 1039, ABV 3.9%)
A pale gold-coloured session bitter with a floral and spicy aroma building upon a crisp and refreshing taste.

Three Shires Bitter (OG 1040, ABV 4%)
Yellow-coloured beer with hop and fruit aroma. Fresh citrus fruit, hops and bitterness in the taste and aftertaste.

Tiger Rut (OG 1040, ABV 4%)
A pale-coloured, hoppy ale with a distinctive citrus/grapefruit aroma.

Stout (OG 1045, ABV 4.5%)
A traditional dry stout; pale chocolate malt, roasted barley and hint of sweetness to the aroma.

Rising Sunsation (OG 1047, ABV 4.7%)
A pale-coloured, dry bitter with hints of pine.

True Grit (OG 1050, ABV 5%)
A well-hopped, strong ale with a mellow bitterness and a citrus/grapefruit aroma.

Milltown SIBA

The Brewery, The Old Railway Goods Yard, Scar Lane, Milnsbridge, West Yorkshire, HD3 4PE ☎ 07946 589645 🌐 milltownbrewing.co.uk

Milltown began brewing in 2011 using a four-barrel plant. Two pubs are owned, the Dusty Miller at Longwood, which acts as the official brewery tap, and the Traveller's Rest, Meltham. **!!**♦

Golden Hop (OG 1037, ABV 3.8%)
Easy-drinking, golden-coloured session bitter with a good malt and hop balance.

Missing Link (NEW)

The Old Dairy, Chiddinglye Farm, West Hoathly, West Sussex, RH19 4QS 🌐 missinglinkbrewing.com

Missing Link was established in 2017 by Jeremy Cook using a five-barrel plant. No real ale.

Mitchell's Hop House

352-354 Meadowhead, Sheffield, South Yorkshire, S8 7UJ
☎ (0114) 274 5587 🌐 mitchellswine.co.uk

Brewing began in 2016 in a converted space at the back of an award-winning off-licence. Beers are available from the brewery shop and a growing number of local pubs. A gin distillery is also operated. RAIB

Mithril

Aldbrough St John, North Yorkshire, DL11 7TL
☎ (01325) 374817 ☎ 07889 167128
✉ mithril58@btinternet.com

Mithril started brewing in 2010 in old stables opposite the brewer's house on a 2.5-barrel plant. Owner/brewer Pete Fenwick, a well-known craft brewer, brews twice a week to supply the local area of Darlington and Richmond. A new beer is brewed every week. ♦

Dere Street (OG 1039, ABV 3.8%)
Amber-coloured bitter with a fruity, malty sweetness and a smooth, hoppy finish.

Flower Power (OG 1040, ABV 3.9%)
A pale ale with a massive citrus, fruity hop flavour. Hints of grapefruit and floral on the tongue from the late addition of elderflowers.

A66 (OG 1041, ABV 4%)
A crisp, refreshing, golden-coloured beer. A dry bitterness with a lingering citrus and spicy hop taste and aroma.

Mix

3 Cemmaes Court Road, Hemel Hempstead, Hertfordshire, HP1 1ST 🌐 mixbrewery.co.uk

A small brewery established in 2013 and based in a domestic garage. Beer is produced in small batches allowing for an ever-changing range.

Mobberley SIBA

Unit 2, Barncroft Farm, Woodend Lane, Mobberley, Cheshire, WA16 7LZ
☎ (01565) 873601 ☎ 07879 771209
🌐 mobberleyfineales.co.uk

Mobberley began brewing in 2011 in an old milking parlour on a working farm in the heart of the Cheshire countryside. Expansion is planned. Beers are contract brewed for Burton Road Brewing Co. ♦

HedgeHopper (OG 1039, ABV 3.8%)
A golden-coloured, refreshing ale; light and aromatic.

RoadRunner (OG 1039, ABV 3.8%)
A pale yellow-coloured ale with a delicate, lightly spicy finish. Sweet-tasting and smooth with a refreshing hop aroma.

Mandalay (OG 1040, ABV 4%)

Maori (OG 1040, ABV 4%)

WhirlyBird (OG 1040, ABV 4%)
A sweet yet full-bodied pale ale with a smooth, subtle zesty finish.

Red Vienna (ABV 4.2%)

Legacy (ABV 4.4%)

1924 (ABV 4.5%)
Amber-coloured, powerful and fruity ale.

Elysium (ABV 4.7%)

Origin (ABV 4.7%)

Moles

See Wickwar

Molson Coors

Molson Coors (Burton): 137 High Street, Burton upon Trent, Staffordshire, DE14 1JZ
☎ (01283) 511000

Molson Coors (Tadcaster): Tower Brewery, Wetherby Road, Tadcaster, LS24 9SD
🌐 molsoncoorsbrewers.com

Molson Coors is the result of a merger between Molson of Canada and Coors of Colorado, US. Coors established itself in Europe in 2002 by buying part of the former Bass brewing empire, when Interbrew (now AB InBev) was instructed by the British government to divest itself of some of its interests in Bass. Coors owns several cask ale brands. It brews 110,000 barrels of cask beer a year (under licensing arrangements with other brewers) and also provides a further 50,000 barrels of cask beer from other breweries. In 2011 Molson Coors bought Sharp's brewery in Cornwall (qv) in a bid to increase its stake in the cask beer sector. No cask ale is produced in Burton or Tadcaster.

Moncada SIBA

37 Humber Road, Dollis Hill, London, NW2 6EN
☎ (020) 8964 0829 🌐 moncadabrewery.co.uk

Moncada began brewing in 2011 using a six-barrel plant. ♦RAIB

Notting Hill Bitter (ABV 3.7%)
Brown-coloured bitter with a good balance of hops and sweetness and a pleasant finish.

Notting Hill Blonde (ABV 4.2%)
Continental-style, golden-coloured beer with a smooth mouthfeel, sweetish with a touch of honey and fruity hops. Short, crisp finish.

Notting Hill Amber (ABV 4.7%)
Full-bodied, creamy, amber-coloured beer with a citrus peel aroma and flavour. Well-balanced by the sweet biscuit character.

Notting Hill Stout (ABV 5%)
A dry, malty beer with roast, caramel and a little malty sweetness. The pleasant aftertaste is long and lingering.

Notting Hill Ruby Rye (ABV 5.2%)
Sweetish ruby-coloured beer with a full, fruity aroma, a creamy mouthfeel and a little roast throughout.

Mondo

86-92 Stewarts Road, South Lambeth, London, SW8 4UG
☎ (020) 7720 0782 ☎ 07453 312170
🌐 mondobrewingcompany.com

The brewery opened in 2015 using a 10-hectolitre brew kit. A taphouse has been added. !!♦

THE BREWERIES

Monty's

Unit 1, Castle Works, Hendomen, SY15 6HA
☎ (01686) 668933 montysbrewery.co.uk

Monty's began brewing in 2009. It leases one pub, the Sportsman in Newtown, through its sister company, Hophouse Inns. The Cottage Inn in Montgomery is owned and acts as the brewery's visitor centre. It also houses a 250-litre plant producing small runs of experimental beers. ♦RAIB GF

Old Jailhouse (OG 1039.5, ABV 3.9%)
Copper-coloured bitter with a good blend of malt and hops.

Best Offa (OG 1040, ABV 4%)
A golden-coloured, toasty bitter.

Moonrise (OG 1040, ABV 4%)
A copper-coloured, gently malty, well-balanced traditional brew.

MPA (OG 1040.5, ABV 4%)
Pale ale with a good bitter character.

Sunshine (OG 1041, ABV 4.2%)
A golden-coloured, hoppy, floral/citrus ale with a pleasantly dry finish.

Masquerade (OG 1046, ABV 4.6%)
A premium, golden-coloured bitter with a tropical fruit flavour and hop aroma.

Mischief (OG 1050, ABV 5%)
Strong golden ale with a good balance of malt and hop bitterness.

Dark Secret (OG 1056, ABV 5.6%)
Oatmeal stout with chocolate and coffee flavours.

Eastbound (OG 1073, ABV 7.3%)

Moody Fox

Hilcote Country Club, Hilcote Lane, Hilcote, Derbyshire, DE55 5HR ☎ 07702 253235
moodyfoxbrewery@gmail.com

Established in 2016, Moody Fox is a microbrewery specialising in traditional ales using the finest hops and barley from around the world.

Cub (ABV 3.8%)
Smooth session bitter with a slightly dry finish.

Pale Tale (ABV 5.4%)
An IPA-style pale ale, full of citrus flavour with a slightly bitter finish.

Moody Goose

King William IV, 114 London Road, Braintree, Essex, CM77 7PU
☎ (01376) 567755 moodygoosebrewery.co.uk

A three-barrel brewery, brewing approximately 15 times a year. The beers are currently only available in the King William IV, where the brewery is located, and select beer festivals.

moogBREW

1 Copeland Cottages, Marsh Lane, Taplow, SL6 0DF
☎ 07941 241954 moogbrew.co.uk

Situated in a converted garden shed, this 100-litre brewery was set up in 2016. The majority of the output is bottle-conditioned with inspiration for the range coming from world-wide beer hunting. Distribution is targeted to within a 10-mile radius of the brewery. !! ♦RAIB

Bastard Bunny Strikes Back (ABV 6%)
A well-balanced, amber-coloured, American-style IPA.

Wigmore's Right Proper Porter (ABV 6.5%)
A robust porter with a complex mix of chocolate, coffee and liquorice flavours.

Moonchild

Church Gate, Petrockstow, Devon, EX20 3HL ☎ 07773 367155 moonchildbrewing.co.uk

Moonchild was established in 2016 by Fred and Sophie Caure. All beers are unfined, unfiltered and unpasteurised and only available in bottle-conditioned format. ♦RAIB

Moonshine

Hill Farm, Shelford Road, Fulbourn, Cambridgeshire, CB21 5EQ ☎ 07906 066794

Office: 28 Radegund Road, Cambridge, CB1 3RS
moonshinebrewery.co.uk

Established in 2004, the brewery produces up to 20 barrels a week. Locally-produced ingredients are used including water from the brewery's own well and barley grown on the farm where the brewery is based. CAMRA beer festivals are supplied throughout the country, with 30 local outlets supplied direct. ♦RAIB

Sundowner (OG 1036, ABV 3.6%)
Light amber-coloured session beer with balanced malt and a rounded hop finish.

Trumpington Tipple (OG 1036, ABV 3.6%)
Deep amber-coloured ale with malty flavours and a fragrant hop aroma.

Cambridge Pale Ale (OG 1038, ABV 3.8%)
Golden-coloured beer, light to the palate with a dryish, citrus finish.

Shelford Crier (OG 1038, ABV 3.8%)
A light-bodied, amber-coloured beer with a citrus fruit bouquet and taste that continues through to a refreshing clean and dry finish.

Spiritual Matter (OG 1037, ABV 3.8%)

Harvest Moon Mild (OG 1040, ABV 3.9%)
A distinctive dark mild, well-balanced and slightly sweet. Smooth fruit notes combine with coffee and chocolate flavours.

Heavenly Matter (OG 1041, ABV 4.1%)
A huge hoppy, citrus flavoured, straw-coloured beer. Tropical fruits tastes with a generous bitter finish.

Cambridge Best Bitter (OG 1041, ABV 4.2%)
A copper-coloured best bitter; the malt and hop aromas carry through to the taste and the finish is rounded with a growing hop bitterness.

Nightwatch Porter (OG 1043, ABV 4.5%)
A well-rounded porter made with local honey. Sweet to start with a dry finish.

Raspberry Porter (OG 1043, ABV 4.5%)
A well-rounded porter with added fruit.

Black Hole Stout (OG 1048, ABV 5%)
Full-bodied stout with a complex malt profile. The roasted flavours are rich, smooth and long-lasting.

Hot Numbers Coffee Stout (OG 1057, ABV 5.5%)
Dark-coloured, roasted coffee milk stout with balanced coffee and hops.

Chocolate Orange Stout (OG 1068, ABV 6.7%)
Full-bodied, well-rounded, soft stout. Loaded with chocolate and coffee flavours with a good hop balance that has a hint of orange on the nose.

Moonstone

Ministry of Ale, 9 Trafalgar Street, Burnley, Lancashire, BB11 1TQ
☎ (01282) 830909 moonstonebrewery.co.uk

A small, three-barrel brewery, based in the front room of the Ministry of Ale pub. Brewing started in 2001 and beer is only available in the pub. ‼

Moor SIBA

Days Road, Bristol, BS2 0QS
☎ (0117) 941 4460 moorbeer.co.uk

Established in 1996, Moor Beer has relocated twice, each time increasing its brewing capacity, resulting in larger premises now located in central Bristol, which feature a shop and brewery tap. All beers are produced without the addition of isinglass finings, so are naturally hazy and suitable for vegans. Moor's canned beers are the first in the UK to be recognised as real ale by CAMRA.
‼ ♦ RAIB V

All-Dayer (ABV 3.5%)
A session IPA with pronounced bitterness.

Revival (OG 1038, ABV 3.8%)
An immensely hoppy and refreshing pale ale.

Nor'Hop (OG 1041, ABV 4.1%)
Golden yellow-coloured unfined beer with spicy hops on the nose. Citrus flavours of grapefruit and lemon, short bitter aftertaste.

So'Hop (OG 1041, ABV 4.1%)

Union Hop (ABV 4.1%)
A pale ale. Zingy, citrus and refreshing with some sweet pale malt to balance.

Raw (OG 1043, ABV 4.3%)
Amber-coloured best bitter with a pineapple aroma. Hoppy bitterness on the tongue balanced with malty sweetness leads to a subtle bitter finish.

Amoor (OG 1045, ABV 4.5%)
Roasted malt and coffee aroma, taste adds chocolate and vanilla impressions before a smooth and almost spicy finish.

Claudia (ABV 4.5%)
Hoppy wheat beer. Flavours of banana, lemon and cloves together with a herbal and citrus hop character.

Dark Alliance (OG 1045, ABV 4.5%)
A hoppy coffee stout.

Illusion (OG 1045, ABV 4.5%)
A powerfully-hopped, session black IPA.

Confidence (OG 1046, ABV 4.6%)
A red-coloured ale with a spicy, peppery flavour. A rustic unpasteurised quality to its taste, with a sweetness given by hints of stone fruit. Pleasant short bitter finish.

Ported Amoor (OG 1047, ABV 4.7%)
Amoor with added reserve port.

Radiance (OG 1048, ABV 5%)
Golden ale with floral aromas of citrus fruit and blossom. Grapefruit palate with an initial tanginess, becoming more sweet. The grapefruit is present in the pleasant lingering aftertaste.

Smokey Horyzon (OG 1050, ABV 5%)
A speciality beer made using smoked rye. Hoppy, pale brown-coloured, strong ale with plenty of body, balanced by sweetness and smokiness.

Stout (OG 1050, ABV 5%)
A classic black-coloured stout. Smoky roast malts and dark fruit aroma with hint of vanilla. Prunes and liquorice notes follow into the taste. Pleasant dark chocolate aftertaste.

Do It Together (ABV 5.2%)
A fruity and easy-drinking beer for its strength. The addition of mango and tea add to the flavour.

PMA (Positive Mental Attitude) (ABV 5.3%)
Hoppy pale ale with oats.

Return of the Empire (OG 1057, ABV 5.7%)
Modern English IPA. Light caramel honey malt with honeydew melon, citrus, apricot and peach notes.

B-Moor (OG 1060, ABV 6%)
Aromas of roasted malt and fruit, bitter chocolate and rich, dark fruit on the palate with a dry bitter aftertaste.

Hoppiness (OG 1065, ABV 6.5%)
All the rich malt and fruit flavours of a barley wine combined with the hoppy crispness of a pale ale.

Old Freddy Walker (OG 1073, ABV 7.3%)
Rich, dark-coloured, strong ale with a fruity complex taste, leaving a fruitcake finish.

Moorhouse's SIBA

The Brewery, Moorhouse Street, Burnley, Lancashire, BB11 5EN
☎ (01282) 422864 moorhouses.co.uk

Established in 1865 as a soft drinks manufacturer, the brewery started producing cask-conditioned ale in 1978. A new brewhouse and visitor centre opened in 2012. Three pubs are owned. ‼♦

Black Cat (OG 1036, ABV 3.4%)
A dark mild-style beer with delicate chocolate and coffee roast flavours and a crisp, bitter finish.

Premier Bitter (OG 1036, ABV 3.7%)
A clean and satisfying bitter aftertaste rounds off this well-balanced hoppy, amber-coloured session bitter.

White Witch (OG 1039, ABV 4%)
Delicate sweet start with gentle bitterness and a drying finish.

Pride of Pendle (OG 1040, ABV 4.1%)
Well-balanced, amber-coloured best bitter with a fresh initial hoppiness and a mellow, malt-driven body.

Blonde Witch (OG 1045, ABV 4.5%)
Well-liked, fruity light ale.

Pendle Witches Brew (OG 1050, ABV 5.1%)
Well-balanced, full-bodied, malty beer with a long, complex finish.

MòR SIBA

Old Mill, Kellas, DD5 3PD ☎ 07884 346351
morbrewing.co.uk

Retired lifeboat coxswain Jim Hughan teamed up with family friend Ross Niven to establish the 2.5-barrel brewery in 2012. Just over a year later it expanded to a 4.5-barrel plant. In 2016 Matt Forrest joined the business as a co-director following Ross' retirement. ‼♦RAIB

Tea Vicar? (OG 1038, ABV 3.8%)
A pale amber-coloured bitter with a pleasant balance of malt and hops. With a malty, fruity aroma and a pronounced bitter finish.

Ish! (OG 1042, ABV 4.2%)
A bright amber-coloured ale with a malty, fruity aroma and a well-balanced and controlled bitter finish.

Please! (OG 1045, ABV 4.5%)
A clean-tasting, full-bodied, golden-coloured bitter bursting with malt and hops.

Mordue SIBA

Units D1 & D2, Narvic Way, Tyne Tunnel Estate, North Shields, Tyne & Wear, NE29 7XJ
☎ (0191) 296 1879 🌐 morduebrewery.com

In 1995 the Fawson brothers revived the Mordue Brewery name (the original closed in 1879). High demand required moves to larger premises and replacing the original five-barrel plant with a 20-barrel one. The beers are distributed nationally and 300 outlets are supplied direct. ‼♦RAIB

Five Bridges (OG 1038, ABV 3.6%)
Crisp, golden-coloured beer with a good hint of hops, the bitterness carries on in the finish. A good session bitter.

Northumbrian Blonde (OG 1040, ABV 4%)
A blonde beer with a citrus aroma and hoppy finish.

Panda Frog Pandarillo (OG 1042, ABV 4.2%)

Workie Ticket (OG 1045, ABV 4.5%)
Complex, tasty bitter with plenty of malt and hops, long satisfying bitter finish.

Panda Frog Project Pils (OG 1047, ABV 4.7%)
Pale straw-coloured, Czech-style Pilsner with a herbal grassy aroma and fruity citrus undertone.

Radgie Gadgie (OG 1048, ABV 4.8%)
Strong, easy-drinking bitter with plenty of fruit and hops.

Panda Frog Project Allelic Drift (OG 1050, ABV 5%)
Pale golden ale featuring floral pine, citrus notes with a clean bitterness.

IPA (OG 1051, ABV 5.1%)
Easy-drinking golden ale with plenty of hops, the bitterness carries on in the finish.

Morgans

See Merry Miner

Morland

See Greene King

Morton

Unit 10, Essington Light Industrial Estate, Essington, Staffordshire, WV11 2BH ☎ 07988 69647

Office: 96 Brewood Road, Coven, WV9 5EF
🌐 mortonbrewery.co.uk

This family run brewery was established in 2006 on a three-barrel, purpose-built plant. Beers are supplied locally, further afield by reciprocal arrangements, to various beer festivals and a selection is always available at the brewery's own micropub, Hail to the Ale. ‼♦

Essington Dark Mild (OG 1036, ABV 3.6%)

Essington Bitter (OG 1037, ABV 3.8%)
Fruity, hoppy session ale.

Merry Mount (OG 1037, ABV 3.8%)

Essington Blonde (OG 1039, ABV 4%)

Essington Ale (OG 1041, ABV 4.2%)

Jelly Roll (OG 1041, ABV 4.2%)

Essington Gold (OG 1044, ABV 4.4%)

Essington Supreme (OG 1046, ABV 4.6%)

Scottish Maiden (OG 1045, ABV 4.6%)

Essington IPA (OG 1046, ABV 4.8%)
Yellow-coloured with lots of hop and fruit aromas. A good mouthful of bitterness with hops and fruit jostling for taste. Lingering bitter finish.

Morton Collins

Star, Standbridge Lane. Sandal, Wakefield, West Yorkshire, WF2 7DY ☎ 07812 111960

Office: 49 Willow Garth, Durkar, WF4 3BX

Set up in 2016 by Ged Morton and Sam Collins using a 100-litre plant in Ged's garage. The brewery produces to demand but can brew every day if required. It took over the lease of the Star, Sandal, in 2016. Several of the beers are named after the nearby Nature Reserve at Wintersett. The brewery kit was upgraded to 200 litres per brew in 2017.

Wintersett Gold (OG 1041, ABV 4.1%)

Amber No. 9 (OG 1048, ABV 4.8%)

Morwell (NEW)

Morwellham Quay, Morwellham, Devon, PL19 8JL
☎ (01822) 832766 🌐 morwellham.org

Established in 2017 at Victorian tourist attraction Morwellham Quay, near Tavistock, by brewer George Lister. Using a 100-litre plant, three bottle-conditioned beers are brewed, which are available in the on-site shop and the Ship Inn, the on-site café, and a growing number of local outlets. RAIB

Moseley

14 Cleveland Court, St Agnes Road, Moseley, B13 9PR
🌐 moseleybeercompany.co.uk

Moseley Beer Company began brewing in 2016, set up by a family of four brothers. **V**

Sightseer Wheat Beer (ABV 4.5%)
A light, refreshing wheat beer with a citrus aftertaste.

Pale Ale (ABV 5%)

Marianna Porter (ABV 8%)
A dark-coloured, roasty porter with a sweet honey kick, based on a Victorian recipe.

Iron Man Stout (ABV 9%)

Moulin

2 Baledmund Road, Moulin, PH16 5EL
☎ (01796) 472196

Office: Moulin Hotel, 11-13 Kirkmicheal Road, Moulin, PH16 5EH moulinhotel.co.uk

The brewery opened in 1995 to celebrate the Moulin Hotel's 300th anniversary. Two pubs are owned and four outlets are supplied. !! RAIB

Mount St Bernard (NEW)

Mount St Bernard Abbey, Oaks Road, Charley, Coalville, Leicestershire, LE67 5UL
☎ (01530) 832298

Monks at this Cistercian abbey launched a beer in 2017, the first monastic beer brewed in England since the Reformation. Tynt Meadow (7.4% ABV) is bottle-conditioned and brewed with all English ingredients. It is available commercially in selected outlets. RAIB

Mountain Hare

Mountain Hare Inn, Brynna Road, Brynnau Gwynion, CF35 6PG
☎ (01656) 860453 mountainhare.co.uk

Paul Jones, licensee of the Mountain Hare, finally realised his ambition of installing a brewery in his family-owned pub. A 1.5-barrel custom-built brewing plant was installed in 2013, supplying only the pub itself. There are plans for expansion to a six-barrel plant to meet demand. V

Mourne Mountains

Milltown East Industrial Estate, Upper Dromore Road, Warrenpoint, BT34 3PN
☎ (028) 4175 2299
mournemountainsbrewery.com

Brewing since 2015 with an extensive and varying range of seasonals, specials and one-off brews produced throughout the year – some may appear in cask format. ♦

Mourne Gold (ABV 4%)
Fruity, session golden ale.

Mouselow Farm

3 Mouselow Farm, Dinting, Derbyshire, SK13 7QQ
☎ 07920 048252 ✉ glossopowl@btinternet.com

Mouselow Farm began brewing in 2013 using a 2.5-barrel plant housed in a converted barn. Brewing is on a part-time basis. Local free houses, clubs and beer festivals are supplied. ♦

Golden Gosling (OG 1037, ABV 3.6%)

Cluckstar (ABV 3.7%)

Udder the Influence (OG 1041, ABV 4%)

Flying Goose (ABV 4.2%)

Mr Bees (NEW)

Unit D, Searsons Farm, Cordys Lane, Trimley, Suffolk, IP11 0UD ☎ 07503 773630 mrbeesbrewery.co.uk

Mr Bees is based on the beautiful Suffolk Coast. All beers contain honey direct from the brewery's own beehives. Around 30 outlets are supplied direct including the Shannon Inn, Bucklesham, Felsto Arms, Felixstowe and the Ramsholt Arms.

Pollen Power (OG 1036.5, ABV 3.8%)
An easy-drinking, fruity beer.

Best BeeR (OG 1038, ABV 4%)

BeeLightful (OG 1040, ABV 4.3%)

BeeClipse (OG 1043.5, ABV 4.5%)

Brewed for the Boardwalk Café Bar, Felixstowe:

Trimley Best Bitter (OG 1036.5, ABV 3.8%)
A fruity ale with caramel notes.

Boardwalk Best (OG 1039.5, ABV 4.2%)

Pier Pint (OG 1044, ABV 4.3%)

Boardside (OG 1044, ABV 4.6%)

Landguard IPA (OG 1049, ABV 5.3%)

Mr Grundy's SIBA

Georgian House Hotel, 34 Ashbourne Road, Derby, DE22 3AD
☎ (01332) 349806 ☎ 07812 812953
mrgrundysbrewery.co.uk

Named after a local WW1 veteran who once resided on the site, the brewery opened in 2010 using a purpose-built 3.5-barrel plant fitted inside a former hotel bedroom. Beers are produced for the two hotels owned by the parent company, GHH Llp, and the free trade. Sales are handled by sister brewery Black Hole (qv). ♦

Passchendaele (OG 1039, ABV 3.9%)
A straw-coloured, sharp bitter with citrus overtones.

Big Willie (OG 1043, ABV 4.3%)
Thirst-quenching golden ale packed with English hops giving a lasting, dry bitter finish.

Bullet (OG 1043, ABV 4.3%)
Dark-coloured ale with a treacle aroma and a smooth, rounded taste.

Sniper (OG 1046, ABV 4.6%)
Amber-coloured, smooth, refreshing bitter with a hint of toffee and a satisfying malty aroma.

Mr Majolica

Units 7a & 15, Thurrock Enterprise Centre, Maidstone Road, Grays, Essex, RM17 6NF ☎ 07834 539761
mrmajolica.co.uk

A family-run microbrewery situated in Grays town centre, Mr Majolica began brewing in 2014 on a 2.5-barrel plant. Pubs and clubs are supplied around Essex, Kent and London.

Buccaneer (OG 1039, ABV 3.8%)

Phantom (OG 1041, ABV 4%)

Vanguard (OG 1041, ABV 4.1%)

Enterprise (OG 1045, ABV 4.5%)

Evolution (OG 1048, ABV 4.8%)

Muckle SIBA

3 Bellister Close, Park Village, Haltwhistle, Northumberland, NE49 0HA ☎ 07711 980086 🌐 mucklebrewing.co.uk

Established in 2016, Muckle Brewing is a tiny brewery in rural Northumberland, close to Hadrian's Wall. Beers are influenced by the local landscape that surrounds the brewery.

Tickle (OG 1039, ABV 4%)

Chuckle (OG 1040, ABV 4.2%)

Moss Stout (OG 1042, ABV 4.3%)

Buster (OG 1043, ABV 4.5%)

Muirhouse

Unit 1, Enterprise Court, Manners Avenue, Manners Industrial Estate, Ilkeston, Derbyshire, DE7 8EW ☎ 07916 590525 🌐 muirhousebrewery.co.uk

Muirhouse was established in 2009 in a domestic garage in Long Eaton. It expanded in 2011 to the present location in Ilkeston and the plant was upgraded in 2016 to 7.5 barrels. ‼♦RAIB

Summit Hoppy (OG 1041, ABV 4%)
Pale-coloured session beer packed hops.

Magnum Mild (OG 1047, ABV 4.5%)

Pirate's Gold (OG 1045, ABV 4.5%)
Pale golden-coloured beer with a hint of caramel.

Hat Trick IPA (OG 1052, ABV 5.2%)

Mumbles SIBA

Unit 14, Worcester Court, Swansea Enterprise Park, Swansea, SA7 9FD ☎ (01792) 792612 ☎ 07757 109938 🌐 mumblesbrewery.co.uk

Mumbles was established in 2011 and began brewing in 2013. In 2014 brewing took place using spare capacity at other local breweries but a permanent home was found in 2015 using a 10-barrel plant. Director/brewer Rob Turner supplies numerous pubs in South Wales and the Bristol area. ♦

Hop Kick (OG 1038, ABV 4%)

Mile (OG 1039, ABV 4%)

Malt Bitter (ABV 4.1%)

Murmelt (ABV 4.2%)

Gold (OG 1042, ABV 4.3%)
A light, refreshing pale ale with lingering lemon and lime flavours.

Oystermouth Stout (OG 1043, ABV 4.4%)
A rich, creamy head and dark roasted malt flavours distinguish this classic stout.

Lifesaver Strong Bitter (OG 1048, ABV 4.9%)
A bronze-coloured, smooth, malty ale with a clean hop finish.

India Pale Ale (OG 1052, ABV 5.3%)
A traditional IPA with a distinct marmalade taste and aroma.

Musket SIBA

Unit 7, Loddington Farm, Loddington Lane, Linton, Kent, ME17 4AG ☎ (01622) 749931 ☎ 07967 127278 🌐 musketbrewery.co.uk

Launched in 2013 with a five-barrel plant, this family owned brewery is based at Loddington Farm, Linton, in the heart of the Kent countryside. Expanding to a 15-barrel plant, Musket Brewery now supplies more than 300 pubs, micropubs and clubs throughout Kent and Medway. ♦

Trigger (OG 1032, ABV 3.6%)
A hoppy, easy-drinking session ale.

Fife & Drum (OG 1034, ABV 3.8%)
A golden ale with flavours and aromas of spice, honey, marmalade, floral and a hint of blackcurrant.

Matchlock (OG 1034, ABV 3.8%)

Ball Puller (ABV 4%)

Flintlock (OG 1037, ABV 4.2%)
A best bitter with spicy orange undertones and a hint of marmalade.

Muzzleloader (OG 1039, ABV 4.5%)
Dark-coloured beer, smoky with a faint, spicy aroma of orange.

Muswell Hillbilly (NEW)

Mews Workshops, 24-26 Avenue Mews, Muswell Hill, London, N10 3NP 🌐 muswellhillbillybrewers.co.uk

Originally homebrewers, premises were acquired in Muswell Hill in 2017. Beer is primarly bottled with one cask-conditioned or keg beer per week.

Myrddins

Church Street, Barmouth, LL42 1EH ☎ (01341) 388060 ✉ myrddins@talktalk.net

Established in 2016, Myrddins is a small brewery within a café bar in the centre of Barmouth.

Nant SIBA

The Outbuildings, Penrhwylfa, Maenan, Llanrwst, LL26 0UB ☎ 07723 036862 🌐 bragdy-nant.com

Nant commenced brewing in 2007 with a plant purchased from the Yorkshire Dales Brewery. Capacity is currently 10-15 nine gallon firkins a week. ♦RAIB

Brenin (OG 1038, ABV 3.8%)
A light golden-coloured session ale with balanced hops and malt.

Prop Hop (OG 1036, ABV 3.8%)

Cwrw Coryn (OG 1042, ABV 4.2%)
Traditional amber-coloured beer. Slightly malty with good bitter overtones.

Chwaden Aur (OG 1043, ABV 4.3%)
Golden orange-coloured ale with a citrus aroma and full mouthfeel. Grapefruit and lemon citrus taste balance with biscuity malt for a long, fruity finish.

Mwnci Nel (OG 1055, ABV 5.5%)
A dark-coloured ale, not excessively sweet but dominated by burnt chocolate flavours, balanced with hops.

NauticAles

Sowell Street, St Peters, Broadstairs, Kent, CT10 6SG
☎ 07552 600919

Office: 347 Margate Road, Ramsgate, CT12 6SG
✉ nauticales@outlook.com

⊗ Beers are only available at the brewery's micropub in Ramsgate and at local beer festivals. ♦

Navigation SIBA

Trent Navigation Inn, 17 Meadow Lane, Nottingham, NG2 3HS
☎ (0115) 986 9877 🌐 navigationbrewery.com

Brewing began in 2012 in the old stable block of the Trent Navigation Inn. The brewery is owned by sister company Great Northern Inns and supplies cask beers to the pubs in its estate. ‼

Patriot (OG 1038, ABV 3.8%)
Tawny-coloured, malty bitter.

New Dawn Pale (OG 1039, ABV 3.9%)
Golden-coloured ale with initial fruit and hops and a bitter finish.

Rebel (ABV 4.2%)

Splendor (OG 1041.8, ABV 4.3%)
A golden-coloured best bitter.

Eclipse (OG 1043.5, ABV 4.4%)
Dark roast stout aroma and aftertaste with bitterness and some sweetness.

Saviour (OG 1054, ABV 5.5%)
Golden in colour with assertive hop aroma and citrus fruit taste throughout with a balanced bitterness.

Naylor's SIBA

Midland Mills, Station Road, Cross Hills, North Yorkshire, BD20 7DT
☎ (01535) 637451 🌐 naylorsbrewery.com

The Naylor brothers started brewing in 2005 at the Old White Bear pub in Cross Hills. The brewery moved to Midland Mills in 2006 and transferred to a larger unit on the same site in 2012. 100 outlets are regularly supplied and around 1,200 on an occasional basis. The on-site bar (the Beer Belly Music Venue & Bar) is open Wednesday to Sunday. ‼ ♦

Yorkshire Ale (OG 1037, ABV 3.8%)
Predominantly malty traditional mid-brown-coloured bitter with subtle fruit and hops on the nose and taste and a growing bitter finish.

Gold (OG 1040, ABV 4%)
Golden-coloured ale, bitter to taste with a classic grapefruit hop finish.

Velvet (OG 1040, ABV 4%)
Chocolate and roast aromas and flavours predominate in this dark brown-coloured mild, which has an increasingly roast bitter finish.

Pinnacle Blonde (OG 1041.5, ABV 4.3%)
Hoppy, fruity aroma followed by grassy hop and tropical fruit flavours. The finish remains hoppy with a bitter, fruity edge.

Black & Tan (OG 1042, ABV 4.4%)
Dark brown-coloured best bitter with a roast edge and hop hit. Liquorice and a malty sweetness lead to a bitter finish.

Old Ale (OG 1054, ABV 5.9%)
A smooth beer with sweet maltiness balanced by subtle bitterness. Strong but easy drinking.

Neath

Endeavour Close, Port Talbot, SA12 7PT ☎ 07772 468436 🌐 neathales.co.uk

Neath Ales was established in 2009 and produces a range of single hop variety beers. Some beers are released under the Black Falls brand name. ♦RAIB V

Firebrick (OG 1042, ABV 4.2%)
Amber-coloured best bitter with a British hop flavour and aroma.

Deliverance (OG 1045, ABV 4.5%)

Welsh Amber Ale (OG 1045, ABV 4.5%)

Dewi Sant (OG 1048, ABV 4.8%)
A pale ale with a well-balanced hop fruit flavour.

Neatishead

White Horse Inn, The Street, Neatishead, Norfolk, NR12 8AD
☎ (01692) 630828
🌐 thewhitehorseinnneatishead.com

⊗ Brewing began in 2015 at the White Horse Inn. The brew kit can be viewed through glass from the restaurant. Beer is only available in the pub at present. A range of semi-regular beers is brewed with at least one ever-changing ale.

Neckstamper SIBA

Unit 3, Cromwell Industrial Estate, Staffa Road, Leyton, London, E10 7QZ
☎ (020) 7018 1760 ☎ 07968 150075
🌐 neckstamper.com

Neckstamper began brewing in 2016 using a 10-barrel plant. No real ale.

Neepsend

Units 1-3, Lion Works, Mowbray Street, Sheffield, South Yorkshire, S3 8EN
☎ (0114) 276 3406 ☎ 07545 323427
✉ gavin@neepsendbrewco.com

Established in 2015 by James Birkett and Gavin Martin after taking over Little Ale Cart Brewery and moving to new premises in Sheffield's 'Valley of Beer'. A 10-barrel plant is used, supplying beers locally, including to the company's own pubs, Sheaf View, the Blake Hotel and the Wellington. Despite only having one core beer, the brewery produces an ever-changing range of hop-forward seasonal ales. An on-site bar is planned. ♦

Blonde (OG 1039, ABV 4%)
Mellow, easy-drinking session pale ale. Low in bitterness with a short finish.

Nelson SIBA

Unit 2, Building 64, The Historic Dockyard, Chatham, Kent, ME4 4TE
☎ (01634) 832828 🌐 nelsonbrewery.co.uk

Based in Chatham's Historic Dockyard and brewing on a nautical theme, the brewery supplies award-winning ales direct to more than 330 outlets. ‼ ♦RAIB

Pieces of Eight (OG 1040, ABV 3.8%)
A light, refreshing ale with full-flavoured hops and a hint of chocolate aftertaste.

Admiral IPA (OG 1040, ABV 4%)
A traditional IPA with a combination of citrus flavours on the palate.

Midshipman Dark Mild (OG 1040, ABV 4%)
A dark mild brewed with a roasted aftertaste on the palate.

Trafalgar Bitter (OG 1040, ABV 4.1%)

Powder Monkey (OG 1043, ABV 4.3%)
A golden ale with a smooth aftertaste, which leaves a sweetness on the palate.

Friggin' in the Riggin' (OG 1046, ABV 4.5%)
A premium bitter with a smooth malt flavour and bittersweet aftertaste.

Pursers Pussy Porter (OG 1051, ABV 4.8%)

Nelsons Blood (OG 1062, ABV 6%)
A strong, malty ale with mellow roast tones. Slightly nutty and fruity with a warm aftertaste.

Nene Valley SIBA

Oundle Wharf, Station Road, Oundle, Northamptonshire, PE8 4DE
☎ (01832) 272776 🌐 nenevalleybrewery.com

⊗ Established in 2011, a bespoke 15-barrel plant was installed in former Water Board premises on expansion in 2012. Further expansion in 2016 has doubled the floorspace. A brewery tap, Tap & Kitchen, opened on the same site in 2014.
!! ⛟ ♦ RAIB GF

Simple Pleasures Ale (OG 1036, ABV 3.6%) ◆

Blonde Session Ale (OG 1036, ABV 3.8%)
A light golden-coloured session ale with a refreshing citrus hop finish.

Dark Horse (OG 1039, ABV 3.8%)
A dark ruby-coloured mild with roasted grains giving hints of chocolate, coffee and liquorice.

Manhattan Project (OG 1037, ABV 4%)
A light beer with lots of citrus and tropical hop flavours.

Bitter (OG 1038, ABV 4.1%) ◆
Floral hop and malt aroma introduces a full, clean biscuit malt taste balanced by bitterness and some fruit, ending with a long malt and bitter finish.

Australian Pale (OG 1041, ABV 4.4%)
A rich golden ale with a floral aroma preceding citrus and tropical fruit flavour from the hops.

Release the Chimps (OG 1043, ABV 4.4%)
A crisp mouthfeel, clean, punchy bitterness and a good deal of hop flavour for this light IPA.

Egyptian Cream (OG 1053, ABV 4.5%)
A milk stout with a velvety mouthfeel and a deep, full malty richness.

Dick's Extraordinary Bitter (OG 1045, ABV 4.6%)
Chestnut in colour with plenty of maltiness. Balanced with late-hopped spicy character.

Big Bang Theory (OG 1048, ABV 5.3%) ◆
Well-balanced pale ale with a huge hop aroma giving way to malty sweetness and a gentle bitter finish.

A Beer Named Leeroy (ABV 5.5%)
Hugely hoppy and fruity pale ale. Lots of oats and aromatic malt added to give the beer a big mouthfeel with a hint of maltiness.

Jim Irving Pale (OG 1053, ABV 5.6%)
Full-bodied beer with a big malty taste backed with heaps of zesty hop flavour.

Supersonic (OG 1055, ABV 6%) ◆
A pale wheat beer brewed with gin and tonic botanicals including lemons, juniper and cardamom.

Bible Black (OG 1063, ABV 6.5%) ◆
An inviting aroma of malt and fruit leads to a rich-tasting beer where blackberry dominates but is balanced by malt, hops and some bitterness. The lingering finish is bittersweet, with fruit assertive.

Mid-week Bender (OG 1072, ABV 7.4%)
Dark amber-coloured beer with flavours of rich malt, molasses and candied orange and a big hop hit throughout.

Neon Raptor

Unit 14, Avenue A, Sneinton Market, Nottingham, NG1 1DT ☎ 07821 586342
🌐 neonraptorbrewingco.com

Established in 2016 Neon Raptor is a small independent brewery that utilised spare capacity at neighbouring breweries. Production commenced in 2018 in a brand new 10-barrel plant in the Sneinton Market area of Nottingham, which also has a licence for a tap room. All beers are unfiltered, unfined and unpasteurised.

Neptune

Unit 1, Sefton Lane Industrial Estate, Maghull, Merseyside, L31 8BX
☎ (0151) 222 3908 🌐 neptunebrewery.com

⊛Neptune began brewing in 2015, upgrading from a one-barrel plant to six barrels. **RAIB V**

Riptide (OG 1038, ABV 3.7%)

Mermaids Purse (OG 1040, ABV 4%)

Shifting Sands (OG 1043, ABV 4.3%)

Triton (OG 1044, ABV 4.4%)

Mosaic (OG 1045, ABV 4.5%)

Abyss (OG 1058, ABV 5%)

On the Bounty (OG 1064, ABV 5.8%)
A chocolate and coconut stout.

Amarillo & Citra IPA (OG 1060, ABV 6.5%)

Nessie

Westoaks, Fort Wiliam Road, Fort Augustus, PH32 4BH

Set up in 2017 this nanobrewery markets to the tourist trade around Fort Augustus.

Nethergate SIBA

The Brewery, Rodbridge Corner, Suffolk, CO10 9HJ
☎ (01787) 377087 🌐 nethergate.co.uk

⊗Nethergate was formed in 1986 by Dick Burge and Ian Hornsey in Clare, Suffolk, and was one of the original UK microbreweries. It was sold in 2010, but in 2014 Dick Burge re-purchased the business and in 2017 a brand new brewery, visitor centre and shop was built at Rodbridge Corner, a couple of miles from its original home. ‼ ◆

Priory Mild (OG 1036, ABV 3.5%)
A 'black bitter' rather than a true mild. Strong roast and bitter tastes dominate throughout.

Venture (OG 1039, ABV 3.7%)
Light-tasting, sweetish and fruity session beer.

Umbel Ale (OG 1039, ABV 3.8%)
Pleasant, easy-drinking bitter, infused with coriander, which dominates.

Suffolk County Best Bitter (OG 1041, ABV 4%)
Dark-coloured bitter with roast grain tones off-setting biscuity malt and powerful hoppy, bitter notes.

Stour Valley Gold (ABV 4.2%)
A light and refreshing golden ale brewed using fragrant citrus hops. A floral aroma with a touch of spice early on and a mellow bitterness at the end.

Old Growler (OG 1051, ABV 5%)
Well-balanced porter in which roast grain is complemented by fruit and bubblegum.

Umbel Magna (OG 1051, ABV 5%)
Old Growler flavoured with coriander. The spice is less dominant than in Umbel Ale, with some of the weight and body of the beer coming through.

New Bristol

20a Wilson Street, Bristol, BS2 9HH ☎ 07837 976871 newbristolbrewery.co.uk

Brothers Noel and Tom have been brewing since 2013. Capacity has increased from five to 15 barrels in recently expanded premises, which now house the Bristol Brewery School. All beers are unfined, unfiltered and unpasteurised. ‼ ◆ RAIB

365 (OG 1041, ABV 4%)
Traditional bitter with malt aroma. Flavours balance the malt with toffee and hop bitterness leading to a bittersweet aftertaste.

Oolala (OG 1040, ABV 4.2%)
An amber-coloured beer balanced by sweet spicy notes with hints of citrus and herbs, and the zest of 60 lemons.

Beer Du Jour (OG 1046, ABV 4.6%)
A bittersweet, strong bitter with citrus fruit aromas and flavours which continue in the aftertaste. Unfined so may be hazy.

New Inn

New Inn, 112 Roberttown Lane, Roberttown, Liversedge, West Yorkshire, WF15 7NP ☎ (01924) 402069 thenewinnroberttown.com

Brewing commenced in 2012 using a half-barrel brew plant located in the cellar of the New Inn, Liversedge. The beer is produced in wood-clad vessels by Andrew Kenyon, the son of ex-brewer at the Riverhead Brewery, Joe Kenyon. ◆

New Lion SIBA

Station Road, Totnes, Devon, TQ9 5JR ☎ (01803) 226277 lioncraftbrewery.com

The original Lion Brewery closed in 1926 and was restarted in 2013 by four local business people. A five-barrel plant is used. Brewery supporters provide hops from a patchwork of hop gardens for annual green hop ale and a series of traditional Belgian-style beers are being re-created. Beer is distributed throughout South Devon. ◆ RAIB

Mane Event (OG 1039, ABV 3.8%)

TQ9 (OG 1042, ABV 4.2%)
A golden-coloured, refreshing ale with a hint of Earl Grey.

Totnes Stout (OG 1045, ABV 4.4%)
Full-bodied stout with roasted malts and some smoky chocolate and liquorice. Dry bitterness finishes.

Pandit IPA (OG 1046, ABV 4.9%)
A citrus and floral nose. These flavours are complemented on the palate by a well-defined, biscuity malt character.

Smokestack Lightning Porter (OG 1067, ABV 6.8%)
A rich, dark-coloured porter with a hint of smoke, chocolate, plums and liquorice.

New Plassey

See Magic Dragon

New River SIBA

Unit 47, Hoddesdon Industrial Centre, Pindar Road, Hoddesdon, Hertfordshire, EN11 0FF ☎ (01992) 446200 newriverbrewery.co.uk

New River commenced brewing in 2015 on a brand new 10-barrel plant. ◆

London Tap (OG 1038, ABV 3.8%)
A refreshing, hoppy pale ale with hints of toffee and light citrus. A dry finish.

Twin Spring (OG 1039, ABV 4%)

Riverbed Red (OG 1041, ABV 4.2%)

Five Inch Drop (OG 1044, ABV 4.6%)
A triple-hopped IPA with a toffee, malty aroma and a pine resin, fruit citrus flavour.

New Wharf SIBA

Hyde Farm, Marlow Road, Maidenhead, SL6 6PQ ☎ 07815 717251 newwharfbrewing.co.uk

A 20-barrel brewery set up in 2017 producing a range of cask-conditioned and KeyKeg beers, which are distributed across the Berkshire area. RAIB

Session (ABV 3.5%)
A session IPA with notes of citrus, pine and tropical fruit.

Pale (ABV 4.3%)
A light brown-coloured, fruity beer with a light finish.

Erin's (ABV 4.5%)
A full-bodied, American-style pale ale with tropical fruit flavours.

Voyage (ABV 5.5%)
A full-bodied, American-style beer with hints of caramel and chocolate, tinged with citrus and berry flavours.

Legends (ABV 5.8%)
An IPA with notes of fresh citrus, earthy pine and tropical fruit.

Transatlantic (ABV 6.3%)

A New England-style black IPA.

Breakfast Stout (ABV 7.5%)

DIPA (ABV 8.5%)

Newark

77 William Street, Newark, Nottinghamshire, NG24 1QU ☎ 07804 609917 🌐 newarkbrewery.co.uk

Established in 2012 on the site of a former maltings using an eight-barrel plant. The bulk of production is supplied to local pubs. Its brewery tap is the Ram in Castle Gate, Newark.

Best (OG 1038, ABV 3.8%)
Deep copper in colour with a biscuity malt nose. Sweet toffee dominates the palate with a long, fruity finish.

NPA (Newark Pale Ale) (OG 1039, ABV 3.8%)
Pale gold in colour, citrus lemon on the nose, leading to a fruity finish.

BLH4 (OG 1040, ABV 4%)

Norwegian Blue (OG 1040, ABV 4%)
Deep gold in colour. Grapefruit and citrus orange on the nose. Malty lemon on the palate with a long finish.

Winter Gold (OG 1040, ABV 4%)
A dry golden ale with bittersweet lemon citrus flavours.

Pure Gold (OG 1045, ABV 4.5%)
A rich gold colour with biscuit, burnt orange on the nose leading to a soft biscuit finish.

Summer Gold (OG 1045, ABV 4.5%)
Deep gold in colour with a strong, sweet citrus nose. The lime character and light malt balance produce a lasting finish.

Phoenix (OG 1048, ABV 4.8%)
Russet brown in colour, slight spice and roasted malt on the nose, with a fruity treacle, full-bodied finish.

5.5 (OG 1055, ABV 5.5%)
Deep, gold-coloured, strong ale. Honey on the nose with sweet soft fruits on the finish.

Newbridge

Unit 3, Tudor House, Moseley Road, Bilston, West Midlands, WV14 6JD ☎ 07970 456052 🌐 newbridgebrewery.co.uk

First established in 2014, the five-barrel plant incorporates six original Grundy cellar tanks. The brewery closes during the winter months and resumes production around March.

Little Fox (OG 1042, ABV 4.2%)

Solaris (OG 1045, ABV 4.5%)

Indian Empire (OG 1051, ABV 5.1%)

Newby Wyke SIBA

Unit 24, Limesquare Business Park, Alma Park Road, Grantham, Lincolnshire, NG31 9SN ☎ (01476) 565682 🌐 newbywyke.co.uk

The brewery is named after a Hull trawler skippered by brewer Rob March's grandfather. It started life in 1998 as a 2.5-barrel plant in a converted garage then moved to premises behind the Willoughby Arms, Little Bytham. In 2009 it moved back to Grantham. !! ♦

Banquo (OG 1036, ABV 3.8%)
A pale blonde ale with a full, hoppy taste and a long, fruity finish.

Orsino (OG 1037, ABV 4%)
Blonde ale with a bright, fruity citrus and mango taste moving to a soft citrus hop finish.

Comet (OG 1039, ABV 4.1%)
Single-hopped, amber-coloured ale. Slight malt undertones with a gooseberry citrus fruit finish.

Kingston Topaz (OG 1039, ABV 4.2%)
A single-hopped ale with floral undertones.

Black Beerd (OG 1040, ABV 4.3%)
Oat malt stout with a balanced malt palate and fruit undertones.

Bear Island (OG 1043, ABV 4.6%)
A blonde beer with a hoppy aroma and a crisp, dry finish.

White Squall (OG 1044, ABV 4.8%)
Blonde-hued with a hoppy aroma. Generous amounts of hop are well-supported by a solid malty undercurrent. An increasingly bittersweet tang makes itself known towards the finish.

Newcastle

Arch 2, Stepney Bank, Ouseburn, Newcastle upon Tyne, NE1 2NP ☎ 07446 011941 🌐 newcastlebrewingltd.co.uk

Mike and Leo Bell initially founded the brewery in the Quayside Development Centre in Ouseburn before moving to new premises under Byker Bridge. !! RAIB

Newtown

25 Victoria Street, Gosport, Hampshire, PO12 4TX ☎ (023) 9250 4294 🌐 newtownbrewery.co.uk

Brewing commenced in 2016 in this nanobrewery with just a half-barrel plant, although the brewer has had many years previous experience of homebrewing. Full mash beers are produced on demand for local pubs and CAMRA beer festivals.

Nightjar SIBA

2 Richmond House, Caldene Business Park, Mytholmroyd, West Yorkshire, HX7 5QL ☎ 07412 008221 🌐 nightjarbrew.co.uk

Nightjar Brew Co is the new name for Slightly Foxed Brewery, which was established in 2011. The 10-barrel brewery is located in an industrial building in Mytholmroyd and supplies around 90 free trade outlets, mainly in Yorkshire and Lancashire. Its extensive beer swaps with other breweries means that its beers can also be found in more distant parts of the country. ♦

Hebden Hop (OG 1039, ABV 3.9%)

Haka Pale (OG 1040, ABV 4%)
A pale ale with gooseberry and fresh apple notes.

Klondike (OG 1042, ABV 4.2%)
A golden session bitter with fresh fruit notes.

Cosmonaut (OG 1044, ABV 4.4%)
A velvety and smooth milk oatmeal Irish-style stout.

Kalifornia (OG 1044, ABV 4.4%)
A West Coast-style pale ale with tropical fruit notes.

Bollywood IPA (OG 1050, ABV 5%)
A classic, punchy and fresh IPA.

Knievel (OG 1064, ABV 6.4%)
A rich, golden-coloured ale with rhubarb and custard and vanilla notes.

Supernova (OG 1069, ABV 6.9%)
A dark-coloured, rich, chocolate milk stout with espresso and dark chocolate flavours.

Nine Standards

See Settle

Nirvana SIBA

Unit T6, Leyton Industrial Village, Argall Avenue, Leyton, London, E10 7QP
☎ (020) 3417 5580 🌐 nirvanabrewer.com

Established in 2017 producing a range of non-alcoholic beers. No real ale.

No. 18 Yard Brewhouse

See Shepherd Neame

No Frills Joe (NEW)

50 Wakefield Road, Greenhithe, Kent, DA9 9JE
☎ 07516 725577

⊗ No Frills Joe is a two-barrel microbrewery spread over an impressive 16m squared, making it one of the smallest breweries in the UK. All beers are produced unpasteurised, unfiltered and unfined. A small on-site taproom is available (restricted opening hours). RAIB V

London Pale Ale (ABV 3.9%)
A well-balanced pale ale with earthy, herbal and spicy hop notes and citrus, apricot and peach aromas and flavours.

Amber Ale (ABV 5%)
Amber-coloured ale with hints of caramel and honey.

Hefeweizen (ABV 5.1%)
German-style wheat beer. Quite sweet with banana and cloves flavours.

American IPA (ABV 6%)
A hoppy IPA with grapefruit, citrus aromas and flavours.

Oatmeal Stout (ABV 7.4%)
A dark-coloured, roasty, chocolaty and coffee stout. Rich, smooth and warming.

Nobby's SIBA

Unit 2, Cottingham Way, Thrapston, Northamptonshire, NN14 4PL
☎ (01832) 730800 🌐 nobbysbrewery.co.uk

Paul 'Nobby' Mulliner started commercial brewing in 2004 on a 2.5-barrel plant at the rear of the Alexandra Arms, Kettering. The brewery relocated to Guilsborough in 2007 and again in 2014 to larger premises in Thrapston. Brewing now takes place on a 12-barrel plant. ‼ ♦ RAIB

Claridges Crystal (OG 1036, ABV 3.6%)
A pale ale, crisp and fresh with a slightly citrus hop finish.

The Guzzler (OG 1036, ABV 3.6%)
An easy-drinking, malty, auburn-coloured ale with a gentle hop finish.

Best (OG 1037, ABV 3.8%)
A session ale with an excellent hop finish.

Goldings (OG 1041, ABV 4%)
A full-bodied, well-balanced golden ale with a traditional hop finish.

Swift Nick (OG 1042, ABV 4.2%)

Plum Porter (OG 1044, ABV 4.4%)
A dark brown-coloured porter with bitterness from hops and plums.

Tow'd Navigation (OG 1067, ABV 6.1%)
Dark-coloured, strong ale. Warming with rich malt and hops.

Nomadic

c/o 29 Skelton Terrace, Leeds, West Yorkshire, LS9 9ES ☎ 07868 345228
✉ nomadicbeers@gmail.com

Nomadic Beers was established in 2017 by Katie Marriott and Ross Nicholson. Beers are produced using spare capacity at other breweries.

Pale (OG 1035, ABV 3.8%)

Strider (ABV 4.4%)

Bandit (ABV 4.8%)

Nook SIBA

Riverside, 7b Victoria Square, Holmfirth, West Yorkshire, HD9 2DN
☎ (01484) 682373 🌐 thenookbrewhouse.co.uk

The Nook Brewhouse is built on the foundations of a previous brewhouse dating back to 1754, next to the River Ribble. Two brewery taps are supplied, one with a restaurant whose dishes are matched with the beer brewed on site. A history room with renovated archives dating back to the 1700s and a brewery shop are planned. ‼

Norfolk Brewhouse SIBA

Moon Gazer Barn, Harvest Lane, Hindringham, Norfolk, NR21 0PW
☎ (01328) 878495 🌐 norfolkbrewhouse.co.uk

⊗ Brewing began in 2012 using a 10-barrel plant. The brewery is owned and run by Rachel and David Holliday. Chalk-filtered water is used from the brewery's own well. ‼ ♦

Moon Gazer Amber Ale (OG 1040, ABV 4%)
Smooth and easy drinking with a sweet malty start. Full bodied with a growing hoppy bitterness.

Moon Gazer Golden Ale (OG 1040, ABV 4%)
Orange peel and honey nose. Marmalade intro bolstered by well defined bitterness. Initial sweetness fades into a sharp, astringent bitterness.

Moon Gazer Ruby Ale (OG 1040, ABV 4%)
Roasty dark fruit nose flows through into the first taste. Increasing malt and caramel. Smooth grainy mouthfeel. Short bitter finish.

Moon Gazer Dark Mild (OG 1051, ABV 4.9%)
Savoury smoky bacon character throughout. Bittersweet dark chocolate nuances give depth. A

THE BREWERIES

smooth and creamy finish with hints of blackcurrant.

Moon Gazer Gold IPA (OG 1050, ABV 5%) ◆
Full bodied with a rich tropical fruit aroma. Oranges in the taste, mixing well with a piquant hoppy bitterness.

North SIBA

Unit 6, Taverner's Walk Estate, Sheepscar Grove, Leeds, West Yorkshire, LS7 1AH
☎ (0113) 345 3290 🌐 northbrewing.com

Brewing began in 2015, originally supplying the North Bar group of bars in Leeds. It has since grown and supplies other outlets. An on-site tap is open at weekends. !! ◆

Prototype (ABV 3.8%) ◆
Light amber-coloured, hoppy beer with an ever present bitterness.

North Blyth

North Blyth Bar & Brewery, Worsdell Street, Blyth, NE24 1SD
☎ (01670) 822012 ☎ 07711 725186
🌐 northblyth.com

Previously known as Northumberland, brewing began in 1996 in Ashington using a five-barrel plant. Relocation and expansion mean that the brewery now uses a 10-barrel plant. Brewing is currently suspended. !! ◆

North Cotswold SIBA

Unit 3, Ditchford Farm, Stretton-on-Fosse, Warwickshire, GL56 9RD
☎ (01608) 663947 🌐 northcotswoldbrewery.co.uk

North Cotswold started in 1999 as a 2.5-barrel plant, which was upgraded in 2000 to 10 barrels. Beers are also contract brewed for Yubberton Brewing Co. ◆ RAIB

Windrush Ale (OG 1036, ABV 3.6%)
A thirst-quenching, amber-coloured session bitter with a malty, slightly sweet palate.

Fosseway Flanker (OG 1038, ABV 3.8%)
A refreshing, pale-coloured, hoppy session ale.

Moreton Mild (OG 1038, ABV 3.8%)
A classic dark mild with a nutty palate.

Cotswold Best (OG 1040, ABV 4%)

Shagweaver (OG 1045, ABV 4.5%)

Hung, Drawn 'n' Portered (OG 1050, ABV 5%)
Strong, dark-coloured porter with a malty finish.

North Riding (Brewery)

Unit 9, Betton Business Park, Racecourse Road, East Ayton, Scarborough, North Yorkshire, YO13 9HD
☎ (01723) 864845 ☎ 07930 843868
🌐 northridingbrewery.com

Having outgrown the brewpub in Scarborough, Stuart Neilson established a 10-barrel brewery in East Alton on the outskirts of Scarborough in 2015. Concentrating on hop-forward beers, distribution is throughout Yorkshire and further afield. ◆ RAIB

USA Session IPA (OG 1037, ABV 3.8%)

Cascade Pale Ale (OG 1040, ABV 4%)
A hoppy pale ale with citrus notes.

Mosaic Pale Ale (OG 1042, ABV 4.3%)
A pale ale with blueberry and citrus flavours.

Citra Pale Ale (OG 1043, ABV 4.5%)
Easy-drinking premium pale ale with a grapefruit, mango and lemon taste and aroma.

North Riding (Brewpub)

North Marine Road, Scarborough, North Yorkshire, YO12 7HU
☎ (01723) 370004 🌐 northridingbrewpub.com

Brewing commenced in 2011 using a two-barrel plant situated in the cellar of the pub, which is now brewing to capacity with three fermenting vessels. ◆

North Yorkshire SIBA

Unit 7, South Gare Court, Tod Point Road, Warrenby, North Yorkshire, TS10 5BN
☎ (01642) 497298 ✉ sales@nybrewery.co.uk

Founded in Middlesbrough in 1989 the brewery moved to Pinchinthorpe Hall, Guisborough in 1998. In 2017, following the purchase of the brewery, the new owner moved the entire operation to new premises on an industrial estate in Warrenby near Redcar, North Yorkshire. ◆ RAIB

Northern Navigator (OG 1036, ABV 3.6%)
A chestnut-coloured, nutty session ale. Medium-bodied and quite hoppy.

Old Jacks Tipple (OG 1038, ABV 3.8%)

Temptation (OG 1038, ABV 3.8%)
A refreshing beer with pleasant bitterness. A citrus and grapefruit nose.

Beckwatter (OG 1040, ABV 4%)
Dark ruby-coloured ale with balanced notes of hops and malt. Full-bodied with a thick, creamy head.

Honey Bunny (OG 1042, ABV 4.2%)
A golden bitter with a hoppy finish. Hints of honey.

NYPA (OG 1046, ABV 4.6%)
An English IPA with an earthy, grassy character.

Flying Herbert (OG 1047, ABV 4.7%)
Smooth, full-flavoured premium bitter with a malty, fruity and dry finish.

Valhalla (OG 1055, ABV 5.5%)
Strong, brown-coloured beer with plenty of hops. A subtle malt taste to finish.

Northbound SIBA

Campsie Industrial Estate, McLean Road, Eglinton, Derry, BT47 3XX 🌐 northboundbrewery.com

Established in 2015, Northbound produce a range of bottle-conditioned beers named after their measurement of bitterness (IBUs). RAIB

Northdown (NEW)

Unit J1C/A, Channel Road, Westwood Industrial Estate, Margate, Kent, CT9 4JS ☎ 07791 441219
🌐 northdownbrewery.co.uk

Northdown began brewing in 2018 using a seven-barrel plant. It is run by Jonny and Katie Spanjar and takes its name from their original intention to run out of the Northdown area of

Margate. The origins of a Northdown brewery date back to the 1600s. ‼ ♦ RAIB

Pale Ale Mary (OG 1040, ABV 4%)
A pale ale with hints of citrus.

Papworth Victory Best Bitter (OG 1046, ABV 4.6%)
A well-rounded mouthfeel with hints of raisin.

HE-BRU IPA (OG 1050.2, ABV 4.9%)
An American-style IPA with hints of pineapple, mango and citrus.

Muggy Porter (OG 1054, ABV 5%)
A dark-coloured, full-bodied, London-style oatmeal porter with hints of coconut.

Northern Alchemy

The Lab, Cumberland Arms, St James Street, Newcastle upon Tyne, NE6 1LD ☎ 07834 386333
wearenorthernalchemy.com

Brewing began in 2014. Production is mostly keg but some cask-conditioned beer is available.

Northern Monk SIBA

The Old Flax Store, Marshalls Mill, Holbeck, Leeds, West Yorkshire, LS11 9YJ
☎ (0113) 243 6430 northernmonkbrewco.com

Based in a Grade II-listed mill building in the centre of Leeds, Northern Monk started brewing as cuckoo brewers in 2013 and set up at its present site in 2014 using a 10-barrel plant. Although most of production is keg, a small amount is available cask-conditioned.

True North (OG 1037, ABV 3.7%)
Hops dominate this light yellow-coloured beer, but there is a bitterness which builds in strength then lingers in the finish.

Northern Monkey SIBA

The Link, Bow Street, Bolton, BL1 2EQ ☎ 07737 125629 northernmonkeybrew.co.uk

Ryan Bailey and Liam Covey were homebrewers for a number of years before setting up Northern Monkey Brew Co in 2016 using a one-barrel plant. Expansion means that a 2.5-barrel plant is now used. The local area and beer festivals are supplied. ♦

The Last Drop (ABV 3.6%)
A classic pale ale, triple-hopped with English hops.

Wilhelmina (ABV 3.8%)
A pale ale with subtle hints of citrus and ginger.

Winter Hill (ABV 3.8%)
A golden ale with a caramel flavour and fruity finish.

Reenys Beans (ABV 4%)
A sweet and creamy coffee mild.

Sheephouse (ABV 4.2%)
A pale ale with subtle peach and lime flavours followed by a hoppy finish.

Dirty Harry (ABV 4.5%)
A rich and malty rye ale.

Funky Monkey (ABV 5.5%)
A hoppy, American-style IPA.

Underdog (ABV 6%)
A chocolate treacle porter.

Northern Whisper

Hill End Mill, Hill End Lane, Cloughfold, Lancashire, BB4 7RN
☎ (01706) 230082
northernwhisperbrewingco.co.uk

Brewing began in 2017.

Blighty (ABV 3.8%)

Oppenchops (ABV 4%)

Yammerhouse (ABV 4.5%)

Beltie (ABV 4.8%)

Northumberland

See North Blyth

Norton

Norton Priory, Tudor Road, Manor Park, Runcorn, Cheshire, WA7 1SX
☎ (01928) 716971 ☎ 07767 354674
nortonbrewing.com

Situated within the grounds of Norton Priory, the brewery was created as a social enterprise by Halton Borough Council to provide employment opportunities for people with learning disabilities, autism and other disabilities. It opened in 2011 with a 2.5-barrel plant.

Noss Beer Works SIBA

Unit 6, Ash Court, Pennant Way, Lee Mill, Devon, PL21 9GE ☎ 07977 479634 nossbeerworks.co.uk

Noss Beer Works, based in Lee Mill, was formed in 2012 using a six-barrel plant. The beers are made from only the finest locally sourced hops and malts. ‼ RAIB

Black Rock (ABV 4%)
Black IPA with liquorice, citrus and caramel notes. Slightly bitter aftertaste.

Church Ledge (OG 1040, ABV 4%)
Bitter dominated by hops and fruit throughout. Hoppy and citrus, slight caramel balances bitter dryness. Slight kick at the end.

Mew Stone (OG 1043, ABV 4.3%)

Ebb Rock (OG 1049, ABV 4.9%)

Nottingham SIBA

Plough Inn, 17 St Peter's Street, Radford, Nottingham, NG7 3EN
☎ (0115) 942 2649 ☎ 07815 073447
nottinghambrewery.co.uk

The former owners of the Bramcote and Castle Rock Breweries re-established the Nottingham Brewery in 2000 in a purpose-built brewhouse behind the Plough Inn. Philip Darby and Niven Balfour set out to revive the brands of the original Nottingham Brewery, closed by Whitbread in the 1950s. Within the LocAle ethos, beers are supplied widely to the local trade including the brewery tap house, the Plough Inn, and its other tied house the Frame Breakers, Ruddington. ‼

Rock Ale Bitter Beer (OG 1038, ABV 3.8%)
A pale-coloured and bitter, thirst-quenching, hoppy beer with a dry finish.

Rock Ale Mild Beer (OG 1038, ABV 3.8%)
A reddish-black-coloured malty mild with some refreshing bitterness in the finish.

Legend (OG 1040, ABV 4%)
A fruity and malty pale brown-coloured bitter with a touch of sweetness and bitterness.

Extra Pale Ale (OG 1042, ABV 4.2%)
A hoppy and fruity golden ale with a hint of sweetness and a long-lasting bitter finish.

Broadway Reel Ale (OG 1044, ABV 4.4%)
Hoppy golden ale with a lingering bitter finish.

Dreadnought (OG 1045, ABV 4.5%)
Well-balanced best bitter. Blend of malt and hops give a rounded, fruity finish.

Bullion (OG 1047, ABV 4.7%)
A refreshing premium golden ale. Brewed with a single malt variety, it is triple-hopped and exceptionally bitter.

Supreme (OG 1052, ABV 5.2%)
A strong, amber-coloured, fruity ale. A touch of malt in the taste is followed by a sweet and slightly hoppy finish.

Brewed for the Trent Bridge Inn, Nottingham:

Trent Bridge Inn Ale (OG 1038, ABV 3.8%)

Nutbrook

6 Hallam Way, West Hallam, Derbyshire, DE7 6LA
☎ 0800 458 2460 nutbrookbrewery.com

Nutbrook was established in 2007. In addition to a regular range, special beers are brewed to order for domestic and corporate clients. The brewery's unique 'Design-a-Beer' system allows customers to design and brew their own beer. On Saturdays cask-conditioned beer is sold at Oakfield Farm, Stanley Common. !! RAIB

The Mild Side (OG 1036, ABV 3.6%)
A golden-coloured mild with a traditional malt taste and fruit tones.

Responsibly (OG 1041, ABV 4%)
A light bronze-coloured, crisp beer with a fruity flavour.

Banter (OG 1040.8, ABV 4.5%)
A light golden yellow-coloured beer with a traditional hoppy taste and floral notes.

Daft Apeth (OG 1050, ABV 4.5%)
A pale yellow-coloured beer with undertones from the addition of maize.

More (OG 1047, ABV 4.8%)
Dark-coloured beer with a subtle red tint, burnt roasted barley taste and sweet bitterness.

Black Beauty (OG 1054, ABV 5%)
A traditional milk stout with undertones of chocolate, honey and nuts.

The Perfect Fifth (OG 1047.8, ABV 5%)
A strong pale ale with honey tones.

Moderation (OG 1057, ABV 5.5%)
A golden ale with subtle hop flavours and medium bitterness.

O'Brien

Unit 13, Enderby Road Industrial Estate, Whetstone, Leicestershire, LE8 6HZ
☎ (0116) 286 3166 dobrienbrewery.co.uk

D. O'Brien commenced brewing in 2016 using a four-barrel plant. One regular beer is produced along with a rotating selection of seasonal and one-off brews. ♦

Rebel Porter (OG 1040, ABV 4%)
Roast malt tastes infused with spicy hops.

O'Connor

12 Lime Road, Faughanvale, Greysteel, BT47 3EH
☎ 07748 004065 oconnorbrewing.com

Brewing began in 2013. No real ale.

Oakham SIBA

2 Maxwell Road, Woodston, Peterborough, Cambridgeshire, PE2 7JB
☎ (01733) 370500 oakhamales.com

The brewery started in 1993 in Oakham, Rutland, and moved to Peterborough in 1998. The brewery's main production site is a 75-barrel plant. An additional six-barrel plant is located at its city-centre brewpub, which makes special and one-off brews. Around 350 outlets are supplied and four pubs are owned. !! ♦ RAIB

JHB (OG 1038, ABV 3.8%)
Straw-coloured golden ale dominated by citrus hop character throughout. Long, dry, slightly astringent finish.

Inferno (OG 1039, ABV 4%)
The citrus hop character of this straw-coloured brew begins on the nose and builds in intensity on the palate. Clean, dry, citrus finish.

Citra (OG 1042, ABV 4.2%)
Refreshing grapefruit and peach aroma and flavour characterise this golden ale. Bittersweet palate gives way to a long, dry aftertaste.

Scarlet Macaw (OG 1043, ABV 4.4%)
Tart gooseberry and soft peach on the nose and intense bitter finish.

Bishops Farewell (OG 1046, ABV 4.6%)
Powerfully citrus, the hops and fruit on the aroma of this golden/yellow-coloured beer become bittersweet on the palate. Zesty citrus aftertaste.

Oaks SIBA

Unit 6, Stanney Mill Industrial Estate, Dutton Green, Ellesmere Port, Cheshire, CH2 4SA ☎ 07890 567582

Cheshire Brew Brothers began brewing in 2013 and was taken into new ownership in 2017. The new proprietors renamed the brewery and are revising the beer range, which will include a series of experimental brews. The beers can be found in free and tied trade across North-west England and West Yorkshire. ♦

Chester Gold (ABV 3.6%)
A fruity, hoppy bitter with a pleasant sweet finish.

Earls Eye Amber (ABV 3.8%)
A smooth beer with balanced malt characteristics.

Cascade Pale (ABV 4%)

Delamere Blonde (ABV 4%)

Oakwood

Northfield Crescent, Wells-next-the-Sea, Norfolk, NR23 1LP ☎ 07512 111211 oakwoodbrewery.com

Oakwood was established in 2015. After producing beers on a small scale from home the brewer decided to turn his hobby into a full-time job. Barley is locally-grown by Teddy Maufe at Branthill Farm on the Holkham Estate in Norfolk. RAIB

Oban Bay

See Argyll

Odcombe

Masons Arms, 41 Lower Odcombe, Odcombe, Somerset, BA22 8TX
☎ (01935) 862591 masonsarmsodcombe.co.uk

Odcombe opened in 2000, but closed a few years later. It re-opened in 2005 with assistance from Shepherd Neame (qv). Brewing takes place once a week and beers are available only in the Masons Arms. ‼ ♦ RAIB

Oddly

Unit 12, Platt's Eyot, Lower Sunbury Road, Hampton, TW12 2HF
☎ (020) 3741 7717 oddlybeer.com

A one man operation located on an island in the River Thames, Oddly started brewing in 2017 using a five-barrel plant. The brewery occupies a building that was formerly part of the Thornycroft works, which produced motor torpedo boats and RAF rescue launches during WWII. ‼ RAIB

Odyssey

Brockhampton Brewery, Oast House Barn, Whitbourne, Herefordshire, WR6 5SH
☎ (01885) 483496 ☎ 07918 553152
odysseybrewco.com/

This six-barrel brewery was bought in 2014 by Alison and Mitchell Evans, who also own the Beer in Hand in Hereford. The original building, a restored barn on a National Trust estate, has been retained.

Syren (OG 1039, ABV 3.9%)

Mo' Citra (OG 1040, ABV 4%)

Little India Pale Ale (OG 1045, ABV 4.5%)

Latte Stout (OG 1062, ABV 5.4%)

Nirvana (OG 1052, ABV 5.4%)

31st State (OG 1049, ABV 5.8%)

Crowd Control (OG 1060, ABV 6%)

Cookie Monster (OG 1045, ABV 6.5%)
A chocolate raisin, cinnamon and oatmeal cookie stout.

Offa's Dyke

Chapel Lane, Trefonen, Shropshire, SY10 9DX
☎ (01691) 656889 trefonen.org/offas-dyke-brewery.html

Established in 2007, the brewery and adjoining pub straddle the old England/Wales border, Offa's Dyke. The Olde Vaults and adjacent Ironworks in Oswestry serve as alternative brewery taps. ‼

Ogwen

5 Rhes Ogwen, Bethesda, LL57 3AY ☎ 07545 684752
cwrwogwen.cymru

The first brewery in the Ogwen Valley for over a century. Beers are named after characters from Welsh folklore.

Cwrw Caradog (OG 1039, ABV 3.9%)

Okell's SIBA

Kewaigue, Douglas, Isle of Man, IM2 1QG
☎ (01624) 699400 okells.co.uk

Founded in 1874 by Dr Okell this is the main brewery on the island and moved in 1994 to a new, purpose-built plant at Kewaigue. All the beers are produced under the Manx Brewers' Act. ‼ ♦

MPA (Manx Pale Ale) (OG 1036, ABV 3.6%)
A golden-coloured, fruity session bitter with background sweetness and a rising hoppy finish.

Bitter (OG 1035, ABV 3.7%)
A gently bittered, sweet beer with some fruit and malt flavours.

Dr Okell's IPA (OG 1044, ABV 4.5%)
A clean, fruity, sweetish bitter with an alcoholic bite.

Old Cannon

86 Cannon Street, Bury St Edmunds, Suffolk, IP33 1JR
☎ (01284) 768769 oldcannonbrewery.co.uk

The St Edmunds Head pub opened in 1845 with its own brewery. Brewing ceased in 1917, and Greene King closed the pub in 1995. It re-opened in 1999 as the Old Cannon Brewery complete with a unique state-of-the-art brewery housed in the bar area. A growing number of local outlets are supplied. ‼ ♦

Best Bitter (OG 1037, ABV 3.8%)
Rich, hoppy aroma and bitterness dominate throughout with just a hint of sweetness in the aftertaste.

Elveden IPA (OG 1038, ABV 3.9%)

Hornblower (OG 1038, ABV 4%)

Black Pig (OG 1042, ABV 4.2%)

Blonde Bombshell (OG 1042, ABV 4.2%)
Subtle citrus flavours with a pleasant bitterness and astringency that grows on the aftertaste. Hoppy, well-balanced and quaffable.

Gunner's Daughter (OG 1052, ABV 5.5%)
A well-balanced strong ale with a complexity of hop, fruit, sweetness and bitterness in the flavour, and a lingering hoppy, bitter aftertaste.

Old Chimneys

Hopton End Farm, Church Road, Market Weston, Suffolk, IP22 2NX
☎ (01359) 221013 oldchimneysbrewery.com

Old Chimneys opened in 1995, moving to a converted farm building in 2001. Some of the beers are named after rare species found nearby. ‼ ♦ RAIB

Military Mild (OG 1035, ABV 3.3%)

A rich, dark mild with good body for its gravity. Sweetish toffee and light roast bitterness dominate, leading to a dry aftertaste.

Great Raft Bitter (OG 1039, ABV 4%)
Pale copper-coloured bitter bursting with fruit. Malt and hops add to the sweetish, fruity flavour, which is rounded off with hoppy bitterness in the aftertaste.

Black Rat Stout (OG 1048, ABV 4.4%)
Roast malt and coffee flavours with body and sweetness from added lactose.

Golden Pheasant (OG 1044, ABV 4.5%)
Pale-coloured, dry bitter with citrus, apple and malt balanced with robust hop bitterness.

Arrowhead (OG 1047, ABV 4.8%)
A premium dark ruby-coloured ale with smooth, malty tones.

Old Cross

Old Cross Tavern, 8 St Andrew Street, Hertford, SG14 1JA
☎ (01992) 583133

The microbrewery was set up in 2008 and is located within the pub. Owner Nigel Beviss brews solely for the Old Cross Tavern. A range of beers is produced during the year including beers brewed with single variety hops. One of these is usually available at the bar. ♦

Old Dairy SIBA

Tenterden Station Estate, Station Road, Tenterden, Kent, TN30 6HE
☎ (01580) 763867 olddairybrewery.com

Old Dairy was founded in 2009. It relocated from Rolvenden in 2014 to larger premises near the Kent & East Sussex Railway in Tenterden in order to increase capacity. !! ♦ RAIB

Red Top (OG 1038, ABV 3.8%)
A sweetish, copper-coloured bitter with hints of caramel and a subtle hop character.

Uber Brew (OG 1038, ABV 3.8%)
Full-bodied, hoppy pale ale with a strong floral aroma.

Copper Top (OG 1041, ABV 4.1%)

Gold Top (OG 1043, ABV 4.3%)
A well-balanced golden ale with a good blend of malt and hops followed by a long, bittersweet finish.

Blue Top (OG 1048, ABV 4.8%)
Rich and full bodied, this pale brown-coloured ale has a long, bittersweet finish and a hint of aroma hop.

Snow Top (OG 1060, ABV 6%)

Old Inn

Old Inn, Flowerdale Glen, Gairloch, IV21 2BD
☎ (01445) 712006 theoldinn.net

Brewing began in 2010 using a 150-litre plant. ♦

Old Laxey

Shore Hotel Brew Pub, Old Laxey, Isle of Man, IM4 7DA
☎ (01624) 863214 shorehotel.im

Beer brewed on the Isle of Man is brewed to a strict Beer Purity Act. Additives are not permitted to extend shelf life, nor are chemicals allowed to assist with head retention. Old Laxey's beer is sold mostly through the adjacent Shore Hotel. !!

Old Luxters

Old Luxters Vineyard, Dudley Lane, Hambleden, Buckinghamshire, RG9 6JW
☎ (01491) 638330 chilternvalley.co.uk

Situated in a 17th-century barn beside the Chiltern Valley Vineyard, Old Luxters is a traditional brewery established in 1990 and was awarded a Royal Warrant of Appointment in 2007. The core range is bottle-conditioned beers. !! ♦ RAIB

Old Market

See Llŷn

Old Mill SIBA

Mill Street, Snaith, East Yorkshire, DN14 9HU
☎ (01405) 861813 oldmillbrewery.co.uk

Opened in 1983 in a 200-year-old former malt kiln and corn mill, the brew-length is 60 barrels. The brewery is building a tied estate, now standing at 18 houses. Beers can be found nationwide through wholesalers and around 80 free trade outlets are supplied direct. !! ♦

Traditional Mild (OG 1034, ABV 3.4%)
A satisfying roast malt flavour dominates this easy-drinking, quality dark mild.

Traditional Bitter (OG 1038.5, ABV 3.8%)
A malty nose is carried through to the initial flavour. Bitterness runs throughout.

Blonde Bombshell (OG 1042, ABV 4%)
An easy-drinking, straw-coloured beer with delicate and refreshing fruity flavours.

Yorkshire Elixir (ABV 4%)

Red Goose (OG 1042, ABV 4.2%)
A rich, ruby-coloured, malty beer.

Old Curiosity (OG 1044.5, ABV 4.5%)
Slightly sweet, amber-coloured brew, malty to start. Malt flavours all the way through.

Bullion (OG 1047.5, ABV 4.7%)
The malty and hoppy aroma is followed by a neat mix of hop and fruit tastes within an enveloping maltiness. Dark brown/amber in colour.

Old Pie Factory SIBA

4 Montague Road, Warwick, CV34 5LW ☎ 07816 413026 josh@oldpiefactorybrewery.co.uk

Brewing began in 2011 using a 5.5-barrel plant and is a joint venture between Underwood Wines, Stratford upon Avon, and the Case is Altered, Five Ways.

Case Bitter (OG 1036, ABV 3.9%)

Pie in the Sky (OG 1042, ABV 4.1%)

Humble Pie (OG 1045, ABV 4.2%)

I Pie A (OG 1040.3, ABV 4.5%)

American Pie (OG 1051, ABV 5.5%)

Old Sawley SIBA

White Lion, 352a Tamworth Road, Sawley, Derbyshire, NG10 3AT ☎ 07722 311209 oldsawley.com

Established in 2013, initially on a 0.5-barrel plant, upgraded to a 10-barrel plant in 2016. Beers are available in the White Lion, at Midlands beer festivals and in outlets across the East Midlands. ‼ ♦

Figaro (OG 1038.5, ABV 4%)
Pale ale with a tropical fruit taste and floral aroma.

Jobber (OG 1042, ABV 4.2%)
Traditional amber-coloured bitter with a good balance of malt and hops to give a smooth, easy-drinking session ale.

Little Jack (OG 1043, ABV 4.3%)
Crisp, refreshing pale ale with a fruity citrus taste from a unique blend of hops.

Tollbridge Porter (OG 1049, ABV 4.5%)
A dark-coloured porter with smooth, subtle flavours of chocolate, coffee and vanilla.

Old School SIBA

Holly Bank Barn, Crag Road, Warton, Lancashire, LA5 9PL ☎ (01524) 740888 ☎ 07515 376700 oldschoolbrewery.co.uk

A 12-barrel brewery, founded in 2012, located in a renovated 400-year-old former school outbuilding overlooking the picturesque village of Warton. Beer is mainly sold to free houses within a 40-mile radius. ‼♦

Hopscotch (OG 1037, ABV 3.7%)
Initially hoppy, astringency builds in this satisfying beer, ending with a bitter finish.

Textbook (OG 1039, ABV 3.9%)

Detention (OG 1041, ABV 4.1%)
Light, malty bitter, sweetish middle with a gentle finish.

Headmaster (OG 1045, ABV 4.5%)
A dark-coloured, strong best bitter. It mixes a complex, malty flavour with a blackcurrant aroma, leaving a subtle, sweet, nutty aftertaste.

Old Spot SIBA

Manor Farm, Station Road, Cullingworth, West Yorkshire, BD13 5HN ☎ (01535) 691144 oldspotbrewery.co.uk

Old Spot, named after the owner's sheepdog, started brewing in 2005. The beers are available locally with the acting brewery tap, the George Hotel in Cullingworth, being the main outlet. ‼♦

Light but Dark (OG 1043, ABV 4%)
Chestnut-coloured bitter with a slight malty taste and pleasant bitter finish. An ideal session beer.

Spot Light (OG 1040, ABV 4.2%)
This smooth-drinking golden ale has a slightly fruity, hoppy aroma leading to a well-balanced fruit hop flavour with hints of pineapple and a long, bittersweet finish.

Inn-Spired (OG 1043, ABV 4.3%)
Light-coloured bitter with a light, hoppy taste and a slight, fruity finish.

OSB (OG 1042, ABV 4.5%)
A golden-coloured, full-bodied bitter.

Spot O'Bother (OG 1060, ABV 5.5%)
Complex porter with a chocolate ice cream taste and slight liquorice bitterness to finish.

Old Street

Arch 11, Gales Gardens, Bethnal Green Road, Bethnal Green, London, E2 0EJ oldstreet.beer

Originally situated in the basement of the Queen's Head pub, brewing began in 2014. In 2018 the brewery moved to a railway arch in Bethnal Green with an on-site taproom. Beer is mainly bottled and keg.

Old Tree

Old Tree, Yachtwerks, 28-29 Richmond Place, Brighton, East Sussex, BN2 9NA ☎ 07413 064346 oldtree.house

A co-operative based in Brighton producing a unique range of small-batch, probiotic and celebration drinks. It supplies its own zero-waste Silo restaurant. Brewing and gardening are combined and a production process is used that contributes to land regeneration. RAIB

Old Vault (NEW)

Old Vault, 12 Market Place, Thorne, South Yorkshire, DN8 5DP ☎ 07809 471355

Production began in 2017. The brewing equipment is in a room at the back of the Old Vault Brewery & Tap micropub in Thorne.

Old Worthy

Broughton, ML12 6HQ ☎ 07955 113083 oldworthybeer.co.uk

Brewing takes place on a 10-barrel plant. The beers are designed to be drunk as a 'half 'n' half', a beer served with a dram of whisky on the side. The malt used is sourced from Scottish whisky distilleries. 200 outlets are supplied.

Wee XP (OG 1045, ABV 4.4%)

Wee Blonde (OG 1048, ABV 4.7%)

The Old Worthy (OG 1050, ABV 5%)

Wild Bill's Aces & Eights (OG 1050, ABV 5%)

A Midnight Caper (OG 1050, ABV 5.5%)

Mighty XP (OG 1060, ABV 6%)

Olde Potting Shed

See TOPS

Olde Swan

Old Swan, 89 Halesowen Road, Netherton, West Midlands, DY2 9PY ☎ (01384) 253075

A famous brewpub best known as Ma Pardoe's after the matriarch who ruled it for years. The pub has been licensed since 1835 and the present brewery and pub were built in 1863. Brewing continued until 1988 and restarted in 2001. ‼♦

THE BREWERIES

Oldershaw SIBA

Heath Lane, Barkston Heath, Lincolnshire, NG32 2DE
☎ (01476) 572135 🌐 oldershawbrewery.com

Oldershaw Brewery has been brewing since 1997. Owned and run by brewster Kathy Britton, it is a nine-barrel plant and brews in the region of 500,000 pints a year. The brewery produces around 20 different beers of varying styles. Beers branded as Home Ales are brewed under contract for Brands Reunited. !! ♦

Heavenly Blonde (OG 1038, ABV 3.8%)
A blonde session beer with zesty tropical fruit flavours and a crisp, dry finish.

Newton's Drop (OG 1041, ABV 4.1%)
Balanced malt and hops but with a strong bitter, lingering taste in this mid-brown-coloured beer.

Grantham Stout (OG 1043, ABV 4.3%)
Dark brown in colour and smooth with rich roast malt notes and warming, fruity, complex flavours.

Mosaic Blonde (OG 1041, ABV 4.3%)
A lager-style beer, powerfully citrus with tropical flavours.

American Hopquad IPA (ABV 4.5%)
A fresh IPA with sharp citrus and herbal notes backed with a warm, toasted malt base. A distinct orange aroma and crisp finish.

Old Boy (OG 1047, ABV 4.8%)
A full-bodied, amber-coloured ale, fruity and bitter with a hop/fruit aroma. The malt that backs the taste dies in the long finish.

Blonde Volupta (OG 1050, ABV 5%)
Straw gold-coloured, zesty premium beer packed with complexity and intense tropical fruit flavours that lead to a crisp, dry finish.

On the Edge

Sheffield, South Yorkshire ☎ 07854 983197
🌐 ontheedgebrew.com

On the Edge started brewing commercially in 2012 using a 0.5-barrel plant in the brewer's home. Brewing takes place once a week. Three local pubs are supplied as well as beer festivals. There is no regular beer list as new brews are constantly being tried.

One Mile End SIBA

Unit 2, Compass West Estate, West Road, Tottenham, London, N17 0XL
☎ (020) 7998 0610 ☎ 07912 411147

Correspondence: White Hart Brewpub, 1-3 Mile End Road, London, E1 4TP 🌐 the-white-hart.co.uk/index.php

One Mile End took over the former premises of the Redemption Brewery (qv) using a 12.5-barrel plant brewing up to four times a week. A three-barrel plant is also in operation at the White Hart in Whitechapel. Beer is also brewed using the Under the Street brand name. !!

Hospital Porter (OG 5.2
Dark brown-coloured porter with a smoky, roasty nose. Sweet mocha, roast and nuts on the palate. Dry, dark roast finish.

Great Tom Mild (ABV 3.8%)
Complex dark mild with hints of coffee, cocoa and vanilla in the taste. Slightly roasty bitter finish.

Opa Hay's

Glencot, Wood Lane, Aldeby, Norfolk, NR34 0DA
☎ (01502) 679144 ☎ 07916 282729
🌐 engelfineales.com

Opa Hay's began brewing in 2008. It is a small, family-run brewery, taking its name from the brewer's great grandfather. Only traditional brewing methods are used, with ingredients that are, where possible, sourced locally. ♦RAIB

Engels Fruity Little Number (ABV 3.6%)
Powerful citrus/grapefruit aroma with malt and hops. Smoky, sweetish flavours with fruit notes, and a fruity, hoppy aftertaste.

Engel's Best Bitter (ABV 4%)
A triple-hopped, aromatic English ale.

Hop Hop Hooray (ABV 4.3%)
Steam beer brewed with American lager yeast.

Matilda's Revenge (ABV 4.3%)

SEMP (Samuel Engels Meister Pils) (ABV 4.8%)
A Pilsner-style beer, light in colour with a hoppy aroma.

Liquid Bread (ABV 5.2%)
Naturally cloudey, Bavarian-style wheat beer with a distinct aroma of cloves and banana.

Bavarian Breakfast Beer (ABV 5.4%)
A cask-conditioned lager with a malty body.

Orbit

Arches 225 & 228, Fielding Street, Walworth, London, SE17 3HD
☎ (020) 7703 9092 ☎ 07885 663842
🌐 orbitbeers.com

Established in 2014, Orbit is a microbrewery producing keg and bottle-conditioned beers. RAIB

Origami

75 North Western Street, Ardwick, Manchester, M12 6DY

Office: 23 Bradshaw Lane, Stretford, Manchester, M32 8WF 🌐 origamibrewingcompany.com

Brewing began in 2016 using its own brew plant on the premises of Beer Nouveau (qv) on the 'Piccadilly Beer Mile'.

Fortune Teller (ABV 4%)

Rabbit Ear (ABV 4.8%)

1000 Cranes (ABV 5%)

Valley Fold (ABV 5.2%)

Arctic Fox (ABV 7%)

Orkney SIBA

Quoyloo, Orkney, KW16 3LT
☎ (01667) 404555 ☎ 07721 013227

Office: Sinclair Breweries Ltd, Cawdor, IV12 5XP
🌐 orkneybrewery.co.uk

Orkney was established in 1988 in an old village school building. Having incorporated sister brewery Atlas (qv), it moved next door in 2010 to enable an increase in capacity and the completion of an award-winning visitor centre in 2012. ‼ ♦

Raven (OG 1038, ABV 3.8%)
A well-balanced, quaffable bitter. Malty fruitiness and bitter hops last through to the long, dry aftertaste.

Dragonhead (OG 1040, ABV 4%)
A strong, dark roasted malt aroma flows into the taste. The roast malt continues to dominate the aftertaste, and blends with chocolate to develop a strong, dry finish.

Northern Light (OG 1040, ABV 4%)
A well-balanced golden ale with a real smack of fruit and hops in the taste and an increasing bitter aftertaste.

Red MacGregor (OG 1040, ABV 4%)
This tawny red-coloured ale has a red fruit, malt and hop mix. Generally a well-balanced bitter.

Corncrake (OG 1042, ABV 4.1%)
A straw-coloured beer with soft citrus fruits and a floral aroma.

Puffin Ale (OG 1045, ABV 4.5%)
Bittersweet mix of malts and plenty of hops.

Dark Island (OG 1045, ABV 4.6%)
A sweetish roast chocolate malt taste leads to a long-lasting roasted, slightly bitter, dry finish.

Skull Splitter (OG 1080, ABV 8.5%)
An intense velvet malt nose with hints of apple, prune and plum. The hoppy taste is balanced by satiny smooth malt with sweet, fruity, spicy edges, leading to a long, dry finish with a hint of nut.

Brewed for Atlas Brewery:

Wayfarer (OG 1044, ABV 4.4%)
Full of citrus fruits and hops with a bitter finish.

Golden Amber (OG 1045, ABV 4.5%)
Refreshing hops, honey, marmalade and grapefruit to the fore with a dry, hoppy finish.

Blizzard (OG 1047, ABV 4.7%)
Light on malts and hops with ginger and spices coming through.

Oscars

Unit 5, Oxhey Trading Estate, Greenbank Street, Preston, Lancashire, PR1 7PH
☎ (01282) 616192 lancashirebeer.co.uk

John Smith started the Hart Brewery at the Cartford Hotel, Little Eccleston in 1995 and moved to Preston in 2010. Brewing ceased in 2016 and the brewery was sold in 2017 to the Lancashire Beer Company, a pub supplies wholesaler in Nelson, Lancashire. John Smith has been retained to brew most of the previous range of beers. In 2018 the brewery name was changed to Oscars and all beers were re-branded.

Bonnie (OG 1040, ABV 4%)
A light blonde beer with crisp hop flavours and a strawberry aroma.

Muddy Paws (OG 1040, ABV 4%)
A bronze-coloured, hoppy beer with a smooth, malty base.

Golden Retriever (OG 1042, ABV 4.2%)
A premium bitter with citrus flavours.

Ossett SIBA

Kings Yard, Low Mill Road, Ossett, West Yorkshire, WF5 8ND
☎ (01924) 261333 ossett-brewery.co.uk

Brewing began in 1998, moving to a new site in 2005. 2017 saw significant investment in brewery improvements and expansion to bring total brewing capacity up to 360 barrels per week. In addition a brand new warehouse and packaging facility was constructed. A visitor centre is planned. The brewery owns 25 pubs, four of which are 'Hop'-branded bars – larger city centre venues based around a concept of real ale and live music. ‼ ♦

Pale Gold (OG 1038, ABV 3.8%)
A light, refreshing pale ale with a hoppy aroma.

Yorkshire Blonde (OG 1040, ABV 3.9%)
A pale-coloured, full-bodied and well-rounded ale. Slightly sweet on the palate with a hoppy aroma.

Big Red Bitter (OG 1042, ABV 4%)
Deep red-coloured, malty Yorkshire bitter.

Silver King (OG 1041, ABV 4.3%)
A lager-style beer with a crisp, dry flavour and citrus fruity aroma.

Excelsior (OG 1051, ABV 5.2%)
A strong pale ale with a full, mellow flavour and a fresh, hoppy aroma with citrus/floral characteristics.

Ostlers (NEW)

White Horse, 2 York Street, Harborne, West Midlands, B17 0HG
☎ (0121) 427 8004 whitehorseharborne.com

Situated at the back of the White Horse in Harborne, the brewery was in occasional production for a few years. It now has a 4.5-barrel plant brewing a small range of core beers alongside frequent specials and seasonal beers. ♦

Other Monkey (NEW)

Three Wise Monkeys, 60 High Street, Colchester, Essex, CO1 1DN
☎ (01206) 543014 othermonkeybrewing.com

Other Monkeys is located in the basement of the Three Wise Monkeys pub. The brewery and pub are separately owned but beer is only brewed for the Three Wise Monkeys and two other outlets in Colchester.

Pale Ale (ABV 4.4%)

Otter SIBA

Mathayes, Luppitt, Devon, EX14 4SA
☎ (01404) 891285 otterbrewery.com

A family-run brewery set high up in the Blackdown Hills. Environmental responsibility lies at the heart of its ethos. Otter's eco cellar has been built underground and is naturally chilled. The beers are made from the brewery's own springs and locally-sourced ingredients. ♦

Bitter (OG 1036, ABV 3.6%)
Well-balanced, amber-coloured session bitter with a fruity nose and bitter taste and aftertaste.

Amber (OG 1038.5, ABV 4%)

Light, refreshing and mellow with hints of citrus hoppiness. Creamy and delicate with hops and fruit.

Bright (OG 1039, ABV 4.3%) ◆
A light and refreshing golden ale with delicate malt and fruit leading through hops to a lingering bitter aftertaste.

Ale (OG 1043, ABV 4.5%) ◆
Malt dominates from nose to throat. Sweet fruit, toffee and caramel with a dry aftertaste, full of flavour.

Head (OG 1054, ABV 5.8%) ◆
Smooth, strong ale. Malt, banana, caramel throughout. Full-bodied with rich, malty fruitiness and a hint of chocolate, leaving a moderately bitter aftertaste.

Out There SIBA

Unit 4, Foundry Lane Industrial Estate, Newcastle upon Tyne, NE6 1LH ☎ 07946 579534
outtherebrewing.com

Out There was established in 2012 by Steve Pickthall. Branding and beer names are themed around the 1950s space race.

Space is the Place (OG 1034, ABV 3.5%)
An amber-coloured beer with aromas of digestive biscuits and bread. Sweet malt flavours with floral notes.

Laika (OG 1049, ABV 4.8%)
A straw-coloured beer, the aroma is citrus with a hint of custard cream biscuits. Flavours of orange peel and spices.

Celestial Love (OG 1051, ABV 5.1%)
A red-coloured beer with caramel and malt loaf aromas and sweet malt tastes with floral and grapefruit hop notes.

Outgang

Kinsley Hotel, Wakefield Road, Kinsley, West Yorkshire, WF9 5EH ☎ 07747 694611
kinsleyhotel.com/Outgang-Brewery.html

Originally established in 2011, brewing ceased but resumed in 2017. Local outlets are supplied as are outlets further afield due to increased production.

Tailgate Ripper (OG 1039, ABV 3.9%)

Pit Bottom (OG 1040, ABV 4%)

Outlaw

See Rooster's

Outstanding SIBA

Units 1 & 2, Foundry, Ordsall Lane, Ordsall, Manchester, M5 3AN
☎ (0161) 873 8090 outstandingbeers.com

Established in 2008, the brewery operates a dual system, brewing on a 15-barrel plant and using a 2.5-barrel plant for special and experimental brews. Originally based in Bury, it moved to Ordsall in 2017. Selected free trade accounts are supplied nationally. ♦

3.9 (OG 1036, ABV 3.9%)

Ultra Pale (OG 1041, ABV 4.1%) ◆
Straw in colour, with a light citrus aroma. Lemony fruit with hop bitterness to taste and a bitter, astringent finish.

Red (OG 1045, ABV 4.4%)
Copper-coloured ale; mellow, biscuity.

Blond (OG 1044, ABV 4.5%)
A pale blonde ale, refreshing with citrus flavours.

IPA (OG 1058, ABV 5.5%)

Stout (OG 1061, ABV 5.5%)
A jet black-coloured stout with roast and liquorice notes.

Imperial IPA (OG 1065, ABV 7.4%)

Oxbrew (NEW) SIBA

Unit 4d, Enstone Airfield, Enstone, Oxfordshire, OX7 4NP
☎ (01608) 677717 ☎ 07789 241084
oxbrew.co.uk

Brewing began in 2017 using an eight-barrel plant. ♦ RAIB

Amber Ale (ABV 4.5%)

Red (ABV 5%)

Oxted

Oxted, Surrey, RH8 ☎ 07867 541700
theoxtedbrewery.co.uk

Oxted Brewery was established in 2015 using a two-barrel plant and occupies a purpose-built extension at the owner's home. Beers are regularly available in the Crown and Wheatsheaf pubs, Old Oxted, and the Hatch, Redhill. Bottles can be found in local off-licences and farm shops. Occasional events are held locally. RAIB

Hop'dfather (OG 1038, ABV 3.8%)

Amber Ale (OG 1039, ABV 3.9%)
Citrus and grapefruit with a light malty finish.

Single Hop (OG 1039, ABV 3.9%)
Light, fresh, mildly-hopped session beer, which may use a different hop for each brew.

BOB (Best Oxted Bitter) (OG 1041, ABV 4%)
Biscuity, mildly chocolate with a smooth finish.

The Black Perle (OG 1044, ABV 4.4%)
Dark roasted flavour with a hint of coffee.

Treehouse IPA (OG 1048, ABV 4.9%)
Well-balanced IPA with citrus and grapefruit to the fore.

Padstow SIBA

The Brewery, Unit 4a, Trecerus Industrial Estate, Padstow, Cornwall, PL28 8RW
☎ (01841) 532169 ☎ 07834 924312
padstowbrewing.co.uk

The brewery started commercially in 2013 using a 0.5-barrel plant. Owners Des and Caron Archer, Caron being the brewster, have since installed a custom-built 10-barrel plant. Beers are available from the brewery shop as well as the town centre brewery off-licence, which includes a tasting room. Beer festivals and an increasing number of local outlets are supplied. !! ♦ RAIB

Pale Ale (OG 1037, ABV 3.6%) ◆

Golden-coloured beer with an assertive hop aroma. Citrus hops dominate the taste with bitterness and dryness. Hoppy, refreshing and crisp finish.

Kor Dorgel (OG 1040, ABV 4%) ◆
Refreshing, gold-coloured ale with fruity hop nose. Crisp citrus, apple and pineapple flavours colour the grassy hop bitterness.

Windjammer (OG 1042, ABV 4.3%) ◆
Copper-coloured best bitter. Dominant biscuit malt with delicate stone fruits and grassy hops. Bitterness grows and lasts well into the finish.

Lobster Tale (OG 1044, ABV 4.5%) ◆
A smooth, yellow-coloured and cloudy wheat beer with fruity aroma. Bitter lemon hop and coriander flavours with light malt.

Pride (OG 1044, ABV 4.5%) ◆
Bronze-coloured beer with honey. Malt dominates throughout with some light roast balanced by bitterness, lemon, plums and hops. Long malt finish.

IPA (OG 1046, ABV 4.8%) ◆
Refreshing IPA. Fully hopped on nose and taste with orange bitterness. Sweet finish with citrus hops and faintly dry.

The Smoke (OG 1049, ABV 4.9%) ◆
Smooth, dark red-coloured stout with gentle roast aroma. Smoky roast and earthy, peaty malt dominates the taste. Long finish.

May Day (OG 1048, ABV 5%) ◆
Golden ale with aromatic citrus hop aroma and flavour. Powerful grapefruit and moderate bitterness. Strong grassy hop finish with dryness.

Sundowner (OG 1060, ABV 6.5%) ◆
American-style IPA with a fruity hop aroma. Dominant marmalade and apricot with citrus hops flavour. Quite bitter, slightly sweet and dry.

Palmers SIBA IFBB

Old Brewery, West Bay Road, Bridport, Dorset, DT6 4JA
☎ (01308) 422396 pælmersbrewery.com

Palmers is Britain's only thatched brewery and dates from 1794. It is situated in Bridport, the heart of the Jurassic Coast in south-west Dorset. The company continues to make substantial investment in its 54 tenanted pubs, all serving cask ale. An additional 400 outlets are supplied within the free trade.

Copper Ale (OG 1036, ABV 3.7%) ◆
Well-balanced, copper-coloured light bitter with a hoppy aroma.

IPA (OG 1040, ABV 4.2%) ◆
Hop aroma and bitterness stay in the background in this predominately malty best bitter, with some fruit on the aroma.

Dorset Gold (OG 1046, ABV 4.5%) ◆
More complex than many golden ales thanks to a pleasant banana and mango fruitiness on the aroma that carries on into the taste and aftertaste.

200 (OG 1052, ABV 5%) ◆
This is a big beer with a touch of caramel sweetness adding to a complex hoppy, fruit taste that lasts from the aroma well into the aftertaste.

Tally Ho! (OG 1057, ABV 5.5%) ◆
A complex, dark-coloured old ale. Roast malts and treacle toffee on the palate lead in to a long, lingering finish with more than a hint of coffee.

Panther

Unit 1, Collers Way, Reepham, Norfolk, NR10 4SW
☎ 07766 558215 pantherbrewery.co.uk

Panther began brewing in 2010 on an industrial estate near the old railway station, formerly the home of Reepham Brewery. RAIB

Mild Panther (OG 1035, ABV 3.3%) ◆
A smooth, malty character and notes of chocolate, which gives this beer plenty of flavour and aroma.

Ginger Panther (OG 1037, ABV 3.7%) ◆
Refreshingly clean ginger wheat beer with a distinct fiery kick.

Golden Panther (OG 1039, ABV 3.7%) ◆
Refreshing orange and malt notes flow through this well-balanced, easy-drinking bitter. Hops and a soft bitterness add depth.

Honey Panther (OG 1044, ABV 4%) ◆
A gentle flowing brew with honey and malt throughout. Amber-coloured with a tapering, bittersweet finale.

Red Panther (OG 1041, ABV 4.1%) ◆
Full-flavoured brew. Solidly malty in both aroma and taste. Hops and a residual sweetness provide balance.

American Pale Ale (OG 1044, ABV 4.4%)
A light malt base lets tropical flavours and aromas shine through, with a crisp, dry finish.

Black Panther (OG 1050, ABV 4.5%) ◆
This dark-coloured ale is full flavoured, smooth and complex. It has a bittersweet balance that leads to a dry finish.

Beast of the East (OG 1052, ABV 5.5%)
An amber-coloured IPA, refreshing with floral and grapefruit notes.

Papworth

24 Earith Business Park, Meadow Drove, Earith, Cambridgeshire, PE28 3QF
☎ (01480) 842442 ☎ 07835 845797
papworthbrewery.com

Brewing began in 2014 in Papworth Everard. The brewery moved to new premises in Earith in 2017 and acquired an 11-barrel plant, significantly increasing its production. The new brewery site is licensed for on and off-sales.

Mad Jack (ABV 3.8%)
A well-balanced session bitter with a light copper colour and gentle citrus aroma. Caramel overtones lead to a long, hoppy finish.

Half Nelson (ABV 4.1%)
A well-balanced, ruby-coloured IPA with a fresh and zesty finish.

Red Kite (ABV 4.4%)
A sweet, ruby-coloured ale with a strong hop finish bursting with tropical fruit flavours.

Crystal Ship (ABV 4.5%)
An amber-coloured ale with a light body and strong citrus finish.

Big Sur (ABV 5%)

THE BREWERIES

A West Coast-style pale ale with a light malt body and a finish of floral and citrus flavours.

Robin Goodfellow (ABV 5.4%)
A dark-coloured and full-bodied ale with a strong hop aroma. Heavy and complex malts softened with dark fruit flavours give way to a smooth yet hoppy finish.

A reddish brown-coloured ale with a good balance of malt and hops.

Poachers Ale (OG 1060, ABV 6%)
Deep ruby red-coloured, full bodied, malty beer.

Baz's Bonce Blower (OG 1098, ABV 12%)
Strong, dark-coloured beer with a rich, malty character. A Christmas pudding ale.

Paradigm SIBA

4d Green End Farm, 93a Church Lane, Sarratt, Hertfordshire, WD3 6HH
☎ (01923) 291215 🌐 paradigmbrewery.com

Founded by two friends, Neil Hodges and Rob Atkinson, Paradigm went into production in 2015. Its five-barrel plant is located in an industrial unit on a farm. One-off beers are also brewed. The brewery and beer names are based on corporate jargon and buzzwords. !! ♦ RAIB

Down Time (ABV 3.6%)
Blackcurrants in the aroma, a malty session beer with a sweet finish.

Watercress Ale (OG 1036, ABV 3.6%)
Produced with locally grown watercress to add a peppery flavour to this bitter, amber-coloured beer.

Low Hanging Fruit (OG 1038, ABV 3.7%)
Refreshing with citrus flavours, particularly tangerine and grapefruit.

Fake News (ABV 3.8%)
A pale-coloured session beer with citrus flavours.

Touch Point (OG 1039, ABV 3.9%)
A light-coloured, hoppy, pale ale.

Juxtaposition (OG 1041, ABV 4%)
An amber-coloured, hoppy beer with a hint of blueberries in the aroma.

Heads Up (ABV 4.1%)
A light golden-coloured beer with fruity and peppery hop notes and a dry aftertaste.

Win-Win (OG 1042, ABV 4.2%)

Best Practice (ABV 4.5%)
A dark ruby-coloured, malty beer with a vanilla flavour.

Old School (ABV 4.8%)
A reddish amber-coloured, malty and sweet strong bitter.

Black Friday (OG 1062, ABV 6%)
A dark-coloured, strong mild. Smooth and sweetish with a hint of smoked malt.

Parish

6 Main Street, Burrough on the Hill, Leicestershire, LE14 2JQ
☎ (01664) 454801 ☎ 07715 369410
✉ bazbrewery@gmail.com

Parish began in 1983 and now operates on a 20-barrel plant, with capacity to brew a further 12 barrels. The brewery is located in a 400-year-old building next to Grants Freehouse, which stocks the full range of beers. Other local outlets are also supplied and one-off brews are produced for beer festivals. !! RAIB

PSB (OG 1038, ABV 3.9%)
Hoppy session beer with a malty aftertaste.

Burrough Bitter (OG 1047, ABV 4.8%)

Park Brew

Unit 10, Brechin Business Centre, Brechin, DD9 6DY
☎ 07905 998740 🌐 parkbrew.com

Established in 2016 by John Leatherbarrow and Andrew Donald.

Park Brewery SIBA

Office: 38 St Georges Road, Kingston, Surrey, KT2 6DN
☎ 07932 624395 🌐 theparkbrewery.com

The Park Brewery was founded in 2014 in a former greengrocer's premises, using a one-barrel plant, increasing in 2015 to four barrels. Beers are available locally as well as across London and are named after locations in Richmond Park. Brewing is taking place using spare capacity at local breweries while new premises are sought. !! ♦ RAIB

Killcat Pale (OG 1037, ABV 3.7%)
Unfined, golden-coloured bitter with grapefruit throughout and a strong, hoppy, bitter flavour and finish, which is dry and slightly tart.

Gallows Gold (OG 1044, ABV 4.4%)
Unfined, hoppy golden ale with citrus notes. Bitterness develops in the taste and finish, which has some pineapple fruitiness.

Spankers IPA (OG 1055, ABV 5.5%)
An amber-coloured, hoppy, citrus, dry golden ale with a similar finish and a touch of dry bitterness.

Parker

Unit 3, Gravel Lane, Banks, Lancashire, PR9 8BY
☎ (01704) 620718 ☎ 07949 797889
🌐 theparkerbrewery.co.uk

Parker was established in 2014 using a 25-litre plant, and has since expanded to a five-barrel plant. !! RAIB

Centurion Pale Ale (OG 1040, ABV 3.9%)
A light, refreshing pale ale with zesty fruit flavours with a crisp, dry and hoppy finish.

Barbarian Bitter (OG 1041, ABV 4.1%)
Amber-coloured traditional ale with notes of caramel. Well-balanced and smooth.

Saxon Red Ale (OG 1046, ABV 4.5%)
Ruby-coloured ale with warm fruit flavours and a subtle hint of spice on the finish.

Viking Blonde (OG 1042, ABV 4.5%)
A blonde ale with subtle hints of blackcurrant leaf and summer berry fruit flavours with a refreshing, full, crisp finish.

Dark Spartan Stout (OG 1052, ABV 5%)
A silky smooth stout with hints of chocolate and coffee.

Partizan

34 Raymouth Road, South Bermondsey, London, SE16 2DB

☎ (020) 8127 5053 🌐 partizanbrewing.co.uk

Partizan began brewing in 2012. Each brew is different, but is based on a variety of international styles and is vegan-friendly. ♦RAIB V

Partners SIBA

Brew House, 589 Halifax Road, Hightown, Liversedge, West Yorkshire, WF15 8HQ
☎ (01924) 457772 🌐 partnersbrewery.co.uk

Partners was formed in 2011 following the purchase of the long-established Anglo Dutch Brewery by Richard Sharp. The brewery moved into newly renovated premises in 2015 and invested in a 15-barrel state-of-the-art brew plant to meet increased demand for its beers. In 2017 Bob's Brewing Co and Partners Brewery were both purchased by Peter Seabourne and his partner Julie Britton. The new owners have changed the name of the company to Partners Brewery Yorkshire. ‼♦

Blonde (OG 1039, ABV 3.9%)
A blonde, crisp, aromatic session beer.

Brown Lion (ABV 3.9%)
An amber-coloured bitter, well-balanced with a full body and pronounced bitter finish.

Black Lion (ABV 4%)

Dark Mild (ABV 4%)

White Lion (ABV 4.3%)

American Craft Ale (ABV 4.5%)
Light and refreshing beer packed with citrus flavours and aromas.

Tabatha (OG 1054, ABV 6%)
Golden-coloured, Belgian-style Tripel with a strong, fruity, hoppy and bitter character. Powerful and warming, slightly thinnish, with a bitter, dry finish.

Patriot

Upcott Farm, Bicknoller, Somerset, TA4 3HZ

Office: Farmer's Arms, Combe Florey, TA4 3HZ
🌐 thepatriotbrewery.co.uk

Patriot began brewing in Warwickshire in 2010 using a four-barrel plant before relocating to Bicknoller, Taunton, in 2015. All beers are available at the Farmer's Arms, Combe Florey, the Blue Ball, Trimscombe, plus a few other local outlets. ‼♦

Somerset Blonde (OG 1038, ABV 3.8%)

Broomsquire (OG 1040, ABV 4%)

Peak SIBA

Barn Brewery, Chatsworth, Derbyshire, DE45 1EX
☎ (01246) 583737 🌐 peakales.co.uk

Opened in 2005 in former derelict farm buildings on the Chatsworth estate aided by a DEFRA Rural Enterprise Scheme grant and support from trustees of Chatsworth Settlement. Main beer production moved to a new facility at Ashford in the Water in 2014 to increase capacity. A new visitor centre opened in 2017 at the original site. A pilot brewery is expected to be built in due course. ‼♦

Swift Nick (ABV 4%)
Easy-drinking, copper-coloured bitter with balanced malt and hops and a gentle, hoppy, bitter finish.

Bakewell Best Bitter (ABV 4.2%)
Full-bodied, tawny-coloured bitter with a hoppy bitterness against a malty background, leading to a hoppy, dry aftertaste.

Chatsworth Gold (ABV 4.6%)
Speciality beer made with honey, which gives a pleasant sweetness leading to a hop and malt finish.

IPA (ABV 6%)
A classic IPA; bold and hoppy with a modern citrus twist.

Peakstones Rock SIBA

Peakstones Farm, Cheadle Road, Alton, Staffordshire, ST10 4DH ☎ 07891 350908 🌐 peakstonesrock.co.uk

Peakstones Rock was established in 2005 with a five-barrel plant located on a farm in the Peak District National Park. The brewery was expanded to 10-barrel capacity in 2009. It supplies an expanding free trade market in the North Midlands and surrounding areas. ‼♦RAIB

Nemesis (OG 1042, ABV 3.8%)
Biscuity aroma with some hop background. Sweet start, sweetish body then hops emerge to give a fruity middle. Bitterness develops slowly to a tongue tingling finish.

Pugin's Gold (OG 1043, ABV 4%)

Chained Oak (OG 1045, ABV 4.2%)
A copper-coloured beer with a bitter finish and hop aroma.

Alton Abbey (OG 1051, ABV 4.5%)

Black Hole (OG 1048, ABV 4.8%)
Grassy aroma with malt background. Hops hit the mouth and intensify. Bitterness lingers with some mouth-watering astringency

Submission (OG 1058, ABV 5%)

Oblivion (OG 1055, ABV 5.5%)

Peerless SIBA

The Brewery, 8 Pool Street, Birkenhead, Merseyside, CH41 3NL
☎ (0151) 647 7688 🌐 peerlessbrewing.co.uk

Peerless began brewing in 2009 and is under the directorship of Steve Briscoe. Beers are sold through festivals, local pubs and the free trade. ‼♦

Pale (OG 1036, ABV 3.8%)
Pale-coloured session ale. Good initial bitterness and a hint of grapefruit on the finish.

Deadbeat (ABV 4%)
A toasted wheat backbone leads to a fruity hop finish.

Triple Blonde (OG 1040, ABV 4%)
A blonde wheat beer with a fruity citrus finish.

Lottie Dod (ABV 4.2%)
An amber-coloured ale with a good malt backbone and a hint of hop bitterness.

Langton Spin (ABV 4.4%)
A well-balanced, dry-hopped golden ale. Initial bitterness with a citrus, crisp, dry finish.

Oatmeal Stout (OG 1050, ABV 5%)
Full-bodied, black-coloured stout with toffee and caramel tones.

Red Rocks (OG 1047, ABV 5%)

Full-bodied, ruby-coloured ale. Rich malt flavours combine with the hops to give fruity overtones.

Knee-Buckler IPA (ABV 5.2%)
Initial hop bitterness matched with a hint of malty sweetness. A distinct fruity hop finish.

Full Whack (OG 1054, ABV 6%)
A hoppy, bitter beer with a fruity finish.

Tectonic (ABV 6.2%)
A deep honey-coloured ale with lots of hop aroma and flavour.

Penistone

White Heart, 77 Gate Bridge Street, Penistone, South Yorkshire, S36 7AH ☎ 07885 251603
thewhiteheart.co.uk/penistone_brewers

Brewing began in 2017 at the back of the White Heart pub, which dates back to 1377. Initially set up to provide cask-conditioned ales for the pub, the brewery now supplies other local outlets and beer festivals. ♦

Ambers Brew (OG 1042, ABV 4.3%)

Blonde Bombshell (OG 1046, ABV 4.7%)

Queen Bee (OG 1046, ABV 4.7%)

Back Oil Tap (OG 1048, ABV 4.9%)

Penlon Cottage

Panteg Farm, New Quay, SA45 9TL
☎ (01545) 561492 penlonbrewery.co.uk

Established in 2004, Penlon is a six-barrel, farm-based brewery situated on the Cardigan coast above Newquay. In 2017 it opened the on-site Granary tap room with stunning views across the Cardigan coastline. Beers are available across Wales. There are plans for further expansion.
!! RAIB

Cardi Bay Best Bitter (OG 1036, ABV 4%)

Hidden Howler (OG 1038, ABV 4.3%)

RSA (OG 1055, ABV 6.2%)

Pennine SIBA

Well Hall Farm, Well, North Yorkshire, DL8 2PX
☎ (01677) 470111 pennine-brewing.co.uk

Originally established in Batley in 2012 and now located in the village of Well near Masham, the brewery has been in production on this site since 2013 using an 18-barrel plant complete with lauter tun. ♦

Amber Necker (OG 1039, ABV 3.9%)
A session beer with a smooth, creamy texture and a hoppy aftertaste.

Best Bitter (OG 1040, ABV 3.9%)

Hair of the Dog (OG 1036, ABV 3.9%)

Real Blonde (OG 1041, ABV 4%)
Well-balanced blonde ale with a fruity aftertaste.

Natural Gold (OG 1043, ABV 4.2%)

Pentrich SIBA

Unit B, Asher Lane Business Park, Asher Lane, Pentrich, Derbyshire, DE5 3RB
☎ (01773) 741700
pentrichbrewingco@gmail.com

Two former homebrewers began producing beer for sale in their garage in Pentrich, before moving to share the plant of the Landlocked Brewing Co (qv) at the Beehive Inn, Ripley, in 2014. In 2016 the brewery moved into its own premises. ♦

Shoot the Servant (OG 1038, ABV 3.8%)
Malt driven, dark-coloured bitter with flavours of toasted caramel and subtle chocolate. English hops add blackcurrant aromas and an understated spicy character.

Soma (OG 1041, ABV 4.1%)
A session pale ale with vibrant citrus and floral flavours.

1817 (OG 1045, ABV 4.5%)
A full-bodied, amber-coloured ale with a dry fruit aroma and pleasing bitter finish.

Kiama (OG 1047, ABV 5%)
A vibrant, hoppy pale ale with punchy citrus flavours and huge stone fruit aromas.

Death Valley (ABV 5.2%)
An American-style pale ale with a subtle caramel malt character and a cocktail of US hops. Huge citrus and tropical flavours power through alongside subtle floral and pine notes.

Dry River (ABV 5.8%)
Huge pine, grapefruit and orange flavours of tropical fruit fuse with big punchy citrus notes. A delicate caramel malt backbone complements these hop flavours.

Three Graves (OG 1060, ABV 6%)

Northfield Garage (ABV 6.5%)

Black Ale (ABV 7.4%)
A black IPA with a silky mouthfeel. Pungent pine and stone fruit flavours.

Penzance

Star Inn, Crowlas, Penzance, Cornwall, TR20 8DX
☎ (01736) 740375
penzancebrewing.wordpress.com

Owner Peter Elvin began brewing in 2008 on a self-built five-barrel plant in the old stable block of the Star Inn. The fermentation capacity has since been expanded, increasing the volume and range of beers produced. Production is now at full capacity of 1,400 barrels a year. Besides the pub, selected outlets and beer festivals are supplied.
!! ♦

Mild (OG 1042, ABV 3.6%)
Creamy dark brown-coloured mild with a smoky malt aroma. Roast coffee and sweet malt dominate the palate, balanced by light bitterness.

Crowlas Bitter (OG 1037, ABV 3.8%)
Refreshing, copper-coloured session bitter with a light malt aroma. Light biscuit maltiness and hops. Lingering finish of malty bitterness with dryness.

Potion No. 9 (OG 1039, ABV 4%)
Refreshing golden ale with floral, grapefruit hops dominating nose and taste. Big bitter taste grows into a complex grapefruit, apricot finish.

Brisons Bitter (OG 1043, ABV 4.5%)
Copper-coloured best bitter with a malt aroma. Malt dominates the taste with sweetness, fruits and bitterness. Malt finish with sweet toffee.

Trink (OG 1048, ABV 5.2%)
Pale-coloured golden ale with a grapefruit nose. Punchy pine-resin hop flavours with grapefruit, marmalade and peaches. Bittersweet and hoppy finish.

IPA (OG 1058, ABV 6%)
Smooth, golden-coloured IPA with a hoppy aroma. Powerful hop bitterness with light malt and tropical fruits, finishing bitter and dry.

Scilly Stout (OG 1067, ABV 7%)
Dark brown-coloured, full-bodied and creamy stout. Burnt malt, liquorice, chicory and prunes taste. Long, bittersweet finish with strong roast malt.

People's

Mill House, Mill Lane, Thorpe-next-Haddiscoe, Norfolk, NR14 6PA
☎ (01508) 548706 ✉ peoplesbrewery@mail.com

A one-barrel brewery associated with the community-owned Queen's Head pub in Thurlton, which takes most of its draught output. Bottle-conditioned beers are supplied to Thurlton Community Stores. RAIB

Northdown Bitter (OG 1038, ABV 3.8%)

Raveningham Bitter (OG 1040, ABV 3.9%)

Thurlton Gold (OG 1042, ABV 4.2%)

Cascade (OG 1043, ABV 4.5%)

Imperial Stout (OG 1072, ABV 7.3%)

Pershore SIBA

Unit 5, Lyttleton Road, Pershore, Worcestershire, WR10 2DF
☎ (01386) 561578 ☎ 07495 578397
pershorebrewery.com

Brewing began in 2016 using a six-barrel plant.

Summertime (OG 1038, ABV 3.8%)

Croft (OG 1042, ABV 4.2%)

Pale Ale (ABV 4.5%)

Black Moon (ABV 5%)

Oh Betty (ABV 5%)

Pheasantry SIBA

High Brecks Farm, Lincoln Road, East Markham, Nottinghamshire, NG22 0SN
☎ (01777) 872728 ☎ 07948 976749
pheasantrybrewery.co.uk

Pheasantry began brewing in 2012 using a new 10-barrel plant from Canada. Situated in a listed barn on a farm, the brewery and visitor centre incorporate a wedding and events venue, with the brewery visible through glass partitions. It supplies some 200 pubs and retail outlets in Nottinghamshire, Lincolnshire and South Yorkshire. !!

Best Bitter (OG 1038, ABV 3.8%)
Smooth-tasting, copper-coloured beer with a light, spicy aroma.

Pale Ale (OG 1040, ABV 4%)
A pale-coloured, smooth-tasting beer with floral and citrus notes and a dry finish.

Ringneck Amber Ale (OG 1041, ABV 4.1%)
Amber-coloured best bitter, initial malt and caramel leading to a brief bitter, dry finish.

Dark Ale (OG 1042, ABV 4.2%)
A smooth, soft, dark-coloured ale with malty flavours, balanced bitterness and a velvety texture.

Lincoln Tank Ale (OG 1042, ABV 4.2%)

Dancing Dragonfly (OG 1050, ABV 5%)
A refreshing blonde ale with exotic fruit flavours.

Philsters

Beehive Brewery, Beehive Cottage, Little Haseley, Oxfordshire, OX44 7LH ☎ 07747 827489
philsters.co.uk

Named after the owner/brewer's nickname, this small 200-litre brewery was established in 2015. It supplies local pubs, including the Plough, Great Haseley and the Bull, Great Milton. There are plans to increase production to five barrels when premises become available. ♦

Glassblower (OG 1035, ABV 3.6%)

Haseley Gold (OG 1039, ABV 4.1%)
A light golden ale with a good balance of malt and hops, giving an initial bright, fresh bitterness, with soft, woody, honey notes following.

Haseley Red (OG 1045, ABV 4.2%)
A deep ruby-coloured ale with a smooth bitterness and a fruity, pine aroma.

Haseley Rising (OG 1040, ABV 4.2%)
A pale-coloured IPA with an earthy bitterness and a big citrus hit.

Boosh (OG 1041, ABV 4.5%)
A light copper-coloured best bitter with an easy-drinking, crisp, dry, bitter finish to balance the rich malts.

Phipps SIBA

Albion Brewery, 54 Kingswell Street, Northampton, NN1 1PR
☎ (01604) 946606 ☎ 07717 078402
phipps-nbc.co.uk

Originally founded in Towcester in 1801, Phipps had been brewing in Northampton since 1817 until taken over by Watney Mann, who closed the brewery in 1974. The company name and recipes were acquired and in 2008 the first Phipps draught beer reappeared after 40 years, brewed to the original recipe at Grainstore Brewery (qv) in Oakham. The Albion Brewery site, once owned by Phipps, was acquired and a new 15-barrel brewing plant installed in 2014 to enable Phipps beers to be once again brewed in the town. Hoggleys brewery, which was established in 2002, merged with Phipps NBC at the end of 2013 and all Hoggleys beers are now brewed on the Phipps plant. !! ♦ RAIB

Diamond Ale (OG 1037, ABV 3.7%)

Red Star (OG 1038, ABV 3.8%)
A red-coloured, nutty bitter.

Cobbler's Ale (ABV 4%)
A chestnut-coloured session bitter with a dry finish.

India Pale Ale (OG 1043, ABV 4.3%)
A residual malt sweetness and grapefruit note from the hops gives a fresh, crisp finish.

Ratliffe's Celebrated Stout (OG 1043, ABV 4.3%)

A creamy, well-balanced stout with just a hint of bitterness.

Becket's Ale (ABV 4.5%)
A sweet, dark-coloured and malty beer brewed with honey.

Bison Brown (OG 1046, ABV 4.6%)

Cascadia (OG 1050, ABV 5%)

Gold Star (OG 1050, ABV 5.2%)

Brewed for Hoggley's Brewery:

Mill Lane Mild (OG 1040, ABV 4%)

Northamptonshire Bitter (OG 1040, ABV 4%)

Reservoir Hogs (OG 1042, ABV 4.3%)

Pump Fiction (OG 1045, ABV 4.5%)

India Pale Ale (OG 1050, ABV 5%)

Solstice Stout (OG 1050, ABV 5%)

Phoenix SIBA

Green Lane, Heywood, OL10 2EP
☎ (01706) 627009 ✉ tony@phoenixbrewery.co.uk

Established in Ellesmere Port in 1982, Oak Brewery moved to the old Phoenix Brewery in Heywood and adopted the name in 1991. It now supplies more than 400 outlets plus wholesalers. Restoration of the old brewery, built in 1897, is ongoing. ♦

Hopsack (OG 1038, ABV 3.8%)
An easy-drinking, hoppy session beer.

Navvy (OG 1039, ABV 3.8%)
Amber-coloured beer with a citrus fruit and malt nose. Good balance of citrus fruit, malt and hops with bitterness coming through in the aftertaste.

Monkeytown Mild (OG 1039, ABV 3.9%)
Dark-coloured mild with fruitiness, bitterness and a smooth, full malt finish.

Arizona (OG 1040, ABV 4.1%)
Yellow in colour with a fruity and hoppy aroma. A refreshing beer with citrus, hops and good bitterness, and a shortish dry aftertaste.

Spotland Gold (OG 1041, ABV 4.1%)
A pale-coloured, hoppy beer with a lingering bitter finish.

Pale Moonlight (OG 1042, ABV 4.2%)
Quite bitter with a lingering grassy hop finish.

Black Bee (OG 1045, ABV 4.5%)
Brewed with honey this porter has a malty aroma, which tastes of dark fruit, honey and a hint of coffee.

White Monk (OG 1045, ABV 4.5%)
Yellow-coloured beer with a citrus fruit aroma, plenty of fruit, hops and bitterness in the taste, and a hoppy, bitter finish.

Thirsty Moon (OG 1046, ABV 4.6%)
Tawny-coloured beer with a fresh citrus aroma. Hoppy, fruity and malty with a dry, hoppy finish.

West Coast IPA (OG 1046, ABV 4.6%)
Golden in colour with a hoppy, fruity nose. Strong hoppy and fruity taste and aftertaste with good bitterness throughout.

Double Gold (OG 1050, ABV 5%)

Wobbly Bob (OG 1060, ABV 6%)
A red/brown-coloured beer with malty, fruity aroma and creamy mouthfeel. Strongly malty and fruity in flavour, with hops and a hint of herbs. Both sweetness and bitterness are evident throughout.

Brewed for Brunning & Price Pub Co:

Original (ABV 3.8%)

Pictish

Unit 9, Canalside Industrial Estate, Rochdale, OL16 5LB
☎ (01706) 522227 pictish-brewing.co.uk

The brewery was established in 2000 and supplies free trade outlets in the North-west and West Yorkshire. Famed for the consistency and clarity of its brews and its ever-changing single hop series of beers. ♦

Brewers Gold (OG 1038, ABV 3.8%)
Yellow in colour, with a hoppy, fruity nose. Soft maltiness and a strong hop/citrus flavour lead to a dry, bitter finish.

Talisman IPA (OG 1042, ABV 4.2%)
Strong, hoppy aroma; hops and fruit in the taste. Some initial sweetness, but with hoppy bitterness throughout.

Alchemists Ale (OG 1043, ABV 4.3%)
Yellow-coloured beer with generous hop and fruit on the nose and palate. Good bitter hop finish.

Piddle SIBA

Unit 24, Enterprise Park, Piddlehinton, Dorset, DT2 7UA
☎ (01305) 849336 ☎ 07730 436343
piddlebrewery.co.uk

Established in 2007, with new owners in 2014. The brewery produces a broad range of beers from their location in the Piddle valley in Dorset. Some beer names reflect this unusual name. Beers are available in pubs and retail outlets across Dorset and beyond. ♦ **GF**

Martyr's Relief (OG 1038, ABV 3.5%)

Dorset Rogue (OG 1038, ABV 3.9%)
A well-balanced, complex, chestnut brown-coloured best bitter. Malty and fruity with a hint of caramel and toffee.

Piddle (OG 1043, ABV 4.1%)
Easy-drinking, amber-coloured session ale. Full-bodied beer that is slightly sweet but malty with a fruity nose and citrus twist.

Cocky (OG 1047, ABV 4.3%)
Golden-coloured, hoppy IPA with a refreshing hoppy zing and crisp grapefruit finish with pine and floral notes.

Bent Copper (OG 1050, ABV 4.8%)
Smooth, strong bitter made with a herbal, grassy aroma.

Slasher (OG 1053, ABV 5.1%)
Light-coloured, lager-style ale. Slightly sweet with a gentle floral aroma and dry finish.

Pied Bull

Pied Bull Hotel, 57 Northgate Street, Chester, CH1 2HQ
☎ (01244) 325829 piedbull.co.uk

Pied Bull began brewing in 2011 using a one-barrel plant. Beer is mainly for in-house consumption but local beer festivals are supplied and occasional brewery swaps occur. ♦

Pig & Porter

18h Chapman Way, Tunbridge Wells, Kent, TN2 3EF
☎ (01424) 893519 🌐 pigandporter.co.uk

Originally brewing at several microbreweries in Sussex and Kent, brewing has taken place on its own plant in Tunbridge Wells since 2013 using a 10-barrel plant. ♦

Ashburnam (ABV 3.8%)

Skylarking (ABV 4%)

Dance First (ABV 4.2%)

Fatal Flaw (ABV 4.5%)

Red Spider Rye (ABV 4.8%)

Pig Iron SIBA

Rowley Village, Rowley Regis, B65 9AT ☎ 07816 018777 🌐 pigironbrewingco.co.uk

Set up in 2015, this three-barrel plant has relocated and is now sited to the rear of the Britannia pub in Rowley village. The brewer, from a former baking family, acquired the kit from Brewmeister in Northern Scotland. The brewery supplies free trade outlets within 15 miles of the brewery and the brewers home, as well as Weavers Real Ale House, Kidderminster. ♦

Blonde (OG 1038, ABV 3.8%)

EPA (OG 1042, ABV 4.2%)
Floral, grapefruit, pine and cedar flavours with a spicy honey aroma give this golden-coloured beer a smooth, light texture.

IPA (OG 1042, ABV 4.2%)

Unbeweavable (OG 1042, ABV 4.2%)

APA (OG 1045, ABV 4.5%)
An American-style pale ale with pronounced citrus, blackcurrant and grapefruit flavours

Brewed under the Britt Brewery brand name:

Brew Britannia (ABV 4.2%)

Pop (ABV 4.9%)

Pig Pub

Pig In Muck, Manor Road, Claybrooke Magna, Leicestershire, LE17 5AY
☎ (01455) 202859 🌐 piginmuck.com/brewery

Brewing began in 2013 using a two-barrel plant, upgraded to a five-barrel plant built by head brewer Kev Featherstone. RAIB

Pigeon Fishers

Unit B1, Devonshire Buildings, Works Road, Hollingwood, Chesterfield, Derbyshire, S43 2PE
☎ 07506 000989 🌐 pigeonfishers.com

Pigeon Fishers was founded by Ade Cole in 2014. Originally brewed in Hollingwood, beers are now cuckoo brewed at Raw Brewing Co (qv). ♦

Rainbrew (ABV 4.4%)

Pigeon Porter (ABV 4.8%)

Pigeon IPA (ABV 5%)

Pilgrim SIBA

11 West Street, Reigate, Surrey, RH2 9BL
☎ (01737) 222651 ☎ 07973 297410 🌐 pilgrim.co.uk

Pilgrim was the first microbrewery in Surrey, set up in 1982 in Woldingham before moving to its current premises in Reigate in 1984. The original owner, Dave Roberts, retired in 2017 selling the brewery to new owners who are developing new ales to complement the current selection, have enlarged to a 12-barrel brew length and opened a tap room. Beers are available in around 40 local outlets. ‼ ♦

Surrey (OG 1038, ABV 3.7%)
Pineapple, grapefruit and spicy aromas. Biscuity maltiness with a hint of vanilla balanced by a hoppy bitterness and refreshing bittersweet finish.

Progress (OG 1041, ABV 4%)
Well-rounded, tawny-coloured bitter. Predominantly sweet and malty with an underlying fruitiness and hint of toffee, balanced with a subdued bitterness.

Quest (OG 1043, ABV 4.3%)
Light on the palate with a mix of hops giving the beer a floral, lime note.

Exile (OG 1050, ABV 5%)
A classic English IPA with an assertive pine, herbal aroma and a deep earthy taste.

Pillars SIBA

Unit 2 Ravenswood Industrial Estate, Shernhall Street, Walthamstow, London, E17 9HQ
☎ (020) 8521 5552 🌐 pillarsbrewery.com

Brewing began in 2016 and is the only exclusively lager brewery and taproom in London. No real ale. ♦V

Pilot Beer

22 Jane Street, Leith, EH6 5HD
☎ (0131) 561 4267 ☎ 07805 760018
🌐 pilotbeer.co.uk

Pilot started brewing in 2013 in an industrial unit in Leith using a salvaged five-barrel plant, which has since been extended. Graduates of the Heriot-Watt University Brewing degree course, the owners infuse a number of flavours in their hop-forward beers. Distribution is to the Edinburgh area. Beers are mostly unfiltered and unfined but much of the current output is keg. RAIB

Pilot Brewery

726 Mumbles Road, Mumbles, Swansea, SA3 4EL
☎ 07897 895511 🌐 thepilotbrewery.co.uk

The Pilot Brewery began production on its 2.5-barrel plant in 2013. It is located at the rear of the Pilot Inn on the Mumbles sea front. The output is mainly for the Pilot Inn but can be found at festivals and other select outlets. A sister brewery, Beer Riff (qv) was established in 2017 (no real ale).

Pin-Up SIBA

Unit 3, Block 3, Chalex Industrial Estate, Manor Hall Road, Southwick, West Sussex, BN42 4NH

☎ (01273) 411127 ☎ 07888 836892
🌐 pinupbrewingco.com

⊗ Pin-Up began brewing in 2011, initially having its beers contract brewed at an Essex brewery. In 2014 it obtained its own plant and began brewing in Southwick, expanding from a five-barrel to a 10-barrel plant in 2015. Its first pub, the United Brethren, Chelmsford, opened in 2016. ♦RAIB

Honey Brown (OG 1039, ABV 4%)

Session IPA (OG 1040, ABV 4.1%)

Summer Pale (OG 1040, ABV 4.1%)

Red Head (OG 1041, ABV 4.2%)

Milk Stout (OG 1044, ABV 4.5%)

Pipes

183a Kings Road, Cardiff, CF11 9DF ☎ 07776 382244
🌐 pipesbeer.co.uk

Formery known as Artisan, the brewery was established in 2008. All beers are unfiltered, without additives or preservatives and suitable for vegans. The main output is bottled and keg beers, although cask-conditioned beers are occasionally produced. ♦V

Pirate

White Lion, Fritwell Road, Fewcott, Oxfordshire, OX27 7NZ
☎ (01869) 346676 🌐 whitelionfewcott.uk

Pirate Brewery set sail in 2017 and is located in a building behind the White Lion in Fewcott. It is a small, family-run brewery and with its 60-litre capacity, beer is brewed once a week, mainly for in-house consumption but local pubs and beer festivals are supplied. The name comes from a large children's pirate play ship in the pub garden. ♦

Pit Top (NEW)

Bridge Cottage, Willimoteswick, NE47 7DD

Brewing commenced in 2015.

Gold Drift (ABV 3.9%)

Wry Tree Bitter (ABV 4%)

Pitchfork

See Epic Beers

Pixie Spring

See Hopcraft

Plain SIBA

17c Deverill Trading Estate, Sutton Veny, Wiltshire, BA12 7BZ
☎ (01985) 841481 🌐 plainales.co.uk

⊗ Plain Ales started production in 2008 on a 2.5-barrel plant in a garage, and expanded to a 10-barrel plant in 2010 to keep up with demand for its award-winning ales. ‼♦

Sheep Dip (OG 1040, ABV 3.8%)
A session ale with a zesty start leading to a dry and hoppy finish.

Innocence (OG 1042, ABV 4%)
A straw-coloured, aromatic bitter.

Innspiration (OG 1042, ABV 4%)
A traditional, copper-coloured, easy-drinking bitter.

Inntrigue (OG 1044, ABV 4.2%)
Ruby-coloured best bitter with flavours of woodland berries and a hint of dark chocolate.

Inncognito (OG 1053, ABV 4.8%)
A stout with sweet, roasted malt, aged port and mature vine fruit flavours.

India Plain Ale (OG 1052, ABV 5.2%)

Inndulgence (OG 1055, ABV 5.2%)
A dark ruby-coloured porter with coffee and chocolate flavours and a hint of smoke.

Plan B

Audley Avenue Enterprise Park, Newport, TF10 7DW
☎ (01952) 810091

Plan B is a family-run brewery set up in 2016 using a 10-barrel plant. Beers are distributed within a 30-mile radius of the brewery and are available from the shop or on-site bar. ‼ RAIB

New Session IPA (ABV 4%)

Newport Pale Ale (ABV 4.4%)

Boscobel Bitter (ABV 4.8%)

Steam Stout (ABV 4.8%)

Platform 5 SIBA

Railway Brewhouse, 197 Queen Street, Newton Abbot, Devon, TQ12 2BS
☎ (01626) 437140 🌐 platform5brewing.co.uk

⊗ Established in 2013 using a six-barrel plant. The Railway Inn is supplied along with Molloys in Teignmouth and Torquay. This family-run brewery is situated in part of an enclosed alley under the disused Platform 5 of Newton Abbot station.

The Coaster (OG 1040, ABV 4%)

The Antelope (OG 1043, ABV 4.3%)

APA (OG 1046, ABV 4.6%)

The Whistleblower (OG 1046, ABV 4.6%)
Complex nose with roast and caramel leading to fruit and sweet hops with bitterness on the tongue. Dry aftertaste.

Western Gold (OG 1048, ABV 4.8%)

Blitzen (OG 1050, ABV 5%)

IPA (OG 1050, ABV 5%)

Plockton

5 Bank Street, Plockton, IV52 8TP
☎ (01599) 544276 ☎ 07823 322043
🌐 theplocktonbrewery.com

The brewery started trading in 2007 and expanded to a 2.5-barrel plant in 2009. ‼♦RAIB

Fiddlers Fancy (OG 1046, ABV 4.6%)
Refreshing grapefruit aroma and taste turning to a more malty finish.

Plockton Bay (OG 1047, ABV 4.6%)

A well-balanced, tawny-coloured best bitter with plenty of hops and malt, which give a bittersweet, fruity flavour.

Starboard! (OG 1052, ABV 5.1%)
A fruity golden ale with a light citrus bitterness. Hop and spicy fruit feature in the nose with a smack of grapefruit in the taste. The bitterness holds well into the aftertaste.

Ring Tong (OG 1056, ABV 5.6%)
A hoppy IPA with a fruity, full flavour.

Poachers

439 Newark Road, North Hykeham, Lincolnshire, LN6 9SP
☎ (01522) 807404 ☎ 07954 131972
poachersbrewery.co.uk

Brewing started in 2001 on a five-barrel plant. In 2006 it was downsized to 2.5-barrel and relocated to outbuildings at the rear of the brewer's home. 2011 saw capacity returned to five barrels. Regular outlets in Lincolnshire and surrounding counties are supplied direct; outlets further afield via wholesalers. !! ♦

Trembling Rabbit Mild (OG 1034, ABV 3.4%)
Rich dark mild with a smooth, malty flavour and a slightly bitter finish. Local honey used.

Shy Talk Bitter (OG 1037, ABV 3.7%)
A crisp, pale golden-coloured beer, refreshing with citrus overtones.

Rock Ape (OG 1038, ABV 3.8%)
Traditional brown-coloured session bitter produced from English ingredients.

Poachers Pride (OG 1040, ABV 4%)

Bog Trotter (OG 1042, ABV 4.2%)
An amber-coloured, full-flavoured, malty beer with a bitter hop aftertaste.

Lincoln Best (OG 1042, ABV 4.2%)
A brown-coloured beer with a floral hop aroma. A well-balanced but bitter taste complements the malt, becoming more apparent in the dry finish.

Billy Boy (OG 1044, ABV 4.4%)

Imp Ale (OG 1044, ABV 4.4%)
Copper-coloured, fruity and floral with a bitter finish.

Black Crow Stout (OG 1045, ABV 4.5%)
A full-bodied stout with a lingering aftertaste. Burnt toffee and caramel flavours to the fore.

Hykeham Gold (OG 1045, ABV 4.5%)

Monkey Hanger (OG 1045, ABV 4.5%)
A ruby-coloured bitter with a smooth, fruity flavour balanced by hop bitterness.

Jock's Trap (OG 1050, ABV 5%)
A strong, pale brown-coloured bitter with a hoppy flavour and aroma. A slightly dry fruit finish.

Trout Tickler (OG 1055, ABV 5.5%)
A strong, ruby-coloured bitter with intense flavour and character, sweet undertones with a hint of chocolate. A rich, malty beer.

Polarity

5 Abbotts Close, Worthing, West Sussex, BN11 1JB
☎ 07872 105300 polaritybrewing.co.uk

A small brewery established in 2016 by two homebrewing enthusiasts.

Rosetta's Comet (OG 1052, ABV 5.4%)
Traditional IPA with a well-balanced malt and hop flavour. A lasting, bitter, fruity finish.

Pomona Island (NEW)

Unit 33, Waybridge Enterprise Centre, Daniel Adamson Road, Salford, M50 1DS ☎ 07972 445474
pomonaisland@gmail.com

Brewery set up in 2017, part owned by the people behind the Gas Lamp in Manchester city centre. Head brewer James Dyer is formerly of Tempest Brew Co (qv). All beers are vegetarian.

Pale (ABV 3.8%)

Session IPA (ABV 4.5%)

Stout (ABV 4.5%)

APA (ABV 5.3%)

NZ Pale (ABV 5.3%)

IPA (ABV 7%)

Pope's Yard

Frogmore Paper Mill, Fourdrinier Way, Apsley, Hemel Hempstead, Hertfordshire, HP3 9RY
☎ (01923) 510850 popesyard.co.uk

Pope's Yard began commercial brewing in 2012 using a one-barrel plant. Relocation in 2015 also meant expansion to a five-barrel plant with a one-barrel pilot plant. In 2018 the brewery relocated to Hemel Hempstead. RAIB

Luminaire (OG 1041, ABV 3.9%)
Hints of citrus, passion fruit and pineapple with a classic bitter finish.

Quartermaster (OG 1044, ABV 4.4%)

Club Hammer Stout (OG 1060, ABV 5.5%)
Chocolate sweetness and rich roastiness are balanced by hoppy bitterness and aroma.

Strong Dark Mild (OG 1063, ABV 6.8%)

Poppyland

46 West Street, Cromer, Norfolk, NR27 9DS
☎ (01263) 513992 ☎ 07887 389804
poppylandbeer.com

Established in 2012 by museum curator and geologist Martin Warren as a working retirement project, the two-barrel Poppyland Brewery produces unfiltered and vegan-friendly beers. Many of the beers are gluten free, most are experimental and some are brewed with local wild ingredients such as damson, sea purslane, wild hops and dandelions. RAIB GF V

East Coast IPA (OG 1069, ABV 7%)

Portobello SIBA

Unit 6, Mitre Bridge Industrial Estate, Mitre Way, North Kensington, London, W10 6AU
☎ (020) 8969 2269 portobellobrewing.com

Portobello began brewing in 2012 using a 10-barrel plant. ♦

Pale (OG 1040, ABV 4%)

THE BREWERIES

Golden-coloured, well balanced best bitter with citrus and spiced hops. Biscuit sweetness fades in the clean, dry finish becoming bitter.

Star (OG 1044, ABV 4.3%) ◆
Pale brown-coloured, malty best bitter with a sweetish nose, a fruity flavour and a bitter finish. Hints of nut on the palate and some hops throughout.

APA (OG 1050, ABV 5%) ◆
Full-bodied, straw-coloured strong ale. The honey sweetness and soft citrus fruit balanced by bitter hops. Dry aftertaste.

Portpatrick

The Neuk, Stoneykirk, DG9 9EF ☎ 07826 542149
portpatrick-brewery.co.uk

The brewery opened in 2015 using a 1.5-barrel plant in converted space in outbuildings. A number of local pubs are supplied. ♦RAIB

16-21 (OG 1040, ABV 3.8%)

Beltie Blonde (OG 1042, ABV 4%)

Rhins Ruby (OG 1043, ABV 4%)

Dark Skies (OG 1045, ABV 4.2%)

Dorn Rock (OG 1046, ABV 4.3%)

Fog Horn (OG 1049, ABV 4.9%)

Potbelly SIBA

Sydney Street Entrance, Kettering, Northamptonshire, NN16 0JA
☎ (01536) 410818 ☎ 07834 867825
potbelly-brewery.co.uk

Potbelly started brewing in 2005 on a 10-barrel plant and supplies some 200 outlets. Beers are also contract brewed for J Church and under the Olde England Ales brand name. !! ♦RAIB GF

Best (OG 1036.9, ABV 3.8%)

Lager Brau (OG 1039, ABV 3.9%)

Hop-Trotter (OG 1041, ABV 4.1%)
Golden-coloured beer with a spicy aroma and citrus notes.

Piggin' Saint (OG 1042, ABV 4.2%)
A pale golden-coloured ale with a dry flavour.

Beijing Black (OG 1045, ABV 4.4%)

Pigs Do Fly (OG 1041, ABV 4.4%)

Hedonism (OG 1045, ABV 4.5%)
A light-coloured bitter with a citrus, hoppy finish, brewed with the help of Bellowhead, a local band.

Crazy Daze (OG 1050, ABV 5.5%)

Contract brewed for J Church Brewing:

Gold Testament (OG 1036, ABV 3.9%)

Powderkeg SIBA

10 Hogsbrook Units, Woodbury Salterton, Devon, EX5 1PY
☎ (01395) 488181 powderkegbeer.co.uk

Powderkeg was established in 2015 brewing small batches of beer. It combines International beer styles with new ingredients sourced from around the world. Beers are also brewed under contract for EMAL.

Speak Easy Transatlantic Pale Ale (OG 1041.5, ABV 4.3%)
Uniting robust malt and fruitiness with balanced bitterness and a clean finish.

Contract brewed for EMAL Brewery:

Castra (ABV 3.7%)
A session pale ale with a light malt base, gentle bitterness and a well-rounded, hoppy finish.

Isca Gold (ABV 4%)
An easy-drinking golden ale balancing a hint of caramel sweetness with a gentle bitter finish and a fruity hop aroma.

Legio (ABV 4.5%)
A full-bodied, mahogany-coloured ale with sweet caramel notes, balanced bitterness and a crisp hop finish.

Poynton

Royal British Legion Club, St George's Road West, Poynton, Cheshire, SK12 1JY ☎ 07771 722403

The Poynton Brewery was established in 2015 by Colin Bavens and Andy King, located at the Poynton Legion Club. Around 20 pubs, clubs and bars are supplied in the Stockport, Altrincham, East Cheshire and Macclesfield areas. There are plans for a tap room in the village. ♦

Hoppy Daze (ABV 3.8%)
A zesty aroma with a crisp, dry finish.

Aurora (ABV 3.9%)
A well-rounded, refreshing bitter with a good dry finish.

Elder Pale (ABV 4%)
A light and refreshing pale ale with the fragrant, floral aroma and sweetness of elderflowers.

Kiwi (ABV 4%)
A light, golden-coloured beer with mellow fruit flavours.

Ginger Vibe (ABV 4.1%)
A straw-coloured beer with added ginger.

Viaduct (ABV 4.1%)
An upfront hoppy bitterness and fruity finish in this golden ale.

Idaho (ABV 4.2%)
A robust, fruity, thirst-quenching pale ale.

Vulcan (ABV 4.2%)

Slow Boat IPA (ABV 4.8%)

Black Pearl Chocolate Stout (ABV 5%)
A rich, dark-coloured and aromatic chocolate stout.

Dark Side (ABV 5.2%)

Prescott SIBA

Unit 1, The Bramery Business Park, Alstone Lane, Cheltenham, Gloucestershire, GL51 8HE ☎ 07526 934866 prescottales.co.uk

Established in 2008, Prescott Ales brews on a 25-barrel plant, clad in wood, brass and copper. It takes its name from the famous Prescott Hill Climb, which is also the home of the UK Bugatti Owners Club. In 2015, a number of craft ales brewed under the Super-6 banner was introduced. !! ♦

Hill Climb (OG 1039.5, ABV 3.8%)
A straw-coloured session beer with a refreshing fruity finish.

Chequered Flag (OG 1042, ABV 4.1%)
A generously-hopped, amber-coloured ale with a malty finish.

Track Record (OG 1044, ABV 4.4%)
A fruity, light copper-coloured best bitter with a slightly sweet finish.

Grand Prix (OG 1050, ABV 5.2%)
A dark amber-coloured strong ale with a rich, smooth finish.

Pressure Drop

Unit 6, Lockwood Industrial Estate, Mill Mead Road, Tottenham Hale, London, N17 9QP
☎ (020) 8801 0616 🌐 pressuredropbrewing.co.uk

Run by three partners who were homebrewers but began commercial brewing in 2013 using a five-barrel plant and a small pilot kit. An on-site brewery tap is open on Saturdays. RAIB

Street Porter (ABV 6.5%)
Roast notes and a bitter character dominate this black-coloured porter.

Pretty Decent (NEW)

Arch 338, Sheridan Road, Forest Gate, London, E7 9EF
☎ 07825 381346 🌐 prettydecentbeer.co

Brewing began in 2017 in a railway arch in Forest Gate. Production is mostly keg and KeyKeg but some cask-conditioned and bottle-conditioned beers are available. An on-site taproom is open Thursday-Sunday. RAIB

Priest Town

139 Ribbleton Avenue, Preston, Lancashire, PR2 6YS
🌐 priesttownbrewing.com

Brewing began in 2017 using a 2.5-barrel plant. RAIB

Prior's Well SIBA

Unit 8, Block 22, Farm Way, Old Mill Lane Industrial Estate, Mansfield Woodhouse, Nottinghamshire, NG19 9BQ
☎ (01623) 632393 ☎ 07970 885204
🌐 priorswellbrewery.co.uk

Originally established in a National Trust building on the Clumber Park Estate, but brewing ceased there in 2014. The brewery was subsequently sold and the five-barrel plant modernised and relocated to a new site in Mansfield Woodhouse in 2016 with an on-site bar. ‼

Citra (ABV 3.9%)

Incensed (ABV 4%)

Silver Chalice (OG 1014.7, ABV 4.2%)
A straw-coloured ale with a balanced hop flavour and good bitterness. Orange peel and coriander seeds add flavour.

Blade (OG 1043.1, ABV 4.7%)

Priory Gold (OG 1045.2, ABV 4.7%)
Pale gold in colour with a citrus aroma, pleasant hop flavours and an intense bitter finish.

Prior's Pale (OG 1047.1, ABV 4.8%)
A pale ale with a lingering bitter finish.

Resurrected (OG 1046.7, ABV 4.8%)
Dark ruby in colour with complex nutty overtones and a dry finish.

Wolfcatcher (OG 1047.1, ABV 4.8%)
American-style pale ale with intense citrus, grapefruit tones.

Dirty Habit (OG 1054.4, ABV 5.8%)
An American-style IPA, deceptively easy to drink for its strength. A complex hop profile complemented by pleasant maltiness.

Problem Child

Wayfarer Inn, Alder Lane, Parbold, Lancashire, WN8 7NL
☎ (01257) 464600 ☎ 07588 736926
🌐 problemchildbrewing.co.uk

Problem Child began brewing in 2013, at the Wayfarer Inn, Parbold, oppostite the Leeds-Liverpool canal aqueduct that spans the River Douglas. Owned by Johnny and Rachel Birkett, a five-barrel plant is used. The brewery is named in honour of Rachel – the eponymous problem child. ‼

Project 88 (NEW)

Beer + Burger, 88 Walm Lane, Willesden Green, London, NW2 4QY
☎ (020) 3019 7575 🌐 beerandburgerstore.com

Established in 2017, Project 88 is a nanobrewery at the Beer + Burger bar in Willesden Green. Beers are also available at the Dalston branch plus a few other local outlets.

Prospect SIBA

Unit 10a, Great George Street, Off Wallgate, Wigan, WN3 4DL
☎ (01257) 421329 🌐 prospectbrewery.com

Prospect was founded as a five-barrel plant in 2007 in the Prospect Hill area of Standish, hence the name, relocating to its current town centre premises in 2017. The brewery owns a popular local bar, Wigan Central, across the road. ‼ ♦

Silver Tally (OG 1037, ABV 3.7%)
A pale golden-coloured bitter with citrus aromas and a full hop flavour with a dry bitter finish.

Whatever! (OG 1040, ABV 3.8%)
Yellow-coloured beer with a light malt/hop aroma. Some malt in taste, but hop and bitterness dominate. Dry, bitter finish.

Nutty Slack (OG 1039, ABV 3.9%)
Dark brown-coloured mild ale with malt and fruit in the aroma. Creamy and chocolaty on the palate, with both malt and fruit in evidence. Malty and moderately bitter finish.

Pioneer (OG 1040, ABV 4%)
A light-bodied, amber-coloured beer with aromas of dry pale malt and earthy hops.

Whatever Next! (ABV 4%)

Cascade Blonde (OG 1039, ABV 4.1%)
A yellow/gold-coloured beer with zesty citrus notes; clean-tasting and refreshing lemon flavours.

Blinding Light (OG 1042, ABV 4.2%)
A pale, refreshing beer with citrus and spicy notes.

Gold Rush (OG 1045, ABV 4.5%)

A deep golden-coloured ale with hoppy and bitter flavours, light fruity notes and a grassy, floral finish.

Big John (OG 1047, ABV 4.8%)
A dark-coloured stout bursting with smoky liquorice flavour with a satisfying bitter aftertaste.

Providence (NEW)

Unit 51, Old Mill Industrial Estate, Bamber Bridge, Lancashire, PR5 6SY ☎ 07811 599147
✉ anne.graham.driver@btinternet.com

Brewing began in 2017 using a 3.25-barrel plant.

Gold Standard (ABV 4.1%)

Pumphouse

Green Man, Church Lane, Toppesfield, Essex, CO9 4DR ☎ 07421 994518
pumphousecommunitybrewery.com

Pumphouse is the first community-owned brewery in the UK. Established in 2015 it uses a two-barrel plant and specialises in session beers with occasional one-off, experimental brews. Pubs, clubs, special events and festivals are supplied within a 10-mile radius as well as its Green Man tap outlet. !! ♦

Bitter (OG 1037, ABV 3.6%)

Toppesfied Tap (OG 1037, ABV 3.6%)

Golden Duck IPA (OG 1040, ABV 3.7%)

St Margaret's Ale (OG 1040, ABV 3.8%)

Old Gold (OG 1042, ABV 3.9%)

Gold (OG 1041, ABV 4.2%)

Punchline (NEW)

Unit 13, Monmore Road, Wolverhampton, WV1 2TZ
☎ (01902) 213063 punchlinebrewery.co.uk

Launched in 2017, this 200-litre nanobrewery is run by a group of beer-loving friends. All brews are named after the punchline to jokes. RAIB

Purity SIBA

The Brewery, Upper Spernal Farm, Spernal Lane, Great Alne, Warwickshire, B49 6JF
☎ (01789) 488007 puritybrewing.com

Brewing began in 2005 in a purpose-designed plant housed in converted barns. The brewery incorporates an environmentally-friendly effluent treatment system. It supplies the free trade within a 70-mile radius, plus London postcodes, and delivers to more than 500 outlets. !! ♦

Bunny Hop (OG 1037, ABV 3.5%)

Pure Gold (OG 1039.5, ABV 3.8%)
An easy-drinking ale with a dry, bitter finish.

Mad Goose (OG 1042.5, ABV 4.2%)
Light copper in colour with a zesty hop character and citrus overtones.

Pure UBU (OG 1044.8, ABV 4.5%)

Purple Cow (NEW)

Alexandra Arms, 39 Victoria Street, Kettering, Northamptonshire, NN16 0BU
☎ (01535) 227306 ☎ (07507 398353)

Purple Cow was established in 2017. It is owned by David Burns, who is also the brewer.

Purple Moose SIBA

Madoc Street, Porthmadog, LL49 9DB
☎ (01766) 515571 purplemoose.co.uk

Established in 2005, Purple Moose is a 40-barrel brewery housed in former iron works in the coastal town of Porthmadog. It owns a brewery shop on Porthmadog High Street plus the Australia pub. The names of the beers reflect local history and geography. !! ♦

Cwrw Eryri/Snowdonia Ale (OG 1035.3, ABV 3.6%)
Golden-coloured, refreshing bitter with citrus fruit hoppiness in aroma and taste. The full mouthfeel leads to a long-lasting, dry, bitter finish.

Cwrw Madog/Madog's Ale (OG 1037, ABV 3.7%)
Full-bodied session bitter. Malty nose and an initial nutty flavour but bitterness dominates. Well-balanced and refreshing with a dry roastiness on the taste and a good dry finish.

Cwrw Ysgawen/Elderflower (OG 1039, ABV 4%)
A pale-coloured and refreshing elderflower beer with a good citrus fruit aroma, bittersweet taste, and a zesty, hoppy, mouthwatering finish.

Cwrw Glaslyn/Glaslyn Ale (OG 1040.5, ABV 4.2%)
Refreshing, light and malty, amber-coloured ale. Plenty of hop in the aroma and taste. Good smooth mouthfeel leading to a slightly chewy finish.

Ochr Tywyll y Mws/Dark Side of the Moose (OG 1045, ABV 4.6%)
A dark-coloured, complex beer, quite hoppy and bitter with roast undertones. Malt and fruit flavours also feature in the smooth taste and dry finish.

Q

16 The Ringway, Queniborough, Leicestershire, LE7 3DL ☎ 07762 300240 qbrewery.co.uk

A microbrewery situated in a converted building behind the house of head brewer Tim Lowe. It was established in 2014 and uses a 0.5-barrel brew kit. Beers are brewed on demand.

Quantock SIBA

Westridge Way, Broadgauge Business Park, Bishops Lydeard, Somerset, TA4 3RU
☎ (01823) 433812 quantockbrewery.co.uk

Quantock is a family-run brewery that started trading in 2008 on an eight-barrel plant. The brewery supplies beers to outlets throughout the South-west and further afield via wholesalers. ♦ RAIB

Ale (OG 1036, ABV 3.8%)
An amber-coloured beer with a fruity, full-bodied flavour and a dry finish.

Ginger Cockney (OG 1037, ABV 4%)
A copper-coloured ale with a hint of fresh ginger.

QPA (OG 1040, ABV 4%)

Rorke's Drift (OG 1039, ABV 4.2%)

A lager-style ale, fruity with a delicate citrus aroma.

Sunraker (OG 1039, ABV 4.2%)
A pale straw-coloured beer, light and refreshing with a delicate, clean, grassy hop finish.

Wills Neck (OG 1040, ABV 4.3%)
A golden-coloured ale with a rich, malty flavour and prominent aroma with hints of grapefruit and cherries. Leaves a lasting bitterness on the palate.

Nightjar (OG 1045, ABV 4.5%)

White Hind (OG 1042, ABV 4.5%)
A chestnut-coloured best bitter with a full-bodied, malty flavour and a dry finish. A biscuity, spicy aroma.

Quantock Stag (OG 1056, ABV 6%)
A copper-coloured beer with a malty and fruity flavour. A smoky aroma with hints of banana and toffee.

UXB (OG 1088, ABV 9%)
A strong, well-hopped beer, slightly sweet with a full malty flavour.

Quartz SIBA

Archers, Alrewas Road, Kings Bromley, Staffordshire, DE13 7HW
☎ (01543) 473965 quartzbrewing.co.uk

Quartz was established in 2005 by Scott and Julia Barnett. Around 50 outlets are supplied direct. !! ♦

Blonde (OG 1038, ABV 3.8%)
Little aroma, gentle hop and background malt. Sweet with unsophisticated sweetshop tastes.

Crystal (OG 1040, ABV 4.2%)
Sweet aroma with some fruit and yeasty Marmite hints. Hoppiness begins but dwindles to a bittersweet finish.

Extra Blonde (OG 1042, ABV 4.4%)
Sweet, malty aroma with a touch of fruit. Sweet start, smooth with a hint of hops in the sugary finish.

Heart (OG 1045, ABV 4.6%)
Pale brown in colour with some aroma of fruit and malt. Gentle tastes of fruit and hops lead to a bitter finish.

Cracker (OG 1050, ABV 5%)
Chestnut in colour with a slight roasted aroma, smooth fruit notes leaving a dry hop finish.

Queen Inn

28 Kingsgate Road, Winchester, Hampshire, SO23 9PG
☎ (01962) 853898 thequeeninnwinchester.co.uk

Brewing began in 2013 using a 2.5-barrel brew plant. Currently brewing once a month and only for the pub.

Queen's Head

See Old Street

Quiet

Buchanan's Bistro, Banchory, AB31 5QA
☎ (01330) 826530 buchananfood.com

Quiet Brewery is situated at Buchanan's Bistro. Beers are available bottle-conditioned only and are supplied to the bistro and local outlets. ♦RAIB

Quirky

Units 3 & 4, Ash Lane, Garforth, Leeds, West Yorkshire, LS25 2HG
☎ (0113) 286 2072 ☎ 07425 133199
quirkyales.com/home.html

Established in 2015, Quirky Ales brews two or three times a week on its 2.5-barrel plant. A tap room and bottle shop opened in 2016.

Porter (ABV 3.5%)
A smooth, dark-coloured ale with a malty finish.

Blonde (ABV 3.8%)
A light, crisp, refreshing beer with a tropical citrus finish.

Pilsner (ABV 3.8%)
A modern Pilsner with a dry,malty backbone.

Bitter (ABV 4%)
An easy-drinking session bitter with well-balanced malt and hops.

Ruby (ABV 4%)
A ruby-coloured ale with a smooth finish.

Intrigue Black IPA (ABV 4.8%)
A hoppy black IPA with a malty backbone.

Hip Hop (ABV 5.5%)
A full-bodied, hoppy beer with a dry, clean malt base.

Radlett

See Watling Street

Radnorshire SIBA

Timberworks, Brookside Farm, Mutton Dingle, New Radnor, LD8 2SU
☎ (01544) 350456 ☎ 07789 909748
radnorhillsholidaycottages.com

Set up in 2012 in a barn on the grounds of a farm offering holiday cottage accommodation, Radnorshire uses its own spring water. Drinkers staying at the cottages are supplied as well as a few local pubs. !!

Whimble Gold (OG 1038, ABV 3.8%)

Four Stones (OG 1040, ABV 4%)
A light amber-coloured ale with a subtle maltiness.

Smatcher Tawny (OG 1042, ABV 4.2%)

Water-Break-Its-Neck (ABV 5.7%)

Ralph's Ruin

c/o Royal Oak, Lower Bristol Road, Bath, BA2 3BW
☎ (01225) 481409

Brewing commenced in 2017 using a two-barrel plant in the old kitchen of the Royal Oak. Beer is only available in the pub.

Ramsbottom Craft

15a Halliwell Business Park, Rossini Street, Bolton, BL1 8DL ☎ 07976 263344 rammycraft.com

THE BREWERIES

Established in a garage in 2011, the brewery began full time production in 2014 with cask ale distribution being around the North-west. It moved to larger premises in 2017. Beers are sold under the Rammy Craft name. ♦RAIB V

Stellar IPA (OG 1040, ABV 3.7%)
Refreshing ale with an intensely fruity finish.

Waterfall Pale (OG 1041, ABV 3.9%)

Bumble's Honeyed Ale (OG 1039, ABV 4%)
An elderflower and honey pale ale.

Rammy Ale (OG 1041, ABV 4%)

Flaori Maori (OG 1042, ABV 4.1%)
A balanced session ale, initial light malt gives way to an increasingly red fruit finish.

Chocolate Porter (OG 1043, ABV 4.2%)
A brown-coloured porter. Cocoa steep giving mocha notes.

Yankie Lip Smacka (OG 1042, ABV 4.2%)

Fat Lady Stout (OG 1043, ABV 4.3%)
Dark brown, almost black-coloured stout with a hint of roast in the aroma and a smooth taste.

Crafty Ram (OG 1045, ABV 4.4%)

Oh Sunny Day (OG 1046, ABV 4.5%)
A pale yellow-coloured, mellow ale with balanced malt sweetness and fruitiness.

Mango Beach (OG 1054, ABV 5.5%)

Ramsbury SIBA

Stockclose Farm, Aldbourne, Wiltshire, SN8 2NN
☎ (01672) 541407 ☎ 07843 289527
ramsbury.com/brewery

The Ramsbury Brewing & Distilling Company started brewing in 2004 using a 10-barrel plant, situated high on the Marlborough Downs in Wiltshire. The brewery uses home-grown barley from the Ramsbury Estate. Expansion in 2014 saw an upgrade to a 30-barrel plant with a visitor centre and a well to provide the water. A distillery that uses grains grown on the estate became operational in 2015. ‼ ♦

Farmer's Best (OG 1036, ABV 3.6%)
A dark amber-coloured beer with subtle floral notes and a delicate rounded flavour.

Same Again (ABV 3.8%)
Pale amber-coloured ale with a citrus finish.

Deerstalker (OG 1040, ABV 4%)
Amber in colour with a pleasing hoppy aroma.

RPA (Ramsbury Pale Ale) (ABV 4%)

Flint Knapper (OG 1042, ABV 4.2%)
A smooth ale, rich amber in colour, with malty overtones.

Gold (OG 1045, ABV 4.5%)
A rich, golden-coloured beer with a light, hoppy aroma and taste.

Red Ram (OG 1045, ABV 4.5%)

Chalk Stream (OG 1050, ABV 5%)

Belapur IPA (OG 1055, ABV 5.5%)
A well-hopped IPA with a fruity, citrus finish.

Ramsgate SIBA

1 Hornet Close, Pyson's Road Industrial Estate, Broadstairs, Kent, CT10 2YD
☎ (01843) 868453 ramsgatebrewery.co.uk

Ramsgate was established in 2002 at the back of a Ramsgate seafront pub. In 2006 the brewery moved to its current location, allowing for increased capacity and bottling. A 25-hectolitre brew plant is used. ‼ ♦RAIB

Gadds' No. 7 (OG 1037, ABV 3.8%)

Gadds' Seasider (OG 1042, ABV 4.3%)

Gadds' No. 5 (OG 1043, ABV 4.4%)

Gadds' No. 3 (OG 1047, ABV 5%)

Gadds' Faithful Dogbolter (OG 1054, ABV 5.6%)

Gadds' Black Pearl Oyster Stout (OG 1062, ABV 6.2%)

RAN SIBA

Unit 8, Ormonde Street, Fenton, Stoke-on-Trent, Staffordshire, ST4 3NP ☎ 07843 092620
ranales.co.uk

Brewing began in 2014 using a one-barrel kit in the garage to the rear of the owner's house. It relocated in 2015 to larger, purpose-built premises nearby, increasing capacity to 2.5 barrels. ♦

Coppa Flya (OG 1040, ABV 4%)
A copper-coloured bitter with a dry finish and a caramel aftertaste.

American Pale Ale (OG 1045, ABV 4.5%)

Flya (OG 1045, ABV 4.5%)
Easy-drinking session ale. Amber in colour with a malty bitterness.

Hedge Hopper (OG 1045, ABV 4.5%)
A light golden-coloured bitter with refreshing fruity notes.

Owd Flya (OG 1050, ABV 5%)
Malt and roast aromas. Liquorice flavours, sweet finish with gentle hops.

Cherry Chilli Stout (OG 1053, ABV 5.3%)

Rum 'n' Raisin Stout (OG 1053, ABV 5.3%)
Chocolate aroma with cocoa. Sweet, fruity start with hoppy background, which develops to a mouthwatering finish.

Stout (OG 1053, ABV 5.3%)
Rich, dark-coloured ale with hints of coffee and chocolate.

Randalls SIBA

La Piette Brewery, St Georges Esplanade, St Peter Port, Guernsey, GY1 3JG
☎ (01481) 720134 randallsbrewery.com

Randalls has been brewing in Guernsey since 1868. The company was bought out in 2006 and moved into a modern, purpose-built brewery in 2008. 19 pubs are owned and a further 70 outlets are supplied. ‼ ♦

Range SIBA

Unit N4, Lympne Industrial Estate, Otterpool Lane, Lympne, Kent, CT21 4LR
☎ (01303) 230842 ☎ 07912 207775
rangealesbrewery.co.uk

Range Ales was planned and set up in 2016 by two friends over a few pints in their local. The brewery name comes from associations with the

Hythe small arms ranges nearby, which provides the names of the beers. A four-barrel plant is used to supply pubs and clubs in the Hythe and Folkestone areas. ‼♦V

Golden Shot (ABV 3.7%)

CQB (ABV 4%)
A pale ale with a sharp, hoppy note to the nose and the tastes of lemon sorbet to follow.

One in the Chambers (ABV 4%)

Double Tap (ABV 4.1%)
Based on an original Burton recipe; sweetish with a gentle hop aftertaste.

Black 'Ops (ABV 4.8%)
Modern black IPA with a smooth, coffee-like finish.

Rat

Rat & Ratchet, 40 Chapel Hill, Huddersfield, West Yorkshire, HD1 3EB
☎ (01484) 542400 ✉ ratandratchet@ossett-brewery.co.uk

The Rat & Ratchet was originally established as a brewpub in 1994. Brewing ceased and it was purchased by Ossett Brewery (qv) in 2004. Brewing re-started in 2011 with a capacity of 30 barrels per week. A wide range of occasional brews with rat themed names supplement the regular beers. ♦

Raw SIBA

Units 3 & 4, Silver House, Adelphi Way, Staveley, Derbyshire, S43 3LJ
☎ (01246) 475445 🌐 rawbrew.com

Raw began brewing in 2010 using a five-barrel plant, upgraded in 2016 to a 15-barrel one. Specials are available including the Xtreme range, which are one-off brews that push the ingredients a little further. ‼♦

Baby Ghost IPA (OG 1039, ABV 3.9%)
A powerfully-hopped session IPA with citrus flavours.

JR Best Bitter (OG 1042, ABV 4.2%)
Traditional brown-coloured bitter with sweet biscuit malt flavours and a smooth, balanced bitterness.

Dark Peak Stout (OG 1045, ABV 4.5%)
Easy-drinking stout with plenty of malt flavours. English hopped for a smooth bitter finish.

Edge Pale Ale (OG 1045, ABV 4.5%)
Pale ale with balanced bitterness and a citrus aroma.

Anubis Porter (OG 1051, ABV 5.2%)
Smooth roast malt and mild coffee flavours with a lingering bitterness and gentle hop aroma.

Grey Ghost IPA (OG 1056, ABV 5.9%)
An American-hopped IPA with citrus and grapefruit flavours. Smooth and deceptively easy to drink.

Reality

127 High Road, Chilwell, Nottingham, NG9 4AT
☎ 07801 539523
✉ alandenismonaghan@hotmail.com

Reality began brewing in 2009 in the unused space of an IT business, hence the pun on Real-ITy. Core beers are mainly themed around the brewery name and can be found locally and at beer festivals across the country. ♦

Virtuale Reality (OG 1039, ABV 3.8%)

No Escape (OG 1043, ABV 4.2%)

Bitter Reality (OG 1044, ABV 4.3%)

Stark Reality (OG 1046, ABV 4.5%)
Amber-coloured bitter with a hint of rum.

Reality Czech (OG 1047, ABV 4.6%)

Rebel SIBA

Century House, Kernick Industrial Estate, Penryn, Cornwall, TR10 9EP
☎ (01326) 379362 🌐 rebelbrewing.co.uk

Rebel began brewing in 2011. It expanded to a nine-barrel plant with a shop and bar in 2012, supplying local pubs. Further expansion occurred in 2015, doubling capacity to meet increased local and national demand. The brewery was sold to the owners of cellar management company, Clear Brew, in 2017. ‼♦RAIB

Surf Bum IPA (OG 1034, ABV 3.5%)
Golden ale with a fruity hop nose. Dominant grassy hop bitterness with grapefruit, apples and apricots. Lingering hop bitterness and a little dryness.

Rebel Gold (OG 1038, ABV 3.8%)
Refreshing golden ale with a light grassy hop and fruit nose. Sweet grapefruit and citrus marmalade throughout. Bitter and hoppy finish.

Bal Maiden (OG 1041, ABV 4%)
Tawny-coloured best bitter with malt aroma. Full malt and bitter ale with apple and lemon flavours. Lingering bitter finish. Dry throughout.

Penryn Pale Ale (OG 1043, ABV 4.3%)
Pale brown-coloured best bitter with a hop aroma. Bitter taste, citrus fruit, and biscuit malt. Short, fresh hop, bitter finish.

Rebel Red (OG 1045, ABV 4.5%)
Red-coloured best bitter with biscuit malt and toffee dominating the taste with bitter hop and light fruit. Light bitter finish.

80/- Scotch Ale (OG 1051, ABV 5%)
Dark brown-coloured porter with a roast malt aroma. Smoky roast and biscuit malt balanced by sweet plum and bitterness. Long finish.

Rebellion SIBA

Rebellion Brewery, Bencombe Farm, Marlow Bottom, Buckinghamshire, SL7 3LT
☎ (01628) 476594 🌐 rebellionbeer.co.uk

Established in 1993, Rebellion has grown steadily with one site move and several expansion projects, including an on-site shop. It currently brews approximately 100,000 pints per week, supplying more than 600 local pubs and clubs within a 30-mile radius of Marlow. Its ever-popular membership club now has over 4,500 active members. ‼♦

IPA (OG 1039, ABV 3.7%)
Copper-coloured bitter, sweet and malty with resinous and red apple flavours. Caramel and fruit decline to leave a dry, bitter and malty finish.

Smuggler (OG 1042, ABV 4.2%)
A reddish-coloured beer, full-bodied and bitter with an uncompromisingly dry, bitter finish.

THE BREWERIES

Roasted Nuts (OG 1046, ABV 4.6%)
A deep ruby-coloured, complex beer packed with intense malt and hop character.

Zebedee (OG 1047, ABV 4.7%)
A clean and fresh, straw-coloured pale ale with a crisp bitterness and tropical fruit aroma.

Recoil

See Copper Dragon

Rectory SIBA

Streat Hill Farm, Streat Hill, Streat, East Sussex, BN6 8RP
☎ (01273) 890570 ✉ rectoryales@hotmail.com

Rectory was founded in 1995 by the Rev Godfrey Broster to generate funds for the maintenance of his three parish churches. 107 parishioners are shareholders. ‼♦

Rector's Pleasure (OG 1037, ABV 3.7%)

Rector's Light Relief (OG 1045, ABV 4.5%)
Golden ale with a fresh, floral aroma and distinctly hoppy, bitter characteristics.

The Rector's Revenge (OG 1050, ABV 5%)
Brown-coloured, strong bitter with a good balance of malt and hops and a long bitter finish.

Red Cat SIBA

Unit 10, Sun Valley Business Park, Winnall Close, Winchester, Hampshire, SO23 0LB
☎ (01962) 863423 ☎ 07824 876489
redcatbrewing.co.uk

Red Cat was established in 2014 by Andy Mansell and Iain McIntosh using an 11-barrel plant. It supplies Hampshire and bordering counties. A small bar in the brewery sells a range of products.

Art of T (OG 1033, ABV 3.6%)
Easy-drinking speciality pale ale with a slight fruit aroma. Refreshing dry astringency and bitterness in the taste and lingering aftertaste.

Prowler Pale (OG 1034.5, ABV 3.6%)
A refreshing, light session bitter, predominantly hoppy with some malt and a dry bitter finish.

Scratch (ABV 4%)
Session pale golden-coloured bitter. Low aroma but well-balanced hop, malt and fruit flavours in the taste and aftertaste.

Mr M's Porter (OG 1050, ABV 4.5%)
A rich, fruity porter, complex flavours with good roast aroma and taste. Well-balanced with fruit flavours throughout.

TomCat (OG 1044.4, ABV 4.7%)
American-style pale ale with a powerful, hoppy fruit aroma, strong hop flavours int he taste leading to a dry aftertaste.

Mosaic Pale (OG 1050, ABV 4.9%)
American-style pale ale with a rich floral aroma leading to balanced fruit and hop flavours, fading to a hop, fruit and bitter finish.

Red Dragon (NEW)

Unit 24, Ard Business Park, New Inn, NP4 0PN

Brewing began in 2018.

Red Fox SIBA

The Chicken Sheds, Upp Hall Farm, Salmons Lane, Coggeshall, Essex, CO6 1RY
☎ (01376) 563123 redfoxbrewery.co.uk

Red Fox began brewing in 2008 and has continued to expand in line with increasing demand. Brewery experience days are available. ‼♦RAIB

Mild (OG 1037, ABV 3.6%)
A dark-coloured, full-flavoured mild with hints of chocolate and a deep roast barley flavour.

IPA (OG 1038, ABV 3.7%)
A copper-coloured beer with a delicate flavour.

Bitter (OG 1039, ABV 3.8%)
A traditional-style bitter, which perfectly balances malt and fruit flavours.

Hunter's Gold (OG 1040, ABV 3.9%)
A golden-coloured beer with a delicate citrus aroma.

Best Bitter (OG 1040, ABV 4%)
A light brown-coloured bitter, full-flavoured with a malty backbone.

Coggeshall Gold (OG 1041, ABV 4%)
An aromatic, golden-coloured beer, packed full of citrus and exotic fruit flavours.

Surrex Gold (OG 1041, ABV 4.1%)
A highly-hopped, aromatic beer. Pink grapefruit and peach aromas abound leading to a slightly bitter finish.

Black Fox Porter (OG 1046, ABV 4.8%)
A rich-flavoured, black-coloured beer packed with malty flavour and undertones of chocolate.

Wily Ol' Fox (OG 1050, ABV 5.2%)
An aromatic, amber-coloured, traditional IPA made from English hops and malt, with a soft, fruity palate.

Ruby Red Mild (OG 1065, ABV 6.9%)
A full mash dark ruby-coloured mild, full-bodied and rounded.

Contract brewed for Harwich Town Brewery:

Bay Bitter (OG 1036, ABV 3.6%)

Ha'Penny Mild (OG 1036, ABV 3.6%)

EPA 100 (OG 1038, ABV 3.8%)

Leading Lights (OG 1038, ABV 3.8%)

Ganges (OG 1040, ABV 4%)

Misleading Lights (OG 1040, ABV 4%)

Bathside Battery Bitter (OG 1042, ABV 4.2%)

Redoubt Stout (OG 1042, ABV 4.2%)

Parkeston Porter (OG 1045, ABV 4.5%)

Lighthouse Bitter (OG 1048, ABV 4.8%)

Phoenix APA (OG 1052, ABV 5%)

Red Hand

38 Main Street, Donaghmore, County Tyrone, BT70 3EZ ☎ 07748 637056

Established in 2013, Red Hand Brewing Company forms part of the award-winning Brewers House pub in Donaghmore, County Tyrone. No real ale.

Red Kite

See Glede

Red Moon (NEW)

25 Holder Road, Yardley, West Midlands, B25 8AP
redmoonbrewery.co.uk

Red Moon Brewery was started in 2015 by two friends. Beer names are inspired by their own life events.

Back Yard BBQ (ABV 4.5%)

Poison's Pleasure (ABV 4.5%)

Screaming Dwarf (ABV 4.5%)
A gold-coloured ale with caramel notes combined with rich hop flavours and a citrus finish.

Coney Island (ABV 4.2%)

Havana Moon (ABV 4.2%)
An oatmeal stout with notes of chocolate, coffee and raisins.

Samba (ABV 4.7%)

Hurricane (ABV 4.8%)
A premium, copper-coloured ale with a bittersweet finish.

Weissbier (ABV 5.3%)
A cloudy wheat beer with big orange and coriander flavours.

Partisan (ABV 5.4%)
Dark chestnut in colour, a smooth and malty finish follows flavours of mocha and caramel.

Red Rock SIBA

Higher Humber Farm, Bishopsteignton, Devon, TQ14 9TD
(01626) 879738 redrockbrewery.co.uk

Red Rock first started brewing in 2006 with a four-barrel plant and upgraded in 2011 to a 7.5-barrel one. It is based in a converted barn on a working farm using locally sourced malt, fresh hops and the farm's own spring water. It has a bar and can accommodate private functions. !! ♦ RAIB

Lighthouse IPA (OG 1038, ABV 3.9%)
A pale ale with a dry finish, floral hop nose and a citrus palate.

Red Rock (OG 1041, ABV 4.2%)

Break Water (OG 1046, ABV 4.6%)
Flavours of roasted malt, balanced with a heavy hop finish.

Red Shoot

Toms Lane, Linwood, Hampshire, BH24 3QT
(01425) 475792 redshoot.co.uk

The 2.5-barrel brewery was commissioned in 1998 and can be viewed from inside the pub. Most of the output is sold in the pub, but sometimes the beers are made available to Wadworth outlets.

Red Squirrel

See Mad Squirrel

Red Star SIBA

54b Stephenson Way, Formby Business Park, Formby, Merseyside, L37 8EG
(01704) 461120 07899 904270
redstarbrewery.co.uk

Production started in 2015 using a 10-barrel plant. Pubs and bars are supplied in Merseyside and the wider North-west region. !!

Formby Blonde/Sandinista (ABV 3.9%)
A light ale with a malty base and orange peel finish.

Formby IPA (ABV 4%)
A well-balanced session IPA with a hint of elderflower.

Lakota (ABV 4.1%)
An amber-coloured ale with a smooth, sweet edge.

Redcastle SIBA

Drummygar Mains, Carmyllie, DD11 2RA
(01241) 860516 07967 226357
redcastlebrewery.co.uk

Established by local farmer and Clydesdale horse breeder John Anderson, Redcastle started brewing in rural Angus in 2016 in a purpose-built brewery on the family farm. The brewery takes its name from the nearby ruined 'red castle' at Lunan Bay and the beers are named accordingly with a historic theme. In addition to the 10-barrel plant, the brewery also includes a bottling line. RAIB

Crusader (OG 1043, ABV 4%)

Red Lady (OG 1044, ABV 4%)

Nobleman (OG 1042, ABV 4.2%)

Tower IPA (OG 1046, ABV 4.8%)
American-style IPA. Fruity aroma with a hint of toffee on the palate.

Redchurch

275-276 Poyser Street, Bethnal Green, London, E2 9RF
(020) 3487 0255 07968 173097
theredchurchbrewery.com

Redchurch was established in 2011 using an eight-barrel plant and is now situated in a pair of units under the railway arches in Bethnal Green. The brewery produces beers in KeyKegs and bottle-conditioned format, for both the domestic and export markets. There are ongoing plans for expansion. An on-site brewery bar is open Thursday and Friday evenings (and often Saturday). ♦ RAIB

Redemption Brew SIBA

Unit 16, Compass West Industrial Estate, 33 West Road, Tottenham, London, N17 0XL
(020) 8885 5227 redemptionbrewing.co.uk

Redemption began brewing in 2010 on a 12-barrel plant. In 2016 it moved into a larger unit with a 30-barrel plant and a tasting room (open to the public on Saturdays). Most of the beer is supplied in cask to pubs in north and central London and to beer festivals. !! ♦ RAIB

Trinity (OG 1036.6, ABV 3%)
Refreshing, golden-coloured beer with strong citrus notes throughout. The strong bitterness is softened by a little sweet malt character.

THE BREWERIES

Pale Ale (OG 1037.5, ABV 3.8%) ◆
Well-balanced, amber-coloured bitter with peppery hops and citrus throughout. Sweet toffee and fruit fades in the slightly dry bitter finish.

Hopspur (OG 1044.5, ABV 4.5%) ◆
Smooth, brown-coloured best bitter. Sweet Coffee roast notes, a little nuttiness with resinous hops on the flavour. Dry bitter finish.

Urban Dusk (OG 1044.5, ABV 4.6%) ◆
Full-bodied, brown-coloured best bitter; chocolate and fudge in the aroma and flavour overlaid with citrus. Lingering, dry bitter finish.

Fellowship Porter (OG 1051.5, ABV 5.1%) ◆
Sweetish, smooth porter. Liquorice, treacle and caramelised fruit balances the dry, dark roast coffee and chocolate notes in the flavour.

Big Chief (OG 1052.5, ABV 5.5%) ◆
Golden ale with a smooth mouthfeel and a strong, fruity aroma, flavour and finish, which is also dry and bitter.

Redscar SIBA

c/o Cleveland Hotel, 9-11 High Street West, Redcar, North Yorkshire, TS10 1SQ
☎ (01642) 513727 ☎ 07828 855146
redscar-brewery.co.uk

Redscar first brewed in 2008. In 2014 it increased its capacity to a five-barrel plant. The brewery supplies the hotel, local pubs and beer festivals. ‼♦

Blonde (ABV 3.8%)

Poison (OG 1040, ABV 4%)

Beach (OG 1050, ABV 5%)

Redwell

7 The Arches, Bracondale, Trowse Millgate, Norwich, NR1 2EF
☎ (01603) 624072 redwellbrewing.com

Redwell was started in 2013 by a group of beer lovers, tracing their beery influences from England and Scotland to Canada, Sweden, Norway, New Zealand and America. It is now under new ownership and has recently appointed Belinda Jennings as its head brewer. ‼

Brewed under the Bullards Brewery name:

No. 4: Session IPA (OG 1041.8, ABV 3.8%)
A golden-coloured, juicy session beer packed full of American hops.

No. 5: Best Red Bitter (OG 1040, ABV 4%)
A deep red-coloured, malty bitter.

No. 1: East Coast Pale Ale (OG 1042, ABV 4.2%) ◆
Punchy tropical fruit nose. Well-balanced with grapefruit, lemon, biscuit and citrus hoppiness. Smooth finish dominated by marmalade and maltiness.

No. 6: Rye Pale Ale (OG 1045, ABV 4.4%)
A brown-coloured rye ale brewed with spicy hops.

No. 3: Amber Ale (OG 1047, ABV 4.7%)
A malty, amber-coloured ale with hints of caramel as well as peppery and fruity hops.

No. 2: India Pale Ale (OG 1058, ABV 6%)
A copper-coloured IPA full of rich caramel and burnt brown sugar flavours with a bitter orange aroma.

RedWillow SIBA

The Lodge, Sutton Garrison, Byrons Lane, Macclesfield, Cheshire, SK11 7JW
☎ (01625) 502315 redwillowbrewery.com

Established in 2010 by homebrewer Toby McKenzie and his wife Caroline. In 2015 brewing moved to a larger, purpose-built unit on the same site. The award-winning beers are distributed nationwide and are available from the brewery's own RedWillow bars in Macclesfield and Buxton. Experimental brews are branded under the Faithless and Clueless labels. ♦

Effortless (OG 1038, ABV 3.7%)
A pale ale with a full, fruity flavour.

Headless (OG 1037, ABV 3.9%)
A straw-coloured, floral pale ale with a restrained orange-led bitterness.

Stateless (OG 1035, ABV 3.9%)

Feckless (OG 1040, ABV 4.1%)
A classic best bitter, rich toffee and malt balanced with subtle hop flavours.

Weightless – Mosaic (OG 1044, ABV 4.2%)

Wreckless (OG 1046, ABV 4.8%)
A pale ale with a big tropical fruit flavour and clean finish.

Sleepless (OG 1052, ABV 5.4%)
An American-style, amber-coloured ale. Rich toffee malt flavours followed by juicy hops with a long, clean bitter finish.

Smokeless (OG 1055, ABV 5.7%)
A smooth, smoky porter infused with chipotles.

Shameless (OG 1054, ABV 5.9%)

Reedley Hallows SIBA

Unit B3, Farrington Close, Farrington Road Industrial Estate, Burnley, Lancashire, BB11 5SH ☎ 07749 414513 reedley-hallows-brewery.co.uk

Brewing started on this four-barrel plant in 2012. Having moved to larger premises the brewery now has nine fermenters to cope with demand. ‼

Old Laund Bitter (OG 1038, ABV 3.6%)
A good session beer, smooth and creamy with a distinctive hoppy aftertaste.

Filly Close Blonde (OG 1040, ABV 3.9%)
A well-balanced ale, bitter and spicy with a fruity finish.

Pendleside (OG 1042, ABV 4%)
A light-coloured beer with hints of tropical fruits and a spicy aftertaste.

Monkholme Premium (OG 1042, ABV 4.2%)
A premium golden ale, smooth with a hoppy taste throughout.

New Laund Dark (OG 1044, ABV 4.4%)
A dark-coloured stout, sweet with a smoky, bitter finish.

Griffin IPA (OG 1045, ABV 4.5%)
Well-hopped, classic IPA balanced with traditional malty sweetness.

Nook of Pendle (OG 1050, ABV 5%)
An amber-coloured ale with a dried fruit and malty aroma. Tropical fruits in the taste with a bittersweet finish.

Regather

57-59 Club Garden Road, Sheffield, South Yorkshire, S11 8BU
☎ (0114) 273 1258 🌐 regather.net/food-drink/regather-brewery

Regather Brewery is one of Sheffield's smallest breweries. It runs as a part of the Regather Co-op. Brewer Dan Robinson has created a series of bottle-conditioned beers that range from traditional favourites to more inventive brews. Beers are available at all Regather events, in local bottle shops and to order online. RAIB

Remedy

10-11 Market Place, Stockport, SK1 1EW
☎ (0161) 477 1842
🌐 remedybarandbrewhouse.co.uk

Opened in 2016, the three-barrel plant is located in a glazed partition in the main bar of the Remedy pub, situated in the historic market place in the heart of the old part of Stockport. Every beer is a one-off recipe, available in the pub only.

Renegade

See West Berkshire

Republic of Liverpool

See Stamps

Reunion SIBA

Units 16 & 17, Vector Park, Forest Road, Feltham, TW13 7EJ
☎ (020) 8890 8309 ☎ 07401 035557
🌐 reunionales.com

Reunion Ales was founded in 2015 by Francis Smedley using a Moeschle 16.5-hectolitre plant. Beers are available across London, from the taproom at the brewery and sometimes further afield. Beers are also available in cans and kegs, unfined, unfiltered and unpasteurised. !! ♦

Opening Gambit (OG 1038, ABV 3.8%)
Traditional bitter with a pleasant balance of biscuit, hop and bitter orange. Bitterness builds strongly in the lingering finish.

Beardtongue (OG 1044, ABV 4.5%)
Reddish brown-coloured best bitter with a chocolate and damson aroma and flavour with some honey. Lingering sweet finish with dry cocoa.

Talwar (OG 1042, ABV 4.5%)
Yellow-coloured beer with sweet earthy hops overlaid with a lemony fruitiness and a touch of spice from the added coriander.

Incredible Pale Ale (OG 1047, ABV 5%)
Smooth, amber-coloured beer with honey sweetness overlaid with a mix of fruits. Earthy hop character is present throughout. Bitter finish.

Revolutions SIBA

Unit B7, Whitwood Enterprise Park, Speedwell Road, Whitwood, West Yorkshire, WF10 5PX
☎ (01977) 552649 ☎ 07503 007470
🌐 revolutionsbrewing.co.uk

Revolutions began brewing in 2010. All beers are musically inspired. The Rewind 33 series of bi-monthly specials references music from 33 years ago. !! ♦

Candidate Session Pale (OG 1039, ABV 3.9%)
A pale-coloured, hoppy session ale.

Grip Yorkshire Ale (OG 1039, ABV 3.9%)

Clash Porter (OG 1048, ABV 4.5%)
A complex, dark-coloured, malty beer, rounded off with a smooth hop finish.

Switch (OG 1044, ABV 4.5%)
Light golden-coloured pale ale with a hop bill that switches every two months.

Swoon Chocolate Fudge Milk Stout (OG 1048, ABV 4.5%)
A sweet stout with flavours of chocolate and fudge.

Marquee US IPA (OG 1053, ABV 5.4%)
A rich, golden-coloured, well-hopped IPA.

Manifesto Stout (OG 1059, ABV 6%)
A stout with berry fruit hop notes.

Rhymney SIBA

Gilchrist Thomas Industrial Estate, Blaenavon, NP4 9RL
☎ (01495) 790456 🌐 rhymneybreweryltd.com

Award-winning brewery established in 2005 and based at the World Heritage Site at Blaenavon, where the world's first steel was developed. Proud of its Welsh industrial heritage, beers are widely available throughout the Valleys and South Wales in its nine freehouses, and through the free trade. Capacity at the 75-hectolitre plant is sufficient for brewing all its own beers and to support a range of other breweries from London to South Wales with contract brewing to help meet their requirements. !! ♦ RAIB

Best (OG 1037, ABV 3.7%)

Hobby Horse (OG 1038, ABV 3.8%)

Dark (OG 1040, ABV 4%)

Bevans Bitter (OG 1042, ABV 4.2%)

General Picton (OG 1043, ABV 4.3%)

Bitter (OG 1045, ABV 4.5%)

Export (OG 1050, ABV 5%)

Richmond SIBA

Station Brewery, Station Yard, Richmond, North Yorkshire, DL10 4LD
☎ (01748) 828266 🌐 richmondbrewing.co.uk

Richmond opened in 2008 in the renovated Victorian station complex beside the River Swale. Producion is split 50/50 between cask-conditioned and bottled beers. The former are available in the local area at the Hildyard Arms, Colburn, and the Castle Tavern, Richmond, as well as direct from the brewery. !! ♦ RAIB

SwAle (OG 1035, ABV 3.7%)
Dark mild brewed using chocolate malt with slightly more bitterness than a traditional mild.

Station Ale (OG 1039, ABV 4%)
Light golden-coloured bitter brewed using hedgerow hops.

Greyfriars Stout (OG 1042, ABV 4.2%)

Dale Strider (OG 1043, ABV 4.5%)

Stump Cross Ale (OG 1046, ABV 4.7%)

Ridgeside SIBA

Unit 24, Penraevon 2 Industrial Estate, Meanwood, Leeds, West Yorkshire, LS7 2AW ☎ 07595 380568 🌐 ridgesidebrewery.co.uk

Ridgeside began brewing in 2010 using a four-barrel plant. Regular outlets are supplied around Leeds and beers can be found across West and North Yorkshire. ♦V

Jailbreak (OG 1038, ABV 3.8%)

Plato (OG 1038, ABV 3.8%)

Cascadia (OG 1041, ABV 4.1%)

Stonegate (OG 1043, ABV 4.4%)
A pale-coloured, cask-conditioned lager. Hoppy with a grassy, floral, refreshing taste.

Black Night (OG 1050, ABV 5%)
A strong, dark-coloured oatmeal stout with a complex malt character and smooth mouthfeel.

Stargazer (OG 1049, ABV 5%)
A light amber-coloured IPA, bitter, pithy and aromatic.

Ridgeway SIBA

Stane Street, North Heath, West Sussex, RH20 1DJ ☎ (01491) 873474 🌐 ridgewaybrewery.co.uk

Set up by ex-Brakspear head brewer Peter Scholey, Ridgeway specialises in bottle-conditioned beers, although cask beers are occasionally available at beer festivals and locally. A new brewery has been operational since 2016, co-located within Hepworth Brewery's new premises near Pulborough, sharing some facilities. RAIB

Rigg & Furrow

Acklington Park Farm, Acklington, Northumberland, NE65 9AA 🌐 riggandfurrow.com

Brewing commenced in 2017 in a former milking parlour. It is a family-run business celebrating the best of home-grown Northumbrian and British produce. More than 60 outlets are supplied direct.

The Pale Ale (ABV 3.8%)

Owl Porter (ABV 4%)

Run Hop Run (ABV 4.2%)

Trickster (ABV 4.3%)

Ringwood

Christchurch Road, Ringwood, Hampshire, BH24 3AP ☎ (01425) 471177 🌐 ringwoodbrewery.co.uk

Ringwood was bought in 2007 by Marston's for £19 million. Production has been increased to 50,000 barrels a year. Some 750 outlets are supplied. Ringwood beers are now available in Marston's pubs all over the country. Part of Marston's PLC. !! ♦

Razorback (OG 1038, ABV 3.8%)
A malty session bitter with strong toffee notes in the aroma, leading to a short, bittersweet finish. Malt tends to dominate throughout.

Boondoggle (OG 1042, ABV 4.2%)
A golden-coloured beer, full of zesty hop flavours and aromas.

Fortyniner (OG 1049, ABV 4.9%)
A caramel, biscuity aroma, with hints of damson, lead to a sweet but well-balanced taste with malt, fruit and hop flavours.

Old Thumper (OG 1055, ABV 5.1%)
A powerful, sweet, copper-coloured beer. A fruity aroma preludes a sweet, malty taste with fruit and caramel and a bittersweet aftertaste.

Ripple Steam

Parsonage Farm, Vale Road, Sutton, Kent, CT15 5DH ☎ 07917 037611 🌐 ripplesteambrewery.co.uk

Ripple Steam began brewing commercially on a farm in Kent in 2012 and has gradually expanded, producing bottled beers as well as cask ales. It also produces a selection of artisan beers according to season. ♦RAIB

Gold (ABV 3.8%)

Best Bitter (ABV 4.1%)

APA (ABV 4.5%)

Classic IPA (ABV 4.5%)

Rising Sun

Rising Sun, 235 Stockport Road, Mossley, OL5 0RQ ☎ (01457) 238236 🌐 risingsunmossley.co.uk

Brewing began in 2016 using a two-barrel plant at the side of the Rising Sun. The beers are primarily produced for sale in the pub. In addition to the regular beer, various other brews are produced on demand.

Rival

60 Theobald Road, Cardiff, CF5 1LQ ☎ (029) 2030 6619

Brewing began in 2017 using a one-barrel plant in a residential garage. No real ale.

River Leven

Lab Road, Kinlochleven, PH50 4SG ☎ (01855) 831519 ☎ 07901 873273 🌐 riverlevenales.co.uk

Established in 2011 in the former carbon bunker of the aluminium smelter factory in Kinlochleven. Only pure malt cask-conditioned ale is produced.

Blonde (OG 1040, ABV 4%)
A clean-tasting, pale golden-coloured beer with hints of citrus.

Traditional IPA (OG 1040, ABV 4%)
A copper-coloured IPA, the distinctive, traditional British hops combine well with the nutty flavours of the malt.

Riverhead

2 Peel Street, Marsden, Huddersfield, West Yorkshire, HD7 6BR ☎ (01484) 841270 (pub) 🌐 ossett-brewery.co.uk

Riverhead is a brewpub that opened in 1995. Ossett Brewing (qv) purchased the site in 2006 but runs it as a separate brewery. It has since opened the Dining Room on the first floor, which uses Riverhead beers in its dishes. Many different beers are produced on a rotating basis. ‼♦

Riverside

Unit 6, Beeding Court Business Park, Shoreham Road, Upper Beeding, West Sussex, BN44 3TN
☎ (01903) 898030 🌐 riversidebreweryltd.co.uk

Riverside began brewing in 2015 using a five-barrel plant. Beers are available locally. RAIB

Rambling Monarch (OG 1036, ABV 3.6%)
A floral, citrus/spicy hop aroma is followed by a bitter hop taste.

Steyning Stinker (OG 1042, ABV 4%)
The hops used give the beer a slight fruity/spicy edge to complement the earthy, smoky flavours.

Beeding Best Bitter (OG 1038, ABV 4.2%)
Pine/floral characteristics with just a hint of liquorice.

Sneaky Steamer (OG 1050, ABV 5.1%)
Pine/floral characteristics with a hint of grapefruit.

Tubbers' Tipple (OG 1051, ABV 5.6%)
A premium bitter with an earthy/spicy character and a hint of honey.

Riviera

4 Yonder Meadow, Stoke Gabriel, Devon, TQ9 6QE
☎ 07857 850110 🌐 rivierabrewing.co.uk

⊗ Riviera started brewing commercially in 2015 using a one-barrel plant.

RBC Best (ABV 3.8%)

Devonian (OG 1039, ABV 4.1%)
A lightly-hopped, amber-coloured ale with a floral finish.

Gold (OG 1040, ABV 4.2%)
A golden-coloured ale, citrus and refreshing.

Torbay Express (OG 1046, ABV 4.8%)
A copper-coloured premium ale with fruity, spicy notes and citrus and pine aromas.

Rivington

Cunliffe Farm, New Road, Anderton, Lancashire, PR6 9EY ☎ 07989 165370 🌐 rivingtonbrewing.co.uk

Established in 2015, operating from a dairy farm with a three-barrel plant. A number of local outlets are supplied direct from the brewery. Approximately 20% of beer is supplied in cask form, but all beers are unpasteurised, unfiltered, unfined and vegan-friendly, normally available in KeyKeg or bottle-conditioned form. ♦RAIB V

Roam SIBA

Unit 9, Porsham Close, Beliver Industrial Estate, Plymouth, Devon, PL6 7DB
☎ (01752) 396052 ☎ 07971 411727
🌐 roambrewco.uk

⊗ Formerly known as Tavy Ales, Roam Brewing Co produces small batch beers using a combination of traditional and modern brewing techniques and local ingredients. A six-barrel plant is used. ‼♦RAIB

Tavy Gold (ABV 4%)
Clean, bright session ale, this balanced beer has a solid hoppy flavour and aroma, backed up with nicely balanced malt.

Tavy Best Bitter (OG 1043, ABV 4.3%)
Malt dominates the nose and taste with caramel, roast and hops overpowering a subtle hint of fruit. A complex aftertaste.

Sound Bitter (OG 1045, ABV 4.5%)

Tavy IPA (OG 1048, ABV 4.8%)
Gold-coloured ale dominated by hops and fruit from start to finish. Slight fruit/straw aroma. Citrus/hoppy dry taste. Dry bitter finish.

Tavy Porter (OG 1052, ABV 5.2%)
Full-bodied porter. Malt, liquorice, chocolate nose. Slightly bitter, fruity taste. Roasted coffee and a touch of vanilla in the aftertaste.

Roath

32 Colchester Avenue, Cardiff, CF23 9BP

Brewing began in 2016. Only bottled beer is produced at present. No real ale.

Robin Hood

Unit 3, Northgate Place, High Church Street, New Basford, Nottingham, NG7 7JT ☎ 07804 499462
🌐 robinhoodbrewery.com

Robin Hood began brewing in 2012, originally using spare capacity at Wirksworth Brewery (qv). It moved to its own premises in 2013 using a 5.5-barrel plant. ♦

Maiden's Pale (OG 1039, ABV 3.9%)
Lightly-hopped, pale-coloured session ale with a fruity aroma and hint of honey taste.

Golden Archer (OG 1042, ABV 4.2%)
Golden ale with a subtle aroma and a moderate fruity hop taste. A mellow finish with a top dressing of orange.

Red Knight (OG 1044, ABV 4.4%)
Red in colour and malty with an aroma of vine fruits and a smooth, complex berry taste.

Broadsword Porter (OG 1045, ABV 4.5%)
Dark brown-coloured and rich with autumn fruit aromas and a sweet malt taste with a slight bitterness to balance.

Little John IPA (OG 1050, ABV 5%)
Deep gold-coloured ale with a big hop aroma and a gentle bitter finish.

The Black Death (OG 1085, ABV 8.5%)
Dark-coloured ale with a strong liquorice aroma and flavours of dark chocolate, coffee and sweet, dark malt.

Contract brewed under the Bendigo Beer name:

Middleweight (OG 1038, ABV 3.8%)
A session pale ale giving a light, malty taste with a jab of fresh, zesty hops to finish.

Bitter (OG 1040, ABV 4%)
Classic amber-coloured English bitter with a rounded malt flavour and a bitter hop finish.

Stout (OG 1045, ABV 4.5%)
A rich stout with slightly smoky flavours and a bittersweet finish.

Red (OG 1048, ABV 4.8%)

THE BREWERIES

A robust ale with smooth, malt flavours and citrus, fruity hops.

Heavyweight (OG 1060, ABV 6%)
A deep gold-coloured IPA with big, punchy hops.

Robinsons SIBA IFBB

Unicorn Brewery, Lower Hillgate, Stockport, SK1 1JJ
☎ (0161) 612 4061 🌐 robinsonsbrewery.com

Robinsons has been brewing since 1838 and the business is still owned and run by the family. It has an estate of around 290 pubs stretching from Cheshire to Cumbria and out to North Wales. In addition to the seasonal range a series of one-off 'White Label' beers are produced every 2-3 months. This year may also see more 'Trooper' beers brewed with Iron Maiden's Bruce Dickinson. In 2017 it took over production of Beacon Hill and Tiger for Everards (qv). !! ♦

Wizard (OG 1037, ABV 3.7%)

Dizzy Blonde (OG 1037, ABV 3.8%)
A light-bodied beer, yellow in colour. It has malt and hops in the taste and a dry bitter finish.

Cumbria Way (OG 1040, ABV 4.1%)
Pale brown in colour with a malty aroma, this beer has a balance of malt, some hops and a little fruit, with sweetness and bitterness throughout.

Cwrw'r Ddraig Aur (OG 1041, ABV 4.1%)

Unicorn (OG 1041, ABV 4.2%)
Amber-coloured beer with a fruity aroma. Malt, hops and fruit in the taste with a bitter, malty finish.

Trooper (OG 1048, ABV 4.8%)
Well-balanced, amber-coloured beer with malt and hops in aroma and taste.

Double Hop (OG 1050, ABV 5%)
Pale brown-coloured beer with malt and fruit on the nose. Full hoppy taste with malt and fruit, leading to a hoppy, bitter finish.

Old Tom (OG 1079, ABV 8.5%)
A full-bodied, dark-coloured beer with malt, fruit and chocolate on the aroma. A complex range of flavours includes dark chocolate, full maltiness, port and fruits that lead to a long, bittersweet aftertaste.

Contract brewed for Everards Brewery:

Beacon Hill (OG 1036, ABV 3.8%)
Light, refreshing, well-balanced pale amber-coloured bitter in the Burton style.

Tiger Best Bitter (OG 1041, ABV 4.2%)
A mid-brown-coloured, well-balanced best bitter with a long, bittersweet finish.

Rock & Roll

Unit 2, 60 Regent Place, Hockley, Birmingham, B1 3NJ ☎ 07922 554181
✉ rnrbrewhouse@outlook.com

Rock & Roll started life as Birmingham's only rooftop pub brewery, set up by experienced brewer Mark Shepherd using a two-barrel plant. In 2014 brewster Lynn Crossland joined and now does all of the brewing. In 2016 the brewery moved and expanded to a six-barrel plant in Birmingham's historic Jewellery Quarter in order to increase capacity. A brewhouse bar is open at weekends. !! ♦

Brew Springsteen (OG 1042, ABV 4.2%)
A pale ale with honey.

Thirst Aid Kit (OG 1042, ABV 4.2%)

Mash City Rocker (OG 1045, ABV 4.5%)

Voodoo Mild (OG 1052, ABV 5%)

Rock Mill

2a Rock Mill Lane, New Mills, Derbyshire, SK22 3BN
☎ 07971 747050

Office: 81-83 Bridge Street, New Mills, SK22 4DN
✉ rbpine@Hotmail.co.uk

Rock Mill is a microbrewery established by Ray Barton, a former homebrewer, in 2016. All the beers are unfined, unpasteurised and suitable for vegetarians.

Mermaids Pool (OG 1035, ABV 3.5%)

Strange Ways (OG 1038, ABV 3.8%)

Back to the Future (OG 1040, ABV 4%)

Cotton Spinner (OG 1040, ABV 4%)

Orangeytang (OG 1044, ABV 4.3%)
A golden-coloured bitter with a hint of orange.

Rock Solid

Office: 25 Thornebank, Blackpool, FY3 8QE ☎ 07963 860080 ✉ rocksolidbrewingcompany@gmail.com

This brewery, based at the owner's home, started brewing in 2017 using a one-barrel plant. ♦

Blonde (ABV 3.9%)

Strawberry Blonde (ABV 3.9%)

Amarillo Gold (ABV 4%)

American Pale (ABV 4.5%)

Rock the Boat SIBA

6 Little Crosby Village, Little Crosby, Merseyside, L23 4TS
☎ (0151) 924 7936 ☎ 07727 959356
🌐 rocktheboatbrewery.co.uk

Rock the Boat began brewing in 2015 in a converted 16th-century wheelwright's workshop in Little Crosby village. A core range of ten beers is produced, all with a name relating to a local theme. The beers can be found in pubs, clubs and bottle shops in the Crosby and Waterloo area, Liverpool city centre, and Chorley, Lancashire. ♦ RAIB V

Liverpool Light (OG 1033, ABV 3.4%)
A blonde ale with subtle bitterness and a delicate hop flavour.

(Sittin' on) The Dock (OG 1039, ABV 3.5%)
Five malts and real treacle are combined to create a beer with nutty and chocolate flavours.

Dazzle (OG 1035, ABV 3.6%)
Pale gold-coloured beer bursting with hop flavour. Smooth in the mouth with a long bitter finish.

Bootle Bull (OG 1040, ABV 3.8%)
A traditional, light brown-coloured bitter. Smooth and malty, balanced with a good hop character.

Mussel Wreck (OG 1040, ABV 3.9%)

A subtle blend of malt and hops creates an easy-drinking, deep golden-coloured ale. Fruity hop flavours with a short bitter finish.

Yellow Submarine Special (OG 1038, ABV 3.9%)
Golden ale brewed with a different British hop each time.

Faith Hope Charity (OG 1041, ABV 4%)
Copper-coloured traditional bitter. A little malt flavour with a bitter edge.

Waterloo Sunset (OG 1044, ABV 4.2%)
Biscuit and toasted malt flavours with subtle orange marmalade hints.

Dragon's Teeth Chocolate Stout (OG 1045, ABV 4.3%)
A stout with a chocolate edge.

Fab Four Liverpool IPA (OG 1043, ABV 4.4%)

Rocket

The Brewery, Garden Farm, Great Staughton, Cambridgeshire, PE19 5BE ☎ 07747 617527
✉ mikeblakesley@virginmedia.com

Originally using spare capacity at King's Cliffe Brewery (qv), Rocket Ales relocated to its own site in 2017.

Rocket Town

c/o Unit 1, Cleveland Industrial Estate, Darlington, DL1 2PB
☎ (01325) 466720 ☎ 07964 301040
rockettownbrewing.com

Rocket Town began brewing in 2015 using spare capacity at Schoolhouse Brewery (qv). In 2017 the Rocket Town Brewhouse brewery tap opened in Darlington.

Rocket Blonde (ABV 3.6%)
Smooth ale with grapefruit notes.

Black India Pale Ale (ABV 3.8%)
Dark-coloured session beer with roasted, malty flavours and a hoppy finish.

Rocket Kolsch (ABV 4%)
Crisp and refreshing Kolsch-style pale ale.

Dirty Bumble (ABV 4.2%)
Roasted chocolate flavours with hints of honey, leading to a rounded finish.

Second Burn (ABV 4.2%)
Golden ale with a fruity richness leading to a hoppy finish.

Maple Dog (ABV 4.4%)
Dark brown-coloured ale with hints of maple syrup.

Lift Off (ABV 4.5%)
Caramel and chocolate flavours with a bitter aftertaste.

Rookie (ABV 4.6%)

DPA (ABV 4.8%)
Pale ale with floral notes.

Rockhopper

1 Forrest Crescent, Luton, Bedfordshire, LU2 9AR
☎ 07879 810558 rockhopperbrew.co

Rockhopper began brewing in 2016 using a two-barrel plant. ♦RAIB V

Rockin' Robin SIBA

Campfield Farm, Haste Hill Road, Boughton Monchelsea, Kent, ME17 4LR
☎ (01622) 747106 ☎ 07787 416110
rockinrobinbrewery.co.uk

Brewing began in 2011 using a one-barrel plant in a garden shed. It moved to its current location in 2014. Outlets throughout Kent, Sussex and the South-east London borders are supplied, including several micropubs. !! ♦

Reliant Robin (OG 1036, ABV 3.7%)
An auburn-coloured classic session bitter. Rich with hoppy notes on the palate and a fresh, spicy finish.

RPA (OG 1038, ABV 3.9%)
An American-style pale ale with a rich lemony flavour.

Robin Redbest (OG 1041, ABV 4%)
Light amber in colour with initial good hop flavour moving to a pleasant malty finish.

Rocka Hula (OG 1039, ABV 4%)
A pale ale with a fruity and slightly spicy taste.

Blizzard of Oz (OG 1046, ABV 4.5%)
A full-bodied, mahogany-coloured old ale with a blend of rich, dark malts and English hops.

Reckless Robin (OG 1044, ABV 4.5%)
A strong bitter that delivers a fresh hoppy punch, well-balanced with soft fruit malt.

Stoutly Robin (OG 1046, ABV 4.5%)
A rich, creamy stout with a smooth, burnt, roasted character.

Crafty Robin (OG 1048, ABV 5%)

Portly Robin (OG 1049, ABV 5%)
Full-bodied deep ruby-coloured porter. Rich fruits promote a vinous character, while liquorice undertones create complex notes.

Really Rockin (OG 1052, ABV 5%)
A full-bodied pale ale with tropical fruit flavours.

Rockingham SIBA

Blatherwycke, Northamptonshire, PE8 6YN
☎ (01832) 280722

Office: 25 Wansford Road, Elton, PE8 6RZ
rockinghamales.co.uk

⊗ Rockingham is a small brewery established in 1997 that operates from a converted farm building near Blatherwycke, Northamptonshire, with a two-barrel plant producing a prolific range of beers. It supplies half a dozen local outlets. ♦

Forest Gold (OG 1039, ABV 3.9%)
A hoppy blonde ale with citrus flavours. Well-balanced and clean finishing.

Hop Devil (OG 1040, ABV 3.9%)
Six hop varieties give this golden ale a bitter start and fruity finish.

White Rabbit (OG 1040, ABV 4%)
Light golden ale with a bitter start and tropical fruit finish.

Saxon Cross (OG 1041, ABV 4.1%)
A red-hued ale with a nutty coffee aroma and fruit and blackcurrant undertones.

Fruits of the Forest (OG 1043, ABV 4.3%)
A multi-layered beer in which summer fruits and several spices compete with a big hop presence.

THE BREWERIES

Dark Forest (OG 1050, ABV 5%)
A dark-coloured and complex beer with malty/smoky flavours that give way to a fruity, bitter finish.

Roebuck (NEW) SIBA

Roebuck, Tobys Hill, Draycott-in-the-Clay, Staffordshire, DE6 5BT
☎ (01283) 703411 ☎ 07757 503851
roebuckdraycott.co.uk

Brewing begain in 2017 using a six-barrel plant. Although situated adjacent to the Roebuck pub the brewery is a separate business. Head brewer Steve Topliss has more than 45 years experience in the industry.

Blonde (OG 1038, ABV 3.7%)

Bitter (OG 1045, ABV 4.5%)
An amber-coloured bitter with well-balanced, mellow, bittersweet flavours.

IPA (OG 1052, ABV 5.2%)
Straw-coloured IPA with an orange citrus flavour and aroma.

Romney Marsh SIBA

Unit 7, Jacks Park, Cinque Ports Road, New Romney, Kent, TN28 8AN
☎ (01797) 362333 ☎ 07796 176011
romneymarshbrewery.com

An award-winning, 12-barrel, family-run brewery founded in 2015 by former Come Dine with Me executive producer Matt Calais. Beer is supplied to outlets throughout Kent and East Sussex. A summer weekend beer garden called Ales by the Rails is operated on the grounds of the Romney Hythe & Dymchurch Railway station in Dungeness, Kent. !! RAIB

Mellow (OG 1036, ABV 3.6%)
American-style pale ale with creamy hop flavours.

Romney Best (OG 1039, ABV 4%)
Biscuit and chocolate malts with blackcurrant hop notes.

Romney Amber Ale (OG 1042, ABV 4.4%)
Tropical hop flavours with a hint of caramel.

Rooster's SIBA

Unit 3, Grimbald Park, Wetherby Road, Knaresborough, North Yorkshire, HG5 8LJ
☎ (01423) 865959 roosters.co.uk

Founded in 1993 by Sean and Alison Franklin, Rooster's is now owned and operated by Ian Fozard and his sons, Tom and Oliver. One-off experimental beers are also brewed under the Outlaw Brewing Co name. ♦

Buckeye (OG 1035.5, ABV 3.5%)
An easy-drinking, well-hopped pale ale with an orange, citrus fruit aroma and a refreshing level of bitterness.

Highway 51 (OG 1036.5, ABV 3.7%)
Juicy, tropical fruit flavours come to the fore in this dry-hopped, session pale ale that's backed up by a hint of citrus and a grapefruit finish.

YPA (Yorkshire Pale Ale) (OG 1039.5, ABV 4.1%)
A pale-coloured, aromatic ale that offers up delicate peachy and berry fruit flavours.

Yankee (OG 1041, ABV 4.3%)
A straw-coloured beer with a delicate, fruity aroma leading to a well-balanced taste of malt and hops with a slight evidence of sweetness, followed by a refreshing, fruity/bitter finish.

TwentyFourSeven (OG 1043, ABV 4.7%)
Aromas of lemon, tangerine and gooseberry, followed by a balanced grapefruit bitterness.

Baby-Faced Assassin (OG 1058, ABV 6.1%)
An IPA with aromas of mango, apricot, grapefruit and mandarin orange, along with a lasting, juicy, tropical fruit bitterness.

Rossendale

Griffin Inn, 84 Hud Rake, Haslingden, Lancashire, BB4 5AF
☎ (01706) 214021 rossendalebrewery.co.uk

The brewery acquired the brew plant previously used by Porter Brewing Co in 2007 and is based in the cellar of the Griffin Inn in Haslingden. The Sportsman in Hyde and many other local outlets are also supplied.

Floral Dance (OG 1040, ABV 3.8%)
A pale and fruity session beer.

Hameldon Bitter (OG 1040, ABV 3.8%)
A dark-coloured, traditional bitter with a dry and assertive character that develops in the finish.

Glen Top Bitter (OG 1040.5, ABV 4%)
A citrus, full-bodied, pale beer. Intentionally not over-hopped with quite a dry aftertaste.

Rossendale Ale (OG 1045, ABV 4%)
A malty aroma leads to a complex, malt dominated flavour, supported by a dry, increasingly bitter finish.

Halo Pale (OG 1045, ABV 4.5%)
A citrus pale ale finishing with a slightly bitter aftertaste.

Pitch Porter (OG 1050, ABV 5%)
A full-bodied, rich beer with a slightly sweet, malty start, counter balanced with sharp bitterness and a roast barley dominance.

Sunshine (OG 1055, ABV 5.3%)
A hoppy and bitter golden-coloured beer with a citrus character. The lingering finish is dry and spicy.

Rother Valley SIBA

Gate Court Farm, Station Road, Northiam, East Sussex, TN31 6QT
☎ (01797) 252922 ☎ 07798 877551
rothervalleybrewery.co.uk

Rother Valley Brewey was established in Northiam in 1993, overlooking the Rother Levels and the Kent & East Sussex Railway. Established and new hop varieties are grown on the farm and also sourced locally. Brewing on a 10-barrel plant, around 100 outlets are supplied direct. ♦

Black Ops (OG 1037, ABV 3.8%)
Black IPA with hints of fruit.

Smild (OG 1038, ABV 3.8%)
A full-bodied, dark-coloured, creamy mild with hints of chocolate.

Level Best (OG 1040, ABV 4%)

Full-bodied, tawny-coloured session bitter with a malt and fruit aroma, malty taste and a dry, hoppy finish.

Copper Ale (OG 1041, ABV 4.1%)
A copper-coloured ale with a good balance of malt and hops.

Hoppers Ale (OG 1044, ABV 4.4%)
A copper-coloured ale. The initial burst of hop is followed by a pleasant caramel taste.

Boadicea (OG 1045, ABV 4.5%)
A straw-coloured beer with a delicate, fruity flavour.

Blues (OG 1050, ABV 5%)
Black-coloured ale with notes of roast malt and chocolate.

Exit (OG 1055, ABV 5.7%)
A strong IPA with complex fruity notes.

Rothes

77 New Street, Rothes, AB38 7BJ ☎ 07336 233634
✉ therothesbrewery@sky.com

Situated in the heart of the Spey Valley, Rothes began producing commercially in 2014. Initially producing only bottle-conditioned beers, cask ales are now also brewed. RAIB

Roundhill SIBA

Unit 1, Lagonda Court, Cowpen Lane Industrial Estate, Cowpen Bewley, TS23 4JF ☎ 07910 567847

Office: 9 Trevine Gardens, Ingleby Barwick, TS17 5HD ✉ roundhillbrewery@outlook.com

Brewing commenced in 2016 on a five-barrel plant. Along with the core and seasonal beers, collaboration brews are produced with local bars. ♦

Bitter (OG 1038, ABV 4.1%)

Pale & Golden (OG 1041, ABV 4.2%)
A citrus burst with a pleasing bitterness.

Midnight Slug (OG 1047, ABV 4.8%)
A dark-coloured, rich, creamy porter.

Brown Ale (OG 1046, ABV 4.9%)

BPA (Billingham Pale Ale) (OG 1047, ABV 5.2%)
A hoppy and zesty IPA-style ale.

Dark Ale (OG 1046, ABV 5.2%)
Rich, ruby-coloured ale with subtle fruit overtones.

Rowditch

Rowditch Inn, 246 Uttoxeter New Road, Derby, DE22 3LL
☎ (01332) 343123

The Rowditch Brewery was established in 2010 and is a 3.75-barrel plant situated on the premises of the Rowditch Inn, where all of the production is currently consumed. Several regular ales and some one-off specials are brewed by the publican, Steve Birkin. ♦

Rowton SIBA

Stone House, Rowton, Shropshire, TF6 6QX ☎ 07854 885870 🌐 rowtonbrewery.com

Rowton Brewery is family-run and was established in 2008 in a converted Victorian cowshed on a farm. The brewing operation is split over two locations, the original brewery is still in the village of Rowton and uses water from a borehole on the farm. A second brewery has been installed at the Pheasant Pub, Wellington. Combined brew length over the two plants is 10 barrels. ♦

Moonstruck Mild (OG 1033, ABV 3.3%)

Starliite (OG 1036, ABV 3.6%)

Pure Gold (OG 1038, ABV 3.8%)

Bitter (OG 1040, ABV 3.9%)

Portly Stout (OG 1045, ABV 4.5%)
A smooth stout fortified with port.

Area 51 (OG 1051, ABV 5.1%)

RPM

118 High Street, Weston-super-Mare, BS23 1HP

Office: 19 Orchard Street, Weston-super-Mare, BS23 1RG

Established in 2015 and operating on a 10-gallon system out of the Brit Bar in Weston-super-Mare. Brewing is currently suspended.

RT

See Velvet Owl

Ruddles

See Greene King

Rudgate SIBA

2 Centre Park, Marston Moor Business Park, Tockwith, York, North Yorkshire, YO26 7QF
☎ (01423) 358382 🌐 rudgatebrewery.co.uk

Established in 1992, the original brewery was a former ammunition building at RAF Marston Moor Airfield, which was home to Halifax Bombers in WWII, expanding to a modern facility in 2011. The old Roman road of Rudgate runs through the airfield and led the Vikings into Jorvik (York), so beer names are Viking themed. ♦

Jorvik Blonde (OG 1036, ABV 3.8%)
Blonde ale with a balanced hoppy bitterness and a crisp, fruity finish.

Viking (OG 1036, ABV 3.8%)
An initially warming and malty, full-bodied beer, with hops and fruit lingering into the aftertaste.

Battleaxe (OG 1040, ABV 4.2%)
A well-hopped bitter with a slightly sweet initial taste and light bitterness. Complex fruit character gives a memorable aftertaste.

Ruby Mild (OG 1041, ABV 4.4%)
Nutty, rich ruby-coloured ale, stronger than usual for a mild.

Valkyrie APA (ABV 5%)
A gold-coloured, American West Coast-style pale ale with a tropical hoppy finish.

York Chocolate Stout (OG 1049, ABV 5%)
Deep, rich stout with complex balanced flavours and a subtle chocolate finish.

THE BREWERIES

Runaway

Unit 4, Millgate, Dantzic Street, Manchester, M4 4JW
☎ (0161) 832 2628 ☎ 07505 237078
🌐 therunawaybrewery.com

Runaway is located in a railway arch outside Manchester Victoria station. It began brewing in 2014 using a 5.5-barrel plant producing KeyKeg and bottle-conditioned beers. All core range beers are unfiltered and unpasteurised and increasing available locally. ‼ ♦ RAIB

Ryedale SIBA

Hardings House, Hardings Lane, Cross Hills, North Yorkshire, BD20 7AD
☎ (01535) 637026 ☎ 07850 510859
🌐 ryedalebrewing.co.uk

Rydale began brewing in 2013 using a four-barrel plant. In 2016 it relocated to Cross Hills. Brewing is currently suspended pending another relocation.

S&P

Homestead, Drayton Lane, Horsford, Norfolk, NR10 3AN ☎ 07552 300768 🌐 spbrewery.co.uk

⊗ Production commenced in 2013 using a 10-barrel plant constructed upon land once owned by prominent Norfolk brewers Steward & Patteson (1800-1965), hence the name. Locally produced malts are used as is water from the brewery's own borehole. ‼

Topaz Blonde (OG 1038, ABV 3.7%)
A golden-coloured beer with a citrus aroma and grapefruit taste. A crisp bitter finish.

Blackberry Porter (OG 1044, ABV 4%)

First Light (OG 1042, ABV 4.1%)
A light golden-coloured beer with a pleasing citrus aroma and deep hoppy flavour, complemented by a lingering bitter finish.

Dennis (OG 1042, ABV 4.2%)
A rich, amber-coloured bitter with a well-balanced, malty sweetness.

Darkest Hour (OG 1047, ABV 4.4%)
Roasted barley gives a faint coffee aroma and taste to this full-bodied, dark-coloured Irish-style stout.

NASHA IPA (OG 1050, ABV 5%) ◈
Strong banana and grapefruit character throughout. A good balance of malt and hop with a bittersweet background.

St Andrews Brewhouse

▤ City Pub Co, 41 St Andrews Street, Norwich, NR2 4TP
☎ (01603) 305995 ☎ 07976 652410
🌐 standrewsbrewhouse.com

⊗ A city centre brewpub opened in 2015 in the premises formerly occupied by Delaney's Irish Bar. ‼ ♦ GF

St Andrews Brewing SIBA

Unit 7 Bassaguard Business Park, St Andrews, KY16 8AL
☎ (01334) 208586
🌐 standrewsbrewingcompany.com

Established in 2012 the St Andrews Brewing Company is a four-barrel plant producing bottle-conditioned, cask and eco-keg beers. The beers are supplied to a number of supermarket chains, local retailers and outlets across Scotland including the brewery tap in St Andrews. In 2017 the brewery took over two outlets in Edinburgh, one of which has been rebranded as the St Andrews Brewing Company. RAIB

The Wee Blonde (OG 1035, ABV 3.7%)
Gentle blonde ale with light citrus hops, hints of fruit and a floral aroma.

Fife Gold (OG 1040, ABV 4.2%)
Straw yellow in colour with a fresh floral aroma backed up with a citrus punch of lemon, lime and grapefruit.

Crail Ale (OG 1043, ABV 4.5%)
A bright golden ale with long-lasting citrus and floral flavours.

Oatmeal Stout (OG 1043, ABV 4.5%)
A smooth, full-bodied Scottish oatmeal stout. Strong coffee, chocolate and dark fruit flavours balanced against a blend of hops to create a rich, silky aftertaste.

Eighty Bob (OG 1046, ABV 4.8%)
A traditional Scottish 80/- . Complex malt flavours dominate.

India Pale Ale (OG 1048, ABV 5%)
Bold IPA with a super hop kick and a depth of orange and tropical fruit flavours that are both refreshing and complex.

Mocha Porter (ABV 6%)
A coffee and chocolate porter.

Notorious BIPA (ABV 6%)
A black IPA with dark stone fruit flavours, particularly cherry.

Yippie IPA (ABV 6%)

St Annes (NEW) SIBA

St Annes Church, Lea Cross, Shropshire, SY5 8JE
☎ (01743) 860296 ☎ 07505 56951

Brewing began in 2017 in a converted church.

St Austell SIBA 👁

63 Trevarthian Road, St Austell, Cornwall, PL25 4BY
☎ (01726) 74444 🌐 staustellbrewery.co.uk

Founded in 1851, St Austell Brewery remains fully independent and family owned. Cask ale is available in all its pubs, and is widely available nationally. A ten-barrel, small batch plant is used to brew monthly specials, including beers for its annual Celtic beer festival in November. In 2016 it purchased Bath Ales (qv). ‼ 🛒 ♦ RAIB

Cornish Best Bitter (OG 1036, ABV 3.5%) ◈
Light, refreshing, tawny-coloured bitter with hop aroma. Gentle biscuit malt and hops flavour with fruity bitterness. Malty, dry finish.

Trelawny (OG 1039, ABV 3.8%) ▣ ◈
Light tawny-coloured bitter with aroma of hops and stone fruits. English hop bitterness develops into caramel malt sweetness. Strong, rising malty finish.

Nicholson's Pale Ale (OG 1040, ABV 4%) ◈

Copper-coloured bitter. Hops dominate the taste with citrus, tropical fruits and malt. Dry bitterness rises in the finish.

Tribute (OG 1043, ABV 4.2%)
Amber-coloured best bitter with a malt and fruity hop aroma. Dominant hop bitterness with sweet malt, ending refreshingly bitter and fruity.

Proper Job (OG 1046, ABV 4.5%)
Golden ale with a resinous hop aroma. Copious citrus fruits with bitterness and a crisp hop bitter and grapefruit finish, becoming dry.

HSD (OG 1051, ABV 5%)
Tawny-coloured strong bitter with a malt nose. Powerful malt and vine fruit flavour with balancing bitterness. Long malty and floral finish.

St George's

The Old Bakery, Bush Lane, Callow End, Worcestershire, WR2 4TF
☎ (01905) 831316 🌐 stgeorgesbrewery.co.uk

The brewery was established in 1998 in an old village bakery premises and acquired in 2006 by Duncan Ironmonger, who owns three nearby pubs. The brewery supplies local free houses and wholesalers for a wider distribution. !! ♦

By George (OG 1036, ABV 3.6%)
Clean-drinking, pale golden ale with a strong floral aroma and citrus notes.

Friar Tuck (OG 1040, ABV 4%)
A golden-coloured ale with a smooth, refreshing bitter and citrus character.

Lazy Days (OG 1042, ABV 4.1%)
A light golden-coloured ale with mellow floral hop aromas followed by a distinctive hoppy taste.

Worcester Sauce (OG 1043, ABV 4.3%)
A chestnut-coloured ale with a hoppy aroma and a strong bitter finish.

Dream Weaver (OG 1045, ABV 4.5%)
A light golden ale with citrus and pine notes.

Charger (OG 1046, ABV 4.6%)
A light golden-coloured beer with a citrus blast and a hint of grapefruit.

Dragons Blood (OG 1048, ABV 4.8%)
A ruby-coloured porter with a hint of chocolate and an earthy, slightly spicy aroma.

St Ives SIBA

Trewidden Road, St Ives, Cornwall, TR26 2BX
☎ (01736) 793467 ☎ 07702 311595
🌐 stives-brewery.co.uk

Owner Marco Amura started the brewery in 2010, though all beers at the time were produced under licence by various local breweries. In 2015 a two-storey brewhouse was constructed with a 10-barrel plant, incorporating a visitor centre and gift shop plus a 60-seat café enjoying panoramic views of St Ives bay. Commercial brewing began in 2016. !! ♦ RAIB

Harbourside Light Ale (OG 1038, ABV 3.8%)
A yellow-coloured golden ale with a citrus hop aroma. Fresh grassy hop, grapefruit and gooseberry flavours with moderate and rising bitterness.

Boilers Golden Ale (OG 1040, ABV 4%)
Amber-coloured bitter with an earthy, hoppy aroma. Strong, bitter hop flavours balanced by biscuit malt and tropical fruits. Bitter, hoppy finish.

XPA (OG 1048, ABV 4.8%)
Golden ale with a grapefruit and lemon aroma and dominant taste. Assertive bitterness and hops throughout with kiwi fruit and peach.

IPA (OG 1051, ABV 5%)
A heavily-hopped IPA with juicy notes and fresh bitterness.

Knill by Mouth (OG 1048, ABV 5%)
Copper-coloured strong bitter with a cherry, hops and malt aroma. Pine and grassy citrus hop flavour with stone fruits and bitterness.

Brewhouse Belgian Golden Ale (OG 1076, ABV 7.3%)
Smooth, copper-coloured barley wine. Oily and alcoholic. Complex flavours of vine and stone fruits, cloves, light malt and rising dry bitterness.

St John at Hackney (NEW)

Arches 16 & 17, Bohemia Place, Hackney, London, E8 1DU 🌐 stjohnathackneybrewery.com

Brewing began in 2018. The brewery is based in two railway arches in Hackney, one contains a 20-barrel plant, the other a taproom.

St Judes

2 Cardigan Street, Ipswich, Suffolk, IP1 3PF
☎ (01473) 413334 ☎ 07879 360879
🌐 stjudestavern.com

The brewery resumed brewing in 2015 on a newly installed 10-barrel plant. Run by Frank Walsh and Colleen Seymour, the beers are sold mainly through their Ipswich tavern, but can occasionally be found further afield through a distribution agreement with Nethergate Brewery (qv). A core range of beers is offered, but the emphasis is on a wide range of one-off and special brews. ♦

Stuffed Canary (OG 1040, ABV 4%)
A well-balanced, hoppy, amber-coloured beer.

Gainsborough Bitter (OG 1044, ABV 4.4%)
An amber-coloured bitter with a good body and hoppy aftertaste.

Honey Slip (OG 1044, ABV 4.4%)
A light, hoppy bitter. Full-flavoured for its strength.

St Marys Stout (OG 1058, ABV 5.5%)
A smooth, malty, dark-coloured stout. Full-flavoured with a long finish.

St Mary's (NEW)

St Mary the Virgin, Elsworthy Road, Primrose Hill, London, NW3 3DJ
☎ (020) 7722 3238 🌐 stmarysbrewery.co.uk

Brewing began in 2016 in the crypt of St Mary's Church in Primrose Hill.

St Oswald's (NEW)

Red Lion, The Green, Guiseley, West Yorkshire, LS20 9BB

Brewing began in 2017.

THE BREWERIES

St Peter's SIBA

St Peter's Hall, St Peter South Elmham, Suffolk, NR35 1NQ
☎ (01986) 782322 🌐 stpetersbrewery.co.uk

St Peter's Brewery is based adjacent to a moated medieval hall near Bungay, Suffolk. Established in 1996 it concentrates in the main on bottled beer/keg (85% of capacity) but has a rapidly increasing cask market. Two pubs are owned. 50% of production is exported to 50 countries worldwide. !! ♦ GF

Best Bitter (OG 1037, ABV 3.7%)
A complex but well-balanced hoppy brew. A gentle hop nose introduces a singular hoppiness with supporting malt notes and underlying bitterness. Other flavours fade to leave a long, dry, hoppy finish.

Mild (OG 1037, ABV 3.7%)
Heady aroma of caramelised blackberries and black toffee. Complex flavours with caramel, blackberries, hops and an astringent bitterness. Long, sustained finish with a roast coffee bitterness, increasingly dry.

Golden Ale (OG 1040, ABV 4%)
Amber-coloured, full-bodied, robust ale. A strong hop bouquet leads to a mix of malt and hops combined with a dry, fruity hoppiness. The malt quickly subsides, leaving creamy bitterness.

Organic Best (OG 1041, ABV 4.1%)
A dry and bitter beer with a growing astringency. Pale brown in colour, it has a gentle hop aroma which makes the definitive bitterness surprising.

G-Free (OG 1048, ABV 4.2%)
A pale gold-coloured ale with aromas of citrus and mandarin.

Ruby Red (OG 1043, ABV 4.3%)
A red-coloured ale with subtle malt undertones and a distinctive spicy hop aroma.

Organic Ale (OG 1045, ABV 4.5%)
A rich toffee apple aroma and a smooth grainy feel. Malt and caramel initially match the dry hoppy bitterness. As the flavours mature, liquorice dryness develops. Full-bodied.

Grapefruit Beer (OG 1047, ABV 4.7%)
Fudge as well as grapefruit on the nose. A refreshing fruit flavour, with hints of grapefruit peel in the aftertaste.

IPA (OG 1055, ABV 5.5%)
A full-bodied, highly-hopped pale ale with a zesty character.

Saddleworth

Church Inn, Church Lane, Uppermill, Oldham, OL3 6LW
☎ (01457) 820902 🌐 churchinnsaddleworth.co.uk

Saddleworth started brewing in 1997 in a 120-year old brewhouse at the Church Inn. Brewery and inn are set above a valley overlooking Saddleworth Moor. Brewing capacity was significantly expanded in 2011 with a new 13-barrel plant. ♦

Mild (OG 1038, ABV 3.6%)

St George's Bitter (OG 1038, ABV 3.8%)
Quite dry and bitter, with some citrus and nutty notes.

Ruby Treasure (OG 1040, ABV 4%)

The Notorious IPA (OG 1045, ABV 4.5%)

Milk of Amnesia (OG 1055, ABV 5.4%)

Shaftbender (OG 1060, ABV 5.4%)

Bitter & Twisted IPA (OG 1065, ABV 6.2%)

Taking the Pith (OG 1065, ABV 6.2%)

Sadler's

Unit 2, Conyers Trading Estate, Station Drive, Lye, West Midlands, DY9 8ER
☎ (01384) 895230 🌐 sadlersales.co.uk

Third and fourth generation brewers John and Chris Sadler re-opened this historic brewery in 2004. The brewery tap house was built and opened in 2006 next to the brewery. Around 250 outlets are supplied. A new 30-barrel plant, visitor centre, shop and tasting room opened in 2015. More than 1,000 outlets are supplied nationwide. !! ♦

JPA (OG 1036, ABV 3.6%)
A pale-coloured, hoppy bitter with a crisp and zesty lemon undertone.

Mellow Yellow (OG 1039, ABV 3.9%)
A pale honey-coloured beer. Uplifting hop character is balanced with a sweet honey finish.

Thin Ice (OG 1042.5, ABV 4.3%)
A pale ale; bitter but with an orange and lemon finish.

Worcester Sorcerer (OG 1041.5, ABV 4.3%)
Hints of mint and lemon, creating a floral aroma and crisp bitterness.

Peaky Blinder (OG 1044, ABV 4.4%)
Black in colour with malt and fruit in the aroma. Smoky bitterness and toffee in the taste with powerful hops lingering.

Boris Citrov (OG 1045, ABV 4.5%)
A punchy orange marmalade ale, hoppy flavours lead to a sweet, crisp and fruity knockout finish.

Hop Bomb (OG 1046, ABV 4.6%)
American-style pale ale. A sweet malt base is lifted by a powerful hop character.

Red IPA (OG 1050, ABV 5%)

Mud City Stout (OG 1061, ABV 6%)
Dark brown in colour. Soft, fruity aroma, malty taste with caramel and raisins, lingering sweet aftertaste with a hint of bitterness.

Saeburh (NEW)

Long Lane, Tendring, Essex, CO16 0BG ☎ 07923 973093 🌐 saeburh.com

Saeburh was established in 2015 by two horticulturalists with a passion for beer. Hops and fruit are grown on the grounds of the estate where the brewery is based. Expansion is planned. RAIB

Amber No. 1 (OG 1040, ABV 4%)
A clean, biscuity, malty ale with medium bitterness.

Citrus Isles (OG 1040, ABV 4%)
Light and crisp with mild citrus flavours.

Black Sails (OG 1048, ABV 5%)

Charge (OG 1048, ABV 5%)
A rich, soft, ruby-coloured mild.

Saffron SIBA

The Cartshed, Parsonage Farm, Henham, Essex, CM22 6AN
☎ (01279) 850923 ☎ 07980 972067
saffronbrewery.co.uk

Founded in 2005, the brewery was upgraded to a 15-barrel plant in early 2008 and re-located to a converted barn at Parsonage Farm, with a purpose-built reed bed for environmentally-friendly disposal of waste products. 40 outlets are supplied direct. **!! ♦ RAIB**

IPA (OG 1036, ABV 3.6%)

Citra (ABV 3.8%)
Light golden ale with grapefruit aromas and a crisp gooseberry finish.

Dawn Til Dusk (ABV 3.8%)
Traditional copper-coloured bitter with hints of citrus and biscuit maltiness.

Ramblers Tipple (OG 1040, ABV 3.9%)
A rich, copper-coloured bitter with toffee and caramel flavours.

Brewhouse Bell (OG 1041, ABV 4%)
Golden amber in colour with citrus and hop flavours balancing well for a clean, fresh finish.

Royal Blue (ABV 4.1%)

Littlebury Lighthouse (OG 1043, ABV 4.2%)

Blonde (OG 1044, ABV 4.3%)
A light golden ale with a delicate balance of citrus and smooth, malty flavours and a crisp finish.

Squires Gamble (OG 1044, ABV 4.3%)
Traditional, copper-coloured ale; soft, mellow, full-flavoured and hoppy with citrus and biscuit hints.

Turpins Temptation (ABV 4.8%)
Warming malty beer with nutty and bittersweet toffee flavours.

Tiddly Vicar (OG 1051, ABV 5.1%)
Traditional dark copper-coloured nutty beer with a light, spicy finish.

Porter (ABV 5.2%)
Ruby-coloured porter with rich chocolate and coffee aromas. Ruby Port and red grape juice create a soft fruit and spice finish.

Saints Row (NEW)

c/o 4 Clayton Court, Bowesfield Crescent, Stockton on Tees, TS18 3QX ☎ 07922 617622

Office: 2 Hawkesbury Mews, Darlington, DL3 6RR

Formerly known as Hells Kettle, Saints Row commenced brewing in 2017 using equipment at Three Brothers Brewing (qv).

Salamander SIBA

22 Harry Street, Dudley Hill, Bradford, West Yorkshire, BD4 9PH
☎ (01274) 652323 salamanderbrewing.co.uk

Salamander first brewed in 2000 in a former pork pie factory. An expansion in 2004 increased capacity to 40 barrels per week. Direct deliveries are made to around 100 outlets in Cumbria, Lancashire, North and East Yorkshire, Manchester and Derbyshire. An open night with live music occurs at the brewery on the first Friday of the month. **!! ♦**

Blondie (OG 1040, ABV 4%)

Mudpuppy (OG 1042, ABV 4.2%)
A well-balanced, copper-coloured best bitter with a fruity, hoppy nose and a bitter finish.

Golden Salamander (OG 1045, ABV 4.3%)
Citrus hops characterise the aroma and taste of this golden premium bitter, which has malt undertones throughout. The aftertaste is dry, hoppy and bitter.

Spectre Stout (OG 1045, ABV 4.5%)
Rich roast malts dominate the smooth coffee and chocolate flavour. Nicely balanced. A dry, roast, bitter finish develops over time.

Bright Black Porter (ABV 4.8%)

Salcombe SIBA

Estuary View, Ledstone, Devon, TQ7 4BL
☎ (01548) 854888 salcombebrewery.com

Formerly known as Quercus, brewing began in 2007 using an eight-barrel plant, before being sold to local residents John Tiner and Mike George in 2012. A complete rebranding occurred in 2016, with the brewery relocating to a new purpose-built twenty-barrel brewery and visitor centre in 2017. **!! ♦**

Devon Amber (OG 1038, ABV 3.8%)
A classic bitter. Amber in colour with a dry hoppy aroma and flavour, with a sweet malt backbone.

Gold (OG 1042, ABV 4.2%)
A straw-coloured ale with a hoppy aroma and taste and a long, hoppy finish.

Shingle Bay (OG 1042, ABV 4.2%)
A light, easy-drinking ale with a fruity aroma and flavour. Smooth to the taste with a crisp finish.

Seahorse (OG 1044, ABV 4.4%)
Toffee malt is evident throughout this complex yet subtle mix of everything you would expect from a best bitter.

Lifesaver (OG 1048, ABV 4.8%)
A refreshing ale, deep copper in colour, with a smack of citrus and orange peel and malty flavour. A dry citrus finish with a taste of liquorice.

Salopian SIBA

The Old Station Yard, Station Road, Hadnall, Shropshire, SY4 3DD
☎ (01743) 248414 salopianbrewery.co.uk

The brewery was established in 1995 in an old dairy on the outskirts of Shrewsbury but moved in 2014 to its new location in an industrial unit in the village of Hadnall, where it now produces more than 150 barrels a week. **!! ♦ RAIB**

Shropshire Gold (OG 1037, ABV 3.8%)
A light, copper-coloured ale with an unusual blend of body and dryness.

Oracle (OG 1040, ABV 4%)
Citrus aromas lead to an impressive dry and increasing citrus taste.

Darwins Origin (OG 1042, ABV 4.3%)
Pale brown-coloured ale in which hops and fruit are dominant. Hops top the aftertaste with a pleasing lingering bitterness.

Hop Twister (OG 1044, ABV 4.5%)
A premium bitter with a citrus flavour and complex hop finish.

THE BREWERIES

Lemon Dream (OG 1043.5, ABV 4.5%)
A light gold-coloured ale subtly flavoured with fresh lemons.

Golden Thread (OG 1048, ABV 5%)
A bright gold-coloured ale. Strong and quite bitter but well-balanced.

Kashmir (OG 1053.5, ABV 5.5%)

Automaton (OG 1068, ABV 7%)
Gold in colour with pine forest aromas and peaches. Syrup with a kick. Dry hints and exotic astringency as hops give a dry finish but sweet balance.

Saltaire SIBA

Unit 6, County Works, Dockfield Road, Shipley, West Yorkshire, BD17 7AR
(01274) 594959 saltairebrewery.co.uk

Launched in 2006, Saltaire is an award-winning brewery based in a former Victorian power station. A mezzanine bar, open on the last Friday of the month, gives visitors views of the brewing plant and a chance to taste the beers. A brewery tap and shop opened in 2014. More than 600 pubs are supplied across West Yorkshire and the north of England.

South Island Pale (OG 1035, ABV 3.5%)
This golden-coloured pale ale has an intensely hoppy aroma, which follows through to a well-balanced fruity, citrus, hop flavour and a long hoppy finish.

Pride (OG 1039, ABV 3.9%)
A deep gold-coloured beer with a toasty, bready, malt flavour and rich, spicy hop flavours.

Blonde (OG 1040, ABV 4%)
This straw-coloured beer is slightly sweet and well-rounded with fruit, malt and hops in the taste and a fruity, hoppy finish.

Elderflower Blonde (OG 1040, ABV 4%)
An easy-drinking, smooth, golden-coloured ale with subtle elderflower aroma leading to a pleasant elderflower fruit taste and a long, refreshing finish.

Raspberry Blonde (OG 1040, ABV 4%)
Refreshing blonde ale infused with a hint of raspberries.

Blackberry Cascade (OG 1046, ABV 4.8%)
A hoppy ale infused with a hint of blackberries.

Cascade Pale Ale (OG 1046, ABV 4.8%)
A well-balanced, golden-coloured American-style pale ale with a smooth mouthfeel, floral hop aromas and pronounced bitterness, culminating in a long, dry finish and dry aftertaste.

Cascadian Black (OG 1046, ABV 4.8%)
A well-rounded, smooth, dark-coloured, strong bitter with a hoppy aroma. The flavour is strong on hops and malt with a slight liquorice hint. The aftertaste is long, liquorice and strongly hoppy.

Triple Chocoholic (OG 1048.5, ABV 4.8%)
A creamy, dark brown-coloured, roast, chocolate stout with a dry bitter finish and a rich chocolate aroma.

Sambrook's SIBA

Units 1-3, Yelverton Road, Battersea, London, SW11 3QG
(020) 7228 0598 sambrooksbrewery.co.uk

Sambrook's was founded in 2008 and supplies its award-winning ales throughout London. The brewery tap hosts various events, is available for private booking and is open as a pub Thursday to Saturday. RAIB

Wandle Ale (OG 1038.5, ABV 3.8%)
Dryness balances the rounded, sweetish malt flavour of this fruity, quaffable pale brown-coloured bitter. Some peach and citrus notes.

Pumphouse Pale Ale (OG 1041.5, ABV 4.2%)
Refreshing, golden-coloured beer with a hint of citrus aroma becoming more pronounced on the palate, lingering into the bitter finish.

Junction Ale (OG 1045.5, ABV 4.5%)
Smooth, full-bodied, brown-coloured best bitter. Fruit and spicy hoppy aroma and flavour, lingering in the dry, slightly bitter finish.

Powerhouse Porter (OG 1050, ABV 4.9%)
Dark brown-coloured porter with a pleasant roasted malt nose with some sultana, blackcurrant and treacle character. Dry roasted finish.

Samphire

118 Sandgate Road, Folkestone, Kent, CT20 2AL
(01303) 250373

Small brewery established in 2015 in a converted back room of a homebrew shop.

George Samuel

See under G

Sandbanks

Unit 6, 4-6 Abingdon Road, Nuffield Industrial Estate, Poole, Dorset, BH17 0UG
(01202) 280405 bournemouthbrewery.co.uk

Previously known as Bournemouth Brewing, it was established in 2013 using a one-barrel plant but has since increased capacity to seven barrels. Most of the beer is sold directly from the brewery bar or from the its two pubs. A small proportion goes to local pubs and beer festivals. RAIB

Bitter (OG 1038, ABV 3.9%)
Session bitter with lingering aftertaste.

Wessex Wobble (OG 1041, ABV 4.3%)
Traditional English ale with a mildly hoppy taste.

Export (OG 1052, ABV 5.7%)
Sweeter, maltier and hoppier version of Sandbanks Bitter.

Battleaxe (OG 1058, ABV 6.3%)
Lots of dark malts rounded off with powerful hops.

Extra Reserve (OG 1059, ABV 6.6%)
Strong and well-aged beer emphasising the hops.

Tempestatum (OG 1068, ABV 7%)
A rich, dark, velvety IPA.

Sandiway

Blakemere Village, Chester Road, Sandiway, Cheshire, CW8 2EB
(01606) 301000 07543 623152
sandiwayales.co.uk

Sandiway began brewing in 2015 using a five-barrel plant in the premises of the former Blakemere Brewery at Blakemere Village Craft Centre. Aimed at local trade, outlets include the on-site shop called 'Wee Howff'. Beers are also available at the No. 4 Bar in Winsford and limited outlets throughout Cheshire and surrounding areas.

Hop Salvo (OG 1037, ABV 3.8%)
Light session bitter with citrus flavours.

Summit (OG 1040, ABV 4%)

Hop Schism (OG 1040, ABV 4.1%)
Golden ale with a hint of orange peel.

Hop Sepia (OG 1041, ABV 4.3%)
Copper-coloured ale with liquorice/caramel hints.

Endo (OG 1043, ABV 4.5%)

Hop Secret (OG 1043, ABV 4.5%)
A dark-coloured porter with coffee notes.

Chain Breaker (OG 1046, ABV 4.8%)

Klunkerz (OG 1047, ABV 5%)
A whisky orange chocolate stout.

Sandstone SIBA

Unit 5, Wrexham Enterprise Park, Preston Road, off Ash Road, North Wrexham Industrial Estate, Wrexham, LL13 9JT
(01978) 664805 07851 001118
sandstonebrewery.co.uk

Sandstone Brewery was established as a four-barrel plant in 2008. It was taken over by the current owners in 2013. Beers are available at around 50 outlets in North-west England and North Wales.

Celtic Light (OG 1044, ABV 3.6%)

Edge (OG 1039, ABV 3.8%)
A satisfying session ale, this pale-coloured, dry, bitter beer has a full mouthfeel and a lingering hoppy finish that belies its modest strength.

Steam Dragon (ABV 3.9%)

Celtic Pride (ABV 4%)

Onyx Dragon (OG 1040, ABV 4%)
Coal black in colour with hints of chocolate, toffee and caramel.

Post Mistress (OG 1046, ABV 4.4%)
A full-bodied, smooth premium bitter, ruby-red in colour, with a rich, mellow taste.ôGood combination of malt, hops and fruit in aroma and initial taste leading to a lasting, satisfying finish.

Twisted Dragon (OG 1058, ABV 5.8%)

Sarah Hughes

See under H

Savour

Office: 10 Stephenson Drive, Windsor, Berkshire, SL4 5LG savourbeer.com

Inspired by the farmhouse beers of Belgium and Northern France, Savour was founded in 2013 and focuses mainly on bottle-conditioned beers. The company is based in Windsor and the beers are brewed in small batches using the kit at Altarnun Brewing (qv) in Cornwall. RAIB

Sawbridgeworth

81 London Road, Sawbridgeworth, Hertfordshire, CM21 9JJ
(01279) 722313 07446 960409
thegatepub.net

Set up in 2000 by owners Tom and Gary Barnett, the brewery is situated behind the Gate Inn. Tom is a former professional footballer whose clubs included Crystal Palace. Special and one-off beers are regularly brewed by Bob Renvoise (ex-Nethergate).

Scarborough SIBA

Unit 21b, Stadium Works, Barry's Lane, Scarborough, North Yorkshire, YO12 4HA
(01723) 367506 scarboroughbrewery.co.uk

Scarborough is a family-run brewery established in 2010 using a one-barrel plant., expanding to 10 barrels in 2011. Beers can be found at its brewery tap, the Valley Bar in Scarborough, the family-owned Rivelyn Hotel, and nationwide via wholesalers. RAIB

Trident (ABV 3.8%)
Pale-coloured session beer with refreshing flavours of lemon and passion fruit.

Citra (OG 1042, ABV 4.2%)
Refreshing pale golden-coloured beer with light citrus aromas.

Sealord (OG 1043, ABV 4.3%)
Golden ale brewed with a combination of hops that give subtle hints of lime, grapefruit and melon.

Ship of Fools (ABV 4.5%)
A pale ale with citrus flavours.

Stout (OG 1046, ABV 4.6%)
Full-bodied, dark-coloured stout brewed using five malts giving depth of flavour and a bitter chocolate aroma.

Old Sailor (ABV 4.9%)
A pale ale packed with hops for tropical flavours and a hoppy aroma.

Schoolhouse SIBA

Unit 1, Cleveland Industrial Estate, Darlington, DL1 2PB
(01325) 461812 07506 034481
gannaway@schoolhousebrewery.co.uk

Schoolhouse began brewing in 2013 on a six-barrel plant. Beer names are school themed and available in local outlets plus wholesalers. The brewery offers group brewing days for social, training or team building events.

Scribbler's

7 Lime Grove, Stapleford, Nottinghamshire, NG9 7GF
(0115) 875 1759 07780 662244
scribblers-ales.com

Scribbler's was established in 2014 by Richard Nettleton, an author (hence the name) and Roger Frost. The 4.5-barrel plant was constructed by the owners, the fermentation and mash tun converted from old ice cream vessels. Beer names are based on classic book titles.

Beerfest at Tiffanys (OG 1046, ABV 3.8%)

Golden-coloured ale with a citrus fruit aroma and taste and a dry bitter finish.

Hoppy Potter & the Goblet of Ale (OG 1048, ABV 4.2%)
Light-coloured ale with with citrus aromas.

Masher in the Rye (OG 1053, ABV 4.8%) ◆
Golden-coloured, delicately-hopped beer, subtle malt, hint of fruit, soft bitterness.

Rubecca (OG 1053, ABV 4.8%) ◆
Dark ruby-coloured ale with a mixture of roast malt, raisin, fruit and chocolate, leading to a gentle bitter finish.

One Brew Over the Cuckoo's Nest (OG 1058, ABV 5.3%)
A premium ale with smooth, sweet hop flavours.

Beyond Reasonable Stout (OG 1068, ABV 6%) ◆
Initial roast malt and coffee giving way to moderate bitternes and a dark fruit finish.

Secret Herb Garden

See Top Out

Sentinel SIBA

178 Shoreham Street, Sheffield, South Yorkshire, S1 4SQ
☎ (0114) 399 9888 🌐 sentinelbrewing.co

Sentinel operates a brewhouse, tap and kitchen in a modern building that used to be a wine warehouse.

Sheffield Bitter (ABV 3.3%)
Full-flavoured session ale. Full malt body with a spicy rye and honeysuckle aroma and tangy orange bitterness.

Summer Gold (ABV 4%)
A refreshing ale with flavours of soft peach and ripe lemons.

Sheffield Best Bitter (ABV 4.4%)

Dry-Hopped Zestfest (ABV 4.5%)

Dry-Hopped Pilsner (ABV 4.6%)

Cologne-Style Kolsch (ABV 4.8%)

American Red (ABV 5.2%)

IPA (ABV 6.5%)

Serious

Unit C5, Fieldhouse Industrial Estate, Fieldhouse Road, Rochdale, OL12 0AA ☎ 07840 301797
✉ jenny@seriousbrewing.co.uk

Established in 2015 and run by a husband-and-wife team. The focus is on producing high quality beers drawing influences from traditional British ales, US craft beers and artisanal Belgian beers. Available nationwide through Direct Drinks. ♦RAIB

Arboria (OG 1036, ABV 3.6%)
A pale ale with a spicy, earthy bitterness and pleasant aroma with floral and pine overtones.

Evergreen (OG 1045, ABV 4.5%)

Moonlight (OG 1045, ABV 4.5%)
A silky smooth stout with chocolate notes and a bitter hop finish.

Redsmith (OG 1045, ABV 4.5%)

Arrakis (OG 1051, ABV 5.1%)
A Belgian-style IPA with a dry and spicy finish.

Goldrush (OG 1056, ABV 5.6%)

Settle SIBA

Unit 2b, The Sidings Industrial Estate, Settle, North Yorkshire, BD24 9RP
☎ (01729) 824936 🌐 settlebrewery.co.uk

Settle Brewery is located in an industrial unit adjacent to Settle railway station. Brewing started in 2013 using a 12-barrel plant. More than 40 outlets across Cumbria, the Yorkshire Dales, West Yorkshire and North Lancashire are supplied. The beers are also available through wholesalers. !!♦

Blonde (OG 1036, ABV 3.6%)
A delicate straw-coloured beer with a subtle blend of fruit and spice flavours and citrus overtones.

Jericho Blonde (OG 1036, ABV 3.6%)

Mainline (OG 1037.5, ABV 3.8%) ◆
Creamy traditional Yorkshire Bitter. Good balance of rich malt and bittering hops, giving a pronounced raspberry fruitiness and hints of nuts in both aroma and taste.

Ribblehead Bitter (OG 1037.5, ABV 3.8%)

Attermire IPA (OG 1041, ABV 4.2%) ◆
Floral hoppy aroma leading to citrus on the tongue. A bitter finish in this full-bodied IPA.

Contract brewed for Nine Standards Brewery:

No. 4 Amber Ale (OG 1037, ABV 3.7%) ◆
Rich biscuity malty taste balanced by bitter hops and a dry finish. Malty aroma and gentle fruitiness.

No. 1 Golden Ale (OG 1040, ABV 4.1%)
A golden ale with a hint of blackcurrant.

No. 2 Pale Ale (OG 1042, ABV 4.3%)
A classic pale ale with a strong hoppy aroma.

No. 3 Porter (OG 1048, ABV 4.7%) ◆
Porter with coffee and dark fruits. Hints of liquorice and plums in the aroma. The finish is bitter and roasty.

Seven Bro7hers SIBA

Unit 63, Waybridge Enterprise Centre, Daniel Adamson Road, Salford, M50 1DS
☎ (0161) 637 9929 ☎ 07968 538572
🌐 sevenbro7hers.com

Brewing began in 2014 using a 10-barrel plant. A new brewhouse and fermentation tanks doubled brewing capacity in 2017 and allowed for the brewing of speciality and one-off beers plus a brewery tap. The Seven Bro7hers Beerhouse in Ancoats opened in 2016. There are plans for expansion. ♦

Session (ABV 3.8%)
A session ale with massive citrus aromas and tropical fruit flavours. Strawberry and elderflower undertones on the palate.

Ruby (ABV 4%)
A ruby-coloured beer with sweet caramel notes. Aromas of tropical fruit, grapefruit and champagne are followed by a subtle combination of tangerine, spiced cherry and herbal vanilla flavours.

Water Melon (ABV 4.5%)

A wheat beer with a subtle infusion of fresh watermelon. Mellow strawberry and pineapple aromas.

EPA (ABV 4.8%)
A pale ale with a floral, tropical fruit aroma. The flavour is sweet with tropical fruit notes and a sweet caramel finish.

IPA (ABV 5%)
An American-style IPA, bitter rather than sweet. Grapefruit and floral undertones with a citrus aroma.

Stout (ABV 5.2%)
A dark-coloured, silky stout with a huge hit of roasted coffee and chocolate. Fruity hop undertones. Star anise is added to give a distinctive but subtle liquorice character.

Severn (NEW)

The Brewery, Tortworth Business Park, Tortworth, Gloucestershire, GL12 8HQ
☎ (01454) 269421 ⊕ s7n.co.uk

⊗ Following a short period of closure, the assets of Combined Brewers were purchased by a drinks distribution company, Foxstead Ltd, in 2017. Steve McDonald, the brewer from Combined, and Kevin Newbould, ex Flying Monk, were brought in to set up the brewing operation. A new range of beers are brewed using the 30-barrel plant, with experimental beers brewed using a smaller five-barrel plant. ‼ ♦

Copper Ale (OG 1038, ABV 3.8%)
A classic English ale with a subtle bitterness balanced with smooth malt notes and fruity hops on the finish.

Double Hopped Pale Ale (OG 1042, ABV 4.2%)
A session pale ale, well-balanced with a smooth, hoppy finish and aroma.

Golden IPA (OG 1045, ABV 4.5%)
Rich and full-bodied IPA with a robust, fruity flavour.

Ruby Porter (OG 1048, ABV 4.8%)
Dark-coloured porter with deep roasted malt flavours, balanced with traditional hops.

Shalford SIBA

PO Box 10411, Braintree, CM7 5WP
☎ (01371) 850925 ☎ 07749 658512
⊕ shalfordbrewery.co.uk

Shalford began brewing in 2007 on a five-barrel plant at Hyde Farm in the Pant Valley in Essex. More than 50 outlets are supplied direct. ♦RAIB

1319 Mild (OG 1037, ABV 3.7%)
Roast malt and chocolate sweetness with a slight bitter finish.

Barnfield Pale Ale (OG 1038, ABV 3.8%)
Pale-coloured but full-flavoured, this is a traditional, hoppy bitter rather than a golden ale. Malt persists throughout, with bitterness becoming more dominant towards the end.

Braintree Market Ale (OG 1040, ABV 4%)
Traditional, easy-drinking session ale with a hoppy, lingering, dry finish.

Levelly Gold (OG 1040, ABV 4%)
Golden-coloured bitter with a pleasant finish.

Stoneley Bitter (OG 1042, ABV 4.2%)
Dark amber-coloured session beer whose vivid hop character is supported by a juicy, malty body. A dry finish makes this beer very drinkable.

Hyde Bitter (OG 1047, ABV 4.7%)
Stronger version of Barnfield, with a similar but more assertive character.

Levelly Black (OG 1048, ABV 4.8%)
A dark-coloured, heavy, well-hopped ale with a grainy toffee taste topped with a thick creamy head.

Rotten End (OG 1065, ABV 6.5%)
Strong beer with slightly sweet, nutty undertones and a bitter edge to finish.

Shardlow

The Old Brewery Stables, British Waterways Yard, Cavendish Bridge, Leicestershire, DE72 2HL
☎ (01332) 799188 ✉ nev@shardlowbrewery.co.uk

On a site associated with brewing since 1819, Shardlow delivers to more than 100 outlets throughout the East Midlands and is also one of the largest UK cider distributors. Reverend Eaton is named after a scion of the Eaton brewing family, Rector of Shardlow for 40 years. The brewery tap is the Blue Bell Inn at Melbourne, Derbyshire. Prolific supplier of beers to local beer festivals. ‼♦RAIB

Chancellors Revenge (OG 1036, ABV 3.6%)
A light-coloured, refreshing, full-flavoured and well-hopped session bitter.

Cavendish Dark (OG 1037, ABV 3.7%)
A mild, well-balanced beer with a hoppy aftertaste.

Golden Hop (OG 1041, ABV 4.1%)
Golden-coloured, sweet-tasting beer with a hoppy aroma.

Kiln House (OG 1041, ABV 4.1%)
A refreshing golden ale with a lingering bitter finish.

Narrow Boat (OG 1043, ABV 4.3%)
A pale amber-coloured bitter with a short, crisp, hoppy aftertaste.

Cavendish Bridge (OG 1045, ABV 4.5%)
Pale amber-coloured premium bitter. Refreshing, clean and fruity with a pleasing bitter finish.

Cavendish Gold (OG 1045, ABV 4.5%)
Pale gold in colour, bright and clean-tasting. A full-bodied ale with pronounced bitterness and complexity.

Reverend Eaton (OG 1045, ABV 4.5%)
A smooth, medium-strong bitter, full of malt and hop flavours with a sweet aftertaste.

Mayfly (OG 1048, ABV 4.8%)
Fruit notes predominate together with a pronounced malty aroma. Easy-drinking but strong.

Five Bells (OG 1050, ABV 5%)
Rich, ruby-coloured ale, powerful and bittersweet to the palate. Coffee notes complete the profile.

Whistlestop (OG 1050, ABV 5%)
A smooth and surprisingly strong, pale-coloured beer.

Sharp's

Pityme Business Centre, Rock, Cornwall, PL27 6NU
☎ (01208) 862121 ⊕ sharpsbrewery.co.uk

THE BREWERIES

⊗ Sharp's was bought for £20 million by Molson Coors in 2011. The brewery was founded in 1994 and within 15 years had grown from producing 1,500 barrels a year to 60,000. £7.5 million of investment from Molson Coors has brought the capacity up to 200,000 barrels a year. The company owns no pubs and delivers beer to more than 1,200 outlets across the south of England via temperature-controlled depots in Bristol and London. Molson Coors has stressed that it will maintain production in Cornwall. Part of Molson Coors PLC. ♦ RAIB

Cornish Coaster (OG 1035.2, ABV 3.6%)
Refreshing, amber-coloured bitter. Gentle balance of biscuit malt, fruit and sweetness. Fruit in the finish with bitterness and faint dryness.

Doom Bar (OG 1038.5, ABV 4%)
Pale brown-coloured bitter with gentle fruit aroma. Balanced taste of biscuit malt, resinous hops with apple, strawberry and plum fruits.

Atlantic (OG 1043, ABV 4.2%)
Amber-coloured best bitter with fragrant hop aroma. Orange citrus with caramel sweetness balanced by malt and bitterness. Tropical fruit hints.

Original (OG 1042.5, ABV 4.4%)
Mid brown-coloured best bitter with a firm malt aroma. Dominant malt taste with apple fruit, bitter, earthy hops and faint roast.

Sea Fury (OG 1050, ABV 5%)
Smooth, red-coloured strong bitter with a malt and fruit aroma. Malty taste balanced by bitter hopping with mixed and roast fruits throughout.

Shed

Broadfields, Pewsey, Wiltshire, SN9 5DT
☎ (01672) 564533 ☎ 07769 812643
shedales.com

Shed Ales was launched in 2012 operating from a one-barrel plant in a converted garden shed. The brewery currently produces three core ales and several bespoke beers, available at selected local outlets including the brewery-owned Shed Alehouse, a micropub in Pewsey. ♦

Dig It (OG 1037.5, ABV 3.7%)

Shed Some Light (OG 1041, ABV 3.8%)
A refreshing blonde ale with a light earthy hop aroma and flavour.

Dibber (OG 1042.5, ABV 4.2%)
Light amber in colour with a biscuit malt and citrus hop aroma. Easy-drinking with a good balance of malt and fruity hop notes and dry finish.

Sheelin

178 Derrylin Road, Bellanaleck, County Fermanagh, BT92 2BA ☎ 07730 432232 sheelin.com

Sheelin was established by brewer and chemist Dr George Cathcart in 2013. Beer is mainly available in bottles.

Sheffield SIBA

Unit 111, JC Albyn Complex, Burton Road, Sheffield, South Yorkshire, S3 8BT
☎ (0114) 272 7256 sheffieldbrewery.com

Established in 2006, Sheffield Brewery Company is situated in a rustic Victorian factory, originally known for making Blanco polish. The 10-barrel plant operates on a gravity-fed tower based system. The brewery has its own on-site tap room. !!

Crucible Best (OG 1038, ABV 3.8%)

Five Rivers (OG 1038, ABV 3.8%)
Easy-drinking, straw-coloured ale with a hoppy aroma that carries through to the finish.

Seven Hills (OG 1039, ABV 4.1%)
A crisp, refreshing, hop-forward session IPA. Full of citrus flavours and a bitter punch.

Blanco Blonde (OG 1042, ABV 4.2%)

Porter (OG 1045, ABV 4.4%)
A dark-coloured porter with a rich chocolate, malty and caramel flavour.

Shepherd Neame IFBB

17 Court Street, Faversham, Kent, ME13 7AX
☎ (01795) 532206 shepherdneame.co.uk

⊗ Shepherd Neame traces its history back to 1698, making it the oldest continuous brewer in the country, though brewing probably began even earlier. The company has 350 tied houses in the South-east, nearly all selling cask ale. More than 2,000 other outlets are also supplied. The cask beers are made with mostly Kentish hops, and water from the brewery's own artesian well. There is a microplant within the brewery to produce speciality ales for special occasions and product development. These beers may be available in selected pubs. The company also brews cask ales under the Faversham Steam Brewery and No. 18 Yard Brewhouse names. !! ♦ RAIB

Master Brew (OG 1032, ABV 3.7%)
A distinctive bitter, mid-brown in colour, with a hoppy aroma. Well-balanced, with a nicely aggressive bitter taste from its hops, it leaves a hoppy/bitter finish, tinged with sweetness.

Whitstable Bay Pale Ale (OG 1038, ABV 3.9%)
A full-bodied, fruity ale with a subtle bitterness and grapefruit and pine aromas.

Kent's Best (OG 1036, ABV 4.1%)
A robust bitter, which merges the biscuity sweetness of English malt with the fruity, floral bitterness of locally-grown hops.

Spitfire Gold (ABV 4.1%)
A well-balanced golden ale with tropical fruit and pine aromas, and a subtle bitterness.

Spitfire (OG 1036, ABV 4.2%)
A well-balanced bitter. Hints of marmalade, red grapes and pepper, with warm, mellow malts. A fruity finish with hints of spice and raspberry.

Bishops Finger (OG 1046, ABV 5%)
A strong ale with a complex hop[aroma reminiscent of lemons, oranges and bananas combined with malt, molasses and toffee. Refreshing, with a good malt character tinged with a lingering bitterness.

Sherfield Village SIBA

Goddards Farm, Goddards Lane, Sherfield on Loddon, Hampshire, RG27 0EL ☎ 07906 060429
sherfieldvillagebrewery.co.uk

Production started in 2011 in a converted barn on a working dairy farm. Using a five-barrel plant, the brewery supplies local pubs and regional festivals. Extensive use is made of New World hops (prefixed SOLO), particularly those from New Zealand. Dry-hopped versions of single-hop beers are usually available. ♦RAIB

Threesome (OG 1030, ABV 3%)
Copper-coloured session beer with a long hoppy finish.

SOLO Southern Gold (OG 1040, ABV 4%)
A golden-coloured beer with a citrus flavour and a floral aroma.

SOLO Green Bullet (OG 1042, ABV 4.3%) ◈
A strong, lemony nose, with hops dominating the taste building to a strong aftertaste with a big astringent hit at the end.

SOLO Single Hop (OG 1042, ABV 4.3%)
A golden ale which uses a single hop variety that changes every month, thereby subtly changing the beer characteristics.

Hoppy Harrington (OG 1046, ABV 4.7%)
A mid-brown-coloured strong bitter with a complex, sweetish flavour and a satisfying, hoppy finish.

Pioneer Stout (OG 1048, ABV 5%)
A black-coloured stout, chocolaty with a hint of vanilla.

Shilling

92 West George Street, Glasgow, G2 1PJ
☎ (0141) 353 1654 🌐 shillingbrewingcompany.co.uk

Brewing began in 2016.

ShinDigger

Office: 170 Vie Building, 185 Water Street, Manchester, M3 4JU 🌐 shindiggerbrewing.co

Established in 2012, ShinDigger's output is predominantly keg and cans supplied to outlets such as restaurants and music venues around Manchester. Music, beer and food events are run. Beers are contract brewed in Cumbria and Lancaster.

Shiny SIBA

Unit 10, Old Hall Mill Business Centre, Little Eaton, Derbyshire, DE21 5EJ
☎ (01332) 902809

Brewing commenced in 2012 using a six-barrel plant sited in the beer garden of the Furnace Inn. After initially brewing solely for the pub, 2014 saw an increase in scale and output, with beers distributed across most of the country. A second 12-barrel brew plant was built in 2015 to increase capacity and host a visitor centre and shop. ♦RAIB

New World (OG 1039, ABV 3.7%)
Golden in colour with powerful citrus hop flavours.

MOA (OG 1038, ABV 3.9%)
An ever-evolving, New Zealand hopped session pale ale.

Wrench (OG 1045, ABV 4.4%)
A stout with six different malts for a complex, rich flavour profile.

4 Wood (OG 1045, ABV 4.5%)
Traditional, well-balanced, light chestnut-coloured ale with a delicate hop finish.

Affinity (OG 1046, ABV 4.6%)
Strong, golden-coloured bitter with lots of fruity hops.

Disco Balls (OG 1050, ABV 5.3%)
A hop-loaded IPA.

Tomahawk (OG 1055, ABV 6%)
An American-style, brown-coloured IPA with a citrus flavour and aroma.

Ship & Mitre

See Flagship

Ship Inn

Ship Inn, Low Newton-by-the-Sea, Northumberland, NE66 3EL
☎ (01665) 576262 🌐 shipinnnewton.co.uk

Brewing commenced in 2008 on a 2.5-barrel plant. The brewery now produces 7.5 barrels per week. All regular beers are brewed in constant rotation but are only available on the premises. A special beer (4.2% ABV) is brewed for every 100 brews. ♦RAIB

Shipstone's SIBA

Little Star Brewery, Fox & Crown, Church Street, Old Basford, Nottingham, NG6 0GA
☎ (0115) 871 6477

Office: 27 Grace Drive, Nottingham, NG8 5AG
🌐 shipstones.com

Set up in 1996, originally as Fiddlers Ales. In 1999 it became Alcazar Brewery on change of ownership. A full mash brewery with a 10-barrel brew length, it is located behind the Fox & Crown. The brewery changed hands in early 2016, when the name of the brewery was changed again and a new portfolio of beers established but this was short lived and it soon reverted back to the name Alcazar. In late 2016 Shipstone's took over brewing, producing its range of beers that had previously been contract brewed at Belvoir Brewery (qv). Beers are also brewed under the Hollow Stone Brewing Co name. ♦

Mild (OG 1038, ABV 3.5%)
A traditional dark mild with aromas of roasted nuts and chocolate caramel. A soft, sweet flavour with a mix of dark, ripe fruits.

Original (OG 1040, ABV 3.8%) ◈
Pale brown-coloured, malty, traditional bitter, well-balanced in both hops and bitterness without either becoming overpowering.

Nut Brown (OG 1042, ABV 4%)
Full-bodied ale with a rich, nut brown colour and a malty finish. Hints of butterscotch and mild liquorice, caramel and roasted flavours.

Gold Star (OG 1043, ABV 4.2%) ◈
Golden in colour with a delicate citrus hop and slightly dry bitter finish.

India Pale Ale (OG 1054, ABV 5.5%)
A hoppy IPA with a fresh, floral aroma with plenty of citrus and grapefruit.

Brewed under the Hollow Stone Brewing Co name:

Oligo Nunk (OG 1041, ABV 4%)

Pale Ale (OG 1043, ABV 4.2%)

Waitomo (OG 1045, ABV 4.5%)

Spelunker (OG 1049, ABV 5%)

Shortts SIBA

Shortts Farm, Thorndon, Suffolk, IP23 7LS ☎ 07900 268100 🌐 shorttsfarmbrewery.com

An award-winning brewery established in 2012 by Matt Hammond on what has been the family farm for over a century. The beers are based around a musical theme and can be found throughout East Anglia. RAIB

The Cure (ABV 3.6%)

Strummer (OG 1038, ABV 3.8%)
An amber-coloured ale, light and hoppy with a malty character.

Two Tone (ABV 3.8%)

Blondie (OG 1040, ABV 4%)

Skiffle (OG 1047, ABV 4.5%)
A chestnut-coloured, complex, malty premium bitter with a good balance of hops over malt.

Indie (OG 1048, ABV 4.8%)

Shotover SIBA

Coopers Yard, Manor Farm Road, Horspath, Oxfordshire, OX33 1SD
☎ (01865) 604620 ☎ 07710 883273
🌐 shotoverbrewing.com

⊗ A family-owned and run brewery four miles from Oxford city centre. It began brewing in 2009 and supplies outlets in the Oxford area. ‼ ♦ RAIB

Prospect (OG 1040, ABV 3.7%)

Trinity (OG 1040, ABV 4.2%)
Pale gold in colour with an intense grapefruit hop character.

Scholar (OG 1047, ABV 4.5%)
Deep copper-coloured premium bitter combining a silky malt base with a mixture of oranges, grapefruit and spiciness.

Shottle Farm

School House Farm, Lodge Lane, Shottle, Derbyshire, DE56 2DS
☎ (01773) 550056 ☎ 07877 723075
🌐 shottlefarmbrewery.co.uk

Located in the hills above Belper, the Grade II-listed farm is part of the Chatsworth Estate. Family-run, Shottle Farm Brewery has been in production since 2011 with a 10-barrel plant. It has an on-site bar (limited opening hours), the Bull Shed, which is the only outlet for its beers. ♦ RAIB

Shugborough

Shugborough Estate, Milford, Staffordshire, ST17 0XB ☎ (01782) 823447 🌐 shugborough.org.uk

Brewing in the original brewhouse at Shugborough, home of the Earls of Lichfield, restarted in 1990, but a lack of expertise led to the brewery being a static museum piece until Titanic Brewery of Stoke-on-Trent (qv) began helping in 1996. ‼

Signal SIBA

8 Stirling Way, Beddington Farm Road, Croydon, CR0 4XN
☎ (020) 8684 6111 🌐 signallager.com

Brewing began in 2016. No real ale.

Signature Brew SIBA

Unit 25, Leyton Business Centre, Etloe Road, Leyton, London, E10 7BT
☎ (020) 7684 4664 🌐 signaturebrew.co.uk

Signature Brew has been brewing beer inspired by music since 2011. Originally using spare capacity at a number of breweries, a successful crowd funding initiative has resulted in it owning its own brewery in Leyton. Special seasonal beers are brewed in collaboration with music artists. ♦ RAIB

Session (OG 1042, ABV 4%) ◆
Refreshing bitter with spicy hop on the nose and palate balanced by a malty sweetness and a lingering bitterness.

Signature Pale (OG 1033, ABV 4.1%) ◆
Golden-coloured beer using pale malts with a little wheat. The American hops give the beer its fruity character.

Black Vinyl Stout (OG 1046, ABV 4.2%) ◆
Rich cocoa roasted notes predominate on the palate balanced by some sweetness and American hops giving lightness to the flavour.

Red Wedge (OG 1047, ABV 4.7%) ◆
Reddish brown-coloured beer with a hoppy, fruity aroma. Flavour is dominated by hops with bitterness coming through later. Tangerine fruit notes.

Backstage IPA (OG 1054, ABV 5.6%) ◆
Amber-coloured, unfined IPA with fruity hops and a bitterness overlaid with some banana and biscuity malty notes. Lingering, dry finish.

Silhill SIBA

Oak Farm, Hampton Lane, Solihull, West Midlands, B92 0JB ☎ 07977 444564

Office: PO Box 15739, Solihull, B93 3FW
🌐 silhillbrewery.co.uk

⊗ Established in 2010, Silhill is a small independent brewery based in premises just outside Solihull town centre using a 10-barrel plant. Bottling operations commenced in 2015. Beers are available in Solihull, Birmingham and Stratford-upon-Avon as well as in Malmaison restaurants. ‼ RAIB

Gold Star (OG 1039, ABV 3.9%)
An amber-coloured ale. Malty and smooth, finishing with a delicate honey note.

Blonde Star (OG 1041, ABV 4.1%)
A refreshing, sweet citrus pale ale.

HOP star (OG 1041, ABV 4.2%)
A golden-coloured, American-style IPA with grapefruit, lemon and tropical fruit zest flavours.

Pure Star (OG 1043, ABV 4.3%)
A chestnut-coloured ale, warm and well-balanced with a hint of chocolate.

Silks SIBA

Wash Farm, Queen Street, Sible Hedingham, Essex, CO9 3RH
☎ (01787) 275513 ☎ 07921 654910
silksbrewery@co.uk

Silks is a five-barrel microbrewery producing hand-crafted ales in small batches. Established in 2015, it is based on a North Essex farm in a converted grain store. ♦RAIB

Molly's Jolly Mild (OG 1036, ABV 3.6%)
A dark-coloured, mellow mild with hints of dark chocolate and roasted coffee.

Veteran Campaigner (OG 1037, ABV 3.7%)
An amber-coloured session ale with a spicy finish.

Whacker Payne (OG 1037, ABV 3.8%)
A crisp, golden-coloured ale with subtle fruity citrus hints.

Old Man Shirv (OG 1043, ABV 4.5%)
A smooth and full-bodied, copper-coloured premium ale with a rich malt flavour.

Pegstar Porter (OG 1048, ABV 4.8%)

Silver Street

Britannia Mill, Cobden Street, Bury, BL9 6AW
☎ 07515 651874
silverstreetbrewingcompany.com

Brewing began in 2014 at the Clarence on Silver Street, Bury. The brewery has since expanded to a 15-barrel plant at Britannia Mill. !!♦

Session (OG 1039, ABV 3.9%)

Fire Island (OG 1040, ABV 4%)

One (OG 1040, ABV 4%)

Ruby, Ruby, Ruby, Ruby (OG 1047, ABV 4.7%)
Deep ruby-coloured ale with a slight treacle undertone and a floral aroma.

Porter (OG 1053, ABV 5%)
An easy-drinking porter with a treacle toffee flavour balanced with American hops.

Red (OG 1055, ABV 5.5%)
A well-balanced IPA with biscuit flavours, floral hops and an intense maltiness.

USA IPA (OG 1056, ABV 5.7%)
Malty caramel undertones and bold American hops.

Silverstone SIBA

Office: Shacks Barn Farm, Silverstone, Northamptonshire, NN12 8TB
☎ (01280) 860288 ☎ 07918 031464
silverstonerealale.com

This traditional tower brewery, which is located near the celebrated motor racing circuit, opened in 2008. With a change of hands in 2015 the brewery re-engineered its range of real ales. !!♦

Ignition (OG 1036, ABV 3.4%)
Floral, hoppy blonde ale with a zesty, powerful flavour.

Pitstop (OG 1040, ABV 3.9%)
Session bitter with a mellow bitter flavour and undertones of lime.

Polestar (OG 1042, ABV 4.1%)
Amber-coloured ale with hints of caramel and toffee and a long, bittersweet finish.

Chequered Flag (OG 1043, ABV 4.3%)
Full-bodied, amber-coloured IPA with a complex taste and a citrus hop finish.

Octane (OG 1047, ABV 4.8%)
A rich ale with hints of honey and toffee and a mellow, slightly coffee aroma.

Classic IPA (OG 1057, ABV 5.6%)
Mildly hoppy with a touch of bitter honey.

Simpsons

White Swan, Eardisland, Herefordshire, HR6 9BD
☎ (01544) 388635 simpsonsfineales.co.uk

Tim Simpson acquired the White Swan in 2011 and set up the brewery at the rear of the pub in 2013. Beers are currently served in the White Swan, and locally to the free trade. A bottling facility is now in operation to supply local county shows. ♦

Golden Cock (OG 1037, ABV 3.7%)

Red Leg (OG 1043, ABV 4.3%)

Black Grouse (OG 1045, ABV 4.5%)

Old English (OG 1047, ABV 4.7%)

Siren Craft SIBA

Unit 1, Hogwood Industrial Estate, Weller Drive, Finchampstead, Berkshire, RG40 4QZ
☎ (0118) 973 0929 sirencraftbrew.com

Established in 2013, Siren is a 40-barrel craft brewery. Rapid growth has necessitated continuous expansion. A state-of-the-art bottling facility and further major expansions to double production were completed in 2017. Siren has had three international head brewers, with the current brewer coming from the US. The Siren Tap Yard opened in 2017. !! ♦RAIB

Yu Lu (OG 1041, ABV 3.6%)
A pale ale made with lemon zest and loose leaf earl grey tea with orange and lemon notes. A hoppy bitterness and a peach and apricot finish.

Undercurrent Oatmeal Pale Ale (OG 1042, ABV 4.5%)
A pale ale with spicy, grassy aromas and a taste of grapefruit and apricot.

Soundwave IPA (OG 1056, ABV 5.6%)
An American-style IPA; golden-coloured and immensely hoppy with grapefruit, peach and mango flavours.

Liquid Mistress Red IPA (OG 1061, ABV 5.8%)
An American-style, red-coloured ale; burnt raisins and crackers balanced by a citrus grapefruit and peach spark.

Broken Dream Breakfast Stout (OG 1072, ABV 6.5%)
A breakfast stout with a gentle touch of smoke, coffee and chocolate.

Six Bells SIBA

Six Bells, Church Street, Bishop's Castle, Shropshire, SY9 5AA
☎ (01588) 638930 sixbellsbrewery.com

Six Bells began brewing in 1997 and was upgraded and modernised in 2010 with a new 12-barrel plant. It supplies customers both within Shropshire and over the border in Wales. !!♦

THE BREWERIES

Noggin' (OG 1037, ABV 3.8%)
A pale, fairly hoppy bitter.

Ow Do! (OG 1040, ABV 4%)
Rich, amber-coloured ale full of spicy, fruity character.

Spikey Blonde (OG 1040, ABV 4%)

Cloud Nine (OG 1043, ABV 4.2%)
Golden ale, well-hopped with citrus notes throughout.

six°north

Reekie House, Aberdeen Road, Laurencekirk, AB30 1AG
☎ (01561) 377047 ☎ 07840 678243
sixdnorth.co.uk

Established in 2013, the brewery brews beers in the Belgian tradition, using a purpose-built 470-hectolitre plant. Depending on beer style, the beers are supplied as cask or keg as appropriate. !! ♦ RAIB

Chopper Stout (ABV 4.1%)
Roasted coffee malted, with background liquorice.

Sixpenny SIBA

The Old Dairy, Holwell Farm, Cranborne, Dorset, BH21 5QP
☎ (01725) 762006 sixpennybrewery.co.uk

Founded in 2007, Sixpenny Brewery has been able to increase its capacity to a 20-barrel plant by moving in 2016 to its present home in renovated Victorian farm buildings near Cranborne. This has allowed for the expansion of the brewery bar and shop (the Sixpenny Tap), which is located next to the brewery in converted stables. More than 50 outlets are supplied. There are plans to use the water from a recently discovered on-site borehole. !! ♦

6d Best Bitter (OG 1042, ABV 3.8%)
A well-balanced ale with a rounded malt flavour that leads to a pleasantly bitter and hoppy finish.

6d Gold (OG 1043, ABV 4%)
A golden ale, slightly citrus flavoured with a distinct hoppy, floral aroma.

6d IPA (OG 1053, ABV 5.2%)
Traditional IPA with a powerful hop character and a long, rounded malt finish.

Skinner's SIBA

Riverside, Newham Road, Truro, Cornwall, TR1 2DP
☎ (01872) 271885 skinnersbrewery.com

Award-winning brewery established in 1997. The brewery moved to bigger premises in 2003, opening a shop and visitor centre. The 25-barrel plant produces 25,000 hectolitres a year, using local Cornish barley. !! ♦

Cornish Trawler (OG 1038, ABV 3.8%)
Refreshing, amber-coloured bitter with a hop, malt and toffee aroma. Grassy, resinous hops with summer fruits. Long and gentle hop-bitter finish.

GTA (OG 1038, ABV 3.8%)
Golden-coloured speciality honey ale. Citrus hop aroma and powerful flavour balanced by bitterness. Persistent hop bitterness finishes with some fruitiness.

Betty Stogs (OG 1040, ABV 4%)
Copper-coloured bitter with a gentle hop aroma. Balance of light citrus hops and apple, sweet malt and bitterness. Long finish.

Hops 'n' Honey (OG 1040, ABV 4%)
Amber-coloured honey beer with a delicate hop aroma. Balance of light citrus, grassy hops, apple, bitterness and sweet malt. Long finish.

Lushingtons (OG 1041, ABV 4.2%)
Smooth golden ale with a citrus hop aroma. Lemon zest and marmalade citrus hop flavours with bitterness and tropical fruits.

Cornish Knocker (OG 1044, ABV 4.5%)
Refreshing, amber-coloured ale with a fragrant hop and malt aroma. Citrus hops, malt and summer fruit flavours. Bitter and dry finish.

Pennycomequick (OG 1046, ABV 4.5%)
Creamy, smooth, black-coloured, sweet stout with a roast grain aroma. Heavy roast coffee, malt, fig and cherry flavours. Roast, dry finish.

Porthleven (OG 1048, ABV 4.8%)
Refreshing golden ale with a citrus hop and pine nose. Assertive citrus hop, bitter and fruity flavour. Bitter citrus hop finish.

7 Hop (OG 1050, ABV 5%)
Smooth golden ale. Strong hop aroma and heavy punch of grapefruit citrus hops throughout. Marmalade and stone fruits. Bitter, dry finish.

Skippool Creek

15 Alexandra Road, Thornton-Cleveleys, Lancashire, FY5 5DB
☎ (01253) 858904 ☎ 07446 219497
skippoolcreek.co.uk

A nanobrewery based in Thornton-Cleveleys on the Fylde coast with a 100-litre brewing capacity. Brewing began in 2016, supplying local pubs and clubs. RAIB

Skipper's Dark Ale (ABV 3.2%)
A dark-coloured ale with a delicate, slightly floral aroma. A balanced malt flavour with overtones of caramelised toffee and a hint of nuts.

Top Sail Pale Ale (ABV 4.2%)
A complex blackcurrant, loganberry and spice note to the aroma with a gentle grapefruit and lime flavour. Light in colour with a crisp, delicate finish.

Black Oar Stout (ABV 4.9%)
Rich, full-bodied stout with an aroma that carries hints of coffee, chocolate, liquorice and molasses.

Slater's SIBA IFBB

St Albans Road, Common Road Industrial Estate, Stafford, ST16 3DR
☎ (01785) 257976 slatersales.co.uk

The brewery was opened in 1995 and in 2006 moved to new, larger premises. It has won numerous awards from CAMRA and SIBA and supplies a large number of outlets. 2015 saw Slater's celebrate its 20th anniversary. !!

Ultra (OG 1035.5, ABV 3.7%)
Amber in colour with a hop and malt aroma. Hoppiness develops into a long dry finish.

Rye IPA (OG 1038.5, ABV 3.8%)

Top Totty (OG 1039, ABV 4%)
Yellow-hued with a fruit and hop nose. Big malty start leads to citrus hints with mouthwatering

edges. Dry finish with tangs of lingering lemon bitterness.

Premium (OG 1042.5, ABV 4.4%) ◆
Pale brown-coloured bitter with a malt and caramel aroma. Malt and caramel taste supported by hops and some fruit provide a warming descent and satisfyingly bitter mouthfeel.

Smoked Porter (OG 1046, ABV 4.8%) ◆
Nose full of smoke, bonfire tastes with bacon. Hops break out to a bitter finish.

Western (OG 1048, ABV 4.9%)
A heavily-hopped pale ale with a chewy, aromatic finish.

Haka (OG 1049, ABV 5.2%) ◆
Exotic aromas of tropical fruits lead to a sweet, fruity start with background bitterness. This erupts into a mouthy bitterness with a long finish.

Slaughterhouse SIBA

Bridge Street, Warwick, CV34 5PD
☎ (01926) 490986 ☎ 07951 842690
slaughterhousebrewery.com

Production began in 2003 on a four-barrel plant in a former slaughterhouse. Around 30 outlets are supplied. The brewery premises are licensed for off-sales direct to the public. In 2010 Slaughterhouse opened its first pub, the Wild Boar in Warwick, adding a two-barrel plant. ‼

Saddleback Best Bitter (OG 1038, ABV 3.8%)
Amber-coloured session bitter with a distinctive hop flavour.

Extra Stout Snout (OG 1044, ABV 4.4%)

Boar D'eau (OG 1045, ABV 4.5%)

Wild Boar (OG 1052, ABV 5.2%)

Slightly Foxed

See Nightjar

Small Beer (NEW)

70-72 Verney Road, South Bermondsey, London, SE16 3DH theoriginalsmallbeer.com

Small Beer Brewery was set up in 2017 as the world's first to specialise exclusively in the production of small beer (0.5-2.8% ABV). RAIB V

Small Paul's

27 Briar Close, Gillingham, Dorset, SP8 4SS
☎ (01747) 823574 ✉ smallbrewer@btinternet.com

Launched in 2006, this half-barrel brewery is located in the owner's garage. There are usually two brews a month. A small number of local pubs, clubs and beer festivals are supplied direct and beers can be designed and brewed to order. ♦

Gylla's Gold (OG 1039, ABV 3.8%) ◆
Mild fruit hop aromas lead to bitter hop flavours and a lingering dry hop aftertaste.

Amber Nectar (OG 1042, ABV 4.2%)
Amber-coloured, full-bodied best bitter. Slightly citrus aroma with balanced malt and spicy hop flavours and a bitter finish.

Invicta (OG 1042, ABV 4.2%)
Pale, aromatic and hoppy with a long bitter finish.

Challenger II (OG 1044, ABV 4.3%)
A copper-coloured, slightly sweet, malty bitter.

Wyvern (OG 1044, ABV 4.4%) ◆
Red-brown-coloured, well-balanced best bitter with malt and caramel flavours and a short, bittersweet finish.

Gillingham Pale (OG 1045, ABV 4.5%) ◆
Fruity, caramel aromas lead to complex bitter flavours and short, dry finish.

Small World SIBA

Unit 10, Barncliffe Business Park, Near Bank, Shelley, West Yorkshire, HD8 8LU
☎ (01484) 602805 smallworldbeers.com

The brewery is situated in the former Barncliffe Mill near the picturesque village of Shelley. The beers are brewed on a 20-barrel plant using spring water from an on-site bore hole. ‼♦

Barncliffe Bitter (OG 1037, ABV 3.7%)
A light bitter with fruit and citrus notes and a lasting bitterness through the finish.

Long Moor Pale (OG 1039, ABV 3.9%)
Pale ale with grapefruit and citrus notes and a light bitter finish.

Spike's Gold (OG 1043, ABV 4.4%)
Smooth, well-balanced golden ale with fruit and hop flavours through to the finish.

Thunderbridge Stout (OG 1051, ABV 5.2%)
Traditional dry stout with roast flavours giving way to smooth coffee undertones and a sharp, dry finish.

Twin Falls (OG 1051, ABV 5.2%)
Full-bodied pale ale with a fruity aroma and a strong tropical fruit and hop taste.

Samuel Smith

The Old Brewery, High Street, Tadcaster, North Yorkshire, LS24 9SB
☎ (01937) 832225 samuelsmithsbrewery.co.uk

Fiercely independent, family-owned company. Tradition, quality and value are important, resulting in brewing without any artificial additives. All real ale is supplied in wooden casks. A bottle-conditioned beer (Yorkshire Stingo, ABV 8%) is only available in specialist off-licences. RAIB V

Old Brewery Bitter (OG 1040, ABV 4%)
Malt dominates the aroma, with an initial burst of malt, hops and fruit in the taste, which is sustained in the aftertaste.

John Smith's

The Brewery, Tadcaster, North Yorkshire, LS24 9SA
☎ (01937) 832091 heineken.com

No real ale. The brewery was built in 1879 by a relative of Samuel Smith (qv). John Smith's became part of the Courage group in 1970 before being taken over by S&N and now Heineken UK. John Smith's cask Magnet has been discontinued. John Smith's Bitter in cask form is brewed by Caledonian Brewery (qv) in Edinburgh.

Snaggletooth

rear of 11 Pole Lane, Darwen, Lancashire, BB3 3LD
☎ 07810 365701 snaggletoothbrewing.com

THE BREWERIES

Snaggletooth was established in 2012 by three beer geeks with a passion for crafting ales. A 2.5-barrel plant is used at the Hopstar Brewery (qv) in Darwen, Lancashire. Beers are available throughout East Lancashire and Manchester.

Allotropic Pale Ale (ABV 3.8%)
A pale ale with floral and citrus notes.

I Ain't Afraid of Noh Ghost (ABV 3.9%)
A session ale with bursts of lemon and pineapple flavours.

Three Amigos (ABV 3.9%)
A pale session ale with citrus hop flavours.

Déjà Brewed (OG 1040, ABV 4%)
A refreshing ale with floral, spicy and citrus flavours.

Rolling Maul (ABV 4.1%)
A pale ale with bursts of floral flavours and a citrus finish.

'Cos I'm a Lobster (OG 1044, ABV 4.2%)
Red-coloured ale with subtle roasted malts and spicy currant and berry hop fruitiness.

Snowdonia

Snowdonia Parc Brewpub & Campsite, Waunfawr, LL55 4AQ
☎ (01286) 650409 ⊕ snowdonia-park.co.uk

Snowdonia started brewing in 1998 in a two-barrel brewhouse. The brewing is now carried out by the owner, Carmen Pierce. The beer is brewed solely for the Snowdonia Park pub and campsite.

Snowhill

Snowhill Cottage, Snow Hill Lane, Scorton, Lancashire, PR3 1BA
☎ (01524) 791352

Snowhill was established in 2015 by Nigel Stokes following several years of small scale brewing. It uses a 1.5-barrel plant. A one-man operation, Nigel brews 3-4 times per month to supply pubs in North-west Lancashire and South Cumbria. An environmentally-friendly set-up sees the spent grain feeding local cattle and waste water treated through a small reed bed. ♦

Pale (OG 1037, ABV 3.7%)
A fruity, pale yellow-coloured beer with a pronounced citrus aftertaste.

Copy Cat (ABV 3.8%)
A light ale, based on a classic, popular 1970s northern cask ale.

Retro Bitter (ABV 3.8%)
A well-balanced session bitter with a clean finish.

Blonded (ABV 3.9%)
A light, fruity, well-hopped blonde ale with a bitter, slightly astringent finish.

Gold (OG 1039, ABV 3.9%)
Fruit and malt dominate, with a dry bitter finish.

Best Bitter (OG 1042, ABV 4.2%)
Smooth, rich and malty with caramel notes leading to a pronounced bitter finish.

Black Magic IPA (OG 1042, ABV 4.2%)
A complex, black-coloured IPA with a hoppy aroma and taste and hints of roast.

Porter (OG 1048, ABV 4.8%)
Dark-coloured and smooth with a liquorice, malty and dry hop taste.

Winter Porter (OG 1050, ABV 4.8%)
Rich and black in colour, the initial roast and malt taste leads to a bitter, fruity and hoppy aftertaste.

Sociable

6-8 Britannia Road, Worcester, WR1 3BQ ☎ 07957 583984 ⊕ thesociablebeercompany.com

A small craft brewery just outside Worcester city centre, established in 2017. An on-site tap room is open Thursday to Saturday.

Solvay Society

Cuckoo Hall Brewery, Unit 8, Aldborough Hall Farm, Aldborough Hatch, Essex, IG2 7TD
☎ (020) 7226 2277 ⊕ solveysociety.com

Solvay Society began brewing in 2014 in the cellar of a Walthamstow pub using a small 0.5-hectolitre kit. In 2015 it transferred the equipment to the Hops & Glory pub in North London. In 2016 the brewery moved again, taking over the old equipment from the Ha'penny Brewery in Aldborough Hatch. Production is mostly keg but bottle-conditioned beer is also available. RAIB

Son of Sid

Chequers, 71 Main Road, Little Gransden, Cambridgeshire, SG19 3DW
☎ (01767) 677348 ⊕ sonofsid.co.uk

Son of Sid was established in 2007. The three-barrel plant is situated in a room at the back of the pub and can be viewed from a window in the lounge bar. It is named after the father of the current landlord, who ran the pub for 42 years. His son has carried the business on as a family-run enterprise. Beer is sold in the pub and at local beer festivals. !! RAIB

Sonnet 43 SIBA

Durham Road, Coxhoe, County Durham, DH6 4HX
☎ (0191) 377 3039 ⊕ sonnet43.com

Sonnet 43 began brewing in 2012. The name and brewing ethos is inspired by the most famous work of poet Elizabeth Barrett Browning, who was born nearby. A limited edition beer range named 'How do I love thee let me count the beers' is brewed comprising original recipes with experimental ingredients. The brewery has seven outlets in the North East and supplies extensively to the free trade.

Abolition (OG 1038, ABV 3.8%)
An amber-coloured ale with sourdough and nut aromas. Malty with a slightly bitter aftertaste.

Seraphim (OG 1041, ABV 4.1%)
A straw-coloured, wheat-style beer with a sweet, delicate, floral aroma.

The Raven (OG 1046, ABV 4.3%)
Bourbon, cocoa and oats give this dark-coloured beer a rich, full-bodied, chocolate bitterness.

The Aurora (OG 1044, ABV 4.4%)
A strong pale ale with a complex hoppy aroma and a delicate fruity malt taste.

Impressment (OG 1055, ABV 5.4%)

Pale bronze-coloured ale with a spicy, peppery hop aroma and a fruity, malty and spicy flavour.

Soul (NEW)

Correspondence: 18 Broomfield Road, Heaton Moor, Stockport, SK4 4ND ☎ 07718 155191
🌐 soulbrewingco.com

⊗ Brewing commenced in 2017 using spare capacity at Manchester Brewing (qv). Beers are supplied to outlets in Greater Manchester and are inspired by Northern Soul music. A move to its own premises is planned. **V**

All Nighter (OG 1038, ABV 3.8%)
A session pale ale with lemon citrus hoppiness, floral notes and a bitter finish.

Magic Touch (OG 1046, ABV 4.7%)
A well-balanced IPA with grape/gooseberry and citrus notes.

The Snake (OG 1052, ABV 5.8%)
An IPA with grapefruit/citrus fruit, earthy spiciness and a malty finish.

Double-O Soul (OG 1060, ABV 5.9%)
A Vermont-style IPA with bags of citrus, peach and tropical fruit flavours.

South Hams SIBA

Stokeley Barton, Stokenham, Devon, TQ7 2SE
☎ (01548) 581151 🌐 southhamsbrewery.co.uk

⊗ The brewery moved to its present site, a milking parlour, in 2003, with a 10-barrel plant and plenty of room to expand. It supplies more than 60 outlets in Plymouth and South Devon. Wholesalers are used to distribute to other areas. The brewery is run by Sam Brooking, the owner's youngest son. **!! ♦ RAIB**

Devon Pride (OG 1039, ABV 3.8%)
A dark amber-coloured beer, smooth to drink with a malty palate.

Wild Blonde (OG 1044, ABV 4.4%) ◆
Subtle notes of malt, roast and caramel, dominated by fruity hops. These persist to a refreshing hint of lemon.

Hopnosis (OG 1046, ABV 4.5%)

Eddystone (OG 1050, ABV 4.8%) ◆
Strong, amber-coloured ale. Hoppy, caramel, slightly citrus nose. Dryer taste with light fruit and hops. Dry yet fruity finish.

Pandemonium (OG 1054, ABV 5%)

South Lakes

Unit 30, Ulverston Auction Mart, North Lonsdale Road, Ulverston, Cumbria, LA12 0AU ☎ 07795 363523
✉ aaronpos1@hotmail.com

South Lakes began brewing on a 1.5-barrel plant in 2016, in a part of the Auction Mart in Ulverston.

4Cs Extra Pale Ale (OG 1040, ABV 3.8%)
An American-style pale ale with hints of grapefruit.

Lucky Dip (OG 1040, ABV 3.8%)
Blonde ale with a simple malt backbone and plenty of hops.

Amacoe (OG 1040, ABV 4%)

Poison Dwarf (OG 1043, ABV 4.1%)

Rakau (OG 1048, ABV 4.7%)
A strong blonde ale bursting with hops and fruit.

American Pale Ale (OG 1050, ABV 4.8%)
A rich golden ale with lots of citrus.

Ripe (OG 1055, ABV 5.5%)

Southbourne

45 Poole Hill, Bournemouth, Dorset, BH2 5PW
☎ (01202) 421190 ☎ 07845 795464
🌐 southbourneales.co.uk

⊗ Jennifer Tingay, former technologist and brewer for Ringwood, began brewing in 2013 using spare capacity at Town Mill brewery. Using crowdfunding she secured the lease of a former nightclub on Bournemouth's West Cliff and in 2017 transferred the brewery there and opened a bar. **!! ♦**

Paddler (OG 1037, ABV 3.6%)
A light but balanced session bitter with only moderate hop characteristics.

Sunbather (OG 1040, ABV 4%) ◆
Dry red-coloured ale with some caramel sweetness and a lingering nutty aftertaste.

Headlander (OG 1043, ABV 4.2%)
Floral aroma and full hop bitterness, balanced with malt.

Beach Comber (OG 1058, ABV 5.7%)
A full-flavoured, brown-coloured ale with a good malt and hop balance.

Southey

21 Southey Street, Penge, London, SE20 7JD
☎ (020) 8659 4033 ☎ 07450 573577
🌐 southeybrewing.co.uk

⊗ The Southey Brewing Company has taken over the premises formerly used by the Late Knights Brewery. Brewing began in 2017 using a five-barrel plant. An on-site brewery tap is open Fridays and Saturdays. Two other outlets are also supplied, the London Beer Dispensary, Brockley, and the Brighton Beer Dispensary. ♦

Southport SIBA

Unit 3, Enterprise Business Park, Russell Road, Southport, Merseyside, PR9 7RF ☎ 07748 387652
🌐 southportbrewery.co.uk

Southport Brewery was established in 2004 on a five-barrel plant. Outlets are supplied in Southport, North-west England and nationally. ♦

Sandgrounder Bitter (OG 1039.5, ABV 3.8%)
Pale, hoppy session bitter with a floral character.

Dark Night (OG 1040.5, ABV 3.9%)

Carousel (OG 1041.5, ABV 4%)
A refreshing, floral, hoppy best bitter.

Golden Sands (OG 1041.5, ABV 4%)
A golden-coloured, triple-hopped bitter with a citrus flavour.

Ruck & Maul (OG 1040, ABV 4%)
A copper-coloured ale with a subtle bitterness leading to a lemon grapefruit flavour.

Natterjack (OG 1043.5, ABV 4.3%)
A premium bitter with fruit notes and a hint of coffee.

Band Stand (OG 1046, ABV 4.5%)

Southsea

Southsea Castle, Clarence Esplanade, Southsea, Portsmouth, Hampshire, PO5 3PA ☎ 07939 063970 🌐 southseabrewing.co.uk

Launched in 2016, Southsea Brewing is located in an old ammunition storage room within the walls of a coastal defence fort built by Henry VIII in 1544. All beers are unfined, unfiltered and unpasteurised and bottled on site. !! RAIB

Southwark SIBA

46 Druid Street, Bermondsey, London, SE1 2EZ ☎ (020) 3302 4190 🌐 southwarkbrewing.co.uk

Established in the Bermondsey brewing scene, Southwark Brewing Company opened in 2014, focussing on cask-conditioned ales. A tap room is open Thursday to Sunday. ♦ RAIB

London Pale Ale (OG 1038.5, ABV 4%)
Pale golden-coloured, smooth beer. Sweet biscuity malt is balanced by pineapple and pithy citrus. Dry aftertaste with a building bitterness.

Potters' Fields Porter (OG 1040, ABV 4%)
Dark brown-coloured porter. Raisins, prunes and cocoa in the flavour and aroma fading in the dry, roast bitter aftertaste.

Bermondsey Best (OG 1042, ABV 4.4%)
A well-balanced best bitter with fruity notes developing in the finish, which is bitter. Some malty notes on the palate.

Harvard (OG 1049, ABV 5.5%)
Honey with sweet orange and grapefruit marmalade character are present in this rich, smooth pale brown-coloured beer. Dry bitter finish.

Spa Town

See Harrogate

Space Cadet

See Velvet Owl

Spartan (NEW)

Arch 8, Almond Road, South Bermondsey, London, SE16 3LR 🌐 spartanbrewery.com

Originally cuckoo brewing at Ubrew (qv), Spartan took over the old Partizan Brewery premises in 2017. An on-site taproom serves the beers.

Spencer's (NEW)

Unit 4, The Old Piggery, Chichester Road, Upper Norton, West Sussex, PO20 9DZ ☎ (01243) 487301 ☎ 07919 487301 🌐 spencers-brewery.co.uk

Brewing began in 2018 using a six-barrel plant. Bottled beers are planned.

Windmill IPA (OG 1043, ABV 4.2%)

Crafty Bitter (OG 1048, ABV 4.7%)
A dark-coloured, malty bitter.

Golden Sunset (OG 1049, ABV 4.8%)
A light, deep golden-coloured ale with a hint of citrus.

Yankee Doodle (OG 1051, ABV 5.4%)

Sperrin

Lord Nelson Inn, Birmingham Road, Ansley, Warwickshire, CV10 9PQ ☎ (0247) 7639 2305 ☎ 07917 772208 🌐 sperrinbrewery.co.uk

Sperrin began brewing in 2012 and is situated by the side of the Lord Nelson Inn. A brewery was first established there in 1868. Beers are also available at its sister pub, the Blue Boar, Mancetter. !! ♦ RAIB

Spey Valley SIBA

Mains of Mulben, Mulben, Keith, AB55 6YH ☎ 07780 655199 🌐 speyvalleybrewery.co.uk

Pilot brewery was established in 2007 at Mulben Mains Farm. Originally using a two-barrel plant from Loch Ness Brewery, it now brews on a 20-barrel plant at a site in Mulben. ♦

Sunshine on Keith (OG 1036, ABV 3.5%)
Golden-coloured, light citrus, bitter hop.

David's Not So Bitter (OG 1046, ABV 4.4%)
Light brown in colour with a good mix of malts, hops and red fruits.

Stillman's IPA (OG 1047.6, ABV 4.6%)
Amber-coloured, hoppy bitter with a whisky background.

1814 (OG 1050, ABV 5%)

Spey Stout (OG 1055, ABV 5.4%)
A good, thick, dark-coloured, malty stout with a smoky blackcurrant background.

Spey's Harware (ABV 6.4%)

Speyside Craft SIBA

2 Greshop Road, Forres, IV36 2GU ☎ (01309) 358082 ☎ 07854 053277 🌐 speysidecraftbrewery.com

Based in a traditional whisky-producing area, Speyside Brewery uses the same water that goes into the region's whisky. A number of local outlets are supplied. A donation from sales of Bottlenose Bitter goes to help support the work of the Whale & Dolphin Conservation Society. ♦

Bow Fiddle Blonde (OG 1038, ABV 3.8%)

Bottlenose Bitter (OG 1041, ABV 4.1%)
Slightly citrus, hoppy bitter.

Randolph's Leap (OG 1049, ABV 4.9%)

Moray IPA (OG 1055, ABV 5.5%)

Findhorn Killer Red IPA (OG 1056, ABV 5.6%)

Spitting Feathers SIBA

Common Farm, Waverton, Cheshire, CH3 7QT ☎ (01244) 332052 ☎ 07974 348325 🌐 spittingfeathers.org

Spitting Feathers was established in 2005. The brewery is located in a sandstone building set around a cobbled yard. Around 200 local outlets are supplied. Seasonal and occasional beers are available, including a new range called Hard Working Beers. ‼♦

Session Beer (OG 1035, ABV 3.6%)

Thirstquencher (OG 1038, ABV 3.9%) ◆
Powerful hop aroma leads into the taste. Bitterness and a fruity, citrus hop flavour fight for attention. A sharp, clean, golden-coloured beer with a long, dry, bitter aftertaste.

Special Ale (OG 1041, ABV 4.2%) ◆
Complex tawny-coloured beer with a sharp, grainy mouthfeel. Malty with good hop coming through in the aroma and taste. Hints of nuttiness and a touch of acidity. Dry, astringent finish.

Old Wavertonian (OG 1043, ABV 4.4%) ◆
Creamy and smooth stout. Full-flavoured with coffee notes in aroma and taste. Roast and nut flavours throughout, leading to a hoppy, bitter finish.

Empire IPA (ABV 5.2%)

Spotlight (NEW)

The Goddards, Goole Road, West Cowick, East Yorkshire, DN14 9DJ ☎ 07713 477069
spotlightbrewing.co.uk

Spotlight is a social enterprise. All beers are brewed, packaged and delivered by people with learning disabilities. A taproom is planned. ‼♦

One More (OG 1038, ABV 3.9%)
A session American-style pale ale with biscuity malts complementing the citrus and fruity hop aroma.

Bollingham Bitter (OG 1045, ABV 4.4%)

Fragile X (OG 1057, ABV 5.8%)

Sprey Point (NEW)

Unit 10, Helmores Yard, Exeter Street, Teignmouth, Devon, TQ14 8JW ☎ 07917 434859
spreypointbrewery.com

Established in 2017, this microbrewery specialises in small batch beers using a wide variety of ingredients, sourced locally and organic where possible. Output is mostly keg but some cask-conditioned beer is available. V

Springhead SIBA

Robin Hood Site, Main Street, Laneham, Nottinghamshire, DN22 0NA
☎ (01777) 228080 ☎ 07720 461655
springhead.co.uk

Springhead Brewery opened in 1990, expanding and moving to bigger premises three years later to meet increased demand. In 2011 the brewery relocated to its current address. Around 500 outlets are supplied direct and the brewery owns three pubs, one of which, the Bees Knees, is adjacent to the brewery. Beers are also available under the Amplified Ales name, mainly for the craft market. ‼♦V

Outlawed (OG 1040, ABV 3.8%)
A triple-hopped, easy-drinking, American-style pale ale with a citrus aroma.

Drop of the Black Stuff (OG 1041, ABV 4%)
A smooth, dark-coloured, easy-drinking porter.

Robin Hood (OG 1041, ABV 4%)
A chestnut-coloured, traditional bitter with a good head and plenty of hops.

Maid Marian (OG 1045, ABV 4.5%)
A pale golden-coloured beer with a fruity orange aroma and a dry finish.

Leveller (OG 1047, ABV 4.8%)
A dark-coloured beer with a smoky flavour and toffee finish.

Roaring Meg (OG 1052, ABV 5.5%)
A smooth, classic IPA. Golden in colour with a citrus honey aroma and dry finish.

Squawk

Unit 4, Tonge Street, Ardwick, Manchester, M12 6LY
☎ 07590 387559
oliverturton@squawkbrewingco.com

Squawk initially cuckoo-brewed on the Hand Drawn Monkey plant in Huddersfield in 2013, with the first brew from the Manchester site being in 2014. The eight-barrel plant is located in a railway arch in Ardwick. Beers are widely available in the North West and Yorkshire but can be found further afield. RAIB

Pavo (ABV 3.8%)

Pica (ABV 4.9%)

Espresso Stout (OG 1060, ABV 6.5%)
A silky smooth, rich beer with an espresso flavour.

Stables

Beamish Hall Country House Hotel, Beamish, County Durham, DH9 0YB
☎ (01207) 288750 beamish-hall.co.uk/stables

Stables was established as part of a £1 million development of an old stable block of Beamish Hall, converting a disused building to a restaurant and eight-barrel microbrewery. The hotel is supplied plus the Sun Inn at Beamish Museum. Beers are also brewed under the Bull Lane Brewery name. ‼♦

Staffordshire

12 Churnet Court, Cheddleton, Staffordshire, ST13 7EF
☎ (01538) 361919 ☎ 07971 808370
staffordshirebrewery.co.uk

No real ale. Brewing started in 2002. The brewery was renamed from Leek Brewery in 2013 at which time cask production ceased, being replaced by filtered, pasteurised bottled beers only. A small pilot plant is sometimes used to contract brew for Wicked Hathern (qv) when time permits. ‼

Contract brewed for Wicked Hathern Brewery:

Albion Special (OG 1042, ABV 4%)
Light copper in colour with a nutty aroma and a smoky, malty taste.

Hawthorn Gold (OG 1045, ABV 4.6%)
A light golden-coloured, easy-drinking beer with a good balance of hops and malt.

Stag (Cheshire)

Stag at Walton, Chester Road, Walton, Cheshire, WA4 6EG
☎ (01925) 261680 thestagatwalton.co.uk

Nanobrewery based at the Stag at Walton, near Warrington. Beers are available in the pub and occasionally at local beer festivals.

Stag (Kent)

Little Engeham Farm, Woodchurch, Kent, TN26 3QY
☎ 07539 974068 ⊕ stagbrewery.co.uk

Stag began brewing in 2016 producing cask and bottle-conditioned ales. RAIB

Roe Buck (ABV 3.8%)

Jane Doe (ABV 4%)

Screaming Sika (ABV 5%)

Staggeringly Good SIBA

Unit 3, St Georges Industrial Estate, Rodney Road, Portsmouth, Hampshire, PO4 8SS
☎ (023) 9229 7033 ⊕ staggeringlygood.com

⊗ Brewing began in 2014, originally using spare capacity at other breweries. In 2015 a 10-barrel plant at its own premises came on stream. There is an on-site shop and tap room with limited opening hours. !! ♦ RAIB V

Staggersaurus (OG 1039, ABV 4%)
A deep golden-coloured ale with summer fruit aromas and grapefruit on the palate.

ThaiRannoCitrus (OG 1048, ABV 5%)
A unique pale ale with distinct lime and peach flavours and aromas, balanced with hoppy bitterness.

Dawn Stealer (OG 1051, ABV 5.2%)

Post Impact Porter (OG 1057, ABV 5.4%)
A rich porter with roasted malts and hints of espresso and dark chocolate.

VelociRapture (OG 1060, ABV 6.5%)
An American-style IPA with a strong fruit character and bitterness.

Stamps SIBA

St Mary's Complex, Waverley Street, Liverpool, L20 4AP ☎ 07779 000094 ⊕ stampsbrewery.co.uk

Brewing began in 2012, producing beers named after famous world postage stamps. The brewery moved to its new site in 2017 on a temporary basis. There are plans to build a brand new brewery and pub. Beers are also contract brewed for the Republic of Liverpool Beer Co. !!

Blonde Moment (OG 1037, ABV 3.6%)
A pale-coloured session beer with a smooth floral and citrus aroma and flavour.

Bondi Blonde (OG 1037, ABV 3.7%)
A pale-coloured, full-flavoured beer with floral and citrus notes.

Ahtanum (OG 1039, ABV 3.9%)

First Class (OG 1039, ABV 3.9%)

Mail Train (OG 1042, ABV 4.2%)
Traditional bitter with a noticeable bitterness and malty character.

Swedish Blonde (OG 1041, ABV 4.3%)
A blonde ale with strong hints of citrus.

Inverted Jenny (OG 1046, ABV 4.6%)
Golden in colour with a grassy and floral bouquet and a noticeable tinge of caramel.

Penny Black (OG 1055, ABV 5.5%)

Stancill SIBA

Unit 2, Oakham Drive, off Rutland Road, Sheffield, South Yorkshire, S3 9QX
☎ (0114) 275 2788 ☎ 07809 427716

Stancill began brewing in 2014 and is named after the first head brewer and co-owner. It is situated on the doorstep of the late Stones' Cannon Brewery, taking advantage of the soft Yorkshire water. !!

Barnsley Bitter (OG 1037.5, ABV 3.8%)

Blonde (OG 1038.5, ABV 3.9%)

India (ABV 4%)

No.7 (OG 1042, ABV 4.3%)

Stainless (ABV 4.3%)

Porter (OG 1042.5, ABV 4.4%)

Black Gold (ABV 5%)

Stannary SIBA

Unit 6. Pixon Trading Centre, Tavistock, Devon, PL19 8DH
☎ (01822) 258130 ☎ 07971 238758
⊕ stannarybrewing.co.uk/

Stannary was established in 2016 by four keen homebrewers using a 2.5-barrel plant. A brewery tap is open on Friday evenings showcasing its unfined and unfiltered craft beers inspired by ingredients around the world. ♦

Stanway

Stanway House, Stanway, Gloucestershire, GL54 5PQ
☎ (01386) 584320 ⊕ stanwaybrewery.co.uk

Stanway is a small brewery founded in 1993 with a five-barrel plant that confines its sales to the Cotswolds area (15 to 20 outlets). The brewery is the only known plant in the country to use wood-fired coppers for all its production. ♦

Stanney Bitter (OG 1042, ABV 4.5%)
A light, refreshing, amber-coloured beer, dominated by hops in the aroma, with a bitter taste and a hoppy, bitter finish.

Star Wing SIBA

Unit 6, Hall Farm, Church Road, Redgrave, Suffolk, IP22 1RJ
☎ (01379) 890586 ⊕ starwingbrewery.com

Brewing began in 2017 after converting an old sawmill into a brewery. Half an acre of hops have been planted with plans to grow more and to convert part of the sawmill into a tap room. Around 75 outlets are supplied direct.

Spire Light (OG 1041, ABV 4.2%)
A straw-coloured pale ale with a floral aroma.

Stardust SIBA

Unit 5, How Lane Farm Estate, Howe Lane, White Waltham, Berkshire, SL6 3JP
☎ (01628) 947325 ⊕ stardustbrewery.co.uk

⊗ An independent, family-owned and run brewery, Stardust was established in 2016. Tucked towards the back of a farm estate, brewing takes place on a six-barrel plant. ♦ RAIB

Easy Pale (OG 1038, ABV 3.8%)
Easy-drinking session pale ale with a subtle blend of hops and a pale malt body.

English Bitter (OG 1041, ABV 4%)
Notes of roasted caramel balanced by a clean bitter finish with a classic hop aroma.

American Pale (OG 1043, ABV 4.5%)
An American-style pale ale with citrus and pine hop aromas giving an aromatic punch, balanced by a light malt body.

PK3 (OG 1051, ABV 5.6%)
An American-style IPA with a complex tropical, spicy and fruity hop profile.

Station 119

Unit 4, Progress Way, Eye, Suffolk, IP23 7HU
☎ (01379) 882230 ⊕ station119.co.uk

Brewing started in 2014 using a two-barrel plant, upgraded in 2018 to a 12-barrel one to meet demand. Beers are available locally. RAIB

Station Works

Camlough Road, Newry, Northern Ireland, BT35 6JP

A sister brewery to Cumberland Breweries, Station Works was bought by the US firm Alltech in 2015.

The Foxes Rock (OG 1042, ABV 4.2%)

Finn (OG 1045, ABV 4.5%)

Stealth SIBA

34 Old Broughton Road, Melksham, Wiltshire, SN12 8BX
☎ (01225) 707111 ☎ (01225) 707111 ☎ 07917 272482 ⊕ stealthbrew.co

Brewing began in 2014 under the name of Kennet & Avon, with beer brewed by Wessex Brewery (qv) while the plant was under construction. It relocated to its current site in 2015 and changed its name to Stealth in 2018. It now brews a range of hop-forward pale ales and dark beers, most of which are unfined and hazy. A beer garden is planned. ‼ ♦ RAIB GF V

Hush (OG 1040, ABV 3.8%)
A single-hopped pale ale with aromas of grapefruit and tropical fruits.

Covert (ABV 3.9%)
A pale-coloured session ale with grapefruit, lime and mango flavours.

Ambush (ABV 4.5%)
Unashamedly bitter with notes of pepper, herbs, pine and stone fruits in the aroma.

Camouflage (ABV 4.7%)

Conceal (ABV 4.8%)
A dark brown-coloured porter infused with raw liquorice root. Well-balanced with a slight sweetness.

Solitude (OG 1.53, ABV 5.3%) ♦
Full-bodied, black-coloured beer with aromas of liquorice, roast coffee and chocolate and a delicate, pleasant aftertaste.

Seclusion (ABV 5.5%)
Full-bodied, pale-coloured ale with aromas of grapefruit, mango and passion fruit.

Steam Town (NEW)

1 Bishopstoke Road, Eastleigh, Hampshire, SO50 6AD ⊕ steamtownbrewco.co.uk

Steam Town is a five-barrel microbrewery with its own craft beer bar and restaurant, established in 2017. Other local pubs, clubs and micropubs are also supplied as well as beer festivals and outlets further afield by special arrangement. ♦

Stoke Pale (OG 1040, ABV 3.8%)
A crisp, fruity pale ale.

Barton Bitter (OG 1042, ABV 4%)

Reefer Express (OG 1045, ABV 4.2%)
Amber-coloured, hoppy session IPA packed with citrus fruit.

Steam Stout (OG 1051, ABV 4.5%)
Milk stout with complex chocolate malt bitterness balanced with lactose and spicy hops.

Steamin' Billy

See Belvoir

Steel City

c/o Lost Industry Brewing, 14a Nutwood Trading Estate, Sheffield, South Yorkshire, S6 1NJ
⊕ steelcitybrewing.co.uk

Steel City was established in 2009 and operates on a cuckoo basis, brewing once or twice a month. Brewing now takes place at Lost Industry Brewing (qv). Much of the Steel City output is collaborations with other like-minded brewers having a little fun producing interesting and experimental beers.

Stewart SIBA

26a Dryden Road, Bilston Glen Industrial Estate, Loanhead, EH20 9LZ
☎ (0131) 440 2442 ⊕ stewartbrewing.co.uk

Established in 2004 by Steve and Jo Stewart, the brewery moved to a larger, custom-built brewery in 2013 with a brand new 50-hectolitre plant. It produces a wide portofolio of beers including collaborations such as the Natural Selection Brewing partnership with the brewing school at Heriot Watt. The on-site 'Craft Beer Kitchen' is a small 80-litre plant providing a brew-it-yourself facility. ‼ ♦ RAIB

Jack Back (OG 1039, ABV 3.7%) ♦
A pale-coloured, hoppy beer with strong citrus and tropical fruit aromas. The taste is light, crisp and refreshing.

Pentland IPA (OG 1040, ABV 3.9%) ♦
A pleasing, hoppy, golden-coloured session ale. The dry bitter taste is well balanced by sweetness from the malt, and fruit flavours. The aftertaste is dry with a lingering bitterness.

Crossfire (OG 1045, ABV 4.3%) ♦
A New World-hopped, golden-coloured IPA. Pine and citrus aromas on the nose with a distinct malt profile and a crisp bitterness in its complex flavour.

80/- (OG 1044, ABV 4.4%) ♦

Traditional Scottish heavy. The complex profile is dominated by malt with fruit flavours giving the sweetish character typical of this beer style. Hops provide a gentle balancing bitterness that intensifies in the dry finish.

Edinburgh Gold (OG 1048, ABV 4.8%) ◆
A full-bodied but easy-drinking golden ale. Bitterness from the hop character is strong in the finish and complemented in the taste by a little sweetness from malt, and fruit flavours.

Sticklegs

Primrose Farm, Hall Road, Great Bromley, Essex, CO7 7TR ☎ 07971 138038
✉ waterhouse.philip@btinternet.com

⊗ Sticklegs was established in 2008 at the Cross Inn, Great Bromley. The brewery expanded and relocated to Elmstead Market, where it continued to grow. In 2016 it moved to Primrose Farm. The brewery is owned and run by Phil Reeve and his wife Linda, the brewster.

Stour Gold (OG 1040, ABV 3.8%)

Bar'King (ABV 4%)

Stocklinch

Unit 3, Manor Farm, Stocklinch, Somerset, TA19 9JG
☎ 07711 479917 ⊕ stocklinchales.co.uk

⊗ Established in 2012 in a converted farm building, Stocklinch uses a five-barrel plant supplying a number of local outlets. The brewery is licensed to open for a few days each month, mainly at weekends, which compensates for the lack of a village pub. ‼ ◆

Ramblers Gold (OG 1038, ABV 3.8%)
Refreshing, light golden-coloured beer with a slight aftertaste of grapefruit.

Jakes (OG 1040, ABV 4%)

Gunner Boyce (OG 1042, ABV 4.2%)

Jucy Lucy (OG 1042, ABV 4.2%)
A golden-coloured beer with a creamy aroma, hints of fruit and a lingering aftertaste.

Jakes Special (OG 1045, ABV 4.5%)

Ramblers Gold Extra (OG 1045, ABV 4.5%)

Rusty Boiler (OG 1045, ABV 4.5%)
Mid brown-coloured best bitter with strong fruity flavours and a lick of caramel.

Black Smock (OG 1050, ABV 5%)
Dark-coloured beer with a strong, rich tastes of chocolate, liquorice and coffee and a hint of blackcurrant.

Stockport SIBA

Arch 14, Heaton Lane, Stockport, SK4 1AQ
☎ (0161) 477 1084 ☎ 07442 530728
⊕ stockportbrewingcompany.com

A former cuckoo brewery, Stockport Brewing installed its own eight-barrel plant in an arch of the iconic Stockport Viaduct in 2014. The beers are available at more than 100 pubs across the North-west including its tap, the Crown on Heaton Lane. ‼ ◆

Cascade (ABV 4%)
Pale-coloured beer with a slight citrus flavour.

Bitter Lemon (ABV 4.2%)
A straw-coloured, hoppy beer with a bitter lemon finish.

Crown Best Bitter (ABV 4.2%)
Amber-coloured ale with a smooth, hoppy taste and a dry finish.

Stock Porter (ABV 4.8%)
Porter with liquorice and malty aromas and coffee and chocolate notes.

Heaton Rifles (ABV 6.6%)
A volley of hops burst through the malt base.

Stockton

28 Light Pipe Hall Road, Stockton on Tees, County Durham, TS18 4AH
☎ (01642) 678334
⊕ stocktonbrewingcompany.co.uk

Stockton started production in 2015 based in an industrial unit. It uses a 2.5-barrel plant. RAIB

Stod Fold SIBA

Stod Fold Farm, Hays Lane, Halifax, West Yorkshire, HX2 8UL
☎ (01422) 245951 ☎ 07568 487182
⊕ stodfoldbrewing.com

Stod Fold was founded by childhood friends Paul Harris and Angus Wood. They designed and built the brewery themselves and the result is a state of the art 10-barrel plant. The brewery is not open to the public but once a month is opened for trade partners only.

Gold (OG 1038, ABV 3.8%) ◆
A refreshing, hoppy and fruity session ale. It has a crisp bitter aftertaste.

Amber (OG 1042, ABV 4.2%) ◆
Well-balanced best bitter. Overtones of fruit and hops. Easy-drinking with a mild bitter finish.

Blonde (OG 1045, ABV 4.5%) ◆
Smooth-tasting, fruity beer with a lingering dry finish.

Dark (ABV 4.9%)

Stokesley

See Wainstones

Stonehenge SIBA

The Old Mill, Mill Road, Netheravon, Wiltshire, SP4 9QB
☎ (01980) 670631 ⊕ stonehengeales.co.uk

⊗ The brewery was founded in 1984 in what was originally a water-driven mill built in 1914. In 1993 the company was bought by Danish master brewer Stig Andersen and now supplies more than 300 outlets. From 2013 a new borehole, accessing the Salisbury Plain aquifer, has been supplying the brewery's water. It is of such pristine quality that the brewery now bottle and sell it under the Stonehenge name. ‼ ◆

Spire Ale (OG 1037, ABV 3.8%) ◆
A pale golden-coloured session bitter with an initial bitterness giving way to a well-rounded bitter aftertaste with discernible fruit balance.

Pigswill (OG 1039, ABV 4%) ◆

A tawny-coloured session bitter with an initial pleasant hop aroma and slight bitterness to the taste moving to a well-rounded bitter finish with slight malt and fruit.

Heel Stone (OG 1042, ABV 4.3%) ◆
A copper-coloured best bitter with some malt and fruit in the aroma continuing into the initial taste along with pleasant hoppiness. Plenty of flavour in the aftertaste with noticeable malt, fruit and hops.

Great Bustard (OG 1046, ABV 4.8%) ◆
A copper-coloured strong bitter. Complex malt and fruit flavours at first with a long fruit and bitter aftertaste.

Danish Dynamite (OG 1048, ABV 5%) ◆
Golden-coloured strong bitter with good hop and fruit aromas. Complex flavours in the initial taste with a beautifully balanced, full-bodied aftertaste with hops and fruit to the fore.

Stonehouse SIBA

Stonehouse, Weston, Shropshire, SY10 9ES
☎ (01691) 676457 🌐 stonehousebrewery.co.uk

Stonehouse is a family-run brewery, established in 2007, operating a 22-barrel plant. It is next to the preserved Cambrian railway line and includes a shop, bar and visitor centre. Direct delivery is within 30 miles of the brewery. ‼

Sunlander (OG 1037, ABV 3.7%)
A pale ale with a good balance of citrus and floral hops.

Station Bitter (OG 1041, ABV 3.9%)
A traditional, amber-coloured session bitter with a good balance of fruity hops and roasted malt.

Zaffir (OG 1038, ABV 4%)
Pale-coloured ale, well-balanced with with hints of tropical fruit hops.

Cambrian Gold (OG 1042, ABV 4.2%)
A deep golden-coloured, fruity beer with a subtle dry finish.

Whitbier (ABV 4.2%)

Tekau (ABV 4.3%)
A pale-coloured, easy-drinking beer with refreshing pine and citrus notes.

Off the Rails (OG 1048, ABV 4.8%)
A rich and malty premium bitter with a hoppy flavour.

Storm SIBA

2 Waterside, Macclesfield, Cheshire, SK11 7HJ
☎ (01625) 431234 🌐 stormbrewing.co.uk

Storm Brewing was founded in 1998. In 2001 it moved to its current location, an old riverside pub building, which until 1937 was called the Mechanics Arms. More than 60 outlets are supplied. ♦RAIB

Beauforts Ale (OG 1038, ABV 3.8%)
Golden brown-coloured, full-flavoured session bitter with a lingering hoppy taste.

Desert Storm (OG 1040, ABV 3.9%)
Amber-coloured beer with a smoky flavour of fruit and malt.

Bosley Cloud (OG 1041, ABV 4.1%) ◆
Dry, golden-coloured bitter with peppery hop notes throughout. Some initial sweetness and a mainly bitter aftertaste.

Ale Force (OG 1042, ABV 4.2%) ◆
Amber-coloured, smooth-tasting, complex beer that balances malt, hop and fruit on the taste, leading to a roasty, slightly sweet aftertaste.

Dexter (OG 1040, ABV 4.2%)

Downpour (OG 1043, ABV 4.3%)
A pale ale with a full, fruity flavour, a hint of apple and a sightly hoppy aftertaste.

PGA (OG 1044, ABV 4.4%) ◆
Light, crisp, lager-style beer with a balance of malt, hops and fruit. Moderately bitter and slight dry aftertaste.

Hurricane Hubert (OG 1045, ABV 4.5%)
A dark-coloured beer with a refreshing, full, fruity hop aroma and subtle bitter aftertaste.

Silk of Amnesia (OG 1047, ABV 4.7%) ◆
Smooth, premium, easy-drinking bitter. Fruit and hops dominate throughout. Not too sweet, with a good lasting finish.

Red Mist (OG 1049, ABV 4.8%)
A dark red-black-coloured porter with fruity notes and a hoppy finish.

Stourton

See Enville

Stowey

Old Cider House, 25 Castle Street, Nether Stowey, Somerset, TA5 1LN
☎ (01278) 732228 🌐 stoweybrewery.co.uk

Somerset's smallest brewery was established in 2006, primarily to supply the owners' guesthouse and to provide beer to participants at events run from the accommodation. The small quantities of beer produced are also supplied to limited outlets in Nether Stowey and Watchet on a regular basis. ‼♦

Nether Ending (OG 1044, ABV 4.2%)

Strands

Strands Inn, Nether Wasdale, Cumbria, CA20 1ET
☎ (01946) 726237 🌐 strandshotel.com

Strands Brewery is a six-barrel plant with a 30-barrel fermentation capacity. Six of the beers are available on the bar of the Strands Inn at all times or in its sister pub, the Screes, across the road. ‼♦RAIB

Pied Piper (OG 1030, ABV 2.7%) ◆
Lots of traditional mild characteristics: malty, caramel, roast, sweet and fruity.

Green Bullet (OG 1037, ABV 3.5%)

Responsibly (OG 1038, ABV 3.7%)
Clean-tasting, heavily-hopped and lightly smoked beer.

Brown Bitter (OG 1039, ABV 3.8%) ◆
A complex-tasting, brown-coloured beer with a lingering bitter aftertaste.

Errmmm... (OG 1038, ABV 3.8%) ◆
A complex, traditional bitter.

Scafell Summit (ABV 3.8%)
Light and crisp with a long, soft hop finish.

Best Bitter (ABV 4.3%)

Red Screes (OG 1047, ABV 4.5%) ◆
A rich-tasting, smooth, strong bitter; full-flavoured with plenty of roast and malt tastes.

T'errmmm-inator (OG 1052, ABV 4.9%) ◆
A smooth, dark brown-coloured, roast-led beer. Full-bodied and well-balanced.

Traditional IPA (OG 1060, ABV 5.9%)

Contract brewed for Independent Lakeland Breweries:

Gold Wing (OG 1040, ABV 4%) ◆
A full-bodied, hoppy, bitter beer with a malty start.

Dark Knight (OG 1050, ABV 5%)

Stratford Upon Avon SIBA

Warwick Road, Stratford-upon-Avon, Warwickshire, CV37 0NT ☎ 07866 495232 🌐 sua-brewery.co.uk

Stratford Upon Avon is the first brewery in Stratford since Flowers in the 1960s. It was established by Richard Williams in 2014 on his family farm, which lies on the River Avon. The brewery has been developed around an environmentally-friendly approach, using the farm's own small solar farm, wind turbine and borehole. ♦

Stratford Gold (OG 1038, ABV 3.8%)

Louis's Pale Ale (OG 1040, ABV 4%)
A hoppy beer with powerful floral flavours.

Stratford Mosaic (OG 1042, ABV 4.2%)

Malty Pig Bitter (OG 1044, ABV 4.4%)
A malty but well-hopped ale with biscuity flavours.

Stratford Porter (OG 1046, ABV 4.6%)
A full-bodied ale with hints of coffee and chocolate.

American Amarillo (OG 1050, ABV 5%)

Immortal (OG 1050, ABV 5%)
A deep amber-coloured beer, fresh with subtle hints of grapefruit and tropical fruits.

Strathaven SIBA

Craigmill Brewery, Sandford Road, Strathaven, ML10 6PB
☎ (01357) 520419 🌐 strathavenales.com

Strathaven Ales is a 10-barrel brewery on the River Avon close to Strathaven and was converted from the remains of a 16th-century mill. The range is distributed throughout Scotland and the north of England. !! ♦

Craigmill Mild (OG 1035, ABV 3.5%)
A black-coloured ale with a chocolate aroma and a subtle orange zest aftertaste.

Clydesdale (OG 1038, ABV 3.8%)
A pale ale with a grapefruit aroma and sweet malt finish.

Duchess Anne (ABV 3.9%)
A straw-coloured clear wheat beer with a floral aroma.

Avondale (OG 1048, ABV 4%)
An amber-coloured ale with a floral aroma and subtle bitter finish.

Line Out (ABV 4%)
An amber-coloured ale with a floral aroma and subtle spicy aftertaste.

Old Mortality (OG 1046, ABV 4.2%)
A chestnut-coloured ale with a well-rounded, malty aroma and a rich, dried fruit flavour.

Claverhouse (OG 1046, ABV 4.5%)
A red-coloured ale with a sweet citrus aroma and lingering malt finish.

Teuchter (ABV 5.6%)
A strong, dark-coloured ale with a chewy toffee aroma, a citrus hop flavour and a satisfying dry finish.

500 (ABV 7%)
A smooth, full-flavoured, amber-coloured ale with subtle tropical fruit and lemon zest tones.

Usquebae Ale (ABV 7%)
A rich, honey-coloured ale, matured in oak casks, exuding a vanilla aroma, chewy toffee palate and a lasting, warming finish.

Strathbraan SIBA

Deanshaugh, Amulree, PH8 0EB
☎ (01350) 725264 ☎ 07747 857908
✉ strathbraan.bry@btinternet.com

Straathbraan began brewing in 2012 using a 10-barrel plant. RAIB

Due South (OG 1038, ABV 3.8%)

Head East (OG 1042, ABV 4.2%)

Strathcarron

Arinackaig, Strathcarron, IV54 8YN
☎ (01599) 577236 🌐 strathcarronbrewery.com

Brewing began in 2016 using a 2.5-barrel plant. Fresh West Highland water is used from an on-site spring. Beer is only available locally. RAIB

Golden Cow (OG 1038, ABV 3.8%)

Black Cow (OG 1042, ABV 4.2%)
A traditional, dark-coloured stout with a toasty malt flavour.

Red Cow (OG 1042, ABV 4.2%)

Stripey Cat

Tiger Inn, 14-16 Barrack Street, Bridport, Dorset, DT6 3LY
☎ (01308) 427543 🌐 tigerinnbridport.co.uk/the-stripey-cat-craft-brewery

Brewing began in 2017 at the Tiger Inn.

Stroud SIBA

Unit 11, Phoenix Works, London Road, Thrupp, Gloucestershire, GL5 2BU
☎ (01453) 887122 🌐 stroudbrewery.co.uk

Established in 2006, Stroud Brewery supports the local economy and does not sell its beers through supermarkets. The ales are sold in 40-50 pubs, independent retailers and its brewery shop. All beers have full organic status. A brewery bar is open Thursday-Saturday evenings. A move to new premises is planned during the currency of this guide. !! ♦ RAIB

Tom Long (OG 1039, ABV 3.8%)

An amber-coloured session bitter. Full-bodied with caramel notes and a spicy orange hop aroma.

OPA (Organic Pale Ale) (OG 1041, ABV 4%)
An easy-drinking, golden-coloured organic pale ale. Refreshing and soft on the palate, with hints of caramel and a delicate apple aroma.

Budding (OG 1045, ABV 4.5%)
A complex pale ale with aromatic citrus notes, a sweet malt backbone and a balanced, grassy bitterness.

Stu Brew

Newcastle University, Room 2.41, Merz Court, Newcastle upon Tyne, NE1 7RU stubrew.com

Stu Brew is Europe's first student-run microbrewery based at Newcastle University. The brewery was set up as part of a research project aimed at reducing waste and costs in all parts of brewing. The university and local pubs are supplied. **V**

Wheat Wanderer (ABV 4.2%)

Lab Session (ABV 4.3%)

Red Brick (ABV 4.8%)

Extended Overdraft (ABV 5.2%)

Into the Black (ABV 5.6%)

Stubborn Mule

Unit 2, Radium Works, Bridgewater Road, Altrincham, WA14 1LZ ☎ 07730 515251 stubbornmulebrewery.com

Brewing began in 2015, producing mainly bottled beers to micro pubs, specialist beer shops and restaurants in the Manchester area. At the end of 2016 the brewery relocated to new premises on the outskirts of Altrincham and expanded to a 10-barrel plant. It now runs regular tap events and tastings. **!! ♦ RAIB**

L'il Napoleon (OG 1038, ABV 3.9%)

Absolute Banker (OG 1047, ABV 4.7%)

Pre-Prohibition Cream Ale (OG 1050, ABV 5.5%)

Single Hop IPA (OG 1054, ABV 5.7%)

Chocolate Stout (OG 1052, ABV 5.8%)

WA15 Magnum IPA (OG 1066, ABV 7.2%)

Stumptail

North Street, Great Dunham, Norfolk, PE32 2LR ☎ (01328) 701042 stumptail@btinternet.com

Stumptail began commercial home-brewing in 2011 using a 100-litre plant. Bottle-conditioned beers are produced with cask-conditioned versions brewed to order. Only the West Norfolk area is supplied. **RAIB**

Suddaby's

See Half Moon and Leeds

Sulwath SIBA

The Brewery, 209 King Street, Castle Douglas, DG7 1DT ☎ (01556) 504525 sulwathbrewers.co.uk

Sulwath started brewing in 1995. The beers are supplied to markets as far away as Devon in the south and Aberdeen in the north. The brewery has a fully licensed brewery tap. Cask ales are sold to around 100 outlets and four wholesalers. **!! ♦ RAIB**

Cuil Hill (OG 1039, ABV 3.6%)
Distinctively fruity session ale with malt and hop undertones. The taste is bittersweet with a long-lasting, dry finish.

Tri-ball (OG 1039, ABV 3.9%)
A fresh, crisp. blonde ale.

The Grace (OG 1044, ABV 4.3%)
A refreshing, rich ale with a full-bodied flavour that balances the caramel undertones.

Black Galloway (OG 1046, ABV 4.4%)

Criffel (OG 1044, ABV 4.6%)
Full-bodied beer with a distinctive bitterness. Fruit is to the fore of the taste with hops becoming increasingly dominant in the taste and finish.

Galloway Gold (OG 1049, ABV 5%)
A cask-conditioned lager that will be too sweet for many despite being heavily hopped.

Knockendoch (OG 1047, ABV 5%)
Dark copper-coloured ale, reflecting a roast malt content, with bitterness from Challenger hops.

Solway Mist (OG 1052, ABV 5.5%)
A naturally cloudy wheat beer. Sweetish and fruity.

Summer Wine

The Old Furnace, Unit 15, Crossley Mills, New Mill Road, Honley, West Yorkshire, HD9 6QB ☎ (01484) 665466 summerwinebrewery.co.uk

Brewing commenced in 2006 on a 10-gallon kit. A 2007 upgrade saw a 0.5-barrel plant installed and in 2008 the brewery expanded to a six-barrel plant. More than 500 outlets are supplied direct. **♦**

Resistance (OG 1037, ABV 3.7%)
Dark ruby-coloured mild with a malty body and hints of caramel, cocoa and bitter roasted barley combined with a light, fruity hop character.

Zenith (OG 1040, ABV 4%)
Pale golden-coloured beer with floral aroma and a crisp bitter finish.

Barista (OG 1048, ABV 4.8%)
A rich coffee-flavoured stout which gets its flavour from ground Aribica added at the end of the boil.

Teleporter (OG 1050, ABV 5%)
A malty porter with a creamy body and cocoa, caramel and vanilla flavours.

Oregon (OG 1055, ABV 5.5%)
American-style pale ale with grapefruit, sherbet, spicy and floral aromas, a malty body and hoppy finish.

Rogue Red Hop Ale (OG 1058, ABV 5.8%)

Diablo (OG 1060, ABV 6%)
A strong IPA with tropical fruit aroma and flavours.

Summerskills SIBA

15 Pomphlett Farm Industrial Estate, Broxton Drive, Billacombe, Plymouth, Devon, PL9 7BG ☎ (01752) 481283 summerskills.co.uk

⊗ Established in a vineyard in 1983 at Bigbury-on-Sea, Summerskills moved to its present site in 1985 and is the oldest brewery in Plymouth. Wholesalers and pub companies provide national distribution and the beers regularly appear in a selection of local outlets. ♦RAIB

Start Point (OG 1036, ABV 3.7%)
Golden ale with a clean and fresh nose. Sweet upfront with a delicate bitter finish.

Westward Ho! (OG 1040, ABV 4.1%)
Malt dominates a light nose. Gentle bitterness introduces its malty-fruit friends. Malt and bitterness remain, with bitterness dominating.

Best Bitter (OG 1042, ABV 4.3%)
A mid-brown-coloured beer with plenty of malt and hops through the aroma, taste and finish. A good session beer.

Tamar (OG 1042, ABV 4.3%)
A tawny-coloured bitter with a fruity aroma and a hoppy taste and finish.

Stout (OG 1044, ABV 4.4%)
The deep colour is provided by roasted malts and barley, which also give a distinctive but smooth flavour.

Devon Dew (OG 1044, ABV 4.5%)
Honey yellow in colour with a floral, clean malty aroma. Sweet lemon upfront, with a long grapefruit finish.

Devon Frost (OG 1044, ABV 4.5%)
A lighter, slightly hoppier version of Devon Dew.

Menacing Dennis (OG 1045, ABV 4.5%)
Golden amber in colour with aromas of dark malt and hops and a slight hint of liquorice.

Bolt Head (OG 1046, ABV 4.7%)
Fruit-hop nose has roast-malt hints. Bitter flavours with sweet malt, roast and hoppiness. Lingering bitter finish with background malt and fruit.

Whistle Belly Vengeance (OG 1047, ABV 4.7%)
Full-flavoured, strong, red-coloured ale. Roast and malt aroma with roasted chestnut taste. Sweetness and bitterness mingle in the aftertaste.

Ninja (OG 1049, ABV 5%)

Plymouth Porter (OG 1050, ABV 5%)
A dark-coloured beer, lightly-hopped with a malty taste.

First Light (OG 1054, ABV 5.5%)
Strong golden ale. Fruity, hoppy aroma. Sweet grapefruit and hops on the palate. Aftertaste continues with fruit and hops.

Indiana's Bones / South Star (OG 1055, ABV 5.6%)
Old ale with a good body. Rich malty roasty aroma bursting with strong, sweet flavours on the tongue. Slightly dryer finish.

Sunbeam

52 Fernbank Road, Leeds, West Yorkshire, LS13 1BU
☎ 07772 002437 ⊕ sunbeamales.co.uk

Sunbeam Ales was established in a house in Leeds in 2009 with commercial brewing beginning in 2011. Since moving, capacity has increased to a two-barrel plant based in a garage. The core range of ales, available in West and North Yorkshire at present, are brewed on rotation up to twice weekly with occasional brews every six weeks or so. ♦

Eclipse (ABV 3.8%)
A stout infused with ground coffee and orange peel.

New Dawn (ABV 4.1%)
A well-balanced, golden-coloured session ale with New Zealand hops.

Dusk (ABV 4.5%)
Smooth, malty, easy-drinking best bitter hopped with traditional spicy English hops.

Foggy Morning (ABV 5.1%)
Delicate lemongrass is set against the banana esters of a cloudy wheat beer.

Helios (ABV 5.8%)
American-style IPA with tropical fruit flavours and aromas.

Sunset (NEW)

Office: 63 The Hurlings, St Columb Major, Cornwall, TR9 6FE
☎ (01637) 881798 ☎ 07702 087256
⊕ sunsetbrewingcompany.co.uk

Established in 2017 by Dan Piper, a bottled beer is contract brewed to Dan's own recipe.

Sunset Taverns (NEW)

Wheatsheaf, 234 High Street, Tunstall, Staffordshire, ST6 5TT
☎ (01782) 922628 ⊕ sunsettaverns.co.uk

Brewing began in 2016.

Surfing Monkey

Correspondence: 31 Fairwater Grove West, Cardiff, CF5 2JN ☎ 07412 365789
⊕ surfingmonkeybrewery.com

Brewing began in 2014 utilising a large garage at the rear of a private house. The company has recently announced that it is to operate as a gypsy brewery. Brewing is currently suspended. **V**

Surrey Hills SIBA

Denbies Wine Estate, London Road, Dorking, Surrey, RH5 6AA
☎ (01306) 883603 ⊕ surreyhills.co.uk

⊗ Surrey Hills began brewing in 2005 near Shere, moving to Dorking in 2011. Nearly 95% of production is sold within 15 miles of the brewery. The beers have won several local and national awards. !! ♦

Ranmore (OG 1039, ABV 3.8%)
A light, flavoursome session beer. An earthy hoppy nose leads into a grapefruit and hoppy taste and a clean, bitter finish.

Shere Drop (OG 1043, ABV 4.2%)
A hoppy ale with some balancing malt. A pleasant citrus aroma and a noticeable fruitiness in the taste, with some sweetness.

Gilt Complex (OG 1047, ABV 4.6%)

Greensand IPA (OG 1047, ABV 4.6%)
A strong-flavoured, easy-drinking IPA with intense grapefruit and hops in the aroma and taste and a soft citrus finish.

Collusion (OG 1053, ABV 5.2%)

Suthwyk

See Bowman

Swan SIBA

Unit 17, Rural Enterprise Centre, Brunel Road, Leominster, Herefordshire, HR6 0LX
☎ (01568) 617709 ☎ 07508 207928
swanbrewery.co.uk

Swan Brewery was established in 2016 by Jimmy Swan and partner Gill Bullock using a 10-barrel plant in Leominster. A 1.3-barrel plant is used to brew bespoke beers for local pubs.

Ruffled Feathers (OG 1040.5, ABV 3.8%)
A session ale with a clean, crisp hop flavour that lingers.

Gold (OG 1042, ABV 4.2%)
A golden ale with floral, herbal and zesty notes.

Swan on the Green

Swan on the Green, West Peckham, Kent, ME18 5JW
☎ (01622) 812271 swan-on-the-green.co.uk

The brewery was established in 2000 in an old coal shed behind the Swan on the Green pub using a two-barrel plant. !! ♦

Swannay SIBA

Swannay Brewery, Swannay by Evie, Orkney, KW17 2NP
☎ (01856) 721700 swannaybrewery.com

Brewing began in 2006 at the redundant Swannay dairy on Orkney mainland's exposed north-western tip. Two brewing plants are utilised, a five and a twenty barrel. Founder Rob is assisted by son Lewis plus a further small team of passionate beer lovers. !! ♦

Orkney Best (OG 1038, ABV 3.6%)
A refreshing, light-bodied, golden-coloured beer bursting with hop, peach and sweet malt flavours. The long, hoppy finish leaves a dry bitterness.

Island Hopping (OG 1039, ABV 3.9%)
Passion fruit hoppiness with some caramel and a lasting, bitter aftertaste.

Dark Munro (OG 1040, ABV 4%)
The nose presents an intense roast hit, which is followed by plums and blackcurrant in the mouth. The strong roast malt continues into the aftertaste.

Scapa Special (OG 1042, ABV 4.2%)
A good copy of a typical Lancashire bitter, full of bitterness and background hops, leaving your mouth tingling in the lingering aftertaste.

Sneaky Wee Orkney Stout (OG 1044, ABV 4.2%)
Bags of malt and roast with a mixed fruit berry background. Dry bitter finish.

Pale Ale (OG 1047, ABV 4.7%)

Orkney IPA (OG 1048, ABV 4.8%)
A traditional bitter with light hop and fruit flavour throughout.

Duke IPA (OG 1053, ABV 5.2%)
Good, refreshing citrus-fruited IPA with background malt.

Orkney Blast (OG 1058, ABV 6%)
Plenty of alcohol in this warming strong bitter/barley wine. A mushroom and woody aroma blossoms into a well-balanced smack of malt and hop in the taste.

Swansea SIBA

Joiners Arms, 50 Bishopston Road, Bishopston, Swansea, SA3 3EJ
☎ (01792) 232658

Opened in 1996, Swansea was the first commercial brewery in the area for almost 30 years. Beers are regularly available at the Joiners and also at the Railway Inn, Killay. !! ♦

Taddington

Blackwell Hall, Blackwell, Buxton, Derbyshire, SK17 9TQ
☎ (01298) 85734

Taddington started brewing in 2007, and brews one Czech-style unpasteurised lager in two different strengths. No real ale.

Tally Ho!

14 Market Street, Hatherleigh, Devon, EX20 3JN
☎ (01837) 810306 ☎ 07532 105871
tallyhobrewery.co.uk

Having stood idle at the rear of the Tally Ho! pub for 14 years, the brewery was recommissioned in 2015 by four brewing enthusiasts using the original copper brewing vessels. As well as the pub, local free houses and other establishments are supplied. ♦

Ruby EPA (OG 1038, ABV 3.8%)
A dark-coloured ale, with a long chocolaty bite.

Ukulale (OG 1042, ABV 4.2%)
Light aroma with hints of hops. Clean hop flavours and bitter taste lead to a sweeter but short lived aftertaste.

Tamworth (NEW)

29 Market Street, Tamworth, Staffordshire, B79 7LR
☎ (01827) 319872 tamworthbrewing.co.uk

Owner/brewer George Greenaway has brought brewing back to Tamworth town centre after a gap of 70 years. Brewing started in 2017. The showcase five-barrel plant sits on open view in a former shop, which dates from Tudor times and also serves as a tap room. !!

Ethelfleda (ABV 4.2%)
A straw-coloured ale with robust hop notes. Grapefruit to the fore.

Hopmaster (ABV 4.2%)
Single-hopped golden ale with overtones of coconut.

Hoppy Poppy (ABV 4.5%)
A golden-coloured beer with a gentle malty sweetness and a well-defined citrus bitterness.

Castle Black (ABV 4.8%)
Easy-drinking, black-coloured ale with roasty flavours and a good hit of hops on the palate.

Whopper (ABV 6.5%)
A strong IPA-style golden ale with an assertive resin hoppiness and a dry bitter finish.

Tankleys

Correspondence: 33 Beech Avenue, Sidcup, Kent, DA15 8NH ☎ 07901 333273 🌐 tankleysbrewery.com

Tankleys is a cuckoo brewery based in South-east London using spare capacity at Beerblefish Brewing (qv). Its Australian brewer has been brewing for 17 years and produces small batch brews, available occasionally around the local area.

English Golden Strong Ale (OG 1040, ABV 4.5%)

TAP

Marsden Estate, Rendcomb, Gloucestershire, GL7 7EX ☎ 07931 920988 🌐 tapbrewerygloucestershire.com

⊗ TAP is a microbrewery established near Cirencester in 2015. It prides itself on sourcing materials and services locally, with malt from Warminster, hops from Worcester and the beer labels produced in Cirencester. Twelve local pubs are regularly supplied. ‼ ♦ RAIB

Old Dairy Mild (OG 1038, ABV 3.2%)

Old Dairy Gold (OG 1040, ABV 3.9%)
A golden ale with a zesty finish.

Old Dairy Bronze (OG 1043, ABV 4.2%)

Tap East SIBA

7 International Square, The Great Eastern Market, Westfield Stratford City, Montfichet Road, Stratford, London, E20 1EE
☎ (020) 8555 4467 🌐 tapeast.co.uk

⊗ Tap East is located in Westfield Stratford City shopping centre opposite the main entrance to Stratford International Station. Brewing began in 2011 using a 2.5-barrel plant. One-off and collaborative beers with other breweries are also produced. Bottle-conditioned beers are planned. ♦

Tap House

See Leatherbritches

Tap It SIBA

Unit 6, Muira Industrial Estate, William Street, Southampton, Hampshire, SO14 5QH ☎ 07484 649425 🌐 tapitbrew.co.uk

The first brew by enthusiastic homebrewer Rob Colmer was in 2018. Tap It is an eight-barrel plant producing eight regular beers mainly in KeyKeg and bottles, but occasional cask-conditioned beers are available. There is an on-site brewery tap and a bar in Southampton is planned. ‼

Tap Social Movement

27 Curtis Industrial Estate, North Hinksey Lane, Oxford, OX2 0LX
☎ (01865) 236330 🌐 tapsocialmovement.com

A 1,000-litre brewery, founded in 2016 to provide training and opportunities for effective rehabilitation for people serving prison sentences. The three co-founders all have a background in the criminal justice system. A popular taproom is open on Thursday and Friday evenings and over the weekend. Beers are supplied in KeyKegs to some local outlets. RAIB

Tapped

Sheffield: Sheffield Tap, Platform 1b, Sheffield Station, Sheaf Street, Sheffield, South Yorkshire, S1 2BP
☎ (0114) 273 7558

Leeds: Leeds Tap, 51 Boar Lane, Leeds, West Yorkshire, LS1 5EL ☎ (0113) 244 1953
🌐 tappedbrewco.com

Brewing began in 2013 after the old Edwardian dining rooms were converted into an on-site brewery with a viewing gallery at the Sheffield Tap pub. The beer is supplied via the company's specialist beer wholesale business, Pivovar. A further on-site brewery opened at the Leeds Tap in 2014.

Ale (OG 1035, ABV 3.5%)

Mojo (OG 1036, ABV 3.6%)

SMASH (Single Malt and Single Hop Bitter) (ABV 3.9%)
A pale-coloured, crisp beer with light, hoppy flavours.

Rodeo (OG 1039, ABV 4%)
An American-hopped, light and fruity session pale ale.

Stout (OG 1041, ABV 4%)
English dry stout with a with hints of coffee and dark chocolate.

Bramling (OG 1042, ABV 4.2%)

Pegler (ABV 4.4%)

USP (ABV 4.5%)

Porter (ABV 5%)

IPA (ABV 5.3%)

Tapstone

11 Bartlett Park, Millfield, Chard, Somerset, TA20 2BB
☎ (01460) 929156 ☎ 07969 651998
🌐 tapstone.co.uk

⊗ Founded in 2015, the brewery was custom built around a unique brewing process that preserves delicate hop oils – making beers with a saturated hop flavour. It is growing Centennial hops about two miles from the brewery.

Zen Garden (OG 1036, ABV 3.6%)

Sea Monster (ABV 4.2%)
Fresh and fruity unfined pale ale with tropical flavours of blueberry, mango and lime.

Soma (OG 1046, ABV 4.6%)
An unfined ale brewed with oats so the fruity hops come to the fore.

Voodoo Juice (OG 1048, ABV 4.8%)
Orange-coloured ale bursting with stone fruit aromas. Unfined and hazy.

Wild Woods (OG 1048, ABV 4.8%)
Loads of grapefruit and sweet pine hop flavours. Unfined and hazy.

Kush Kingdom (OG 1050, ABV 5%)
An orange-coloured beer with fruity, citrus flavours. Unfined and hazy.

Sledge Hammer (OG 1060, ABV 6%)

A double IPA with a powerful hop flavour.

Tarn Hows SIBA

Low Bield, Knipe Fold, Outgate, Cumbria, LA22 0PU
☎ (01539) 422290 ☎ 07852 881105
tarnhowsbrewery.com

A microbrewery near Hawkshead specialising in traditional British ales. Oak casks may be used for occasional specials to provide further dimension to the beer flavour. ♦

Beertrix Porter (OG 1042, ABV 4%)
A well-balanced, fruity beer with some liquorice aromas and a lasting finish of bitterness and roast.

Extra Pale (OG 1043, ABV 4%)

Blueberry & Vanilla Oatmeal Stout (OG 1054, ABV 5%)
A fruit-dominated stout with intense chocolate, coffee, blueberry and vanilla flavours leading to a fruity finish.

Tarn51 (NEW)

Robin Hood, 10 Church Road, Altofts, West Yorkshire, WF6 2NJ
☎ (01924) 892911 ✉ realale@tarn51brewing.co.uk

Tarn51 uses a three-barrel plant situated at the Robin Hood in Altofts. Expansion is planned. Five other outlets are supplied. RAIB V

Tatton SIBA

Unit 7, Longridge Trading Estate, Knutsford, Cheshire, WA16 8PR
☎ (01565) 750747 ☎ 07738 150898
tattonbrewery.co.uk

Tatton is a family-run business based in the heart of Cheshire. Brewing commenced in 2010 using a steam-fired, custom-built 15-barrel brewhouse. It supplies pubs throughout Cheshire and the North-west. !! ♦

Ale (OG 1036, ABV 3.7%)
An easy-drinking session ale with a rich copper colour. It has a full malty/toffee flavour balanced by a soft bitterness and a hoppy, fruity taste and aroma.

Blonde (OG 1039, ABV 4%)
A clean-tasting, smooth pale ale with a fine hop aroma.

Best (OG 1040.5, ABV 4.2%)
A classic, light amber-coloured best bitter with a clean malt flavour and fine hop character.

Gold (OG 1046, ABV 4.5%)
A golden-coloured special ale with a maltiness backed by robust hop character.

Tavernale

Bridge Tavern, 7 Akenside Hill, Newcastle upon Tyne, NE1 3UF
☎ (0191) 232 1122 thebridgetavern.com

A two-barrel plant supplying beers to the Bridge Tavern only. All beers brewed are one-offs. ♦

Tavy

See Roam

Timothy Taylor SIBA IFBB

Knowle Spring Brewery, Keighley, West Yorkshire, BD21 1AW
☎ (01535) 603139 timothy-taylor.co.uk

An independent, family-owned company established in 1858, it has occupied the Knowle Spring site since 1863. Pennine spring water is used to brew its award-winning ales on both the established main plant and a 10-barrel plant introduced in 2017 to develop new beers, including occasional specials. ♦

Dark Mild (OG 1034, ABV 3.5%)
Malt and caramel dominate throughout in this sweetish beer with background hop and fruit notes.

Golden Best (OG 1033, ABV 3.5%)
Refreshing, amber-coloured, traditional Pennine mild. A delicate fruity, hoppy aroma leads to a fruity taste with underlying hops and malt. Fruity finish.

Boltmaker (OG 1038, ABV 4%)
Tawny-coloured bitter combining hops, fruit and biscuity malt. Lingering, increasingly bitter aftertaste. Formerly and sometimes still sold as Best Bitter.

Knowle Spring (OG 1041, ABV 4.2%)
A golden ale with a floral aroma, malty with grassy hops and a finish of bitter lemon.

Landlord (OG 1042, ABV 4.3%)
A moreish bitter combining citrus peel aromas, malt and grassy hops, marmalade sweetness and a long bitter finish.

Ram Tam (OG 1043, ABV 4.3%)
A black-coloured beer with red highlights topped by a coffee-coloured head. Burnt caramel on the nose, sweetish caramel taste leading to a light, sweet finish

Taylor Illingworth (NEW)

21 Harwood Court, Riverside Park Industrial Estate, Middlesbrough, TS2 1PU ☎ 07562 248707

Brewing began in 2017 using a four-barrel plant.

Taylors

London Tavern, Church Street, Attleborough, Norfolk, NR17 2AH ☎ 07983 178799
✉ taylorsbrewery@gmail.com

Brewing began in 2014, primarily to supply the London Tavern but the beers are now supplied to beer festivals and the free trade.

Number One (ABV 3.9%)

Second Coming (ABV 3.9%)

Dogtooth (ABV 4%)

English Pale Ale (ABV 4%)

Remember Me (ABV 4.4%)
A malty beer with caramel notes and a dry finish.

Stitched Up (ABV 4.7%)

Teignworthy SIBA

The Maltings, Teign Road, Newton Abbot, Devon, TQ12 4AA
☎ (01626) 332066 teignworthybrewery.com

THE BREWERIES

⊗ Teignworthy Brewery opened in 1994 within the historic Tucker's Maltings building. The 20-barrel plant produces 50 barrels a week and supplies around 300 outlets in Devon and Somerset. It diversified in 2017 with the addition of a gin distillery. !! ◆ RAIB

Neap Tide (OG 1038, ABV 3.8%)
A pale-coloured, fruity bitter.

Reel Ale (OG 1039.5, ABV 4%)
Subtle aromas. The taste is gentle with malt and fruit dominating the hops. The aftertaste is dry.

Gun Dog (OG 1043.5, ABV 4.3%)
Easy-drinking, session best bitter. Fruity throughout. Dry aftertaste lingers; sweetness and fruit over malt and caramel, progressing into hoppiness.

Spring Tide (OG 1043.5, ABV 4.3%)
A full and well-rounded, mid-brown-coloured beer with a dry, bitter taste and aftertaste.

Old Moggie (OG 1044.5, ABV 4.4%)
Best bitter. Hoppy and bitter with fruity undertones. Complex aftertaste with a balance of malt, hops and fruit.

Beachcomber (OG 1045.5, ABV 4.5%)
A pale brown-coloured beer with a light, refreshing fruit and hop nose, grapefruit taste and a dry, hoppy finish.

Teme Valley SIBA

Talbot, Bromyard Road, Knightwick, Worcestershire, WR6 5PH
☎ (01886) 821235 ☎ 07792 394151
temevalleybrewery.co.uk

Teme Valley was established in 1997 to brew beer for the Talbot, Knightwick. Only hops grown in Herefordshire and Worcestershire are used in brewing. Beers are supplied throughout the West Midlands and Marches. !! ◆ RAIB

T'Other (OG 1035, ABV 3.5%)
Refreshing, amber-coloured bitter offering an abundance of flavour with a fruity aroma, followed by a short, dry bitterness.

This (OG 1037, ABV 3.7%)
Amber-coloured ale with a vivid hop aroma and a hint of chocolate malt.

That (OG 1041, ABV 4.1%)
A chestnut-coloured best bitter with a robust malt flavour balanced by powerful hops.

Talbot Blonde (OG 1042, ABV 4.4%)

Tempest SIBA

Block 11, Units 1 & 2, Tweedbank Industrial Estate, Tweedbank, TD1 3RS
☎ (01896) 759500 tempestbrewingco.com

Based in a former dairy, Tempest was set up in 2010 by Gavin Meiklejohn, brewer and co-proprietor of the Cobbles Inn in Kelso, which is the brewery tap. In 2015 the brewery moved from Kelso to new premises at Tweedbank. !! ◆ RAIB

Pemberton Pale (OG 1037, ABV 3.7%)
An American-style pale ale, straw-like in colour with a refreshing hop character. Aromas of lemon and lime, some tropical notes and subtle spice.

Armadillo (OG 1039, ABV 3.8%)
Waves of zesty citrus amplified with hops for added flavour.

Cascadian (OG 1039, ABV 3.9%)
Light, citrus, hoppy session ale.

White Light (OG 1047, ABV 4.7%)
American hop hitter with a smooth citrus finish.

Tenby SIBA

Unit 15, The Salterns, Tenby, SA70 8EQ
☎ (01834) 218090 ☎ 07410 169447
tenbybrewingco.com

Formerly known as Preseli, Tenby Brewing Co uses a six-barrel plant. Beer is supplied to outlets in Pembrokeshire, neighbouring counties and further afield. Spent grain is fed to animals at a local eco-farm and through energy savings the brewery plans to become carbon neutral. RAIB

West Coast Rocks (OG 1040, ABV 3.8%)
A malty body with a hint of spiced blackberry.

Pembrokeshire Promise (OG 1046, ABV 4.5%)
Hints of caramel, complex grain and mellow bitter hops.

Barefoot Blonde (OG 1041, ABV 4.6%)
A refreshing, clean, crisp blonde infused with Kaffir lime leaves.

Black Flag Porter (OG 1055, ABV 5.6%)
Full of character, with coffee and chocolate and a hint of vanilla spiced rum.

Tenby Harbour

See Harbwr Tenby

Test (NEW)

Old Stables, Greyhound Inn, High Street, Broughton, Hampshire, SO20 8AA
☎ (01794) 301573 ☎ 07831 746725
testbrewing.co.uk

⊗ Brewing started in 2017 in redundant stables behind, and independent of, the Greyhound Inn, using a four-barrel plant. There are four part-time brewers. Two local pubs as well as around 12 pubs in Andover and Basingstoke are supplied.

Anton Bitter (OG 1037, ABV 3.8%)

Wallop Gold (OG 1042, ABV 4.3%)

Thame

East Street, Thame, Oxfordshire, OX9 3JS
☎ (01844) 218202
thamebrewery@btinternet.com

⊗ This one-barrel brewery was set up in 2009 by Peter Lambert and Oak Taverns in the old stables at the Cross Keys. Beer is produced for the Cross Keys and includes many one-off brews.

Thames Side SIBA

Unit 7, Tims Boatyard, Timsway, Staines-upon-Thames, Surrey, TW18 3JY
☎ (01784) 409887 ☎ 07749 204242
thamessidebrewery.co.uk

⊗ Thames Side was founded in 2015 by CAMRA member Andy Hayward using a four-barrel plant situated in an old boatyard on the banks of the river. Beer is supplied to the local area as well as into central London. Beers are named after birds found on or near the River Thames. ♦

Harrier Bitter (ABV 3.4%)

Heron Ale (ABV 3.7%)

White Swan Pale Ale (OG 1041, ABV 4.2%)

Egyptian Goose India Pale Ale (ABV 4.8%)

Wryneck Rye IPA (OG 1055, ABV 5.6%)

Theakston

The Brewery, Masham, North Yorkshire, HG4 4YD
☎ (01765) 680000 theakstons.co.uk

After several years under the control of other companies Theakston is now owned by four brothers, grandsons of Thomas Theakston, the son of the company's founder who built the brewery in 1875. A new fermentation room was built in 2004 to provide additional flexibility and capacity, and further capacity was added in 2006. All Theakston beers are now brewed in Masham. !! ♦

Best Bitter (OG 1038, ABV 3.8%)
A golden-coloured beer with a full flavour that lingers pleasantly on the palate. With a good bittersweet balance, this beer has a robust hop character, citrus and spicy.

Black Bull Bitter (OG 1037, ABV 3.9%)
A distinctively hoppy aroma leads to a bitter, hoppy taste with some fruitiness and a short bitter finish.

Lightfoot (OG 1041, ABV 4.1%)

XB (OG 1044, ABV 4.5%)
A sweet-tasting bitter with background fruit and spicy hop. Some caramel character gives this ale a malty dominance.

Old Peculier (OG 1057, ABV 5.6%)
A full-bodied, dark brown-coloured, strong ale. Slightly malty but with hints of roast coffee and liquorice. A smooth caramel overlay and a complex fruitiness leads to a bitter chocolate finish.

Third Eye SIBA

The Mill, Hurst House Farm Barn, Halfpenny Lane, Heskin, Lancashire, PR7 5PR ☎ 07871 870015
thirdeyebrewery.co.uk

Third Eye began brewing in 2015 using a 1.5-barrel plant. Brewing is currently suspended.

Thirst Class

Unit 16, Station Road Industrial Estate, Reddish, Stockport, SK5 6ND
☎ (0161) 431 3998 thirstclassale.co.uk

Thirst Class opened in 2014 in the centre of Stockport using a purpose-built two-barrel plant. In 2016 the brewery relocated to larger premises and installed a 10-barrel plant. ♦ RAIB

High 5 (OG 1053, ABV 4.2%)
A session pale ale with a citrus aroma and flavour.

Stocky Oatmeal Stout (ABV 4.7%)
Smooth, full-bodied oatmeal stout with notes of coffee and chocolate.

Any Porter in a Storm (ABV 4.8%)
Smooth, full-bodied porter with a rich taste and finish.

Green Bullet Pale Ale (ABV 4.8%)
A traditional-style English pale ale with an earthy hop, floral flavour.

American Brown Ale (ABV 5.6%)
An American-style, brown-coloured ale; hoppy but with a pronounced roasted maltiness.

Hoppy Couple IPA (ABV 6.2%)
Rich copper-coloured, American-style IPA with a big citrus hop aroma and flavour.

Thomas Guest

See Black Country

John Thompson

Ingleby, Derbyshire, DE73 7HW
☎ (01332) 862469 johnthompsoninn.com

Established by John Thompson in 1977 as an addition to the John Thompson Inn, which he converted from a 15th-century farmhouse in 1968, and is now run by his son Nick. John Thompson Special (formerly JTS XXX) is Derbyshire's longest continuously brewed ale. !!

Thorley & Sons

30 East Street, Ilkeston, Derbyshire, DE7 5JB ☎ 07899 067723 dylan.thorley1@yahoo.co.uk

Thorley & Sons began brewing commercially in 2016 on a 1.5-barrel plant located in an old coach house at the rear of brewer Dylan Thorley's house.

Pale & Interesting (ABV 4.5%)
Easy-drinking pale ale with a subtle hint of citrus in the taste.

Thornbridge SIBA

Riverside Business Park, Buxton Road, Bakewell, Derbyshire, DE45 1GS
☎ (01629) 815999 thornbridgebrewery.co.uk

The first Thornbridge craft beers were produced in 2005 using a 10-barrel brewery, housed in the grounds of Thornbridge Hall. The beers have gained considerable success with over 300 consumer and industry awards won. A 30-barrel brewery opened in Bakewell in 2009. The original site continues to develop new, seasonal and speciality beers. 200 outlets are supplied direct. 12 pubs are managed and owned. !! ♦ RAIB

Wild Swan (OG 1035, ABV 3.5%)
Pale-coloured yet flavoursome and refreshing beer. Plenty of lemony citrus hop flavour, becoming increasingly dry and bitter in the finish and aftertaste.

Brother Rabbit (OG 1035, ABV 4%)
Lemon zest in colour with a clean, hoppy aroma, a resinous finish and some bitterness.

Lord Marples (OG 1041, ABV 4%)
Smooth, traditional, easy-drinking bitter. Caramel, malt and coffee flavours fall away to leave a long, bitter finish.

Ashford (OG 1043, ABV 4.2%)
A brown-coloured ale with a floral hoppiness, a smooth, malty kick and a delicate coffee finish.

Kipling (OG 1050, ABV 5.2%) ♦
Golden-coloured, pale bitter with aromas of grapefruit and passion fruit. Intense fruit flavours continue throughout, leading to a long bitter aftertaste.

Jaipur IPA (OG 1055, ABV 5.9%) ♦
Flavoursome IPA packed with citrus hoppiness that's nicely counterbalanced by malt and underlying sweetness and robust fruit flavours.

Saint Petersburg Imperial Russian Stout (OG 1073, ABV 7.4%) ♦
Smooth and easy to drink with raisins, bitter chocolate and hops throughout, leading to a lingering coffee and chocolate aftertaste.

Thousand Trades

Unit 5, 270 Lakey Lane Hall Green, Birmingham, B28 8RA ☎ 07768 454741
🌐 thousandtradesbrewing.co.uk

Brewing began in 2016 but is currently suspended. ♦

Three B's

Black Bull, Brokenstone Road, Blackburn, Lancashire, BB3 0LL
☎ (01254) 581381 ☎ 07563 573199
🌐 threebsbrewery.co.uk

Robert Bell acquired the Black Bull in 2011 and the brewpub now supplies 50 outlets. !! ♦ RAIB

Bee Thrifty (OG 1036, ABV 3.4%)

Stoker's Slake (OG 1038, ABV 3.6%) ♦
Lightly roasted coffee flavours are in the aroma and the initial taste. A well-rounded, dark brown-coloured mild with dried fruit flavours in the long finish.

Honey Bee (OG 1039, ABV 3.7%)
A golden-coloured honey beer with honey apparent in both aroma and taste.

Bobbin's Bitter (OG 1038, ABV 3.8%)
A golden-coloured bitter with warm aromas of nutty grain and a full, fruity flavour with a light, dry finish.

Bee Blonde (OG 1041, ABV 4%)
A distinctive, pale-coloured bitter with a light, dry balance of grain and hops and a delicate finish with citrus fruits.

Black Bull (OG 1042, ABV 4%)
Dark ruby-coloured bitter with a rich character and a hint of chocolate.

Tackler's Tipple (OG 1044, ABV 4.3%)
A dark-coloured best bitter with a full hop flavour, biscuit tones on the tongue and a deep, dry finish.

Black Bull Lager (ABV 4.5%)

Doff Cocker (OG 1045, ABV 4.5%) ♦
Yellow in colour with a hoppy aroma and initial taste giving way to subtle malt notes and orchard fruit flavours. Crisp, dry finish.

Pinch Noggin (OG 1046, ABV 4.6%)
A dark-coloured, strong best bitter with a full hop flavour and long aftertaste.

Knocker Up (OG 1047, ABV 4.8%) ♦
A smooth, rich, creamy porter. The roast flavour is foremost without dominating and is balanced by fruit and hop notes.

Shuttle Ale (OG 1050, ABV 5.2%)

Three Blind Mice

Unit W10, Black Bank Business Park, Black Bank Road, Little Downham, Cambridgeshire, CB6 2UA
☎ (01353) 864438 ☎ 07912 875825
🌐 threeblindmicebrewery.com

Brewing began in 2014. A seven-barrel plant is used, supplying regularly to the Drayman's Son micropub, Ely, plus other outlets in Ely, Cambridgeshire and further afield. The name comes from the three owners/brewers, who reckoned they didn't have a clue what they were doing when they first started brewing. ♦

Lonely Snake (ABV 3.5%)

Juice Rocket (ABV 4.5%)

Old Brown Mouse (ABV 4.7%)

Milk Worm (ABV 5.3%)

Three Brothers SIBA

Unit 4, Clayton Court, Bowesfield Crescent, Stockton on Tees, TS18 3QX
☎ (01642) 678084 🌐 threebrothersbrewing.co.uk

The brewery is the vision of Kit Dodd after brewing for five years with another local brewery. He established it in 2016, together with his brother Dave and brother-in-law Chris. !! ♦ RAIB

The Ex Wife (OG 1037, ABV 3.7%)
A bitter beer brewed in a traditional way with a modern, slightly fruity twist

Honeysuckle Smash (OG 1040, ABV 4%)
A delicate golden ale brewed with North Yorkshire honey.

ThaiPA (OG 1041, ABV 4.1%)
A full-flavoured, lemongrass infused, hoppy pale ale.

Au (OG 1042, ABV 4.2%)
A refreshingly crisp, lightly-hopped golden ale with light citrus notes.

Ruby Revolution (OG 1046, ABV 4.6%)
Robust, traditional-style, ruby-coloured ale. Packed with chocolate and crystal malts.

Short & Stout (OG 1050, ABV 5%)

The Beginning (OG 1055, ABV 5.5%)

Three Castles

Unit 12, Salisbury Road Business Park, Pewsey, Wiltshire, SN9 5PZ
☎ (01672) 564433 ☎ 07725 148671
🌐 threecastlesbrewery.co.uk

Three Castles is an independent, family-run brewery established in 2006. It delivers direct to around 80 pubs and independent retailers. Wholesalers and beer festivals are also supplied. !! ♦ RAIB

Chain Mail Pale (OG 1038, ABV 3.8%)
This clean, zesty pale ale has a citrus fruit cocktail flavour and a bittersweet finish.

Barbury Castle (OG 1039, ABV 3.9%)
A well-balanced, easy-drinking pale ale with a hoppy, spicy palate.

Armour Plated (OG 1040, ABV 4%)

Saxon Archer (OG 1040, ABV 4%)
A well-balanced, easy-drinking session ale with a good aroma and a hoppy, fruity palate.

Heritage (OG 1042, ABV 4.2%)
A bronze-coloured best bitter with a smooth taste.

Uffington Castle (OG 1042, ABV 4.2%)
A dark brown-coloured ale with a malty and nutty palate and a pleasant bitterness. The hop comes through well with a big, spicy aroma.

Vale Ale (OG 1043, ABV 4.3%)
Golden-coloured ale with a fruity palate and strong floral aroma.

Corn Dolly (OG 1047, ABV 4.7%)
Honey-coloured, easy-drinking ale with a slightly floral, delicate aroma.

Three Daggers SIBA

Westbury Road, Edington, Wiltshire, BA13 4PG
☎ (01380) 830940 threedaggersbrewery.com

Three Daggers Brewery was established in 2013 using a 2.5-barrel brew plant in a farm shop next to a popular roadside pub. Malt is sourced locally from Warminster Maltings and hops from Charles Faram in Herefordshire. Hops are grown on-site for use in seasonal beers. !! ♦ RAIB

Daggers Blonde (OG 1037, ABV 3.6%)

Daggers Ale (OG 1041, ABV 4.1%)
A refreshingly malty ale with a dry hoppy finish.

Daggers Edge (OG 1047, ABV 4.7%)

Three Engineers (NEW)

Cow Byers, Winterbourne Medieval Barn, Church Lane, Winterbourne, BS36 1SE
threeengineersbrewery@gmail.com

Three Engineers is a nanobrewery established in 2017. Relocation is planned.

Beluga Wheat Beer (ABV 3.9%)
A wheat beer with subtle fruity flavours.

Corsair American Pale Ale (ABV 4.1%)
A session American-style pale ale with a mellow, fruity character.

Gladiator (ABV 4.4%)
A classic British best bitter with a rich, malty flavour and a hint of sweetness from Belgian hops.

Crosswind Pale Ale (ABV 5%)

Spannered (ABV 5.1%)
A dark-coloured, smooth porter with a rich, malty flavour.

Harvest Ale (ABV 5.2%)
A light and fruity American-style pale ale.

Mustang IPA (ABV 5.4%)

Three Fiends

Brookfield Farm, 148 Mill Moor Road, Meltham, West Yorkshire, HD9 5LN ☎ 07810 370430
threefiends.co.uk

The brewery was set up by three friends in 2015 and is based in one of the outbuildings at Brookfield Farm. The current two-barrel plant is in the process of being upgraded. Beers are available around Huddersfield and at CAMRA beer festivals.

Two Face (OG 1041, ABV 4%)
An easy-drinking session ale with floral, citrus and honey-like tones.

Bad Uncle Barry (OG 1042, ABV 4.2%)

Boomer (OG 1043, ABV 4.3%)
A heavily-hopped, big-tasting, malty beer.

Mok Titi (OG 1045, ABV 4.6%)

Dark Side (OG 1053, ABV 5.3%)
A black IPA with a smooth, chocolaty start, leading to an increasingly bitter finish.

Little Devil (OG 1051, ABV 5.3%)

Voodoo (OG 1061, ABV 6%)
A chocolate chilli stout.

Panic Attack Espresso Stout (OG 1071, ABV 6.8%)

Bukowski (OG 1065, ABV 7%)

Three Hills

Woodford, Northamptonshire, NN14 4HY
threehillsbrewing.com

Named after the ancient communal tombs that stand on the outskirts of the village of Woodford, Three Hills is a small batch brewery established in 2016. RAIB

Three Kings SIBA

14 Prospect Terrace, North Shields, NE30 1DX
☎ 07580 004565 threekingsbrewery.co.uk

Three Kings started in 2012 using a 2.5-barrel plant, upgrading to a five-barrel one in 2013. Four house beers are brewed for local pubs. In 2016 the brewery upgraded to a 10-barrel plant and expanded into the adjacent unit. ♦

Shieldsman (ABV 3.8%)
Easy-drinking session ale with medium bitterness and tropical fruit flavours.

Billy Mill Ale (OG 1040, ABV 4%)

Darkside of the Toon (OG 1042, ABV 4.1%)
A dry, dark-coloured, roast, bitter, creamy stout with hints of chocolate and coffee.

Ring of Fire (OG 1045, ABV 4.5%)
A golden-coloured, American-style pale ale with floral, citrus and grapefruit tones.

Silver Darling (OG 1053, ABV 5.6%)
A strong pale ale with long-lasting bitterness and a spicy, pine, citrus and grapefruit aroma.

Three Legs

Unit 1, Burnt House Farm, Udimore Road, Broad Oak, East Sussex, TN31 6BX ☎ 07939 997622
thethreelegs.co.uk

Three Legs was started in 2015 by two friends who met studying wine-making and viticulture at university. Initially a nanobrewery, it has expanded to a four-barrel plant, in a converted farm barn. 20 local pubs and several local bottle shops are supplied. The brewery is also home to a thriving brewery tap. !! RAIB

Pale (OG 1033, ABV 3.7%)
A light, pale ale with an aromatic nose. Crisp with low bitterness.

Dark (OG 1045, ABV 4%)
A dark-coloured ale with a huge roasted character, chocolate and coffee flavours and a dry finish.

Columbus Pale (ABV 4.2%)
Orange and grapefruity, zesty pale ale with an American hop bitterness.

Black Pale (OG 1040, ABV 4.3%)
Hopped heavily as a pale ale with added roasted malts to give hints of a stout.

Session IPA (OG 1041, ABV 4.5%)
Aromatic hops give a punch of fruit and spice.

English IPA (OG 10417, ABV 5%)
Locally-grown hops give a citrus and orange punch and an assertive bitterness.

Three Peaks

Scar Top, Buck Haw Brow, Settle, North Yorkshire, BD24 0DJ
☎ (01729) 822939 ☎ 07795 358932

Office: 7 Craven Terrace, Settle, BD24 9DB
threepeaksbrewery.co.uk

Formed in 2006 using a five-barrel plant, Three Peaks is run by husband and wife team Colin and Susan Ashwell assisted by Andrew Murphy. ♦

Pen-y-Ghent Bitter (OG 1040, ABV 3.8%)
The malty character of this mid-brown-coloured session bitter is balanced by fruit in the aroma and taste. The finish is malty and hoppy.

Ingleborough Gold (OG 1041, ABV 4%)
This golden-coloured best bitter is hoppy throughout with fruit in the aroma and taste and a hoppy, bitter finish.

Whernside Pale Ale (OG 1042, ABV 4.2%)

Three Shires

See Wintrip

Three Sods SIBA

Bethnal Green Working Men's Club, 42 Pollard Row, Bethnal Green, London, E2 6NB ☎ 07544 422236
threesodsbrewery.com

Based in a working men's club in East London, Three Sods is run by head brewer David Jonsson-Buttery and specialises in small batch beers.

Three Tuns SIBA

Salop Street, Bishop's Castle, Shropshire, SY9 5BN
☎ 07973 301099

Office: 16 Market Square, Bishop's Castle, SY9 5BW
threetunsbrewery.co.uk !! ♦ RAIB

Mild (OG 1040, ABV 3.4%)
Tawny-coloured beer of rich maltiness with burnt and roasted flavours.

Rantipole (OG 1036, ABV 3.7%)

1642 Bitter (OG 1042, ABV 3.8%)
A golden ale with a light, nutty maltiness and spicy bitterness.

Solstice (OG 1037, ABV 3.9%)
Pale straw-coloured beer, lightly malty with a crisp, fruity bitterness and citrus flavours.

XXX (OG 1046, ABV 4.3%)
A pale-coloured, sweetish bitter with a light hop aftertaste that has a honey finish.

Stout (OG 1048, ABV 4.4%)
Dark brown to black in colour. Mixed dried fruit aroma with yeast. Bitter start, fruity with roast. Balanced finish with fruit and sweetness among the hops.

Cleric's Cure (OG 1059, ABV 5%)
A light tan-coloured ale with a malty sweetness. Strong and spicy with a floral bitterness.

Steampunk (OG 1065, ABV 6.5%)
Rich, dark-coloured and fiery, smooth barley wine with flavours of liquorice, ginger, caramel and roasted malts, lasting through into the strong bitter finish.

Three Tuns XXXXXXX Strong Ale (OG 1095, ABV 9.5%)
Brandy, full spiced, strong old ale.

Three Valleys (NEW)

290-292 Rochdale Road, Todmorden, West Yorkshire, OL14 7LP ☎ 07736 061150
threevalleysbrewery@yahoo.com

This five-barrel brewery is located in the building previously occupied by Bare Arts Brewery. It started selling beers to other outlets in 2018 and is run by two enthusiastic and accomplished home brewers. New beers are being developed and existing beers have already been sold in the Calderdale area and across the border in Lancashire. ♦ RAIB

Pale Ale (OG 1036, ABV 3.6%)
A pale-coloured, lightly-hopped ale.

Stout (OG 1043, ABV 4.3%)
Smooth, dark-coloured and rich stout, brewed using chocolate malt.

Cascade (OG 1053, ABV 5.3%)
An ale with a distinct citrus flavour.

IPA (OG 1062, ABV 6.2%)

Thurstons (Horsell)

The Courtyard, 102c High Street, Horsell, Surrey, GU21 4ST
☎ (01483) 729555 ☎ 07789 936784
thurstonsbrewery.co.uk

Originally based in the Crown, Horsell, Thurstons moved next door in 2014 when the brewery upgraded to a 4.5-barrel plant. The brewery supplies pubs across Surrey. ♦ RAIB

Horsell Best (OG 1040, ABV 3.8%)
Traditional, well-balanced bitter, initially malty with strong caramel flavours throughout and balancing bitterness, becoming drier in the finish.

Horsell Gold (OG 1040, ABV 3.8%)
Light, fruit and slightly nutty aroma, leads to some bitterness and malt, which soon fades into a light bitter finish.

Stedmans Ale (OG 1042, ABV 4.1%)
Golden in colour with citrus and caramel aroma, and malt and hops more pronounced in the taste.

Milk Stout (OG 1055, ABV 4.5%)
Smooth, sweet stout, with a chocolaty flavour. A sweet, malty flavour with a pleasant sharpness and a slightly dry finish.

Un-American Pale Ale (OG 1045, ABV 4.6%)
A well-hopped American-style pale ale with grapefruit and pineapple on the nose and palate. This is balanced by a strong malt backbone and a good bitter finish.

Thwaites IFBB

Myerscough Road, Mellor Brook, Blackburn, Lancashire, BB2 7LB
☎ (01254) 686868 thwaites.co.uk

Founded in 1807, Thwaites brewed in the centre of Blackburn until 2018 when it moved operations some five miles away to a rural site in the Ribble Valley. Brewing takes place on a 20-barrel plant and is exclusively for the company's own properties. While all of these can sell the regularly-brewed beers, members of the 1807 Cask Club are also able to select up to four monthly brews from the seasonal ales range. The arrangement with Marston's, which bought the company's Wainwright and Lancaster Bomber brands, free trade business and distribution facility in 2015, is still in place and all licensees continue to be able to sell designated Marston's beers. The estate is comprised of around 240 tenanted pubs , 11 managed Inns of Character, eight hotels and two lodges. ♦RAIB

Nutty Black (OG 1036, ABV 3.3%)
Traditional, malty, dark mild with caramel notes and a slightly bitter finish.

Original (OG 1036, ABV 3.6%)
A classic, copper-coloured, traditional session bitter with balance between malt flavour and hop bitterness.

TBC (Thwaites Best Cask) (OG 1038, ABV 3.8%)
A chestnut-coloured bitter, malty and sweet, balanced by delicate hops.

Wit (OG 1045, ABV 4.5%)

Tigertops

22 Oakes Street, Flanshaw, Wakefield, West Yorkshire, WF2 9LN
☎ (01229) 716238 ☎ 07951 812986
✉ tigertopsbrewery@hotmail.com

Tigertops was established in 1995 by Stuart Johnson and his wife Lynda who, as well as owning the brewery, run the Foxfield brewpub in Cumbria (qv). The brewery is run on their behalf by Barry Smith, supplying five regular outlets. ♦

Tiley's

Salutation Inn, Ham, Gloucestershire, GL13 9QH
☎ (01453) 810284 sallyatham.com

This 2.5-barrel microbrewery was established in an outbuilding of the award-winning Salutation Inn in 2015. It concentrates on producing small batches of award-winning beer, predominantly in cask with some in KeyKeg. Most of the brewery's output is sold on-site at the Salutation Inn with the rest going to selected pubs in the local area.

Tilford

Duke of Cambridge, Tilford Road, Tilford, Surrey, GU10 2DD ☎ 07710 500967
✉ genesiscraftales@hotmail.com

Tilford Brewery was started in 2017 using a 2.5-barrel plant in an old coaching house on the site of the Duke of Cambridge pub. A shop, tasting room and mini maltings are planned for the upstairs of the building. Beer is supplied to pubs in Surrey and Hampshire. !!

Red Mist (ABV 3.7%)

Rushmoor Ripper (OG 1044, ABV 4.4%)

Tillingbourne SIBA

Old Scotland Farm, Staple Lane, Shere, Surrey, GU5 9TE
☎ (01483) 222228 tillybeer.co.uk

Tillingbourne began in 2011 on a farm site previously used by Surrey Hills Brewery using its old 17-barrel plant. Around 25 local outlets are supplied. !! ♦

The Source (OG 1033, ABV 3.3%)
Light and crisp golden ale with strong grapefruit flavours.

Black Troll (OG 1035, ABV 3.7%)
A black-coloured bitter in which initial roast notes are eventually overpowered by citrus hop through to the finish.

Bouncing Bomb (ABV 3.8%)

AONB (OG 1036, ABV 4%)
Golden ale in which citrus hop dominates throughout. Some balancing malt in the aroma and taste.

Falls Gold (OG 1037, ABV 4.2%)
Whilst hops dominate, balancing malt is evident throughout. Hints of grapefruit in the aroma and taste lead to a dry finish.

Whakahari (ABV 4.6%)

Hop Troll (OG 1045, ABV 4.8%)
Golden ale with big hop flavours together with peach and apricot. Sweet, fruity taste leads to a floral bitter finish.

Summit (ABV 6%)

Time & Tide

Statenborough Farm, Felderland Lane, Eastry, Kent, CT14 0BX ☎ 07739 868256
timeandtidebrewing.co.uk

Time & Tide began brewing in 2013 using spare capacity at Ripple Steam Brewery (qv). In 2015 it obtained its own 20-barrel brewhouse. No real ale. ♦

Tindall

Toad Lane, Seething, Norfolk, NR35 2EQ

Tindall Ales began brewing in 1998. It was originally based in Ditchingham but moved to its current location towards the end of 2001. ♦

Best Bitter (OG 1037, ABV 3.7%)

Fuggled Up (OG 1037, ABV 3.7%)

Mild (OG 1037, ABV 3.7%)

Liberator (OG 1038, ABV 3.8%)

Alltime (OG 1040, ABV 4%)

Mundham Mild (OG 1040, ABV 4%)

Ditchingham Dam (OG 1042, ABV 4.2%)

Seething Pint (OG 1043, ABV 4.3%)

Norwich Dragon (OG 1046, ABV 4.6%)

Honeydo (OG 1050, ABV 5%)

Tinpot

See Wash House

Tintagel SIBA

Condolden Farm, Tintagel, Cornwall, PL34 0HJ
☎ (01840) 213371 🌐 tintagelbrewery.co.uk

⊗ Established in 2009 in a redundant milking parlour on the highest farm in Cornwall, using a 7.5-barrel plant. A new purpose-built brewery, shop, restaurant and visitor centre opened in 2017. Around 80 outlets are supplied direct. !! ♦

Castle Gold (OG 1038, ABV 3.8%)
Refreshing golden ale with little aroma. Light citrus, apples and soft fruit flavours with faint malt. Short hop bitter finish.

Cornwall's Pride (OG 1040, ABV 4%)
Copper-coloured bitter with a caramel malt aroma. Sweet, grainy malt with toffee and summer fruit flavours. Late dried fruit and coffee hints.

Arthur's Ale (OG 1044, ABV 4.4%)
Light copper-coloured best bitter with an initial assertive earthy hop flavour. Balanced biscuit malt and bitter hop with some fruit and toffee.

Pendragon (ABV 4.5%)
Smooth golden ale with a powerful citrus hop nose. Refreshing strong hop bitterness taste with moderate dryness. Citrus fruit and grape flavours.

Poldark Ale (OG 1045.8, ABV 4.5%)
Tawny-coloured strong mild. Assertive malty flavour with light caramel, roast notes and sweetness balanced by fruity hop bitterness. Caramel malt finish.

Harbour Special (OG 1048.9, ABV 4.8%)
Brown-coloured strong bitter with ripe fruity, malty aroma. Rich, nutty malt, stone fruits and esters taste, finishing bitter and malty.

Merlins Muddle (OG 1052, ABV 5.2%)
Copper-coloured, smooth strong bitter. Malt dominates the taste throughout with hop bitterness and a complex mixture of fruit flavours.

Excaliber (OG 1058, ABV 5.8%)
Black-coloured old ale, smooth, rich winter warmer. Steeped in chocolate with heavy roast, creamy maltiness, but silky, roast, sweet aftertaste.

Tinworks (NEW)

Llys Cerdd, Heol Gelli Fawr, Llanelli, SA15 5EQ
☎ 07595 841958 🌐 tinworksbrewery.co.uk

Tinworks commenced brewing in 2018. Bottled beers are produced, named after the local industry.

Tiny Rebel SIBA

Wern Industrial Estate, Rogerstone, NP10 9FQ
☎ (01633) 547378 🌐 tinyrebel.co.uk

◎ Established in 2012, Tiny Rebel moved to new, bespoke premises in 2017 having outgrown its previous site. Originally using a 12-barrel plant, the brewery now operates a dual-stream 30-barrel plant, and consists of 23 fermentation tanks and four conditioning tanks, supplying its three tied pubs as well as numerous outlets across the UK. !! ♦

Dutty (OG 1052, ABV 4.2%)
A session IPA with a smooth texture and mouthfeel.

Cwtch (OG 1045, ABV 4.6%)
A well-balanced, red-coloured ale that combines caramel malt flavours with citrus hops.

Stay Puft (OG 1053, ABV 5.2%)
A marshmallow porter with classic roasty qualities of a dark-coloured ale and a smooth sweetness.

Tiny Vessel (NEW)

Unit 505, Platts Eyot, Hampton, TW12 2HF
🌐 tinyvessel.co.uk/home.html

Brewing began in late 2016 on Platts Eyot, an island on the River Thames near Hampton. All beers are unfiltered and unfined. **V**

Summit Else (ABV 5.2%)
A full-bodied, complex, amber-coloured beer with a rich hop aroma.

Summit Pink (ABV 6.8%)
A full-flavoured pale ale with a light hop aroma and grapefruit taste.

Double Date (ABV 7.4%)
A strong, brown-coloured ale with date syrup added. Notes of biscuit and jam.

Tipples

Unit 3, The Mill, Wood Green, Salhouse, Norfolk, NR13 6NY
☎ (01603) 721310 🌐 tipplesbrewery.com

⊗ Tipples was established in 2004 on a six-barrel brew plant. In addition to a full range of cask ales, an extensive range of bottled beers is produced, which can be found in some farmers markets and supermarkets in Norfolk. ♦RAIB

Hanged Monk (OG 1038, ABV 3.8%)
Strong roast and malt notes dominate the aroma and taste. A grainy mouthfeel with caramel and a growing vinous finish.

Sundown (OG 1040, ABV 3.9%)
Berries and malt introduce this smooth, creamy bitter. Bitterness gives depth to the fruity malt core as it slowly sweetens.

Redhead (OG 1042, ABV 4.2%)
Malt and hops in both nose and palate. Toffee in the initial taste gives way to an increasing bitterness.

Brewers Progress (OG 1046, ABV 4.6%)
Solid and malty with strong caramel and vanilla support. Smooth and creamy with added depth by a bitter blackcurrant fruitiness.

Moonrocket (OG 1050, ABV 5%)
A complex golden-coloured brew. Malt, hop bitterness and a fruity sweetness swirl round in an ever-changing kaleidoscope of flavours.

Tipsy Angel

Unit 20, Manor Industrial Estate, Lower Wash Lane, Latchford, Warrington, Cheshire, WA4 1PL
☎ (01925) 653326 ☎ 07909 893912
✉ andycharlie1@hotmail.co.uk

◎ Relocated from the Lower Angel pub in Warrington to the nearby 4Ts Brewery (qv) using its original 0.5-barrel plant. Some recipes are based on those from the now defunct Walker's of Warrington brewery.

Angels Mild (OG 1038, ABV 3.8%)
A dark mild, faithfully brewed from the old Walkers recipe.

George Shaws Premium (OG 1043, ABV 4.3%)
A well-balanced, complex, amber-coloured bitter.

Angels Folly (OG 1052, ABV 5.2%)
A strong, dark-coloured, complex beer, rich in texture with an aroma of strong malted barley and a lingering finish.

Taipur (OG 1059, ABV 5.9%)
A well-balanced, golden-coloured beer brewed with hops from the southern hemisphere.

Tír Dhá Ghlas

Cullins Yard, 11 Cambridge Road, Dover, Kent, CT17 9BY
☎ (01304) 211666 🌐 cullinsyard.co.uk

Brewing began in 2012 using a two-barrel plant. Beers are only available in the bar/restaurant and occasionally at the nearby Royal Cinque Ports Yacht Club, particularly at beer festivals.

Tirril SIBA

Red House, Long Marton, Cumbria, CA16 6BN
☎ (01768) 361846 🌐 tirrilbrewery.co.uk

Established in 1999, Tirril Brewery has twice outgrown its premises. It has more than 170 outlets, 100 of which regularly stock the beer. One pub is owned. Contract brewing is also carried out for Bitter End Brewery. ‼♦

Original Bitter (OG 1038.5, ABV 3.8%)

Ullswater Blonde (OG 1038.5, ABV 3.8%)

Langdale Light (OG 1039, ABV 3.9%)

Old Faithful (OG 1040, ABV 4%)
Initially bitter, gold-coloured ale with an astringent finish.

1823 (OG 1041, ABV 4.1%)
A full-bodied session bitter with a gentle bitterness.

Academy Ale (OG 1041.5, ABV 4.2%)
A dark-coloured, full-bodied, traditional rich and malty ale.

Borrowdale Bitter (OG 1041.5, ABV 4.2%)

Windermere IPA (OG 1043, ABV 4.3%)

Red Barn Ale (OG 1043, ABV 4.4%)
A ruby red-coloured ale with a strong hop finish.

Titan

c/o Golden Eagle, 6 St Katherine's Court (off Agard Street), Derby, DE22 3AY
☎ (01332) 298465 ☎ 07749 556837
🌐 titanbrewery.co.uk

Titan was set-up by former Mr Grundy's brewers in 2014. A pub has been acquired, the Golden Eagle, Derby. It is in the process of obtaining a second pub in order to set up a brewery there but at present the beers are brewed using spare capacity at Mr Grundy's Brewery (qv).

Bitter (OG 1036.8, ABV 3.8%)

Pale (OG 1038.7, ABV 4%)

Gold (OG 1043.5, ABV 4.5%)

Ruby (OG 1044.6, ABV 4.6%)
Ruby-coloured ale with malt and coffee notes and a slightly spicy aroma.

Stout (OG 1066, ABV 4.8%)

IPA (OG 1048.5, ABV 5%)

Titanic SIBA

Callender Place, Burslem, Stoke-on-Trent, Staffordshire, ST6 1JL
☎ (01782) 823447 🌐 titanicbrewery.co.uk

Founded in 1985 and named after Captain Smith, a Potteries man and the captain of the Titanic. One of the earliest microbreweries, Titanic has grown into a local brewer with a small, constantly expanding tied pub estate and supplies free trade customers across the Midlands and the North-west. 2014 saw a major investment in the brewery and brewhouse creating a brewery shop and sample room. ‼♦RAIB

Mild (OG 1036, ABV 3.5%)
Fresh, fruity hop aroma leads to a caramel start then a rush of bitter hoppiness ending with a lingering, dry finish.

Steerage (OG 1039.5, ABV 3.8%)
Pale yellow-coloured bitter. Flavours start with hops and fruit but become zesty and refreshing in this light session beer with a long, dry finish.

Lifeboat (OG 1040, ABV 4%)
Dark brown in colour with fruit, malt and caramel aromas. Sweet start, malty and caramel middle with hoppiness developing into a fruity and dry, lingering finish.

Anchor Bitter (OG 1042, ABV 4.1%)
Amber-coloured beer with a spicy hint to the fruity start that says go to the rush of hops for the dry bitter finish.

Iceberg (OG 1042, ABV 4.1%)
Yellow gold-coloured sparkling wheat beer with a flowery start leading to a great hop crescendo.

Cherry Dark (OG 1045, ABV 4.4%)

Cappuccino Stout (OG 1046, ABV 4.5%)

Chocolate & Vanilla Stout (OG 1047, ABV 4.5%)
Chocoholic paradise with real coffee and vanilla support. Cocoa, sherry and almonds lend depth to this creamy stout.

Stout (OG 1046, ABV 4.5%)
Roasty, toasty with tobacco, autumn bonfires, chocolate and hints of liquorice; perfectly balanced with a bitter, dry finish reminiscent of real coffee.

White Star (OG 1048, ABV 4.5%)
Hints of cinnamon apple pie are found before the hops take over to give a bitter edge to this well-balanced, refreshing, fruity beer.

Plum Porter (OG 1051, ABV 4.9%)
Dark brown in colour with a powerful fruity aroma. A sweet plum fruitiness gives way to a gentle bitter finish.

Captain Smith's Strong Ale (OG 1054, ABV 5.2%)
Red brown-coloured and full-bodied, lots of malt and roast with a hint of honey but a strong bittersweet finish.

Titsey (NEW)

Botley Hill Farmhouse, Limpsfield Road, Titsey, Surrey, CR6 9QH ☎ 07850 914189
titseybrewingco.com

A microbrewery established in 2017 on the Titsey Estate. It supplies two associated pubs, the Botley Hill Farmhouse and the White Bear at Fickleshole. Ales are named after historic owners of the Titsey Estate. Expansion is planned with a move to larger premises on the estate to further these aims.

Gresham Hopper (OG 1040, ABV 3.7%)
Golden ale with citrus, refreshing pine notes and some bitterness.

Leveson Buck (OG 1040, ABV 3.7%)
Session IPA with citrus, passion fruit and grapefruit notes.

Gower Wolf (OG 1042, ABV 4%)
Caramel and honey sweetness contrast with spicy flavours in this best bitter.

Toll End

c/o Waggon & Horses, 131 Toll End Road, Tipton, West Midlands, DY4 0ET ☎ 07903 725574

The four-barrel brewery opened in 2004. With the exception of Phoebe's Ale, named after the brewer's daughter, all brews commemorate local landmarks, events and people. !! RAIB

Tollgate SIBA

Unit 1, Southwood House Farm, Staunton Lane, Calke, Derbyshire, LE65 1RG
☎ (01283) 229194 tollgatebrewery.co.uk

This six-barrel brewery was founded in 2005 on the site of the old Brunt & Bucknall Brewery in Woodville, but relocated to new premises on the National Trust's Calke Park estate in 2012. Around 180 outlets are supplied direct, mainly in the North Midlands. The brewery operates three micropubs: Queens Road Tap, Leicester, Tap at No.76, Ashby-de-la-Zouch, and Town Street Tap, Duffield. !! ♦ RAIB

Stand & Deliver (OG 1036, ABV 3.8%)
Traditional session bitter; medium malts with a smooth finish.

Hackney Blonde (OG 1036, ABV 3.9%)
Crisp, pale-coloured, lager-style session ale, refreshing with a citrus finish.

Melbourne Bitter (OG 1038, ABV 4%)
A golden-coloured, mellow bitter with a hint of citrus in the finish.

California Steam (OG 1041, ABV 4.2%)

Eclipse BIPA (OG 1040, ABV 4.2%)
Low gravity dark-coloured IPA with malted rye.

Red Storm (OG 1040, ABV 4.2%)
Based on an Irish recipe, red-coloured with soft malts and complex hops.

Tollgate Bitter (OG 1041, ABV 4.3%)
Golden-coloured English bitter with a light malt base and a fruity, hoppy finish.

Duffield Amber (OG 1042, ABV 4.4%)
A traditional amber-coloured bitter with English hops and malts.

Ashby Pale (OG 1043, ABV 4.5%)
A light, refreshing traditional English pale ale with a citrus finish.

Kalika IPA (OG 1043, ABV 4.5%)

Old Rasputin (OG 1043, ABV 4.5%)
Dark in colour with a hint of sweet creaminess, balanced with a smooth, slightly bitter finish.

Red Star IPA (OG 1043, ABV 4.5%)
Traditional IPA with smooth, hoppy flavours.

Billy's Best Bitter (OG 1044, ABV 4.6%)
A smooth-drinking, dark amber-coloured best bitter with good malt flavours balanced with fruity hops.

High Street Bitter (OG 1045, ABV 4.7%)
A dark, strong, smooth English bitter, brewed with rich malts.

Spark IPA (OG 1050, ABV 5.6%)
Dark, hoppy, strong golden ale, brewed with north American hops.

Tolly Cobbold

See Greene King

Tom Herrick's

See under H

Tombstone SIBA

6 George Street, Great Yarmouth, Norfolk, NR30 1HR ☎ 07584 504444
tombstonebrewery.co.uk

Established in 2013, the brewery is run by former homebrewer Paul Hodgson. The original brewery backed onto the town cemetery, inspiring the name, but it has now relocated to the rear of its brewery tap, the Tombstone Saloon. Around 30 outlets are supplied around Norwich. ♦

Ale (OG 1038, ABV 3.7%)
Banana toffee aroma. Piquant bitter hoppy beginning softened by a biscuity maltiness. Dry bitter finish.

Arizona (OG 1040, ABV 3.9%)
Malt and lemon nose. Initial lemongrass and sweet biscuit beginning quickly fades. Sweet, watery finish enhanced by malt.

Texas Jack (OG 1040, ABV 4%)
Toffee apple and vanilla aroma. Caramel leads the smooth complex mix of flavours. A bittersweet fruitiness continues to the end.

Regulators (OG 1040, ABV 4.1%)
Golden-coloured hoppy ale with a bitter, dry finish.

Gunslinger (OG 1044, ABV 4.3%)
Golden in colour with a caramel, nutty finish.

Lone Rider (OG 1044, ABV 4.3%)
A deep ruby-coloured, hoppy ale.

Stagecoach (OG 1044, ABV 4.4%)
Smooth, dark-coloured and malty ale with a hit of liquorice.

Cherokee (OG 1045, ABV 4.5%)
Malty nose with plum and cherry. Initial mix of biscuit and roasty bitterness gently changes to a slightly spicy maltiness.

Santa Fe (ABV 5%)

Sweet and fruity.

Big Nose Kate (OG 1054, ABV 5.3%)
Ruby-coloured ale. Malty and fruity with a subtle passion fruit taste.

6 Shooter (ABV 6.6%)
Fresh orchard fruits, floral with citrus undertones.

Brewed for Brunning & Price Pub Co:

Blackfoot (ABV 4.8%)

Tomos A Lilford SIBA

Unit 11b, Vale Business Park, Llandow, CF71 7PF
☎ (01446) 796905 ☎ 07779 132647

Office: 117 Boverton Road, Llantwit Major, CF61 1YA
✉ tomos.lilford@gmail.com

⊗ Tomos A Lilford was launched in 2013 by homebrewers Rolant Tomos and brothers Rob and James Lilford. The brewery supplies pubs and clubs across the Vale of Glamorgan and further afield. All point of sale material is bilingual. ♦

Cob (OG 1040, ABV 4%)
Malty session beer with creamy, nutty notes.

Annwyl (OG 1050, ABV 5%)

Gaucho (OG 1050, ABV 5%)
An IPA brewed to an old recipe using wheat and a South American herb tea.

OPA (OG 1050, ABV 5%)

Rosemary Ale (ABV 5%)
A pale-coloured, refreshing ale bursting with the flavours of honey and rosemary.

Hay (OG 1052, ABV 5.2%)
An English-style IPA with added hay for sweetness and aroma.

Tonbridge SIBA

Unit 19, Branbridges Industrial Estate, East Peckham, Kent, TN12 5HF
☎ (01622) 871239 🌐 tonbridgebrewery.co.uk

⊗ Tonbridge Brewery was launched in 2010 using a four-barrel plant, expanding in 2013 to a 12-barrel plant. It is owned and run jointly by Paul Bournazian and Mark Gardner. Pubs, clubs and shops are supplied throughout Kent and also parts of Surrey, Sussex, Essex and South-east London. ‼

Golden Rule (OG 1036.5, ABV 3.5%)
Hoppy golden ale with a light, crisp body and delicate floral aroma.

Traditional Ale (OG 1038, ABV 3.6%)
Easy-drinking and refreshing ale with a light, fruity taste and aroma.

Coppernob (OG 1039.5, ABV 3.8%)
A fairly dry, rich copper-coloured ale with robust fruity flavours.

Countryman (OG 1041, ABV 4%)
Classic best bitter with a light, malty taste and a refreshing spice and fruit finish.

Rustic (OG 1041.5, ABV 4%)
Deep bronze-coloured, rich-tasting ale. Lightly-hopped, giving a delicate spicy taste and aroma.

Blonde Ambition (OG 1043.5, ABV 4.2%)
Crisp, refreshing blonde ale with spicy and citrus notes.

Old Chestnut (OG 1045, ABV 4.4%)
Full-bodied, chestnut-coloured ale with a malty base and a berry/honey finish.

American Pale (OG 1050, ABV 5%)
Classic, full-bodied American-style pale ale with a refreshing citrus finish.

Toolmakers SIBA

6-8 Botsford Street, Sheffield, South Yorkshire, S3 9PF
☎ 07956 235332 🌐 toolmakersbrewery.com

Toolmakers is a family-run brewery established in 2013 in an old tool-making factory. Beers are brewed on a five-barrel plant and are available within a 40-50 mile radius of the brewery. The adjoining Forest pub is owned. ‼♦

Lynch Pin (OG 1038, ABV 4%)
A dark-coloured best bitter with chocolate and caramel undertones.

Ramataz (OG 1040, ABV 4.2%)
A pale-coloured bitter with citrus and grapefruit flavours.

Flange Noire (OG 1046, ABV 4.8%)
A full-bodied, smooth, dark-coloured ale with a subtle hint of spice.

Top-Notch

Haywards Heath, West Sussex, RH16 1UQ ☎ 07963 829368 🌐 topnotchbrewing.co.uk

This 0.5-barrel brewery is situated in a converted residential outbuilding in Haywards Heath. RAIB

Hop Festival (OG 1039, ABV 3.9%)

Royal Fanfare (OG 1046, ABV 4.6%)

Top Out SIBA

Unit 3, 6b Dryden Road, Loanhead, EH20 9LZ
☎ (0131) 440 0270 ☎ 07742 234970
🌐 topoutbrewery.com

Brewing began in 2013 using a six-barrel plant. Initially focusing on bottle-conditioned beers, the brewery has expanded into brewing cask beer for the on-trade. Branding has a topographical theme. Top Out also contract brews for Secret Herb Garden, a visitor attraction in Edinburgh. ♦RAIB

Copperheid (ABV 3.4%)

Eldorado (ABV 3.6%)

Staple (OG 1037, ABV 4%)

Altbier (ABV 4.5%)

Smoked Porter (OG 1060, ABV 5.6%)

South Face IPA (ABV 5.9%)

The Cone (OG 1058, ABV 6.8%)

Top Rope (NEW)

Unit 14, Engineer Park, Babbage Road, Sandycroft, CH5 2QD

Top Rope commenced brewing on a small scale in Merseyside in 2016 and expanded in 2018, moving to the former Deva Craft brewery in North East Wales. Output is mainly keg but some cask-conditioned beer is also produced, including some of the original Deva Craft range.

TOPS (The Olde Potting Shed)

High Spen, Tyne & Wear

TOPS began brewing in 2013 using a five-barrel plant with a small test kit for experimental beers. Pubs are suppllied direct within a 30-mile radius of the brewery.

Blondie (ABV 3.8%)

Torrside

New Mills Marina, Hibbert Street, New Mills, Derbyshire, SK22 3JJ ☎ 07539 149175
🌐 torrside.co.uk

Established by three friends in 2015, Torrside brews a wide range of beers on a 10-barrel plant, under the tagline 'Hops, Smoke, Monsters'. A changing line-up of largely hop-driven, smoked and strong beers are sold to pubs, bars and bottle shops within a 50-mile radius. All beers are unfined. ♦ RAIB V

Sto Lat (OG 1028, ABV 2.8%)

Candlewick (OG 1047, ABV 4%)

West of the Sun (OG 1044, ABV 4.5%)

I'm Spartacus (OG 1063, ABV 6.8%)

Totally Brewed

Units 8 & 9, Meadow Lane Fruit & Veg Market, Clarke Road, Nottingham, NG2 3JJ ☎ 07702 800639
🌐 totallybrewed.com

Totally Brewed began brewing in 2014 using a seven-barrel plant previously used at White Dog Brewery. A diverse range of hop-forward beers are produced. ♦

Guardian of the Forest (OG 1037, ABV 3.8%)

Slap in the Face (OG 1040, ABV 4%)
Golden-coloured ale with citrus fruit hop aroma and taste with a dry bitter finish.

Crazy Like a Fox (OG 1045, ABV 4.5%)
Copper-coloured, malty best bitter with a caramel aroma and a gentle bitter finish.

Papa Jangle's Voodoo Stout (OG 1046, ABV 4.5%)
Full-bodied, dark-coloured stout oozing complex malt tastes throughout.

Punch in the Face (OG 1047, ABV 4.8%)
Golden-coloured ale, assertive hop aroma leading to grapefruit and malt taste with a hoppy bitter finish.

Four Hopmen of the Apocalypse (OG 1047, ABV 5.2%)
Immensely hoppy, fruity golden ale, moderate bitterness with a lasting hoppy finish.

Captain Hopbeard (OG 1050, ABV 5.5%)
Amber-coloured ale with citrus hops aplenty and a strong bitter finish.

Totnes

59a High Street, Totnes, Devon, TQ9 5PB
☎ (01803) 849290 ☎ 07974 828971
✉ richard.kidd@idnet.net.uk

Brewing began in 2014 at a family-run pub at the foot of Totnes Castle. The brewery is situated immediately behind the bar. Beers are available almost exclusively at the pub. ♦V

Towcester Mill SIBA

The Mill,, Chantry Lane, Towcester, Northamptonshire, NN12 6AD
☎ (01327) 437060 ☎ 07812 366369
🌐 towcestermillbrewery.co.uk

A five-barrel brew plant situated at the Old Mill in Towcester. There is a brewery tap on site and a shop off site at the Bell Plantation in Towcester. !! ♦

Crooked Hooker (OG 1038, ABV 3.8%)
Amber-coloured session ale with a satisfying bitter finish.

Mill Race (OG 1040, ABV 3.9%)
Blonde beer with a herbal and grapefruit finish.

Bell Ringer (OG 1044, ABV 4.4%)
Golden ale with a blend of malts giving the beer subtle malt tones with hops giving orange and citrus notes.

Black Fire (OG 1050, ABV 5.2%)
Dark-coloured beer with dark fruit hop aromas.

Roman Road (OG 1050, ABV 5.2%)

Tower

Old Water Tower, Walsitch Maltings, Glensyl Way, Burton upon Trent, Staffordshire, DE14 1PZ
☎ (01283) 562888 ☎ 07771 926323
🌐 towerbrewery.co.uk

Tower was established in 2001 by John Mills, formerly a brewer at Burton Bridge, in a converted derelict water tower, originally built for Thomas Salt's Brewery in the 1870s. The conversion was given a Burton Civic Society award for the restoration of an industrial building. Tower has 20 regular outlets. !! ♦

Salt's Burton Ale (OG 1035, ABV 3.5%)

Bitter (OG 1042, ABV 4.2%)
Gold-coloured with a malty, caramel and hoppy aroma. A full hop and fruit taste with the fruit lingering. A bitter and astringent finish.

Gone for a Burton (OG 1046, ABV 4.6%)
An amber-coloured beer with a malt/hop aroma.

Imperial IPA (OG 1050, ABV 5%)
A premium IPA, light golden in colour with a rich, citrus fruity flavour and a floral hoppy aroma.

Townes

Speedwell Inn, Lowgates, Staveley, Derbyshire, S43 3TT
☎ (01246) 472252

Townes Brewery, which started in 1994, has been situated in the rear of the Speedwell Inn at Staveley since 1997. After the retirement of brewer Alan Wood in 2013, Lawrie and Nicoleta Evans have continued brewing to the same recipes on the five-barrel plant. ♦

Townhouse

Units 1-4, Townhouse Studios, Townhouse Farm, Alsager Road, Audley, Staffordshire, ST7 8JQ ☎ 07976 209437 ✉ j.nixon2@btinternet.com

Townhouse was set up in 2002 with a 2.5-barrel plant. In 2004 the brewery scaled up to five barrels. ♦

Enigma (OG 1035, ABV 3.5%)

Styrian Pale (OG 1035, ABV 3.5%)

Rye Pale Ale (OG 1035, ABV 3.6%)

Flowerdew (OG 1039, ABV 4%)
Golden in colour with a wonderful floral aroma. Flavour of flowery hops delivering a crisp, hoppy bite and presenting a lingering taste of flowery citrus waves.

Meridian Mild (OG 1039, ABV 4%)

Barney's Stout (OG 1043, ABV 4.5%)
Roast chocolate and toffee nose atop this black-coloured stout. Sweet start becoming bitter at the end, with velvety roast throughout.

Armstrong Ale (OG 1045, ABV 4.8%)
A rich, fruity, ruby red-coloured beer with a hoppy, dry finish.

Gladstone Strong Ale (OG 1048, ABV 5%)

Track

5 Sheffield Street, Manchester, M1 2ND
☎ (0161) 273 4832 ☎ 07725 692096
trackbrewing.co

Track Brewing Co was established in 2014 and is based in a railway arch underneath Manchester's Piccadilly railway station. Since its inception the brewery has expanded considerably in size and now produces a wide variety of beer styles. ‼

Sonoma (OG 1040, ABV 3.8%)
A pale ale with citrus flavours and juicy fruit aromas.

Zaka (OG 1045, ABV 4.2%)
A pale ale with lemon and pine notes.

Mojave (ABV 4.3%)

Ozark (OG 1044, ABV 4.4%)
An American-style pale ale with a malty backbone complemented by juicy hop flavours.

Toba (OG 1054, ABV 5.6%)
Oatmeal stout with a chocolate and coffee flavour.

Pekoe (ABV 5.9%)

Going to the Sun (ABV 7%)
A pale ale with rolled oats giving a dense mouthfeel. Hazy and unfined.

Tractor Shed SIBA

Tractor Shed, Calva Brow, Workington, Cumbria, CA14 1DB
☎ (01900) 68860 tractor-shed.co.uk

Renamed from Mitchell Krause in 2014 and having previously had its beers brewed under contract, brewing started in an old tractor shed on the family farm in 2013. After initially focusing on bottled and kegged continental-style beers, the first cask-conditioned beer was produced in 2014. The brewery contract brews various beers for Shindigger (qv), mostly for bottle and keg. ‼ RAIB

Clocker Stout (OG 1043, ABV 4%)

Traffic Street Specials

See Castle Rock

Traquair House SIBA

Traquair House, Innerleithen, EH44 6PW
☎ (01896) 830323 traquair.co.uk/traquair-house-brewery

The 18th century brewhouse is based in one of the wings of the 1,000-year-old Traquair House, Scotland's oldest inhabited house. All the beers are oak-fermented and 60% of production is exported. ‼ ♦

Bear Ale (OG 1050, ABV 5%)

Treboom SIBA

Millstone Yard, Main Street, Shipton-by-Beningbrough, North Yorkshire, YO30 1AA
☎ (01904) 471569 ☎ 07761 608662
treboom.co.uk

Established in 2011 this 10-barrel brewery produces five core beers alongside monthly seasonal specials using water from its own borehole. Beers are distributed throughout Yorkshire. ‼ ♦ RAIB

Tambourine Man (OG 1038.5, ABV 3.9%)
A golden ale with a hint of maltiness complemented by fruit flavours.

Yorkshire Sparkle (OG 1039, ABV 4%)
A pale ale with a fresh citrus taste.

Kettle Drum (OG 1042, ABV 4.3%)
Copper-coloured ale with a distinct fruitiness and robust hop flavours leading to a clean finish.

Hop Britannia (OG 1047.5, ABV 5%)
A hoppy, strong pale ale. Honey in colour with intense citrus fruit and spice notes.

Baron Saturday (OG 1049, ABV 5.2%)
A strong, dark-coloured porter with flavours of coffee and liquorice.

Treen's

Unit 3, Viaduct Works, Frog Hill, Ponsanooth, Cornwall, TR3 7JW ☎ 07552 218788

Office: 18 St Michaels Road, Ponsanooth, Cornwall, TR3 7EA treensbrewery.co.uk

This family-run brewery was founded in 2016, initially using spare capacity at other local breweries. It now has its own premises using a 12-barrel plant. Bottling was introduced in 2018. ♦

Essential (ABV 3.8%)
Gold-coloured bitter with grassy and resinous hops and light malt flavours. Citrus and plum fruit notes. Long, bitter finish.

Classic (ABV 4.3%)
Brown-coloured best bitter with a light malt nose. Bitterness dominates with citrus/earthy hops and biscuit malt. Molasses, coffee and dried fruit notes.

Sunbeam (ABV 4.8%)
Golden ale with a complex nose and well-balanced body. Full citrus aroma with spicy and floral notes on top of a malt base of grain and caramel.

Resolve (ABV 5.2%)

THE BREWERIES

A black-coloured, sweet stout with a dark chocolate aroma. Dominant smoky coffee, bitter chocolate and molasses flavours with malt and fruit undertones.

Tremethick

Tremethick Brewery, Grampound, Cornwall, TR2 4QY
☎ 07726 427775 🌐 tremethick.co.uk

Tremethick began brewing in 2015. Having brewed in small batches in a garage or using spare capacity at other breweries, a new building was completed and 5.5-barrel plant commissioned in 2016. Regular brewery open evenings are held. !! RAIB

Pale Ale (OG 1043, ABV 4.3%) ◆
Yellow-coloured golden ale with aromas of cider and sherbet. Refreshing grassy citrus hops, bitterness and apple fruit. Lemon grainy aftertaste.

Dark Ale (ABV 4.6%) ◆
Red-coloured strong mild with a coffee malt nose. Sweet taste with coffee-roast malt, liquorice, caramel and fruits. Faintly bitter and hoppy.

Tring SIBA

Dunsley Farm, London Road, Tring, Hertfordshire, HP23 6HA
☎ (01442) 890721 🌐 tringbrewery.co.uk

Founded in 1992, Tring Brewery moved to its present site in 2010. It brews more than 130 barrels a week, producing a core range of ten beers augmented by monthly and seasonal specials, most taking their names from local myths and legends. !! ♦ RAIB

Side Pocket for a Toad (OG 1035, ABV 3.6%)
A straw-coloured ale with citrus notes and floral aroma with a crisp, dry finish.

Brock Bitter (OG 1036, ABV 3.7%)
A mid-brown-coloured session ale with a hint of sweetness and caramel.

Mansion Mild (OG 1036, ABV 3.7%)
Smooth and creamy dark ruby-coloured mild with a fruity palate and gentle late hop.

Drop Bar Pale Ale (OG 1039, ABV 4%)
A dry-hopped pale ale with a biscuit malt base and citrus aroma.

Ridgeway (OG 1039, ABV 4%)
Balanced malt and hop flavours with a dry, floral hop aftertaste.

Moongazing (OG 1042, ABV 4.2%)
Amber-coloured ale with a rounded bitterness and hoppy aftertaste.

Pale Four (OG 1048, ABV 4.6%)

Tea Kettle Stout (OG 1047, ABV 4.7%)
Rich and complex traditional stout with a hint of liquorice and moderate bitterness.

Colley's Dog (OG 1051, ABV 5.2%)
A dark-coloured ale with a long, dry finish and overtones of malt and walnuts.

Death or Glory (OG 1074, ABV 7.2%)
A strong, dark-coloured, aromatic barley wine.

Trinity

5 Church Road, Gisleham, Suffolk, NR33 8DS
☎ (01502) 743121 🌐 trinity-ales.co.uk

⊗ Trinity Ales was launched in 2009 using a four-barrel plant. It uses pure spring water from its own ancient well along with locally sourced ingredients. Pubs, restaurants, retail outlets and festivals are supplied throughout Suffolk and beyond. RAIB

Wishing Well (OG 1039, ABV 3.8%)

High Light (OG 1040, ABV 4%)

Black Street Smithy (OG 1045, ABV 4.5%)

Gisleham Gold (OG 1045, ABV 4.5%)

Gold (OG 1045, ABV 4.5%)

Triple fff SIBA

Magpie Works, Station Approach, Four Marks, Alton, Hampshire, GU34 5HN
☎ (01420) 561422 🌐 triplefff.com

⊗ Established in 1997 close to a stop on the Watercress Line, the brewery and all the beers except Alton's Pride are named following a musical theme. The fff refers to fortissimo, meaning louder or stronger. Brewing on a 50-barrel plant since 2006, multiple CAMRA awards have been won. Two pubs are owned: the Railway Arms, Alton, and the White Lion, Aldershot. !! ♦ RAIB

Alton's Pride (OG 1039, ABV 3.8%) ◆
Full-bodied session biter. An initially malty flavour fades as citrus notes and hoppiness take over, leading to a lasting hoppy/bitter finish.

Pressed Rat & Warthog (OG 1039, ABV 3.8%) ◆
Toffee aroma with hints of blackcurrant and chocolate lead to a well-balanced flavour with roast, fruit and malt vying with the hoppy bitterness.

Moondance (OG 1042, ABV 4.2%) ◆
An aromatic citrus hop nose, balanced by bitterness and sweetness in the mouth. Bitterness increases in the finish as fruit declines.

True North

47 Eldon Street, Sheffield, South Yorkshire, S1 4GY
☎ (0114) 272 0569

Office: 127-129 Devonshire Street, Sheffield, S3 7SB
🌐 truenorthbrewco.uk

True North began brewing in 2012 using spare capacity at Welbeck Abbey Brewery (qv). It opened its own plant in Sheffield in 2016. 10 pubs are owned.

Session Pale (ABV 3.6%)
A light straw-coloured pale ale. Fresh grapefruit aroma and citrus flavours with limes predominating.

Best Bitter (ABV 3.8%)
A malty, sweet, traditional brown-coloured ale, which is balanced with hoppy spice and bitterness.

Blonde (ABV 4%)
A golden ale with smooth vanilla and floral flavours.

Pale Ale (ABV 4.3%)
Light straw-coloured pale ale packed with citrus and floral flavours.

Red Rye (ABV 4.7%)

A red-coloured ale with a malty background of toffee but a burst of bitterness and orange/apricot flavours from the hops.

Truman's SIBA

The Eyrie, 2 & 3 Stour Road, Hackney Wick, London, E3 2NT
☎ (020) 8533 3575 trumansbeer.co.uk

The legendary East London brewery Truman's was reborn in 2013, 24 years after the original Brick Lane brewery's closure in 1989. The new brewery is a 45-barrel plant in Hackney Wick, just a stroll down the Roman Road from the original site and close to the Queen Elizabeth Olympic Park. The original Truman's yeast, recovered from the National Collection of Yeast Cultures, is used. ♦RAIB

Swift (OG 1040.5, ABV 3.9%)
Well-balanced, golden-coloured bitter with hops and a trace of grapefruit on the nose and palate and a bitter finish.

Runner (OG 1040, ABV 4%)
Traditional brown-coloured best bitter with a spicy, hoppy aroma and flavour fading in the dry aftertaste. Some marmalade fruity notes.

Lazarus (OG 1043, ABV 4.2%)
Well-balanced, pale-coloured golden ale with a peaches and straw aroma, refreshing grassy and citrus flavour, continuing into the short finish.

Zephyr (ABV 4.4%)
Pale brown-coloured, smooth beer with a slightly dry roasted character on palate and a bitter finish. Touch of orange and hops.

Tryst SIBA

Lorne Road, Larbert, FK5 4AT
☎ (01324) 554000 trystbrewery.co.uk

Tryst started production in 2003. A large range of beers is produced. !! ♦RAIB

Brockville Pale (OG 1039, ABV 3.9%)
A pale golden-coloured session ale, smooth on the palate.

Hop Trial (OG 1040, ABV 3.9%)

Carronade Pale Ale (OG 1043, ABV 4.2%)
A pale ale bursting with citrus flavours.

Drovers 80/- (OG 1044, ABV 4.3%)

Sherpa Porter (OG 1044, ABV 4.4%)

German Hops Pils (OG 1045, ABV 4.5%)

V.I.P (OG 1046, ABV 4.5%)
Light brown-coloured best bitter with a deep hop taste and floral aroma.

RAJ IPA (OG 1055, ABV 5.5%)
Exclusively English hopped with balanced flavours and a hoppy aroma and palate.

Tudor SIBA

Unit A, Llanhilleth Industrial Estate, Llanhilleth, NP13 2RX
☎ (01495) 214808 ☎ 07971 015844
tudorbrewery.co.uk

Tudor is a family-run, four-barrel plant that began brewing in 2007 in Abergavenny before moving in 2012 to Llanilleth. Several local pubs are supplied, in addition to others further afield. RAIB

Blorenge (OG 1038, ABV 3.8%)
A pale ale with fresh citrus undertones.

Black Mountain Stout (OG 1039, ABV 4%)

IPA (OG 1039, ABV 4%)
A classic IPA with a sharp, hoppy, grapefruit finish.

Skirrid (OG 1040, ABV 4.2%)
A full-flavoured, dark-coloured beer with a hoppy taste.

Sugarloaf (OG 1044, ABV 4.7%)
A rounded, full-bodied ale with smooth, caramel undertones.

Winter Cheer (OG 1046, ABV 5%)
A dark-coloured ale infused with ground ginger, lemon rind, honey, cinnamon and nutmeg.

Black Rock (OG 1050, ABV 5.6%)
A dark-coloured ale with a rich aroma and a smooth chocolate/coffee finish.

Tunnel SIBA

Correspondence: Red House Farm, Nuneaton Road, Ansley, Nuneaton, Warwickshire, CV10 0QU ☎ 07765 223110 tunnelbrewery.co.uk

Beers are brewed at various breweries under the Tunnel and Battlefield Brewery brand names. !! ♦RAIB

Percheron (OG 1037, ABV 3.7%)
A refreshing, citrus, pale-coloured golden ale.

Late Ott (OG 1040, ABV 4%)
Dark golden-coloured session bitter with a fruity nose and perfumed hop edge. The finish is dry and bitter.

Trade Winds (OG 1045, ABV 4.6%)
An aromatic, copper-coloured beer with a hoppy aroma and a clean, crisp hint of citrus, followed by fruity malts and a dry finish full of scented hops.

Shadow Weaver (OG 1046, ABV 4.7%)
A dark-coloured stout with chocolate and roasted coffee on the tongue, developing through slight fruit into a dry, mellow, bitter finish.

Nelson's Column (OG 1051, ABV 5.2%)
A ruby red-coloured, strong old English ale.

East India Pale Ale (OG 1058, ABV 5.9%)
Robust in flavour with a good hit of hops.

Brewed under the Battlefield Brewery brand name:

Let Battle Commence (OG 1041, ABV 4%)
An amber-coloured bitter with well-balanced malt and hops.

Richard III (OG 1042, ABV 4%)
A pale ale with a sweet start and dry finish.

Henry Tudor (OG 1050, ABV 5%)
A chestnut-coloured ale with a fruit and malt nose and a mellow hop finish.

Turning Point (NEW)

34 Dove Way, Kirkby Mills Industrial Estate, Kirkbymoorside, YO62 6QR
☎ (01751) 431132 turningpointbrewco.com

Two friends, Cameron Brown and Aron McMahon, began brewing in 2017 on a 12-barrel plant, utilising the water from a well beneath the brewery. All beers are unfined and unfiltered.

Avalon (ABV 3.8%)

Lucid Dream (ABV 5%)
Cookie cream stout with a smooth mouthfeel and body. Cacao nibs, chocolate and a touch of vanilla are added to give a unique taste.

Disco King (ABV 5.1%)
A hoppy beer with a subtle malt base.

Turnstone

20 West Cliff, Whitstable, Kent, CT5 1DN ☎ 07807 262662 ✉ turnstoneales@outlook.com

⊗ Turnstone Ales is a small, 0.5-barrel home-based brewery set up in 2014. The brewery has a regular stall at the Best of Faversham market. Beers are supplied to a few local pubs and shops in Whitstable, Tankerton and Canterbury. RAIB

Turpin

Turpins Lodge, Lodge Farm, Tadmarton Heath Road, Hook Norton, Oxfordshire, OX15 5DQ
☎ (01608) 737033
✉ turpinbrewery@btconnect.com

⊗ Brewing started in 2013. A number of local pubs are supplied regularly, as well as a few pubs further afield in Rugby and Birmingham. ♦

Golden Citrus (OG 1042, ABV 4.2%)
A bright golden-coloured beer with a pronounced citrus character. Full-tasting yet easy drinking, it has a good body and a strong, lasting bitter hop finish.

Turpin's SIBA

Unit 13b, Sawston Trade Park, London Road, Pampisford, Cambridgeshire, CB22 3EE
☎ (01223) 833883 🌐 turpinsbrewery.co.uk

Turpin's opened in 2015 at the Med pub in Cambridge, but due to increased demand brewing has moved to Pampisford.

Meditation (ABV 4.3%)
Smooth pale ale with citrus aromas.

Cambridge Black (ABV 4.6%)

Tweed SIBA

Unit D1C, Newton Business Park, Talbot Road, Newton, Hyde, SK14 4UQ
☎ (0161) 368 8608 🌐 tweedbrewing.com

Tweed began brewing in 2014 and expanded to bottle production in 2015. Beers are available in Manchester, particularly the Northern Quarter. Its micropub opened in 2017 in Hyde town centre and serves as the brewery tap. ♦

Sorachi (ABV 3.7%)

Pale Ale (ABV 3.8%)
Delicate pine and cedar notes with a sweet honey finish.

Hopster (ABV 3.9%)
A single-hopped, pineapple infused pale ale with citrus flavours and a rounded body.

Orange County IPA (ABV 4.3%)
A well-balanced ale with added Orange County oranges.

Twice Brewed (NEW) SIBA

Twice Brewed Inn, Bardon Mill, NE47 7AN
☎ (01434) 344534 🌐 twicebrewedinn.co.uk

Brewing commenced on a five-barrel plant in 2017. Due to the close proximity of Hadrian's Wall, beer names have a Roman theme. Beers are available at the Twice Brewed Inn as well as other outlets.

Best Bitter (ABV 3.8%)

Sycamore Gap (ABV 4.1%)

Caesar (ABV 4.2%)

Vindolanda Excavation IPA (ABV 5.3%)

Twickenham SIBA

Unit 6, 18 Mereway Road, Twickenham, TW2 6RG
☎ (020) 8241 1825 🌐 twickenham-fine-ales.co.uk

⊗ Established in 2004, Twickenham Fine Ales is London's oldest microbrewery. Operating a 25-barrel plant, it is the first brewery in Twickenham since the 1920s. !! ♦

Sundancer (OG 1037.5, ABV 3.7%)
Light, zesty golden ale with citrus notes dominating from beginning to end. Finish is bitter but balanced by biscuity sweetness.

Grandstand Bitter (OG 1038, ABV 3.8%)
Pale brown-coloured beer with peach, citrus and malt on the palate, fading in the bitter, slightly dry finish.

Redhead (OG 1041, ABV 4.1%)
A creamy, chestnut brown-coloured best bitter with interesting sweet caramel hints and a mild, short, roasted bitter finish.

Naked Ladies (OG 1044, ABV 4.4%)
Refreshing, dark golden-coloured ale with a touch of spicy hop in the flavour but fruit dominates with a lasting bitterness.

Twin Taff (NEW)

Unit 4, Star Yard, Merthyr Tydfil, CF47 8EB ☎ 07564 187945 ✉ twintaffbrewery@outlook.com

Twin Taff was established in 2018 by twin brothers Darryl and Daniel Williams. It is Merthyr Tydfil's first town centre microbrewery.

Penydarren Mild (ABV 3.8%)

Iron King Pale (ABV 4%)

Cyfarthfa Bitter (ABV 4.2%)

Twisted SIBA

Unit 8, Commerce Business Centre, Commerce Close, Westbury, Wiltshire, BA13 4LS
☎ (01373) 864441 ☎ 07512 261914
🌐 twisted-brewing.com

⊗ Twisted began brewing in 2014 using a new six-barrel plant. Outlets in west Wiltshire and north Somerset are supplied. ♦

Three and Sixpence (OG 1036, ABV 3.6%)

WTF (OG 1038, ABV 3.8%)
A light chestnut-coloured ale with a bucket full of hops providing the balance to a caramel base.

Rider (OG 1041, ABV 4%)

A triple-hopped, amber-coloured ale balanced with biscuit malt flavours.

Conscript (OG 1043, ABV 4.2%)
A golden-coloured ale with a soft fruit aroma and floral notes.

Pirate (OG 1043, ABV 4.2%)
A classic English best bitter, pale copper-coloured with an aroma of roasted malt and coffee. Undertones of nutty fruit cake.

Gaucho (OG 1048, ABV 4.6%)
Ruby-coloured ale with aromas of soft fruits, coffee and a hint of chocolate, with a long-lasting finish.

Twisted Angel (NEW) SIBA

Unit 2, Beckside Court, Annie Reed Road, Beverley, East Yorkshire, HU17 0LF
☎ (01482) 888509 ☎ 07432 588159
twistedangelbrewing.com

Twisted Angel is a five-barrel microbrewery established in 2017.

Clockwork Bitter (OG 1035, ABV 3.6%)

Shapeshifter (OG 1042, ABV 4%)

Gargoyle (OG 1044, ABV 4.8%)

Impaler (OG 1053, ABV 5.1%)

Daywalker (OG 1058, ABV 5.8%)

Berserker (OG 1067, ABV 7.5%)

Twisted Barrel

Unit 11, Fargo Village, Far Gosford Street, Coventry, CV1 5ED
☎ (024) 7610 1701 twistedbarrelale.co.uk

Commencing commercial production as a picobrewery in 2013, Twisted Barrel expanded to a six-barrel brewery and moved to Fargo Village in 2015 with an on-site tap house open at weekends. Continued growth resulted in another move to larger premises on the same site in 2017 and increased opening hours. Beers are distributed to Birmingham, Yorkshire, London, the North-west and are exported to the Far East. !! ♦ RAIB

Beast of a Midlands Mild (OG 1044, ABV 3.5%)

The Great Went (ABV 4%)

Detroit Sour City (ABV 4.5%)

God's Twisted Sister (OG 1050, ABV 4.5%)

Inspired (OG 1046, ABV 4.5%)

Sine Qua Non (OG 1046, ABV 4.5%)

The Morgul Path (ABV 4.5%)

Naido (ABV 5%)

Saison From Another Place (ABV 5.5%)

Twisted Oak SIBA

Yeowood Farm, Iwood Lane, Wrington, Bristol, BS40 5NU
☎ (01934) 310515 twistedoakbrewery.co.uk

Twisted Oak began brewing in 2012 using a five-barrel plant. It is a family-run business situated in a former agricultural building on a working farm in the North Somerset countryside. It crafts small batches of unique ales. One pub is owned, the Fallen Tree, Clevedon. ♦RAIB

Fallen Tree (OG 1039, ABV 3.8%)
Bittersweet session bitter. Aroma and flavour of hops and ripe fruit. Complex and satisfying bitter astringent finish.

Crack Gold (OG 1039, ABV 4%)

Wild Wood (OG 1041, ABV 4%)
Little aroma. Smooth, with flavours of hops and fruit and a little malt. Minimal aftertaste.

Crack Hops (OG 1040, ABV 4.2%)

Junction Lock IPA (OG 1039, ABV 4.2%)

Old Barn (OG 1044, ABV 4.5%)
Fruity red-coloured ale. Well-balanced flavour with a long bitter finish.

Spun Gold (OG 1043, ABV 4.5%)
Classic golden ale with a soft mouthfeel. Spicy notes to the fruity malt aroma and flavour. Hops in the aroma develop into a bitter finish.

Leveret (OG 1043, ABV 4.6%)
Amber-coloured best bitter with a light hop aroma. Initial pale malt flavours combine with hoppy bitterness that continues into the aftertaste.

Sheriff Fatman (OG 1048, ABV 5%)
Amber-coloured ale with hops dominant on both the nose and the slightly citrus palate, also in the bitter finish.

Slippery Slope (OG 1054, ABV 5.3%)

Two by Two

Unit 19, Point Pleasant Industrial Estate, Wallsend, NE28 6HA ☎ 07723 959168

Office: 14 Albany Gardens, Whitley Bay, NE26 2DY
twobytwobrewing@gmail.com

Brewing began in 2014 using a five-barrel plant. RAIB

Session IPA (OG 1040, ABV 4%)

Leap Frog (OG 1041, ABV 4.1%)

Foxtrot Pale (OG 1045, ABV 4.5%)

Snake Eyes Pale (OG 1046, ABV 4.6%)

Dragonfly (OG 1055, ABV 5.5%)

Sitting Duck (OG 1057, ABV 5.7%)

American Pale Ale (OG 1058, ABV 5.8%)

South Paw IPA (OG 1062, ABV 6.2%)

Two Cocks SIBA

Church Lane, Enborne, Berkshire, RG20 0HB
☎ (01635) 37777 ☎ 07831 201533
twococksbrewery.com

The brewery was established in 2011 after wild hops were found growing in the farm's hedgerows. A 180-feet deep borehole supplies water for the brewery. During the English Civil War, the 1st Battle of Newbury (1643) was fought on the surrounding land and most of the beer names refer to it in some way.

Diamond Lil' (OG 1035, ABV 3.2%)
A light and fruity golden ale.

1643 Cavalier (OG 1039, ABV 3.8%)

1643 Leveller (OG 1040, ABV 3.8%)

1643 Roundhead (OG 1042, ABV 4.2%)

1643 Puritan (OG 1049, ABV 4.5%)

A dark-coloured stout with notes of caramel and chocolate.

1643 Viscount (OG 1054, ABV 5.6%)
An unusually fruity, strong beer.

Two Drifters (NEW)

61 Huntingdon Way, Sketty, Swansea, SA2 9HN

Two Drifters Brewery is run by a husband-and-wife team, producing a range of bottled beers.

Two Finches

Finchley Cricket Club, 1 Arden Cottages, 33-45 East End Road, Finchley, London, N3 2TA
🌐 twofinchesbrewery.co.uk

Brewing began in 2015, originally brewing just for the cricket club. No real ale.

Two Rivers SIBA

2 Sluice Bank, Denver, Norfolk, PE38 0EQ
☎ (01366) 380131 ☎ 07518 099868
🌐 denverbrewery.co.uk

Two Rivers was established in 2012 by John Nash. Bottled-conditioned ale has been available since the establishment of the brewery and cask ales have been produced since 2013. !! ♦ RAIB V

Miners Mild (OG 1032, ABV 3.1%)
Easy-drinking, tawny-coloured mild with a good malt character, light finish and chocolate notes.

Hares Hopping (OG 1041, ABV 4.1%)
Refreshing, clean-tasting bitter with a distinctive late bitterness and dry finish.

Kiwi Kick (ABV 4.1%)
A golden-coloured bitter with a pleasant hop aroma and zesty hop finish.

Denver Diamond (OG 1047, ABV 4.4%)
Bitter with a full-bodied, malty finish. A rounded bitter and malty taste with a grassy, slightly floral aromatic character.

Porters Pride (OG 1050, ABV 5%)
A full-bodied, rich porter with a slight sweetness cutting through the smooth malt. Coffee and chocolate aromas and taste, with a liquorice/ vanilla finish.

Norfolk Stoat (OG 1050, ABV 5.8%)
A full-bodied, silky oatmeal stout with a subtle burnt edge.

Two Roses SIBA

Unit 9, Darton Business Park, Barnsley Road, Darton, South Yorkshire, S75 5QX ☎ 07780 701254
🌐 tworosesbrewery.co.uk

Two Roses started brewing in 2011 using an eight-barrel plant. It has since been taken over by a local brewer, who has rebranded. Beers can be found in local pubs and clubs. !! ♦

Full Nelson (OG 1038, ABV 3.8%)

Chinook (OG 1040, ABV 4%)

Marynka (OG 1040, ABV 4%)

Heron Porter (OG 1041, ABV 4.2%)

Legacy (OG 1041, ABV 4.2%)

Two Thirsty Men SIBA

74 High Street, Grantown-on-Spey, PH26 3EL
☎ (01479) 872246 🌐 twothirstymen.com

Brewing began in 2016 in a garage at the back of a café bar.

Spey IPA (ABV 3.5%)
A refreshing citrus aroma with hints of grassy, lemon and spicy aromas.

Angus Pale Ale (ABV 4%)
A lightly-hopped ale with aromas of sweet fruits and woody, grassy notes.

No. 74 (ABV 4.5%)
An amber-coloured ale with roasted malts and fruity, slightly spicy hop notes with a hint of orange.

Two Tone (NEW)

Tor View, Hayes Cross, Shebbear, Devon, EX21 5SW
☎ 07450 745338

Home-based nanobrewery run by Gary Seaton, an ex Coventrian, hence the Two Tone record label connection, and Paul Scantlebury, originally from Bristol. Bottle-conditioned beer is produced in small batches. RAIB V

Two Towers SIBA

29 Shadwell Street, Birmingham, B4 6HB
☎ (0121) 439 3738 ☎ 07795 247059
🌐 twotowersbrewery.co.uk

Established in 2010, the 10-barrel brewery moved to its current location behind its tap house, the Gunmakers Arms, in 2016 and is visible from the beer garden. The brewery also undertakes bespoke brewing for special events, mainly local in nature. !! ♦ RAIB V

Baskerville Bitter (OG 1038, ABV 3.8%)

Hockley Gold (OG 1041, ABV 4.1%)
A bitter with a fruity aroma and hoppy characteristics.

Complete Muppetry (OG 1043, ABV 4.3%)
An aromatic beer with powerful hop characteristics. Well-balanced with orange, fruity notes.

Chamberlain Pale Ale (OG 1042, ABV 4.5%)
A crisp, light ale loaded with grapefruit flavours and a long, hoppy finish.

Peaky Blinders Mild (ABV 4.5%)

Jewellery Porter (OG 1049, ABV 5%)
A full-bodied stout with a thick, slightly chocolate texture underlined with hops.

Two Tribes

Tileyard Studios, Tileyard Road, King's Cross, London, N7 9AH
☎ (020) 3955 6782 🌐 twotribesbrewing.com

Two Tribes, formerly of Horsham, has moved into its new home in King's Cross using a 10-hectolitre brew kit, although brewing still takes place at the Horsham site. An on-site taproom is open daily.

Non Stop Hits Modern Lager (ABV 5%)

Twt Lol SIBA

Unit B27, Trefforest Industrial Estate, Pontypridd, CF37 5YB ☎ 07966 467295 🌐 twtlol.com

Established in 2015 using a 10-barrel plant, the brewery has a capacity of 80 firkins a week, with the potential to expand to 160. All of its branding is produced in both Welsh and English. ‼ ♦

Glog (OG 1043, ABV 4%)
A bitter, caramel/toffee, malty beer.

Cwrw'r Afr Serchog/Horny Goat Ale (OG 1039, ABV 4.2%)
A golden ale with pine and citrus flavours. A hint of Horny Goat Weed is also used in the brew.

Glo in the Dark (OG 1045, ABV 4.5%)
A dark-coloured beer with crisp, fresh hoppy notes.

Pewin Ynfytyn/Crazy Peacock (OG 1045, ABV 4.8%)
Hoppy golden amber-coloured beer made with a hint of caramel malt.

Tydd Steam SIBA

Manor Barn, Kirkgate, Tydd Saint Giles, Cambridgeshire, PE13 5NE
☎ (01945) 871020 ☎ 07932 726552
🌐 tyddsteam.co.uk

Established in 2007 in a converted agricultural barn, the brewery is named after two farm steam engines. A 15-barrel plant was installed in 2011. Around 70 outlets are supplied direct. ‼ ♦ RAIB

Barn Ale (OG 1038, ABV 3.9%)
A golden-coloured bitter that has a good biscuity malt aroma and flavour, balanced by spicy hops. Long, dry, fairly astringent finish.

Piston Bob (OG 1044, ABV 4.6%)
Malt and faint hops on the aroma progress through to a malty flavour complemented by a balance of hops and fruit. A long, dry finish rounds off this amber-coloured, strong bitter.

Tyne Bank

375 Walker Road, Newcastle upon Tyne, NE6 2AB
☎ (0191) 262 2828 ☎ 07989 426604
🌐 tynebankbrewery.co.uk

Tyne Bank began brewing in 2011. It moved and expanded in 2016 due to a successful crowd-funding initiative. It features an on-site brewery tap. The SMaSH (Single Malt and Single Hop) series of ales is now available. ‼ ♦

Single Blonde (OG 1037, ABV 3.5%)
Light ale, slightly dry bitterness with hints of vanilla.

EPA (OG 1040, ABV 3.8%)

Summer Breeze (OG 1040, ABV 3.9%)

West Coast IPA (OG 1040, ABV 4%)
A pale ale with a light citrus character.

Monument Bitter (OG 1041, ABV 4.1%)
Smooth, balanced bitter with a berry fruit character.

80 Degrees North (OG 1046, ABV 4.5%)
Rich, malty character with a dry finish.

Northern Porter (OG 1047, ABV 4.5%)
A subtly smoky porter, aged in oak.

Northern Warmth (OG 1046, ABV 4.5%)
A cinnamon spiced, dark-coloured session ale.

Silver Dollar (OG 1050, ABV 4.9%)
Hoppy American-style ale with lasting bitterness and a citrus kick.

Helix (OG 1050, ABV 5%)
Czech-style lager with a crisp, clean finish and bold malty taste.

Ubrew

Arches 29-30 Old Jamaica Business Estate, Old Jamaica Road, Bermondsey, London, SE16 4AW
🌐 weareubrew.com

Ubrew is a an open membership brewery where anyone can brew their own beer. It also features an on-site homebrew shop and taproom. A range of its own beer is also available. RAIB V

Uffa

White Lion Inn, Lower Street, Lower Ufford, Suffolk, IP13 6DW
☎ (01394) 460770 🌐 uffordwhitelion.co.uk/brewery

Uffa began brewing in 2011 using a 2.5-barrel plant. It is situated next to the White Lion pub in a converted coach house. ♦

Uley

The Old Brewery, 31 The Street, Uley, Gloucestershire, GL11 5TB
☎ (01453) 860120 🌐 uleybrewery.com

Brewing at Uley began in 1833 as Price's brewery. After a long gap, the premises were restored and Uley Brewery opened in 1985, and now uses a ten-barrel plant. It has its own spring water, which is used to mash Tucker's Maris Otter malt, and boiled with Herefordshire hops. Uley delivers to 40-50 outlets in the Cotswold area while brewing to capacity. ♦

Hogshead Cotswold Pale Ale (OG 1035, ABV 3.5%)
A pale-coloured, hoppy session bitter with a good hop aroma and a full flavour for its strength, ending in a bittersweet aftertaste.

Bitter (OG 1040, ABV 4%)
A copper-coloured beer with hops and fruit in the aroma and a malty, fruity taste, underscored by a hoppy bitterness. The finish is dry, with a balance of hops and malt.

Laurie Lee's Bitter (OG 1045, ABV 4.5%)
A copper-coloured, full-flavoured, hoppy bitter with some fruitiness and a smooth, long, balanced finish.

Old Spot Prize Strong Ale (OG 1050, ABV 5%)
A ruby-coloured ale with an initial strong malty sweetness that develops into a smooth, dry, malty finish. A beer that is deceptively easy to drink.

Pig's Ear Strong Beer (OG 1050, ABV 5%)
A golden-coloured pale ale with an initial refreshing taste with a hint of fruitiness that develops into a light, malty finish. A smooth, quaffable, strong ale.

Brewed for the Old Spot Inn, Dursley:

Old Ric (OG 1045, ABV 4.5%)

A full-flavoured, hoppy bitter with some fruitiness and a smooth, balanced finish. Distinctively copper-coloured.

Ulverston

Lightburn Road, Ulverston, Cumbria, LA12 0AU
☎ (01229) 586870 ☎ 07840 192022
🌐 ulverstonbrewingcompany.co.uk

The brewery occupies the octagonal bullring of the old livestock market. There is a bar that overlooks the brew-plant which opens by prior arrangement and during some local festivals. Some beers have a Laurel and Hardy theme: Stan Laurel was born in Ulverston. ‼ ♦

Flying Elephants (OG 1037, ABV 3.7%)
Clean, refreshing, yellow-coloured bitter, sweet and fruity with a dry citrus finish.

Celebration Ale (OG 1039, ABV 3.9%)
Yellow-coloured, fruity bitter with hints of tangerine and a notably sustained dry finish.

Harvest Moon (OG 1039, ABV 3.9%)
A well-balanced, pale-coloured, hoppy bitter.

Another Fine Mess (OG 1040, ABV 4%)
A refreshing, gold-coloured bitter. Initially fruity but with a rising bitterness.

Laughing Gravy (OG 1040, ABV 4%)
Smooth and grainy, brown-coloured bitter with a good mix of flavours.

Lonesome Pine (OG 1042, ABV 4.2%)
A fresh and fruity pale gold-coloured beer; honeyed, lemony and resiny with an increasingly bitter finish.

Fra Diavolo (OG 1043, ABV 4.3%)

Unbarred

The Old Dairy, Chiddinglye Farm, West Hoathly, East Sussex, RH19 4QS ☎ 07850 070471

Office: 33 Bolsover Road, Hove, BN3 5HQ
🌐 unbarredbrewery.com

UnBarred has upscaled from a purpose-built brewery in the owner's garden and has teamed up with Missing Link Brewing (qv) in West Hoathly. It has a core range of beers, almost exclusively in can and keg, but also brews small batches and occasional casks for festivals and a small number of local pubs. RAIB

Under the Street

See One Mile End

Unity

Unit 10, Belgrave Industrial Estate, Belgrave Road, Southampton, SO17 3EA
☎ (023) 8067 7070 🌐 unitybrewingco.com

Founded in 2016, Unity Brewing Co is a six-barrel brewery. It produces beers influenced by Belgian and North East American styles using traditional techniques and modern ingredients. Output is mainly keg or bottles, including 750ml bottle-conditioned versions. ♦RAIB

Local Table Pale (OG 1040, ABV 3.8%)
An easy-drinking session pale ale with a changing hop profile.

Unity Brew House

See Hop Shed

Unsworth's Yard SIBA

4 Unsworth's Yard, Ford Road, Cartmel, Cumbria, LA11 6PG ☎ 07810 461313 🌐 unsworthsyard.co.uk

Unsworth's Yard opened in 2011, brewing on a five-barrel plant. The brewery produces beers named after historic figures and legends associated with the Cartmel area. Beers are available in Cartmel pubs and other local outlets as well as the brewery's tap bar ‼

Cartmel Peninsula (OG 1039, ABV 3.8%)
A mellow and sweet English bitter brewed with Kentish hops.

Crusader Gold (OG 1041, ABV 4.1%)
A crisp and refreshing golden ale with a subtle citrus finish.

Cartmel Wharf Sandpiper Cask (OG 1038, ABV 4.3%)
A crisp, light blonde beer from lager malt and delicately flavoured German hops.

Sir Edgar Harrington's Last Wolf (OG 1045, ABV 4.5%)
Well-balanced, rich and fruity, tawny-coloured ale with gentle bitterness.

The Flookburgh Cockler (OG 1057, ABV 5.5%)
Smooth, rich and dark in colour with roasted grain and mocha flavours.

Untapped SIBA

Unit 6, Little Castle Farm Business Park, Raglan, NP15 2BX
☎ (01291) 690074 ☎ 07988 197794
🌐 untappedbrew.com

Brewing started in 2009 at Newent but transferred to its current premises in Raglan in 2013. A wide range of beers is brewed, including a range primarily aimed at the bottled market. Recently the brewery has achieved a certificate for organic brewing. Beers are also contract brewed for Whittingtons Brewery. ‼ ♦RAIB

Border Awesome Amber Ale (OG 1036.8, ABV 3.8%)

Sundown (OG 1038.8, ABV 4%)

Monnow (OG 1038.3, ABV 4.2%)

Whoosh (OG 1038.3, ABV 4.2%)

UPA (OG 1043.6, ABV 4.5%)

Guardian (OG 1045.5, ABV 4.7%)

Triple S (OG 1048.4, ABV 4.9%)

Ember (OG 1050, ABV 5.2%)

Crystal (OG 1052.3, ABV 6%)

Coldharbour (OG 1062, ABV 6.5%)

Up Front

Office: 1.1, 27 Skirving Street, Glasgow, G41 3AB
☎ 07526 088973 🌐 upfrontbrewing.com

Established in 2016, Up Front is a gypsy brewery producing canned beers. Cask-conditioned beers are occasionally available.

Upham SIBA

Stakes Farm, Cross Lane, Upham, Hampshire, SO32 1FL
☎ (01489) 861383 🌐 uphambrewery.co.uk

Upham began brewing in 2009 and expanded to a 30-barrel plant in 2013. It manages 16 pubs and supplies more than 250 outlets. ♦ RAIB

Tipster (OG 1036, ABV 3.6%)
An easy-drinking and light golden ale. Initial hoppiness and fruit is balanced by maltiness that lasts into the finish.

Punter/Sam FM Ale (OG 1039, ABV 4%)
Light amber-coloured ale with a sweet and floral hop aroma. A balanced flavour of refreshing bitterness and maltiness with a dry, fruity finish.

Urban Chicken

Ilkeston, Derbyshire, DE7 5EH ☎ 07976 913395
🌐 urbanchickenale.co.uk

A nanobrewery producing small batches of beer for local pubs, restaurants, bottle shops and beer festivals. Registered as a commercial brewery in 2016. ♦

Urban Gold (ABV 4.5%)
Single Hop Series. A session pale ale with a simple grain bill, allowing the character of the hop to shine.

Earthquake (ABV 4.6%)
An earthy, rich oatmeal stout.

Pit Pony (ABV 4.9%)

Rooster Juice (ABV 5%)

Take Me To The Circus (ABV 5.1%)
A brown-coloured, American-style ale with roast flavours and a citrus hop finish.

Bantam (ABV 5.4%)
A well-balanced, American-style pale ale with tropical fruit flavours.

Urban Island SIBA

Unit 28, Limberline Industrial Estate, Limberline Spur, Portsmouth, Hampshire, PO3 5DZ
☎ (023) 9266 8726 🌐 urbanislandbrewing.uk

Urban Island began production in 2015 on a bespoke five-barrel, purpose-built plant. The range is distributed throughout Hampshire and the South East and expanding further afield. The brewery also features an on-site taproom. !!

Urban Pale (OG 1040, ABV 3.8%)
Hoppy pale ale with aromas of orange and pink grapefruit.

DSB (Dolly's Special Beer) (OG 1045, ABV 4.6%)
A light, refreshing ale, slightly fruity with a bitter hop finish.

Citra (OG 1050.6, ABV 5%)
A smooth, single-hopped, American-style ale with floral and grapefruit aromas.

Porter 28 (OG 1056, ABV 5%)
A combination of seven malts giving gentle hints of smokiness and chocolate with a roasted finish.

High & Dry – West Coast IPA (OG 1056, ABV 5.5%)
An American-hopped IPA with an earthy base and citrus finish.

Uttoxeter SIBA

27 Demontfort Way, Uttoxeter, Staffordshire, ST14 8XY ☎ 07734 392321
🌐 uttoxeterbrewingcompany.com

A nanobrewery set up in 2016, exploiting the famous Burton upon Trent hard water.

Full Gallop (ABV 4.4%)
A brown-coloured ale, malty and spicy with slight sweetness and a toffee note.

Dr Johnson's Contrafibularity (ABV 4.5%)
A hoppy IPA with an orange citrus flavour.

Earthmover (ABV 4.5%)
Traditional English bitter, hoppy with a good malty flavour and a fruity finish.

Final Furlong (ABV 4.5%)
A smooth, spicy and floral best bitter with a caramel flavour.

Uxonian (ABV 4.5%)
An amber-coloured ale with white grape and tangerine flavours.

Earthmover Gold (ABV 4.7%)
A light-coloured golden ale. Hoppy yet fruity.

Ground Breaker (ABV 4.7%)
A golden-coloured beer with a grassy, earthy aroma and pineapple flavours.

Paddock Porter (ABV 4.8%)
A chocolaty porter with a distinctive dark roasted grain flavour and a slight sweetness.

American IPA (ABV 5.6%)
An American-style IPA. Powerful, bitter and fruity.

Vale SIBA

Tramway Business Park, Ludgershall Road, Brill, Buckinghamshire, HP18 9TY
☎ (01844) 239237 🌐 valebrewery.co.uk

Established in 1995 and initially based in Haddenham, Vale moved to Brill in 2007. In 2010 it expanded to a 20-barrel brew plant. Five pubs are owned, including the Hop Pole where sister brewery the Aylesbury Brewhouse (qv), opened in 2011. !! ♦ RAIB

Brill Gold (OG 1035, ABV 3.5%)
Golden-coloured session ale with a full malt flavour, well-balanced with fruity, slightly citrus hop aromas and a soft bitterness.

Best IPA (OG 1036, ABV 3.7%)
This pale amber-coloured beer starts with a slight fruit aroma. This leads to a clean, bitter taste where hops and fruit dominate. The finish is long and bitter with a slight hop note.

Black Swan Mild (OG 1038, ABV 3.9%)
Dark-coloured and smooth with hints of chocolate and coffee on the nose and a malty, dry finish.

Wychert Ale (OG 1038, ABV 3.9%)
Woody flavours are notable in this malty beer with a finish of port and berries on the nose.

VPA (Vale Pale Ale) (OG 1042, ABV 4.2%)
An assertive, dry, hoppy ale with a citrus nose, combined with a pronounced malt background.

Red Kite (OG 1043, ABV 4.3%)
Chestnut-coloured beer with a bitter finish.

Black Beauty Porter (OG 1044, ABV 4.4%)

A dark-coloured ale, the initial aroma is malty. Roast malt dominates initially and is followed by a rich fruitiness, with some sweetness. The finish is increasingly hoppy and dry.

Gravitas (OG 1047, ABV 4.8%)
A strong pale ale packed with hop and citrus flavours, rounded off by a dry, malty, biscuit finish.

Valhalla

Haroldswick, Unst, Shetland, ZE2 9TJ
☎ (01957) 711658 🌐 valhallabrewery.co.uk

Valhalla was set up by husband and wife team Sonny and Sylvia Priest in 1997. A new brewery building was officially opened in 2012, converted from part of the former RAF SaxaVoord camp at Haroldswick. In 2018 ownership of the brewery transferred to Alistair Morgan of Viking Mead Ltd. Brewing is only taking place occasionally at present and there are plans for relocation. ‼♦

White Wife (OG 1038, ABV 3.8%) ◆
Predominantly hop and citrus fruit, which remain on the palate. The aftertaste is increasingly bitter.

Old Scatness (OG 1038, ABV 4%)
A light bitter brewed with an ancient strain of barley called Bere.

Simmer Dim (OG 1039, ABV 4%) ◆
A light golden ale. The sulphur features do not mask the fruits and hops of this well-balanced beer.

Island Bere (OG 1044, ABV 4.2%) ◆
Original Bere barley used with some citrus hops.

Auld Rock (OG 1043, ABV 4.5%) ◆
A full-bodied, dark-coloured, Scottish-style best bitter, it has a rich malty nose but does not lack bitterness in the long, dry finish.

Sjolmet Stout (OG 1048, ABV 5%) ◆
Full of malt and roast barley, especially in the taste. Smooth, creamy, fruity finish, not as dry as some stouts.

Velvet Owl (NEW)

c/o Unit 2e, Pontygwindy Estate, Caerphilly, CF83 3HU
☎ (01452) 901492 ☎ 07415 933486

Office: 33 Snetterton Heath, Kingsway, Gloucester, GL2 2HE 🌐 velvetowlbrew.co.uk

Velvet Owl began brewing in 2017, initially using spare capacity at other breweries. In 2018 a five year lease was signed to use the plant of Lines Brew Co (qv) in Caerphilly. It mostly produces keg and bottled beers with the occasional cask-conditioned ale. Beers are also produced under the RT Ales and Space Cadet brand names.

Verdant

Unit 6, Tressidder Close, Tregoniggie Industrial Estate, Falmouth, Cornwall, TR11 4SP
☎ (01326) 619117 ☎ 07970 503574
🌐 verdantbrewing.co

Brewery established in 2014 by keen homebrewers using a 10-barrel plant. No real ale. ‼

Vibrant Forest SIBA

Unit 3, Gordleton Business Park, Hannah Way, Bowling Green, Lymington, Hampshire, SO41 8JD
☎ (01590) 681094 ☎ 07921 753109
🌐 vibrantforest.co.uk

⊗ Located in the New Forest, Vibrant Forest began brewing commercially in 2011 using a one-barrel plant. This award-winning brewery has progressed to a 10-barrel capacity. ‼ ♦ RAIB

Summerlands (OG 1036, ABV 3.5%)
An IPA-style bitter, well-hopped with balanced malt flavours. An easy-drinking session beer.

Nova Foresta (OG 1038, ABV 3.8%)
A refreshing, well-hopped bitter with spicy fruitiness balanced by pleasant maltiness.

Outlander (OG 1040, ABV 4%)
Citrus on the nose, warm malt follows, with long waves of hoppy bitterness.

Flying Saucer (OG 1041, ABV 4.3%)
A golden ale with fruity, floral and citrus flavours. Fresh and hoppy with a long bitter finish.

Cydonia (OG 1046, ABV 4.7%)
Grapefruit, citrus and pine flavours balanced with a sweet maltiness.

Black Forest (OG 1051, ABV 4.9%)
A flavoursome porter with notes of coffee and chocolate. Full bodied on the palate with a good balance of roasted bitterness.

Farmhouse (OG 1043, ABV 5%)
Golden ale with slightly peppery and spicy aromas, subtle bitter and fruity flavours and a dry finish.

Single Hop Pale Ale (OG 1047, ABV 5%)

Kick-Start (OG 1060, ABV 5.7%)
A jet black-coloured, rich stout made with freshly roasted Colombian coffee beans. Oats add a smooth texture.

Metropolis (OG 1100, ABV 6%)
A hoppy black IPA with flavours of citrus and tropical fruits, undertones of chocolate and a balanced bitterness.

Kaleidoscope (OG 1060, ABV 6.5%)
Massively-hopped American-style IPA with intense citrus flavours.

Umbral Abyss (OG 1086, ABV 8.8%)

Victoria Inn

Roch, SA62 6AW
☎ (01437) 710426 ☎ 07814 684975
🌐 thevictoriainnroch.com

⊗ A four-barrel brewery in a separate building on the same site as the pub. At present the only outlet for the beers is the pub itself. ‼

Village Brewer

See Hambleton

Village Brewer: Brew 22

Number Twenty 2, 22 Coniscliffe Road, Darlington, DL3 7RG
☎ (01325) 354590 🌐 villagebrewer.co.uk

One-barrel microbrewery, established in 2013, which has been brewing on a regular basis since

2015. The plant is also used to produce the malt wash for the distilling of gin and vodka on site. The beer strength and style varies from brew to brew and complement the Village Brewer beers produced by Hambleton Ales (qv) since 1992.

Villages

21-22 Resolution Way, Deptford, London, SE8 4NT
☎ (020) 3489 1143 🌐 villagesbrewery.com

Established in 2016 by brothers Archie and Louis Village. Beers are currently only available in keg and can, but occasional cask-conditioned specials are produced. An on-site tap room is open on Fridays and Saturdays. ♦

Vine Inn

Vine Inn & Brewery, Sheep Fair, Rugeley, Staffordshire, WS15 2AT
☎ (01889) 574443 ✉ oli@thevinebrewery.com

Brewery based within the Vine Inn, parts of which date back to the 16th century. Its beers can be found in a number of pubs in the Cannock Chase area.

Session Ale (OG 1039, ABV 3.8%)
Light ale with subtle fruity hints.

EPA (OG 1045, ABV 4%)

Vanilla Porter (OG 1046, ABV 4.5%)
A dark-coloured porter with coffee undertones, with rising sweetness from the vanilla.

Grapefruit IPA (OG 1045, ABV 4.8%)
Well-hopped IPA with fresh grapefruit, giving it a balanced bitterness.

Violet Cottage

Gwaelod-y-Garth Inn, Main Road, Gwaelod y Garth, CF15 9HH
☎ (029) 2081 0408

The brewery was established in 2012 in a converted outbuilding at the rear of the Gwaelod-y-Garth Inn, within the grounds of the licensee's private house. All brews are subject to availability as the brewer decides. Most of the production is sold within the pub. Beers are badged as Room with a View after the view across the Taff valley. ♦

VIP

See Hawk Wing

Vision (NEW)

Unit 12, Burma Drive, Marfleet Lane, Hull, East Yorkshire, HU9 5SD ☎ 07921 905503
✉ shaune@visionbrewingco.co.uk

Vision Brewing was established in 2018 using a purpose-built 20-barrel plant. Shaun was a homebrewer who has expanded his hobby into a full-time pursuit. Beers are available across Hull.

H-Eye Brass (OG 1038, ABV 3.5%)
A hoppy, fruity, easy-drinking session beer.

Dark Argus (OG 1042, ABV 4%)
A malty beer based on an Irish red ale.

Vocation SIBA

Unit 8, Craggs Country Business Park, New Road, Cragg Vale, Hebden Bridge, West Yorkshire, HX7 5TT
☎ (01422) 410810 🌐 vocationbrewery.com

Vocation began brewing in 2015 on a bespoke 20-barrel plant. The brewery is located high above Hebden Bridge. In 2017 it opened its first bar in Hebden Bridge called Vocation & Co. Brewing capacity trebled to 45 barrels in 2018 due to increased demand. ♦

Bread & Butter (ABV 3.9%)
A feast of floral hops with citrus aroma and taste. Robust bitter aftertaste.

Heart & Soul (ABV 4.5%)
A golden ale with a strong citrus aroma. Hops dominate taste and aftertaste.

Pride & Joy (ABV 5.3%)
Flavoursome IPA packed with citrus hoppiness. A hint of sweetness gives way to a mellow aftertaste.

Life & Death (OG 1061, ABV 6.5%)
American-style IPA with flavours of tropical and citrus fruits with a lingering bitterness set against a smooth, malty backbone.

VOG SIBA

Unit 8a, Atlantic Trading Estate, Barry, CF63 3RF
☎ (01446) 730757 🌐 vogbrewery.co.uk

Created in 2005, the founders handed over the reins to a new team in 2015 who have rebranded the brewery and refreshed the beer range. Beers can be found in a number of South Wales pubs as well as occasionally throughout the country due to brewery beer swaps. A micro bar on the outskirts of Cardiff opened is due to open. ♦RAIB

Paradigm Shift (OG 1042, ABV 4.2%)
A classic English bitter reworked; amplified malt and dry-hopped.

South Island (OG 1042, ABV 4.2%)
A pale ale; dry, bitter and refreshing with a big punch from heavy late hopping.

Dark Matter (OG 1044, ABV 4.4%)
A blackcurrant porter. Rich and smooth with liquorice and chocolate notes.

Speak Easy IPA (OG 1046, ABV 4.6%)
An American-hopped IPA with a big malt character and bitter tropical citrus finish.

Lady Liberty (OG 1048, ABV 4.8%)
An American-style pale ale with a refreshing, clean bitterness supporting a juicy, resinous hop character.

Volden SIBA

35a Neville Road, Croydon, CR0 2DS
☎ (020) 8684 4492 🌐 volden.co.uk

Volden produce beer for the Antic pub group in South London. ♦

Session Ale (OG 1037, ABV 3.8%)
Amber-coloured bitter with a caramel and orange aroma. Lemon marmalade and sweetish malty biscuit that fades to a bitter, dryish finish.

Pale Ale (ABV 4.6%)

Dry, bitter, floral hop flavour with a slight hint of fresh orange peel, becoming more bitter on drinking. A little malt.

Wadworth SIBA IFBB

Northgate Brewery, Devizes, Wiltshire, SN10 1JW
☎ (01380) 723361 🌐 wadworth.co.uk

Established in 1875 by Henry Alfred Wadworth, this impressive family-owned brewery has a modern brewhouse and a microbrewery, which enables it to create unique small batch beers. Its traditional horse-drawn drays deliver beer daily around Devizes. Wadworth has more than 200 pubs in the South-west of England. !! ♦ RAIB

IPA (OG 1035, ABV 3.6%)
A classic session beer with malt-led flavours.

Horizon (OG 1039, ABV 4%)
A pale gold-coloured beer with zesty citrus and hop aromas and a crisp, tangy finish on the palate.

6X (OG 1040.5, ABV 4.1%)
Copper-coloured ale with a malty and fruity nose and some balancing hop character. The flavour is similar, with some bitterness and a lingering malty, but bitter finish.

Bishops Tipple (OG 1048, ABV 5%)
A golden-coloured beer with well-balanced hop bitterness and a clean finish.

Swordfish (OG 1047.5, ABV 5%)
A full-bodied, deep copper-coloured ale flavoured with Pussers Rum.

Wagtail

New Barn Farm, Wilby Warrens, Old Buckenham, Norfolk, NR17 1PF
☎ (01953) 887133 🌐 wagtailbrewery.com

Wagtail Brewery went into full-time production in 2006. All beers are only available bottle-conditioned. RAIB V

Wainstones SIBA

1 North Side, Hutton Rudby, North Yorkshire, TS15 0DA ☎ 07885 240226
🌐 stokesleybrewing.co.uk

Wainstones began brewing in 2010 using a 2.5-barrel plant set up in an industrial unit in Stokesley, trading as the Stokesley Brewing Company. It moved to new premises in Hutton Rudby in 2017, where the plant is also used to brew beers under the Bay Brewery name.

Amber (OG 1038, ABV 3.8%)
Distinctive light golden-coloured ale with moderate bitterness and a pleasant floral aroma.

Chinook (ABV 3.9%)
A pale ale with grapefruit and spruce zest hop notes.

Sandstone (OG 1040, ABV 4%)
Traditional brown-coloured ale with moderate bitterness and a pleasant aftertaste.

Ironstone (OG 1042, ABV 4.2%)
A rich, full-flavoured ale made with English malts and complex hops, giving a smooth aftertaste.

Copper (OG 1043, ABV 4.3%)

Steel River (OG 1043, ABV 4.3%)
Traditional chestnut-coloured ale with medium bitterness and a full, hoppy flavour.

Jet (OG 1045, ABV 4.5%)
Unusual black-coloured ale, full-flavoured with a hoppy aftertaste.

Transporter (OG 1045, ABV 4.5%)
A dark-coloured porter with a creamy head and a deep malty taste.

Brewed under the Bay Brewery name:

Saxon 1086 (ABV 3.8%)

Hutton Blonde (ABV 4%)
A light golden ale with moderate bitterness and a pleasant floral nose.

Sailmakers (ABV 4%)

Haymakers (ABV 4.2%)

Rudby Ruby (ABV 4.3%)
A traditional chestnut-coloured ale with a full, hoppy flavour.

Smugglers (ABV 4.3%)

Dark Horse (ABV 4.4%)

Walled City

70 Ebrington Square, Londonderry, BT47 6FA
☎ (028) 7134 3336 🌐 walledcitybrewery.com

Restaurant-based brewery established in 2015.

Wander Beyond

98 North Western Street, Manchester, M12 6HR
☎ (0161) 661 3676
✉ sales@wanderbeyondbrewing.com

Set up in 2016 in a railway arch under Piccadilly Station as Dan's Brewery, mainly to supply house beers to the Knott Bar, Manchester city centre, the Macc, Macclesfield and Chorlton Tap, Chorlton. Renamed as Wander Beyond Brewing with extended distribution in 2017.

Peak (ABV 3.8%)

Northern Night (ABV 4.1%)
A session porter. Well-balanced and complex with flavours of ginger cake and sweet malts.

Great Rift (ABV 6%)

Finders Keepers (ABV 6.2%)

Wantsum SIBA

Kent Barn, St Nicholas Court Farm, Court Road, St Nicholas at Wade, Kent, CT7 0PT
☎ (01227) 910135 🌐 wantsumbrewery.co.uk

Wantsum Brewery, established by James Sandy in 2009, takes its name from the nearby Wantsum Channel. Previously located in Hersden near Canterbury, the brewery relocated to a farm site in 2017. It has an extensive range of beers, named after pivotal events in Kent's history. Outlets are supplied throughout the South of England. An on-site taproom showcases the beers. !! ♦ RAIB

More's Head (OG 1034, ABV 3.5%)
A chestnut-coloured bitter with malt and roasted grains balanced against fruit and floral hops with a hint of citrus.

1381 (OG 1036, ABV 3.8%)

A light amber-coloured IPA with delicate citrus and herbal aromas.

Black Prince (OG 1036.5, ABV 3.9%)
A rich, full-bodied mild, smooth on the palate with subtle hop notes.

Imperium (OG 1037, ABV 4%)
A deep amber-coloured best bitter; smooth biscuit malts and a rich, hoppy nose.

Montgomery (OG 1037, ABV 4%)
Amber in colour with spicy citrus aromas.

Fortitude (OG 1039, ABV 4.2%)
A full-bodied beer with a pronounced hop finish.

One Hop (OG 1040, ABV 4.2%)

Dynamo (OG 1043, ABV 4.3%)
A crisp, light golden ale, fruity and floral with an orange citrus twist.

Turbulent Priest (OG 1041, ABV 4.4%)
A full-bodied best bitter offering chocolate and coffee notes on top of a sweet malt base. Bitterness is tempered with deep, fruity hop aromas.

Yellow Tail (OG 1043, ABV 4.5%)
A pale-coloured ale with mild malt flavours and a sweet floral taste. Fruity with a hint of vanilla.

Black Pig (OG 1044, ABV 4.8%)
Smooth with burnt chocolate and smoky malt notes. Delicate hop bitterness and floral notes.

Hengist (OG 1045, ABV 5%)
A golden-coloured pale ale with flavours of biscuit malt balancing a deep, mellow, fruity nose.

Red Raddle (OG 1049, ABV 5%)
Ruby-coloured premium bitter, biscuit and toasted malt base supporting a hoppy, smooth finish.

Golgotha (OG 1047, ABV 5.5%)
A rich, deep malt base gives this stout a long, smooth finish. Hops are prominent on the nose with blackcurrant, liquorice and cedar.

Ravening Wolf (OG 1052, ABV 5.9%)
A light amber-coloured, strong pale ale; toasted biscuit and rye malt flavours support a pine lemon hop crispness with a hint of vanilla.

Warwickshire SIBA

Bakehouse Brewery, Queen Street, Cubbington, Warwickshire, CV32 7NA
☎ (01926) 450747 warwickshirebeer.co.uk

A six-barrel brewery in a former village bakery which has been in operation since 1998. Bottled beers are available from local farm shops, garden centres, wine specialists, supermarkets, as well as from the brewery direct and its four pubs. ♦ RAIB

Shakespeare County (OG 1034, ABV 3.4%)
A deep copper-coloured ale with a fruity, spicy and floral aroma. Full-bodied, soft and hoppy to taste.

Fusilier (OG 1039, ABV 3.9%)
A traditional bitter with a fruity, hoppy, malty aroma and sharp, light and malty taste.

Darling Buds (OG 1041, ABV 4%)

Duck Soup (OG 1043, ABV 4.2%)
A copper-coloured beer with rich, malty overtones.

Lady Godiva (OG 1042, ABV 4.2%)
A golden ale with honey and malt on the nose. Slightly sweet, biscuity maltiness is balanced by the rounded bitterness of the hops. A lingering bitter finish.

Golden Bear (OG 1049, ABV 4.9%)
An assertive golden brown-coloured beer characterised by a long-lasting, slightly resinous bitterness. The finish is fruity and warming with hints of spice and orange.

Ball Stitcher (OG 1051, ABV 5%)

Kingmaker (OG 1055, ABV 5.5%)
A rich, fruity beer, amber in colour. A fruity, malty, toffee aroma leads onto a palate with overtones of spice and caramel.

Wash House

Allanwater Brewhouse, Queens Lane, Bridge of Allan, FK9 4NY
☎ (01786) 834555 ☎ 07831 224242
bridgeofallan.co.uk

Originally named Tinpot, Wash House Brewery was established in 2009 using a one-barrel plant designed to brew speciallity beers, expanding in 2014 to a 1.5-barrel one. The beer range varies depending on season and demand, which is increasing every year. !! ♦ RAIB GF

Watermill SIBA

Watermill Inn, Ings, Cumbria, LA8 9PY
☎ (01539) 821309 ☎ 07831 873300
lakelandpub.co.uk

Watermill was established in 2006 in a purpose-built extension to the inn. The beers have a doggy theme – dogs are allowed in the main bar. The brewery was extended in 2008 with a new brewery planned within the grounds. Also produces beers under the Windermere Brewery name. !! ♦

Tomos Watkin SIBA

Unit 3, Alberto Road, Century Park, Valley Way, Swansea Enterprise Park, Swansea, SA6 8RP
☎ (01792) 797280 tomoswatkin.com

Brewing began in 1995, originally in Llandeilo behind the Castle Hotel. The brewery moved to Swansea in 2000 and was taken over by Hurns Water Mineral Company in 2002. More than 60% of production is bottled beers (not bottle conditioned). !! ♦

Delilah (OG 1040, ABV 4%)
Light, golden-coloured ale with zesty citrus flavours and a hint of spice.

OSB (Old Style Bitter) (OG 1045, ABV 4.5%)
Amber-coloured with an inviting aroma of hops and malt. Full-bodied; hops, fruit, malt and bitterness combine to give a balanced flavour continuing into the finish.

IPA (OG 1049, ABV 4.8%)
Full-bodied, crisp IPA with floral bitterness and aromas of peach and mandarin.

Pecker Wrecker (OG 1052, ABV 5%)
A rich, amber-coloured, fruity beer with a gentle hop finish.

THE BREWERIES

Watling Street SIBA

2a Greycane Road, Watford, Hertfordshire, WD24 7GP ☎ 07713 841936 🌐 watlingstreetbeer.com

Brewing began in 2015 in Aldenham and relocated to an old farm building on Hilfield Farm in 2016 to allow for expansion to a 10-barrel plant. The brewery relocated again to North Watford in 2017. An on-site tap room is open six days a week. !!

Sir Newton Golden Ale (ABV 3.8%)

Queen Boudicca Premium Ale (ABV 4.2%)

Miss Shelley Pale Ale (ABV 4.3%)

Mr Ripper Red Ale (ABV 4.6%)

Wat Tyler Pale Ale (ABV 4.8%)

Watson's

Old Heath, Colchester, Essex, CO1 2HD ☎ 07804 641267 🌐 watsonsbrewery.co.uk

Small batch home brewery set up in 2016 using a 100-litre brew plant. Local pubs, festivals and bottle shops are supplied with one-off beers.

Watts Brewing?

Magnet Freehouse, 51 Wellington Road North, Stockport, SK4 1HJ ☎ (0161) 429 6287 🌐 themagnetfreehouse.co.uk

Brewing began in 2014 on the premises of the Magnet freehouse. No regular beers. Speciality beers are brewed to suit the season, and are mostly sold in the pub. ♦

Waveney

Queen's Head, Station Road, Earsham, Norfolk, NR35 2TS ☎ (01986) 892623 ✉ lyndahamps@aol.com

Established at the Queen's Head in 2004, the five-barrel brewery produces three beers, regularly available at the pub along with other free trade outlets. ♦

Way Outback

144 Seabourne Road, Southbourne, Dorset, BH5 2HZ 🌐 thewayoutback.co.uk

Started in 2017 and born in a shed but now based in a lovingly restored building, which includes a tap room, the Way Outback is run by owner and head brewer Rich Brown with help from his able assistant Arthur.

Working like a Dog (ABV 3.6%)
A session pale ale with fruity flavours.

Take Me to Valhalla (ABV 4%)
A pale ale with aromas of blueberry, citrus and tropical fruit.

Hopposites Attract (ABV 5.6%)
A double-hopped pale ale with aromas of passion fruit, grapefruit and gooseberry.

Weal SIBA

Unit 6, Newpark Business Park, London Road, Chesterton, Staffordshire, ST5 7HT ☎ (01782) 565635 ☎ 07980 606966 🌐 wealales.co.uk

Weal Ales is an award-winning microbrewery established in 2014 on a one-barrel plant. It expanded to a six-barrel plant in 2015 and is now also bottling its beers. Its first pub, Wellers, opened in Newcastle under Lyme in 2016. RAIB

Sqweal (OG 1039, ABV 3.9%)
A refreshing golden ale, smooth and full-bodied with a slight hoppy flavor and a hint of caramel in the aftertaste.

Weally Hopper (OG 1042, ABV 4.2%)
A light and refreshing pale ale. It has a defining floral and citrus aroma with a dry bitter finish.

Weller Weal (OG 1046, ABV 4.6%)
A hoppy pale ale with a citrus finish.

Robin Wealiant (ABV 4.7%)
A triple-hopped pale ale with a distinct fruit and floral aroma.

Noir (OG 1048, ABV 4.8%)
A rich, warming porter with a roast malt flavour throughout and a subtle hint of spice.

Centwealial Milk Stout (OG 1059, ABV 4.9%)
A sweet, creamy milk stout with a rich chocolate taste and silky smooth finish.

Ginger Weal (ABV 5.5%)
A strong golden ale with a spicy ginger kick.

Lemon & Ginger Weal (ABV 5.5%)
A strong golden ale with distinct citrus and spicy ginger flavours.

Potters Weal (OG 1055, ABV 5.5%)
Complex aroma of biscuit, chocolate and roast. Taste belies the strength of this brown-coloured beer. Smooth and sweet but a slightly acidic bitter edge evident then a bittersweet finish.

Weard'ALE

Hare & Hounds, 24 Front Street, Westgate, DL13 1RX ☎ (01388) 517212

Brewing commenced in the Hare & Hounds in 2010. The beers are mainly sold on the premises but some have found their way to nearby beer festivals and other local pubs.

Weatheroak

Unit 7, Victoria Works, Birmingham Road, Studley, Warwickshire, B80 7AP ☎ (0121) 445 4411 (eve) ☎ 07798 773894 🌐 weatheroakbrewery.co.uk

The brewery was set up in 1997 at Weatheroak Hill. It is now in a spacious factory unit in Studley. Around 40 outlets are supplied direct. !!♦

St Udley Mild (OG 1034, ABV 3.4%)

Ale (OG 1041, ABV 4.1%)
The aroma is dominated by hops in this golden-coloured beer. Hops also feature in the mouth and there is a rapidly fading dry aftertaste.

Victoria Works (OG 1043, ABV 4.3%)
A pale-coloured, hoppy bitter with a citrus finish.

Redwood (OG 1047, ABV 4.7%)
A rich, tawny-coloured, strong but mellow beer with a short-lived sweet fruit and malt balance.

Keystone Hops (OG 1050, ABV 5%)

A golden yellow-coloured beer. Fruity hops are the dominant flavour without the commonly associated astringency.

Weatheroak Hill SIBA

Coach & Horses, Weatheroak Hill, Alvechurch, Worcestershire, B48 7EA
☎ (01564) 823386

Weatheroak Hill Brewery is located at the busy Coach & Horses pub and restaurant near Alvechurch. ‼♦

Websters

Graham's Place, 73 Bridgnorth Road, Wollaston, West Midlands, DY8 3PZ
☎ (01384) 440315 ✉ info@grahams-place.co.uk

Microbrewery set up to the side of Graham's Place in 2014. Currently brewing with malt extract, full mash beers are planned. All beers are sold though the pub including some one-off specials. ♦

Weetwood SIBA

The Brewery, Common Lane, Kelsall, Cheshire, CW6 0PY
☎ (01829) 752377 weetwoodales.co.uk

Weetwood Ales, which originally began brewing in 1992 in a barn, now operates out of a modern 30-barrel plant close to Kelsall. Following a change of ownership in 2014, not only has the beer range broadened but monthly Thursday evening brewery tours have been introduced as well as an on-site shop. Cask-conditioned ales can be found in pubs across Cheshire, the North-west, North Midlands and throughout North Wales. ‼

Southern Cross (ABV 3.6%)
A hoppy session beer. Pale golden in colour with pine and lemon hop characteristics.

Bitter (OG 1038.5, ABV 3.8%)
Pale brown-coloured beer with an assertive bitterness and a lingering dry finish. Despite initial sweetness, peppery hops dominate throughout.

Mad Hatter (OG 1038.5, ABV 3.9%)
A red-brown-coloured beer with fruity and malty flavours throughout. Spicy and floral hop notes.

Cheshire Cat (OG 1040, ABV 4%)
Pale-coloured, dry bitter with a spritzy lemon zest and a grape aroma. Hoppy aroma leads through to the initial taste before fruitiness takes over. Smooth, creamy mouthfeel and a short, dry finish.

Eastgate (OG 1043.5, ABV 4.2%)
Well-balanced and refreshing, clean, amber-coloured beer. Citrus fruit flavours predominate in the taste and there is a short, dry aftertaste.

Old Dog (OG 1045, ABV 4.5%)
Robust, well-balanced, amber-coloured beer with a slightly fruity aroma. Rich malt and fruit flavours are balanced by bitterness. Some sweetness and a hint of sulphur on nose and taste.

Oregon Pale (ABV 4.5%)
Pale-coloured ale with big citrus and grapefruit hop flavours.

Weighbridge

Penzance Drive, Swindon, Wiltshire, SN5 7JL
☎ (01793) 881500 weighbridgebrewhouse.co.uk

A microbrewery established in 2011 and based within the Weighbridge Brewhouse Restaurant and Bar, in the building which was formerly the home of Archer's brewery and once part of Swindon Railway Works. It was acquired by Upham Brewery (qv) of Hampshire, but remains separate to that company. ‼♦

Weird Beard SIBA

Unit 5, Boston Business Park, Trumpers Way, Hanwell, W7 2QA
☎ (020) 3645 2711 weirdbeardbrewco.com

Brewing began in 2013 on an industrial estate in Hanwell. The plant has expanded again with two new 20-barrel fermenters in addition to six 10-barrel ones. Beer is mostly sold bottle-conditioned or in KeyKeg, but some is available cask-conditioned. RAIB

Dark Hopfler (OG 1043, ABV 2.5%)
A hoppy, dark-coloured beer with pine and chocolate on the nose. Roasted malt and sweet cocoa flavours carry into the taste, which is balanced with resinous hop bitterness.

Black Perle (OG 1053, ABV 3.8%)
Coffee milk stout with roast notes throughout this full-favoured, sweetish, black-coloured beer. Finish has some roast bitter dryness.

Little Things That Kill (OG 1044, ABV 3.9%)
Hoppy, fruity golden ale which varies in flavour as the hops that are used can alter.

Hops Maiden England (OG 1047, ABV 4.5%)
An oatmeal pale ale with varying hops.

Mariana Trench (OG 1048, ABV 5.3%)
Passion fruit and citrus are noticeable throughout this malty, sweet, golden-coloured beer. Bitterness builds and lingers, overlaid by dryness.

Decadence Stout (OG 1062, ABV 5.5%)
Orange with some black treacle sweetness balances the dry chocolate and coffee character that lingers pleasantly with the bitterness developing.

K*ntish Town Beard (OG 1054, ABV 5.5%)

Fade to Black (OG 1063, ABV 6.5%)
Well-balanced black IPA with some fruitiness. Roast coffee notes throughout.

Five O'clock Shadow (OG 1065, ABV 7%)
Highly-hopped American-style IPA, big on mouthfeel with citrus and floral notes balanced by a classic malt backbone.

Welbeck Abbey SIBA

Brewery Yard, Welbeck, Nottinghamshire, S80 3LT
☎ (01909) 512539 ☎ 07921 066274
welbeckabbeybrewery.co.uk

Welbeck Abbey opened in 2011. The microbrewery is housed in a listed barn at the centre of the traditional landed Welbeck estate. General manager Claire Monk trained at the Kelham Island Brewery after studying microbiology at Sheffield University. ‼

Henrietta (OG 1035, ABV 3.6%)
A clean-tasting, delicate golden ale with notes of honeysuckle and fresh hay.

Red Feather (OG 1040, ABV 3.9%)

A robust auburn-coloured ale with bold walnut and bittersweet caramel flavours.

Kaiser (ABV 4.1%)
A pale-coloured beer with biscuity sweet notes and a refreshing herbal flavour.

Harley (OG 1038, ABV 4.3%)
A honey-coloured ale with orange blossom and fresh zesty notes at the front and subtle sweetness behind.

Portland Black (OG 1043, ABV 4.5%)
Black-coloured ale with a roast malt aroma and taste throughout, and a well-balanced bitterness.

Cavendish (OG 1046, ABV 5%)
Golden in colour with a smooth, hoppy and malt mouthfeel and a lingering hoppy bitter finish.

Weldon

Bencroft Grange, Bedford Road, Rushden, Northamptonshire, NN10 0SE
☎ (01536) 601016

Office: 12 Chapel Road, Weldon, NN17 3HP
weldonbrewery.co.uk

Weldon originally started brewing in 2014 on a two-barrel plant at the Shoulder of Mutton, after which the brewery was originally named. In 2016 the premises and 3.5-barrel kit of the former Copper Kettle brewery in Rushden were purchased and became the main production facility, with the brewery being renamed Weldon. The original plant at the Shoulder of Mutton has been retained and is used for small runs and test batches. ♦

Essanell (OG 1038, ABV 3.8%)

Dragline (OG 1040, ABV 3.9%)
Golden ale, light and crisp with delicate fruit and floral notes.

Stahlstadt (OG 1040, ABV 4%)
A blonde ale, light and refreshing with delicate hints of lemon and fragrant garden herbs.

Galvy Stout (OG 1042, ABV 4.2%)
A classic stout with hints of coffee, chocolate and liquorice.

Rosie's Sweatbox (OG 1042, ABV 4.2%)
A deep ruby-coloured ale, fruity in character with hints of toffee and wood smoke.

Windmill (OG 1042, ABV 4.2%)

Roman Mosaics (OG 1044, ABV 4.6%)
A robust, hoppy pale ale with deep complex flavours of stone fruit.

Well Drawn SIBA

Unit 5, Greenway Workshops, Bedwas House Industrial Estate, Caerphilly, CF83 8HW ☎ 07376 556745 welldrawnbrewing.co.uk

This six-barrel brewery opened in 2017 in a small industrial unit near Caerphilly, supplying direct to local pubs as well as through a number of regional wholesalers. ♦RAIB

Pale Ale (ABV 3.8%)
Pale gold-coloured session ale with a floral aroma and hints of elderflower.

Classic Bitter (ABV 4.2%)
Classic bitter with a malty flavour coming through traditional bittering hops.

Gold (ABV 4.4%)
Golden-coloured session ale with a toffee hint and floral, hoppy aromas.

Charles Wells

See Eagle

Weltons SIBA

1 Mulberry Trading Estate, Foundry Lane, Horsham, West Sussex, RH13 5PX
☎ (01403) 242901 weltonsbeer.co.uk

Ray Welton moved the brewery into a factory unit in 2003. More than 70 different beers are brewed every year. Pubs throughout the South-east and London are supplied. !! ♦RAIB

Pride 'n' Joy (OG 1028, ABV 2.8%)
A light brown-coloured bitter with a slight malty and hoppy aroma. Fruity with a pleasant hoppiness and some sweetness in the flavour, leading to a short malty finish.

Horsham Pale (OG 1037, ABV 3.7%)
Amber-coloured, bitter but with a huge aroma.

Sussex Pride (OG 1040, ABV 4%)

Old Cocky (OG 1043, ABV 4.3%)

American Graffiti (OG 1045, ABV 4.5%)
A pale ale with citrus bitterness and a powerful, lingering aroma.

Old Harry (OG 1051, ABV 5.2%)

Churchillian Stout (OG 1066, ABV 6.6%)
Hints of burnt toast balanced by good levels of hops with a long finish.

Wensleydale SIBA

Unit 4, Badger Court, Leyburn, North Yorkshire, DL8 5BF
☎ (01969) 622463 ☎ 07765 596666
wensleydalebrewery.co.uk

Wensleydale was set up in 2003 and recently moved to larger premises in Leyburn with plans for further expansion. Around 100 outlets are supplied direct. !! ♦RAIB

Lidstone's Rowley Mild (OG 1032, ABV 3.2%)
Chocolate and toffee aromas lead into what, for its strength, is an impressively rich and flavoursome taste. The finish is pleasantly bittersweet.

Bitter (OG 1036, ABV 3.7%)
Intensely aromatic, straw-coloured ale offering a superb balance of malt and hops on the tongue.

Falconer Session Bitter (OG 1038, ABV 3.9%)
A fruity, malt-based session ale, copper in colour, with a long, bitter, dry finish.

Semerwater Summer Ale (OG 1040, ABV 4.1%)
A pale-coloured ale with citrus aromas. The clean, hoppy nose is balanced by a light, malty sweetness.

Coverdale Gamekeeper (OG 1042, ABV 4.3%)
A copper-coloured best bitter with huge spicy hop and juicy malt flavours.

Black Dub Oat Stout (OG 1043, ABV 4.4%)
Black-coloured, silky stout brewed with oats and four different malts.

Gold (OG 1044, ABV 4.5%)

A light golden-coloured best bitter with aromatic and spicy hop flavours.

Coverdale Poacher IPA (OG 1048, ABV 5%)
Citrus flavours dominate both aroma and taste in this pale-coloured, smooth, refreshing beer; the aftertaste is quite dry.

Wessex

Rye Hill Farm, Longbridge Deverill, Wiltshire, BA12 7DE
☎ (01985) 844532
wessexbrewery@tinyworld.co.uk

Wessex was estabished in 2001 and moved to its current location in 2004. Five local outlets are supplied as well as selected wholesalers. Beers are occasionally contract brewed when capacity permits. ♦

Stourton Pale Ale (OG 1038, ABV 3.5%)
A pale-coloured, hoppy session beer.

Potter's Ale (OG 1038, ABV 3.8%)

Longleat Pride (OG 1040, ABV 4%)

Kilmington Best (OG 1041, ABV 4.2%)
Slightly sweet, amber-coloured best bitter with balanced malt and hop characteristics.

Warminster Warrior (OG 1045, ABV 4.5%)

Golden Apostle (OG 1048, ABV 4.8%)

Beast of Zeals (OG 1066, ABV 6.6%)

Russian Stoat (OG 1080, ABV 9%)

WEST

Binnie Place, Glasgow Green, Glasgow, G40 1AW
☎ (0141) 550 0135 westbeer.com

Brewery-bar and restaurant, producing German-style beer to the Bavarian Purity Law. Beers are usually served under pressure, but not pasteurised. In 2017 a bottle-conditioned beer was introduced to the range. !! ♦ RAIB

West Berkshire SIBA

The Old Dairy, Yattendon, Berkshire, RG18 0XT
☎ (01635) 767090 wbbrew.com

West Berkshire was established in 1995. In 2017, following a £6M investment from new shareholders, capacity has been increased threefold. The new state-of-the-art brewery is located in a former dairy building. The site also includes a shop, café and brewery tap. Beers are available throughout the South of England. Craft beers are produced under the Renegade brand name. !! ♦ RAIB

Mr Chubb's Lunchtime Bitter (OG 1041, ABV 3.7%)
Well-balanced session bitter. A malty caramel note dominates aroma and taste and is accompanied by a nutty bittersweetness and a hoppy aftertaste.

Maggs' Magnificent Mild (OG 1041, ABV 3.8%)
Silky, full-bodied dark mild with a creamy head. Roast malt aroma is joined in the taste by caramel, sweetness and mild, fruity hoppiness. Aftertaste of roast malt with balancing bitterness.

Good Old Boy (OG 1043, ABV 4%)
Well-rounded, tawny-coloured bitter with malt and hops dominating throughout. A balancing bitterness accompanies the taste and aftertaste.

Mr Swift's Pale Ale (OG 1043, ABV 4%)
A golden-coloured, fruity session bitter.

Dr Hexter's Healer (OG 1051, ABV 5%)
An amber-coloured strong bitter with malt, caramel and hops in the aroma. Taste is a balance of malt, caramel, fruit, hops and bittersweetness. Caramel, fruit and bittersweetness dominate the aftertaste.

West by Three

Unit 19, St Lukes Court, Swansea, SA1 7ER ☎ 07291 253227 westbythree.com

West by Three was established in 2016 and brews small batch beers available in bottles, keg and cask. All beers are unfined.

West Coast

See Conwy

West Coast Rock (NEW)

1877 The Brew Room, 137-139 Church Street, Blackpool, FY1 3NX

Historic Blackpool pub, which reopened as a specialist beer outlet in 2017 and first brewed in 2018 using a six-barrel plant.

West End

68-70 Braunstone Gate, Leicester, LE3 5LG
☎ 07875 745302 thewestendbrewery.co.uk

The West End Brewery is Leicester city centre's original brewpub, which opened in 2016 using a 2.5-barrel plant. Beers are available in the pub and occasionally in other local outlets. ♦ RAIB

Westerham SIBA

Beggars Lane, Westerham, Kent, TN16 1QP
☎ (01732) 864427 westerhambrewery.co.uk

The brewery was established in 2004 at the National Trust's Grange Farm, and is housed in a former dairy. More than 500 outlets are supplied in Kent, Surrey, Sussex and London. In 2017 more than £1.6m was invested in a new building, which houses the brewery, tap room, shop and the tasting room for the Squerryes Estate Winery. !! ♦ RAIB GF V

Finchcocks Original (OG 1036.2, ABV 3.5%)
Gold-coloured session beer. Citrus notes on the palate with a hint of biscuit and resiny hoppiness.

Grasshopper Kentish Bitter (OG 1039, ABV 3.8%)
A dark-coloured, malty bitter with nutty, roasted notes from the chocolate malt.

Summer Perle (OG 1038.5, ABV 3.8%)
Golden ale with a spicy, refreshing finish.

Spirit of Kent (OG 1039.5, ABV 4%)
Crisp golden ale with floral and fruity notes. Complex tropical fruit and citrus flavours blend with the sweet malt.

British Bulldog (OG 1040, ABV 4.1%)

A rich, full-bodied best bitter with a massive aroma and palate of jammy fruit, biscuity malt and bitter hop resins.

1965 Special Bitter Ale (OG 1047.5, ABV 4.8%)

Hop Rocket India Pale Ale (OG 1052, ABV 5.5%)
Traditional IPA with plum jam and blackcurrant aroma and palate, balanced by sappy malt and a long, lingering bitter, fruity finish.

Audit Ale (OG 1061, ABV 6.2%)

Brewed for the Spirit Pub Company:

Taylor Walker 1730 Special Pale Ale (OG 1040, ABV 4%)
Lemon balm, honey and blackcurrant flavours, combined with grassy, earthy and botanical tones.

Westmorland

Kendal, Cumbria ☎ 07554 562662

Office: Mint Street, Kendal, LA9 6DS
✉ westmorlandbrewery@gmail.com

Westmorland began brewing in 2016 using a one-barrel plant.

Wetherby (NEW)

Beer Station, York Road Industrial Estate, Wetherby, West Yorkshire, LS22 7SU
☎ (01937) 584637 ☎ 07725 850654
wetherbybrewco.com

Wetherby was established in 2017 under the direction of head brewer Sean White, brewing on a 1.25-barrel plant. The brewery incorporates a tap room and bottle shop selling its own beers and guest casks. ♦

WH Buckley

See Evan Evans

Wharfe

See Hambleton

Wharfedale SIBA

Back Barn, 16 Church Street, Ilkley, West Yorkshire, LS29 9DS
☎ (01943) 609587 wharfedalebrewery.com

Wharfedale began brewing in 2012 using spare capacity at Five Towns brewery in Wakefield. Brewing moved to Ilkley in 2013 using a 2.5-barrel plant located at the rear of the Flying Duck pub, creating Wharfedale's first brewpub.

Whim SIBA

Whim Farm, Hartington, Derbyshire, SK17 0AX
☎ (01298) 84991 whimales.co.uk

Whim opened in 1993 in outbuildings at Whim Farm. The beers are available in 50-70 outlets and the brewery's tied house, Wilkes Head, Leek. ♦

Marynka (ABV 3.3%)

Arbor Light (OG 1035, ABV 3.6%)
Light-coloured bitter, sharp and clean with lots of hop character and a delicate, light aroma.

Hartington Bitter (OG 1039, ABV 4%)
A light, golden-coloured, well-hopped session beer. A dry finish with a spicy, floral aroma.

Earl Grey Bitter (OG 1042, ABV 4.2%)
Traditional, full-bodied, golden-coloured ale. Complex malt and dry hop flavours.

Hartington IPA (OG 1045, ABV 4.5%)
Pale-coloured and smooth on the palate, allowing malt to predominate. Slightly sweet finish combined with distinctive light hop bitterness.

Flower Power (OG 1053, ABV 5.3%)
Light, golden-coloured beer with a flowery hop aroma, citrus with mild spice on the palate and a dry, bitter finish.

Whitacre (NEW)

Dog Inn, Dog Lane, Nether Whitacre, Warwickshire, B46 2DU
☎ (01675) 481318 ☎ 07977 393833
thedoginnwhitacre.co.uk

Established in 2017 by licencees Gary and Joanne Webb to supply the adjacent Dog Inn. The nine-gallon brewery is situated in an outbuilding. All the beer names are dog themed as the owners are dog lovers with two Shih Tzus, Ted and Chicco.

Whitby SIBA

East Cliff, Whitby, North Yorkshire, YO22 4JR ☎ 07516 116377 whitby-brewery.com

Whitby Brewery was established in 2012 under the Conquest name by a local team who built the brewery from scratch. It expanded in 2016 to a new site in the shadow of Whitby Abbey, with a 20-barrel capacity and an on-site tap room. Local outlets are supplied. !!

Abbey Blonde (OG 1036, ABV 3.6%)
A golden-coloured blonde ale with a zesty finish and strong notes of toffee.

Whaler (OG 1040, ABV 4%)
A fruity pale ale with a malty, citrus flavour and a mild bitter finish.

Saltwick Nab (OG 1044, ABV 4.2%)
A full-bodied, ruby-coloured ale with a pleasantly fruity finish.

Smugglers Gold (ABV 4.2%)
Golden ale with a smooth maltiness lifted by spicy hop flavours.

Black Death (OG 1045, ABV 4.5%)
Stout with a robust taste full of liquorice with hints of chocolate and coffee.

Jet Black (OG 1047, ABV 4.5%)
A well-balanced porter packed with liquorice, coffee and sweet toffee flavours.

IPA (ABV 5.2%)
Hoppy IPA with strong notes of passion fruit and grapefruit.

Brewed for Station Inn, Whitby:

Platform 3 (OG 1038, ABV 3.6%)
Nutty pale ale with a smooth citrus finish.

White Hart

White Hart Hotel & Restaurant, 15 High Street, Halstead, Essex, CO9 2AP

☎ (01787) 475657 🌐 whitehartbrewery.co.uk

⊗ Brewing began in 2017 in old stables at the back of the White Hart. Both the brewery and pub are owned by father and son, Charles and Hugo Townsend. Beers are available in the pub and at local beer festivals.

White Hart Tap

White Hart Tap, 4 Keyfield Terrace, St Albans, Hertfordshire, AL1 1QJ
☎ (01727) 860974 🌐 whiteharttap.co.uk

Brewing began in 2015. Beers are only available in the pub.

White Horse SIBA

3 Ware Road, White Horse Business Park, Stanford in the Vale, Oxfordshire, SN7 8NY
☎ (01367) 718700 🌐 whitehorsebrewery.co.uk

⊗ White Horse was founded in 2004. The brewery has a major outlet in Oxford, the Royal Blenheim, as well as supplying outlets nationally. A number of one-off beers are brewed in collaboration with Titanic brewery (qv) under the Luna brand name. ♦

Oxfordshire Bitter (OG 1038.7, ABV 3.7%)
Golden-coloured bitter, well-hopped with a clean, fruity finish.

Black Beauty (OG 1043.2, ABV 3.9%)

Village Idiot (OG 1041.8, ABV 4.1%)
A blonde ale with a complex hop aroma and taste.

Dark Blue Oxford University Ale (OG 1045, ABV 4.3%)

Wayland Smithy (OG 1047.1, ABV 4.4%)
A red-brown-coloured ale with a biscuit flavour balanced by a spicy hop finish.

White Park

Three Cups, Newnham Street, Bedford, MK40 3JR
☎ (01234) 352153 🌐 whiteparkbrewery.co.uk

⊗ White Park, established in 2007 in Cranfield on a 4.5-barrel plant, supplies direct to regional and local outlets. The brewery relocated in 2018 to the Three Cups, Bedford – its flagship pub. ♦

Park Light (ABV 3.6%)
A nutty English IPA. A sweet hop aroma balanced with a crisp, dry taste.

White Gold (OG 1037, ABV 3.8%)
A golden-coloured session ale. Gentle malt flavour giving rise to floral hoppiness.

Cranfield Best (ABV 4.2%)
A traditional best bitter with a complex, biscuity malt flavour.

Oast House (ABV 4.8%)
A light yellow-coloured, zesty pale ale with four varieties of hop.

Malt Store (OG 1047, ABV 5%)
A malty, strong English ale.

Moonshine (OG 1050, ABV 5.2%)
A citrus strong ale.

White Rock SIBA

Units 6 & 7, Dysons Complex, Southside, St Sampsons, Guernsey, GY2 4QJ
☎ (01481) 249920 ☎ 07911 760302
🌐 whiterockbrewery.gg

White Rock began brewing in 2013 in a modern industrial unit and supplies the limited free trade on the island as well as a small number of tied houses. ‼♦

Pushang (OG 1038, ABV 3.8%)
Golden ale with a light floral aroma and subtle sweetness.

Wonky Donkey (OG 1047, ABV 4.7%)
A distinctive hoppy bitter with hints of citrus.

Lost Tourist (OG 1050, ABV 5.3%)
A hoppy, citrus IPA with a slightly caramel flavour.

White Rose SIBA

7 Doncaster Road, Mexborough, South Yorkshire, S64 0HL ✉ whiterose.brewery@btinternet.com

Established in 2007 by Gary Sheriff, former head brewer at Wentworth Brewery. Formerly sharing premises with Little Ale Cart, White Rose then brewed in Mexborough, sharing premises with Imperial Brewery (qv). In 2018 it moved to its own premises using a new seven-barrel plant. ‼♦

Original Blonde (OG 1040, ABV 4%)
A golden ale with a citrus aroma and bitterness on the palate.

Stairlift to Heaven (OG 1042, ABV 4.2%)

Raven (OG 1048, ABV 4.9%)
A dark-coloured classic stout, rich and fruity.

Whitechapel

See Haworth Steam

Whitewater

40 Tullyframe Road, Kilkeel, Northern Ireland, BT34 4RZ
☎ (028) 4176 9449 🌐 whitewaterbrewery.com

Established in 1996, Whitewater is now the biggest brewery in Northern Ireland. One pub is owned, the White Horse in Saintfield, Co Down. ‼♦

Copperhead (OG 1037, ABV 3.7%)

Crown & Glory (OG 1038, ABV 3.8%)

Belfast Black (OG 1042, ABV 4.2%)

Belfast Ale (OG 1046, ABV 4.5%)

Maggie's Leap IPA (OG 1047, ABV 4.7%)
Triple-hopped IPA with powerful hop and fruit aromas. Full-bodied, rich and complex.

Clotworthy Dobbin (OG 1050, ABV 5%)

Whitley Bay

The Brewery, 2-4 South Parade, Whitley Bay, NE26 2RG ☎ 07392 823480
✉ whitleybaybrewingcompany@gmail.com

Brewing commenced in 2016 on a five-barrel plant and relocated to larger premises (the brewery tap), a former Fitzgeralds pub in the centre of Whitley Bay, in 2018. Around 40 local outlets are supplied.

Slow Joe (ABV 3.9%)
Pilsner with a hint of magnolia.

Warrior (ABV 3.9%)
A well-balanced pale ale, initial malt flavours are followed by a pleasant bitter aftertaste.

Spanish City Blonde (ABV 4.2%)
A light golden ale with a hint of grapefruit and citrus.

Ghost Ships (ABV 4.3%)

55 Degrees North (ABV 5.5%)

Whitstable SIBA

Little Telpits Farm, Woodcock Lane, Grafty Green, Kent, ME17 2AY
☎ (01622) 851007 🌐 whitstablebrewery.co.uk

Whitstable Brewery was founded in 2003. It currently provides all the beer for the Whitstable Oyster Company's three restaurants, their hotel and a brewery tap as well as supplying cask ale to pubs all over Kent, London and Surrey. ♦

Native Bitter (OG 1036, ABV 3.7%)
A classic copper-coloured Kentish session bitter with a hoppy aroma and a long, dry bitter hop finish.

Renaissance Ruby Mild (OG 1038, ABV 3.7%)
Deep ruby in colour, this classic mild has a nutty taste with a gentle roast malt aroma.

East India Pale Ale (OG 1040, ABV 4.1%)
A well-hopped, golden-coloured IPA with good grapefruit aroma, hop character and lingering bitter finish.

Oyster Stout (OG 1045, ABV 4.5%)
Rich, dry, deep chocolate, coffee and roast malt flavours.

Pearl of Kent (OG 1043, ABV 4.5%)
A well-rounded premium golden ale with a subtle bitterness and hints of tropical fruit.

Winkle Picker (OG 1042, ABV 4.5%)
A well-balanced, amber-coloured best bitter. A pleasant maltiness is offset by a firm but not overpowering bitterness and hints of orange.

Kentish Reserve (OG 1047, ABV 5%)
Reddish-amber-coloured premium bitter. Malty notes with flavours of peaches and plums, ending on a note of rich ruby port.

Whittingtons

See Untapped

Why Not

27 Redfern Road, Norwich, NR7 9RB
☎ (01603) 300786 🌐 thewhynotbrewery.co.uk

Why Not began brewing in 2005 on a 1.5-barrel plant located to the rear of the house of proprietor Colin Emms. In 2006 the brewery was extensively upgraded, doubling in capacity. In 2011 the brewery was moved to a new location in Thorpe St Andrew. RAIB

Wally's Revenge (OG 1040, ABV 4%)
An overtly bitter beer with a hoppy background. The bitterness holds on to the end as an increasing astringent dryness develops.

Roundhead Porter (OG 1045, ABV 4.5%)

Cavalier Red (OG 1047, ABV 4.7%)
Explosive fruity nose belies the gentleness of the taste. The summer fruit aroma dominates this red-gold-coloured brew. A sweet, fruity start disappears under a quick, bitter ending.

Norfolk Honey Ale (OG 1050, ABV 5%)
A golden-coloured beer with a honey nose. A definite hop edge leaves a honey aftertaste.

Chocolate Nutter (OG 1056, ABV 5.5%)

Wibblers SIBA

Goldsands Road, Southminster, Essex, CM0 7JW
☎ (01621) 772044 🌐 wibblers.com

Wibblers was established in 2007 and expanded to a 20-barrel plant in 2009. In 2016 the brewery moved to new premises in Southminster with a tap room. Production is currently 70 barrels per week. More than 100 outlets are supplied including many Gray & Sons pubs. ♦ RAIB GF

Dengie IPA (OG 1037, ABV 3.6%)
Malty and full flavoured with gentle bitterness and balanced sweetness.

Apprentice (OG 1039, ABV 3.9%)
Amber-coloured session beer with a hoppy aroma and light, malty taste.

Dengie Dark (OG 1039, ABV 4%)
Smooth, light and malty beer with subtle bitterness and balancing sweetness.

Dengie Gold (OG 1040, ABV 4%)
Golden in colour with a refreshing hop punch, citrus aroma and balanced bitterness.

Hop Black (OG 1041, ABV 4%)
A dark-coloured bitter that tastes light and hoppy.

Crafty Stoat (OG 1056, ABV 5.3%)

Wicked Hathern

See Staffordshire

Wickwar SIBA

Old Brewery, Station Road, Wickwar, Gloucestershire, GL12 8NB
☎ (01454) 292000 🌐 wickwarbrewing.co.uk

Wickwar was established as a 10-barrel brewery in 1990. In 2004 it expanded to 50 barrels. Moles Brewery and pubs were acquired in 2017, bringing its pub estate up to 20. 350 outlets are supplied on a regular basis and the beers are available nationally through most distributors and SIBA. ♦

BOB (OG 1040, ABV 4%)
Amber-coloured, this has a distinctive blend of hop, malt and apple/pear citrus fruits. The slightly sweet taste turns into a fine, dry bitterness, with a similar malty-lasting finish.

Cotswold Way (OG 1042, ABV 4.2%)
Amber-coloured, it has a pleasant aroma of pale malt, hop and fruit. Good dry bitterness in the taste with some sweetness. Similar though less sweet in the finish, with good hop content.

Falling Star (OG 1045, ABV 4.2%)
A golden-coloured premium beer with a floral aroma and a light malty finish.

Station Porter (OG 1061, ABV 6.1%)
Aromas of roasted malt, coffee, chocolate and rich fruits, and flavours of chocolate, liquorice, coffee and smoke. Smooth and warming roast and slightly sweet finish.

Brewed under the Moles brand name:

Gold (OG 1038, ABV 3.8%) ◆
Golden hoppy beer with subtle citrus fruit aroma & flavour derived from the Brewers Gold hops, with a malty background

Best (OG 1040, ABV 4%) ◆
An amber-coloured bitter, clean, dry and malty with some bitterness, and a delicate floral hop flavour.

Elmo's (OG 1044, ABV 4.4%) ◆
Medium-bodied bitter with subtle fruit aroma and flavours, leading to a long bitter finish.

Wigan (NEW)

The Old Brewery, Brewery Yard, off Wallgate, Wigan, WN1 1JU
☎ (01942) 234976

Local businessman Martin Blythe leased the now-defunct AllGates Brewery premises in 2018, including the acquisition of beers formerly brewed by AllGates. He will also be featuring some of his own beer recipes, developed by head brewer Jonathan Provost with Martin's input. !! ♦

Tag (OG 1036, ABV 3.6%) ◆
Dark brown-coloured beer with a malty, fruity aroma. Creamy and malty in taste, with blackberry fruits and a satisfying aftertaste.

California (OG 1037, ABV 3.8%) ◆
A pale yellow-coloured beer with a restrained hoppy and fruity aroma. It is clean and fresh-tasting, with hops and fruit in the mouth and a bitter, hoppy finish.

Junction (OG 1038, ABV 3.9%)
A full-flavoured, golden-coloured bitter with tastes of fruit and vanilla balanced by a resinous hop character.

Dry Bones (OG 1040, ABV 4%)
Light, golden-coloured and hoppy with tropical fruits and hints of melon.

Git Pit (ABV 4.3%)
A saffron-coloured ale with a smooth malt balance and floral aroma. A dry, spicy finish from the juniper berries and other gin botanicals.

Wild Beer SIBA

Lower Westcombe Farm, Evercreech, Somerset, BA4 6ER
☎ (01749) 838742 ☎ 07968 721841
wildbeerco.com

Brewing began in 2012 using a 24-hectolitre plant. Set on a Somerset farm, the brewery shares premises with Westcombe Dairy in an adjacent building. A wide range of beers is produced, including sour beers using alternative fermentation methods and unusual yeasts, alongside barrel-aging and a blending program. Seasonal wild ingredients are also foraged. Two pub restaurants are owned. ♦RAIB

Bibble (OG 1042, ABV 4.2%)
Pale ale with tropical fruits and mangos. Unfined and naturally hazy.

Scarlet Fever (OG 1048, ABV 4.8%)
A well-balanced ale with hops complementing the caramel and bready sweetness of the malts.

Fresh (OG 1055, ABV 5.5%)

Madness IPA (OG 1068, ABV 6.8%)

Wild Boar

Wild Boar, Crook Road, Bowness-on-Windermere, Cumbria, LA23 3NF ☎ 08458 504604
englishlakes.co.uk

Brewing began in 2013 at the Wild Boar, a large, traditional Lakeland luxury hotel. The hotel is part of the English Lakes Hotels group and supplies beers to hotels within the group. ♦

Wild Card SIBA

Unit 2, Lockwood Way, Blackhorse Road, Walthamstow, London, E17 5RB ☎ 07982 402650
wildcardbrewery.co.uk

Wild Card began brewing in 2013, initially using spare capacity at several breweries in and around London. It now has its own six-barrel plant in Walthamstow.

Pale Amrarillo (ABV 3.4%)

Jack of Clubs (ABV 4.5%) ◆
Complex ruby-coloured best bitter with a malty nose. Flavour has hints of chocolate, citrus and malt and a slightly bitter finish.

King of Hearts (ABV 4.5%) ◆
Easy-drinking beer with a lager character in the lemony flavour, which is sweet and biscuity. Clean, dry finish.

Ace of Spades (ABV 4.7%) ◆
Black-coloured porter with a fruity nose overlaid with a little roast. Liquorice, caramelised fruit and roasted malt flavour. Lingering dryness.

Queen of Diamonds (ABV 5%) ◆
Smooth golden ale with strong citrus aroma and flavour alongside biscuit notes. The finish is dry with a little bitterness.

Wild Horse SIBA

Unit 4, Cae Bach Builder Street, Llandudno, LL30 1DR
☎ (01492) 868292 wildhorsebrewing.co.uk

Small brewery concentrating on supplying KeyKeg and bottled beers to local bars and off-licences. All products are unfiltered and unpasteurised. ♦

Wild Weather SIBA

Unit 19, Easter Park, Benyon Road, Aldermaston, Berkshire, RG7 2PQ
☎ (0118) 970 1837 wildweatherales.com

Wild Weather was established in 2012 on the Hampshire/Berkshire border. !! ♦V

Serendipity (OG 1037, ABV 3.9%)
A fruity golden ale.

Betrayal (OG 1039, ABV 4%)
Tropical fruity flavours of limes, pineapple, mango and orange with a long-lasting hop tang.

Obscure 80's Reference (ABV 5%)
A smooth, hazy beer bursting with passion fruit, pine and berry flavours.

Shepherd's Warning (OG 1056, ABV 5.6%)
A smooth, rich IPA with strong hoppy flavours of grapefruit, peach and mango.

Wildcraft

Foragers' Rest, Buxton, Norfolk, NR10 5JD
☎ (01603) 278054 ☎ 07584 308850
🌐 wildcraftbrewery.co.uk

Wildcraft was set up in 2016 and uses as much foraged and locally sourced ingredients as possible to produce its beers.

Wilde Child

Armley Road, Leeds, West Yorkshire, LS12 2DR
☎ 07908 419028 🌐 wildechildbrewing.co.uk

Microbrewery that produces strong keg and cask ales with a wide variety of flavours. The majority of beers are in excess of 6% ABV and the emphasis is on bold tasting IPAs. A move to a larger unit has enabled production to increase substantially.

Wilderness (NEW)

Unit 54, Mochdre Industrial Estate, Newtown, SY16 4LE
☎ (01686) 449020

Wilderness began brewing in 2018 using a custom-made five-barrel plant. The brewery focuses on seasonal, barrel-aged and mixed fermentation beers. Belgian and farmhouse-style beers make up the majority of the range. ♦V

Motueka Grisette (ABV 3.8%)

Southern Pale (ABV 4.3%)

Keller Weiss (ABV 5.1%)

Equinox Saison (ABV 5.2%)

Wildside

See Brightside

Williams Bros SIBA

New Alloa Brewery, Kelliebank, Alloa, FK10 1NT
☎ (01259) 725511 🌐 williamsbrosbrew.com

A brotherhood of brewers, creating unique beers. Bruce and Scott Williams started brewing Heather Ale in 1988. A range of indigenous, historic ales have been added since. Hundreds of cask ale outlets are supplied worldwide. Contact the brewery for the latest cask beers available. ‼♦

Harvest Sun (OG 1041, ABV 3.9%)

Williams Gold (OG 1040, ABV 3.9%)
Golden-coloured session beer with a crisp mouthfeel and lemon hop aromas.

Fraoch Heather Ale (OG 1041, ABV 4.1%)
The unique taste of heather flowers is noticeable in this beer. A fine floral aroma and spicy taste give character to this speciality beer.

Williams Black (OG 1042, ABV 4.2%)
A light-bodied, rich, dark-coloured ale in the style of Czech dark lagers. Aromatic and full-flavoured with coffee and chocolate undertones and a blackcurrant aroma.

Birds & Bees (OG 1044, ABV 4.3%)
A bright golden ale with a late infusion of elderflowers and lemon zest. Fruity and aromatic.

Cock O' the Walk (OG 1042, ABV 4.3%)

Kelpie (OG 1045, ABV 4.4%)
A rich, dark chocolate ale, which has the aroma of a fresh sea breeze and a distinctive malty texture.

Williams Red (OG 1045, ABV 4.5%)
A rich, amber-coloured beer with aromas of caramel, malt and sweet berries giving way to a palate of biscuit malts, woody and fruity hops.

Joker IPA (OG 1050, ABV 5%)
A well-balanced IPA. Gold-coloured and fruity on the nose with hints of cedar.

Seven Giraffes (OG 1051, ABV 5.1%)
A golden-coloured IPA with aromas of elderflower and citrus hops, followed by sweet caramel. On the tongue the biscuity malts are perfectly balanced with the bitterness of the hops.

Midnight Sun (OG 1058, ABV 5.6%)
A rich, black-coloured, smooth porter with an after-bite of fresh root ginger.

Willy's

17 High Cliff Road, Cleethorpes, Lincolnshire, DN35 8RQ
☎ (01472) 602145

The brewery opened in 1989 to provide beer mainly for its in-house pub in Cleethorpes, although some beer is sold in the free trade. It has a five-barrel plant with maximum capacity of 15 barrels a week. The brewery can be viewed at any time from pub or street. ‼♦

Willy's Brew (NEW)

Rose & Crown, 2 Oxford Road, Stone, Buckinghamshire, HP17 8PB
☎ (01296) 749160 🌐 roseandcrownstone.co.uk/willys-brew.asp

A microbrewery based at the Rose & Crown, Stone. Brewing began in 2017 on an 80-litre plant.

Wily Fox SIBA

1 Kellet Close, Wigan, WN5 0LP
☎ (01942) 215525 🌐 wilyfoxbrewery.co.uk

Brewing commenced in 2016 in Wigan. The head brewer was formerly from Thwaites (qv). ‼♦

Blonde Vixen (OG 1039.5, ABV 3.8%)
A blonde session ale, light and refreshing with a spicy citrus character and grapefruit overtones.

Prohibition APA (OG 1041, ABV 3.9%)
A classic American-style pale ale with pungent grapefruit notes.

Crafty Fox (OG 1042.5, ABV 4%)
A full-bodied bitter ale with a spicy, earthy aroma.

The Fox Hat (OG 1044, ABV 4.2%)
A hop-infused golden ale that is bitter and zesty with spicy citrus and grapefruit notes.

Karma Citra (OG 1044.5, ABV 4.3%)
A complex golden ale with intense citrus and tropical fruit flavours.

Wimbledon SIBA

8 College Fields, Prince George's Road, Colliers Wood, London, SW19 2PT
☎ (020) 3674 9786 🌐 wimbledonbrewery.com

Set up by Mark Gordon after a 23 year career in the City, Wimbledon began production in 2015 with former Young's brewer Derek Prentice at the helm of a brand new 30-barrel plant. The brewery expanded in 2017 with two new 60-barrel fermenters. !! ♦ RAIB

Common PA (ABV 3.7%)
Well-balanced, gold-coloured bitter with mandarin and hoppy flavours and aroma. Floral note in the lingering finish with some dry bitterness.

Copper Leaf (OG 1040, ABV 4%)
Burst of citrus, floral and tropical flavours overlay the complex malt characters of rye, caramel and spice. A refreshingly dry finish.

Tower SPA (ABV 4.6%)
Fruit and honey aroma. Flavour has a balanced malt and hoppy character with a bittersweet finish with some fading orange notes.

Quartermaine IPA (ABV 5.8%)
Amber-coloured beer with slight sweetness complementing citrus and summer fruits plus spicy hops. Fruit, spice and bittersweet finish. Hoppy nose.

Wincle SIBA

Tolls Farm Barn, Dane Bridge, Wincle, Cheshire, SK11 0QE
☎ (01260) 227777 ☎ 07701 075368
🌐 winclebeer.co.uk

Wincle Beer Company was set up in 2008 in a redundant milking parlour on a working farm located within the Peak District National Park. The brewery now operates a 15-barrel plant in Wincle using water from its own borehole. !! ♦ RAIB

Waller (OG 1038, ABV 3.8%)
A pale-coloured and refreshing beer with a distinctive hop character.

Rambler (ABV 4%)
A well-balanced beer with autumn fruit hoppiness.

Sir Philip (OG 1041, ABV 4.2%)

Wibbly Wallaby (OG 1043, ABV 4.4%)
A full-bodied, golden-coloured beer with fruity, hoppy overtones and a dry, slightly biscuity finish.

Burke's Special (ABV 5%)
A chestnut-coloured English special bitter with a full malty and fruity taste.

Windermere

See Watermill

Windmill SIBA

Standish Hall Farm, Beech Walk, Standish, WN6 0YQ
☎ (01257) 472482 ☎ 07831 225656
🌐 windmillbrewery.co.uk

Brewing began in 2016 in converted farm buidlings near Standish. Run by the owner of the Windmill pub in Parbold, beers are supplied to the Windmill and other local free trade outlets, mainly in Merseyside, West Lancashire and Wigan. !!

Deckhand (OG 1038, ABV 3.8%)

Autumn Gold (ABV 3.9%)
Medium bitterness and a refreshing hoppy flavour.

Duke of Lancaster's Ale (ABV 4%)

Anderson Amber Bitter (OG 1046, ABV 4.4%)

Liverpool Porter (OG 1049, ABV 4.5%)
A creamy, bitter porter.

Taonga (ABV 4.5%)

Windmill Hill (NEW) SIBA

Garage Unit, 11 Williams Road, Radford Semele, Warwickshire, CV31 1UR
☎ (01926) 355450 🌐 whbrewery.co.uk

Windmill Hill is an independent microbrewery using a one-barrel plant brewing small batch beers. Around 30 outlets are supplied direct. RAIB V

Pump Room Porter (OG 1042, ABV 4%)

Chesterton IPA (OG 1043, ABV 4.2%)

American Session IPA (OG 1046, ABV 4.5%)

Grindstone APA (OG 1046, ABV 4.5%)

Windsor & Eton SIBA

Unit 1, Vansittart Estate, Duke Street, Windsor, Berkshire, SL4 1SE
☎ (01753) 854075 🌐 webrew.co.uk

Four friends, including two fully-qualified brewers, set up the brewery in 2010 though their brewing experience goes back to the original Courage Brewery. In 2018 it was granted a Royal Warrant as Brewer to Her Majesty the Queen. The purpose-built plant is 18 barrels, which supplies around 300 outlets in London and the Thames Valley area. Craft beers are produced under the Uprising name. !! ♦ RAIB

ParkLife (OG 1037, ABV 3.2%)
A full-flavoured, light ale with a citrus aroma and taste.

Knight of the Garter (OG 1036.5, ABV 3.8%)
Hoppy golden ale with grapefruit notes. Dry, refreshing finish.

Windsor Knot (OG 1039, ABV 4%)
Amber-coloured ale with a grapefruit aroma. An initially sweet malt and fruit taste followed by a mild bitter finish.

Guardsman (OG 1041, ABV 4.2%)
A tangy best bitter with a fresh hoppy finish.

Conqueror (OG 1049, ABV 5%)
A black IPA. Malty and hoppy with berry notes. A full, rounded, slightly dry finish.

Conqueror 1075 (OG 1075, ABV 7.4%)
A black IPA, the taste is chocolate and roasted malts, dominated by hop aroma and flavour.

Brewed under the Uprising brand name:

All Day Pale Ale (ABV 2.7%)
A pale ale with a huge hoppy character.

Windswept SIBA

Unit B, 13 Coulardbank Industrial Estate, Lossiemouth, IV31 6NG
☎ (01343) 814310 ☎ 07896 897944
🌐 windsweptbrewing.co.uk

THE BREWERIES

Windswept began brewing in 2012 using a 10-barrel plant installed by John Trow of Oban Ales. It is situated near the gates of RAF Lossiemouth and run by two former Tornado pilots who are CAMRA members. ‼ RAIB

Blonde (OG 1039, ABV 4%)
Smooth, golden, citrus hoppy brew with hints of peach. Slight malty background.

APA (OG 1046, ABV 5%)
Good mix of malts and grapefruited hop throughout. Tangy finish.

Weizen (OG 1052, ABV 5.2%)
Cloudy wheat beer full of bananas and pear drops with a hint of spices.

Wolf (OG 1064, ABV 6%)
Dark-coloured, strong-tasting, slightly sweet, roasted malty brew with chocolate and a vanilla coffee background.

Windy SIBA

Volunteer Inn, New Road, Seavington St Michael, Somerset, TA19 0QE
☎ (01460) 240126 thevolly.co.uk

The brewery was established at the Volunteer Inn in 2011 using a four-barrel plant. The name stems from the time when alterations were carried out to the back of the pub and the workmen suffered extremes of varying weather conditions. All beers are named with a weather theme. ‼ ♦

Winster Valley

Brown Horse Inn, Winster, Cumbria, LA23 3NR
☎ (01539) 443443 winstervalleybrewery.co.uk

Winster Valley was established in 2009 using a 2.5-barrel plant at the Brown Horse Inn in Winster. Brewing is currently suspended. ‼

Winter's

8 Keelan Close, Norwich, NR6 6QZ
☎ (01603) 787820 wintersbrewery.com

Winter's was established in 2001 by David Winter, who had previous award-winning success as a brewer for both Woodforde's and Chalk Hill breweries. Winter's ales have won many awards, with David now passing his brewing knowledge to his son, Mark, an award-winning brewer in his own right. ♦

Mild (OG 1036.5, ABV 3.6%)
A long-lasting, biscuity roast backbone. Caramel notes give depth as a growing hoppy bitterness adds complexity to the finish.

Cloudburst (OG 1037.5, ABV 3.7%)
Copper-coloured with a malty nose. A bitter beginning with malt and hop notes ends in a long, dry finale.

Bitter (OG 1038.5, ABV 3.8%)
Gentle, easy-drinking beer with a soft strawberry bouquet. Sweet biscuity notes develop to augment the hoppy, increasingly citrus base.

Geniuss (OG 1041.5, ABV 4.1%)
A dark brown-coloured stout that has a smooth mouthfeel with a grainy edge. Roast dominates throughout but is balanced by a mix of malt, a bittersweet fruitiness and an increasingly nutty finish.

Golden (OG 1041.9, ABV 4.1%)
Just a hint of hops in the aroma. The initial taste combines a dry bitterness with a fruity apple buttress. The finish slowly subsides into a long, dry bitterness.

Revenge (OG 1047.9, ABV 4.7%)
Blackcurrant notes give depth to the inherent maltiness of this pale brown-coloured beer. A bittersweet background becomes more pronounced as the fruitiness gently wanes.

Storm Force (OG 1053, ABV 5.3%)
A well-defined, sweetish brew. Hops and vine fruit give depth to the malty backbone of this pale brown-coloured strong beer. All flavours hold up well as the finish develops a warming softness.

Wintrip

7 Copenhagen Street, Worcester, WR1 2HB ☎ 07964 196194 wintripbrew.co

Wintrip began brewing in 2014 as Three Shires Brewery on a hand-built plant in Worcester before moving to new premises and subsequent name change. Local outlets are supplied.

Kenelm (OG 1041, ABV 3.8%)
Golden in colour, a smoky aroma and initial sweetness gives way to a malt whiskey flavour with peat and fruit undertones. Dry hop and peaty finish.

Hafren (OG 1043, ABV 4%)
Tawny in colour, butterscotch aroma with caramel flavours predominating balanced by a slightly hoppy finish.

Wiper and True SIBA

2 – 8 York Street, St Werburghs, Bristol, BS2 9XT
☎ (0117) 941 2501 wiperandtrue.com

Originally launched in 2012 by Michael Wiper as a cuckoo brewery, Wiper and True has operated since 2015 using its own 20-barrel plant. It produces an ever-changing range of bottle-conditioned beers, with a small amount going into casks. The beers are available locally in Bristol/Bath, nationally and internationally. ‼ RAIB

Wishbone SIBA

2a Worth Bridge Industrial Estate, Chesham Street, Keighley, West Yorkshire, BD21 4LG ☎ 07867 419445 wishbonebrewery.co.uk

Established in 2015 and run by a husband and wife team with many years previous experience in the brewing industry, beers are brewed on a modern 10-barrel brew plant. The on-site bar is open to the public two days each month.

Blonde (OG 1037, ABV 3.6%)
A hoppy golden ale with with a strong citrus character. A bitter, hoppy and slightly astringent finish.

Volk (OG 1038, ABV 3.9%)

Flux (OG 1041, ABV 4.1%)

Drover (OG 1043, ABV 4.2%)

Tiller Pin (OG 1041, ABV 4.2%)

Abyss (OG 1048, ABV 4.3%)
Caramel and coffee bean aroma in a stout of chocolate and liquorice leading to a malty finish.

Gumption (OG 1046, ABV 4.5%) ◆
Well-balanced, amber-coloured best bitter. Look for hints of dried fruit, biscuit and nuts, underpinned by dry hoppiness, leading to a bitter finish.

Witham

c/o The Chicken Sheds, Upp Hall Farm, Salmons Lane, Coggeshall, Essex, CO6 1RY
☎ (01376) 563123 ☎ 07824 698235
✉ glennackerman15@gmail.com

Brewing started in 2012, using a 0.5-barrel plant at the Woolpack Inn, Witham. In 2015 it began using spare capacity at the Red Fox Brewery (qv). The beer continues to be available at the Woolpack.

Scruffy (OG 1041, ABV 3.9%)

Witham Gold (OG 1041, ABV 4.1%)
A light, refreshing, golden-coloured beer with a citrus aftertaste.

No Name (OG 1043, ABV 4.3%)
Malty roasted flavours giving way to a surprisingly hoppy best bitter.

Withnell's SIBA

Unit 35, The Old Mill Industrial Estate, School Lane, Bamber Bridge, PR5 6SY
☎ (01254) 830989 ☎ 07787 567471
🌐 withnells.co.uk

Withnell's was established in 2016 using a five-barrel plant. Beers are supplied direct to pubs within a 20-mile radius of the brewery and occasionally beyond.

Hoppy Fettler (ABV 4.3%)
A hoppy pale ale packed with tropical hops.

Push Iron (ABV 4.5%)

Wizard (NEW)

Unit 4, Lundy View, Mullacott Cross Industrial Estate, Ilfracombe, Devon, EX34 8PY ☎ 07584 093470
✉ wizardbrewery@gmail.com

Originally established in 2003 in Warwickshire, Wizard relocated to Devon in 2007 and was sold to Carly O'Callaghan in 2017. !! ♦

Lundy's Gold (OG 1042, ABV 4.1%)

Druid's Fluid (OG 1048.5, ABV 5%)

Wobbly

Unit 22c, Beech Business Park, Tillington Road, Hereford, HR4 9QJ
☎ (01432) 355496 ☎ 07702 739357

Wobbly began brewing in 2013 using a 2.5-barrel plant. There is an on-site bottling/canning plant in production, which undertakes contract work. A new 30-barrel plant is operational and the brewery has recently taken on the tenancy of a local pub.
!! ♦ RAIB

Gold (OG 1036.5, ABV 4.2%)

Welder (OG 1046.5, ABV 4.8%)

Wold Top SIBA

Hunmanby Grange, Wold Newton, East Yorkshire, YO25 3HS
☎ (01723) 892222 🌐 woldtopbrewery.co.uk

An integral part of Hunmanby Grange Farm, Wold Top brewed its first ale in 2003 and uses home and Wolds-grown malting barley and chalk filtered water from the farm's own borehole. Now brewing on a 40-barrel plant, the range includes special edition cask and bottled beers plus three gluten-free beers. The brewery installed a bottling line in 2007 and contract bottles for other breweries. !! ♦ GF

Bitter (OG 1036, ABV 3.7%)
A crisp, clean, aromatic session bitter. Full-flavoured with a long, hoppy finish.

Anglers Reward (OG 1039, ABV 4%)
A refreshing, golden-coloured pale ale with a fruity bitterness and lingering aftertaste.

Wolds Way (OG 1039, ABV 4%)
A golden-coloured pale ale, triple-hopped to give a fruity bitterness.

Headland Red (OG 1042, ABV 4.3%)
A full-bodied, mellow and malty dark red-coloured ale.

Wold Gold (OG 1046, ABV 4.8%)
A light-coloured beer with a soft, fruity flavour and a hint of spice.

Wolf SIBA

Decoy Farm, Old Norwich Road, Besthorpe, Norfolk, NR17 2LA
☎ (01953) 457775 🌐 wolfbrewery.com

The brewery was founded in 1995 on a 20-barrel plant, which was upgraded to a 25-barrel plant in 2006. It moved to its current site in 2013. More than 300 outlets are supplied. ♦

Edith Cavell (OG 1037, ABV 3.7%) ◆
Hoppy, peppery nose flows into taste. Malt, caramel and bitterness give depth and complexity. Crisp finish with a hoppy edge.

Golden Jackal (OG 1039, ABV 3.7%) ◆
A hoppy, citrus nose and first taste. Increasingly dry bitter ending as citrus notes fade.

Wolf in Sheep's Clothing (OG 1039, ABV 3.7%) ◆
Strong, fruity nose with roast. A strong caramel beginning with a bitter roast counterpoint. Gently tapering finish. Increasing raspberry sweetness.

Lavender Honey (OG 1038, ABV 3.8%) ◆
Malty caramel aroma leads into a bittersweet beginning with background honey notes. A long, drying finish.

Ale (OG 1039, ABV 3.9%)

Battle of Britain (OG 1039, ABV 3.9%)
A copper-coloured, full-bodied best bitter with English hops. A donation is made from each sale to the RAF Association Wings appeal.

Lupus Lupus (OG 1042, ABV 4.2%) ◆
Hops, with a citrus edge, dominate both aroma and taste. A biscuity background disappears quickly in a short, sharp finish.

Sirius Dog Star (OG 1044, ABV 4.4%) ◆
Roast, coffee and caramel aroma flows into a similar first taste. Big mouthfeel with a slightly sour caramel-enhanced finale.

Sly Wolf (OG 1041, ABV 4.4%)
A light-coloured blonde beer with hints of lime.

Straw Dog (OG 1045, ABV 4.5%) ◆

Delicately flavoured with a fruity character. A redcurrant aroma gives way to marmalade and hops. A strong, increasingly bitter finale.

Mad Wolf (OG 1048, ABV 4.7%)
A smooth, malty dark ale with a moreish aftertaste.

Granny Wouldn't Like It (OG 1049, ABV 4.8%) ◆
Complex, with a malty bouquet. Increasing bitterness is softened by malt as a gentle, fruity sweetness adds depth.

Woild Moild (OG 1048, ABV 4.8%) ◆
Heavy and complex with malt, vine fruit, bitterness and roast notes vying for dominance. Increasingly dry finish.

Contract brewed for City of Cambridge Brewery:

Boathouse (OG 1037, ABV 3.7%)
A light copper-coloured session bitter with a pleasant aroma from the unique blend of hops and malt.

Hobson's Choice (OG 1041, ABV 4.2%)
A light golden ale with a refreshing flowery nose and slightly citrus aftertaste.

Atom Splitter (OG 1045, ABV 4.5%)
An amber-coloured beer bursting with hoppiness and character.

Parkers Piece (OG 1050, ABV 5%)
A dark, rich, ruby-coloured, fruity bitter.

Wood

Wistanstow, Shropshire, SY7 8DG
☎ (01588) 672523 ⊕ woodbrewery.co.uk

The brewery opened in 1980 in buildings next to the Plough Inn, the brewery's only tied house. Steady growth over the years included the acquisition of the Sam Powell Brewery in 1991. Around 200 outlets are supplied. !! ♦

Parish Bitter (OG 1038, ABV 3.8%) ◆
A blend of malt and hops with a bitter aftertaste.

Shropshire Lass (OG 1040, ABV 4%)
A golden ale with zesty bitterness.

Beauty (OG 1042, ABV 4.2%)
A fusion of fruity hops give a lingering bitter aftertaste together with a well-rounded maltiness.

Shropshire Lad (OG 1045, ABV 4.5%)

Tom Wood's

See Lincolnshire Craft

Woodcote Manor

Kidderminster Road, Dodford, Worcestershire, B61 9DY
☎ (01527) 558141 ☎ 07779 166174
⊕ woodcotemanor.com

⊗ Opened in 2015 in former dairy outbuildings attached to the brewer's house. The one-barrel plant can produce 20 firkins a week. It is run by a keen homebrewer who turned his hobby into a business, using locally sourced ingredients including own grown hops. The regular beers are distributed to a number of local pubs. ♦ RAIB

SSS (OG 1038, ABV 3.8%)

Half Cut (OG 1042, ABV 4.2%)

Single Hop (OG 1044, ABV 4.4%) ◆
Well-balanced, golden-coloured bitter, light hop aromas with subtle melon, the initial sweetness is followed by a hint of ginger with hops predominating. Long and smooth hoppy finish.

Weavers Exclusive (OG 1044, ABV 4.4%) ◆
Straw-coloured, golden-coloured bitter in which dry hop flavours predominate throughout, noticeable grapefruit background in the taste and a long, dry finish.

IPA (OG 1046, ABV 4.6%) ◆
Golden-coloured, well-balanced and hoppy, grapefruit aromas are followed by a pronounced hop and slightly spicy taste, with a lingering bitter finish.

Oatmeal Stout (OG 1049, ABV 4.9%) ◆
Dark in colour, roasted malt, chocolate and coffee tones are evident in the aroma and flavour, leading to a satisfying, slightly bitter finish.

Woodforde's SIBA

Broadland Brewery, Woodbastwick, Norfolk, NR13 6SW
☎ (01603) 720353 ⊕ woodfordes.co.uk

⊗ Founded in 1981 by two members of the Homebrewers' Society, Woodforde's is named after Parson Woodforde, the 18th century Norfolk diarist with a penchant for real ale. In 1989 the brewery moved to its current home at Woodbastwick, where it has its own boreholes and brews using locally-grown Maris Otter. Investment in 2001 and 2008 more than doubled the production capacity. The brewery tap, the Fur & Feather, is located next door, and more than 600 outlets are supplied on a regular basis. !! ♦ RAIB

Mardler's (OG 1036, ABV 3.5%) ◆
Full, malty aroma with hop and caramel. Sweet biscuit flavour with a bitter hoppiness. Caramel notes and sweet malty finish.

Wherry (OG 1037.5, ABV 3.8%) ◆
Malty aroma infused with summer fruits. Smooth and creamy with a huge biscuit base and peachy elements. Hoppy bittersweet ending.

Once Bittern (OG 1040, ABV 4%) ◆
A light malty nose. A dark marmalade tang gives an edge to the dominant malt character. Long, bittersweet ending.

Sundew (OG 1039, ABV 4.1%) ◆
Hops emerge from a mix of malt, fruit and bitterness to provide a cutting edge to both taste and aroma.

Reedlighter (OG 1040, ABV 4.2%) ◆
A hop, lemon and biscuit nose. Well-balanced with citrus and hop softened by a biscuity background. Short lemon ending.

Bure Gold (OG 1043, ABV 4.3%) ◆
A bouncy orange and biscuit bouquet. A bittersweet hoppy beginning develops into a full-bodied marmalade ending.

Nelsons Revenge (OG 1045, ABV 4.5%) ◆
Malt aroma with hop. Initially malt and caramel float over a slightly hoppy, sweetish character. Tapering biscuity finish with caramel.

Norfolk Nog (OG 1047, ABV 4.6%) ◆
Echoes of Pontefract cake dominate. A plummy sweetness is aided by a dry bitterness and a hint of caramel.

Woodman's

Unit 5, Viaduct Works, Frog Lane, Ponsanooth, Cornwall, TR3 7JW ☎ 07941 069890
🌐 woodmanswildale.com

Stuart Woodman is well regarded as a forager. In 2016 he took over Verdant Brewery's former premises to start brewing beers in small batches featuring foraged ingredients. Regular beer and food events are held and brewery visits welcomed. ‼ ♦ RAIB

Wooha

Upper Hempriggs Farm, Kinloss, IV36 2UB
☎ (01667) 459929 ☎ 07811 260732
🌐 woohabrewing.com

Wooha opened in 2015 using a 10-barrel plant. It specialises in producing bottle-conditioned ales. Cask-conditioned beers are brewed on demand for beer festivals. Pubs and retail outlets are supplied locally, in Nairn, and across Scotland. In 2017 the brewery moved to larger premises. RAIB

IPA (ABV 6.2%)
Malty background but with a strong peachy hop character in this pale brown-coloured IPA.

Worcester

Arch 49, Cherry Tree Walk, Worcester, WR1 3AU
☎ 07906 432049 🌐 worcesterbrewingco.co.uk

A small brewery in the heart of Worcester and home to Sabrina Ales. A range of beers brewed in rotation using traditional British hops, with a loose association to the English Civil War.

Holy Ground (OG 1042, ABV 4.2%)

Powick Porter (ABV 4.5%)

1651 (ABV 5.1%)

Sabrina's Dark Ruby Ale (ABV 5.5%)

Working Hand SIBA

Three Horseshoes, Pit House Lane, Leamside, DH4 6QQ
☎ (0191) 584 2394 ☎ 07703 337556
🌐 threehorseshoesleamside.co.uk

Brewing began in 2012 using a 2.5-barrel plant. Beers are available at the Three Horseshoes as well as the four other pubs in the group. The brewery was renamed the Working Hand Brewery in 2016 when Matthew Booth took over the brewing. In 2018 it upgraded to a seven-barrel plant.

World's End

Crown Inn, 60 Wilcot Road, Pewsey, Wiltshire, SN9 5EL
☎ (01672) 562653 🌐 thecrowninnpewsey.com

⊗ World's End Ales was established in 2009 on a one-barrel plant at the rear of the Crown Inn in Pewsey. World's End is the 18th-century name for the area in which the brewery is located. ‼ ♦

Worsthorne SIBA

Unit 11, Siberia Mill, Holgate Street, Briercliffe, Lancashire, BB10 2HQ
☎ (01282) 422588 ☎ 07815 708289
🌐 worsthornebrewingcompany.co.uk

Worsthorne began brewing in 2011 using a 5.5-barrel plant. The brewery moved to larger premises behind the original building in 2014. An expansion to a 10-barrel plant was carried out in 2016, including a licensed visitor centre. More than 150 outlets are supplied. ‼ ♦

Gold (OG 1036, ABV 3.6%)
Lightly bittered golden ale with a spicy aroma.

Packhorse (OG 1037, ABV 3.7%)
Pale amber-coloured ale with a subtle earthy bitterness and floral spicy finish.

Some Like It Blond (OG 1039, ABV 3.9%)
A blonde beer brewed using German hops with a lingering, dry aftertaste.

Redman (OG 1042, ABV 4.2%)
Smooth, light bitter. Overtones of honey and citrus with a satisfying aftertaste and subtle lingering bitterness.

Old Trout (OG 1045, ABV 4.5%)

Blackthorn Stout (OG 1049, ABV 4.9%)
Rich, dark-coloured stout with distinct chocolate and liquorice flavours. A hint of ripe berries and a smooth bitter aftertaste.

Colliers Clog (OG 1055, ABV 5.5%)
A strong pale ale lightly bittered with spicy overtones and a citrus finish.

Worthington's

See Heritage

Wrexham Lager

42 St Georges Crescent, Wrexham, LL13 8DB
☎ (01978) 266222 🌐 wrexhamlager.co.uk

Brewing began in 2011. No real ale.

Wriggle Valley SIBA

Unit 4, The Sidings, Station Road, Stalbridge, Dorset, DT10 2RQ
☎ (01963) 363343 ☎ 07952 198777
🌐 wrigglevalleybrewery.co.uk

⊗ Wriggle Valley began brewing in 2014 based in a converted garage at the owner's house but relocated in 2017 to an industrial unit using a three-barrel plant. Beers are mainly supplied within a 15-mile radius of the brewery. ♦ RAIB

Golden Bear (ABV 4%)

Ryme Rambler (OG 1040, ABV 4%)

Dorset Pilgrim (ABV 4.2%)
Session bitter with a good level of bitterness and some fruit.

Copper Hoppa (OG 1047, ABV 4.5%)
A full-bodied, dark copper-coloured ale with big fruit aromas and flavour.

Valley Gold (ABV 4.5%)
An orange-coloured best bitter with citrus flavours.

Wriggly Monkey

Bicester Heritage Centre, Launton, Oxfordshire, OX26 5HA ☎ 07590 749062
🌐 wrigglymonkeybrewery.com

⊗ Based at a car heritage centre and named after a component of a chain-drive mechanism, the brewery was established in 2018.

George Wright SIBA

Unit 11, Diamond Business Park, Sandwash Close, Rainford, Merseyside, WA11 8LY
☎ (01744) 886686 🌐 georgewrightbrewing.co.uk

George Wright started production in 2003. The original 2.5-barrel plant was replaced by a five-barrel one, which has since been upgraded again to 25 barrels. ‼ ♦

Drunken Duck (OG 1040, ABV 3.9%)
Fruity, gold-coloured bitter beer with good hop and a dry aftertaste. Some acidity.

Longboat (OG 1040, ABV 3.9%)
Good hoppy bitter with grapefruit and an almost tart bitterness throughout. Some astringency in the aftertaste. Well-balanced, light and refreshing with a good mouthfeel and long, dry finish.

Blonde Moment (OG 1040, ABV 4%)
A premium blonde beer. Light in colour, herbal nose with a sweet aftertaste.

Mild (OG 1042, ABV 4%)

Pipe Dream (OG 1044, ABV 4.3%)
Refreshing, hoppy best bitter with a fruity nose and grapefruit to the fore in the taste. Lasting dry, bitter finish.

Pure Blonde (OG 1045, ABV 4.6%)
A premium blonde ale, light with an earthy hop flavour.

Cheeky Pheasant (OG 1047, ABV 4.7%)
Light amber in colour, distinctive fruit, malty taste with a sweet aftertaste.

Roman Black (OG 1047, ABV 4.8%)
A dark-coloured premium ale, smooth and creamy leaving a long, malty,sweet taste.

Blue Moon (OG 1048, ABV 5%)
Easy-drinking, strong, gold-coloured beer. Good malt/bitter balance and well hopped.

Mocne Piwo (OG 1051, ABV 5%)
Strong ale, light amber in colour with a hoppy aftertaste.

Northern Lights (OG 1049, ABV 5.1%)
Strong ale, amber in colour. A strong citrus taste balanced by the bitter hop.

Wychwood

Eagle Maltings, The Crofts, Witney, Oxfordshire, OX28 4DP
☎ (01993) 890800 🌐 wychwood.co.uk

Wychwood brewery is located in the Cotswold market town of Witney. The brewers take inspiration from the myths and legends associated with the ancient medieval Wychwood forest. Part of Marston's PLC. ‼ ♦ RAIB

Hobgoblin Gold (OG 1042, ABV 4.2%)
Full of malty flavours. A mix of hops gives a refreshing bitterness and zesty aroma.

Hobgoblin (OG 1045, ABV 4.5%)

Wye Valley SIBA

Stoke Lacy, Herefordshire, HR7 4HG
☎ (01885) 490505 ☎ 07970 597937
🌐 wyevalleybrewery.co.uk

Founded in 1985 in the back of a village pub, this award-winning brewery is now producing around 250,000 pints per week and delivers direct to more than 1,200 pubs, including eight of its own. Its products are also available through selected wholesale and retail stockists. ‼ RAIB

Bitter (OG 1037, ABV 3.7%)
A beer whose aroma gives little hint of the bitter hoppiness that follows right through to the aftertaste.

The Hopfather (OG 1039, ABV 3.9%)
A smooth-bodied ale featuring a spicy, honey-pine and grapefruit flavour.

HPA (OG 1040, ABV 4%)
A pale, hoppy, malty brew with a hint of sweetness before a dry finish.

Golden Ale (OG 1042, ABV 4.2%)
A light, gold-coloured ale with a good hop character throughout.

Butty Bach (OG 1046, ABV 4.5%)
A burnished gold-coloured, full-bodied premium ale.

Wholesome Stout (OG 1046, ABV 4.6%)
A smooth and satisfying stout with a bitter edge to its roast flavours. The finish combines roast grain and malt.

IPA (OG 1058, ABV 6%)
A strong golden ale with a pronounced hop character.

Wylam SIBA

Palace of Arts, Exhibition Park, Newcastle upon Tyne, NE2 4PZ
☎ (0191) 650 0651 🌐 wylambrewery.co.uk

Wylam commenced brewing in 2000 on a 4.5-barrel plant. Originally brewing in Heddon-on-the-Wall in Northumberland, the brewery moved to Newcastle upon Tyne in 2016 with a new 30-barrel brew kit with an on-site brewery tap. ‼ ♦

Galatia (OG 1039, ABV 3.9%)
Light session pale ale with fresh orange shred stone fruit flavours and a clean, dry, fresh pine kick to the finish.

Gold Tankard (OG 1040, ABV 4%)
Fresh, clean flavour, full of hops. This golden ale has a hint of citrus in the finish.

Collingwood (OG 1041, ABV 4.1%)
Honey-coloured ale with a sweet tangerine aroma. Light and soft-bodied with a citrus zest, fresh pine flavour and a dry and bitter finish.

Angel (OG 1044, ABV 4.3%)
A pale copper-coloured ale with a citrus character aroma and finish.

Red Kite (OG 1046.5, ABV 4.5%)
A ruby-coloured ale where the hops are balanced by residual maltiness.

Swipe Right (OG 1049.2, ABV 4.7%)

A session pale ale with tropical hop notes of grapefruit, pineapple and kiwi.

Remain in Light (OG 1048, ABV 5%)

Le Saisonnier (OG 1052, ABV 5.4%)
Lemon balm and rosemary saison.

Puffing Billy (OG 1055, ABV 5.5%)
A smoked, black-coloured bitter with a mellow blend of malts. Notes of coffee, tobacco and dark chocolate with a hoppy finish.

Wyre Piddle

See Ambridge

XT SIBA

Notley Farm, Chearsley Road, Long Crendon, Buckinghamshire, HP18 9ER
☎ (01844) 208310 🌐 xtbrewing.com

⊗ XT started brewing in 2011 using an 18-barrel plant. It supplies direct to pubs in Buckinghamshire, Oxfordshire and the Midlands. Its brewery taproom sells a range of draught beers along with bottles and other gifts. A range of limited edition, one-off brews is produced under the Animal Brewing Co name. !! ♦ RAIB

Four (OG 1037, ABV 3.8%)
A balanced, mellow, session amber-coloured ale with pine and citrus hop notes.

Hop Kitty (OG 1038, ABV 3.9%)
A hugely hoppy, golden-coloured ale, bursting with intense tropical and citrus flavours.

One (OG 1041, ABV 4.2%)
Blonde beer with dry citrus, lemon and spice notes.

Three (OG 1041, ABV 4.2%)
An American-style pale ale with citrus and pine flavours, light biscuit malt character.

Two (OG 1041, ABV 4.2%)
Golden ale with chewy, juicy malts and a mellow, balanced hop character.

Eight (OG 1045, ABV 4.5%)
A full-bodied, dark-coloured porter with roast malt, coffee and bitter chocolate notes.

Fifteen (OG 1044, ABV 4.5%)
A pale amber-coloured IPA with caramel malt notes and a lasting floral, grassy hop character.

Six (OG 1045, ABV 4.5%)
A rich, ruby-coloured beer with a strong malt character and soft citrus hop finish.

Thirteen (OG 1044, ABV 4.5%)
A red-coloured ale, brewed with a range of citrus aromatic hops.

Five (OG 1052, ABV 5.5%)
An American-style, amber-coloured ale with intense hop character on a full-bodied malt base.

XPA (OG 1055, ABV 5.9%)
An American-style IPA. Clean malt character with an intense mix of aromatic fruity hops.

Xtreme

Unit 21, Alfric Square, Maxwell Road, Woodston, Peterborough, Cambridgeshire, PE2 7JP ☎ 07427 661839 🌐 xtremeales.com

⊗ Family-run, small, independent brewery, which supplies a wide range of beers to local pubs and beer festivals. In addition to its regular beers, it specialises in developing one-off brews for different festivals and occasions including the annual Whittlesea Straw Bear festival in January. Bumbling Brewery beers are also brewed for the Bumble Inn micropub, Peterborough. !! ♦

Pigeon Ale (OG 1043, ABV 4.3%)

Chocolate Stout (OG 1050, ABV 5%)

Evil Pigeon (OG 1055, ABV 5.5%)

Yaarbrew

c/o Pleasure Boat, Staithe Road, Hickling, Norfolk, NR12 0YW ☎ 07708 430230 🌐 yaarbrew.co.uk

⊗ Formed in 2016 by four work colleagues who had been keen homebrewers and real ale enthusiasts for a number of years. The 1.5-barrel plant is located in the former Post Office next to the Pleasure Boat Inn at Hickling Broad. Beer is available around Norfolk and further afield. RAIB

Ginger Porter (OG 1048, ABV 4.2%)
Rich, dark-coloured porter with root ginger added to give the beer some heat and sweetness.

Robust Porter (OG 1048, ABV 4.2%)
Rich, dark-coloured, full-bodied porter.

Citrus Gold (OG 1046, ABV 4.5%)
A rich, golden-coloured session beer with hints of orange, grapefruit and a scent of pine.

Smoked Chilli IPA (OG 1046, ABV 4.5%)
A smoky IPA with a touch of heat thanks to the green chillies added to the brew.

Yard of Ale

Surtees Arms, Chilton Lane, Ferryhill, DL17 0DH
☎ (01740) 655724 ☎ 07540 733513
🌐 thesurteesarms.co.uk

Established in 2008, the 2.5-barrel microbrewery supplies ales to its brewery tap, the Surtees Arms, beer festivals and to a growing number of pubs. !! ♦ RAIB

Reach for the Yard (ABV 3.8%)

Yard Dog Brown Ale (ABV 4%)

One Foot in the Yard (OG 1044, ABV 4.5%)
Premium golden ale. Fruity on the nose and palate with a sweet finish.

Yates' SIBA

Unit 4c, Langbridge Business Centre, Newchurch, Isle of Wight, PO36 0NP
☎ (01983) 867878 🌐 yates-brewery.co.uk

Brewing started in 2000 on a five-barrel plant at the Inn at St Lawrence. In 2009 it moved to Newchurch and upgraded to a 10-barrel plant. In 2015 the brewery was moved on to the same site as the wholesale unit at Newchurch. !! ♦ RAIB

Golden Bitter (OG 1040, ABV 4%)
Light, refreshing, golden-coloured bitter with fruity after tones and a subtle bitter finish.

Islander (OG 1040, ABV 4%)
An easy-drinking, amber-coloured ale with a full-bodied taste.

Beachcomber (OG 1043, ABV 4.3%)

Straw-coloured, easy-drinking ale with a distinctive fresh aroma and a crisp, clean hoppy finish.

Holy Joe (OG 1050, ABV 4.9%)
Amber-coloured ale with a bittersweet aftertaste. Ground coriander is added to the brew to give it an extra citrus, spicy finish.

Dark Side of the Wight (OG 1049, ABV 5%)
Malty milk chocolate at first in the nose, then plenty of orange fruit. Bitter, malty and toasted to taste, with perfumed bitter orange notes present.

Yelland Manor

Lower Yelland Farm, Yelland, Devon, EX31 3EN
☎ 07770 267592 ✉ yellandmanor@gmail.com

⊗ Located on the Taw Estuary and close to the Tarka Trail, this is a five-barrel plant in a converted milking parlour. The brewery began production in 2013 and now supplies a small number of local pubs and hotels. ♦

The Tarka Special (OG 1040, ABV 4.1%)

Standard (OG 1043, ABV 4.2%)

Yeovil SIBA

Unit 5, Bofors Park, Artillery Road, Lufton Trading Estate, Yeovil, Somerset, BA22 8YH
☎ (01935) 414888 🌐 yeovilales.com

⊗ Yeovil Ales was established in 2006 using an 18-barrel plant. More than 300 pubs are supplied in the South West. !! ♦ RAIB

Hopkandi (OG 1038, ABV 3.8%)
A pale-coloured bitter with citrus hops and a dry finish.

Star Gazer (OG 1042, ABV 4%)
Easy-drinking, tawny-coloured bitter. Malt and toffee in the aroma lead to a predominantly sweet flavour. Short bitter finish.

Summerset (OG 1041, ABV 4.1%)
Blonde ale with a fruity hop finish.

Lynx Wildcat (OG 1044, ABV 4.3%)
A bronze-coloured, full-bodied, hoppy bitter. Specialist malt provides a sweetness which is accompanied by grapefruit hop flavours.

Stout Hearted (OG 1045, ABV 4.3%)
A smooth, dark-coloured stout, full-bodied with rich roast flavours.

Ruby (OG 1047, ABV 4.5%)
Red-coloured bitter with rich malt depth.

POSH IPA (OG 1052, ABV 5.4%)
A strong IPA with a fruity body and hoppy finish.

Yetman's

Bayfield Farm Barns, Bayfield Brecks Farm, Bayfield, Norfolk, NR25 7DZ ☎ 07774 809016 🌐 yetmans.net

A 2.5-barrel plant built by Moss Brew was installed in restored medieval barns near Holt in 2005. The brewery supplies local free trade outlets. Bottle-conditioned beers are available in many Waitrose stores throughout the East Anglian area. RAIB

Red (OG 1036, ABV 3.8%)

Orange (OG 1042, ABV 4.2%)

Stout (OG 1042, ABV 4.2%)

Green (OG 1048, ABV 4.8%)

York SIBA

12 Toft Green, York, North Yorkshire, YO1 6JT
☎ (01904) 621162 🌐 york-brewery.co.uk

York started production in 1996. It was the first brewery in the city for 40 years and was acquired by Mitchell's of Lancaster in 2008. Five pubs are owned in York and Leeds. The 20-barrel plant has a viewing platform overlooking the conditioning and fermenting rooms. !! ♦

Guzzler (OG 1036, ABV 3.6%)
Refreshing golden ale with dominant hop and fruit flavours developing throughout.

Hansom Blonde (OG 1039, ABV 3.9%)
Creamy, fruity and refreshing beer with a light bitterness and hints of tropical fruit and citrus on the aftertaste.

Yorkshire Terrier (OG 1041, ABV 4.2%)
Refreshing and distinctive amber/gold-coloured beer where fruit and hops dominate the aroma and taste. Hoppy bitterness remains assertive in the aftertaste.

Centurion's Ghost Ale (OG 1051, ABV 5.4%)
Dark ruby in colour, full-tasting with a mellow roast malt character balanced by light bitterness and autumn fruit flavours that linger into the aftertaste.

Yorkshire SIBA

Brewery Wharf, 70 Humber Street, Fruit Market, Hull, East Yorkshire, HU1 1TU
☎ (01482) 618000 ☎ 07850 494990
✉ guy@yorkshirebrewing.co.uk

Brewing started in 2012 in the Fruit Market Arts Quarter of Hull using a six-barrel plant. Two of the beers are named in honour of Hull Minster. A bottling plant, tours and a retail outlet are established. Festivals and local outlets are supplied. !! ♦ RAIB

Mutiny (OG 1036, ABV 3.6%)
Based upon an old 1750 London porter recipe. Has a distinctive coffee aroma and chocolate flavour.

Supernatural Blonde (OG 1041, ABV 4.1%)

Mosaic (OG 1042, ABV 4.2%)
Easy-drinking session bitter with a mango, peach and tangerine finish.

Blackjack (OG 1046, ABV 4.5%)
A complex stout fortified with fresh blackberries, providing lasting fruit and chocolate characteristics.

Moondance (OG 1045, ABV 4.5%)
A blonde ale infused with passion fruit for a refreshing taste.

Oregon Gold (OG 1045, ABV 4.5%)
A cloudy, Belgian-style wheat beer with added coriander and curacao oranges.

Passion (OG 1045, ABV 4.5%)

Raspberry Tipple (OG 1048, ABV 4.8%)
A cloudy, Belgian-style wheat beer infused with raspberries.

Strawberry Blonde (OG 1048, ABV 4.8%)
A cloudy, Belgian-style wheat beer infused with strawberries.

Waverider (OG 1052, ABV 5.2%)

Shangri-la (OG 1067, ABV 6.7%)
A double IPA with tropical flavours and a lingering grapefruit finish.

Yorkshire Brewhouse (NEW)

The Brewery, Goulton Street, Hull, East Yorkshire, HU3 4DD
☎ (01482) 755199 🌐 yorkshirebrewhouse.com

Founded in 2017 by Jon Constable and Simon Cooke. Around 20 outlets are supplied direct. !! RAIB V

YPA (Yorkshire Pale Ale) (OG 1037, ABV 3.4%)
A hoppy, slightly spicy, refreshing pale ale.

Ey Up (OG 1040, ABV 3.8%)
A refreshing beer with a spicy hop aroma and malty bitter finish.

Reet (OG 1039, ABV 3.8%)
Powerful peppery hops, light malt background and a long, dry bitter finish.

Red Robin (OG 1049, ABV 4.8%)
A stout with a malty chocolate finish.

Faithful (OG 1050, ABV 4.9%)
Rich, malty stout with a fruity bitter finish.

Yorkshire Dales

Abbey Works, Askrigg, North Yorkshire, DL8 4LP
☎ (01969) 622027 ☎ 07818 035592
🌐 yorkshiredalesbrewery.com

Situated in the heart of the Yorkshire Dales, brewing started in a converted milking parlour in 2005. In 2016 the brewery moved to larger premises. More than 150 pubs are supplied throughout the north of England. A tap and bottle shop opened at the brewery in 2017. ♦RAIB

Butter Tubs (OG 1037, ABV 3.7%)
A pale golden-coloured beer with a dry bitterness complemented by strong citrus flavours and aroma.

Askrigg Bitter (OG 1038, ABV 3.8%)

Bainbridge Blonde (OG 1038, ABV 3.8%)

Buckden Pike (OG 1040, ABV 3.9%)
A refreshing blonde beer with a crisp, fruity finish.

Nappa Scarr (OG 1041, ABV 4%)
A golden ale with citrus and peach flavours.

Muker Silver (OG 1041, ABV 4.1%)
A lager-style ale. Crisp with a sharp, hoppy finish.

Askrigg Ale (OG 1043, ABV 4.3%)
A pale golden ale with intense aroma, a crisp, dry flavour and a long, bitter finish.

Garsdale Smokebox (OG 1057, ABV 5.6%)
A complex ale created by smoked and dark malts. Deep, rich chocolate and coffee flavours are complemented by the smokiness.

Yorkshire Heart SIBA

The Vineyard, Pool Lane, Nun Monkton, YO26 8EL
☎ (01423) 330716 ☎ 07838 030067
🌐 yorkshireheart.com

Yorkshire Heart has been brewing since 2011 and is situated adjacent to the Yorkshire Heart vineyard and winery, not far from York. !! ♦ GF

Lightheart (OG 1033, ABV 3.3%)
A pale ale with citrus and spice flavours.

Off the Wheaten Path (OG 1035, ABV 3.5%)

Hearty Bitter (OG 1037, ABV 3.7%)
A chestnut-coloured bitter with toffee flavours.

Rhubarbeer (OG 1037, ABV 3.7%)
A rhubarb flavoured, dark-coloured ale.

Dark Heart (OG 1039, ABV 4%)
Coffee-coloured ale with a smooth treacle flavour.

Silver Heart IPA (OG 1039, ABV 4%)
Amber-coloured ale with a citrus and spice flavour.

JRT Golden Best Bitter (OG 1041, ABV 4.2%)
Golden ale with a caramel and citrus flavour.

Blackheart Stout (OG 1047, ABV 4.8%)
Stout with a roasted coffee flavour.

Platinum EPA (OG 1047, ABV 5%)
Pale ale with zest and spice flavours.

Young's

See Eagle

Yubberton

See North Cotswold

Zapato

Correspondence: 2 Pollard Lane, Leeds, West Yorkshire, LS13 1EY 🌐 zapatobrewery.co.uk

Small company, established in 2016, that cuckoo brews in the Leeds area. It produces innovative beers based on traditional European styles.

Zepto (NEW)

Graig Fawr Lodge, Blackbrook Road, Caerphilly, CF83 1NF ☎ 07951 505524 🌐 zeptobrew.co.uk

Established in 2016, Zepto is a 100-litre brewery set up by CAMRA member Chris Sweet. Although production is mainly bottled, cask-conditioned beers are occasionally brewed.

Zerodegrees SIBA

Blackheath: 29-31 Montpelier Vale, Blackheath, London, SE3 0TJ

Bristol: 53 Colston Street, Bristol, BS1 5BA ☎ (0117) 925 2706

Cardiff: 27 Westgate Street, Cardiff, CF10 1DD ☎ (029) 2022 9494

Reading: 9 Bridge Street, Reading, RG1 2LR ☎ (0118) 959 7959

Brewing started in 2000 in Blackheath, London and now four brewpubs are owned, each incorporating a state-of-the-art, computer-controlled, German plant producing unfiltered and unfined ales and lagers. All beers use natural ingredients, are suitable for vegetarians, and are served from tanks using air pressure (not CO2). ♦

Zymurgorium

Unit 19, Irlam Business Centre, Soapstone Way, Irlam, M44 6RA 🌐 zymurgorium.com

The UK's first craft meadery and Manchester's first distillery. In combination with the brewery it was established in Irlam in 2013. Most of its output is in bottled form.

Closed breweries

The following breweries have closed or gone out of business since the 2018 Guide was published:

3 Potts, Southport, Merseyside
Alchemist (Contract brewery)
AleCraft (Cuckoo brewery)
Allsaints (Cuckoo brewery)
Artisan, Newcastle upon Tyne, Tyne & Wear
Ashdown, Withyham, East Sussex
Ashleyhay, Wirksworth, Derbyshire
Bad Bunny, Derby, Derbyshire
Baildon, Baildon, West Yorkshire
Ballard's, Nyewood, Hampshire
Barrell & Sellers, St Cross South Elmham, Suffolk
Bartrams, Rougham, Suffolk
Beachy Head, East Dean, East Sussex
Bear North, Denby Dale, West Yorkshire
Beardface & Bines, Cardiff, Glamorgan
Beardy Monkey, Melton Mowbray, Leicestershire
Biggleswade, Biggleswade, Bedfordshire
Bishop's Stortford (Cuckoo brewery)
Black Tap, Redditch, Worcestershire
Blackmore, Stourton Caundle, Dorset
Bolthole, Westbury on Trym, Gloucestershire & Bristol
Borough, Lancaster, Lancashire
Bridestones, Hebden Bridge, West Yorkshire
Cannon Royall, Uphampton, Worcestershire
Carbon Smith, Manchester, Greater Manchester
Castles, Caldicot, Gwent
Chadwick's, Kendal, Cumbria
Chew Valley, Pensford, Somerset
Chippenham, Chippenham, Wiltshire
Coppertown, Amlwch, North West Wales
Cottage, Lovington, Somerset
Cryptic, Stockport, Greater Manchester
De Brus, Dunfermline, Kingdom of Fife
Decent, Addlestone, Surrey
Deva Craft, Sandycroft, North East Wales
Deverells, Grays, Essex
Dickens, Reading, Berkshire
Edenfield, Edenfield, Lancashire
Emmanuales, Sheffield, South Yorkshire
Ewhurst, Ewhurst Green, East Sussex
Faringdon, Faringdon, Oxfordshire
Felstar, Felsted, Essex
Firefly, Worcester, Worcestershire
Five Oh, Prestwich, Greater Manchester
Free Radical (Cuckoo brewery)
Funfair, Elston, Nottinghamshire
Gas Dog, Melton Mowbray, Leicestershire
Golden Owl, Leeds, West Yorkshire
Golden Valley, Hereford, Herefordshire
Goldstone, Hove, East Sussex
Goosnargh, Goosnargh, Lancashire
Grill & Grain, Hoghton, Lancashire
Hardknott, Millom, Cumbria
Hastings, St Leonards on Sea, East Sussex
Hawk Hill, Dundee, Tayside
Hedge Row, Bradford, West Yorkshire
Hellhound, Bramford, Suffolk
Hen House, Whitchurch-on-Thames, Oxfordshire
Here Be Monsters, Holmbridge, West Yorkshire
Hewitt's (Cuckoo brewery)
Hope, Grays, Essex
Hoxne, Palgrave, Suffolk
Hurst, Hurstpierpoint, West Sussex
Idle Valley, Retford, Nottinghamshire
James & Kirkman, Pontefract, West Yorkshire
Kelpaul, Holmer, Herefordshire
Kendrick's, Claybrooke Magna, Leicestershire
Laine @ Aeronaut, W3: Acton, Greater London
LAM, Kennington, Oxfordshire
Landlord's Friend, Luddendenfoot, West Yorkshire
Langwith, Mansfield, Nottinghamshire
Leazes Lane, Newcastle upon Tyne, Tyne & Wear
Leyden, Nangreaves, Greater Manchester
Little Bush, Marehay, Derbyshire
Little Dragon, Milford Haven, West Wales
Liverpool Organic, Liverpool, Merseyside
Long Arm, W5: Ealing, Greater London
Long Hop, Louth, Lincolnshire
Maidstone, Maidstone, Kent
Market Harborough, Market Harborough, Leicestershire
Mayflower, Wigan, Greater Manchester
Moles, Melksham, Wiltshire
Moorstone, Horndon, Devon
Ness, Nesscliffe, Shropshire
New Religion, Cwmbran, Gwent
North Union, Sheffield, South Yorkshire
North Wales, Abergele, North West Wales
Northallerton, Northallerton, North Yorkshire
Northern FC, Gosforth, Tyne & Wear
Oast House (Cuckoo brewery)
Occasional, Silverton, Devon
Offbeat, Crewe, Cheshire
Old Bog, Headington, Oxfordshire
Old Forge, Coleshill, Oxfordshire
Otley, Pontypridd, Glamorgan
Oud Craft, Manchester, Greater Manchester
Ouseburn Valley, Newcastle upon Tyne, Tyne & Wear
Paradise, Hayle, Cornwall
Pells, Lewes, East Sussex
Pokertree, Carrickmore, Northern Ireland
Pope's, Worcester, Worcestershire
Red, Great Staughton, Cambridgeshire
Rocky Head, SW18: Wandsworth, Greater London
Roseland, Truro, Cornwall
Rowett, North Thoresby, Lincolnshire
RT, Cardiff, Glamorgan
Seal Bay, Cardigan, West Wales
Six O'Clock, Manchester, Greater Manchester
Joseph Herbert, Smith, Hanley Broadheath, Worcestershire
Spire, Sutton Scarsdale, Derbyshire
Steampunk, Castleford, West Yorkshire
Stoney Ford, Ryhall, Rutland
Streatham, SW16: Streatham, Greater London
Stringers, Ulverston, Cumbria
Tanners, Wiveliscombe, Somerset
Target, Roden, Shropshire
Ticketybrew, Stalybridge, Greater Manchester
Topsham, Topsham, Devon
Totem, Newton Abbot, Devon
Trinity, Wakefield, West Yorkshire
Two Beach, Shaldon, Devon
Tydwals, Llangorse, Mid Wales
Valve, Edinburgh, Edinburgh & the Lothians
Westwood, Denton, Greater Manchester
Whaley Bridge, Furness Vale, Derbyshire
Whippet, Leeds, West Yorkshire
Willy Good Ale, Winsley, Wiltshire
Winning Post, Worcester, Worcestershire
Woodbury, Woodbury Salterton, Devon
Wooden Hand, Truro, Cornwall
Worcestershire, Hartlebury, Worcestershire
Yates, Westnewton, Cumbria
Zeitgeist, Manchester, Greater Manchester

Future breweries

The following new breweries have been notified to the Guide and will start to produce beer during 2018/2019. In a few cases, they were in production during the summer of 2018 but were too late for a full listing:

4 Mice, Bolton-by-Bowland, Lancashire
Braybrooke, Braybrooke, Northamptonshire
Brewhouse & Kitchen, Hoxton, Greater London
BrewIT, W1: Fitzrovia, Greater London
Buswell, Burbage, Leicestershire
Chicken Foot, Bonsall, Derbyshire
Duration, West Acre, Norfolk
Earth Station, E16: North Woolwich, London
Eel Pie, Twickenham, Greater London
Fonthill, Tunbridge Wells, Kent
Fountain, EC1, Greater London
German Kraft, SE1: Borough, Greater London
Glasshouse, Stirchley, West Midlands
Glenelg, Glenelg, Highlands & Western Isles
Goose Island, E1: Shoreditch, Greater London
Grumpy's, Darton, South Yorkshire
Hop Forge, Lledrod, West Wales
IT's, Melksham, Wiltshire
Kegworth, Kegworth, Leicestershire
Kentish Town, NW5: Kentish Town, Greater London
Kitchen, SW15: Putney, Greater London
Liquid Light, Nottingham, Nottinghamshire
Lowland, Lockerbie, Dumfries & Galloway
Oak Tavern & Tap House, Sevenoaks, Kent
Oyster Inn, Butley, Suffolk
PopCity, Leeds, West Yorkshire
Progress, Kirkham, Lancashire
Purple Donkey, Wraysbury, Berkshire
Ride, Glasgow, Greater Glasgow & Clyde Valley
Round Corner, Melton Mowbray, Leicestershire
St David's, St David's, West Wales
Splott, Cardiff, Glamorgan
Taw Valley, North Tawton, Devon
Three Legged Fox, Darlington, Durham
Toast, SE1: Southwark, Greater London
Vine, Tarring, West Sussex
Watchmaker's Arms, Hove, East Sussex

Indexes & Further Information

Places index

C

D

E

T

PLACES INDEX

Beers index

These beers refer to those in bold type in the breweries section (beers in regular production) and so therefore do not include seasonal, special or occasional beers that may be mentioned elsewhere in the text.

A

BEERS INDEX

BEERS INDEX

E

BEERS INDEX

F

H

I

J

K

L

M

N

O

S

T

Award winning pubs

Local CAMRA Pubs of the Year

The Pub of the Year competition is judged by CAMRA members. Each of the CAMRA branches votes for its favourite pub: criteria include the quality and choice of real ale, atmosphere, customer service and value. The pubs listed below are the current winners of the title; look out for the 🏆 next to the entries in the Guide.

England

🏆 Bedfordshire
Engineers Arms, Henlow
Black Lion, Leighton Buzzard
Polhill Arms, Renhold

🏆 Berkshire
Old Manor, Bracknell
Craufurd Arms, Maidenhead
Catherine Wheel, Newbury
Nag's Head, Reading

🏆 Buckinghamshire
Chequers, Fenny Stratford
Royal Standard, Wooburn Common

🏆 Cambridgeshire
Maypole, Cambridge
Draymans Son, Ely
Chequers, Little Gransden
Bumble Inn, Peterborough

🏆 Cheshire
Bhurtpore, Aston
Olde Cottage Inn, Chester
Prince of Wales, Congleton
Ring o' Bells, Daresbury
Costello's Bar, Stockton Heath

🏆 Cornwall
Front, Falmouth

🏆 Cumbria
Manor Arms, Broughton-in-Furness
Punch Bowl Inn, Great Broughton
Drovers Rest, Monkhill

🏆 Derbyshire
White Hart, Bargate
Rose & Crown, Chesterfield
Smithfield, Derby
Town Street Tap, Duffield
Miners Arms, Hundall
York Chambers, Long Eaton
Thorn Tree Inn, Matlock
Devonshire Arms, South Normanton

🏆 Devon
Bridford Inn, Bridford
Bell Inn, Chittlehampton
Royal Oak Inn, Meavy
Beer Engine, Newton St Cyres

🏆 Dorset
George, Askerswell
Spyway Inn, Askerswell
Micro Moose, Bournemouth
Sixpenny Tap, Cranborne

🏆 Durham
Quakerhouse, Darlington
Victoria Inn, Durham
Three Horseshoes, Leamside
Golden Smog, Stockton-on-Tees

🏆 Essex
Victoria Arms, Brentwood
Railway Tavern, Chelmsford
New Inn, Colchester
Plough, Debden
Carpenters Arms, Maldon
Mawson's Micro Pub, Southend-on-Sea
Woodbine Inn, Waltham Abbey
White Hart, Weeley Heath

🏆 Gloucestershire & Bristol
Chums, Bristol: Redland
Jolly Brewmaster, Cheltenham
Inn at Fossebridge, Fossebridge
Fleece Inn, Hillesley

🏆 Hampshire
Lawrence Arms, Portsmouth
Guide Dog, Southampton
Wonston Arms, Wonston

🏆 Hertfordshire
Rising Sun, Berkhamsted
Land of Liberty, Peace & Plenty, Heronsgate
Old Cross Tavern, Hertford
Red Lion, Preston

🏆 Isle of Wight
Bargeman's Rest, Newport

🏆 Kent
New Inn, Canterbury
Lanes, Dover
Bell & Jorrocks, Frittenden
Past & Present, Gillingham
Bowl Inn, Hastingleigh
Old House, Ightham Common
Two Halves, Margate
Admiral's Arm, Queenborough
George, Tunbridge Wells

🏆 Lancashire
Bar 19, Blackpool
Bowland Beer Hall, Clitheroe
Little Bare, Morecambe
Cricketers, Ormskirk
Guild Ale House, Preston

🏆 Leicestershire
Geese & Fountain, Croxton Kerrial
Elbow Room Ale & Cider House, Hinckley
Blue Boar, Leicester
Needle & Pin, Loughborough

🏆 Lincolnshire
Red Lion, Newton

🏆 Greater London
Broken Drum, Blackfen
Star & Garter, Bromley
Hope, Carshalton
Olde Rose & Crown, E17: Walthamstow
Little Green Dragon, N21: Winchmore Hill

Bhurtpore, Aston, Cheshire

Beer Engine, Newton St Cyres, Devon

White Hart, Weeley Heath, Essex

Land of Liberty, Hertfordshire

Old House, Ightham Common, Kent

Hope, Carshalton, Greater London

Tapping The Admiral, NW1: Camden Town
Roebuck, Richmond
Blythe Hill Tavern, SE23: Forest Hill
Antelope, Surbiton
Trafalgar, SW19: South Wimbledon
Upminster TapRoom, Upminster
Dodo Micropub, W7: Hanwell
Harp, WC2: Charing Cross

Greater Manchester

Old Packet House, Altrincham
Queen Anne, Golborne
Blue Bell, Levenshulme
Brink, Manchester: City Centre
Flying Horse Hotel, Rochdale
New Oxford, Salford
Beer School, Westhoughton
Wigan Central, Wigan

Merseyside

Grasshopper, Hillside
Lazy Landlord Ale House, Liscard
Cask, Liverpool: Stoneycroft
Cricketers Arms, St Helens

Norfolk

Tombstone Saloon, Great Yarmouth
Fat Cat Brewery Tap, Norwich
King's Arms, Shouldham

Northumberland

Curfew, Berwick upon Tweed

Nottinghamshire

Dandy Cock Ale House, Kirkby-in-Ashfield
Brew Shed, Retford

Oxfordshire

Rose & Crown, Charlbury
White Hart, Oxford
Flowing Spring, Playhatch
Royal Oak, Wantage

Rutland

Green Dragon, Ryhall

Shropshire

Red Lion, Market Drayton
Bailey Head, Oswestry
White Hart, Shifnal
Lion O'Morfe, Upper Farmcote

Somerset

Raven, Bath
Crossways Inn, West Huntspill

Staffordshire

Dog Inn, Burton upon Trent
Linford Arms, Cannock
Crown Joule's, Codsall
Cat Inn, Enville
Fountain Inn, Leek
Beerbohm, Lichfield
Hopinn, Newcastle-under-Lyme
Swan Inn, Stone
Horse & Dove, Uttoxeter

Suffolk

Vine, Hopton
Fox, Pakenham
Fox, Shadingfield
Wheatsheaf, Tattingstone

Surrey

Jolly Sailor, Farnham
Running Horse, Leatherhead
Surrey Oaks, Newdigate
Barley Mow, Shepperton

East Sussex

Brewers Arms, Lewes
King's Arms, Rotherfield
Standard Inn, Rye

West Sussex

White Horse, Maplehurst
Crab Pot, Selsey
Green Man Ale & Cider House, Worthing

Tyne & Wear

Town Mouse Ale House, Newcastle upon Tyne: City Centre
Steamboat, South Shields

Warwickshire

Turk's Head, Alcester
Angel Ale House, Atherstone
Old Bakery, Kenilworth
Lord Hop, Nuneaton
Seven Stars, Rugby
Old Post Office, Warwick

West Midlands

Inn on the Green, Birmingham: Acocks Green
Bishop Vesey, Boldmere
Broomfield Tavern, Coventry: Spon End
Wagon & Horses, Halesowen
Ale Rooms, Knowle
Beacon Hotel, Sedgley
Black Country Arms, Walsall
Hail to the Ale, Wolverhampton

Wiltshire

Bell Inn, Lacock
Victoria & Albert, Netherhampton
Five Bells, Royal Wootton Bassett
Benett Arms, Semley

Harp, WC2 Charing Cross, G. London

Rose & Crown, Charlbury, Oxfordshire

Running Horse, Leatherhead, Surrey

Beacon Hotel, Sedgley, W. Midlands

Dragon Inn, Worcester, Worcestershire

Rook & Gaskill, York, N. Yorkshire

Worcestershire
Fleece Inn, Bretforton
Weavers Real Ale House, Kidderminster
Alestones, Tardebigge
Dragon Inn, Worcester

East Yorkshire
Marine Bar, Bridlington
Goodmanham Arms, Goodmanham
George Hotel, Hull
Jemmy Hirst at the Rose & Crown, Rawcliffe

North Yorkshire
Falcon Inn, Arncliffe
Starling Independent Beer & Coffee House, Harrogate
George & Dragon, Hudswell
Infant Hercules, Middlesbrough
Sun Inn, Pickering
North Riding Brewpub, Scarborough
Rook & Gaskill, York

South Yorkshire
Arcade Alehouse, Barnsley
Doncaster Brewery Tap, Doncaster
Kelham Island Tavern, Sheffield: Kelham Island
Wath Tap, Wath-upon-Dearne

West Yorkshire
Horse & Jockey, Birstall
Fighting Cock, Bradford
Victorian Craft Beer Café, Halifax: Town Centre
Corner, Huddersfield
Sair, Linthwaite
Harry's Bar, Wakefield

Wales

Glamorgan
Grange, Cardiff
Cross Inn, Cwmfelin
Pilot Inn, Mumbles
Pencelli Hotel, Treorchy

Gwent
Queen's Head, Chepstow
Goose & Cuckoo, Upper Llanover

Mid-Wales
New Inn, Bwlch
Arvon Ale House, Llandrindod Wells
Ancient Briton, Penycae

North-East Wales
Mold Alehouse, Mold
Bridge End Inn, Ruabon

North-West Wales
Black Boy Inn, Caernarfon
Bay Hop, Colwyn Bay

West Wales
Rhos yr Hafod Inn, Cross Inn (Llanon)
Salutation Inn, Llandeilo
Buccaneer Inn, Tenby

Scotland

Aberdeen & Grampian
Krakatoa, Aberdeen

Ayrshire & Arran
Fraser's Bar, Millport: Isle of Cumbrae

Dumfries & Galloway
Clachan Inn, Dalry

Edinburgh & the Lothians
Volunteer Arms (Staggs), Musselburgh

Greater Glasgow & Clyde Valley
State Bar, Glasgow
Bull Inn, Paisley

Highlands & Western Isles
Dores Inn, Dores

Kingdom of Fife
Hillend Tavern, Hillend

Loch Lomond, Stirling & the Trossachs
White Stag, Strathyre

Tayside
Green Room, Perth

Northern Ireland

Errigle Inn, Belfast

Channel Islands

Jersey
Lamplighter, St Helier

Isle of Man

White House Hotel, Peel

Kelham Island Tavern, S. Yorkshire

Sair, Linthwaite, W. Yorkshire

White House Hotel, Peel, Isle of Man

Readers' recommendations

Suggestions for pubs to be included or excluded

All pubs are regularly surveyed by local branches of the Campaign for Real Ale to ensure they meet the standards required by the *Good Beer Guide*. If you would like to comment on a pub already featured, or on any you think should be featured, please fill in the form below (or a copy of it), and send it to the address indicated. Alternatively, email **gbgeditor@camra.org.uk**. Your views will be passed on to the branch concerned. Please mark your envelope/email with the county where the pub is, which will help us to direct your comments efficiently.

Pub name:

Address:

Reason for recommendation/criticism:

Pub name:

Address:

Reason for recommendation/criticism:

Pub name:

Address:

Reason for recommendation/criticism:

Your name and address:

Please send to: [Name of county] Section, Good Beer Guide,
230 Hatfield Road, St Albans, Hertfordshire AL1 4LW

Outside influences

Monks, collaborations and a wine maker's twist

Brewers share a sense of community – coming together to share ideas and techniques with fellow enthusiasts. When a new Trappist brewery started in the UK, the monks looked to the international brewing community for help, whilst other brewers are creating collaborative brews closer to home.

Holy beers

In the world of beer there are indeed many heaven-blessed brews, but some of best must be those brewed by the Trappist breweries.

The term Trappist is a designation of origin rather than a style. Breweries can only use the Trappist appellation if the beers have been brewed within the enclosed community of a monastery of the Order of Cistercians of the Strict Observance (known as Trappists), and the monks have element of control over process, with the largest part of proceeds used for the social good.

All the brewing abbeys share a common commitment to quality. The monastic communities pride themselves on using the highest quality brewing equipment. The abbeys where Trappist monastic brewing takes place include six in Belgium, two in the Netherlands, and one each in Austria, Italy and the USA.

There is no such thing as a Trappist style, though there are some shared characteristics between all the monastic brews, including a deeply held conviction to brew the best beers with the finest ingredients. Between them, the monks and their secular workers produce more than 20 beers. All are top fermenting, likely to be strong and bottle conditioned, and full of yeast, fruity and aromatic flavours.

Now a 12th monastery, and the first in the UK, has joined their ranks. Mount Saint Bernard Abbey in Leicestershire has become Britain's first Trappist brewery, after years of research, experimentation and no doubt some sampling.

Monks at the abbey began investigating the idea after giving up their dairy business in 2013, which was no longer economically viable. The abbey, which is home to 27 monks, is the first permanent monastery to be founded in England since the Reformation, and the only Cistercian house in England.

As part of their research, the Brothers visited ten of the eleven existing Trappist breweries, and engaged the help of a Dutch master brewer, Constant Keinemans. They began producing experimental brews of twenty litres at a time. The first was on St Lutgarde's Day; Saint Lutgardis of Aywières was known for conducted seven-year fasts, surviving on bread and weak beer alone.

The final result, Tynt Meadow, comes in at 7.4% ABV. The name comes from the field where monks established a small church in the 1830s before moving a short distance to the site of the present abbey built in grey stone Gothic style.

Dom Erik Varden, abbot of Mount Saint Bernard, said he was 'very relieved' to see the brewery up and running, and hoped it could help them extend their community work.

'Beer is a good, honest, nurturing drink – our Belgian friends said more than once it should be liquid bread and not coloured water, and that's what we're aiming to live up to,' he said.

He stressed that the Belgian brewers who had helped and advised him had urged him not to produce a Belgian-style beer. So the result is an 'English Trappist ale'.

Any profits made from the venture will go to the trustees of Mount St Bernard, a charity responsible for maintaining the abbey and paying the monks' living expenses.

Tynt Meadow is an English Trappist ale, named after the original location of the monastery

Collaborations

Led by the US craft brewing movement, collaboration brews have become a common sight in the UK. You will often find them in brewery taps – interesting offerings from brewers large and small who have worked together, merging their styles and techniques to create a beer. Indeed, some pubs hold festivals dedicated to collaborations.

The concept behinds these "collabs" is to show that there is a craft beer ethos, which sees companies and individuals

Jenn Marrick (centre) and the brewing team behind Rhubarb: A User's Guide

coming together to promote common values rather than fighting over market share.

Now, thirty women have collaborated to make a rhubarb flavoured beer – Rhubarb: A User's Guide.

Led by brewing expert Jenn Merrick of Earth Station brewery, brewers, and students from Heriot-Watt University's Brewing and Distilling programme, gathered at Pressure Drop brewery in north London for just one day to create the kettle sour beer, which celebrates female brewing's past, present and future.

American-born Merrick, who was head brewer with Beavertown for a number of years, wants to see a fundamental shift in beer culture. In previous generations, brewing was dominated by white, able-bodied, middle-class men – brewers and drinkers – now it has become something more diverse.

The beer was brewed using a pale grist with a high proportion of wheat, quick-soured in the kettle overnight with the help of lactic acid and then blended with freshly juiced rhubarb.

Merrick said: 'It was such an inspiring day to see so many women who contribute to the beer industry all in one place, making a beer that drew on the skills of these industry leaders and connecting them with the next generation of brewers.'

Other breweries have also been keen to celebrate women's place in brewing. Brewster Aneta Izdebska, from Marston's DE14 nanobrewery joined forces with Ritchie Bosworth, head brewer of Coventry's Twisted Barrel Ale brewery, to brew Mathilde, a 4.8% abv Hazy Belgian Session IPA in celebration of International Women's Day.

Marston's marketing manager Joanne Wyke said 'back to the middle ages, it was women who were the powerhouse of brewing in Britain. By the 19th and 20th century, that had died away, with brewing being seen as man's work; but over the last 10 years, brewers like Marston's have been addressing that imbalance, with women rising naturally to the top like a finely chiselled bubble on a pint of ale.'

Izdebska adds: 'In the world of wine, women are recognised as having more accurate palates than men; so, I am thrilled to work alongside the highly inventive team Twisted Barrel to add my own tastes and talents to a great new brew. This collaboration will be a mini testament to the rise of women in beer.'

Taking inspiration from wine

Curious Brewery, the brewery owned by England's leading winemaker, Chapel Down has worked with London-based brewery Brew By Numbers to make a series of limited edition batch beers, each produced with a winemaker's twist.

The first beer in the brewery's Curiouser & Curiouser series – named Chapter 1 – mimics the flavours of Bacchus grapes, the classic English grape varietal which Chapel Down has developed a strong reputation with in its wines and sparkling wines.

The Bacchus grape produces fruit and floral notes and is often acidic. These notes are complemented perfectly by the dry and fruity qualities of Brew By Numbers' house saison yeast, which are amplified by the delicate vinous, floral and soft fruity notes of hallertau blanc and huell melon hops.

Their second offering, Chapter 2, is delicately refined elderflower saison.

Chapel Down head winemaker, Josh Donaghay-Spire said: 'We have strived to create a new, exciting, and forward-thinking beer that is as focused on quality as it is drinkability, crafted with our winemaker's care and finesse.

'Whether it's developing new styles, adapting established ones, or shining a light on more enigmatic techniques, Brew By Numbers crafts each beer with the same level of care, attention and respect that we pride ourselves with here at Chapel Down. Brew By Numbers align perfectly with our own goals of producing great, high-quality beer and of always staying curious.'

Chapel Down's wine-inspired beer Chapter 2

Books for beer lovers

CAMPAIGN FOR REAL ALE

CAMRA Books publishes a range of other titles on beer, pubs and brewing. Some of our latest titles are detailed below. You can buy our books – and a selection of beer-related titles from other publishers – from us direct, by visiting our online bookshop at **www.camra.org.uk/books** or calling **01727 867 201**. Discounts are available for CAMRA members.

Essential Home Brewing

Andy Parker

Whether you're taking your first steps in home brewing, or you're a more experienced home brewer entering competitions or following a dream of brewing commercially, this book contains everything you need to know. From understanding and selecting your ingredients, through to equipment, the brewing process, and troubleshooting, this is a step-by-step guide to brewing your own great-tasting beer. Featuring 30 exciting recipes from world-leading, innovative craft breweries, with hints and tips on adapting the brews to make them your own.

RRP £11.99 ISBN 978-1-85249-351-6

Good Beer Guide Belgium

Joe Stange & Tim Webb

The definitive, totally independent guide to one of the world's top beer nations, the *Good Beer Guide Belgium* is CAMRA's essential guide to the beers of Belgium, the brewers who make them, and where to enjoy them, both in Belgium and around the world. This eighth edition is fully revised and updated, guiding you to the very best places to drink Belgian beer – from cosy cafés to specialist beer bars, and from brewery taps to world-renowned beer festivals.

RRP £14.99 ISBN 978-1-85249-341-7

Peak District Pub Walks

Bob Steel

Bob Steel's classic *Peak District Pub Walks* has been tempting people into the magnificent hills, dales and inns of the national park for over a decade. Now fully revised, this third edition introduces many completely new routes, revealing the wonderful diversity of the Peak landscape, and exploring of the area's abundant industrial heritage. An indispensable guide to the scenic highlights and some of the best pubs of the region for the outdoor enthusiast and real-ale lover alike.

RRP £12.99 ISBN 978-1-85249-353-0

Wild Pub Walks

Daniel Neilson

The ideal book for hill walkers who enjoy long days out followed by a refreshing beer in a welcoming pub. Join author Daniel Nielson on 22 walks in beautiful remote or mountain landscapes, each with one or more great pubs at journey's end. The areas covered are: Peak District; Lake District; North York Moors and Yorkshire Dales National Parks; the Scottish Highlands and Islands; Scottish Borders; Snowdonia; Pembrokeshire and South Wales. The walks vary in the level of challenge, from long walks in lower-lying areas to Grade 1 scrambles.

RRP £11.99 ISBN 978-1-85249-340-0

CAMRA'S Home-Brewing Problem Solver

Erik Lars Myers

Real ale and other craft beers have become increasingly popular over the past few years, and as a result more people have been compelled to try making their own home-brew. However, while the concept behind making beer is simple, the execution can at times seem complex and confusing. CAMRA's *Home-brewing Problem Solver* provides the information you need to nip problems in the bud – and, better still, to avoid them in the first place.

RRP £12.99 ISBN 978-1-85249-347-9

So You Want to Be a Beer Expert

Jeff Evans

More people than ever are searching for an understanding of what makes a great beer. This book meets that demand by presenting a hands-on course in beer appreciation, leading to an understanding of world beer styles, beer flavours, how beer is made, the ingredients, buying and storing beer, and more. The novelty of this book is that it doesn't just relate the facts, but helps readers reach conclusions for themselves, with interactive tasting sessions that show readers – through their own tasting experiences – what beer is all about.

RRP £12.99 ISBN: 978-1-85249-322-6

Historic Coaching Inns of the Great North Road

Roger Protz

The Great North Road is a UK icon, the Route 66 of Britain, but instead of gas stations and diners, we have magnificent coaching inns. Taking in the history of these buildings, as well as the literature that has celebrated them – from Charles Dickens through to JB Priestley – Roger Protz describes these coaching houses with an expert and discerning eye, producing not only a great pub guide but also a gazetteer of the history and culture that are draped along this iconic road.

RRP £12.99 ISBN 978-1-85249-339-4

Britain's Best Real Heritage Pubs (2nd edition)

Geoff Brandwood

This definitive listing is the result of 25 years' research by CAMRA to discover pubs that are either unaltered in 70 years or have features of truly national historic importance. Fully revised, this latest edition boasts updated information and a new set of evocative illustrations. Among the 260 pubs, there are unspoilt country locals, Victorian drinking palaces and mighty roadhouses. The book has features describing how the pub developed, what's distinctive about pubs in different parts of the country, and how pubs provided take-out sales in the pre-supermarket era.

RRP £9.99 ISBN 978-1-85249-334-9

Good Beer Guide digital editions

The *Good Beer Guide* is also available in digital formats, including a mobile app, an e-book and a sat-nav Points of Interest (POI) download. Together, these offer the perfect solution to pub-finding on the move.

Good Beer Guide e-book

The *Good Beer Guide 2019* is available as an e-book in ePUB and Kindle formats from major online e-book retailers. Key features of the e-book include the following (**depending on the device*):

- Portable, electronic version of the printed Guide
- Fully interactive, searchable content
- Full-colour features and images from the printed edition* as well as complete pubs and breweries listings
- Active e-mail and web links within entries*
- Postcode links to Google maps to help you navigate*

Good Beer Guide app

The recently updated Good Beer Guide mobile app provides detailed information on the latest *Good Beer Guide* pubs, breweries and beers wherever you are or wherever you are going. It also provides basic information for 31,000 other real ale pubs all over the UK, collated by CAMRA. Social media integration lets you share your beer experiences with other users and you can record your pub visits, tasted beers and your own personal reviews in 'My Guide'. For more information see p1046 or visit **www.camra.org.uk/gbg-mobile**

Good Beer Guide POI files

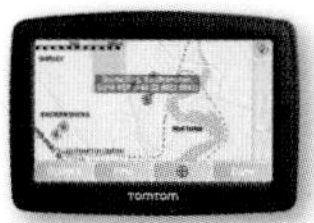

The Good Beer Guide POI (Points of Interest) file allows users of TomTom, Garmin and Navman sat-nav systems to find the locations of all 4,500 current *Good Beer Guide* pubs and all the UK's real-ale breweries and plan routes to them. To download the POI file visit **www.camra.org.uk/gbg-sat-nav**

An offer for CAMRA members
Join the Good Beer Guide Privilege Club

CAMRA members can take advantage of an even bigger discount on the *Good Beer Guide*, and get further benefits, by joining the *Good Beer Guide* Privilege Club.

- Pay just £10 (RRP £15.99) for your copy, with free p&p
- Receive your copy hot off the press and in advance of other purchasers
- Receive ocassional special Club offers and discounts on other CAMRA books and merchandise
- Stay up-to-date every year with CAMRA's *Good Beer Guide* as everything is taken care of with one simple Direct Debit
- Help to fund CAMRA directly, allowing us to continue to campaign for real ale and community pubs

For further details and to sign up visit **www.camra.org.uk/gbg-privilege-club** and follow the online instructions.

CAMRA Shop

Books & merchandise

CAMRA's online shop is the ideal place to visit for anyone looking for beer- and pub-related books, clothing or merchandise for themselves or fellow beer lovers.

With an ever-changing list of new and established titles from CAMRA Books and a carefully curated selection of titles from a variety of other publishers and authors, the CAMRA Shop is the go-to destination for anyone looking for books on pubs, beer bars, beer and brewing. Whether you are looking for a basic introduction to the world of beer or to deepen your knowledge; or whether you are after a consumer guide to the best local pubs or some authoritative industry insight, we have something for you on our shelves.

The Shop also stocks a range of CAMRA-branded and beer-themed clothing and products, all chosen with the keen beer drinker in mind.

- Browse the full range of CAMRA Books titles within categories including: beer knowledge; beer travel; history, heritage & culture; home brewing; miscellany & gift; and pub walks
- Discover our growing selection of beer-related titles from other publishers
- Shop among our expanding range of clothing and merchandise
- Get upcoming CAMRA titles in advance of publication at special pre-order prices
- As a CAMRA member, log in to receive further discounts

Visit us at: **camra.org.uk/shop**

Join the Campaign!

CAMPAI
FOR
REAL A

CAMRA, the Campaign for Real Ale, is an independent not-for-profit, volunteer-led consumer group. We promote good-quality real ale and pubs, as well as lobbying government to champion drinkers' rights and protect local pubs as centres of community life.

CAMRA has over 190,000 members from all ages and backgrounds, brought together by a common belief in the issues that CAMRA deals with and their love of good-quality British beer. From just £25 a year – that's less than a pint a month – you can join CAMRA and enjoy the following benefits†:

- Access to *What's Brewing* news and the award-winning *BEER* magazine, containing features and updates about beer, pubs and brewing.
- Free or reduced entry to over 200 national, regional and local beer festivals.
- Money off many CAMRA products and publications including the *Good Beer Guide*.
- Exclusive member benifits include 10% discount with Cottages.com, Cotswold Outdoor, Beer Hawk and man
- £20 worth of J D Wetherspoon™ real ale vouchers*
  (40 x 50 pence off a pint).
- Discounts in thousands of pubs across the UK through the CAMRA Real Ale Discount Scheme
- 15 months membership for the price of 12 for new members paying by Direct Debit**

This pub offers CAMRA members a discount
See inside for more details

For more details about member benefits please visit **www.camra.org.uk/benefits**

If you feel passionately about your pint and about pubs, join us by visiting **www.camra.org.uk/join** or calling **01727 798 440**

For the latest campaigning news and to get involved in CAMRA's campaigns visit **www.camra.org.uk/campaigns**

† Membership prices and benefits are subject to change.

* Joint members receive £20 worth of J D Wetherspoon™ vouchers to share.

** 15 months membership for the price of 12 is only available the first time a member pays by Direct Debit.